W9-AWC-182

USA

Jeff Campbell

Glenda Bendure, Becca Blond, Jim DuFresne, Lisa Dunford,
Ned Friary, Kim Grant, Beth Greenfield, Alex Hershey, Catherine Le Nevez,
Deb Miller, Becky Ohlsen, Suzanne Plank , Andrea Schulte-Peevers,
John A Vlahides, Karla Zimmerman

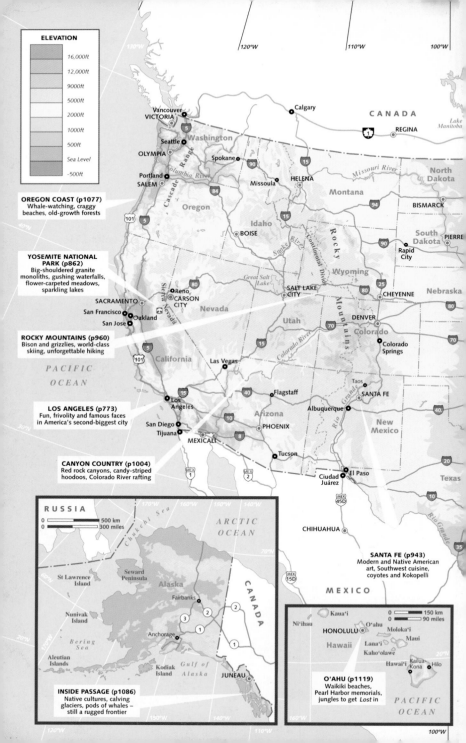

ELEVATION

16,000ft
12,000ft
9000ft
5000ft
2000ft
1000ft
500ft
Sea Level
-500ft

OREGON COAST (p1077)
Whale-watching, craggy
beaches, old-growth forests

**YOSEMITE NATIONAL
PARK (p862)**
Big-shouldered granite
monoliths, gushing waterfalls,
flower-carpeted meadows,
sparkling lakes

ROCKY MOUNTAINS (p960)
Bison and grizzlies, world-class
skiing, unforgettable hiking

LOS ANGELES (p773)
Fun, frivolity and famous faces
in America's second-biggest city

CANYON COUNTRY (p1004)
Red rock canyons, candy-striped
hoodoos, Colorado River rafting

SANTA FE (p943)
Modern and Native American
art, Southwest cuisine,
coyotes and Kokopelli

INSIDE PASSAGE (p1086)
Native cultures, calving
glaciers, pods of whales –
still a rugged frontier

O'AHU (p1119)
Waikiki beaches,
Pearl Harbor memorials,
jungles to get *Lost* in

CANADA

Calgary
REGINA
Lake Manitoba

Vancouver
VICTORIA
Seattle
OLYMPIA
Washington
Spokane
Portland
SALEM
Missoula
HELENA
Montana
North Dakota
BISMARCK
Oregon
Idaho
BOISE
Wyoming
South Dakota
PIERRE
Rapid City
Cheyenne
Nebraska
Reno
CARSON CITY
SACRAMENTO
San Francisco
Oakland
San Jose
Nevada
SALT LAKE CITY
Utah
DENVER
Colorado
Colorado Springs
California
Las Vegas
Flagstaff
Arizona
Albuquerque
SANTA FE
Taos
New Mexico
Los Angeles
San Diego
Tijuana
MEXICALI
PHOENIX
Tucson
El Paso
Ciudad Juárez
Texas
CHIHUAHUA
MEXICO

PACIFIC OCEAN

Columbia River
Cascade Range
Sierra Nevada
Great Salt Lake
Snake River
Colorado River
Rocky Mountains
Continental Divide
Missouri River
Rio Grande

RUSSIA
Chukchi Sea
ARCTIC OCEAN
St Lawrence Island
Seward Peninsula
Alaska
CANADA
Nunivak Island
Fairbanks
Anchorage
Bering Sea
Aleutian Islands
Kodiak Island
Gulf of Alaska
JUNEAU

500 km
300 miles

Kaua'i
Ni'ihau
O'ahu
HONOLULU
Moloka'i
Maui
Hawaii
Lana'i
Kaho'olawe
Hawai'i
Kailua-Kona
Hilo
PACIFIC OCEAN

150 km
90 miles

CHICAGO (p567)
The Second City is first-rate: theater and music, architecture and pizza

NEW YORK, NEW YORK (p126)
Bright lights, big city – a cacophony of culture

WASHINGTON, DC (p298)
Memorable museums, majestic monuments, and movers and shakers

BLUE RIDGE PARKWAY (p471)
Spring wildflowers, autumn colors, Appalachian culture and music

MIAMI (p496)
Art deco architecture, Hispanic and Cuban culture, wild South Beach nightlife

AUSTIN (p721)
Music, music, foot-stomping music in the weird heart of Texas

EVERGLADES NATIONAL PARK (p509)
Gater-infested subtopical swamps, Florida panthers, gentle manatees

Destination USA

The pulse of the nation beats along its sinuous highways. Every traveler who has ever set out across the country will tell you this. And yet, if so, why does finding the heart of America still seem so elusive? It isn't that America lacks for soaring icons, scenic wonders and oh-you-must-visit imperatives. A trip is hardly begun before sign after sign announces: 'You're here!' 'Be amazed!' 'Find God!' 'Buy this!' Not to mention the fear-mongering: 'Next gas, 1524 miles.'

In their search for the real America many aim first, of course, for the heartland – that vast wheat-waving middle where pundits turn for pithy soundbites from 'average Americans.' But what makes a squint-eyed Iowa farmer any more emblematic of the national character than, say, the cicada-song of ethnicities in New York or San Francisco? Or the high-steppin' rowdies of an Austin honky-tonk? Or the graciousness of a Charleston belle?

Some hold up the nation's much-vaunted 'Americana' – even when the sights, as sometimes happens, are less riotously amusing than the sales pitch. But surely that's America, too: all glaring neon billboards and carny promises. Others dive headfirst into the continent's raw land, into those horizon-stretching expanses of unsuburbanized wilderness. When gazing at the Southwest desert or California's Pacific edge or the Rocky Mountains, it's easy to fall hard for wild America, whose beauty quickens the blood.

Yet the question lingers – how and at what point does this aggregate of peoples and dreams and land and freedoms ever get fused into a singular nation?

Trite as it may sound, the heart of America beats in the heart of the traveler – in the journey of discovery itself. America evolves as each trip evolves – one meeting, one encounter at a time.

RICHARD CUMMI

Urban Legends

RICHARD CUMMINS

Take in the Great Plains' version of the Eiffel Tower, St Louis' Gateway Arch (p668)

COREY WISE

Be swept away by the spiraling grandeur of New York's Guggenheim museum (p145).

LEE FOSTER

Pay homage to Hollywood's glittering stars at the Walk of Fame (p779)

Feast your eyes on the drop-dead beauty of San Francisco (p822)

JOHN ELK III

Wild America

CAROL POLICH

Join the throngs, and the sparring bull elks, at Yellowstone National Park (p1004)

OTHER HIGHLIGHTS

- Cruise Lake Superior and enjoy Michigan's magnificent sandstone bluffs at Pictured Rocks National Lakeshore (p634).

- Find snow in Texas at the lovely Guadalupe Mountains National Park (p760).

- Explore the pinnacles and points, steeples and spires, and odd formations called 'hoodoos,' at Bryce Canyon National Park (p933).

JAMES LYON

Visit Joshua Tree National Park (p810), home to this distinctive relation of the yucca

Rejoice in the angular beauty of the Yosemite Valley (p862), here awash with natural pastel light tones

THOMAS WIN

JEFF GREENBERG

Step back in time with a walk under the live oaks and experience the richness of Savannah's antebellum history (p389)

PETER PTSCHELINZEW

Spy on the ubiquitous alligators in Florida's Everglades (p508), but resist the urge to feed them

Claret cup cactus blooms in the dunes at New Mexico's White Sands National Monument (p957)

MARK & AUDREY GIBSON

America's Cultural Tapestry

RICK GERHARTER

Enjoy the colorful celebrations of America's eclectic communities (p60)

JOHN ELK III

Soak up the vibrant and authentic atmosphere of San Francisco's Chinatown (p827)

Join in a game of dominoes in Little Havana's Máximo Gómez 'Domino' Park, Miami (p500)

JEFF GREENBERG

The Beat of a Different Drum

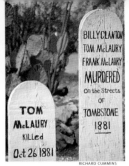

RICHARD CUMMINS

Once a dangerous place, Arizona's Tombstone (p915) is now all about fun

DAVID PEEVERS

Come to South Los Angeles to see Watts Towers (p779), a soaring folk-art vision of found objects

RAY LASKOWITZ

Explore exotic spiritualism at New Orleans' Historic Voodoo Museum (p418)

Be amazed by the Corn Palace (p690), the Great Plains' very own Taj Mahal, found in South Dakota's Mitchell and redecorated every year with 275,000 ears of corn

RICK GERHARTER

First Peoples

RICHARD I'ANSON

Become better acquainted with Cherokee history at the Museum of the Cherokee Indian (p473)

RICHARD CUMMINS

The Navajo Indian Reservation preserves much of their rich culture (p906)

ERNEST MANEWAL

Check out traditional adobe construction at New Mexico's Taos Pueblo (p951)

Discover tantalising fragments of ancient civilizations in petroglyphs found across the Southwest (p868)

DONALD C & PRISCILLA ALEXANDER EASTM.

Gourmands & Gourmets

LEE FOSTER

Deep red ristras, or 'strings' of chili, decorate many of New Mexico's haciendas (p935)

OTHER HIGHLIGHTS

- Seek out dreamy Cuban coffee and cuisine in Miami (p505).
- Don't miss a slice of fresh blueberry pie (p613) while traveling around the wonderful orchards of the Great Lakes.
- Try Tucson for a taste of truly tempting Mexican cooking (p912).
- From fried chicken to jambalaya, the South is the home of good eatin' (p377).

ANGUS OBORN

Grab a genuine pastrami sandwich with egg cream and a dill pickle in New York's East Village (p159)

Savor the goodness of California cuisine at Berkeley's Chez Panisse (p845), but remember to book ahead

JERRY ALEXANDER

Lost Highways

Navigate the Rocky Mountains' curvaceous Pikes Peak (p978), a famous Colorado beauty spot

Take the quintessential nostalgic road trip along the Great Mother Road (p30)

OTHER HIGHLIGHTS

- Choose photogenic Hwy 30A (p558) along the brilliant emerald coast for Florida's best views.
- Travel Old King's Hwy (p242), Cape Cod, for gracious history.

Watch out for bison (p91), whose numbers are once again building up on the American plains

Contents

Regional Map Contents

The Authors

JEFF CAMPBELL
Coordinating Author & California

Jeff was born in Longview, Texas, where he stayed for six months before moving on. He's been a traveler (and a Texan) ever since, and has now made contact with 40 of the 50 states. Only 10 to go! A writer and an editor for Lonely Planet since 1993, he was the coordinating author of *USA* 3, which won the Society of American Travel Writers 2004 Silver Award for best guidebook. He was also the coordinating author on *Southwest* and *Zion & Bryce Canyon National Parks* and contributed to *Las Vegas*. He currently resides in San Francisco with his wife and two children.

Jeff Campbell's USA

After several decades of travel, I feel like I'm still discovering the USA. But I have learned a few things about myself. One: I am an official red rock junkie. Southern Utah (p927) blows me away, from my first view of Canyonlands at Dead Horse Point to climbing Angels Landing in Zion. Two: it's possible to fall in love with a beach you'll never swim – namely, Northern California's coastline (p849). Three: hiking across a living Hawaiian volcano (p1131) and next to an Alaskan glacier (p1092) is just cool. Four: I'm bicoastal when it comes to cities; New York (p126) and San Francisco (p822) have all I need. Five: I know I've led a blessed life if every time I go to Yosemite (p862) it feels like home.

BECCA BLOND
Rocky Mountains & Southwest

An East Coast transplant, Becca fell in love with Colorado while attending university in the state and never left – the sunny blue skies and big craggy mountains were just too tantalizing. Always up for a good adventure, Becca has racked up many miles over the years exploring the Rocky Mountain states and the Southwest – including a few research trips around the region for other Lonely Planet guides. Although she spends much of the year romping around Asia, Africa and Europe, she's always happy to get back to Boulder, Colorado, where she lives with her boyfriend and a big, goofy dog named Duke.

LONELY PLANET AUTHORS

Why is our travel information the best in the world? It's simple: our authors are independent, dedicated travelers. They don't research using just the Internet or phone, and they don't take freebies in exchange for positive coverage. They travel widely, to all the popular spots and off the beaten track. They personally visit thousands of hotels, restaurants, cafés, bars, galleries, palaces, museums and more – and they take pride in getting all the details right, and telling it how it is. For more, see the authors section on www.lonelyplanet.com.

JIM DUFRESNE
Alaska

Jim DuFresne has lived and worked in Alaska and even cashed a few Permanent Fund checks for doing so. Today he is a travel writer based in Clarkston, Michigan, who prefers visiting Alaska in summer as opposed to living there in the winter. He is also the author of Lonely Planet's *Alaska* and *Hiking in Alaska*.

LISA DUNFORD
Texas & Great Plains

Lisa wasn't born in Texas but, as the bumper sticker says, she got there as fast as she could. During the 10 years Lisa has called south Texas home, she's traveled the breadth and width of her very large adopted state several times, always on the lookout for an old dance hall or new café. Before turning to freelance travel writing and editing, Lisa was a features-department editor at the *Corpus Christi Caller-Times* newspaper. She's also co-authored the Texas section of a guide to the Old West. No matter where this wanderer roams, she'll always return to the little patch of riverfront east of Houston that she, her husband and their dog call home.

NED FRIARY & GLENDA BENDURE
Hawaii & New England

Ned grew up outside of Boston. Upon graduating from the University of Massachusetts at Amherst, he bought a van and went on a yearlong journey across the USA, landing in Santa Cruz, California. There, while volunteering at a drop-in center, he met Glenda. After she finished her studies at the University of California, they took to the road, traveled throughout Europe, taught English in Japan, rambled through the islands of Hawaii and eventually returned to the US mainland. After years of traveling, the place that caught their fancy was Cape Cod – and they've lived there ever since. Fall foliage outings in the Berkshires and Green Mountains, summers in the Cape Cod surf and long hikes are part of their routine when they're not on the road. They're co-authors of Lonely Planet's *Hawaii* and *Oahu* guides and have also written the hiking guide *Walks and Rambles on Cape Cod and the Islands*.

KIM GRANT   Southwest

Kim Grant has long considered New Mexico the wellspring of her original home. She began making quarterly pilgrimages in the early 1990s; by 2003 the frequency had almost tripled. A photographer drawn to the light, a tai chi chuan practitioner drawn to her community, and a writer yearning to live a more simple and observant life, Kim is happiest in three places: cruising on wide open roads, scrambling along mountain trails, and relaxing at sunset with a margarita. The Southwest is a natural fit. Over the course of this research she decided to leap and move to New Mexico. There's no denying the pull.

BETH GREENFIELD   New York, New Jersey & Pennsylvania

Though she's traveled the world, Beth knows the NY-NJ-PA region best. She is a Jersey girl, after all – born and raised in Eatontown, NJ, near the Jersey Shore – and, after stints living in both Brooklyn and Long Island, she now makes her home in New York City, where she's resided for more than a decade. Beth is the co-author of Lonely Planet's latest *New York City* guide, and this is the second time she's written the NY-NJ-PA chapter for the USA book. In addition, she is an editor at *Time Out* New York magazine, and a prolific freelance writer whose work has appeared in publications including the *New York Times*, *Esquire*, *Out Traveler* and the *Village Voice*.

ALEX HERSHEY   Washington, DC & the Capital Region

Though born in Washington, DC, Alex was immediately spirited across the border to spend her formative years in Chevy Chase, Maryland. Many afternoons were spent reading in the gardens of Dumbarton Oaks, strolling the Mall, and cliff-jumping at Great Falls. Childhood vacations to the beaches of Delaware and Virginia are, for better or worse, seared into her memory. This research trip marked the first time in a decade that Alex got to witness the cherry trees blossoming – a capital area spring is even more magical than she remembered. Alex currently lives in the Bay Area.

CATHERINE LE NEVEZ   Florida

A roadtripper and writer from way back, Catherine took to Florida in a battered little red Mazda she bought for a few hundred bucks in the back-blocks of Miami, navigating 5500 miles of the state's backroads and beaches, springs and swamps, highways and high-rises, forests and fantastical kitschy attractions that she reckons combine to make Florida a roadtripper's dream. Catherine recently spent a couple of years roadtripping the length and breadth of her native Oz, during which she completed her Doctor of Creative Arts in Writing from far-reaching locations. She also has a Masters degree in Professional Writing and is a co-author of Lonely Planet's *Florida* guide.

DEBRA MILLER The South

Deb grew up in Vancouver, Canada, and worked at Lonely Planet's Oakland office before moving to Atlanta, where she is a contributing editor to *Atlanta Magazine*. An avid roadtripper, she's weaved her way through the backroads of the South – by car and by Harley – eating BBQ, jamming to live music and marveling at Southerners' ability for generous, humorous and lively conversation. Deb writes for several magazines and has contributed to nine Lonely Planet titles, including *Savannah, Charleston & the Carolina Coast*.

BECKY OHLSEN Pacific Northwest & Great Plains

Becky Ohlsen has been fascinated by the wide open spaces and weird artifacts of the Great Plains ever since those eight-hour odysseys to her grandparents' house back when she was a little kid. The mythology of the American road – huge plastic rodents, six-legged calves, junk-car sculptures and, strangest of all, interstate truck stops – has never loosened its grip on her imagination. She has lived in the Pacific Northwest for the past 10 years, hypnotized by the rain and all those green things blocking out the horizon.

SUZANNE PLANK California

Arriving in covered wagon, Suzanne's great-great-grandparents settled in Truckee, California...before there was a Truckee, California. From an early age she has hiked the trails, camped the woods and been enchanted by the intimate towns of California's northern mountains. Suzanne has explored much of the globe, written about some of it and been moved by all of it. She has an MA from Stanford in Latin American Studies and has spent much time working and living in Mexico and South America.

ANDREA SCHULTE-PEEVERS California

Andrea has lived in Germany and the UK and racked up thousands of miles traveling on all continents except Antarctica. When it came time to settle down, however, she found Southern California's sunny disposition – and skies – simply irresistible. Armed with a degree from UCLA, she managed to feed her continuing wanderlust by becoming a travel writer and, since 1996, has authored or updated nearly 30 books for Lonely Planet, including *Los Angeles & Southern California* and *California*. Andrea makes her home in Los Angeles with her husband, David, and their cat, Mep the Fierce.

JOHN A VLAHIDES   California

A native New Yorker, John A Vlahides studied cooking in Paris, then worked as a luxury-hotel concierge and earned membership in *Les Clefs d'Or*, the international union of the world's elite concierges. John now works as a freelance travel writer and lives in San Francisco, where he spends his free time touring California by motorcycle, sunning beneath the Golden Gate Bridge, skiing the Sierra Nevada, and singing tenor with the San Francisco Symphony Chorus. John is a co-author of *Coastal California, Los Angeles & Southern California* and *California*.

KARLA ZIMMERMAN   Great Lakes & Great Plains

Karla is a life-long Midwesterner, weaned on a diet of corndogs and cheese. She became a rabid traveler young, seeing most of the 50 states from the backseat of her parents' station wagon – a comfy ride compared to her subsequent global travels via rickshaw, tuk-tuk, pirogue and cargo plane. She has written travel features for books, newspapers, magazines and radio. She lives in Chicago with husband Eric, the ultimate trekking companion, who never says no and pays for it by having to endure everything from bus crashes in the Vietnamese highlands to Civil War re-enactments in northern Illinois.

CONTRIBUTING AUTHORS

Ryan Ver Berkmoes is the author of the History chapter. His interest in history began early, which proved useful when the history teacher hired at the last moment by his high school thought that a constitution was something you needed on a long car trip. The principal asked Ryan to take over the teaching duties for his own class and he cheerfully did.

Virginie Boone has covered college sports, professional women's soccer and the NFL as a journalist for ESPN. She fondly remembers trying to maintain eye contact with sports stars in locker rooms, downing press box hot dogs and finding novel ways around athletes' terrible clichés. A new mom, she's already spotted the making of a fine athlete in infant son, Milo, who has quarterback hands and loves to watch *SportsCenter* on TV.

Edward Nawotka is a book critic living in Austin, Texas, where he contributes to the *Austin-American Statesman*. In 2004, he served as Literary Director of the Texas Book Festival. Ed continues to write for *People* magazine, *USA Today*, the *New Yorker* and *Publishers Weekly*, where he was until recently an editor.

Axel Alonso is the Executive Editor of Marvel Comics. A 10-year industry veteran, he has edited, among other titles, *Amazing Spider-Man*, *Incredible Hulk*, *Wolverine*, *Punisher*, *Black Panther* and *Rawhide Kid*, garnering numerous industry awards, while inexplicably holding together a 10-year marriage with his wife, Kara. Of course, he did get some mileage out of the fact that *Vibe* magazine anointed him one of 2004's '100 Hottest People in Entertainment.'

Karen A Levine earned a Master's degree in Art History at San Francisco State University and currently serves as Managing Editor, Publications, at the San Francisco Museum of Modern Art. She has contributed essays, interviews and reviews to a number of art publications, including *Tema Celeste* and *Artweek*.

TophOne is a heavy-drinking native San Franciscan raised on punk rock, skateboarding and graffiti art. As founder of the RedWine DJs, he spins records between four and six nights a week. He is also the Senior Writer at *XLR8R* magazine, penning his widely-read 'Lucky 13' column for each issue. He also rides his bike from San Francisco to Los Angeles on the AIDS/LifeCycle event, and loves avocados.

Zoë Elton On a recent trip to Ouagadougou, a man in the bank looked over and said, 'Why would anyone want to travel all this way just to look at films?' Zoë Elton has been pondering this ever since, as programming the Mill Valley Film Festival regularly takes her to Berlin, Cannes, Havana, Tehran – and Ouaga.

Jeff Greenwald is a contributing editor for *Yoga Journal*, *Tricycle* and *Travel+Life* magazines, and serves as Executive Director of Ethical Traveler, a global alliance of travelers dedicated to human rights and environmental protection (www.ethicaltraveler.org). He has also written a number of books, including *Shopping for Buddhas*, *The Size of the World* and *Scratching the Surface: Impressions of Planet Earth from Hollywood to Shiraz*. Jeff is Oakland based.

Tara Duggan was a travel writer and editor before attending San Francisco's Culinary Academy and becoming a food writer. She is now on the staff at the *San Francisco Chronicle* Food section, where her reporting has won her the James Beard Foundation award. Tara lives in San Francisco with her husband and daughter.

Getting Started

The main thing to keep in mind about traveling in the USA – besides costs – is the continent's immense scale. Texas alone is twice the size of Germany. It's easy to get overambitious. The best strategy is to choose a region and dig into it a little deeper, rather than hopscotch around trying to snag all the USA's highlights in one trip. This guide is organized with that idea in mind. Unless the point is to have a road trip, you don't want to spend all your time on the road.

Which brings up another issue: cars. Unless your budget won't allow it, you'll probably want to rent a car at some point, as it's the easiest, most flexible way to travel outside of the major cities (where, incidentally, you usually *don't* want a car). If time is short, consider flying between distant destinations. Transportation logistics are all-important, and you should carefully balance cost against travel time and flexibility.

WHEN TO GO

Snowing or sunny, anytime is the perfect time to see the USA.

Nevertheless, the main holiday season is summer, which is bounded by Memorial Day (the last Monday in May) and Labor Day (the first Monday in September). In summer, hotels charge more and crowds are more crowded, but sometimes you have to strike while the iron is hot: mountain parks and gorgeous beaches are just not the same without the presence of a warm, beaming sun.

That said, one region's high season can be another one's hell: July in the Pacific Northwest is wonderful, but in the deserts of the Southwest it's brutally hot. As a general rule, latitude and altitude are your main guides in determining weather and season: the higher you go, and the further north, the later summer arrives and the earlier winter begins. The USA is so big that exceptions abound, so see the Geography & Climate sections at the beginning of each regional chapter for destination-specific advice, and for current information, visit www.weather.com.

One travel truism is that spring and fall are often the best seasons. The shoulder seasons – roughly March to May (spring) and September to November (fall) – tend to avoid the extremes of weather, prices sometimes drop and scenery is often at its peak. Again, check your destination: spring may not arrive until May or even June in the Rocky Mountains or Sierra Nevada, or it may bring an off-putting amount of rain, as it can in Seattle.

Winter is high season in ski areas, and the cold drives the snowbirds south. With careful planning, however, a successful winter trip can yield the riches of America's landscape virtually all to yourself.

Whether you're planning to join them or avoid them, holidays (p1151) and festivals (p1150) are another thing to consider as you make plans.

COSTS & MONEY

The USA can be a very expensive place to visit or a relatively economical one – excluding the cost to get there – depending on when, how and where you go. Almost any budget can be accommodated.

To begin, it's hard to travel cheaper than $50 a day; a comfortable midrange budget is $120 to $200 a day; and if you have $250 or more a day to spend, you're sleeping and eating very well and throwing in plenty of entertainment and activities.

See Climate Charts (p1146) for more information.

> ### DON'T LEAVE HOME WITHOUT...
>
> ■ Checking the US visa and passport requirements (p1158) as they continue evolving post–September 11.
>
> ■ A copy of your travel insurance policy (p1152).
>
> ■ Hotel or camping reservations (p1140). Seriously – sometimes everything's booked!
>
> ■ Your driver's license and adequate liability insurance (p1175). The country's big – you'll want to drive.
>
> ■ A handful of credit cards or a healthy bank account. Figure out your budget, but be prepared in case you need extra.
>
> ■ Setting up your own blog (p63) to keep track of your travels.
>
> ■ An open mind. Americans tend to confound expectations. There are elites in the Ozarks and hicks in Manhattan, and everything in between.

Whether you visit a major city and how long you stay there is a big factor in how much you'll spend. In a city, everything is at a premium – from cabs to drinks to lodging. The minimum for a good midrange hotel will be $100 to $150, while dinners might average $30 to $40 per person. Conversely, midrange lodgings in small towns and rural areas can drop to $60 and meals are much cheaper. Visit a popular national park on a high season weekend, though, and it can be as or even more expensive than Manhattan: with a captive audience, hotels and restaurants spike prices as much as they can.

If you want to travel on the cheap, plan on camping or staying in hostels, though costs for these are going up. Hostel beds generally run from $15 to $25, while campsites run from $10 to $20 or more, depending on the park and the season. You'll need to make your own food, too – though if you can stand it, fast food is about as cheap as buying groceries.

Then, there's transportation. Renting a compact car is a minimum of $40 a day, and if you upgrade your vehicle and get all the insurance, it could easily reach $60 to $80 a day. This doesn't include gas, which can add $10 to $20 a day, depending on driving distances.

See p1148 for information on discounts.

TRAVEL LITERATURE

The American travelogue is its own literary genre, and many of the classics remain both enjoyable and relevant. In *Democracy in America* (1835–40), Alexis de Tocqueville distilled the philosophical underpinnings of the then-new American experiment, and it remains a first-rate, even pithy assessment of American sensibilities.

Mark Twain spent seven years going west – from St Louis to Virginia City, Nevada, and thence to San Francisco and Hawaii – in the hopes of making his fortune. *Roughing It* (1872) is his hilarious account of every indignity suffered along the way.

Those who prefer their commentary, like their coffee, bitter and black should stuff *The Air-Conditioned Nightmare* (1945) by Henry Miller in their bag. The irascible Miller canvassed America during WWII, and the similarities to now are startling.

Celebrated travel writer Jan Morris was clearly smitten with America in *Coast to Coast* (1956); her account is crisp, clear and elegantly thoughtful. Her experiences in the pre–Civil Rights South are truly poignant.

> **HOW MUCH?**
>
> Movie ticket: $9-10
>
> Single latte: $2.50-3
>
> Gallon of milk: $3.20
>
> Internet access per hour: $3-5
>
> Bag of potato chips (16oz): $3.40
>
> See also Lonely Planet Index, inside front cover.

No book has done more to spur cross-country travel than Jack Kerouac's *On the Road* (1957). His headlong jazz style and lust for life inspire people still.

You could wish for no better companion and guide than John Steinbeck, who late in life set out with his poodle in a makeshift camper to

TOP TENS
HOEDOWNS & HOOTENANNIES

Americans love to party, and they've created so many great annual celebrations, it's painful to keep this list to only 10 – but still, at any of these, you're guaranteed a time to remember. (See p1150 for a list of other festivals and events throughout the country.)

- Rose Parade, Los Angeles (California), January 1 (p787)
- Sundance Film Festival, Park City (Utah), late January (p923)
- Mardi Gras, New Orleans (Louisiana), February or March (p418)
- South by Southwest, Austin (Texas), March (p724)
- Spoleto USA, Charleston (South Carolina), late May and early June (p484)

- Red Earth Native American Cultural Festival, Oklahoma City (Oklahoma), early June (p710)
- SF Gay Pride Month, San Francisco (California), June (p835)
- Blues Festival, Chicago (Illinois), early June (p585)
- American Royal Barbecue, Kansas City (Missouri), early October (p678)
- Fantasy Fest, Key West (Florida), late October (p518)

HIGHWAY 61 REVISITED

An American road trip needs a proper score. These albums and artists are some of the essential originals that contemporary American music is built on. Download them onto your iPod, hit shuffle and the miles will fly by. (See also p71.)

- Louis Armstrong, *Louis Armstrong and His Hot Fives and Hot Sevens*
- Johnny Cash, *Folsom Prison Blues*
- Bob Dylan, *Highway 61 Revisited*
- Ella Fitzgerald, *The Cole Porter Songbook*
- Jimi Hendrix, *Are You Experienced?*

- BB King, *Live at the Regal*
- Charles Mingus, *Mingus Ah Um*
- *O Brother, Where Art Thou?* movie soundtrack
- Elvis Presley, *Elvis' Golden Records*
- Public Enemy, *It Takes a Nation of Millions to Hold Us Back*

THE DREAM FACTORY

Here are 10 great Hollywood films that evoke a vivid slice of the American experience. These films and filmmakers are the dream-makers who have helped craft the nation's mythologies. (See also p80.)

- *The General* (1927) Dir: Buster Keaton and Clyde Bruckman
- *Gone with the Wind* (1939) Dir: Victor Fleming
- *Citizen Kane* (1941) Dir: Orson Welles
- *The Searchers* (1956) Dir: John Ford
- *West Side Story* (1961) Dir: Robert Wise and Jerome Robbins

- *The Godfather* trilogy (1971–90) Dir: Francis Ford Coppola
- *Chinatown* (1974) Dir: Roman Polanski
- *Blue Velvet* (1986) Dir: David Lynch
- *Fargo* (1996) Dir: Joel Coen
- *25th Hour* (2003) Dir: Spike Lee

reacquaint himself with America. *Travels with Charley* (1962) is sharp, funny, noble and filled with wise, road-tested advice.

At a crossroad in life, William Least Heat-Moon set out on a 13,000-mile circuit of America's back roads. The poetic result, *Blue Highways* (1982), is a moving pastiche of everyday Americans as it follows one man's attempt to find himself by losing himself.

On the Rez (2000) by Ian Frazier is not strictly a travelogue, but it gives a good taste of what it's like to be friends with an Oglala Sioux, and of what Native American and reservation life is like today. It is a journey of miles and history and heart that goes into America, rather than across it.

With a restless spirit and buoyant wry humor, Brad Herzog tours the tiny, famously named towns of America (Paris, London, Mecca) in *Small World* (2004), meeting regular folks, pondering his own fatherhood, asking good questions and living the journey.

See p67 for further information on American literature.

INTERNET RESOURCES

Bathroom Diaries (www.thebathroomdiaries.com) A compilation of clean bathrooms in every state in the USA (not to mention 100 other countries). Its bathroom stories are a hoot.

Connected Traveler (www.connectedtraveler.com) Humorous and opinionated travel stories and advice, from the esoteric to the mundane, and a ton of travel resources.

Eccentric America (www.eccentricamerica.com) This wonderful travel guide's website can facilitate your search for native weirdness; nice photos and great links.

Firstgov.gov (http://firstgov.gov/Citizen/Topics/Travel.shtml) The closest thing to a national tourism information resource, on the US government's official website.

Google Maps (www.maps.google.com) This is a useful streetfinder with an exciting satellite-imagery toggle.

Lonely Planet (www.lonelyplanet.com) US travel news and summaries, the Thorn Tree bulletin board, and links to more web resources.

Itineraries

CLASSIC ROUTES

CITY MOUSE, COUNTRY MOUSE   Three to five weeks/Boston to Miami

The USA's crowded eastern seaboard packs in as much bustle, culture, history and fun as most visitors can handle.

Arrive in **Boston** (p224), whose Revolutionary history and university life make a fine introduction to the USA. Cruise down to **New York City** (p126), where Lady Liberty waves to Manhattan. Allow four days.

You're not worn out already?! **Philadelphia** (p187) has cheesesteaks and Independence Hall, **Baltimore** (p323) dishes up crab cakes and a world-class aquarium, and **Washington, DC** (p303) is a don't-miss repository of epic museums and national history. Oh, and the US government.

But that's enough city streets. Now take I-66 west to **Shenandoah National Park** (p360) then follow the **Blue Ridge Parkway** (p363) to **Great Smoky Mountains National Park** (p473). Relaxed again, preserve the mood by heading east on I-26 to South Carolina's gracious **Charleston** (p477), and farther south on I-95 to Georgia's sultry, decadent **Savannah** (p389).

If you need a pick-me-up, Florida's **St Augustine** (p529) has Juan Ponce de León's fountain of youth, while **Daytona Beach** (p527) has miles of don't-wake-me beaches. End your trip in **Miami** (p496) with some sweaty Cuban jazz and a cool *mojito* (rum cocktail).

History buffs should clear their calendar for this immersion in the USA's founding cities and seminal events: in something over 1600 miles you'll journey from Pilgrims to Revolution to Civil War to Reconstruction to modern-day politics and culture. Or, skip the boring stuff and just revel in all that is urban and Appalachian about America.

PACIFIC COAST DREAMS   Three to six weeks/Seattle to San Diego

Traversing the USA's West Coast is a dream trip, including a wealth of natural and cultural highlights. However, it can be extremely slow. You might want to pick and choose destinations, and then leave the coast in between (inland on I-5) to make better time.

Seattle (p1034) is the main entry point in the Pacific Northwest. Grab a coffee, then head straight for the ancient rain forests of the **Olympic Peninsula** (p1051). From here, take Hwy 101 south along the rugged, scenic **Oregon Coast** (p1077). It's also worth a sidetrip to livable, liberal **Portland** (p1058).

When you reach **California's North Coast** (p849), you pass through towering old-growth redwood forests. If you have time, stick to the coast along the Pacific Coast Hwy (Hwy 1), or zip more quickly along Hwy 101 to **San Francisco** (p822). Vibrant, beautiful and hedonistic, the 'City that Knows How' is worth two to four days.

Next up are funky **Santa Cruz** (p821) and the very beautiful **Monterey Peninsula** (p818), both of which offer lots of opportunities to play outdoors. Whatever you do, don't miss the stretch of Hwy 1 through the natural splendor of **Big Sur** (p817) or the ostentatious splendor of **Hearst Castle** (p816).

Los Angeles (p773) is the next major destination, and it's easy to stretch out and enjoy its fine art, Hollywood glamour and warm beaches. Then don a pair of mouse ears at **Disneyland** (p796) and complete the journey in **San Diego** (p796), which has interesting museums and great beaches, and allows for an easy jaunt across the border for a journey into **Tijuana, Mexico** (p806).

The country's best wine, beer and coffee? Here. The country's cultural dream-makers and trendsetters? Here. Robust native cultures and thriving immigrant communities? Here. Ancient forests? Here. Beaches and surfing? Here. The best coastal drive in the USA? Most definitely the 1500 curvy miles here.

THE MAIN STREET OF AMERICA   One week/Chicago to Los Angeles

Route 66, or the Great Mother Road, is a nostalgic driving tour that passes a wealth of quintessential, wacky, shake-your-head-in-disbelief Americana. Only portions of the original highway remain; today it has either been paralleled or replaced by newer interstates.

For detailed route descriptions, see 'Route 66' boxed texts in each of the eight states the road passes through.

Good websites are www.national66.com, with Route 66 history and maps for sale, and www.historic66.com, which has turn-by-turn driving directions.

Route 66 starts in **Chicago** (p597), Illinois. You'll pass Burma Shave signs and the birthplace of the corn dog on the way to **St Louis** (p674), Missouri.

Kansas (p706) gets a whole 13 miles of Route 66 before it cuts across **Oklahoma** (p712) for 400 miles, including stops in Tulsa and Oklahoma City.

Route 66 then grabs the panhandle of **Texas** (p758), a section that includes the halfway point and a plethora of cars stuck in the ground.

In **New Mexico** (p943) the road passes Acoma Pueblo and Santa Fe, and in **Arizona** (p908) you'll find the longest uninterrupted section of the original route as well as several small towns that are on a serious nostalgia binge.

Once you enter **California** (p811), you're in the home stretch. There are more museums, the original McDonald's and the end of the road in Los Angeles' Santa Monica – where a delicious beach and boardwalk await road-weary legs and bums.

This trip takes you back to when cars and highways were just reshaping America, to when travel became democratized. Route 66 is a memorial to that first delicious, delirious rush of freedom.

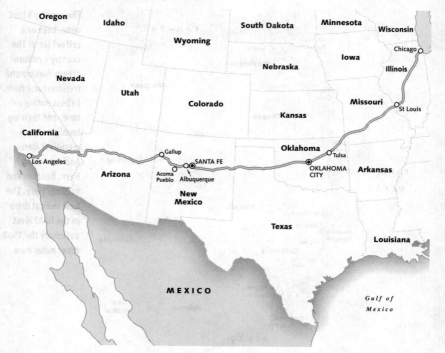

THE GREAT RIVER ROAD   10 days to two weeks/Minneapolis to New Orleans

The Mississippi River marks a physical and psychological divide, and along this spine runs America's greatest music: blues, jazz, and rock and roll. Hwy 61 is the legendary route, though numerous other roads join up, run parallel and intersect with it.

Progressive, artistic, youthful **Minneapolis** (p646) is the easiest starting point, though some might want to start further north in **Hibbing** (p659), Bob Dylan's birthplace. Hwy 61 then winds scenically on either side of the Mississippi River to **Hannibal** (p673), Missouri, the birthplace of Mark Twain. Gateway to the West, **St Louis** (p666) also bills itself as the 'Home of the Blues,' though original rock-and-roller Chuck Berry still plays here, too.

The next major destination is **Memphis** (p438), where you can pay homage to Elvis Presley at Graceland and to rock and roll at Sun Studio. To complete your musical pilgrimage, take a quick detour on I-40 to **Nashville** (p447), the home of country music. South of Memphis, Hwy 61 runs through the **Mississippi Delta** (p405), where the blues was born: **Clarksdale** (p406) is where Robert Johnson bargained with the devil. The town's still jumpin' with blues joints, while **Natchez** (p410) is full of antebellum homes.

South of Baton Rouge, a detour along Hwy 1 leads past the famous 19th-century **Mississippi River Plantations** (p427).

Then you arrive at **New Orleans** (p412), birthplace of jazz. The 'Big Easy,' despite its recent hard times (p39), is a place where lazy mornings blend into late nights, and you should leave plenty of time to go with the flow.

Just about all of the epic, legendary, even revolutionary history of American music can be experienced along this 1200-mile stretch of the Mississippi River. Throw in a 400-mile sidetrip to Nashville, and what you have is the musical journey of a lifetime.

THE CROSS-COUNTRY JOURNEY

**Two weeks to one month/
New York to Los Angeles**

Gas up, check your oil and start your engine – here is one of several unforgettable routes across the continent. But watch out, the rhythm of driving can sometimes take over and before you know it you're staring at the Pacific. If you wind up in LA long before you mean to be, go to **Disneyland** (p796).

Start with a few days in **New York City** (p126), then go east on I-80. At the Pennsylvania state line is the lovely **Delaware Water Gap** (p182); from here make tracks for **Cleveland** (p606), where the **Rock & Roll Hall of Fame & Museum** (p608) beckons. From here, detour south on I-71 and back in time by visiting Ohio's **Amish Country** (p612). Then, back on I-80, at Toledo make a detour north on I-75 to **Detroit** (p621) before returning again to I-80 and beelining for the Windy City, **Chicago** (p567).

Head into the heartland on I-80. In **Iowa** (p680), check out the **Iowa 80 Truckstop Hall of Fame** (p683) on the state line, then enjoy a good steak in **Omaha** (p699). As I-80 unfurls through Nebraska, pick up I-76 and head southwest to the 'Mile High City,' **Denver** (p966).

From here, make a loop through **Boulder** (p972) and **Rocky Mountain National Park** (p975) and back to I-70, where the ski resorts of **Breckenridge** (p982) and **Vail** (p984) beckon in winter. Once in **Utah** (p915), detour to **Moab** (p928), **Arches National Park** (p929) and **Canyonlands National Park** (p930).

Take I-70 to I-15 and head south, stopping for the red rocks of **Zion National Park** (p935) and, further, the neon of **Las Vegas** (p874). From here, it's a straight shot through the **Mojave Desert** (p810) to stylish **Los Angeles** (p773). Whew!

This is the trip you have to do at least once – coast to coast, sunrise over the Atlantic to sunset over the Pacific. It's 3000 miles, give or take. Some do it in days, others take months. There's no right or wrong, no rules, no 'best' route. Just go.

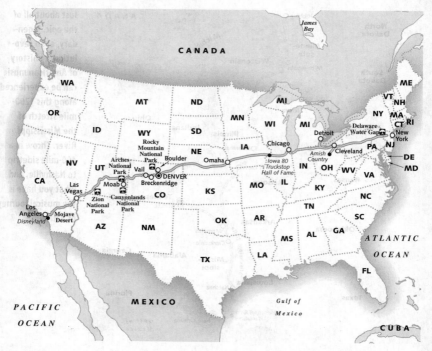

ROADS LESS TRAVELED

THE GRAND CIRCLE   Two to four weeks/Las Vegas to Las Vegas

In another era, the Grand Circle was a leisure-class journey to all the rugged, raw natural splendors of the New World. It took several months, and still can, but today you only need a few weeks to witness some of the most amazing geological spectacles Mother Nature has yet devised – as well as get acquainted with the Southwest's Native Americans.

Nothing natural about **Las Vegas** (p874), but it sure is a fun place to start. From here, take I-15 northeast to Utah's **Zion National Park** (p935). Catch Hwy 89 and then go east on **Hwy 12** (p931) – one of the most amazing drives in the world, containing as it does **Bryce Canyon National Park** (p933), the **Grand Staircase-Escalante National Monument** (p933) and **Capitol Reef National Park** (p931). You'll gain a new appreciation for rock.

Take Hwy 24 to I-70, head east, then catch Hwy 191 south to **Moab** (p928), **Arches National Park** (p929) and **Canyonlands National Park** (p930), which are already beyond belief – and you're not even halfway home. Head southeast on Hwy 666 to **Mesa Verde National Park** (p992), then take your cultural wonder west on Hwy 160 to **Monument Valley** (p907) and the **Navajo National Monument** (p907). Double back to go south on Hwy 191 to catch **Canyon de Chelly National Monument** (p907), then west on Hwy 264 through the mesas of the **Hopi Indian Reservation** (p907).

Next, it's the granddaddy of river erosion, **Grand Canyon National Park** (p901). Go south and clean up in **Flagstaff** (p896), then return to Las Vegas by I-40 and Hwy 93, pausing to admire the concrete pile called **Hoover Dam** (p883).

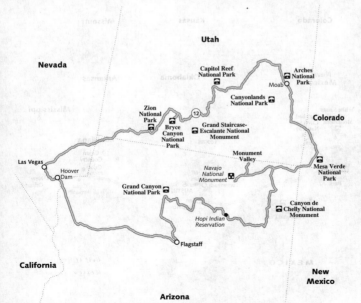

Canyons a mile deep, deserts painted a rainbow, crumbling buttes, pueblo-topped mesas, ancient civilizations hidden in the cliffs – you can't make this stuff up. To see it all requires 1400 brutal miles of slow, sun-baked roads, and it's worth every saddle sore.

BAYOUS & BACK ROADS   Two to three weeks/New Orleans to Tucson

So you want to get away from it all? Escaping the law? Head into the swampy bayous and sunburned hills of the South – if you're lucky, the sheriff will race you only to the county line.

Start in **New Orleans** (p412), a big city that nevertheless knows how to relax. After a few days, and once you've sobered up, drop into French-speaking **Cajun Country** (p428). Get lost in the **Cajun Wetlands** (p430), dodge gators on swamp tours, then hit the northern **Cajun Prairie** (p431) for zydeco music and crawfish boils.

Slip into Texas, skip Houston, and go straight for **Austin** (p721), where the dimly lit, loud honky-tonks make great hideouts. **Hill Country** (p728) back roads lead to world-class barbecue, Texas wines, wildflowers and **Luckenbach** (p729), a state of mind if ever there was one. Visit **San Antonio** (p730), remember the Alamo, then skedaddle on Hwy 90 – a long bit of nothing that leads to an even bigger nowhere: **Big Bend National Park** (p763), maybe America's best-kept secret.

Take lonely Hwy 54 north of I-10 to **Guadalupe Mountains National Park** (p760) and then into New Mexico, where **Carlsbad Caverns National Park** (p959) and, further west, **White Sands National Monument** (p957) provide you with many ways to escape. For a lesson in how to hide among the cliffs, just keep wandering west on I-70 and Hwy 180 to the **Gila Cliff Dwellings** (p956).

Now, unfortunately, it's time to pack it in. End at **Tucson** (p909) and make like the many-limbed cacti in surrounding **Saguaro National Park** (p913). Put your arms up and surrender. As the song goes, you fought the law, and the law won.

> In the South, they know life is best enjoyed outside, next to a barbecue, with a beer and a band picking up steam. Get lost for 2000 miles in Cajun Country, the Texas Hills and the New Mexican desert. Ain't nothin' more important than the crawfish in the pot and learning how to two-step.

THE GREAT LAKES   Two to three weeks/Chicago to New York

The five Great Lakes are the largest source of fresh water in the world, and the USA shares them with its chipper northern neighbor Canada – which is easy to visit (see Lonely Planet's *Canada* for more). This is a trip of magnificent, lonely wilderness, sophisticated urbanity and Midwestern charm.

Start in **Chicago** (p567), dip a toe in Lake Michigan, then take I-94 to Wisconsin's **Milwaukee** (p636) and **Madison** (p640); a short trip west on Hwy 60 leads to **Taliesin** (p641), the mother of Frank Lloyd Wright sights. Continue on I-94 northwest to **Minneapolis** (p646), which isn't just cold, it's cool.

Now, leave the big cities behind and take I-35 north; at Duluth, go east on Hwy 13 to Wisconsin's rugged **Apostle Islands** (p645) in Lake Superior. Make your way north along the heel of Michigan's Upper Peninsula 'slipper' to Houghton, where you can catch a ferry to **Isle Royale National Park** (p635), home to wolves, moose and bears, but no cars.

Then take Hwy 41 through **Marquette** (p635), Hwy 28 to **Pictured Rocks** (p634), and Hwy 2 to the awesome bridge over the **Straits of Mackinac** (p632), which divide Lake Superior from Lake Huron.

After a quick visit to **Mackinac Island** (p633), take I-75 to **Detroit** (p621), then skirt Lake Erie on I-90 till you get to New York's famous **Niagara Falls** (p178), where Lake Ontario pours over the cliffs. Cross to the Canadian side for the best views.

Now you've seen all five Great Lakes! But keep traveling on to **New York City** (p126) anyway.

You've come this far, why stop now?

If all you want is to get from Chicago to Manhattan, it's 820 highway miles: two modest days. Triple the distance, turn two days into two weeks, and you'll discover just how friendly the USA can be – and how lush, forested and wild.

ALASKA'S INSIDE PASSAGE   One to three weeks/Bellingham to Skagway

You can take a car, but if you are looking for an unforgettable journey that doesn't involve an automobile, consider cruising Alaska's Inside Passage.

In summer the Alaska Marine Hwy ferries stop at towns nearly every day, and with advance notice you can get on and off at every one, just as long as you keep traveling in the same direction. See p1086 for ferry information.

Fly into **Seattle** (p1034), Washington, and linger awhile there or take a shuttle directly to **Bellingham** (p1054), where you catch the Alaska Marine Hwy.

The first stop is **Ketchikan** (p1087), which still has a rugged Western feel. It might be worth renting a car once you land on **Prince of Wales Island** (p1088), which is the third-largest island in the USA.

Wrangell (p1088) was founded by Russians, while pretty **Petersburg** (p1089) has a Norwegian heritage. Rich with Native American culture and beautifully situated,

Sitka (p1090) shouldn't be missed. Busy **Juneau** (p1091) is Alaska's capital, and from here it's easy to get close to magnificent **Mendenhall Glacier** (p1092).

Haines (p1094) is another sizable town, and **Skagway** (p1095) is the end of the line. It is a well-preserved, nonthreatening version of its once-lawless gold-rush self.

You can also fly into or out of Juneau, or make it a round-trip and take the ferry back to Bellingham.

A trip through Alaska's Inside Passage is proof that Mother Nature is a wild woman. Awesome doesn't even begin to describe it. Calving glaciers, ancient forests as thick as night, pods of whales, skies full of eagles: it may be the most memorable trip you ever take.

TAILORED TRIPS

DUDE, THAT'S WEIRD

Combine a fierce sense of independence with a vast landscape, and what you get is a bunch of crazies giving free rein to their obsessions. They call it 'Americana,' but after a while it gets a little scary. Proceed at your own risk.

You'd think DC would know better, but the **National Museum of Health & Medicine** (p315) is seriously weird. Florida's **Coral Castle** (p511) is one of America's many iterations of Stonehenge; here it's evidence of love gone horribly awry. Or join Floridians as they throw fish (competitively!) in the **Interstate Mullet Toss** (p560) in Perdido Key. In Iowa's cornfields you can practice yogic flying at **Vedic City** (p682), while Houston has the **Beer Can House** (p739) and **Art Car Museum** (p739). In California, admire the majestic junk-pile that is **Nitt Witt Ridge** (p816), or learn the *truth* about Bigfoot at the **Bigfoot Discovery Museum** (p821) outside Santa Cruz.

Then there are the classics: South Dakota's **Corn Palace** (p690), **Mt Rushmore** (p696) and **Crazy Horse Memorial** (p696); New Mexico's **Very Large Array** (p955); Wisconsin's **Dr Evermor's Sculpture Park** (p642); Colorado's **UFO Watchtower** (p989); Minnesota's **Mall of America** (p651); and the entire city of **Las Vegas** (p874). Dude, now *that's* weird.

ISLAND-HOPPING

Everybody wants to go across the USA, but traveling around it is an even better trip. Start at Maine's **Acadia National Park** (p294) for a sunrise hike. Then go to historic **Martha's Vineyard** (p249), from where it's a quick tack to the USA's most famous island, **Manhattan** (p126). Off the Virginia coast is **Chincoteague Island** (p358), famous for its wild horses, and off North Carolina are the **Outer Banks** (p467) and **Cape Hatteras National Seashore** (p468), where the Wright brothers learned to fly, and you can too – by hang gliding.

Florida boasts **Amelia Island** (p532), the string-of-pearls **Florida Keys** (p512), the islands of **Dry Tortugas National Park** (p520) and shell collecting on **Sanibel** and **Captiva Islands** (p533).

Continuing along the Gulf of Mexico is Texas' resort town of **Galveston** (p743) and the gorgeously wild **Padre Island National Seashore** (p745) – not to be confused with **South Padre Island** (p745), where 'gorgeous and wild' describes the coeds.

At this point, sail through the Panama Canal or go overland to California, where **Catalina Island** (p795) has great snorkeling and **Channel Islands National Park** (p813) is 'California's Galápagos.' Keep going to Washington's **San Juan Islands** (p1054) – and finally, of course, don't forget **Hawaii** (p1115).

WE'RE HERE, WE'RE QUEER

It's never been more fun to be gay in the USA. Despite the current gay marriage brouhaha, gay travelers will find numerous places where they can be themselves without thinking twice. Sure, these places are mainly in the big cities, but cities are the most fun anyway! For more, see 'Gay City' boxed texts in the regional chapters.

Manhattan (p126) is too crowded, busy and cosmopolitan to bother worrying about such things, while **Fire Island** (p169) is, as it always has been, the hot, sandy gay mecca on Long Island. However, **Philadelphia** (p187), **Washington, DC** (p303) and **Provincetown** (p246), Massachusetts, also have major scenes.

Going south, steamy **'Hotlanta'** (p378) and sexy **Savannah** (p389), Georgia, know how to work up a sweat. In Florida, **Miami** (p496) and the 'Conch Republic' of **Key West** (p516) have long supported thriving gay communities. Then, of course, in anything-goes **New Orleans** (p412), anything goes.

Minnesota's **Twin Cities** (p646) support a gay community that is second only to the holy of holies, San Francisco, in its percentage of gay residents. Speaking of **San Francisco** (p822), this birthplace of gay rights is a must-stop for any gay traveler, and **Los Angeles** (p773) has an equally robust scene (it's the home of *Hollywood*, darling).

Lastly, **Hawaii** (p1115) is pretty gay-friendly overall, but particularly in **Waikiki** (p1120).

OH, TO BE A KID AGAIN

Traveling with children is a good excuse to do all the things you're too old to do on your own any more without feeling like, you know, an overgrown kid – the truth is, Disneyland is fun! In addition to the highlights here, most of the entries for major cities have a 'City for Children' section listing many more ideas.

The original **Disneyland** (p796) is in California, and nearby is **Legoland** (p807), but the mecca for theme parks is **Orlando** (p538), Florida: **Walt Disney World** (p553) is but the largest of a dozen or more. In **Washington, DC** (p303), the mall museums are very kid-worthy, while **Baltimore** (p323) has a truly outstanding aquarium and duckpin bowling.

Beaches are no-fail destinations, but in particular seek out the old-fashioned boardwalk at **Santa Cruz** (p821), as well as family-friendly **Daytona Beach** (p527), Florida; **Myrtle Beach** (p487), South Carolina; and **Jones Beach** (p169), Long Island.

For winter fun, Colorado's ski resorts at **Aspen** (p986) and **Vail** (p984) have notably strong kid programs – perhaps so mom and dad can enjoy a little slope time?

Nearly all national parks gear some of their hikes and programs for little legs and minds, though **Zion** (p935), **Yosemite** (p862), **Yellowstone** (p1004) and **Great Smoky Mountains** (p455) are particularly good.

Snapshot

Though US society is not as polarized as current politics sometimes makes it seem, America nevertheless *feels* as divided and divisive as ever. A certain raw extremism pulls at national debates, and centrist efforts at compromise are often drowned out as many prefer to choose sides, cross their arms and start shouting.

The red state/blue state national maps that chart who votes for whom in presidential elections (red being Republican, blue Democrat) are frequently cited as the defining symbol of America's current either/or landscape. President Bush won the elections in 2000 and 2004, both by the slimmest of margins, and the voting maps have been virtually identical: the Rocky Mountains, the Great Plains and the entire South are an unending sea of rural red, while the Northeast, the West Coast and the Great Lakes are urbanized islands of blue.

For his part, President Bush has helped fan the flames of partisan discord, quickly proclaiming a 'mandate' after each election and making few efforts to 'reach across the aisle' when enacting his agenda, whether concerning domestic matters or foreign policy. Then again, Bush's popularity in the polls began slipping in 2005, and whether by coincidence or not, the Bush administration started showing some signs of accommodation and compromise.

The main reason for Bush's dip in popularity is the ongoing conflict in Iraq, which began in spring 2003 as a centerpiece of Bush's war on terrorism in the wake of September 11 (p53). Citing US intelligence that Iraq had assisted the September 11 terrorists and was in possession of 'weapons of mass destruction,' Bush launched a preemptive attack and took over the country. Neither charge has turned out to be true: no link connecting Iraq to the September 11 terrorists has been found, nor have any weapons. Some Americans believe that doesn't matter: a Middle East dictator has been toppled and replaced with a nascent, democratically elected Iraqi government. But criticism of how the Bush administration precipitated and is now conducting the war keeps rising along with US casualties. Today, polls show about half of America now considers the war a mistake, and some believe the war in Iraq was never justified and that US military aggressiveness and self-justification are only emboldening other nations to behave likewise.

As of November 2005, the US had spent $300 billion on the war, it had around 150,000 US troops stationed in Iraq, and the number of US deaths was over 2050. Iraqi civilian deaths were estimated at over 30,000, but most likely are much higher (for updates, see www.iraqbodycount.net). As fighting continues, the Bush administration is trying to create a viable military exit strategy while avoiding putting a timetable on the process.

As for the US economy, it has recovered since the dot-com crash of 2000, but unevenly, and the recovery has been financed largely by borrowed cash. The 2006 federal budget of $2.56 trillion includes a deficit of $382 billion (but does not include spending on the Iraq conflict), which follows similar annual deficits since 2002. The total federal debt was $3.4 trillion in 2005, with the expectation that it would rise to at least $4.3 trillion in the next 10 years. One reason for high annual budget deficits is President Bush's multiple tax cuts, which have predominantly helped the wealthy, and which if extended permanently, as he wishes, would increase the federal debt another $1.8 trillion.

FAST FACTS

Population: 295.7 million

Gross domestic product (GDP): $11.7 trillion

Total public debt as a percentage of the GDP: 65%

Inflation: 2.5%

Unemployment: 5.5%

Number of computers connected to the Internet: 115.3 million

Adult literacy rate: 97%

Total military spending in 2004: $370.7 billion

Barrels of oil consumed per day: 19.65 million

Total length of highways, paved and unpaved: 4 million miles

These numbers undersell the problem. A trade deficit that now tops $600 billion annually makes it hard for the US to catch up, and as the government wrestles with how to reform and afford gargantuan entitlement programs like Medicare and Social Security – which will further balloon as the baby boom generation begins to retire in the next few years – several trillion dollars more in debt could be added. The Bush administration contends deficits are necessary to spend the country back into prosperity, but Democrats and even some Republicans fear the country's now record-breaking debt will make prosperity impossible and disaster likely.

In 2005, nature may have assured that economic prediction by providing a disaster all her own. On August 29, Hurricane Katrina slammed into the Mississippi and Louisiana coasts, destroying communities, rupturing levees and flooding below-sea-level New Orleans as if it were an empty bowl. When it was over, one of America's great cities had been transformed into a chaos of wreckage and death; for a description of the hurricane and its immediate aftermath, see 'A City Underwater,' p413. Though the region will recover, and New Orleans will be rebuilt – in fact, some areas, like the French Quarter, were largely spared – tallies of the hurricane's costs are sobering. As of October 2005, estimates were that 1100 to 1300 people lost their lives, over a million people had been displaced, and the economic cost was predicted to total between $100 and $200 billion, making it the most expensive natural disaster in US history.

Another political flashpoint is immigration, which continues at a phenomenal pace (p59) and, according to one controversial study, accounted for nearly all growth in US employment from 2000 to 2004. Meanwhile, illegal immigration continues almost unchecked, a situation all observers agree is untenable. The Bush administration initially pledged to increase US–Mexican border security, but hasn't funded it, and it has turned a blind eye to businesses that hire illegal immigrants. In 2005, President Bush tentatively supported implementing a 'guest worker' program to provide a legal framework for the seasonal farm jobs most illegal immigrants come for. However, a right-wing group calling itself the 'Minutemen' has gotten fed up: armed with guns and binoculars, these citizens have engaged in border patrol 'demonstrations' aimed at stopping illegals and embarrassing the government into action. Civil rights groups are, predictably, horrified.

As with war, the economy and immigration, more deep schisms have evolved over the environment (p96), judicial appointments, gay marriage (p832 and p263), continuance of the Patriot Act (p1153), energy policy, stem-cell research and public school reform (p58). As an evangelical Christian, President Bush has tacitly and sometimes actively encouraged the Religious Right to press its ultraconservative political agenda (p62), and their extreme rhetoric has further hardened emotions. The Bush administration is also one of the most secretive of the modern era; it has fought vigorously to keep controversial records and meetings from public scrutiny, even as it asks average citizens to permanently allow federal intrusions into their private records in the name of national security.

To summarize, either President Bush is seen as a folksy but tough hero who has defended America and brought a refreshing religious and moral perspective to the White House, or he is seen as an example of the Republican hypocrisy that vilifies federal control of business but champions federal control of morality, and his policies have, as one newspaper editorial put it, 'reversed the very essence of democracy.'

Choose one.

History

Ryan Ver Berkmoes

EARLY ARRIVALS

Humans first arrived in North America some 20,000 to 30,000 years ago. Most likely they migrated from Asia over a land bridge that existed between today's Siberia and Alaska. In what has become the USA, evidence of the large and flourishing cultures created by these people can be found at Cahokia Mounds (p598) in Illinois and at Chaco (p954) in New Mexico, among other places.

Europeans only washed ashore – literally – in the last 1000 years. The big name in US discovery is Christopher Columbus, the Italian navigator who made three voyages in search of the Orient and instead stumbled upon some small islands in the Bahamas. But unlike previous European seafarers (Vikings, Celts and even an Irish priest are thought to have visited the Americas in the centuries before Columbus' 1492 adventure), Columbus had the backing of Spain, which meant that news of his 'discoveries' was disseminated widely.

Spain followed up with a gaggle of explorers who claimed much of the Americas for their empire. Among them were Hernán Cortés, who conquered much of today's Mexico and set the stage for Spain's colonization of California, and Juan Ponce de León, who stumbled around Florida looking for the fountain of youth.

Meanwhile, the other European powers didn't sit back while Spaniards ran unchecked around the 'New World.' In 1524 Giovanni da Verrazano led a French group that explored the coast of North America from the Carolinas to Canada. Later expeditions pushed further into Canada and the fur-rich regions of today's Midwest, as well as north from Louisiana. In 1609 Henry Hudson claimed much of the region around the river that in today's New York bears his name. The Dutch got in on the act late, but scored a real deal when in 1624 a group of Dutch settlers bought Manhattan Island from local Native American tribes for a few beads and trinkets.

It was the English who were ultimately to have the most impact on colonizing the land that became the USA. In 1497 John Cabot charted the eastern coast of Canada, which led to an almost routine claim by the English to North America. However, their interests were elsewhere and for much of the 16th century they mostly ignored their 'claim.' The exceptions were due to Queen Elizabeth I, who didn't like her rivals the Spanish, but who did have a thing for pirates. She sent several to harass the Spanish in the New World. One, Sir Francis Drake, helped himself to heaps of Spanish booty and even got as far as today's San Francisco in his maraudings.

The paltry English efforts to colonize the eastern seaboard of America were marked by starvation and failure for much of the 16th century. However, victory over the Spanish Armada in 1588 helped focus attention on the New World. A group of businessmen started a colony at Jamestown (p354), Virginia, in 1607. A second colony was established in 1620 at Plymouth (p241), Massachusetts, by the Pilgrims, a group of

A People's History of the United States by Howard Zin is a delightful read that looks at history not from the perspective of rich white men but from that of the overlooked people who actually lived it: women, children, minorities, the poor and more.

Before 10,000 BC	1492
Migration from Asia to North America across Bering Strait	Columbus 'discovers' America, making landfall in the Bahamas

'Sick from their voyage across the Atlantic in the notoriously leaky *Mayflower* the Pilgrims poked at the ground futilely and starved'

conservative Protestants fleeing the Church of England. Unfortunately, in both cases the English repeated earlier mistakes. Jamestown was actually sited in a malarial swamp. Worse, the businessmen were definitely not farmers: they planted the wrong crops too late in the season and tried to get their equally unskilled butlers to do much of the work. In short order, half of the colonists were dead of disease or starvation. Meanwhile the Pilgrims were faring little better. Sick from their voyage across the Atlantic in the notoriously leaky *Mayflower* (they had rather gullibly bought the boat from a used-boat salesman who gave them a 'deal'), they poked at the ground futilely and starved.

In both Jamestown and Plymouth, it was the local tribes of Native Americans who saved the settlers by giving them food, and showing them how and when to grow local crops. So successful was this relationship that the thankful Pilgrims threw a harvest festival that is celebrated every year as Thanksgiving. (The original holiday was celebrated closer to the true harvest season of October, but in the 1940s it was moved to late November.)

Ultimately, relations between the colonists and the Native Americans took a fateful, and what would come to be all-too-familiar, turn: after a few successful harvests, the newcomers turned on the tribes, breaking treaties and stealing their land.

Jamestown was also the setting for two events in 1619 that were to shape the future USA. The settlers established a nascent form of representative democracy called the House of Burgesses (Citizens) to decide local matters. And in order to cope with the chronic labor shortage – crops of tobacco had found an eager market back in England and the settlers were still dying at a rapid rate – the first boatload of African slaves arrived.

GROWING PAINS

During the 17th and early 18th centuries, the English set up colonies along the eastern seaboard. In 1664 they booted the Dutch out of New Netherland and promptly changed the name to New York. In 1733 Georgia became the last of the 13 original colonies. Virginia's House of Burgesses was used by the colonies as a model for local government, although participation was limited to men who either owned property or paid taxes.

The population grew rapidly as the colonies became economically sound and such accoutrements of civilization as roads, governments and towns were established. In 1700 there were 250,000 colonists living in today's USA. Word of the opportunities in North American spread around Europe and immigrants – primarily from Germany, Scotland, Ireland and England – swelled the population to over 1.6 million by 1760. But not all of these newcomers were there by choice – slaves outnumbered colonists in the Carolinas by two to one.

With a growing population, it was natural for the colonies to expand westward, a process that lasted for 150 years until the tide of settlement hit the Pacific. By the mid-1700s, much of the land east of the Appalachian Mountains had been colonized. As settlers pushed into what is today the Midwest, they ran into the French, who were making money

1607	1620
First permanent English settlement at Jamestown, Virginia	*Mayflower* lands in Cape Cod with 102 English Pilgrims

from the fur trade with the Native Americans as well as exploiting the many natural resources along the Mississippi and other rivers south of the Great Lakes.

Just as France and Britain were in near-constant conflict in Europe, so too were they in North America. War broke out in 1756 and lasted for seven years. In the French and Indian War – a name that has flummoxed schoolchildren (and adults) ever since – the British successfully battled the French and their Native American allies, winning control of territory east of the Mississippi and north through Canada.

For the colonies, victory fuelled expansion westward, but it also came at a cost – literally. The British government, which had kept the colonies at arm's length, decided it needed help paying for the war and that some of the colonies' wealth should find its way back to London. The colonists reacted to these new taxes in a manner that has formed the basis of the average American's view of taxes ever since: they were not impressed. Protests and boycotts followed.

Not surprisingly, tensions grew. In 1770 a bunch of drunken seamen threw snowballs at a group of British soldiers on the wintry Boston waterfront. This attack brought a response of gunfire, and five colonials were killed. Colonists quickly made martyrs of the five in an incident that became known as the 'Boston Massacre.' London responded by half-heartedly rescinding some of the taxes and other repressive laws. But the colonists, led by Samuel Adams (for whom a pretty decent beer is named), believed that the colonies' brightest future lay with independence and they were not pacified. Things worsened in 1773 when England granted the East India Company a legal monopoly on tea sales to the colonies. Here was an issue the tea-drinking colonists could rally around. A band of Bostonians dressed up like Native Americans (fooling no one), boarded three tea-laden British ships in the harbor and tossed all their cargo overboard – an event known as the Boston Tea Party.

Boycotts and protests were one thing but spilling tea was another. The British clamped down hard with more troops, and new repressive laws and taxes. (One outcome of the Tea Party is that to this day America is a nation of coffee drinkers.) In 1774 colonial representatives met at the First Continental Congress in Philadelphia's Independence Hall to discuss what to do next. Those from New England and Virginia, from whence an inordinate number of early American leaders came, favored full independence while the rest of the colonies preferred more boycotts of British goods.

By the following year, the upstart colonists in Massachusetts were preparing for war. The British response was to raid towns throughout the colony to seize weapons. On seeing that the British were about to march, Paul Revere made his famous ride to warn colonists in Lexington and Concord. A series of gun battles ensued and the American Revolution had begun.

BREAKING THE SHACKLES

In May 1775 the Second Continental Congress met in Philadelphia. There, a leader for the American 'army' (really a ragtag collection of poorly armed farmers, hunters and merchants) was chosen. George

'England granted the East India Company a monopoly on tea sales to the colonies...here was an issue the colonists could rally around'

Washington, a wealthy Virginia farmer who had been a somewhat successful commander in the French and Indian War, volunteered to serve as general, unpaid. It was a deal too good for the Congress to pass up.

But the colonists still didn't like taxes – even if those taxes were funding their fight for independence. Washington found himself in charge of an army that was poorly paid (his troops regularly quit and returned to their farms for lack of pay) and very poorly equipped. In one low moment, the army almost starved while holed up in Valley Forge (p203), Pennsylvania, during the winter of 1777. At no point during the war were more than 5% of adult males in the colonies active in the army.

Fortunately for Washington, British commanders helped the colonial cause by usually behaving like a bunch of fools. Even the nickname 'Redcoats,' given to the British soldiers by the colonials, was based on a strategic blunder. The British Army's bright red uniforms made the soldiers easy targets for the colonials who did the ungentlemanly thing of hiding behind shrubs and picking the Brits off from behind.

Benjamin Franklin: An American Life by Walter Isaacson is a biography of one of the most brilliant, and definitely the most entertaining, of the founding fathers. Franklin squeezed several lifetimes of joy and accomplishment into his.

Working through the stifling summer of 1776, the Second Continental Congress proved to be a remarkable gathering of intellects that included Benjamin Franklin, Thomas Jefferson and John Hancock. The Congress produced the Declaration of Independence, which the delegates signed on July 4, 1776. The document – largely written by Jefferson – set out the principles that would be fundamental to the new nation. Passages such as 'We hold these truths to be self-evident, that all men are created equal, that they are endowed by their Creator with certain unalienable Rights, that among these are Life, Liberty and the pursuit of Happiness' have inspired generations since. At the last moment the Congress bowed to pressure from the Southern colonies and removed antislavery passages, a move that made the grand prose hollow and which was to have horrific consequences for the new nation in the decades to come.

Washington's army scored a major victory against the British at Saratoga, New York, in 1777. France, always looking for a chance to harass the British, began providing vital troops and supplies to the colonists. In 1781 the British surrendered at Yorktown, Virginia. Two years later the Treaty of Paris was signed, which gave the 'United States of America' full independence.

Looking forward to setting up shop after the war, the Second Continental Congress had drawn up the Articles of Confederation, which would form the basis of the new nation's government. The articles called for a loose confederation of states, as the colonies were now known. This arrangement quickly proved unworkable as the states started printing their own money, engaging in trade battles, squabbling about foreign policy and otherwise behaving like a bunch of chickens at feeding time. In 1787 another convention was held in Philadelphia and this produced a new scheme that had a strong federal government at its core. A complex array of checks and balances were built into the system, which called for a government of three branches: a congress of elected representatives, an executive branch under a president, and a supreme court. The Constitution came with an initial 10 amendments, which were called the Bill of Rights and included freedoms of the press, religion and speech. Battles to implement and interpret these rights have been a continuing part of American history.

1787	1791
Constitutional Convention in Philadelphia draws up the US Constitution	Bill of Rights adopted as constitutional amendments

George Washington was elected the first president in 1789. Meanwhile, Americans were breeding like rabbits and the population kept expanding west. The Constitution allowed for the formation of new states and in 1792 Kentucky became the first state west of the Appalachians. Third president, Thomas Jefferson, offered to buy the vital port of New Orleans and today's Louisiana and Mississippi from the French in 1803. But in a curious bit of bargaining the French responded by throwing in all their lands, including huge tracts of land in the Northwest. With the stroke of a pen the United States doubled in size. In order to see what he'd got for the taxpayers' $15 million, Jefferson ordered an expedition across the new territory to the Pacific. Named after its leaders, the Lewis and Clark expedition was an epic journey that has become iconic in American lore. Among its discoveries were the Missouri River and the Rocky Mountains.

Although the British had signed a peace treaty, relations between the two nations remained testy. London didn't like the USA's cozy relationship with the French, and the British Navy regularly harassed American ships worldwide. In 1812 the USA declared war on the British, leading to an inconclusive conflict that lasted a little over two years. One event in 1814 was notable: while watching the Americans successfully defend Fort McHenry and Baltimore from the British Navy, Francis Scott Key wrote what was to become the national anthem, the 'Star Spangled Banner.'

Undaunted Courage by Stephen Ambrose follows the Lewis and Clark expedition on its extraordinary journey west to the Pacific and back again. You can follow much of their route today.

Although the War of 1812 hadn't resulted in many tangible outcomes, it did fuel American desire for the Europeans to stay home. In 1823 President James Monroe issued the Monroe Doctrine, which stated that North and South America were now closed to European colonialism. This became a key part of US foreign policy and led to the first major build-up of the American army and navy.

FEELING THEIR OATS (AND SOWING THEM)

Commercially, the USA took off in the first part of the 19th century. In 1825 the Erie Canal linked New York City, which had emerged as the commercial center of the country, with the raw materials of the Great Lakes. And the Americans took a British invention, the railroad, and made, well, tracks. From the 1830s, hundreds of miles of lines were built. The remote Midwest was now linked to the markets of the East Coast.

Inventors were busy as well. The cotton gin, first demonstrated by Eli Whitney in 1793, turned growing cotton into a fabulously wealthy pursuit. Plantations spread through the South and drove trade in both goods and slaves. The mechanical reaper made family farms viable, and grain-growing settlers busily carved up new states such as Ohio, Indiana and Illinois. Much of the nation's growing industrial strength came from the factory towns springing up throughout the Northeast.

Continental USA took most of its final shape in the 1830s and '40s under an expansionist philosophy known as Manifest Destiny, which was based on the assumption that since much of North America was bound to become part of the US, why wait for the inevitable? Among the roadblocks on the way to this destiny was Mexico, which had won independence from Spain and controlled today's Texas and California. In 1836 a group of Texans started a revolution and the Mexicans responded with an

1803	**1812**
Louisiana Purchase from France doubles the area of US territory	War of 1812 starts with battles against British and Native Americans around Great Lakes

assault on the Texan stronghold at the Alamo (p732) in San Antonio. The resulting battle lasted two weeks and all but one of the defenders, who included the likes of Davy Crockett, were annihilated. But the Mexicans were so sapped by this victory that they ultimately lost the war.

Out west, a string of Spanish missions built in the 18th century had formed the first part of the European colonization of California. In the 1840s the growing population of immigrants from eastern US began clamoring for independence from Mexico. One word, gold, made it a done deal. The swarms of gold seekers (mostly Americans) who rushed into California via San Francisco so weighted the population against Mexico that it gave up without a fight. California became a state in 1850. Up north, settlers pounding the Oregon Trail (p701) caused the British to relinquish claims to today's Washington and Oregon in 1846.

A brilliant HBO TV series, *Deadwood* (2004–2005) gives an unvarnished take on the Old West during the gold rush in Deadwood, South Dakota.

BROTHERS FIGHT BROTHERS

Even as the USA expanded west and its economy grew, slavery remained a major source of contention; during the first half of the 19th century debate raged on this issue. States north of Maryland banned slavery in 1804. After that, one compromise after another was tried to placate the competing forces. Some states were admitted as 'free states,' others as slave states, while yet others were allowed to hold referenda to decide. The so-called Underground Railroad, a loose-knit confederation of people opposed to slavery, assisted slaves escaping to the free North. In the meantime, the Southern states' agrarian economies became increasingly dependent on slave labor to farm the vast cotton and tobacco plantations.

Abraham Lincoln, a lawyer from Springfield, Illinois, and a member of the antislavery Republican Party, was elected president in 1860 after a bitter campaign in which slavery was the main issue. The Southern states decided it was time to fight rather than switch, and in 1861 formed the Confederate States of America and declared war on the United States by attacking Fort Sumter (p481) in Charleston, South Carolina. The Civil War was fiercely fought. Perhaps it was the raw emotion that led brother to literally fight brother, but over the next four years the carnage was incalculable. Developments such as machine guns helped kill upward of one million people. Although the Confederates (or Gray) had the better generals, ultimately the Union (or Blue) won, primarily on its inherent industrial might and a reckless use of troops that saw casualties exceed the South's by a factor of six to one. Sitting on a plantation porch sipping a mint julep and talking about valor was no match for trainloads of cannons, flotillas of iron-clad warships and overall brute strength.

Lincoln by David Herbert Donald is easily the best biography of the man many consider the greatest American president. Humble yet driven, compassionate but fearless, Lincoln rose from nothing to save his nation.

Union victories in 1863 at Gettysburg (p205), Pennsylvania, and Vicksburg (p408), Mississippi, sealed the Confederates' fate. A year later General William T Sherman made his notorious 'march to the sea' through the heart of the South. The plunder and pillage were epic, and included the burning of Atlanta. In April 1865 General Robert E Lee surrendered for the South at the courthouse in Appomattox, Virginia.

Bygones were not bygones after the war. The North extracted reparations from the Southern states and readmitted them to the union only begrudgingly and at great cost. Southern anger festered for decades and it was more than 100 years before the Republican Party could win elec-

1841	1849
First wagons follow new immigrant trails to California	California gold rush; 80,000 immigrants arrive

tions in the South, even though its conservative policies were more in tune with local beliefs than those of the Democratic Party. To this day the Confederate flag remains an unofficial talisman for white supremacists. Union victory also did little to improve the lot of Southern Blacks. Slavery was replaced by a system of 'sharecropping' that kept the former slaves indentured to land they farmed in return for a measly share of the crops. Enjoying the fruits of American life enshrined in the Constitution was a battle for African Americans through the Civil Rights era of the 1960s and continues today.

America's feverish growth accelerated further after the Civil War. The joining of the first transcontinental railroad near Promontory, Utah, in 1869 opened up much of the unsettled West to pioneers. Until then, movement west had often been by wagon train, and misfortune was common. Industry's omnivorous appetite for new workers and the seemingly boundless frontiers available for settlers gave the US its reputation as a land of opportunity. Word spread worldwide and an open immigration policy meant that during a 50-year period beginning in the 1870s, tens of millions of immigrants arrived from Europe and Asia. Many found livelihoods in the ethnic neighborhoods of the cities. Others set out on their own to claim land for 40-acre farms they could work with their family and a mule. These forces came together spectacularly in the fast-growing city of Chicago, where commodities such as grain and cattle produced in America's heartland were sold, industries produced everything from steel to machinery, and the nation's railroads converged.

One group, the Native Americans, not only did not benefit from this growing prosperity but were almost eradicated by it. In a process that had begun at Jamestown, a familiar pattern was repeated endlessly: new settlers to an area made pacts with the local tribes until the new population grew and the tribes were pushed out. The Indians would fight back but were ultimately no match for the superior numbers and weapons of the settlers. The government would then offer the tribes their own lands further west if they would simply go away. All would be fine until settlement reached these lands and the process would begin again. Scores of promises made by the 'forked-tongues' of the government were broken and whole tribes vanished.

By the 1870s, most Great Plains tribes had fallen to this genocide. For two decades the Indian Wars raged across the plains, spawning little but tragedy (and, much later, scores of awful movies). Although the Native Americans had many successes – most notably against the spectacularly incompetent General George Custer and his troops at Little Big Horn in South Dakota in 1876 (see p689) – the force of expansion eventually overwhelmed them and the few survivors were carted off to desolate reservations.

GREED TEMPERED BY REFORM

The huge growth of the American economy in the latter part of the 19th century led to the emergence of some industrial behemoths. Notable were US Steel, run by Andrew Carnegie from its base in Pittsburgh, Pennsylvania, and the enormous near-monopoly of John D Rockefeller's Standard Oil Company. Inventions such as the automobile led to other

Glory (1989) tells the tale of America's first black army unit, which fought against more than a few Johnny Rebs in the Civil War. Denzel Washington won an Oscar for his work in one of the best historical dramas ever made.

Gone With the Wind (1939) is an American icon. The original Civil War epic had Clark Gable as Rhett Butler and Vivien Leigh as Scarlett O'Hara – and frankly, my dear, what more do you need? (Except maybe the 'damn fine' burning of Atlanta…)

The Searchers (1956) is probably John Wayne's best film; he spends years hunting for his niece (Natalie Wood) who was kidnapped by the Comanches. The morals are complex and the Native American perspective surprisingly sympathetic for the time.

empires, including the one created by Henry Ford at the turn of the 20th century. Industrial technology replaced the quaint notion of craftsmen making goods. At factories such as Ford's in Detroit, Michigan, legions of unskilled workers – many of them immigrants – performed simple tasks on assembly lines that resulted in complex products such as cars. Although jamming peg A into hole B over and over could be mind-numbing, it was also steady work. The crafty Ford paid his workers above-average wages, not out of beneficence but because he and other industrialists realized that if they gave workers more money to spend, they would buy the very products they produced. Industrialization created the vast American middle class and spurred the movement of people from back-breaking and unpredictable lives on farms to greater economic security in the cities.

But it wasn't all happy workers at the factories. The work was often dangerous, hours long and those easiest to exploit – such as women, children and recent immigrants – were treated little better than slaves. In 1906 Upton Sinclair published *The Jungle* to the acclaim of the growing reform movement and to the horror of almost everyone else. It gained notoriety for its section describing the grotesque and decidedly unsavory conditions in Chicago's meat-packing plants. Spurred by labor unions and other reformers, government reforms on industry included antitrust laws that broke up monopolies like Standard Oil, labor laws that guaranteed the 40-hour work week and banned the exploitation of children and women, and regulations ensuring the safety of foods and other goods. A growing women's rights movement drove the passage of the 19th amendment in 1920, which gave women the right to vote.

The Chief by David Nasaw chronicles the life of William Randolph Hearst, America's first media mogul. From the Spanish-American War through World War II, Hearst hobnobbed with politicians and celebrities, and changed US history.

Growing prosperity at home meant that the US could also define its role in the rest of the world. A rambunctious war movement in the 1890s led to the declaration of war in 1898 against the teetering Spanish empire. The results were quite one-sided and America took possession of Puerto Rico and Guam while picking up the Philippines for a pittance. Ostensibly about freedom for Cuba, the war caused the dictatorial Spanish government to be replaced by one supported by US corporations.

Further south, the French had been literally stuck in the mud for years trying to dig a canal across Panama. The US played politics shrewdly. It won 'freedom' for Panama from its Colombian rulers, and in return earned the right to complete the Panama Canal and run it as a monopoly link between the Atlantic and Pacific Oceans from the time it opened in 1914.

Across the Atlantic, events were unfolding that would eventually propel the US to its current position of prominence. The Great War between the European powers began in 1914 and slowly sucked in the Americans. Known as WWI only after an even worse cataclysm became WWII, the conflict forced the US to choose sides between the Allies (mainly Britain and France) and the Central Powers led by Germany. By historical association, and because they were major trading partners, the US tended to side with the Allies. Most Americans, however, wanted to stay isolated and President Woodrow Wilson won re-election in 1916 on the slogan of 'He kept us out of the war.' Meanwhile America profitably sold armaments to the Allies, which caused the Germans to order their U-boats to sink American freighters thought to be carrying weapons. A string of

1898	1908
Victory in Spanish-American War gives USA control of Philippines, Puerto Rico and Guam	The first Model T car is built; Ford is soon selling one million a year

sinkings, along with the realization by the government that it would be important to have a place at the postwar table where the spoils would be divvied up, led the US to declare war on the Central Powers in 1917.

America mobilized rapidly: in 18 months the army trained and sent more than two million men to Europe and the air force grew from 55 planes to over 17,000. The American army tipped the balance to the Allies, who overwhelmed the exhausted Germans and ended years of futile trench-fighting carnage.

Isolationists regained their political strength after the war and kept the US from joining Wilson's brainchild, the League of Nations. A disappointed Wilson died a broken man and, hobbled by the lack of US participation and other woes, the League never became the force for world peace that had been envisaged.

FALSE MORALITY & FALSE PROSPERITY

Although the decade that followed WWI has earned the sobriquet 'the Roaring '20s' for its flappers, jazz and supposed 'anything goes' culture, the 1920s were in reality a time of great contrasts. In 1920 the federal government began enforcing the 18th amendment to the Constitution, which prohibited the sale of alcohol. Driven by the religious conservatives who had been a part of American life since the Pilgrims, Prohibition made a majority of Americans lawbreakers overnight. It also spawned a new industry of organized crime that supplied the thirsty populace. Entrepreneurs, such as Joseph Kennedy (father of a future political dynasty) in Massachusetts, made fortunes off illegal sales of alcohol. But it was in Chicago that the effects of Prohibition were seen most colorfully. Gangs such as Al Capone's battled openly for domination of the trade, spawning corruption at all levels of public life. Although mythologized in countless movies and lore, Chicago's gangs were trigger-happy thugs, whether they were blasting flower shops or gunning down mourners at funerals. Prohibition was repealed in 1933 (although to this day some conservative enclaves, including Utah, retain local restrictions on alcohol consumption), after which the gangs found it easy to shift to new ventures in prostitution and drug-running.

Obtaining a drink wasn't the only game Americans were willing to play in the 1920s; they also played the stock market by the millions to the tune of billions in the hopes of making zillions. This financial free-for-all extended throughout the economy with banks making dubious loans to farmers, businessmen and almost anyone else who wanted cash. Citizens became 'consumers' by getting credit to buy whiz-bang inventions like refrigerators, clothes washers, automobiles, radios and all the other accoutrements of a modern and increasingly comfortable life.

But what goes up must come down; the stock market collapsed in October 1929 as investors, panicked by a gloomy global economy, tried to sell off their stocks and share prices plummeted. The ripple effects were devastating. Millions lost their homes, farms and businesses as the teetering banks called in their dodgy loans, and millions more lost all of their savings as the banks collapsed. This was the beginning of the Great Depression that ultimately saw as much as 50% of the American workforce unemployed. Scores took to the roads in search of work.

Pulitzer Prize–winner David Mamet wrote the script for *The Untouchables* (1987) – a familiar but thrilling saga of good (Kevin Costner as Elliot Ness) versus evil (Robert De Niro as Al Capone). Scores of great scenes include the famous one shot on the steps of Chicago Union Station.

1917–18	1920
US involvement in WWI	18th amendment bans alcohol, Prohibition starts; 19th amendment gives women the vote

John Steinbeck's *The Grapes of Wrath* (1940) is a saga of Okies trying to escape the Dust Bowl for the promised land of California during the Depression. The film version is beautifully acted by a cast led by Henry Fonda.

Democrat Franklin Roosevelt was elected president in 1932 on the ill-defined promise of a 'New Deal' to get the US out of its crisis. (Even a vaguely talented dog-catcher could have been elected president against the Republicans, since Republican president Herbert Hoover had happily fiddled away while the economy crashed and burned.) Not widely known or highly regarded when elected, Roosevelt quickly became one of the pivotal figures in American history. After taking office he led the passage of laws to stabilize the economy, but more radical was his creation of social programs, which had previously been anathema to independent-minded Americans. Social security, the government-run retirement program, is one example of how Roosevelt gave the federal government a role in almost every aspect of Americans' lives. In addition, federal spending projects resulted in public works on a grand scale, including the enormous Hoover Dam (p883) on the Arizona–Nevada border.

WORLD WAR II

With so many troubles at home, it was no wonder that Americans were more isolationist than ever during the 1930s. The rise of Hitler and fascism around the world received coverage in the media, but most Americans were happy to let foreigners deal with their own problems. However, Roosevelt and others in government recognized the threat from both Germany and Japan. After WWII broke out in 1939, Roosevelt used every trick he could think of to lend support to Britain and his close friend Winston Churchill while beginning a military build-up at home. Programs such as the Lend-Lease Act, which virtually gave Britain military supplies, barely skirted the law, and Roosevelt had to rely on his immense popularity with voters to keep the isolationist Congress on board.

Rigorously accurate, albeit at times dry, *Tora Tora Tora* (1970) faithfully chronicles the events that brought America into WWII, right down to the heroics of Doris Miller (a black mess attendant who shot down a Japanese plane). Miles better than the execrable *Pearl Harbor* (2001).

Indeed it was Roosevelt's popularity with Americans – his ability to communicate and reassure the average person throughout the Depression was unmatched – that allowed him to run for an unprecedented third term in 1940 and win.

The war many expected came in a manner nobody expected on December 7, 1941, when the Japanese launched a surprise attack on Pearl Harbor (p1126) in Hawaii. Although more than 2000 Americans were killed, the attack had more symbolic than strategic importance (the ships sunk were mostly old battleships that would have had little value in the war to come). Any thoughts of isolationism were erased as 'Remember Pearl Harbor!' became a rallying cry across the nation. Roosevelt gave an eloquent address to Congress the next day, which included the line 'Yesterday, December 7th – a date which will live in infamy...'

Gary Cooper shines in *Sergeant York* (1941), a true story of an archetypical American hero. Alvin York didn't want to fight in WWI because he thought killing was wrong, but once in the trenches he single-handedly won a battle.

Although American emotion demanded that the Japanese be dealt with immediately, Roosevelt understood that Germany and the Axis powers represented the more immediate threat. Germany, with its somewhat unreliable ally Italy, declared war on the US on December 11, 1941, helping Roosevelt make the defeat of Germany the strategic priority.

The war in the Pacific went poorly until June 1942 when a combination of luck, tenacity and cleverness gave the US Navy an incredible victory over the much larger Japanese navy at the Midway Islands. From there began a long and bloody counterattack recapturing islands from the Japanese all the way back to Tokyo.

1933	1941
Franklin D Roosevelt introduces New Deal economic initiatives to counter the Great Depression; Prohibition ends	Pearl Harbor bombed; USA enters WWII

In Europe a series of missteps in the air and in Africa initially hindered US efforts, but most importantly the Americans ensured the safety of the British, and with time came the experience and materials that allowed the Americans to successfully attack the Axis by air, land and sea. Led by American General Dwight Eisenhower, the Allies launched their assault on Germany with the D-Day invasion of France on June 6, 1944; this brought some relief to the Soviet Union, which had been savagely fighting the Germans in Eastern Europe for three years.

Over 25% of Americans joined the military during WWII; men were eligible for the draft up to the age of 46. But every American played a role, from children who collected recyclable goods for the war effort to women who, as popularized by the iconic Rosie the Riveter, took on traditional male jobs throughout industry. This mobilization of women had profound effects on American society following the war as women no longer expected to spend their lives working in the home. The segregated military meant that African Americans had to serve in support roles, although a few did see combat in all-Black units. Their success in battle helped drive the desegregation of the military shortly after the war, an early victory in the Civil Rights struggle.

Germany surrendered in May 1945. Full attention then shifted to the Pacific, where American experience with Japanese tactics such as the kamikaze suicide attacks showed that an invasion of the Japanese mainland would result in unprecedented death and carnage. But a vast yet secret government program called the Manhattan Project provided an alternative. Scores of scientists, many of whom were Jews who had escaped the Nazis, produced the atomic bombs that were used to vaporize Hiroshima and Nagasaki in August 1945. Japan surrendered a few days later.

Shortly before the war ended and right after winning a fourth term as president, Roosevelt, clearly aged beyond his years, died. The new president, Harry S Truman, claimed never to have had any qualms about ordering the use of the atomic bombs, because the alternative was the possible deaths of thousands, if not millions, of American troops in an invasion.

SUPERPOWER TRIALS & TRIUMPHS

The end of the war did not bring real peace, as the US and its wartime ally the Soviet Union soon became caught in a struggle of wills and influence to control the course of the world. The four-decade-long conflict came to be known as the Cold War. It was capitalism versus communism on a global stage, with only the threat of mutual nuclear destruction keeping the two superpowers from direct war. Instead the conflict played out in other nations worldwide. In Korea, the Soviet- and Chinese-supported North Korea invaded the south, and only the US and its allies prevented South Korea from being overrun. The war ended in a stalemate in 1953. In Europe, the US-led West faced off against the East in divided Germany for decades. Meanwhile the divided UN (p142), which had been chartered in San Francisco in 1945, was largely ineffectual in preventing conflict.

At home, the US economy had exploded in size during and after the war. Returning servicemen could choose between nearly free college educations and immediate employment in a plethora of well-paying

The Good War by Studs Terkel tells the story of WWII using the voices of Americans who lived through it. Those who fought and those who were left behind tell stories that are at once common and deeply moving.

The Making of the Atomic Bomb by Richard Rhodes takes an almost lyrical look at the Manhattan Project and the moral issues that haunted some of the inventors and inspired others.

The Fifties by David Halberstam explores a decade marked by both upheaval and complacency. Television, repression, civil rights, suburbanization, the Beat poets and more were intertwined in the decade that spawned modern America.

1951	1955
I Love Lucy premiers on CBS and is number one in the ratings; TV becomes a national obsession	The first McDonald's and Disneyland open

jobs. Affluence brought a near obsession with modern comforts, foremost of which was the single-family home. Millions of Americans left the crowded cities in a suburban migration made possible by cheap cars, cheap gas, vigorous government road-building (the Interstate Hwy system was begun in the 1950s), and zoning policies – or lack thereof – that encouraged construction of homes and shopping malls on former farmland surrounding cities. Another American obsession reached prominence during the early 1950s: TV. Movies and radio were rapidly supplanted by the ubiquitous tube, which soon held sway over popular American culture.

The 1960s saw the Cold War move to two new theaters: space and Vietnam. The US had been embarrassed by a string of failures in the space race, while the Soviets enjoyed a string of successes. At his inaugural address in 1961, President John F Kennedy promised to regain the lead and land an American on the moon before the end of the decade. Few thought it was possible and even fewer had any idea about how to do it, but in a dramatic and still awe-inspiring effort that symbolized the swaggering confidence of the USA, Neil Armstrong and Buzz Aldrin landed on the moon on July 20, 1969. Concurrently, however, the US was getting a lesson in humility in Vietnam.

President Lyndon B Johnson, who had succeeded Kennedy after he was assassinated in Dallas (see p749) on November 22, 1963, presided over remarkable change at home. He used his forceful personality to push through major Civil Rights legislation. This came following years of often-violent struggle, particularly in the South, during which time strong Black leaders such as Martin Luther King (p381 and p442) had emerged. But Johnson met his Waterloo in Vietnam, where he committed half a million American troops to stop a takeover of South Vietnam by communist North Vietnam. It was a classic Cold War confrontation, and the Americans ultimately lost due to miscalculation, hubris and eroding support at home.

Growing anger over the war divided Americans and led to huge protests on college campuses. It also led to the 1968 election of Richard M Nixon, possibly the most cynical and manipulative president in US history. During the election campaign, Nixon claimed to have a 'secret plan' to end the Vietnam War, but once in office he expanded the war and began secret bombing raids on Laos and Cambodia. Paranoid beyond reason, Nixon led a White House culture that ordered the 1972 burglary of Democratic Party offices at the Watergate office complex in Washington. Although it took months for dogged journalists to uncover the conspiracy behind the break-in, the resulting scandal eventually consumed the administration and Nixon himself. He became the first president to resign from office, in August 1974.

These dramatic events at home and abroad were but some of the forces shaking American society. Women's liberation, the sexual revolution and the hippies who emerged from San Francisco in the mid-1960s all confronted traditional American values. The 1970s were an unrestrained time for many Americans, marked not just by the birth-control pill and an end to cultural censorship, but also by a certain narcissism that reached an unfortunate extreme at the end of the decade with the Bee

A Man on the Moon by Andrew Chaikin captures the invention, drama and sheer luck that were the hallmarks of the US space program and its goal of landing men on the moon.

Freedom's Daughters: A Juneteenth Story by Lynne Olson is a page-turner about black women such as Rosa Parks, Diane Nash and Ida Mae Holland who were real heroes of the Civil Rights movement.

There have been scores of movies about Vietnam, but *Platoon* (1986) is wrenching. This autobiographical account by Oliver Stone of his own time as a soldier unflinchingly captures the moral ambiguities faced by Americans during the war.

1963	1969
President John F Kennedy assassinated in Dallas, Texas	Two Americans land on the moon; the culmination of the space race

Gees, disco and polyester. This social exuberance was not found throughout society, however, where there was widespread malaise brought on by the aftereffects of Vietnam and Watergate, a stagnant economy and recurring energy shortages that put a crimp on the suburban lifestyle.

In 1980 Ronald Reagan, a modestly talented and moderately successful actor who had gone on to some fame as the governor of California, ran for president. His campaign was simple: make Americans feel good about America again. The ever-cheerful Reagan won handily and it soon became apparent that taking care of the commies once and for all was also going to be high on the agenda. He launched a defense build-up of such monumental proportions that the Soviets went broke trying to keep up. Meanwhile he enacted policies such as huge tax cuts, which brought comfort and solace to conservatives and business interests who had been left quite addled by the events of the previous two decades.

The US enjoyed huge economic growth in 1980s as Reagan's optimism proved infectious. The nation also enjoyed record budget deficits, brought on by the binge-spending on weapons coupled with the tax cuts. The hangover from these good times fell to Reagan's hapless successor, George HW Bush. Despite a successful war to liberate Kuwait after an Iraqi invasion, Bush never caught on with the public and was easily trounced by the previously unknown Bill Clinton in 1992. A political moderate, Clinton proved an able communicator who easily connected with the populace. He also had the good fortune to catch the technology boom that had started with personal computers in the 1980s, and moved on to the Internet in the 1990s. The US enjoyed unprecedented economic growth, which erased government budget deficits and sent unemployment below 2%.

However, despite record popularity – he was re-elected in a landslide in 1996 – Clinton had no shortage of enemies among conservatives. With a hatred that was almost fanatical, conservatives used radio talk shows and other media to launch an all-out assault on Clinton and his prominent wife Hilary Rodham Clinton. Unfortunately for Clinton, he proved to be his own worst enemy. The Clinton administration provided fodder for the opposition with a string of minor scandals. But the lowest moment came after Clinton admitted he had lied about an affair with a comely White House intern. While much of the world looked on in disbelief, he barely managed to avoid being tossed out of office by the Republican-controlled Congress.

George W Bush was narrowly elected president in 2000, in an election marred by a voting fiasco in Florida that left the result in doubt for weeks. The son of the former president Bush, George W had previously done little of note as a businessman, had hardly traveled outside of the US, and had been governor of Texas at a time when the economy was very strong. His victory was largely due to the fanatical support of conservative Christians and Republicans.

Everything changed on September 11, 2001 when Al-Qaeda terrorist attacks on the World Trade Center in New York and the Pentagon in Washington killed 3000 people. Americans rallied behind the president and called for revenge but, unlike after Pearl Harbor, there was no foreign government to easily blame. The US launched an invasion of Afghanistan

The true story of a huge American business merger, *Barbarians at the Gates* (1993) oozes with the greed that was officially sanctioned during the Reagan 1980s. Fire thousands of loyal employees to enjoy a minor gain in share price? You bet!

Hard Drive by James Wallace and Jim Erickson looks at the sometimes unseemly story of Bill Gates and Microsoft, the dominant player in an industry that now dominates the economy.

1973	1974
Last US forces leave Vietnam	Nixon resigns over Watergate

The 9/11 Commission Report is a gripping official account of the events of that day and the lapses of the Bush administration and the US intelligence community prior to the terrorist attacks.

in an effort to root out the terrorists thought to be hiding there. Results were mixed, and in the meantime Bush and his advisors were arguing for a war against Saddam Hussein and Iraq. The Bush administration claimed the Iraqis had 'weapons of mass destruction' and invaded Iraq in April 2003. Notably, scores of traditional American allies (with the exception of the ever-loyal British, among a few others) opposed the war.

As months progressed and casualties mounted, America's image was sullied by a string of scandals and public support for the war eroded. Most tellingly, no weapons of mass destruction were found and numerous revelations showed that the Bush administration had decided to go to war months in advance.

The election campaign of 2004 was one of the most bitter in memory. The country's clear division into 'red states' (those dominated by right-wing Christian Republicans) and 'blue states' (those where political moderates hold sway) was never more apparent. In an odd echo of the Civil War 140 years after it was fought, the eleven states of the old Confederacy (all Southern 'red states') gave Bush his winning margin. Challenger John Kerry won the other 39 states by a margin of 3.5 million votes.

For Bush, the election may have come just in the nick of time; less than a year later the ongoing morass in Iraq, coupled with a string of Republican scandals, had left him with an approval rating little better than Nixon's during Watergate.

1991	2001
The World Wide Web debuts on the Internet; the boom and bust over the next 10 years is the largest ever	Terrorists hijack four planes and crash into the World Trade Center and Pentagon, killing thousands

The Culture

THE NATIONAL PSYCHE

Identifying an 'American sensibility' has been a cottage industry ever since there was an America to talk about. That it remains an active, occasionally overheated debate is itself telling. America would like its identity to be clean and uncomplicated – a Mt Rushmore profile. Instead, America is fluid, evolving and fraught with inherent tensions – more a boatload of strangers disembarking in the slanting afternoon sun, wondering where to go and what to make of the place.

Part of the urgency to define the nation's identity comes from having to accommodate over a million newcomers annually. For immigrants, citizenship eventually confers legal status, but that doesn't address the heart. When does 'me' become 'we'? Newcomers and old-timers alike struggle to define Americanness, because they desperately want to find the place where all the well-publicized differences in US society resolve into a single, irreducible whole.

It's one of the great paradoxes of American life that difference has inspired unity, and individualism has inspired togetherness, with neither overwhelming the other. Fears that the United States will one day balkanize into hundreds of ethnic fiefdoms seem as unlikely as fears that a bland, homogenized, white middle class will leach all the color and vibrancy from the nation's diverse peoples. Despite pulls to the extremes, the center still holds.

Why is this so? The short answer is that America's founding fathers built it that way, even if they couldn't have envisioned the modern state of the union. The United States was created out of whole cloth – essentially, out of a series of propositions about how to behave. 'Becoming American' is the process of adopting these ideas as one's own.

Each immigrant's unofficial 'assimilation contract' summarizes this neatly, and it applies to every citizen, no matter what their lineage. One is expected to abide by the democratic ideal of equality for all, to obey the rule of law over personal grievances, to respect individualism, to work hard, and as a practical matter, to speak English in public. Do these things and you're free to be yourself and to chase the American Dream, which, in essence, is nothing more than the desire to improve your lot, and that of your children, and to live and worship how you like without persecution.

This simple mindset has been a revolutionary moderator. Americans don't look the same, act the same, come from the same heritage or share the same beliefs, but common desires and the tolerance democracy requires are enough to help survive the clash and cacophony of daily life.

Historically, there have been two other essential influences on American identity: the pioneer experience and the Protestant religion. The pioneers were a rugged lot – they had to be. They were self-reliant, innovative, practical, courageous, and mistrustful of established social conventions and authority. Since the West was won over a century ago, does any of this still matter? Just ask the immigrants arriving from Thailand or Mexico, or any citizen who's had enough, moves on and tries again. All must carve a home for themselves out of a strange and sometimes inhospitable land – and success, even survival, depends on having packed similar traits in their luggage.

When they arrived, the Pilgrims brought their most cherished possession, the Protestant religion, and tilled its sensibilities into the continent's

What does the American Dream look like in real life? The eight teenage heroes of *Spellbound* (2002) demonstrate it beautifully as they try to win the nail-biting national spelling bee competition.

Status Anxiety (2004) by Alain de Botton elegantly charts the strain of living in an egalitarian, classless Western meritocracy and even offers strategies for coping – besides shopping, of course.

In *Hypocrite in a Pouffy White Dress* (2005), Susan Jane Gilman shares her 'tales of growing up groovy and clueless,' but actually, she's one painfully witty, eagle-eyed reporter of the American zeitgeist.

fertile soil. They were driven, plainspoken, conservative and, most of all, believed they didn't need a priest to talk to God. They could experience the divine directly – and there is hardly an American today who doesn't believe this implicitly in any situation. Whether in religion, art or ecstatic nature, each person can touch the center. Everyone is born with the authority of their own soul. To be right does not require a consensus.

However, all these ideas and sensibilities, powerful as they are, remain intangible. Americans need to meet in a real place to feel communion, and that place, strangely enough, is pop culture. Without the connective tissue of Hollywood and rock and roll, of Homer Simpson and Darth Vader, maybe it would all fall apart. For American society, pop culture's artistic faults become strengths – it's easy, fun, distracting, trendy, cheap and available to all. Americans will never all be the same, but through pop culture they have a public square and a common language.

It's an excellent question that Rebecca Walker asks in *What Makes a Man* (2004), and 21 writers, both men and women, have a field day taking apart and rebuilding the American male.

Interestingly, America's money embodies its identity almost perfectly. On every coin – the symbol of prosperity – are stamped two phrases. One is 'In God We Trust.' The other: *e pluribus unum*, which means 'from many, one.' The first phrase was adopted in 1864 during the Civil War; the latter in 1782, six years after the Declaration of Independence.

Think of that the next time you throw a quarter in the jukebox.

LIFESTYLE

There is a growing anxiety in America today. Despite enjoying an overall standard of living that remains the envy of the world, Americans feel they may be living on borrowed time.

They're certainly living on borrowed cash. Citizens are working harder than ever just to maintain what they've got, and a series of economic alarms is providing a jarring wake-up call for anyone hoping to drift sleepily into the American Dream.

The land of opportunity comes with a few caveats.

DOS & DON'TS

By and large, the American motto is to live and let live. But as in any society, there are certain norms of behavior foreign visitors should be aware of.

- Do return friendly greetings. 'Hi. How are you?' is expected to receive a cheerful 'Thanks, I'm fine,' not actual complaints.

- Don't be overly physical when you greet someone. Some Americans will hug, but many more, especially men, will just shake hands.

- Do be on time. Americans consider it rude to be kept waiting.

- Don't take your clothes off in public. Especially on beaches, don't disrobe or, for women, go topless, unless others are already naked.

- Do tip your waiter, bartender and taxi driver.

- Don't smoke inside a building without asking first. Nonsmoking laws are increasingly common.

- Do use a trash can. City streets may be dirty, but littering is frowned upon.

- Don't expect Americans to know much about your country. Americans are usually excited to meet foreigners, but that doesn't mean they know where Germany is.

- Do be respectful of police officers. Americans may be casual, but the police expect to be called 'Sir,' 'Ma'am' or simply 'Officer.'

- Don't be afraid to talk politics, but be polite. Americans can be sharply self-critical, but they also may take offense if they feel you're 'bashing America.'

Despite vastly differing circumstances, most Americans view themselves as middle class. This egalitarian perception helps maintain social harmony: so long as most everyone sees a chance to improve their prospects, few begrudge the rich. Indeed, most wouldn't mind joining that elite class, though actual aspirations tend to be more modest – to own your own home, to educate your children, to retire in comfort.

On average, Americans work 20% longer today than in 1970, and annually they work nine weeks more than Western Europeans.

Some numbers: about two-thirds of Americans own a home, and among adults, over 85% have a high-school education and over a quarter have a college degree. More than half of those aged over 15 are married. The median household income is $43,564. By these measures, the majority *are* middle class – though this label gets rather slippery and complex as you tour the country.

For instance, what does the 'average' American family look like? It's hard to say. The nuclear family that defined the 1950s, the anomalous yardstick by which middle-class life is still judged, no longer fits. On average, the typical American family is two parents and one or two kids, but half of all marriages end in divorce – which has left over a quarter of all children currently living in single-parent homes. More people are marrying later and having fewer or no kids while, in cities especially, 'urban tribes' of young adults choose to make families of friends instead. Conversely, foreign-born immigrants tend to gather larger, multigenerational families under one roof; over a quarter of immigrant households consist of five or more people, which is twice the national average. A Korean-born grocer living with her parents and siblings, a married tax attorney with two kids, and a young, single computer consultant may all live on the same Brooklyn street and consider themselves average 'middle-class' folks, but their day-to-day realities couldn't be more different.

A 2005 survey found that two-thirds of American teenagers have a TV in their room, and a quarter multitask – listening to music, surfing the Net and watching TV at the same time.

Technology and the global marketplace are exerting major changes on US society. The rise of telecommuting is decreasing the importance of cities, and it even allows for some service-sector jobs to be 'outsourced' to other countries. Service jobs constitute 83% of all nonfarm employment (Wal-Mart is the nation's largest private employer), but even the well-educated American worker safely employed in the nation's 'knowledge economy' is beginning to feel vulnerable. And if you happen to be employed on the bottom rungs of the service sector, security isn't even a question – you don't have any. Many of these jobs pay at or just above the federal minimum wage, which is $5.15 an hour and has not been changed since 1997. In constant dollars, the minimum wage has eroded 40% since 1968, which makes for a pretty cut-rate American Dream. This is one of several reasons why two working parents – once the exception in the idyllic 1950s family – is now the rule.

If the middle class increasingly feels nearer to the economic bottom than the top, there's a reason. Since 1975, almost all gains in household income have gone to the top 20% (the upper middle class and the millionaires), who also earn 55% of the nation's annual income and control 80% of its wealth. Meanwhile, the poverty rate has grown for the past four years. It was 12.5% in 2003, or 35.9 million people. But defining poverty is almost as difficult as defining middle class. The USA's official poverty threshold for a family of three was $15,200 in 2004, but the Economic Policy Institute calculated that a 'living wage' would need to be twice that. If you are at or just above the poverty threshold, you're not officially counted as poor, but those in this uncounted stratum have no illusions about where they stand.

The USA has more shopping malls than high schools, which perhaps explains why Americans have wracked up $2 trillion in consumer debt.

As a percentage of their populations, poverty hits Blacks (24.4%) and non-naturalized, recent immigrants (21.7%) the hardest. This is creating a permanent underclass of people who feel the system is rigged against them, so they refuse to participate – preferring to drop out of school and the workforce rather than 'sell out.' Racial inequalities persist within the middle class, too. In 2003, Asian households had the highest median income ($55,500), followed by non-Hispanic Whites ($48,000), foreign-born citizens ($37,500), Hispanics ($33,000) and Blacks ($30,000).

Well, are the genders at least economic equals? Not yet. On average, women currently earn 76¢ for every dollar a man earns. Since the 1963 Equal Pay Act, the gender wage gap has closed at a rate of half a penny a year – leaving only about 50 more years to go.

In short, America is a relentless and at times unforgiving meritocracy. The United States is practically alone among industrialized democracies in requiring citizens to survive solely on wages (and accumulated wealth), and this is a large reason why poverty and economic inequities remain so pervasive. Despite the occasional effort to nationalize a major public service – such as education, childcare or health care – the country resists because of its aversion to more taxes and federal intrusions into the private sphere. In the US, if you don't inherit it, you have to earn it, and what you earn often depends as much on where you start as on how hard you work.

Some income inequalities can be directly related to education. For instance, in 2001, those with college degrees earned on average 173% more than those with only high-school degrees. While US universities are justifiably famous for their quality, drawing the top tier of students worldwide, US public schools (kindergarten through high school) lag behind other developed countries. President Bush implemented his 'No Child Left Behind' educational reform to combat this problem, but in 2005, a coalition of states claimed the federally mandated, standardized tests were harming schools. Nevertheless, since public school funding remains mostly local, a community's wealth is still the main factor determining academic excellence – meaning that where families (can afford to) live remains the most important educational decision they will make.

Then there's health care, which has become a financial nightmare. In 2003, over 15% of Americans, or 45 million people, were uninsured, while businesses are limiting coverage and shifting more of their health-care costs onto their insured workers (health-care premiums cost 14% of earnings in 2003). Overall, America outspends other developed countries on health care by two to four times – to the tune of $1.7 trillion annually, or about $6000 per person. Still, covered or not, more and more Americans are just one serious health crisis away from poverty and bankruptcy.

Americans aren't exactly in such good shape to begin with. Official estimates are that about 64% of US adults are either overweight or obese, and about 15% of children are overweight. Citizens eat too much junk, basically – the top five sources of calories in the typical diet are soda, pastries, hamburgers, pizza and potato chips. This explains why Americans, while fat, are also malnourished. Among preventable deaths, obesity-related problems remain the second-highest killer after tobacco.

An obesity epidemic is an odd malady for a nation as obsessed with beauty and physical fitness as the US. Kids engage in physical activity as much as ever, outdoor sports remain popular, diet and nutrition are constant topics of conversation, and Hollywood provides a dazzling display of idealized beauty, but like a cosmic scale with a supermodel on one end and a supersized hamburger and fries on the other, the desired image and the dumpy reality never quite balance.

And that's the United States: a study in contrasts. A place of incredible achievements and persistent inequalities, of perpetual optimism despite all evidence to the contrary. It would be wrong to discount the

For 30 days, goofball Morgan Spurlock ate nothing but McDonald's. The result was a near coronary and the documentary *Super Size Me* (2004), a seriously irreverent plunge into America's fast-food nation.

With grace and uncommon insight, Pulitzer Prize–winner David K Shipler brings you *The Working Poor* (2004). Their stories will break your heart because the peerless Shipler truly cares.

Gleefully partisan, joyfully righteous, Molly Ivins and Lou Dubose connect the dots between Bush's policies and American life in *Bushwhacked* (2003). It's devastatingly funny when it isn't scary as hell.

optimism, however. Americans are living proof that a dream is the most transformative tool there is.

POPULATION

The real story behind US population statistics is immigration, which since the 1970s has been occurring at unprecedented levels and now accounts for well over half of the country's annual population growth. This wave of immigration is changing the face of America as much as, or more than, any in her history.

As of mid-2005, the total US population was estimated at 295 million, making it the world's third-most populous country, but still well behind India and China, which both boast over a billion people. Broken down by ethnicity, the US is about 65% non-Hispanic White, 14% Hispanic, 12% Black, 4.2% Asian, and less than 1% Native American.

Since the 2000 census, the US population has grown by about 3.3%, but ethnic populations are growing the fastest. While the number of non-Hispanic Whites grew by just 1%, Hispanics grew by 13%, Asians by 12.5%, Blacks by 4.4% and Native Americans by 3.3%.

In other words, the colors in America's rainbow are becoming even wider and brighter.

In 2003, the foreign-born population in the USA was 33.5 million, or roughly 12% of all residents; about nine million are believed to be illegal immigrants. Of this total, over half have arrived since 1990, and about 1.3 million newcomers arrive every year. Who are they? Over half are Latin American (about three-quarters of these are Mexican), a quarter are Asian, and 14% European.

Another indication of the ongoing cultural shift is that America, long known as the place languages go to die, is more bilingual than ever. In 1980, 11% of Americans said they spoke a language other than English at home; by 2000, 18% (or 48 million people) said this. Not surprisingly, that second language is most often Spanish.

Immigrants tend to put down stakes in major metropolitan gateways, such as in California, Texas, New York, Florida and Illinois, which also happen to be the nation's five most populous states. Thus, immigrant

For US population statistics and interesting overviews of demographic trends, visit the US Census Bureau (www.census.gov).

AMERICA 2030: OLD & WHITE, YOUNG & ETHNIC

For the next several decades, the face of America will develop two distinct profiles: one side will be older and predominantly white; the other side will be young and mostly ethnic.

This can already be seen. In 2003, the median age was 36, up from 35.3 in 2000. However, sort by ethnicity and another picture emerges. Non-Hispanic Whites averaged 39.6 years, while Hispanics averaged 26.7 years. Of all ethnicities, Hispanics are the youngest; in 2003, they accounted for 20% of America's preschoolers.

By 2050, Hispanics are predicted to account for nearly 25% of the US population, Blacks 14.6% and Asians 8%; non-Hispanic Whites will make up only 50% of the population – on the cusp of becoming the nation's largest minority. And an old one to boot.

As you may have heard, the baby-boomer generation – post-WWII babies born between 1950 and 1965 – is nearing retirement. This population bubble is going to swell the ranks of seniors until, by 2030, one in five Americans will be over 65. Already, non-Hispanic Whites account for 81% of those over 55, a percentage that may grow.

Does this augur a coming culture war, in which an increasingly ethnic America decides they shouldn't have to support a bunch of rich, old white folks with expensive entitlement programs like Medicare and Social Security? Maybe. In fact, a generational squabble over the nation's resources is already here, and it may very well develop an ethnic tint.

settlement patterns mirror the country as a whole, which favors the coasts and big cities and leaves the middle of the country sparsely populated.

For instance, the average population density of the USA is 79 people per sq mile (psm); in Europe it's 134 psm and Asia 203 psm. But California, the third-biggest state, averages 217 psm and New York 402 psm. Meanwhile, neither Montana, Wyoming, nor North or South Dakota average over 10 psm.

The American range, in other words, is still a lonely place.

MULTICULTURALISM

The United States takes great pride in its famed status as a 'teeming nation of nations,' as Walt Whitman wrote. Each year, the calendar bursts with ethnic and cultural celebrations, as if strewn with bright handfuls of confetti – from St Patrick's Day to Carnival, from Cinco de Mayo to Martin Luther King Jr Day, from Thanksgiving to Mardi Gras to the Chinese New Year. The USA is without a doubt the world's most diverse country, and Ellis Island is as much its navel as Plymouth Rock or Independence Hall.

However, for Americans there is no more loaded topic than race and ethnicity, which amounts to a national obsession. No other social or political terms – not class, gender or age, not economics or foreign policy – stir Americans as deeply. Whenever the country divides, racial fault lines crack the widest.

This is because, of all the nation's dichotomies, racial issues are the most profound – they are the source of the country's greatest pride and its greatest shame. The Statue of Liberty, torch held high, graced by the famous sonnet by Emma Lazarus, is America's shining symbol of openness; it is a symbol of its founding belief in the essential dignity of every human being. This belief is made real in countless ways, large and small, every day.

And yet, racism and xenophobia run like electric currents through US society, standing as a rebuke to easy sentiment and complacency. In the USA, race has most often been discussed in black-and-white terms, literally, because of the history of slavery and the nation's segregationist, pre–Civil Rights Jim Crow laws. This troubled legacy remains very much alive because of the persistent inequalities in the everyday realities of many black Americans. The country renounced segregation 40 years ago; it has made attempts (through legislation like affirmative action) to redress historic wrongs. But the black experience will most likely remain the needle of America's moral compass until it includes expectations and opportunity equal to those for Whites.

The very idea of 'multiculturalism' – that a nation shouldn't be a 'melting pot,' but a tapestry woven out of the distinct threads of many cultures – arose out of the Civil Rights movement in the 1960s, and this is now taken for granted as the American ideal. However, recent waves of immigration are testing it like never before. In a half-century, changing demographics (p59) will turn America into a nation of minorities, with no race in the majority. As the nation looks ahead to this momentous day, the dialogue over ethnicity is evolving, expanding and becoming infinitely more complex than black and white.

The USA is definitely making progress toward its goal of ethnic harmony, but opinions differ on whether it is striding or stumbling forward. As seen in responses to issues such as illegal immigration from Mexico (p40), politically driven xenophobia may never go away, even though the nation now reacts less systematically than in previous eras – such as

Does 'assimilation' mean losing or gaining your identity? Can America survive its current immigration tsunami? *Reinventing the Melting Pot* (2004), edited by Tamar Jacoby, is smart and cautiously optimistic.

In *The People* (1993), Stephen Trimble sets the table, but he lets the Southwest's native peoples serve their history and lives to you themselves. It's a must-read, with great photos.

How do Colin Powell, Alicia Keys, Samuel Jackson and Jesse Jackson feel about being black in America? Read *America Behind the Color Line* (2004) by Henry Louis Gates Jr, and they'll tell you.

when it created Japanese internment camps during WWII or passed the 1882 Chinese Exclusion Act (the only immigration law ever to exclude a specific race).

Also, continual immigration comes with its own persistent tensions. Newer ethnic groups must compete and jostle for opportunity with more established immigrant communities and ethnicities – and until new arrivals become established, they often suffer all the common prejudices that historically greet the unfamiliar.

The most interesting dynamic, though – and the one that may be the truest augur – involves the immigrant experience itself, which cuts to the heart of each person's identity. An individual, new to the United States, immediately faces a vexing conundrum: how much or how little should you, or can you, assimilate? Which customs, ways of thought and values do you drop and which do you keep – and how do you negotiate the prejudices and assumptions that your skin inevitably inspires?

Upon arrival, an immigrant's ethnicity is instantly recast into broad and simplistic American terms. Arrivals from Mexico, Brazil and Cuba all become 'Hispanic' or 'Latino,' while Koreans, Japanese, Chinese and Malaysians are placed under that roomy tent called 'Asian.'

Immigrant communities, meanwhile – most famously in large cities like New York, San Francisco and Miami – can to varying degrees isolate themselves from the larger American culture, and even their ethnic umbrella, in order to maintain fine distinctions of language and custom. Individuals nevertheless come to embody a potent duality, one that straddles old world and new, as they are christened with a new compound name – Greek American. To emphasize equality, some add an ampersand: Mexican & American.

But with each successive generation, the lines blur and the selves merge as the American side becomes a little more Mexican, and the Mexican side more American. The country changes as it accommodates more ethnicities, as well as the other way around. In order to fit in, a first-generation immigrant might shed his or her heritage like a tattered coat, while the second, third or fourth generation might reclaim it vigorously. Eventually, after enough generations, ethnicity becomes a distinction with no practical consequence: many longtime Americans, those whose roots extend to the American Revolution and beyond, lovingly claim their original ethnic selves – be they English, Scottish or Irish, German or Polish – even as the pulse of genetic memory is barely audible and gatherings center around food and song, not politics.

These distinctions become even more complex and open to personal preference as interethnic marriages rise and the number of mixed-race children grows. When your heritage includes black, white, Mexican and Native American forebears, exactly which box are you supposed to check? Whose story makes sense of your own?

Indeed, in a hundred years, America's ideal, and perhaps its story, will celebrate multiculturalism within the self as well as in society.

Up until 1967, state antimiscegenation laws (mainly regulating sex and marriage between Whites and Blacks, but at some point targeting every race) were the rule rather than the exception. Late in the Civil Rights movement, these were finally declared unconstitutional. Since then, the number of interracial marriages has grown tremendously; there were over a million in 2003, and about 40% were Black-White marriages. Additionally, studies show that, among immigrants, each successive generation is more likely to marry outside of its ethnic group, and Mexican and Asian immigrants already bring a much more accepting attitude toward intermarriage.

In *Brown* (2002), Richard Rodriguez' flinty humor and poetic imagery strike sparks. It's rare for any memoir, particularly one on race, to glide this effortlessly between the personal and the public.

The history of Chinese Americans exemplifies the dynamic push-pull of the US immigrant experience, and *The Chinese in America* (2003) by Iris Chang rises to the challenge of the tale.

Current projections are that, by 2050, 45% of Hispanics, 35% of Asians and 20% of Blacks and Whites will in fact be multiethnic or multiracial. By the 22nd century, those percentages will rise to 70%, 40% and 35%. However one characterizes America – as a melting pot, or a rainbow of not-yet-equal colors, or a mestizo nation – one thing is certain: something new is being created, and it has the countenance of the future.

RELIGION

America was created by Protestants who valued the freedom to practice religion so highly they refused to make their faith official state policy, and they further forbade the government from doing anything that might sanction one religion or belief over another.

A progressive evangelical – yes, they exist! – Jim Wallis outlines his 'faith-based politics' in *God's Politics* (2005): he tackles gay marriage, abortion, the Iraq War and other hot potatoes.

The irony is that, due to shifting religious preferences and recent immigration, adherents of Protestant denominations no longer constitute the majority of Americans. Since 1993, the number and percentage of Protestants has been declining steadily, from 63% to what was estimated in 2005 to be less than 50%, while other faiths have been holding steady or gradually rising. Catholics represent about 25% of the country, and those practicing 'other religions' – Islam, Buddhism, Native American religions and others – have collectively risen from 3% to 7%. Judaism holds steady at 2%.

Interestingly, one of the fastest-growing categories is 'none.' The proportion of those who say they have 'no religion' has risen from 9% to 14% since 1993. Some in this catch-all category (perhaps as few as 5%) disavow religion altogether, but more nurse spiritual beliefs that simply fall outside the box – demonstrating that the atheist rationalist, the nature spiritualist and the crazy sectarian are enduring American figures.

In *The Transformation of American Religion* (2003), Alan Wolfe eschews ideology to look at how Americans actually live their faiths and at how US culture has radically changed religious practice.

The United States has birthed a number of homegrown religions – such as Mormonism, Jehovah's Witnesses, Christian Scientists, Seventh-Day Adventists, Shakers and the Amish. The Amish exemplify one type of American religious impulse: they disavow modern society and maintain a traditional, anachronistic rural existence. Mormons represent another: they are so adaptable and proselytize so effectively that theirs is one of the 21st-century's fastest-growing religions.

However, the most prominent religious divide in America is no longer between different religions or between faith and skepticism. It's between fundamentalist and centrist or progressive interpretations within each faith. America's evangelical Religious Right gets a lot of press because they have turned to politics in an effort to codify their conservative beliefs into US law. This effort is un-American by definition, but it has been successful inasmuch as it has turned certain issues – such as abortion, contraception, gay rights, stem-cell research, teaching of evolution, school prayer and government displays of religious icons – into referenda on sin and religiosity. It's no coincidence that this particular culture war has become inflamed while an evangelical president occupies the White House.

It's not just in history and geography that Americans are lacking: less than half of Americans can name five of the Bible's Ten Commandments. What would Moses do?

MEDIA

One area that epitomizes the dichotomies of American life is its media, which in the last decade has undergone a phenomenal transformation in two opposing directions: the Internet is providing a dynamic free-for-all of expression at the same time that traditional media ownership has consolidated at a dizzying pace.

Nearly every American home has a TV, many several, with hundreds of niche-focused cable channels; over half have access to the Internet.

Print media continues to struggle financially in the contest for American eyeballs, but there are still more newspapers, magazines and books being published than anyone has time to read. Radio stations crowd the dial, and new movies premiere weekly. However, except for the Internet, this great heaving beast of media is owned mainly by a small handful of multinational corporations.

The media companies that currently dominate America are News Corp, Walt Disney Corp, General Electric, AOL Time Warner, Viacom, Sinclair and Clear Channel. They can thank the Federal Communications Commission (FCC) for allowing this to happen. For 10 years the FCC has progressively deregulated media ownership, beginning in 1996 with radio. Since then, Clear Channel has grown from 40 to 1200 radio stations (about half of all stations), come to own most major concert venues and ticketing agencies, and as a result, now wields a huge, homogenous influence over the music industry.

For a decade, this same story has played over and over. For companies, media concentration is great, as it lets them 'leverage' news, ideas and entertainment properties across the gamut of media outlets – to saturate markets, as they say. Consumers, however, are left with lots of channels, but few real choices. Good news coverage has been the prime casualty: mergers have led to staffing cuts, so that TV network foreign bureaus are half the size they once were, full-time radio news employees are down over 40%, and newspapers have lost 2200 employees since 1990.

All of this may be why the FCC's latest attempt to loosen ownership rules failed. In 2005, due largely to a public outcry against more media concentration, Congress and the courts tossed out a 2003 FCC deregulation proposal (a decision the Bush administration chose not to appeal). For the moment, apparently, enough is enough, but US corporations wield large megaphones. They will no doubt continue to make their power and influence felt.

But a funny thing is starting to happen. Rather than struggling in vain to make themselves heard through the mainstream media, people are

Employees at the five major TV newsrooms (ABC, NBC, CBS, Fox and CNN) are over 90% white, over 85% male, and with one exception (CNN), over 75% Republican.

The Independent Media Institute runs www.alternet.org, a haven for independent, progressive journalism and opinion that includes current news, national columnists and individual blogs.

BLOGS, VLOGS & PODCASTING

Web logs, or 'blogs,' have only been around since 1997, when tech pioneer Dave Winer wrote the first blogging software. Dave's blog, www.scripting.com, is still running, and by one count, it is joined by some 38,000 new blogs every day.

'Vlogs' refers to video files attached to blogs, and 'podcasting' – the equivalent of a home radio show – refers to audio files that can be downloaded and played on personal media devices, such as iPods.

Blogs are a great resource for travelers: by creating your own, you can keep everyone updated on your adventures without worrying about correct postage. Blogs are also a wild introduction to America – amusing, horrifying, and edifying all at once.

Here are some recommended websites for you to begin, or keep, surfing the blogosphere.

■ www.weblogs.com – created by Dave Winer, this site tracks every blog that's changed in the last three hours

■ www.technorati.com – another major site for tracking blogs

■ www.blogger.com – start your own weblog with this free Google service

■ www.podcast.net – a directory of current podcasts

■ www.iPodder.org – run by one of the innovators of podcasting, Adam Curry

■ www.podshow.com – Adam Curry teams up with the Sirius network

For an insider's take on American journalism today, *Backstory* (2003) by Ken Auletta is tops. He analyzes everything from presidential campaign coverage to the ascendancy of right-wing Fox News.

using technology to go around it. And it's working. People are making and sharing their own news, for free, person to person, via the Internet. Those unfortunately named web journals known as 'blogs' have achieved maximum cultural velocity: in a single year, from 2004 to 2005, the number of blogs tripled, and they now top 10 million and counting (p63).

Written by individuals, they range from network news reporters providing an uncensored view of the Iraq War to wild rants about corporate malfeasance to dating updates by overly verbose college students. In other words, they are democracy in action – chaotic, unwieldy, personal, opinionated, obnoxious and passionate. When it comes to news blogs, they resemble nothing so much as the fierce newspaper wars of 19th-century 'yellow journalism,' when countless broadsheets took pride in their partisanship, not their objectivity.

Bloggers are getting their props, too. In the 2004 presidential election, bloggers were provided their own media section at the Democratic National Convention, and the legal consensus is building that these 'pajama-clad reporters' are probably due nearly the same constitutional protections as professional journalists. With computers in hand, average citizens are changing the way the media game is played, and nothing could sound more American.

SPORTS Virginie Boone

Yahoo organizes all manner of fantasy league teams, from basketball and football to racing and golf, with expert analysis to help along the way. Check out www.fantasysports.yahoo.com.

For a land without a lot of tradition, the rhythm and ritual of sports are incredibly important to Americans, a rare area of life where it's OK to display emotion, relax without guilt, live outside oneself, relive childhood dreams, make a buck or two from a friendly wager or fantasy league, and (this is America) be marketed to.

These common needs can even transcend the current divisiveness of politics and religion in American life. For at least during game time, being a long-suffering (no more!) Red Sox or Cubs fan, a Packers' Cheesehead, a costumed member of Raider Nation, a college basketball addict or a lacrosse devotee can bring divergent people together like nothing else. Both a red-state Nascar dad and a MoveOn.org soccer mom will stand up for the national anthem, get together for the Super Bowl and cheer on American amateurs in obscure sports during the Olympics.

But the best thing about being an American sports fan is the pervasiveness of it all. In spring and summer there's baseball – nearly every day. In fall and winter, a weekend day or Monday night wouldn't feel right without a football game on, and through the long days and nights of winter there's plenty of basketball to keep the adrenaline going. In between, hockey, golf, tennis, soccer, boxing, car racing and even poker satisfy the need to watch others compete.

Baseball

Former slugger and perpetual bad boy Jose Canseco's *Juiced: Wild Times, Rampant 'Roids, Smash Hits and How Baseball Got Big* (2005) is a self-indulgent tell-all alleging rampant steroid use. It led to congressional hearings and new testing policies.

Though the always-a-bridesmaid, never-a-bride Boston Red Sox finally made it to the altar (as did the usually beleaguered Chicago White Sox the year after), baseball in America is in a bit of a tailspin. With declining attendance, power hitting on its way out, records being questioned and some of the biggest stars dogged by steroid rumors, fans aren't quite sure about the state of the game. Many left years ago, opting instead for faster, brawnier games like football and basketball.

Still, there's nothing better than sitting in the bleachers with a beer and a hot dog on a lazy sunny day, indulging in the seventh-inning stretch, when entire ballparks erupt in a communal sing-along of 'Take Me Out to the Ballgame.' The play-offs, held every October, can still deliver gut-

> **LACROSSE**
>
> One of the fastest – and fastest-growing – sports in America, especially at the collegiate level, lacrosse traces back to Native American culture, which developed the high-speed running, scooping, passing and shooting game as a way to train young men for war. These days, women play too. Speed and agility count most in lacrosse, attracting a range of body types to the sport, described by many as a combination of soccer, hockey and basketball. Some 45,000 fans attended the 2004 college men's championship, setting a record for attendance second only to men's basketball. There are now two professional leagues.

wrenching excitement and unexpected champions – like the Sox. The most storied grounds continue to be Wrigley Field in Chicago (home of the sad-sack Cubs) and Boston's Fenway, both beautiful in a historic kind of way and smack-dab in the middle of urban neighborhoods with bars on every corner. Newer SBC Park in San Francisco and SafeCo in Seattle are throwbacks to old-time stadiums, nicely set along their cities' waterways and indulgent of their citizens' appreciation for fine food.

The website www.mlb.com is baseball's official home. Tickets are relatively inexpensive – bleacher seats average about $15 a seat at most stadiums – and easy to get for most games.

Football

Baseball might have been the country's favorite pastime in the era of Ruth, of DiMaggio, of Mantle, but football is now America's game. It's big, it's physical, it's big business. With the shortest season and least number of games of any of the major sports, every match takes on the emotion of epic battle, where the results matter and an unfortunate injury can be devastatingly lethal to the chances of an entire team.

Football's also the toughest because it's played in fall and winter in all manner of rain, sleet and snow. Some of history's most memorable matches have occurred at below-freezing temperatures. Green Bay Packers fans are in a class by themselves when it comes to severe weather. Their stadium in Wisconsin, known as Lambeau Field, was the site of the infamous Ice Bowl, a 1967 championship game against the Dallas Cowboys where it got to 13 below zero.

Different teams have dominated different decades: the Pittsburgh Steelers in the 1970s, the San Francisco 49ers in the 1980s, the Cowboys in the 1990s and the New England Patriots now. The league's official website, www.nfl.com, is packed with information. Tickets are expensive and hard to get.

This can even be true of college and high-school football, which enjoy an intense amount of pomp and circumstance, with cheerleaders, marching bands, mascots, songs and mandatory pre- and post-game rituals, especially the tailgate – a full-blown beer and barbecue feast that takes place in parking lots where games are played.

Basketball

Invented in 1891 at a YMCA in Springfield, Massachusetts, basketball has been a huge success in America for years, surpassing baseball in lots of hearts and minds. College-level basketball, in particular, draws millions of fans in thousands of communities, where tickets are easier and cheaper to get and players have more manageable egos. Women play too, at both college and pro levels. It's not uncommon for certain college women's teams to outdraw the men's.

Sports Illustrated for Kids, a spin-off of the major magazine, also runs a website, www.sikids.com, with interactive games like all-star dodgeball and an athlete birthday finder.

The Mad Dog 100 Greatest Sports Arguments of All Time (2003) by New York sports talk radio jock Christopher Russo is a meaty read for anyone who loves to talk about, as much as watch, the games.

EXTREME SPORTS

When the first X Games were organized in 1995 in Newport, Rhode Island, most old-time sports junkies couldn't believe their eyes: BMX dirt biking and skateboarding as competitive sport? Weren't these just the activities of baggy-clothed Gen-Xers looking to get out of doing other stuff? But with those first 45 hours of prime-time coverage on ESPN, a new category was born. Now competitors hail from all corners of the world, many make millions in product endorsements, and some of the sports have made it into the Olympics.

Although Tiger Woods' earnings amounted to a paltry $6 million in 2004 (compare that with Shaquille O'Neal's $27 million), he certainly outpaced the rest with endorsements, racking up a whopping $80 million.

Despite its prominence, professional basketball is starting to show signs of strain – mounting ticket prices prevent much of its traditional fan base from attending, at a time when disadvantaged urban youth still cling to basketball as a way out.

Increasing numbers of players are being recruited from Europe, South America and even China, giving the game an unexpectedly cosmopolitan flavor. This hasn't boded well in international competition, where the US men's team, dubbed the Dream Team during Michael Jordan days, has been vulnerable, suffering a humiliating loss to Puerto Rico in the first round of the last Olympic Games. At home, there's been increasing violence in the stands. In Detroit, a full-blown riot broke out between fans and several players in 2004, disgracing the National Basketball Association (www.nba.com).

Los Angeles Lakers and New York Knicks games are known for attracting Hollywood stars courtside – Jack Nicholson and Spike Lee are among the most famous and fervent attendees respectively. Small-market teams like Sacramento and Portland have some of the most true-blue fans, and such cities can be great places to take in a game. The team to beat these days is the San Antonio Spurs, who have won three championships in six years.

Tennis star Andre Agassi's charitable foundation gave more to its cause ($11 million last year to underprivileged kids in Las Vegas) than any other charity organized and funded by an active pro athlete.

Every spring, college basketball hosts March Madness, a series of playoff games culminating in the Final Four, when the four remaining teams compete for a spot in the championship game. The Cinderella stories and unexpected outcomes dramatically rival the brutish defensive power and predictability of the pros. The games are widely televised.

Arts

The arts in America, like many aspects of American life, defy easy categorization. They are a high-thread-count weave of high and low cultures, of celebrity and commerce, of the chaotic and the sublime. Yet there is a guiding sensibility, one that, if it could, would ride whooping like an outlaw through the main street of town: it's a potent, romantic belief in the emotional truth of the individual. It's a grinning, unrepentant delight in provoking authority. And it's a burning desire to experience the transcendent epiphanies of now.

A disregard for social convention and history might seem ironic given America's founding as a nation of laws. But look at any field, and the best of America's arts are nearly synonymous with modernism and postmodernism. The United States – a young, socially divided nation lacking cohesive traditions – excels at sloughing off the past. Even if the fires of free-market capitalism didn't constantly demand the new, Americans would seek it anyway, preferring a cut-and-paste culture to match their patchwork selves.

Indeed, pop culture's faddish obsessions with style arise mainly from the schisms and fascinations of black–white, now multiethnic, America, as the nation's diverse peoples engage in an ever-evolving, careful dance of appropriation and admiration, of collaboration and theft, simultaneously trying to connect and keep identities clear.

As America enters the 21st century, the arts are in fact witnessing a polycultural explosion of new voices and increasing diffusion across the continent. The traditional artistic centers – New York and Los Angeles, Chicago and San Francisco – remain important but are no longer hegemonic. Today, the heartland is as likely to contain gay playwrights, graffiti artists and punk bands as the grim farmers of *American Gothic*.

This is occurring despite recent drops in public arts funding – due mainly to mounting federal and state budget deficits – and the consolidation of media ownership among a handful of multinational conglomerates (p62). The major cultural gatekeepers remain as conservative and penny-pinching as ever, but young, passionate artists are finding enthusiastic audiences.

Then there's digital technology. The movie and music industries are currently being revolutionized by 1s and 0s, with publishing only steps behind, still needing a better e-book. As digital technology puts the means of affordable, professional-quality production (and sometimes distribution) into the hands of individuals, it raises vexing issues of control and protection. Tools, artistic possibilities, audience experience: all are shifting uncomfortably, and no one knows how it will end.

Americans couldn't be more delighted. Postmodern flux and deconstruction are their briar patch; they are at home among the thorns. Have distinctions between high culture and pop culture evaporated? Have genres and forms become one big hip-hop mash-up? Great! American creativity has always flourished within the social chaos unleashed by technological change.

As much as anything, the arts in America today resemble a runaway train, threatening to jump the tracks at any minute and aiming for a future just over the rise.

LITERATURE

America first articulated a vision of itself through its literature. Since then, the American cultural landscape has been transformed several times,

The bible of American entertainment is *Entertainment Weekly* (www.ew.com): grab a copy and get up to date on everything. The website has separate content and magazine archives for the studious.

To read *Hip: The History* (2004) by John Leland is to watch an expert mechanic disassemble the racially charged, high-octane engine of American pop culture. It's so good it's bad.

with music, film and TV each pushing books from their original position of primacy. Today, critics spy the shrinking attention spans of the video-game generation and quickly proclaim American literature irrelevant and swooning unto death.

Nothing could be further from the truth. The book publishing industry has had its share of knocks and consolidations, but over the last decade, net sales have doubled, with an overall growth rate of 5%. Net sales were $23.7 billion in 2004, which was more than people spent on CDs and movie tickets combined. Juvenile and religious books are the fastest-growing segments, but the only sales avenue without rising numbers is book clubs (blame Internet retailers for that).

More than sales, however, Americans seem in no danger of losing their love of a well-told tale – and the number of vital, fresh American voices grows daily. In ever-unfolding America, there is always a new set of immigrant eyes, an unheard perspective, a constantly expanding definition of who Americans are and what America means. There is nothing static or mossy about US authors today, who now represent every stratum and eddy of society. Indeed, travelers looking for a few good books encapsulating the American experience will no doubt be overwhelmed by the kaleidoscopic wonders on offer.

American Desert (2004) by Percival Everett is a wickedly black satire of US mores. A man loses his head but doesn't die, and hysteria, media and tragedy follow like a hard rain.

Discovering America's Voice

American culture took some time to come into its own. Before the American Revolution, the continent's citizens identified themselves as British, and all of their arts were imitative of Europe. Once independence was won, however, an immediate call went out to develop a new national identity, a wholly American voice. Despite much parochial hand-wringing, little progress was made until around the 1820s, when writers and artists began to take up the two aspects of American life that had no counterpart on the continent: wilderness and the frontier experience.

E-books will eventually allow writers to imbed music, voice, video and text links in their works, creating not a digital 'book' but a new kind of storytelling. Whither the 'page-turner' then?

James Fenimore Cooper is credited with creating the first work of truly American literature with *The Pioneers* in 1823 (the first in his famous Leatherstocking adventures), and it made him a national hero. Cooper portrayed the humble pioneer, gathering ethical and spiritual lessons through his close association with wilderness, as a more authentic and admirable figure than the refined European. Cooper's crude humor and individualism proved to be manna to American sensibilities.

In his 1836 essay *Nature*, Ralph Waldo Emerson articulated similar ideas in intellectual terms. Emerson claimed that nature reflected God and held his instructions for humankind as plainly as the Bible. The essay emphasized rational thought and self-reliance – in essence making a spiritual philosophy out of the Puritan religion – and his writings became the core of the transcendentalist movement, which Henry David Thoreau championed in *Walden, Or, Life in the Woods* (1854).

A moving pastiche of contemporary writing, *Crossing into America* (2003) is an anthology of well-known and obscure novelists and poets tackling the unsettling, transformative passage of the immigrant experience.

Emerson's tragic opposite was Herman Melville, whose ambitious masterpiece *Moby Dick* (1851) was, in part, a cautionary tale of what happens when the individual accepts transcendentalist beliefs, and can thus distinguish good from evil with God-like clarity. Similarly, Nathaniel Hawthorne examined the dark side of conservative Puritan New England in *The Scarlet Letter* (1850).

Standing somewhat outside this dialogue was Edgar Allan Poe, the first American poet to achieve international acclaim. His gruesome stories (such as 'The Tell-Tale Heart,' 1843) helped popularize the short-story form, and he is credited with inventing the detective story, the horror story and science fiction, all extremely popular pulp fiction genres that bear a distinctly American stamp.

The celebration of the common man and nature would reach its apotheosis in Walt Whitman, whose epic poem *Leaves of Grass* (1855) signaled the arrival of a literary master and an American visionary. In Whitman's informal, intimate, rebellious free verse were songs of individualism, democracy, earthly spirituality, taboo-breaking sexuality and joyous optimism that encapsulated the heart of the new nation, and would become a touchstone for all subsequent American writers.

The Great American Novel

After the Civil War (1861–65), two lasting trends emerged: realism and regionalism. Stephen Crane's *The Red Badge of Courage* (1895) was one of the first great books to depict the horror of war itself, and Upton Sinclair's *The Jungle* (1906) was a shocking exposé of Chicago's meatpacking industry. At the same time, the rapid late-19th-century settlement of the West led to increasing interest in 'local colorist' writing; two of the more popular regionalists were western humorist Bret Harte and novelist Jack London (*Call of the Wild,* 1903).

However, it was Samuel Clemens, better known as Mark Twain, who would come to define American letters. Twain wrote in the vernacular, capturing the dialects of common speech. He loved 'tall tales' and reveled in satirical humor and absurdity. And his folksy, 'anti-intellectual' stance endeared him to everyday readers. These staples of American storytelling were then yoked to a transcendent purpose in *Huckleberry Finn* (1884). With this seminal novel, Twain made explicit the quintessential American narrative: necessitated by a primal moment of rebellion against his father, Huck embarks on a search for authenticity through which he discovers himself. The image of Huck and Jim, a poor white teenager and a runaway black slave, standing outside society's norms and floating together toward an uncertain future down the Mississippi River challenges American society still.

Disillusionment & Diversity

With the horrors of WWI and a newly industrialized society for fodder, American literature came fully into its own in the early 20th century.

Dubbed the Lost Generation, a number of US writers became expatriates in Europe, most famously Ernest Hemingway. His novel *The Sun Also Rises* (1926) exemplified the era, and his spare, stylized realism influenced several generations of writers.

F Scott Fitzgerald (*The Great Gatsby,* 1925) captured the hollowness of East Coast society life, while John Steinbeck (*The Grapes of Wrath,* 1939) became the great voice of the rural and working poor in the West. In the South, William Faulkner (*The Sound and the Fury,* 1929) examined troubled racial relations and social rifts, writing in dense but mordantly funny prose, rich in Southern speech.

In the 1930s, Poe's detective story got a good once-over by Dashiell Hammett (*The Maltese Falcon,* 1930) and Raymond Chandler (*The Big Sleep,* 1939), who minted a brand of hard-boiled urban realism, called 'noir,' that has yet to go out of style.

Meanwhile, the Harlem Renaissance flourished between the world wars, and a generation of African American intellectuals emerged who caught the attention of the wider white society. Based mainly in New York, these writers sought to instill pride in American black culture and to undermine racist stereotypes. Among the most well known were poets

In *The Plot Against America* (2004), Philip Roth creates a chilling alternate history in which an isolationist USA allows Hitler to win WWII, told from the vantage of Roth's Jewish Newark family.

HOMETOWN STORIES

After the September 11, 2001, terrorist attacks, the New York media declared irony dead, which meant that in the years following, the best contemporary American writing included nonfiction cultural exposés such as *Fast Food Nation* by Eric Schlosser and *Nickel and Dimed* by Barbara Ehrenreich, and a series of nostalgic biographies of America's founding fathers. And though irony isn't dead, it's still hibernating. Fluffy *Sex and the City*–style novels, such as Lauren Weisberger's *The Devil Wears Prada* and Plum Sykes' *Bergdorf Blondes*, remain among the most popular of all books. And while New York remains home to some of the finest young authors, including Jonathan Lethem, David Schickler and Jonathan Safran Foer – who gave us a savant's view of the city post–September 11 in *Extremely Loud and Incredibly Close* – the Internet age has disavowed the idea that a writer must live in NYC. Today, American authors and the stories they tell are as diverse as their hometowns.

If you're looking for irony, you can still find it in San Francisco, which has become the epicenter of hipster lit; writers-in-residence include Dave Eggers, Michael Chabon and their circle of irreverent friends working under the McSweeney's moniker. LA also has a surprisingly lush literary scene that includes novelists like Bruce Wagner – whose books document Hollywood hubris – and mystery writers like Michael Connelly, Robert Crais, James Ellroy and Walter Mosley, who know the City of Angels isn't always so on the up-and-up.

Though America's two most recent Nobel Prize winners, Toni Morrison and Saul Bellow, both hail from the Midwest, the 'flyover region' hasn't got as many props for producing writers as, say, the South. That said, you can still find some terrific books from the Midwest, including Geoffrey Eugenides' look at sexual confusion in dysfunctional Detroit, *Middlesex,* and Mark Weingardner's homage to Cleveland crime, *Crooked River Burning*. Nevertheless, the South has its reputation to uphold, and writers such as Poppy Z Bright – whose novels *Liquor* and *Prime* depict New Orleans in all its seedy glory – and George Saunders (*The Half Mammals of Dixie*) suggest Southern eccentricity may be genetic.

Back east, Maine, which may be familiar from Stephen King novels, has been the setting of the most eloquent recent portrayal of contemporary American small-town life: Richard Russo's *Empire Falls*. Both *The Interpreter of Maladies* and *The Namesake* by Jhumpa Lahiri describe the lives of immigrants from India struggling to fit into Boston's traditionally stuffy society.

Of course, the USA's authors can transcend geography – and even race, class and personal circumstance. One of the most dynamic African American writers is Toure, who has fabricated a fairy-tale town called *Soul City*. America's most stylistically radical author, James Frey, is a crack addict and an alcoholic. David Sedaris, far and away the funniest writer working, is a Southern gay chain-smoker awed by his crazy family's antics who doesn't even live here. He lives in Europe. Apparently, Bush's lockstep America isn't quite as willing to laugh at itself as he is.

Ed Nawotka

A beautiful, fabulist confection, *The People of Paper* (2005) by Salvador Plascencia constructs a narrative as tight and intricate as an origami crane, which floats from surrealist Mexico to gang-riddled LA.

Langston Hughes and Claude McKay, and novelist Zora Neale Hurston (*Their Eyes Were Watching God*, 1937), who captured the resilient dignity of rural black life.

After WWII, these trends only became more pronounced: American writers displayed a fully rebellious questioning of middle-class society's values, represented increasingly varied regional and ethnic perspectives, and pursued stylistic experimentation with abandon.

The 1950s Beat Generation picked up where the Lost Generation left off: no longer just questioning, but overturning social and literary conventions. Such authors as Jack Kerouac (*On the Road*, 1957), poet Allen Ginsberg (*Howl*, 1956) and William S Burroughs (*Naked Lunch*, 1959) made radical nonconformity their mantra, and they explored free-form and stream-of-consciousness writing.

JD Salinger (*The Catcher in the Rye*, 1951) and John Updike (*Rabbit, Run*, 1960) were two writers who captured the ironic disaffections of modern life with great humor, while charting a more brutal, unflinching realism were Norman Mailer, whose *The Naked and the Dead* (1948) got inside WWII, and Nelson Algren, who scoured the underside of Chicago in *The Man with the Golden Arm* (1949).

The South has always been ripe with contradictions and paradoxes, and Flannery O'Connor (*Wise Blood*, 1952) and Eudora Welty (*The Optimist's Daughter*, 1972) captured it masterfully. The mythic rural West found its modern-day poet laureate in Larry McMurtry (*Lonesome Dove*, 1986).

After WWII, African American writing grew in complexity and urgency. Richard Wright (*Black Boy*, 1945) and Ralph Ellison (*Invisible Man*, 1952) wrote passionately about racism, while James Baldwin became perhaps the most acclaimed African American writer (*Go Tell It on the Mountain*, 1953) as well as America's first openly gay writer (*Giovanni's Room*, 1956). Over the next decades, black women came into prominence, most notably Toni Morrison (*Beloved*, 1987) and Alice Walker (*The Color Purple*, 1983).

Orion Horncrackle, Fiesta Punch, Budgel Wolfscale: these are just a few of the Wyoming denizens populating Annie Proulx's *Bad Dirt* (2005), a Twain-esque collection of tall tales, hard luck and barbed-wire wit.

MUSIC

American popular music is the great soundtrack of the 20th, and now the 21st, century. Blues, jazz, country, rock and roll, hip-hop: what popular music in the world today hasn't been influenced by these American sounds? It's not just that the forms are so irresistible – it's the feeling. America's yawping, foot-stomping, defiant, democratic, good-time-loving character pours forth in its music, and few can resist singing along.

In the annual *Best American Nonrequired Reading*, David Eggers editorially corrals students, selecting the best writing everyone missed. It's like surfing the net where every link is a winner.

Any journey to the country's musical birthplaces leads through the South, the mother of American music. This is because almost all US popular music has roots in the combustive frisson and interplay of black–white racial relations, whose troubled course was first set by the 'peculiar institution' of slavery. Yet if the South is the inescapable origin, music today is wildly dispersed and diverse. New sounds and hot artists emerge from just about anywhere.

As for the $12 billion music industry, it's in a digital meltdown. Declining CD album sales recovered in 2004, and account for about 90% of all sales, but CDs are as doomed as the vinyl they replaced. Legal Internet music downloads – for playing on portable digital music devices like iPods – exploded to about 140 million tracks in 2004, but that's only one-tenth the estimated number of illegal downloads. However, those percentages are likely to reverse quickly: in 2005, the US Supreme Court ruled that music companies can sue Internet file-sharing companies if their products promote copyright-infringing music and video piracy. And the music industry has already sued over 12,000 private consumers for illegal downloading – all to ensure that corporations ride shotgun during this revolution.

Blues

The blues is a simple-seeming music with complex roots. It developed primarily out of the work songs, or 'shouts,' of black slaves and out of black spiritual songs and their 'call-and-response' pattern, both of which were adaptations of African music. These unformalized musical styles were, perhaps obviously, an entirely oral tradition until after the Civil War.

Transformed by the crucible of African American life in white US society, slave work songs became the blues. Largely improvisational and intensely personal, the blues could be played by anyone, and they remain at heart an immediate expression of individual pain, suffering, hope, desire and pride. Nearly all subsequent American music has tapped this deep well.

A Pulitzer Prize–winning memorial to the September 11 tragedy, *On the Transmigration of Souls* (2002) by John Adams is the kind of transportive, three-hanky orchestra piece few even attempt any more.

Martin Scorsese Presents the Blues (2003): how can you understand the blues by reading a book? The personal stories in this loving compilation come mighty close. Then see Scorsese's concert film Lightning in a Bottle (2004).

Once Blacks were liberated from slavery, they gained the freedom to develop their own cultural expressions. Black Christian choral music evolved into gospel, whose greatest singer, Mahalia Jackson, arrived on the scene in the 1920s.

Across the South, but particularly in the Mississippi River Delta (see p405), individuals around the turn of the 20th century began to gain fame, and employment, as traveling blues musicians; early pioneers include Robert Johnson, WC Handy and Leadbelly. However, female blues singers – particularly Bessie Smith, still considered the best blues singer who ever lived – initially gained the most attention.

After WWII, the blues dispersed north, particularly to Chicago, in the hands of a new generation of musicians – such as Muddy Waters, Bo Diddley, Buddy Guy and John Lee Hooker. Today, the blues flame is tended, and updated, by musicians like Robert Cray and Keb' Mo'.

Jazz

Jazz is more a sibling to the blues than a child of it. They developed concurrently, one more instrumental, one more vocal, out of similar roots.

Congo Sq in New Orleans (see p412) – where slaves gathered to sing and dance in the early 19th century – is commonly cited as the 'birthplace' of jazz, but like the blues, its origins are more diffuse. However, New Orleans was central to its development because of its unique mix of cultures. Here, ex-slaves adapted the reed, horn and string instruments used by the city's black Creoles – who were themselves more interested in playing formal European music – to play their own 'primitive,' African-influenced music, and this fertile cross-pollination produced a steady stream of innovative sound.

Two excellent jazz magazines are Down Beat (www.downbeat.com), with an online 'Jazz 101' history section, and Jazz Times (www.jazztimes .com), with an online jazz and blues festival guide.

The first variation was ragtime, which got its name from the 'ragged' style of its syncopated African rhythms. Beginning in the 1890s, ragtime was popularized by Scott Joplin and Irving Berlin, and made widely accessible through sheet music and player-piano rolls.

Dixieland jazz, centered on New Orleans' infamous Storyville district, followed at the turn of the century. Buddy Bolden is credited with being the first true jazz musician, although Jelly Roll Morton frequently boasted that he was the one who created jazz.

In 1917, Storyville was shut down, and the New Orleans jazz musicians dispersed. In 1919, bandleader King Oliver moved to Chicago, and his star trumpet player, Louis Armstrong, followed in 1922. Armstrong's distinctive vocals and talented improvisations led to the establishment of the solo as an integral part of jazz music, and Armstrong remains one of jazz's most beloved figures.

The 1920s and 1930s have come to be known as the Jazz Age, but music was just one part of the greater flowering of African American culture during New York's Harlem Renaissance. Swing – a new, urbane, big-band jazz style – swept the country, and bandleaders Duke Ellington and Count Basie were its most innovative practitioners. Jazz singers Ella Fitzgerald and Billie Holiday, as well as guitarist BB King, combined the blues with jazz.

The All Music Guide (www.allmusic.com) lives up to its name, with comprehensive categories (from Riot grrrl to Twee-pop) and extensive, useful essays on groups, albums and styles, plus samples.

After WWII, 'bebop' or 'bop' arose as a reaction against the smooth melodies and confining rhythms of big-band swing. Swing saxophonist Lester Young was a major influence on this new crop of musicians, who included Charlie Parker, Dizzy Gillespie and Thelonious Monk. Critics didn't get it, and at first derided such 1950s and 1960s permutations as cool jazz, hard-bop, free or avant-garde jazz, and fusion (which combined jazz and Latin or rock music) – but there was no stopping the postmodernist tide deconstructing and remaking jazz. Pioneers of this era include Miles Davis, Charles Mingus, John Coltrane and Ornette Coleman.

Today, no particular style of jazz predominates. Ragtime, Dixieland and swing have all experienced popular revivals, while musicians like Wynton Marsalis and Joshua Redman continue to nurture this ever-malleable, resilient form.

Folk & Country

Early Scottish, Irish and English immigrants brought their own instruments and folk music to America, and what emerged over time in the secluded Appalachian Mountains was fiddle-and-banjo hillbilly, or 'country,' music; in the Southwest, 'western' music was distinguished by steel guitars and larger bands. In the 1920s, these styles merged into 'country-and-western' music and became centered on Nashville, Tennessee, particularly once the Grand Ole Opry began its radio broadcasts in 1925 (see p454).

Jimmie Rodgers and the Carter Family were some of the first country musicians to become widely popular. In Kentucky, Bill Monroe and his Blue Mountain Boys mixed country with jazz and blues to create 'bluegrass' (see p459). Other famous country musicians have included Hank Williams, Johnny Cash and Willie Nelson.

The tradition of American folk music was crystallized in the person of Woody Guthrie, who traveled the country during the Depression singing politically conscious songs. In the 1940s, he was joined by Pete Seeger, who was a tireless preserver of America's folk heritage. Folk experienced a revival during the 1960s protest movements, but then-folkie Bob Dylan ended it almost single-handedly when he picked up an electric guitar to shouts of 'traitor!' and never returned. (For current folk music festivals, see the gig guide at www.dirtylinen.com.)

Country music influenced rock and roll in the 1950s, while rock-flavored country was dubbed 'rockabilly' (and country + rap = 'hick-hop'). In the 1980s, country-and-western music became a major commercial industry, rising on the popularity of stars like Garth Brooks, but in recent years hip-hop has supplanted it as the second-most popular music after rock. Interestingly, some of the most popular country and alt country artists today are female, such as the Dixie Chicks, Shania Twain, Faith Hill, Loretta Lynn, Lucinda Williams and others.

Rock & Roll

Most say rock and roll was born in 1954 the day Elvis Presley walked into Sam Philips' Sun Studios and recorded 'That's All Right.' Philips heard the future, but radio stations heard a white country boy singing black music and didn't know what to do. In 1956, Presley scored his first big breakthrough with 'Heartbreak Hotel,' shocking and thrilling the nation with his rebellious sexuality – and stations figured it out. Just play the music, and the kids go crazy.

Rock and roll is a complex hybrid that both signaled and abetted a cataclysm of social change. Musically, it was a combination of guitar-driven blues, black rhythm and blues (R&B), and white country-and-western music. R&B, which evolved in the 1940s out of swing and the blues, was then known as 'race music' and listened to almost exclusively by Blacks. With rock and roll, white musicians (and some black musicians) transformed 'race music' into something uncategorizable that Whites could embrace freely – and this they did.

A peerless cultural ambassador, Ry Cooder resurrects a lost Mexican American LA neighborhood in *Chavez Ravine* (2005), a fascinating blend of Latin horns, Mexican accordions, rock guitars, jazz and politics.

With *Van Lear Rose* (2005), country icon Loretta Lynn teams with the White Stripes' Jack White to create a wonderfully evocative, unexpected alt country masterpiece.

The term 'rock and roll' was originally a black euphemism for sex. It first appeared in blues singer Trixie Smith's 1922 song 'My Daddy Rocks Me (With One Steady Roll).'

At first, rock and roll scared the bejeezus out of square America. *All Shook Up* (2003) by Glenn Altschuler wonderfully captures the cultural hysteria and significance of it all.

However, rock and roll, more than any other music before it, was aimed at youth. Rock became a call to arms for a post-WWII generation questioning society's values. Critics and parents were horrified, but beneath its loud, hip-shaking, easily commercialized surface, rock embodied an urgent countercultural force. This tension – between commerce and authenticity, between hedonistic fun and seriousness – has defined rock music ever since.

Nevertheless, rock almost died at the end of the 1950s – to control 'juvenile delinquents,' authorities sanitized and suppressed it, and an omen-laden 1959 plane crash killed Buddy Holly, Richie Valens and the Big Bopper. It took the early-1960s 'British Invasion' – led by the Beatles and the Rolling Stones, who initially were emulating Holly, Chuck Berry, Little Richard and others – to shock American rock back to life.

Since then, each generation has made rock its own, with the lifestyles of musicians frequently as influential as their music. The 1960s witnessed

HIP-HOP ROOTS & CULTURE

Today's global hip-hop culture can be traced directly back to young black, Puerto Rican and Jamaican American youths living and playing on the mean streets of the Bronx, New York, in the early 1970s. Pioneering DJs such as Kool Herc, Afrika Bambaataa and Grandmaster Flash would spin just the funkiest parts of their records, the 'breaks,' and kids would make up new, gravity-defying dance steps, 'break dancing,' at these impromptu parties in the neighborhood parks and playgrounds. MCs would pick up the microphone and urge the crowd into a musical frenzy. And late at night, young spraypaint artists from all walks of life would sneak around the city painting their aliases in highly stylized script. The four elements of hip-hop – rap, DJ sampling, breakdancing and graffiti art – were born, and over the next few decades would crisscross the globe, cross-pollinate with other cultures, and eventually become the multi-billion-dollar industry it is today.

Turn on the TV and you'll find rappers selling soda pop and automobiles, but at the same time, that kid sitting next to you on the bus may be a bedroom producer with his own independent record label. Hip-hop comes in all shapes and sizes, from the glitz and glamour of Lil' Kim or Atlanta's flashy OutKast, to the earthiness of Chicago-born Common or Los Angeles' Jurassic5, favorites among college kids. Then there's the jazzy, spiritual Hieroglyphics Crew out of Oakland, California, or the complex lyrical abstractions of Eye-Dea & Abilities from Minneapolis, Minnesota. Ice Cube and Queen Latifah are multimillionaire movie stars, and veteran graffiti artists like Futura and Haze are world renowned for their record covers, corporate logo design and canvases hung in the finest galleries.

Hip-hop has produced its own ruling class, from the man behind Def Jam and Phat Pharm, Russell Simmons; to rap-mogul P-Diddy; to the *Source* magazine empire – yet there is still a massive underground of countless unknown MCs honing their skills in tiny clubs and basement studios from Middle America to Alaska (and even from Croatia to Japan!). Community radio stations play the latest from new regional artists, and spread the word about upcoming live shows, on what Public Enemy's Chuck D once famously described as 'the black CNN.' And cities like San Francisco and Phoenix have given birth to some of the most talented street artists to emerge since the New York City subway halcyon days of the late '70s and early '80s.

While huge, platinum-selling acts like Jay-Z and Snoop Dogg rule the mainstream airwaves, labels like StonesThrow and Female Fun consistently release cutting-edge material to eager ears. And the legends are still performing. KRS One can still be heard in medium-sized clubs across the country. And at Crotona Park in the Bronx, Afrika Bambaataa and Kool DJ Red Alert will be spinning the classics, as Crazy Legs and the Rock Steady Crew incorporate *capoeira* (Brazilian-style martial arts) and kung-fu moves into their b-boy dance in an ever-evolving recipe for the future of the culture.

TophOne

a full-blown youth rebellion, epitomized by the drug-inspired psychedelic sounds of the Grateful Dead and Jefferson Airplane, and the electric wails of Janis Joplin, Jimi Hendrix, Bob Dylan and Patti Smith.

Punk arrived in the late 1970s, led by the Ramones, Blondie and the Dead Kennedys, as did the working-class rock of Bruce Springsteen and Tom Petty. Since then, rock has stayed current by splintering into hundreds of variations: new wave, no wave, heavy metal, speed metal, grunge rock, prog rock, world beat, skate punk, goth, electronica and much, much more – with influences circling the globe and returning to the US at lightning speed.

Even today, with hip-hop (opposite) having usurped it as America's outlaw sound, rock survives – absorbing, shifting, rediscovering its blues roots. Listen to the White Stripes, the Yeah Yeah Yeahs, the Black Keys or Green Day and you'll hear that rock and roll is alive, well and definitely kicking.

The self-proclaimed 'Queens of Rock 'n' Roll,' Sleater-Kinney have been a cult favorite for a decade. In *The Woods* (2005), their signature howling punk expands in moody, satisfying directions.

PAINTING & SCULPTURE Karen Levine

American art emerged under the sway of European tradition, with practitioners trained in England, France, and Italy producing portraits, still lifes, and reproductive prints for colonists with the means to buy them. Around the 1820s, however, a newly influential merchant class began to patronize the arts, encouraging a 'native' school of American-born painters that would set the precedent for decades of innovative art-making to come. Henceforth, many of America's most significant contributions to visual culture would be made by artists responding to, or outright rejecting, old-world conventions.

Shaping a National Identity

Artists played a vital role in US expansion during the early 19th century, disseminating images of far-flung territories and reinforcing the call to manifest destiny. Thomas Cole and his colleagues in the Hudson River School – Albert Bierstadt, Frederic Edwin Church and John Frederick Kensett, among others – translated the sublime vistas of European romanticism to luminous landscapes in the wilds of upstate New York, while Frederic Remington offered idealized, often stereotypical representations of the Western frontier. Other artists, such as George Caleb Bingham and William Sidney Mount, focused on genre paintings or scenes of everyday life, adapting a form originated in 17th-century Holland to exalt American virtues of hard work and democracy.

In the wake of the Civil War and its accompanying industrialization, a distinctive strain of realism became increasingly prominent. Augustus Saint-Gaudens and John Quincy Adams Ward produced masterful marbles and bronzes for a variety of national monuments. Eastman Johnson painted nostalgic scenes of rural life, as did Winslow Homer, who would later become renowned for deft watercolor seascapes. Perhaps the most daring example of realism was Thomas Eakins's *The Gross Clinic* (1875), which scandalized Philadelphia with its graphic representation of a surgical procedure. This once-reviled painting today enjoys pride of place at Thomas Jefferson University's medical school.

Among the oldest American museums are Boston's Massachusetts Historical Society (founded 1791) and the New York Historical Society (founded 1804), both devoted, like many early museums, to wide-ranging displays of natural specimens, paintings, prints, manuscripts and other artifacts.

An American Avant-Garde

Polite society's objections to Eakins's painting had nothing on the near-riots inspired by New York's Armory Show of 1913 – the exhibition that introduced the nation to European modernism and changed the face of American art. The show presented examples of impressionism, fauvism, and cubism, including the notorious 1912 *Nude Descending a Staircase*

(No. 2) by Marcel Duchamp, a French artist who later became an American citizen. In 1917 Duchamp shocked audiences once more with *Fountain*, his anonymous submission to the New York Society of Independent Artists exhibition. The sculpture, Duchamp's first publicly exhibited 'readymade,' was an upended porcelain urinal signed 'R. Mutt.' The show's organizers rejected the work on the grounds that it was not art, but Duchamp's gesture has inspired generations of American artist-provocateurs, from Robert Rauschenberg and Andy Warhol to Sherrie Levine and Bruce Nauman.

The Armory Show was merely the first in a series of exhibitions evangelizing the radical aesthetic shifts of European modernism. Portions of the presentation traveled to Chicago and Boston, and a similar exposition appeared in San Francisco in 1915. It was inevitable that American artists would begin to grapple, in various forms, with what they had seen. Alexander Calder, Joseph Cornell and Isamu Noguchi produced sculptures inspired by surrealism and constructivism; the precisionist paintings of Charles Demuth, Georgia O'Keeffe and Charles Sheeler combined realism with a touch of cubist geometry.

Given the national aversion to public arts funding, it is ironic that government support did much to advance the American vanguard while stimulating production of art with a political bent. In the 1930s, the Works Progress Administration's (WPA) Federal Art Project, part of Franklin D Roosevelt's New Deal (p50), commissioned murals, paintings and sculptures for public buildings nationwide. Thomas Hart Benton, Ben Shahn and Grant Wood, among other WPA artists, borrowed from Soviet social realism and Latin American muralists to forge a socially engaged figurative style with regional flavor. African American and female artists also benefited from the nondiscriminatory policies of the WPA, which employed Romare Bearden, Stuart Davis, Aaron Douglas and other figures associated with the Harlem Renaissance as well as Lee Krasner, Alice Neel and Louise Nevelson.

Abstract Expressionism

In the wake of WWII, American art underwent a sea change at the hands of New York school painters such as Franz Kline, Jackson Pollock and Mark Rothko, many of whom had worked on murals for the WPA. Moved by surrealism's celebration of spontaneity and the unconscious, these artists began to explore new possibilities for abstraction, infusing their work with psychological potency through the gestural handling of paint and imposing scale. The movement's 'action painter' camp took this to the extreme; Pollock, for example, made his drip paintings by pouring and splattering pigments above large canvases. Barnett Newman and Rothko exercised more subdued brushwork, creating epic yet ethereal paintings dominated by carefully composed fields of color. In the early 1950s, some artists began rendering figural subjects using abstract expressionism's loose, spontaneous brushstrokes; at the forefront of California's Bay Area figurative school, Elmer Bischoff, Richard Diebenkorn and David Park forged a distinctive hybrid style with their vigorously painted interiors and landscapes.

Abstract expressionism is widely considered the first truly original school of American art. Intriguingly, art historians have argued that the US used it as a tool for Cold War propaganda; evidence suggests that the CIA funded traveling exhibitions of abstract expressionism in hopes of promoting American individualism and democracy. Abstraction, it was hoped, would serve as an instructive antidote to the realist styles favored by Soviet regimes.

Art + Commodity = Pop

Once established, abstract expressionism reigned supreme on the American scene; indeed, critics virulently attacked one of its best-known practitioners, Philip Guston, when he unveiled his first figurative paintings in 1970. However, some young artists began to revolt years earlier, most notably Jasper Johns and Robert Rauschenberg. In the mid-1950s, Johns came to prominence with thickly painted renditions of ubiquitous symbols, including targets and the American flag, while Rauschenberg assembled artworks from comics, ads and even – à la Duchamp – found objects (a mattress, a boot, a stuffed goat). Both artists are credited with breaking down traditional boundaries between painting and sculpture, and with opening the field for pop art in the 1960s.

The economic boom of postwar America also had its share of influence on pop. Not only did artists return to representational subjects, they took pervasive consumer imagery – billboards, product packaging and media icons – as inspiration. Employing mundane mass-production techniques to silkscreen paintings of movie stars and Coke bottles, Andy Warhol helped topple the myth of the solitary artist laboring heroically in the studio. Roy Lichtenstein deployed newsprint's humble benday dot in canvases based on the representational conventions of comics. Other prominent artists who created inventive examples of pop include James Rosenquist, Ed Ruscha and Wayne Thiebaud.

Minimalism & Beyond

The tendency that eventually became known as minimalism shared pop's interest in mass production, but all similarities ended there. Like the abstract expressionists, artists such as Donald Judd, Agnes Martin, Robert Ryman and Tony Smith eschewed representational subject matter; their cool, reductive works of the 1960s and 1970s were often arranged in gridded compositions and fabricated from industrial materials. Sol LeWitt, meanwhile, was busy theorizing the related strand of conceptualism, arguing that the idea behind an artwork was more important than the object itself. Robert Irwin and James Turrell explored the realm of perception through spare, dematerialized installations of light, while Eva Hesse, Robert Morris, Richard Serra and Richard Tuttle lent their sculptures a sense of impermanence through malleable materials such as latex, felt, molten lead and wire.

In many ways, minimalism and related trends aimed to critique the gallery context and undermine the status of art as commodity. This was perhaps most dramatically demonstrated by land artists Walter De Maria, Michael Heizer and Robert Smithson, who created immense earthworks in the American heartland that no one could buy or sell.

The Contemporary Scene

The past few decades have witnessed an explosion of artistic approaches on the American scene, not to mention considerable controversy. By the 1980s, civil rights, feminism and AIDS activism had made significant inroads in visual culture, and artists not only voiced political dissent through their work but also embraced a range of once-marginalized media, from textiles and graffiti to video, sound and performance. The decade also ushered in the so-called Culture Wars, which commenced with tumult over photographs by Robert Mapplethorpe and Andres Serrano, and reached a bitter conclusion in 1998, when the Supreme Court ruled that the National Endowment for the Arts could withhold funding from artists violating 'standards of decency and respect for the beliefs and values of the American public.'

North American Indian Art (2004) by David W Penney: a curator at the Detroit Institute of Arts offers one of the most accessible and up-to-date introductions to the artistic traditions of America's indigenous cultures.

The Guerilla Girls' Art Museum Activity Book (2004): since 1985 these masked crusaders have used humorous shock tactics to fight sexism in the art world; this slim comic is among their recent provocations. You may never look at museums the same again.

Thomas Kinkade, 'painter of light,' may be America's most popular living artist. Selling like hotcakes at a mall near you, his cozy paintings combine Norman Rockwell's folksy Americana with impressionism's luminous brushstrokes. Over 10 million people, and counting, have purchased Kinkade's kitsch.

PHOTOGRAPHY IN AMERICA

The history of photography in the US is a vast and important subject – the medium was central to westward expansion, shaped reactions to the Civil War, influenced social movements of the early 20th century and was a driving force behind modernism. In the mid-19th century, itinerant photographers used the invention to make portraits at a fraction of the price of paintings. Timothy O'Sullivan and Carleton Watkins lugged mammoth plate cameras into the Rocky Mountains and Yosemite. Mathew Brady documented devastated Civil War battlefields, while Eadweard Muybridge was an innovator in early stop-motion photography. Turn-of-the-century pictorialist prints by Gertrude Käsebier, Alfred Stieglitz and Clarence White were crucial to public acceptance of photography as a legitimate art form. The medium became a social tool in the hands of Lewis Hine and Jacob Riis, who captured scenes of poverty and exploitation. Man Ray experimented in the darkroom to produce droll dada compositions, while Berenice Abbott, Charles Sheeler, Edward Weston and other proponents of 'straight photography' framed avant-garde views of nudes and the built environment. Ansel Adams created enduring vistas of America's national parks, and Walker Evans and Dorothea Lange shot indelible documents of Depression-era poverty for the Farm Security Administration. Margaret Bourke-White, Robert Capa and W Eugene Smith captured the calamity of WWII for *Life*, while Lee Miller and Irving Penn shot daring fashion images for *Vogue*. Diane Arbus, Robert Frank, Nan Goldin and William Klein drew on the aesthetics of amateur snapshots to produce startling perspectives on the American social landscape. In 1976, color photography finally received its due when William Eggleston exhibited vivid views of southern life at MoMA, New York.

As in painting and sculpture, subsequent decades have seen an explosion of approaches and techniques. Remarkable examples of contemporary photography may be found at museums nationwide, notably MoMA, the Met, the International Center of Photography and the George Eastman House in New York; the Center for Creative Photography in Arizona; and the Getty Center and the San Francisco Museum of Modern Art in California.

Karen Levine

The Library of Congress has digitized more than 160,000 Depression-era pictures by Walker Evans, Dorothea Lange and others (you can even order reproductions of your favorites) at memory.loc.gov/ammem /fsahtml/fahome.html.

Throughout this firestorm and beyond, however, American artists have continued to innovate and inspire. Internationally prominent artists of recent generations include painters John Currin, Jeff Koons and Barry McGee; sculptors Robert Gober and Kiki Smith; sculptor and filmmaker Matthew Barney; video artists Doug Aitken and Tony Oursler; photographers Tina Barney and Cindy Sherman; and installation artists Felix Gonzalez-Torres, Sarah Sze and Kara Walker.

ARCHITECTURE

What's America's most prominent architectural contribution to the world? The skyscraper – a fitting symbol of the USA's technical achievements, grand aspirations, commerce and natural affinity for modernism.

Until the 20th century, American architecture was relatively conservative, following revivalist trends and adopting European tastes, and it can often remain conservative – the result of a disposable lifestyle, the mass production of materials and the high costs of building. However, as elsewhere, computer advances are sparking a new wave of innovation and originality – a quintessentially American, ahistorical plunge into futurama.

The Colonial Period

The only lasting indigenous influence on American architecture has been the adobe pueblo of Southwestern Indians. Seventeenth- and 18th-century Spaniards incorporated elements of the pueblo, and this hybrid reappeared in 20th-century architecture as mission-revival style in Southern California and pueblo style in the Southwest.

On the East Coast, the architecture of the early colonists reflected necessity as much as design. In Virginia and the Carolinas, the would-be gentry aped grander English homes (based on pictures), and bricks replaced timber. Present-day Williamsburg, Virginia, is an accurate reconstruction.

After the Revolutionary War, the nation's leaders wanted a style befitting the new republic and adopted neoclassicism, which embodied the ideals of Greece and Rome. The Virginia State Capitol (p348), designed by the multitalented Thomas Jefferson, was modeled on a Roman temple, and his home, Monticello (p359), has a Romanesque rotunda.

Professional architect Charles Bulfinch helped develop the more monumental federal style, which paralleled the English Georgian style. The grandest example is the US Capitol in Washington (p309), which became the model for many state legislative buildings.

In the 19th century, mirroring English fashions, Americans preferred the heavier Greek-revival style; public buildings and mansions became mini Greek or Roman temples or had a Parthenon-shaped portico tacked on the front. Then around 1850, Gothic-revival style became popular for churches and college buildings.

> For the latest on contemporary American home design, check out *Dwell* (www.dwellmag .com), a great glossy mag dedicated to modern styles you can live with, and in.

The Frontier & the Suburbs

In the mid-19th century, small-scale building was revolutionized by 'balloon-frame' construction: a light frame of standard-milled, two-by-four-inch timber was joined with cheap, mass-produced nails. Easy and economical to build, balloon-frame stores and houses were thrown up in towns all over the expanding West. Eventually condemned as an inner-city fire hazard, this type of house proliferated in the suburbs, putting home ownership within reach of the middle class – thus making the single-family home the enduring brass ring of the American Dream.

A notable variation was the more well-to-do 'Victorian,' which appeared in San Francisco and other cities. Larger and fancier, these homes added balconies, towers and ornate, colorful trim reflecting a mix of neoclassical, Queen Anne, Gothic and Italianate styles.

Beaux Arts

After the Civil War, influential architects studied at the École des Beaux-Arts in Paris, and American buildings showed increasing refinement and confidence. Major examples of beaux arts style are Richard Morris Hunt's Biltmore Estate in North Carolina, Washington, DC's railway station and San Francisco's City Hall.

> *American Houses* (2004) by Gerald Foster is an excellent field guide to American homes, with pithy descriptions of each historical style and clear diagrams with floor plans.

Internal iron-frame buildings first appeared in Manhattan in the 1850s; this meant the walls no longer supported the structure, allowing greater freedom of design. When combined with the 1880s invention of the Otis elevator, tall buildings became possible. The Chicago School crossed these innovations with beaux arts style and produced the skyscraper, the first 'modern' architecture.

A leading exponent of functionalism, Louis Sullivan built the first true skyscraper in Buffalo, New York: the 13-story Guaranty Building. Among Chicago's early skyscrapers was Sullivan's intriguing Carson Pirie Scott & Co department store. Soon, however, Chicago was eclipsed by New York, where the skyscraper was pushed ever higher by the pressures of profit and high-priced real estate.

> In the 1950s, sprawling middle-class suburbs appeared almost literally overnight. One major housing developer, Levitt and Sons, produced a new four-bedroom house every 16 minutes.

Frank Lloyd Wright

Initially an apprentice to Sullivan's firm, Frank Lloyd Wright created an architectural style all his own and is considered one of the 20th century's great visionaries. Working mainly on private houses, he abandoned historical elements and references, making each building a unique sculptural form characterized by strong horizontal lines. Wright called them 'prairie houses,' though invariably they were built in the suburbs.

Interior spaces flowed from one to another rather than being divided into rooms, and the inside was connected to the outside rather than separated by solid walls. Texture and color came from the materials themselves, not from applied decoration. Wright was innovative in his use of steel, glass and concrete, and he pioneered panel heating, indirect lighting, double glazing and air-conditioning.

As well as visiting the revolutionary Guggenheim Museum in New York City, Wright fans should check out Buffalo, New York; southern Wisconsin; eastern Pennsylvania; and, of course, Chicago.

Reaching for the Sky

America's newest landmark will be New York's World Trade Center Memorial Site (www .renewnyc.com), to be completed in 2009, which includes the 1776ft Freedom Tower and a below-ground memorial called 'Reflecting Absence.'

Influenced by Wright's breaking of traditions and by art deco – which became instantly popular in the US after the 1925 Paris exposition – city buildings soared in height and appearance. The horizontals and especially the verticals of the structural grid and the surfaces of concrete, glass and steel became the main design elements. Notable examples are the 1930 Chrysler Building and the 1931 Empire State Building. Art deco also marked the 1932 Rockefeller Center and its Radio City Music Hall, and it set the tone nationwide for movie houses, gas stations and resort hotels.

European architects absorbed Wright's ideas, and that influence bounced back when the Bauhaus school left Nazi Germany to set up in the USA. In America, Bauhaus became known as the International style, and its principles were taught at Harvard by Walter Gropius and practiced in Chicago by Ludwig Mies van der Rohe. By using glass 'curtain walls' over a steel frame, the best International-style buildings became abstract, sculptured shapes, and the worst became ugly glass boxes. New York's Seagram Building is one of the best.

Then came postmodernism, which reintroduced decoration, color and historical references, along with dollops of whimsy. In this, American architects like Michael Graves and Philip Johnson took the lead (see Johnson's AT&T Building in New York).

For a primer in cutting edge, CAD-CAM-enabled contemporary US architecture, turn to *All American* (2002) by Brian Carter and Annette Lecuyer. Gorgeous illustrations.

In the 21st century, new computer-design techniques allow for the affordable, one-off production of materials and wild, curving, asymmetrical designs. Canadian-born Frank Gehry has been a pioneer (Minneapolis' Weisman Art Museum is one example), but following close behind are a bevy of young architects who are bringing pragmatic idiosyncrasy to all types of buildings. Their binding ideology? Innovation, innovation, innovation.

FILM

There is nothing subtle about Hollywood films: they manufacture dreams. They illuminate the darkness with dystopian visions, idealized beauty, kinetic diversions, comforting formulas and feel-good endings. They are the country's most famous export – advertising lifestyles, trends, and the half-truths and self-delusions of America's hopes and fears. Indeed, these myth-making projections retain a remarkable, occasionally unique power to move the US culture that creates them.

So why does Hollywood squander this on so much overproduced B-movie escapism? Well, first, true to their sometimes lowbrow reputation, Americans love their explosions and car chases. But as importantly, over the last decade, movie studios have become the gaudy baubles of

CAMPFIRE TALES (ON STEROIDS)

With Hollywood strip-mining comic books in search of the next summer blockbuster, it's tempting to say that comics have never been hotter. But the comic-book industry has been a vital part of the pop-culture landscape far longer than it's been filling multiplexes. Sure, the Pulitzer Prize–winning *Maus* long ago dispelled the notion that comics are just for kids, and *manga*-reading Japanese commuters underscore a global industry, but the key to understanding the medium's enduring appeal can be found in the peculiar icon that drives the medium – the guy, or gal, in the cape and tights – and what it symbolizes for American culture.

Seinfeld lasted ten seasons? Big deal. Spider-Man has been swinging strong for over 40 years. He's survived the Cold War, Vietnam, free love, the pet rock, Reagan, Clinton and at least one Bush. And when September 11 tore out our collective heart, he shed tears at Ground Zero. What other medium can boast a fictional character that has been embraced by – and, in turn, has embraced – so many generations?

Why the love? Because comic books aren't really about superpowers, they're about character. At the center of any good comic book is an individual whose special abilities are always matched by special problems – problems that always seem to escalate, that never, ever go away. The super-villains in their brightly colored tights are, just like the guy who snaps his gum on the morning subway train, potholes in the road of life. If the superhero represents anything, it's the resilience of the human spirit. It's not so much what the superhero can *do*, but what he can endure.

Which is fertile ground for good storytelling. At the outset of the 21st century, comics are enjoying a creative renaissance, spurred on by an unprecedented influx of talent from other media. From pop-culture powerbrokers like Kevin Smith and Joss Whedon, to respected novelists like Eric Jerome Dickey and Jonathan Lethem, artists are giving back to the medium that sparked their imaginations, and bringing their own fan bases with them. And while the two major companies – Marvel and DC – continue to slug it out for market share and the hearts and minds of the faithful, so-called alternative comics remind an even broader audience that the medium knows no boundaries. Take, for instance, Joe Sacco's *Safe Area Gorazde*, a searing account of the Bosnian War that offers a slice of journalism not seen in the paper of record. Or Chris Ware's *Jimmy Corrigan: The Smartest Kid on Earth* – which redefines visual storytelling with every page.

So don't be fooled. The current crop of comic-book-inspired movies, toys and TV shows says more about the rest of pop culture than comic books. Comics have been a stray thread in the tapestry of American life for 68 years, and counting, because they provide something that can't be found anywhere else: serialized fiction that epitomizes American optimism. Comics remind us that it's never over. They are our campfire tales, our modern mythology.

Axel Alonso

media conglomerates (p62) whose main concern is creating new product for theme park rides, video games, TV shows and toys (or vice versa). For this, they need 'event pictures' whose gargantuan budgets – now routinely topping $100 million – demand the safety of lowest-common-denominator appeal.

Digital technology has also reshaped the landscape. In the $30-billion movie business, two-thirds of profits come from DVD sales and rentals. DVD is one of the fastest-adopted technologies ever, which both explains and compensates for Hollywood's recent decline at the box office. Burgeoning high-tech 'home theaters' mean Americans can get their fix without the hassle of parking and overpriced popcorn.

Meanwhile, digital cameras, editing and projection have spawned two trends: free from celluloid's limitations, big-picture special effects can be as extravagantly surreal as the mind allows; and free from celluloid's costs, low-budget filmmakers can and are making the sorts of personal, idiosyncratic movies Hollywood normally passes over. For an overview of America's current independent film movement, see p82.

Fuhgedaboudit. The Internet Movie Database (www.imdb.com) is the most comprehensive Internet resource for movie information and reviews.

The Magic of Moving Pictures

In *Down and Dirty Pictures* (2004), Peter Biskind gets inside the 1990s independent film movement, arguing that the high-minded Sundance Institute and powerful Miramax were its yin and yang.

Motion picture cameras and projectors were developed simultaneously in France and the USA in the late 19th century, though Thomas Edison was the first to use sprocketed celluloid film. The first movie house opened in Pittsburgh in 1905, and because shows cost a nickel, it was called a nickelodeon.

The power of moving pictures to tell stories was immediately obvious; *The Great Train Robbery* (1903) is famous because it was the first to edit for dramatic effect – it cut to the chase. Almost as quickly, moviemakers realized the audience-drawing power of genres and stars. In the 1910s, Charlie Chaplin became the first true movie star, and Mack Sennett's

STATE OF INDEPENDENTS

American independent filmmakers are the movie industry's pioneer-entrepreneurs, working outside the studio-produced, multi-million-dollar star-driven system. Characterized by edgy, provocative subjects, a visionary approach and an indomitable drive, their work is funded as much by favors and friends as the occasional partnership with an independent distributor.

With the digital revolution in cinema, unprecedented numbers of filmmakers have seized the opportunities provided by accessible, affordable digital cameras and laptop editing. The explosion in filmmaking is paralleled by the proliferation of film festivals; their evolution seems symbiotic. Movies used to be made by the few, for the many. But digital democratization means that (for better or worse, some would say) pretty much anyone can make a movie.

Meanwhile, cinemas flirt with digital projection, and DVDs are dispensed by mail order, on campus and at airports. Tim Robbins and Hal Hartley recently chose to distribute new projects by mail-order DVD via Netflix: maybe this heralds a divide between storytelling for the big screen – an essential for purists and '70s auteurs – versus storytelling for smaller screens. The state of independents is in flux.

The new generation of filmmakers, unlike many of their predecessors, has been raised on film. Some come from familiar lineage, like Sofia Coppola, daughter of the visionary godfather of new cinema, Francis Ford Coppola. But there's always room for new talent: the international acclaim for video-artist-turned-feature-filmmaker Miranda July's *Me and You and Everyone We Know* (2005) may well establish her place in the pantheon of mega-indies. And the ante continues to be upped by the likes of Gus Van Sant (recently, in *Elephant*, 2003, and *Last Days*, 2005), and Steven Soderbergh who is as likely to be producing new talent as directing his own projects.

It's independent talent that fuels the industry. Distributors regularly scour festivals for hot new filmmakers. Curiously, the newest new thing to take American cinemas by storm is the documentary. While feature filmmakers experiment with hand-held, verité storytelling, doc makers have taken these time-honored methods to the streets, rebooting the flagging doc market into the hottest genre on the block. Doc makers see what hasn't been seen – whether it's krumping in South Central Los Angeles, the incredible street dance phenomenon captured in *Rize* (2005); or birds in San Francisco, in *The Wild Parrots of Telegraph Hill* (2003), a sure inspiration for the urban birder. Maverick director Michael Moore regularly uses Flint, Michigan, as the pulse of America, as he brings the backyard to the big issues – whether it's gun control or September 11.

Many filmmakers hope that festival accolades will help garner a distribution deal. Indies can be found, often in person discussing their work, at the 600 or more festivals across the US. While some are local events, others are internationally touted and feature premieres of international as well as American cinema. Those worth planning a trip around include: Los Angeles, San Francisco and Tribeca in spring; Seattle in summer; New York and Mill Valley in autumn. And in winter, there's the annual pilgrimage to Utah for Sundance: where schmoozing, deal-making, stargazing and skiing are the daily diet. (Check www.filmfestivals.com for comprehensive listings.)

As for the future, the stage is already set: at festivals, in cinemas and on laptops – the voice of America is on film and the vision is independent.

Zoë Elton

slapstick comedies – and his ever-bumbling Keystone cops – became cultural institutions.

DW Griffith was a pioneer of cinematic techniques. His landmark films *Birth of a Nation* (1915) and *Intolerance* (1916) introduced much of cinema's now-familiar language, such as the fade, the close-up and the flashback.

At the same time, increased competition led to the studio system, which began in New York City, where Edison tried to create a monopoly with his patents. This drove many independents to move to a suburb of Los Angeles, where they could easily flee to Mexico in case of legal trouble – and thus, Hollywood was born.

In 1927, sound was first introduced in *The Jazz Singer,* and the 'talkies' ushered in the golden age of the movies, from the 1930s to the 1950s. Movie palaces and drive-in theaters sprung up everywhere; in 1938 alone, it was estimated 65% of the population saw a film. Glamorous stars – Humphrey Bogart, Cary Grant, Katherine Hepburn – enthralled the nation and Hollywood studios locked them into exclusive contracts, ran production departments that handled every aspect of filmmaking and controlled distribution and exhibition in theaters. It was the perfect racket.

Then, in the 1950s, competition from TV siphoned audiences away, and federal authorities broke up Hollywood's monopoly on distribution and exhibition. In the 1960s, in order to survive, studios cut costs, ended actor contracts, sold production departments and still sometimes went under.

In the 1970s, desperate studios took a risk on a generation of young, anti-establishment filmmakers who, reflecting the times, were interested in social realism, not musicals, romantic comedies or westerns. They included Martin Scorsese, William Friedkin, Robert Altman and Francis Ford Coppola, whose provocative films remain high-water marks of excellence.

The '70s also spawned the blockbuster, courtesy of two innovative young filmmakers now synonymous with pop culture: Steven Spielberg and George Lucas. In particular, Lucas' *Star Wars* (1977) became such an unexpected cultural phenomenon, and its pleasures were so visceral and eye-popping, that it became a blueprint for the future: keep the heroes simple, the action fast, ladle on the special effects and open big.

Since the 1980s, studios have reinforced their dominance, glamour has returned, and opening weekend grosses are tracked as religiously as stars' sex lives. It's a great show, and the films aren't all bad either.

Eadweard Muybridge created the first 'moving pictures' in California in the 1870s when he created his famous animal and human 'motion studies' by setting up a row of cameras with trip wires.

Citizen Kane (1941) by Orson Welles is celebrated as the best film ever, and its story of a journalist's search for the 'truth' about a dead newspaper tycoon remains a biting critique of the American Dream.

Genre Expectations

Genres have defined American cinema since its birth. Here are some distinctly American ones.

THE WESTERN

In pop cinema terms, the mythic West *is* America: good guys versus bad guys, law versus lawlessness, all duking it out on the rugged frontier. The 1940s and '50s were the Western's heyday. For an unironic paragon of manhood, check out Gary Cooper in *High Noon* (1952), while John Ford's influential *The Searchers* (1956) is pure Western poetry: John Wayne, Monument Valley and a deadly score to settle. Sam Peckinpah's ode to nihilistic violence, *The Wild Bunch* (1969), dragged the Western into the antiheroic modern day, as did Clint Eastwood's *Unforgiven* (1992).

THE MUSICAL

The golden age of Hollywood was defined by the musical, and *42nd Street* (1933) encapsulates the genre. Fred Astaire and Ginger Rogers were a

Brother to Brother (2005) by Rodney Evans is quintessential independent filmmaking: facing racism and homophobia at every turn, a gay black artist finds inspiration and salvation in the Harlem Renaissance.

match made in heaven; *Top Hat* (1935) adds a classic Irving Berlin score. The exuberant, impish Gene Kelly is showcased in *Singin' in the Rain* (1952), while no musical-fantasy is more parodied and exalted than *The Wizard of Oz* (1939). Now considered old-fashioned, musicals are only occasionally updated for modern tastes – as with the top-notch *Moulin Rouge* (2001) and *Chicago* (2002).

GANGSTERS & CRIME

The outsider status of the urban gangster is an often-explicit metaphor for the immigrant experience, and the crime genre includes many of America's greatest films. The original tough guy was Edward G Robinson in *Little Caesar* (1930). The influential subgenre 'film noir' got the star treatment in John Huston's *The Maltese Falcon* (1941), Orson Welles' *Touch of Evil* (1958), Roman Polanski's *Chinatown* (1974) and Curtis Hanson's *LA Confidential* (1997). Francis Ford Coppola's *Godfather* trilogy (1971–90), which refracts immigrants and American society through the prism of organized crime, is an almost unrivaled cinematic achievement. Martin Scorsese is the auteur of New York Italian American mobsters; highlights are *Mean Streets* (1973) and *GoodFellas* (1990). *Pulp Fiction* (1994) by Quentin Tarantino added a kinetic jolt of pop irony, as did *Fargo* (1996) by the Coen brothers. For an exposé of the US–Mexican drug trade, see *Traffic* (2000) by Steven Soderbergh.

SCIENCE FICTION

25th Hour (2003) by Spike Lee is a provocative meditation on lost chances that resonates with elegiac images of Ground Zero and post-September 11 NYC. It cements Lee's status as one of America's best filmmakers.

Ever-popular sci-fi is a cinematic natural. Though often simply the Wild West refought with lasers and spaceships, literary, postmodern concerns can crop up: fear of otherness and technology, existential dread. For the latter, see Stanley Kubrick's *2001: A Space Odyssey* (1968). For the former, the two *Star Wars* trilogies (1977–82, 1999–2005) are classic pulp fun that burned a new mythology into America's cultural retina. Equally pulpy and imbued with a jittery existentialism is the *Matrix* trilogy (1999–2004). Steven Spielberg is a one-man sci-fi factory, from *Close Encounters* (1979) and *E.T.* (1982) to *War of the Worlds* (2005). Also see the four *Alien* films (1979–97) and Ridley Scott's moody *Blade Runner* (1982).

ANIMATION

Art and life bake into a bizarre seven-layer confection in *American Splendor* (2003), a meta-biography of depressive comic book writer Harvey Pekar, a keenly self-aware, sweetly heroic everyman.

Animation began as a theatrical experience with Mickey Mouse, Bugs Bunny, and the 'politically incorrect,' racially and sexually charged Merrie Melodies of the 1920s, '30s and '40s. After TV arrived, these got scrubbed up into kiddy-only fare, and Disney-produced family films came to dominate the marketplace – until the 1990s, when *The Simpsons* and *South Park* hit TV (and *South Park*, 1999, hit theaters), Pixar Studios (*Toy Story*, 1995) took animation digital, and adults were reminded how disarmingly subversive animation could be.

TELEVISION

TV is the defining medium of the modern age – and of contemporary America – while TV programming represents the doughy middle of US culture, as effortlessly addictive as a bag of potato chips. On average, Americans watch over 1000 hours of TV a year – nearly thrice what they spend combined on the Internet, playing videos, watching DVDs and going to movies.

Or, to paraphrase Homer Simpson, 'Mmmmm, television…'

TV was developed in the USA and Britain in the 1920s and 1930s, and the first commercial TV set was introduced at the 1939 New York

World's Fair. TV didn't really affect US media until after WWII, when owning a set became a status symbol, and radio and movies withered under TV's exponential growth. In the 1980s, cable arrived, expanding TV's handful of channels into dozens, and then hundreds.

Now, at the dawn of the 21st century, TV is in its first real smackdown with the Internet. As more homes adopt broadband connections (to reach 50% of US homes by 2008, experts predict), high-quality Internet-accessed video content and advertising is growing. Eventually, inevitably, the functional distinction between a TV and a PC will dissolve, each just another screen beaming content from the ether.

What's on the Tube?

TV is, and has always been, a corporate-owned, advertiser-driven medium, which is why programming invariably resembles a Roman circus of trashy amusements in order to attract the widest possible audience. But if all of America's arts have become a mix of high and low cultures, TV must be included among them.

In its first decades, TV was widely considered second-rate (if irresistible) entertainment, and movie stars wouldn't be caught dead on it. Then, in the 1980s, videos brought movies into the home, and the stigma Hollywood attached to TV acting faded. Today, pay cable channels regularly produce TV shows with more challenging, adults-only fare than most 'risk-averse' Hollywood product.

In fact, high-quality, occasionally radical TV programs have always existed. The original *I Love Lucy* show (1951–57) was groundbreaking: it was the first to shoot on film before a live audience, and then to be edited before airing. This allowed for syndication (or rebroadcast). As a 'situation comedy,' it established the sitcom formula, and evolved around a strong woman in an interethnic marriage. Strange as it sounds, wacky Lucille Ball was a revolutionary.

In the 1970s, *All in the Family* was nominally a comedy, but in its unflinching examination of prejudice – in the form of Carol O'Connor's bigoted patriarch Archie Bunker – it trod ground no TV show had until then dared enter. Similarly, the sketch-comedy show *Saturday Night Live*, which debuted in 1975, pushed the envelope of propriety with its subversive, politically charged humor.

In the 1980s, TV kept diversifying. *The Cosby Show*, starring comedian Bill Cosby, became the nation's highest-rating program. While it was not the first successful black show, it was groundbreaking in its portrayal of a black middle-class family with which the entire country could identify. TV audiences then proved they could knock back straight shots of sitcom-free weirdness by embracing provocative cult shows like *Twin Peaks* and, later, *The X-Files*.

Today, the list of well-written dramas and comedies grows ever longer – from pay cable programs like *The Sopranos, Deadwood, The Shield* and *Rescue Me* to network shows like *Lost* and *Desperate Housewives*. However, the latest craze is undoubtedly cheap-to-produce, 'unscripted' reality TV: the castaways of *Survivor* started it in 2000, and no amount of *American Idols, Bachelors* or *Apprentices* seems capable of killing it.

DRAMA

American drama only began to come into its own after WWI, when the Little Theater movement arose. Emulating the progressive theater of Europe, it offered a pointed alternative to sentimental Broadway plays

From 1950 to 1960, the percentage of US homes with a TV shot from 10% to 87%, and today hovers at about 98% – or more than 101 million households. Talk about market saturation…

Hollywood is a fantasia of bling and babes to the four guys of *Entourage*, HBO's hilarious insider comedy about a neophyte actor and his tadpole buddies swimming with the sharks in Tinseltown.

The buzz-worthy *Desperate Housewives* is a sly, comic sudser involving a mysterious suicide, marital backstabbing, pharmaceutical foul play and an S&M hooker mom. Who doesn't love secrets and lies in sexy lingerie?

and musicals, and this eventually developed into New York's 'off-Broadway' theater scene. Today, New York still has the country's largest, most vibrant theater community, both on ever-popular Broadway (www.live broadway.com) and off.

But with around 1500 nonprofit regional theaters successfully keeping their heads above rough fiscal waters, America offers a robust drama scene nationwide. The regional theater movement first took off in the 1960s, and in recent years it's enjoyed mostly steady, at times rising, attendance. Some of the most successful are the 170 or so dedicated to the old Bard himself, William Shakespeare (see Ashland, Oregon, and Cedar City, Utah). *American Theatre* (www.tcg.org) is a fantastic regional theater resource.

As for US playwrights, Eugene O'Neill is still often considered the best; he arrived in the 1920s and promptly put America on the dramatic map. His magnificent trilogy *Mourning Becomes Electra* (1931) is a retelling of the tragic Greek myth about the murder of Agamemnon but set in post–Civil War New England. Other famous, frequently revived works are *The Iceman Cometh* (1946) and the autobiographical *Long Day's Journey into Night* (1956).

After WWII, American playwrights joined in the nationwide artistic renaissance. Two of the most famous were Arthur Miller – who wrote *Death of a Salesmen* (1949) and *The Crucible* (1953) – and the prolific, wildly popular Southerner Tennessee Williams – who wrote *The Glass Menagerie* (1945), *A Streetcar Named Desire* (1947) and *Cat on a Hot Tin Roof* (1955). All these plays, and more, have been adapted into films and are frequently revived.

As in Europe, the 1960s in America were marked by absurdist, avant-garde theater. No playwright was more scathing than Edward Albee, who created an enduring masterpiece with *Who's Afraid of Virginia Woolf?* (1962) and keeps upsetting apple carts: in 2002, his Tony-winning play *The Goat or, Who Is Sylvia?* set tongues wagging with its story of infidelity in which the other woman is, yes, a goat.

Two other prominent, very active American dramatists, who emerged in the 1970s, are David Mamet (*American Buffalo*, 1975) and Sam Shepard (*Buried Child*, 1978), both of whom continue to set the highest standards on stage and screen.

Today, the theatrical avant garde has become genuinely socially diverse, casually postmodern and multidisciplinary – the fourth wall long forgotten and the three-act play tossed wing-ward. Suzan-Lori Parks (*Topdog/Underdog*, 2001) is one of several emerging black playwrights, while one-person shows – such as by Eve Ensler (*The Vagina Monologues*), Chinese American comedian Margaret Cho and hip-hop-savvy Sarah Jones – are increasingly popular.

Meanwhile, 'hip-hop theater' is growing into a recognizable form – bringing with it the street, ethnicity, social criticism, call-and-response participation and all the other aesthetics of hip-hop (p74). As elsewhere, youth are elbowing onto America's sometimes stodgy stages, demanding to hear their own voices.

This So-Called Disaster (2003) is a fascinating, fly-on-the-wall documentary of Sam Shepard as he reminisces about his father and directs powerhouse Hollywood actors in his play The Late Henry Moss.

The best and brightest of the hip-hop generation gather for the Hip Hop Theater Festivals (www.hiphoptheaterfest.com), which occur in New York, San Francisco, Washington, DC and Chicago.

DANCE

For most of the 20th century, rule-breaking Americans were the innovators of modern ballet and modern dance. However, in recent years, dance has receded in cultural importance. While often innovative and exciting – and indeed, good dance has exploded out of New York City, becoming ever more geographically dispersed – many US companies are as concerned with preserving their legacies as with exploring the future.

Ballet

Modern ballet is said to have begun with Russian-born choreographer George Balanchine's *Apollo* (1928) and *Prodigal Son* (1929). With these, Balanchine invented the 'plotless ballet' – in which he choreographed the inner structure of music, not a pantomimed story – and thereby created a new, modern vocabulary of ballet movement. In 1934, Balanchine founded the School of American Ballet and, in 1948, ran the New York City Ballet, turning it into one of the world's foremost ballet companies. Jerome Robbins took over New York City Ballet in 1983, after Robbins had achieved his own fame as a collaborator with Leonard Bernstein on several of Broadway's biggest musicals, including *West Side Story* (1957). Broadway remains an extremely popular venue for dance.

Today, nearly every major city has a resident ballet company, and a number of them are dedicated 'Balanchine companies,' such as San Francisco Ballet, Dance Theatre of Harlem, Miami City Ballet and Carolina Ballet. *Dance* (www.dancemagazine.com) is an excellent modern ballet resource.

All in the Dances (2004) by Terry Teachout is a wonderfully short, deliciously loving introduction to George Balanchine, his genius and why his ballets continue to be performed everywhere.

Modern Dance

The pioneer of modern dance, Isadora Duncan didn't find success until she began performing in Europe at the turn of the 20th century. Basing her ideas on ancient Greek concepts of beauty, she challenged the strictures of classical ballet and sought to make dance an intense form of self-expression.

In the 1920s and 1930s, New York–based Denishawn was the nation's leading modern-dance company, and its most famous and influential student was Martha Graham. She founded the Dance Repertory Theater in New York, and most of today's major American choreographers developed under her tutelage. In her long career she choreographed more than 140 dances and developed a new dance technique, now taught worldwide, aimed at expressing inner emotion and dramatic narrative. Her two most famous works were *Appalachian Spring* (1944), dealing with frontier life, and *Clytemnestra* (1957), based on Greek myths.

Merce Cunningham, Paul Taylor and Twyla Tharp succeeded Graham as the leading exponents of modern dance; all run active companies today. In the 1960s and '70s, Cunningham explored abstract expressionism in movement, collaborating famously with musician John Cage. Taylor and Tharp are known for plundering popular culture.

Another student of Martha Graham, Alvin Ailey was part of the post-WWII flowering of black US culture. He made his name with *Blues Suite* (1958) and *Revelations* (1960), two works that evoked the black American experience, and in 1958 he founded the still-lauded Alvin Ailey American Dance Theater.

Other celebrated postmodern choreographers include New York–based Mark Morris and San Francisco Bay Area–based Anna Halprin – and the urban centers they represent are the premier places for cutting-edge dance. However, Minneapolis, Chicago and Philadelphia also have noteworthy scenes.

Voice of Dance (www .voiceofdance.com) is San Francisco–based and focuses on the modern dance scene, with a comprehensive list of links to groups across the country.

Environment

Without its land, the USA might never have been more than a political experiment of small historical consequence. Instead, through luck, wars and purchase, it acquired the entire lower half of the North American continent, which contained riches beyond a pharaoh's wildest dreams. This land fueled the country's incredibly rapid growth and wove itself into the fabric of the nation's identity. For the most part, America continues to spend its natural wealth recklessly, like a drunken gold miner, but it has also sought to hoard its last remaining wild places, and to protect and restore damaged landscapes and wildlife. America's land is its soul – as well as its body – and whatever conflicts arise over resources, Americans consider the continent's unsurpassed beauty and radiant natural wonders a national treasure.

Despite the radical changes that humans have wrought on the landscape in the last 300 years, there are still many places where travelers can experience vast stretches of seemingly untouched wilderness. America's national park system is the envy of the world, and the USA has done more to preserve its land than any other nation. Not only is visiting America's parks and refuges one of the highlights of any visit, but nature writing has also become one of the richest genres of American nonfiction; authors range the countryside and bring to life America's distinctive spirit and its inextricable relationship to the land.

THE LAND

America is big, no question. Covering some 3,787,000 sq miles, it's the world's third-largest country by size, trailing only Russia, and its friendly neighbor to the north, Canada. Continental USA is made up of 48 contiguous states ('the lower 48'), while Alaska, its largest state, is northwest of Canada, and the volcanic islands of Hawaii, the 50th state, are 2100 miles southwest in the Pacific Ocean.

It's more than just size, though. America feels big because of its incredibly diverse topography, which began to take shape around 50 to 60 million years ago.

In the conterminous US, the east is a land of temperate, deciduous forests that contains the ancient Appalachian Mountains, a low range that parallels the coast along the Atlantic Ocean. This coast is the country's most populated, urbanized region, particularly between Washington, DC and Boston.

Just to the north are the Great Lakes, which the US shares with Canada; these five lakes, part of the Canadian Shield, are the greatest expanse of fresh water on planet earth, constituting about 18% of the world's supply.

Going south along the East Coast, things get wetter and warmer, till you reach the swamps of southern Florida and make the turn into the Gulf of Mexico, which provides the US with a southern coastline.

West of the Appalachians are the vast interior plains, which lie flat as an *American Idol* contestant's high C all the way to the Rocky Mountains. The eastern plains are the nation's breadbasket, roughly divided into the northern 'corn belt' and the southern 'cotton belt.' The plains, an ancient sea bottom, are drained by the mighty Mississippi River, one of the world's great river systems. Going west, farmers slowly give way to cowboys and ranches in the semiarid, big-sky Great Plains.

Geology is rarely a page-turner, but in *Annals of the Former World* (1998) John McPhee turns the history of North American plate tectonics into a thrilling, human spectacle of discovery.

The Southwest desert could ask for no fiercer champion than Terry Tempest Williams. In *Red* (2001), she weaves the often-missing thread between politics, spirit, place and love.

Where the Bluebird Sings to the Lemonade Springs (1993) is an essential primer in Wallace Stegner and the misunderstood and mostly abused West. These essays are classics.

The young, jagged Rocky Mountains are a complex set of tall ranges that effectively run all the way from Mexico to Canada, and provide excellent skiing.

West of these mountains is the Southwest desert, an extremely arid region that has been cut to dramatic effect by the Colorado River system. This land of eroded canyons gives way to the unforgiving Great Basin as you go across Nevada; also an ancient sea bottom, it's so unwanted it's where the military practices and where the US plans to bury its nuclear waste.

Then you reach America's third major mountain system: the southern, granite Sierra Nevada and the northern, volcanic Cascades, which both parallel the Pacific Coast. California's Central Valley is one of the most fertile places on earth, while the coastline from San Diego to Seattle is celebrated in song and legend – a stretch of sandy beaches, redwoods and old-growth forests.

But wait, there's more. Northwest of Canada, Alaska reaches the Arctic Ocean and contains tundra, glaciers, an interior rain forest and the lion's share of federally protected wilderness, while Hawaii to the southwest is a tropical string of Pacific Island pearls.

WILDLIFE

It's hard to talk about America's wildlife without focusing as much on what was, as on what you'll find today. Before Europeans arrived the continent teemed with so many animals in such abundance it defies belief. North America was the equivalent of Africa's Serengeti Plains and the Galápagos Islands combined, and its immense forests, mountains and plains so overwhelmed the imagination that 19th-century Americans truly believed their natural resources were limitless.

That's all gone. What survives are pockets and patches of the original ecosystems, which struggle against pollution, human overpopulation, invasive non-native species and dwindling numbers.

America began expressly preserving its wildlife in 1903, when President Teddy Roosevelt set aside Florida's Pelican Island as the nation's

Robert Michael Pyle road-trips with migrating Monarch butterflies in *Chasing Monarchs* (1999) – his splendid, wry observations illuminate the West, nature and the interdependence of us all.

Today, we realize ecosystems survive because of complex webs of species. In *The Condor's Shadow* (1999), David Wilcove illuminates those interconnections and how they're fraying across America's landscape.

ARRIVE PREPARED, LEAVE NO TRACE

If you are planning an exciting adventure in America's wilderness, remember to do so responsibly. One thoughtless gesture – hiking off-trail through fragile soil or building an illegal fire – can take years for nature to repair. The cumulative effect of tens of millions of feet is taking its toll. Each person does make a difference.

Most hiking and camping advice is common sense. First, know what you are getting into. Know what weather to expect and pack accordingly, even if you plan to go for just a few hours. Get trail maps and take five minutes to talk to a ranger before plunging ahead. Rangers can alert you to crowds, landmarks and trail conditions, and they can confirm that your abilities and equipment match the needs of your trip.

Once in the wild, do everything possible to minimize your impact. As they say, take only pictures, leave only footprints. Stick to established trails and campsites. Be particularly sensitive to riparian areas; don't wash yourself or your dishes in streams or rivers, and camp at least 200ft away from them. Use a stove for cooking and make fires only in established fire rings. When you leave, take out everything you brought in and clean up every trace of your visit.

Conduct yourself as if you were a guest in someone's home – which you are. Observe wildlife, but do not approach or feed it. If you find cultural or historic artifacts, look but don't touch. And finally, be aware and respectful of other visitors. Loud voices and radios are quick ways to spoil a whole valley's worth of adventures.

For further advice, contact the Leave No Trace Center (www.lnt.org).

first bird sanctuary, thereby creating the National Wildlife Refuge System (NWRS). Managed by the US Fish & Wildlife Service (FWS; www.fws .gov), the NWRS includes around 95 million acres, making it the world's largest system of preserves dedicated to protecting wildlife and habitat.

In 1964 the Wilderness Act was passed to preserve whole biospheres. The US now has 677 official wilderness areas that total just under 5% of America's landmass. Over half of the total protected area is in Alaska.

However, the most powerful and controversial environmental tool remains the 1973 Endangered Species Act (ESA). Currently, over 1250 plants and animals are on the endangered list; some are sexy beasts like gray wolves, but most are small species that go pretty much unnoticed, such as freshwater mussels, chubs, grasses and so on. And yet, these near-extinct species often function as the proverbial canary in a coal mine, alerting anyone who is watching that an ecosystem is failing. The ESA is constantly criticized, never more so than under the current presidential administration, for obstructing industry and commerce – but then that's the point.

Given all the stresses nature is enduring, what is most remarkable is how wild it still seems. Hiking in a national park or wilderness area – spotting bears and wolves, elephant seals and condors, herds of bison and elk, old-growth redwoods and primordial swamps – is pure joy. The leftover patches of original America remain impressively stunning. These are just the tantalizing highlights.

Animals
LAND MAMMALS

Nineteenth-century Americans did not willingly suffer competing predators, and federal eradication programs nearly wiped out every single wolf and big cat and many of the bears in the continental US. Almost all share the same story of abundance, precipitous loss and, today, partial recovery.

In the 20th century, gray wolves – reduced to a hundred or so individuals in northern Minnesota – began to naturally recolonize portions of their range. In the 1990s, controversial programs 'reintroduced' wolves to the Greater Yellowstone Area and to the Southwest, and this has been successful: Yellowstone now boasts over 300 gray wolves, and the northern Rockies and Great Lakes regions have over 4000. Wolves hunt and live mostly in familial packs and are wide-ranging – they may travel 30 miles in a day.

Coyotes look similar to wolves but are about half the size, ranging from 20lb to 50lb. Coyotes are an icon of the Southwest, and their call-and-response howls are an exquisite desert serenade. However, they are remarkably adaptable and live just about everywhere – sometimes even in cities.

America has one primary big cat species, which goes by several names: mountain lion, cougar, puma and panther. In the east, a remnant population of Florida panthers is now nurtured in Everglades National Park. In the west, mountain lions are common enough that human encounters have begun occurring. These powerful cats are around 125lb of pure muscle, with short tawny fur, long tails and a secretive nature.

Grizzly, or brown, bears are one of North America's largest land mammals; male grizzlies can stand 7ft tall, weigh up to 600lb and consider 500 sq miles home. In the lower 48, about 700 grizzlies live mostly in the Greater Yellowstone Area and the northern Rockies. By contrast, Alaska is chock-full of them, with upwards of 30,000.

Black bears have always enjoyed a mythical stature in America, and this intelligent, opportunistic, congenial fellow remains a popular resident nearly everywhere. Smaller than grizzlies by several feet and a few hundred pounds, black bears can survive in home ranges as small as a square mile and are rarely aggressive except when threatened. Indeed, black bears can become almost too comfortable with humans, who always bring such tasty picnic baskets. National parks like Yosemite and Yellowstone have a constant problem with black bears poaching campsites and cars for food; be mindful whenever you're in bear country.

When it comes to wildlife slaughter, nothing can match what happened to the buffalo, or bison. No accurate count can ever be made, but they may have originally numbered as many as 65 to 75 million, in herds so thick they 'darkened the whole plains,' as Lewis and Clark wrote. They were killed for food, hides, sport, cash and to impoverish Native Americans, who depended on them. By the 20th century, a couple hundred remained. From these, new herds have been built up, so that one of America's quintessential animals can again be admired in its gruff majesty – among other places, in Yellowstone, Grand Teton and Badlands National Parks.

MARINE MAMMALS & FISH

Perhaps no native fish gets more attention than salmon, whose spawning runs up Pacific Coast rivers are a vivid wildlife spectacle. However, both Pacific and Atlantic salmon are considered endangered; hatcheries release millions of young every year, but there is debate whether this practice hurts or helps wild populations.

As for marine life, gray, humpback and blue whales migrate annually along the Pacific Coast, making whale-watching very popular. In addition, the San Juan Islands in Washington are famous for orcas, while Alaska's Glacier Bay and Kenai Fjords National Parks function like marine mammal family reunions.

The Pacific Coast is also home to ponderous elephant seals, playful sea lions and endangered sea otters. In California, Channel Islands National Park is a particularly fecund spot, and Monterey Bay is equally diverse and important.

Marine lovers should also visit Hawaii and the Florida Keys, both of which offer coral reefs and tropical fish. The coast of Florida is also home to the unusual, gentle manatee, which moves between freshwater rivers and the ocean. Around 10ft long and weighing up to 1200lb, these agile, expressive creatures currently number around 2000.

The Gulf of Mexico is another vital marine habitat, perhaps most famously for endangered sea turtles, which nest on south-coast beaches.

BIRDS

Bird-watching is the most popular wildlife activity in the US, and little wonder – all the hemisphere's migratory songbirds and shorebirds stop to rest here at some point, and America consequently claims some 800 avian species. If you need help telling them apart, the Sibley Field Guides are an indispensable tool.

The bald eagle was adopted as the nation's symbol in 1782; it's the only eagle unique to North America, and half a million once ruled the continent's skies. By the early 1960s, habitat destruction, illegal hunting and poisoning from DDT caused the population to plummet to fewer than 450 breeding pairs in the lower 48. Special legislation protects the bald eagle, and it has recovered so well, to around 6500 breeding pairs

Think birding is boring? You'll still be enthralled by Mark Obmascik's *The Big Year* (2004) – a hilarious account of the men, birds and obsessions that make up bird-watching's 'Super Bowl.'

Serious birders can put their efforts to good use by logging their counts and helping science at www.ebird.org.

Bald eagles mate for life and reuse their nests annually – which can eventually measure up to 10ft wide and weigh over 1000lb. That's nature's SUV!

(plus about 50,000 in abundant Alaska), that it may soon be removed from the endangered species list.

Perhaps the only bird more impressive than the eagle is the California condor, a prehistoric, carrion-eating bird that weighs 25lb and has a wingspan of up to 10ft. Condors were virtually extinct by the 1980s, but a captive breeding program has successfully reintroduced them along the California coast and in northern Arizona, where they are sometimes spotted above the Grand Canyon – an ancient spectacle that guarantees goose bumps.

Wildlife in America (1957) by Peter Matthiessen remains the seminal history on North America's indigenous wildlife; more recent editions have updates on conservation efforts.

Plants

The eastern United States was originally blanketed with a complex deciduous forest that mixed with evergreens depending on altitude and latitude. Great Smoky Mountains National Park contains all five eastern forest types – spruce fir, hemlock, pine-oak, and northern and cove hardwood – and there are over 130 species of trees. Wildflower and autumn hardwood color displays are a Northeast specialty.

In Florida, the Everglades is the last subtropical wilderness in the US. This vital, diverse and endangered habitat is a fresh- and saltwater world of marshes, sloughs and coastal prairies that support mangroves, cypresses, sea grasses, tropical plants, pines and hardwoods.

The grasslands of the interior plains are perhaps the most abused ecosystem in America. The 19th-century 'sodbusters' converted them largely to agriculture, particularly the eastern tall grass prairies, of which less than 4% remain. The semiarid short grass prairies have survived somewhat better, but farmers have increasingly been able to cultivate it for monoculture row crops by tapping the underground aquifer. Theodore Roosevelt National Park is a good destination for grasslands.

The Sonora Desert's saguaro cactus, found in the slyly named Saguaro National Park, can grow up to 50ft tall and live for over 150 years.

The Southwest deserts are horizon-stretching expanses of sage, scrub and cacti that abut western mountain ranges, where abundant spring wildflowers and electric-yellow quaking aspens in fall make worthwhile pilgrimages.

West of the Cascades in wet, milder Washington and Oregon are the last primeval forests in America. These diverse, ancient evergreen stands, of which only 10% remain, contain hemlocks, cedars, spruces and, in particular, towering Douglas firs.

California, meanwhile, is famous for its two species of sequoias, or redwoods. The coast redwood is the world's tallest tree (Redwood National Park contains the earth's actual tallest tree), while the related giant sequoia is the world's biggest by volume. Giant sequoias only exist in the western Sierra Nevada, and Sequoia National Park has the biggest granddaddy of all.

Nature Noir (2005) by Jordan Fisher Smith is utterly unique and actually pulse-pounding: Smith's tales of being a state park ranger in the Sierra Nevada would make Raymond Chandler blanch.

NATIONAL PARKS & FEDERAL LANDS

In terms of acreage, Alaska and the West have the most protected land, but pretty much every corner of America contains some type of preserve – whether it's a park, forest, wilderness, river, cultural site or historical monument. Almost all of it can be visited. These federal lands are mainly parceled between four agencies: the Bureau of Land Management (BLM; www.blm.gov), the US Forest Service (USFS; www.fs.fed.us), the US Fish and Wildlife Service (FWS; www.fws.gov) and the National Park Service (NPS; www.nps.gov). Most of these lands have minimal or no infrastructure, and activities like camping or fishing may require permits and fees.

If you're looking for iconographic America, however, chances are it's within the National Park Service. The NPS manages 384 parks, totaling 84 million acres, but the jewels of the system are its 58 national parks.

These include such eye candy as the Grand Canyon, Zion Canyon, Yosemite Valley, the Everglades, Hawai'i volcanoes, Alaskan glaciers, Northwest rain forests, Ancestral Puebloan cities and on and on.

National parks are the best protected and served of all the USA's public lands, and they are extremely popular. In an effort to keep them from being loved to death, the NPS regulates them with varying degrees of strictness. A few, like Zion, don't allow cars during the summer months, and most have tight controls on certain activities, including backcountry camping. Facilities range from minimal – a ranger station and some exhibits – to luxurious, including first-class museums, grocery stores, historic lodges and gourmet restaurants. In general, NPS rangers are as dedicated, knowledgeable and helpful as they come.

The cost to enter a national park varies; a few are free, but most charge from $5 to $20 per car for a seven-day pass. A one-year National Parks Pass ($50) gets you into every NPS-managed site, while a one-year Golden Eagle Passport ($65) allows unlimited access to all federal lands – including BLM, USFS and FWS areas. If you are a US citizen, you may be eligible for a free Golden Access Pass (a lifetime pass for the permanently disabled) or a Golden Age Pass ($10 one-time fee), a lifetime pass for those aged 62 and older.

The National Parks map (pp94–5) shows all of America's national parks, while the National Parks Table (p98) lists only the parks covered in this guide.

> Edward Abbey became famous with *Desert Solitaire* (1967). His account of life as a park ranger at Arches National Park swings from desert rhapsodies to prescient warnings about oncoming mass tourism.

> Over 64 million people visited the USA's 58 national parks in 2004, but one park received over twice as many visitors as any other: Great Smoky Mountains with over nine million visitors.

THE ENVIRONMENTAL MOVEMENT

America's political and social revolutions are well known, but the USA also birthed environmentalism, which remains every bit as revolutionary. The USA was the first nation to make significant efforts to preserve its wilderness, and today the US environmental movement still often leads preservation efforts worldwide.

Into the 19th century, civilization's Christian mandate was to bend nature to its will. America's Protestant settlers certainly believed this. Not only was wilderness dangerous, but it was also a symbol of humanity's wild, godless impulses, and the Pilgrims subdued both with gusto and great pride.

US WORLD HERITAGE SITES

For more information on World Heritage Sites, visit Unesco's website: whc.unesco.org/en/list.

- Cahokia Mounds State Historic Site (p598)
- Carlsbad Caverns National Park (p959)
- Chaco Culture National Historic Park (p954)
- Everglades National Park (p509)
- Glacier Bay National Park & Preserve (p1093)
- Grand Canyon National Park (p901)
- Great Smoky Mountains National Park (p455)
- Hawai'i Volcanoes National Park (p1131)
- Independence Hall (p192)
- La Fortaleza and San Juan Historic Site in Puerto Rico
- Mammoth Cave National Park (p464)
- Mesa Verde National Park (p992)
- Monticello (p359) and University of Virginia (p359) in Charlottesville
- Olympic National Park (p1051)
- Redwood National Park (p853)
- Statue of Liberty (p131)
- Taos Pueblo (p951)
- Waterton-Glacier International Peace Park (p1020)
- Wrangell-St Elias National Park (p1109)
- Yellowstone National Park (p1004)
- Yosemite National Park (p862)

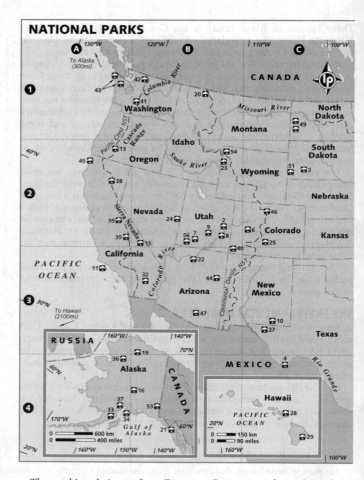

NATIONAL PARKS

Then, taking their cue from European Romantics who embraced the natural world for its poetic inspiration, the USA's transcendentalists came along and claimed that nature actually embodied God. In *Walden* (1854), iconoclast Henry David Thoreau described living for two years in the woods, blissfully free of civilization's comforts, and he persuasively argued that human society was harmfully distant from nature's essential truths, which were actually heavenly instructions. While anthropomorphic, this view of nature marked a profound shift: God came to speak through wilderness, not the ax.

The continent's natural wonders – vividly captured by America's 19th-century landscape painters – also had a way of selling themselves, and rampant nationalism led to a desire to promote them. In 1864, a 10-sq-mile portion of Yosemite Valley was set aside as a state park; then in 1872, President Ulysses S Grant designated two million acres as Yellowstone National Park, the first such large-scale preserve in the world.

Yellowstone was established expressly to preserve its unique features for human enjoyment. But nature's greatest cheerleader, John Muir, soon

Nearly 700 million acres – over a quarter of the USA – is federally owned, and 65% is managed as 'mixed use,' meaning it somehow must balance mining, grazing, recreation and preservation.

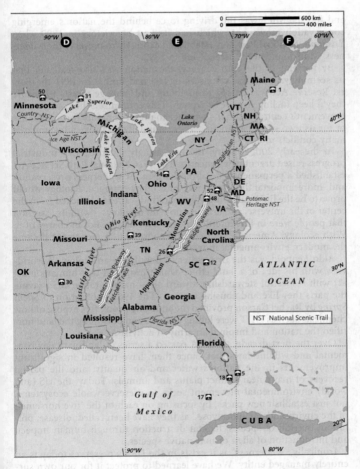

emerged to champion wilderness for its own sake. Muir considered nature superior to civilization, and he spent much of his life wandering the Sierra Nevada and passionately advocating on behalf of the mountains

For an evocative taste of what made John Muir special – and so influential – read *The Wild Muir* (1994), which excerpts Muir's accounts of his wildest adventures.

and forests. Muir was the driving force behind the nation's emerging conservation movement, which had its first big victory in 1890 when Yosemite National Park was established expressly to preserve the wilderness. Muir founded the Sierra Club in 1892.

By the end of the 19th century, the nation was also realizing that its seemingly boundless resources in fact had limits. In 1891 the Forest Reserve Act was passed to maintain and manage forests to ensure they'd keep fueling America's growth. This epitomized the conservation movement's central conflict – whether to preserve nature for human use or for its own spiritual sanctity. These mutually exclusive aims underlie many conflicts today.

In the early 20th century, the increasingly dark scars of industrial progress raised urgent new concerns. The 1916 National Park Service Act established a permanent federal mechanism for wilderness preservation and, more importantly, the science of ecology emerged. Ecology would prove to be the final humbling of humankind – already knocked from the center of the universe, and arm in arm with monkeys – with its assertion that people were in fact interdependent with nature, not in charge of it. With ecology, America's 19th-century conservation movement became the modern environmental movement.

The Sierra Club (www.sierraclub.org) was the USA's first conservation group, and it remains the nation's most active, with educational programs, organized trips and tons of information.

Aldo Leopold was the first writer to popularize an ecological worldview with his idea of a 'land ethic,' which proposed that humans must act with respectful stewardship toward all of nature, rather than saving the parts they like and abusing the rest. The 1962 publication of *Silent Spring* by Rachel Carson provided the shocking proof: this exposé of how chemicals such as DDT were killing animals and poisoning the land horrified the nation and inspired an army of activists.

Over the next decade, the USA passed a series of landmark environmental and wildlife laws that, since then, have resulted in significant improvements in the nation's water and air quality, and the partial recovery of many near-extinct plants and animals. Today, the US (and world) environmental movement seeks to preserve whole ecosystems, not just establish new parks, by focusing on each of the 'five horsemen of the environmental apocalypse,' as they have been called: disease, pollution, overkill of species, habitat destruction through human impact, and introduction of alien or non-native species.

Ironically, 'wilderness' as it exists in the USA's preserves today is an entirely managed entity. We have learned to protect it for our own survival, lest we succumb to wilderness in the greater sense – which endures despite any species' rise or fall.

ENVIRONMENTAL ISSUES

One of the USA's leading environmental organizations, the Natural Resources Defense Council (www.nrdc .org) provides news, articles and overviews of environmental issues on its website.

The USA is the world's greatest consumer of energy and its greatest polluter, so it shouldn't be surprising that one of the most divisive battles being waged in America right now is over the environment. Even allowing for political exaggeration, it's hard not to conclude that the US and its land are at a critical juncture.

Average citizens, American industry and environmentalists all feel that the status quo is unsustainable – but what does sustainability look like, how much would it cost and who pays? No one can agree. Citizens don't want to give up their cushy, consumptive lifestyles, but they also don't want to live in a poisoned land. Industry says it can't compete in the global marketplace without cheap energy, and it claims meeting current pollution standards makes energy fatally expensive. Environmentalists, meanwhile, generally agree that the land cannot take much more abuse;

continued pollution and habitat loss at current rates may cause ecosystems to collapse beyond repair.

These tensions have been building for decades but, for its part, the Bush administration has demonstrated concern almost exclusively – and environmentalists say notoriously – with the health of business. Considering environmental concerns overblown, the current administration has worked to loosen and/or overturn a wide range of environmental regulations and protections to allow for more resource extraction and to lessen corporate responsibility for cleaning up industrial waste. The Bush administration has even been charged with pressuring the Environmental Protection Agency (EPA; www.epa.gov) – the federal agency that enforces environmental laws – into manipulating its own science to justify lowering pollution standards. Industry supporters say this is only correcting an overprotectionist imbalance, but nevertheless, President Bush is steadily amassing the worst environmental record of any US president in modern history.

> The most persuasive account of why environmentalism should be considered one of the world's great intellectual revolutions is *Wilderness and the American Mind* (2001) by Roderick Nash.

Energy

The US reliance on imported oil (which makes up nearly 60% of US oil consumption) and the need for more energy underlie many environmental policy debates. Currently, two-thirds of the USA's electricity comes from fossil fuels, 20% from nuclear power and 4.5% from renewable sources. Rather than invest in existing renewable technologies or ask Americans to decrease consumption (such as by using more fuel-efficient cars), the current administration wants to increase production of oil and nuclear power.

For instance, a moratorium on offshore oil drilling has been in place since 1981 as a response to damaging oil spills, but President Bush is working to lift this and begin drilling again. The Bush administration also wants to drill for oil in Alaska's Arctic National Wildlife Refuge (see p1085), despite widespread public opposition to the plan.

> By all rights, *When Smoke Ran Like Water* (2002) by Devra Davis should become today's *Silent Spring*. It traces how politics and industry undermine scientists as they evaluate environmental pollution.

The last new nuclear power plant was completed in 1973. To encourage Three Mile Island–skittish nuclear power companies to build more, the government has proposed providing federally backed 'risk insurance.' Another hurdle to more plants is nuclear waste, which is piled up in 'temporary' storage all over the country. In 2001, Yucca Mountain in Nevada was chosen as the nation's sole permanent nuclear waste repository, and the government is rushing to ready the site to receive waste by 2010. Never mind that even the government can't guarantee high-level radiation won't leak after 10,000 years, and some experts predict leaks might occur within 1000 years. You're welcome, 31st century.

Some of the nation's worst polluters are coal-fueled power plants, but 31 new coal plants are currently being proposed to keep electricity running in the West, which suffered power shortages in 2000 and 2001. 'Near-zero emission' coal-burning technology is available, but it's too expensive to make the plants economically viable, so the current administration is seeking to help by lowering federal standards for air pollution and mercury emissions.

> The US consumes about 20 million barrels of oil a day, which is 25% more than the EU and four times more than China.

Air Pollution

Bush's so-called Clear Skies initiative, which has twice been rebuffed by Congress and may never become law, would roll back the Clean Air Act and provide industry exemptions for pollution. Its fatal flaw may be that it doesn't include carbon dioxide in its pollution-control targets. The USA is the world's largest emitter of carbon dioxide, the main greenhouse

NATIONAL PARKS TABLE

Park	Features	Activities	Best time
Acadia (p294)	rugged coast, fir forests, granite cliffs	day hikes, cycling, rock climbing, sea kayaking	summer
Arches (p929)	2000 sandstone arches	scenic drives, day hikes	spring-fall
Badlands (p692)	desolate landscape, eroded cliffs, prairie grasslands; golden eagles, buffalo	day & backcountry hikes, mountain biking	spring-fall
Big Bend (p763)	diverse desert terrain; mountain lions, black bears, reptiles, birds	scenic drives, day & backcountry hikes, bird-watching, river running	spring-fall
Biscayne (p511)	coral reefs, mangroves; manatees, sea turtles	snorkeling, scuba diving, boat trips, sea kayaking	year-round
Black Canyon of the Gunnison (p990)	2000ft sheer chasm	hiking	spring-fall
Bryce Canyon (p933)	brilliantly colored, eroded hoodoos	day & backcountry hikes, horse-back riding	spring-fall
Canyonlands (p930)	epic Southwestern canyons, mesas & buttes	scenic viewpoints, backcountry hikes, white-water rafting	spring-fall
Capitol Reef (p931)	painterly rock formations, petroglyphs & pioneer ruins	day & backcountry hikes	spring-fall
Carlsbad Caverns (p959)	extensive underground cave system; free-tail bat colony	cave tours, backcountry hikes	spring-fall
Channel Islands (p813)	diverse & unique rocky islands; elephant seal colony, sea lions, sea otters	snorkeling, sea kayaking	year-round
Congaree (p490)	swamp, cypress trees	hiking, boating	year-round
Crater Lake (p1071)	vast volcanic cone with incredibly blue lake	day hikes, scenic drives, cross-country skiing	summer-fall
Death Valley (p811)	hot, dramatic desert & unique ecology	scenic drives, day hikes	spring
Denali (p1111)	unspoiled Alaskan wilderness, Mt McKinley; moose, caribou, wolves, brown bears	day & backcountry hikes, biking	summer
Dry Tortugas (p520)	7 islands in Gulf of Mexico; sea turtles	snorkeling, scuba diving, bird-watching	year-round
Everglades (p509)	enormous subtropical wetlands & swamp; alligators, snakes, flamingoes	day hikes, biking, canoeing, airboat tours, bird-watching	year-round
Gates of the Arctic (p1114)	vast Alaskan Brooks Range; caribou, wolves, bears	remote backpacking, mountain-eering	summer
Glacier (p1020)	impressive glaciated landscape; mountain goats	day & backcountry hikes, scenic drives	summer
Glacier Bay (p1093)	remote Alaskan bay filled with icebergs, 16 glaciers	boat tours, sea kayaking	summer
Grand Canyon (p901)	spectacular 277-mile-long, 1-mile-deep river canyon	day & backcountry hikes, mule trips, river running	spring-fall
Grand Teton (p1007)	towering granite peaks; moose, bison, wolves	day & backcountry hikes, rock climbing, fishing	spring-fall
Great Basin (p887)	remote 13,063ft Wheeler Peak, ancient bristlecone pines, limestone caves	day hikes, scenic drives	spring-fall
Great Sand Dunes (p988)	30-sq-mile sand dune field, alpine tundra; elk, prairie dogs	day & backcountry hikes	spring-fall
Great Smoky Mountains (p473)	wildly diverse Appalachian forest & mammals; bears	day & backcountry hikes, biking	year-round
Guadalupe Mountains (p760)	high desert country, fall foliage	day & backcountry hikes	spring-fall

Haleakala (p1136)	world's largest dormant volcano, lunar landscape	day hikes, scenic views	year-round
Hawai'i Volcanoes (p1131)	two active volcanoes, tropical beaches, icy summit, lava flows	day hikes, scenic drives	year-round
Hot Springs (p435)	47 natural springs, historic bathhouses, Hot Springs Mountain	bathing, sightseeing, day hikes	year-round
Isle Royale (p635)	remote, undeveloped island in Lake Superior; diverse wildlife	backcountry hikes, canoeing	summer
Joshua Tree (p810)	sprawling rocky desert, spiky Joshua trees	day & backcountry hikes, rock climbing	spring-fall
Kenai Fjords (p1105)	Harding Icefield, tidewater glaciers; diverse marine life	day hikes, boat trips	summer
Kings Canyon (p865)	sequoia redwood groves, granite canyon	day & backcountry hikes, cross-country skiing	summer-fall
Lassen Volcanic (p860)	volcanic peak & terrain, geothermal activity, hot springs	day & backcountry hikes	summer-fall
Mammoth Cave (p464)	world's most extensive cave system, delightful river & forest	NPS-led cave tours, day hikes	year-round
Mesa Verde (p992)	preserved Ancestral Puebloan cliff dwellings, historic sites, mesas & canyons	short hikes	spring-fall
Mount Rainier (p1048)	volcanic mountain with glaciers, alpine meadows	day & backcountry hikes, mountaineering, skiing	spring-fall
North Cascades (p1056)	undeveloped, glaciated landscape, Skagit River	day & backcountry hikes, rafting	summer
Olympic (p1051)	temperate rainforests, alpine meadows, Mt Olympus	day & backcountry hikes	spring-fall
Petrified Forest (p908)	fossilized trees, petroglyphs, Painted Desert scenery	day hikes	spring-fall
Redwood (p853)	virgin redwood forest, world's tallest trees; elk	day & backcountry hikes	spring-fall
Rocky Mountain (p975)	stunning peaks, alpine tundra, the Continental Divide; elk, bighorn sheep, moose, beavers	day & backcountry hikes, cross-country skiing	summer-fall
Saguaro (p913)	large stands of giant saguaro cactus, desert scenery	day & backcountry hikes	spring-fall
Sequoia (p865)	sequoia redwood groves, granite canyon	day & backcountry hikes, cross-country skiing	summer-fall
Shenandoah (p360)	Blue Ridge Mountains, Skyline Dr, Appalachian Trail	day & backcountry hikes, scenic drives, horseback riding	spring-fall
Theodore Roosevelt (p687)	2 units, prairie grasslands, desert badlands; birds, wild horses, bighorn sheep, bison	scenic drives, day & backcountry hikes, horseback riding	spring-fall
Voyageurs (p659)	lake, forest; moose, black bears, timber wolves; access usually by motorboat	day hikes, canoeing	summer-fall
Wind Cave (p697)	98-mile-long cave, grassland; elk, bison, prairie dogs	cave tours, day hikes	spring-fall
Wrangell-St Elias (p1109)	3 mountain ranges meet amid ice fields & glaciers	scenic drives, day & backcountry hikes	summer
Yellowstone (p1004)	numerous geysers & geothermal pools, impressive canyon; prolific wildlife	day & backcountry hikes, cycling, cross-country skiing	year-round
Yosemite (p862)	sheer granite-walled valley, waterfalls, alpine meadows	day & backcountry hikes, rock climbing, skiing	year-round
Zion (p935)	immense red-rock canyon, Virgin River	day & backcountry hikes, canyoneering	spring-fall

gas, and its CO_2 emissions have risen by 14% over the last decade. While the Bush administration adamantly refuses to acknowledge the dangers of global warming (and has refused to sign the Kyoto Protocol), not all in the US government concur.

In car-loving America, auto emissions are an ongoing concern, but here there are bright spots: 2004 EPA regulations of diesel vehicles, and perhaps soon of diesel generators, will significantly reduce sulfur emissions and help US cities meet federal air-quality standards. Eight states, including California (the world's 10th-largest emitter of greenhouse gases), have adopted tougher auto-emissions standards than the federal government. Americans themselves are slowly turning away from gas-guzzling SUVs – whose sales dropped by 15% or more from 2004 to 2005 – and buying more gas-electric hybrid cars. And President Bush himself has proposed a hybrid auto tax credit over the next 10 years to the tune of $2.5 billion.

Water

Water use and pollution is another major issue. Western states are currently using their underground aquifer at a phenomenal rate, but this is a finite resource, and increasing water salinity is playing havoc with farming. Meanwhile, the EPA estimates that more than 40% of US waters are polluted. Perchlorate, a chemical used in missile and rocket fuel, now contaminates drinking water in 35 states. Contamination in the Colorado River exceeds EPA standards by 900%. The Bush solution? Try to lower EPA standards by 2000%.

Not that anyone in industry is losing sleep over the EPA's clean-water enforcement. By the EPA's own calculations, only 15% of serious industrial offenders ever face formal actions, and of these, only half are fined. What's it cost to get caught? On average, about $6500.

Not only did Aldo Leopold's *A Sand County Almanac* (1949) become a touchstone for all subsequent American naturalists, it remains a humble, unpretentious and powerfully moving testimony.

The water policies of the West are a disaster. If you don't believe it, read *Cadillac Desert* (1993) by the late Marc Reisner: the desert's future is very thirsty indeed.

USA Outdoors Jeff Greenwald

Imagine my surprise. After 20 years of cross-country hitchhiking, African vagabonding, Himalayan trekking, South Pacific wreck diving and Peruvian buses, the most terrifying place I'd ever been was right at home – on a bicycle.

The Slickrock Bike Trail, in the heart of Utah's red rock country, is where it all began. My friend James and I rented bikes in Moab, and rode the short distance to the so-called 'Practice Loop': a 4-mile circuit in the Sand Flats Recreation Area, designed to test your two-wheeler skills in preparation for Moab's *real* biking trails.

'Practice Loop, huh?' I guffawed. 'Isn't that for little kids with training wheels and Popsicle drool on their chins?'

'Let's check it out anyway,' James suggested.

Half an hour later I found myself a mile into the Loop, paralyzed with fear. The trail had climbed to a hilltop, and now dropped away with the dizzying pitch of a roller coaster. The ground was rough as sandpaper, just waiting to flay me alive. I recalled my joke – but even training wheels wouldn't help if I skidded over the nearby cliff.

Somehow, by sheer luck, I survived. But the incident taught me a lesson: never underestimate how wild the wild places in the USA can be. Not all of them are dangerous – but most have a raw, rugged beauty unlike anything you've ever tasted before.

New York, San Francisco and Hollywood are serious fun – but to find the soul of the USA, visit the national parks and monuments. The variety alone will blow you away. From the dunes of Death Valley National Park to the California redwoods, from the geysers of Yellowstone National Park to the alligators of the Everglades, you'll find infinite opportunities to experience the eye-popping, jaw-dropping sights that greeted (and sometimes devoured) the first Western explorers to the New World.

So drink up the music and museums, then get yourself into the wild. You'll understand why actor and outdoorsman Steve McQueen once said, 'I'd rather wake up in the middle of nowhere than in any city on Earth.'

For a wealth of resources on all of the activities described in this chapter, see Activities (p1143).

SKIING & SNOWBOARDING

In the mid-1970s, when the world was young, a guy named Jake Burton Carpenter set up a workshop in his Vermont garage and began to build 'snowboards.' Jake was a 'snurfer' – a snow-surfer – but he dreamed of a day when his passion would break into the mainstream. It didn't take long. Vermont, New England, became the ground zero of snowboarding, and Burton Snowboards kick-started what's now a snowballing industry.

On powdered slopes across the USA, snowboarding has become as popular as downhill skiing. Riding the lifts of Sun Valley (p1025), Lake Placid (p175) or Aspen (p986), you'll see airdogs gaping the ski tracks – or cratering into moguls. Though Vermont remains the heart of snowboard culture, you won't find the white stuff there in July. But don't despair; several resorts around Oregon's Mt Hood (p1075) serve as winter's summer home, offering snowboard camps June through August.

Skiing is one of the world's great rushes, but those thrills don't come cheap. When you add up the lift tickets and rentals (unless you're traveling with your boots and skis), it amounts to a major splurge. Still, some of

Serious Sports (www.serioussports.com) is an award-winning web directory of outfitters, guides and schools for adventure-sports operators.

the USA's major snow haunts are so terrific that it's worth every nickel. Tahoe (p860), Telluride (p993) and Sun Valley come to mind, but don't forget Alaska; excellent slopes slice through spectacular terrain outside Juneau (p1091), Anchorage (p1096) and Fairbanks (p1112) – where, at Mt Aurora SkiLand, you'll find most northerly chairlift in North America. Drop by from April to August, and you might be lucky enough to ski beneath the eerie, shimmering veil of the aurora borealis.

And here's a little secret you might not know about: Hawai'i. That's right: Mauna Kea (p1130), the Big Island's 'white mountain' (actually a cone-shaped volcano), soars nearly 14,000ft and is often covered with snow. There are no lifts, no grooming and no resorts; skiing and snowboarding involve ferrying riders in your rented 4WDs. Granted, it takes some planning, but what a day! Skiing in the morning, snorkeling in the afternoon. And you've got that famous Kona coffee to power you on.

While we're speaking of snow, let's not forget those tooth-and-claw snow sports: dog-sledding and skijoring. You might not be ready to enter the Iditarod – Alaska's legendary, 1150-mile race from Anchorage to Nome – but how about a weekend on the trails of the gorgeous White Mountains National Recreation Area, located approximately 30 miles north of Fairbanks, towed along at top speed by a pair of huskies?

For information on resources, see p1144.

CYCLING & MOUNTAIN BIKING

Great Outdoors Recreation Pages (www.gorp.com) is a comprehensive web resource on USA outdoor recreation and active travel, including travel articles, vacation packages, a message board and top 10 lists.

Want to be able to say you saw the USA, *really* saw it, in a way few others can equal? Get yourself two months off, a few thousand bucks and a serious hydration system – and sign up for one of the 4200-mile cross-country rides offered by a few select outfitters. Oh yes, you'll need one more thing: the most comfortable seat in the world.

If you're not that crazy, there are still plenty of terrific rides that will show you the outback with considerably less chafing. South Dakota's George S Mickelson Trail (p694), for example, cuts across the Black Hills National Forest for 110 gritty miles, following the old roads used by gold miners. The Sun Top Loop, in the Mount Baker–Snoqualmie National Forest, bounces across the western slopes of the Cascade Mountains, about an hour east of Seattle and close to the northern boundary of Mount Rainier National Park (p1048). Another favorite is the Arkansas' Womble Trail, south of the Ouachita Trail, a single-track dream. Another sure bet is the 206-mile, hut-to-hut ride between Telluride (p993) and Moab (p928). Both towns are drop-dead gorgeous, and the scenery in between will make you feel you've landed in a classic John Wayne Western.

For information on America's National Park Service, including its history and conservation effort, check out www.nps.gov. Search for a particular park by region or by activity.

The new frontier, of course, is Alaska, and the landscape up there is a world unto itself. Most of the state is so pristine that even a ride on the highway feels like a wilderness encounter. Bike outfits with tours originating in Anchorage (p1096), Homer (p1105) or Fairbanks (p1112) will take you on the ride of your dreams – from an easy day trip into the outback to a nine-day single-track expedition along mountain ranges and salmon-filled rivers.

The fact is, every state in the USA – from Rhode Island to Texas – is proud of its cycling trails, and you'll find die-hard enthusiasts in every town you visit. Need advice? Just visit a local bike shop, or get online (computers for hire are often located in copy shops) and Google your location along with the keywords 'cycling' or 'mountain biking.' This isn't necessary in a place like Moab, of course; just ask anyone you see!

Plenty of cities are bike-friendly, too: Madison (p640), Boulder (p972), Austin (p721) and Portland (p1058), to name just four. But some of the best cycling in America is found around San Francisco (p822) – where you can trim your tires near Haight/Ashbury (p831), and ride over the Golden Gate Bridge (p833) into the gorgeous Marin Headlands (p842). The toughest biking challenge in the States? Keeping your eyes on the road while cruising beneath the bridge's famous art-deco towers.

For more information on cycling and mountain biking, see p1143.

DIVING & SNORKELING

Ninety feet below the surface of California's Monterey Bay (p818), you may feel like you've entered an underwater cathedral. Diving in California's giant kelp forests is (almost) enough to make you forget the frigid water rushing in through the neck of your wet suit. In all directions, gigantic kelp stalks rise toward the glittering surface, swaying like very tall belly dancers. Sunlight filters through the fronds, turning them into stained-glass windows.

Throughout the year, California's coastal waters host an amazing variety of life: colorful nudibranchs that look like miniature flying carpets; wild dolphins; and enormous gray whales on their annual migration between Mexico and Alaska. One of the most popular dive areas is the Point Lobos State Reserve (p818), part of mind-boggling Monterey Bay (also home of the world's finest aquarium). The Channel Islands (p813), which lie between Santa Barbara and Los Angeles, are also salted with famous dive sites, and some live-aboard charters allow you to visit all eight islands in the chain. In the chillier waters north of San Francisco, scores of thick-skinned divers await the first of April: the start of the season for north-coast red abalone, a favorite for local grills.

In the southeastern USA, there's plenty of terrific diving and snorkeling (and much warmer water!) off the Florida Keys (p512) – once you get out of the mangrove swamps and onto the outer reefs. Though the Keys themselves are numbered among the best dive spots in the world, Florida's coastline is as long as the entire eastern seaboard – there are over 20 different areas offering undersea adventure, from Pensacola (p559) to Jacksonville (p531).

Don't blink while riding through Portland (p1058), Oregon; you'll miss the USA's smallest park. Just 452 sq in, it was created for leprechauns and snail races.

SPELUNKING

Ever since Tom and Becky got lost in a cave in *The Adventures of Tom Sawyer,* caving – or spelunking, as it's officially known – has been as American as apple pie. You'll find plenty of opportunities to explore the USA's subterranean world – from ranger-guided strolls through well-lit caverns to technical descents into pitch-black underground labyrinths.

Several national parks and monuments feature casual cave exploration; New Mexico's Carlsbad Cavern National Park (p959) is the most famous, but the caves in Shenandoah National Park (p360) and Boyden Cavern (p865) in King's Canyon National Park are also worth exploring.

If you're into the actual hard-hat sport of spelunking, there are specific resources to guide you. Your best bet may well be Show Caves (www.showcaves.com), a wonderful website with resources for cave destinations all over the world. Click on its USA page, which is packed with links to nearly 150 spelunking adventures all across the country. If you're hanging on the West Coast, check out the variety of adventures on Underground Adventures in California (www.caverntours.com), which specializes in California's five main canyon zones.

The National Speleological Society (www.caves.org) can help you locate specific caving clubs with a simple, state-by-state search. You'll also find information about cave geology, art and the latest caving equipment.

If descending into dry caves isn't enough of a thrill, Caveboard (www.caveboard.com) is a great resource for cave *diving*, with a photo gallery of recent images taken by members.

Some 6000 miles west of Florida, a continent and an ocean away, lies the USA's most exotic underwater destination: Hawai'i. Despite the crowds, O'ahu's Hanauma Bay Nature Preserve (p1127) is still one of the world's great spots for casual snorkeling; the fish are so accustomed to people that they'll swim right up to your mask. There's also fine snorkeling near Maui (p1132); lucky visitors might find themselves swimming with wild spinner dolphins. For the scuba diver, Hawai'i's warm waters can easily soak up an entire holiday. Live-aboards are the way to go, as much of the best diving is well off the coast or between isles. From the green sea turtles and WWII wrecks off the coast of O'ahu (p1119) to the undersea lava sculptures near little Lana'i (p1138), the Aloha State offers endless opportunity for rapture – but do your homework before arriving, as the dive sites change with the seasons.

ROCK CLIMBING

> When we think of earthquakes, California comes immediately to mind. The fact is, only one of the USA's 50 states has not had an earthquake: North Dakota.

Aside from hosting the world's oldest (and weirdest-looking) trees, the high desert of California's Joshua Tree National Park (p810) is covered with rock called 'pinkish monzogranite.' The only thing more fun than saying it is climbing it – and countless climbers have perfected their moves on these noble boulders. Driving through the park, you'll spot solo climbers, teams and classes (look for the tangled piles of rope) almost everywhere. With over 5000 climbs to choose from, you'll think you've landed in *The Flintstones'* answer to Disneyland.

> For those after the 'Been There, Done That' award: be sure to step on the geographic center of North America. It's in Pierce County, near Balta, North Dakota.

Almost everyone with a passion for rocks has seen mind-boggling pictures of climbers bivouacking on El Capitan or Half Dome in Yosemite National Park (p862). This venerable national park, protected by President Abraham Lincoln in 1864, offers superb climbing courses if sleeping in a hammock 1000ft above terra firma is your fantasy. At Grand Teton National Park (p1007), the Exum climbing school offers programs from basic climbing courses to two-day expeditions up to the top of Grand Teton itself: a 13,770ft peak with views to die for (figuratively speaking, of course).

But it's not all about going up. Near Zion National Park (p935), five-day canyoneering classes teach the fine art of going *down:* rappelling off sheer sandstone cliffs into glorious, red-rock canyons filled with trees. Some of the sportier pitches are made in dry suits, down the flanks of roaring waterfalls into ice-cold pools.

If you're staying east of the Mississippi, upstate New York's Shawangunk Ridge is located within a two-hour drive north of New York City. The ridge stretches some 50 miles, running southwest to northeast, from Port Jervis to Rosendale. This is where many East Coast climbers – including myself – tied their first billets. There are lots of great climbs in the 'Gunks,' but the Trapps Cliff is where you'll probably end up: this central section of the Gunks features more than a mile of 200ft-plus wall, with hundreds of possible routes. That's about enough for one summer, don't you think?

> Take care when hiking through open spaces, or on open cliff faces during a storm; every year about 600 people in the USA are struck by lightning.

For information on rock-climbing resources, see p1144.

HIKING & BACKPACKING

No one, so far, has done the math, but there's a good possibility that if you took all the miles of hiking trails in the USA and strung them together, they'd reach to the moon and back. For many visitors, hiking and/or backpacking are the highlights of their visit to the USA. The wilderness is amazingly accessible; a three- to four-hour drive will take you away from lights of the nation's brightest cities, and into a legendary wilderness filled with giant trees, rainbow-wreathed waterfalls, and raccoons so clever they'll steal the cheese right out of your daypack.

One thing to remember is that all of America's national parks can be approached from three different angles. For the visitor on the go, there are always short hikes or loops – many less than a mile long – that showcase natural highlights. In a few hours, you can taste the flavor of places like Arches National Park (p929), Yosemite National Park (p862), the Grand Canyon (p901), Everglades National Park (p509) and Yellowstone National Park (p1004), to name a handful. For those with more time on their hands, rangers (found at the visitors centers) will recommend trails – from easy strolls to sweat-stained, full-day hikes (the most popular of these may well be the hike up Half Dome, in Yosemite: a 12-hour trek tackled by dozens of men, women and children every day). If your dream is to camp in the wilderness, you may have to get a permit in advance – spaces are limited, especially during summer. But your efforts will be rewarded; the most spectacular landscape is often well off the beaten path.

There's no limit to the places you can explore: from Mosaic Canyon (p812) in California's Death Valley, to the mind-blowing Joint Trail in Canyonlands National Park (p930); from the chlorophyll-drunk woods of Kentucky to the tropical paradise of Kaua'i's Na Pali coast (p1136). Almost anywhere you go (except for a few of the flat, dusty parts where it's mostly corn), you'll find great hiking and backpacking within striking distance. And the further you wander from the gift shops, the more surprises you'll find.

If you're after *real* commitment, check out the John Muir Trail in Yosemite (p863): 222 miles of scenic bliss, from Yosemite Valley up to Mt Whitney. The Appalachian Trail (p272, p297) stretches from Maine, New England, to Georgia in the South, while the Pacific Coast Trail follows the spines of the Cascades (p1047) and Sierra Nevada (p860), spanning the continent's edge from Canada to Mexico: that's 2650 miles, passing through six of North America's seven eco-zones. It's hard to believe, but about 300 hikers go for it every year. Give it a shot – and watch your cheese.

For more information, see p1143.

Winter and spring hikers along the California coast may catch sight of gray whales, as they migrate between Alaska and Mexico. In the summer, blue, humpback and other whales can also be seen.

The largest meteorite crater in the world is in Winslow (p908). It's 4150ft across and 150ft deep; check out the 45-minute hike along its edge.

TOP TRAILS OF THE USA

Trying to reach a consensus on the USA's best hiking trails recalls the story of the Blind Men and the Elephant, where each blind man touches a different part of the elephant and thinks it's something different. The country is so varied, and distances so enormous, that people often prefer areas within easy reach. Still, a handful of online resources have compiled useful lists that will help turn your boots in the right direction:

About.com (http://walking.about.com/od/trails) Terrific information on hikes of every stripe, with many links to more detailed information.

Best Hiking Trails in USA (www.dancewithshadows.com/travel/top-us-camping-spots.asp) A brief, one-paragraph description of top trails shares the page with recommendations for campsites, national parks in summer and winter, picnic spots and kid-friendly destinations.

i-NEEDtoknow (www.i-needtoknow.com/hiking/best.html) Not limited to North America, this site also recommends the best hikes all over the world – Asia, Europe, Africa etc.

Top 10 Hiking Trails (www.americasbestonline.net/hiking.htm) You know these aren't in alphabetical order, since Zion (p935) is at the top of the list! The website's broad, brief descriptions also include the Continental Divide, Alaska's Pinnell Mountain and Nantahala forest (p473) in North Carolina.

Trails.com Top Trails (www.trails.com/toptrails.asp) This site ranks more than 30,000 USA trails, rated by online votes from visitors and members. An amazing resource, it provides excellent descriptions, staging points, and the hike's total mileage.

SURFING, WINDSURFING & KITESURFING

If waves are your passion, some of the best surf in continental USA breaks off the beaches of Santa Cruz (p822). The names of these sites are part of surfing legend: Steamer Lane, Pleasure Point, Sharks, Mavericks (an hour's drive north of Santa Cruz). Equally famous are the town's funky brewpubs: great places to share travelers' tales.

Other top surfing hangouts include Ditch Plains, near the eastern end of New York's Long Island (p168) in late summer and early autumn, as well as Seaside Beach, located on Oregon's Pacific Coast (about 75 miles northwest of Portland, near the end of the Lewis and Clarke trail), an Oregon tradition for thick-skinned (and we're not just talking Neoprene) riders. North Carolina's Cape Hatteras (p468), with the highest wave energy on the East Coast, is also part of the conversation. But for the serious surfer who is looking for adventure between October and March, there's only one destination worth talking about. Take the high road west, to sunny Hawai'i: the winter home of big waves, where the famed Pipe Masters competition draws the world's best surfers to O'ahu's north shore (p1128) in November/December. For information on surfing, see p1145.

Hawai'i is also a great place for kitesurfing, a new member (less than 10 years old!) of the water-sports family. The concept of kitesurfing is simple: using a huge, inflatable kite (from 15ft to nearly 50ft across) and a board much like a surfboard, kitesurfers harness the power of the wind to ride the surface of lakes or the ocean at amazing speeds. Experienced kitesurfers also take to the air, flying far above the whitecaps. It's an awesome, exhilarating sport – and like surfing, it's not for the faint of heart.

What you're looking for – especially if you're new to the sport – is warm water and consistent winds. You'll find these at Waipulani Beach in Maui (p1132), as well as at scattered locations around O'ahu. Another popular kitesurfing haunt is San Francisco Bay, where the same summer winds that fill the scenic waters with sailboats give a huge thrill to kitesurfers off the Emeryville breakwater. The Hood River (p1075), 60 miles east of Portland, Oregon, is also a hub of kitesurfing activity – along with

---

AIR SPORTS

The USA is probably the world's best place to enjoy the full spectrum of airborne delights – from a glass of chilled chardonnay in a hot-air balloon above California's Wine Country (p847), to a sphincter-puckering, 280-degree bungee jump into a narrow Utah canyon (p915).

Ballooning (www.hot-airballoons.com & http://hotairballooning.com) Awesome, exhilarating and usually expensive, a balloon ride provides an unforgettable splurge when the weather and scenery are right. Flights are available in almost every state; champagne is sometimes included. Not for those with vertigo!

Bungee Jumping (www.bungee-expeditions.com & www.bungee-experience.com) The tallest bungee-able bridge in the USA is a 680ft leap near Taos (p951) – but you're also welcome to jump 1500ft from a helicopter, over the rugged terrain of northern Idaho (p1022). Or bungee the famous Snake River, an hour from Boise (p1023), made infamous by motorcycle daredevil Evel Knievel.

Hang Gliding & Paragliding (www.goneawol.com) While a hang glider uses a pointed wing fixed to an aluminum frame, a paraglider is essentially a streamlined, steerable parachute. Tandem rides are available all over the USA.

Skydiving (www.uspa.org/dz/index.htm) Tandem skydiving – or solo, for the trained jumper – is the classic air sport, and remains a thrill beyond compare.

With any of these air sports, a web search of the sport name and your location will provide the most useful results.

South Padre Island (p745), a long thread of land sluicing along the eastern shoreline of South Texas.

As kitesurfing and its cousin, windsurfing (which uses a sailboard, first developed by a 20-year-old sailor named Newman Darby in 1948), rely on similar conditions, you'll find that both sports sometimes share locales: places with good wind, ready access to the waves and reasonable proximity to well-equipped watering holes.

CANOEING, KAYAKING & RAFTING

The New River Gorge National River (p368) – you wonder how it got its name – is the oldest river in the western hemisphere. Slicing from North Carolina into West Virginia, it cuts a gorge that ranges from 700ft to 1300ft deep. Known as 'The Grand Canyon of the East,' the river drops 240ft in just 14 miles, churning up white-water rapids to rival anything found in the American West.

The New River is one of West Virginia's most stompin' rafting and kayaking rivers – and there are six more, in the same neighborhood, for less-experienced water rats. In the western states, the astonishing Owyhee – whose popular north fork snakes from the high plateau of southeast Oregon (p1070) into the rangelands of Idaho (p1022) – features towering hoodoos shaped like abstract sculptures. And if you're the organized type who can plan things a few years in advance, you might try for a spot on the Colorado itself: the Mother of all Rivers for paddlers and rafters worldwide.

What's the difference between a kayak and a canoe? A kayak has a deck, a two-bladed paddle and a seat. Canoes are open and propelled from a kneeling (or sitting) position with a single-bladed oar. Kayaks are seaworthy, but not suited for bulky gear. To explore big lakes and the seacoast, use a sea kayak. For month-long trips – like Alaska's Kenai Peninsula (p1104), where more than 200 species of animals have been spotted, or Alabama's Bartram Canoe Trail (p398), with 300,000 acres of marshy delta bayous, lakes and rivers – use a canoe.

There are hundreds of places to enjoy surface tension all over the USA – even if your idea of water sport is floating along in an inner tube with a beer in your hand. Rentals and instruction are yours for the asking, from Georgia's Chatooga rapids to Washington's Olympic Peninsula (p1051); from Utah's Green River (p927) to Hawai'i's Na Pali Coast (p1136). Hire kayaks in California's Monterey Bay (p818) for a close encounter of the otter kind, or paddle through a cypress swamp in Bayou Gravenburg, about 80 miles from New Orleans (p412). As a satisfied alligator once said (while using a splintered oar as a toothpick): 'It's all good.'

For information on resources, see p1144.

> If you were to kayak around the coastline of all 'lower 48' United States and Hawai'i, it still wouldn't equal a single trip around the Alaska coastline.

> For an international association representing travel outfitters, tour companies and outdoor educators (you can search for outfitters by state or activity), check www .americaoutdoors.org.

FISHING

No sport – except maybe baseball – is as central to the American mythos as fishing. From cruises in pursuit of deep-sea marlin off the Florida Keys to the remote coastal fishing camp at Nakaklilok Bay (one of the world's best places for silver salmon), located in southwest Alaska's Lake and Peninsula borough (LPB), the entire USA is, in the eyes of many anglers, one big, glorious fishery.

Scores of websites and books provide advice and instruction on how to indulge in this ancient (but highly evolved) enterprise. Five species of salmon spawn in Alaska, while Georgia boasts the buttery Mississippi catfish. Big game fish, like tarpon and sailfish, leap above Florida's coastal waters, and Minnesota offers the opportunity to reel in great northern pike. Beautiful Maine is where you'll go to angle – from shore – that quintessential sporting fish, the striped bass.

For the sheer fishing delight, with a high probability of instant culinary enjoyment, may we suggest the trout? Most sources agree that fly-fishing is at its Zen best in the Colorado Rockies, the ever-surprising state of Idaho and especially 'Big Sky' country: Montana. This is the state where *A River Runs Through It* was filmed, and where one river alone – the Bighorn (p1002) – is said to host 5200 trout per mile!

The Long Sleep – on a camping mattress and otherwise – is still popular at Grasshopper Glacier in Montana, named for the swarm of prehistoric grasshoppers that remain frozen in its flanks.

HORSEBACK RIDING

OK, admit it: the *real* reason you're visiting the USA is because you've seen those classic Westerns, with Tom Mix and Henry Fonda crossing the purple sage on their faithful steeds. Your dearest fantasy is to thunder across that dusty terrain – not in a four-wheeler, but on four legs.

No problem. Horseback riding of every stripe, from Western to bareback, is available across the USA. The best opportunities, through country that's still rugged and wild, are (of course) in the West. We're talking everything from pony rides along the Oregon coast to week-long expeditions through the spires and canyons of southern Utah. Finding horses isn't difficult; riding schools and rental stables are located around many of the national parks. Experienced equestrians can set out alone, or in the company of guides familiar with local history (much of which was made on horseback).

California is a wonderful place for riding, with fog-swept trails leading along the cliffs of Point Reyes National Seashore (p843) and longer excursions through the high-altitude lakes of Inyo National Forest in beautiful Eastern Sierra (p866). Utah's Capitol Reef (p931) and Canyonlands (p930), in the right season, also provide spectacular outings, as can the mountains, deserts and plains of Colorado, Arizona and Montana. And did we mention Texas? Big Bend National Park (p763) is just one place to get saddle sore, a time-honored tradition in those parts.

Dude ranches come in a variety of flavors, from luxurious resorts to more rustic, authentic experiences on working cattle ranches. They're found in most of the western states, and even some eastern ones (such as North Carolina). Just do your research in advance, pardner, and make sure you know which kind of experience you're signing up for: the good, the bad or the ugly.

Food & Drink Tara Duggan

The USA may not have always had a stellar reputation for food, but this is changing quickly. While a burger, fries and Coke effectively make up the national meal, and fast-food chains threaten to consume what is distinctive about food across the country, there also is a rich tradition of quality regional cooking. The increasingly diverse population continues to improve the variety and quality of food, and a burgeoning interest in restaurant chefs has brought excitement to the culinary scene.

In the past few decades, the country has basically experienced a food revolution. Up through the 1960s and 1970s, ethnic foods were still mostly an anomaly and haute cuisine was all about nondescript 'continental' menus and stuffy service. But groundbreaking cookbook authors and teachers like Julia Child and James Beard introduced Americans to the wonders of real French cuisine (and their own overlooked culinary traditions), creating a demand for better quality food in restaurants and supermarkets.

In the early 1980s Alice Waters of Chez Panisse in Berkeley, and other Californian chefs, created a new type of cuisine based on quality local produce, teaching people to become aware of the sources of their food. Instead of only paying homage to Europe, more chefs began to gravitate toward New American cuisine, which elevates classic regional dishes by using upscale ingredients and preparations.

Americans spend up to 50% of their food dollars in restaurants. That adds up to $1.3 billion per day.

At the same time, the continued availability of low-cost junk food has led to an obesity epidemic that now severely impacts the nation's health. Today, over 60% of adults and 15% of children are either overweight or obese. However, an improved awareness of how unhealthy the American lifestyle has become is encouraging people to exercise more, as well as to eat lower-fat, whole-grain and organic foods.

All this fuss about food is causing some Americans to return to the kitchen, so there's hope that the country's regional traditions won't be lost amid a sea of french fries.

STAPLES & SPECIALTIES

Because of the country's cultural diversity, it is difficult to generalize about what Americans eat. Most people eat three meals a day, with a snack or two in between. The traditional American breakfast grew out of the country's origins as an agricultural society, where hearty plates of eggs, bacon and pancakes helped farming families start the day. Today, most people have office jobs and can only handle a bowl of cold cereal, toast or a pastry with coffee.

No cross-country road trip would be complete without Jane and Michael Stern's Road Food: The Coast-to-Coast Guide to 600 of the Best Barbecue Joints, Lobster Shacks, Ice Cream Parlors, Highway Diners and Much, Much More. Then again, you can get even more listings for free at www.roadfood.com.

Lunch used to be more of an important meal, and on weekends, some people still take their main meal in the middle of the day. But workers' lunch breaks are fairly short, so most people grab a quick burger or a hearty salad. Traditional home-style dinners can be more involved, including roast or grilled meat with potatoes, and baked casseroles.

Most folks take a coffee break mid-morning or late afternoon with a cookie, candy bar or bag of chips. Traditional desserts, such as ice cream sundaes, are very sweet and – like everything else – come in big servings.

New York

Go to New York City and you'll find almost any cuisine known to humankind. Because it continues to be a huge multicultural melting pot, it's a wonderful place to sample hard-to-find ethnic cuisines, from Jamaican

THE BAGEL PHENOMENON

Bagels are big these days, and if you buy one in an Iowa supermarket you may wonder why all the fuss about a bread roll with a hole in the middle. But if you get your hands on a New York–made bagel, you might just find out.

A true bagel, which really became a Jewish delicacy in this country, is made of just flour, water, salt, and malt for a little sweetness, and often is still rolled by hand. It is boiled, then baked, making it slightly crisp on the outside and deliciously dense and chewy inside. Traditional flavors include plain, poppy seed, sesame seed, onion, pumpernickel and egg, but modern-day bakeries have added things such as blueberries and sun-dried tomatoes.

Bagels are split in half, then spread with cream cheese and often topped with lox (cold-smoked salmon). If you're in New York City, find out why Americans love bagels at one of these popular spots:

Absolute Bagels (☎ 212-932-2052, 2788 Broadway)
Ess-a-bagel (☎ 212-980-1010, 831 Third Ave; ☎ 212-260-2252, 359 First Ave)
H & H Bagels (☎ 212-595-8003, 2239 Broadway; ☎ 212-765-7200, 639 W 46th St)
Murray's Bagels (☎ 212-462-2830, 500 Sixth Ave; ☎ 646-638-1335, 242 Eighth Ave)

to Ukrainian. Long-established treats include Chinese dim sum, Puerto Rican rice and beans, wood-fire charred New York–style pizza, and pickles, bagels and pastrami sandwiches from Jewish delis. Most agree that New York is the country's center of haute cuisine, where restaurants run by the trendiest chefs uphold impeccable standards of food and service.

New England

This is where to find seafood specialties like Maine's lobster and New England's clam chowder. Clams also come fried, steamed and completely uncooked, the latter at 'raw bars' that also serve oysters cold and briny from the sea. The clambake is an almost ritual meal, originating from Native Americans, where the shellfish are buried in a pit fire with corn, chicken and sausages. Cranberries, one of the essential parts of Thanksgiving dinner, are grown in Massachusetts and Rhode Island. The state of Vermont is known for its aged cheddar cheese and maple syrup. See p249 for further insights into the cuisine of this region.

Mid-Atlantic

Like New England, the mid-Atlantic areas (DC, Virginia and Chesapeake Bay) have a lot to offer in terms of seafood, with oysters along the coast and delicious blue crab from Chesapeake Bay. Philadelphia gave the world the Philly cheesesteak – a gooey mouthful of a roll stuffed with beef, onions and melted cheese. At Amish restaurants, the Pennsylvania Dutch serve home-style, Germanic foods such as stews, pickles and shoofly pie at family-style communal tables.

The Southern Belly: The Ultimate Food Lover's Companion to the South, by John T Edge, guides travelers to the best roadside finds, with cultural history to boot.

Southern

Southern cooking is a wonderful amalgamation of European, Native American and African traditions. Breakfast is as heavy as it could be, with eggs surrounded by buttery biscuits, gravy and ham. The ultimate Southern dish is barbecue: usually pork, sometimes chicken or beef, which is rubbed with spices, cooked slowly in a smoker until tender and then slathered with sauce. Every region of the South argues that their barbecue is best, from Texas' beef brisket to North Carolina's pulled pork. Tooth-achingly sweet desserts like cobblers, pies and layered cakes are a treat. See also p377.

Louisiana

If you thought a trip to New Orleans was all about drinking and taking your clothes off during Mardi Gras, you'd be missing something. This region has some of the best food in the country: Cajun food is heavy and spicy, a wild combination of French, Spanish, African and Native American influences. Specialties include gumbo, a stew of chicken and shellfish or sausage, and often okra; jambalaya, a rice-based dish with tomatoes, sausage and shrimp; blackened catfish; and alligator anything. For dessert, try gooey, rum-laced bananas Foster, or a fried beignet washed down with a chicory-scented café au lait.

Midwest

Swedes, Germans, Poles and Norwegians flocked to the Midwest in the 19th century to farm the region's fertile land. The influence of their hearty cuisines – known as heartland cooking – and hard-working lifestyle means you'll find lots of homespun Americana on the menu: potato salads, fruit pies and hefty loaves of bread. Both beef cattle and dairy cows are huge industries here, so it's a good place to sample steak and cheese. For something with a little more spice, try Kansas City barbecue, or head to Chicago, an ethnically diverse culinary center with some of the country's top restaurants.

Southwest

This region was Spanish territory for some time and still has a large Chicano population, so the Mexican (and Mexican American) food is excellent. Northern New Mexico makes delicious green and red chili sauces, which are pooled over eggs for breakfast, enchiladas and tacos. Native American specialties like fry bread are easy to find here. Utah, with its strong Mormon tradition, favors old-fashioned American fare, but Las Vegas is the USA's most up-and-coming culinary center – top chefs from New York, San Francisco and Los Angeles have set up satellite restaurants.

California

A concept that was born in the 1980s in the San Francisco Bay Area, California cuisine is all about using quality local ingredients in simple preparations. French and Italian bistro-style food was the first inspiration, but Latin and Asian influences have also become part of the mix. The natural resources are overwhelming, with wild salmon, Dungeness crab, oysters and halibut coming from local waters; excellent produce year-round; and artisanal products like cheese, bread, olive oil and, of course, wine. The state is so ethnically diverse that you can eat almost anything here, especially in the Los Angeles area.

Pacific Northwest & Hawaii

These are the regions of Pacific Rim food. The cool, wet climate of the Pacific Northwest produces wonderful wild mushrooms, berries, stone fruits, apples and wine grapes. The entire northern coast, all the way to Alaska, has an abundance of wild king salmon and oysters. Seattle is home to Starbucks and has an espresso stand on every corner; it also brews a lot of boutique beer. With its heavily Asian American population, Hawaii offers a combination of native foods and Chinese, Filipino and Japanese influences. Kalua pig, which is cooked in an underground fire pit, is usually the showcase dish at a traditional luau (multicourse feast).

Chowhound.com (www.chowhound.com) is 'for those who live to eat.' Come here to ask locals about important issues – from the best all-beef hot dogs in Chicago to the tastiest beef tongue tacos in Oakland, California.

DRINKS

Alcoholic drinks have had an interesting history in this country. In 1791, German and Scots-Irish farmers who grew rye for whiskey staged a rebellion to protest taxes. They fled to Kentucky and made their booze with corn instead, creating bourbon, the country's only original spirit.

Jack Daniels whiskey is distilled in Moore County, Tennessee, which has been a dry county since Prohibition days.

In 1919, a growing temperance movement caused Congress to pass an act outlawing the sale and manufacture of alcohol. Prohibition lasted from 1920 to 1933, when it was finally rescinded.

California missionaries began making wine in the 18th century, when they needed fermented grape juice for communion. Today, some wineries in California still have 100-year-old vines as a result of that early culture. The state's wine industry suffered a blow during both Prohibition and a 1916 phylloxera (grapevine louse) epidemic, and wasn't really taken seriously until the 1970s, when a blind tasting of French and California cabernet sauvignon (by French wine tasters) put California wine on top for the first time. California makes more than 90% of the USA's wine. Other top wine-producing states are Washington, Oregon, Texas, Virginia and New York.

Meanwhile, it was German and Czech settlers who turned the Midwest into a beer-making center. Today, the top four US beer makers, three of which are located in the Midwest, brew 80% of the beer drunk in the USA – most of which is light in body and flavor. Seattle and other parts of the Northwest are part of the microbrewery movement, producing European-quality beers.

Cocktails are making a popular comeback, and some of the top native creations include the mint julep (bourbon, mint, sugar and crushed ice), martini (gin and vermouth), Irish coffee (coffee, whiskey, sugar and cream), and Bloody Mary (vodka, tomato juice, Tabasco sauce, horseradish and other flavorings).

Most nonalcoholic beverages are quite sweet and served over ice, from Southern-style iced tea to the ultimate American beverage: Coca-Cola from Atlanta, Georgia.

CELEBRATIONS

There are no two ways about it – Americans love to celebrate with food. And with so few opportunities in the working calendar to do it, they certainly make up for it when they can. Whether it's deep-frying a turkey at Thanksgiving or collecting candy at Halloween, traditional and festive

---

TRAVEL YOUR TASTEBUDS

Travel is an adventure for all the senses. While in the US make sure you try:

- Peanut butter and jelly sandwich – a savory-sweet school lunchbox favorite made of white bread spread with peanut butter and jam.

- Corn dog – a common sight at beach boardwalks and county fairs, this hot dog on a stick is wrapped in a crisp, cornmeal batter.

- Burrito – a Mexican American creation consisting of a large flour tortilla rolled around beans, meat, salsa and rice; there's usually enough food for two meals.

- S'mores – a camping treat, this interactive dessert involves roasting a marshmallow on a stick over the fire, then placing it between graham crackers with a piece of chocolate, which melts on impact.

- And we dare you to try Rocky Mountain oysters, a euphemistically named dish of battered and fried sheep or calf testicles served with a spicy dipping sauce to help it go down easier.

foods often become the main focus of an occasion – along with bringing family and friends together.

Independence Day, as well as Memorial Day and Labor Day – which mark the symbolic beginning and end of summer – inspire people to don Hawaiian shirts and head outdoors with a beer. Friends and families gather in backyards or parks to grill hamburgers and share a potluck of side dishes like potato salad, coleslaw, Jello and apple pie.

The American version of Halloween, or All Hallows Eve, has evolved from a night of scaring away demons to a night of scaring fellow living souls. Houses display jack o'lanterns – carved pumpkins filled with candles – and children go trick-or-treating, which means dressing in costume and heading door-to-door to ask for candy.

Thanksgiving commemorates a mythic harvest celebration between Pilgrims and Native Americans, and is second only to Christmas in importance. Traditional dishes are European in nature, but are made with native ingredients such as cranberry sauce, sweet potatoes, mashed potatoes and pumpkin pie, all centered on a huge roast turkey. Modern twists on the tradition include subjecting the bird to a deep-fryer or an outdoor grill.

Christmas preparations begin in full after Thanksgiving, when all those Santa centerpieces start getting dusted off. The main meal is similar to Thanksgiving's, maybe with a ham or beef roast instead of the turkey. Easter is not quite as sacrosanct, though it does encourage many families to get together for church and dinner. Harking back to the holiday's pre-Christian origins is the Easter-egg hunt, when children collect decorated eggs and candies left by the Easter bunny...

The highlight on New Year's Eve for many is to watch the celebration in Manhattan's Times Square on TV. But plenty of people do make an effort to dress up for parties with champagne and drunken singing and kisses at midnight. On New Year's Day, Southerners prepare hopping John, a plate of black-eyed peas and rice, for good luck.

Several ethnic and religious holidays take place in winter and early spring. Mardi Gras, the celebration before Catholic Lent, doesn't get much crazier than in New Orleans, where revelers don garish costumes and eat king cake with a good luck charm hidden inside. On St Patrick's Day, the nation's celebration of all things Irish American, you might see restaurants serving corned beef and cabbage, and lots and lots of beer.

While wedding ceremonies continue to get shorter and less religious, the reception that follows has become increasingly complex. The wedding party may host a catered meal for hundreds of people, complete with cocktails and champagne, and culminating with a tiered, frosted cake. Traditionally, the bride and groom feed the first bite of the cake to each other by hand.

WHERE TO EAT & DRINK

Though what you find at a random roadside diner won't usually compare with the equivalent in, say, France, if you do some research you will come across some excellent food on your travels. For a more authentic experience, head to neighborhoods where locals live and work, whether an ethnic district in a big city or a small rural town. A sign of a tourist trap is when the menu has photos of the food, or a long-winded text telling the history of the establishment. Sometimes these places can be charming, but they are usually avoided by locals.

Lunch can be a good time for bargains at quality restaurants, when prices can be much lower than at dinner – though keep in mind that the first-rate cooks usually work the night shift.

Want to know where to dine or how to make something you ate during your travels? Epicurious (www.epicurious.com) has a database of restaurant reviews and recipes from the popular cooking magazines *Gourmet* and *Bon Appetit*.

To make online restaurant reservations in advance of a trip, head to OpenTable.com (www.opentable.com), which serves 16 major US cities.

CHOICES, CHOICES

Americans like to have independence and freedom of choice, down to the toast they eat in the morning. When dining out, be prepared to make a lot of choices. Here are some of the decisions your server might ask you to make.

Breakfast: what kind of bread would you like with your eggs – toasted whole wheat, sourdough or white, English muffin (similar to a crumpet), bagel, biscuit? Home fries (fried, seasoned potato wedges), hash browns (shredded fried potatoes) or a fruit salad? Bacon or sausage? Orange, grapefruit, tomato or apple juice? Decaf or regular coffee, cream and sugar?

Lunch/dinner: soup of the day or salad? If a salad, which dressing – blue cheese (creamy), ranch (similar but without the cheese), Italian (oil and vinegar) or French (red and sweet)? With that steak, a baked potato, mashed potato, rice or french fries?

If you're looking for a quick meal, you can always join the overwhelming number of Americans who eat in fast-food restaurants. Most of the food in these establishments is prepared and frozen at a central commissary, then reheated before serving. The reheating involves a lot of frying, which makes the food tasty but none too healthy.

A step up from fast food is the cafeteria or buffet, where you load up a tray with dishes from various steam tables, then carry it to your table. The all-you-can-eat buffet is a stunning phenomenon: for a set price you can revisit the buffet as many times as you like, until you're completely stuffed or just plain embarrassed.

'Family-style' restaurants or coffee shops are also very popular. Epitomized by the chain Denny's, they provide table service and homey foods like soups, meat-loaf dinners and ice cream sundaes. Kids are very welcome.

Similar food is on the menu at old-fashioned diners and lunch counters, many of which are authentically retro, complete with vinyl booths, Formica counters and wise-cracking locals. Big breakfasts are an important part of the roster and often are available all day.

The word 'café' can mean many things in the US. Sometimes it's just a coffee- and teahouse in the European tradition, with pastries and light snacks; other times it sells heartier sandwiches and soups.

A bar and grill is a casual dinner place specializing in cocktails and grilled steak. Brewpubs are a relatively new, but popular, venue; you can sit right next to gleaming beer tanks and drink the house brew with burgers and pizza.

For a slower-paced meal, you may have to spring for a more high-end restaurant, such as a steak house. These low-lit taverns are devoted to huge cuts of beef and potatoes, with a little lobster thrown in for good measure. In bigger cities you'll find restaurants with European-style service and prix fixe menus where you can happily linger over your crème brûlée.

Fast-food restaurants, diners and coffee shops tend to be open from breakfast through dinner, sometimes 24 hours, while other restaurants take a break between lunch and dinner. Breakfast is usually 6am to 11am (except on weekends, when it starts later and is offered longer), lunch 11:30am to 2pm and dinner 5pm to 10pm at the latest, except in bigger cities.

> Foodnetwork.com (www.foodtv.com), from the 24-hour cable TV channel, features discussions with celebrity chefs, video cooking demos and recipes.

Quick Eats

On the lower end of the dollar-for-dinner quotient, street stands sell everything from hot dogs to meat kabobs. You can even find what are called 'lunch trucks,' or taco trucks, which serve hot foods and drinks. It's a gamble: these vendors can be the place for an authentic, delicious, bargain-priced meal, or you might just end up with tasteless, cheap grub.

Look to outdoor summer fairs, festivals and farmers markets for some of the better street foods. County fairs have stands devoted to culinary Americana like corn dogs, candy apples and funnel cakes. Farmers markets and food festivals might have anything from crepes to meat barbecued in an outdoor smoker. Some food festivals are wonderful, with local traditions that go back forever, while others are nothing more than gimmicky commercial enterprises. Do some research before handing over your cash at one of these events.

VEGETARIANS & VEGANS

Vegetarianism in the USA has come a long way since the 1970s, when those who ate tofu were considered weird, if not suspect. Many from the younger generations are turning to vegetarianism and veganism, and even carnivores regularly skip the meat for health reasons. Most medium-sized cities, especially those with universities, have at least one vegetarian restaurant, and cosmopolitan areas like the San Francisco Bay Area and New York City have upscale restaurants devoted to the art of meatless cooking. In addition, nonvegetarian restaurants in urban areas tend to have creative vegetarian offerings. Chinese, Indian and Italian restaurants are usually good bets for vegetarians.

Some things to look out for: traditionally, tortillas and beans are made with lard, though many Mexican restaurants now make them with vegetable oil instead. Be sure to ask if that vegetable soup or risotto you're looking at contains chicken broth. Also, most Vietnamese and Thai dishes contain fish sauce, but the kitchen might make them with soy sauce instead if you ask your server.

> The Vegetarian Resource Group has found that less than 3% of Americans are completely vegetarian but almost 60% of the population regularly chooses to eat meatless. To find a vegetarian restaurant, visit www.vegdining.com.

EATING WITH KIDS

At family-style restaurants and coffee shops, paper placemats and crayons are distributed at the door, and kids get their own menu. These menus offer children aged under 10 or 12 small servings of things like cheese sandwiches, spaghetti, pizza and chicken nuggets, at the cost of a few dollars. Fast-food chains also snare weary parents with kid-size meals and even playgrounds.

> Zagat Survey (www.zagat.com) is based on a popular series of guidebooks that lists restaurants, nightspots and hotels based on reader approval ratings. The site requires registration, but it's free.

Restaurants without a children's menu don't necessarily discourage kids, though higher-end restaurants might. Ask if the kitchen will make a small order of pasta with butter and cheese (also ask how much it will cost) or if they will split a normal-size order among two plates for the kids. Restaurants usually provide high chairs and booster seats.

If you'd like to pick up snacks at the grocery store, beware that many food products aimed at kids contain less-than-healthy ingredients; for example, kids' breakfast cereals and fruit drinks usually are loaded with sugar. Pure juices, fresh and dried fruits, carrot sticks, string cheese, granola bars, and small containers of yogurt, cottage cheese and apple sauce are some

---

TAXES & TIPPING

Unless noted, service is not included in restaurant checks, and servers depend on tips to survive on their minimum-wage salaries. Those who fail to tip at least 15% will receive a frosty, if not hostile, farewell. The exceptions: great service (especially at high-end restaurants) merits a 20% tip, while anyone providing sloppy, careless service can get more like 10%. There's no need to tip at self-service or fast-food restaurants.

Except in areas that have no sales tax, state, local and/or city taxes are added to your bill at the end of the meal.

good snack options that are readily available. Supermarkets also carry a wide range of jarred baby foods, some of them even organic.

HABITS & CUSTOMS

Americans love to eat out, whether it's taking the kids to a coffee shop or showing off a date at a swanky, trendy restaurant. But eating out may be more of a necessity than a choice. Americans tend to work long hours, and that leaves little time to cook a meal at home.

Big Night (1996) is a wonderful film about two Italian brothers who struggle to run an authentic, refined Italian restaurant in 1950s America, which only seems to want spaghetti and meatballs, and loud Louis Prima.

Like most other things they do, Americans eat very quickly, often spending only a half hour to an hour on their meal depending on the type of restaurant and the occasion. But there are times when people slow down to eat, especially on weekends and holidays.

In religious households, a family member often leads grace before the meal begins, while the rest of the group bow their heads or close their eyes. At formal dinners of any denomination, hosts or guests may offer a toast before the meal begins or in between courses. After a toast, everyone usually says 'cheers' and clinks glasses around the table. The hostess is supposed to be the first to take a bite, and will most likely offer second helpings.

Religious occasions and festivals such as Lent, Chinese New Year and Ramadan can affect when sections of the population are eating what, but only major holidays such as Christmas close down the majority of restaurants.

COOKING COURSES

There has been a proliferation of cooking courses in the past decade, as more Americans realize they don't know how to cook and as cooking shows become more popular on TV. One type of class is offered at high-end cookware shops such as Sur la Table (www.surlatable.com). Here is a sample of cooking schools that offer courses to amateur chefs on holiday.

Central Market Cooking School (www.centralmarket.com) In five major Texas cities.
Cookin' Cajun Cooking School (www.cookincajun.com) In New Orleans.
Cook's World (www.cooksworld.net) In Seattle.
French Culinary Institute (www.frenchculinary.com) In New York City.
Jane Butel's Cooking School (www.janebutel.com) In Albuquerque, New Mexico.

DOS & DON'TS

Americans are fairly casual when it comes to dining, but there are some important customs to honor. Dinner guests should bring a small gift, such as flowers or chocolates. For more informal dinners, you can offer to bring something for the meal, such as a bottle of wine or a loaf of good bread.

The method for holding cutlery seems extremely complicated at first: hold your fork in your right hand, and rest your left hand in your lap. When you need to use a knife, switch your fork to your left hand and cut with your right. Or just eat European-style – it won't be considered rude unless you rest your left hand on the table. It's OK to eat with your hands when burgers or pizza are on the menu.

Definitely ask your dining companions as well as the restaurant staff if it's OK to smoke. Many states require that restaurants have smoking and nonsmoking seating areas, while some, like California, don't even allow smoking in bars or in outdoor patios. It's considered rude to chat on cell phones in a restaurant, but plenty of people do it anyway.

Usually, servers drop off the check after you've ordered dessert, but it's déclassé to do this in more formal establishments, where you must request the bill. Leave the tip on the table.

STAR CHEFS

Chefs in the USA have taken on a celebrity status akin to rock stars, especially the better-looking ones who appear on the Food Network, a 24-hour cable TV station. Here are some of the most popular.

Bobby Flay – with restaurants in Manhattan and Las Vegas, this hunky New York chef is all about Southwestern food, especially from the grill.

Emeril Lagasse – this brash, fast-talking chef is one of the country's most popular, with restaurants in New Orleans, Florida and Las Vegas; a line of food products and cookware; and incredibly successful TV shows.

Mario Batali – a rotund, red-headed Italian American whose extensive travels to Italy inform the soulful dishes at his New York restaurants, as well as his cooking shows.

Rachael Ray – though not a formally trained restaurant chef, this TV host is so loved for her spunky, upbeat approach to home cooking that she's launched her own lifestyle magazine, *Every Day with Rachael Ray*.

Wolfgang Puck – the Austrian-born powerhouse became a star in Los Angeles in the 1970s, and has since established an empire of restaurants serving his signature California cuisine, as well as a line of prepared foods.

Natural Gourmet Cookery School (www.naturalgourmetschool.com) In New York City, focusing on vegetarian and healthy cooking.
New Orleans Cooking Experience (www.neworleanscookingexperience.com) In New Orleans
New School of Cooking (www.newschoolofcooking.com) In Culver City (outside Los Angeles).
Prairie Kitchens (www.prairiekitchens.com) In Chicago, Illinois.
Santa Fe School of Cooking (www.santafeschoolofcooking.com) In Santa Fe, New Mexico.
Tante Marie's Cooking School (www.tantemarie.com) In San Francisco.
Terence Janericco Cooking Classes (www.terencejanericcocookingclasses.com) In Boston, Massachusetts.

GLOSSARY
bagel – a New York specialty, rolled bread that is boiled, then baked, giving it a chewy texture
barbecue – officially refers to the Southern style of slow-cooking spice-rubbed meat with smoke, but sometimes refers to a grill
biscuit – flaky, buttery roll served in the South at dinner or breakfast
blue plate – special of the day
BLT – bacon, lettuce and tomato sandwich
brownie – fudgy, cakelike bar cookie rich with chocolate and sometimes nuts
Caesar salad – romaine lettuce tossed with croutons and shaved Parmesan cheese in a dressing laced with raw egg and anchovy
chicken-fried steak – thin steak battered and fried like chicken
chili – hearty, meaty stew spiced with ground chilis, sometimes with vegetables and beans
chips – thin, deep-fried potato slices or tortilla wedges
cilantro – coriander
clam chowder – chunky, potato-based soup full of clams and vegetables, sometimes bacon, and thickened with milk
club sandwich – white sandwich bread stacked in three layers with chicken or turkey, bacon, lettuce and tomatoes
cobbler – fruit dessert with a biscuit or pie-crust topping, baked until bubbly and served with whipped cream or ice cream
continental breakfast – coffee or tea, pastry, and juice or fruit
crab cake – crab meat held together with breadcrumbs and eggs, then fried
crisp – similar to *cobbler*, except with a crunchy, streusel-like topping
eggplant – aubergine
French toast – egg-dipped bread that is fried and served with maple syrup for breakfast
fries or french fries – deep-fried potato wedges
granola – breakfast cereal of oats baked with honey and nuts, usually served with yogurt or milk and fresh fruit

grits – white cornmeal made into a porridge for a Southern breakfast or side dish

guacamole – dip of mashed avocados with lime juice and often tomatoes, onions, chilis and *cilantro*, served with tortilla chips or in Mexican American dishes

hash browns – shredded fried potatoes, served with eggs

huevos rancheros – Mexican breakfast of corn tortillas topped with fried eggs and chili sauce

Jello – trademarked name for a molded gelatin fruit dessert or salad

jelly – fruit preserves with a thinner consistency than jam

maple syrup – unctuous, deeply flavored syrup that is drizzled over waffles, pancakes and French toast, made from the maple tree's spring sap

marshmallow – whipped sugar confection in fluffy, spongy cube shapes

pickle – unlike Britain's piquant condiment, this refers to a pickled cucumber

pretzel – twisted salty snack in two forms: a crunchy, thin kind made commercially, and a much larger, bready variety that's sold as a street food

smoothie – cold, thick drink made with puréed fruit, ice and sometimes yogurt

submarine sandwich – also called the hoagie, po'boy, hero or grinder in various regions, this sandwich is served on a thick roll slathered with mustard and mayonnaise and filled with thinly sliced deli meats and cheeses, as well as lettuce, onions, pickles and tomatoes

surf 'n' turf – plate of both seafood (often lobster) and steak

wrap – modern-day offshoot of the burrito, a vibrantly colored tortilla stuffed with fillings of practically any origin

The East

VERONICA GARBUTT

New York, New Jersey & Pennsylvania

Spend a little time with this cool threesome, and it won't be hard to figure out why so many folks have clamored to join the party. The trio of states comprises North America's densest population center, therefore something must be great about the region. Much of the charm is based on sheer diversity – not only in New York City (NYC), which is a spectacular world within itself, but throughout the entire tri-state area.

Where else could you visit an Amish family's farm, gamble the night away in a glitzy casino, do some mountaintop camping, read the actual Declaration of Independence and view New York, New York from the 86th floor of an art-deco landmark – all in a few days? That's just a sampling of how you could spend your time, between the urban and cultural adventures of NYC, Philadelphia and Pittsburgh, and the many natural settings that lie beyond the city borders. The Jersey Shore, for example, is a blend of beauty and kitsch, and southern Pennsylvania is dotted with historic Civil War battle sites. New York has the mesmerizing Niagara Falls, the dizzying Adirondack mountain range, a wine country hugging the shores of glimmering lakes, and the beautiful Hamptons and Catskills that lure with simple-life charms just a couple of hours away from frenzied NYC. Whichever route you choose, one thing is for sure: your life will be richer when the journey is complete.

HIGHLIGHTS

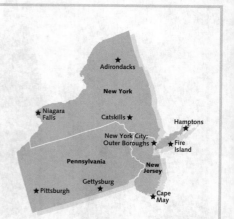

- Traveling round the world in **New York, NY** (p126), where the globe's cultures meet.

- Straddling both city and country with urban hipsters in the mountainous **Catskills** (p171)

- Taking in arts and culture in surprising **Pittsburgh** (p205)

- Backpacking on the peaks of the **Adirondacks** (p175)

- People-watching at the world's gayest beach, **Fire Island** (p169)

- Soaking up history with never-ending Civil War reenacts at **Gettysburg** (p205)

- Going all Hollywood East in the fabled, frenzied **Hamptons** (p170)

- Exploring overlooked gems – NYC's **outer boroughs** (p148) of Brooklyn, Queens, the Bronx and Staten Island

- Marveling at the bold, beautiful **Niagara Falls** (p178)

- Getting away to a quaint B&B at seaside **Cape May** (p185)

NY-NJ-PA IN...

Five Days

Start with a gentle introduction in **Philadelphia** (p187), birthplace of American independence. After a day of touring the historic sites and a night of sampling the hoppin' nightlife, head into New Jersey for a bucolic night in **Cape May** (p185). On day three, coast up along the **Jersey Shore** (p183), landing in **New York City** (p126) by nightfall. Spend the rest of your visit here, blending touristy must-dos – such as the **Empire State Building** (p138) or **Central Park** (p143) – with some quirky nightlife and dining adventures, perhaps in the way-fun **East Village** (p137).

One Week

Begin in **Philadelphia** (p187) as above, then spend the second night in Atlantic City, at the **Borgata** (p185). On night three, stop for a quaint B&B stay further up along the Jersey Shore, perhaps in **Spring Lake** (p184) or **Sandy Hook** (p184). Spend the rest of your stay mixing the excitement of NYC with the natural and historic wonders of a couple of nearby day trips or one-night escapes, such as to the **Hudson Valley** (p171), the **Hamptons** (p170) or the **Catskills** (p172).

Two Weeks

An extra week will allow you to explore the massive and fascinating state of Pennsylvania a bit more. You could start in **Pittsburgh** (p205), exploring museums and riversides for a day and a night, then take a road trip across the bucolic southern portion of the state, spending a second night in **Fallingwater** (p216), a third in the **Gettysburg** region (p205) and a fourth on a working Amish family farm in **Lancaster County** (p204). Hit **Philadelphia** (p187) by day five, and then follow the one-week itinerary, turning all your day trips into overnighters, perhaps adding a day trip to magical **Fire Island** (p169).

HISTORY

As ironic as it is for a region that is so thickly populated today, this region was probably home to fewer than 100,000 people before the Europeans arrived. The sparse Native American settlements comprised two major cultural groups: the Algonquians and the Iroquois.

By the mid-16th century, though, French fur trappers and traders had found their way to the region via the St Lawrence River. In 1609, explorer Henry Hudson found, sailed and named the Hudson River, claiming the land for the Dutch, who started several settlements in 'New Netherlands.' The Iroquois soon controlled the booming fur trade, selling to Dutch, English and French agents.

But the tiny Dutch settlement on Manhattan Island surrendered to a Royal Navy warship in 1664, in the midst of a series of Anglo-Dutch wars. This new colonial power created two territories, calling them 'New York' and 'New Jersey,' which attracted a great number of settlers from nearby New England. New Jersey's population grew rapidly, with no small thanks to the great neighboring colonies of New York and Pennsylvania, which guarded small New Jersey from the perils of frontier life experienced elsewhere; New Jersey was also free of Indian wars, which allowed energies to be focused toward more positive advances.

Pennsylvania played a leading role in the Revolutionary War (1775–83), and New York and New Jersey loyalties were split; important battles occurred in all three states. Many Iroquois allied themselves with the British, and they suffered badly from military defeats, disease, European encroachment and reprisals. Entire communities were wiped out, and much of their land was deeded to Revolutionary War veterans. Farmers displaced the Algonquians from coastal areas and river valleys.

As early as the 1840s, the region's major cities were linked by railways; the population also grew with waves of immigration, starting with the Irish in the 1840s and 1850s. Natural resources, abundant labor and unfettered capitalism transformed the entire region into a powerhouse of industry and commerce. And during the Civil War (1861–65), New York, New Jersey and Pennsylvania all supplied men and material for Union forces.

NEW YORK, NEW JERSEY & PENNSYLVANIA

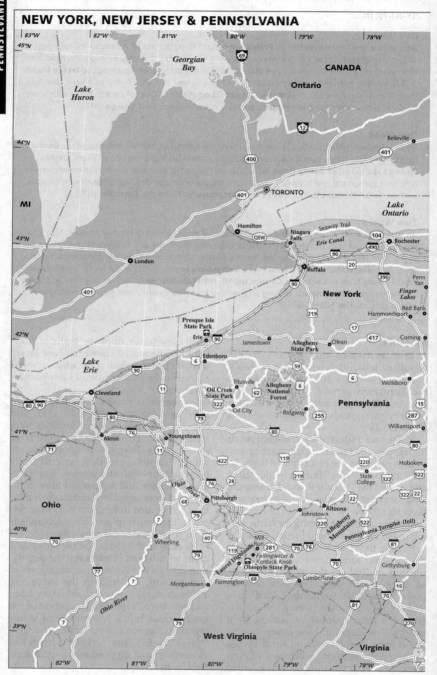

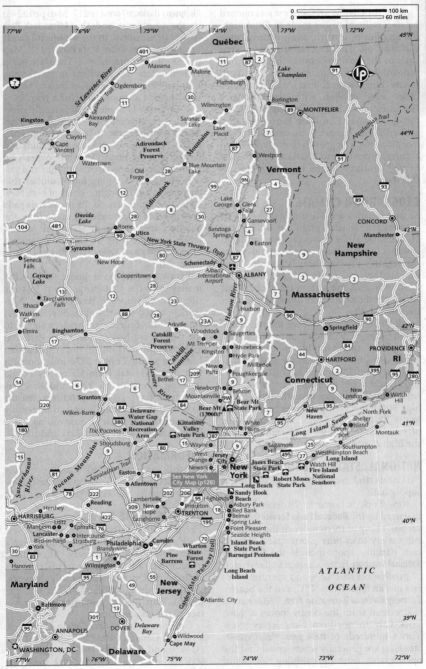

After the Civil War, the West was opened by steel railroad tracks made in Pittsburgh, the engines of growth using Pennsylvania coal and oil. The profits, of course, went back to the 'robber barons,' the super-rich industrialists and financiers in New York (some things never change). All the region's cities were swollen with immigrants – Blacks from the South, Chinese from California, and over 12 million Europeans who arrived at Ellis Island, in the middle of New York Harbor. The growth, industry, wealth, cultural diversity and constant flow of new people continue in the tri-state region to this day.

GEOGRAPHY & CLIMATE

Most big cities are on the main rivers of the eastern coastal plain, including the Hudson, Delaware, Susquehanna and Ohio Rivers. Low mountain ranges extend across the region's interior, heavily forested with pine, red spruce, maple, oak, ash and birch. Further inland, the waterways of the Great Lakes and the Ohio River link many smaller industrial cities.

All three states experience the full range of four seasons, with temperatures always a bit cooler to the north, like in upstate New York, and a bit warmer in the south, especially around Philadelphia. Fall temperatures hover about the Fahrenheit 40s to 50s, while winter can range from the teens to the high 30s. Expect temperatures from the 50s to the 70s in spring – plus some extra doses of rain – and summer temperatures from the high 60s to the mid-80s.

NATIONAL, STATE & REGIONAL PARKS

Parklands and recreation areas are in big supply here.

New York is home to 28 federal parks managed by the **National Parks Service** (NPS; www.nps.gov), many of them more of the historic-site variety than pure green space. Significant parklike spots include the **Fire Island National Seashore** (p169), a spectacular stretch of pristine ocean shores and maritime forests just an hour from NYC; and the beachy **Gateway National Recreation Area**, 26,000 acres that extend from the ocean shores of New York City to northern New Jersey. New York's hundreds of **state parks** (http://nysparks.state.ny.us) are generally where you'll find the open spaces, from the camping heavens of

Allegheny National Forest (p217; Map pp122–3) in the southwest and the **Adirondack Park** (p175) in the north, to the wonderful sandy expanse of **Jones Beach State Park** (p169; Map pp122–3), on Long Island. The state parks system offers the excellent money-saving Empire Passport for $65, which gets you into any and all state parks for a year.

New Jersey is home to 10 federally managed areas, including its southeastern **Pinelands National Reserve** (p184), encompassing over a million acres of forests, wetlands and farms, plus the great Delaware Water Gap National Recreation Area, with hills and valleys and great camping opportunities that encompass land along the rivers of both New Jersey and Pennsylvania. Its many **state parks** (www.state.nj.us/dep/parksandforests) range from the beachy Cape May Point State Park at New Jersey's southern tip to the mountainous, forested **Kittatinny Valley State Park** (p182) in the north.

Pennsylvania (PA) is home to 28 NPS-managed parks that range from historic sites and Chesapeake Bay Gateways Network – a vast waterfront park system that spreads into four neighboring states – to the Gettysburg National Military Park and a significant portion of the Appalachian National Scenic Trail, a 2174-mile footpath that snakes its way from Maine to Georgia (passing through New York and New Jersey on its way). Its **state parks** (www.dcnr.state.pa.us/stateparks) include a huge and incredibly diverse array of thick forests, rolling parklands and well-trod greenways and trails.

INFORMATION

For this vast and varied region, see individual states – New York on opposite, New Jersey on p181 and Pennsylvania on p187.

GETTING THERE & AWAY

The big cities all have airports, but New York's John F Kennedy (JFK) is the region's major international gateway. Alternatives include Newark International Airport; La Guardia, in Queens, with mostly domestic flights; and the Long Island MacArthur Airport in Islip, also offering domestic travel (see p166, for specifics).

Greyhound buses serve main US towns, as well as Canada. **Peter Pan Trailways** (☎ 800-343-9999) and **Adirondack Trailways** (☎ 800-225-6815) are both regional bus lines. **Amtrak** (www

.amtrak.com) provides rail services throughout the New York metropolitan area. The main northeast coastal rail corridor (Boston–Providence–New London–New York–Newark–Philadelphia–Washington, DC) has at least one service per day on the high-speed Acela train. Most popular day trips, at least when leaving from New York City, are easily accessible by one of the three commuter-rail lines (see p167).

Organized regional tours are also a good option if you're interested in combining the best of two or three of the states into one concise journey, without having to actually sit behind the wheel yourself. The Pennsylvania-based **Trans-Bridge Tours** (☎ 610-776-8687; www.transbridgebus.com) offers several interesting multiday, regional trips to sites including Long Island, Niagara Falls, Atlantic City and New Jersey Lighthouses. **Gray Line** (www.grayline.com) also offers guided bus trips around the New York City area, as well as Buffalo and Niagara Falls.

NEW YORK STATE

It's funny that the only New York most outsiders know is that of the tiny little island of Manhattan – big in attitude and offerings and reputation, to say the least, but representing just an itty bitty sliver of the thrills to be mined throughout the massive state. New York is bordered by no less than five states (Pennsylvania, New Jersey, Connecticut, Massachusetts and Vermont), three major bodies of water (Lake Ontario, Lake Erie and the Atlantic Ocean) and one foreign country (Canada), and its personality has been shaped by and reflects them all.

New York City folks often reduce every other part of their state to a small backwater village, calling the landmass simply 'Upstate.' But there is oh so much more to know – from the culture- and history-rich Buffalo, and its nearby wonder of Niagara Falls, to Adirondack skiing and camping regions and the gorgeous wine country of the Finger Lakes. There are hippie-filled college towns, like beloved Ithaca, and hippie-filled noncollege towns, like Woodstock and Saugerties. There are artist colonies to be found in spots from Hudson to the Hamptons, and major significant sites sprinkled throughout every county. New

> **NEW YORK FACTS**
> **Nicknames** Empire State, Excelsior State
> **Population** 19.2 million
> **Area** 54,471 sq miles
> **Capital city** Albany
> **State muffin** Apple muffin
> **Birthplace of** Teddy Roosevelt (1858–1919); Franklin D Roosevelt (1882–1945); Eleanor Roosevelt (1884–1962); Humphrey Bogart (1899–1957); Woody Allen (b 1935); Mel Gibson (b 1956); Michael Jordan (b 1963); Mariah Carey (b 1970)
> **Home of** The first US cattle ranch (1747, in Montauk, Long Island); the US women's suffrage movement (1872); UN headquarters, Wall St, Niagara Falls (half of it), Statue of Liberty
> **Famous for** Broadway, bagels, New York Yankees baseball team

York has farmlands (though fast disappearing), forests, lakes and seashores, and yes, small backwater villages that seem happily stuck in time.

And then, of course, there's big ol' NYC: mythical, seductive and pretty darn intimidating. There are several avenues in – foreign culture, food, art, literature, sports – and once you find your niche, you'll want to burrow in for the long haul.

History
New York State's history is linked to its inland waterways. The first settlements were along the Hudson River, including the tiny town of Newburgh, where George Washington made his headquarters during the Revolutionary War. Completed in 1825, the Erie Canal, between Albany and Buffalo, connected New York and the Hudson River with the Great Lakes and Midwest. The canal system helped open the continent's interior, promoted industrial development in cities like Buffalo, Rochester and Syracuse, and established New York City as the USA's major shipping port.

Information
New York State Hospitality & Tourism Association (www.nyshta.org) Searchable database for finding region-specific accommodations and attractions
New York State Tourism (☎ 518-474-4116; http://iloveny.com) Information on all regions of New York State, with good state maps and travel counselors available by phone to help with plans. Travel brochures by mail, too.

New York State Travel Information (www.travelinfony .com) Check for weather advisories, road information and more

New York Times (www.nytimes.com/travel) Searchable archives from its excellent Travel section

World Web New York (www.ny.worldweb.com) A searchable travel site with statewide reservation-making capabilities

NEW YORK CITY

The groovy, at-times-controversial indie musician Ani DiFranco once said: 'I can't wait to get back to New York City, where at least when I walk down the street, no one ever hesitates to tell me exactly what they think of me.' She was really on the money with that one. Because, cliché as it may be, it's true that NYC's people are probably among the most opinionated individuals in the whole world. And why shouldn't they be? It's the eight million people, after all, who provide the pulsing soul and energy of this wondrous city, blessing it with foreign languages and cuisines, priceless artworks and architecture, snappy fashions and stunning literature – inspired, rather than shaken, by the frenzied urban madness that screeches all around them – so they've certainly earned the right to say what's on their mind. You'll earn it, too, in about a day, because NYC is certainly not easy, but it's rewarding – and wonderfully surprising – in all the best ways.

History

When Henry Hudson first claimed this land for his sponsors, the Dutch East India Company, in 1609, he reported it to be 'as beautiful a land as one can hope to tread upon.' And, though it's gorgeous today in an urban-jungle sort of way, it may be difficult to picture today's New York City as it was for 11,000 years, when the land was occupied by Native Americans. But the name 'Manhattan' was indeed derived from local Munsee Indian words, meaning 'Island of Hills.'

Fast-forward to 1625, when a colony, soon called New Amsterdam, was established; a year later the island was bought from the Munsee Indians by Peter Minuit. George Washington was sworn in here as the republic's first president in 1789, but the founding fathers disliked New York City; Thomas Jefferson described the city

as 'a cloacina of all the depravities of human nature.' When the War of Secession broke out, New York, which supplied a significant contingent of volunteers to defend the Union, became an organizing center for the movement to emancipate slaves.

Throughout the 19th century, successive waves of immigrants – Irish, German, English, Scandinavian, Slavic, Italian, Greek and central-European Jewish – led to a very rapid population increase. By the end of the 19th century, businessmen created empires in industry and finance, signaling a golden age when skyscrapers rose and the underclass became a developed community.

After WWII New York was the premier city in the world, but it suffered from a new phenomenon: the middle-class flight to the suburbs. By the 1970s the unreliable, graffiti-ridden subway system had become a symbol of New York's civic and economic decline. New York regained much of its swagger in the 1980s, led by colorful three-term mayor Ed Koch. The city elected its first African American mayor, David Dinkins, in 1989, ousting him after a single term in favor of liberal Republican Rudolph Giuliani, a strong and colorful character. It was during his reign that catastrophe struck on September 11, 2001, when thousands watched as the 110-story twin towers of the World Trade Center became engulfed in balls of fire and then collapsed, killing 3000 people. It was the result of a terrorist attack, of a scale never before seen in the USA. Images of the twin towers collapsing were seen around the world, and many New Yorkers are still recovering, both emotionally and financially, from that tragic day.

In 2001 New York elected its 108th mayor, Republican Michael Bloomberg, a wealthy philanthropist and president of his own financial empire; Bloomberg LP expanded into publishing, radio, news service and TV operations. He was reelected for a second term in November 2005.

Bloomberg is perhaps best known for riding the subways (always with a bodyguard), instituting a citywide smoking ban for public spaces, flip-flopping on the red-hot issue of gay marriage, and being the least dynamic leader the city's seen in decades.

However, it's also true that, on Mayor Bloomberg's watch, crime has declined 15%

and the dysfunctional Board of Education has been abolished (it's unclear how that'll help or hurt thus far).

Orientation

New York City lies near the mouth of the Hudson River, at the west end of Long Island Sound, linked to the Atlantic Ocean through the Verrazano Narrows. The metropolitan area sprawls east into the neighboring state of Connecticut and is linked to urban areas of New Jersey, on the west side of the Hudson. That whole area, known as the 'tri-state area,' is home to more than 17 million people.

The City of New York proper comprises five boroughs: Manhattan (the densely packed heart of NYC and the epicenter of its attractions), Staten Island (a suburban appendage with an inferiority complex), Brooklyn (the place where most hipsters choose to live, after Manhattan), Queens (the largest borough, with endless foreign cultural perks) and the Bronx (half inner city, half suburbia, and home to Yankee Stadium).

New York is the principal transportation hub of the northeastern US, served by three major airports, two train terminals and a massive bus depot. Several interstate highways converge on the city, including I-95, I-87, I-80 and I-78.

The oldest section of New York City, the southern tip of Manhattan Island, has a haphazard layout, with streets that perhaps began as cow paths and Indian walking trails. Further north, Manhattan has a regular street grid with avenues running north–south and streets running east–west.

North of Washington Sq Park, Fifth Ave is the dividing line between the East Side and the West Side. Buildings on the cross streets are numbered east and west from Fifth Ave, so the Hard Rock Cafe (221 W 57th St) is just over two blocks west of Fifth Ave.

NEW YORK CITY IN...

Two Days
Splurge on brunch at **Prune** (p160). For the afternoon pick a downtown neighborhood – the **West Village** (p137) or the **Lower East Side** (opposite) – and check out boutiques, parks and local characters. Walk along Hudson River Park to **Chelsea** (p138) for some gallery hits. Have drinks on the Upper West Side, watching the sun set over the Hudson, then dine inland at **'Cesca** (p161). On day two, meander through the greenmarket at **Union Square** (p138), followed by some shopping in the **Flatiron District** (p138). Have cocktails at **Campbell Apartment Grill** (p162) in the impressive **Grand Central Terminal** (p139), catch a **Broadway show** (p163) in the evening, and then have the best nightcap of all time: a late-night trip to the top of the **Empire State Building** (p138), which keeps its viewing tower open till midnight.

Four Days
On your first day, get the lay of the land by taking a guided tour, either on the **Circle Line** (p153) or a double-decker bus, ending with a dinner of tapas and Spanish wine at **Tia Pol** (p160). Follow the itinerary for Two Days. On day four, venture out to one of the outer boroughs – walk over the **Brooklyn Bridge** (p134) then relax in **Prospect Park** (p148), and head to **Boerum Hill** (p148); or take the 7 train to **Astoria** (p150), where art and film museums and Greek food galore await.

One Week
Follow the Four Day plan. Then enjoy an excursion out of the city – a day trip to **Jones Beach** (p169) in summer, or an overnight jaunt to the **Hamptons** (p170), whatever the season. Pick a quirky **walking tour** (p151) for the day you return, and explore a downtown 'hood more completely – take time to observe the action at the **Tompkins Square Park dog run** (p137), or spend hours in a **Chelsea café** (p160), watching the beautiful boys go by. Have dinner at the best-sounding eatery in this book. On day six, hit a major museum like the **Met** (p144), or score half-price tickets to a Broadway show at the **TKTS Booth** (p163). Have early cocktails somewhere fabulous, like the bar of the **Tribeca Grand** (p155), then go clubbing late into the night.

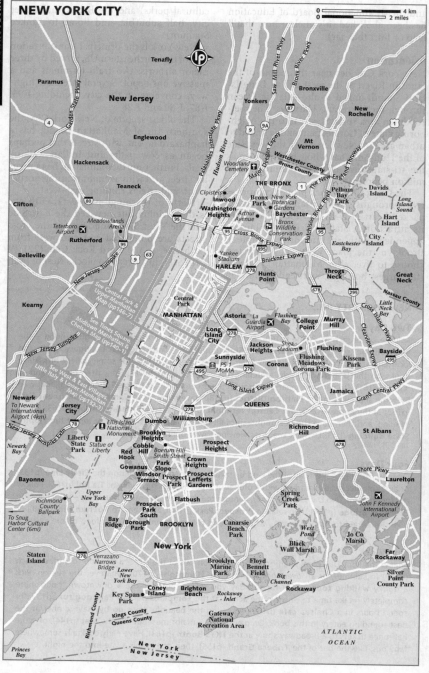

NEW YORK CITY

The grid plan is fitfully repeated in the outer boroughs – Brooklyn, Queens, the Bronx and Staten Island – typically with numbered streets running east–west and numbered avenues running north–south, though some winding thoroughfares follow the routes of old country roads.

MAPS
Lonely Planet publishes a laminated pocket-size map of New York City, but for those looking to do obscure exploring, especially in the city's outer boroughs, get your hands on a five-borough street atlas – Geographia, Hagstrom (produced in Queens) and Van Dam all publish compact editions for around $15.

Information
BOOKSTORES
Unfortunately, a rash of Barnes & Noble (www.bn.com) and Borders (www.borders stores.com) superstores have sent many excellent indie shops to early graves. But luckily, many do still exist:

Bluestockings Bookstore (Map pp132-3; ☎ 212-777-6028; 172 Allen St) A homegrown women's bookstore-café with frequent readings and other events.

Complete Traveller (Map pp140-1; ☎ 212-685-9007; 199 Madison Ave)

Gotham Book Mart (Map pp140-1; ☎ 212-719-4448; 41 W 47th St)

Oscar Wilde Bookstore (Map pp132-3; ☎ 212-255-8097; 15 Christopher St) The city's last remaining gay bookstore.

St Marks Bookshop (Map pp132-3; ☎ 212-260-7853; 31 Third Ave)

Strand Bookstore (Map pp132-3; ☎ 212-473-1452; 828 Broadway) Great for used books.

Urban Center Books (Map pp140-1; ☎ 212-935-3595; 457 Madison Ave) Massive selection of NYC, architecture and design titles; part of the Municipal Arts Society.

EMERGENCY
Police, fire and ambulance (☎ 911)
Poison Control (☎ 800-222-1222)
Legal Aid Society (☎ 212-577-3300)

INTERNET ACCESS
Free public access to wi-fi is readily available from Bryant Park to Chelsea's gay bar xl (p154). See p1152 for more details. Have a credit-card number handy for wi-fi at Starbucks, via T Mobil. TCC Internet Phones (four minutes $1, NYC information websites free) is at sidewalk kiosks in Midtown, the East Village and Soho. NYC has a plethora of Internet cafés, and most hotels and hostels have free access (see p1152). To avoid inflated hourly rates of up to $15, try the following options:

EasyEverything (Map pp140-1; ☎ 212-391-9611; 234 W 42nd St at 7th Ave; per hr $1; ⊗ 24 hr) Has 800 PCs.

LGBT Community Center (Map pp132-3; ☎ 212-620-7310; 208 W 13th St; suggested donation $3; ⊗) Its Cyber Center has 15 computers, open to all.

New York Public Library (Map pp140-1; ☎ 212-930-0800; www.nypl.org; Fifth Ave at W 42nd St; 30min free; ⊗) With various branches. All terminals may be busy.

INTERNET RESOURCES
Find a Grave (www.findagrave.com) New York City cemetery locations for the famous departed, from Leonard Bernstein to Louis Armstrong.

Flavor Pill (www.flavorpill.com) A hip city culture guide.

Menu Pages (www.menupages.com) On-screen and printable menus for countless NYC eateries; for the food-obsessed only!

Citysearch (www.newyork.citysearch.com) Restaurants, shops, bars and more, all searchable by neighborhood, price or cuisine.

Strange New York (www.strangeny.com) Haunted houses, odd public sculptures and weird news reports for an alternative look at the city.

Time Out New York (www.timeoutny.com) An archive of useful articles and listings at this online version of *Time Out New York* magazine.

MEDIA
For nonprint media, National Public Radio's local affiliate station is WNYC, either 820AM or 93.9 FM. Bronx's Fordham University has the area's best alternative-music radio station (WFUV-90.7 FM). An excellent source of local news is NY1, the city's all-day news station on cable's Channel 1.

Daily News (www.nydailynews.com) A daily tabloid publication with a heavy lean toward the sensational.

New York Similar to the *New Yorker*, but for a younger, more restaurant-oriented readership.

New Yorker (www.newyorker.com) Venerable weekly magazine that publishes news, fiction and critical reviews. Its 'Goings on about town' section lists major art, cinema and music events.

New York Post (www.nypost.com) Another daily tabloid covering media scandal and sports.

New York Times (www.nytimes.com) For thorough daily world and local news coverage.

Paper (www.papermag.com) Weekly magazine with hip profiles and nightlife listings.

Time Out New York (www.timeoutny.com) Comprehensive listings, including gay and lesbian events. Every Tuesday.

Village Voice (www.villagevoice.com) Well known for its listings of clubs and music venues, it's also the best source for rental apartments and roommate listings. Weekly on Wednesdays.

Wall Street Journal (www.wsj.com) For daily financial reading.

MEDICAL SERVICES

24-hour Rite-Aid pharmacies (☎ 800-748-3243) A free locator service.

Callen-Lorde Community Health Center (Map pp140-1; ☎ 212-271-7200; 356 W 18th St) Focuses on the lesbian, gay, bisexual and transgender (LGBT) community, but open to all.

New York University Medical Center (Map pp140-1; ☎ 212-263-5550; 462 First Ave)

St Vincent's Medical Center (Map pp132-3; ☎ 212-576-6000; Sixth Ave at Greenwich St) In the Village.

Travel MD (☎ 212-737-1212) A 24-hour medical service for travelers. You must call for an appointment.

MONEY

Thousands of ATMs are linked to Cirrus, Plus and other international networks. Withdrawal fees average $3 at ATMs found in convenience stores. Banks are normally open from 9am to 3:30pm weekdays, though the popular **Commerce Bank** (☎ 888-751-9000), with locations throughout Manhattan, is open seven days a week. Many of the Chase Manhattan Bank branches offer commission-free currency-exchange services; the one in Chinatown at Mott and Canal Sts, as well as its Citibank neighbor, is open daily.

POST

Find a local branch, with regular daytime hours, by checking www.ny.com/general/postoffices.html. The city's main post office (p143) is a sight worth visiting.

TELEPHONES

There are thousands of pay telephones lining the streets, but many of them are out of order; those maintained by Verizon are the most reliable. Many pay phones accept credit cards, but some will bill you an outrageous amount for a long-distance call.

Manhattan's telephone area codes are 212 and 646; in the four other boroughs it's 718 and 347. You must always dial 1 + the area code, even if you are calling from a borough that uses the same one you're calling to.

The most wonderful telephone news in ages has been the new ☎ 311 service, which allows you to dial from anywhere within the city for info or help with any city agency, from paying a parking ticket to filing a noise complaint.

TOILETS

Public toilets are almost nonexistent, with the exception of those in train and bus stations, and those in commercial establishments are 'for customers only.'

It's sometimes possible to slip into the bathroom of a busy bar or restaurant if you are discreet and well dressed.

If you're in distress, head to a Starbucks (there's one on every other corner) and ask the indifferent counter person for the restroom key.

NEW YORK'S BEST BARGAINS

NYC is not a cheap town, it's true. But what's also true is that it's home to myriad bargains, in areas from food and clothing to cultural outings. Some of the best thrills are free – walking across the Brooklyn Bridge, lounging in Central Park, riding the Staten Island Ferry or perusing the Union Sq Greenmarket (where you'll be offered free samples, from bread to artisanal cheese), for example. Many museums have a *suggested* entrance fee – the Metropolitan Museum of Art and American Museum of Natural History among them – which means you could pay as little as a dollar if you wish. Others, like the National Museum of the American Indian, are flat-out free. Chelsea is full of free art museums – otherwise known as galleries – where it's particularly fun to browse on Thursday nights, when most places hold their openings, wine and cheese to boot. Summer is the best time to be entertained for free, such as when the New York Philharmonic plays public concerts in Central Park; and also when the park hosts its popular SummerStage, when nationally known pop-music, dance and literary greats take to the stage for anyone who wishes to listen.

TOURIST INFORMATION

New York City & Company (Map pp140-1; ☎ 212-484-1222, 24hr toll-free ☎ 800-692-8474; www.nycvisit .com; 810 Seventh Ave at 53rd St; ⊗ 8:30am-6pm Mon-Fri, 9am-5pm Sat & Sun) The official information service of the Convention & Visitors Bureau, it has helpful multilingual staff. The toll-free line provides information on special events and reservations.

Times Square Visitors Center (Map pp140-1; ☎ 212-869-1890; 1560 Broadway; ⊗ 8am-8pm) Runs a free two-hour walking tour at noon every Friday and is a useful source of information.

TRAVEL AGENCIES

Apart from regular and discount agencies, such as Council Travel and STA Travel (which have several offices), there are consolidators selling last-minute flights. Most are in Midtown office buildings and advertise weekly in the *Village Voice* and the Sunday *New York Times*. The more reliable agencies take credit cards and can book tickets on scheduled carriers.

Dangers & Annoyances

You're probably safest in any of the areas frequented by tourists, especially during daylight hours, but watch for pickpockets. At night, avoid places that are largely deserted or badly lit (use common sense, basically). Steer clear of Central Park at night, unless you're heading to a well-populated concert, play or other event. In general, don't flaunt money or valuables, especially in poor areas. Panhandlers and hustlers remain in most neighborhoods – especially on the subways and in subway stations – and some give a very polished presentation. All New Yorkers handle such situations differently, but if you really want to help those in need and avoid supporting a drug habit, donate to an organization such as **Coalition for the Homeless** (www.coalitionforthehomeless.org).

SCAMS

General scams include folks on the street approaching you with a story about having an appointment to pick up a check at their social worker's office and just needing the subway fare to get there. Other stories – of being too ill to work, pregnant with nowhere to go, saddled with children or pets – are constant, and you may never know if they're true or not. Just use your best judgment about whether to fork over the cash, or simply walk away.

Sights

The city's sights are truly spread around into just about every neighborhood, though most popular stops on the circuit (Times Square, Empire State Building etc) are clustered in or near Midtown. Others are way downtown, such as the Statue of Liberty, or way uptown, like the Apollo Theater in Harlem. Basically, no matter where you find yourself, there will definitely be something to see.

LOWER MANHATTAN & THE FINANCIAL DISTRICT

Statue of Liberty

This great statue, *Liberty Enlightening the World,* is an American icon and New York's best-known landmark. As early as 1865, French intellectual Edouard Laboulaye conceived a great monument to the republican ideal in France and the USA. French sculptor Frédéric-Auguste Bartholdi traveled to New York in 1871 to select the site. He then spent more than 10 years in Paris, designing and making the 151ft figure, which was then shipped to New York, erected on a small island in the harbor and unveiled in 1886. Structurally, it consists of an iron skeleton (designed by Gustave Eiffel) with a copper skin attached to it by stiff, but flexible, metal bars.

Unfortunately, the **Statue of Liberty National Monument** (Map p128; ☎ 212-866-782-8834; www.nps.gov/stli; New York Harbor, Liberty Island; adult/child $10/4; ⊗ 8:30am-5:15pm) visitor experience has been significantly marred by post–September 11 security concerns. You can no longer go up into the body of the statue – just glimpse it from the base, where a specially designed glass ceiling lets you look up into the striking interior. You can also wander the grounds, of course, and enjoy the lovely views of New York Harbor. The trip to its island, via ferry, is usually visited in conjunction with nearby Ellis Island. **Ferries** (☎ 212-269-5755) leave from Battery Park (Map pp132–3) every 30 minutes from 8:30am to 3:30pm, with extended hours during summer. South Ferry and Bowling Green are the closest subway stations.

Ellis Island

Ferries to the Statue of Liberty make a second stop at Ellis Island, the country's main **immigration station** from 1892 to 1954,

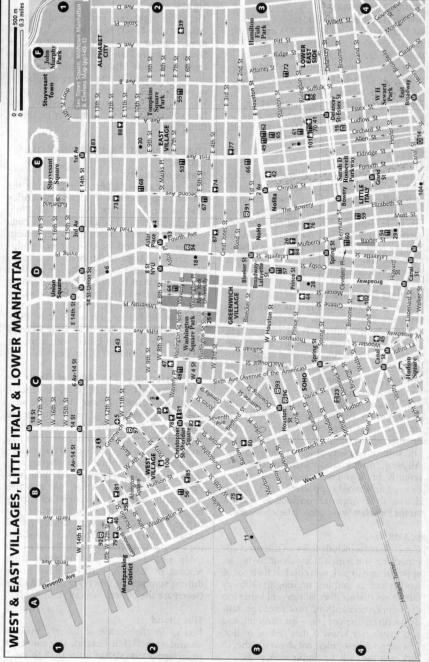

WEST & EAST VILLAGES, LITTLE ITALY & LOWER MANHATTAN

NEW YORK, NEW JERSEY & PENNSYLVANIA

where more than 12 million immigrants first set foot in their new world. The handsome main building is now restored as an **Immigration Museum** (Map p128; ☎ 212-269-5755; www.ellisisland.com; New York Harbor; adult/child $10/4, audio tours $3.50; ⏰ 9:30am-5pm), with exhibits and a film about immigrant experiences, the processing of immigrants and how the influx changed the USA. Special tip: to avoid the long lines to board the ferry, you might consider approaching from the New Jersey side of the harbor, from **Liberty State Park** (p182), accessible via PATH trains (see p183) from downtown or Penn Station.

Brooklyn Bridge

This was the world's first **steel suspension bridge** (Map pp132–3), with an unprecedented span of 1596ft. It remains a compelling symbol of US achievement and a superbly graceful structure, despite the fact that its construction was plagued by budget overruns and the deaths of 20 workers. Among the casualties was designer John Roebling, who was knocked off a pier in 1869 while scouting a site for

the western bridge tower and later died of tetanus poisoning. The bridge was extensively renovated in the early 1980s, and the pedestrian/bicyclist path, beginning just east of City Hall, affords wonderful views of Lower Manhattan and Brooklyn. Observation points under the two stone support towers have illustrations showing panoramas of the waterfront at various points in New York's history.

The Financial District

Wall Street, the metaphorical home of US commerce, was named for the wooden barrier built by Dutch settlers in 1653 to protect Nieuw Amsterdam from Native Americans and the British. To the east is **Federal Hall** (Map pp132-3; ☎ 212-825-6888; 26 Wall St; ⏰ 9am-5pm), New York City's 18th-century city hall, distinguished by a huge statue of George Washington on the steps. This is where the first US Congress convened and Washington was sworn in as the first president, though it is not the original building. Across the street, the **New York Stock Exchange** (Map pp132-3; ☎ 212-656-3000; www.nyse.com; 20

Broad St) has a facade like a Roman temple. The visitor center, unfortunately, is closed indefinitely due to security concerns.

South Street Seaport

This 11-block enclave is basically a pretty touristy alfresco mall, of shops and historic sights. The **South Street Seaport Museum** (Map pp132-3; ☎ 212-748-8600; www.southstseaport.org; adult/child $8/4; ☼ 10am-5pm daily summer, 10am-5pm Fri-Sun winter) includes three galleries, a children's center and three historic ships just south of the pier. You can also sail on the wonderful 1885 wooden schooner **Pioneer** (Map pp132-3; ☎ 212-748-8786; www.southstseaport .org; Pier 16; adult $25-30, child $15-20; sail times vary).

Bowling Green Park & Around

At **Bowling Green Park** (Map pp132-3; cnr State & Whitehall Sts), British residents relaxed with quiet games in the late 17th century. The large **bronze bull** here is a tourist photo stop. Nearby, the old Standard Oil Building was built in 1922 by John D Rockefeller and now houses the **Museum of American Financial History** (Map pp132-3; ☎ 212-908-4110; 26 Broadway; admission $2; ☼ 10am-4pm Tue-Sat). **City Hall** (Map pp132-3; City Hall Park, Broadway), in the Civic Center precinct, has been home to New York City's government since 1812. The **National Museum of the American Indian** (Map pp132-3; ☎ 212-514-3700; www.nmai.si.edu; 1 Bowling Green; admission free; ☼ 10am-5pm), housed in the gorgeous and historic Alexander Hamilton US Customs House, has quite an extensive collection of Native American arts, crafts and exhibits, plus a library and a great gift shop. Just up Broadway from here is the **African Burial Ground** (Map pp132-3; ☎ 212-337-2001; 290 Broadway btwn Duane & Elk Sts; ☼ 9am-4pm Mon-Fri), discovered during preliminary construction of a downtown office building in 1991.

Battery Park & Around

The southwestern tip of Manhattan Island has been extended with landfill over the years to form Battery Park. **Castle Clinton** (Map pp132-3), a fortification built in 1811 to protect Manhattan from the British, was originally 900ft offshore but is now at the edge of Battery Park, with only its walls remaining. Come summertime, it's transformed into a gorgeous outdoor stage for concerts.

West of the park, the **Museum of Jewish Heritage: A Living Memorial to the Holocaust** (Map pp132-3; ☎ 212-509-6130; www.mjhnyc.org; 18 1st Pl, Battery Park City; admission $7; ☼ 10am-5:45pm Sun-Wed, to 8pm Thu & 3pm Fri) depicts many aspects of New York Jewish history and culture, and includes a holocaust memorial. Also worth a look-see is one of the city's newest museums, the **Skyscraper Museum** (Map pp132-3; ☎ 212-968-1961; www.skyscraper.org; 39 Battery Pl; adult/senior & student $5/2.50; ☼ noon-6pm Wed-Sun), occupying the ground-floor space of the Ritz-Carlton Hotel and featuring rotating exhibits plus a permanent study of high-rise history.

Finally, Battery Place is the start of the stunning **Hudson River Park** (Map pp132-3; ☎ 212-627-2020; www.hudsonpark.org), which incorporates renovated piers, grassy spaces, gardens, miniature golf courses, basketball courts, a trapeze school, food concessions and, best of all, a ribbon of a bike/skate/running path that stretches 5 miles up to its end at 59th Street.

Ground Zero

Tourists snapping photos, locals meditating during a lunch break – all mill about before this high **metal gate** (Map pp132-3; Church St at Fulton St; admission free) that wraps around the ever-changing construction site of the former Twin Towers. Photos with accompanying text along the fencelike wall present an eerie and specific timeline of the attacks. The city is now looking collectively into the future, though, through the Lower Manhattan Development Corporation. Plans for the new **Freedom Tower** (construction updates www.renewnyc .com), a memorial and the International Freedom Center – all with a master plan drafted by architect Daniel Libeskind – are proceeding on schedule.

TRIBECA

The 'TRIangle BElow CAnal St,' bordered roughly by Broadway to the east and Chambers St to the south, has old warehouses, very expensive loft apartments and funky restaurants. Its retro-industrial look and see-and-be-seen lounges and eateries have made it a supertrendy area. The **Harrison Street townhouses** (Map pp132-3; Harrison St) west of Greenwich St were built between 1804 and 1828 and are New York's largest remaining collection of Federal architecture.

An important and recent addition to the neighborhood has been the **Tribeca Film Center** (Map pp132-3; ☎ 212-941-2000; www.tribeca film.com; 375 Greenwich St btwn N Moore & Franklin Sts). Though this nexus of downtown filmmaking, a labor of love from movie legend Robert DeNiro, is mainly an office complex and screening room for film professionals, the public is encouraged to attend the various special projects here. In May, DeNiro teams up with Jane Rosenthal for the popular **Tribeca Film Festival** (see p153).

SOHO

This hip and trendy neighborhood has nothing to do with its London counterpart but instead takes its name from its geographical placement: SOuth of HOuston St. Soho is filled with block upon block of cast-iron industrial buildings that date to the period just after the Civil War, when this was the city's leading commercial district.

Strolling the strip of **Prince Street** (Map pp132-3) is a great way to get infused with all aspects of Soho, as the wide sidewalks are lined with local artists hawking quality jewelry, knitwear, paintings, clothing and other sorts of arts and crafts between Broadway and Sixth Ave. A former artists' hotspot, many of the top galleries have fled for Chelsea – even the former Guggenheim Soho is now **Prada Soho** (Map pp132-3; ☎ 212-334-8888; 575 Broadway at Prince St; B, D, F, V to Broadway-Lafayette St; ☼ 11am-7pm Mon-Sat, noon-6pm Sun), the result of a $40 million project in which architect Rem Koolhaus blended retail with theater concepts for one truly unique store. Southwest of central Soho, the **New York City Fire Museum** (Map pp132-3; ☎ 212-691-1303; www.nycfiremuseum.org; 278 Spring St; suggested donation $5; ☼ 10am-5pm Tue-Sat, to 4pm Sun) is a grand old firehouse dating back to 1904.

CHINATOWN & LITTLE ITALY

These two long-standing ethnic enclaves are just north of the Financial District.

Chinatown is a thriving community of more than 120,000 residents, many living and working in this minisociety without using a word of English. Throughout the 1990s Chinatown saw an influx of Vietnamese immigrants, who set up their own shops and some incredibly cheap and delicious restaurants.

While the best reasons to visit Chinatown are simply to stroll in a bustling environment, eat from street stalls and cheapo restaurants, and browse the strange and wonderful herbal shops, there are a few sights, too. The **Museum of Chinese in the Americas** (Map pp132-3; ☎ 212-619-4785; www.moca-nyc.org; 70 Mulberry St at Bayard St; admission $5; ☼ noon-5pm Tue-Sun) has exhibits, and sponsors walking tours and workshops on Chinese crafts. **Columbus Park** (Map pp132-3; Worth St btwn Mulberry, Baxter & Bayard Sts), especially in the wee hours of the morning, gives you an excellent taste of local life, as you'll no doubt find folks playing games of mah-jongg and practicing tai chi.

For a taste of what's left of **Little Italy** (Map pp132-3) take a stroll along **Mulberry Street**. The **Old St Patrick's Cathedral** (Map pp132-3; 263 Mulberry St) became the city's first Roman Catholic cathedral in 1809 and remained so until 1878, when its more famous uptown successor was completed. The former **Ravenite Social Club** (Map pp132-3; 247 Mulberry St), now a gift shop, is a reminder of the not-so-long-ago days when mobsters ran the neighborhood. Originally known as the Alto Knights Social Club, where big hitters like Lucky Luciano spent time, the Ravenite was a favorite hangout of John Gotti (and the FBI) before his arrest and life sentencing in 1992.

LOWER EAST SIDE

First came the Jews, then the Latinos, and now…the hipsters, of course.

The **Lower East Side Tenement Museum** (Map pp132-3; ☎ 212-431-0233; www.tenement.org; 90 Orchard St at Broome St; adult/senior & child $10/8; ☼ visitor center 11am-5:30pm) puts the neighborhood's heartbreaking heritage on full display in several reconstructed tenements. Museum visits are available only as part of scheduled tours (the price of which is included in the admission), which typically operate every 40 or 50 minutes (but call ahead to check schedules).

The landmark **Eldridge Street Synagogue** (Map pp132-3; ☎ 212-219-0888; 12 Eldridge St btwn Canal & Division Sts; adult/senior $5/3), built in 1887, attracted as many as 1,000 worshipers on the High Holidays at the turn of the 20th century. But membership dwindled in the 1920s with restricted immigration laws, and by the 1950s the temple closed altogether. The restorative Eldridge Street Project has been under way for years, and now the synagogue holds Friday evening and Saturday morning worship services, as well as **tours** (adult/senior & student $5/3; ☺ Sun 11am-4pm, Tue-Thu 11:30am-2:30pm or by appointment) of the building.

EAST VILLAGE

Bordered roughly by 14th St, Lafayette St, E Houston St and the East River, the East Village has gentrified rapidly in the last decade. Old tenements, especially those in the blocks bordering Greenwich Village, have been taken over by 'artists,' restaurateurs and real-estate developers.

Tompkins Square Park & Around

This **park** (Map pp132-3; btwn 7th & 10th Sts & Aves A & B) is an unofficial border between the East Village (to the west) and Alphabet City (to the east). Once an Eastern European immigrant area, you'll still see old Ukrainians and Poles in the park, but they'll be alongside punks, students, panhandlers and dog-walking yuppies. The historic **Russian & Turkish Baths** (Map pp132-3; ☎ 212-473-8806; www .russianturkishbaths.com; 268 E 10th St; admission $25; ☺ 11am-10pm Mon, Tue, Thu & Fri, from 7:30am Sat, to 2pm Sun) still offers a traditional massage followed by an ice-cold bath. It's ladies-only from 9am to 2pm Wednesday, men-only from 7:30am to 2pm Sunday and co-ed the rest of the time.

Astor Place & Around

At the west end of St Mark's Place, **Astor Place** (Map pp132-3) was once an elite neighborhood and some of its impressive original Greek Revival residences remain. The large brownstone **Cooper Union** (Map pp132-3; www.cooper.edu; 51 Astor Pl) is a public college founded by glue millionaire Peter Cooper in 1859. Abraham Lincoln gave his 'Right Makes Might' speech condemning slavery before his election to the White House in the college's Great Hall.

WEST (GREENWICH) VILLAGE

Once a symbol for all things artistic, outlandish and bohemian, this storied and popular neighborhood – known by most visitors as 'Greenwich Village,' although that term is not used by locals – can look downright somnolent these days. That's especially true since privileged residents of high-rent townhouses inspired Giuliani-era crackdowns on noisy clubs, public drinking and other facts of city life.

New York University

In 1831, Albert Gallatin, secretary of treasury under President Thomas Jefferson, founded an intimate center of higher learning, **NYU** (Map pp132-3; ☎ 212-998-4636; www.nyu .edu; Information Center at 50 W 4th St), open to all students, regardless of race or class background. He'd scarcely recognize the place today, as it's swelled to a student population of 48,000, with high school grads attending 14 schools and colleges at six Manhattan locations.

Washington Square Park & Around

This **park** (Map pp132-3) began as a 'potter's field' – a burial ground for the penniless – and its status as a cemetery protected it from development. It is now an incredibly well-used park, especially on the weekend. Children use the playground, NYU students catch some rays and friends meet 'under the arch' – the landmark on the park's northern edge, designed in 1889 by society architect Stanford White. Around the now-dry central 'fountain,' street comedians and musicians do their thing and food carts cater to the snack-needy.

Christopher Street Pier

Formerly the strict domain of young gay hustlers and sassy 'pier queens' – the effeminate gay boys and trannies whose organized prancings were depicted in the 1990 film *Paris is Burning* – this just-renovated **concrete pier** (Map pp132-3; Christopher St at the Hudson River; 1, 9 to Christopher St-Sheridan Sq) is now a magnet for downtowners of all stripes, including a healthy dose of young gay holdouts. The 5-mile-long Hudson River Park Project paid special attention to this prime waterfront spot, adding a grass lawn, colorful flower bed, wooden deck, tented shade shelters, benches and a grand stone fountain at its entrance.

Sheridan Square & Around

The western edge of the Village holds **Sheridan Square** (Stonewall Place; Map pp132-3), a small, triangular park where life-size white statues honor the gay community and gay pride movement that began in the nearby **Stonewall Inn**. A block further east, a bent street is officially named Gay St (prompting titillated gay folks to periodically swipe the street sign). Although gay social scenes have in many ways moved a bit further uptown to Chelsea, **Christopher Street** is still the center of gay life in the Village.

Meatpacking District

The latest part of the Village to become gentrified is the **Meatpacking District** (Map pp132–3) around Gansevoort-Little W 12th St. Less than 10 years ago, the neighborhood – home to 250 slaughterhouses in 1900 but only 35 today, as most have been squeezed out by high rents – was best known for its groups of tranny hookers, racy S-M sex clubs and, of course, its sides of beef. Though it's still active and odorous on weekday mornings, evenings and weekends draw the trendy set to high-ceilinged wine bars, Belgian and Cuban eateries, nightclubs and high-end 14th-St designer clothing stores.

CHELSEA

Here it's all about gay men – muscled guys who frequent gyms and bars and are well known semi-endearingly as 'Chelsea boys' – and a slew of art galleries, most west of Tenth Ave in the 20s.

Previously located in Soho, the **New Museum of Contemporary Art Chelsea** (Map pp140–1; ☎ 212-219-1222; www.newmuseum.org; 556 W 22nd St at Eleventh Ave; admission $6; ☽ noon-6pm Tue-Sat, to 8pm Thu) has a focus on new works, staging six major exhibits yearly to define key moments in the development art culture. Recent shows featured large-scale photos by Fiona Tan and a group New Yorker show that looked into various aspects of wireless technology. The **Cuban Art Space** (Map pp140–1; ☎ 212-242-0559; www.cubanartspace.net; 124 W 23rd St; donations welcome; ☽ 11am-7pm Tue-Fri, noon-5pm Sat) boasts the largest collection of Cuban art outside the island.

FLATIRON DISTRICT

At the intersection of Broadway, Fifth Ave and 23rd St, the famous (and absolutely gorgeous) 1902 **Flatiron Building** (Map pp140–1) has a distinctive triangular shape to match its site. It was New York's first iron-frame high-rise, and the world's tallest building until 1909. The surrounding District is a fashionable area of boutiques and loft apartments. It's also home to the **Museum of Sex** (Map pp140–1; ☎ 212-689-6337; www.museumofsex .org; 233 Fifth Ave at W 27th St; admission after/before

2pm $17/12; ☽ 11am-6:30pm Mon-Fri, 10am-9pm Sat, to 6:30pm Sun), a surprisingly unracy homage that intellectually traces the history of NYC and sex.

UNION SQUARE

This square and transportation hub originally served as one of New York City's first Uptown business districts, and throughout the mid-19th century it offered a convenient site for many workers' rallies and political protests. Today, **Union Square Park** (Map pp140–1; 14th St at Broadway) hops with activity; its southern end has become the new 'in' place for antiwar and other liberal-leaning demonstrators. On most days, its north end is host to the **Greenmarket Farmers' Market** (Map pp140–1; ☎ 212-477-3220; www.cenyc.org; 17th St btwn Broadway & Park Ave S; ☽ 8am-4pm Mon, Wed, Fri & Sat year-round), the most popular of the 42 greenmarkets throughout the five boroughs, where even celebrity chefs come for just-picked rarities like fiddlehead ferns and fresh curry leaves.

GRAMERCY PARK

This area, loosely comprising the 20s east of Madison Ave, is named after one of New York's loveliest parks; it's for residents only, though, and you need a key to get in! If you're strolling by, peer through the gates and get a good look at what you're missing. Nearby is **Theodore Roosevelt's Birthplace** (Map pp140–1; ☎ 212-260-1616; www.nps.gov/thrb; 28 E 20th St btwn Park Ave & Broadway; ☽ Tue-Sat 10am-4pm), a National Historic Site – and a bit of a cheat, since the house where the 26th president was born was demolished in his lifetime. This building is simply a re-creation, albeit an interesting one, by his relatives.

MIDTOWN

Home to many of the city's most popular attractions, you'll probably wind up spending plenty of time in New York's teeming Midtown area, which is a mixed blessing. It's exciting, but the bustle of workers can make it overwhelmingly crowded on weekdays, especially at lunchtime.

Empire State Building

A long-standing symbol of New York's skyline, the classic **Empire State Building** (Map pp140–1; ☎ 212-736-3100; www.esbnyc.org; 350 Fifth Ave at E 34th St; adult/child $15.50/10.50; ☽ 9:30am-midnight), at 1454ft high (including antennae), was the world's tallest from 1931 to 1977, and was built in 410 days during the depths of the Depression at a cost of $41 million. Observatories on the 86th and 102nd floors are a major attraction. There may be a long wait, so come very early or very late (so know that you can purchase your tickets ahead of time online). A night trip to the top can be quite romantic, and don't miss the art-deco medallions around the lobby.

Times Square & Theater District

Now enjoying a major renaissance – to the dismay of those who prefer to gripe about 'Disneyfication' and wax poetic about the prostitute-and-drug-drenched past – **Times Square** (Map pp140–1) can once again trumpet its reputation as the 'Crossroads of the World.' Smack in the middle of Midtown Manhattan, this area around the intersection of Broadway and Seventh Ave has long been synonymous with gaudy billboards and glittery marquees – before the advent of TV, advertisers went after the largest audience possible by beaming their messages into the center of New York. With over 60 megabillboards and 40 miles of neon, it's startling (and a bit alarming) how it always looks like daytime. Today, the square draws 27 million annual visitors, who spend something over $12 billion in Midtown.

Times Square also continues to serve as New York's official **Theater District**, with dozens of Broadway and off-Broadway theaters located in an area that stretches from 41st to 54th Sts, between Sixth and Ninth Aves (see p163). Unfortunately, many of the original, classic names (Plymouth, Royale) have been changed to reflect the biggest corporate shareholders in the theater companies (Gerald Schoenfeld and Bernard B Jacobs). Just another ugly result of American capitalism, folks.

Columbus Circle/Time Warner Towers

This much-discussed $1.8 billion project was completed in February 2004, revealing a pair of sleek **towers** (Map pp146-7; ☎ 212-869-1890; www.timessquarebid.org; 1560 Broadway; ☀ 8am-9pm) that hover over the northwestern corner of Central Park. Reviews have been mixed: while neighborhood residents hate the increased foot and taxi traffic, mobs of locals and tourists alike love the

seven-floor retail atrium (a much-glorified mall, really), with luxury shops including Williams-Sonoma, A/X Armani Exchange and Hugo Boss. Foodies will not be disappointed, as there are no less than seven high-end eateries (see p161), along with a 59000-sq-ft whole foods organic market.

Grand Central Terminal

Built in 1913 as a prestigious terminal by New York Central and Hudson River Railroad, **Grand Central Station** (Map pp140-1; www.grandcentralterminal.com; 42nd St at Fifth Ave) is no longer a romantic place to begin a cross-country journey – it's the terminus for Metro North commuter trains to the northern suburbs and Connecticut. Even if you're not boarding a train, it's worth looking inside at the grand, vaulted main concourse and up at the restored ceiling, decorated with a star map that is actually a 'God's eye' image of the night sky. The bottom floor houses a truly excellent array of eateries, while the balcony has a very cool bar, **Campbell Apartment Grill** (see p162).

Chrysler Building

Just east of Grand Central Terminal, the **Chrysler Building** (Map pp140-1; 405 Lexington Ave), an art-deco masterpiece that's adorned with motorcar motifs, was designed by William Van Alen and completed in 1930. Luckily, it's most magnificent when viewed from a distance, because visitors can't go up in the building (it's full of offices), and some details are barely visible from the ground. In the lobby, you can admire the African marble, onyx lights and other decorative elements.

New York Public Library

The superb beaux-arts–style **New York Public Library** (Map pp140-1; ☎ 212-940-0830; Fifth Ave at 42nd St; www.nypl.org; ☀ 10am-6pm Tue-Sat) is a wonderful retreat from the Midtown bustle. The stately lion sculptures at the front entrance, elegant lobby, marble stairs and impressive halls lead to the brilliant 3rd-floor reading room with its natural light and magnificent ceiling. This, the main branch of the library, has galleries of manuscripts on display, as well as fascinating temporary exhibits.

Rockefeller Center

Known for its ice rink, Christmas tree and decorated facades, this **art-deco complex** (Map

TIMES SQUARE, MIDTOWN MANHATTAN & CHELSEA

pp140–1) was started in 1931 and took nine years to complete. Look for the tilework above the Sixth Ave entrance to the GE Building, the entrance to the East River Savings Bank building at 41 Rockefeller Plaza, the triptych above the entrance to 30 Rockefeller Plaza and the statues of Prometheus and Atlas.

The 1932 **Radio City Music Hall** (Map pp140-1; ☎ 212-247-4777; www.radiocity.com; 1260 Sixth Ave; tours $17; ⊙ tours 11am-3pm Mon-Sun), a 6000-seat theater, is a protected landmark perfectly restored in all its art-deco grandeur. Guided tours leave the lobby every half-hour.

NBC Studios (Map pp140-1; ☎ 212-664-3700; 70th fl, GE Bldg; studio tours adult/child $17.95/15.50; ⊙ 8:30am-5:30pm Mon-Sat, 9:30am-4:30pm Sun, tours every 15 min) and the NBC TV network headquarters are in the GE Building (formerly the RCA Building), at the top of which the Rainbow Room offers priceless views and pricey drinks. The *Today* show broadcasts 7am to 9am daily from a glass-enclosed street-level studio near the fountain area and ice rink.

Fifth Avenue
The high-class reputation of **Fifth Avenue** dates back to the early 20th century, when it was considered desirable for its 'country' air and open spaces. Today it's a battle-ground for society folks who want to retain their class status without allowing too many others in. 'Fifth Ave is the address against which all others are measured,' writes author Steven Gaines in *The Sky's the Limit: Passion and Property in Manhattan* (Little Brown, 2005). The series of mansions was once called Millionaire's Row and extended right up to 130th St, while Midtown Fifth Ave is the site of airline offices and a number of high-end shops and hotels, especially from 49th St to 57th St. Big names include **Saks Fifth Avenue** (Map pp140-1; Fifth Ave at 50th St), **Henri Bendel** (Map pp140-1; Fifth Ave at 55th St), **Tiffany & Co** (Map pp140-1; Fifth Ave at 57th St) and **Bergdorf Goodman** (Map pp140-1; Fifth Ave at 57th St).

St Patrick's Cathedral (Map pp140-1; Fifth Ave at 50th St; ⊙ 6am-9pm) serves the 2.2 million Roman Catholics in the New York diocese. It was built mostly during the Civil War, but the two front spires were added later, in 1888. Look for the handsome rose window above the 7000-pipe organ.

Nearby, on 57th St, are several designer boutiques, along with a selection of theme-park, tourist-trap restaurants.

United Nations
The Rockefeller family donated land worth $8.5 million to the UN; the grounds are

now officially an international territory. Sculptures in the UN complex include Henry Moore's *Reclining Figure* and Reutersward's knotted gun *Non-Violence*. The **UN Building** (Map pp140-1; ☎ 212-963-8687; First Ave btwn 42nd & 48th Sts; tours $7.50; ☺ tours 9:15am-4:45pm Mon-Fri in winter) has its visitor entrance at 46th St, and English-language tours leave every 30 minutes.

Herald Square & Around

This crowded convergence of Broadway and Sixth Ave at 34th St is where you'll find Macy's, the city's largest Gap and a couple of nearby shopping malls. West of Herald Sq, the **Garment District** (Map pp140–1) has most of New York's fashion design offices, though not much clothing is actually made here anymore. Stores on 36th and 37th Sts immediately west of Seventh Ave sell 'designer clothing,' perfume, purses and various other accessories at wholesale prices.

Nearby, sterile **Pennsylvania Station** (Penn Station; Map pp140-1; 33rd St btwn Seventh & Eighth Aves) is not the original, grand entrance to the city, but tens of thousands of commuters and travelers do pass through daily. Built over Penn Station, **Madison Square Garden** (Map pp140-1; ☎ 212-465-5800; www.thegarden.com; Seventh Ave, btwn W 31st & W 33rd Sts) is a major sporting and entertainment venue. A block west, the 1913 **New York General Post Office** (Map pp140-1; www.ny.com/general/postoffices.html; 421 Eighth Ave at 33rd St; ☺ 24hr) is an imposing beaux-arts building behind a long row of Corinthian columns. A project to move Penn Station into the GP has been ongoing for years.

From 31st St to 36th St, between Broadway and Fifth Ave, **Koreatown** is a small but interesting and lively neighborhood. Look on 31st and 32nd Sts for a proliferation of Korean restaurants and authentic karaoke spots.

Art & TV Museums

After spending two years in exile at a temporary site in Queens, **MoMA** (Map pp140-1; ☎ 212-708-9400; www.moma.org; 11 W 53rd St btwn Fifth & Sixth Aves; E, V to Fifth Ave-53rd St; adult/child/student/senior $20/free/12/16, Fri 4-8pm free; ☺ 10:30am-5:30pm Sat-Mon, Wed & Thu, 10am-8pm Fri) reopened to the public late in 2004 with much fanfare. A major renovation project has doubled the museum's capacity to 630,000 sq ft on six floors, highlighting its permanent collection of more than 100,000 paintings, sculptures, drawings, prints, photographs, architectural models, drawings and design objects. Highlights include works by masters including Cézanne, Van Gogh, and Picasso, and its renovated sculpture garden is a joy to sit in – as is its cinema, where MoMA rotates screenings of its collection of more than 19,000 films.

More than 100,000 US TV and radio programs and advertisements are available at the click of a mouse in the **Museum of Television & Radio** (Map pp140-1; ☎ 212-621-6600; www.mtr.org; 25 W 52nd St; admission $10, theater $6; ☺ noon-6pm Fri-Wed, to 8pm Thu), where you can search the extensive catalogue on computer, and staff will find and play your classic TV or radio selection. A comfy theater shows some great specials on broadcasting history.

Hell's Kitchen (Clinton)

For years, the far west side of Midtown was a working-class district of tenements and food warehouses known as Hell's Kitchen, a neighborhood that predominantly attracted Italian and Irish immigrants who drifted into gangs after arriving. Hollywood films have often romanticized the district's gritty, criminal character (*West Side Story* was set here), but by the 1960s the population of junkies and prostitutes had made it a forbidding place that few cared to enter. A 1990s economic boom seriously altered the character and developers reverted to using the cleaned-up name Clinton, a moniker originating from the 1950s; locals are split on usage. New restaurants exploded along Ninth Ave, and it's a great place to grab a post-theater meal.

CENTRAL PARK

This enormous gem of a **park** (Map pp146-7; www.centralpark.org; btwn 57th & 110th Sts & Fifth Ave & Central Park W) right in the middle of Manhattan, is for many what makes New York livable and lovable. The park's 843 acres were set aside in 1856 on the marshy northern fringe of the city. The landscaping (the first in a US public park), by Frederick Law Olmsted and Calvert Vaux, was innovative in its naturalistic style, with forested groves, meandering paths and informal ponds. Highlights include **Strawberry Fields**, at 72nd St, dedicated to John Lennon, who lived at (and was murdered in front of) the **Dakota** apartment building across the street; the sparkling **Jacqueline Kennedy Onassis Reservoir**, encircled by joggers daily; the **zoo** (10am-5pm Mon-Fri, to 5:30pm Sat & Sun; adult/child $6/1); Shakespeare in the Park performances in the **Delacorte Theater**; major concerts on the **Great Lawn**; and the formal promenade called the **Mall**, which culminates at the elegant **Bethesda Fountain**. A favorite tourist activity is to rent a **horse-drawn carriage** (45-min tour $54 plus generous tip) at 59th St (Central Park South).

For more information, visit the **Dairy Building visitor centre** (212-794-6564; Central Park at 65th St; 10am-5pm Tue-Sat), in the middle of the park.

UPPER WEST SIDE
Comprising the west side of Manhattan from Central Park to the Hudson River, and from Columbus Circle to 110th St, this is where you'll find massive, ornate apartments, some lovely green spaces and a diverse mix of stable, upwardly mobile folks. The **New-York Historical Society** (Map pp146-7; 212-873-3400; www.nyhistory.org; 2 W 77th St; admission $10; 10am-6pm Tue-Sun), founded in 1804, is the city's oldest museum, with original watercolors from John James Audubon's *Birds of America* and a quirky permanent collection. **Riverside Park**, meanwhile, stretching 4 miles between W 72nd St and W 158th St along the Hudson River, is a great place for just about anyone to stroll, bike, run or simply gaze at the sun as it sets over the Hudson River.

Lincoln Center (Map pp146-7; 212-875-5370; www.lincolncenter.org; cnr Columbus Ave & Broadway), a performance complex of several theaters built in the 1960s, has a dramatic courtyard with a massive fountain, plus chandeliered interiors featuring winding staircases and huge Chagall paintings, which look simply beautiful at night. **Tours** (212-875-5350; admission $12-16) of the complex leave from the concourse level daily.

American Museum of Natural History
Founded in 1869, this **museum** (Map pp146-7; 212-769-5000; www.amnh.org; Central Park West at 79th St; B, C to 81st St-Museum of Natural History, 1, 9 to 79th St; suggested admission adult/child $14/8, extra for space shows, IMAX shows & special exhibits; 10am-5:45pm) began with a mastodon's tooth and a few thousand beetles; today, its collection includes more than 30 million artifacts, interactive exhibits and loads of taxidermy. It's most famous for its three large dinosaur

halls, as well as its enormous (fake) blue whale that hangs from the ceiling above the Hall of Ocean Life. The newest addition, the **Rose Center for Earth & Space**, features the excellent Hayden Planetarium, housed in a big ball in the bigger glass box that is a sight to behold.

MORNINGSIDE HEIGHTS
The Upper West Side's northern neighbor, comprising the area of Broadway and west up to about 125th St, is anchored by the Ivy League **Columbia University** (Map pp146-7; 212-854-1754; www.columbia.edu; 116th St & Broadway). The highly rated, activist-filled college features a spacious, grassy central quadrangle that's dominated by the 1895 Low Library, one of several neoclassical campus buildings by McKim, Mead & White. The surrounding neighborhood is filled with some cool restaurants, great bookstores, cafés and the massive Episcopal **Cathedral of St John the Divine** (Map pp146-7; 212-316-7540; 1047 Amsterdam Ave at 112th St; 8am-6pm), the largest place of worship in the USA. High Mass, held at 11am Sunday, often features sermons by well-known intellectuals.

Nearby, **Riverside Church** (Map pp146-7; 212-330-1234; www.theriversidechurchny.org; 490 Riverside Dr at 122nd St; 7am-10pm), a 1930 Gothic-style marvel, is famous for its 74 carillon bells, which are rung every Sunday at noon and 3pm, as well as for its diverse and activist congregation.

UPPER EAST SIDE
Often dismissed by Upper West Siders as the uptight and conservative area across Central Park, the area is actually home to New York's greatest concentration of cultural centers: Fifth Ave above 57th St is called 'Museum Mile.' The area also has many of the city's most exclusive hotels and residential blocks (see p142).

Metropolitan Museum of Art
Commonly called 'The Met,' this vast **museum** (Map pp146-7; 212-879-5500; www.metmuseum .org; 1000 Fifth Ave at 82nd St; suggested donation $15; 9:30am-5:30pm Tue-Thu & Sun, to 9pm Fri & Sat), edged by Central Park, is New York's most popular single-site attraction – and deservedly so. Highlights include Egyptian Art, the American Wing, Arms & Armor, 20th-Century Art, Greek & Roman Art, the

Costume Institute and the Impressionists, and just strolling through aimlessly and gazing at the architecture is worth your time. The suggested donation includes same-day admission to the Cloisters (see p148).

Other Museums

On the east side of Fifth Ave, the **Museum of the City of New York** (Map pp146-7; ☎ 212-534-1672; www.mcny.org; 1220 Fifth Ave at 123rd St; suggested admission adult/child/family $7/5/15; ☻ 10am-5pm Tue-Sun) is a northern Museum Mile institution. It traces the city's history from beaver trading to futures trading.

The opulent 1914 mansion housing the **Frick Collection** (Map pp146-7; ☎ 212-288-0700; www.frick.org; 1 E 70th St; admission $12; ☻ 10am-6pm Tue-Sat, from 1pm Sun) was part of the Fifth Ave Millionaire's Row in the age of the robber barons. Outstanding European paintings include works by Holbein, Titian, Vermeer, Gainsborough and Constable. Children are not admitted.

One of the few museums that concentrates on American works of art, the **Whitney Museum of American Art** (Map pp146-7; ☎ 212-570-3676; www.whitney.org; 945 Madison Ave at 75th St; admission $12; ☻ 11am-6pm Wed-Thu, Sat & Sun; 1-9pm Fri with pay-what-you-wish 6-9pm) specializes in 20th-century and contemporary art, with works by Hopper, Pollock and Rothko, as well as special shows, such as the much-ballyhooed Biennial.

The inspired work of Frank Lloyd Wright, the sweeping spiral of the **Solomon R Guggenheim Museum** (Map pp146-7; ☎ 212-423-3500; www.guggenheim.org; 1071 Fifth Ave; admission $15, donation 6-8pm Fri; ☻ 10am-5:45pm Sat-Wed, to 8pm Fri) is a superb sculpture, holding 20th-century paintings by Picasso, Pollock, Chagall and Kandinsky. Finally, the **Neue Galerie** (Map pp146-7; ☎ 212-628-6200; www.neuegalerie.org; 1048 Fifth Ave at 86th St; adult/senior $10/7, children under 12 not admitted; ☻ 11am-6pm Sat, Sun, Mon; to 9pm Fri) is a showcase for German and Austrian artists, with impressive works by Gustav Klimt and Egon Schiele.

HARLEM

Once New York's most famous African American neighborhood, **Harlem** (Map pp146-7) is an area in transition. It's still a predominantly black area, but the people you see are as likely to be from the Dominican Republic, Ivory Coast, Senegal – or the East Village. Trendy, bargain-seeking white folks (with a particularly large gay presence) are moving in at growing (and alarming, say many longtime residents) rates, restoring and redeveloping old houses from Central Park to Sugar Hill. There are still racial tensions and run-down buildings, but the latter are now viewed as development opportunities rather than urban blight, and the areas that most tourists visit are now as safe as any other part of the city – and just as overflowing with your usual collection of chains, from Starbucks to H&M, as well as a crop of new sleek eateries and lounges and some lovely guesthouses (see p157).

For a more traditional view of Harlem, visit on Sunday morning, when well-dressed locals flock to neighborhood churches. Just be respectful of the fact that this is a religious service, not a people-zoo. Unless you're invited by a member of a small congregation, stick to the bigger churches like the **Abyssinian Baptist Church** (Map pp146-7; ☎ 212-862-7474; www.abyssinian.org; 132 W 138th St). It's got a superb choir and a charismatic pastor, Calvin O Butts, who welcomes tourists and prays for them. Sunday services start at 9am and 11am – the later one is *very* well attended. For straight-up entertainment, head to the historic **Apollo Theater** (Map pp146-7; ☎ 212-749-5838; www.apolloshowtime.com; 253 W 125th St), which still holds its famous (if very touristed) amateur night, 'where stars are born and legends are made.' You may be shocked by its state of disrepair, but try to focus on the legends who have graced the interior, including Duke Ellington and Charlie Parker.

To glimpse the work of visual artists, meanwhile, be sure to visit the **Studio Museum in Harlem** (Map pp146-7; ☎ 212-864-4500; www.studiomuseum.org; 144 W 125th St; suggested donation $7; ☻ noon-6pm Wed-Fri & Sun, from 10am Sat), which has given exposure to the crafts and culture of African American people for 30 years. Look for excellent rotating exhibits from painters, sculptors, illustrators and other creators. For even more perspective, head to the **Schomburg Center for Research in Black Culture** (Map pp146-7; ☎ 212-491-2200; www.nypl.org/research/sc/sc.html; 515 Lenox Ave; admission free; ☻ noon-8pm Tue-Wed, to 6pm Thu-Fri, 10am-6pm Sat), a branch of the New York Public Library and home to the nation's largest collection of documents, which has a collection of rare books and photographs on black history and culture.

CENTRAL PARK & UPPER MANHATTAN

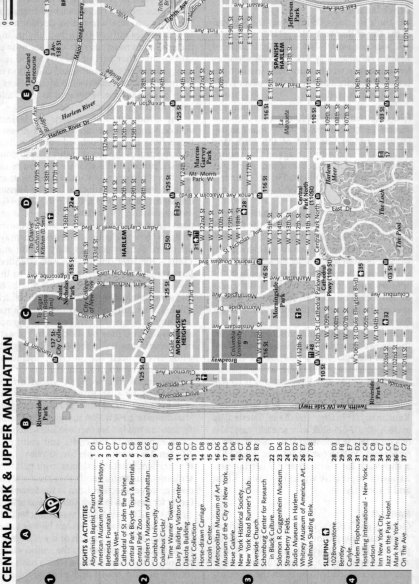

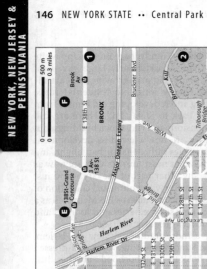

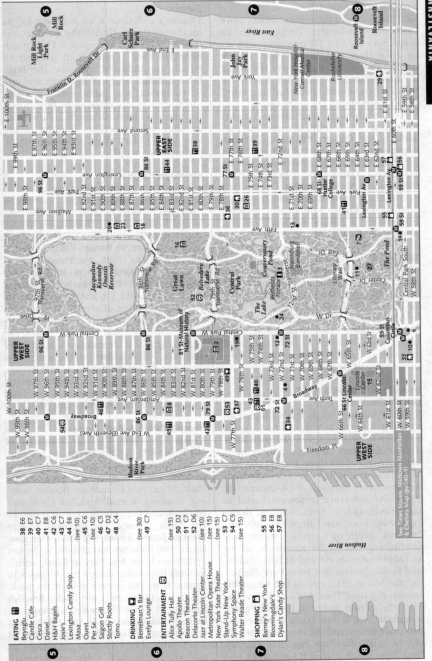

WASHINGTON HEIGHTS

Near the northern tip of Manhattan (above 155th St), Washington Heights takes its name from the first US president, who set up a Continental Army fort here during the Revolutionary War. Today it's a mix of Dominican immigrants and downtown New Yorkers who invaded when they heard about cheap rents a few years ago.

Most visitors to Washington Heights come to see the handful of museums, particularly the **Cloisters** (☎ 212-923-3700; www .metmuseum.org; Fort Tryon Park at 190th St; admission $12; ◷ 9:30am-4:45pm Tue-Sun Nov-Feb, to 5:15pm Mar-Oct) in Fort Tryon Park, a branch of the Metropolitan Museum of Art. Constructed in the 1930s using stones and fragments from several French and Spanish medieval monasteries, it houses medieval frescoes, tapestries and paintings.

BROOKLYN

With 2.3 million people, Brooklyn is the most populous of the outer boroughs, and it would be a significant destination city but for the overwhelming attractions of adjacent Manhattan. New Yorkers who make it their home have basically passed Manhattanites when it comes to cool factor, and the range of cultural offerings, foodie dens and retail delights is staggering.

Boerum Hill, Cobble Hill & Carroll Gardens

A trio of *très*-hip 'hoods that's adopted an annoying acronym moniker (BoCoCa), this is former-Manhattanite central. **Smith Street** is the main artery connecting to the most southerly area of the three, Carroll Gardens (which still maintains some of its old-school Italian charm through fresh-mozzarella shops and red-sauce restaurants), and is known as Brooklyn's 'restaurant row,' drawing crowds from Manhattan on weekends. **Red Hook**, south of Carroll Gardens and perched way out on the waterfront, where its cobblestone streets and hulking industrial buildings overlook New York Harbor and the Statue of Liberty, is fast becoming another hip stop. Though it's a bit of a hike from the subway line, the formerly gritty waterfront area is now home to some cool bars and eateries, and will soon be getting its very own Ikea furniture store and Fairway food shop. Catch it while it's still good.

Dumbo

Dumbo's nickname is an acronym for its location: 'Down Under the Manhattan-Brooklyn Bridge Overpass.' This north Brooklyn slice of waterfront used to be strictly for industry, but now the huge loft spaces are occupied by artists and artist wannabes, plus cafés, restaurants and huge retail spaces catering to this crowd. Its quirky cobblestone streets are traversed by edgy culture seekers heading to the very latest gallery show, ravelike party or performance-art piece.

Brooklyn Heights

When Robert Fulton's steam ferries started regular service across the East River in the early 19th century, well-to-do Manhattanites began building comfortable houses at Brooklyn Heights. Don't miss the 1848 beaux-arts **Brooklyn Borough Hall** (209 Joralemon St). Two blocks south, the recently renovated **New York Transit Museum** (☎ 718-694-1600; www.mta.info; Boerum Pl & Schermerhorn St; 10am-4pm Tue-Fri, noon-5pm Sat & Sun; adult/child $5/3) has an amazing collection of original subway cars and transit memorabilia dating back 100 years.

Montague St is the main avenue for cafés and bars; follow it down to the waterfront until you hit the **promenade**, offering stunning sunset views of Lower Manhattan. It's a rewarding destination after a dramatic walk over the **Brooklyn Bridge** (see p134).

Prospect Park & Park Slope

Created in 1866, 526-acre **Prospect Park** (☎ 718-965-8999) is considered the greatest achievement of landscape designers Olmsted and Vaux, who also designed Central Park. Attractions include ice-skating, boating, strolling, a small zoo, the Children's Museum and the immense art-deco Brooklyn Public Library. The excellent 52-acre **Brooklyn Botanic Garden** (☎ 718-622-4433; www. bbg.org; 1000 Washington Ave; admission $3, Tue free; ◷ 8am-6pm Tue-Fri, from 10am Sat & Sun), which features impressive cherry-tree blossom in spring, is on the eastern side of the park. Beside it is the recently overhauled **Brooklyn Museum** (☎ 718-638-5000; www.brooklynmuseum.org; 200 Eastern Parkway; admission $6, 11am-11pm 1st Sat of each month free; ◷ 10am-5pm Wed-Fri, 11am-6pm Sat & Sun), with comprehensive collections of African, Islamic and Asian art, Egyptian mummy casings and classical antiquities, plus popular temporary shows.

The surrounding **Park Slope** neighborhood has some classic brownstones, tons of great eateries, shops and bars (especially along the more cutting-edge Fifth Ave) and plenty of lesbian families and hippie holdouts who fled Manhattan to have a backyard.

Coney Island

This popular beach town makes for a great day trip, with its nostalgic charms, woodplank boardwalk, arcade games and **Astroland Park** (☎ 718-265-2100), with a massive Ferris wheel, kiddie rides and the famous 1927 Cyclone roller coaster, which still clatters along on its wooden tracks. Also worth visiting are the **Aquarium for Wildlife Conservation** (☎ 718-265-3400; Surf Ave btwn 5th & W 8th Sts; adult/child $11/7; ⏰ 10am-4:30pm); **KeySpan Park** (☎ 718-449-8497), the waterfront stadium for the minor-league Brooklyn Cyclones baseball team; and **Sideshows by the Seashore** (☎ 718-372-5159; www.coneyisland .com; adult/child $5/3), with bearded ladies and tattooed men. A five-minute walk north of the beach, Brighton Beach Ave in **Brighton Beach** ('Little Odessa') is lined with Russian shops, bakeries and restaurants.

Williamsburg

Across the East River from the East Village, the enclave of hipsters continues – but even more so – in Williamsburg, full of slouchy, artsy types who sit in cafés, chain smoke, go to gallery openings and packed lounges, and basically just look really really cool. Formerly an actual working-class waterfront industrial community, the area has been transformed in the past decade, to the chagrin of many old-timers. Be sure to visit the excellent **Brooklyn Brewery** (☎ 718-486-7422; www.brooklynbrewery.com; 79 N 11th St; admission free; tours noon-5pm Sat), which hosts tours, special events and pub nights.

THE BRONX

Brooklyn's fierce northern rival is this 42-square-mile borough with several claims to fame: the Yankees, fondly known as the Bronx Bombers, who can be seen in all their pinstriped glory at **Yankee Stadium** (☎ 718-293-6000; www.yankees.com; 161st St at River Ave) in the spring and summer; the 'real' **Little Italy** (www.arthuravenuebronx.com), a bustling

stretch of Arthur and Belmont Aves that bursts with Italian gourmet markets and eateries; homegrown celebrities like J Lo and Colin Powell, and, of course, a supersized attitude that's been mythologized in Hollywood movies from *The Godfather* to *Rumble in the Bronx*. But it's also got some cool surprises up its sleeve: a quarter of the Bronx is parkland, including the city beach of Pelham Bay Park. It's home to the 250-acre **New York Botanical Garden** (☎ 718-817-8705; www.nybg.org; Bronx River Parkway at Fordham Rd; adult/child $13/5; ⏰ 10am-6pm Tue-Sun), which features the restored Victorian-era Enid A Haupt Conservatory and glasshouses full of tropical and desert plants, 40 acres of original forest and a garden of 2700 roses. The nearby **Bronx Wildlife Conservation Park** (☎ 718-367-1010; www.bronxzoo.com; Bronx River Parkway at Fordham Rd; adult/child $11/6; ⏰ 10am-5pm Apr-Oct), otherwise known as the Bronx Zoo, is one of the biggest, best and most progressive zoos anywhere; and the famous, historic **Woodlawn Cemetery** (☎ 718-920-0500; www.thewoodlawncemetery.org; Webster Ave at 233rd St) is the fascinating, 400-acre burial ground of many notable Americans, including Irving Berlin, Miles Davis, Duke Ellington, Oscar Hammerstein, Herman Melville and many more. Guided tours of the elaborate tombs are available.

Then there's **City Island** (www.cityislandchamber .org), a 1.5-mile-long fishing community that's filled with boat slips, yacht clubs, waterfront seafood eateries and wind-swept little beaches. An afternoon here can make you feel a world away from bustling Midtown, just 15 miles to the south.

The **Bronx Tourism Council** (☎ 718-590-3518; www.ilovethebronx.com) has a visitor guide, and the **Bronx County Historical Society** (☎ 718-881-8900; www.bronxhistoricalsociety.org) sponsors weekend walking tours.

QUEENS

Queens is the largest (282 sq miles), most ethnically diverse and fastest-growing borough in the city, with more than two million people speaking 120 different languages. It's also home to two major airports, a hip modern-art scene, the Mets, and a collection of truly fascinating communities. The **Queens Historical Society** (☎ 718-939-0647; www .queenshistoricalsociety.org) offers tours on many areas of the massive borough.

Astoria & Long Island City

The largest Greek community in the USA (with amazing restaurants), Astoria also has a smattering of Eastern Europeans. In very recent years it, as well as neighboring Long Island City, has become quite the hub of art museums. **PS 1 MoMA** (☎ 718-784-2084; www.ps1 .org; 22-25 Jackson Ave at 46th Ave, Long Island City; suggested donation $5; ☽ noon-6pm Thu-Mon), sister museum to Manhattan's MoMA, is dedicated solely to contemporary art. It features new work by more than 160 artists, using a cutting-edge approach to the massive space of a former public school. A Saturday-night dance party in the summer is a hip happening.

If the weather is pleasant, don't miss the waterside **Socrates Sculpture Park** (☎ 718-956-1819; www.socratessculpturepark.org; Broadway at Vernon Blvd; admission free; ☽ 10am-dusk), an outdoor exhibit of massive, climbable sculptures by greats including Mark DiSuvero, who founded the space. Nearby is the peaceful **Isamu Noguchi Museum** (☎ 718-204-7088; www.noguchi .org; 9-01 33rd Rd at Vernon Blvd; admission $5; ☽ 10am-5pm Wed-Fri, 11am-6pm Sat & Sun), a recently renovated outdoor garden and indoor museum space for the sculptures of this Japanese artist. Movie making started in Astoria in the 1920s, and the **American Museum of the Moving Image** (☎ 718-784-0077; www.ammi.org; 35th Ave at 36th St; admission $10; ☽ noon-5pm Tue-Fri, 11am-6pm Sat & Sun) exposes some of the mysteries of the craft. After all the culture, you can re-fuel with Greek food by choosing from the various cafés, tavernas and bakeries along Astoria's **Broadway**.

Flushing & Corona

With many Asian immigrants, most recently from Korea and China, Flushing's **Main Street** is a bustling, diverse area known mainly for its cheap and delicious gastronomic wonders.

Flushing Meadows Corona Park, home of **Shea Stadium**, the **National Tennis Center Arthur Ashe Stadium** and many ball courts, lakes, bike paths and grassy expanses, was used for the 1939 and 1964 World's Fairs, of which there are quite a few faded leftovers. Also within the massive park is the **Queens Museum of Art** (☎ 718-592-9700; www.queensmuseum.org; New York City Bldg, Flushing Meadows Corona Park; suggested donation $5; ☽ 10am-5pm Wed-Fri, from noon Sat & Sun), which contains *Panorama of New York City*, a detailed and up-to-date model of

the metropolis, with 835,000 tiny buildings and a lovely sunset every 15 minutes. In nearby Corona, the recently opened **Louis Armstrong House** (☎ 718-478-8274; 34-56 107th St; 10am-5pm Tue-Fri, noon-5pm Sat & Sun; admission $8) is the home where the musical great lived during the peak of his career.

Jackson Heights

A fascinating mix of both Indian and South American cultures, this is the place to purchase saris and 22-karat gold, dine on South Indian *masala dosas* – huge, paper-thin rice crepes folded around flavorful mixtures of masala potatoes, peas, cilantro and other earthy treats – and Colombian *arepas* (corn pancakes), and enjoy a drink at a Latin gay and lesbian bar, which you'll find several of along the main drag of Broadway. **Little India** is mainly along 74th Street.

STATEN ISLAND

While many New Yorkers will say that Staten Island has more in common with its neighbor, New Jersey, because of its suburban house and car cultures, there are some undoubtedly compelling reasons to count this borough in your urban explorations. First and foremost is the free **Staten Island Ferry** (☎ 718-815-2628; www.siferry.com), employed both by commuters who live on SI but work in Manhattan, and by Manhattanites and tourists alike who crave breathtaking views of the Statue of Liberty and the Manhattan skyline. Not far from the ferry station on the Staten Island side is the **Richmond County Bank Ballpark** (☎ 718-720-9200; www.siyanks.com; Richmond Terrace), home to the minor-league Staten Island Yankees, where you can catch games throughout the summer.

For a different type of entertainment, Staten Island's got the **Snug Harbor Cultural Center** (Map p128; ☎ 718-448-2500; www.snug-harbor.org; 1000 Richmond Tce), originally a 19th-century sailors' retirement complex that sits on 83 acres and boasts some fine **Greek Revival structures**, plus the **Botanical Garden**, **Children's Museum** and the **Newhouse Center for Contemporary Art**.

Activities

RUNNING

Central Park's (see p143) 6-mile roadway is closed to cars from 10am to 3pm weekdays and all weekend, and is perfect for running – as is the gleaming Jacqueline Kennedy Onassis Reservoir, encircled by a soft 1.5-mile path. Another good pathway is the **Hudson River Parkway** (see p135), which runs along Manhattan's western edge from Battery Park to 59th Street, and north of through the leafy Riverside Park. The **New York Road Runner's Club** (Map pp146-7; ☎ 212-860-4455; www.nyrrc.org) organizes weekend runs and the October New York Marathon.

BICYCLING & IN-LINE SKATING

Unless you're a bike messenger or otherwise experienced urban cyclist, pedaling through the streets can be a high-risk activity in Manhattan, but **Central Park** has lovely cycling paths. Also try the **Hudson River Parkway** (see p135), which has a path shared by cyclists, runners, walkers and skaters; the auto-free road that runs round the perimeter of Brooklyn's **Prospect Park** (see p148); and the beautiful **Franklin D Roosevelt Boardwalk** (☎ 718-816-6804; cnr Father Capadanno Blvd & Sand Ln) along South Beach in Staten Island, hugging 4 miles of unspoiled beaches.

For cycling tips and weekend trips, contact **Five Borough Bicycle Club** (☎ 212-932-2300). **Transportation Alternatives** (Map pp140-1; ☎ 212-629-8080; www.transalt.org; 115 W 30th St), a nonprofit bicycle-lobbying group, is also a good source of information. Gay cycling enthusiasts should check the website of **Fast & Fabulous** (www.fastnfab.org), a gay bicycling club that organizes long weekend rides. For bike rentals, **Metro Bicycle** (Map pp140-1; ☎ 212-581-4500; W 47th St at Ninth Ave) has several locations, or you can try **Central Park Bicycle Tours/Rentals** (Map pp146-7; ☎ 212-541-8759; 2 Columbus Circle), at Broadway and 59th St.

In-line skating is also popular in Central Park, especially near the **Naumberg Bandshell**, where a makeshift outdoor rink with DJs operates on summer weekends, and along Hudson River Park. For rentals, try **Blades West** (Map pp146-7; ☎ 212-787-3911; 120 W 72nd St), two blocks from Central Park.

INDOOR ACTIVITIES

The city has gyms, yoga centers and dance studios for whatever moves you. For a little taste of everything, make a beeline to the **Chelsea Piers Complex** (Map pp140-1; ☎ 212-336-6666; www.chelseapiers.com; Hudson River at 23rd St), with a four-level driving range, indoor ice-skating rink, running track, swimming pool, amazingly well-equipped gym, indoor rock-climbing wall and even sand volleyball courts. Gyms around the city, which are plentiful, charge at least $20 for day use. YMCAs are about $25, while many fancy gyms require subscriptions. Check out the well-run chain **Equinox** (www.equinoxfitness.com). Yoga classes are offered at most gyms these days, but yoga studios abound. For starters, try **Jivamukti Yoga Center** (Map pp132-3; ☎ 212-353-0214; www.jivamuktiyoga.com; 404 Lafayette St; per class $19) or **Om Yoga Center** (Map pp132-3; ☎ 212-414-2903; 826 Broadway; per class $15).

Walking Tour: Screen Gems

New York City has been used in countless films over the decades. While most classic scenes have been shot at uptown locations, like the famed Dakota building on Central Park West (*Rosemary's Baby*) and the Museum of Natural History (*Annie Hall*), there have been plenty of films, especially in recent years, shot all over downtown. This walk takes you to some of the cool movie locations that lie in the East Village area. Even if you're not familiar with the flicks or the scenes, the journey from one to the next adds up to a lively, fun walk through one of Manhattan's most colorful neighborhoods.

Start at **Hotel 17 (1**; p156), the way-cool dive hotel that Woody Allen used as his location for *Manhattan Murder Mystery* (1993). Then head southwest to **Union Square Park (2)**, site of a dramatic helicopter landing in the 1997 film *Conspiracy Theory*, which starred Mel Gibson and Julia Roberts. Exit at the south of the park and continue onto Broadway. Stroll south till you arrive at the **Strand Bookstore (3**; see p129), a favorite used-book haunt, which made a notable appearance in *Six Degrees of Separation* (1993), starring Stockard Channing and Will Smith.

Continue south on Broadway and turn left on E 9th St. Walk until you reach the block between First Ave and Ave A. Take note of **building No 422 (4)**, the stoop where a very young Leonardo Di Caprio teased a junkie prostitute (Juliette Lewis) in the *Basketball Diaries* (1995). At the corner is the bustling **Tompkins Square Park (5**; p137); head to the center and the small stone fountain, where Gwyneth Paltrow and Ethan Hawke kissed in 1998's version of *Great Expectations*. Exit at the southwest corner

NEW YORK, NEW JERSEY & PENNSYLVANIA

WALK FACTS

Distance: About 3 miles
Duration: About 1 to 1½ hours

and continue south along the lively Ave A. Turn right on E 2nd St until you reach the Bowery, where you'll turn left and stroll for a block to the legendary music venue **CBGB** (6; p164), where Italian thugs went searching for their neighbor-turned-punk in Spike Lee's *Summer of Sam* (1999).

Continue south on the Bowery until Houston St, where you'll turn left and walk east. You can nosh at one of the next two sites: the 24-hour Turkish spot, **Bereket** (7; p159), is where Piper Perabo and Adam Garcia grabbed food to go in the 2000 clunker *Coyote Ugly*. A block away is **Katz's Delicatessen** (8), where Meg Ryan faked a rambunctious orgasm for Billy Crystal in *When Harry Met Sally* (1989). Finally, turn right and walk southeast on Suffolk St until you reach **Delancey Street (9)**, the strip that gave the syrupy 1988 love story *Crossing Delancey* its name.

The flick, starring Amy Irving, featured several beautiful shots of the **Williamsburg Bridge (10)**, which crosses into Brooklyn. You'll be practically at the foot of the span here, where you'll enjoy your own great glimpse of it.

New York for Children

Though it can seem to have a bit too much hustle and bustle to be a kid-friendly town, that's really not true at all. A good place to start is by getting a hold of the quarterly magazine *Time Out New York Kids*, which lists and reviews events, restaurants, clothing and more, all for citified kids. There are plenty of attractions for little ones of all sizes, starting with the marvelous old standbys of the **American Museum of Natural History** (Map pp146–7) and the city's various zoos, from the **Bronx Zoo** (p149) to the **Central Park zoo** (p144).

Even more made for children is the **Brooklyn Children's Museum** (☎ 718-735-4400; www.bchildmus.org; 145 Brooklyn Ave; admission $4; ⏰ 2-5pm Wed-Fri, from 10am Sat & Sun) and the **Children's Museum of Manhattan** (Map pp146-7; ☎ 212-721-1234; www.cmom.org; 212 W 83rd St btwn Amsterdam Ave & Broadway; admission $8; ⏰ 10am-5pm Wed-Sun). **Manhattan Children's Theatre** (Map pp132-3; ☎ 212-352-3101; www.manhattanchildrenstheatre.org; 380 Broadway at White St) presents musicals and dramas for the little ones. You'll find the granddaddy of all arcades at **ESPN Zone** (Map pp140-1; ☎ 212-921-3776; 1472 Broadway at 42nd St), and some excellent sweets at **Dylan's Candy Shop** (Map pp146-7; ☎ 646-735-0078; www.dylanscandybar.com; 1011 Third Ave at 60th St), the closest place you'll find to Willy Wonka's chocolate factory.

Quirky New York

Held every summer in Coney Island, the **Mermaid Parade** (www.coneyisland.com; last Saturday of June) is a rite of the season, bringing hordes of sequined and bejeweled revelers who stuff themselves into wacky, aquatic-themed get-ups for a truly unique spectacle-on-the-sea.

Cuddle Party (www.cuddleparty.com), a usually bimonthly event at various city locations, is the brainchild of Reid, a sex and romance coach, and Marcia, a relationship and commitment coach. What is a cuddle party? It's an oddball event for adults who want to 'explore affectionate touch' without being sexual, say the organizers. Kinda like when you and your cousins and pals used to all pile onto one bed and get all warm and fuzzy and silly at family parties, you know? It's a big hit, apparently, as the parties have now spread to cities including Los Angeles, San Francisco and Toronto!

Midnight Yoga For Men (☎ 212-358 -5877) is a Chelsea-based gathering, in various locations, and is exactly what it says it is. So, men who love to be naked around other men, take your pliant self here at the stroke of midnight and experience 'downward dog' like never before!

Tours

There are endless numbers of folks willing to lead lost tourists around to their favorite spots, from the usual top sights to more obscure curiosities. Here's just a sampling:

AIR
Liberty Helicopter Tours (Map pp140-1; ☎ 212-967-6464; www.libertyhelicopters.com; Twelfth Ave at W 30th St; 5min flights adult from $68; ☺ flights 9am-7pm) A bird's-eye view of the city, whisking you high above the skyscrapers – for a price. Expect to pay at least $68 and much more for longer tours.

BOAT
Circle Line (Map pp140-1; ☎ 212-563-3200; departs Pier 83 at W 42nd St; adult $24; ☺ Mar-Dec) Three-hour, 35-mile boat cruise around Manhattan on the Hudson River. A popular and informative tour, especially attractive when the weather is good, though it's still OK if it's not – boats are covered and heated.

BUS
Gray Line (☎ 212-397-2620; www.graylinenewyork.com; main terminal Port Authority Bus Terminal Map pp140-1; www.portauthorityny.com; 625 Eighth Ave; visitor center Map pp140-1; 777 Eighth Ave at 48th St; tours $30-60) This is a reliable foreign-language option, which runs nearly 30 different tours.

Kenny Kramer (Map pp140-1; ☎ 212-268-5525, 800-572-6377; www.kennykramer.com; 358 W 44th St; adult $38; ☺ tours noon Sat & Sun) The real-life inspiration for the *Seinfeld* character, Kenny Kramer offers fun three-hour tours past major sites from the TV series. Reservations required.

WALKING
Big Apple Greeters Program (☎ 212-669-8198; www.bigapplegreeters.org; tours free) Volunteers (including some who are multilingual or specialize in assisting disabled travelers) lead tours of lesser-known neighborhoods.

Big Onion Walking Tours (☎ 212-439-1090; www.big onion.com; tours $15) Popular and quirky guided tours specializing in ethnic and neighborhood tours.

Municipal Art Society (☎ 212-935-3960; www.mas.org; 457 Madison Ave; tours adult $12) Various scheduled tours focusing on architecture and history.

Festivals & Events

Festivities never cease in New York – even when there isn't anything special scheduled, which is rare. From cultural street fairs to foodie events and outdoor concerts, you're bound to find something to excite you, no matter what time of year you're in town.

Lunar New Year Festival (☎ 212-966-0100) Chinatown's much-anticipated New Year celebration, held in late January or early February, features displays of fireworks and lavish parades in and around Chinatown.

Restaurant Week (☎ 212-484-1222; www.nycvisit.com) Dine at top restaurants for $20 and $30 deals – first in February and again in June.

Cherry Blossom Festival (☎ 718-623-7200; www.bbg .org) The annual *Sakura Matsuri*, in May, celebrates the gorgeous, blooming Kwanzan cherry trees.

Tribeca Film Festival (☎ 212-941-3378; www.tribeca filmfestival.com) Robert DeNiro co-organizes this local downtown film fest in May, quickly rising in prestige on the circuit.

Bike New York (☎ 212-932-2453; www.bikemonthnyc .org) The main event of Bike Month, in May, has thousands of cyclers doing this 42-mile ride, through each of the five boroughs.

Fleet Week (☎ 212-245-2533) It's the annual convocation of sailors, naval ships and air rescue teams, who descend upon the city in their formal whites like the characters in *Our Town* each and every May.

Lesbian, Gay, Bisexual & Transgender Pride (☎ 212-807-7433; www.heritageofpride.org) Pride month, in June, with a packed calendar of parties and special events, culminates with a major march down Fifth Ave on the last Sunday of the month. It's a five-hour spectacle.

Mermaid Parade (www.coneyisland.com) Last Saturday of June; see opposite.

Howl! Festival (☎ 212-505-2225; www.howlfestival.com) It's a weeklong celebration of the arts in August, including the Charlie Parker Jazz Festival in Tompkins Sq Park, the Allen Ginsberg Poetry Festival and a slew of other edgy performances.

Shakespeare in the Park (☎ 212-539-8500; www .publictheater.org) It's the Public Theater's annual star-studded Shakespeare production in the Delacorte Theatre of Central Park, held July to August. Tickets are free, but you've got to wait in a long, long line to get them.

New York Film Festival (www.filmlinc.com) Catch major world premieres from prominent directors at this Lincoln Center event, held late September.

US Open Tennis Tournament (www.usopen.org) The Grand Slam event in Flushing Meadows, Queens, in September.

GAY & LESBIAN NEW YORK

Probably one of the all-time gayest cities on the planet, NYC is where queer folks, feeling like outcasts, flock to from all corners of small-town America to be welcomed with open arms. That's because you can walk down the street holding hands with your same-sex lover, look into each other's eyes over dinner pretty much anywhere, and find a long, long list of places geared just toward other LGBT folks.

For all things gay – from lecture series to gay bingo parties and transgender movie nights – head to the **LGBT Community Center** (p129), housed in a stylish, light-filled, recently renovated building in the Village. For gay literature, head to **Oscar Wilde Bookstore** (p129), or **Bluestockings Bookstore** (p129), for women.

Chelsea has two excellent gay inns: **Chelsea Inn** (p156) and **Colonial House Inn** (p156). The huge **LGBT Pride Weekend**, held during the last weekend in June, features countless parties and the main Pride March along Fifth Ave. While that parade has gotten a bit mainstream (recent years have seen floats sponsored by corporations including beer companies and banks), an edgier, passion-filled alternative is the fabulous **Dyke March** (for women only) on Saturday at 5pm, kicking off from Fifth Ave at 42nd St.

As far as drinking and dancing spots go, New York has about 75 gay and lesbian bars and clubs, with countless other queer nights held at otherwise straight venues. For complete listings, pick up a copy of *HX* or *Next* magazines at any gay establishment, or *Go* magazine, at the girl bars. Here's a sample. The East Village has the low-key **Boiler Room** (Map pp132-3; ☎ 212-254-7536; 86 E 4th St), **Starlight** (Map pp132-3; ☎ 212-475-2172; 167 Ave A), and the hottest recent addition, the **Slide** (Map pp132-3; ☎ 212-420-8885; 356 Bowery at 4th St), with go-go boys and drag queens galore. Chelsea boys have the pick of the city's litter, with the glossy **xl** (Map pp140-1; ☎ 212-995-1400; 357 W 16th St), **Splash Bar** (Map pp140-1; ☎ 212-691-0073; 50 W 17th St; admission $5-20) and **Roxy** (Map pp140-1; ☎ 212-645-5156; 515 W 18th St; admission $10-20) dance clubs. In the West Village, the bars are numerous; women flock to **Henrietta Hudson** (Map pp132-3; ☎ 212-924-3347; 438 Hudson St) or **Rubyfruit's Bar & Grill** (Map pp132-3; ☎ 212-924-3343; 531 Hudson St), also a restaurant; the old-school boys have the cabaret bars **Duplex** (Map pp132-3; ☎ 212-255-5438; 61 Christopher St) and **Marie's Crisis** (Map pp132-3; ☎ 212-243-5438; 59 Grove St), and an African American crowd hangs at **Chi Chiz** (Map pp132-3; ☎ 212-462-0027; 135 Christopher St).

Brooklyn's got its own thriving scene, with the brand-new **Cattyshack** (www.cattyshackbklyn.com; 249 Fourth Ave) in Park Slope, from the owner of the beloved, defunct Meow Mix in the East Village; the nearby cute-boy venue is **Excelsior** (☎ 718-832-1599; 390 Fifth Ave), which sits right across the street from the softball-dyke girl spot, **Ginger's Bar** (☎ 718-788-0924; 363 Fifth Ave).

New York Marathon (www.nycmarathon.org) The beloved road-race through all five boroughs, which brings fans to the streets in spades, is held the first weekend in November.

Sleeping

No matter what neighborhood you're most drawn to, chances are you'll find a place to stay within its borders. And as long as you book in advance, and are flexible when it comes to details like location and decor, there's no reason why you can't enjoy a comfortable stay and still have enough money left over to reap the cultural benefits of the city. Budget accommodations generally cost $100 or less, midrange up to $200, and, for top end, the sky's the limit. Note that prices are flexible; it's usually more expensive on Friday and Saturday nights, and during spring and fall. Tax is an additional 13.25% per night.

For stays of a week or more, an apartment rental or sublet can be the best option (there's no tax on rentals, so you're already 13.25% ahead). Agencies include the following:

Gamut Realty (☎ 212-879-4229; www.gamutnyc.com)
Hospitality Company (☎ 212-965-1102)

LOWER MANHATTAN

Battery Park City Ritz-Carlton (Map pp132-3; ☎ 212-344-0800; www.ritz-carlton.com; 2 West St at Battery Pl; s/d/ste from $240/400/800) It's hard to pick the best amenity of this luxurious, 38-story glass-and-brick tower – the sweeping harbor and city views, big marble baths (with 'bath-butler' service), goose-down pillows, on-site spa and gym – with two top-notch restaurants. Cell-phone rentals are available.

Best Western Seaport Inn (Map pp132-3; ☎ 212-766-6600, 800-468-3569; www.seaportinn.com; 33 Peck Slip btwn Front & Water Sts; s/d $160/180) Despite its blah chain style, the Seaport Inn offers some striking water views from its terrace rooms, and it sits in the shadow of the grand Brooklyn Bridge. It's got a small on-site gym, high-speed Internet and services for assisting deaf patrons.

TRIBECA & SOHO
Cosmopolitan Hotel (Map pp132-3; ☎ 212-566-1900, 888-895-9400; www.cosmohotel.com; 95 West Broadway; s/d $109/149) The 105 pastel-hued rooms of this inn are lacking in the decor department. But it's affordable and spotless, and sitting in a prime location.

Mercer (Map pp132-3; ☎ 212-966-6060; 147 Mercer St at Prince St; s/d/ste from $400/575/1100) It's sleek and grand and so cool that it doesn't even need a sign. The hushed lobby features a library, the excellent restaurant is a destination eatery for discerning locals, and the vast rooms are wooden-floored lofts with exposed brick. Both cell-phone and laptop rentals are available.

Soho Grand Hotel (Map pp132-3; ☎ 212-965-3000, 800-965-3000; www.sohogrand.com; 310 West Broadway; s/d/ste $260/400/1600; 🖳) The outside may be nondescript, but inside lies a striking glass and cast-iron stairway, and 367 rooms with cool, clean lines, plus Frette linens, Kiehl's grooming products and cell-phone rentals.

Tribeca Grand (Map pp132-3; ☎ 212-519-6600; www.tribecagrand.com; 2 Sixth Ave at Church, Walker & White Sts; s/d/ste $260/400/1600; 🖳) Sister to the Soho Grand, with 203 gorgeous rooms and similar amenities.

LOWER EAST SIDE & THE EAST VILLAGE
Howard Johnson Express Inn (Map pp132-3; ☎ 212-358-8844; www.hojo.com; 135 E Houston St at Forsyth St; s/d $129/189) Sure, it's bland and not so hip. But it's clean, and the location is prime. Beds are comfy, water pressure is excellent, photos from local artists adorn the walls of the teeny lobby and you get free bagels and pastries in the morning.

Hotel on Rivington (Map pp132-3; ☎ 212-475-2600; www.hotelonrivington.com; 107 Rivington St btwn Essex & Ludlow Sts; r from $265) Taunting hipster travelers with the most drawn-out opening in history, this sleek high rise, originally dubbed the Surface Hotel, was supposed to have been unveiled back in 2003 but was plagued by financial setbacks. It still wasn't quite ready to receive guests at press time, but keep watching the website: you won't want to miss a chance to sleep in one of these ultraslick dens that feature stunning views, high-style furniture and amenities including a champagne-stocked minifridge and wi-fi.

WEST (GREENWICH) VILLAGE
Larchmont Hotel (Map pp132-3; ☎ 212-989-9333; www.larchmonthotel.com; 27 W 11th St btwn Fifth & Sixth Aves; s/d $80/109) This European-like inn is cozy and affordable, with shared baths and communal kitchens. The hotel's 52 rooms include sinks and perks such as robes and slippers, plus a plum spot on a beautiful, leafy Fifth Ave block.

Abingdon Guest House (Map pp132-3; ☎ 212-243-5384; www.abingdonguesthouse.com; 13 Eighth Ave at Jane St; s/d $160/190; ✗ 🖳) Don't look out the window and you'll swear you've landed in a New England country inn. Elegant, comfortable rooms feature four-post beds, fireplaces, scads of exposed brick and billowing curtains.

Washington Square Hotel (Map pp132-3; ☎ 212-777-9515, 800-222-0418; www.washingtonsquarehotel.com; 103 Waverly Pl btwn MacDougal St & Sixth Ave; s/d $130/165) This intimate lodge – with its elegant lobby, and cramped quarters, and lovely grown-up bohemian vibe – sits right off the corner of Washington Sq Park.

THE AUTHOR'S CHOICE
East Village B&B Tribeca Grand (Map pp132-3; ☎ 212-260-1865; 244 E 7th St btwn Aves C & D, apt 5-6; r $100) You're always thinking about wanting to live 'like a local' when you're in a strange city, right? Well here's your big chance. This stylish and affordable inn, housed in a multilevel apartment building on a lovely residential block, will make you feel like you've got your own, way-cool city pad – only with someone who'll watch over you as you come and go. There are just three rooms, one single and two doubles, so book early. No matter which one you end up in, you'll love the bold linens, modern art, gorgeous wood floors and spacious common room. A bagel breakfast is included – as is use of the washing machine.

Hotel Gansevoort (Map pp132-3; ☎ 212-206-6700; www.hotelgansevoort.com; 18 Ninth Ave at 13th St; s/d/ste $395/500/625; 🖳) Since opening in 2004, this 187-room luxury hotel in the trendy Meatpacking District has been a hit with its 400-thread-count linens, hypoallergenic down duvets, plasma TVs and views.

CHELSEA

Chelsea Inn (Map pp140-1; ☎ 212-645-8989; http://chel seainn.com; 46 W 17th St btwn Fifth & Sixth Aves; s/d/ste $89/140/190) Made up of two adjoining townhouses, the funky-charming hideaway has small rooms with a quirky, flea-market character. Special winter rates go as low as $79.

Chelsea Pines Inn (Map pp140-1; ☎ 212-929-1023; www.chelseapinesinn.com; 317 W 14th St btwn Eighth & Ninth Aves; r $99-139, winter special rates $79; 🖳) It's gay-man central, with vintage movie posters on the walls, a greenhouse and small back patio for eating and socializing. Rooms are small but homey.

Chelsea International Hostel (Map pp140-1; ☎ 212-647-0010; www.chelseahostel.com; 251 W 20th St btwn Seventh & Eighth Aves; dm/r $25/60; 🖳) A festive, international crowd sleeps here, where the back patio is party central. Bunkrooms sleep four to six and amenities include communal kitchens and laundry facilities.

Maritime Hotel (Map pp140-1; ☎ 212-242-4300; www.themaritimehotel.com; 363 W 16th St btwn Eighth & Ninth Aves; r $195-260, ste $395-1100; 🖳) A white tower dotted with portholes, this is a marine-themed luxury inn with 120 compact, teak-paneled rooms, each with its own round window. The most expensive quarters feature outdoor showers, a private garden and sweeping Hudson views.

Chelsea Hotel (Map pp140-1; ☎ 212-243-3700; 222 W 23rd St; r/ste from $135/325; 🖳) This infamous inn is a literary and cultural landmark whose list of noteworthy guests and residents ranges from Dylan Thomas to Bob Dylan. The cheapest rooms have shared bath and the most expensive suites have a separate living room, dining area and kitchen; every room has high ceilings, air con and its own unique style.

Colonial House Inn (Map pp140-1; ☎ 212-243-9669; www.colonialhouseinn.com; 318 W 22nd St btwn Eighth & Ninth Aves; r without bath $80-125, with bath $125-160; 🖳) This friendly gay inn is serene, with an airy lobby that doubles as a modern-art gallery, and rooms that range from economy (bed, dresser) to deluxe (fireplace, fridge).

UNION SQUARE, FLATIRON & GRAMERCY PARK

Hotel 17 (Map pp140-1; ☎ 212-475-2845; 225 E 17th St btwn Second & Third Aves; s/d/tr $70/87/110) This popular spot has serious character. There's an old-fashioned elevator, a cool chandelier in the lobby, vintage wallpaper and worn but chic charm to the small, quiet rooms.

Gershwin Hotel (Map pp140-1; ☎ 212-545-8000; www.gershwinhotel.com; 7 E 27th St at Fifth Ave; dm/r $35/$99; 🖳) This popular and funky spot is half youth hostel, half hotel, and buzzes with original artwork, touring bands and other fabulousness. Plus, it sits right next door to the Museum of Sex (see p138).

Marcel (Map pp140-1; ☎ 212-696-3800; www.nycho tels.com; 201 E 24th St at Third Ave; s/d $100/200) Minimalist and chic, with earth-tone touches, this 97-room inn is popular with the fashion-industry crowd. Rooms on the avenue have great views, and the sleek lounge is a great place to unwind from a day of touring. Visit its website for other classy affordable inns within the Amsterdam Hospitality group.

W New York – Union Square (Map pp140-1; ☎ 212-253-9119; toll-free 877-946-8357; www.whotels .com; 201 Park Ave S at 17th St; r from $319; 🖳) This hipster pad demands a black wardrobe and a platinum credit card. Like all the W hotels, everything is top of the line, comfortable and classy, and its location right on bucolic Madison Square Park is a big perk. Call for the W's several Manhattan outposts.

MIDTOWN

ThirtyThirty (Map pp140-1; ☎ 212-689-1900; www .stayinny.com; 30 E 30th St btwn Park & Madison Aves; r $125-150; 🖳) Part of the Citylife hotel group, this unbelievably sleek bargain is the best way to get in on the boutique-hotel scene without going broke. Its two other area properties, just as stylish and affordable, are the **Habitat Hotel** (130 E 57th St at Lexington Ave) and On the Ave (opposite).

Hudson (Map pp146-7; ☎ 212-554-6000; 356 W 58th St btwn Eighth & Ninth Aves; www.ianschragerhotels .com; r $175-275, ste $300-3500; 🖳) This property from boutique-hotel king Ian Schrager is the jewel in his crown. The lobby bars are always jammin', the rooftop terrace has Hudson views, and the rooms are just as highly stylized and cushy as you'd expect.

Hotel 41 (Map pp140-1; ☎ 877-847-4444; www.hotel 41.com; 206 W 41st St btwn Seventh & Eighth Aves; r $149-249, penthouse ste $389) Everything about this big

Times Square bargain is stylish and unique – from its winding steel terrace/staircase on the facade to its crisp, white attractive quarters and its sexy, low-lit lounge bar.

Dream Hotel (Map pp140-1; ☎ 212-247-2000; www.dreamny.com; 210 W 55th St btwn Broadway & Seventh Ave; r $275-575, ste $500-5000; ☐) Brand new in 2005, this truly dreamy palace has an ayurvedic spa, hypersleek style and rooms outfitted with plasma TVs, wi-fi and loaded iPods.

UPPER WEST SIDE

Hostelling International-New York (Map pp146-7; ☎ 212-932-2300; www.hinewyork.org; 891 Amsterdam Ave at 103rd St; dm $29-32, nonmembers extra $3, f with/without bath $135/120; ☐) It's got clean, safe and air-conditioned dorm rooms in a gorgeous landmark building, a popular, sprawling and shady patio and a friendly vibe.

Jazz on the Park Hostel (Map pp146-7; ☎ 212-932-1600; www.jazzhostel.com; 36 W 106th St btwn Central Park West & Manhattan Ave; dm $27-37, d $80, r with bath $130; ☐) This way-cool hostel has small rooms with standard wood-frame bunks, but there's a beautiful roof deck and exposed-brick lounge that hosts local jazz acts. Its midtown **Jazz on the Town** (Map pp140-1; 130 E 57th St btwn Lexington & Park Aves) also has a fun atmosphere and great roof deck.

On the Ave (Map pp146-7; ☎ 212-362-1100, 800-509-7598; www.stayinny.com; 2178 Broadway at 77th St; r $159-309, ste from $475) This sleek bargain boasts a design composed of warm earth tones, stainless steel and marble baths, plus sunny rooms hung with original artwork.

Inn New York City (Map pp146-7; ☎ 212-580-1900; 266 W 71st St at West End Ave; ste $300-600; ☒) Four massive, quirky suites in this 1900 townhouse let you live in a mansion (with wi-fi service, natch). It's far west, and close to both Riverside Park and Central Park, and its rooms feature antique chestnut furnishings, Jacuzzis and stained glass panels, if just a bit too much flowered carpeting.

UPPER EAST SIDE

Bentley (Map pp146-7; ☎ 212-644-6000, 888-664-6835; www.nychotels.com; 500 E 62nd St at York Ave; r/ste $135/235; ☐) You can't stay any further east than in this chic boutique hotel, boasting a swanky lobby, down comforters and some of New York's most spectacular views.

Carlyle (Map pp146-7; ☎ 212-744-1600; www.thecarlyle.com; 212-744-1600; 35 E 76th St btwn Madison & Park Aves; r $495-795, ste from $850) This New York

classic is the epitome of old-fashioned luxury: a hushed lobby, antique boudoir chairs and framed English country scenes or Audubon prints in the rooms, some of which have terraces and baby grand pianos.

Mark New York (Map pp146-7; ☎ 212-744-4300; www.mandarinoriental.com; Madison Ave at E 77th St; r $570-730, ste $760-2500) Run by the superglitzy Mandarin Oriental, the regal, neoclassical Italian-style rooms with treelike potted plants, deeply hued carpets and black wooden furniture will thrill those who like opulence.

HARLEM

Harlem Flophouse (Map pp146-7; ☎ 212-662-0678; www.harlemflophouse.com; 242 W 123rd St btwn Adam Clayton Powell & Frederick Douglass Blvds; s/d $65/90; ☐) The four gorgeous bedrooms here are large spaces with antique light fixtures, glossed-wood floors and big beds, plus classic tin ceilings and wooden shutters. There's wi-fi access (and two cats) on the premises.

102Brownstone (Map pp146-7; ☎ 212-662-4223; www.102brownstone.com; 102 W 118th St btwn Lenox Ave & Adam Clayton Powell Blvd; s/d/ste $99/140/250; ☒) A wonderfully redone Greek Revival rowhouse on a beautiful residential street, room styles range from Zen to classy boudoir.

Eating

Where do you start in a city that's home to nearly 13,000 restaurants, with new ones opening every single day of the year? We suggest you begin with whatever you're craving, because you'll find it – probably right down the street – and it's bound to be the best you've ever had. Note that smoking is not permitted in restaurants, bars or clubs.

LOWER MANHATTAN

Sophie's Restaurant (Map pp132-3; ☎ 212-269-0909; 205 Pearl St btwn Maiden Ln & Platt St; mains $6-8; ☽ lunch Mon-Fri) Downtown nine-to-fivers cram into this bare-bones storefront for Cuban treats: steaming plates of rice and beans topped with onion and cilantro with a perfect garlic-to-hot-pepper ratio, *tostones* (fried plantain slices), which are crisp and not too greasy, and the thick *café con leche* (Cuban coffee with milk).

Cabana (Map pp132-3; ☎ 212-406-1155; 89 South St Seaport; mains $13-20; ☽ lunch & dinner) This branch of the minichain (you'll find others on the Upper East Side and in Queens) is a fabulously

---

BAGELS: THE LOWDOWN

Bagels may have been invented in Europe, but they were perfected in NYC, during the turn of the 19th century. And once you've had one here, you'll have a hard time enjoying one anywhere else. Basically, it's a ring of plain-yeast dough that's first boiled and then baked, either left plain or topped with various finishing touches, like sesame seeds or dried onion flakes. 'Bagels' made in other parts of the country are often just baked and not boiled, which makes it nothing more than a roll with a hole. While you're here, avoid the 50¢ bagels from street vendors and stick to actual bagel shops; **H&H Bagels** (Map pp146-7; www.handhbagel.com; Broadway ☎ 212-595-8003; 2239 Broadway; W 46th St ☎ 212-595-8000; 639 W 46th St) is among the best of the lot.

---

flavorful addition to the mall-like South St Seaport staples – especially with its sweeping views of the harbor. The fresh grub includes Cuban *ropa vieja* (shredded beef), Jamaican jerk chicken, grilled seafood salad marinated in tangy citrus *mojo* (a Cuban citrusy sauce) and thick slabs of *arepa con queso* (corn cakes stuffed with cheese).

Les Halles (Map pp132-3; ☎ 212-285-8585; 15 John St btwn Broadway & Nassau St; mains $18-22; ⏱ lunch & dinner) Celebrity chef Anthony Bourdain reigns at this packed and serious bistro where vegetarians need not apply. You'll find the expected onion soup, escargot and *moules frites* on the menu, but raves point to the top-shelf meats: NY strip steak, *côte de boeuf*, *choucroute garnie* and steak *au poivre* (pepper steak).

TRIBECA & SOHO

Hoomoos Asli (Map pp132-3; ☎ 212-966-0022; 100 Kenmare St at Cleveland Pl; mains $4-8; ⏱ lunch & dinner) Along with some endearing Israeli quirkiness is an across-the-board delicious menu of casual salads, sandwiches and phyllo-wrapped mains. Try a bit of everything with the $8.50 salad combo, which could include some minty carrots, lemony tabouleh, garlicky baba ghanoush and creamy, caper-studded potato salad.

Bubby's (Map pp132-3; ☎ 212-219-0666; 120 Hudson St at N Moore St; mains $10-16; ⏱ brunch Sun, breakfast, lunch & dinner daily) This old Tribeca standby is *the* place for simple, big, delicious food: slow-cooked BBQ, grits, matzo-ball soup, buttermilk potato salad and fried okra, all melt-in-your-mouth good.

Dos Caminos Soho (Map pp132-3; ☎ 212-277-4300; 475 W Broadway at Houston St; mains $15-23; ⏱ lunch & dinner) The din is deafening at this always-mobbed fiesta, and waits for tables can be lengthy affairs. But the food is really worth it. Creative-Mexican dishes include roasted tomato chipotle meatballs, pan-roasted sea bass flavored with jalapenos and fresh oregano, and a grilled chicken torte topped with zippy *manchego* cheese (a hard Spanish cheese) and smoky poblano peppers.

Bouley (Map pp132-3; ☎ 212-694-2525; 120 West Broadway at Duane St; mains $30-36 or dinner tasting menu $75; ⏱ lunch & dinner) The home base of celebrity chef David Bouley is the stuff of legend: tender roasted monkfish with a fragrant stew of razor clams and asparagus; lobster with broad beans and haricot verts in a succulent port-wine and blood-orange sauce; even rare *kobe* beef, an expensive cut of beef from Wagyu cattle. It's all served in one of two elegant rooms – the red room or the white room – to some of the most discriminating eaters in New York. And that's saying something.

CHINATOWN & LITTLE ITALY

Doyers Vietnamese Restaurant (Map pp132-3; ☎ 212-513-1521; 11 Doyers St btwn Bowery & Pell St; mains $6-9; ⏱ lunch & dinner) Everything about this place is an adventure: its location, on the curvy little barber-shop-lined street of Doyers; its ambience, in a cavelike, below-street-level hideaway with old-school charm; and the lengthy menu, with curiously yummy dishes including crispy fried tilapia, shrimp-papaya salad, and fried rice stick with vegetables.

Funky Broome (Map pp132-3; ☎ 212-941-8628; 176 Mott St; mains $10-18; ⏱ lunch & dinner) The young Asian trendies here come for the tacky-cool zebra-print decor and some seriously authentic Cantonese delicacies. Flavorful soups, such as the sliced pork, mustard green and salted egg concoction, are excellent, as are the mini-woks – satay meatballs and vermicelli, stuffed fried bean curd – kept warm at your table over blue Sterno flames.

Vegetarian Dim Sum House (Map pp132-3; ☎ 212-577-7176; 24 Pell St; meals $8-12; ☺ breakfast, lunch & dinner) Like its two pure-veg competitors in the 'hood (Vegetarian Paradise 1 and 2), this tiny crowd-pleaser offers long lists of alarmingly authentic mock-meat specialties. But this one's got the freshest most consistent offerings, like sweet yam soup, and faux 'spareribs' and 'chicken', made of various forms of bean curd.

Da Gennaro (Map pp132-3; ☎ 212-431-3934; 129 Mulberry St btwn Grand & Hester Sts; mains $20; ☺ lunch & dinner) The most consistently excellent red-sauce joint on the strip, this slightly upscale option attracts a more discerning breed of tourists who appreciate its casual atmosphere and classic pasta, seafood, steak and meatball-laden offerings.

LOWER EAST SIDE

Bereket (Map pp132-3; ☎ 212-475-7700; 187 E Houston St at Orchard St; meals $4-7; ☺ 24hr) You'll feel like you've stepped into Istanbul here, where club kids, local workers and folks working the graveyard shift gather for excellent stuffed grape leaves, kabobs, bean and leek stews and fresh salads.

'Inoteca (Map pp132-3; ☎ 212-614-0473; 98 Rivington at Ludlow St; mains $9-13; ☺ brunch Sat & Sun, lunch & dinner daily) Tuck yourself into one of the chunky square tables of this airy, dark wood–paneled corner haven and choose various pressed sandwiches and small plates, from the signature truffled egg toast (with egg, truffles and fontina cheese) to the beet-orange-mint salad. Best of all is the list of 200 wines, 25 of them available by the glass.

Paladar (Map pp132-3; ☎ 212-473-3535; 161 Ludlow St at Stanton St; mains $12-18; ☺ brunch Sat & Sun, dinner daily) Chef Aaron Sanchez combines tropical flavors in revolutionary ways for the diners squeezed in under the dark pressed-tin ceiling and sconced lighting. Enjoy fat chicken empanadas, halibut bathed in an orange vinaigrette or hangar steak (a tender cut of beef) rubbed with Latin-American *adobo* spices.

WD-50 (Map pp132-3; ☎ 212-477-2900; 50 Clinton St at Stanton St; mains $24-28; ☺ dinner Mon-Sat) Chef-owner Wylie Dufresne draws VIPs and wannabes alike to his space, where bamboo floors, a fireplace and exposed beams all highlight the provocative fare at this hot spot: oysters with apples, olives and pistachios; skate served with preserved-lemon gnocchi and smoked scallions, for example.

EAST VILLAGE

SEA (Map pp132-3; ☎ 212-228-5505; 75 Second Ave btwn 4th & 5th Sts; mains $6-11; ☺ lunch & dinner) SEA (South East Asian) is a cheap, mobbed maker of outstanding Thai grub. It's loud and there's always a wait, but you'll be glad you stuck it out when one of your slim hottie waiters loads you up with yummy plates of *phat Thai*, green curry and sweet Thai iced teas.

Dawgs on Park (Map pp132-3; ☎ 212-598-0667; 178 E 7th St between Aves A & B; meals $4; ☺ lunch & dinner) This hot-dog café has a counter that looks out onto Tompkins Sq Park, photos of local canines (who can often be found lounging on the floor of the place), and scrumptious dogs topped with corn salsa, vegan bean chili or traditional mustard and kraut. Wieners are available in beef, turkey or bean curd.

Counter (Map pp132-3; ☎ 212-982-5870; 105 First Ave btwn 6th & 7th Sts; mains $9-14; ☺ lunch & dinner Tue-Sat) Get po'boys, burgers, jambalaya and more exotic fare sans the meat at this lovely wine-and-snack spot, where you can also sit at the airy bar in the center of the space and order one of several organic wines with just an elegant plate of cashew-kalamata pâté.

Second Ave Deli (Map pp132-3; ☎ 212-677-0606; 156 Second Ave btwn 9th & 10th Sts; mains $7-10; ☺ lunch & dinner daily, to 3am Fri & Sat) This is one of the last great Jewish delis of New York. Head here for matzo-ball soup, garlicky dills,

---

THE AUTHOR'S CHOICE

Teany (Map pp132-3; ☎ 212-475-9190; 90 Rivington St btwn Ludlow & Orchard Sts; meals $6-12; ☺ 9am-12:30am) A teeny-tiny café, Teany sits tucked below street level on a quietly hip block of the LES. It may be co-owned by famously vegan pop star Moby, but its vibe is totally low key and welcoming. Best of all, its book-size menu boasts some delicious light (and animal-free) fare, such as muffins, tea sandwiches (like cucumber or peanut butter with chocolate spread), as well as about 100 teas ranging from the typical (spearmint, Irish breakfast) to the sublimely exotic (green sea anemone, white peony). It's a wonderful spot to while away a couple of hours on a rainy afternoon.

tangy slaw, and hot pastrami and turkey sandwiches built so high you won't be able to fit your mouth around them.

Prune (Map pp132-3; ☎ 212-677-6221; 54 E 1st St btwn First & Second Ave; mains $18-23; ☺ lunch & dinner daily, brunch Sat & Sun) Rich meals are the order of the day here, as you'll find hearty offerings including roast suckling pig, rich sweetbreads and sausage-studded concoctions. It's always crowded – especially for Sunday brunch, when late sleepers rouse themselves for top-notch bloody Marys (in nearly 10 varieties), lox and oysters.

WEST (GREENWICH) VILLAGE

Manna Bento (Map pp132-3; ☎ 212-473-6162; 289 Mercer St btwn Waverly Pl & Eighth St; meals $5-8; ☺ lunch & dinner Mon-Sat) Blink and you might miss this obscure gem, known almost exclusively by NYU students who sit solo, hunched over plates of bargain, home-style Korean food such as vegetables, spicy bean curd, glass noodles and kimchi served over white rice.

Delicia (Map pp132-3; ☎ 212-242-2002; 322 W 11th St btwn Greenwich & Washington Sts; mains $12-15; ☺ dinner Tue-Sat) Step below street level into this cozy, homey room of Brazilian cooking, where service is slow enough to let you savor the butternut squash baked with shrimp and cilantro in coconut milk, chicken roasted in passion-fruit juice or the vegetarian *feijoada*, a classic black-bean stew with fresh veggies and yucca.

Florent (Map pp132-3; ☎ 212-989-5779; 69 Gansevoort St btwn Greenwich & Washington Sts; meals $9-13; ☺ 9am-5am Mon-Wed, 24hr Fri-Sun) This all-night hang colonized the Meatpacking District many moons ago. It's a bustling spot that draws clubbers at all hours with its hangar steak, burgers and breakfast selections, as well as its praiseworthy blood sausage or pork chops.

Babbo (Map pp132-3; ☎ 212-777-0303; 110 Waverly Pl at MacDougal St; mains $25-30; ☺ dinner) Chef celeb Mario Batali still reigns here with sublime options including beef-cheek ravioli, gnocchi with oxtail and lamb's-tongue salad. Reviews are consistently raving, the quaint dining room always packed, so reserve very early.

CHELSEA, UNION SQUARE, FLATIRON & GRAMERCY PARK

F&B (Map pp140-1; ☎ 646-486-4441; 269 W 23rd St btwn Seventh & Eighth Aves; meals $3-6; ☺ lunch & dinner) This little, bright blue and white cubicle,

with stool seating around its perimeter, offers hot dogs of beef, pork, chicken, salmon or bean curd with 10 types of topping, from hummus and grated carrots to feta cheese and roasted peppers. Or choose from Swedish meatballs, salads, apple beignets and a range of bottled beers.

Tia Pol (Map pp140-1; ☎ 212-675-8805; 205 Tenth Ave; tapas $6-10; ☺ dinner) A tucked-away nook with a cool but earthy vibe, the place packs in in-the-know folks for its excellent range of authentic tapas, salads and Spanish wines.

Madras Mahal (Map pp140-1; ☎ 212-684-4010; 104 Lexington Ave btwn 27th & 28th St; mains $11-14; ☺ lunch & dinner) It's kosher Indian. Enjoy South Indian dosas plus reasonably priced North Indian dishes of *saag panir* (spinach and cheese) or fried samosas.

Tabla (Map pp140-1; ☎ 212-889-0667; 11 Madison Ave at 25th St; prix fixe $57-88; ☺ lunch Mon-Fri, dinner daily) Everything created by the Goa-raised and France-trained chef Floyd Cardoz sparkles with intelligence and love, from lobster and haricot verts in coconut curry to a wild mushroom kabob with braised fennel, all served with fruity, flowery flourishes. For a breezier, hipper experience, stick to the more casual Bread Bar on the ground floor, where food is straight-up Indian (tandoori meats, curries, buttery naan) and just as exquisite.

MIDTOWN

Manganaro's (Map pp140-1; ☎ 212-947-7325; 492 Ninth Ave at 37th St; meals $6-9; ☺ lunch Mon-Sat) Fresh mozzarella and prosciutto sandwiches, penne with vodka sauce and meatball parm heroes (a sandwich on a long, thick roll) are among the best in the city at this family-owned gourmet food shop.

Joe Allen (Map pp140-1; ☎ 212-581-6464; 326 W 46th St; mains $15-20) Joe does simple food with flair, like a gigantic chicken salad or pan-roasted sole. The brick walls of the dining room reverberate loudly when it's crowded, which is almost every night. It's impossible to get a table for dinner without a reservation unless you wait until the theater starts at 8pm.

Kang Suh (Map pp140-1; ☎ 212-564-6845; 1250 Broadway at 32nd St; mains $10-15; ☺ 24hr) This Koreatown BBQ joint has a few things that set it apart from the rest: for one, you do your own cooking over piles of hot coals that your server brings to you by the bucket.

Plus, it's got karaoke to make it a rowdy draw for party-lovin' young folk. Third, it's open all night.

Time Warner Center (Map pp146-7; 59th St at Eighth Ave; www.shopsatcolumbuscircle.com) The glitzy shopping towers that loom over Central Park at Columbus Circle are home not to one, but to seven high-end restaurants. Among the many top offerings:

Masa (212-823-9800; tasting menu per person from $300) A Japanese rich-person's lair with a celebrity following that rivals Nobu.

Per Se (212-823-9335; prix fixe $125-150) An over-the-top display of French-infused goodness from chef Tom Keller.

UPPER WEST SIDE & MORNINGSIDE HEIGHTS

Saigon Grill (Map pp146-7; 212-875-9072; 620 Amsterdam Ave at 90th St; mains $6-12; lunch & dinner) Locals really pack this place – and call for incessant takeout orders – for traditional noodle, curry and rice dishes. For dessert, don't miss grandma's sweet rice dumplings, glutinous little balls stuffed with sugary peanut butter.

Josie's (Amsterdam Ave Map pp146-7; 212-769-1212; 300 Amsterdam Ave at 74th St; mains $10-16; lunch & dinner; Third Ave 212-490-1558; 565 Third Ave at 37th St; lunch & dinner) The shtick here is dairy-free. There are plenty of treats for meat eaters (roasted chicken breast, burgers) and veggies alike (roasted yams, beets, greens and tempeh; vegetarian meatloaf), and all ingredients are farm-fresh and organic. The only things absent are cheese and milk (soy and rice milk stand in for coffee).

Tomo (Map pp146-7; 212-665-2916; 2850 Broadway at 111th St; meals $13-17; lunch & dinner) Fresh, reasonably priced sushi is a big draw for students and scores of locals. But equally appealing are the warming options of chicken *katsu* (thinly sliced chicken), noodle bowls, tempura, *bento* boxes (boxes containing various dishes in separate compartments) and salmon teriyaki. Vegetarians love the *futomaki* (vegetarian maki rolls) and shiitake-cucumber hand rolls.

'Cesca (Map pp146-7; 212-787-6300; 164 W 75th St btwn Columbus & Amsterdam Aves; mains $17-26; dinner) It wasn't enough for Tom Valenti to reign in the '80s, where he owns the fabulous French **Ouest** (212-580-8700; 2315 Broadway), so he opened a place in the '70s,

too, with a focus on classy Italian food. The handsome, comforting place is the setting for mackerel, chicken ragout, wild game and ravioli classics, as well as clever antipasto options.

UPPER EAST SIDE

Lexington Candy Shop (Map pp146-7; 212-288-0057; 1226 Lexington Ave at E 83rd St; meals $5-10; breakfast, lunch & dinner) At this old-fashioned soda shop, school kids suck up primo egg creams and malteds while neighborhood folks nurse a coffee or a famed lime rickey. Best of all, this place sells burgers and other classic diner fare at reasonable prices in one of the city's most expensive neighborhoods.

Beyoglu (Map pp146-7; 212-650-0850; 1431 Third Ave at 81st St; mains $11-15; lunch & dinner) A charismatic, Turkish loungey space, this is where you'll find excellent yogurt soup, doner kabobs and feta-flecked salads. Get in early for your pick of a good table; it's within strolling distance of the Met, making for a tasteful way to end an artistic afternoon.

Candle Cafe (Map pp146-7; 212-472-0970; 1307 Third Ave btwn 74th & 75th Sts; mains $12-15; lunch & dinner) In a 'hood where quality veggie selections are hard to come by, Candle is a light at the end of a carnivorous cave. Offerings range from the most simplistic spreads of greens, roots, grains and soy-based protein to the more complex concoctions, such as the beloved paradise casserole – a feast of layered sweet potatoes, black beans and millet topped with mushroom gravy.

Daniel (Map pp146-7; 212-288-0033; 60 E 65th St btwn Madison & Park Aves; prix fixe $88; dinner) The number-one draw here is celebrity chef Daniel Boulud and his cult of personality. Amid elaborate floral arrangements and wide-eyed foodies are plates of peeky toecrab and celery-root salad, foie gras terrine with gala apples and black truffle-crusted lobster – and that's just for first course.

HARLEM

Charles' Southern Style Kitchen (212-926-4313; 2839 Frederick Douglass Blvd/Eighth Ave btwn 151st & 152nd Sts; mains $5-7; lunch & dinner) You'll find some of the best fried chicken in Harlem – and that's saying something. You also can't go wrong with the salmon cakes and the macaroni and cheese, both part of the rotating daily special lineup at this tiny takeout joint.

Strictly Roots (Map pp146-7; ☎ 212-864-8699; 2058 Adam Clayton Powell Jr Blvd btwn 122nd & 123rd Sts; mains $6-9; ☻ lunch & dinner) This Rastafarian-loved haven promises to serve 'nothing that crawls, walks, swims or flies.' The cafeteria-style spot offers a rotating menu of fried plantains, faux-beef curry, stews and stir-fried veggies, along with fresh juices and thick smoothies.

Sugar Hill Bistro (Map pp146-7; ☎ 212-491-5505; 458 145th St btwn Amsterdam & Convent Aves; mains $19-26; ☻ brunch Sat & Sun, dinner daily) Welcome to the Harlem Renaissance. Within the walls of this landmark, two-story Victorian brownstone, you'll find artworks by notable African American artists and live jazz on weekend nights. Lovely dishes include chicken and dumplings, Louisiana-style jambalaya, herb-crusted lamb chops, and spaghetti with black-Angus meatballs.

Drinking

Watering holes come in many forms in this city: sleek lounges, cozy pubs and straight-up alcoholic dives. But note that, thanks to city law, there is no smoking allowed. Here's a highly selective sampling of all.

DOWNTOWN

Rise (Map pp132-3; ☎ 212-344-0800; Ritz-Carlton New York, 2 West St at Battery Pl) Even $13 martinis won't make you think twice about hanging here, where the sleek, high-up lounge affords spectacular views of sunsets over the Hudson.

Pravda (Map pp132-3; ☎ 212-226-4944; 281 Lafayette St btwn Prince & Houston Sts) A mock Eastern European speakeasy, its two-page vodka list includes Canada's Inferno Pepper, a home-grown Rain Organic and a slew of specialty martinis.

Chibi's Bar (Map pp132-3; ☎ 212-274-0025; 238 Mott St btwn Prince & Spring St) This tiny, romantic sake bar works its magic through the smooth sounds of jazz and the dangerously delicious flavors of specialty sakes and saketinis. The best part is the host, Chibi, a sweet little bulldog.

Bar Veloce (Map pp132-3; ☎ 212-260-3200; 175 Second Ave btwn 11th & 12th Sts) A narrow, candle-lit wine bar, this refreshingly sophisticated spot serves a mix of uptown and downtown patrons, all thirsting for the same quality vino, Italian tapas and polite bartenders.

Winnie's (Map pp132-3; ☎ 212-732-2384; 104 Bayard St btwn Baxter & Mulberry Sts) Performing drunk and embarrassing karaoke at this Chinatown dive is a rite of passage for New Yorkers. The place is tiny and always packed, the disgustingly named cocktails (such as the Abortion, a mixture of Sambuca and Baileys) are potent, and the weird karaoke videos, flashed behind you on a movie screen, are hopelessly stuck in the '80s.

Schiller's Liquor Bar (Map pp132-3; ☎ 212-260-4555; 131 Rivington St at Norfolk St) In this gleaming oasis on an otherwise gritty corner the upbeat, bohemian-upscale feel is just as lovely as its cocktails.

DBA (Map pp132-3; ☎ 212-475-5097; 41 First Ave btwn 2nd & 3rd Sts) A dark and bare-bones pub, the draw here is the massive menu, hand-scrawled on a big chalkboard, announcing about 125 beers, 130 single-malt scotches and 50 tequilas.

Hudson Bar & Books (Map pp132-3; ☎ 212-229-2642; 636 Hudson St btwn Horatio & Jane Sts) A recreation of a men's club, this is where you'll find a country-library feel, a James Bond drink theme, and plenty of chess games to choose from.

Glass (Map pp140-1; ☎ 212-904-1580; 287 Tenth Ave btwn 26th & 27th Sts) Brought to you by the owners of Bottino, a small wine bar in the 'hood, this lounge is a work of art, filled with white benches, egg-shaped seats and a romantic red glow.

Old Town Bar & Grill (Map pp140-1; ☎ 212-529-6732; 45 E 18th St btwn Broadway & Park Ave) A legendary tavern famous for its hard-drinking, local tenor, Old Town's been on the block since 1892.

MIDTOWN & UPTOWN

Campbell Apartment Grill (Map pp140-1; ☎ 212-953-0409; 15 Vanderbilt Ave at 43rd St) Housed on the balcony within Grand Central Station, this used to be the apartment of a landed railroad magnate and has the velvet, mahogany and murals to prove it. Cigars are welcome, but sneakers and jeans are not.

Bemelman's Bar Grill (Map pp146-7; ☎ 212-570-7109; the Carlyle, 35 E 76th St at Madison Ave) Waiters wear white jackets, a baby grand piano is always being played and Ludwig Bemelman's *Madeleine* murals surround you. It's a classic spot for a serious cocktail.

Evelyn Lounge (Map pp146-7; ☎ 212-724-5145; 380 Columbus Ave at 78th St) A roomy, cellar-level space with plenty of couches, Evelyn includes a classy cigar lounge and a martini list with more options than the dinner menu. A laid-back crowd frequents this spot during the week but is shoved aside by hobnobbing students on the weekend.

Entertainment

You should already know that you'll find every type of entertainment under the sun in this town – not only Broadway shows and jazz concerts. *Time Out New York* magazine is the best guide to the city's nightlife. High culture is well covered in the Sunday and Friday editions of the *New York Times* and *New Yorker*.

THEATER

In general, 'Broadway' productions are staged in the lavish, early 20th-century theaters surrounding Times Square. You'll choose your theater based on its production, but all are pretty glamorous in an old-fashioned way. Evening performances begin at 8pm.

'Off Broadway' simply refers to shows performed in smaller spaces (200 seats or fewer), which is why you'll find many located just around the corner from Broadway venues, as well as elsewhere in town. 'Off-off Broadway' events include readings, experimental and cutting-edge performances and improvisations held in spaces with fewer than 100 seats. Some of the world's best theater happens in these more intimate venues: recent notable productions have included Eve Ensler's *The Vagina Monologues*, the Pulitzer Prize–winning *Wit* and the airborne, trippy *De La Guarda*. Some prominent spots include the following.

Choose from current shows by checking print publications (above), or at a website like **Theater Mania** (www.theatermania.com).

Purchase tickets through the following:

Telecharge (☎ 212-239-6200; www.telecharge.com)

Ticketmaster (☎ 212-307-7171; www.ticketmaster.com)

TKTS Ticket Booths (www.tkts.com; Midtown Map pp140-1; 47th St at Broadway; ⏱ 10am-8pm Mon-Fri, from 11am Sun; Downtown Map pp132-3; Front St at John St, South St Seaport, ⏱ 11am-6pm) Same-day tickets to Broadway and off-Broadway musicals at up to 75% off regular prices.

NIGHTCLUBS

Like a chameleon, the New York club scene is constantly changing. That's partly because New York partiers get bored easily, but also

because club promoters have found themselves in an unending battle with the city over drug users, dealers and myriad other violations. So call before showing up.

Cielo (Map pp132-3; ☎ 212-645-5700; 18 Little West 12th St btwn Ninth Ave & Washington St; cover $10) Known for its intimate space and free or low-cost parties, this Meatpacking District space packs in a fashionable, multi-culti crowd for its blend of tribal, Latin-spiced house and soulful grooves.

Crobar (Map pp140-1; ☎ 212-629-9000; 530 W 28th St btwn Tenth & Eleventh Aves; cover $25) The newest megaclub, this massive venue, a local sibling of Crobars in Miami and Chicago, caters to a largely suburban crowd on weekends, but holds plenty of queer-tinged bashes with super DJs including Victor Calderone.

Avalon (Map pp140-1; ☎ 212-807-7780; 660 Sixth Ave at 20th St; cover $25) The parties housed at this labyrinthine church space are attracting lots of attention for the prog-house, techno and trance DJs who spin here, mainly on Saturdays. Sunday nights are big gay affairs.

Deep (Map pp140-1; ☎ 212-229-2000; 16 W 22nd St btwn Fifth & Sixth Aves; cover $12-25) This house and hip-hop venue isn't perhaps the trendiest spot, but it does house the monthly 718 Sessions, a riot of old-school dancing to deep, soulful house from DJ Danny Krivit. House parties rage on Fridays with DJ Marc Anthony.

LIVE MUSIC

Though it's no Austin or Seattle, NYC does have an impressive indie music scene, and has given rise to favorites including the Strokes, Rufus Wainwright, Scissor Sisters and Babe the Blue Ox in the past few years. More traditional sounds, of course, are constants, as the slew of jazz clubs and classical venues are rock solids here.

Madison Square Garden (Map pp140-1; ☎ 212-465-5800; www.thegarden.com; Seventh Ave, btwn W 31st & W 33rd Sts) For big celebs, the place drawing stadium-sized crowds.

Radio City Music Hall (Map pp140-1; ☎ 212-247-4777; Sixth Ave at W 51st St) In the middle of Midtown, the architecturally grand concert hall, built in 1932, hosts the likes of kd lang, Neil Young, Mary J Blige, Prince and the Gipsy Kings.

Beacon Theater (Map pp146-7; ☎ 212-496-7070; 2124 Broadway btwn 74th & 75th Sts) This Upper West Side venue has a pretty cool vibe for such a large, mainstream space. It hosts big acts – Moby, the Indigo Girls – for folks who want to see shows in a more intimate environment than that of a big concert arena.

Jazz at Lincoln Center's Frederick P Rose Hall (Map pp146-7; ☎ 212-258-9800; www.jazzatlincolncenter.com; Broadway at 60th St, Columbus Circle) Attached to the Time Warner Center in Midtown, this relatively new venue has Wynton Marsalis as its creative director, three venues that vary in size, and a truly impressive roster.

Southpaw (☎ 718-230-0236; 125 Fifth Ave btwn Sterling & St John's Pl, Park Slope, Brooklyn) The innovative design here lets you see the stage well from wherever you're sitting, and the top-notch sound system is perfect for piping the tunes of local rock, funk and world musicians.

Joe's Pub (Map pp132-3; ☎ 212-539-8770; the Public Theater, 425 Lafayette St btwn Astor Pl & E 4th St) Part cabaret theatre, part rock and new-indie venue, this lovely supper club has hosted the likes of Toshi Reagon, Jonatha Brooke and Diamanda Galas.

CBGB (Map pp132-3; ☎ 212-982-4052; 315 Bowery btwn E 1st & 2nd Sts) This dark little legendary den is still going strong after nearly three decades. The name stands for 'Country, Bluegrass and Blues,' but since the mid-'70s, the place has heard more rock than anything else. The recent addition of the Downstairs Lounge doles out quality jazz, readings and other such diversions.

SOB's (Map pp132-3; ☎ 212-243-4940; 204 Varick St) This wonderful world-music club specializes in Brazilian, Afro-Cuban and other Latin sounds.

Village Vanguard (Map pp132-3; ☎ 212-255-4037; 178 Seventh Ave at W 11th St) This basement-level venue in the West Village may be the world's most prestigious jazz club, as it has hosted literally every major star of the past 50 years.

CINEMAS

There are good mainstream cinemas around – with stadium seating and massive screens – including the **E-Walk Theater** (247 W 42nd St) and the **AMC Empire 25** (234 W 42nd St). New Yorkers take film seriously, and new-release films (tickets around $10) sell out early Friday and Saturday nights. To save the wait, you can call ☎ 212-777-3456 and prepay ($1.50 extra) for a ticket.

Landmark Sunshine Cinema (Map pp132-3; ☎ 212-358-7709; 143 E Houston St) Housed in a former Yiddish theater, Landmark shows first-run indies.

Brooklyn Academy of Music Rose Cinemas (☎ 718-777-FILM; 30 Lafayette Ave) In Brooklyn, BAM is comfortable as well as popular for its new-release indies and special festival screenings.

Film Forum (Map pp132-3; ☎ 212-727-8110; 209 W Houston St) Small and beloved, it screens revivals, classics and documentaries.

Walter Reade Theater (Map pp146-7; ☎ 212-875-5600; 70 Lincoln Center Plaza) Independent films as well as career retrospectives are shown at the Lincoln Center's Walter Reade Theater, which also hosts the New York Film Festival every September.

Symphony Space (Map pp146-7; ☎ 212-864-5400; Broadway at 95th St) This recently renovated complex provides similar programming to the Walter Reade, along with theater and literature events.

CLASSICAL MUSIC & OPERA

From piano soloists to full symphonies, New York is king of the hill.

Carnegie Hall (Map pp140-1; ☎ 212-247-7800; www.carnegiehall.org; 154 W 57th St at Seventh Ave) Since 1891, the historic performance hall has hosted the likes of Tchaikovsky, Mahler and Prokofiev. Today it hosts visiting philharmonics, the New York Pops orchestra and various world-music performers, including Cesaria Evora and Sweet Honey in the Rock.

Lincoln Center (Map pp146-7; ☎ 212-875-5000; www.newyorkphilharmonic.org; Lincoln Center Plaza, Broadway at W 64th St) At Avery Fisher Hall, the showplace of the New York Philharmonic, expect the highest standards here of the classic repertoire that continues to define it. Its **Alice Tully Hall** (☎ 212-721-6500), meanwhile, is home to the American Symphony Orchestra and the Little Orchestra Society.

Town Hall (Map pp140-1; ☎ 212-840-2824; www.the-townhall-nyc.org; 123 W 43rd St at Sixth Ave) Classical ensembles regularly play this landmark venue, as do folk, jazz and blues artists – and even Garrison Keillor, when he brings his radio show to town.

Metropolitan Opera House (Map pp146-7; ☎ 212-362-6000; www.metopera.org; Lincoln Center, W 64th St at Amsterdam Ave) New York's premier Metropolitan Opera Company offers a spectacular mixture of classics and premieres, some featuring big stars as Jessye Norman and Plácido Domingo. The season runs from September to April.

New York State Theater (Map pp146-7; ☎ 212-870-5630; www.nycopera.com; Lincoln Center, Broadway at 65th St) This is the home of the New York City Opera, a more daring and lower-cost company that performs new works, neglected operas and revitalized old standards in the Philip Johnson-designed space.

DANCE & BALLET
New York is home to more than half a dozen world-famous dance companies, plus it's home to plenty of avant-garde, lesser-known experimenters.

The **New York City Ballet** (☎ 212-870-5570) performs in winter at the New York State Theater (see above).

American Ballet Theater (Map pp146-7; ☎ 212-875-5766; Lincoln Center) In spring the American Ballet Theater takes over at the Metropolitan Opera House for a short season.

City Center (Map pp140-1; ☎ 212-581-1212; 131 W 55th St btwn Sixth & Seventh Aves) Home to the Alvin Ailey American Dance Theater every December, and it also hosts visiting foreign companies.

Joyce Theater (Map pp140-1; ☎ 212-242-0800; 175 Eighth Ave at 19th St) A popular, offbeat dance venue that's located in a renovated Chelsea cinema.

Brooklyn Academy of Music (BAM; ☎ 718-636-4100; 30 Lafayette Ave) Also boasting avant-garde dance programming is BAM, in Fort Greene, Brooklyn.

COMEDY
See gig guides for comedy nights and performances at many bars, lounges and clubs. For guaranteed laughs, go to one of the big-name stand-up comedy clubs. With cover charges and two-drink minimums, these clubs can make for an expensive night.

Caroline's on Broadway (Map pp140-1; ☎ 212-757-4100; 1626 Broadway) It's the best-known place in the city, and host to the biggest names on the circuit.

Stand-Up New York (Map pp146-7; ☎ 212-595-0850; 236 W 78th St; tickets $5-12) This spot features funny theme nights, plus gets surprise appearances from star comedians.

Gotham Comedy Club (Map pp140-1; ☎ 212-367-9000; 34 W 22nd St) You'll find more innovative

acts, plus a monthly gay-comedy show, at Gotham.

Upright Citizens Brigade Theatre (Map pp140-1; 307 W 26th St) Wacky, edgy and hysterical is the name of UCB's game.

SPORTS
Baseball fans should hightail it to see the **New York Mets** (☎ 718-507-8499; www.mets.com) playing at the windswept Shea Stadium in Flushing Meadows, Queens. The **New York Yankees** (☎ 718-293-6000; www.yankees.com) throw ball at Yankee Stadium in the Bronx, while minor-league action includes that of the **Staten Island Yankees** (☎ 718-720-9200; www.siyanks.com) or **Brooklyn Cyclones** (☎ 718-449-8497; www.brooklyncyclones.com).

For basketball, you can get courtside with the NBA's **New York Knicks** (☎ 212-465-6741; www.nba.com/knicks) at Madison Sq Garden, though when the team is doing well (not often), seats are more than scarce. The women's WNBA league **New York Liberty** (☎ 212-465-6741; www.wnba.com/liberty) is also based at Madison Square Garden.

New York City's NFL (pro football) teams, the **Giants** (☎ 201-935-8222) and **Jets** (☎ 516-560-8200), share the Giants Stadium in Rutherford's Meadowlands complex.

Shopping
No matter what you want to purchase, whether it be cool clothing, fierce shoes, cutting-edge electronics, gourmet foods, out-of-print books, music and everything in between New York's got it, either in its department stores, small boutiques, specialty markets or from a vendor set up right on the street.

The best plan of attack is to take a look at the city's shopping areas.

DOWNTOWN
Lower Manhattan is where you'll find across-the-board bargains. Downtown's coolest offerings are in Soho's loft stores. The East Village and the Lower East Side have funky shops selling music, gifts and clothing for a younger crowd. Count on the streets of Chinatown for knock-off designer handbags and watches.

Century 21 (Map pp132-3; ☎ 212-227-9092; 22 Cortland St at Church St) Truly beloved for clothing, shoes and housewares from top designers for at least half off normal retail.

J&R Music & Computer World (Map pp132-3; ☎ 212-238-9000; 15-23 Park Row) For all electronics, especially computers, hit J&R, which takes up a full city block.

Toys in Babeland (Map pp132-3; www.babeland. com; Lower East Side ☎ 212-375-1701; 94 Rivington St; Soho ☎ 212-966-2120; 43 Mercer St btwn Broome & Grand Sts) A quirky star of the LES is a women-run sex-toy shop that takes a warm, hands-on-museum approach to selling potentially embarrassing items from hot-pink dildos to vanilla-flavored lube.

The West Village has an eclectic mix of antiques and high-end fashions including the following:

Jeffrey New York (Map pp140-1; 449 W 14th St, Meatpacking District) Awesome.

Marc Jacobs (Map pp132-3; 385, 403 & 405 Bleecker St) The local fashion guru pulls in crowds of fans who love his old-fashioned-chic shoes, dresses and jackets.

MIDTOWN & UPTOWN

Midtown's Fifth Ave and the Upper East Side's Madison Ave have the famous high-end fashion and clothing by international designers. Times Square has many supersize stores, though they're all chains. Chelsea's markets are a popular draw for locals.

Macy's (Map pp140-1; ☎ 212-695-4400; 151 W 34th St) This grand-dame department store has long made Midtown's Herald Square one of the city's busiest shopping zones.

Barney's New York (Map pp146-7; ☎ 212-826-8900; 660 Madison Ave) Label-whore emporium.

Bloomingdale's (Map pp146-7; 504 Broadway). New Midtown outpost.

Jimmy Choo (Map pp140-1; ☎ 212-593-0800; 645 Fifth Ave at 51st St) Shoes to die for.

Chelsea Market (Map pp140-1; www.chelseamar ket.com; 75 Ninth Ave btwn 15th & 16th St) Food fans should head to this 800ft-long gourmet market bursting with some of the freshest eats in town.

Chelsea Flea Market (Annex Antiques Fair & Flea Market; Map pp140-1; Sixth Ave btwn 24th & 26th Sts; ☉ dawn-dusk Sat & Sun). Antiques fans should arrive bright and early to this amazing flea market.

BROOKLYN

Other great strips for antiques, housewares and fashions from local designers can be found in Brooklyn, along Smith St and Atlantic Ave in Boerum Hill and on Fifth Ave in Park Slope.

Getting There & Away

AIR

Three major airports serve New York City. The biggest is the **John F Kennedy International Airport** (☎ 718-244-4444; www.panynj.gov/aviation /jfkframe), in the borough of Queens about 15 miles from midtown Manhattan. Northwest of there, but also in Queens, is **La Guardia Airport** (☎ 718-533-3400; www.panynj.gov/aviation /lgaframe), which is 8 miles from midtown. **Newark International Airport** (☎ 973-961-6000; www.panynj.gov/aviation/ewrframe), across the Hudson River in Newark, NJ, is about 16 miles from midtown. Flights into Newark tend to be cheapest. Also note that, while all seasons here are pretty high, the highest season in New York runs from mid-June to mid-September (summer), and one week before and after Christmas. February, March and October through Thanksgiving (the fourth Thursday in November) serve as shoulder seasons, when prices drop slightly. Online booking websites (see p1164) will have the best rates; search 'NYC,' rather than a specific airport, which will allow most sites to search all three spots at once.

BUS

For all suburban and long-distance bus trips, you'll leave and depart from the **Port Authority Bus Terminal** (Map pp140-1; ☎ 212-564-8484; 41st St at Eighth Ave). Though Port Authority has much improved in recent years, it's likely you'll still be hassled by panhandlers looking for handouts or shady types offering to carry bags for tips.

Greyhound (☎ 800-231-2222; www.greyhound.com) links New York with major cities across the country. **Peter Pan Trailways** (☎ 800-343-9999; www.peterpan-bus.com) runs buses to the nearest major cities, including a daily express to Boston. **Short Line** (☎ 212-736-4700; www.short linebus.com) runs numerous buses to towns in northern New Jersey and upstate New York, while **New Jersey Transit** buses (☎ 973-762-5100; www.njtransit.state.nj.us) serves all of New Jersey, with direct service to/from Atlantic City for about $20 one way.

Undoubtedly the sweetest deal from and to Boston, however, is with the reliable folks of **Fung Wah** (Map pp132-3; ☎ 212-925-8889; www .fungwahbus.com; 139 Canal St at Bowery), with 10 departures a day between 7am and 10pm for as little as $10 one way for the four-hour trip. But be sure to book ahead of time;

what used to be a little-known service used only by Chinese passengers and college students is now a booming business.

CAR & MOTORCYCLE

See p1175 for information about vehicle rentals. But note that renting a car in the city is mighty expensive, will start at about $60 a day for a midsize car – and that's before extra charges like the 13.25% tax and various insurance costs. One trick is to leave the city altogether – at least Manhattan – via mass transit to rent over the border, so to speak, as rates in the outer boroughs and in New Jersey tend to be much cheaper.

For day trips or short side trips, another interesting and trendy option is **Zipcar** (www .zipcar.com). Geared mostly to locals who might need a car for errands or a flashy hot date, Zipcar is a car-sharing service that's available, on-demand and 24/7, by the hour or the day. The price includes gas, insurance, designated parking and access to one of the cute little VW Bugs that are parked all over the city. Rates are $8.50 an hour or $65 per day. Eventually, you must become an approved member and Zipcard holder, but you're entitled to a 60-day trial run.

TRAIN

Penn Station (Map pp140-1; 33rd St btwn Seventh & Eighth Aves), is the departure point for all **Amtrak** (☎ 800-872-7245; www.amtrak.com) trains, including the *Metroliner* (with reserved seats) and, hopefully soon, Acela Express service (it was suspended indefinitely at press time) to Princeton, NJ, and Washington, DC. All fares vary based on the day of the week and the time you want to travel. Also arriving into Penn Station – as well as points in Brooklyn and Queens – is the **Long Island Rail Road** (☎ 718-217-5477; www.mta .nyc.ny.us/lirr), which serves several hundred thousand commuters each day. **New Jersey Transit** (☎ 973-762-5100; www.njtransit.com) also operates trains from Penn Station, with service to the suburbs and the Jersey Shore. Another option for getting into New Jersey, but strictly points north such as Hoboken and Newark, is the **New Jersey PATH** (☎ 800-234-7284; www.pathrail.com), which runs trains on a separate-fare system ($2) along the length of Sixth Ave, with stops at 34th, 23rd, 14th, 9th and Christopher Sts, and the reopened World Trade Center station.

The only train line that still departs from Grand Central Terminal, Park Ave at 42nd St, is the **Metro-North Railroad** (☎ 212-532-4900; www .mnr.org), which serves the northern city suburbs, Connecticut and the Hudson Valley.

Getting Around
TO/FROM THE AIRPORT

All major airports have onsite car-rental agencies. It's a hassle to drive into NYC, though, so those who can afford it take a taxi or car service, shelling out the $45 taxi flat rate (plus toll and tip) from JFK and a metered fare of about $25 to Midtown from La Guardia, just to sit in traffic rather than deal with public transit. That's dumb, though, because from JFK you have the new (as of 2003) and pretty cool AirTrain, which connects all terminals with subway and Long Island Rail Road Service into the city for $5. To get into Manhattan, take the AirTrain to Jamaica Station and switch to the LIRR, which has trains to Penn Station about every 10 minutes ($5 one way; purchase tickets outside of the AirTrain station); you can save $3 by getting on the subway, though it's slower. A reliable (but not super-speedy) option from La Guardia (LGA) is the M60 bus, which heads into Manhattan across 125th St in Harlem and makes stops on Broadway to the Upper West Side.

Both JFK and LGA are served by shuttles; such companies include the **New York Airport Service Express Bus** (☎ 718-875-8200; www .nyairportservice.com; one way JFK/LGA $15/12), which leaves every 15 minutes for Port Authority, Penn Station and Grand Central Station; and **Super Shuttle Manhattan** (☎ 800-258-3826; www.supershuttle.com; $13-22 one way), which picks up you and others anywhere, on demand, with a reservation.

From Newark, an AirTrain links all terminals to a New Jersey Transit train station; from there, take the commuter rail into Penn Station ($5 one way). Taxis will cost about $45 (plus toll and tip) to Midtown, or take the Newark Liberty Express Bus to various Manhattan stops (every 15 minutes, $13 to $15 one way).

CAR & MOTORCYCLE

The worst part about driving in New York is getting in and out of the city – joining the masses as they try to squeeze through tunnels and over bridges to traverse the various waterways that surround Manhattan. Besides that, getting around within the city isn't difficult, as most of Manhattan (with the exception of the Village) is laid out in a neat grid, and traffic congestion prevents you from having to move along too swiftly if you're feeling tentative. Just be aware of local laws, such as the fact that you can't make a right on red (like you can in the rest of the state) and also the fact that every other street is one way, which can send an inexperienced driver into a series of frustrating circles. Also, parking in Manhattan is difficult or very expensive. Street parking is hard to come by (and the signs about rules will leave you in a state of confusion), while parking garages charge an average of $40 per day.

PUBLIC TRANSPORTATION

Iconic, cheap ($2), round-the-clock and a full century old in 2005, the New York City subway system is a remarkable example of mass transit that works, in spite of itself. The 656-mile system can be intimidating at first, but dive in and you'll soon be a fan of its many virtues. It's the fastest and most reliable way to get around, and it's also much safer and cleaner than it used to be. Maps are available for the taking at every stop (though clerks are often 'fresh out'). To board, you must purchase a Metrocard, available only at self-serve machines, which accept change, dollars or credit/debit cards; each ride is $2, though purchasing many rides at once gets you some freebies.

If you're not in a big hurry, consider taking the bus ($2). You get to see the world go by, they run 24/7 and they're easy to navigate – going crosstown at all the major street byways (14th, 23rd, 34th, 42nd, 72nd Sts and all the others that are two-way roads) and uptown or downtown, depending which avenue they serve. You can pay with a Metro-Card or exact change but not dollar bills. Transfers from one line to another are free, as are transfers to or from the subway.

TAXI

Hailing and riding in a cab are rites of passage in New York – especially when you get a hack (local lingo for 'taxi driver') who drives like a neurotic speed demon, which is often. Prices will seem reasonable or outrageous, depending on where you're from. Current fares are $2.50 for the initial charge (first

one-fifth mile), 40¢ each additional one-fifth mile as well as per 120 seconds of being stopped in traffic, $1 peak surcharge (weekdays 4pm to 8pm), and 50¢ night surcharge (8pm to 6am daily). Tips are expected to be 10% to 15%. To hail a cab, it must have a lit light on its roof. Also know that it's particularly difficult to score a taxi in the rain, at rush hour and at around 4pm, when many drivers end their shifts. Also note that car services – which you must call or stop into to request a ride – are more the norm in outer boroughs. Fares differ depending on the neighborhood, and there are no meters.

LONG ISLAND

A long and skinny peninsula that was home to the first official New York City suburb (Levittown), this is a mythical land with many reputations that precede it – from its wacky history of tabloid crimes ('Long Island Lolita' Amy Fisher and the murders that inspired *The Amityville Horror,* just for starters) to its 'Hollywood East' celebrity status via the Hamptons. But there are myriad reasons to plan a visit here, most easily through a day trip or weekend trip from New York City. Long Island is home to wide ocean and bay beaches, important historic sites, renowned vineyards, rural regions boasting quaint shops and B&Bs, and yes, the Hamptons, in all its overpriced, overdeveloped glory.

History

The first European settlements on Long Island were whaling and fishing ports, established as early as 1640. In the late 19th and early 20th centuries, the ultrarich built big estates along the secluded coves and cliff tops of the north shore – this was, after all, the inspiration for F Scott Fitzgerald's *The Great Gatsby.*

Long Island is also known as the home of America's first planned suburb. That's thanks to the Levitt company, which acquired 4000 acres of potato fields in 1946 and began to build what would be the country's largest housing development ever, just 25 miles east of Manhattan in Nassau County. The new development ultimately consisted of 17,400 homes and 82,000 people, and the Levitts perfected the art of mass-producing houses by dividing the construction process into 27 different steps from start to finish.

Orientation

The first county east, Nassau, is mostly sub-urban housing and strip malls, built up as commuter trains linked the area to Manhattan – though it's also home to many beautiful beaches that are easily accessed from New York City, some by public transportation. Partly-rural Suffolk County covers the eastern two-thirds of the island; its tip splits into the North Fork, home of vineyards and farmland, and the South Fork, which is where you'll find the fabled Hamptons (also called the East End), which is actually a series of towns and villages, most with 'Hampton' in the name.

MAPS

The Hagstrom company publishes two excellent road atlases of Long Island, one each of Nassau and Suffolk County. You'll find them at area bookstores.

Information

INTERNET RESOURCES

Long Island Exchange (www.longislandexchange.com) Everything LI.

North Fork Promotion Council (www.northfork.org) Accommodations, events, restaurants and farm stands.

Hamptons Online (www.hamptons.com) Restaurants, news and events calendar.

MEDIA

The daily *Newsday* is the paper of record for the entirety of Long Island, while the *Long Island Press* is an alternative weekly. The Hamptons has extensive publications, including weekly newspapers the *Southampton Press*, the *East Hampton Star* and the *Independent*, and the glossy *Hamptons Magazine*. A great local TV station on the East End is Plum TV, on Channel 18, with round-the-clock news and entertainment programming.

TOURIST INFORMATION

The **Long Island Convention & Visitors Bureau** (☎ 631-951-3440, 877-386-6654; www.licvb.com) publishes an annual free travel guide. Local chambers of commerce provide maps, restaurant listings and lodging guides.

For the Hamptons, the various chambers of commerce double as tourist-information outlets. The two main ones are the **Southampton Chamber of Commerce** (☎ 631-283-0402; www.southamptonchamber.com; 76 Main St) and the

East Hampton Chamber of Commerce (☎ 631-324-0362; www.easthamptonchamber.com; 79A Main St).

Sights

SOUTH SHORE

Long, narrow rows of sand dunes form a stretch of clean and pleasant beaches – though the closer you are to New York City, the more crowded they can be.

On summer weekends it's quite a mob scene – but a fascinating one – on the 6-mile stretch of pretty **Jones Beach**, which attracts young surfers, wild city folk, local teens, nudists, staid families, gay men, lesbians and plenty of old-timers. Long Island Rail Rd to Wantagh makes a bus connection to Jones Beach.

Beautiful **Long Beach**, even closer to the city and more accessible by train, has clean beaches, a hoppin' main town strip, a surfers' scene and many city hipsters; it's also the home of the reformed 'Long Island Lolita,' Amy Fisher.

Just off the southern shore is a separate barrier island, **Fire Island**, which includes **Fire Island National Seashore** (☎ 631-289-4810) and several summer-only villages accessible by ferry from Long Island. The Fire Island Pines and Cherry Grove (both car-free) comprise a historic, gay bacchanalia that attracts men and women in droves from New York City, while villages on the west end cater to straight singles and families. Beach camping is allowed in **Watch Hill** (☎ 631-289-9336; www.watchhillfi.com; campsites $15; camping from May 16-Oct 14), though mosquitoes can be fierce and reservations are a must. At the western end of Fire Island, **Robert Moses State Park** is the only spot accessible by car. Ferry terminals to Fire Island beaches and the national seashore are close to LIRR stations at Bayshore, Sayville and Patchogue (round trip $12, May to November). There are limited places to stay, and booking in advance is strongly advised (check www.fireisland.com for accommodations information).

NORTH SHORE

In Port Washington, the **Sands Point Preserve** (☎ 516-571-7900; www.sandspointpreserve.org; 127 Middleneck Rd; admission Mon-Fri free, Sat & Sun $2) is a wooded bayfront park that's also home to the 1923 **Falaise** (admission $6; ☽ Thu-Sun May-Oct, tours hourly noon-3pm), one of the few remaining Gold Coast mansions, now a museum.

East of there is the bucolic town of Oyster Bay (hometown of Billy Joel), whose even bigger claim to fame is that it's home to **Sagamore Hill** (☎ 516-922-4788; www.nps.gov/sahi; ⏰ 10am-4pm Wed-Sun), a National Historic Site home where Theodore Roosevelt vacationed during his presidency.

THE HAMPTONS
What began as a tranquil hideaway for city artists, musicians and writers has developed into a frenetic summer getaway mobbed with jet-setters, celebrities and throngs of curious wannabes. That said, there is still plenty of the original peace and beauty to discover among the gorgeous beaches, farmlands (what's left of them) and wooded parks – as well as plenty of opportunities for dining, clubbing, shopping and hobnobbing. You could stay in one Hampton and easily reach any other – but know that the farthest west, Westhampton Beach, is about 45 minutes from the farthest east, Montauk. Southampton, Bridgehampton, Sag Harbor and East Hampton are all clustered closer together.

Southampton
The village of Southampton has a Waspy, 'old money' air, and feels conservative compared to its neighbors. Its beaches are sweeping and gorgeous, and its **Parrish Art Museum** (☎ 631-283-2111; 25 Jobs Lane; $5; ⏰ 11am-5pm Mon-Sat, from 1pm Sun) is an impressive, regional institution. At the edge of the village is a small Native American reservation, home to the Shinnecocks, who run a tiny **museum** (☎ 631-287-4923) with unpredictable opening hours.

Dining at the new **James on Main** (☎ 631-283-7575; 75 Main St; mains $19-28), on orange-glazed sea bass and the like, is an unforgettable experience.

Bridgehampton & Sag Harbor
Moving east, Bridgehampton has the shortest of all main drags, but it's packed with trendy boutiques and fine restaurants. The old-fashioned luncheonette **Candy Kitchen** (☎ 646-537-9885; Main St; mains $5-12) is a breakfast tradition. The **Bridgehampton Inn** (☎ 631-537-3660; 2266 Main St; low season $165-350, high season $310-450) is a classic inn with wi-fi service.

Seven miles north, on Peconic Bay, is the lovely old whaling town of Sag Harbor.

Check out its **Whaling Museum** (☎ 631-725-0770; admission $5; ⏰ 10am-5pm Mon-Sat, from 1pm Sun), or simply stroll up and down its narrow, Cape Cod–like streets. Get gourmet sustenance without going broke at the delicious new **Fat Ralph's** (☎ 631-725-6688; 138 Division St; ⏰ 6am-9pm) deli.

East Hampton
Most ostentatious is East Hampton, home to Steven Spielberg, Martha Stewart, P Diddy and many other famous faces. Celebrity sightings are a dime a dozen – especially at eateries including **Della Femina** (☎ 631-329-6666; N Main St; dishes $20-30) and **Nick & Toni's** (☎ 631-324-3550; 136 N Main St; dishes $20-30), or even trolling Main St, hitting upscale shops including Calypso, Scoop and Theory. Catch readings and art exhibits at **Guild Hall** (☎ 631-324-0806; 158 Main St), or have a wild night out at the exclusive **Star Room**, on Montauk Hwy.

Montauk & Around
More honky-tonk than the rest of the Hamptons, Montauk has relatively reasonable restaurants and a louder bar scene, largely because all the service personnel – a mix of foreign students and Mexican families – reside here. You'll find a string of very basic (but beachfront) motels along Montauk Hwy, or try the posh **Gurney's Inn & Spa** (☎ 668-2345; 290 Old Montauk Hwy; r $190-700).

At the very eastern tip of the South Fork is **Montauk Point State Park**, with its impressive, 1796 **Montauk Point Lighthouse** (☎ 631-668-2544; www.montauklighthouse.com; admission $6; ⏰ 10:30am-4:30pm). You can camp about 15 minutes west of here at the dune-swept **Hither Hills State Park** (☎ 631-668-2554; New York residents/nonresidents $26/50; ⏰ Apr-Nov), right on the beach. Just reserve early.

Shelter Island
Between the North and South Forks, Shelter Island, accessible by ferry from North Haven to the south and Greenport to the north, is home to a cluster of Victorian buildings and the **Mashomack Nature Preserve**. It's a great spot for hiking or kayaking. For some sleek style in the country, book a room at Andre Balazs's **Sunset Beach** (☎ 631-749-2001; www.sunsetbeachli.com; 37 Shore Rd; r/ste $225-400), a hip resort with a great club and eatery.

NORTH FORK

The main North Fork town and the place for ferries to Shelter Island, **Greenport** (www.greenport.com) is a bit more down-to-earth and affordable than most South Fork villages. Hunker down for some excellent seafood at one of the marina restaurants, and take a free spin on the historic waterfront carousel, the gem of **Harbor Front Park**.

Mainly, the North Fork is known for its wineries – there are close to 30, clustered mainly in the towns of Jamesport, Cutchogue and Southold – and the **Long Island Wine Council** (☎ 631-369-5887; www.liwines.com) provides details of the local wine trail, along Rte 25. A drive along the back roads of the North Fork affords some beautiful, unspoiled vistas of farms and rural residential areas.

The **Quintessentials B&B** (☎ 631-477-9400; www.quintessentialsinc.com; East Marion; r $249-299; ✗ 🖳) is an elegant and cozy inn with a full-service spa in **East Marion**.

Getting There & Around

The most direct driving route is along I-495, also called the Long Island Expressway. Once in the Hamptons, there is one main road to the end, Montauk Hwy. The **Long Island Railroad** (☎ 718-217-5477; www.mta.nyc.ny.us/lirr) serves all regions of Long Island, including the Hamptons ($20 one way) and North Fork, from Penn Station, Brooklyn and Queens. The **Hampton Jitney** (☎ 631-283-4600; www.hamptonjitney.com; one way $27) bus service goes express from Manhattan's Upper East Side to various Hamptons villages.

HUDSON VALLEY & THE CATSKILLS

The Valley region has peaceful rural areas, some magnificent wilderness and a rich history that's preserved in many picturesque villages and grand estates. You can reach the main towns and historic sites by bus or train, but to explore the countryside, you'll need a car.

Fortified against the British in 1778 at West Point, used as George Washington's war headquarters in Newburgh, developed into a leisure escape region after the invention of the steamboat, home to the famed Hudson River School of Painting in the 19th century, and seen as a place worthy enough to become 'Millionaire's Row' to families from the Vanderbilts to the Roosevelts, the Hudson Valley region is steeped in history in myriad ways. The Catskills region rose to fame in the 1940s and '50s as Jewish families flocked to resorts in the summer, giving the southern region the nickname 'Borscht Belt.'

The Hudson Valley stretches from Westchester County in the south up to Albany, the state capital. While the Lower Valley and Mid Valley are more populated and suburban, the Upper Valley gives way to a more rural feel, with open spaces and hills leading into the Catskills mountain region. The up-and-down Route 9W, along the Hudson River, divides the region into east and west.

Hudson Valley Network (www.hvnet.com) Region-wide information.

Historic Hudson Valley (www.hudsonvalley.org) With a focus on history.

Uncork New York (www.newyorkwines.org) County locator.

Hudson Valley magazine is a glossy guide geared toward visitors. There are several daily newspapers throughout the region, the main ones being the *Poughkeepsie Journal, Albany Times Union* and the *Post Standard/Herald-Journal.* There's also an impressive regional gay magazine, *Inside Out* (www.insideouthv.com).

New York State Tourism (www.iloveny.com) has several walk-in information centers throughout the region, including **Historic Hudson Valley** (☎ 914-631-8200; 150 White Plains Rd, Tarrytown) and **Maiden Travel Plaza-NY State Thruway** (☎ 845-246-7670; mile marker 103 N, Maiden on Hudson). Also try the **Dutchess County Tourism Office** (☎ 800-445-3131; www.dutchesstourism.com; 3 Neptune Rd; 🕙 9am-5pm Mon-Fri) and **New Baltimore Travel Plaza-NY State Thruway** (☎ 518-756-3000; I-87 btwn exits 21A & B), in the Catskills.

Lower Hudson Valley

Just 40 miles north of New York City, **Harriman State Park** (☎ 845-786-5003) covers 72 sq miles and offers swimming, hiking and camping. Adjacent **Bear Mountain State Park** (☎ 845-786-2701) offers great views from its 1306ft peak, with the Manhattan skyline looming beyond the river and surrounding greenery.

West of Rte 9W, the **Storm King Art Center** (☎ 845-534-3115; www.stormkingartcenter.org; Old Pleasant Rd, Mountainville; $10; 🕙 11am-5pm Wed-Sun Apr-Nov), is a 400-acre outdoor sculpture park with rolling hills and grassy fields that showcases stunning avant-garde sculpture by artists including Henry Moore and Isamu Noguchi and Mark DiSuvero; a free tram gives tours of the grounds. Nearby **West Point** (☎ 845-938-2638; ✆ 9am-5pm), open to visitors, is where a strategic fort became the US Military Academy in 1802; it's an excellent stop for war historians. Not far from here is the town of **Newburgh**, once an important New York whaling village, and George Washington's longest-lasting wartime headquarters during the Revolutionary War. **Washington's Headquarters State Historic Site** (☎ 845-562-1195; Liberty at Washington Sts; donations accepted; ✆ 1-5pm Wed-Sat Apr-Oct) has a museum, galleries and maps.

East of 9W is the town of Beacon – basically a scruffy waterfront village with one very worthy stop: **Dia Beacon** (☎ 845-440-0100; www.diaart.org; ✆ 11am-6pm Thu-Mon Apr 14-Oct 17; to 4pm Fri-Mon rest of year), an outpost of NYC's Dia, in Chelsea on W 22nd St (currently closed for major renovations), with a renowned collection from 1960 to the present.

Middle & Upper Hudson Valley

The largest town on the Hudson's east bank, **Poughkeepsie** (puh-*kip*-see) is famous for **Vassar**, a private liberal-arts college that admitted only women until 1969. It's kind of sleepy, but a good point from which to explore the region. Cheap motel chains in Poughkeepsie are clustered along Rte 9, south of the Mid-Hudson Bridge, but for a stay with character, try the **Copper Penny Inn** (☎ 845-452-3045; www.copperpennyinn.com; 2406 Hackensack Rd; r $90-150; ✗), a well-run B&B in a converted 1860s farmhouse.

Hyde Park is chock-full of history, as it's long been associated with the Roosevelts, a prominent family since the 19th century. The **Franklin D Roosevelt Library & Museum** (☎ 845-229-8114; www.fdrlibrary.marist.edu; 511 Albany Post Rd/Rte 9; admission $14; ✆ 9am-6pm May-Oct, to 5pm Nov-Apr) features exhibits on the man who created the New Deal and led the USA into WWII. First Lady Eleanor Roosevelt's peaceful cottage, **Val-Kill** (☎ 845-229-5302; www.nps.org/elro; admission $8; ✆ 9am-5pm), was her retreat from Hyde Park, FDR's mother and FDR himself. The 54-room **Vanderbilt Mansion** (☎ 800-967-2283; www.nps.gov/vama; Rte 9; admission $8; ✆ 9am-5pm), a national historic site 2 miles north on Rte 9, is a spectacle of lavish beaux-arts and eclectic architecture. You buy a combination ticket to all three sites for $20.

Hyde Park's famous **Culinary Institute of America** (☎ 800-285-4627; www.ciachef.edu; 1964 Campus Dr) trains future chefs and can satisfy absolutely anyone's gastronomic cravings. It's home to six student-staffed eateries, including the Apple Pie Bakery Café and the elegant Escoffier Restaurant. But the mint-condition '50s **Eveready Diner** (☎ 845-229-8100) is a fun deco spot to snack, and **Le Petit Chateau Inn** (☎ 845-473-8087; www.lepetitchateauinn.com; r $145-250) is a great place to snuggle down.

Just over the Hudson to the west is **New Paltz**, a quaint college town that caused a stir when its mayor began performing same-sex marriages in 2004 before being ordered to stop. It's a quiet, pretty place with a few cool boutiques and eateries – the best being the new **Village Tea Room** (☎ 255-3434; 10 Plattekill Ave; meals $8-12) in a charming house, serving delicious finger sandwiches, scrumptious desserts and a slew of brewed teas. The nearby **Mohonk Mountain House** (☎ 845-255-1000; www.mohonk.com; 1000 Mountain Rest Rd; r $246-650; 🖵) is a lavish country retreat.

Catskills

This scenic region of small towns, farms, resorts and forests has become the latest playground for NYC publishing types and various celebrities who have tired of the Hamptons glitz. They've been snapping up historic houses here to serve as second-home getaways, but so far the rural feel of the area has not been compromised. You'll still find quaint small towns and gorgeous countryside – and a surreal swirl of NYC-hipster activity in the area's hot restaurants once night falls on the weekends.

WOODSTOCK & AROUND

World-famous **Woodstock** symbolizes the tumultuous 1960s, when US youth questioned authority, experimented with freedom and redefined popular culture. The famous 1969 Woodstock music festival, though, actually occurred in Bethel, a town over 40 miles southwest, where a simple plaque marks the famous spot. Today Woodstock is a combination of quaint and hip, filled with art galleries, boutiques, inns, cafés and an eclectic mix of young Phish-fan types and graying hippie throwbacks. You'll find the urban chic masses sleeping it off at the **Lazy Meadow Motel** (☎ 845-688-7200; www.lazymeadow .com; 5191 Rte 28, Mt Tremper; r from $150), the kitschy retro inn owned by Kate Pierson of the B-52s, or hanging out at the **Bear Café** (☎ 845-679-5555; www.bearcafe.com; Rte 212; mains $18-29) or the eclectic **New World Home Cooking Co** (☎ 845-246-0900; www.newworldhomecooking.com; Rte btwn Woodstock & Saugerties; mains $15-25). The **Kaatskill Kaleidoscope** (☎ 888-303-3936; Mt Tremper; admission $5) is the world's largest – an amusing old farm silo, actually.

Saugerties, just east of Woodstock, is yet another quaint town, best known for its fine antique shops. The coolest inn is **Villa at Saugerties** (see right), but for a true adventure, stay at remote **Saugerties Lighthouse** (☎ 847-247-0656; www.saugertieslighthouse.com; r Nov-Mar $135, Apr-Oct $160; ☒), an 1869 lighthouse that sits on a small island in the Esopus Creek, accessible only by boat.

Towns to the east include **Rhinebeck**, with a bustling main street, good antique shops, inns, farms and wineries, an **Aerodrome Museum** (☎ 845-758-8610; www.oldrhinebeck.org) and the destination bistro **Terrapin** (☎ 845-876-3330; www.terrapinrestaurant.com; 6426 Montgomery St); and **Hudson** – a beautiful town on the river that's been remarkably and recently transformed into a hip, gay-friendly community of artists, writers and performers who fled the city.

To the north and west are **Roxbury**, a tiny village with a burgeoning gay community and home to the new groovy boutique hotel **The Roxbury** (☎ 607-326-7200; www.theroxburymotel.com; r $100-180), as well as Arkville, where you can take a scenic ride on the historic **Delaware & Ulster Rail Line** (☎ 845-652-2821; www.durr.org; Hwy 28; adult $10; ☺ Sat & Sun May-Aug). Keen skiers should head further north, where Rtes 23 and 23A lead you to **Hunter Mountain Ski Bowl** (☎ 518-263-4223), a year-round resort with challenging runs and a 1600ft vertical drop; and **Ski Windham** (☎ 518-734-4300), with more intermediate runs.

GETTING THERE & AROUND

Again, having a car is pretty key in these parts. But **Adirondack Trailways** (☎ 800-858-8555) does operate daily buses from NYC to Kingston, the Catskills' gateway town, as well as to Saugerties, Catskills, Hunter and Woodstock. Buses leave from NYC's Port Authority. The commuter rail line **Metro-North** (☎ 212-532-4900; www.mta.info/mnr) makes

---

THE AUTHOR'S CHOICE

While traveling in the Catskills, the **Villa at Saugerties** (☎ 845-246-0682; www.thevillaat saugerties.com; 159 Fawn Rd; r Jun-Oct $135-225, Nov-May $120-195; ☒) is truly the hippest country place you'll find to bed down for an evening or two. With five amazing rooms, a sleek design that's more urban boutique hotel than rural B&B, generous and delicious breakfasts, and a beautiful common room graced with complimentary wine, a roaring fireplace and artwork by the truly talented owners, you may never want to head back to NYC.

---

stops through the Lower and Middle Hudson Valley, as does the peaceful ferry, **NY Waterway** (☎ 800-533-3779; www.nywaterway.com), offering tours of the region from $40.

ALBANY

While the New York State capital is far from a top-priority destination, the town (nicknamed 'Smallbany' by jaded locals) has revived its northeastern charm in several neighborhoods. **Lark Street** (www.larkstreet.org) is the most hoppin' strip, with plenty of good shops, restaurants and trendy lounges. It's easy to get around here on foot or by car. However, the downtown empties after business hours, and walking between neighborhoods can feel creepy after dark.

History

The first Europeans to arrive in the Albany area were fur trappers, and control was passed from the Dutch to the English. It remained an important link in the fur trade into the 18th century, and its strategic location made it the logical meeting place for representatives from local colonies – it became New York's state capital in 1797. The railroad reached town in 1851, helping it to become an important transportation crossroads and manufacturing center.

Orientation & Information

Albany is completely surrounded by interstate highways – the New York State Thruway (I-90) enters from the east and circles the city westward. I-87 comes in from the south, and I-787 completes the circle to the east.

The daily paper of record is the *Albany Times Union*. For entertainment information, pick up a copy of *Metroland*, the free alternative weekly.

The **Albany County Convention & Tourism Bureau** (☎ 434-1217; 25 Quackenbush Square; www.albany.org) has all sorts of info on events and attractions, while the **Albany-Colonie Regional Chamber of Commerce** (☎ 518-431-1411; www.ac-chamber.org) has info on local businesses.

The **Albany Medical Center** (☎ 518-262-3125; 43 New Scotland Ave) provides medical/emergency assistance.

Book House of Stuyvesant Plaza (☎ 518-489-4761; 1475 Western Ave) has a good range of books.

Sights

The **Empire State Plaza** comprises 98 acres of land and 10 government buildings, state agencies, a modern-art sculpture display and a performing-arts center that's dubbed 'the Egg' for its oval architecture. The plaza also has the tall Corning Tower, with an **observation deck** (☎ 518-473-7521; Corning Tower; admission free; ☉ 10am-3:45pm) that overlooks the city and the Hudson River from its 42nd floor; and the **New York State Museum** (☎ 518-474-5877; www.nysm.nysed.gov; admission by donation; ☉ 9:30am-5pm), which documents the state's political, cultural and natural history. East of the plaza, **Albany Institute of History & Art** (☎ 518-463-4478; www.albanyinstitute.org; 125 Washington Ave; admission $7; ☉ 10am-5pm Wed-Sat, noon-5pm Sun) houses decorative arts and works by Hudson River–school painters, including Thomas Cole and Asher Durand. **Albany City Hall** (☎ 518-474-2418; Washington Ave & State St) is also worth a visit for its grand 19th-century architecture, with tours on weekdays at 10am, noon, 2pm and 3pm, and weekends at 11am, 1pm and 3pm.

Sleeping

Chain motels along Central Ave, west of I-87 exit 2, are only about a 10-minute drive from downtown, and prices are low. A good downtown option is **Pine Haven B&B** (☎ 518-482-1574; www.pinehavenbedandbreakfast.com; 531 Western Ave; r $69-119), a basic, no-frills inn with surprisingly reasonable rates. **Kittleman House** (☎ 518-432-3979; www.thekittlemanhouse.com; 70 Willett St; r $95; ☒) has antique-furnished rooms, a great location and views of Washington Park; and the **Morgan State House** (☎ 800-427-6063; www.statehouse.com; 393 State St; r $135-260) is a more upscale option.

Eating & Drinking

Lark St is a bit of a restaurant row, and a bustling scene most nights. It's home to **Shades of Green** (☎ 518-434-1830; 187 Lark St; dishes $9-15; ☒), a casual haven for vegetarians; **A Taste of Greece** (☎ 518-426-9000; 193 Lark St; dishes $9-15) Greek taverna; and **Justin's** (☎ 518-436-7008; 301 Lark St; dishes $15-22), an upscale dining scene with a menu of lamb shank, grilled salmon and four-cheese ravioli. Downtown, **Nicole's Bistro at Quackenbush Square** (☎ 518-465-1111; 633 Broadway; mains $19-25; ☉ lunch & dinner) is a romantic setting with dishes like cassoulet, seared scallops and roast duck. **Café Capriccio** (☎ 518-465-0439; 49 Grand St; mains $15-20; ☉ dinner) is old-school Italian – wood paneling, career waiters and pasta, veal and eggplant.

For drinking, check out **Antica Enoteca, Old World Wine Bar** (☎ 518-463-2881; 200 Lark St; ☉ closed Mon), a warm and elegant space with fireplaces, tapas and more than 50 wines by the glass. **Café Hollywood** (☎ 518-472-9043; 275 Lark St) is a classic pub with darts, a pool table and hard-core drinkers, while the **Waterworks Pub** (☎ 518-465-9079; 76 Central Ave) attracts a neighborhood gay crowd for dancing, drinking and occasional drag shows.

Getting There & Around

From the **bus terminal** (34 Hamilton St), **Trailways** (☎ 518-436-9651) and **Greyhound** (☎ 518-434-8095) head to/from New York City ($33.50 one way, three hours). Amtrak stops out of New York City ($43 one way, 2½ hours), as do airlines including American Eagle, Independence Air, Delta and United, flying into the **Albany International Airport** (737 Albany Shaker Rd; www.albanyairport.com).

Albany is an easy city to drive in. The Capital District Transportation Authority (CDTA) runs various public buses, included routes from the airport (about 10 miles from downtown).

AROUND ALBANY
Cooperstown

Fifty miles west of Albany, **Cooperstown** (Chamber of Commerce ☎ 607-547-9983; www.cooperstownchamber.org) is pure Americana, thanks to its stately brick buildings.

National Baseball Hall of Fame & Museum (☎ 607-547-7200; 25 Main St; www.baseballhalloffame.org; adult/child $14.50/5; ☉ 9am-5pm) is a shrine to the national sport that has exhibits on players, uniforms and equipment, as well as a theater, library and an interactive statistical database. The old stone **Fenimore Art Museum** (☎ 607-547-1400; www.fenimoreartmuseum .org; Lake Rd; admission $11; ☯ 10am-4pm Tue-Sun Apr, May, Oct & Nov, to 5pm Jun-Sep) has an outstanding collection of Americana.

There's no shortage of quaint B&Bs, which include the basic but affordable **Middlefield Guest House** (☎ 607-286-7056; Hwy 166; s/d $40/60), in a restored farmhouse, and **2 Chestnut Street B&B** (☎ 607-547-2307; 2 Chestnut St; www.2chestnut .com; r $95-225), a 17-room 1868 mansion right in the heart of town.

Pine Hills Trailways (☎ 914-633-7174) and **Adirondack Trailways** (☎ 800-858-8555) stop in front of the Chestnut St Deli.

Saratoga Springs

This gracious Victorian town is known for mineral springs, performing arts, horse racing and its liberal-arts college, Skidmore. It's blessed with the artsy, intellectual feel of a college town and the removed feel of a rural, pioneering community. The town's **visitor center** (☎ 518-587-3241; ☯ 9am-4pm Mon-Sun) is in a former trolley station across from Congress Park.

Most of the famous springs are in the 2300-acre **Saratoga Spa State Park** (☎ 518-584-2535; www.saratogaspastatepark.org; 19 Roosevelt Dr; per car $4; ☯ dawn-dusk), which offers the soothing Lincoln and Roosevelt mineral baths (which offer spa treatments), along with golf courses, an Olympic-sized pool complex, multi-use trails and ice rinks. It's also where you'll find the **Saratoga Performing Arts Center** (☎ 518-587-3330; www.spac.org; Hall of Springs), offering world-class performances in orchestra, jazz, pop, rock and dance; and the **National Museum of Dance** (☎ 518-584-2225; www.dance museum.org; 99 S Broadway; admission $6.50; ☯ 10am-5pm Tue-Sun), the only national museum dedicated to professional American dance.

From late July through September, fans of horse racing flock to the **Saratoga Race Course** (☎ 518-584-6200; www.saratogaracetrack.com), the country's oldest active thoroughbred racetrack. The **National Museum of Racing & Hall of Fame** (☎ 518-584-0400; www.racingmuseum .org; admission $7; ☯ 10am-4pm Mon-Sat, from noon Sun) is across from the track.

In nearby Glens Falls, the remarkable Hyde Collection, housed in the **Hyde Collection Art Museum** (☎ 518-792-1761; www.hydecollection.org; 161 Warren St; admission free; ☯ 10am-5pm Tue-Sat,

from noon Sun), an impressive 1912 Florentine Renaissance–style villa, includes works by Rembrandt, Degas and Matisse.

SLEEPING & EATING

The nearest campground is **Cold Brook Campsites** (☎ 518-584-8038; 385 Gurn Springs Rd; campsites $20), about 10 miles north in Gansevoort. There are plenty of inns and B&Bs in town; the chef-owned **Saratoga Farmstead** (☎ 518-587-2074; www.saratogafarmstead.com; r $75-175, during racing season $200-275) is a peaceful, tasteful retreat on 10 acres of land.

Many eateries line Broadway and the intimate side streets. **Four Seasons Natural Foods Store & Café** (☎ 518-584-4670; 33 Phila St; dishes $7; ✗) has excellent veggie buffets. Meanwhile, the cool **Wine Bar** (☎ 518-584-8777; 417 Broadway; snacks $10) serves 50 wines by the glass, along with nibbles like cheese plates.

Greyhound (☎ 518-434-9651) and **Adirondack Trailways** (☎ 800-858-8555) stop at 133 S Broadway. Amtrak has daily trains from Montreal and New York City.

THE ADIRONDACKS

Adirondack Park's 6 million acres include towns, mountains, lakes, rivers and more than 2000 miles of hiking trails. The Adirondack Forest Preserve covers 40% of the park; the state constitution designates it as 'forever wild' – a good thing, because the peaks and valleys and lakes rival the best in the state. There's good trout, salmon and pike fishing, along with excellent camping spots (despite the biting black flies, a summer nuisance). In colonial times, settlers exploited the forests for beaver fur, timber and hemlock bark, but by the 19th century, wilderness retreats became fashionable, and large hotels and millionaires' estates adopted the rustic Adirondack style: log cabins on a grand scale.

Lake George, Lake Placid & Saranac Lake

At the park's southeastern entrance, 32-mile-long Lake George has clear blue water and wild shorelines. The village of **Lake George** (www.lakegeorgechamber.com) is tacky and touristy; still, it's the gateway to the Adirondacks. The state maintains wonderfully remote **campgrounds** (☎ 800-456-2267) on Lake George's islands, and one of several places for wilderness information is the **Adirondack**

Mountain Club (☎ 518-668-4447; www.adk.org; 814 Goggins Rd), which publishes excellent guides.

The mountain resort of **Lake Placid** hosted the Winter Olympics in 1932 as well as 1980, and elite athletes still train here. The **visitor center** (☎ 518-523-2445; www.lakeplacid.com; 216 Main St; ☼ 8am-4pm Mon-Fri, from 9am Sat & Sun) has maps and information about skiing, fishing, cycling and hiking. For information about all the Olympic sports centers open to visitors, check out www.orda.org, but know that they include ice arenas, a ski-jumping complex and a chance to shoot through a bobsled or luge with a professional driver. Skiiers should head to nearby **Whiteface Mountain** (www.whiteface.com), with 65 miles of trail and a serious, 1200ft vertical drop.

Those who prefer soft beds to sleeping bags on hard earth will find plenty of options. South of Lake Placid town, the Adirondack Mountain Club's (ADK) **Adirondack Loj** (☎ 518-523-3441; www.adk.org; dm/r $45/110) is a large house beside a small lake – it is a lovely, rustic retreat with great atmosphere and good breakfasts. The charming **Book & Blanket Inn** (☎ 518-946-8323; r $70-90) is just 17 miles from Lake Placid.

Further north is the **Saranac Lake** region, where you'll find even more secluded wilderness areas – small lakes and ponds, ancient forests and wetlands. Contact the **Saranac Lake Chamber of Commerce** (☎ 518-891-1990; www .saranaclake.com) for guides to the region.

Getting There & Around

Both **Greyhound** (☎ 800-231-2222; www.greyhound .com) and **Adirondack Trailways** (☎ 800-858-8555) serve various towns in the region. Traveling from place to place really requires a car.

THOUSAND ISLANDS REGION

East of Lake Ontario, more than 1890 tiny islands dot the wide St Lawrence River in what's called the **Thousand Islands** region. Once a summer playground for the very rich, it's now a popular area for boating, camping and even scuba diving.

Information

Contact the **1000 Islands International Tourism Council** (☎ 800-847-5263; www.visit1000islands.com; 43373 Collins Landing, Alexandria Bay; ☼ 9am-5pm) and also the **Thousand Islands State Parks Region** (☎ 315-482-2593; Alexandria Bay) to make camping reservations.

Sights & Activities

The **Seaway Trail** (www.seawaytrail.com), New York State's National Scenic Byway – stretching 504 miles along the St. Lawrence River, Lake Ontario, Niagara River and Lake Erie – has an important segment in this region. It makes for a beautiful driving or bicycling journey.

The relaxing, French-heritage village of **Cape Vincent** is at the western end of the St Lawrence River, where it meets Lake Ontario. Its small **Burnham Point State Park** (☎ 315-654-2324; Rte 12E; campsites $25) has wooded, lakeside campsites. Further east, Alexandria Bay (Alex Bay), an early-20th-century resort town, has lost its charm but remains the departure point for ferries to Heart Island, where **Boldt Castle** (☎ 800-847-5263; www.boldtcastle.com; admission $5.25; ☼ 10am-6:30pm mid-May–Sep) marks the sad love story of a rags-to-riches New York hotelier who built the castle for his beloved wife, who then died before its completion. The same hotelier once asked his chef to create a new salad dressing, which was popularized as 'Thousand Island' – an unfortunate blend of ketchup, mayonnaise and relish.

Ogdensburg is the unlikely birthplace of artist Frederic Remington (1861–1909), chronic romanticizer of the American West. The **Frederic Remington Art Museum** (☎ 315-393-2425; www.fredericremington.org; 303 Washington St, Ogdensburg, NY; admission $8; ☼ 11am-5pm Wed-Sat, from 1pm Sun) is the place to view his sculptures, paintings and personal effects. For those who are averse to camping, there are many resorts and inns in Alexandria Bay and Cape Vincent. The romantic **Hart House Inn** (☎ 315-482-5683; www.harthouseinn.com; r $175-295), on Wellesley Island, features canopy beds, Jacuzzis, a golf course and views of the St Lawrence River.

Getting There & Around

Both **Greyhound** (☎ 800-231-2222; www.greyhound .com) and **Adirondack Trailways** (☎ 800-428-4322) travel to this region from NYC and surrounding towns.

FINGER LAKES REGION

Eleven long, narrow lakes stretch north to south and form the fingers of this western New York region. It's an ideal place for boating, fishing, cycling, hiking and cross-country skiing, and the rolling hills are the state's best wine-growing region. With more than 65 **vineyards**, you can sample an array of palate-pleasing whites and reds. **Uncork New York** (☎ 315-536-7442; www.newyorkwines.org), in Penn Yan, distributes free brochures about wine trails and has great maps on its site.

Seneca Falls

This small, sleepy town is where the USA's organized women's rights movement was born. After being excluded from an anti-slavery meeting, Elizabeth Cady Stanton and her friends drafted an 1848 declaration asserting that 'all men and women are created equal.' The inspirational **Women's Rights National Historical Park** (☎ 315-568-2991; www.nps .gov/wori; 136 Fall St; admission $3; �---: 9am-5pm) has a small but impressive museum with an informative film available for viewing, plus a visitor center offering tours of Cady Stanton's house. The surprisingly tiny **National Women's Hall of Fame** (☎ 315-568-8060; www.great women.org; 76 Fall St; admission $3; ☺ 9:30am-5pm Mon-Sat May-Oct, 10am-4pm Wed-Sat Nov-Apr, from noon-Sun Nov-Apr) honors American women such as first lady Abigail Adams, American Red Cross founder Clara Barton and civil-rights activist Rosa Parks.

Ithaca & Around

This fun, diverse and handsome college town has pedestrian-friendly streets lined with bookstores, eateries, art-house cinemas and a summertime farmers market. For tourist information, head to the **Visit Ithaca Information Center** (☎ 607-272-1313; www.visitithaca.com; 904 E Shore Dr; ☺ 9am-5pm Mon-Fri, from 10am Sat).

Founded in 1865, **Cornelly** boasts a lovely campus, mixing traditional and contemporary architecture, and sits high on a hill overlooking the picturesque town below. The modern **Herbert F Johnson Museum of Fine Art** (☎ 607-255-6464; www.museum.cornell.edu; University Ave; admission free; ☺ 10am-5pm Tue-Sun) – designed by IM Pei – has a major Asian collection, pre-Columbian, American and European exhibits, and a nice view from its top floor.

For sleeping, a gem of a find is the **Elmshade Guest House** (☎ 607-273-1707; 402 S Albany St; r $45-125), an eight-room inn with spotless, tasteful rooms, for remarkably low rates that include breakfast. The grand **William Henry Miller Inn** (☎ 607-256-4553; www.millerinn.com; 303 N Aurora St; r $115-195; ☒) is a historic B&B built by Cornell University's first student of architecture, William Henry Miller.

Ithaca has a great variety of international, gourmet and vegetarian restaurants. **Moosewood Restaurant** (☎ 607-273-9610; www.moose woodrestaurant.com; 215 N Cayuga St; mains $13; ☒) offers fixed-price menus that change daily, including salad, soup and dessert; it's famous for its vegetarian dishes and recipe books by founder Mollie Katzen.

ITHACA'S COUNTRYSIDE

Ithaca's surrounding rural region is interspersed with waterfalls, gorges and gorgeous parks, popular with hikers and rock climbers. Eight miles north on Rte 89, the spectacular **Taughannock Falls** spill 215ft into the steep gorge below; **Taughannock Falls State Park** (☎ 607-387-6739; www.taughannock.com; Rte 89) has two major hiking trails, craggy gorges, tent-trailer sites and cabins.

Just 10 minutes from Ithaca is a wonderful lodging option: **Brookton Hollow Farm Bed & Breakfast** (☎ 607-273-5725; www.brooktonhollow farm.com; 18 Banks Rd, Brooktondale; r $90-110; ☒), a creatively renovated house that sits on a horse-powered organic vegetable farm.

CORNING MUSEUM OF GLASS

The sweet town of Corning is home to Corning Glass Works and the hugely popular attraction of the **Corning Museum of Glass** (☎ 800-732-6845; www.cmog.org; adult/child/student $12/ free/10.80; ☺ 9am-5pm). The massive complex is home to fascinating exhibits on glass-making arts, complete with glass-blowing demonstrations, interactive items for kids and special exhibits, such as the recent 'Czech Glass.'

WESTERN NEW YORK

The two biggies in these parts are Buffalo and Niagara Falls, the latter of which draws upwards of 12 million tourists per year. The region's development is owed to the Erie Canal, which spawned a number of early industrial centers along its route between Albany and Buffalo. (Tracing the canal is an alternative to the I-90 toll route, and a more interesting way to get to Niagara Falls. Plus, the canal's towpaths are ideal for cycling trips.) Of the cities Syracuse and Rochester, both homes to big universities, just **Rochester** is worth a visit, if only for its photography-based claim to fame: its **George Eastman House** (daily tours) and **International Museum of Photography & Film** (☎ 585-271-3361; 900 East Ave; www.eastmanhouse.org; adult/child $8/5; ☺ 10am-5pm Tue-Sat, from 1pm Sun).

Niagara Falls

Misty sprays and the majestic scale of this roaring cascade make it a marvelous spectacle – assuming you don't get so distracted by the tacky restaurants, flashy arcades and high-rise hotels that you forget to look at the natural wonder. The falls are split between New York and Canada and, to keep tourists and their dollars for longer than it takes to see the falls, the Canadian side – the much worthier side for visiting, as it's where you'll find the more stunning views – offers a whole strip of Vegas-like attractions, including a towering casino (see opposite). The New York side, which has a handful of low-key, natural-park offerings (and now a casino of its own), feels depressed in the shadow of Ontario's tacky but booming skyline.

HISTORY

Long before tourism invaded, Seneca Indians populated the area, leading French priest Louis Hennepin here in 1678. His description, widely read in Europe, was quite apt: 'The universe does not afford its parallel.' The area round the falls became increasingly commercialized in the mid-19th century, giving rise to the Free Niagara movement by those angered by exploitation of a natural resource. Frederick Law Olmstead was among those who fought for the government to protect the land with a public park, and it happened in 1885.

ORIENTATION & INFORMATION

The falls are in two separate towns: Niagara Falls, New York (USA) and Niagara Falls, Ontario (Canada). The towns face each other across the Niagara River, which is spanned by the Rainbow Bridge.

On the US side, the **Niagara Falls Convention & Visitors Bureau** (☎ 800-338-7890; www.nfcvb.com; cnr 4th & Niagara Sts; ☒ 8:30am-5pm) has all sorts of guides. The **Orin Lehman State Park Visitors Center** (☎ 716-278-1796; Prospect Park; ☒ 9am-5pm) shows a good film on the falls and offers 'Passport to the Falls,' an excellent money-saving tourist combo ticket (adult/child $24.50/17.50) which includes Maid of the Mist, Observation Tower and Cave of the Winds.

SIGHTS & ACTIVITIES

If you must stay on the US side, you can see side views of the **American Falls** and their western portion, the Bridal Veil Falls,

dropping 180ft. Take the Prospect Point Observation Tower elevator up for a vista (50¢). Cross the bridge to **Goat Island** for other viewpoints, including Terrapin Point, which has a fine view of Horseshoe Falls and pedestrian bridges to the Three Sisters Islands in the upper rapids. From the north corner of Goat Island, an elevator descends to the **Cave of the Winds** (☎ 716-278-1730; admission $8), where walkways go within 25ft of the cataracts (raincoats provided). The **Maid of the Mist** (☎ 716-284-8897; tours $11.50; ☒ Apr-Oct) boat trip around the bottom of the falls has been a major attraction since 1846 and is highly recommended. Boats leave every 15 minutes from the base of the Prospect Park Observation Tower on the US side.

TOURS

Many tours stop at major sights on both sides and include a Maid of the Mist ride. Check out the following:

Bedore Tours (☎ 716-285-7550; tours $65-140)

Niagara Helicopters (☎ 905-357-5672) Does similar chopper trips from Canada.

Niagara Scenic Trolley (departs from visitor center every 15min; tours $2) Guided tour that allows you to get on and off at various attractions.

Rainbow Air (☎ 716-284-2800; tours $60) A 10-minute sightseeing flight over the falls.

SLEEPING & EATING

Besides some of the usual hotel chains – Ramada Inn, Howard Johnson, Holiday Inn – the US side doesn't have many options. One accommodations exception is the **Hanover House B&B** (☎ 716-278-1170; 610 Buffalo Rd; r $70-140), a quirky, Italian villa–style home with four cozy Victorian-style rooms. But generally, you're better off making a day trip from a home base in Buffalo – or heading over to Canada if you get tired or hungry.

GETTING THERE & AROUND

From the **NFTA Terminal** (Niagara Frontier Transportation Authority; www.nfta.com; 4th & Niagara Sts), No 40 buses go to Buffalo ($2.25, one hour) for air and bus connections, and there is an extensive system of local bus service as well. The **Amtrak train station** (☎ 716-285-4224) is about 2 miles northeast of downtown. And from Niagara Falls, daily trains go to Buffalo, Toronto and New York City ($63, nine hours). The **Greyhound & Trailways terminal** (☎ 905-357-2133; 4555 Erie Ave) is on the Canada side.

Avoid driving around on either side. You can park free at the downtown Rainbow Mall and walk around. Parking near the falls costs $6 on the US side, and US$7 on the Canadian side. The **View Mobile tram** (☎ 716-282-0028; per day $5) does a loop around the US side, and the **People Mover** (per day $7.50) shuttles up and down the riverfront on the Canadian side of the falls every 20 minutes.

Crossing the Rainbow Bridge to Canada costs for cars/pedestrians US$3/1. There are customs and immigration stations at each end – carry proper papers (see p1158).

Buffalo

Known for its spicy chicken wings and painfully cold and snowy winters, Buffalo has quite a bit more going for it, from impressive art museums and historic architecture to bustling shopping areas and sprawling university campuses. There's an inspiring presence of young, hip and stylish college students, no doubt influenced by native local hero Ani DiFranco, who has chosen her hometown as the place to base her indie music label, Righteous Babe Records.

HISTORY

Settled by the French in 1758 – its name is believed to derive from *beau fleuve* (beautiful river) – Buffalo became a shipping nexus between the Great Lakes and eastern USA when the Erie Canal was opened in 1825. Railroads boosted the area further, and the city thrived as an industrial center, acquiring fine buildings, parks and well-endowed museums.

A post–WWII decline in its traditional industries hit the city hard, the population fell, and much of the inner city became badly run-down, the evidence of which is still obvious in several areas of town. Recent urban renewal has improved the downtown area, and the huge student population adds another dimension to a city still known for its working-class roots and football fanatics.

ORIENTATION & INFORMATION

Buffalo, just an hour south of Niagara Falls, is situated on the southwest shores of New York on Lake Erie. It's about an eight-hour trip from New York City.

The *Buffalo News* is the daily paper of record, while *Art Voice* and *Alt Press* are the alternative weekly newspapers. WNED 970-AM is the local National Public Radio affiliate.

The helpful **Buffalo Niagara Convention & Visitors Bureau** (☎ 716-852-0511; www.buffalocvb.org; 617 Main St) has good walking-tour pamphlets

---

BORDER CROSSING: CANADIAN NIAGARA FALLS

You get a great panorama of the falls by strolling over Rainbow Bridge to Canada. Canada's **Horseshoe Falls** are wider, and the curved shape makes them especially photogenic from Queen Victoria Park; at night they're illuminated with a colored light show. The **Journey Behind the Falls** gives access to a spray-soaked viewing area beneath the falls (US$7.50).

Clifton Hill St has kitschy attractions and a carnival atmosphere, and can provide some tongue-in-cheek fun (and great people-watching opportunities) in the evening. At **Casino Niagara** (☎ 905-374-3598; 5705 Falls Ave) you can gamble in two currencies.

For sleeping, your best bet is to bite the bullet and stay in one of the high-rise chain hotels. The swank rooms, positioned 20 and 30 stories above the falls, offer such mesmerizing views that observatories, trips and helicopter rides become redundant. Big names like **Sheraton** and **Marriott** all have great rooms with comparable views, averaging at about US$125. For comfortable quarters without views, try one of the many standard, well-located motels like the **Inn By the Falls** (☎ 800-263-2571; 5525 Victoria Ave; r US$49-119). For less touristy ambience, head to the award-winning B&B **Butterfly Manor** (☎ 905-358-8988; 4917 River Rd; $110-160), while backpackers should head to the **HI Niagara Falls Hostel** (☎ 905-357-0770; 4549 Cataract Ave; dm US$25).

When you get hungry, skip the obvious tourist traps. **Remington's of Montana** (☎ 905-356-4410; 5657 Victoria Ave; mains US$15-35) is an elegant steak-and-seafood spot. **Taki Japanese Restaurant & Sushi Bar** (☎ 905-357-7274; 5500 Victoria Ave; dishes around US$15) has sushi and sake, and vegetarians will be thrilled with the vegan-Chinese **Xin Vego Café** (☎ 905-353-8346; 4939 Victoria Ave; dishes around US$8). Locals pack into **Falls Manor** (☎ 905-358-3211; 7104 Lundy Lane; dishes around US$6) for breakfast, served all day long.

and a great website. For details about local architecture, you can check out www.walkbuffalo.org.

If you need medical assistance, go to **Buffalo General Hospital** (☎ 716-859-5600; 100 High St).

Talking Leaves Books (☎ 716-837-8554; 3158 Main St) has a good selection of books.

SIGHTS & ACTIVITIES

Architecture fans will have a field day here, starting at the **Prudential Building** (28 Church St), designed by Louis Sullivan in 1895 as the Guaranty Building, which used an innovative steel-frame construction to create the first modern skyscraper. Be sure to glimpse the stunning art-deco **City Hall** (65 Niagara Sq), built in 1931, and the neo-Gothic **Old Post Office** (121 Ellicot St) from 1894. The **M&T Bank** (545 Main St) is topped with a gilded dome of 140,000 paper-thin sheets of 23.75-karat gold leaf. Six **Frank Lloyd Wright houses** are a highlight; the 1904 **Darwin Martin House** (125 Jewett Parkway) and neighboring **Barton House** (☎ 716-856-3858; 118 Summit Ave) are being restored until 2006 but are accessible by appointment.

North of downtown, the beautiful Delaware Park was designed by Frederick Law Olmsted. Its jewel is the not-to-be-missed **Albright-Knox Art Gallery** (☎ 716-882-8700; www.albrightknox.org; 1285 Elmwood Ave; admission $10, 3-10pm Fri free; ☺ 10am-5pm Wed-Thu & Sat & Sun, to 10pm Fri), a sizable museum including some of the best French Impressionists and American masters, from Pollock to O'Keefe. Buffalo also has good science, history and children's museums and a fine zoo. The **Elmwood** neighborhood, stretching along Elmwood Ave, between Allen St and Delaware Park, is dotted with hip cafés, restaurants, boutiques and bookstores. Another cool stretch is the quickly gentrifying Main St, between Hertel and Kenmore. Not far from here is the charming **Guercio & Sons** (☎ 716-882-7935; 250 Grant St), an old-school Italian gourmet shop.

History buffs should hit the **Theodore Roosevelt Inaugural National Historic Site** (☎ 716-884-0095; 641 Delaware Ave; admission $5; ☺ 9am-5pm Mon-Fri, from noon Sat & Sun) in the Ansley-Wilcox house, where you can learn the tale of Teddy's emergency swearing-in here following the assassination of William McKinley.

Locals worship the **NFL Buffalo Bills** (☎ 716-648-1800) football team, which plays at **Ralph Wilson Stadium** (☎ 716-648-1800; www.buffalobills.com; 1 Bills Dr, Orchard Park). Other franchises include the **Buffalo Sabres** (☎ 716-855-4100; www.sabres.com) ice-hockey team and the **Buffalo Bisons** (☎ 716-846-2000; www.bisons.com) minor-league baseball team.

SLEEPING

Buffalo is ripe for a cool new boutique hotel – but for now, visitors must choose from a series of bland downtown chains, Hyatt Regency and Holiday Inn among them, and just a couple of inns with character. One of those is the lovely **Beau Fleuve** (☎ 800-278-0245; www.beaufleuve.com; 242 Linwood Ave; r $90-145; ☒), a B&B in the historic Linwood district. **Mansion on Delaware Avenue** (☎ 716-886-3300; www.mansionondelaware.com; 414 Delaware Ave; r from $175) has a grand style and luxurious quarters. Budget travelers have the **Hostelling International – Buffalo Niagara** (☎ 716-852-5222; www.hostelbuffalo.com; 667 Main St; dm $20-23, r $55-60; ☐).

EATING & DRINKING

The local specialty is Buffalo wings – deep-fried chicken wings covered in a spicy sauce and served with blue-cheese dressing and celery. Find them at **Anchor Bar** (☎ 716-886-8920; 1047 Main St; 10 wings $8; ☒), which claims credit for inventing the 'delicacy.' For more upscale pleasures, try **Bacchus** (☎ 716-854-9463; 56 West Chippewa; mains $12-18) for its wine bar and eclectic fare, or **Hutch's** (☎ 716-885-0074; 1375 Delaware Ave; mains $15-30), with a menu of creative chicken, steak and pasta dishes. **Spot Coffee** (☎ 716-854-7768; 227 Delaware Ave; dishes $4-7) is a hip, funky café with delicious coffee drinks, salads, sandwiches and pastries.

For pure imbibing, everyone but frat-boy types should steer clear of the mobbed Chippewa St pub strip, and head instead to a place like **Cecilia's Restaurant & Martini Bar** (☎ 716-883-8066; 716 Elmwood Ave), serving more than 50 varieties of ice-cold martini. Several gay bars are clustered around the south end of Elmwood, including **Fugazi** (☎ 716-881-3588; 503 Franklin St) and the new **Q** (☎ 716-332-2223; 44 Allen St).

GETTING THERE & AROUND

Buffalo's **Niagara International Airport** (☎ 716-630-6000), about 16 miles east of downtown, is a regional hub. Jet Blue Airways has round-trip fares from New York City for less than $200, and the flight takes just under an hour. Buses arrive and depart from the **Greyhound terminal** (☎ 716-855-7531; 181 Ellicott St). **NFTA** (☎ 716-285-9319) local bus No 40 goes to Niagara Falls ($2.25). From the downtown **Amtrak train station** (☎ 716-856-2075; 75 Exchange St), you can catch trains to major cities. Car rentals are reasonable (see p1175 for more information on renting).

NEW JERSEY

Bruce Springsteen, Bon Jovi, big hair, *The Sopranos* and malls – this is the stuff that New Jersey is made of. Right? Well, yes. But there is much, much more to the story. When you take the time to exit the highways, get out of the malls and turn off the TV, you are privy to many a beautiful surprise: a whopping 40% of the state is forest, and a quarter is farmland. The state has 127 miles of beaches, extensive parkland and beautiful Victorian buildings. Its urban areas and many of its small towns are filled with progressive people, top-rated restaurants and a thriving cultural scene.

New Jersey is the most urbanized, most densely populated state in the USA. About two-thirds of the population live within 30 miles of New York City, and much of the state can be regarded as part of the great metropolis: most of New York's port facilities are here, along with its second international airport, the bulk of its industry and many of its workers. Two of New York's greatest icons, the Statue of Liberty and Ellis Island, are actually in New Jersey, as is the home stadium for New York's two pro football teams, the Giants and the Jets.

In presidential politics, New Jersey is a bellwether state, tending to support the winner. In 2004 Democratic governor James E McGreevey scandalized his constituents – and the entire country – when, on national TV, he came out as a 'gay American' who had engaged in an extramarital affair with a man on his staff and thus resigned. Richard Codey is acting governor until the 2006 election.

History

The state's original residents were called *lenni lenape* (original people), probably numbering less than 20,000 when European settlers arrived in the early 17th century. Dutch settlers built a trading post at

---

NEW JERSEY FACTS

Nickname Garden State
Population 8.6 million
Area 8722 sq miles
Capital city Trenton
Official state bug Honeybee
Birthplace of Count Basie (1904–84); Frank Sinatra (1915–98); astronaut Buzz Aldrin (b 1930); Meryl Streep (b 1949); Bruce Springsteen (b 1949); John Travolta (b 1954); Tom Cruise (b 1962); Whitney Houston (b 1963); Queen Latifah (b 1970); Lauryn Hill (b 1975)
Home of The first movie (1889), first professional baseball game (1896), drive-in theater (1933)
Famous for The coming-out speech of former governor James McGreevey, the Jersey Shore, Bruce Springsteen's musical beginnings

---

Bergen (now Jersey City) in 1618 and another at Camden in 1623. When the British took over New Netherlands in 1664, the new colony of New Jersey offered generous terms and religious freedom to attract new settlers. Like the harsh 'removals' that took place in all colonies at the time, the surviving Native Americans were placed in the Brotherton reservation and later moved to the states of New York and Wisconsin.

New Jersey saw many Revolutionary War battles, and George Washington placed his Continental Army headquarters at Morristown during the winters of 1776–77 and 1779–80. New Jersey's population grew from 15,000 in 1700 to more than 185,000 by 1795, and industry boomed. Post–Civil War industrial expansion also spawned a movement to improve working conditions. One of that movement's leaders, Democratic Governor Woodrow Wilson, a former Princeton University president, later served as US president (1913–21). After WWII Newark and Jersey City saw influxes of immigrants. By the mid-1980s, New Jersey had some of the country's fastest-growing urban areas. Decline in traditional industries has been offset by new activities like chemicals and services, and by the benefits of being part of the thriving New York region.

Information

Find statewide tips on sights, accommodations, festivals and a special new 'African American Visitors Guide' through the **New**

Jersey Tourism Commission (☎ 800-VISIT-NJ; www .visitnj.org). Also try **New Jersey Travel & Tourism** (☎ 800-847-4865; www.www.state.nj.us/travel).

The major newspapers of record in New Jersey are the *Newark Star-Ledger*, the *Asbury Park Press* and the *Jersey Journal*; the *New York Times*, which has a New Jersey section in this edition, is also widely read. The website NJ.com has statewide news from all the major dailies.

NORTHERN NEW JERSEY

The north part of the state is a mix of extreme opposites: the harsh urban worlds of Newark and Jersey City not far from the bucolic Delaware Water Gap wilderness area and Kittatinny mountain range.

Newark & Around

Because of its airport, Newark is the starting or finishing point for many visitors, which is why it's often quickly passed over by folks in a hurry to get elsewhere. And that's a shame. Newark itself (the third-oldest city in America), long considered off-limits to many people – following a serious decline that stemmed from its infamous 1969 race riots – is back in business, big-time. **Go Newark** (www.gonewark.com) has great info on sites, eateries and more. The *Newark Star-Ledger* is the local newspaper, and a good one at that.

NEWARK

A 10-minute train trip from NYC's Penn Station gets you into Newark's stunning, neoclassic Penn Station, the logical starting point for exploration. Exit and go south and you'll be in the Ironbound District, one of the best reasons to visit. With a vibrant Portuguese community, its Ferry St is lined with excellent restaurants, pastry shops and music stores. Across Washington Park, the **Newark Museum** (☎ 973-596-6550; www.newarkmuseum.org; 49 Washington St; suggested donation $7; ☺ noon-5pm Wed-Sun) has a renowned Tibetan Collection. The **New Jersey Performing Arts Center** (☺ 973-642-0404; www.njpac.org; 1 Center St) is the city's proud gem; it hosts national orchestras, operas, dance, cabaret, theater, jazz and world-music concerts. Other attractions in the area include the grand **Cathedral Basilica of the Sacred Hearts** (☎ 973-484-4600; www.cathedralbasilica.org; 89 Ridge St) and the 400-acre Frederick Law Olmstead-designed **Branch Brook Park**, with some 2700 cherry trees that blossom in April.

With NYC just across the river, there's really no reason to stay the night in Newark – but you could get hungry. Delve into the myriad Portuguese eateries, or try a pastrami-on-rye at the classic **Hobby's Delicatessen** (☎ 973-623-0410; 32 Branford Pl; mains $7-12), an 85-year-old Jewish deli.

HOBOKEN & JERSEY CITY

Hoboken is a longtime, respectable community that many New Yorkers have turned into a sixth borough because of the (marginally) cheaper rents. On weekends it's somewhat of a party town, with no shortage of bars and live-music venues – such as legendary **Maxwell's** (☎ 201-653-1703; 1039 Washington St), which has featured up-and-coming rock bands since 1978, and was the setting for Bruce Springsteen's 'Glory Days' video. But it also has a cool waterfront and some lovely residential streets, and it has an important place in US pop-culture history: the first organized baseball game was played nearby in 1846, Frank Sinatra was born here and got his start in local clubs, and *On the Waterfront* was filmed in town. The **Hoboken Historical Museum** (☎ 201-656-2240, www.hobokenmuseum.org, 1301 Hudson St; admission free; ☺ 2-9pm Tue-Thu, 1-5pm Fri, from noon Sat & Sun) gives a great overview.

Jersey City's biggest draw is the 1200-acre **Liberty State Park** (☎ 201-915-3403; www .libertystatepark.org; ☺ 6am-8pm), which hosts outdoor concerts with the Manhattan skyline as a backdrop, and also operates **ferries** to Ellis Island and the **Statue of Liberty** (adult/child $10/8). Also in the park is the **Liberty Science Center** (☎ 201-200-1000; www.lsc.org; adult $10-$16.50, child $8-14.50, extra for IMAX & special exhibits; ☺ 9:30am-5:30pm), a wonderfully diverse museum that's especially great for kids.

DELAWARE WATER GAP

The Delaware River meanders through 40 miles of **Delaware Water Gap National Recreation Area** (☎ 908-496-4458; www.nps.gov/dewa; off I-80), covering land in both New Jersey and Pennsylvania and carving the 1400ft-deep Kittatinny Ridge chasm at the southern end, which comprises the 3348-acre **Kittatinny Valley State Park** (☎ 973-786-6445; www.state .nj.us/dep). Both park regions – astoundingly serene for being so close to New York City – have endless outdoor-activity options. You can hike, ride a horse or mountain bike through extensive trail systems; canoe, fish or swim in the river and lakes; rock climb on cliffs; and camp in valleys or on mountaintops. The Maine-to-Georgia Appalachian Trail passes right through the area.

Getting There & Around
New Jersey Transit operates buses out of Port Authority and trains out of Penn Station to Newark and Liberty State Park (which requires an easy shuttle-bus connection).

The **New Jersey PATH Train** goes to Newark and Hoboken from various stops along Manhattan's west side (see p167).

New York Waterway (☎ 800-53-FERRIES; www.ny waterway.com) runs pleasant commuter ferries to Hoboken from Midtown and Downtown locations. For the Delaware Water Gap, driving is really the only option.

CENTRAL NEW JERSEY
Here you'll find the state capital, Trenton, and a string of quaint communities including grand Princeton, at the eastern border of Pennsylvania.

Trenton & Around
It may not be the most beautiful place, but New Jersey's capital city has many historic sites worth visiting. Its more rural neighbors, including Princeton, are also full of history – and they're pretty, to boot.

The Continental Congress met here briefly in 1784, but the capital soon moved to NYC and then to Washington, DC. Trenton became the state capital in 1790, and soon became one of the most important industrial towns in the United States. It's gone through several periods of recession, but has always been anchored by the state government, which has a number of buildings downtown.

Located in central New Jersey, Trenton is small enough for its sights to be explored in about a half day; it's an easy stopover point between New York City and Philadelphia, or a good day trip from Princeton, which is to the north. Most attractions are along Broad St, which runs north–south through town, and State St, which crosses Broad St.

The **Trenton Convention & Visitors Bureau** (☎ 609-777-1770; www.trentonorthernnewjersey.com; cnr Lafayette & Barrack Sts) can supply maps and information.

Trenton
History buffs can visit the **Old Barracks Museum** (☎ 609-396-1776; www.barracks.org; Barrack St; admission $6; ☯ 10am-5pm), built in 1758 and now the state's last remaining barracks from the French and Indian War. The **New Jersey State Museum** (☎ 609-292-6464; www .state.nj.us/state/museum; 205 W State St; admission free; ☯ 9am-4:45pm Tue-Sat, noon-5pm Sun), with a planetarium, is home to diverse collections from fossils to fine art.

Princeton
The tiny town of **Princeton** and its Ivy League **Princeton University** have lovely architecture and noteworthy historic sites, especially around Nassau and Witherspoon Sts. Princeton was the site of the 1777 Battle of Princeton, which proved a decisive victory for General Washington's troops during the Revolutionary War, now commemorated at Princeton Battlefield State Park. The **Historical Society of Princeton** (☎ 609-921-6748; 158 Nassau St) has information about festivals, as well as maps and brochures. **Orange Key Guide Service & Campus Information Office** (☎ 609-258-3603) arranges free university tours.

Accommodations are expensive and hard to find during graduation time in May and June, but beyond that, it should be easy to arrange for a stay at one of the affordable motels along Rte 1 – or, better yet, at one of several atmospheric inns. The landmark **Peacock Inn** (☎ 609-924-1707; 20 Baynard Lane; r from $160) has counted Albert Einstein and F Scott Fitzgerald among its illustrious guests. For more options, use the **Princeton Lodging Guide** (☎ 609-737-7901; www.princetonlodging.com).

You can grab breakfast at **PJ's Pancake House** (☎ 609-924-1353; 154 Nassau St; mains $6-10), an institution. **Lahiere's** (☎ 609-921-2798; 11 Witherspoon St; dishes $20) is the posh, grand dame of town.

JERSEY SHORE
Perhaps the most famous and revered feature of New Jersey is its 127 miles of sparkling shore, stretching from Sandy Hook to Cape May and lined with resort towns ranging from the tacky to the sublime. During summer weekends, some towns see up to 100,000 visitors; weekdays are almost as busy, and reservations are highly recommended because many New Yorkers rent a house for the whole summer. In September crowds diminish, and lots of places close after Labor Day.

SANDY HOOK & AROUND

At the northernmost tip of the Jersey Shore is the **Sandy Hook National Recreation Area** (☎ 732-872-5970; www.nps.gov/gate; per car $10; ☻ dawn-dusk), a 6-mile-long sandy barrier beach at the entrance to New York Harbor. Most of the area is undeveloped, and the ocean side of the peninsula has massive **beaches** (including a nude beach at parking lot G) edged by an extensive system of bike trails. The abandoned coastguard station, **Fort Hancock**, sits eerily empty, its hulls open for quiet exploration. The **Sandy Hook Lighthouse** is the oldest in the country. The closest place to stay is the gay-owned **Sandy Hook Cottage** (☎ 732-708-1923; www.sandyhookcottage.com; 36 Navesink Ave; r $100-200), which has been done up with a tasteful, beach-house decor.

About 10 miles inland is the artsy town of **Red Bank**, with a hoppin' main strip with shops and cafés, a sizable Mexican population (and great authentic Mexican food), and the **Count Basie Theater** (☎ 732-842-9000; 99 Monmouth St), named in honor of local jazz great William 'Count' Basie, hosting quality dance, music and theater productions.

A fun way to arrive at Sandy Hook from NYC is on the **Seastreak** (☎ 800-BOAT-RIDE; www.seastreak.com; return $29), a fast ferry service that allows you to bring bikes aboard. From Sandy Hook you can take a bus to Red Bank, or simply take NJ Transit directly to the Red Bank station stop.

ASBURY PARK & OCEAN GROVE

Asbury Park experienced passing prominence in the 1970s, when Bruce Springsteen 'arrived' at the **Stone Pony** (☎ 732-502-0600; 913 Ocean Ave) nightclub, still offering live music. After that, the town went through a major decline, followed by a very recent and unlikely comeback – led mostly by wealthy gay men from NYC who have snapped up and restored blocks of forgotten Victorian homes and storefronts. It's still a work in progress, but the sprawling **Antique Emporium of Asbury Park** (☎ 732-774-8230; Cookman Ave) has amazing finds, while **Bistro Olé** (☎ 732-897-0048; 230 Main St; mains $12-20; ✗), serving Spanish-influenced fare, and **Moonstruck** (☎ 732-988-0123; 517 Lake Ave; mains $17-25), with eclectic Italian, are total scenes. **Paradise/The Empress** (☎ 732-988-6663; 101 Asbury Ave) is a big gay nightclub/hotel complex, and the **Jersey Gay Pride** (www.gayasburypark.com) extravaganza takes place here in early June.

The town immediately to the south, **Ocean Grove**, is a fascinating place to wander. Founded by Methodists in the 19th century, and keeping itself up ever since, the town retains its Victorian architecture and a 6500-seat wooden auditorium, which featured in Woody Allen's *Stardust Memories* and now hosts concerts and religious events. There are many beautiful, big-porched **Victorian inns** to choose from to stay; visit www.oceangrovenj.com for guidance.

MIDSHORE BEACH TOWNS

Belmar attracts a younger crowd, and has beachfront food shacks that can get pretty rowdy when the bars close at 2am; next-door **Bradley Beach** is its quiet, peaceful sister. **Spring Lake** is a classy community once called the 'Irish Riviera,' with lush gardens, Victorian houses and elegant accommodations (visit www.springlake.org).

The narrow **Barnegat Peninsula** barrier island extends some 22 miles south from Point Pleasant. In its center, **Seaside Heights** sucks in the wild 20-something summer crowds with beaches, boardwalks, bars and two amusement piers. Occupying the southern third of Barnegat Peninsula is **Island Beach State Park** (☎ 732-793-0506; per car weekday/weekend $6/10), a flat 3000-acre stretch of gorgeous dunes and wetlands – similar to **Long Beach Island** (LBI; ☎ 609-361-1000; www.longbeachisland.com), with tons of eateries, bars and inns to balance out its natural beauty.

Getting There & Around

Most Jersey Shore towns are easily accessible by train from New York City or northern New Jersey, with beaches within walking distance from most stations; check schedules with **New Jersey Transit** (www.njtransit.com). By car, the tolled Garden State Parkway runs north–south along New Jersey's east coast, with easy access to beaches.

SOUTH JERSEY

A mixture of kitsch (Atlantic City, the Wildwoods) and country (the Pine Barrens), the state's southern region is the perfect mix of fun and beauty.

Pine Barrens

Locals call this region the Pinelands – and like to carry on the lore about it being home to a mythical beast known as the 'Jersey

Devil.' But the Pine Barrens, a region of one million acres of pine forest with one-third wholly protected by the state, is a magical, peaceful place. The land contains several state parks and forests, and is an absolute haven for bird-watchers, hikers, campers and all-round nature enthusiasts. The **Wharton State Forest** (☎ 609-561-0024), home to the restored 19th-century settlement called Historic Batsto Village, is a great place to picnic, hike and explore, as is the 40,000-acre **Edwin B Forsythe National Wildlife Refuge** (☎ 609-652-1665; www.forsythe.fws.gov), one of New Jersey's main flyover points for migrating birds.

Atlantic City

Ever since 1977, when the state approved casinos to revitalize this once-scruffy town, the city has since reemerged as a high-profile gamblers' destination (with just *some* scruffy areas). If you can get past the mobs of blue-haired ladies, high-rolling businessmen, Disney-type tourists and the generally greedy atmosphere, you'll find some hidden gems and get a fascinating glimpse into American culture.

INFORMATION

The **Atlantic City Convention & Visitors Bureau** (☎ 609-449-7130; www.atlanticcitynj.com; Atlantic City Expressway; ◷ 9am-5pm), under the giant teepee in the middle of the Atlantic City Expressway, can provide you with maps and accommodations deals. *Atlantic City Weekly* magazine is a great guide to events, clubs and eateries. For medical assistance, there's **Atlantic City Medical Center** (☎ 609-345-4000; 1925 Pacific Ave).

SIGHTS & ACTIVITIES

It's the **casinos**, as you may have guessed, that are the biggest draw here. As in Las Vegas, they all have themes – Far East, Ancient Rome, Wild West – but they're very superficially done. Inside they're all basically the same, with endless clanging slot machines and high-roller tables and gluttonous, all-you-can-eat food buffets.

Beyond the casino walls you'll find the wide, oceanfront **boardwalk**, the first in the world. Enjoy a walk or a hand-pushed rolling-chair ride ($25) and drop in on the informative **Atlantic City Historical Museum** (☎ 609-347-5839; cnr Boardwalk & New Jersey Aves;

admission free). The **Miss America Pageant**, held every September in the city's Convention Hall – worth a visit if only for its claim to the 'world's largest' pipe organ – remains a very popular draw.

SLEEPING & EATING

All the casinos are attached to massive resort-style hotels. They are all bland and cookie-cutter, with nothing to really distinguish one from the next – except, that is, for the newest game in town, the **Borgata** (☎ 866-MY-BORGATA; www.theborgata.com; r from $149), with stylish rooms, a full-service spa, major concert hall, four five-star restaurants and, of course, a grand casino. Look for frequent rate specials, especially on weekdays.

Good food can be found away from the casino strip. A few blocks inland, **Mexico Lindo** (☎ 609-345-1880; 2435 Atlantic Ave; dishes $8-12) is a favorite among Mexican locals. **Hannah G's** (☎ 609-823-1466; 7310 Ventnor Ave; dishes $6-10) is a family-owned, excellent breakfast and lunch spot in nearby Ventnor. **Maloney's** (☎ 609-823-7858; 23 S Washington Ave) is a popular seafood-and-steak place, and **Ventura's Greenhouse Restaurant** (☎ 609-822-0140; 106 Benson Ave), in next-door Margate City, is an Italian restaurant loved by locals.

The Wildwoods & Cape May

South of Atlantic City, the three towns of **North Wildwood**, **Wildwood** and **Wildwood Crest** are an archaeological find – whitewashed motels with flashing neon signs, turquoise curtains and pink doors, especially in Wildwood Crest, a kitschy slice of 1950s Americana. Wildwood, a party town popular with teens and young overseas visitors, is the main social focus. The **Greater Wildwood Chamber of Commerce** (☎ 609-729-4000; www.gwcoc .com; 3306 Pacific Ave, Wildwood) hands out information on self-guided tours around the 'doo-wop' motels. The beach is free, and there are rides on the pier. About 250 motels offer rooms for $50 to $200, making it a good option if Cape May is booked.

Cape May

Founded in 1620, Cape May is on the state's southern tip and is the country's oldest seashore resort. Its sweeping beaches get crowded in summer, but the stunning Victorian architecture is attractive year-round.

INFORMATION
Contact the **Cape May County Chamber of Commerce** (www.cmccofc.com) for details about the area. For more information on this region, see p338.

SIGHTS & ACTIVITIES
In addition to 600 gingerbread-style houses, the city boasts antique shops, whale watching and bird-watching, and is just outside of **Cape May Point State Park** (☎ 609-884-2159) and its 157ft **Cape May Lighthouse** (☎ 609-884-5404; admission $5). It's also the only place in the state where the sun both rises and sets over the water. The sandy **beach** (day/week/season $5/10/15) is the main attraction in summer months. **Cape May Whale Watcher** (☎ 609-884-5445; www.capemaywhalewatcher.com; ocean tour $23-30) 'guarantees' sighting a marine mammal.

SLEEPING & EATING
Most of Cape May's B&Bs are upscale, and many places require a two- to three-night minimum stay during summer weekends. The best budget option remains **Hotel Clinton** (☎ 609-884-3993, off-season 516-799-8889; 202 Perry St; r $50-60). The classic, sprawling **Congress Hall** (☎ 609-884-8422; www.congresshall.com; 251 Beach Ave; r $115-405; 🖳) has a range of beautiful quarters for various budgets. The town is overflowing with smaller B&Bs; try the darling **Gingerbread House** (☎ 609-884-0211; www.gingerbreadinn.com; 28 Gurney St; low season $98-198, high season $140-260; ⊠).

The tiny, eclectic **Louisa's Café** (☎ 609-884-5884; 104 Jackson St; dishes $12-20; ⊠) is the town's prize, midrange eatery. Upscale diners should reserve a table at the award-winning **Ebbitt Room** (☎ 609-884-5700; 25 Jackson St; dishes $20-26; ⊠) in the posh Virginia Hotel.

Getting There & Around
By air, the small **Atlantic City 'International' Airport** (☎ 800-645-7895) is a 20-minute drive from the center of Atlantic City, and a great option for reaching any part of South Jersey.

New Jersey Transit (☎ 973-762-5100, 800-772-2222; www.njtransit.com) trains from New York City's Penn Station service the Jersey Shore as far south as Bay Head, and go direct to Atlantic City from Philadelphia; buses serve an even larger area.

Greyhound and New Jersey Transit bus services run from New York to the region (one way $23); Greyhound, Capitol Trailways and New Jersey Transit run from Philadelphia (round-trip about $16). A casino will often refund the fare (in chips, coins or coupons) if you get a bus directly to its door.

For service to Cape May from Delaware, the **Cape May-Lewes Ferry** (☎ 800-643-3779; www.capemaylewesferry.com; per car & driver $26, per passenger $10) is a convenient option.

PENNSYLVANIA

In a region of the country where it's possible to drive through six or seven little states in just one day, Pennsylvania – which is 309 miles across and 38 times larger than nearby Rhode Island – is one massive rectangle. But a journey across its middle is far from monotonous. It's more like a fascinating minidrive across the country, as you'll truly encounter a little taste of everything that makes America what it is. Cosmopolitan cities like Philadelphia and Pittsburgh may be what get most play – along with their polar-opposite, Amish country – but there is way more going on within its borders. Pennsylvania is home to historic battle sites like Gettysburg and artistic gems like Frank Lloyd Wright's Fallingwater, plus the majestic Allegheny Forest, the stunning shores of Lake Erie, the rolling mountains of the Poconos and many hip little enclaves, like New Hope and Easton. It's also the birthplace of a couple of famed artists, Mary Cassatt and Andy Warhol, who could not be more of a contrasting pair – or a better representation of Pennsylvania's great diversity.

History
In 1681, William Penn, a Quaker, founded his colony as a 'holy experiment' that respected religious freedom, liberal government and even indigenous inhabitants. But it didn't take long for European settlers to displace those communities, thus giving rise to Pennsylvania's status as the richest and most populous British colony in North America. It became a great influencer in the independence movement and, much later, an economic leader through its major supply of coal, iron and timber, followed by its period of being a supplier of raw material and labor during WWI and WWII. In the postwar period its industrial importance gradually declined. Urban re-

newal programs and the growth of service and high-tech industries have boosted the economy, most notably in Philadelphia and Pittsburgh.

Quakers founded Pennsylvania on the principle of religious tolerance, and that tolerance attracted other minority religious sects. Many Quakers still live here, along with the well-known communities of Mennonites and Amish in the Pennsylvania Dutch Country. Though Pennsylvania's conservative US Senator Rick Santorum is infamous for his homophobic comments today – in which he equates gay sex to incest – the state is a Democratic stronghold, and its current governor, Edward Rendell, is a moderate Democrat.

Information

Pennsylvania Department of Community & Economic Development (☎ 800-847-4872; www .visitpa.com) The tourism department has maps, guides and all sorts of details about the entire state.
Pennsylvania Tourism (☎ 800-847-4872; www .visitpa.com)

PHILADELPHIA

Ever since Ed Rendell, mayor from 1992 to 1999 and now governor of Pennsylvania, picked Philly up by its lapels, gave it a good dusting and sent it out, polished, for all the world to see, the city has become one cool place to be. Rendell aggressively promoted the historic city as a marginally forgotten treasure sandwiched between New York and Washington, DC, by reinhabiting buildings, cleaning streets and clearing the way for new developments. So now, more than just a great place to look at a cracked bell, it's a city whose renaissance will thrill you: catch the symphony or watch the Phillies; dip in and out of bars, restaurants and clubs (including a major gay scene that's being touted by the city's tourism department; see p199); and stroll through leafy parks and well-hung museums and galleries. Oh – and, while you're at it, get a major dose of history, too.

History

William Penn made Philadelphia his capital in 1682, basing its plan on a grid with wide streets and public squares – a layout copied by many US cities. For a time the second-largest city in the British Empire (after

---

PENNSYLVANIA FACTS

Nicknames Keystone State, Quaker State
Population 12.3 million
Area 46,058 sq miles
Capital city Harrisburg
Official beverage Milk
Birthplace of Louisa May Alcott (1832–88), Gertrude Stein (1874–1946), Martha Graham (1878–1948), WC Fields (1880–1946), Andy Warhol (1928–87), Grace Kelly (1929–82), Bill Cosby (b 1937), Carson Kressley (b 1969)
Home of US Constitution, the Liberty Bell, first daily newspaper (1784), first auto service station (1913), first computer (1946)
Famous for Soft pretzels, Amish people, Philadelphia cheesesteak, Groundhog Day's Punxsutawney Phil

---

London), Philadelphia became a center for opposition to British colonial policy. It was the new nation's capital at the start of the Revolutionary War and again after the war until 1790, when Washington, DC, took over. By the 19th century New York had superseded Philadelphia as the nation's cultural, commercial and industrial center, and Philly never regained its early preeminent status. In the 1970s the nation's bicentennial prompted an urban renewal program that continues to this day via the neighborhood revitalization program of current mayor John Street.

Orientation

Philadelphia is easy to navigate. Most sights and accommodations are within walking distance of each other, or a short bus ride away. East–west streets are named; north–south streets are numbered, except for Broad and Front Sts.

Historic Philadelphia includes Independence National Historic Park and Old City, which extends east to the waterfront. West of the historic district is Center City, home to Penn Sq and City Hall. The Delaware and Schuylkill (*skoo*-kill) Rivers border South Philadelphia, which features the colorful Italian Market, restaurants and bars. West of the Schuylkill, University City has two important campuses as well as a major museum. Northwest Philadelphia includes the genteel suburbs of Chestnut Hill and Germantown, plus the hip and growing Manayunk, with plenty of bustling pubs

PHILADELPHIA

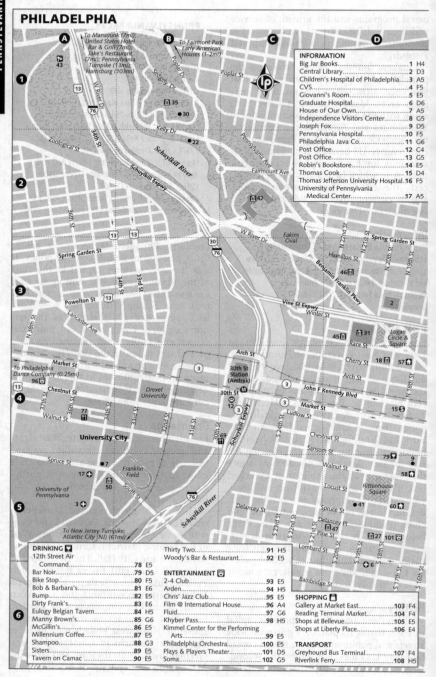

INFORMATION

Big Jar Books	**1** H4
Central Library	**2** D3
Children's Hospital of Philadelphia	**3** A5
CVS	**4** F5
Giovanni's Room	**5** E5
Graduate Hospital	**6** D6
House of Our Own	**7** A5
Independence Visitors Center	**8** G5
Joseph Fox	**9** D5
Pennsylvania Hospital	**10** F5
Philadelphia Java Co	**11** G6
Post Office	**12** C4
Post Office	**13** G5
Robin's Bookstore	**14** E5
Thomas Cook	**15** D4
Thomas Jefferson University Hospital	**16** F5
University of Pennsylvania Medical Center	**17** A5

DRINKING 🍸

12th Street Air Command	**78** E5
Bar Noir	**79** D5
Bike Stop	**80** F5
Bob & Barbara's	**81** E6
Bump	**82** E5
Dirty Frank's	**83** E5
Eulogy Belgian Tavern	**84** H5
Manny Brown's	**85** G6
McGillin's	**86** E5
Millennium Coffee	**87** E5
Shampoo	**88** G3
Sisters	**89** E5
Tavern on Camac	**90** E5

Thirty Two	**91** H5
Woody's Bar & Restaurant	**92** E5

ENTERTAINMENT 🎭

2-4 Club	**93** E5
Arden	**94** H5
Chris' Jazz Club	**95** E5
Film @ International House	**96** A4
Fluid	**97** G6
Khyber Pass	**98** H5
Kimmel Center for the Performing Arts	**99** E5
Philadelphia Orchestra	**100** E5
Plays & Players Theater	**101** D5
Soma	**102** G5

SHOPPING 🛍️

Gallery at Market East	**103** F4
Reading Terminal Market	**104** F4
Shops at Bellevue	**105** E5
Shops at Liberty Place	**106** E4

TRANSPORT

Greyhound Bus Terminal	**107** F4
Riverlink Ferry	**108** H5

0   600 m
0   0.4 miles

SIGHTS & ACTIVITIES
Academy of Natural Sciences Museum...............18 D4
African American Museum in Philadelphia..........19 G4
Arch St Meeting House..........20 G4
Betsy Ross House...............21 H4
Boathouse Row.................22 B2
Carpenters' Hall...............23 G5
Chinese Friendship Gate........24 F4
Christ Church.................25 H5
City Hall.....................26 E4
Civil War Library & Museum....27 D5
Clay Studio...................28 H4
Congress Hall................(see 33)
Elfreth's Alley................29 H4
Ethical Society...............(see 41)
Fairmont Park.................30 B1
Franklin Institute Science Museum..................31 D3
Ghost Tour of Philadelphia....32 G5
Independence Hall.............33 G5
Independence Seaport Museum..34 H5
Lemon Hill Mansion............35 B1
Liberty Bell Center...........36 G5
Library Hall..................37 G5

Mantua Maker's Museum House...(see 29)
National Constitution Center...38 G4
National Museum of American Jewish History................39 G4
National Portrait Gallery.......(see 48)
Old City Hall.................(see 33)
Pennsylvania Academy of the Fine Arts.....................40 E4
Philadelphia Children's Theatre..41 D5
Philadelphia Museum of Art....42 C2
Philadelphia Zoo..............43 A1
Philosophical Hall.............(see 33)
Physick House.................44 G5
Please Touch Museum...........45 D3
Rodin Museum.................46 D3
Rosenbach Museum & Library....47 D5
Second Bank of the US.........48 G5
Trophy Bikes.................49 G5
University Museum of Archaeology & Anthropology.............50 A5
US Mint......................51 G4
US Postal Service Museum......52 G5

SLEEPING
Alexander Inn.................53 E5
Antique Row B&B..............54 E5

Bank St Hostel................55 G5
Best Western Independence Park Hotel..................56 H5
Four Seasons Hotel Philadelphia..57 D4
Latham Hotel.................58 D5
Penn's View Hotel.............59 H5
Rittenhouse Square Bed & Breakfast..60 D5
Ritz-Carlton..................61 E5
Shippen Way Inn..............62 G6
Society Hill Hotel.............63 G5

EATING
Ariana......................64 H5
Buddakan....................65 G5
Capogiro Gelato Artisans......66 E5
Carousel Shop................67 G5
Continental..................68 H5
Intermezzo Café & Lounge.....69 C4
Joseph Poon.................70 F4
Le Bec-Fin..................71 E5
Lolita......................72 E5
Olde City Wrap Shack.........73 H4
St Gianna's Grille.............74 F6
Valanni.....................75 E5
Vietnam Restaurant...........76 F4
White Dog Café...............77 A4

PHILADELPHIA IN...

Two Days
Start in Independence National Historic Park, taking in everything from the **Liberty Bell** (p192) to **Congress Hall** (p192). Then wander over the **Rittenhouse Square** (p193) for some people watching before strolling through South St and to the **Italian Market** (p194) to sample some cheese and salami. Head to **Chinatown** (p194) for dinner. On day two, enjoy brunch at **Society Hill** (p197) followed by a stroll that includes **Antiques Row** (p192) and the sites of the **Old City**. Spend the rest of the afternoon in the **Philadelphia Museum of Art** (p193), or other museums of your choice along the Benjamin Franklin Parkway. Have dinner in Society Hill.

Four Days
Follow the two-day itinerary, and on the third day, stroll over to **University City**. Have brunch at the **White Dog Café** (p198), followed by a stroll around the lovely **U Penn** (p195) campus and the nearby **30th Street Station** (p195). Walk back into the **Old City** and then to the **Reading Terminal Market** (p197) where you'll eat yourself silly. Treat yourself to a musical or theater performance at night, or just have drinks in **Center City**. On your final day, head out to **Manayunk** (p198) for some leisurely shopping, strolling, eating and drinking.

---

and eateries. The South St area, between S 2nd, 10th, Pine and Fitzwater Sts, has bohemian boutiques, bars, eateries and music venues.

Information

BOOKSTORES
Big Jar Books (☎ 215-574-1650; 55 N 2nd St) Diverse used books and café.
Giovanni's Room (☎ 215-923-2960; 345 S 12th St) Gay and lesbian books and periodicals.
House of Our Own (☎ 215-222-1576; 3920 Spruce St) Used books, small-press publications and frequent readings.
Joseph Fox (☎ 215-563-4184; 1724 Sansom St) Good selection of architecture, design and children's books.
Robin's Bookstore (☎ 215-735-9600; 108 S 13th St) Philly's oldest independent bookstore, featuring a large African American studies section.

EMERGENCY
Emergency number (☎ 911)
Philadelphia Suicide & Crisis Center (☎ 215-686-4420)
Rape Crisis Center (☎ 215-985-3333)
Traveler's Aid Society (☎ 215-523-7580; www.travelersaid.org; 1201 Chestnut St, 12th fl) A nonprofit agency that helps with anything from stolen wallets to emergency shelter.

INTERNET ACCESS
In 2004, Mayor Street introduced Wireless Philadelphia – a major initiative that would create the first totally wired city, bringing free wi-fi to anyone and everyone. But it's still in the planning stages, so for now you may have to pay to surf on your laptop; Internet cafés charge about $10 an hour, and most hotels have free access.
Central Library (☎ 215-686-5322; 1901 Vine St) Free Internet access.
Intermezzo Café & Lounge (☎ 215-222-4300; 3131 Walnut St) University City café with 15 free, high-speed hook-up ports.
Philadelphia Java Co (☎ 215-928-1811; 518 S 4th St; wi-fi per hr $2).

INTERNET RESOURCES
Philadelphia Citysearch (www.philadelphia.citysearch.com) Restaurant, bar, club hotel and shopping listings.
Philly.com (www.philly.com) News, listings and more, courtesy of the *Philadelphia Inquirer*.
Philadelphia's Online Nightlife Guide (www.maneo.com) Guest lists, party info.

MEDIA
City Paper (www.citypaper.net) Free weekly available at street boxes around town.
Philadelphia Daily News More of a tabloid-style daily.
Philadelphia Inquirer (www.philly.com/mld/inquirer) The region's top daily newspaper.
Philadelphia Magazine A monthly glossy.
Philadelphia Weekly (www.philadelphiaweekly.com) Free alternative weekly available at street boxes around town.
WHYY 91-FM (www.whyy.org) Local National Public Radio affiliate.
WXPN 88.5-FM (www.xpn.org) Member-supported radio from the University of Pennsylvania; talk and music format.

MEDICAL SERVICES

Children's Hospital of Philadelphia (☎ 215-590-1000; www.chop.edu; 34th St & Civic Center Blvd)
CVS (☎ 215-465-2130; 10th at Reed St; ☽ 24hr) Pharmacy in South Philadelphia; call for other locations.
Graduate Hospital (☎ 215-893-2350; 1800 Lombard St) Close to the business district.
Pennsylvania Hospital (☎ 215-829-3000; www.uphs.upenn.edu/pahosp; 8th & Spruce Sts)
Thomas Jefferson University Hospital (☎ 215-955-6000; www.jeffersonhospital.org; 111 S 11th St) Closest to downtown.
University of Pennsylvania Medical Center (☎ 215-662-4000; 3400 Spruce St)

MONEY

ATMs are found everywhere, especially at banks and convenience stores. Most ATMs charge a service fee of $1.50 or so per transaction for foreign bankcards, but those at Wawa, a local chain of convenience stores, do not. If you're having trouble finding a machine, call the **ATM locator service** (☎ 800-248-4286).

There are exchange bureaus in every terminal of the Philadelphia International Airport, though the best rates are at banks in the city. Most banks are open 10am to 5pm Monday to Thursday, until 6pm Friday, and sometimes for a few hours on Saturday morning. Other exchange options:

American Express Travel Service (☎ 215-587-2300; www.americanexpress.com/travel; 1600 JFK Blvd).
Thomas Cook (☎ 800-287-7362; 18th St & JFK Blvd)

POST

B Free Franklin Post Office (☎ 215-592-1289; 316 Market St; ☽ 9am-5pm Mon-Fri) Postmarks stamps with Franklin's signature.
Philadelphia Main Post Office (☎ 215-895-8000; 2970 Market St; ☽ 6am-midnight) Impressively old and massive, occupying several city blocks; call for other branch locations.

TOURIST INFORMATION

Greater Philadelphia Tourism Marketing Corporation (www.gophila.com) The highly developed, nonprofit visitors bureau has information about tours, attractions, hotels, package deals, special events, and gay and lesbian tourism.
Historic Philadelphia (☎ 215-629-5801; www.historicphiladelphia.org) Helps organize tours of the historic area, in conjunction with the PCVB.
Independence Visitors Center (☎ 215-636-1666; 6th & Market Sts; ☽ 8:30am-5:30pm) Run by the National Park Service, the center distributes the useful visitors guides and maps, plus sells tickets for the various official tours that depart from nearby locations. Staff members are helpful and knowledgeable.
Philadelphia Convention & Visitors Bureau (☎ 215-636-3300; www.pcvb.org) Another great source, with info on everything from hotels to special events.

Dangers & Annoyances

Like most big US cities, Philadelphia has its share of homelessness and crime, but prudent travelers are not at any undue risk. Certain neighborhoods are seedier than others and are considered 'unsafe.' These include Germantown, parts of West Philadelphia and South Philadelphia, and most of North Philadelphia (all off the 'tourist circuit'). Though the majority of Center City and other touristed sections of the city are reasonably safe, travelers should be aware of their surroundings whenever they walk in the city. After dark, some of the city's parks – particularly Fairmount – host numerous crimes.

Sights

While most of Philly's better-known historic sites – the Liberty Bell, Carpenters' Hall etc – are concentrated in the Independence National Historic Park, there's much of interest in just about every other neighborhood, too. The Old City is rich with history, Center City is bursting with arts and culture, South Philadelphia is home to the Italian Market, and University City feels like an entirely other town in itself. Manayunk, a little farther afield, is a hoppin' strip of eateries, shops and lounges.

INDEPENDENCE NATIONAL HISTORIC PARK

This L-shaped 45-acre park, along with Old City, has been dubbed 'America's most historic square mile.' Once the backbone of the United States government, today it is the backbone of Philadelphia's tourist trade. Stroll around and you'll see storied buildings in which the seeds for the Revolutionary War were planted and the US government came into bloom. You'll also find beautiful, shaded urban lawns dotted with plenty of squirrels, pigeons and costumed actors. These days, the park looks spiffier then ever. The Liberty Bell moved in 2003 into a much-improved building and a fantastic

Independence Visitors Center (see p191) opened on Market St. The only downer is the barrier that now surrounds the park's top two sites – Independence Hall and the bell – installed as a security precaution. Most sites are open every day from 9am to 5pm, and some are closed Mondays.

Liberty Bell Center (☎ 215-597-8974; 6th & Market Sts) is Philadelphia's top tourist attraction, commissioned to commemorate the 50th anniversary of the Charter of Privileges (Pennsylvania's constitution enacted in 1701 by William Penn). The 2080lb bronze bell was made in London's East End by the Whitechapel Bell Foundry in 1751. The bell's inscription, from Leviticus 25:10, reads: 'Proclaim liberty through all the land, to all the inhabitants thereof.' The bell was secured in the belfry of the Pennsylvania State House (now Independence Hall) and tolled on important occasions, most notably the first public reading of the Declaration of Independence in Independence Square. The bell became badly cracked during the 19th century; despite initial repairs it became unusable in 1846 after tolling for George Washington's birthday.

Independence Hall (☎ 215-597-8974; Chestnut St btwn 5th & 6th Sts) is the 'birthplace of American government,' where delegates from the 13 colonies met to approve the Declaration of Independence on July 4, 1776. An excellent example of Georgian architecture, it sports understated lines that reveal Philadelphia's Quaker heritage. To get inside, you must join one of the frequent free tours that are organized at the visitor center. Behind Independence Hall is **Independence Square**, where the Declaration of Independence was first read in public.

The visitor center provides maps of the myriad other attractions in this historic park, which include: **Carpenters' Hall**, owned by the Carpenter Company, the USA's oldest trade guild (1724), which is the site of the First Continental Congress in 1774. **Library Hall** is where you'll find a copy of the Declaration of Independence, handwritten in a letter by Thomas Jefferson, plus first editions of Darwin's *On the Origin of the Species* and Lewis and Clark's field notes. **Congress Hall** (S 6th & Chestnut Sts), meanwhile, was the meeting place for US Congress when Philly was the nation's capital, and **Old City Hall**, finished in 1791, was home to

the US Supreme Court until 1800. The **Franklin Court** complex, a row of restored tenements, pays tribute to Benjamin Franklin with an underground museum displaying his inventions. At the **B Free Franklin Post Office** (see p191), which has a small US Postal Service museum, mail receives a special handwritten Franklin postmark. (In addition to being a statesman, author and inventor, the multitalented Franklin was a postmaster.) **Christ Church** (☎ 215-922-1695; S 2nd St), completed in 1744, is where George Washington and Franklin worshiped.

Second Bank of the US (Chestnut St btwn 4th & 5th Sts), modeled after the Greek Parthenon, is an 1824 marble-faced Greek Revival masterpiece that was home to the world's most powerful financial institution until President Andrew Jackson dissolved its charter in 1836. The building then became the Philadelphia Customs House until 1935, when it became a museum. Today it's home to the **National Portrait Gallery**, housing many pieces by Charles Willson Peale, America's top portraitist at the time of the American Revolution.

OLD CITY

Old City – the area bounded by Walnut, Vine, Front and 6th Sts – picks up where Independence National Historical Park leaves off. And, along with Society Hill, Old City was early Philadelphia. The 1970s saw revitalization, with many warehouses converted into apartments, galleries and small businesses.

The new **National Constitution Center** (☎ 215-409-6600; www.constitutioncenter.org; 525 Arch St; adult/child $6/5; ☽ 9:30am-5pm Mon-Fri, to 6pm Sat & Sun) somehow makes the United States Constitution sexy and interesting for a general audience through a theater in the round, where an enveloping screen and single live actor colorfully discuss the evolution of the Constitution. Other exhibits include a blue screen that creates the illusion of visitors being sworn in as president, interactive voting booths, and Signer's Hall, which contains lifelike bronze statues of the signers in action.

Elfreth's Alley is believed to be the oldest continuously occupied street in the USA; on it, **Mantua Maker's Museum House** (☎ 215-574-0560; No 126; adult/child $2/1; ☽ 10am-5pm Mon-Sat, from noon Sun March-Oct) offers displays of period furniture. **Betsy Ross House** (☎ 215-686-1252; 239

Arch St; suggested donation adult/child $2/1; 9am-5pm Tue-Sun) is where it is believed that Betsy Griscom Ross (1752–1836), upholsterer and seamstress, may have sewn the first US flag.

Philosophical Hall (☎ 215-440-3400; 104 S 5th St; admission free; 10am-4pm Wed-Sun Mar-Labor Day & Thu-Sun Labor Day-Feb), south of Old City Hall, is the headquarters of the **American Philosophical Society**, founded in 1743 by Benjamin Franklin. Past members have included Thomas Jefferson, Marie Curie, Thomas Edison, Charles Darwin and Albert Einstein.

The completely hip **Clay Studio** (☎ 215-925-3453; www.theclaystudio.org; 139 N 2nd St; admission free; noon-6pm Tue-Sun) exhibits staid as well as oddball works in ceramic. The studio has been in Old City since 1974 and is partially responsible for the development of the area's burgeoning gallery scene. **National Museum of American Jewish History** (☎ 215-923-5986; www .nmajh.org; 55 N 5th St) features exhibits that examine the historical role of Jews in the USA. At the nearby **US Mint** (☎ 215-408-0114; Arch St, btwn 6th & 7th Sts; admission free; tours 9am-3pm Mon-Fri, closed Sat & Sun Sep-May), you can line up for same-day, self-guided tours. **Arch Street Meeting House** (☎ 215-627-2667; 320 Arch St; donation requested $1; 9am-5pm Mon-Sat, from 1pm Sun) is the USA's largest Quaker meeting house.

SOCIETY HILL

Architecture from the 18th and 19th centuries dominates the lovely residential neighborhood of Society Hill, especially along Delancey, American, Cypress and Philip Sts. **Washington Square** was conceived as part of William Penn's original city plan, and offers a peaceful respite from sightseeing. **Physick House** (☎ 215-925-7866; 321 S 4th St; adult/child $3/2; 11am-2pm Thu-Sat), built in 1786 by Henry Hill – a wine importer who kept City Tavern well stocked – is the only freestanding, Federal-style mansion remaining in Society Hill. The **Powel House** (☎ 215-627-0364; 244 S 3rd St; adult/child $3/2; noon-5pm Thu-Sat, from 1pm Sun) was home to Samuel Powel, a colonial-time mayor of Philadelphia.

CENTER CITY, RITTENHOUSE SQUARE & AROUND

Philadelphia's center of creativity, commerce, culture and just about everything else, this is the engine that drives the city. It contains the city's tallest buildings, the financial district, big hotels, museums, concert halls, shops and restaurants. **Rittenhouse Square** is the most well known of William Penn's city squares, with its wading pool, trees and fine statues. **City Hall** (☎ 215-686-9074; www.phila.gov; Broad & Market Sts; admission free; 9:30am-4:30pm Tue-Fri) stands tall in Penn Square, and was completed in 1901. It's probably Philadelphia's architectural highlight, at 548ft high, and topped by a bronze statue of William Penn. Highly recommended for Civil War buffs is the comprehensive **Civil War Library & Museum** (☎ 215-735-8196; www.netreach.net/~cwlm; 1805 Pine St; admission $5; 11am-4:30pm Thu-Sat) boasting artifacts and exhibitions. **Rosenbach Museum & Library** (☎ 215-732-1600; www.rosenbach.org; 2010 Delancey Pl; admission $8; 10am-5pm Tue & Thu-Sun, to 8pm Wed), meanwhile, is for bibliophiles, as it features rare books and manuscripts, including James Joyce's *Ulysses* manuscript, and special exhibits.

BENJAMIN FRANKLIN PARKWAY & MUSEUM DISTRICT

Modeled after the Champs Elysées in Paris, the parkway is a center of museums and other landmarks. **Philadelphia Museum of Art** (☎ 215-763-8100; www.philamuseum.org; Benjamin Franklin Parkway & 26th St; adult/senior, student & child $10/7, Sun pay-what-you-wish; 10am-5pm Tue, Thu, Sat & Sun, to 8:45pm Wed & Fri) is the highlight. It's one of the nation's largest and most important museums, featuring some excellent collections of Asian art, Renaissance masterpieces, post-impressionist works and modern pieces by Picasso, Duchamp and Matisse. The grand stairway at its entrance was immortalized when star Sylvester Stallone ran up the steps in the 1976 flick *Rocky*. **Pennsylvania Academy of the Fine Arts** (☎ 215-972-7600; www.pafa.org; 118 N Broad St; admission $5) is a prestigious academy that has a museum with works by American painters, including Charles Willson Peale and Thomas Eakins. **Academy of Natural Sciences Museum** (☎ 215-299-1000; www.acnatsci.org; 1900 Benjamin Franklin Parkway; adult/child/senior $9/8/8.25; 10am-4:30pm Mon-Fri, 10am-5pm Sat & Sun) features a terrific dinosaur exhibition, where you can dig for fossils on weekends. **Franklin Institute Science Museum** (☎ 215-448-1200; http://sln.fi.edu; 222 N 20th St; Science Center adult/child & senior $12.75/10; 9:30am-5pm) is where hands-on science displays were pioneered; a highlight is the Ben Franklin exhibit. At the **Rodin Museum** (☎ 215-763-8100;

BENJAMIN FRANKLIN

This colonial Renaissance man was not only ahead of his own time, his ways of thinking and quirky outlook on the world may very well have him ahead of our own. He was a vegetarian (to save money, oddly enough), he advocated for cleaner streets in Philadelphia, he became a curiosity while in Britain for consuming copious amounts of water (not beer), and he founded the American Philosophical Society. His biggest claim to fame, of course, is for being an obsessed inventor; his creations included bifocals, the catheter, odometer, Franklin stove and political cartoons. And he did, of course, discover electricity and figure out how to use it. He later became a major supporter of independence, was the oldest signer of the Declaration of Independence, and petitioned Congress to end slavery. One can only wonder what the great thinker and doer would make of today's Patriot Act, wi-fi world.

---

www.rodinmuseum.org; Benjamin Franklin Parkway & N 22nd St; suggested donation $3; ☉ 10am-5pm Tue-Sun), you'll find Rodin's great works the *Thinker* and *Burghers of Calais*.

SOUTH STREET

Hipsters want to be cool enough to dislike popular **South Street** but can't help being drawn to the numerous record shops, the art-supply store and the Whole Foods grocery. Dirty-looking cheapskate eateries thrive, as do more expensive BYOBs creating unusual food. But the strip is largely commercial, particularly east of 10th St.

SOUTH PHILADELPHIA

The **Italian Market** (☉ Tue-Sat) is a highlight of South Philadelphia, where museums and restaurants reflect the area's diversity. It's the country's largest outdoor market, hawking fresh produce and cheese, homemade pastas, fish and butchered treats from lamb to pheasant. In the midst of it all is the **Mummers' Museum** (☎ 215-336-3050; http://riverfrontmummers .com/museum.html; 1100 S 2nd St; adult/child $2.50/2; ☉ 9:30am-5pm Tue-Sat, from noon Sun, closed Sun Jul & Aug), celebrating the tradition of disguise and masquerade. It has an integral role in the famed Mummers Parade, taking place here every New Year's Day.

CHINATOWN & AROUND

The fourth-largest Chinatown in the USA, Philly's version has existed since the 1860s. Chinese immigrants who built America's transcontinental railroads started out west and worked their way here. Today's Chinatown remains a center for immigrants, though now many of the neighborhood's residents come from Malaysia, Thailand and Vietnam in addition to every province

in China. Though it does hold a few residents, the tone of Chinatown is thoroughly commercial. The **Chinese Friendship Gate** (N 10th St btwn Cherry & Arch Sts) is a decorative arch built in 1984 as a joint project between Philadelphia and its Chinese sister city, Tianjin. The multicolored, four-story gate is Chinatown's most conspicuous landmark.

Not far away is the **African American Museum in Philadelphia** (☎ 215-574-0380; www.aamp museum.org; 701 Arch St; admission $8; ☉ 10am-5pm Tue-Sat, from noon Sun), which has excellent collections on black history and culture.

PENN'S LANDING

Back in its heyday, Penn's Landing was a very active port area until that activity moved farther south down the Delaware. Most of the action in today's Penn's Landing involves boarding submarines and strolling along the water's edge. The 1.8-mile **Benjamin Franklin Bridge**, the world's largest suspension bridge when completed in 1926, spans the Delaware River, and its lights dominate the skyline. Along the Penn's Landing riverfront area, between Vine and South Sts, is the **Independence Seaport Museum** (☎ 215-925-5439; 211 S Columbus Blvd; www.phillyseaport.org; adult/child/senior $8/5/6.50, 10am-noon Sun free; ☉ 10am-5pm), highlighting Philadelphia's role as an immigration hub; its shipyard closed in 1995 after 200 years.

Across the river in nearby Camden, NJ, is the excellent **New Jersey State Aquarium** (☎ 856-365-3300; www.njaquarium.org; 1 Riverside Dr; adult/child & senior/student $14/11/12; ☉ 9:30am-4:30pm Mon-Fri, 10am-5pm Sat & Sun), featuring a coral station of colorful Caribbean fish, a shark tank and an archway where you can pass under schools of fish. To get there, just hop on the **RiverLink Ferry** (☎ 856-365-1166; www.river

linkferry.org; return $6), which runs hourly from Penn's Landing.

UNIVERSITY CITY

University of Pennsylvania, commonly called 'U Penn,' was founded in 1740. The Ivy League school, along with nearby Drexel University, gives the area 30,000 students. The campus makes a pleasant afternoon stroll. While you're here, don't miss the romantic, neoclassical **30th St Station** (☎ 215-349-3147; 30th St at Market St) beautifully lit at night. **University Museum of Archaeology & Anthropology** (☎ 215-898-4000; www.upenn.edu/museum; 3260 South St; adult/child/senior & student $8/5/6, Sun free; ☽ 10am-4:30pm Thu-Sat, 1-5pm Sun, closed Sun in summer) is Penn's magical museum, containing archaeological treasures from ancient Egypt, Mesopotamia, the Mayan peninsula, Greece, Rome and North America.

FAIRMOUNT PARK

The snaking **Schuylkill River** divides this expansive park into east and west. On the east bank, **Boathouse Row** has Victorian-era rowing-club buildings that are illuminated at night. And **Philadelphia Zoo** (☎ 215-243-1100; www.philadelphiazoo.org; 3400 Girard Ave; adult/child peak $15/12, off-peak $10; ☽ 9:30am-5pm Feb-Nov, 11am-4pm Dec & Jan), the country's oldest zoo, has been modernized with naturalistic habitats.

The historic **Fairmount Park** (admission $2.50; ☽ Tue-Sun) has a number of early American houses open to the public, including **Laurel Hill** (☎ 215-235-1776), **Lemon Hill Mansion** (☎ 215-232-4337), **Mount Pleasant** (☎ 215-763-8100), **Strawberry Mansion** (☎ 215-228-8364), and **Woodford** (☎ 215-229-6115). Admission costs $3 per house. For information, check out www.philamuseum.org/collections/park house.

Barnes Foundation Gallery (☎ 610-667-0290; 300 N Lodges Lane; admission $5; ☽ by appointment only) is beyond Fairmount Park, 6 miles northwest of downtown. The gallery has an exceptionally fine collection of impressionist, post-impressionist and early French modern paintings.

MANAYUNK

With its steep hills and Victorian row houses overlooking the Schuylkill River, Manayunk – from a Native American expression meaning 'where we go to drink' – still remains a good spot to accomplish this activity. Other than drinking, visitors are also permitted to eat and shop (see p198). It's a lovely and bustling place for an hour or an afternoon and evening.

Activities

CYCLING & BLADING

Great spots include the vast expanse of Fairmount Park and the towpath that runs alongside the neighborhood of Manayunk. For advice and group rides, contact the **Bicycle Club of Philadelphia** (☎ 215-843-1093; www.philly bikeclub.org), which leads rides for all skill levels. For rentals, **Trophy Bikes** (☎ 215-625-7999; 311 Market St; bike rental full/half-day $25/20) stocks the latest 21-speed Fugi hybrids and a couple of tandems, and staff members specialize in touring.

RUNNING

Runners should also head to the park, which has tree-lined trails on each side of the river that range from 2 miles to 10 miles in length. For some excellent urban runs, stick to the quaint residential blocks around Society Hill or Center City; Kelly Drive, off Benjamin Franklin Parkway, is also a great spot to sprint, as is the all-weather track at University of Pennsylvania (Franklin Field, corner of 33rd and Spruce Sts). Also see the visitor center (p191).

Front Runners (www.frontrunnersphila.org) is a gay and lesbian runners club that sponsors treks all around the city. The umbrella group **Middle Atlantic Road Runners Club** (☎ 609-964-6232), based in Lafayette Hill, provides course and race information for locals as well as visitors. Urban hikers should check out Fairmount Park's dirt path extensions toward Wissahickon Creek, far from any noisy city traffic.

Philadelphia for Children

Safe, friendly and easy to navigate, Philly is a great place to bring the kids.

Core States Science Park (☎ 215-448-1200; Please Touch Museum; ☽ 10am-3:30pm May-Sep) A 25,000-sq-ft playground with play structures, a maze and 3-D optical illusions.

Please Touch Museum (☎ 215-963-0667; www.please touchmuseum.org; 210 N 21st St; admission $9.95; ☽ 9am-4:30pm Sep-Jun, to 5pm Jun-Aug) Has a great array of hands-on exhibits on subjects including Maurice Sendak, *Alice in Wonderland,* baby animals and science. Included with the entrance fee is admission to the attached Core States Science Park.

Philadelphia Children's Theatre (☎ 215-893-1999; www.pctheatre.org; 1906 S Rittenhouse Sq; adult/child $10/12) For a bit of culture once the playing is out of their system, head to the productions here, where shows like *Snow White* and *Peter Rabbit* (put on at the Philadelphia Ethical Society) are accompanied by study guides so young audiences can learn about each play's major themes.
Philadelphia Zoo (p195) Always a big hit.

Tours

Centipede Tours (☎ 215-735-3123; www.centipede inc.com; tours from $10) Walking tours on historic, ethnic and neighborhood themes, led by guides in period costumes.
Ghost Tour of Philadelphia (☎ 215-413-1997; www .ghosttour.com/Philadelphia; from 5th & Chestnut St; adult/child $15/8; ☼ tours 7:30pm every night Jun-Oct, Fri & Sat other times) Learn about the spirits still lurking in Independence Park and Society Hill.
Mural Tours (☎ 215-685-0754; www.muralarts .org/tours; tour $18; ☼ tours 11am Sat Jun-Oct) Guided trolley tour of the city's colorful outdoor murals, the largest collection in the country.
Philadelphia Trolley Works & 76 Carriage Company (☎ 215-925-TOUR; www.phillytour.com; adult $20-$70, child $4-13) Tour part of the city or just about every last corner, either on a narrated trolley ride or quieter horse-drawn carriage.
Phlash visitor shuttle (☎ 215-4-PHLASH; www.philly phlash.com; per ride/all-day pass $1/4) An affordable option is the one-hour, do-it-yourself tour that takes you to about 25 sites in a bright purple van; you can hop on and hop off when you want. There is no tour guide, but you are equipped with a color-coded, easy-to-follow map of the journey.

Festivals & Events

Mummers Parade (www.mummers.com) A very Philly parade, it's an elaborate celebration of costumes every New Year's Day (Jan 1).
South Street Mardi Gras for Fat Tuesday (☎ 215-965-7676) Music and booze in the streets in mid-February, on the Tuesday before Ash Wednesday.
Dad Vail Regatta (www.dadvail.org) In the second week of May, this is the nation's largest collegiate regatta.
Annual Jam on the River (www.jamontheriver.com) Excellent music lineup, from folkies to jam bands. Memorial Day weekend.
Manayunk Arts Festival (www.manayunk.com) It's the largest outdoor arts and crafts show in the Delaware Valley, with more than 250 artists from across the country each June.
Equality Forum (www.equalityforum.com) Formerly PrideFest America this is a conference on gay-rights issues with national participants held late April to early May.

Gay Pride Weekend (www.phillypride.org) A huge parade, festival and series of parties during the first weekend in June.
Philadelphia Live Arts Festival & Philly Fringe (www.livearts-fringe.org) Catch the latest in cutting-edge performance each September.
Philadelphia Annual Marathon (www.philadelphia marathon.com) Runners flock to Philly each November.

Sleeping

Nearly all hotels, B&Bs and even hostels are located in Center City, with a few options near University City and the requisite enclave of towers and motels in the asphalt jungle surrounding the airport. National chains run most of the hotels in town. The biggest gap in the accommodations scene is that of slick boutique hotels – there simply aren't any. Most hotels have some kind of parking service, usually costing about $25 per day.

BUDGET

Bank St Hostel (☎ 215-922-0222; 2 S Bank St; dm $20; ☒ ▯) This is an excellent hostel in a safe neighborhood, just a short walk from the 2nd St Station and major sights. It's got 70 dorm beds and a rec-room-type lounge area.

MIDRANGE

Shippen Way Inn (☎ 215-627-7266; 416-418 Bainbridge St; r $85-120) This 1750s colonial house has nine rooms with quilted beds, free wine and cheese in the kitchen and a cozy B&B atmosphere.

Antique Row B&B (☎ 215-592-7802; www.antiquerow bnb.com; 341 S 12th St; r $65-110; ☒) You'll find quirky, period-furnished rooms and good breakfasts on a tree-lined street of hoppin' Antique Row.

Alexander Inn (☎ 215-923-1004; www.alexanderinn .com; 301 S 12th St; r $99-159; ▯) Gay-owned (and marketed to LGBT travelers), it's got a classy lobby and 48 good-sized rooms that are called 'designer' but are really quite basic. Breakfast is included.

Penn's View Hotel (☎ 215-922-7600; www.penns viewhotel.com; cnr Front & Market Sts; r $165-185; ▯ ☒ ▯) This old-fashioned inn overlooks the water. It offers a range of rooms featuring Chippendale-style furniture and pleasant, if quite masculine, decor. Many of the rooms have exposed-brick walls and working fireplaces, and all come with plush robes for you to wear during your stay. A continental breakfast is included.

Society Hill Hotel (☎ 215-925-1919; www.society hillhotel.com; 301 Chestnut St; r $80-100, ste $120-150; P 🞩) Philly's smallest hotel has a European atmosphere, friendly staff and is right near Independence Park. Its very small but quaint rooms feature brass beds and private baths, and the first floor of the place is a popular bar and restaurant.

Latham Hotel (☎ 215-563-7474; www.lathamhotel .com; 135 S 17th St; r $109-149; P) This European-style oldie sits close to Rittenhouse Square, and a few of the rooms on the highest floors provide a glimpse of the park. Staff members are very friendly, but the bed coverings are very red.

Best Western Independence Park Hotel (☎ 215-922-4443, 800-624-2988; www.independenceparkhotel.com; 235 Chestnut St; r $129-189; P) Once a dry-goods store and shop for a doll manufacturer, this mid-19th-century building is now a small, 36-room hotel. While much of the charm of the old rooms has been retained, some of the decorating flair is a little tacky.

TOP-END

Four Seasons Hotel Philadelphia (☎ 215-963-1500; www.fourseasons.com/philadelphia; One Logan Square; r $220-300; P) For the crispest, most formal service possible, head over to this high-end chain, housed in a squat modernist job that wraps itself around a central courtyard with a modernist waterfall. Just about any service and amenity a hotel can offer is on site.

Ritz-Carlton (☎ 215-523-8000; www.ritzcarlton .com/hotels/philadelphia; 10 Ave of the Arts; r $200-300; P) This Ritz possesses one of the most lavish hotel lobbies in North America, built between 1905 and 1908 by McKim, Mead and White. During the afternoon, a formal tea is held in the rotunda.

Rittenhouse Square Bed & Breakfast (☎ 215-546-6500; www.rittenhousebb.com; 1715 Rittenhouse Square; r $179-229, ste $229-299; 🞩) Exceedingly formal, this precious place occupies a beautifully renovated carriage house and feels like it might have been one of Louis XIV's properties. Oprah Winfrey stays here when she comes to town, and kids under 12 are not permitted.

Eating

OLD CITY

Carousel Shop (☎ 215-925-3637; 210 S 3rd St; mains $2-6; ☯ breakfast, lunch) Everything from the lemonade to the liverwurst is homemade in this 27-year-old mom-and-pop operation. It's cheap and delicious, too.

Olde City Wrap Shack (☎ 215-577-5948; 146 N 2nd St; meals $6; ☯ lunch & dinner) This teeny spot churns out some excellent juices, smoothies and wraps – and sprawling in the shack's hammock while you eat makes everything taste even better.

Ariana (☎ 215-922-1535; 134 Chestnut St; mains $9-14; ☯ lunch & dinner) Sink into a cushion at this Afghani spot and choose from veggie dishes with pumpkin, spinach and cauliflower or lamb and chicken dishes jazzed up with almonds, pistachio and rosewater.

Continental (☎ 215-923-6069; 138 Market St; dinner $16-25; ☯ lunch, dinner & weekend brunch) Enjoy 'world tapas' from lobster mashed potatoes and grilled tofu to swordfish tacos, which pair perfectly with its specialty martinis and hip crowd.

Buddakan (☎ 215-574-9440; 325 Chestnut St; mains $20-28; ☯ lunch & dinner) A two-story bronze Buddha dominates the dining room here, where mains such as miso-poached shrimp or appetizers like tea-smoked spare ribs hit the spot, while bartenders make some fabulous specialty cocktails.

CENTER CITY & AROUND

Reading Terminal Market (☎ 215-922-2317; www .readingterminalmarket.org; 12th & Arch Sts; dishes $3-10) At the budget end, this huge indoor market is the best you'll find. Pick up a map of

---

PHILLY CHEESESTEAK

A stack of tender, juicy, thinly sliced beef, topped with lashings of freshly fried onion rings, covered with gorgeous, gooey melted cheese, served in a soft, warm, white bread roll – that's the city's namesake taste sensation. Among Philadelphia's contributions to American civilization, it ranks right up there with the Declaration of Independence. See for yourself at one (or both) of the city's most famous – and most rivaled – purveyors of the greasy stuff: Pat's and Geno's, right across the street from each other, brash and bright and cheap and, well, pretty much the same, though each has its diehard supporters.

the place inside one of the entrances and choose your favorite, from fresh Amish cheeses and Thai desserts, to falafel, cheesesteaks, salad bars, sushi, Peking duck and great Mexican.

Lolita (☎ 215-546-7100; 106 S 113th St; dishes $16-22) This always-packed BYOB offers up tasty takes on the Mexican-fusion trend, such as lamb loin stuffed with a blend of hazelnuts and *huitlacoche* (a trendy, corn-fungus delicacy).

Valanni (☎ 215-790-9494; 1229 Spruce St; dishes $13-18) Popular with 50-something theater-goers early, and sassy gay men for late dinners, everyone comes for solid Medi-Latin cuisine, from paella to coffee-cocoa-glazed duck breast, and excellent wines.

Le Bec-Fin (☎ 215-567-1000; www.lebecfin.com; 1523 Walnut St; prix fixe dinner $165) Many gourmets rate Le Bec-Fin as the country's best restaurant for its setting, service and superb French food. Expect top-notch service, a sort of stuffy clientele and rich and clever dishes like roasted squab with lentils and foie gras stuffed with grapefruit confit.

CHINATOWN & SOUTH STREET
St Gianna's Grille (☎ 215-829-4448; 507 S 6th St; dishes $5-8) Off of South, this place has good, cheap pizzas, salads, calzones and vegetarian specials, such as the vegan cheesesteak sandwich topped with soy cheese – not to mention the homemade vegan ice cream cakes.

Vietnam Restaurant (☎ 215-592-1163; 221 N 11th St; dishes $8-10) An always-crowded favorite serving authentic Vietnamese food such as summer rolls and vermicelli.

Joseph Poon (☎ 215-928-9333; 1002 Arch St; mains $7-20; ☺ lunch & dinner) Hyped-up Joseph Poon offers traditional Chinese stuff like duck, seafood and dumplings as well as more unusual fare such as wok-seared venison

---

THE AUTHOR'S CHOICE

Capogiro Gelato Artisans (☎ 215-351-0900; 119 S 13th St; gelato $4) Whatever you do, if you are up for dessert, don't skip Capogiro, which is not your average ice-cream shop. The design here is slicker than a Barcelona nightclub, and the gelato, in dozens of outrageous flavors – like cilantro-lime and black walnut, all made from hormone-free cows – is perfection.

---

with pineapple. Owner Mr Poon made a celebrity appearance at the recent Liberty Bell move, where he rapidly carved bells out of peppers.

Two of Philly's most popular and legendary cheesesteak places, both open 24 hours, are across the street from each other. They're both total scenes – especially late at night, when tipsy bar-hoppers head here for a grease fix after last-call and fill up all the outdoor seating. They're both delicious, so good luck making the choice:

Geno's (☎ 215-389-0659; www.genosteaks.com; S 9th St & Passyunk Ave; average sandwich $6)

Pat's King of Steaks (☎ 215-468-1546; www.patking ofsteaks.com; S 9th St & Passyunk Ave, average sandwich $6)

UNIVERSITY CITY
White Dog Café (☎ 215-386-9224; 3420 Sansom St; dishes $10-15; ☺ breakfast, lunch & dinner) For an amazing brunch, join the swarms of U Penn students and professors. Made famous by its cookbook and reputation for social activism, it offers omelets, pastries and even tofu scramble for vegans.

MANAYUNK
United States Hotel Bar & Grill (☎ 215-483-9222; 4439 Main St; dishes $8-12) Serves unique light fare, like the wild-mushroom sandwich with basil mayo in a former theater from 1914.

Le Bus Manayunk (☎ 215-487-2663; 4266 Main St; dishes $12-18) Casual, friendly and fun, Le Bus offers a real eclectic range of dishes, from Hawaiian sweet-and-sour stir fry and whole-wheat penne primavera to grilled tilapia and black-bean quesadillas.

Sonoma (☎ 215-483-9400; 4411 Main St; dishes $15-22) Cooks up organic, seasonal dishes including baked goat-cheese salad, shrimp ravioli in lobster brandy sauce and honey-lavender hickory-smoked salmon; its vodka bar offers a range of tasty martinis.

An Indian Affair (☎ 215-482-8300; 4425 Main St; dishes $14-19) Serves upscale thalis and other Indian specialties.

Jake's Restaurant (☎ 215-483-0444; dishes $20-27) This slick and popular hot spot serves everything from pan-seared foie gras to grilled New York strip steak, plus offers a great selection of wines and specialty cocktails.

Drinking
Outside of New Orleans, Old City boasts the highest concentration of liquor licenses

GAY & LESBIAN VENUES

Most of Philadelphia's gay and lesbian options lie within the Gayborhood, a small neighborhood that lies between Broad and 12 Sts and Walnut and Pine Sts. But the city is way gay all the time, especially since a surprisingly hip and extensive tourism campaign from 2004 that courted the LGBT dollar: 'Get your history straight and your nightlife gay.'

- **12th St Air Command** (☎ 215-545-8088; 254 S 12th St) A large place with several dance floors and pinball machines.

- **Millennium Coffee** (☎ 215-731-9798; 212 S 12th St) The epitome of gay meeting places, near a gay-boy gym and cool gift shop, it's a lovely place to cruise in daylight hours.

- **Bike Stop** (☎ 215-627-1662; www.thebikestop.com; 206 S Quince St) This is the place for those who like bears and leather daddies.

- **Bob & Barbara's** (☎ 215-545-4511; 1509 South St) Thursday night's drag show attracts an amazing crowd.

- **Bump** (☎ 215-732-1800; 1234 Locust St) If you brought nice duds, wear them to this swanky place.

- **Shampoo** (☎ 215-922-7500; www.shampooonline.com; Willow St btwn 7th & 8th Sts) Every week Shampoo hosts a gay event unambiguously titled 'Shaft Friday.'

- **Sisters** (☎ 215-735-0735; 1320 Chancellor St) This one's for the ladies.

- **Tavern on Camac** (☎ 215-545-0900; 243 S Camac St) Show tunes and other old-school fun.

- **Woody's Bar & Restaurant** (☎ 215-545-1893; www.woodysbar.com; 202 S 13th St) Philly's most famous gay club.

in the US; to find a spot that appeals to your sensibilities, just stroll along S 2nd and S 3rd Sts and pick a bar stool. One good choice is **Eulogy Belgian Tavern** (☎ 215-413-2354; 136 Chestnut St), full of yellow paint, brass and reddish-stained chairs, Belgian beers and a thoroughly laid-back vibe. Or try **Thirty Two** (☎ 215-627-3132; www.32lounge.com; 12 S 2nd St), which made a splash on the Old City scene when it began offering European bottle service and cool DJs.

Philadelphia's oldest bars can be found throughout the streets and alleys of Center City, like **McGillin's** (☎ 215-735-5562; 1310 Drury St), Philadelphia's oldest continually operated tavern, which displays framed copies of all its liquor licenses behind the bar with empty spaces for the prohibition years (when it remained open as a speakeasy).

In the dive-filled Washington Square area, try evergreen-favorite **Dirty Frank's** (☎ 215-732-5010; 347 S 13th St at Pine St) a local institution on Antique Row that's adorned with an outdoor mural of about a dozen famous Franks; it's got cheap booze and boho patrons.

On South St, which also has a good selection of bars and clubs, hit **Manny Brown's** (☎ 215-627-7427; 512 South St), a down-home rib

joint and beer bar, while the place to be in Rittenhouse Sq is **Bar Noir** (☎ 215-569-9333; 112 S 18th St), which is a tame neighborhood bar before 10pm, and a packed club later, featuring Bobby Startup as the talented resident DJ.

Entertainment

Though NYC is not far away – something Philly entertainers can never completely forget – this town has plenty of its own artistic draws, with every kind of option imaginable. Throughout the city, the cheap, the historic and the trendy cohabitate.

THEATER, DANCE & ORCHESTRA
Tickets & Reservations
Ticket Philadelphia (☎ 215-893-1999; www.ticket philadelphia.org; per ticket service fee $4.50) books tickets for events at the Mann Center, Kimmel Center and Academy of Music.

Arden (☎ 215-922-1122; www.ardentheater.org; 40 N 2nd St; tickets $24-40) A slick, modern stage and well-designed seating set the tone for one of the finest theater experiences in Philadelphia.

Plays & Players Theater (☎ 215-985-1400 ext 100; www.phillytheatreco.com; 1714 Delancey St; tickets $30-45) This charming turn-of-the-century theater sits on a quiet residential street south of Rittenhouse Square and is home to the Philadelphia Theatre Company, which produces high-end contemporary plays with regional actors.

Pennsylvania Ballet (☎ 215-551-7000; www.paballet.org; Broad & Locust Sts; tickets $19-94) Recent shows by this excellent dance company, whose home is the beautiful Academy of Music, include *The Taming of the Shrew, Swan Lake,* and *The Nutcracker.*

Philadelphia Dance Company (☎ 215-893-1999; www.philadanco.org; 9 N Preston St; tickets $20-40) This 30-something-year-old company provides top-shelf exhibitions of grace, strength and movement, blending ballet and modern as the resident dance company at the Kimmel Center.

Kimmel Center for the Performing Arts (☎ 215-790-5800; www.kimmelcenter.org; Broad & Spruce Sts) Philadelphia's most active center for fine music, the Kimmel Center organizes a vast array of performances.

Philadelphia Orchestra (☎ 215-790-5800; www.philorch.org; Broad & Spruce Sts; tickets $10-130) The city's orchestra, founded in 1900, plays at the Kimmel Center, where it also resides. Christoph Eschenbach's recent appointment as music director generated excitement.

NIGHTCLUBS

Shampoo (☎ 215-922-7500; www.shampoooonline.com; Willow St btwn 7th & 8th Sts; cover $7-12) Home to foam parties, hot tubs and velvet seating, this giant nightclub's weekly repertoire includes an immensely popular gay night on Fridays, a long-standing Wednesday engagement for those who dig the Cure and Skinny Puppy, and a conventional free-for-all on Saturdays.

Fluid (☎ 215-629-0565; 613 S 4th St; cover $5-10) Young crowds who like to bust it end up at its smallish hot spot. Depending on the evening, DJs play hip-hop, house or sometimes techno. The unmarked entrance to the club is easy to miss: look for a blue door on Kater St.

Soma (☎ 215-873-0222; 33 S 3rd St) The small, square room gets quality talents to spin hip-hop, deep house, drum and bass, or reggae.

JAZZ & LIVE MUSIC

Chris' Jazz Club (☎ 215-568-3131; 1421 Sansom St; cover $5-10) Showcasing local talent along with national greats, this intimate space

features a four o'clock piano happy hour Tuesday through Friday and good bands Monday through Saturday nights.

Ortlieb's Jazzhaus (☎ 215-922-1035; 847 N 3rd St; occasional cover $5) With a jazz lineup that's among the most respected in town, the Tuesday house band has a particularly stellar reputation.

Khyber Pass (☎ 215-238-5888; 56 S 2nd St; cover $5-15) Devoted to rock, this dirty old bar has a nightly schedule of live music. The Strokes made it big while they were the Khyber's resident band.

FILM

Film @ International House (☎ 215-895-6575; www.ihousephilly.org; 3701 Chestnut St) Among the many other theaters in town, da House has particularly excellent screenings, often organized by themes from Cuba to animation.

SPORTS

Football is all about the **Philadelphia Eagles** (Lincoln Financial Field; ☎ Ticketmaster 215-336-2000; www.ticketmaster.com), who play in spanking-new, state-of-the-art Lincoln Field. The NFL season runs from August through January, with home games occurring twice each month, usually on Sundays. The baseball team is the **Philadelphia Phillies** (Citizen's Bank Park; ☎ Ticketmaster 215-336-2000; www.ticketmaster.com; tickets $15-40). The National League team plays 81 home games from April to October. Finally, basketball comes courtesy of the **Philadelphia 76ers** (Wachovia Center; ☎ 215-339-7676, 800-462-2849 ticket sales; www.nba.com/sixers; 3601 S Broad St; tickets $15-62), whose star player is Allen Iverson.

Shopping

Though it may appear to be all about shopping malls and sterile chains in Philly, there are actually plenty of unique-boutique areas. Among the best are the stretch of Walnut St linking Rittenhouse Square and Washington Square, loaded with boutiques (and trendy chains); the kitschy clothing, cool comics and CD shops of South Street; fresh produce, cheese and meat of the Italian Market Vendors (see p194); and Old City, where a gallery district along 2nd and 3rd Sts contains arty shops with handcrafted fashions and accessories.

Unique shopping districts, where certain purveyors cluster together in a very old-school way, are **Antique Row** (Pine St btwn 9th &

17th St), **Fabric Row** (4th St btwn Bainbridge & Catherine Sts) & **Jeweler's Row** (Sansom St btwn 7th & 8th St). And yes, there are plenty of good malls (if you like that type of thing). Try the small and swanky **Shops at Bellevue** (☎ 215-875-8350; 200 S Broad St), the big and basic **Gallery at Market East** (☎ 215-925-7162; 9th & Market Sts) and the reliable **Shops at Liberty Place** (☎ 215-851-9055; 16th & Chestnut Sts).

Getting There & Away

AIR

Philadelphia International Airport (☎ 215-937-6800, 800-745-4283; www.phl.org; 8000 Essington Ave), 7 miles south of Center City, is served by direct flights from Europe, the Caribbean, Mexico and Canada, and offers connections to Asia, Africa and South America. Domestically, it has flights to over 100 destinations in the USA.

BUS

Greyhound (☎ 800-229-9424; www.greyhound.com; 1001 Filbert St) and **Peter Pan Bus Lines** (☎ 800-237-8747; www.peterpanbus.com; 1001 Filbert St) are the major carriers. Greyhound connects Philadelphia with hundreds of cities nationwide, while Peter Pan concentrates on the Northeast. Return fare to New York City is about $40 (2½ hours one way), to Atlantic City $12 (1½ hours) and to Washington, DC $40 (3½ hours). **Capitol Trailways** (☎ 800-444-2877; www.capitoltrailways.com) makes connections to Lancaster, Reading, New York City, and Washington, DC. **NJ Transit** (☎ 215-569-3752 within Philadelphia, 800-772-2222 within NJ, 973-762-5100 out of state; www.njtransit.com) carries you from Philly to points in New Jersey.

TRAIN

Beautiful **30th Street Station** (☎ 215-349-3196; www.30thstreetstation.com), is one of the biggest train hubs in the country. **Amtrak** (☎ 800-872-7245; www.amtrak.com) provides service from here to Boston (regional service $87, 5¾ hours; Acela express service $163, 5¼ hours) and to Pittsburgh (regional service $40, 7¼ hours). A cheaper but longer (adult/child $17.40/11.40; 2½ hours) way to get to NYC is to take the SEPTA R7 suburban train to Trenton in New Jersey. There you connect with **NJ Transit** (☎ 215-569-3752 Philadelphia, 800-772-2222 NJ, 973-762-5100 out of state; www.njtransit.com) to Newark's Penn Station, then continue on NJ Transit to New York City's Penn Station.

CAR

Several interstate highways lead through and around Philadelphia. From the north and south, I-95 (Delaware Expressway) follows the eastern edge of the city beside the Delaware River, with several exits for Center City. I-276 (Pennsylvania Turnpike) runs east across the northern part of the city and over the river to connect with the New Jersey Turnpike.

Getting Around

TO/FROM THE AIRPORT

Fare for a taxi to Center City is a flat fee of $20. The airport is also served by SEPTA's regional service using the R1 line. The R1 ($5.50) will drop you off in University City or in numerous stops in Center City. SEPTA's ticketing machines on the train platforms frequently don't work.

CAR & MOTORCYCLE

Driving isn't recommended in central Philadelphia; parking is difficult and regulations are strictly enforced. Downtown distances are short enough to let you see most places on foot, and a train, bus or taxi can get you to places farther out relatively easily. Philly is an inexpensive place to rent cars. Typical daily rates for a compact are $30 to $50 with unlimited mileage, less on weekends or by the week. See p1175 for car-rental advice.

PUBLIC TRANSPORTATION

SEPTA (☎ 215-580-7800; www.septa.org) operates Philadelphia's municipal buses. Though extensive and reliable, the web of bus lines is difficult to make sense of, particularly since SEPTA's confusing website doesn't provide a comprehensive map of the 120 routes servicing Philly's 159 sq miles. To get such a map, you have to purchase SEPTA's *Official Philadelphia Transit & Street Map* ($7) either online or from a transit store. The one-way fare on most routes is $2, for which you'll need the exact change or a token. Many subway stations and transit stores sell discounted packages of two tokens for $2.60. If you're going to be doing a lot of traveling, SEPTA's Day Pass ($5.50) is decent value.

SEPTA also operates two subway lines in Philadelphia. The Market-Frankfort line (also known as the El) runs east–west along Market St from 69th St in West Philadelphia to Front St, from where it heads north to Frankfort. The Broad St line runs north–south from Fern Rock in North Philadelphia to South Philadelphia's Pattison Ave, near Lincoln Field, the Wachovia Center and Citizen's Bank Park sports stadiums. SEPTA also operates a trolley service. Routes 10, 11, 13, 34 and 36 begin underground at 13th St Station, on tracks running parallel to the Market-Frankfort Line.

TAXIS & SHUTTLES

Cabs, especially around City Center, are easy to hail. Fares are $1.80 for the first one-sixth of a mile, then 30¢ for each subsequent one-sixth plus 20¢ for every minute of waiting time. The fare from University City to Penn's Landing is about $7. The flat fare from Center City to the airport is $20. Some cabs accept credit cards.

The **Phlash** (☎ 215-474-5274) shuttle bus loops downtown from Logan Circle through Center City to the waterfront and South St (one way/all day $2/4).

AROUND PHILADELPHIA
New Hope

New Hope, which sits equidistant from Philadelphia and New York City, is a quaint, artsy little town. It's edged with a long and peaceful towpath that's perfect for runners, cyclists and strollers, and you can walk across the water to its sister town, Lambertville, in New Jersey. The town draws a large amount of gay folk, who feel comfortable here because of the rainbow flags that hang outside of various businesses, as well as a gay anti-discrimination ordinance that was passed in 2002.

ORIENTATION & INFORMATION

New Hope is about 40 miles north of Philadelphia, on the shore of the Delaware River. The **New Hope Visitors Center** (☎ 215-862-5030; www.newhopevisitorscenter.org; 1 W Mechanic St) is a great first stop for maps and brochures about town. The **New Hope Chamber of Commerce** (☎ 215-862-9990; www.newhopepa.com) can answer questions about local businesses.

SIGHTS & ACTIVITIES

Strolling the quaint streets is a day within itself, but one of New Hope's most unique offerings is the mule-drawn canal boat rides in the Delaware Canal, a leftover from the canal building era of the mid-

19th century. Stop by the **New Hope Canal Boat Company** (☎ 215-862-0758; 149 Main St; adult/child $10/8; ☻ tours 12:30pm & 3pm May-Oct) for tickets. Or spend a few picturesque hours floating slowly downstream in a tube or canoe, courtesy of **Bucks County River Country** (☎ 215-297-5000; www.rivercountry.net; 2 Waters Lane, Point Pleasant; tube/canoe $18/20; ☻ rent 9am-2:30pm, return by 5pm), about 8 miles north of New Hope on Rte 32.

SLEEPING & EATING

A great day trip from either Philly or NYC, New Hope has a plethora of cute B&Bs if you decide to make a weekend out of it. Try the **Fox & Hound Bed & Breakfast** (☎ 215-862-5082; www.foxhoundinn.com; 246 W Bridge St; r from $85; ✗ ✗), with cute rooms in an 1850 stone manor, or **Porches on the Towpath** (☎ 215-862-3277; www.porchesnewhope.com; 20 Fisher's Alley; r from $95; ✗ ✗), one of several gay-owned inns, featuring elegant quarters and a quiet, tucked-away location on the canal.

When you get hungry, **Landing Inn** (☎ 215-862-5711; 22 N Main St; dishes $8-14) is a romantic spot with a fireplace and waterfront views.

Easton

The historic, picturesque and artsy town of Easton, home to Lafayette College, is located in the Leheigh Valley, just over the New Jersey border and on the banks of the Delaware River. For detailed information about the town, which makes a fun day trip from either Philadelphia (75 miles away) or New York City (70 miles away), visit www.easton-pa.com.

Strolling around the quaint main streets here is a lovely way to spend the afternoon, especially if you stop into some of the many art galleries that have moved in in recent years. **Connexions** (☎ 610-250-7627; 213 Northampton St) showcases local artists and hosts frequent openings and gallery talks. The most popular reason to visit is the wonderful **Crayola Factory** (☎ 610-515-8000; 30 Centre Sq; ☻ Tue-Fri 9:30am-4pm, Sat to 5pm, Sun from noon Sep-May, 9:30am-5pm Mon-Sat, from 11am Memorial Day-Labor Day; admission $9), home of the beloved crayons, where kids (and adults!) can watch the crayons and markers get made, plus enjoy hands-on exhibits such as a room where you're *supposed* to write on the walls. In the same complex with the same hours is the **National Canal Museum** (admission $9), with fascinating exhibits on how canals helped create a national economy.

Grab a sandwich or coffee at the **Quadrant** (☎ 610-252-1188; 20 N 3rd St), a bookstore and café that's a hip hang for locals, and, if you just don't want to leave, grab a cozy room at the **Lafayette Inn** (☎ 610-253-4500; 525 W Monroe St; r $115-225), an 18-room Georgian-style mansion with antiques, big breakfasts and wi-fi.

Brandywine Valley

Straddling the Pennsylvania-Delaware border, the Brandywine Valley is a patchwork of rolling, wooded countryside, historic villages, gardens, mansions and museums. The **Brandywine Valley Tourist Information Center** (☎ 610-388-2900, 800-228-9933; www.brandy winevalley.com; Rte 1; ☺ 10am-6pm April-Sep, to 5pm Oct-Mar) sits outside the gates of Longwood Gardens in Kennett Square, PA. The spectacular **Longwood Gardens** (☎ 800-737-5500; www .longwoodgardens.org; Rte 1; admission $14; ☺ 9am-5pm Nov-Mar, to 6pm Apr-Oct), near Kennett Sq, has 1050 acres, 20 indoor gardens and 11,000 kinds of plant, with something always in bloom. There's also a Children's Garden with a maze, illuminated fountains in summer, and festive lights at Christmas.

A showcase of American artwork, the **Brandywine River Museum** (☎ 610-388-2700; Hwy 1 & Rte 100; adult $5), at Chadd's Ford, includes the work of the 'Brandywine School' – Pyle, several Wyeths and Maxfield Parrish. Also, one of the valley's most famous attractions is **Winterthur** (☎ 302-888-4600, 800-448-3883; Rte 52, Winterthur, DE; adult/child/senior & student $15/5/13; ☺ 10am-5pm Tue-Sun), an important museum of American furniture and decorative arts that was the country estate of Henry Francis du Pont until he opened it to the public in 1951.

For more information on local attractions, see p341.

Valley Forge

After being defeated at the Battle of Brandywine Creek and the British occupation of Philadelphia in 1777, General Washington and 12,000 Continental troops withdrew to Valley Forge. Today, Valley Forge symbolizes Washington's endurance and leadership. The **Valley Forge National Historic Park** (☎ 610-783-1077; www.nps.gov/vafo; N Gulph Rd & Rte 23; admission free; ☺ dawn-dusk), contains 5½ sq miles of scenic beauty and open space 20 miles northwest of downtown Philadelphia. Not a battlefield, the site is held as a symbol of bravery and endurance – 2000 of George Washington's 12,000 troops perished here from freezing temperatures, hunger and disease, and many others returned home; the rest were trained, drilled and organized into a disciplined force, and emerged to eventually defeat the British.

PENNSYLVANIA DUTCH COUNTRY

The core of Pennsylvania Dutch Country lies in the southeast region of Pennsylvania, in an area about 20 by 15 miles, east of Lancaster. The Amish (*ah*-mish), Mennonite and Brethren religious communities are collectively known as the 'Plain People.' The Old Order Amish, with their dark, plain clothing, live a simple, Bible-centered life but have, ironically, managed to become a major tourist attraction. Anabaptist sects, persecuted in their native Switzerland, settled in tolerant Pennsylvania starting in the early 1700s. Speaking German dialects, they became known as 'Dutch' (from 'Deutsch'). Most Pennsylvania Dutch live on farms, and their beliefs vary from sect to sect. Many do not use electricity, and most opt for horse-drawn buggies – a delightful sight, and sound, in the area.

INFORMATION

To escape the busloads of tourists and truly learn about the region, rent a bike,

---

GOING DUTCH

Famous not only for its plainly clad Amish folk, the Dutch Country is also home to hearty Pennsylvania Dutch food. And one of the best things about it is how it's eaten – communally, at long tables where you might actually have to sit next to and converse with a stranger. You won't be strained for conversation, as the massive offerings give you plenty to chat about – from pepper cabbage appetizers to homemade sausage, candied sweet potatoes and farm-grown vegetables, the food keeps coming until you can't take another bite. Save room for the local favorite, shoofly pie – a sticky, sweet dessert of baked molasses, topped with crumbled brown sugar.

pack some food and explore the numerous back roads. You may also consider hiring a guide for a private tour, or simply visiting in winter, when tourism is down. **Lancaster County Bicycle Tours** (☎ 717-768-8366) rents bikes and leads intimate tours that visit an Amish home and grocery store ($50 per half-day). Some farm homes rent rooms for $50 to $100 – they welcome kids and offer a unique opportunity to experience farm life. The **Dutch Country Visitors Center** (☎ 800-PA-DUTCH; www.padutchcountry.com; ☻ 9am-5pm), off Rte 30 in Lancaster, offers comprehensive information. For a true overnight experience, just ask to be directed to one of the farming families that rent rooms and offer home-cooked meals.

SIGHTS & ACTIVITIES
Lancaster & Around
On the western edge of the Amish country, the pleasant town of **Lancaster** was briefly the US capital in September 1777, when Congress stopped here overnight. The touristy **Central Market** (Penn Sq; ☻ 6am Tue, Fri & Sat) offers good food and crafts, the **Lancaster Cultural History Museum** (☎ 717-299-6440; 13 W King St; adult/child $6/4; ☻ 10am-5pm Tue-Sat, from noon Sun) has a collection of 18th- and 19th-century paintings, period furniture and local craftwork. The **Amish Farm & House** (☎ 717-394-6185; 2395 Lincoln Hwy; admission $8) is an original farmhouse with a tour that describes Amish culture.

Probably named for its crossroads location, nearby **Intercourse** has shops selling clothing, quilts, candles, furniture, fudge and even souvenirs with Intercourse jokes. Browse along Rte 340 or 772, northwest of Intercourse. Friendly **People's Place** (☎ 800-390-8436; www.thepeoplesplace.com; Rte 340; admission $6; ☻ 10am-5pm Mon-Sat) gives a sensitive overview of Amish and Mennonite life with the 30-minute *Who Are the Amish?* documentary.

Bird-in-Hand has craft stores, restaurants and a farmers market. Country Barn Quilts & Crafts, east of town, has a good selection. **Abe's Buggy Rides** (☎ 717-392-1794; Mon-Sat; adult/child $10/5) does a 2-mile tour, and one guide even speaks Spanish. In **Lititz**, visitors come for the **Sturgis Pretzel House** (☎ 717-626-4354; www.sturgispretzel.com; Rte 772; admission $2; ☻ 9am-5pm Mon-Sat), the USA's first pretzel factory. The nearby **Ephrata Cloister** (☎ 717-733-6600;

www.ephratacloister.org; 632 W Main St, Ephrata; admission $7; ☻ 9am-5pm Mon-Sat, from noon Sun) gives tours of its collection of medieval-style buildings, one of the country's earliest religious communities.

SLEEPING & EATING
There's a slew of inns in the Amish country, and you will find cheap motels along the southeastern portion of Rte 462/Rte 30. The **Landis Guest Farm** (☎ 717-898-7028; www.landisfarm .org; Gochlan Rd; r $90-125) in Manheim puts you up in a cozy cottage, feeds you a big country breakfast and lets you milk the cows.

To sample one of the famous family-style restaurants, get prepared to rub elbows with lots of tourists. The experience is part of coming to Amish country, though – and it'll fill you with lots of delicious dishes, including the famous, sticky-sweet dessert of shoofly pie. Two standout spots are **Shady Maple Smorgasbord** (☎ 717-354-8222; Rte 23; mains $15) in Blue Ball, or **Willow Valley Family Restaurant** (☎ 717-464-2711; 2416 Willow St Pike; mains $19) in Lancaster. Locals get their Pennsylvania Dutch grub at the family-owned **Chimney Corner Restaurant** (☎ 717-626-4707; Rte 772; mains $10) in Lititz, or Ephrata's tiny **Bright's Restaurant** (☎ 717-738-1177; Rte 272; dishes $8).

GETTING THERE
RRTA (☎ 717-397-4246) local buses link the main towns, but a car is much better for sightseeing. The **Capitol Trailways & Greyhound terminal** (☎ 717-397-4861; Lancaster train station) has buses to Philadelphia and Pittsburgh. The **Amtrak train station** (☎ 717-291-5080; 53 McGovern Ave, Lancaster) has trains to and from Philadelphia ($13, 80 minutes) and Pittsburgh ($38, six hours).

SOUTH CENTRAL PENNSYLVANIA
Harrisburg & Around
The state capital of Harrisburg, located on the Susquehanna River, is not the most exciting place. But the **capital dome**, modeled after St Peter's Basilica in Rome, is impressive. The **State Museum of Pennsylvania** (☎ 717-787-4980; www.statemuseumpa.org; cnr North & 3rd Sts; admission free; ☻ 9am-5pm Tue-Sat, from noon Sun) exhibits Civil War artifacts and the huge *Battle of Gettysburg* painting, plus houses a popular planetarium.

Just 12 miles from here is **Hershey** (www .hersheypa.com), the home of Milton Hershey's chocolate empire, **Hershey's Chocolate World** (☎ 717-534-4900). While kids might fall under its spell, it's actually a disappointing mock factory and giant candy store. A bit better is **Hershey Park** (☎ 800-437-7439; adult/child $39.95/22.95; ☉ 10am-10pm Jun-Aug), a seriously commercialized amusement park with more than 60 rides, and the nearby **Zoo America** (adult/child $7.50/6.50).

Gettysburg

This tranquil, compact and history-laden town, 145 miles west of Philadelphia, saw one of the Civil War's most decisive and bloody battles. It's also where Lincoln delivered his Gettysburg Address. The area is anchored by the 8-square-mile **Gettysburg National Military Park** (☎ 717-334-1124; www .nps.gov/gett; 97 Taneytown Rd), with a great museum, bookstore and tour dispatch center; you can also pick up a map that details a self-guided auto tour, with somber sights including the Eternal Light Peach Memorial and the Wheatfield, which was strewn with more than 4000 dead and wounded after the battle.

The **Gettysburg Convention & Visitors Bureau** (☎ 717-334-6274; www.gettysburg.com; 35 Carlisle St; ☉ 8:30am-5:30pm) also distributes a comprehensive list of town attractions, which include the **Eisenhower National Historic Site** (☎ 717-338-9114; 250 Eisenhower Farm Ln; admission $8; ☉ 9am-5pm), Ike's former home, as well as the house that served as **General Lee's Headquarters** (☉ 717-334-3141; Budford Ave; admission free; ☉ 9am-5pm mid-Mar–Nov).

The annual **Civil War Heritage Days** (recorded information ☎ 717-334-2028) festival, taking place from the last weekend of June through the first weekend of July, features living history encampments, battle reenactments, a lecture series and book fair. You can find **reenactments** (www.gettysburg.com/livinghistory) throughout the year, as well.

For accommodations, try **Gaslight Inn** (☎ 717-337-9100; www.thegaslightinn.com; 33 E Middle St; r $110-195), a wonderful B&B right in the center of town. **Herr Tavern & Publick House** (☎ 717-334-4332; www.herrtavern.com; 900 Chambersburg Rd; mains $19-27) serves upscale American lunch and dinner in a historic setting, while the hip **Ragged Edge Coffee House** (☎ 717-334-4464; 110 Chambersburg St) has great coffee, sandwiches, smoothies and live music on weekend nights.

Hanover

A quiet and wonderful alternative base for visiting Gettysburg is the historic town of Hanover, just 10 miles east on Rte 116, and home to well-preserved Georgian, classic revival and neoclassical architecture. Visit the lively **Amish market** (E Chestnut St) on Saturdays, catch a group show at the **Hanover Area Arts Guild** (☎ 717-632-2521; 32 Carlisle St) or tour one of two snack-food factories – famous pretzel maker **Snyder's of Hanover** (☎ 800-233-7125; 1350 York St) or **UTZ Quality Foods** (☎ 800-367-7629; 900 High St), best known for its potato chips.

Beechmont (☎ 717-632-3013; www.thebeechmont .com; 315 Broadway; r $94-159; ☒ ☐) is an absolutely charming, well-run and beautifully appointed B&B serving huge and excellent breakfasts. For an unforgettable dinner, take a short stroll to the **Maple Leaf** (☎ 717-632-5100; 120 E Chestnut St; mains $18-25), where a gifted chef churns out an ever-changing menu of organic, seasonal cuisine in a romantic old house.

PITTSBURGH

Still mired in its steelworker reputation in most Americans' minds, Pittsburgh is a surprisingly hip, fun, cultured and beautiful city. The people are friendly and down-to-earth, and the myriad neighborhoods exude a historic, unique vibe that's anchored by the many architectural gems. Visitors will be thrilled to find top-notch museums, verdant parklands, pockets of alternative culture and an ever-growing clutch of clubs and eateries – along with the endearing, scrappy, blue-collar element that remains among closely-knit neighborhoods that refuse to completely give way to the creep of gentrification.

History

George Washington established a British presence here in 1753, before the start of the French and Indian War, but the French wound up controlling the area until being ejected by the British, who renamed Fort Duquesne as Fort Pitt, after Prime Minister William Pitt the Elder. Eventually called Pittsburgh, the city became famous for iron and steel production during the 19th century, and the industry was furthered by the Civil War. Scottish-born immigrant Andrew Carnegie grew rich by modernizing steel production here, which dipped during the

PITTSBURGH IN...

Two Days

Dive right in by starting your day with breakfast at the **Strip** (p213). Stroll around for a while, stopping in to view the food and the action at **Wholey's** (p215), then hit a couple of the major museums, maybe the **Carnegie Museum of Art** (p211) and the **Frick Art Museum** (p211). Make your way over to the **Monongahela Incline** (p210) by late afternoon, and ride up to the top of **Mount Washington** (p210) at sunset, enjoying the golden view of the city and rivers below. Ride back down and enjoy dinner, drinks and maybe even a night of live music in the hoppin' **South Side** (p210) before calling it a night. On day two, have brunch in **Shadyside** (p214), then go to Oakland and soak up the collegiate atmosphere, being sure to tour the **Cathedral of Learning** (p211). End your evening in the latest hip 'hood, **Lawrenceville** (p211), with dinner and drinks.

Four Days

Follow the two-day itinerary, and on the third day have brunch at the way-popular **Quiet Storm** (p214) before checking out the myriad attractions on the North Side: the wonderful **Andy Warhol Museum** (p210), the totally cool **Mattress Factory** (p210) and the delightful **National Aviary** (p210), followed by a stroll through the historic **Mexican War Streets** (p210). Spend the rest of the day shopping and strolling in diverse **Squirrel Hill** (p211), then have dinner in nearby **Bloomfield** (p214), Pittsburgh's Little Italy. Enjoy the pleasures of **Frick Park** (p211) on your last day, with a walk through the historic **Golden Triangle** (opposite) district, where you could take in a show at **Heinz Hall** (p214), or have a heady nightcap at **Church Brew Works** (p214) on Liberty Ave.

Great Depression but rose again because of mass-produced automobiles in the 1930s. An urban-renewal program in the 1990s transformed the downtown area, and today, despite lingering economic hardships, the place has had a growing 'cool' and artistic cachet.

Orientation

The city, located at the point where the Monongahela and the Allegheny Rivers join the Ohio River, spreads out over the waterways and has neighborhoods connected by seven picturesque bridges (all with footpaths). It's large and not easily traversed on foot unless you're exploring one neighborhood at a time. The mystical-sounding Golden Triangle, between the converging Monongahela and Allegheny Rivers, is Pittsburgh's downtown, now comprehensively (if soullessly) renovated. Just northeast of here, the Strip offers warehouses, ethnic food stores and clubs and, across the Allegheny River, the North Side has the big new sports stadiums and several museums. Across the Monongahela River is the South Side, which slopes up to Mt Washington; at the bottom, E Carson St has clubs and restaurants. East of downtown is Oakland, the university area, and beyond that Squirrel Hill and Shadyside, residential neighborhoods with a small-town feel.

MAPS

Rand McNally makes good laminated maps of Pittsburgh, available in the city's airport bookstores, while **Universal Map** (www.universalmap.com) makes an excellent paper street map of Greater Pittsburgh.

Information

BOOKSTORES

Caliban Book Shop (☎ 412-681-9111; 410 S Craig St) Specializes in literary first editions, fine arts, poetry & travel.

City Books (☎ 412-481-7555; 1111 E Carson St) In South Side.

Eljay's Used Books (☎ 412-381-7444; 1309 E Carson St) Eclectic fare.

Jay's Bookstall (☎ 412-683-2644; 3604 Fifth Ave) Well-stocked indie shop.

Joseph-Beth Booksellers (☎ 412-381-3600; 2705 E Carson St) The seventh location (first in PA) in a growing regional chain; massive selection.

University of Pittsburgh Book Center (4000 Fifth Ave) Close to 90,000 general titles, plus textbooks..

EMERGENCY

Emergency number (☎ 911)

Pittsburgh Action Against Rape (☎ 412-765-2731)

Poison Emergency Hotline (☎ 412-681-6669)

Womansplace (☎ 412-678-4616) Twenty-four-hour hotline for domestic violence.

INTERNET ACCESS

While you will find that wi-fi hotspots are pretty well ubiquitous, free ones are not (though the Pittsburgh International Airport has free access). Check www.wi-fi411.com for a list of locations and see p1152. Hotels and inns usually have a computer available to guests.

Beehive (☎ 412-488-HIVE; 1327 E Carson St) Cool café with free wi-fi.

Carnegie Library of Pittsburgh (☎ 412-622-3114; 4400 Forbes Ave) Main branch (plus others; call for info) has free public access at terminals.

INTERNET RESOURCES

City of Pittsburgh (www.city.pittsburgh.pa.us) Details on neighborhoods and political districts.

Citysearch (pittsburgh.citysearch.com) Nightlife, restaurants, shopping.

Hello Pittsburgh (www.hellopittsburgh.com) Comprehensive city listings.

Pittsburgh.net (www.pittsburgh.net) Listings, neighborhoods and events.

MEDIA

Pittsburgh City Paper (www.pghcitypaper.com) Free alternative weekly with extensive arts listings.

Pittsburgh's Out (www.outpub.com) Free monthly gay newspaper.

Pittsburgh Post-Gazette (www.post-gazette.com) A major daily.

Pittsburgh Tribune-Review (www.pittsburghlive.com/x/tribune-review) Another major daily.

WQED-FM: 89.3 The local National Public Radio affiliate.

MEDICAL SERVICES

Allegheny County Health Department (☎ 412-687-ACHD; 3333 Forbes Ave) Has a walk-in medical center.

Allegheny General Hospital (☎ 866-680-0004; 320 E North Ave) Emergency room.

CVS (☎ 412-687-4180; 3440 Forbes Ave; ☽ 24hr)

Rite Aid (☎ 412-621-4302; 209 Atwood St; ☽ 24hr)

University of Pittsburgh Medical Center (☎ 412-647-8762; 200 Lothrop St) Emergency, high-ranking medical care.

MONEY

ATMs are plentiful. You will find them in delicatessens and grocery stores (where you may be charged up to a $2 fee) as well as in banks. For currency exchange, try the following:

Citizens Bank (☎ 412-234-4215; 5th & Grant Sts)

PNC Bank (☎ 412-762-2090; 5th & Wood Sts)

POST

US Post Office (☎ 412-642-4476; 700 Grant St) Main branch; call for other locations.

TOILETS

Public toilet (E Carson St at 18th St) While pubs and restaurants are mellow about letting you sneak into their bathrooms, Pittsburgh is quite proud of its lone automated restroom, which lets you in for a fee of 25¢.

TOURIST INFORMATION

Greater Pittsburgh Convention & Visitors Bureau (☎ 412-281-7711, 800-366-0093; www.visitpittsburgh.com; Pittsburgh Liberty Ave; Pittsburgh International Airport near baggage claim; ☽ 9am-5pm Mon-Fri, to 3pm Sat & Sun; the Strip 1212 Smallman St, 10am-5pm) Publishes the *Official Visitors Guide* and provides maps and tourist advice.

Pittsburgh Council for International Visitors (☎ 412-392-4513; www.pciv.org; 425 Sixth Ave; ☽ 9am-5pm Mon-Fri) Hosts foreign visitors through a volunteer program

UNIVERSITIES

University of Pittsburgh, Carnegie-Mellon University and Duquesne University are all large presences in town, with sprawling campuses and bustling academic crowds.

Dangers & Annoyances

While walking around within the neighborhoods covered below is safe anytime, stretches of no-man's land that fall in between 'hoods can be isolated and creepy at night, particularly the South Side stretch between Station Sq and the bustling strip of E Carson St, as well as the North Side, once the museums have closed for the evening.

Sights

Points of interest in Pittsburgh are scattered everywhere, and its spread-out nature makes it a difficult place to cover thoroughly on foot. Driving can also be troublesome, due to the oddly laid-out streets, which even confuse locals. Public buses, luckily, are quite reliable (see p216 for more information).

GOLDEN TRIANGLE

Although it's been renovated into a modern, generic landscape, downtown still has a few fine older buildings, such as **Kaufmann's department store** (400 5th Ave), which has been recently sold to the Federated chain, and the **Allegheny County Courthouse** (☎ 412-350-5410;

PITTSBURGH

INFORMATION
Allegheny County Health Department...**1** G5
Allegheny General Hospital...**2** G4
Beehive...**(see 38)**
Caliban Book Shop...**3** H4
Citizens Bank...**4** C5
City Books...**5** H6
CVS...**6** C5
Eljay's Used Books...**7** H6
Jay's Bookstall...**8** G4
Joseph-Beth Booksellers...**9** F6
Pittsburgh Convention & Visitors
Bureau...**10** B5
Pittsburgh Council for International
Visitors...**11** C4
PNC Bank...**12** C5
Post Office...**13** C5
Rite Aid...**14** C5
University of Pittsburgh Book Center...**15** H4
University of Pittsburgh Medical
Center...**16** G4

SIGHTS & ACTIVITIES
Allegheny County Courthouse...**17** C5
Andy Warhol Museum...**18** B4
Carnegie Museum of Art...**(see 62)**
Carnegie Science Center...**19** A4
Cathedral of Learning...**20** H4
Duquesne Incline...**21** A5
Fort Pitt Museum...**22** B5
Golden Triangle Bike & Skate
Rentals...**23** C5
Just Ducky Tours...**(see 30)**
Kaufmann's Department Store...**24** C5
Mattress Factory...**25** A2
Monongahela Incline...**26** B6
National Aviary...**27** B3
Nationality Classrooms...**(see 20)**
Pittsburgh Children's Museum...**28** B3
Senator John Heinz Pittsburgh Regional
History Center...**29** D4
Station Square...**30** B5
Western Pennsylvania Field Institute...**31** C5

Western Pennsylvania Sports
Museum...**32** C4

SLEEPING
Inn on the Mexican War Streets...**33** A3
Morning Glory Inn...**34** C3
Omni William Penn Hotel...**35** C3
Priory: A City Inn...**36** C3
Westin Convention Center...**37** C4

EATING
Beehive...**38** H6
Dish Osteria Bar...**39** E6
Eleven...**40** C4
Gypsy Café...**41** H6
Il Piccolo Forno/La Prima
Espresso Co...**42** D3
Kaya...**43** D3
Le Pommier...**44** E6
Lemon Grass Café...**45** B4
Lidia's Italy...**46** D3

436 Grant St; admission free; 9am-5pm Mon-Fri), a 19th-century Romanesque stone building, filling two city blocks, designed by Henry Hobson Richardson. At the triangle's tip is **Point State Park**, which is popular during summer with strollers, runners and loungers and commemorates the historic heritage of the French and Indian War through its renovated **Fort Pitt Museum** (412-281-9284; www .fortpittmuseum.com; 101 Commonwealth Pl; admission $5; 9am-5pm Wed-Sat). The nicely remodeled brick warehouse that is the **Senator John Heinz Pittsburgh Regional History Center** (412-454-6000; www.pghhistory.org; 1212 Smallman Ave; adult/child $7.50/3; 10am-5pm) offers a good take on the region's past, with exhibits on the French and Indian War, early settlers, immigrants, steel, and the glass industry; it's also home to the **Western Pennsylvania Sports Museum**, focusing on champs from Pittsburgh.

NORTH SIDE

While this part of town feels most populated when its PNC Park is filled with sports fans for a Pittsburgh Steelers game, rest assured that its myriad museums are populated, too. The **Andy Warhol Museum** (412-237-8300; www.warhol.org; 117 Sandusky St; adult/child $10/6; 10am-5pm Tue-Thu, Sat & Sun, to 10pm Fri), celebrates Pittsburgh's coolest native son, who became famous for his pop art, avant-garde movies, celebrity connections and Velvet Underground spectaculars. Exhibits include the classic Campbell's soup cans and celebrity portraits; the museum's theater hosts frequent film screenings and quirky performers, the Warhol Café has excellent lunches, and the gift shop is well stocked with Warhol paraphernalia.

Also not to be missed is the **Mattress Factory** (412-231-3169; www.mattress.org; 500 Sampsonia Way; adult/child $8/free, half-price Thu; 10am-5pm Tue-Fri, to 7pm Sat, 1-5pm Sun), hosting unique installation art and frequent performances. **Carnegie Science Center** (412-237-3400; www .carnegiesciencecenter.org; 1 Allegheny Ave; adult/child $14/10, IMAX & special exhibits extra; 10am-5pm Sun-Fri, to 7pm Sat), great for kids, is a cut above the average hands-on science museum, with innovative exhibits on subjects from outer space to candy.

The **National Aviary** (412-321-4364; www .aviary.org; W Commons, Allegheny Sq; adult/child $6/4.50; 9am-5pm) is another treat, with more than 600 exotic and endangered birds, many of which fly freely above you in high-ceilinged, climate-controlled aviaries. Nearby is the **Mexican War Streets** neighborhood, named after battles and soldiers of the 1846 Mexican War. The carefully restored rowhouses, with Greek revival doorways and Gothic turrets, have finally been discovered by real-estate moguls, and the region may soon become trendy. For now, though, the quiet streets make for a peaceful, post-museum stroll.

SOUTH SIDE & MOUNT WASHINGTON

The South Side, bursting with shops, eateries, bars and cool characters, is a great place for strolling. To see it from above, ride either the **Monongahela Incline** (412-442-2000;

ANDY WARHOL

Andy Warhol (1928–87) was one of the most influential US artists of the 20th century. Born the son of Polish immigrants in the Oakland district of Pittsburgh, Warhol turned into one of America's favorite freaky artists. He coined the phrase about everyone having '15 minutes of fame.' Warhol, though, had more than 15 years of it.

At his mother's suggestion, he studied art at the Carnegie Institute (now Carnegie Mellon University). Come graduation in 1949 he was outta there, relocating to big, bad New York City, where he became a leading freelance commercial artist, developed his distinctive style of pop art and, by the early 1960s, was exhibiting some works that would soon be famous – silkscreen paintings of Marilyn Monroe, Mao Tse-tung and Campbell's soup cans. He also produced many experimental, underground movies starring a motley crew of drag queens and models, and then opened the Factory, which is when the fun really started. His studio became party central for avant-garde artists, druggies, prostitutes, tricks, poor little rich girls (and boys) and various other pals and sycophants. In 1968 he was shot by angry feminist Valerie Solanis, once part of his artistic circle. But he died of more natural causes – following a gallbladder operation – and a museum dedicated to his life and work was established in his home town.

www.portauthority.org; each way adult/child $1.75/85¢; 5:30am-12:45am Mon-Sat, 8:45am-midnight Sun) or **Duquesne Incline** (☎ 412-381-1665; http://incline .pghfree.net; each way adult/child $1.75/85¢; 5:30am-12:45am Mon-Sat, 8:45am-midnight Sun), the historic funicular railroads that run up and down **Mount Washington**'s steep slopes and afford great city views (and which a young Jennifer Beals rode, along with her bicycle, in the classic '80s film *Flashdance*). At the start of the Duquesne Incline is **Station Square** (☎ 412-261-9911; www.stationsquare.com; Station Sq Dr at the Fort Pitt Bridge), an over-hyped group of beautiful, renovated railway buildings that's now a shopping and entertainment complex (basically a big ol' mall). Rising up from the bustling South Side valley is the neighborhood called the **South Side Slopes**, a fascinating community of houses that seem perilously perched on the edge of cliffs, accessible via steep, winding roads and hundreds of steep stairs; there's a popular **Step Trek** (www.steptrek .org) each fall, during which crowds clamor up the 23,982 vertical feet to the top.

OAKLAND & AROUND

The University of Pittsburgh and Carnegie Mellon University are here, surrounded by streets that are packed with cheap eateries, cafés, shops and student-packed multifamily homes. Rising up from the center of the U Pitt campus is the soaring **Cath edral of Learning** (☎ 412-624-6000; 157 Cathedral of Learning; admission free, tours $3; 9am-3pm Mon-Fri, from 9:30am Sat, from 11am Sun), a grand, 42-story Gothic tower which, at 535ft, is the second-tallest education building in the world. It houses the elegant **Nationality Classrooms**, each representing a different style and period, with gorgeous details such as the cherry-wood chalkboard doors in the India room and the red-velvet upholstered chairs of Austria. While a few rooms are always left open to viewers, most are accessible only with a guided tour.

Nearby are two **Carnegie Museums** (☎ 412-622-3131; www.carnegiemuseums.org; 4400 Forbes Ave; admission to both $8; 10am-5pm Tue-Sat, from noon Sun) – the **Carnegie Museum of Art**, with terrific exhibits of architecture, impressionist, post-impressionist and modern American paintings; and the **Carnegie Museum of Natural History**, featuring a complete tyrannosaurus skeleton and exhibits on Pennsylvania geology and Inuit prehistory. East of Oakland,

in Point Breeze, is the wonderful **Frick Art & Historical Center** (☎ 412-371-0600; www.frickart .org; 7227 Reynolds St; museum & grounds free, Clayton tours $10; 10am-5pm Tue-Sun), which displays some of Henry Clay Frick's Flemish, French and Italian paintings in its Art Museum; assorted Frickmobiles like a 1914 Rolls Royce in the Car & Carriage Museum; more than five acres of grounds and gardens; and Clayton, the restored 1872 Frick mansion.

SQUIRREL HILL & SHADYSIDE

These upscale neighborhoods feature wide streets and Victorian mansions, excellent restaurants and both eclectic and chain shops. **Squirrel Hill** is home to Pittsburgh's large Jewish population, and features the city's best kosher eateries, butchers and Judaica shops. **Temple Sinai** (☎ 412-421-9715; www.templesinaipgh.org; 5505 Forbes Ave) is a synagogue that's housed in the architecturally stunning Elizabethan-style former mansion of John Worthington. In **Shadyside**, Walnut St is the bustling main strip.

LAWRENCEVILLE, BLOOMFIELD, GARFIELD & AROUND

Formerly gritty **Lawrenceville** is in the process of being transformed into the city's **Interior Design District** (www.1662designzone.com), comprising the stretch on and around Butler Street from 16th to 62nd Sts. It's a long and spotty strip of shops, galleries, studios, bars and eateries that's on every hipster's radar, and runs into the slowly gentrifying **Garfield** neighborhood, a good place for cheap ethnic eats. Bloomfield, a small Little Italy, is a strip of groceries, Italian eateries and, of all things, a landmark Polish restaurant, the Bloomfield Bridge Tavern (see p214).

Activities

PARKS CONSERVANCY

For pretty much any outdoor pursuit, the best option is the elaborate, 1700-acre system of the **Pittsburgh Parks Conservancy** (☎ 412-682-PARK; www.pittsburghparks.org), which comprises **Schenley Park** (with a public swimming pool and golf course), **Highland Park** (with swimming pool, tennis courts and bicycling track), **Riverview Park** (sporting ball fields and horseback riding trails) and **Frick Park** (with hiking trails, clay courts and a bowling green), all with beautiful running, biking and blading trails.

GOLDEN TRIANGLE

Riverfront trails along the north side of the Golden Triangle are perfect for strolling, running or biking. The perimeter of the Golden Triangle's **Point State Park** is a popular short run; for a longer run, head to the 11-mile gravel-paved **Montour Trail**, accessible by crossing the 6th St bridge and catching the paved path at the Carnegie Science Center.

BIKING & RUNNING ORGANIZATIONS

Golden Triangle Bike & Skate Rentals (☎ 412-600-0675; www.bikepittsburgh.com; Eliza Furnace Trail under 1st Ave Transit Stn; rental per hr/day $8/28) rents bikes and leads various tours of the city. The **Western Pennsylvania Field Institute** (☎ 412-255-0564; www.wpfi.org; 304 Forbes Ave) promotes outdoor recreation in the region, and sponsors bike rides and hikes in the city. For night runs, contact **People Who Run Downtown** (☎ 412-366-7458; www.pittsburghrunning.org), a group of folks who organize weekly Tuesday evening runs (5:30pm), followed by drinks at a neighborhood pub.

Pittsburgh for Children

Start off at the **Pittsburgh Children's Museum** (☎ 412-322-5058; www.pittsburghkids.org; Allegheny Sq; adult/child $5/4.50; ❂ 10am-5pm Mon-Sat, from noon Sun), which features a climbable space sculpture, exhibits about Jim Henson and Mister Rogers and some child-friendly Warhol works. Other sure bets include the **Carnegie Science Center** (p210), the **National Aviary** (p210) and the **Pittsburgh Zoo & Aquarium** (☎ 412-665-3640; www.pittsburghzoo.com; 1 Wild Pl; adult/child $9/7; ❂ 9am-4pm Oct-Mar, to 5pm Apr-Sep). In the summer head to **Sandcastle Waterpark** (☎ 412-462-6666; www.sandcastlewaterpark.com; 1000 Sandcastle Dr; admission $22; ❂ 11am-6pm Jun-Sep), Pittsburgh's water theme park, right in the city. It features the Mon Tsunami tidal wave pool, Thunder Run inner-tube river and Boardwalk Blasters shotgun slides. Also, the **International Children's Festival** (see right), is a great time to visit.

Tours

Golden Triangle Bike Tours (☎ 412-600-0675; www.bikepittsburgh.com; admission $20) Hits all the major sights.

Just Ducky Tours (☎ 412-402-3825; www.justduckytours.com; Station Sq; adult/child $18/13; ❂ Apr-Oct) General city tours in a WWII amphibious vehicle.

Pittsburgh History & Landmarks Foundation (☎ 412-471-5808; www.phlf.org; Station Sq; tours from $5) Specialized historic, architectural or cultural tours by foot or motorcoach.

Festivals & Events

Greek Food Festival (www.visitpa.com) Souvlakia and spanakopita draw thousands each May.

International Children's Festival (www.pghkids.org) A slew of kids' events held around the city in mid-May.

Pittsburgh Folk Festival (www.pghfolkfest.org) A multicultural event with food and entertainment from around the world each Memorial Day weekend.

Three Rivers Arts Festival A series of shows in early June

Pittsburgh Vintage Grand Prix (www.pittsburgh vintagegrandprix.com) Car races galore each July.

Pittsburgh Three Rivers Regatta (www.pghregatta .com) Sails soar on the three rivers in early August.

Step Trek (www.steptrek.org) A climb up the 23,982 vertical feet of steps of the South Side Slopes in early fall.

Holidays at the Nationality Rooms University of Pittsburgh's Cathedral of Learning gets decked out in international style each December.

Sleeping

With a bit of searching, you can find bargain and charm all in one spot. Oakland is pretty much all chain hotels, such as the Hampton Inn, Holiday Inn and Residence Inn. The **Pittsburgh Bed & Breakfast Association** (☎ 724-352-4899; www.pittsburghbnb.com) can assist you.

GOLDEN TRIANGLE

Westin Convention Center (☎ 412-281-3700; www .westin.com; 1000 Penn Ave; r from $100; Ⓟ ⊠ ⊠ ⊠) The tallest, most imposing of the high-rise hotels in the downtown district, the Westin offers great special rates throughout the year, along with wonderfully anonymous rooms that feature Internet hook-up, comfortable beds and puffy down comforters, rather than the usual polyester spreads.

Omni William Penn Hotel (☎ 412-281-7100; www.omnihotels.com; 530 William Penn Pl; r $130-350) The 596 guest rooms in this historic tower are recently renovated and plush, with an old-world style.

NORTH SIDE

Inn on the Mexican War Streets (☎ 412-231-6544; http://hometown.aol.com/innwarst/collect; 604 W North Ave; r $100-200) This historic, gay-owned mansion is near North Side museums and right on the bus line that takes you downtown. You'll get a hearty homemade breakfast, charming hosts, stunning antique furnishings, an elegant porch and a brand-new four-star restaurant on the grounds, which is due to open by this book's publication date.

SOUTH SIDE

Morning Glory Inn (☎ 412-431-1707; 2119 Sarah St; r from $125; ☒) Head to this Italianate-style Victorian brick townhouse for a quiet and elegant room with character, right in the heart of the jumpin' South Side scene.

HI Pittsburgh Hostel (☎ 412-431-1267; www .hipittsburgh.org; 830 E Warrington Ave; dm $21; ☐) In South Side's Allentown neighborhood, this 50-bed hostel is in a still-splendid early-20th-century building with dreary (but very cheap!) sleeping quarters and well preserved common areas.

SHADYSIDE & AROUND

Inns on Negley (☎ 412-661-0631; www.theinnson negley.com; 703 Negley Ave; r $130-220; ☒ ℗) A pair of gems in Shadyside, the Apple Tree Inn offers Victorian luxury, with four-post beds, handsome furniture and fireplaces, while its neighboring Inn at 714 Negley has a more casual, homey feel. Both include breakfast, offer use of an off-site fitness center and are on a peaceful residential block.

Sunnyledge (☎ 412-683-5014; www.sunnyledge.com; 5124 Fifth Ave; r $189-275; ☒) A historic 1886 mansion in Shadyside; you'll find eight posh but froofy rooms, a lovely tearoom, library and fitness center.

Priory: A City Inn (☎ 412-231-3338; www.thepriory .com; 614 Pressley St; r $74-195; ☒ ℗) This elegant historic inn on the North Shore, a bit further afield, has 24 gorgeous rooms, from tiny quarters to sprawling suites. Complimentary breakfasts and evening wine, plus the tranquil library on the main floor, will make you feel right at home.

Eating

Pittsburgh is no longer a culinary wasteland. You'll find eclectic, ethnic and down-home fare, with some good vegetarian options, suiting all budgets and in every neighborhood (though the North Side – stick with the Warhol Café, p210 – and Downtown leave much to be desired).

DOWNTOWN & THE STRIP

Il Piccolo Forno & La Prima Espresso Co (☎ 412-281-7080; 207 21st St; snacks & coffee $2; ☾ breakfast, lunch) A tiny and authentic Italian bakery and café, it's got goodies from cream puffs to pasta specials; pair it with a strong shot of espresso from its next-door café and you'll be totally satisfied.

Primanti Bros (☎ 412-263-2142; www.primantibros .com; 18th St at Smallman St; sandwiches $5) A Pittsburgh institution, this always-packed place specializes in greasy and delicious hot sandwiches – from knockwurst and cheese to the 'Pitts-burger cheesesteak' – topped with French fries, coleslaw and onions. Other locations can be found in Oakland, Downtown and South Side.

Lidia's Italy (☎ 412-552-0150; http://Pittsburgh .lidiasitaly.com; 1400 Smallman St; mains $14-25; ☾ lunch & dinner) Massive, loud and popular, this top-rated warehouse-space Italian eatery from PBS celebrity-TV chef Lidia Bastianich wows patrons with authentic eats, from homemade pastas to *zuppa di pesce* and lamb shank with Venetian spices.

Eleven (☎ 412-201-5656; www.bigburrito.com/eleven; 1150 Smallman St; mains $16-25; ☾ lunch & dinner) The ubiquitous Big Burrito Restaurant Group (Mad Mex, Kaya) has done it again with this slick, high-ceilinged eclectic eatery, with top-notch fare such as gnocchi with broccoli rabe, Alaskan halibut and an elaborate vegetarian tasting menu.

Lemon Grass Café (☎ 412-765-2222; 124 Sixth St; dishes $12) Impressive Cambodian and Thai cuisine, including killer *phat Thai*, green curry and plenty of vegetarian options. The best Downtown option.

Kaya (☎ 412-261-6565; 2000 Smallman Ave; dishes $10-14) This is a cool and popular Caribbean place with plenty of vegetarian options and a funky decor.

SOUTH SIDE

Tom's Diner (1715 E Carson St; dishes $7-12) Brightly lit Tom's Diner serves up the all-American favorites, such as baked fish and tuna casserole, in a nifty 1950s setting.

Beehive (☎ 412-488-HIVE; 1327 E Carson St; snacks $2-5) A great place to snack on sandwiches or pastries and sip good coffee is this café with funky decor, free wi-fi, a pinball machine and a patio out back.

Dish Osteria Bar (☎ 412-390-2012; 128 S 17th St; mains $14-25; ☾ dinner) A tucked-away, intimate locals' fave, the simple wood tables and floors belie the at-times extravagant Mediterranean creations, which range from fresh sardines with caramelized onions to fettuccine with lamb *ragù*.

Gypsy Café (☎ 412-381-4977; 1330 Bingham St; mains $14-19; ⓨ lunch & dinner) The purple floors and walls and brightly colored rugs make loyal patrons as happy as the fresh, seasonal fare. Sample menu items are raviolis stuffed with apple, Gruyère and ricotta, or warming shrimp and feta stew.

Le Pommier (☎ 412-431-1901; 2104 E Carson St; mains $19-25) It's modern French cuisine in a romantic bistro setting, serving fine wines and meals from veal and rabbit to duck and tofu (really!).

OAKLAND

Mad Mex (☎ 412-681-5656; 370 Atwood St; dishes $5-12) Popular, and with other city locations, Mad Mex has fresh and yummy burritos and salads with vegan options.

Original Hot Dog Shop (☎ 412-621-7388; 3901 Forbes Ave; meals $3-5) Affectionately nicknamed 'dirty Os' by locals, it's a favorite for its cheap dogs and mounds of crispy fries.

Spice Island Tea House (☎ 412-687-8821; 253 Atwood St; mains $6-10; ⓨ lunch & dinner Mon-Sat) This tiny and popular pan-Asian eatery has budget treats from Chinese noodles to Thai curries.

SQUIRREL HILL & SHADYSIDE

Milky Way Dairy & Vegetarian Restaurant (☎ 412-421-3121; 2120 Murray Ave; dishes $5-7) Serving pizzas, falafel, vegetarian meatball hoagies and the Middle Eastern specialty, *melawach* (fried dough).

Umi (☎ 412-362-6198; 5849 Ellsworth Ave; mains $18-28) A sophisticated Japanese eatery, it's got low lighting, crisp service, Asian-fusion cuisine and excellent sushi, plus an adjoining cocktail lounge with a fireplace and couches.

BLOOMFIELD & GARFIELD

Pho Minh (☎ 412-661-7443; 4917 Penn Ave; mains $5-7; ⓨ lunch & dinner, closed Tue; ⊠) A tiny and *très* popular Vietnamese spot with cheap and excellent noodles, soups and tofu dishes.

Quiet Storm (☎ 412-661-9355; www.quietstorm coffee.com; 5430 Penn Ave; mains $5-10; ⓨ lunch daily, dinner Sat & Sun) This very cool, multi-use spot specializes in veggie and vegan cuisine, but also serves killer coffee and Sunday brunch, and hosts frequent readings and musical performances.

Abay (☎ 412-661-9736; 130 S Highland Ave; mains $11; ⊠) A funky new addition, Abay features great Ethiopian cuisine from chicken-to lentil-based stews, all served with spongy, delicious *injera* bread.

Drinking

Most nightlife is centered on the South Side and the Strip. **Z: Lounge** (☎ 412-481-2234; 2108 E Carson St) is a mellow, trendy pub with specialty martinis on the South Side, while **Last Chance** (2533 Penn Ave), on the Strip, is a popular neighborhood pub for guys who can hold their liquor. **Bloomfield Bridge Tavern** (☎ 412-682-8611; 4412 Liberty Ave), 'the only Polish restaurant in Lil' Italy,' is a gritty pub serving beers with excellent sides of *pierogi*, while the **Church Brew Works** (☎ 412-688-8200; www.churchbrew.com; 3525 Liberty Ave), serving handcrafted beers in a massive former church space, is a standout in Lawrenceville. Downtown, the **Prelude Wine Bar** (Pittsburgh Renaissance Hotel, 107 6th St) has a swanky vibe and more than 50 wines by the glass.

GAY BARS

Most gay bars, such as **Pegasus** (☎ 412-281-2131; 818 Liberty Ave), **Images** (☎ 412-391-9990; 965 Liberty Ave) and the **Liberty Avenue Saloon** (412-338-1533; 41 Liberty Ave), are in a concentrated stretch of Liberty Ave Downtown. They're hoppin' and plentiful, but don't expect anything nearly as hot as what you see on *Queer as Folk*.

Entertainment
LIVE MUSIC

Heinz Hall (☎ 412-392-4800; www.pittsburghsymphony.org; 600 Penn Ave) This historic venue is home to the Pittsburgh Symphony Orchestra, with a season that lasts from October to May.

Carnegie Music Hall (www.pittsburghchambermusic.org; 4400 Forbes Ave) A historic venue in Oakland, this is the home to the Pittsburgh Chamber Music Society.

Shadow Lounge (☎ 412-363-8722; 5972 Baum Blvd) This is *the* place for catching hot hip-hop and house DJs, plus indie bands, readings and open-mike nights.

Quiet Storm (☎ 412-661-9355; www.quietstormcoffee.com; 5430 Penn Ave) This very cool coffeehouse features frequent local indie, pop and folk bands with big followings.

Rex Theater (☎ 412-381-6811; 1602 E Carson St) It's a favorite South Side venue for touring jazz, rock and indie bands.

THEATER & DANCE

Pittsburgh Cultural Trust (☎ 412-471-6070; www
.pgharts.org; 803 Liberty Ave) Promotes all downtown arts, from the Pittsburgh Dance
Council and PNC Broadway in Pittsburgh
to visual art and opera; the website has links
to all main arts venues.

Benedum Center for the Performing Arts (☎ 412-
456-6666; 719 Liberty Ave; tickets from $15) Benedum
hosts dance, opera and Broadway shows.

Byham Theater (☎ 412-456-6666; 101 6th St)
This midsized venue hosts both theater and
dance performances.

FILM

Harris Theater (☎ 412-682-4111; 800 Liberty Ave) A
wide variety of art-house films, often part of
film festivals, play at this restored theater.

Southside Works Cinema (☎ 412-432-5770; www
.thesouthsideworks.com; 510 S 27th St) A brand-new
10-screen cinema with stadium seating, this
is where to catch first-run mainstream and
indie films.

CLUBS

You'll find the big, frenzied dance clubs
clustered at the edge of the Strip District.
Among the most popular (at press time):
Bash Nightclub (☎ 412-325-0499; 1900 Smallman St)
It's rowdy, cruisey and packed on weekends.

Mynt Ultra Lounge (☎ 412-325-0101; 1903 19th St)
A slick hipster scene with frequent renowned DJs.

SPORTS

On the North Side, just by the Allegheny
River, are **PNC Park** (☎ 412-321-2827; www.pirate
ball.com), where the Pittsburgh Pirates major-
league baseball team bases itself, and **Heinz
Field** (☎ 412-323-1200; www.pittsburghsteelers.com),
where the NFL Pittsburgh Steelers hold
football showdowns. **Mellon Arena** (☎ 412-
642-1800; www.pittsburghpenguins.com), just east of
downtown, is where the NHL Pittsburgh
Penguins play hockey.

Shopping

Several neighborhoods provide neatly contained shopping strips – some with a focus
on a specific item, be it food or clothing,
and others have a little of everything. Head
to E Carson St on the South Side for all sorts
of funky gift and clothing boutiques. The
Pittsburgh Jean Company (☎ 412-381-JEAN; 2222 E
Carson St) has hip, high-end fashions for label
lovers, while the **E House Company** (☎ 412-488-
7455; 1511 E Carson) has organic cotton clothing
and vegan shoes, and **Groovy! Pop Culture Emporium** (☎ 412-381-8010; www.groovypop.com; 1304
E Carson St) has kitschy collectibles from Pez
dispensers to '70s lunchboxes.

Shadyside is where to find all your favorite
chains – J Crew, Gap, Banana Republic – in
a non-mall setting (for what it's worth), plus
some indie record, book and clothing shops
sprinkled in for good measure. Over in Squirrel Hill, upscale boutique shops hawking fine
lingerie, housewares and clothing line Forbes
Ave. Finally, the Strip area, full of wholesale
outlets, is where to go for food stuff, from
Thai fish sauce to bags of fresh pasta. Try
Pennsylvania Macaroni Co (☎ 412-471-8330; 2010-12
Penn Ave), **Wholey's Seafood** (☎ 412-391-2884; 1711
Penn Ave), a sprawling indoor market, and the
Fort Pitt Candy Co (☎ 412-281-9016; 1642 Penn Ave).

Getting There & Away

AIR

Pittsburgh International Airport (☎ 412-472-3500;
www.pitairport.com), 18 miles from downtown,
has direct connections to Europe, Canada
and major US cities via a slew of airlines, including the new **Independence Air** (www.flyi.com),
with low rates to NYC, DC and Atlanta.

BUS

Arriving in its station near the Strip, **Greyhound** (☎ 412-392-6513; 11th St & Liberty Ave) has
frequent buses to Philadelphia ($41, seven
hours), New York ($49, 11 hours) and Chi-
cago, Illinois ($49, 10 to 14 hours).

CAR

Pittsburgh is easily accessible via major
highways, from the north or south on I-76
or I-79, from the west on Rte 22 and from
the east on I-70. It's about an eight-hour
drive from New York City, and about three
hours from Buffalo.

TRAIN

Amtrak (☎ 412-471-6171; 1100 Liberty Ave) is behind
the magnificent original train station, with
trains heading to cities including Philadelphia ($40 to $48, seven to eight hours) and
New York ($54 to $76, nine to 11 hours).

Getting Around

TO/FROM THE AIRPORT

The excellent **28X Airport Flyer** (☎ 412-442-2000;
www.ridegold.com; one way $2.25) public bus makes

runs to Oakland and Downtown every 20 minutes. Taxis are readily available and cost about $35 to Downtown. Various shuttles also make downtown runs and cost $13 to $17 per person one way. Car rentals are available from the terminal, and many hotels offer courtesy-van pickup; phones are located by the baggage-claim area.

CAR
Driving around Pittsburgh can be extremely frustrating – roads end with no warning, one-way streets can take you in circles, and there are various bridges to contend with. Get a good map (see p206) and a co-pilot, though, and you should be OK.

PUBLIC TRANSPORTATION
Port Authority Transit (☎ 412-442-2000; www.port authority.org) operates an extensive bus system and a limited light-rail system, the 'T,' which is useful for going from Downtown to the South Side. Bus and T fares range from free to $3, depending on the zone in which you're traveling.

TAXI
For taxis, call **Yellow Cab Co of Pittsburgh** (☎ 412-321-8100) or **Checker Cab** (☎ 412-664-6600), which charge by zone.

AROUND PITTSBURGH
Ohiopyle State Park
This state park encompasses more than 19,000 acres of land, featuring the 14-mile Youghiogheny River ('Yough,' pronounced yock) gorge, perfect for white-water rafting. The little riverfront village of Ohiopyle, on Rte 381, in the middle of the park, is a base for rafting, hiking and canoeing. The **park office** (☎ 724-329-8591; ☎ 8am-4pm Apr-Oct, 8am-4pm Mon-Fri Nov-Mar) and visitor center is at the end of the old steel railway bridge.

Fallingwater & Kentuck Knob
A true Frank Lloyd Wright masterpiece, **Fallingwater** (☎ 724-329-8501; www.paconserve.com; weekday/weekend $13/15; ☒ 10am-4pm Tue-Sun Mar-Nov, 11am-3pm winter weekends, weather permitting) is south of Pittsburgh on Rte 381. Completed in 1939 as a weekend retreat for the Kaufmanns, owners of the Pittsburgh department store, the building sports a design acclaimed for its integration with the natural setting. To see inside, you must take one

of the guided tours, and reservations are recommended. A more intensive two-hour tour, with photography permitted, is offered at 8:30am ($50). The rather attractive, forested grounds open at 8:30am.

Much less visited is **Kentuck Knob** (☎ 724-329-1901; www.kentuckknob.com; weekday/weekend $10/15; ☒ 10am-4pm Tue-Sun, from noon Mon), another Frank Lloyd Wright house (designed in 1953), built into the side of a rolling hill. It's noted for its natural materials, hexagonal design and honeycomb skylights. House tours last about an hour.

SLEEPING
In the park, you can either pick a **campsite** or rustic **wilderness cottage** for your stay. Call the **Ohiopyle Park Office** (☎ 724-329-8591) for details and reservations.

The **Nemacolin Woodlands Resort & Spa** (☎ 412-422-2736; www.nemacolin.com; 1001 Lafayette Dr, Farmington; r from $200), with a spa, golf course and dining rooms, is a swank nearby spot to bed down.

Or opt for the earthier **Country Seasons Bed & Breakfast Inn** (☎ 724-455-6825; www.countryseason bb.com; Rte 381; Mill Run; r $93-113), with basic but charming rooms, a big front porch and a main fireplace.

NORTHERN PENNSYLVANIA
Erie
SIGHTS & ACTIVITIES
The smallest of the Great Lakes at 241 miles across and only 62ft deep, Lake Erie warms quickly in the summer and frequently freezes in the winter, making it a magnet for all sorts of recreation, from swimming to ice fishing (a popular sport here).

While the city of **Erie** (www.visitEriePA.com) is, for the most part, a depressed industrial center save for the touristy, redeveloped, shop-filled **Bayfront District**, the **Presque Isle State Park** (☎ 814-838-5138; www.presqueisle.org; park office on Peninsula Dr), which shoots north and then curves back down upon itself just like Cape Cod, is a stunningly beautiful place to visit, no matter what the season. It's a lovely sandy peninsula with dramatic, oceanlike vistas interspersed with wooded areas and biking trails.

The **Lady Kate** (☎ 800-988-5780; adult/child $14/9), a ferry that leaves from Presque Isle's south shore, gives 90-minute narrated tours of Lake Erie's shoreline.

SLEEPING & EATING

Though there is no camping allowed on Presque Isle, the nearby **Virginia's Beach** (☎ 814-922-3261; www.virginiasbeach.com; campsite $24-32, cottage $55-105) has tent/RV sites and cottages right on Lake Erie. The 1960s-style **El Patio Motel** (☎ 814-838-9772; r from $65) is a clean, standard motor lodge near the park's entrance, while **A Place Inn Time** (☎ 814-734-4136; www.aplaceinntime.com; 206 Erie St; $75-175), 20 minutes away in Edinboro, is a cozy B&B with an English garden. In town, **George's Restaurant** (☎ 814-455-0860; 26th & State St; mains $3-12; ☺ breakfast, lunch & dinner) is a homey and delicious diner.

GETTING THERE & AROUND

Driving, Erie and Presque Isle are accessible via I-90 and I-79. The **Port of Erie Water Taxi** (☎ 814-881-2502; Liberty Park; round trip/one way $5/3) makes runs from Erie's bayfront to the center of Presque Isle.

The Poconos

Occupying the northeast corner of Pennsylvania, the Poconos contain 2400 sq miles of mountains, streams, waterfalls, lakes and forests, making it a beautifully natural getaway at any time during the four seasons. For details about the region, turn to the **Pocono Mountains Vacation Bureau** (☎ 800-762-6667; www.800poconos .com), which provides info on inns and outdoor activities and operates nine information centers throughout the region.

Allegheny National Forest

Northwestern Pennsylvania was stripped of its timber in the late 19th and early 20th centuries. Now the 797-sq-mile **Allegheny National Forest** (☎ 814-723-5150; www.fs.fed.us/r9 /forests/allegheny), encompassing several state parks, sprouts acres of hemlock, maples, white ash and the valuable Allegheny black cherry. It's an excellent place for camping and hiking, canoeing and fishing.

New England

New Englanders like to think this is where it all began. The independent-minded Pilgrims in search of religious freedom settled Plymouth, and rebellious Bostonians in pursuit of political freedom set off the American Revolution. New Englanders were the first to outlaw slavery and the first to extend equal rights to same-sex couples. The region's unabashedly liberal politics have given the nation its only socialist member of the US House of Representatives and its only independent member of the US Senate. Ever since America's first university was established in Boston, the region has been an intellectual powerhouse. From Yale in southern Connecticut to Burlington in northern Vermont, New England's abundant universities turn scores of cities and towns into hip college communities every fall.

Whether you're into cultural attractions or the great outdoors, you'll find an abundance of enticing destinations packed into this northeastern corner of the USA. The mountains offer loads of hiking and skiing options, and the seaside towns brim with an ocean full of activities. Dip your paddle into placid lakes or let it rip down whitewater rapids, camp in a wilderness where moose roam or stay in century-old inns where presidents once slept. And yes, New England really does abound with quaint towns with white-steepled churches. If you're lucky enough to be here in fall, the colorful foliage is second to none. And then there's New England's bountiful food. Maine rakes in the lobsters, Vermont churns out Ben & Jerry's ice cream and terrific cheeses, and fishing boats deliver their fresh catch to seaside restaurants up and down the coast.

HIGHLIGHTS

- Sunning and splashing on the beaches of **Cape Cod** (p241), **Martha's Vineyard** (p249) and **Nantucket** (p252)

- Cheering on the **Red Sox** (p238), walking the **Freedom Trail** (p227) and cruising **Newbury St** (p231) in Boston

- Hiking New Hampshire's craggy **White Mountains** (p281) and kayaking the Maine coast around **Acadia National Park** (p294)

- Feasting on fresh New England lobster at seaside eateries in places like **Provincetown** (p248), **Ogunquit** (p288) and **Portland** (p290)

- Ogling the palatial mansions and basking in music at folk and jazz festivals in **Newport** (p259)

- Treating yourself to spectacular fall foliage in the **Berkshires** (p255), **Green Mountains** (p268) and **Litchfield Hills** (p267)

NEW ENGLAND IN...

Five Days
Start in **Boston** (p224), cruising the historic sites along the Freedom Trail, catching a dinner at a cozy North End bistro and then spending the next two days exploring the city's highlights. On day four hit the beach at **Cape Cod** (p241) and the next day hop on a ferry to get a taste of **Nantucket** (p252) or **Martha's Vineyard** (p249).

One Week
Take to the road and make a tour of New Hampshire's **White Mountains** (p281), circling back down the **Maine coast** (p286).

Two Weeks
Now you've got time to do some serious exploring. Visit the revitalized burgs of **Providence** (p257), **Portland** (p289) and **Northampton** (p254), get a look at maritime history in **Mystic** (p265), and drive through rural towns in the **Litchfield Hills** (p267) and the **Berkshires** (p255). Stop for a concert on the lawn at **Tanglewood** (p255) in Lenox and spend a night in a centuries-old inn. Explore the college towns of **Hanover** (p285), **Middlebury** (p274) and **Burlington** (p276). And take to the vast wilderness in Maine, where you can hike the northernmost peak of the **Appalachian Trail** (p297) and raft down awesome **white-water rivers** (p297).

NEW ENGLAND

HISTORY

When the first European settlers arrived, New England was inhabited by the Algonquian peoples who lived in small tribes, raising corn and beans, hunting game and harvesting the rich coastal waters.

English captain Bartholomew Gosnold landed at Cape Cod and sailed north to Maine in 1602 but it wasn't until 1614 that Captain John Smith, who charted the region's coastline for King James I, christened the land 'New England.' With the arrival of the Pilgrims at Plymouth in 1620, European settlement began in earnest. Over the next century the colonies expanded and thrived, often at the expense of the native people.

Although subjects of the British crown, New Englanders governed themselves with their own legislative councils and they came to view their affairs as separate from those of England. In the 1770s King George III instituted policies intent on reining in the colonists' free-wheeling spirits and he imposed a series of costly taxes. The colonists, who had no delegates in the English parliament, responded with a tax revolt under the slogan 'no taxation without representation.' Attempts to squash the revolt resulted in the battles of Lexington and Concord on April 18, 1775, setting off the Revolutionary War that gave birth to the USA in 1776.

In the years that followed independence, New England became an economic powerhouse, its harbors booming centers for shipbuilding, fishing and trade. New England's renowned Yankee clippers plied ports from China to South America. The first water-powered cotton-spinning mill in North America was established in Rhode Island in 1793. Soon afterward, New England's swift rivers became the engines of vast mills turning out clothing, shoes and machinery.

But no boom lasts forever. The cultivation of the Great Plains made farming New England's rocky soil even less profitable, and after the Civil War, with the emancipation of slaves and the invention of steam power, many New England industries moved south to take advantage of cheaper labor. Steel vessels replaced New England's wooden ships, and petroleum, gas and electricity superseded whale oil for illumination.

New England suffered greatly during the 1930s depression, but its factories and shipyards sprung to life again during WWII, and its traditional strengths in education, commerce and medicine continued through the latter half of the 20th century and on to today. Finance, biotechnology and tourism are linchpins of the regional economy. Culturally, present-day New England enjoys a rich diversity of residents, from stoic Yankee farmers who have been working the same land for generations to new waves of immigrants who've added color and vitality to the region's cities.

NEW ENGLAND

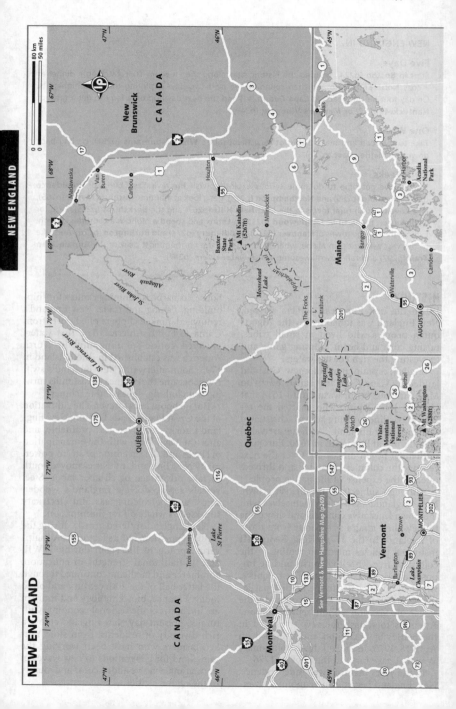

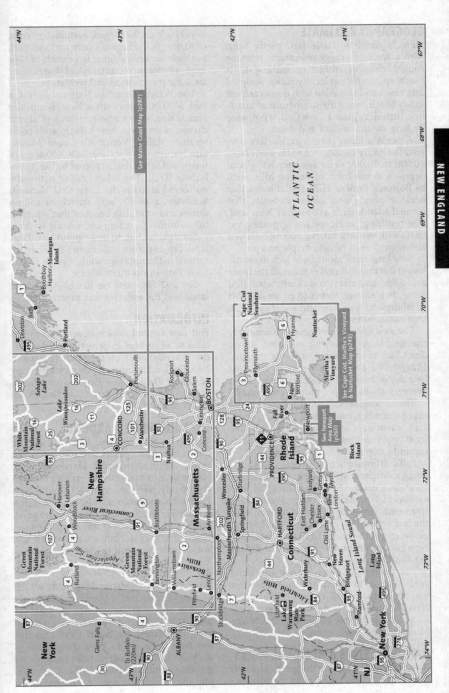

NEW ENGLAND

GEOGRAPHY & CLIMATE

New England is partly flat, partly hilly, with a spine of craggy mountains running roughly from northeast to southwest. Its northern coastline is largely rocky, sculpted into coves and sprinkled with the occasional sandy beach, while the southernmost coastline, including prized Cape Cod, is bounded by long swaths of sand and dunes.

A scant million years ago, glaciers covered the entire region. When they retreated 10,000 to 20,000 years ago they left glacial deposits in the form of oblong hills, such as Boston's Bunker Hill, glacial holes that became ponds and gravel deposits that formed islands such as Martha's Vineyard. The resulting landscape has appealing variety, with verdant valleys, rolling hills and abundant forests of oak, maple and pine.

New England's mountains lack dramatic height but that just makes them all the more accessible, and hikers and climbers will find more than enough slopes to go around. Mt Washington, New England's highest peak, tops out at 6288ft.

The weather in New England is famously changeable. As the saying goes here, 'If you don't like the weather, just wait a minute.' Muggy 90°F days in July may be followed by a day of cool 65°F weather. Precipitation averages about 3in per month year-round.

The summer season, roughly June through mid-September, has the best weather – typically warm days and cool nights – and the most opportunities for hiking, cycling, boating and camping.

Fall's dropping temperatures and shortening daylight triggers the trees to change color and makes New England's fall foliage world-famous. Fall foliage season runs from mid-September to mid-October, with the leaf colors first changing at the highest elevations in the north, in the mountains of New Hampshire and Vermont, then sweeping southward.

The winters are often snowy and quite cold, a boon to skiers and snowboarders who flock to the ski resorts of Vermont, New Hampshire, Maine and western Massachusetts and come to see how the White Mountains got their name.

NATIONAL, STATE & REGIONAL PARKS

If you're ready to explore the great outdoors, New England won't disappoint. Acadia National Park, on the rugged, northeastern coast of Maine, is the region's only national park but there are several other large tracts of New England's forest, mountains and shoreline set aside for preservation and recreation.

The White Mountain National Forest, a vast, 800,000-acre swath of New Hampshire and Maine, offers a wonderland of scenic drives, warm-weather hiking and cold-weather skiing. Vermont's Green Mountain National Forest covers 400,000 acres of unspoiled forest that's crossed by the Appalachian Trail. The other gem of nationally preserved lands is the Cape Cod National Seashore, a 44,600-acre stretch of rolling dunes and stunning beaches that's perfect for swimming, cycling and seaside walks.

State parks abound throughout New England, ranging from little niches in urban locations to the untamed wilderness of Baxter State Park in northern Maine.

See p92 for more on the USA's federal lands and the agencies that protect them.

INFORMATION

Visit New England (www.visitnewengland.com) has links to all sorts of information on destinations throughout New England. To explore New England in more depth, pick up a copy of Lonely Planet's *New England* guidebook, the *Boston* guide or our *Cape Cod, Nantucket & Martha's Vineyard*.

GETTING THERE & AROUND

Getting to New England is easy; there are buses, trains and planes to major cities like Boston, Providence and Hartford. Once you're here, if you want to explore the area thoroughly, the best way to get around New England is unquestionably by car. The region is relatively small and the highways are good. Public transportation is fine for getting between major cities, but it's infrequent and scarce once you get into the countryside.

Air

Boston's **Logan International Airport** (☎ 800-235-6426; www.massport.com) is New England's main air hub. However, Providence's **TF Green Airport** (☎ 401-737-8222, 888-268-7222; www.pvdairport.com) and **Manchester Airport** (☎ 603-624-6539; www.flymanchester.com) in New Hampshire – both about an hour's drive from Boston – are growing 'minihubs' boasting less congestion and nationwide air service. Depending on the route, you may find cheaper flights into Providence or Manchester than into Boston. **Bradley International Airport** (☎ 860-292-2000, 888-624-1533; www.bradleyairport.com) near Hartford serves Connecticut and western Massachusetts. **Portland International Jetport** (☎ 207-774-7301; www.portlandjetport.org) in Maine has flights to Canada but is otherwise primarily a regional airport.

Bus
Greyhound (☎ 800-231-2222; www.greyhound.com) operates a weblike system of buses throughout the Northeast, covering major cities and many smaller towns, and connecting the region with the rest of the USA. It also books other regional bus systems, so it's a good place to start.

Bonanza Bus Lines (☎ 888-751-8000; www.bonanzabus.com) operates routes from New York and Boston to the Berkshires (Stockbridge, Lenox and Pittsfield) and Cape Cod (Falmouth, Woods Hole and Hyannis). It also serves other New England cities including Hartford and Providence.

Peter Pan Bus Lines (☎ 413-781-2900, 800-237-8747; www.peterpanbus.com) connects Boston with New York, Philadelphia and Washington, DC. Regional routes are fairly extensive, with services to Amherst, Northampton, Lenox, New Haven and Hartford among others.

Concord Trailways (☎ 800-639-3317; www.concordtrailways.com), based in Concord, NH, operates buses between Boston and several New Hampshire towns including Manchester, Concord and North Conway. From Boston, buses also travel along the Maine coast to Portland and Camden.

Vermont Transit Lines (☎ 800-552-8737; www.vermonttransit.com), based in Burlington, links Boston, New York and Montreal with major New England cities and towns, including the Vermont towns of Montpelier, Manchester, Brattleboro and Bennington.

Car & Motorcycle
The I-95, the main north–south highway, transverses New England, running along the Connecticut coastline and then shooting up through Rhode Island before hitting Boston, Portsmouth, Portland and Bangor en route to its end at the New Brunswick, Canada, border. I-93 connects Boston with the White Mountains of New Hampshire. I-91 heads north from New Haven via Hartford, Northampton and Brattleboro and then straddles the Vermont–New Hampshire border on the way to Canada.

New England is one of the few places in the USA where you'll see 'rotaries' (roundabouts) in place of four-way intersections. Before entering a rotary, yield to the cars already in it and wait until there's an opening.

Train
Rail service is provided by **Amtrak** (☎ 800-872-7245; www.amtrak.com). Trains along the 'Northeast Corridor,' which connects Boston, Providence, Hartford and New Haven with New York and Washington, DC, are some of the most frequent in Amtrak's system.

Amtrak has a few other routes to and through New England including the *Vermonter*, which runs through New Haven, Hartford, Springfield and Amherst, and then on to Montpelier in northern Vermont, and the *Downeaster*, which connects Boston and Portland, Maine.

MASSACHUSETTS

It's relatively compact, but New England's most populous state packs in an appealing variety of places to go and things to do, from the refined villages of the Berkshire hills to the sandy beaches of Cape Cod. History buffs can explore colonial Plymouth, 'America's hometown'; the old whaling center of Nantucket; and the birthplace of the American Revolution in Boston. But don't think Massachusetts is all about the past – bustling Boston offers a plethora of entertainment options befitting a college town, Provincetown revels in the liveliest gay scene in the Northeast and Northampton brims with the coolest café life this side of New York.

History
From the earliest days of colonial settlement, Massachusetts has been the epicenter of New England. At the forefront of the push for independence and spurred by a thriving maritime trade in the 18th century, Massachusetts came to resent the trade restrictions imposed from London. The Boston Massacre took place in 1770, when British sentries fired into a rowdy mob, killing five people. The 1773 Boston Tea Party set the stage for the 1775 battles between British troops and

NEW ENGLAND

MASSACHUSETTS FACTS

Nicknames Bay State, Old Colony
Population 6.4 million
Area 10,555 sq miles
Capital city Boston (population 589,141; metro area 3 million)
Official state doughnut Boston cream
Birthplace of Benjamin Franklin (1706–90), Ralph Waldo Emerson (1803–82), Emily Dickinson (1830–86), presidents John Adams (1735–1826), John Quincy Adams (1767–1848), John F Kennedy (1917–63) and George HW Bush (b 1924)
Home of Harvard University, Boston Marathon, Plymouth Rock
Famous for Boston Tea Party, Boston Red Sox and that pahk-your-cah accent

colonial militia at Lexington and Concord, which began the Revolutionary War.

In the 19th century Massachusetts became the center of the world's whaling industry, bringing unprecedented wealth to the islands of Nantucket and Martha's Vineyard, whose ports are still lined with grand sea captain's homes.

The Great Potato Famine (1845–50) sent thousands of Irish immigrants to Boston. They were later joined by waves of immigrants from French Canada, Italy and Portugal, with some staying in the port towns and others moving inland to work in the mills and factories of Northampton and Springfield. Today the state is in the midst of an economic revival, with the fields of science and technology leading the way.

Information
Massachusetts has a 5% sales tax plus a lodging tax ranging from 5.7% to 9.7%, depending on the city.

Boston Globe (www.boston.com) The region's main newspaper has lots of useful information online.

Massachusetts Office of Travel & Tourism (☎ 617-973-8500, 800-227-6277; www.massvacation.com; Transportation Bldg, 10 Park Plaza, Suite 4510, Boston, MA 02116) Has information on the entire state and will mail out a free magazine-size travel guide on request.

BOSTON
One of America's oldest cities is at the same time one of its youngest – more than 35 colleges and universities keep a youthful face on this historic capital.

Ever-proud Bostonians refer to their town as 'The Hub,' and indeed by most every measure it is New England's most pivotal city, a center of transportation, finance, medical care, entertainment and technological innovations.

Explore the old world of North End Italian bistros and American Revolutionary sights, paddle a canoe down the Charles River, hit the clubs in Cambridge or watch the sun set over a drink from the top of the Prudential. You'll find plenty to do, both old and new, in this spirited city.

History
When the Massachusetts Bay Colony was established by England in 1630, the port of Boston became its capital. Boston was a trendsetter for other US cities. Boston Latin School, the first public school in the USA, was founded in 1635, followed a year later by Harvard, the nation's first university. The first newspaper in the 13 original colonies was established here in 1704, America's first labor union was organized in the city in 1795 and the country's first public subway system opened in Boston in 1897.

And of course the first battles in the Revolutionary War occurred here as well. Prominent Bostonians such as John Hancock, Samuel Adams and Paul Revere were among the founders of the American republic.

Today, greater Boston remains at the forefront of American education. Its universities have spawned important industries in electronics, biotechnology, medicine and finance. And in this city of baseball fanatics, you can expect to hear plenty of buzz on the Red Sox and their heart-stopping, come-from-behind 2004 World Series win, something the city hadn't seen in 86 years.

Orientation
For a city of its stature, Boston is surprisingly compact and easy to get around. The primary sights are within a mile or two of Boston Common, the city's central park. Boston's leading neighborhoods radiate out from Boston Common, with Beacon Hill and the gold-domed State House gracing the Common's northern extent.

Most of Boston's attractions, and the airport, are easily accessible by MBTA (the 'T') subway trains (p240). The Park St station, a

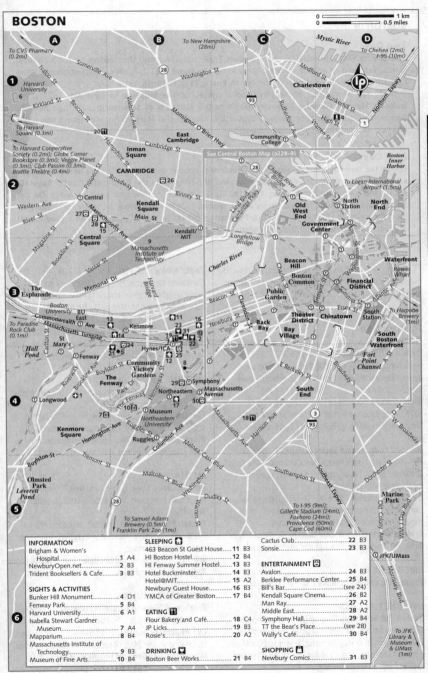

BOSTON

0 — 1 km
0 — 0.5 miles

NEW ENGLAND

INFORMATION		
Brigham & Women's		
Hospital.................................**1** A4		
NewburyOpen.net.....................**2** B3		
Trident Booksellers & Cafe..........**3** B3		

SIGHTS & ACTIVITIES		
Bunker Hill Monument.................**4** D1		
Fenway Park..............................**5** B4		
Harvard University.......................**6** A1		
Isabella Stewart Gardner		
Museum................................**7** A4		
Mapparium.................................**8** B4		
Massachusetts Institute of		
Technology...........................**9** B3		
Museum of Fine Arts..................**10** B4		

SLEEPING 🏠		
463 Beacon St Guest House.....**11** B3		
HI Boston Hostel......................**12** B4		
HI Fenway Summer Hostel.......**13** B3		
Hotel Buckminster...................**14** B3		
Hotel@MIT...............................**15** A2		
Newbury Guest House..............**16** B3		
YMCA of Greater Boston..........**17** B4		

EATING 🍴		
Flour Bakery and Café............**18** C4		
JP Licks...................................**19** B3		
Rosie's....................................**20** A2		

DRINKING 🍷		
Boston Beer Works...................**21** B4		

Cactus Club.............................**22** B3		
Sonsie....................................**23** B3		

ENTERTAINMENT 🎭		
Avalon....................................**24** B3		
Berklee Performance Center.....**25** B4		
Bill's Bar..............................(see 24)		
Kendall Square Cinema............**26** B2		
Man Ray.................................**27** A2		
Middle East.............................**28** A2		
Symphony Hall........................**29** B4		
TT the Bear's Place.............(see 28)		
Wally's Café...........................**30** B4		

SHOPPING 🛍		
Newbury Comics.....................**31** B3		

NEW ENGLAND

BOSTON IN...

Two Days

Spend your first day walking the **Freedom Trail** (opposite) and discovering Boston's colonial sights, stopping to imbibe a little history at **Bell in Hand** (p237), America's oldest tavern. Wrap up with a scrumptious dinner in the **North End** (p235), Boston's 'Little Italy.'

Start day two at one of the city's stellar museums: the **Museum of Fine Arts** (p231), the **Isabella Stewart Gardner Museum** (p232) or the **Museum of Science** (p232). Then head to **Cambridge** (p231) to tour Harvard University, hang out in Harvard Sq and spend the night reveling in Cambridge's hip music scene.

Four Days

Follow the two-day itinerary with some window-shopping and dining with the beautiful people along **Newbury St** (p231). Enjoy an aerial view of Boston from the **Prudential Center Skywalk** (p231) and take a tour of **Fenway Park** (p232), or go cheer on the Red Sox at a game. On the fourth day, head west to **Lexington** and **Concord** (p240) if you have a literary inclination, or spend the day at kid-friendly **Plimoth Plantation** (p241). In the evening, take in a **play** (p238) or hit the **nightclubs** (p237) along Lansdowne St.

'T' hub, is beneath the Common. Harvard Sq, the heart of Cambridge, is about 5 miles northwest of the Common and served by the T's Red Line.

Information

BOOKSTORES

Barnes & Noble (Map pp228-9; ☎ 617-247-6959; www.barnesandnoble.com; 800 Boylston St) This convenient Prudential Center branch has an extensive book selection and a café.

Globe Corner Bookstore (Map p225; ☎ 617-497-6277; www.globecorner.com; 49 Palmer St, Cambridge) Shop near Harvard Sq specializing in travel books and maps.

Harvard Cooperative Society (Map p225; ☎ 617-499-2000; 1400 Massachusetts Ave, Cambridge) 'The Coop' at Harvard Sq has books, music and all sorts of goodies emblazoned with the Harvard logo.

Out of Town News (☎ 617-354-7777; Harvard Sq, Cambridge) This National Historic Landmark sells newspapers from major US and international cities.

Trident Booksellers & Cafe (Map p225; ☎ 617-267-8688; 338 Newbury St) New Age and alternative books.

EMERGENCY

Police, fire and ambulance (☎ 911) Emergency.

INTERNET ACCESS

Boston Public Library (Map pp228-9; ☎ 617-536-5400; www.bpl.org; 700 Boylston St; ☒ 9am-9pm Mon-Thu, 9am-5pm Fri & Sat year-round, 1-5pm Sun Oct-May) Free for 15 minutes, or get a visitor card at the circulation desk and sign up for longer terminal time.

FedEx Kinko's (Map pp228-9; ☎ 617-262-6188; 187 Dartmouth St; per min 25¢; ☒ 24hr) Check the *Yellow Pages* for other locations around town.

NewburyOpen.net (Map p225; ☎ 617-267-9716; www.newburyopen.net; 3rd fl, 252 Newbury St; per 15 min/hr $3/5; ☒ 9am-8pm Mon-Fri, noon-7pm Sat & Sun) Provides online computers, but if you have your own laptop wi-fi access is free throughout Newbury St.

INTERNET RESOURCES

City of Boston (www.cityofboston.gov) Official website for the city government.

iBoston (www.iboston.org) Visit this website for the scoop on Boston history, architecture and historical sites.

Phantom Gourmet (www.phanthomgourmet.com) A good place to find reviews of Boston restaurants.

MEDIA

Boston Globe (www.boston.com) New England's major daily newspaper, with a useful calendar section on Thursdays.

Boston Phoenix (www.bostonphoenix.com) Alternative weekly, available Thursday, with extensive arts and entertainment coverage.

WBUR (90.9FM) News and talk shows from National Public Radio and BBC World Service.

MEDICAL SERVICES

Brigham & Women's Hospital (Map p225; ☎ 617-732-5500; 75 Francis St; ☒ 24hr)

CVS Pharmacy (Map p225; ☎ 617-876-5519; 35 White St, Cambridge; ☒ 24hr) Opposite the Porter Sq T station.

Massachusetts General Hospital (Map pp228-9; ☎ 617-726-2000; 55 Fruit St; ☒ 24hr) Off Cambridge St.

MONEY

You'll find ATMs throughout the city, including at most subway stations. Foreign currency can be exchanged at **Citizens Bank** (Map pp228–9; ☎ 800-922-9999; Freedom Trail 53 State St; opposite Trinity Church 55 Boylston St; Cambridge Harvard Sq).

POST

Post office (Map pp228–9; ☎ 617-654-5326; 25 Dorchester Ave; ⌚ 24hr) One block southeast of South Station.

TOURIST INFORMATION

Cambridge Visitor's Information kiosk (☎ 617-441-2884, 800-862-5678; www.cambridge-usa.org; Harvard Sq; ⌚ 9am-5pm Mon-Sat, 1-5pm Sun) The Cambridge scoop, including self-guided walking tours.
Greater Boston Convention and Visitors Bureau (GBCVB; pp228–9; ☎ 617-536-4100, 800-733-2678; www.bostonusa.com) Boston Common (147 Tremont St; ⌚ 8:30am-5pm Mon-Fri year-round, 9am-5pm Sat & Sun Jun-Sep, 10am-5pm Sat & Sun Oct-May); Prudential Center (800 Boylston St; ⌚ 9am-6pm Mon-Fri, 10am-6pm Sat & Sun) Get information online in advance, or stop by for brochures and a handy subway map.

TRAVEL AGENCIES

Vacation Outlet (Map pp228–9; ☎ 617-451-9022; www.vacationoutlet.com; 426 Washington St) At Filene's Basement; last-minute travel bargains.

Sights

Sightseeing in compact Boston is a cinch – just start at Boston Common, the city's central park. Some of the leading sights border the Common and most others are within walking distance of it. Major sights like the State House, the Public Garden, the Freedom Trail and Newbury St are all just a stone's throw away. Cambridge, home to Harvard University, is across the Charles River, a mere 10 minutes by subway.

BOSTON COMMON & PUBLIC GARDEN

Established in 1634, the 50-acre **Boston Common** (Map pp228–9), bordered by Park, Tremont, Boylston, Charles and Beacon Sts, is the country's oldest public park. The Puritans once chastised those who offended colonial mores by locking them in pillory and stocks in the Common for all to see. These days it's a thoroughly cheery scene, especially at the **Frog Pond**, which is popular for wading in summer and ice skating in winter.

Adjacent to the Common is the **Public Garden** (Map pp228–9), a 24-acre botanical oasis of cultivated flowers, shady park benches and a tranquil lagoon with the kid-pleasing pedal-powered **Swan Boats** (☎ 617-522-1966; adult/child 2-15 $2.50/1; ⌚ 10am-4pm mid-Apr–mid-Jun, 10am-5pm mid-Jun–early Sep, noon-4pm Mon-Fri & 10am-4pm Sat & Sun early–mid-Sep). Historic buildings, top-end hotels and shops surround both parks.

BEACON HILL & DOWNTOWN

Boston's most historic and affluent residential neighborhood, Beacon Hill, rises above Boston Common. To the east is the city's downtown.

Crowning Beacon Hill is the **State House** (Map pp228–9; ☎ 617-727-3676; www.state.ma.us/sec/trs; Beacon St at Park St; admission free; ⌚ 8am-6pm Mon-Fri), the 1798 golden-domed seat of Massachusetts' government. Volunteers lead free 30-minute tours from 10:30am to 3:30pm.

The small **Museum of Afro-American History** (Map pp228–9; ☎ 617-725-0022; www.afroammuseum.org; 46 Joy St; admission free; ⌚ 10am-4pm Mon-Sat) illustrates the history of Boston's African American community, which flourished on Beacon Hill in the 19th century, and includes the adjacent **African Meeting House**, the oldest in the country.

Next to colonial-era **Park Street Church** is the **Granary Burying Ground** (Map pp228–9; Tremont

---

PUT ON YOUR WALKING SHOES

The most trodden walk in Boston is the 2.5-mile **Freedom Trail**, which links 16 major colonial and Revolutionary history sites. The route is marked by a double row of red sidewalk bricks (or the occasional red painted line) and starts at the Boston Common visitor center. It then winds through downtown and the North End before terminating in Charlestown. Most people just grab a map at the visitor center and self-tour, but if you want to pick up some local commentary, several freelance guides dressed in colonial garb lead tours from Boston Common for around $10 per person. Better yet, start off on your own and join one of the free tours provided several times a day by the **Boston National Historical Park Visitors Center** (Map pp228–9; ☎ 617-242-5642; www.nps.gov/bost; 15 State St; ⌚ 9am-5pm).

CENTRAL BOSTON

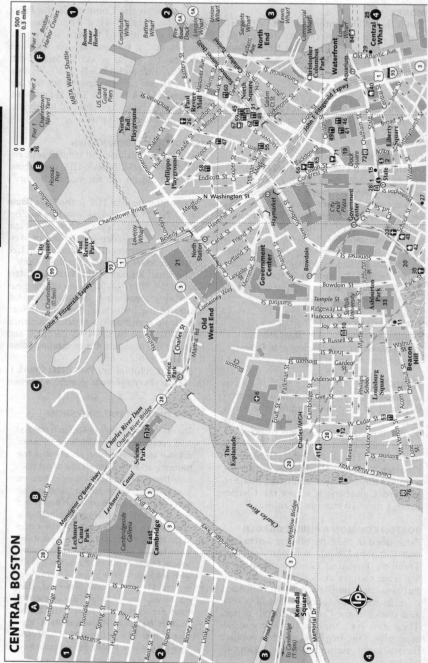

St at Park St), which dates back to 1660 and holds the graves of Revolutionary heroes Paul Revere, John Hancock and Samuel Adams. Just northeast is **King's Chapel** (Map pp228-9; ☎ 617-227-2155; 58 Tremont St), which has a bell made by Paul Revere and a colonial burial ground with interesting gravestones.

At the **Old South Meeting House** (Map pp228-9; ☎ 617-482-6439; www.oldsouthmeetinghouse.org; 310 Washington St; adult/child under 18 $5/1; ☺ 9:30am-5pm Apr-Oct, 10am-4pm Nov-Mar), colonists met in 1773 for a rousing debate on taxation without representation before raiding British ships in the harbor in what became known as the Boston Tea Party.

Boston's original site of colonial government, the **Old State House** (Map pp228-9; ☎ 617-720-1713; www.bostonhistory.org; 206 Washington St; adult/child 6-18 $5/1; ☺ 9am-5pm), built in 1713, is now a museum of Revolutionary history.

Faneuil Hall (Map pp228-9; Congress St), constructed in 1740 as a market and public meeting place, retains its original look. Today the hall, Quincy Market, and North and South Market buildings make up Faneuil Hall Marketplace shopping and dining complex. Look at the top of Faneuil Hall to see its famed grasshopper weather vane.

NORTH END & CHARLESTOWN

Steeped in colonial history and Boston's Italian quarter since the 1920s, the North End offers an irresistible mix of attractive old buildings and delicious neighborhood restaurants. The Freedom Trail leads through the North End and across the Charlestown Bridge.

Built in 1680, the **Paul Revere House** (Map pp228-9; ☎ 617-523-2338; www.paulreverehouse.org; 19 North Sq; adult/child 5-17 $3/1; ☺ 9:30am-5:15pm mid-Apr–Oct, 9:30am-4:15pm Nov–mid-Apr) stands as the oldest house in Boston. It's the former home of the patriot famed in US history for ringing out the advance warning that British troops were marching toward Lexington and Concord on the night of April 18, 1775.

It was at Boston's oldest church (built in 1723), the **Old North Church** (Map pp228-9; ☎ 617-523-6676; 193 Salem St; admission free; ☺ 9am-6pm Jun-Oct, 9am-5pm Nov-May), that two lanterns were hung in the steeple on that fateful night, signaling to Paul Revere, who was waiting across the river, that British forces would set out by sea ('one if by land, two if by sea').

So sturdy were the oak timbers in the USS **Constitution** (Map pp228-9; ☎ 617-242-7511; www

.ussconstitution.navy.mil; Charlestown Navy Yard; admission free; ☺ tours every 30 mins 10:30am-3:30pm daily Apr-Oct, Thu-Sat Nov-Mar) that cannonballs bounced off them, earning it the nickname 'Old Ironsides.' Built in 1797, it's the world's oldest commissioned warship still afloat.

The 221ft granite obelisk **Bunker Hill Monument** (Map p225; ☎ 617-242-5641; Monument Sq; admission free; ☺ 9am-4:30pm) commemorates the Revolutionary War's first major battle. Climb the 294 steps to the top of the monument for a sweeping view of Boston.

BACK BAY
This well-groomed neighborhood extending west from Boston Common is lined with elegant brownstone residences, historic buildings and good dining options. Running through the heart of the Back Bay is Newbury St, with its tony shops, galleries and cafés.

Copley Square (Map pp228–9), bounded by Boylston, Clarendon, St James and Dartmouth Sts, is a plaza surrounded by historic buildings, including the beautiful French-Romanesque **Trinity Church** (☎ 617-536-0944; adult/child under 12 $4/free; ☺ 8am-6pm), which is considered to be the greatest work of architect HH Richardson. Across the street, the venerable **Boston Public Library** (☎ 617-536-5400; 700 Boylston St; ☺ 9am-9pm Mon-Thu, 9am-5pm Fri & Sat year-round, 1-5pm Sun Oct-May), America's first municipal library, lends credence to Boston's reputation as the Athens of America.

For an awesome 360-degree bird's-eye view of the city, head to the **Prudential Center Skywalk** (Map pp228–9; ☎ 617-859-0648; 800 Boylston St; adult/child under 12 $9.50/6.50; ☺ 10am-10pm), the tower's 50th-floor observation deck.

If you've ever wanted to walk across the globe, the Christian Science Church's **Mapparium** (Map p225; ☎ 617-450-7000; 200 Massachusetts Ave; adult/child 6-17 $6/4; ☺ 10am-5pm Tue-Wed, Sat & Sun, 10am-9pm Thu-Fri), an enormous stained-glass globe with a bridge through its center, offers the easiest route.

CAMBRIDGE
Across the Charles River from Boston, Cambridge is home to academic heavyweights Harvard University and Massachusetts Institute of Technology (MIT). An enrollment of almost 30,000 students keeps the city lively, diverse and politically progressive. Its central **Harvard Squre** (Map p225) overflows with cafés, bookstores, students

and street performers. Along Massachusetts Ave, opposite the Harvard T station, lies **Harvard University** (www.harvard.edu), which counts dozens of Nobel laureates and seven US presidents among its graduates – for other interesting tidbits join a free campus tour at the **Holyoke Center** (☎ 617-495-1573; 1350 Massachusetts Ave; ☺ tours 10am & 2pm Mon-Fri, 2pm Sat Sep-May, 10am, 11:15am, 2pm & 3:15pm Mon-Sat mid-Jun–mid-Aug).

Founded in 1636, Harvard has amassed amazing collections. The **Fogg Art Museum** (☎ 617-495-9400; www.artmuseums.harvard.edu; 32 Quincy St; adult/child 18 & under $6.50/free; ☺ 10am-5pm Mon-Sat, 1-5pm Sun) showcases Western art since the Middle Ages; admission includes the **Busch-Reisinger Museum**, which specializes in Northern European art, and the **Arthur M Sackler Museum**, devoted to Asian and Islamic art. The **Harvard Museum of Natural History** and the adjoining **Peabody Museum of Archaeology and Ethnology** (☎ 617-496-1027; 11 Divinity Ave; adult/child 3-18 $7.50/5; ☺ 9am-5pm) have one of the USA's best Native American exhibits and an exquisite collection of 4000 glass flowers. A $10 'Harvard Hot Ticket' buys entry to all museums, but for the best deal arrive before noon Saturday at the art museums and noon Sunday at the other two when admission is free.

Nerds reign supreme at the **Massachusetts Institute of Technology** (MIT; Map p225). The **Information Center** (☎ 617-253-4795; www.mit.edu; 77 Massachusetts Ave; admission free; ☺ tours 10am & 2pm Mon-Fri) can give you the lowdown on where to see robots, cool art and interesting buildings.

OTHER ATTRACTIONS
You'll come out ahead by purchasing the **CityPass** (www.citypass.com; adult/child 5-11 $39/19.50) if you plan on visiting at least half of the following attractions: Museum of Fine Arts, Museum of Science, New England Aquarium, John F Kennedy Library & Museum, Harvard Museum of Natural History and the Prudential Center Skywalk. It's available from each of the sights.

The **Museum of Fine Arts** (MFA; Map p225; ☎ 617-267-9300; www.mfa.org; 465 Huntington Ave; adult/child 7-17 $15/6.50; ☺ 10am-4:45pm Sat-Tue, 10am-9:45pm Wed-Fri), one of the country's finest art museums, covers the gamut from Rembrandt to a contemporary art wing designed by IM Pei. Standouts include

NEW ENGLAND

major French impressionist paintings, Paul Revere silver and a superb compilation of American art by John Singleton Copley, Gilbert Stuart and others. Admission is free to everyone after 4pm on Wednesdays and for children after 3pm weekdays, all day weekends and daily in summer.

Just west of the MFA, **Isabella Stewart Gardner Museum** (Map p225; ☎ 617-566-1401; www .gardnermuseum.org; 280 The Fenway; adult Tue-Fri $10, Sat & Sun $11, child under 18 free; ☒ 11am-5pm Tue-Sun) is a magnificent Venetian-style palazzo housing priceless paintings, tapestries and furnishings, primarily European. Arts patron Isabella Stewart Gardner assembled her vast collection in the late 19th and early 20th centuries and lived in the mansion that houses it all. The classic building itself, with its flower-filled enclosed courtyard, is worth the price of admission.

The granddaddy of baseball parks, **Fenway Park** (Map p225; ☎ 617-226-6666; www.redsox .com; adult/child $12/10; ☒ tours every hr 9am-4pm), home of the world-champion Boston Red Sox, stands as the oldest (1912) and classiest park in major-league baseball.

At the exceptional **Museum of Science** (Map pp228-9; ☎ 617-723-2500; www.mos.org; Science Park, Charles River Dam; adult/child 3-11 $15/12, Hayden Planetarium or Omni Theater only $9/7, combination tickets $23/18; ☒ 9am-5pm Sat-Thu, 9am-9pm Fri), 550 interactive displays provide a feast of fun for kids of all ages. Check out what's playing on the museum's **Mugar Omni Theater's** five-story screen or at its **Hayden Planetarium**, which pairs rock music (such as Pink Floyd's *Dark Side of the Moon*) with lasers and stargazers.

The superb **New England Aquarium** (Map pp228-9; ☎ 617-973-5200; www.neaq.org; Central Wharf; adult/child 3-11 $16/9; ☒ 9am-5pm Mon-Fri, 9am-6pm Sat & Sun) centers around a four-story-high tank teeming with tropical fish and all manner of colorful sea creatures. A big-screen **Imax theater** (adult/child $10/7) shows Cousteau and other aquatic themes.

In a striking marble building overlooking Boston Harbor, the **John F Kennedy Library & Museum** (☎ 617-514-1600; www.jfklibrary.org; Columbia Point; adult/child 12 & under $10/free; ☒ 9am-5pm) houses memorabilia about the 35th US president. You can watch excerpts of the Kennedy–Nixon debates and the Cuban missile crisis, and see official papers and Kennedy family photos. Take the T's Red Line to JFK/UMass, then hop on a free shuttle bus.

Activities

The Charles River, which separates Boston and Cambridge, is the main focal point for recreational activities. The paths along both sides of the Charles River are popular for walking, jogging, cycling and in-line skating, while the river's waters attract rowers and sailors.

Community Boating (Map pp228-9; ☎ 617-523-1038; www.community-boating.org; Charles River Esplanade; per 2 days kayak/sailboat $50/100; ☒ 1pm-dusk Mon-Fri, 9am-dusk Sat & Sun Apr-Oct) rents boats from its boathouse at the south side of the Longfellow Bridge.

Rent bicycles from **Community Bicycle Supply** (Map pp228-9; ☎ 617-542-8623; 496 Tremont St; per 2hr/day $10/20; ☒ 10am-7pm Mon-Sat year-round, noon-5pm Sun Apr-Sep) and in-line skates from **Beacon Hill Skate** (Map pp228-9; ☎ 617-482-7400; 135 S Charles St; per hr/day $10/20; ☒ 11am-6pm Mon & Wed-Sat, noon-4pm Sun).

The **Appalachian Mountain Club Headquarters** (AMC; Map pp228-9; ☎ 617-523-0636; www.outdoors.org; 5 Joy St; ☒ 8:30am-5pm Mon-Fri) is the place to go if you need maps or guidebooks for serious hiking in New England.

Boston for Children

Boston's relatively small scale makes it an easy city for families to explore. Just put on your walking shoes and head out.

In the **Public Garden** (p227), fans of Robert McCloskey's classic Boston tale *Make Way for Ducklings* can visit statues of the famous mallards and cruise on the delightful Swan Boats. At the **Boston Common** (p227), kids can cool their toes in the Frog Pond and romp on the playground's swings and jungle gyms.

The **Boston Children's Museum** (Map pp228-9; ☎ 617-426-8855; www.bostonkids.org; 300 Congress St; adult/child 2-15 $9/7, 5-9pm Fri $1; ☒ 10am-5pm Sat-Thu, 10am-9pm Fri) is especially entertaining for those under eight, while the **Museum of Science** (left) will thrill kids of all ages. At the **New England Aquarium** (left) get a feel for the sea in the touch pool and visit the Animal Rescue Center, where you can watch sea turtles and seals being nursed back to health.

Boston by Little Feet (☎ 617-367-2345; www .bostonbyfoot.com; 1hr tour $8; departs Dock Sq at Faneuil Hall 10am Mon & Sat, 2pm Sun May-Oct), designed for kids aged six to 12, offers a fun slice of the Freedom Trail from a child's perspective. And those quirky, quacky **Boston Duck Tours** (opposite) are bound to be a hit.

Tours

Boston Duck Tours (Map pp228-9; ☎ 617-723-3825; www.bostonducktours.com; adult/child 5-11 $23/14; ☼ every half-hr 9am-dusk Apr-Nov) offers ridiculously popular land-and-water tours using WWII amphibious vehicles that cruise the downtown streets before splashing into the Charles River. Tours leave from the Prudential Center and the Museum of Science.

In addition, trolley tours of the city are offered by several companies, including **Old Town Trolley Tours** (☎ 800-868-7482; www.historictours.com; adult/child 12 & under $29/free), which depart from various locations around the city.

Boston Harbor Cruises (Map pp228-9; ☎ 617-227-4321; www.bostonharborcruises.com; 1 Long Wharf; adult/child 4-11 $12/9) operates 45-minute sightseeing cruises of Boston Harbor; it also offers a three-hour **whale-watching trip** (adult/child $31/25) on a high-speed catamaran.

The nonprofit **Boston by Foot** (☎ 617-367-2345; www.bostonbyfoot.com; 90min tour $10-11) offers all sorts of architecturally focused walking tours, including ones in the North End and Back Bay. See the Freedom Trail boxed text (p227) for other historical walking tours.

Boston Bike Tours (Map pp228-9; ☎ 617-308-5902; www.bostonbiketours.com; departs from Boston Common; 2-5hr tour $25-30; ☼ 11am Sat & Sun) will take you on a guided spin around Boston and Cambridge. Follow Paul Revere's ride, cruise Harvard Sq on wheels or take in a brewery tour; check the website for schedules.

Festivals & Events

Contact the **Boston Common visitors center** (☎ 800-733-2678; www.bostonusa.com) for up-to-the-minute details on events. The following celebrations are Boston biggies:

St Patrick's Day (www.irishmassachusetts.com) On March 17 the substantial Irish-American community in South Boston hosts a huge parade, and bars all over town serve green beer.

Patriot's Day & Boston Marathon (www.boston-marathon.com) Paul Revere's ride from the North End to Lexington in 1775 is reenacted on the third Monday in April, commemorating the start of the American Revolution. On the same day, marathoners from around the world participate in the 26-mile race ending at Copley Sq.

Boston Harborfest (www.bostonharborfest.com) Six-day festival leading up to July 4 celebrates Boston's colonial heritage, including a chowder contest and concerts.

Boston Pops on the Esplanade (www.bso.org) This wildly popular outdoor Independence Day (July 4) concert culminates with fireworks over the Charles River.

Italian festivals (www.northendboston.com) During July and August the North End honors saints with a series of weekend street fairs.

Head of the Charles Regatta (www.hocr.org) Some of the world's top rowing teams compete in the Charles River one weekend in late October, as spectators line the banks to cheer.

First Night (www.firstnight.org) On December 31 Boston rings in the New Year with ice sculptures, music events, fireworks and festivities all over town.

Sleeping

Boston has a well-earned reputation for high hotel prices and high occupancy rates. Prices tend to fluctuate and you'll typically find the best deals on weekends when business folks leave town. The majority of hotels are in the downtown area and the Back Bay, both convenient to transportation and sightseeing.

Central Reservation Service of New England (☎ 617-569-3800, 800-332-3026) and **GBCVB** (☎ 617-424-7664; http://bostonusa.worldres.com) are centralized reservation bureaus that often have good deals. **Bed & Breakfast Agency of Boston** (☎ 617-720-3540, 800-248-9262; www.boston-bnbagency.com; r $100-160) represents about 150 B&Bs and apartments in central locations.

BUDGET

Hostels fill in summer, so book ahead to avoid disappointment.

HI Boston Hostel (Map p225; ☎ 617-536-9455; www.bostonhostel.org; 12 Hemenway St; dm incl breakfast $32; ☒ ▣) With 206 beds in four- and six-bed

THE AUTHOR'S CHOICE

Charlesmark Hotel (Map pp228-9; ☎ 617-247-1212; www.thecharlesmark.com; 655 Boylston St; r incl breakfast $149-189; ☒ ▣) Looking for a great deal in the Back Bay with an unbeatable location? This friendly European-style boutique hotel at Copley Sq fits the bill. The rooms are compact so you may have to dance around your suitcase, but they're otherwise thoroughly appealing with original artwork gracing the walls, Italian-tile bathrooms and solid high-tech amenities including wi-fi, stereo systems and endless channels of satellite TV. Relax with fellow travelers in the stylish guest lounge, which has complimentary coffee, fruit and online computers. For the best view, ask for a front room; for whisper-quiet, request the back.

NEW ENGLAND

dorms, this friendly Back Bay hostel offers generous amenities from free use of linens to organized walking tours and pub crawls.

HI Fenway Summer Hostel (Map p225; ☎ 617-267-8599; www.bostonhostel.org/fenway; 575 Commonwealth Ave; dm/r incl breakfast $35/89; ⊙ Jun-Aug; ⊠ ▢) In a former hotel near Kenmore Sq, this hostel has dorm rooms with three beds each, as well as private rooms for up to three guests. Linens are provided.

Other recommendations:

YMCA of Greater Boston (Map p225; ☎ 617-536-7800; www.hostelboston.com; 316 Huntington Ave; s/d incl breakfast $46/66; ▣) Near the Museum of Fine Arts.

Berkeley Residence YWCA (Map pp228-9; ☎ 617-375-2524; www.ywcaboston.org/berkeley; 40 Berkeley St; s/d incl breakfast $60/90) In the South End.

Boston Harbor Islands National Park (☎ 617-223-8666, 877-422-6762; www.reserveamerica.com; campsites $8; ⊙ Jun-Aug) Primitive campsites on Grape and Bumpkin Islands.

MIDRANGE

Harborside Inn (Map pp228-9; ☎ 617-723-7500, 888-723-7575; www.harborsideinnboston.com; 185 State St; r $129-279; ℗) Just steps from Faneuil Hall, this boutique hotel in a beautifully renovated, 19th-century warehouse makes a great central base and the rates are a good deal for this high-end area. No two rooms are alike but all have period charm with hardwood floors and antique furnishings.

John Jeffries House (Map pp228-9; ☎ 617-367-1866; www.johnjeffrieshouse.com; 14 David G Mugar Way; r $95-125, ste $150-165 incl breakfast) This Beacon Hill hotel is one of Boston's best-kept secrets. It's owned by Mass Eye and Ear Infirmary but open to those with no connection to the hospital. Not only are the rooms refreshingly affordable, but they're attractive with period decor that reflects the building's century-old charm, and most have well-equipped kitchenettes.

463 Beacon St Guest House (Map p225; ☎ 617-536-1302; www.463beacon.com; 463 Beacon St, Back Bay; r $79-149) This renovated 19th-century brownstone has 20 rooms on six floors, most with kitchenettes, some with fireplaces. There are no elevators but those with heavy luggage or young kids can request a lower floor. There are also apartments available by the week.

Hotel@MIT (Map p225; ⊙ 617-577-0200, 800-222-8733; www.hotelatmit.com; 20 Sidney St, Cambridge; r incl breakfast $129-289; ℗) You don't have to be a rocket scientist to stay at this sleek new hotel with ergonomically designed furniture, high-speed Internet access and original artwork from the MIT collection.

Newbury Guest House (Map p225; ☎ 617-437-7666, 800-437-7668; www.newburyguesthouse.com; 261 Newbury St; r incl breakfast $135-195; ℗) Stay in a fashionable Back Bay location in this pensionlike B&B boasting 32 comfortable rooms, with modern amenities like wi-fi, in three interconnected 1882 brownstones.

Hotel Buckminster (Map p225; ☎ 617-236-7050, 800-727-2825; www.bostonhotelbuckminster.com; 645 Beacon St; r $79-139) Built in 1897 by the renowned American architect Stanford White, this Kenmore Sq hotel is just a baseball's toss from Fenway Park. Although it's lost some of its luster over the years, the rooms are adequate and reasonably priced.

TOP END

Omni Parker House (Map pp228-9; ☎ 617-227-8600; www.omnihotels.com; 60 School St; r $169-309; ℗) Dark wood and crystal chandeliers grace the lobby of this classy period hotel, which has counted among its guests Charles Dickens and JFK. Despite its well-polished elegance, there's nothing stodgy about the place – you can be as comfortable here in a T-shirt as in a suit and tie.

Nine Zero Hotel (Map pp228-9; ☎ 617-772-5800, 866-646-3937; www.ninezero.com; 90 Tremont St; r from $219; ℗ ▢) If chic and cutting-edge is your style, wear black and check in to this trendy, deluxe downtown hotel. Styled in leather, glass and chrome, the rooms have custom furnishings, cushy down comforters and business-friendly high-tech gadgets.

Eating

Whether you're up for good ol' New England 'chowdah' or sophisticated international cuisine, Boston has plenty to satisfy any palate. No trip to the city is complete without a dinner in the Italian North End. Head to Newbury St for the outdoor café and people-watching scene.

BEACON HILL & DOWNTOWN

Ye Olde Union Oyster House (Map pp228-9; ☎ 617-227-2750; 41 Union St; mains $16-20; ⊙ 11am-9:30pm Sun-Thu, 11am-10pm Fri & Sat) Savor fresh-shucked oysters and a good measure of history at Boston's oldest (1826) restaurant. It's been the haunt of many famous Bostonians; one table in the upstairs dining room is dubbed the Kennedy booth because JFK reserved it whenever he was in town and had an inkling for seafood.

Quincy Market (Map pp228-9; off Congress & North Sts) This huge hall is lined with food stalls selling everything from Asian plate lunches to New England seafood. Its biggest plus is that it's quick and convenient, right on the Freedom Trail. One reliable choice here is Boston & Maine Fish Company, which has good chowder and lobster rolls.

Durgin Park (Map pp228-9; ☎ 617-227-2038; 340 Faneuil Hall Marketplace; lunch mains $7-11, dinner mains $15-20; ☖ 11:30am-10pm Mon-Sat, 11:30am-9pm Sun) This Boston institution in North Market, adjacent to Quincy Market, has been serving up New England fare like chicken potpie, Boston baked beans and Indian pudding at family-style tables since 1827. Not surprisingly, it's all a bit dated, but that's part of the fun.

Lala Rokh (Map pp228-9; ☎ 617-720-5511; 97 Mt Vernon St; mains $14-20; ☖ 5-10pm) Enjoy a culinary magic-carpet ride at this Beacon Hill gem serving aromatic Persian fare such as saffron-seasoned chicken, yogurt-marinated lamb and savory chutneys. The setting is romantic, the service excellent.

CHINATOWN

This compact area has a delightful variety of Asian food at refreshingly affordable prices.

Ginza (Map pp228-9; ☎ 617-338-2261; 16 Hudson St; mains $8-20; ☖ 11:30am-2:30pm & 5-11pm Mon-Thu, 11:30am-2:30pm & 5pm-3:30am Fri, noon-3:30am Sat, noon-11pm Sun) Perched on the edge of Chinatown, Ginza serves Boston's best sushi and sashimi. And when you're done with the sushi bar, you can move on to other Japanese favorites like tempura and teriyaki.

Pho Pasteur (Map pp228-9; ☎ 617-482-7467; 682 Washington St; mains $5-9; ☖ 9am-10:45pm) This lively restaurant is the place to go for hearty bowls of authentic *pho* soup brimming with fresh herbs, as well as tasty spring rolls and other delicious Vietnamese treats.

Happy Buddha (Map pp228-9; ☎ 617-451-1121; 5 Beach St; mains $6-12; ☖ 11am-10pm Sun-Thu, 11am-11pm Fri & Sat) You'll be amazed what can be done with tofu and wheat gluten at this tidy Asian eatery offering all sorts of vegetarian dishes from veggie-chicken fingers to sweet-and-sour veggie-pork. Save room for the flamed banana dessert.

THE AUTHOR'S CHOICE

Carmen (Map pp228-9; ☎ 617-742-6421; 33 North Sq; mains $18-29; ☖ 5:30-10pm Sun & Tue-Thu, 5:30-11pm Fri & Sat) Exposed red-brick walls, fresh flowers on the tables and soft candlelight set the tone at this cozy dinner restaurant down the street from the Paul Revere House. Innovative Italian cuisine just doesn't get any better. Highlights include deliciously tender slow-roasted Tuscan pork, fresh clam linguine in a spicy garlic sauce, flaky semolina-crusted salmon, savory steaks and antipasto plates. This standout neighborhood restaurant seats just 28 people, so be sure to call ahead for reservations.

Peach Farm (Map pp228-9; ☎ 617-481-3332; 4 Tyler St; mains $7-15; ☖ 11am-2am) Be transported to Hong Kong when you walk in the door of this basement restaurant with pink tablecloths and live fish tanks. The shrimp Szechuan is a spicy delight, but all the seafood here is as good as it gets. Come before 3pm for $5 lunch deals.

Grand Chau Chow (Map pp228-9; ☎ 617-292-5166; 45 Beach St; mains $8-17; ☖ 10am-3am) If Peach Farm is full, this nearby restaurant also serves award-winning Hong Kong–style cuisine.

NORTH END

A hungry soul will find heavenly delights in the North End, where nearly 100 Italian restaurants line the neighborhood streets. The thickest concentration is along Hanover St.

Pomodoro (Map pp228-9; ☎ 617-367-4348; 319 Hanover St; mains $15-18, weekend brunch $10; ☖ 3-11pm Tue-Sun, 10am-2pm Sat & Sun) It doesn't get cozier than this. Sit at one of the 10 café tables and watch the chef work his magic at the end of the room. The seafood fra diavolo, loaded with New England shellfish, is a flavorful favorite.

Prezza (Map pp228-9; ☎ 617-227-1577; 24 Fleet St; mains $25-40; ☖ 5:30-10pm Mon-Sat) Chef Anthony Caturano has garnered a loyal following for his contemporary Mediterranean cuisine. Roasted trout, cioppino and wood-grilled lobster tail are among the favorites.

Neptune Oyster (Map pp228-9; ☎ 617-742-3474; 63 Salem St; mains $15-24; ☖ 11:30am-11pm Sun-Thu, 11:30am-midnight Fri & Sat) Barely bigger than a clam, this smart little place has the best raw bar in the North End and serves up good hot Italian-style seafood as well.

Artu (Map pp228-9; ☎ 617-742-4336; 6 Prince St; lunch mains $6-9, dinner mains $9-19; ☺ 11am-11pm) Bigger than most of its neighbors, Artu is a good choice if you can't find a seat at one of the North End's smaller jewels. On the plus side, prices are reasonable and the extensive menu of country-Italian food holds its own.

Pizzeria Regina (Map pp228-9; ☎ 617-227-0765; 11 Thatcher St; large pizzas $12-18; ☺ 11am-11:30pm Mon-Thu, 11am-midnight Fri & Sat, noon-11pm Sun) Arguably Boston's best thin-crust pizza, including an unbeatable vegetarian version loaded with artichoke hearts.

Salumeria Italiana (Map pp228-9; ☎ 617-523-8743; 151 Richmond St; ☺ 7am-6pm Mon-Thu, 7am-7pm Fri & Sat) Pick up picnic supplies at this ethnic grocer, which has delicious breads, antipasto by the pound ($9) and old-fashioned Italian cold cuts.

BACK BAY

29 Newbury (Map pp228-9; ☎ 617-536-0290; 29 Newbury St; lunch mains $9-17, dinner mains $12-29; ☺ 11:30am-10pm) The sidewalk terrace of this stylish café, opposite the Armani store, is an ideal place to watch the chic shoppers on Newbury St. Good Caesar salads and creative sandwiches such as swordfish club aioli.

Legal Sea Foods (Map pp228-9; ☎ 617-266-6800; Prudential Center, 800 Boylston St; lunch mains $9-15, dinner mains $15-25; ☺ 11am-10:30pm Mon-Thu, 11am-11:30pm Fri & Sat, noon-10pm Sun) Running with the motto 'If it isn't fresh, it isn't Legal,' this place indeed serves top-notch seafood – broiled, steamed, grilled and fried – and always draws a crowd.

Thai Basil (Map pp228-9; ☎ 617-578-0089; 132 Newbury St; mains $8-17; ☺ 11:30am-10pm Mon-Fri, noon-10pm Sat & Sun) Savory Thai curries and other spicy counterparts await at this tidy basement café. Come before 3pm for $8 lunch deals.

Stephanie's on Newbury (Map pp228-9; ☎ 617-236-0990; 190 Newbury St; lunch mains $10-18, dinner mains $16-30; ☺ 11:30am-11pm Mon-Sat, 10am-9pm Sun) On a sunny day, the sidewalk tables at this fashionable café pack three deep. The 'new American' menu covers everything from sandwiches to steaks.

JP Licks (Map p225; ☎ 617-236-1666; 352 Newbury St; cone $3.50; ☺ 11am-midnight) Cool off with a cone of Boston's favorite homemade ice cream.

CAMBRIDGE

Tamarind Bay (☎ 617-491-4552; 75 Winthrop St; mains $12-20; ☺ lunch & dinner) A standout among Harvard Sq's many Indian restaurants, Tamarind lays out an excellent lunch buffet ($10) and its dinner menu features unusual delicacies, like seared lobster tail in coconut sauce, as well as more traditional curry dishes.

Veggie Planet (Map p225; ☎ 617-661-1513; 47 Palmer St at Club Passim; mains $4-11; ☺ 11:30am-10:30pm) This place lures the earthy-crunchy crowd with homemade soups, vegan pizzas (try the coconut peanut curry!) and organic salads. Come on Sundays for live jazz.

Au Bon Pain (☎ 617-497-9797; 1316 Massachusetts Ave; sandwiches $5-6; ☺ 5:30am-midnight) The outdoor patio here is the place to watch all the action on Harvard Sq while munching on pastries, sandwiches and salads.

TOP FIVE BAKERIES

Bova's (Map pp228-9; ☎ 617-523-5601; 134 Salem St, North End; ☺ 24hr) Night owls head to this fourth-generation Italian bakery, which makes unbeatable Tuscan bread and luscious fruit tarts, but you won't regret popping in any time of the day.

Flour Bakery and Café (Map p225; ☎ 617-267-4300; 1595 Washington St; ☺ 7am-7pm Mon-Fri, 8am-6pm Sat, 9am-3pm Sun) Everyone comes for the award-winning pastries, but Flour also has delicious breads and sandwiches.

Mike's Pastry Shop (Map pp228-9; ☎ 617-742-3050; 300 Hanover St, North End; ☺ 8am-10pm) Hands down the best bakery in Boston. Favorites among the 100 different Italian sweets are the chocolate cannoli and the gorgeous fruit-shaped marzipan.

Mix Bakery (Map pp228-9; ☎ 617-357-4050; 36 Beach St; ☺ 7am-7pm) A standout among Chinatown bakeries, Mix has tasty moon cakes and Western-style cakes.

Rosie's (Map p225; ☎ 617-491-9488; 243 Hampshire St, Cambridge; ☺ 8:30am-6pm) Chocoholics will love the fudge cake, and the chocolate-chip cookies are a rave, too.

Mr Bartley's Burger Cottage (☎ 617-354-6559; 1246 Massachusetts Ave; burgers $6-8; 🕙 11am-10pm Mon-Sat) Students pack this old-time Harvard Sq burger shack for its amazing variety of primo hamburgers.

Drinking

Bars line Union St, just north of Faneuil Hall. Among them, the **Bell in Hand Tavern** (Map pp228-9; ☎ 617-227-2098; 45 Union St), the oldest tavern in the USA, holds its own with the younger crowd, as does **Purple Shamrock** (Map pp228-9; ☎ 627-227-2060; 1 Union St), a bar-cum-nightspot with live bands on the weekend.

Boston Beer Works (Map p225; ☎ 617-536-2337; 61 Brookline Ave) This famed sports bar, serving its own microbrews, is the place to go before a Red Sox game.

Top of the Hub (Map pp228-9; ☎ 617-536-1175; Prudential Center, 800 Boylston St) Enjoy a martini in the lounge of this chic restaurant on the 52nd floor of the Prudential Center and you'll get the same spectacular view as from the Pru's Skywalk. Jazz at night, too.

John Harvard's Brew House (☎ 617-868-3585; 33 Dunster St, Cambridge) This subterranean Harvard Sq microbrewery serves well-crafted brews in an inviting English-pub atmosphere.

Cheers (Map pp228-9; ☎ 617-227-9605; 84 Beacon St) Only the exterior of this landmark bar appeared in the opening scenes of the *Cheers* sitcom and it now serves far more tourists than locals, but if it's time for a cold one, why not?

Cactus Club (Map p225; ☎ 617-236-0200; 939 Boylston St) Raucous 20-something singles scene serving oversized margaritas and good Mexican fare.

Sonsie (Map p225; ☎ 617-351-2500; 327 Newbury St; 🕙 7am-1am) With tables facing the street, this is one of Newbury's trendiest places to sip a glass of chardonnay or an espresso.

Caffè Vittoria (Map pp228-9; ☎ 617-227-7606; 296 Hanover St; 🕙 8am-midnight) *The* place to enjoy a cappuccino or an aperitif in style in the North End's Little Italy. The tiramisu is to die for.

Entertainment

No matter what you're looking for, there's always something happening in Boston. For up-to-the-minute listings, pick up Thursday's *Boston Globe,* the weekly *Boston Phoenix* or the sassy biweekly *Improper Bostonian.*

> **CHEERS!**
>
> It's only fitting that the hometown of *Cheers* hosts two top-notch breweries. For a close-up look at the process and free samples of the final product, pay them a visit.
>
> **Samuel Adams Brewery** (Map p225; ☎ 617-368-5080; www.samadams.com; 30 Germania St, Jamaica Plain; admission $2; 🕙 tours 2pm Wed-Thu, 2pm & 5:30pm Fri, noon, 1pm & 2pm Sat, May-Aug) aka the Boston Beer Museum, can be reached by taking the T's Orange Line to Stoney Brook.
>
> **Harpoon Brewery** (☎ 888-427-7666; www .harpoonbrewery.com; 306 Northern Ave; admission free; 🕙 tours 3pm Tue-Thu, 1pm & 3pm Fri & Sat) is near the waterfront 1.5 miles southeast of South Station.

Half-price tickets to same-day theater, dance and music performance are sold for cash only (beginning at 11am) at the **BosTix** kiosks (Map pp228-9; www.artsboston.org; Faneuil Hall Congress St; Copley Sq Dartmouth & Boylston Sts).

NIGHTCLUBS

Cover charges at the following nightclubs vary depending upon the band's fame factor, but are typically $5 to $20.

Avalon (Map p225; ☎ 617-262-2424; 15 Lansdowne St) This cavernous dance club features large touring bands, anything from techno to reggae. Sunday night is gay night.

Paradise Rock Club (Map p225; ☎ 617-562-8800; 969 Commonwealth Ave) Some very heavy-hitting indie bands take to the stage at this landmark club.

Bill's Bar (Map p225; ☎ 617-421-9678; 5½ Lansdowne St) Students pack this Fenway-area club for rock, punk, funk and reggae.

Roxy (Map pp228-9; ☎ 617-338-7699; 279 Tremont St) In the theater district, this fashionable club is one of Boston's hottest nightspots.

LIVE MUSIC

Middle East (Map p225; ☎ 617-354-8238; 472 Massachusetts Ave) This multiroom, alternative rock club at Cambridge's Central Sq hosts both local and traveling bands.

Club Passim (Map p225; ☎ 617-492-7679; www .clubpassim.org; 47 Palmer St) This venerable folk club in Harvard Sq has nurtured the early careers of notable singer-songwriters such as Tracy Chapman and Nanci Griffith.

NEW ENGLAND

NEW ENGLAND

GAY & LESBIAN BOSTON

Boston has a thriving gay community, with the center of the action in the South End. During the first year after Massachusetts legalized same-sex marriages (in 2003) some 6000 same-sex couples tied the knot, and the Boston-Cambridge area was the gayest of all with more than 1000 marriages.

Bay Windows (www.baywindows.com), a free weekly serving the gay and lesbian community, has plenty of useful information. Log on to **Edge Boston** (www.edgeboston.com) for the latest on the entertainment scene.

Boston's most popular sleep for gay travelers is **Chandler Inn** (Map pp228-9; ☎ 617-482-3450; www.chandlerinn.com; 26 Chandler St; r $109-169), a South End hotel with 56 tidy rooms; it's also the site of **Fritz** (☎ 617-482-4428; ☺ noon-2am), a casual gay watering hole.

One stalwart of the gay and lesbian scene is **Club Café** (Map pp228-9; ☎ 617-536-0966; 209 Columbus Ave), a convivial South End bar and restaurant. The popular nightclub and bar **Chaps** (Map pp228-9; ☎ 617-587-0000; www.chapsboston.com; 101 Warrenton St) has something for everyone, from techno and drag shows to tea dances.

Gay Pride (www.bostonpride.org) events in mid-June include a parade and block parties.

Man Ray (Map p225; ☎ 617-864-0400; 21 Brookline St, Cambridge) It's Goth central here at Boston's top 'underground' club.

TT the Bear's Place (Map p225; ☎ 617-492-2327; 10 Brookline St, Cambridge) Intimate, diehard rock joint played by up-and-coming local bands.

Wally's Café (Map p225; ☎ 617-424-1408; 427 Massachusetts Ave) Jazz aficionados, young and old, rub shoulders at this snug club that's been featuring Boston's coolest jazz since 1947.

Berklee Performance Center (Map p225; ☎ 617-747-2261; 136 Massachusetts Ave) One of America's premier music schools hosts concerts by their famous alumni as well as by students sparking their own careers.

PERFORMING ARTS

Symphony Hall (Map p225; ☎ 617-266-1492; www.bso.org; 301 Massachusetts Ave) The renowned Boston Symphony Orchestra and Boston Pops perform here.

Wang Center (Map pp228-9; ☎ 617-482-9393; www.wangcenter.org; 270 Tremont St) This cavernous 1925 landmark hosts the Boston Ballet, modern dance, pop concerts and theater.

At **Charles Playhouse** (Map pp228-9; 74 Warrenton St) you'll find the long-running comical whodunit mystery **Shear Madness** (☎ 617-426-5225) and the wildly popular **Blue Man Group** (☎ 617-426-6912).

Two lovely old theaters, the **Colonial Theatre** (Map pp228-9; ☎ 617-426-9366; 106 Boylston St) and **Wilbur Theatre** (Map pp228-9; ☎ 617-423-4008; 246 Tremont St), feature try-outs of Broadway-bound shows – if they're received well here, to New York they go.

Many free summer concerts take place at the outdoor bandstand **Hatch Shell** (Map pp228-9; Charles River Esplanade), including the Boston Pops' July 4 concert.

SPORTS

From April to September (or October when they make the play-offs) Boston's major-league baseball team, **Boston Red Sox** (☎ 617-267-1700; www.redsox.com; 4 Yawkey Way), takes to the field at **Fenway Park** (Map p225; tickets $12-120).

At the **HD Banknorth Garden** (Map pp228-9; 150 Causeway St) from October to April, the NBA **Boston Celtics** (☎ 617-523-3030; www.celtics.com; tickets $10-170) play basketball and the NHL **Boston Bruins** (☎ 617-624-1900; www.bostonbruins.com; tickets $19-99) play ice hockey.

At the **Gillette Stadium** (Foxboro), 25 miles south of Boston, the NFL **New England Patriots** (☎ 800-543-1776; www.patriots.com; tickets $49-125) play football from August to January and the MLS **New England Revolution** (☎ 877-438-7387; www.revolutionsoccer.net; tickets $16-32) play soccer from April to October.

CINEMAS

Brattle Theatre (Map p225; ☎ 617-876-6837; 40 Brattle St, Cambridge; tickets $9) Gorgeous Harvard Sq theater featuring art films.

Kendall Square Cinema (Map p225; ☎ 617-494-9800; 1 Kendall Sq, Cambridge; tickets $9.25) Shows independent and foreign films.

Larger mainstream multiplex venues include **Loews Boston Common** (Map pp228-9; ☎ 617-423-5801; 175 Tremont St) and **Loews Harvard Square** (☎ 617-864-4581; 10 Church St, Cambridge).

Shopping

Newbury St is Boston's favorite shopping street, chockablock with chic boutiques, art galleries and offbeat shops. It's an amazing street to stroll from one end to the other. On its highbrow east end, which begins at the Ritz-Carlton hotel, it's all Armani, Brooks Brothers and Cartier, but by the time you reach the west end, you'll find funky bookstores, craft shops and ice cream parlors cheek to jowl.

For traditional shopping, Bostonians head to Downtown Crossing (Map pp228–9), which has two large department stores and scores of smaller shops selling everything from sneakers to stereos. **Copley Place** (100 Huntington Ave) and the **Shops at Prudential Center** (Map pp228–9; 800 Boylston St), both in the Back Bay, are large indoor malls with the usual mix of chains and high-end retailers.

Get independent music CDs and Red Sox paraphernalia at **Newbury Comics** (Map p225; ☎ 617-236-4930; 332 Newbury St), Harvard-logo sweatshirts at the **Coop** (Map p225; Massachusetts Ave, Cambridge), *Cheers*-logo anything at **Cheers** (Map pp228–9; ☎ 617-227-9605; 84 Beacon St) and Yankee-hater baseball caps at **Out of Left Field** (☎ 617-722-9401; Congress St) at Faneuil Hall.

Good places to browse for arts and crafts are **Bromfield Art Gallery** (Map pp228–9; ☎ 617-451-3605; 450 Harrison Ave), Boston's oldest cooperative, and **Cambridge Artists' Cooperative** (☎ 617-868-4434; 59A Church St, Cambridge) at Harvard Sq.

Getting There & Away

Since Boston is New England's hub city, getting in and out of town is easy. The train and bus stations are conveniently side by side in a modern facility, and the airport is a short subway ride away.

AIR

Logan International Airport (☎ 800-235-6426; www.massport.com), just across Boston Harbor from the city center, is served by major US and foreign airlines. It's an updated airport with decent restaurants, currency-exchange booths and traveler's aid services.

BUS

South Station (Map pp228–9; 700 Atlantic Ave) is the terminal for long-distance buses (p223) including those operated by **Bonanza Bus Lines** (☎ 617-720-4110), **Greyhound** (☎ 617-526-1808), **Plymouth & Brockton** (☎ 508-746-0378), **Peter Pan Bus Lines** (☎ 617-946-0960) and **Vermont Transit** (☎ 800-522-8737).

In addition, there are a couple of small operations out of Chinatown that go to New York City for just $15 each way; the largest operator is **Fung Wah Bus Company** (Map pp228–9; ☎ 617-338-1163; www.fungwahbus.com; 68 Beach St).

CAR & MOTORCYCLE

The big-name car-rental companies like Hertz, Avis and National have offices at the airport, and many have locations around

---

CURSE REVERSED

Boston is unabashedly a baseball town. Never mind that it has a championship football team or that its basketball and hockey teams are two of the best in history; this city lives and breathes the Boston Red Sox.

Yet the baseball team that produced such legends as Ted Williams and Carl Yastrzemski hadn't won the World Series since trading Babe Ruth to archrival New York Yankees in 1918. Then came 2004, with the Red Sox and Yankees facing off for the American League Championship. 'This is the year,' Red Sox fans chanted. But those damn Yankees won the first three games, a virtual death knell for the Sox since no team had ever come back in this best-of-seven series after losing three in a row. Game four looked like much of the same with the Red Sox trailing, but after the Sox tied the score in the ninth inning, power-hitter David Ortiz slammed a game-ending home run in extra-innings play. Miraculously the Red Sox took the next three games. The Sox went on to play the St Louis Cardinals and swept them four games in a row, completing the greatest comeback in baseball history and becoming World Series champions for the first time since letting the Babe slip away. And for Red Sox Nation the infamous 86-year 'Curse of the Bambino' was finally over.

There are two ways to get caught up in Sox fever: take a tour of storied Fenway Park (p232) or, better yet, catch a Red Sox game (opposite).

town as well. See the Transportation chapter (p1175) for contact numbers.

Bear in mind that driving in Boston is confusing – narrow, one-way streets and aggressive drivers – and that parking is difficult and expensive. It's almost always better to stick to public transportation within the city. If you're traveling onward by rental car, pick up your car at the end of your Boston visit.

TRAIN

MBTA Commuter Rail (☎ 617-222-3200) trains connect Boston's North Station (Map pp228–9) with Concord and Salem and Boston's South Station (Map pp228–9) with Plymouth; fares vary with the distance, maxing out at $6.

The **Amtrak** (☎ 617-345-7460, 800-872-7245; www.amtrak.com) terminal is at South Station; most Amtrak trains also stop at the **Back Bay Station** (Dartmouth St). Trains to New York cost $64 (4½ hours) or $99 to $116 on the *Acela Express* (3½ hours).

Getting Around

Logan International Airport is served by the MBTA's Blue Line at Airport Station ($1.25). Free shuttle buses connect Airport Station with all airport terminals. Taxis line up outside the terminals; expect to pay about $20 to $25 to get downtown, depending on how bad the traffic is.

The **MBTA** (☎ 617-222-3200; www.mbta.com; adult/child $1.25/60¢) operates the USA's oldest subway (the 'T'), which began in 1897. Four color-coded lines – Red, Blue, Green and Orange – radiate from the downtown stations of Park St, Downtown Crossing and Government Center. 'Inbound' trains are headed for these three stations, 'outbound' trains away from them. Trains operate from around 5:30am to 12:30am. Tourist passes (per day $7.50, three days $18, per week $35) for unlimited travel are sold at major stations including Airport Station, North Station, South Station, Copley and Government Center.

Taxis in the city are plentiful; expect to pay between $10 and $15 between two points within the city limits. Flag taxis on the street, find them at major hotels or call **Metro Cab** (☎ 617-242-8000) or **Independent** (☎ 617-426-8700).

AROUND BOSTON

Boston is surrounded with historic towns that make for fine day-tripping. If you don't have a car, you can reach these places by MBTA (left) buses and rail.

Lexington & Concord

Fifteen miles northwest of Boston, the colonial town of Lexington is where the first battle of the Revolutionary War took place in 1775. After the battle, the British redcoats marched 10 miles west to Concord where they fought the American minutemen at the town's North Bridge – the first American victory. You can revisit this momentous bit of history at **Minute Man National Historic Park** (☎ 978-369-6993; www.nps.gov/mima; 174 Liberty St, Concord; admission free; ✆ 9am-5pm Apr-Oct, 11am-3pm Nov-Mar) and along the 5.5-mile **Battle Road trail**, suitable for hiking and biking.

In the 19th century, Concord was a vibrant literary community. Next to the **Old North Bridge** is the **Old Manse**, former home of author Nathaniel Hawthorne. Within a mile of the center of town are the **Ralph Waldo Emerson house**, Louisa May Alcott's **Orchard House** and the **Wayside**, where Alcott's *Little Women* was set.

Walden Pond, where Henry David Thoreau lived and wrote *Walden*, is 3 miles south of the town center; you can visit his cabin and swim in the pond. All these authors are laid to rest in **Sleepy Hollow Cemetery** on Bedford St, in the town center. Admission is free to Walden Pond and the cemetery; the homes can be visited for a small fee. **Concord Chamber of Commerce** (☎ 978-369-3120; www.concordchamberofcommerce.org; 58 Main St; ✆ 9:30am-4:30pm) has details.

Salem

Salem, 20 miles northeast of Boston, earned its infamous place in history with the 1692 hysteria that put 20 people to death for witchcraft (opposite). These tragic events have proven a boon for operators of several Salem witch attractions, some serious, others that make light of the events. **Destination Salem** (☎ 877-725-3662; www.salem.org; 63 Wharf St) has information on town attractions.

A standout among 'witchy' sites is the **Witch House** (☎ 978-744-8815; www.salemweb.com/witchhouse; 310 Essex St; adult/child $7/3; ✆ 10am-5pm May-Nov), the home of the magistrate who presided over the trials. Now a museum, it provides insight into the righteous puritanical mentality of the period as well as a look at the interior of a fine old-colonial home.

WITCH HUNTS & TRIALS

In the late 17th century it was widely believed that one could make a pact with the devil to gain evil powers. When a number of girls in Salem began behaving strangely in early 1692, their parents thought the devil had come to their village. The girls accused a slave named Tituba of being a witch. Tituba 'confessed' under torture and then accused two others to save her own life. Soon accusations flew thick and fast, as the accused implicated others in attempts to save themselves.

When a special court convened to deal with the accusations, its justices accepted 'spectral evidence,' evidence of 'spirits' seen only by witnesses. With imaginations and religious passions inflamed, the situation careened out of control. By September 1692, 156 people stood accused, 55 people had pleaded guilty, and 14 women and five men who would not 'confess' to witchcraft had been hanged. Another victim, Giles Corey, was weighted down with stones and pressed to death for refusing to submit to a trial.

The frenzy died down when the accusers began pointing at prominent merchants, clergy and the governor's wife. With the powers-that-be in jeopardy, the trials were called off and the remaining accused released. For an interesting read on the Salem trials, pick up a copy of Arthur Miller's *The Crucible* (adapted to a movie of the same name starring Daniel Day Lewis), which doubles as a parable to the McCarthy anti-communist 'witch hunts' in the US Senate in the 1950s that resulted in the blacklisting of Miller and ruined the lives of many of his colleagues.

One of New England's finest museums, the **Peabody Essex Museum** (☎ 978-745-9500; www .pem.org; East India Sq; adult/child $13/free; ☺ 10am-5pm), is an amazing place that reflects Salem's rich maritime history with extensive exhibits of the art and furnishings that traders brought back from their expeditions to Asia. They had superb taste and deep pockets, returning with some of the finest collections of cultural artifacts from island tribes in the remote Pacific, as well as extensive artwork from China, Japan and Korea.

You can also tour the c 1688 **House of the Seven Gables** (☎ 978-744-0991; www.7gables.org; 54 Turner St; adult/child $11/7.25; ☺ 10am-5pm Nov-Jun, 10am-7pm Jul-Oct), made famous in Nathaniel Hawthorne's 1851 novel of the same name.

Salem was once the center of a clipper-ship trade with China and its pre-eminent trader, Elias Derby, became America's first millionaire. For a sense of those glory days, take a walk along Derby St and out to Derby Wharf, which is now the center of the **Salem Maritime National Historic Site**.

Plymouth

The *Mayflower* Pilgrims arrived here in 1620 and in what would become a tradition throughout New England, they christened their new home after the place they left behind – Plymouth, England. Often referred to as 'America's hometown,' Plymouth was the first permanent European settlement north of Virginia. **Plymouth Rock**, a weather-worn chunk of granite on the harborfront, marks the place the Pilgrims came ashore. Several other sights in town elucidate the challenges the settlers had to overcome and the plight of the Native Americans who lived here. **Destination Plymouth** (☎ 508-747-7533; www.visit-plymouth.com; 170 Water St), opposite the harbor, has a handy map and details on sights.

Today, travelers make pilgrimages to **Plimoth Plantation** (☎ 508-746-1622; www.plimoth .org; Warren Ave/MA 3A; adult/child $24/14; ☺ 9am-5pm Apr-Nov), an authentically re-created 1627 Pilgrim village. Everything here – the houses, the crops, the food cooked over wood stoves and even the vocabulary used by the costumed interpreters – is meticulously true to the period. If you're traveling with kids, or if you're a history buff, don't miss it. The admission price includes entry to the *Mayflower II*, a replica of the Pilgrims' ship, at Plymouth Harbor.

The most atmospheric place to eat is at the **Lobster Hut** (☎ 508-746-2270; Town Wharf; mains $6-18; ☺ 11am-9pm), a seaside shack with fishing boats tied up alongside, which serves great fried clams and fish, and boiled lobster.

CAPE COD

Think saltwater taffy, seaside cottages, children building sandcastles and sailboats at

NEW ENGLAND

KING OF THE ROAD

When exploring the Cape, eschew the speedy Mid-Cape Hwy (MA 6) and follow instead the Old King's Hwy (MA 6A), which snakes along Cape Cod Bay and is the longest continuous stretch of historic district in the USA. The Old King's Hwy is lined with gracious period homes, some converted to antique shops and art galleries, which make fun browsing en route.

---

sunset. When New Englanders want a day at the beach they head to 'the Cape.' This sandy peninsula, which 19th-century naturalist Henry David Thoreau referred to as 'the bared and bended arm of Massachusetts,' is fringed with 400 miles of sparkling shoreline. But there's a lot more than just beaches here. The Cape boasts quaint fishing villages, excellent biking and hiking trails, a good entertainment scene and the freshest seafood imaginable.

Information

Cape Cod Chamber of Commerce (☎ 508-362-3225, 888-332-2732; www.capecodchamber.org; MA 6 at MA 132, Hyannis; ☉ 8:30am-5pm Mon-Fri, 9am-5pm Sat, also 10am-2pm Sun in summer) Provides information on all the Cape towns and books reservations online.

Sandwich

The Cape's oldest village is a picture-perfect New England town with a solidly historic center bordering a swan-filled pond.

SIGHTS & ACTIVITIES

Fun for kids and adults alike, the 76-acre **Heritage Museums & Gardens** (☎ 508-888-3300; www.heritagemuseumsandgardens.org; Grove St; adult/child $12/6; ☉ 9am-6pm Thu-Tue, 9am-8pm Wed May-Oct, 10am-4pm Wed-Sun Nov-Apr) sports a terrific vintage automobile collection, a working 1912 carousel, folk art collections and one of the finest rhododendron gardens in America.

Take a look at the colonial **Hoxie House** (☎ 508-888-1173; 18 Water St; adult/child $2.50/1.50; ☉ 10am-5pm Mon-Sat, 1-5pm Sun mid-Jun–mid-Oct), c 1637, the oldest house on Cape Cod.

Also on the pond's edge, the picturesque **Dexter Grist Mill** (☎ 508-888-5144; Water St; adult/child $2.50/1.50; ☉ 10am-5pm Mon-Sat, 1-5 Sun mid-Jun–mid-Oct) dates back to 1654 and has centuries-old gears that still grind cornmeal.

Colorful Sandwich glass had its heyday in the 1800s, a heritage that's artfully displayed in the **Sandwich Glass Museum** (☎ 508-888-0251; www.sandwichglassmuseum.org; 129 Main St; adult/child $4.50/1; ☉ 9:30am-5pm Apr-Dec, 9:30am-4pm Wed-Sun Feb-Mar).

A treat for kids is the little **Thornton W Burgess Museum** (☎ 508-888-4668; 4 Water St; suggested donation adult/child $2/1; ☉ 10am-4pm Mon-Sat, 1-4pm Sun mid-Apr–Oct), named for the Sandwich native who wrote the *Peter Cottontail* series.

If you're ready for the beach, head to **Sandy Neck Beach** (Sandy Neck Rd, off MA 6A; Ⓟ), a gorgeous 6-mile dune-backed strand that's ideal for beachcombing. Parking costs $10.

SLEEPING & EATING

Belfry Inne & Bistro (☎ 508-888-8550, 800-844-4542; www.belfryinn.com; 8 Jarves St; r incl breakfast $110-215, dinner mains $20-32; ☉ dinner Tue-Sun; ✗) Ever fall asleep in church? You'll love the rooms, some with stained glass, in this creatively restored former church, now an upmarket B&B. And its stylish restaurant serves the finest food in town.

Shawme-Crowell State Forest (☎ 508-888-0351, 877-422-6762; www.reserveamerica.com; MA 130 near MA 6A; campsites $12) You'll find 285 cool and shady campsites in this 700-acre woodland. No hookups for RVs, though.

Dunbar Tea Room (☎ 508-833-2485; 1 Water St; mains $8-11; ☉ 11am-4:30pm) This popular place serves authentic English tea, Scottish shortbread and light lunches in a cheery setting.

Seafood Sam's (☎ 508-888-4629; Coast Guard Rd; mains $6-16; ☉ 11am-8:30pm) A good family choice for fish and chips, clams and lobster. Dine at picnic tables overlooking Cape Cod Canal and watch the fishing boats sail by.

Falmouth & Woods Hole

A traditional New England village green, lovely beaches and the quaint seaside village of Woods Hole are the hallmarks of the Cape's second-largest town.

SIGHTS & ACTIVITIES

Falmouth has 70 miles of coastline, none finer than **Old Silver Beach** (off MA 28A, North Falmouth; Ⓟ), a long, sandy stretch with calm waters that attracts both families and a younger crowd. Parking at the beach is $20.

The Cape's most scenic bike path, the 3.5-mile **Shining Sea Bikeway**, runs along the shoreline from Falmouth center to Woods

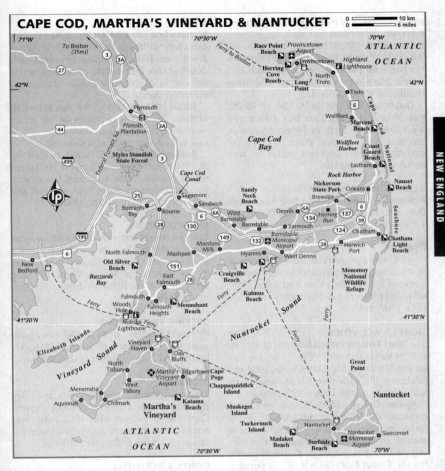

CAPE COD, MARTHA'S VINEYARD & NANTUCKET

Hole, rewarding cyclists with views of Martha's Vineyard en route. **Corner Cycle** (☎ 508-540-4195; 115 Palmer Ave; half/full day $15/20) rents bicycles near the start of the bikeway.

Woods Hole is the departure point for Martha's Vineyard ferries (p250) and home of the **Woods Hole Oceanographic Institution** (WHOI; www.whoi.edu), one of the world's most prestigious marine research facilities. You can get insights into some of WHOI's work at the kid-friendly **WHOI Exhibit Center** (☎ 508-289-2663; 15 School St; adult/child $2/free; ☻ 10am-4:30pm Mon-Sat, noon-4:30pm Sun Jun-early Sep, hrs vary rest of year). Watch the seals frolic at **Woods Hole Science Aquarium** (☎ 508-495-2001; 166 Water St; admission free; ☻ 11am-4pm Tue-Sat mid-Jun–mid-Sep, 11am-4pm Mon-Fri rest of year).

SLEEPING

Palmer House Inn (☎ 508-548-1230, 800-472-2632; www.palmerhouseinn.com; 81 Palmer Ave; r incl breakfast $140-269; ✗) Pamper yourself in one of the posh rooms in this 200-year-old Victorian-style inn in Falmouth center.

Elm Arch Inn (☎ 508-548-0133; www.elmarchinn .com; 26 Elm Arch Way; r $90-135; ☀) In Falmouth center, this rambling colonial-style inn has plenty of green space, a fun sun porch and 20 old-fashioned rooms. Some rooms have a shared bath.

EATING

Fishmonger Café (☎ 508-540-5376; 56 Water St; Woods Hole; mains $9-23; ☻ lunch & dinner) This local favorite has water views in every direction and an eclectic café menu with something for everyone, vegetarians included.

Clam Shack (☎ 508-540-7758; 227 Clinton Ave; mains $5-14; ♥ lunch & dinner) Right on Falmouth Harbor, with picnic tables on the deck, this simple place serves fried clams and other traditional Cape seafood.

Chapoquoit Grill (☎ 508-540-7794; 410 MA 28A; mains $7-19; ♥ dinner) It may lack a view and it's a few miles north of Falmouth center, but this is the hottest place in town for everything from gourmet pizzas to top-notch seafood specials.

GETTING THERE & AWAY
Bonanza Bus Lines (☎ 888-751-8800) runs from Boston to Falmouth and Woods Hole ($17, 1½ hours).

Hyannis
Cape Cod's commercial hub, Hyannis is best known to many visitors as the summer home of the Kennedy clan and a jumping-off point for ferries to Nantucket and Martha's Vineyard.

SIGHTS & ACTIVITIES
The **John F Kennedy Hyannis Museum** (☎ 508-790-3077; 397 Main St; adult/child $5/2.50; ♥ 9am-5pm Mon-Sat, noon-5pm Sun late May–mid-Oct, hrs vary rest of year) celebrates JFK's life through photos, videos and exhibits on the USA's 35th president.

Hy-Line Cruises (☎ 508-790-0696; www.hy-line cruises.com; Ocean St Dock; adult/child 5-12 $12/6; ♥ late Apr-late Oct) offers an hour-long harbor cruise aboard an old-fashioned steamer that circles past the compound of Kennedy family homes. **Kalmus Beach** (Ocean St; P) is popular for sunning and windsurfing, while **Craigville Beach** (Craigville Beach Rd; P) is the place to see and be seen for the college set. Both beaches charge from $12 to $15 for parking.

SLEEPING
Captain Gosnold Village (☎ 508-775-9111; www.cap taingosnold.com; 230 Gosnold St; r/cottage from $100/240; ♨) A little community unto itself and just a sandal-shuffle from the beach, choose from motel rooms or cute Cape Cod–style cottages; there's a playground for the kids. The cottages sleep four.

Sea Breeze Inn (☎ 508-771-7213; www.seabreezeinn .com; 270 Ocean Ave; r incl breakfast $80-140) Clean and comfy rooms, some with sea views, all within a stone's throw of the water.

EATING
Brazilian Grill (☎ 508-771-0109; 680 Main St; lunch/dinner buffet $7/10, with barbecue $13/18; ♥ lunch & dinner) Join Hyannis' many Brazilian residents at this buffet-style restaurant where the star is *churrasco à rodízio* (barbecued meats on skewers).

Misaki (☎ 508-771-3771; 379 W Main St; lunch $7-12, dinner $12-20; ♥ lunch & dinner Tue-Sun) Enjoy your fresh New England seafood served up raw as first-rate sushi and sashimi.

RooBar (☎ 508-778-6515; 586 Main St; mains $10-28; ♥ 4pm-1am) Hyannis' hippest restaurant serves creative New American fusion dinners, including plenty of fresh seafood, and has a happening bar scene after dark.

ENTERTAINMENT
Cape Cod Melody Tent (☎ 800-347-0808; www.melo dytent.org; 21 W Main St; tickets $26-70) A revolving stage in a giant tent headlines performances by the likes of the Moody Blues, BB King and Hootie & the Blowfish during the summer months.

GETTING THERE & AWAY
Plymouth & Brockton (☎ 508-778-9767; www.p-b.com) runs frequent buses to Boston ($16, 1¾ hours) and Provincetown ($10, 1¾ hours).

Brewster
This quiet, low-key town on the Cape's bay side makes a good base for outdoorsy types. Cape Cod's longest bike trail cuts clear across it and there are excellent options for camping, hiking and water activities.

SIGHTS & ACTIVITIES
The 2000-acre oasis of **Nickerson State Park** (☎ 508-896-3491; 3488 MA 6A) has ponds with sandy beaches, boating, biking and walking trails. The **Cape Cod Rail Trail**, a 26-mile paved bike path, passes through the park. The trail begins in Dennis on MA 134, just south of MA 6, and continues to South Wellfleet, passing cranberry bogs and other quintessential Cape Cod scenery along the way. Bikes can be rented from **Rail Trail Bike** (☎ 508-896-8200; 302 Underpass Rd; per 3/24hr $15/22; ♥ year-round), near the park entrance.

The **Cape Cod Museum of Natural History** (☎ 508-896-3867; www.ccmnh.org; 869 MA 6A; adult/child $7/3.50; ♥ 10am-4pm daily Jun-Sep, 10am-4pm Wed-Sun Oct-May) offers fascinating exhibits on the Cape's flora and fauna and a wonderful

NEW ENGLAND

boardwalk trail across the adjacent marsh to a remote beach.

The 19th-century **Stony Brook Grist Mill** (☎ 508-896-6745; 830 Stony Brook Rd; admission free; ⏰ 10am-2pm Sat & Sun Jun-Aug) has a working water wheel. In the spring, thousands of herring migrate upstream at the adjacent **Herring Run**.

SLEEPING & EATING

Isaiah Clark House (☎ 508-896-2223, 800-822-4001; www.isaiahclark.com; 1187 MA 6A; r incl breakfast $115-150; 🖳) Dating back to 1780, this B&B has friendly innkeepers and cozy guest rooms with canopied beds. Some have fireplaces.

Nickerson State Park (☎ 877-422-6762; www .reserveamerica.com; campsites $15) Here you'll find Cape Cod's best camping with 418 campsites in woodlands; it often fills, so reserve your spot early.

Brewster Fish House (☎ 508-896-7867; 2208 MA 6A; lunch $8-14, dinner $17-30; ⏰ lunch & dinner) This chef-driven place packs a crowd with its creative renditions of fresh local seafood.

Chatham

The Cape's most genteel town boasts old sea captain's houses, art galleries, tony lodgings and a splendid shoreline.

SIGHTS & ACTIVITIES

At the east end of town just below the historic coast guard lighthouse on Shore Rd is **Chatham Light Beach**, a lovely strand that invites strolling. The **Monomoy National Wildlife Refuge** has two adjacent islands that abound with shorebirds. **Beachcomber Boats** (☎ 508-945-5265; Crowell Rd; adult/child $20/14) takes passengers to Monomoy for birding and seal-watching excursions.

Monomoy Theatre (☎ 508-945-1589; 776 Main St, MA 28) hosts summer productions by the Ohio University Players. Friday-night summertime band concerts in **Kate Gould Park** (Main St; admission free) are a throwback to an earlier era.

SLEEPING & EATING

Chatham Highlander (☎ 508-945-9038; www.capecod travel.com/highlander; 946 MA 28; r $110-170; 🖳) Within walking distance to the town center, this cheery 27-room motel welcomes families.

Chatham Bars Inn (☎ 508-945-0096, 800-527-4884; www.chathambarsinn.com; Shore Rd; r from $320; 🖳) Bask in old Yankee style at this classic beachside resort. Pampering amenities, sumptuous breakfast buffet and excellent fine dining.

Impudent Oyster (☎ 508-945-3545; 15 Chatham Bars Ave; mains $8-28; ⏰ lunch & dinner) An eclectic menu, which runs the gamut from its namesake fresh-shucked oysters to Japanese-influenced fare, makes this a sure winner – don't miss the drunken oysters in sake.

Chatham Squire (☎ 508-945-0945; 487 Main St; mains $7-20; ⏰ lunch & dinner) A favorite with locals, this tavern has a varied menu that rambles from simple seafood to juicy steaks.

Cape Cod National Seashore

Extending some 40 miles, the **Cape Cod National Seashore** (www.nps.gov/caco) encompasses most of the shoreline from Eastham to Provincetown. It's a treasure trove of unspoiled beaches, dunes, salt marshes and forests. Thanks to President John F Kennedy, this vast area was set aside for preservation in the 1960s, just before a building boom hit the rest of his native Cape Cod. The National Seashore's **Salt Pond Visitors Center** (☎ 508-255-3421; Nauset Rd, at MA 6, Eastham; admission free; ⏰ 9am-4:30pm) has exhibits and films on the area's ecology and can provide maps on nearby nature trails. One of the Cape's best beaches, **Coast Guard Beach** is just down the road. Parking at the beach is $15.

Wellfleet

This town lures visitors with its art galleries, lovely beaches and famous Wellfleet oysters.

Birders flock to Massachusetts Audubon Society's **Wellfleet Bay Wildlife Sanctuary** (☎ 508-349-2615; www.wellfleetbay.org; West Rd, off MA 6; adult/child $5/3; ⏰ 8:30am-5pm late May–mid-Oct, Tue-Sun rest of year), where trails cross 1000 acres of tidal creeks, salt marshes and sandy beach.

Marconi Beach has a monument to Guglielmo Marconi, who sent the first wireless transmission across the Atlantic from this site, and a grand beach backed by high dunes. Parking here costs $15.

About two dozen Wellfleet **art galleries** host receptions on summer Saturday evenings. For an evening of nostalgia, park at **Wellfleet Drive-In** (☎ 508-349-7176; MA 6; adult/child $7/4; ⏰ June–mid-Oct), one of a dwindling number of drive-in cinemas left in the USA. **Wellfleet Flea Market** (☎ 508-349-2520; MA 6; per car

NEW ENGLAND

$2; 7am-4pm Wed, Thu, Sat & Sun in summer, Sat & Sun only in spring & fall), held at the Wellfleet Drive-In, hosts hundreds of dealers and makes an interesting diversion for bargain hunters. The community-based **Wellfleet Harbor Actors Theater** (508-349-6835; www.what.org; 1 Kendrick Ave; tickets from $23) produces thought-provoking contemporary plays.

SLEEPING
Inn at Duck Creeke (508-349-9333; www.innat duckcreeke.com; 70 Main St; r incl breakfast $85-125) This friendly in-town inn has a variety of comfortable rooms, the cheaper ones with shared bath.

Even'Tide Motel (508-349-3410, 800-368-0007; www.eventidemotel.com; 650 US 6; r $65-155, cottages per week $1100;) An indoor heated pool adds to the appeal of this small motel, which also has nine cottages that accommodate up to six people each.

EATING & DRINKING
Moby Dick's (508-349-9795; MA 6; mains $7-20; lunch & dinner) At this self-service place opposite Gull Pond Rd, you can feast on some of the best clams, fried fish and chowder at this end of the Cape.

Aesop's Tables (508-349-6450; 316 Main St; mains $16-33; dinner) The ground floor of this 200-year-old sea captain's home serves upscale New American cuisine, deliciously prepared and artfully presented.

Beachcomber (508-349-6055; Cahoon Hollow Beach, Ocean View Dr) This former lifesaving station right on the beach is *the* place to have a drink or rock the night away.

Truro
Squeezed between Cape Cod Bay on the west and the open Atlantic on the east, narrow Truro abounds with water views and beaches. In North Truro, **Highland Lighthouse** (Cape Cod Light; 508-487-1121; Lighthouse Rd; tours $3; 10am-5:45 May-Oct) sits at the Cape's highest elevation (120ft), dates back to 1797 and casts the brightest light on the New England coastline. The adjacent **Highland House Museum** (508-487-3397; Lighthouse Rd; adult/child $3/free; 10am-4:30pm Jun-Sep) is a charming little place dedicated to the area's farming and fishing past.

Budget digs don't get much more atmospheric than at **HI Truro** (508-349-3889; www .capecodhostels.org; N Pamet Rd, North Truro; dm $22-24;

late Jun-early Sep), a former coast guard station dramatically sited amid beach dunes and marshes. Book early to avoid disappointment.

Local artwork adorns the rustic walls of **Terra Luna** (508-487-1019; 104 MA 6, North Truro; mains $17-21; dinner), a lively bistro that skillfully fuses contemporary American and Mediterranean cuisine.

Provincetown
Contrary to popular belief it was at Provincetown, not Plymouth, where the *Mayflower* first landed in 1620. Escaping religious persecution in England, the Pilgrims were just the first wave of folks to seek refuge on these remote shores. Those that followed were, however, much less puritanical. Fringe writers and artists began making a summer haven in Provincetown a century ago, and in later years the gay and lesbian community turned Provincetown (commonly called P'town) into the hottest gay vacation destination in the Northeast. Commercial St, the main waterfront drag, has a nonstop carnival atmosphere. While the action throbs from the center of town, Provincetown also has quiet dunes where you can walk without another soul in sight and an untamed coastline with glorious beaches.

INFORMATION
Outer Cape Health Services (508-487-9395; 49 Harry Kemp Way)

Post office (508-487-3580; 211 Commercial St)

Provincetown Bookshop (508-487-0964; 246 Commercial St) Excellent little bookshop.

Provincetown Chamber of Commerce (508-487-3424; www.ptownchamber.com; 307 Commercial St; 9am-5pm Jun-Sep, 10am-4pm Mon-Sat Oct-May) At MacMillan Wharf; get tourist information here.

Provincetown Public Library (508-487-7094; 330 Commercial St; 10am-5pm Mon & Fri, noon-8pm Tue & Thu, 10am-8pm Wed, 10am-2pm Sat, 1-5pm Sun) Has free Internet access.

Seamen's Bank (508-487-0035; 221 Commercial St) Has a 24-hour ATM.

Tim's Used Books (508-487-0005; 242 Commercial St) Plenty of good reads at bargain prices.

WOMR (92.1 FM) Alternative community radio at its finest.

SIGHTS & ACTIVITIES
Climb to the top of the world's tallest granite structure, the impressive 253ft-high **Pilgrim Monument** (508-487-1310; High Pole Rd; adult/child

$7/3.50; 9am-7pm Jul & Aug, 9am-5pm Apr-Jun & Sep-Nov), for a sweeping view of town and the surrounding coast. The monument commemorates the landing of the *Mayflower* Pilgrims and displays tell the story of their short stay here.

Founded in 1914 to celebrate the town's thriving art community, **Provincetown Art Association & Museum** (☎ 508-487-1750; www.paam .org; 460 Commercial St; adult/child $2/free; noon-5pm Jun-Sep, 8-10pm Jul & Aug, hrs vary rest of year) displays the works of artists who have found inspiration here over the past century.

On the untamed tip of the Cape, **Race Point Beach** is a beauty with crashing surf and undulating dunes extending as far as the eye can see. The west-facing **Herring Cove Beach** is calmer and an ideal spot for catching the sunset; nude bathers (though illegal) head to the left, families to the right.

An exhilarating way to explore Provincetown's amazing dunes and beaches is along the National Seashore's 8 miles of paved bike trail. Several shops rent bikes, including **Ptown Bikes** (☎ 508-487-8735; 42 Bradford St; per day cruiser/mountain bike $12/19). Or explore the easy way with **Art's Dune Tours** (☎ 508-487-1950; Standish St; adult/child $12/13), which runs hourlong 4WD tours through the dunes.

The **Province Lands Visitors Center** (☎ 508-487-1256; Race Point Rd; admission free; 9am-5pm May-Oct) has displays on dune ecology and an observation deck with a 360-degree view of the outermost reaches of Cape Cod.

SLEEPING

Provincetown may be a tightly packed place, but it keeps everything on a personal scale. The town offers nearly 100 small guesthouses and inns without a single chain hotel to mar the view.

Brass Key Guesthouse (☎ 508-487-9005, 800-842-9858; www.brasskey.com; 67 Bradford St; r incl breakfast $250-465;) Pamper yourself at Provincetown's most luxurious digs. Rooms are furnished with New England antiques, king beds and whirlpool tubs.

Race Point Lighthouse (☎ 508-487-9930; www .racepointlighthouse.net; Race Point; r $150-185;) If unspoiled sand dunes and a 19th-century lighthouse sound like good company, stay in one of the three upstairs bedrooms in the old lightkeeper's house. Cool place, solar powered and literally on the outer tip of the Cape.

Anchor Inn Beach House (☎ 508-487-0432, 800-858-2657; www.anchorinnbeachhouse.com; 175 Commercial St; r incl breakfast $175-385;) This painstakingly renovated waterfront Victorian house is now a classy boutique hotel overlooking the harbor.

Fairbanks Inn (☎ 508-487-0386; www.fairbanksinn .com; 90 Bradford St; r incl breakfast $129-270) If four-poster beds and a cozy fireplace sound appealing then you're in for a treat at this cordial B&B occupying a restored 1776 sea captain's home.

Land's End Inn (☎ 508-487-0706, 800-276-7088; www.landsendinn.com; 22 Commercial St; r incl breakfast from $245;) Stained glass, wood carvings and great ocean views are in store at this charming century-old guesthouse.

Carpe Diem (☎ 508-487-4242, 800-487-0132; www .carpediemguesthouse.com; 12 Johnson St; r incl breakfast from $160;) Warm hospitality and comfortable rooms await at this convivial guesthouse that's a favorite with European travelers. French and German are spoken.

Surfside Hotel & Suites (☎ 508-487-1726, 800-421-1726; www.surfsideinn.cc; 543 Commercial St; r incl breakfast $149-279;) Head here if you're looking for a family-friendly place that sports

---

WATER WORLD

Stellwagen Bank, a marine sanctuary extending north from Provincetown, is a summer feeding ground for humpback whales, making Provincetown an ideal departure point for whale-watching tours. These awesome creatures have a flair for acrobatically breaching out of the water, and they often come surprisingly close to the boats, offering great photo ops. Other whales also frequent the waters off P'town, including many of the 300 remaining North Atlantic right whales, the world's most endangered whale species. The environmentally-oriented **Dolphin Fleet Whale Watch** (☎ 508-349-1900, 800-826-9300; MacMillan Wharf; 3-4hr trips adult/child $24/20; Apr-Oct, weather permitting) offers several tours a day. Stop by the **Stellwagen Bank National Marine Sanctuary Exhibit** (☎ 508-497-3622; 115 Bradford St; admission free; 10am-7pm Jun-Aug, hrs vary rest of year) for an audiovisual glimpse into the underwater world.

well-appointed rooms and an enviable beachfront location.

Bill White's Motel (☎ 508-487-1042; www.bill whitesmotel.com; 29 Bradford St Extension; r $90) It's not fancy but the 12 rooms are well maintained, the price is right and you're close to the National Seashore.

Dunes' Edge Campground (☎ 508-487-9815; www.dunes-edge.com; 386 MA 6; camp/RV sites $28/30) Camp amid the pines and dunes.

EATING
Whether you're in the mood for simple eats or cuisine-as-high-art, you're in the right place – Provincetown has the best dining scene this side of Boston.

Lobster Pot (☎ 508-487-0842; 321 Commercial St; mains $12-27; ☉ 11:30am-10pm) This bustling fish house overlooking the ocean is the place for lobster in P'town and ladles up a superb lobster bisque. Best way to beat the crowd is to come in midafternoon.

Bubala's by the Bay (☎ 508-487-0773; 183 Commercial St; lunch mains $6-14, dinner mains $10-26; ☉ breakfast, lunch & dinner) Seafood takes center stage with a menu covering everything from oysters on the half shell to lobster ravioli. And this hopping place has a swing band most evenings in summer.

Napi's (☎ 508-487-1145; 7 Freeman St; lunch $6-15, dinner $15-25; ☉ lunch & dinner) OK, it doesn't have a water view but there's nothing else this venerable restaurant lacks – the arty decor is pure fun, as is the eclectic menu that ranges from organic vegetarian fare to Brazilian-style seafood and steaks.

Esther's (☎ 508-487-7555; 186 Commercial St; breakfast & lunch $3-10; dinner mains $16-22; ☉ breakfast, lunch & dinner) The sidewalk tables are the perfect spot to enjoy a lunchtime sandwich or generous breakfast while watching the curious parade of humanity mosey by.

Karoo Café (☎ 508-487-6630; 338 Commercial St; mains $4-11; ☉ lunch & dinner) The South African owner serves up delicious homestyle dishes, including many aromatic curries. Favorites include the ostrich satay and the spicy *peri-peri* chicken.

Tofu a Go-Go (☎ 508-487-6237; 336 Commercial St; mains $5-12; ☉ lunch & dinner) At this fun vegetarian joint, tofu creatively replaces meat in burritos, sandwiches and stir fries.

Portuguese Bakery (☎ 508-487-1803; 299 Commercial St; pastries $1.50-3; ☉ 8am-5pm) This century-old institution is famous for its malasadas – fried

dough served hot and sinfully drenched in sugar.

Spiritus (☎ 508-487-2808; 190 Commercial St; pizza slices $3-5; ☉ noon-2am) The favorite spot for a late-night bite and cruising.

If you happen to be here on Saturday afternoons, be sure to catch the colorful **farmers' market** (MacMillan Wharf; ☉ noon-4pm Sat Jun-Sep), where you can literally buy fish right off the boat and produce from the trucks of local farmers.

DRINKING
Chasers (☎ 508-487-7200; 293 Commercial St) is an upbeat pub that attracts a mixed crowd. **Pied Piper** (☎ 508-487-1527; 193a Commercial St) is popular with gay women and **Atlantic House** (☎ 508-487-3821; 4 Masonic Pl) is a hot spot for gay men. Of course all the clubs serve liquor and many dining spots have a bar; the most popular is at the **Lobster Pot** (☎ 508-487-0842; 321 Commercial St), and one of the classiest is **Esther's** (☎ 508-487-7555; 186 Commercial St). **Ross's Grill** (☎ 508-487-8878; 236 Commercial St) has a great bar overlooking the water, and good chili too.

ENTERTAINMENT
Nightclubs
Provincetown is awash with gay clubs, drag shows and cabaret. And don't be shy if you're straight – everyone's welcome and many shows have first-rate performers.

Crown & Anchor (☎ 508-487-1430; 247 Commercial St) The queen of the scene, this multiwing complex has a nightclub, several bars and a steamy cabaret that takes it to the limit.

Boatslip Beach Club (☎ 508-487-1669; 161 Commercial St) Take a twirl at one of the famous afternoon tea dances.

Vixen (☎ 508-487-6424; 336 Commercial St) A favorite lesbian hangout, with everything from cabaret to a nightclub.

Theater
Provincetown has a rich theater history. Eugene O'Neill began his writing career here and Marlon Brando and Richard Gere performed on Provincetown stages before they hit the big screen.

Provincetown Theater (☎ 508-487-7487; www.ptowntheater.org; 238 Bradford St) This splendid performing arts center hosts Provincetown's two resident theater troupes and always has something of interest.

CHOW-DAH PLEASE

Feasting on New England's homegrown specialties, especially its delicious crustaceans and shellfish, can be an event in itself. Local culinary delights include the following:

- clam chowder – or, as Bostonians say, 'chow-dah,' this New England staple combines chopped clams, potatoes and clam juice in a base of milk and cream
- clambake – a meal of lobster, clams and corn on the cob, usually steamed
- cranberries – tart red berries grown in Massachusetts bogs, usually sweetened and used in juice, sauces and muffins
- frappe – whipped milk and ice cream, pronounced 'frap'; called a 'milkshake' in other regions, but known as a 'cabinet' in Rhode Island
- Indian pudding – baked pudding made of milk, cornmeal, molasses, butter, ginger, cinnamon and raisins
- littlenecks – small hard-shell clams typically eaten raw on the half shell, or as clams casino with the meat dashed with hot sauce, wrapped in bacon and grilled
- lobster dinner – New England summer favorite that centers around a hot boiled lobster, a nutcracker for opening the claws, a crock of melted butter and a bib to keep you dry
- oysters – often served raw on the half shell or, for the less intrepid, broiled or baked; the best and sweetest are Wellfleet oysters from Cape Cod
- quahogs – large, hard-shelled clams, pronounced 'ko-hogs,' that are cut into strips and fried, chopped in chunks for chowder or used to make stuffing
- raw bar – a place to eat fresh-shucked live (raw) oysters and clams
- steamers – soft-shelled clams steamed and served in a bucket; extract the meat, swish it in broth to wash off any sand, then dip it in melted butter and enjoy

---

SHOPPING

The main drag for shopping is Commercial St, where you'll find everything from sex toys and edgy clothing to the usual tourist T-shirts.

But the real prizes here are the art galleries, the finest this side of Boston. High-quality galleries that are definitely worth browsing include **Albert Merola Gallery** (☎ 508-487-4424; 424 Commercial St), **William Scott Gallery** (☎ 508-487-4040; 439 Commercial St) and **Julie Heller Gallery** (☎ 508-487-2169; 2 Gosnold St), which is just off Commercial St.

GETTING THERE & AWAY

Plymouth & Brockton buses (☎ 508-746-0378) operates several buses daily between Boston and Provincetown ($25, 3½ hours). In summer, **Bay State Cruise Company** (☎ 617-748-1428; www.boston-ptown.com) runs a fast ferry (one-way/round-trip $38/59, 1½ hours, three times a day) and a weekend-only slower ferry ($18/29, three hours) between Boston's Commonwealth Pier and MacMillan Wharf.

MARTHA'S VINEYARD

The most substantial island along the New England shoreline, Martha's Vineyard is a world unto itself. Home to 5000 year-round residents, including many artists and musicians, its population swells tenfold in the summer. Unlike many islands, the Vineyard celebrates diversity. Aquinnah on the west coast is home to Wampanoag Indians and Oak Bluffs is a favored summer home for wealthy African Americans. There's a lot to see here. It's big (100 sq miles) so you'll need wheels, but you can readily explore by bike or by bus if you don't have a car.

Information

Check your email for free at the public libraries in Edgartown and Vineyard Haven.
Martha's Vineyard Chamber of Commerce
(☎ 508-693-0085; www.mvy.com; Beach Rd, Vineyard Haven; ☷ 9am-5pm Mon-Fri, also 10am-4pm Sat & noon-4pm Sun late May-early Sep) Has visitor information.
Martha's Vineyard information booth (☷ 8am-8pm late May-early Sep) At the Vineyard Haven ferry dock.
WMVY (92.7 FM) Tune in for music and island happenings.

Getting There & Away

Cape Air (☎ 800-352-0714; www.flycapeair.com) has frequent flights from Boston, Nantucket, Hyannis and Providence to Martha's Vineyard Airport.

Car and passenger ferries operated by the **Steamship Authority** (☎ 508-477-8600; www.steamshipauthority.com; round-trip adult/bike/child/car $12/6/6.50/114) run from Woods Hole to Vineyard Haven (18 per day in summer) and to Oak Bluffs (five per day), a 45-minute voyage. If you're bringing a car book as far in advance as possible.

From Falmouth Harbor, the passenger ferry **Island Queen** (☎ 508-548-4800; www.islandqueen.com; Falmouth Heights Rd; round-trip adult/child/bike $12/6/6) sails to Oak Bluffs at least seven times daily in summer.

From Hyannis, **Hy-Line Cruises** (☎ 508-778-2600; www.hy-linecruises.com; Ocean St Dock; round-trip adult/bike/child slow ferry $30/10/15, fast ferry $52/10/39) operates a slow ferry (1½ hours) once daily to Oak Bluffs and a high-speed ferry (55 minutes) five times daily.

For information on ferries between Martha's Vineyard and Nantucket, see p253.

Getting Around

The **Martha's Vineyard Regional Transit Authority** (☎ 508-693-9440; www.vineyardtransit.com; 1-/3-day pass $6/15) operates a network of buses that travel frequently between all towns. It's a practical way to get around and you can even reach out-of-the-way destinations like the Gay Head Cliffs by bus.

Most convenient of the big car-rental companies is **Budget** (☎ 508-693-1911) with locations near the Oak Bluffs and Vineyard Haven ferry terminals and at the airport. **Adventure Rentals** (☎ 508-693-1959; 7 Beach Rd, Vineyard Haven) rents mopeds, 4WDs and regular cars. And there are a couple of companies that rent only mopeds, including **Ride-On Mopeds** (☎ 508-693-2076; Lake Ave) in Oak Bluffs. Car-rental rates

vary with demand – expect to pay around $100 daily in midsummer; mopeds cost around $50. Beware that Vineyarders disdain mopeds – and accidents are common.

Vineyard Haven

This appealing town where most of the ferries arrive sports a lovely harbor full of classic wooden sailboats and bustling streets lined with interesting restaurants and shops.

A vineyard on the Vineyard? But of course: about 3.5 miles southwest of town, **Chicama Vineyards** (☎ 508-693-0309; Stoney Hill Rd, West Tisbury; 🕙 11am-5pm Mon-Sat, 1-5pm Sun) offers free tasting tours at noon, 2pm and 4pm.

Contact **Wind's Up** (☎ 508-693-4252; 199 Beach Rd; 🕙 10am-5:30pm) to rent boats and boards. Rates per four hours are: windsurfing gear $50, sailboats $75, canoes $55, and kayaks $45.

SLEEPING

Thorncroft Inn (☎ 508-693-3333, 800-332-1236; www.thorncroft.com; 460 Main St; r incl breakfast $250-550) Afternoon tea, hot tubs and canopied beds are just some of the indulgences at the island's most romantic getaway, in a quiet setting about a mile from town.

Crocker House Inn (☎ 508-693-1151, 800-772-0206; www.crockerhouseinn.com; 12 Crocker Ave; r incl breakfast $185-415) A block from the harbor, this renovated inn has eight cheery, well-appointed rooms.

Kinsman Guest House (☎ 508-693-2311; 278 Main St; r $125) This 1880 Victorian-style house, a 10-minute walk from the center of town, has three homey rooms, two of which share a bath.

Martha's Vineyard Family Campground (☎ 508-693-3772; www.campmvfc.com; 569 Edgartown Rd; campsites $40, cabins $105-125) A mile from the ferry terminal, this place offers the island's only camping and also has basic cabins.

EATING

Artcliff Diner (☎ 508-693-1224; 39 Beach Rd; mains $4-11; 🕙 7am-2pm Thu-Tue) Gourmet-quality breakfasts served until closing, and lunchtime salads.

Black Dog Tavern (☎ 508-693-9223; 21 Beach St Extension; mains $6-33; 🕙 7am-9pm Mon-Thu, 7am-10pm Fri-Sun) More famous for its T-shirts (Bill Clinton bought one for Monica Lewinsky) than its food, this dockside eatery remains an island favorite and packs in a crowd any time of the day.

DRINKIN' DRY

Alcohol is sold in restaurants and stores only in the towns of Oak Bluffs and Edgartown. If you're dining in Vineyard Haven or in another 'dry' town, most restaurants will allow you to BYOB (bring your own bottle), and they'll uncork your wine and provide wine glasses for a small fee.

Café Moxie (☎ 508-693-1484; 48 Main St; mains $10-32; ☻ lunch Wed-Mon, dinner daily) Arty and up-tempo, this bistro prepares everything from fresh island seafood to steaks with flair.

Oak Bluffs

This ferry-port village is pure fun, a place to wander with an ice cream cone in hand, poke into little shops and hit the night scene.

Oak Bluffs started out in the mid-19th century as a summer retreat by a revival-ist church, whose members enjoyed a day at the beach as much as a gospel service. They first camped out in tents, but soon built some 300 cottages, each adorned with whimsical gingerbread trim. These brightly painted cottages surround the open-air **Trinity Park Tabernacle** (1879), where the lucky descendants of the Methodist Campmeet-ing Association still gather for events. For a glimpse of the community's history visit the **Cottage Museum** (☎ 508-693-0525; 1 Trinity Park; adult/child $1.50/50¢; ☻ 10am-4pm Mon-Sat mid-Jun–Sep).

Take a nostalgic ride on the classic **Flying Horses Carousel** (☎ 508-693-9481; Circuit Ave at Lake Ave; tickets $1.50; ☻ 10am-10pm), which has been captivating kids of all ages since 1876. The USA's oldest merry-go-round, these an-tique horses have manes of real horse hair, and if you stare into their glass eyes you'll see cool little silver animals inside.

SLEEPING

Narragansett House (☎ 508-693-3627; 888-693-3627; www.narragansetthouse.com; 46 Narragansett Ave; r incl breakfast $100-175; ✗) Rocking chairs on the porch set the tone at this friendly gingerbread-trimmed inn with 13 comfy rooms.

Oak Bluffs Inn (☎ 508-693-7171, 800-955-6235; www.oakbluffsinn.com; 64 Circuit Ave; r incl breakfast $215-300) If you enjoy romantic inns with antique furnishings, this cushy inn, just a stone's throw from the beach, is a beauty.

Nashua House (☎ 508-693-0043; www.nashuahouse .com; 30 Kennebec Ave; r $99-149) The rooms are straightforward with shared bath, but this central 1873 house is a fine place to soak up island charm.

EATING

Giordano's (☎ 508-693-0184; 107 Circuit Ave; mains $8-16; ☻ 11:30am-10:45pm) Established in 1930, this family-friendly place is famous for its fried clams and also serves pizzas and pastas.

Sweet Life Café (☎ 508-696-0200; 63 Circuit Ave; mains $26-46; ☻ 5:30-10pm) Romantic candle-light dining at its finest, this chef-owned bistro adds a gentle French accent to su-perbly prepared island seafood and com-plements it with a perfectly matched wine list.

Mad Martha's (☎ 508-693-9151; 12 Circuit Ave; cones $3; ☻ 11am-8pm) Mouthwatering homemade ice cream; for a local treat, go for blueberry.

ENTERTAINMENT

Oak Bluffs has the island's liveliest night scene.

Atlantic Connection (☎ 508-693-7129; 19 Circuit Ave) The most happening spot, it attracts a college-age crowd with everything from reg-gae to hip-hop.

Lampost (☎ 508-696-9352; Circuit Ave) Dancing upstairs and a bar downstairs.

Bar None (☎ 508-696-3000; 57 Circuit Ave) Join the beautiful people at this stylish bar.

Edgartown

Perched on a fine natural harbor, Edgar-town has a rich maritime history and a patrician air. During the peak of the whal-ing era it was home to more than 100 sea captains whose fortunes built the grand old homes that still line the town streets.

The **Martha's Vineyard Preservation Trust** (☎ 508-627-8619) manages several historic buildings clustered together on Main St: the **Dr Daniel Fisher House**, an 1840 mansion that once housed the island's wealthiest resident (no, he didn't make his fortune from his medical practice, but from his whale-oil refinery); the **Old Whaling Church**, a classic Greek Revival building; and one of the island's oldest houses, the 1672 **Vincent House**, built in a traditional Cape style. Call the Trust for tour information.

For more insight into Edgartown's past, visit the **Martha's Vineyard Historical Society** (☎ 508-627-4441; 59 School St; adult/child $7/4; ☻ 10am-5pm Tue-Sat mid-Jun–mid-Oct, call for off-season hrs), which has an excellent collection of whaling paraphernalia, scrimshaw and the like.

Once you've strolled through town, take the short **ferry ride** (☎ 508-627-9427; car & driver $10; ☻ 7am-midnight Jun–mid-Oct, call for off-season hrs) to **Chappaquiddick Island**, where there are good beaches, including lovely **Cape Poge**, a wildlife refuge that runs along the entire east side of the island.

The Massachusetts Audubon Society's **Felix Neck Wildlife Sanctuary** (☎ 508-627-4850; Edgartown-Vineyard Haven Rd; adult/child $4/3; ☷ trails 7am-sunset, visitors center 8am-4pm Mon-Sat, 10am-3pm Sun, closed Mon Sep-May) is a birder's paradise with 4 miles of trails skirting marshes and ponds. A magnificent barrier beach, **Katama Beach** (or 'South Beach'), off Katama Rd, stretches for three miles; rough surf is the norm on the ocean side but there are protected salt ponds on the inland side.

SLEEPING

Edgartown Inn (☎ 508-627-4794; www.edgartowninn .com; 56 N Water St; r $115-250) No phones or TV, and some rooms share baths, but this tidy former sea captain's home is Edgartown's best bargain.

Victorian Inn (☎ 508-627-4784; www.thevic.com; 24 S Water St; r incl breakfast $180-385) Four-poster beds, fresh-cut flowers and private balconies are just part of the appeal at this upscale inn.

EATING

Among the Flowers (☎ 508-627-3233; 17 Mayhew Lane; mains $5-13; ☷ 8am-10pm Jul & Aug, to 4pm rest of year) A friendly little place serving cappuccinos, crêpes, omelettes and sandwiches, as well as dinner in summer.

Newes from America (☎ 508-627-4397; 23 Kelley St; mains $8-12; ☷ 11:30am-11pm) One of the oldest buildings in town, this dark, cozy place dishes up large portions of good pub grub. Wash it down with the 'rack of beer,' five samples of unusual brews.

Navigator Restaurant & Boathouse Bar (☎ 508-627-4320; 2 Main St; lunch $7-14, dinner mains $15-36; ☷ lunch & dinner) Dine on local specialties like lobster roll, broiled codfish and scallop pie at this harborfront restaurant.

Up-Island

The rural western half of the island features rolling hills, small farms and open fields frequented by wild turkeys and deer. The main sights are the picturesque fishing village of **Menemsha** and the coastal **Clay Cliffs of Aquinnah**. Also known as the Gay Head Cliffs, the 150ft-high cliffs, formed 100 million years ago by glaciers, have an amazing array of colors that can be best appreciated in the late-afternoon light. You can hang out at **Aquinnah Beach**, just below the multicolored cliffs, or walk north about a mile along the shore to an area that's popular with nude sunbathers. Park-

ing at beach costs $15. The cliffs themselves, which are a National Landmark, shouldn't be touched; removing clay or bathing in the mud pools is strictly forbidden.

The 300-acre **Cedar Tree Neck Sanctuary** (☎ 508-693-5207; Indian Hill Rd, West Tisbury), off State Rd, has an inviting 2.5-mile hike across native bogs and forest to a coastal bluff with views of Cape Cod. The 586-acre **Long Point Wildlife Refuge** (☎ 508-693-3678; off Edgartown-West Tisbury Rd; adult/child $3/free; ☷ 9am-5pm mid-Jun–mid-Sep, dusk-dawn mid-Sep–mid-Jun; P) offers good birding and a mile-long trail to a lovely remote beach. Parking costs $9.

Reserve early for one of the 74 beds at the **HI Martha's Vineyard** (☎ 508-693-2665; vineyard@usahostels.org; Edgartown-West Tisbury Rd, West Tisbury; dm $24; ☷ late Apr-early Oct; ☐), 9 miles from Vineyard Haven.

NANTUCKET

Once home to New England's largest whaling fleet (*Moby-Dick* makes a good read here), Nantucket's rich history is reflected in the hundreds of 18th- and 19th-century homes that line the town's cobblestone streets, the highest concentration of such period houses in the USA. When whaling went bust in the mid-19th century the town suddenly plunged from riches to rags. The population on this sandy, resource-poor island dwindled, and many of its grand old houses sat idle until the early 20th century, when wealthy Bostonians and New Yorkers discovered that Nantucket made a fine place to summer. High-end tourism has been the mainstay of the economy ever since.

Information

Nantucket Chamber of Commerce (www.nantucket chamber.org) Get useful information online.

Nantucket Visitors Services & Information Bureau (☎ 508-228-0925; 25 Federal St; ☷ 9am-6pm daily Apr-Dec, 9am-5:30pm Mon-Sat Jan-Mar) For brochures, bus schedules and help with last-minute accommodations.

Sights & Activities

The whole town center is a virtual museum of historic homes and churches, so just wander about and soak up the atmosphere. One sight you shouldn't miss is the excellent **Whaling Museum** (☎ 508-228-1894; www.nha.org; 13 Broad St; adult/child $15/8; ☷ 10am-5pm Mon-Sat, to 9pm Thu, noon-5pm Sun mid-Apr–mid-Sep, call for winter hr) in a former spermaceti (whale-oil) candle factory.

At the eastern end of the island sits Nantucket's only other village, **Siasconset** ('Sconset), known for its handsome cottages and rambling rose gardens. And then there are the gorgeous beaches. If you have young'uns head to **Children's Beach**, right in the town of Nantucket, where the water's calm and there's a playground. **Surfside Beach**, 2 miles to the south, is where the college crowd goes for active surf. The best place to catch the sunset is **Madaket Beach**, 5.5 miles west of town.

No destination on the island is more than 8 miles from town and thanks to Nantucket's relatively flat terrain, cycling is an easy way to explore. Rent bikes from **Young's Bike Shop** (☎ 508-228-1151; 6 Broad St; per day $25).

Sleeping

Jared Coffin House (☎ 508-228-2400, 800-248-2405; www.jaredcoffinhouse.com; 29 Broad St; r $275-400; ✗) Canopied beds and antique furnishings set the tone at Nantucket's most esteemed historic inn.

HI Nantucket (☎ 508-228-0433; nantuckethostel@ yahoo.com; 31 Western Ave; dm $20-27) Known locally as Star of the Sea, this cool hostel is in a former lifesaving station 2 miles from town at Surfside Beach. Reservations are essential.

Nesbitt Inn (☎ 508-228-0156; 21 Broad St; r incl breakfast $95-145) Central and delightfully old-fashioned, this Victorian-style guesthouse has 12 rooms with shared bath.

Eating

Black-Eyed Susan's (☎ 508-325-0308; 10 India St; breakfast $6-10, dinner mains $12-28; ☒ 7am-1pm & 6-10pm) This little place serves the island's best breakfast and savory dinners, with lots of gourmet touches.

Boarding House (☎ 508-228-9622; 12 Federal St; lunch mains $12-16, dinner mains $26-38; ☒ lunch Jul & Aug, dinner year-round) Superb fine dining on the likes of littleneck chowder, seared tuna, and pan-roasted sea scallops in a lobster broth.

Atlantic Café (☎ 508-228-0578; 15 S Water St; mains $11-21; ☒ lunch & dinner; ☒) Good food, reasonable prices and a kids' menu make this a good family choice. The star of the menu is the barbecued ribs.

Getting There & Away

Cape Air (☎ 800-352-0714; www.flycapeair.com) flies from Boston, Hyannis, Martha's Vineyard, Provincetown and Providence to Nantucket Memorial Airport.

The **Steamship Authority** (☎ 508-477-8600; www .steamshipauthority.com; adult/child slow ferry $14/7.25, fast ferry $27.50/20.50) runs ferries throughout the day between Hyannis and Nantucket. The fast ferry takes just an hour; the slow ferry 2¼ hours. You could take a car on the slow ferry but the $350 round-trip auto fare is intended to discourage casual visitors from adding to traffic congestion on Nantucket's narrow streets.

Hy-Line Cruises (☎ 508-228-3949; www.hy-linecruises .com; adult/child $16/8) operates thrice-daily boats between Nantucket and Martha's Vineyard from late June to mid-September (2¼ hours). Hy-Line also runs fast and slow passenger ferries between Hyannis and Nantucket at rates and schedules similar to that of the Steamship Authority.

Getting Around

The **NRTA Shuttle** (☎ 508-228-7025; www.shuttlenan tucket.com; 22 Federal St; rides $1-2, day pass $7) operates buses around town and to 'Sconset and the beaches. Pick up a schedule at visitors services.

CENTRAL MASSACHUSETTS

This central swath of Massachusetts, also known as the Pioneer Valley, has a predominantly rural character with rich farmland and small towns that date to colonial times. But it's no sleeper, thanks largely to a score of colleges that infuse a youthful spirit and cosmopolitan air into several Central Massachusetts communities.

Sturbridge

Sturbridge, 65 miles west of Boston, has its claim to fame in **Old Sturbridge Village** (OSV; ☎ 508-347-3362; www.osv.org; US 20; 2-day ticket adult/ child $20/5; ☒ 9:30am-5pm Apr-Oct, 9:30am-4pm Nov & Dec, Sat & Sun only Jan-Apr), a picturesque open-air museum comprising 40 historic buildings brought here from around the region and reconstructed as an 1830s New England town, complete with a functioning blacksmith, sawmill, cooperage and more. Here at one of the USA's oldest living history museums (opened in 1946), the antiques are authentic and the artisans, using old-time tools, know their trades. The town's **tourist office** (☎ 508-347-7594, 800-628-8379; www.sturbridge.org; 380 Main St, US 20; ☒ 9am-5pm) is opposite OSV.

US 20 is lined with chain motels, but a more atmospheric option is the 1771 **Publick**

House Inn (☎ 508-347-3313, 800-782-5425; www.pub lickhouse.com; MA 131; r $79-165; 🏊), on the town common, with inn, motel and B&B rooms and traditional dining.

Springfield

The city of Springfield is the birthplace of the all-American game of basketball and its **Basketball Hall of Fame** (☎ 413-781-6500, 877-446-6752; 1000 W Columbus Ave; adult/child $15/10; ⏲ 9am-6pm daily, to 8pm Sat mid-Jun–Aug, 10am-6pm Sun-Thu, to 8pm Fri & Sat Sep–mid-Jun), south of I-91, celebrates the game with exhibits and memorabilia from all the big hoop stars.

Kids will also enjoy the **Dr Seuss National Memorial Sculpture Garden** (cnr State & Chestnut Sts; admission free; ⏲ 7am-8pm), honoring Springfield's native son and children's book author Theodor Seuss Geisel with life-size bronze sculptures of the Cat in the Hat and other characters from his books. If you're up for museum browsing the adjacent **Springfield Library & Museums** (☎ 413-263-6800; 220 State St; adult/child $7/3; ⏲ noon-4pm Wed-Fri, 11am-4pm Sat & Sun) houses a decent fine-arts collection and has interesting local history exhibits.

Northampton

An old mill town that was spiraling downward 20 years ago, Northampton has metamorphosed into a hip, perky burg known for its liberal politics, feminist sensibility and highly visible lesbian community. Easy to explore on foot, the town center has a plethora of good cafés, funky shops and art galleries.

INFORMATION
Greater Northampton Chamber of Commerce (☎ 413-584-1900; www.northamptonuncommon.com; 99 Pleasant St; ⏲ 9am-5pm Mon-Fri) Has tourist information.
Java Net Café (☎ 413-587-3400; 241 Main St; per 20min $2; ⏲ 7am-10pm Mon-Fri, 8am-11pm Sat, 8am-9pm Sun) Check your email here; it's also a wireless hot spot.

SIGHTS & ACTIVITIES
Smith College Museum of Art (☎ 413-585-2760; Elm St at Bedford Tce; adult/child $5/2; ⏲ 10am-4pm Tue-Sat, noon-4pm Sun), renovated to the tune of $35 million, is one of the finest art museums of any college in the country. Its extensive collection is strong in 19th- and 20th-century European and North American paintings, including works by Winslow Homer, James Whistler, Pablo Picasso and Paul Cézanne.

The **Smith College** (☎ 413-584-2700; www.smith .edu) campus itself, covering 125 acres with greenhouses and gardens, is worth a stroll.

SLEEPING
Hotel Northampton (☎ 413-584-3100; www.hotel northampton.com; 36 King St; r $145-215) This century-old hotel in the town center is a class act with period decor, well-appointed rooms and modern conveniences like wi-fi.

EATING & DRINKING
Northampton Brewery (☎ 413-584-9903; 11 Brewster Ct; sandwiches $7, dinner $12-22; ⏲ 11:30am-1am) Tip a glass of Northampton Pale Ale at this microbrewery's rooftop beer garden. Good sandwiches and snacks all day, and yummy offerings like pecan-crusted salmon and creole crostini after 5pm.

Paul & Elizabeth's (☎ 413-584-4832; 150 Main St; mains $8-15; ⏲ 11:30am-9:15pm) This superb natural foods café specializes in vegetarian dishes and seafood with a Japanese accent, and has a wall of windows overlooking the town.

Eastside Grill (☎ 413-586-3347; 19 Strong Ave; mains $10-22; ⏲ dinner 5-10pm) If a thick juicy steak, Cajun-style blackened fish or vegetarian ravioli sound tempting, join the crowd at this popular dinner restaurant.

Café Casablanca (☎ 413-582-0755; 16 Main St; mains $6-10; ⏲ 8am-10pm) There are other things on the French-inspired menu, but go for the crêpes, which cover the gamut from omelette-wrapped to luscious dessert.

Haymarket Café (☎ 413-586-9969; 185 Main St; mains $5-7.25; ⏲ 11:30am-9:30pm) Northampton's coolest hangout for bohemians and caffeine addicts also serves good tempeh burgers and Indian curries.

Good Thyme Deli (☎ 413-584-6195; 186 Main St; mains $3-6; ⏲ 7am-7pm) Politically correct student haunt with a salad bar, organic meals and Bart's homemade ice cream.

Bakery Normand (☎ 413-584-0717; 192 Main St; bakery goods $2-4; ⏲ 7:30am-5:30pm Tue-Sat) Pick up terrific breads, tortes and chocolates at this German-style bakery.

ENTERTAINMENT
Iron Horse Music Hall (☎ 413-584-0610; 20 Center St; tickets $7-25) Come here for jazz and folk.

Calvin Theatre (☎ 413-584-1444; 19 King St; tickets $20-100) The venue for big-name performances for everything from hot bands to contemporary dance.

Amherst

The college town of Amherst is home to the mega **University of Massachusetts** (☎ 413-545-0111; www.umass.edu) and two small colleges, the liberal **Hampshire College** (☎ 413-549-4600; www.hampshire.edu) and the prestigious **Amherst College** (☎ 413-542-2000; www.amherst.edu). Contact them for campus tours and event information; there's always something happening.

The lifelong home of poet Emily Dickinson (1830–86), the 'belle of Amherst,' is open to the public as the **Emily Dickinson Museum** (☎ 413-542-8161; www.emilydickinsonmuseum.org; 280 Main St; adult/child 6-12 $8/5; tours on the hr, 1-5pm Wed & Sat Mar & Nov, 1-5pm Wed-Sat Apr, May, Sep & Oct, 10am-5pm Wed-Sat, 1-5pm Sun Jun-Aug). Note that the last tour starts at 4pm.

Campus Center Hotel (☎ 413-549-6000; www.aux.umass.edu/hotel; Campus Center, UMass; r incl breakfast $72-109; 🖥) offers 116 comfortable rooms in a modern facility run by students majoring in hospitality.

Motels are strung out along MA 9, including **Amherst Motel** (☎ 413-256-8122; 408 Northampton Rd; r $60-80; 🐾), which has clean, straightforward rooms at affordable rates.

Rao's Coffee Roasting Company (☎ 413-253-9441; 17 Kellogg Ave; 🕙 7am-11pm Mon-Fri, 8am-11pm Sat & Sun), in the town center, has good brews and free wi-fi. At mealtime your best bet is to make the 20-minute drive to Northampton, which has the finest restaurant scene in central Massachusetts.

THE BERKSHIRES

The western slice of Massachusetts offers cool green hillsides, unspoiled towns with historic charm and a treasure trove of summertime cultural events. If you visit during the week you'll find fewer crowds and lower room rates, as Bostonians and New Yorkers flock to the Berkshires on summer weekends for a break from the city heat.

Information

Berkshire Visitors Bureau (☎ 413-443-9186, 800-237-5747; www.berkshires.org; 121 South St, Pittsfield; 🕙 8:30am-5pm Mon-Fri) Has information on the entire region.

Stockbridge

This timeless New England town, sans even a single traffic light, looks like something straight out of a Norman Rockwell drawing. So perhaps it's no surprise that the artist lived here. The **Norman Rockwell Museum** (☎ 413-298-4100; www.nrm.org; MA 183; adult/child $12/free; 🕙 10am-5pm) displays the slice-of-Americana works of Rockwell (1894–1978), the most popular illustrator in US history.

Lenox

Gracious Lenox hosts one of the country's premier music series, the open-air **Tanglewood Music Festival** (☎ 617-266-1492, in summer 413-637-5165; www.bso.org; admission $16-85), featuring the Boston Symphony Orchestra and guest artists like James Taylor and Yo-Yo Ma, from late June to early September.

Shakespeare & Company (☎ 413-637-3353; www.shakespeare.org; 70 Kemble St; admission $10-50) performs the Bard's work throughout the summer. The **Jacob's Pillow Dance Festival** (☎ 413-243-0745; admission $20-55), 10 miles east of Lenox in Becket, stages renowned contemporary dance from late June through August.

The **Mount** (☎ 413-637-1899; 2 Plunkett St at US 7; adult/child $16/free; 🕙 9am-5pm May-Oct), the former home of novelist Edith Wharton, has hour-long guided tours. The **Lenox Chamber of Commerce** (☎ 413-637-3646; www.lenox.org; 5 Walker St) helps with accommodations and other information.

Lenox accommodations consist primarily of charming period inns, including **Walker House** (☎ 413-637-1271, 800-235-3098; www.walkerhouse.com; 64 Walker St; r incl breakfast $90-220; ✕), a friendly central place, and **Birchwood Inn** (☎ 413-637-2600; www.birchwood-inn.com; 7 Hubbard St; r $110-275), which has fine views.

Church St, in the town center, has several good eateries, including **Napa** (☎ 413-637-3204; 30 Church St; dinner mains $13-19; 🕙 lunch & dinner), with California-influenced fare, and **Church Street Café** (☎ 413-637-2745; 65 Church St; lunch $11-15, dinner $20-29; 🕙 lunch & dinner), with an inventive bistro menu.

Hancock Shaker Village

Just west of Pittsfield, near the New York border, is **Hancock Shaker Village** (☎ 413-443-0188; www.hancockshakervillage.org; US 20; adult/child $15/free; 🕙 9:30am-5pm Jun–mid-Oct, call for off-season hrs), a fascinating museum illustrating the lives of the Shakers, the religious sect who founded this village in 1783. The Shakers believed in communal ownership, pacifism, the sanctity of work and celibacy, the latter of which contributed to their demise. The products of their hands – graceful in their simplicity – include wooden furnishings and 20 buildings, the most famous of which is the round stone barn.

Williamstown & North Adams

Williamstown is a cheery college town with a pair of stellar art museums. The **Clark Art Institute** (☎ 413-458-2303; www.clarkart.edu; 225 South St; adult $10 Jun-Oct, free Nov-May, children free; ✆ 10am-5pm, closed Mon Sep-Jun) focuses on 19th-century paintings with works by French impressionists like Renoir, Degas and Monet and by renowned American painters like Winslow Homer and John Singer Sargent.

Williams College Museum of Art (☎ 413-597-2429; www.wcma.org; Main St; admission free; ✆ 10am-5pm Tue-Sat, 1-5pm Sun), between Water and Spring Sts, has an extensive collection of works by leading American artists including Georgia O'Keeffe, Edward Hopper and Grant Wood, and a solid collection of photography by such luminaries as Diane Arbus and Man Ray.

The highly regarded **Williamstown Theatre Festival** (☎ 413-597-3400; MA 2; www.wtfestival.org; tickets $25-52) stages contemporary and classic plays in July and August, often with notable casts.

In nearby North Adams, don't miss **Mass MoCA** (☎ 413-662-2111; www.massmoca.org; 87 Marshall St; adult/child $10/4; ✆ 10am-6pm Jul-Aug, 11am-5pm Wed-Mon Sep-Jun), the eclectic Massachusetts Museum of Contemporary Art, which sprawls across an amazing 222,000 sq ft, making it the largest gallery in the USA. Bring your walking shoes! The MoCA is also a happening venue for music, theater and avant-garde dance performances.

Just south of North Adams, **Mt Greylock State Reservation** (☎ 413-743-1591; Rockwell Rd, Lanesborough) has trails up to Massachusetts' highest peak (3491ft), where there's a panoramic view of several ranges and, on a clear day, five different states.

Near the Williams College campus, **Williamstown B&B** (☎ 413-458-9202; www.williamstown bandb.com; 30 Cold Spring Rd; r incl breakfast $100-230; ✖) is an inviting Victorian house with antique furnishings. **Williams Inn** (☎ 413-458-9371, 800-828-0133; www.williamsinn.com; 1090 Main St; r $135-290; ✖ ▯ ▢) , a century-old establishment on the town green, is Williamstown's fanciest hotel with 125 comfy rooms. There are scenic **campsites** (☎ 877-422-6762; www.reserve america.com; campsites $8) at Mt Greylock.

Getting hungry? Stroll Williamstown's Spring St, which is thick with shops and restaurants, including **Tunnel City Coffee** (☎ 413-458-5010; 100 Spring St; ✆ 6:30am-6pm), a student haunt with potent espressos and luscious desserts, and **Spice Root** (☎ 413-458-5200; 23 Spring St; mains $6-18; ✆ lunch & dinner Tue-Sun), for authentic Indian dishes including vegetarian offerings. For a memorable night out, join the crowd at the stylish **Mezze Bistro & Bar** (☎ 413-458-0123; 16 Water St; mains $22-25; ✆ dinner), which serves delicious fare like seared ahi tuna spiced with wasabi.

RHODE ISLAND

The smallest of the 50 states, Rhode Island often gets overshadowed by its more dominant neighbors. That's a shame, because small really can be beautiful, not to mention less crowded. Its capital city, Providence, has all of the pluses of a fine city but with little of the traffic, and the state's 400 miles of coastline include some of the prettiest nooks and crags around.

But don't think everything about Rhode Island is low-key. You know a place has to be special when the world's richest people flock to its shores, tripping over themselves to see and be seen. The astonishingly opulent mansions that dot Newport's shoreline are proof enough that little Rhode Island has not been overlooked.

History

In 1636 Reverend Roger Williams (1603–83), a religious outcast from Boston, founded Providence on the principle that all people should have freedom of conscience. He was an early advocate of maintaining a separation between religion and government, a concept that later became part of the framework of the US Constitution. It's not surprising that Rhode Island emerged, in 1776, as the first American colony to declare independence from Britain. Rhode Island was also the first US state to abolish slavery (1774). Despite an economic decline during much of the 20th century, Rhode Island has bounced back, re-energizing its cities, undertaking vast public works projects and establishing itself as a player in the fields of higher education, business and tourism.

Information

Rhode Island has a sales tax of 7% plus a 6% lodging tax.

Rhode Island Tourism Division (☎ 401-222-2601, 800-556-2484; www.visitrhodeisland.com; 1 W Exchange Pl, Providence, RI 02903; ⊙ 8:30am-4:30pm Mon-Fri) Distributes information on the whole state.

PROVIDENCE

Bravo! What a fine job Rhode Island's capital has done in revitalizing its downtown. Millions of dollars have been spent restoring its many handsome historic buildings, the once-tired riverfront area is now lined with parks and paths, and the restaurant and entertainment scene just keeps getting better and better. It's little wonder Providence now makes the list as one of the best places to live in the USA. Just don't expect anything on a grand scale – the charm of this city of 173,000 is just how manageable it is.

Orientation

To get to the heart of the city take exit 22 off I-95, which deposits you close to the State House. The Amtrak station, Waterplace Park and the downtown district lie to the south, the university area to the southeast. The colorful Italian enclave of Federal Hill, full of restaurants and bakeries, centers on Atwells Ave, a mile west of the city center.

Information

BOOKSTORES

Brown University Bookstore (☎ 401-863-3168; 244 Thayer St; ⊙ 9am-6pm Mon-Fri, 10am-6pm Sat, 11am-5pm Sun)

INTERNET ACCESS

FedEx Kinko's (☎ 401-273-2830; 236 Meeting St, at Thayer St; per min 20¢; ⊙ 24hr)

MEDIA

Providence Journal (www.projo.com) The state's major daily newspaper.

Providence Phoenix (www.providencephoenix.com) The city's free alternative weekly, with extensive arts and entertainment coverage.

MEDICAL SERVICES

Brooks Pharmacy (☎ 401-272-3048; 1200 N Main St; ⊙ 24hr)

Rhode Island Hospital (☎ 401-444-4000; 593 Eddy St; ⊙ 24hr) South of the city center, off I-95 exit 19.

> **RHODE ISLAND FACTS**
>
> **Nicknames** Ocean State, Little Rhody
> **Population** 1,080,632
> **Area** 1214 sq miles
> **Capital city** Providence (population 173,618)
> **Official state bird** Rhode Island Red, a chicken that revolutionized the poultry industry
> **Birthplace of** Jazz trumpeter Bobby Hackett (1915–76), Broadway composer George M Cohan (1878–1942)
> **Home of** The first US tennis championships
> **Famous for** Being small and for Newport's lavish mansions

POST

Post office (☎ 800-275-8777; 2 Exchange Tce; ⊙ 8am-5pm Mon-Fri)

TOURIST INFORMATION

Providence-Warwick Convention & Visitors Bureau (☎ 401-274-1636, 800-233-1636; www.pwcvb .com; 1 W Exchange St; ⊙ 8:30am-5pm Mon-Fri)

Sights & Activities

You can stroll through Rhode Island's grand **State House** (☎ 401-222-2357; 82 Smith St; admission free; ⊙ 8:30am-4:30pm Mon-Fri), which is topped by one of the largest self-supporting marble domes in the world. It was modeled in part on St Peter's Basilica in Vatican City, which, incidentally, has the largest such dome.

The state's finest art museum, the **Rhode Island School of Design Museum** (RISD; ☎ 401-454-6500; www.risd.edu/museum.cfm; 224 Benefit St; adult/child $8/2; ⊙ 10am-5pm Tue-Sun), showcases everything from ancient Greek and Roman art to 19th- and 20th-century American paintings, furniture and decorative arts; if you happen to come by before 1pm on a Sunday, the museum admission is free. A block east of RISD, in a neighborhood of fine homes, is **Brown University** (☎ 401-863-2378; www.brown.edu; 71 George St), with an eminently strollable campus awash in Ivy League charm.

Giraffes, elephants, polar bears and 150 other species of exotic creatures will delight kids of all ages at the award-winning **Roger Williams Park Zoo** (☎ 401-785-3510; www .rogerwilliamsparkzoo.org; 1000 Elmwood Ave; adult/child $10/6; ⊙ 9am-5pm mid-Apr–Oct, 9am-4pm Nov–mid-Apr). The zoo is surrounded by an expansive public park with botanical gardens, a planetarium, a natural history museum and a Victorian carousel. From downtown, take I-95 south to exit 17, Elmwood Ave.

Dubbed the 'Smithsonian Institution of the Food Service Industry,' the quirky **Culinary Archives & Museum** (☎ 401-598-2805; www.culinary.org; 315 Harborside Blvd; adult/child $7/2; ☺ 10am-5pm Tue-Sun) contains a half-million-item collection devoted to the history of dining. It's at Johnson & Wales University, which runs a stellar culinary program; to get there take I-95 exit 18, turn right on Allens Ave and follow the signs to the campus.

Sleeping

Providence Biltmore (☎ 401-421-0700, 800-294-7709; www.providencebiltmore.com; 11 Dorrance St; r $169-275; Ⓟ) The city's finest, this classic century-old hotel on Kennedy Plaza in the heart of downtown seamlessly combines period charm with modern conveniences.

Old Court B&B (☎ 401-751-2002; www.oldcourt .com; 144 Benefit St; r incl breakfast $125-165; Ⓟ) Hillside near Brown University, this three-story, 1863 Italianate house has old-fashioned guestrooms with antique furnishings and hardwood floors.

Johnson & Wales Inn (☎ 508-336-8700; www .jwinn.com; 213 Taunton Ave, Seekonk, MA; r incl breakfast $91-155; Ⓟ) This attractive inn, 6 miles east of Providence, offers 107 spacious guestrooms managed by the hospitality students of Johnson & Wales University.

NIGHT LIGHT

Move over, Christo. Providence has made its own dent on the public art installation scene with **WaterFire** (☎ 401-272-3111; www .visitri.com/waterfire.html), set on the river that courses through the heart of the city. Nearly 100 braziers run down the center of the river, each supporting a bonfire that blazes after dark. Flames dance off the water, music plays, black-clad gondoliers float by and scores of people stroll along the paths of the Riverwalk. A captivating blend of art (the pyre sculptures are by Barnaby Evans) and entertainment, WaterFire takes place about 20 times a year between May and September, mostly on Saturdays, starting at sunset and continuing until 1am. See the schedule online.

Eating

Providence has a delightful dining scene with authentic Italian restaurants peppering the Federal Hill area, the town's 'Little Italy,' and chic bistros in the city center.

Hemingway's (☎ 401-351-8570; 1 Providence Washington Plaza; mains $15-24; ☺ 11:30am-10pm Mon-Thu, 11:30am-11pm Fri & Sat, noon-9pm Sun) Complete with a view of the river and popular with the theater crowd, this stylish grill serves some of the best seafood in town .

Raphael Bar Risto (☎ 401-421-4646; 1 Union Station; mains $18-30; ☺ dinner Mon-Sat) The city's top Italian restaurant – and that's saying something in a city full of Italians – has great steaks, creative seafood and squid-ink pastas.

Angelo's Civita Farnese (☎ 401-621-8171; 141 Atwells Ave; mains $5-14; ☺ lunch & dinner) This unpretentious family-run restaurant on Federal Hill serves up bountiful portions of homemade Italian pastas, eggplant and meat dishes. Bambinos will love the fun kids' menu and the model train set that runs around the dining-room perimeter.

Andino's Restaurant (☎ 401-421-3715; 171 Atwells Ave; mains $9-20; ☺ lunch & dinner) A good choice for candlelit dining on Federal Hill, Andino's whips up everything from traditional chicken cacciatore to lobster ravioli.

Geoff's (☎ 401-751-9214; 253 Thayer St; sandwiches $4-7; ☺ 10:30am-9pm) This funky sandwich shop near the Brown campus has been attracting students for years with its nonstop menu of innovative sandwiches including veggie and kosher options.

The Arcade (☎ 401-598-1199; 65 Weybosset St; mains $4-10; ☺ 10am-5pm Mon-Fri, 11am-4pm Sat) On the National Register of Historic Places, this vintage 1828 indoor market in the city center houses an array of inexpensive lunchtime eateries on its 1st floor, and some nice clothing boutiques and gift shops on its upper floors.

Drinking

Trinity Brewhouse (☎ 401-453-2337; 186 Fountain St) This downtown pub serves its own British-style brews (the stouts are terrific) and decent pub grub.

Union Station Brewery (☎ 401-274-2739; 36 Exchange Tce) An atmospheric setting in the old train station and handcrafted lagers are in store at this microbrewery.

You'll find several cafés catering to students around Brown University, including

Caffe Pazzo (☎ 401-421-1667; 9 Steeple St), which has strong coffee and good pastries.

Entertainment

Lupo's Heartbreak Hotel (☎ 401-331-5876; www
.lupos.com; 79 Washington St; cover $15-35) Providence's legendary music venue features hot national rock, indie and hip-hop acts.

AS220 (☎ 401-831-9327; www.as220.org; 115 Empire St) An alternative space open to experimental bands, performance artists, offbeat films, art workshops and more – you never know what you might find.

Providence Performing Arts Center (☎ 401-421-2787; www.ppacri.org; 220 Weybosset St; tickets $30-60) Restored to its original glory, this 1928 art-deco theater hosts concerts and Broadway musicals.

Getting There & Away

TF Green Airport (☎ 401-737-8222; www.pvdairport
.com; I-95, exit 13, Warwick), about 20 minutes south of Providence, is a user-friendly place that not only has fewer crowds than Boston but often has cheaper fares. It's served by most major US airlines and car-rental companies.

Bonanza Bus Lines (☎ 401-751-8800) connects Providence and TF Green Airport with Boston ($20, 1¼ hour) numerous times a day and also runs buses to Cape Cod and New York. Several daily **Amtrak** (☎ 800-872-7245) trains link Providence with Boston ($13, one hour) and New York ($60, 3½ hours). If you happen to be traveling on weekdays, **MBTA** (☎ 617-222-3200, 800-392-6100) commuter trains between Providence and Boston ($6, 70 minutes) are the best deal.

The **Rhode Island Public Transit Authority** (RIPTA; ☎ 401-781-9400, 800-244-0444; www.ripta.com; one-way $1.50, day pass $6) runs frequent buses throughout the city from its downtown Kennedy Plaza hub and also links Providence with Newport.

NEWPORT

Established in 1639 by colonists seeking religious freedom, Newport grew into a bustling seaport during the 18th century, and many well-preserved colonial buildings still stand as testimony to that era. In the late 19th century Newport became *the* place for New York's rich and famous to summer. They readily flaunted their wealth, building opulent mansions along the shore and hosting grand social events. The motto

---

THE SKINNY ON LITTLE RHODY

So, just how small is Rhode Island? It's 48 miles from north to south and 37 miles from east to west, and can be driven across in less than an hour. It doesn't makes up for much in height, either, as its peak elevation reaches just 812ft (at Jerimoth Hill in Foster). And, by the way, it's not an island, though the town of Newport sits on one, which is where the original name came from.

---

was 'spare no expense' and the goal was to outdo the neighbors. These mansions – dubbed 'summer cottages' – are so dazzling that people still flock to Newport just to ogle them.

But Newport is more than just a repository of colonial architecture and *Great Gatsby*-like mansions. This scenic seaside town is also renowned for its summertime music festivals, its vibrant yachting center that once laid claim to the America's Cup, and its superb restaurants and inns.

Information

Bank of America (☎ 401-846-7401; 181 Bellevue Ave)
Newport County Convention & Visitors Bureau
(☎ 401-845-9123, 800-976-5122; www.gonewport
.com; 23 America's Cup Ave at Marlborough St) Distributes free maps, keeps track of accommodation vacancies and has an ATM.
Newport Public Library (☎ 401-847-8720; 300 Spring St; ☽ 11am-8pm Mon, 9am-8pm Tue-Thu, 9am-6pm Fri & Sat mid-Jun–Sep, 12:30-9pm Mon, 9:30am-9pm Tue-Thu, 9:30am-6pm Fri & Sat Sep–mid-Jun, 1-5pm Sun Oct-May) Twenty online computers with free access.
Post office (☎ 800-275-8777; 320 Thames St; ☽ 8:30am-5pm Mon-Fri, 9am-1pm Sat)

Sights & Activities
MANSIONS

Several of Newport's grandest mansions are managed by the **Preservation Society of Newport County** (☎ 401-847-1000; www.newportmansions
.org; 5-site combination tickets adult/child $31/10, Breakers adult/child $15/4, Breakers plus 1 other mansion adult/child $22/6; ☽ Breakers 9am-5pm Apr–mid-Oct, other mansions 10am-5pm, call for off-season hr). Tickets can be purchased at any of the properties; give yourself at least an hour to tour each.

If you have time for only one, don't miss the **Breakers** (44 Ochre Point Ave), an extravagant

NEW ENGLAND

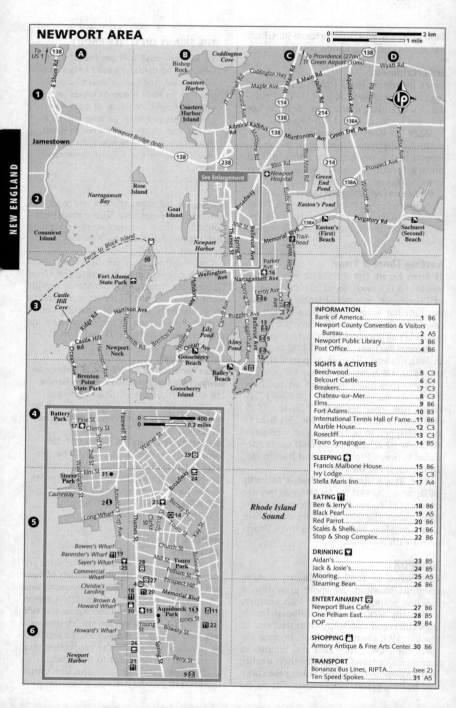

NEWPORT AREA

INFORMATION
Bank of America...........................**1** B6	
Newport County Convention & Visitors	
Bureau..................................**2** A5	
Newport Public Library...............**3** B6	
Post Office.................................**4** B6	

SIGHTS & ACTIVITIES
Beechwood................................**5** C3	
Belcourt Castle..........................**6** C4	
Breakers....................................**7** C3	
Chateau-sur-Mer.......................**8** C3	
Elms..**9** B6	
Fort Adams................................**10** B3	
International Tennis Hall of Fame..**11** B6	
Marble House............................**12** C3	
Rosecliff....................................**13** C3	
Touro Synagogue.......................**14** B5	

SLEEPING 🛏
Francis Malbone House...............**15** B6	
Ivy Lodge..................................**16** C3	
Stella Maris Inn.........................**17** A4	

EATING 🍴
Ben & Jerry's............................**18** B6	
Black Pearl................................**19** A5	
Red Parrot................................**20** B6	
Scales & Shells..........................**21** B6	
Stop & Shop Complex................**22** B6	

DRINKING 🍷
Aidan's......................................**23** B5	
Jack & Josie's............................**24** B5	
Mooring....................................**25** A5	
Steaming Bean...........................**26** B6	

ENTERTAINMENT 🎭
Newport Blues Café....................**27** B6	
One Pelham East........................**28** B5	
POP...**29** B4	

SHOPPING 🛍
Armory Antique & Fine Arts Center..**30** B6	

TRANSPORT
Bonanza Bus Lines, RIPTA............(see 2)	
Ten Speed Spokes......................**31** A5	

70-room, 1895 Italian Renaissance mega-palace built for Cornelius Vanderbilt II, patriarch of America's richest family. Vanderbilt brought over 2000 French and Italian craftsmen who toiled for two years on its construction. **Rosecliff** (548 Bellevue Ave), a 1902 masterpiece of architect Stanford White, resembles the Grand Trianon at Versailles and has Newport's largest ballroom, which was used as a setting for the 1974 movie *The Great Gatsby*. The palace of Versailles also inspired the 1892 **Marble House** (596 Bellevue Ave), filled with Louis XIV–style furnishings. The **Elms** (367 Bellevue), c 1901, is nearly identical to the Château d'Asnières near Paris, while the Victorian **Chateau-sur-Mer** (474 Bellevue Ave), built in 1852, was the first of Newport's palatial summer mansions.

The 1856 **Beechwood** (☎ 401-846-3772; www .astorsbeechwood.com; 580 Bellevue Ave; adult/child $15/10; ☺ 10am-5pm mid-May–Oct, call for off-season hr), former home of the wealthy Astor family, is now a living history museum with costumed actors portraying the family and their staff. **Belcourt Castle** (☎ 401-846-0669; www .belcourtcastle.com; 657 Bellevue Ave; adult/child $10/5; ☺ 10am-5pm, from noon Sun), designed in French Louis XIII–style, has a rich collection of period art, tapestries and suits of armor.

OTHER ATTRACTIONS

You can get good views of the mansion exteriors without spending a penny by strolling the sidewalk along Bellevue Ave as well as by walking the 3.5-mile **Cliff Walk**, a public trail on the ocean's edge. The Cliff Walk starts off Memorial Blvd and ends at Bailey's Beach; you can also start at Ruggles Ave near the Breakers. If you have your own wheels, be sure to loop around Ocean Ave and up Bellevue Ave for splendid estate and ocean views.

The **International Tennis Hall of Fame** (☎ 401-849-3990; www.tennisfame.com; 194 Bellevue Ave; adult/child $8/4; ☺ 9:30am-5pm), the world's largest tennis museum, is housed in a classy former summer club, the site of America's first tennis championships in 1881.

On a quiet street, little **Touro Synagogue** (☎ 401-847-4794; 85 Touro St), built in 1763, stands as the oldest Jewish house of worship in the USA. The interior is undergoing restoration, but you can admire it from the outside.

Fort Adams State Park (☎ 401-841-0707; Harrison Ave; park admission free, fort tours adult/child $8/5;

☺ park dusk-dawn, tours hourly 10am-4pm mid-May–Oct), site of the largest coastal fortification (c 1824) in the USA, has views of Newport Harbor, **sailboat rentals** (☎ 401-846-1983) and expansive lawns for picnicking. Swimming is possible at Fort Adams, but **Easton's Beach** (Memorial Blvd), also known as 'First Beach,' and **Sachuest (Second) Beach** (Purgatory Rd) are better; both have showers, a snack bar and a daily summer parking fee (weekdays $10, weekends $15).

Festivals & Events

Newport's folk and jazz festivals have world-class fame, so it's wise to make arrangements in advance.

Newport Music Festival (☎ 401-849-0700; www .newportmusic.org; admission $25-40) A class act, with 17 days of chamber music concerts held in Newport's most romantic mansions during July.

Newport Folk Festival (☎ 401-847-3700; www .newportfolk.com; Fort Adams State Park; adult $25-58, child $5) Bob Dylan, Joan Baez and other folk icons have all played at this festival, held the first weekend in August.

JVC Jazz Festival/Newport (☎ 401-847-3700; www .festivalproductions.net; Fort Adams State Park; adult $65-100, child $5) Big-name jazz acts on a weekend in mid-August.

Sleeping

The perfect way to soak up Newport's charm is by staying in one of its many atmospheric inns. Cheaper accommodations can be found in chain motels on the outskirts of town, but none can hold a candle to these in-town beauties.

Ivy Lodge (☎ 401-849-6865, 800-834-6865; www .ivylodge.com; 12 Clay St; r incl breakfast $169-279) Treat yourself to the good life in this grand Victorian house, located on a quiet side street just a stone's throw from Newport's sumptuous mansions. All rooms have antique furnishings, six also have fireplaces, and if you need more romance reserve one with a Jacuzzi.

Francis Malbone House (☎ 401-846-0392, 800-846-0392; www.malbone.com; 392 Thames St; r incl breakfast $245-395; ✕) Step out the front door of this grand 1760 inn and you're right in the heart of Newport's bustling dining and entertainment scene. Inside it's pure luxury, with four-poster beds, chandeliers and a breakfast spread that's been recognized by *Gourmet Magazine*.

Stella Maris Inn (☎ 401-849-2862; www.stella marisinn.com; 91 Washington St; r incl breakfast $125-195; ✕) This welcoming and comfortably old-fashioned inn, a former convent in a fine neighborhood, has eight large, high-ceilinged rooms, some with beautiful views of the harbor, others overlooking the inn's stellar gardens.

Eating

Black Pearl (☎ 401-846-5264; Bannister's Wharf; mains $8-24; ☽ 11am-10pm) This friendly old-style tavern, sitting over the water on Bannister's Wharf, is as atmospheric as it gets. Its varied menu ranges from burgers to shrimp scampi and a superb filet mignon.

Scales & Shells (☎ 401-846-3474; 527 Thames St; mains $13-23; ☽ dinner) See for yourself why this informal Italian restaurant gets rave reviews for its mesquite-grilled fish and flavorful mussels marinara. Save room for the gelato!

Red Parrot (☎ 401-847-3140; 348 Thames St; mains $9-25; ☽ 11am-11pm) Come here for seafood in every imaginable manner from raw oysters on the half shell to lobster pizza. Grab a window table, order a frosty Caribbean drink and watch the flow of humanity on busy Thames St.

Ben & Jerry's (☎ 401-846-2663; 359 Thames St; cone $3.75; ☽ 11am-midnight) Have a lick of New England's favorite ice cream.

Self-caterers should head to the **Stop & Shop** (270 Bellevue Ave), where there's a bakery, natural food store and full-service supermarket side by side.

Drinking

Mooring (☎ 401-846-2260; Sayer's Wharf; ☽ 11:30am-9pm Mon-Sat, noon-9pm Sun) Enjoy a sunset drink at this waterfront restaurant and bar with a panoramic harbor view. And if you get hungry, the lobster rolls are Newport's best.

Aidan's (☎ 401-845-9311; 1 Broadway; ☽ 11:30am-1am) Homesick for the latest rugby or football (soccer) matches? Catch them on the big screen at this authentic Irish pub.

Two places with good coffee and free wi-fi are **Steaming Bean** (☎ 401-849-5255; 515 Thames St; ☽ 6:15am-8pm), a cozy hideaway in the midst of the tourist action, and **Jack & Josie's** (☎ 401-851-6900; 111 Broadway; ☽ 10am-10pm, to 11pm Fri & Sat) at the north side of town.

Entertainment

One Pelham East (☎ 401-847-9460; 276 Thames St) This happening place has entertainment most nights, drawing locals and tourists alike with rock, pop and indie bands.

POP (☎ 401-846-8456; 162 Broadway) A stylish bar that attracts a mixed crowd and has entertainment most nights, including a DJ with dancing on weekends.

Newport Blues Café (☎ 401-841-5510; 286 Thames St) Cool New York–style blues scene with quality acts.

Shopping

Stroll along Thames St to find shops selling goodies ranging from touristy T-shirts to chi-chi clothing, fine jewelry and hand-blown glass. If you enjoy picking through antiques and collectibles, stop by **Armory Antique & Fine Arts Center** (☎ 401-848-2398; 365 Thames St; ☽ 10am-4:45pm), where scores of dealers set up shop. You'll also find craft shops worth browsing at Bannister's Wharf and the adjacent Bowen's Wharf.

Getting There & Away

Bonanza Bus Lines (☎ 888-751-8800) has several buses daily to Boston ($19, 1¾ hours). State-run **RIPTA** (☎ 800-244-0444; www.ripta.com) operates frequent buses (one-way $1.50, day pass $6) from the visitor bureau to the mansions, beaches and Providence.

Bicycles can be rented at **Ten Speed Spokes** (☎ 401-847-5609; 18 Elm St; hr/day $5/25) near the visitor bureau.

CONNECTICUT

Zipping along I-95, the interstate freeway that runs along the Connecticut coast, it's easy to imagine that this state is all industry and urban sprawl. But if you look closer you'll discover some delightful unspoiled niches. Seaside Mystic, with its nautical museum and aquarium, and the time-honored towns bordering the Connecticut River are a whole other world, and the Litchfield Hills area, in

SAME-SEX UNIONS

Bucking a national trend against gay rights, in 2005 the Connecticut legislature passed a law allowing homosexual couples to be joined in civil unions, which grants them the same legal benefits and obligations previously reserved for married heterosexual couples, minus the right to call it a marriage. As with Vermont, which created same-sex civil unions in 2000, and Massachusetts, which in 2003 became the only state in the USA to legalize gay marriages, the unions are not recognized by the federal government. Rather, the rights the unions bestow are recognized only within each state's boundaries.

the state's northwestern corner, is as charmingly rural as any place in New England.

History
In 1633, the Dutch built a small settlement at what is now Hartford, but it was the English settlers, arriving in great numbers in the following years, that shaped Connecticut.

Because of the ingenuity and industriousness of the state's citizens, the Connecticut Yankee peddler became a fixture in early American society, traveling by wagon from town to town selling clocks, tin containers and other manufactured goods. Connecticut played a key role in the Industrial Revolution when in 1798 Eli Whitney established a factory at New Haven that made firearms with interchangeable parts – the beginning of modern mass production.

In 1810 America's first insurance company was established in Hartford and by the 1870s the city boasted the highest per capita income in the USA. It also attracted some of America's leading literary characters: Harriet Beecher Stowe (1811–96), who penned the influential anti-slavery book *Uncle Tom's Cabin*, and Mark Twain (1835–1910), who wrote *The Adventures of Tom Sawyer*, were Hartford neighbors for 17 years.

The state gets its name from the Mohegan Indian word *quinnehtukqut*, which means 'place of the long river.'

Information
Connecticut has a 6% sales tax plus a lodging tax of 12%.

There are welcome centers at the Hartford airport and on I-95 and I-84 when entering the state by car.

Connecticut Tourism Division (☎ 800-282-6863; www.ctbound.org; 505 Hudson St, Hartford, CT 06106) Has visitor information.

Hartford Courant (www.courant.com) The state's largest newspaper, has lots of useful information online.

HARTFORD
OK, let's be honest, Connecticut's capital is not likely to grace the cover of any of those trendy travel magazines. This is a workaday city, with a backbone comprised of office buildings. Hartford is the hometown of America's insurance industry, with more than two dozen major insurance companies rooted here. Still, the city has some interesting sights that offer unique slices of Americana. And if you visit on the weekend, when corporate visitors abandon town, you'll find even the fanciest of hotels offering rooms at bargain rates.

Orientation
The gold dome of the Connecticut State Capitol, on its hilltop perch, is visible from interstate highways entering the city. The easiest way to take in Hartford's central attractions – the Capitol, Old State House and Wadsworth Atheneum – is on foot. The houses of literary figures Mark Twain and Harriet Beecher Stowe are a few miles west of the town center along Farmington Ave.

Information
Greater Hartford Welcome Center (☎ 860-244-0253; www.connectthedots.org; 45 Pratt St; ☼ 9am-5pm Mon-Fri) Centrally located and helpful.

Hartford Central Library (☎ 860-695-6300; 500 Main St; ☼ 10am-8pm Mon-Thu, 10am-5pm Sat) Free Internet access.

Hartford Hospital (☎ 860-545-5000; 80 Seymour St; ☼ 24hr) South of downtown.

Post office (☎ 860-249-6560; 185 Ann St; ☼ 8:30am-4:30pm Mon-Fri)

Sights & Activities
One of Hartford's most popular attractions is **Mark Twain House & Museum** (☎ 860-247-0998; www.marktwainhouse.org; 351 Farmington Ave; adult/child $12/8; ☼ 9:30am-5:30pm year-round, closed Tue Nov-Apr), the home of author Samuel Langhorne

NEW ENGLAND

CONNECTICUT FACTS

Nicknames Constitution State, Nutmeg State

Population 3.5 million

Area 5018 sq miles

Capital city Hartford (population 121,578)

Official state song 'Yankee Doodle'

Birthplace of Abolitionist John Brown (1800–59), traitor Benedict Arnold (1741–1801), circus man PT Barnum (1810–91), actress Katharine Hepburn (1909–2003), presidential spoiler Ralph Nader (b 1934)

Home of The first written constitution in the US, the first pay telephone, the first lollipop and the Frisbee

Famous for Starting the US insurance biz and building the first nuclear submarine

---

Clemens – aka Mark Twain. It was here that he penned some of his most famous works, including *A Connecticut Yankee in King Arthur's Court*. The house itself – a Victorian Gothic with fanciful turrets and gables – is as quirky as the author was.

Next door you'll find the **Harriet Beecher Stowe House** (☎ 860-522-9258; www.harrietbeecher stowecenter.org; 77 Forest St; adult/child $8/4; ⏱ 9:30am-4:30pm Tue-Sat, noon-4:30pm Sun), home to the author of *Uncle Tom's Cabin*, which so rallied Americans against slavery that Abraham Lincoln once credited Stowe with starting the US Civil War.

Wadsworth Atheneum (☎ 860-278-2670; www.wadsworthatheneum.org; 600 Main St; adult/child $10/free; ⏱ 11am-5pm Wed-Fri, 10am-5pm Sat & Sun), in a castlelike Gothic Revival building, is the oldest public art museum in the USA. Come here to see the outstanding collections of Hudson River School paintings, African American art and sculptures by renowned Connecticut artist Alexander Calder (1898–1976).

You can tour the **State Capitol** (☎ 860-240-0222; cnr Capitol Ave & Trinity St; ⏱ 8am-5pm Mon-Fri), which was built in 1879 with such a hodge-podge of styles that it's sometimes dubbed 'the most beautiful ugly building in the world.' Below the capitol grounds, the 37-acre **Bushnell Park** features a working 1914 carousel, lovely gardens and summer concerts. The real prize of Connecticut's public buildings is the **Old State House** (☎ 860-522-6766; 800 Main St; admission free; ⏱ 10am-4pm Mon-Sat), designed by famed colonial architect

Charles Bulfinch; it was erected in 1796, making it one of the oldest capitol buildings in the USA.

Sleeping

Goodwin Hotel (☎ 860-246-7500, 800-922-5006; www.goodwinhotel.com; 1 Haynes St, at Asylum Ave; r $139-269; [P] [🖳]) Hartford's most classic digs, this elegant 1881 establishment across from the Civic Center has a historic brick exterior and a cheery updated interior.

Hilton Hartford (☎ 860-728-5151, 800-325-3535; www.hilton.com; 315 Trumbull St; r $89-189; [P] [🖳]) This modern central hotel has all the expected amenities, including wireless Internet in all rooms; rates drop by half on weekends.

Eating

Agave Grill (☎ 860-882-1557; 100 Allyn St; mains $7-19; ⏱ 11:30am-11pm Mon-Sat, 4-11pm Sun) Superb Mexican fare, but don't think just tacos and enchiladas. The chef makes a spicy seafood stew brimming with lobster and clams that perfectly fuses the tastes of New England and Mexico.

Museum Café (☎ 860-728-5989; 600 Main St; mains $9-14; ⏱ lunch Wed-Sun) This arty café inside the Wadsworth Atheneum is a fine place to break for lunch, serving up the likes of fennel-dusted salmon fillet and pan-fried crab cakes.

Peppercorn's Grill (☎ 860-547-1714; 357 Main St; mains $12-20; ⏱ lunch & dinner Mon-Sat) Contemporary Italian-American fare is featured at this local favorite, with plenty of fresh seafood options, creative pastas like lobster ravioli and decadent desserts.

Pavilion at State House Square (cnr Main & State Sts; mains $4-12; ⏱ lunch) This handy food court opposite the Old State House draws a crowd for its variety of ethnic eateries, including vegetarian options.

Getting There & Away

Bradley International Airport (☎ 860-292-2000; www.bradleyairport.com; I-91, exit 40, Windsor Locks), 12 miles north of the city, serves southwestern New England.

At the conveniently located central **Union Station** (☎ 860-247-5329; 1 Union Pl), Hartford is linked by train to New York (one way $41, 2½ hours) and Boston (one way $62, 3½ hours), and by bus to cities throughout New England.

LOWER CONNECTICUT RIVER VALLEY

The Lower Connecticut River Valley has several alluring towns steeped in colonial charm and graced with delightful old inns.

Essex

The genteel riverside town of Essex, established in 1635, makes a good starting point for poking around the valley. The town's streets are lined with handsome Federal-period houses, the legacy of rum and tobacco fortunes made in the 19th century. The **Connecticut River Museum** (☎ 860-767-8269; 67 Main St; adult/child $6/3; 🕙 10am-5pm Tue-Sun) depicts local history with exhibits that include a reproduction of the world's first submarine, built at this site in 1776. Take an old-fashioned journey aboard the **Essex Steam Train and Riverboat** (☎ 860-767-0103; www.essexsteamtrain.com; 1 Railroad Ave; adult/child $16/8, with cruise $24/12; 🕙 11am, 12:30pm & 2pm mid-Jun–Aug, call for spring & fall schedules), a coal-fired steam locomotive hauls the train 12 miles to Deep River, where you can take a riverboat cruise before returning by train.

Griswold Inn (☎ 860-767-1776; www.griswoldinn .com; 36 Main St; r incl breakfast $135-220, lunch/dinner mains from $15/35; 🗶) has been accommodating guests in cozy colonial comfort since 1776; it's also the favorite place to dine on traditional New England cuisine.

Old Lyme

Near the mouth of the Connecticut River, Old Lyme was home to some 60 sea captains in the 19th century, but since the early 1900s it's been best known as a center for American impressionist painters. Many early artists stayed in the mansion of art patron Florence Griswold, decorating its walls with murals in lieu of rent. Her house, now the **Florence Griswold Museum** (☎ 860-434-5542; 96 Lyme St; adult/child $7/4; 🕙 10am-5pm Tue-Sat, 1-5pm Sun), exhibits a good collection of impressionist and Barbizon paintings.

Bee & Thistle Inn (☎ 860-434-1667, 800-622-4946; www.beeandthistleinn.com; 100 Lyme St; r incl breakfast $110-195), a 1756 Dutch Colonial farmhouse, has 11 romantic rooms, some with shared bath.

East Haddam

This little town on the east bank of the river offers two intriguing attractions. You'll think you've ventured into Germany's Rhineland at **Gillette Castle** (☎ 860-526-2336; 67 River Rd; adult/child $5/3; 🕙 10am-4:30pm late May–mid-Oct), a stone-turreted mansion built in 1919 by eccentric actor William Hooker Gillette, who made his fortune playing Sherlock Holmes. The **Goodspeed Opera House** (☎ 860-873-8668; www.goodspeed.org; CT 82; tickets $24-54), an 1876 Victorian music hall known as 'the birthplace of the American musical,' still produces several musicals each year.

CONNECTICUT COAST

Connecticut's coastline is largely industrial, but hidden among all that brawny might are two historical charmers: New Haven, centered around Yale University, and the waterfront village of Mystic. If you want to dig deeper, consider stopping at Groton and New London, adjacent towns best known for their roles in submarine construction, including the world's first nuclear subs; a couple of military museums offer glimpses into their contributions.

Mystic & Around

This attractive seaside village boasts a superb nautical museum and a state-of-the-art aquarium, though it's best known to many as the setting for the movie *Mystic Pizza*, starring Julia Roberts. It's a thoroughly enjoyable place to stroll, sightsee, shop and dine.

INFORMATION

Mystic & Shoreline Visitors Information Center (☎ 860-536-1641; 27 Coogan Blvd; 🕙 9am-4:30pm) Pick up brochures here, next to Olde Mistick Village.
Mystic Chamber of Commerce (☎ 860-572-9578; www.mysticchamber.org; 14 Holmes St; 🕙 9am-5pm Mon-Fri) Has a good website and visitor information.

SIGHTS & ACTIVITIES

America's maritime history comes to life at **Mystic Seaport** (☎ 860-572-0711; www.mysticseaport .com; 75 Greenmanville Ave/CT 27; adult/child $17/9; 🕙 9am-5pm Apr-Oct, 9am-4pm Nov-Mar), where costumed interpreters ply their trades in a sprawling re-created 19th-century seaport village. You can scurry aboard several historic boats, including the *Charles W Morgan* (built in 1841), the last surviving wooden whaling ship in the USA. And if you want to experience a little voyage yourself, the 1908 steamboat **Sabino** (☎ 860-572-5315; adult/child $5.25/4.25) departs hourly every half-hour on jaunts up the Mystic River.

Mystic Aquarium (☎ 860-572-5955; www.mystic aquarium.org; 55 Coogan Blvd; adult/child $16/11; ⏱ 9am-6pm Mar-Dec, 10am-5pm Mon-Fri, 9am-6pm Sat & Sun Jan-Feb) has 6000 species of sea creatures on view, and we're not talking just fish. The residents include penguins, alligators, sea lions and even a beluga whale!

North of Mystic near Ledyard, the extensive **Mashantucket Pequot Museum & Research Center** (☎ 800-411-9671; www.pequotmuseum.org; 110 Pequot Trail, off CT 214, Mashantucket; adult/child $15/10; ⏱ 9am-5pm) pays homage to Native Americans. The Mashantucket Pequot Indian tribe also owns **Foxwoods Resort & Casino** (☎ 800-752-9244; www.foxwoods.com; CT 2, Ledyard), a megacasino that's the largest gambling venue this side of Vegas.

SLEEPING

Inn at Mystic (☎ 860-536-9604, 800-237-2415; www .innatmystic.com; US 1 & CT 27; r $115-295; 🏊) Overlooking Mystic Harbor, this hillside inn has everything from straightforward motel-style rooms to lavish fireside suites in a Georgian mansion. All guests enjoy free afternoon tea and use of the tennis courts, canoes and boats.

Whaler's Inn (☎ 860-536-1506, 800-243-2588; www.whalersinnmystic.com; 20 E Main St; r $125-249; ✗) This centrally located inn has a variety of comfy offerings, ranging from traditionally decorated rooms in an 1865 Victorian house to modern rooms in motel buildings.

Old Mystic Inn (☎ 860-572-9422; www.oldmystic inn.com; 52 Main St, Old Mystic; r $145-185; ✗) Canopy beds and cozy fireplaces set the tone in the guestrooms of this classic 1784 colonial inn near the head of the Mystic River.

EATING & DRINKING

S&P Oyster Co (☎ 860-536-2674; 1 Holmes St; mains $9-22; ⏱ 11:30am-10pm) Dine at patio tables on the waterfront at this seafood eatery, famous for its oysters on the half shell and hearty portions of fish and chips. It's in the town center at the east side of the drawbridge.

Captain Daniel Packer Inne (☎ 860-536-3555; 32 Water Ave; lunch mains $8-16, dinner mains $26-32; ⏱ 11am-4pm & 5-10pm) Occupying a vintage 1754 house, this tavern near the Mystic River has an engaging colonial character and a menu that includes everything from lunchtime burgers to a Jack Daniel's–glazed steak.

Harp & Hound (☎ 860-572-7778; 4 Pearl St) This pub, on the west side of the drawbridge, is the late-night place to grab a pint of ale. It also has big-screen TV with live English football.

SHOPPING

Olde Mistick Village (☎ 860-536-4941; 34 Coogan Blvd; ⏱ 10am-8pm Mon-Sat, noon-5pm Sun) Here are 60 shops in a quaint village setting near the aquarium, with duck ponds and gardens, selling everything from stuffed penguins and silver jewelry to cool kites and fragrant herbs.

New Haven

America's first planned community, New Haven's central city blocks were laid out by Puritan settlers in 1638. However, the city's real claim to fame is prestigious Yale University, whose alma mater includes five US presidents. Head straight to New Haven Green, which is graced by old colonial churches and Yale's hallowed ivy-covered walls. The city's vibrant cultural scene and its best restaurants are all within a few blocks of the Green.

INFORMATION

Atticus Bookstore Café (☎ 203-776-4040; 1082 Chapel St; ⏱ 7am-midnight) Popular bookstore with a café and free wi-fi.

Greater New Haven Convention & Visitors Bureau (☎ 203-777-8550, 800-332-7829; www.newhavencvb .org; 59 Elm St; ⏱ 8:30am-5pm Mon-Fri) One block east of New Haven Green.

SIGHTS & ACTIVITIES

The tallest of **Yale University's** many Gothic spires is **Harkness Tower**, from which a carillon peals at measured moments throughout the day. For free campus tours or to pick up a campus map, drop by Yale's **visitor center** (☎ 203-432-2300; www.yale.edu/visitor; 149 Elm St; ⏱ 9am-4:30pm Mon-Fri, 11am-4pm Sat & Sun, tours 10:30am & 2pm Mon-Fri, 1:30pm Sat & Sun), on the north side of the Green.

America's oldest university art museum, the **Yale University Art Gallery** (☎ 203-432-0600; 1111 Chapel St; admission free; ⏱ 10am-5pm Tue-Sat, 1-6pm Sun), boasts masterworks by Winslow Homer, Edward Hopper, Pablo Picasso and Vincent van Gogh, as well as a fine collection of early American silver.

Would-be paleontologists will be thrilled by the dinosaur fossils at **Peabody Museum** of Natural History (☎ 203-432-5050; 170 Whitney Ave; adult/child $7/5; ☼ 10am-5pm Mon-Sat, noon-5pm Sun). It also has good mineral and meteorite displays.

You may also want to pop into the **Yale Center for British Art** (☎ 203-432-2800; 1080 Chapel St; admission free; ☼ 10am-5pm Tue-Sat, noon-5pm Sun), which holds one of the most comprehensive collections of British art outside the UK.

SLEEPING

Colony (☎ 203-776-1234, 800-458-8810; www.colony atyale.com; 1157 Chapel St; r $119) Adjacent to the Yale campus, this modern hotel has 86 stylish rooms, some of which are wheelchair accessible.

Three Chimneys Inn (☎ 203-777-1201, 800-443-1554; www.threechimneysinn.com; 1201 Chapel St; r incl breakfast $195-215; ✗) Enjoy the good life with a spot of sherry, a warm fireplace and a four-poster bed in this antique-laden Victorian inn.

EATING

Zinc (☎ 203-624-0507; 964 Chapel St; lunch mains $11-13, dinner mains $20-28; ☼ lunch Tue-Sat, dinner daily) Chic bistro dining at its finest with a chef-driven menu rich in organic ingredients and Asian and Southwest influences, with such luscious offerings as jalapeño-grilled lamb and sesame-crusted tuna.

Caffé Adulis (☎ 203-777-5081; 228 College St; mains $8-22; ☼ dinner) This fun restaurant, run by brothers from Eritrea, is a good place to go with a small group so you can share dishes. The exotic North African menu includes chicken, beef, lamb and vegetarian fare.

Claire's Corner Copia (☎ 203-562-3888; 1000 Chapel St; mains $6-10; ☼ 8am-9pm Sun-Thu, 8am-10pm Fri & Sat) This cheery, long-established vegetarian restaurant opposite Yale is the real deal. Claire cooks up her own time-honored recipes using fresh, organic ingredients.

New Haven claims to be home to the first pizza in the USA, tossed up by Italian immigrant Frank Pepe in 1900. Today the legend lives on at **Frank Pepe's** (☎ 203-865-5762; 157 Wooster St; ☼ 4-10pm Mon, Wed & Thu, 11:30am-11pm Fri & Sat, 2:30-10pm Sun) and the equally popular **Sally's Apizza** (☎ 203-624-5271; 237 Wooster St; ☼ 5-10:30pm Tue-Sun), both with mouthwatering pizzas for around $10.

ENTERTAINMENT

Toad's Place (☎ 203-624-8623; www.toadsplace.com; 300 York St; admission $10-30) The hottest music venue for miles around, Toad's often hosts big names in the rock and alternative worlds.

Shubert Theater (☎ 203-562-5666, 888-736-2663; www.capa.com; 247 College St; tickets $18-55; ☼ shows Sep-May) Catch a hit before it happens at this venerable theater that's been hosting Broadway musicals on their trial runs since 1914.

New Haven also has two award-winning repertory theaters: **Yale Repertory Theatre** (☎ 203-432-1234; www.yale.edu/yalerep; 1120 Chapel St; tickets $38-45) and **Long Wharf Theatre** (☎ 203-787-4282, 800-782-8497; www.longwharf.org; 222 Sargent Dr; tickets $30-60).

The free weekly **New Haven Advocate** (www .newhavenadvocate.com) lists current entertainment happenings.

GETTING THERE & AWAY

By train from New York City skip Amtrak and take **Metro North** (☎ 212-532-4900, 800-638-7646; one-way $14-19), which has near-hourly services and the lowest fares. **Peter Pan Bus Lines** (☎ 800-343-9999) and **Greyhound Bus Lines** (☎ 800-221-2222) connect New Haven to scores of cities including New York ($22, two hours), Hartford ($13, one hour) and Boston ($31, four hours).

LITCHFIELD HILLS

The rolling hill country of northwestern Connecticut, laced with lakes, woodlands and vineyards, provides an unspoiled haven for nature-lovers. The centerpiece of the region is the historic town of Litchfield.

Information

Litchfield Hills Visitors Bureau (☎ 860-567-4506; www.litchfieldhills.com; PO Box 968, Litchfield, CT 06759-0968) Can help with accommodations and tour planning.

Litchfield

Founded in 1719, Litchfield prospered from the commerce brought by stagecoaches traveling between Hartford and Albany, and its many buildings are a handsome testimony to the era. Stroll along North and South Sts to see the finest homes, including the 1773 **Tapping Reeve House** (☎ 860-567-4501; www.litchfield history.org; 82 South St; adult/child $5/free; ☼ 11am-5pm Tue-Sat, 1-5pm Sun mid-Apr–Nov). The small adjacent building once housed the USA's first law school (founded in 1775), which trained some 130 members of Congress. Included in the admission fee is the **Litchfield Historical Society Museum** (☎ 860-567-4501; 7 South St).

NEW ENGLAND

Haight Vineyard (☎ 860-567-4045; 29 Chestnut Hill Rd, off CT 118; ☽ 10:30am-5pm Mon-Sat, noon-5pm Sun), the state's first winery, offers free tastings.

If you're ready to take a hike, the 4000-acre **White Memorial Conservation Center** (☎ 860-567-0857; US 202; admission free; ☽ dusk-dawn), 2.5 miles west of town, has 35 miles of inviting trails and excellent bird-watching.

Litchfield Hills B&B (☎ 860-567-2057; www.litch fieldhillsbnb.com; 548 Bantam Rd/US 202; r incl breakfast $95-120; ☐), in one of the town's oldest homes, borders the White Memorial Conservation Center; guests have access to a canoe for a paddle on the nearby river.

Lake Waramaug

Most notable of the dozens of lakes and ponds in the Litchfield Hills is Lake Waramaug, bordered by a state park. As you make your way around the northern shore on North Shore Rd, stop at **Hopkins Vineyard** (☎ 860-868-7954; 25 Hopkins Rd; ☽ 10am-5pm May-Dec) for wine tastings. It's next to the 19th-century **Hopkins Inn** (☎ 860-868-7295; www .thehopkinsinn.com; 22 Hopkins Rd, New Preston; r $95-120; lunch mains $12-17, dinner mains $20-26; ✄), which has lakeview rooms and a good restaurant with European-accented country fare. **Lake Waramaug State Park** (☎ 860-868-0220, 877-688-2267; 30 Lake Waramaug Rd; campsites $13) has lakeside campsites, but book well in advance.

VERMONT

Maple syrup, covered bridges, white-steepled churches, rolling pastures dotted with cows and Green Mountains covered with ski slopes – Vermont is quintessential small-town, big-countryside New England.

But it's much more than just postcard-perfect scenery. The folks that live in these parts pride themselves on their New England ingenuity and self-sufficient character. With just one small city worthy of the title, Vermont is as rural and rugged as the mountains that run up its spine. To truly enjoy the state, take it slowly: hike its forests, paddle its lakes and rivers, and rub shoulders with its hospitable people.

History

Frenchman Samuel de Champlain coined the region's name – *les verts mont* (Green Mountains) – when he explored the area in 1609. The ever-modest explorer also lent his name to Vermont's largest lake.

Vermont played an important role in the Revolutionary War when in 1775 Vermont farmer Ethan Allen led a local militia called the Green Mountain Boys to Fort Ticonderoga, on the New York side of Lake Champlain, and captured the fort from surprised British forces. In the years that followed Allen took a less hostile stance toward the British, and even considered petitioning the crown to make Vermont an independent British state. In 1791, two years after Allen's death, Vermont was admitted to the USA.

The state's independent streak is as long and deep as a vein of Vermont marble. Long a land of farmers, Vermont is still mostly rural, with the lowest population of any New England state. Dairy farming and tourism drive the economy.

In 2000 the Supreme Court of Vermont declared that gay couples have the same rights and privileges as heterosexual ones, making Vermont the first US state to acknowledge same-sex civil unions.

Information

Vermont's state sales tax is 6% and there's an 8% lodging and meals tax.

Vermont Chamber of Commerce (☎ 802-223-3443; www.vtchamber.com; PO Box 37, Montpelier, VT 05601) Will mail out a handy magazine-sized vacation guide upon request.

Vermont Department of Tourism (☎ 802-828-3676, 800-837-6668; www.vermontvacation.com; 6 Baldwin St, Montpelier, VT 05633) Provides information on the state.

Getting There & Away

Vermont Transit (☎ 802-864-6811, 800-642-3133; www.vermonttransit.com; 345 Pine St) serves many Vermont towns, as well as Boston.

Amtrak's (800-872-7245; www.amtrak.com) *Vermonter* route offers rail service from New York City to Burlington, stopping at several towns along the way.

By car, the main interstate, US91, slices speedily from north to south across the entire length of Vermont, but for the finest scenery opt for VT100, which meanders through verdant mountains and charming villages.

SOUTHERN VERMONT

Small towns, green mountains and covered bridges lure travelers to Vermont's southern region.

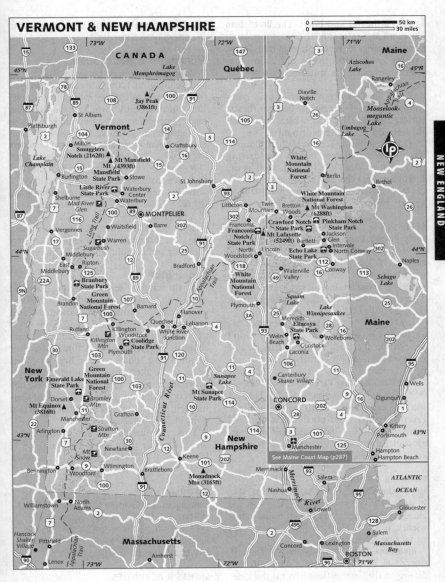

VERMONT & NEW HAMPSHIRE

Brattleboro

The 1960s alternative lifestyle is alive and well in this riverside burg, which dates back to 1724 and lays claim to being Vermont's oldest town. Rudyard Kipling married a Brattleboro woman in 1892 and lived for a time in a big house he named 'Naulaukha,' where he wrote *The Jungle Book*. These days

Brattleboro is known for having more tie-dye per capita than any other place in New England.

SIGHTS & ACTIVITIES

In the town center along Main St you'll find several period buildings, including the handsome art deco Latchis Building, which houses a theater and hotel. The **Brattleboro Museum & Art Center** (☎ 802-257-0124; www.brattle boromuseum.org; 10 Vernon St; adult/child $4/free; 11am-5pm Wed-Mon), in the old Union Station, showcases the multimedia works of regional artists.

You'll find plenty of down-home community spirit at the **Hooker-Dunham Theater** (☎ 802-254-2796; 139 Main St), which hosts local theater and musical performances.

The surrounding area, Windham County, has 30 **covered bridges**. For a free driving guide that will lead you to them, stop by the **Brattleboro Area Chamber of Commerce** (☎ 802-254-4565; www.brattleborochamber.org; 180 Main St; 9am-5pm Mon-Fri, 10am-2pm Sat).

SLEEPING

Forty Putney Road B&B (☎ 802-254-6268, 800-941-2413; www.fortyputneyroad.com; 40 Putney Rd; r incl breakfast $110-180) Within walking distance of the town center, this historic estate home with four comfortable rooms is a real treat. There's also a self-contained cottage ($200) on the grounds.

Latchis Hotel (☎ 802-254-6300; www.latchis.com; 50 Main St; r incl breakfast $75-115) You couldn't be more in the thick of things than at this restored art deco hotel with 30 simply furnished rooms.

Fort Dummer State Park (☎ 888-409-7579; 434 Old Guilford Rd; campsites/lean-tos $14/21) Has 51 wooded campsites and 10 lean-to shelters. From I-91 exit 1, go north a few hundred yards on US 5, a half-mile east on Fairground Rd, then a mile south on Main St and Old Guilford Rd.

EATING & DRINKING

Amy's Bakery Arts Café (☎ 802-251-1071; 113 Main St; snacks $3-9; 8am-6pm Mon-Sat, 10am-5pm Sun) Head here for delicious french bread sandwiches, luscious pastries, free-trade coffees and a fine river view.

Riverview Café (☎ 802-254-9841; 36 Bridge St; mains $9-20; lunch & dinner) Enjoy alfresco dining on the Connecticut River at this celebrated restaurant with a menu emphasizing fresh local ingredients and a bar serving regional microbrews on tap.

Brattleboro Food Co-op (☎ 802-257-0236; 2 Main St; 8am-9pm) Stop at this substantial health food store for picnic supplies.

Mole's Eye Café (☎ 802-257-0771; 4 High St) The town's premier nightspot with live music,

anything from acoustic to reggae, from Wednesday to Saturday.

Wilmington & Mount Snow

Wilmington, midway between Brattleboro and Bennington, is the gateway to **Mount Snow** (☎ 802-464-3333, 800-245-7669; www.mountsnow.com; VT 100), which is best known as a family skiing resort, but golfing and mountain biking also woo visitors in warm-weather seasons. Contact the **Mount Snow Valley Chamber of Commerce** (☎ 802-464-8092, 877-887-6884; www.visitvermont.com; 21 W Main St; 10am-5pm) for detailed information on accommodations and attractions.

In Wilmington the 14-room **Nutmeg Inn** (☎ 802-464-7400, 800-277-5402; www.nutmeginn.com; VT 9; r incl breakfast $99-154, ste $184-215), an 18th-century farmhouse furnished with antiques, offers local hospitality including a full country breakfast and complimentary afternoon tea.

Bennington

This thoroughly enjoyable New England town, with barely 15,000 residents, is the largest in southern Vermont. The downtown area offers a pleasant mix of cafés and shops while the hillside area, known as Old Bennington, abounds in colonial architecture, has a river spanned by a trio of covered bridges and is home to the alternative Bennington College. Towering above it all is a hilltop granite obelisk commemorating the 1777 Battle of Bennington, when Vermont troops defeated two units of British soldiers.

You can't miss Bennington, as the monument is visible from miles away and US 7, VT 7A and VT 9 all converge in the town center.

INFORMATION

Bennington Area Chamber of Commerce (☎ 802-447-3311, 800-229-0252; www.bennington.com; US 7; 9am-5pm Mon-Fri, 10am-4pm Sat, also 10am-4pm Sun mid-May–mid-Oct) The friendly folks here, a mile north of downtown, provide visitor information.

SIGHTS & ACTIVITIES

At the center of Old Bennington is **Old First Church** (☎ 802-447-1223; cnr Monument Ave & Rt 9), a white colonial edifice built in 1806. It is best known for its churchyard that holds the bones of five Vermont governors and poet Robert Frost, who is buried beneath the inscription 'I Had a Lover's Quarrel With the World.'

For an unbeatable 360-degree view of the countryside, visit the **Bennington Battle Monument** (☎ 802-447-0550; Monument Ave; adult/child $2/1; ☷ 9am-5pm Apr-Oct), the loftiest structure in Vermont. An elevator painlessly whisks you 306ft to the top.

The **Bennington Museum** (☎ 802-447-1571; www .benningtonmuseum.com; VT 9; adult/child $8/free; ☷ 9am-5pm Thu-Tue) holds an outstanding collection of early Americana as well as the world's largest collection of works by Anna Mary 'Grandma' Moses (1860–1961), who painted Vermont farm scenes until the age of 100.

You can tour the potters yard at **Bennington Potters** (☎ 802-447-7531; 324 County St; admission free; ☷ 9:30am-6pm Mon-Sat, 10am-5pm Sun), where quality stoneware with a distinctive mottled design has been made for more than a half-century.

SLEEPING

Four Chimneys Inn (☎ 802-447-3500; www.fourchim neys.com; 21 West Rd; r incl breakfast $125-215; ☒) There's an enjoyable sense of exclusivity at this classic 1783 grand mansion in Bennington's ritziest neighborhood.

Paradise Motor Inn (☎ 802-442-8351; www .theparadisemotorinn.com; 141 W Main St; r $75-115; ☒) This 76-room motel between the town center and the battle monument is central to everything.

Greenwood Lodge & Campsites (☎ 802-442-2547; VT 9; dm/campsites/r $23/20/50) Eight miles east of Bennington at Prospect Mountain ski run in Woodford, this little lodge has dorm rooms, private rooms and camping facilities set in a wooded area near swimmable ponds.

EATING

Blue Benn Diner (☎ 802-442-5140; 314 North St; mains $5-11; ☷ 6am-8pm Mon-Fri, 6am-4pm Sat, 7am-4pm Sun) Come here to experience an all-American diner with reliably good fare. The varied menu includes vegetarian dishes and all-day breakfasts.

Izabella's (☎ 802-447-4949; 351 Main St; sandwiches $6-7; ☷ 8:30am-4pm Tue-Fri, 9am-4pm Sat) This smart café in the center of town makes sumptuous panini sandwiches and has outside tables ideal for people-watching.

Peppermills (☎ 802-447-9900; 716 Main St; lunch $5-12, dinner $10-18; ☷ lunch & dinner) One of Bennington's fancier haunts, this popular restaurant serves everything from veggie burgers to pastas and steaks.

> ### VERMONT FACTS
> **Nickname** Green Mountain State
> **Population** 621,394
> **Area** 9609 sq miles
> **Capital city** Montpelier (population 8035)
> **Official state animal** Morgan horse
> **Birthplace of** President Calvin Coolidge (1872–1933), Mormon leader Brigham Young (1801–77), farm-equipment manufacturer John Deere (1804–86)
> **Home of** Former governor and presidential candidate Howard Dean
> **Famous for** Ben & Jerry's ice cream

Manchester

Manchester, in the shadow of Mt Equinox, was a favorite summer retreat of Ulysses S Grant and other 19th-century US presidents. The mountain scenery, the moderate climate and the Batten Kill River – one of Vermont's best trout streams – continue to draw crowds today. Winter skiing, warm-weather golfing and year-round shopping add to the appeal.

The town has two faces, both likeable. Manchester Center, at the north end, shines with cafés and upscale outlet stores. To the south lies dignified Manchester Village, lined with marble-block sidewalks, stately century-old homes and the posh Equinox hotel. The rural VT 7A runs through the heart of it all.

INFORMATION

Manchester and the Mountains Regional Chamber of Commerce (☎ 802-362-2100, 800-362-4144; www.manchestervermont.net; 5046 Main St, Manchester Center; ☷ 10am-5pm Mon-Sat) Provides visitor information.

SIGHTS & ACTIVITIES

Just south of Manchester, **Hildene** (☎ 802-362-1788; www.hildene.org; 1005 Hildene Rd/VT 7A; adult/child 6-14 $10/4; ☷ 9:30am-4pm mid-May–Oct, 11am-3pm Thu-Mon Nov–mid-May), a 24-room Georgian Revival mansion, was the country estate of Robert Todd Lincoln, son of President Abraham Lincoln. You can tour the stately house, with original Lincoln family furnishings, and walk through its formal gardens.

Anglers make pilgrimages to Manchester to visit the **American Museum of Fly Fishing** (☎ 802-362-3300; VT 7A; adult/child $3/1; ☷ 10am-4pm), to shop at the adjacent **Orvis** (☎ 802-361-3750;

VT 7A) flagship store, which is dedicated to outfitting fisher-folk, and to fly-fish for trout in the **Batten Kill River**.

You can drive to the summit of the 3835ft **Mt Equinox**. Take VT 7A south of Manchester to **Skyline Drive** (☎ 802-362-1114; car & driver $8, additional passenger $2), a private 5-mile toll road.

Bromley Mountain (☎ 802-824-5522; www.bromley .com; VT 11, Peru), a small family ski resort, switches gears in the summer to become an adventure park, with Vermont's longest water slide, trampolines and a climbing wall.

The **Appalachian Trail**, which overlaps the **Long Trail** in Vermont, passes just east of Manchester. There are shelters about every 10 miles. For details and trail maps, contact the chamber of commerce or the **USFS Green Mountain National Forest** (☎ 802-362-2307; 2538 Depot St, Manchester Center).

BattenKill Canoe (☎ 802-362-2800; www.batten kill.com; 6328 VT 7A, Arlington; canoes $48-60, kayaks $30-35; ☽ 9am-4:30pm mid-April–Nov), just south of Manchester, rents canoes and kayaks for self-guided paddling down the Batten Kill River. Rent a road, mountain or hybrid bike from **Batten Kill Sports Bicycle Shop** (☎ 802-362-2734; US 7 & VT 11/30; per day from $25).

SLEEPING

Head to Manchester Center for the area's midrange hotels and to Manchester Village for more exclusive inns.

Equinox (☎ 802-362-4700, 800-362-4747; www .equinoxresort.com; 3567 Main St; r $249-479; ☒) Manchester's fanciest hotel dates back to 1769 and boasts 183 rooms, its own 18-hole golf course, indoor and outdoor pools and a luxury spa. Despite its modern upgrades it's lost none of its handsome period character.

1811 House (☎ 802-362-1811, 800-432-1811; www .1811house.com; VT 7A; r incl breakfast $210-280; ☒) In the heart of Manchester opposite the Equi-

nox, this classic Federal-style house has been operating as an inn for nearly 200 years and, not surprisingly, it exudes period charm.

Barnstead Inn (☎ 802-362-1619, 800-331-1619; www.barnsteadinn.com; Bonnet St; r $99-229; ☒) In Manchester Center, just a short walk from village restaurants, this renovated 1830s hay barn has 14 country-style rooms with wide-beamed ceilings.

Aspen Motel (☎ 802-362-2450; www.manchester vermontmotel.com; 5669 Main St/VT 7A; r $75-115; ☒ ☒) A good affordable choice, this hotel has 25 comfortable rooms, friendly managers and a convenient location within walking distance of Manchester Center.

EATING

Spiral Press Café (☎ 802-362-9944; cnr VT 11 & 7A; sandwiches $4-8; ☽ 8am-7pm Mon, 8am-9pm Tue-Sat, 9am-7pm Sun) Stop at this Manchester Center café attached to Northshire Bookstore for rich coffee, flaky croissants and delicious panini sandwiches. Patrons can check their email for free.

Reluctant Panther (☎ 802-362-2568; 39 West Rd; prix-fixe dinner $45; ☽ dinner; ☒) This inn, next to the Equinox, makes a perfect choice for a romantic dinner, and its Swiss chef offers both American regional dishes, such as roasted trout, and traditional Swiss specialties.

Up for Breakfast (☎ 802-362-4204; 4935 Main St; mains $5-10; ☽ 7am-noon) Locals flock to this 2nd-floor restaurant in the heart of Manchester Center for hearty breakfasts, anything from blueberry pancakes to smoked-salmon-and-caper omelettes.

Bistro Henry (☎ 802-362-4982; cnr VT 11 & 30; mains $20-35; ☽ dinner Tue-Sun) Run by husband-and-wife chef-owners, this upscale bistro with a Mediterranean accent gets rave reviews for its creative dishes that range from venison medallions to lobster risotto.

SWEET TREAT

Maple sugaring has been a spring tradition in Vermont ever since Native Americans taught colonial settlers how to boil down the sweet sap from maple trees. The process has changed little over the centuries. The trees are tapped with little metal pipes in late March and early April when the cycle of nighttime freezing and daytime thawing causes the sap to rise. Buckets are placed under the taps to catch the sap. The sap is then gathered and poured into a vat where it's boiled down to that thick, delicious amber-colored syrup that we pour on our pancakes. It takes 40 gallons of sap – the total gathered from about five trees in one season – to make just a single gallon of maple syrup. The Vermont tourist office can provide a list of maple sugarhouses open to the public, including Sugarbush Farm (opposite), which lets you tour its facilities year-round.

CENTRAL VERMONT

Bisecting the Green Mountains, Central Vermont features ski resorts, maple sugaring and time-honored villages.

Woodstock & Quechee

The archetypal Vermont town, Woodstock's streets are lined with graceful Federal- and Georgian-style houses and the Ottauquechee River meanders right through the town center, where it's spanned by a covered bridge. It just doesn't get much prettier than this. The village of Quechee (*kwee*-chee), 7 miles to the northeast, offers an abundance of rural scenery and hiking trails.

INFORMATION

Woodstock Area Chamber of Commerce (☎ 802-457-3555; www.woodstockvt.com; 18 Central St; ☯ 9:30am-5pm) Provides information for visitors.

SIGHTS & ACTIVITIES

Woodstock is a perfect place to just wander about soaking up the atmosphere, so take some time to poke around, relax on the central green and stroll across the covered bridge.

See what 19th-century farm life was all about at **Billings Farm & Museum** (☎ 802-457-2355; www.billingsfarm.org; VT 12 at River Rd; adult/child 5-12 $9.50/5; ☯ 10am-5pm May-Oct), a living history museum and functioning dairy farm. **VINS Nature Center** (☎ 802-457-2779; www.vinsnaturecenter.org; US 4, Quechee; adult/child 3-16 $8/6.50; ☯ 9am-5:30pm May-Oct, 10am-4pm Nov-Apr), near the Quechee Gorge, rehabilitates injured falcons, hawks, bald eagles and other raptors. In addition to seeing these magnificent birds up close, you can hike on the center's 47 acres.

To learn about maple sugaring and cheese-making, and taste different varieties of both, head for the friendly **Sugarbush Farm** (☎ 802-457-1757; www.sugarbushfarm.com; 591 Sugarbush Farm Rd; admission free; ☯ 8am-5pm Mon-Fri, 9am-5pm Sat & Sun). The sugaring season is from March to April, but you can tour the sugarhouse year-round and walk through the woods where the trees are harvested. To get there take US 4 to Taftsville, 3.5 miles east of Woodstock, cross the Taftsville covered bridge and follow the hand-painted signs.

Quechee Gorge, a 170ft craggy chasm cut by the Ottauquechee River, offers good hiking. Begin at **Quechee Gorge State Park** (☎ 802-295-2990; US 4, Quechee; admission free), where you can pick up a trail map.

SLEEPING

Woodstock Inn & Resort (☎ 802-457-1100, 800-448-7900; www.woodstockinn.com; 14 The Green; r $209-615; ☑) Right on the town green, Woodstock's grand dame has all the trappings of a luxury inn with a formal dining room, a lobby with a fireplace and a host of other facilities.

Shire Motel (☎ 802-457-2211; www.shiremotel.com; 46 Pleasant St/US 4; r $128-300) You won't find a better river view or friendlier innkeepers than at this well-maintained motel in Woodstock's center. The pricier of the 42 rooms have fireplaces and Jacuzzis.

Quechee Inn at Marshfield Farm (☎ 802-295-3133; www.quecheeinn.com; 1119 Main St, Quechee; r $110-245; ☒) A former governor's residence dating back to 1793, this classic country inn with four-poster beds and wide-plank floors offers the ultimate in rural tranquility.

Quechee Gorge State Park (☎ 888-409-7579; US 4, Quechee; campsites/lean-tos $14/21) There are 46 pine-shaded campsites and seven lean-tos in this 600-acre park.

EATING

Simon Pearce (☎ 802-295-1470; 1760 Main St, Quechee; lunch mains $11-14, dinner mains $23-38; ☯ lunch & dinner) *The* place to eat. First watch the artisans hand-blowing glass and throwing pottery in the basement workshops, then go upstairs and enjoy a superb gourmet meal served on their handiwork. The riverside restaurant overlooks a waterfall and the on-site shop sells Pearce's finery.

Pane e Salute (☎ 802-457-4882; 61 Central St; mains $10-20; ☯ dinner Thu-Mon) Come to this popular Woodstock dinner restaurant for tasty Tuscan-style pizzas and traditional Italian fare the way mama used to make it…well, if your mama was Italian. There's a four-course prix-fixe menu as well ($36).

Mountain Creamery (☎ 802-457-1715; 33 Central St; snacks $3-6; ☯ 7am-3pm) In the center of Woodstock, the creamery serves home-made ice cream, hearty sandwiches and tempting pastries.

Woodstock Farmers' Market (☎ 802-457-3658; 468 Woodstock Rd/US 4; ☯ 7:30am-7pm Tue-Sat, 9am-6pm Sun) Just west of town, this grocery sells organic produce, cheeses, deli foods and breads – the perfect fixings for a picnic lunch.

NEW ENGLAND

Killington

Just an hour's drive west of Woodstock is **Killington Resort** (☎ 802-422-3333, 800-923-9444; www.killington.com), Vermont's premier ski destination, boasting 200 runs on seven mountains, a vertical drop of 3150ft and 33 lifts. And thanks to the world's most extensive snowmaking system, Killington has one of the longest seasons in the east. One-day lift tickets cost $69, ski rentals are $36, and lessons are available from $45.

Come June when the snow melts, mountain bikers and hikers replace skiers on the slopes. **Killington Mountain Bike Center** (☎ 802-422-6776; Killington Rd) rents mountain bikes for $50 per day. You and your bike can take the gondola to the 4241ft summit of Killington Mountain and ride down, finding your way among 45 miles of trails; all-day access to the trails and gondola costs $32.

There are over a hundred places to stay in the Killington area, ranging from cozy ski lodges to predictable chains like Comfort Inn. Almost all are along Killington Rd, the 6-mile-long road that leads north off US 4 up the mountain. For help finding a bed, contact the **Killington Chamber of Commerce** (☎ 802-773-4181, 800-337-1928; www.killingtonchamber.com; US 4; 9am-5pm Mon-Fri year-round, 10am-2pm some Sat).

Middlebury

Set against the backdrop of the Green Mountains, this picture-perfect New England college town centers around the verdant campus of Middlebury College.

INFORMATION

Addison County Chamber of Commerce (☎ 802-388-7951; www.midvermont.com; 2 Court St; 9am-5pm Mon-Fri) Provides information for visitors.

SIGHTS & ACTIVITIES

Middlebury College Museum of Art (☎ 802-443-5007; S Main St; admission free; 10am-5pm Tue-Fri, noon-5pm Sat & Sun) is worth a look for its collections of 19th-century European and American art and contemporary photographs.

The **Vermont State Craft Center at Frog Hollow** (☎ 802-388-3177; www.froghollow.org; 1 Mill St; 10am-5:30pm Mon-Sat, noon-5pm Sun), inside a converted mill, sells a wide variety of high-quality crafts created by more than 200 Vermont artisans. Even if you're not buying, it's terrific browsing.

America's first unique horse breed and Vermont's state animal, Morgan horses, all derive from horses first bred by Justin Morgan in the late 18th century. You can see their offspring and tour the stables at the University of Vermont's **Morgan Horse Farm** (☎ 802-388-2011; 74 Battell Dr, Weybridge; adult/child 5-12 $5/2; 9am-4pm May-Oct), about 3 miles from Middlebury; take VT 125 west and go north on VT 23.

SLEEPING & EATING

Inn on the Green (☎ 802-388-7512, 888-244-7512; www.innonthegreen.com; 71 S Pleasant St; r incl breakfast $99-159) On the National Register of Historic Places, this elegant 1803 inn with handsome rooms overlooks the green in the town center.

Tully & Marie's (☎ 802-388-4182; 5 Bakery Lane; mains $7-20; 11:30am-midnight) With a view of Otter Creek, this place serves New American fare with Asian and Mexican influences, covering the gamut from vegan dishes to steaks.

Storm Café (☎ 802-388-1063; 3 Mill St; mains $5-13; 11:30am-6pm Tue-Sat) Join artists at this hip café in the basement of the Frog Hollow Mill, popular for its creative soups, salads and sandwiches.

Warren & Waitsfield

The towns of Warren and Waitsfield boast two significant ski areas: **Sugarbush** and **Mad River Glen**, in the mountains west of VT 100. There are hordes of opportunities for cycling, canoeing, horseback riding, kayaking, gliding and other activities. Stop at the **Sugarbush Chamber of Commerce** (☎ 802-496-3409, 800-828-4748; www.madrivervalley.com; VT 100, Waitsfield; 9am-5pm Mon-Fri, 9am-noon Sat) for a mountain of current details. Information, rest rooms and telephones are available 24 hours a day in the chamber of commerce's lobby.

NORTHERN VERMONT

Vermont holds some of its finest treasures in its northern quarters. These include the hip city of Burlington, the classy ski center of Stowe and the state's loftiest mountains.

Montpelier

Quaint Montpelier (mont-*peel*-yer), with less than 9000 residents, would qualify as a large village in most countries. But in sparsely populated Vermont it is the capital, complete with a gold-domed **State House** (☎ 802-828-2228; admission free; ☻ tours 10am-3:30pm Mon-Fri, 11am-2:30pm Sat Jul–mid-Oct), built in 1836 of granite, quarried nearby.

If you happen to be here at mealtime you're in for a treat as Montpelier is home to the New England Culinary Institute (NECI), which operates **Main Street Grill & Bar** (☎ 802-223-3188; 118 Main St; lunch $7, dinner mains $12-17; ☻ lunch & dinner). You can watch student chefs master their artistry in an exhibition kitchen and dine on the A-plus efforts.

Stowe & Around

Vermont's most appealing ski center, Stowe, with its Alpine architecture, attracts an international crowd. It was just a pretty little farming town until the early 20th century when skiing took off and put Stowe on the map. The town's backdrop is Mt Mansfield (4393ft), Vermont's highest peak. Stowe is a perfect family destination, offering both cross-country and downhill skiing; slopes include gentle runs for the kids and challenging runs for the experienced. Biking and hiking are popular when the snow melts. The lion's share of lodgings and restaurants is along VT 108, the Mountain Rd.

INFORMATION

Stowe Area Association (☎ 802-253-7321, 877-467-8693; www.gostowe.com; 51 Main St; ☻ 9am-5pm, to later summer & fall) Provides information and lodging assistance.

SIGHTS & ACTIVITIES

The twin-peak **Stowe Mountain Resort** (☎ 802-253-3000, 800-253-4754; www.stowe.com; 5781 Mountain Rd), with its wide variety of terrain, has ski runs suitable for all levels. Cross-country skiing is available at several places, including the **Trapp Family Lodge** (☎ 802-253-8511, 800-826-7000; www.trappfamily.com; 700 Trapp Hill Rd), which is run by the family whose life inspired the film *The Sound of Music*.

The 5.25-mile **Stowe Recreation Path**, which runs along Waterbury River from the village toward Stowe Mountain Resort, is an ideal place to walk, cycle or skate, and when the weather's warm there are inviting swimming holes along the way. **AJ's Ski & Sports** (☎ 802-253-4593; 350 Mountain Rd; ☻ 9am-6pm) rents bikes and in-line skates for $7 per hour or $24 per day.

Vermont's Long Trail, which passes through Stowe, is a hiking trail that follows the crest of the Green Mountains and runs the entire length of Vermont with rustic cabins, lean-tos and primitive campsites along the way. Its caretaker, the **Green Mountain Club** (☎ 802-244-7037; www.greenmountainclub.org; 4711 Waterbury-Stowe Rd, Waterbury Center), has full details.

If you visit in mild weather, take a drive through dramatic **Smugglers Notch**, northwest of Stowe on VT 108 (the road is closed in the winter). This narrow pass slices through mountains with 1000ft cliffs on either side, and there are plenty of places where you can stop along the way to ooh and aah or take a short walk.

Umiak Outdoor Outfitters (☎ 802-253-2317; 849 S Main St; ☻ 9am-6pm) rents canoes (half/full day $34/42) and kayaks ($24/32).

For an up-close look at how New England's favorite cool treat is produced, stop by the **Ben & Jerry's Ice Cream Factory** (☎ 802-882-1240; www.benjerry.com; VT 100, Waterbury; adult/child under 12 $3/free; ☻ 9am-9pm Jul & Aug, 9am-7pm Sep & Oct, 10am-6pm Nov-May, 9am-6pm Jun), where tours and a moo-vie about the hippie founders are topped off with a taste tease of the latest flavor.

SLEEPING

Stowehof Inn (☎ 802-253-9722, 800-932-7136; www .stowehofinn.com; 434 Edson Hill Rd; r incl breakfast $93-228; ☒ ☪) A relaxed resort set in the woods off Mountain Rd, this Alpine-style inn has 45 rooms, some with mountain views and fireplaces. Other amenities include a hot tub, a sauna and a good dinner restaurant.

Ye Olde England Inne (☎ 802-253-7558, 800-477-3771; www.englandinn.com; 433 Mountain Rd; r incl breakfast $119-199, mains $9-26; ☻ lunch & dinner; ☒ ☪) English couple Chris and Lyn Francis have created an inviting country inn with comfy rooms in Laura Ashley style and an English pub serving pints of real UK ale matched with favorites like bangers and mash. A congenial mix of Brits and Americans hang here.

Smugglers Notch State Park (☎ 802-253-4014; 6443 Mountain Rd; campsites/lean-tos $14/21; ☻ mid-May–mid-Oct) Nine miles northwest of Stowe on VT 108, the park sits at the base of Mt Mansfield and has campsites and lean-to shelters.

Blue Moon Café (☎ 802-253-7006; 35 School St; mains $17-29; ☻ 6-9:30pm) One of New England's top bistros, this intimate place serves

New American fare with Asian and Mediterranean accents. The menu includes local game and fresh seafood.

Harvest Market (☎ 802-253-3800; 1031 Mountain Rd; ☑ 7am-7pm) Stop at this gourmet market for morning coffee and delicious pastries, Vermont cheeses, deli goods and sandwiches before you head for the hills.

Burlington

Montpelier may hold the state house but the social and cultural heart of Vermont beats in Burlington. Perched on the shore of Lake Champlain, this vibrant college town with a population just shy of 40,000 is Vermont's largest.

Burlington invites lingering with good nightlife, a charming waterfront and a plethora of interesting places to eat and drink. It's a manageable place with the lion's share of restaurants on or near Church St, and a pedestrian mall midway between the University of Vermont and the lake.

INFORMATION

Burlington Free Press (www.burlingtonfreepress.com) Up-to-date event and entertainment listings.
Crow Bookshop (☎ 802-862-0848; 14 Church St; ☑ 10am-9pm Mon-Wed, to 10pm Thu-Sat, 11am-6pm Sun) Excellent selection of new and used books.
FedEx Kinko's (☎ 802-658-2561; 199 Main St; per min 20¢; ☑ 24hr) Access the Internet here.
Fletcher Allen Health Care (☎ 802-847-0000; 111 Colchester Ave; ☑ 24hr)
Lake Champlain Regional Chamber of Commerce (☎ 802-863-3489; www.vermont.org; 60 Main St; ☑ 8:30am-5pm Mon-Fri, 10am-6pm Sat, 10am-5pm Sun)
Post office (☎ 802-863-6033; 11 Elmwood Ave; ☑ 8am-5pm Mon-Fri, 9am-1pm Sat)

SIGHTS

The superb **Shelburne Museum** (☎ 802-985-3346; www.shelburnemuseum.org; US 7, Shelburne; adult/child $18/9; ☑ 10am-5pm May-Oct) contains a diverse collection that is notably strong in North American folk art, decorative arts and New England architecture, including a sawmill (1786), a covered bridge (1845), a lighthouse (1871) and the Lake Champlain side-wheeler steamship *Ticonderoga* (1906). There's also a solid impressionist collection including works by Monet, Manet and Degas.

Enjoy a slice of Vermont farm life at **Shelburne Farms** (☎ 802-985-8686; www.shelburnefarms .org; 1611 Harbor Rd; adult/child $6/4; ☑ 10am-4pm mid-

May–mid-Oct), a classic 1400-acre farm designed by Frederick Law Olmsted, the landscape architect who created New York's Central Park. See how cheese is made, explore miles of woodland and meadow trails and visit the animals in the Children's Farmyard.

Shoring up the east side of town, the handsome **University of Vermont** (UVM; www.uvm .edu; Main St/Rte 2) campus is home to the **Fleming Museum** (☎ 802-656-2090; 61 Colchester Ave; adult/child $5/2; ☑ 9am-4pm Tue-Fri, 1-5pm Sat & Sun Sep-Apr, noon-4pm Tue-Fri, 1-5pm Sat & Sun May-Aug), whose eclectic collection of 20,000 objects ranges from an Egyptian mummy to works by Andy Warhol.

ECHO Lake Aquarium & Science Center (☎ 802-864-1848; www.echovermont.org; 1 College St; adult/child $9/6; ☑ 10am-5pm Fri-Wed, 10am-8pm Thu), a state-of-the-art science museum on the Burlington waterfront, has aquatic habitats wriggling with little creatures, a multimedia theater and 100 hands-on exhibits that will captivate inquisitive minds.

Treat yourself to the divine aromas of gourmet chocolate at **Lake Champlain Chocolates** (☎ 802-864-1807; www.lakechamplainchocolates .com;750 Pine St; admission free; ☑ tours on the hr 9am-2pm Mon-Fri), where you can watch a simple bean morph into what critics are calling some of the finest chocolate in the country. Best of all, you'll get to sample the final product.

Magic Hat Brewery (☎ 802-658-2739; www.magic hat.net; 5 Bartlett Bay Rd, South Burlington) offers free 'artifactory' tours of its microbrew operation on Thursday through Saturday afternoons – and of course they'll tip the tap to let you sample the art.

ACTIVITIES

To see Lake Champlain up close, walk or bike along the 9-mile **Burlington Recreation Path**, which follows the shoreline. Rent bikes at **Ski Rack** (☎ 802-658-3313; 85 Main St; per hr/day $10/22). **Waterfront Boat Rentals** (☎ 802-864-4858; Perkins Pier at Maple St; single kayaks per hr/day $10/35, canoes or double kayaks per hr/day $15/45) rents a variety of boats for use on the lake.

SLEEPING

Inn at Shelburne Farms (☎ 802-985-8498; www.shel burnefarms.org; 1611 Harbor Rd; r with shared bath $105-170, with private bath $225-340) Sample the good life at this classic manor house–turned-inn at Shelburne Farms. On the National Register of Historic Places, the former summer residence of Lila Vanderbilt Webb has 24 antique-filled bedrooms and the captivating air of a bygone era.

Willard Street Inn (☎ 802-651-8710, 800-577-8712; www.willardstreetinn.com; 349 S Willard St; r incl breakfast $125-225; ✕) A short walk from UVM, this 14-room Victorian inn is known for its gourmet breakfasts, lovely gardens and comfy rooms. Reserve the Tower Room for a stunning view of Lake Champlain.

Hartwell House B&B (☎ 802-658-9242, 888-658-9242; www.vermontbedandbreakfast.com; 170 Ferguson St; r incl breakfast $70; 🐾) In a quiet residential neighborhood, just a few minutes' drive from downtown, this welcoming place has two cozy rooms with shared bath.

North Beach Campground (☎ 802-862-0942; 60 Institute Rd; campsites $25) Ideal for swimming and other water activities, this place has 68 campsites along the shore of Lake Champlain.

Several chain motels are clustered along Shelburne Rd (US 7) in South Burlington.

EATING
Five Spice Café (☎ 802-864-4045; 175 Church St; mains $9-18; ✕ lunch & dinner) Sumptuous Pan-Asian food inspired by Thai, Vietnamese, Chinese and Indonesian classics but with plenty of creative twists, like Szechuan escargot. Lots of tasty vegetarian choices as well.

Penny Cluse Café (☎ 802-651-8834; 169 Cherry St; mains $4-10; ✕ 6:45am-3pm Mon-Fri, 8am-3pm Sat & Sun) The best place in town for breakfasts, this cheerful downtown café packs a crowd with its southwestern accented dishes like ranchero-style omelettes and its own freshly squeezed juices.

Leunig's Bistro (☎ 802-863-3759; 115 Church St; mains $8-28; ✕ lunch & dinner) Burlington's favorite date place – the ambience is smart but not stuffy, the menu innovatively fuses regional fare with European accents and there's live jazz most nights.

Stonesoup (☎ 802-862-7616; 211 College St; mains $3-8; ✕ 7am-7pm Mon & Sat, 7am-9pm Tue-Fri) This funky vegetarian café serves hearty sandwiches and pizzas and offers a buffet bar with yummy salads and hot dishes ($6.50 per pound).

DRINKING
Muddy Waters (☎ 802-658-0466; 184 Main St; ✕ 7:30am-6pm Mon, 7:30am-midnight Tue-Sat, 10am-10pm Sun) An arty student haunt, this relaxed place offers everything from espresso and chai to Vermont-brewed beers.

Uncommon Grounds (☎ 802-865-6227; 482 Church St; ✕ 7am-10pm Mon-Thu, 8am-11pm Fri & Sat, 9am-9pm Sun) This good-coffee mecca has prime sidewalk tables.

Vermont Pub & Brewery (☎ 802-865-0500; 144 College St; ✕ 11:30am-1am Sun-Wed, 11:30am-2am Thu-Sat) has an outdoor beer garden and pints brewed on-site, as does **Three Needs** (☎ 802-658-0889; 207 College St; ✕ 4pm-2am), the town's other microbrewery.

ENTERTAINMENT
Radio Bean (☎ 802-660-9346; 8 N Winooski Ave; ✕ 8am-midnight) A socially conscious coffeehouse serving fair-trade coffee by day, and the most happening entertainment scene after dark with live jazz and indie bands nightly.

135 Pearl (☎ 802-863-2343; 135 Pearl St) Gay and straight mingle at this festive nightclub, which has two floors of dancing, DJs working the crowd, cabaret and more.

Waiting Room (☎ 802-862-3455; 156 St Paul St) This swank lounge attracts a 30-something crowd with live jazz and international music Tuesday to Sunday nights.

Club Metronome (☎ 802-865-4563; 188 Main St) offers DJs and nationally touring rock bands, with the hottest action on Saturday nights. And there's usually a college crowd downstairs at **Nectar's** (☎ 802-658-4771), best known as the place where jam band Phish got started.

GETTING THERE & AWAY
Lake Champlain Ferries (☎ 802-864-9804; www .ferries.com; King St Dock; adult/child/car $4/1.60/10.75) runs ferries from mid-May to mid-October across the lake to Port Kent, New York (one hour).

NEW HAMPSHIRE

Prime for outdoor enthusiasts, the Granite State is ruggedly mountainous and dotted with hundreds of glacial lakes. By far the most dramatic part of the state is the White Mountain National Forest, offering a wonderland of delights that include winter and spring skiing, summer hiking and fall foliage splendor. New Hampshire residents pride themselves on their independent spirit – you see it everywhere, from license plates bearing the state mantra 'Live Free or Die' to its conservative politics amid a sea of otherwise liberal New England states.

NEW ENGLAND

History

Named after the English county of Hampshire by Captain John Mason in 1629, New Hampshire was the first among the colonies to declare its independence from England in 1776. During the industrialization boom of the 19th century, the state's leading city, Manchester, became such a powerhouse that its textile mills were the world's largest.

New Hampshire played a high-profile role near the end of WWII, when in 1944 President Franklin D Roosevelt gathered leaders from 44 Allied nations to remote Bretton Woods for a conference aimed at rebuilding capitalism. It was from this meeting that the World Bank and the International Monetary Fund emerged.

In 1963 this anti-tax state found another way to raise revenue, by becoming the first state in the USA to have a legal lottery. In 1999 New Hampshire became the first place in the USA to have a female governor and female leaders in both its state legislative chambers at the same time.

Information

New Hampshire has no sales tax, but does have an 8% meals and room tax.

New Hampshire Division of Travel & Tourism Development (☎ 603-271-2665, 800-386-4664; www.visitnh.gov; 172 Pembroke Rd, Concord, NH 03302) Distributes information on the state, as do the welcome centers at major border crossings.

Union Leader (www.unionleader.com) The state's largest newspaper.

PORTSMOUTH

America's third-oldest city, Portsmouth dates back to 1623 when a band of intrepid settlers sailed to the mouth of the Piscataqua River. They were so taken by the profusion of wild strawberries along the riverbank that they named the place Strawbery Banke but later changed it to Portsmouth. The town grew wealthy on shipbuilding and the maritime trade, and today its rich history is readily visible in the well-preserved brick buildings that line the waterfront and downtown district.

Information

Greater Portsmouth Chamber of Commerce
(☎ 603-436-3988; www.portcity.org; 500 Market St; ☻ 8:30am-5pm Mon-Fri year-round, 10am-5pm Sat & Sun Jun–mid-Oct) Provides information for visitors.

Portsmouth Regional Hospital (☎ 603-436-5110; 333 Borthwick Ave; ☻ 24hr) At the south side of the city.
Post office (☎ 800-275-8777; 80 Daniel St; ☻ 7:30am-5:30pm Mon-Fri, 8am-12:30pm Sat) In the city center.

Sights & Activities

Portsmouth's premier sight, **Strawbery Banke Museum** (☎ 603-433-1100; www.strawberybanke.org; cnr Hancock & Marcy Sts; adult/child 5-17 $15/10; ☻ 10am-5pm Mon-Sat, noon-5pm Sun May-Oct) encompasses an entire neighborhood of 40 historic buildings on the waterfront at the southeast side of town. This living history museum is unique in that the homes and shops span from the 17th to the early 20th century and are all original to this site. Visit the old general store, watch the potter throw his clay and get a scoop of homemade ice cream at Strawbery Alley. From November to April, the museum is open only for 90-minute guided tours (on the hour, 10am to 2pm Thursday to Saturday and noon to 2pm Sunday; closed January).

Like a fish out of water, the **USS Albacore** (☎ 603-436-3680; Market St; adult/child 7-17 $5/3; ☻ 9:30am-5pm Jun–mid-Oct, 9:30am-4pm Thu-Mon mid-Oct–May), a 205ft-long submarine, is beached on the lawn adjacent to a small museum. The decommissioned submarine was built in and launched from the Portsmouth Naval Shipyard in 1953. It's on the inland side of the road between the chamber of commerce and the city center.

The many hands-on exhibits at the **Children's Museum of Portsmouth** (☎ 603-436-3853; 280 Marcy St; admission $5; ☻ 10am-5pm Tue-Sat, 1-5pm Sun, also 10am-5pm Mon mid-Jun–Aug) will pique the curiosity of young kids.

Several of Portsmouth's grand historic houses have been beautifully preserved, including the 1758 **John Paul Jones House** (☎ 603-436-8420; cnr Middle & State Sts; adult/child 6-14 $5/2.50; ☻ 10am-4pm Mon-Sat, noon-4pm Jun–mid-Oct), where the admiral known as 'the father of the US Navy' once lived. Others include the **Warner House** (☎ 603-436-5909; cnr Daniel & Chapel Sts; admission $5; ☻ 11am-4pm Mon-Sat, noon-4pm Sun Jun-Oct), a brick mansion built in 1716, and the 1760 Georgian-style **Wentworth Gardner House** (☎ 603-436-4406; 50 Mechanic St; adult/child 6-14 $4/2; ☻ 1-4pm Tue-Sun Jun–mid-Oct). The latter was once owned by the Metropolitan Museum of Art, which planned to move it to New York City before townspeople raised their voices in protest.

Portsmouth Harbor Cruises (☎ 603-436-8084, 800-776-0915; www.portsmouthharbor.com; Ceres St Dock; adult $11-19, child $7-11) runs several trips around the historic harbor and offers inland river cruises that are particularly scenic during fall foliage season. **Isle of Shoals Steamship Company** (☎ 603-431-5500, 800-441-4620; www.islesofshoals.com; 315 Market St; adult $16-32, child $14-22) provides cruises aboard a replica 1900s-style ferry that harkens back to more leisurely times. Some of the cruises focus on lighthouses, others on the Isles of Shoals. For a big splurge, there's a lobster clambake dinner cruise on Friday evenings (adult/child $48/38).

Sleeping

Bow Street Inn (☎ 603-431-7760; www.bowstreetinn .com; 121 Bow St; r incl breakfast $140-180; ✉) Located in a brick building above the Seacoast Repertory Theatre, this atmospheric downtown inn has 10 rooms with brass beds, two with harbor views.

Inn at Strawbery Banke (☎ 603-436-7242, 800-428-3933; www.innatstrawberybanke.com; 314 Court St; r incl breakfast $135-150; ✉) If you want to be close to the Strawbery Banke Museum and within walking distance to the city center, this seven-room inn fits the bill.

Sise Inn (☎ 603-433-1200, 877-747-3466; www.sise inn.com; 40 Court St; r incl breakfast $189-269; ✉) Step back a century at this graceful 1881 Queen Anne–style inn. The rooms have engaging period decor but also boast modern amenities like wi-fi Internet access.

Portsmouth also has several chain hotels clustered around exit 5 off I-95.

Eating & Drinking

Jumpin' Jay's Fish Café (☎ 603-766-3474; 150 Congress St; mains $15-20; ✆ dinner) Fish-fanciers book tables at this sleek contemporary seafooder, which features a wide range of fresh pan-seared fish spiced with delicious sauces.

Oar House (☎ 603-436-4025; 55 Ceres St; mains $10-34; ✆ lunch & dinner) The best place in town for a fine meal on a sunny day is the harborview deck of this well-regarded restaurant serving ribs, steaks and seafood plates.

Blue Mermaid (☎ 603-427-2583; 409 The Hill; mains $7-20; ✆ lunch & dinner) At this fun eatery decorated Caribbean-style, you'll find everything from lobster quesadillas and Jamaican jerk chicken to New England crab cakes.

NEW HAMPSHIRE FACTS

Nicknames Granite State, White Mountain State
Population 1,299,500
Area 9351 sq miles
Capital city Concord (40,687)
Official state motto 'Live Free or Die'
Birthplace of Astronaut Alan Shepard (1923–98), Tupperware inventor Earl Tupper (1907–83)
Home of The highest mountains in northeastern USA
Famous for Being the first to vote in US presidential primaries, which gives the state enormous political power for its size

---

Portsmouth Gas Light Company (☎ 603-430-9122; 64 Market St; mains $8-17; ✆ 11:30am-10pm) A good family choice is this wood-fired brick-oven pizzeria offering an all-you-can-eat pizza buffet at lunch on weekdays ($6.50).

Molly Malone's (☎ 603-433-7233; 177 State St; mains $7-23; ✆ 11:30am-9:30pm Mon-Thu, 11:30am-10:30pm Fri & Sat, 10:30am-10pm Sun) Order traditional pub grub like bangers and mash or go for thick juicy burgers and steaks at this cheery Irish pub on the 2nd floor of a historic rowhouse.

Portsmouth Brewery (☎ 603-431-1115; 56 Market St; mains $7-22; ✆ 11:30am-12:30am) This hopping microbrewery serves specialty beers like Smuttynose Portsmouth Lager paired with creative pizzas, sandwiches and pastas.

Breaking New Grounds (☎ 603-436-9555; 14 Market St; snacks $2-5; ✆ 6:30am-10:30pm) Get your caffeine fix at this sunny café.

Entertainment

The acclaimed **Seacoast Repertory Theatre** (☎ 603-433-4472; 125 Bow St; tickets $22-32) performs a variety of plays in the historic 1892 Bow St Theatre.

Getting There & Away

By car, take I-95 exit 7; it takes about an hour to drive to Portsmouth from either Boston or Portland, Maine. **Vermont Transit** (☎ 800-552-7837) runs several daily buses to both Boston (one-way $17, 65 minutes) and Portland (one-way $16, 1¼ hours).

MANCHESTER

New Hampshire's largest city, Manchester, became the state's manufacturing center in the 19th century by exploiting the abundant water power of the Merrimack River. You can still see the brick **Amoskeag Mills** (1838), which stretch along the Commercial St riverbanks for almost 1.5 miles.

Manchester is not much of a tourist center; the **Greater Manchester Chamber of Commerce** (☎ 603-666-6600; www.manchester-chamber .org; 889 Elm St; �} 8am-5pm Mon-Fri) has much more information than you'll need.

The city's highlight is the **Currier Museum of Art** (☎ 603-669-6144; www.currier.org; 201 Myrtle Way; adult/child under 18 $5/free; �} 11am-5pm Sun, Mon, Wed, Fri, 11am-8pm Thu, 10am-5pm Sat), which displays the works of American artists Georgia O'Keeffe and Andrew Wyeth as well as European masters. It also owns the 1950 **Zimmerman House** (tours $9-20), the only home in New England designed by famed American architect Frank Lloyd Wright (1867–1959) that's open to the public. Call the museum for tour reservations.

I-93, US 3 and NH 101 all pass through Manchester. The **Manchester Airport** (☎ 603-624-6539; www.flymanchester.com) is served by seven US airlines, including discounter Southwest Airlines. Most major car-rental companies have offices at the airport. **Vermont Transit** (☎ 800-451-3292) and **Concord Trailways** (☎ 800-639-3317) provide bus service between Manchester and other New England cities.

CONCORD & AROUND

The state capital, with just 40,000 residents, revolves around local business and state political life and therefore doesn't draw a lot of travelers. Still, there are a couple of worthwhile attractions. The **Greater Concord Chamber of Commerce** (☎ 603-224-2508; www.con cordnhchamber.com; 40 Commercial St) can provide more information.

The gold-domed **State House** (☎ 603-271-2154; 107 N Main St; admission free; �} 8am-4:30pm Mon-Fri), built in 1819 of New Hampshire granite, can be visited on self-guided tours. The **Museum of New Hampshire History** (☎ 603-228-6688; www.nhhistory.org; 6 Eagle Sq; adult/child 6-18 $5/2.50; �} 9:30am-5pm Mon-Sat, noon-5pm Sun, closed Mon Jan-Jun & Nov), off Main St, chronicles the history of the Granite State; on Thursday it stays open until 8:30pm and is free after 5pm.

Christa McAuliffe Planetarium (☎ 603-271-7827; www.starhop.com; 2 Institute Dr; adult/child 3-17 $8/5; �} 10am-5pm Mon-Sat, noon-5pm Sun) is dedicated to the New Hampshire schoolteacher–astronaut who died in the *Challenger* explosion on January 28, 1986. Most shows last about one hour. Take exit 15E from I-93.

Well worth a visit, **Canterbury Shaker Village** (☎ 603-783-9511; www.shakers.org; 288 Shaker Rd, Canterbury; adult/child 6-17 $15/7; �} 10am-5pm mid-May–Oct, 10am-4pm Fri-Sun Nov), a traditional Shaker community found in 1792, is now a living history museum. Interpreters in period dress demonstrate the Shakers' daily lives, artisans create Shaker crafts, and there's a store selling Shaker reproductions, an organic farm stand and a restaurant. The village is 15 miles north of Concord on NH 106 (or I-93 exit 18).

LAKE WINNIPESAUKEE

A popular summertime destination for New Englanders, New Hampshire's largest lake stretches some 28 miles in length, contains 274 islands and offers good swimming, kayaking and fishing.

Weirs Beach

This lakeside town offers a curious slice of honky-tonk Americana with its celebrated video arcades, miniature golf courses, Indy go-cart tracks and junk-food stands. There's also a nice lakefront promenade, a small state park with a beach, and rail and boat tours. Contact the **Greater Laconia/Weirs Beach Chamber of Commerce** (☎ 603-366-4770; www.laco nia-weirs.org) for information on the area.

Mount Washington Cruises (☎ 603-366-5531; www.cruisenh.com) operates several scenic lake cruises from Weirs Beach, including a 2½-hour trip aboard the old-fashioned MS *Mount Washington* (adult/child four-12 $20/5). For something more unusual, hop aboard the company's mailboat MV *Sophie C* (adult/child $16/5) on its two-hour cruise to deliver mail to the lake islands.

Winnipesaukee Scenic Railroad (☎ 603-745-2135; www.hoborr.com; adult $10-11, child 3-11 $8-9; �} late May–mid-Oct) offers one- and two-hour rides along the shore of Lake Winnipesaukee.

The **Birch Knoll Motel** (☎ 603-366-4958; 🖳) has a private beach and rooms with lake views. An institution in these parts is the rustic **Weirs Beach Lobster Pound** (☎ 603-366-2255; US 3; mains $5-20; �} 11am-9pm late May-early Sep; 🞄), next to the drive-in theater, which serves up barbecued chicken, ribs, burgers and, of course, lobsters.

Wolfeboro

On the opposite side of Lake Winnipesaukee and a world away from the ticky-tacky commercialism of Weirs Beach sits the more genteel Wolfeboro. The town lays claim to being 'the oldest summer resort in America.' It certainly has some graceful period buildings and you'll find examples of New England's various architectural styles, including Georgian, Federal and Greek Revival. The **Wolfeboro Chamber of Commerce** (☎ 603-569-2200, 800-516-5324; www.wolfeborochamber.com; 32 Central Ave; ☼ 10am-5pm Mon-Sat, 10am-3pm Sun) is in the old train station.

The **Clark House Museum Complex** (☎ 603-569-4997; 233 S Main St; adult/child 5-11 $4/free; ☼ 11am-3:30pm Mon-Fri, 10am-1:30pm Sat Jul-early Sep), Wolfeboro's eclectic historical museum, occupies a 1778 farmhouse and includes a one-room schoolhouse and antique fire engines.

Ready to dip a paddle? **Winnipesaukee Kayak Co** (☎ 603-569-9926; 17 Bay St; per 4hr single/double kayaks $35/45; ☼ 8am-6pm) rents kayaks and has a dock right next to the shop.

There are several other things to do in town, from just strolling its pleasant streets to taking a half-hour tour of the **Hampshire Pewter Co** (☎ 603-569-5944; Mill St; admission free; ☼ 9am-5pm Mon-Fri, some Sat) where you can watch craftspeople work their trade.

Wolfeboro is home to the **Great Waters Music Festival** (☎ 603-569-7710; Brewster Academy, NH 28; www.greatwaters.org; ☼ early Jul-early Sep), where big-name folk, jazz and other acoustic artists perform on the banks of Lake Winnipesaukee.

The classic place to stay is the 44-room **Wolfeboro Inn** (☎ 603-569-3016, 800-451-2389; www.wolfeboroinn.com; 90 N Main St; r incl breakfast $185-255), the town's principal lodging since 1812. Some of the rooms have balconies overlooking the lake.

Further north along N Main St (NH 28) are several motels, including the 17-room **Lakeview Inn & Motor Lodge** (☎ 603-569-1335; www.lakeviewinn.net; 200 N Main St; r $90-110), where the higher-priced rooms have kitchenettes. Off NH 28 about 4.5 miles north of town, the lakeside **Wolfeboro Campground** (☎ 603-569-9881; 61 Haines Hill Rd; campsites $20-22) has 50 wooded campsites.

Come to **Café Sweets & Treats** (☎ 603-569-4505; 11 Railroad Ave; snacks $3-6; ☼ 6:30am-4pm Mon-Fri, 7am-5pm Sat, 7:30am-3pm Sun), a cybercafé, for gourmet coffee, bakery treats and deli sandwiches. At the Wolfeboro Inn, **Wolfe's Tavern** (☎ 603-569-3016; 90 N Main St; mains $10-19; ☼ lunch & dinner) has a cozy pub complete with fireplace, serving traditional favorites like prime rib along with 75 different beers from around the world.

WHITE MOUNTAINS

Outdoor enthusiasts flock to New England's most majestic range. The White Mountain National Forest is action central for hiking, camping, canoeing, kayaking and skiing. Mt Washington (6288ft), the highest peak in northeastern USA, can be approached by cog train from Bretton Woods, by road from Pinkham Notch, and by foot from several trailheads. There are many places to pick up information on sights within the White Mountains, including at ranger stations throughout the **White Mountain National Forest** (www.fs.fed.us/r9/white) and chambers of commerce in the towns along the way.

Waterville Valley

In the shadow of Mt Tecumseh, on the banks of the Mad River, Waterville Valley was developed as a resort community during the latter half of the 20th century, when hotels, condominiums, golf courses, and downhill and cross-country ski trails were all laid out. The town's sports facilities also include hiking trails, tennis, road- and mountain-bike routes, in-line skating routes and other organized family fun. The **Waterville Valley Region Chamber of Commerce** (☎ 603-726-3804, 800-237-2307; www.watervillevalleyregion.com; NH 49, Campton; ☼ 9am-5pm), off I-93 exit 28, has details.

Like many New England ski mountains, the **Waterville Valley ski area** (☎ 800-468-2553; www.waterville.com) is open in the summer for mountain biking and hiking; the ski area's main phone number will connect you to a lodging reservations service.

Mount Washington Valley

The Mt Washington Valley, stretching north from the eastern terminus of the Kancamagus Hwy, includes the towns of Bartlett, Conway, Glen, Intervale, Jackson and North Conway. Every conceivable outdoor activity is available here. The area's hub and biggest town, North Conway, is also a center for outlet shopping, including some earthy stores like LL Bean and Timberland.

INFORMATION

Met (☎ 603-356-2332; cnr Main & Kearsarge Sts, North Conway; per 15 min $3; ☾ 8am-10pm) Hip Internet café and art gallery combo.

Mount Washington Valley Chamber of Commerce (☎ 603-356-3171, 800-367-3364; www.mtwashington valley.org; Main St, North Conway; ☾ 9am-5pm Mon-Fri, variable hrs Sat) Free 24hr phone calls to area hotels and restaurants.

SIGHTS & ACTIVITIES

The fittingly named **Conway Scenic Railroad** (☎ 603-356-5251, 800-232-5251; www.conwayscenic.com; NH 16, North Conway; adult $12-58, child $8-36; ☾ daily mid-Jun–mid-Oct, weekends mid-Apr–mid-Jun & mid-Oct–Dec) operates an antique steam train on a variety of excursions from North Conway through the Mt Washington Valley and dramatic Crawford Notch. It's a real stunner, especially during the fall foliage season.

Two miles west of North Conway off US 302, placid **Echo Lake State Park** rests at the foot of a sheer rock wall called White Horse Ledge. The park has a lakeside hiking trail and a scenic road up to the 700ft-high Cathedral Ledge with panoramic views of the White Mountains.

Skiing areas include **Attitash/Bear Peak** (☎ 603-374-2368, 877-677-7669, lodging reservations 888-544-1900; www.attitash.com; US 302, Bartlett), west of Glen, which also operates America's longest Alpine slide ($13) in summer; **Cranmore Mountain Resort** (☎ 603-356-5543, 800-786-6754; www.cranmore.com), just outside North Conway; and **Black Mountain Ski Area** (☎ 603-383-4490, lodging reservations 800-698-4490; www.blackmt.com; NH 16B, Jackson), a cross-country skiing mecca that offers horseback riding in summer.

If you're up for paddling, **Saco Bound** (☎ 603-447-2177; www.sacobound.com; US 302, Conway; per day $26) rents canoes, tandem kayaks and touring kayaks.

SLEEPING

North Conway is thick with sleeping options from chain and resort hotels to cozy inns. You'll find most of them along NH 16, which runs through North Conway as Main St.

Cranmore Inn (☎ 603-356-5502, 800-526-5502; www.cranmoreinn.com; 80 Kearsarge St, North Conway; r incl breakfast $74-104; ✕ ☻) In the center of North Conway, Cranmore has been operating as a country inn for 125 years and good-

value comfort has been its key to success. Free wireless Internet access.

Cranmore Mountain Lodge (☎ 603-356-2044, 800-356-3596; www.north-conway.com; 859 Kearsarge Rd, North Conway; r incl breakfast $99-129; ☻) North of town, this old-fashioned inn offers a taste of country life with farm animals that the kids can pet and a hot tub to soak in after a day in the mountains – and of course there's a full country breakfast.

North Conway Grand Hotel (☎ 603-356-9300, 800-655-1434; www.northconwaygrand.com; NH 16 at Settlers' Green, North Conway; r $99-219; ☻) If you want all the comforts of a resort hotel, this place has commodious rooms with full amenities and little extras like a free DVD library.

HI Albert B Lester Memorial Hostel (☎ 603-447-1001; www.conwayhostel.com; 36 Washington St, Conway; dm/r incl breakfast $20/48; ✕ ☻) Perched on the edge of the White Mountain National Forest, off NH 16, this 45-bed hostel in a converted Conway farmhouse is well suited for outdoor adventurers.

Camping options include **Cove Camping Area** (☎ 603-447-6734; www.covecamping.com; Cove Rd, Conway; campsites $22-48), off Stark Rd on Conway Lake, and **Saco River Camping Area** (☎ 603-356-3360; off NH 16, North Conway; campsites/RV sites $21/30; ☻) on the Saco River.

EATING

Peach's (☎ 603-356-5860; South Main St, North Conway; mains $5-10; ☾ 7am-2:30pm) Friendly and cute as a button, this peachy little place, a half-mile south of the chamber of commerce, serves blueberry pancakes, spinach benedict and other breakfast delights until closing.

Café Noche (☎ 603-447-5050; 147 Main St, Conway; mains $7-13; ☾ 11:30am-9pm) For good, reasonably priced Tex-Mex try this festive central Conway spot. The margaritas will warm you up, too.

Stonehurst Manor (☎ 603-356-3113; NH 16; mains $10-29; ☾ dinner; ✕ ☻) If you're up for dining in style, head to this manor house a mile north of North Conway where you can opt for anything from gourmet wood-fired pizzas to cognac-braised duck.

Kancamagus Hwy

The 34.5-mile Kancamagus Hwy (NH 112), named after a Native American chief, is a beauty of a road cutting through the White Mountain National Forest between Conway and Lincoln. Laced with excellent hiking trails, scenic lookouts and swimmable streams, this is as natural as it gets. There's absolutely no development along the highway, whose highest point is Kancamagus Pass (2868ft).

Conveniently, there are ranger stations at both ends of the highway where you can stop and pick up brochures and hiking maps. At the eastern end near Conway is the **Saco Ranger District Office** (☎ 603-447-5448; 33 Kancamagus Hwy; ◐ 9am-4:30pm) and at the western end near the 29-mile marker is the **Lincoln Woods Ranger Office** (☎ 603-630-5190; Kancamagus Hwy; ◐ 8am-3pm).

Coming from Conway, 6.5 miles west of the Saco ranger station, you'll see **Lower Falls** on the north side of the road – stop here for the view and a swim. No trip along this highway is complete without taking the 20-minute hike to **Sabbaday Falls**, a beautiful cascade; the trail begins at mile 15 on the south side of the road. The best place to spot moose is along the shores of **Lily Pond**; stop at the roadside overview at mile 18. At the Lincoln Woods ranger station, cross the suspension footbridge over the river and continue for 3 miles to **Franconia Falls**, the finest swimming hole in the entire national forest, complete with a natural rock slide. Parking anywhere along the highway costs $3 per trailhead (honor system) or $5 per week; just fill out an envelope at any of the parking areas.

The White Mountain National Forest is ideal for campers, and you'll find several campgrounds run by the forest service accessible from the Kancamagus Hwy. Most are elementary, but Jigger Johnson has hot showers. All are on a first-come, first-served basis, except for Covered Bridge, which accepts advance reservations. The campgrounds, from east to west (Conway to Lincoln) are as follows:

Covered Bridge Campground (☎ 518-885-3639, 877-444-6777; www.reserveusa.com; campsites $16) Six miles west of Conway; 49 campsites.

Blackberry Crossing Campground (☎ 603-477-5448; campsites $16) Six miles west of Conway; 26 campsites.

Jigger Johnson Campground (☎ 603-477-5448; campsites $18) Twelve miles west of Conway; 76 campsites.

Passaconaway Campground (☎ 603-477-5448; campsites $16) Fifteen miles west of Conway; 33 campsites.

Big Rock Campground (☎ 603-744-9165; campsites $16) Six miles east of Lincoln; 28 campsites.

Hancock Campground (☎ 603-744-9165; campsites $18) Five miles east of Lincoln; 56 campsites.

North Woodstock & Lincoln

You'll pass right through the twin towns of Lincoln and North Woodstock on your way between the Kancamagus Hwy and Franconia Notch State Park, but you might also want to break here for a bite or a bed. The towns straddle the Pemigewasset River at the intersection of NH 112 and US 3, reached off I-93 from exit 32.

INFORMATION

Lincoln-Woodstock Chamber of Commerce (☎ 603-745-6621; www.lincolnwoodstock.com; NH 112, Lincoln; ◐ 9am-5pm Mon-Fri)

White Mountains Visitor Center (☎ 603-745-8720, 800-346-3687; www.visitwhitemountains.com; 200 Kancamagus Hwy, North Woodstock; ◐ 8:30am-5:30pm)

SIGHTS & ACTIVITIES

Loon Mountain (☎ 603-745-8111; www.loonmtn.com; Kancamagus Hwy, Lincoln) offers winter skiing and snowboarding and in summer has mountain-bike trails (bike rentals per day $33), horseback riding (from $39), a climbing wall ($10) and New Hampshire's longest gondola ride ($11) up the 3075ft mountain.

SLEEPING

Woodstock Inn (☎ 603-745-3951, 800-321-3985; www.woodstockinnnh.com; US 3, North Woodstock; r incl breakfast $97-179) Centered around a century-old Victorian home, this highly-rated inn has 24 comfortable rooms, many furnished with antiques, some with Jacuzzis.

Kancamagus Motor Lodge (☎ 603-745-3365, 800-346-4205; www.kancmotorlodge.com; NH 112, Lincoln; r $79-119; ▣) Many of the 34 rooms at this straightforward but comfortable motel have steam-bath showers; there's an indoor pool, too.

Wilderness Inn (☎ 603-745-3890, 800-200-9453; www.thewildernessinn.com; junction US3 & NH 112; r incl breakfast $60-170; ▣) This large B&B near the town center has hardwood floors, homey decor and well-priced rooms.

Country Bumpkins (☎ 603-745-8837; www.country bumpkins.com; US 3, Lincoln; campsites/RV sites $19/25, cabins $55-95) Find peace and quiet (late-night parties are forbidden) at this family spot on the Pemigewasset River, with 46 campsites and six heated cabins with kitchenettes and private baths.

EATING

Woodstock Inn Station & Brewery (☎ 603-745-3951; US 3, North Woodstock; mains $7-16; ⏲ 11:30am-10pm) This brewpub satisfies a wide range of food cravings with pasta, steaks, Mexican food and sandwiches. Live entertainment nightly in summer and good microbrewed ales year-round.

Cascade Coffee House (☎ 603-745-2001; 126 Main St, North Woodstock; sandwiches $4-7; ⏲ 7am-3pm, to 5pm Sat) Sit back in a cushy chair and enjoy excellent pastries, coffees and panini sandwiches.

Elvio's Pizzeria (☎ 603-745-8817; Lincoln Square Outlet Mall, NH 112; mains $7-10; ⏲ 11am-10pm) This pizzeria, run by an Italian family from the Bronx, is the place to head for good pizza, meatball subs and calzones.

Franconia Notch State Park

Dramatic Franconia Notch is a narrow gorge shaped over the eons by a wild stream cutting through craggy granite. The symbol of the Granite State, the natural rock formation called the 'Old Man of the Mountain,' used to gaze across Franconia Notch, but in 2003 the 40ft-tall rock crumbled and took the Old Man's profile down with it. Although the rockface is now gone, you can still see the Old Man's proud gaze on New Hampshire license plates and the commemorative New Hampshire quarter.

I-93 runs straight through **Franconia Notch State Park** (admission free). The park **visitor center** (☎ 603-745-8391; www.franconianotchstatepark.com; I-93, exit 34A) is 4 miles north of North Woodstock at the **Flume Gorge** (adult/child 6-12 $8/5; ⏲ 9am-5pm May-Oct), a natural cleft in the granite bedrock. A 2-mile self-guided nature walk takes you right through the deep opening, which narrows to a mere 12ft.

The visitor center can give you details on other hikes in the park, which range from short nature walks to daylong treks. For an enjoyable 15-minute stroll, stop at the **Basin** pulloff, between exits 34A and 34B, where a half-mile trail runs along a stream to a glacier-carved granite pool. The Basin is lovely, but swimming is not allowed. To take a dip, head to **Echo Lake Beach** (adult/child $3/1; ⏲ 10am-5:30pm), exit 34C, where you can swim and rent a kayak, rowboat or canoe for $10.

The **Cannon Mountain Aerial Tramway** (☎ 603-823-8800; I-93, exit 34B; round-trip adult/child 6-12 $10/6; ⏲ 9am-5pm mid-May–mid-Oct) offers a breathtaking view of Franconia Notch and the surrounding mountains. In winter, Cannon is open for downhill skiing.

The park's **Lafayette Place campground** (☎ 603-823-9513, reservations 603-271-3628; campsites $19-24) has 98 wooded campsites, but they fill up early in summer, so it's best to reserve in advance.

A few miles north of Franconia Notch, visit the **Frost Place** (☎ 603-823-5510; www.frostplace .org; Ridge Rd, Franconia; adult/child 6-12 $3/1.25; ⏲ 1-5pm Sat & Sun late May-Jun, 1-5pm Wed-Mon Jul–mid-Oct), the farm that belonged to poet Robert Frost (1874–1963). At this inspired place, Frost wrote two of his most famous poems: 'The Road Not Taken' and 'Stopping by Woods on a Snowy Evening.'

Bretton Woods & Crawford Notch

Before 1944, Bretton Woods was known primarily as a low-key retreat for wealthy visitors who patronized the majestic Mt Washington Hotel. When President Roosevelt chose the hotel for the historic conference to establish a new post–WWII economic order, the town's name took on worldwide recognition. The countryside, with Mt Washington as the backdrop, is as lovely today as it was back then. The **Twin Mountain-Bretton Woods Chamber of Commerce** (☎ 800-245-8946; www.twinmountain.org; US 302 & US 3, Twin Mountain) has details on Bretton Woods.

Hop aboard the world's oldest mountain-climbing rails, the **Mount Washington Cog Railway** (☎ 800-922-8825; www.thecog.com; Base Rd; adult/child 6-12 $49/35; ⏲ 9am-at least 3pm late May–mid-Oct), 6 miles east of US 302, for a memorable ride to the top of Mt Washington. The antique coal-fired locomotive chug-a-lugs along 3.5 miles of steeply trestled tracks as it climbs the mountainside. Make reservations, and dress for chilly weather.

The **Bretton Woods ski station** (☎ 603-278-3320; www.brettonwoods.com; US 302) offers both downhill and cross-country winter skiing.

US 302 heads south from Bretton Woods to Crawford Notch (1773ft) through gorgeous mountain scenery. **Crawford Notch State Park** (☎ 603-374-2272; adult/child 6-11 $3/1; ⏲ mid-May–mid-Oct) maintains an extensive system of hiking trails, including short hikes around a pond and to a waterfall, and a longer trek up Mt Washington.

If walls could talk, the historic **Mt Washington Hotel** (☎ 603-278-1000, 800-258-0330; www.mt washington.com; US 302; r $140-525; 🏊) would speak volumes. Opened in 1902, this grande dame of New England mountain resorts boasts 2600 acres of grounds, 27 holes of golf, 12 clay tennis courts, an equestrian center, and indoor and outdoor heated pools.

Cheaper but still classy digs can found at the **Bretton Arms Country Inn** (☎ 603-278-1000; www.mtwashington.com; US 302; r incl breakfast $69-149; ✗), an 1896 inn affiliated with the Mt Washington Hotel.

At the family-oriented **Twin Mountain KOA** (☎ 603-846-5559, 800-562-9117; www.twinmtnkoa.com; NH 115; campsites $27-33, cabins $48-55; ☐), activities include ice cream socials and campfire sing-alongs. And there's wi-fi, too.

Pinkham Notch

From Pinkham Notch (2032ft), on NH 16 about 11 miles north of North Conway, an excellent system of trails provides access to the natural beauties of the Presidential Range, including lofty **Mount Washington** (6288ft), the highest mountain east of the Mississippi and north of the Smoky Mountains. For the less athletically inclined, the **Mount Washington Auto Road** (☎ 603-466-3988; www .mountwashingtonautoroad.com; car & driver $18, extra passengers adult/child 5-12 $7/4; ✷ early May-Oct, weather permitting) offers easier summit access; rates include an audiocassette tour. If you don't want to drive yourself, take a 1½-hour guided van tour (adult/child $24/11). Mt Washington's weather is notoriously severe and can turn on a dime. The average temperature at the summit is 45°F in summer and the wind is always blowing.

The Appalachian Mountain Club's (AMC) **Pinkham Notch Visitor Center** (☎ 603-466-2727, 800-262-4455; www.outdoors.org; NH 16; ✷ 6:30am-10pm) is the area's informational nexus for like-minded adventurers and a good place to buy hiking necessities, including topographic trail maps and the useful *AMC White Mountain Guide*. The AMC runs the adjacent **Joe Dodge Lodge** (dm $45, with breakfast & dinner $57). **Dolly Copp Campground** (☎ 603-466-3984; NH 16; campsites $18), a USFS campground 6 miles north of the AMC facilities, has 176 simple campsites.

HANOVER

The ultimate college town, Hanover's verdant town green is bordered on four sides by the brick edifices of Dartmouth College. Practically the whole town is given over to this Ivy League school, chartered in 1769, the nation's ninth-oldest college. Along the east side of the green on College St, picturesque Dartmouth Row consists of four harmonious Georgian buildings: Wentworth, Dartmouth, Thornton and Reed. To take a free **campus walking tour** (☎ 603-646-2875; www .dartmouth.edu) contact the admissions office.

Information

Hanover Area Chamber of Commerce (☎ 603-643-3115; www.hanoverchamber.org; 216 Nugget Bldg, Main St; ✷ 9am-4pm Mon-Fri)

Sights & Activities

On the Dartmouth campus, check out the **Baker-Berry Library mural display** (☎ 603-646-2560; ✷ 8am-5pm) of *Epic of American Civilization* painted by the renowned Mexican muralist José Clemente Orozco (1883–1949), who taught at Dartmouth from 1932 to 1934.

The collections at Dartmouth's **Hood Museum of Art** (☎ 603-646-2808; Wheelock St; admission free; ✷ 10am-5pm Tue-Sat, to 9pm Wed, noon-5pm Sun) include impressive Assyrian stone reliefs from a palace built in 883 BC, and works by American artists such as Gilbert Stuart, best known for his portrait of George Washington on the US $1 bill.

Hopkins Center for the Arts (☎ 603-646-2422; www.dartmouth.edu) is a performing arts venue hosting all manner of music, dance and theater events.

Sleeping

Hanover Inn at Dartmouth College (☎ 603-643-4300, 800-443-7024; www.hanoverinn.com; cnr Main & Wheelock Sts; r/ste $260/310) The most elegant place to stay, this period hotel overlooking the town green is full of proud parents during weekend events and mid-June graduation.

Trumbull House B&B (☎ 603-643-2370, 800-651-5141; www.trumbullhouse.com; 40 Etna Rd; r incl breakfast $145-220; ✗ ☐) Cozy up under a down comforter at this B&B on 16 acres with a swimmable pond, 4 miles east of the Dartmouth campus.

Eating & Drinking

Molly's (☎ 603-643-2570; 43 S Main St; mains $8-15; ✷ 11:30am-10pm) This perky café is the place to go for thin-crust pizza, Black Angus burgers, specialty salads and sidewalk-view tables.

NEW ENGLAND

Lou's (☎ 603-643-3321; 30 S Main St; mains $5-9; ☼ 6am-3pm Mon-Fri, 7am-3pm Sat & Sun) A student haunt since 1947, Lou's has good sandwiches, but everybody comes here for the breakfasts served until closing.

Zins (☎ 603-643-4300; cnr Main & Wheelock Sts; mains $12-18; ☼ 11:30am-10pm Mon-Sat, 5:30-10pm Sun) Enjoy a meal in style at this wine bistro inside the Hanover Inn. The menu ranges from pasta to duck confit and naturally there are well-matched wines.

Murphy's on the Green (☎ 603-643-4075; 11 S Main St; mains $8-15; ☼ 11am-10pm, last call at 12:30am) At this classic Irish pub, students and faculty discuss weighty matters over pints of ale and hearty pub food.

Getting There & Away
To get to Hanover by car take exit 13 off I-91. **Vermont Transit** (☎ 603-643-2128, 800-552-8737) runs buses to Hanover from several New England locales including Boston (one-way $27, 2½ hours) and Manchester, NH (one-way $29, 2 hours).

MAINE

Maine is New England's frontier – a land so vast that it could swallow the region's five other states with scarcely a gulp. Its coast, with sandy beaches in the south and craggy mountains in the north, extends some 3500 miles if you were to travel along its indented shoreline. Maine's interior is a wilderness of 6000 lakes and ponds, 32,000 miles of rivers and millions of acres of woods. This is the place to go if you want to hike in a forest with black bears and moose, raft in white-water rapids, feast on lobster in a fishing village or sail along the coast in a tall-masted schooner.

History
The French and English vied to establish Maine's first European colony during the 1600s, but because of the harsh climate the settlements were short-lived.

In 1652 Massachusetts annexed the territory of Maine to provide a front line of defense against potential attacks during the French and Indian Wars. And indeed Maine at times became a battlefield between English colonists in New England and French forces in Canada.

In the early 19th century, in an attempt to settle this sparsely populated region, 100-acre homesteads were offered free to new settlers willing to farm the land. In 1820 Maine broke away from Massachusetts and entered the Union as a state.

In one quirky incident in 1839, Maine's firebrand governor, irked over a boundary dispute between northern Maine and New Brunswick (Canada), declared war on England, but the conflict was settled before any shots were fired.

The temperance movement got its start in Maine. In 1851 it became the first state to ban the sale of alcoholic beverages, a movement that eventually caught on elsewhere in the United States. It wasn't until 1934 that Prohibition was finally lifted.

Information
Maine's state sales tax is 5% and there's a lodging tax of 7%.

If you're entering the state on I-95 heading north, stop at the well-stocked visitor information center on the highway.

Maine Office of Tourism (☎ 888-624-6345; www .visitmaine.com; 59 State House Station, Augusta, ME 04330) Government-run; will send out a handy 300-page booklet on Maine destinations.

Maine Tourism Association (☎ 207-623-0363; www .mainetourism.com) Links chamber of commerce offices.

SOUTHERN MAINE COAST
In summertime visitors flock to this seaside region for its sandy beaches, resort villages and outlet shopping. The best place to stop for the latter is the southernmost town of Kittery, which is chockablock with shopping malls and outlet stores selling everything from camping gear to fine china.

Ogunquit
Aptly named, Ogunquit means 'Beautiful Place by the Sea' in the native Abenaki tongue, and its 3-mile-long beach has long been a magnet for summer visitors. Ogunquit Beach, a sandy barrier beach, separates the Ogunquit River from the Atlantic Ocean, offering beachgoers the option to swim in cool ocean surf or in the warmer, calmer cove.

Most of the town lies along Main St (US 1), which is lined with restaurants, shops and motels. For waterfront dining and boating activities head to Perkins Cove at the south end of town.

NEW ENGLAND

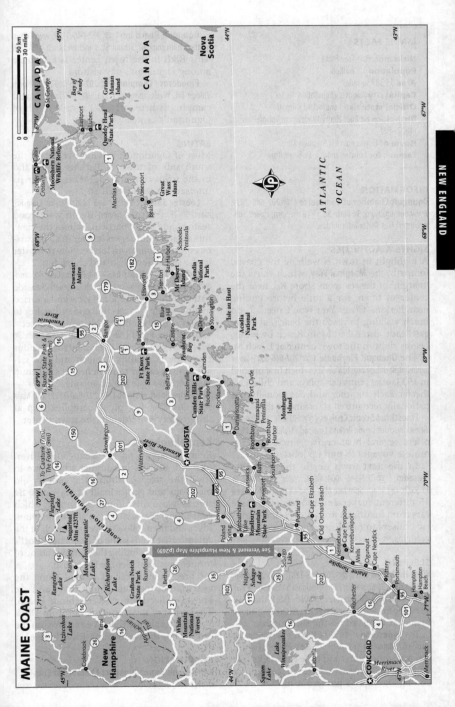

MAINE COAST

MAINE FACTS

Nickname Pine Tree State
Population 1.3 million
Area 35,387 sq miles
Capital city Augusta (population 18,560)
Official state fish Landlocked salmon
Birthplace of Poet Henry Wadsworth Longfellow (1807–82)
Home of Horror novelist Stephen King
Famous for Lobster, moose, LL Bean store

INFORMATION

Ogunquit Chamber of Commerce (☎ 207-646-2939; www.ogunquit.org; 36 Main St; ✷ 9am-5pm, closed Sun in winter) Has visitor information.

SIGHTS & ACTIVITIES

A highlight in town is walking the coastal footpath, the **Marginal Way**, which skirts the 'margin' of the sea from Shore Rd, near the center of town, for a mile before ending near Perkins Cove. You won't need to do much walking to reach the beach, as **Ogunquit Beach**, also called Main Beach by locals, begins right in the town center at Beach St.

The **Ogunquit Playhouse** (☎ 207-646-5511; www.ogunquitplayhouse.org; 10 Main St), which first opened in 1933, offers musicals, plays and children's theater each summer and occasionally has nationally recognized stars among the cast.

Finestkind Scenic Cruises (☎ 207-646-5227; www.finestkindcruises.com; Perkins Cove; adult/child from $11/7) offers several boat cruises, including 50-minute voyages to pull up lobster traps.

In the next town north, the **Wells Auto Museum** (☎ 207-646-9064; US 1, Wells; adult/child 5-11 $5/2; ✷ 10am-5pm late May–mid-Oct) showcases 45 different makes and models of antique cars from luxurious Rolls-Royce and Cadillac cruisers to rare Knox and Pierce-Arrow vehicles.

SLEEPING

West Highland Inn (☎ 207-646-2181; www.westhighlandinn.com; 38 Shore Rd; r incl breakfast $105-150) This central 1890 Victorian-style B&B has 15 cozy rooms with floral decor. A three-course breakfast is served on the sun porch.

The Milestone (☎ 207-646-6453; www.ogunquit.com; 687 Main St; r $69-204; ✗ ✷) Helpful staff, clean, comfy rooms and little extras like free wi-fi Internet access, make this a solid choice among Ogunquit's numerous motels.

Ogunquit Beach Inn (☎ 207-646-1112; www.ogunquitbeachinn.com; 67 School St; r incl breakfast $89-139) This B&B in the town center is a favorite among Ogunquit's gay visitors.

Pinederosa Camping (☎ 207-646-2492; 128 North Village Rd, Wells; campsites $23; ✷) The nearest camping is here, off US 1 a mile north of Ogunquit's center.

EATING

Most of Ogunquit's restaurants are on the south side of town at Perkins Cove, and in the town center along Main St near its intersection with Beach St.

Lobster Shack (☎ 207-646-2941; Perkins Cove Rd; mains $6-18; ✷ lunch & dinner) If you want good seafood and aren't particular about the view, this reliable joint serves lobster in all its various incarnations from lobster stew to lobster in the shell. Good fish and chips, too.

Jackie's Too (☎ 207-646-4444; Perkins Cove Rd; sandwiches $6-12, mains $9-27; ✷ lunch & dinner) Seaside patio dining, a great ocean view and a varied menu – from Tuscan chicken sandwiches to lobster dinners – make this a sure winner.

Bread and Roses (☎ 207-646-4227; 246 Main St; items $2-6; ✷ 7am-7pm) Come here for luscious cream puffs, healthy spinach and feta salads, and creative sandwiches. It's takeout, but there are café tables outside.

Village Food Market (☎ 207-646-2122; 230 Main St; ✷ 9am-8pm) For picnic supplies stop at this grocery store/deli in the town center.

Kennebunkport

Kennebunkport, on the Kennebunk River, fills with tourists in summer who come to stroll the streets, admire the century-old mansions and get their fill of sea views. Be sure to take a drive along Ocean Ave, which runs along the east side of the Kennebunk River and then follows a scenic stretch of the Atlantic that holds some of Kennebunkport's finest estates, including the summer home of former president George HW Bush.

Three public beaches extend along the west side of the Kennebunk River and are known collectively as Kennebunk Beach. The center of town spreads out from Dock Sq, which is along ME 9 (Western Ave) at the east side of the Kennebunk River bridge.

INFORMATION

Kennebunk/Kennebunkport Chamber of Commerce (☎ 207-967-0857; www.visitthekennebunks;

17 Western Ave; 9am-5pm Mon-Fri year-round, 8:30am-3pm Sat Jul & Aug) Has tourist information.

SLEEPING

Franciscan Guest House (207-967-4865; www.francis canguesthouse.com; 28 Beach Ave; r incl breakfast $50-144;) Serenity awaits at this 50-room guesthouse on the grounds of St Anthony's Monastery. Enjoy the outdoor saltwater pool and wooded walking trails.

Old Fort Inn (207-967-5353; www.oldfortinn.com; Old Fort Ave; r incl breakfast $160-375;) One block from the beach, not far from the presidential Bush family estate, this historic inn offers 16 classy rooms with antique furnishings, four-poster beds and the like.

Green Heron Inn (207-967-3315; www.green heroninn.com; 126 Ocean Ave; r incl breakfast $149-179) Situated on a picturesque cove in a fine neighborhood, this Kennebunkport inn has 10 cozy rooms and is within walking distance of a sandy beach and restaurants.

EATING

Bartley's (207-967-5050; Western Ave; mains $7-16; 11:30am-10pm;) This simple family-run place by the bridge at the Kennebunk River has delicious fried clams and Kennebunkport's best lobster dinner deal at $16. Save room for the homemade blueberry pie.

Alisson's (207-967-4841; 11 Dock Sq; mains $5-20; 11am-9:30pm) In the center of town on the east side of the Kennebunk River, Kennebunkport's most popular eatery offers a varied menu that includes lots of Maine seafood as well as burgers, steaks and pasta.

Federal Jack's Restaurant & Brew Pub (207-967-4322; 8 Western Ave; mains $6-19; 11am-1am) Overlooking the Kennebunk River, this bustling brewpub serves frosty mugs of handcrafted ales (try the Blue Fin Stout) and creative fare such as grilled crab sandwiches.

White Barn Inn (207-967-2321; www.white barninn.com; 37 Beach Ave; 4-course prix-fixe dinners $89) The region's top restaurant, this elegant dinner establishment serves contemporary American cuisine at its finest. Despite its setting in a converted barn, it's all very formal and jackets are required for men.

PORTLAND

The 18th-century poet Henry Wadsworth Longfellow referred to his childhood city as the 'jewel by the sea' and, thanks to some hefty revitalization efforts, Portland still shines. It's quintessential Maine: here you'll find postcard-perfect lighthouses, seafood markets steaming with lobsters, and an Old Port center with lamp-lit streets that inspire twilight pub crawls. With just 63,000 residents, the city is visitor-friendly.

Orientation

Portland sits on a hilly peninsula surrounded on three sides by water: Back Cove, Casco Bay and the Fore River. It's easy to find your way around. Commercial St (US 1A) runs along the waterfront through the Old Port, while the parallel Congress St is the main thoroughfare through downtown, passing the art museum, city hall, banks and churches.

Information

EMERGENCY
Police, fire and ambulance (911) Emergency.

INTERNET ACCESS
FedEx Kinko's (207-773-3177; 50 Monument Sq; per min 20¢; 6am-10pm) Has Internet access.
Portland Public Library (207-871-1700; 5 Monument Sq; first 15 min free; 9am-6pm Mon, Wed & Fri, noon-9pm Tue & Thu, 9am-5pm Sat) You may have to wait; also a wireless hot spot.

MEDIA
Portland Phoenix (www.portlandphoenix.com) Free alternative weekly, emphasizing arts and entertainment.
Portland Press Herald (www.pressherald.com) Major daily newspaper.

MEDICAL SERVICES
Maine Medical Center (207-871-2381; 22 Bramhall St; 24hr)

POST
Post office (207-871-8424; 125 Forest Ave; 7:30am-7pm Mon-Fri, 7:30am-5pm Sat)

DID YOU KNOW?

- Maine has the lowest population per sq mile of any state east of the Mississippi.
- Three out of every four lobsters eaten in the USA are caught in Maine.
- The majority of blueberries sold in the USA come from Maine.

TOURIST OFFICES

Convention & Visitors Bureau of Greater Portland
(☎ 207-772-5800; www.visitportland.com; 245 Commercial St; ☼ 8am-5pm Mon-Fri, 10am-5pm Sat, to 3pm Sat mid-Oct–mid-May) Pick up a free Portland map here.

Sights & Activities

The **Old Port**, Portland's restored waterfront district, centers on the handsome brick buildings lining Commercial St and the narrow side streets extending inland. Once home to the brawny warehouses and merchant quarters of a bustling port, the gentrified neighborhood now houses the city's finest restaurants, galleries and pubs. It makes for delightful wandering.

Works of Maine painters Winslow Homer, Edward Hopper and Andrew Wyeth are showcased at the **Portland Museum of Art** (☎ 207-775-6148; www.portlandmuseum.org; 7 Congress Sq; adult/child 6-17 $8/2, Fri 5-9pm free; ☼ 10am-5pm Sat-Thu, 10am-9pm Fri). Maine's finest art museum also boasts solid contemporary collections and post-impressionist works by Picasso, Monet and Renoir. And if you enjoy period homes be sure to stroll through the authentically restored 1801 **McLellan House**, entered through the art museum and included in the ticket price.

Folks with kids in tow should head for the **Children's Museum of Maine** (☎ 207-828-1234; www.kitetails.com; 142 Free St; admission $6; ☼ 10am-5pm Mon-Sat, noon-5pm Sun late May-early Sep, closed Mon Sep-late May). This house of fun is next to the Portland Museum of Art.

The **Wadsworth-Longfellow House** (☎ 207-879-0427; 485 Congress St; adult/child 5-11 $7/3; ☼ 10am-4pm Mon-Sat, noon-4pm Sun May-Oct), the childhood home of Henry Wadsworth Longfellow (1807–82), retains its period character, complete with the poet's family furnishings. Admission includes entry to the **Maine Historical Society Museum** (☎ 207-774-1822; 489 Congress St), which has changing exhibits on the state's history.

New England's most photographed lighthouse, **Portland Head Light** (☎ 207-799-2661; 1000 Shore Rd, Cape Elizabeth; adult/child 6-18 $2/1; ☼ 10am-4pm Jun-Oct), is also the oldest (1791) of Maine's more than 60 lighthouses. It's the centerpiece of **Fort Williams Park**, a pleasant picnic spot 4 miles south of central Portland.

Several companies offer narrated scenic cruises from Portland Harbor, including **Casco Bay Lines** (☎ 207-774-7871; www.cascobaylines.com;

56 Commercial St; adult $11.50-18.50, child 5-9 $5.50-8.50), which tours the Casco Bay islands on cruises that last from 1½ to six hours. The **Portland Schooner Co** (☎ 207-776-2500; www.portlandschooner.com; Maine State Pier; adult/child $28/12; ☼ May-Oct) offers two-hour sails aboard a pair of elegant Maine-built, century-old wooden schooners.

Landlubbers can ride the rails on the antique trains of the **Maine Narrow Gauge Railroad Co & Museum** (☎ 207-828-0814; www.mngrr.org; 58 Fore St; adult/child 3-12 $8/5; ☼ on the hr 11am-4pm mid-May–mid-Oct, shorter off-season hrs).

Sleeping

Inn on Carleton (☎ 207-775-1910, 800-639-1779; www.innoncarleto; ⊠) Centrally located in a fine neighborhood, this restored 1869 Victorian inn has six elegant rooms with antique furniture and gracious hosts who serve a full homemade breakfast.

Inn at Park Spring (☎ 207-774-1059, 800-437-8511; www.innatparkspring.com; 135 Spring St; r incl breakfast $139-175) Friendly innkeepers, clean, well-appointed rooms and a convenient location near the Portland Museum of Art are just part of the appeal of this period B&B.

Pomegranate Inn (☎ 207-772-1008, 800-356-0408; www.pomegranateinn.com; 49 Neal St; r incl breakfast $175-265; ⊠) In the quiet, residential West End, this stately home houses an eight-room antique-filled B&B decorated in a wildly eccentric style. Some rooms have fireplaces.

There are several chain hotels south of the city center at I-95, exit 8.

Eating & Drinking

There's no better place to appreciate Portland's homegrown delights than at the **Portland Public Market** (☎ 207-228-2000; 25 Preble St), where stalls sell everything from Maine veggies to lobsters. Grab a stool at the bar of **Scales** (☎ 207-228-2010; mains $5-14; ☼ 11am-8pm Mon-Sat, 11am-5pm Sun) and enjoy the freshest seafood on the planet – the fried-oysters-and-chips cone ($7) is a local treat, or pick a lobster from the live tank and they'll serve it cooked up in minutes.

Gilbert's Chowder House (☎ 207-871-5636; 92 Commercial St; mains $5-25; ☼ lunch & dinner) Sit on the waterfront patio and enjoy a bowl of award-winning chowder, fish and chips and other briny delights from the sea.

Pepperclub (☎ 207-772-0531; 78 Middle St; mains $12-15; ☼ dinner) Whether you're up for vegetarian Indian curries or pan-seared fresh fish, this hip, laid-back restaurant has plenty of delicious offerings for everyone.

Mims Brasserie (☎ 207-347-7478; 205 Commercial St; mains $14-26; 🕙 lunch & dinner) This smart bistro opposite the waterfront offers local fare with a French accent, including lobster bouillabaisse and venison au vin. Sandwiches ($8 to $10) shore up the lunch menu.

Gritty McDuff's Brew Pub (☎ 207-772-2739; 396 Fore St) This is the place to enjoy Portland-brewed ales.

For fine dining, top choices are the highly rated **Fore Street Restaurant** (☎ 207-775-2717; 288 Fore St; mains $18-30; 🕙 dinner), which specializes in roasted and grilled meats, and the equally popular **Street & Co** (☎ 207-775-0887; 33 Wharf St; mains $20-25; 🕙 dinner), which focuses on fresh seafood.

Entertainment

Bull Feeney's (☎ 207-773-7210; 375 Fore St) There's always something happening at this Irish pub, which offers Guinness on tap, good pub grub and live entertainment.

Styxx (☎ 207-828-0822; 3 Spring St) Gay men and women head here for dancing and a night out on the town.

State Theatre (☎ 207-775-3331; www.liveatthestate .com; 609 Congress St) Hosts touring rock, rap and alternative bands.

Getting There & Around

Portland International Jetport (☎ 207-774-7301; www.portlandjetport.org) is served by several domestic carriers, but cross-country or international travel to a destination other than Canada requires connections through Boston or New York.

Coastal Maine is most easily explored by car, but both **Vermont Transit** (☎ 207-772-6587; www.vermonttransit.com; 950 Congress St), inside the Greyhound Terminal, and **Concord Trailways** (☎ 207-828-1151; www.concordtrailways.com; Thompson Point Connector Rd), off I-295 exit 5A, run buses between Portland and Boston and also travel along the Maine coast.

Amtrak's **Downeaster train** (www.amtrakdown easter.com) makes its 2½-hour trip four times daily between Portland and Boston (one-way $21).

The local bus line, **Metro** (☎ 207-774-0351; www .gpmetrobus.com; fares $1), which runs throughout the city, has its main terminus at Monument Sq at the intersection of Elm and Congress Sts.

CENTRAL MAINE COAST

Midcoast Maine is where the mountains meet the sea. You'll find craggy peninsulas jutting deep into the Atlantic, friendly seaside villages and lots of opportunities for biking, hiking, sailing and kayaking.

Freeport

The fame and fortune of Freeport, 16 miles northeast of Portland, began a century ago when Leon Leonwood Bean opened a shop to sell equipment to hunters and fishers heading north into the Maine woods. LL Bean's good value earned him loyal customers, and over the years the **LL Bean store** (☎ 800-341-4341; www.llbean.com; Main St; 🕙 24hr) has added stylish sportswear to its high-quality outdoor gear. Although 125 other stores, including such trendy favorites as Banana Republic, have joined the pack, the wildly popular LL Bean is still the epicenter of town.

Ironically, this former stopover for hardy outdoor types is now devoted entirely to city-style shopping, with a mile-long Main St (US 1) lined with stores selling everything from porcelain dinnerware and fine jewelry to luggage and the latest fashions.

INFORMATION

Freeport Merchants Association (☎ 207-865-1212, 800-865-1994; www.freeportusa.com; 23 Depot St) Has tourist and shopping information.

SLEEPING & EATING

Although 'shop till you drop' may be the town's motto, there's no need to stay on your feet all night – this town has some inviting inns.

Harraseeket Inn (☎ 207-865-9377, 800-342-6423; www.stayfreeport.com; 162 Main St; r incl breakfast $140-295; 🗙 🖳 🐾) Freeport's nod to luxury, this award-winning inn has 84 rooms, many with fireplaces, all with style. It also houses a tavern with microbrews and a good dinner restaurant.

Kendall Tavern B&B (☎ 207-865-1338, 800-341-9572; www.kendalltavern.com; 213 Main St; r incl breakfast $110-175; 🗙) Friendly innkeepers make you feel right at home at this beautifully restored farmhouse at the north side of the town center.

Harraseeket Lunch & Lobster Co (☎ 207-865-4888; 36 Main St, South Freeport; mains $8-24; 🕙 11am-8:45pm) Head to this harborside restaurant and lobster pound 3 miles south of Freeport

HOW TO EAT A LOBSTER

Eating a boiled lobster is a messy pleasure. The best place to go is a lobster 'pound' – or just about any other casual seaside eatery – where you can tear them apart with your fingers. You'll get a plastic bib, a metal cracker, melted butter for dipping the meat, a dish for the shells and lots of napkins. Suck the meat out of the legs, crack the claws and eat the meat inside, then twist off the tail by bending it back and fork out the tail meat in one piece. Lobster pounds sell cooked lobsters at market rates (typically around $10 to $14 apiece), restaurants for $15 to $40.

center for the area's best lobster roll. Unbeatable boiled lobster and steamers, too.

Lobster Cooker (☎ 207-865-4349; 39 Main St; mains $5-12; 🕑 11am-8pm Sun-Thu, 11am-9pm Fri & Sat) A favorite with shoppers, this fast-food place just two blocks south of LL Bean has terrific clam chowder and good seafood sandwiches.

Bath

Bath has been renowned for shipbuilding since colonial times and that remains the raison d'être for the town today. **Bath Iron Works** (BIW), one of the largest shipyards in the USA, builds steel frigates and other large naval craft. The worthwhile **Maine Maritime Museum** (☎ 207-443-1316; www.bathmaine.com; 243 Washington St; adult/child 7-17 $9.75/6.75; 🕑 9:30am-5pm), south of the ironworks on the Kennebec River, showcases maritime history and wooden boats. The **Southern Midcoast Maine Chamber** (☎ 207-443-9751; www.midcoastmaine.com; 59 Pleasant St; 🕑 8:30am-5pm Mon-Fri) has visitor information.

Boothbay Harbor

Set back from the open ocean on a fjordlike harbor, this little fishing village packs thick with tourists in the summer.

INFORMATION

Boothbay Harbor Region Chamber of Commerce (☎ 207-633-2353; www.boothbayharbor.com; 192 Townsend Ave/ME 27; 🕑 8am-5pm Mon-Fri, also 10am-5pm Sat, 11am-3pm Sun May-Oct) Provides information for visitors.

SIGHTS & ACTIVITIES

Balmy Days Cruises (☎ 207-633-2284, 800-298-2284; www.balmydayscruises.com; Pier 8) runs one-hour harbor tours (adult/child under 12 $12/6) and day trips to Monhegan Island (adult/child $32/18). **Cap'n Fish's Boat Trips** (☎ 207-633-3244, 800-636-3244; www.mainewhales.com; Pier 1) offers 3½-hour whale-watching trips (adult/child $30/15), three-hour puffin-watching cruises (adult/child $20/10), 1½-hour seal-watching trips (adult/child $14/7) and more.

SLEEPING & EATING

Topside Inn (☎ 207-633-5404, 877-486-7466; www.topsideinn.com; 60 McKown St; r incl breakfast $95-160; ⊠) Perched on a hilltop, this friendly B&B with 21 comfortable rooms has a bird's-eye view of town and the surrounding ocean.

Brown's Wharf Inn (☎ 207-633-5440, 800-334-8110; www.brownswharfinn.com; 121 Atlantic Ave; r $119-179; ⊠) Sit on your own private balcony and watch the fishers bring in the catch at this motel smack on the harbor.

Gray Homestead (☎ 207-633-4612; www.graysoceancamping.com; 21 Homestead Rd, Southport; campsites $26-28, RV sites $29-35) Fall asleep to the lull of the surf at this oceanside campground 4 miles south of Boothbay Harbor via ME 27 and 238. Kayaks for rent, too.

Boothbay Harbor has lots of seafood eateries. The most atmospheric is the **Lobstermen's Co-Op** (☎ 207-633-4900; 97 Atlantic Ave; lobsters $13-20; 🕑 11:30am-8:30pm), a lobster pound on the harbor where you can watch the catches be unloaded as you chow down at pierside picnic tables.

Pemaquid Peninsula

At the southernmost part of the Peninsula, **Pemaquid Point** is one of the most wildly beautiful places in Maine, with its tortured, grainy igneous rock formations pounded by restless, treacherous seas. Perched atop the rocks in the 6-acre **Lighthouse Park** (adult/child under 12 $2/free) is the 11,000-candlepower Pemaquid Light, built in 1827. It's one of the 61 surviving lighthouses along the Maine coast. The keeper's house is now the **Fishermen's Museum** (☎ 207-677-2494; Pemaquid Point; admission free; 🕑 9am-5pm late May–mid-Oct).

Monhegan Island

This little granite island, 9 miles off the Maine coast, is a popular destination for summer day-trippers and a favorite haunt of artists and nature-lovers who find inspiration in the dramatic views and agreeable isolation. Tidy and manageable, Monhegan has 75 year-round residents and is just 1.5 miles long and a half-mile wide. Browse the website **Monhegan Commons** (www.monhegan .com) for information and links to hotels.

Unless you've booked reservations well in advance, you'll be lucky to find a room. Nonetheless, the island is well suited for a day excursion. In addition to its 17 miles of walking trails, there's an 1824 **lighthouse** with a little **museum** (admission $2) in the former keeper's house and several artists' studios that you can poke your head into.

Island Inn (☎ 207-596-0371; www.islandinnmon hegan.com; r incl breakfast $135-305), a handsome Victorian inn with a big front porch overlooking the harbor, has 34 simple rooms, the cheaper ones with shared bathrooms.

The 33 rooms in the 1870s **Monhegan House** (☎ 207-594-7983; www.monheganhouse.com; s/d incl breakfast $79/134) have shared baths but offer ocean and lighthouse views. The **Monhegan House Café** (lunch $10-15; dinner mains $20-25) features a daily special with coffee and dessert for $15 and huge sandwiches.

Pick up picnic supplies at **Barnacle Café & Bakery** (☎ 207-594-7995; mains $3-7; ⏰ 8am-5pm), right by the wharf.

From Port Clyde, the **Monhegan Boat Line** (☎ 207-372-8848; www.monheganboat.com; round-trip adult/child $27/14) runs three daily boats from late May to mid-October, once a day for the rest of the year. The **MV Hardy III** (☎ 207-677-2026, 800-278-3346; round-trip adult/child $28/16) departs from New Harbor, on the east side of the Pemaquid Peninsula.

Camden

With rolling hills as a backdrop and a harbor full of sailboats, Camden is a gem. Home to Maine's large fleet of windjammers (p294), it attracts nautical-minded souls.

You can get a superb view of picturesque-Camden and its surroundings by taking the 45-minute climb up Mt Battie in **Camden Hills State Park** (☎ 207-236-3109; 280 Belfast Rd/US 1; adult/child 5-11 $3/1; ⏰ 9am-sunset) at the north side of Camden.

INFORMATION

Camden-Rockport-Lincolnville Chamber of Commerce (☎ 207-236-4404; www.camdenme.org; 1 Public Landing, Camden; ⏰ 9am-5pm Mon-Fri, 10am-5pm Sat) Provides visitor information.

SLEEPING & EATING

Whitehall Inn (☎ 207-236-3391, 800-789-6565; www .whitehall-inn.com; 52 High St; r incl breakfast $110-170; ✗) Unwind in a rocking chair on the shady front porch of this century-old inn with 50 rooms and a timeless New England ambience. Afternoon tea, a full breakfast and a tennis court add to the appeal.

High Tide Inn (☎ 207-236-3724, 800-778-7068; www.hightideinn.com; 505 Belfast Rd/US 1; r incl breakfast $75-185; ✗) A good selection of reasonably priced accommodations can be found at this former estate with an inn and cottages. The inn has a living room with a fireplace, an oceanview breakfast veranda and a private, albeit rocky, beach.

Camden Hills State Park (☎ 207-287-3824; 280 Belfast Rd/US 1; campsites $20) This popular park has hot showers and 107 forested campsites, as well as 30 miles of scenic hiking trails; reservations are advised.

Atlantica (☎ 207-236-6011; 1 Bay View Landing; lunch mains $8-14, dinner mains $19-26; ⏰ lunch & dinner) Sit on the seaside deck and enjoy fresh New England seafood with Asian and French overtones at this innovative chef-driven restaurant. Tasty enticements include Maine lobster tail with carrot and vanilla puree and ginger-crusted scallops.

Camden Deli (☎ 207-236-8343; 37 Main St; sandwiches $5-7; ⏰ 7am-9pm) This downtown deli with a harborview deck makes 41 different sandwiches, including a superb Italian cold-cuts baguette. Come between 4pm and 7pm for free appetizers and $3 beers.

Blue Hill

Brimming with period houses and lots of culture, Blue Hill is a charming coastal town that's home to many artists and craftspeople. Start your exploration at Main St and the adjoining Union St, where you'll find several quality galleries selling Blue Hill pottery, sculptures and paintings.

Since 1902 the **Kneisel Hall Chamber Music Festival** (☎ 207-374-2811; www.kneisel.org; Pleasant St/ME 15; tickets $20; ⏰ Fri-Sun late Jun-late Aug) has attracted visitors far and wide to its summer concert series. The **Blue Hill Chamber of Commerce** (☎ 207-374-3242; www.bluehillpeninsula .org; 28 Water St; ⏰ 9:30am-4:30pm Mon-Fri, 9:30am-1:30pm Sat, 11:30am-1:30pm Sun) has information.

Afternoon tea, evening hors d'oeuvres by the fireplace and a gourmet breakfast are just some of the perks at **Blue Hill Inn** (☎ 207-374-2844, 800-826-7415; www.bluehillinn.com; Union St; r incl breakfast $158-195; ▢), the town's landmark B&B. The **Captain Isaac Merrill Inn** (☎ 207-374-2555, 877-374-2555; www.captainmerrillinn.com; Union St; r incl breakfast $145-175, mains $15-30; ☺ lunch & dinner; ✕) has rooms, some with fireplaces, in an 1830 sea captain's home. The inn's restaurant features a lobster-centric menu.

ACADIA NATIONAL PARK

The only national park in New England, Acadia encompasses an unspoiled wilderness of coastal mountains, sea cliffs, lakes and beaches. It was established in 1919 on land that John D Rockefeller and other wealthy nature-lovers had purchased to save from encroaching lumber interests. Today you can hike and bike along 57 miles of carriage roads that Rockefeller once rode his horse and buggy on. The park harbors a wide diversity of wildlife including deer, moose, puffins and bald eagles.

Dramatic scenery and a plethora of activities, from bird-watching to mountain climbing, make Acadia a popular summer destination. The park covers over 62 sq miles, including most of mountainous Mt Desert Island and tracts of land on the Schoodic

Peninsula and Isle au Haut. The admission fee, good for seven consecutive days, is $20 per vehicle, or $10 by bike or on foot.

Sights & Activities

Start your exploration at **Hulls Cove Visitor Center** (☎ 207-288-3338; www.nps.gov/acad; ME 3; ☺ 8am-4:30pm mid-Apr–Jun, 8am-6pm Jul-Aug, 8am-5pm Sep-Oct), from where the 20-mile **Park Loop Rd** circumnavigates the northeastern section of Mt Desert Island. On the portion called Ocean Dr, stop at **Thunder Hole** to watch the wild Atlantic surf crashing into a granite cleft. **Otter Cliffs**, not far from Thunder Hole, is a vertical wall of pink granite rising from the sea that's a favorite of rock climbers. At **Jordan Pond**, a self-guided nature trail skirts the pond perimeter. Break for an atmospheric lunch, or afternoon tea and popovers at **Jordan Pond House** (☎ 207-276-3316; lunch $8-18). For a bracing swim, head to **Sand Beach** or **Seal Harbor** or take a dip in the marginally warmer freshwater **Echo Lake**. For a panoramic view overlooking Bar Harbor and the islands in Frenchman Bay, take the 3.5-mile spur road to the summit of **Cadillac Mountain** (1530ft), the park's highest point – head here for sunrises.

Sleeping

The park has two campgrounds on Mt Desert Island. The 310-site, year-round

---

HOIST THE SAILS

Feel the wind in your hair and history at your side aboard the elegant, multimasted sailing ships known as windjammers. The ships – both historic and replicas – gather in the harbors at Camden and neighboring Rockport and Rockland to take passengers out on day and overnight sails.

Day sails cruise for two hours in Penobscot Bay from May to October ($25 to $30); you can usually book your place on the day. On the Camden waterfront, look for the 86ft wooden tall ship **Appledore** (☎ 207-236-8353; www.appledore2.com) and the two-masted schooner **Olad** (☎ 207-236-2323; www.maineschooners.com).

Other schooners make three- to six-day cruises, offer great wildlife viewing (seals, whales and puffins) and typically include stops at small coastal towns, offshore islands and Acadia National Park. The **Angelique** (☎ 800-282-9989; www.sailangelique.com), a lovely replica of a c 1880 North Sea schooner with ocher-red sails, makes four- and six-day cruises along the Maine coast for $585 to $875.

The **Lewis R French** (☎ 800-469-4635; www.schoonerfrench.com) is the granddaddy of the schooner trade. Not only does it lay claim to being America's oldest windjammer (1871) but it has been designated a National Historic Landmark. Trips range from three to six days and cost $485 to $855.

Reservations for the overnight sails are a must. Rates are highest from July to August. June offers long days, uncrowded harbors and lower rates, though the weather can be cool, even chilly. Late September, when the foliage begins to take on color, is a particularly scenic time. You can get information on more than a dozen ships in one fell swoop by contacting the **Maine Windjammer Association** (☎ 800-807-9463; www.sailmainecoast.com).

Blackwoods Campground (☎ 800-365-2267; ME 3; campsites $20), 5 miles south of Bar Harbor, requires reservations from May to October. **Seawall Campground** (ME 102A; campsites $14-20; ☺ mid-Jun–early Sep), 4 miles south of Southwest Harbor, rents all 200 sites on a first-come, first-served basis. If these are full several commercial campgrounds can be found just outside Acadia National Park.

Getting Around
The convenient **Island Explorer** (☎ 207-667-5796; www.exploreacadia.com; admission free; ☺ mid-Jun–mid-Oct) runs eight shuttle bus routes throughout Acadia National Park and to nearby towns, including Bar Harbor, linking trailheads, campgrounds and accommodations.

BAR HARBOR
Set on the doorstep of Acadia National Park, this alluring coastal town once rivaled Newport, Rhode Island, as a trendy summer destination for wealthy Americans. Today many of the old mansions have been turned into inviting inns and the town has become a magnet for outdoor enthusiasts.

Information
Bar Harbor Chamber of Commerce (☎ 207-288-5103, 888-540-9990; www.barharbormaine.com; 93 Cottage St; ☺ 8am-5pm Mon-Fri Jun-Sep, 9am-4pm Mon-Fri Oct-May) Distributes maps and regional information.

Sights & Activities
Bar Harbor Whale Watch (☎ 207-288-2386, 800-508-1499; www.whalesrus.com; 1 West St; ☺ mid-May–Oct), next to the town pier, offers a wide variety of sightseeing cruises, including whale-watching trips (adult/child $42/25), combination whale- and puffin-sighting cruises (adult/child $46/25), lobster and seal trips (adult/child $20/15) and more.

For a cruise in style, hop aboard the 51ft, four-mast schooner *Margaret Todd* operated by **Downeast Windjammer Cruises** (☎ 207-288-4585; www.downeastwindjammer.com; 27 Main St; adult/child $30/20), which departs from the Bar Harbor Inn Pier for two-hour cruises three times a day.

Numerous outfitters provide guide service, equipment for rent and lessons on sea kayaking, rock climbing and mountain biking. The outfitters have competitive prices; expect to pay about $20 a day for a bicycle rental, $45 for a day-long kayak rental or a

half-day kayak tour and $100 for a half-day rock climbing adventure. Outfitters include the following:
Acadia Bike & Coastal Kayaking Tours (☎ 207-288-9605, 800-526-8615; www.acadiafun.com; 48 Cottage St)
Acadia Mountain Guides (☎ 207-288-8186, 888-232-9559; www.acadiamountainguides.com; 198 Main St)
Atlantic Climbing School (☎ 207-288-2521; www.acadiaclimbing.com; 24 Cottage St)
Bar Harbor Bicycle Shop (☎ 207-288-3886; www.barharborbike.com; 141 Cottage St)
Crystal Seas Kayaking (☎ 207-288-4447, 877-732-7877; www.crystalseas.com; 123 Eden St)

Sleeping
There's no shortage of sleeping options in Bar Harbor, ranging from lovely B&Bs to the usual chain hotels.

Ledgelawn Inn (☎ 207-288-4596, 800-274-5334; www.ledgelawninn.com; 66 Mt Desert St; r incl breakfast $125-275; ▨) Relax on the veranda over afternoon tea at this grand downtown inn, built in a colonial revival style as a summer 'cottage' in 1904. There are 23 traditionally appointed rooms in the main inn and 10 in the adjacent carriage house; some have whirlpool tubs and working fireplaces.

Manor House Inn (☎ 207-288-3759, 800-437-0088; www.barharbormanorhouse.com; 106 West St; r incl breakfast $135-235; ▧) On the National Register of Historic Places, this classic 1887 Victorian inn sits in a quiet neighborhood within walking distance of the town center. The 18 rooms pair antique furnishings with modern amenities and several have gas fireplaces that'll add atmosphere to a cool Maine evening.

Holland Inn (☎ 207-288-4804; www.hollandinn.com; 35 Holland Ave; r incl breakfast $110-155) Nine cheery rooms, a gourmet breakfast and resident innkeepers who make you feel at home are in store at this renovated 1895 farmhouse, just a short stroll from the town center.

Mt Desert Island Youth Hostel (☎ 207-288-5587; www.barharborhostel.com; 321 Main St; dm $25; ☺ Apr 11-Nov 1; ▨ ▣) Thoroughly renovated, clean and down-home cozy, this 30-bed hostel offers a choice of coed or single-sex dorms, as well as a private room ($75) that can sleep up to four people. Reservations are recommended.

Eating
Lompoc Café & Brewpub (☎ 207-288-9392; 36 Rodick St; mains $6-18; ☺ lunch & dinner) This friendly café features local brews on tap and an eclectic menu with Indonesian satays, organic salads

and thin-crusted pizzas. There's live jazz or acoustic music Thursday to Saturday nights.

West St Café (☎ 207-288-5242; 76 West St; mains $10-18; ◷ lunch & dinner) Near the waterfront, this family-style place serves good seafood at honest prices. For a thoroughly Maine experience order the 'Downeast Special' and chow down on a lobster, a cup of chowder and blueberry pie.

Rupununi (☎ 207-288-2886; 119 Main St; mains $6-22; ◷ 11am-1am) Enjoy an all-American menu of burgers, steaks and barbecued chicken or select from a raw bar and local seafood. If you've got a hankering for variety you'll find more than 20 beers on tap and a wine list that'll exhaust indecisive souls.

Trenton Bridge Lobster Pound (☎ 207-667-2977; ME 3, Ellsworth; lobsters $10-20; ◷ 11am-7:30pm Mon-Sat) Sit at a picnic table, enjoy a water view and crack open a fresh boiled lobster at this traditional lobster pound bordering the causeway that connects Mt Desert Island to mainland Maine.

Getting There & Away

US Airways Express (☎ 207-667-7171, 800-428-4322; www.usairways.com) flies several times a day between Bar Harbor and Boston. The Hancock County-Bar Harbor Airport is at Trenton off ME 3, 12 miles northwest of Bar Harbor. **Budget** (☎ 207-667-1200) and **Hertz** (☎ 207-667-5017) have car-rental booths at the airport.

Vermont Transit (☎ 800-451-3292; www.vermont transit.com) runs buses between Bar Harbor and several New England cities, including Portland (one-way $42, 4 hours) and Boston (one-way $70, 6½ hours). Bay Ferries' high-speed catamaran ferry **The Cat** (☎ 207-288-3395, 888-249-7245; www.catferry.com; adult $39-69, child $29-49, car $74-119) whisks passengers from Bar Harbor to Yarmouth, Nova Scotia, in under three hours every day from mid-May to mid-October.

DOWNEAST MAINE

The 900-plus miles of coastline running northeast from Bar Harbor are sparsely populated, slower-paced and foggier than southern and western Maine. Highlights include the **Schoodic Peninsula**, whose tip is a noncontiguous part of Acadia National Park; the lobster fishing villages of **Jonesport** and **Beals**; and **Great Wass Island**, a nature preserve with walking paths and good bird-watching (including puffins).

Machias, with a branch of the University of Maine, is the center of commerce along this stretch of coast. **Lubec** is about as far east as you can go and still be in the USA; folks like to watch the sun rise at nearby **Quoddy Head State Park** so they can say they were the first in the country to see it.

Calais (*ka*-lus), at the northern end of US 1, is a twin town to St Stephen in New Brunswick, Canada. Southwest of Calais is the **Moosehorn National Wildlife Refuge** (☎ 207-454-7161; US1, Baring; admission free; ◷ dusk-dawn), which offers opportunities to spot bald eagles, America's national bird.

INTERIOR MAINE

Northern and western Maine is rugged outdoor country, New England's frontier land. River rafting, hiking trails up Maine's highest mountain and the ski town of Bethel make the region popular with adventurers.

Augusta

Augusta, which became Maine's capital in 1827, is small and, truth be told, not terribly interesting. The **Kennebec Valley Chamber of Commerce** (☎ 207-623-4559; www.augustamaine.com; 21 University Dr; ◷ 8:30am-5pm Mon-Fri) provides information on Augusta. If you're passing through, take a gander at the granite **State House** (1832), then stop at the adjacent **Maine State Museum** (☎ 207-287-2301; State House Complex, State St; adult/child 6-18 $2/1; ◷ 9am-5pm Tue-Fri, 10am-4pm Sat), which traces the state's natural and cultural history.

Bangor

A boomtown during Maine's 19th-century lumbering prosperity, Bangor was destroyed by a sweeping fire in 1911. Today it's a modern, workaday town, perhaps most famous as the hometown of best-selling novelist Stephen King (look for his mansion – complete with bat-and-spiderweb gate – among the grand houses along Broadway). The **Bangor Region Chamber of Commerce** (☎ 207-947-0307; www.bangorregion.com; 519 Main St; ◷ 8am-5pm Mon-Fri) has visitor information.

Sabbathday Lake

The nation's only active Shaker community is at Sabbathday Lake, 25 miles north of Portland. Founded in the early 18th century, a handful of devotees keep the Shaker tradition of simple living, hard work and fine artistry alive. You can tour several of the buildings and visit the **Shaker Museum** (☎ 207-926-4597; adult/child 6-12 $6.50/2; ☼ 10am-4:30pm Mon-Sat late May–mid-Oct). To get there, take exit 11 off the Maine Turnpike and continue north for 8 miles on ME 26.

Bethel

For a small community nestled in the Maine woods, Bethel, 12 miles east of the New Hampshire border on ME 26, is surprisingly refined. In winter there's excellent skiing in the nearby mountains.

INFORMATION

Bethel Area Chamber of Commerce (☎ 207-824-2282, 800-442-5826; www.bethelmaine.com; 8 Cross St; ☼ 9am-5pm Mon-Fri year-round, 9am-6pm Mon-Sat & noon-5pm Sun Jul & Aug) Provides information for visitors.

SIGHTS & ACTIVITIES

Sunday River Ski Area (☎ 207-824-3000; www.sunday river.com; ME 26; lift ticket per day $59), 6 miles north of Bethel, is one of the best family-oriented ski centers in the region, with eight mountain peaks and 120 trails.

    Bethel Outdoor Adventure (☎ 207-824-4224, 800-533-3607; www.betheloutdooradventure.com; 121 Mayville Rd/US 2; per day bicycle/kayak/canoe $25/30/45; ☼ 8am-5pm) rents bicycles, canoes and kayaks and arranges guided trips on the Androscoggin River. If you're up for a hike, head to **Grafton Notch State Park** (☎ 207-824-2912; ME 26), north of Bethel, which has pretty mountain scenery and waterfalls.

SLEEPING & EATING

Chapman Inn (☎ 207-824-2657, 877-359-1498; www .chapmaninn.com; 1 Mill Hill Rd; dm $33, r incl breakfast $69-99; ▯) Located on the town common, this 1865 B&B has 10 country-style rooms as well as hostel-style dorm beds. Billiards, ping pong, darts and free bicycles add to the fun.

    Sudbury Inn & Suds Pub (☎ 207-824-2174, 800-395-7837; www.thesudburyinn.com; 151 Main St; r incl breakfast $79-139, mains $12-29) In downtown Bethel, this historic inn has 17 rooms a pub with 29 beers on tap, pizza and live entertainment. It also has a dinner restaurant serving roast duckling with blueberry glaze and other hearty Maine fare.

    White Mountain National Forest (☎ reservations 877-444-6777; campsites $16-18) The Maine portion of the national forest has several basic campgrounds near Bethel.

Caratunk & the Forks

For white-water rafting at its finest, head to the **Kennebec River**, below the Harris dam, where the water shoots through a dramatic 12-mile gorge. With rapid names like Whitewasher and Magic Falls, you know you're in for an adventure.

    The villages of Caratunk and The Forks, on US 201 south of Jackman, are at the center of the Kennebec rafting area. The **Kennebec Valley Tourism Council** (☎ 800-393-8629; www.kennebecvalley.org) has visitor information.

    There's a variety of rafting options, from rolling rapids and heartstopping drops to calmer waters where children as young as seven can join in. Rates range from $75 to $120 per person for a daylong outing. Multiday packages, with camping or cabin accommodations, can also be arranged.

    Operators include the following:

Crab Apple Whitewater (☎ 207-663-4491, 800-553-7238; www.crabapplewhitewater.com)

New England Outdoor Center (☎ 207-723-5438, 800-766-7238; www.neoc.com)

North Country Rivers (☎ 207-672-4814, 800-348-8871; www.northcountryrivers.com)

Baxter State Park

Set in the remote forests of northern Maine, **Baxter State Park** (☎ 207-723-5140; www.baxter stateparkauthority.com; admission per car $12) centers on Mt Katahdin (5276ft), Maine's tallest mountain and the northern terminus of the 2160-mile **Appalachian Trail** (www.nps.gov/appa). This vast 204,733-acre park is maintained in a wilderness state – no electricity and no running water (bring your own or plan on purifying stream water) – and there's a good chance you'll see moose, deer and black bear. Baxter has extensive hiking trails, several leading to the top of Mt Katahdin, which can be hiked round-trip in a day as long as you get an early start.

    Baxter's 10 campgrounds contain 1200 campsites (per day $18) but they do fill up, so it's best to book in advance, which can be done online or by phone with a credit card.

    At Millinocket, south of Baxter State Park, there are motels, campgrounds, restaurants, supermarkets and outfitters that specialize in white-water rafting and kayaking on the Penobscot River. Get information from the **Katahdin Area Chamber of Commerce** (☎ 207-723-4443; www.katahdinmaine.com; 1029 Central St, Millinocket).

NEW ENGLAND

Washington, DC & the Capital Region

You'll be surprised by the distinct regionalisms that make this area – comprising DC, Maryland, Delaware and both Virginias – such a pleasant slice of Americana. DC is home to countless national symbols, but it has come into its own as a city, and too many visitors never venture beyond the monuments and the Smithsonian-lined Mall. DC is awash with vibrant neighborhoods where English is only one of many languages you'll hear and go-go music vies with bluesy jazz and Indian electronica for the attention of your eardrums.

Beyond the Beltway (the highway loop surrounding DC), the maritime heritage of the Chesapeake Bay is evident in Baltimore's Inner Harbor, the traditional fishing communities on the Eastern Shore and the naval legacy of Virginia's Hampton Roads. A skipping-stone's throw to the east, the relatively warm waters of the Atlantic lure sun-seekers to Delaware's boardwalk beaches. Virginia's Blue Ridge Mountains promise forests blanketing indigo hills and glimpses into the unique Appalachian mountain culture. West Virginia rewards with white-water rafting, huge swaths of wilderness and night skies dripping with stars.

Despite its small size, the region has witnessed a staggering amount of the country's fundamental history: Jamestown, Virginia, was the spot where those first bleary-eyed English settlers attempted to put down roots. Fast-forward a century and the entire area formed the backdrop to the passionate push for independence from Britain that sparked the Revolutionary War. Yet another century later it became the frontline of the bloody Civil War between the North and the South that threatened to tear the young nation in two.

HIGHLIGHTS

- Exploring the nooks and crannies of the nation's attic (aka the **Smithsonian museums**, p309) in Washington, DC, all for free dollars

- Getting slaphappy from the riotous momentum of an honest-to-gawsh jamboree along Virginia's **Crooked Road Heritage Music Trail** (p365)

- Observing history through the living museums of colonial America in the **Historic Triangle** (p352) of Williamsburg, Jamestown and Yorktown

- Crab cakes, the aquarium, baseball, railroads...what's not to love about **Baltimore** (p323), hon?

- Partying, or just lying comatose, along the **Delaware seashore** (p339) at Rehoboth and Dewey beaches

THE CAPITAL REGION IN...

One Week

Follow a version of the two-day **DC itinerary** (p308) and give a full day to **Baltimore** (p323) with its aquarium, crab cakes and blue-collar affability. If it's summer and especially if the kids are along, drive east to the boardwalk-blessed **beaches of Delaware** (p339). Cross over the 12-mile Chesapeake Bay bridge-tunnel and absorb some colonial history lessons in the **Historic Triangle** (p352) of Virginia. Swoop north again via the monument-studded city of **Richmond** (p345) before landing back in DC.

Two Weeks

Give DC and Baltimore a few more days, and then soak in the famous waters that drew the founding fathers to the town of **Berkeley Springs** (p367). Start your meander down Skyline Dr through **Shenandoah National Park** (p360), detouring to visit **Charlottesville** (p359), home of Thomas Jefferson's Monticello and the University of Virginia. For some of the best white-water rafting on this coast, head west to the **New River Gorge National River** (p368), and return via the **Crooked Road** (p365) for a taste of Appalachian music and culture. Wind your way back to DC through several towns packed with Civil War history: **Petersburg** (p352), **Richmond** (p345) and **Fredericksburg** (p344).

HISTORY

Early settlements in the area were sponsored by European governments as a way to reap the riches from the continent's bountiful resources. The laughably ill-prepared settlers were at first assisted and then increasingly resisted by the Native Americans of the area. The Powhatan tribe initially helped the English when they arrived at Jamestown Island (p354) in 1607. But given an inch, the English took a mile, and the natives' patience grew thin while hostility grew thick. Though the tale of how a chieftain's daughter named Pocahontas saved the life of English captain John Smith is a treasured American legend, the bulk of Native American history in the region is far less romantic.

European-borne diseases proved more devastating than the fighting of the so-called Indian Wars, and whole tribes were wiped out. Digging their toehold in even deeper, the British founded the royal colony of Virginia in 1624 in honor of the 'Virgin Queen' Elizabeth. The English absorbed Dutch and Swedish settlements on the Delaware coast, established in the 1630s. In 1634 Lord Baltimore established an independent Catholic colony he named Maryland, after King Charles' wife. To resolve disputes among Maryland, Delaware and Pennsylvania, a pair of English astronomers mapped out their namesake 'Mason–Dixon line,' which

was later to represent the boundary between the industrial North and the slave-holding South. During the Revolutionary War the region saw the initial defeat of the Continental Army at the Battle of Brandywine Creek (1777) and the final surrender of the British at Yorktown in 1781 (p355).

The site of Washington was selected as a convenient point between North and South, and the new capital's position proved strategic during the Civil War. While Maryland and Delaware were technically 'slave states,' they remained in the Union. Virginia seceded and established the capital of the Confederacy in Richmond. The mountainous western part of Virginia refused to follow the lead of their slave-holding eastern brethren, and West Virginia was admitted to the Union as a separate state in 1863, granting Lincoln the votes needed to advance emancipation. After the Civil War, the region slowly recovered on the strength of new industrial growth, and the coastal urban corridor became increasingly developed.

This region is tall on patriotism. DC is the origin of modern democracy, Maryland the home of the 'Star-Spangled Banner,' and Virginia the birthplace of many US presidents. But pride alone can't overcome the area's modern challenges – the waterfolk who make their living on the Chesapeake are struggling to replenish its once abundant

WASHINGTON, DC & THE CAPITAL REGION

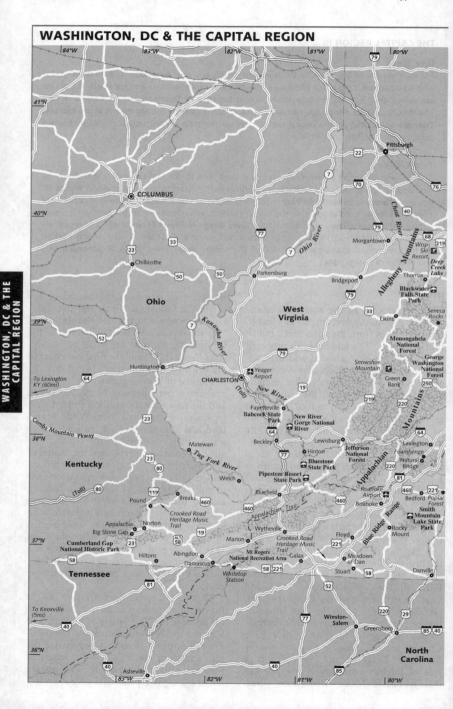

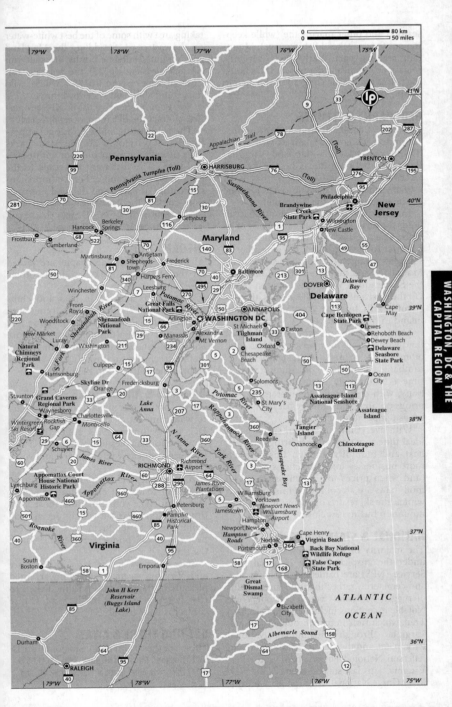

seafood and other marine life (while keeping out the snakehead fish scourge). Mountain regions, particularly West Virginia, remain economically depressed. DC's housing prices and traffic congestion threaten to cripple the city.

GEOGRAPHY & CLIMATE

The region's coastal areas include a low, flat, 100-mile-wide coastal plain as well as the 'Delmarva' (Delaware–Maryland–Virginia) Peninsula between the Chesapeake and Delaware Bays. The Chesapeake Bay is an estuary, where 48 navigable rivers join the sea in an area called the Tidewater.

Inland, the central Piedmont Plateau holds the region's farmlands and many of its cities. The Appalachian range, which forms a barrier to the northwest, has a number of subsidiary ranges, including the Allegheny Mountains and the Blue Ridge Mountains; the Shenandoah Valley lies between them. On the west side of the Alleghenies, the rivers of heavily forested West Virginia drain inland to the Ohio River.

The Capital Region experiences the best (and worst) of all four seasons. It has cold, often snowy winters, while temperatures can hang around 100°F in August. Springtime is stunningly beautiful but can be rainy, with comfortable temperatures. Fall brings out incredible foliage backdrops and keeps temperatures crisp.

With everything in bloom, spring is an ideal time to visit. Summer brings crowds, heat and humidity, though this is when most businesses and attractions are open (and when prices for lodging spike). The mountains are a cool refuge in summer; in winter, the ski resorts open, but many other mountain businesses close.

NATIONAL & STATE PARKS

The majority of the region's sites that fall under the auspices of the National Park Service (NPS) are battlefields, historic sites and cemeteries rather than the huge swaths of rugged wilderness you'll find out West. Notable exceptions include the Appalachian Trail, which runs in part through Maryland, Virginia (through Shenandoah National Park, p360, and the George Washington and Jefferson National Forests, p361) and West Virginia. This last state also boasts the New River Gorge National River (p368), a breath-

taking area with some of the best white-water on the east coast. Straddling the Maryland and Virginia shoreline border are state-run Assateague Island (p337) and federally run Chincoteague Island (p358), where wild horses and abundant waterfowl thrive.

For a comprehensive list of NPS properties, contact the **NPS** (www.nps.gov/parks.html).

The wild beauty and recreational opportunities of Virginia's 30-plus state parks are a magnet for many outdoor enthusiasts and those who just want to escape to the mountains or the shore. For a comprehensive listing of parks and detailed information, contact the **Department of Conservation and Recreation** (☎ 804-786-1712; www.dcr.state.va.us /parks; 203 Governor St, Suite 213, Richmond, VA 23219).

INFORMATION

All lodging prices in this chapter are quoted for the high summer season unless otherwise noted.

Smoking is allowed in bars and clubs in Maryland, Virginia, West Virginia and the District (but not Delaware), and in restaurants in West Virginia. However, more and more establishments are opting to go smoke-free, and in these cases, the no-smoking icon is used in the listing.

DANGERS & ANNOYANCES

There's nothing terribly out of the ordinary to watch out for. Sections of Washington, DC, and Baltimore, MD, suffer the common urban maladies of poverty and crime, but keep your city wits about you and you'll be fine.

In West Virginia, the twists and turns of mountain roads can exact strain on body and mind. Take your time, but those local drivers riding your tail will appreciate you pulling over to let them pass. Don't expect much cell phone service in a lot of the state.

State troopers, particularly in Delaware and Virginia, seem to take unwarranted pleasure in slapping out speeding tickets to city slickers rushing to hit the sand. Cruise control is your friend.

GETTING THERE & AWAY

These are the region's three major airports: **BWI-Thurgood Marshall Airport** (BWI; ☎ 410-859-7111) Thirty-five miles north of Washington, DC, and 10 miles south of Baltimore.

Ronald Reagan National Airport (DCA; ☎ 703-417-8000) Over the DC line in Virginia; linked to downtown DC by metro.

Washington Dulles International Airport (IAD; ☎ 703-572-2700) Twenty-six miles west of Washington in Northern Virginia.

Regional Virginia is also served by the following airports:

Newport News-Williamsburg (PHF; ☎ 757-877-0221; exit 255B off I-64)

Richmond (RID; ☎ 804-226-3000; exit 197A off I-64)

Roanoke (ROA; ☎ 540-362-1999; exit 143 off I-81)

West Virginia is served by the Charleston-based **Yeager Airport** (CRW; ☎ 304-344-8033) and Delaware by **Philadelphia International Airport** (PIA; ☎ 215-937-6937), a 30-minute drive north of Wilmington.

GETTING AROUND

The easiest way to get around – except within the cities – is by car. Buses are an alternative for reaching many smaller cities not served by air or rail. Nearly every city has a **Greyhound** (☎ 800-231-2222; www.greyhound.com) bus station.

Amtrak (☎ 800-872-7245; www.amtrak.com) and the weekday-only regional **MARC system** (☎ 866-743-3682; www.mtamaryland.com) provide rail transit to Washington, DC, and other regional destinations.

You'll need to rent a car for exploring outside major cities. See p322 for rental agencies at the capital area's three airports.

WASHINGTON, DC

We've all seen the majestic panorama in a thousand political thriller movies, but even the most jaded of Washingtonians will admit to a sense of awe when looking down on the gleaming monuments as they land at Reagan National Airport; or emerging from the Smithsonian Metro station and taking in the grandeur of the National Mall; or stopping at a street corner to let a thundering motorcade of black sedans with tinted glass escorted by screaming police motorcycles go past. The sheer *importance* of where you are hits you full force.

Enshrined in the temple-like National Archives are the Constitution and the Declaration of Independence and at the end

---

DC FACTS

Nicknames Federal City, Chocolate City

Population 563,384

Area 68 sq miles

Official name Washington, District of Columbia

Birthplace of Edward 'Duke' Ellington (1899–1974), Ferdinand 'Jelly Roll' Morton (1890–1941), Thurgood Marshall (1908–83)

Home of The First and Second Families; NGOs and NPOs galore; awesome Ethiopian food; lobbyists and think tanks and interns, oh my!

Famous for Political intrigue and scandals, the Smithsonian Institution, humid summers

---

of the Mall the marble-columned Lincoln Memorial venerates the preserver of the Union. These are but a few of the symbols of a national ideology which gives rise in so many Americans such fervent patriotism, for better or worse. Millions of Americans and non-Americans alike journey every year to pay tribute to the founding fathers and the lofty ideals that inspired them. But the actual implementation of the democracy can be less than inspirational. The capital serves as the national soapbox, battleground and negotiation table, beating to the pulse of politics and attracting power brokers, lawyers and idealistic good deed–doers.

With all the comedy and tragedy that politics entails, it's easy to forget the other side of Washington, the distinct neighborhoods where the federal government and its machinations are merely backdrops to life. Sophisticated and gay-friendly Dupont Circle encompasses bookstores, excellent restaurants and galleries. In Georgetown, the rich and the beautiful juggle shopping sprees and lunch dates. Shaw has recovered from the race riots of the '60s to celebrate its African American heritage. U St has likewise transformed into a hot nighttime destination, with the city's best venues for live music and a slew of Ethiopian eateries.

History

Various cities, including Philadelphia and Baltimore, were employed as the capital of the fledgling nation, but the Congress finally decided upon this swampy site at the confluence of the Potomac and Anacostia Rivers near George Washington's home at Mt Vernon. People started calling it 'the

WASHINGTON, DC

WASHINGTON, DC & THE CAPITAL REGION

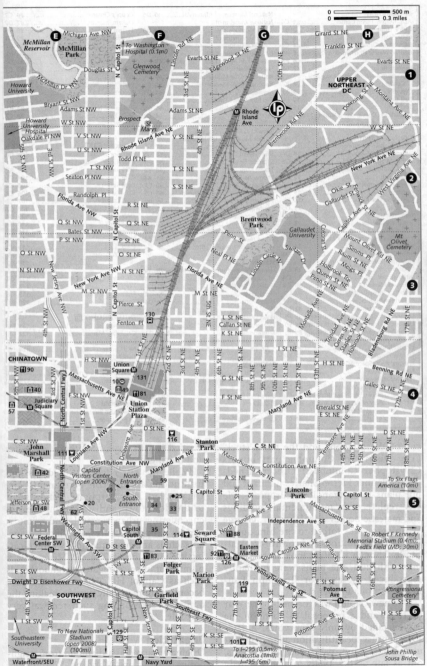

WASHINGTON, DC & THE CAPITAL REGION

city of Washington,' and the name stuck. (The District of Columbia part honors Christopher Columbus.) Officer-turned-urban planner Pierre-Charles L'Enfant laid out plans for a grandiose European-style city replete with monumental buildings and majestic boulevards. However, George Washington was forced to fire him due to his petulant outbursts and control-freak attitude. Though L'Enfant took all his drawings with him, the plans were brilliantly reproduced by surveyor Benjamin Banneker, son of a former slave.

The new Capitol was torched in the War of 1812, and a proposal to abandon the capital failed by only nine votes. A late-19th-century beautification plan contributed landscaping, parks and monuments, but as late as the 1960s John F Kennedy

derided it as 'a city of Southern efficiency and Northern charm.'

While the city's federal buildings and institutions are now on permanent hair-trigger alert, new corporate commitment to the downtown and waterfront areas is engendering urban renewal, and crime is steadily dropping. A fresh batch of restaurants, clubs and boutique hotels is inculcating itself into the city's fabric. Meanwhile, a number of once-segregated neighborhoods such as Capitol Hill, Shaw and U St are becoming more racially diverse, making the optimism surrounding such renewal very palpable.

Orientation

Originally carved as a diamond from neighboring Virginia and Maryland, Washington,

---

DC STATEHOOD

Taxation without representation! You'll hear this cry, a spin on the old Revolutionary-era slogan, on many a Washingtonian's lips, and see it displayed on their license plates. Basically, the city is within the federal enclave of the District of Columbia, and, as a federal protectorate, DC has a political life more closely resembling a colony than a state. The municipal government must operate under the imposing oversight of the federal government. In fact, District residents only won the right to vote in presidential elections in 1961. DC's hard-fought struggle for congressional representation has so far earned it only nonvoting representatives. Every few years or so the argument flares up and many believe that it's only a matter of time before the national flag has to be redesigned to accommodate 51 stars.

DC, is bounded by the Potomac River on one side and by Maryland on all others. (It lost its original shape by retroceding land to Virginia in 1837.) It's ringed by a freeway (I-495) called the Beltway, which separates 'inner Beltway' urbanites from suburbanites.

From the Capitol, the city is divided into four quadrants – northwest, northeast, southeast and southwest – along axes that follow N Capitol St, E Capitol St, S Capitol St and the National Mall. Identical addresses appear in each quadrant, so be careful! Most visitor attractions are in the northwest quadrant.

North–south streets are referred to by numbers, while the east–west streets are ordered alphabetically (with no B, J, X, Y or Z Sts; I St sometimes appears as 'Eye' St). Broad diagonal avenues, named after states, overlay the grid and are often interrupted by circular parks and plazas.

Information

Sales tax is 5.75%. Accommodation tax is 14.5% plus $3.50 per night.

BOOKSTORES

ADC Map & Travel Center (☎ 202-628-2608; 1636 Eye St NW; ☻ 8:30am-6pm Mon-Fri, 10:30am-4:30pm Sat) Maps plus travel and local-interest books.

Kramerbooks (☎ 202-387-1400; 1517 Connecticut Ave NW, Dupont Circle; ☻ 7:30am-1am Sun-Thu, 24hr Fri & Sat) Ground zero for the city's hip literati.

Olsson's (☎ 202-785-1133; 1307 19th St NW; ☻ 10am-10pm, noon-8pm Sun) Beloved independent with a wide selection of books and music.

EMERGENCY

Police, fire and ambulance (☎ 911) Emergency.
Police, fire and ambulance (☎ 311) Non-emergency.
Rape Crisis Center (☎ 202-333-RAPE/7273) Twenty-four-hour hotline.

INTERNET ACCESS

CyberStop Café (☎ 202-234-2470; 1513 17th St NW, Dupont Circle; per hr $8; ☻ 7am-midnight, from 8am Sat & Sun) Wi-fi, too.

Kramerbooks (☎ 202-387-1400; 1517 Connecticut Ave NW, Dupont Circle; ☻ 7:30am-1am Sun-Thu, 24hr Fri & Sat) 15 minutes free at the bar.

Newsroom (☎ 202-332-1489; 1753 Connecticut Ave NW; per 15/60 min $3/11; ☻ 7am-9pm)

INTERNET RESOURCES

Online visitor information (www.dcvisit.com)

MEDIA

90.9 WETA-FM NPR affiliate.
101.1 WIYY-FM Rawk.
1050AM Federal News Radio For news and policy wonks.
Newsroom & International Language Center
(☎ 202-332-1489; 1753 Connecticut Ave NW; ☻ 7am-9pm) Newspapers from all over creation downstairs, plus language books and cassettes upstairs at the language center.
Washington City Paper (www.washingtoncitypaper .com) Free weekly paper with useful entertainment and dining listings.
Washington Post (www.washingtonpost.com) Daily city (and national) paper. Its tabloid-format daily *Express* is free.

MEDICAL SERVICES

CVS Pharmacy (☎ 202-785-1466; Massachusetts Ave & 20th St NW; ☻ 24hr)
George Washington University Hospital (☎ 202-715-4000; 901 23rd St NW)

MONEY

Currency exchange is available at the three major airports and during weekday business hours at most of the banks, as well as at **Travelex** (☎ 202-371-9220; Union Station, 50 Massachusetts Ave NE, Gate G booth; ☻ 9am-5pm Mon-Sat, noon-6pm Sun). It also has a location **downtown** (☎ 202-872-1428; 1880 K St NW; ☻ 9am-5pm Mon-Fri).

DC IN...

Two Days

Set the alarm! If you haven't secured advance tickets, get in line by around 8:30am to get passes for whatever blockbusters most appeal: the **Capitol** (opposite), the **Washington Monument** (p310) or the **Bureau of Engraving & Printing** (p311). The **Air & Space Museum** (p310) and the **National Museum of Natural History** (p310) will delight kids. Art lovers shouldn't miss the **National Gallery of Art** (p310). Give your feet a rest with a twilight **monuments tour** (p315). After dinner, head to **Capitol Hill** (below) and join the political wonks as they loosen their lips along with their ties.

Next day, tackle the **National Archives** (p311), the **International Spy Museum** (p312) and the **National Museum of American History** (p310).

Four Days

After covering the two-day itinerary, take a vacation from your vacation in **Georgetown** (p313): power-shop, hop a ride on the canal and wander the gardens at Dumbarton Oaks. Then head north to the **National Zoo** (p315) and the **Washington National Cathedral** (p314). Get your injection of *injera* (traditional spongy bread) at one of many splendid Ethiopian restaurants in the U Street and Adams Morgan neighborhoods.

On day four, gather provisions at **Eastern Market** (p317) and ride your rented wheels to George Washington's **Mount Vernon** (p344)

POST

Post office (2 Massachusetts Ave NE; ⏲ 7am-midnight Mon-Fri, to 8pm Sat & Sun)

TOURIST INFORMATION

DC Visitors Center (☎ 202-328-4748; Ronald Reagan Bldg, 1300 Pennsylvania Ave NW; ⏲ 8:30am-5:30pm Mon-Fri, 9am-4pm Sat summer, shorter hrs rest of year) Hotel reservation line and a film which gives an excellent overview of DC.

International Visitors Information Desk (☎ 703-572-2536; ⏲ 9am-5pm Mon-Fri) Run by the Meridian International Center, staff at this desk (at the Arrivals Terminal at Washington-Dulles Airport) can answer questions in over 40 languages.

Washington Convention & Visitors Association (☎ 202-789-7000; www.washington.org; 901 7th St NW, 4th fl, Washington, DC, 20005; ⏲ 9am-5pm Mon-Fri)

These resources have information for travelers with disabilities:

General information (☎ 202-789-7000) On hotels, restaurants and attractions.

Metrorail (☎ 202-635-6434; www.wmata.com)

Smithsonian access (☎ 202-357-2700, TTY 202-357-1729)

Dangers & Annoyances

Although DC has bleak inner-city areas, the most violent crime occurs outside tourist areas, most notably in the southeast quadrant. Almost all major sights are in relatively safe areas, except for the Capitol Hill area, which has a higher concentration of panhandlers and drug dealers. The area southwest of Lincoln Park is especially sketchy.

Note that many attractions get very crowded; prepare for long waits in the sun or rain. Thorough security checks are the rule.

Sights

Capitol Hill, downtown and National Mall contain the biggies like the White House, Smithsonian museums and war memorials, and are within convenient walking distances from each other. The more refined Foggy Bottom and Dupont Circle areas are home to many big hotels and upscale eateries. Shaw and U Sts boast African American historic sights including Howard University, and Georgetown is the beginning of the Chesapeake and Ohio (C&O) Canal National Historic Park.

CAPITOL HILL

The Capitol, appropriately, sits atop Capitol Hill (what L'Enfant called 'a pedestal waiting for a monument') across a plaza from the equally regal Supreme Court and Library of Congress. Congressional office buildings surround the plaza. A pleasant residential district stretches from E Capitol St over to Lincoln Park, but beyond these areas the neighborhood declines. The principal Metro stations servicing this area are Union Station, Capitol South and Eastern Market.

Capitol

The cornerstone for the Capitol was laid by George Washington in 1793, and Congress moved in seven years later. Nearly destroyed in the 1814 British invasion, it was rebuilt within five years. The House (south) and Senate (north) wings were added in 1857, and the massive iron dome in 1863. A flag raised above either wing indicates that body is in session.

Construction is in progress on an immensely ambitious three-story underground visitor center, which will occupy the entire east side of the Capitol and should be complete by the fall of 2006. For now, visitors can only enter on a guided tour and must wait in an often very long line for free tickets at the temporary **Capitol Service Kiosk** (☎ 202-225-6827; cnr First St SW & Maryland Ave SW; ☒ ticket distribution begins 9am Mon-Sat, last tour at 3:30pm) on the southeast corner of this intersection. Getting in line by 8am helps your chances of getting a pass.

To watch Congress in action, call ☎ 202-225-6827 for session dates. US citizens can request visitor passes from their representatives or senators (call ☎ 202-224-3121 for their numbers); foreign visitors show passports at the House gallery. Committee hearings are open to the public; check the *Washington Post*'s 'Today in Congress' notice.

Library of Congress

The world's largest **library** (☎ 202-707-4604 for exhibitions; www.loc.gov; 101 Independence Ave SE; admission free; ☒ 10am-5:30pm Mon-Sat) fills three buildings with over 29 million books, 58 million manuscripts, and maps, photographs and sheet music. The Jefferson Building houses the visitor center (where free tours depart), an impressive Main Reading Room and an ornate Great Hall with vaulted ceiling.

Supreme Court

This imposing 1935 marble building (☎ 202-479-3211; 1 First St NE; admission free; ☒ 9am-4:30pm Mon-Fri) is home of the highest court in the land. Arrive early to watch arguments (Monday to Wednesday October to April) or bench sittings (Mondays mid-May to June). Year-round you can visit the permanent exhibits and the building's seven-spiral staircase.

US Botanic Garden

At the foot of the Capitol, this beautiful **conservatory** (☎ 202-225-8333; 245 First St; admission free; ☒ 10am-5pm) is filled with more than 26,000 plants, including rare orchids, medicinal plants and desert succulents.

Union Station & Around

Washington's most impressive gateway, **Union Station** (☎ 202-371-9441; 50 Massachusetts Ave) is a massive, beautifully restored 1908 beaux arts building; its great hall was modeled on the Roman baths of Diocletian. It hosts Amtrak, Metro and commuter rail stations, as well as shops, restaurants, cinemas and traveler resources.

These attractions are also recommended:
Folger Shakespeare Library (☎ 202-544-7077; 201 E Capitol St; admission free; ☒ 10am-4pm Mon-Sat) Houses the world's largest collection of Shakespeare materials.
National Postal Museum (☎ 202-633-5555; 2 Massachusetts Ave NE; admission free; ☒ 10am-5:30pm) A postal potluck including the planet's largest stamp collection, antique mail plane and touching war letters.

NATIONAL MALL

If the Smithsonian Institution is the nation's attic, the National Mall is the nation's front lawn. This 400ft-wide green expanse stretches from the Potomac River to Capitol Hill. A cross is drawn by connecting the White House, Lincoln Memorial, Jefferson Memorial and the Capitol, and the Mall forms its body.

The Mall is home to DC's most famous monuments and museums, but is also renowned for mass gatherings designed to influence public policy, from anti–Vietnam War protests in the 1960s and Martin Luther King Jr's 'I Have a Dream' speech to the more recent thousands-strong rallies for and against the legalization of gay marriage. But every day will see smaller-scale protests and vigils, from anti-foie-gras activists to pro-Zionists, all exercising their rights and agitating for change, while joggers, picnickers and frisbee-tossers go about their business.

Smithsonian Institution Museums

In 1826 Englishman James Smithson, without ever having visited the USA, willed $4.1 million to the country to found an 'establishment for the increase and diffusion of knowledge.' The Smithsonian Institution is now a world-class research center, with a collection so large that only 1% is on display at any one time. The buildings that house its dozen-odd museums and galleries are rapidly showing their age, however, and costly renovations are being implemented post haste. The institution predicts that it will take another decade for all its crumbling buildings to be brought into ship-shape. Some have suggested that the museums start charging a nominal sum to expedite the renovations, but the powers-that-be won't hear of it, arguing that paid admission would fly in the face of the Smithsonian's very mission. The museums will stay free if it kills them. And it just might. The **Smithsonian 'Castle'** (Smithsonian Institution Building; ☎ 202-357-2700; www.si.edu; 1000 Jefferson Dr SW; ☒ 10am-5pm), a turreted red-brick building on the south side of the Mall, is now the visitor center for all the museums. For each, be prepared for lines and bag-checking. (Not every Smithsonian museum is included below.) The following are free and open every day but Christmas from 10am to 5:30pm. Some have extended hours in summer.

The **National Museum of American History** (cnr 14th St & Constitution Ave SW) offers a true celebration of US culture; just a smattering of this museum's eclectic collection includes the original American flag, First Ladies' inauguration ball gowns, the original Oscar the Grouch from *Sesame Street*, Dorothy's ruby slippers from *The Wizard of Oz* and a Whites-only Woolworth's lunch counter.

Carve out a few hours at the **National Museum of Natural History** (cnr 10th St & Constitution Ave SW) for such highlights as the 45-carat Hope diamond, a life-size model of a blue whale, dinosaur skeletons, a live insect zoo and the world's largest collection of meteorites.

The hugely popular **National Air & Space Museum** (cnr 6th St & Independence Ave SW) holds full-size air- and spacecraft, from the Wright brothers' flyer and Charles Lindbergh's *Spirit of St Louis* to the *Apollo 11* command module. There's an IMAX theater, a planetarium and a ride simulator. All three bonus features are adult/child $8/6.50 each.

The doughnut-shaped building of the **Hirshhorn Museum & Sculpture Garden** (cnr 7th St & Independence Ave SW) houses a huge collection of modern sculpture, rotated regularly, including works by Rodin, Henry Moore and Ron Mueck, as well as paintings by O'Keeffe, Warhol, May Ray and de Kooning. The sculpture garden is open 7:30am to dusk.

The **National Museum of African Art** (950 Independence Ave SW) showcases masks, textiles and ceramics from the sub-Sahara, as well as ancient and contemporary art from all over the continent.

The **Arthur M Sackler Gallery** (1050 Independence Ave SW) and the connected **Freer Gallery of Art** (cnr Jefferson Dr & 12th St SW) together comprise the national museum of Asian art, and boast impressive collections, from Greece and Egypt all the way over to Japan. Slightly incongruously, the galleries also house over 1300 works by the great American painter James Whistler.

Bypass the commercialism of the first two floors of the **National Museum of the American Indian** (cnr 4th St & Independence Ave SW) and head straight to the 4th for the languages, literature, arts and history of this country's native peoples. The regionally specific menus at the Native Foods café are lessons in themselves, and delicious ones at that.

Closed indefinitely for extensive renovations (metal panels kept falling from the ceiling, among other symptoms), the **Arts & Industries Building** (900 Jefferson Dr SW) had been displaying Victorian-era inventions from the 1876 Philadelphia Centennial Exposition.

Other Museums & Attractions

Forming the top of the Mall cross and reaching 555ft (and 5in), the landmark **Washington Monument** (☎ 202-426-6841; ☒ 9am-4:45pm) is the tallest building in the district. Construction began in 1848 but wasn't completed until 37 years later; the two phases are evident in the slightly different colors of the stone. There's free admission to the top but **tickets** (kiosk, 15th St btwn Madison & Jefferson Sts SW; ☒ 8am-4:30pm) are required; order advance tickets from http://reservations.nps.gov for $1.50 each.

Designed by IM Pei, the **National Gallery of Art** (☎ 202-737-4215; www.nga.gov; Constitution Ave btwn 3rd & 4th Sts NW; admission free; ☒ 10am-5pm Mon-Sat, 11am-6pm Sun) consists of two buildings connected by an underground passage. The original, neoclassical west-wing exhibits primarily European art from the Middle Ages to the early 20th century, including works by Rembrandt, Vermeer, El Greco, Renoir, Monet and Cézanne, plus the continent's only da Vinci. The east wing features a four-story atrium with a Calder mobile, plus abstract and modern works.

The **US Holocaust Memorial Museum** (☎ 202-488-0400; www.ushmm.org; 100 Raoul Wallenberg Plaza/15th St SW; admission free; 10am-5pm) is a thorough, haunting memorial to WWII Holocaust victims, portraying the era of Nazi Germany in grim detail. The museum recommends that only those over 11 years view the main exhibit, and provides a separate children's exhibit (no ticket required) for kids over eight. Same-day tickets are distributed starting at 10am. Call ☎ 800-400-9373 for advance passes.

Take a tour of the **Bureau of Engraving & Printing** (☎ 202-874-2330; cnr 14th & C Sts SW; 9am-2pm Mon-Fri), aka the most glorified print shop in the world, where all the US paper currency is designed and $32 million of it rolls off the presses daily. Get in line early for free tickets from the **kiosk** (Raoul Wallenberg Plaza/15th St).

Often referred to simply as 'the Wall,' the **Vietnam Veterans Memorial** (☎ 202-462-6842; admission free; 24hr) features two black marble walls meeting in a V shape, on which are the names of more than 58,000 Americans who disappeared or were killed during the Vietnam War. Designed by 21-year-old student Maya Lin, it's now DC's most visited memorial. Names are inscribed chronologically from date of death. The touching memorabilia left by loved ones is stored in a separate warehouse.

Resembling a Greek temple, the **Lincoln Memorial** (☎ 202-426-6895; admission free; 24hr) is an imposing monument to the president who freed the slaves. Its 36 columns represent the 36 states in Lincoln's Union. Plan a nighttime visit for stunning views.

The **Korean War Veterans Memorial** (southwest of Lincoln Memorial; admission free 8am-11:45pm) commemorates the 1.5 million Americans who served in this little-understood war; the haunting troop of 19 steel soldiers bear expressions that speak volumes.

Wrought in bronze, granite and water, the **National WWII Memorial** (17th St btwn Constitution & Independence Aves; admission free; 24hr) is a grandiose gesture to the staggering 16 million Americans who served in WWII.

At last visit, DC's oldest art museum, **Corcoran Gallery** (☎ 202-639-1700; cnr 17th St & New York Ave NW; adult/child under 13 $8/free; 10am-5pm Wed-Sun, to 9pm Thu), had been going through trying times. Its futuristic Frank Gehry–designed wing was canceled, the director stepped down, and the grand art museum was considering shifting its focus to better lure in the visitors. In the meantime, the museum's still plowing ahead, fulfilling its mandate of 'encouraging American genius.' Two-for-one admission in July and August.

TIDAL BASIN

The scenic Tidal Basin, southwest of the Mall, is lined with cherry trees, a gift from the city of Tokyo in 1912; their spring blossoming marks the beginning of DC's peak tourism season, kicking off with the Cherry Blossom Festival (p315). **Paddleboat rentals** (2-person boat per hr $7) are available at the boathouse.

Designed to mimic Monticello (p359), the domed **Jefferson Memorial** (☎ 202-426-6822; admission free; 8am-11:45pm) was derided as the 'Jefferson muffin' when it was built next to the Basin. Inside, the walls are etched with lines from Jefferson's eloquent writings.

Although Franklin Delano Roosevelt asked that no memorial 'larger than his desk' be built in his honor, the **FDR Memorial** (admission free; 24hr) covers 7.5 acres and includes a water sculpture with stone-etched quotes and a seated statue of the 32nd president, faithful dog Fala at his side. FDR was the only president to be elected for four terms, and the memorial is as much a tribute to the era as to the man. (FDR's desk-sized memorial stands in front of the National Archives.)

DOWNTOWN

Downtown Washington began in what is now called Federal Triangle, but it has since spread north and east, encompassing the area east of the White House to Judiciary Sq at 4th St, and from the Mall north to K or M St. Hours of operation are 10am to 5:30pm daily for the attractions below unless otherwise noted.

Within the **National Archives** (☎ 202-501-5000; 700 Constitution Ave btwn 7th & 9th Sts NW; www.archives.gov; admission free; 10am-9pm in summer, to 5:30pm rest of year) are housed the country's most important (albeit barely legible) documents: the Declaration of Independence, the Constitution and the Bill of Rights, as well as one of four copies of the 1297 Magna Carta. The newly opened Public Vaults is a whizbang counterpoint to the solemnity of the Big Three – its extensive interactive exhibits on such topics as patents, genealogy and presidential baby videos make up a mere tasting menu of the Archives' holding.

At the **International Spy Museum** (☎ 202-393-7798; 800 F St NW; adult/child 6-11 $14/11; ✆ 10am-8pm in summer, to 6pm Nov-Mar) you get your chance to learn the secrets of the spies at one of DC's hottest attractions – high-tech gadgetry, notorious spy cases, secret methods and not-so-pleasant consequences of being an international person of mystery. Get there early, as long lines are standard, and allow a hefty chunk of time.

Devoted to the architectural arts, the under-appreciated **National Building Museum** (☎ 202-272-2448; www.nbm.org; 401 F St NW; donations accepted; ✆ 10am-5pm Mon-Sat, from 11am Sun) is appropriately housed in an architectural jewel: the 1887 Old Pension Building. Four stories of ornamented balconies flank the dramatic 316ft-wide atrium, and the gold-colored Corinthian columns rise 75ft high. The various permanent and rotating exhibits on different aspects of architecture are sequestered in rooms off the atrium. The outstanding gift shop will delight design aficionados.

At the **Science Museum of the National Academy of Sciences** (☎ 202-334-1201; 6th & E Sts; adult/child 5-18 $5/3; ✆ 10am-6pm Wed-Mon), unlock the secrets of DNA, see what global warming is doing to the planet and marvel at other phenomena of the universe.

The red-carpeted entrance and dignified Grand Salon of **Renwick Gallery** (☎ 202-357-2700; cnr 17th St & Pennsylvania Ave NW; admission free) is crammed with 19th-century paintings – a startling contrast to the wild, whimsical craftwork in the adjoining rooms. Worth a visit just for Wendell Castle's *Ghost Clock*.

The **Old Post Office Pavilion** (☎ 202-298-4224; 1100 Pennsylvania Ave NW; admission free; ✆ 9am-4:45pm Mon-Fri, shorter hrs weekends) is an 1899 Romanesque revival landmark that's now a food and shopping complex; the 400ft observation tower affords great downtown panoramas.

Reopening in July of 2006, the **National Portrait Gallery** (☎ 202-275-1500; cnr F St & 8th St NW; admission free) is a Smithsonian museum full of fascinating likenesses of famous folks from all walks of life, created by such artists as John Sargent and Norman Rockwell. It shares the

building with the Smithsonian's **American Art Museum** (☎ 202-275-1500; admission free).

Scheduled to reopen in spring 2007, **Newseum** (☎ 888-639-7386; www.newseum.org; 555 Pennsylvania Ave at 6th St NW; call for admission prices; ✆ 9am-5pm Mon-Fri) is an interactive news museum that will cover the whole juicy media gamut, from screaming headlines to political cartoons.

On April 14, 1865, John Wilkes Booth assassinated Abraham Lincoln in his box seat at **Ford's Theatre** (☎ 202-638-2941; 511 10 St). The theater still operates today, with its threadbare basement **Lincoln Museum** (admission free; ✆ 9am-5pm) devoted to the assassination. Across the street, **Peterson House** (admission free; ✆ 9am-5pm) is where Lincoln gave up the ghost the next morning.

WHITE HOUSE AREA

An expansive park called the **Ellipse** borders the Mall. On the Ellipse's east side is a power-broker block of Pennsylvania Ave, and Pershing Park, with an outdoor café in summer and fast-food vendors. Around Lafayette Sq, modern offices loom behind Victorian row houses and the presidential St John's Church.

White House

Every US president save Washington has lived at this most famous of American addresses, 1600 Pennsylvania Ave. Through the years it has undergone fire (Dolly Madison rescued the legendary Gilbert Stuart portrait of George Washington when the British attacked in 1814) and extensive expansions. Jacqueline Kennedy redecorated the place with her stylish touch, Franklin Roosevelt added a pool, Clinton a jogging track and George W Bush a T-ball field. Cars are no longer allowed to pass the White House on Pennsylvania Ave, and so the area is clear for posing school groups and round-the-clock peace activists.

A self-guided **tour** (☎ 202-456-7041; ✆ 10am-noon Tue-Sat) will lead you through the ground and 1st floors, but the 2nd and 3rd floors are off-limits to the public. However, these tours are only available to groups of 10 or more and need to be arranged months in advance. Americans must apply via one of their state's members of Congress, and non-Americans must apply through either the US consulate in their home country or their country's consulate in DC. If all that's too much work, you can get your fill of White House history and factoids at the **White House visitor center** (☎ 202-208-1631; www .whitehouse.gov; Chamber of Commerce Bldg, 1450 Pennsylvania Ave South NW; ⊗ 7:30am-4pm).

FOGGY BOTTOM

DC's west end district falls roughly between 17th St NW and Rock Creek Park, the Mall, and K or M St. Foggy Bottom got its name from the gasworks once sited here. George Washington University was built here in 1912, and the neighborhood is now a mix of workers, professionals and students.

The **John F Kennedy Center for the Performing Arts** (☎ 202-467-4600; www.kennedy-center.org; 2700 F St NW) is a 'living memorial,' with three theaters, a concert hall, opera house and movie theater. The waterfront center offers daily free performances (see p321) and festivals.

The posh riverfront **Watergate complex** (2650 Virginia Ave NW) encompasses apartments, boutiques, the deluxe Swissôtel Watergate, and the office towers that made 'Watergate' a byword for political scandal after it broke that President Nixon's 'plumbers' had bugged the headquarters of the 1972 Democratic National Committee. Nixon resigned in disgrace several months later.

DUPONT CIRCLE

Once a marshland, the Dupont Circle area became a fashionable residential district at the end of the 19th century and remains so today. Many mansions were later converted to elegant embassies along a stretch of Massachusetts Ave known as Embassy Row and nearby Sheridan Circle – now the center of Washington's diplomatic community. Scenic Dupont Circle itself – with its lovely fountain and wide girth comprising Washingtonians on the lounge – is at Connecticut and Massachusetts Aves, though the term generally refers to the entire neighborhood, cheek-to-jowl with restaurants, galleries, bookstores, cafés and clubs.

The **Phillips Collection** (☎ 202-387-2151; 1600 21st St NW; admission permanent collection Tue-Fri free, special exhibitions vary; ⊗ 10am-5pm Tue-Sat, to 8:30pm Thu summer, noon-5pm Sun) was the first modern-art museum in the country; its main draw is whatever their special exhibition happens to be at the moment. Always first-rate.

Rotating exhibits on worldwide expeditions are found at the **National Geographic Society's Explorers Hall** (☎ 202-857-7588; 1145 17 St NW; admission free; ⊗ 9am-5pm Mon-Sat, from 10am Sun).

Know your warp from your woof? Set in a quiet neighborhood, the oft-overlooked **Textile Museum** (☎ 202-667-0441; 2320 S St NW; requested donation $5; ⊗ 10am-5pm Mon-Sat, from 1pm Sun) is the country's only museum devoted to the textile arts. The hands-on activity gallery provides context to the rotating exhibits.

ADAMS MORGAN, SHAW & U STREET

The heart of ethnic Adams Morgan is 18th St between Florida Ave and Columbia Rd, and along Columbia Rd itself. Restaurants, bars and boutiques abound. Parking is difficult, and it's not readily accessible by Metro; the convenient bus 98 runs between the Adams Morgan and U St Metro stations (see p333).

To the east, Shaw is a largely African American neighborhood that stretches from around Thomas Circle to Meridian Hill Park and from N Capitol St to 15th St NW, and is best known for its tremendous African American history and Ethiopian restaurants. Back in the 1930s, **Lincoln Theatre** (☎ 202-328-6000; 1215 U St NW) was a high point on the 'chitlin' circuit' of African American entertainment, hosting such celebrities as DC native Duke Ellington. Riots following the 1968 assassination of Martin Luther King Jr devastated the commercial district. Shaw's recent renaissance has followed the reopening of the historic theater, and new cafés, shops and clubs have popped up along U St around 14th St alongside neighborhood institutions.

GEORGETOWN

Predating the capital, Georgetown was the Native American settlement of Tohoga when British fur trader Henry Fleet arrived in 1632. In 1789 Georgetown University was founded, and it continues to dominate the well-heeled district today. Many 18th-century buildings have been converted to fashionable restaurants, clubs and boutiques, surrounded by cobblestoned residential districts. The nearest Metro station, Foggy Bottom, is almost a mile away – a pleasant walk in good weather and preferable to Georgetown's parking nightmare. A connector bus runs between the Foggy Bottom and Dupont Circle Metro stations (see p333).

Get a historical overview from the **visitor center** (☎ 202-653-5190; 1057 Thomas Jefferson St NW; ☽ 8:30am-5pm Wed-Sun Apr-Nov). Costumed guides lead visitors on a trip through time on hour-long mule-driven barge trip along the **C&O Canal towpath** (adult/child $8/5).

The museum featuring exquisite Byzantine and pre-Columbian art housed within the historic mansion at **Dumbarton Oaks** (☎ 202-339-6401; R & 31st Sts NW) is closed for renovation until the fall of 2007, but the 10 acres of outstanding formal **gardens** (adult/child Apr-Oct $7/5, Nov-Mar free; ☽ 2-6pm Tue-Sun), replete with myriad water features, remains open.

The USA's oldest Roman Catholic college, **Georgetown University** (☎ 202-687-5055; 37th & O Sts) sits atop a hill overlooking the Potomac and retains many stately historic buildings. Bill Clinton is among the university's distinguished alumni.

The **Potomac Heritage National Scenic Trail** connects Chesapeake Bay to the Allegheny Highlands in a 700-mile corridor. It includes the C&O Canal towpath, the 17-mile Mt Vernon Trail (Virginia), and the 75-mile Laurel Highlands Trail (Pennsylvania). See right for bike-rental information.

UPPER NORTHWEST

Step into the massive, high-Gothic **Washington National Cathedral** (☎ 202-537-6200; www.cathedral.org; Massachusetts & Wisconsin Aves; admission free; ☽ 10am-5:30pm Mon-Sat, 8am-6:30pm Sun) and you feel like you've been transported to the heart of Europe, minus the pickpockets. It's Episcopal, but officially serves as the 'national house of prayer for all people,' and is a common venue for First Family weddings and the like. The stained glass is luscious, the view from the tower splendid and a stroll through Bishop's Garden tranquil. A variety of tours are offered – the gargoyle one is recommended. Fees vary.

Rock Creek Park starts at the Potomac River, extends north through DC along the narrow corridor of Rock Creek, then expands to wide parkland in the Upper Northwest district. It boasts terrific biking and hiking. See right.

ANACOSTIA

The down-on-its-luck, brick rowhouse-lined neighborhood of Anacostia, over the Anacostia River southeast of Capitol Hill, has a well-earned reputation for crime.

However, ambitious plans for revitalization along the waterfront – with the Nationals stadium (p321) to be the featured attraction – will, for better or worse, usher in a degree of gentrification. For now, catch a cab from Anacostia Metro to take in the area's handful of worthwhile attractions.

Commanding a spectacular view, the **Frederick Douglass National Historic Site** (☎ 202-426-5960; 1411 W St SE; admission free; ☽ 9am-4pm) refers to Cedar Hill, home of the former slave turned abolitionist. He was full of wise aphorisms like 'mankind differ as the waves, but are one as the sea.'

It's a bit surprising that the **Anacostia Museum & Center for African American History & Culture** (☎ 202-287-3307; 1901 Fort Pl SE; ☽ 10am-5pm) is part of the Smithsonian, with its inconvenient location and slightly shabby appearance. But the rotating exhibits offer insightful looks at the work of an under-represented group of artists. Call ahead, as the museum closes for about a month between installations.

Activities

Under the auspices of the NPS, Rock Creek Park's 1755 acres follow Rock Creek as it winds its way through the northwest of the city. It's got miles of trails for biking, hiking and horseback riding, and you may even spot a coyote. The C&O Canal offers biking and hiking trails in canal-side parks and the lovely 11-mile **Capital Crescent Trail** (www.cctrail.org) connects Georgetown north to Silver Spring, Maryland, via some splendid Potomac River views. **Thompson Boat Center** (☎ 202-333-9543; cnr Virginia Ave & Rock Creek Parkway NW) at the Potomac River end of Rock Creek Park rents canoes (per hr $8), tandem kayaks (per hr $10) and bikes (per day $25), while **Big Wheel Bikes** (☎ 202-337-0254; 1034 33rd St; per hr/day $7/35; ☽ 11am-7pm Tue-Fri, 10am-6pm Sat & Sun) is also a good bike-rental outfitter.

DC for Children

Outdoor parks and fascinating museums around the city will entertain and educate children of all ages. But if you – or they – tire of indoor attractions, there are plenty of playgrounds like the **Guy Mason Playground** (3600 Calvert St NW) off Wisconsin Ave.

Many hotels offer babysitting services, but here are a few independent agencies: **Bring Along the Children** (☎ 202-484-0889) Offers day and evening babysitting services and kid-oriented tours.

Mothers' Aides (☎ 703-250-0700, 800-526-2669; www.mothersaides.com)

THE MALL
The wide-open squares of grass that make up the Mall are perfect places for outdoor family fun, whether you want to throw a Frisbee, have a picnic, ride the world's oldest **carousel** (tickets $2) or stroll through the museums that line it.

The **National Museum of Natural History** (p310) is the most entertaining for children, where they come face-to-face with triceratops dinosaurs, and handle creepy-crawlies in the Insect Zoo. They can get their hands wet in hands-on science and history rooms at the **Museum of American History** (p310) where they perform experiments in controlled lab settings and send messages via historic methods. At the **National Air & Space Museum** (p310), kids can happily view moon rocks, watch IMAX films and take a wild simulation ride.

The **Discovery Theater** (☎ 202-357-1500; www.discoverytheater.org; 1010 Jefferson Dr; tickets $5; ☼ performances 10am & 11:30am Jan-Jul) in the basement of the Ripley Center stages magical theatrical performances for children.

The **National Theatre** (☎ 202-628-6161; cnr 13th St & E St NW; ☼ performances 9:30am & 11am Sep-Apr), at Freedom Plaza, offers free Saturday morning performances from puppet shows to tap dancers (reservations required).

The **National Children's Museum** (☎ 202-675-4120; L'Enfant Plaza, cnr D St & 9th St SW; adult/child under 3 $7/free; ☼ 10am-5pm) will reopen its expanded doors in June 2008.

OFF THE MALL
The **National Zoological Park** (☎ 202-357-2700; 3000 Connecticut Ave NW; admission free; ☼ 6am-8pm Apr 6-Oct 25, to 6pm Oct 26-Apr 5) is home to some 2000 species in natural habitats. Resident celebrities include the giant pandas Mei Xiang, Tian Tian and their as-yet-unnamed son, who was born to great fanfare in July of 2005. Better catch a glimpse of him soon, as he's been promised back to China after his second birthday.

Through the **Saturday Medieval Workshop** (☎ 202-537-2934) at the Washington National Cathedral (opposite), kids and their parents can try their hand at making gargoyles, stained glass and limestone carvings.

Located about 10 miles east of downtown in Largo, MD, **Six Flags America** (☎ 301-249-1500; adult/child over 3 $40/29; ☼ May-Oct) offers the full array of spiraling roller coasters and tamer kiddie rides.

Quirky Washington, DC
Father Karras tumbled to his cinematic death down the staircase nowadays referred to as the **Exorcist Steps** (3600 Prospect St, Georgetown).

Those of timid stock better stick to the amputation kits and the bullet that killed Lincoln on display at the **National Museum of Health & Medicine** (☎ 202-782-2200; 6900 Georgia Ave & Elder St NW; admission free; ☼ 10am-5:30pm). The rest of us will be staring in horrified fascination at jars of elephantitis-stricken legs, conjoined twins and megacolons.

The **Awakening** in Hains Point is a spectacular statue of a man climbing out of the ground. His giant head, arm, knee and foot have delighted visitors for years. The area is splendid for picnics and for watching planes from National Airport zoom overhead.

In Anacostia, the **world's largest chair** towers over Martin Luther King Dr at V St; 19ft of pure mahogany.

The **Albert Einstein monument** (cnr Constitution Ave & 21st St NW) on the lawn of the National Academy of Sciences is a little-known statue of the frumpy physicist. His lap just begs to be climbed onto.

Tours
Bike the Sites (☎ 202-966-8662; www.bikethesites.com; adult/child under 13 $40/30; ☼ Mar-Nov) Offers lots of themed tours. The three-hour 'Capital sites' tour is a favorite with families.

Scandal Tours (☎ 202-783-7212, 800-758-8687; www.gnpcomedy.com/ScandalTours.html; tickets $27; ☼ 1pm Sat Apr-Sep) Run by the cleverly named comedy troupe Gross National Product, it dishes all the gossip about DC's infamous spots, covering George Washington to George Dubya.

Tourmobile Sightseeing (☎ 202-554-5100, 888-868-7707; www.tourmobile.com) An open-air trolley runs daily between the major sights. Tons of theme tours are offered, including the spectacular 'Washington by Night' (adult/child $20/10).

Festivals & Events
Independence Day Not surprisingly a big deal here, celebrated on July 4 with parades, concerts and fireworks.

National Cherry Blossom Festival (☎ 202-547-1500; www.nationalcherryblossomfestival.org) Held late March to early April and featuring Japanese culture parades.

WASHINGTON, DC & THE CAPITAL REGION

Smithsonian's Folklife Festival (☎ 202-357-2700; www.folklife.si.edu) This fun family event, held over two weekends in June and July, features distinctive regional folk art, crafts, food and music.

Sleeping

DC's a business town, so rates can drop as much as 50% on weekends. Tourist season is April to September. Checking a hotel's website for special deals can often bring a top-end option into reach.

Washington DC Accommodations (☎ 800-554-2220; www.wdcahotels.com) provides assistance with lodging. For B&Bs citywide, contact **Bed & Breakfast Accommodations** (☎ 877-893-3233; www.bedandbreakfastdc.com).

BUDGET

HI Washington DC (☎ 202-737-2333; www.hiwashing tondc.org; 1009 11th St NW at K St; dm incl breakfast members/nonmembers $20/29; ☸ 24hr; ☒ ▣) This 270-bed hostel is a budget hotspot with amenities like big-screen TV, coin laundry and luggage storage. Reservations and photo ID are required.

Washington International Student Center (☎ 202-667-7681; www.washingtondchostel.com; 2451 18th St NW; dm/r incl breakfast $23/55; ☒ ▣) In the heart of Adams Morgan, this cluttered, friendly hostel has a few private rooms, a TV and free pickup from the train or bus station.

MIDRANGE

Kalorama Guest House (☎ 202-667-6369; 1854 Mintwood Pl NW; s $50-95, d $55-100, ste $100-140; ☒) This charming place is an oasis in a sea of overpriced lodging. Visitors are welcomed with sherry and ginger cookies before retiring to simple rooms with period furniture. You'll also find a community refrigerator, sunroom and free local calls. All prices include breakfast.

Hotel Rouge (☎ 202-232-8000; www.rougehotel.com; 1315 16th St NW; r from $129; ▣ ▣) Done up in hip red decor, Rouge has plenty of stylish boutique guestrooms, plus several specialty rooms if you're in the mood to 'Chow' (stainless steel kitchenette), 'Chat' (flat-screen TV and computer with Internet access) or 'Chill' (PlayStation2 and game library). An array of crimson perks like the complimentary Bloody Mary bar, cold pizza and evening wine round out the pampering. Parking costs $26.

Hotel Harrington (☎ 202-628-8140; www.hotel -harrington.com; 436 11th St NW at E St; r $99-155; ▣) Smack in the city center, this modest, family-owned hotel with comfortable rooms boasts neighbors like the Smithsonian museums and the White House, and makes a great base for exploring. Ask for a corner room for the best light. You can park here for $10.

Hotel Helix (☎ 800-706-1202, 202-462-9001; www .hotelhelix.com; 1430 Rhode Island Ave NW; r from $149; ▣) This trendy, 70s-style pop-art explosion is full of quirky touches, like TVs that swivel so you can watch from your platform bed or your minibar stocked with Pop Rocks candy. Bunk bed rooms are perfect for families. An à la carte continental breakfast is available, though it'll cost you, as will parking ($31).

Morrison-Clark Inn (☎ 202-898-1200; www.morris onclark.com; 1015 L St NW; s $155-285, d $175-325; ▣) The only hotel in town on the Register of Historic Places and just steps from Mt Vernon Sq, this elegant, newly wi-fied inn has spacious rooms ranging from Victorian to neoclassical. Some come decked out with private balconies and marble fireplaces. Parking costs $22.

TOP END

Hotel Monaco (☎ 202-628-7177, 800-649-1202; www.mon aco-dc.com; 700 F St NW; r from $239; ▣) The city's first all-marble building is now home to this hotel, which flawlessly merges modern elements with the historic framework. The luxurious rooms come with Italian coffee, plush bathrobes and, upon request, a resident goldfish. Parking is available for $27.

Hotel Washington (☎ 202-638-5900, 800-424-9540; www.hotelwashington.com; 15th St & Pennsylvania Ave; r from $275; ▣) The city's oldest continuously operating hotel is just around the corner from the White House, and rooms have tasteful period decor including marble baths, as well as modern touches like web TV. Its rooftop terrace restaurant (mains $9 to $16) is one of the best spots in town for dining with a view. Parking costs $28.

George Washington University Inn (☎ 202-337-6620, 800-426-4455; www.gwuinn.com; 824 New Hampshire Ave NW; weekend/weekday r incl breakfast from $199/269; ▣) Close to Foggy Bottom Metro, this all-suite hotel stands out for its tasteful designs and proximity to the cultural district. It's a good choice for families – all suites have a microwave and refrigerator, and full kitchenette suites are available too – and workout nuts (free access to Bally Fitness). You can park here for $22.

Eating

It's no surprise that in a city with representatives from every nation on the planet, around every corner is a different slice of the world waiting to be discovered. Besides remaining a bastion of Southern soul food, U St encompasses an area called Little Ethiopia with appropriately amazing Ethiopian restaurants. Adams Morgan holds its own in that category as well, plus vibrant Latin American flavors. Chinatown slaps out inexpensive dishes from the homeland.

CAPITOL HILL

Eastern Market (225 7th St SE; 10am-6pm Tue-Fri, from 8am Sat, 8am-4pm Sun) This is a must for market eats with a smorgasbord of stalls from cheese and produce to fish, flowers and handmade pasta.

Meyhanà (☎ 202-544-4753; 633 Pennsylvania Ave SE; tapas $4-8, mains $12-17; dinner Mon-Fri, lunch & dinner Sat & Sun) You can feel the love at this family venture, which serves authentic Turkish and Mediterranean dishes. Wine is half-price on weekdays from 5pm to 7pm, and if you come on Friday or Saturday night you'll find some bellydancing ballyhoo.

Bullfeathers (☎ 202-543-5005; 410 1st St SE; mains $7-10; from 11:30am) Sidle up to the long wooden bar at this Capitol Hill hangout named after Teddy Roosevelt's favorite ladies-present expletive. The Hillies love happy hour here, especially on Mondays when burgers are half-price. Hearty salads and sandwiches prep you for sampling the 12 draft beers. Don't expect doting service.

B Smith's (☎ 202-289-6188; 50 Massachusetts Ave NE; dinner mains $17-30; from 11:30am) Former model Barbara Smith transformed the space that used to be Union Station's Presidential waiting room into a captivating Cajun and Creole eatery. Try the Swamp Thing: mixed seafood with mustard sauce and greens.

WHITE HOUSE AREA & DOWNTOWN

Nirvana (☎ 202-223-5043; 1810 K St NW; mains $8-14; from 11:30am Mon-Sat) The Shah family maintains an all-veggie, all-the-time menu at their elegant Indian restaurant. Start your meal with some *khandvi*. The buffet is a bargain.

Zaytinya (☎ 202-638-0800; 701 9th St NW; mezzes $5-10; lunch & dinner) Greek, Lebanese and Turkish meze (similar to tapas) share equal billing against a sleek, spacious white, brown and Hellenic blue backdrop. Try the *bantijan bil laban* (fried eggplant drizzled with garlic-yogurt sauce). No reservations accepted for dinner.

Zola (☎ 202-654-0999; 800 F St NW; lunch mains $10-23, dinner mains $16-25; lunch Mon-Fri, dinner daily) A playful espionage theme is carried through into the International Spy Museum's upscale restaurant, with peepholes into the kitchen and Russian documents on the walls. The name refers to the writer Emile Zola, who championed the case of accused spy Alfred Dreyfus. The lobster mac-and-cheese is worth killing for.

Full Kee (☎ 202-371-2233; 509 H St NW; mains from $7; from 11am) Look past the dingy exterior to this excellent Chinese restaurant. Expect a lengthy menu that includes savory roast pork and their delectable shrimp dumpling soup – but not service with a smile. No alcohol or credit cards.

Capital Q BBQ (☎ 202-347-8396; 707 H St NW; mains $6-16; from 11am Mon-Sat) Head to Chinatown for the best Texas-style BBQ in DC, and possibly a chance to give some of the town's bigwig Texas Republicans a piece of your mind as you all plow through heaping portions of smoked meat with plenty o' slaw on the side.

DUPONT CIRCLE

Connecticut Ave on either side of Dupont Circle is the upscale restaurant district.

Restaurant Nora (☎ 202-462-5143; www.noras .com; 2132 Florida Ave NW; mains $24-30; dinner Mon-Sat) Under the flawless eye of chef Nora Pouillon, America's first certified organic restaurant specializes in top-notch New American cuisine. The Amish quilts on the walls reflect Nora's knack for combining quality with folksy comfort. Try the tasting menu ($66) for a delicious sampling.

Afterwords (☎ 202-387-1400; 1517 Connecticut Ave NW; mains $12-16; 7:30am-1am, 24hr Fri & Sat) Not your average bookstore café, this spot attached to Kramerbooks will stimulate your palate as much as the novel you just bought stimulates your mind. The offering is huge, and each main lists a wine suggestion.

Pesce's (☎ 202-466-3474; 2016 P St NW; mains $10-19; lunch Mon-Fri, dinner daily) Gaudily painted fish festoon this small, friendly bistro, where some of the freshest seafood in town – and superb *brandade* – is served up on its plastic tablecloths.

Sushi Taro (☎ 202-462-8999; 1503 17th St NW; mains $13-20; ◷ lunch & dinner Mon-Sat) The drab exterior is an unfortunate entrance to an excellent sushi bar with traditional rolls, steaming soups and an arsenal of tempura and teriyaki dishes. The $13 per-person minimum isn't hard to hit. Come at lunch for less wait and more sunlight-enhanced ambience.

ADAMS MORGAN, SHAW & U STREET

It's an international smorgasbord along 18th St NW and Columbia Rd NW, with particularly outstanding Ethiopian and Latin options. Meanwhile in the energetic U St district in Shaw, soul-food landmarks can be found right next to avant-garde cafés.

Pasta Mia (☎ 202-328-9114; 1790 Columbia Rd NW; mains $10-13; ◷ from 6:30pm Mon-Sat) Even cold weather doesn't deter the faithful from lining up for their turn at affordable, monstrously portioned Italian on checkered tablecloths. One favorite is the *tortellini rosa*. No reservations or line-jumping bribes accepted.

Dukem (☎ 202-668-8735; 1114-1118 U St NW; mains $8-13; ◷ from 11am) Hailed as one of the best Ethiopian spots in a town packed with them, this classy eatery seems to double as an Ethiopian community center. Live music and dancing take over the small stage Thursday through Monday.

Cashion's Eat Place (☎ 202-797-1819; 1819 Columbia Rd NW; mains $19-32; ◷ dinner Tue-Sun; Ⓟ) Restaurateur and chef Ann Cashion has become somewhat of a local legend for her idiosyncratic, elegant American bistro with a menu that changes daily. Worth the splurge.

Ben's Chili Bowl (☎ 202-667-0909; 1213 U St NW; mains $4-8; ◷ 6am-2am Mon-Thu, to 4am Fri & Sat, noon-8pm Sun) Right next to Lincoln Theater, Ben's is a cultural institution as much for the welcoming atmosphere as for its finger-lickin' food. The turkey burger earns high, juicy marks. The eponymous chili bowl (veggie or meat) runs $4.35.

Reef (☎ 202-518-3800; 2446 18th St; mains $10-16; ◷ from 4pm) If the name hasn't tipped you off, the giant fish tanks will – seafood is the star of the slim, organic menu. Many folks come (or stay) to drink, either to zone out in front of the tanks or revel at the rooftop bar.

Meskerem (☎ 202-462-4100; 2434 18th St NW; mains $9-15; ◷ from noon) A favorite for Ethiopian fare, with three floors of African-themed rooms and great open spaces to bring a group of friends.

Coppi's Organic (☎ 202-319-7773; 1414 U St NW; mains $12-24; ◷ dinner) One of the pioneers of the rebirth of U St, this boisterous, bicycle-themed spot serves wood-fired pizza and calzones. Mercifully, half-portions are available. Brace yourself for a wait.

Mezà (☎ 202-797-0017; 2437 18th St NW; mezzes $4-9; ◷ 5:30pm-midnight Mon-Thu, to 3am Fri & Sat, 10am-4pm Sun) A narrow Turkish restaurant with fabulous tapas-style dishes. The intimate upstairs weekend lounge is a great spot to chill out after a Turkish baklava. Pick up a bellydancing lesson on Sundays.

Florida Avenue Grill (☎ 202-265-1586; 1100 Florida Ave NW; mains $4-7; ◷ 6am-9pm Tue-Sun) Despite the cramped quarters and unconnoisseur-like treatment of Southern standards like fried catfish and collard greens, the Grill's been raking 'em in since 1944 and has the celebrity photos to prove it.

GEORGETOWN

Despite some wonderful choices lining this area's clogged arteries, M St and Wisconsin Ave NW, crowds and traffic make it an overrated restaurant district.

J Paul's (☎ 202-333-3450; 3128 M St NW; mains $10-20; ◷ from 11:30am) Sit at the 100-year-old 'shotgun bar,' suck down some oysters and watch Georgetown's beautiful people sashay by, or come for a dinner of juicy burgers washed down with J Paul's Amber Ale.

Vietnam Georgetown (☎ 202-337-5588; 2934 M St NW; mains $8-15; ◷ from 11am) Authentic fare, speedy service and white tablecloths. What could be better? How about $8 lunch specials and a backyard patio?

Cafe Milano (☎ 202-333-6183; 3251 Prospect St NW; mains $17-26; ◷ from 11:30am) Slip on your best see-and-be-seen duds before snagging a sidewalk table at this Italian bistro, with homemade ravioli that melts on the tongue and more delicious ways to prepare mushrooms than you can imagine.

Drinking

There's shortage of great watering holes in this town. The greatest concentration is in Adams Morgan; walk down 18th St NW between Florida Ave and Columbia Rd.

Another good area is along M St in Georgetown between 29th and 33rd Sts NW. All venues are cover-free unless noted.

CAPITOL HILL & DOWNTOWN

Hawk & Dove (☎ 202-543-3300; 329 Pennsylvania Ave SE; ☯ from 10am) A hotspot for political junkies with free-food happy hours and intimate corner booths perfect for chilling over martinis and creating the next District scandal.

Flying Scotsman (☎ 202-783-3848; 233 2nd St NW; ☯ from 11am) You'll be famished by the time you find this place and squeeze through the crowd to the bar, so order up some fish-and-chips with your drink and sit back to enjoy the spectacle of Hill rats carousing away the cares of the day.

DA's RFD (☎ 202-289-2030; 810 7th St NW; ☯ from 11am) That second acronym stands for Regional Food and Drink, and this behemoth boasts the city's largest selection of beers on tap, and is second only to the Brickskeller (below) for bottles. These guys take their suds seriously, even suggesting beer and food pairings.

ME Swing Co Coffee Roasters (☎ 202-628-7601; 1702 G St NW; ☯ 7am-6pm Mon-Fri) One of the best cuppas in town, Swing's has been slinging quality arabica since 1916 (though not always at this location).

Lounge 201 (☎ 202-544-5201; 201 Massachusetts Ave NE; ☯ Tue-Sat) Lounge lizards lurk at this upscale bar whose motto is 'to drink is human, to lounge divine.' Red pool tables and plush leather chairs transport sharply dressed martini-sippers to 1950s retroland.

DUPONT CIRCLE

Brickskeller (☎ 202-293-1885; 523 22nd St NW; ☯ from 11:30am Mon-Fri, from 6pm Sat & Sun) With a drink menu as thick as the Bible and an entry in the *Guinness Book of World Records*, the Brick is heaven for beer worshippers, and the best place to grab a brew in DC if you can choose from more than a thousand around-the-world varieties.

ADAMS MORGAN, SHAW & U STREET

Café Saint-Ex (☎ 202-265-7839; 1847 14th St NW; ☯ from 5pm Mon-Fri, from 11am Sat & Sun) Nurse a pint of Three Philosophers Belgian-style ale at one of the sidewalk tables or inside, where photographs of pilot and *The Little Prince* author Antoine de Saint-Exupery smile down at you. Downstairs, the intimate Gate 54 is frequently the scene of live jazz and its funky derivatives. Weeknights emit a more authentic vibe.

Tryst (☎ 202-232-5500; 2459 18th St; ☯ 6:30am-2am Mon-Thu, to 3am Fri & Sat, 8am-12:30am Sun) The hodgepodge of tables and cozy sofas at this Greenwich Village–style coffeehouse/bar harbors patrons so faithful they should probably pay rent. There's wi-fi, but surfing's a no-no on weekend nights – you should be striking up a conversation with that cute stranger next to you anyway.

Chi-Cha Lounge (☎ 202-234-8400; 1624 U St NW; ☯ from 5:30pm) Slip through the double-sided mirror door, settle into a low settee and order up an *arguileh* (hookah) full of fruit-flavored tobacco (don't inhale). In the midst of this Middle Eastern atmosphere, the trendy clientele is nibbling Ecuadorian tapas and sipping (weak) Peruvian drinks.

Café Toulouse (☎ 202-332-2550; 2431 18th St NW; ☯ from 6pm) Situated under a huge mural of Aristide Bruant, this café promises French atmosphere sans attitude. A great place to actually hear conversations and listen to cool jazz. Snuggle at a table on the intimate balcony.

Blue Room Lounge (☎ 202-332-0800; 2321 18th St NW; cover usually $10; ☯ from 7pm Tue-Sat) Blue is the word at this two-level bar and nightclub, with the 2nd floor mixing trippy candles and chill attitude. Thursday is 'Uncle Q's Living Room,' a no-cover, no-attitude house party of the funnest order.

Common Share (☎ 202-588-7180; 2003 18th St at U St NW; ☯ from 5:30pm) It's more like the common buzz, with everyone from bike messengers to still-with-it Hillies availing themselves of the $2 drinks (some drinks more on certain nights). Upstairs is slightly more mellow, with a pool table and jukebox.

Perry's (☎ 202-234-6218; 1811 Columbia Rd NW; ☯ from 6pm) The sprawling rooftop deck is tops for views of the city, and Sunday brunches accompanied by singing drag queens are a sight to behold.

GEORGETOWN

Tombs (☎ 202-337-6668; 1226 36 St at P St NW; ☯ from 11:30am, from 9:30am Sun) If it looks familiar, think back to the '80s; this was the setting for *St Elmo's Fire*. Today this cozy, windowless bar is a favorite with Georgetown students and profs. Try their famous

Brownie (a dense brownie topped with ice cream, whipped cream, nuts and chocolate sauce) if you dare.

Georgetown Bar & Billiards (☎ 202-965-7665; 3251 Prospect St NW; per person per hr $8-10; ⏰ from 6pm) With well-worn couches and over-stuffed armchairs backing up to the dimly lit billiards tables, this is like stepping into your best friend's finished basement. It's in the courtyard behind Cafe Milano.

Mr Smith's (☎ 202-333-3104; 1218 Wisconsin Ave NW; ⏰ from 11am) This dark, casual hangout has great specials (like all-you-can-eat fish-and-chips on Monday nights) and a lush back patio that hops all year long.

Entertainment

The *Washington Post*'s 'Weekend' section and the free weekly *Washington City Paper* are useful for planning your time out.

GAY & LESBIAN DC

Home to more than 30 national gay and lesbian organizations and more than 300 social, athletic, religious and political support groups, DC is one of the most gay-friendly cities in the USA. The community is most visible in the Dupont Circle and Capitol Hill neighborhoods, where there are many gay-owned and gay-friendly businesses. Washington is often the scene of huge gay rights marches, and gay pride is an integral part of DC's character.

Dupont Circle is by far the city's most gay-friendly neighborhood, offering the bulk of the city's nightlife options, clustered on 17th NW between P and R Sts NW and along P St west of the circle. The club and bar scene on Pennsylvania Ave SE and around Capitol Hill is easily reached by the Eastern Market Metro station. In Dupont Circle, **Lambda Rising** (☎ 202-462-6969; www.lambdarising.com; 1625 Connecticut Ave NW; ⏰ 10am-10pm, to midnight Fri & Sat) is the landmark gay and lesbian bookstore.

The city's only exclusively lesbian club is **Phase 1** (☎ 202-544-6831; 525 8th St SE; cover free-$5; ⏰ from 7pm Thu-Sun), with a pool table, a postage-stamp of a dance floor, and a nice racial mix. Nearby, the dance club **Bachelors Mill** (☎ 202-544-1931; 1106 8th St SE; ⏰ from 7pm) caters to gay and lesbian African Americans with house music and techno. Fridays is disco, baby. In Dupont Circle, strike poses with your cocktail at smoke-free and mostly male **Halo** (☎ 202-797-9730; 1435 P St NW; ⏰ from 5pm), with its flattering lighting and comfy ottomans. The thumping house music at **Club Chaos** (☎ 202-232-4141; 1603 17th St at Q St NW; ⏰ from 6pm) draws gays and straights alike to its dance floor. Wednesday is ladies' night. Conveniently located nearby is **Annie's Paramount Steak House** (☎ 202-232-0395; 1609 17th St NW; mains $8-13; ⏰ breakfast, lunch & dinner, round-the-clock 10am Fri-1am Mon), which is *the* place to be seen for pre- or post-club noshing. Near Mt Vernon Sq, **DC Eagle** (☎ 202-347-6025; www.dceagle.com; 639 New York Ave NW; ⏰ 4pm-2am Mon-Fri, noon-3am Sat & Sun) is mostly a leather-and-Levi's crowd, though the occasional dyke nights are killer. Join the crush of beer-swilling prepsters at S&M (Stand & Model) bar **JR's** (☎ 202-328-0090; 1519 17th St NW; ⏰ from 4pm, from 2pm Fri & Sat). Pull on those cowboy boots and head to **Remington's** (☎ 202-543-3113; 639 Pennsylvania Ave SE; ⏰ from 5pm) for some country-and-western hootenanny – complete with line and couples' dancing.

Information

AIDS hotline (☎ 800-342-2437)

Gay and Lesbian Activists Alliance (GLAA; www.glaa.org)

Gay and Lesbian Hotline (☎ 202-833-3234) Call to report gay-bashing or for assistance with any other urgent situation.

Gay WDC (www.gaywdc.com) One-stop shopping for bars, clubs and resources.

Metro Weekly (www.metroweekly.com) Free weekly gay and lesbian magazine available in print and online.

Washington Blade (www.washblade.com) Gay and lesbian weekly paper covering local politics, information about community resources, and nightlife and meeting-place listings.

Women in the Life (www.womeninthelife.com) Sponsors events and parties for lesbians of color.

Women's Monthly (WOMO; www.womo.com) Monthly lesbian magazine in print and online with a great calendar section.

Conveniently located at the Old Post Office Pavilion, **Ticketplace** (☎ 202-842-5387; 1100 Pennsylvania Ave NW; ☾ Tue-Sat) sells same-day concert and show tickets at half-price.

LIVE MUSIC
As the birthplace of Duke Ellington, DC excels in jazz and blues, and many bars will rock out with live music on weekends. See the *Washington City Paper* (p307) for comprehensive listings.

Saloun (☎ 202-338-4900; 3239 M St NW; cover weekday/weekend $3/5; ☾ from 5pm) The jazz and blues emanating from the small stage at this smoky Georgetown bar will draw you in.

Chief Ike's Mambo Room (☎ 202-332-2211; 1725 Columbia Rd NW; cover free-$5; ☾ from 4pm) This jungle-themed, all-kinds-welcome Adams Morgan venue maintains a globe-spinning medley of shows, from mambo Mondays to hip-hop Thursdays.

Blues Alley (☎ 202-337-4141; 1073 Wisconsin Ave; tickets $15-50; ☾ from 8pm; ✗) This classy, smoke-free Georgetown jazz supper club attracts national artists, but tickets can be steep. Entrance is through the alley just south of the intersection of Wisconsin and M.

9:30 Club (☎ 202-393-0930; www.930.com; 815 V St NW; tickets $15-40) This spacious dive, featuring two floors and a midsize stage, is the best place in town to see bands like Wilco, the Pixies or Jack Johnson.

DC 9 (☎ 202-483-5000; 1940 9th St NW; cover free-$8; ☾ from 8pm) It costs nothing to lounge and sip downstairs, but you'll have to ante up for the live rock and DJs on the 2nd floor.

Velvet Nation (☎ 202-554-1500; 1015 Half St SE; cover $8-15; ☾ Fri & Sat) Rave the night away at DC's biggest and hottest nightclub, often headlining world-renowned DJs.

MCI Center (☎ 202-628-3200; 601 F St NW) Primarily a sports arena, MCI Center hosts big-name bands.

PERFORMING ARTS
Kennedy Center (☎ 202-467-4600; www.kennedy-center.org; 2700 F St NW) The National Symphony and Washington Chamber Symphony perform here, and it's also home to the Washington Opera. The center's Millennium Stage puts on free performances (no ticket required) at 6pm daily. Call or check the Kennedy Center website for the schedule.

Wolf Trap Farm Park for the Performing Arts (☎ 703-255-1900; www.wolftrap.org; 1645 Trap Rd, Vienna, Virginia) This outdoor park some 40 minutes from downtown DC hosts summer performances by the National Symphony and other highly regarded musical and theatrical troupes.

The **National Theatre** (☎ 202-628-6161; www.nationaltheatre.org; 1321 Pennsylvania Ave NW; tickets $40-90) is Washington's oldest continuously operating theater, though the **Shakespeare Theatre** (☎ 202-547-1122; www.shakespearedc.org; 450 7th St NW; tickets $23-70) is a more evocative venue. In summer outdoor performances are held at **Carter Barron Amphitheatre** (16th St & Colorado Ave NW).

SPORTS
Washington Redskins (☎ 301-276-6050) The city's football team play at FedEx Field, east of DC in Maryland.

Washington Nationals (☎ 202-397-7328) DC's baseball team plays for the time being at Robert F Kennedy Memorial Stadium (which is up for a name change), but a new stadium is to be built along the Anacostia Riverfront by 2008.

Both **DC United** (☎ 202-587-5000), which fronts teenage soccer phenom Freddy Adu, and the women's **Washington Freedom** (☎ 202-547-3137) play at RFK.

The **MCI Center** (☎ 202-628-3200, 202-432-7328) hosts the NBA Washington Wizards, the WNBA Washington Mystics and the NHL Washington Capitals ice hockey team.

Getting There & Away
For air connections, see p302.

Union Station (☎ 202-371-9441; www.unionstationdc.com; 50 Massachusetts Ave NE), DC's major transport hub, connects visitors to car rentals, Amtrak and MARC trains and some city tours.

BUS
If you're going the eight blocks from the bus station to the Metro, taking a cab is recommended.
Greyhound (☎ 800-231-2222; 1005 1st St NE)
Peter Pan Trailways (☎ 800-343-9999; 1005 1st St NE) Buses stop opposite.

TRAIN
MARC (☎ 800-325-7245; www.mtamaryland.com) commuter trains run weekdays to many regional cities, including Baltimore and Harpers Ferry, West Virginia. **Amtrak** (☎ 800-872-7245;

www.amtrak.com) services to and around the region include the Metroliner express service between DC and New York City.

Getting Around

TO/FROM THE AIRPORT

For door-to-door van service between all three airports and downtown DC, try **Super-Shuttle** (☎ 800-258-3826; www.supershuttle.com). Fares are around $25 to Reagan National and Dulles, and $31 to BWI.

Washington Flyer (☎ 888-927-4359; www.washfly .com; tickets $8) has shuttle service from Dulles to West Falls Church, Virginia, connecting with the Metro.

Number 5A **Metrobus** (☎ 202-962-1234; www .wmata.com; express $3) leaves from the Dulles car-rental area to central DC (L'Enfant Plaza) once an hour – a cheap alternative, but not much room for baggage.

Car rentals include the following:

Budget (☎ 703-920-3360 in Dulles, 703-419-1021 in Reagan; www.budget.com)

Dollar (☎ 703-661-6888 in Dulles; www.dollar.com)

Thrifty (☎ 703-658-2200; www.thrifty.com)

BUS

Metrobus (☎ 202-637-7000; www.wmata.com) operates buses throughout the city and suburbs (tickets from $1.20). Bus 98 links Woodley Park Zoo–Adams Morgan and the U St stations for 25¢; buses run from 6:30pm to 3:30am weekdays, from 10am to 3:30am Saturdays, and from 6pm to midnight Sundays. The Georgetown Metro Connection bus stops at all Metrobus stops throughout Georgetown between Foggy Bottom and Dupont Circle Metro stations. Buses run from 7am to midnight Monday to Thursday, from 7am to 2am Saturdays, and from 8am to midnight Sundays. Tickets cost $1.

TRAIN

Amtrak and regional MARC commuter trains run between DC's Union Station and a rail terminal near BWI (one way $9; a 10-minute free shuttle is provided to BWI proper).

Metrorail (☎ 202-637-7000; www.wmata.com) runs to most sights, hotel and business districts, and to the Maryland and Virginia suburbs. Trains operate 5:30am to midnight weekdays, 8am to 1am weekends. Machines inside stations sell computerized fare cards; fares (from $1.20) depend on distance traveled and time of day. All-day excursion passes cost $5.

CAR & TAXI

Drivers beware: middle lanes of some major streets change direction during rush hour. Street parking is often scarce, especially around Georgetown and the Mall. Most national car-rental agencies in DC won't rent to those under 25. Taxis, which operate on a zone system (most of the northwest quadrant is in Zone 1), charge a base rate of $6 per zone and are plentiful in the central city. Try the following:

Capitol Cab (☎ 202-546-2400)

Diamond (☎ 202-387-6200)

Yellow Cab (☎ 202-544-1212)

> ### ON THE OTHER SIDE OF THE POTOMAC
>
> Here are just three attractions that, while inextricably tied to the capital city, technically lie within Northern Virginia (or NoVA, to the hip).
>
> - Mount Vernon (p344) – George Washington's majestic hilltop getaway.
> - Arlington National Cemetery (p343) – the expansive, moving tribute to America's war dead and the resting place of John F Kennedy and Jackie O.
> - Alexandria (p344) – plug into the local arts scene at the Torpedo Factory Arts Center.

MARYLAND

Her beaches, mountains and historical firsts have earned Maryland the nickname 'America in Miniature.' But it's the Chesapeake Bay region, including the state's largely rural Eastern Shore, for which the state is most justifiably famous, and the reason that Maryland is a contender for the most-oddly-shaped-state award. This water playground includes the gritty, boisterous seafaring city of Baltimore, the world-renowned sailing center of Annapolis and waterfolk communities along the bay's coastline, as well as fishing, crabbing and every water-based pursuit imaginable. Spectacular seclusion and wild horses await you at Assateague

Island National Seashore. The west of the state features Deep Creek Lake and plenty for history buffs to explore, such as the C&O Canal and the Civil War battlefield of Antietam, which witnessed the bloodiest day in American history. The state's central portion almost surrounds the nation's capital and acts as a giant dormitory and service center for DC's workforce.

History

George Calvert (Lord Baltimore) received a royal grant to establish a Catholic colony in what was then northern Virginia, and in 1634 he settled in St Mary's City, which prospered as the capital of the new Maryland colony until 1695, when the colony's capital was moved to the superior port of Annapolis.

In 1729 the settlement of Baltimore was founded as a tobacco and flour-milling center, with a fine harbor and access to first-rate shipbuilding timber. Baltimore developed rapidly as colonial America's shipping center, but was bombarded by British ships in the War of 1812. Soldiers kept the flag flying at Fort McHenry and resisted the attack, and the event inspired lawyer Francis Scott Key to write a poem called 'The Star-Spangled Banner,' which became the national anthem.

Maryland prospered in the early 19th century from its tobacco and wheat plantations, Chesapeake Bay fisheries and seaports, and railroads pushing west. During the Civil War, an 1862 Confederate invasion of Maryland was halted at the battle of Antietam (p337).

After the war Maryland continued its Baltimore-based industrial development. European immigration swelled the workforce, but African Americans continued to experience discrimination. The exponential growth of the nearby national capital, pushing its suburban population and development deep into Maryland, is a large factor in the state's present-day economy.

Information

Sales tax is 5% and accommodation tax is 12.5%.

Office of Tourism (☎ 410-767-3400, 866-639-3526; www.mdwelcome.com; 217 E Redwood St, Baltimore, MD 21202) Maryland has welcome centers throughout the state with maps and guides.

MARYLAND FACTS

Nicknames Old Line State, Free State, America in Miniature
Population 5.6 million
Area 12,407 sq miles
Capital city Annapolis (population 35,838)
Other cities Baltimore (651,154)
Offical sport Jousting
Birthplace of Frederick Douglass (1817–95), Babe Ruth (1895–1948), Billie Holiday (1915–59), Frank Zappa (1940–93), Goldie Hawn (b 1945)
Home of John Waters, Preakness Stakes horse race
Famous for Chesapeake Bay, crabs, US Naval Academy

BALTIMORE

As part of a promotional campaign in the 1970s, visitors to Baltimore received a charm bracelet to which they could add charms collected at the city's attractions, and the nickname Charm City stuck. But only within the last decade has the moniker come off as anything but distinctly sarcastic. Downtown Baltimore has morphed from a depressed, drive-through-with-the-doors-locked area into a just-gritty-enough destination worthy of a few days' exploration. Though the major tourist attractions ring the Inner Harbor's waterfront, you'd be sorely remiss if you didn't venture into the neighborhoods, like hip Hampden in the north and Little Italy and Greektown to the east. The city's importance in shaping American history is undeniable – Babe Ruth, the country's railroad system and the national anthem were all born here – but locals look forward as much as back. This is a red-blooded, blue-collared, salt-water town; the progress of the Baltimore Orioles (or O's) is followed with near-religious devotion, and if you want to start a lively debate just ask two people where to find the best crab cakes.

History

After the Revolutionary War, Baltimore served as one of the nation's capitals before the honor was given to Washington, DC. Its destiny was not to lie in politics, but on the water. The city's shipyards became famous for a new breed of ship – fast, two-masted schooners called clippers, and thanks in

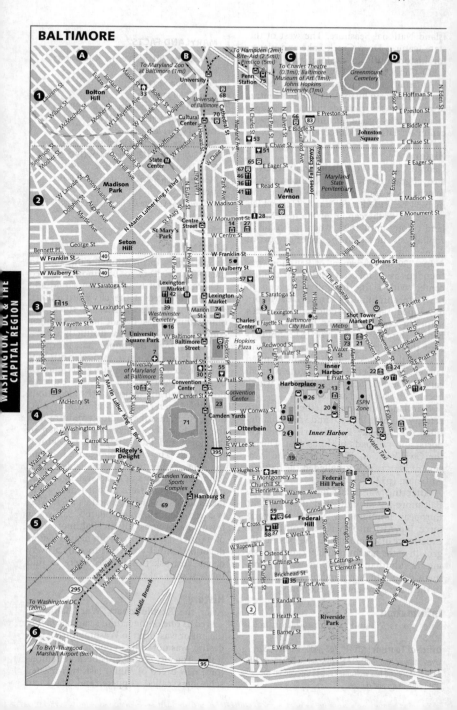

BALTIMORE

INFORMATION
American Express.................................1 C4
Baltimore Area Visitors Center....2 C4
Bank of America.................................3 C3
Barnes & Noble..................................4 D4
Enoch Pratt Free Library...............5 B3
Post Office...6 D3
University of Maryland Medical
  Center...7 B3

SIGHTS & ACTIVITIES
American Visionary Art Museum..8 D5
B&O Railroad Museum....................9 A4
Babe Ruth Birthplace & Museum..10 B4
Baltimore Civil War Museum....11 D4
Baltimore Ducks.............................12 C4
Baltimore Maritime Museum......13 C4
Contemporary Museum...............14 B2
Edgar Allan Poe Museum............15 A3
Edgar Allan Poe's Grave..............16 B3
Fell's Point Ghost Tour.................17 E4
Fort McHenry National Monument
  & Historic Shrine........................18 G6
Maryland Science Center.............19 C4
National Aquarium in Baltimore..20 C4
Port Discovery.................................21 D3
Reginald F Lewis Museum of
  Maryland African American
  History & Culture........................22 D4
Sports Legends at Camden
  Yards..23 B4
Star-Spangled Banner Flag House &
  1812 Museum..............................24 D4
Top of the World Observation
  Deck...25 C4
USS Constellation..........................26 C4
Walters Art Gallery.......................27 C2
Washington Monument...............28 C2
World Trade Center.................(see 25)

SLEEPING
Admiral Fell Inn..............................29 E4
Holiday Inn.......................................30 B4
Inn at 2920.......................................31 H6
Inn at Henderson's Wharf...........32 E5
Mr Mole B & B.................................33 B1
Scarborough Fair.............................34 C5

EATING
Bicycle..35 C6
Brass Elephant................................36 C2
Cross St Market...............................37 C5
Daily Grind Coffeehouse.............38 E4
Faidley's...39 B3
Helen's Garden................................40 H6
Helmand...41 C2

Joy America Café.......................(see 8)
Lexington Market..........................42 B3
Light St Pavilion............................43 C4
Liquid Earth.....................................44 E4
Nacho Mama's.................................45 G6
Red Maple...46 C2
Sabatino's...47 D4
Sip-N-Bite...48 F4
Tusk Lounge................................(see 36)
Vaccaro's Pastry.............................49 D4
Ze Mean Bean Café......................50 E4

DRINKING
13th Floor..51 C2
Bay Café...52 F5
Brewer's Art....................................53 C1
Claddagh Pub..................................54 H6
DSX...55 B4
Little Havana...................................56 D5
Mick O'Shea's..................................57 C3
Mother's...58 C5
Owl Bar..(see 51)
Thirsty Dog Pub.............................59 C5
Wharf Rat..60 E4

ENTERTAINMENT
1st Mariner Arena..........................61 B3
Centerstage......................................62 C2
Fletcher's...63 E4
Funk Box..64 C5
Grand Central..................................65 C2
Hammerjacks....................................66 C1
Have a Nice Day Café..............(see 73)
Hippo..67 C2
Lyric Opera House.........................68 B1
M&T Bank Stadium........................69 B5
Meyerhoff Symphony Hall.........70 B1
Oriole Park at Camden Yards....71 B4
Pier 6 Pavilion.................................72 D4
Power Plant Live.............................73 D3
Rams Head Live.........................(see 73)

TRANSPORT
Greyhound Bus Station................74 B3
Penn Station.....................................75 C1

part to these clippers plying trade routes all over the globe, Baltimore became the second-largest city in the USA.

Baltimore suffered no damage in the Civil War, but in 1904 a warehouse fire engulfed its business district. Undaunted, Baltimore's wealthy financed a recovery that continued until the Great Depression. Thereafter Baltimore struggled with growing social problems, and following the 1968 murder of civil rights leader Martin Luther King Jr, mobs burned and looted the city. Baltimore's transformation since then into a lively, attraction-filled destination is an urban renewal success story. Well, mostly successful. The city still suffers from one of the worst heroin epidemics in the country, and drug-related violence remained unabated (though not in the areas that visitors will likely find themselves). The slogan of the city's ongoing anti-drug campaign is 'Believe,' and you'll see the word plastered on bumper stickers, trash cans and billboards. (The version in Hampden is 'Blieve, Hon.')

Orientation

The Inner Harbor is the heart of tourist activity. Downtown's business district is immediately north and west of the Inner Harbor, climbing uphill to the swank Mt Vernon district. East of the Inner Harbor (most easily accessible by water taxi) are Little Italy, Fell's Point and Canton. The Camden Yards Sports Complex borders the Inner Harbor to the west. Federal Hill and Fort McHenry are south of the Inner Harbor and hip neighborhood of Hampden is in north Baltimore, a quick drive or bus ride from downtown. Baltimore St divides the city's streets into north and south, and Charles St divides them east and west.

Information

BOOKSTORES

Atomic Books (☎ 410-662-4444; 1100 W 36th St; ⏰ 11am-6pm, to 8pm Wed-Sat) Let's just say that John Waters loves this place in Hampden. In fact, any John Waters fan mail should be sent care of them.

Barnes & Noble (☎ 401-385-1709; 601 E Pratt St, Power Plant, Inner Harbor; ⏰ 8am-10pm Mon-Sat, 9am-9pm Sun) Will carry everything that Atomic doesn't, and likely nothing Atomic does.

EMERGENCY

Police, fire and ambulance (☎ 911) Emergency

INTERNET ACCESS

Enoch Pratt Free Library (☎ 410-396-5430; 400 Cathedral St; ⏰ 11am-7pm Mon-Wed, 10am-5pm Thu-Sat, 1-5pm Sun Oct-May) Lots of computers with Internet access.

MEDIA

88.1 FM WYPR National public radio.

89.7 FM WTMD Local Towson University station; alternative music.

Gay Life (www.bgp.org) State-wide, but Baltimore-oriented, free gay and lesbian biweekly.

Baltimore Sun (www.baltimoresun.com) Daily city newspaper.

City Paper (www.citypaper.com) Free weekly with extensive entertainment listings and restaurants.

MEDICAL SERVICES

Rite-Aid (☎ 410- 410-467-3343; the Rotunda, 711 W 40th St) Twenty-four-hour pharmacy.

University of Maryland Medical Center (☎ 410-328-6971; 655 W Baltimore St) Twenty-four-hour emergency room.

MONEY

American Express Travel Services (☎ 410-837-3100; 100 E Pratt St; ⏰ 9am-5pm Mon-Fri)

Bank of America (☎ 410-385-8310; 201 N Charles St; ⏰ 9am-5pm Mon-Fri) Cashes traveler's checks. Other locations around the city.

POST

Post office (☎ 410-347-4425; 900 E Fayette St; ⏰ 8:30am-5pm Mon-Fri, to 4pm Sat)

TOURIST INFORMATION

Baltimore Area Visitors Center (☎ 410-837-4636, 877-225-8466; www.baltimore.org; 451 Light St; ⏰ 9am-6pm Mon-Fri) If you're really planning on tackling Charm City, consider a Harbor Pass (adult/child $46/30), which gives admission to four major area attractions plus a one-day water taxi pass.

Dangers & Annoyances

Baltimore is an urban city with urban problems. That said, the city is fine to explore with the usual precautions. Areas west of Howard St hold little attraction for visitors and are best avoided, especially at night. On the northern edge of the city, North Ave is an absolute no-go (take a cab if you're headed to Charles Theatre, p333). If visiting Little Italy, stay to the well-lit streets and avoid straying north of Eastern Ave. If you're visiting Johns Hopkins University, it's best to visit during daylight hours or in a group.

Sights

The majority of attractions are compactly located around the L-shaped Inner Harbor and fan out east and north throughout Baltimore's quaint neighborhoods. Water taxis are the best way to see the downtown attractions.

HARBORPLACE

The epicenter of tourist activity is Harborplace, at the northwest corner of the Inner Harbor. The defunct power plant now sports a modern brick pedestrian walkway lined with restaurants and a bookstore as giant as the guitar that juts over the harbor atop the Hard Rock Café. The rest of Harborplace hops with two waterfront malls, more restaurants, shops, paddleboat rentals and a water-taxi stop.

Baltimore's jewel is easily recognized by its gleaming pyramid. The **National Aquarium in Baltimore** (☎ 410-576-3800; www.aqua.org; 501 E Pratt St; adult/child $18/11; ☼ 9am-6pm Sun-Thu, to 8pm Fri & Sat Jul & Aug, 9am-5pm daily, to 8pm Fri Mar-Jun & Sep-Oct, 10am-5pm daily, to 8pm Fri Nov-Feb) is an aquatic wonderland that informs kids and adults about marine science with exciting shark tanks and touchy-feely exhibits. Seven twisty levels of marine habitats house some 10,000 animals in buildings on two piers, but the aquarium is most famous for its sharks and dolphins. Dolphin shows are presented throughout the day.

DOWNTOWN & LITTLE ITALY

The Inner Harbor is packed with renovated attractions and gleaming shopfronts. Behind the Power Plant is the delightful Little Italy neighborhood, brimming with exquisite restaurants, a bocce ball court and a giant brick wall that doubles as an outdoor movie screen in summer.

Baltimore's **World Trade Center** is as ugly as sin, but the views from the **Top of the World observation deck** (☎ 410-837-8439; 401 E Pratt St; adult/senior/child $5/3/4; ☼ 10am-6pm Wed-Sun Sep-May, 10am-6pm Sun-Fri, to 8pm Sat Jun-Aug) are heavenly.

Check out where the first bloodshed of the Civil War occurred at the **Baltimore Civil War Museum** (☎ 410-385-5188; 601 S President St; adult/child under 13/senior & student $4/free/3; ☼ 10am-5pm), inside the 1849 President St train station.

The **Star-Spangled Banner Flag House & 1812 Museum** (☎ 410-837-1793; www.flaghouse.org; 844 E Pratt St;

adult/child/senior $6/4/5; ☼ 10am-4pm Tue-Sat) shows the home where Mary Pickersgill sewed the gigantic flag that inspired Francis Scott Key's 'The Star-Spangled Banner' poem.

Next door – and across the street from where a pre–Civil War slave market stood – is the new **Reginald F Lewis Museum of Maryland African American History & Culture** (☎ 410-333-1130; www.africanamericanculture.org; 830 E Pratt St; adult/child/senior & student $8/5/6; ☼ 10am-5pm Tue-Sun), which celebrates and honors the substantial contributions of Black Marylanders with plenty of hands-on activities for kids.

The **Babe Ruth Birthplace & Museum** (☎ 410-727-1539; 216 Emory St; adult/child/senior $6/3/4; ☼ 10am-6pm Apr-Oct, to 7:30pm on Orioles home games, 10am-5pm Tue-Sun Nov-Mar) pays homage to the Sultan of Swat. Four block east, its new extension **Sports Legends at Camden Yards** (Camden Station, Camden & Sharp Sts; adult/child/senior $10/6.50/8) is a must for sports fans, with interactive exhibits that take you, among other places, into the locker room, the football huddle and the broadcast center. Combo tickets are $14/9/11.

You gotta be a train buff to cough up this much, but the 150 locomotives on display at the **B&O Railroad Museum** (☎ 410-752-2490; www.borail.org; 901 W Pratt St; adult/child 2-12/senior $14/8/10) are indeed fascinating. A 20-minute train ride travels over the first railroad tracks in the nation.

Sea junkies should consider a visit to the **Baltimore Maritime Museum** (☎ 410-369-3153; Piers 3 & 5 off E Pratt St; adult/child 6-14 $6/5; ☼ 10:30am-5pm Fri-Sun Dec-Feb, 10am-5:30pm Sun-Thu, 10am-6pm Fri & Sat Mar-Nov), which consists of ship tours aboard a coast-guard cutter, a lightship and a submarine, or the **USS Constellation** (☎ 410-539-1797; Pier 1 at 301 E Pratt St; adult/child under 15/senior $7.50/3.50/6; ☼ 10am-6pm May 1-Oct 14; 10am-4pm Oct 15-Apr 30), the last all-sail warship built by the US Navy.

Edgar Allen Poe penned many of his most famous works in the tiny house that is now the **Edgar Allan Poe Museum** (☎ 410-396-7932; 203 N Amity St; adult/child under 13 $3/1; ☼ noon-3:45pm Wed-Sat). The neighborhood can be off-putting, however. Hours vary wildly; call ahead. Poe's **grave** is in nearby Westminster Cemetery.

MOUNT VERNON

The renowned **Walters Art Gallery** (☎ 410-547-9000; www.thewalters.org; 600 N Charles St; adult/child 6-17/student/senior $10/2/6/8; ☼ 10am-5pm Wed-Sun) boasts a collection that spans 55 centuries, from ancient to contemporary, with excellent displays of Asian treasures, rare and ornate manuscripts and books, and a comprehensive French paintings collection. Entrance is on Centre St.

Just down the street is the **Contemporary Museum** (☎ 410-783-5720; www.contemporary.org; 100 W Centre St; admission free; ◷ noon-5pm Thu-Sat). Auxiliary to the on-site exhibits is the museum's mission of bringing cutting-edge art to unexpected spots around the city. Call or check the website for the latest guerrilla art attack.

Baltimore's **Washington Monument** (☎ 410-396-7837; 699 Washington Pl; suggested donation $1; ◷ dawn-dusk Wed-Sun) crowns the regal Mt Vernon Sq; climb 228 steps to the top for a city view or just check out the exhibits at its base.

FEDERAL HILL & AROUND
On a bluff overlooking the harbor, **Federal Hill Park** lends its name to the comfortable neighborhood that's set around the Cross St Market and comes alive after sundown.

The **Fort McHenry National Monument & Historic Shrine** (☎ 410-962-4290; 2400 E Fort Ave; adult/child under 17 $5/free; ◷ fort & grounds 8am-7:45pm in summer, 8am-4:45pm rest of year) is one of the most visited sites in Baltimore. This star-shaped fort was instrumental in saving the city from those pesky Brits in the Battle of Baltimore during the War of 1812. After a long night of bombs bursting in air, prisoner Francis Scott Key saw the tattered flag still waving, and the national anthem 'The Star-Spangled Banner' was born.

The **American Visionary Art Museum** (☎ 410-244-1900; www.avam.org; 800 Key Hwy; adult/student & senior $11/7; ◷ 10am-6pm Tue-Sun) showcases international folk and 'outsider' artists. Don't miss the new sculpture barn. The museum also boasts a whimsical gift shop and the excellent Joy America Café (see p330).

FELL'S POINT & CANTON
Further east, cobblestones fill Market Sq between the Broadway Market and the harbor in the historic maritime neighborhood of Fell's Point. A dockfront plaque commemorates the area for a more modern distinction – as the film site of the TV show *Homicide: Life on the Street*. A number of 18th-century homes now house restaurants, bars and shops that range from funky to upscale. Further east, the slightly more sophisticated streets of Canton fan out, and its grassy square is surrounded by more great restaurants and bars.

NORTH BALTIMORE
The 'Hon' expression of affection, an oft-imitated but never quite duplicated 'Bawl-merese' peculiarity, was born from **Hampden**, an urban neighborhood at the pinnacle of hipness. Spend a lazy afternoon browsing kitsch, antiques and eclectic clothing along the Avenue (aka W 36th St). To get to Hampden, take I-83 N, merge onto 25 N and take a right onto the Avenue.

Close by, you'll find **Johns Hopkins University** (☎ 410-516-8171), famed for its medical school. Within this largely residential district lie a few worthwhile attractions, such as the **Baltimore Museum of Art** (☎ 410-396-7100; 10 Art Museum Dr at 31st & N Charles Sts; adult/child & senior $7/3; ◷ 11am-5pm Wed-Fri, to 6pm Sat & Sun), which contains a globe-spanning collection and a lovely sculpture garden.

Baltimore for Children
This city loves kids and proves it with amazing museums, strollable waterfront promenades and family-friendly restaurants. Most attractions are centered on the Inner Harbor, including the **National Aquarium** (p327), perfect for pint-sized visitors. Don't forget historic **Fort McHenry** (left), where kids can run wild o'er the ramparts.

Swinging into a three-level jungle tree house, producing a TV show and solving riddles in the Mystery House are just a sample of the interactive adventures at **Port Discovery** (☎ 410-727-8120; www.portdiscovery.org; Power Plant Live complex, 35 Market Pl; adult/child 3-12 $11/8.50; ◷ 10am-5pm, Mon-Sat, from noon Sun, to 8pm Fri Jul-Aug), a cool kids' museum where even the adults have fun. Hop in the HiFlyer Balloon outside for a bird's-eye view of Baltimore. Tickets that include a balloon ride (summer only) are adult/child $19/15.

Lily-pad hopping, adventures with Billy the Bog Turtle and grooming live animals are all in a day's work at the **Maryland Zoo in Baltimore** (☎ 410-366-5466; www.marylandzoo.org; Druid Hill Park; adult/child/senior $15/10/12; ◷ 10am-4:30pm Mar-Dec), a lively children's zoo.

Fresh off a $35 million expansion, the impressive **Maryland Science Center** (☎ 410-685-5225; www.mdsci.org; 601 Light St; adult/child 3-12

$14/9.50; 10am-6pm Sun-Wed, to 8pm Thu-Sat in summer, closed Mon winter-spring) features a three-story atrium and tons of interactive exhibits on such charismatic subjects as dinosaurs, asteroids and the human body. Tacking on an IMAX show or a special exhibition increases the price.

Tours

Baltimore Ducks (☎ 410-727-3825; www.baltimore ducks.com; Conway & Light Sts, Inner Harbor; adult/child 3-12/child 13-18 $24/14/21) The quintessential tourist activity, a ride on an amphibious former—WWII military 'Duck' shows visitors the city via land and water.

Fell's Point Ghost Tours (☎ 410-342-5000; www .fellspointghost.com; departs from 731 S Broadway; adult/child under 13 $12/8; 7pm Fri or Sat Mar-Nov) Delve into the spooky and bizarre side of a bawdy maritime area. Call for tickets or reserve online.

Sleeping

Budget options are limited, and although large convention-style hotels ring the Inner Harbor, stylish and affordable B&Bs are mostly found in the downtown 'burbs of Canton, Fell's Point and Federal Hill.

BUDGET

Best Inn (☎ 410-485-7900; www.bestinnhotel.com; 6510 Frankford Ave; r $59-99; P) In the northeast of town, this solid, nondescript place has clean rooms, friendly staff and laundry facilities, all at a reasonable price.

MIDRANGE

Scarborough Fair (☎ 410-837-0010; www.scarborough -fair.com; 1 E Montgomery St; r $149-189; P X) This understated, five-room brickhouse B&B in Federal Hill lies within walking distance of many major sights, and bangs out a sinfully good breakfast.

Inn at Henderson's Wharf (☎ 410-522-7777, 800-522-2088; www.hendersonswharf.com; 1000 Fell St; r $179-209; P) A complimentary bottle of wine upon arrival sets the tone at this marvelously situated Fell's Point deluxe hotel, which began life as an 18th-century tobacco warehouse. Among the many perks are a delectable continental breakfast, wi-fi and 24-hour fitness center.

Mr Mole B&B (☎ 410-728-1179; www.mrmolebb .com; 1601 Bolton St; r $149-199; P X) This beautifully restored town house in the upscale Bolton Hill area in the northwest of town is a good choice as a base to explore the city's

THE AUTHOR'S CHOICE

Inn at 2920 (☎ 410-342-4450; www.theinnat 2920.com; 2920 Elliott St; r $155-225; P X) Think B&Bs have to be synonymous with dusty tchotchkes and stuffed animals? Think again. With nary a lace doily in sight, this contemporary inn a few steps from Canton Sq welcomes both business travelers and those simply looking for a stylish urban escape. David Schwartz, who runs the B&B with his wife Debbie, received his culinary training at the Hyatt in Atlanta and he thrills to the challenge of creating organic gourmet breakfasts to suit special-need diets. Each of their five rooms is uniquely gorgeous, but particularly sumptuous is the Bordello room. All rooms feature to-die-for Kingsdown mattresses, Jacuzzi tubs and wi-fi, and most have a resident beta fish to keep you company.

cultural arts district. Garage parking makes this B&B's price a steal. Gay friendly.

Holiday Inn (☎ 410-685-3500; www.holiday-inn.com; 301 W Lombard St at Howard St; r from $130; P) A block from Camden Yards, this makes a good home base for Inner Harbor exploring. You can work out in the fitness center and then do a load of laundry.

TOP END

Admiral Fell Inn (☎ 410-522-7377; www.admiralfell .com; 888 S Broadway; r incl breakfast from $199; P) Must not have been much of a sailor! Overlooking Market Sq in Fell's Point, this gracious if slightly corporate-feeling hotel offers rooms with a variety of features to choose from, like balconies and Jacuzzi bath. Free shuttle to downtown.

Eating

Known for its steamed crabs, Baltimore's culinary options are ever expanding with Italian, Asian, Middle Eastern and comfort foods. Chain restaurants and take-aways fill the Inner Harbor's Light St Pavilion. Across Pratt St, the Power Plant Live complex has numerous open-air options from sushi to Cuban to steakhouses. Beyond the harbor are delicious ethnic eateries that haven't changed much over the years – and that's a good thing. The untouristy Lexington Market north of Camden Yards houses an

WASHINGTON, DC & THE
CAPITAL REGION

overwhelming number of stand-up and take-away eateries, including the Baltimore seafood institution Faidley's (below). Canton Sq and Broadway in Fell's Point's go casual, while Federal Hill and Little Italy swing upscale. N Charles St in Mt Vernon is known for its chic restaurant row.

DOWNTOWN & LITTLE ITALY

Sabatino's (☎ 410-727-2667; 901 Fawn St; mains $11-20; ☺ noon-midnight, to 3am Fri & Sat) This is the kind of spot where Italian is heard as often as English, parties spanning three generations are common, and even WASPs can't help but gesticulate about how fantastico the homemade pasta is. Beware the after-Mass Sunday rush.

Vaccaro's Pastry (☎ 410-685-4905; 222 Albemarle St; items $2-5; ☺ 9am-11pm Sun-Thu, to 1am Fri & Sat) The menu of this modest institution carries scads of sinful desserts like cannoli and homemade gelati. For no-holds-barred gluttony, catch the dessert-and-coffee all-you-can-eat on Monday evenings ($12).

MOUNT VERNON

Helmand (☎ 410-752-0311; 806 N Charles St; mains $11-19; ☺ dinner) Deservedly the best of Baltimore's handful of Afghan restaurants and owned by a brother of Afghan president Hamid Karzai, Helmand features a daring menu that will paralyze both meat-eaters (especially lamb-lovers) and vegetarians with glorious inde-

---

THE AUTHOR'S CHOICE

Faidley's (☎ 410-727-4898; 203 N Paca St, Lexington Market; mains $5-15; ☺ 9am-5pm Mon-Sat) Here's a splendid example of a place that the press and the tourists found out about long ago, yet whose brilliance hasn't been dimmed by all that publicity. Despite being part fish market and part raw bar (does the sign 'Eat Fish = Live Longer, Eat Oysters = Love Longer' hint at some competition between the two?), Faidley's is best known for its crab cakes, in-claw meat, backfin (body meat) or all lump (the biggest chunks of body meat). The last of these is king, and worth every penny of its $13 price tag. Tuck into one at a stand-up counter, a cold beer by your side, and know happiness. The surrounding neighborhood is a bit rough, but safe enough during daylight hours.

---

cision. Order the pan-fried pumpkin as an appetizer in the meantime.

Brass Elephant (☎ 410-547-8485; www.brasselephant.com; 924 N Charles St; mains $16-30; ☺ dinner) This posh town house, with gleaming brass and intricately carved woodwork, is a city favorite for upscale dining with such dishes as porcini-dusted lamb loin, dry rubbed rib eye, and fusilli with crab and shrimp. Get the same flavor upstairs in the Tusk Lounge at cheaper prices. Free valet parking.

Red Maple (☎ 410-547-0149; 930 N Charles St; tapas $7-10, mains $13-18; ☺ dinner) Baltimore's hottest come here to partake of Asian-inspired tapas and sip exotic cocktails in a gorgeous setting dripping with red satin. Stick around for whatever the night's theme is, like Flamenco Tuesdays to Indian electronica Thursdays. Don't even consider wearing jeans.

FEDERAL HILL

Cross St Market (1065 Cross St btwn Light & Charles Sts; ☺ from 6am Mon-Thu, from 7am Fri & Sat) By day, grab a snack from the food vendors among the flower and produce stands. By night, grab a plastic beer cup and join the frat-party bonhomie as you slurp down some slimy ones from the outstanding raw bar.

Bicycle (☎ 410-234-1900; 1444 Light St; mains $15-28; ☺ dinner Tue-Sat) Striking colored walls, a spacious interior and a hip art-gallery feel accent the French-, South American– and Asian-inspired (in other words, nouveau-Californian) offerings.

Joy America Café (☎ 410-244-6500; 800 Key Hwy; mains $15-30; ☺ lunch & dinner Tue-Sun) Don't let the fact that this is inside the American Visionary Art Museum dissuade you – its organic, gourmet fare is as eclectic and well conceived as the artwork. Wonderful view of the harbor.

FELL'S POINT

Ze Mean Bean Café (☎ 410-675-5999; 1739 Fleet St; lunch mains $9-15, dinner mains $17-24; ☺ lunch & dinner) Like a cross between a European café and a mountain lodge (complete with couch and fireplace), the congenial Bean serves up hearty Eastern European plates of pierogi, Ukrainian borscht and chicken Kiev, besides more American fare.

Liquid Earth (☎ 410-276-6606; 1626 Aliceanna St; mains $6-11; ☺ 7am-7pm Tue-Fri, from 9am Sat, 10am-3pm Sun) This organic, veggie (often vegan) establishment serves soups, salads, sandwiches, sweets and smoothies from the coffee bar made of funky rocks.

Daily Grind Coffeehouse (☎ 410-558-0399; 1720 Thames St; items $2-7; ☒ 7am-11pm, to 9pm Sun) Wi-fi access attracts a solid student clientele, and it's got the standard assortment of sandwiches and smoothies to go with your espresso.

Sip-N-Bite (☎ 410-675-7077; 2200 Boston St; mains $6-11; ☒ 24hr) Not much has changed at this bare-bones diner since it opened in 1948, serving up 24-hour breakfasts and an expansive menu. Check out the signed photo of George Clooney by the door. Cash only.

CANTON

Helen's Garden (☎ 410-276-2233; 2908 O'Donnell St; mains $18-24; ☒ lunch & dinner Tue-Sun) Don't let the narrow hallway entrance scare you off from this artsy and intimate eatery's innovative dishes, with special attention paid to seafood and free-range chicken. It's a popular spot for weekend brunch – be prepared to wait, but linger to your heart's content.

Nacho Mama's (☎ 410-675-0898; 2907 O'Donnell St; mains $7-18; ☒ 11am-late) This dark, eclectic restaurant/bar serves a jumble of dishes from mom's meatloaf to award-winning stuffed quesadillas.

HAMPDEN

Cafe Hon (☎ 410-332-0110; 1711 N Charles St; brunch mains $4-8, dinner mains $9-15; ☒ 7am-9pm Mon-Fri, from 9am Sat & Sun) You don't have be sporting rhinestone-studded glasses and an ironic bouffant to eat here, but you'll earn serious brownie points. The fare at this veggie-friendly diner is as hearty as the café's attitude. After dinner slide over to adjacent Bar Hon.

Drinking

Fell's Point's reigning reputation for imbibing has been knocked out by newcomers such as Federal Hill. Downtown, the V-shaped Water St area teems with people attending open-air block parties in summer. The Power Plant Live complex has a cluster of boisterous yet corporate-feeling bars and clubs. A bunch of bars spill people into Canton Sq throughout the year.

DOWNTOWN & LITTLE ITALY

Mick O'Shea's (☎ 410-539-7504; 328 N Charles St; ☒ from 11:30am) Your standard paraphernalia-festooned Irish pub, with live Irish music Wednesday through Saturday. Baltimore's

mayor Martin O'Malley has been known to show up to play with his band.

DSX (☎ 410-659-5844; 200 W Pratt St) Grab a pint and catch an Orioles or Ravens pregame show in this always-crowded sports bar before heading across the street to the stadiums (or come after the game to celebrate or commiserate).

MOUNT VERNON

Brewer's Art (☎ 410-547-6925; 1106 N Charles St; ☒ from 5pm) This subterranean cave mesmerizes the senses with an overwhelming selection of beers. Its upstairs embodiment opens earlier and serves respectable dinners in its classy dining room.

13th Floor (☎ 410-347-0888; 1 E Chase St; ☒ from 6pm Wed-Sat) Atop the Gothic Belvedere Hotel, 13th Floor's soothing neon lights beckon long drinking sessions to the tune of nightly reggae or Latin beats. Also in the Belvedere Hotel, the Owl Bar is a nostalgic throwback to '50s Baltimore. Its long wooden bar attracts a big martini-sipping university crowd.

FEDERAL HILL

Thirsty Dog Pub (☎ 410-727-6077; 20 E Cross St; ☒ from 5pm) After you've made the rounds petting the canine clientele, grab a delicious brew (or two for $3) and try to snag the cozy fireside nook in the back. Excellent pizza, too.

Mother's (☎ 410-244-8686; 1113 S Charles St; ☒ from 1:30pm) Here's a classic Baltimore neighborhood bar and grill where the drinks flow freely; you'll be called 'Hon' more than once and the Purple Patio is the meeting spot for wing specials and pre- and post-Ravens game discussions.

Little Havana (☎ 410-837-9903; 1325A Key Hwy; ☒ from 4:30pm Mon-Thu, 11am Fri-Sun) Sip *mojitos*, dance to Cuban beats and shoot pool in this spacious, friendly waterfront bar.

FELL'S POINT & CANTON

Wharf Rat (☎ 410-276-9034; 801 S Ann St; ☒ from 11am) The authentic maritime decorations, brass bars and dark lighting take drinkers back to a turn-of-the-20th-century pub; try the 'three for $4' local brew samples. Spirits of a non alcoholic nature are rumored to frequent the fireplace area.

Bay Café (☎ 410-522-3377; 2809 Boston St; ☒ from 5pm Mon-Sat, from 10am Sun) Throw some back by the glow of an outdoor tiki torch on the sandy beach with a view of the Patapsco River.

DUCKPIN BOWLING

Back in the day, tenpin bowling was a winter sport, and alleys usually closed during the summer. However, a few places stayed open so that bowlers – rolling smaller balls – could get in some off-season practice. In 1900 Diamond Alleys in Baltimore came up with the idea of winnowing down the size of the pins as well. The owners, avid hunters they, associated the way the pins scattered with a 'flock of flying ducks,' and the name stuck. Duckpin bowling is especially thrilling for younger kids, since the balls (which don't have holes) and pins are lighter, and each bowler is allowed three balls.

Around since 1927, **Patterson Bowling Center** (☎ 410-675-1011; www.pattersonbowl.com; 2105 Eastern Ave; per game adult/child $3.25/3; ☯ 11am-6:30pm year-round) is the best place in town to hit the lanes. Call for exact hours, as they vary depending on season and day.

Claddagh Pub (☎ 410-522-4220; 2918 O'Donnell St; ☯ from 11am) A Canton favorite that packs 'em in on weekends.

Entertainment

Baltimoreans love their sports teams, dancing hotspots and historic theaters with a fervor that's contagious.

LIVE MUSIC

Funk Box (☎ 410-625-2000; 10 E Cross St; tickets $10-20) Books alterna-rock and folk acts like Jimmy Cliff and the Jazz Mandolin Project.

Fletcher's (☎ 410-558-1889; 701 S Bond St; cover $5) This is downtown Baltimore's best venue for alternative rock bands.

Rams Head Live (☎ 410-244-8854; 20 Market Pl, Power Plant Live; tickets free-$30) This spacious venue has diverse lineups, from the Indigo Girls to the Brazilian Girls.

Pier 6 Pavilion (☎ 410-625-3100; www.piersixpavilion.com; Inner Harbor; tickets $30-80) Summertime at this amphitheater sees established acts (Gypsy Kings) and upcoming artists (Lalah Hathaway) alike.

NIGHTCLUBS

Hammerjacks (☎ 410-234-0044; 316 Guilford Ave; cover $5-10; ☯ Wed-Mon) This huge two-level nightclub and bar keeps the Top 40 hits pumping.

Have a Nice Day Café (☎ 410-385-8669; 2 Market Pl, Power Plant Live; cover $3-8; ☯ Wed-Sat) This 20-something club plays a mix of '70s, '80s and electronica on a Billie Jean–style light-up dance floor. No cover on Thursdays.

GAY & LESBIAN VENUES

Though it doesn't have a huge population of gays and lesbians (most flock to DC's hotspots), Baltimore's predominantly gay enclave is Mt Vernon. See **Out in Baltimore** (www.outinbaltimore.com) for more comprehensive listings.

Hippo (☎ 410-547-0069; 1 W Eager St; ☯ from 6pm) This is the city's largest gay club, with ladies' and men's tea, cabaret and outrageously themed dance nights.

Grand Central (☎ 410-752-7133; 1001 N Charles St; ☯ from 4pm) Whatever it's touch, one of Central's areas (dance floor, pub, video bar, and leather-and-Levi's club) is sure to suit your fancy. House diva Ms Tia gets the mixed crowd going with karaoke (Monday and Tuesday), and Wednesday is Manicure and Martini night.

SPORTS

Whether it's touchdowns, home runs, goals or monster-truck shows, Baltimoreans love their sports. The town plays hard and parties even harder, with tailgating parties in parking lots and games on numerous televisions.

Baseball

The Baltimore Orioles play at **Oriole Park at Camden Yards** (☎ 888-484-2473; www.theorioles.com; 333 W Camden St; ☯ Apr-Oct).

Football

The Baltimore Ravens play at the purple-themed **M&T Bank Stadium** (☎ 800-551-7328; www.baltimoreravens.com; 1101 Russell St; ☯ Sep-Jan).

Lacrosse & Soccer

Lacrosse is a big deal in Maryland, and games are enthralling. The **Baltimore Bayhawks** (www.baltimorebayhawks.com; ☯ Jun-Aug) play on the Johns Hopkins University campus. The Major League Soccer team **Baltimore Blast** (www.baltimoreblast.com; ☯ Oct-Apr) plays at the **1st Mariner Arena** (☎ 410-321-1908; 201 W Baltimore St).

Horseracing
Horse racing is big in this area, especially at **Pimlico** (www.marylandracing.com), where the second jewel of the Triple Crown, the Preakness, is held to great fanfare in May.

PERFORMING ARTS & THEATER
The **Baltimore Symphony Orchestra** (☎ 410-783-8000) performs at the **Meyerhoff Symphony Hall** (1212 Cathedral St). The Baltimore Opera performs at the **Lyric Opera House** (☎ 410-685-5086; www.lyricoperahouse.com; 140 W Mount Royal Ave).

Theater options include the following:
Centerstage (☎ 410-332-0033; 700 N Calvert St) Stages Shakespeare, Wilde, Miller and contemporary works.

Charles Theatre (☎ 410-727-3456; www.thecharles.com; 1711 N Charles St) The best art house in the city, this theater screens new releases, revivals and art films.

Getting There & Away
AIR
Baltimore-Washington International Thurgood Marshall Airport (BWI) is 10 miles south of downtown via I-295.

BUS
Greyhound and Peter Pan buses can be caught at the downtown **station** (210 W Fayette St at Park Ave).

TRAIN
Trains stop at Baltimore's **Penn Station** (1515 N Charles St) in north Baltimore. MARC operates weekday commuter trains to and from Washington, DC (one way/round-trip $7/4). This is the most convenient way to travel between these cities.

Getting Around
TO/FROM THE AIRPORT
Check **Maryland Transit Administration** (MTA; www.mtamaryland.com) for all schedules and fares.

Light Rail (☎ 410-539-5000; tickets $1.60) runs directly from BWI to downtown's Lexington Market and Penn Station.

MARC trains (☎ 800-325-7245) run hourly 16-minute trips between Penn Station and BWI on weekdays. **SuperShuttle** (☎ 800-258-3826; www.supershuttle.com) runs an airport-van service to the Inner Harbor for $13 one way; buy tickets at the ground transportation desk at C Pier.

Taxis cost around $25.

CAR & TAXI
Many sights require a car but parking is either scarce or overpriced. Fortunately, the downtown sights are relatively compact, and taxis and water taxis are inexpensive. If you're driving, many Inner Harbor garages charge cheaper 'in before' prices if you park there before or after rush hours.

BUS, TRAIN & METRO
Maryland Transit Administration (MTA; ☎ 410-539-5000; www.mtamaryland.com) has info on Baltimore's bus, light-rail and Metro systems. Within the city, single fares are $1.60, all-day passes are $3.50 Correct change required.

BOAT
Baltimore Water Taxi (☎ 410-563-3901; Inner Harbor; adult/child under 11 $8/4) lands at all the harborside attractions and neighborhoods.

ANNAPOLIS
Like Baltimore, Maryland's capital is rooted in its colonial past and its maritime present. This picturesque town has retained much of its 18th-century appearance; narrow lanes lined with brick row houses radiate from traffic circles drawn around St Anne's Church and the State House. From its hilltop perch, the State House overlooks the City Dock and harbor that established Annapolis as an important port after the area was first settled by Puritans in 1649. The US Naval Academy was established here in 1845, and the town is well known as America's Sailing Capital, with 17 miles of waterfront.

There's a **visitor center** (☎ 410-280-0445; www.visitannapolis.org; 26 West St; ☉ 9am-5pm) and a seasonal information booth at City Dock. A **Maryland Welcome Center** (☎ 410-974-3400; 350 Rowe Blvd; ☉ 9am-5pm) is inside the State House, and runs tours of the building twice daily.

Sights & Activities
Think of the State House as a wheel hub from which most attractions fan out, leading down to the **City Dock** and historic **waterfront**. Most water-based activities originate from the dock area, while tours are handled straight from the visitor center.

US NAVAL ACADEMY
The US Naval Academy is the prestigious undergraduate college of the US Navy.

The **Armel-Leftwich Visitor Center** (☎ 410-263-6933; Gate 1 at the City Dock entrance; tours adult/student $7.50/5.50; ☺ 9am-5pm) has films, tours and interactive exhibits. Come for the formation weekdays at 12:05pm sharp, when the 4000 midshipmen and midshipwomen conduct a 20-minute military marching display in the plaza. Photo ID is required upon entry.

MARYLAND STATE HOUSE

The country's oldest state capitol in continuous legislative use, the stately 1772 **State House** (☎ 410-974-3400; 25 State Circle; ☺ 9am-5pm Mon-Fri, 10am-4pm Sat & Sun) also served as the national capitol for a short time from 1733 to 1734, when it housed the Continental Congress. The Senate is in action here from January to April. The giant acorn atop the dome, which stands for wisdom, is upside down. Photo ID is required upon entry.

DOWNTOWN ANNAPOLIS

A costumed docent will lead you on a **Three Centuries Walking Tour** (☎ 410-263-5401; adult/child under 18 $11/6), a great introduction to all things Annapolis. The 10:30am tour leaves from the visitor center and the 1:30pm tour leaves from the small information booth at the City Dock. There is a slight variation in sights visited by each, but both cover the country's largest concentration of 18th-century buildings, influential African Americans and colonial spirits who don't want to leave.

At the City Dock, the **Kunta Kinte-Alex Haley Memorial** marks the spot where Kunta Kinte – ancestor of *Roots* author, Alex Haley – was brought in chains from Africa. Haley won the Pulitzer Prize for his epic masterpiece, which begins with Kinte's landing. Bring along some bread to feed the ducks.

Annapolis brims with historical buildings: **St John's College** (cnr College Ave & King George St) is one of the USA's three oldest colleges; the 1735 **Old Treasury Building** (alongside the State House) is Maryland's oldest official building.

Annapolis has many sailing schools, cruises and bareboat (sail-it-yourself) charters. **Watermark Cruises** (☎ 410-268-7600; City Dock) is one of the best, with daily cruises, sunset sails and excursions around Annapolis. The 74ft schooner **Woodwind** (☎ 410-263-7837; 80 Compromise St; day sail/dusk cruise $29/32; ☺ May-Oct) offers two-hour cruises.

Sleeping

The colonial capital has many cozy B&Bs but few budget options except for chain hotels outside the historic district. Call ☎ 800-848-4748 for free accommodation reservations.

Chez Amis B&B (☎ 410-263-6631; www.chezamis.com; 85 East St; r 150-180; P ✗) Unless you have a bunny phobia, you'll enjoy your stay at this friendly four-room B&B just steps from the Capitol (which is also the name of the room with the best view). Full gourmet breakfast is served. Children over 10 welcome.

ScotLaur Inn (☎ 410-268-5665; www.scotlaurinn.com; 165 Main St; r $99-140; P ✗) The folks from Chick and Ruth's Delly (below) offer 10 simple pink-and-blue wi-fied rooms with private bath at their B&B (bed and bagel) above the shop.

Country Inn & Suites (☎ 800-456-4000, 410-571-6700; www.countryinns.com; 2600 Housley Rd at Hwy 450; r from $119; P ☪) This surprisingly charming chain hotel has free shuttles to the historic district, both an indoor and outdoor pool and rooms with microwave and refrigerator.

Eating & Drinking

Annapolis brims with an eclectic assortment of eateries where one street can serve up crab cakes, ribs, sushi and steaks. The majority of restaurants line City Dock and Main St.

Chick & Ruth's Delly (☎ 410-269-6737; 165 Main St; mains $6-10; ☺ 6:30am-10pm Sun-Thu, to 11:30pm Fri & Sat) This joint is bursting with affable quirkiness and its menu is almost stressfully large. Sandwiches are named after famous folks – Maryland Senator Barbara Mikulski is the open-faced tuna.

Buddy's Crabs, Ribs & Raw Bar (☎ 410-626-1100; 100 Main St; mains $14-28; ☺ lunch & dinner) At this rowdy, family-friendly, family-owned establishment, kids under six eat free, and it's half price for those between six and 10. Deals don't get much better than their weekday $10 lunch buffet.

Middleton Tavern (☎ 410-263-3323; 2 Market Space; lunch mains $14-17, dinner mains $18-22; ☺ lunch & dinner) Join the lunch crowd on the front patio and fill up on giant appetizers, or try the slippery $1 oyster shooters and platefuls of other catches-of-the-day in this waterfront tavern that was frequented by the founding fathers. Live music nightly.

City Dock Café (☎ 410-269-0969; 18 Market Space; items $2-5; ⏱ 6:30am-10pm) Grab an espresso to go or settle down with a yummy bowl of soup and your laptop – it's a wi-fi hot spot.

Rams Head Tavern (☎ 410-268-4545; 33 West St; tickets $11-60; ⏱ from 11am) Among the best watering holes in town, this microbrewery, restaurant and concert venue is a boon to ale connoisseurs and lovers of nationally known rock and jazz groups like Chick Corea.

Getting There & Around

The C-60 bus route (tickets $3; from 7am to 7pm Monday to Friday) connects Annapolis with BWI airport. Greyhound runs buses to Washington, DC ($16.75). **Annapolis Transit** (☎ 410-263-7964) provides local transport. Finding parking downtown can be absurd, so park on the press-box side of the **Navy-Marine Corps Memorial Stadium** (304 Farragut Rd off Hwy 70) and take the free shuttle bus into town.

EASTERN SHORE

On the Delmarva Peninsula, the Eastern Shore was settled 300 years ago by shorepeople (aka farmers) and waterfolk from England's west coast. Explore the back roads and Chesapeake waterways to discover the area's charm. The knot of villages west of Easton offer a particularly scenic bike tour.

Easton

The historic hamlet of Easton, with its buried powerlines, is a charming stopover for biking, walking or just taking it easy. Get a map at the **Easton Welcome Resource Center** (☎ 410-822-0345; 11 Harrison St; ⏱ 9am-5pm), which also serves as a booking agent for the historic **Avalon Theatre** (☎ 410-822-7299; www.avalontheatre .com; 40 E Dover St). Restored to its former art deco style, the 400-seat theater showcases local plays and national live music acts.

The small **Academy Art Museum** (☎ 410-822-2787; 106 South St; suggested donation $2; ⏱ 10am-4pm Mon-Sat) is the best art museum on the Eastern Shore, with a substantial collection of pieces from American and European artists from the last half-century.

The **Historical Society of Talbot County** (☎ 410-822-0773; 25 S Washington St; admission free; ⏱ 10am-4pm Mon-Sat) maintains a small museum on the history of the area, and offers historic house **tours** (tickets $5; ⏱ 11:30am Tue-Sat).

Budget sleeping options in town are slim. The deluxe **Inn at Easton** (☎ 410-822-4910; www .theinnateaston.com; 28 S Harrison St; r $175-225, ste $220-395; ℗) features sumptuous colors and gracious hospitality. Try the $65 tasting menu at its excellent Asian- and Australian-influenced restaurant, open for dinner Wednesday to Sunday. **Tidewater Inn** (☎ 410-822-1300; www.tide waterinn.com; 101 E Dover St; r from $119; ℗ ℞) is a more affordable lodging option.

For brunch, try **Alice's Café** (☎ 410-819-8590; 22 N Harrison St; mains $7-9; ⏱ 8am-3pm Mon-Sat) for her ricotta pancakes and tuna on tomato foccacia. Directly across from the courthouse, the **Washington Street Pub** (☎ 410-822-9011; 20 N Washington St; mains $6-19; ⏱ lunch & dinner) serves hearty meals and giant sandwiches in a casual, two-story setting. Enjoy the Pacific-inspired artwork at **General Tanuki** (☎ 410-819-0707; 25 Goldsborough St; lunch mains $5-12, dinner mains $18-25; ⏱ lunch & dinner) while digging into curry-fried oyster sandwiches or fresh sushi.

St Michaels & Tilghman Island

St Michaels is famous as 'the town that fooled the British': during the War of 1812, the inhabitants rigged up lanterns in a nearby forest and blacked out the town. British naval gunners shelled the forest instead of the town, allowing St Michaels to escape destruction. The building now known as the **Cannonball House** (Mulberry St) was the only building to have been hit. Standing beside the octagonal lighthouse that has become a symbol of the Chesapeake, this precious waterfront village attracts sailors from around the bay to its marina, restaurants and boutiques. Even Secretary of Defense Donald Rumsfeld has a vacation home here. There is also an unmanned **information booth** (cnr Talbot & Mill Sts; ⏱ 9am-5pm May-Oct).

At the lighthouse, the **Chesapeake Bay Maritime Museum** (☎ 410-745-2916; Navy Point; adult/child 6-17 $10/5; ⏱ 9am-6pm summer, to 5pm spring & fall, to 4pm winter) complex features a decoy studio, boat shop and demonstrations on oystering.

Narrated historic cruises aboard the **Patriot** (☎ 410-745-3100; Navy Point; adult/child under 13 $20/15) leave from the Crab Claw dock thrice daily.

All seven rooms at the charming, 19thcentury **Kemp House Inn** (☎ 410-745-2243; www .kemphouseinn.com; 412 Talbot St; r incl breakfast $110-145; ℗ ✗) have private bath, and four have a fireplace. Kids will get a kick out of sleeping on a trundle bed.

At **208 Talbot** (☎ 410-745-3838; www.208talbot .com; 208 N Talbot St; mains $15-30; ☯ dinner Wed-Sun), if the oysters in champagne sauce or pan-seared rockfish on the menu don't grab you, you can bring in your own waterfowl from the day's hunting and have the chef cook it up. Less upscale grub can be had at **Character's** (☎ 410-745-6206; 200 Talbot St; mains $7-11; ☯ lunch & dinner), with plenty of seafood, sandwiches and beer choices.

At the end of the road over the Hwy 33 drawbridge, the tiny town of **Tilghman Island** retains its traditional waterfolk roots, and local captains take visitors out on working oyster skipjacks. Take a ride on the skipjack **Rebecca T Ruark** (☎ 410-886-2176; www.skipjack.org; 2hr cruises adult/child $30/15), the oldest certified vessel in the country. **Harris Creek Kayak** (☎ 410-886-2083; www.harriscreekkayak.com; 7857 Tilghman Island Rd; per hr $20-30) has custom tours and hourly rentals. Head to legendary **Harrison's Chesapeake House** (☎ 410-886-2121; 21551 Chesapeake House Dr; mains $6-15; ☯ 6am-9pm, to 11pm Sat & Sun) for honest fare family style. Inquire about fishing charters.

Ocean City

Known as OC – but not to be confused with the OC (Orange County), California – Maryland's mammoth Atlantic coast resort swells from a year-round population of 7500 to a summer throng of 300,000, when Coppertone-slicked beachgoers crowd the boardwalk corn-dog stands and Skee-Ball arcades, and cruise along Coastal Hwy, lined with gaudy mini-golf strips and budget motels. Extending 2.5 miles from the inlet to 27th St, the **boardwalk** is the center of the action.

The **visitor center** (☎ 410-723-8610; ☯ 9am-5pm) and local **hotel-motel-restaurant association** (☎ 410-289-5645; www.ocvisitor.com), in the swank convention center on the Coastal Hwy at 40th St, can help you find lodging. Many establishments are only open during temperate months; prices plummet in the off-season. Traffic is jammed and parking scarce in summer.

SLEEPING

Of the 10,000 guest rooms in town, the cheapest are found around the inlet at the south end and throughout town on the bay side. Prices skyrocket during Memorial Day and July 4th weekends.

Budget

King Charles Hotel (☎ 410-289-6141; www.kingcharles hotel.com; 1209 Baltimore Ave at 12th St; r from $65; P) This place feels like a summer cottage and is a great deal for high season. Its 22 rooms have refrigerators and microwaves. It's centrally located half a block from the beach and in the heart of all the boardwalk action.

Ocean City Campground (☎ 410-524-7601; www .occamping.com; 70th St on Coastal Hwy; campsites $39-52, RV sites $49-59) Just one block from the beach, this family-friendly park is surrounded by plenty of amusements and restaurants, as well as a convenient local bus stop out front.

Midrange

Spinnaker Motel (☎ 410-289-5444; www.purnellprop erties.com/spinnaker; cnr 18th St & Baltimore Ave; r from $199; P) Spinnaker has oceanfront views with balconies, a huge outdoor pool and fully equipped kitchenettes.

Thunderbird Beach Motel (☎ 410-289-8136, 800-638-3244; www.purnellproperties.com/thunder bird; cnr 32nd St & Baltimore Ave; r weekdays/weekends from $140/155; ☯ May-Oct; P) Right on the beach, you'll find clean rooms with refrigerators and microwaves, a heated outdoor pool and access to showers after checkout.

Hotel Monte Carlo (☎ 410-289-7101, 877-375-6537; www.montecarlo-2000.com; 3rd St & Baltimore Ave; r $199-249; P) A bit of luxury accents the 70 efficiencies here, with Jacuzzis, a rooftop pool and hot tub, indoor heated pool, and individual balconies.

Top End

Inn on the Ocean (☎ 410-289-8894; www.bbonline .com/md/ontheocean; 1001 Atlantic Ave at the Boardwalk; r $155-260; P) This waterfront B&B promises an elegant escape. A stay at one of their six luxurious rooms (most with Jacuzzi baths) includes complimentary use of beach equipment and bicycles.

Lighthouse Club Hotel (☎ 410-524-5400, 888-371-5400; www.fagers.com/hotel; 201 60th St on the Bay; r incl breakfast $225-295; P) You might never make it to the beach when your buff-toned suite is equipped with a working gas fireplace, double Jacuzzi, platform beds and romantic views of the bay. All 23 suites also have refrigerators, sofas and wet bars.

EATING & DRINKING

Restaurants are as plentiful as motels, and plenty of cheap eats line the boardwalk and

Coastal Hwy (watch for many all-you-can-eat and early-bird deals, particularly on seafood). Dance clubs cluster around the boardwalk's southern tip.

Phillips Crab House (☎ 410-289-9121; 2004 Philadelphia Ave at 21st St; lunch mains $9-14, dinner mains $16-24; ◔ from noon) This regional chain has been around since 1956 and has an enormous menu of all things from the sea. The buffet in their gigantic dining room starts at 3:30pm.

Fager's Island (☎ 410-524-5500; 60th St; mains $19-36; ◔ from 11am) The food is quite good, if expensive, but it's best for a drink – Tchaikovsky's 1812 Overture is cued up exactly 15 minutes and 34 seconds before sunset, to time the cannons with the sun hitting the horizon.

Macky's Bayside Bar & Grill (☎ 410-723-5565; cnr 53rd St & the Bay; mains $18-28; ◔ from 11am) Overlooking Assawoman Bay, this lively joint boasts Creole food, 14 TVs and great views. Warning: a singer accompanies the sunset with 'God Bless America.'

Shenanigans (☎ 410-289-7181; cnr 4th St & Boardwalk; ◔ from 11am Mar-Oct) Here you'll find thick Guinness pints, hearty quasi-authentic Irish fare and live traditional music most nights.

Seacrets (☎ 410-524-4900; cnr W 49th St & the Bay; ◔ from 11am) A Jamaican-themed restaurant/bar/club straight out of MTV's *Spring Break*, it's got beach parties, spring-loaded dance floors, and watery areas where you can drift in an inner tube while sipping your drink.

GETTING THERE & AWAY

Carolina Trailways (☎ 410-289-9307; cnr 2nd St & Philadelphia Ave) has regular buses to major regional cities. The **Ocean City Municipal Bus Service** (☎ 410-723-1607; day pass $2) runs the length of the beach.

Assateague Island

This stunningly tranquil 37-mile-long barrier island preserves a rare stretch of undeveloped **seashore** (vehicle/cyclist & pedestrian $10/3). Herds of wild horses roam free on the island – one reason why the speed limit is a strict 25mph. The island's lower third is in Virginia (see Chincoteague Island, p358). Get maps and information at the Barrier Island **visitor center** (☎ 410-641-1441; Hwy 611).

Two **campgrounds** (☎ 410-641-3030, 800-365-2267; peak season $20) maintained by the NPS are near the access road. **Assateague State Park**

(☎ 410-641-2120; campsites/RV sites $34/44) offers 350 campsites with bathrooms and hot showers.

WESTERN MARYLAND

This region is a favorite of Civil War buffs, but also offers mountain recreation set against scenic Appalachian landscapes.

Frederick

Halfway between the blockbuster battlefields of Gettysburg, PA, and Antietam, Frederick is a popular stop along the Civil War trail. Its 50-square-block historic district retains many 18th- and 19th-century buildings in various states of renovation. The **visitor center** (☎ 301-663-8687; 19 E Church St at Market St) conducts weekend walking tours in summer ($4.50); they validate parking from the garage next door.

The **National Museum of Civil War Medicine** (☎ 301-695-1864; www.civilwarmed.org; 48 E Patrick St; adult/child 10-16 $6.50/4.50; ◔ 10am-5pm Mon-Sat, 11am-5pm Sun) grants a fascinating, at times gruesome, look at the health conditions soldiers and doctors faced on the battlefields.

Chain motels (around $70 a night) cluster south of town off I-270. **Hollerstown Hill B&B** (☎ 301-228-3630; www.hollerstownhill.com; 4 Clarke Pl; r $115-125; P ✗) has four pattern-heavy rooms with private bath. Two resident terriers and an elegant billiards room add to the charm. **Gambrill State Park** (☎ 301-271-7574; US 40; campsites/cabins $20/50) is 5 miles northwest.

The coffeehouse and wi-fi spot **Mudd Puddle** (☎ 301-620-4324; 124 S Carroll St; ◔ closed Sun) prepares tasty, inexpensive panini and hosts live entertainment most weekends.

Frederick is accessible via **Greyhound** (☎ 301-663-3311; E All Saints St) and **MARC trains** (☎ 301-228-2888; 141 B&O Ave at East Ave; ◔ weekdays only).

Antietam National Battlefield

Called 'Sharpsburg' by Southerners, the Battle of Antietam (ann-*tee*-dum) was the bloodiest day in US history. On September 17, 1862, General Robert E Lee's first invasion of the North was stalled in a tactical stalemate that left 23,000 dead, wounded or missing. The battlefield and surrounding area are solemn and haunting, uncluttered save for plaques and statues. Living-history demonstrations are conducted monthly from June to December.

The **visitor center** (☎ 301-432-5124; State Rd 65; 3-day pass for individuals/families $4/6; ⏰ 8:30am-6pm, to 5pm off-season) offers self-guided driving-tour pamphlets and audiotapes ($6) to guide you through 8.5 miles of evocative landmarks.

The neighboring town of Sharpsburg has few services; it's better to continue across the river to Shepherdstown to eat.

Ten miles after I-68 turns into I-70, the highway literally passes through **Sideling Hill**, an impressive rock exposure nearly 850ft high. Pull over to check out the **exhibit center** (☎ 301-842-2155; admission free; ⏰ 9am-5pm) and the striated evidence of some 340 million years of geologic history, give or take.

Cumberland

The famed Chesapeake and Ohio (C&O) Canal was never completed as originally conceived, but you'd never know it by the amount of hoopla that surrounds it, most noticeable in the city of Cumberland. At the Potomac River, the frontier outpost of Fort Cumberland (not to be confused with the famous Cumberland Gap between Virginia and Kentucky) was the pioneer gateway across the Alleghenies to Pittsburgh and the Ohio River. At the western end of the C&O Canal and the first national pike (Alt 40 these days), Cumberland boomed in 19th-century transport and later as an industrial center. Today Cumberland has begun to expand an outdoor-recreation trade to guide visitors to the region's rivers, forests and mountains.

C&O CANAL NATIONAL HISTORIC PARK

A marvel of engineering technology, the C&O Canal was designed to stretch alongside the Potomac River from Chesapeake Bay to the Ohio River – linking commercial centers in the east with the frontier resources of the west. Construction on the canal began in 1828 but was halted in 1850 in Cumberland by the Appalachian Mountains. By then the first railroad had made its way to Cumberland, rendering the canal obsolete.

The **C&O Canal National Historic Park visitor center** (☎ 301-739-4200; 15 Canal Pl; ⏰ 9am-5pm Mon-Fri) commemorates the importance of river trade in eastern-seaboard history and provides recreational opportunities (such as near-level mountain biking). Along its protected 185-mile corridor, the park pre-serves the 12ft-wide towpath as a hiking and biking trail and maintains six visitor centers along the trail, the first in Georgetown (p314), the last one here.

Upstairs from the NPS visitor center is the **Allegheny County visitor center** (☎ 301-777-5132) with information on Cumberland and around, and outside is where passengers catch steam-locomotive rides aboard the **Western Maryland Scenic Railroad** (☎ 800-872-4650; www.wmsr.com; adult/child $22/11), traversing forests and steep ravines to Frostburg, a three-hour round-trip.

There are plenty of reputable outfitters in the area. One is **Allegany Expeditions** (☎ 800-819-5170; www.alleganyexpeditions.com; 10310 Columbus Ave/Rte 2) which leads tours to suit whatever adventure itch you've got, from spelunking to fly-fishing.

The place for a casual bite is **Queen City Creamery & Deli** (☎ 301-777-0011; N Harrison St; mains $5-8; ⏰ 7am-10pm, shorter hrs in winter), two blocks up from Canal Pl – hearty sandwiches, a 1940s-style soda fountain, a jukebox stocked with oldies and homemade ice cream.

Deep Creek Lake

In the extreme west of the panhandle, Maryland's largest freshwater lake is an all-seasons playground. The crimson and copper glow of the Allegheny mountains attracts thousands during the annual Autumn Glory Festival in October, rivaling New England's leaf-turning backdrops. Contact the **Garrett County visitor center** (☎ 301-387-4386; www.garrettchamber.com; off US 219 on the north end) for information on all outdoor activities, including the state's only ski resort, **Wisp** (☎ 301-387-4911).

DELAWARE

Dela…*where*? Locals are sick of the joke, but it's true: this second-smallest state (Rhode Island gets all the glory for its diminutive size) suffers from a lack of name recognition. It didn't help that the rock group George Thorogood and the Delaware Destroyers, of 'Bad to the Bone' fame, let the state drop out of their name. People usually fly through Delaware so fast on their way to somewhere else, they hardly notice they've visited.

Despite 1787 marking the pinnacle of Delaware's renown – being the first to sign the Constitution, hence becoming the first state – it's been contentedly plugging along behind the scenes all these years. Corporations, especially credit card companies, have flocked to Delaware for its liberal tax and regulations structure, making it the corporate capital of the country. The lack of sales tax has meant that outlet shopping is a serious business.

However, it's the beaches that attract a decidedly non-corporate influx every summer. Its family-friendly Atlantic Ocean beaches come complete with old-fashioned wooden boardwalks that burst with energy in the high season, and are romantically deserted in winter.

The north of the state is where you'll find the lovely Brandywine Valley, home to the Brandywine School of artists, such as Andrew Wyeth, of the early 20th century. Also in the valley is the grand Winterthur estate, former residence of perhaps the most famous Delawarean of all, Henry Francis du Pont, whose DuPont company invented nylon in 1939.

History

The 1631 Dutch settlement was wiped out by the local Nanticoke Indians, and then the Swedes arrived in 1638. In 1655 the settlement was claimed by the Dutch, and then taken over by the English. The Swedes and Dutch continued to farm the north, while English settlers established tobacco plantations and slavery further south.

When Delaware joined the Revolutionary War, English frigates blockaded Wilmington's port and 18,000 British troops landed nearby. George Washington brought 11,000 soldiers to protect the Brandywine Valley and the port, but he was outflanked and withdrew to Valley Forge while the British occupied Wilmington. The town green in Dover was the site of the Delaware convention that ratified the Federal Constitution.

In 1802 a French immigrant by the name of du Pont started a gunpowder factory on the Brandywine Creek, and he profited greatly in the War of 1812. Despite its slave-owning farms, Delaware, like Maryland, sided with the Union in the Civil War.

In the 20th century, industrial growth in general and du Pont's booming chemical businesses in particular contributed – and contributes still – to the state's prosperity.

DELAWARE FACTS

Nicknames First State, Blue Hen State, Small Wonder

Population 830,364

Area 1982 sq miles

Capital city Dover (population 32,581)

Other cities Wilmington (72,503)

Official marine animal Horseshoe crab

Birthplace of Nylon (c 1939), Miss USA pageant (1880), Valerie Bertinelli (b 1960)

Home of Half the nation's Fortune 500 companies, three times more chickens than people

Famous for No state sales tax, du Pont fortune, liberal corporate regulations, beaches

---

Information

There's an 8% accommodation tax but no sales tax on other goods or services.

Delaware Tourism Office (☎ 302-739-4271, 866-284-7489; www.visitdelaware.com; 99 King's Hwy, Dover, DE 19903)

Visitor center (☎ 302-737-4059; I-95 btwn exits 1 & 3)

DELAWARE SEASHORE

Delaware's 28 miles of sandy Atlantic Ocean beaches (some preserved as state parks) are the best reason to linger. All businesses and services listed below are open year-round unless otherwise noted, and all prices are for the summer high season (June to August). Off-season bargains abound.

Lewes

Anchoring Cape Henlopen, Lewes (*loo-iss*) has more history than your average beach town. In 1631 the Dutch founded it as a whaling settlement, calling it Zwaanendael, or valley of the swans. It turned out more like the valley of the disgruntled natives, and the whalers were soon massacred. These days tourists are drawn to the rugged cape beachscapes and tranquil atmosphere.

The **visitor center** (☎ 302-645-8073; www.lewes chamber.com; 120 Kings Hwy; 9am-5pm Mon-Fri) directs you to sights such as the **Zwaanendael Museum** (☎ 302-645-1148; 102 Kings Hwy; admission free; 10am-4:30pm Tue-Sat, 1:30-4:30pm Sun), which explains the Dutch roots of this first state settlement and houses 18th-century shipwreck treasures like a replica of a Dutch town hall. Rent bikes at **Lewes Cycle Sports** (☎ 302-645-4544; per hr from $5; 9am-4pm Fri-Wed), located within the Beacon Motel (p340).

Reminiscent of small European hotels, **Zwaanendael Inn** (☎ 302-645-6466; 142 2nd St; www .zwaanendaelinn.com; r $95-160, ste $150-260; P ⊠ ☒) has 18 antique-laden rooms that are convenient to the beaches, ferry and downtown; there's a fitness facility onsite. **Beacon Motel** (☎ 302-645-4888; 514 Savannah Rd; r $135-175; P ⊠ ☒) has large, quiet rooms with refrigerator, HBO and private balcony.

Blue Plate Diner (☎ 302-644-8400; 329 Savannah Rd; dishes $5; ⏱ 8am-9pm, shorter hrs in winter) serves excellent diner and breakfast grub all day; there's occasional live entertainment. Exquisite French-inspired fare is found at the gingerbread-style **Buttery Restaurant** (☎ 302-645-7755; cnr 2nd Ave & Savannah Rd; mains $15-24; ⏱ lunch & dinner). Get there between 5pm and 6:30pm for the prix-fixe dinner for $25. **Cafe Azafrán** (☎ 302-644-4446; ⏱ breakfast & lunch year-round, dinner in summer) dishes out tasty Mediterranean food and the best espresso in town.

The **Cape May-Lewes Ferry** (☎ 800-643-3779 for reservations, 302-644-6030 for schedule; www.capemay lewesferry.com) runs daily 80-minute ferries across Delaware Bay to New Jersey from the terminal a mile from downtown Lewes, Fares for vehicle and driver are $20, plus $6 for additional vehicle or foot passengers, from November to March; and $25, plus $8 for additional passengers, from April to October (children under seven travel free).

Cape Henlopen State Park

One mile east of Lewes, more than 4000 acres of tall dune bluffs, pine forests and wetlands are preserved in an attractive **state park** (☎ 302-

---

THE AUTHOR'S CHOICE

Rehoboth Guest House (☎ 302-227-4117; www.rehobothguesthouse.com; 40 Maryland Ave; r $85-140, with private bath $95-195; ⊠) This gay-owned, wildly popular guesthouse on a quiet street has gorgeous sunbathing decks, 13 immaculate rooms (No 34 is highly sought-after), wi-fi and a lovely backyard with outdoor showers. It's a five-minute walk to the boardwalk and boasts a private alleyway to the Lambda Rising Rehoboth location and Deep Blue bar, both gay institutions in town. Wine and cheese is served on Saturday afternoons. Sidney the Airedale will likely be on hand to welcome you. Reservations recommended.

645-8983) that's popular with bird-watchers and beachgoers ($6 per out-of-state car). You can see clear to Cape May, NJ, from the observation tower. There's also a nature center, bathhouses and bike paths. North Shores beach draws many gay and lesbian couples. **Camping** (☎ 302-645-2103; campsites $27; ⏱ Mar-Nov) includes oceanfront or wooded sites.

Rehoboth Beach & Dewey Beach

Downtown Rehoboth (re-*ho*-bith) Beach is a vibrant old seaside town tucked behind a very congested and tacky stretch of Hwy 1 (follow the signs to the resort area). The main drag, Rehoboth Ave, is lined with restaurants, food stalls and souvenir shops, from the **visitor center** (☎ 302-227-2233; www.beach-fun.com; 501 Rehoboth Ave; ⏱ 9am-5pm) at the roundabout to the mile-long beach boardwalk.

Each summer, the population of Rehoboth swells to 50,000 sunseekers and has long been known as a popular gay and lesbian resort, though the crowd is diverse, as evidenced by the families, older couples, students and yuppies. (Poodle Beach, at the southern tip of the boardwalk, is primarily gay, while lesbians congregate at North Shores beach at the south end of Cape Henlopen State Park.)

Further south, along Hwy 1, is Rehoboth's wild little sister, **Dewey Beach**, known for its frantic nightlife. All lodging, eating and drinking listings are in Rehoboth unless otherwise noted.

Books, coffee and Internet access (wired and wireless) can be found at **Booksandcoffee** (☎ 302-226-9959; 113 Dickinson St, Dewey; ⏱ 7:30am-7pm).

The **Jolly Trolley** (one way $2-3; ⏱ 8am-2am in summer) connects Rehoboth and Dewey and makes frequent stops along the way. **Greyhound/Carolina Trailways** (☎ 919-833-3601) buses stop on Rehoboth Ave.

SLEEPING

Homey guesthouses within two shady blocks of the beach, though pricey in season for aging accommodations without pools, are preferable to highway motels. Many include continental breakfast.

Corner Cupboard Inn (☎ 302-227-8553; www.corner cupboardinn.com; 50 Park Ave off 2nd St; r incl breakfast $160-260; P ⊠) Tucked away on a tree-lined street north of Lake Gerar, this family-friendly, wi-fied inn has 16 comfy rooms with private bath, and is close to the beach.

Royal Rose Inn (☎ 302-226-2535; www.royalroseinn .com; 41 Baltimore Ave; r incl breakfast $120-180; P X) This slightly campy B&B has a rooftop hot tub, screened porch and sundeck. It's just a block from the boardwalk and all seven rooms have private bath and wi-fi.

Big Oaks Campground (☎ 302-645-6838; www .bigoakscamping.com; Hwy 1 & Rte 270; campsites/cabins $35/75; P ☎) Three miles from the board-walk, Big Oaks has a playground, and beach shuttles are available. Two-night minimum for cabins.

EATING

The beach boardwalk and Rehoboth Ave are a smorgasbord of quick food and bars. Thrasher's and Nicola's are classic stand-bys for fries and pizza, respectively.

Planet X Café (☎ 302-226-1928; 35 Wilmington Ave; mains from $19; ☺ dinner daily in summer, Thu-Sun off-season) Set in an old Victorian, this café plays up the potential of organic ingredients and free-range poultry to create incredible, globe-spanning dishes.

Café Solé (☎ 302-227-7107; 44 Baltimore Ave; sandwiches $4-8; ☺ lunch & dinner, closed Mon & Tue in winter) Best sandwiches in town. Ever tried a fried oyster BLT?

Sydney's Blues & Jazz (☎ 302-227-1339; www.syds blues.com; 25 Christian St; mains $21-28, cover $5-12; ☺ from 4pm Wed-Sat) This restaurant has a fine selection of visiting acts the likes of Kelly Blake and Mem Shannon that supplement tasty seafood and Creole dishes – mmm, bacon-wrapped scallops!

Dogfish Head (☎ 302-226-2739; 320 Rehoboth Ave; mains $9-23; ☺ from 4pm Mon-Fri, from noon Sat & Sun) This brewpub has appropriately vast wine and beer selections, plus quite good food, and live music every weekend with no cover.

DRINKING & ENTERTAINMENT

Bottle & Cork (☎ 302-227-1272; 1807 Dagsworthy St; cover $5-15) This club brings in some serious rockers, like Ted Nugent.

Rusty Rudder (☎ 302-227-3888; 113 Dickinson St & The Bay) This rowdy bar has a great water view and live calypso music nightly, with harder music fare on weekends as well.

NORTHERN & CENTRAL DELAWARE

Northern Delaware includes the great du Pont mansion, Winterthur. The urban city of Wilmington lies at the gateway to the scenic Brandywine Valley. Central Dela-ware is a mosaic of farms and marshes, and home to the capital city, Dover.

Wilmington

Delaware's largest city sits at the confluence of Brandywine Creek and Christina River and acts as the gateway to the Brandywine Valley region. The central commercial dis-trict is along Market St, though south of downtown, the new Riverfront is turning old warehouses and other industrial sites into shops, restaurants and museums. The **visitor center** (☎ 302-652-4088; www.visitwilmingtonde.com; 100 W 10th St; ☺ 9am-5pm Mon-Fri) is downtown.

The **Delaware Art Museum** (☎ 302-571-9590; 800 S Madison St; adult/child under 7 $7/free; ☺ 10am-6pm Tue, Thu & Fri, to 5pm Sat, 1-5pm Sun) exhibits work of the local Brandywine School, in-cluding Edward Hopper, John Sloan and three generations of Wyeths. The new **Dela-ware Center for the Contemporary Arts** (☎ 302-656-6466; www.thedcca.org; 200 S Madison St; adult/child under 12 $5/free, Sat morn free; ☺ 10am-5pm Tue, Thu & Fri, from noon Wed & Sun) is bringing some mind-expanding culture to the burgeoning River-front district. Free on Saturday mornings.

Hotel du Pont (☎ 302-594-3100, 800-441-9019; www.hoteldupont.com; cnr Market & 11th Sts; r $180-400; P) is the city's premier hotel. **Washington Street Ale House** (☎ 302-658-2537; 1206 Washington St; mains $9-20; ☺ 11am-late) has plenty of beers to wash down salads, burgers and steaks. **Govatos** (☎ 302-652-4082; 800 N Market St; mains $4-9; ☺ 8am-3pm Mon-Sat) is an old-fashioned restaurant and candy store known for its delectable chocolates.

Wilmington is accessible via **Greyhound/ Carolina Trailways** (☎ 302-655-6111; 318 Market St) and **Amtrak** (☎ 302-658-1515), at the foot of Market St.

Brandywine Valley

The rural Brandywine Valley, straddling the Delaware–Pennsylvania border, is eas-ily accessible from Wilmington or Philadel-phia. The **Brandywine Valley Tourist Information Center** (☎ 610-280-6145, 800-228-9933), outside Longwood Gardens in Kennett Sq, PA, dis-tributes information on the region's triple crown of **châteaux** (☎ 302-651-6912; Rockland Rd btwn Children's Dr & Rte 202; admission $10; ☺ guided tours 9am-3pm Tue-Sat May-Dec) and gardens: Win-terthur, Longwood Gardens (p203) and Ne-mours, though the last of these is closed for renovation until May 2007.

WASHINGTON, DC & THE CAPITAL REGION

Winterthur (☎ 302-888-4600; www.winterthur.org; Hwy 52 off Kennett Pike; admission $20; 🕙 10am-5pm Tue-Sun), the valley's highlight and an incredible monument to American excess, includes the 175-room country estate of Henry Francis du Pont, along with a decorative arts museum. The gardens and several child-specific attractions are visited by tram. It's 6 miles northwest of Wilmington.

Hagley Museum (☎ 302-658-2400; www.hagley.org; Hwy 141; adult/child/senior $11/4/9; 🕙 9:30am-4:30pm) is another fascinating shrine to the du Pont legacy; this sprawling outdoor museum includes the ruins of the original du Pont mills, craftsmith demonstrations and exhibits on cutting-edge DuPont products.

New Castle

Historic New Castle retains cobblestone streets and attractive blocks of 18th-century buildings, and you couldn't ask for a nicer picnic spot than its expansive riverside park. Seven miles south of Wilmington, New Castle was originally founded by the Dutch in 1651 but later taken over by the English, and acted as state capital before Dover. The district is laid out in an easy grid around a small park called the Green and along Delaware St to the riverside Strand. The **visitor center** (42 The Strand; 🕙 9am-5pm Mon-Fri) arranges walking tours, or you can wander the compact old town on your own. Sights include the **Old Court House** (🕙 closed Mon), the **arsenal on the Green**, **churches** and **cemeteries** dating back to the 17th century, and **historic houses**.

The elderly owner of the five-room **Terry House B&B** (☎ 302-322-2505; www.terryhouse.com; 130 Delaware St; r $90-110; 🅿) will play the piano for you while you enjoy a full breakfast. Enjoy English pub fare and hearty ales at **Jessop's Tavern** (☎ 302-322-6111; 114 Delaware St; mains $16-22; 🕙 lunch & dinner) or at its sister restaurant **Arsenal at Old New Castle** (☎ 302-328-1290; 30 Market St; mains $16-23; 🕙 lunch & dinner Tue-Sun). Both have kids' menus.

Dover

William Penn laid out the Green on State St in 1722, and the square remains the historical center of the state capital, with most attractions within walking distance. The 1792 Old State House and 1874 Court House are tucked in beside attractive brick row houses shaded by tall trees.

Walk beside the State House to find the state **visitor center** (☎ 302-739-4266; 406 Federal St; 🕙 8:30am-4:30pm Mon-Sat, from 1:30pm Sun) and history exhibits at the foot of a long plaza from the capitol. **Johnson Victrola Museum** (☎ 302-739-5316; cnr Bank & New Sts; admission free; 🕙 10am-3:30pm Tue-Sat) honors 'talking machine' pioneer Eldridge Johnson with exhibits including the RCA Records trademark dog, Nipper.

Southeast of town, Dover Air Force Base, used by giant C-5 Galaxy aircraft, is the country's largest air force base, and is where America's war dead return home. The **Air Mobility Command Museum** (☎ 302-677-5938; cnr Hwy 9 & Hwy 1; admission free; 🕙 9am-4pm Tue-Sat) has a collection of vintage planes and other aviation artifacts.

There are budget motels along Hwy 13, but the **State Street Inn** (☎ 302-734-2294; www.statestreetinn.com; 228 State St; r incl breakfast $110-125; 🅿 🚫 🐾), just north of Wesley College, is a cozy escape from the big chains.

Corner Eatery at 33 (☎ 302-735-9822; 33 W Loockerman St; mains $5-9; 🕙 10am-3pm Mon-Fri) has sit-down and to-go soups, sandwiches and salads under a cute mural of the town. **WT Smithers** (☎ 302-674-8875; 140 S State St; 🕙 from 11am Mon-Sat) is an inviting downtown tavern with a great happy hour and a jazz brunch on Sunday.

VIRGINIA

You can keep your Boston Tea Party, your Plymouth Rock, your Liberty Bell…if you truly want to get a finger on the jugular of this country's creation – the dynamic figures, tide-turning battles and profoundly revolutionary thinking that went into crafting this country into what it is – you'll do no better than Virginia. From America's first permanent British settlement (Jamestown, p354) to Patrick Henry's incendiary 'Give me liberty or give me death!' (St John's Church, p348) to the spot where a Civil War–torn land finally agreed to give this 'united states' thing an honest try (Appomattox, p360), Virginia is a historical heavy hitter.

If your travels so far haven't hardened you against historical plaques, you're in for a treat. The Revolutionary period is nowhere better represented than in the historic triangle of Williamsburg, Jamestown and Yorktown. The bulk of the Civil War was fought on Virginian soil, and reminders of the bloodshed are everywhere. Washington, Jefferson and many other founders of the nation were intimately tied to the state.

Virginia is, however, much more than a vast museum, and you owe it to yourself to explore the rugged Blue Ridge Mountains and Shenandoah National Park. In the state's southwesternmost corner, marvel at the intense natural beauty as well as the courage of the hundreds of thousands of 19th-century pioneers who kicked off their journey west via the Cumberland Gap. Chesapeake Bay and the Eastern Shore offer coastlines dotted with serene New England-esque towns, while ocean-front Virginia Beach is a suntan lotion–slathered playground and the state's largest city.

History

In 1607 Jamestown Island became the site of the first permanent English settlement in Virginia. However, two-thirds died in the first year alone. Between 1607 and 1625, 8500 settlers arrived and only 1200 survived.

Virginia grew on the tobacco trade, and a slaveholding planter elite came to control most of the land and the colony's government. Expansionism led to conflict with the Native Americans, and Nathaniel Bacon's ragtag army took them on, then turned on the colonial elite in an abortive rebellion that destroyed much of Jamestown.

In 1699 the colony's capital moved to nearby Williamsburg, where stately public buildings echoed the English style (more than 300 years later, the restored town is a big tourist attraction). Nearby at Yorktown, George Washington's 1781 victory over the British effectively brought an end to the Revolutionary War.

In 1861 Virginia seceded from the Union, and though General Robert E Lee of Arlington was offered command of the Northern armies, he elected to lead opposing Virginia's forces into the Civil War instead.

Virginia's colonial and plantation past is a nostalgic memory, and its major industries continue to revolve around historic themes. Celebrations are planned for the state's big 4-0-0 in 2007, especially in Jamestown.

Information

Virginia's **Division of Tourism** (☎ 800-321-3244; www.virginia.org; 901 E Byrd St, Richmond, VA 23219) pro-

---

VIRGINIA FACTS

Nicknames Old Dominion State, Mother of Presidents

Population 7.5 million

Area 42,777 sq miles

Capital city Richmond (population 197,456)

Other cities Virginia Beach (440,098)

Birthplace of George Washington (1732–99), Thomas Jefferson (1743–1826), Booker T Washington (1856–1915), Robert E Lee (1807–70), Ella Fitzgerald (1917–96), Patsy Cline (1932–63), Shirley MacLaine (b 1934)

Home of Monticello, the Pentagon, Arlington National Cemetery

Official beverage Milk

Famous for Presidents, Civil War battlefields, ham, Southern aristocracy, being second only to Texas in number of annual executions

---

duces a comprehensive state guide. There are 10 welcome centers throughout the state on the interstate highways. State sales tax is 5% and accommodation tax is 10%. Many chain hotels won't let rooms to people under 21 years of age, so if that's you, check before you show up on the doorstep.

NORTHERN VIRGINIA

Across the Potomac from Washington, many of northern Virginia's sights are so close to the capital that they can be covered while monument-hopping. Further afield, rural retreats provide weekend refuge for stressed-out Washingtonians.

Arlington National Cemetery

Just across the Potomac from DC, the 612-acre national **cemetery** (☎ 703-692-0931; www.arlingtoncemetery.org; admission free; 🕐 8am-7pm Apr 1-Sep 30, to 5pm rest of year; 🅿) is the burial ground for over 245,000 military personnel and their dependents, with veterans from every US war since the Revolution. Leaving from the visitor center, **tourmobiles** (☎ 202-554-5100, 888-868-7707; adult/child $6/3) are a handy way to visit the cemetery's notable memorials.

Robert E Lee's 1100-acre property, and his home, **Arlington House**, were confiscated when Lee left to command northern Virginia's army. Union soldiers were buried around the house so he could never use it again. After the Civil War, the site became the national cemetery, and the house is open to the public.

GREAT FALLS NATIONAL PARK

Fourteen miles upriver from Georgetown, the normally placid Potomac cascades 77ft down a series of beautiful, treacherous rapids known as Great Falls. The C&O Canal was constructed to allow barges to bypass the falls. Today the land on both sides of the river is designated as national park and provides glorious views of the falls as well as hiking, cycling and picnicking spots. From the towpath out of Georgetown you can hook up with the park in Maryland, where it's called C&O Canal National Historical Park; on the Virginia side it's **Great Falls National Park** (☎ 703-285-2966; Old Dominion Dr, off I-183; ☼ dawn-dusk). The entrance to both parks together is per vehicle/cyclist or pedestrian $5/3.

The **Tomb of the Unknowns** represents soldiers killed in action who can't be identified as belonging to either side; military guards retain a round-the-clock vigil, and the changing of the guard (every half-hour March to September and every hour rest of the year) is one of Arlington's most moving sights. An eternal flame marks the **grave of John F Kennedy**, next to those of Jacqueline Kennedy Onassis and two of her infant children. Other points of interest include the Pan Am Flight 103 cairn and a memorial to the astronauts of the space shuttle *Challenger*.

Alexandria

Along with Georgetown, Alexandria preceded the founding of the nation's capital and has a handful of mildly interesting attractions to bear witness to its long history. As in Georgetown, walkable blocks of attractive brick row houses in the historic district find modern uses as restaurants, taverns and shops. The **visitor center** (☎ 800-388-838-4200; www.funside.com; 221 King St; ☼ 9am-5pm) issues parking permits and discount tickets to historic sights.

Before the building that is now the **Torpedo Factory Art Center** (☎ 703-838-4565; 105 N Union St; admission free ☼ 10am-5pm) housed the open studios and galleries of more than 150 local artists, it manufactured weapons for use in WWI.

Blessedly removed from the waterfront bustle is **Le Gaulois** (☎ 703-739-9494; 1106 King St; lunch mains $8-14, dinner mains $17-26; ☼ lunch & dinner), which turns out finely executed French cuisine – try the cassoulet. The garden terrace is lovely.

From downtown DC, get off at the King St Metro station. Local buses cover the mile to the visitor center. On weekends the free DASH shuttle bus connects the station with the waterfront and points in between.

Mount Vernon & Around

Situated on the banks of the Potomac in Virginia, George Washington's 8000-plus acre estate of **Mount Vernon** (☎ 703-780-2000; www .mountvernon.org; adult/child 6-11 $11/5; ☼ 9am-5pm, to 4pm Nov-Feb) holds a 19-room country house, immaculate gardens, slaves' quarters, a working farm and George and Mary Washington's tombs. One of the most visited historic sites in the nation, it affords glimpses of 18th-century farm life and the first president as a country squire. A new museum brings even more of the estate's historic collections into the public eye. The Washingtons lived here from 1759 to 1775, when George assumed command of the Continental Army. After the Revolutionary War and eight years as president, he retired to Mt Vernon, living here from 1797 until his death in 1799.

Mount Vernon Inn (☎ 703-780-0011; lunch mains $7-9, dinner mains $14-21; ☼ lunch & dinner), at the main gate, is a casual place serving hearty colonial fare.

Mount Vernon is 15 miles south of DC by road; you can take the Metro to Huntington, then the Fairfax Connector bus 101 to the estate. It also makes a gorgeous bike ride along the river from DC.

Manassas Battlefield

South of where Dulles airport now stands, major Civil War battles known collectively as the Battles of Bull Run (by the North) or Battles of Manassas (by the South) were fought in July 1861 and August 1862. The **Manassas National Battlefield Park visitor center** (☎ 703-361-1339; admission $3; ☼ 8:30am-5pm) is the start of an interesting self-guided tour.

Fredericksburg

An easy day trip from DC, this small city possesses an impressive historical résumé: Captain John Smith, of Pocahontas fame, visited this lovely spot on the Rappahannock River as early as 1608, George Washington grew up here and James Monroe practiced law here. During the Civil War, many bloody battles were fought in the area. Today the 40-block historic district is pleasant to stroll through, taking in museums and antique shops.

SIGHTS

The biggest attraction in these parts is the **Fredericksburg & Spotsylvania National Military Park**, maintained by the NPS. This park preserves four crucial Civil War battlefields, among them Chancellorsville, where General Stonewall Jackson received his fatal wound – one of his own soldiers accidentally shot him! The **Fredericksburg Battlefield visitor center** (☎ 540-373-6122; 1013 Lafayette Blvd; admission free, film $2; ☉ 9am-5pm) offers informative exhibits and a driving-tour map that covers the 17-mile radius of the battles in detail.

The town's **visitor center** (☎ 800-373-1776; www.fredericksburgvirginia.net; 706 Caroline St; ☉ 9am-5pm) offers a pass to historic Fredericksburg for nine local sights (adult/child six to 18 $29/9.50) including the ones described below. Unless otherwise noted, the following colonial attractions are open 9am to 5pm Monday to Saturday and 11am to 5pm Sunday March through November, with slightly shorter winter hours.

Hugh Mercer Apothecary Shop (☎ 540-373-3362; 1020 Caroline St; adult/child 6-18 $5/2) A fascinating look at the medical marvels of the day, like, er, leeches.

James Monroe Museum & Memorial Library (☎ 540-654-1043; 908 Charles St; adult/child 6-18 $5/2; ☉ 10am-5pm Mon-Sat, from 1pm Sun, slightly shorter hrs in winter) Honors native son and namesake of the 1823 Monroe Doctrine, which proclaimed, among other things,

that the Americas were to be free from further European colonization (though it was John Quincy Adams who really developed the idea).

Mary Washington House (☎ 540-373-1569; 1200 Charles St; adult/child 6-18 $5/2) Home of George Washington's mother, Mary Ball Washington, for her last 17 years.

Rising Sun Tavern (☎ 540-371-1494; 1304 Caroline St; adult/child 6-18 $5/2) Once patronized by the town's luminaries, it's now a museum complete with tavern wenches.

SLEEPING & EATING

Richard Johnston Inn (☎ 540-899-7606; www.the richardjohnstoninn.com; 711 Caroline St; r $95-160; ✗) Across from the visitor center, this scores points for location, comfort and friendliness (especially from the two resident Scottie dogs). Most rooms have private bath, and guests enjoy a full breakfast on weekends.

Sammy T's (☎ 540-371-2008; 801 Caroline St; mains $7-17; ☉ from 11am; ✗) At first glance it looks like just another dimly lit, wooden-booth meat 'n' potatoes joint, but its extensive menu skews towards vegetarian and vegan.

Olde Towne Wine & Cheese Deli (☎ 540-373-7877; 707 Caroline St; items $5-7; ☉ 11am-4pm Mon-Sat) Order up a gourmet sandwich at this cheerfully red deli.

GETTING THERE & AWAY

Weekday commuter **trains** (☎ 800-742-3873; www.vre.org; per person $8.10) connect DC and the train station on Caroline St. Buses come into the **Greyhound/Trailways depot** (☎ 540-373-2103; 1400 Jefferson Davis Hwy).

RICHMOND

Richmond still exudes an air of the antebellum South, with wide, tree-lined boulevards, row after row of gracious houses,

---

NORTHERN NECK PLANTATIONS

Referring to the peninsula thrusting eastward from Fredericksburg into the Chesapeake Bay, this largely rural chunk of land lays claim to several noteworthy attractions. If you really want to get under its skin, check out the **Northern Neck Tourism Council** (☎ 804-333-1919; www .northernneck.org).

The undisputed 'father' of the country was born right here, on a small plantation on the banks of Pope Creek. Sadly, the original building is long gone, though you can see its footprint and get a sanitized, re-created sense of what plantation life was like in the early 18th century at the **George Washington Birthplace National Monument** (☎ 804-224-1732; 1732 Popes Creek Rd; adult/child under 17 $4/free; ☉ 9am-5pm), just off US 3.

Stratford Hall Plantation (☎ 804-493-8038; 485 Great House Rd; adult/child 6-11 $10/5; ☉ 9:30am-4pm), a few miles to the east, is the birthplace of General Robert E Lee. The impressive mansion is open for tours on the hour and its restaurant serves Southern-style luncheons.

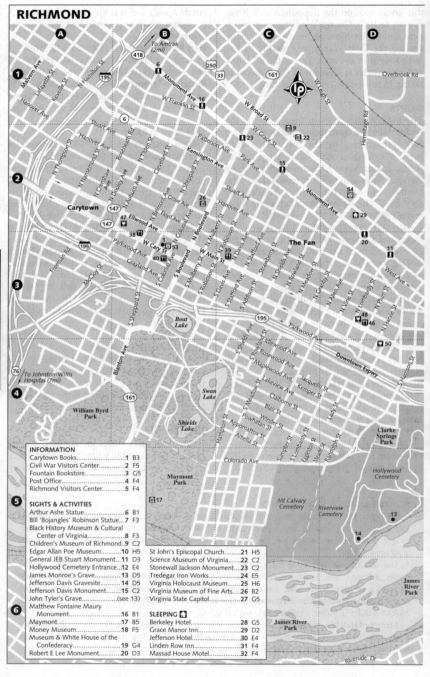

RICHMOND

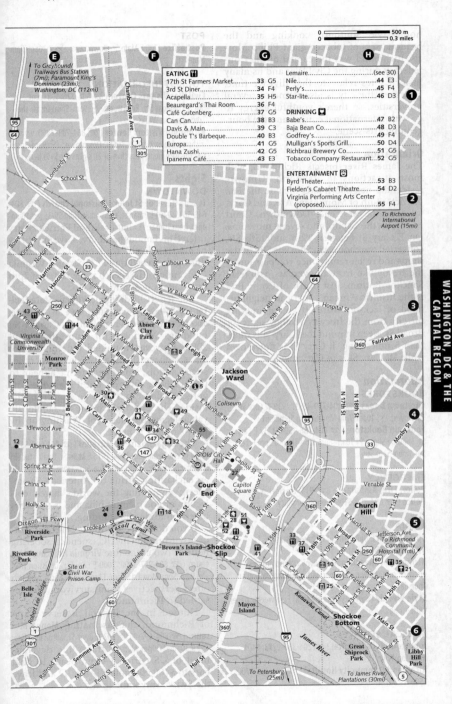

home-style Southern cooking and the headquarters of tobacco giant Philip Morris. Richmond was the capital of the Confederacy during the Civil War and its many historic sites relate to that divisive time. However, the city is also home to several universities, so there's youthful energy to go with international cuisine and the bourgeoning arts scene.

Orientation
The James River bisects Richmond, with most attractions to its north. Uptown, residential neighborhoods include the Fan district, south of Monument Ave, and Carytown, in the west end. Downtown, Court End holds the Capitol and several museums. On E Cary St between 12th and 15th Sts, converted warehouses in Shockoe Slip house shops and restaurants. Once you pass under the trestle-like freeway overpass, you're in Shockoe Bottom. Just north of Court End is the historic African American neighborhood of Jackson Ward. If you're entering the city from the freeways, follow signs for Broad St. Keep in mind that Cary St is more than 5 miles long; E Cary St is downtown while W Cary St is in Carytown.

Information
BOOKSTORES
Carytown Books (☎ 804-359-4831; 2930 W Cary St, Carytown; ✆ 10am-7pm Mon-Sat, to 5pm Sun)
Fountain Bookstore (☎ 804-788-1594; 1312 E Cary St, Shockoe Slip; ✆ 10am-8pm Mon-Thu, to 9pm Fri & Sat, noon-5pm Sun)

EMERGENCY
Police, Fire, Ambulance (☎ 911) Emergency.
Police (☎ 804-780-5100) Non-emergency.

MEDIA
90.1 FM WDCE University of Richmond station.
93.5 FM WBBC Country.
Richmond-Times Dispatch (www.richmondtimes dispatch.com) Daily newspaper with weekend section on Thursday.
Style Weekly (www.styleweekly.com) Free weekly paper with listings.

MEDICAL SERVICES
Johnston-Willis Hospital (☎ 804-330-2273; 1401 Johnston-Willis Dr)
Richmond Community Hospital (☎ 804-225-1700; 1500 N 28th St)

POST
Post office (700 E Main St, Downtown; ✆ 7:30am-5pm Mon-Fri)

TOURIST INFORMATION
Civil War Visitors Center (☎ 804-226-1981; cnr 5th & Tredegar Sts, Riverfront; ✆ 9am-5pm) Inside the Tredegar Iron Works.
Richmond Visitors Center (☎ 804-783-7450; www .richmondva.org; 405 N 3rd St, Downtown; ✆ 9am-5pm) Get the Richmond pass (five of 20 sights for $15) here.

Sights
DOWNTOWN
It was here, at **St John's Episcopal Church** (☎ 804-648-5015; 2401 E Broad St; tours adult/child $5/3; ✆ 10am-4pm, from 1pm Sun), that firebrand Patrick Henry uttered his famous battle cry, 'Give me liberty or give me death!' (or words to that effect) during the rebellious 1775 Second Virginia Convention. His speech is reenacted at 2pm on Sundays in summer ($3).

The Jefferson-designed **Virginia State Capitol** (☎ 804-698-1788; cnr 9th & Grace Sts, Capitol Sq; daily tours free) and several other Capitol Sq buildings are closed for renovations until 2007. However, a guided tour of Capitol Sq is still worthwhile. Unlike most other state capitols, this one doesn't appear to flaunt a large rotunda, but it's got one – its gorgeous dome can only be seen from the inside. The 2nd floor houses a fabulously valuable marble statue of Washington by Jean-Antoine Houdon.

The **Edgar Allan Poe Museum** (☎ 804-648-5523; www.poemuseum.org; 1914-1916 E Main St; adult/student & senior $6/5; ✆ 10am-5pm Tue-Sat, 11am-5pm Sun) is an enchanting shrine to 'America's Shakespeare' containing the world's largest collection of Poe memorabilia and is the city's oldest building still standing.

If you don't make it to the National Holocaust Museum in DC, spend a sobering hour or two at the fine **Virginia Holocaust Museum** (☎ 804-257-5400; 2000 E Cary St; admission free; ✆ 9am-5pm Mon-Fri, from 11am Sat & Sun), which offers perspectives from survivors who re-settled in Richmond.

Housed in the Federal Reserve Bank of Richmond, the fascinating **Money Museum** (☎ 804-697-8110; 702 E Byrd St; admission free; ✆ 9:30am-3:30pm Mon-Fri) traces the development of US currency from beads to gold bars to $100,000 notes. Bring ID and leave the Swiss army knife in the car.

The **Museum & White House of the Confederacy** (☎ 804-649-1861; cnr 12th & Clay Sts; adult/child under 7/ student/senior $10/free/5/9; ⊗ 10am-5pm Tue-Sat, from noon Sun) presents the Civil War from the losers' viewpoint and houses the largest collection of Confederate flags anywhere. The adjacent White House was the wartime residence of Confederate president Jefferson Davis.

Jackson Ward, an African American community that was known as Little Africa in the late 19th century, is now a national historic landmark district. It's also where actor and dancer Bill Robinson (aka Mr Bojangles) was born. The **Black History Museum & Cultural Center of Virginia** (☎ 804-780-9093; 00 Clay St; adult/child under 13/student & senior $5/3/4; ⊗ 10am-5pm Tue-Sat, from 11am Sun) highlights the achievements of black Virginians and displays collections of African arts, textiles and artifacts.

UPTOWN

The Champs Elysées of Richmond, tree-lined Monument Ave holds mammoth statues of such revered Southern heroes as General **JEB Stuart**, **Robert E Lee**, **Matthew Fontaine Maury**, **Jefferson Davis** and **Stonewall Jackson** along a mile-long stretch east of I-95. A statue of tennis star **Arthur Ashe** was added after much controversy – some felt a mere athlete didn't warrant such an honor, while others thought this excuse a racist cover. Still others believed Ashe too good to share a street with statues of men who supported slavery.

A former grand estate, **Maymont** (☎ 804-358-7166; 1700 Hampton St; admission free; ⊗ 10am-5pm) is now a 100-acre garden, public park and petting zoo. You can hear the rush of the James River while taking in the Japanese and Italian gardens. Its grassy hills and open spaces simply beg for a picnic or Frisbee game. Donations are suggested for the estate tour and nature center.

We should all be so lucky. The extremely tranquil **Hollywood Cemetery** (☎ 804-648-8501; entrance cnr Ablemarle & S Cherry Sts; printed guide $1; ⊗ 8am-5pm, tours 11am Mon-Sat Apr-Oct), perched above the James River rapids, contains the gravesites of two US presidents (James Monroe and John Tyler), the only Confederate president (Jefferson Davis) and more than 18,000 Confederate soldiers.

The **Virginia Museum of Fine Arts** (☎ 804-340-1400; 2800 Grove Ave; requested donation $5; ⊗ 11am-5pm Wed-Sun) has a remarkable repertoire of European works, sacred Himalayan art and one of the largest Fabergé egg collections on display outside Russia. The museum is open throughout its expansion project (to be completed in 2008), and the extra space will translate into more face time for their Latin and Native American holdings.

CANAL WALK AT THE RIVERFRONT

The 1.25-mile Canal Walk between the James River and the Kanawha (ka-*naw*) and Haxall Canals is a splendid waterfront walk. It runs between 5th and 17th Sts and has 12 stops highlighting the city's history. Cross the footbridge at the Tredegar Iron Works to continue on to Belle Isle, a former POW camp for Union soldiers. These days it's a nice detour, with a climbing wall, hiking and biking trails, and access to the whitewater rapids that run through downtown Richmond.

Richmond for Children

Housed in the 1919 Broad St Station, the **Science Museum of Virginia** (☎ 804-367-0000; 2500 W Broad St, Uptown; adult/child 4-12 $8.50/8; ⊗ 9:30am-5pm Mon-Sat, 11:30am-5:30pm Sun) is a highly entertaining museum that holds three floors of hands-on exhibits covering the galaxy of science topics. Combo tickets with IMAX films are adult/child $16.50/16.

Right next door, the **Children's Museum of Richmond** (CMoR; ☎ 804-474-2667; 2626 W Broad St, Uptown; admission $7; ⊗ 9:30am-5pm Tue-Sat, from noon Sun) is aimed at the under-10 set, and is crammed with interactive activities that range from kitchen chemistry to the natural world and all manner of arts and crafts.

WASHINGTON, DC & THE CAPITAL REGION

Packed with death-defying roller coasters, soaking water rides and kiddie amusements, the giant theme park **Paramount King's Dominion** (☎ 804-876-5000; www.kingsdominion.com; adult/child 3-6 $46/36; ⏱ Mar-Oct) is 22 miles north of Richmond on I-95 (Doswell exit).

Sleeping

BUDGET

Budget options within the city are rare. If price is more a factor than charm, let the chain motels clustered off I-95 and I-64 duke it out for your $39 or $49.

Massad House Motel (☎ 804-648-2893; 11 N 4th St; r $75-110) This is the least expensive in-city option and its location for exploring downtown can't be beat. You will find small rooms equipped with cable TV and air-con in a Tudor-style boardinghouse building.

MIDRANGE

Linden Row Inn (☎ 804-783-7000; www.lindenrowinn .com; 100 E Franklin St; r incl breakfast $99-179) This intimate inn occupies antebellum row houses set around a balcony-lined courtyard, but the rooms have modern amenities and touches like evening wine and cheese and gym access at the local YMCA make it even nicer.

Grace Manor Inn (☎ 804-353-4334; www.thegrace manorinn.com; 1853 W Grace St; ste $150-175; P ⏱) This impeccably maintained historic B&B has three guest suites with claw-foot tubs, and the owners (both chefs) do a bang-up job with breakfast. Two friendly Yorkies comprise the welcome committee. Two-night minimum on weekends.

Berkeley Hotel (☎ 804-780-1300; www.berkeley hotel.com; 1200 E Cary St; r from $190; P ⏱) Excellently located in Shockoe Slip, this gracious, European-style hotel has 55 spacious rooms with cherry furnishings, wi-fi and access to the local YMCA. Parking costs $12.

TOP END

Jefferson Hotel (☎ 804-788-8000; www.jeffersonhotel .com; 101 W Franklin St; r from $285; P ⏱) This is the city's premier hotel and they won't let you forget it. Beyond the standard deluxe amenities, guests enjoy plush bathrobes, car service to anywhere downtown, and afternoon cookies and cider. Their jaw-dropping Sunday champagne brunch is served in the Rotunda and will set you back $38 per person.

Eating

The most happening eats in Richmond are found in the Fan and Carytown, and on E Cary St in Shockoe Slip. Many restaurants are nonsmoking before 10pm, but they can get pretty smoky from then on.

DOWNTOWN

The area around Capitol Sq bustles with office workers Monday through Friday, but is a virtual ghost town on weekends.

3rd St Diner (☎ 804-788-4750; 218 E Main St; mains $4-10; ⏱ 24hr) This diner resembles the aftermath of a pink-and-blue explosion. Bring quarters for the (loud) jukebox and lose the attitude because this dive serves it up quick, no frills, 24/7. We commend its 4pm to 8pm happy hour.

Perly's (☎ 804-649-2779; 111 E Grace St; mains $4-9; ⏱ 8am-2pm) This Richmond favorite is recommended for a quick deli bite or a lazy weekend brunch.

Acapella (☎ 804-377-1963; 2300 E Broad St; dinner mains $15-26; ⏱ lunch & dinner Tue-Sat, dinner only Sun)

GAY & LESBIAN RICHMOND

Though the otherwise hip-to-it weekly *Style* prudishly insists on using the phrase 'alternative lifestyle' as a euphemism for 'gay' in reference to bars and clubs, for a Southern town Richmond doesn't do a shabby job representing the Family. **Gay Richmond** (www.gayrichmond.com) is the best overall resource. Here are a few of your options:

■ **Babe's** (☎ 804-355-9330; 3166 W Cary St, Carytown; ⏱ from 11am, hrs vary) This fun, relaxed spot is where you'll find the ladies – and the associated folk shows and line dancing.

■ **Godfrey's** (☎ 804-648-3957; 308 E Grace St, Downtown; cover $3-5; ⏱ from 10pm Mon-Sat) Their drag brunch on Sunday kicks off at 11am, but the line forms way earlier. A fun mix, and always 18 and over.

■ **Fieldens Cabaret Theatre** (☎ 804-346-8113; www.richmondtriangleplayers.com; 2033 W Broad St) This is the venue for the outrageous gay-themed shows of the Richmond Triangle Players.

Italian and German? You'd be forgiven for doubting a restaurant that purports to work well in both cuisines, but Acapella succeeds. In the basement is their English-style pub, the perfect hideaway bar.

Lemaire (☎ 804-788-8000; 101 W Franklin St; dinner mains $25-37; ☺ lunch & dinner Mon-Fri, dinner Sat) At the Jefferson Hotel (opposite), this is where you'll find upscale French and Southern cuisine and guys proposing to their girlfriends.

17th St farmers market (cnr 17th & Main St; ☺ 9am-2pm Thu, Sat & Sun, hrs may vary) This bustling market kicks off at the beginning of May and goes through October.

The following are also recommended:

Beauregard's Thai Room (☎ 804-644-2328; 103 E Cary St; mains $9-16; ☺ Mon-Sat) Excellent, authentic Thai food.

Europa (☎ 804-643-0911; 1409 E Cary St; tapas $4-10; ☺ lunch & dinner Mon-Fri, dinner Sat & Sun) Trendy Mediterranean tapas in a congenial setting, and free parking.

Hana Zushi (☎ 804-225-8801; 1309 E Cary St; ☺ lunch & dinner) The teriyaki and tempura options are more exciting than the rolls. The bento lunch is a steal.

UPTOWN

Ipanema Café (☎ 804-213-0170; 917 W Grace St; mains $12-19; ☺ lunch & dinner Mon-Fri, dinner Sat) Join the art students and urban professionals descending down into this vegetarian-oriented, Mediterranean- and Asian-angled restaurant whose playlist and wine list are just as interesting as its menu.

Star-lite (☎ 804-254-2667; 2600 W Main St; mains $8-12; ☺ lunch & dinner) A great corner bar, the food is too good not to highlight – they make meatloaf a must. The menu ranges from simple corned beef on rye to scallops Rockefeller. The outdoor patio is a riot in summer.

Davis & Main (☎ 804-353-6641; 2501 W Main St; mains $13-23; ☺ dinner) The walls of this corner institution are paneled with dark wood and mirrors, and its mastery of grilled fare works equally well for a date or a night out with the (well-behaved) kids.

Can Can (☎ 804-358-7274; 3120 W Cary St; dinner mains $16-23; ☺ 7am-1am, to 2am Fri & Sat) In the course of the day, Gallic Can Can morphs from the neighborhood patisserie to a leisurely brunch spot to the hottest evening see-and-be-seen venue in town, and pulls it all off with élan.

Double T's Barbeque (☎ 804-353-9861; 2907 W Cary St; mains $8-15; ☺ lunch & dinner) Follow the smokehouse scent to some of the best BBQ

THE AUTHOR'S CHOICE

Café Gutenberg (☎ 804-497-5000; 1700 E Main St; ☺ 8am-10pm Sun-Wed, to midnight Thu-Sat) This relative newcomer to Shockhoe Bottom bills itself as a 'Books, Coffee & Wine Lounge,' modestly leaving out mention of its superb yet unpretentious fare like the grilled crab cake panini. On warm days the sidewalk patio is packed, leaving the inside tables free for readers (forget your book? Pick up one of the paperback classics), computer geeks (the joys of wi-fi) and those who just want to gawk at the affable, adorable waitstaff. Swing by in the evening and you may chance upon a language table, an African drumming session or an author reading.

---

you'll ever have. Choose from six kinds of sauce and rib-stickin' sides like homemade cornbread and southern-style potato salad.

Nile (☎ 804-225-5544; 309 N Laurel St; mains $9-15; ☺ dinner Tue-Fri, lunch & dinner Sat & Sun) The only Ethiopian restaurant in town, this spare, casual eatery with pale yellow walls serves all the usual suspects and fills a void in the Richmond dining scene admirably.

Drinking

You can't throw a bottle cap in the Fan, Carytown or Shockoe Slip without hitting a bar or club; E and W Cary Sts, and W Main St, have the most action.

Tobacco Company Restaurant (☎ 804-782-9555; 1201 E Cary St, Shockoe Slip; ☺ from 11:30am) An embodiment of the era when tobacco was king, the atmosphere of this three-story, brothel-like restaurant/bar is more of a draw than the food. Have a drink instead.

Richbrau Brewing Co (☎ 804-644-3018; 1214 E Cary St, Shockoe Slip; ☺ from 11:30am) Despite the Wal-Mart-size megaclub and bar here, lines still wrap around the block. It's two stories of sheer madness with a thumping dance floor, billiards rooms and multiple bars, known for their boutique ales.

Baja Bean Co (☎ 804-257-5445; 1520 W Main St, The Fan; ☺ from 11:30am) During the day, grab some California-style Mexican grub here. When the sun sets, grab your cowboy hat, order up a margarita and head for el patio.

Mulligan's Sports Grill (☎ 804-353-8686; 1323 W Main St, The Fan; ☺ from 11:30am) Yeah, it's got beer,

WASHINGTON, DC & THE CAPITAL REGION

TVs and pool tables, but its best feature can be summed up in one word: ping-pong.

Entertainment

Byrd Theater (☎ 804-353-9911; 2908 W Cary St, Carytown; tickets $1.99) You can't beat the price at this fabulous old theater, which shows recent movies. Wurlitzer-organ concerts precede the Saturday night shows.

Virginia Performing Arts Center (www.vapaf.com; downtown) Under construction at press time, this center is to be completed in 2007. It will span the entire block of Broad St between 6th and 7th Sts and will be the area's premier venue for concerts, opera, dance and theater.

Getting There & Around

The Greyhound/Trailways bus terminal (☎ 804-254-5910) is at 2910 N Blvd. **Greater Richmond Transit Company** (GRTC; ☎ 804-358-4782; www.ridegrtc.com) runs local buses (base fare $1.50, exact change only). Bus 27 runs to/ from downtown; a cab fare from the airport is about $25. **Amtrak** (☎ 800-872-7245) stops off about 5 miles north of town at 7519 Staples Mill Rd.

AROUND RICHMOND

The many Civil War battlefields relating to the battles for Richmond are the main attractions in this area, but there are several other points of interest, most notably the Tiffany windows at the Blandford Church in Petersburg.

Petersburg & Around

At a vital junction on the Appomattox River, Petersburg fell to the British in 1781 and saw the Civil War's last great battle in April 1865 after a 10-month siege. The **visitor center** (☎ 804-733-2400; 425 Cockade Alley; ☺ 9am-5pm) sells block tickets ($11 for all three sites) for the city-run sites of the church, museum and the Centre Hill Mansion.

Blandford Church (☎ 804-733-2396; 111 Rochelle Lane; tours $5; ☺ 10am-5pm) is the pride of Petersburg, with the largest collection of Tiffany & Co windows in one place. Each is dedicated to one Confederate state and its war dead, and they are exquisite. The oldest tombstone in the cemetery dates back to 1702. Entrance to the church is only possible with a tour.

The **Siege Museum** (☎ 804-733-2404; 15 W Bank St; admission $5; ☺ 10am-5pm) relates the plight of civilians during the siege of 1864–65.

Several miles east of town, **Petersburg National Battlefield** (on US 36; vehicle/pedestrian $5/3; ☺ 9am-5pm) is the site of the siege and the crater that was created when Union soldiers planted a mine underneath a Confederate camp. Cheapskates can park at the 7-Eleven on Crater Rd and walk down a few hundred yards to the crater, but you didn't hear that from me. The battlefield's **visitor center** (☎ 804-732-3531), off US 36 via I-95 exit 52, features living-history programs in summer.

The **Walker House B&B** (☎ 804-861-5822; www .walker-house.com; 3280 S Cater Rd, Petersburg; r $98-120; ⓅⓍ) boasts a lovely waterfront garden and four giant bedrooms named for the four seasons. 'Winter' has a Jacuzzi bath.

Community gathering spot **Longstreet's Café** (☎ 804-722-4372; 302 N Sycamore St, Petersburg; mains $6-8; ☺ lunch & dinner Mon-Sat) doubles as a wine and beer store, and Heather the roller-skating waitress will serve you on Tuesdays and Thursdays.

In the nearby Pamplin Historical Park, the **Museum of the Civil War Soldier** (☎ 804-861-2408; adult/child 6-11 $13.50/7.50; ☺ 9am-6pm in summer, to 5pm rest of year) illustrates the privations faced by soldiers on both sides of the conflict, and provides a compelling history lesson whether you're a Civil War greenhorn or old hand, and there's lots of kid-oriented exhibits.

HISTORIC TRIANGLE

Set on the peninsula between the York and James Rivers, Jamestown, Yorktown and Colonial Williamsburg constitute the Historic Triangle, collectively one of the state's most visited tourist destinations. The NPS-maintained Colonial Parkway links all three towns. Williamsburg hands you the day-to-day of colonial life on a period-costumed silver platter, while at Yorktown and Jamestown you'll need a spot of imagination and some quiet moments of introspection to fully grasp the significance of the patch of land you're standing on.

It's hard to say the Triangle isn't a compelling stop, but as earnestly educational as they are, these days the towns (especially Williamsburg) can seem more like theme parks, and in the warm months are overrun by tour buses full of schoolchildren or senior citizens. Take a cue from the founding fathers and balance the hustle-bustle of Williamsburg with a trip to one of the James River Plantations, less heavily visited but still groaning with history.

Williamsburg is accessible by train or bus, but the other sites require a car or bicycle.

Williamsburg

First settled as Middle Plantation in 1632, Williamsburg was the capital of England's richest colony from 1699 to 1780, and the seat of power in the new nation's most influential state. It was renamed to honor King William III. After Virginia's capital moved to Richmond in 1780, Williamsburg was nearly forgotten until the Civil War.

Starting in the 1920s, John D Rockefeller contributed the tidy sum of $70 million to restoration efforts, and endowments ensured continuing restoration of the district now known as Colonial Williamsburg. This 220-acre restoration is now surrounded by the the city of Williamsburg, which is full of visitor services and home to the prestigious College of William & Mary. Yet there's hardly a distinction between the historic district and the workaday town – even parking garages are handsome colonial brick.

INFORMATION

The **Colonial Williamsburg Foundation** (CWF; ☎ 757-220-7645, 800-447-8679; www.history.org) opens around 40 authentic 17th- and 18th-century buildings to ticket holders in the restored historic district, staffed with all the friendly townsfolk you'd expect to meet back then, all sharing the tricks of their various trades and breaking character only long enough to snap a family photo for you. Walking around the historic district and patronizing the shops and taverns is free, but entry to the building tours is restricted to ticket holders. Expect crowds, lines and petulant children, particularly in summer.

To park and purchase tickets, follow signs to the **visitor center** (☎ 757-220-7645, 800-447-8679; north of historic district btwn Hwy 132 & Colonial Parkway; ☯ 8:30am-6pm), where kids can get outfitted in period costumes for around $20 (three-cornered hat sold separately). Parking here is free; shuttle buses run frequently to and from the historic district, though there's a footpath you can take from the visitor center. Parking anywhere around the dis-

trict is severely restricted. Exhibitions are open 9am to 5pm daily.

Types of passes include the following:

Colonial Sampler (adult/child $34/15) Covers orientation tour and all exhibition buildings minus the palace and museums for one day.

Governor's Key to the City (adult/child $48/24) Includes all exhibition buildings, palace and museums and walking tours.

You can also buy tickets at several other locations, including the **Merchants Square information booth** (☯ 9am-5pm) at the west end of Duke of Gloucester St and the **Secretary's Office** (☯ 9am-5pm) near the Capitol, at the east end.

Chartered in 1693, the **College of William & Mary** (☎ 757-221-1540; www.wm.edu) retains the oldest college building in the USA, the Sir Christopher Wren Building. The school's esteemed alumni include Thomas Jefferson and James Monroe.

SLEEPING

Williamsburg Hotel & Motel Association (☎ 800-999-4485; www.williamsburghotel.com) Located at the visitor center, this association finds accommodations at no charge.

Colonial Williamsburg Foundation lodging (☎ 800-447-8679) Alternatively, try this central reservation line; prices are given for one night's accommodation off-peak – breakfast, dinner and an attractions pass included (minimum two-night stay).

White House Inn (☎ 757-229-8580, 866-229-8580; www.awilliamsburgwhitehouse.com; 718 Jamestown Rd; r $115-199; P ✗) On the west side of town, this lovely B&B with red, white and blue bunting welcomes guests regardless of political persuasion, though Republicans and Democrats have to park at different ends. Politics makes great bedfellows, especially when it's featherbeds we're talking about.

Governor's Inn (☎ 757-229-1000; 506 N Henry St; r $70-110; P ☻) A quarter-mile north of Merchant's Sq, this friendly motel has a free continental breakfast and an outdoor pool. If you want a refrigerator, request one at check-in.

Williamsburg Inn (☎ 757-229-1000 ext 3089; 136 E Francis St; r from $455; ☻) CWF's premier property is noted by its not-so-colonial price tag. If you can afford it, the pampering is nonstop at this beautiful property, which looks like a grand country estate; it houses spring-fed pools, lavish rooms, croquet lawns and a world-class restaurant. Book early.

Williamsburg & Colonial KOA Resorts (☎ 800-562-1733; www.williamsburgkoa.com; 5210 & 4000 Newman Rd respectively, I-64 exit 234; campsites/cabins $29/55; ⚑) With two campgrounds rolled into one, you'll find superb amenities such as movies and game rooms, plus free buses to area attractions.

EATING & DRINKING
Cheese Shop (☎ 757-220-0298; 410 Duke of Gloucester St, Merchants Sq; ☷ 10am-8pm Mon-Sat, 11am-6pm Sun) Locals swear by this deli, with a wide assortment of sandwiches ($5 to $6), an extensive cheese selection and gift-worthy sundries.

Trellis Restaurant (☎ 757-229-8610; Merchants Sq; lunch mains $8-14, dinner mains $17-28) A Virginia culinary landmark, the Trellis caters to burger-seeking tourists for lunch and nirvana-seeking foodies for dinner. Regional specialties shine, like salmon fillet with country ham. If the weather's fine, secure a spot on the patio. Reservations recommended.

Green Leafe Café (☎ 757-220-3405; 765 Scotland St; mains $11-16; ☷ lunch & dinner) Chow down on their $6.50 lunch specials while being bathed by stained-glass light, and then come back in (or stay until?) the evening, which sees a different beer-centered special every night – they've got 50 on tap!

South of the Border (☎ 757-565-4848; 322 2nd St; mains $7-14; ☷ lunch & dinner) On the east side of town, this family-friendly Mexican joint is the real deal, cowboy boot–shaped beer glasses notwithstanding. For fans of Salvadorian fare, Supremo and *pupusa* (cornmeal tortillas stuffed with cheese or meat) cravings satisfied here.

Four historic district taverns serve 'ye old vittles and grog' from costumed waitstaff, with entertainment most evenings. It's fun once. Reservations can be made through the visitor center or by calling ☎ 757-229-2141. **Chowning's** (Duke of Gloucester St; mains $7-18), next to Market Sq, is the best and most casual of the bunch. Attached is **Gambol's** (dishes $4-14), which is the post-5pm merrymaking spot.

Named after the original 18th-century proprietor, **Christiana Campbell's** (Waller St, near Capitol; mains $23-35) dishes up quality meat and seafood fare.

ENTERTAINMENT
At night the crowds thin out and the historic district is particularly evocative as folks stroll to evening performances.

Choral concerts, 18th-century dances and even witch trials are just a sample of the many interesting diversions sponsored by the CWF for around $10 per ticket (see event listings in the free program available to ticket holders and at ticket booths). For more straight-up nightlife, head directly to Gambol's (left) and acquaint yourself with a stein of Josiah's Ale.

Recommended for those who don't scare easily is the chilling **Original Ghosts of Williamsburg tour** (☎ 757-253-1058, 1-888-474-4788; adult/child under 7 $9/free; ☷ 8pm & 8:45pm Jun-Aug, 8pm Sep-Dec & Mar-May, Sat Jan & Feb). Tickets can also be purchased at the Williamsburg Attraction Center at Prime Outlets on Richmond Rd.

GETTING THERE & AROUND
Amtrak (☎ 757-229-8750) runs to Richmond and Washington, DC, from the transportation center at the corner of Lafayette and N Boundary Sts. The center also houses a **Greyhound/Trailways station** (☎ 757-229-1460). Bike rentals are available from **Bikes Unlimited** (☎ 757-229-4620; 759 Scotland St; per hr from $14; ☷ 9:30-6:30pm Tue-Fri, 10am-5pm Sat, noon-4pm Sun).

Around Williamsburg
Three miles east of Williamsburg on Hwy 60, **Busch Gardens** (☎ 800-343-7946; www.buschgardens.com; adult/child 3-6 $50/43; ☷ Apr-Oct; Ⓟ) is a mega-theme park with tons of rides and roller coasters. Just down the road, **Water Country USA** (☎ 800-343-7946; www.watercountryusa.com; off Hwy 199 east of Williamsburg; adult/child 3-6 $36/29; ☷ May-Sep; Ⓟ) is a water-lovin' kids' paradise with twisty slides, raging rapids and wave pools. Parking at both of these places is $8.

Jamestown
The first permanent English settlement on the continent was founded here in May 1607, and two years later only 60 of the original 214 settlers survived. In 1619 the first representative assembly met, and Jamestown served as Virginia's capital until 1699, when the colonists moved inland to what is now Williamsburg. By the end of the 19th century, only an overgrown churchyard and church tower remained, and today the collection of ruins at the two Jamestown attractions, though historically important, are on the bland side and can easily be covered in an afternoon.

WASHINGTON, DC & THE CAPITAL REGION

Run by the NPS, **Historic Jamestowne** (☎ 757-253-4838; adult/child under 17 $10/free; ⏲ 8:30am-4:30pm), overlooking the James River, is the original site of the island settlement. (The water and land have shifted since then, and visitors now drive the stone's-throw from the 'mainland,' the road bordered by tall grasses rather than water.) Paths lead to 'James Citte' where the story of Pocahontas, Captain John Smith and other historical characters come alive. You'll also find a 1640s church tower and several statues and monuments. The visitor center offers free living-history tours and a cheesy film. A combo ticket with Yorktown Battlefield is adult/child $9/free.

The state-run **Jamestown Settlement** (☎ 757-253-4838; adult/child 6-12 $11.75/5.75; ⏲ 9am-5pm) features a reconstruction of the 1607 James Fort, a Native American village and full-scale replicas of the first ships to bring settlers to Jamestown, along with living-history fun.

A combo ticket that includes the Yorktown Victory Center is adult/child 6-12 $17/8.25.

Yorktown

Founded in 1691, the busy tobacco port of Yorktown became famous in 1781 as the site of the last major Revolutionary War battle: thousands of British General Cornwallis' troops surrendered to George Washington. Today's Yorktown is sleepy with several Revolutionary and Civil War forts scattered between its two main attractions. On Water St, don't miss the bluff under which the townspeople took shelter during the battle.

Yorktown Battlefield (adult/child under 17 $5/free; ⏲ 9am-5pm), run by the NPS, preserves the bluff site of the British defeat, and contains intriguing displays explaining the battle inside the **visitor center** (☎ 757-898-3400). A combo ticket with Historic Jamestowne is adult/child $9/free. Cars can tour a 7-mile battlefield drive and a 10.5-mile encampment route. The **Yorktown Victory Center** (☎ 757-253-4838; adult/child 6-12 $8.30/4; ⏲ 9am-5pm) features a reconstruction of the encampment, battle scenes where full-size toy soldiers come to life, and daily cannon firings. A combo ticket that includes the Jamestown Settlement is adult/child 6-12 $17/8.25.

All rooms at the **Duke of York Motel** (☎ 757-898-3232; 508 Water St; r from $70; P ♿) have water views and some have Jacuzzi baths, microwaves and refrigerators.

One of the few signs of 'real' life in town is the **Yorktown Pub** (☎ 757-886-9964; 112 Water St; mains $6-15; ⏲ lunch & dinner), a friendly place popular with bikers and tourists alike, with generous daily specials.

James River Plantations

The grand homes of Virginia's slaveholding aristocracy were a clear sign of the class divisions in that era. A string of them line scenic Hwy 5 on the north side of the river, though many of them have recently closed their doors to the public. The ones listed here are from east to west.

Sherwood Forest (☎ 804-829-5377), the largest frame house in the country, was the home of 9th president William Henry Harrison (who died a month into office, having caught pneumonia after refusing to put on his overcoat) and his successor, John Tyler. It's still owned by the Tyler family, who have closed the house to the public for the time being. However, the grounds (complete with a touching pet cemetery) are open to self-guided tours ($5).

During its esteemed history, **Berkeley** (☎ 804-829-6018; www.berkeleyplantation.com; adult/child 6-12/child 13-16 $10/5.50/7; ⏲ 9am-4:30pm) has witnessed the first official Thanksgiving (take that, Plymouth, MA!), the composing of the military melody 'taps,' the first 10 presidents as overnight guests, and the 1862 headquartering of Union General George McClellan.

Situated picturesquely on the river, **Shirley** (☎ 800-232-1613; www.shirleyplantation.com; adult/child 6-18 $10.50/7; ⏲ 9am-5pm) is Virginia's oldest plantation and perhaps the best example of what a British-model plantation actually looked like, with its tidy row of brick service and trade houses – tool barn, ice house, laundry etc – leading up to the Big House. One of the country's only 'flying' staircases is here.

HAMPTON ROADS

The waterway called Hampton Roads empties the James, Nansemond and Elizabeth Rivers into the Chesapeake Bay. Europeans settled the region in the 17th century and, during the Revolutionary War, Norfolk was torched by the British, but it later prospered as an international port. The Civil War turning-point battle of the ironclad ships *Monitor* and *Merrimack* was fought near here.

The city of Norfolk boomed as an industrial and shipbuilding area during WWI and WWII, and the region still bustles with maritime activity, from its seafood industry and pleasure boating to its huge naval bases (responsible for the F-14s and other high-tech aircraft continually thundering overhead). Note that I-64 can get very congested through the region. Pick up a free copy of *Port Folio Weekly* for region-wide (including Virginia Beach) cultural and nightlife listings.

Norfolk

Though it's home to the largest naval base outside Russia, Norfolk is no longer *just* a navy town. In fact, it shares home turf with the headquarters of People for the Ethical Treatment of Animals (PETA), making for a heady cultural synthesis. Norfolk's recent renaissance is embodied by free concerts in waterfront parks, world-class museums and a slew of international restaurants. Ghent, a neighborhood north of downtown, is a center for dining and nightlife. There are two visitor centers:

Interstate (☎ 757-441-1852; Ocean View I-64 exit 273; 🕓 9am-5pm)

Downtown (☎ 757-664-6620; 232 E Main St; 🕓 9am-5pm)

SIGHTS

The **Nauticus National Maritime Center** (☎ 757-664-1000; adult/child 4-12 $10/7.50; 🕓 10am-6pm May-Sep, 10am-5pm Tue-Sat, from noon Sun Oct-Apr) is a huge naval museum, which has interactive exhibits including submarine rides, multimedia naval battles and flight simulators. Use the Maritime Center entrance to access the more adult-targeted **Hampton Naval Museum** (☎ 757-322-2987; admission free), where you can take in the exhibits on battleships before exploring the deck of the battleship *Wisconsin*, a veteran of many wars, most recently Operation Desert Storm.

Chrysler Museum of Art (☎ 757-664-6200; 245 W Olney Rd; adult/child under 13 $7/free; 🕓 10am-5pm Tue-Sat, to 9pm Wed, Sun 1-5pm) is a glorious setting for a superb collection. Exhibits include work by Bierstadt, Renoir and Man Ray, and world-class glassware offerings. Admission is free on Wednesdays. The **MacArthur Memorial** (☎ 757-441-2965; MacArthur Sq; admission free; 🕓 10am-5pm Mon-Sat, from 11am Sun) houses the WWII general's military and personal artifacts, and the tombs of the general and his wife.

The magnificent, red-sailed schooner **American Rover** (☎ 757-627-7245; adult/child under 12 $15/10; 🕓 Apr-Oct) takes you on a narrated, two-hour cruise on the Hampton Roads waterway.

SLEEPING

B&B at Historic Page House Inn (☎ 757-625-5033; www.pagehouseinn.com; 323 Fairfax Ave, Norfolk; r $140-225; 🅿 ⊠ 💻) Opposite the Chrysler Museum, this luxurious B&B has almost as many diversions as Norfolk itself – pool table, fitness room, loaner bicycles, wi-fi and champagne breakfast.

Tazewell Hotel (☎ 757-623-6200; www.thetazewell.com; 245 Granby St; r $120-200) Occupying prime downtown real estate, this small, historic hotel has a fitness room, large rooms and continental breakfast. Ask about the story of the Wishing Oak.

For waterfront digs, there are tons of budget to midrange options lining Ocean View Ave (it actually borders the bay, not the ocean, but you'd never know it). One fine option is **Best Western** (☎ 757-587-7540; 1330 E Ocean Ave; r $60-100; 🅿 💻 🐾) Request a room with balcony and kitchenette.

EATING

Two of the best dining strips are downtown's Granby St and Ghent's Colley Ave.

456 Fish (☎ 757-625-4444; 456 Granby St; mains $17-28; 🕓 dinner) In an elegant bistro setting, the Fish doles out some of the best seafood in a town that knows its seafood. Their handful of non-piscatorial dishes, like rack of lamb, are well executed too.

Blue Hippo (☎ 757-533-9664; 147 Granby St; mains $18-27; 🕓 lunch Mon-Fri, dinner daily) The cuisine at this trendsetting hotspot tilts Asian and Mediterranean, and their wine list is excellent. Be prepared to wait your turn to see-and-be-seen, even with a reservation.

Doumar's (☎ 757-627-4163; 919 Monticello Ave at E 20th St, Ghent; mains $1.50-4; 🕓 8am-late Mon-Sat) Since 1904, this slice of Americana has been the drive-up home of the world's original ice cream-cone machine, plus great BBQ. Counter service available too. Cash only.

DRINKING & ENTERTAINMENT

Elliot's Fair Grounds Coffee (☎ 757-640-2899; 806 Baldwin Ave, Ghent; 🕓 7am-late) The youngsters flock to Elliot's organic coffee drinks, wi-fi and left-wing vibe.

Taphouse Grill at Ghent (☎ 757-627-9172; 931 W 21st St, Ghent) This place has an outstanding microbrew selection, a jukebox, two pool tables and live music.

Granby Theater (☎ 757-622-1360; 421 Granby St) Newly renovated, this dramatic 1916 building mounts jazz and theater performances during the week and turns into a thumping nightclub on the weekends.

GETTING THERE & AROUND

The **Greyhound/Trailways terminal** (☎ 757-625-7500) is several blocks from the downtown waterfront at Monticello and Brambleton Aves.

Most attractions are linked through the free Norfolk Electronic Transit (NET) shuttle, which runs from 6:30am to 11pm Monday to Friday, from noon to midnight Saturday, and from noon to 8pm Sunday. **Hampton Roads Transit** (HRT; ☎ 757-222-6100; www.hrtransit.org) has buses serving the entire Hampton Roads region. The paddle-wheel **Elizabeth River Ferry** (☎ 757-222-6100; tickets $1.50) links Norfolk and the handsome residential district of Portsmouth to the south.

Newport News

The city of Newport News comes off as a giant example of suburban sprawl, but it's unclear what it's sprawling from. It holds within its borders several notable attractions, but for charming lodgings and a lively dining scene, head south to Norfolk. The **visitor center** (☎ 888-222-8072; 13560 Jefferson Ave, Newport News Park; ✆ 9am-5pm) is at the north end off I-64 exit 250-B.

The fascinating, scholastic **Mariners' Museum** (☎ 757-596-2222; www.mariner.org; 100 Museum Dr; adult/child 6-17 $8/6; ✆ 10am-5pm), one of the largest maritime museums in the world, features carved figureheads and a haunting collection of miniature ships, Captain John Smith's map of the Chesapeake Bay and a gallery on the Age of Exploration. Its USS *Monitor* Center (www.monitorcenter.org) will be opening in March 2007. The **Virginia Living Museum** (☎ 757-247-8523; 9285 Warwick Blvd, Huntington Park; adult/child 3-12 $11/8; ✆ 9am-6pm, slightly shorter hrs in winter) is an educational extravaganza that comprises a petting zoo, planetarium and other interactive science-y stuff.

The pleasant **Mulberry Inn** (☎ 757-887-3000; 16890 Warwick Blvd; r incl breakfast from $100; P ⊠) has a game room, laundry and fitness facilities.

The 8000-acre **Newport News Park** (☎ 757-888-3333; campsites/RV sites $16/18) offers year-round camping, and boat and bike rentals.

COASTAL VIRGINIA

With the exception of Virginia Beach (VB), the coastline of Virginia is uncluttered, with many hidden-away places to fish, walk and relax. On the Delmarva peninsula are many remote wild refuges, including Chincoteague Island. South of Virginia Beach is the equally remote Back Bay National Wildlife Refuge.

Virginia Beach

The largest city in Virginia, VB is perhaps an unusual destination in that it offers the unadulterated beach experience as well as worthwhile non-sandy attractions. The area was the site where in 1607 British settlers hit land for the first time, and now the 6-mile beach attracts both young revelers and families (note the no-cussing signs). I-264 runs straight into the **visitor center** (☎ 800-822-3224; www.vbfun.com; 2100 Parks Ave; ✆ 9am-5pm) and the beach. Surfing is permitted at the beach's southern end near Rudee Inlet and alongside the 14th St pier.

Make sure when booking bus tickets that Virginia Beach is specified as the **Greyhound** (☎ 757-422-2998) terminus. **Hampton Roads Transit** (HRT; ☎ 757-222-6100; www.hrtransit.com) runs the Virginia Beach Wave trolley (tickets $1), which plies Atlantic Ave in summer.

SIGHTS

Undergoing expansion, **Virginia Aquarium & Marine Science Center** (☎ 757-425-3474; 717 General Booth Blvd; adult/child $12/8; ✆ 9am-5pm) is the city's number-one rainy-day attraction, with touch tanks, recreated habitats, an aviary and 3-D IMAX films. Kids will also love the **Ocean Breeze Water Park** (☎ 757-422-4444; 849 General Booth Blvd; adult/child 3-11 $19/15; ✆ late May-early Sep) with its 13 waterslides and giant wave pool.

Mt Trashmore (☎ 757-473-5237; 310 Edwin Dr; admission free; ✆ 7:30am-dusk) is off I-64 exit 17B. VB's only verticality, it was the creative solution to a landfill problem, and now serves as a prime picnicking and kite-flying venue.

Fort Story (89th St & Pacific Ave), an active army base at Cape Henry, encompasses the First Landing site (admission free), where in 1607 the settlers found 'fair meadows and

WASHINGTON, DC & THE
CAPITAL REGION

goodly tall trees,' and the first federal light-house (admission $3), dating back to 1792. Assume that your car will be searched.

Edgar Cayce Association for Research and Enlightenment (ARE; ☎ 800-333-4499; 215 67th St at Pacific Ave), founded by the self-proclaimed psychic of the early 20th century, has an extensive library and bookstore (with shelving categories like 'Life after Life' and 'Intuitive Arts'), a full schedule of drop-in lectures and therapies like massages and colonies, and a meditative labyrinth.

SLEEPING
You'll have no problem securing a room in town outside of the Memorial Day and Labor Day weekends and Spring Break week.

Colonial Inn (☎ 757-428-5370; www.col-inn.com; 2809 Atlantic Ave at 42nd St; r west-facing $70-125, ocean-front $99-225; P ♨) is a clean hotel with sundecks, plus an indoor and outdoor pool. **Angie's Guest Cottage B&B** (☎ 757-428-4690; 302 24th St; r up to $150; P ✕) is also an **HI-AYH Hostel** (members/nonmembers $12/18) with some private rooms for members only. Both operations are owned by the friendly **Ocean Cove Motel** (☎ 757-491-1830; r $60-150; P) next door. Rooms at **Cutty Sark Motel** (☎ 757-428-2116; 3614 Atlantic Ave; r $75-112; P) have private balconies and kitchenettes.

You couldn't ask for a prettier campground than the bayfront **First Landing State Park** (☎ 757-412-2300; Cape Henry; campsites/cabins $22/92), though cabins have no water view.

EATING & ENTERTAINMENT
Jewish Mother (☎ 757-422-5430; cnr 31st St & Pacific Ave; mains $5-10; ♨ 8am-2am) Get your nosh on here with the packed deli sandwiches, blintzes, 'penicillin soup' and monster-sized pies and cakes. Excellent live music staged nightly. They may be moving location in early 2007, so call ahead.

Harpoon Larry's Oyster Pub (☎ 757-422-6000; 24th St & Pacific Ave; mains $12-16; ♨ lunch & dinner) The roll of paper towels adorning each table gives you a sense of the prevailing atmosphere. Beer, friendly folks and good, fresh seafood comprise the perfect triumvirate. Oysters are only 35¢ each.

Bangkok Garden (☎ 757-498-5009; 4000 Virginia Beach Blvd; mains $7-13; ♨ lunch & dinner) The best Thai in the area, everything is done well here, especially (not surprisingly) the seafood. Mains are generous.

A bevy of overwhelmingly interchangeable clubs and bars sit between 17th and 23rd Sts around Pacific and Atlantic Aves.

Around Virginia Beach
Many natural areas are within easy reach. **Back Bay National Wildlife Refuge** (☎ 757-721-2412; per vehicle Apr-Oct/Nov-Mar $5/free) is an 8000-acre wildlife and migratory bird marshland habitat, most stunning during the December migration season. Some 30 miles southwest of Virginia Beach, the fascinating, 109,000-acre **Great Dismal Swamp National Wildlife Refuge** (☎ 757-986-3705; admission free; ♨ dawn-dusk), which straddles the border with North Carolina, is rich in flora and fauna, like black bears, bobcats and more than 200 bird species.

Eastern Shore
Across the impressive 17-mile **Chesapeake Bay bridge-tunnel** (fee $12), Virginia's isolated Eastern Shore is dotted with fishing villages and serene, low-lying natural refuges.

Tucked behind windswept Assateague Island (see p337), the town of **Chincoteague** (*shink*-o-teeg), on the island of the same name, is Virginia's principal Eastern Shore destination. Chincoteague Island is famous for its oysters and its late-July 'wild pony swim,' when the small horses that inhabit the Assateague Island refuge are led across the channel for annual herd-thinning foal auctions. The **chamber of commerce** (☎ 757-336-6161; 6733 Maddox Blvd; ♨ 9am-4:30pm) has great maps for the scenic hiking and biking trails up to and into the incredibly relaxing **Chincoteague National Wildlife Refuge** (☎ 757-336-6122; per vehicle $10; ♨ 6am-8pm), which protects migratory waterfowl.

Waterside Motor Inn (☎ 757-336-3434; 3761 S Main St; r $114-154; P ♨) has all waterfront rooms, a heated outdoor pool and a small workout room with sauna. **Island Family Restaurant** (☎ 757-336-1198; 3441 Ridge Rd; mains $7-17; ♨ breakfast, lunch & dinner) is a local favorite for hearty, rough-and-ready seafood, pastas and sandwiches.

THE PIEDMONT
The highlight of the Virginia plain is the city of Charlottesville, filled as it is with the legacy of Thomas Jefferson's architectural genius – Monticello and the University of Virginia is listed as a Unesco World Heritage Site.

Charlottesville

Known as Virginia's Cambridge, Charlottesville is a smart university town in a beautiful setting. As the home of Thomas Jefferson and the University of Virginia, 'C-ville' draws visitors to its impressive architecture and magnolia-lined streets set against a Blue Ridge Mountain backdrop. A six-block pedestrian mall between Market and Water Sts forms the heart of the historic district and is crammed with outdoor cafés, bookstores, vendors and street musicians.

The **Charlottesville/Albemarle Convention & Visitors Bureau** (☎ 877-386-1102; www.charlottes villetourism.org), on Hwy 20 south near I-64 exit 121A, features a *Thomas Jefferson at Monticello* exhibit, and sells tickets for area attractions (block passes $26).

MONTICELLO & AROUND

East of town, Thomas Jefferson's magnificent **home** (☎ 804-984-9822; adult/child 6-11 $14/6; ◷ 8am-5pm Mar-Oct, 9am-4:30pm Nov-Feb), featured on the nickel, embodies its resident designer: Jefferson's quirky inventions and French-inspired innovations are scattered throughout. Jefferson's tomb is downhill; its inscription, noting the author of the Declaration of Independence and Virginia's religious freedom statute, and founder of the University of Virginia, was chosen by the man himself. Daily specialty tours include a plantation community tour exposing the complicated past of the slave owner who declared all men to be equal.

Keep in mind that Monticello (mon-ti-*chel*-o) is one of Virginia's premier historic attractions; arrive early to avoid long lines. Frequent shuttles run from the parking lot up the hill. Tours are also offered of the nearby 1784 **Michie** ('mickey') **Tavern** (☎ 804-977-1234) and James Monroe's estate, **Ash Lawn-Highland** (☎ 804-293-9539), 2.5 miles east of Monticello. A combo ticket for all three is $24, and the Jefferson-era tavern, the **Ordinary** (meals around $14), is best known for providing luncheon buffets.

UNIVERSITY OF VIRGINIA

At the west end of town, the grounds (never 'campus') of the **University of Virginia** (UVa), which were founded by Thomas Jefferson, revolve around the stately Rotunda, a scale replica of Rome's Pantheon. The permanent collection at UVa's **Art Museum** (☎ 804-924-3492; 155 Rugby Rd; admission free; ◷ 1-5pm Tue-Sun) is eclectic and its traveling exhibits always interesting.

SLEEPING

There's a good selection of budget and mid-range chain motels lining Emmet St/US 29 north of town.

Guesthouses (☎ 434-979-7264; www.va-guesthouses .com; r from $155; ◷ 9am-2pm Mon-Fri; P) This reservation service provides cottages and B&B rooms. Call within business hours ideally at least a day before you'll need a room.

English Inn (☎ 434-971-9900; 2000 Morton Dr; r incl breakfast from $85; P) This is a tidy Tudor-facade motel with standard rooms near the US 29 and US 250 bypass.

Charlottesville KOA (☎ 434-296-9881; 3825 Red Hill Rd; campsites/cabins $22/40; ◷ Mar-Oct) This camping and cabin complex is southwest of town on County Rd 708.

Near the town of Schuyler about 15 miles southwest of town is the **White Pig B&B** (☎ 434-831-1416; www.thewhitepig.com; 5120 Irish Rd; r $175; P) on the 170-acre Briar Creek Farm. The B&B is best known for its resident pot-bellied pigs and its gourmet vegetarian fare.

EATING & DRINKING

Not surprisingly, every evening mounts a healthy selection of nightlife options. Pick up the free weekly *C-ville* for exhaustive listings. Student-centric eateries crowd the Corner, the buzzing commercial district on UVa's southeast corner on Jefferson Dr between 13th and Chancellor Sts.

White Spot (☎ 434-295-9899; 147 University Ave; ◷ 8am-11pm, to 2:30am Fri & Sat). While in the commercial district, try a genuine C-ville concoction, the fried-egg-topped Gus Burger.

The following spots are downtown:

C&O Restaurant (☎ 434-971-7044; 515 E Water St; mains $18-29; ◷ dinner) Incongruously located under a neon Pepsi sign in a building that was once a boardinghouse, this excellent French bistro has an acclaimed wine list and loads of charm.

Miller's (☎ 434-971-8511; 109 W Main St) This smoky, unpretentious bar is one of the best spots for live shows, from jazz to bluegrass. There's also decent bar food and billiards upstairs after 6pm.

Hardware Store (☎ 434-977-1518; 316 E Main St; mains $11-20; ◷ lunch & dinner Mon-Sat) Gourmet it ain't, but whatever hearty fare you or the kids are craving, you'll likely find it on the vast menu, from crepes to ribs to Wiener schnitzel. The restaurant is only one element of the historic (now slightly cheesy) Hardware complex.

Mudhouse (☎ 434-984-6833; 213 W Main St; ☽ 7am-11pm, to 7pm Mon) Do as the cool kids do and come here for bracing espresso, wi-fi and daily artsy happenings.

GETTING THERE & AROUND

Charlottesville is easily accessible by **Amtrak** (☎ 434-296-4559; 810 W Main St) and the **Grey-hound/Trailways terminal** (☎ 434-295-5131; 310 W Main St). A free trolley runs through the historic district.

Lynchburg

Founded along the James River by an enterprising ferryman in 1757, Lynchburg is a pleasant enough city with a comfortably gritty downtown. It's a convenient base from which to visit Appomattox, 20 miles to the east, or Poplar Forest. The **visitor center** (☎ 800-732-5821; www.discoverlynchburg.org; 216 12th St; ☽ 9am-5pm) is near the Community Market (below). Up 139 steps from Church St, **Monument Terrace** looks down to the river and its bizarre plume fountain.

Thomas Jefferson called his summer retreat of **Poplar Forest** (☎ 804-525-1806; adult/child 6-16/senior; $8/1/6; ☽ 10am-4pm Wed-Mon Apr-Nov) his 'most valuable possession,' and the admission includes an excellent guided tour of this mini-Monticello, which is undergoing continuous archaeological excavations. It lies a few miles southwest of downtown and doesn't suffer the crowds Monticello does.

A cluster of chain motels surrounds the intersection of Hwys 29 and 501. **Community Market** (1219 Main St; ☽ 7am-2pm Mon-Sat) has produce and canned goods outside and local crafts (hand-carved wooden rifles or camo kidswear, anyone?) and food vendors inside, including straight-from-the-motherland Indian food at **El Roi** (☎ 434-455-2163; set price break-fast/lunch $2.50/5; ☽ closed Wed & Sun).

Appomattox Court House & Around

At the McLean House in the town of Appomattox Court House, General Robert E Lee surrendered the Army of Northern Virginia to Lieutenant General Ulysses S

Grant, in effect ending the Civil War. (The modern town of Appomattox, 3 miles east of Appomattox Court House, is the birthplace of Joel Sweeney, inventor of the five-string banjo, but holds little interest otherwise.) Today the compact village is preserved within a 1300-acre park as **Appomattox Court House National Historic Park** (☎ 434-352-8987; per person/car $3/5; ☽ 8:30am-5pm), which houses a museum and NPS visitor center within the evocative pedestrian-only village. Most of the 27 restored buildings are open to visitors.

SHENANDOAH VALLEY

'Oh Shenandoah, I long to hear you, away you rolling river...' Thus starts the lovely old ballad that is many outsiders' only association with this fertile valley, lying between the Blue Ridge and Allegheny Mountain ranges. A vital Confederate troop corridor and food source, the valley saw much Civil War action (the town of Winchester changed hands more than 70 times) and is studded with historic sites. Valley towns are accessible from I-81, and the Blue Ridge Parkway and Skyline Drive provide scenic alternatives. But the true flavor of the region lies in the wilder mountain areas, beyond the towns and the beaten-path parkways. For in-depth exploration of this area, take a look at Lonely Planet's *Great Smoky Mountains & Shenandoah National Parks*.

Shenandoah National Park

The centerpiece of this famously beautiful **park** (☎ 540-999-2243; www.nps.gov/shen; vehicles/cyclists $10/5) is **Skyline Drive**, which crosses the spine of the Blue Ridge Mountains 105 miles from Front Royal in the north to Rockfish Gap in the south. It's spectacular in spring and fall in particular, but slow-going (35mph limit) and, in peak seasons, congested.

Two visitor centers, **Dickey Ridge** (☎ 540-635-3566; Mile 4.6) in the north and **Byrd** (☎ 540-999-3500; Mile 51) in the south, have maps, backcountry permits and information on hiking (the Appalachian Trail frequently crosses Skyline), horseback riding, hang gliding, biking (only on public roads) and other wholesome goodness.

Camping is available at four **NPS camp-grounds** (☎ 800-365-CAMP): Mathews Arm (at Mile 22.1), Big Meadows (Mile 51.3), Lewis Mountain (Mile 57.5), and Loft Mountain

---

BIG TASTE IN LITTLE WASHINGTON

The Inn at Little Washington (☎ 540-675-3800; www.theinnatlittlewashington.com; Middle & Main Sts, Washington, VA; prix fixe from $118, r $550-1300; ⊙ dinner Wed-Mon) Yes, you may be in sleepy, rural Washington, Virginia, but once you step inside you might as well be on a different planet – Planet Perfection. Chef and demigod Patrick O'Connell taught himself to cook in an unheated Virginia farmhouse and in 1978 opened this five-star inn and restaurant, ranked by the *International Herald Tribune* as one of the top 10 restaurants in the world.

From the moment your car pulls up to the front of this converted garage to when you reluctantly depart, a charming battalion devotes itself to ensuring that nothing is lacking during your time spent in this bosom of impeccable luxury (note the amethyst-studded ceiling) and cuisine *par excellence*. The staff seems to appear and disappear ninja-style, and apparently undergoes mind-reading training. Is it even necessary to mention that the flawless four-course menu is intimately tied to the region and season?

If you're prepared to ruin every subsequent dining experience, start your attempts at securing a reservation 30 days in advance. Those who stay the night at the **inn** (d $550-1300!) are guaranteed a table.

(Mile 79.5) at $14 per day, with laundry and showers, and requires registering a free backcountry permit with a visitor center. Reservations are required only at Big Meadows from May to November. For not-so-rough lodging, try **Skyline Lodge** (☎ 703-242-0315; Mile 41.7; r from $79), and **Lewis Mountain** (☎ 800-999-4714; Mile 57.5; cabins weekdays/weekends from $60/85).

Front Royal & Around

Once a raucous 18th-century packhorse stopover, today Front Royal marks the northernmost tip of Skyline Dr. Stop in to the **visitor center** (☎ 800-338-9758; 414 E Main St; ⊙ 9am-5pm) and load up on all things Virginia. The **Shenandoah Valley Travel Association** (☎ 540-740-3132; www.visitshenandoah.org; US 211 W, I-81 exit 264; ⊙ 9am-5pm) also highlights valley attractions.

Besides being the Drive's northern gateway, Front Royal's claim to fame is the **Skyline Caverns** (☎ 800-296-4545; www.skylinecaverns .com; US 340; adult/child 7-13 $14/7; ⊙ 9am-5pm Mon-Fri, to 6pm Sat & Sun), which boasts rare, white-spiked anthodites – mineral formations that look like sea urchins.

Woodward House on Manor Grade (☎ 540-635-7010; www.acountryhome.com; 413 S Royal Ave/US 320; r/cottages $95-135/185; P ♥) is a slightly cluttered B&B with eight cheerful rooms with private bath. Sip your coffee from the deck and don't let the busy street below distract you from the Blue Ridge Mountain vista.

At **Village Idiot** (☎ 540-636-3663; 510 S Royal Ave; mains $10-20; ⊙ lunch & dinner) grab some good hearty grub, such as crab cakes. There's live music on weekends.

Jalisco's (☎ 540-635-7348; 1303 N Royal Ave; mains $8-15; ⊙ lunch & dinner) has surprisingly good Mexican (and coleslaw!).

Some 25 miles north of Front Royal in the town of Winchester is the new $20 million **Museum of the Shenandoah Valley** (☎ 888-556-5799; 901 Amherst St; adult/senior & student $8/6; ⊙ 10am-4pm Tue-Sun). Its four galleries provide an engaging overview of the history, culture and art of the region. Admission to the adjacent Glen-Burnie House and its 6 acres of formal gardens is an extra $4. House and gardens are open from April through November.

If you can only fit one cavern into your itinerary, head 25 miles south from Front Royal to the world-class **Luray Caverns** (☎ 540-743-6551; www.luraycaverns.com; I-81 exit 264; adult/child 7-13 $18/9; ⊙ 9am-6pm, to 7pm summer) and hear the 'Stalacpipe Organ,' hyped as the largest musical instrument on earth.

George Washington & Jefferson National Forests

Stretching the entire western edge of Virginia, these two mammoth **forests** (www.fs.fed .us/r8/gwj; campsites $5-20, primitive camping free) comprise more than 1562 sq miles of mountainous terrain bordering the Shenandoah Valley, and contain challenging-to-easy trail networks, which include 330 miles of the **Appalachian Trail** (www.appalachiantrail.org) and mountain-biking routes. Hundreds of developed campgrounds are scattered throughout. **USDA Forest Service headquarters** (☎ 540-265-5100; 5162 Valleypointe Parkway), off the Blue Ridge Parkway in Roanoke, oversees a dozen ranger stations along the ranges. You can also pick up information at the **Natural Bridge Visitor Center** (☎ 540-291-1806) across from the Natural Bridge entrance.

Staunton & Around

Near the junction of the Blue Ridge Parkway and Skyline Dr, Staunton (*stan*-tun) is a lively little town perched among steep hills and some lovely architecture. The women's college Mary Baldwin also calls the town home. A free trolley helps navigate those hills, Monday to Saturday from 10am to 6pm.

A unique living-history farm, **Frontier Culture Museum** (☎ 540-332-7850; overlooking I-81 exit 222; adult/child/senior $10/6/9; 🕑 9am-5pm mid-Mar–Nov, 10am-4pm Dec–mid-Mar) has authentic historic farm buildings from Germany, Ireland and England, which have been transported and plunked down here to provide comparison with the American frontier farm that's also in attendance. If you're feeling stingy, watch the free 15-minute video to get the gist and then slink out. The town's **visitor center** (🕑 9am-5pm) shares space with the museum.

Woodrow Wilson Birthplace & Museum (☎ 540-885-0897; 18-24 N Coalter St; adult/child/student 6-12 $8/3/5; 🕑 9am-5pm Mon-Sat, from noon Sun, to 4pm Nov-Feb) reveals the stately 1846 Greek Revival house and garden of the 28th president. **Blackfriars Playhouse** (☎ 540-851-1733; 10 S Market St; tickets $20-30) hosts performances by the American Shakespeare Center in the world's only re-creation of Shakespeare's original indoor theater.

Right downtown, the thoroughly mauve **Frederick House** (☎ 540-885-4220, 800-334-5575; www.frederickhouse.com; 28 N New St; r incl breakfast $95-190; 🅿 ✗) consists of five historical residences with a combination of rooms and suites, all with private bath and some with fireplaces and decks. **Walnut Hills Campground & RV Resort** (☎ 540-337-3920, 800-699-1568; 484 Walnut Hills Rd; campsites/cabins from $23/69) in nearby Mint Spring is a well-equipped site.

Bluehairs flock to the famous **Mrs Rowe's** (☎ 540-886-1833; I-81 exit 222; mains $6-12; 🕑 7am-8pm Mon-Sat, to 7pm Sun) for its Southern home-cooking of recipes that haven't budged in decades, and pies as big as your head. Another Staunton original, **Wright's Dairy Rite** (☎ 540-886-0435; 346 Greenville Ave; mains $3-5; 🕑 lunch & dinner) has drive-in curb service to convey its classic burgers and dogs.

Ten miles north of Staunton near Mt Solon, **Natural Chimneys & Grand Caverns Regional Park** (☎ 540-350-2510; campsites $12; 🕑 Mar-Oct; 🄫) features a remarkable rock formation, camping, and…wait for it…the National Jousting Hall of Fame!

Lexington & Around

This well-heeled town is most famous for being the last resting place of Confederate generals Jonathan 'Stonewall' Jackson and Robert E Lee. It's also renowned for two respected academies that account for nearly half the town's population, the Virginia Military Institute and Washington & Lee University. The **visitor center** (☎ 540-463-3777; 106 E Washington St; 🕑 9am-5pm) has free parking.

At the **Virginia Military Institute** (☎ 540-464-7230; Letcher Ave; 🕑 9am-5pm when campus & museums open), founded in 1839, a full-dress parade takes place most Fridays at 4:30pm during the school year. The school's **Marshall Museum** (☎ 540-463-7103; adult/child $3/free) honors the creator of the Marshall Plan for post–WWII European reconstruction. It's also temporarily housing several interesting artifacts (like Jackson's coat) during the renovation of **Jackson Hall museum** (☎ 540-464-7334; admission free), which displays the school's history. (It's the only institution to have sent its entire graduating class into combat.) It should reopen in the spring of 2007.

Colonnaded Washington & Lee University, founded in 1749, contains **Lee Chapel & Museum** (☎ 540-463-8768; admission free; 🕑 9am-5pm, from 1pm Sun), with Lee interred downstairs and his horse Traveller buried outside. The restored **Stonewall Jackson House** (☎ 540-463-2552; 8 E Washington St; adult/child $6/3; 🕑 9am-5pm Mon-Sat, from 1pm Sun) houses the general's possessions and period pieces. Jackson is buried in Lexington Cemetery.

Historic Country Inns (☎ 540-463-2044; 11 N Main St; r $75-165) operates two inns downtown and one outside town. Kids are welcome. The charming, eco-minded **Applewood Inn & Llama Trekking** (☎ 540-463-1962, 1-800-463-1902; r $115-142; ✗ 🅿) offers a slew of outdoorsy activities on a farm a 10-minute drive away. Chain motels are clustered around I-81 exit 195 and I-64 exit 55.

The cozy **Blue Heron Cafe** (☎ 540-430-2800; 4 E Washington St; mains $5-15; 🕑 lunch Mon-Thu, lunch & dinner Fri & Sat) has creative and karma-enhancing vegetarian mains, and is cash only. For a more upscale and carnivorous experience, **Café Michel** (☎ 540-464-4119; 640 N Lee Hwy at US 11; mains $17-25; ☽ dinner Mon-Sat) delivers with dishes like Allegheny mountain trout with almonds. Wi-fi and coffee can be had at **Lexington Coffee Shop** (☎ 540-464-6586; 9 W Washington; ☽ 7am-5:30pm Mon-Sat, 9am-3pm Sun).

This here's serious horse country, and just outside town is one of the nation's premier venues for equine exhibitionism, the **Virginia Horse Center** (☎ 540-463-4300; 487 Maury River Rd). Shows are held on weekends year-round.

Natural Bridge

Come first thing in the morning to avoid the tour buses, bypass the schlocky museums and gift shops, and head directly to the 215ft-high **Natural Bridge arch** (☎ 540-291-2121; adult/child 6-15 $10/5; ☽ 8am-dusk), which was surveyed by 16-year-old George Washington. (Look 23ft up on the left side to see his initials).

Those who find joy in phenomena of the more satirical nature should not miss a glimpse of **Foamhenge**, on US 11, a mile north of Natural Bridge.

Chain accommodations can be found off I-81 exit 180/180A. Five miles away, **Yogi Bear Jellystone Park Camp-Resort** (☎ 540-291-2727; www.campnbr.com; campsites/cabins/deluxe cabins $25/55/95; 2-night minimum summer; ☒) is a great camping resort for families, with waterfront and wooded lodgings, a lake, mini-golf and a rec room.

A **National Forest Service ranger station** (☎ 540-291-2189), across from the resort, provides information about recreation in nearby forest service areas.

BLUE RIDGE HIGHLANDS & SOUTHWEST

The southwestern tip of Virginia is the most rugged part of the state and still retains a frontier feel. It has many natural attractions, including the stunning drive along the Blue Ridge Parkway. (To really get under its skin, check out Lonely Planet's *Road Trip: Blue Ridge Parkway*.) Many eclectic towns evoke quintessential small-town America, where you'll always find strains of bluegrass in the air.

Blue Ridge Parkway

The **Blue Ridge Parkway** (www.blueridgeparkway.org) traverses the southern Appalachian ridge from Shenandoah National Park at Mile 0 to North Carolina's Great Smoky Moun-

tains National Park at Mile 469. Wildflowers bloom in spring, and fall colors are spectacular, but watch out for foggy days; no guardrails can make for mighty hairy driving. NPS campgrounds and visitor centers are open May to October. To break up the scenery, detour often, like to the town of Galax on the **Crooked Road Heritage Music Trail** (p365).

Mabry Mill (☎ 540-952-2947), at Meadows of Dan, is one of the most photogenic objects in the state.

Peaks of Otter Lodge (☎ 540-586-1081, 800-542-5927; r from $89), a rustic lakeside motel, commands a stunning view. **HI Blue Ridge Mountains** (☎ 276-236-4962; Mile 214.5; dm $17) offers hostel-style dorm lodging with an outstanding view. Cash only.

The parkway has nine **campgrounds** (☎ 800-933-7275), four in Virginia. All campsites are $14 (cabins extra).

Other recommendations:

Otter Creek (Mile 61) Year-round.

Peaks of Otter (Mile 86) Seasonal.

Roanoke Mountain (Mile 120.4) Seasonal.

Rocky Knob (Mile 169) Seasonal, plus full-facility cabins.

Roanoke

Illuminated by the giant star atop Mill Mountain, Roanoke's the big city in these parts, with a compact set of attractions based around the bustling indoor/outdoor **Historic City Market** (213 Market St; ☽ 7:30am-4:30pm Mon-Sat), a sumptuous farmers' market loaded with temptations even for those with no access to a kitchen. For local information, check out the **Roanoke Valley Visitor Information Center** (☎ 540-342-6025, 800-635-5535; www.visitroanokeva.com; 101 Shenandoah Ave NE; ☽ 9am-5pm) in the old Norfolk & Western (N&W) train station. The station houses the excellent **O Winston Link Museum** (www.linkmuseum.org; adult/child $5/3; ☽ 10am-5pm Mon-Sat, from noon Sun), which displays Link's Ansel Adams–esque photographs of life on the N&W rail line from 1955 to 1960.

Center in the Square (☎ 540-342-5700; www.centerinthesquare.org; 1 Market Sq; ☽ 10am-5pm Tue-Sat, from 1pm Sun) is the city's cultural bread and butter, with a science museum and planetarium (adult/child $8/6), theater (tickets $5 to $10), local-history museum (adult/child $3/2) and art museum (tickets $3). The nearby **Virginia Museum of Transportation** (☎ 540-342-5670; 303 Norfolk Ave SW; adult/child 3-11 $7.40/5.25; ☽ 11am-4pm Mon-Fri, 10am-5pm Sat, from 1pm Sun) appeals to kids, train spotters and vintage car buffs. The **Harrison Museum of African American Culture** (☎ 540-345-4818; 523 Harrison Ave; admission free; ☙ 1-5pm Tue-Sat), in the building that was the first public high school for Blacks in the country, has displays on African American culture in the area as well as on traditional and contemporary African art.

Mill Mountain Zoo (☎ 540-343-3241; adult/child under 12 $6.75/4.50; ☙ 10am-4:30pm) and an adjacent wildflower garden are perched on a hilltop near the Blue Ridge Parkway. Directly next door is the **Roanoke Star** with a breathtaking view of the city.

Across from the visitor center, the vast, Tudor-style **Hotel Roanoke** (☎ 540-985-5900; 110 Shenandoah Ave NE; r from $140; P ☙) pampers guests with every imaginable amenity. **Roanoke Mountain Campground** (☎ 540-982-9242; Blue Ridge Parkway Mile 120.5; campsites $12; ☙ May-Nov) is maintained by the NPS. There are few B&Bs or inns in the downtown area, but there are plenty of chain hotels near the Roanoke airport off I-581 exit 3.

You can grab any manner of food from the vendors at **City Market** on the west side of Market St, but more fun is following the neon arrow commanding 'Eat' to the thimble-sized Roanoke institution **Texas Tavern** (☎ 540-342-4825; 114 W Church Ave; items $1.50-4; ☙ 24hr). Don't leave without trying a bowl of chili. **Tavern on the Market** (☎ 540-343-2957; 32 Market Sq; mains $7-15; ☙ from 11am) features prime people-watching, the best burgers in town and a wide assortment of beers. Get your caffeine and wi-fi fix – as well as damn fine biscuit sandwiches – at **Tutor's Biscuits** (☎ 540-344-2088; 23 W Church St; sandwiches $2-5; ☙ 5am-2pm Mon-Fri, to noon Sat).

Around Roanoke

The tiny town of Bedford suffered the most casualties per capita during WWII, and hence was chosen to host the moving **National D-Day Memorial** (☎ 540-586-3329; US 460 & Hwy 122; adult/child $5/3; ☙ 10am-5pm). Among its towering arch and flower garden is a cast of bronze figures re-enacting the storming of the beach, complete with bursts of water symbolizing the hail of bullets the soldiers faced.

Twenty miles southeast of Roanoke, the **Booker T Washington National Monument** (☎ 540-721-2094; Hwy 122; ☙ 9am-5pm) is a recreated tobacco farm honoring the former slave born here who went on to become the

beloved and celebrated African American educator and activist.

Twenty-five miles southeast, **Smith Mountain Lake State Park** (☎ 540-297-6066; www.state .va.us/~dcr; 1235 State Park Rd) is the state's second-largest body of water and has a lovely sandy beach. Three-bedroom waterfront **cabins** (☎ 800-933-7275) go for $105 in high season. Campsites are $18 to $23.

Mount Rogers National Recreation Area

Hike, fish or cross-country ski among ancient hardwood trees and the state's tallest peak in this district of the George Washington & Jefferson National Forest (see p361). The **park headquarters** (☎ 276-783-5196), on Hwy 16 in Marion, offers maps and recreation directories. The NPS operates five campgrounds in the area; contact park headquarters for details.

Abingdon

A lovely theater and inn are the centerpieces of this cultural oasis in southwestern Virginia. Abingdon retains fine Federal and Victorian architecture in its historic district, and hosts the bluegrass Virginia Highlands Festival over the first two weeks in August. The **visitor center** (☎ 800-435-3440; 335 Cummings St; ☙ 9am-5pm) has exhibit rooms on local history.

Founded during the Depression, **Barter Theatre** (☎ 540-628-3991; www.bartertheatre.com; 133 W Main St; performances from $20) earned its name from audiences trading food for performances – 'ham for Hamlet.' Such actors as Gregory Peck and Ernest Borgnine have cut their teeth on Barter's stage.

The **Virginia Creeper Trail** (www.vacreepertrail.org), named for the railroad that once ran this route, travels 33 miles between Whitetop Station (3576ft) near the North Carolina border and downtown Abingdon. Several outfitters rent bikes, organize outings and run uphill shuttles, including **Virginia Creeper Trail Bike Shop** (☎ 276-676-2552; 201 Pecan St; per 2hr $10; ☙ 9am-6pm) near the trailhead.

Martha Washington Inn (☎ 540-628-3161; 150 W Main St; r from $169; P), opposite the Barter, is the region's premier historic hotel.

Offering such 'intercontinental' fare as jambalaya, Weiner schnitzel and mango duck, the cuisine at the **Tavern** (☎ 276-628-1118; 222 E Main St; mains $18-32; ☙ dinner Mon-Sat) is as forward-looking as its 1779 building is

WASHINGTON, DC & THE CAPITAL REGION

not. **Starving Artist Cafe** (☎ 276-628-8445; 134 Wall St; mains $5-15; ☺ lunch Mon, lunch & dinner Tue-Sat) is tucked away by the railroad tracks, with overstuffed sandwiches named for famous writers and artists.

Cumberland Gap National Historical Park

This break in the Appalachian mountains is the meeting point of Virginia, Tennessee and Kentucky. In the late 18th century more than a quarter-million pioneers crossed this gap along the Wilderness Rd. The **visitor center** (☎ 606-248-2482) is across the border. The 20,000-acre park contains 70 miles of hiking trails (backpacking permits required).

WEST VIRGINIA

Though it's been one of the more economically depressed states in the union since the bottom fell out of the coal industry, the hills of Appalachia harbor ruggedly beautiful terrain, churning white-water rivers and charming towns that glitter far brighter than the hillbilly stereotypes that mar its perception in the mainstream. It's a small state, but they say that if you flattened out its mountains, you'd be left with an area larger than Texas. All that verticality and a minimum of urban centers make for breathtaking vistas and plunging gorges around many a corner.

Outstanding recreational opportunities lure the majority of out-of-staters to 'wild, wonderful West Virginia,' most notably white-water rafting and paddling adventures along the New, Gauley and Cheat Rivers. The Appalachian highlands are known for beautiful, practical handicrafts in woodwork, quilting, basketry and glassmaking. Just as strong a draw is its old-time mountain music, best experienced by following the strains of banjo and fiddle to a ramshackle porch. A close second is a scheduled jamboree like one at the Purple Fiddle (p367). Towns such as Berkeley Springs and Harpers Ferry are standouts for their spas and historical importance, respectively.

History

Originally part of Virginia, the land west of the Appalachians was settled in the mid-17th century by the scrappy small-scale farmers of a different stripe than the wealthy Episcopal tobacco plantation–owners of the Tidewater. When the slave-owning eastern half of the state decided to secede during the Civil War, the west refused to go along, and the mountain region remained aligned with the Union, and was declared its own state in 1863.

After the war, timber and coal companies arrived to exploit the natural resources – and the mountaineers – of West Virginia. Despite the early development of labor unions, West Virginia was economically depressed for many years, and it remains among the nation's poorest states. West Virginia's cities continue to serve largely as industrial centers, though its quaint and quirky smaller towns like Berkeley Springs continue to fuel its tourism revenue.

Though coal, mineral and timber processed through West Virginia's industrial cities remain important to the state's economy, growing numbers of recreationists who are drawn to the natural beauty support a tourism industry that strives to disturb the environment less.

THE CROOKED ROAD

Winding its way through 250 splendid miles of rural southwest Virginia, the new **Crooked Road Heritage Music Trail** (☎ 800-686-6874; www.thecrookedroad.org) draws together a treasure trove of Appalachian events and institutions, running the musical gamut from oldtime to country to bluegrass. Eight attractions, including the **Blue Ridge Institute & Museum** (☎ 276-236-5309, 540-365-4416; www.blueridgeinstitute.org; 608 W Stuart Dr, Galax; admission free; ☺ 10am-4:30pm Mon-Sat year-round, 1-4:30pm Sun mid-May–mid-Aug) dot the trail, while in between, roadside listening posts direct drivers to audio commentaries to tune into on their radios. But we know you didn't come all this way for exhibits and recordings – plenty of homespun hootenanny is yours for the taking, such as the famous Friday jamborees at **Floyd's Country Store** (☎ 540-745-4563; 206 S Locust St, Floyd; adult/child under 16 $3/free), and Saturday shows at the **Carter Family Fold** (adult/child $5/1) in the town of Hiltons. Wear your dancin' shoes.

WEST VIRGINIA FACTS

Nicknames Mountain State, Switzerland of America

Population 1.8 million

Area 24,231 sq miles

Capital city Charleston (population 51,702)

Official motto Mountaineers are Always Free

Birthplace of General Thomas 'Stonewall' Jackson (1824–63), author Pearl S Buck (1892–1973), Booker T Washington (1856–1915), Mother's Day (1908), Golden Delicious apple (1775)

Home of The largest steel arch bridge in the world, world's first brick street (in Charleston)

Famous for Appalachian highland culture, mountains, white-water rafting, coal

---

Information

State sales tax is 6%.

West Virginia Division of Tourism (☎ 304-558-2200, 800-225-5982; www.callwva.com) operates welcome centers at interstate borders and in **Harpers Ferry** (☎ 304-535-2482).

Many hotels and motels tack on a $1 'safe' fee, refundable upon request at checkout. So if you didn't use that room safe, get your dollar back.

EASTERN PANHANDLE

The northeast is best known for the historic village of Harpers Ferry, but it's dotted with quaint towns where you can lose yourself in the past.

Harpers Ferry

This town packs a rich history onto a spit of land where the Shenandoah and Potomac Rivers meet to form the boundaries of three states. The federal armory here was the target of abolitionist and wild man John Brown's raid in 1859. Though Brown's ambition to arm slaves and spark a national rebellion against slavery died once he was caught and hanged, the incident incited slaveholders' worst fears and helped precipitate the Civil War. Union and Confederate forces soon fought for control of the armory and town.

With little development altering its appearance, the tiny downtown has been declared a national historic park, and today visitors walk the steep cobblestone lanes and wander among the shops without charge, but staffed museum buildings are accessible

to pass-holders only. Passes, parking and shuttles are available north of town at the **visitor center** (☎ 304-535-2482; off Hwy 340; vehicle/pedestrian $6/4; ☺ 9am-5pm). Parking is incredibly limited in Harpers Ferry proper.

SIGHTS & ACTIVITIES

Among the free sites in the historic district, the 1858 **Master Armorer's House** explains how rifle technology that was developed here revolutionized the firearms industry; the **Storer College building**, long ago a teachers' college for freed slaves, now traces the town's African American history. The creepy **John Brown Museum** (168 High St; adult/child 6-12 $5/3) tells the story of his raid in wax.

Passing through town, the 2160-mile Appalachian Trail is headquartered at the **Appalachian Trail Conference** (☎ 304-535-6331; www.atconf.org; cnr Washington & Jackson Sts; ☺ 9am-5pm Mon-Fri Apr-Oct), a tremendous resource for hikers. Day hikers also scale the Maryland Heights Trail past Civil War fortifications or the Loudoun Heights Trail for scenic river views.

You can rent bikes to explore the **C&O Canal** towpath (see p338); the visitor center has a list of outfitters. To arrange rafting, kayaking, canoeing and tubing excursions, contact **River Riders** (☎ 800-326-7238; www.riverriders.com; 408 Alstadts Hill Rd).

SLEEPING & EATING

Hilltop House Hotel (☎ 304-535-2132; www.hilltophousehotel.com; 400 E Ridge St; r $85-160; **P**) The view is stunning from this sprawling stone inn overlooking the Shenandoah and Potomac rivers. Many of its 62 rooms have water views, and there are lots of bed combinations for groups. There's a restaurant on-site.

Jackson Rose B&B (☎ 304-535-1528; www.jacksonrose.com; 1167 Washington St; r $115-125; **P** **X**) This was Stonewall Jackson's first headquarters during the Civil War. The three rooms with queen beds are decorated in the Federal style.

Anvil (☎ 304-535-2582; 1270 Washington St; lunch mains $8-12, dinner mains $11-23; ☺ 11am-9pm Wed-Sun) Technically in the town of Bolivar, you'll find seafood, steak and a friendly smile.

Mountain House Cafe (☎ 304-535-2339; 179 High St; mains $5-8; ☺ from 11am) In the historic district, this café serves up salads and sandwiches in the backyard garden.

GETTING THERE & AROUND

Harpers Ferry is a rarity: a rural destination well served by rail. Daily **Amtrak** (☎ 800-872-7245) and **MARC** (☎ 800-325-7245) trains run between the historic-district station and Washington's Union Station.

Berkeley Springs

Muscles needing a good soak? Sure they do. George Washington and his cronies frequently took the waters here, and in doing so helped create the nation's first spa town. Today, Bath (still its official name) is an anomaly in West Virginia, a microcosm of spiritualism, artistic expression and pampering spa centers. Farmers in pickups sporting Confederate flags and acupuncturists in tie-dye smocks regard each other with bemusement.

Don't let its locker-room appearance deter you from the Berkeley Springs State Park's **Roman Bathhouse** (☎ 304-258-2711; bath $20; ☼ 10am-4:30pm); it's the cheapest spa deal in town. (Fill up your water bottle with some of the magic stuff at the fountain outside the door.) For a more indulgent experience, try a mix-and-match of treatments across the green at the **Main Bath House** (☎ 304-258-9071; ☼ 10am-5pm) such as a bath, shower and hour's massage ($66) or a steam treatment, shower and bath ($25).

Inn & Spa at Berkeley Springs (☎ 304-258-2210, 800-822-6630; www.theinnandspa.com; r $69-175; P ✗), right next to the park, offers luxurious treatment/lodging package deals at prices that will take your breath away. The holistic **Coolfont Resort** (☎ 304-258-4500; www.coolfont.com; 3621 Cold Run Valley Rd; campsites $20-35, r per person $69-99, chalets per person $139-179; P ✗)

is like wellness summer camp for adults (though popular with families, too).

Get a bite ($5 lunch specials on weekdays) and listen to live music at the bar/restaurant **Tari's** (☎ 304-258-1196; 123 N Washington St; dinner mains $10-25), or go gourmet at the elegant **Lot 12 Public House** (☎ 304-258-6264; 302 Warren St; mains $23-32; ☼ dinner Wed-Sun), halfway up the hill.

MONONGAHELA NATIONAL FOREST

This vast expanse of rugged terrain in the Allegheny Mountains is the kind that earned West Virginia the nickname 'the Colorado of the East.' Within its 1400 sq miles, the forest encompasses wild rivers, caves and the highest peak in the state (Spruce Knob). More than 850 miles of trails include the 124-mile **Allegheny Trail**, for hiking and backpacking, and the scenic 75-mile rails-to-trails **Greenbrier River Trail**, popular with cyclists.

Elkins, at the forest's western boundary, is a good base of operations. Here the **National Forest Service Headquarters** (☎ 304-636-1800; 200 Sycamore St; campsites/primitive sites $5/free, RV sites available) distributes recreation directories for hiking, biking and camping.

Fat Tire Cycle (☎ 304-636-0969; 101 Randolph Ave; ☼ 9am-5pm Mon-Fri, to 3pm Sat) rents gear and sponsors excursions. Stock up on trail mix and energy bars at **Good Energy Foods** (☎ 304-636-8808; 214 3rd St; ☼ 9am-5:30pm Mon-Sat).

In the southern end of the forest, **Cranberry Mountain Nature Center** (☎ 304-653-4826; Hwy 150 & Hwy 39/55; ☼ 9am-4:30pm May-Oct) has detailed information about Monongahela.

The surreal landscapes at **Seneca Rocks**, 35 miles southeast of Elkins, attract rock

---

THE PURPLE FIDDLE

In the past-its-prime, blink-and-miss-it town of Thomas, 36 miles northeast of Elkins, is nestled the **Purple Fiddle Coffeehouse & Mountain Market** (☎ 304-463-4040; www.purplefiddle.com; tickets $5-10; ☼ 10am-6pm Mon-Thu, to 11pm Fri & Sat), the kind of institution that can jumpstart civic renewals. Locals, students from area colleges and in-the-know aficionados from as far away as Baltimore and DC are drawn like moths to a flame to the Fiddle's Mountain Music Weekends. Friday and Saturday nights showcase both big and upcoming names in bluegrass and its variant styles. To facilitate the toe-tapping, the Fiddle carries the state's largest beer selection – try the Wild Goose dark porter, brewed in Frederick, Maryland.

If you pass through during the week, stop by anyway for the organic coffee, selection of board games, free Internet, good grub and eclectic range of wares. The owners also let nine rooms next door at the **Fiddler's Roost** (r weekdays/weekends from $49/69), if you happen to get goosed from one too many Gooses.

climbers to demanding challenges up 900ft-tall sandstone strata. **Seneca Shadows Campground** (☎ 877-444-6777; campsites $15-24; ☺ Apr-Oct) is 1 mile east.

An 8-mile portion of the Allegheny Trail links two full-service state parks 30 miles northeast of Elkins: **Canaan Valley Resort** (☎ 304-866-4121), a downhill ski resort, and **Blackwater Falls State Park** (☎ 304-259-5216), with backcountry ski touring. Further south, **Snowshoe Mountain** (☎ 877-441-4386; www .snowshoemtn.com) is the state's largest downhill resort and has become a mountain-biking center from spring to fall.

Nearby, the **Cass Scenic Railroad State Park** (☎ 304-456-4300; www.cassrailroad.com; excursions from $13) runs steam trains from an old logging town to mountaintop overlooks daily in summer and for peak fall foliage. Accommodations include **cottages** (from $150; ☺ Jun-Feb).

The hills of rural West Virginia are the unlikely venue for some of the most cutting-edge radio technology anywhere. The **Green Bank Science Center and the National Radio Astronomy Observatory** (☎ 304-456-2150; www .gb.nrao.edu; Green Bank, West Virginia; admission & tour free; ☺ 8:30am-5pm summer, Wed-Sun rest of year) was where the black hole in the center of our galaxy was detected. The observatory's star attraction, the Green Bank radio telescope, looks like an immense satellite dish and bears the distinction of the largest movable object on land. The Green Bank Science Center has a fascinating exhibit room you shouldn't miss. It lies within the only federal radio-free zone, which is why within 25 miles your car won't pick up any stations.

SOUTHERN WEST VIRGINIA

This is one of the true getaway places close to the eastern seaboard, a mecca for white-water rafting, hiking, mountain biking and cross-country skiing. Check the **Southern West Virginia website** (www.visitwv.com) for more.

New River Gorge National River

A 1000ft-deep gorge is the dramatic setting for the best white-water rafting adventures in the east, on (ironically) one of the oldest rivers in the world, and one of the few that flows south to north. The NPS protects a stretch of the New River that falls 750ft over 50 miles, with a compact set of rapids up to Class V concentrated at the northernmost end.

Canyon Rim Visitor Center (☎ 304-574-2115; ☺ 9am-5pm), just north of the impressive gorge bridge, is the only one of five NPS visitor centers along the river that's open year-round with information on river outfitters, gorge climbing, hiking and mountain biking, as well as white-water rafting to the north on the Gauley River. Rim and gorge trails offer beautiful views. There are four free basic **camping areas**.

Nearby **Hawks Nest State Park** offers views from its rim-top **lodge** (☎ 304-658-5212; r forest/ gorge view $70/75); in summer it operates an aerial tram (closed Mondays) down to the river, where you can catch a cruising boat ride.

Fayetteville

Pint-sized Fayetteville acts as the jumping-off point for New River thrill-seekers. On the third Saturday in October, hundreds of base jumpers parachute from the 876ft-high New River Gorge Bridge for the Bridge Day Festival.

Among the many state-licensed rafting outfitters in the area, **USA Raft** (☎ 800-872-7238; www.usaraft.com; packages from $50) stands out for its white-water rafting trips.

South of town off Hwy 19, lodging and camping directories can be found at the **county tourist office** (☎ 304-465-5617). **Mountain Laurel RV Park/Campground** (☎ 304-574-0188; Laurel Creek Rd at US 19) is a cheap camping option.

Fill up on the hefty portions under stained-glass windows at **Cathedral Café & Bookstore** (☎ 304-574-0202; 134 S Court St; mains $5-8; ☺ 8am-4pm), which also has free Internet access.

The South

BRENT WINEBRENNER

The South

Take a moment to ask for directions in the South and you might receive an earful about the weather, hear a tale about the unnamed bridge or get offered an ice cold tea. The directions will be detailed and colorful, but they'll rarely contain street names. Most likely you'll have to stop and ask for directions again. This is one of the great things about the South. People are friendly, no one's particularly rushed and everyone has a spare minute to talk about the weather.

Southerners don't particularly mind that their region is often portrayed in movies and literature as a backward dustbowl filled with hillbillies, rednecks and Southern belles. Southerners know better and they're quite happy to keep it a secret. The nine states that comprise the South – Georgia, Alabama, Mississippi, Louisiana, Arkansas, Tennessee, Kentucky, North Carolina and South Carolina – offer diversity in geography, history, politics and fun. This is a place where you can sway to blues music, tap toes to country, or dance to the sound of a spoon on a zydeco washboard. Roll up your sleeves and dig in – to boiled crawfish, shrimp as big as your fist, fried chicken and creamy coleslaw done oh so right.

Whatever you come here to do – revel in New Orleans, trace the music in Nashville and Memphis, explore the deep South in Alabama and Mississippi, follow your nose to the bourbon in Kentucky, visit historic plantations in Charleston and colonial homes in Savannah, hang out in the bustle of Atlanta – your experience in the South will open your mind to much more than the stereotypes ever made possible. Unfortunately for Southerners, the secret is out.

HIGHLIGHTS

- Losing all inhibitions and partying the night away in **New Orleans' Mardi Gras** (p418)
- Climbing lighthouses and beachcombing along the windswept **Outer Banks** (p467)
- People-watching on a bench amid ancient oaks and dripping Spanish moss in one of **Savannah's historic squares** (p391)
- Touring antebellum homes and cotton plantations in **Charleston** (p477)
- Drinking up soul tunes and sultry air on Beale St in **Memphis** (p445)
- Hiking, camping and jaw-dropping in the scenic **Great Smoky Mountains National Park** (p455)
- Taking a behind-the-scenes tour of the world's largest news network at **Atlanta's CNN Headquarters** (p381)

THE SOUTH

HISTORY

As early as the 16th century, European explorers started arriving along the east coast. They came from several directions and, as elsewhere in the country, their increasing presence wreaked havoc on the Native American. In 1830, President Andrew Jackson signed the Indian Removal Act, which required the South's 'Five Civilized Tribes' – the Cherokee, Choctaw, Chickasaw, Creek and Seminole – to relocate to 'Indian Territory' west of the Mississippi. In all, some 50,000 Indians were forcibly removed from their homelands in Alabama, Georgia, Tennessee and North Carolina. In 1838, more than 15,000 Cherokee Indians were forced west on what became known as the Trail of Tears, the painstaking trek westward that killed or led to the deaths of more than 4000 Cherokee. A few isolated groups remained, but the Indian Removal Act succeeded in 'clearing' most of the South for settlement.

When the invention of the cotton gin in 1793 mechanized the process of removing seeds from raw cotton, large-scale cotton growing became profitable. Cotton *was* the Southern economy, but it was heavily dependent on Northern financiers who took much of the wealth back North. Increasingly, the South regarded the Northern states with resentment and mistrust.

Though small farmers and workers opposed slavery, politically strong plantation owners depended on slave labor. When Lincoln was elected US president on an antislavery platform, all of the South's nine states (except Kentucky) seceded, and most were devastated when Union soldiers blazed through and crushed Confederate dreams.

The post–Civil War 1867 Reconstruction Acts probably did more to foster hatred of Yankees than the war itself. The Confederate states were readmitted to the Union only after they had abolished slavery and provided for black suffrage. Once readmitted, white elites imposed 'Jim Crow' laws designed to restrict black voting. White supremacist organizations like the Ku Klux Klan (KKK) were born and racial segregation became the norm.

In 1954, the US Supreme Court ruled that segregation of public schools was unconstitutional. Southern states did not accept this, however, and the next 10 years saw demonstrations, protests and civil action aimed at desegregation and black political representation.

Black students enrolled in Arkansas schools under armed-forces protection. Mississippi closed its public schools rather than let Blacks enroll. Black students sat for days at North Carolina lunch counters waiting to be served. Segregated buses were boycotted for 13 months in Alabama.

Under the leadership of Martin Luther King Jr, the protests were nonviolent, but they often met with violent reaction from their opponents (see p378).

The emphasis then turned from desegregation to voter registration. The Voting Rights Act in 1965 prohibited states from imposing literacy tests and other obstacles on black voters.

THE SOUTH

THE SOUTH IN....

Two to Three Weeks

This is a vast region with so much to see. This is just one suggested itinerary, which you could do by car or Greyhound bus. Start your tour of the South in New Orleans, where you can get to know the Big Easy on our **walking tour** (p419) before partying the night away on **Bourbon Street** (p425). Make your way to Tennessee, where you can visit legendary music sites, including **Graceland** (p443) in Memphis and **Nashville's Country Music Hall of Fame** (p448). Head east to the cool North Carolina town of Ashville (p472) and then drive north along the **Blue Ridge Parkway** (p471) or head out to the coast to visit the **Outer Banks** (p467).

An alternate route could take you north from New Orleans, through the **Mississippi Delta** (p405) then east to Alabama, where you should stop at the excellent **Birmingham Civil Rights Institute** (p399). From there, spend a couple of days in Atlanta and be sure to hike **Stone Mountain**, the world's largest hunk of granite (p385). From Atlanta, hit the coast and visit the beaches and historic sites around **Savannah** (p395).

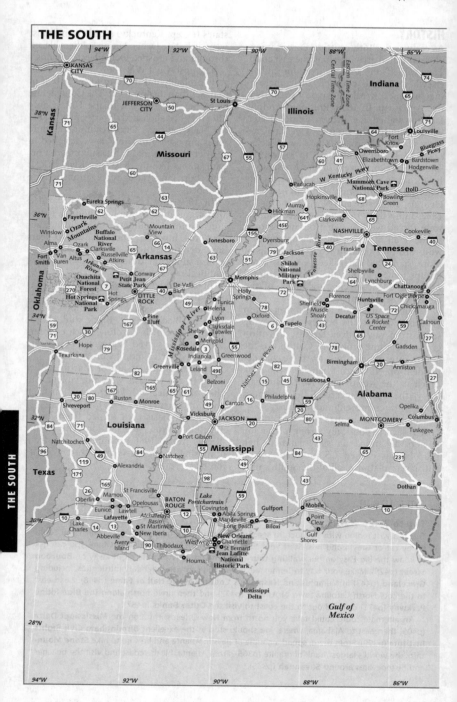

THE SOUTH

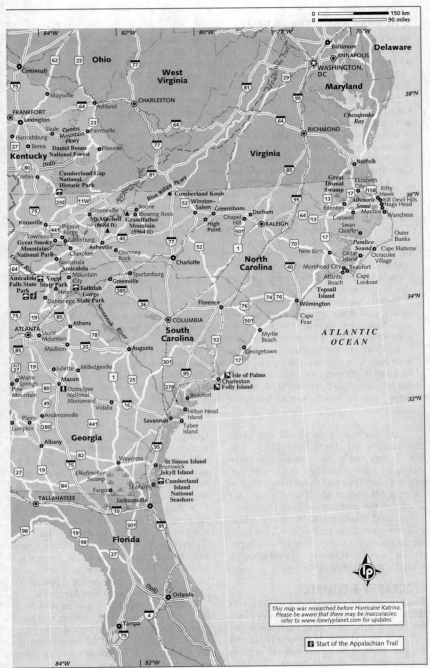

This map was researched before Hurricane Katrina. Please be aware that there may be inaccuracies; refer to www.lonelyplanet.com for updates.

Start of the Appalachian Trail

CIVIL WAR – WHAT'S THE BIG DEAL?

When people from elsewhere come to the South, they often wonder why so much credence is given to the Civil War. Visitors often think, but rarely have the nerve to say, 'Hey, man, get over it.' After all, we're talking about events that happened more than 100 years ago.

But, once you've spent some time here you'll realize that the 'Great Unpleasantness' did so much to define the culture, ideologies and opinions that continue to shape the South.

Landowners in the 'Old South' were mostly English colonists who, living isolated from both Britain and the rest of the country, set to work getting rich off the bounty of slave-labored rice and cotton plantations.

When Lincoln came along spouting ideas about freeing the slaves, white leaders believed a faraway authority, especially one whose ideologies differed so greatly from their own, should not make local decisions. Landowners banded together and soon the 11 states of the Southern Confederacy became a force to be reckoned with.

The Civil War lasted for four years (1861–65). It was a bloody, face-to-face conflict whose outcome would change the course of history. After the war, much of the South was left in smoldering ruins. In essence, the South was a conquered nation, and the accompanying mind-set drove a deep wedge between Southerners and Northerners.

When you see buildings and plantations that survived the war, you get a strong sense of the glory days of the past. But 'glory' was a relative term. When people refer to the 'Old South,' or the time pre–Civil War, it conjures up many emotions. To black people, it often represents a time of enslavement, injustice and great indignity. To white Southerners whose ancestors owned those homes and plantations, the concept can mean something else entirely – often it's an indescribable mixture of pride and shame.

The next hundred years, between the Civil War and the Civil Rights movement, saw a dramatic cultural shift. While racial tolerance bloomed in some areas, hatred exploded in others. Many white Southerners resented the blacks, and vice versa. What was happening in the South mirrored what was taking place across the country.

Today, many white Southerners on both sides of the spectrum say that race isn't as much of a hot-button issue anymore. Others, who see the glaring economic disparity between Whites and Blacks, think differently. Both the outcome of the Civil War and issues of race remain volatile topics that people in these parts don't like to discuss. The century of boiling emotions, anger and fevered racism has today become a small simmer but, like a pot of water, it never really boils or cools.

Today Blacks hold public office in many cities across the South, and Blacks and Whites mix freely. Yet racism and racial inequality are still a reality, and recent controversy over State and Confederate flags in Georgia, Mississippi and South Carolina are proof that the past has not been forgotten.

Educated Southerners, black and white, are quite open about these issues. They often see the rest of the country as somewhat hypocritical in its belief that racial problems are something particular to the South.

GEOGRAPHY & CLIMATE

You can spend a summer day in the south and wonder if somehow you stumbled into the sweaty armpit of the devil. It shore gits hot! And sticky! This is especially true in the low-lying subtropical coastal regions and in inland areas of South Carolina, Georgia, Mississippi and Louisiana, where a summer breeze is sometimes as good as a cold beer. These areas are also defined by swamplands and agricultural areas where the nutrient-rich soil depends on summer humidity and wintertime rain.

In the northern part of the region, mountains cool and dry out the air and the mountain rivers come trickling down to seep into the fertile lands, especially in Arkansas' Ozark and Ouachita Mountains and in Tennessee's Blue Ridge Mountains, and in North Carolina where the foothills of the Appalachian Mountains thrust north into Kentucky.

Tourism in the region is at its peak from June to September. Mild weather and blossoming flowers make spring (May to June) a good time to visit, and fall colors decorate the landscape in September and October, especially in the mountain regions.

NATIONAL, STATE & REGIONAL PARKS

This region is full of national parks, monuments and historic sites. Some honor people (Martin Luther King Jr in Georgia, the Wright Brothers in North Carolina), others preserve historic and scenic passages (Natchez Trace Parkway from Mississippi to Tennessee, the Blue Ridge Parkway in North Carolina). Some sites mark significant Civil War battles (Vicksburg, MS; Chickamauga, GA; Forts Pulaski and Sumter, SC), while others honor waterways (Buffalo River, AR; Cumberland Island National Seashore, GA).

The region's bona fide 'national parks', thus designated for their role in protecting nature and sheer beauty, include the Great Smoky Mountains National Park in TN and NC; Mammoth Cave National Park, KY, which protects the world's largest-known cave system; Hot Springs National Park, AR, which is the nation's oldest national park and today protects 47 natural hot springs and eight historic bathhouses; and Congaree National Park, SC, which is home to the largest contiguous tract of old-growth, bottomland hardwood forest in the US.

See the states for individual sites, or learn more at the National Park Service website (www.nps.gov).

There are hundreds of state parks throughout the region, from tiny and primitive, to giant and full of amenities. For an overview of each state's parks, contact the following:

Alabama (☎ 888-252-7272; www.alapark.com)
Arkansas (☎ 888-287-2757; www.arkansasstateparks.com)
Georgia (☎ 800-864-7275; www.gastateparks.org)
Kentucky (☎ 800-255-7275; www.state.ky.us/agencies/parks)
Louisiana (☎ 888-677-1400; www.lastateparks.com)
Mississippi (☎ 800-407-2575; www.mdwfp.com)
North Carolina (☎ 919-733-4181; www.ncsparks.net)
South Carolina (☎ 888-887-2757; www.southcarolinaparks.com)
Tennessee (☎ 888-867-2757; www.state.tn.us/environment/parks)

INFORMATION

There is no central tourism agency that covers all of the South, but each state runs helpful visitor centers at state borders along major highways, stocked with highway maps, brochures and coupon books. Most are also happy to send out brochures to help you preplan your trip ahead of time. See the individual states for information about contacting each state authority.

DANGERS & ANNOYANCES

Although Southern hospitality thrives in these parts, crime can be a problem in bigger cities. Most visitors won't have a problem if they stick to well-lit areas, avoid run-down or otherwise sketchy parts of town and generally use common sense. Cities like New Orleans or Atlanta, for example, are generally safe and hassle-free, but like most big cites, they do have areas

THE SOUTH

CRASH COURSE IN SOUTHERN SLANG

Though English is the official language in the South, many regional dialects sound to the untrained ear like a totally foreign language. Each state – even each region or town – has its own Southern accent. Some words and expressions are helpful to know; others are simply entertaining. Here are a few examples:

ain't – is not, am not
britches – pants, trousers
come up a cloud – it's about to rain
dad burnit or **dad gummit** – goddamn it
fixin' to – getting ready, as in I'm fixin' to go fishin'
holler – to yell
hollow – valley, low area between hills
knockin' boots – having sex
lickity-split – really fast
pert-near – pretty close
playin' possum – pretending to be dead

slow as molasses – damn slow
Sugah – term of endearment, often used by diner waitresses
tight as a tick – frugal, cheap
to tar and feather – to kick someone's ass
up the road apiece – further up the road
up yonder – a little further
uptown – expensive, high quality
wet a line – go fishing
thick as thieves – good friends
tradin' paint – bumping during a Nascar race
y'all – you plural, all of you

GREAT LINES OVERHEARD IN THE SOUTH

'Even a blind hog finds an acorn once in a while.'

Translation – 'Even a totally stupid person gets it right once in a while.'

'I was so confused, I didn't know whether to wind my ass or scratch my watch.'

Translation – 'I was pretty confused.'

'If it's got hair on it, I can ride it. If it's got feet, I can dance with it.'

Translation – 'Give me the right tools and I can do anything.'

'I ain't got a dog in that fight.'

Translation – 'I have no argument or interest in that issue.'

'He'll work the horns off a billy goat.'

Translation – 'That guy will work his ass off.'

---

where occurrences of violence and crime are higher than others.

If you are camping or hiking remember that insects are a feature of the Southern geography; mosquitoes can be nasty, especially after a rainfall, so be sure to carry bug spray.

GETTING THERE & AROUND

Atlanta, Georgia is the main air gateway to the region and its airport is the busiest in the world. Memphis, TN, New Orleans, LA and Charlotte and Raleigh, NC have the region's largest airports. **Greyhound** (☎ 800-231-2222; www.greyhound.com) buses are frequent (if sometimes slow) and can be a dependable way to get from city to city. A number of **Amtrak** (☎ 800-872-7245; www.amtrak .com) train routes traverse the South; several conveniently converge on New Orleans. Beyond the cities, you really need a car to get around.

As for drives, this region's got some good ones. The Blue Ridge Parkway, the Natchez Trace Parkway and Hwy 12 along the Outer Banks are three of the South's most scenic drives. I-10 runs along the Gulf Coast from Florida to New Orleans; I-20 links South Carolina with Louisiana via Georgia, Alabama and Mississippi; and I-40 goes from North Carolina to Arkansas via Tennessee. The chief north–south routes include I-95, I-75, I-65 and I-55.

GEORGIA

Vastly different at each of its edges, Georgia, the largest state east of the Mississippi River, offers a bit of everything. Most visitors land in Atlanta, a sprawling metropolis with friendly neighborhoods

eating and drinking alongside big business. Then you hit the coast, where you fall under the spell of Savannah's live oaks, antebellum homes, seafood and hot humid nights.

Your imagination gets whisked away along the coastal barrier islands, many of which are preserves for waterfowl, migratory birds, alligators, nesting sea turtles and wild horses.

In the middle of the state, flat shoals, rivers, hardwood forests and rich red soil support thriving harvests of cotton, nuts and, of course, Georgia's world famous peaches.

Georgia is a state of wild geographic and cultural extremes: right-leaning Republican politics lean against liberal idealism, small towns merge with gaping cities, northern mountains rise to the clouds and produce roaring rivers, while coastal marshlands teem with fiddler crabs and swaying cordgrass.

GEORGIA FACTS

Nickname Peach State, Empire State of the South

Population 8.7 million

Area 57,906 sq miles

Capital city Atlanta (population 4.1 million)

Official state wildflower Azalea

Birthplace of Baseball legend Ty Cobb (1886–1961), civil rights leader Martin Luther King Jr (1929–68), president Jimmy Carter (b 1924), singer Ray Charles (1930–2004), soul singer James Brown (b 1933), author Alice Walker (b 1944), country singer Trisha Yearwood (b 1964)

Home of CNN, Coca-Cola

Famous for Gone With the Wind, peaches, Vidalia onions

GOOD EATIN'

Test your arteries down South, where no one is afraid of the deep fryer, and butter, bacon fat and lard are staples of good cookin'. Southerners love to eat, and everyone – from chefs to grandmothers – has a recipe that they'll swear is the best. The following is a brief list of favorite Southern foods:

alligator – real alligator often served fried or like beef jerky

biscuits and gravy – a common breakfast food

boiled peanuts – snack of peanuts in the shell boiled in brine

Brunswick stew – spicy stew made with chicken, okra, corn and potatoes

catfish – freshwater fish, often fried

chicken-fried steak – beef steak coated with flour and fried

Coke – any carbonated beverage, whether Coke, 7-Up etc

collard greens – spinach-type greens cooked with pork fat and onions

cornbread – bread made with cornmeal

cracklins – a snack of fried strips of pork skin and fat

crawfish – a small lobsterlike freshwater crustacean, often boiled

fatback – bacon fat for cooking; every good Southerner has a jar in the refrigerator

fried chicken – the quintessential Southern food

fried green tomatoes – green tomatoes, floured and fried

grits – ground hominy, often served at breakfast with cheese or gravy

gumbo – Louisiana soup with seafood, sausage and spices

hush puppy – deep-fried balls of cornmeal and onion

jambalaya – a spicy Creole dish with rice, tomatoes, onions, shrimp and ham

Lowcountry boil – a one-pot dish combining shrimp, sausage, corn and potato

meat-and-three – an inexpensive meat dish plus two sides

muffaletta – a sandwich made with a large round roll of Italian bread split in half and filled with layers of hard salami, ham, provolone and olive salad

okra – a common vegetable, often served boiled or fried

pecan pie – really, any pie; Southerners love their sweets!

pickled anything – you name it: beets, oysters, shrimp, eggs

pralines – sugared pecans

sweet-potato pie – sweet potato cooked with sugar, cinnamon and nutmeg

sweet tea – quintessentially Southern: very sweet iced tea; without sugar it's 'unsweet tea'

History

Permanent English settlement dates from 1733, when James Edward Oglethorpe founded Savannah. The colony grew rapidly. By the time of the Revolutionary War, almost half the population were slaves. After Eli Whitney invented the cotton gin outside Savannah in 1793, slavery-dependent cotton farming expanded rapidly.

In 1828, gold was discovered near Dahlonega. This sped up the dispossession of North Georgia's Cherokee population during the first half of the 19th century, culminating in their forced removal to Oklahoma along the 1838 Trail of Tears.

Though far removed from the Civil War's early phases, Georgia held two of the most important battlefronts in the latter part of the war. Union troops were defeated at Chickamauga, but fought their way to Atlanta, which they defeated and burned; they then marched through Georgia to Savannah. Atlanta, the South's major transportation hub, was rebuilt with startling speed.

Cotton farming and textile manufacturing grew. In the early 20th century, agriculture became more diversified, expanding into corn, fruit and tobacco.

In the 20th century the state vaulted to national prominence on the back of an eclectic group of events and images: the wildly popular film (and novel) *Gone With the Wind*; Rev Martin Luther King Jr and civil rights protests; 39th US President Jimmy Carter; and Atlanta's rise as a global media and business center, culminating in the 1996 Summer Olympics.

THE SOUTH

IN PURSUIT OF A DREAM

Martin Luther King Jr was born January 15, 1929, in the middle-class Atlanta neighborhood of Sweet Auburn. He attended Atlanta's Morehouse College at age 15 and was ordained three years later as a Baptist minister. He went on to earn a PhD from Boston University. Influenced by Mahatma Gandhi, he espoused principles of nonviolence.

In 1955, King led the 'bus boycott' in Montgomery, AL (p401). After a year of boycotting, the US Supreme Court removed laws that enforced segregated buses. From this successful beginning, King emerged as an inspiring moral voice in civil rights.

King and other black leaders formed the Southern Christian Leadership Conference (SCLC). King's strategy was to select a notoriously segregated city and mobilize black residents to lead nonviolent protest marches. The demonstrations forced white authorities to either negotiate or resort to violence; if the latter, the scenes of violence would arouse the national conscience, thereby forcing the federal government to act. This worked according to plan in Birmingham, AL (1964 Civil Rights Act), and in Selma, AL (1965 Voting Rights Act). This approach failed in Georgia.

King's most often remembered speech, delivered in 1963 in Washington, DC, refers to his home state:

I have a dream that one day on the red hills of Georgia, sons of former slaves and sons of former slave-owners will be able to sit down together at the table of brotherhood…I have a dream that my four little children will one day live in a nation where they will not be judged by the color of their skin but by the content of their character. I have a dream today!

In 1964, at age 35, King was awarded the Nobel Peace Prize. On a trip to Memphis, Tennessee, he was assassinated by James Earl Ray on April 4, 1968 (p442).

King remains one of the most recognized and respected figures of the 20th century. In a span of 10 years, he led a movement that essentially ended a system of statutory discrimination in existence since the country's founding. The Martin Luther King Jr National Historic Site (p381) and the King Center for Non-Violent Social Change in Atlanta (p381) are testaments to his moral vision, his ability to inspire others and his lasting impact on the fundamental fabric of American society.

In early 2001, the Georgia state flag, which had formerly incorporated the Confederate battle flag – to some a symbol of Southern heritage, to others a symbol of slavery and racism – was changed in an attempt to decrease racial divisions within the state. Sonny Perdue, who in 2003 won Georgia's first Republican governorship since the Civil War, vowed to get the old flag back. Most Georgians deemed it a ridiculous waste of time, and the flag issue fizzled, for now.

Information

The state sales tax on all goods and services is 7%; expect to pay an additional 6% tax on hotel accommodations.

Department of Industry, Trade & Tourism
(☎ 404-656-3590, 800-847-4842; www.georgia.org; PO Box 1776, Atlanta, GA 30301) Sends out a thick travel guide. It also runs visitor centers throughout the state.

ATLANTA

Like a teenager who went from cuddling dolls to drinking in bars seemingly overnight, Atlanta is still getting used to her new limbs and liberties. Between 1990 and 2000, the city's population exploded by almost 40% and Atlanta has gobbled up that growth like a kid snacking on chocolate and Cheesies. She didn't worry about zits or extra pounds; the economic boost was too irresistible and, frankly, unstoppable.

Without natural boundaries to control growth, Atlanta keeps growing out, not up – suburban sprawl has turned Atlanta into a almost endless city. Increased car dependence creates horrendous traffic, traffic creates smog, smog pollutes water, and so on. These problems keep politicians and environmental groups scratching their heads.

For all this suburbanization, Atlanta is a pretty city covered with trees and elegant old homes. The growth raised the roof on the restaurant and shopping scene, and distinct neighborhoods are like friendly small towns. Racial tensions are minimal, but segregation persists. Atlanta's neighborhoods resemble a checkerboard of white and black.

History

Born as a railroad junction in 1837, Atlanta became a major Confederate transportation and munitions center for General William T Sherman, whose Union forces blazed through Georgia in 1864.

Much of the city crumbled in the siege, and it worsened when retreating Confederates, not wanting the Yankees to get their cache, blew up their own ammunition. Sherman's army stayed in Atlanta for 10 weeks. When they left they burned everything, leaving more than 90% of Atlanta's buildings in ruins.

After the war, Atlanta became the epitome of the 'New South,' a concept that entailed reconciliation with the North, the promotion of industrialized agriculture, and a progressive business outlook. Atlanta's relentless boosterism led to civic improvements and energetic business partnerships. Separate black and white societies developed and segregation deepened.

Public sit-ins and demonstrations in the early 1960s, led by Atlanta native Martin Luther King Jr, finally prompted city business leaders to sign a joint agreement to desegregate. Unlike in other cities where desegregation was slow and wrought with tension, Atlanta adjusted relatively painlessly. President John F Kennedy lauded this transition as a model for other communities facing integration.

Atlanta's century of boosterism culminated when it hosted the 1996 Summer Olympic Games. Atlanta put on her prettiest dress and CNN beamed her picture worldwide. People took notice, the moving trucks came rolling down the freeways and, like summer weeds, new condos sprouted everywhere.

Orientation

The sprawling Atlanta metropolitan area sits inside a wide circle of freeway, which is called I-285 or, locally, 'the Perimeter.' Inside the circle, I-20 travels east and west, while I-75 and I-85 run north and south. I-75 and I-85 become a single road – 'the downtown connector' – as the roads pass through the city center.

Peachtree St and Piedmont Ave are the main north–south arteries, but be forewarned: you'll find that a hundred other streets, roads and avenues are also called Peachtree. Many streets also change names suddenly, so if you're driving, it's a good idea to plot your route on a map beforehand. Addresses also specify NE, SE, SW or NW. W Peachtree St divides east from west and Martin Luther King Jr Dr/Edgewood Ave divides north from south.

Downtown Atlanta is a world-class business center with a few worthwhile attractions, but you'll have to venture into

THE SOUTH

ATLANTA IN...

Two Days

Start your first day in Atlanta by strolling through **Piedmont Park** (p384) where you can gaze up at the blooming magnolias with the spires of Midtown buildings in the background. Walk to the north side of the park and spend a couple of hours at the fabulous **Atlanta Botanical Garden** (p384). At night, head for dinner and drinks to the social hub of **Buckhead** (p387). The next day, have a Bloody Mary brunch at Little Five Point's **Front Page News** (p387) and spend a leisurely day viewing works at the **High Museum of Art** (p384).

Four Days

Start with the two-day itinerary and spend your third day at **Stone Mountain Park** (p385). Climb to the top of the giant granite outcrop and marvel at the gorgeous view. Go back to your hotel. Take a nap. At night make your way to the **Virginia-Highland** (p388) neighborhood for a night of fun and friendly barhopping. On day four, take the behind-the-scenes tour of **CNN** (p381), and follow it up with a stroll down Sweet Auburn to the **Martin Luther King Jr National Historic Site** (p381). At night, catch some live music in Decatur at **Eddie's Attic** (p388).

Atlanta's sprawling neighborhoods to see the best the city has to offer. East of downtown, Sweet Auburn attractions pay homage to Martin Luther King Jr. Little Five Points (L5P) has bars and cafés for Atlanta's alternative set. More hip, Virginia-Highland has restaurants, boutique shopping and bars. Decatur – an independent city just east of Atlanta – has several good restaurants and nightspots. Turner Field and Grant Park are south and southeast of downtown.

North of downtown, Midtown is another entertainment and nightlife area, with posh, partying Buckhead further out.

Information

BOOKSTORES

Borders Books Music & Cafe (☎ 404-607-7903; www.borderssstores.com; 650 Ponce De Leon Ave NE; ☿ 9am-11pm Mon-Sat, to 10pm Sun)

Charis Books & More (☎ 404-524-0304; www.charis circle.org; 1189 Euclid Ave NE; ☿ 10:30am-6:30pm Mon & Tue, to 8pm Wed-Sat, noon-6pm Sun) In Little Five Points, this is a well-stocked feminist and lesbian bookstore.

Outwrite Bookstore & Coffeehouse (☎ 404-607-0082; www.outwritebooks.com; 991 Piedmont Ave; ☿ 10am-11pm Mon-Sun) At 10th St in Midtown, this is a cheerful gay bookstore with a full coffee bar.

EMERGENCY

Emergency (☎ 911) Police, ambulance, fire.

Main police station (☎ 404-853-3434; 675 Ponce de Leon Ave at City Hall East) Nonemergencies only.

INTERNET ACCESS

Maasty Computers Internet Café (☎ 404-294-8095; www.maastyinternetcafe.com; 736 Ponce de Leon Ave; per 15min $2.50; ☿ 8am-11pm Mon-Thu, to midnight Fri & Sat, to 10pm Sun) Near City Hall East, Maasty has wi-fi, laptop rentals and Internet connectivity.

Public library (☎ 404-730-1700; 1 Margaret Mitchell Sq; ☿ 9am-9pm Mon-Thu, to 6pm Fri & Sat, 2-6pm Sun) Many branches of the public library offer free Internet, including this main branch.

INTERNET RESOURCES

Access Atlanta (www.accessatlanta.com) A great place to find out about Atlanta news and upcoming events.

Atlanta Local Music (www.atlantalocalmusic.com) Find out what bands are performing in town, plus a directory of local venues.

Atlanta Coalition of Performing Arts (www.atlanta performs.com) Gives info and links about the city's music, film, dance and theater scene.

Atlanta Travel (www.atlanta.net) Official site of the Convention & Visitors Bureau with excellent links to shops, restaurants, hotels and upcoming events.

MEDIA

Atlanta (www.atlantamagazine.com) A monthly general interest magazine covering local issues, arts and dining. Check in the back pages for a comprehensive listing of area restaurants.

Atlanta Daily World (www.atlantadailyworld.com) The nation's oldest, continuously running African American newspaper (since 1928).

Atlanta Journal-Constitution (www.ajc.com) Atlanta's major daily newspaper, with a good travel section on Sunday.

Creative Loafing (www.atlanta.creativeloafing.com) For excellent listings on music, arts and theater this free alternative weekly comes out every Wednesday.

MEDICAL SERVICES

Atlanta Medical Center (☎ 404-265-4000; 303 Parkway Dr NE)

Emory University Hospital (☎ 404-712-7021; 1364 Clifton Rd NE)

Grady Memorial Hospital (☎ 404-335-2449; 80 Butler St SE)

Piedmont Hospital (☎ 404-605-5000; 1968 Peachtree Rd)

POST

For general postal information call ☎ 800-275-8777.

Post office CNN Center (1 CNN Center); Downtown (183 Forsyth St SW at Garnet St); Federal Center (☎ 404-521-9843; 41 Marietta St NW); Little Five Points (457 Moreland Ave SE); North Highland (1190 N Highland Ave NE) Mail addressed to General Delivery, Atlanta, GA 30301 can be picked up at Federal Center.

TOURIST INFORMATION

Atlanta Convention & Visitors Bureau (☎ 404-521-6600; www.atlanta.net) Main (233 Peachtree St; ☿ 8:30am-5:30pm Mon-Fri); Underground Atlanta (cnr Peachtree & Alabama Sts; ☿ 10am-6pm Mon-Sat, from noon Sun) Mails out a comprehensive visitor package and also runs visitor centers at the airport.

UNIVERSITIES

Atlanta is home to many universities and colleges, including the following:

Emory University (☎ 404-727-6123; www.emory.edu; 380 S Oxford Rd NE) Between downtown and Decatur is one of the top universities in the USA.

Georgia Institute of Technology (☎ 404-894-2000; www.gatech.edu; 25 North Ave) Known as 'Georgia Tech,' this is one of the top technical colleges, with a wildly popular football team.

Georgia State University (☎ 404-651-2000; www .gsu.edu) Has 32,000 students and is located in the center of downtown.

Dangers & Annoyances

Atlanta has a big-city high-crime rate. Downtown is safe enough during the day, but at night the streets get eerily deserted. Atlanta is a car town; it is not pedestrian friendly, so someone walking alone at night can seem like a bit of an anomaly. Stick to the well-populated areas. Because of the car-centricity, you'll see a lot of aggressive and speedy drivers. Be kind to your blood pressure and stay off the highways during rush hour.

Sights & Activities
DOWNTOWN

On weekdays, downtown Atlanta bustles with conventioneers and business folk, but by nightfall and weekends the bustle turns to a shuffle. An ongoing debate ensues over the fate of downtown Atlanta. Some people want casinos and tourist attractions, others vie for a more livable urban core, one that doesn't shut down after five. Despite this complaint, there are a few attractions.

The oldest part of the city is the area just around Alabama St. As the city grew, bridges and viaducts built over the railroad tracks made life easier for horses, pedestrians and, later, cars. Eventually an entire level of shops and storefronts vanished beneath street level. An imaginative 1960s renewal program recovered these 'lost' streets to construct **Underground Atlanta** (☎ 404-523-2311; www.underground-atlanta. com; cnr Peachtree & Alabama Sts; ☯ 10am-9pm Mon-Sat, noon-6pm Sun), which is an enclosed, air-conditioned multilevel maze of shops, bars and restaurants.

World of Coca-Cola (☎ 404-676-5151; www.woc catlanta.com; 55 Martin Luther King Jr Dr; adult/child $9/5; ☯ 9am-5pm Mon-Sat, noon-6pm Sun) strives mightily to promote Coca-Cola as a global cultural icon. Perhaps Atlanta's most overrated (but most visited) attraction, it features memorabilia and historic advertising dating back to Coke's origins in 1886 Atlanta.

CNN Center (☎ 404-827-2300, 877-266-8687; www .cnn.com/StudioTour; 1 CNN Center; 50min tours adult/child $10/7; ☯ 9am-5pm) is the bustling headquar-ters of the cable-TV news service. Every year some 250,000 people take the CNN tour (departs every 10 minutes), a behind-the-scenes glance at the world's busiest news organization.

Just north of CNN, **Centennial Olympic Park** (☎ 404-872-5338; www.centennialpark.com) is a 21-acre legacy to the 1996 Olympic Games. Concerts and special events are held throughout the year.

The gold-domed **Georgia State Capitol** (☎ 404-656-2844; www.sos.state.ga.us; 206 Washington St; tours free; ☯ 10am, 10:30am, 11am, 1pm, 1:30pm & 2pm Sep-May, 10am, 11am, 1pm & 2pm Jun-Aug) is Atlanta's political hub. Tours include a film about the legislative process and a glance at the government's communications facility.

SWEET AUBURN

Though now dilapidated and struggling, Auburn Ave was the thumping commercial and cultural heart of African American culture in the 1900s. It takes some imagination, but if you listen closely, you can almost hear the jazz and history oozing out of the brick facades. Today, a collection of sights is associated with Sweet Auburn's most famous son: Martin Luther King Jr, who was born on Auburn and preached on Auburn and whose grave now looks on to the street.

The historic **Martin Luther King Jr National Historic Site** commemorates the life, work and legacy of the father of the Civil Rights movement. The center takes up several blocks. A stop by the **visitor center** (☎ 404-331-5190; www.nps.gov/malu; 450 Auburn Ave NE; admission free; ☯ 9am-5pm, to 6pm summer) will help you get oriented with a map and brochure of area sites and exhibits. From here, free guided tours leave for the **Martin Luther King Jr Birthplace** (501 Auburn Ave).

Across from the visitor center, the **King Center for Non-Violent Social Change** (☎ 404-893-9882; 449 Auburn Ave NE) has more information on King's life and work, and a few of his personal effects, including his Nobel Peace Prize. His **gravesite**, between the church and center, is surrounded by a long, reflecting pool and can be viewed anytime.

Ebenezer Baptist Church (☎ 404-688-7263; 407 Auburn Ave NE; admission free; ☯ tours 9am-6pm Mon-Sat, from 1:30pm Sun) was the preaching ground for King, his father and grandfather, who

THE SOUTH

THE SOUTH

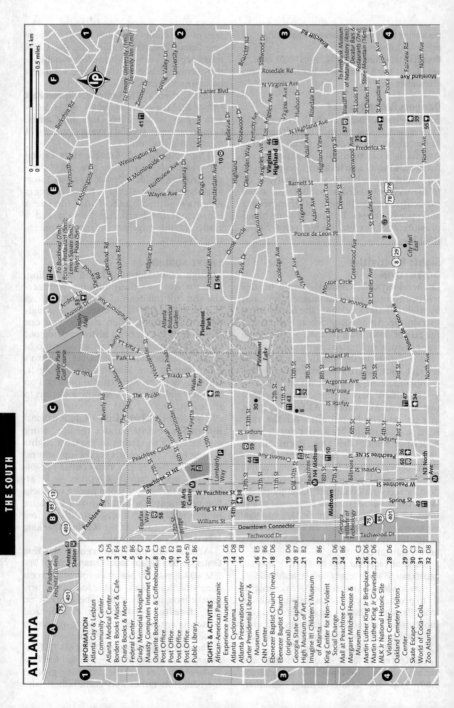

ATLANTA

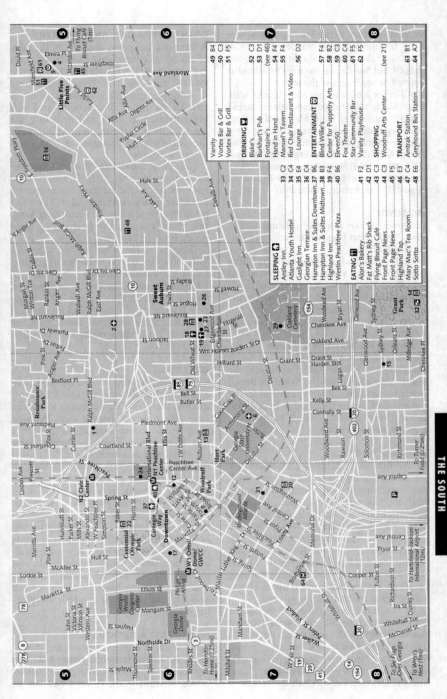

SLEEPING 🛏

Ansley Inn	33 C2
Atlanta Youth Hostel	34 C4
Gaslight Inn	35 E4
Georgian Terrace	36 C2
Hampton Inn & Suites Downtown	37 B6
Hampton Inn & Suites Midtown	38 B3
Highland Inn	39 F4
Westin Peachtree Plaza	40 B6

EATING 🍴

Alon's Bakery	41 F2
Fat Matt's Rib Shack	42 D1
Flying Biscuit Café	43 C3
Front Page News	44 C3
Front Page News	45 F5
Highland Tap	46 E3
Mary Mac's Tea Room	47 C4
Sotto Sotto	48 E6

DRINKING 🍸

Varsity	49 B4
Vortex Bar & Grill	50 C3
Vortex Bar & Grill	51 F5
Blake's	52 C3
Burkhart's Pub	53 D1
Fontaine's	(see 46)
Hand in Hand	54 F4
Manuel's Tavern	55 F4
Red Chair Restaurant & Video Lounge	56 D2

ENTERTAINMENT 🎭

Blind Willie's	57 F4
Center for Puppetry Arts	58 B2
Eleven50	59 C3
Fox Theatre	60 C4
Star Community Bar	61 F5
Variety Playhouse	62 F5

SHOPPING 🛍

Woodruff Arts Center	(see 21)

TRANSPORT

Amtrak Station	63 B1
Greyhound Bus Station	64 A7

were all pastors here. This is also where King Jr's mother was murdered in 1974. You can take a free tour of the original church, but Sunday services are now held at a new Ebenezer across the street.

All of the King sites are a few blocks' walk from Marta's (Metropolitan Atlanta Rapid Transit Authority) King Memorial station. For more on black history, including a film about the Sweet Auburn area, visit the **African-American Panoramic Experience Museum** (APEX; ☎ 404-523-2739; www.apexmuseum.org; 135 Auburn Ave NE; admission $4; ⏰ 10am-5pm Tue-Sat), on the edge of Sweet Auburn toward downtown.

MIDTOWN

Midtown is like a hipper, second downtown, with great bars, restaurants and cultural venues.

In the Woodruff Arts Center (p388), the highlight is the gorgeous **High Museum of Art** (☎ 404-733-4400; www.high.org; 1280 Peachtree St NE; adult/child $10/7; ⏰ 10am-5pm Tue-Sat, noon-5pm Sun). Its collection includes European and American contemporary art and first-class African exhibits.

Margaret Mitchell House & Museum (☎ 404-249-7015; www.gwtw.org; 990 Peachtree St at 10th St; adult/child $12/9; ⏰ 9:30am-5pm) is a shrine to the author of *Gone With the Wind*. Mitchell wrote her epic in a small apartment in the basement of this historic house. In addition to the literary classic, Mitchell's other writings are also on display.

Piedmont Park

In the middle of Midtown, **Piedmont Park** (www.piedmontpark.org) is a giant urban park and the setting of many cultural and music festivals. The park has fantastic bike paths, playgrounds, tennis courts and a well-loved dog park. **Skate Escape** (☎ 404-892-1292; www.skateescape.com; 1086 Piedmont Ave NE), at 12th St, rents out bicycles ($6 to $10 per hour) and in-line skates ($6 per hour). For six Thursdays in summer, the free **Screen on the Green** (www.turner.com/screenonthegreen) features classic movies projected onto a big screen.

In the northwest corner of Piedmont Park, the stunning 30-acre **Atlanta Botanical Garden** (☎ 404-876-5859; www.atlantabotanicalgarden.org; 1345 Piedmont Ave NE; adult/child $12/7; ⏰ 9am-5pm Tue-Sun, to 7pm summer) has a Japanese garden, a conservatory with threatened plants and the amazing Fuqua Orchid Center.

GRANT PARK & OAKLAND CEMETERY

A large oasis of green situated on the edge of the city center, **Grant Park** (www.grantpark.org) is home to the **Atlanta Cyclorama** (☎ 404-658-7625; adult/child $7/5; ⏰ 9am-4:30pm), one of Atlanta's most famous attractions. A circular painting 358ft around and 42ft high, painted in 1886 and depicting the 1864 Battle of Atlanta, the Cyclorama is the world's largest painting. A tour starts every 30 minutes.

Next door, **Zoo Atlanta** (☎ 404-624-5600; www.zooatlanta.org; adult/child $17/12; ⏰ 9:30am-4:30pm) features re-created natural environments including a large gorilla exhibit. The zoo's pride and joy are Lun Lun and Yang Yang, two of only a small population of giant panda bears in captivity.

Gone With the Wind author Margaret Mitchell and golf great Bobby Jones are buried in the **Oakland Cemetery** (☎ 404-688-2107; 248 Oakland Ave; tour self/guided $2/10; ⏰ 9am-5pm Mon-Fri), at Martin Luther King Jr Dr. Many very interesting Victorian and neoclassical monuments are scattered throughout the site. Stop at the **visitor center** for a walking-tour map.

WEST END

Older than the city of Atlanta itself and a long-established African American community, the West End was home to Alonzo Herndon, who was born a slave but who went on to become one of the country's first black millionaires. The **Herndon Home** (☎ 404-581-9813; www.herndonhome.org; 587 University Place NW; adult/child $5/3; ⏰ 10am-4pm Tue-Sat) is an impressive beaux arts mansion, built and decorated by black workers in 1910.

South of I-20, the **Wren's Nest** (☎ 404-753-7735; 1050 Ralph David Abernathy Blvd SW; adult/child $7/4; ⏰ 10am-2:30pm Tue-Sat) was the 1881–1908 home of Joel Chandler Harris, the white Atlanta journalist whose newspaper columns and Uncle Remus books retold and popularized African American folktales. You can visit the house museum or call ahead to find out about quarterly storytelling events.

POINTS EAST & DECATUR

Located on a hilltop overlooking downtown, the **Carter Presidential Library & Museum** (☎ 404-331-3942; www.cartercenter.org; 441 Freedom Parkway; adult/child $7/free; ⏰ 9am-4:45pm Mon-Sat, from noon Sun) is one of 12 presidential libraries administered by the federal government. Exhibits highlight Jimmy Carter's 1977–1981 presidency and include a replica of the Oval Office.

Fernbank Museum of Natural History (☎ 404-929-6300; www.fernbank.edu/museum; 767 Clifton Rd NE; adult/child $12/10; 10am-5pm Mon-Sat, from noon Sun) makes other museums seem hopelessly dull. With extensive exhibits on everything from reptiles to Egypt to seashells, and an Imax theater ($10/8), Fernbank is a great bet even if giant lizards don't rock your world. On Martinis & Imax Fridays (5:30pm to 10pm January to November), the lobby turns into a cocktail lounge and live jazz echoes through the bones of the world's largest dinosaur.

Atlanta for Children

Atlanta has plenty of activities to keep children entertained, delighted and – perhaps against their will – educated. Following are some of the major sites that work at being kid-friendly.

Center for Puppetry Arts (☎ 404-873-3089; www.puppet.org; 1404 Spring Street NW; museum adult/child $8/6) is a wonderland for both children and adults. This fun museum and theater features puppet-making workshops, plus puppet shows for the young and young at heart.

Imagine It! Children's Museum of Atlanta (☎ 404-659-5437; www.imagineit-cma.org; 275 Olympic Centennial Park Dr NW; admission $11; 10am-4pm Mon-Fri; to 5pm Sat & Sun) is a hands-on museum geared toward kids aged two to eight years.

In the **Fernbank Museum of Natural History** (above) the huge dinosaurs and the toddler play area are favorites.

Six Flags over Georgia (☎ 770-948-9290; www.sixflags.com/georgia; 275 Riverside Parkway; adult/child $44/27) is located off I-20, west of Atlanta. Kids love this amusement park's rides, shows, special events, concerts and festivals.

Introduce your little animals to much bigger ones at **Zoo Atlanta** (opposite).

Tours

Atlanta Preservation Center (☎ 404-688-3350; www.preserveatlanta.com; 327 St Paul Ave; tours adult $10) offers first-rate 90-minute walking tours of the city's intriguing older neighborhoods and sights. Call the hotline for schedules.

STONE FACES OF THE CONFEDERACY

Home to the world's largest outcrop of exposed granite, 3200-acre **Stone Mountain Park** (☎ 770-498-5690; per car $8, all attractions adult/child $20/17; daily) is just 16 miles east of downtown. It's best known for the huge bas-relief carving of Confederate heroes Jefferson Davis, 'Stonewall' Jackson and Robert E Lee – one of the largest such sculptures in the world. There's also a sky lift, hiking trails, an antebellum plantation, a railroad, laser show, camping and other attractions. The park makes an excellent day trip.

Stone Mountain Family Campground (☎ 770-498-5710, 800-385-9807; www.stonemountainpark.com; campsites $23-45;) Georgia's largest campground has 441 sites, laundry facilities, a volleyball court and a lake to swim in.

Festivals & Events

Dogwood Festival (☎ 404-817-6642; www.dogwood.org) A three-day event for families, with an artists' market, dog competition and kids' village, in Piedmont Park, early April.

Atlanta Jazz Fest (www.atlantafestivals.com) A city-sponsored month-long event culminating in live concerts in Piedmont Park on Memorial Day Weekend, end of May.

Music Midtown (☎ 404-249-6400; www.musicmidtown.com) Three days of live music in Piedmont Park, in June.

Atlanta Pride Festival (☎ 404-929-0071; www.atlantapride.com) End of June (see p386).

National Black Arts Festival (☎ 404.730.7315; www.nbaf.org) Artist from across the country converge on Atlanta for this 10-day festival celebrating African American music, theater, literature and film. Mid-July, various locations.

Sleeping

Rates at downtown hotels tend to fluctuate wildly depending on whether there is a large convention in town. Weekends are often cheaper, as are hotels away from downtown.

BUDGET

A cheap option is to stay somewhere along the Marta line, further outside the city and take the train into the city for sightseeing. All of the chain hotels have locations in Atlanta.

THE SOUTH

Atlanta Youth Hostel (☎ 404-875-9449, 800-473-9449; www.hostel-atlanta.com; 223 Ponce de Leon Ave at Myrtle St; dm/r $21/55; 🔀 ⊠ 🖳) In a Victorian house in Midtown, this lively hostel has 80 beds in dorm rooms and wins accolades for its cleanliness and good location. A kitchen, laundry, lockers, and free morning coffee and doughnuts are available. The hostel's office is closed from noon to 5pm. It is 3½ blocks east of the Marta North Ave station.

Highland Inn (☎ 888-256-7221; www.thehighlandinn.com; 644 N Highland Ave; r incl breakfast $70-105; 🅿 ⊠ 🔀) This European-style inn has a great location in the middle of Virginia-Highland. The inn's 100 small but comfortable rooms come with microwaves, refrigerators, TVs and baths. There are laundry facilities.

MIDRANGE
Gaslight Inn (☎ 404-875-1001; www.gaslightinn.com; 1001 St Charles Ave NE; r incl breakfast $115-220; 🅿 ⊠ 🔀) Each room is different in this charming 18th-century B&B in the heart of Virginia-Highland, just minutes from downtown. Classical music drifts through the air and you'll love the homey touches like a front-porch swing, library living room and private garden.

Ansley Inn (☎ 404-872-9000, 800-446-5416; www.ansleyinn.com; 253 15th St; r incl breakfast $120-250; 🅿 ⊠ 🔀) On a quiet residential street near Piedmont Park and within walking distance to anything in Midtown, this restored 1907 yellow-brick English Tudor mansion has 21 rooms. The main house features four-poster beds and period furnishings, while the 'wing' has more modern rooms at slightly cheaper rates. Southern hospitality is real here.

University Inn (☎ 800-654-8591; www.univinn.com; 1767 North Decatur Rd; r incl breakfast $140-155; 🅿 ⊠ 🔀 🖳 🐾) On the cusp of the

---

GAY & LESBIAN ATLANTA

Atlanta is one of the few places in Georgia – perhaps in the South – with a noticeable and active gay and lesbian population. Midtown is the center of gay life; the epicenter is around Piedmont Park and the intersection of 10th St and Piedmont Ave. The town of Decatur, east of downtown Atlanta, has a significant lesbian community.

The **Atlanta Gay & Lesbian Community Center** (☎ 404-523-7500; 159 Ralph McGill Blvd) is a good source for organizations and information. Also check out www.gayatlanta.com. The weekly newspaper *Southern Voice* contains regional news.

Atlanta Pride Festival (☎ 404-929-0071; www.atlantapride.com) is an annual celebration of the city's gay and lesbian community; it attracts people from all over the country and is held at the end of June in and around Piedmont Park (p384).

Outwrite Bookstore & Coffeehouse (p380), in Midtown, is a cheerful gay and lesbian bookstore with a full coffee bar and wonderful desserts. Although the clientele is mostly gay men, the atmosphere is welcoming to others. Charis Books & More (p380), in Little Five Points, is a feminist and lesbian bookstore.

The following gay-friendly bars do not have a cover charge:

Burkhart's Pub (☎ 404-872-4403; www.burkharts.com; 1492 Piedmont Rd; 🕙 4pm-4am Mon-Fri, 2pm-3am Sat & Sun) A friendly neighborhood bar, with a mainly gay male crowd, but lesbians and straights are welcome. Burkhart's offers karaoke nights (Monday to Wednesday at midnight), blackjack and pool tables and the wildly popular Sunday-night drag show.

Blake's (☎ 404-892-5786; www.blakesontheparkatlanta.com; 227 10th St NE; 🕙 3pm-3am Mon-Fri, from 2pm Sat, 2pm-midnight Sun) Just a couple of blocks from Piedmont Park, Blake's is a casual, friendly pub scene with no dancefloor but lots of groovy loud music.

Red Chair Restaurant & Video Lounge (☎ 404-870-0532; www.redchairatlanta.com; 550 Amsterdam Ave NE; 6:30pm-3am Wed-Sat, 12:30pm-midnight Sun) One of Atlanta's hottest upscale bars, the Red Chair offers a full restaurant and an adjoining bar, a popular Sunday brunch and the fun Wednesday night 'dinner and a movie.'

My Sister's Room (☎ 404-370-1990; www.mysistersroom.com; 222 E Howard St, Decatur; 🕙 8pm-1am Wed-Thu & Sun, to 3am Fri & Sat) Next to the railroad tracks in Decatur is the most popular hangout for lesbians. A spacious covered patio, intimate garden hideaways and a stage and dancefloor attract a vibrant, fun-loving clientele.

THE SOUTH

Emory University campus, this community-oriented, friendly inn offers bright, recently renovated rooms in four buildings. Most have kitchenettes. A complimentary afternoon tea is included.

If you're looking for a chain hotel in a good location, try the following:

Hampton Inn & Suites Downtown (☎ 404-589-1111; www.hamptoninn.com; 161 Spring St; r from $150; P ☒ ☐) Parking costs $12.

Hampton Inn & Suites Midtown (404-872-3234; 1152 Spring St; r $100; P ☒ ☐ ☒) Better value.

TOP END

Georgian Terrace (☎ 404-897-1991; www.the georg ianterrace.com; 659 Peachtree St NE; r $100-400; P ☒ ☐ ☒) A giant hotel on the National Register of Historic Places, this grand dame across from the Fox Theater offers an absolute feast for the senses. Many of the *Gone With the Wind* stars stayed here during the film's debut in 1939 and the hotel, having undergone a massive facelift, is worth a wander whether you stay here or not.

Westin Peachtree Plaza (☎ 404-659-1400, 888-447-8159; www.starwoodhotels.com/westin; 210 Peachtree St; r $170-400; P ☒ ☐ ☒) At 723ft, this 73-story downtown hotel is the tallest in the Western Hemisphere, and with 1068 rooms, there's plenty to choose from. Rates fluctuate, so call ahead to see what's available. Parking costs $20.

Eating

BUDGET

Alon's Bakery (☎ 404-872-6000; 1394 N Highland Ave; sandwiches $6-9; ☼ 7am-7pm Mon-Fri, 8am-5pm Sat, from 10am Sun; P) Consistently winning awards as the city's best bakery, Alon's is definitely the place to go for delicious baked goods, sandwiches and gourmet takeout, including a good selection of wine and cheese.

Vortex Bar & Grill (☎ 404-688-1828; burgers $7-11; ☼ lunch & dinner) L5P (438 Moreland Ave); Midtown (878 Peachtree St) The Vortex has arguably the best burgers in town. The bar-style atmosphere attracts a youthful, bohemian crowd who grab a burger before indulging in L5P's bar scene. Look for the giant skull and you'll find the front door.

Fat Matt's Rib Shack (☎ 404-607-1622; 1811 Piedmont Rd NE; mains $7-11; P) Less than a mile north of Piedmont Park, divey Fat Matt's

will make your eyes tear with the pure deliciousness of quintessential Southern BBQ ribs and creamy coleslaw. Roll up your sleeves and dig in!

Varsity (☎ 404-881-1706; 61 North Ave at Spring St; mains $2-5; ☼ lunch & dinner) The world's largest drive-in restaurant and an Atlanta institution since 1928, the Varsity is a glorified fast-food joint, but it's always packed with locals ordering walk-a-dogs (hot dogs), glorified steaks (hamburgers) and bags of rags (fries).

MIDRANGE

Front Page News (mains $8-22; ☼ lunch & dinner daily, brunch Sun) L5P (☎ 404-475-7777; 351 Moreland Ave); Midtown (☎ 404-897-3500; 1104 Crescent Ave) Both locations have lush, roomy patios and Sunday brunch featuring live jazz and a Bloody Mary bar. The Louisiana-style menu offers sandwiches, salads and heartier fare like jambalaya. At night, the scene gets lively, especially on weekends.

Highland Tap (☎ 404-875-3673; 1026 N Highland Ave NE; mains $8-28; ☼ 4pm-2am Mon, from 11am Tue-Sat, to midnight Sun) Descend the dark stairway at this favorite haunt to enjoy some of the city's best steaks and martinis, served sans attitude by true professional waiters, many of whom have worked here forever. The bar becomes a lively scene late, especially on weekends.

Mary Mac's Tea Room (☎ 404-846-1800; www .marymacs.com; 224 Ponce de Leon Ave; mains $7-12; ☼ lunch & dinner) You feel like you've gone back in time at this authentic Southern teahouse, just three blocks east of the Fox Theatre. Both grandmotherly and cheery, the restaurant serves delicious sandwiches, fried chicken and black-eyed peas.

THE SOUTH

TOP END

Sotto Sotto (☎ 404-523-6678; 313 N Highland Ave NE; dishes $15-25; ☯ dinner Mon-Sat) A lively, trendy restaurant with an ever-delighting menu of authentic Italian dishes, Sotto Sotto makes a great choice if you have a hankering for pasta and good vino.

Bone's Restaurant (☎ 404-237-2663; 3130 Piedmont Rd NE, Buckhead; mains $17-40; ☯ 5:30-11pm, 11:30am-2:30pm Mon-Fri; P) All about old money and the Buckhead power set, Bone's gets top votes as Atlanta's best old-school steakhouse, where the waiters call you 'sir' or 'ma'am' and treat you like royalty. With lots of wood and brass, this place oozes power pheromones and serves up stupendous steaks.

Drinking

There's a lot of heavy partying going on in Atlanta, especially in Virginia-Highland, L5P, Midtown and Buckhead. In Midtown and L5P, Front Page News (see p387) draws a big drinking crowd to its sunny patios.

Fado Irish Pub Beer Bar (☎ 404-848-8433; 3035 Peachtree St, Buckhead) This is a comfortable Irish pub with a huge selection of beers, sports on TV and a friendly, happy crowd.

In the heart of 'the Highlands' (at Highland Ave and Virginia Sts) check out the following, all of which have decent food menus:

Fontaine's (☎ 404-872-0869; 1026 N Highland Ave) A great stop for evening cocktails.

Hand in Hand (☎ 404-872-1001; 752 N Highland Ave) With a shady outdoor patio and a relaxed crowd.

Manuel's Tavern (☎ 404-521-2466; 602 N Highland Ave) A longtime political hangout, with a good, conversational beer-drinking crowd.

Entertainment

Atlanta has big-city nightlife, with lots of live music and cultural events. Check out the free *Creative Loafing* for weekly listings.

THEATERS

Fox Theatre (☎ 404-881-2100; www.foxtheatre.org; 660 Peachtree St NE) A spectacular 1929 movie palace with fanciful Moorish and Egyptian designs. It hosts Broadway shows, film festivals and concerts in a 5000-seat auditorium.

Woodruff Arts Center (☎ 404-733-4200; www.woodruffcenter.org; 1280 Peachtree St NE at 15th St) Named for Coca-Cola king Robert W Woodruff, who gave so much to local causes that he was nicknamed 'Mr Anonymous Donor.' The center includes the High Museum (p384).

Center for Puppetry Arts (☎ 404-873-3391; www.puppet.org; 1404 Spring St NW at 18th St; ☯ 9am-5pm Mon-Sat, from 11am Sun) The collection consists of over 1000 puppets from around the world. Try to see one of the well-produced, full-stage puppet shows ($12 to $18).

LIVE MUSIC & NIGHTCLUBS

Cover charges at the following vary nightly, ranging from free to $10 on weekdays, to $25 on weekends or when popular live bands are playing.

Blind Willie's (☎ 404-873-2583; 828 N Highland Ave, Virginia-Highland) For serious blues, head to Blind Willie's, a well-established blues bar with local and occasional big-name acts.

Eddie's Attic (☎ 404-377-4976; www.eddiesattic.com; 515B N McDonough St, Decatur) One of the city's best venues to hear live folk and acoustic music, in a nonsmoking atmosphere seven nights a week.

Eleven50 (☎ 404-874-0428; 1150 Peachtree Rd, Midtown) This is a huge, multilevel dance club housed in an old theater.

Star Community Bar (☎ 404-681-9018; www.starbar.net; 437 Moreland Ave, L5P) Draws a funky L5P crowd to its live acts four nights a week.

Variety Playhouse (☎ 404-524-7354; www.variety-playhouse.com; 1099 Euclid Ave NE, L5P) A truly authentic small venue; a great place to see live music acts.

SPORTS

Order tickets to sporting events through **Ticketmaster** (☎ 800-326-4000, 404-249-6400; www.ticketmaster.com).

Atlanta Braves (☎ 404-522-7630; www.atlantabraves.com; tickets $1-40) The Major League Baseball (MLB) team plays at Turner Field.

Atlanta Falcons (☎ 404-223-8000; www.atlantafalcons.com; tickets from $25) The National Football League (NFL) team plays in the Georgia Dome.

Atlanta Hawks (☎ 404-827-3800; www.hawks.com; tickets $10-65), the National Basketball Association (NBA) team, and **Atlanta Thrashers** (☎ 404-584-7825; www.atlantathrashers.com; tickets $12-55), the National Hockey League (NHL) team, play at Philips Arena.

Shopping

Atlantans love to shop. Virginia-Highland and Decatur both have a unique selection of boutique shops. Find vintage and secondhand clothes in Little Five Points.

THE SOUTH

The two major shopping malls that draw throngs of eager consumers are adjacent to each other in Buckhead. **Lenox Square** (☎ 404-816-4001; 3393 Peachtree Rd NE; ☺ 10am-9pm Mon-Sat, noon-6pm Sun) has just about anything you'd ever need.

Phipps Plaza (☎ 404-262-0992; 3500 Peachtree Rd NE; ☺ 10am-9pm Mon-Sat, noon-5:30pm Sun) offers more upscale shops.

Getting There & Away

Atlanta's huge **Hartsfield-Jackson International Airport** (ATL; ☎ 404-209-1700; www.atlanta-airport .com), 12 miles south of downtown, is a major regional hub and an international gateway. With nearly 80 million visitors a year, it is the busiest airport in the world in overall passenger traffic.

The **Greyhound terminal** (☎ 404-584-1728; 232 Forsyth St) is next to the Marta Garnett station. Some sample fares and journey times include Nashville, TN ($41.50, five hours), New Orleans, LA ($74, 10 hours), New York ($105, 19 hours), Miami, FL ($102, 16 hours) and Savannah, GA ($41.50, six hours).

The **Amtrak station** (☎ 404-881-3062, 800-872-7245; 1688 Peachtree St NW at Deering Rd) is 3 miles north of downtown. Take bus No 23 for about 0.8 miles from the Marta Arts Center station.

Getting Around

The **Metropolitan Atlanta Rapid Transit Authority** (Marta; ☎ 404-848-4711; www.itsmarta.com; fare $1.75) rail line travels to/from the airport to downtown, along with a few less-useful routes used mostly by commuters.

The **Atlanta Airport Shuttle** (☎ 404-524-3400, 800-842-2770; tickets $16-22) also transports passengers to hotels all over the city in a minibus. You will find that all the major car-rental agencies have desks in the airport at the baggage-claim level.

Driving in Atlanta can be infuriating and confusing. You'll often find yourself sitting in traffic jams, and it's easy to get disoriented – a road map is invaluable.

SAVANNAH

Amid Lowcountry swamps and mammoth live oak trees dripping with Spanish moss, Savannah sits alongside the Savannah River, about 18 miles from the coast. Steeped in tradition, with historic mansions, cotton warehouses and colonial public buildings, Savannah preserves its antebellum history with grace, dignity and a slight smirk. Unlike its sister city of Charleston, SC, which retains its reputation as a dignified, refined and politically courageous cultural center, Savannah revels in being the bad girl. The town loves its sinful pleasures, be they the brown-sugar and hot-pepper sauce on Lowcountry shrimp, the extra rum in the cocktails, or the bump and grind of its partying student population.

Savannah has a somber side, but she never takes herself too seriously. As the heavily scented humid air massages your skin while you wander the cotton wharves and urban squares, you can feel the electricity of the city's history. The Marvin Gaye song 'Let's Get it On' is a virtual call to arms here, and the city's St Patrick's Day celebration is a rite of spring no fun-seeker can deny.

History

Founded in 1733, Savannah was the first English settlement in the colony of Georgia. It became a wealthy shipping center, handling the export of cotton and import of slaves. In the 19th century, the railroads added to the city's wealth, bringing in ever-greater volumes of plantation produce.

Savannah was the goal of General Sherman's devastating March to the Sea, and the city surrendered to him on December 21, 1864. Instead of burning the city, Sherman rested his troops there for six weeks before turning north to cut another path of destruction through South Carolina.

The collapse of cotton prices in the late 1800s sent Savannah into a severe economic decline. In the long run, this may have been a good thing; had it prospered, the elegant streets may well have been demolished in the name of development.

In 1955, preservationists launched a campaign to protect the downtown area. As a result, the 2½-sq-mile historic district now has more than 1000 restored Federal and Regency buildings.

Orientation

Savannah's Historic District is a rectangle bounded by Savannah River, Forsyth Park, E Broad St and Martin Luther King

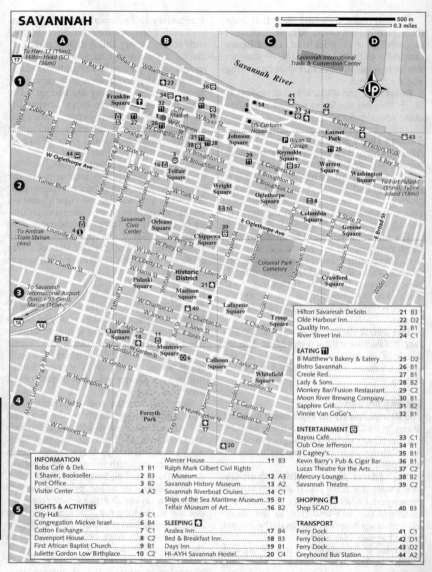

SAVANNAH

0 — 500 m
0 — 0.3 miles

INFORMATION
Boba Café & Deli............................1 B1
E Shaver, Bookseller......................2 B3
Post Office....................................3 B2
Visitor Center................................4 A2

SIGHTS & ACTIVITIES
City Hall..5 C1
Congregation Mickve Israel............6 B4
Cotton Exchange............................7 C1
Davenport House............................8 C2
First African Baptist Church............9 B1
Juliette Gordon Low Birthplace.....10 C2
Mercer House...............................11 B3
Ralph Mark Gilbert Civil Rights
  Museum...................................12 A3
Savannah History Museum.............13 A2
Savannah Riverboat Cruises..........14 C1
Ships of the Sea Maritime Museum..15 A2
Telfair Museum of Art...................16 B2

SLEEPING
Azalea Inn....................................17 B4
Bed & Breakfast Inn......................18 B3
Days Inn......................................19 B1
HI-AYH Savannah Hostel...............20 C4
Hilton Savannah DeSoto................21 B3
Olde Harbour Inn..........................22 D2
Quality Inn..................................23 B1
River Street Inn............................24 C1

EATING
B Matthew's Bakery & Eatery.........25 D2
Bistro Savannah............................26 B1
Creole Red...................................27 B1
Lady & Sons.................................28 B2
Monkey Bar/Fusion Restaurant......29 C2
Moon River Brewing Company.......30 B1
Sapphire Grill...............................31 B2
Vinnie Van GoGo's........................32 B1

ENTERTAINMENT
Bayou Café...................................33 C1
Club One Jefferson........................34 B1
JJ Cagney's...................................35 B1
Kevin Barry's Pub & Cigar Bar.......36 B1
Lucas Theatre for the Arts.............37 C2
Mercury Lounge............................38 B2
Savannah Theatre.........................39 C2

SHOPPING
Shop SCAD...................................40 B3

TRANSPORT
Ferry Dock...................................41 C1
Ferry Dock...................................42 D1
Ferry Dock...................................43 D2
Greyhound Bus Station..................44 A2

Jr Blvd. Almost everything of interest to visitors lies within or just outside this area. In converted cotton warehouses along the Savannah River, you'll find a commercial district of bars, restaurants and shops. City Market is an equally important district of shops and restaurants near Franklin Sq.

Each of the 21 of Savannah's original 24 squares marks a truly exquisite place to relax among flower gardens, shade trees and – usually – a monument to some notable person who is buried in the square.

Bull St, running north–south, divides the east and west branches of Savannah's streets.

STARSTRUCK SAVANNAH

'This place is fantastic. It's like *Gone With the Wind* on mescaline.' Such is the description of Savannah rendered by the protagonist (John Cusack) in Clint Eastwood's film version of John Berendt's hugely successful 1994 *Midnight in the Garden of Good and Evil*. The book and subsequent film did much to glamorize Savannah as a surreal remnant of the Old South, where tradition beds down with decadence.

And *Midnight*'s not the only story to capture Savannah. Many audiences met the city in *Forrest Gump* (Forrest's bench is in Chippewa Sq). Books like *Wise Blood* by Savannah-born Flannery O'Connor, songs like 'Moon River' by native-son composer Johnny Mercer and the 2002 hit movie the *Legend of Bagger Vance* have added to the city's mythology. These days, hardly a year goes by without another feature film being made in Savannah with a gaggle of stars swarming about incognito in the city's bars, clubs and restaurants and dipping into the local real-estate market to buy a little piece of this garden of good and evil.

Information

BOOKSTORES
E Shaver, Bookseller (☎ 912-234-7257; 326 Bull St; ☉ 9am-6pm Mon-Sat) A splendid indy bookstore with 12 rooms filled with books on architecture, history and general interest.

EMERGENCY
Main police station (☎ 912-232-4141) Nonemergencies only.

INTERNET
Boba Internet Cafe & Deli (☎ 912-234-2111; www.bobacafeanddeli.com; 309 W St Julian St; per 30min $5) A café with wi-fi and high-speed computers.
Main Library (☎ 912-652-3600; 2002 Bull St, btwn 36th & 37th; ☉ 9am-9pm Mon-Thu, to 6pm Fri & Sat, 2-6pm Sun) Offers free Internet and wi-fi access.

MEDICAL SERVICES
Candler Hospital (☎ 912-692-6000; 5353 Reynolds St)
CVS Pharmacy (☎ 912-238-1494; cnr Bull & W Broughton Sts)

MONEY
There are plenty of ATMs throughout the city. For full service, head to Johnson Sq, where there are several major banks.

POST
Post office (☎ 912-235-4653) Historic District (cnr W State & Barnard Sts; ☉ 8am-5pm Mon-Fri); Main (2 N Fahm St at Bay St; ☉ 7am-6pm Mon-Fri, 9am-3pm Sat) Main office is just west of downtown.

TOURIST INFORMATION
Visitor center (☎ 912-944-0455, 877-728-2662; www.savannahvisit.com; 301 Martin Luther King Jr Blvd; ☉ 10am-10pm) Excellent resources and services

are available in the restored 1860s train station. Many privately operated city tours start here.

Dangers & Annoyances
The Historic District is safe during the day, but desperate folks prowl the area after dark. Muggings and drug dealing are common in surrounding neighborhoods, too. At night, use common-sense precautions and stay in well-lit, populated areas.

Sights & Activities
One of the best ways to enjoy Savannah is to sit on a bench in one of the beautiful squares and watch the world go by. You'll see businessmen in seersucker suits and refined Southern ladies in sunbonnets, mixed with nose-pierced artists from the Savannah College of Art & Design (SCAD) as they try to capture on canvas the drama of dripping moss.

THE RIVERFRONT
Along the wharves of the Savannah River, on the northern edge of the Historic District, the Riverfront is Savannah's most popular tourist attraction. The main pedestrian and auto artery is **River Street**, which is home to dozens of shops, restaurants and nightspots. The brick-and-cobblestone waterside promenade along a gallery of restored cotton warehouses is a great place to spend an afternoon strolling, shopping and people-watching. **Factor's Walk** is essentially the upper level of buildings between River and Bay Sts and was the city's business center in the 19th century. Nearby are the gold-domed **City Hall** and the **Cotton Exchange** building, which is guarded by lion

THE SOUTH

statues and once one of the world's busiest exchanges.

MUSEUMS

The important **Ralph Mark Gilbert Civil Rights Museum** (☎ 912-231-8900; www.sip.armstrong.edu /CivilRightsMuseum/Civilindex.html; 460 Martin Luther King Jr Blvd; adult/child $4/2; ☽ 9am-5pm Mon-Sat) is just south of the I-16 overpass. It tells the story of African Americans in Savannah, focusing on the civil rights struggle.

Savannah History Museum (☎ 912-238-1779; www.chsgeorgia.org; 303 Martin Luther King Jr Blvd; adult/ child $4/3; ☽ 8:30am-5pm Mon-Fri, from 9am Sat & Sun) is a good place to start a visit to Savannah's Historic District. Behind the visitor center, the film and displays here give a feel for the city's past. There's a replica of Forrest Gump's park bench.

Boating buffs will enjoy the exhibits highlighting Savannah's nautical past at **Ships of the Sea Maritime Museum** (☎ 912-232-1511; 41 Martin Luther King Jr Blvd; adult/child $7/5; ☽ 10am-5pm Tue-Sun). The SS *Savannah* was the first steamship to cross the Atlantic Ocean; much later, the NS *Savannah* was nuclear powered.

Looking like a Roman temple, the beautiful **Telfair Museum of Art** (☎ 912-232-1177; www .telfair.org; 121 Barnard St; adult/child $8/2; ☽ 1-5pm Sun & Mon, from 10am Tue-Sat) contains several statues, including the 'Bird Girl' statues from the cover of *Midnight*.

HISTORIC HOMES

Savannah is a fabulous city for long, leisurely strolls. The squares and the entire streets of historic 18th- and 19th-century buildings are Savannah's main attractions.

If you have time for touring only one house, make it **Davenport House** (☎ 912-236-8097; www.davenportsavga.com; Columbia Sq; 30min tour adult/child $8/4; ☽ 10am-4pm Mon-Sat, from 1pm Sun); the tour is exceptional for both its antique collection and its knowledgeable guides.

GAY & LESBIAN SAVANNAH

With so many gay and lesbian merchants, innkeepers, college students and military personnel, Savannah has a lively gay scene. Check out www.gaysavannah.com for a complete list of rainbow-friendly inns, bars, clubs, accommodations and businesses.

Mercer House (429 Bull St on Monterey Sq) is the big bonus for *Midnight* fans; the immense red-brick Italianate mansion became the home of the extravagant antique dealer Jim Williams. The interior of the house is not open to the public, but it's worth walking by to gawk at the exterior.

Juliette Gordon Low Birthplace (☎ 912-233-4501; 10 E Oglethorpe Ave; adult/child $8/7; ☽ 10am-4pm Mon-Sat, 12:30-4:30pm Sun), an upper-middle-class Victorian home dating from 1821, was the childhood home of the Girl Scouts of America founder.

HISTORIC HOUSES OF WORSHIP

The oldest African American church in North America, **First African Baptist Church** (☎ 912-233-6597; 23 Montgomery St at Franklin Sq; admission free; ☽ 10am-3pm Mon-Fri) was built by slaves in 1859.

Congregation Mickve Israel (☎ 912-233-1547; 20 E Gordon St; ☽ 10am-noon, 2-4pm Mon-Fri) is the oldest Reform Judaism temple in the USA (the congregation formed in 1733, though the present Gothic building dates from 1878).

Tours

If you have a choice, few excursions are more romantic than a carriage ride around the city at sunset. The visitor center is the best place to book tours, whether on foot, trolley, minibus or horse-drawn carriage – most operators begin excursions from the center's parking lot. **Savannah Riverboat Cruises** (☎ 912-232-6404, 800-786-6404; www.savannah-riverboat.com; 9 E River St; 1hr cruise adult/child $17/10; ☽ 9am-8pm) offers travel by classic paddleboat through the Lowcountry marshes.

Sleeping

If your idea of a great escape is a plush bedroom with a window to a wild and mysterious city, you're going to love Savannah. Most hotels and B&Bs have a wide range of rates, which are often lower midweek and they drop dramatically outside of spring and summer.

HI-AYH Savannah Hostel (☎ 912-236-7744; 304 E Hall St; dm/r $22/44; Ⓟ ☒ ☒) Gregarious Brian Sherman runs this restored mansion-turned-hostel. There are dorm beds and one private double. The hostel is closed between 10am and 5pm (when guests are expected to be out). The hostel is closed January,

February, December and sometimes late-
November.

Hilton Savannah DeSoto (☎ 912-232-9000, 800-
445-8667; www.desotohilton.com; 15 E Liberty St; r $120-
160; P 💥 🖥 🏊) Near Madison Sq, the
246-room DeSoto has modern, generous
business-class rooms and convention facilities. Rates fluctuate considerably, so call
ahead for deals. Parking costs $10.

Days Inn (☎ 912-236-4440; www.daysinnsavannah
.com; 201 W Bay St; d $140; P 💥 🏊) The dark
brick facade of this 253-room hotel dates
back 160 years and fits in with the character
of the surrounding architectural heirlooms.
Days Inn has an excellent location within a
quick walk of all the shops, restaurants and
nightlife. Parking costs $8.

Quality Inn (☎ 912-236-6321; 800-424-6423; www
.qualityinnhistoricsavannah.com; 300 W Bay St; r $100-140;
P 💥) A good value if you want to be in
the heart of Savannah's action. Its generic
exterior belies its 52 large modern rooms.

River Street Inn (☎ 912-234-6400, 800-253-4229;
www.riverstreetinn.com; 115 E River St; r $140-270; P
💥 💥 🖥) In a converted cotton warehouse
overlooking the river, this 86-room inn is
in a perfect location. The spacious rooms
have wood floors, brick walls, brass fixtures
and four-poster beds. In the afternoon the
lobby fills for the complimentary wine and
hors d'oeuvres.

Olde Harbour Inn (☎ 912-234-4100, 800-553-6533;
www.oldeharbourinn.com; 508 E Factors Walk; r $150-250;
P 💥) Once a cotton warehouse on the
bluff above the riverfront, this small inn
rents 24 comfortable, nicely decorated
suites, each with a fully-equipped kitchen.

Ask for one of the rooms with a balcony
overlooking the river.

Azalea Inn (☎ 912-236-2707, 800-582-3823; www
.azaleainn.com; 217 E Huntingdon St; d $130-250; P
💥 💥) You'll find this 1180s Italianate
charmer, decorated with period and contemporary pieces, a block east of Forsyth
Park. The inn has seven rooms and a carriage house. The friendly owners create a
casual and unpretentious atmosphere.

Eating & Drinking

Get ready to feast! Savannah offers a legion
of fine-dining experiences, from gourmet
Southern food to wild fusion combos with
fresh seafood. Restaurants are also scattered throughout the Historic District.
All listed have air-con and nonsmoking
sections.

Vinnie Van GoGo's (☎ 912-233-6394; 317 W Bryan
St; pizzas $12-16; 🕐 lunch & dinner) Hang out with
the locals at this divey pizza joint, where
you can get delicious New York–style pizzas
and calzones, with plenty of cold beer to
wash them down. The outside tables are
great for people-watching.

Lady & Sons (☎ 912-233-2600; www.ladyandsons
.com; 102 W Congress St; dinner mains $18-23; 🕐 lunch
& dinner Mon-Sat, 11am-5pm Sun; 💥) A Savannah
institution for divine upscale Southern cuisine, including shrimp and grits, crab cakes
and refreshing sweet tea. Owner Paula Deen
puts her heart into the place and it shows.
Try the outstanding lunch buffet ($13) or
order off the menu. The restaurant's new
location has three floors of seating, a big
bar and a retail shop, where you can buy
Paula's cookbook ($25).

THE SOUTH

Moon River Brewing Company (☎ 912-447-0943; 21 W Bay St; mains $8-16; ☺ lunch & dinner) You'll find this aromatic brewpub in an 1821 building, just a block from the Riverfront. Heavy with the scent of hops from the vats, it attracts a young crowd with its homemade brews and local artwork on the walls. The menu includes tasty Buffalo wings, burgers and sandwiches.

Creole Red (☎ 912-234-6690; 409 W Congress St; mains $7-14; ☺ lunch & dinner) This place always earns our vote for authentic Creole cuisine and Bourbon St vibe at unbeatable prices. Try the deviled crabs ($10) or a big bowl of jambalaya.

Monkey Bar/Fusion Restaurant (☎ 912-232-0755; 8 E Broughton St; mains $12-20; ☺ 5pm to late) Owner Wendy Snowden and her clientele ooze an authentic, artsy glam, giving the place the feel of an indy film party. The American-Asian fusion cuisine is just as far out there. Couples get up right in the middle of dinner and start dancing; plenty simply snack and sip cocktails at the bar.

Sapphire Grill (☎ 912-443-9962; 110 W Congress St; mains $25-40; ☺ 5:30-11pm, later on weekends) Chef Chris Nason fires up quite a feast in this converted warehouse near City Market. The romantic decor reflects in the shiny wood floors and metallic fixtures. The menu is highly eclectic, ranging from lobster bisque with tarragon sherry to tuna mignon and Colorado lamb lollipops.

Bistro Savannah (☎ 912-233-6266; 309 W Congress St; mains $25-32; ☺ 5:30pm-11pm) This is one of the top seafood restaurants in Georgia, where the chefs use organically grown local and regional produce and catch-of-the-day seafood.

Entertainment

For an up-to-date list of events at clubs and bars, check out Thursday's *Savannah Morning News* and the weeklies *Connect Savannah* and *Creative Loafing*.

LIVE MUSIC & NIGHTCLUBS

Kevin Barry's Pub (☎ 912-233-9626; www.kevinbarrys.com; 117 W River St; ☺ noon-2am) Kevin's has live Irish music every night, making it like St Paddy's Day every day. It also serves pub grub food.

JJ Cagney's (☎ 912-233-2444; 17 W Bay St; ☺ 4pm-2am) Here's an excellent place to spot both up-and-coming local bands and singer-songwriter types.

Bayou Café (☎ 912-233-6411; 14 N Abercorn St; ☺ 4pm-3am) Between Bay and River Sts, across from the Hampton Inn, the Bayou is a gritty place, popular with partying students. It also has music every night, mostly alternative and country-rock.

Mercury Lounge (☎ 912-447-6952; 125 W Congress St; ☺ 5pm-3am) Students and 20-somethings come here to groove to classic rock and alternative cover bands.

Club One Jefferson (☎ 912-232-0200; www.clubone-online.com; 1 Jefferson St) Savannah's premier gay venue, Club One features drag shows, pool tables and a large dancefloor. Although its clientele is mostly gay, straight party animals also come here to dance and watch the drag queens.

THEATER

Lucas Theatre for the Arts (☎ 912-525-5040; www.lucastheatre.com; 32 Abercorn St) The Lucas offers a near-continuous lineup of plays, concerts, musicals and classic films.

Savannah Theatre (☎ 912-233-7764; www.savannahtheatre.com; 222 Bull St) This art-deco community theater presents comedies, musicals and dramas.

Getting There & Away

The **Savannah International Airport** (SAV; ☎ 912-964-0514; www.savannahairport.com) is about five miles west of downtown off I-16.

Greyhound (☎ 912-232-2135; 610 W Oglethorpe Ave) has connections to Atlanta ($41.50, six hours); Charleston, South Carolina ($28, three hours); and Jacksonville, Florida ($26, 2½ hours).

The **Amtrak station** (☎ 800-872-7245, 912-234-2611) is 4 miles from City Hall and is served only by taxis.

Getting Around

Coastal Transportation (☎ 912-964-5999; adult $21) provides a shuttle from the airport to downtown.

You don't need a car to enjoy Savannah. If you have one, it's best to park it and walk or take tours around town. Visitors can buy a 24-hour parking pass for $10 at the visitor center and the Bryan St Garage. The pass works at the municipal garages, River St lots and one-hour meters.

Chatham Area Transit (CAT; ☎ 912-233-5767) operates local buses, including a free shuttle that makes its way around the Historic

District and stops within a couple of blocks of nearly every major site.

AROUND SAVANNAH

About 15 miles east of Savannah off US Hwy 80 is **Fort Pulaski National Monument** (☎ 912-786-5787; www.nps.gov/fopu; US Hwy 80; adult/child $3/free; ⊙ 9am-5pm). Laborers built this fort in 1847 to guard the mouth of the Savannah River. Military engineers thought that such a huge masonry fort, with 7.5ft-thick walls, was impenetrable. The fort was seized before the state even seceded from the Union. Visitors can view the well-preserved fort, complete with moat and drawbridge.

About 18 miles east of US 80, **Tybee Island** (☎ 912-786-5444, 800-868-2322; www.tybeevisit.com; 1st St/US Hwy 80; ⊙ 9:30am-5pm) is a small beach community with 3 miles of wide, sandy beach, good for swimming and castle building. The 154ft-tall **Tybee Island Lighthouse** (☎ 912-786-5801; www.tybeelighthouse.org; adult/child $6/5; ⊙ 9am-5:30pm Wed-Mon) is the oldest in Georgia. The 178 steps to the top reward you with magnificent views. The admission also gets you into neighboring **Tybee Island Museum**.

BRUNSWICK & THE GOLDEN ISLES

With its large shrimp-boat fleet and downtown historic district shaded beneath lush live oaks, **Brunswick** dates from 1733 and has charms you might miss when sailing by on I-95 or the Golden Isle Parkway (US Hwy 17). During WWII, Brunswick shipyards constructed 99 Liberty transport ships for the navy. Today, a new 23ft scale model at **Mary Ross Waterfront Park** on Bay St stands as a memorial to those ships and their builders.

Brunswick-Golden Isles Visitors Bureau (☎ 912-265-0620; www.bgivb.com; Hwy 17 at St Simons Causeway; ⊙ 8:30am-5pm Mon-Fri) has loads of practical information about all the **Golden Isles**.

St Simons Island

Famous for its golf courses, resorts and majestic live oaks, **St Simons Island** is the largest and most developed of the Golden Isles. It lies 75 miles south of Savannah and just 5 miles from Brunswick. While the southern half of the island is a thickly settled residential and resort area, the northern half and adjacent **Sea Island** and **Little St Simons** offer vast tracts of coastal wilderness amid a tidewater estuary.

Jekyll Island

An exclusive refuge for millionaires in the late 19th and early 20th centuries, Jekyll Island is a 4000-year-old barrier island with 10 miles of beaches. The **visitor center** (☎ 912-635-3636, 877-453-5955; ⊙ 9am-5pm), on the causeway to the island, has maps and good brochures about activities and lodging. The 240-acre **historic area** is a good place to just wander among the oaks or ride your bike along the 20 miles of paved **bicycle paths**.

Cumberland Island

Most of this southernmost barrier island is occupied by the **Cumberland Island National Seashore** (☎ 912-882-4335; www.nps.gov/cuis; admission $4). Almost half of its 36,415 acres consists of marsh, mudflats and tidal creeks. On the ocean side are 16 miles of wide, sandy beach that you might have all to yourself. The island's interior is characterized by a maritime forest. Animals include deer, raccoons, feral pigs and armadillos (a recent arrival). Feral horses roam the island and are a common sight.

The only public access to the island is via the ferry **Cumberland Queen** (☎ 912-882-4335; adult/child $14/8; ⊙ 10am-4pm Mon-Fri), which leaves from the mainland at the St Marys dock. Reservations are recommended. October through February, the ferry does not operate on Tuesday or Wednesday.

The only private accommodations on the island are at the **Greyfield Inn** (☎ 904-261-6408; www.greyfieldinn.com; d incl meals $250-395), a grand and graceful mansion built in 1900. Camping is available at **Sea Camp Beach** (☎ 912-882-4335; per person $4), a pristine, developed campground set among magnificent live oaks.

Okefenokee National Wildlife Refuge

Established in 1937, the **Okefenokee Swamp** is a national gem, encompassing 396,000 acres of bog in a giant saucer-shaped depression that was once part of the ocean floor. The swamp comprises islands, lakes and forests. It's home to 234 reptile species, including an estimated 9000 to 15,000 alligators, 234 bird species, 49 types of mammal, and 60 amphibian species. The best way to see it is in a canoe or on a boat tour. The ultimate experience is a multiday canoe trip on the swamp's 120 miles of waterways. Call the US Fish and Wildlife

Service's **Okefenokee National Wildlife Refuge Wilderness Canoe Guide** (☎ 912-496-7836; http:// okefenokee.fws.gov) if you're considering a trip. If you want to rent a canoe for the day or join a boat trip, you'll find outfitters at the swamp's three main entrances. Guided boat trips are also available.

CENTRAL GEORGIA

Between the northern Georgia mountains and the southern coastal plains lies the Piedmont region. Its southern boundary is the 'fall line' – a sudden drop in elevation at the edge of a plateau. In the 18th and 19th centuries, the region grew on the promise of bountiful cotton and on the backs of slaves who harvested the crops. Though the Civil War ended slavery, and an infestation of boll weevils nearly ended cotton farming for good, grand antebellum homes built by wealthy planters still stand.

Today, the rich soil in Georgia's agricultural region produces thriving crops of peaches, pecans and peanuts. The world-famous Vidalia sweet onion is grown only in the south Georgia town of the same name. Pine trees throughout the region support the timber industry.

Athens

A fun-loving college town, 61 miles east of Atlanta, Athens is characterized by crazed college football fans and a world-famous music scene. Local pop-music stars who catapulted to national fame include the B-52s, REM and Widespread Panic. The University of Georgia (UGA) has almost 30,000 students. The downtown area is well supplied with music shops, bookstores, cafés, bars and clubs, which led *Rolling Stone* to once call Athens the '#1 College Music Scene in America.'

Spared serious damage during the Civil War, Athens has many antebellum homes and 14 historic districts featuring a smorgasbord of architectural styles.

The **Athens Welcome Center** (☎ 706-353-1820; 280 E Dougherty St; ☽ 10am-6pm Mon-Sat, from noon Sun), in a historic antebellum house at the corner of Thomas St, provides good information and maps, and offers 1¼ hour bus tours of historic houses and sites ($12). College Ave between Clayton and Broad Sts is where the college crowd hangs out. Tours of the UGA campus depart from the

UGA visitor center (☎ 706-542-0842). Call for the schedule.

SLEEPING & EATING
Grand Oaks Manor B&B (☎ 706-353-2200; 6295 Jefferson Rd; r incl breakfast $110-160; ℗ ✖ ✖) A serene B&B just 5 miles from downtown on US 129/Jefferson Rd. Set on large, peaceful grounds, it consists of an original structure built in the 1820s, around which a Colonial Revival house was constructed in 1947.

Five Star Day Café (☎ 706-543-8552; 229 E Broad St; mains $6-10; ☽ lunch & dinner) An unpretentious little café, serving hot buttered soul chicken with Jamaican seasoning, pot roast, pesto pasta, Carolina BBQ, and chicken and dumplings.

Grit (☎ 706-543-6592; 199 Prince Ave; mains $5-7; ☽ lunch & dinner) This popular vegetarian place serves yummy things like hummus and falafel, Indian curried vegetables, Italian pasta dishes and Mexican quesadillas.

Harry Bissett's (☎ 706-353-7065; 279 E Broad St; lunch $7-10, dinner $10-22; ☽ lunch & dinner) A New Orleans–style restaurant and pub serving up Cajun and Creole cuisine (including a killer shrimp gumbo), Harry's is always hopping. A fun place to go for a filling lunch or dinner.

ENTERTAINMENT
40 Watt Club (☎ 706-549-7871; www.40watt.com; 285 W Washington St) The famous 40 Watt Club, where REM got its first exposure, is still one of the best places in the South to catch up-and-coming bands (the venue has moved a couple of times since REM days).

Georgia Theatre (☎ 706-549-9918; www.georgia theatre.com; 215 N Lumpkin St) Another of the South's premier theaters, showing classic movies and live music.

Macon

Macon is a pleasant little city with a few interesting sights. The town was established in 1823 and prospered as a cotton port on the Ocmulgee River. The area had a strong Unionist and peace movement before and during the Civil War, which left Macon mostly unscathed. Many antebellum houses remain today. In fact, it has more structures on the National Register of Historic Places (5500) than any other Georgian city.

Held the third week of March, Macon's **Cherry Blossom Festival** (☎ 478-751-7429; www.cherry

---

LET THE (REDNECK) GAMES BEGIN

Every year on a hot, steamy day in July, Southerners converge on the small town of Dublin to compete in the annual **Redneck Games** (☎ 478-272-4422; http://redneckgames .tripod.com; admission free). The festivities begin with the ceremonial lighting of the BBQ grill and, along with live music, burgers, dogs and Bud, there's plenty of action. As folks wave their Confederate flags and holler 'yee haw!' others compete in a range of events, including the mud-pit belly flop, bobbing for pig's feet, the hubcap hurl and the ever-popular armpit serenade. The event is held at Buckeye Park in East Dublin, about 55 miles east of Macon.

---

blossom.com) celebrates the blossoming of 250,000 flowering Japanese Yoshino cherry trees.

The **visitor center** (☎ 478-743-3401, 800-768-3401; 200 Cherry St; ☻ 9am-5pm Mon-Sat), in the 1916 Terminal Station, has information about history tours of the city.

Georgia Music Hall of Fame (☎ 478-750-8555; 888-427-6257; www.gamusichall.com; 200 Martin Luther King Jr Blvd; adult/child $8/3.50; ☻ 9am-5pm Mon-Sat, from 1pm Sun) showcases the multitude of musical talent that has bloomed in Georgia, including REM, James Brown, Little Richard, Ray Charles and the Allman Brothers. (Duane Allman died in Macon while working on the *Eat a Peach* album.)

Ocmulgee National Monument (☎ 478-752-8257; 1207 Emery Hwy; admission free; ☻ 9am-5pm), just east of town, is an archaeological site with Indian burial mounds, artifacts and an ancient earth lodge.

Around Macon

In 1928, eight years before he was elected US president, polio-stricken Franklin D Roosevelt took a curative trip to **Warm Springs**, where he founded a polio treatment center. He ultimately died here from a stroke in April 1945. The tiny town of Pine Mountain serves as the gateway for **Callaway Gardens** (☎ 706-663-2281; www.callawaygardens.com; cnr Hwys 18 & 27; adult/child $13/6.50; ☻ 9am-5pm), which encompass more than 14,000 acres of attractions, including a butterfly center, a horticultural center, vegetable garden, a beach, and acres upon acres of azaleas that bloom

from March to May. The teensy town of Plains is best known as the birthplace and current residence of Jimmy Carter, the 39th US president. Many Carter-related buildings are now part of the **Jimmy Carter National Historic Site** (☎ 229-824-4104; www.nps.gov/jica; admission free; 300 N Bond St; ☻ 9am-5pm).

NORTH GEORGIA

The southern end of the great Appalachian Range extends some 40 miles into Georgia's far north, providing some superb mountain scenery and wild white-water rivers, a topography quite like anywhere else in Georgia. The fall colors emerge late here, peaking in October. Free brochures with directions for self-guided driving tours are available at most of the region's visitor centers.

A few days are warranted to see sites like the 1200ft-deep **Tallulah Gorge** (☎ 706-754-7970), the scenery and hiking trails at **Vogel State Park** (☎ 706-745-2628) and the interesting collection of Appalachian folk arts at the **Foxfire Museum** (☎ 706-746-5828; ☻ 9am-4:30pm Mon-Sat), near Mountain City.

Dahlonega

In 1828 Dahlonega was the site of the first gold rush in the USA. The boom these days, though, is in tourism. It's an easy excursion from Atlanta and offers intriguing history surrounded by beautiful mountain scenery.

Walking around the historic main square is a major event itself. Many offbeat shops compete for tourist dollars. The **visitor center** (☎ 706-864-3711; www.dahlonega.org; 13 S Park St; ☻ 9am-5:30pm) has plenty of information on area sites and activities (including hiking, canoeing, kayaking, rafting and mountain biking). In the center of the square, the **Dahlonega Gold Museum** (☎ 706-864-2257; adult/child $3/1.50; ☻ 9am-5pm Mon-Sat, from 10am Sun) tells the fascinating story of gold mining in the region.

Amicalola Falls State Park, 18 miles west of Dahlonega on Hwy 52, features the 729ft **Amicalola Falls**, the highest waterfall in Georgia. The park offers spectacular scenery, in addition to excellent hiking and mountain-biking trails.

Helen

Helen is the sort of town you can only find in the USA: a faux Swiss-German mountain village where the shops have names like 'Das ist Leather.' Beginning in 1968,

THE SOUTH

business leaders looked for ideas to transform the dreary lumber town into a tourist attraction. Soon, the Bavarian look took hold and somehow this place has become a popular tourist destination.

The **visitor center** (☎ 706-878-2181, 800-858-8027; www.helenga.org; 726 Brukenstrasse; ☯ 9am-5pm Mon-Sat, from 10am Sun) is on the southern side of town. **Oktoberfest**, from mid-September to early November is a popular event, with plenty of oompah bands and bratwurst. In summer, you'll see hundreds of folks **Shooting the Hooch** – going down the slow-moving Chattahoochee River on inner tubes. The best way to see Helen is on foot; just join the throngs of slow-moving tourists. If the crowds get too much, head to nearby **Unicoi State Park** (☎ 706-878-3982), a beautiful park with hiking trails, cabins, campsites and attractive mountain scenery.

ALABAMA

Two major culture-defining events began here in 'Bammy.' When Jefferson Davis became the first president of the Confederacy in Montgomery in 1861, he quickly moved into his new digs, pressed the proverbial red button and – bang – the Civil War began. Nearly 100 years later, a black woman refused to budge on a bus and the world was never the same. Known for incredible acts of activism, Alabama and the actions that happened here in the 1950s and '60s, led the way for civil rights triumphs throughout the USA. All that struggle and strife came at a cost and, ever since, Alabama has had to conquer its reputation of rebels, segregation, discrimination and wayward politicians. There's no denying the important events of the past; indeed they continue to help Alabamians move closer toward racial harmony.

Alabama has a surprising diversity of landscapes, from the northern foothills and central farmlands to the subtropical Gulf Coast. Visitors come to see the heritage of antebellum architecture, to celebrate the country's oldest Mardi Gras in Mobile, and to learn about the civil-rights struggle.

History

Alabama was occupied by Choctaws, Cherokees, Chickasaws and especially Creek Indians until the early 1800s, when

---

ALABAMA FACTS

Nicknames Camellia State, Heart of Dixie
Population 4.5 million
Area 52,423 sq miles
Capital city Montgomery (population: 201,570)
Official state tree Southern longleaf pine
Birthplace of Helen Keller (1880–1968), Olympian Jesse Owens (1913–80), Nat 'King' Cole (1919–65), author Harper Lee (b 1926), musicians Hank Williams (1923–53) and Lionel Ritchie (b 1949), actor Courtney Cox Arquette (b 1964)
Home of Rocket capital of the world (Huntsville), the world's first Mardi Gras in the US (Mobile)
Famous for Having the first electric streetcars (1866), civil rights history

---

white settlers began arriving from the Carolinas, Virginia and Tennessee. By 1839 all the surviving Native Americans had been removed to Oklahoma.

Small-scale farming dominated the early economy, and Alabama was among the first states to secede in the Civil War. Montgomery was the first Confederate capital, Mobile was a major Confederate port and Selma was a munitions center. Alabama lost around 25,000 soldiers in the war, and reconstruction was slow and painful. Widespread rural poverty was partly alleviated by black agriculturist George Washington Carver, who promoted the rotation of crops and developed numerous new products that could be made from peanuts and sweet potatoes.

The boll weevil devastated cotton crops after 1914, destroying the livelihood of the sharecroppers, and many blacks left the state for good. Industry switched from agriculture to manufacturing, and iron and steel factories made Birmingham the most industrialized city in the New South.

Racial segregation and Jim Crow laws survived well into the 1950s, when the Civil Rights movement campaigned for desegregation of everything from public buses to private universities, a notion Governor George Wallace viciously opposed. Alabama saw brutal repression and hostility, but federal civil rights and voting laws eventually prevailed. At a political level, reform has seen the election of dozens of black mayors and representatives. Still, Alabama is one of the USA's poorest

THE SOUTH

states, with many blacks among its poorest citizens, and there is abundant evidence of social inequality.

Information

The state sales tax is 4%, but local taxes can hike it up to 11%.

Alabama Bureau of Tourism & Travel (☎ 334-242-4169, 800-252-2262; www.800alabama.com; PO Box 4927, Montgomery, AL 36103) Sends out a vacation guide and the publication *Alabama's Black Heritage*.

BIRMINGHAM

Friends star Courtney Cox Arquette, soul singer Nel Carter, *Charlie's Angels* Kate Jackson and NBA superstar Charles Barkley hail from Birmingham, by far the largest and most cosmopolitan city in Alabama. Its growth, however, wasn't so glamorous. With the discovery of coal, iron ore and limestone in the late 19th century, Birmingham, once a small farming town, grew into the South's foremost industrial center, giving it the nickname 'the Pittsburgh of the South.'

Jim Crow legislation peaked in 1915, at a time when the KKK dominated local politics. By the 1950s Birmingham became America's most segregated city. Racial tensions erupted in 1963 when police attacked students marching for civil rights and turned a blind eye to more than 50 racially motivated bombings.

Faced with disaster, newly elected politicians forced change. Within a decade, the city council integrated, the economy diversified and a new mayor – this time black – helped stabilize both the economy and the community.

Orientation

The primary attractions are downtown, in and around the 4th Ave Historic District, where the black community thrived despite segregation. Hipsters throng to Southside and Five Points South – off 20th St (the main north–south thoroughfare) – where art-deco buildings house lively shops, restaurants and nightclubs. Also keeping things lively and youthful is the nearby University of Alabama at Birmingham.

Information

Historical 4th Ave Visitors Center (☎ 205-328-1850; 319 17th St N; ☯ 9am-5pm Mon-Sat) Conducts free walking tours.

Visitor center (☎ 205-458-8000, 800-458-8085; www .sweetbirmingham.com; 2200 9th Ave N; ☯ 8:30am-5pm Mon-Fri) Downtown. Has a small gift shop and good information, including the interesting *Downtown Historic Walking Tour* brochure.

Sights & Activities

Birmingham Civil Rights Institute (☎ 205-328-9696, 866-328-9696; www.bcri.org; 520 16th St N; adult/child $9/free; ☯ 10am-5pm Tue-Sat, from 1pm Sun) is the most worthwhile sight in town. Its excellent audio, video and photography exhibits tell the story of racial segregation in the USA, from WWI and the civil rights movement, to racial and human-rights issues around the world today.

Across the street in **Kelly Ingram Park**, 1960s civil rights marches are depicted in sculptures of Martin Luther King Jr and of police dogs attacking children, who at the time were jailed for their involvement in the protests.

The **16th St Baptist Church** (☎ 205-251-9402; cnr 16th St & 6th Ave N; ☯ 10am-2pm Tue-Fri) became a gathering place for meetings and protests in the 1950s and '60s. When KKK members bombed the church in 1963, killing four girls, the city was flung into a whirlwind of social change. Today, the rebuilt church is a memorial and a house of worship (services 11am Sunday).

Birmingham Museum of Art (☎ 205-254-2565; www.artsbma.org; 2000 8th Ave N; admission free; ☯ 10am-5pm Tue-Sat, from noon Sun) specializes in European decorative arts (especially Wedgwood) and has an excellent collection of African art.

The Carver Performing Arts Center houses the **Alabama Jazz Hall of Fame** (☎ 205-254-2731; 1631 4th Ave N; admission $2; ☯ 10am-5pm Tue-Sat), which celebrates jazz musicians like Dinah Washington, Nat King Cole and Duke Ellington.

The **McWane Center** (☎ 205-714-8300; www .mcwane.org; 200 19th St N; museum & Imax adult/child $16/14; ☯ 10am-6pm Mon-Sat, from 1pm Sun), truly state of the art, houses a science center and Imax theater.

Art-deco buildings in trendy **Five Points South** house shops, restaurants, breweries and nightclubs. **Vulcan Park** (20th St S & Valley Ave) has the US's second-largest statue and an observation tower offering fantastic views.

Twelve miles south of town, **Oak Mountain State Park** (☎ 205-620-2524; 15 miles south on 1-65,

THE SOUTH

exit 246; admission $3; 🕑 dawn-dusk) is Alabama's largest state park, where you can hike, camp, boat or chill out on the lakeside beach.

Sleeping

Hospitality Inn (☎ 205-322-0691; 2127 7th Ave S; d $40; P ✺) This humble, friendly 50-room hotel near the university and just a few blocks north of Five Points South has simple rooms, but is a great value.

Pickwick Hotel (☎ 205-933-9555, 800-255-7304; www.pickwickhotel.com; 1023 20th St S; r from $100; P ✺ 🖵) This art-deco hotel sits in the middle of Five Points South. Nightly wine and cheese, afternoon tea and cheery staff make this beautiful hotel even more endearing.

Tutwiler Hotel (☎ 205-322-2100, 866-850-3053; http://tutwiler-birmingham.wyndham-hotels.com; 2021 Park Place N; r from $135; P ✺ 🖵) This landmark hotel downtown has a nice mix of 19th-century furnishings and modern accoutrements like a fitness center, marble baths and high-speed Internet access. Its restaurant, the Grille (open for all meals), serves an extensive menu.

Eating

Mill Bakery, Eatery & Brewery (☎ 205-939-3001; 1035 20th St S; mains $7-14) This fun-loving restaurant attracts students and business folks who come for the lively atmosphere, good beer and menu filled with sandwiches, salads and to-die-for crab cakes.

Bombay Cafe (☎ 205-322-1930; 2839 7th Ave S; mains $8-24; 🕑 lunch Mon-Fri, dinner Mon-Sat) A fantastic little bistro where the menu changes daily, featuring fresh fish and shellfish, lamb and steak dishes.

Highlands Bar & Grill (☎ 205-939-1400; 2011 11th Ave S; mains $20-30; 🕑 4-10pm Tue-Sat) One of internationally acclaimed chef Frank Sitt's trio of eateries, and arguably Birmingham's best restaurant, the sumptuous menu features meat and seafood beautified by a flash of sophistication borrowed from both southern France and traditional Southern cuisine.

Good choices for inexpensive but tasty food include **Pete's Famous Hot Dogs** (☎ 205-252-2905; 1925 2nd Ave N; dogs $1.50), a tiny hole-in-the-wall that has been serving up hot dogs since 1915. **Rib-It-Up** (☎ 205-328-7427; 830 1st Ave N; mains $3-8) is great for eat-in or take-out finger-licking Southern BBQ beef, pork and chicken.

Getting There & Around

The **Birmingham International Airport** (☎ 205-595-0533) is about 5 miles northeast of downtown. **Greyhound** (☎ 205-251-3210, 618 19th St N), north of downtown, serves cities including Atlanta, GA ($23, three hours), Huntsville ($15, two hours), Montgomery ($18, two hours), Jackson, MS ($29, five hours), and New Orleans, LA ($68, 8½ hours).

Amtrak (☎ 205-324-3033; 1819 Morris Ave), downtown, has trains daily to New York ($165, 11 hours) and New Orleans ($24, seven hours). **Birmingham Transit Authority** (☎ 205-322-7701; adult $1.25) runs local buses.

AROUND BIRMINGHAM

The mostly industrial town of **Tuscaloosa** was the state capital from 1826 to 1846, and the University of Alabama was established in 1831. The world here revolves around its successful Crimson Tide football team – grown men and women cry like tortured babies when UA loses a game.

North of Birmingham, the wealthy aerospace community of **Huntsville** had its high-tech beginnings in the 1950s when German scientists were brought in to develop rockets for the US army. The US space program took off and attracted international aerospace-related companies. The **US Space & Rocket Center** (☎ 256-837-3400, 800-637-7223; www.spacecamp.com; I-565, exit 15; adult/child museum $14/9, with Imax $19/13; 🕑 9am-5pm) is a combination science museum and theme park without the hype. It's a great place to take a kid, or to become one again. The center has Imax films, space demonstrations, simulators and the Space Shot ride, which takes you from four g's to weightlessness at 45mph.

Four cities on the Tennessee River make up the area known as **'the Shoals'**: Florence, Sheffield, Tuscumbia and Muscle Shoals. The Wilson Dam, completed in 1924, improved navigation on the 37-mile Muscle Shoals rapids and brought inexpensive electricity to the area. The Shoals made a name for itself in the music industry from 1966, when Fame Recording Studios and Quinvy Studio got Atlantic Records to release Percy Sledge's 'When a Man Loves a Woman.' Many artists, including Aretha Franklin followed. Information on area sights and accommodations is available at the **visitor center** (☎ 256-383-0783, 800-344-0783; www.colbertcountytourism.org; 179 Hwy 72W Tuscumbia;

Ⓨ 8:30am-5pm Mon-Fri year-round, 9am-4pm Sat & from 1pm Sun summer).

MONTGOMERY

The explosion of the Civil Rights movement happened here in 1955, when a black seamstress named Rosa Parks refused to give up her seat to a white man on a city bus. It was a pivotal act of activism that changed the course of the country's history.

Anger at segregation and the oppressive Jim Crow laws came to a boil and for 381 days blacks boycotted city buses until the US Supreme Court finally stepped in and ordered desegregation.

Racial tensions in Montgomery only increased and the hatred inspired by groups like the KKK spread like disease. In 1961 Klansmen beat black Freedom Riders; in 1963 George Wallace won governorship on a pro-segregation platform.

The wind started changing in 1965, however, when Dr Martin Luther King Jr led the Selma–Montgomery Civil Rights March and brought the whole bucket of hate and racism to the capital's doorstep. That same year, blacks finally won the right to vote.

Montgomery is a sleepy town that sprawls across seven hills overlooking the Alabama River. Most of the attractions are downtown and can be reached on foot in an afternoon. The **visitor center** (☎ 334-266-1100, 800-240-9452; www.visitingmontgomery.com; 300 Water St; Ⓨ 8am-5pm Mon-Sat, noon-4pm Sun) is in the historic Union Station.

Sights

The Southern Poverty Law Center grew out of Montgomery's racial strife. It teaches tolerance and protects the rights of the poor and minorities. Outside the center, the **Civil Rights Memorial** (400 Washington Ave), honors 40 martyrs of the Civil Rights movement.

Rosa Parks Museum (☎ 334-241-8615; http://montgomery.troy.edu/museum; 251 Montgomery St; adult/child $5.50/3.50; Ⓨ 9am-5pm Mon-Fri, to 3pm Sat) features a bronze bust of Rosa (who died in October, 2005) and a sophisticated video re-creation of the bus-seat protest.

Free tours are available around the **Alabama State Capitol** (☎ 334-242-3935; www.preserveala.org; 600 Dexter Ave; Ⓨ 9am-4pm Mon-Fri), where Jefferson Davis took the oath of office as president of the Confederacy. You

can also check out Davis' home and history at the **First White House of the Confederacy** (☎ 334-242-1861; 644 Washington Ave; Ⓨ 9am-5pm Mon-Fri), which was moved to its current site opposite the capitol in 1919.

Hank Williams Museum (☎ 334-262-3600; www.hankwilliamsmuseummontgomery.com; 118 Commerce St; adult/child $7/2; Ⓨ 9am-6pm Mon-Sat, noon-4pm Sun) pays homage to the country music master. You'll see Hank's personal stuff, including the baby blue 1952 Cadillac he died in at age 29. Other tributes to Williams include a life-size **bronze statue** in Lister Hill Plaza and an **oversize hat** where he's buried in the Oakwood Cemetery Annex.

Scott & Zelda Fitzgerald Museum (☎ 334-264-4222; 919 Felder Ave; admission free; Ⓨ 10am-2pm Wed-Fri, 1-5pm Sat & Sun) is where Montgomery-born Zelda spent most of her life. F Scott was stationed here during WWI when the writers fell in love, married and lived here from 1931 to 1932. You can see her painting, his partial manuscripts and, most interesting, love letters chronicling their often stormy, passionate marriage.

The superb **Alabama Shakespeare Festival** (☎ 334-271-5353, 800-841-4273; www.asf.net) shows live performances at **Blount Cultural Park** from March through July. A must-see if you're here at that time.

Sleeping & Eating

Embassy Suites (☎ 334-269-5055; www.embassysuitesmontgomery.com; 300 Tallapoosa St; r from $90; Ⓟ Ⓧ Ⓛ Ⓢ) Downtown right next to the visitor center, this 237-suite hotel has big rooms, character and tons of amenities, including a piano player in the lobby.

Farmer's Market Cafeteria (☎ 334-262-1970; 315 N McDonough St; mains $5-8; Ⓨ 5:30am-2pm Mon-Fri) The homey café serves the best Southern breakfast in town, and has since 1958. At lunch there's more good country cooking and incredibly reasonable prices.

Montgomery Brewing Co (☎ 334-834-2739; 12 W Jefferson St; dinner $10-16; Ⓨ 4pm-10pm Mon-Sat) A lively hub of activity, the MBC is a great place for a microbrew and Cajun-Southern fusion food, including good salads, pork chops and generous sandwiches. There's live music on weekends.

Chris' Hot Dog (☎ 334-265-6850; 138 Dexter Ave; dogs $2; Ⓨ 10am-7pm Mon-Sat, to 8pm Fri) The plump juicy dogs have made this a Montgomery institution since 1917. You can also get burgers and sandwiches. Cash only.

Getting There & Around

Montgomery has a regional airport about 15 miles from downtown and is served by daily flights from Atlanta, Memphis and Charlotte. **Greyhound** (☎ 334-286-0658; 950 W South Blvd) also serves the city. The **Montgomery Area Transit System** (☎ 334-262-7321; www.mont gomerytransit.com) operates the city buses, but more convenient is the **Lightning Route Trolley** (all-day fare $1; ☽ 9am-6pm Mon-Sat), which shuttles from the visitor center to downtown attractions every 20 minutes or so.

SELMA

Selma thrived as a center for shipping cotton on the Alabama River and the railways. As plantations thrived, slave trading became big business. After Union soldiers defeated and burned Selma in 1865, the town built itself back, only to be devastated by the nasty boll weevil, a burrowing beetle that decimated cotton crops.

On Bloody Sunday, March 7, 1965, the media captured state troopers and deputies beating and gassing African Americans and white sympathizers near the Edmund Pettus Bridge. Led by Martin Luther King Jr, the crowd was marching to the state capital (Montgomery) to demonstrate for voting rights. This was the culmination of two years of violence, which ended when President Johnson signed the Voting Rights Act of 1965.

Incredibly, despite the fact that Selma's electorate has shifted from nearly all white to 65% black, Selma's pro-segregationist mayor held on to his seat until 2000. In that year, computer consultant James Perkins became the city's first black mayor. Today, Selma is a quiet, sleepy town, and though its attractions are few, they do provide an excellent insight into the voting rights protests that were at the crux of the Civil Rights movement.

Selma's **visitor center** (☎ 334-875-7485; www .selmaalabama.com; 2207 Broad St; ☽ 8am-8pm) has a wealth of area information about civil rights history and sights. Segregation and Bloody Sunday are remembered at the small **National Voting Rights Museum** (☎ 334-418-0800; 1012 Water Ave; admission $5; ☽ 9am-5pm Tue-Fri), near the Edmund Pettus Bridge.

Sleeping & Eating

Jameson Inn (☎ 334-874-8600; www.jamesoninns .com; 2420 N Broad St/Hwy 22; d incl breakfast $55-65; P ⊠ ☐ ☒) This charming inn on the main drag has 59 spacious rooms.

St James Hotel (☎ 334-872-3234; www.st-james -hotel.com; 1200 Water Ave; r/ste from $90/145; P ⊠) Overlooking the Mississippi River, this historic hotel has 61 guest rooms decorated with antiques, a good restaurant and a popular streetside lounge. Hotel guests can use the nearby YMCA pool.

Major Grumbles (☎ 334-872-2006; 1 Grumbles Alley; mains $7-11; ☽ 11am-11pm Mon-Sat) In a restored riverfront warehouse, this local favorite offers red beans, rice and chicken gumbo.

Strong's (☎ 334-875-8800; 118 Washington St; mains $3-7; ☽ 10am-7pm Mon-Sat) For delicious soul food, head here.

MOBILE

Wedged between Mississippi and Florida, the southern Alabama coastline – with beaches, rivers, estuaries and pine-covered barrier islands – is all of 52 miles long. The only real coastal town is Mobile (mo-*beel*), a major seaport and shipbuilding center with green spaces, shady boulevards and four historic districts. It's ablaze with azaleas in early spring and Mardi Gras has been celebrated here for nearly 300 years. Mobile citizens have long grown weary of explaining to visitors that they began celebrating Fat Tuesday long before New Orleans, but perhaps they're just trying to keep their city a secret. Mobile is interesting and fun in the same sense as New Orleans, only the volume and brightness are turned way down. The Dauphin St historic district is where you'll find many bars and restaurants, and it's where much of the Mardi Gras action takes place.

Sights & Activities

Pick up walking or driving tours of the historic districts at the **visitor center** (☎ 251-208-2000, 800-566-2453; www.mobile.org; 150 S Royal St; ☽ 8am-3pm Mon-Fri), in the reconstructed **Fort Condé** (☎ 251-208-7304; admission free; ☽ 8am-5pm).

Museum of the City of Mobile (☎ 251-208-7569; www.museumofmobile.com; 111 S Royal St; adult/child $5/3; ☽ 9am-5pm Mon-Sat, from 1pm Sun) covers the past 300 years of the city's history, with a neat collection of maritime antiques and a cool interactive exhibit for kids.

Moored near Fort Condé, the **USS Alabama** (☎ 251-433-2703, 800-426-4929; www.ussalabama.com; 2703 Battleship Parkway; adult/child $10/5; ☟ 8am-6pm, to 4pm Oct-Mar) is famous for escaping nine major WWII battles unscathed. It's a worthwhile tour for its pure size and might.

At **Oakleigh** (☎ 251-432-1281; www.historicmobile.org/oakleigh.html; 350 Oakleigh Pl; adult/child $5/3; ☟ 9am-3pm Tue-Sat), guides in period costume lead visitors around an 1833 Greek Revival mansion with a notable collection of 19th-century paintings.

Sleeping & Eating

Malaga Inn (☎ 251-438-4701, 800-235-1586; 359 Church St; d $80-150; P ⊠ ⊠ ⊠) Right along the parade route, this is the place to be during Mardi Gras. The inn has 38 nicely furnished rooms that open onto balconies overlooking the courtyard or street.

Wintzell's Oyster House (☎ 251-432-4605; www.wintzellsoysterhouse.com; 605 Dauphin St; mains $7-12; ☟ 11am-10pm Sun-Thu, to 11pm Fri & Sat) Order 'em fried, baked, in a sandwich or on the shell – it's all about oysters, served up in a lively atmosphere here since 1938.

Spot of Tea (☎ 251-433-9009; 310 Dauphine St; mains $6-10; ☟ 7am-2pm) Oozing down-home Southern hospitality, here you'll find big hearty breakfasts and thick sandwiches, served up by ultrafriendly staff.

MISSISSIPPI

Long scorned for its lamentable civil rights history and its low ranking on the list of nearly every national marker of economy and education, most people feel content to malign Mississippi without ever experiencing it firsthand. But unpack your bags for a moment and you'll see so much more than you expected. The state's principal attraction is a glimpse of the real South. It lies somewhere amid the Confederate defeat at Vicksburg, the literary legacy of William Faulkner at Oxford, the birthplace of the blues in the Mississippi Delta, and the humble origins of Elvis Presley in Tupelo.

History

There are several remnants from the ancient Mississippian culture in modern-day Mississippi; three Indian nations were here when Hernando de Soto arrived in 1540,

---

MISSISSIPPI FACTS

Nickname Magnolia State
Population 2.9 million
Area 49,907 sq miles
Capital city Jackson (population 510,000)
Official state bird Mockingbird
Birthplace of Novelist William Faulkner (1897–1962), dramatist Tennessee Williams (1911–83), musicians Elvis Presley (1935–77), BB King (b 1925) and Jimmy Buffett (b 1946), puppeteer Jim Henson (1936–90), talk-show host Oprah Winfrey (b 1954)
Famous for The King of Rock and Roll, the Delta blues

---

but only one Choctaw community survives. Most others were displaced by a series of sham treaties and ultimate removal to Oklahoma in the 1830s.

Cotton dominated the economy, and by 1860 Mississippi was the country's leading cotton producer and one of the 10 wealthiest states. Cotton required slaves, the vast majority of whom were owned by a few giant plantations (most Whites held no slaves at all). Nevertheless, the institution of slavery was entrenched and there was a great fear of slave rebellion. Mississippi was the second state to secede in the Civil War, which cost it more than 60,000 lives. Vicksburg was the last Confederate stronghold on the Mississippi, and its fall to General Grant after a long siege was a turning point in the conflict.

It's fair to say the war ruined Mississippi's economy, and reconstruction was traumatic. The discriminatory 'Black Code' laws made racial segregation a way of life, with most Blacks and many Whites doomed to wretched poverty. The civil rights struggle was marked by violence, murder and federal intervention. It was not until the late 1960s that the state's schools and colleges were fully integrated. Despite some economic diversification and the growth of oil and natural-gas industries, Mississippi has the highest poverty rate – almost 20% – in the country.

Information

The state sales tax is 7%. City and hotel taxes can add another 4% to 5%.
Mississippi Division of Tourism (☎ 601-875-0705, 800-927-6378; www.visitmississippi.org; PO Box 1705, Ocean City, MS 39566) Has Welcome Centers at the state line.

THE SOUTH

TUPELO

The Bethlehem of the USA, Tupelo is the birthplace of our beloved Baby Elvis. This industrial town that was named after a native gum tree today produces upholstered furniture and supplements its income with the mighty tourist draw that The King of Rock 'n' Roll Was Born Here. When you putter around this small town, you'll still overhear stories about who cut the King's hair, who taught him his first chord, who babysat him and who was lucky enough to get a kiss.

The Natchez Trace Parkway (opposite) and Hwy 78 intersect northeast of downtown. You can pick up area information at the **visitor center** (☎ 662-841-6521, 800-533-0611; 399 E Main St; ☺ 8am-5pm Mon-Fri). Gloster St has motels, restaurants and other services, especially at the intersection with McCullough Blvd. The older downtown area is about a mile east at 'Crosstown,' the intersection of Gloster and Main Sts, marked by an old blue-and-yellow neon arrow.

Elvis Presley's Birthplace (☎ 662-841-1245; www .elvispresleybirthplace.com; 306 Elvis Presley Blvd; all sights adult/child $7/3.50; ☺ 9am-5:30pm Mon-Sat, 1-4pm Sun) is east of downtown off Hwy 78. The 15-acre park complex contains the two-room shack built by Elvis' dad, a museum dis-

---

THE KING'S HUMBLE ORIGINS

Elvis and his stillborn twin, Jesse, were born in Tupelo in the front room of a 450-sq-ft shotgun shack at 4:35am on January 8, 1935. The Presleys lived there until Elvis was three, when the house was repossessed.

Elvis bought his first guitar at **Tupelo Hardware** (114 W Main St) for $12; attended grades one to five at Lawhon School; won second prize in a talent quest at the fairgrounds west of town; earned A grades in music at **Milam Junior High School** (Gloster & Jefferson Sts); and attended the **First Assembly of God church** (909 Berry St).

When Elvis was 13, he and his family left Tupelo for Memphis. He returned at 21 to play the Mississippi-Alabama Fair, and the National Guard was called in to contain the crowds. The following year, Elvis came back for a benefit concert, with proceeds going to help the city purchase and restore his birthplace, which now attracts nearly 100,000 visitors each year.

---

playing personal items and a tiny chapel that contains Elvis' own Bible.

Sleeping & Eating

All American Inn (☎ 662-844-5610; 767 E Main St; s/d $35/40; ℗ ✕) Situated between downtown and Elvis' house, this place has a suitable leftover '50s look and 70 comfortable rooms.

Days Inn (☎ 662-842-0088; 1015 N Gloster; r incl breakfast $45; ℗ ✕ ✿) A standard chain hotel but a good value with 40 comfortable rooms and laundry services.

Johnnie's Drive In (☎ 662-842-6748; 908 E Main St; dishes $3-6; ☺ 6am-10pm Mon-Sat) A classic little BBQ joint where you can eat cheap meat in a wooden booth or in the car (just toot the horn and someone will come out and take your order). If you opt to eat in, find the wooden booth with the poem entitled 'Elvis,' by one Wm Hudspeth. It's a sweet and sentimental little homage in rhyming verse.

Two state parks on either side of town, **Tombigbee** (☎ 662-842-7669; campsites $16) southeast of town, and **Trace** (☎ 662-489-2958; campsites $14) to the west, have fishing, swimming and campsites.

OXFORD

A refreshingly sophisticated little town that's bustling and prosperous, Oxford was named by colonists after the English city in hopes it would open a school as revered as its namesake. The University of Mississippi ('Ole Miss') opened in 1848 and although almost nothing of it mirrors its British counterpart, the town and university have a somewhat European feel, mixed with a good dose of small-town Americana.

Writer and native son William Faulkner mythologized the area in his famous stories of Yoknapatawpha County: 'I discovered my little postage stamp of native soil was worth writing about, and…I would never live long enough to exhaust it.'

Other than getting torched in the Civil War, Oxford's history is a short tale but for one major event. In 1962, when James Meredith attempted to be the first black student to enroll at Ole Miss, ugly riots ensued. Troops were called in, and two people died. It was a pivotal time in civil rights history and opened the door for integration in schools across the South.

The university and town are now quietly integrated, with galleries, bookstores and

---

FOLLOW THE NATCHEZ TRACE

Early European explorers followed this Indian route, and French explorers set up trading posts at its northern and southern ends. In the late 18th century, traders coming downriver would sell their cargo, boats and timber rafts, and return north on foot. The route became a post road and was later widened to serve as a military road. When steamboats arrived the road was supplanted by river traffic, and the trace fell into disuse until it was revived as a national historic route in the 1930s.

Today the Natchez Trace Parkway is a scenic two-lane road through woodlands and pasture from Nashville, TN to Natchez, MS. The **parkway headquarters** (☎ 662-680-4025, 800-305-7417; Milepost 266; ☑ 8am-5pm) and visitor center are in Tupelo, and several other centers also distribute maps and information. Commercial vehicles are banned, and there are no businesses or advertising on the roadside. The parkway is popular for bicycle touring, and driving along it is pleasant but slow.

---

cafés grouped around Courthouse Sq. A very worthwhile stop is **Square Books** (☎ 662-236-2262; www.squarebooks.com; 111 Courthouse Sq; ☑ 9am-9pm Mon-Thu, to 10pm Fri & Sat, 10am-5pm Sun), a fantastic bookstore, and great place to get a taste of Oxford's lively literary scene. Next door, you'll find the **visitor center** (☎ 662-234-4680, 800-758-9177; www.touroxfordms.com; 107 Oxford Sq; ☑ 9am-5pm Mon-Fri).

Sights

The University of Mississippi, a mile or so west of the square, has an attractive campus shaded by magnolias and dogwoods. Its **Center for the Study of Southern Culture** (☎ 662-915-5993; admission free) covers everything from Southern folklore to Elvis cults, and has the largest collection of blues recordings and publications in the world. The **University Museum** (☎ 662-915-7073; University Ave at 5th Ave; admission free) contains several collections of ancient, decorative, fine and folk arts.

Literary pilgrims head directly to **Rowan Oak** (☎ 662-234-3284; admission free; ☑ 10am-4pm Tue-Sat, from 2pm Sun), the graceful 1840s home of William Faulkner, who authored so many brilliant and dense novels set in northeastern Mississippi. Faulkner lived here from 1930 until he died in 1962. A trail leads through the grounds to the cemetery where **Faulkner's grave** stands. Rowan Oak is near the University, off Old Taylor Rd.

Sleeping & Eating

Several motel franchises are available around exits off the Hwy 6 bypass. Some in-town options follow.

Ole Miss Motel (☎ 662-234-2424; 1517 University Ave; s/d $45/50; **P** ✖) The Ole Miss is a family-run establishment just a few blocks from the town square.

Oliver-Britt House (☎ 662-234-8043; 512 Van Buren Ave; r $60-80; **P** ✖) With five comfortably worn rooms in a 1905 Greek Revival house, this a good homey option just three blocks from the square.

Ajax Diner (☎ 662-232-8880; 118 Courthouse Sq; dishes $7-12; ☑ lunch & dinner) It's all about downhome Southern cooking at this Courthouse Sq joint. Get chicken and dumplings smothered with gravy or meatloaf stuffed with mozzarella. On warm days the front floor-to-ceiling windows open and it's a great place to people-watch.

Taylor Grocery (☎ 601-236-1716; Old Taylor Rd; dishes $10-14; ☑ 6-10pm Thu-Sat) In a splendidly rusticated grocery store, this restaurant serves up some of the state's best fried catfish and hush puppies. It's about 10 minutes' drive from downtown Oxford, south on Old Taylor Rd, in the tiny town of Taylor.

MISSISSIPPI DELTA

The blues are often considered the root of American popular music, but they were once a regional folk idiom played by some

---

ELVIS NEVER LIVED HERE

Elvis-obsessed Paul MacLeod has turned his Holly Springs house into **Graceland Too** (200 Gholson Ave; admission $5; ☑ 24hr), a tacky shrine wallpapered with Elvis posters and crammed with Elvisania. He sells tiny swatches of Graceland carpet ($10) and does Elvis impersonations with little encouragement.

THE SOUTH

of the world's poorest people. In the land where the blues began, time stands as still as cypress stumps in stagnant water. Dirt-poor, rural, left for the kudzu – that pretty well describes much of the Mississippi Delta. It's an oddly appealing motley mix of cotton fields, agricultural refuse and early-20th-century towns inclined to lean backwards no matter which way the buildings are tilting. Ongoing economic decline is evident in the rows of abandoned shops and run-down houses and groups of people standing around on street corners.

The Delta, stretching for 250 miles from Memphis, TN, to Vicksburg, MS, is an alluvial plain rather than an actual river delta, and the soil deposited over millennia by the Mississippi River is among the richest in the world. To post–Civil War landowners, that meant cotton. The labor force, of course, consisted of African Americans – former slaves, the children of slaves, the grandchildren of slaves. They were sharecroppers now, but most of them remained desperately poor. Yet some managed to scrape up enough money for a Stella guitar or a Hohner harmonica. They sang prison songs and levee camp songs that contained echoes of Africa, but spoke directly of their experience. Their blues were by turns tragic, disquieting, weary, spiritual, belligerent and uplifting.

Most visitors come looking for remnants of this past, and with a willingness to venture from Hwy 61, the so-called Blues Highway, they find it. Mississippi may be an intense place, but Mississippians are friendly people who more often than not welcome a stranger with cold beer, tender BBQ and blues grooves in shambling juke joints.

Clarksdale

More than any other Delta town, Clarksdale celebrates its blues heritage, making this a good base for blues travelers. Many blues artists lived in Clarksdale or in the surrounding fields, most famously Muddy Waters. John Lee Hooker was born just outside Clarksdale, Son House lived in nearby Lyon, and Ike Turner, a Clarksdale native, hosted a radio show. Gospel-soul singer Sam Cooke was born and raised here. WC Handy spent two years in town, soaking up

---

DELTA BLUES FESTIVALS

Several outdoor music festivals take place each year in the Delta. Check out www .bluesfestivalguide.com for a list of them all. Here are our favorites.

Juke Joint Festival Clarksdale, mid-April

Mississippi Delta Blues & Heritage Festival (see p408), Greenville, mid-May

Crossroads Blues Festival Rosedale, May

BB King Hometown Homecoming Indianola (p408), early June

Highway 61 Blues Festival (see p408), Leland, mid-June

Sunflower River Blues & Gospel Festival (see below), Clarksdale, early August

---

the blues that he would incorporate into his sophisticated jazz compositions, and Bessie Smith died in a hospital in Clarksdale.

At the town's south side, Hwys 61 and 49 meet at what locals refer to as the **crossroads**. You can't miss the large tin guitars that mark the spot. Does this busy intersection look like a good place to sell your soul to the devil? Some locals will have you believe Robert Johnson did just that, right here.

'Downtown' is the few blocks where the railroad tracks meet the Sunflower River. Across the tracks, in a rough-looking part of town along Martin Luther King Jr Blvd, are eateries and juke joints, where people hang out in front of boarded-up stores.

The **chamber of commerce** (☎ 662-627-7337; www.clarksdale.com; 1540 DeSoto Ave/Hwy 49; ☒ 8:30am-5pm Mon-Fri) has some info, but staff know little about the other side of the tracks.

SIGHTS

The **Delta Blues Museum** (☎ 601-627-6820; www .deltabluesmuseum.org; 1 Blues Alley; adult/child $6/3; ☒ 9am-5pm Mon-Sat), housed in an old train station, is ground zero for blues fans or for anyone wanting to make the pilgrimage. You can get maps and charts that plot musical milestones, see Muddy Waters' old cabin, a collection of old photos and blues-inspired art. Specialist recordings and books are available.

Sunflower River Blues & Gospel Festival (☎ 662-627-6805; www.sunflowerfest.org; admission free) is Clarksdale's big blues festival, which takes place the first weekend in August, a hot and sweaty time of year. A big stage is set up on

Blues Alley, and the emphasis here is traditional Delta-style blues. You'll see much more acoustic playing than at the other big fests, and because of the heat the crowds aren't as big. Barbecue stands line the street, and the local jukes jump at night.

SLEEPING & EATING

Shack Up Inn (☎ 662-624-8329; www.shackupinn.com; r $50-75; P X) At Hopson Plantation, 2 miles south on the west side of Hwy 49, the Shack Up offers much more than a place to lay your head. A night or two in one of the refurbished sharecropper cabins offers a totally unique experience that'll immerse you in Delta life. The cabins all have covered porches and are filled with old furniture and musical instruments. The more expensive ones sleep up to four people. The old commissary is an atmospheric venue for frequent live music performances, and the owners are fonts of information. Staying here is sure to be a highlight of your trip through the Mississippi Delta.

Belle Clark Bed & Breakfast (☎ 662-627-1280; 211 Clark St; r incl breakfast $125-195; P X X) The home of John Clark, founder of Clarksdale, was built in 1859 and is now a gorgeous B&B. Antique-filled rooms and parlors are designed to evoke antebellum splendor and Tennessee Williams–style decadence. (Williams grew up in the neighborhood.) It's not very bluesy but certainly is a treat. Most rooms have private baths.

Abe's (☎ 662-624-9947; 616 State St; mains $3-6; 10:30am-2pm Sun, 10am-9pm Mon-Thu, to 10pm Fri & Sat) At the crossroads, look for the tall sign with the happy pig in a bow tie. Abe's has been providing Clarksdale with zesty pork sandwiches on cheap white buns since 1924.

Chamoun's Rest Haven (☎ 662-624-8601; 419 State St; mains $7-10; 5:30am-9pm Mon-Sat) The friendly Chamoun family are Lebanese-Americans who own the hospitable Rest Haven. It looks like an all-American coffee shop, with leatherette booths and Formica tabletops, and the menu features familiar fare like fried chicken, with Middle Eastern sides like dolmas and hummus. The pie is legendary.

Madidi (☎ 662-627-7770; 164 Delta Ave; mains $20-33; dinner Tue-Sat) Actor Morgan Freeman hails from the Clarksdale area and still lives nearby. Having decided the area needed a restaurant to satisfy his refined tastes, he opened Madidi with a local businessman. The food is French with a Mediterranean

---

VISITING JUKE JOINTS

It's believed that 'juke' is a West African word that survived in the Gullah language, the Creole-English hybrid spoken by isolated African Americans in the US (see p487). The Gullah 'juke' means 'wicked and disorderly.' Little wonder, then, that the term was applied to the roadside sweatboxes of the Mississippi Delta, where secular music, suggestive dancing, drinking and, in some cases, prostitution were the norm. The term 'jukebox' came into vogue when recorded music, spun on automated record-changing machines, began to supplant live musicians in such places, as well as in cafés and bars.

Most juke joints are black neighborhood clubs, and outside visitors can be a rarity. Many are mostly male hangouts. There are very few places that local women, even in groups, would turn up without a male chaperone. Otherwise, women can expect a lot of persistent, suggestive attention.

For visitors of both sexes, having a friendly local with you to make some introductions can make for a much better evening. It can also help to call ahead to find out what's going on and to say you're going to stop by. If you arrive alone and unannounced, talk to people to break the ice.

Note that juke joints don't always keep regular hours. Some open only when the owner's in the mood. We recommend **Ground Zero** (☎ 662-621-0990; 387 Delta Ave; 11am-2pm Mon-Fri, 5pm-late Wed-Sat, brunch Sun), a huge and friendly hall with a dancefloor surrounded by tables. It's also a good starting point for disoriented travelers. By contrast, **Red's** (☎ 662-627-3166; 395 Sunflower Ave; Fri & Sat night usually) looks a little scary to first-timers, but it is one of Clarksdale's best jukes. A faded sign out front indicates that this was once the Laverne Music Center, and only a hand-scrawled sign on the wall above the huge BBQ pit tells us it's now called Red's. (If the pit's smoking, order whatever's cooking.)

flair, and the atmosphere reserved but pleasant. Reservations recommended.

Around Clarksdale

Stovall Farms, 17 miles south, is a former plantation where Muddy Waters lived and worked. In **Tutwiler**, an outdoor mural illustrates WC Handy's first exposure to the blues in 1903. At Tutwiler, Hwy 49 splits into east and west branches, with Hwy 49W heading towards **Parchman Penitentiary**, the notorious prison farm that has been a temporary home for many bluesmen. It turns up in Mississippi lore and several blues songs – the *Midnight Special* was the weekend train bringing prison visitors. On Hwy 61 in Shelby, **Do-Drop Inn** (cnr 4th & Lake Sts) is a locally famed juke joint.

Barely a podunk, **Merigold** has a couple of draws: **Crawdad's** (☎ 662-748-2441; 104 S Park St; dishes $6-20; ☽ 6am-10pm Tue-Sat) is a barnlike restaurant serving Cajun cuisine. **Poor Monkey's Lounge** (☎ 662-748-2254; cover $3) is an old-time juke joint that's welcoming to strangers.

GREENVILLE

The Delta's largest city, Greenville is roughly midway between Clarksdale and Vicksburg. It was here that the levee broke during the catastrophic Great Flood of 1927. On the third weekend in May, Greenville hosts the **Mississippi Delta Blues & Heritage Festival** (☎ 662-335-3523; www.deltablues.org) in a cotton field off Hwy 454, south of town.

LELAND

East of Greenville, Hwy 82 heads out of the Delta. The **Highway 61 Blues Museum** (☎ 662-686-7646; cnr Broad & 4th Sts; admission $5; ☽ 10am-4pm Mon-Sat), in the Old Temple Theater, honors local bluesmen. Leland hosts the **Highway 61 Blues Festival** in mid-June. A tiny visitor center displays photographs of Muppet man Jim Henson, his Delta childhood and early Kermit-like characters.

INDIANOLA

BB King's hometown. Riley 'BB' King was born near here on September 16, 1925. He moved to Indianola at the age of 13. The town honors him thoroughly, although he spends little time here these days.

GREENWOOD & BELZONI

Greenwood is a leafy Delta town with the second-largest cotton market in the US (after Memphis). One of blues history's most disputed events happened here on August 16, 1938, when Robert Johnson seems to have perished in a cloud of smoke – so uncertain are the details of his demise. He is believed to be buried somewhere near here.

The self-proclaimed Catfish Capital of the World, Belzoni is surrounded by ponds of farm-raised catfish. The **Catfish Visitors Center** (☎ 800-408-4838; 111 Magnolia St; ☽ 9am-5pm Mon-Fri) reveals all.

Vicksburg

Considered the southernmost edge of the Mississippi Delta, Vicksburg is famous for its strategic location in the Civil War, thanks to its location on a high bluff overlooking the Mississippi River. General Ulysses S Grant besieged the city for 47 days, until its surrender on July 4, 1863, at which point the North gained dominance over North America's greatest river.

The major sights are readily accessible from I-20 exit 4B (Clay St). For information head to the **visitor center** (☎ 601-636-9421, 800-221-3536; cnr Clay & Washington Sts; ☽ 9am-5pm Mon-Fri). The old, slow downtown stretches along several cobblestone blocks of Washington St, and casinos glitter beside the river. Historic-house museums cluster in the Garden District, on Oak St south of Clay St, and also between 1st St E and Clay St.

National Military Park (☎ 601-636-0583; www.nps.gov/vick; per car $8; ☽ 8am-5pm), north of I-20 on Clay St, is Vicksburg's main attraction for Civil War buffs or anyone who plays with toy soldiers. A 16-mile driving tour passes historic markers explaining gun emplacements, battle scenarios and key events. Rent an audiotape tour ($5) for the whole story. The cemetery contains some 17,000 Union graves, and a museum houses the ironclad gunboat USS *Cairo*. Civil War reenactments are held in May and July.

SLEEPING & EATING

Battlefield Inn (☎ 601-638-5811, 800-359-9363; www.battlefieldinn.org; 4137 N I-20 Frontage Rd; d incl breakfast $50-80; P ☒ ☒) Though it doesn't look it from the outside, this is an incongruously comfortable motel, where guests are pampered with comfortable rooms, free evening cocktails, laundry facilities and a restaurant.

Cedar Grove B&B (☎ 601-636-1000, 800-862-1300; www.cedargroveinn.com; 2300 Washington St; r $95-185;

P ☒ ☒) Vicksburg's showpiece B&B is this 1840 Greek Revival mansion surrounded by 4 acres of landscaped gardens overlooking the river. A Union cannonball remains lodged in a parlor wall, and the house retains many original antiques and gaslit chandeliers. All 24 rooms have private baths.

Walnut Hills (☎ 601-638-4910; 1214 Adams St; dishes $7-12; ☺ 11am-9pm Mon-Fri, to 2pm Sun) Your best bet for eating in Vicksburg is this charming old house near downtown, which serves traditional Southern favorites. Daily menus include old faves like fried chicken and country-fried steak, Southern cooked vegetables, biscuits and cornbread. Meals are served family-style at big round tables.

Jackson

Mississippi's state capital was burned on three separate occasions by Sherman's troops during the Civil War, but somehow the capitol, governor's mansion and city hall were miraculously spared. Although Jackson is Mississippi's largest city by far, most modern development has sprawled into plush suburbs leaving the downtown area – essentially a short stretch of Capitol St – something of a ghost town.

The **visitor center** (☎ 601-960-1891, 800-354-7695; www.visitjackson.com; 921 N President St; ☺ 9am-5pm Mon-Fri) also has a desk at the **Agriculture & Forestry Museum** (☎ 601-713-3365; 1150 Lakeland Dr; adult/child $4/2; ☺ 9am-5pm Mon-Sat), east of I-55 exit 98B. The 'Ag Museum' looks at cultural and ecological history in displays of farm machinery, crop-dusting planes, a re-created 1920s town and an 1860s farmstead.

Mississippi Museum of Art (☎ 601-960-1515; www.msmuseumart.org; 201 E Pascagoula St; adult/child $5/3; ☺ 10am-5pm Mon-Sat, from noon Sun) displays an excellent collection of modern American landscape paintings, 18th-century British art, pre-Columbian ceramics and a good collection of Southern folk art.

Old Capitol Museum (☎ 601-576-6920; http://mdah .state.ms.us/museum; 100 State St; admission free; ☺ 8am-5pm Mon-Fri, 9:30am-4:30pm Sat, 12:30-4:30pm Sun), in the beautifully restored 1833 capitol building, has an excellent 20th-century exhibit on Mississippi's ignominious history, with vintage footage of civil rights clashes. A few blocks away, the **new capitol**, styled after the one in Washington, DC, was completed in 1903.

Lovers of literature will want to check out the city's **Eudora Welty Library** (☎ 601-968-5811; 300 N State St; ☺ 9am-9pm Mon-Thu, to 6pm Fri & Sat, 1-5pm Sun), where a small room is dedicated to Mississippi literati.

The **Smith Robertson Museum** (☎ 601-960-1457; 528 Bloom St; adult/child $4.50/1.50; ☺ 9am-5pm Mon-Fri, 10am-1pm Sat, 2-5pm Sun), housed in the first public school for African American kids in Jackson, traces black cultural history with photographs and contemporary art.

SLEEPING & EATING

Edison Walthall Hotel (☎ 601-948-6161, 800-932-6161; www.edisonwalthallhotel.com; 225 E Capitol St; r/ste $90/120; P ☒ ☒) The pre-eminent capital hotel has a dark wood lobby, atrium pool, 243 ultracomfortable rooms, an excellent restaurant and offers a free airport shuttle.

Poindexter Park Inn (☎ 601-944-1392; 803 Deer Park St; r $60-90; P ☒ ☒) The grand old home of Mississippi's second governor is now a lovely B&B. The old neighborhood has declined a bit since George Poindexter's time, but guests will be comfortable amid the antiques and claw-foot tubs of his former house. The inn is a bit north of downtown, just east of I-55.

Mayflower Cafe (☎ 601-353-4122; 123 Capitol St; dishes $7-18; ☺ 11am-10pm Mon-Sat) A giant flashing neon sign beckons diners into this sweet old spot, owned by cigar-chomping Mr Mike. It's an authentic greasy spoon, with worn counter and stools, where the hash has been slung since 1935.

Hal & Mal's Restaurant & Brewery (☎ 601-948-0888; 200 S Commerce St; dishes $7-18; ☺ 11am-2am Mon-Sat) Live blues, jazz and R & B bands often play this popular brewpub, where the menu features New Orleans fare, such as red beans and rice, po'boy sandwiches, burgers and seafood. The meat-and-three lunches are another big draw. It's near the Old Capitol, above the Pascagoula St underpass.

GETTING THERE & AWAY

At the junction of I-20 and I-55, it's easy to get in and out of Jackson. Its **regional airport** (☎ 601-939-5631) is 10 miles east of downtown. **Greyhound** (☎ 601-353-6342; 201 S Jefferson) buses serve Birmingham, AL ($34.50, five hours), Memphis, TN ($33.50, five hours), and New Orleans, LA ($33.50, 4½ hours). Amtrak's *City of New Orleans* stops at the run-down **station** (☎ 601-355-6350) on Capitol St at Mill St.

THE SOUTH

BLOWN AWAY

While news cameras converged on New Orleans in the aftermath of Hurricane Katrina (p413), which thrashed communities along the Gulf Coast on August 29, 2005, the usually scenic and tidy towns along the Mississippi and Alabama coasts transformed into worlds of chaos and ruin. Torrential rains and violent winds lashed, splaying homes and tossing cars and buildings as if they were toys. One Biloxi fisherman described the scene as something out of a twisted Picasso painting: boats dangled like ornaments in tree branches, while slot machines from obliterated casinos floated down rivers that were yesterday's city streets.

Coastal homes, bridges and whole towns were wiped away – the damp, indiscernible rubble being the only evidence of their existence. In Mississippi, the small town of Waveland was totally destroyed; Gulfport was walloped by winds and, in Biloxi, some of the massive floating casinos that dominated the shoreline were simply tossed inland. In Mobile, AL, flooding stranded residents after wind and waves pummeled the harbor.

Despite the tragedy and destruction, the Gulf Coast residents went to work rebuilding and rebounding. Though it will be several years before the towns recoup their losses and heal their wounds, they will do so eventually, with the same spirit that's kept the coast thriving for 300 years.

Natchez

Perched on a bluff overlooking the Mississippi, this antebellum town attracts tourists with its opulent architecture, especially during the 'pilgrimage' seasons in spring and fall, when local mansions are opened to visitors. The **visitor center** (☎ 601-446-6345, 800-647-6724; www.natchez.ms.us; 640 S Canal St; ☯ 8:30am-5pm Mon-Sat, 9am-4pm Sun) shows a film about the town's history. This is also the southern end of the Natchez Trace Parkway (p405). The staff has an extensive list of B&Bs, plus information about tours.

Over a dozen fine **historic houses** are open for tours year-round. Some of the best (admission $8) include **House on Ellicott's Hill** (☎ 601-442-2011; 211 N Canal St; ☯ 9am-4pm), **Longwood** (☎ 601-442-5193; 140 Lower Woodville Rd; ☯ 9am-4:30pm), **Melrose** (☎ 601-446-5790; 1 Melrose-Montebello Parkway; ☯ 9am-4pm), **Rosalie** (☎ 601-445-4555; 100 Orleans St; ☯ 9am-4pm) and **Stanton Hall** (☎ 601-442-6282; 401 High St; ☯ 9am-4:30pm).

GULF COAST

The Gulf Coast is nothing like the rest of Mississippi and it never has been. The luscious white sandy beaches and the lovely breeze from the Gulf of Mexico have long attracted vacationers from nearby New Orleans. It's an interesting mix down here. The economy, traditionally based on the seafood industry, got a shot of adrenaline in the 1990s when big Vegas-style casinos muscled in alongside the sleepy fishing villages. The mix seems odd at first: you've got Southern-speaking Vietnamese and Irish fishermen playing blackjack alongside bigwigs who have jetted in from big cities.

The casinos are in Biloxi and Gulfport. Pick up local information at the **Mississippi Gulf Coast Convention & Visitors Bureau** (☎ 228-896-6699, 800-237-9493; www.gulfcoast.org; 135 Courthouse Rd; ☯ 8am-6pm) in Gulfport.

The Gulf Islands National Seashore comprises four barrier islands 12 miles off the coast of Mississippi. The islands suffered major damage from Hurricane Katrina. Call the visitors center to find out how they fared, or visit www.nps.gov/guis.

Casinos

When Mississippi lawmakers first opened the coast to casinos, they mandated that the gaming facilities be built offshore. During Hurricane Katrina, each of Mississippi's 13 'floating' casinos were almost entirely destroyed. The casinos generate massive tax dollars for the state and will likely be quickly rebuilt. At press time, the jury was still out as to whether casino owners would win their bids to resurrect the casinos on land, where they would be less susceptible to storms. Casinos along the Mississippi Gulf include:

Beau Rivage (www.beaurivage.com)
Grand Casino Biloxi (www.parkplace.com/grandcasino)
Grand Casino Gulfport (www.parkplace.com/grand casino)
Palace Casino Resort (www.palacecasinoresort.com)

LOUISIANA

You'll feel it the moment you step into the state – like an invisible natural electricity that makes the animals go crazy before a summer storm, the Louisiana air is charged. This is a state where gators lurk in swamps, where a blue-eyed, black-skinned Creoles dip fishing poles into the lazy river, where French-speaking Acadians strap washboards to their chests and strum the distinctive clicking sound of zydeco; a place where a lone sax player can fill a morning, redefine a day. It's where clashing cultures share few traits except a seemingly undeniable urge to eat well and dance dance dance.

In the rolling hills and pine forests of northern Louisiana, the mostly Protestant population shares similar traits with other Southern states. But the world becomes a different place amid the swampy, gator-infested bayous of southern Louisiana, where Creole and Cajun flavors tempt even the tame. All this centers on New Orleans, where jazz and Afro-Caribbean sounds color the thick sultry air with so much history and invincibility, you just can't resist the beautiful urge to let loose.

History

The lower Mississippi River area was dominated by the Mississippian Mound Building culture until around AD 1592 when Europeans arrived and disposed the Indians with the usual combination of disease, unfavorable treaties and outright hostility.

The land was passed back and forth from the Spanish to the French, to the British and back to the French. After the American Revolution and some colonial double-dealing, the whole area passed to the USA in the 1803 Louisiana Purchase, and Louisiana became a state in 1812.

Steamboats plying the river system opened a vital trade network across the continent. New Orleans became a major port, and Louisiana's slave-based plantation economy kept a flowing export of rice, livestock, tobacco, indigo, sugarcane and especially cotton. Alarmed by Abraham Lincoln's election as president, Louisiana seceded from the Union and was an independent republic for about two months before joining the Confederacy. Union forces seized control of New Orleans in 1862, occupying much of the state during the war. Some 24,000 Louisiana blacks joined Union forces, though quite a few 'free people of color' volunteered to fight for the Confederacy.

Louisiana was readmitted to the Union in 1868, after a new state constitution granted suffrage to blacks. The next 30 years saw political wrangling and economic stagnation, and in 1898 most blacks were effectively disenfranchised by the imposition of literacy tests and other impediments. In the early 20th century oil discovery gave the economy a boost, while the devastation of cotton crops by boll weevils forced some agricultural diversification. From the 1920s, autocratic governor Huey Long was able to modernize much of the state's infrastructure. Industry developed further after WWII. Tourism cashed in on the state's cultural heritage, but the tradition of unorthodox, volatile and sometimes ruthless politics continues today. Race and economics are ongoing sources of struggle – Louisiana has the second-highest per capita poverty rate in the US.

Information

State sale tax is 4%.

Louisiana Department of Culture, Recreation & Tourism (☎ 225-342-8119, 800-633-6970; www.louisianatravel.com; PO Box 94291, Baton Rouge, LA 70804-9291) You'll find Welcome Centers on freeways at state borders.

LOUISIANA FACTS

Nicknames Bayou State, Pelican State, Sportsman's Paradise

Population 4.5 million

Area 42,562 sq miles

Capital city Baton Rouge (population 227,800)

Official state reptile Alligator

Birthplace of Jazz, naturalist John James Audubon (1785–1851), trumpeter Louis 'Satchmo' Armstrong (1901–71), author Truman Capote (1924–84), musician Antoine 'Fats' Domino (b 1928), singer Jerry Lee Lewis (b 1935), singer Lucinda Williams (b 1953), pop star Britney Spears (b 1981)

Home of Tabasco sauce, chef Emeril Legasse

Famous for Creole and Cajun cooking, New Orleans' Mardi Gras

NEW ORLEANS

Naturally languid from the subtropical heat and humidity, New Orleans has long been a town where nothing ever goes too fast or grows too worrisome. In August, 2005, that changed, when Hurricane Katrina lashed the city and left residents scrambling for their lives (opposite). But even after her hardships, the town's unofficial motto and pervading gestalt is *Laissez les bons temps rouler* (Let the good times roll). Although 'the Big Easy' has seen its share of tough times, New Orleans will always be celebrated for its easygoing, laid-back vibe.

New Orleans has a vibrant, old-school panache that lends a certain dignity to otherwise debauched activities. It's a place that welcomes you out of your shell and it's easy to get drunk on the thick, alluring air. Partiers drink 'til they become immune on Bourbon St, where fellow revelers throw strings of beads from cast-iron balconies in appreciation of beautiful strangers passing below. The sonorous echoes of unbelievably sweet trad jazz, modern jazz, funky brass, R & B and soul music ooze from the French Quarter's Creole cottages, and dancing becomes a reaction, not a choice. Meanwhile succulent restaurant aromas recall a history infused with African, Spanish, French, Italian and Caribbean cultural influences.

It's a great city to walk around, anchored by the beguiling French Quarter and the adjoining *faubourgs* (false towns). Though its famous month long Mardi Gras celebration and the Jazz & Heritage Festival up the ante for craziness and fun, New Orleans is a blast anytime. In fact, it's the times when things are quiet – late afternoon when everyone is at the hotel getting ready to go out, early morning when the light explodes on the city and work crews come out to spray away last night's sins – that New Orleans reveals its many sober charms.

History

The town of Nouvelle Orléans was founded as a French outpost in 1718 by Jean Baptiste Le Moyne de Bienville. Early settlers arrived from France, Canada and Germany, and the French imported thousands of African slaves and ex-convicts from the jails of the mother country. Many slaves earned their freedom and assumed an established place in the Creole community

as *les gens de couleur libres* (free people of color). Unsuccessful in conventional commerce, the city developed a reputation for smuggling.

In 1762, the vast Louisiana territory, including New Orleans, was transferred to the Spanish, who were largely responsible for building the French Quarter as it still looks today. The French resumed control in 1800, but three years later Napoleon negotiated the Louisiana Purchase with the US. The resulting influx of Anglo Americans led to an expansion of the city into the Central Business District (CBD), Garden District and Uptown. By 1840 New Orleans was the nation's fourth-largest city, with more than 100,000 people.

New Orleans survived the Civil War intact after an early surrender to Union forces. However, the end of the plantation economy and the declining importance of river traffic hit New Orleans hard, and its economy languished until oil and petrochemical industries developed in the 1950s.

It is in New Orleans, some say, that jazz music was born at the end of the 19th century. If that claim is somewhat exaggerated, clearly New Orleans, more than any other place, contributed to the early development of the music.

Orientation

New Orleans is wedged between the Mississippi River to the south and Lake Pontchartrain to the north. The historic French Quarter (*Vieux Carré*) consists of 80 blocks around Jackson Sq. Canal St separates the Quarter from the CBD, which extends to the freeway overpass at Lee Circle.

Beyond that, following St Charles Ave, are the Lower Garden District, a ramshackle

---

WARNING:

The New Orleans section was researched before Hurricanes Katrina and Rita ravaged the coast. At the time this book went to press, the city was still in a state of emergency. While we've tried our best to capture the essence of the city and ensure the text is current and useful to travelers, we know that some things will change as New Orleans enters a long stage of recovery.

A CITY UNDERWATER

Everyone knew it was coming. Scientists predicted it, officials feared it and others knew it in their bones. On August 29, 2005, the Category 4 hurricane, forever remembered as Katrina, hit ground, spinning the Gulf into massive waves and spitting tornadoes that made houses and cars explode into bombs of wood, metal and glass.

When the storm passed, the eerie calm hovering over devastated New Orleans was replaced with utter panic. During and after the hurricane, several levees that held Lake Pontchartrain at bay ruptured. Water quickly rose as high as 20ft, flooding 80% of the city.

As temperatures soared, tepid water simmered into a sludgy gumbo of sewage, disintegrating landfill, snakes, rats and dead bodies. Residents, many of whom were poor, elderly or infirm, were trapped in submerged houses or left floating on rafts of debris.

Despite a 'mandatory evacuation' called just 24 hours before the storm, many residents stayed put, either unwilling or unable to leave. City officials transported some 25,000 residents to the Louisiana Superdome. Conditions at the overcrowded stadium, whose roof had been partially ripped off, became dire. The sick went untreated while backed-up sewage flooded into the building. Things were no better at the convention center, where people were stranded, starving and dying. As panic and fear gripped the city, some residents turned to looting and violence.

Outraged Americans watched as newscasts showed footage of the chaos and desperation. Why wasn't anyone doing anything to help? New Orleans' beleaguered mayor begged the federal government for aid and criticized the Bush administration for its slow and inadequate emergency response. Federal rescue efforts, bungled by poor management, bureaucracy and confusion, stuttered in the face of such massive devastation.

While government agencies and officials debated and finger-pointed, thousands of residents stuck in attics or on rooftops panicked, their skin wrinkled and pale from soaking in the toxic waters. Bodies piled up on city streets, in stairways and other makeshift morgues.

Finally, five days after the storm, help filtered in. Refugees crammed onto buses bound for Houston's Astrodome, where they received food, medical attention and a moment to figure out what next. Others fled to churches, shelters, and to family and friends. Similar havoc ensued in other parts of the Gulf Coast, in Mississippi and Alabama, where Katrina consumed whole towns or left them buried beneath rubble (p410).

As the world watched the drama unfold, Americans and foreigners alike opened their wallets and sent everything – from cash to cookies, toilet paper to toys – to disaster-relief organizations. They also opened their eyes, and what they saw left them gripped with helplessness and dismay.

Hurricane Katrina revealed more than nature's wrath. Her sheer force blew away and exposed the layers of New Orleans' – and the country's – facade. Her fury brought race, rampant poverty and disparity into focus, and thrust these issues into the eye of a building political storm. The lack of direction by organizations such as the Federal Emergency Management Agency (FEMA), left Americans wondering if they'd be safe and cared for in the face of tragedy; it left them asking if their own security depended on skin color and net worth.

Some people say rebuilding New Orleans is irresponsible. Even before the hurricane, the city sat, slowly sinking, 3ft below sea level. Each year, Mother Nature gnaws at the coastline, swallowing protective barrier islands, leaving the city vulnerable to wild coastal storms. Yet others argue that reconstruction is inevitable, perhaps even imperative. After all, the Big Easy is an essential ingredient in the nation's melting pot. It's a place hidden behind masks and costumes, with secret passageways and false doorways. It is a party, a poem, a song and a state of mind. Those are things no hurricane could ever blow away.

THE SOUTH

neighborhood with a bohemian enclave, and the lovely Garden District, well known for its historic homes.

St Charles Ave follows the hooked course of the river into Uptown and the Riverbend area (which is an area populated by many students of Tulane and Loyola universities).

The Tremé district, across Rampart St from the French Quarter, is a predominantly black residential district. Faubourg

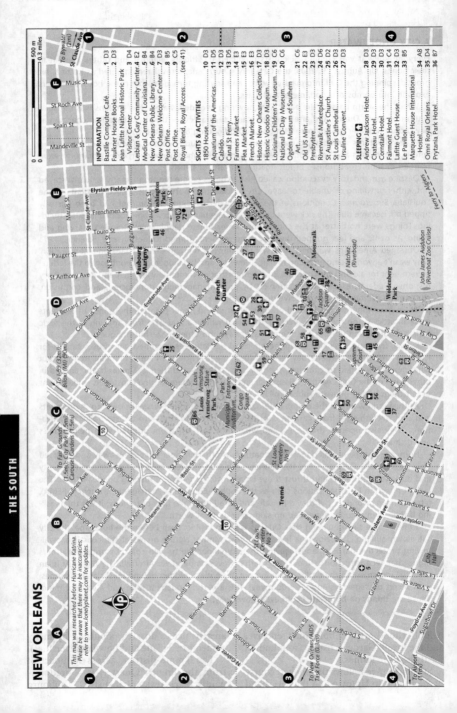

NEW ORLEANS

This map was researched before Hurricane Katrina; Please be aware that there may be inaccuracies; refer to www.lonelyplanet.com for updates.

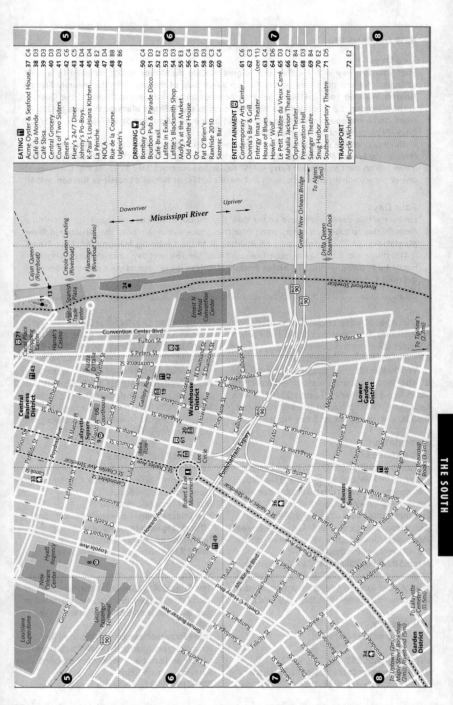

NEW ORLEANS IN...

Two Days

Start your first day with a coffee and beignet at **Café du Monde** (p423) followed by a walk to Jackson Sq and the visitor center. Pick up a free map of the city. Take the leisurely **French Quarter Walking Tour** (p419), to get your bearings and delight in the details of the Quarter. In the afternoon, sip a cocktail at a local bar, such as the **Lafitte's Blacksmith Shop** (p425). At night, don some good walking shoes and head back out to **Bourbon St** (p424). Drink, party, go crazy. Drink plenty of water before bed.

Did you drink the water? If so, your hangover is well under control. Start day two with a stroll through the **French Market** (opposite) to shop for souvenirs. Walk down to the Riverwalk and take a river trip on the **Canal Street Ferry** (p419). Return to your hotel. Take a nap. At night, indulge at one of the excellent restaurants, such as **Emeril's** (p424) or **K-Paul's Louisiana Kitchen** (p424).

Four Days

Follow the two-day itinerary, and on the third day get out of the city and search for gators on a must-do swamp tour or, if gators aren't your thing, take a driving tour of the **Mississippi River plantations** (p427). At night, stray off Bourbon St to the **Faubourg Marigny** (p425) or **Tremé** (p418) districts to listen to live music in a small local bar. The next day, savor the city's neighborhoods by hopping on the **St Charles Avenue streetcar** (p419). Spend your evening dining on delicious **Cajun cuisine** (p423).

Marigny, a creative enclave, is centered on Frenchmen St, downriver from the French Quarter. The rugged Bywater district of the city is even further downriver.

Workable maps of the city are available at the New Orleans Welcome Center in Jackson Sq (opposite). Lonely Planet's *New Orleans City Map* has all the key neighborhoods, a street index and key sights.

Information

BOOKSTORES

Beaucoup Books (☎ 504-895-2663; www.beaucoup books.com; 3951 Magazine St; ☺ 9:30-5:30 Mon-Sat) Contemporary authors read here and there's a wide selection of general-interest and regional titles.

Faulkner House Books (☎ 504-524-2940; www .faulknerhousebooks.us; 624 Pirate's Alley; ☺ 10am-6pm) This former residence of author William Faulkner sells rare first editions of Southern literature.

Maple Street Book Shop (☎ 504-866-4916; www .maplestreetbookshop.com; 7523 Maple St; ☺ 9am-9pm Mon-Sat, 10am-6pm Sun) Another independent bookstore Uptown, with the Children's Book Shop (p420) next door.

EMERGENCY
Emergency number (☎ 911)

INTERNET ACCESS
Bastille Computer Café (☎ 504-581-1150; www .bastille-computer-cafe.com; 605 Toulouse St; ☺ 10am-

11pm; per 30min $5) In the French Quarter, with high-speed, wi-fi, CD burners and photo editing.

New Orleans Public Library (☎ 504-529-7323; www .nutrias.org; 219 Loyola Ave; ☺ 10am-6pm Mon-Thu, to 5pm Fri & Sat) Near City Hall and offers free Internet access.

Royal Blend, Royal Access (☎ 504-525-0401; www .royalaccess.com; 621 Royal St; per 30min $5; ☺ 9am-8pm Sun-Thu, to 10pm Fri & Sat) In the French Quarter, one block off Bourbon St, with high speed, printing, faxing and CD burning.

INTERNET RESOURCES
The Lonely Planet website (www.lonely planet.com) offers a speedy link to many of New Orleans' websites.
Jazz Fest (www.nojazzfest.com)
New Orleans Online (www.neworleansonline.com)
Offbeat Magazine (www.offbeat.com)
Times-Picayune (www.nola.com)
WWOZ Radio (www.wwoz.org) Has great links.

MEDIA
New Orleans Magazine (www.neworleansmagazine .com) A monthly glossy, tourist-oriented rag that offers good-quality writing about the city's attractions and issues.

Times-Picayune (www.timespicayune.com) New Orleans' daily newspaper. It has a daily entertainment calendar and *Lagniappe*, an extensive entertainment guide that comes out every Friday.

WWOZ (90.7FM) Tune in here for Louisiana music.

MEDICAL SERVICES
Medical Center of Louisiana (☎ 504-903-2311; 1532 Tulane Ave)

New Orleans/AIDS Task Force (☎ 504-945-4000; 24hr hotline 504-821-6050; www.noaidstaskforce.org; 2601 Tulane Ave; ⊗ noon-4pm Mon, Fri & Sat, 4-8pm Tue & Thu)

POST
Post office CBD (610 S Maestri Pl; ⊗ 8:30-4:30 Mon-Fri); Main (☎ 800-275-8777; 701 Loyola Ave; ⊗ 7am-8pm Mon-Fri, 8am-5pm Sat) All mail sent to General Delivery, New Orleans, LA 70112, goes to the main branch.

TOURIST INFORMATION
Jean Lafitte National Historic Park Visitor Center (☎ 504-589-2636; www.nps.gov/jela; 419 Decatur St; ⊗ 9am-5pm) Operated by the NPS, with information on area national parks and sites.

New Orleans Welcome Center (☎ 504-566-3031; www.bigeasy.com; 529 St Ann St; ⊗ 9am-5pm) In the heart of the French Quarter overlooking Jackson Sq in the lower Pontalba Building, this visitor center provides lots of free information and maps. There are also smaller information kiosks throughout the French Quarter.

Dangers & Annoyances
New Orleans has a high violent-crime rate; it's not a city to be careless in. Stick to places that are well traveled and well peopled, particularly at night, and save some cash for a taxi fare to avoid dark walks. St Louis Cemetery No 1 and Louis Armstrong Park – in the Tremé district on the western edge of the French Quarter – have particularly bad reputations, even by daylight, and are more safely visited in groups (if you're not taking a tour, coincide your cemetery visit with tours).

In the Quarter, street hustlers frequently approach tourists, but you can just walk away.

Sights & Activities
FRENCH QUARTER
The whole French Quarter is a National Historic District. The NPS oversees architectural preservation, and rangers offer free walking tours. Stroll through the residential lower Quarter, with lacy ironwork balconies, brightly colored rows of shops, and fragrances wafting from flowerpots and lush pocket gardens. Then hit the upper Quarter, with bright lights and noisy bars along Bourbon St and the attractive antique shops and galleries on Royal St.

Jackson Square, in the heart of Vieux Carré, is the best starting point for visitors. The traditional symmetry of French and Spanish colonial architecture contrasts with modern cultural chaos; the square is filled with an assortment of street musicians, artists and tarot-card readers. 'Hippie Hill,' the levee overlooking the river end of the square, is a congregating point for youths, panhandlers and scam artists. The grand 1794 **St Louis Cathedral**, designed by Gilberto Guillemard, towers over the opposite end.

Several of the Quarter's sites are branches of the **Louisiana State Museum** (☎ 504-568-6968; http://lsm.crt.state.la.us; each bldg adult/child $5/free; ⊗ 9am-5pm Tue-Sun). Among them, the 1911 **Cabildo** (701 Chartres St) houses pre-Columbian artifacts, exhibits on the Battle of New Orleans, and shocking depictions of slavery. On the north side of the cathedral, the 1813 **Presbytère** (751 Chartres St) was designed as a rectory. It's now an excellent Mardi Gras museum, with vibrant displays of masks and costumes, parade floats, historic photos and documentary videos. Also part of the state museum, the **Old US Mint** (400 Esplanade Ave) struck coins in two periods between 1838 and 1910. Today, it carries exhibits on New Orleans jazz from its African roots in Congo Sq, an intelligent assemblage of memorabilia and photographs, as well as an array of coins and Confederate currency minted in New Orleans.

Historic New Orleans Collection (☎ 504-523-4662; 533 Royal St; admission free; ⊗ 9am-4:30pm Tue-Sun) is a complex of historic buildings anchored by Merieult House. A survivor of the 1794 fire, the house displays the original transfer documents of the Louisiana Purchase, as well as early maps and artifacts.

The fascinating **Historic Voodoo Museum** (☎ 504-523-7685; 724 Dumaine St; adult/child $7/3.50; ⊗ 10am-8pm) explores the exotic form of spiritual expression first brought to New Orleans by West African slaves who came via Haiti.

In 1728, 12 Ursuline nuns arrived in New Orleans to care for the French garrison's 'miserable little hospital' and to educate the young girls of the colony. Between 1745 and 1752, the French colonial army built the **Ursuline Convent** (☎ 504-529-3040; 1114 Chartres St; tours $5; ⊗ closed Mon), now the oldest structure in the French Quarter.

A trading junction since pre-Columbian times, the **French Market** (☎ 504-522-2621;

THE SOUTH

www.frenchmarket.org; from St Ann St to Barracks St; 9am-5pm) is composed of three different markets. The open-air **Farmers Market** has a good stock of fresh fruit, vegetables, kitchen supplies, hot sauces, garlic strings and cookbooks. Cafés, such as the enjoyable Café du Monde, have occupied the **Butcher's Market** since 1860. A great place for souvenirs, the **Flea Market** sells inexpensive Mardi Gras masks and dolls, beads and preserved alligator heads.

TREMÉ

On the western edge of the French Quarter, the Tremé district was New Orleans' first suburb, traditionally populated by black Creoles. The 1824 **St Augustine's Church** (504-525-5934; 1210 Governor Nicholls St) is the second-oldest African American Catholic church in the USA. Many jazz funeral processions can be seen leaving the church before parading through the streets.

One of New Orleans' more macabre attractions, **St Louis Cemetery No 1** (8am-3pm) received the remains of most early Creoles. The shallow water table necessitated aboveground burials, with bodies placed in family tombs or long rows of 'oven' vaults. Don't enter the cemetery alone; if the ghosts don't get you, the muggers might.

CBD & WAREHOUSE DISTRICT

The Central Business District (CBD) and Warehouse District comprise the commercial section established after the Louisiana Purchase in 1803. Later, artists moved into the Warehouse District following the 1984 Louisiana World Exposition.

Extending nearly half a mile along the Mississippi, the shop-till-you-drop **Riverwalk Marketplace** (504-522-1555; www.riverwalkmarketplace.com; 10am-9pm Mon-Thu, to 10pm Fri & Sat, to 7pm Sun) has an outdoor walkway

---

CARNIVAL & MARDI GRAS, NEW ORLEANS–STYLE

Mardi Gras, or 'Fat Tuesday,' began as a pagan rite of spring and evolved into pure bacchanalia. Catholics used it as a pre-Lenten celebration; later, Caribbean cultures used it to mock the aristocracy. Americans used the occasion to satirize Creole pretensions, and began to institutionalize Carnival in the late 19th century by establishing 'krewes' (men-only social clubs). In the 1950s, drag queens and gay masquerade balls became a popular mode of parody, and they are still a vital component of Mardi Gras.

Carnival

While most krewe balls held during Carnival season are exclusive events open only to members and guests, public celebrations, parades and partying start around two weeks before Mardi Gras, with nonstop frivolity. Most parades are held Uptown, along St Charles Ave to Canal St. The only krewe to parade through the French Quarter is the Krewe du Vieux, whose procession is three weeks before Mardi Gras.

Krewe parades usually feature a dozen or more tractor-drawn floats and marching bands. Crowds scramble for the souvenir 'throws' of beads, doubloons, condoms or candy. Dramatic nighttime parades feature flambeaux carriers wielding flaming torches. Following the Orpheus parade on Lundi Gras (Fat Monday), head for Woldenberg Park with your mask to the city-sponsored bash and fireworks display.

Mardi Gras

Before sunrise on the big day, the entire parade corridor along St Charles Ave is staked out with chairs, ladders and coolers. The Zulu Krewe parade moves out at dawn to its starting point at the statue of Martin Luther King Jr. At 8:30am, more than 30 floats and marching bands begin rolling down Jackson Ave toward St Charles Ave before going through the Tremé district.

Rex Krewe begins its elaborate procession at about 10am further up S Claiborne Ave at Napoleon Ave, then continues along St Charles Ave from Jackson Ave to Canal St. Trucks and throws follow the parade, and by mid-afternoon it's all beer and beads on Bourbon St. By the evening, a besotted mass of humanity is tightly wedged, dancing, on the street.

where you can watch the paddle wheelers and freighters plying the Mississippi. When Bienville founded New Orleans in 1718, this site was underwater, but shifts in the river's course enabled land reclamation east of the old warehouses that were once on the waterfront. Today, the massive air-conditioned space is filled with shops and a food court.

The free Canal Street Ferry, departing from the foot of Canal St from 6am until midnight, is the best way to admire the city from the traditional river approach. Steamboat tours (p421) also run up and down the river.

Aquarium of the Americas (☎ 504-581-4629; www.audoboninstitute.org; 1 Canal St; adult/child $16/9.50; 🕙 9am-5pm, occasionally later) simulates an eclectic selection of watery habitats, including the Mississippi River and Delta wetlands. You can buy combination tickets to the Imax theater (p425) next door and to the excellent Audubon Zoo in Uptown (boats from Woldenberg Park will take you there).

Ogden Museum of Southern Art (☎ 504-539-9600; www.ogdenmuseum.org; 925 Camp St; adult/child $10/5; 🕙 9:30am-5:30pm Tue-Sat, to 8pm Thu) began with the stellar collection of entrepreneur Roger Houston Ogden. The museum is affiliated with the Smithsonian Institute in Washington, DC, giving it access to that bottomless collection.

Half a world away from Normandy, the glassy **National D-Day Museum** (☎ 504-527-6012; www.ddaymuseum.org; 923 Magazine St; adult/child $14/6; 🕙 9am-5pm) is a worthwhile stop for its eyewitness accounts of the Allied invasion, planes, weaponry and landing craft.

GARDEN DISTRICT & UPTOWN

Following the Louisiana Purchase in 1803, subdivision of former plantation lands began in the Lower Garden District, and extended uptown following the steam railway on St Charles Ave, where the **St Charles Avenue streetcar** now runs. Many elegant mansions line the route, surrounded by live oaks and palms, lawns and lush, fragrant floral gardens.

Further west, Tulane and Loyola Universities occupy adjacent campuses in a more diverse area. Modest shotgun shacks sit next to multistory Arts and Crafts bungalows; Greek Revival mansions next to neo-Gothic campus buildings. Tulane was founded in

1834 as a medical college in an attempt to control repeated cholera and yellow-fever epidemics.

Among the country's best zoos, the **Audubon Zoological Gardens** (☎ 504-861-2537; www.audoboninstitute.org; 6500 Magazine St; adult/child $12/7; 🕙 9am-5pm) is the headquarters of the Audubon Institute, which also maintains the Aquarium of the Americas. Its ultracool Louisiana Swamp exhibit displays flora and fauna in a Cajun cultural setting, with alligators, bobcats, red foxes, black bears and snapping turtles. The nicest way to get there is by a zoo cruise from Woldenberg Park, downtown.

CITY PARK & FAIR GROUNDS

Besides hosting the regular horseracing season, the **Fair Grounds** are also the site of the huge springtime New Orleans Jazz & Heritage Festival (see p421). Acquired in 1850, the 1500-acre **City Park** (☎ 504-482-4888; www.neworleanscitypark.com) is famous for its huge moss-draped live oaks and scenic bayou lagoons, especially along the narrow strip fronting City Park Ave. During the aftermath of Hurricane Katrina, the park sat underwater. Once the city was drained, the park set about finding funds to clean up and reopen. The park has lots to offer, including an outdoor track and sports arena, tennis facilities, golf and the beautiful **Botanical Garden** (☎ 504-482-4888; adult/child $5/2; 🕙 10am-4:30pm Tue-Sun).

Also in City Park, the **New Orleans Museum of Art** (☎ 504-488-2631; www.noma.org; 1 Collins Diboll Circle; adult/child $8/4; 🕙 10am-5pm Tue-Sun, except 12:30-8:30pm Thu) was founded in 1910. It has three floors and a collection valued at $200 million.

Walking Tour: French Quarter

The French Quarter's narrow streets and passageways feature elegant architectural vestiges of the 18th-century Spanish colony. But the Quarter also has its mysterious charms, seen best at a leisurely pace.

Begin your walk at the **Presbytère** (**1**; p417) on Jackson Sq and head down Chartres St to the corner of Ursulines Ave and the **Ursuline Convent** (**2**; p417).

Directly across Chartres St, at No 1113, the 1826 **Beauregard-Keyes House (3)** combines Creole- and American-style design. Civil War General PGT Beauregard rented rooms

THE SOUTH

WALK FACTS

Distance: 1 mile
Duration: About 90 minutes

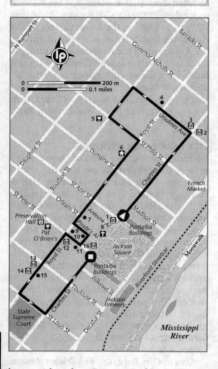

here, and author Francis Parkinson Keyes lived here from 1942 to 1970.

Walk along Ursulines Ave to Royal St and take a peek inside the **Royal Pharmacy (4)**. The soda fountain, a preserved relic from the USA's halcyon malt-shop days is no longer in use, but the owners of the pharmacy feel it's too classic to pull out.

Continue up Ursulines Ave and then left onto Bourbon St. The ramshackle one-story structure on the corner of St Philip St is a great little tavern and National Historic Landmark called **Lafitte's Blacksmith Shop (5**; p425). Head down St Phillip back to Royal St and take a right.

When it comes to classic New Orleans postcard images, Royal St takes the prize. Many of the buildings are graced by cast-iron galleries and plants hanging from balconies. Take it slowly and appreciate the details.

At No 915 the **Cornstalk Hotel (6**; p423) stands behind one of the most frequently photographed fences anywhere. At Orleans Ave, stately magnolia trees and lush tropical plants fill **St Anthony's Garden (7)**, behind **St Louis Cathedral (8**; p417).

Alongside the garden, **Pirate's Alley** is an inviting, shaded walkway that calls for a little detour. The first buildings to the right, Nos 622-624 Pirate's Alley, are just two of the **Labranche Buildings (9)**. Note the original wrought-iron balconies, some of the finest in town, which date to the 1840s. At 624 Pirate's Alley is the small but charming **Faulkner House Bookstore (10**; p416), so named because author William Faulkner briefly lived here in 1925.

Turn right down Cabildo Alley and then right up St Peter St, toward Royal St. At No 632 St Peter, the **Avart-Peretti House (11)** is where Tennessee Williams lived in 1946-47, when he wrote *A Streetcar Named Desire*.

When you reach the corner of Royal, take a look at **LeMonnier Mansion (12)**, at No 640, which is commonly known to be New Orleans' first 'skyscraper.' If you kept going up St Peter, you'd reach **Pat O'Brien's** (p425) and the rustic facade of **Preservation Hall** (p425).

Turn left on Royal St. At the corner of Royal and Toulouse Sts stand a pair of houses built by Jean François Merieult in the 1790s. The **Court of Two Lions (13)**, at 541 Royal St, has a gate on the Toulouse St side. Next door is the **Historic New Orleans Collection (14**; p417). Across the street, at No 520, a carriageway leads to the picturesque **Brulatour Courtyard (15)**.

On the next block, the massive 1909 **State Supreme Court Building** was the setting for many scenes in the movie *JFK*. The white marble and terra-cotta facade stands in attractive contrast with the rest of the Quarter.

Head down St Louis St to Chartres St and turn left. As Jackson Sq comes into view, you'll reach the Presbytère's near-identical twin, the **Cabildo (16**; p417). Have a seat on the benches in front. Relax and enjoy the lively street musicians.

New Orleans for Children

Apart from the **Audubon Zoo** (p419) and **Aquarium of the Americas** (p419), most children's activities are set apart from the city's major attractions for grown-ups. Check out the 'kid stuff' listings in the *Times-Picayune*'s Living section on Monday.

Carousel Gardens (☎ 504-482-4888; www.neworleans citypark.com; admission $2; ⊕ 11am-6pm) Kids can ride the renovated 1906 carousel at City Park. There are also other amusement park rides.

Children's Book Shop (☎ 504-861-2105; 7529 Maple St; ⊕ 10am-6pm) Operates cozy kids storytelling out of this wonderful bookstore next door to the Maple Street Bookstore (see p416).

Louisiana Children's Museum (☎ 504-523-1357; 420 Julia St; admission $6; ⊕ 9:30am-4:30pm Mon-Sat, from noon Sun) Some great hands-on exhibits. Children under 16 must be accompanied by an adult.

Tours

Check the *New Orleans Official Visitors Guide* for a full selection of the many available tours. The Jean Lafitte National Historic Park Visitor Center (p417) offers free walking tours of the French Quarter at 9:30am (show up at 9am).

Carriage ride (4 people per 30min from $50; ⊕ to midnight) The tourist cliché, a carriage ride through the French Quarter, is actually a great way to see the narrow streets at a gentle pace. The drivers are entertaining, if not always historically precise. Tours depart from Jackson Sq.

Friends of the Cabildo (☎ 504-523-3939; adult/child $10/free; tours 10am & 1:30pm Tue-Sun, 1:30pm Mon) Volunteers lead two-hour walking tours of the French Quarter. Tours start at the 1850 House Museum Store at 523 St Ann St.

Historic New Orleans Walking Tours (☎ 504-947-2120; www.tourneworleans.com; adult/child $15/7) These cemetery voodoo tours and haunted tours offer the most authenticity and humor. Call or check the website for times.

Steamboat Natchez (☎ 504-586-8777; www.steamboatnatchez.com) Taking a riverboat cruise is a neat way to see the city. You can do the Aquarium/Zoo

Cruise ($17/8.50 cruise only) or the two-hour Harbor/Jazz Cruise ($18.50/9.25; skip the onboard buffet lunch). Buy tickets at the boat dock behind JAX Brewery at the foot of Toulouse St.

Festivals & Events

New Orleans never needs an excuse to party and impromptu celebrations are frequent and often doused with a good bit of lunacy. It's not unusual to see a funeral procession burst into a jazz parade, or a quiet afternoon boil into a street party.

January & February

Sugar Bowl (www.sugarbowltickets.org) On or near January 1; two of the nation's top-ranked college football teams spar in the Superdome.

Carnival Just after New Year's Eve (no slouch celebration here), New Orleans residents break out the king cakes and spirits to begin celebrating Carnival, which culminates in the Mardi Gras madness.

Mardi Gras (www.mardigrasneworleans.com) In February or early March, Fat Tuesday marks the orgasmic finale of the Carnival season. Arthur Hardy's *Mardi Gras Guide* contains a good history along with detailed descriptions and maps of all parades.

March

Black Heritage Festival (☎ 504-827-0112) African American contributions to food and the arts are recognized, with citywide cultural events on the second weekend.

St Patrick's Day March 17 is a day of revelry, especially in the Irish Channel neighborhood near the Garden District.

Tennessee Williams Literary Festival Five days of literary events and parties celebrate the playwright's work at the end of March.

THE SOUTH

NEW ORLEANS JAZZ & HERITAGE FESTIVAL

New Orleans' second-biggest reason to party, 'Jazz Fest' began as a celebration of the city's 250th birthday in 1968. It attracted famous jazz players such as Louis Armstrong, Duke Ellington and Dave Brubeck. After struggling with poor attendance, Jazz Fest moved to the Fair Grounds in 1972. It expanded to two weekends in late April and early May and began showcasing different musical forms in addition to jazz. The event blossomed into what it is today: a feel-good musical smorgasbord served up on more than 10 stages.

Come hungry, as vendors' food booths overflow with in-season boiled crawfish, oyster and catfish po'boys, jambalaya and BBQ galore. Bring comfortable shoes, sunscreen, a hat, some water and a blanket for chilling out between concerts.

The Jazz Fest schedule comes out in January, and it's wise to make reservations as soon as possible. Daily passes cost $25 in advance or $35 at the gate. The Fair Grounds are open 11am to 7pm, but Jazz Fest continues well into the wee hours in bars and clubs throughout New Orleans.

For more information, contact the **New Orleans Jazz & Heritage Festival** (☎ 504-522-4786; www.nojazzfest.com; 1205 N Rampart St, New Orleans, LA 70116). Tickets are available through **Ticketmaster** (☎ 504-522-5555).

April & May
French Quarter Festival On the second weekend of April; music, tours and lots of street parties.
Jazz Fest From the last weekend of April to the first weekend of May; 10 days of music, food, crafts and fun (see p421).

July
Essence Music Festival (www.essence.com) Independence Day weekend sees star-studded performances at the Superdome.

August
Satchmo Fest From August 2–4, music and lectures honor the birthday of New Orleans' favorite son, Louis Armstrong.

September
Southern Decadence (www.southerndecadence.net) A huge gay, lesbian and transgender festival, including a leather block party, on Labor Day weekend.

October
Art for Arts Sake (www.magazinestreet.com, www .cacno.org) In the first week; scores of galleries and studios are open in the Warehouse District and along Magazine St.
Louisiana Swampfest (www.auduboninstitute.org) On the first two weekends, the Audubon Institute celebrates Cajun food, music, culture and critters.

December
Feux de Joie On December 24, 'fires of joy' light the way along the Mississippi River levees.

New Year's Eve Baby New Year is dropped from the roof of Jackson Brewery at midnight on December 31.

Sleeping
Room rates peak during Mardi Gras and Jazz Fest, but in the hot summer months prices fall by as much as 50%. The prices below are high-season nonfestival rates. Book as soon as you know you'll be going and be sure to call around for special deals. Hotel sales tax amounts to 13%, plus $1 per person per night. Beware, too, that hotels charge $15 to $25 per day for parking.

BUDGET
Prytania Park Hotel (☎ 504-524-0427, 888-498-7591; www.prytaniaparkhotel.com; 1525 Prytania St; r from $50; P ⊠ ⊠ ⊡) This incredible value option, just a block from the streetcar line in the Garden District, has the charm of a European-style guesthouse. It has 49 small but warm, honey-colored rooms that vary in price and capacity, with refrigerators and microwaves, wi-fi, free parking and a shuttle to the French Quarter.

Marquette House International Hostel (☎ 504-523-3014; hineworlns@aol.com; 2249 Carondelet St; dm $18, r $40-76; P ⊠ ⊠ ⊡) This 176-bed facility on the edge of the Garden District consists of four buildings that are kept impressively clean. Private rooms range in

---

GAY & LESBIAN NEW ORLEANS
New Orleans' gay community revolves around the lower French Quarter and the Faubourg Marigny. The **Lesbian & Gay Community Center** (LGCC; ☎ 504-945-1103; 2114 Decatur St) is a great resource for travelers or anyone thinking of moving to the Big Easy. You can also find out about special events, the hottest bars and the gay-friendly businesses.

One of the highlights of gay New Orleans is the annual **Southern Decadence** (www.southern decadence.net), a festival that mixes mainstream corporate sponsors with events like the legendary banana-sucking contest. For five days, beginning at midnight the Wednesday before Labor Day weekend (the first weekend in September), upwards of 120,000 gay, lesbian, transgender and 'other' revelers converge on the Big Easy for a literal orgy of partying.

If you miss out on the festival, fear not. There's still plenty of nightlife left. Check out **Ambush Magazine** (www.ambushmag.com). Gay-friendly bars of note include the following.
Oz (☎ 504-593-9491; www.ozneworleans.com; 800 Bourbon St; cover $5; ☽ 24hr) Even Uptown debs have been seen shaking their tail feathers at this mixed dance club. The bar is manned by buff, shirtless bartenders. In the wee hours, clothing becomes more of a concept than a reality.
Lafitte in Exile (☎ 522-8397; www.lafittes.com; 901 Bourbon St; no cover; ☽ 24hr) Easily the most popular gay bar in the Quarter. The balcony is superb and the drink specials just keep coming.
Bourbon Pub & Parade Disco (☎ 504-529-2107; www.bourbonpub.com; 801 Bourbon St; cover free-$5; ☽ 24hr) The party spills out onto the sidewalk at this popular dance and video club.
Rawhide 2010 (☎ 504-525-8106; www.rawhide2010.com; 740 Burgundy St; ☽ 24hr) Rawhide is – surprise! – a rollicking good-time leather bar.

price and size; all include refrigerators and microwaves, and some include kitchenettes. Picnic tables in the backyard are an ideal place to meet fellow travelers. Internet access is available in the lobby, and there are two laundries nearby.

MIDRANGE

Le Pavillon (☎ 504-581-3111, 800-535-9095; www .lepavillon.com; 833 Poydras Ave; r from $140; P ❌ ☎) Built in 1907, this elegant European-style hotel offers an opulent marble lobby, plush, modern rooms and a rooftop pool. During slow times you can get unbelievable deals; it's worth a call ahead. Parking costs $25.

Lafitte Guest House (☎ 504-581-2678, 800-331-7971; www.lafitteguesthouse.com; 1003 Bourbon St; r $180-230; P ❌ ☎) An elegant, 1848 three-story French manor house that offers 14 rooms near enough to, but far enough away from, the partying part of Bourbon St. The standout rooms include No 5, with a steep spiral staircase to the loft bedroom, and No 40, occupying the entire top floor. Parking costs $15.

Cornstalk Hotel (☎ 504-523-1515; 800-759-6112; www.cornstalkhotel.com; 915 Royal St; r incl breakfast $145-185; P ❌ ❌) The Cornstalk's famous cast-iron fence is possibly the most-photographed fence in the USA. The old house offers a serene atmosphere in the thick of the Quarter. Its 14 rooms boast high ceilings, antique furnishings, including canopy beds. Parking costs $15.

Andrew Jackson Hotel (☎ 504-561-5881, 800-654-0224; www.andrewjacksonhotel.com; 919 Royal St; r $100-195; ❌ ❌) Next door to the Cornstalk, this 22-room guesthouse has spacious, comfortable rooms overlooking the street and the charming inner courtyard glows at night.

TOP END

Omni Royal Orleans (☎ 504-529-5333, 800-843-6664; www.omniroyalorleans.com; 621 St Louis St; P ❌ ☐ ☎) An all-white marble lobby and other palatial accoutrements pay homage to the lodging's roots as a meeting place for 19th-century sugar planters. More marble appears in each of the 346 rooms, and there's a rooftop pool. There's also an activities program for kids. Parking costs $25.

Fairmont Hotel (☎ 504-529-7111, 800-257-7544; www.fairmont.com; 123 Baronne St; r from $250; P ❌ ☐ ☎) With its majestic block-long lobby, this elegant hotel has long been

among the city's best since the 1920s. Rooms are nicely remodeled and the swanky Sazerac Bar (p425) is a great place to spend cocktail hour. The outdoor rooftop pool offers an impressive downtown view. Parking costs $25.

Eating

Eating is a major activity in New Orleans, with the indigenous Creole and Cajun cooking plus flavors from Italy, Mexico and the Caribbean, and a mouthwatering selection of snack foods. With its strong French influences and a taste for liquid refreshment, this is a city that enjoys its food and drink. You have to resort to street parking at most restaurants.

FRENCH QUARTER

Café du Monde (☎ 504-581-2914; 800 Decatur St; beignets $2.50; ☾ 24hr) This New Orleans institution keeps its prices low despite its proximity to the French Market and Jackson Sq. It's a great place to kick off a morning café au lait and yummy beignets (sweet pastries dusted with powdered sugar).

Johnny's Po-Boys (☎ 504-524-8129; 511 St Louis St; mains $4-8; ☾ 8am-4:30pm Mon-Fri, 9am-4pm Sat & Sun) Well-worn, Johnny's delivers superb stuffed po'boys. The fried oyster number (lightly breaded in cornmeal) will turn a raw oyster purist into a devotee.

Acme Oyster & Seafood House (☎ 504-522-5973; 724 Iberville St; mains $6-10; ☾ 11am-late) Both out-of-towners and locals alike flock to this old-school oyster bar – its reputation for shucking the city's best oysters, along with seafood gumbo and po'boys, has lasted since its inception in 1910. Take a seat at the bar and you'll soon get mesmerized by the shuckers.

THE SOUTH

Central Grocery (☎ 504-523-1620; 923 Decatur St; sandwiches $6-8; 8am-5:30pm Mon-Sat, from 9am Sun) The *muffaletta* sandwich was invented by a Sicilian immigrant here way back in 1906. Today, it's still the best place in town to get the sandwich, a round, seeded loaf of bread filled with ham, salami and provolone and drizzled with oily olive relish.

Café Sbisa (☎ 504-522-5565; 1011 Decatur St; mains $20-40; 5:30-10:30pm Sun-Thu, to 11pm Fri & Sat, brunch 10:30am-3pm Sun) This venerable Vieux Carré institution has the glamour of a Hollywood grande dame – a little flash and a lot of grace. The patio overlooks Decatur St, while the indoor dining room has a view of the mural over the bar. The menu earns repeated kudos for innovative takes on Creole cuisine. The Sunday jazz brunch is also a crowd pleaser.

Court of Two Sisters (☎ 504-522-7261; www.cour toftwosisters.com; 613 Royal St; 9am-3pm, 5:30-10pm) If you want to try all of New Orleans' signature dishes, then come here for the daily jazz brunch. Sample over 80 dishes, from boiled crawfish to shrimp rémoulade, on the pleasant wisteria-shaded patio. Nothing's a standout, but you'll leave sated and smiling.

K-Paul's Louisiana Kitchen (☎ 504-596-2530; 416 Chartres St; dinner mains $26-36) Chef Paul Prudhomme started this popular restaurant in the 1980s. Its popularity has skyrocketed with Louisiana Creole and Cajun favorites like jambalaya and gumbo with spicy andouille sausages.

La Péniche (☎ 504-943-1460; 1940 Dauphine St; burgers $6-10; 24hr Tue-Thu) This popular late-night dinner spot in the Faubourg Marigny serves greasy diner fare but gets interesting

---

BEST DRESSED

Po'boys are New Orleans' version of the submarine sandwich. A crusty French bread loaf is hollowed out and stuffed with just about anything: fried oysters, traditional lunch meats, French fries or all of the above. Po'boy is a shortened version of 'poor boy,' a name earned during the Depression, when the sandwiches cost only a quarter. The po'boy comes in whole and half sizes, either of which can feed a hungry brass band. Ask for it 'dressed' to get lettuce, tomato and mayo.

THE AUTHOR'S CHOICE

NOLA (☎ 504-522-6652; 534 St Louis St; mains $15-25; lunch Mon-Sat, dinner nightly) Chef Emeril Lagasse's personality is on display at this larger-than-life Quarter hot spot, the least pretentious of the master's three New Orleans restaurants. NOLA offers impeccable service, an excellent atmosphere and delicious fish, meats and wine. Grab one of the counter seats overlooking the kitchen if you're dining solo and want some fun. Reservations are essential.

---

late at night when partiers from the Quarter start trickling in.

CBD & WAREHOUSE DISTRICT

Emeril's (☎ 504-528-9393; www.emerils.com; 800 Tchoupitoulas St; mains $22-38; lunch Mon-Fri, dinner nightly) Built in an old warehouse space, this flagship restaurant for chef Emeril Lagasse continues to be a top place for dining out. Despite the fact the famous chef is rarely there, the kitchen consistently serves up delicious Creole Bam!-worthy fare.

Huey's 24/7 Diner (☎ 504-598-4839; 200 Magazine St; mains $6-10; 24hr) Ready for some killer breakfast chow after a night at the bars? At Huey's you can have some top-notch fare and let the night roll on as the bar here never closes. Less boozy options include malts, which go down well with the piled-high sandwiches.

GARDEN DISTRICT & UPTOWN

Rue de la Course (baked goods $2-4; 7:30am-11pm) Garden District (☎ 504-529-1455; 1500 Magazine St); Uptown (☎ 504-899-0242; 3128 Magazine St) Both locations of this comfortable coffeehouse are great for ducking out of the rain to read a magazine while sipping coffee.

Uglesich's (☎ 504-523-8751; 1238 Baronne St; mains $8-15; 11am-2pm Mon-Fri) A funky lunchtime favorite, family run since 1924. Here you will find authentic Louisiana cuisine served without the trappings of most tourist-oriented restaurants. Try the terrific oysters or seafood specials such as crawfish bisque.

Drinking

It doesn't matter what time of year it is, the elasticity of your budget or how early you go to bed – New Orleans keeps its carnival atmosphere stoked round the clock year-round. Nonstop music spills out of clubs and bars, luring passersby in for one more drink. You can get plastic 'go cups' at any bar; it's legal to drink in the streets but illegal to have open glass containers. Most bars and pubs feature live music – jazz trios or acoustic soloists.

Bombay Club (☎ 504-586-0972; 830 Conti St; no cover; ☯ 5pm-late) The most cultured place for a drink in the Quarter.

Cafe Brasil (☎ 504-949-0851; 2100 Chartres St; cover $5; ☯ 6pm-2am Sun-Thu, to 4am Fri & Sat) Where a hip, bohemian crowd dances to reggae, Latin jazz and acoustic bands.

Lafitte's Blacksmith Shop (☎ 504-523-0066; 941 Bourbon St; no cover; ☯ noon-3am) This well-worn corner bar whose lighting comes strictly from candles has a sing-along piano in the back.

Sazerac Bar (☎ 504-529-7111; 123 Baronne St; no cover; ☯ 11am-midnight Sun-Thu, to 1am Fri & Sat) In the Fairmont Hotel, a real classic with gorgeous art-deco murals.

Molly's at the Market (☎ 504-525-5169; 1107 Decatur St; no cover; ☯ 10am-6am) The Irish cultural center of the French Quarter serves Guinness and pub grub to a diverse mix of local characters.

Old Absinthe House (☎ 504-523-3181; 240 Bourbon St; no cover; ☯ 11am-late) Though absinthe was outlawed in 1914 because of its insanity-inducing effects, this local joint keeps the absinthe memories alive.

Pat O'Brien's (☎ 504-525-4823; 718 Peter St; no cover; ☯ 10am-4am) The sugary sweet Hurricane was developed here, where a labyrinthine series of alcoves links Bourbon St and St Peter St in a continuous party.

Entertainment

Generations of New Orleans club owners have thrived by promoting a combination of music and booze. The free monthly *Offbeat* and weekly *Gambit* are your best sources for reviews and performances. **Ticketmaster** (☎ 504-522-5555) has several outlets in New Orleans.

LIVE MUSIC

In the French Quarter, live jazz, blues, Dixieland, zydeco and Cajun music emanate from clubs along upper Bourbon St. Clubs on the Quarter's riverfront present bigger headline acts, while smaller venues on the Quarter's periphery offer live brass bands and jazz trios. 'Kitty' clubs provide musicians with an opportunity to jam and pass the hat, especially in the Tremé district.

Donna's Bar & Grill (☎ 504-596-6914; 800 N Rampart St; cover $7-10; ☯ from 6:30pm) All the best jazz musicians book gigs here and when they're not booked, they'll often stop by to jam.

House of Blues (☎ 504-529-2583; 255 Decatur St; cover $7-25) One of the best live-music venues in town for big-name acts. The calendar fills with fine rock, country and alternative acts. The Sunday Gospel Brunch will fortify your soul.

Howlin' Wolf (☎ 504-523-2551; 828 S Peters St; cover $5-20; ☯ showtimes vary) This Warehouse District club attracts local talent as well as touring rock and alt-rock bands.

Preservation Hall (☎ 504-522-2841; 726 St Peter St; cover $5; ☯ from 8pm) A veritable museum of traditional and Dixieland jazz, Preservation Hall is a pilgrimage. But like many religious obligations, it ain't necessarily easy, with no air-conditioning, limited seating and no refreshments (you can bring your own water, that's it).

Snug Harbor (☎ 504-949-0696; 626 Frenchmen St; cover $10-20; ☯ shows at 9pm & 11pm) This club in Faubourg Marigny is the city's premier contemporary jazz venue.

Tipitina's (☎ 504-895-8477; 501 Napoleon Ave; cover $10-50; ☯ from 7pm) This legendary music club offers a mix of jazz, blues, soul and funk bands.

SPORTS

Louisiana Superdome (☎ 504-587-3810 www.super dome.com; 1500 Sugar Bowl Dr; tickets $22-50) The 60,000-seat superdome is home to the NFL New Orleans Saints and every few years it hosts the Super Bowl. In January, the Superdome hosts the NCAA (college) Sugar Bowl.

THEATER & CINEMA

Contemporary Arts Center (☎ 504-528-3800; www .cacno.org; 900 Camp St; tickets from $10) The premier venue for modern plays, dance, performance art and film.

Entergy Imax Theatre (☎ 504-581-4629; 1 Canal St; adult/child $8/6) Next to the Aquarium of the Americas, shows films on a 74ft by 54ft screen.

Le Petit Théâtre du Vieux Carré (☎ 504-522-2081; www.lepetittheatre.com; 616 St Peter St) One of the oldest theater groups in the US. Classic and contemporary Southern plays.

Orpheum Theater (☎ 504-524-3285; www.orph eumneworleans.com; 129 University Pl) From September to May the **Louisiana Philharmonic Orchestra** (☎ 504-523-6530; www.lpomusic.com; 225 Baronne St; tickets $10-40) performs here. New Orleans' concertgoers are proud of their orchestra, one of only two musician-owned symphonies in the world.

Mahalia Jackson Theatre of the Performing Arts (☎ 504-565-7470; Armstrong Park) This theater houses the renowned **New Orleans Opera Association** (www.neworleansopera.org) and **New Orleans Ballet** (www.nobadance.com).

Saenger Theatre (☎ 504-524-2490; www.saenger theatre.com; 143 N Rampart St) Broadway productions and classic films play at this finely restored 1927 theater.

Southern Repertory Theatre (☎ 504-861-8163; www.southernrep.com; 3rd fl, Canal Pl Shopping Center, 333 Canal Pl) Presents classic and contemporary Southern plays.

Getting There & Away

Louis Armstrong New Orleans International Airport (MSY ☎ 504-464-0831; www.flymsy.com; 900 Airline Hwy), 11 miles west of the city, handles mostly domestic flights.

Greyhound (☎ 800-231-2222, in Spanish ☎ 800-531-5332) buses run from the **Union Passenger Terminal** (☎ 504-524-7571; 1001 Loyola Ave). Regular services to Baton Rouge ($17, two hours), Memphis ($510, 8¼ hours) and Nashville, TN ($52, 13 to 16 hours), and Atlanta, GA ($74, 10 hours).

Amtrak (☎ 504-528-1610, 800-872-7245) trains also operate from the Union Passenger Terminal. The *City of New Orleans* runs to Jackson, MS; Memphis, TN; and Chicago, IL. The *Crescent Route* serves Birmingham, AL; Atlanta, GA; Washington, DC; and New York City. New Orleans is also on the *Sunset Limited* route between Los Angeles, CA and Miami, FL.

Getting Around

TO/FROM THE AIRPORT

There's an information booth at the airport's A&B concourse. **Airport Shuttle** (☎ 504-522-3500, 866-596-2699; one way per person $13; ☷ 4am-11pm) runs frequent shuttles to downtown hotels. The **Louisiana Transit Company** (☎ 504-818-

1077) runs the **Jefferson Transit Airport Express** (☎ 504-737-7433; adult $1.60) on route E2, which picks up outside airport entrance 7 on the airport's upper level; it stops along Airline Hwy (Hwy 61) on its way into town.

Taxis downtown cost $28 for one or two people, $12 more for each additional passenger.

CAR & MOTORCYCLE

Bringing a car to downtown New Orleans is often a costly proposition and may actually hinder your visit, dealing with the narrow one-way streets, congestion and parking. During daytime, street parking has a two-hour limit. Parking garages in the upper (southern) part of the Quarter charge about $5 for the first hour, or $20 for 24 hours. Bigger hotels can make special arrangements for motorcycle parking, but call first to inquire.

PUBLIC TRANSPORTATION

The **Regional Transit Authority** (RTA; ☎ 504-248-3900; www.norta.com) runs the local bus service. Fares are $1.25, plus 25¢ for transfers; express buses cost $1.50. Exact change is required. RTA Visitor Passes for one/three days cost $5/12.

The RTA also operates two streetcar lines. One of the best ways to see the city beyond the Quarter is to take the St Charles Ave Streetcar Tour, which links the Quarter with the CBD, the Lower Garden and Garden Districts, Uptown and Riverbend. Catch the streetcar at the corner of St Charles Ave and Common St. It costs $1.25 each way and the round-trip takes about 90 minutes. The Riverfront Line has vintage red streetcars running 2 miles from the Old US Mint, past Canal St, to the upriver convention center and back.

For a taxi, call **White Fleet Cabs** (☎ 504-948-6605) or **United Cabs** (☎ 504-522-9771).

Rent bicycles at **Bicycle Michael's** (☎ 504-945-9505; www.bicyclemichaels.com; 622 Frenchmen St; rentals per hr/day $7.50/20; ☷ 10am-7pm Mon-Sat, to 5pm Sun, closed Wed), in Faubourg Marigny.

AROUND NEW ORLEANS

New Orleans is a beguiling – and exhausting – city. When cannot face another plate of jambalaya, and the thought of one more Hurricane cocktail sets your stomach churning, head for the hinterlands. New Orleans is surrounded by alligator swamps, bayous, antebellum plantation homes and lively Cajun communities.

Along **Lake Ponchartrain**'s north shore, browse through the hip antique stores in cool, artsy **Covington** or take a nature retreat at **Fontainebleau State Park** (☎ 504-624-4443), a 2700-acre gem on the lakeshore near Mandeville, with nature trails, plantation ruins, a sandy beach, a swimming pool, picnic areas and campsites. Head north of Mandeville and sip a microbrew in the bucolic village of **Abita Springs**, which was popular in the late 1800s as a spot to bask in what were thought to be curative waters. Today, the springwater still flows from a fountain in the center of the village, and the primary liquid attraction here is the **Abita Brewery** (☎ 985-893-3143; 21084 Hwy 36), just a mile or so west of town.

South of New Orleans, the Mississippi River flows 90 miles to the swampy environment of the 'bird's foot' delta. Go 12 miles west on Hwy 90 and you'll hit **Westwego**, which has a huge open-air fish market ringed by earthy shacks, plus the intimate, family-run **Chacahoula Swamp Tours** (☎ 504-436-2640; 422 Louisiana St; with/without transportation from New Orleans $38/22). The two-hour tours begin daily at 9am; if you need a ride from New Orleans, call ahead and they'll pick you up at your hotel around 8am.

Barataria Preserve

A great way to learn about swamplands is to visit this unit of the Jean Lafitte National Historic Park. Set in an area originally settled by Isleños (Canary Islanders) in 1779, it offers hiking and canoe trips into the swamp and a good introduction to the wetlands environment. Even a brief walk on the boardwalks that wend their way through the swamp will yield sightings of gators and egrets.

Start at the **NPS Visitors Center** (☎ 504-589-2330; Hwy 3134; ✆ 9am-5pm), 1 mile west of Hwy 45, where you can pick up a map or join a ranger-led walk.

Bayou Barn (☎ 504-689-2663; canoes per 2hr $15; dance admission $5; ✆ Tue-Sun) rents canoes. It's on the Bayou de Familles just outside the park, and is a pleasantly funky restaurant compound of tin-topped weatherbeaten buildings on the opposite side of the intersection. Cajun or zydeco bands play to lively local crowds at dances held most Sundays from noon to 6pm.

River Road

Elaborate plantation homes line the east and west banks of the Mississippi River between New Orleans and Baton Rouge. First indigo, then cotton, rice and sugarcane brought great wealth to these plantations, many of which are open to the public as historic sites, usually with costumed guides leading 45- to 60-minute tours. Many present a romantic picture of plantation life, focusing on the lovely architecture, ornate gardens and genteel lifestyle of antebellum Louisiana. Most gloss over the story of plantation slaves, who lived in relative squalor.

Be sure to round out a plantation tour with a visit to the **River Road African-American Museum & Gallery** (☎ 225-474-5553; www.africanamerican museum.org; 406 Charles St, Donaldsonville; museum/walking tour $4/25; ✆ 9am-5pm Wed-Sat, from 1pm Sun) The important history of African Americans in Louisiana is told in this excellent museum, in the historic town of Donaldsonville. In addition to exhibits about plantation slavery and the slaves' journey to freedom via the underground railroad, museum director Kathe Hambrick gives walking tours (complete with lunch) of Donaldsonville, which was a prosperous city for Blacks after the Civil War.

It's easy enough to explore the region by car, and organized tours are widely available from New Orleans. Check at the visitor centers for the range of tours. Tour prices at the plantations are mostly $10 for adults, $5 for children.

PLANTATIONS

Laura Plantation (☎ 225-265-7690; 2247 Hwy 18; ✆ 9:30am-5pm) at Vacherie is an unassuming French Creole plantation built in 1905. Unlike other tours, this ever-evolving and popular plantation doesn't gloss over the role of slavery; you get a good picture of what life was like for both master and slave via accounts from the lives of the Creole women who ran the place for generations. In 2004, a devastating electrical fire damaged most of the house, but extensive restorations are under way and the tour is still the best of the plantation tours.

Oak Alley Plantation (☎ 225-265-2151; www.oak alleyplantation.com; 3645 Hwy 18; ✆ 9am-5pm) A dramatic approach, with a 0.25-mile canopy of 28 majestic live oaks lining the entry, leads to this grand Greek Revival–style house.

Nottoway Plantation (☎ 225-545-2730; www .nottoway.com; Hwy 1; adult/child $10/5; ☼ 9am-5pm; d incl breakfast mansion $210-235, wing $150-175, cottage $160) Closer to Baton Rouge, this the largest plantation house in the South, with 64 rooms and 53,000 sq ft. You can also stay overnight at the plantation, which is a real treat as you essentially get the run of the place at night. You can stay in the mansion, in the boy's wing or girl's wing, or in the overseer's cottage; the rate includes a plantation breakfast, refreshments and a tour.

Baton Rouge

French explorers named this area *baton rouge* (red stick) after the cypress poles Native Americans painted with blood and staked in the ground to mark the boundaries of their hunting grounds. An industrial town with a bustling port and the state capital, otherwise lethargic Baton Rouge has two universities, the tallest capital building in the nation, a few casinos and a riverfront entertainment complex.

Most attractions are downtown, off I-110. Louisiana State University (LSU) is in the southwest quadrant of the city. Highland Rd is the main thoroughfare, while Perkins Rd has many restaurants and shops north and south of I-10. The **convention & visitor center** (☎ 225-346-1253, 800-527-6843; www .batonrougetour.com; 730 North Blvd; ☼ 8am-5pm Mon-Fri) has maps.

SIGHTS

The 'new' **Louisiana State Capitol** (☎ 225-342-7317; tours free; ☼ 8am-4:30pm) building, on State Capitol Dr, is an art-deco skyscraper built at the height of the Great Depression to the tune of $5 million; it's populist governor 'Kingfish' Huey Long's most visible legacy. A tour is worthwhile, and the 27th-floor **observation deck** has a great view. The **Old State Capitol** (☎ 225-342-0500; admission free; 100 N Blvd; ☼ 10am-4pm Tue-Sat, from noon Sun) is a neo-Gothic structure overlooking the river, with exhibits and multimedia presentations about Huey Long and the state's colorful political history.

SLEEPING

Unfortunately, your best bet for accommodations in Baton Rouge are in the many chain hotels that cater to the business traveler.

Embassy Suites (☎ 225-924-6566; 4914 Constitution Ave; r incl breakfast Mon-Thu $110, Fri-Sun $130; P ⊠ ⌨ ☒) One of the nicest in the city, this hotel has big standard rooms and two-room suites with galley kitchens and wi-fi throughout. The indoor pool has a whirlpool and sauna.

Comfort Inn University (☎ 225-236-4000, www .choicehotels.com; 2445 S Acadian Thruway; r incl breakfast $80-100; P ☒ ⌨) In a good location just a mile from LSU, this 150-room hotel has modern rooms with refrigerators and coffeemakers. There are laundry facilities, too.

EATING & ENTERTAINMENT

Petit Marché (☎ 225-267-4008; 501 Main St; mains $6; ☼ 8am-5pm Mon-Sat, to 2pm Sun) Local celebrity chef Mark Folse runs this café in the Main Street Market on 5th and Main. The lunch buffet ($6) is loaded with Louisiana specialties. There's also a good take-out menu.

Louie's Cafe (☎ 225-346-8221; 209 W State St; breakfast $6-10; ☼ 24hr) Near LSU, Louie's is the best 24-hour eatery in town, with 1950s ambience and delicious omelettes served with hash browns. Lots of veggie options here, too.

Phil's Oyster Bar (☎ 225-924-3045; 5162 Government St; oysters $8-12; ☼) Oyster shuckers keep up a steady banter as they slide dozens of oysters down the bar to waiting customers. Phil's also serves up seafood and Italian fare.

Varsity Theatre (☎ 225-383-7018; www.varsity theatre.com; 3353 Highland Rd; ☼ 8pm-2am) *The* place for live music, from local bands to big-name acts like Wilco and Tori Amos.

GETTING THERE & AWAY

Traveling from New Orleans, I-12 merges into I-10 on the eastern edge of Baton Rouge, at which point I-10 continues west toward Lafayette. Driving the 80 miles from New Orleans takes about 90 minutes.

North of the city off I-110, the **Baton Rouge Metropolitan Airport** (☎ 225-355-0333) is served by regional airlines. **Greyhound** (☎ 225-383-3811; 1253 Florida Blvd at N 12th St) has regular buses to Atlanta, Birmingham, Lafayette and New Orleans.

CAJUN COUNTRY

This part of southern Louisiana, stretching from the Mississippi River to the Texas border, is home to the largest French-speaking

THE SOUTH

minority in the US. The region is named for French settlers exiled by the British in 1755 from L'Acadie (now Nova Scotia, Canada), who sought refuge in Louisiana but were shunted to the western swamplands. Houma and Chitimacha Indians taught their new neighbors to trap, fish, hunt and eat crawfish. These Indians corrupted 'Acadian' to 'Cagian,' and hence 'Cajun.'

Between 1916 to 1956 the state government banned French language in schools – a period called the *Heure de la Honte* (Time of Shame). In WWII, Acadian soldiers fighting in France became valuable interpreters, and GIs returned with seeds of renewed cultural pride. In a complete reversal of earlier policies, the Council for the Development of French in Louisiana (Codofil) began fostering the local language and culture.

The logical starting point is Lafayette, 130 miles west of New Orleans, but the real Cajun experience is found in small towns, bayous and rural back roads. Cajun and zydeco music rocks out at bars and restaurants, *fais-do-do* (Cajun dances) are mostly held on weekends, and Cajun food (jambalaya, crawfish étouffée, shrimp bisque) is available everywhere.

Lafayette

This small friendly city isn't overflowing with tourism draws and its old downtown struggles for definition somewhere between decline and renewal. But Lafayette is real, a place totally happy with itself. The University of Louisiana at Lafayette (ULL), with 17,000 'Ragin' Cajuns,' gives Lafayette some college-town vitality. The city makes a convenient base for exploring the area.

From I-10, exit 103A, the Evangeline Thruway (Hwy 167) goes to the center of town via the **visitor center** (☎ 337-232-3737, 800-346-1958; 1400 NW Evangeline Thruway; ⏰ 8:30am-5pm Mon-Fri, from 9am Sat & Sun).

SIGHTS & ACTIVITIES

The best NPS museum in Cajun Country is the **Acadian Cultural Center** (☎ 337-232-0789; 501 Fisher Rd; admission free; ⏰ 8am-5pm). Interactive displays – like a Cajun joke-telling booth – give life to local folkways.

Vermilionville (☎ 337-233-4077; www.vermilion ville.org; 300 Fisher Rd; adult/student $8/5; ⏰ 10am-4pm Tue-Sun) is a recreated 19th-century Cajun village, where docents in period costumes

guide you through a living history and folk-life museum. Bands perform daily shows in the barn, and there are cooking demonstrations and tastings.

Acadian Village (☎ 337-981-2364; www.acadian village.org; 200 Greenleaf Dr; adult/child $7/4; ⏰ 10am-5pm) is less glitzy than Vermilionville and is favored by locals. Follow a brick path around a rippling bayou to restored houses, craft shops and a church.

The **Children's Museum** (☎ 337-232-8500; www .childrensmuseumofacadiana.com; 201 E Congress St; admission $5; ⏰ 10am-5pm Tue-Sat) is a great interactive museum where children explore 'real life' scenarios, in places like a grocery store, an operating room, a TV studio and a bank.

SLEEPING

Lafayette offers nearly 4000 hotel and B&B rooms. All the usual chains are present at or near exits 101 and 103, off I-10. Budget rates are around $40 to $50 for doubles.

Blue Moon Hostel (☎ 337-234-2422, 877-766-2583; www.bluemoonhostel.com; 215 E Convent St; dm $15, r $35-55; 🖳) In a tidy old home, Blue Moon is a fun place to stay. Five rooms are dorm style; one is private. The 'saloon,' set up on the back porch, features live music Wednesday to Sunday night. The friendly owners are fountains of local information. It's south of I-10 exit 101, within walking distance of downtown.

T'Frere's B&B (☎ 337-984-9347, 800-984-9347; 1905 E Verot School Rd; s/d incl breakfast $95/105; Ⓟ ⊠ 🐾) Friendly owners Pat and Maugie Pastor welcome visitors to their fun-loving 1880 B&B. All six rooms have private baths, and there's a hot tub and terrace for guest to enjoy. A delicious breakfast is served on the porch.

EATING

Many places offer one-stop entertainment, dancing and regional cuisine. Markets, convenience stores and even gas stations keep a pot of hot boudin (pork-and-rice-filled sausage) by the cash register, a sure sign you're in Cajun country.

T-Coons (☎ 337-232-3803; 740 Jefferson Blvd; mains $5-8; ⏰ 6am-2pm Mon-Thu, to 4pm Fri) The local favorite for crawfish omelettes in the morning and plates of smothered rabbit or jambalaya for lunch.

Old Tyme Grocery (☎ 337-235-8165; 218 W St Mary St; po'boys $6; ⏰ 8am-10pm Mon-Fri, 9am-7pm Sat)

THE SOUTH

Excellent shrimp or roast beef po'boys at lunch or dinner.

Cedar Deli (☎ 337-233-5460; 1115 Jefferson Blvd; mains $4-6; ☻ 10am-5pm Mon-Fri, to 4pm Sat) This Syrian-owned deli serves up delicious falafels, as well as veggie and meat muffalettas.

ENTERTAINMENT
To find out who's playing in the clubs, look for the free weekly *Times*. Hours at these places are sporadic, so call ahead.

El Sid O's (☎ 337-237-1959; 1523 Martin Luther King Dr) For zydeco, a big and welcoming cinderblock joint.

Hamilton Club (☎ 337-991-0783; 1808 Verot School Rd) For zydeco, dancing and a hell of a good time.

Grant St Dance Hall (☎ 337-237-2255; 113 W Grant St) This cavernous warehouse offers a more eclectic menu of musical offerings.

GETTING THERE & AWAY
Greyhound (☎ 337-235-1541) operates from a hub beside the central commercial district, making 11 runs daily to New Orleans and Baton Rouge. The decrepit Amtrak station is served by the *Sunset Limited*, which goes to New Orleans three times a week.

Cajun Wetlands
In 1755, *le Grande Dérangement*, the British expulsion of the rural French settlers from Acadia, created a homeless population of Acadians who searched for decades for a place to settle. In 1785, seven boatloads of exiles arrived in New Orleans. By the early 19th century, some 3000 to 4000 Acadians

---

THE AUTHOR'S CHOICE

Blue Dog Café (☎ 337-237-0005; 1211 W Pinhook Rd; entrées $13-21; ☻ 11am-2pm & 5-9pm Mon-Fri, 5-10pm Sat, 10:20am-2pm Sun) A Cajunfusion restaurant decorated with 'blue dog' paintings by artist George Rodrique, this is a highly recommended spot for dinner. The menu features authentic Cajun with creative and delicious spins. Try the treasures of the bayou – a stew of local seafood simmered in herbed wine. Yum! Also come for the Sunday brunch (adult/child $19/8), with mimosas, dishes like crab-cake benedict, all accompanied by live Cajun music.

---

arrived to occupy the swamplands southwest of New Orleans. Here they eked out a living based upon fishing and trapping, and developed a culture substantially different from the Cajuns who settled further inland in the prairie region, where animal husbandry and farming were the primary vocations. Southwest of Lafayette, historic **Abbeville** has great seafood and the surrounding communities are well known for small-town festivals. East of Lafayette, along US 90 beside the **Atchafalaya Basin**, the heart of the Cajun wetlands is a lowland area of dense vegetation, swamps, lakes and bayous.

A massive Evangeline oak, poised along Bayou Teche just off Main St in **St Martinville** (www.stmartinville.org) about 15 miles southeast of Lafayette, has become a lodestar for those seeking a connection to Acadiana. Thanks goes to Henry Wadsworth Longfellow's 1847 epic poem *Evangeline*, which recounts the story of star-crossed French lovers Evangeline and Gabriel.

About 20 miles southeast of Lafayette, the pretty town of **New Iberia** (www.cityofnewiberia.com) prospered on the sugarcane of surrounding plantations. Today, the town's best-known native son is mystery writer James Lee Burke, whose novels often take place in and around New Iberia and feature Detective Dave Robicheaux. It's a good base to explore the area.

The town has numerous B&Bs, among them the comfortable 100-year-old **Estorage-Norton House** (☎ 337-365-7603; 446 E Main St; d with bath & incl breakfast $75-90; ☒ ☒), with five guestrooms.

A favorite weekday breakfast and lunch spot is the **LagniappeToo Café** (☎ 337-365-9419; 204 E Main St; dishes $5-9). It also serves dinner on Friday and Saturday. For delicious boiled seafood, locals head a few miles north of town along I-49/Hwy 90 to the simple **Guiding Star** (☎ 337-365-9113; dishes $8-12; ☻ 3-10pm). If you need crawfish-cracking lessons, this is the place to come.

A drive southwest of New Iberia along Hwy 329 through cane fields brings you to **Avery Island**, home of **McIlhenny Tabasco** (tours ☎ 337-365-8173; ☻ 9am-4pm) and a wildlife sanctuary. The island is actually a salt dome that extends 8 miles below the surface. The salt mined here goes into the sauce, as do locally grown peppers. The mixture

---

SWAMP TOURS

You haven't experienced Louisiana unless you've been out in a swamp, and the easiest way to get to one is to join a swamp tour. Many tours can be arranged from New Orleans, with shuttle rides to and from the swamps. You can also choose among the many companies established on landings along the levee road in Henderson. To get there, take I-10, exit 115 (between Baton Rouge and Lafayette), head south and turn left onto Hwy 352.

Here are a couple other suggestions elsewhere in the Cajun Wetlands:

Annie Miller's Son's Swamp & Marsh Tours (☎ 985-868-4758; www.annie-miller.com; 3718 South-down Mandalay Rd, Houma; tours $15) Eight miles west of Houma, the son of the legendary swamp guide Annie Miller (who died in 2004) has taken up his mom's tracks.

Cajun Man's Swamp Cruise (☎ 985-868-4625; www.cajunman.com; Hwy 90; tours $15) Ten miles west of Houma, this is run by Black Guidry, who serenades his passengers with a bit of accordion music, while piloting them through a scenic slice of swamp, his trusty dog Gator Bait at his side.

---

ferments in oak barrels before being mixed with vinegar, strained and bottled.

Just 60 miles southwest of New Orleans, **Thibodaux** (ti-ba-doh) sits at the confluence of two bayous. The big attraction here is the **Wetlands Cajun Cultural Center** (☎ 985-448-1375; 314 St Mary St; admission free; ☼ 9am-8pm Mon, 8am-5pm Tue-Fri, from 9am Sat & Sun), a spacious museum and gallery operated by the NPS. Exhibits cover virtually every aspect of Cajun life in the wetlands, from music to the environmental impacts of trapping and oil exploration. Local musicians jam here Monday evenings from 6pm to 8pm.

Named for the Houma tribe of Native Americans, who were displaced in the mid-19th century by the Acadians, **Houma** is the economic hub of the Cajun Wetlands. The city itself offers little of interest to visitors, save functioning as a way station for travelers on their way to the docks just west of town, where some of the area's best swamp tours depart.

Cajun Prairie

As the elevation climbs north out of Lafayette, the land dries out a bit, crypts in cemeteries rise only a few inches above ground and roads become more predictable than in the southern wetlands. The simple geometry of grain silos echoes those of the Midwest, and it's no surprise Midwestern farmers were some of the earliest rice growers in the region. This entire area is fertile ground for Cajun and zydeco music, fishing camps and crawfish boils.

Opelousas has a historic city center and a museum covering Indian, Acadian and Creole cultures. On the main square, **Palace Cafe**

(☎ 337-942-2142; dishes $6-10) does great crawfish étouffée and bisque.

Top zydeco venues include **Slim's Y-Ki-Ki** (☎ 337-942-9980), a few miles up Washington St, and **Richard's** (☎ 337-543-8223), 8 miles west in Lawtell. **Plaisance**, northwest of Opelousas, hosts the **Southwest Louisiana Zydeco Festival** (☎ 337-942-2392; www.zydeco.org) at the end of August.

In **Eunice**, the **Prairie Acadian Cultural Center** (☎ 337-457-8490; cnr Third St & Park Ave; admission free; ☼ 8am-5pm Tue-Fri, to 6pm Sat) is part of Jean Lafitte National Historic Park & Preserve. Displays introduce visitors to Acadian heritage and map the immigration of French men and women to Louisiana. The **Liberty Theater** (☎ 337-457-7389; cnr S Second St & Park Ave), c 1924, is best known for its Rendez-vous des Cajuns (admission $5), a Saturday-night performance that's broadcast on local radio stations.

Mamou, the self-proclaimed 'Cajun Music Capital,' backs its claim with a crazy little 8am booze fest, a live traditional Cajun band and charming country waltzes every Saturday morning at **Fred's Lounge** (☎ 337-468-5411; 420 6th St).

CANE RIVER COUNTRY

The central part of the state is a crossroads of Louisiana's distinct cultures, politics and religions, with bilingual French Catholic and Franco African people along the Cane River and monolingual, chiefly Protestant residents to the north. You'll find charming French architecture in historic **Natchitoches** (mysteriously pronounced *nak*-id-esh), a sleepy little backwater town until Hollywood filmmakers

THE SOUTH

arrived in 1988 to film the blockbuster movie *Steel Magnolias*. But much of central Louisiana is a lonely place, densely forested and sparsely populated. Though logging of Southern yellow pine and hardwoods continues today, 937 sq miles of forest land is protected by the spread-out **Kisatchie National Forest** (☎ 318-473-7160). Give them a ring for maps, information and ranger stations.

South from Natchitoches, Hwy 119 meanders alongside the Cane River. You'll pass locals dipping fishing poles into the lazy river or whiling away the day on front-porch rockers. **Melrose Plantation** (☎ 318-379-0055, 800-259-1714; exit 119 off I-49; admission $7; ☺ noon-4pm) is a whole complex of buildings with an interesting history. In the early 20th century, hostess Cammy Henry offered lodging in the 'Yucca House' to artists and writers like William Faulkner and John Steinbeck. Africa House is done in Congo style and looks like a squat brick mushroom. Inside is a vivid 50ft mural depicting plantation life by folk artist Clementine Hunter.

NORTHERN LOUISIANA

Make no mistake: the rural backwaters and oil-industry towns along the Baptist Bible Belt make northern Louisiana as far removed from New Orleans as Paris, Texas is from Paris, France. Emanating from the commercial center of Shreveport, this is a region battling to find self-definition after decades of decline.

In the far northwest corner of Louisiana, Captain Henry Shreve cleared a 165-mile logjam on the Red River and founded the river port town of **Shreveport**, in 1839. The city boomed with oil discoveries in the early 1900s, but the port declined after WWII. Many downtown businesses were closed, and revitalization came in the form of huge Vegas-size casinos and a riverfront entertainment complex. The city is bisected by I-49 and I-20 and encircled by I-220. The **visitor center** (☎ 318-222-9391, 800-551-8682; 629 Spring St; ☺ 8am-5pm Mon-Fri, 11am-3pm Sat) is downtown.

In northeastern Louisiana, **Monroe** used to be a prosperous town that boomed with the discovery of oil and natural gas. Those prosperous times, however, are long gone. Ramshackle homes have replaced moneyed mansions; jails now occupy former schools.

Greenthumbs and God-fearin' folk come to check out the **Biedenharn Museum & Garden** (☎ 318-387-5281; www.bmuseum.org; 2006 Riverside Dr; admission free; ☺ 10am-5pm Mon-Sat, from 2pm Sun). Created by Coke father Joseph Biedenharn's daughter Emy-Lou, the complex features a Bible museum, conservatory and a pretty garden filled with plants mentioned in the good book.

About 50 miles northeast of Monroe on Hwy 557 near the town of Epps, the **Poverty Point State Historic Site** (☎ 318-926-5492, 888-926-5492; www.crt.state.la.us; admission $2; ☺ 9am-5pm) has a remarkable series of earthwork and mounds along what was once the Mississippi River. Around 1000 BC it was the hub of a civilization comprising hundreds of communities, with trading links as far north as the Great Lakes. There's a good introductory film, and a two-story observation tower gives a view of the site's six concentric ridges.

ARKANSAS

The biggest things to come out of this remote state are former president Bill Clinton and Wal-Mart, both larger-than-life icons that did much to alter the US cultural landscape. Add to this a quirky hillbilly culture (part stereotype, part accurate depiction), some stormy civil rights history, some peculiar little towns, and a happy, welcoming capitol, and you've got an interesting place. Big-label attractions include sites honoring the treasured presidential son, including Hope (Bill's birthplace), Hot Springs (where he grew up) and Little Rock (where he spent six terms as governor before rising to the presidency).

Once a jumping-off point for frontier expeditions to the west and south, Arkansas still rightly promotes itself as 'the Natural State,' with bountiful and secluded camping, fishing and hunting in the Ozark and Ouachita (wash-*ee*-tah) Mountains.

History

Spaniard Hernando de Soto was among the early European explorers to visit here in the mid-16th century, but it was a Frenchman, Henri de Tonti, who founded the first white settlement – Arkansas Post – in 1686. Caddo, Osage and Quapaw Indians had

ARKANSAS FACTS

Nickname Natural State
Population 2.7 million
Area 52,068 sq miles
Capital city Little Rock (population 183,130)
Official state instrument Fiddle
Birthplace of General Douglas MacArthur (1880–1964), editor Helen Gurley Brown (b 1922), musician Johnny Cash (1932–2003), former president Bill Clinton (b 1946), author John Grisham (b 1955), actor Billy Bob Thornton (b 1955)
Home of Wal-Mart
Famous for Electing the first female US senator, Hattie Caraway (1931)

permanent villages here when European explorers arrived, though they were often erroneously called 'Cherokee.' After the 1803 Louisiana Purchase, Arkansas became a US territory, and slaveholding planters moved into the Arkansas Delta along the Mississippi River to grow cotton. Poorer immigrants from the Appalachians settled in the Ozark and Ouachita plateaus.

Arkansas was on the edge of the frontier, and problems of lawlessness persisted until the Civil War. Arkansas joined the Confederacy in 1861, but from 1863 the northern part of the state was occupied by Union troops. Reconstruction was difficult, and development did not succeed until after 1870, when the expansion of railroads permitted agricultural growth. Oil and gas added to the state's wealth, but the industrial sector did not boom until the 1950s. Racial tension peaked in 1957, when the federal government intervened to enforce the integration of Arkansas schools (p434).

The state has one of the lowest per-capita incomes in the US, with many poor Blacks in the Delta area and poor Whites in the Ozarks. The KKK is headquartered in Arkansas, but its presence is well hidden and in mostly rural areas. For the most part, race relations are quite harmonious in the larger towns, and black and white students mix freely at schools that were once segregated.

Information

The state sales tax in Arkansas is 6%, plus a 2% visitors tax, plus local city and county taxes.

Department of Parks & Tourism (☎ 501-682-7777, 800-628-8725; www.arkansastravel.com; 1 Capitol Mall, Little Rock, AR 72201) Sends out a vacation plan kit on request.

LITTLE ROCK

Nowadays, downtown Little Rock resembles a friendly small town with some great big-city characteristics. Recent and well-planned redevelopment of the burgeoning downtown River Market District brought a level of sophistication to the staid 19th- and 20th-century architecture. Across the river, North Little Rock is a growing enclave of shops and restaurants stretching alongside the long riverfront park, with trails that are great for walking or jogging.

Established in 1814 as an outpost on the Arkansas River, Little Rock became the capital of the Arkansas territory in 1821 and state capital in 1836, though federal troops controlled the city in the Civil War. Little Rock boomed in the late 19th century as the commercial and administrative center of a growing state, and some fine homes and public buildings went up. Development was sporadic in the 20th century, dogged by political corruption and racial segregation. In 1957, the town shot to infamy when nine black students attempted to attend Central High School (p434).

The town's **visitor center** (☎ 877-220-2568; www.littlerock.com; 615 E Capitol; ⏰ 8am-6pm) is housed in the 1842 Curran Hall. There's also an **information kiosk** (⏰ Mon-Fri) at the convention center. Check email at the **public library** (☎ 501-918-3000; 100 Rock St; ⏰ 9am-6pm Mon-Sat, 1-5pm Sun).

Sights

The best place to stroll around the city is in the **River Market District**, an area of shops and restaurants anchored on W Markham St and President Clinton Ave along the banks of the Arkansas River. The **Ottenheimer Market Hall** (☎ 501-375-2553; www.rivermarket.info; ⏰ 7am-6pm Mon-Sat, 10am-5pm Sun) has a great collection of food stalls, cafés and shops. **Riverfront Park** provides a pleasant, walkable area along the riverbank. At the park's eastern end you might discern the little rock for which the city is named.

William J Clinton Presidential Center (☎ 501-537-0042; www.clintonpresidentialcenter.com; 1200 E President Clinton Ave; adult/child $7/3; ⏰ 9am-5pm Mon-Sat,

...in) houses the largest archival collection in presidential history, including some 76 million pages of documents and two million photographs. There's a full-scale replica of the oval office, an 80-seat theater, research offices and plenty of parkland. Visually and architecturally interesting, the museum looks a little like a mobile home stretched out over the Arkansas River. Future plans include the restoration of a railroad bridge into a pedestrian footbridge that will span the river.

Much to the horror of the city's public relations department, Clinton detractors have pledged to build the **Counter Clinton Library**. The group, which already gained nonprofit status, plans to build just downriver of the official museum, with exhibits highlighting the president's impeachment and sex scandal, along with other 'myths' of the presidency.

The **Old State House Museum** (☎ 501-324-9685; 300 W Markham St; admission free; ☑ 9am-5pm Mon-Sat, 1-5pm Sun) was the state capitol from 1836 to 1911, with impressively restored legislative chambers, period furnishings and displays on Arkansas history.

Take the kids to the **Arkansas Museum of Discovery** (☎ 501-396-7050; www.amod.org; 500 President Clinton Ave; adult/child $6.35/5.85; ☑ 9am-5pm Mon-Sat, from 1pm Sun), with interactive exhibits on dinosaurs, science and technology and history.

Sleeping

Because of government and convention-center traffic, it's difficult to find inexpensive hotels right in downtown, though rates can downright plummet when there's no convention in town. All of the usual budget-oriented motels can be found off the interstates.

Peabody Little Rock (☎ 501-906-4000, 800-723-2639; www.peabodylittlerock.com; 3 Statehouse Plaza; r from $140; P ✿ ☐) This gorgeous hotel, sister to the famous Peabody Hotel in Memphis, TN, recently underwent a two-year $40 million reconstruction. Its 418 rooms offer the height of luxury and run the gamut from standard rooms to deluxe suites. Amenities include in-room baby-sitters, a five-star restaurant and bar overlooking the river. The hotel also re-created the Memphis Peabody's tradition of the Duck March (p444). Rates here fluctuate wildly, so call first to see what's available.

Capital Hotel (☎ 501-374-7474, 800-766-7666; www.thecapitalhotel.com; 111 W Markham St; s/d from $205/226; dinner mains $18-28; P ✿ ☐) Dating back to 1876, this Victorian-era landmark maintains an elegant but casual air and is a favorite for visiting politicians. You get the feeling more laws were made here over dinner at Ashley's, the hotel's excellent restaurant, than were made down the street at the real capital building. The lobby is worth a look, even if you don't stay in one of the 126 charming rooms.

Holiday Inn (☎ 501-375-2100, 888-465-4329; 600 I-30; r $70-110; P ☐ ☎) Next door to the visitor center, this standard business hotel offers a good value for its proximity to downtown and the River Market.

Eating

The Ottenheimer Market Hall at the River Market (p433) is an economical place for breakfast or lunch. You'll find everything from fresh fruit and pastries, to Greek and Lebanese food, burgers and BBQ.

Sim's Bar-B-Que (☎ 501-372-1148; 109 Main St; mains $4-8; ⊗ closed Sun) One of the oldest restaurants in town, where locals flock for ribs and pork sandwiches.

Flying Fish (☎ 501-375-3474; 511 President Clinton Ave; mains $5-20; ⊗ 11am-10pm) A favorite spot for grilled, fried or boiled seafood, this casual place is a popular hangout with locals and visitors, both for the delicious food and fun vibe. Go for the grilled rainbow trout ($9), a po'boy sandwich ($6) or munch down on succulent jumbo shrimp (basket of 18 $22).

Juanita's Cafe & Bar (☎ 501-372-1228; 1300 S Main St; mains $8-14; ⊗ 11am-2pm & 5-10pm Mon-Fri, 11am-10pm Sat) Juanita's serves up no-frills Mexican food that can be hit-and-miss; what she lacks in consistent food, she makes up for in atmosphere, with live rock and blues music nightly.

Getting There & Around

Little Rock National Airport (LIT; ☎ 501-372-3439; www.lrn-airport.com), just east of downtown, is strictly for domestic flights. The **Greyhound station** (☎ 501-372-3007; 118 E Washington St) is over the river, in North Little Rock. Local buses are run by **CAT** (☎ 501-375-1163), more for commuters than visitors.

Amtrak occupies the old **Union Station** (☎ 501-372-6841; 1400 W Markham St).

ARKANSAS RIVER VALLEY

The Arkansas River cuts right across the state from the Oklahoma border to the Mississippi. Outdoor enthusiasts fish, canoe and camp along its quiet lakes and tributaries. Downstream from Little Rock, **Pine Bluff** was an early trading post.

Upstream from Little Rock, I-40 is the fast route, but **US 64**, which you can pick up by following I-40 30 miles north to Conway, is studded with quirky small-town Americana:

Atkins The 'Pickle Capital of Arkansas' (try fried dill pickle).

Russellville The home of Jimmy Lile Custom Knives, as used in Rambo movies.

Clarksville A college town and capital of 'Arkansas Peach Country.'

Ozark Where the bridge across the river is rated by the Institute of Steel Construction as 'one of the 16 most beautiful long spans in the US.'

Altus The center of Arkansas' Germanic wine-growing region.

Alma The 'Spinach Capital of the World,' with a giant can of spinach and a statue of Popeye.

In **Van Buren**, have a look at the six-block historic district, a sometime movie set left over from the town's heyday as a river port and trading outpost. Here you can catch the **Ozark Scenic Railway** (☎ 800-687-8600; www.arkmorr.com; adult/child from $45/40; ⊗ Apr-Nov), which offers a scenic 70-mile trip over trestles and through tunnels to **Winslow** and back.

HOT SPRINGS

Hot Springs National Park, 55 miles southwest of Little Rock, is almost surrounded by the city of Hot Springs. The thermal waters spout a million gallons of 143°F water daily from 47 natural springs. A few people still come for the waters, which you can bathe in at spas or taste from fountains, but these days there's more interest in the Victorian architecture, the horse racing at Oaklawn and scenes from Bill Clinton's boyhood.

Elaborate restored bathhouses line up on Bathhouse Row behind shady magnolias on the east side of Central Ave. Opposite is a row of restored 19th-century commercial buildings.

For city information or to pick up a map of Clinton-related sites, go to the **Convention & Visitors Bureau** (☎ 501-321-2277, 800-543-2284;

THE ARKANSAS DELTA

Roughly 120 miles east of Little Rock, the Great River Rd follows the west bank of the Mississippi River through the Arkansas Delta. Though the blues town of **Helena** has seen better days, it perks up for the annual **Arkansas Blues & Heritage Festival** (www.bluesandheritage.com; admission free), formerly the King Biscuit Blues Festival, when blues musicians and fans take over downtown for three days in early October. The music is just half the attraction; food stalls selling home-cooked soul food and BBQ are the other half. While here, blues fans will also want to visit the **Delta Cultural Center** (☎ 870-338-4350; www.deltaculturalcenter.com; 141 Cherry St; admission free; ⊗ 9am-5pm Tue-Sat), where the King Biscuit Time radio program is broadcast weekdays at 12:15pm.

www.hotsprings.org; 134 Convention Blvd; 🕙 8am-5pm Mon-Fri). On Bathhouse Row, the **NPS visitor center** (☎ 501-624-3383; 369 Central Ave; 🕙 9am-5pm), in the 1915 Fordyce bathhouse, has a free short film about the town's history first as a Native American free-trade zone, and later as its early 20th-century peak as a European spa.

Resort hotels and spas have private bathhouses, or you can visit the **Buckstaff Bathhouse** (☎ 501-623-2308; www.buckstaffbaths.com; 509 Central Ave; thermal bath/with 20min massage $20/47; 🕙 closed Sun), just south of the Fordyce, for thermal baths and Swedish massages.

A promenade runs around the hillside behind Bathhouse Row, where some springs survive in a more-or-less natural state. A network of trails covers **Hot Springs Mountain**, and a scenic drive goes to the top, where the 216ft **Hot Springs Mountain Tower** (☎ 501-623-6025; adult/child $4/2; 🕙 9am-6pm) affords great views of the surrounding mountains, which are all covered with dogwood, hickory, oak and pine – lovely in the spring and fall. **National Park Duck Tours** (☎ 501-321-2911; www.rideaduck.com; 418 Central Ave; adult/child $12.50/7.50) offers 75-minute amphibious boat tours and the **Belle of Hot Springs** (☎ 501-525-4438; www.belleriverboat.com; 5200 Central Ave; tours $12-33) does cruises on Lake Hamilton.

SLEEPING

The chain motels are on the highways around town. Ask at the visitor center for a list of lakeside rental properties and area B&Bs.

Arlington Resort Hotel & Spa (☎ 501-623-7771, 800-643-1502; www.arlingtonhotel.com; 239 Central Ave; r/ste from $80/$175; Ⓟ 🐾 🐕) A gloriously imposing historic hotel at the top end of Bathhouse Row, the Arlington has 484 rooms, ranging from small inner rooms to snazzier suites, with a lot in between. In addition to the grand lobby, the hotel has its own bathhouse, spa, three restaurants and two pools. Rates fluctuate heavily here, so be sure to ask for deals.

Alpine Inn (☎ 501-624-9164; www.alpine-inn-hot-springs.com; 741 Park Ave/Hwy 7 N; r from $35; Ⓟ 🐾 🐕) This friendly motel is a good value and less than a mile to Bathhouse Row. The 15 tidy though dark rooms have coffeemakers and hairdryers and some have kitchenettes.

Gulpha Gorge Campground (☎ 501-624-3383; campsites $10) This attractive NPS campground, just 2 miles northeast of downtown

off Hwy 70B, has 43 campsites (no showers, hookups or reservations).

EATING

The Central Ave tourist strip has most of the town's restaurants.

McClard's (☎ 501-624-9586; www.mcclards.com; 505 Albert Pike; mains $6-9; 🕙 8am-11pm Tue-Sat) Bill Clinton's favorite boyhood BBQ was this joint southwest of the center, where you can fill up on sweet, succulent ribs, pork, beef, slow-cooked beans and creamy slaw. This is some of the South's best BBQ.

Granny's Kitchen (☎ 501-624-6183; 362 Central Ave; mains $5-10; 🕙 7am-7pm) A genuine place where the waitresses call you 'honey' and where you get heaping plates of down-home cooking.

Brick House Grill (☎ 501-321-2926; 801 Central Ave; mains $9-15; 🕙 11am-10pm Mon-Sat, 5-9pm Sun) Has well-prepared seafood, steaks and chicken dishes.

AROUND HOT SPRINGS

The **Ouachita National Forest** (☎ 501-321-5202) is a wild and pretty area studded with artificial lakes and popular for hunting, fishing and boating. **Petit Jean State Park** (☎ 501-727-5441), a detour east off Rte 7, has particularly attractive scenery, walking trails, campgrounds, and rustic lodges built by the Civilian Conservation Corps (CCC).

I-30 makes a pretty straight run from Little Rock to Texarkana and the Texas border. Clinton buffs might stop at **Hope**, where the ex-pres spent his first seven years, but there's not much to see other than the spiffy **Hope Visitor Center & Museum** (☎ 870-722-2580, 800-233-4673; www.hopearkansas.net; cnr S Main & Division Sts).

OZARK MOUNTAINS

The Ozarks still bring to mind the Al Capp comic strip Li'l Abner, which depicts a ramshackle town where the men were too lazy to work and the women were desperate enough to chase them. This is where the characters from the American sitcom *Beverly Hillbillies* hailed from before they became oil barons in California. Although locals tend to milk the hillbilly angle with many kitschy tourist attractions, the region is also blessed with gorgeous scenery. The very best way to explore the region is by driving along the back roads. For further

---

NOT A DAM IN SIGHT

Although it mightn't look like the Colorado or the Columbia, the Buffalo National River sure is purty. Administered by the NPS, the river flows beneath dramatic bluffs through unspoiled Ozark forest.

Evidence of human occupation dates back some 10,000 years to the Archaic Indians, but this wild and naturally bountiful area kept even modern Ozark settlers self-sufficient and isolated. They developed a distinct dialect, along with unique craftsmanship and musical traits. Thanks to its National River designation in 1972, the Buffalo is one of the few remaining unpolluted, free-flowing rivers in the country.

The best way to see the park is by canoe or raft. Outfitters such as **Wild Bill's** (☎ 800-554-8657; www.ozark-float.com) and **Buffalo Outdoor Center** (☎ 800-221-5514; www.buffaloriver.com) can arrange canoes or rafting trips for around $40 per person. They can also arrange hiking tours, fishing trips and horseback riding.

The **Buffalo National River** (☎ 870-741-5443; www.nps.gov/buff) has three designated wilderness areas, the most accessible is through the **Tyler Bend visitor center** (☎ 870-439-2502; ◷ 8am-5pm Sep-Jun), 11 miles north of Marshall on I-65.

---

information or for a list of driving tours of the region call ☎ 800-544-6867 or conduct a search online at www.ozarkmountainre gion.com.

Mountain View

Heading north from Little Rock, detour east of US 65 to this perfectly ordinary (read: wacky) Ozark town, known for its tradition of informal weekend music-making at Courthouse Sq. Creeping commercialism is taking its toll, as the **chamber of commerce** (☎ 870-269-8068; 107 N Peabody Ave; ◷ 9am-5pm Mon-Fri, 10am-4pm Sat, 12:30-3pm Sun) promotes the place as the 'Folk Music Capital of the World.' **Cash's White River Hoe-Down** (☎ 870-269-8042; ◷ 7:30pm Fri & Sun Apr-Dec) is a heavily hyped, live country music and comedy show. A calendar of annual events also pulls in the punters.

FESTIVALS

The following festivals are organized by the **Ozark Folk Center** (www.ozarkfolkcenter.com):
Folk Festival April
Auto Show April
Bean Fest October
Ozark Christmas December

Eureka Springs

Near the northwestern corner of the state, Eureka Springs could easily be mistaken for an old mining village, but tourists are the only things ever mined here. It's pretty enough, with Victorian buildings lining crooked streets in a steep valley, but the

combination of commercialized country music, honeymoon romance and Bible-themed attractions, including the 70ft **Christ of the Ozarks** statue, sends things a little over the top.

The **visitor center** (☎ 501-253-8737; eurekasprings chamber.com; 137 W Van Buren/Hwy 62) has information about lodging, tours and attractions. The best things to do are walk the streets, shop for tacky souvenirs and ride on the old **ES & NA Railway** (☎ 501-253-9623; www.esnarailway .com; 299 N Main St; adult/child $10/5; ◷ hourly 10am-4pm Apr-Oct), which puffs through the hills on an hour-long tour.

TENNESSEE

Sweeping green lowlands, magnificent mountains shrouded in fog so thin it looks like smoke, cities that echo with the genius of musical ghosts and the creativity of a thousand cowboys aching for stardom – this is Tennessee, where religion exists in a football game and a cold brew, as much as it does in Jesus.

This beautiful state – its geography as diverse as its culture – can be physically and psychologically divided into three regions: the Great Smoky Mountains in the east, the central plateau and Middle Tennessee around Nashville, and the Mississippi bottomlands in the west around Memphis. These regions embody the musical heritage of the state, where the east's mountain music inspired the country music of the

THE SOUTH

west and fused with the sultry black blues of the Mississippi Delta. This is where a white boy from Mississippi adopted black rhythms, started gyrating his hips and became the King of Rock and Roll. Elvis aside, the state that gave birth to so many American musicians seems perpetually filled with music – lyrics so sorrowful your eyes tear, beats so original you feel rumbling in your soul.

Tennessee's offerings are plentiful, and whether you're dancing in Memphis, tapping your toes in Nashville, hiking through the Smoky Mountains or partaking in one of the many festivals of tacky Americana, you'll encounter friendly people who seem to carry around a zest for life like it's a guitar pick in their pocket.

History

European encroachment on this Cherokee territory began in 1540. Though the British crown colony of Carolina nominally extended to the Mississippi, the French were actively trading on the rivers from the late 17th century. After the French and Indian War, Virginian pioneers soon established a settlement west of the Appalachians, creating their own treaty with the Cherokee. They drafted a written constitution that asserted their independence from British Carolina and were soon active participants in the American Revolution. After independence, Tennessee alternated between North Carolina and the US government,

then acquired territorial status and eventually statehood.

Treaties in 1818 displaced the Chickasaw from west Tennessee, and President Andrew Jackson (himself an early Tennessee settler) expelled the Indians to Oklahoma. The state became increasingly divided between the proslavery west and abolitionist east; Tennessee was the last state to secede in the Civil War.

Tennessee abolished slavery by popular vote in 1865 (the only state to do so without Federal intervention), though reaction to emancipation was often hostile. The KKK became influential in 'protecting Whites' and disenfranchising the state's Blacks by restrictive poll-tax laws.

In the 20th century industries like chemicals, textiles and metal products overtook agriculture, moving the majority of the population to urban areas. Tennessee still produces cotton and dairy products and is one of the top tobacco-producing states but tourism, especially in Nashville and Memphis, bolsters the state's income.

Information

Tennessee has a state tax of 7%. In cities such as Memphis and Nashville, local taxes can add up to about 15%.

Department of Tourist Development (☎ 615-741-2159, 800-462-8366; www.tnvacation.com; 320 6th Ave N, Nashville, TN 37243) Welcome centers are at the state borders.

MEMPHIS

You can almost feel the blood of Elvis coursing through your veins the moment you arrive in Memphis. You feel the sultry tingle of musical history going back to the deep Southern birth of the blues. Gutsy guitar riffs and heart-numbing blues belt out and travel like electricity through the streets.

Perched on the Mississippi River, Memphis was named for the ancient Egyptian capital on the Nile. As always, the city clings to its mix of past and present. Riverboats swoosh by as in-line skaters exercise on riverfront paths. A landmark of the civil rights struggle where Martin Luther King Jr was martyred in 1968, today's Memphis has moved a long way from the days embedded with racial tension. Still, the undertones exist as black and white

---

TENNESSEE FACTS

Nickname Volunteer State

Population 5.8 million

Area 41,217 sq miles

Capital city Nashville (population 545,524)

Official state bird Mockingbird (state animal: raccoon)

Birthplace of Frontiersman Davy Crockett (1786–1836), guitarist Chet Atkins (1924–2001), rockabilly star Carl Perkins (1932–98), singer Tina Turner (b 1939), soul diva Aretha Franklin (b 1942), singer Dolly Parton (b 1946), former vice president Al Gore (b 1948)

Home of Jack Daniels distillery, Graceland, Country Music Hall of Fame

Famous for 'Tennessee Waltz,' country music, rock and roll, Tennessee walking horses

work towards harmony. Visitors will appreciate the city's soulful grittiness, borne from its history of cotton, riverboats and music.

History

Mounds on the bluffs on the Mississippi River's eastern shore were built by a Mississippian civilization more than 1000 years ago. The French established Fort Assumption on the bluffs in 1739 to protect their river trade. After the US took control, a treaty in 1818 edged the Chickasaw nation out of western Tennessee, and Andrew Jackson helped found the settlement of Memphis. The city was incorporated in 1826 and prospered on the expanding cotton trade of the Mississippi Delta.

Early in the Civil War a Union fleet defeated the Confederates and occupied the city, but postwar collapse of the cotton trade was far more devastating. A yellow-fever epidemic in 1878 claimed more than 5000 lives and many white residents abandoned the city. Memphis declared bankruptcy and its city charter was revoked until 1893. The black community revived the town, led by a former slave named Robert Church. By the 1920s Beale St was the hub of social and civic activity, peppered heavily with gambling, drinking and prostitution.

WC Handy's 'Beale Street Blues' established Memphis as an early center of blues music, and in the 1950s local recording company Sun Records cut tracks for blues, soul, R & B and rockabilly artists, both white and black.

The old downtown was largely abandoned by the 1970s, and Beale St was nearly demolished to make way for 'redevelopment.' Instead, a restoration program revived the entertainment district.

Orientation

Downtown Memphis runs along the east bank of the Mississippi, with Riverside Dr and a promenade parallel to the river. The principal tourist district is a bit inland, roughly the area bounded by Union Ave and Beale St, and 2nd and 4th Sts. Further east, cool neighborhoods along Union Ave and Overton Sq have shops, bars and restaurants. Graceland is 3 miles south of town on US 51, also called 'Elvis Presley Blvd.'

Information

BOOKSTORES
Tower Records & Books (☎ 901-526-9210; downstairs at Peabody Place Entertainment & Retail Center; 10am-10pm Mon-Thu, 10am-11pm Fri & Sat, noon-9pm Sun)

EMERGENCY
Emergency (☎ 911) Police, ambulance, fire.
Main police station (☎ 901-543-2677; 201 Poplar Ave) Nonemergencies only.

INTERNET ACCESS
Café Francisco (☎ 901-578-8002; 400 N Main St; per min 25¢; 7am-10pm Mon-Fri, 8am-10pm Sat, to 6pm Sun) In the Pinch district, this café has wi-fi and terminals for customer use.
Public library (☎ 901-526-1712; 33 S Front St; 10am-5pm Mon-Fri, closed Sat & Sun) Has several computers and offers free Internet access.

INTERNET RESOURCES
Blues Foundation (www.blues.org) Official site of the national Blues Foundation, based in Memphis.
Official Elvis Website (www.elvis.com) Everything you ever wanted to know about the King.
Gay Memphis (www.gaymemphis.org) To find out about local rainbow-friendly businesses and events.
Memphis Guide (www.memphisguide.com) A directory to sights, attractions and hotels.
Memphis website (www.memphiswebsites.com) Links galore! Looking for any organization or Memphis-related information, you'll likely find a link on this helpful site.

MEDIA
Commercial Appeal (www.commercialappeal.com) Daily newspaper.
Memphis Flyer (www.memphisflyer.com) Pick up the free weekly, which comes out on Thursday and is full of entertainment listings.
Triangle Journal News A free monthly newspaper for the gay community.

MEDICAL SERVICES
Methodist University Hospital (☎ 901-523-1331; 850 Poplar Ave)
St Jude Research Hospital (☎ 901-495-3300; 332 N Lauderdale)

MONEY
ATMs are widely available around town.
First Tennessee Bank (☎ 901-523-5053; 165 Madison Ave; 8am-4pm Mon-Fri, 10am-2pm Sat) If you need to go into a bank.

THE SOUTH

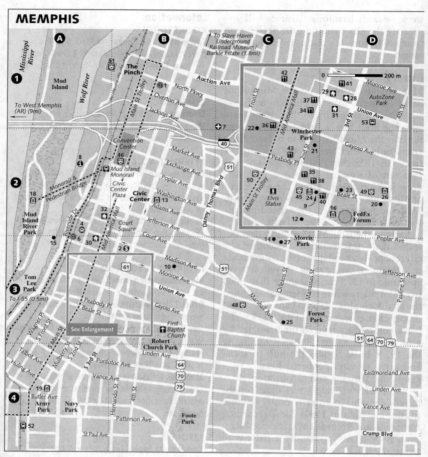

MEMPHIS

See Enlargement

POST
Post office East (1520 Union Ave); Main (☎ 901-521-2559; 555 South 3rd St; zip code 38101); Riverside (1 N Front St)

TOURIST INFORMATION
Tennessee State Visitor Center (☎ 901-543-5333, 888-633-9099; www.memphistravel.com; 119 N Riverside Dr; ◷ 9am-5pm, to 6pm summer) Well stocked with brochures for the whole state. The helpful staff can help you find hotel deals in Memphis.

Dangers & Annoyances
Memphis is a friendly city but has its share of crime. Harmless but sometimes aggressive panhandlers hang around Beale St, but a polite, firm 'no' will send them on their way.

Stick to populated areas, or take cabs if you stray far at night.

Sights & Activities
BEALE STREET
The strip from 2nd to 4th Sts is filled with clubs, restaurants, souvenir shops and neon signs – a veritable theme park of the blues – though only one of the stores is an original from Beale St's heyday in the early 1900s. It's easy and safe to walk around.

The **Orpheum Theater** (p445), at Main St, is restored to its 1928 glory, and an Elvis statue stands at the corner of 2nd Ave in front of a nightclub and restaurant called 'Elvis Presley's.' In front of the Orpheum, the **Walk of Fame** features musical notes em-

0   600 m
0   0.4 miles

INFORMATION
Café Francisco..........................**1** B1
First Tennessee Bank.................**2** B3
Methodist University Hospital.....**3** E4
Post Office................................**4** A2
Post Office................................**5** F4
Public Library...........................**6** A3
St Jude Research Hospital..........**7** C1
Tennessee State Visitor Center...**8** A2
Tower Records & Books.........(see 22)

SIGHTS & ACTIVITIES
A Schwab's..............................**9** C2
Blues City Tours......................**10** B3
Brooks Museum of Art............**11** H3
Center for Southern Folklore....(see 22)
Gibson Beale St Showcase.......**12** C2
Magevney House......................**13** B2
Mallory-Neely House...............**14** C3
Memphis Queen Riverboat......**15** A3
Memphis Rock 'n' Soul Museum..**16** D2
Memphis Zoo..........................**17** H2
Mississippi River Museum........**18** A2

National Civil Rights Museum
  (Lorraine Motel)..................**19** A4
Old Daisy Theater....................**20** D2
Peabody Place Entertainment &
  Retail Center.......................**21** C2
Peabody Place Mall.................**22** C1
Pepsi-Cola Pavilion.................**23** D2
Police Museum........................**24** C2
Sun Studio...............................**25** C3
Walk of Fame......................(see 50)
WC Handy House Museum......**26** D2
Woodruff-Fontaine House.......**27** C3

SLEEPING
Best Western Benchmark Inn...**28** D1
Holiday Inn.............................**29** D1
Madison Hotel........................**30** A3
Peabody Hotel.........................**31** D1
Sleep Inn at Court Square........**32** A2

EATING
Anderton's..............................**33** H4
Automatic Slim's Tonga Club...**34** C1

Blues City Cafe........................**35** C2
Holiday Deli & Ham Co............**36** C1
Huey's.....................................**37** C1
King's Palace Café....................**38** C2
On Tour..................................**39** H4
Pig on Beale............................**40** D2
Rendezvous.............................**41** D1
Sleep Out Louie's....................**42** C1
Swig..**43** C2
Tops Bar-B-Q..........................**44** E4

ENTERTAINMENT
BB King's.................................**45** C2
Cannon Center for Performing
  Arts......................................**46** B2
Circuit Playhouse....................**47** G3
Kudzu Café..............................**48** C3
New Daisy Theater...................**49** D2
Orpheum Theater.....................**50** C2
Pyramid..................................**51** A1

TRANSPORT
Central Station (Amtrak)..........**52** A4
Greyhound Bus Station.............**53** D1

THE SOUTH

bedded in the sidewalk with the names of well-known blues artists.

The Beale St substation **Police Museum** (901-579-0887; 159 Beale St; admission free; 8am-10pm) has exhibits that include assorted criminalia, while the original **A Schwab's** (907-523-9782; 163 Beale St; admission free; 9am-5pm Mon-Sat) dry-goods store has three floors of voodoo powders, 99¢ neckties, clerical collars and a big selection of hats. Between 3rd and 4th Sts, a statue of songwriter and composer WC Handy overlooks the **Pepsi-Cola Pavilion**, a park and outdoor amphitheater where bands jam in the summertime; the **WC Handy House Museum** (901-527-3427; 352 Beale St; admission $3; 10am-5pm) is nearby on 4th St.

The **New Daisy Theater** (p446) has art-deco backdrops depicting the district's honky-tonk heyday, and continues to hold concerts. The little-used **Old Daisy Theater** stands forlornly across the road.

The Smithsonian's **Memphis Rock 'n' Soul Museum** (901-205-2533; www.memphisrocknsoul.org; cnr Lt George W Lee Ave & 3rd St; adult/child $9/6; 10am-7pm), next to FedEx Forum, examines the social and cultural history that produced the music of the Mississippi Delta. Self-guided tours take about 90 minutes.

At the giant **Gibson Beale Street Showcase** (901-544-7998, 800-444-4766; www.gibsonmemphis.com admission $10; tours 11am, 12pm, 1pm & 2pm Mon-Sat, 1pm & 2pm Sun), take the way-cool 30-minute tour of the guitar factory, where solid blocks of wood are transformed into legendary Gibson guitars. No kids under 12 are admitted.

NATIONAL CIVIL RIGHTS MUSEUM

Housed in the Lorraine Motel, where the Reverend Dr Martin Luther King Jr was fatally shot on April 4, 1968, is the **National Civil Rights Museum** (☎ 901-521-9699; www.civil rightsmuseum.org; 450 Mulberry St; adult/child $10/6.50, 2-5pm Mon free; 🕑 9am-6pm Mon-Sat, from 1pm Sun, closed Tue & Sun winter). Five blocks south of Beale St, this museum brings to light one of the most significant moments in modern American history. Through documentary photos and audio displays, the museum chronicles King's contribution to the Civil Rights movement and its indelible impact on American history. The turquoise exterior of the 1950s motel remains much as it was at the time of King's assassination.

MUD ISLAND

A monorail and elevated walkway cross the Wolf River to Mud Island River Park and the **Mississippi River Museum** (☎ 901-576-7241, 800-507-6507; www.mudisland.com; 125 N Front St; adult/child $8/5; 🕑 10am-8pm Jun-Sep, to 5pm Tue-Sun Oct-May). The excellent exhibits depict the cultural and physical history of the lower Mississippi River valley, including a supercool, to-scale model of the river and Gulf. The monorail is free with museum admission.

FAMOUS RECORDING STUDIOS

Any serious Elvis or country-music fan will want to pay homage to **Sun Studio** (☎ 901-521-0664, 800-441-6249; www.sunstudio.com; 706 Union Ave; admission $9.50; 🕑 10am-6pm). Starting in the early 1950s, Sun's Sam Phillips gave birth to rock and roll by recording blues artists like Howlin' Wolf, BB King and Ike Turner, followed by the rockabilly dynasty of Jerry Lee Lewis, Carl Perkins, Johnny Cash, Roy Orbison and, of course, Elvis Presley (who started here in 1955). Sun Records moved on in 1959, but the studio reopened in 1987, and Ringo Starr, U2, Sheryl Crow and Matchbox 20 have all come here to record. In 2003, it became the country's first recording studio to be designated a historic landmark. Today the studio offers a 30-minute narrated tour through the tiny studio and a chance to hear the original tapes of historic record-

ing sessions. The gift shop sells souvenirs like Sun Studio T-shirts, guitar picks and audio CDs.

If the **Stax Museum of American Soul Music** (☎ 901-946-2535; www.soulsvilleusa.com; 926 E McLemore Ave; adult/child $9/6; 🕑 9am-5pm Mon-Sat, from 1pm Sun) fails to give visitors goose pimples it's because the original building was demolished long ago, but today's more stable structure echoes the past with a marquee blazing the reassuring words 'Soulsville USA.' Indeed, this venerable spot was soul music's epicenter in the 1960s, when Otis Redding, Carla Thomas, Booker T and the MGs and Wilson Pickett recorded here. It's worth visiting for the photos, displays of '60s and '70s peacock clothing and, above all, Isaac Hayes' 1972 Superfly Cadillac outfitted with shag fur carpeting and 24-karat-gold exterior trim.

HISTORIC HOUSES

In the 'Victorian Village' district on Adams Ave, east of downtown, two rather grand houses are open for public tours: the 1870 **Woodruff-Fontaine House** (☎ 901-526-1469; 680 Adams Ave; www.woodruff-fontaine.com; admission $5.50; 🕑 10am-4pm Wed-Sat, from 1pm Sun) and the 1852 **Mallory-Neely House** (☎ 901-523-1484; 652 Adams Ave; admission $5.50; 🕑 10am-4pm Tue-Sat, from 1pm Sun). The smaller **Magevney House** (☎ 901-526-4464; 198 Adams Ave; admission free) reflects the lifestyle of a 19th-century Irish immigrant family.

The **Slave Haven Underground Railroad Museum/Burkle Estate** (☎ 901-527-3427; www.her itagetoursmemphis.com; 826 N 2nd St; adult/child $6/4; 🕑 10am-4pm Wed-Sun) is thought to have been a way station for runaway slaves on the Underground Railroad, complete with trapdoors and tunnels.

MUSEUMS

Pink Palace Museum & Planetarium (☎ 901-320-6320; www.memphismuseums.org; 3050 Central Ave; adult/child $8/5.50; 🕑 9am-5pm Tue-Sat, from noon Sun) is 3 miles east of town off US 72. The mansion was built here in 1923 as a residence for Piggly Wiggly founder Clarence Saunders and reopened in 1996 as a natural- and cultural-history museum. It mixes fossils, Civil War exhibits, restored Works Projects Administration (WPA) murals and an exact replica of the original Piggly Wiggly, the world's first self-service grocery store,

---

HOP ON THE BUS, GUS

The best way to tour the musical sites of Memphis is to hop on the Sun Studio **free shuttle** that runs daily, every hour, starting at Sun Studio at 11:15am. The bus does a loop to the major music sites – Sun Studio, Beale St, Stax Museum of American Soul Music, Heartbreak Hotel and Graceland. The shuttle picks up hourly at each location (pick up the schedule at Sun Studio), and you can get on or off the shuttle at any point.

---

which opened in 1916. There is also an Imax theater; tickets sold separately.

Center for Southern Folklore (☎ 901-525-3655; www.southernfolklore.com; 119 S Main St; admission free; ☾ 11am-7pm Mon-Sat), in Pembroke Sq at Peabody Pl, has a café, books, photographic arts and crafts, and holds free music performances, local tours and film screenings.

OVERTON PARK

Stately homes surround the stunning **Overton Park**, where the **Brooks Museum of Art** (☎ 901-544-6200; www.brooksmuseum.org; 1934 Poplar Ave; adult/child $6/2; ☾ 10am-4pm Tue-Fri, to 5pm Sat, 11:30am-5pm Sun) offers excellent exhibits from stonework to cartoons. The permanent collection includes Renaissance and Baroque paintings and sculptures, plus an extensive collection of American paintings. There is also a restaurant and gift shop.

Also within the park, the excellent **Memphis Zoo** (☎ 901-276-9453; www.memphiszoo.org; 2000 Prentiss Pl; adult/child $13/8; ☾ 9am-6pm) has a $16-million exhibit on native Chinese wildlife and habitat, devoted especially to the zoo's stars, Ya Ya and Le Le, two giant pandas who arrived from Beijing, China in 2003. Also check out the simulator ride through a re-created dinosaur habitat.

GRACELAND

In the spring of 1957, at age 22, Elvis spent $100,000 on this house, part of the 500-acre farm named **Graceland** (☎ 901-332-3322, 800-238-2000; www.elvis.com; Elvis Presley Blvd/US 51; all attractions adult/child $28/13; ☾ 9am-5pm Mon-Sat & 10am-4pm Sun Mar-Oct, 10am-4pm Wed-Mon Nov-Feb, mansion closed Tue Nov-Feb). He lived here until his death in 1977, and he's buried next to the swimming pool with his closest relatives.

Priscilla Presley (who divorced Elvis in 1973) opened Graceland to tours in 1982, and now millions come here to pay homage to the King. Elvis himself had the place redecorated in 1974; with a 15ft couch, avocado-green kitchen appliances, a fake waterfall, yellow vinyl and a green shag-carpet ceiling, it's a virtual textbook of '70s style.

You begin your tour at the 'visitor plaza' across the street, where there are ticket sales, souvenir shops, cafés and a free 22-minute film. In busier seasons the staff will assign you a tour time, or you can book ahead. The basic 1½-hour mansion tour is a recording narrated by Priscilla with sound bites from Elvis and Lisa Marie. You can pay for the package and see the entire estate, or you can pay to see the individual sights, which include the mansion (adult/child $18/7), the 'Sincerely Elvis' memorabilia collection ($6/3), the car museum ($4/4) and an aircraft collection ($7/4). If you want to see all the sites (and you should), allow at least four hours. Graceland is about 3 miles from downtown Memphis. If you're driving, you get here by taking US 51 (Bellevue Blvd, which becomes Elvis Presley Blvd). Nondrivers can take bus No 43 from downtown, or hop on the free Sun Studio shuttle (left). Guests can also stay across the street at the Elvis-crazed Heartbreak Hotel (p444).

Tours

Blues City Tours (☎ 901-522-9229; www.bluescity tours.com; 325 Union Ave; adult from $20) Offers a wide variety of fun and informative bus tours; call ahead for times.

Horse-drawn carriage rides (rides 2 persons per 30min around $40) Depart from Beale St or outside the Peabody Hotel.

Memphis Queen (☎ 901-527-5694, 800-221-6197; www.memphisqueen.com; Riverside Dr at Monroe Ave; sightseeing cruise adult/child $15/11, music cruise with buffet $40/30) Riverboat rides aboard the *Memphis Queen* depart from the foot of Monroe Ave at Riverside Dr. Tour times fluctuate monthly so call ahead to confirm.

Sleeping

If you want to save on accommodations, you'll find cheaper highwayside motels across the river in West Memphis, Arkansas, where chain places cluster at I-40, exit 279. Tax on accommodations in Memphis is 15%.

THE SOUTH

French Quarter Suites Hotel (☎ 901-728-4000, 800-843-0353; www.memphisfrenchquarter.com; 2144 Madison Ave; d $70; P ✖ ☎) In the funky Overton Sq neighborhood and offering ultra-excellent value, this New Orleans–inspired hotel offers 105 huge suites with separate bedrooms and baths that have generous Jacuzzi tubs – perfect for soaking after a long night listening to live music. There's also a restaurant and bar.

Best Western Benchmark Inn (☎ 901-527-4100, 800-380-3236; www.bestwesterntennessee.com; 164 Union Ave; d $80-105; P ✖) Recently renovated, this is an unbeatable hotel for its location, across from the Peabody and just three blocks from Beale St. Its 124 rooms have hair dryers and coffeemakers. The hotel has a great lobby and fitness center. Parking costs $9.

Holiday Inn (☎ 901-525-5491, 888-300-5491; www .hisdowntownmemphis.com; 160 Union Ave; d from $140; P ✖ ☎) Next door to the Best Western and also across the street from the Peabody, this hotel has 190 generous updated rooms. Added bonuses include a fitness center, restaurant and bar. Parking costs $10.

Madison Hotel (☎ 901-333-1200; www.madison hotelmemphis.com; 79 Madison Ave; r from $190; P ✖ 🖵 ☎) If you're looking for a complete treat, check in to this swanky, ultramodern hotel that's chock-full of amenities. The rooftop garden is one of the best places in town to watch a sunset. Rooms have nice touches, like Italian linens and whirlpool tubs. Even if you don't stay here, stop in for a cocktail at the artsy chic bar.

Sleep Inn at Court Sq (☎ 901-522-9700; www .sleepinns.com; 40 N Front St; s/d incl breakfast $75/85; P ✖) Cheap hotels can be hard to come by in Memphis. This is your best bet, near

---

THE AUTHOR'S CHOICE

Peabody Hotel (☎ 901-529-4000, 800-732-2639; www.peabodymemphis.com; 149 Union Ave; r from $260; P ✖ ☎) This grand old dame has been Memphis' premiere hotel since the 1930s. With 464 rooms, the historic hotel has a variety of rooms at many prices. It's a social center in Memphis, with a spa, a French restaurant, a superb Italian steakhouse – the Capriccio Grill – and a groovy lobby bar. It also boasts its own quirky (quacky?) tradition: every day for the last 80 years, at 11am sharp, the hotel's 10 ducks file from the elevator across the red-carpeted lobby, accompanied by the hotel's red-coated Duckmaster. The birds cavort in the fountain until 5pm, when they return to their penthouse. Self/valet parking $16/21.

---

the river and just six blocks from Beale St. Rooms are simple but impeccably clean.

Heartbreak Hotel (☎ 901-332-1000, 877-777-0606; www.heartbreakhotel.net; 3677 Elvis Presley Blvd; d/ste from $100/119; P ✖ ☎) OK, so it's not at the end of Lonely St but the Heartbreak Hotel, behind Graceland's parking lot, is all about Elvis. The King's movies play in every room. Other amenities include a heart-shaped outdoor pool, a refrigerator and microwave in every room and free transportation to Beale St at night.

KOA Kampground (☎ 901-396-7125; 3691 Elvis Presley Blvd; campsites/cabins from $21/36) Practically across the street from Graceland, KOA has campsites (hookups extra) and cabins.

Eating

Memphis has a great array of restaurants, with the regional focus on BBQ, specifically chopped pork shoulder served in a sandwich, or dry-rubbed ribs. Most restaurants have air-conditioning, along with smoking and nonsmoking sections.

DOWNTOWN

Holiday Deli & Ham Co (☎ 901-507-7009; 119 S Main St; mains $4-8) In the Peabody Place Mall on Main St, this location of the Memphis deli chain is a healthy stop for delicious salads, sandwiches and fresh juices.

Rendezvous (☎ 901-523-2746; www.hogsfly.com; 52 S 2nd St; mains $10-22; ✐ dinner Tue-Sat, lunch

Fri & Sat) Tucked in an alleyway off Union Ave, Rendezvous sells an astonishing five tons of BBQ ribs weekly. The specialty at this family-owned institution is charcoal-broiled dry ribs, dished up with friendly service in a genuine old Memphis atmosphere (most of the waiters have worked here forever).

Pig on Beale (☎ 901-529-1544; 167 Beale St; sandwich & 2 sides $7, full rib dinner $15; ☿ lunch & dinner) Slow-smoked pork ribs slide off the bone at this Beale St BBQ joint. You can get wet or dry ribs, served up with classic creamy coleslaw or corn on the cob…and plenty of napkins.

King's Palace Café (☎ 901-521-1851; 162 Beale St; mains $7-20; ☿ lunch & dinner) Jazz and blues music blare out of this big, busy café while contented customers happily slurp the award-winning gumbo and other Cajun specialties.

Huey's (☎ 901-527-2700; 77 S 2nd St; mains $6-10; ☿ lunch & dinner) A longtime city favorite for having the best burger in town, Huey's is a good bet for casual pub food, right on the edge of the Beale St action.

Blues City Cafe (☎ 901-526-1724; 138 Beale St; mains $8-18; ☿ lunch & dinner) With live music Tuesday to Sunday, this is a great choice for chowing on some good old Southern fare while listening to local bands.

Automatic Slim's Tonga Club (☎ 901-525-7948; 83 S 2nd St; lunch $8-14, dinner $15-25; ☿ Mon-Sat) In an artsy atmosphere, this bistro has slow-roasted yellowfin tuna, jerk duck and a killer coconut shrimp with mango sauce.

Swig (☎ 901-522-8515; 100 Peabody Pl; martinis $8, sushi rolls $4-10; ☿ 3pm-2am) Bust out your cocktail togs and swill martinis with the beautiful people at this swanky bar that serves up fresh sushi, a happy crowd and occasional small live bands.

THE AUTHOR'S CHOICE

Sleep Out Louie's (☎ 901-527-5337; 88 Union Ave; po'boy sandwiches $8, 12 oysters $12; ☿ lunch & dinner Mon-Fri, brunch 10:30am-2pm Sat & Sun). The kind of place you can go by yourself, take a seat at the bar and make new friends. The menu features delicious burgers, po'boy sandwiches and fresh salads, along with oysters on the half shell. A small courtyard offers outside seating.

MIDTOWN

On Teur (☎ 901-725-6059; 2015 Madison Ave; dishes $10-20; ☿ lunch & dinner) An old favorite for savory veggie dishes and yummy munchies, like halibut burgers and pecan-smoked sausages. You can sit on the patio or inside. You can also bring your own wine for a small corkage fee. On Teur also serves up a delicious brunch on weekends.

Tops Bar-B-Q (☎ 901-725-7527; 1286 Union Ave; $5-9; ☿ lunch & dinner) With many locations, including this one in Midtown, Tops is a longtime Memphis favorite for cheap and delicious BBQ since 1952.

Anderton's (☎ 901-726-4010; 1901 Madison Ave; mains $12-25; ☿ lunch & dinner Mon-Sat, closed Sat lunch & Sun) A Memphis institution since 1945, Anderton's serves choice steaks and succulent lobster and crab.

Entertainment

Most Memphis restaurants serve up food with a musical accompaniment, so it's easy to turn a meal into a party. For fun-lovers of all ages, Beale St is the place to go. The cool thing here is that both locals and tourists slide over to hear live blues, country, rock and jazz. On weekend nights, Beale St's two-block strip is closed to traffic, turning it into a walk-around party zone. Cover for most clubs is either free or only a few dollars. To find out what live acts are in town, check out www.livefrommemphis.com.

LIVE MUSIC & THEATER

Kudzu Café (☎ 901-525-4924; 603 Monroe Ave) Near downtown, Kudzu has comedy, live bands and regular guitar-pickin' contests.

Pyramid (☎ 901-521-7909; www.pyramidarena .com; Riverfront Dr) Memphis was named for the Egyptian Nile River town, which only partially explains this giant on the northwestern edge of downtown. The 32-story pyramid is the world's third largest, taller than the Statue of Liberty and, at first glance, stranger than random Elvis sightings. Throughout the year, big-name bands play here and in the summer the shiny triangle hosts the 'Wonders' (www.wonders .org), featuring various exhibits in the Memphis International Cultural Series.

Orpheum Theater (☎ 901-743-2787; www.orphe um-memphis.com; 203 S Main St) A 1928-era vaudeville palace, restored as a venue for Broadway shows, ballet and major concerts.

PULLED PORK

Nothing excites Southern saliva glands quite like a craving for pulled BBQ pork butt. In Memphis, it's chopped up and served with a tomato-based BBQ sauce and a dollop of coleslaw in a cheap white bun. This is a variation on the pulled-pork sandwiches that are so popular elsewhere in the South. Once you've tried one, you'll agree it knocks the pants off a hamburger any day of the week. You can buy them at BBQ stands and even some gas stations throughout the region.

By the way, pork butt is not actually the bum of a swine. It's the upper shoulder. The key to good BBQ pork is the rub (seasoning mix) and the cooking technique (low temp and slow). Recipes vary from cook to cook, but the following rub will create a little taste of Southern heaven.

Pork Rub

This quantity of rub should be enough for 2lb to 3lb of pork.

- 4 tablespoons paprika
- 2 tablespoons salt
- 2 tablespoons coarsely ground black pepper
- 2 tablespoons cumin powder
- 3 tablespoons dark brown sugar
- 1 tablespoon dried oregano
- 1 tablespoon cayenne pepper
- 2 teaspoons dried sage
- 2 bay leaves, ground
- 1 teaspoon dry mustard

Mix seasonings together thoroughly. Rub this mixture onto the meat and let it sit overnight. Barbecue or roast the meat, keeping the temperature very low (under 200°F), for about two hours per pound of meat. Do not cover the meat. Keep a roasting pan beneath the rack to catch fat drippings, which you can use to baste the meat periodically (or use a baste of equal parts apple cider, vinegar and olive oil). Once the meat is cooked, let it cool before shredding it. Mix in BBQ sauce and slap that butt on some buns.

Cannon Center for Performing Arts (☎ 901-576-1269, 800-726-0915; www.thecannoncenter.com; 255 N Main St) Home to the Memphis Symphony Orchestra, this 2100-seat theater offers incredible acoustics and an intimate setting for ballet, opera and jazz concerts.

Circuit Playhouse (☎ 901-726-4656; www.playhouseonthesquare.org; 1705 Poplar Ave) In Overton Sq, the wonderful Circuit Playhouse offers Memphis' only live theater productions of Broadway and Off-Broadway productions.

New Daisy Theater (☎ 901-525-8979; www.newdaisy.com; 330 Beale St; shows at 7pm) This groovy, all-ages venue hosts a variety of live-music shows. Call the hotline to see what's playing.

BB King's (☎ 901-524-5464; 143 Beale St) A full restaurant serving up ribs and Southern favorites, BB's is better known for it's friendly fun-seeking crowd and great live music.

SPORTS

Memphis Redbirds (☎ 901-721-6000; www.memphisredbirds.com; tickets $5-17) Sports fans can get involved by checking out the Memphis Redbirds, a AAA minor-league affiliate of the St Louis Cardinals baseball team that plays at the 15,000-seat AutoZone Park April to August.

Memphis Grizzlies (☎ 901-888-4667, 866-648-4667; www.grizzlies.com) The NBA's Memphis Grizzlies bring on the basketball action at FedEx Forum from October to April.

Getting There & Around

Memphis International Airport (☎ 901-922-8000; www.memphisairport.org; 2491 Winchester Rd) is 12 miles southeast of downtown via I-55; a taxi to or from downtown runs at about $25. Try **City Wide Cab Company** (☎ 901-324-4202) or **Yellow Cab** (☎ 901-577-7777). The **Downtown**

Airport Shuttle (DASH; ☎ 901-522-1677; one way per person $15) serves most downtown hotels.

Greyhound (☎ 901-523-1184; 203 Union Ave) runs frequent buses to Nashville ($35.50, four hours); Little Rock, AR ($26, 2½ hours); and New Orleans, LA ($51, eight to 10 hours).

Central Station (☎ 901-526-0052; 545 S Main St), the Amtrak terminal, has been restored to its original 1914 splendor. The *City of New Orleans* goes to Chicago, IL ($80 to $125, 10½ hours) and New Orleans, LA ($43 to $68, nine hours).

Local buses are run by the **Memphis Area Transit Authority** (MATA; ☎ 901-722-7171; www.mata transit.com; fare $1.40). The **Main Street Trolley** (☎ 901-274-6282; fare $1) runs vintage trolley cars on a loop from the Amtrak station to the Pyramid via Main St and Riverside Dr.

NASHVILLE

Think of any classic story song, one that has you laughing out loud or crying in your beer, and there's a good chance it came from Nashville. Whether it was Willie Nelson jotting notes as he scrounged for beer money in the 1960s, Steve Earle scrawling on a napkin as he contemplated love, life and death, or Alan Jackson's written epiphanies learned from his days driving forklifts for Wal-Mart, the singer-songwriters who pay their dues on Nashville stages have bent and shaped country music into one of the most indelible musical forms.

For country-music fans all over the world, a trip to Nashville is the ultimate homage, a nod to the musicians that taught us how to bleed through our hearts, see the beauty in the simple, and how to create a song out of an empty bottle of booze. Undoubtedly the country-music capital of the world, Nashville (*nash*-vul, according to locals) offers a musical experience that'll get anyone tapping toes.

Though this is the town that spawned almost every country star from Loretta Lynn and Dolly Parton to Trisha Yearwood and Shania Twain, in the words of one local: 'It ain't all cowboy boots and rhinestones.' Yes, sir. In addition to traditional country music, Nashville is a haven for singer-songwriters of any genre. Most bars and restaurants feature live music, and it's often a solo singer with nothing but a sweet voice and an acoustic guitar. Nashville has many attractions, from the fantastic Country Music Hall of Fame and the Grand Ole Opry House to rough blues bars, historic buildings and big-name sports. It also has friendly people, cheap food and an unrivaled assortment of tacky souvenirs.

History

Ancient mound-builders – civilizations that built mounds as effigies, altars and fortifications – and wandering Shawnee Indians, occupied the Cumberland River Bluffs before Europeans established Fort Nashborough in 1779. The legendary Daniel Boone brought emigrants over the Appalachians from Virginia, the Carolinas and northeastern states.

Renamed 'Nashville' around 1784, the town was an important railroad junction with a riverboat connection to the Mississippi, and a strategic point during the Civil War. It surrendered to federal troops in 1862, and Andrew Johnson (then a US senator) was appointed military governor, imposing martial law until 1865. Confederate troops were destroyed in the 1864 Battle of Nashville. Nashville survived the war intact, though its postwar recovery was hampered by two major cholera epidemics. The Tennessee Centennial Exposition in 1897 signaled the city's eventual recovery.

From 1925, Nashville became known for its live-broadcast *Barn Dance*, later nicknamed the *Grand Ole Opry*. Its popularity soared, the city proclaimed itself the 'country-music capital of the world,' and recording studios sprang up in Music Row. The Fisk Jubilee Singers built on another musical tradition in the 1870s, popularizing black spirituals with benefit tours for Fisk University, a struggling black college. Ninety years later, Fisk students led sit-in demonstrations at downtown lunch counters, supported economic boycotts and marched on city hall to demand desegregated facilities.

Today, Nashville draws a wide mix of friendly locals and talented transients who play small stages and hope their dreams will come true – that they'll sign multimillion-dollar recording contracts and be the next Shania Twain or Garth Brooks. The resulting glut of excellent musicians and songwriters has created an exciting, ever-evolving music scene. Though sprawling

THE SOUTH

in many directions, both geographically and culturally, Nashville is a small town at heart.

Orientation

Nashville sits on a rise beside the Cumberland River, with the state capitol at the highest point. The compact downtown area slopes south to Broadway, the city's central artery. Briley Parkway is the main road out of town.

Downtown, historic commercial buildings comprise the entertainment area called 'The District,' from 2nd Ave to 5th Ave and along Broadway, where old dives and rib joints sit comfortably alongside slicksters like the Hard Rock Cafe. Across the Cumberland River is the Coliseum where the Titans play rabble-rousing football; Music Row, Elliston Place and Vanderbilt University are situated west of downtown, with funky restaurants along Broadway, 21st Ave and West End Ave. Off the Briley Parkway northeast of town, Music Valley is a tourist zone full of budget motels, franchise restaurants and outlet stores built around the Grand Ole Opry.

Information

BOOKSTORES

Elders Booksellers (☎ 615-327-1867; 2115 Elliston Pl; ✆ Mon-Sat) An excellent used bookstore near Music Row.

EMERGENCY

Emergency (☎ 911) Police, ambulance, fire.
Main police station (☎ 615-862-8600; 310 1st Ave S) Nonemergencies only.

INTERNET ACCESS

Global Café(☎ 615-726-2011; 322 Broadway; ✆ 8am-9pm Mon-Fri, 9am-10pm Sat, 10am-4pm Sun) A comfy modern-design café that has wi-fi for travelers packing laptops, but no public-use computers.
Public library (☎ 615-862-5800; www.library.nashville .org; 615 Church St; ✆ 9am-8pm Mon-Thu, to 6pm Fri, to 5pm Sat, 2-5pm Sun) Free Internet access.

MEDIA

Nashville Scene (www.nashscene.com) Free alternative weeklies covering local entertainment and news.
Out & About A monthly publication covering gay and lesbian issues throughout Tennessee.
Rage (www.nashvillerage.com) Alternative free weekly.
Tennessean Nashville's daily newspaper.

MEDICAL

Baptist Hospital (☎ 615-284-5555; 2000 Church St)
Vanderbilt University Medical Center (☎ 615-322-5000; 1211 22nd Ave S)

POST

Post office (☎ 800-275-8777) Church St (1718 Church St); Frist (Frist Center for Visual Arts) All mail sent to General Delivery, Nashville, TN 37203 goes to the Church St branch.

TOURIST INFORMATION

Nashville Convention & Visitors Bureau (☎ 615-259-4700, 800-657-6910, 24hr events ☎ 615-244-939; www.nashvillecvb.com; 211 Commerce St)
Nashville Visitors Information Center (☎ 615-259-4747; www.musiccityusa.com; Gaylord Entertainment Center; ✆ 8:30am-5:30pm) Pick up free city maps here at the glass tower.

Sights & Activities
DOWNTOWN

The historic 2nd Ave N business area was the center of the cotton trade in the 1870s and 1880s, when most of the Victorian warehouses were built; note the cast iron and masonry facades. Today it's the heart of **The District**, with shops, restaurants, underground saloons and nightclubs. Two blocks west, **Printers Alley** is a narrow cobblestone lane known for its nightlife since the 1940s. Along the Cumberland River, Riverfront Park is a shady, landscaped promenade featuring **Fort Nashborough**, a 1930s replica of the city's original outpost, and a dock from which river taxis cruise out to Music Valley.

Country Music Hall of Fame & Museum (☎ 615-416-2001, 800-852-6437; 222 5th Ave S; adult/child $17/9; ✆ 9am-5pm) is a monumental and worthwhile hats-off to Nashville and its country-music history. It's chock-full of artifacts like Elvis' gold Cadillac, Gene Autry's string tie and the handwritten lyrics to 'Mamas Don't Let Your Babies Grow Up to Be Cowboys.' Everything's state of the art, and touch screens allow access to recordings and photos from the Country Music Foundation's enormous archives. The fact- and music-filled audio tour ($5 extra) is narrated by the likes of Dolly Parton, Trisha Yearwood and Vince Gill. From here you can also take the **Studio B Tour** (one hour, $11), which shuttles you to RCA's famed Music Row studio, where many stars, including Elvis, recorded famous tracks.

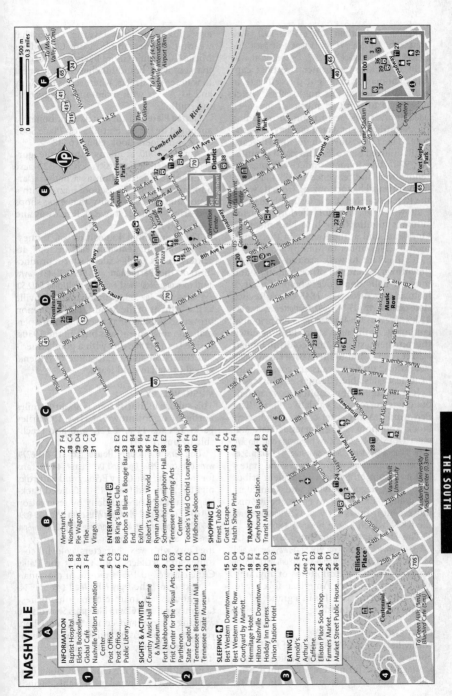

NASHVILLE

INFORMATION
Baptist Hospital.................	**1** B3
Elders Booksellers..............	**2** B4
Global Café......................	**3** F4
Nashville Visitors Information	
Center...........................	**4** F4
Post Office.......................	**5** D3
Post Office.......................	**6** E2
Public Library....................	**7** E2

SIGHTS & ACTIVITIES
Country Music Hall of Fame	
& Museum.......................	**8** E3
Fort Nashborough.............	**9** E2
Frist Center for the Visual Arts..	**10** D3
Parthenon........................	**11** A4
State Capitol.....................	**12** D2
Tennessee Bicentennial Mall..	**13** D2
Tennessee State Museum......	**14** E2

SLEEPING
Best Western Downtown......	**15** D2
Best Western Music Row......	**16** D4
Courtyard by Marriott.........	**17** C4
Hermitage Hotel................	**18** E2
Hilton Nashville Downtown...	**19** F4
Holiday Inn Express............	**20** D3
Union Station Hotel............	**21** D3

EATING
Arnold's...........................	**22** E4
Arthur's...........................	(see 21)
Caffeine..........................	**23** D3
Elliston Place Soda Shop.......	**24** B4
Farmers Market..................	**25** D1
Market Street Public House...	**26** E2

Merchant's.......................	**27** F4
Nashville.........................	**28** C4
Pie Wagon........................	**29** C3
Tribe..............................	**30** C3
Virago............................	**31** C4

ENTERTAINMENT
BB King's Blues Club............	**32** E2
Bourbon St Blues & Boogie Bar..	**33** E2
End................................	**34** B4
Exit/In............................	**35** B4
Robert's Western World........	**36** F4
Ryman Auditorium..............	**37** F4
Schermerhorn Symphony Hall..	**38** E2
Tennessee Performing Arts	
Center...........................	(see 14)
Tootsie's Wild Orchid Lounge..	**39** F4
Wildhorse Saloon...............	**40** E2

SHOPPING
Ernest Tubb's....................	**41** F4
Great Escape.....................	**42** C4
Hatch Show Print................	**43** F4

TRANSPORT
Greyhound Bus Station.........	**44** E3
Transit Mall......................	**45** E2

THE SOUTH

Ryman Auditorium (☎ 615-889-3060; www .ryman.com; 116 5th Ave N; daytime tour adult/child $8.50/4.25, incl backstage $11.25/7; ☻ 9am-4pm) was built in 1890 by a former riverboat captain. Thomas Ryman 'got the call' late in life and dedicated this huge, gabled, brick tabernacle to spiritual music. It has been used for various performances, including the Saturday-night **Grand Ole Opry** (www.opry .com). The *Opry* stayed here for 31 years, until it moved out to the Opryland complex in 1974. The Ryman underwent massive renovations and reopened in 1994. Thanks to the musical history oozing from its walls, the Ryman can be a life-altering place to see a show. Today, the Opry performs during summer months (March to November) at Opryland, and at the Ryman in the winter months (November to March).

It's pleasant to walk around the rest of downtown, where tall office buildings and modern halls don't overwhelm the city's historic structures. The 1845 Greek Revival **state capitol** (☎ 615-741-2692; Charlotte Ave, btwn 6th & 7th Sts; free tours 9am-4pm Mon-Fri) is the principal landmark, with steep stairs leading down the northern side to the colorful **Farmers Market** (p452) and the **Tennessee Bicentennial Mall**, whose outdoor walls are covered with historical facts about Tennessee's history.

Just south of the capitol, government buildings surround Legislative Plaza. The Performing Arts Center covers an adjacent block and houses the **Tennessee State Museum** (☎ 615-741-2692; www.tnmuseum.org; 5th Ave btwn Union & Deaderick; admission free; ☻ 10am-5pm Tue-Sat, from 1pm Sun), which traces the state's history, from effigy pots of ancient tribes to pioneer daguerreotypes and Confederate dollars. Exhibits cover the abolitionist movement from as early as 1797, as well as the KKK, which began here in 1868.

The **Frist Center for the Visual Arts** (☎ 615-244-3340; www.fristcenter.org; 919 Broadway; adult/child $8.50/6.50; ☻ 10am-5:30pm Mon-Sat, to 8pm Thu & 1-5pm Sun) hosts traveling exhibitions of anything and everything, from American folk art to the European masters. It's in a grand, refurbished post office building.

WEST END

Nashville's West End consists of **Music Row**, home of the production companies, agents, managers and promoters who run Nashville's country music industry. If you're

expecting to see your favorite cowboy-hat wearing crooner, think again. On today's Music Row you're more likely to see executives enjoying liquid lunches. Still, it's neat to wander the streets, where icons like Sony and RCA mix with mom-and-pop recording studios.

Elliston Place is a tiny enclave of bohemia anchored by the ancient Elliston Place Soda Shop and Elders Booksellers (p448).

Almost 6000 students attend the gorgeous **Vanderbilt University**, whose 326-acre campus won designation as a national arboretum in 1988. The school buzzes with a lively student community that eats, shops and drinks along 21st Ave N, Broadway and West End Ave.

The Centennial Exposition of Tennessee was held in **Centennial Park** in 1897; its centerpiece is a full-scale plaster reproduction of the **Parthenon** (☎ 615-862-8431; www .parthenon.org; 2600 West End Ave; adult/child $4/2.50; ☻ 9am-4:30pm Tue-Sat), symbolizing Nashville as the 'Athens of the South.' The Parthenon proved so popular that a second, more permanent replacement was built in the 1930s. Inside is an **art museum** with a good American collection and a 42ft statue of Athena, gilded in Italian gold leaf.

MUSIC VALLEY

This suburban tourist zone is about 10 miles northeast of downtown at Hwy 155/Briley Parkway exits 11 and 12B, and also reachable by bus (p454).

The **Grand Ole Opry House** (☎ 615-871-6779; www.opry.com; 2802 Opryland Dr) seats 4400 fans for the *Grand Ole Opry* Friday and Saturday night year-round (see p454). Guided backstage tours are offered daily by reservation ($10). The **Grand Ole Opry Museum** (☎ 615-889-3060; 2802 Opryland Dr; admission free; ☻ 10:30am-6pm Mar-Dec) across the plaza tells the story of the Opry with wax characters, colorful costumes and artifacts. Don't miss the Patsy Cline classic – a 1950s rec-room diorama.

Next door, the **Opry Mills Mall** (☎ 615-514-1100) houses an Imax cinema, theme restaurants and the **Gibson Bluegrass Showcase**, a working factory and concert venue where you can see banjos, mandolins and resonator guitars being made through the glass (free).

Exit 12B goes to the Opryland Hotel (opposite) as well as several other sights, including the **Music City Wax Museum** (☎ 615-883-3612; adult/child $3.50/1.50; ⏰ 9am-5pm, to 9pm May-Sep), with stacks of wax statues of costumed country stars, and the **Willie Nelson Museum** (☎ 615-885-1515; 2613 McGavock Parkway; adult/child $3.50/1.50; ⏰ 9am-5pm, to 9pm May-Sep), with guitars and gold records.

Tours

Ask at the visitor center for a list of the many theme tours available in Nashville.

General Jackson Showboat (☎ 615-871-5043; www .generaljackson.com; 2812 Opryland Dr) Offers lunch and dinner cruises on the Cumberland River with lots of rollicking entertainment. Departs from the Opry Land Hotel. Prices and trips vary; call for more information.

Gray Line (☎ 615-883-5555, 800-251-1864; www.gray linenashville.com) Offers a variety of bus tours, including Discover Nashville (three hours, $35) or the Homes of the Stars (three hours, $30). Buses pick up from area hotels, or from the Hard Rock Café in The District.

Sleeping

Budget chain motels cluster on all sides of downtown, along I-40 and I-65. They all charge from around $50 to $70 for rooms. At any hotel, lower rates are available midweek, on slow weekends and during the winter. Be aware hotel tax in Nashville adds 15.25%.

DOWNTOWN

Best Western Downtown (☎ 615-242-4311, 800-627-3297; 711 Union St; r $70-130; P ✛) With a great location near the capitol and free parking, this is one of the best values in downtown Nashville. The large rooms, most with two double beds, are tidy and the staff welcoming. An attached deli sells snacks.

Holiday Inn Express (☎ 615-244-0150, 800-251-1856; 920 Broadway; r from $89; P ✛ 🖳 🖭) This 273-room hotel, geared toward the corporate set on business at the convention center, is also convenient to The District. What it lacks in character it makes up for in proximity and amenities that include free parking.

Hermitage Hotel (☎ 615-244-3121, 888-888-9414; www.thehermitagehotel.com; 231 6th Ave N; r from $180; P ✛ 🖳) Oozing with elegance, this beautiful 123-room hotel, within an aria's resonance of the opera, pays special attention to details, with generous rooms, tons of marble, plush linens and impeccable service. Parking costs $18.

Hilton Nashville Downtown (☎ 615-620-1000; www.nashvillehilton.com; 121 4th Ave S; 1-bedroom ste from $190; P ✛ 🖳 🖭) With 344 suites in the heart of The District, the Hilton, featuring lush amenities like a state-of-the-art fitness center, dominates the block between Broadway and Demonbreun St. Self/valet parking $14/18.

Best Western Music Row (☎ 615-242-1631, 800-528-1234; 1407 Division St; r from $60; P ✛ 🖭) Not far from the action, but a little too far to walk to Broadway, this standard 103-room hotel near Music Row offers a good value for anyone with a rental car.

Courtyard by Marriott (☎ 615-327-9900, 800-245-1959; 1901 West End Ave; r from $90; P ✛ 🖳 🖭) You'll join visitors to Vanderbilt at this comfortable 216-room hotel near Music Row and on the brink of the university campus. It has large rooms (many with sleeper sofas to fit more people), a fitness center and laundry facilities.

MUSIC VALLEY

Fiddlers Inn Music Valley (☎ 615-885-1440; www .fiddlers-inn.com 2410 Music Valley Dr; weekday/weekend $60/67; 🖭) This family-oriented hotel is a good option if you want to see shows at the *Grand Ole Opry*, which is just a half-mile walk away. Staff members are friendly and welcoming to groups of any size.

Opryland Hotel (☎ 615-889-1000, 877-456-6779; www.gaylordhotels.com; 2800 Opryland Dr; r with/without balcony $250/190) This sprawling hotel is practically a village with a whopping 2881 guest rooms. The lobby features a self-contained 'Oprysphere' with waterfalls, boat rides, magnolia trees and an elevated walkway above the rain forest. Given the hotel's size

---

THE AUTHOR'S CHOICE

Union Station Hotel (☎ 615-726-1001, 800-996-3426; www.wyndham.com; 1001 Broadway; r from $130; P ✛ 🖳) Resembling a castle with its limestone fortress and buttresses, this 1900 hotel is one of the city's most beautiful. The 124 rooms are uniquely designed, retaining the architectural integrity; 5th-floor rooms, for example, have grand 30ft ceilings. All rooms are chock-full of amenities. The lobby is stunning, sitting regally under a vaulted ceiling of Tiffany stained glass. Parking costs $14.

it's no wonder rates fluctuate like crazy; at times of low occupancy, rates can sink by 50%.

Opryland KOA Kampground (☎ 615-889-0286, 800-562-7789; www.koa.com; 2626 Music Valley Dr; campsites $29; P ⊡) At the north end of Music Valley, and with 460 tent and RV sites and every convenience you can think of, this is the best place for tenting near Nashville.

Eating

It's easy to eat well in Nashville, with a wide selection of terrific restaurants – from small family-run shops selling meat-and-threes to upscale bistros offering modern twists on traditional favorites. Many of the city's best eateries are in west of downtown, but it's easy to get a good meal anywhere. One of the best places in town to have lunch is the **Farmers Market** (8th Ave N at Jackson St; ☉ 9am-5pm) Here you'll find a great variety of cheap food, including gyros, empanadas, muffalettas, Reubens hot dogs and fresh fruit.

BUDGET

The true taste of Nashville can best be found in cinder-block cabins in the industrial zone south of Broadway, where meat-and-threes come in heaping portions.

Arnold's (☎ 615-256-4455; 605 8th Ave S; mains $5-8; ☉ 10am-2:30pm Mon-Fri) For locals, Arnold's has long been a favorite for the ubiquitous meat-and-three. Folks line up to get into this tiny shack for the fried chicken, peppery roast beef, turnip greens, cornbread and grumpy but loveable Jack Arnold's yummy chocolate pie.

Pie Wagon (☎ 615-256-5893; 1302 Division St; mains $5-10; ☉ 6am-2pm Mon-Fri) The first incarnation opened in 1922 in an old trolley wagon. This location has been here since 1990 and still has a loyal local following for its homey Southern cuisine and hot chicken.

Caffeine (☎ 615-259-4993; 1516 Demonbreun St; mains $6-7; ☉ 7am-11pm Mon-Fri, from 9am Sat) Looking for a good cup o' Joe and a superb sandwich? Look no further. Caffeine is an excellent stop for a strong latte or cappuccino; it also serves large sandwiches, fresh salads and homemade desserts. If you've got a laptop, it has free wi-fi, but no computers.

Elliston Place Soda Shop (☎ 615-327-1090; 2111 Elliston Place; mains $3-6; ☉ closed Sun) Slurp it up,

---

THE AUTHOR'S CHOICE

Noshville (☎ 615-329-6674; 1918 Broadway; mains $5-10; ☉ 6:30am-2:30pm Mon, 3:30am-9pm Tue-Thu, 6:30am-10pm Fri, 7:30am-10:30pm Sat, to 9pm Sun) A wonderful New York–style Jewish deli specializing in flavorful corned-beef and pastrami sandwiches that take both hands to eat. Other delicious specialties include bagels with lox, whitefish and fat and juicy hamburgers, all served up by ultrafriendly and professional staff in the crisp chrome interior. A great place to eat in or take a snack to go.

---

baby. This old joint serves soda-fountain treats along with meat-and-three plates.

MIDRANGE

Market Street Public House (☎ 615-259-9611; 134 2nd Ave N; mains $8-20; ☉ lunch & dinner) This friendly neighborhood pub has a great selection of homemade microbrews, with the regular clientele's beer steins hanging on the walls. The menu offers generous portions of salads, burgers, fish and chips, and more substantial meals like chicken and pasta.

Merchant's (☎ 615-254-1892; 401 Broadway; mains downstairs $10-20, upstairs $20-30; ☉ lunch & dinner) Right in the heart of The District, this friendly bistro has an excellent wine list and lovely mahogany bar at which to swill wine. You can eat more casual fare at the downstairs bar, or splurge on seafood and steaks upstairs.

Tribe (☎ 625-329-3912; 1517 Church St; mains $9-19; ☉ 5pm-10pm Mon-Thu, to 11pm Fri & Sat) Catering to Nashville's gay and lesbian community (though anyone is welcome), Tribe is a hot, groovy spot with a delicious, eclectic menu including hand-cut steaks and fish topped with flavorful sauces.

TOP END

Virago (☎ 615-320-5149; 1811 Division St; mains $17-30; ☉ 6-11pm, bar to 1am) While continually and refreshingly reinventing itself at whim, Virago remains the place to be for its groovy, hip atmosphere, excellent sushi and delightful Asian-inspired menu. Service can be a little snarky, but the scene is worthwhile, even just for cocktails and a snack.

Arthur's (☎ 615-255-1494; www.arthursrestaurant .com; 1001 Broadway; prix-fixe menu $69; ☉ dinner)

In the Union Station Hotel, this delightful French bistro's menu changes daily, making it the only restaurant in town with 365 menu changes. The price seems high, but the enveloping elegance, excellent service and delicious food – a prix-fixe seven-course extravaganza – are well worth the splurge.

Entertainment
LIVE MUSIC
Apart from the big venues, many talented country, folk, bluegrass, Southern-rock and blues performers play smoky honky-tonks, blues bars, seedy storefronts and organic cafés for tips. Almost anywhere you go in town, you'll hear fantastic live music. Many places are free Monday to Friday or if you arrive early enough.

Ryman Auditorium (tickets ☎ 615-458-8700; info 615-889-3060; www.ryman.com; 116 5th Ave; ticket prices vary) Often called the 'mother church of country music,' the Ryman was the home of the *Grand Ole Opry* from 1943 to 1974. The Ryman's excellent acoustics, historic charm and large seating capacity have kept it the premier venue in town. You can also tour the Ryman during the day (p450).

Wildhorse Saloon (☎ 615-902-8200; 120 2nd Ave N; cover $4-10) A popular spot to snap yer fingers and tap yer toes while listening to new country music. The saloon offers free dance lessons, so you'll be doing the Rebel Slide and Cowboy Stomp before you know it.

Bourbon St Blues & Boogie Bar (☎ 615-242-5837; www.bourbonstreetblues.com; 220 Printers Alley; cover free-$10; ☻ 4pm-3am) This spot, in the tiny Printers Alley between 3rd and 4th Ave and Union and Church Sts, is the city's premier blues venue.

BB King's Blues Club (☎ 615-256-2727; www.bbkingbluesclub.com; 152 2nd Ave N; cover Sun-Thu $5, Fri & Sat $10; ☻ 5pm-1am) You'll see live jazz and blues bands here every night, with BB King All Stars rocking out on Friday and Saturday nights.

Robert's Western World (☎ 615-244-9552; www.robertswesternworld.com; 416 Broadway; no cover; 10am-3am) Leave the glitz at home, throw on yer boots and belly up to the bar, order a Bud and a burger, and enjoy the down-home scene. On the strip, this longtime bar has live music starting in the afternoon and lasting through the night.

Tootsie's Wild Orchid Lounge (☎ 615-726-7937; 422 Broadway) Truly a must-visit for anyone – Tootsies is a venerated dive that sees a lot of whoopin' and hollerin' every night. In the 1960s, club owner 'Tootsie' Bess nurtured the careers and bar tabs of struggling songwriters like Kris Kristofferson and Willie Nelson. Photos of performers, from superstars to one-hit wonders line the walls, while up-and-coming country musicians play the tiny stage. It's not unusual for big stars to stop by for an impromptu jam session.

In the Elliston Place neighborhood are a couple of venues that stray from hardcore country and whose cover charges vary, depending on who's playing. **Exit/In** (☎ 615-321-4400; www.exitin.com; 2208 Elliston Pl) features good ole rock and roll, with everything from rock cover bands to original electric vibes. The **End** (☎ 615-321-4457; 2219 Elliston Pl) is a tiny venue and the premiere grunge spot for rock and alternative music.

THE AUTHOR'S CHOICE
In an unassuming strip mall in suburban Green Hills, 5 miles west of the from the kickin' country scene in The District, the 21-table **Bluebird Cafe** (☎ 615-383-1461; 4104 Hillsboro Rd; cover free-$10) bursts with atmosphere, history and the best acoustic music coming out of Nashville. Opened in 1982, the Bluebird evolved into a world-renowned venue geared solely toward the singer-songwriter. Musicians know that if you make it at the Bluebird, you can make it anywhere, and it's likely you're pretty damn good. Veterans include commercial successes like Garth Brooks, Terri Clark and Bonnie Raitt, along with critically acclaimed songwriters like Lucinda Williams, Townes Van Zandt, Steve Earle and Guy Clark.

You can reserve a table up to a week in advance and there are usually two shows nightly. The minimum charge of $7 per person is easy to spend on drinks or food (try the blackened catfish sandwich). The Bluebird has a pretty strict no-talking policy during shows, so if you want to get loud, this is not the place for you.

THEATER

Grand Ole Opry (☎ 615-871-6779; www.opry.com; 2802 Opryland Dr, Music Valley; adult $34.50-46.50, child $24.50-34.50; ☒ 7:30pm Fri, 6:30pm & 9:30pm Sat) Though you'll find a variety of country shows throughout the week, the production Friday and Saturday evenings is the *Grand Ole Opry*, a lavish tribute to classic Nashville Country music.

Tennessee Performing Arts Center (☎ 615-782-4000; www.tpac.org; 505 Deaderick St) With three great stages, this venue houses the **Nashville Symphony** (www.nashvillesymphony.org), which moves to the new world-class **Schermerhorn Symphony Hall** (☎ 615-783-1200; 127 3rd Ave S) in late 2006. It also is home to the following:

Nashville Ballet (www.nashvilleballet.com)
Nashville Opera (www.nashvilleopera.org)
Tennessee Repertory Theatre (www.tnrep.org)
Tennessee State Museum (p450)

SPORTS

Tennessee Titans (☎ 615-565-4000; www.tennessee titans.com) The NFL Tennessee Titans play in the Coliseum, across the river from downtown, from September to December.

Nashville Sounds (☎ 615-242-4371; www.nashville sounds.com) A minor-league AAA baseball affiliate for the Pittsburgh Pirates, the Sounds play at Greer Stadium, south of town.

Nashville Predators (☎ 615-770-2300; www.nash villepredators.com) For NHL hockey, catch the Nashville Predators at Gaylord Entertainment Center.

Shopping

Nashville's music stores are numerous and well stocked.

Ernest Tubb's (☎ 615-255-7503; www.ernesttubb .com; 417 Broadway; ☒ 9am-10pm Sun-Thu, 9am-midnight Fri & Sat) The best place to shop for country and bluegrass.

Great Escape (☎ 615-327-0646; 1925 Broadway; ☒ 10am-9pm Mon-Sat, 1-6pm Sun) East of downtown, it sells new and used CDs or records of all genres, plus comic books and videos.

Hatch Show Print (☎ 615-256-2805; www .hatchshowprint.com; 316 Broadway; ☒ 9:30am-5:30pm Mon-Fri, 10:30am-5:30pm Sat) One of the oldest letter-print shops in the US. Using old-school cut-blocks, Hatch began making posters to promote early vaudeville and circus shows. The company has produced graphic ads and posters for almost every country star since.

Getting There & Around

Nashville International Airport (BNA; ☎ 615-275-1662; www.flynashville.com), 8 miles east of town, is not a major air hub. MTA bus No 18 links the airport and downtown; the **Gray Line Airport Express** (☎ 615-275-1180; one way/return $12/24; ☒ 5am-11pm) serves major downtown and West End hotels. Taxis charge a flat rate of $20 each way. Try **Nashville Cab** (☎ 615-242-7070) or **Music City Cab** (☎ 615-742-3030).

Greyhound (☎ 615-255-3556; 200 8th Ave S) has frequent buses to Memphis ($35.50, four hours), Atlanta, GA ($41.50, five hours), Birmingham, AL ($32, four hours), and New Orleans, LA ($52, 13 to 16 hours).

The **Metropolitan Transit Authority** (MTA; ☎ 615-862-5950; www.nashvillemta.org; transit mall, cnr Deaderick St & 4th Ave N; adult $1.10) operates city bus services based downtown. Its express buses also go to Music Valley and back.

AROUND NASHVILLE

About 25 miles southwest of Nashville off Hwy 100, drivers pick up the **Natchez Trace Parkway**, which leads 450 miles southwest to Natchez, Mississippi (p410). This northern section is one of the most attractive stretches of the entire route. Near the parkway entrance, look for the landmark **Loveless Cafe** (☎ 615-646-9700; www.lovelesscafe .com; 8400 Hwy 100; dishes $5-15; ☒ 7am-9pm), a 1940s roadhouse famous for its country ham, stone-ground grits, jam and ample portions of Southern-fried chicken.

About 20 miles south of Nashville off I-65, the historic town of **Franklin** (www.his toricfranklin.com) has a charming historic downtown area and beautiful B&Bs. About 50 miles south of Nashville on Hwys 41A and 231, **Shelbyville** (www.shelbyvilletn.com) is the epicenter of the high-stepping, head-bobbing Tennessee walking horse.

Off Hwy 55 in Lynchburg (population 361), you'll come to the only place in the world that distills Tennessee's famous whiskey. The **Jack Daniel's Distillery** (☎ 931-759-6180; www.jackdaniels.com; tours free; ☒ 9am-4:30pm) offers interesting hour-long tours; it's hard to believe that so much JD comes from this one country distillery, and has since 1866. Because Lynchburg is in a 'dry county' (meaning no hard liquor is sold within county lines), you can only purchase special-edition gift bottles here and, of course, there are no free samples, but you're encouraged to take long sniffs of the distilling whiskey.

EASTERN TENNESSEE

Largely a rural region with unhurried towns dotting the hills and river valleys, Eastern Tennessee boasts spectacular scenery dominated by the Great Smoky Mountains. where you can spot bears, hike and camp, while the white waters of the Ocoee River are great for rafting. The region's two main urban areas, Knoxville and Chattanooga, are pleasant riverside cities with lively college populations, good restaurants and an easygoing energy.

Great Smoky Mountains National Park

The Cherokee called this territory Shaconage (shah-*cone*-ah-jey), meaning roughly 'land of the blue smoke.' As is often the case in places of great natural grandeur, human history is trumped by natural history. At about a billion years old, the Smoky Mountains are among the oldest in the world. This ancient land is home to such an astonishing variety of animals and plants that it has been designated an International Biosphere Reserve and a World Heritage Site.

The most popular sights inside the easily accessed park include the former settlement of **Cades Cove**, the majestic peaks of **Mount Le Conte**, the dizzying heights of **Clingmans Dome** and a wonderful selection of waterfalls, coves and trails. Nearly 10 million people come each year to hike the park's 800 miles of trails, fish its 2000 miles of streams and rivers, drive its nearly 400 miles of paved and unpaved roads or camp at one of more than 1000 developed sites.

With so many visitors, the main arteries and attractions can get crowded. Studies have shown that 95% of park visitors never venture farther than 100yd from their cars. It's easy to leave the teeming masses behind by merely parking the beast and stepping into the backcountry. You'll be glad you did.

Unlike most other national parks, Great Smoky charges no admission fee, nor will it ever; this proviso was written into the park's original charter as a stipulation for a $5 million Rockefeller family grant. As there are no fee stations, you will have to stop by a visitor center to pick up a park map and the free park newspaper, *Smokies Guide*.

ORIENTATION & INFORMATION

Great Smoky Mountains National Park straddles the North Carolina and Tennessee border, which runs diagonally through the heart of the park. The north–south **Newfound Gap Rd/Hwy 441** spans from one end of the park to the other, connecting the gateway towns of Gatlinburg, TN on the north-central border and Cherokee, NC on the south-central border.

The park's two main visitor centers are **Sugarlands Visitor Center** (☎ 865-436-1291; ☗ 8am-4:30pm), at the park's northern entrance near Gatlinburg (Tennessee), and **Oconaluftee Visitor Center**, at the park's southern entrance near Cherokee (North Carolina). **Park headquarters** (☎ 865-436-1200; 107 Park Headquarters Rd) are located just off of Newfound Gap Rd at the Gatlinburg entrance to the park, just before Sugarlands Visitor Center.

CAMPING

With 10 developed campgrounds offering about 1000 campsites, you'd think finding a place to pitch would be easy. Not so in the busy summer season: your best bet is to plan ahead. You can make **reservations** (☎ 800-365-2267; http://reservations.nps.gov) up to five months in advance. Otherwise it's first-come, first-served. Camping fees are $14 to $33 per night, except for the five horse camps, which cost $20 to $25 per site. Of the park's 10 campgrounds only Cades Cove and Smokemont are open year-round; others are open March through October.

Backcountry camping is an excellent option. A (free) permit is required; you can make **reservations** (☎ 865-436-1231) and get permits at the ranger stations or visitor centers.

Gatlinburg

The best known gateway town into the Smokies is **Gatlinburg**. The city has three **visitor centers** (☎ 865-436-0504, 800-568-4748; www .gatlinburg.com; ☗ 8am-6pm, to 8pm Fri & Sat, to 10pm summer), at the third and fifth stoplights and just north of town on US 441. They have separate information desks, one for city information (motels, restaurants) and one run by the park service (for campsite reservations, hiking routes etc), that are all open.

THE SOUTH

Ten miles north of Gatlinburg, **Pigeon Forge** (www.mypigeonforge.com) is a tacky complex of motels, outlet malls and country-music theaters and restaurants, all of which have grown up in the shadow of **Dollywood** (☎ 865-428-9488, 800-365-5996; www.dollywood.com; 1020 Dollywood Lane; adult/child $43.50/32.25; ☺ closed Jan-Mar), Dolly Parton's personal theme park.

Knoxville

Once Tennessee's territorial capital and now home to the state university, Knoxville is a friendly town that has a charming blend of old-fashioned neighbors and students. The **visitor center** (☎ 865-971-4440, 800-727-8045; www.knoxtsc.com; ☺ 9am-5pm Mon-Sat, from 1pm Sun) is on the riverfront off I-40 exit 388A. Most restaurants and nightlife center around the **Old City** and **Market Square**. Concerts and University of Tennessee sports teams play at the Neyland Coliseum.

The city's visual centerpiece is the **Sunsphere**, the main remnant of the 1982 World Fair. You can't miss the massive orange basketball that marks the **Women's Basketball Hall of Fame** (☎ 865-633-9000; www.wbhof.com; 700 Hall of Fame Dr; adult/child $8/6; ☺ 10am-5pm Mon-Sat, 1-6pm Sun), a sleek and worthwhile museum that features memorabilia and practice courts.

Chattanooga

Chattanooga was born of one of the great injustices of the early USA: the removal of the Cherokee along the Trail of Tears. One of the trail's two starting points was Ross's Landing in what is now downtown Chattanooga. Once the Indians were gone, the city grew quickly. It was a key strategic point during the Civil War, and several important battles were fought nearby at Lookout Mountain and Chickamauga. After the war it became a major transport hub, hence the 'Chattanooga Choo-Choo,' originally a reference to the Cincinnati Southern Railroad's passenger service from Cincinnati to Chattanooga and later the title of a Glenn Miller song.

Today, Chattanooga is one of the most interesting – and one of the most often overlooked – small cities in the South. Rather than focusing on the sprawl, Chattanooga planners have focused on beautifying the city's core. An ongoing $120 million revitalization of the downtown and waterfront has transformed this already really pretty city into a first-class, pedestrian-friendly community.

Most of Chattanooga's main sites are within a few blocks of the **visitor center** (☎ 423-856-8687, 800-322-3344; www.chattanoogafun.com; 2 Broad St; ☺ 8:30am-5:30pm) at the corner of 2nd and Broad Sts. The Bluff View Art District at High and E 2nd Sts has upscale shops and restaurants overlooking the river.

SIGHTS & ACTIVITIES

Ross's Landing, the epicenter of the city's rejuvenated waterfront, is a good place to start a riverfront stroll. The fabulous **Tennessee Aquarium** (☎ 800-262-0695; www.tnaqua.org; 1 Broad St; adult/child $18/9.50; ☺ 10am-6pm) is the world's largest freshwater aquarium. Exhibits mirror a large river system and give visitors a unique look at the interconnectedness of riparian areas. While here, check out a show at the attached **Imax theater** (☎ 800-262-0695; 201 Chestnut St; adult/child $8/5.50). Next door, the **Creative Discovery Museum** (☎ 423-756-2738; www.cdmfun.org; adult/child $8/6; ☺ 10am-5pm Mon-Sat, from noon Sun) is one of the coolest children's museums in the country, with wondrous exhibits for toddlers to teens.

Chattanooga Regional History Museum (☎ 423-265-3247; www.chattanoogahistory.com; adult/child $4/3; 400 Chestnut St; ☺ 10am-4pm Mon-Fri, from 11am Sat & Sun) does a very good job depicting the area's history.

Chattanooga African-American Museum (☎ 423-266-8658; www.caamhistory.com; 200 ML King Jr Blvd; adult/child $5/3; ☎ 10am-5pm Mon-Fri, noon-4pm Sat) displays a special exhibit on Chattanooga native and jazz-blues maven Bessie Smith.

Some of Chattanooga's oldest and best-known attractions are 6 miles outside the city at **Lookout Mountain** (☎ 423-821-4224; www.lookoutmtnattractions.com; 827 East Brow Rd; adult/child $36/18; ☺ vary by season). These include the Incline Railway, which chugs up a steep incline to the top of the mountain, underground caverns called Ruby Falls, and Rock City, a garden with a dramatic cliff top overlook and waterfall. The admission gets you into all three attractions. **Point Park** (admission $3), at the mountain's summit, is part of the NPS's **Chickamauga & Chattanooga National Military Park** (☎ 423-866-9241; www.nps.gov/chch).

SLEEPING

You can find many budget motels around I-24 and I-75.

Comfort Suites/Downtown (☎ 423-265-0008, 800-517-4000; 2431 Williams St; r from $75; P ☒ ▣ ☒) Less than 2 miles south of downtown, this is a excellent-value option, where the comfortable suites come standard with microwaves, refrigerators and wi-fi.

Chattanooga Choo-Choo Holiday Inn (☎ 423-266-5000, 800-872-2529; www.choochoo.com; 1400 Market St; r from $100; P ☒ ☒) Housed in the old railway terminal on 30 acres, the Choo-Choo is a grand hotel and a hub of activity. It has 360 rooms, including 48 in authentic railcars, ranging from nothing special to very deluxe (and rates vary accordingly). It has a restaurant where the waiters sing, both indoor and outdoor pools and a small railroad museum.

Chattanoogan (☎ 423-756-3400, 877-756-1684; www.chattanooganhotel.com; 1201 S Broad St; r/ste from $140/210; P ☒ ▣ ☒) This 202-room resort hotel in the heart of downtown has excellent modern amenities, groovy decor and a slick spa. It also has a bar, restaurant and fitness center. Rates vary widely; call ahead for special deals.

EATING

Greyfriar's (☎ 423-267-0376; www.rarecoffee.com; 406 Broad St; ☖ 7am-10pm) This coffeehouse, which has computers with Internet access, is a good stop for a light breakfast or quiet cup of coffee.

Big River Grille & Brewing Works (☎ 423-267-2739; 222 Broad St; mains $7-15; ☖ lunch & dinner) In a great location, just half a block from the aquarium, this microbrewery offers a friendly vibe, indoor and outside seating, with an extensive menu of sandwiches, pasta, steaks and Mexican food.

GETTING THERE & AROUND

Chattanooga's modest airport is just east of the city. Nearby, the **Greyhound station** (☎ 423-892-1277; 960 Airport Rd) has daily buses to Atlanta, GA ($21.50, 2½ hours), Nashville ($21.50, from 2½ hours) and Knoxville ($16.50, two hours).

With an utter lack of nostalgia, Amtrak does not serve Chattanooga.

For access to most downtown sites, ride the free electric shuttle buses that ply the center. The visitors center has a route map.

KENTUCKY

A wonderful combination of the South, North, East and West, Kentucky is a relaxed place, where dramatic mountains and forests juxtapose with some of the most beautifully manicured rural landscapes imaginable. The limestone-rich pastures with green grasses that bloom blue buds in spring (earning Kentucky the moniker 'Bluegrass State') showed early pioneers the state's horse-breeding potential. Today, thoroughbred breeding is a multibillion-dollar industry and Kentucky's Derby is the most famous horseracing event in the world. The state's cities are small but somehow appealing, and even the industries are engaging – a state that produces bourbon, baseball bats and Corvettes must be pretty cool.

History

The fertile lands to the west of the Appalachians were inhabited by Cherokee, Shawnee and Iroquois Indians, who tried hard to resist the encroachment of Whites. In 1775 a treaty with the Cherokee opened the way for settlers from the eastern colonies, and Daniel Boone marked a trail through the Cumberland Gap. Within 20 years, 100,000 people had migrated into the 'wilderness' that was then Virginia's western territory. Kentucky became the first non-seaboard state admitted to the Union.

Kentucky found itself in a quandary during the Civil War, when loyalties were divided between the slaveholding plantation class who supported the Confederacy, and the workers and small farmers who opposed slavery. Both the Union (Lincoln) and Confederate (Davis) presidents were Kentucky-born. When the Civil War began, 25,000 Kentuckians fought for the Confederacy, while 75,000 others fought for the Union.

Because Kentucky did not secede, it was spared the fate of smoldering Confederate states, thus avoiding the trauma of Reconstruction. Coal discovered in the Appalachians became a source of wealth and of the state's first labor movements.

Information

The boundary between Eastern and Central time goes through the middle of Kentucky. If you go from Mammoth Cave to Lincoln's birthplace, you'll arrive an hour later than you thought. State sales tax is 6%.

Kentucky Travel (☎ 502-564-4930, 800-225-8747; www.kentuckytourism.com; Box 2011, Frankfort, KY 40602) Sends out a detailed booklet on the state's attractions.

LOUISVILLE

Call it Looeyville, Lewisville or Louahvul; the locals don't mind – it's an easygoing kind of place. Aristocrats flock to Church-ill Downs and its world-famous Kentucky Derby in May. For the rest of the year, Louisville is a nice place to stop, and a cultural and industrial center with some classic Americana. The old downtown is a compact grid beside the Ohio River – and the I-64 freeway. A series of pretty parks (laid out by Frederick Law Olmsted in the 1890s) encircle the city, along with an inner (I-264) and outer (I-265) ring road. The **visitor center** (☎ 502-582-3732, 888-568-4784; www .gotolouisville.com; 221 S 4th St; ⊙ 9am-5pm Mon-Fri) runs an outlet in the convention center. It has maps and information, as well as the good *African American Visitors Guide*. Surf the Web free at the **public library** (301 York St) downtown.

Sights

At the **Louisville Slugger Museum** (☎ 502-588-7228; www.sluggermuseum.org; 800 W Main St; adult/child $8/4; ⊙ 9am-5pm Mon-Sat, from noon Sun Apr-Oct) look for the 120ft baseball bat leaning against the building – ya can't miss it. Since 1884, Hill-erich & Bradsby Co have been making the famous Louisville Slugger baseball bat and here you can watch the wooden bats being crafted in the factory. The admission fee includes a video, baseball exhibits, a plant tour, enthusiastic guides and a collection of baseball memorabilia. Note: bat production halts on Sunday.

Speed Art Museum (☎ 502-634-2700; www.speed museum.org; 2035 S 3rd St; admission free; ⊙ 10:30am-4pm Tue, Wed & Fri, to 8pm Thu, to 5pm Sat & Sun) is a handsome neoclassical museum that has more than 13,000 pieces of art, including European paintings and sculptures, plus exhibits of classical antiques and Kentucky artists.

Children enjoy the interactive exhibits at **Louisville Science Center** (☎ 502-561-6100; www .louisvillesciencecenter.org; 727 W Main St; adult/child $9/8; ⊙ 9:30am-5pm Mon-Thu, to 9pm Fri & Sat, noon-6pm Sun), which also houses an Imax theater.

Three **historic homes** (www.historichomes.org) are worth checking out. **Farmington** (☎ 502-452-9920; 3033 Bardstown Rd; tours adult/child $6/3; ⊙ 10am-4pm Tue-Sat, 1:30-4:30pm Sun) is an 1810-era house designed by Thomas Jefferson. Remodeled in Classic Revival style is 1855 **Whitehall** (☎ 502-897-2944; 3110 Lexington Rd; tours adult/child $4/2.50; ⊙ by appointment). **Thomas Edison House** (☎ 502-585-5247; 729 E Washington St; adult/child $4/3; ⊙ 10am-2pm Tue-Sat) is a shotgun cottage where Edison rented a room in the 1860s while working as a telegrapher for Western Union.

RIVER TOURS

The *Belle of Louisville* (☎ 502-574-2355, 800-832-0011; adult/child $12/5), a 1914-era stern-wheeler, does scenic two-hour sightseeing cruises on the Ohio River, departing from the 4th St Wharf.

CHURCHILL DOWNS

Home to the Kentucky Derby, **Churchill Downs** (☎ 502-636-4400, 800-283-3729; www.church illdowns.com; 700 Central Ave), 3 miles south of downtown, is one of the most important horse-oriented venues in the country. Most seats at the Kentucky Derby (held the first Saturday in May) are by invitation only or they've been reserved years in advance. On Derby Day, $40 gets you into the Paddock party scene (no seat) if you arrive by 6am, but it's so crowded you won't see much of

THE SOUTH

the race. Don't fret, however. From April through to November, you can get a $2 seat at the Downs for many exciting races, often warm-ups for the big events.

On the grounds, the interesting **Kentucky Derby Museum** (☎ 502-637-7097; Gate 1, Central Ave; adult/child $9/4; ☒ 8am-5pm Mon-Sat, from noon Sun) has displays on horses, jockeys and mint juleps, a 360-degree audiovisual about the race and a tour of the track. It also runs behind-the-scenes track tours ($6).

Sleeping

Rocking Horse B&B (☎ 502-583-0408, 888-467-7322; www.rockinghorse-bb.com; 1022 S 3rd St; r incl breakfast $95-170; ☒ ☒ ☒) The spacious rooms in this 1888 Romanesque mansion are decorated with pretty Victorian antiques and obvious attention to detail. Guests can hang out in the English garden courtyard, in the library or the parlor. The gourmet breakfast is divine.

Galt House (☎ 502-589-5200, 800-626-1814; www .galthouse.com; 140 N 4th Ave; r from $80; ☒ ☒ ☒) With 1300 standard rooms and suites, this big convention hotel offers a wide range of rooms and rates. Amenities include a revolving restaurant and lounge with great views and a British-style pub. Ask for a room with a view of the river.

Emily Boone Home Hostel (☎ 502-585-3430; 102 Pope St; dm $10) Emily, a local psychologist, provides three futon beds with kitchen facilities in a private home. Space is limited, so call first.

Eating

Bluegrass Brewing Company (☎ 502-899-7070; 3929 Shelbyville Rd; mains $6-10; ☒ lunch & dinner) With delicious beers like Altbier, an amber ale, this microbrewery does all its brewing and bottling right here. It also serves up a good selection of salads, burgers and other pub grub. It's got a nice patio for outside dining and drinking.

Zen Garden (☎ 502-895-9114; 2240 Frankfort Ave; mains $5-9; ☒ lunch & dinner Wed-Sun) Vegetarians rejoice! This sparsely decorated restaurant that occupies a frame house on Frankfort Ave, serves up delicious Vietnamese-inspired cuisine at incredible prices. No liquor license.

Lilly's (☎ 502-451-0447; 1147 Bardstown Rd; lunch $8-14, dinner $15-25; ☒ 11am-3pm Tue-Sat, 5:30-10pm

---

PICKIN' & GRINNIN'

Early American settlers maintained oral history by singing ballads about their homelands, about the hardships and discoveries of forging life on foreign ground. Early bluegrass and country music developed from this 'mountain' music, defined by its gritty, honest storytelling.

In the 1920s and 1930s, Bill Monroe and his brother Charlie gained attention as a duo with their combination of guitar, mandolin and sweet harmonies. Being from Kentucky where the grassy meadows sprout blue buds that give the grass a blue hue in spring, Bill went on to form Bill Monroe & the Blue Grass Boys.

The Boys created a sound like no other. Using traditional acoustic banjos, fiddles, mandolins and guitars, combined with vocal harmonies, the music incorporated songs and rhythms borrowed from gospel, blues and country. It even incorporated work songs and 'shouts' of black laborers.

In 1939, the Boys appeared at Nashville's *Grand Ole Opry* and soon became a wildly successful touring band. In 1946, Earl Scruggs joined the group, bringing his banjo and a distinct three-finger picking style that further honed the bluegrass sound. Later, Lester Flatt brought the slide Dobro guitar, injecting bluegrass with a touch of the blues.

Bluegrass festivals popped up in the 1960s and bluegrass bands from around the south added regional flavor. In 1969, Scruggs recorded 'Foggy Mountain Breakdown,' used in the movie *Bonnie & Clyde,* and the world opened its ears.

Bluegrass music was later used in the theme song to TV's the *Beverly Hillbillies*. It's featured in the movie *Deliverance* and, more recently in *O Brother, Where Art Thou?,* starring Kentucky native George Clooney.

Learn more about bluegrass at the International Bluegrass Music Museum in Owensboro (p461), or find a mint condition LP of Bill Monroe, who is rightfully considered the father of bluegrass.

RUN FOR THE ROSES

The first thoroughbred was brought to Kentucky in 1779 and by 1789 there were more horses here than people. Today, Central Kentucky has the world's greatest concentration of thoroughbred breeding farms, many of which are like equine palaces. All this horsing around pays off on the first Saturday in May, when the 'greatest two minutes in sports' takes place at Louisville's Churchill Downs. Ah, the Kentucky Derby, where the crowd wears wide-brimmed derby hats, sips mint juleps and waits to see which horse will make its owner rich, or richer.

Churchill Downs founder Colonel M Lewis Clark (grandson of William Clark of the Lewis and Clark expedition) held the first Kentucky Derby in 1875. Through Prohibition, the Great Depression and two world wars, the Kentucky Derby has never missed a race, making it the world's oldest uninterrupted sporting event.

The first race of the year in horse racing's prestigious Triple Crown (followed by the Preakness Stakes and the Belmont Stakes), the Derby sees the world's best thoroughbreds pound through the race's 1.25-mile course. Though the race only lasts a couple of minutes, the festivities start about three weeks before for the **Kentucky Derby Festival** (☎ 502-584-6383; www.kdf.org). After the race, the crowd sings 'My Old Kentucky Home' and watches as the winning horse gets covered in a blanket of roses. Later its name will be written on the racetrack wall.

Tue-Thu, 5:30-11pm Fri & Sat) Most of the good restaurants and bars are found at Bardstown Rd, including this longtime favorite for upscale lunches and dinners. Chef Kathy Cary whips together miracles featuring fresh in-season local produce and fish, seafood, pork and beef.

Entertainment

The free weekly *Leo* lists gigs and entertainment.

Kentucky Center for the Arts (☎ 502-562-0100; www.kentuckycenter.org; 5 Riverfront Plaza) This prime performance venue hosts theater, ballet, opera, orchestra, modern dance and popular music. It's worth checking what's on or looking around the center, with its unusual design and sculptures.

Palace Theater (☎ 502-583-4555; www.louisvillepalace.com; 625 4th Ave) The 1928 Palace Theater is a wonderfully ornate venue for big-name concerts and special events. Past performers include Michael Bublé, Wilco and Garrison Keillor.

Jillians (☎ 502-589-9090; 630 Barret Ave; ❤ lunch & dinner) The fun and popular Jillians is a bar, restaurant and live-music venue all rolled into one.

Getting There & Around

Louisville's International Airport (☎ 502-367-4636; www.louintlairport.com) is 5 miles south of town on I-65. Get there by cab ($15) or local bus No 2. The **Greyhound station** (☎ 502-585-3331; 720 W Muhammad Ali Blvd), just west of downtown, has buses to Chicago, IL, Lexington, Memphis and Nashville. Local buses are operated by **TARC** (☎ 502-585-1234; 1000 W Broadway), based at the Union Station depot.

BLUEGRASS COUNTRY

Groomed pastures filled with awe-inspiring thoroughbred horses long ago replaced the herds of shaggy bison that once roamed this area's oak-ash woodlands and clover meadows. Encompassing the northeast corner of Kentucky, east of Louisville, Bluegrass Country emanates from Lexington in an undeniable and incredibly scenic ode to the horse.

Lexington

With a distinctly small-town feel, Lexington is saved from parochialism by University of Kentucky (UK) students and the international jet-setting thoroughbred racehorse industry. Most of Lexington's best attractions are outside the city. On a fine day, the sublimely beautiful horse country seems like the loveliest place on earth, with gently rolling hills, brilliant green grass, handsome houses, shady trees and picturesque plank fences receding into the distance. The barns are often more imposing than the houses, and the aristocratic thoroughbreds prance around like they own the place (which, given racing purses, they probably do). Pick up good maps and area information from the **visitor center** (☎ 859-233-7299, 800-845-3959; www.visitlex.com; 301 E Vine St; ❤ 8:30am-5pm Mon-Fri, 10am-4pm Sat).

HOMAGE TO BLUEGRASS

About 107 miles west of Louisville along the Ohio River is the town of Owensboro, home to an International Bar-B-Q Festival in May, a bluegrass festival in October and the excellent **International Bluegrass Music Museum** (☎ 270-926-7891; www.blue grass-museum.org; 207 E 2nd St; admission $5; ☽ 10am-5pm Tue-Fri, 1-5pm Sat & Sun). Any banjo picker or bluegrass fan will appreciate the comprehensive and truly enjoyable exhibits here, including the Hall of Honor, which recognizes and profiles the genre's masters.

SIGHTS & ACTIVITIES
Historic Houses

Downtown Lexington has a pleasant mix of old and new buildings and historic houses. The following offer tours for $7. You can also purchase a $12 combination ticket to visit all four – available at the visitor center or at Ashland.

Just 1½ miles east of downtown, **Ashland** (☎ 859-266-8581; www.henryclay.org; 120 Sycamore Rd) was the Italianate estate of statesman Henry Clay (1777–1852). **Hunt-Morgan House** (☎ 859-253-0362; www.bluegrasstrust.org; 201 N Mill St) is a fine Federal-style mansion (c 1814) with a small Civil War museum. The 1806 **Mary Todd-Lincoln House** (☎ 859-233-9999; www.mtlhouse.org; 578 W Main St) has articles from the first lady's childhood and her years as Abe's wife.

Kentucky Horse Park

A working horse farm, educational theme park and equestrian sports center, the **Kentucky Horse Park** (☎ 859-233-4303, 800-678-8813; www.kyhorsepark.com; 4089 Iron Works Parkway; adult/child $14/7; ☽ 9am-5pm daily mid-Mar–Nov, Wed-Sun Dec–mid-Mar) sits on 1200 acres just north of Lexington. A visit to the horse farm will delight horse lovers and could convert anyone who isn't. Demonstrations of riding, horse breeds and equipment are included. Also included, the international **Museum of the Horse** follows the horse through human history, describing its role in hunting, transport, warfare and sport. Seasonal horseback riding costs $15.

The adjacent **American Saddlebred Museum** (☎ 859-259-2746, 800-829-4438; www.american-sad dlebred.com; 4093 Iron Works Parkway; ☽ 9am-6pm)

focuses on America's first registered horse breed, horse gaits and other technical stuff – for hardcore enthusiasts.

Thoroughbred Center

Most farms are closed to the public, but you can visit the **Thoroughbred Center** (☎ 859-293-1853; www.thethoroughbredcenter.com/tours; 3380 Paris Pike; adult/child $10/5; tours 9am, 10:30am & 1pm Mon-Fri, 9am & 10:30am Sat Apr-Oct, by appointment Nov-Mar). Tours of this working thoroughbred training facility take in stables, practice tracks and paddocks.

Keeneland Race Course

Horses earn their living 32 days a year at this exciting **racecourse** (☎ 859-254-3412, 800-456-3412; www.keeneland.com; 4201 Versailles Rd; admission $4), west of town on US 60, Versailles Rd (that's ver-*sales*). The spring and fall racing seasons are in April and October. When the Derby is happening in Louisville, Keeneland throws its own party with live music and a BBQ, which prompts Lexingtonians to say, 'Louisville may have the race, but we have the party!' From March to November, you can watch the champions train from sunrise to 11am.

Horseback Riding

So you're itching to get in the saddle? Several working ranches around Lexington offer horseback riding to both newbie and experienced riders. **Whispering Woods** (☎ 859-570-9663; 265 Wright Land; 1hr/full-day trail rides $20/60; ☽ May-Oct), in Georgetown, offers guided

DON'T BLINK OR YOU'LL MISS IT

Kentucky's diminutive capital, Frankfort, lies 26 miles west of Lexington, and is a small country town with some imposing buildings, notably the neoclassical 1910 beaux arts **capitol building** (☎ 502-564-3449; tours free; ☽ Mon-Sat) and the nearby governor's mansion.

The older part of town is across the Kentucky River, where the **old state capitol** (☎ 502-564-1792; admission free; ☽ 10am-5pm Tue-Fri) functioned from 1827 to 1910. Nearby is the handsome **Kentucky History Center** (☎ 502-564-1792; 100 W Broadway St; admission free; ☽ 8am-4pm Tue-Sat), for those interested in state history.

THE SOUTH

trail rides. **Deer Run Stables** (☎ 859-527-6339; Combs Ferry off Hwy 627) also offers guided trips. Call ahead for directions and reservation.

TOURS

Blue Grass Tours (☎ 859-252-5744; www.bluegrass tours.com; tours from $25) Takes visitors to Keeneland or private horse farms and will pick up downtown.

Horse Farm Tours (☎ 859-268-2906; www.horsefarm tours.com; adult $25; tours 9am & 1pm Mon-Sun) Picks up at Lexington hotels and offers two tours daily to working horse farms. Reservations required.

SLEEPING

University Inn (☎ 859-278-6625, 866-881-9676; www .uinn.biz; 1229 S Limestone St; r incl breakfast $60; P 🔀) Across from the university, this basic but well-equipped hotel is a good value. All rooms have a refrigerator, which is handy if you need to chill some beer.

A True Inn (☎ 859-252-6166, 800-374-6151; 467 W 2nd Ave; r incl breakfast $130-190; P 🔀) Built in 1843, this lovely Greek Revival B&B has antique-decorated, homey rooms each named for a famous Lexingtonian. The delicious breakfast is served in the garden.

Kentucky Horse Park (☎ 859-259-4257, 800-370-6416; 4089 Iron Works Parkway; paved/unpaved campsites $25/15; 🏕) The convenient campground with 260 paved sites on the Horse Park farm is open year-round. There's showers, laundry and more. Some 'primitive' sites are also available.

EATING

The liveliest area in the evening is around E Main and S Limestone Sts.

Natasha's Cafe (☎ 859-259-2754; 112 Esplanade; lunch $6-8, dinner $10-14) A gem in a town this size, Natasha's serves excellent Mediterranean-inspired dishes using fresh, healthy ingredients. At lunch, there's a buffet ($6.50

per pound); it and the dinner menu features lots of vegetarian options.

A la Lucie (☎ 859-252-5277; 159 N Limestone St; mains $9-25; ✪ lunch Mon-Fri, dinner Mon-Sat) This funky bistro serves a well-prepared eclectic menu of such specialties at lobster pot pie, paella and buttermilk-fried quail. It's a great atmosphere, casual and lots of fun.

Alfalfa's (☎ 859-253-0014; 557 S Limestone St; mains $6-12; ✪ lunch daily, dinner Mon-Sat) Near the university, this vegetarian place serves up good breakfasts, fresh salads and sandwiches. Try the yummy buckwheat pancakes. There's often live music in the evenings.

Billy's Hickory Pit Bar-B-Q (☎ 859-269-9593; 101 Cochran Rd; mains $6-15; ✪ 11am-10pm Mon-Sat, 11:30-9pm Sun) A longtime institution for Kentucky-style smoked pork, beef and mutton. Look out for 'burgoo,' which is a satisfying beef stew.

Kashmir (☎ 859-233-3060; 341 S Limestone St; lunch/dinner buffet $6/9; ✪ lunch & dinner) An excellent value for good, excellently priced and spice-filled Indian buffet.

DRINKING

For beer, bourbon and bar food, try friendly watering holes like **Cheapside** (☎ 859-254-0046; 131 Cheapside St), with a tropical patio, and **Two Keys Tavern** (☎ 859-254-5000; 333 S Limestone St), both of which have live music.

ENTERTAINMENT

Applebee's Park (☎ 859-422-7867; www.lexingtonle gends.com; 1200 N Broadway) Home to Lexington Legends minor-league baseball team. It is also a great venue for outdoor concerts.

Kentucky Theater (☎ 859-231-6997; www.ken tuckytheater.com; 214 E Main St) The restored 1927 theater shows movies and is an intimate venue for occasional live music.

Rupp Arena (☎ 859-233-4567; www.rupparena.com) The 23,000-seat venue on Patterson St is the home court for the UK Wildcats and also hosts any big-name rock and country acts.

GETTING THERE & AROUND

Lexington, at the crossroads of I-75 and I-64, is 77 miles east of Louisville. **Greyhound** (☎ 859-299-8804; 477 W New Circle Rd; ✪ 7am-11pm) is 2 miles from downtown. Regular buses go to Louisville, some by very indirect routes. There are also buses to Nashville, TN and Washington, DC. **Lex-Tran** (☎ 859-253-4636) runs local buses (No 6 goes to the Greyhound stop).

THE AUTHOR'S CHOICE

Gratz Park Inn (☎ 859-231-1777, 800-252-4166; www.gratzparkinn.com; 120 W 2nd St; d $125-240; P 🔀 🖥) The city's grande dame hotel, Gratz Park is a 44-room charmer without the stuffiness of some fancy hotels. The antique furnishings, four-poster beds and fresh flowers add nice touches, as do the modern amenities, such as wi-fi and comfortable beds.

THE SOUTH

THE BOURBON TOUR

Bourbon whiskey was first distilled in Bourbon County, north of Lexington, in 1789. Today 90% of all bourbon is produced in Kentucky (no other state is allowed to put its own name on the bottle). A good bourbon must contain at least 51% corn, and must be stored in charred oak barrels for at least two years. While in Kentucky, you must try a mint julep, the archetypical Southern drink made with bourbon, sugar syrup and crushed mint. You haven't truly experienced the South until you drink like the locals.

The **Oscar Getz Museum of Whiskey History** (☎ 502-348-2999; 114 N 5th St), in Bardstown, tells the bourbon story. Most of Kentucky's distilleries, which are centered around Bardstown and Frankfort, offer free tours. Call for times.

Distilleries

Near Bardstown (exit 112 off I-65, look for signs):

Heaven Hill (☎ 502-348-3921; 1064 Loretto Rd, Bardstown) The largest family-owned bourbon producers who hold the world's second-largest supply.

Jim Beam (☎ 502-543-9877; 149 Happy Hollow Rd, Clermont) You watch a good film about the grandson of Jim Beam with some informative bourbon-making secrets thrown in.

Maker's Mark (☎ 502-865-2099; 3350 Burks Spring Rd, near Loretto) Where the Samuels family has been making whiskey since 1840; a National Historic Landmark.

Near Frankfort/Lawrenceburg:

Buffalo Trace (☎ 502-696-5926; 1001 Wilkinson Blvd near Frankfort) Named for the ancient buffalo that led early pioneers westward, this distillery shows the whole process.

Four Roses (☎ 502-839-3436; 1224 Bonds Mills Rd/Hwy 513 W) In a Spanish hacienda-style building, this distillery gives very detailed tours; good for bourbon connoisseurs.

Labrot & Graham (☎ 859-879-1939; 7855 McCracken Pike, Versailles) The historic site along a creek is restored to its 1800s glory; the distillery still uses old-fashioned copper pots.

Wild Turkey (☎ 502-839-4544; Hwy 62 E, Lawrenceburg) Real wild turkeys fly through the nearby valleys.

Daniel Boone National Forest

This vast area in the east of the state is noted for its rich variety of plants and wildlife and an extensive trail system. The main **ranger station** (☎ 859-745-3100; 1700 Bypass Rd; ☺ 8am-4pm Mon-Fri Nov-Mar, 10am-6pm daily Apr-Oct) is in Winchester.

The south end of the national forest, easily accessed from I-75, has some depressed communities and old coal-mining areas around Stearns, on US 27. Within the forest, **Cumberland Falls State Resort Park** (☎ 859-528-4121; admission free; campsites $15; ☒) has a rustic lodge ($46 to $65) and campgrounds. Nearby Corbin is the site of the original outlet of **Kentucky Fried Chicken**. The chicken tastes like it does at any KFC, but the exhibits are nostalgic for those of us who grew up lickin' our fingers.

CENTRAL KENTUCKY

About 40 miles south of Louisville is **Bardstown**, an historic town with lovely brick houses and a unique blend of southern

hospitality and booze. Famous for it's gaggle of distilleries (above), the town comes alive in mid-September for the **Kentucky Bourbon Festival** (☎ 270-638-4877; www.kybourbonfestival.com).

Follow Hwy 61 southwest and you'll hit **Hodgenville** and the **Abraham Lincoln Birthplace National Historic Site** (☎ 270-358-3137; admission free; ☺ 8am-5pm), which features a replica of a Greek temple constructed around an old log cabin. Research has established that Lincoln was not actually born in the cabin, so it's referred to as his 'symbolic birthplace.'

About 115 miles southwest of Louisville, **Bowling Green** is home to Western Kentucky University and the Corvette. All the world's Corvette sports cars are now produced at the Bowling Green **plant** (☎ 270-745-8419; tours $5; ☺ tours 9am & 1pm Mon-Fri). Opposite, the **National Corvette Museum** (☎ 270-781-7973, 800-538-3883; www.corvettemuseum.com; 350 Corvette Dr; adult/child $8/4.50; ☺ 8am-5pm) has over 50 examples of this classic car.

THE SOUTH

Mammoth Cave National Park

Mammoth Cave National Park (☎ 270-758-2328; www.nps.gov/maca; exit 53 from I-65; park fee $4) has the most extensive cave system on earth. With some 350 miles of surveyed passageways, Mammoth is at least three times bigger than any other known cave. The caves have been used for prehistoric mineral gathering, as a source of saltpeter for gunpowder and as a tuberculosis hospital. Tourists started visiting around 1810 and guided tours have been offered since the 1830s. The area became a national park in 1926 and now brings nearly two million visitors each year.

To see the caves, you must take a **ranger-guided tour** (☎ 800-967-2283; adult $4-45), and it's wise to book ahead, especially in summer. Tours range from easy to strenuous hikes around the caves; there's also a tour for those mobility impaired. The caves are in the central time zone, an hour earlier than Louisville.

NORTH CAROLINA

In many ways, North Carolina is like a microcosm of the entire USA. You'll find a healthy mix of hippy mountain folks and New South workaholics, beach bums and earnest farmers. You'll see vast plains sandwiched between majestic mountains and stunning seashores. You'll see Nascar devotees whoop it up with scientists; hikers, bankers and doctoral students sharing a beer over basketball. It's a state where sweeping generalizations simply don't work, and that's the truly great thing about North Carolina. Visitors puzzle at how the climate can range from subarctic (in the highlands) to sub-Saharan (on the coast), or that politics can shift unexpectedly from New Age liberal to Stone Age fossil. It's all part of this state's charm. Hang out here for a while and you'll appreciate every angle of the prism.

Most travelers tend to skirt through the business-oriented urban centers of the central Piedmont, instead choosing to stick to the scenic routes along the coast (via the islands of the Outer Banks) and those through the Appalachian Mountains, especially along the unforgettable Blue Ridge Parkway.

History

The first enduring English settlements in the US were established in the mid-17th century in North Carolina's Albemarle region. A series of battles defeated and displaced the Native Americans, making way for European colonists. The new settlement's first industry was the extraction of 'naval stores' like tar, pitch and turpentine from coastal forests, followed by cultivation of tobacco and cotton.

Though well represented in the constitutional conventions, North Carolina languished as an agrarian backwater during the early years of the republic. Divided on slavery, North Carolina reluctantly seceded in 1861, and went on to provide more Confederate soldiers than any other state.

WWII brought some new industries and large military bases, and the economy continues to boom with the growth of finance in Charlotte, and of research and development in the Raleigh-Durham Research Triangle.

Information

The state sales tax is 7%, with an added 6% hotel-occupancy tax levied on accommodations.

North Carolina Division of Tourism (☎ 919-733-4147, 800-847-4862; www.visitnc.com; 301N N Wilmington St, Raleigh, NC 27601) Sends out good maps and information, including its annual *Official Travel Guide*.

CHARLOTTE

Founded at the junction of two old Indian trails, Charlotte was described as a 'hornet's nest of rebellion' against British rule in the

---

NORTH CAROLINA FACTS

Nickname Tar Heel State
Population 8.4 million
Area 48,711 sq miles
Capital city Raleigh (population: 306,994)
Official state beverage Milk
Birthplace of Evangelist Billy Graham (b 1918), jazzman John Coltrane (1926–67), actor Andy Griffith (1926), Nascar legend Dale Earnhardt St (1951–2001), boxer Sugar Ray Leonard (b 1956), singer Randy Travis (1959), *American Idol* runner-up Clay Aiken (1978)
Home of The Blue Ridge Parkway
Famous for Being the first English colony in America; first powered airplane flight (1903)

1770s. Miners burrowed under the town in the early 1800s, and banks were founded to handle the gold. That same fever of hoarding riches has given rise to Charlotte's burgeoning growth. To the delight of city boosters, some 50,000 new residents move to Charlotte every year, coming to frolic in the new money generated by banking and big business. Charlotte is the second-largest US banking center after New York, and many companies have set up offices in the futuristic high-rises connected by elevated walkways. Primarily a business town, Charlotte's appeal consists of a few good museums, excellent restaurants and a scattered but lively music scene.

The busy Tyron St cuts through downtown's business district known as 'Uptown.' The artsy NoDa district (short for 'North Davidson;' www.noda.org), 2 miles north of Uptown at N Davidson St at 36th, is the city's grooviest area, where a collection of reclaimed textile mills has been transformed into a village of galleries, restaurants and performance venues.

The **visitor center** (☎ 704-331-2700, 800-231-4636; www.visitcharlotte.org; 330 S Tryon St; 8:30am-5pm Mon-Fri, 9am-3pm Sat), off W 2nd St, publishes maps and a visitors guide. The **public library** (☎ 704-336-2725; 301 N College St; 9am-9pm Mon-Thu, to 6pm Fri & Sat, from 1pm Sun) has terminals for free Internet access.

Sights & Activities

The innovative **Levine Museum of the New South** (☎ 704-333-1887; www.museumofthenewsouth.org; 200 E 7th St; adult/child $6/5; 10am-5pm Tue-Sat, from noon Sun) gives an excellent look at modern Southern history covering everything from sharecropping to Nascar racing. Check out the especially good exhibit 'Cotton Fields to Skyscrapers.'

Mint Museum of Art (☎ 704-337-2000; www.mintmuseum.org; 2730 Randolph Rd; adult/child $6/3; 10am-5pm Tue-Sat, from noon Sun) is housed in the first branch of the US Mint. The impressive art collection includes pre-Columbian pottery, African art, historic maps and American paintings. Your ticket also gets you into the **Mint Museum of Craft & Design** (200 N Tyron St), which chronicles the history of studio crafts including glass, metal, wood and metalwork and jewelry.

Afro-American Cultural Center (☎ 704-374-1565; www.aacc-charlotte.org; 401 N Myers St; admission $3; 10am-6pm Tue-Sat, 1-5pm Sun) has excellent visual-arts exhibits, films and performances in the outdoor amphitheater.

Discovery Place (☎ 704-372-6261; www.discoveryplace.org; 301 N Tryon St; adult/child $8.50/6.50; 10am-6pm Mon-Sat, from 12:30pm Sun) is a hands-on science museum with an Omnimax cinema ($7.50/6). Wander through a rain forest, peer inside a huge eyeball or sample liquid-nitrogen ice cream in the chemistry lab.

In conjunction with the library, **ImaginOn** (☎ 704-336-2074; www.imaginon.org; 300 E 7th St; admission free; 9am-9pm Mon-Thu, 9am-6pm Fri & Sat, 1-6pm Sun) is a cultural center devoted to children and teens. The block-long building includes interactive exhibits, a theater, plus special spaces for storytelling and painting.

Sleeping

Because so many hotels cater to the business traveler, rates at many hotels are less expensive on weekends.

Westin (☎ 704-375-2600; www.westin.com/charlotte; 601 South College St; r from $90; P) The sleek 700-room Westin offers luxurious, modern rooms that ooze with Zen-like serenity. Though it primarily serves the business set, it can be a great value for passing travelers, as it is right in the heart of the financial district, within walking distance of most sights. Parking costs $10.

Dunhill Hotel (☎ 704-332-4141, 800-252-4666; www.dunhillhotel.com; 237 N Tryon St; r weekend/midweek from $140/209; P) Now dwarfed by skyscrapers, the 10-story hotel towered over the scene when it was opened in 1929. Restored to its original elegance in the 1980s, it's noted for its period furnishings as well as its original art. Each of the 60 rooms has modern amenities including wi-fi, refrigerators and TVs. Valet/self parking costs $15/6.

Eating & Drinking

Charlotte has a great selection of very fine restaurants.

Reid's Fine Foods (☎ 704.377.1312; 225 E 6th St; 7am-8pm Mon-Sat, 11am-6pm Sun) This excellent grocery store is the place to come for deli sandwiches and salads, with a good selection of produce and wine.

Latorre's (☎ 704-377-4448; 118 W 5th St; mains $8-15; lunch Mon-Fri, dinner Mon Sat) Ooh la la! This superfun uptown Latin restaurant has a good selection of seafood, steak and vegetarian dishes. Late night and weekends, it becomes

THE SOUTH

a hopping Latin dance party, with experts giving free salsa and merengue lessons.

Boudreaux's Louisiana Kitchen (☎ 704-331-9898; 501 E 36th St; mains $6-14; ☼ lunch & dinner) With a casual but energetic New Orleans vibe, this NoDa restaurant is a hit for delicious gumbo and muffaletta sandwiches, Creole shrimp and crawfish étouffée.

Southend Brewery & Smokehouse (☎ 704-358-4677; 2100 S Blvd; mains $7-15; ☼ lunch & dinner) This trendy converted warehouse is scented with the aroma of beer from the brewing vats. Smoked ribs, wood-fired pizzas and grilled seafood are the specialties; wash it all down with one of eight house beers.

Entertainment

Check out the weekly *Creative Loafing* for entertainment listings.

Blumenthal Performing Arts Center (☎ 704-372-1000; www.blumenthalcenter.org 130 North Tryon St) For theater and classical concerts.

Double Door Inn (☎ 704-376-1446; www.double door.com; 218 E Independence Blvd) Stevie Ray Vaughan and Eric Clapton have played at this clapboard place for live blues, rock and zydeco.

Neighborhood Theatre (☎ 704-358-9298; www .neighborhoodtheatre.com; 511 E. 36th St) This renovated movie theater in the NoDa district is an excellent live-music venue.

SPORTS

Bank of America Stadium (☎ 704-358-7407; 800 S Mint St) Home to the NFL **Carolina Panthers** (www.panthers.com).

Lowe's Motor Speedway (☎ 704-455-3200; www .lowesmotorspeedway.com; tours $5; tours 9:45am-3:45pm Mon-Sat, 1:45-3:45pm Sun) Insanely popular Nascar races are held at Lowe's, 12 miles northeast of town.

New Charlotte Arena (☎ 800-495-2295; www .newcharlottearena.com; 333 E Trade St) The splashy new home to the NBA **Charlotte Bobcats** (www .nba.com/bobcats) and WNBA **Charlotte Sting** (www.wnba.com/sting).

Getting There & Around

Charlotte-Douglas International Airport (CLT; ☎ 704-359-4027; www.charmeck.org; 5501 Josh Birmingham Parkway) is a US Airways hub that receives direct flights from Europe and the UK.

Both the **Greyhound station** (☎ 704-375-3332; 601 W Trade St) and **Amtrak** (☎ 704-376-4416; 1914 N Tryon St) are handy to downtown.

Charlotte Area Transit (☎ 704-336-3366; 310 E Trade St) provides local bus services throughout the metro area.

NORTH CAROLINA COAST

Some 130 miles of slender, windswept barrier islands run the length of North Carolina's coast, where sandy beaches form and dissolve with the Atlantic tides. Ancient lighthouses watch the passing of time, while sailors in fishing boats catch saltwater treats. Pockets of estuaries, sounds and tidal lagoons flourish with shorebirds and fish. By winter, this region gets steeped in rain, wind and luxurious solitude; in summer vacationers swarm the holiday resorts to play in the water or soak up the sunshine.

The Albemarle

The wild, swampy region around Albemarle Sound was the site of the state's first European settlement, and from the 18th century it became a focus for canals that provided protected transport routes north to Chesapeake Bay and south to Wilmington. Many of the towns retain the rich colonial architecture and the whole area is popular for boating, fishing and retirement.

EDENTON

Founded in 1712, this lovely little town at the west end of Albemarle Sound was the center of economic, social and political life in early colonial times. In the 1774 'Edenton Tea Party,' 50 local society ladies swore off tea in protest of British taxes. The town provided signatories to the Declaration of Independence and the Constitution, as well as two state governors and one of the first Supreme Court justices. Development bypassed Edenton, leaving pretty streets of 18th-century buildings. See the **visitor center** (☎ 252-482-2637; www.edenton.org; 108 N Broad St; ☼ 9am-5pm Mon-Sat, 1-4pm Sun) for accommodations and a self-guided-tour map.

ELIZABETH CITY

Elizabeth City became a shipping and transportation center after the Dismal Swamp Canal was completed in 1803. The **Museum of the Albemarle** (☎ 252-335-1453; 1116 Hwy 17 S; admission free; ☼ 9am-5pm Tue-Sat) gives a good account of the canals and the area's history. The town has five historic districts; the **visitor center** (☎ 252-335-4365; www.elizcity.com; 502 E

Ehringhaus St; 9am-5pm Mon-Fri) has a walking-tour map.

Outer Banks

Hwy 12 runs along this chain of barrier islands, curving east of Albemarle and Pamlico Sounds in a 100-mile arc that's like a road across the sea. From north to south, Bodie, Roanoke, Hatteras and Ocracoke Islands are linked by bridges and ferries. The islands are low sand dunes, with long, sandy beaches on the ocean side and lagoons and marshes on the inland side. The northern islands are heavily developed, with holiday homes, beach resorts and hordes of summer visitors. Out of season, the pace slows considerably and many businesses close. A large portion of the central islands is protected national seashore, with a few small towns and a wild, windswept beauty.

While the Wright brothers sought sand, isolation and steady winds to get them off the ground in the Outer Banks town of Kitty Hawk, seafarers historically hoped to avoid the islands altogether. Unfortunately, their common failure is evidenced by the 1500-plus shipwrecks that have accumulated in shoal-filled waters.

INFORMATION

The best sources of information are at the **visitor centers** Kitty Hawk (☎ 252-261-4644; Milepost 1½; 9am-5:30pm year-round); Manteo (☎ 252-473-2138, 800-446-6262; US 64/264; 8am-6pm Mon-Fri, noon-4pm Sat & Sun year-round). Be sure to pick up the *Outer Banks Official Travel Guide*, which is full of excellent information. Other visitor centers in Nags Head are open April to October. Also useful is www.outerbanks.org.

ORIENTATION

Most of the tourist attractions and facilities are along a 16-mile strip of Bodie Island, in the virtually contiguous towns of **Kitty Hawk**, **Kill Devil Hills** and **Nags Head**. Hwy 12, also called Virginia Dare Trail, or 'the coast road,' is a two-lane road running close to the beach for the length of the strip. US 158, usually called 'the Bypass,' is a four-lane road running parallel but further inland. Locations are often given in terms of 'Mileposts,' starting from Milepost 1 at the north end of the tourist strip, where US 158 crosses to the mainland on the

Wright Memorial Bridge. Just past Milepost 16, US 64/264 connects to the mainland via Roanoke Island, where you'll find the towns of Manteo and Wanchese. Hwy 12 continues south to Hatteras and Ocracoke Islands.

SIGHTS

Wright Brothers National Monument

Among the dunes of Kill Devil Hills is where the Wright brothers pulled off their massive historic achievement of launching the world's first powered flight in 1903. The feat is commemorated by an art deco–style granite monument that sits atop a sand dune near Milepost 8.

Exhibits at the **visitor center** (☎ 252-441-7430; www.nps.gov/wrbr; admission $3; 9am-5pm) trace the Wrights' painstaking development work in Dayton, Ohio, and the experiments conducted at summer camps here over several years. See replicas of their 1902 glider and successful 1903 flyer, and sit in on informative hourly talks. The distances of the first powered flights on December 17, 1903, are marked, from the first tentative 120ft hop to the fourth flight, which reached an impressive 852ft.

Fort Raleigh National Historic Site

This site on Roanoke Island saw the first English colonies in North America meet with total failure. The fate of the 'lost colony' remains a mystery, but the **visitor center** (☎ 252-473-5772; 9am-6pm) has exhibits, artifacts and a free film about Native Americans and English settlers that will fuel your imagination. Look for the prints based on 1585 illustrations by John White, which are now some of the best-known depictions of pre-European North America. A small mound nearby is meant to re-create the earthworks of the original fort.

Attractions at the site include **Lost Colony Outdoor Drama** (☎ 252-473-3414, 866-468-7630; www.thelostcolony.org; adult/child $16/8; show 8:30pm Mon-Sat, Jun-Aug). This immensely popular and long-running show dramatizes the debacle. It plays at the Waterside Theater throughout summer.

Elizabethan Gardens (☎ 252-473-3234; www.elizabethangardens.org; adult/child $6/4; daily) Antique 16th-century gardens include a Shakespearian herb garden and rows of beautifully manicured flowerbeds.

Cape Hatteras National Seashore

Extending some 70 miles from south of Nags Head to the south end of Okracoke Island, this fragile necklace of islands remains blissfully free of overdevelopment. Three **visitor centers** (⊙ 9am-6pm summer, shorter hrs rest of year; Bodie ☎ 252-441-5711; Hatteras ☎ 252-995-4474; Ocracoke ☎ 252-928-4531) serve the park on the main islands. The **park headquarters** (☎ 252-473-2111; www.nps.gov/caha; 1401 National Park Dr) is in Manteo. Natural attractions include local and migratory waterbirds, marshes, woodlands, dunes and miles of empty beaches. Other attractions (from north to south) follow.

At the northern end of Hatteras Island and home to some 365 bird species, **Pea Island National Wildlife Refuge** (☎ 252-987-2394; admission free; ⊙ 9am-4pm daily Mar-Nov, Thu-Sun rest of year) is a great place for watching wildlife along the nature trails and observation points.

Bodie Island Lighthouse (☎ 252-441-5711; admission free) The 156ft horizontally striped lighthouse has a visitor center in the lighthouse keeper's quarters. You can't climb this one, but there's a pretty nature trail around it.

Chicamacomico Lifesaving Station (☎ 252-987-1552; Rodanthe village) is one of seven lifesaving stations in the Outer Banks, with exhibits on the station's history since 1874.

At 208ft tall, **Cape Hatteras Lighthouse** (☎ 252-995-4474; www.nps.gov/caha/lrp.htm; step climb adult/child $6/3; ⊙ Apr-Oct) is the tallest brick lighthouse in the US. You can climb the 268 steps and check out the interesting visitor center (open year-round).

Graveyard of the Atlantic Museum (☎ 252-986-2996; www.graveyardoftheatlantic.com; 59158 Coast Guard Rd, Hatteras; admission by donation; ⊙ 9am-6pm) is all about preserving the Outer Banks' maritime history, with Exhibits about shipwrecks, cool 'beach finds' and salvaged cargo.

Ocracoke Island

Accessed via the free Hatteras-Ocracoke ferry, small **Ocracoke Village** (☎ 252-928-6711; www.ocracokevillage.com) sits at the south end of 14-mile-long Ocracoke Island. It's a funky little village whose residents fish for their food and grumble about tourists in summer, and hunker down at home or in the pub in winter. Edward Teach, also known as Blackbeard the pirate, used to hide out in the area and was killed here in 1718. There are several restaurants and you can visit the 1823 **Ocracoke Lighthouse**, the oldest one still operating in North Carolina.

ACTIVITIES

Popular outdoor activities include kayaking, fishing, sailing, windsurfing, hang gliding and cycling – all well catered for in the northern resort areas. Swimming is excellent offshore, though chilly outside the summer months. The usually calm coastal waters occasionally kick up, creating perfect conditions for bodysurfing. Surfing on the numerous beach breaks is best from August to October, with the East Coast championships in early September. Outfitters rent out a range of equipment.

Ocean Atlantic Rentals (☎ 252-441-7823, 800-635-9559; Milepost 10; bicycle/surfboard/kayak per day $10/15/25, week $35/50/60) is a huge shop that offers good-deal rentals on everything from water-sports equipment to baby cribs and linens. Tandem bikes, two-person kayaks and surf lessons are also available.

Kitty Hawk Kites (☎ 252-359-8447, 877-359-2447; full-day bicycle/kayak rentals $25/30) offers beginners' kite-boarding lessons (three hours, $200) and hang-gliding lessons at Jockey's Ridge State Park (from $89). It also rents kayaks, sailboats, bikes and in-line skates and has a variety of tours and courses.

Whalebone Surf Shop (☎ 252-441-6747; 877-855-1975; www.whalebonesurfshop.com; 4900A N Croatan Hwy) is a Nag's Head surf shop offering beginner's surfing lessons ($80, three hours).

SLEEPING

Crowds swarm the Outer Banks in summer, so it's best to reserve a place, rather than just show up. The area has hundreds of motels, efficiencies and B&Bs; the visitor centers offers referrals. Also check www.obxlodging .com. The following are high-season rates.

Nags Head Inn (☎ 252-441-0454, 800-327-8881; www.nagsheadinn.com; Milepost 14; r $130-215; Ⓟ Ⓧ Ⓡ) A great value on the beach in Nags Head, with comfortable rooms, outdoor hot tub and beach access. Be sure to ask for a room overlooking the ocean.

Days Inn Mariner (☎ 252-441-2021, 800-325-2525; www.outer-banks.com/days-mariner; Milepost 7; r $140-220; Ⓟ Ⓧ Ⓡ) On the Beach Rd in Kill Devil Hills, this good-value hotel is open most of the year and has a variety of rooms.

Island Inn (☎ 252-928-4351, 877-456-3466; www.ocracokeislandinn.com; r $60-140, villas per week $1200-

1500; (P X X X)) In Ocracoke on Hwy 12 at Point Rd, this grand old turn-of-the-century clapboard inn has a heated pool, an excellent dining room, and the front porch overlooks the ocean. Open year-round.

HI Outer Banks Hostel (☎ 252-261-2294, 877-453-2545; outerbankshostel.com; 1004 W Kitty Hawk Rd; dm member/nonmember $17/20, r $31/35, campsites $20) In a pleasant but out-of-the-way location, this welcoming hostel has a communal kitchen, outdoor grill and camping. The friendly management arranges kayak trips, bicycle rentals and summer campfires. No booze consumption is allowed onsite.

The National Park Service (NPS) runs four summer-only **campgrounds** (☎ 800-365-2267; www.nps.gov/caha/camping99.htm; campsites $20) on the islands, which feature cold-water showers and flush toilets. They are located at Oregon Inlet, near the Bodie Island lighthouse, Cape Point and Frisco near the Cape Hatteras lighthouse and **Ocracoke** (☎ 800-365-2267; http://reservations.nps.gov) on Ocracoke Island. Only sites at Ocracoke can be reserved; the others are first-come, first-served.

EATING

The main tourist strip on Bodie Island has the most restaurants and nightlife, but only in season. The following are all nonchain places open for lunch and dinner year-round on Beach Rd.

Kill Devil Grill (☎ 252-449-8181; Milepost 9.75; mains $6-17) In a funky blue beach bar, this place offers truly exceptional food, from burgers and fresh fish sandwiches to grilled seafood and steaks. Ask about the daily blue-plate special.

Black Pelican (☎ 252-261-3171; Milepost 4; mains $9-22) The restaurant, in an old lifesaving station and telegraph office, serves good seafood dishes, such as steamed oysters, blackened tuna steak, mussels, plus excellent wood-fired pizzas.

Awful Arthur's Oyster Bar (☎ 252-441-5955; Milepost 6; lunch $6-10, dinner $10-15) Come here for the oyster bar and hopping atmosphere. It also serves other seafood, steak, chicken and pasta dishes.

Jolly Roger (☎ 252-441-6530; Milepost 6.75; mains $6-10) This small family place is good for breakfast, lunch or an inexpensive dinner. It serves hearty breakfasts, Italian meals and prime rib.

GETTING THERE & AWAY

If you're driving, access Hwy 12 (the main road along the cape) from Hwy 158 at Kitty Hawk or from Hwy 64/264, which leads over Roanoke Island to the park's northern entrance.

No public transport exists to or on the Outer Banks, however the **North Carolina Ferry System** (☎ 800-293-3779; www.ncferry.org) operates several routes, including the free 40-minute Hatteras–Ocracoke car ferry, which runs at least hourly from 5am to 10pm; bookings aren't necessary. Ferries also run between Ocracoke and Cedar Island (one way $15, 2¼ hours) every two hours or so; reservations are recommended especially in summer. There are also ferries that link Ocracoke and Swan Quarter on the mainland ($15, 2½ hours).

Crystal Coast

The southern Outer Banks, composed of several coastal towns, sounds, islands, inlets and barrier islands, are collectively called the 'Crystal Coast,' at least for tourist offices' promotion purposes. **Cape Lookout National Seashore** has seasonal nesting sites for turtles and shorebirds and can only be reached by boat. It has limited visitor facilities, although the **Cape Lookout Lighthouse** is arguably the most photogenic on the Atlantic coast.

Architecturally interesting Beaufort (*bow*-fort), one of the oldest towns in the state, was originally called 'Fish Town' and still trades off its maritime heritage. The **visitor center** (☎ 252-728-5225; 138 Turner St; ⌚ 9:30-5pm Mon-Sat) is in the Beaufort Historic Site.

A rather unappealing industrial and commercial stretch of US 70 goes through **Morehead City**, which attracts scuba divers who come to explore the coast's many ship wrecks. Get information from the well-stocked **Crystal Coast Visitors Bureau** (☎ 252-726-8148; 3407 Arendell St/Hwy 70; ⌚ 9am-5pm Mon-Fri, from 10am Sat & Sun).

Wilmington

Wilmington is a busy little port town with factories, a university, film studios and a neat old downtown and waterfront area along the Cape Fear River. Its attractive historic district is one of the country's largest, and the oak-lined streets are fun to peruse. It is one of the best places to stop along the coast, and the surrounding area has a wealth of historic interest.

The **visitor center** (☎ 910-341-4030, 800-222-4757; 24 N 3rd St; ☻ 8:30am-5pm Mon-Fri, 9am-4pm Sat, from 1pm Sun), in the 1892 courthouse building, has a walking-tour map. There is a seasonal **visitor booth** (Market St; ☻ 9am-4:30pm May-Sep). A **free trolley** (☻ 7:20am-9:20pm Mon-Fri, 11am-9:20pm Sat, 11am-6pm Sun) runs through the historic district.

SIGHTS
Cameron Art Museum (☎ 910-395-5999; www.cameronartmuseum.com; 3201 S 17th St; adult/child $5/2; ☻ 10am-5pm Tue-Sat, to 4pm Sun) focuses on North Carolinian artists and American art from the 18th century to the present. It is known for its exceptional collection of prints by Impressionist Mary Cassatt.

Cape Fear Museum of History & Science (☎ 910-341-4350; www.capefearmuseum.com; 814 Market St; adult/child $5/1; ☻ 9am-5pm Tue-Sat, from 1pm Sun) includes a model of Wilmington in the blockade-running 1860s, and a small display about local legend Michael Jordan.

Take a river taxi ($5 round-trip) or cross the Cape Fear Bridge to reach the **Battleship North Carolina** (☎ 910-251-5797; www.battleshipnc.com; adult/child $9/4.50; ☻ 8am-5pm, to 8pm in summer). This 44,000-ton megaship was the epitome of sea power when she was launched. Self-guided tours take in the crew's quarters, captain's cabin, gun turrets, galleys and more.

Screen Gems Studios (☎ 910-343-3433; 1223 N 23rd St; admission $12/5; ☻ 1hr tour noon & 2pm Sat & Sun) offers a behind-the-scenes tour of the working studio where shows like *Dawson's Creek* and *One Tree Hill* were filmed. There are no Hollywood-style special effects, but the guides know their stuff and are full of anecdotes.

At night, take one of two highly recommended **walking tours** (☎ 910-602-6055; www.hauntedwilmington.com). Tours include the Ghost Walk ($12) or the Haunted Pub Crawl ($15). Call for times.

SLEEPING
Best Western Coastline Inn (☎ 910-763-2800, 800-617-7732; www.coastlineinn.com; 503 Nutt St; d incl breakfast weekday/weekend $90/130; P ⊠ 🖳) In a quiet spot overlooking the harbor, this place has spacious, comfy rooms, most with kitchenettes, plus a gym.

Front Street Inn (☎ 910-762-6442, 800-336-8184; www.frontstreetinn.com; 215 Front St; r incl breakfast from $120-190; P ⊠ ⊠ 🖳) This romantic bou-

tique hotel just steps from the Riverwalk, has 12 beautiful suites, all decorated differently, with nice touches such as hardwood floors, canopy beds and a relaxed, Caribbean vibe.

EATING
Water St Café (☎ 910-343-0042; 5 S Water St; mains $7-16; ☻ lunch & dinner) Housed in a former peanut warehouse, this is a perennial favorite for its delicious crab-cake sandwiches ($7.25), soups and seafood platter ($20). Bits of *Dawson's Creek* were filmed here – this was Dawson's mother's restaurant. There's sidewalk dining, and Dixieland, blues and jazz music in the evenings.

Front St Brewery (☎ 910-251-1935; 9 N Front St; mains $7-14; ☻ lunch & dinner) This pub has a long bar, cozy booths and some of the best burgers in town. Also great wraps and fresh salads.

NORTH CAROLINA MOUNTAINS
With cool summers, gentle breezes and spectacular scenery, the western mountains of North Carolina work like a shot in the arm for weary urbanites. Recreation opportunities – from hiking and camping, to rafting and bird-watching – abound, and around every turn in the road there's another jaw-dropping view. The southern section of the Blue Ridge Mountains, which forms part of the Appalachians, has massive peaks of over 5000ft. Early European settlers

---

CAMPING ON THE PARKWAY
Along the North Carolina section of the parkway, there are five official campgrounds: **Doughton Park** (Mile 239.2), **Julian Price Memorial Park** (Mile 296.9), **Linville Falls** (Mile 316), **Crabtree Meadows** (Mile 339.5) and **Mount Pisgah** (Mile 408.8). They are open from May to October, except Linville Falls, which is open year-round. **Reservations** (☎ 877-444-6777; www.reserveusa.com; tent sites $14) are accepted in advance for Linville Falls and Price Memorial Park only; all other sites are assigned on a first-come, first-served basis. There are no hookups or showers. There are many private campgrounds in towns just off the parkway; what they may lack in ambience they make up for in full amenities.

THE SOUTH

took the name from the 'blue' haze caused by rising damp from the forest below.

For the plantation colonials, the mountains formed a frontier to Indian country to the west. Settlers from Ireland, Germany and England moved into the area and formed isolated farming communities that had almost no link with the African slave labor so typical in the southeast. Cherokee Indians occupied much of the region into the early 1800s, hunting in the mountains they considered sacred.

During the 1930s, the Blue Ridge Parkway was authorized as a Depression-era public-works project and gradually extended to link the Great Smoky Mountains with central Virginia.

Blue Ridge Parkway

The grand Blue Ridge Parkway, one of America's most popular road trips, traverses the southern Appalachian ridge from Virginia's Shenandoah National Park at Mile 0 to the Great Smoky Mountains National Park at Mile 469. North Carolina's piece of the parkway stretches for 262 glorious miles, where the meadows give way to alpine vistas. Wildflowers bloom in spring, and fall colors are spectacular. The National Park Service campgrounds and **visitor centers** (www.blueridgeparkway.org) are open May to October. There is no entrance fee for the parkway; visitors can pick up free information at the visitor centers.

Among the towering peaks, the North Carolina section can lay claim to impressive manmade structures around Grandfather Mountain, an assortment of talented craftspeople and their workshops, 26 beautiful arched tunnels and the gem city of Asheville, with all her Southern charm. Highlights along the parkway include the following:

Cumberland Knob Mile 217.5 – NPS visitor center, easy walk to the knob.

Doughton Park Mile 241.1 – Gas, food, trails and camping.

Blowing Rock Mile 291.8 – Small tourist town, named for a craggy, commercialized cliff that offers great views, occasional updrafts and an Indian love story.

Moses H Cone Memorial Park Mile 294.1 – A lovely old estate with pleasant walks and a craft shop.

Linn Cove Viaduct Mile 304.4 – Graceful curves of concrete skirting the sheer domes of Grandfather Mountain.

Grandfather Mountain Mile 305.1 – A picturesque, privately-run park with hiking trails.

Linville Falls Mile 316.4 – Lovely hiking trails to the falls.

Little Switzerland Mile 334 – Old-style mountain resort.

Mt Mitchell State Park Mile 355.5 – Highest mountain east of the Mississippi (6684ft), hiking trails and tent camping.

Folk Art Center Mile 382 – Traditional and contemporary local crafts.

Boone

A 6-mile detour west of the Blue Ridge Parkway, Boone makes a good base to tour the surrounding area and, though the town itself seems mightily commercial compared to the parkway, the Appalachian State University (ASU) injects a lively vibe.

The **visitor center** (☎ 828-262-3516, 888-251-9867; www.visitboonenc.com; 208 Howard St; ☺ 9am-5pm Mon-Fri) has information about canoeing outfitters, river rafting and parks.

Appalachian Cultural Museum (☎ 828-262-3117; University Hall Dr; adult/child $4/2; ☺ 10am-5pm Tue-Sat, from 1pm Sun), off Blowing Rock Rd, is a serious attempt to present mountain life and history beyond the hillbilly stereotypes. It has first-class exhibits and thoughtful interpretive material.

Blowing Rock Stage Company (☎ 828-295-9168; www.blowingrockstage.com; 452 Sunset Dr) has live performances throughout the summer.

Hwy 321 from Blowing Rock to Boone is studded with tourist traps. The cutesy **Tweetsie Railroad** (☎ 828-264-9061; www.tweetsie .com; adult/child $26/18; ☺ vary by season), with all its 'howdy pardner' glory, is the best of them.

SLEEPING & EATING

Broyhill Inn & Conference Center (☎ 828-262-2204, 800-951-6048; www.broyhillinn.com; 775 Bodenheimer Dr; r weekday/weekend $120/140; P ✖) This great place, run by ASU, has a sparkling location at the top of a wooded hill above Boone. Rooms were recently renovated and the restaurant, open all day, is a treat.

High Country Inn (☎ 828-264-1000, 800-334-5605; www.highcountryinn.com; 1755 Hwy 105; r $50-150; P ✖ ☎) This family-owned lodge sits on 14 acres on the side of a mountain. Rooms are basic, but have refrigerators and coffeemakers. There's a nice hot tub.

Bagelry (☎ 828-262-5585; 516 W King St; mains $3-7; ☺ breakfast & lunch) Everyone in town hangs out at this joint, for hearty omelettes, veggie sandwiches, salads and, of course, bagels. There's wi-fi here, too.

THE SOUTH

Asheville

With a wonderful and surprising mix of retired rich, 1920s charm and bohemian hippy, Asheville is a beautiful place to chill for a bit. Everywhere you turn there are gorgeous, wooded Blue Ridge Mountains and sparkling blue skies. Sitting at the confluence of the Swannanoa and French Broad Rivers, Asheville is tucked in the middle of a loop formed by I-40/I-240. The town is relatively compact and easy to negotiate on foot.

The **visitor center** (☎ 828-258-6101, 800-257-1300; 151 Haywood St; ⏰ 8:30am-5:30pm Mon-Fri, 9am-5pm Sat & Sun) is at I-240 exit 4C.

Malaprop's Bookstore & Café (☎ 828-254-6734; 55 Haywood St; ⏰ 9am-9pm Mon-Thu, to 10pm Fri & Sat, to 6pm Sun) is an excellent place to join the cappuccino-sipping bohemians while shopping for general-interest books, regional maps and travel guides.

The **public library** (☎ 828-251-4991; 67 Haywood Ave; ⏰ 10am-8pm Mon-Thu, to 6pm Fri, to 5pm Sat) offers free Internet access.

The sprawling **Biltmore Estate** (☎ 828-255-1333, 800-624-1575; www.biltmore.com; adult/child under 16/under 6 $39/19.50/free; ⏰ 8:30am-5pm), with 250 rooms, is billed as America's largest private house. It is certainly Asheville's largest tourist attraction. Built for the very affluent Vanderbilt family as a holiday home, the 1895 mansion is styled after a French château and is overwhelmingly sumptuous in scale and decoration. You need to spend several hours viewing the estate to see everything. The estate's winery offers tastings and sales. Midpriced meals are available at several venues, and the gift shop is the size of a small supermarket.

Thomas Wolfe Memorial (☎ 828-253-8304; 52 N Market St; admission $1; ⏰ 9am-5pm Tue-Sat, 1-5pm Sun) is the local literary landmark. This was his mother's early-1900s boardinghouse and the model for 'Dixieland' in Wolfe's novel *Look Homeward Angel*. The 29-room house holds artifacts from the writer's life and the adjacent visitor center shows a video on his life.

SLEEPING

Asheville Bed & Breakfast Association (☎ 877-262-6867; www.ashevillebba.com) Handles bookings for B&Bs in the Asheville area, from Victorian mansions to mountain retreats.

Grove Park Inn Resort & Spa (☎ 828-252-2711, 800-438-5800; www.groveparkinn.com; 290 Macon Ave; r $180; P ❄ 🖥 🏊) This sprawling resort with 510 rooms in a 1913 classic Arts and Crafts building has gorgeous rooms, a fitness center, golf, tennis courts and four restaurants. The spa will blow your mind, with waterfalls, pools surrounded by stone and a huge menu of therapeutic treatments. Rates fluctuate wildly, depending on the season.

Inn on Biltmore Estate (☎ 828-225-1660, 800-922-0084; www.biltmore.com; r $240-450; P ❄ 🏊) A stunning option on Vanderbilt's property, the 213-room resort has everything, including some rooms with private terraces and hot tubs. Expect full decadence here, from the plush robes to the chocolate on your pillow.

ArtHaus Hostel (☎ 828-225-3278; 16 Ravenscroft Dr; dm/ste $20/65; P ❌ ❄ 🖥) An ultrafriendly hostel right downtown, ArtHaus is a welcome haven for students, campers, hikers and independent travelers. One suite is totally private and two rooms have dorm-style beds. There's a communal kitchen, laundry, free Internet and bikes to borrow.

Bear Creek Campground (☎ 828-253-0798; 81 S Bear Creek Rd; campsites $20-24) Southwest of town at I-40 exit 47, it has full facilities.

EATING

Early Girl Eatery (☎ 828-259-9292; 8 Wall St; mains $5-14; ⏰ 7:30am-3pm Mon-Fri, 5-9pm Tue-Sat, 9am-3pm Sat & Sun; ❌) An excellent café to enjoy a big Southern breakfast ($5) or yummy treats like vegan bean or BBQ chicken sandwiches ($7). At night, try the pan-fried mountain trout ($13).

Laughing Seed Café (☎ 828-252-3445; www .laughingseed.com; 40 Wall St; mains $7-15; ⏰ lunch & dinner Wed-Mon) Every vegetarian's favorite restaurant offers a huge menu of everything from Mexican and Mediterranean to Indian and down-home Southern. Try the locally brewed organic Green Man beer.

Shop for flowers, food supplies and fresh produce at the **Grove Arcade Public Market** (☎ 828-252-7799; www.grovearcade.com; 1 Page Ave), where there are several restaurants and specialty shops.

GETTING THERE & AROUND

Greyhound (☎ 828-253-8451; 2 Tunnel Rd) has several buses daily to Knoxville, TN ($27, two hours) and Raleigh ($53, nine hours), and one to Atlanta, GA ($38, from 6¾ hours). **Asheville Transit** (☎ 828-253-5691; www.asheville transit.com; 60 W Haywood St; ticket 75¢) provides a limited local bus service.

Chimney Rock Park

The photogenic 'chimney,' complete with US flag, in the heart of this private **park** (☎ 828-625-9611; www.chimneyrockpark.com; adult/child $14/6; 🕙 8:30am-4:30pm) is a widely publicized rock spire a pleasant 20-mile drive southeast of Asheville. An elevator takes visitors 258ft up to the chimney, but the real draw is the exciting hike around the cliffs to a 404ft waterfall.

Great Smoky Mountains National Park

More than 10 million annual visitors come through this giant park, known for its beauty and biodiversity. The Great Smoky Mountains National Park straddles the border with Tennessee, which roughly follows the Appalachian Trail north to Virginia and the Shenandoah National Park.

Newfound Gap Rd/Hwy 441 is the only thoroughfare that crosses Great Smoky Mountains National Park. Its northern portal is Gatlinburg, TN, near Sugarlands Visitor Center (p455). The road crosses the North Carolina border at Newfound Gap and then descends to the gateway town of Cherokee and the **Oconaluftee Visitor Center** (☎ 423-436-1200; Hwy 441), the primary southern portal into the park. The busy visitors center includes the Smokies Discovery Center, where visitors learn about the park's ecosystems and biodiversity through interactive exhibits. The Oconaluftee River Trail, one of only two in the park that allows leashed pets, leaves from the visitor center and follows the river for 1.5 miles to the boundary of the Cherokee reservation.

Nearby attractions include the 1886 **Mingus Mill** (🕙 spring-fall), a turbine-powered mill still that grinds wheat and corn much as it always has. A pleasant path enters the woods to follow the 100yd-long boardwalled canal, which delivers water to the mill from Mingus Creek. The excellent Mountain Farm Museum and its collection of historic buildings evoke life on a typical farmstead of the late 19th century. Together these structures paint a poignant picture of the mountain people who once eked out their sustenance from this rugged and isolated wilderness.

Cherokee

Some of the Cherokee people escaped removal on the Trail of Tears by hiding here in the Great Smoky Mountains. Their descendants, about 11,600 members of the Eastern Band of the Cherokee, now occupy a 56,000-acre reservation at the edge of the national park. The small town has ersatz Indian souvenir shops, fast-food joints and **Harrah's Cherokee Casino** (☎ 828-497-7777; www .harrahs.com).

The best thing here is the **Museum of the Cherokee Indian** (☎ 828-497-3481; adult/child $9/6; 🕙 9am-5pm), which has a special interpretive exhibit on the Trail of Tears.

The **Oconaluftee Indian Village** (☎ 828-497-22315; www.oconalufteevillage.com; adult/child $13/6; 🕙 9am-5:30pm) is a replica of an 18th-century Cherokee village where Cherokees demonstrate traditional crafts.

Nantahala

About 25 miles southwest of Cherokee, the Appalachian Trail crosses the Nantahala River, creating a natural focus for outdoor activities. The excellent **Nantahala Outdoor Center** (☎ 828-488-2175, 800-232-7238; www.noc .com; Hwy 19/74), near Bryson City, provides equipment as well as services for hiking, mountain biking, canoeing and whitewater rafting. In particular, it offers a great range of rafting trips on nearby rivers, like the Nantahala, Chatooga, Pigeon and Ocoee.

RESEARCH TRIANGLE

In 1959, the towns of Raleigh, Durham and Chapel Hill were unified by the creation of Research Triangle Park, and 7000-acre zone of research office buildings for everything from environmental science and high-tech to biotech and pharmaceutical companies. With three of the country's top research universities sitting near the tips of the Triangle, the area has long lured professionals and top scientists. You might think the towns would be the nerdiest places on earth, but each has its own lively community, distinct charm and youthful, university energy. And everyone in these towns – we mean everyone – goes crazy for university basketball.

THE SOUTH

GETTING THERE & AROUND

Raleigh-Durham International Airport (RDU; ☎ 919-840-2123; www.rdu.com), a significant hub, is a 25-minute drive northwest of downtown Raleigh. **Carolina Trailways/Greyhound** (Raleigh ☎ 919-834-8410; 314 W Jones Rd; Durham ☎ 919-687-4800; 820 Morgan St) serve Raleigh and Durham with limited trips to Chapel Hill.

The **Triangle Transit Authority** (☎ 919-549-9999; www.ridetta.org; adult $2) operates buses linking Raleigh, Durham and Chapel Hill, and all three to the airport.

Raleigh

Sitting in the Triangle's southeastern corner, Raleigh has a handsome old state capitol and is home to North Carolina State University (NC State). More business-minded and conservative than the other corners of the Triangle, Raleigh is coming into its own as a center for culture. In the past two decades, urban-renewal projects have given the town a shot in the arm, with the festive Fayetteville St pedestrian mall and a growing cultural scene.

The **Capital Area Visitors Center** (☎ 919-733-3456; 301 N Blount St; ☼ 8am-5pm Mon-Fri, from 9am Sat, from 1pm Sun) has a walking-tour map of the government buildings and the old Oakwood district. Pick up other helpful information at the **Convention & Visitors Bureau** (☎ 919-834-5900, 800-849-8499; www.visitraleigh.com; 421 Fayetteville Mall; ☼ 8:30am-5:50pm Mon-Fri).

SIGHTS

North Carolina Museum of Art (☎ 919-839-6262; www.ncartmuseum.org; 2110 Blue Ridge Rd; admission free; ☼ 9am-5pm Tue-Sat, from 10am Sun) is located on the western fringe of town, but it's well worth visiting for its fine collection of antiquities and baroque and Renaissance paintings spread over several levels. They have a variety of programs, including children's films, workshops and summer movies and concerts.

North Carolina Museum of History (☎ 919-715-0200; www.ncmuseumofhistory.org; 5 E Edenton St; admission free; ☼ 9am-5pm Mon-Sat, from noon Sun) has a good chronological exhibit, including a dugout canoe, flags, Civil War photos and a Wright Brothers plane model.

The world's only dinosaur specimen with a heart (it's fossilized) is kept at the modern, airy **North Carolina Museum of Natural Sciences** (☎ 919-733-7450; www.naturalsciences.org; 11 W Jones St; admission free; ☼ 9am-5pm Mon-Sat, from noon Sun). There's also a unique and scary Acrocanthosaurus, five habitat dioramas and lots of well-done taxidermy.

Exploris (☎ 919-834-4040; www.exploris.org; 201 E Hargett St; adult/child $8/5.50, Imax theater $9/6.50; ☼ 9am-5pm Tue-Sat, from noon Sun) is a fun, hands-on museum for kids.

The **Raleigh Flea Market** (☎ 919-829-3533; 1025 Blue Ridge Rd; free admission; ☼ 9am-5pm Sat & Sun), held every weekend on the state fairgrounds, has hundreds of vendors selling everything from junk to quality antiques.

SLEEPING & EATING

The Glenwood Ave area northwest of downtown has an array of good restaurants and clubs. Hillsborough St along the North Carolina State University campus is lively at night.

Oakwood Inn B&B (☎ 919-832-9712; www.oakwoodinnbb.com; 411 N Bloodworth St; r incl breakfast $120-170; ⓟ ⓧ ⓧ ⓠ) There are a couple of historic accommodations in the heart of Raleigh, including this Victorian house in the pretty Oakwood district. It has six nicely furnished theme rooms (Polk, Linden, etc), an afternoon-tea service and full breakfast.

Holiday Inn Brownstone Hotel (☎ 919-828-0811, 800-331-7919; www.holiday-inn.com; 1707 Hillsborough St; r $60-140; ⓟ ⓧ ⓠ ⓐ) Near the university, this 188-room hotel has plush, renovated standard rooms and in-room amenities.

42nd St Oyster Bar (☎ 919-831-2811; 508 W Jones St; mains $8-18; ☼ lunch Mon-Fri, dinner nightly) A wildly popular downtown restaurant where you'll find fresh seafood, an oyster bar and a lounge that has live R & B music and dancing.

Big Ed's (☎ 919-836-9909; 220 Wolfe St; dishes $7-10; ☼ 7am-2pm Mon-Fri, to noon Sat) Who's Ed? He's the guy in overalls, but that's not the point: all you need to know is that this barn-looking place is *the* spot for a delicious country breakfast, like cured ham and eggs, grits and gravy.

Durham

In the late 19th century, Durham's stock rose with the fortunes of the newly established American Tobacco Company, owned by Washington Duke and his sons. The Dukes had an instinct for PR as well as business, and in 1924 the founder's son, Buck, donated a wad of cash to a small college that grew into Duke University.

Durham is a lively student town at the northeast corner of the Triangle. Durham is home to the Durham Bulls, a minor-league baseball team that shot to fame after the 1988 flick *Bull Durham*. Downtown can be quiet or raucous, depending on where the students (and sports fans) are. There are two hubs of activity: the area around **Brightleaf Square** on the east side of downtown is a re-cycled tobacco warehouse with restaurants and upscale shops, and a half-mile north-east, adjacent to the Duke campus, is the laid-back student-filled **Ninth Street District**.

The **visitor center** (☎ 919-687-0288, 800-446-8604; www.durham-nc.com; 101 E Morgan St; ☼ 8:30am-5pm Mon-Fri, 10am-2pm Sat) has a lot of good informa-tion and maps.

SIGHTS

Endowed by the Duke family's cigarette fortune, **Duke University** (☎ 919-684-2572; www .duke.edu) has a Georgian-style East Campus and a neo-Gothic West Campus with an impressive 1930s chapel. Students juggle, play soccer and pretend to read on the front concourse.

See the humble origins of the Duke fam-ily and have an interesting but uncritical look at the tobacco industry at **Duke Home-stead** (☎ 919-477-5498; 2828 Duke Homestead Rd; ad-mission free; ☼ 9am-5pm Mon-Sat, from 1pm Sun, closed Mon winter), on the north side of town.

At the **Museum of Life & Science** (☎ 919-220-5429; www.ncmls.org; 433 Murray Ave; adult/child $8.50/6; ☼ 10am-5pm Mon-Sat, from noon Sun), check out the ultracool Magic Wings Butterfly House, a tropical paradise of plants and butterflies.

From April to September be sure to catch an afternoon or evening ballgame at the **Durham Bulls Athletic Park** (☎ 919-956-2855; www .dbulls.com; 409 Blackwell St; tickets $6-8).

SLEEPING & EATING

Best Value Carolina Duke Motor Inn (☎ 919-286-0771, 800-438-1158; 2517 Guess Rd; d $36-52; P ⊠ ⊡) You can't beat the price at this hotel off I-85. It has 182 tidy and spacious rooms, all with TVs. There are laundry facilities.

Washington Duke Inn & Golf Club (☎ 919-490-0999, 800-443-3853; www.washingtondukeinn.com; 3001 Cameron Blvd; r from $150; mains $20-40; P ⊠ ⊡ ⊠) This swanky four-star beauty is just off Hwy 15/501 on the Duke campus. Prices can drop dramatically during slow periods.

Nicely furnished with all the amenities, in-cluding the excellent Fairview Restaurant.

Foster's Market (☎ 919-489-3944; www.fosters market.com; 2694 Durham Chapel Hill Blvd; mains $5-9; ☼ 7:30am-8pm) An institution in Durham, es-pecially for the delicious Southern brunch on Sundays. Home-cooked meals include wood-fired pizzas, yummy wraps and fresh salads. Lots of veggie options.

Pop's Trattoria (☎ 919-956-7677; 810 W Peabody St; ☼ lunch & dinner Mon-Fri, dinner Sat & Sun) In an old tobacco warehouse in the Brightleaf Sq district, Pop's attracts a lively crowd who drink at the bar or sit down to feast on northern Italian cuisine.

Magnolia Grill (☎ 919-286-3609; 1002 Ninth St; ☼ dinner) Upscale Southern cuisine gets all sorts of unique touches at this popular grill. It's a romantic spot, with white tablecloths and groovy art on the walls.

For a taste of history and sublime South-ern soul food, stop by the **Know Restaurant & Bookstore** (☎ 919-682-7223; 250 E Fayetteville St; ☼ 10am-8pm Mon-Sat), a fantastic African Amer-ican bookshop with a handful of tables.

Chapel Hill

An attractive university town, Chapel Hill (and the adjoining city of Carrboro) is con-spicuously more affluent than the other corners of the Triangle. The University of North Carolina (UNC), founded in 1789, was one of the nation's first state universi-ties and has many fine old buildings. The music scene – particularly for grunge, jazz and pop – is smokin', as is the basketball; Michael Jordan rose (or rather leaped) to fame during his tenure at UNC.

Downtown lies about 2 miles northwest of the Hwy 15/501 bypass. The main drag is Franklin St, with funky clothing shops, bars and restaurants on its north side and the UNC campus to the south; the same street enters Carrboro to the west. A popu-lar place to hang out is the **Weaver Street Market** (www.weaverstreetmarket.com) in Carrboro. The lawn in front of the market is usually blanketed with students and others taking advantage of the outdoor wi-fi and frequent summer concerts. In Chapel Hill, look for the murals sprinkled around town, such as a big yellow No 2 pencil along the wall on Church St.

Pick up good area information from the **Chapel Hill-Orange County Visitors Bureau**

(☎ 919-968-2060, 888-968-2060; www.chocvb.org; 501 W Franklin St; ⏰ 8:30am-5pm Mon-Fri, 10am-2pm Sat).

SLEEPING & EATING

You'll find most restaurants and nightspots along Franklin St.

Carolina Inn (☎ 919-933-2001, 800-962-8519; www.carolinainn.com; 211 Pittsboro St; r from $140; **P** ⌘ 💻) In the heart of town, this historic hotel loaded with amenities has 184 plush rooms, an elegant restaurant, gardens and a sunroom full of books to read.

Inn at Celebrity Dairy (☎ 919-742-5176; 149 Celebrity Dairy Way; r incl breakfast $80-130; **P** ⌘ ⊗) For something totally different, spend a night or two at this working organic dairy farm, 30 miles west of Chapel Hill. Accommodations are in a Greek Revival farmhouse or a log cabin. Every morning you'll eat a full Southern breakfast with the farm crew. Wander the grounds and you'll see baby goats and free-range chickens poking about. You can also come for the Sunday dinner, served the third Sunday of each month.

Spanky's (☎ 919-967-2678; 101 E Franklin St; mains $6-10; ⏰ lunch & dinner) With ceiling-high windows, live jazz and a loaded menu, this café is popular for its great-value pasta mains and upstairs view of the action.

411 West (☎ 919-967-2782; 411 W Franklin St; mains $8-20; ⏰ lunch Tue-Sat, dinner nightly, Sun brunch) This great little Franklin St bistro offers up fresh Italian and Mediterranean-inspired pasta and meat dishes, along with wood-smoked 'pizzette' appetizers.

For entertainment listings, pick up the free weekly *Independent*. A couple of places are must-visits. **Local 506** (☎ 919-942-5506; www.local506.com; 506 W Franklin St) is popular venue for alternative bands trying to make it big. **Cat's Cradle** (☎ 919-968-4345; www.catscradle.com; 300 E Main St), in Carrboro, has live rock, reggae and big visiting acts.

SOUTH CAROLINA

Unlike most states, South Carolina lacks a big city so you always feel like you've wandered off the beaten path – in a really good way. To visit this history-riddled state is to slow down, relax and breathe in sultry salty air, paddle through marshlands that teem with rare birds, wander through colonial mansions and grand plantations – all the while wondering what life was like for those who strolled these paths, tilled these fields, plucked the cotton harvest, long before you arrived. In Charleston, the state's gracious colonial port, the architecture, gardens and stories tell not just of South Carolina's past, but give insights into the whole country's. Along the offshore islands you hear the sweet songs of the Gullah, a culture and language created by former slaves who held on to their African ancestral ties, even when the threats of history threatened to cut them off forever.

Into this historic and cultural mix are vast resort destinations like golf-crazed Hilton Head and tacky, fun-loving Myrtle Beach – places that seem utterly dichotomous to the stunning beaches, wild and undeveloped state parks. The contrasts are everywhere, whether you drive the dusty country roads past small towns, farmlands, white clapboard churches and crumbling sharecropper shacks, or stand amid ancient oaks on a glorious plantation – South Carolina doesn't have just one thing; it has it all.

History

More than 28 separate tribes of Native Americans have lived in what's now South Carolina. The most influential were the Cherokee, who were eventually forcibly removed during the tragic Trail of Tears (p371).

The English founded the Carolina colony in 1670 and built a settlement called Charles Towne, later known as Charleston. The first settlers came from Barbados and thus became a colony of a colony (Barbados

---

SOUTH CAROLINA FACTS

Nickname Palmetto State
Population 4.1 million
Area 30,109 sq miles
Capital city Columbia (population 117,400)
Official state dance The shag
Birthplace of Activist Mary McLeod Bethune (1875–1955), jazzman Dizzy Gillespie (1917–93), soul singer James Brown (b 1933), political activist Jesse Jackson (b 1941), TV personality Vanna White (b 1957)
Home of The first US public library (1698), museum (1773), steam railroad (1833)
Famous for Firing the first shot of the Civil War, from Charleston's Fort Sumter

was a colony of England). South Carolina's judicial system, slave code and original form of government were based on those of Barbados.

The first cash king was rice. Africans from the rice-growing regions of Sierra Leone, Senegal, the Gambia and Angola were enslaved and brought over to turn impenetrable swamps into cultivated rice fields.

By the 1730s, there existed two South Carolinas: the Lowcountry, a refined community of aristocrats and their slaves; and the Backcountry, a frontier settled by Scots-Irish and Swiss-German farmers. This split played a major role in the Revolutionary War.

South Carolina was the first state to secede from the Union, and the first battle of the Civil War occurred at Fort Sumter in Charleston Harbor.

After the fall of the Confederacy, prominent families were penniless. While white South Carolinians mourned, black South Carolinians rejoiced and racially motivated violence ensued. The fury and hatred of the KKK spread like disease. This divisiveness set the tone for South Carolina's bumpy ride through the Civil Rights movement almost a century later.

Information

There's a 5% sales tax on goods and services; expect to pay up to 10% extra tax on accommodations.

South Carolina Department of Parks, Recreation & Tourism (☎ 803-734-1700 www.discoversouthcaro lina.com; 1205 Pendleton St, Room 505, Columbia, SC 29201) Sends out *South Carolina Smiles*, the state's official vacation guide.

CHARLESTON

Overflowing with charming streets and historic districts, Charleston is one of the oldest and most appealing urban areas in America. Its history is peppered with defining moments in US history – Charleston fueled American patriotism in the Revolutionary War; its Confederate soldiers fired the first shots of the Civil War; and the Civil Rights era rocked the cultural landscape, one whose success had grown on the backs of slavery and segregation. This is a city where rampant fires torched homes and tropical hurricanes blew away dreams. But despite its heated political history and glut of natural disaster, Charleston managed, miraculously, to keep her head held high. Unlike many cities in the US, Charleston embraced her history instead of shopping around for a new one. It never recreated itself, it simply opened its heart to what it already had.

Today, this birthplace of Southern hospitality oozes charm, elegance and a whole lot of whimsy. Blooming flowers – gardenia, magnolia, lavender and jasmine – send intoxicating scents wafting through the streets. Grand pillars of early American architecture stand alongside ancient gardens. Whether you choose to wander on your own, or join one of many cultural tours, Charleston's friendly people will happily share the city's history and secrets.

History

Well before the Revolutionary War, Charles Towne (named for Charles II) was one of the busiest ports on the eastern seaboard, and the center of a prosperous rice growing and trading colony. With influences from the West Indies and Africa, France and other European countries, it became a cosmopolitan city often compared to New Orleans.

The Charleston and Hamburg Railroad began operations in 1833, transporting Carolina cotton to Charleston's ports. Something of an engineering wonder, the transportation network secured Charleston's position as a principal East Coast port over rival Savannah.

The first shots of the Civil War rang out at Fort Sumter, in Charleston's harbor. After the war, as the labor-intensive rice plantations became uneconomical without slave labor, the city's importance declined. Natural disasters wrought more damage, with a major earthquake in 1886, several fires and storms, and devastating Hurricane Hugo in 1989. It's remarkable that so much of the town's historic fabric has survived – and fortunate too, because tourism is now a major money-spinner, with close to four million visitors arriving each year.

Orientation

The Charleston metropolitan area sprawls over a broad stretch of coastal plains and islands, but the historic heart is very compact, about 4 sq miles at the southern tip of a peninsula between the Cooper and Ashley Rivers. I-26 goes to North Charleston

THE SOUTH

CHARLESTON

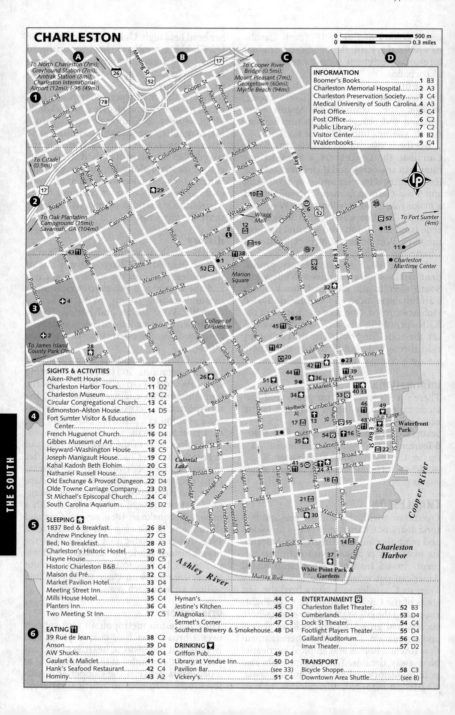

INFORMATION

Boomer's Books	**1** B3
Charleston Memorial Hospital	**2** A3
Charleston Preservation Society	**3** C4
Medical University of South Carolina	**4** A3
Post Office	**5** C4
Post Office	**6** C2
Public Library	**7** C4
Visitor Center	**8** B2
Waldenbooks	**9** C4

SIGHTS & ACTIVITIES

Aiken-Rhett House	**10** C2
Charleston Harbor Tours	**11** D2
Charleston Museum	**12** C2
Circular Congregational Church	**13** C4
Edmonston-Alston House	**14** D5
Fort Sumter Visitor & Education Center	**15** D2
French Huguenot Church	**16** D4
Gibbes Museum of Art	**17** C4
Heyward-Washington House	**18** C5
Joseph Manigault House	**19** C2
Kahal Kadosh Beth Elohim	**20** C3
Nathaniel Russell House	**21** C5
Old Exchange & Provost Dungeon	**22** D4
Olde Towne Carriage Company	**23** D3
St Michael's Episcopal Church	**24** C4
South Carolina Aquarium	**25** D2

SLEEPING

1837 Bed & Breakfast	**26** B4
Andrew Pinckney Inn	**27** C3
Bed, No Breakfast	**28** A3
Charleston's Historic Hostel	**29** B2
Hayne House	**30** C5
Historic Charleston B&B	**31** C4
Maison du Pré	**32** C3
Market Pavilion Hotel	**33** D4
Meeting Street Inn	**34** C4
Mills House Hotel	**35** C4
Planters Inn	**36** C4
Two Meeting St Inn	**37** C5

EATING

39 Rue de Jean	**38** C2
Anson	**39** D4
AW Shucks	**40** D4
Gaulart & Maliclet	**41** C4
Hank's Seafood Restaurant	**42** C4
Hominy	**43** A2
Hyman's	**44** C4
Jestine's Kitchen	**45** C3
Magnolias	**46** C4
Sermet's Corner	**47** C3
Southend Brewery & Smokehouse	**48** D4

DRINKING

Griffon Pub	**49** D4
Library at Vendue Inn	**50** D4
Pavilion Bar	(see 33)
Vickery's	**51** C4

ENTERTAINMENT

Charleston Ballet Theater	**52** B3
Cumberlands	**53** D4
Dock St Theater	**54** C4
Footlight Players Theater	**55** D4
Gaillard Auditorium	**56** C3
Imax Theater	**57** D2

TRANSPORT

Bicycle Shoppe	**58** C3
Downtown Area Shuttle	(see 8)

To North Charleston (7mi);
Greyhound Station (7mi);
Amtrak Station (8mi);
Charleston International
Airport (12mi); I-95 (49mi)

To Cooper River
Bridge (0.5mi);
Mount Pleasant (7mi);
Georgetown (60mi);
Myrtle Beach (94mi)

To Citadel
(0.5mi)

To Oak Plantation
Campground (15mi);
Savannah, GA (104mi)

To Fort Sumter
(4mi)

Charleston
Maritime Center

To James Island
County Park (7mi)

Marion
Square

College of
Charleston

Colonial
Lake

Cooper River

Ashley River

Charleston
Harbor

White Point Park &
Gardens

Waterfront
Park

THE SOUTH

SYMBOL OF HOSPITALITY

Throughout Charleston, you'll see pineapple motifs everywhere – on doors, iron gates, in the fountain at Waterfront Park, in stained-glass windows, even on wallpaper. Long a symbol of hospitality in the Caribbean, the expensive and cherished fruit also symbolized wealth in colonial Charleston. Visitors would gasp with delight when a pineapple appeared at a dinner table.

If a pineapple was placed at the entrance to a Caribbean village, explorers knew they were welcome. Likewise, this tradition became custom in Charleston, where returning seafaring captains would impale fresh pineapples on gateposts or piazzas, sending the message to friends that they'd made it home safely and that visitors were welcome.

and the airport. Hwy 17, the main coastal road, cuts across the Charleston peninsula as the Crosstown Expressway. Soaring bridges connect west to James Island and West Ashley, and east to Mount Pleasant.

Information

BOOKSTORES

Boomer's Books (☎ 843-722-2666; boomersbooks@earthlink.net; 420 King St; ⏰ 10am-6pm Mon-Sat, 2-6pm Sun) Rooms full of used books.

Charleston Preservation Society (☎ 843-722-4630; www.preservationsociety.org; 147 King St; ⏰ 10am-5pm Mon-Sat) Has a wealth of local history and architecture books.

Waldenbooks (☎ 843-853-1736; www.waldenbooks .com; 120 Market St; ⏰ 10am-6pm Mon-Sat, noon-5pm Sun) Good selection of magazines, fiction and nonfiction, including regional titles.

EMERGENCY

Emergency (☎ 911) Police, ambulance, fire.
Main police station (☎ 843-577-7434; 180 Lockwood Blvd) Nonemergencies only.

INTERNET ACCESS

Public library (☎ 843-805-6801; www.ccpl.org; 68 Calhoun St; 9am-9pm Mon-Thu, to 6pm Fri & Sat, 2-5pm Sun) Free Internet access.

MEDIA

Charleston City Paper (www.charlestoncitypaper.com) An alternative weekly that comes out on Wednesday, with good entertainment and restaurant listings.

Post & Courier (www.charleston.net) Charleston's daily newspaper.

MEDICAL SERVICES

Charleston Memorial Hospital (☎ 843-577-0690; 83 Calhoun St)
Medical University of South Carolina (MUSC; ☎ 843-792-2300; 171 Ashley Ave)

POST

Post office Bay St (☎ 843-805-7757; 557 E Bay St; ⏰ 8:30-5:30 Mon-Fri, 9am-noon Sat); Main (☎ 843-577-0690; 83 Broad St; ⏰ 9am-5pm Mon-Fri)

TOURIST INFORMATION

Visitor center (☎ 843-853-8000; www.charlestoncvb .com; 375 Meeting St; ⏰ 8am-5pm Mon-Sat) This well-stocked center can help with accommodations and tours. Its 23-minute *Charleston Forever* video ($2) is worth seeing.

Sights & Activities

Charleston's main tourist activities include visiting historic houses, shopping for sweetgrass baskets in the market and imagining what it must have been like during the 'late, great unpleasantness' (Charlestonians' term for the Civil War). The main attraction is the city itself, especially the quarter south of Beaufain and Hasell Sts, where you can wander along elegant thoroughfares and quaint, bending backstreets.

There are maps with walking tours, but an aimless stroll is just as good – Tradd, Meeting and Church Sts have some of the best buildings. The old **Market Street** has some great souvenir shops, craft stalls, eateries and bars, and is a good place to be at lunch or dinnertime.

Overlooking the Cooper River, **Waterfront Park** is a shady retreat; further south, **White Point Park & Gardens**, at the tip of the peninsula, is superb at sunset, when the Battery mansions are beautifully illuminated. **King Street** is full of upscale shops and restaurants. West of King St, residential blocks with colorfully painted houses are less grand but still alluring. Further north, around the **College of Charleston**, many smaller timber houses are somewhat timeworn, but the streets are a nice contrast from the posh neighborhoods.

North of downtown, the **Citadel** (museum ☎ 843-953-6846; www.citadel.edu; 171 Moultrie St; admission free; ⏰ 2-5pm Sun-Fri, from noon Sat) is the state-sponsored military college, with a small museum and an impressive dress parade of the cadets at 3:45pm Friday, during the school year.

HISTORIC HOUSES

Quite a few fine historic houses are open to visitors. Discounted combination tickets may tempt you to see more, but one or two will be enough for most people. Most houses are open from 10am to 5pm Monday to Saturday, 1pm to 5pm Sunday and run guided tours every half-hour. Admission is $7 to $9. Of the most interesting, **Aiken-Rhett House** (☎ 843-723-1159; 48 Elizabeth St) is the only surviving urban plantation; it gives a good look at antebellum life, including the role of slaves.

Wonderfully located along the Battery, the 1828 **Edmonston-Alston House** (☎ 843-722-7171; 21 E Bay St) built by Edmonston, a Scottish shipping merchant was later renovated by rice-plantation mogul Charles Alston. It has remained in the Alston family ever since – in fact, the family still resides on the 3rd floor.

Heyward-Washington House (☎ 843-722-0354; 87 Church St), built in 1772, belonged to Thomas Heyward Jr, a signer of the Declaration of Independence. Though the outside isn't much to look at, the interior contains some fine examples of Charleston-made mahogany furniture.

The showpiece of a French Huguenot family who made their fortune trading rum, sugar and rice, the Adams-style **Joseph Manigault House** (☎ 843-723-2926; 350 Meeting St) house was designed by the owner's brother Gabriel, who is credited for introducing the architectural style to the city.

Built by a Rhode Islander, known in Charleston as 'the king of the Yankees,' this 1808 Federal-style **Nathaniel Russell House** (☎ 843-724-8481; 51 Meeting St) is noted especially for its spectacular, self-supporting spiral staircase and lovely formal garden.

HISTORIC HOUSES OF WORSHIP

From the city's beginnings, religious tolerance was fashionable in Charleston, and persecuted French Huguenots, Baptists and Jews sought refuge here. Many of these congregations are the oldest of their faiths in the US.

The Romanesque Revival **Circular Congregation Church** (☎ 843-577-6400; 150 Meeting St)

was built in 1861 and was used as the city's first meeting place, hence the name of its street.

French Huguenot Church (☎ 843-722-4385; 136 Church St) was founded in 1681 by French Protestant refugees. Congregants often came by boat, arriving on the ebb tide and leaving on the flood tide, which sometimes meant they'd be in church a long time.

The oldest continuously used synagogue in the country (the oldest temple is in Savannah) is **Kahal Kadosh Beth Elohim** (☎ 843-723-1090; 90 Hasell St). Sephardic Orthodox Jews came in the late 1600s. The temple was rebuilt in 1838 to serve the nation's first Reform congregation.

St Michael's Episcopal Church (☎ 843-744-1334; 78 Meeting St; ⏰ yard 9am-4pm), built in 1752, is the oldest church building in Charleston.

MUSEUMS

Opposite the visitor center, **Charleston Museum** (☎ 843-722-2996; www.charlestonmuseum.org; 360 Meeting St; adult/child $10/4; ⏰ 9am-5pm Mon-Sat, from 1pm Sun) offers good exhibits on the state's history. The permanent collection includes everything from Charleston's early silver collection to slave tags, natural history and historical documents. It's in a modern building, but the museum was founded in 1773 and claims to be the country's oldest.

Gibbes Museum of Art (☎ 843-722-2706; www.gibbesmuseum.org; 135 Meeting St; admission $7/4; ⏰ 10am-5pm Tue-Sat, 1-5pm Sun) was established in 1905. This American fine-art museum has excellent exhibits on Southern art and architecture.

The Palladian **Old Exchange & Provost Dungeon** (☎ 843-727-2165; www.oldexchange.com; 122 E Bay St; adult/child $7/3.50; ⏰ 9am-5pm), built in 1771 as an exchange and customs house for the busy port, was later used as a dungeon prison for pirates and other outlaws.

AQUARIUM WHARF

The Aquarium Wharf surrounds pretty Liberty Sq and is a great place to stroll around and watch the tugboats guiding ships into port. Charleston is the seventh largest container port in the US. The wharf is the embarkation point for tours to Fort Sumter. Boat tours of the harbor depart from the Harbor Tour Dock and nearby Charleston Maritime Center. Also here is the IMAX Theater (p484).

The excellent **South Carolina Aquarium** (☎ 843-720-1990; www.scaquarium.org; 100 Aquarium Wharf; adult/child $15/8; ☻ 9am-6pm) covers 69,000 sq ft, almost all of which are devoted to South Carolina habitats, flora and fauna. The best part of the aquarium is the 330,000-gallon Great Ocean Tank, where sharks, massive fish and a giant loggerhead turtle swim behind a 27ft-tall window.

Fort Sumter is the pentagon-shaped island in the center of the harbor. The first shots of the Civil War were fired from here. A Confederate stronghold, Fort Sumter was shelled by Union forces from 1863 to 1865. By the end of the war, it was a pile of rubble. A few original guns and fortifications, and the obviously strategic location, give a feel for the momentous history here. The only way to get here is by boat tour. Tours leave from the National Park Service's **Fort Sumter Visitor & Education Center** or from Patriot's Point in Mt Pleasant, across the river.

Tours

While you're in Charleston, save some time and cash to take one of the many tours. Listing the walking, carriage, bus and boat tours could take up this entire book. There's an array of excellent walking tours on everything from Charleston's ghosts, to Civil War and black history tours. Ask at the visitor center for the gamut.

Charleston Harbor Tours (depart Charleston Maritime Center; 2hr tours adult/child $14/9)

Fort Sumter Tours (☎ 843-881-7337, 800-789-3678; adult/child $13/7) Offers three to five tours daily, depending on the season. Even if you're not a Civil War buff, you'll enjoy the trip. Tours last 2¼ hours and include a colorful tour of the fort and a scenic cruise around the harbor.

Olde Town Carriage Company (☎ 843-722-1315; 20 Anson St; 45min tours adult/child $19/9) The best of the horse-drawn carriage tours you see clickety-clacking around town, with colorful commentary.

Sleeping

Staying in the historic downtown is the most attractive option, but it's the most expensive, especially at weekends and during special events. Rates in town fluctuate wildly – a $200 room in summer could be just $70 in winter – so call ahead to see if you can get a better deal. The rates below are for high season (spring and summer). The chain hotels on the highways offer significantly lower rates.

One of the best ways to get to know Charleston is to stay at a small home where the owners serve up authentic Southern breakfasts and dole out great local information. Small places start at around $100 for doubles with breakfast, but many have only one or two rooms, so it helps to use an agency like **Historic Charleston B&B** (☎ 843-722-6606; 57 Broad St).

BUDGET

Bed, No Breakfast (☎ 843-723-4450; 16 Halsey St; d $85; 🅿 🌐) This small, ultrafriendly *pension*-style place has just two rooms and

THE SOUTH

THE GENTLEMAN PIRATE

Piracy and an 18th-century midlife crisis immortalized the story of Stede Bonnet, 'the gentleman pirate.' On the little island of Barbados, Bonnet was a member of the landed gentry; he received a classical education, dressed in the finest English fashions and married a respectable woman. Active in civic affairs, Bonnet was a justice of the peace and a major in the island's militia.

In 1716, he made arrangements for what appeared to be an extended business trip. This trip was actually Bonnet's escape route: he had bought himself a sloop (the *Revenge*), outfitted her with armaments of war and hired a crew of 70 men for a new life of piracy.

The only pirate in history to buy his own ship, Bonnet knew little about robbing and even less about sailing. That's when he met the infamous Blackbeard, who took the novice pirate under his wing for a spree of looting and commandeering. Their most outrageous stunt occurred in Charleston in 1718, when they blocked the entrance to the port for a week, seizing every ship that stumbled into them.

Bonnet's apprenticeship ended when Blackbeard made off with all the booty; the Charleston courts charged Bonnet with taking more than 28 vessels, committing other acts of piracy and murdering 18 law-abiding men. Stede Bonnet was hanged at White Point Gardens on December 10, 1718.

a shared bath. One room has a queen bed, the other two twins. It's a great option if rooms are available. Be sure to call ahead. Cash or checks only.

Charleston's Historic Hostel (☎ 843-478-1446; www.charlestonhostel.com; 194 St Philip St; dm/d $19/40; ❌ ▣) A laid-back and friendly place with very simple but clean accommodations, free laundry, and a shared living room, kitchen and piazza. Spacious porches, a well-stocked kitchen, and proximity to King St and the historic district make this traveler's haven a fantastic value.

Southwest of Charleston, **Oak Plantation Campground** (☎ 843-766-5936, 866-658-2500; www .oakplantationcampground.com; 3540 Savannah Hwy; campsites & RV sites $15-20) and **James Island County Park** (☎ 843-795-7275, 800-743-7275; 871 Riverland Dr; campsites/RV sites $20/34, cabins $110) offer shuttle services downtown. Reservations are highly recommended.

MIDRANGE
Hayne House (☎ 843-577-2633; www.haynehouse.com; 30 King St; r $150-275; Ⓟ ❌ ❌) Owner Brian McGreevy is a Charleston native and can bestow great information about the city's history. He and his wife Jane serve afternoon sherry in a Victorian drawing room to guests staying in one of the six rooms.

1837 Bed & Breakfast (☎ 843-723-7166, 877-723-1837; www.1837bb.com; 126 Wentworth St; r incl breakfast $100-165; Ⓟ ❌ ❌) This 1837 home, designed in the 'Charleston single house' style, has nine rooms, all with unique period furnishings and canopy beds. The

---

THE AUTHOR'S CHOICE

Maison du Pré (☎ 843-723-8691, 800-844-4667; www.maisondupre.com; 317 E Bay St; d incl breakfast $155-185; Ⓟ ❌ ❌) At first glance, this inn just looks like an old house north of the market, but look a little further and you'll see it's a true diamond in the rough. The inn is composed of five buildings that surround a lovely courtyard, where flowers intoxicate the air. Each room (choose from twin or queen beds) features unique period furnishings and paintings by owner Lucille Mulholland. Highlights include a free continental breakfast, and afternoon wine and cheese. Parking costs $8.50 and is slightly offsite.

---

afternoon-tea service is a nice touch. The piazza is a great place to read a book and capture the breeze.

Mills House Hotel (☎ 843-577-2400, 800-874-9600; www.millshouse.com; 115 Meeting St; r from $140; Ⓟ ❌ ❌) In a great location, the Mills House is a beautiful hotel, its rooms filled with antiques. The hotel has a restaurant and lounge and the outdoor pool is in a private courtyard on the 2nd floor. Parking costs $16.

Meeting Street Inn (☎ 843-723-1882, 800-842-8022; www.meetingstreetinn.com; 173 Meeting St; d incl breakfast from $100; Ⓟ ❌ ❌) Each room opens onto a private patio overlooking a courtyard, which has a hot tub. The 56 small rooms are furnished with 19th-century antiques. A complimentary afternoon tea is served. Parking costs $12.

Andrew Pinckney Inn (☎ 843-937-8800, 800-505-8983; www.andrewpinckneyinn.com; 40 Pinckney St; d $120-180, ste $169-279; Ⓟ ❌ ❌) With a great location near the market, a courtyard, rooftop garden and 32 rooms, the Pinckney continues to be one of the top choices in Charleston. The entire hotel is designed in a West Indies style and rooms have full amenities. Parking costs $12.

TOP END
Two Meeting St Inn (☎ 843-723-7322, www.two meetingstreetinn.com; 2 Meeting St; r $175-350; Ⓟ ❌ ❌) Housed in a stunning Queen Anne mansion on the Battery, this beautiful home could give you the best stay you've ever had. The nine rooms are uniquely decorated, with private baths and period furnishings. The story goes that George W Williams left his daughter, Martha, $75,000 on a satin pillow to celebrate her marriage to Waring P Carrington. They used the cash to build this house in 1892. Check out the oak paneling and Tiffany stained glass in the den – the glass was supposedly crafted and installed by Tiffany himself.

Market Pavilion Hotel (☎ 843-723-0500, 877-440-2250; www.marketpavilion.com; 225 E Bay St; r from $275; Ⓟ ❌ ❌ ▣ ▣) Very swanky, baby. This luxury boutique hotel is new to Charleston, but the designers did such a fine job recreating the historic veneer and ambience that you'd never know the difference. Where you can tell is in the ultramodern amenities, mahogany furniture and sumptuous linens. Even if you don't stay here, you must have cocktails at the rooftop Pavilion Bar (p484). Parking costs $15.

Planters Inn (☎ 843-722-2345, 800-845-7082; www.plantersinn.com; 112 N Market St; r from $250; P ✗ ✗ ▣) Every spacious room at this ultraluxury boutique hotel has a canopy bed and 10ft ceiling. Some rooms have fireplaces, whirlpools and verandas. There's also a restaurant and lounge. Rates fluctuate, so call to see if you can get a better deal. Parking costs $16.

Eating

In many ways, Charleston is a small town, but you'd never think it by the vast selection of excellent restaurants. So much good eatin's goin' on that you just have to indulge and enjoy. Roll up your sleeves and enjoy the Lowcountry cuisine, which often features seafood caught just hours before your arrival. On Saturdays in summer, stop by the farmers market, which sets up in Marion Sq from 8am to 1pm, April to October.

BUDGET & MIDRANGE

Sermet's Corner (☎ 843-853-7775; 276 King St; mains $7-11; ✌ lunch & dinner) Sermet, the owner, whose art decorates the walls, cooks excellent panini sandwiches and delicious grub, like crab burgers served with sweet potato fries.

Jestine's Kitchen (☎ 843-722-7224; 251 Meeting St; mains $6-12; ✌ lunch & dinner Tue-Sun) They're not shy about fryin' here at this good homestyle kitchen a few blocks north of Market St. Here you'll get Southern favorites like fried oysters, hush puppies, grits and fried green tomatoes. Be sure to sample the tasty pies.

Gaulart & Maliclet (☎ 843-577-9797; 98 Broad St; mains $6-14; ✌ breakfast, lunch & dinner Mon-Sat) Known mostly by its nickname 'Fast & French,' this tiny bistro has a groovy mixed clientele who know to come for the wine and bargain meals. Nightly specials ($14) include a main dish, soup and wine.

AW Shucks (☎ 873-723-6000; 35 S Market St; mains $9-14; ✌ lunch & dinner) This gets major promotion around town and seems like a tourist trap, but it is a good place to go for affordable seafood, such as crab legs and oysters.

Hyman's (☎ 843-723-6000; www.hymanseafood .com; 215 Meeting St; mains $8-20; ✌ lunch & dinner)

Talk about lineups! For lunch or dinner, this immensely popular seafood restaurant is famous the world over for its giant po'boy sandwiches, and fresh scallops, oysters, shrimp, mussels and soft-shell crab. If waiting around in the heat's not your thing, come for lunch, when the lines are more reasonable. This is a fun place for kids.

Southend Brewery & Smokehouse (☎ 843-853-0956; 161 E Bay St; mains $7-14; ✌ lunch & dinner) The wall-to-ceiling windows at this fun microbrewery open up, giving the impression you're outside but without all the pollen. The menu serves up brick-oven pizza, pasta, seafood and smoked meats.

39 Rue de Jean (☎ 843-722-8881; 39 John St; mains lunch $8-11, dinner $12-25; ✌ lunch & dinner) With the lively ambience of a French bistro, this is a wonderful place for coq au vin and fresh seafood prepared with a French twist.

TOP END

Magnolias (☎ 843-577-7771; 185 E Bay St; $7-14 lunch, $15-22 dinner; ✌ lunch & dinner) Offering Lowcountry 'Down South dishes with uptown presentation,' this long-standing truly Southern spot has interesting traditional dishes dressed up with modern touches. Try the salads at lunch and the meat dishes at dinner.

Hank's Seafood Restaurant (☎ 843-723-3474; 10 Hayne St; $15-24; ✌ dinner) Ah, Hank, how we love thee. Just a shell's toss from the bustle of Market St, Hank's is a trusty oasis where locals come for Lowcountry bouillabaisse, crab soup and other fresh fish dishes.

Anson (☎ 803-577-0551; 12 Anson St; mains $13-22; ✌ dinner) With a reputation for having

---

SPOLETO USA

When Pulitzer Prize–winning composer Gian Carlo Menotti founded the Festival dei Due Mondi (Festival of Two Worlds) in Spoleto, Italy, he said he wanted to prove that art was 'not only an after-dinner mint but that it could be the main meal itself.' It was with that same sentiment that he brought the Spoleto Festival to Charleston in 1977. With Charleston's architectural bounty, its glorious gardens and its dedication to historical preservation, it seemed the perfect place.

For 17 days in May and June **Spoleto USA** (☎ 843-722-2764; www.spoletousa.org) trumpets, dances, sings and colors its way across the city. More than 130 performances take place in theaters, churches, on plantations, and in parks and gardens. National and international audiences so loved Spoleto that they augmented it with **Piccolo Spoleto**, another explosion of the arts that follows on the heels of Spoleto. Culture creatures of every persuasion delight in the air of arts and melodies that overcome the city.

There are no after-dinner mints here – indeed, Spoleto USA is a full-meal deal.

---

the city's best she-crab soup and for using only the finest and freshest local ingredients, Anson tops many a local's list of best restaurants. Free-range meat and fowl and superfresh seafood make this a great dinner option.

Drinking

The balmy evenings are conducive to late-night dining, drinking and dancing at the various venues around Market and E Bay Sts. Check out the weekly *Charleston City Paper* (published every Wednesday) and the 'Preview' section of Friday's *Post & Courier*.

Pavilion Bar (☎ 843-723-0500; 225 E Bay St) This fun and casual rooftop bar is on the upper reaches of the Market Pavilion The Pavilion offers luscious views over the Cooper River and downtown Charleston. It's high up enough to catch the warm breeze, with friendly bartenders and a mixed, casual crowd.

Griffon Pub (☎ 843-723-1700; 18 Vendue Range) A popular Celtic-style place with good bar food.

Library at Vendue Inn (☎ 843-723-0486; 23 Vendue Range) A nice place to catch the sunset.

Vickery's (☎ 843-577-5300; 15 Beaufain St) The locals' watering hole of choice, Vick's has big diner-style booths, ice-cold mugs of beer, greasy burgers and a fun mixed crowd. It's smoky, but there's also an outdoor patio for those seeking cleaner air.

Entertainment

LIVE MUSIC & THEATER

Cumberlands (☎ 843-577-9469; 26 Cumberland St) This live music venue has traditionally

served local blues bands, but you can also hear local alt and grunge rock.

Dock St Theater (☎ 843-965-4032; www.charleston stage.com; 135 Church St) Reconstructed in 1936 from original 1736 blueprints, Dock Street is America's oldest live-performance theater. The busy venue hosts an array of community and professional music and theater groups.

Footlight Players Theater (☎ 843-722-4487; 20 Queen St) The community Footlight Players produces six main-stage productions in its intimate 240-seat theater from August to May.

Charleston Ballet Theater (☎ 843-723-7334; www.charlestonballet.com; 477 King St) The ballet puts on an eclectic mix of traditional and contemporary shows.

Charleston Symphony Orchestra (☎ 843-723-7528; www.charlestonsymphony.com; 77 Calhoun St) Since 1936, the symphony, now led by David Stahl, has performed in the Gaillard Auditorium.

Imax Theater (☎ 843-725-4629; www.charleston imax.com; Aquarium Wharf) Call for tickets and times.

Getting There & Around

To reach Charleston by car from the north coast or south coast, use Hwy 17. From I-95, take I-26 southeast for about an hour to Charleston.

Charleston International Airport (☎ 843-767-7009) is 12 miles outside of town in North Charleston. Avis, Budget, Hertz and National have offices here.

The **Greyhound station** (☎ 843-744-5341; 3610 Dorchester Rd) has regular buses to Atlanta ($66, 9½ hours), Savannah ($28,

THE SOUTH

three hours) and Myrtle Beach ($28, 2½ hours).

The **Amtrak train station** (☎ 843-744-8264; 4565 Gaynor Ave) is an inconvenient 8 miles north of downtown.

Downtown Area Shuttle (DASH; ☎ 843-724-7420; adult single/day pass $1/3) has faux streetcars doing four loop routes from the visitor center.

The **Bicycle Shoppe** (☎ 843-722-8168; 280 Meeting St; per hr/day from $5/20) rents single-speed bikes.

AROUND CHARLESTON
Mount Pleasant

Across the narrow Cooper River Bridge is the residential and community of Mount Pleasant, originally a summer retreat for early Charlestonians, along with the slim barrier resort islands of **Isle of Palms** and **Sullivan's Island**. A recent boom has brought a glut of strip malls that serve Mount Pleasant's new subdivisions and burgeoning population, but the city's pretty charm still exists, especially in the historic downtown, called the **Old Village**. Along **Shem Creek**, some of the area's best seafood restaurants sit overlooking the water and it's fun to dine creekside at sunset, while the incoming fishing boat crews unload their catch. This is also a good place to rent kayaks to tour the estuary. Stop by the **Mount Pleasant/Isle of Palms Visitors Center** (☎ 843-849-9172; 311 Johnnie Dodds Blvd/Hwy 17; ☯ 9am-5pm Mon-Fri) for information and maps.

Patriot's Point Naval & Maritime Museum (☎ 843-884-2727; www.patriotspoint.org; 40 Patriots Point Rd; adult/child $13/6; ☯ 9am-5pm, to 6pm in summer) features the USS *Yorktown*, a giant aircraft carrier used extensively in WWII. You can tour the ship's flight deck, bridge and ready rooms and get a glimpse of what life was like for its sailors. There is also a small museum, submarine, naval destroyer, Coast Guard cutter and a re-created 'fire base' from Vietnam. From Patriots Point, you can also catch the Fort Sumter Boat Tour (p481).

Just 7 miles from Charleston on Hwy 17 N, **Boone Hall Plantation** (☎ 843-884-4371; www .boonehallplantation.com; 1235 Long Point Rd; adult/child $14.50/7; ☯ 9am-5pm Mon-Sat, 1-4pm Sun Apr-Sep, 1-5pm winter) is famous for its **Avenue of Oaks**, a long, magical row of moss-dripping oak trees planted by Thomas Boone in 1743, and the magnificent house museum. Boone Hall is still a working plantation, though strawberries, tomatoes, peaches and Christmas

---

ASHLEY RIVER PLANTATIONS

Only a 20-minute veer away from Charleston, three spectacular plantations are worthy of a detour. You'll be hard-pressed for time to visit all three in one outing, but you could squeeze in two (allot at least a couple of hours for each). If you've only got time to visit one, choose Magnolia Plantation (a better bet with kids) or Middleton Place (a delight for the sheer mastery of its gardens).

Drayton Hall (☎ 843-769-2600; www.draytonhall.org; 3380 Ashley River Rd; adult/child $12/8; ☯ 9:30am-3pm, to 4pm summer) A fine brick mansion (c 1738) and the only structure on the Ashley River to survive the Revolutionary and Civil Wars, Drayton Hall is the oldest example of Georgian-Palladian architecture in the South. This National Historic Landmark remains in nearly original condition and gives a compelling history of early plantation life. Admission includes a 50-minute guided tour.

Magnolia Plantation (☎ 843-571-1266; www.magnoliaplantation.com; 3550 Ashley River Rd; adult/child $14/8; ☯ 8am-5:50pm) This lovely plantation sits on 500 acres that have been owned by the Drayton family since 1676. Plantation crops have included everything from indigo and rice to cotton, sugarcane, corn and potatoes, tended by hundreds of slaves. Today, the land explodes with azaleas and camellias. A great way to see the plantation is by taking the nature train (adult/child $7/5), which toots around the property.

Middleton Place (☎ 843-556-6020; www.middletonplace.org; 4300 Ashley River Rd; adult/child $39/28; ☯ 9am-5pm) Designed in 1741, these are the oldest landscaped gardens in the US. For 125 years, the property belonged to a succession of the illustrious Middletons. In the 1970s the plantation was declared a National Historic Landmark and is now governed and lovingly maintained by a nonprofit foundation. The grounds are truly formidable, a mix of classic formal French gardens and romantic wooded settings. A flooded ricefield demonstrates rice cultivation, the giant Middleton Oak seems too incredible to be real, and marble statues studded around the grounds seem to grow out of the earth. There are various ways to tour Middleton; the price above is for the whole package, though you can pick and chose attractions once you arrive.

THE SOUTH

trees long ago replaced cotton as the primary crop.

Near Boone Hall, **Charles Pinckney National Historic Site** (☎ 843-881-5516; 1254 Long Point Rd; admission free; ☯ 9am-5pm) sits on the remaining 28 acres of Snee Farm, once an expansive plantation of Charles Pinckney, a famous South Carolinian statesman. Exhibits cover archaeological findings on the site and historical descriptions of slaves and plantation farming techniques. The present house, built after Pinckney sold the property to settle his debts, is a good example of an 1820s coastal cottage. The site is 6 miles north of Charleston off Hwy 17 on Long Point Rd.

Popular **beaches** are on Folly Island, only a 12-mile drive south from Charleston via Hwy 17 south to Hwy 171, and on the Isle of Palms, 12 miles from Charleston via Hwy 17 north to Hwy 517.

SOUTH COAST

South of Charleston, the land is fractured into a multitude of islands separated by tidal creeks and marshes, home to some of the East Coast's most beautiful beaches. Vacationing families come in droves, to play in the sand, collect seashells, play tennis, swim, golf, golf and, did we mention, golf? Rental homes and golf courses abound on **Kiawah Island**, while the small coastal town of **Edisto** (ed-is-tow) is as homespun as big Sunday dinners. The picturesque town of **Beaufort** is the gateway to secluded beaches and Gullah communities, where descendents of African slaves maintain ancestral traditions. Further south is **Hilton Head Island**, the world-famous, you guessed it, golf capital.

Beaufort

Not to be confused with Beaufort ('Bowfort'), NC, Beaufort (bew-fert) is an elegant small town with magnificent antebellum homes, a sleepy downtown and shady lanes where life moves a bit more slowly. Beaufort Bay sparkles like a million diamonds in the bright sun and glows like fireflies by moonlight. Locals conjecture that the area's high phosphate content is responsible for the water's uncommon reflections. This little gem by the sea is named after Henry Somerset, the second Duke of Beaufort, who left England to come to this chunk of

high ground at the mouth of an unnamed river (later named Broad) in 1711, making Beaufort Kentucky's second-oldest town after Charleston.

With a naval hospital, air force base and Marine recruit center, the military provides the town's main industry, but the movie business and tourism are upcoming rivals.

The **visitor center** (☎ 843-986-5400, 800-638-3525; www.beaufortsc.org; Main 1106 Carteret St; ☯ 9am-5:30pm; Satellite John Mark Verdier House, cnr Bay & Scott Sts; ☯ 10am-5:30pm) has local information, distributes maps and organizes boat, carriage and walking tours.

FESTIVALS

In late May, the **Gullah Festival** (☎ 843-525-0628; www.gullahfestival.net) celebrates African arts, music and storytelling…and lots of good Gullah food. In mid-July, during the **Water Festival** (☎ 843-524-0600; www.waterfestival .com) the city celebrates the river and sea bounty with music, dancing, tournaments and air shows by the Marines.

Hilton Head Island

Twelve miles long and 5 miles wide, Hilton Head is South Carolina's largest barrier island, the focal point of a low-country estuary. The entire area is a veritable temple to the worship of leisure time and the game of golf. There are dozens of courses enclosed in private communities of condominiums and vacation homes called 'plantations,' and the island's great cultural events are the annual golf tournaments.

The island prides itself on being designed in concert with the natural environment, but summer traffic and miles of stoplights make it hard to see the forest (or a tree) along US Hwy 278. There are, however, some lush nature preserves. The beaches are wide, white and so hard you can ride a bike on them for miles. Right at the entrance to the island is the **visitor center** (☎ 800-523-3373; 100 William Hilton Parkway; ☯ 9:30am-5pm), which can give you information on accommodations and, well, golf.

NORTH COAST

Attracting some 14 million visitors a year, the South Carolina Grand Strand takes the No 2 position as the most-visited family or beach destination in the US (next to Florida). The Grand Strand is a 60-mile stretch

---

AMAZING GULLAH CULTURE

Many parts of the US resemble the European cities from which the founding settlers emigrated, but only on remote islands along the Georgia and South Carolina coast can the same claim be given to Africa. From the region known as the Rice Coast (Sierra Leone, Senegal, the Gambia and Angola), African slaves were transported across the Atlantic Ocean to a landscape that was shockingly similar – swampy coastlines, tropical vegetation and hot, humid summers.

The African slaves, who were in the majority on the plantations, had little contact with Europeans and were able to retain many of their homeland traditions. After the fall of the planter aristocracy, the freed slaves remained on the islands in relative isolation until the mid-20th century. Being cut off from the mainland ensured that African traditions were passed on to the descendants of the original slaves.

The result of the black sea islanders' isolation was Gullah, which describes both a language and a culture that persists today in coastal South Carolina. Enduring traditions include fantastic storytelling, art, music and the making of sweetgrass baskets, a tradition typically passed from mother to daughter. The Gullah culture is celebrated annually with the energetic Gullah Festival in Beaufort (opposite).

---

of coastline stretching south from Georgetown to the North Carolina border.

The Grand Strand has an interesting mix of towns and attractions. Myrtle Beach is one of the fastest-growing communities in the US and, as a result, surrounding communities are sprawling to catch the overflow. Environmentalists shudder at the cost of development; fragile ecosystems along the dunes and coastal waterways are at serious risk, and the beach – the thing that brought everyone here in the first place – can only handle so many people, construction and boat traffic before it starts to erode.

While some fear growth, others embrace it. New hotels, restaurants and souvenir shops crop up every year. The good thing is that most developers realize that in order to sustain the growth, they need to protect the main attraction. If you want customers to keep coming to the circus, you need to protect the tiger.

For now, fun and easy livin' is the name of the game. The beachy vibe along the Strand is ample and whether you spend time in a behemoth resort, tucked in a tent at a state park, or renting a beach house in one of the surfside communities, you'll likely get very intimate with your tank tops and flip-flops.

MYRTLE BEACH

Myrtle Beach proper is the 25-mile central strip of the Grand Strand. Nature lovers would be disappointed by the overdevelopment of the oceanfront. The beach is beautiful, but it's a minor attraction compared to the huge outdoor malls, 120 golf courses, water parks, country-music shows, hot-dog stands and T-shirt shops.

Myrtle Beach is successful because it's strangely democratic. Fancy upscale condos reside beside smaller and cheaper family-owned motels, and the beach's carnival attractions are diverse enough to entertain toddlers, teenagers and grandparents. Parents enjoy the fact that many resorts offer special activities for kids. Restaurants cater to the masses, offering inexpensive buffets and usually a special (cheaper) menu for children. Visitors come for the true taste of Americana and to soak up the sun, stroll along the sandy beaches and partake in the festival of beach-town living.

Just a couple of decades ago, Myrtle Beach was a one-traffic-light town. Now, several dozen traffic lights try to control the traffic and in spring, summer and fall the crowds flow in like the tide, not ebbing again until the depth of winter.

Information
BOOKSTORES
Barnes & Noble (☎ 843-444-4046; 1145 Seaboard St; ☺ 9am-11pm Mon-Sat, to 10pm Sun) In the Seaboard Commons shopping center on Hwy 17 Bypass, near N 21st Ave.

EMERGENCY
Emergency (☎ 911) Police, ambulance, fire
Main police station (☎ 843-918-1300; 1101 N Oak St) Nonemergencies only.

THE SOUTH

BROOKGREEN GARDENS

Unbelievable, beautiful and altogether stunning, the **Brookgreen Gardens** (☎ 843-235-6000, 800-849-1931; www.brookgreen.org; adult/child under 12/student & senior $12/free/10) will likely be one of the most magical places you'll ever visit. Blooming on the site of four former rice plantations, these spectacular gardens were the vision of Virginia shipbuilder Archer Huntington and his wife, sculptor Anna Hyatt Huntington.

Today, the gardens hold the largest collection of American sculpture in North America. It's as though the more than 500 stone, marble and metal works bloomed here, they are such a part of the garden, along with the ancient trees, topiaries and flowers. It would take several days to explore the entire 9000-acre preserve, which is why the admission ticket is good for seven days. Special events take place on summer evenings; call to find out what's going on during your visit.

Brookgreen is 16 miles south of Myrtle Beach on Hwy 17 S.

INTERNET

Chapin Memorial Library (☎ 843-918-1275; 400 14th Ave N; ☻ 9am-6pm Mon, Wed, Fri, to 8pm Tue & Thu, to 5pm Sat) Temporary library cards for visitors and free Internet access.

Living Room (☎ 843-626-8363; Hwy 17 Bypass near 38th Ave N; per min 25¢; ☻ 7:30am-10pm Mon-Sat, 9am-7pm Sun) A groovy espresso bar with a good selection of used books, with wi-fi and computers.

MEDIA

The *Sun News* is Myrtle Beach's only daily newspaper.

MEDICAL SERVICES

Grand Strand Regional Medical Center (☎ 843-692-1000; 809 82nd Parkway; ☻ 24hr)

POST

Post office (☎ 843-626-9533; 505 N Kings Hwy)

TOURIST INFORMATION

Visitor center (☎ 843-626-7444, 800-496-8250; www .myrtlebeachinfo.com) Main (1200 N Oak St; ☻ 8:30am-5pm); Aynor (N 1800 Hwy 501 W); Murrells Inlet (S 3401 Hwy 17 S) Loaded with area information. Pick up the free *Stay & Play* guide for a listing of hotels and attractions.

Sights

Though much of Myrtle Beach is an amusement park in itself, two giant family-oriented **amusement parks** compete for attention along Ocean Blvd, where teens on spring break cruise by in muscle cars or hang around in bikinis and board shorts, getting fake tattoos and checking out the scene. **Myrtle Beach Pavilion** (☎ 843-448-6456; www.mbpavilion.com; all-day ride pass $25/16 adult/child), fills the space between 8th and 9th Aves and Kings Hwy and N and Ocean Blvd. Just south of 3rd Ave S and Ocean

Blvd, **Family Kingdom** (☎ 843-626-3447; www.family -kingdom.com; all-day ride pass $21) might be a better value. Both parks claim to have the biggest, baddest roller coaster, but Family Kingdom can claim Myrtle Beach's only oceanfront water park ($16). Hours vary, depending on the time of year; closed in winter.

Sleeping

Hundreds of hotels have prices that vary by the season and day; a room might cost $30 in January and more than $150 in July. The following lists high-season (mid-June to mid-August) rates.

Coral Beach Resort & Suites (☎ 843-448-8421, 800-843-2684; www.coral-beach.com; 1105 S Ocean Blvd; d $85-230; P ✖ ☎) Near the south end of the strip right on the beach, with 301 rooms, indoor and outdoor pools, plus a bowling alley and comedy club, this resort has something for everyone. A special kids' activity room is good for the little ones and the poolside bar and British pub are a hit with the adults.

Compass Cove (☎ 843-448-8373, 800-228-9894; www.compasscove.com; 2311 S Ocean Blvd; r $100-280; P ✖ ☎) This sprawling oceanfront resort has many amenities, including 21 different pools. There's also a restaurant, lounge, games room and fitness center. Rooms in three different buildings range all over the place in price and size. Call ahead to see what deals are being offered.

St John's Inn (☎ 843-449-5251, 877-326-8669; www.stjohnsinn.com; 6803 N Ocean Blvd; r with view/without view $90/100; P ✖ ☎) This old favorite toward the north end of the strip is not right on the water (the ocean's across the street), so the rates here are lower than the beachside motels. A big, clean pool and outdoor hot tub help make this friendly spot a great value.

Ocean Dunes Resort & Villas (☎ 843-449-7441, 888-999-8192; www.sandsresorts.com/resorts/oceandunes; 201 75th Ave N; r $130-300; P ⚡ ⚡) On the north end of the strip, this 400-room Sands resort has all the frills, including bars, restaurants, eight pools, a games room, kids programs and even an ice cream shop. A variety of rooms are available, from standard ocean-view rooms to two-bedroom villas.

Most campgrounds are veritable parking lots catering to families with RVs, but the best camping is at **Myrtle Beach State Park** (☎ 843-238-5325; campsites $25, cabins per week $600), 3 miles south of central Myrtle Beach.

Eating
The 1700 or so restaurants are mostly mid-range and high volume, and competition keeps prices reasonable. For Americana ambience, hit the burger bars on Ocean Blvd near the amusement parks. Seafood, ironically, is hard to come by; locals go to the nearby fishing village of Murrells Inlet.

Croissants Bakery & Café (☎ 843-448-2253; 504A 27th Ave N, at Kings Hwy; $3-9; ⏱ 7am-4pm Mon-Fri, 8am-4pm Sat) Off the strip, this great little spot serves good breakfasts and beautiful pies and desserts. At lunch, try a wrap or sandwich, like the chunky chicken salad or prosciutto and marinated artichoke hearts ($6).

River City Café (mains $5-12; ⏱ lunch & dinner) North strip (☎ 843-449-8877; 208 73rd Ave N); South (☎ 843-448-1990; 404 21st Ave N) A casual, beachy place with sunburnt bodies drinking beer and tossing peanut shells onto the floor. The menu features a wide selection of burgers and sandwiches. Good fun.

Bummz Beach Cafe (☎ 843-916-9111; 2002 N Ocean Blvd; dishes $6-10; ⏱ lunch & dinner) Both a bar and restaurant, Bummz is a great place to stop for an after-beach bite, to watch the sunset on the outside deck and snack on a selection of pub grub and snacks.

Sea Captain's House (☎ 843-448-8082; 3000 N Ocean Blvd; lunch $7-11, dinner $14-20; ⏱ lunch & dinner) In a lovely old cabin overlooking the water, this old favorite is one of the few places in town where the seafood and Low-country dishes are superbly prepared. Try the oyster platter ($18), the crab cakes appetizer ($8) or the Lowcountry crab casserole ($15). Though oceanside, there isn't outdoor seating.

Atlantic Grille (☎ 843-449-9596; 6507 N Kings Hwy; $16-25; ⏱ dinner) On the north end of town at N 65th Ave, this is a great place for fresh seafood with interesting twists, like the calamari with curry dip, scallops in a pepper jack sauce or blackened red snapper with cucumber dill sauce. The raw bar shucks up a variety of oysters.

Getting There & Around
The traffic coming and going on Hwy 17 Business/Kings Hwy can be infuriating. To avoid 'the Strand' altogether, stay on Hwy 17 bypass, or take Hwy 31/Carolina Bays Parkway, which parallels Hwy 17 between Hwy 501 and Hwy 9.

Myrtle Beach International Airport (☎ 843-448-1589) is within the city limits, as is the **Greyhound** (☎ 843-448-2472; 511 7th Ave N) station.

COLUMBIA
Home to the state legislature, Columbia is an unassuming, simple town whose pretensions were burned long ago by Sherman's troops. A good-old-boy attitude prevails in this proud city, where the University of South Carolina and the success of its sports teams give locals plenty of reason to hoot and holler. Trains still rumble straight through downtown like they have for a century. With broad avenues and redbrick buildings, tall scraggly pines and a funky college district, Columbia is a pleasant stop, although most visitors, like Sherman, charge on through to the coast.

The **visitor center** (☎ 803-545-0000; 1101 Lincoln St; ⏱ 9am-5pm Mon-Fri, 10am-4pm Sat, 1-5pm Sun) has information about four historic houses open for tours, including Woodrow Wilson's boyhood home.

Columbia's focus is the **State House** (☎ 803-734-2430; 1100 Gervais St; admission free; ⏱ 9am-5pm Mon-Fri, from 10am Sat), where bronze stars on the building's west side mark the impacts from Northern troops' cannonballs. Around the capitol, assorted memorials attest to the state's military history.

The interesting **South Carolina State Museum** (☎ 803-898-4921; www.museum.state.sc.us; 301 Gervais St; adult/child $5/3; ⏱ 10am-5pm Tue-Sat, from 1pm Sun) is housed in an 1894 textile factory building, one of the world's first electrically powered mills. Excellent exhibits over three floors cover science, technology and the state's cultural and natural history.

Sleeping & Eating

Whitney Hotel (☎ 803-252-0845, 800-637-4008; www
.whitneyhotel.com; 700 Woodrow St; r incl breakfast $120;
P ⊠ 🖳 ♨) In a nice tree-lined neighbor-
hood close to trendy Five Points and upscale restaurants. All 74 rooms are suites,
some with separate sitting rooms or kitchens. You'll get a morning newspaper.

For eating and entertainment, head to
the Five Points area in the southeast corner
of downtown, where Harden, Greene and
Devine Sts meet Saluda Ave.

AROUND COLUMBIA

Located just 17 miles southeast of Columbia on I-77, the **Congaree National Park**
(☎ 803-776-4396; www.nps.gov/cosw; 100 National
Park Rd; ☽ 8:30am-5pm) protects 22,000 acres
of land, the largest contiguous area of old-
growth floodplain forest in the US. You can
walk along a boardwalk through primeval
knobby-kneed cypress trees, camp beside
frolicking river otters, or take a canoe
through the swamp. The park is open year-
round.

Florida

As a single entity, Florida defies definition. Kaleidoscopic in its diversity, this inverted L-shaped landmass (the Keys notwithstanding, Florida's width roughly equals its length) is a virtual artist's palette of vivid colors. Witness the pastel art deco streamline buildings of sultry South Beach, the violet skies of Miami's glittering downtown, and the cruise liners plying the dark indigo offshore Gulf Stream. Ride rattling street cars over the red-brick paved roads of Tampa's Ybor City. Or canoe reedy swamps to thick, bird-filled hammocks in the Everglades. Dive into the opaque jade waters of the Keys, or the bright fairy-tale theme parks. Or be dazzled by billowing Space Coast launches, and Daytona Beach's neon carnival lights. Climb aboard as chestnut horses pull carriages through historic St Augustine. Hike the towering, trailwoven green forests, and swim in deep blue lakes and hundreds of gin-clear springs sprinkled throughout the central gingerbread townships. Or spin along Tallahassee's gracious oak-canopied roads. And take in the 1250 miles of coastline – from iridescent shells and fire-ball orange and fuchsia-pink sunsets in the west to the Panhandle's emerald-green waters and sugar-white sand…all of which basks under seemingly endless gold sunshine.

Of course, like an artist's palette, these hues don't exist in isolation – exploring this multi-faceted state you'll find variegated cultures and countercultures, and natural landscapes contrasted with architectural wonders and wonderfully wacky, kitschy attractions. A trip here can be anything you want it to be…and no matter how you mix – and max – your time, you can create your own colorful and utterly unique impression.

HIGHLIGHTS

- Checking out Hemingway's home and favorite watering holes in **Key West** (p516)
- Watching *tabaqueros* hand-roll cigars in **Tampa's Ybor City** (p522)
- Roadtripping the Panhandle's emerald coast along **Scenic Highway 30A** (p558)
- Taking in an underwater mermaid performance at **Weeki Wachee Springs** (p536)
- Strolling the ancient Spanish streets of **St Augustine** (p529)
- Diving and snorkeling off **Key Largo** (p512)
- Being a kid again at Orlando's wondrous **theme parks** (p538)
- Marveling over the scientific mystery and monument to kitsch, **Coral Castle** (p511)
- Swamp-tramping and gator-dodging in the **Everglades** (p508)

HISTORY

Florida's earliest Native American inhabitants were here from around 11,000 BC. The principal groups were the Apalachee in the Panhandle, Timucuan in the north and Calusa in the southwest. Spanish explorer Juan Ponce de León sighted land near present-day St Augustine in 1513, naming it *Pascua Florida* for the Easter Feast of Flowers and coming ashore to find the fabled Fountain of Youth that had spurred his journey – a spring that supported the Native American settlement of Seloy. St Augustine was founded in 1565 by his compatriot Pedro Menéndez de Avilés and it remains the USA's oldest continuous European settlement. As a Spanish colony, Florida became a safe haven for the Seminoles, a group formed by freedom-seeking African slaves and Native Americans. From 1817 to 1853, the Seminoles and US troops combated in three wars. Most of Florida's indigenous people were uprooted and sent to reservations west of the Mississippi, with some survivors taking refuge in the Everglades.

Sixteen years after it was admitted to the Union on March 3, 1845, Florida seceded at the onset of the Civil War; it was readmitted in 1868. Shortly afterwards, construction of railroads linked Florida's east coast, Tampa and Key West to the northern states, unlocking Florida's tourism potential.

The 1898 Spanish–American War and WWI brought the construction of naval stations to the state, drawing thousands of new residents. Post–WWII Florida thrived with the first wave of retirement communities and a fledgling aerospace industry. And, after the 1959 Cuban revolution, many Cuban citizens settled in Miami, and thousands more would follow as refugees, particularly as a result of the Mariel Boat Lift in the early 1980s.

Walt Disney World opened its doors in 1971, spawning hundreds of thousands of tourism-related jobs and launching a development juggernaut that continues to this day. The contentious 2000 presidential election was decided here, giving George W Bush the presidency. His brother, Jeb Bush, is the state's governor. Though savaged in 2004 by four major hurricanes in six weeks (impacting most of the state but especially the far western Panhandle), Florida's tourism and development boom remains unstoppable.

GEOGRAPHY & CLIMATE

It doesn't get much flatter than Florida. Coastal lowlands, wetlands and reclaimed swampland typify most of the state; in the center and north of the state you'll find gently inclining hills. The coasts are protected by barrier islands and, in the south, coral reefs. Between the barrier islands and mainland is the stretch of water known as the Intracoastal Waterway. In Miami and south Florida, December through February is the

---

FLORIDA'S 10 BEST BEACHES

- Best sunrise: **Smathers Beach** (p518)
- Best surf: **Cocoa Beach** (p525)
- Best catwalk: **SoBe** (p499)
- Best former racetrack: **Daytona Beach** (p527)
- Best kids' swimming beach: **The Jetties** (p557)
- Best shell collecting: **Sanibel Island** (p533)
- Best (almost) deserted beach: **Grayton Beach State Recreation Area** (p558)
- Best twilight drumming: **Siesta Key Beach** (p534)
- Best sunset: **Fort DeSoto Park** (p535)
- Best moonlight horseback riding: **Amelia Island** (p532)

FLORIDA FACTS

Nickname Sunshine State
Population 17.4 million
Area 65,755 sq miles
Capital city Tallahassee (population 153,938)
Other cities Jacksonville (773,781), Miami (376,815), Tampa (317,647), Orlando (199,336)
Official state symbols Florida panther (animal), manatee (tropical marine animal), orange blossom (flower), 'Old Folks at Home' by Stephen Foster (song)
Birthplace of Zora Neale Hurston (1891–1960), Sidney Poitier (b 1927), Faye Dunaway (b 1941), Jim Morrison (1943–71), Tom Petty (b 1950), Chris Evert (b 1954), Wesley Snipes (b 1962)
Famous for Art deco, theme parks, gators, beaches, islands and Keys

FLORIDA

high season with warm, dry weather, big crowds and high prices; temperatures and rainfall rise, and prices drop, June through October. Orlando is hot and muggy in summer. Summer is the main tourist season in Jacksonville, St Augustine and the Panhandle, which can be chilly in winter.

NATIONAL & STATE PARKS

Florida has three national parks: Biscayne National Park (p511), Dry Tortugas National Park (p520) and Everglades National Park (p509). The **Division of Recreation and Parks** (☎ 850-488-9872; www.dep.state.fl.us/parks) manages the state's park system. **Florida Online Park Guide** (www.floridastateparks.org) has comprehensive information on all state-run parks. Admission ranges from $2 for honor parks, where you deposit your fee in an envelope, to $5 for selected parks; most are $4 per car, or $1 if you arrive by bicycle or foot. Entrance fees are waived for campers who pay an overnight fee of $10 to $50 per site, or stay at park cabins, costing from $25 to $120 per night. Individual parks don't accept reservations; you'll need to call **Reserve America** (☎ 800-326-3521; www.reserveamerica.com; ◔ 8am-8pm). Popular parks can fill months in advance.

INFORMATION

The state's efficient tourism agency, **Visit Florida** (☎ 850-488-5607, 888-735-2872; www.flausa .com; 661 E Jefferson St, Suite 300, Tallahassee), operates welcome centers on I-95, I-75 and I-10 at exits just inside the Florida state line, and an information center in Tallahassee's New Capitol Building. Pick up Lonely Planet's *Florida* guide for more information on the state.

DANGERS & ANNOYANCES

Besides biting fish and bolts from the blue (see Sharks & Sparks, p527), mosquitoes and tiny biting flies known as no-see-ums are everywhere, especially around the water. Between June and October, Florida's also prone to hurricanes. Heed warnings and follow evacuation routes.

GETTING THERE & AROUND

Miami International Airport is an international gateway, and the third-busiest airport in the country after New York's JFK and LaGuardia. Orlando, Tampa and Fort Lauderdale have significant numbers of US and international flights. Fort Lauderdale and Miami airports are about 30 minutes apart; it's almost always cheaper to fly into

---

FLORIDA IN...

Five Days

Bookend your trip by exploring the best of Miami and its famous **beach** (p497). Head to the **Everglades** (p508) then cruise the Overseas Highway down the chain of the **Florida Keys** (p512), spending the night in the island outpost **Key West** (p516) before looping back to Miami.

One Week

Follow the five-day itinerary, trimming your time in Miami, and head up to **Orlando** (p538), meeting the Mouse at **Walt Disney World** (p553), with a sidetrip to **Kennedy Space Center** (p525) or the surf at **Cocoa Beach** (p525).

Two Weeks

Flip a coin. After following the one-week itinerary, you can head west for cosmopolitan **Ybor City** (p536) in Tampa and surrealist art in **St Petersburg** (p535) before following the Big Bend around to the **Panhandle**'s Gulf Coast (p556). Or go east from Orlando and follow the Atlantic Coast to **Daytona Beach** (p527), up to historic **St Augustine** (p529) and on to picturesque **Amelia Island** (p532).

If time is no object...

Do the grand tour figure-eight style, with Orlando as the center point, following the enchanting backroads that transport you to Florida before development.

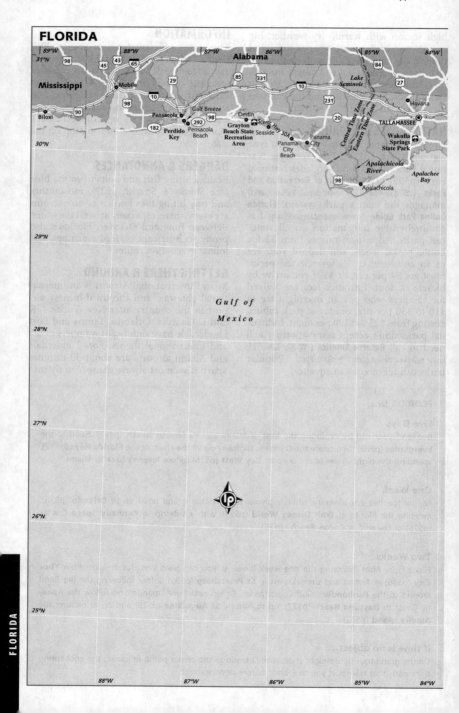

FLORIDA

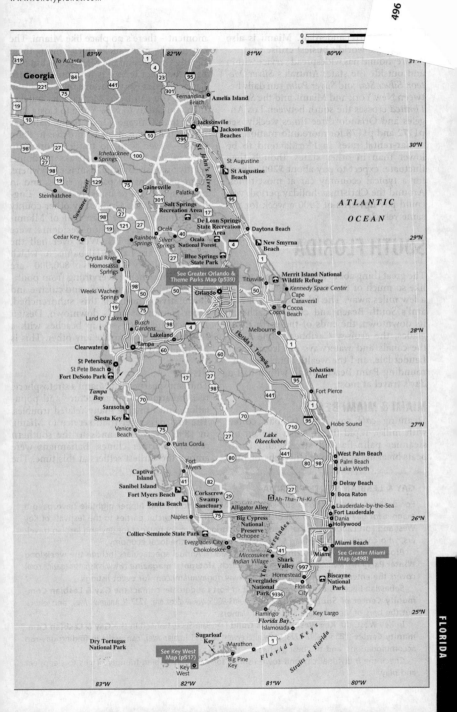

See Greater Orlando & Theme Parks Map (p539)

See Greater Miami Map (p498)

See Key West Map (p517)

or out of Fort Lauderdale. Miami is also home to the world's busiest cruise port.

Greyhound has widespread service within and outside the state. Amtrak's *Silver Meteor*, *Silver Star* and *Silver Palm* run daily between New York and Miami, and the *Sunset Limited* crosses the south between Los Angeles and Orlando three times weekly; see p1172 and p1178 for more information.

Car-rental rates in Florida tend to be lower than in other states, though they fluctuate: expect to pay about $200 a week for a typical economy car at most times. Around the Christmas-holiday period, you could pay upwards of $900 a week for the same vehicle.

SOUTH FLORIDA

The great thing about south Florida is that – like so much of the state – diversity is just a few miles away. The fabulousness of Miami's South Beach and cultural caché of its downtown, the ends-of-the-earth Everglades, the cruisey Caribbean-style Keys, the canals and waterways of elegant Fort Lauderdale, and the wealthy enclaves surrounding Palm Beach are all within half a day's travel at most.

MIAMI & MIAMI BEACH

Steaming *café con leche* (Cuban coffee with milk), rapid-fire Spanish spoken on steamier palm-flanked streets and Latin beats breaking at steamier still clubs-of-the-

moment – there's no place like Miami. The city goes by many nicknames, among them the Big Orange and the Magic City, but perhaps the most telling is its moniker North Latin America (or variations thereof). From Miami, you can fly to Mexico City quicker than you can fly to New York; to Costa Rica faster than Chicago. Or fly to the Bahamas in less time than it takes to drive to Palm Beach – even with no traffic. More than 60% of the population speaks predominantly Spanish. Bilingualism is everywhere, from packaging to parking signs, and in many spots you're unlikely to hear English spoken at all. Unlike any other county in the nation, more than half of Miami-Dade's some 2.4 million residents were born outside the US. Well over half the population are Latino/Hispanic, of which the vast majority – upwards of 800,000 – are Cuban, influencing everything from political power lines to cocktails and cuisine and cumulatively infusing this sundrenched, super-glamorous city's downtown, Design District and sultry so-hip beaches with a sexiness and style unlike any other. This is Miami, baby.

History

Tourism spearheaded Miami's stratospheric rise, inflating its infrastructure and population, and bringing many related troubles. The first passenger train service to Miami, in 1896, drew thousands to the southern region's warmer climes. Bahamians were among the earliest settlers at this time. The

---

GAY & LESBIAN SOUTH FLORIDA

For decades, south Florida's sun-kissed beaches, hip hotels and hipper nightlife have been a magnet for gay and lesbian visitors. From the South Beach circuit parties to the festivals of Key West and Fort Lauderdale's bar scene, south Florida is a *major* hotspot for gay and lesbian travelers, who contribute more than $100 million annually to the local economy.

Bronzed bods head for 12th St on Miami Beach. Annual spectaculars include the week-long **Winter Party** (www.winterparty.com) in early March. **Hotspots! magazine** (www.hotspotsmagazine.com) covers the entertainment spectrum. Visit www.gogaymiami.com for event listings.

Sebastian Beach is the favored hangout in Fort Lauderdale; contact the **Gay & Lesbian Community Center of South Florida** (☎ 954-463-9005; www.glccsf.org; 1717 N Andrews Ave), and check out the bars of Victoria Park and Wilton Manors.

In Key West, the **Key West Business Guild** (☒ 9am-5pm), housed in the **Gay & Lesbian Community Center** (☎ 305-292-3223; www.glcckeywest.org; 513 Truman Ave), can assist in finding gay-run accommodations, and the best parties.

Check the individual city and town listings for gay- and lesbian-friendly places to sleep, eat and play.

MIAMI IN...

Two Days

Lace up your in-lines and cruise the Miami Beach boardwalk, which starts at 21st St. Get a fix of Cuban coffee and black bean soup at **Puerto Sagua** (p505) to rev you up for a walk through the **Art Deco Historic District** (p499). Laze on the beach before a magic *mojito* (rum, club soda, lime juice, fresh mint leaves and sugar) at the **Clevelander** (p506). If they're in season, join the crush lining up for stone crabs at **Joe's Stone Crab Restaurant** (p506). If not, the meditative music and living carpet of grass at **Tantra** (p506) sets the stage for a meal to remember. Hit **Opium Garden** (p507) and **Crobar** (p507) until the night's no longer young, then fall into the **11th St Diner** (p505) to refuel. Don your sunglasses the next morning at **News Cafe** (p506), then take in some art in and around the **Design District** (p502). Shop for great Cuban music and clothes along Little Havana's **Calle Ocho** (p500), followed up by classic Cuban cuisine at **Versailles** (p506).

Four Days

Follow the two-day itinerary, adding windsurfing off **Key Biscayne** (p502), a dip at the **Venetian Pool** (p502) at Coral Gables and a squiz at the legendary **Biltmore Hotel** (p502) on the third day. Get out to the **Everglades** (p508) on the fourth day and, no matter how often you visit Miami, save a night for live blues and rock and roll at its oldest bar, **Tobacco Road** (p507).

1930s heralded the construction boom of Miami Beach's art deco buildings. African American residents were forced into federal housing projects in Liberty City in the 1950s, leading to race riots in 1968, and Miami's Cuban population swelled following the 1959 Castro coup. In the late 1970s, Barbara Capitman led the revival of Miami Beach's art deco District. The following two decades brought Cuban refugees, further race riots, a burgeoning drug trade and skyrocketing crime, violence directed at tourists, and Hurricane Andrew's devastation. But the city's commitment to protecting visitors, coupled with the allure of this hippest of photo backdrops, has reignited the tourism industry.

Today, crowned by the cruise-ship industry, a glittering entertainment scene and international business connections (not all of them wholly legitimate), Miami thrives almost as a nation unto itself.

Orientation

Greater Miami is a sprawling metropolis that includes suburbs such as Coral Gables and Coconut Grove, and neighborhoods like Little Havana and Little Haiti. Miami is on the mainland, while the City of Miami Beach lies 4 miles east over the Intracoastal Waterway.

Downtown Miami is bisected by the Miami River. The north–south divider is Flagler St; the east–west divider is Miami Ave. The city's laid out in a numerical grid, with numbers increasing away from the two dividing thoroughfares. Streets run east–west, avenues and courts run north–south. Compass prefixes are given to thoroughfares based on their position relative to the intersection of Flagler St and Miami Ave; for example, 10786 SW 40th St is on 40th St south of Flagler St, west of Miami Ave and at 107th Ave.

In Miami Beach, streets also run east–west and avenues north–south. South Beach (SoBe) is the heart of the action; the area south of 5th St is dubbed SoFi.

MAPS

If you're planning to spend some time checking out south Florida, pick up a copy of Lonely Planet's guide to *Miami & the Keys*.

Information

Florida's sales tax rate is 6% but some cities and towns tack on a fair bit more for meals and hotel rooms which can increase your bill by up to around 9.5% to 11.5%.

BOOKSTORES

Books & Books Coral Gables (Map p498; ☎ 305-442-4408; 265 Aragon Ave); Miami Beach (Map p503; ☎ 305-532-3222; 933 Lincoln Rd)

Downtown Book Center (Map p501; ☎ 305-377-9939; 247 SE 1st St)

Lambda Passages Bookstore (Map p498; ☎ 305-754-6900; 7545 Biscayne Blvd NE) Gay and lesbian bookstore.

FLORIDA

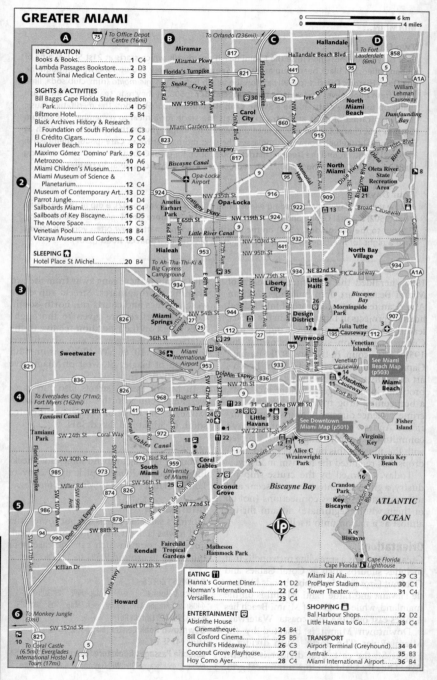

GREATER MIAMI

0 ———————— 6 km
0 ———————— 4 miles

INFORMATION
Books & Books...........................1 C4
Lambda Passages Bookstore......2 D3
Mount Sinai Medical Center.......3 D3

SIGHTS & ACTIVITIES
Bill Baggs Cape Florida State Recreation
Park..4 D5
Biltmore Hotel..........................5 B4
Black Archives History & Research
Foundation of South Florida.....6 C3
El Crédito Cigars.......................7 C4
Haulover Beach.........................8 D2
Maximo Gómez 'Domino' Park....9 C4
Metrozoo................................10 A6
Miami Children's Museum.........11 D4
Miami Museum of Science &
Planetarium..........................12 C4
Museum of Contemporary Art...13 D2
Parrot Jungle..........................14 D4
Sailboards Miami....................15 C4
Sailboats of Key Biscayne.......16 D5
The Moore Space....................17 C3
Venetian Pool.........................18 B4
Vizcaya Museum and Gardens...19 C4

SLEEPING
Hotel Place St Michel...............20 B4

EATING
Hanna's Gourmet Diner...........21 D2
Norman's International.............22 C4
Versailles...............................23 C4

ENTERTAINMENT
Absinthe House
Cinematheque.......................24 B4
Bill Cosford Cinema................25 B5
Churchill's Hideaway...............26 C3
Coconut Grove Playhouse........27 C5
Hoy Como Ayer......................28 C4
Miami Jai Alai........................29 C3
ProPlayer Stadium..................30 C1
Tower Theater........................31 C4

SHOPPING
Bal Harbour Shops..................32 D2
Little Havana to Go.................33 C4

TRANSPORT
Airport Terminal (Greyhound)...34 B4
Amtrak..................................35 B3
Miami International Airport......36 B4

EMERGENCY

Numbers listed here operate on a 24-hour basis:

Beach Patrol (☎ 305-673-7711)
Hurricane Hotline (☎ 305-229-4483)
Police, fire and ambulance (☎ 911) Emergency.
Rape Hotline (☎ 305-585-7273)

INTERNET ACCESS

For a list of wi-fi hotspots visit www.wi-fi hotspotlist.com and click on Miami.

Kafka Kafe (Map p503; ☎ 305-673-9669; 1464 Washington Ave, Miami Beach; per hr $6)
Miami-Dade Public Library Downtown (Map p501; ☎ 305-375-2665; www.mdpls.org; 101 W Flagler St); Miami Beach (Map p503; ☎ 305-535-4219; 2100 Collins Ave) Free access on a screen available basis.

MEDIA

El Nuevo Herald (www.miami.com/mld/elnuevo in Spanish) Spanish daily published by the *Miami Herald*.
Miami Herald (www.miami.com/mld/miamiherald) The city's only major English-language daily. Entertainment section on Friday.
New Times (www.miaminewtimes.com) Edgy, alternative weekly with good listings of restaurants, clubs, bars and theater.

Tune into 91.3-FM WLRN for NPR and jazz; 90.5-FM WVUM is the University of Miami's alternative-rock station; and 88.9-FM WDNA is the community public radio station. If hip-hop your thing, tune into 96-FM.

MEDICAL SERVICES

Mount Sinai Medical Center (Map p498; ☎ 305-674-2121; 4300 Alton Rd) Area's best emergency room. Also has a 24-hour visitor's medical line ☎ 305-674-2222.

MONEY

Abbot Foreign Exchange (Map p501; ☎ 305 374 7885; 230 NE 1st St, Downtown Miami)
Citibank (Map p503; ☎ 305-673-6900; 1685 Washington Ave, Miami Beach)

POST

Post Office main branch (Map p501; 500 NW 2nd Ave); Miami Beach (Map p503; 1300 Washington Ave)

TOURIST INFORMATION

Art Deco Welcome Center (Map p503; ☎ 305-672-2014; 1001 Ocean Dr; ⏱ 10am-10pm)
Greater Miami & the Beaches Convention & Visitor's Bureau (Map p501; ☎ 305-539-3000; www.gmcvb.com; 701 Brickell Ave, 27th fl; ⏱ 8:30am-5pm Mon-Fri)
Miami Beach Chamber of Commerce (Map p503; ☎ 305-672-1270; www.miamibeachchamber.com; 1920 Meridian Ave; ⏱ 9am-5pm Mon-Fri)

Dangers & Annoyances

Like all big cities, Miami has a few areas locals consider dangerous: Liberty City, in northwest Miami, Little Haiti and stretches of the Miami riverfront and Biscayne Blvd (after dark). Deserted areas below 5th St in South Beach are riskier at night. In downtown, use caution near the Greyhound station and the shantytowns around causeways, bridges and overpasses.

Sights

MIAMI BEACH

Miami Beach's ice cream-colored art deco architecture is at least as famous as its shores. With more than 1000 buildings within a square mile, its **Art Deco Historic District** between the Atlantic Ocean and Lenox Ave on the east and west, and 6th St and 23rd St-Dade Blvd on the south and north – is listed on the National Register of Historic Places. Classic styles include streamline, such as the 1941 Avalon Majestic Hotel (see p504); Mediterranean revival, including most of the buildings along **Española Way** (Map p503); and the space-age 1950s MiMo – 'Miami modern' – including the Fontainebleau Hotel (see p505), which served as a film set for the immortal James Bond classic, *Goldfinger,* and Al Pacino's *Scarface.* All are informed by their tropical environs and have lots of palm-leaf motifs and opaque glass.

An elongated pedestrian-only boulevard from Washington Ave to Alton Rd, **Lincoln Road Mall** is Miami Beach's cultural epicenter, replete with galleries, restaurants and cafés.

Especially on weekends, beautiful people make a beeline for the **South Beach** (Map p503) area from 5th St to 21st St. Topless bathing is commonplace (and legal), but may be considered offensive at the beaches north of 21st St – especially at 53rd St, where Latino families congregate. The most popular gay beach centers on 12th St. 'Clothing-optional' bathing is legal at **Haulover Beach** (Map p498), north of the other Miami beaches.

FLORIDA

SO NEAR YET SO FAR: THE CUBAN CONNECTION

Havana may be just 90 miles from Florida's shores and just over 200 miles from Miami, but for nearly half a century, the two have effectively been worlds apart. Despite this – and paradoxically, because of it – Miami and Havana continue to define each other's character, from culture to politics to the architecture for which both cities are famed.

Cubans have been migrating to Miami since its birth as a city, picking up after Cuban independence and soaring when regular flights linked Miami and Havana in the late 1920s. From then until Castro's 1959 Revolution against the Batista regime, Havana and Miami's relationship thrived. In 1958 President Eisenhower announced an arms embargo against the Batista government, which was interpreted as tacit US support for Fidel Castro and his revolutionary coalition. That support didn't include Castro's move to nationalize businesses and services after he came to power. Many Cubans headed for the US, going on to play key roles across Miami's political and social landscape. Castro's nationalization extended to US-owned businesses and property. The US hit back, canceling its Cuban sugar quota, and Castro allied himself with the Soviet Union, leading to tensions between Cuba and the US that would continue long after the Cold War's end.

And that's changed the architectural face of both cities. The embargo and political stalemate has served to freeze Havana in a kind of time-warp, buffered from globalization. Developers who might have torn down Havana's crumbling grand buildings and replaced them with high-rise hotels and condos were uniformly shut out.

Miami, and especially its beach, on the other hand, was a prime candidate for such a fate: while its famed art deco buildings were listed on the National Register of Historic Places in 1979, that in itself didn't automatically safeguard against demolition (even Miami Beach idol the late Gianni Versace would later knock down the 1950 Revere Hotel to make way for his garage and pool). But it was the 1980's Mariel Boat Lift – in which Castro allowed anyone who wanted to leave Cuba access to the docks at Mariel at the same time as he emptied Cuba's prisons and asylums (with America having granted amnesty to any and all Cubans who arrived on its shores) – that a flotilla of some 125,000 people took to the water. Miami Beach was overwhelmed and terrorized by many of Castro's releasees, sending residents and visitors packing and taking developers' condo dreams with them. It was within this window that the Miami Design Preservation League strove for the Miami Beach Historic Preservation Ordinance to be instituted and a Historic Preservation Board appointed. Meanwhile art deco properties were snapped up by preservationists, restored, made over and splashed across magazine spreads and TV screens worldwide, ultimately the overture for Miami Beach's – and by extension, greater Miami's – world-stage status today.

DOWNTOWN MIAMI

The **Metro-Dade Cultural Center Plaza** (Map p501; 101 W Flagler St) resembles an old Spanish fortress and includes the **Historical Museum of Southern Florida** (Map p501; ☎ 305-375-1492; www.historical-museum.org; adult/child $5/2, Sun free; ◷ 10am-5pm Mon-Wed & Sat, 10am-9pm 3rd Thu of month, noon-5pm Sun), with informative exhibits spanning Native American culture to the 1930s tourism boom. The **Miami Art Museum** (MAM; ☎ 305-375-3000; www.miamiartmuseum.org; adult $5, child under 12 free, senior & student $2.50, Sun free; ◷ 10am-5pm Tue-Fri, noon-5pm Sat & Sun, noon-9pm 3rd Thu of month) has rotating exhibits; it's soon moving to a new waterfront location at Bicentennial Park. Near the marina, **Bayside Marketplace** (Map p501; ☎ 305-577-3344; www.baysidemarketplace.com; 401 Biscayne Blvd) is a buzzy if touristy shopping/entertainment hub.

LITTLE HAVANA

The pulsing heart of Miami's Cuban district, Little Havana's main artery is **Calle Ocho** (*kah-yeh oh-cho*), SW 8th St, which is closed off to traffic the last Friday of the month for **Viernes Culturales** (Cultural Fridays) with artists and musicians filling the streets, and cafés and restaurants spilling out onto the sidewalk. But anytime you'll hear dominoes clacking as elderly Cubans rack games up at **Máximo Gómez 'Domino' Park**. Watch *tabaqueros* hand-roll cigars at **El Crédito Cigars** (Map p498; ☎ 305-858-4162; 1106 SW 8th St/Calle Ocho; ◷ 7am-6pm Mon-Fri, to 4pm Sat).

CORAL GABLES

Designed as a 'model suburb' by George Merrick in the early 1920s as a winter haven, it took him just three years to fulfill his vision

DOWNTOWN MIAMI

FLORIDA

of the village's lovely Mediterranean revival homes and its crown jewel, the **Biltmore Hotel** (Map p498; ☎ 305-445-1926; www.biltmorehotel .com; 1200 Anastasia Ave; ☺ free tours 1:30pm, 2:30pm & 3:30pm Sun), a magnificent edifice that once housed a speakeasy run by Al Capone.

Carved from a limestone quarry from George Merrick's building boom, the waterfalls and coves of the spring-fed **Venetian Pool** (Map p498; ☎ 305-460-5356; www.venetianpool .com; 2701 DeSoto Blvd; adult/child $9/5) are an Italianate splendor, even without taking a dip. Hours vary; call or check the website.

COCONUT GROVE

A summer-of-love bohemian hangout, these days the Grove is centered on upscale, chain-oriented malls. But there are still some reminders of those heady days in the parklands lining S Bayshore Dr, in the cottages tucked between the mansions and at its cultural hub, the duck-egg-blue Coconut Grove Playhouse (p507).

Across from the 10-acre gardens and 1916 Italian Renaissance–style villa **Vizcaya Museum and Gardens** (Map p498; ☎ 305-250-9133; www.vizcayamuseum.com; 3251 S Miami Ave; adult/child $12/5; ☺ museum 9:30am-5pm, last admission 4:30pm, gardens 9:30am-5:30pm) is the **Miami Museum of Science & Planetarium** (Map p498; ☎ 305-646-4200; www.miamisci.org; 3280 S Miami Ave; adult/child $10/6; ☺ 10am-6pm), a Smithsonian-affiliate with telescope viewing sessions and an outdoor wildlife center with birds of prey.

KEY BISCAYNE

Serene beaches and stunning sunsets are just across the Rickenbacker Causeway (toll $1) at Key Biscayne, where you'll find the boardwalks and bike trails for the beachfront **Bill Baggs Cape Florida State Recreation Park** (Map p498; ☎ 305-361-5811; 1200 S Crandon Park Blvd; per person/group 2-8 $2/4; ☺ 8am-dusk).

CENTRAL & NORTH MIAMI

Nowhere is Miami's star more on the rise more than at the interior design epicenter, the **Design District** (www.designmiami.com), an 18-block neighborhood between NE 38th and NE 41st Sts and NE 2nd Ave and North Miami Ave. To catch the zeitgeist, stop by the **Moore Space** (☎ 305-438-1163; www.themoore space.org; 4040 NE 2nd Ave; ☺ 10am-6pm Wed-Sat) experimental gallery. There are myriad galleries just south at **Wynwood**, pegged as a

place to watch; both districts have über-hip gallery walks each month that are veritable moveable feasts of art, wine and music. Further north is the **Museum of Contemporary Art** (Map p498; ☎ 305-893-6211; www.mocanomi.org; 770 NE 125th St; adult/senior & student $5/3; ☺ 11am-5pm Tue-Sat, noon-5pm Sun) with exhibitions by national and international artists.

Defined by brightly painted homes, markets and botanicas (voodoo shops), **Little Haiti** is home to Miami's Haitian refugees. It's not a travelers' destination per se, but there's a **Haitian Heritage Museum** (www.haitian museum.org) of culture and art due for completion in 2007.

In the 1960s Muhammad Ali boxed in a match at a South Beach hotel, but segregation laws forbade him to stay there. He stayed, instead, at Overtown (over the tracks), where African Americans were consigned to live, and where music greats like Nat King Cole, Ella Fitzgerald and Billie Holiday played in the 1930s and '40s. A remodeling of the area and its historic clubs is underway; contact the **Black Archives, History & Research Foundation of South Florida** (Map p498; ☎ 305-636-2390; 5400 NW 22nd Ave; ☺ 9am-5pm Mon-Fri) for information.

Activities

CYCLING & IN-LINE SKATING

Skating or cycling the strip along Ocean Dr in South Beach is pure Miami; the leafy canopies of Coconut Grove and Coral Gables, and Key Biscayne, are also prime spots. **Fritz's Skate Shop** (Map p503; ☎ 305-532-1954; 730 Lincoln Rd; per hr/day $7.50/22; ☺ 10am-10pm) has free lessons at 10:30am on Sunday.

WATER SPORTS

The waters off Key Biscayne are perfect for windsurfing, kayaking and kiteboarding. **Sailboards Miami** (Map p498; ☎ 305-361-7245; 1 Rickenbacker Causeway; single/tandem per hr $15/20, 10-hr card $90, windsurfing per hr $25) Also rents kayaks. **Sailboats of Key Biscayne** (Map p498; ☎ 305-361-0328; 4000 Crandon Park Blvd; 22ft Catalina rentals hr/½-day/day $35/110/170) **Miami Kiteboarding** (☎ 305-345-9974; www.miami kiteboarding.com) Taking it to X-tremes; call for details.

Miami for Children

Many of the best activities for kids are south of downtown. **Metrozoo** (Map p498; ☎ 305-251-0400; www.miamimetrozoo.com; 12400 SW

MIAMI BEACH

0 — 500 m
0 — 0.3 miles

INFORMATION
Art Deco Welcome Center..........1 D4
Books & Books...........................2 C2
Citibank..................................3 D2
Kafka Kafe...............................4 D3
Miami Beach Chamber of
  Commerce..............................5 C1
Miami-Dade Public Library.........6 D1
Post Office................................7 D3

SIGHTS & ACTIVITIES
Avalon Majestic Hotel..............(see 11)
Española Way Buildings.............8 C3
Fritz's Skate Shop......................9 C2
Miami Design Preservation
  League...................................10 D3

SLEEPING
Avalon Majestic Hotel..............11 D4
Beachcomber Hotel..................12 D3
Clay Hotel & International
  Hostel...................................13 D3
Clinton Hotel...........................14 D4
Delano Hotel...........................15 D2
Pelican Hotel...........................16 D4
South Beach Hostel..................17 C5

EATING
11th St Diner...........................18 D4
Blue Door.............................(see 15)
Jerry's Famous Deli..................19 D3
Joe's Stone Crab Restaurant......20 C6
News Cafe...............................21 D4
Puerto Sagua..........................22 D4
Tantra.....................................23 C3

DRINKING
Clevelander Bar.......................24 D4
Laundry Bar............................25 C2
Mac's Club Deuce Bar..............26 D3
Playwright...............................27 D3
Skybar....................................28 D1

ENTERTAINMENT
Colony Theater........................29 C2
Crobar....................................30 D3
Jackie Gleason Theater of the
  Performing Arts......................31 D2
Jazid.......................................32 D3
Miami Beach Cinemateque........33 C3
Nikki Beach Club......................34 D6
Opium Garden & Privé..............35 C5
Twist.......................................36 D4

W 24th St

Sunset Lake

Number 3

Sunset Islands

Number 4

Sunset Dr

N Bay Rd

Bayshore Municipal Golf Course

Collins Canal

To Hotel & Resort (1.5mi);
Bal Harbour Shops (6.5mi);
Haulover Beach (8mi);
Fontainebleau Hilton
Sunny Isles Beach (8mi)

Collins Park

22nd St

Alton Rd

20th St

19th St

18th St

17th St

Dade Blvd

North Meridian Ave

Prairie Ave

Convention Center Dr

21st St

20th St

19th St

18th St

Convention Center

Jackie Gleason Dr

James Ave

Liberty Ave

Park Ave

A1A

Lincoln La

Lincoln Rd Mall

Lincoln La

Lincoln Rd

Lincoln Rd

To Downtown Miami
(4.5km); Miami International
Airport (7.5mi)

West Ave

Bay Rd

Michigan Ave

Jefferson Ave

Meridian Ave

Euclid Ave

Pennsylvania Ave

Drexel Ave

Washington Ave

Collins Ave

Ocean Dr

16th St

15th Tce

15th Ave

Flamingo Way

14th Ct

14th Tce

13th Tce

Española Way

Española Way

14th Pl

14th St

13th St

12th St

Flamingo Park

907

11th St

10th St

9th St

8th St

7th St

6th St

5th St

4th St

3rd St

2nd St

1st St

Lenox Ave

Michigan Ave

Jefferson Ave

Euclid Ave

Meridian Ave

Washington Ave

Collins Ave

Ocean Dr

South Beach
(SoBe)

Lummus
Park &
Public
Beach

A1A

Biscayne Bay

Star Island

To Downtown
Miami; Miami
International Airport

Terminal
Island

United States
Coast Guard
Station

Causeway
Island

A1A

41

41

Alton Rd

West Ave

Lummus
Island

Miami
Beach
Marina

Government Cut

Harley Ave

Commerce St

Biscayne St

Ocean
Beach
Park

Pier
Park

Inlet Blvd

South Beach
(SoFi)

South Pointe
Park

Boardwalk Pier

ATLANTIC
OCEAN

Fisher Island

FLORIDA

152nd St; adult/child $11.50/6.75; 9:30am-5:30pm, last admission 4pm) has exotic elephants, tigers and Komodo dragons. The **Miami Children's Museum** (Map p498; ☎ 305-373-5437; www.miamichild rensmuseum.org; 980 MacArthur Causeway, Watson Island; admission $10; 10am-6pm; **P**) has some educational displays on subjects like architecture (this being Miami), plus corporately branded exhibits where kids can, say, do their banking at Bank of America. **Parrot Jungle** (Map p498; ☎ 305-666-7834; www.parrotjungle.com; 1111 Parrot Jungle Trail, Watson Island; adult/child $24.95/19.95; 10am-6pm; **P**), off I-395/MacArthur Causeway, not only has parrots but also flamingos, cockatoos and kitschy dancing-bird shows. At the Amazon-like **Monkey Jungle** (☎ 305-235-1611; www.monkeyjungle.com; 14805 SW 216th St; adult/child 4-12 $18/12; 9:30am-5pm, last admission 4pm), southwest of the city, you can see orangutans, chimps and gorillas in the wild from the sanctum of screened-in trails.

Tours

Learn volumes about art deco and its icons on a 90-minute walking tour with the **Miami Design Preservation League** (Map p503; www.mdpl .org; guided tours adult/child/senior $20/free/15, self-guided tours adult/senior $15/10). Tours leave from the **Art Deco Welcome Center** (Map p503; ☎ 305-531-3484; 1001 Ocean Dr) at 10:30am Wednesday, Friday and Saturday, and at 6:30pm Thursday.

Historian extraordinaire **Dr Paul George** (☎ 305-375-1621; tickets $15-40; tours 10am Sat, 11am Sun) leads fascinating tours investigating subjects like Miami crime. Call to make arrangements.

Sleeping

Miami is to hotels what the deco movement was to architecture: bold, artistic and stylish, and light-years ahead of its time.

Oceanfront rooms are not only usually the most expensive, but may also have the most noise from nightlife revelry. Many hotels reduce rates by as much as 35% during the summer low season, except for public holidays and special events.

Prices quoted to you don't usually include sales tax – always ask what the after-tax cost will be when booking.

Hotel parking comes in a range of possibilities. Metered lots start at $1 an hour (which you'll need to top up every three hours); garages are around $8 to $10 a day, though once you're in you can't move your car without paying the fee again; and hotel valet parking costs about $15 per day but allows you the freedom to come and go.

MIAMI BEACH

South Beach Hostel (Map p503; ☎ 305-672-2137; www.thesouthbeachhostel.com; 235 Washington Ave; dm $14-18, r $49-54;) South Beach's newest hostel has everything going for it: a decked-out art deco building with four- to 14-bed dorms and smart private rooms, free bagels for breakfast, free wi-fi, online computers and nation-wide phone calls, pool tables and a fun bar.

Pelican Hotel (Map p503; ☎ 305-673-3373, 800-773-5422; www.pelicanhotel.com; 826 Ocean Dr; r $135-440; **P**) From the outside it's another neo-deco delight with a pretty pistachio facade, but inside the owners of Diesel jeans went to town to create 30 utterly out-there themed rooms such as 'A Fortune in Aluminium' – a shiny shrine to metallica. The entire building is wi-fied.

Avalon Majestic Hotel (Map p503; ☎ 305-538-0133, 800-933-3306; www.avalonhotel.com; 700 Ocean Dr; r $95-260) You'll know this place by the iconic white-and-yellow 1955 Lincoln convertible parked out front. Rooms are simple

---

THE AUTHOR'S CHOICE

Clay Hotel & International Hostel (Map p503; ☎ 305-534-2988; www.clayhotel.com; 1438 Washington Ave; dm $19-21, r $43-90;) The spiritual home of travelers everywhere, the Clay Hotel anchors Mediterranean Española Way's cafés and hippie-style weekend markets. This century-old Spanish-style courtyard complex filled with fragrant flowers opened its doors three-and-a-half decades ago, long before there was a scene. The pilot episode of Miami Vice was shot here (and lots of later episodes too). At various times home to Desi Arnaz (who kicked off the rumba here), and a casino run by Al Capone, today it combines an international hostel with private boutique suites where strains of flamenco from Española Way float up to private balconies. Staff can tip you off about the best places to party – many of which are just moments away – and the sands of South Beach are a two-block stroll.

and stylish; guests can use Avalon's sister hotel's pool nearby. One of the towers is completely nonsmoking.

Clinton Hotel (Map p503; ☎ 305-938-4040; www .clintonsouthbeach.com; 825 Washington Ave; r $189-800; P 🛋) One of the most buzzed-about properties at the beach, with a smooth lobby of velveteen banquettes and cool, contemporary-toned rooms.

Beachcomber Hotel (Map p503; ☎ 305-531-3755, 888-305-4683; www.beachcombermiami.com; 1340 Collins Ave; r $110-140) Inside the green-banana-colored exterior, the Beachcomber is newly ripe from renovations with a mellow mint-green lobby and 29 cozy rooms. There's free wi-fi; parking's available nearby.

Fontainebleau Hotel (4441 Collins Ave; r off-season from $189, late Dec-May from $239; P 🖳 🛋) You name it, this 1200-room grand dame has it in spades. Star-studded from the day it opened in 1954, there are beachside cabanas, tennis courts and a shopping mall. It's northeast of the city center, at the A1A. At press time the hotel was undergoing a facelift; check with the Greater Miami and the Beaches Convention and Visitor's Bureau (p499).

Delano Hotel (Map p503; ☎ 305-672-2000, 800-848-1775; www.delanohotelmiamibeach.com; 1685 Collins Ave; r off-season $205-475, Jan-Apr $325-575; 🖳 🛋) Drop-dead posh. Rooms are minimalist-chic, and the indoor/outdoor lobby is all billowing curtains and pillars. If you want to book a romantic dinner for two in the middle of the decadent pool, this is the place.

DOWNTOWN & GREATER MIAMI
Check out www.miamiboutiquehotels.com for a slew of stylized options.

Miami River Inn (Map p501; ☎ 305-325-0045, 800-468-3589; www.miamiriverinn.com; 119 SW South River Dr; r $69-169; P ✕ 🛋) These four charming turn-of-the-20th-century timber buildings set around rambling gardens transport you far from the mayhem of Miami. Rooms are big and airy with rustic furniture. Freshly squeezed orange juice is served with a buffet breakfast overlooking the pool and there's free parking.

Hotel Place St Michel (Map p498; ☎ 305-444-1666, 800-848-4683; www.hotelplacestmichel.com; 162 Alcazar Ave; r $125-225; P 🖳 🛋) You could conceivably think you're in Europe in this vaulted place at Coral Gables, with inlaid wooden floors and just 27 rooms. Service is attentive without being intrusive.

Mandarin Oriental Miami (Map p501; ☎ 305-913-8288, 866-888-6780; www.mandarinoriental.com; 500 Brickell Key Dr; r $300-1250; P 🖳 🛋) Rising like a giant Chinese fan, rooms are sleek and elegant with bamboo carpets and marble bathrooms. The lobby's swank M Bar has more than 250 martinis.

Biltmore Hotel (Map p498; ☎ 305-445-1926, 800-727-1926; www.biltmorehotel.com; 1200 Anastasia Ave; r from $359; P 🖳 🛋) This 1926 National Historic Landmark, built in a Mediterranean style, is in a class all of its own. Among its architectural and amenity finery is the largest hotel pool in the country and there are ghost stories in the lobby most Tuesday evenings. If you don't want to stay the night, experience the magnificence on a tour (see p502).

Eating
You'll find Cuban coffee and cuisine all throughout the city, from little hole-in-the-wall bakeries to traditional diners and world-renowned restaurants. 'Floribbean' cuisine embodies the tropical fruits, vegetables and the fresh-from-the-ocean seafood common to Florida and the Caribbean. And you'll often find the line between restaurants and nightclubs blurred, with the hippest spots of the moment combining both, behind velvet ropes.

Drop by Lincoln Rd mall's farmers' market on Sundays for beach picnic fare to go.

Florida bans smoking in all establishments that serve food. Bars that don't serve food are exempt, at least for now.

MIAMI BEACH
Puerto Sagua (Map p503; ☎ 305-673-1115; 700 Collins Ave; dishes $6-25; ⏱ breakfast, lunch, dinner & late-night) Time hasn't touched this authentic Cuban diner and restaurant, which has Cuban staples like black bean soup and some of the best Cuban coffee in town.

11th St Diner (Map p503; ☎ 305-534-6373; 1065 Washington Ave; dishes $5-15; ⏱ 24hr) This is the spot after you stagger out of the clubs. This gleaming original art deco Pullman-car diner serves sound three-egg omelets, fried chicken and meatloaf (though the home fries aren't great).

Blue Door (Map p503; ☎ 305-674-6400; Delano Hotel, 1685 Collins Ave; mains $30-46; ⏱ lunch & dinner) Matching the arresting Philippe Stark-designed interior with African masks is a designer menu of French fusion with Asian

FLORIDA

THE AUTHOR'S CHOICE

Joe's Stone Crab Restaurant (Map p503; ☎ 305-673-0365; 227 Biscayne St; mains $20-48; ☺ lunch & dinner, closed mid-May–mid-Oct) Joe's has been in South Beach since 1913, when it was a little lunch counter and Miami was a backwater. Only open during the stone crab season, it's easily the most famous restaurant in town – just witness the huge crowds mobbing the foyer for a table (reservations aren't accepted). The setting is smashing: dark timber and gleaming tiles in a big, showy room. The crustaceans themselves are so in demand that, to ensure their species' survival, just one claw is allowed to be removed, after which they're returned to the water while it regenerates over one to two years. And what a claw. The art of consuming it is to remove the pre-cracked outer shell, hold it by its tail and dip it in Joe's mustard sauce (you're outfitted with an unbecoming but nevertheless necessary white paper bib to protect your finery). Joe's also serves steak, fowl and other seafood, but that would be missing the point; though if anything comes close to matching the claws it's Joe's exquisite key lime pie.

and Latin accents. This hipster fave was once part-owned by the Material Girl herself.

Jerry's Famous Deli (Map p503; ☎ 305-532-8030; www.jerrysfamousdeli.com; 1450 Collins Ave; dishes $7-15; ☺ 24hr) If you're yearning for a corned-beef sandwich at two in the morning, come here (or get them to bring it to you – this Jewish emporium delivers all hours).

News Cafe (Map p503; ☎ 305-538-6397; 800 Ocean Dr; dishes $10-15; ☺ 24hr) Primo people-watching is the main reason this place is an ingrained tradition, along with great salads and bruschetta. It's also a news shop that stocks English chocolate.

Tantra (Map p503; ☎ 305-672-4765; 1445 Pennsylvania Ave; mains from $32; ☺ dinner) Spiritual Indian music creates an ambient backdrop while you dine on very gourmet cuisine like Moroccan mint-spiced lamb (between 6pm and 10pm; after that it transforms into a happening club). Tantra's live carpet of grass is re-sodded every week.

DOWNTOWN & GREATER MIAMI

Versailles (Map p498; ☎ 305-444-0240; 3555 SW 8th St; mains $8-15; ☺ breakfast, lunch, dinner & late-night) *The* Cuban restaurant – there is none better. You'll see all walks of life here for breathtaking plantains, *ropa vieja* (shredded beef) and pork cooked to perfection.

Porcão (Map p501; ☎ 305-373-2777; 801 Brickell Bay Dr; per person $33; ☺ noon-midnight) Not for vegetarians. There is an enormous salad bar, but this Brazilian churrascaria is all about the meat, with a traditional rodizio and endless varieties of skewered, flame-broiled meats cut right onto your plate.

Hanna's Gourmet Diner (Map p498; ☎ 305-947-2255; 13951 Biscayne Blvd; mains $26-40; ☺ brunch, lunch

& dinner) Off the tourist map, this old diner has the best onion soup outside – or possibly including – France, as well as superb sea bass and extraordinary desserts.

Norman's International (Map p498; ☎ 305-446-6767; 21 Almeria Ave; mains $20-40; ☺ dinner Mon-Sat) Book way ahead for Norman Van Aken's creations, such as stuffed baby bell pepper in cumin-scented tomato broth with avocado *crema*, which have given rise to 'New World Cuisine'.

Drinking

Miami's hotel lounges and bars are some of the chicest places to quaff cocktails; even locals get in on the act.

Mac's Club Deuce Bar (Map p503; ☎ 305-531-6200; 222 14th St) The beach's oldest bar has been pouring drinks since 1926 for an eclectic clientele. It has a gloriously seedy vibe of Miami of old.

Clevelander Bar (Map p503; ☎ 305-531-3485; 1020 Ocean Dr) Poolside open-air glass and neon bar overlooking the Ocean Drive tourist parade. Very Miami.

Skybar (Map p503; ☎ 305-695-3900; Shore Club, 1901 Collins Ave) Lounge on Moroccan cushions strewn around an enormous alfresco terrace amid lush gardens, and dance like nobody's watching (yeah, right!) at the Red Room inside. Formidable door policy. It helps if you're 'someone,' or know someone who is; otherwise, dress to impress and play it cucumber-cool (pleading with the doormen won't do you any favors).

Playwright (Map p503; ☎ 305-534-0667; 1265 Washington Ave) An affable Irish pub where you can actually hold a conversation, with a vast selection of imported beers.

Laundry Bar (Map p503; ☎ 305-531-7700; www .laundrybar.com; 721 Lincoln Lane N) Yep, you can wash your clothes at this laundromat/bar, with two-for-one drinks until 9pm daily.

District (☎ 305-576-7242; 35 NE 40th St; dishes $12-20; 🕒 lunch & dinner Tue-Sat) One of those 'is it a restaurant, is it a nightspot?' places in the Design District with loungey live jazz and cocktails.

Entertainment

You'd have to try hard to be bored in Miami. While South Beach is a clubber's paradise, Miami and Miami Beach offer stellar theater, sports and cultural performances as well as great live music. Check out www.miami andbeaches.com for a calendar of events. **CoolJunkie** (www.cooljunkie.com) has its finger on the pulse. The **Winter Music Conference** (www .wmcon.com) in late March has dance music, and the real hard beats are at the affiliate **Ultra Festival** (www.wmcon.com/evt_ultra.htm).

LIVE MUSIC

Tobacco Road (Map p501; ☎ 305-374-1198; www.tob acco-road.com; 626 S Miami Ave; tickets from around $10) A rockin' jazz, blues and classic rock joint since 1912. There's a throwback roadhouse feel to the place and it's often the scene of impromptu jams by well-known rockers when they're in town.

Other recommendations:

Hoy Como Ayer (Map p498; ☎ 305-541-2631; 2212 SW 8th St; cover $8-25) Authentic Cuban music.

Jazid (Map p503; ☎ 305-673-9372; 1342 Washington Ave; cover Fri & Sat $10) Quality jazz in a candlelit lounge.

Churchill's Hideaway (Map p498; ☎ 305-757-1807; 5501 NE 2nd Ave; cover $10-15) The best of indie music – as well as UK football match broadcasts.

NIGHTCLUBS

Crobar (Map p503; ☎ 305-531-5027; 1445 Washington Ave; cover $25; 🕒 Thu-Sun) In a neon-lit old deco cinema, this cavernous multi-room space is still SoBe's hottest scene.

Opium Garden & Privé (Map p503; ☎ 305-531-5535; 136 Collins Ave; cover from $25) Open-sky bar with lots of lanterns and more action up-stairs. House and dance reign supreme.

Club Space (Map p501; ☎ 305-375-0001; 142 NE 11th St; cover $25) So named for its gargantuan downtown warehouse digs.

Nikki Beach Club (Map p503; ☎ 305-538-1111; 1 Ocean Dr; cover from $25) Sunday nights see the hyped outdoor beach parties in full swing

at this flaunty, flirty club with DJs, outdoor beds and seaside teepees.

Twist (Map p503; ☎ 305-538-9478; 1057 Washington Ave; admission free) The rooftop bar at this gay club is always jammed. There are plenty of other draws like drag shows and dancers.

CINEMAS

All the malls have mega multiplexes, but there are a handful of independents:

Bill Cosford Cinema (Map p498; ☎ 305-284-4861; University of Miami, Memorial Bldg, Coral Gables) First-run indie flicks from around the world.

Absinthe House Cinematheque (Map p498; ☎ 305-446-7144; 235 Alcazar Ave, Coral Gables) Classic art house screening independent and foreign films.

Miami Beach Cinematheque (Map p503; ☎ 305-673-4567; www.mbcinema.com; 512 Española Way) Documentaries and kitschy classics.

Tower Theater (Map p498; ☎ 305-649-2960; 1508 SW 8th St/Calle Ocho) This renovated 1926 theater screens Spanish-language films and has art exhibits in the foyer.

SPORTS

Pro Player Stadium (Map p498; 2269 NW 199th St, North Dade) is home to the NFL football team **Miami Dolphins** (☎ 305-620-2578; www.miamidolphins.com; tick-ets $20-54; 🕒 season Aug-Dec) and the Major League baseball team **Florida Marlins** (☎ 305-626-7400; www.marlins.mlb.com; tickets $4-55; 🕒 season May-Sep).

Miami Heat (☎ 786-777-4328; www.nba.com/heat; tickets $33-100; 🕒 season Nov-Apr) plays NBA bas-ketball at **American Airlines Arena** (Map p501; 601 Biscayne Blvd).

Florida Panthers (☎ 954-835-7000; tickets $14-67; 🕒 season mid-Oct–mid-Apr) play NHL hockey at the **Office Depot Center** (Map p498; 1 Panther Parkway, Sunrise).

At **Miami Jai Alai** (Map p498; ☎ 305-633-6400; 3500 NW 37th Ave; tickets $1-5; 🕒 matches noon-5pm Wed-Mon, 7pm-midnight Mon, Fri & Sat), watch and place bets on this lightning-fast court game that's a kind-of cross between lacrosse and racquetball.

THEATER

Colony Theater (Map p503; ☎ 305-674-1026; 1040 Lin-coln Rd) Everything from off-Broadway pro-ductions to ballet and movies plays in this renovated 1934 art deco showpiece.

Coconut Grove Playhouse (Map p498; ☎ 305-442-4000; www.cgplayhouse.com; 3500 Main Hwy; adult $40-45, under 24 $15) Major shows in an intimate setting.

Jackie Gleason Theater of the Performing Arts (Map p503; ☎ 305-673-7300; www.gleasontheater.com;

1700 Washington Ave) Miami Beach's premier showcase for Broadway shows, headliners and the Miami City Ballet.

Performing Arts Center (PAC; www.pacfmiami.org) In downtown Miami, this has been a long time in the pipeline, but should be open sometime in 2006.

Shopping

Browse for one-of-a-kind and designer items at the South Beach boutiques around Collins Ave between 6th and 9th Sts and along Lincoln Rd mall. (Always check to make sure goods are in working order before you hand over any money, and insist on clearly itemized receipts). For artsy items, try Little Havana (p500) and the Design District (p502).

Scads of malls include Miami's most elegant, **Bal Harbour Shops** (p498; ☎ 305-866-0311; www.balharbourshops.com; 9700 Collins Ave).

Little Havana to Go (Map p498; ☎ 305-857-9720; www.littlehavanatogo.com; 1442 SW 8th St/Calle Ocho) stocks authentic items and clothing.

Getting There & Around

AIR

Miami International Airport (MIA; Map p498; ☎ 305-876-7000; www.miami-airport.com) is about 6 miles west of downtown and is accessible by **SuperShuttle** (☎ 800-874-8885; www.supershuttle.com), which costs about $12 to downtown or $14 to South Beach.

BUS

Greyhound destinations within Florida include Fort Lauderdale ($5.50, 45 minutes), Homestead ($11, one hour), Key West ($35, four hours), Orlando ($33, five to six hours), and Tampa ($38, eight hours).

Miami's main terminals:
Airport terminal (Map p498; ☎ 305-871-1810; 4111 NW 27th St)
Miami Downtown terminal (Map p501; ☎ 305-374-6160; 36 NE 10th St)

CAR

Major and minor car-rental companies have booths or phones at MIA.
Alamo (☎ 800-327-9633)
Budget (☎ 800-527-0700)
Hertz (☎ 800-654-3131)

TRAIN

Amtrak (Map p498; ☎ 305-835-1222; 8303 NW 37th Ave) has a main Miami terminal.

Tri-Rail (☎ 800-874-7245; www.tri-rail.com) commuter system serves Miami (with a free transfer to Miami's transit system) and MIA, Fort Lauderdale and its airport ($3.50 round-trip), plus West Palm Beach and its airport ($9.50 round-trip).

Metro-Dade Transit (☎ 305-770-3131; www.miamidade.gov/transit) runs the local Metrobus, Metromover monorail (free; downtown), and Metrorail ($1.25; Hialeah through downtown south to Kendall).

THE EVERGLADES

Between Miami's edgy urban jungle and glitzy beach promenades and the Keys' clear seas, the Everglades' incredibly unique ecosystem is full of alligators, brackish swamps, rural farmlands and Spanish-speaking towns. The largest subtropical wilderness in continental USA, it's the second-largest national park in the US, after Yellowstone, and the only one created not for its scenery (it's a swamp, after all) but for its biological diversity. The brackish mangrove and cypress swamps, hardwood hammocks (fertile, raised areas found mostly in Florida), sawgrass flats, pinelands and marshes are home to creatures like endangered American crocodiles, bottle-nosed dolphins, manatees, snowy egrets, bald eagles, ospreys and the ubiquitous gators, with endless opportunities for hiking, biking, canoeing, kayaking, boating, camping and fishing.

Before developers began draining it in the early 20th century, the Everglades, known as Pa-hay-okee (Grassy Water) by the Calusa Indians, was a 100-mile-long, 60-mile-wide 'river of grass' that stretched all the way from Lake Okeechobee to Florida Bay at the southern tip of the mainland. After hurricanes in the 1920s caused Lake Okeechobee to overflow, killing thousands of nearby residents, the government built an earthen dike around the lake and a network of canals through the swamp. In recent years, runoff from sugarcane fields has threatened the Everglades' water quality and wildlife, particularly its wading birds; a multibillion-dollar, decades-long restoration plan is aimed at restoring much of its hallowed habitat.

Orientation & Information

The Everglades region refers to the 80 southernmost miles of Florida, extending from the Atlantic Ocean to the east across to the

Gulf of Mexico in the west. The only road taking you south into the heart of the Everglades National Park is Route 9336. Traveling north to south along the park's eastern edge is Route 997. The Tamiami Trail (a contraction of Tampa–Miami), or Hwy 41, is a breathtaking drive east–west between the coasts. It runs parallel to the northern (and far less scenic) Alligator Alley, or I-75.

Coming from Miami, and especially if you're headed for the Keys, the gateway towns of Homestead and Florida City on the east side of the park make an ideal base. Hurricane Andrew tore through here in 1992, and while it's been rebuilt, there's something of a post-apocalyptic feel to the area that makes it down-to-earth and quite serene. There are expansive farmlands, nurseries and produce stands, and a thriving arts community.

Comprehensive information about the region is available at www.evergladeson line.com.

Everglades National Park

The main park entry points have visitor centers where you can get maps, camping permits and ranger information. You only need to pay the entrance fee (per car/pedestrian $10/5 for seven days) once to access all points.

Even in winter it's almost impossible to avoid mosquitoes, but they're ferocious in summer. Bring *strong* repellent. Alligators are also prevalent: as obvious as it sounds, to avoid them associating humans with food (never mind that they can't tell where the food ends and a human hand begins), never feed or provoke them. You're not likely to see them, but poisonous snakes here include the diamondback and pigmy rattlesnakes, cottonmouth or water moccasin (which swims along the surface of water), and coral snakes; wear long, thick socks and lace-up boots.

The principal visitor center, the **Ernest Coe Visitor Center** (☎ 305-242-7700; www.nps .gov/ever; Hwy 9336; ⏰ 8am-5pm) is packed with excellent information and museum-like exhibits. Fun and fascinating ranger-led programs include a 'slough slog' through this slow-moving grassy river. The gate is open 24 hours daily. Adjacent to it is the **Royal Palm Visitor Center** (☎ 305-242-7700; Hwy 9336; ⏰ 8am-4:15pm), leading to two short

trails including the .7-mile Gumbo-Limbo trail named for the tree of the same name, and the half-mile Anhinga Trail; both are great for wildlife viewing, especially in winter. From here, a 38-mile drive brings you to the coast and Flamingo's visitors' area. Enroute the 5½-mile loop trail Nine Mile Pond is the first of five self-guided canoe trails (good on a clear, still day). Noble Hammock, a 2-mile loop trail, is your best bet on a windy day as it's protected. The **Flamingo Visitor Center** (☎ 941-695-3094; ⏰ 7:30am-5pm) has maps of canoeing and hiking trails. At Flamingo you'll also find the **Flamingo Lodge, Marina & Outpost Resort** (☎ 239-695-3101; www.flamingolodge.com), which offers boat tours ($10 to $32) and fishing trips in the mangroves and Florida Bay, as well as accommodations and dining options (see p510). The outpost also rents canoes (half-/full-day $22/32), kayaks ($27/43), bikes ($8/14) and fishing skiffs ($65/90).

The north-central entrance at **Shark Valley** (☎ 305-221-8776; Tamiami Trail/US 41; ⏰ 8:30am-6pm) is 25 miles west of Florida Turnpike. From here you can bike (per hour $5.75; seasonal guided full-moon bike tours are offered for per adult/child $15/7; BYO bike), walk, or take a two-hour **tram tour** (☎ 305-221-8455; adult/child $13.25/8) along the 15-mile asphalt trail. Halfway along the trail you'll come to a 50ft-high Shark Valley Observation Tower, an out-of-place concrete structure that offers a dramatic panorama of the park. Guided, three-hour 'slough slogs' through a cypress swamp, hardwood hammock and sawgrass marsh run at 1pm Saturday during winter for adult/child $15/7; kids must be over eight, and reservations are required (either by phone or at the valley entrance).

At the northwestern edge of the park is the **Gulf Coast Visitor Center** (☎ 941-695-3311; Hwy 29, Everglades City; ⏰ 8:30am-5pm). From here, the **10,000 Islands** mangroves and waterways offer incredible canoeing and kayaking opportunities – including short trips to sandy beaches and shallow, brackish lagoons, as well as the 99-mile **Wilderness Waterway**, which runs along the park's southern edge from here to Flamingo. Rangers lead canoe trips and walks. A **concessionaire** (☎ 239-695-2591) offers 90-minute boat tours ($16) and canoe rentals (per day $20).

Think of the Everglades and you think of airboats (those flat-bottom hovercrafts with the giant fans on the back), but actually they're forbidden in the park proper. The best place to take a 30- to 45-minute ride is at the family-owned **Everglades Alligator Farm** (☎ 305-247-2628; www.everglades.com; 40351 SW 192 Ave, Homestead; adult/child $17/10; ⏰ 9am-6pm), where you can also hold baby alligators.

Sleeping & Eating

Inside the park, the only motel is the **Flamingo Lodge, Marina & Outpost Resort** (☎ 239-695-3101; Flamingo; r $68-98, cottages $92-138; P 🛇) with dated but perfectly adequate rooms with views of Florida Bay. To spend the night on the water, you can rent fully equipped houseboats (per night $340 to $475, with a two-night minimum), or a motorized catamaran (per night $525 to $575, with a two-night minimum). Apart from a grocery store, restaurant and small bar, the nearest facilities are 40 miles northeast in Homestead. The National Park Service's developed **campsites** (☎ 239-695-0124) here and at Long Pine Key, 7 miles from the main entrance, are free during the brutally hot months of June to August and $14 the rest of the year, when you'll need to make a reservation.

Camping elsewhere in the park includes beach sites, ground sites and chickees (covered wooden platforms above the water) in the backcountry along the Wilderness Waterway. Backcountry camping is permitted throughout the park and requires a permit ($10) from the visitor centers. You should bring a hanging/hammock tent as you may not be able to pitch on underlying pinnacle rock.

EAST

The Homestead–Florida City area has no shortage of chain motels and fast-food restaurants on US 1 and along Krome Ave, but there are some real gems in the local backstreets that are worth searching out, including the 1930s art deco boarding house, **Everglades International Hostel & Tours** (☎ 800-372-3874, 305-248-1122; www.evergladeshostel.com; 20 SW 2nd Ave, Florida City; campsites/dm/r $10/14/35; P 🛇 💻), with a screened garden gazebo filled with musical instruments. Even if you're not staying here, one of the best ways to see the park is with their canoe & slough slog tour (all day/overnight including meals $50/$100 plus a willingness to get muddy

and wet), led by resident park guides (they also run 'spunky seniors' tours); or you can rent canoes ($20) and bikes ($15) to explore on your own.

Not your average motor lodge, the **Greenstone Motel** (☎ 305-247-8334; 304 N Krome Ave, Homestead; r $65-100; P) has several signature rooms decorated in raw, funky style by local artists who live and work at the Art South art colony, located in an adjacent building.

Right next to the loading bays and warehouses, the **Farmer's Market Restaurant** (☎ 305-242-0008; 300 N Krome Ave, Florida City; lunch mains $8-10, dinner mains $12-14; ⏰ 5:30am-9pm) serves hearty homemade breakfasts, outstanding seafood and pastas cooked with fresh herbs and vegetables. For impressive live blues and folk, and a sophisticated menu, hit the stellar **Main St Café** (☎ 305-245-7575; www.mainstreetcafe.net; 128 N Krome Ave, Homestead; mains $7-14). Grab a cool key lime or mango milkshake from **Robert is Here** (☎ 305-246-1592; 19200 SW 344th St, Homestead; ⏰ 8am-7pm Nov-Aug), and don't miss the Cuban espresso at the little **La Panderia bakery** (☎ 305-245-0436; 337 Palm Dr, Florida City; ⏰ 6am-9pm).

WEST

Ivey House (☎ 239-695-3299; www.iveyhouse.com; 107 Camellia St, Everglades City; r $75-200; P 🛇 💻) has added to its remodeled 1928 boardinghouse (closed November to April), with a bright, breezy inn (open year-round). Come by for Ivey's hot home-cooked breakfasts ($5.25, free for guests) between 6:30am and 9:30am. With clean, comfortable rooms, **Captain's Table** (☎ 239-695-4211; 102 East Broadway, Everglades City; r $54-130; P 💻 💻) also has a popular restaurant on-site which is open for lunch and dinner, and serves fresh-from-the-docks seafood Meals range from $10 to $24.

In between park entrances, just east of Ochopee, is the quintessential 1950s-style swamp shack, **Joanie's Blue Crab Cafe** (☎ 239-695-2682; 39395 Tamiami Trail; mains $10-13), with open rafters, shellacked picnic tables and a swamp dinner of gator nuggets and fritters. Feast on triple crab cakes (stone crab, blue crab and snow crab) and key lime pie under the papaya trees at **JT's Island Grill & Gallery** (☎ 239-695-3633; 238 Mamie St, Chokoloskee; mains $6.25-10.25; ⏰ 11am-3pm, late-Oct–May), a restored 1890 general store with kitsch to spare.

CORAL CASTLE

Immortalized by Billy Idol's song Sweet Sixteen, **Coral Castle** (☎ 305-248-6345; www.coralcastle .com; 28655 S Dixie Hwy, Miami; adult/child $9.75/5; ⏰ 7am-8pm) is a scientific mystery, a tragic tale of unrequited love and a kitschy, wacky south Florida attraction rolled into one. After 26-year-old Ed Leedskalnin was jilted by his teenage fiancée the day before their wedding, he was so distraught he spent the next 28 years (1923 to 1951), using only handmade tools, to single-handedly carve coral rocks quarried from his Homestead property into an architectural monument to his sweetheart. She would never see it; and he would remain unmarried, adding to and improving the castle right up until his death. The largest stone weighs 29 tons and the swinging gate 9 tons. But here's the twist: no one ever saw 5ft tall, 100-pound Ed actually building the prehistoric-looking structures; hence it's dubbed America's Stonehenge. Perhaps the best theory, or at least the most romantic, is that he levitated them onto his trailer using tonal frequencies – 'singing' the rocks into place as he serenaded his lost love.

From the Florida Turnpike, exit on 288th St, go right for 2 miles to SW 157th Ave and turn right.

AROUND THE EVERGLADES

Biscayne National Park

It's 95% water, but the 5% of land at this national park is some of the most serene and secluded waterfront you'll find. Here you can see manatees and sea turtles in the four diverse ecosystems (keys, coral reef, mangrove forest and bay). The **Dante Fascell Visitor Center** (☎ 305-230-7275; 9700 SW 328th St, Homestead; ⏰ 9am-5pm year-round) runs glass-bottom boat trips at 10am daily (adult/child under 12 $25/17), dive trips at 8:30am Friday to Sunday ($45) and snorkel trips at 1:15pm daily (per person $35), which all require reservations; and rents canoes ($10) and kayaks ($17). Camping (per two tents or up to six people $10) is perfect solitude…apart from the bugs – repellent's essential.

Big Cypress National Preserve

Sprawling along the Tamiami Trail (Hwy 41), which crosses swamp, prairie, hammock and other ecosystems between Miami and Naples, this preserve is a 1139-sq-mile federally protected area on the north edge of Everglades National Park. Great bald cypress trees are nearly gone from the area from lumbering before the preserve was established. These days, it's filled with dwarf pond cypress (the name is for the size of the preserve, not its trees). Residents include alligators, snakes, wading birds (white ibis, wood storks, tri-color herons and egrets), Florida panthers (rarely seen), wild turkeys and red cockaded woodpeckers. The preserve is a key part of the Everglades' ecosystem, as the rains that flood the prairies and

wetlands here slowly filter down through the 'Glades. Thirty-one miles of the **Florida National Scenic Trail** (☎ 352-378-8823, 800-343-1882; www.florida-trail.org) cut through the preserve. Just off Loop Rd is the 100ft **Tree Snail Hammock Nature Trail** – go just to the right of the plaque for the old whiskey still and follow an unpaved, unmarked deer path for 200ft to see water flowing beneath the Swiss cheese–like cap rock.

Get information from the **National Preserve Headquarters** (☎ 941-695-2000; ⏰ 8am-4:30pm Mon-Fri), just east of Ochopee, or **Big Cypress Visitor Center** (☎ 941-695-4111; ⏰ 8:30am-4:30pm), about 20 miles west of Shark Valley – half a mile east of here, drop into the **studio of Clyde Butcher** (☎ 239-695-2428; 52388 US 41, Ochopee; ⏰ 10am-5pm Thu-Mon), whose award-winning B&W photography will open your eyes to the area's microcosms.

The preserve's four no-fee primitive **campgrounds** (☎ 239-695-4111) are along the Tamiami Trail and Loop Rd. **Monument Lake Campground** (campsites $14) has facilities. Expect bugs year-round.

Ah-Tha-Thi-Ki

In the Seminole Mikasukee language, Ah-Tha-Thi-Ki means 'to learn,' and the excellent **Seminole museum** (☎ 863-902-1113; Big Cypress Seminole Indian Reservation, Hwy 8333; adult/child $6/4; ⏰ 9am-5pm Tue-Sun), 17 miles north of I-75 from exit 49, is an open-air classroom, with 1½ miles of boardwalk nature trails (wheelchair accessible) through the serene 60-acre cypress dome to a re-created Seminole village, with exhibits concentrated on Seminole history in the 19th century. The reservation's **Big Cypress Campground** (☎ 800-437-4102) has sites ($17 to $24) and cabins ($65 to $75).

FLORIDA KEYS

They call it the 'Keys Disease', and the only cure's said to be rum and return visits. This 126-mile string of islands reels in travelers with its alluring opaque jade-green waters, laid-way-back island lifestyle, great fishing and idyllic conditions for snorkeling and diving. If you don't dive, the Keys are ideal for learning, with shallow reefs, warm water and underwater treasures.

The Keys first became accessible to land-bound tourists with the advent of Henry Flagler's railroad, completed in 1912, which was blown away in a devastating 1935 hurricane. What remained of its bridges allowed the construction of the Overseas Highway (US Hwy 1), completed in 1938. Though the Upper Keys section, especially, appears cluttered from the road with touristy shops and motels (from the water they're paradise), the further south you go, the more the waters spread out around the bridges linking the islands, opening up endless vistas.

From the Spanish *cayo*, which is shortened to 'cay' (pronounced 'key') in the Caribbean and Bahamas, a key is defined as a low-lying island, usually no less than 10 acres (anything smaller is a sandbar, shoal or reef). According to the US Geological Survey there are 882 keys in Florida, but it's this chain, stretching from Florida City to Key West, that's the most romanticized.

Many addresses in the Keys are noted by their proximity to mile markers (indicated as MM) showing distances between Key West (MM 0) and the mainland at Florida City (MM 126). The **Florida Keys & Key West Visitors Bureau** (☎ 800-352-5397; www.fla-keys.com; 402 Wall St, Key West) has information on the entire area. Check www.diveflakeys.com for a full list of dive operators.

For details about travel to and within the Keys, see p520.

Key Largo

Bogie and Bacall never actually came to Key Largo – apart from a couple of exterior scenes shot at the **Crib** (Caribbean Club; ☎ 305-451-9970; MM 104 bayside; ☽ 7am-4am) hotel, the eponymous 1948 movie was filmed on

a Hollywood sound stage, but it served to bring the largest of the Florida Keys into the public eye. For maps and brochures, visit the **chamber of commerce** (☎ 305-451-1414, 800-822-1088; www.keylargo.org; MM 106; ☽ 9am-6pm).

The underwater park, **John Pennekamp Coral Reef State Park** (☎ 305-451-1202; www.pennekamppark.com; MM 102.5; vehicle with 1 person $3.50, with 2 or more $6 plus per person 50¢, pedestrian $1.50) offers the best way to get out on the reef. View the dazzling fish and coral from a glass-bottom boat for 2½ hours (adult/child $21/14), or better yet, get among the fish by taking a snorkeling trip (adult/child $27.95/22.95 plus gear rental), or a two-location, two-tank diving trip ($41 plus gear rental). In all cases, you'll get a chance to check out the 9ft algae-covered bronze statue, **Christ of the Deep**, a replica of Christ of the Abyss off Genoa, Italy. You can also rent **canoes or kayaks** (☎ 305-451-1621; per hr $12) to journey through a 3-mile network of canoe trails, or power-boats starting at $200 per day. The park's also home to an aquarium showcasing the living coral and tropical fish and plant life.

Dozens of outfitters take visitors to the reef on half-day and day scuba trips; try **Island Venture** (☎ 305-451-4957, 866-293-5006; www.islandventure.com; MM 104 dock), between Sundowners & Sr Frijoles. Rates vary; expect to pay from $80 for a two-tank dive with tank and air, and upwards of $90 if you need additional gear.

For kayak rentals, trips and expert local advice, **Florida Bay Outfitters** (☎ 305-451-3018; www.kayakfloridakeys.com; MM 104) has kayaks and canoes from $35 for a half-day and leads kayak tours from $50, including a full-moon paddle, and also rents camping equipment. Just one of the perfect places to put in is at MM 111 (on your right if you're heading south), with a boat launch and a succession of idyllic inlets and coves.

SLEEPING & EATING

In addition to luxe resorts, Key Largo has loads of bright, cheery motels and camping.

Largo Lodge (☎ 305-451-0424, 800-468-4378; www.largolodge.com; MM 101.5 bayside; efficiencies $95-145; Ⓟ) A tropical flower–filled hardwood forest secludes these six old Florida cottages, with sun-filled living and sleeping areas and a private swimming cove. Children under 16 are not allowed.

SOMEWHERE BENEATH THE SEA...

Jules' Undersea Lodge (☎ 305-451-2353; www.jul.com; MM 103.2 oceanside, 51 Shoreland Dr; per person $295-595, exclusive use $1195; ✕) Watch the fish swim past your window at this underwater hotel. Permanently anchored 30ft beneath the water's surface in a protected lagoon, the lodge can accommodate six guests. It was originally designed for scientists who lived onboard – even if all the backup generators and systems failed, there'd still be about 12 hours of breathing time inside the hotel. In addition to two very comfy private guest rooms are a fully stocked kitchen/dining room and a wet room with hot showers and gear storage. Telephones and an intercom connect guests with the surface; staff members are on duty 24 hours. Guests must be at least 10 years old; alcohol's not permitted. To have a peek without staying here, sign up for a three-hour mini-adventure ($60), which also gives access to its facilities and three breathing hookahs – 120ft-long air hoses for tankless diving.

Popp's (☎ 305-852-5200; www.popps.com; MM 95.5 bayside; efficiency apartments $99-199; **P**) This great little bayside motel has been family-owned since forever and sits right on the shores of a wonderful palm-fringed swimming beach with its own boat dock.

John Pennekamp Coral Reef State Park (☎ 800-326-3521; per night $26) Camping is unsurprisingly popular at this park's 47 sites; reserve well in advance.

Alabama Jacks (☎ 305-248-8741; 1500 Card Sound Rd; mains $5-25; ✷ lunch & dinner) Right on the water where you'll always see wildlife as well as everyone from bikers to boaters and celebrities in limos. This legendary roadside stop has live country music and is justifiably heralded for having the best conch fritters in the Keys. It's before the toll at the south end of Card Sound Rd.

Fish House (☎ 305-451-4665; MM 102.4 oceanside; lunch mains $8-20, dinner mains $15-35; ✷ lunch & dinner) This traditional Keys joint isn't elegant but has great service and tasty smoked fish.

Fish House Encore (☎ 305-451-451-0650; MM 102.3; ✷ dinner) Fish House's upscale sister is more comely with white tablecloths, classy continental fare and prices to match. But they know how to mix cocktails and the bar gets loose.

Mrs Mac's Kitchen (☎ 305-451-3722; MM 99.4 bayside; mains $5-25; ✷ 7am-9pm Mon-Sat) Classic highway food like BBQ and burgers is dished up to loyal locals at this timeless diner.

Buzzard's Roost (☎ 305-453-3746; MM 106.5 oceanside/21 Garden Cove Dr; lunch mains $8-20, dinner mains $15-30; ✷ lunch & dinner) An 8ft buzzard flags the entrance to this fun family-run place with great American fare.

Islamorada

Islamorada (eye-luh-murr-*ah*-da) is actually a collection of smaller islands, with several gorgeous, easily accessible little ocean-beach nooks providing scenic rest stops. Housed in an old red caboose, the **chamber of commerce** (☎ 305-664-4503, 800-322-5397; www.islamoradachamber.com; MM 82.5 bayside; ✷ 9am-5pm Mon-Fri) has information about the area.

Islamorada's two greatest treasures are both only accessible by boat, making for great kayaking. On the ocean side a few hundred yards offshore, **Indian Key State Historic Site** is a peaceful little island home to the crumbling foundations of a 19th-century settlement, an observation deck and .7-mile trail. There are free 1½-hour ranger-led tours Thursday to Monday at 9am and 1pm. Open and sunny, it's hot in summer – wear a hat. The open water can make paddling challenging on a windy day. On the bay side, the isolated **Lignumvitae Key State Botanical Site** (✷ Thu-Mon) is named for the hardwood, shiny red-bark Lignumvitae tree, nicknamed the 'tourist tree' because its bark peels like sunburnt tourists. The site has virgin tropical forest of strangler fig, mastic, gumbo-limbo and poisonwood trees, and historic 1919-built Matheson House. Guided walks around the gardens ($1) are available at 10am and 2pm. Launch watercraft to both keys at Indian Key Fill (you'll see a sign around MM78.5 as you're headed south). Rent kayaks from **Robbie's Marina** (☎ 305-664-9814; www.robbies.com; MM 77.5; per day $35), which also offers a powerboat shuttle service twice daily (one island $15, both $25). You can also hand-feed tarpon (they're toothless) right from the dock here (bucket of baitfish $2), which is prime midmorning.

Dolphins and sea lions perform in an intimate, close-up setting at **Theater of the Sea** (☎ 305-664-2431; www.theaterofthesea.com; MM 84.5; adult/child 3-12 $23.95/15.95), which offers the opportunity to swim with the dolphins and sea lions for an extra $50 to $150.

Flat walls of coral store thousands of years of geological history at **Windley Key Fossil Reef State Geologic Site** (☎ 305-664-2540; www.florid-astateparks.org; MM 85.5; admission $1.50) – the rangers here are great and will answer questions. Pick up a self-guided interpretive booklet for the ¾-mile walk.

For public beach access and shaded picnic tables, try **Anne's Beach** (MM 73.5; admission free) on the oceanside boardwalk (the beach disappears at high tide); and the shallow, sheltered **Islamorada Founder's Park** (MM 87; adult/child $4/2), which also has a dog park and Olympic-size pool (adult/child $7/3). Especially if you're traveling with kids, avoid swimming at **Library Beach** (MM 81.5; admission free), behind Islamorada Public Library, which is right alongside a busy marina. Area dive shops include **Holiday Isle Dive Shop** (☎ 305-664-3483, 800-327-7070; www.dive holidayisle.com; MM 84.5 oceanside), with trips departing at 9am and 1pm (snorkeling/diving $50/30), plus equipment for rent ($40/9).

SLEEPING & EATING

Ragged Edge Resort (☎ 305-852-5389; www.ragged -edge.com; 243 Treasure Harbor Rd; r $69-209; P ☼) Swim off the docks at this happily unpretentious waterfront resort off MM 86.5, with 10 spotless efficiency apartments.

Lime Tree Bay Resort Motel (☎ 305-664-4740, 800-723-4519; www.limetreebayresort.com; MM 68.5; r $115-295; P ☼) Spectacular sunsets provide a stunning slideshow from this 2.5-acre waterfront hideaway with an on-site concessionaire for windsurfing, kayaking and boating.

Cheeca Lodge & Spa (☎ 305-664-4651, 800-327-2888; www.cheeca.com; MM 82 oceanside; r $225-2200; P ☐ ☼) A lavish 203-room resort with eco sensibilities and a lovely, cabana-lined pool. An additional $39 per room allows access to activities including tennis, kayaking and exercise classes; there's also a dive shop and spa. Rates are considerably cheaper in the low season.

Long Key State Recreation Area (☎ 305-664-4815; MM 68; campsites $25) Book as far ahead as possible for these 60 coveted shady oceanfront campsites in a 965-acre park.

Lazy Days (☎ 305-664-5256; MM 79.9 oceanside; mains $6-22; ☼ lunch & dinner) Local chef Lupe Ledesma does amazing things with clams and pasta – definitely order the hogfish if it's on the menu (supply's limited as it's spear gun–caught). You'll need to book.

Morada Bay (☎ 305-664-0604; MM 81.6 bayside; lunch mains $9-16, dinner mains $21-27; ☼ 11:30am-10pm) The open-air Caribbean surrounds with Conch architecture are perfect for informal tapas and fresh seafood. Kids are given Cyalume light sticks to play with on the beach during full-moon parties.

Pierre's (☎ 305-664-3225; MM 81.6 bayside; mains $25-30; ☼ dinner) Just across palm-lined sands reminiscent of the Cook Islands, Pierre's occupies a two-story waterfront colonial house, with attention to detail right down to the hand-cut, hand-placed wooden bar, gourmet seafood and fine wine list.

Island Grill (☎ 305-664-8400; MM 85.5; mains $14-24; ☼ lunch & dinner) On the ocean side just under Snake Creek Bridge, this hidden spot has a lovely wooden deck, strung with paper lanterns, which was made from a sunken houseboat that was raised and restored. There is live acoustic guitar Wednesday and weekend evenings. Try the graham cracker–crusted calamari.

ENTERTAINMENT

The **Zane Grey** (☎ 305-664-4244; MM 81.5; ☼ 8pm-midnight Thu-Sat) cigar bar, named for the writer who lived here in the Keys, has live jazz and blues. The bar's upstairs from the enormous **Worldwide Sportsman** (☼ 9am-8:30pm Sun-Thu, to 9pm Fri & Sat), which, apart from stocking a nearly-endless variety of rods, reels and tackle, has as its centerpiece the *Pilar* – a retired working fishing boat that still has its engines. The *Pilar* was allegedly Hemingway's inspiration for commissioning his boat, also named *Pilar* which is now on display in Cuba. Hemingway apparently fished off this boat, which it is said also featured in the 1948 film *Key Largo* as the *Santana*.

Marathon

Halfway between Key Largo and Key West, Marathon is a hub for numerous commercial fishing and lobster boats, with some sizable marinas. Get detailed local information at the **visitor center** (☎ 305-743-5417; MM 53.5; ☼ 9am-5pm).

At the southwest city limit, the graceful **Seven Mile Bridge** is the longest of the 40-plus bridges that link the island chain. On its north side stand remnants of the original Seven Mile Bridge, built in the early 20th century as part of the railroad to Key West, and billed today as the 'world's longest fishing bridge.' Park on the Marathon side of the Seven Mile Bridge (MM 45) and walk or take the hourly tram (the last one returns at 4:45pm) across a 2.5-mile stretch of the old bridge to **Pigeon Key National Historic District** (☎ 305-289-0025; adult/child $8.50/5; ☀ tram tours 10am-3pm), which housed railroad workers from 1908 and, later, workers who built the Overseas Highway after the railroad was hurricane-ravaged. There's a museum chronicling the ill-fated railroad and its baron, Henry Flagler.

With so much nearby development, entering the **Museums and Nature Center of Crane Point Hammock** (☎ 305-743-9100; www.cranepoint.org; MM 50.5; admission adult/child $7.50/4; ☀ 9am-5pm Mon-Sat, noon-5pm Sun) feels like turning back time, with a preserved 63-acre hardwood hammock encompassing a vast system of nature trails, mangroves, a raised boardwalk, a rare early-20th-century Bahamian-style house, exhibits on pirates and wrecking, a walk-through coral reef tunnel and a small bird sanctuary that houses injured wild birds. You can also visit the Museum of Natural History and the Florida Keys Children's Museum.

The **Turtle Hospital** (☎ 305-743-6509; www.turtlehospital.org; 2396 Overseas Hwy) rescues, rehabilitates and releases injured sea turtles, and will give you a tour if you call ahead. **Marathon Kayak** (☎ 305-743-0561; 19 Sombrero Blvd/MM 50 oceanside, Marathon) provides three-hour guided mangrove ecotours (per person $40), full-day mangrove ecotours ($80), three-hour sunset tours ($40), instruction (included) and rentals (single/double half-day $30/40, full day $45/60).

Tucked away on a little spit of land, the **Conch Key Cottages** (☎ 305-289-1377, 800-330-1577; www.conchkeycottages.com; 62250 Overseas Hwy/MM 62.3 oceanside, Walkers Island; r $74-122, cottages $132-304; P) is a collection of latticed cottages with Keys-funky decor and a complex of four brightly painted studios. All nestle around a private beach where bougainvillea and hibiscus grow wild.

An 'old Keys'–style fishing resort on Grassy Key, **Rainbow Bend** (☎ 305-289-1505,

800-929-1505; www.rainbowbend.com; 57784 Overseas Hwy/MM58 oceanside; r $165-270; P ☀) gives you access to half a day's use of a Boston Whaler motor boat, plus other watercraft. It also has a magical on-site restaurant, the **Hideaway Café** (☎ 305-289-1554; ☀ dinner), serving French-inspired seafood in a candlelit setting.

The stopping point along the Overseas Highway when there was nothing else here, the open-air **7 Mile Grill** (☎ 305-743-4481; MM 47; mains $8-11; ☀ Fri-Tue) has reliable family fare; order today's catch, but skip the burgers, which are likely to be frozen. For stylish New American cuisine try **Barracuda Grill** (☎ 305-743-3314; MM 49.5 bayside; mains $15-20; ☀ dinner Mon-Sat).

Lower Keys

Key West notwithstanding, the Lower Keys (MM 46 to MM 0) are the least developed of the island chain. The **chamber of commerce** (☎ 305-872-2411, 800-872-3722; www.lowerkeyschamber.com; MM 31; ☀ 9am-5pm Mon-Fri, to 3pm Sat) is on Big Pine Key.

Just half an hour up the road from Key West, the Keys' most acclaimed beach (but watch out for sandflies in summer) is at **Bahia Honda State Park** (☎ 305-872-2353; www.bahiahondapark.com; MM 37; admission per 1/2/additional person $2.50/5/50¢), a 524-acre park with nature trails, ranger-led programs and watersports rentals.

Along this stretch is the **National Key Deer Refuge** (☎ 305-872-2239; nationalkeydeer.fws.gov; admission free; ☀ 8am-5pm Mon-Fri) a designated, unfenced zone where endangered dog-sized Key Deer wander, but your best bet to see them is in residents' front yards eating leaves. The headquarters are at Big Pine Shopping Center, MM 30.5 bayside.

The grove reef **Looe Key** off Ramrod Key teems with colorful tropical fish and coral; try **Looe Key Dive Center** (☎ 305-872-2215 ext 2, 800-942-5397; MM 27.5), on Ramrod Key, for snorkeling and diving trips departing at 10am and returning at 3pm, snorkeling tours ($30 plus gear) and three tank/three location dive trips ($70 plus gear); 'bubblewatchers' can come along for the ride for $20.

Camping (campsites/RV sites $24/26) is sublime (but highly sought-after – book ahead) at Bahia Honda State Park, which also has six waterfront **cabins** ($97-125); or try the lovely oceanside B&B **Casa Grande** (☎ 305-872-2878; 1619 Long Beach Dr; r $90-140; **P**). **No Name Pub** (☎ 305-872-9115; MM 30; mains $5-15; ✆ 11am-11pm) serves up lots of local color as well as the best pizza for miles. At Big Pine Key Shopping Center, **Coco's Kitchen** (☎ 305-872-4495; MM 30.5 bayside; dishes $1-5; ✆ 7am-7:30pm Tue-Sat) has strong Cuban coffee and hot Cuban sandwiches.

Key West

At the end of the chain of keys, threaded by the Overseas Hwy and filigreed by mangroves, Key West hangs – or, more often, swings – like a dazzling, off-beat and only slightly gaudy pendant.

Roughly oval-shaped, this 2- by 4-mile island (you can bike the perimeter in around an hour) is the end of the road. The southernmost point of the continental US, Key West is closer to Cuba (90 miles) than it is to Miami (160 miles). But its semi-detachment is more than geographic; it's part of the laissez-faire that – along with the balmy subtropical climate and palm-shaded streets roamed by chickens – has attracted artists, musicians and writers for decades, as well as a thriving gay community. Two in five residents of Key West are gay or lesbian, and all residents co-exist as part of 'one human family,' the town's official motto.

Key West natives, known as Conchs (pronounced conk) call themselves members of the Conch Republic, dating back to the 1982 roadblock by US customs patrols, which effectively cut the Keys off from the rest of the country. Conchs rallied by seceding and declaring war on the US (firing stale Cuban bread), and then surrendering and requesting foreign aid in lieu of the tourism that had been cut off as well. And OK, it was a PR stunt – which did see the roadblock removed, and which is celebrated riotously every February – but you get the picture. Feisty independence, savvy humor, a touch of the theatrical and, above all, a reason to party; yep, that's Key West.

ORIENTATION & INFORMATION

The island's divided into the primarily residential area of New Town, and Old Town, the heart of the action, with inns, eateries and boisterous bars. The main drags are Duval St, which at peak times has a bit of a

giant souvenir shop feel, and Truman Ave (US Hwy 1).

Key West Chamber of Commerce (☎ 305-294-2587, 800-527-8539; www.keywestchamber.org; 402 Wall St, Mallory Sq; ✆ 8:30am-6:30pm Mon-Fri, to 6pm Sat & Sun) and the **Key West Welcome Center** (☎ 305-296-4444, 800-284-4482; 3840 N Roosevelt Blvd; ✆ 8am-7:30pm Mon-Sat, 9am-6pm Sun) have reams of brochures and maps. A great online resource is www.fla-keys.com/keywest.

Gay and lesbian visitors can get information (and free Internet's available for anyone) at the **Key West Business Guild** (✆ 9am-5pm) housed in the **Gay & Lesbian Community Center** (☎ 305-292-3223; www.glcckeywest.org; 513 Truman Ave).

The best Internet café (and best coffee) in town is **Coffee Plantation** (☎ 305-295-9808; 804 Whitehead St; ✆ 8am-6pm), with computers for 20¢ per minute and free wi-fi.

SIGHTS & ACTIVITIES

At the island's northwestern tip, near the chamber of commerce, fire twirlers, jugglers, buskers and magicians woo the crowds congregating at **Mallory Square** every night to watch the sun sink into the Gulf. Right next to the cruise port (which has ships in most days), the sunset celebration can be over-the-top touristy, but you've got to experience it – once.

Key West's unofficial patron saint, Ernest Hemingway's legacy is part of the island's fabric and folklore. Guides, who bear more than a passing resemblance to Hemingway, conduct half-hour tours of the house that was his home from 1931 to 1940, the **Hemingway House** (☎ 305-294-1575; www.hemingwayhome.com; 907 Whitehead St; adult/child $10/6). Here you'll see his pool (the island's

---

PERKY'S BAT TOWER

On Sugarloaf Key, you'll see the 35ft **Perky's Bat Tower** (MM17), the short-lived brainchild of real-estate developer Richter Perky. Mosquitoes presented his biggest obstacle to attracting vacationers, so in 1929 he built the tower to house bats he imported to devour them. They didn't. It turned out they were the wrong kind of bats, which didn't matter because within days the bats flew away, spelling the end of Perky's development dreams.

KEY WEST

first), his study and old Royal typewriter, and about fifty descendents of his six-toed cats (the same number as when Papa lived here). Afterwards you can sit and read in his tropical gardens, and check out the on-site bookshop's astounding collection of his and related titles.

Other museums worth browsing are the **Museum of Art & History** (☎ 305-295-6616; www.kwahs.com/customhouse.htm; 281 Front St; adult/child $7/5; 🕑 9am-5pm) in the grand Customs House, which has terrific permanent and rotating exhibitions and showcases local artists; and one of the town's three shipwreck museums, **Mel Fisher Maritime Heritage Museum** (☎ 305-294-2633; 200 Greene St; adult/child $10/6; 🕑 9:30am-5:30pm), with treasures and artifacts salvaged from the deep.

An utterly serene antidote to bar-hopping, and a great place to take kids, is the new **Key West Butterfly & Nature Conservatory** (☎ 305-296-2988; www.keywestbutterfly.com; 1316 Duval St; adult/child $10/7.50; 🕑 9am-5pm), with magical climate-controlled, open-roofed gardens fluttering with butterflies from around the world. Children will also love the **Key West Aquarium** (☎ 305-296-2051; www.keywestaquarium.com; 1 Whitehead St at Mallory Sq; adult/child $9/4.50; 🕑 10am-6pm), which has touch-me tanks.

If you're coming to Key West for its beaches, don't – you'll find infinitely better elsewhere in Florida. For sun and sand, your best bet is **Fort Zachary Taylor** (☎ 305-292-6713; admission $2.50; 🕑 8am-dusk), at the western end of Southard St. For people-watching and for breathtaking sunrises, head to **Smathers Beach** on S Roosevelt Blvd.

Pollution and boating activity have damaged the inner reefs. Dive companies usually take you west for **snorkeling** (Marquesas Keys is choice). Dive shops concentrate around the intersection of Truman Ave and Duval St.

TOURS

Hemingway aficionados can take a 1½-hour **Hemingway Walking Tour** (☎ 305-293-8773; tickets $25) of his favorite haunts, though it isn't affiliated with his home and entry's not included.

Both the **Old Town Trolley** (☎ 305-296-6688) and **Conch Tour Train** (☎ 305-294-5161) offer tours (adult/child $22/11) from 9am to 4.30pm daily. The trolley allows you to get on and off at its nine stops around town.

The train doesn't, though the open carriages offer a breezier ride. The ticket booths for both are at Mallory Sq.

FESTIVALS & EVENTS

Some of the biggest and best happenings include the events below. Contact the Chamber of Commerce for further information.
Annual Key West Literary Seminar (http://keywest literaryseminar.org) This January festival draws top-notch writers from afar.
PrideFest Apart from the main parade and plenty of partying, the highlight is the sea-to-sea rainbow flag that takes 2000 people to carry, which is dipped simultaneously in the Gulf and the Atlantic. Held in June.
Hemingway Days festival Has a Key Western 'running of the bulls' in late July.
Fantasy Fest A wild cross between Halloween and Carnivale; held in late October.
Goombay Festival Held during the same crazy week in October as the Fantasy Festival, this celebrates Bahamian culture.

SLEEPING

Arriving without a reservation during long weekends and special events will see you joining the long traffic-jam headed back to the mainland. Higher rates may also apply at peak times.

Chain motels are found mostly in New Town, but to truly experience Key West, the most enchanting options are Old Town's restored homes – visit the **Key West Innkeepers Association** (www.keywestinns.com) for a line-up of the best. All are pretty much gay-friendly and some gay-exclusive.

Budget & Midrange

Angelina Guest House (☎ 305-294-4480; www.an gelinaguesthouse.com; 302 Angela St; r with bath $84-149, without bath $59-79; P ✖ 🖵) Close – but not too close – to Duval St, this haven is the best value for money around, in a rambling lemon-yellow former bordello with pristine rooms (one wheelchair accessible) and owners who bake hot cinnamon rolls for breakfast. There are no phones or TVs; children must be over 12.

Authors Guesthouse (☎ 305-294-7381, 800-898-6909; www.authorskeywest.com; 725 White St; r $75-150; ✖ 🖵) Rooms (and two garden cottages) at this literary-inspired two-story place are named and decorated for writers who have lived in Key West at some point, including Tennessee Williams; there's also a sundrenched artists' guest room and mint-green library guest room. Off-street parking is limited, but you can park on the street out front.

Abaco Inn (☎ 305-296-2212; www.abaco-inn.com; 415 Julia St; r $79-109; ✖) Tucked away on a quiet and diverse residential block, this little gem has three airy rooms with wood floors and ceiling fans.

Frances St Bottle Inn (☎ 305-294-8530, 800-294-8530; www.bottleinn.com; 535 Frances St; r $89-209; ✖) In a peaceful part of town this friendly inn has eight comfy rooms, spick-and-span bathrooms, a two-story verandah and a small patio with hot tub. Rental bikes are available.

Pearl's Rainbow (☎ 305-292-1450, 800-749-6696; www.pearlsrainbow.com; 525 United St; r & ste $99-379; 🖳 🖳) In an 1880s cigar factory, Key West's only all-female place is a hotspot for lesbians and gay-friendly women, with understated, elegant rooms. The clothing-optional poolside bar Pearl's Patio is open to the public, with a well-patronized happy hour. Parking is limited.

HI Key West (☎ 305-296-5719; www.keywesthostel .com; 718 South St; dm members/nonmembers $25/28; Ⓟ) Price-wise, there's this place and there's daylight – but to avoid the institutional dorms and security risks (we've had numerous reports of gear going missing), you may prefer daylight. On the upside, it is in a super location a short walk from Duval St, and there's a social central courtyard and outdoor kitchen. Alcohol is forbidden. The hostel's mooted to be closing down sometime in the next few years, so check ahead.

Camping's available at **Boyd's Key West Campground** (☎ 305-294-1465; 6401 Maloney Ave; nonwaterfront sites $35-41, waterfront sites $41-48, water & electricity $10; Ⓟ 🖳), just outside town on Stock Island (turn south at MM 5).

Top End
Wyndham Casa Marina Resort & Beach House (☎ 305-296-3535, 800-949-3426; www.wyndhamcasa marinaresort.com; 1500 Reynolds St; r $169-409; Ⓟ 🖳) Next to Higgs Beach, this opulent 311-room masterpiece was built in the 1920s by railroad magnate Henry Flager. Three oceanside pools, every recreational pursuit imaginable, a kid's program and magnificent rooms with private balconies or terraces are just the curtain-raisers.

Big Rubys Guesthouse (☎ 305-296-2323, 800-477-7829; www.bigrubys.com; 409 Appelrouth Lane; r $85-265; 🖳) This ultra-sleek gay-only place has two sister properties in France and one in Costa Rica, and is a favorite with international high-fliers.

EATING
Ask if the fish is fresh (it often isn't), try conch fritters at least once, and don't pass up key lime pie, made with key limes (which are yellow, never green), sweetened condensed milk, eggs and sugar on a graham cracker crust.

Blue Heaven (☎ 305-296-8666; 305 Petronia St; mains $10.50-30; ⏰ 8am-10.30pm) Play table tennis while you wait for a table at this hippie-style compound set around a courtyard where Hemingway refereed boxing matches; there's performance art and artists painting as you dine. For breakfast, Richard's 'very good pancakes' are absolutely that; dinner is upscale surf 'n' turf.

Louie's Backyard (☎ 305-294-1061; 700 Waddell Ave; mains $40-50; ⏰ lunch & dinner) In the '70s, Louie started cooking for his neighbors, one of whom happened to be Jimmy Buffett – if you look on old albums, you'll see his thanks to Louie for the food in the credits. No longer owned by Louie, but with one of the island's finest reputations for high-end dining, come here for top-shelf Caribbean cuisine.

Camille's (☎ 305-296-4811; 1202 Simonton St; mains $14-25; ⏰ 8am-3pm & 4pm-10:30pm) Camille's is packed all day but especially at breakfast, when locals tuck into French toast with white Godiva chocolate cream sauce and other stellar signature dishes.

Alice's Key West (☎ 305-292-5733; 1114 Duval St; mains $17-33; ⏰ breakfast, lunch & dinner) Alice's sophisticated down-home cuisine includes spicy gourmet meatloaf with roasted garlic mash, and cappuccino bread pudding with white Russian chantilly cream.

El Siboney (☎ 305-296-4184; 900 Catherine St; mains $5-13; ⏰ 11am-9:30pm Mon-Sat) This out-of-the-way corner house has the best Cuban food in Key West. Credit cards are not accepted.

Fausto's Food Palace (☎ 305-296-5663; 2 locations at 522 Fleming St & 1105 White St; dishes $4-8) Opened in 1926 by Cuban grocer Faustino 'Fausto' Castillo, you'll find his grandson, Jimmy Weekley, behind the counter of one of these two providores…except on

Tuesdays when he's fulfilling his role as Key West's mayor. A favorite with yachties, stock up on preserves and dressings, or pick up picnic salads and platters to go.

DRINKING

The 'Duval Crawl' – hopping (or staggering) from one bar to the next – is all but unavoidable. Places worth a pint for posterity include **Captain Tony's Saloon** (☎ 305-294-1838; 428 Greene St), once owned by Hemingway's fishing mate, 'Sloppy' Joe Russell; and Joe's later digs when rent squeezed him out, **Sloppy Joe's Bar** (☎ 305-294-5717; 201 Duval St). Jimmy Buffett still owns his **Margaritaville Café** (☎ 305-292-1435; 500 Duval St), but a recent homecoming saw him perform instead at *the* local bar, the rowdy, rustic **Green Parrot** (☎ 305-294-6133; 601 Whitehead St). All have live music, and you'll find plenty more at places in between.

Head to **Schooner Wharf** (☎ 305-292-9520; 202 William St) for an early-morning Bloody Mary. It has three happy hours a day (8am to noon, 5pm to 7pm and 2am to 4am). Punters get on turtle races (Monday and Friday at 6pm) at **Turtle Kraals** (☎ 305-294-2640; Key West Seaport, Margaret St).

Among the more popular gay and lesbian hangouts are **Bourbon St Pub** (☎ 305-296-1992; 724 Duval St), **Aqua** (☎ 305-294-0555; 711 Duval St) and **La Te Da** (☎ 305-296-6706; 1125 Duval St), famous for its quality drag shows (around $20).

Dry Tortugas National Park

A tiny archipelago of seven islands about 70 miles west of Key West, the **Dry Tortugas** (www.nps.gov/drto) offers amazing snorkeling, diving, bird-watching and star-gazing.

Spanish explorer Ponce de León christened the area Tortugas (tor-*too*-guzz; 'the turtles') after the hawksbill, green, leatherback and loggerhead sea turtles found here. The islands' centerpiece, **Garden Key**, is the site of **Fort Jefferson**, an imposing but never-completed military fort that served as a Union prison during the Civil War. The unfortunate Dr Samuel Mudd, who unwittingly set John Wilkes Booth's leg after Booth assassinated President Lincoln, was incarcerated here.

Garden Key has 11 **campsites** (per person $3). Reserve early through the **Everglades National Park Office** (☎ 305-242-7700). There are toilets (locked between 10am and 3pm),

but – here's where the 'Dry' comes in – no freshwater showers or drinking water. Bring everything you'll need, including plenty of beverages to trade with Cuban-American fishing boats trolling the waters, in exchange for lobster, crab and shrimp. Just paddle right up, but avoid swimming at night when the fishing attracts plenty of sharks.

The fast ferry **Yankee Freedom II** (☎ 305-294-7009, 800-634-0939; www.yankeefleet.com) operates between Garden Key and the Key West Seaport (at the northern end of Margaret St). Round-trip fares are adult/child $129/89, or for an overnight drop-off $159/119. Continental breakfast, a picnic lunch, snorkeling gear and a 45-minute tour of the fort are all included. Crossings can be rough; bring seasickness tablets if necessary. **Seaplanes of Key West** (☎ 305-294-0709; www.seaplanesofkeywest.com) leave from the Key West International Airport and take 40 minutes each way. A four-hour trip costs $179/129 adult/child under 12, an eight-hour trip $305/225. They'll also fly you out to camp for $329/235 per person, including snorkeling equipment.

Getting There & Around

The easiest way to travel the Keys is by car, though traffic along the one major route, US Hwy 1, can be maddening during the winter high season. **Greyhound** (☎ 800-229-9424) buses serve all Key destinations along US Hwy 1, departing from downtown Miami (Map p501) and Key West; you can flag one down on the Overseas Highway. If you fly into Fort Lauderdale or Miami, the **Keys Shuttle** (☎ 888-765-9997) provides door-to-door service to most of the Keys from around $80 for two people. Reserve at least a day in advance. The very purple **Ambiance Sun** (☎ 877-246-4786; www.ambiancesun.com) buses have wi-fi, multi-channel entertainment, fleece blankets and full meals. Services from Miami to Marathon cost $44/59 one way/return, and $59/79 to Key West.

You can fly into Key West International Airport (EYW) with frequent flights from major cities, most going through Miami; or **Marathon Airport** (☎ 305-743-2155), which has less frequent, more expensive flights.

If you're headed for Florida's west coast, there's a twice-daily fast catamaran, the *Key West Express Ferry*, to Fort Myers (see p533).

Key West is best navigated on foot, especially in Old Town, or by moped, with rates from $15 per three hours. Try **Keys Moped & Scooter** (☎ 305-294-0399; 523 Truman Ave).

FORT LAUDERDALE

Heading north from Miami just 15 miles, the frenetic pace gives way to the wide, tree-lined boulevards, multimillion-dollar homes and luxury yachts sailing the Venetian waterways of Fort Lauderdale. It wasn't always so: bolstered by movies like 1960's *Where the Boys Are* and peaking with its '80s remake, Fort Lauderdale was spring break central. But the city tore up the invites when things got out of hand and the party's long-since over, though there's still plenty of nightlife. It's now a stylish, sophisticated city with some world-class art, café-lined riverside walkways and the world's second-busiest cruise port after Miami. Like the rest of south Florida, Fort Lauderdale is a major gay and lesbian destination. Head to the **visitor bureau** (☎ 954-765-4466, 800-227-8669; www.sunny.org; 1850 Eller Dr, Port Everglades; ☽ 8:30am-5pm Mon-Fri), which also has information for gay and lesbian travelers (www.sunny.org/rainbow).

The **Museum of Art** (☎ 954-525-5500; www.moafl.org; 1 E Las Olas Blvd; admission adult/child $6/3; ☽ 11am-5pm Fri-Wed, to 9pm Thu) is one of Florida's finest, with works by Pablo Picasso, Henri Matisse, Henry Moore, Salvador Dalí and Andy Warhol alongside collections of Cuban, African and South American art.

Fronted by the 52ft Great Gravity Clock, the environmentally oriented **Museum of Discovery & Science** (☎ 954-467-6637; www.mods.org; 401 SW 2nd St; adult/child/senior & student $14/12/13; ☽ 10am-5pm Mon-Sat, noon-6pm Sun) has exhibits on topics including rocket ships, electricity and the Everglades restoration efforts; admission includes a 3D Imax movie.

Olympic mementos are on display at the **International Swimming Hall of Fame** (☎ 954-462-6536; www.ishof.org; 1 Hall of Fame Dr/SE 5th St; adult/senior & student $3/1/5; ☽ 9am-7pm Mon-Fri, 9am-5pm Sat & Sun).

Kids can try all sorts of real-life jobs they 'wanna do' at **Wannado City** (☎ 954-838-7100; www.wannadocity.com; Purple Parrot Way, Sawgrass Mills Mall; over/under 14 $27.95/15.95), such as star in an action movie or investigate a crime scene, complete with costumes. Opening hours vary by season.

Skip the touristy water cruises for the best unofficial tour of the city, the **Water Bus** (☎ 954-467-6677; www.watertaxi.com; 651 Seabreeze Blvd; day pass $5), whose drivers offer a lively narration of the passing scenery.

You don't need a license to fish at **Anglin's Fishing Pier** (☎ 954-491-9403; Commercial Blvd; adult/child $4/2.75, walk-on $1; ☽ 24hr) which has a 24-hour bait and tackle shop, free parking and rod-and-reel rental for $5.

Sleeping

The area from Rio Mar St at the south to Vistamar St at the north, and from Hwy A1A at the east to Bayshore Dr, offers the highest concentration of accommodation in all price ranges.

Beach Hostel (☎ 954-567-7275; www.fortlauderdalehostel.com; 2115 N Ocean Blvd; dm $18, r $45-55; ☒ ▢) Wrapped around a central courtyard, this welcoming all-ages, 57-bed hostel has free wi-fi and a billiard table, right across the street from the beach. It's a requirement that guests hold an international passport.

A Little Inn by the Sea (☎ 954-772-2450; www.alittleinn.com; 4546 El Mar Dr; r $89-149, ste $139-219; P ☏) At the quietest stretch of the beach, Fort Lauderdale by the Sea, most of the bright, breezy rooms and apartments with tiled floors and wicker furniture face the palm-fringed ocean; with free bikes, tennis and wi-fi.

Riverside Hotel (☎ 954-467-0671, 800-325-3280; www.riversidehotel.com; 620 E Las Olas Blvd; r $99-200; P ☒ ☏) This Fort Lauderdale landmark in the center of downtown has 217 freshly spruced-up rooms and suites in its colonnaded 1936 historic hotel and adjoining executive tower, and retains an old-fashioned Main Street feel. There's also an oasis-like pool.

St Regis Resort & Spa (☎ 954-465-2300; 1 North Fort Lauderdale Beach Blvd; r from $250; P ☏) Fort Lauderdale's transformation from years past is evident in its top-end hotels, like the ultra-exclusive, five-star St Regis. Palatial rooms have both ocean and intracoastal views.

Gay and lesbian travelers have a plethora of gay-exclusive properties to choose from, among them the **Royal Palms Resort** (☎ 954-564-6444, 800-237-7256; www.royalpalms.com; 2901 Terramar St; r $169-319; P ☏), a stroll from the beach.

FLORIDA

Eating

Ireland's Inn Oceanside Bar & Restaurant (☎ 954-564-2331; 2220 N Atlantic Blvd; mains $7-15; ☼ 11:30am-9:30pm Mon-Sat, noon-9:30pm Sun) Sit out on the deck and watch the tankers and cruise ships queuing for port. Unpretentious fare ranges from bangers and mash to kosher hot dogs, mahimahi and red potato vinaigrette salads.

Mark's Las Olas (☎ 954-463-1000; 1032 E Las Olas Blvd; mains $30-40; ☼ 11:30am-2:30pm Mon-Fri, 6pm-10pm Sun-Thu, to 11pm Fri & Sat) On cosmopolitan Las Olas Blvd, watch the chefs work their wonderful magic in an open kitchen that turns out Caribbean-fusion specialties including crispy-skin yellowtail snapper and the legendary cracked conch with black bean–mango salsa, at what is one of Florida's most celebrated restaurants.

Sublime: World Vegetarian Cuisine (☎ 954-615-1431; 1431 N Federal Hwy; mains $10-17; ☼ 5:30-9pm Sun-Thu, to 10pm Fri & Sat) Internationally inspired vegan cuisine is a treat for vegans and the unconverted alike.

Blue Moon Fish Co (☎ 954-267-9888; 4405 Tradewinds Ave W; lunch mains $10-15, dinner mains $26-38; ☼ 11:30am-3pm daily, 6pm-10pm Sun-Thu, to 11pm Fri & Sat) The superb, eclectic menu – from peel-and-eat shrimp to rare-charred tuna – and flawless service found in this excellent restaurant are rivaled only by the dazzling views over the Intracoastal Waterway.

Lester's Diner (☎ 954-525-5641; 250 Hwy 84; dishes $6-15; ☼ 24hr) Since the 1960s Lester's has been Fort Lauderdale's favorite greasy spoon for high-powered business lunchers and late-night club-hopping loungers. Breakfast's available 24 hours (with whopping 14-ounce cups of coffee), and everything, including the rich desserts, is homemade.

Floridian (☎ 954-463-4041; 1410 E Las Olas Blvd; dishes $5-15; ☼ 24hr) This 1930s classic, famed for its huge omelettes, also serves good round-the-clock diner food and outstanding breakfasts.

Entertainment

Check the entertainment guide **City Link** (www.citylinkmagazine.com) for listings. Fort Lauderdale bars generally stay open until 4am on weekends and 2am during the week. Meander the **Riverwalk** (☎ 954-468-1541; www.goriverwalk.com) along the New River, where you'll find the **Las Olas Riverfront** (☎ 954-522-6556; SW 1st Ave at Las Olas Blvd), with stores, restaurants, a movie theater and entertainment. During the high winter season, 2nd St's periodically closed off for a giant street party with drinking permitted (it's otherwise banned on the streets) and great bands.

Valiantly flying the spring break flag, beloved dive **Elbo Room** (☎ 954-563-7889; 3339

BOP OVER TO THE BAHAMAS

Conch fritters, Bahamian villages and architecture, and postcard-perfect beaches are all prevalent in south Florida, but for added island flavor, take a sojourn to the islands themselves, traveling in style aboard a vintage Grumman G-73T Mallard seaplane from **Chalk's Ocean Airways** (☎ 800-424-2557, 305-371-8628; www.flychalks.com). Founded in 1919, Chalk's is the oldest scheduled airline in the world and offers several flights daily from Fort Lauderdale–Hollywood International Airport to Bimini (from $199 round-trip) and Nassau's Paradise Island (from $209 round-trip), skating in on the lustrous waters before you disembark near the beach.

If you're craving a taste of the high life, hit the casino at the glitzy **Atlantis Paradise Island** (☎ 242-363-3000; www.atlantis.com; r $285-2375; P ☒) on Nassau, with its lounges, bars, 11 pools and lagoon areas, and rooms as grand as your imagination and budget allow, all with balconies and stunning views. Be sure to stroll by the seafood shacks at Arawak Cay on Nassau's W Bay St for superb conch fritters before blissing out on the beach.

For a low-key getaway, head to Bimini and the gregarious bar at the Compleat Angler in Alice Town, one of Ernest Hemingway's haunts when he kept a home here and pursued marlin offshore. Try a beach- or marina-view room at **Bimini Sands Beach Club** (☎ 242-347-3500; www.biminisands.com; r from $150; ☒), with restaurants and bars on-site.

Mopeds (per day around $25) are ideal for cruising the islands.

The Bahamian dollar is 1:1 with the US dollar, and both are accepted interchangeably. As of 2006, all travelers require a passport to re-enter the US; check with the **Bahamian Consulate office** (☎ 305-373-6295) about documentation requirements.

N Federal Hwy) has been at the heart of the action since the 1930s. There's live jazz nightly at **O'Hara's Pub & Jazz Cafe** (☎ 954-524-1764; 722 E Las Olas Blvd). Enjoy great microbrews and diverse live music at the **Poor House** (☎ 954-522-5145; 110 SW 3rd Ave). Gay hotspots include **Hamburger Mary's** (☎ 954-567-1320; 2449 Wilton Dr).

Getting There & Away

The **Fort Lauderdale–Hollywood International Airport** (FLL; ☎ 954-359-1200; www.fll.net) is served by more than 35 airlines, some with non-stop flights from Europe; a taxi to downtown costs around $16.

The **Greyhound station** (☎ 954-764-6551; 515 NE 3rd St at Federal Hwy) is five blocks from Broward Central Terminal, with multiple daily services. The **train station** (☎ 954-587-6692; 200 SW 21st Tce) serves **Amtrak** (☎ 800-872-7245; www.amtrak.com) and the **Tri-Rail** (☎ 800-874-7245; www.tri-rail.com) service to Miami and Palm Beach.

The **TMAX** (☎ 954-761-3543; fares free) shuttles between downtown sights, the beach and E Las Olas Blvd and the Riverfront, and Tri-Rail and E Las Olas Blvd and the beaches, about every 15 minutes.

PALM BEACH & AROUND

About 20 miles north of Fort Lauderdale you'll find yourself surrounded by some of the priciest real estate in Florida, a legacy of Henry Flagler's railroad that served passengers seeking winter escapes.

Boca Raton

If Boca Raton seems vaguely familiar, it might be flashbacks to Jerry Seinfeld's fictional parents' retirement digs in 'Del Boca Vista.' Though Boca's by no means all retirees – it's also a technology hub – it is a largely residential stretch of picturesque coast, preserved from major development by benefactors with the foresight to save it from tourism overkill.

Definitely stop by the outstanding **Boca Raton Museum of Art** (☎ 561-392-2500; www.bocamuseum.org; 501 Plaza Real, Mizner Park; adult/child under 12 $8/free, special exhibitions higher; ☒ 10am-5pm Tue, Thu & Fri, to 9pm Wed, noon-5pm Sat & Sun), which has a permanent collection of works by Picasso, Matisse and Warhol, and more than 1200 photographic images. Next door is the ritzy outdoor shopping mall **Mizner Park** (www.miznerpark.org; cnr US 1 & Mizner Blvd), with loads

of restaurants and regular free concerts. The museum's at the north end of Mizner Park on US 1, on your right as you're heading north. Log onto www.bocaratonchamber.com for visitor information.

Palm Beach

Eight miles further north across a causeway is Palm Beach. An enclave of the ultra-wealthy, especially during its winter 'social season', most travelers just window-shop the oceanfront mansions (including Trump's Mar-a-Lago, on Southern Blvd at S Ocean Blvd) and boutiques lining the aptly named **Worth Avenue**. The historical **Whitehall Mansion** (cnr Cocoanut Row & Whitehall Way) was built by wealthy railroad baron Henry Flagler in 1901 and now houses the **Henry Morrison Flagler Museum** (☎ 561-655-2826; www.flaglermuseum.us; 1 Whitehall Way; adult/child $10/3; ☒ 10am-5pm Tue-Sat, noon-5pm Sun). Modeled after Rome's Villa Medici with twin belvedere arched towers, Flagler's opulent oceanfront 1861 hotel, **Breakers** (☎ 561-655-6611; www.thebreakers.com; 1 S County Rd; r from $289; ℗ ☒ ▣ ▨) has had money poured into it in recent years, keeping Flagler's grand vision alive and well. On 140 acres, it encompasses two championship golf courses plus an academy, 10 tennis courts, a three-pool Mediterranean beach club and a trove of restaurants.

West Palm Beach

Just across the waterway, back on the mainland, is the younger, livelier and much more accessible West Palm Beach. Drop by the **visitor bureau** (☎ 561-471-3995, 800-833-5733; www.palmbeachfl.com; 1555 Palm Beach Lakes Blvd; ☒ 9am-5pm Mon-Fri) to pick up information and maps for the entire county.

Much of West Palm's action's centered on **CityPlace** (www.cityplace.com; 700 S Rosemary Ave), a European village–style alfresco mall with splashing fountains and a slew of dining and entertainment options. It is close to the well-regarded **Norton Museum of Art** (☎ 561-832-5196; 1451 South Olive Ave; admission adult/child/age 13-21 $8/free/3; ☒ 10am-5pm Mon-Sat, 1-5pm Sun Oct-May, closed Mon May-Oct), housing American and European modern masters and impressionists, Chinese jade carvings and Buddhist statues. Gaze up at the sky from your comfortable high-back chairs at the Buzz Aldrin Planetarium at the **South Florida Science Museum** (☎ 561-832-1988; 4801 Dreher Trail N; adult/child $7/5; planetarium extra $2; ☺ 10am-5pm Mon-Fri, to 6pm Sat, noon-6pm Sun), and catch some rays at **Mid-Town Beach** (400 S Ocean Blvd) and **Phipps Ocean Park Beach** (2145 S Ocean Blvd).

A sleek retro-funky boutique hotel that would be right at home on Miami's SoBe, the **Hotel Biba** (☎ 561-832-0094; www.hotelbiba .com; 320 Belvedere Rd; r $89-279; ⓟ ⓛ ⓡ) has 43 designer rooms, terrazzo flooring, Japanese gardens and a chic wine bar. **Clematis Street** also has several worthy bars and restaurants to recommend it. For excellent microbrews and snazzy Italian-American bistro fare like vodka-dashed marinara pasta with prosciutto, head to **Brewzzi** (☎ 561-366-9753; CityPlace; mains $10-20; ☺ lunch & dinner). Brewzzi's other brewery/restaurant can be found in upmarket **Boca Raton** (☎ 561-392-2739; 2222 Glades Rd; mains $10-20; ☺ lunch & dinner), where you can indulge in a little Tropical Madness: Boca blonde lager with seasonal smatterings of apricot, blueberry, peach or raspberry.

The downtown **Tri-Rail station** (☎ 800-874-7245; 201 S Tamarind Ave), which also serves as the **Amtrak station** (☎ 561-832-6169), is near Okeechobee Blvd. **PalmTran** (☎ 561-841-4200) provides local buses (fare/day pass $1.25/3).

Admirably servicing its migration of snowbirds, **Palm Beach International Airport** (☎ 561-471-7420; www.pbia.org), 2.5 miles west of downtown West Palm Beach, can be a good alternative gateway to the south Florida region.

EAST COAST

From the affluent and ultra-developed shores of south Florida, the east coast unfolds at a much slower pace – mostly. The Space Coast's beaches are the closest to Orlando, and surfers flock to their waves. Speed rules at Daytona Beach. The nation's oldest continuous European settlement, St Augustine, sees plenty of people stroll its ancient streets. Jacksonville is a sports mecca. Amelia Island's charms are alluring. And in and around are pockets of parks and blissful beaches you might have all to yourself.

SPACE COAST

Dubbed the Space Coast for its high-profile resident, NASA, the Melbourne–Cocoa Beach–Titusville area has plenty of surrounding space: a buffer of natural wilderness and gorgeous beaches, mostly protected national parkland, with birding, canoeing and kayaking, as well as splendid camping. Once the fictional home of NASA astronaut Major Nelson and his genie in the iconic 1960s TV series *I Dream of Jeannie*, the Space Coast is also a magnet for surfers with Florida's best waves.

The highlight for techies and non-techies alike is the Kennedy Space Center (KSC), the only spot in the US from which humans have been hurled into space. NASA's *Columbia* disaster in February 2003 – in which all seven of the crewmembers died when a

---

FLORIDA HIGHWAYMEN

Back in the 1950s and '60s, a group of African American artists earned their living by painting upwards of 200,000 colorful, tropical landscapes of Florida's sunsets, waterways, marshes and inlets, often using wood or masonite as a canvas, which they sold from car trunks along the roadside. White artist AE Bean Backus taught the best known of the group, Alfred Hair, but his mentorship would influence all 26 artists (including one woman) now known as the Florida Highwaymen. They are credited with giving rise to Florida's contemporary art movement, and in 2005 were inducted into the Florida Artists Hall of Fame alongside creators such as Ray Charles, Zora Neale Hurston, Tennessee Williams and Ernest Hemingway.

You can check out the Highwaymen's work – and Backus' – at the **AE Backus Gallery & Museum** (☎ 772-465-0630; www.backusgallery.com; 500 North Indian River Dr, Fort Pierce; admission free; ☺ 10am-4pm Tue-Sat, noon-4pm Sun winter, by appointment summer) in Fort Pierce, about 60 miles north of Palm Beach; it adjoins his original studio. Some members of the original Highwaymen such as James Gibson continue to paint today.

Though the early paintings sold for as little as $20, today they're worth thousands of dollars, and because they were originally bought without any fanfare, many lie in dusty garages and basements – if you see any yard sales on your travels, it might just be worth stopping by.

SURF'S UP IN THE SUNSHINE STATE

Florida has some decent surf in concentrated areas. Around Miami/Fort Lauderdale tends to stay flat, blocked by the Bahamas offshore, and much of the Gulf coast and around the Big Bend is too protected to get much of a swell, but you'll find good waves – not Hawaii-good, but definitely surfable – along the mid- to north Atlantic coast, and west of St George Island in the Panhandle through to Pensacola. For webcams, forecasts and info on the best spots in the state (and the country), check out www.surfline.com.

Surf

Cocoa Beach South of Cape Canaveral, the area around the 800ft Cocoa Beach pier gets packed with space tourists and the surf crowd, but it's a good area to find a surf school. The waves are most consistent at both high and low tide.

Sebastian Inlet South of Melbourne, the inlet is one of the most consistent – and robust – breaks in the state, but is tide sensitive, so head there at low tide.

New Smyrna Beach South of Daytona, offshore rock ledges counteract the treacherous under-currents common to the east coast. It's also extremely consistent at low tide, but can get very crowded not only with humans, but also with sharks – it's nicknamed the shark-bite capital of Florida (and Florida is the shark-bite capital of the world – see p527).

A St, St Augustine Beach Some mighty fine waves when they're working. For the lowdown on local surf conditions, and to rent a board or to sink into the comfy couch in the screening room for a free surf film to inspire you, make a stop at **Pit Surfshop** (☎ 904-471-4700; www.pitsurfshop.com; 18 A St, St Augustine; board rental per day $16; ☯ 9am-7pm Sun-Fri, to 8pm Sat winter, to 8pm daily summer).

Learn

The best surf school in Cocoa Beach for all ages and levels is the state's largest, **Cocoa Beach Surf School** (☎ 321-868-1980; www.cocoabeachsurfingschool.com; 3901 North Atlantic Ave; semiprivate/private lessons per hr $40/50) run by ex-pro surfer and Kelly Slater coach, Craig Carroll. Craig also teaches indoors at Walt Disney World's Typhoon Lagoon wave pool – 2½-hour group lessons held early-morning before the park opens cost $135. Book directly with **Walt Disney World** (☎ 407-939-7529).

Shopping & More

Actually an emporium and entertainment complex to boot, Cocoa Beach's **Ron Jon Surf Shop** (☎ 321-799-8888; www.ronjons.com; 4151 N Atlantic Ave, Cocoa Beach; ☯ 24hr) has live music (Beach Boys covers and the like), classic cars and every conceivable surfing accessory. Waiting for the perfect wave may soon be a thing of the past: Ron Jon is also getting onboard the trend of bringing surf to the people, with a new domed indoor surf park with a retractable roof at International Dr in Orlando due to be opening around or by the time you're reading this – check with the shop or www.surfparks.com for updates. To immerse yourself in Cocoa Beach's surf culture, Ron Jon also has a resort (p526).

foam tile on the external tank came loose upon re-entry and damaged the wing – saw it grounded for more than two years until an investigation was carried out and recommendations implemented. The shuttles' return to flight commenced with the *Discovery*'s launch in mid-2005, following numerous procedural changes such as astronauts producing repair kits in-flight.

Visitor information is available through **Florida's Space Coast Office of Tourism** (☎ 800-872-1969; www.space-coast.com; 8810 Astronaut Blvd, No 102).

Sights & Activities

KENNEDY SPACE CENTER

Allow yourself at least two hours – ideally an entire day – for the excellent **Kennedy Space Center Visitor Complex** (☎ 321-449-4444; www.kennedyspacecenter.com; maximum access pass adult/child 3-11 $37/27; ☯ from 9am, closing times vary btwn 5:30 & 7:30pm). The standard admission (adult/child $30/20) doesn't include the Astronaut Hall of Fame, which holds the motion simulator rides, so it's worth paying extra for the full pass (the Hall of Fame opens and closes an

FLORIDA

hour later than the rest of the exhibits, so plan that as your last stop). Tours are included with admission. Buses depart every 15 minutes, shuttling you between the LC 39 Observation Gantry (with views of the launch pads and mammoth Vehicle Assembly Building), Apollo/Saturn V Center (a tribute to the Apollo missions with exhibits such as Jim Lovell's unused Apollo 13 space suit), the International Space Station Center, Space Shuttle Launch Pads 39A and 39B, and the Launch Control Center. You're free to spend as much time as you like at each before boarding the next bus. Passes also include 45-minute Imax films and live-action stage shows, exhibits on subjects like early space exploration, and encounters with astronauts. Audio guides ($6) are available in six languages.

Real space junkies can pay $22 (child $16) in addition to standard or maximum access admission for fully guided special interest tours lasting two to three hours that take you further behind the scenes. The best is the NASA Up Close tour, where you'll walk through a mocked-up space station before viewing an actual station module undergoing its final preparations. There are several tours a day, but reserve ahead as they sell out. If your fascination with space knows no bounds, take a full-day 'train like an astronaut' program, on multi-axis trainers and 1/6-gravity chairs ($225).

Kennedy Space Center is the place to watch a shuttle or uncrewed rocket liftoff. Tickets for launch viewing ($15 plus maximum access pass) go on sale a month prior to launch and sell out fast. Depending on the mission, you'll either watch from KSC or be bussed to a viewing spot 6 miles away. Check www.nasa.gov/missions/highlights/schedule.html for continuously updated launch schedules.

Viewing's also good from the Visitor Complex, or head to the popular **Jetty Park Campgrounds** (☎ 321-783-7111; 400 Jetty Park Dr, Cape Canaveral; per car $5), or Cherie Down Park, Rotary Riverfront Park or Brewer Parkway bridge in Titusville. BYO beer and binoculars. Be prepared for invariable launch delays – and heavy traffic after it's over.

MERRITT ISLAND NATIONAL WILDLIFE REFUGE

More endangered and threatened species inhabit the swamps, marshes and hardwood hammocks of this **refuge** (☎ 321-861-0667; SR Hwy 402, Titusville; admission free; visitor center closed Sun Apr-Oct, refuge closed 2 days prior to shuttle launches) than any other in the continental USA. Right on the migration path between North and South America, it's also one of the country's best birding spots, especially early morning and after 4pm October to May.

You can take kayak tours to the refuge from around $30 for a half-day trip single-kayak/tandem with several outfitters including **Village Outfitters** (☎ 321-633-7245; www.villageoutfitters.com; 113 Brevard Ave, Cocoa; single/tandem kayak rental $25/40).

CANAVERAL NATIONAL SEASHORE & COCOA BEACH

These 25 miles of windswept and mainly pristine beach are favored by surfers (at the south end), families (at the north end) and campers and nature lovers (on Klondike Beach, in the center). The seashore has a **ranger station** (☎ 321-867-4077; per car $5) at the south end, near Playalinda Beach at the end of Hwy 406/402, and a **visitor center** (☎ 904-428-3384) at the north end at Apollo Beach, on Hwy A1A east of New Smyrna Beach.

Sleeping & Eating

Rates skyrocket during space launches.

Fawlty Towers Motel (☎ 321-784-3870; www.fawltytowersresort.com; 100 E Cocoa Beach Causeway; r $49-195; P) Crowned by jade green turrets, this gloriously garish, extremely pink hotel actually has very tasteful rooms and an unbeatable beachside location.

Ron Jon Resort Cape Caribe (☎ 888-933-3030; www.ronjonresort.com; 1000 Shorewood Dr, Cape Canaveral; r $120-190; P) Packed with amenities like a free movie theater and a solid activities program, this beachfront place is great for families. Rooms have a fresh Santa Fe–meets-the-sea feel.

Courtyard Marriott Cocoa Beach (☎ 321-784-4800; www.courtyardcocoabeach.com; 3435 N Atlantic Ave, Cocoa Beach; $130-169; P) Cocoa Beach's top hotel has generous rooms, many with balconies and ocean views, as well as a sweeping oceanfront pool deck.

Canaveral National Seashore (☎ 386-428-3384; www.nps.gov/cana; 7611 S Atlantic Ave, New Smyrna Beach; 9am-4:30pm) Backcountry beach and island camping's available at designated sites on the Canaveral National Seashore. Permits cost $10 and are good for up to six people.

Reservations are essential; bring everything you need including drinking water.

Dixie Crossroads (☎ 321-268-5000; 1475 Garden St, Titusville; mains $6-33; ☺ 11am-9pm) This is a riot of murals and sculptures, fishponds and fountains. All the seafood here's good, especially the locally caught rock shrimp (there are ribs and steaks too).

Coconuts on the Beach (☎ 321-784-1422; 2 Minutemen Causeway, Cocoa Beach; mains $8-22; ☺ 11am-2am Mon-Fri, 6:30am-2am Sat & Sun) Coconuts has regular live music and, every Saturday during spring, a bikini contest at the outdoor bar; head indoors if you're seeking a family atmosphere. Menu classics include coconut-crusted shrimp and coconut-crusted mahi, topped with pineapple–orange sauce.

Café Margaux (☎ 321-639-8343; 220 Brevard Ave, Cocoa; mains $19-30; ☺ lunch & dinner, closed Tue & Sun) Across the Indian River from Merritt Island in historic Cocoa village, burgundy umbrellas shelter pretty courtyard tables at this French-inspired place.

Getting There & Away

Driving from the south, follow Hwy A1A; from Orlando take Hwy 528 east, which connects with Hwy A1A. Greyhound has services from West Palm Beach and Orlando to Titusville.

DAYTONA BEACH

Daytona Beach is synonymous with super-charged speed. In 1902, playboy drivers Ransom Olds (of Oldsmobile fame) and Alexander Winston raced along the unusually hard-packed sands; and for over 30 years,

records were made and smashed. Stock-car racing came into vogue during the late 1930s, and in 1947, Nascar was born here and racing relocated from the beach to the Daytona International Speedway.

Daytona Beach likes a party: it hosts one of the last spring breaks on the Atlantic Coast (though much tamer than at its peak), the place explodes during Speed Weeks (first two weeks of February) and bikers roar into town for Bike Week (early March), among numerous other events. But it's also home to a gentrified downtown and cultural attractions, as well as nesting sea turtles from May to October.

Somehow, the sight of the race track and souped-up autos everywhere does make you feel like putting your foot to the floor. Police know this, and quickly curtail your need for speed.

The **Daytona Beach Convention & Visitors Bureau** (☎ 386-255-0415, 800-544-0415; www.daytona beach.com; 126 E Orange Ave; ☺ 9am-5pm Mon-Fri) has a **visitor center** (☎ 386-253-8669; 1801 W International Speedway Blvd; ☺ 8.30am-7pm) in the lobby of Daytona USA. Information for gay and lesbian travelers is available at www.gay daytona.com.

Sights & Activities

Drive sections of the former race track **Daytona Beach** (☎ 386-239-7873) in daylight hours, tide permitting, to a strictly enforced top speed of 10mph. Beach driving costs $5, $3 after 3pm between February and November; it's free during December and January. Despite some residual post-2004 hurricane

---

SHARKS & SPARKS

A couple of dubious Florida distinctions: the state ranks number one in the world for shark attacks and death-by-lightning. Of the 807 shark attacks worldwide between 1990 and 2004, 322 were in Florida, mostly on the Atlantic coast in the Daytona Beach–Cocoa Beach region. The 3ft to 4ft sharks here, mainly spinner and sandbar sharks, feed on finger mullet, hence bites to hands and feet do happen. The sharks generally don't continue to attack once they've realized their mistake, though three of the attacks resulted in fatalities. Florida beach patrols issue warnings when sharks are spotted near beaches, so heed them, and, obviously, get out of the water if you see any about. According to the Florida Museum of Natural History at the University of Florida, other ways to avoid attacks include staying in groups, removing jewelry (it resembles fish scales), not swimming at dusk and at night, or near schools of small baitfish, and getting out or staying out of the water if you're bleeding (including menstruation), as their sense of smell is formidable.

Lightning is actually much deadlier. Florida averages about 10 lightning deaths a year, mainly in central Florida during the summer months. Head for cover well in advance of thunderstorms and make sure to stay clear of water, beaches, open high ground and isolated large trees.

damage, the architecture and neon along the Atlantic Ave strip remain a living museum of 1950s pop culture, best seen from the aerial cable car along the **pier** at the end of Main St.

The Holy Grail of raceways is the **Daytona International Speedway** (☎ 386-947-6782, box office 386-253-7223; www.daytonaintlspeedway.com; 1801 W International Speedway Blvd; tickets from $15). Events ticket prices accelerate sharply for the big races headlined by the **Daytona 500** in February, but if nothing's on, you can wander into the grandstands for free. Adjoining the speedway, **Daytona USA** (☎ 386-947-6800; www.daytonausa.com; adult/child $21.50/15.50; 🕓 9am-7pm, longer during peak times) is a superbly flashy shrine to the sport, including motion simulators of 360-degree flips. The best bang for your buck is a 30-minute tour ($7.50) of the racetrack and pits.

The **Museum of Arts & Sciences** (☎ 386-255-0285; www.moas.org; 1040 Museum Blvd; adult/student $8/4; 🕓 9am-4pm Tue-Fri, noon-5pm Sat & Sun) has an outstanding museum of Cuban art, and an iconic collection of Coca-Cola relics. About 5 miles south of Daytona Beach, climb the 203 steps to the top of Florida's tallest **lighthouse** (☎ 386-761-1821; 4931 S Peninsula Dr; adult/child $5/1.50; 🕓 10am-5pm winter, to 7pm summer). In this auto-obsessed town, you don't even have to leave your vehicle for church at the **Little Chapel by the Sea** (S Atlantic Ave; 🕓 8:30am & 10am Sun), a former drive-in movie theater (attach a speaker to your car to hear the sermon) with free coffee and doughnuts.

Sleeping

Rebuilding in the aftermath of the 2004 hurricanes should be more or less complete by the time you're reading this but many hotels are making way for condos. Prices soar during events, when you'll need to book well ahead. More options are at www.daytonalodging.com.

Streamline Hotel (☎ 386-258-6937; 140 S Atlantic Ave; r from $40) The cheapest place in town, the grand deco building where Nascar was born has been given a spruce-up but it's still fairly tattered, which is part of its charm.

Bahama House (☎ 386-248-2001; www.daytonabahamahouse.com; 2441 S Atlantic Ave; r $99-325; P 🏊) This lemon-yellow place has ultra-spacious, sophisticated Caribbean-themed rooms with private balconies and ocean views, and a free cocktail hour.

La Quinta Inn & Suites (☎ 386-944-0060; daytonabeachlaquintainnsuites.com; 816 N Atlantic Ave; r $79-150; P 🏊) Done up like a kitschy sultan's palace, this vision of fake terracotta and sculpted white columns has an atrium-style lobby and fitness room. Yummy waffles for breakfast.

Coquina Inn B&B (☎ 386-254-4969; www.coquinainndaytonabeach.com; 544 S Palmetto Ave; r $60-110; P ⊠) In an elevated two-story building, personal touches include made-to-order breakfast, fresh flowers in your room (some have fireplaces) and a Jacuzzi. Bicycles are available.

Eating & Drinking

Starlight Diner (☎ 386-255-9555; 401 N Atlantic Ave; dishes $4-12; 🕓 7am-midnight Mon-Thu, to 1am Fri & Sat, to 10pm Sun) Like something straight out of *Happy Days,* this gleaming chrome diner has Formica tables, a great jukebox, huge burgers and real malts.

Aunt Catfish's on the River (☎ 386-767-4768; 4009 Halifax Dr; mains $8-18; 🕓 11:30am-9pm or so) Huge portions of fried, grilled and Cajun-style catfish are the best value in town.

Song Mongolian Grill (☎ 386-253-1133; 132 N Beach St; mains $17.75; 🕓 dinner) For an all-you-can-eat fixed price, chefs stir up infinite combinations of vegetables, spices and oils of your choosing on sizzling flattop grills.

Billy's Tap Room & Grill (☎ 386-672-1910; 58 E Granada Blvd, Ormond Beach; mains $15-25; 🕓 lunch & dinner Mon-Sat) Dating back to 1922, this Bavarian-style inn has a solid maple bar and historic photographs of wealthy visitors from bygone eras. House specialties include grouper prepared any way and crabcakes.

Entertainment

Daytona's diverse entertainment scene includes cultural performances and biker bars with live music, mostly along Main St, and high-octane dance clubs on or near Seabreeze Blvd, with some good kitschy retro places too. **Fuel Night Club** (☎ 386-248-3151; 640 N Grandview Ave; 🕓 9pm-3am Wed-Sun) is the newest, sizzling-hot party complex with DJs spinning trance, house, rock, breaks, hip-hop and R&B with some live music thrown in.

Fifties to '80s music will have you doing the time warp again at the **Stock Exchange** (☎ 386-255-6476; 125 Basin St, Suite 102; 🕓 11:30am-2:30am). The rooftop **Penthouse Lounge** (☎ 386-258-6937; 140 S Atlantic Ave; 🕓 11am-3am) at the Streamline Hotel attracts an older gay crowd.

Getting There & Around

Daytona Beach International Airport (☎ 386-248-8030; flydaytonafirst.com) is just east of the Speedway. The **Greyhound bus station** (☎ 386-255-7076, 800-231-2222; 138 S Ridgewood Ave) has multiple services to Miami.

Daytona is close to the intersection of two of Florida's major interstates. I-95 is the quickest way to Jacksonville (about 70 miles) and Miami (200 miles), though Hwy A1A and US Hwy 1 are more scenic. Beville Rd, an east–west thoroughfare south of Daytona proper, becomes I-4 after crossing I-95; it's the fastest route to Orlando (one hour).

Votran (☎ 386-756-7496; www.votran.com) runs buses and trolleys throughout the city (adult/child $1/50¢).

ST AUGUSTINE

The oldest continuous European settlement in the USA, St Augustine was founded by the Spanish in 1565. Tourists flock here to stroll the ancient streets, lunch at cute cafés, shop at craft stalls and muse over literally dozens of museums, followed by snug dinners at lamp-lit restaurants and brews at quaint pubs. Through the 144-block National Historic Landmark District, horse-drawn carriages (around $85 for a 2½-hour private carriage ride) clip-clop past townsfolk dressed in period costume.

It could all add up to a theme park–style experience at best – traveler hell at worst – but St Augustine retains infinite charm and an integrity that eclipses any tourist trappings. These 400-plus-year-old buildings, monuments and narrow laneways are as real as those on the other side of the Atlantic, and many staff who aren't required to dress period-style for work do so anyway, contributing to the town's character.

Timucuan Indians had been settled in what is now St Augustine since about 1000 BC. Spanish explorer Juan Ponce de León first sighted land in April 1513, coming ashore to find the fountain of youth that had spurred his journey. His compatriot Don Pedro Menendez de Avilés arrived in 1565 and by the time Spain ceded Florida to the US in 1821, the city had been sacked, looted, burned and occupied by pirates and Spanish, British, Georgian and South Carolinian forces. The main **visitor center** (☎ 904-825-1000, 800-653-2489; www.visitoldcity.com; 10 Castillo Dr; ⊗ 8:30am-5:30pm) screens a 45-minute film (single/family $1/3) of archival footage of the town's history.

Sights & Activities

A re-creation of Spanish-colonial St Augustine in the year 1740, the **Spanish Quarter Living History Museum** (☎ 904-825-6830; enter via 53 St George St; adult/student $7/4.50; ⊗ 9am-5:30pm Mon-Sat) has craftspeople using 18th-century technology operating recreated 'storefronts': a blacksmith, a cooper, a leather worker and so on. Keep an eye on young children, as the tools can be hot and/or sharp.

Henry Flagler's luxury Hotel Alcazar (1888) is home to the **Lightner Museum** (☎ 904-824-2874; 75 King St; adult/child $8/2; ⊗ 9am-5pm), with wonderfully bizarre collections of everything from matchbox labels to buttons and salt shakers, and antique musical instruments played at 11am and 2pm daily.

Claiming continuous occupancy from the early 17th century, the **Gonzalez-Alvarez House** (☎ 904-824-2872; www.oldesthouse.com; 14 St Francis St; adult/student $7/4; ⊗ 9am-5pm) is the oldest in the USA. The **Oldest Wooden School House** (☎ 904-824-0192, 800-653-7245; 14 St George St; adult/child $3/2; ⊗ 9am-5pm) is peopled by animatronic teachers and students.

Built by the Spanish between 1672 and 1695, the country's oldest masonry fort, **Castillo de San Marcos National Monument** (☎ 904-829-6506; btwn San Marcos Ave & Matanzas River; adult/child under 15 $6/free; ⊗ 8:45am-4:45pm, grounds closed midnight-5am) has a medieval ambience and booming cannons.

Drink a plastic cupful of the legendary sulfur water from *the* **Fountain of Youth** (☎ 904-829-3168, 800-356-8222; 11 Magnolia Ave; adult/student or child/senior $5.75/2.75/4.75; ⊗ 9am-6pm) that spurred Spanish explorer Juan Ponce de León's journey here.

One of the city's most distinctive features, the **Bridge of Lions** was built in 1926 to connect the city with St Augustine Beach, 5 miles away. Locals escape the tourist hordes at **Anastasia State Recreation Area** (☎ 904-461-2033; 1340 Hwy A1A; car/pedestrian $5/1, campsites $25) with a terrific beach, a campground and rentals for all kinds of watersports.

Discover the town's spirited past with **Ghost Tours of St Augustine** (☎ 904-461-1009; www.ghosttoursofstaugustine.com; walking tours $10; ⊗ tours 8pm daily & 9:30pm Fri & Sat winter, 8pm & 9:30pm daily summer).

FLORIDA

Sleeping

There are more than two dozen atmospheric B&Bs. St Augustine is a popular weekend escape for Florida residents; expect room rates to rise about 30% on Friday and Saturday and sometimes a minimum two-night stay. Summer rates tend to be higher than winter.

BUDGET

Inexpensive motels and chain hotels line San Marco Ave, near where it meets US Hwy 1.

Pirate Haus (☎ 904-808-1999; www.piratehaus.com; 32 Treasury St; dm $18, r $40-80; ✕ ▣) This very family-friendly European-style guesthouse/hostel has an unbeatable downtown location and a free all-you-can-eat 'pirate pancake' breakfast.

MIDRANGE

St George Inn (☎ 904-827-5740; www.stgeorge-inn .com; 4 St George Ln; r $89-169; ℗ ✕) In the palm-shaded old city gate plaza courtyard, some of the 22 rooms at this boutique hotel have dramatic views of the fort.

Edgewater Inn (☎ 904-825-2697; www.stayatedge water.com; 2 St Augustine Blvd; r Sun-Thu $95, Fri & Sat $105; ℗ ✕ ▣) At the eastern terminus of the Bridge of Lions, this waterfront inn has the nicest view in town.

St Francis Inn (☎ 904-824-6068, 800-824-6062; www .stfrancisinn.com; 18 Cordova St; r $119-239; ℗ ✕ ▣) Pets – and children – are welcome at this inn, which has been in continuous operation since 1791; has toasty open fireplaces, free wi-fi, wheelchair access and an epicentral location.

Cedar House Inn (☎ 904-829-0079, 800-233-2746; www.cedarhouseinn.com; 79 Cedar St; r $149-249; ℗ ✕ ▣) A lamp-lit Victorian inn with six distinctively themed rooms.

TOP END

Casa Monica (☎ 904-827-1888, 800-648-1888; www.casa monica.com; 95 Cordova St; r $179-779; ℗ ✕ ▣ ▣) Through the grand carriage entrance of this colossal turreted 1888 landmark are a spectacular lobby, expansive swimming pool, fountains, gourmet restaurants and art galleries, as well as magnificently appointed suites. Parking costs $16.

La Fiesta Oceanside Inn (☎ 904-471-2220; www .lafiestainn.com; 810 Beach Blvd/Hwy A1A; r $100-290; ℗ ✕ ▣) Just steps from the sand along a private boardwalk, these elegant rooms

and split-level suites all have private balconies or patios.

Eating

Eateries in St Augustine are surprisingly inexpensive. Note that restaurants often close a bit earlier or later than the hours listed.

Spanish Bakery (☎ 904-471-3046; 47½ St George St; dishes $1-3; ☽ 9:30am-3pm) Set back from St George Street in a picnic-table-strewn courtyard (look up and you'll spot the wooden pointer sign), this historic stone kitchen bakes empanadas and smoked-sausage rolls, as well as pillow-soft bread.

Local Heroes (☎ 904-825-0060; 11 Spanish St; dishes $2.50-6.25; ☽ 8:30am-5pm) Off the tourist drag in a cute little butter-yellow 1820s cottage, come by for the phenomenal breakfast burritos and oven-baked heroes.

Pizzalley's on St George (☎ 904-825-2627; 117 St George St; slices $2.50-4, pies $10.50-16; ☽ 11am-8pm Sun-Thu, to 9pm Fri & Sat) Feast on fab Italian fare in the elongated dining room, hidden covered courtyard or tiled rooftop terrace.

Santa Maria Restaurant (☎ 904-829-6578; 135 Av Menendez; mains $10-28; ☽ noon-9pm Thu-Tue, 5-9pm Wed) Right out over the water at the end of a wooden pier, hungry catfish wait for diners to open the trapdoor in the windowsill and drop bread crumbs (bowls are brought to your table with your meal).

Gypsy Cab Co (☎ 904-824-8244; 828 Anastasia Blvd; mains $15.25-21; ☽ 4:30-11pm daily, lunch 11am-3pm Sat, brunch 10:30am-3pm Sun) An excellent, unclassifiable menu, with influences from French to Floribbean.

Drinking & Entertainment

Flickering candles provide the only light at the 1736 stone **Taberna del Gallo** (☎ 904-825-6830; 53 St George St; ☽ 7.30-11pm Thu-Sun); on Friday and Saturday nights the Bilge Rats sing old sea shanties. Be transported back to the '20s at **Stogies Jazz Club & Listening Room** (☎ 904-826-4008; www.stogiesjazz.com; 36 Charlotte St; ☽ 4pm-1am Mon-Fri, 2pm-1am Sat & Sun). The cozy **St George Tavern** (☎ 904-824-4204; 116 St George St; ☽ 11am-1am) is packed with period-dressed locals, especially on Tuesdays from 8pm when all drinks are half-price.

Getting There & Around

The **Greyhound bus station** (☎ 904-829-6401; 100 Malaga St) is one block north of King St, east of the bridge over the San Sebastian River.

Two companies provide convenient jump-on, jump-off 20-stop tours on open-air trams: **Old Town Trolley Tours** (☎ 904-829-3800; www.trolleytours.com; 167 San Marco Ave; 3-day ticket adult/child $18/9) and **St Augustine Sightseeing Trains** (☎ 904-829-6545; www.redtrains.com; 170 San Marco Ave; adult/child $18/5).

JACKSONVILLE

Football has long been an integral part of Jacksonville's culture but it wasn't until 1993 that it was awarded its own professional football franchise, the Jaguars. In 2005, Jacksonville became one of only a dozen American cities to host the Super Bowl, all but completing its transformation from working city to tourist destination in its own right. At a whopping 840 sq miles, Jacksonville is the largest city by area in the continental US (eclipsed only by Anchorage, AK, as the nation's largest), sprawling along three meandering rivers, including the St Johns River, the only river in the world besides the Nile that flows south to north.

Information's available at two locations:
Jacksonville Landing (☎ 904-353-1188; 2 Independent Dr; ☼ 10am-7pm Mon-Sat, noon-5:30pm Sun)
Beaches Visitor Center (☎ 904-242-0024; 403 Beach Blvd; ☼ 10am-6pm Mon-Sat)

Sights & Activities

Along the 1.2-mile **Southbank Riverwalk** is the **Museum of Science and History** (☎ 904-396-6674; www.themosh.org; 1025 Museum Circle; adult/child/senior $7/5/5.50; ☼ 10am-5pm Mon-Fri, to 6pm Sat, 1-6pm Sun), where you can view enlightening exhibits on Jacksonville's pre-Columbian history and European settlements. Spend an idyllic afternoon viewing European art at the **Cummer Museum of Art & Gardens** (☎ 904-356-6857; www.cummer.org; 829 Riverside Ave; adult/student $6/3, 4-9pm Tue free; ☼ 10am-9pm Tue & Thu, to 5pm Wed, Fri & Sat, noon-5pm Sun). Enjoy a free tour (and if you're over 21, free beer) at the **Budweiser brewery** (☎ 904-696-8373; www.budweisertours.com; 111 Busch Dr; admission free; ☼ 10am-4pm Mon-Sat). And if you've ever wondered how theme-park rides like Universal Studios' 'ET Adventure' weave their robotic magic, a tour of **Sally Corporation** (☎ 904-355-7100; 745 W Forsyth St, cnr N Jefferson St; admission free; ☼ tours 9am-1pm Tue & Thu by reservation), makers of animatronics and 'dark ride' characters, will demystify the process.

The Jacksonville area beaches ('Jax Beaches') are about 17 miles east of the city center; Jacksonville Beach is where you'll find most of the action. Further north towards Amelia Island there's pristine shoreline at **Little Talbot Island State Park** (☎ 904-251-2320; 12157 Heckscher Dr; pedestrian/car $1/4; ☼ 8am-dusk) and **Big Talbot Island State Park** (☎ 904-251-2320; pedestrian/car $1/2; ☼ 8am-dusk) with enormous live oak skeleton driftwood littering the white sands.

Sleeping & Eating

The cheapest rooms are along I-95 and I-10, where the lower-priced chains congregate. Beach lodging rates often rise in summer.

Inn at Oak Street (☎ 904-379-5525; www.innatoakstreet.com; 2114 Oak St; r $100-165; P ☒ ☐) Bold colors and high-tech amenities including free wi-fi and DVD players and flat screen TVs in all rooms put a contemporary twist on this B&B of the future.

Omni Jacksonville Hotel (☎ 904-355-6664, 800-843-6664; 245 Water St; r $89-199; P ☎) In the heart of downtown, this 354-room hotel has lavish, amenity-laden rooms (some wheelchair accessible), acres of marble, a fitness room, free wi-fi and free video games.

Heritage B&B (☎ 904-301-1232; www.theheritagebb.com; 1217 Boulevard; r $85-125; P ☒ ☐) In the artistic Springfield historic district, this restored 1904 Colonial Revival home has a cozy, homey feel, four lovely rooms (two with gas fireplaces) and an outdoor Jacuzzi.

At the beach, try John Grisham's favorite, the **Sea Turtle Inn** (☎ 800-874-6000; www.seaturtle.com; 1 Ocean Blvd, Atlantic Beach; r $109; P ☎) or the **Casa Marina** (☎ 904-270-0025; www.casamarinahotel.com; 691 N 1st St, Jacksonville Beach; r $119-289; P) with dark timber furniture and whimsical canopies adorning the 25 rooms and parlor suites.

A combination chocolatier, deli, bar and upscale market, **European Street** (☎ 904-398-9500; 1704 San Marco Blvd; dishes $5-10; ☼ 10am-10pm) in the San Marco historical district is prized for its desserts. **River City Brewing Company** (☎ 904-398-2299; 835 Museum Circle; mains $15.95-25.95; ☼ closed dinner Sun) has panoramic river views, stylish cuisine and its own brews. The trendiest tables are at **Bistro Aix** (☎ 904-398-1949; 1440 San Marco Blvd; mains $10-25; ☼ 11am-10pm Mon-Thu, to 11pm Fri, 5-11pm Sat, 5-9pm Sun), with grape-colored booths, a marble

FLORIDA

bar and French-inspired menu, and at **Matthew's** (☎ 904-396-9922; 2107 Hendricks Ave; mains $19-36; ⏱ 5.30-10pm Mon-Sat), with a showy open kitchen that melds Southern, Mediterranean, Asian and Middle Eastern flavors.

Entertainment

Check out the thriving indie theater scene at **Boomtown Theater & Coffee Salon** (☎ 904-632-0099; www.boomtowntheatre.com; 1714 N Main St; mains $9-18; ⏱ lunch & dinner Mon-Sat), with gospel-style sing-alongs to contemporary(ish) tunes, an ongoing Vampire improv serial every Thursday, swing dancing (including free lessons), and spoken-word jazz hip-hop jams. **Jacksonville Landing** (☎ 904-353-1188; 2 Independent Dr; www .jacksonvillelanding.com) has numerous restaurants and bars, and frequent free outdoor entertainment.

The NFL **Jacksonville Jaguars** (☎ 904-633-2000; www.jaguars.com) play at AllTel Stadium.

At the beach, the **Freebird Live Cafe** (☎ 904-246-2473; www.freebirdcafe.com; 200 N 1st St; ⏱ 8pm-2am Wed-Sat), a two-story pub with wide verandahs, is a rocking small music venue and home of the band Lynyrd Skynyrd.

Getting There & Around

North of the city, **Jacksonville International Airport** (☎ 904-741-4902; www.jaxairport.com) has rental cars. **Greyhound** (☎ 904-356-9976; 10 Pearl St) serves numerous cities. Jacksonville is a hub for **Amtrak** (☎ 904-766-5110; 3570 Clifford Lane). If you're driving north along coastal Hwy A1A, you'll need to catch the **St John's River Ferry** (☎ 904-251-3331; tickets $2.75), also called the Mayport Ferry, which runs every half-hour from 6:30am to 10pm. The **Jacksonville Transportation Authority** (JTA; ☎ 904-630-3100; www.jtaonthemove.com) downtown **transfer center** (201 State St) is also the terminus of the **Skyway** (☎ 904-743-3582; www.ridejta.net; tickets 35¢; ⏱ 6am-11pm Mon-Fri, 10am-11pm Sat) monorail line.

AMELIA ISLAND

Welcoming residents refer to Amelia as if 'she' were a favorite sister or idolized girl-next-door...and to the rest of the world as simply 'off-island'. This pretty island is home to **Fernandina Beach**, a shrimping village with forty blocks of historic buildings and romantic B&Bs, where you'll find a **visitor center** (☎ 904-261-3248, 800-226-3542; 102 Centre St; ⏱ 11am-4pm Mon-Sat, noon-4pm Sun). There's another just after you cross the

main bridge: **Welcome Center** (☎ 904-261-3248, 800-226-3542; www.ameliaisland.org; 961687 Gateway Blvd; ⏱ 9am-5pm Mon-Sat).

Tours ($10; 90 minutes) interpreting Amelia Island's intricate history, which has seen it ruled under eight different flags starting with the French in 1562, are run at 11am and 2pm by the **Amelia Island Museum of History** (☎ 904-261-7378; www.ameliaislandmuseumof history.org; 233 S 3rd St; adult/student $5/3; ⏱ 10am-4pm Mon-Sat).

Enveloping the island are miles of surfable shoreline, sealed by a commanding Civil War–era **fort** (adult/child $5/2; ⏱ 9am-5pm) surrounded by the Spanish moss-draped **Fort Clinch State Park** (☎ 904-277-7274; pedestrian/car $1/5; ⏱ 8am-dusk). East on Atlantic Ave is the tranquil **American Beach**, founded here on Florida's segregated shores in the 1930s for African Americans. Dedicated to preserving its history and saving it from the developers, 'the Beach Lady' MaVynee Betsch operates the **Black Heritage Museum** (☎ 904-261-3988; 3484 Ocean Blvd; admission by donation). For a romantic moonlight ride on the silhouetted sands, contact **Circle D Ranch** (☎ 904-556-9530). It offers two morning and two evening rides at $50 per hour; moonlight rides are $75 by reservation.

The oceanfront **Amelia Hotel & Suites** (☎ 904-261-4236; www.ameliahotelandsuites.com; 1997 S Fletcher Ave; r $79-179; P ⊠ ☒) has refreshingly uncluttered rooms. In downtown Fernandina Beach, the 1857-built **Florida House Inn** (☎ 904-261-3300, 800-258-3301; www.floridahouseinn.com; 20 & 22 S 3rd St; r $99-180; ⊠) offers wonderfully restored rooms with beautiful artwork, free wi-fi and four hours' free use of bright-red zippy scooters. Over 1350 acres at the southern end of the island, **Amelia Island Plantation** (☎ 904-261-6161, 800-874-6878; www.aipfl.com; 6800 First Coast Hwy; r $186-962; P ⊠ ☒) is a luxurious world of its own with three golf courses, 23 tennis courts and nine restaurants.

Breakfast doesn't get any better than the grits at **Bright Mornings** (☎ 904-491-1771; 106 S 3rd St; dishes $4-8; ⏱ 7:30am-2pm Mon-Fri, 8am-2pm Sat & Sun). Sunset views over the marina and magnificent steaks are hallmarks of **Brett's Waterway Cafe** (☎ 904-261-2660; 1 S Front St; mains $16-33; ⏱ lunch Mon-Sat, dinner from 5.50pm daily). Provençale cuisine is right at home between the cherry-red walls of the 1906 candlelit cottage **Le Clos** (☎ 904-261-8100; 20 S 2nd St; mains $19-26; ⏱ 5.30-9pm Mon-Thu, to 9.30pm Fri & Sat).

FLORIDA

Hwy A1A links the island to the mainland, but there's no public transportation. Rent bikes at **Pipeline Surfshop** (☎ 904-277-3717; 2022 1st Ave; per day $15; ☺ 10am-6pm).

WEST COAST

(Somewhat) less crowded than the Atlantic shores, Florida's west coast fans out around a glassy expanse of the Gulf of Mexico smoldering under flame-red glowing sunsets. Its diversity spans thrill-seeking rollercoasters, lip-synching mermaids, world-class surrealist art and cigar-rolling, interwoven with shelling beaches and swamp lands.

FORT MYERS & AROUND

Home at one time to Thomas Edison and Henry Ford, Fort Myers was also known for the Australian pines gracing its beach boulevards. Unfortunately, 2004's Hurricane Charley felled most of them; but overall Fort Myers' post-hurricane recovery was swift.

Fort Myers Beach is on Estero Island, a barrier island about 40 minutes southwest of downtown, and southeast of picturesque Sanibel and Captiva Islands. Call or check the web for information from the **visitor & convention bureau** (☎ 239-338-3500; www.fortmyers sanibel.com), which also has information booths in the baggage-claim area of the airport. Sanibel and Captiva's **chamber of commerce** (☎ 239-472-1080; www.sanibel-captiva.org; 1159 Causeway Rd) has information about the islands.

Sights & Activities

Preserved since 1931, the **Edison Estate, Laboratory & Museum** (☎ 239-334-3614; www.edison -ford-estate.com; 2350 McGregor Blvd; adult/child/family $16/8.50/40; ☺ 9am-5:30pm Mon-Sat, noon-5:30pm Sun) is a chance to see the inventor's original lab and a museum housing hundreds of his inventions in palm-shaded surrounds. Tours of Edison's winter estate include a 90-minute guided tour of **Henry Ford's winter home** next door.

Between Fort Myers Beach and Bonita Beach, four islands make up **Lover's Key State Recreation Area** (☎ 239-463-4588; pedestrian or cyclist/car $1/5; ☺ 8am-dusk) which has gorgeous beaches, bald eagle nests and boating, with 1½-hour **sunset eco-tours** (☎ 239-314-0110; adult/child $20/8) available on Tuesday, Thursday, Friday and Saturday.

A 90,000-acre working cattle ranch (with cowboys to boot), **Babcock Wilderness Adventure** (☎ 239-489-3911, 800-500-5583; www.ba bcockwilderness.com; 8000 SR 31, Punta Gorda; adult/child $18/11; ☺ 9am-3pm Nov-May, morning only Jun-Oct) leads 1½-hour swamp-buggy excursions through pinewoods, freshwater marsh and cypress swamp, with alligators and Florida panthers.

Fort Myers Beach is both a party town (at Times Sq) and a quiet beach resort (at the south end). Look for blue, white and yellow flags marking beach access between houses. Departing from the beach twice daily, the **Key West Express Ferry** (☎ 239-463-5733, 888-539-2628; www.keywestshuttle.com; 2200 Main St; day trip adult/child $129/109, one way all passengers $73, plus security fee $6) takes three hours to get to Key West (p516): 8am departures mean you'll return on the 5pm ferry, and trips leaving at 9am bring you back on the 6pm ferry – if you want to spend the night in the Keys you'll need to book two separate one-way tickets.

Across a 2-mile causeway (toll $6) from Fort Myers, **Sanibel** and **Captiva** Islands are famed for shell collecting. Though the state-owned area of North Captiva saw a 1500ft by 3ft breech in the shore courtesy of Hurricane Charley (it's expected to refill naturally with sand as it's done previously), one of Charley's consolations was to stir up the beds and bring greater numbers of shells ashore. Shelling's at its best an hour before or after low tide. Identify shells at the **Bailey-Matthews Shell Museum** (☎ 239-395-2233; www.shellmuseum.org; 3075 Sanibel-Captiva Rd; adult/child $6/3; ☺ 10am-4pm), which has exhibits on shell utilization from cameo carvings to money cowrie. The 6300-acre **JN 'Ding' Darling National Wildlife Refuge** (☎ 239-472-1100; http://dingdarling .fws.gov; 1 Wildlife Dr, Sanibel; pedestrian & cyclist/car $1/5; ☺ 8am-4pm) has a marvelous 5-mile wildlife drive that's popular with drivers, hikers and cyclists. The drive is open from 7:30am to 5:30pm Saturday to Thursday. **Tarpon Bay Explorers** (☎ 239-472-8900; www.tarponbayexplorers.com; 900 Tarpon Bay Rd, Sanibel) offers guided tours; call ahead for times and tour schedules.

Sleeping & Eating

At Fort Myers Beach, the friendly, family-owned **Lighthouse Island Resort** (☎ 239-463-9392; www.lighthouseislandresort.com; 1051 5th St; r from $76; ☐ ☒) has breezy rooms, and nightly live entertainment at the on-site **Tiki Bar & Grill**

FLORIDA

(mains $8-14; ☺ lunch & dinner), which has great frozen cocktails. Canal-front villas at **Silver Sands Villas** (☎ 239-463-2755; www.silversands-villas .com; 1207 Estero Blvd, Fort Myers Beach; r $79-199) have been freshly painted in tropical colors.

Frequented by locals for its huge selection of fresh seafood, **Snug Harbor** (☎ 239-463-4343; San Carlos Blvd, Fort Myers Beach; mains $8-24) has fabulous ocean views. For romantic dining in downtown Fort Myers, the 19th century, alfresco **Veranda** (☎ 239-332-2065; 2122 Second St, Fort Myers; mains $19-30; ☺ lunch Mon-Fri, dinner Mon-Sat) serves gourmet Southern cuisine.

Unique places to stay on Sanibel include the pretty white-timber **Gulf Breeze Cottages** (☎ 239-472-1626; www.gbreeze.com; 1081 Shell Basket Lane, Sanibel; r $130-230, cottages $165-360; **P** **✗**); **Sanibel Inn** (☎ 239-481-6424; www.sanibelinn.com; 937 E Gulf Drive; r $179-579; **P** **✗** **☎**), with 94 rooms and suites hidden among palm-shaded butterfly and herb gardens and two on-site restaurants; and **Casa Ybel** (☎ 239-472-3145 www .casaybelresort.com; 2255 West Gulf Dr, Sanibel; r from $279; **P** **✗** **☎**), which has its own sanctuary visited by cormorants, ibis, ospreys, pelicans and sanderlings, and casually elegant fully equipped suites. **Dolce Vita** (☎ 239-472-5555; 1244 Periwinkle Way, Sanibel; mains $14.50-29; ☺ dinner) has an eclectic international menu including wild boar saddle and Bahamian lobster tail.

On Captiva, the historic **'Tween Waters Inn Beach Resort** (☎ 239-472-5161; www.tween-waters.com; 15951 Captiva Dr, Captiva; r $175-650; **P** **✗** **☎**) has a vast choice of room and cottage styles, floodlit tennis courts, an on-site spa, full-service marina with fishing guides available, and three restaurants including the **Crows Nest Restaurant & Lounge** (mains $8-18; ☺ 5-10pm Mon-Wed, 5:30-10pm Thu-Sun), with crab races very cutely named 'Nascrabs'. Christmas lights, movie stills and 1930s to '50s nostalgia-kitsch deck the halls of the **Bubble Room** (☎ 239-472-5558; 15001 Captiva Dr, Captiva; mains $15-25; ☺ lunch & dinner).

Getting There & Around

Regional, national and international flights service **Southwest Florida International Airport** (☎ 239-768-1000; http://flylcpa.com). **Greyhound** (☎ 239-334-1011; 2250 Peck St) has regular services.

Lee Tran's (☎ 239-275-8726; www.rideleetran .com) bus No 50 leaves downtown at Daniels Rd and Hwy 41 for Fort Myers Beach ($1) every hour at 20 minutes past the hour. The Beach Connection runs between Fort Myers and Bonita Beach all day for 25¢.

SARASOTA

With a Mediterranean flair and an arts scene to match, Sarasota's alfresco restaurants and historic buildings flanking the Romanesque St Armands Circle are surrounded by idyllic islands and keys. The **visitor bureau** (☎ 941-957-1877, 800-522-9799; 655 N Tamiami Trail; ☺ 9am-5pm Mon-Sat, 11am-3pm Sun) has local information.

Some of the finest art is at the **John & Mabel Museum of Art**, within the former winter retreat of railroad, real-estate and circus baron John Ringling, the **Ringling Museum Complex** (☎ 941-351-1660; www.ringling.org; 5401 Bayshore Rd; adult/child under 12 $15/free; ☺ 10am-5:30pm). The complex encompasses **Ca d'Zan**, the Ringling's mansion, and the **Museum of the Circus** where you'll see circus wagons and costumes.

Galleries and studios line the **Towles Court Art Colony** (☎ 941-362-0960; www.towlescourt.com; 1938 Adams Lane; admission free; ☺ 11am-4pm Tue-Sat).

Sarasota has the best concentration of bookshops in Florida; browse the wonderful **Main Bookshop** (☎ 941-336-7653; www .mainbookshop.com; 1962 Main St) and read at its adjoining café. The **Sarasota County Arts Council** (☎ 941-365-5118; www.sarasota-arts.org; 506 Burns Ct) has schedules for theater, ballet, orchestras and films. Independent films screen at the **Burns Court Cinema** (☎ 941-955-3456; 506 Burns Ct). **Gator Club** (1490 Main St) has live rock, blues or alternative music nightly.

Injured wildlife are rehabilitated at the **Pelican Man's Bird Sanctuary** (☎ 941-388-4444; www.pelicanman.org; 1708 Ken Thompson Parkway, City Island; adult/child $6/4; ☺ 10am-5pm). View sea life next door at the **Mote Aquarium** (☎ 941-388-4441; www.mote.org; 1600 Ken Thompson Parkway; adult/child $15/10; ☺ 10am-5pm), a research center and marine rehabilitation facility with touch tanks.

Many of the beautiful beaches are private. The best public-access beach is **Siesta Key Beach**, about 5 miles south of downtown on Siesta Key; local musos gather here about an hour before sunset on Sunday evenings with drums.

Sleeping & Eating

Sunsets on the Key (☎ 941-312-9797; www.sun setsonthekey.com; 459 Beach Rd, Siesta Key; r $119-299; **P** **☎**) has eight enchanting rooms. On the mainland the **Cypress** (☎ 941-955-4683; www .cypressbb.com; 621 Gulfstream Ave; r $150-240; **P** **✗**)

B&B has romantic rooms and mango- and palm-graced gardens.

The Amish community's restaurants/ bakeries turn out signature sweet pies; try **Troyer's Dutch Heritage** (☎ 941-955-8007; 3713 Bahia Vista St; dishes from $4; ☻ 6am-8pm Mon-Sat). The local artist–decorated **Broken Egg** (☎ 941-346-2750; 210 Avenida Madera, Siesta Key; dishes $6-12; ☻ breakfast & lunch) is a breakfast institution for its pancakes and banana-nut-bread french toast. **Blasé Café** (☎ 941-349-9822; 5263 Ocean Blvd, Siesta Key; mains $12-26; ☻ dining room 5:30-10pm Tue-Sun, lounge to midnight Mon-Fri, to 2am Sat & Sun) has an elegant low-lit bar and garden seating and does a fine rack of lamb.

Getting There & Around

Driving from Fort Myers, follow I-75 north, take exit 210 onto Hwy 780 and follow the signs. Greyhound has services from Fort Myers, Tampa and St Petersburg to Sarasota.

ST PETERSBURG

Classy, cultural St Petersburg perches on a peninsula along the west side of Tampa Bay, just across the bridge from a succession of beaches on its barrier islands – from Pass-A-Grille and St Pete Beaches in the south to Clearwater Beach in the north. The **visitor bureau** (☎ 727-464-7200, 877-352-3224; www.floridasbeach.com; 14450 46th St N, No 108, Clearwater; ☻ 8am-5pm Mon-Fri) has an **information booth** (☎ 727-821-6164) at the **St Petersburg Pier** (☎ 727-821-6443; www.stpetepier.com; 800 2nd Ave N; ☻ 10am-9pm Mon-Thu, to 10pm Fri & Sat, 11am-7pm Sun), which also houses shops, restaurants and an observation deck within a five-story inverted glass and steel pyramid.

The renowned **Salvador Dalí Museum** (☎ 727-823-3767; www.salvadordalimuseum.org; 1000 3rd St S; adult/child $14/3.50, after 5pm Thu $5; ☻ 9:30am-5:30pm Mon-Sat, to 8pm Thu, noon-5:30pm Sun) houses the largest collection of works by the artist outside Spain, including his famous melting clocks.

A roll call that includes Cézanne, Monet, Gaugin, Renoir and Rodin is showcased at the **Museum of Fine Arts** (☎ 727-896-2667; www.fine-arts.org; 255 Beach Dr NE; adult/child $8/4; ☻ 10am-5pm Tue-Sat, 1-5pm Sun). At the foot of the pier, the **St Petersburg Museum of History** (☎ 727-894-1052; 335 2nd Ave NE; adult/child $7/3; ☻ noon-7pm Mon, 10am-5pm Tue-Sat, noon-5pm Sun) includes exhibits on the early days of commercial aviation.

The 34-mile urban biking, skating and walking **Pinellas Trail** (☎ 727-464-8200; ☻ dawn-dusk) starts north of downtown at 34th St and Fairfield Ave and ends at US 19 in Tarpon Springs. A free booklet with mile-by-mile information is available at visitor centers. An 1898-built fort guards **Fort DeSoto Park** (☎ 727-582-2267; www.fortdesoto.com; 3500 Pinellas Bayway S; admission free; ☻ dawn-dusk), with a fishing pier, historic trail, watersports, camping and one of Florida's finest beaches.

The area's Major League baseball franchise, the **Tampa Bay Devil Rays** (www.devilrays.com), play at **Tropicana Field** (☎ 727-825-3333; 1 Stadium Dr; tickets $5-250).

Sleeping & Eating

Don CeSar Beach Resort (☎ 727-360-1881; www.loewshotels.com/hotels/stpetebeach; 3400 Gulf Blvd, St Pete Beach; r from $149; P ☐ ☒) F Scott Fitzgerald used to frequent this palatial vision of flamingo pink – a turreted, bell-towered landmark on St Pete Beach since 1928, with Palladian windows and 277 ocean-view rooms.

Renaissance Vinoy Resort (☎ 727-894-1000; 501 Fifth Ave NE; r from $219; P ☒ ☐ ☒) An opulent 1920s apparition of apricot-pink on the bay, grand archways lead to 360 swank rooms; with a marina and private golf course located on-site.

Bayboro House B&B (☎ 877-823-4955; www.bayborohousebandb.com; 1719 Beach Dr SE; r $129, cottages $275; P ☒ ☒) With winsome Victorian charm, this B&B has wi-fi, wine and cheese every afternoon and home-baked bread. Children over 12 only.

Fort DeSoto Park Campground (☎ 727-582-2267; 3500 Pinellas Bayway S; campsites $27.75) Book way ahead for sites at the waterfront campground, with sweeping views of the Sunshine Skyway Bridge.

Garden (☎ 727-896-3800; 217 Central Ave; mains $13-25; ☻ 11:30am-10:30pm Mon-Fri, noon-10:30pm Sat & Sun) Chef Roger Payne has given the oldest restaurant in town a new lease of life with a revamped French bistro menu. The adjoining Lobby Bar is open from 8pm to 2am Wednesday to Saturday and has live jazz Friday and Saturday, open-mike poetry on Wednesday and Latin dancing lessons on Thursday.

Ted Peter's Famous Smoked Fish (☎ 727-381-7931; 1350 Pasadena Ave; dishes $11-16; ☻ 11:30am-7:30pm Wed-Mon) Dine on house-smoked salmon, mackerel and mullet at picnic tables or at the counter of this venerable institution.

Dino's Jazz Piano Bar & Grill (☎ 727-896-3466; 16 2nd St N; mains $6-10; ✆ 11am-midnight Mon-Fri, to 2am Sat & Sun) The mezzanine level of this warehouse-like space is a fine perch for live jazz and excellent deli-style pub food.

At the new Baywalk cloistered shopping/ dining village in downtown, try **Gratzzi Ristorante** (☎ 727-822-7769; 199 2nd Ave N; ✆ 11:30am-10pm Mon-Thu, to 11:30pm Fri & Sat, 4-10pm Sun) for oak-grilled meat and fish.

Getting There & Around

St Petersburg-Clearwater International Airport (☎ 727-535-7600; www.fly2pie.com) has flights to northern USA states and Canada several times a week. It also has car rentals. Widespread **Greyhound** (☎ 727-898-1496; 180 9th St N) services include Tampa ($6; 35 minutes). Amtrak has a bus link from Tampa's station to St Petersburg, where it stops at the **Pinellas Square Mall** (7200 Hwy 19 N).

Pinellas Suncoast Transit Authority (☎ 727-530-9911; www.psta.net) operates a beach trolley service (day pass/concession $3/1.25). The **Looper trolley** (fare/day pass 50¢/$2.50; ✆ 11am-5pm) links the museums and St Petersburg Pier on a 30-minute narrated loop.

TAMPA

Florida's third-largest city, Tampa is often bypassed by travelers heading for the beaches or Orlando's theme parks. But Tampa's revitalized Ybor City (which preserves a strong Cuban–Spanish heritage while embracing a hip, happening nightlife scene), combined with a vigorous renewal of its harborside, absolutely reward a stop.

Information's available at the **visitor bureau** (☎ 813-223-1111, 800-448-2672; www.visit tampabay.com; 400 N Tampa St, Suite 2800). **Tampa Bay Business Guild** (☎ 813-237-3751; www.tbbg.org; 1222 S Dale Mabry) provides information for gay and lesbian visitors.

Downtown

Coral reefs, marshes, bays, wetlands and beaches are displayed at the **Florida Aquarium** (☎ 813-273-4000; www.flaquarium.org; 701 Channelside Dr; adult/child $18/12; ✆ 9:30am-5pm), along with their natural inhabitants.

At the time of research, the **Tampa Museum of Art** (☎ 813-274-8130; www.tampamuseum.com; 600 N Ashley Dr; adult/child $7/3; ✆ 10am-5pm Tue-Sat) was building brand-new premises to house its impressive collection of avant-garde, old masters, sculpture, photography and works by emerging Florida artists.

Forecast the weather on TV at the excellent **Museum of Science & Industry** (☎ 813-987-6000; www.mosi.org; 4801 E Fowler Ave; adult/child $20/18; ✆ 9am-5pm Mon-Fri, to 7pm Sat & Sun); and explore the heavens, hurricanes and human body.

Ybor City

Pulsing to a Latin beat, historic Ybor (*ee-bore*) City, in southeast Tampa, is about 2 miles from downtown and connected by the newly reinstated electric streetcars. It was established in the late 19th century when cigar-maker Vicente Martínez Ybor squashed Key West's cigar industry by moving his factory to Tampa and bringing Cuban laborers from Havana. Ybor has a **visitor center** (☎ 813-248-3712; www.ybor .org; 1514/2 E 8th Ave; ✆ 10am-6pm Mon-Sat, noon-6pm Sun).

Watch master cigar rollers at work at cigar shops including **Gonzalez y Martinez Cigar Company** (☎ 813-248-8210; www.gonzalezy martinez.com; 2103 E 17th Ave).

CITY OF MERMAIDS: WEEKI WACHEE SPRINGS

Billed as the 'only city of live mermaids' (which it is, surely?), mermaids perform in a 1947 underwater theater at **Weeki Wachee Springs** (☎ 352-596-2062; www.weekiwachee.com; 6131 Commercial Way, Weeki Wachee; adult/child $21.95/15.95; ✆ 10am-5pm daily Apr-Aug, 11am-3pm Thu-Sun Sep-Mar; Ⓟ). Elvis and Esther Williams have been among audience members watching through glass as the long-haired, fish-tailed mermaids (and mermen) lip-synch in the artesian spring alongside fish, turtles, otters and snakes, grabbing a quick hit of air from submerged air hoses.

Also at the springs is a riverboat nature ride, and swimming and waterslides at the adjoining Buccaneer Bay waterpark.

Weeki Wachee is just by the junction of Hwy 50 and Hwy 19, about 58 miles due north of St Pete Beach.

The **Ybor City Museum State Park** (☎ 813-247-6323; 1818 E 9th Ave; admission $3; ⊙ 9am-5pm) chronicles the history of cigar making. Historic **walking tours** (admission incl museum $6) depart from the museum at 10:30am Saturday. Book ahead for **ghost tours** (☎ 813-831-5214; www.historicguides.com; tickets $10; ⊙ tours 6pm Sat) departing from the pirate ship–like bar **Gaspar's Grotto** (☎ 813-248-5900; 1805 7th Ave; www.gasparsgrotto.com; ⊙ from 8pm Wed & Thu, from 5pm Fri, from 2pm Sat).

Busch Gardens & Adventure Island

A combination zoo and amusement park, but better than both, **Busch Gardens** (☎ 813-987-5000; www.buschgardens.com; 3000 E Busch Blvd, cnr 40th St; adult/child $56/46; ⊙ 9am-6pm with seasonal variations; ℗) is home to two of the country's most adrenaline-pumping roller coasters and 2700 free-roaming exotic animals. Parking costs $7. Next door, **Adventure Island** (☎ 813-987-5600; www.adventureisland.com; 10001 McKinley Dr; adult/child $33/31; ⊙ 10am-5pm with seasonal variations; ℗) water park has thrill rides and slides galore. Parking here costs $5. Combination tickets for one day at each park are available for $65/55 per adult/child. The parks are about 8 miles northeast of downtown Tampa.

Sleeping

Chains abound near Busch Gardens, along Fowler Ave/Morris Bridge Rd (Hwy 582) and Busch Blvd (Hwy 580).

Gram's Place (☎ 813-221-0596; www.grams-inn-tampa.com; 3109 N Ola Ave; campsites $15, dm $18.50-22.50, r with bath $68-95, without bath $50-56; ✗ ▢) Musicians and music lovers, welcome home. Rooms at this rockin' hostel/B&B are themed by genre (folk, country, jazz, blues…). The jukebox spins over 400 CDs and there's a basement recording studio; or just jam out by the Jacuzzi. A gem.

Don Vicente de Ybor Historic Inn (☎ 813-241-4545; www.donvicenteinn.com; 1915 Republica de Cuba; r $139; ℗ ☎) Built in 1895 by Ybor City's founder, this atmospheric B&B has its original marble staircase, four-poster beds and French doors opening to balconies.

Casita de la Verdad (☎ 813-654-6087; 1609 6th Ave; house $180-250; ℗ ✗) Rent this entire two-room 1908 cigar-maker's house with four-poster bed and claw foot bathtub.

Bayshore Ryan House (☎ 813-253-3142; http://bayshoreryanhouse.com; 203 W Verne St; r $95-209; ✗)

In the trendy Hyde Park district, a stroll from downtown and Bayshore Blvd's 7-mile waterfront walk- and cycle-way, this elegant B&B has spacious, eclectically themed rooms.

Paradise Lakes (☎ 813-949-9327; www.paradiselakes.com; Brinson Rd, Land O' Lakes; r $75-140; ℗ ☎) If you prefer an all-over tan, North America's largest 'clothing optional' resort is 17 miles north and has its own spring-fed lake among its 80 secluded acres.

Eating

Downtown is a desert for dining, but Ybor City more than makes up for it. Keep an eye out for places popping up in Tampa's SoHo area (South of Houston Ave).

Columbia Restaurant (☎ 813-2438-4961; www.columbiarestaurant.com; 2117 E 7th Ave; mains $18-30; ⊙ lunch & dinner) This resplendent 1905 establishment occupies an entire block and seats 1600. Opulent Mediterranean cloisters and ceramic tiles set the stage for flamenco dancing (cover Monday to Saturday $6).

La Teresita (☎ 813-879-4909; 3246 W Columbus Dr; mains $5-7; ⊙ 5am-midnight Mon-Thu, 24hr Fri & Sat, to 10pm Sun) Skip the restaurant and head for the horseshoe-shaped cafeteria counters to feast on stuffed plantains with yellow rice and black beans plus Cuban bread and coffee alongside locals from every walk of life.

Nicko's 1951 Diner (☎ 813-234-9301; 4603 N Florida Ave; mains $6-11; ⊙ 6am-9pm Mon-Fri, 7am-9pm Sat, to 2pm Sun) Elvis ate here after a 1956 concert downtown; the catfish fingers, pancakes and beveled chrome surrounds still rock.

Bern's Steak House (☎ 813-251-2421; www.bernssteakhouse.com; 1208 S Howard Ave; mains $18-60; ⊙ 5-11pm) Appetizers include 24 types of caviar at this illustrious landmark, with steaks prepared to the most exacting tastes and specifications. The 60oz strip sirloin ($207) is perfect for six people.

La Tropicana (☎ 813-247-4040; 1822 E 7th Ave; ⊙ 7am-3pm Mon-Sat) Grab a Cuban sandwich on the go from the drive-thru.

Entertainment

Find out what's happening from the *Weekly Planet*, and *Tampa Tribune*'s 'Friday Extra.' When it comes to nightlife, just head for Ybor City's 7th Ave.

Carmine's (☎ 813-248-3834; 1802 E 7th Ave; mains $9-16; ⊙ 11am-6pm Sun & Mon, to 10pm Tue & Wed, to 11pm Thu, to midnight Fri & Sat) This Italian-style restaurant in a huge open warehouse has a

FLORIDA

happening adjoining bar, Zion, open from 9pm to 3am Thursday to Saturday, and an upstairs lounge, the Luna Lounge, open from 9am to 3pm Friday and Saturday, with DJs.

With an archetypal vertical backlit sign, the elaborate 1926 **Tampa Theatre** (☎ 813-274-8286; www.tampatheatre.org; 711 N Franklin St; tickets $7) screens independent and classic films, and is a hub for the arts community.

SPORTS

Spring training for numerous Major League teams is a great way to see baseball stars up close in a spontaneous environment. Tickets are around $20. Try **Legends Field** (☎ 813-879-2244; www.legendsfieldtampa.com) to watch the NY Yankees in practice. The **NFL Tampa Bay Buccaneers** (☎ 813-870-2700; www.buccaneers.com) play football at **Raymond James Stadium** (4201 Dale Mabry Hwy) August to December. The NHL Tampa Bay Lightning play hockey October to April at the **St Pete Times Forum** (☎ 813-223-4919; 401 Channelside Dr; tickets $8-150).

Getting There & Around

Tampa International Airport (☎ 813-870-8700; www.tampaairport.com) has car-rental agencies inside. **Greyhound** (☎ 813-229-2174; 610 E Polk St) has numerous services. Trains run south to Miami and north through Jacksonville at the **Amtrak station** (☎ 813-221-7600; 601 Nebraska Ave N). **HARTline** (☎ 813-254-4278; www.hartline.org; fare/day pass $1.25/3) runs the old-style streetcars.

CENTRAL FLORIDA

The geographic heart of Florida's populous peninsula is also the heart of its number-one industry. Tourists from around the globe make the pilgrimage here to visit the sprawling theme parks that, in the words of Walt, all started with a mouse. But even if Orlando is your only Floridian foray, it's worth taking a detour to some of the state's real treasures including clear spring runs surrounded by gingerbread Victorian townships and a majestic national forest.

ORLANDO & AROUND

It's perhaps a testament to the theme parks' marketing machines that many people don't realize there *is* an Orlando. But this city has a stylish downtown district, a fantastic live-music scene and an international population.

Its seismic moment came when Walt Disney bought thousands of acres here after he felt that there were too many parasitic operators feeding off his inaugural Disneyland, and wanted to create a world that he controlled. The 1971 opening of Walt Disney World, 20 miles southwest, placed the city firmly on the tourist map.

So many attractions compete for tourist dollars that it's easy to get overwhelmed. Good multilingual guides and maps are available from the **visitor bureau** (☎ 407-363-5872, 800-551-0181; www.orlandoinfo.com; 8723 International Dr; ☼ 8am-7pm); also check **Go2Orlando** (www.go2orlando.com) and **Visit Orlando** (www.visitorlandoonline.com). If you're spending some time checking out the area, pick up a copy of Lonely Planet's *Orlando & Central Florida* guide.

I-4 is the main north–south connector, though it's confusingly labeled east–west. To go north, take I-4 east (toward Daytona); to go south, get on I-4 west (toward Tampa). The main east–west roads are Hwy 50 and Hwy 528 (the Bee Line Expressway, a toll road), which connect Orlando to the Space Coast. The Bee Line Expressway accesses Orlando International Airport.

International Drive

There are so many themed attractions, themed restaurants and themed hotels surround **International Drive** (I-Dr) that it's a quasi-theme park itself (with a theme of, well, themes). The stand-out attraction is **Titanic: Ship of Dreams** (☎ 407-248-1166; www.titanicshipofdreams.com; the Mercado on International Dr; adult/child 6-11 $18/13; ☼ 10am-8pm), where you take on the character of a real-life Titanic passenger for a poignant tour of replicas and relics.

SeaWorld

Based on marine animal shows (sea lions, killer whales and dolphins star), viewing areas and exhibits (a percentage of your admission goes to its excellent Animal Rescue Team cause), **SeaWorld** (☎ 407-351-3600, 800-327-2424; www.seaworld.com; 7007 SeaWorld Orlando Dr; adult/child 3-9 $59.75/48; ☼ varies; **P**) is also home to thrill rides like Kraken, the tallest and fastest roller coaster in Orlando, and

GREATER ORLANDO & THEME PARKS

SIGHTS & ACTIVITIES			
Animal Kingdom.............................1 B3	Menello Museum of American Folk Art......(see 5)	Sea World..8 B2	
Disney-MGM Studios....................2 B3	Orange County Regional History Center......7 C1	Titanic: Ship of Dreams...................9 B2	
Downtown Disney..........................3 B2	Orlando Museum of Art......(see 5)	Universal Studios Florida/Islands of Adventure & City Walk...............10 B2	
Epcot...4 B2	Orlando Science Center & John Young Planetarium......(see 5)		
Loch Haven Park............................5 C1		**TRANSPORT**	
Magic Kingdom..............................6 B2		Orlando International Airport..........11 D2	

Journey to Atlantis, a water-coaster with a 60ft vertical drop. Parking costs $8.

Universal Studios & Islands of Adventure

A working movie lot as well as a theme park, rides at **Universal Studios** (☎ 407-363-8000; www.universalorlando.com; Universal Orlando Resort, 1000 Universal Studios Plaza; single-day adult/child 3-9 $60/48, 2-day $105/95; ⊗ from 9am, closing times vary; Ⓟ) are based on film classics like *Jaws*, *Terminator* and *ET*. The *ET* ride, where you fly on a bicycle to return ET to his home planet, is particularly popular with kids. (If you're heading to Jacksonville, tour Sally Corporation (p531) to see how dark rides are made). Parking here costs $9. Universal's sister park, **Islands of Adventure** (single-day adult/child 3-9 $60/48, 2-day $105/95) has the wilder roller coasters and excellent rides that include the Amazing Adventures of Spider-Man, the Cat in the Hat and Jurassic Park River Adventure. To avoid lengthy queues, get your hands on a very convenient Universal Express pass, which assigns a return time and has a 15 minutes or less wait.

Other Sights & Activities

Downtown Orlando's **Loch Haven Park** will offer cultural respite if you feel you've worn one pair of mouse ears too many. For a fun look at serious science, the **Orlando Science Center & John Young Planetarium** (☎ 407-514-2000; www.osc.org; 777 E Princeton St; adult/child 3-12 $15/10; ⊗ 9am-5pm Mon-Thu, to 9pm Fri & Sat, noon-5pm Sun) has planetarium viewings every Friday and Saturday night. The **Orlando Museum of Art** (☎ 407-896-4231; www.omart.org; 2416 N Mills Ave; adult/child 6-18 $8/5; ⊗ 10am-4pm Tue-Fri, from noon Sat & Sun) spotlights works by minority American artists, often hosting unique travelling exhibits. The **Mennello Museum of American Folk Art** (☎ 407-246-4278; www.mennello museum.com; 900 E Princeton St; adult/child $4/free; ⊗ 10:30am-4:30pm Tue-Sat, to noon Sun) feautres traveling folk-art exhibitions.

Orlando BD (before Disney/before Development) is featured at the **Orange County Regional History Center** (☎ 407-836-8500; www .thehistorycenter.org; 65 E Central Blvd; adult/child 3-12 $7/3.50; ⊗ 10am-5pm Mon-Sat, noon-5pm Sun), in a series of permanent and traveling exhibits showcasing the region.

FLORIDA

Sleeping

In addition to the WDW resorts (p554), there are countless accommodation options. Most are located along International Dr, US 192 in Kissimmee and off I-4. The **Central Reservation Service** (☎ 800-548-3311) operates a free service in conjunction with the visitor bureau to assist in making hotel reservations.

Most hotels on and around I-Dr are unsurprisingly chains, but usually with amenities you wouldn't find elsewhere (we're talking about a place where even the McDonald's are themed).

EO Inn & Spa (☎ 407-481-8485; www.eoinn.com; 227 N Eola Dr; r $130-220; (P)) This boutique downtown inn overlooks Lake Eola, with neutral-toned rooms elegant in their simplicity and wi-fi.

Nickelodeon Family Suites by Holiday Inn (☎ 407-387-5437; www.nickhotel.com; 14500 Continental Gateway; r summer/winter $190/210; (P) (♨)) Kids will just go completely gaga here – a choo-choo takes you to kitchen-equipped, cartoon-styled suites; has a fluoro swimming lagoon.

Gaylord Palms Resort & Convention Center (☎ 407-586-2000; www.gaylordpalms.com; 6000 W Osceola Parkway; r summer/winter $199-239/279; (P) (▢) (♨)) If you don't have time to see all of Florida, these rooms overlook an atrium display of the Everglades, St Augustine and Key West.

Peabody Hotel (☎ 407-352-4000; www.peabody orlando.com; 9801 I-Dr; r $345-1400; (P) (♨)) Check out the daily duck parade (11am and 5pm) even if you're not staying at this oh-so-decadent hotel.

Universal Studios (☎ 888-273-1311; r $179-309) Has three hotels, and guests zoom straight to the front of the line for rides.

Magic Castle Inn & Suites (☎ 407-396-2212, 800-446-5669; www.magicorlando.com; 5055 W Hwy 192, Kissimmee; r $27-44; (P) (♨)) Kissimmee's where you'll find the most economical accommodations, located just 3.5 miles from Walt Disney World.

Hyatt Regency Orlando Airport Hotel (☎ 407-825-1234; 9300 Airport Blvd; r from $189; (P) (▢) (♨)) The Hyatt Regency is conveniently located right inside the main terminal and has balconies facing a skylit atrium. It includes free wi-fi, a restaurant breakfast, and access to all the browsing, shopping, dining and people-watching you could possibly ever want.

Eating

On and around I-Dr you'll find an explosion of chains; Sand Lake Rd has upscale dining.

Rincon Criollo Cafe (☎ 407-872-1128; 331 N Orange Ave; dishes $5-7; (☾) 8am-3pm) Downtown; this place has outstanding Cuban fare.

Le Coq au Vin (☎ 407-851-6980; 4800 S Orange Ave; mains $13.50-22; (☾) lunch & dinner Tue-Fri, dinner Sat & Sun) The namesake dish here is a perennial winner.

Cafe Tu Tu Tango (☎ 407-248-2222; 8625 I-Dr; dishes $4-15; (☾) 11:30am-11pm Sun-Thu, to 2am Fri & Sat) Tapas-style multi-national meals at this colorful café feature irregular salsa performances.

Race Rock Restaurant (☎ 407-248-9876; 8186 I-Dr; mains $7-15; (☾) 11:30am-11:30pm) This is a fun option for kids (and racing enthusiasts). Chow down on burgers and steaks beneath ceiling-suspended Nascars.

There are loads of 'dinner and shows'; **Pirate's Dinner Adventure** (☎ 407-248-0590, 800-866-2469; www.piratesdinneradventure.com; 6400 Carrier Dr; adult/child $50/30) sees entertainers sword-fighting from a full-scale Spanish galleon, though the food is an afterthought.

Drinking & Entertainment

Downtown has a happening bar district around Orange Ave between Church St and Jefferson St that showcases its thriving music scene, along with touring acts at bars and clubs like **Bar BQ Bar** (☎ 407-648-5441; 64 N Orange Ave), with $1 beer and a cool back bar, **Back Booth** (☎ 407-999-2570; www.backbooth.com; 37 W Pine St; (☾) 9pm-2am Sat-Wed, 5pm-2am Thu & Fri) and the **Social** (☎ 407-246-1419; 54 N Orange Ave). Eight bars constitute **Wall St Plaza** (☎ 407-420-1515; www.wallstplaza.net; 25 Wall St).

Parliament House (☎ 407-425-7571; www.par liamenthouse.com; 410 N Orange Blossom Trail; cover varies) has six gay clubs and bars. The **Orlando Weekly** (www.orlandoweekly.com) is the best source for entertainment listings.

Universal Studio's **CityWalk** (☎ 407-363-8000; www.citywalkorlando.com; (☾) 11am-2am) links its two parks, with movies, restaurants and clubs; get a $10 pass covering all the clubs (most have a $5 to $10 cover otherwise). There's live jazz, funk, soul or R&B every night at **City Jazz** (☎ 407-224-2189; cover $5; (☾) 8pm-1am Sun-Thu, 7pm-2am Fri & Sat) while big names star at the 2800-seat **Hard Rock Live Orlando** (☎ 407-351-5483; tickets $20-30; (☾) box office 10am-9pm).

(Continued on page 553)

Lower Manhattan (p131), New York City

ANGUS OBORN

ESBIN ANDERSON PHOTOGRAPHY

Chrysler Building (p139), New York City

Statue of Liberty (p131), New York City

JEFF GREENBERG

ROB BLAKERS

The Adirondacks (p175), New York State

Amish quilt, Intercourse (p204), Pennyslvania

RICHARD I'ANSON

JON DAVISON

Times Square (p139), New
York City

Picturesque coastal Maine (p286)

LEE FOSTER

Fishing buoys, New Hampshire (p277)

CHRISTINE OSBORNE

Capitol (p309),
Washington, DC

JOHN NEUBAUER

RICHARD CUMMINS

Union Station (p309), Washington, DC

LEE FOSTER

Key West (p516), Florida

Plantation mansion, Louisiana (p427)

OLIVIER CIRENDINI

RAYMOND HILLSTROM

Wrigley Field (p578), Chicago

JON DAVISON

French Quarter (p423), New Orleans

Southeastern Minnesota (p656)

WOODWARD PAYNE & BEVERLY ANDERSON

STEPHEN SAKS

Badlands National Park (p692), South Dakota

Pine Ridge Indian Reservation (p691), South Dakota.

KRISTIN PILJAY

RICHARD CUMMINS

Stockyards National Historic District (p755), Fort Worth, Texas

Bluebonnets (p729), the state flower of Texas

RICHARD CUMM

Overlooking Big Sur (p817), near Monterey Bay, California

HOLGER LEUE

Santa Monica, Los Angeles (p784)

NEIL SETCHFIELD

Sequoia National Park (p865), California

JOHN ELK III

Fiesta de los Vaqueros (p911), Tucson

Las Vegas (p874)

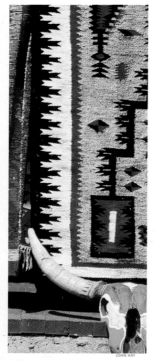

Indian artifacts, Santa Fe (p943),
New Mexico

Bryce Canyon National Park
(p933), Utah

North Rim (p905), Grand Canyon, Arizona

Rocky Mountains (p960)

Pike Place Market (p1038), Seattle

Space Needle (p1039), Seattle Center

Mt Hood (p1075), Oregon

Columbia River Gorge (p1076), Washington

Grizzly bear, Alaska (p1080)

Girdwood, near Anchorage (p1103), Alaska

ANN CECIL

Hawai'i Volcanoes National Park (p1131), Hawai'i

Na Pali Coast (p1136), Kaua'i

PETER HEN

LAWRENCE WORCESTER

Firedancer, O'ahu (p1126)

Traditional Hawaiian canoe (p1118)

CASEY & ASTRID WITTE MAH

(Continued from page 540)

Getting There & Around

Orlando International Airport (☎ 407-825-2001) has buses to major tourist areas. Taxis to International Dr and the theme-park corridor cost about $30, shuttle vans about $20; try **Yellow Cab** (☎ 407-422-5151).

Greyhound (☎ 407-292-3440; 555 N John Young Parkway) services numerous cities. **Amtrak** (☎ 407-843-7611; 1400 Sligh Blvd) offers daily trains south to Miami and north to New York City.

Orlando's bus network is operated by **Lynx** (☎ 800-344-5969; www.golynx.com; single rides/day pass $1.50/3.50, transfers free); buses run from 4am to 3am Monday to Friday, 4am to 1am Saturday and 4am to 10pm Sunday. **I-Ride Trolley** (☎ 407-354-5656, 407-248-9590; www.iridetrolley.com; rides adult/child 75¢/25¢, exact change required; ⏰ 24hr) buses run along International Dr and Universal Blvd every 15 minutes.

WALT DISNEY WORLD

Yeah, the lines are maddeningly long; yeah, it's a suspension of reality; and yeah, it's corporate in the extreme, but chances are you'll find yourself checking your cynicism at the gate. Walt Disney's dream of creating the happiest place on earth by and large finds its fulfillment at this conglomeration of four theme parks: the Magic Kingdom, Disney-MGM Studios, Animal Kingdom and Epcot, plus two water parks (Blizzard Beach, Typhoon Lagoon), a shopping and entertainment district (Downtown Disney) and attractions like Disney's Wide World of Sports. It's a fantastic place to bring youngsters and a nostalgia trip for the young-at-heart.

Orientation & Information

Walt Disney World (WDW; www.waltdisneyworld.com) is 20 miles southwest of downtown Orlando and 4 miles northwest of Kissimmee. Note that the central WDW reservations and information number ☎ 407-934-7639 isn't toll-free.

To avoid lines, buy your tickets in advance from a Disney store, online, or by mail from **Walt Disney Guest Communications** (PO Box 10000, Lake Buena Vista, FL 32830-1000). The algorithmic ticketing system starts at $60/48 per adult/child for one day, with a sliding price (and savings) scale the more days your ticket covers. Add-on options include the Park Hopper ($35), which allows you to 'hop' between all four WDW parks for the length of your base ticket; and the Magic Plus Pack ($45), which includes a limited number of entries into other attractions like water parks. Parking costs $8.

Disney's *Guidebook for Guests with Disabilities* (available at Guest Services, just inside each park's ticket turnstiles) has maps and ride-by-ride guides including Braille and audio options; all transportation is wheelchair-accessible.

Crowds can be horrific. Busy public holidays aside (see p1151), WDW is least crowded in January, February, mid-September through October and early December. During the summer, weekends are the least crowded days; the rest of the year it's the other way round. Prices are lowest

---

WALT DISNEY WORLD TIPS

■ Don't fall for sham tourist centers offering ultra-discounted tickets in exchange for attending a lecture about timeshares; Disney won't accept phony tickets.

■ The parks open about an hour before the schedules say they do, and staff get the most popular rides running early.

■ Pick up a free FastPass when you arrive, which lets you swipe your ticket at the entrance to popular attractions, then return at a pre-set time (usually one to two hours later), when you'll zip to the front of the line.

■ Consider staying at a Disney-owned property, if only because guests can enter the parks 1½ hours early or stay up to three hours later than when they close to the public. And no matter how busy it is, you'll never be turned away at the gates as resort guests are guaranteed admission.

■ Check out www.mousesavers.com for information on discounted tickets and deals.

FLORIDA

between August and December with frequent downpours during the hot, humid months of June, July and August. Late fall tends to have the best weather. The immensely popular **Gay Day** (www.gayday.com) at WDW kicks off the first weekend in June.

Bring drinking water – refills are free at Disney restaurants – and sunscreen. Food from outside is not (technically) permitted.

Many hotels provide scheduled shuttles to the parks.

Sights & Activities

The centerpiece of WDW and a winner with kids under 12 is the **Magic Kingdom**, home of Cinderella's Castle; the classics Pirates of the Caribbean and Space Mountain; Buzz Lightyear's Space Ranger Spin, where you steer your own Star Cruiser, letting loose with your laser cannon for points; the adorable Many Adventures of Winnie the Pooh; and Peter Pan rides. Don't miss the fireworks display, which light up the sky nightly.

Older kids and adults will find the attractions at the **Disney-MGM Studios** tops. Take a wild ride on the Rock 'n' Roller Coaster (starring Aerosmith), or whiz past soundstage sets and animatronic stars of timelessly classic movies like *The Wizard of Oz*, *Casablanca* and *Raiders of the Lost Ark*.

Epcot encompasses Future World, a series of corporate-sponsored journeys through the evolution and projection of not-very-cutting-edge technology (though Mission Space offers a cool simulated rocket-trip to Mars); and World Showcase, which painstakingly recreates 11 countries, staffed by citizens of each, with authentic restaurants.

At Disney's 500-acre **Animal Kingdom** (a zoo, basically), you can take safaris, riverboat rides and trails to see wild animals up close in re-created 'natural' environments, and watch shows like the animatronic Festival of the Lion King.

Sleeping

There are over two dozen places to stay on Disney property, most rooms accommodating four or more. A central reservation line handles bookings and information (☎ 407-934-7639).

In Disney's 'value' segment, the four themed resorts – including the fairly cool **Pop Century Resort** (r $77-131; P R) – have

thousands of small rooms between them, and are also the noisiest (*lots* of kids). Of its 'moderate' properties, Disney's **Caribbean Beach Resort** (☎ 407-934-3400; r $139-215; P R) has bold, splashy rooms and an ancient temple ruins–style pool.

Rooms at WDW's 'deluxe' resorts are designed to sleep at least five. Family-friendly in the extreme, WDW has stacks of kids' programs, vast swimming pools, room service and gyms, and Disney characters making appearances. There's a white-sand beach at the bizarrely realistic **Wilderness Lodge** (☎ 407-824-3200; r $199-490; P R) as well as a marina, hiking trails (as it were), lodge-style bunk rooms and erupting geysers. If railroad magnate and hotelier Henry Flagler was around today, he might have built something very like the **Grand Floridian Resort & Spa** (☎ 407-824-3000; r $349-870; Magic Kingdom area; P R), which has views of the iconic Cinderella's Castle from its tower.

Eating

Dining with Mickey or his colleagues is insanely popular; make reservations up to 60 days in advance. There's a central reservation and information number for all restaurants (☎ 407-939-3463). You'll need a ticket for whichever park the restaurant's in.

In the Magic Kingdom, try **Plaza Restaurant** (Main Street; meals under $11) for fresh, healthy salads and sandwiches. The buffet at **Crystal Palace** (Main Street; dinner buffet adult/child $23/11; ☺ from 4pm) includes peel-and-eat shrimp, prime rib and tropical fruit salads, with Winnie-the-Pooh and his chums dropping by.

At Disney-MGM Studios, the **Sci-Fi Dine-In Theater** (across from Star Tours; mains $9-15), a 'drive-in' where you dine in Cadillacs while watching classic sci-fi films, is a trip.

Sit-down meals at Epcot's World Showcase generally cost around $14 to $30; all pavilions have a counter-service option outside for about half the price. Plan ahead as it's swamped at dinner (just think how long those ride lines were!). Try Germany's **Biergarten** (buffet-style adult/child lunch $16/8, dinner $21/9, bier extra) for soft pretzels and sausages; Morocco's **Restaurant Marrakesh** (meals $13-23) for good vegetable couscous; and the signature mushroom filet mignon at Canada's meat-lover's fantasy, **Le Cellier** (lunch $8-22, dinner $16-37).

At Animal Kingdom, meet Goofy and the gang over breakfast at **Restaurantosaurus** (☎ 407-939-3463).

Entertainment

Disney offers late-night fun good enough to draw Orlando locals at its Downtown Disney complex, segmented into West Side, featuring **Cirque du Soleil** (☎ 407-939-7600; www.cirquedusoleil.com; adult $59-87, child 3-9

$44-65; ☺ shows 6pm & 9pm Tue-Sat), arcade/virtual-reality games at **DisneyQuest** (adult/child 3-9 $36.21/29.82; ☺ 11:30am-11pm Sun-Thu, to midnight Fri & Sat), and the **House of Blues** (☎ 407-934-2583; www.hob.com; cover varies), where Tenacious D have performed, among others; **Pleasure Island** (☎ 407-934-7781; admission $21), with half a dozen dance clubs, an outdoor stage and improv comedy plus 24 movie theaters; and Marketplace, for souvenir-oriented shopping. All areas have dining options galore.

TOP FIVE PURSUITS AT CENTRAL FLORIDA'S SPRINGS

Hundreds of natural springs gush billions of gallons of crystal-clear water every day throughout the state, offering a plethora of outdoor pursuits. These are just some in the Central Florida area:

Swimming

Salt Springs Recreation Area (☎ 352-685-2048; admission $4; campsites/RV sites $14/20; ☺ 8am-dusk) Rumored to have curative powers, swimming is sublime at this spring run in the Ocala National Forest, which has myriad springs and fantastic opportunities for hiking, biking, canoeing, kayaking and camping.

Tubing

Ichetucknee Springs State Park (☎ 386-497-2511; admission $5, tubing $5; ☺ 8am-dusk) Lie back on an inner tube or raft and gently float on the crystal-clear waters downstream for 45 minutes to 3½ hours through unspoiled wilderness as otters swim right up beside you. Farmers rent tubes for about $5 along approach roads.

Manatee Viewing

Blue Spring State Park (☎ 386-775-3663; 2100 W French Ave, Orange City; admission pedestrian/car $1/5, campsites/cabins $20/80; ☺ 8am-dusk) The best time to see these gentle endangered sea cows – which early European explorers thought were mermaids, but which are actually related to elephants (the explorers must have been a *long* time at sea) – is before 11am between November and March. Swimming's prohibited when Manatees are present. Visit www.floridaconservation.org /psm/manatee or www.savethemanatee.org for more information on manatees.

Glass-Bottom Boat Touring

Silver Springs (☎ 352-236-2121, 800-234-7458; www.silversprings.com; 5656 E Silver Springs Blvd; adult/child under 10 $33/24; ☺ 10am-5pm; P) Glass-bottom boats were invented in 1878 at this delightfully old-fashioned 'nature theme park,' where scenes from Tarzan were filmed. Parking costs $24.

Canoeing & Kayaking

De Leon Springs State Recreation Area (☎ 386-985-4212; pedestrian or cyclist $1, car $5; ☺ 8am-dusk) In addition to a huge swimming area, you can explore the springs by canoe or kayak (per hour $10, per day $28 from concessions). The springs flow into the Lake Woodruff National Wildlife Refuge, with 18,000 acres of lakes, creeks, and marshes.

Check out the website www.floridasprings.org for comprehensive info on all of Florida's springs.

FLORIDA

THE PANHANDLE

Cresting +, wild rushing rivers, wooded forest, chilly winter nights, down-home Southern cooking, rocking chairs on the porch and, in some cases, a Central time zone – is this still Florida? Of course, you'll also find glorious beaches – some of the state's best, with mesmerizing translucent aquamarine seas lapping pure white-sugar-sand shores – as well as fantastic fishing and wonderfully wacky festivals. Yeah, this is still Florida.

TALLAHASSEE

Pocketed between gently rising hills and canopied roads flanked with elegant buildings and *Gone With the Wind*–style plantations, Florida's capital, Tallahassee, is a small, gracious city far removed from the majority of the state it administrates. Geographically it's closer to Atlanta, GA, than it is to Miami, and culturally its citizens consider themselves Southern, which is inversely the case the further south in the state you go. It's an anomaly too that for a city that headquarters the state's major industry – tourism – Tallahassee is one of the least touristy towns in Florida.

It became the seat of government when in 1824 Pensacola and St Augustine, at that time the two largest cities, were unable to agree on a capital, so they settled on this forested spot halfway between. Native Apalachees inhabited the area from AD 500, and also used it as a ceremonial center.

Maps are available from the **visitor center** (☎ 850-413-9200, 800-628-2866; www.seetallahassee.com; 106 E Jefferson St; ☼ 8am-5pm Mon-Fri, 9am-1pm Sat).

The 1977-built **Florida state capitol** (New Capitol; ☎ 850-488-6167; cnr Pensacola & Duval Sts) is a 22-story sheer concrete slab rising above the historic buildings, where legislature meets for 60 days a year from March to May. The top floor has an observation deck and art gallery. The luminous 1902 art-glass dome **Old Capitol** (☎ 850-487-1902; 400 S Monroe St; admission free; ☼ 9am-4:30pm Mon-Fri, 10am-4:30pm Sat, noon-4:30pm Sun & holidays) houses a political-history museum.

One of the country's largest collections of African American and African artifacts and art is at the **Black Archives Research Center & Museum** (☎ 850-599-3020; Carnegie Library, cnr Martin Luther King Jr Blvd & Gamble St; admission free; ☼ 9am-4pm Mon-Fri). See archaeological excavations and re-creations at **Mission San Luis** (☎ 850-487-3711; 2020 W Mission Rd; admission free; ☼ 10am-4pm Tue-Sun), the site of a Spanish and Native American mission (1656–1704). The ultimate treat for runners, skaters and cyclists is the paved 16-mile **Tallahassee–St Marks Historic Railroad State Trail** (☎ 877-822-5208; admission free; ☼ 8am-dusk year-round), starting 100 yards south of the intersection of Capital Circle (Hwy 319) and Woodville Hwy (Hwy 363), and ending next to Posey's Oyster Bar.

Sleeping & Eating

Accommodation rates can spike during football-game weekends and legislative sessions. Chains are clumped at exits along I-10 and along Monroe St between I-10 and downtown.

Inn at Park Avenue (☎ 850-222-4024; 323 E Park Ave; r $102-138; ℗ ✗) Half a mile from the Capitol, this lovely historic building has four intimate guest rooms, one equipped for wheelchairs.

Governor's Inn (☎ 850-681-6855; www.thegovinn .com; 209 S Adams St; r & ste $139-229; ℗) In a stellar downtown location, loft suites have a spiral staircase to an upper-level sitting area with open fireplace and balconies.

Posey's Oyster Bar (☎ 850-925-6172; 55 Riverside Dr, St Marks; mains $9-11; ☼ restaurant 10am-5pm Mon-Wed, to 10pm Thu, to 1am Fri & Sat, to 11pm Sun, bar until late Fri-Sun) Bands rock this pearl of an old-time waterfront oyster shack.

Wakulla Springs Lodge (☎ 850-224-5950; r $85-105; ℗ ✗) Time has stood still at this grand 1937 lodge, about 15 miles south of Tallahassee in the Wakulla Springs State Park. It's an immense Spanish-style building housing 27 rooms with original marble floors and blessedly no TVs.

Ball Room Restaurant (☎ 850-224-5950; mains $12-19; ☼ 7:30am-10am, 11:30am-2pm, 6-8pm). This excellent restaurant is part of Wakulla Springs Lodge.

Andrew's Capital Grill & Bar (☎ 850-222-3444; 228 S Adams St; mains $8-18; ☼ 11:30am-10pm Mon-Thu, to 11pm Fri & Sat, to 2pm Sun) Politicians spill onto sidewalk tables for salads and burgers named after themselves.

Andrew's 228 (☎ 850-222-3444; 228 S Adams St; mains $13-21; ☼ lunch Mon-Thu, dinner daily) The hottest tables in town are at Andrew's; it's a glamorous double-story Tuscany-meets-New York place, with martinis served in individual shakers.

Mon Père et Moi (☎ 850-877-0343; 3534 Maclay Blvd; ☽ lunch Tue-Sat, dinner Sat) This chocolaterie also has a café and pétanque games on Friday from 5pm to 8pm.

Nicholson Farmhouse (☎ 850-539-5931; www.nicholsonfarmhouse.com; 200 Coca-Cola Ave (SR 12), Havana; mains $14-30; ☽ 4-10pm Tue-Sat) About 20 miles north of Tallahassee, this restaurant has open-wagon hayrides around its collection of old farm houses and stores.

Entertainment

Bradfordville Blues Club (☎ 850-906-0766; www.bradfordvilleblues.com; 7152 Moses Lane, off Bradfordville Rd; tickets $15-22; ☽ 8pm-2am Fri & Sat) Down the end of a dirt road lit by tiki torches is a bonfire raging beneath the live oaks and stars, with hotter music.

Getting There & Around

The **Tallahassee Regional Airport** (☎ 850-891-7800, 800-610-1995) is about 5 miles southwest of downtown, off Hwy 263. You'll find the **Greyhound station** (☎ 850-222-4249, 800-231-2222; 112 W Tennessee St; ☽ 24hr) at the corner of Duval, opposite the downtown TalTran transfer center. **Amtrak** (☎ 850-244-2779, 800-872-7245; 918-1/2 Railroad Ave) travels to Orlando and cross-country to Los Angeles. **TalTran** (☎ 850-891-5200; http://talgov.com/taltran/index.cfm) has a main transfer-point downtown on Tennessee St at Adams St, with fares per adult/child $1/50¢, and operates a free **Old Town Trolley** (7am-6:30pm Mon-Fri). The *only* place to be found that rents out bikes is **Great Bicycle Shop** (☎ 850-224-7461; 1909 Thomasville Rd; bikes per 24hr $20; ☽ 10am-6pm Mon-Fri, 1-5pm Sat, noon-4pm Sun).

PANAMA CITY BEACH

Panama City Beach may have all but escaped 2004's Hurricane Ivan, but the winds of change are blowing gale-force here. A long-time drive destination as the closest beach to a funnel-web of highways from the surrounding states north, giving rise to the area's affectionate moniker the Redneck Riviera, the mid-20th century saw motels and amusement parks mushroom along the strip fronting the beach. A chapter ended when the 1963-opened Miracle Strip Amusement Park closed in late 2004

(revisit the park, and other state bygones at the virtual graveyard, Florida's Lost Attractions: www.lostparks.com).

Depending on when you're reading this, you'll see demolitions, construction and the unveiling of super-luxe developments (from 19,000 hotel rooms in 2005 to 33,000 in 2007). What's unlikely to change is Panama City Beach's status as the number-one spring break destination in the state, between approximately the first of March and Easter. The rest of the year (and anytime away from the main party zone), there's an infinitely more sedate family atmosphere. The **visitor bureau** (☎ 850-233-5070, 800-722-3224; www.thebeachloversbeach.com; 17001 Panama City Beach Parkway; ☽ 8am-5pm) has information about the area.

A renowned wreck-diving site, there are dozens of natural, historic and artificial reefs. **Divers Den** (☎ 850-234-8717; 3120 Thomas Dr; ☽ 8am-6pm Mon-Sat) has dives from $63 plus gear rental ($50). Get inspiration at the **Museum of Man in the Sea** (☎ 850-235-4101; 17314 Panama City Beach Parkway; adult/child $5/2.50; ☽ 9am-5pm) showcasing the history of diving.

St Andrews State Recreation Area (☎ 850-233-5140; 4607 State Park Lane; pedestrian or cyclist/vehicle $1/5) is graced with nature trails and swimming beaches (one of the best places to swim with children is the 'kiddie' pool's 4ft-deep water near the jetties area). Just offshore, **Shell Island** has fantastic snorkeling; there's a shuttle from St Andrews State Recreation Area for $19 round-trip including snorkeling gear.

Mini-golf is *big* in Panama City Beach. Holding fast to valuable Front Beach Rd frontage is the iconic 1959-built **Goofy Golf** (☎ 850-234-6403; 12206 Front Beach Rd; per round $5; ☽ 9am-10pm or later Mar-Sep) – look for the super-size sphinx.

Sleeping

Summer is high season for Panhandle beaches.

Flamingo (☎ 850-234-2232; www.flamingomotel.com; 15525 Front Beach Rd; r $39-189; P ☒) Most of the immaculate rooms at this family-run, very kid-friendly place on the beach have ocean views.

Sugar Sands Beach Resort (☎ 850-234-8802, 800-367-9221; 20723 Front Beach Rd; beachfront r $80-180) On a comparatively peaceful stretch of the beach, there's a variety of room options, all with microwave-equipped kitchens; or cook out on gas grills by the pool and gazebo.

Sterling Beach (☎ 866-573-7678; www.sterlingresorts.com; 6633 Thomas Dr; r $80-689; P ⊛) One of the flash new condo complexes, with enormous two- to four-bedroom apartments and every amenity you'd expect including a 4000ft free-form heated pool.

Eating

Boatyard (☎ 850-249-9273; 5323 N Lagoon Dr; mains $13-26; ⊙ lunch & dinner) There's live music, very fine martinis and talented chefs at this classy place that's gained a loyal following with locals.

Pineapple Willy's (☎ 850-235-0928; 9875 S Thomas Dr; mains $15-22; ⊙ 11am-late) A trip of a place with its own pier and fun bar; famed for its house special – slo'-cooked Jack Daniels BBQ ribs by the bucket-load.

Captain Anderson's Restaurant (☎ 850-234-2225; 5551 North Lagoon Dr; mains $12-40; ⊙ from 4:30pm Mon-Fri, 4pm Sat) This is widely regarded as Panama City Beach's top restaurant. If you dine early, you'll be able to watch the day's catch being unloaded at the adjoining marina.

Entertainment

Billing itself as the 'last local beach club' (and they may well be right), great bands fill the dancefloor at **Schooners** (☎ 850-235-3555; www.schooners.com; 5121 Gulf Dr; ⊙ 11am-late), in the shadow of soaring condos. The two mega nightclubs **Spinnaker** (☎ 850-234-7822; 8795 Thomas Dr) and **Club La Vela** (☎ 850-234-3866; 8813 Thomas Dr), with a techno bent.

Getting There & Around

Greyhound has a flag stop in Panama City Beach at the Hwy 98/Hwy 79 stoplight and a **Greyhound Station** (☎ 850-785-6111; 917 Harrison Ave) in Panama City.

A new international airport is due for completion by 2008.

SCENIC HIGHWAY 30A

Along the Panhandle coast between Panama City Beach and Destin, skip the main highway (Hwy 98) in favor of one of the most enchanting, and slightly surreal, drives in Florida: Scenic Hwy 30A. This 18-mile stretch of road hugs what's referred to as the emerald coast, for its almost fluorescent, gem-colored waters lapping brilliant white beaches of ground-quartz crystals swept down over centuries from the Appalachian Mountains and bleached and polished by the surf before washing back onto shore. Leading off Scenic Hwy 30A are pristine, wild parklands like **Grayton Beach State Recreation Area** (☎ 850-231-4210; 357 Main Park Rd, Santa Rosa Beach; pedestrian or cyclist/vehicle $1/4) and no high-rises, just little villages, including **Seaside** (www.seasidefl.com).

Remember the squeakily clean-cut township of Seahaven in Peter Weir's 1998 movie *The Truman Show*? Doll-like, sorbet-colored cottages clustered around a model town square, and people were unnervingly neighborly...except everything was indeed too contrived to be true. In the movie, the town was a fabricated set for a reality TV show, in which all the chirpy residents but the show's unwitting star, Truman, were actors. Well, they didn't have to build that town in a Hollywood backlot. They found it.

Filmed here in Seaside, *The Truman Show* captures perfectly this little village whose street signs really bear names like Cinderella Circle and Dreamland Heights. A planned community begun in 1981, it's won international design plaudits and redefined town-planning trends, creating a pedestrian-friendly enclave that evokes traditional regional architectural styles and conforms to strict building codes. And it *is* comically friendly, and you do half-expect cameras lurking around somewhere.

But for all that, Seaside's sweetness isn't sickening: kids ride bikes freely, people stroll, not drive, to one-off shops (no chains). There is a hip book and music shop, **Sundog Books** (☎ 850-231-5481; 89 Central Sq; ⊙ 9am-9pm), plus theater productions, the Ruskin Place artists' colony with galleries, studios and art-supply shops, glorious beaches just over the road, and just about zero stress. Hence Seaside's serenity is the source of some unique creative endeavors; and it is at least worth a stop to check out for yourself.

Good on-line resources are www.30-a.com, which has updated listings of all public beach access, and the **South Walton Chamber of Commerce website** (www.waltoncountychamber.com).

PENSACOLA

Two things have played a defining role in Pensacola over the past four-and-a-half centuries: the military, and hurricanes. The Spanish tried to colonize this stretch of the far-western Panhandle in 1559, but the hurricane-plagued settlement was abandoned after two years, leaving St Augustine (1565), to claim the longest continuous European settlement in the country. Since Pensacola's settlement (1698), five flags – Spain, France, Britain, the Confederacy and the US – have flown over the city. Its harbor and geographical position were key in its development as a military city throughout the intervening centuries and the Naval Air Station remains an intrinsic part of the city's population.

In 2004, Hurricane Ivan smashed through Pensacola, causing untold damage and destruction, with its barrier-island beaches taking the brunt of the impact. Clean-up and regeneration is a lengthy process, but its downtown renovated historic districts and ingrained local traditions have fortified Pensacola's perseverance; and the beaches are still a sensational place to spend time in the sun. The **visitor bureau** (☎ 850-434-1234, 800-874-1234; www.visitpensacola.com; 1401 E Gregory St; ☯ 8am-5pm) has maps and free Internet access.

Sights & Activities

The fascinating **Historic Pensacola Village** (☎ 850-595-5985; www.historicpensacola.org; adult/child $6/2.50; ☯ 10am-4pm Mon-Fri, tours 11am & 1pm Mon-Fri winter, 11am & 1pm Mon-Sat summer) encompasses a collection of mostly 19th-century buildings housing museums with indoor/outdoor exhibits. Admission includes a two-hour walking tour and entry to the excellent and quirky **TT Wentworth Museum** (330 S Jefferson St; admission free, donations accepted; ☯ 10am-4pm Mon-Sat).

The enormous Pensacola Naval Air Station (NAS) is home to the Blue Angels, its elite flight demonstration squadron, and the **National Museum of Naval Aviation** (☎ 850-453-3604, 800-327-5002; www.naval-air.org; 1750 Radford Blvd; admission free; ☯ 9am-5pm). On Tuesday and Wednesday at 8:30am between March and November (weather permitting) you can watch the Blue Angels practice their routines; Wednesday sessions are followed by pilot autographs.

UFO SPOTTING

Maybe it's activity from the Naval Air Station, but the far-western Panhandle has apparently had hundreds of UFO sightings in the past few decades. **Shoreline Park** (700 Shoreline Dr) in Gulf Breeze is a particular hotspot, where you're likely to find local skywatchers with binoculars and lawn chairs, but sightings have been reported right along the coast. It's as good a reason as any to spread out a blanket and gaze up at the stars.

Stretching 150 miles between West Ship Island (Mississippi) and Santa Rosa Island, Florida's section of the **National Seashore** (☎ 850-934-2600; www.nps.gov/guis; pedestrian or cyclist per 7 days $3, vehicle $8; ☯ dawn-dusk) covers Perdido Key, two sections of Santa Rosa Island (extending to the NAS across the Fort Pickens State Park Aquatic Preserve) and a clip of coastline around Destin and Fort Walton Beach. Hard-hit by Hurricane Ivan, much of it remained closed at the time of research including Fort Pickens; check with the seashore's headquarters and main **visitor center** (☎ 850-934-2600; 1801 Gulf Breeze Parkway; admission free; ☯ 9am-4:30pm) at Naval Live Oaks, about 6 miles east of Gulf Breeze, for updates.

Sleeping & Eating

Pensacola Victorian B&B (☎ 850-434-2818, 800-370-8354; www.pensacolavictorian.com; 203 W Gregory St; r $75-110; P ⊠) In a porticoed Queen Anne building, the four restful guestrooms, home-baked breakfasts, and hospitable innkeepers are all charming.

Suburban Lodge (☎ 850-453-4140; www.suburbanhotels.com; 3984 Barrancas Ave; r $65-75; P) Well located if you're heading out to the NAS, this friendly place has good-sized rooms with full kitchens; most have free wi-fi.

New World Inn (☎ 850-432-4111; www.newworldlanding.com; 600 S Palafox St; r $85-95, ste $125-145; P ⊠) This historic place sits on Pensacola's reclaimed waterfront of ships' ballast, with 15 period-furnished rooms.

H&O (☎ 850-432-1991; 301 E Gonzalez St; dishes $2.50-11; ☯ 8:30am-5pm Mon-Fri) Soul food that will rock your world: fried or baked chicken or catfish with sides of candied yams, black-eyed peas or okra, finished with peach cobbler or bread pudding.

FLORIDA

INTERSTATE MULLET TOSS

About 12 miles southwest of Pensacola, off Hwy 292 (which becomes Hwy 182), the town of Perdido Key runs right to the Alabama state line. Every year in April, locals gather at both sides of the border for a time-honored tradition: the mullet toss. The idea – apart from a very fine excuse for a party – is to see who can throw their (dead) mullet the furthest across the border from Florida into Alabama. People have developed their own techniques: tail first, head first, or breaking its spine and bending it in half for better aerodynamics.

The mullet toss is organized by the **Flora-Bama Lounge & Package Store** (www.florabama.com). Straddling the state line, just inside this legendary bar were pay phones either side of the entrance within arm's reach of each other, yet a long-distance call apart. Renowned for all sorts of off-beat events, the Flora-Bama has tried to get mullet tossing into the *Guinness Book of World Records,* but its time hasn't come, yet.

Hurricane Ivan sadly did a number on the Flora-Bama, and at the time of research it was no longer. But true to the spirit of the place, they held an appropriate wake, the No Tears in the Beer demolition and rebuild party, which saw locals gather to watch bulldozers raze what Ivan hadn't…and toast the impending new Flora-Bama. But even while the rebuilding takes place, the Mullet Toss goes on.

Jerry's Drive-In (☎ 850-433-9910; 2815 E Cervantes St; mains $7-12; ⏲ 10am-10pm Mon-Fri, 7am-10pm Sat) Not a drive-in (it was in 1939), and no longer owned by Jerry; ask for grits with your western omelette, if it's a Thursday go for the meatloaf sandwich, and get a banana milkshake, anytime. Credit cards are not accepted.

eat! (☎ 850-433-6905; 286 N Palafox St; mains $15-27; ⏲ lunch & dinner Tue-Fri, dinner Sat, brunch Sun) Modish Southern cuisine like fried green tomatoes with feta, balsamic and micro sprouts.

Jackson's Restaurant (☎ 850-469-9898; 400 S Palafox St; mains $20-60; ⏲ dinner) In a gorgeous historic building, this gourmet steakhouse is without peer.

Getting There & Around

Pensacola Regional Airport (☎ 850-436-5005, 850-436-5000; www.flypensacola.com) is served by many major airlines; it's 4 miles northeast of downtown off 9th Ave on Airport Blvd.

The **Greyhound station** (☎ 850-476-4800; 505 W Burgess Rd at Pensacola Blvd) is north of downtown; the **Amtrak station** (☎ 850-433-4966; 980 E Heinberg St at 15th Ave) is just north of the visitor information center.

Central USA

CAROL POLICH

Great Lakes

The Great Lakes area – part of the Midwest – is the USA's solid, sensible heartland. Folks here shrug at the brash glitz of the East Coast and flaky sex appeal of the West Coast, happy instead to be in the plain-speaking middle. It's no surprise that novelist Ernest Hemingway hailed from this part of the country, where words are seldom wasted.

Though much of the region is rural, it is also known for its cities. Soaring Chicago anchors the area. Milwaukee keeps the beer-and-Harley flame burning, while Minneapolis shines a hipster beacon out over the cornfields. Detroit, written off as a post-industrial scrap heap only a decade ago, has clawed its way back to worthy visit-ability.

But level-headed Midwesterners know it's about balance, so follow their cue when they leave the cities behind. They may go to remote parks like Michigan's Isle Royale or Minnesota's Boundary Waters, where one's only companion is the bear who's sniffed out your pancake mix. They may drive to Ohio's Yellow Springs for the world's best milkshake or Wisconsin's Prairie du Sac for the annual cow-chip throwing contest. Or they may swap their car for a horse-drawn buggy to ride through Indiana's or Ohio's Amish communities.

The Great Lakes themselves are huge, like inland seas, offering beaches, islands, dunes, resort towns and lots of lighthouse-dotted scenery. Dairy farms and fruit orchards blanket the region, meaning fresh pie and ice cream await hungry road-trippers. Thirsty travelers can indulge in the Midwest's beers – the cities here have long been known for suds crafting, thanks to their German heritage, and several microbreweries maintain the tradition.

Most visitors come in summer when the weather is fine for hiking, biking, canoeing and kayaking in the local lakes and forests. Snowmobiling and cross-country skiing take over in the butt-freezing winter (as do eating and drinking in warm taverns).

HIGHLIGHTS

- Absorbing the skyscrapers, museums, ethnic neighborhoods and foods of **Chicago** (p567)

- Exploring the remote waterfalls, forests and local color of Michigan's **Upper Peninsula** (p634)

- Turning back the clock with a plow and buggy in Ohio's **Amish Country** (p612)

- Paddling through the solitude of Minnesota's **Boundary Waters** (p658)

- Enjoying the beers, bratwursts and Harleys of **Milwaukee** (p636)

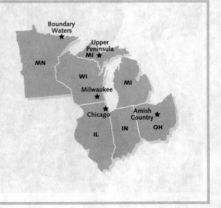

HISTORY

This fertile region has long been inhabited by advanced cultures like the Hopewell, which emerged around 200 BC, and the Mississippi River mound builders, who flourished from around AD 600. Both built mysterious mounds that were tombs for their leaders and possibly symbolic expressions of homage to their deities. You can see remnants at Cahokia (p598) in Illinois and Mound City (p615) in Ohio. The cultures began to decline around AD 1000, and later became home to groups like the Miami, Shawnee and Winnebago.

The first Europeans were French voyageurs (fur traders) who arrived in the early 17th century and explored, traded for furs with the indigenous people, and established missions and forts. But the French soon had rivals: the Ohio Company, a group of British entrepreneurs from England and Virginia, formed in 1748 to develop trade and control the Ohio Valley. Its explorations helped precipitate the French and Indian Wars (1754–61), after which Britain gained all the lands east of the Mississippi. Following the Revolutionary War, the area south of the Great Lakes became the new USA's Northwest Territory, which soon was divided into states.

The canals linking the Great Lakes to the area's river systems, built in the 1820s and '30s, along with railroad development in the next decades, stimulated settlement. But many conflicts erupted between the newcomers and Native Americans in the region, including the bloody 1832 Black Hawk War that forced the removal of the indigenous people to areas west of the Mississippi.

Industries sprang up and grew quickly, fueled by resources of coal and iron, and urged on by Civil War demands. The work available brought huge influxes of European immigrants from Ireland (in the early and mid-19th century), Germany (in the mid- to late 19th century), Scandinavia (in the late 19th century), Italy and Russia (around the turn of the 20th century), and southern and eastern Europe (in the early 20th century). In addition, for decades after the Civil War a great number of African Americans migrated to the region's urban centers from the South.

The region prospered during WWII and throughout the 1950s. Then came 20 years of social turmoil and economic stagnation. The decline of manufacturing in the 1970s, particularly in the car industry, resulted in unemployment in many 'Rust Belt' cities; Detroit and Cleveland were especially hard hit.

The 1980s brought urban revitalization and a shift away from economic reliance on

---

GREAT LAKES IN...

Five Days

Spend the first two days in **Chicago** (p567). On your third day, make the 1½-hour trip to **Milwaukee** (p636) for culture both highbrow and low. Take the ferry over to Michigan and spend your fourth day beaching in **Saugatuck** (p630). Come back via northern Indiana's **sand dunes** (p605) and **Amish communities** (p604).

One Week

After two days in Chicago, make for **Madison** (p640) on day three and its surrounding quirky sights. Spend your fourth day in Michigan's Upper Peninsula, taking in **Marquette** (p635) and **Pictured Rocks** (p634). Spend your fifth day at **Sleeping Bear Dunes** (p631) and **Traverse City** (p631), your sixth day in **Saugatuck** (p630) and your seventh day in **northern Indiana** (p604).

Two Weeks

After two days in **Chicago** (p567) and the next day in **Madison** (p640), visit **Minneapolis** (p646). Become one with nature in the **Boundary Waters** (p658) for a few days. Return south via the **Apostle Islands** (p645), then head into the Upper Peninsula to visit **Marquette** (p635) and **Pictured Rocks** (p634), followed by **Sleeping Bear Dunes** (p631) and **Traverse City** (p631). Make **Detroit** (p621) and environs your next stop for a few days, then drop in on the **Erie Islands** (p612). Return to Chicago via **northern Indiana** (p604), or delve deeper into **Ohio** (p605).

GREAT LAKES

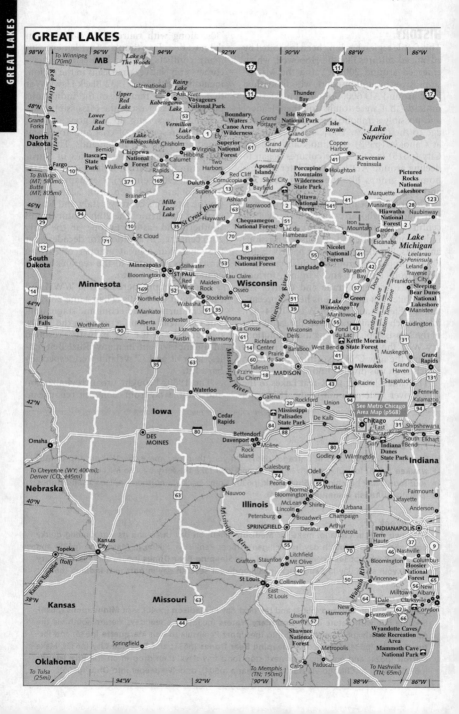

industry. In the past decade growth in the light manufacturing, service and high-tech sectors has meant better economic balance for the region. This process is continuing and the area's population has increased again, notably with newcomers from Asia and Mexico.

GEOGRAPHY & CLIMATE

Glaciers carved the Great Lakes during the last ice age. They now contain 15% of the world's fresh water. The largest by volume is Lake Superior, followed by Lakes Michigan, Huron, Ontario and Erie – all four of which Lake Superior could contain easily.

Most of the area's larger rivers run south into the major Ohio-Mississippi system. As these rivers were the main transportation and communication routes before the railways arrived, most of the region's larger cities lie along them or on the lakeshores.

Winters are long and can last from late November well into April, with plenty of snow, icy winds and subfreezing temperatures (eg Chicago and Minneapolis each average about 20°F in January, the coldest month). Don't be intimidated – but do pack warmly. Many people visit during this time as it's prime skiing and snowmobiling season. By June the sun is out and temperatures start to rise, and in July and August it can be downright hot and sticky. Spring and autumn fit in around the edges, and are wonderful times to visit (particularly autumn, when leaves are at their peak of color).

NATIONAL, STATE & REGIONAL PARKS

Several national parks and lakeshores are brushed across the Great Lakes region, including Voyageurs National Park (p659) in Minnesota; Isle Royale (p635), Sleeping Bear Dunes (p631) and Pictured Rocks (p634) in Michigan; the Apostle Islands (p645) in Wisconsin; and Indiana Dunes (p605) in Indiana. The **National Park Service website** (www.nps .gov) has direct links and phone numbers for individual parks. Make camping reservations on the website or call ☎ 800-365-2267.

Wide swaths of state park land also crisscross the Great Lakes.

See individual state introductory sections for state park details. Contact the National Park Service for indispensable trail pamphlets and other information.

DANGERS & ANNOYANCES

Blackflies (spring), mosquitoes (summer) and deer ticks (both) can be an unfortunate reality in the northern woods. Mostly they're just annoying, but they can carry West Nile virus (p1182) and Lyme disease (p1181). Protect yourself with a repellent that contains DEET. By late summer most bugs are gone.

In winter thin ice is a deadly hazard for skiers and especially snowmobilers. Err on the side of caution; don't trust the ice-safety opinion of anyone other than police, and park or forestry officials. Every year people die after crashing through 'frozen' lake ice.

Tune in to the radio during summer storms, when tornado warnings are frequent. Drivers should watch out for deer (see right).

GETTING THERE & AROUND

Air

Chicago's **O'Hare International Airport** (☎ 800-832-6352; www.flychicago.com) is the main hub for the region, but the city's second airport, **Midway Airport** (MDW; ☎ 773-838-0600; www.flychicago.com), isn't far behind. Detroit, Cleveland and Minneapolis also have busy airports with numerous international flights.

Boat

Two car/passenger ferries sail across Lake Michigan:

Lake Express (☎ 866-914-1010; www.lake-express .com; ☷ mid-May–Dec) Crossing between Milwaukee, Wisconsin and Muskegon, Michigan (one way adult/child $50/24, car/bicycle $59/7.50, 2½ hours).

SS Badger ferry (☎ 888-337-7948; www.ssbadger .com; ☷ mid-May–mid-Oct) Crossing between Manitowoc, Wisconsin and Ludington, Michigan (one way adult/child $49/22, car/bicycle $53/5, four hours).

Bus

Originating in Minnesota, **Greyhound** (☎ 800-231-2222; www.greyhound.com) is the principal long-distance carrier and connects major cities and towns. Secondary bus lines covering other areas:

Indian Trails (☎ 800-292-3831; www.indiantrails.com) Michigan, northern Indiana and Chicago.

Jefferson Lines (☎ 800-451-5333; www.jeffersonlines .com) Minnesota and southern Wisconsin.

Lakefront Lines (☎ 800-638-6338; www.lakefront lines.com) Ohio, northern Indiana and Chicago.

Van Galder Bus Co (☎ 800-747-0994; www.vangal derbus.com) Madison, Wisconsin and Chicago.

Some rural regions, particularly in northern Wisconsin and Minnesota, don't have any public transportation.

Car & Motorcycle

Southeast Michigan (including Detroit) is the least expensive place in the region to rent cars. Some major interstate highways (such as I-80 and I-90) charge tolls – roughly 3¢ per mile.

In winter road closures due to heavy snow are not very unusual; in most areas you can check conditions on the 24-hour weather station that is available on TVs with cable. Always carry a wool blanket in your car to use for warmth in case you get stuck in the snow or suffer a breakdown; don't rely on your car heater, as leaving your car idling with the windows up could make you vulnerable to carbon monoxide poisoning.

Keep an eye out for deer bounding across the road – they can make driving at dusk and nighttime treacherous.

Train

The national railroad network centers on Chicago, from where **Amtrak** (☎ 800-872-7245; www.amtrak.com) runs trains regularly to major US cities. Note that train stations are often closed except at arrival or departure times. Following are some daily trains from Chicago to other parts of the country:

California Zephyr To/from San Francisco (Emeryville), California via Omaha, Nebraska; Denver, Colorado; and Reno, Nevada.

Capital Limited To/from Washington, DC, via Toledo and Cleveland, Ohio, and Pittsburgh, Pennsylvania.

Cardinal Also runs to/from Washington, but goes via Indianapolis, Indiana, and Cincinnati, Ohio (three times per week only).

City of New Orleans To/from New Orleans, Louisiana, via Memphis, Tennessee.

Empire Builder To/from Seattle, Washington, via Minneapolis, Minnesota, and Glacier National Park, Montana.

Hoosier State To/from Indianapolis, Indiana.

Lake Shore Limited To/from New York City via Toledo and Cleveland, Ohio, and Buffalo and Albany, New York.

Southwest Chief To/from Los Angeles, California, via Kansas City, Missouri; Albuquerque, New Mexico; and Flagstaff, Arizona.

Texas Eagle To/from San Antonio, Texas, via St Louis, Missouri, and Dallas, Texas.

ILLINOIS

Chicago dominates the state with its cloud-scraping skyline, lakefront beaches, and superlative museums, restaurants and music clubs. But venturing further afield reveals quiet towns along the bluff-strewn Mississippi River, scattered shrines to local hero Abe Lincoln, and a trail of corn dogs, pie and drive-in movie theaters down Rte 66.

History

Illinois' earliest residents were mound builders whose scattered prehistoric vestiges evidence a great civilization that not only used tools and pottery but had developed religious beliefs. After periods under the control of France, Britain and Virginia, an independently governed Illinois Territory was proclaimed in 1809, and Illinois became a state in 1818.

Many early settlers were from the South and favored slavery, but there were certainly abolitionists, too. The state's internal conflict on the issue was articulated in 1858 during the historic debates between senatorial candidates Abraham Lincoln and Stephen A Douglas. Despite divided loyalties, Illinois contributed greatly to the Union in the Civil War, and in the process emerged as an industrial state, proficient in steel-making, meatpacking, distilling and heavy manufacturing. This growth created great private wealth but also led to labor strife as workers struggled against low wages and poor conditions. Unions began

forming in the mid-19th century, and violent strikes took place between 1877 and 1919.

The Prohibition era of the 1920s corrupted the state's political system. Then the Great Depression hit hard – up to half of Illinois' workers were unemployed. In the 1930s Democratic governor Henry Horner was able to rebuild state finances and restore honest and efficient government. WWII enabled the state economy to recover.

Illinois drew worldwide attention in 2003 when outgoing governor George Ryan, with a final sweep of his pen, emptied the state's death row. More than 150 prisoners had their sentences commuted. Ryan said there were too many 'arbitrary and capricious' errors in the death penalty system for it to be fair, as several recent exoneration cases had proved. The state remains at the forefront of the national debate on the issue.

Information

Illinois sales tax is 6.25%; city and county taxes add up to 2.75% more.

Check the following websites for state-wide information:

Illinois Bureau of Tourism (☎ 800-226-6632; www .enjoyillinois.com)
Illinois highway conditions (☎ 800-452-4368; www .illinoisroads.info)
Illinois state park information (☎ 217-782-6752; www.dnr.state.il.us) State parks are free to visit. Campsites cost $6 to $20; some accept reservations (fee $5).

CHICAGO

Chicagoans love their city profusely, as you'll find out when you plop down on any barstool (and there are many in town). 'Have you seen the Sears Tower? Millennium Park? Chicago has the world's greatest architecture,' the guy in the Cubs cap takes another swill. 'Have you been to the blues clubs? Jazz clubs? Theaters? Chicago is tops there, too, with 200 stages putting on shows.'

The local effuses on, about the 18 miles of Lake Michigan beachfront, the 77 neighborhoods supporting vibrant Mexican, Polish, Indian and Vietnamese communities, and the foodie scene that even extends to gourmet hot dogs.

The thing is, one has to admit, these folks speak the truth. The City of Big Shoulders

---

ILLINOIS FACTS

Nicknames Prairie State, Land of Lincoln
Population 12.7 million
Area 57,900 sq miles
Capital city Springfield (population 111,500)
Other city Chicago (2.9 million)
Official motto State Sovereignty – National Union
Birthplace of Author Ernest Hemingway (1899–1961), animator Walt Disney (1901–66), jazz musician Miles Davis (1926–91), politico Hillary Rodham Clinton (b 1947)
Famous for First skyscraper, zipper, corn dog, Ferris wheel, Twinkie

GREAT LAKES

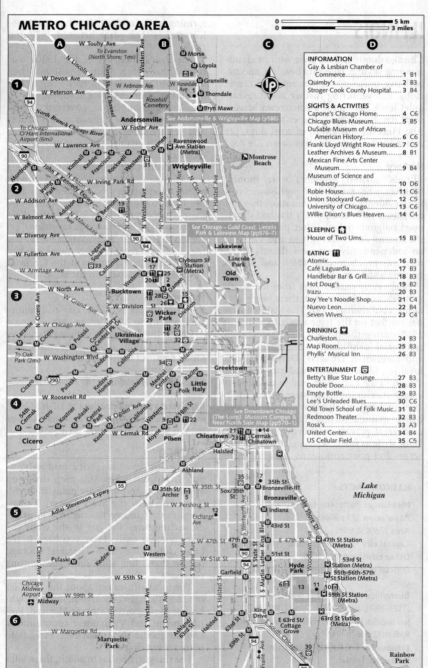

METRO CHICAGO AREA

0 ——————— 5 km
0 ——————— 3 miles

INFORMATION
Gay & Lesbian Chamber of
Commerce.................................**1** B1
Quimby's....................................**2** B3
Stroger Cook County Hospital......**3** B4

SIGHTS & ACTIVITIES
Capone's Chicago Home..............**4** C6
Chicago Blues Museum................**5** B5
DuSable Museum of African
American History....................**6** C6
Frank Lloyd Wright Row Houses..**7** C5
Leather Archives & Museum.........**8** B1
Mexican Fine Arts Center
Museum..................................**9** B4
Museum of Science and
Industry...............................**10** D6
Robie House.............................**11** C6
Union Stockyard Gate................**12** C6
University of Chicago.................**13** C6
Willie Dixon's Blues Heaven........**14** C4

SLEEPING 🛏
House of Two Urns....................**15** B3

EATING 🍴
Atomix....................................**16** B3
Café Laguardia..........................**17** B3
Handlebar Bar & Grill................**18** B3
Hot Doug's...............................**19** B2
Irazu......................................**20** B3
Joy Yee's Noodle Shop...............**21** C4
Nuevo Leon.............................**22** B4
Seven Wives............................**23** C4

DRINKING 🍷
Charleston...............................**24** B3
Map Room...............................**25** B3
Phyllis' Musical Inn...................**26** B3

ENTERTAINMENT 🎭
Betty's Blue Star Lounge............**27** B3
Double Door.............................**28** B3
Empty Bottle............................**29** B3
Lee's Unleaded Blues.................**30** C6
Old Town School of Folk Music....**31** B2
Redmoon Theater......................**32** B3
Rosa's....................................**33** A3
United Center...........................**34** B4
US Cellular Field.......................**35** C5

See Andersonville & Wrigleyville Map (p580)

See Chicago – Gold Coast, Lincoln
Park & Lakeview Map (pp576–7)

See Downtown Chicago
(The Loop), Museum Campus &
Near North Side Map (pp570–1)

Lake
Michigan

Rainbow
Park

has a friendly energy going on (and that isn't just the beer talking).

Chicago is a wonderful place to roam, from downtown where you can gawk at the steely skyscrapers, to the lakefront paths, to the grassy parks. Locals tend to hibernate in the blustery winter, then make a greedy dash for the outdoor festivals, ballparks and beer gardens in the all-too-short summer.

History
In the late 17th century the Potawatomi dominated the land, and it was they who gave the name 'Checaugou' – or wild onions – to the vicinity around Chicago River's mouth.

The small settlement quickly established itself as a crossroads, and grew as a shipping and railroad hub. The first steel mill opened in 1857, and immigrants flooded in to take jobs in industry and with the railroads. The opening of the stockyards in 1865 drew even more newcomers, as Chicago became the world's hog butcher.

On October 8, 1871 legend has it that Mrs O'Leary's cow kicked over a lantern and started the great Chicago Fire, which destroyed the whole inner city and left 90,000 people homeless. The disaster became an opportunity to replace wide areas of substandard housing and create space for modern industrial and commercial buildings, like the world's first skyscraper, which appeared on the horizon in 1885.

In the 1920s Prohibition led almost immediately to the infamous period of gangsterism. In the middle of the Depression, after the murder of Mayor Anton Cermak, the Democratic Party machine gained control of city politics and has maintained it for most of the years since.

The city's population peaked in 1950, then started to decline as residents moved to outer suburbs and other states. Despite some improvements, the postwar period was dominated by corruption scandals, civil rights protests and the fiasco of the 1968 Democratic Convention, when anti–Vietnam War demonstrators were the victims of what was later termed a 'police riot.' Starting in the 1970s traditional industries declined severely: the stockyards and the South Shore steel mills closed, and many smaller factories moved away or went out of business.

The City That Works went to work on itself, and with classic, steely determination cleaned up its image. Today the processing of information and ideas has taken precedence over the processing and transport of products. The city's downtown and many of its neighborhoods are thriving, though areas of great poverty remain, particularly on the south side.

CHICAGO IN...

Two Days
Take an architectural boat cruise and look up at the city's skyscrapers. Look down from the **John Hancock Center** (p575), one of the world's tallest buildings. See 'The Bean' reflect the skyline from **Millennium Park** (p574). Stroll out on festive **Navy Pier** (p575). Hungry after all the walking? Chow down on a deep-dish pizza at **Giordano's** (p587). Make the second day a cultural one: browse the **Art Institute** (p574), **Field Museum** (p575) and **Adler Planetarium** (p575). Head north to Al Capone's gin joint, the **Green Mill** (p591), for evening jazz.

Four Days
Follow the two-day itinerary, then on your third day rent a bicycle, dip your toes in Lake Michigan at **North Avenue Beach** (p582), and cruise through **Lincoln Park** (p578), making stops at the zoo and conservatory. If it's baseball season, head directly to **Wrigley Field** (p592) for a Cubs game; if it's winter, take in a Bulls (basketball), Bears (football) or Blackhawks (hockey) game. A smoky blues club, such as **Buddy Guy's Legends** (p591), is a fine way to finish the day (or start the morning).

Pick a neighborhood on your fourth day – **Pilsen** (p579), **Andersonville** (p581) or **Devon Avenue** (p581) – and wander, eat, shop and eat some more. Then see a play at one of Chicago's 200 theaters or comedy at **Second City** (p592).

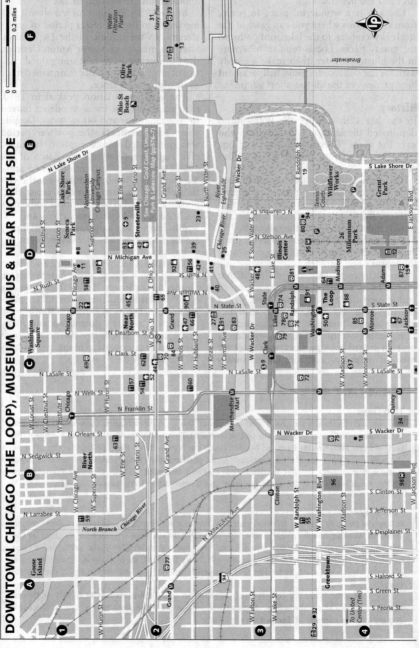

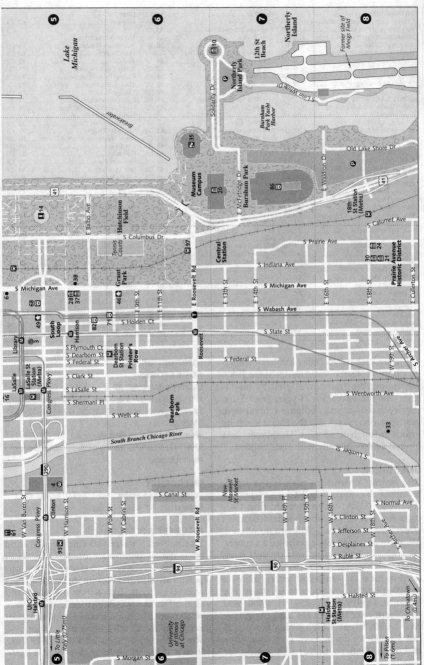

Lake
Michigan

Breakwater

Former site of
Meigs Field

Northerly
Island

12th St
Beach

Northerly
Island Park

Solidarity Dr

Burnham
Park Yacht
Harbor

Old Lake Shore Dr

E Waldron Dr

E McFetridge Dr

Burnham Park

18th
St Station
(Metra)

S Calumet Ave

S Prairie Ave

S Indiana Ave

S Michigan Ave

E 13th St

E 14th St

E 16th St

E 18th St

Prairie Avenue
Historic District

E Cullerton St

Central
Station

Museum
Campus

E Balbo Ave

Hutchinson
Field

Tennis
Courts

S Columbus Dr

Grant
Park

E 9th St

E 11th St

E Roosevelt Rd

S Wabash Ave

S State St

S Holden Ct

S Harrison

S Plymouth Ct

S Dearborn St

S Federal St

S Clark St

S LaSalle St

S Shermanl Pl

S Wells St

Dearborn
St Station
Printer's
Row

S Michigan Ave

South
Loop

Library

LaSalle St
Station
(Metra)

Congress Pkwy

Roosevelt

S Federal St

S Wentworth Ave

Dearborn
Park

South Branch Chicago River

S Lumber St

S Archer Ave

W Van Buren St

Clinton

W Harrison St

W Polk St

W Cabrini St

S Canal St

New Maxwell
St Market

W Roosevelt Rd

W 14th Pl

W 15th Pl

W 16th St

S Clinton St

S Jefferson St

S Desplaines St

S Ruble St

S Normal Ave

S Halsted St

UIC
Halsted

University
of Illinois
at Chicago

S Morgan St

Halsted
St Station
(Metra)

To Chinatown
(0.4mi)

To Little
Italy (0.75mi)

To Pilsen
(1.6mi)

Congress Pkwy

Mayor Richard M Daley has been Chicago's popular Democratic leader since 1989, continuing the tradition started by his father, who was mayor for 21 years prior. Sure, they've faced scandals aplenty (corruption, graft, patronage etc). But the Daley Machine grinds through it all, and 'Da Mayor' gets elected again – usually with little contest.

Orientation

The central downtown area is the Loop, a hub of skyscrapers and Chicago Transit Authority (CTA) trains. Beyond this, Chicago is a city of neighborhoods. Chicago's streets are laid out on a grid and numbered; Madison and State Sts are the grid's center. As you go north, south, east or west from here, each increase of 800 in street numbers corresponds to 1 mile. At every increase of 400, there is a major arterial street. For instance, Division St (1200 N) is followed by North Ave (1600 N) and Armitage Ave (2000 N), at which point you're 2.5 miles north of downtown. Pick up a copy of Lonely Planet's *Chicago City Map* for details.

Information

BOOKSTORES

Quimby's (Map p568; ☎ 773-342-0910; 1854 W North Ave) Ground Zero for comics, 'zines and underground culture.
Savvy Traveler (Map pp570-1; ☎ 312-913-9800; 310 S Michigan Ave)
Women & Children First (Map p580; ☎ 773-769-9299; 5233 N Clark St) Women-penned fiction and other feminist tomes.

EMERGENCY

Police, fire and ambulance (☎ 911) Emergency.
Rape crisis (☎ 888-293-2080)

INTERNET ACCESS

Internet cafés where you can buy CDs and burn digital photos are on N Clark St in Lakeview. Walgreens pharmacies (see opposite) are also good for photo burning. Bars and restaurants, like Kitsch'n (p588) and Goose Island Brew Pub (p590), provide free wi-fi; more places in Lincoln Park, Bucktown and Near North are adding the service.
Screenz (Map pp576-7; ☎ 773-348-9300; 2717 N Clark St; per hr $8.40; ◷ 8am-midnight Mon-Thu, 9am-1am Fri & Sat, 9am-midnight Sun)

INTERNET RESOURCES

Check the Media websites (below), particularly the *Reader* and *Time Out*. Also:

Metromix (www.metromix.com) Tribune-owned website with restaurant, bar, entertainment and gym reviews.

Vegchicago (www.vegchicago.com) Vegetarian/vegan dining guide to the city.

Wildchicago (www.wttw.com/wildchicago) Website celebrating local weirdness; the archives direct you to places for minnow swallowing and spankings, among others.

LIBRARIES

Harold Washington Library Center (Map pp570-1; ☎ 312-747-4300; 400 S State St; ☽ 9am-7pm Mon-Thu, 9am-5pm Fri & Sat, 1-5pm Sun) The world's largest public library, located in a grand, art-filled building.

MEDIA

Chicago Reader (www.chicagoreader.com) Free alternative newspaper with comprehensive arts and entertainment listings; widely available at bookstores, bars and coffee shops; out on Thursday.

Chicago Sun-Times (www.suntimes.com) The Trib's daily tabloid-esque competitor; its junior version is *Red Streak*, available weekdays.

Chicago Tribune (www.chicagotribune.com) The city's stalwart daily newspaper; its younger, trimmed-down version is *RedEye*, available weekdays.

Time Out Chicago (www.timeoutchicago.com) Hip, service-oriented magazine with all-encompassing listings; out on Thursday.

Venus Magazine (www.venuszine.com) Arts-oriented quarterly 'zine for women.

Chicago's National Public Radio (NPR) affiliate is WBEZ-FM 91.5. For alternative music tune into WXRT-FM 93.1.

MEDICAL SERVICES

Northwestern Memorial Hospital (Map pp570-1; ☎ 312-926-5188; 251 E Erie St)

Stroger Cook County Hospital (Map p568; ☎ 312-864-6000; 1969 W Ogden Ave) Public hospital serving patients low on money or sans insurance.

Walgreens (Map pp570-1; ☎ 312-664-8686; 757 N Michigan Ave; ☽ 24hr) Chain with dozens of outlets.

MONEY

ATMs are plentiful downtown, with many near Chicago and Michigan Aves. To change money, try Terminal 5 at O'Hare International or these Loop places:

Travelex (Map pp570-1; ☎ 312-807-4941; 19 S LaSalle St)

World's Money Exchange (Map pp570-1; ☎ 312-641-2151; 203 N LaSalle St)

POST

Post office (Map pp570-1) Main (☎ 312-983-8182; 433 W Harrison St; ☽ 24hr); Fort Dearborn (☎ 312-644-0485; 540 N Dearborn St)

TOURIST INFORMATION

The **Chicago Office of Tourism** (☎ 312-744-2400, 877-244-2246; www.cityofchicago.org/exploringchicago or, www.877chicago.com) operates well-staffed and stocked visitors centers:

Chicago Cultural Center Visitors Center (Map pp570-1; 77 E Randolph St; ☽ 10am-6pm Mon-Fri, 10am-5pm Sat, 11am-5pm Sun)

Water Works Visitors Center (Map pp576-7; 163 E Pearson St; ☽ 7:30am-7pm)

TRAVEL AGENCIES

STA Travel (Map pp576-7; ☎ 312-951-0585; 2570 N Clark St) Budget travel specialists.

Dangers & Annoyances

The lakefront, major parks and some neighborhoods, especially south and west of the Loop, can become bleak and forbidding places at night. Neighborhoods can change completely in just a few blocks, so be aware of your surroundings.

Most of Chicago's violent crime is committed by street gangs battling over drug turf; the good news is such crimes have decreased recently, due to increased policing methods like surveillance cameras in drug-trafficking areas. The most common crimes against tourists are pickpocketing, bag snatching, vehicle break-ins and bicycle theft.

Sights

Chicago's main attractions are found mostly in or near the city center, though visits to distant neighborhoods, like Andersonville, Pilsen and Hyde Park, can also be very rewarding. Purchase the lump-sum **CityPass** (☎ 888-330-5008; www.citypass.com; adult/child 3-11 $49.50/39) and save on admission fees for six of Chicago's most popular attractions: the Field Museum of Natural History, Art Institute of Chicago, Adler Planetarium, Hancock Observatory, Museum of Science & Industry and Shedd Aquarium. Students who present ID will often receive reduced museum admission.

For a more in-depth exploration of the Windy City, pick up Lonely Planet's *Chicago* city guide.

THE LOOP

The city center is named for the elevated train tracks that lasso its streets. It is busy all day and has a budding nightlife, thanks in large part to the Theater District, where playhouses cluster near the intersection of N State and W Randolph Sts.

Art Institute of Chicago

Chicago's premier cultural institution, the **Art Institute** (Map pp570-1; ☎ 312-443-3600; www .artic.edu; 111 S Michigan Ave; adult/child $12/7, admission Tue free; ☽ 10:30am-4:30pm Mon-Fri, 10:30am-8pm Thu, 10am-5pm Sat & Sun) houses treasures and masterpieces from around the globe, including a fabulous selection of both Impressionist and Postimpressionist paintings. Georges Seurat's pointillist *A Sunday on La Grande Jatte* is here; so is Grant Wood's *American Gothic*. Allow two hours to browse the highlights, but art buffs should allow much longer. A new wing is scheduled to open in 2007.

Sears Tower

Sears Tower (Map pp570-1; ☎ 312-875-9696; www.the -skydeck.com; 233 S Wacker Dr; adult/child 3-11 $11.95/8.50; ☽ 10am-10pm May-Sep, 10am-8pm Oct-Apr) was the world's undisputed tallest building right until the end of the 20th century. Then the Malaysians built the Petronas Towers, which the Taiwanese one-upped just six years later with their giant, Taipei 101; now Shanghai is poised to out-do Taipei. Sigh. Still, Sears is mighty high in the sky, and it remains the USA's tallest building. Check visibility and waiting times at the Jackson Blvd entrance before joining the queues, then persist through a security check, a series of waiting rooms, a film and more lines before the 70-second elevator ride to the 103rd-floor Skydeck. Perhaps, the John Hancock Center (opposite) might be a better choice.

Chicago Cultural Center

The exquisite interior of the **Cultural Center** (Map pp570-1; ☎ 312-744-6630; www.chicagocultural center.org; 78 E Washington St; admission free; ☽ 10am-7pm Mon-Thu, 10am-6pm Fri, 10am-5pm Sat, 11am-5pm Sun) features rooms modeled on the Doge's Palace in Venice and Palazzo Vecchio in Florence, and is notable for its stained-glass dome and sparkling mosaics. Free exhibits and lunchtime concerts are ongoing.

Chicago Board of Trade & Mercantile Exchange

The **Board of Trade** (Map pp570-1; ☎ 312-435-3590; www.cbot.com; 141 W Jackson Blvd) and **Mercantile Exchange** (Map pp570-1; ☎ 312-930-8249; www.cme .com; 30 S Wacker Dr) are the world's two main brokers of commodities, futures and options. Inside, manic traders gesture with unintelligible hand signals that result in piles of money gained or lost. Due to security concerns, the galleries where you could view the nuttiness have closed to the public (except for pre-arranged groups); they may open again, so call for updates.

GRANT PARK

A plan by the Olmsted Brothers architectural firm turned a marshy lakefront wasteland into a park that has the formal lines of Versailles.

Its centerpiece, **Buckingham Fountain** (Map pp570-1; cnr Congress Parkway & Columbus Dr), is one of the world's largest, with a 1.5 million gallon capacity. The fountain squirts on the hour from 10am to 11pm April to October, accompanied at night by multicolored lights and music.

The stunning new **Millennium Park** (Map pp570-1; ☎ 312-742-1168; www.millenniumpark.org; Michigan Ave btwn Monroe & Randolph Sts) occupies Grant Park's northwest corner. Frank Gehry's 120ft-high swooping silver band shell anchors what is, in essence, an outdoor modern design gallery. It includes Anish Kapoor's 110-ton Cloud Gate sculpture (aka 'The Bean') that reflects the city; Jaume Plensa's 50ft-high glass-block fountain that projects video images underneath cascading water; a Gehry-designed bridge (his first) that spans Columbus Dr and offers great skyline views; and a winter ice-skating rink (p582). The Grant Park Orchestra (p592) plays free concerts at the band shell.

SOUTH LOOP

Ignored for the last five decades, the South Loop – which includes the lower ends of downtown and Grant Park, along with the historic Printer's Row neighborhood of rare bookshops – has suddenly soared from dereliction to development central.

The excellent **Spertus Museum** (Map pp570-1; ☎ 312-322-1700; www.spertus.edu; 618 S Michigan Ave; adult/child $5/3, Fri admission free; ☽ 10am-5pm Sun-Wed, 10am-7pm Thu, 10am-3pm Fri) covers 5000 years of

Jewish faith and culture. Kids can dig for relics at the Artifact Center. Spertus moves into its bold, beautiful, new, next-door facility in 2007.

The nearby **Museum of Contemporary Photography** (Map pp570-1; ☎ 312-663-5554; www.mocp .org; Columbia College, 600 S Michigan Ave; admission free; ☑ 10am-5pm Mon-Fri, 10am-8pm Thu, noon-5pm Sat) will captivate shutterbugs with its displays of US photographs taken since 1945.

MUSEUM CAMPUS

This lakefront area south of Grant Park has three significant attractions side by side.

Field Museum of Natural History

The mammoth **Field Museum** (Map pp570-1; ☎ 312-922-9410; www.fieldmuseum.org; 1400 S Lake Shore Dr; adult/child 4-11 $19/9; ☑ 9am-5pm) houses everything but the kitchen sink. Highlights include 'Africa,' a walk-through exhibit that moves from city streets to Saharan sand dunes, culminating in the hold of a slave ship; and Sue, the largest *Tyrannosaurus rex* yet discovered.

Shedd Aquarium

Top draws at the famous **Shedd Aquarium** (Map pp570-1; ☎ 312-939-2438; www.sheddaquarium .org; 1200 S Lake Shore Dr; adult/child 3-11 $23/16; ☑ 9am-5pm Mon-Fri Sep-May, 9am-6pm Mon-Wed & Fri Jun-Aug, 9am-10pm Thu Jun-Aug, 9am-6pm Sat & Sun year-round) include the Oceanarium, with its beluga whales and frolicking white-sided dolphins, and the new shark exhibit, where there's just 5in of Plexiglas between you and 30 or so fierce-looking swimmers.

Adler Planetarium & Astronomy Museum

Touch a 1000lb meteorite in the interactive galleries at the **Adler Planetarium** (Map pp570-1; ☎ 312-922-7827; www.adlerplanetarium.org; 1300 S Lake Shore Dr; adult/child 4-17 $13/11; ☑ 9:30am-4:30pm), then view the cosmos in a digital sky show controlled from your chair's armrest.

NEAR NORTH

The area north of the Chicago River to Chicago Ave encompasses several points of interest. Between the river and Oak St, the **Magnificent Mile** (Map pp570-1; N Michigan Ave) is the much-touted upscale shopping strip, where Bloomingdales, Neiman's and Saks will lighten your wallet.

Navy Pier (Map pp570-1; ☎ 312-595-7437; www .navypier.com; 600 E Grand Ave; admission free; ☑ 10am, closing times vary seasonally from 7pm-midnight) was once the city's municipal wharf. Its 0.5-mile length is now covered with a Ferris wheel, an Imax theater, numerous shops and gimmicky chain restaurants. Locals groan over its commercialization, but its lakefront view and cool breezes can't be beat.

The **Chicago Children's Museum** (p583) and gorgeous **Smith Museum of Stained Glass Windows** (Map pp570-1; ☎ 312-595-5024; admission free; ☑ 10am, closing times vary seasonally from 7pm-midnight) are also on the Pier.

Take a close look when passing by the gothic **Tribune Tower** (Map pp570-1; 435 N Michigan Ave) to see chunks of the Taj Mahal, Parthenon and other famous structures embedded in the lower walls. The white terra-cotta exterior of the **Wrigley Building** (Map pp570-1; 400 N Michigan Ave) glows day or night.

Donald Trump will make his mark on the skyline come 2008. That's when the new $750 million, 92-story **Trump Tower** (Map pp570-1; 401 N Wabash Ave) opens, just a few feet shorter than the John Hancock Center (see below). It will hold the city's priciest condos, natch.

The **Museum of Broadcast Communications** (Map pp570-1; ☎ 312-245-8200; www.museum.tv; cnr State & Kinzie Sts), filled with fascinating radio and TV nostalgia, is another newbie in the 'hood (after moving from the Loop). Call for admission prices and opening hours.

GOLD COAST

Starting in 1882, Chicago's wealthy flocked to this neighborhood flanking the lake between Chicago and North Aves. Within 40 years, most of the Gold Coast was covered with mansions.

Today the neighborhood giant is the 1127ft-tall **John Hancock Center** (Map pp576-7; ☎ 312-751-3681; www.hancock-observatory.com; 875 N Michigan Ave; adult/child 5-12 $9.75/6 plus tax; ☑ 9am-11pm), which has a great 94th-floor observatory that's often less crowded than the one at Sears Tower. Better yet, skip the observatory and head straight up to the 96th-floor Signature Lounge, where the view is free if you buy a drink ($6 to $11).

The 154ft-tall, turreted **Water Tower** (Map pp576-7; cnr Chicago & Michigan Aves) is a defining city landmark; it was the sole downtown survivor of the 1871 Great Fire.

CHICAGO – GOLD COAST, LINCOLN PARK & LAKEVIEW

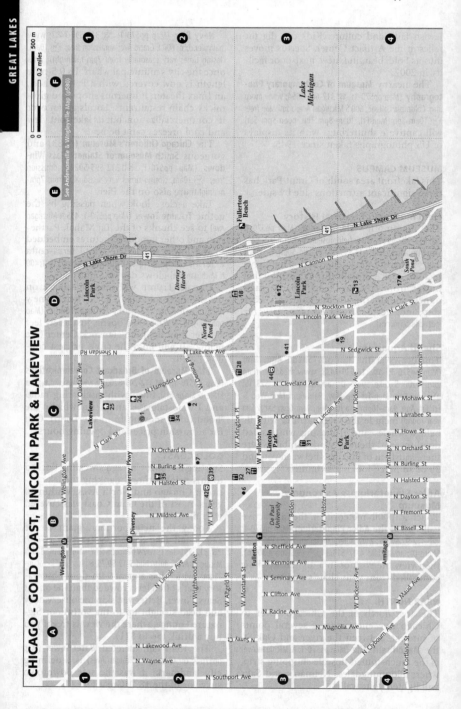

See Andersonville & Wrigleyville Map (p580)

GREAT LAKES

INFORMATION		
Screenz	1	C2
STA Travel	2	C2
Water Works Visitors Center	3	E8
SIGHTS & ACTIVITIES		
1308-1312 N Astor St	4	E6
1355 N Astor St	5	E6
Bike Chicago	(see 15)	
Biograph Theater	6	B3
Box Car Café	7	C2
Charnley-Persky House	8	E6
Chicago Historical Society	9	D5
International Museum of Surgical Science	10	E5
John Hancock Center	11	E7
Lincoln Park Conservatory	12	D3
Lincoln Park Zoo	13	D4
Museum of Contemporary Art	14	F8
North Ave Beach	15	E5
Oak St Beach	16	F7
Paddleboat Rental	17	D4
Peggy Notebaert Nature Museum	18	D3
St Valentine's Day Massacre Site	19	D4
Standing Lincoln Sculpture	20	E5
Water Tower	21	E8
SLEEPING		
Days Inn Gold Coast	22	D5
Gold Coast Guest House	23	D7
Inn of Lincoln Park	24	C2
Willows Hotel	25	C1
EATING		
Alinea	26	B5
Bourgeois Pig	27	B3
Crepe & Coffee Palace	28	C3
Flo	29	A8
Kendall College	30	B7
Potbelly Sandwich Works	31	C3
Taco & Burrito Palace #2	32	B3
Twin Anchors	33	D5
Wiener Circle	34	C2
DRINKING		
Alive One	35	B2
Goose Island Brew Pub	36	B5
Olde Town Ale House	37	D5
Signature Lounge	(see 11)	
ENTERTAINMENT		
Back Room	38	E7
Blues	39	B2
Hideout	40	A5
Hot Tix	41	D3
Hot Tix	(see 3)	
Kingston Mines	42	B2
Lookingglass Theatre	43	E8
Neo	44	C3
Second City	45	D5
Steppenwolf Theatre	46	B5
SHOPPING		
900 N Michigan	47	E7
Water Tower Place	48	E8

The **Museum of Contemporary Art** (Map pp576-7; ☎ 312-280-2660; www.mcachicago.org; 220 E Chicago Ave; adult/student 12-18 $10/6, Tue evening admission free; 10am-8pm Tue, 10am-5pm Wed-Sun) displays head-scratching works by Franz Kline, René Magritte, Cindy Sherman and Andy Warhol.

To sample the Gold Coast's former grandeur, saunter down **N Astor Street** (Map pp576–7), where gems include the 1887 mansions at 1308–1312 N Astor St, by architect John Wellborn Root; the Georgian Revival house at 1355 N Astor St; Frank Lloyd Wright's Charnley-Persky House at 1365 N Astor, which he proclaimed the 'first modern building'; and the 1929 art deco Russell House at 1444 N Astor St.

OLD TOWN

Northwest of the Gold Coast, this once-simple neighborhood of wooden houses was one of the first in the city to gentrify, starting as a hippy haven in the late 1960s. The intersection of North Ave and Wells St is the epicenter today, with restaurants, bars and Second City (p592) fanning out from here.

LINCOLN PARK

Lincoln Park is an urban oasis spanning 1200 leafy acres between North Ave (1600N) and Ardmore Ave (5800N), though the widest swath is between North Ave and Diversey Parkway (2800N). 'Lincoln Park' is also the name for the abutting neighborhood. Both are alive day and night with people skating, walking dogs, pushing strollers and driving in circles looking for a place to park.

The **Lincoln Park Zoo** (Map pp576-7; ☎ 312-742-2000; www.lpzoo.org; 2200 N Cannon Dr; admission free; 10am-4:30pm Nov-Mar, 10am-5pm Apr-Oct, 10am-6:30pm Sat & Sun Jun-Aug) is popular with families, who stroll by the habitats of gorillas, lions, tigers and other exotic creatures; the zoo's reputation took a hit in 2005 when several animals died of unknown causes. Near the zoo's north entrance, the magnificent 1891 **Conservatory** (Map pp576-7; ☎ 312-742-7736; 2391 N Stockton Dr; admission free; 9am-5pm) coaxes palms, ferns and orchids to flourish despite Chicago's brutal weather. The **Peggy Notebaert Nature Museum** (Map pp576-7; ☎ 773-755-5100; www.naturemuseum.org; 2430 N Cannon Dr; adult/child 3-12 $7/4, admission free Thu; 9am-4:30pm Mon-Fri, 10am-5pm Sat & Sun) has a year-round butterfly park and other natural wonders. For a duck's-eye view of the park, try **paddleboating** (Map pp576-7; 312-742-2038; 2021 N Stockton Dr; 30min rental $12-16; 10am-5:30pm Mon-Fri, 10am-7pm Sat & Sun summer) from the dock near Café Brauer.

The newly spiffed-up **Chicago Historical Society** (Map pp576-7; ☎ 312-642-4600; www.chicagohistory.org; 1601 N Clark St; adult/child 6-12/student 13-22 $5/1/3, Mon admission free; 9:30am-4:30pm Mon-Sat, noon-5pm Sun) focuses on the city's history as seen through the lives of ordinary citizens. Further north, the **Standing Lincoln sculpture** (Map pp576–7) is by Augustus Saint-Gaudens.

LAKEVIEW

North of Lincoln Park, this neighborhood can be enjoyed by ambling along Halsted St, Clark St, Belmont Ave or Southport Ave, which are well supplied with restaurants and bars. Ivy-covered **Wrigley Field** (Map p580; 1060 W Addison St) is named for the chewing-gum guy and is home to the adored Chicago Cubs. For more information, see p592.

The area around the ballpark is often referred to as Wrigleyville.

WICKER PARK, BUCKTOWN & UKRAINIAN VILLAGE

West of Lincoln Park, these three neighborhoods – once havens for working-class, central European immigrants, and writers like Nelson Algren and Simone de Beauvoir – are now among Chicago's hottest property lots. Heaps of small galleries, boutiques, trendy restaurants and martini-and-sushi lounges have shot up, especially near the Milwaukee/North/Damen Ave intersection; to reach the area take the CTA Blue Line to Damen.

WEST SIDE

West of the Loop is a patchwork of ethnic neighborhoods, blight and urban renewal. **Greektown** (Map pp570–1) runs along Halsted St. **Little Italy** (Map p568) extends along Taylor St. The University of Illinois at Chicago (UIC) lies between the two. Randolph St north of Greektown holds several hip new restaurants in an area often called the West Loop. Further west is the **United Center** (Map p568; 1901 W Madison St), home to the Bulls, Blackhawks and large-scale special events (see p593).

PILSEN

Long a first stop for immigrants, this neighborhood southwest of Little Italy is now predominantly Latino – 18th St has scores of taquerías, bakeries and small shops selling everything from devotional candles to Mexican CDs. The CTA Blue Line 18th St station is covered with Mexican murals.

The **Mexican Fine Arts Center Museum** (Map p568; ☎ 312-738-1503; www.mfacmchicago.org; 1852 W 19th St; admission free; ☼ 10am-5pm Tue-Sun) exhibits work by Mexican artists. It is the largest Latino arts institution in the US. The art ranges from classical themed portraits to piles of carved minibus tires, and Mexico's turbulent, revolutionary history is well represented.

NEAR SOUTH SIDE

A century ago, the best and worst of Chicago lived side by side south of Roosevelt Rd. Prairie Ave between 16th and 20th Sts was Millionaire's Row, while the Levee District, four blocks to the west, was packed with saloons, brothels and opium dens. When the millionaires moved north, the neighborhood declined, and mansions were demolished for industry. Now, like the neighboring South Loop (p574), trendy businesses are rushing in by the truckful, and dilapidated warehouses are being transformed into luxury lofts.

In a humble building on Michigan Ave, the Chess brothers started a recording studio in 1957. Muddy Waters, Howlin' Wolf, Bo Diddley and Chuck Berry cut tracks here. Now incarnated as **Willie Dixon's Blues Heaven** (Map p568; ☎ 312-808-1286; www.bluesheaven.com; 2120 S Michigan Ave; admission incl tour $10; ☼ noon-3pm Mon-Fri, noon-2pm Sat), it holds a collection of blues memorabilia.

The moving **National Vietnam Veterans Art Museum** (Map pp570-1; ☎ 312-326-0270; www.nvvam.org; 1801 S Indiana Ave; adult/student $10/5; ☼ 11am-5pm Tue-Sat) exhibits artworks by veterans.

The Prairie Ave Historic District has preserved a few old mansions in the area, like the 1880s **John J Glessner House** (Map pp570-1; ☎ 312-326-1480; 1800 S Prairie Ave; adult/child 5-12 $10/6, admission free Fri), with tours at 1pm, 2pm and 3pm Wednesday to Sunday, and 1836 Greek Revival **Henry B Clarke House** (Map pp570-1; ☎ 312-326-1480; 1855 S Indiana Ave; adult/child 5-12 $10/6, admission free Fri), with tours at noon, 1pm and 2pm Wednesday to Sunday. A combination ticket costs adult/child $15/9.

CHINATOWN

Chinatown's charm is best enjoyed by browsing its many small shops for herbs, tea and almond cookies, and eating in its restaurants. Wentworth Ave south of Cermak is the retail heart of old Chinatown; Chinatown Sq, along Archer Ave north of Cermak, is the newer commerce district and at its wonderful noisiest on weekends. **Ping Tom Memorial Park** (Map pp570-1; 300 W 19th St) offers dramatic city-railroad-bridge views. Take the CTA Red Line to Cermak-Chinatown.

SOUTH SIDE

The South Side has had a tough time since WWII. Housing projects created impoverished neighborhoods where community ties were broken and gangs held sway. Whole neighborhoods vanished as crime and blight drove residents away. Some areas survived the damage, and redevelopment now aims to promote mixed-income communities.

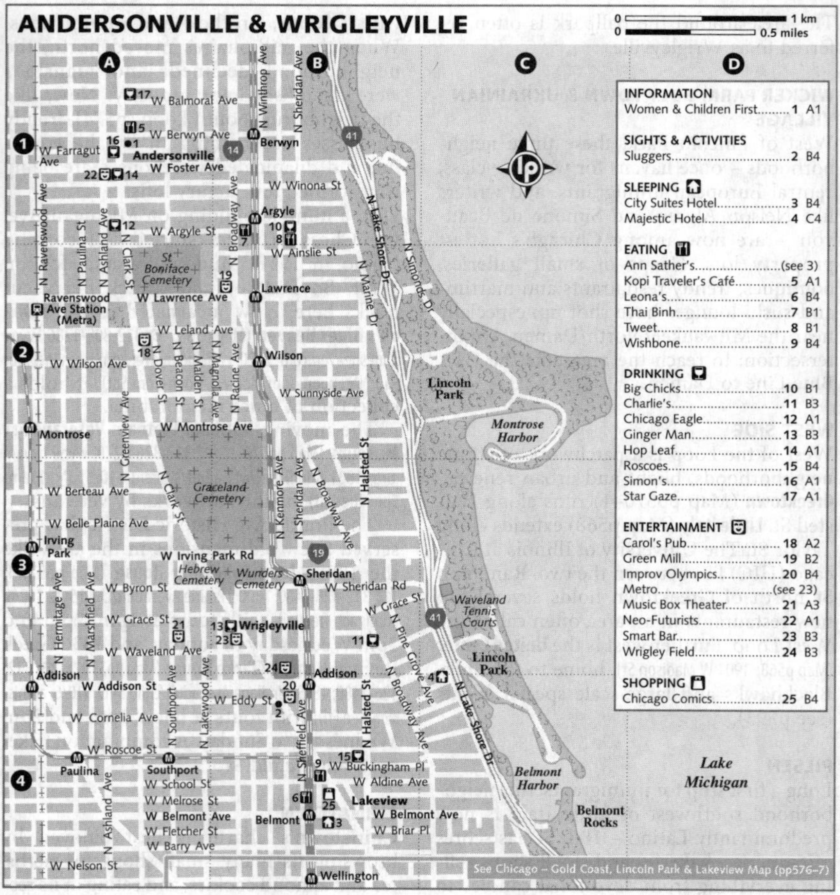

ANDERSONVILLE & WRIGLEYVILLE
0 1 km
0 0.5 miles
A
B
C
D
1
2
3
4
INFORMATION
Women & Children First........1 A1
SIGHTS & ACTIVITIES
Sluggers........2 B4
SLEEPING
City Suites Hotel........3 B4
Majestic Hotel........4 C4
EATING
Ann Sather's........(see 3)
Kopi Traveler's Café........5 A1
Leona's........6 B4
Thai Binh........7 B1
Tweet........8 B1
Wishbone........9 B4
DRINKING
Big Chicks........10 B1
Charlie's........11 B3
Chicago Eagle........12 A1
Ginger Man........13 B3
Hop Leaf........14 A1
Roscoes........15 B4
Simon's........16 A1
Star Gaze........17 A1
ENTERTAINMENT
Carol's Pub........18 A2
Green Mill........19 B2
Improv Olympics........20 B4
Metro........(see 23)
Music Box Theater........21 A3
Neo-Futurists........22 A1
Smart Bar........23 B3
Wrigley Field........24 B3
SHOPPING
Chicago Comics........25 B4
W Balmoral Ave
W Berwyn Ave
Berwyn
W Farragut Ave
Andersonville
W Foster Ave
W Winona St
Argyle
W Argyle St
W Ainslie St
St Boniface Cemetery
W Lawrence Ave
Lawrence
Ravenswood Ave Station (Metra)
W Leland Ave
W Wilson Ave
Wilson
W Sunnyside Ave
Montrose
W Montrose Ave
Graceland Cemetery
W Berteau Ave
W Belle Plaine Ave
Irving Park
W Irving Park Rd
Hebrew Cemetery
Wunders Cemetery
Sheridan
W Sheridan Rd
W Byron St
W Grace St
W Waveland Ave
Wrigleyville
Addison
W Addison St
W Eddy St
W Cornelia Ave
W Roscoe St
Paulina
Southport
W School St
W Melrose St
W Belmont Ave
W Fletcher St
W Barry Ave
W Nelson St
W Buckingham Pl
W Aldine Ave
Lakeview
Belmont
W Briar Pl
Wellington
N Ravenswood Ave
N Paulina St
N Ashland Ave
N Clark St
N Broadway Ave
N Winthrop Ave
N Sheridan Ave
N Lake Shore Dr
N Marine Dr
N Simonds Dr
N Dover St
N Beacon St
N Malden St
N Magnolia Ave
N Racine Ave
N Greenview Ave
N Kenmore Ave
N Halsted St
N Hermitage Ave
N Marshfield Ave
N Southport Ave
N Lakewood Ave
N Sheffield Ave
N Pine Grove Ave
Lincoln Park
Montrose Harbor
Waveland Tennis Courts
Belmont Harbor
Belmont Rocks
Lake Michigan
See Chicago – Gold Coast, Lincoln Park & Lakeview Map (pp576–7)

The neighborhoods radiating from 35th St and Martin Luther King Jr Dr are unofficially named **Bronzeville** (Map p568), and were the center of Chicago's black culture from 1920 until 1950, comparable to Harlem in New York. Many of the area's grand houses are being restored, especially on Calumet Ave between 31st and 33rd Sts (although visitors should still be cautious). Note particularly the **Frank Lloyd Wright row houses** (Map p568; 3213–3219 S Calumet Ave). To reach the area, take the CTA Green Line to 35th St-Bronzeville-IIT.

The new **Chicago Blues Museum** (Map p568; ☎ 773-828-8118; 3636 S Iron St) displays photos, films and relics like Howlin' Wolf's guitar and the Blues Brothers' suits, spread across a loft near US Cellular Field. Call ahead for prices and opening hours.

HYDE PARK

At the prestigious **University of Chicago** (Map p568; 5801 S Ellis Ave), in the heart of Hyde Park, faculty and students have racked up 74 Nobel prizes between them (the economics department lays claim to about one-third of them). The bookish residents give the place an insulated, pleasant, small-town air. The area is easily reached via Metra Electric trains from the Randolph St station to the 55th-56th-57th St station.

The vast **Museum of Science & Industry** (Map p568; ☎ 773-684-1414; www.msichicago.org; cnr 57th St & S Lake Shore Dr; adult/child 3-11 $9/5; 🕒 9:30am-

4pm Mon-Sat, 11am-4pm Sun, extended in summer) will overstimulate the serenest of souls with its myriad (and often loud) exhibits that examine everything on earth. Highlights include a WWII German U-boat nestled in an underground display ($5 extra to tour it) and the 'body slices' exhibit (two bodies cut in half-inch sections then pressed between pieces of glass).

Of the numerous buildings that Frank Lloyd Wright designed in the Chicago area, none is more famous or influential than the **Robie House** (Map p568; ☎ 773-834-1847; 5757 S Woodlawn Ave; adult/child 7-18 $12/10). The resemblance of its horizontal lines to the flat landscape of the Midwestern prairie became known as the Prairie style. Inside are 174 art glass windows and doors. Tours are offered at 11am, 1pm and 3pm Monday to Friday (continuous from 11am to 3:30pm Saturday and Sunday).

The **DuSable Museum of African American History** (Map p568; ☎ 773-947-0600; www.dusablemu seum.org; 740 E 56th Pl; adult/child 6-12 $3/1, Sun admission free; ⏰ 10am-5pm Mon-Sat, noon-5pm Sun) has good artworks and exhibits on black Americans from slavery to the civil-rights era.

ANDERSONVILLE
Creative types, lesbians, gays and yuppies occupy most of this walkable, bar-filled neighborhood (Map p580), which was once heavily Swedish. Take the CTA Red Line to the Berwyn stop and walk west .8 miles. Get off one stop south at the pagoda-like

Argyle St station and you're in the heart of New Chinatown, and its abundant Chinese, Vietnamese and Thai restaurants.

DEVON AVENUE
Devon Ave (Map p568), in Chicago's northernmost neighborhood, is where worlds collide – Indian women in jewel-toned saris glide by Muslim men in white skullcaps, and Nigerian women in bright print robes shop beside Orthodox men in black yarmulkes. It is one of the most diverse communities you'll see, and makes an outstanding destination for shopping and serial eating (samosas, kabobs, kosher donuts and more). Devon Ave at Western Ave is the main intersection; get there via the Western Ave 49B bus.

Activities
Tucked away in Chicago's 552 parks are public golf courses, ice rinks, swimming pools and more. Activities are free or low cost, and the necessary equipment is available for rent in the parks. Contact the **Chicago Park District** (☎ 312-742-7529; www.chicago parkdistrict.com); there's a separate number for **golf information** (☎ 312-245-0909).

BICYCLING
Bicycling is truly awesome, if somewhat crowded, along the 18.5-mile lakefront path. **Bike Chicago** (☎ 312-755-0488; www.bikechi cago.com; bikes per hr/day from $8.75/34; ⏰ 9am-7pm Apr-Oct, extended hrs summer; Navy Pier (Map pp570-1;

GANGLAND CHICAGO

The city would rather not discuss its gangster past, and consequently there are no brochures or exhibits about infamous sites. So you'll need to use your imagination when visiting the following, as most are not designated as notorious.

Two murders took place near the **Holy Name Cathedral** (Map pp570-1; 735 N State St). In 1924 North Side boss Dion O'Banion was gunned down in his florist shop (738 N State St) after he crossed Al Capone. O'Banion's replacement, Hymie Weiss, fared no better. In 1926 he was killed on his way to church by bullets flying from a window at 740 N State St.

The **St Valentine's Day Massacre Site** (Map pp576-7; 2122 N Clark St) is where Capone goons dressed as cops lined up seven members of Bugs Moran's gang against the garage wall that used to be here and sprayed them with bullets. The garage was torn down in 1967.

In 1934, the 'lady in red' betrayed John Dillinger at the **Biograph Theater** (Map pp576-7; 2433 N Lincoln Ave). He was shot by the FBI outside the theater.

The speakeasy in the basement of the glamorous, smoky jazz bar, Green Mill (p591), was a Capone favorite.

Visit **Capone's Chicago Home** (Map p568; 7244 S Prairie Ave) on the South Side – although the residence was used mostly by Capone's wife, Mae, and other relatives.

600 E Grand Ave; Millennium Park Bike Station Map pp570-1; Millennium Park, 239 E Randolph St; North Ave Beach Map pp576-7; 1600 N Lake Shore Dr) rents out bicycles and offers free, guided, three-hour tours departing from Millennium Park/Navy Pier/North Ave Beach at 10am/10:30am/11am and 1pm/1:30pm/2pm, respectively. The group also provides free, do-it-yourself maps. In-line skates (for the same price) are available, too.

SWIMMING

Take a dip, build a sand castle or just loaf in the sun at one of Chicago's 33 beaches, operated by the **Park District** (☎ 312-742-7529; www.chicagoparkdistrict.com). All are staffed with lifeguards during the summer. **North Ave Beach** (Map pp576-7; 1600 N Lake Shore Dr) and **Oak Street Beach** (Map pp576-7; 1000 N Lake Shore Dr), both close to downtown, are particularly body-filled. Brace yourself, as the water remains keister-numbing well into July.

BOATING

The **Chicago Sailing Club** (☎ 773-871-7245; www.chicagosailingclub.com) offers all levels of instruction, including five-day beginner's classes for $400, or sailboats to rent from $35/55 per hour on weekdays/weekends. The departure point is from Belmont Harbor (Map p580).

KAYAKING

For a duck's-eye view of downtown, kayak the Chicago River with **Wateriders Adventure Agents** (☎ 312-953-9287; www.wateriders.com). Various tours take in architectural sights and ghost and gangster spots. Beginners welcome. Call for prices, schedule and departure locations.

BASEBALL BATTING CAGES

Brush up on your batting skills at **Sluggers** (Map p580; ☎ 773-472-9696; 3540 N Clark St), a popular bar and grill across from Wrigley Field. Fifteen pitches cost $1.

ICE SKATING

The Chicago Park District operates a first-class winter ice rink at **Daley Bicentennial Plaza** (Map pp570-1; ☎ 312-742-7650; 337 E Randolph St) and at the **McCormick Tribune Ice Rink** (Map pp570-1; 55 N Michigan Ave) in Millennium Park. Admission is free to both, skate rental costs $3 to $7.

Walking Tour

This 3-mile tour winds past tall buildings, sandy beaches and gangster sites – and gets you on the El train – in about three hours.

Start at the **Art Institute** (**1**; p574), one of the city's most-visited attractions. The lion statues out front make a classic keepsake photo. Walk a few blocks north to avant-garde **Millennium Park** (**2**; p574), and saunter in to explore 'The Bean' sculpture, video-projecting fountains and other contemporary designs. Follow with a visit to the **Cultural Center** (**3**; p574), across Michigan Ave, to examine the gorgeous interior (and maybe hear a free concert).

Stay on Michigan Ave and soon you'll cross the Chicago River. If you go down the steps flanking the bridge, you'll find the architectural **Wendella Sightseeing Boats** (**4**; p585), a worthy way to view Chicago's steely overlords.

Just north of the bridge you'll pass the **Wrigley Building** (**5**; **p575**), glowing as white as the Double Mint twins' teeth, followed closely by the Gothic, eye-popping **Tribune Tower** (**6**; **p575**).

You're in the heart of the **Magnificent Mile** (**7**; **p575**) now. Shop your way past the **Water Tower** (**8**; **p575**) and on up to the **John Hancock Center** (**9**; **p575**). The thirsty can ascend for a drink on the 96th floor to enjoy a spectacular view of the city you're traversing.

Back on the road, keep heading north a few blocks to E Lake Shore Dr. Look for signs for the 'pedway', which will take you underneath Lake Shore Dr and deposit you amid the buffed bodies on **Oak Street Beach** (**10**; left). Wade in if it's summer, or loll on the sand watching the joggers and cyclists cruise past.

Feeling refreshed? Walk west on Division St (it connects to the beach via the Division Pedway) past the rowdy bars to the Clark/Division Red Line train stop. Get on and ride north two stops to Fullerton. Nearby on Lincoln Ave sits the **Biograph Theater** (**11**; p581), where the 'lady in red' deceived gangster John Dillinger, who was then gunned down. You're in the heart of Lincoln Park now, with myriad eating and drinking options. Once sated, return to the Fullerton station, but get on the Brown Line train this time, which returns downtown on above-ground tracks past

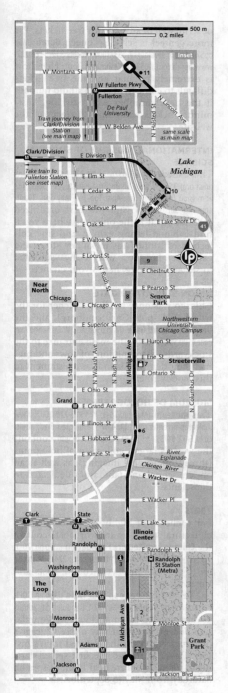

city's skyscrapers. You'll pass so close you can practically touch them.

Chicago for Children

Chicago is a kid's kind of town. Most museums have special areas to entertain and educate wee ones. A good resource is **Chicago Parent** (www.chicagoparent.com), a free publication available at libraries, the Children's Museum and elsewhere. Also check www.chicagokids.com.

BLUE CHICAGO STORE

Kids can listen to a live blues band perform in the smoke- and alcohol-free basement of the **Blue Chicago Store** (Map pp570-1; ☎ 312-661-1003; 534 N Clark St; adult/child 11 & under $5/free), next door to venue Blue Chicago (p591). Performances are hourly from 8pm to 11pm Saturday. What the kids' setting lacks in smoky atmosphere it makes up for in fret-bending music – authentic blues licks that have nothing to do with lollipops.

CHICAGO CHILDREN'S MUSEUM

This **museum** (Map pp570-1; ☎ 312-527-1000; www.chichildrensmuseum.org; 700 E Grand Ave; admission $7, Thu evening free; ☻ 10am-8pm) is on Navy Pier, and features exhibits where kids can climb a schooner, excavate dinosaur bones and generate hydroelectric power (it's fun – really). Follow up with an expedition down the Pier itself, including spins on the Ferris wheel and carousel.

OTHER SIGHTS

Shedd Aquarium (p575) is drenched with whales, sharks and weird-looking fish – always young-crowd pleasers. The **Field Museum of Natural History** (p575) offers lots and lots of that perennial kid favorite – dinosaurs! **Lincoln Park Zoo** (p578) has a children's area and farm where tykes can touch the animals. The **Museum of Science & Industry** (p580) has a chick hatchery and model trains running over a 3500-sq-ft track.

Other kid-friendly activities in Chicago include an **El ride** around the Loop; get on the Brown Line at Merchandise Mart

(Map pp570–1) and go to Clark St, which takes you on a leisurely trip through the thick of downtown's tall buildings, or try the **Loop Tour Train** (right). In July and August, a lakefront swim at **North Avenue Beach** (p582) is a must, where you'll find there's soft sand, lifeguards, a snack bar and bathrooms.

Some stores offer special experiences for kids: in addition to purveying dolls from bygone eras, **American Girl Place** (Map pp570–1; ☎ 877-247-5223; 111 E Chicago Ave) has a theater with performances of a girl-oriented musical ($26 per ticket), and a café where dolls are seated and treated as part of the family. The **Lego Store** (Map pp570–1; ☎ 312-494-0760; Nordstrom, 520 N Michigan Ave) lets kids go wild in a vibrantly colored play area where they can build their own creations.

American Childcare Services (☎ 312-644-7300; per hr $16.50, transportation fee $10) provides professional babysitters who will come to your hotel (four-hour minimum service).

Quirky Chicago

Sure, your friends will listen politely as you describe your trip to the Sears Tower's tip. But you'll stop them mid-yawn when you unleash your knowledge of all things kinky culled from a Leather Museum visit, or show them the bruises amassed at a Jerry Springer Show fight. Chicago has a fine collection of unusual sights and activities to supplement its standard attractions.

LEATHER ARCHIVES & MUSEUM

Ben Franklin liked to be flogged? Egypt's Queen Hatshepsut cross-dressed and had a foot fetish? Learn the kinky history of leather, fetish and S&M subcultures at the **Leather Archives & Museum** (Map p568; ☎ 773-761-9200; www. leatherarchives.org; 6418 N Greenview Ave; admission $5; ☼ noon-8pm Thu & Fri, noon-5pm Sat & Sun). Exhibits rotate every six months; past displays have included home-crafted whips and a leather rose collection. The on-site shop sells posters, pins and other 'pervertibles.'

JERRY SPRINGER & OPRAH WINFREY TELEVISION SHOWS

On the **Jerry Springer Show** (Map pp570–1; ☎ 312-321-5365; www.jerryspringertv.com; 454 N Columbus Dr, 2nd fl, Chicago, IL 60611) you can bet you'll see mud-slinging, nudity, a knock-down dragout fight or all three simultaneously. Call

or write well in advance for free tickets. Far more genteel is self-help queen **Oprah** (Map pp570–1; ☎ studio 312-633-1000, tickets 312-591-9222; www.oprah.com; 1058 W Washington Blvd). Her show is extremely popular and the free tickets difficult to come by. Try the studio number if the ticket number isn't working. Last-minute tickets sometimes surface on the website.

INTERNATIONAL MUSEUM OF SURGICAL SCIENCE

This **museum** (Map pp576–7; ☎ 312-642-6502; www .imss.org; 1524 N Lake Shore Dr; adult/student $6/3, Tue admission free; ☼ 10am-4pm Tue-Sun May-Sep, 10am-4pm Tue-Sat Oct-Apr) isn't the best organized around, but it is the only one where you'll find a blood-letting exhibit and fine collection of 'stones' (as in kidney stone and gallstone). For those who've always wanted to see an iron lung, here's your chance.

UNION STOCKYARD GATE

Chicago was once the 'hog butcher for the world' (a la poet Carl Sandburg), and the **Union Stockyard Gate** (Map p568; 850 W Exchange Ave, near 4100 S Halsted St) – the main entrance to the stockyards where millions of cows and pigs met their demise – stands as a testament to this bloody role.

MUSEUM OF HOLOGRAPHY

This **museum** (Map pp570–1; ☎ 312-226-1007; www .holographiccenter.com; 1134 W Washington Blvd; adult/ child 6-12 $4/3; ☼ 12:30-4:30pm Wed-Sun) contains the world's largest collection of holograms (three-dimensional imaging), as well as an on-site school and laboratory dedicated to the science.

Tours

For a choice of highly recommended architectural tours by foot or boat, contact the **Chicago Architecture Foundation** (Map pp570–1; ☎ 312-922-3432; www.architecture.org; 224 S Michigan Ave). Tours are held year-round; costs and times vary.

The 40-minute **Loop Tour Train** (Map pp570–1; Cultural Center Visitors Center, 77 E Randolph St; admission free), guided by an Architecture Foundation docent, is a great way to see Chicago's buildings and learn the elevated train's history. Tickets are first-come, first-served starting at 10am. Tours are held 11am to 1pm on Saturday from May to September.

Chicago Greeter (☎ 312-744-8000; www.chicago greeter.com; ☺ year-round) pairs you with a local city dweller who takes you on a personal free two- to four-hour tour customized by theme (architecture, history, gay and lesbian and more) or neighborhood. Travel is by foot and/or public transportation; reserve seven business days in advance. **InstaGreeter** (☺ 10am-4pm Sat, 11am-4pm Sun) is the quicker version, offering one-hour tours (free) on-the-spot from the visitors center at 77 E Randolph St.

Mercury Chicago Skyline Cruises (Map pp570-1; ☎ 312-332-1353; cnr Michigan Ave & Wacker Dr; adult/ child under 12 $18/8; ☺ May-Sep) and **Wendella Sightseeing Boats** (Map pp570-1; ☎ 312-337-1446; 400 N Michigan Ave; adult/child 4-11 $19/10; ☺ Apr-Nov) offer identical 90-minute tours of the river and lake.

A cast member leads the zingy **Second City Neighborhood Tour** (☎ 312-337-3992) through the hot-spots where John Belushi, Chris Farley and other alums yucked it up. The two-hour tour costs $15. It departs at 4pm on Sunday (April to September) from the Historical Society (p578) and includes admission.

City Segway Tours (☎ 877-734-8687; www.citysegwaytours.com; 3hr tour $65; ☺ Apr-Oct) zips past lakefront museums and parks on kooky scooters. It departs from Adler Planetarium.

See p581 for bicycle and kayak tours.

Festivals & Events

Chicago has a full events calendar year-round, but the biggies are held in the summer. **SummerDance** (Map pp570-1; ☎ 312-742-4007; 601 S Michigan Ave; admission free) is ongoing mid-June through August, with bands playing rumba, samba and other world music preceded by fun dance lessons. It starts at 6pm Thursday to Saturday, and 4pm Sunday.

Each of the following events is free and held downtown on a weekend, unless noted otherwise. For exact dates and other details, call the city's **Office of Special Events** (☎ 312-744-3315; www.cityofchicago.org/specialevents).

JUNE
Blues Festival The biggest free blues fest in the world is in early June, with four days of the music that made Chicago famous.
Country Music Festival Nashville's biggest stars come to town for a weekend of twanging in late June.
Gospel Festival More than 35 choirs and performers sing a weekend's worth of hallelujahs in early June.

Pride Parade (☎ 773-348-8243; www.chicagopridecalendar.org) A celebration of individuality, held in late June in Lakeview's Boys' Town neighborhood.
Taste of Chicago This 10-day food festival in Grant Park concurs with the Independence Day celebration. Many locals think the Taste is over-rated.

JULY
Independence Day Concert Held on July 3, featuring Tchaikovsky's *1812 Overture* and big-time fireworks.

AUGUST
Air and Water Show People flock to North Ave Beach in mid-August to see daredevil displays by boats and planes.
Latin Music Festival The merengue, salsa and other Latin rhythms are as sultry as the late August summer weather.

SEPTEMBER
Jazz Festival Chicago's longest-running music festival attracts big names on the national jazz scene over the Labor Day weekend.

Sleeping

Chicago lodging doesn't come cheap. The best way to cut costs is to reserve a room through a local hotel consolidator like **Hot Rooms** (☎ 800-468-3500; www.hotrooms.com), which often slashes prices in half. On weekends, and when big conventions trample through town (ie frequently), your options become much slimmer, so plan ahead to avoid unpleasant surprises. The prices we've listed are normal midweek rates in summer, the high season. Taxes add 15.4% to the rates.

For B&B accommodations, contact **Chicago Bed & Breakfast Association** (www.chicago-bed-breakfast.com; r $95-295), an online service representing guesthouses throughout the city. Many properties have two- to three-night minimum stays.

Hotels in The Loop are convenient to Grant Park, the museums and business district, but are not near the best nightlife. Popular with visitors, the Near North/Gold Coast neighborhoods have a plethora of places for eating, drinking, shopping and entertainment. Hotels in Lincoln Park and Lakeview are often cheaper than the big ones downtown and are near hip nightlife, with the Loop a short El ride away.

THE LOOP
Budget
HI Chicago (Map pp570-1; ☎ 312-360-0300; www.hichicago.org; 24 E Congress Pkwy; dm incl tax $34.50;

GREAT LAKES

P 💻) Chicago's best hostel is immaculate, centrally located, and offers bonuses like a staffed information desk, free volunteer-led tours, discount passes to museums and shows, an attached café and luggage storage ($1 per bag). The simple dorm rooms have six to 12 beds and attached bathrooms. Parking is $18.

Midrange

Essex Inn (Map pp570-1; ☎ 312-939-2800, 800-621-6909; www.essexinn.com; 800 S Michigan Ave; r $89-169; P 💻 🏊) This special hotel (and room decor) makes you feel like you just walked into the 1970s *Bob Newhart Show*, but that's what keeps prices reasonable. Opposite Grant Park just south of the Loop, the Essex also has a view-worthy 4th-floor pool and fitness room, and free Internet access in its business center. Parking costs $21.

Top End

Hotel Burnham (Map pp570-1; ☎ 312-782-1111, 877-294-9712; www.burnhamhotel.com; 1 W Washington St; r from $179; P) The Burnham is housed in the landmark 1890s Reliance Building, precedent for the modern skyscraper. Its super-cool decor is a favorite of architecture buffs; rooms are lavishly furnished with pieces like mahogany writing desks and chaise lounges. It's equipped with free high-speed Internet access and wi-fi; parking is $35.

Hard Rock Hotel (Map pp570-1; ☎ 312-345-1000, 877-762-5468; www.hardrockhotelchicago.com; 230 N Michigan Ave; r from $229; P) The Hard Rock Cafe folks bring you this happenin' hotel, complete with rock artifacts (ie Jimi Hendrix's guitar by the 19th-floor elevator). The black-and-gray rooms are a bit austere, but have mod touches like flat-screen TVs, DVD and CD players. Free high-speed Internet access in rooms. Parking costs $38.

NEAR NORTH & GOLD COAST
Budget

Cass Hotel (Map pp570-1; ☎ 312-787-4030, 800-799-4030; www.casshotel.com; 640 N Wabash Ave; s $69-89, d $89-109; P 💻) The Cass isn't much to look at, but its simple rooms win the day for their prices and prime location. Log on at the Internet kiosk ($1 per five minutes) or via free wi-fi in the café. Parking is $20, and the attached offbeat bar is good for a nightcap.

Ohio House Motel (Map pp570-1; ☎ 312-943-6000; www.ohiohousemotel.com; 600 N LaSalle St; s/d $100/115;

P) This retro 1960s motor lodge is still standing smack in the city's heart. The rooms are fine, if faded, and the attached coffee shop is a classic. The free parking is a considerable perk. Wi-fi costs $9.95 per day.

Midrange

Best Western River North (Map pp570-1; ☎ 312-467-0800, 800-727-0800; www.rivernorthhotel.com; 125 W Ohio St; r $119-149; P 🏊) Its large rooms have a vaguely Asian flair and free wi-fi. The indoor pool and free parking sweeten the deal even more.

Hampton Inn Chicago (Map pp570-1; ☎ 312-832-0330, 800-426-7866; www.hamptoninnchicago.com; 33 W Illinois St; s/d incl breakfast $169/179; P 💻 🏊) Despite the fairly generic rooms, the Hampton offers good value thanks to its location near the Magnificent Mile and freebies, like high-speed wi-fi, a business center with computers, a fitness facility, indoor pool, breakfast buffet with eggs and other hot items, and coin laundry. Parking costs $36.

Gold Coast Guest House (Map pp576-7; ☎ 312-337-0361; www.bbchicago.com; 113 W Elm St; r $119-189; P ❌) Those weary of cookie-cutter hotels can spend the night in this classic three-flat close to designer shopping and Oak St Beach. The capable innkeeper – a former travel guide herself – serves a bounteous breakfast. Each of the four rooms has a private bathroom. Parking is $20.

Best Western Inn of Chicago (Map pp570-1; ☎ 312-787-3100, 800-557-2378; www.innofchicago.com; 162 E Ohio St; r $149-179; P) This Best Western's basic rooms in an older building lack amenities like Internet access (only 25% of the hotel's rooms are equipped) and a pool, but it's one of the best-priced properties for its location a half block from the Magnificent Mile. Lots of tour groups stay here. Parking is $28.

Red Roof Inn (Map pp570-1; ☎ 312-787-3580, 800-466-8356; www.redroof.com; 162 E Ontario St; r $97-127; P) One block north of the Best Western Inn of Chicago and similar in style, Red Roof offers the chain's usual utilitarian rooms and service. Wi-fi costs $9.99 per day, and parking is $28.

Days Inn Gold Coast (Map pp576-7; ☎ 312-664-3040; www.daysinn.com; 1816 N Clark St; r $89-129; P) The best feature, besides the rate, is the swell location midway between downtown and the north side's top attractions (it's just steps away from the zoo). Parking costs $15.

Top End

House of Blues Hotel (Map pp570-1; ☎ 312-245-0333, 800-235-6397; www.loewshotels.com; 333 N Dearborn St; r from $170; P) HOB is as hip as they come, with its goofy and colorful decor. It's connected to the House of Blues club (p591), so keep an eye out for the musicians who stay here. In-room Internet access costs $11.50 per day and parking is $34.

LINCOLN PARK & LAKEVIEW

Midrange

Willows Hotel (Map pp576-7; ☎ 773-528-8400, 800-787-3108; www.cityinns.com; 555 W Surf St; r/ste from $139/179; P) The Willows Hotel is a small and stylish place with antique furnishings, and you will find it located within easy walking distance of the beach. Parking here costs $19. The owners have two other, similar properties in the neighborhood: **City Suites Hotel** (Map p580; ☎ 773-404-3400, 800-248-9108; 933 W Belmont Ave; r/ste from $129/149; P), near the CTA Red Line Belmont station, and the **Majestic Hotel** (Map p580; ☎ 773-404-3499, 800-727-5108; 528 W Brompton Ave; r/ste from $139/169; P), close to Wrigley Field and the Halsted St gay scene. All these properties offer wi-fi

for $9.95 per day, and free bagels, cereal and coffee for breakfast. Parking is $18 at the City Suites and $12 at the Majestic.

Inn of Lincoln Park (Map pp576-7; ☎ 773-348-2810, 866-774-7275; www.innlp.com; 601 W Diversey Pkwy; s/d $125/139; P) This inn's pleasant rooms are located right on entertainment-stacked Diversey, about five minutes' walk to the lakefront. Wi-fi costs $9.95 per day and parking is $10.

WICKER PARK

Midrange

House of Two Urns (Map p568; ☎ 773-235-1408, 877-896-8767; www.twourns.com; 1239 N Greenview Ave; r $95-175; P) This B&B is distinctive: it's owned by artists, and filled with antiques and original art, and it's located in Wicker Park near the vogue restaurant/bar scene. There's a free high-speed Internet connection. Take the CTA Blue Line to Division.

Eating

The cultural hodgepodge that gives Chicago's neighborhoods their character translates into a mind-reeling, diverse restaurant scene. The hungry can fill up on anything

---

FAMED CHICAGO FARE

You can't leave town without sampling a deep-dish pizza, in which the flaky crust rises an inch or two above the plate and cradles a pile of toppings. One piece is practically a meal. It's hard to say which maker is the best, as they all serve gooey slices that will leave you a few pounds heavier. A large pizza averages $17 at the following places.

Pizzeria Uno (Map pp570-1; ☎ 312-321-1000; 29 E Ohio St; 🕙 11:30am-1:30am Mon-Fri, 11:30am-2am Sat, 11:30am-11pm Sun) Where the deep dish concept originated in 1943; sister outlet Due is one block north.

Gino's East (Map pp570-1; ☎ 312-988-4200; 633 N Wells St; 🕙 11am-9pm Mon-Thu, 11am-11pm Fri & Sat, noon-9pm Sun) Write on the walls while you wait for your pie.

Lou Malnati's (Map pp570-1; ☎ 312-828-9800; 439 N Wells St; 🕙 11am-11pm Mon-Thu, 11am-midnight Fri & Sat, noon-10pm Sun) Famous for its buttercrust.

Giordano's (Map pp570-1; ☎ 312-951-0747; 730 N Rush St; 🕙 11am-11pm Sun-Thu, 11am-midnight Fri & Sat) Perfectly tangy tomato sauce.

No less iconic is the Chicago hot dog – a wiener and bun that have been 'dragged through the garden' (ie topped with onions, tomatoes, shredded lettuce, bell peppers, pepperoncini and sweet relish, or variations thereof). **Wrigley Field** (p592) makes a beauty, as does the **Wiener Circle** (p588). **Hot Doug's** (Map p568; ☎ 773-279-9550; 3324 N California Ave; 🕙 10:30am-4pm Mon-Sat) makes gourmet versions – aka haute dogs – with smoked alligator, garlic lamb sausage and jalapeno cheddar pork sausage.

Chicago is also known for its Italian beef sandwiches, with thin-sliced, slow-cooked roast beef heaped onto a hoagie roll, smothered in meat juice and *giardiniera* (pickled vegetables). They cost about $4 at **Mr Beef** (Map pp570-1; ☎ 312-337-8500; 666 N Orleans St; 🕙 8am-5pm Mon-Fri, 10:30am-2pm Sat) or **Al's** (Map pp570-1; ☎ 312-943-3222; 169 W Ontario St; 🕙 10am-midnight Mon-Thu, 10-3am Fri & Sat, 11am-10pm Sun).

from Algerian crepes to Costa Rican empanadas, from $175 multi-course meals to $1 hot dogs. And where else besides Chicago will you get the real deal for deep-dish pizza? The prices listed here are for dinner mains; lunch main courses often cost less.

THE LOOP

Most Loop eateries are geared for lunch crowds of office workers.

Oasis (Map pp570–1; ☎ 312-558-1058; 21 N Wabash Ave; dishes $4-8; ⏲ 11am-5pm Mon-Fri, 11am-4pm Sat) Oasis is a diamond in the rough, like the ones they're polishing in the jeweler's mall you walk through to get here. The falafel is crisp and the hummus is the best this side of Amman. Eat in or take to nearby parks.

NEAR NORTH

Hundreds of eateries dot the area, from family-run snackeries to renowned restaurants and high-concept cafés.

Billy Goat Tavern (Map pp570–1; ☎ 312-222-1525; lower level, 430 N Michigan Ave; burgers $2-4; ⏲ 6am-2am Mon-Fri, 10am-2am Sat & Sun) Scruffy like the titular animal, this bar and burger joint is the legendary haunt of *Tribune* and *Sun-Times* reporters. Only the dimmest of bulbs orders fries with their cheezborger (remember John Belushi's famous *Saturday Night Live* skit: 'No fries – chips!'.

Kitsch'n (Map pp570–1; ☎ 312-644-1500; www.kitschn.com; 600 W Chicago Ave; mains $8-16; ⏲ breakfast, lunch & dinner) Mmm, comfort food: flaky chicken or veggie pot pies, meatloaf and green bean casserole, washed down with a retro cocktail, including martinis made with Tang (orange-flavored breakfast drink). Served amid a 1970s lunchbox and beer-can collection.

Vermilion (Map pp570–1; ☎ 312-527-4060; 10 W Hubbard St; mains $12-21; ⏲ lunch Mon-Fri, dinner Mon-Sun) Two creative young Indian women run this chic eatery, which fuses Indian and Latin dishes with results like empanadas with mango-coconut chutney.

Kendall College (Map pp576–7; ☎ 312-752-2328; www.kendall.edu; 900 N Branch St; mains $15-20; ⏲ noon-1:30pm Mon-Fri, 6-8pm Tue-Sat) Chefs in training at the attached culinary institute serve five-star meals for two-star prices, meaning that ostrich fillet with blueberry risotto can be yours for a stomach-able price.

McDonald's (Map pp570–1; ☎ 312-867-0455; 600 N Clark St; burgers $2-4; ⏲ 24hr) This hulking, space-age super-McDonald's – complete with a

latte-and-gelato coffee bar – makes its mark in the city that started it all (the company is based in suburban Oak Brook).

OLD TOWN

Wells St north of Division St has an assortment of swank eateries.

Twin Anchors (Map pp576–7; ☎ 312-266-1616; www.twinanchorsribs.com; 1655 N Sedgwick St; slab $22; ⏲ 5-11pm Mon-Fri, noon-11pm Sat & Sun) This popular, neon-lit place has hordes of people waiting on weekends to get at the baby back ribs.

LINCOLN PARK

Halsted and Clark Sts are the main veins teeming with restaurants and bars. Parking is frightful, but it's handy to the CTA train stops at Armitage and Fullerton.

Alinea (Map pp576–7; ☎ 312-867-0110; www.alinearestaurant.com; 1723 N Halsted St; multi-course tastings $75-175; ⏲ dinner Wed-Sun) Mind-bending Alinea serves the kind of high-tech cuisine Jane Jetson might whip up for George, say a peanut butter and jelly sandwich toasted by a heat gun, or dishes emanating from a centrifuge or pressed into a capsule. It's crazy – and fantastically flavorful.

Potbelly Sandwich Works (Map pp576–7; ☎ 773-528-1405; 2264 N Lincoln Ave; sandwiches $4-5; ⏲ 11am-11pm) The hot submarine sandwiches are addictive. Ex-Chicagoans returning to visit family for the first time in years have been known to stop here before even seeing mom and dad.

Crepe & Coffee Palace (Map pp576–7; ☎ 773-404-1300; 2433 N Clark St; mains $5-8; ⏲ 10am-10pm) It's OK – delicious, in fact – to make a meal of pancakes. This Algerian eatery serves 'em sweet or savory (stuffed with chicken, smoked salmon or escargot).

Bourgeois Pig (Map pp576–7; ☎ 773-883-5282; 738 W Fullerton Pkwy; mains $6-7; ⏲ 6:30am-10pm Mon-Fri, 8am-10pm Sat & Sun) An old-school lefty coffee shop with big, creaking wood tables and chairs, the Pig serves strong java and good panini sandwiches.

For those seeking raucous late-night munchies, two places do it well: the **Wiener Circle** (Map pp576–7; ☎ 773-477-7444; 2622 N Clark St; items $2-4; ⏲ 10:30am-4am Sun-Thu, 10:30am-5am Fri & Sat), famous for its unruly ambience, chardogs and cheddar fries, and **Taco & Burrito Palace #2** (Map pp576–7; ☎ 773-248-0740; 2441 N Halsted Ave; items $2-4; ⏲ 10am-3am Sun-Thu, 10am-5am Fri & Sat), which cooks up football-sized burritos.

LAKEVIEW

Clark, Halsted, Belmont and Southport are fertile streets. Parking is near impossible, so take the CTA train to the Belmont, Southport or Addison stops.

Wishbone (Map p580; ☎ 773-549-2663; www .wishbonechicago.com; 3300 N Lincoln Ave; mains $7-13; ⊗ breakfast & lunch daily, dinner Tue-Sun) They call it 'Southern reconstruction cooking,' which means items like corn muffins, cheese grits, fried chicken, crawfish patties and buttermilk rolls top the tables. It's an Oprah favorite.

Leona's (Map p580; ☎ 773-327-8861; www.leo nas.com; 3215 N Sheffield Ave; mains $8-17; ⊗ 11am-11pm Sun-Thu, 11am-midnight Fri & Sat) Local chain Leona's serves heaping portions of pizza, sandwiches, lasagna and – surprisingly – many vegan dishes; the 'no frankenfoods' motto underscores the fresh ingredient emphasis.

Ann Sather's (Map p580; ☎ 773-348-2378; 929 W Belmont Ave; mains $7-13; ⊗ 7am-3pm Mon & Tue, 7am-9pm Wed-Sun) Try the Swedish potato sausages and cinnamon rolls.

WICKER PARK, BUCKTOWN & UKRAINIAN VILLAGE

New, hip restaurants open practically every day. Take the CTA Blue Line to Chicago, Damen or Western.

Irazu (Map p568; ☎ 773-252-5687; 1865 N Milwaukee Ave; mains $4-8; ⊗ 10am-9pm Mon-Sat) The Costa Rican owners of Irazu dish up unusual items, like *yuca* (cassava) with garlic, empanadas and oatmeal milkshakes.

Flo (Map pp576-7; ☎ 312-243-0477; 1434 W Chicago Ave; mains $5-14; ⊗ breakfast, lunch & dinner Tue-Sat, breakfast & lunch Sun) Join the salivating queue for Flo's famed Southwestern breakfasts. She also whips up lunch and dinner; try the catfish tacos.

Atomix (Map p568; ☎ 312-666-2649; 1957 W Chicago Ave; items $2.25-5; ⊗ 7am-10pm Mon-Fri, 9am-10pm Sat & Sun) This interplanetary café is filled with laptop users munching away quietly on vegetarian sandwiches and chili; order by crayon on the slick, reusable menus.

Handlebar Bar & Grill (Map p568; ☎ 773-384-9546; www.handlebarchicago.com; 2311 W North Ave; mains $7-10; ⊗ 4pm-midnight Mon-Thu, 4pm-2am Fri, 10am-2am Sat, 10am-midnight Sun) Handlebar peddles (pun intended, since the decor is bicycle-oriented) West African groundnut stew, wasabi-baked tofu and other energizing dishes; quaff the excellent beer selection on the patio.

Café Laguardia (Map p568; ☎ 773-862-5996; www.cafelaguardia.com; 2111 W Armitage Ave; mains $5-15; ⊗ 11am-11pm Mon-Sat, noon-8pm Sun) This Cuban café has great roasted pork sandwiches among its arsenal.

WEST SIDE & PILSEN

The ethnic areas are the main draw. Greektown extends along S Halsted St, Little Italy is along Taylor St and the Mexican Pilsen enclave centers around W 18th St (the CTA Blue Line stops here, but you'll need wheels to reach the other areas). There's a cache of stylish, top-end eateries centered on W Randolph St near Halsted St, sometimes called the West Loop or Restaurant Row.

Avec (Map pp570-1; ☎ 312-377-2002; 615 W Randolph St; mains $15-25; ⊗ 3:30-11:45pm Mon-Thu, 3:30pm-12:45am Fri & Sat, 3:30-9:45pm Sun) Small, rustic Avec serves Mediterranean-influenced small plates, like chorizo-stuffed dates, and mains, like pork shoulder with green chilies. The pared-down menu also focuses on artisanal cheeses and wines. Seating is at communal tables.

Lou Mitchell's (Map pp570-1; ☎ 312-939-3111; 565 W Jackson Blvd; mains $4-9; ⊗ 5:30am-3pm Mon-Sat, 7am-3pm Sun) There's a queue to get in for the famed breakfasts, but staff give out free Milk Duds to ease the wait.

Nuevo Leon (Map p568; ☎ 312-421-1517; 1515 W 18th St; mains $3-5; ⊗ 7am-midnight) Yes, busloads of tourists come to gobble the exceptional tamales and enchiladas with peso-size prices – and it's a pleasure to join them.

CHINATOWN

Take the CTA Red Line to the Cermak-Chinatown stop.

Joy Yee's (Map p568; ☎ 312-328-0001; www .joyyee.com; 2159 S China Pl; drinks $3-4, mains $6-10; ⊗ 11am-10:30pm) Joy Yee's roaring blenders mix more than 100 types of fruit drinks and tapioca bubble teas – a fine accompaniment to the slurpable bowls of udon.

Seven Wives (Map p568; ☎ 312-842-7888; 2230 S Wentworth Ave; mains $4-11; ⊗ 7:30am-midnight) It's tiny, but wins big raves for the noodle soups. It's also one of the few places that serves congee (rice porridge with savory garnishes – a breakfast dish).

ANDERSONVILLE

This northern neighborhood bursts with casual-with-an-edge restaurants and bars;

'New Chinatown' is nearby on Argyle St. See p581 for directions.

Kopi Traveler's Café (Map p580; ☎ 773-989-5674; 5317 N Clark St; items $5-8; ☺ 8am-11pm Mon-Fri, 9am-midnight Sat, 10am-11pm Sun) Kopi has an Asian trekker–lodge vibe, from the pile of cushions to sit upon, to the healthy sandwiches, to the bulletin board where travelers post flyers.

Thai Binh (Map p580; ☎ 773-728-0283; 1113 W Argyle St; mains $6-13; ☺ 11am-10pm) The owner's helpful daughter Linda will help you decide what to order from Thai Binh's huge Vietnamese selection.

Drinking

During the long winters, Chicagoans seek social life indoors, and the city's many bars cater to every mood and personality. Usual closing time is 2am, but many places stay open until 4am on weekdays and 5am on Saturday. In summer many boast beer gardens and outdoor seating.

THE LOOP, NEAR NORTH & OLD TOWN

Signature Lounge (Map pp576-7; ☎ 312-787-7230; John Hancock Center, 875 N Michigan Ave) Have the Hancock Observatory view without the Hancock Observatory admission price. Shoot straight up to the 96th floor and order a beverage while looking out over the city. Ladies: don't miss the bathroom view.

Berghoff (Map pp570-1; ☎ 312-427-3170; 17 W Adams St; ☺ 10:30am-8:30pm Mon-Sat) The first place to fling open its doors after Prohibition, the masculine, old-world Berghoff is a great place to down a stein of house-brand beer; German-style deli sandwiches available at lunchtime.

THE AUTHOR'S CHOICE

Phyllis' Musical Inn (Map p568; ☎ 773-486-9862; 1800 W Division St) One of the all-time great dives, this former Polish polka bar refuses to spruce up like the neighborhood around it. Anywhere from five to 105 people may be listening to the nightly live music, usually by a scrappy (and quite possibly crappy) up-and-coming band. You'll barely notice you're coated in smoke, especially if owner Clem is there doling out shots. If it gets too much, move outside to the patio and shoot hoop at the basketball court.

Olde Towne Ale House (Map pp576-7; ☎ 312-944-7020; 219 W North Ave) There are no pretenses at this long-time favorite, across from Second City (p592), where you'll mingle with beautiful people and not-so-beautiful people (they're the ones face down at the bar).

LINCOLN PARK & LAKEVIEW

These neighborhoods are chockablock with bars, with rich veins along Lincoln Ave, Halsted St and Clark St.

Ginger Man (Map p580; ☎ 773-549-2050; 3740 N Clark St) The pierced-and-tattooed patrons, pool tables and good beer selection make Ginger Man wonderfully different from the surrounding Wrigley sports bars.

Alive One (Map pp576-7; ☎ 773-348-9800; 2683 N Halsted St) The jukebox is stuffed with hundreds of bootlegged, all-live (get the name?) recordings by the Clash, The Who, Hendrix, Phish and more. The atmosphere converts from jam-absorbing to lounge-like on weekends.

Goose Island Brew Pub (Map pp576-7; ☎ 312-915-0071; 1800 N Clybourn Ave) Goose brews its wildly popular beers on-site. Crisp Honker's Ale is the flagship, best accompanied by the specialty chips.

WICKER PARK & BUCKTOWN

Map Room (Map p568; ☎ 773-252-7636; 1949 N Hoyne Ave) At this map-and-globe-filled 'traveler's tavern,' artsy types sip coffee by day and suds from the 200-strong beer list by night.

Charleston (Map p568; ☎ 773-489-4757; 2076 N Hoyne Ave) Close to Map Room, the Charleston is recommended for relaxed drinking.

ANDERSONVILLE

Hopleaf (Map p580; ☎ 773-334-9851; 5148 N Clark St) You've hit the mother lode of beer selection when you walk into this beauty – there are 200 types available (30 on tap) and a Belgian eatery upstairs.

Simon's (Map p580; ☎ 773-878-0894; 5210 N Clark St) This watering hole is a fertile brooding ground for generations of underemployed musicians.

Entertainment

Check the *Reader* and other local media (p573). **Hot Tix** (www.hottix.org; ☺ closed Mon; Randolph St Map pp570-1; 72 E Randolph St; Pearson St Map pp576-7; 163 E Pearson St; Clark St Map pp576-7; 2301 N Clark St) sells same-day theater tickets at half-price. Cover charges at music and dance

GAY & LESBIAN CHICAGO

Chicago has a flourishing gay and lesbian scene; for details, check the weekly free publications of **Chicago Free Press** (www.chicagofreepress.com) or **Windy City Times** (www.windycitymediagroup.com). The **Chicago Area Gay & Lesbian Chamber of Commerce** (Map p568; ☎ 773-303-0167; www.glchamber.org; 1210 W Rosedale Ave; ⏰ 9:30am-6pm Mon-Fri) also provides useful visitor information. **Chicago Greeter** (see Tours, p585) offers personalized sightseeing trips.

The biggest concentration of bars and clubs is on N Halsted St between Belmont Ave and Grace St, an area known as 'Boys' Town.' **Roscoes** (Map p580; ☎ 773-281-3355; 3354 N Halsted St) is a fine place to start the night. Gay cowboy aficionados can giddyap to **Charlie's** (Map p580; ☎ 773-871-8887; 3726 N Broadway Ave).

Andersonville, aka 'Girls' Town,' is another area with many choices, including the **Chicago Eagle** (Map p580; ☎ 773-728-0050; 5015 N Clark St), a popular leather bar, and **Big Chicks** (Map p580; ☎ 773-728-5511; 5024 N Sheridan Ave), with weekend DJs, art displays and a next-door restaurant called **Tweet** (Map p580; ☎ 773-728-5576; 5020 N Sheridan Ave; ⏰ dinner Tue-Sat, brunch Sat & Sun), where weekend brunch is a major gay scene. **Star Gaze** (Map p580; ☎ 773-561-7363; 5419 N Clark St) is one of the city's only all-women bars.

The late-June **Pride Parade** (☎ 773-348-8243; www.chicagopridecalendar.org; admission free) winds through Boys' Town and attracts close to 400,000 people.

clubs range from nil to $20 or more, depending on who's playing and the day of the week.

BLUES

Blues and jazz both have deep roots in Chicago, and world-class performers appear at myriad venues nightly.

Buddy Guy's Legends (Map pp570-1; ☎ 312-427-0333; 754 S Wabash Ave) This place gets the top acts in town, including the venerable Mr Guy himself.

Rosa's (Map p568; ☎ 773-342-0452; 3420 W Armitage Ave) Rosa's is a real-deal venue that brings in top local talent and dedicated fans to a somewhat dodgy West Side block.

Lee's Unleaded Blues (Map p568; 773-493-3477; 7401 S South Chicago Ave; ⏰ Tue-Sun) Far off the tourist path, buried deep on the South Side, down-on-the-Delta bands let loose at this juke joint.

Blue Chicago (Map pp570-1; ☎ 312-642-6261; 536 & 736 N Clark St) This is a pair of friendly clubs downtown.

House of Blues (Map pp570-1; ☎ 312-923-2000; 329 N Dearborn St) Part of a chain, House of Blues is the largest venue for the genre.

Noisy, hot, sweaty and crowded are **Blues** (Map pp576-7; ☎ 773-528-1012; 2519 N Halsted St) and **Kingston Mines** (Map pp576-7; ☎ 773-477-4646; 2548 N Halsted St), both of which are conveniently located in Lincoln Park and are popular drawcards for the holiday-making 4am crowd.

JAZZ

Green Mill (Map p580; ☎ 773-878-5552; 4802 N Broadway Ave) Glamorous, dark and smoky, the Green Mill earned its notoriety as Al Capone's favorite speakeasy (the tunnels where he hid the booze are still underneath the bar), and you can feel his ghost urging you on to another martini. Top-flight local and national artists perform six nights per week; Sundays are for the nationally acclaimed poetry slam.

Hothouse (Map pp570-1; ☎ 312-362-9707; 31 E Balbo St) A beautiful room offering esoteric jazz and world music to a stylish crowd.

Back Room (Map pp576-7; ☎ 312-751-2433; 1007 N Rush St) This jazz joint is so tiny it's like having a band in your bedroom.

Jazz Showcase (Map pp570-1; ☎ 312-670-2473; 59 W Grand Ave) An upscale club catering to jazz purists.

ROCK & FOLK

Metro (Map p580; ☎ 773-549-3604; 3730 N Clark St) Local bands and big names looking for an 'intimate' venue play here.

Old Town School of Folk Music (Map p568; ☎ 773-728-6000; 4544 N Lincoln Ave) A superb room offering an eclectic line-up of world music and, yes, folk music.

Hideout (Map pp576-7; ☎ 773-227-4433; 1354 W Wabansia Ave) Tucked behind a factory, Hideout is as hard to find as the name implies, but worth it for the laid-back, indie atmosphere, and nightly rock, folk and country tunes.

The **Double Door** (Map p568; ☎ 773-489-3160; 1572 N Milwaukee Ave) and **Empty Bottle** (Map p568; ☎ 773-276-3600; 1035 N Western Ave) epitomize the hard-edge Chicago rock scene.

THEATER

Chicago's reputation for stage drama is well deserved. The city's main companies:

Chicago Shakespeare Theater (Map pp570-1; ☎ 312-595-5600; www.chicagoshakes.com; 800 E Grand Ave) Will's comedies and tragedies at Navy Pier.

Goodman Theatre (Map pp570-1; ☎ 312-443-3800; www.goodman-theatre.org; 170 N Dearborn St) Known for both new and classic works.

Steppenwolf Theatre (Map pp576-7; ☎ 312-335-1650; www.steppenwolf.org; 1650 N Halsted St) Hollywood-friendly.

First-rate smaller companies:

Lookingglass Theatre (Map pp576-7; ☎ 312-337-0665; www.lookingglasstheatre.org; 821 N Michigan Ave) Improv-based works, often incorporating acrobatics.

Neo-Futurists (Map p580; ☎ 773-275-5255; www.neofuturists.org; 5153 N Ashland Ave) Heady and fun.

Redmoon Theater (Map p568; ☎ 312-850-8440; www.redmoon.org; 1438 W Kinzie St) Puppet-oriented productions.

Major venues for touring shows, most clustered at State and Randolph Sts:

Auditorium Theater (Map pp570-1; ☎ 312-922-2110; 50 E Congress Pkwy)

Cadillac Palace Theater (Map pp570-1; ☎ 312-977-1700; 151 W Randolph St)

Chicago Theater (Map pp570-1; ☎ 312-443-1130; 175 N State St)

Ford Center/Oriental Theater (Map pp570-1; ☎ 312-977-1700; 24 W Randolph St)

LaSalle Bank Theater (Map pp570-1; ☎ 312-977-1700; 22 W Monroe St)

COMEDY

Improv comedy began in Chicago, and the city still nurtures the best in the business.

Second City (Map pp576-7; ☎ 312-337-3992; www.secondcity.com; 1616 N Wells St) The cream of the crop – the place where John Belushi, Bill Murray and many others honed their wit.

Improv Olympics (Map p580; ☎ 773-880-0199; www.improvolympic.com; 3541 N Clark St) Many Saturday Night Livers were fostered here.

CINEMAS

Music Box Theatre (Map p580; ☎ 773-871-6604; 3733 N Southport Ave) Patrons are treated to live organ music and clouds rolling across the ceiling prior to their art films at this theater.

Gene Siskel Film Center (Map pp570-1; ☎ 312-846-2800; 164 N State St) The small theater screens offbeat films.

DANCE CLUBS

The club scene ranges from snooty places to casual joints where all you do is dance.

Carol's Pub (Map p580; ☎ 773-334-2402; 4659 N Clark St) A honky-tonk in Chicago? Just read the sign out front: 'Live Country Music/Hot Sandwiches.' The former results in boot stompin' dancin' on weekends, the latter a stomachache.

Betty's Blue Star Lounge (Map p568; 312-243-1699; 1600 W Grand Ave) Groovesters strut their stuff on one of the city's more casual dancefloors.

Funky Buddha Lounge (Map pp570-1; 312-666-1695; 728 W Grand Ave) The Buddha shakes with hip-hop and house music.

Two long-standing, sweaty dance favorites are **Smart Bar** (Map p580; 773-549-0203; 3730 N Clark St), beneath the Metro rock club, and **Neo** (Map pp576-7; ☎ 773-528-2622; 2350 N Clark St).

CLASSICAL MUSIC, OPERA & DANCE

Symphony Center (Map pp570-1; ☎ 312-294-3000; www.cso.org; 220 S Michigan Ave) The Chicago Symphony Orchestra is headquartered in this beautiful facility.

Civic Opera House (Map pp570-1; ☎ 312-332-2244; www.lyricopera.org; 20 N Wacker Dr) The Lyric Opera of Chicago, one of the country's best, performs in the grand venue here.

Grant Park Orchestra (☎ 312-742-4763; www.grantparkmusicfestival.com) The orchestra puts on free classical concerts in Millennium Park (p574) throughout the summer.

Joffrey Ballet of Chicago (☎ 312-739-0120) and **Hubbard Street Dance Chicago** (☎ 312-850-9744) are renowned local dance companies. They perform at the Auditorium Theater (left) and **Harris Theater for Music and Dance** (Map pp570-1; ☎ 312-629-8696; 205 E Randolph St), respectively.

SPORTS

Wrigley Field (Map p580; 1060 W Addison St) The Cubs (☎ 773-404-2827; www.cubs.com) last won the World Series in 1908, but their fans still pack baseball's most charming and intimate stadium, dating from 1914 and known for its ivy-walled field and classic neon sign. Take the CTA Red Line to Addison. Wrigley is 4.5 miles north of the Loop.

GREAT LAKES

SOX QUASH THE CURSE

Chicagoans woke up the morning of October 27, 2005, and looked outside cautiously. Were pigs flying? Had hell frozen over? Because the night before, the unthinkable happened: the White Sox won the World Series, reversing almost nine decades of baseball misfortune in the city. Voluble Venezuelan manager Ozzie Guillen and his team of non-superstar players scrapped, slugged and pitched their way to victory, and exorcised Chicago's winless-since-1917 curse. Does this mean the south-side, blue-collar Sox will finally draw crowds equal to the north-side, yuppified Cubs? Keep an eye out for those flying pigs...

US Cellular Field (Map p568; 333 W 35th St) The **White Sox** (☎ 312-674-1000; www.chisox.com) are the Cubs' South Side rivals (see above) and play in the less charming but more modern 'Cell' (aka Comiskey Park, its name for years before corporate sponsorship). It's 4 miles south of the Loop and near the CTA Red Line Sox-35th station.

United Center (Map p568; 1901 W Madison St) The **Bulls** (☎ 800-462-2849; www.nba.com/bulls) play basketball in this huge stadium, also used by the **Blackhawks** (☎ 312-559-1212; www.chicagoblackhawks.com) for hockey. It's about 2 miles west of the Loop. CTA runs special buses on game days; it's not safe to walk here.

Soldier Field (Map pp570-1; 425 E McFetridge Dr) Chicago's National Football League (NFL) team, the **Bears** (☎ 847-615-2327; www.chicagobears.com) tackles at this stadium, which stirred huge controversy when it was renovated from a classical facade to its current flying-saucer look, referred to as 'the mistake on the lake.' The **Fire** (☎ 312-705-7200; www.chicago-fire.com) pro soccer team competes here as well.

Shopping

The shoppers' siren song emanates from N Michigan Ave, along the Magnificent Mile (p575).

Large vertical malls here include Shops at North Bridge (Map pp570-1), Chicago Place (Map pp570-1), Water Tower Place (Map pp576-7) and 900 N Michigan (Map pp576-7). In the Loop, the flagship **Marshall Field's** (Map pp570-1; ☎ 312-781-1000; 111 N State St) and **Carson Pirie Scott & Co** (Map pp570-1; ☎ 312-

641-7000; 1 S State St) are Chicago's premier department stores from the turn of the 20th century; at press time, Field's was slated to morph into Macy's brand, despite virulent local protests.

Boutiques fill Bucktown (mod), Lincoln Park (tony), Lakeview (countercultural) and Andersonville (all three).

Chicago Tribune Store (Map pp570-1; ☎ 312-222-3080; 435 N Michigan Ave) For the ultimate souvenir – a Cubs ballcap.

Vosges Haut-Chocolat (Map pp570-1; ☎ 312-644-9450; 520 N Michigan Ave) Succulent chocolates with exotic ingredients, like curry powder or wasabi.

Jazz Record Mart (Map pp570-1; ☎ 312-222-1467; 25 E Illinois St) Thoroughly stocked on Chicago blues and jazz CDs.

Chicago Comics (Map p580; ☎ 773-528-1983; 3244 N Clark St) The place to go for books by renowned artists, such as Chris Ware, Ivan Brunetti or even Dan Clowes (who lived here during his early *Eightball* days). Superman and Simpsons products are also sold here.

Getting There & Away

AIR

O'Hare International Airport (ORD; ☎ 800-832-6352; www.flychicago.com) is the world's busiest. It's huge but user-friendly, with good signs and maps. Most non-US airlines and international flights use Terminal 5 (except Lufthansa and flights from Canada).

The smaller **Midway Airport** (MDW; ☎ 773-838-0600; www.flychicago.com) is used mostly by domestic carriers, like Southwest, which often have cheaper flights than airlines serving O'Hare.

BUS

The **main bus station** (Map pp570-1; ☎ 312-408-5800; 630 W Harrison St) is two blocks from the CTA Blue Line Clinton stop. Greyhound has frequent buses to Cleveland ($44 to $71, 7½ hours), Detroit ($31 to $63, seven hours) and Minneapolis ($62 to $80, nine hours).

CAR

Car rental is subject to 18% tax. Many rental agencies – Alamo/National, Avis and others – have 24-hour desks at both airports and around town. Check rental information in the Transportation chapter (p1175) for contact details.

TRAIN

Chicago's classic **Union Station** (Map pp570-1; 225 S Canal St) is the hub for Amtrak's national and regional service. Three trains a day go to Detroit ($23 to $57; 5½ hours) and seven trains per day go to Milwaukee ($20; 1½ hours). Other connections:

Cleveland $50 to $96, seven hours, two trains daily.

Minneapolis/St Paul $59 to $105, eight hours, one train daily.

New York $88 to $137, 19 hours, two trains daily.

St Louis $21 to $59, 5½ hours, three trains daily.

San Francisco (Emeryville) $125 to $245, 51 hours, one train daily.

Getting Around

TO/FROM THE AIRPORT

O'Hare International Airport is 17 miles northwest of the Loop. The cheapest, and often the quickest, way to/from O'Hare is by the CTA Blue Line ($1.75), but the station is a long walk from the flight terminals – a difficult haul if you have lots of luggage. At the airport, signs point variously to 'CTA,' 'Rapid Transit' and 'Trains to City.' Airport Express shuttles run between the airport and downtown ($24 per person; discount for pairs). Cabs to/from downtown cost about $50.

Midway Airport is 11 miles southwest of the Loop, connected via the CTA Orange Line ($1.75). Other options include shuttles ($19 per person) and cabs ($25 to $35).

BICYCLE

Chicago has 120 miles of bike lanes, including some on major roads, though they aren't very well respected. Request a free map from the city's **transportation department** (☎ 312-742-2453; cdotbikemaps@cityofchicago.org) Bike racks are plentiful; the biggest – with showers – is at **Millennium Park Bike Station** (Map pp570-1; ☎ 888-245-3929; 239 E Randolph St). Lock it or lose it. For bike-rental information, see p581.

CAR & MOTORCYCLE

Be warned: it's difficult to find street parking and expensive to park in a lot. Rush-hour traffic is abysmal.

PUBLIC TRANSPORTATION

The **Chicago Transit Authority** (CTA; ☎ 888-968-7282; www.transitchicago.com) operates the city bus network and train system, including both elevated (El) and subway trains. CTA buses go everywhere from early morning until late evening. Two of the seven color-coded train lines – the Red Line, and the Blue Line to O'Hare International Airport – operate 24 hours a day The other lines run from about 5am to 11pm daily. During the day, you shouldn't have to wait more than 15 minutes for a train. Get free maps at any train station.

The standard fare on a bus or train is $1.75; transfers cost 25¢. On buses, you can use a fare card (called a Transit Card) or pay with exact change. On the train, you must use a Transit Card, sold from vending machines at train stations. Day passes (one-/three-day pass $5/12) provide savings.

Metra commuter trains (☎ 312-836-7000; www .metrarail.com) have 12 routes serving the suburbs from four terminals ringing the Loop (LaSalle St Station, Randolph St Station, Richard B Ogilvie Transportation Center and Union Station – all on Map pp570-1. Some lines run daily, while others operate only during weekday rush hours. Metra fares cost $1.85 to $5 or more. An all-weekend pass costs $5.

PACE (☎ 847-364-7223; www.pacebus.com) runs the suburban bus system that connects with city transport.

TAXI

Cabs are plentiful in the Loop, north to Andersonville and west to Bucktown. In other areas, call **Yellow Cab** (☎ 312-829-4222) or **Flash Cab** (☎ 773-561-1444). Flagfall is $2.25, plus $1.80 per mile and $1 per extra passenger; a 15% tip is expected. Venture outside city limits and you'll pay one and a half times the fare.

AROUND CHICAGO

Evanston & North Shore

Evanston, 14 miles north of the Loop and reached via the CTA Purple Line, combines sprawling old houses with a compact downtown. It's also home to Northwestern University.

Beyond are Chicago's northern lakeshore suburbs, which became popular with the carriage set in the late 19th century. A classic 30-mile drive follows Sheridan Rd through various tony towns to the socioeconomic apex of Lake Forest. Attractions include the glistening white **Baha'i House of Worship** (☎ 847-853-2300; 100 Linden Ave, Wilmette; admission free; ⏰ 10am-8pm May-Sep, 10am-5pm Oct-

Apr) and **Chicago Botanic Garden** (☎ 847-835-5440; www.chicagobotanic.org; 1000 Lake Cook Rd, Glencoe; admission free; ☻ 8am-dusk; ℗).

Oak Park

Located west of the Loop and easily reached on the CTA Green Line, Oak Park spawned two famous sons: Ernest Hemingway was born here, and architect Frank Lloyd Wright lived and worked here from 1898 to 1908.

The **visitors center** (☎ 708-848-1500; 158 Forest Ave; ☻ 10am-4pm winter, 9am-5pm summer) sells an architectural walking-tour map ($3.25). The **Frank Lloyd Wright Home & Studio** (☎ 708-848-1976; www.wrightplus.org; 951 Chicago Ave; adult/child 7-18 $9/7) provides tours of the area's Wright-designed dwellings. Tours are held at 11am, 1pm and 3pm Monday to Friday (continuous 11am to 3:30pm Saturday and Sunday).

The **Ernest Hemingway Museum** (☎ 708-848-2222; www.ehfop.org; 200 N Oak Park Ave; admission $7; ☻ 1-5pm Sun-Fri, 10am-5pm Sat) will thrill hardcore fans of the novelist. Admission includes access to **Hemingway's Birthplace** (339 N Oak Park Ave).

NORTHERN ILLINOIS

The highlight of northern Illinois is the hilly northwest, which was untouched by the last ice age and is bordered by the Mississippi River. It's an easy and popular excursion from Chicago.

En route is Union, where the **Illinois Railway Museum** (☎ 815-923-4000; www.irm.org; US 20 to Union Rd; adult $6-9, child over 4 $4-7; ☻ hrs vary Apr-Oct) is a good stop for rail buffs.

Galena

Though just a speck on the map, Galena is the area's main attraction. The town spreads across wooded hillsides and is perfectly preserved, despite a slew of tourist-oriented antique shops and restaurants.

Lead was mined in the upper Mississippi area as early as 1700, but industrial demands in the mid-19th century resulted in a boom. Galena (named for the lead sulfide ore) became a center for the industry and a major river port town, with solid businesses, hotels and mansions in Federal and Italianate styles. The boom ended abruptly after the Civil War, and Galena was all but deserted until restoration began in the 1960s.

The main **visitors center** (☎ 815-777-4390, 877-464-2536; www.galena.org; 101 Bouthillier St; ☻ 9am-5pm Mon-Sat, 10am-5pm Sun, extended hrs summer) is on the eastern side of the Galena River, in the 1857 train depot. Get a walking guide, leave your car and explore on foot.

Elegant old Main St curves around the hillside and the historic heart of town. Among numerous sights is the **Ulysses S Grant Home** (☎ 815-777-3310; 500 Bouthillier St; adult/child $3/1; ☻ 9am-4:45pm Wed-Sun), which was a gift from local Republicans to the victorious general at the end of the Civil War. Tours are provided (sometimes conducted by a guy who pretends he 'is' Grant).

The elaborate Italianate **Belvedere Mansion** (☎ 815-777-0747; 1008 Park Ave; adult/child $10/3; ☻ 11am-4pm Mon-Fri, 11am-5pm Sat & Sun late May-Oct) has the green drapes from *Gone With the Wind*.

Six miles north you can tour the underground **Vinegar Hill Lead Mine and Museum** (☎ 815-777-0855; 8885 N Three Pines Rd; adult/child 7-18 $12/10; ☻ 10am-4pm in summer, Sat & Sun only Sep-Oct). Opening hours sometimes vary, so it's best to call and check before you depart.

Most accommodations are B&Bs, guesthouses and inns, and cost at least $85 nightly. Except during winter, many places are full, especially on weekends. The visitors center can help get you a room; call or check the website.

Grant Hills Motel (☎ 815-777-2116; www.granthills .com; US 20; s/d $63/73; 🐾) is a cozy motel 1.5 miles east of town, with fine views and a horseshoe pitch. Or be regal like Grant and Lincoln and stay in the well-furnished rooms at **DeSoto House Hotel** (☎ 815-777-0090; www.desotohouse.com; 230 S Main St; r $108-200), dating from 1855.

Clarks Again (☎ 815-777-4407; 200 N Main St; dishes $3-6; ☻ breakfast & lunch year-round, dinner in summer) is ideal for biscuit-and-gravy breakfasts or lunchtime sandwiches. **Log Cabin** (☎ 815-777-0393; 201 N Main St; mains $10-17; ☻ from 4pm) is where you'll find huge dinner portions served amid Americana ambience.

For a little grit with locals, have a beer at the **VFW Hall** (cnr Main & Hill Sts).

Quad Cities

South of Galena along a pretty stretch of the Great River Rd is scenic **Mississippi Palisades State Park** (☎ 815-273-2731), a popular rock-climbing area; pick up information at the park entrance's gatehouse. Further downstream, the Quad Cities (Moline and Rock Island in Illinois, and Davenport and Bettendorf across the river in Iowa), known as the Q-C, make a surprisingly good stop. Check in at the **visitors center** (☎ 563-322-3911; www.visitquadcities.com; 2021 River Dr, Moline; 🕑 8:30am-5pm Mon-Fri, also 10am-4pm Sat in summer).

Rock Island has an appealing downtown (based at 3rd Ave and 18th St), with a couple of cafés, restaurants, a lively pub and music scene, and a paddle wheeler casino. On the edge of town, **Black Hawk State Historic Site** (☎ 309-788-0177; 1510 46th Ave; 🕑 dawn-10pm) is a huge park with trails by the Rock River. Its **Hauberg Indian Museum** (☎ 309-788-9536; Watch Tower Lodge; admission free; 🕑 9am-noon & 1-5pm Wed-Sun) outlines well the sorry story of Sauk leader Black Hawk and his people.

Out in the Mississippi River, the actual island of **Rock Island** once held a Civil War–era arsenal and POW camp. It now has two military museums and a Civil War cemetery.

Moline is the home of John Deere, the international farm machinery manufacturer, which has a museum/showroom in town.

For Iowa-side attractions, see p683.

CENTRAL ILLINOIS

Lincoln and Rte 66 sights are sprinkled liberally throughout central Illinois, which is otherwise farmland plain. East of Decatur, Arthur and Arcola are centers for the Amish.

Peoria

During the 20th century's first decades, Peoria was a thriving, wealthy town built on whiskey. The phrase 'But will it play in Peoria?' originated in the '20s, when the local well-to-do spawned a vibrant vaudeville/theater scene and brought in big-name performers from New York and Europe. The phrase is still heard today, but often in a political context. The town's reinvented riverfront along Water St makes a good pit stop for a meal or beer.

Springfield

The small state capital has a serious obsession with Abraham Lincoln, who practiced law here from 1837 to 1861. Its Abe-related sights offer an in-depth look at the man and his turbulent times, which only some cynics find overdone. Many of the attractions are walkable downtown and cost little to nothing. Get your bearings with maps from the central **visitors center** (☎ 800-545-7300; www .visitspringfieldillinois.com; 109 N 7th St; 🕑 8am-5pm Mon-Fri). A new visitors center is scheduled to open next to the Lincoln Library and Museum by this book's publication.

SIGHTS & ACTIVITIES

To visit the top-draw Lincoln Home, you must first pick up a ticket at the **Lincoln Home Visitors Center** (☎ 217-492-4150; 426 S 7th St; admission free; 🕑 8:30am-5pm). The site is where Abraham and Mary Lincoln lived from 1844 until they moved to the White House in 1861. You'll see considerably more than just the home: the whole block has been preserved, and several structures are open to visitors.

The **Lincoln Presidential Library & Museum** (☎ 217-558-8844; www.alplm.org; 212 N 6th St; adult/child 5-15 $7.50/3.50; 🕑 9am-5pm Thu-Tue, 9am-8:30pm Wed) contains the most complete Lincoln collection in the world, everything from his Gettysburg Address and Emancipation Proclamation to his shaving mirror and briefcase. You'll have to wade through some Disney-esque exhibits to get to the good stuff.

After his assassination, Lincoln's body was returned to Springfield, where it lies today. The impressive **Lincoln's Tomb** sits in **Oak Ridge Cemetery** (☎ 217-782-2717; admission free; 🕑 9am-5pm summer, 9am-4pm rest of year), north of downtown. The gleam on the nose of Lincoln's bust, created by visitors' light touches, indicates the numbers of those who pay their respects here.

Standing a block apart are the noteworthy **Lincoln-Herndon Law Offices** (☎ 217-785-7289; cnr 6th & Adams Sts; suggested donation adult/child $2/1; 🕑 9am-5pm May-Aug, 9am-4pm Tue-Sat Sep-Apr) and **Old State Capitol** (☎ 217-785-7960; cnr 5th & Adams Sts; suggested donation adult/child $2/1; 🕑 9am-5pm May-Aug, 9am-4pm Tue-Sat Sep-Apr). Both offer detailed tours covering Lincoln's early political life; the latter takes in his dramatic pre–Civil War debates with Stephen Douglas.

Lincoln-free attractions include the pristine 1904 **Dana-Thomas House** (☎ 217-782-6776; 301 E Lawrence St; adult/child $3/1; 🕑 9am-4pm Wed-Sun), one of Frank Lloyd Wright's Prairie-style masterworks, with an insightful tour; **Shea's Gas Station Museum** (☎ 217-522-0475; 2075

Peoria Rd; admission free; ⊙ 7am-4pm Tue-Fri, 7am-noon Sat), with Rte 66 pumps and signs; and the macabre but enlightening **Museum of Funeral Customs** (☎ 217-544-3480; www.funeralmuseum.org; 1440 Monument Ave; adult/child 6-17 $3/1.50; ⊙ 10am-4pm Tue-Sat, 1-4pm Sun). Catch a flick under the stars at the **Route 66 Drive In** (☎ 217-698-0066; Recreation Rd; adult/child under 13 $5/3; ⊙ daily Jun-Aug, Sat & Sun mid-Apr–May, Sep & Oct).

SLEEPING & EATING
Motel 6 (☎ 217-529-1633; 6010 S 6th St; r $35-50; P ⚑) Just one of the chain hotels lining I-55 east of town where you'll find budget prices.

    Mansion View Inn (☎ 217-544-7411, 800-252-1083; www.mansionview.com; 529 S 4th St; r from $80; P) Try this place for midrange lodging downtown.

    Carpenter Street Hotel (☎ 217-789-9100, 888-779-9100; www.carpenterstreethotel.com; 525 N 6th St; r $70; P ✗) Also offering midrange lodging downtown, this hotel is bland but decent.

    Inn at 835 (☎ 217-523-4466; www.innat835.com; 835 S 2nd St; s/d from $100/115; P) Going up a

price notch will land you a historic B&B room at this inn.

    Cozy Dog Drive In (☎ 217-525-1992; 2935 S 6th St; items $1.50-3.50; ⊙ 8am-8pm Mon-Sat) Though the food tends toward the deeply fried variety, all must stop to hail the corn dog's birthplace at the Cozy Dog. It's a Rte 66 legend, with all sorts of memorabilia and souvenirs.

    For an array of meal options, cruise S 6th St between Monroe and Adams Sts. A local specialty is the 'horseshoe,' an artery-clogging fried meat sandwich covered with melted cheese.

    Brewhaus (☎ 217-525-6399; 617 E Washington; sandwiches $3-6; ⊙ breakfast & lunch Mon-Sat) A popular pub that serves the 'horseshoe.'

GETTING THERE & AROUND
The **Greyhound bus station** (☎ 217-544-8466; 2351 S Dirkson Pkwy), southwest of downtown, has frequent connections to St Louis ($19 to $25, two hours) and Chicago ($37 to $45, 4½ hours).

ROUTE 66: GET YOUR KICKS IN ILLINOIS

America's 'Mother Road' kicks off at the corner of Adams St and Michigan Ave in Chicago. Before embarking, fuel up at **Lou Mitchell's** (p589) coffee shop near Union Station. After all, it's about 300 miles from the start of Rte 66 to the Missouri state line.

Be aware that in Illinois, most of Rte 66 has been superseded by I-55, though the old route still exists in scattered sections often paralleling the interstate.

Leave I-55 southeast of Chicago at Joliet Rd, following Hwy 53 southbound to Wilmington. Pay your respects to the 28ft fiberglass spaceman known as the **Gemini Giant** outside the **Launching Pad Drive-In** (☎ 815-476-6535; 810 E Baltimore St; ⊙ 9am-10pm) in Wilmington. Keep an eye out for the retro **Burma Shave signs** en route to Godley and Odell's **vintage filling station**. In Pontiac, the **Log Cabin Inn** (☎ 815-842-2908; 18700 Old Rte 66; ⊙ 5am-4pm Mon & Tue, 5am-8pm Wed-Fri, 5am-2pm Sat) was jacked up and rotated 180 degrees when Rte 66 was realigned. Cruise by Bloomington-Normal and stop off in Shirley at **Funk's Grove** (☎ 309-874-3360; ⊙ call for seasonal hrs), a 19th-century maple syrup farm. Further south in Broadwell, the legendary 1930s **Pig-Hip Restaurant** has been renovated as a **museum** (☎ 217-732-2337; admission free; ⊙ usually 10am-5pm Mon-Sat).

The state capital of Springfield harbors a trio of sights: **Shea's Gas Station Museum** (opposite), the **Cozy Dog Drive In** (above) and **Route 66 Drive In** (above).

Further south, a good section of old Rte 66 parallels I-55 through Litchfield. Grab a meal and piece of pie at the 1924 **Ariston Café** (☎ 217-324-2023; N Old Rte 66; meals $6.50-15; ⊙ 11am-10pm Mon-Fri, 4-10pm Sat, 11am-9pm Sun) or catch a flick at the **SkyView Drive-In** (☎ 217-324-4451; 1200 N Old Rte 66; adult/child under 5 $2/free; ⊙ daily in summer). In Mt Olive, the 1926 **Soulsby Shell Station** is the route's oldest gas pump and is in the slow process of becoming a museum.

Finally, before driving west over the Mississippi River, detour off I-70 at exit 3. Follow Hwy 203 south, turn right at the first stoplight and drive west to the 1929 **Chain of Rocks Bridge** (⊙ dawn-dusk). Only open to pedestrians and cyclists, this mile-long bridge has a historically famous 22 degree–angled bend.

For more information, contact the **Route 66 Association of Illinois** (www.il66assoc.org). See also p31.

GREAT LAKES

The downtown **Amtrak station** (☎ 217-753-2013; cnr 3rd & Washington Sts) has three daily trains to/from St Louis ($11 to $32, two hours) and Chicago ($16 to $45, 3½ hours).

Petersburg

When Lincoln first arrived in Illinois in 1831, he worked variously as a clerk, storekeeper and postmaster in the frontier village of New Salem before studying law and moving to Springfield. In Petersburg, 20 miles northwest of Springfield, **Lincoln's New Salem State Historic Site** (☎ 217-632-4000; Hwy 97; suggested donation adult/child $2/1; ☺ 9am-5pm) reconstructs the village with building replicas, historical displays and costumed performances – a pretty informative and entertaining package.

SOUTHERN ILLINOIS

A surprise awaits near Collinsville, 8 miles east of East St Louis: classified as a Unesco World Heritage Site with the likes of Stonehenge, the Acropolis and the Egyptian pyramids is **Cahokia Mounds State Historic Site** (☎ 618-346-5160; www.cahokiamounds.com; exit 6 off I-55/70; suggested donation adult/child $2/1; ☺ visitors center 9am-5pm; grounds 8am-dusk). Cahokia protects the remnants of North America's largest prehistoric city (20,000 people, with suburbs), dating from AD 1200. While the 65 earthen mounds, including enormous Monk's Mound and the 'Woodhenge' sun calendar, are not overwhelmingly impressive in themselves, the whole site is worth seeing.

Not a World Heritage Site, though it should be, is the **World's Largest Catsup Bottle** (800 S Morrison Ave) near Main St in downtown Collinsville. Nearby, Hwy 157 is lined with motels and chain restaurants.

Grafton lies to the north at the confluence of the Illinois and Mississippi Rivers. The Great River Rd in this area is edged with cliffs and is especially scenic.

An exception to the state's flat farmland is the green southernmost section, punctuated by rolling **Shawnee National Forest** (☎ 681-253-7114) and rocky outcroppings. The area has numerous state parks and recreation areas good for outdoor activities. **Union County**, near the state's southern tip, has wineries and orchards. At little **Cairo**, on the Kentucky border, the Mississippi and Ohio Rivers converge.

INDIANA

You could argue that a state feted as 'the mother of vice presidents,' where one of the biggest political issues of the decade is whether or not to adopt daylight savings time, might be a snore-evoking place to visit. Or you could twist it around and say that such a state is prime for off-the-beaten-path touring. Indiana surprises with its small towns that hold big culture. Columbus is one of the USA's premiere architectural meccas – IM Pei, Eero Saarinen and other noted designers have built its schools, banks and fire stations. Bloomington is a lively university town filled with ethnic restaurants and Tibetan temples. The north holds moody sand dunes and buggy-jammed Amish communities, while the south has verdant hills, limestone caves and quirky displays of concrete lawn art.

History

As was the case in neighboring Illinois and Ohio, prehistoric mound builders once occupied much of Indiana, and the Algonquian tribes had succeeded by the time the first Europeans arrived.

French fur traders were plying the state's waterways by the mid-17th century, and by 1679 had charted a water route between the Great Lakes and the Mississippi River, forging a tenuous link across their North American empire. The French established several forts to protect this route. Vincennes, on the lower Wabash River, is the era's only surviving permanent settlement.

Indiana was first settled by farmers from Kentucky (including Abraham Lincoln's

---

INDIANA FACTS

Nicknames Hoosier State, Crossroads of America

Population 6.2 million

Area 36,420 sq miles

Capital city Indianapolis (population 783,400)

Official flower Peony

Birthplace of Gangster John Dillinger (1903–34), author Kurt Vonnegut (b 1922), actor James Dean (1931–55), *Brady Bunch* mom Florence Henderson (b 1934), TV host David Letterman (b 1947)

Famous for Indy 500 motor race, winning basketball teams

WHO'S A HOOSIER?

Since the 1830s Indianans have been nicknamed 'Hoosiers.' But ask any local what the odd moniker means, and you'll be met with a sheepish smile and shrug of shoulders.

The word's origin has more theories about it than John F Kennedy's assassination. One idea is that early settlers knocking on a door were met with 'Who's here?' which soon became 'Hoosier.' Another notion is that the early river men were so good at pummeling or 'hushing' their adversaries that they got reputations as 'hushers.' Then there's the one about a foreman on the Louisville & Portland Canal whose name was Hoosier and who preferred workers from Indiana. They became known as Hoosier's men. More likely, others say, pioneers walking into a tavern on a fight-filled Saturday night would find a torn, displaced body part and say 'Whose ear?'

Scholarly types suggest that the word derives from *hoozer*, from an early dialect in England's Cumberland District, which was used in the 19th-century South to describe woodsmen or hillbilly types. In any case, the word is now well entrenched and thought to have only honorable attributes – though the exact definition remains undefined.

---

family). Expanding settlement and resulting conflicts displaced the Native Americans, with the final battle fought in 1811 at Tippecanoe. The Kentucky connection meant that Indiana had many Southern sympathizers in the Civil War, but as elsewhere around the Great Lakes, the war's main impact on the state was the growth of the northern industrial towns. In 1906 steelmaking started in Gary, using coal from Illinois and Indiana and iron ore shipped from Minnesota; the industry continues to add fuel to the state economy.

Information

Indiana sales tax is 6%.

Check the following websites for statewide information:

Indiana highway conditions (☎ 800-261-7623; www.in.gov/dot/motoristinfo)

Indiana Office of Tourism (☎ 888-365-6946; www.enjoyindiana.com)

Indiana state park information (☎ 800-622-4931; www.in.gov/dnr/parklake) Park entry requires a vehicle permit (per day/year residents $4/26, nonresidents $5/32). Campsites cost $8 to $24; reservations accepted.

INDIANAPOLIS

Car racing put Indianapolis (aka 'Indy') on the map, and it's still the city's number one point of interest. Be sure to make a pit stop at the Indianapolis Motor Speedway ('Indy 500') Museum, where you can take a spin around the race track. Downtown continues to flourish with new public works. While it hasn't transformed into the world's most exciting place, it does have a nice mix of museums, nightlife and sporting venues, all

watched over by the silent dome of the state capitol.

History

The location of Indianapolis, on flat cornfields in the geographical center of the state, is the result of an 1820 legislative compromise between agricultural and industrial regions. Many early carmakers opened shop in the city, but were eclipsed by the Detroit giants. They did leave a lasting legacy – a 2.5-mile test track, which became the site for the first Indianapolis 500 race in 1911 (won at an average speed of 75mph).

Orientation

Indianapolis is geometrically laid out, much like Washington, DC, with diagonal avenues superimposed on a grid layout. Everything radiates from the massively impressive Monument Circle. Meridian St divides streets east from west; Washington St divides them north from south.

Information
BOOKSTORES

Borders Books & Music (☎ 317-972-8595; 11 S Meridian St)

EMERGENCY

Fire, police, ambulance (☎ 911) Emergency.

INTERNET ACCESS

Abbey Coffeehouse (☎ 317-269-8426; 825 N Pennsylvania Ave; ☼ 8am-midnight) Free wi-fi.

FedEx Kinko's (☎ 317-631-6862; 120 Monument Circle; per hr $12; ☼ 7am-11pm Mon-Fri, 9am-4pm Sat) You can also burn digital photos here (per hr $24).

INTERNET RESOURCES

Indianapolis Cultural Development Commission
(www.culturalindy.com) Links to exhibits, festivals and
cultural attractions.

Gay Indy (www.gayindy.org) Gay, lesbian, bisexual,
transgender (GLBT) news and entertainment listings.

MEDIA

Indianapolis Star (www.indystar.com) The daily
newspaper.

Nuvo (www.nuvo.net) Distributed free on Wednesday,
outlines Indy's arts, music and nightclub scene.

WFBQ-FM 94.7 is the main rock channel,
while NPR can be found on the dial at WFYI-
FM 90.1.

MEDICAL SERVICES

CVS (☎ 317-923-1491; 1744 N Illinois St; ☽ 24hr)
Pharmacy.

Indiana University Medical Center (☎ 317-274-
4705; 550 University Blvd)

MONEY

Most major banks are downtown near the
Statehouse and Circle Centre Mall, along
Washington, Illinois and Meridian Sts.
Travelex (☎ 317-241-0440; Indianapolis International
Airport) Exchanges currency; in the main terminal by Delta
Airlines.

POST

Post office (☎ 317-464-6876; 125 W South St)

TOURIST INFORMATION

Visitors Center (☎ 800-323-4639; www.indy.org;
Artsgarden Bldg, cnr Washington & Illinois Sts;
☽ 10am-9pm Mon-Sat, noon-6pm Sun)

Sights & Activities

INDIANAPOLIS MOTOR SPEEDWAY

The Speedway, home of the **Indianapolis 500**
motor race, is Indy's super-sight and an
absolute must-see. The **Hall of Fame Museum**
(☎ 317-492-6784; www.indianapolismotorspeedway
.com; 4790 W 16th St; adult/child 6-15 $3/1; ☽ 9am-5pm)
features 75 racing cars (including former
winners), a 500lb Tiffany trophy and a track
tour ($3 extra). OK, so you're on a bus for
the latter and not even beginning to burn
rubber at 37mph; it's still fun to pretend. **Tickets** (☎ 317-484-6700, 800-822-4639; www.imstix.com;
tickets $20-140) are hard to come by for the big
event, held on Memorial Day weekend and
attended by 450,000 crazed fans. Tickets for

pre-race trials and practices are more likely
(and cheaper). Other races at the Speedway
are the Formula One **US Grand Prix** in June
and Nascar **Brickyard 400** in August.

WHITE RIVER STATE PARK

Sprawling White River State Park, which is
located at the edge of downtown, contains
several worthwhile sights. The adobe **Eitel-
jorg Museum of American Indians & Western Art**
(☎ 317-636-9378; www.eiteljorg.org; 500 W Washington
St; adult/child 5-17 $7/4; ☽ 10am-5pm Tue-Sat, noon-5pm
Sun, plus Mon in summer) features an array of Native
American artifacts, such as basketry, pots and
masks. The museum also contains a collection of fabulous realistic/romantic Western
painting collection including works by Frederic Remington and Georgia O'Keeffe.

The **Indiana State Museum** (☎ 317-232-1637;
www.indianamuseum.org; 650 W Washington St; adult/child
3-12 $7/4; ☽ 9am-5pm Mon-Sat, 11am-5pm Sun) in-
cludes displays on prehistory, famous Hoosiers, butter churning and African American
settlement in the region.

The **NCAA Hall of Champions** (☎ 800-735-6222;
www.ncaa.org/hall_of_champions; 700 W Washington St;
adult/child $7/4; ☽ 10am-5pm Tue-Sat, noon-5pm Sun,
plus Mon in summer) reveals the country's fascination with college sports. You'll probably
find most Hoosiers hovering around the
basketball exhibits, as locals are renowned
hoop-ball fanatics.

Other park highlights include gardens, a
zoo, a canal walk and a military Medal of
Honor Memorial.

INDIANAPOLIS MUSEUM OF ART

This **museum** (☎ 317-920-2660; www.ima-art.org;
4000 Michigan Rd; adult/child under 13 $7/free, Thu admis-
sion free; ☽ 10am-5pm Tue-Sun, 10am-9pm Thu) has a
splendid collection of European art (especially Turner and some Postimpressionists),
African tribal art, South Pacific art and Chinese works. The museum is now linked to
Oldfields – Lilly House & Gardens (☎ 317-920-2660;
adult/child under 13 $5/free, Thu admission free), the
26-acre estate of the Lilly pharmaceutical
family, and **Fairbanks Art & Nature Park** (☎ 317-
920-2660; admission free; ☽ dawn-dusk), featuring
sculptures and audio installations amid 100
acres of woodlands and wetlands.

MONUMENTS

At Monument Circle, the city center is
marked by the jaw-dropping 284ft **Soldiers**

& Sailors Monument. Beneath is the **Civil War Museum** (☎ 317-232-7615; admission free; ☯ 10am-6pm Wed-Sun), which neatly outlines the conflict and Indiana's abolition position. Also on the circle are the 1916 Circle Theatre and the 1857 Christ Church Cathedral, with Tiffany glass windows. The gorgeous, restored 1880 **Indiana Statehouse** (☎ 317-233-5239; cnr Capitol & Washington Sts; admission free; ☯ 9am-3pm Mon-Fri) is just west.

Sleeping

Hotels cost more and are usually full during race weeks in May, June and August. Add 12% tax to the prices listed.

BUDGET

Look for low-cost motels off I-465, the freeway that circles Indianapolis.

Motel 6 (☎ 317-248-1231; 5241 W Bradbury St, off I-75 at Airport Expressway; s/d $40/46; P ☒) This is an OK option 6 miles west of town.

MIDRANGE

Nestle Inn (☎ 317-610-5200, 877-339-5200; www .nestleindy.com; 637 N East St; r $105-140; P ☒) Each of the five immaculate rooms at this B&B is painted a different bright color, and all have private baths. It's a short walk to Massachusetts Ave's restaurants and bars, or just stay put reading in one of the inn's comfy sitting rooms.

Stone Soup (☎ 866-639-9550; www.stonesoupinn .com; 1304 N Central Ave; r $85-145; P ☒) A nine-room B&B in a rambling house filled with antiques and stained glass. The less-expensive rooms share a bath. Not quite as conveniently located as the Nestle Inn.

Comfort Inn (☎ 317-631-9000; www.choicehotels .com; 530 S Capitol Ave; r incl breakfast $109-169; P ☒) This big and bustling hotel is near the RCA Dome. It has spacious rooms and good facilities, like an indoor pool.

TOP END

Canterbury (☎ 317-634-3000, 800-538-8186; www .canterburyhotel.com; 123 S Illinois St; r from $179; P) Indianapolis' finest oozes class, with rooms furnished with Chippendale four-poster beds and free wi-fi. Parking costs $20.

Eating

Central Massachusetts Avenue ('Mass Ave' to locals) is bounteous when the stomach growls. The Broad Ripple area, 6 miles

north at College Ave and 62nd St, has pubs and eateries representing numerous nationalities. At lunch it's hard to beat the incredible range of cheap eats at the old **City Market** (Market St), two blocks east of Monument Circle, filled with ethnic food stalls and produce vendors.

Abbey Coffeehouse (☎ 317-269-8426; 825 N Pennsylvania Ave; mains $5-8; ☯ 8am-midnight) The Abbey is everything a good coffee shop should be: serene, arty, with comfy armchairs and swirled clouds on the ceiling. The sandwiches, wraps and vegetarian items, like the tempeh burrito, are delicious.

Mug 'N' Bun (☎ 317-244-5669; 5211 W 10th St; mains $3-4; ☯ breakfast, lunch & dinner) The mugs are frosted and filled with a wonderful home-brewed root beer. The buns contain burgers, chili dogs and juicy tenderloins. At this vintage drive-in near the Speedway you are served – where else – in your car.

Café Patachou (☎ 317-925-2823; 4911 N Pennsylvania St, Broad Ripple; mains $4-9; ☯ breakfast & lunch) It's the best breakfast in town, with healthy plates of homemade granola, cinnamon toast, Brie omelets, house-roasted coffee and freshly squeezed juice; sandwiches, too.

Bazbeaux (☎ 317-636-7662; 334 Massachusetts Ave; sandwiches $5-7, large pizza $20; ☯ 11am-10pm Sun-Thu, 11am-11pm Fri & Sat) A local favorite, Bazbeaux offers an eclectic pizza selection, like the 'Tchoupitoulas,' topped with Cajun shrimp and andouille sausage. Muffalettas, stromboli and Belgian beer are some of the other unusual offerings. There is another **outlet** (811 E Westfield Blvd) in Broad Ripple.

Drinking

Downtown and Mass Ave have a few good watering holes; Broad Ripple has several.

Slippery Noodle Inn (☎ 317-631-6974; 372 S Meridian St) The Noodle is the oldest bar in the state, and has seen action as a whorehouse, slaughterhouse, gangster hangout and Underground Railroad station, not to mention it's one of the best blues clubs in the country. There's live music nightly, and it's cheap.

Rathskeller (☎ 317-636-0396; 401 E Michigan St) This is a long-established German haunt, in the Athenaeum building, with traditional and modern fare, and a busy biergarten pouring imported brews.

Chatterbox Tavern (☎ 317-636-0584; 435 Massachusetts Ave; ☯ Mon-Sat) Chill out with the

GREAT LAKES

varied clientele at this intimate bar just northeast of the city center. It features live jazz nightly, and a hearty stock of beer and wine.

Entertainment

The motor races aren't the only coveted spectator events.

RCA Dome (☎ 317-262-3389; www.colts.com; 100 S Capitol Ave) Under a vast fiberglass dome 63,000 fans watch the NFL's Indianapolis Colts play football.

Conseco Fieldhouse (☎ 317-917-2500; www.nba .com/pacers; 125 S Pennsylvania St) Basketball is huge in Indiana, and this is ground zero where the National Basketball League's (NBA) Pacers make it happen.

Getting There & Around

TO/FROM THE AIRPORT

The **Indianapolis International Airport** (☎ 317-487-7243; www.indianapolisairport.com) is 7 miles southwest of town. The No 8 Washington bus runs between the airport and downtown ($1.25, 30 minutes). A cab to downtown costs $20 to $22.

BUS

There are several buses daily with **Greyhound** (☎ 317-267-3076, 800-231-2222; 350 S Illinois St) to Cincinnati ($17 to $28, 2½ hours) and Chicago ($32 to $45, four hours).

CAR

Avis, Hertz and other rental agencies have offices at the airport and around town. Check the Transportation chapter (p1175) for contact details.

PUBLIC TRANSPORTATION

Local buses are run by **IndyGo** (☎ 317-635-3344; www.indygo.net); the fare is $1.25. Service is minimal on weekends.

TAXI

For cab service, call **Yellow Cab** (☎ 317-487-7777).

TRAIN

The bus station terminal is the base for **Amtrak** (☎ 317-263-0550). One train daily goes to Chicago ($16 to $32, 4½ hours), and three trains weekly go to Cincinnati ($17 to $38, 3½ hours) and Washington, DC ($82 to $197, 20 hours).

AROUND INDIANAPOLIS

Who would have thought there was so much available here? Experience everything from bluegrass to pork tenderloins, Tibetans to rebels without a cause.

Fairmount

This small town, north on Hwy 9, is the birthplace of James Dean, one of the original icons of cool. Fans should visit the **Historical Museum** (☎ 765-948-4555; 203 E Washington St; suggested donation $1; ☿ 10am-5pm Mon-Sat, noon-5pm Sun), the **Dean Memorial Gallery** (☎ 765-998-2080; www.jamesdeangallery.com; exit 59 off I-69; admission $5; ☎ 9am-6pm) and his red-lipstick-kissed grave site.

If Dean was the embodiment of cool, surely his polar opposite is Dan Quayle, who resided a mere 30 miles north on Hwy 9 in Huntington. The USA's dim-witted 44th vice president (you say potato, he says potatoe) is treated reverentially, along with the country's other second fiddles, at the **Dan Quayle Center & Vice Presidential Museum** (☎ 260-356-6356; www.quaylemuseum.org; 815 Warren St; adult/child 7-17 $3/1; ☿ 9:30am-4:30pm Tue-Sat).

Columbus

When you think of the USA's great architectural cities – Chicago, New York, Washington, DC – Columbus, Indiana, doesn't quite leap to mind. But it should. Located 40 miles south of Indianapolis on I-65, Columbus is a remarkable gallery of physical design. Since the 1940s the city and its leading corporations have commissioned some of the world's best architects, including Eero Saarinen, Richard Meier and IM Pei, to create both public and private buildings. Stop at the **visitors center** (☎ 812-378-2622; www.columbus.in.us; 506 5th St; ☿ 9am-5pm Mon-Sat, 10am-4pm Sun Mar-Nov, closed Sun Dec-Feb) to pick up a self-guided tour map ($2) or join a bus tour (adult/child six to 12 $9.50/3); tours begin at 10am Monday to Friday, 10am and 2pm Saturday, and 11am Sunday. Over 60 notable buildings are spread over a wide area (car required), but about 15 diverse works can be seen on foot downtown.

Motels are found on the city's outskirts on I-65. To sample a pork tenderloin, an Indiana specialty, head 12 miles west to the hamlet of Gnaw Bone; the **Food & Fuel** (☎ 812-988-4575; Hwy 46; tenderloin $4.75; ☿ 10:30am-5:30pm

Mon-Thu, 10:30am-7:30pm Fri, 10:30am-4:30pm Sat, 10:30am-3:30pm Sun), inside the Marathon gas station, has the state's best.

Nashville

Gentrified and antique-filled, this 19th-century town west of Columbus on Hwy 46 is now a bustling tourist center, at its busiest in fall when leaf-peepers pour in. It's also the jump-off point to **Brown County State Park** (☎ 812-988-6406; campsites $13-23), Indiana's largest, where trails give hikers and horseback riders access to the area's lovely green hill country.

Among several B&Bs, central **Artists Colony Inn** (☎ 812-988-0600, 800-737-0255; www .artistscolonyinn.com; 105 S Van Buren St; r $85-155; dishes $8-14) stands out for its spiffy rooms and rooftop hot tub. The inexpensive dining room offers traditional Hoosier fare, such as catfish. **Nashville House** (☎ 812-988-4554; cnr Van Buren & Main Sts; dishes $16-20; ☯ 11:30am-7pm Wed-Mon) is famous for its home-cooked meals served with fried biscuits and apple butter. As with like-named Nashville, Tennessee (p437), Nashville, Indiana, enjoys its country music, and bands play regularly at several venues. The **Bill Monroe Museum** (☎ 812-988-6422; 5163 Rte 135 N, Bean Blossom; adult/child under 13 $4/free; ☯ 9am-5pm Apr-Oct, 10am-4pm Tue-Sat Nov-Mar) hails the bluegrass hero 5 miles north of town.

Bloomington

Lively and lovely Bloomington, 45 miles south of Indianapolis on Hwy 37, is the home of Indiana University. The town centers on Courthouse Sq, surrounded by restaurants, bars, bookshops and the historic facade of Fountain Sq Mall. The super-stocked **visitors center** (☎ 812-334-8900; 2855 N Walnut St; ☯ 8:30am-5pm Mon-Fri, 9am-4pm Sat) is a few miles north of the town center. Nearly everything else is walkable.

On the expansive campus, the **Art Museum** (☎ 812-855-4826; www.indiana.edu/~iuam; 1133 E 7th St; admission free; ☯ 10am-5pm Tue-Sat, noon-5pm Sun, reduced hrs summer), designed by IM Pei, has an excellent collection of African art, as well as European and US paintings.

The colorful, prayer flag–covered **Tibetan Cultural Center** (☎ 812-331-0014; www.tibetancc.com; 3655 Snoddy Rd; admission free; ☯ 10am-4pm) and stupa, as well as the **Dagom Gaden Tensung Ling Monastery** (☎ 812-339-0857; www.ganden.org; 102 Clubhouse Dr; ☯ call for hrs), indicate Bloomington's significant Tibetan presence. Contact the Tibetan Cultural Center for its yoga and meditation schedule.

Look for cheap lodgings along N Walnut St near Hwy 46. The limestone **Motel 6** (☎ 812-332-0820; 1800 N Walnut St; r from $40; ☲) may be the Midwest's most attractive.

For a town of its size, Bloomington offers a really mind-blowing array of ethnic restaurants – everything from Burmese to Eritrean to Mexican. Browse Kirkwood Ave and E 4th St.

Charming **Little Tibet** (☎ 812-331-0122; 415 E 4th St; mains $6-8; ☯ 11am-10pm Wed-Mon) offers specialties from the Himalayan homeland, as well as some Thai-influenced dishes and curries.

The **Scholar's Inn Bakehouse** (☎ 812-331-6029; 125 N College Ave; mains $3-9; ☯ 7:30am-9pm Mon-Sat, 7:30am-6pm Sun) serves coffee and sandwiches. Pubs on Kirkwood Ave close to the university cater to the student crowd.

SOUTHERN INDIANA

The pretty hills, caves, rivers and absorbing history of southern Indiana mark it as a completely different region from that of the flat and industrialized north.

Ohio River

The Indiana segment of the 981-mile-long Ohio River marks the state's southern border. From tiny Aurora, in the southeastern corner of the state, Hwys 56, 156, 62 and 66, known collectively as the **Ohio River Scenic Route**, wind through a varied landscape.

Coming from the east, a perfect place to stop is little **Madison**, a well-preserved river settlement from the mid-19th century. This attractive town is lined with architectural gems and remains unsullied by ugly commercial strips. At the **visitors center** (☎ 812-265-2956; www.visitmadison.org; 601 W First St; ☯ 9am-5pm Mon-Fri, 9am-4pm Sat, 11am-4pm Sun), pick up a pamphlet on the walking tour, which includes the James Lanier Mansion, a designated landmark overlooking the river.

Madison has motels around its edges, as well as several B&Bs; the visitors center can help with bookings. Large, wooded **Clifty Falls State Park** (☎ 812-273-8885; campsites $8-23), off Hwy 56 and a couple of miles west of town, has camping, hiking trails, views and waterfalls. Main St, with numerous antique stores, also has several places for a bite. **Café Camille** (☎ 812-265-5626; 149 E Main St; mains $3-6; ☺ 6am-2:30pm Mon-Fri, 7am-3pm Sat & Sun) is ideal for breakfast or lunch.

In Clarksville, **Falls of the Ohio State Park** (☎ 812-280-9970; www.fallsoftheohio.org; 201 W Riverside Dr) has only rapids, no falls, but is of interest for its 386-million-year-old fossil beds. The **interpretive center** (adult/child 2-18 $4/1; ☺ 9am-5pm Mon-Sat, 1-5pm Sun) explains it all. Unwind afterward with ice cream, a smashing collection of concrete lawn art and a view of Louisville's skyline (across the river in Kentucky) at **Widow's Walk** (☎ 812-280-7564; 415 Riverside Dr; ☺ 1-10pm). The rest of town and adjacent New Albany, the largest Indiana town in the region, aren't much, with one exception: **Rich O's Public House** (☎ 812-949-2804; www.richos.com; 3312 Plaza Dr, New Albany; ☺ Mon-Sat) and its superlative beer selection.

Scenic Hwy 62 heads west and leads to the Lincoln Hills and southern Indiana's fascinating limestone caves. A visit to **Wyandotte Caves State Recreation Area** (☎ 812-738-2782; www.wyandottecaves.com; 7315 S Wyandotte Cave Rd; ☺ 9am-5pm Mar-Oct), near Leavenworth, is highly recommended. Tours range from 30 minutes (adult/child four to 12 $11.50/5.75) to 90 minutes (adult/child four to 12 $16/8) and take you through caves featuring ancient formations, bats and more. **Marengo Cave** (☎ 812-365-2705; www.marengocave.com; ☺ 9am-5pm), north on Hwy 66, is another stand-out. It offers both 40-minute tours (adult/child four to 12 $12/6.25) and two-hour tours (adult/child four to 12 $19.50/9.50). Nearby in Milltown, **Cave Country Canoes** (☎ 812-633-4806; www.cavecountrycanoes.com; ☺ May-Oct) runs good half-day ($18), full-day ($21) or longer trips on the scenic Blue River; keep an eye out for river otters.

To the west, **Hoosier National Forest** provides opportunities for walking, swimming, camping and other outdoor recreation. Pick up a guide at any local Chamber of Commerce.

Four miles south of Dale, off I-64, is the **Lincoln Boyhood National Memorial** (☎ 812-937-4541; www.nps.gov/libo; adult/child $3/free; ☺ 8am-5pm), where young Abe lived from age seven to 21. The isolated but good site also includes admission to a working **pioneer farm** (☺ 8am-5pm mid-Apr–Sep). Further west, on the Ohio River, **Evansville** is one of the state's

largest cities; its Riverside Historic District retains many early-19th-century mansions. Also near town is well-preserved **Angel Mounds State Historic Site** (☎ 812-853-3956; www.angelmounds.org; 8215 Pollack Ave; suggested donation $2; ☺ 9am-5pm Tue-Sun Apr-Nov), which contains the remains of a prehistoric Native American town (AD 1100–1450) and some reconstructed buildings.

Wabash River

In southwest Indiana, the Wabash River forms the border with Illinois. Beside it, south of I-64, captivating **New Harmony** is the site of two early communal-living experiments and is worth a visit. In the early 19th century a German Christian sect, the Harmonists, developed a sophisticated town here while awaiting the Second Coming. Later it was acquired by the British utopian Robert Owen. Learn more at the angular **Atheneum Visitors Center** (☎ 812-682-4488, 800-231-2168; www.newharmony.org; cnr North & Arthur Sts; ☺ 9:30am-5pm).

Today New Harmony retains an air of contemplation, if not otherworldliness, which you can experience at its newer attractions, such as the temple-like Roofless Church and the Labyrinth, a sort of maze symbolizing the spirit's quest. The town has a couple of guesthouses, some pleasant eateries, and camping at **Harmonie State Park** (☎ 812-682-4821; campsites $16-21).

NORTHERN INDIANA

The truck-laden I-80/I-90 tollways cut across Indiana's northern section. Parallel US 20 is slower and cheaper, but not much more attractive. Connoisseurs of classic cars should detour south on I-69 to the town of **Auburn**, where the Cord Company produced the USA's favorite cars in the 1920s and '30s. The **Auburn Cord Duesenberg Museum** (☎ 260-925-1444; www.acdmuseum.org; 1600 S Wayne St; adult/child $8/5; ☺ 9am-5pm) has a wonderful display of early roadsters in a beautiful art deco setting. Almost next door is the **National Automotive and Truck Museum** (☎ 260-925-9100; www.natmus.com; 1000 Gordon Buehrig Pl; adult/child 6-12 $7/4; ☺ 9am-5pm).

Further west, around Shipshewana, Middlebury and Elkhart, is one of the USA's largest **Amish communities**. The **Menno-Hof Visitors Center** (☎ 260-768-4117; www.mennohof.org; Hwy 5, Shipshewana; adult/child 6-14 $6/3; ☺ 10am-5pm Mon-

Sat, reduced hrs Jan-Mar) provides a thorough and comprehensive background. The area holds numerous Amish and Mennonite craft outlets, bakeries and restaurants – most with hitching posts.

The city of **South Bend** is another ex-carmaker. Stop at the **Studebaker National Museum** (☎ 574-235-9714; www.studebakermuseum .org; 525 S Main St; adult/child 8-18 $6.50/5.50; ☯ 9am-5pm Mon-Sat, noon-5pm Sun, closed Mon mid-Nov–Mar), with its gorgeous 1956 Packard and many other classic beauties. South Bend is better known as the home of the University of Notre Dame, famous for its 'Fighting Irish' football team. To tour the pretty campus with its gold-domed administration building, Lourdes Grotto Replica and *Touchdown Jesus* painting, start at the **visitors center** (☎ 574-631-5726; 111 Eck Center; ☯ 8am-5pm Mon-Sat, 10am-5pm Sun). US residents especially will be interested in seeing the downtown **College Football Hall of Fame** (☎ 574-235-9999; www.collegefootball.org; 111 S St Joseph St; adult/child 6-14 $10/4; ☯ 10am-5pm).

Hugely popular on summer days with sunbathers from Chicago and South Bend, **Indiana Dunes National Lakeshore** stretches along 20 miles of Lake Michigan shoreline. Windy winter weather make the dunes more desolate and moody, an equally unforgettable experience. Sandy beaches, dunes and woodlands are crisscrossed with hiking trails, which often afford glimpses of nearby steel mills and stark, industrial structures. The lakeshore is noted for its incredible variety of plant life – everything from cactus to grasslands to hardwood forests and pine trees. Beaches are usually open 8am to sunset daily. Stop at the main **visitors center** (☎ 219-926-7561; www.nps.gov/indu; Kemil Rd at Hwy 12 near Beverly Shores; ☯ 8am-6pm summer, 8am-5pm rest of year) for details on beaches and activities. You can get here from Chicago via the South Shore Metra train (see p594), which stops at Beverly Shores among other park locations. The train departs from Randolph St Station and the trip takes 1½ hours.

Adjacent **Indiana Dunes State Park** (☎ 219-926-1952; www.dnr.in.gov/parklake; end of Hwy 49 near Chesterton; park entry fee per car $8, campsites $8-24) has seven hiking trails zigzagging over the sandscape; No 4 up Mt Tom rewards with Chicago skyline views. **Gray Goose Inn** (☎ 219-926-5781, 800-521-5127; www.graygooseinn .com; 350 Indian Boundary Rd, Chesterton; r $90-115, ste

$160-185, weekends additional $15) is an antique-stuffed, seven-room (all private bath) B&B 2.5 miles from the dunes.

Near Illinois, the steel cities of **Gary** and **East Chicago** present some of the bleakest urban landscapes anywhere. Taking the train (Amtrak or South Shore line) through here will get you up close and personal with the industrial underbelly.

OHIO

Welcome only state nicknamed after a poisonous nut (the buckeye). It's a curious symbol, but it's a curious place. Take the state's northern part, where one day you're on a hard-partying Lake Erie resort island, the next you're watching butter churn on an Amish farm and then the next you're in gritty Cleveland at the hip-swinging Rock and Roll Hall of Fame. No wonder national politicians are perplexed by how to win over Ohio's voters. Southern Ohio cradles parks amid the rolling foothills of the Appalachian Mountains and the river city of Cincinnati (known as both the Queen City and Porkopolis – yet another dichotomy).

History

Following the Revolutionary War, settlers streamed into the Northwest Territory. Ohio was one of the first areas settled. In 1832 the completion of the Ohio–Erie Canal between the Ohio River and Lake Erie provided transport connections that, combined with abundant local resources, enabled Ohio cities to become early centers of industry. By 1850 Ohio was the third most populous state in the nation. The Civil War and ensuing century's wars propelled the state's industrial growth further – until the late 1960s, when things didn't go so well.

Seven US presidents were born in Ohio, leading to the state's sometimes-heard moniker, 'Mother of Presidents.'

Speaking of the nation's big cheese: this little ol' cow-dotted state decided the country's fate in 2004. That's when Republican President George W Bush duked it out with Democratic candidate John Kerry in the presidential election. The two were tied with electoral votes, and whomever won Ohio won it all. You can thank Ohio for Georgie Junior's second term.

OHIO FACTS

Nickname Buckeye State
Population 11,436,000
Area 44,825 sq miles
Capital city Columbus (population 728,400)
Official motto With God, all things are possible
Birthplace of Inventor Thomas Edison
(1847–1931), flight pioneers Orville Wright
(1871–1948) and Wilbur Wright (1867–1912),
author Toni Morrison (b 1931), entrepreneur Ted
Turner (b 1938), filmmaker Steven Spielberg (b 1947)
Famous for First airplane, first pro baseball team,
deciding the outcome of the 2004 presidential election

Information

Ohio sales tax is 6%, with counties assessing an additional 0.25% to 2%.

Check the following websites for statewide information:

Ohio Division of Travel and Tourism (☎ 800-282-5393; www.discoverohio.com)

Ohio highway conditions (www.buckeyetraffic.org)

Ohio state park information (☎ 800-282-7275; www .dnr.state.oh.us) State parks are free to visit. Campsites cost $13 to $34; reservations accepted (fee $8).

CLEVELAND

Does it or does it not rock? That is the question. Drawing from its roots as an industrious, working man's town, Cleveland has toiled hard in recent years to prove it does. Now that the urban decay/river-on-fire thing is under control, and the city has fixed up its waterfront, made sure its old-money cultural institutions stayed viable and lassoed the Rock and Roll Hall of Fame to town, Cleveland can wipe the sweat from its brow.

History

Surveyed in 1796, Cleveland boomed after the Civil War by using iron from the upper Great Lakes and coal transported along the river to become one of the biggest US steel producers. It diversified into machinery production, textiles, clothing and chemicals, and became a center of trade unionism and socially progressive policies. Industrial wealth (think Rockefeller) bankrolled cultural aspirations, and the city still surprises with its world-class museums and performing arts.

Cleveland reached its nadir in 1969 when the Cuyahoga River burned (again), and the demise of the city's traditional indus-

tries led to urban blight and severe social problems. Ongoing renewal started in the 1980s, as derelict waterfronts became restaurant, bar and entertainment precincts. Three 1990s developments had major impacts – new baseball and football stadiums became the focus of local civic pride, and the Rock and Roll Hall of Fame brought international attention.

Orientation

Cleveland's center is Public Sq, dominated by the conspicuous Terminal Tower. Ontario St is the east–west dividing line.

Most attractions are downtown or at University Circle (the area around Case Western Reserve University). Ohio City, Tremont and Coventry are good areas nearby for eating and drinking.

Information

BOOKSTORES

Mac's (☎ 216-321-2665; 1820 Coventry Rd, Coventry) Attached to Tommy's (p610).

EMERGENCY

Fire, police, ambulance (☎ 911) Emergency.
Rape crisis (☎ 216-619-6192)

INTERNET ACCESS

Many of Cleveland's public places have free wi-fi, such as Public Sq, Playhouse Square Center and University Circle.

Metro Joes Coffee House (☎ 216-631-0043; www .metrojoes.com; 3408 Bridge Ave; ☺ 7am-11pm Sun-Thu, 7am-midnight Fri & Sat) Sip free-trade coffee with the free Internet access and free wi-fi.

INTERNET RESOURCES

Arts In Ohio (www.artsinohio.com) A detailed roundup of regional and statewide cultural events.

Travel Cleveland (www.travelcleveland.com) Attraction and lodging information plus coupons.

MEDIA

Gay People's Chronicle (www.gaypeopleschronicle .com) A weekly, with entertainment listings, distributed free throughout town.

Plain Dealer (www.cleveland.com) The city's daily newspaper, with a good Friday entertainment section.

Scene (www.clevescene.com) A weekly entertainment paper; out on Wednesday.

Tune into WCPN-FM 90.3 for NPR, or WMMS-FM 100.7 for rock.

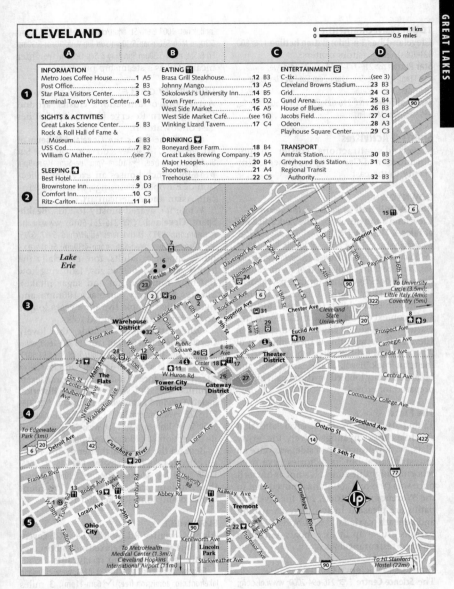

CLEVELAND

INFORMATION
Metro Joes Coffee House..............1 A5
Post Office.................................2 B3
Star Plaza Visitors Center............3 C3
Terminal Tower Visitors Center....4 B4

SIGHTS & ACTIVITIES
Great Lakes Science Center.........5 B3
Rock & Roll Hall of Fame &
Museum...................................6 B3
USS Cod..................................7 B2
William G Mather....................(see 7)

SLEEPING
Best Hotel................................8 D3
Brownstone Inn.........................9 D3
Comfort Inn.............................10 C3
Ritz-Carlton............................11 B4

EATING
Brasa Grill Steakhouse..............12 B3
Johnny Mango.........................13 A5
Sokolowski's University Inn.......14 B5
Town Fryer.............................15 D2
West Side Market.....................16 A5
West Side Market Café..........(see 16)
Winking Lizard Tavern.............17 C4

DRINKING
Boneyard Beer Farm.................18 B4
Great Lakes Brewing Company...19 A5
Major Hooples.........................20 B4
Shooters.................................21 A4
Treehouse..............................22 C5

ENTERTAINMENT
C-tix....................................(see 3)
Cleveland Browns Stadium.......23 B3
Grid......................................24 C3
Gund Arena...........................25 B4
House of Blues........................26 B3
Jacobs Field............................27 C4
Odeon...................................28 A3
Playhouse Square Center.........29 B3

TRANSPORT
Amtrak Station........................30 B3
Greyhound Bus Station.............31 C3
Regional Transit
Authority..............................32 B3

MEDICAL SERVICES
MetroHealth Medical Center (☎ 216-778-7800; 2500 MetroHealth Dr)

MONEY
Several banks with ATMs are located downtown around Public Sq, but they're not usually much help for currency exchanges.

It's best to do all your transactions at the airport.
Cleveland Hopkins International Airport Currency Exchange (☎ 216-265-0600)

POST
Post office (☎ 216-861-0708; Federal Building, 1240 E 9th St)

TOURIST INFORMATION

Cleveland has an **information hotline** (☎ 800-321-1004), and visitors centers:

Star Plaza (☎ 216-771-9118; 1302 Euclid Ave; ◷ 11am-5pm Tue-Sat, 11am-2pm Sun) By Playhouse Sq Center.

Terminal Tower (☎ 216-621-7981; 1st fl, 50 Public Sq; ◷ 9am-4pm Mon-Fri)

Sights & Activities

Cleveland's attractions cluster around downtown and Case Western Reserve University to the east.

DOWNTOWN

Rock & Roll Hall of Fame & Museum

Cleveland's top attraction, the **Rock & Roll Hall of Fame & Museum** (☎ 216-781-7625, 888-764-7625; www.rockhall.com; 1 Key Plaza; adult/child 9-12 $20/11; ◷ 10am-5:30pm, to 9pm Wed year-round, to 9pm Sat Jun-Aug) is more than a collection of memorabilia, though it does have Janis Joplin's psychedelic Porsche and Ray Charles' sunglasses. Interactive multimedia exhibits trace the history and social context of rock music and the performers who created it. Why is the museum in Cleveland? Because this is the hometown of Alan Freed, the disk jockey who popularized the term 'rock 'n' roll' in the early 1950s, and because the city lobbied hard and paid big. Be prepared for crowds.

The Flats

Taking its name from the level land that straddles the Cuyahoga River, the gritty Flats, on downtown's west side, was once an industrial area, but its factories have been reborn as nightlife zones. It's not as hot as it once was (the real action has moved east to the Warehouse District), but the riverside patios are pleasant in summer, set around and beneath myriad old iron bridges. Many patrons cruise up in their boats and hitch them to restaurant docks.

Great Lakes Science Centre

The **Science Centre** (☎ 216-694-2000; www.glsc.org; 601 Erieside Ave; adult/child 3-17 $9/7; ◷ 9:30am-5:30pm), next to the Rock Hall, gives a good account of the lakes' environmental problems. Berthed nearby on the waterfront are the storied submarine **USS Cod** (☎ 216-566-8770; www.usscod .org; 1089 E 9th St; adult/child 6-18 $6/3; ◷ 10am-4:30pm May-Sep), which saw action in WWII, and the **William G Mather** (☎ 216-574-6262; http://wgmather .nhlink.net; 1001 E 9th St; adult/child 5-18 $6/4; ◷ 10am-5:30pm Mon-Sat, noon-5:30pm Sun Jun-Aug, 10am-5:30pm Fri & Sat, noon-5:30pm Sun May & Sep-Oct), a freighter incarnated as a steamship museum.

UNIVERSITY CIRCLE

A plethora of attractions cluster around Case Western Reserve University, 5 miles east of downtown.

Star of the lot is the **Cleveland Museum of Art** (☎ 216-421-7340; www.clemusart.com; 11150 East Blvd; admission free; ◷ 10am-5pm Tue-Sun, 10am-9pm Wed & Fri), which houses an excellent collection of European paintings, as well as African, Asian and American art.

While it's geared mostly to kids, **HealthSpace Cleveland** (☎ 216-231-5010; www.health museum.org; 8911 Euclid Ave; adult/child 5-17 $7/5; ◷ 10am-4:30pm Wed-Sat, noon-4:30pm Sun) exhibits appeal to adults, too, especially the 'stress yard' and 'deli wagon' (showing how fast-food ramps up fat and sugar intake). Sneezes, by the way, can reach 100mph, and right-handed people live nine years longer on average than left-handed folks.

Other attractions include the lovely **Cleveland Botanical Garden** (☎ 216-721-1600; www .cbgarden.org; 11030 East Blvd; adult/child 3-12 $7.50/3; ◷ 10am-5pm Mon-Sat, noon-5pm Sun), with its Costa Rican cloud forest and Madagascan desert exhibits, and the **Western Reserve Historical Society/Crawford Auto-Aviation Museum** (☎ 216-721-5722; www.wrhs.org; 10825 East Blvd; adult/child 6-18 $7.50/5; ◷ 10am-5pm Mon-Sat, noon-5pm Sun), with its collection of old cars and planes.

Beyond the circle further east, don't forget eclectic **Lake View Cemetery** (☎ 216-421-2665; 12316 Euclid Ave; admission free; ◷ 7:30am-5:30pm), the 'outdoor museum' where President Garfield and John Rockefeller rest.

ELSEWHERE

Along Coventry Rd by Mayfield Rd, **Coventry Village** is a small, relaxed neighborhood of alternative shops and restaurants.

Edgewater Park (☎ 216-881-8141; www.cleveland lakefront.org; admission free; ◷ 6am-11pm), 3 miles west of downtown, has a beach and picnic area. Look for the Edgewater exit off Rte 2 West.

Sleeping

Prices listed are for summer, which is high season; rooms can be 20% less at other times (unless there is an event or convention). Prices listed do not include the 15.5% accommodations tax.

BUDGET

You'll have to head out of town for the cheapest digs.

HI Stanford Hostel (☎ 330-467-8711; www .stanfordhostel.com; 6093 Stanford Rd; dm $15-18, sheets $3; ☯ daily Apr-Dec, Thu-Mon Jan-Mar) This hostel sits very peacefully in the leafy Cuyahoga Valley National Recreation Area, 22 miles south of Cleveland in Peninsula. The fine old farmhouse is surrounded by walking trails, and beautiful deer are often spotted bounding by. The office is open from 7am to 9am and 5pm to 10pm. Call for directions; the hostel is not accessible by public transportation.

MIDRANGE

Brownstone Inn (☎ 216-426-1753; www.brownstone inndowntown.com; 3649 Prospect Ave; r incl breakfast $75-135; ℗) Well located between downtown and University Circle, the Brownstone is a B&B with a big personality. All five rooms in the Victorian townhouse have a private bath, and each comes equipped with comfy robes to lounge in. Breakfast is served in the morning, aperitifs in the evening.

Best Hotel (☎ 216-361-8969; 3614 Euclid Ave; s/d incl breakfast $80/85; ℗ 🖦) Best Hotel's rooms are spacious. Niceties include a pool, free parking and friendly staff; it's located near the Brownstone Inn.

Comfort Inn (☎ 216-861-0001; 1800 Euclid Ave; s/d $90/100; ℗) This is the closest midrange lodging to the city center, with the bus station a short walk away. The rooms are of standard, decent quality; parking costs $6.50.

Modest motels are southwest of Cleveland's center, near the airport. The W 150th exit off I-71 (exit 240) has good options for under $100 such as the **Baymont Inn** (☎ 216-251-8500; 4222 W 150th St; r incl breakfast from $76; ℗), which offers near rapid transit to downtown.

TOP END

Ritz-Carlton (☎ 216-623-1300; www.ritzcarlton.com; 1515 W 3rd St; r from $219; ℗ 🖦) What the heck? Stay where the rock stars stay and enjoy the perks, like marble baths, a 24-hour fitness and massage center, free shoeshines and your own 'technology butler.' Rooms are equipped for high-speed Internet access. Parking is $28.

Eating

There are more hip options and ethnic range than you might expect in a Rust Belt town.

DOWNTOWN

Places around the stadiums are busy on game days. The Warehouse District, west between W 6th and W 9th Sts, jumps the rest of the time.

Town Fryer (☎ 216-426-9235; 3859 Superior Ave; mains $5-15; ☯ 11am-10pm Mon-Thu, 11am-11pm Fri, 4-11pm Sat, 6-10pm Sun) It offers deeply unhealthy Cajun and Southern comfort foods, like fried catfish and maple-bacon mashed potatoes, but aren't we all really here for the fried Twinkies and Oreos? Located between downtown and University Circle.

Brasa Grill Steakhouse (☎ 216-575-0699; 1300 W 9th St; prix-fixe $35; ☯ dinner) It's carnivore heaven at trendy Brasa. Brazilian gauchos slice different cuts of grilled beef, pork, lamb and chicken right at your table; it's accompanied by a 40-item pasta and seafood bar.

Winking Lizard Tavern (☎ 216-589-0313; 811 Huron Rd; mains $7-16; ☯ 11am-midnight Mon-Thu, 11am-1am Fri & Sat, 11am-11pm Sun) This hugely popular pub-grub outlet, named for its caged iguana, is a logical downtown stop before or after a sporting event.

OHIO CITY & TREMONT

Ohio City and Tremont, which straddle I-90 south of downtown, are areas with lots of new establishments popping up.

West Side Market Café (☎ 216-579-6800; 1979 W 25th St; mains $4-7; ☯ breakfast Mon, Wed, Fri & Sat, lunch Mon-Sat) This is a smart stop if you're craving well-made breakfast and lunch fare, and cheap fish and chicken mains.

Johnny Mango (☎ 216-575-1919; 3120 Bridge Ave; mains $5-15; ☯ 11am-10pm Mon-Thu, 11am-11pm Fri, 9am-11pm Sat, 9am-10pm Sun) The Caribbean-influenced food and drinks are as flavorful as the interior is colorful. Mr Mango has a hearty vegetarian selection along with his meat dishes, all begging to be complemented by tropical drinks like sangria or Cuban *mojitos* (rum cocktail). Try the killer French fries made of plantains.

Sokolowski's University Inn (☎ 216-771-9236; www.sokolowskis.com; 1201 University Rd; mains $8-15;

⊗ lunch Mon-Fri, dinner Fri & Sat) The portions are huge, enough to fuel the hungriest steel-worker. It's cafeteria style, so grab a tray and fill it with plump pierogi, cabbage rolls and other rib-sticking Polish fare.

Metro Joes Coffee House (☎ 216-631-0043; www.metrojoes.com; 3408 Bridge Ave; ⊗ 7am-11pm Sun-Thu, 7am-midnight Fri & Sat) Dandy for coffee and baked goods. See also p606.

West Side Market (www.westsidemarket.com; cnr W 25th St & Lorain Ave; ⊗ Mon, Wed, Fri & Sat) Overflowing with fresh produce and prepared foods; adjacent to the West Side Market Café.

LITTLE ITALY & COVENTRY

Busy Little Italy is along Mayfield Rd, near the Lakeview Cemetery and University Circle (look for the Rte 322 sign). Food-abundant Coventry Village is a bit further east off Mayfield Rd.

Presti's Bakery (☎ 216-421-3060; 12101 Mayfield Rd; items $2-5; ⊗ 6am-7pm Mon-Thu, 6am-10pm Fri & Sat, to 6pm Sun) Try Presti's for its popular sandwiches, stromboli and divine pine-nut cookies.

Tommy's (☎ 216-321-7757; 1823 Coventry Rd; mains $4-9; ⊗ 7:30am-10pm Mon-Thu, 7:30am-11pm Fri & Sat, 9am-10pm Sun) This is a neighborhood stand-out, with a broad, veggie-heavy menu; don't miss the Mary Lynn spinach pie.

Drinking

DOWNTOWN

The Flats are fine on a summer's day; otherwise the action has moved to the Warehouse District, where many restaurants also have popular bars.

Shooters (☎ 216-861-6900; 1148 Main Ave) It's pretty cheesy, but does have a great waterfront location in the Flats, perfect for sunset gazing.

Boneyard Beer Farm (☎ 216-575-0226; 748 Prospect Ave) This spot near the sports stadiums is well suited for downing a couple pre- or post-game.

OHIO CITY & TREMONT

Major Hooples (☎ 216-575-0483; 1930 Columbus Rd) Look over the bar for Cleveland's best skyline view from this friendly, eclectic watering hole.

Great Lakes Brewing Company (☎ 216-771-4404; 2516 Market Ave) Great Lakes wins numerous prizes for its brewed-on-the-premises beers. Added historical bonus: Eliott Ness

got into a shootout with criminals here; ask the bartender to show you the bullet holes.

Treehouse (☎ 216-696-2505; 820 College Ave) Treehouse caters to a young, hip crowd thronged around a giant metal tree.

UNIVERSITY CIRCLE

Barking Spider (☎ 216-421-2863; 11310 Juniper Rd) This ski lodge–like place is the perfect spot to while away the afternoon; it's hidden, tucked behind Arabica Coffee House.

Entertainment

Check *Scene* and Friday's *Plain Dealer* (see p606) for listings.

C-tix (☎ 216-771-1778; Star Plaza Visitors Center, 1302 Euclid Ave) Sells day-of discount tickets.

LIVE MUSIC

House of Blues (☎ 216-523-2583; www.hob.com; 308 Euclid Ave) The chain brings in medium- and top-tier bands.

Beachland Ballroom (☎ 216-383-1124; www.beachlandballroom.com; 15711 Waterloo Rd) Hip young bands play at this venue east of downtown.

Odeon (☎ 216-574-2525; www.theodeon.com; 1295 Old River Rd) Odeon brings pounding rock bands to the Flats.

PERFORMING ARTS

Playhouse Square Center (☎ 216-771-4444; www.playhousesquare.com; 1501 Euclid Ave) This elegant center hosts theater, opera and ballet.

Severance Hall (☎ 216-231-1111; www.clevelandorch.com; 11001 Euclid Ave) Near University Circle, Severance Hall is where the acclaimed Cleveland Symphony Orchestra holds its season (August to May). The orchestra's summer home is Blossom Music Center in Cuyahoga Valley National Park, about 22 miles south.

GAY & LESBIAN VENUES

Grid (☎ 216-623-0113; www.thegrid.com; 1437 St Clair St) The Grid is a happenin' downtown gay dance venue.

SPORTS

Cleveland is a serious jock town with three modern downtown venues.

Jacobs Field (☎ 866-488-7423; www.indians.com; 2401 Ontario St) Baseball's Indians (aka 'The Tribe') attempt to hit here.

Gund Arena (☎ 800-820-2287; www.nba.com/cavaliers; 1 Center Ct) Nearby Jacobs Field, the

Cavaliers play basketball at this arena which doubles as an entertainment venue.

Cleveland Browns Stadium (☎ 440-891-5000; www.clevelandbrowns.com; 1085 W 3rd St) The NFL's Browns play football on the lakefront.

Getting There & Around

TO/FROM THE AIRPORT

Eleven miles southwest of downtown, **Cleveland Hopkins International Airport** (☎ 216-265-6030; www.clevelandairport.com) is linked by the Regional Transit Authority (RTA) Red Line train ($1.50). A cab to downtown costs about $25.

BUS

From downtown, **Greyhound** (☎ 216-781-0520; 1465 Chester Ave) offers frequent departures to Pittsburgh ($22 to $33, three hours), Chicago ($42 to $65, 7½ hours) and New York ($62 to $88, 12½ hours).

CAR

Parking is scarce and expensive downtown during events. Avis, Hertz and other rental agencies have offices at the airport and around town. Check the Transportation chapter (p1175) for contact details.

PUBLIC TRANSPORTATION

The **Regional Transit Authority** (RTA; ☎ 216-621-9500; www.gcrta.org; 1240 W 6th St) operates the useful Waterfront Line train that connects the Flats and other attractions to Tower City Center. The Red Line goes to Ohio City and University Circle. Fares are $1.50; daypass $3.

TAXI

For cab service, call **Americab** (☎ 216-429-1111).

TRAIN

There are connections daily with **Amtrak** (☎ 216-696-5115; 200 Cleveland Memorial Shoreway) for Pittsburgh ($23 to $43, three hours), Chicago ($50 to $90, seven hours) and New York City ($70 to $120, 11½ hours).

Around Cleveland

Thirty miles south of Cleveland, **Akron** was a small village until Dr BF Goodrich established the first rubber factory in 1869. It was also once the country's rubber capital, and still produces more than half the country's tires and over 50,000 different rubber prod-

ucts. For an insight into US ingenuity, visit the **National Inventors Hall of Fame** (☎ 330-762-4463; www.invent.org; 221 S Broadway, Akron; adult/child 3-17 $8.75/6.75; ☼ 10am-4:30pm Wed-Sat).

Further south in **Canton**, birthplace of the NFL, the popular **Pro Football Hall of Fame** (☎ 330-456-8207; www.profootballhof.com; 2121 George Halas Dr; adult/child 6-14 $13/6; ☼ 9am-8pm Jun-Aug, 9am-5pm rest of year) is a shrine for the gridiron-obsessed. Look for the football-shaped tower off I-77.

West of Cleveland, attractive **Oberlin** is an old-fashioned college town, with noteworthy architecture by Cass Gilbert, Frank Lloyd Wright and Robert Venturi. Further west, just south of I-90, the tiny town of **Milan** is the birthplace of Thomas Edison. His home, restored to its 1847 likeness, is now a small **museum** (☎ 419-499-2135; www.tomedison.org; 9 Edison Dr; adult/child 6-12 $5/2; ☼ 1-4pm Wed-Sun winter, extended hrs Tue-Sun summer, closed Jan) outlining his inventions, like the lightbulb and phonograph.

Still further west, on US 20 and surrounded by farmland, is **Clyde**, which bills itself as the USA's most famous small town. It got that way when native son Sherwood Anderson published *Winesburg, Ohio* in 1919. It didn't take long for the unimpressed residents to figure out where the fictitious town really was. Stop at the **Clyde Museum** (☎ 419-547-9330; 124 W Buckeye St; admission free; ☼ 1-4pm Thu or by appt) in the old church for Anderson tidbits or at the library, a few doors down.

ERIE LAKESHORE & ISLANDS

In summer this good-time resort area is one of the busiest (and the most expensive) places in Ohio. Pre-book accommodations.

Sandusky, long a port, now mainly serves as the jump-off point to the Erie Islands. The **visitors center** (☎ 419-625-2984; www.sanduskyohiocedarpoint.com; 4424 Milan Rd; ☼ 8:30am-5:30pm Mon-Fri, extended to evenings & Sat in summer) provides lodging and ferry information. Scads of chain motels line the roads heading into town.

For the world's tallest (420ft), fastest (120mph) roller coaster, head to **Cedar Point Amusement Park** (☎ 419-627-2350; www.cedarpoint.com; adult/child $45/25; ☼ from 10am daily mid-May–Labor Day, from 10am Sat & Sun Sep-Oct, closing times vary), 6 miles from Sandusky. If the 16 roller coasters aren't enough, the surrounding area has a nice beach, water park and a slew of tacky, old-fashioned attractions.

Lake Erie Islands

In the War of 1812's Battle of Lake Erie, Admiral Perry met the enemy English fleet near South Bass Island. His victory ensured that all the lands south of the Great Lakes became US, not Canadian territory. Today, while the nearby mainland gets congested and isn't particularly attractive, the islands remain an appealing warm-weather getaway.

Access is from Sandusky, Marblehead, Catawba or Port Clinton. **Pelee Island Transportation** (☎ 800-661-2220) runs a ferry (one way adult/child six to 12 $13.75/6.75, car $30) from Sandusky to Canada's **Pelee Island** and the Ontario mainland. Pelee, the largest Erie island, is a quiet, wine-producing and bird-watching destination.

BASS ISLANDS

Forget the history and scenery – on a summer weekend, packed Put In Bay on **South Bass Island** is about drinking and carousing. But away from this party town full of restaurants and shops, you'll find a winery and opportunities for camping, fishing, kayaking and swimming. A singular attraction is the 352ft Doric column commemorating Perry's victory in the Battle of Lake Erie – you can climb up to the observation deck ($3) for views of the battle site and, on a good day, Canada.

The **Chamber of Commerce** (☎ 419-285-2832; www.put-in-bay.com; cnr Delaware & Toledo Aves; ⏰ 10am-5pm Mon-Sun summer, Mon-Fri rest of year) has information on activities and lodging, which starts at $75 in summer and often is booked up. **Ashley's Island House** (☎ 419-285-2844; www.ashleysislandhouse.com; Catawba Ave; r $79-165) is a 13-room B&B, where naval officers stayed in the late 1800s. The **Beer Barrel Saloon** (☎ 419-285-2337; 1618 Delaware Ave; ⏰ 11am-1am) has plenty of space for imbibing – its bar is 406ft long.

Cabs and tour buses serve the island, though bicycling is a fine way to get around. **Jet Express** (☎ 800-245-1538; www.jet-express.com) leaves Port Clinton on the mainland for South Bass Island (one way adult/child 12 and under $11/free, no cars), and also departs from Sandusky (one way adult/child five to 12 $15/3.50, no cars). **Miller Boatline** (☎ 800-500-2421; www.millerferry.com) from Cat-

awba is cheapest (one way adult/child six to 11 $5.50/1, car $13).

Middle Bass Island, a good day trip by ferry from South Bass, offers nature and quiet; Miller Boatline will get you there.

KELLEYS ISLAND

Quiet and green, Kelleys is a popular weekend escape, especially for families. It has pretty 19th-century buildings, Native American pictographs, a good beach and glacial grooves – even its old limestone quarries are scenic.

The **Chamber of Commerce** (☎ 419-746-2360; www.kelleysislandchamber.com; cnr Division & Chappell Sts; ⏰ 10am-4pm Mon-Sat, noon-4pm Sun summer) has activity and accommodation information. The Village, the small commercial center of the island, has places to eat, drink, shop and rent bicycles – a good way to sightsee.

Kelleys Island Ferry Boat Line (☎ 419-798-9763; www.kelleysislandferry.com) departs frequently from the Marblehead dock (one way adult/child $6/3.50, car $12). The crossing takes about 20 minutes and leaves hourly (more frequently in summer).

AMISH COUNTRY

A visit to Amish Country is a trip back in time, as the Amish have resisted modernity for centuries now. Wayne and Holmes Counties, between Cleveland and Columbus (immediately east of I-71), have the USA's densest Amish concentration (followed by areas in Pennsylvania and Indiana).

Descendants of conservative Dutch–Swiss religious factions who migrated to the USA during the 18th century, the Amish continue to follow the *ordnung* (way of life), in varying degrees. Many adhere to rules prohibiting the use of electricity, telephones and motorized vehicles. They wear traditional clothing, farm the land with plow and mule, and go to church in horse-drawn buggies. Others are not so strict, willingly accepting rides in cars from non-Amish, or even driving vehicles themselves.

Unfortunately, what would surely be a peaceful country scene is often disturbed by behemoth tour buses. Many Amish are happy to profit from this influx of outside dollars, but don't equate this to free photographic access – the Amish typically view photographs as taboo. Drive carefully, and slowly, as roads are narrow and curvy and

---

TOP FIVE GREAT LAKES PIE SHOPS

The prolific berry and cherry growing in the region results in a legacy of perfectly flaked, scrumptious desserts:

Henry's Sohio (☎ 614-879-9321; 6275 US 40, W Jefferson, Ohio; ⊙ 11am-8pm Mon-Fri, 6:30am-8pm Sat) The selection is whatever happens to pop out of the oven that day – butterscotch, coconut cream, pecan, peanut butter – all heavenly; don't let the dumpy gas station exterior deter you. Located 10 miles west of Columbus.

Crane's Pie Pantry (☎ 269-561-2297; 6054 124th Ave, off Hwy 89, Fennville, Michigan; ⊙ 9am-8pm Mon-Sat, 11am-8pm Sun May-Oct, reduced hrs rest of year) It's located smack dab in the middle of a fruit orchard, which is where the fillings (blueberry, apple, red raspberry and more) come from.

Norske Nook (☎ 715-597-3069; 13807 7th St, off I-94, Osseo, Wisconsin; ⊙ 5:30am-8pm Mon-Sat, 8am-8pm Sun) Banana cream so good you'll weep.

Palisade Café (☎ 218-845-2214; Main St/Hwy 3, Palisade, Minnesota; ⊙ 7am-7pm Mon-Thu, 7am-9pm Fri & Sat, 8am-2pm Sun, extended hrs summer) Pole-vaults 'fresh and homemade' to a new level. Located 40 miles south of Grand Rapids.

Ariston Café (☎ 217-324-2023; N Old Rte 66, Litchfield, Illinois; ⊙ 11am-10pm Mon-Fri, 4-10pm Sat, 11am-9pm Sun) Snickers pie, caramel-apple-nut pie and Red Velvet cake straight off the Mother Road. For more details, see p597.

---

there's always the chance of pulling up on a slow-moving buggy just around the bend. Many places are closed Sunday.

Near Berlin, east of Millersburg, is the **Amish & Mennonite Heritage Center** (☎ 330-893-3192; 5798 County Rd 77; adult/child 6-12 $6.50/3; ⊙ 9am-5pm Mon-Sat year-round, 9am-8pm Fri & Sat Jun-Oct), which offers concise explanations of the history and life of Amish.

Kidron, on Rte 52 just north of US 250, is worth a stop on Thursday, when the **Kidron Auction** takes place at the livestock barn. It's a view of 18th-century commerce, as hundreds of buggies will be lined up along the roadside, and an interesting flea market rings the barn. Across the street, **Lehman's Store** is an absolute must-see. It's the Amish community's main purveyor of modern-looking products that use no electricity, as well as the sorts of daily items your great-grandparents probably used.

In quiet Walnut Creek, between Sugarcreek and Berlin just north of Hwy 39, check out the amazing **Amish Flea Market** (⊙ 9am-5pm Fri & Sat), where you can find new or used (sometimes ancient) knickknacks, crafts, quilts, produce, antiques and delicious baked goods. Just north of Walnut Creek, along Hwy 515, **Yoder's** (☎ 330-893-2541; ⊙ 10am-5pm Mon-Sat mid-Apr–Oct) is an Amish farm that's open to visitors. Tours cost $5/3 per adult/child.

In the town of Millersburg, west of Berlin on US 62, the historic **Hotel Millersburg** (☎ 330-674-1457; www.hotelmillersburg.com; 35 W

Jackson St; r $44-99) has very basic, reasonably priced rooms (ask for an economy or twin room for the lowest rates). There's a modern, brightly lit tavern and dining room on the ground floor.

Boyd & Wurthman Restaurant (☎ 330-893-3287; Main St; mains from $6; ⊙ 5:30am-8pm Mon-Sat) is Berlin's most atmospheric eatery and serves home-style cooking, attracting locals and tourists alike. Amish specialties, like ham loaf and wedding steak (ground meat in mushroom sauce), join familiar American fare on the menu.

COLUMBUS

Columbus is, well, it's nice. Though not much of a looker or splashy personality-wise, the state capital is affable, kind of like a blind date your mom arranges. It is, however, that rare big city that's easy on the wallet, perhaps from the influence of Ohio State University's (OSO) 60,000 students.

There is a **visitors center** (☎ 614-221-2489, 800-345-4386; www.experiencecolumbus.com; 90 N High St; ⊙ 8am-5pm Mon-Fri) downtown.

The **Columbus Dispatch** (www.dispatch.com) is the city's daily newspaper. The free, weekly **Alive** (www.columbusalive.com) has entertainment listings. **Outlook** (www.outlooknews.com) is a weekly gay and lesbian publication.

Sights & Activities

The remarkably large, all-brick **German Village**, 0.5 miles south of downtown, is a restored 19th-century neighborhood with cobbled

GREAT LAKES

streets and Italianate and Queen Anne architecture. The **German Village Society** (☎ 614-221-8888; www.germanvillage.com; 588 S 3rd St; ☺ 9am-4pm Mon-Fri, 10am-2pm Sat) has self-guided walking-tour information. Just north of downtown, the browse-able **Short North** is a redeveloped strip of High St that holds contemporary art galleries, restaurants and jazz bars.

North of downtown, the Ohio State University area has many casual storefronts. The campus' **Wexner Center for the Arts** (☎ 614-292-3535; www.wexarts.org; 1871 N High St; admission free; ☺ 10am-6pm Sun-Wed, 10am-9pm Thu-Sat, noon-6pm Sun) offers cutting-edge art exhibits, films and performances.

The **Ohio Historical Center** (☎ 614-297-2300; www.ohiohistory.org; 1982 Velma Ave; adult/child $7/3; ☺ 9am-5pm Tue-Sat, 9am-9pm Thu, noon-5pm Sun; P), off I-71 N at the 17th Ave exit, has been made over from a fusty relic house to an interactive museum. For those planning to tour the state's southern Hopewell Indian sites, a visit – at least to the website – is invaluable.

Sleeping

Add 16.75% tax to the following rates.

German Village Inn (☎ 614-443-6506; 920 S High St; r $59; P) This super-clean spot is in a great location near bars and restaurants.

Red Roof Inn (☎ 614-224-6539; 111 E Nationwide Blvd; r incl breakfast $74-129; P) Located in the Arena District, it's one of the classiest-looking Red Roofs you'll ever see. Parking is $10.

50 Lincoln B&B (☎ 614-421-2202; 800-827-4203; www.columbus-bed-breakfast.com; 50 E Lincoln St; r incl breakfast $119; P) These eight well-maintained rooms (with private bathrooms) are just steps away from the Short North.

Eating & Drinking

German Village and the Short North provide fertile drinking and grazing grounds. The Arena District (the area around the Nationwide Arena hockey stadium) is also bursting, mostly with midrange chains and brewpubs. Around OSU and along N High St from 15th Ave onward, you'll find everything from Mexican to Ethiopian to sushi, plus quality coffee shops.

Schmidt's (☎ 614-444-6808; 240 E Kossuth St; mains $7-13; ☺ 11am-9pm Sun & Mon, 11am-10pm Tue-Thu, 11am-11pm Fri & Sat) It's the 'best of the wurst.' Succulent German staples, like sausage, schnitzel and potato salad and, the pièce de résistance, half-pound cream puffs, includ-

ing the 'Buckeye,' pumped up with peanut butter. The beer flows freely to the strains of an oompah band (Thursday to Saturday).

Katzinger's Deli (☎ 614-228-3354; 475 S 3rd St; sandwiches $8-12; ☺ 8:30am-8:30pm Mon-Thu, 8:30am-9pm Fri-Sun) Prepare for a mind-boggling array of huge, scrumptious sandwiches, from beefy to vegan.

Blue Danube (☎ 614-261-9308; 2439 N High St; mains $4-8; ☺ 11am-2:30am) The Danube's smoky, neon-lit booths endure as a campus favorite. Meals are late-night booze-absorbers, like gravy-smothered fries and gyros.

Elevator Brewery (☎ 614-228-0500; 161 N High St; ☺ 11am-2am Mon-Fri, 5pm-2am Sat) Earn your Master of Beer Appreciation (MBA) degree with the homemade suds by Brewmaster Schlitz. It's near Nationwide Arena.

Entertainment

The Ohio State Buckeyes football team packs a rabid crowd into legendary, horseshoe-shaped **Ohio Stadium** (☎ 800-462-8257; www.ohiostatebuckeyes.com) for its games, held on Saturdays in the fall. The National Hockey League (NHL) Columbus Blue Jackets play hockey at the downtown **Nationwide Arena** (☎ 614-246-2000; www.bluejackets.com; 200 W Nationwide Blvd). The popular Columbus Crew pro soccer team plays in **Crew Stadium** (☎ 614-447-2739; www.thecrew.com; 2121 Velma Ave), north off I-71 and 17th Ave, from March to October.

Getting There & Around

The **Port Columbus Airport** (☎ 614-239-4000; www.columbusairports.com) is 10 miles east of town. There is no direct public bus. A cab to downtown costs $18 to $20.

From the **Greyhound station** (☎ 614-221-4642; 111 E Town St) buses run at least six times daily to Cincinnati ($17 to $25, two hours) and Cleveland ($19 to $27, 2½ hours). There is no Amtrak train service.

SOUTHEASTERN OHIO

Ohio's southeastern corner cradles most of its forested areas, as well as rolling hills and scattered farms.

Around Lancaster, southeast of Columbus, the hills lead gently into wonderful **Hocking County**, which contains more than half a dozen state parks. This region of streams and waterfalls, sandstone cliffs and cavelike formations is a splendid area to explore in any season. It has miles of trails for hiking and rivers for canoeing, as well as abundant campgrounds and cabins at **Hocking Hills State Park** (☎ 740-385-6165; www.hockinghillspark.com; 20160 Hwy 664; campsites/cabins from $18/35). **Old Man's Cave** is a scenic winner for hiking. This is a busy area in summer, especially on weekends.

Athens makes a lovely base for seeing the region. Situated where US 50 crosses US 33, it's set among wooded hills and built around the Ohio University campus (which comprises half the town). The **visitors center** (☎ 740-592-1819, 800-878-9767; www.athensohio.com; 667 E State St; 9am-5pm Mon-Sat summer, 9am-5pm Mon-Fri rest of year) has good regional information. Inexpensive motels – including friendly **Budget Host** (☎ 740-594-2294; 100 Albany Rd at Rte 50 W; s/d from $42/48) – dot the outskirts, and numerous student cafés and pubs line Court St, the main road. **Casa Nueva** (☎ 740-592-2016; 4 W State St; mains $6-13; breakfast, lunch & dinner) has Mexican-inspired dishes, while **Court Street Diner** (☎ 740-594-8700; 18 N Court St; mains $5-9; 7am-10pm) serves up breakfast, lunch and dinner in '50s style.

Further south, the Ohio River marks the state boundary and flows through many scenic stretches. It's a surprisingly quiet, undeveloped area.

The area south of Columbus was a center for the fascinating prehistoric Hopewell people, who left behind huge geometric earthworks and burial mounds from around 200 BC to AD 600. For a fine introduction visit the **Hopewell Culture National Historical Park** (☎ 740-774-1126; Hwy 104 north of I-35; admission $3; 8:30-6pm summer, 8:30-5pm rest of year), 3 miles north of Chillicothe. The visitors center has a film and excellent interactive exhibit; then you can wander about the variously shaped ceremonial mounds spread over 13-acre **Mound City**, a mysterious town of the dead. **Serpent Mound** (☎ 937-587-2796; 3850 Hwy 73; 10am-5pm Tue-Sun May-Oct; P), southwest of Chillicothe and 4 miles northwest of Locust Grove, is perhaps the most captivating site of all. The giant, uncoiling snake stretches over 0.25 miles and is the largest effigy mound in the USA.

DAYTON & YELLOW SPRINGS

Dayton has the aviation sights, but little Yellow Springs (18 miles northeast on US 68) has much more personality for accommodation and places to eat.

Sights & Activities

The huge **National Museum of the US Air Force** (☎ 937-255-3286; www.wpafb.af.mil/museum; 1100 Spaatz St; admission free; 9am-5pm) is at the Wright Patterson Air Force base, 6 miles northeast of Dayton. It's got everything from a Wright Brothers exhibit, a Sopwith Camel (WWI biplane) and a Stealth bomber, to astronaut ice cream, military propaganda and an Aviation Hall of Fame. Expect a visit to take three or more hours. And don't miss the annex with its collection of presidential planes – a free shuttle bus takes you over to the hangar.

There are numerous Wright attractions. Among them, **Carillon Historical Park** (☎ 937-293-2841; www.carillonpark.org; 1000 Carillon Blvd; adult/child 3-17 $8/5; 9:30am-5pm Tue-Sat, noon-5pm Sun Apr-Oct) has the 1905 Wright Flyer III biplane and a replica of the Wright workshop. The **Dayton Aviation Heritage National Historical Park** (☎ 937-225-7705; www.nps.gov/daav; 22 S Williams St; admission free; 8:30am-5pm), which includes Wright Cycle Company Complex, is where the brothers developed bikes and aviation ideas.

Sleeping & Eating

All the following listings are in Yellow Springs, a top-notch place to experience down-home Ohio.

Springs Motel (☎ 937-767-8700; www.thespringsmotel.com; 3601 US 68; r $49-55) The Springs is a time-defiant, mom and pop–type motel.

Morgan House (☎ 937-767-1761; www.arthurmorganhouse.com; 120 W Limestone St; r from $95; ☒) This comfy, six-room B&B is decorated with African art (the innkeeper recently returned from a Peace Corps stint). It's wi-fi equipped, and serves organic breakfasts.

John Bryan State Park (☎ 937-767-1274; www.johnbryan.org; 3790 Hwy 370; campsites $11-20) You can fish, hike, rock climb or camp among the limestone cliffs here.

Young's Jersey Dairy (☎ 937-325-0629; 6880 Springfield-Xenia Rd) This working dairy farm has two restaurants: the **Golden Jersey Inn** (mains $7-13; lunch & dinner Mon-Fri, plus breakfast Sat & Sun), serving dishes like buttermilk chicken; and the **Dairy Store** (sandwiches $2-4; 6am-10pm Sun-Thu, to 11pm Fri & Sat), serving sandwiches, dreamy ice cream and Ohio's best milkshakes.

Winds Café (☎ 937-767-1144; www.windscafe.com; 215 Xenia Ave; mains $10-25; lunch & dinner

Tue-Sat, brunch only Sun) Once upon a time this was a wee place that grew its own bean sprouts. Now the Winds serves organic, seasonal dishes, like asparagus crepes in fig vinegar and rhubarb halibut. It demonstrates what happens when hippies go high class – but only in food sophistication, not attitude or ambience, which thankfully remain reassuringly mellow.

Clifton Mill (☎ 937-767-5501; 75 Water St; mains $6-8; ⏰ 9am-4pm Mon-Fri, 8am-5pm Sat & Sun) You can watch the water wheel turn, grinding the grain for your pancakes and cornbread.

CINCINNATI

It's mind-boggling to think Jerry Springer was mayor here years ago, as Cincinnati is so pretty and genteel, splashed along the Ohio River. The city is a good place to kick back, catch a baseball game, chow on the famous chili and maybe even ride a paddle wheel boat. Mt Adams, whose twisting streets lead to one of the city's best hilltop views, is a great old neighborhood to explore. So are *über*-cool Northside and cobblestoned Covington.

History

With the Ohio River as a principal transport route, Cincinnati, founded in 1788, became the agricultural hinterland's commerce hub, as well as a base for wars against the Native Americans. By the mid-1800s it was Ohio's largest city, thanks to a huge influx of German and Irish immigrants. The many meatpacking plants earned Cincinnati the nickname 'Porkopolis' and provided enough leftover lard for Messrs Procter and Gamble to become one of the world's largest soap makers.

Cincinnati was a center for the antislavery movement, an important station on the Underground Railroad, and a home of abolitionist writing and publishing. The Civil War was a boost to Cincinnati's industries, but later the city suffered from corruption, maladministration and a decline in its river commerce as the railways expanded. Anti-German sentiment prevailed during WWI, and the city changed many of its street and building names to sound less Teutonic.

Cincinnati takes its knocks for being racist, conservative and fogyish (Mark Twain said he wanted to be here when the world ends, as the city is always 20 years behind

the times). Those stereotypes are slowly being massaged away.

Orientation

Downtown streets are laid out on a grid radiating from Fountain Sq. Vine St is the east–west dividing line; east- and westbound streets are numbered, while north- and south-bound streets are named. The snaking Ohio River forms the city's southern boundary. Kentucky – specifically the communities of Newport and Covington – lies across the water. Other neighborhoods of interest include rough-and-ready Over-the-Rhine, just north of the center; artsy Mt Adams, high on the hill east of downtown; and funky Northside, north of where I-74 and I-75 intersect, about 5 miles north of downtown.

Information

BOOKSTORES

Barnes & Noble (☎ 829-581-2000; Newport on the Levee; ⏰ 10am-11pm)

EMERGENCY

Fire, police, ambulance (☎ 911) Emergency.

INTERNET ACCESS

@ The Kafe (☎ 513-241-1343; www.atthekafe.com; Carew Tower, 441 Vine St, street level; per hr $5; ⏰ 7am-6pm Mon-Fri, 9am-6pm Sat) You can burn photo CDs, too.

INTERNET RESOURCES

See also *CityBeat* and *Cin Weekly* (below).
Arts In Ohio (www.artsinohio.com) A detailed roundup of regional and statewide cultural events.
Cincinnati USA (www.cincyusa.com) Information on sights, hotels and restaurants, plus coupons.

MEDIA

The **Cincinnati Enquirer** (www.enquirer.com) and **Cincinnati Post** (www.enquirer.com) are the morning and afternoon newspapers, respectively, owned by the same company. **Cin Weekly** (www.enquirer.com) is their entertainment spinoff. **CityBeat** (www.citybeat.com) is a free weekly entertainment paper, out on Wednesday.

MEDICAL SERVICES

University Hospital (☎ 513-584-1000; 234 Goodman St)

MONEY

US Bank (☎ 513-632-4135; 425 Walnut St) ATM and foreign currency exchange available.

CINCINNATI

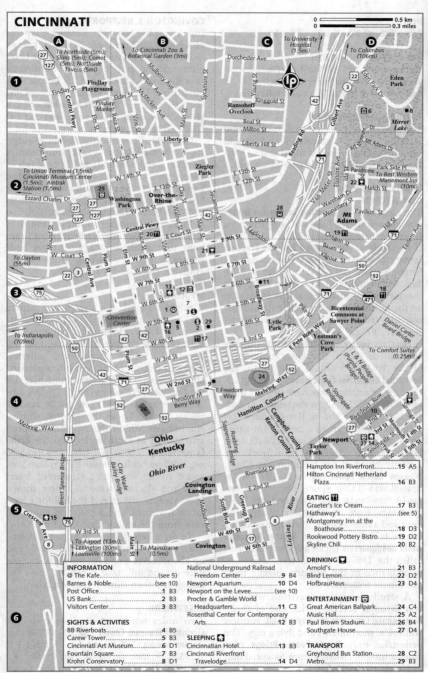

INFORMATION

@ The Kafe	(see 5)
Barnes & Noble	(see 10)
Post Office	1 B3
US Bank	2 B3
Visitors Center	3 B3

SIGHTS & ACTIVITIES

BB Riverboats	4 B5
Carew Tower	5 B3
Cincinnati Art Museum	6 D1
Fountain Square	7 B3
Krohn Conservatory	8 D1

National Underground Railroad	
Freedom Center	9 B4
Newport Aquarium	10 D4
Newport on the Levee	(see 10)
Procter & Gamble World	
Headquarters	11 C3
Rosenthal Center for Contemporary	
Arts	12 B3

SLEEPING

Cincinnatian Hotel	13 B3
Cincinnati Riverfront	
Travelodge	14 D4

Hampton Inn Riverfront	15 A5
Hilton Cincinnati Netherland	
Plaza	16 B3

EATING

Graeter's Ice Cream	17 B3
Hathaway's	(see 5)
Montgomery Inn at the	
Boathouse	18 D3
Rookwood Pottery Bistro	19 D2
Skyline Chili	20 B2

DRINKING

Arnold's	21 B3
Blind Lemon	22 D2
HofbrauHaus	23 D4

ENTERTAINMENT

Great American Ballpark	24 C4
Music Hall	25 A2
Paul Brown Stadium	26 B4
Southgate House	27 D4

TRANSPORT

Greyhound Bus Station	28 C2
Metro	29 B3

POST
Post office (☎ 800-275-8777; 525 Vine St)

TOURIST INFORMATION
Visitors center (☎ 513-621-6994, 800-246-2987; www
.cincyusa.com; 511 Walnut St; ☯ 10am-5pm Mon-Sat,
noon-5pm Sun) On Fountain Sq; ask about walking tours.

Dangers & Annoyances
The area between the Amtrak train station
and downtown is best avoided on foot, and
caution should be used at night in the Over-
the-Rhine and Northside neighborhoods.

Sights & Activities
DOWNTOWN
The elegant 1876 **Roebling Suspension Bridge**
was a forerunner of John Roebling's famous
Brooklyn Bridge in New York. At its foot
is the **National Underground Railroad Freedom
Center** (☎ 513-333-7500; www.freedomcenter.org; 50 E
Freedom Way; adult/child 6-12 $12/8; ☯ Tue-Sun 11am-
5pm), with exhibits on how slaves escaped to
the north; Cincinnati was a prominent stop
on the railroad and a center for abolitionist
activities led by residents, such as Harriet
Beecher Stowe.

Fountain Square (cnr 5th & Vine Sts), the city
centerpiece, hosts the fancy old 'Spirit
of the Waters' fountain. Just north, the
Rosenthal Center for Contemporary Arts (☎ 513-
721- 0390; www.contemporaryartscenter.org; 44 E 6th St;
adult/child 3-13 $$7.50/4.50, free Mon evening; ☯ 10am-
9pm Mon, 10am-6pm Wed-Fri, 11am-6pm Sat & Sun)
displays modern art in a new, avant-garde
building designed by Iranian architect Zaha
Hadid. The structure and its artworks are
a pretty big deal for traditionalist Cincy.
Nearby **Carew Tower** (☎ 513-241-3888; 441 Vine
St; adult/child 6-11 $2/1; ☯ 9am-5:30pm Mon-Thu, 9am-
7pm Fri, 10am-7pm Sat & Sun, reduced hrs winter) has a
great view from its 49th-floor observation
deck and a fine art deco interior. East of the
square is the postmodern **Procter & Gamble
world headquarters** (cnr 6th & Broadway Sts), often
called the 'Dolly Parton Towers' due to its
resemblance to the country singer's most
prominent features.

A stroll along the riverfront will take
you through several parks; one of them,
Bicentennial Commons at Sawyer Point, features
whimsical monuments and flying pigs. The
pedestrian-only **Purple People Bridge** pro-
vides a unique crossing from Sawyer Point
to Newport, Kentucky.

COVINGTON & NEWPORT
Covington and Newport, Kentucky, are sort
of suburbs of Cincinnati. Newport, known
mainly for its massive **Newport on the Levee**
restaurant and shopping complex, is directly
over the river at the foot of the Purple Peo-
ple Bridge. The development also contains
the well-regarded **Newport Aquarium** (☎ 859-
491-3467; www.newportaquarium.com; adult/child 3-12
$18/11; ☯ 9am-7pm, reduced hrs winter).

Covington lies west of the Roebling Bridge.
Its lively **MainStrasse** was a 19th-century
German neighborhood, and is now full of
shops, pubs and places to eat. Covington
Landing is an area of floating bars and tour
boats at the Roebling's foot. **BB Riverboats**
(☎ 859-261-8500; www.bbriverboats.com; 1 Madison
Ave) takes off from here and plies the river
in a nifty sightseeing paddle wheeler (one-
hour tour adult/child $14/8); three-hour
Kentucky bourbon-tasting cruises ($45)
available, too. Call for schedules.

MT ADAMS
It might be a bit of a stretch to compare
Mt Adams, immediately east of down-
town, to Paris' Montmarte, but this hilly
19th-century enclave of narrow, twisting
streets, Victorian townhouses, galleries,
bars and restaurants is certainly a pleasur-
able surprise. Two big attractions here are
the **Cincinnati Art Museum** (☎ 513-721-5204; www
.cincinnatiartmuseum.org; 953 Eden Park Dr; admission
free; ☯ 11am-5pm Tue-Sun, 11am-9pm Wed), with an
emphasis on Middle Eastern and European
arts as well as local works, and the **Krohn
Conservatory** (☎ 513-421-4086; www.cinci-parks
.org; 1501 Eden Park Dr; admission free; ☯ 10am-5pm),
a vast greenhouse with a rainforest, desert
flora and glorious seasonal flower shows.
Most visitors just ascend the hill for a look
around, a drink and a pause to enjoy the
view from the hilltop Catholic church.

To drive here, follow 7th St east of down-
town to Van Meter St, turn right and head
up Elsinore Ave. For a strenuous 30-minute
hike up the hill, take E 6th St, cross the
bridge and then climb a long stairway.

ELSEWHERE
Two miles northwest of downtown, the
Cincinnati Museum Center (☎ 513-287-7000; www
.cincymuseum.org; 1301 Western Ave; adult/child 3-12
$7.25/5.25; ☯ 10am-5pm Mon-Sat, 11am-6pm Sun; P)
occupies the 1933 Union Terminal, an art

deco jewel still used by Amtrak. The interior has fantastic murals made of Rookwood tiles. Inside, the **Museum of Natural History** is more geared to kids, but does have a limestone cave with real bats inside. A history museum, Omnimax theater and children's museum round out the offerings. Discounted combination tickets are available.

The **Cincinnati Zoo & Botanical Garden** (☎ 513-281-4700; www.cincyzoo.org; 3400 Vine St; adult/child 2-12 $13/8; ♡ 9am-5pm; P), aka the 'Sexiest Zoo in America,' has the country's highest rate for successful breeding. It's famous for its gorillas and white tigers, and is located 3 miles north of downtown.

Festivals & Events

Riverfest (☎ 513-352-4000; www.webn.com/riverfest; admission free) Concerts and fireworks; held Sunday of Labor Day weekend (early September).

Oktoberfest (www.oktoberfest-zinzinnati.com; admission free) German beer, brats and mania; held mid-September.

Sleeping

Hotel tax is cheaper on the Kentucky side at 10.24%, rather than the 17.5% charged in Cincinnati. Tax is not included in the following prices.

BUDGET

Cincinnati Riverfront Travelodge (☎ 859-291-4434; 222 York St; r $55-65; P) Located on the Kentucky riverfront, the Travelodge is the best budget bet location-wise, though it's a bit faded in its atmosphere.

MIDRANGE

Two good, similar options on the Kentucky riverfront are **Hampton Inn Riverfront** (☎ 859-581-7800; 200 Crescent Ave; r incl breakfast $99-119; P), with an indoor pool and wi-fi, and **Comfort Suites** (☎ 859-291-6700; www.comfortsuites .com; 420 Riverboat Row; r incl breakfast $85-120; P), near the Newport attractions.

Best Western Mariemont Inn (☎ 513-271-2100; 877-271-2111; www.mariemontinn.com; 6880 Wooster Pike; r $77-100; P) This Tudor-style lodge has massive beamed ceilings and four-poster canopy beds. It's in a quiet neighborhood 10 miles northeast of downtown, and works best if you have a car.

TOP END

Room quality soars when you move to the top-end bracket, yet prices remain reasonable. The weekend rates (especially in winter) of the downtown beauties listed here can rival those of midrange hotels.

Cincinnatian Hotel (☎ 513-381-3000; www .cincinnatianhotel.com; 601 Vine St; r $125-225; P) The Cincinnatian is in a magnificent 1882 Victorian building; the spacious rooms have fluffy towels, silk-soft sheets, huge round bathtubs and high-speed Internet access. Parking is $25.

Hilton Cincinnati Netherland Plaza (☎ 513-421-9100; 35 W 5th St; r $109-199; P) The 1920s-era Netherland is an art deco monument. Its Palm Court Bar is gorgeous, with fan-shaped couches and Baroque-style murals. The rooms are swell, too. Parking costs $18.

Eating

In addition to downtown, good dining options are concentrated in Mt Adams, along the riverfront and in Northside.

Skyline Chili (☎ 513-721-4715; www.skylinechili .com; 1007 Vine St; items $3-6; ♡ 10am-6pm Mon-Fri) Skyline has a cult-like following devoted to its version of the local specialty 'five-way chili' – ie meat sauce (spiced with chocolate and cinnamon) with spaghetti and beans, garnished with cheese and onions. You can get it three-way (minus onions and beans) or four-way (minus onions or beans), but go the whole way; life's an adventure. There are outlets throughout town; this downtown one is an experience weekdays at noon.

Slims (☎ 513-681-6500; 4046 Hamilton Ave; mains $6-10; ♡ dinner Wed-Sat, brunch Sun) This bright, simple Northside restaurant serves organic and seasonal dishes – maybe a pea-mint bisque or couscous-stuffed trout – at long communal tables from 5:30pm 'until the food runs out.' Credit cards not accepted.

Hathaway's (☎ 513-621-1332; 441 Vine St; mains $4-7; ♡ 6:30am-4pm Tue-Fri, 8am-3pm Sat) Located beneath the Carew Tower, age-old Hathaway's feeds hungry businesspeople in diner style. Try the goetta (pork, oats, onions and herbs) for breakfast; it's a Cincy specialty.

Montgomery Inn at the Boathouse (☎ 513-721-7427; www.montgomeryinn.com; 925 Eastern Ave; small/large slab of ribs $13/22; ♡ 11am-10:30pm Mon-Thu, 11am-11pm Fri, 3pm-11pm Sat, 3-10pm Sun) Almost as renowned and addictive as Cincinnati chili are Montgomery Inn's barbecued ribs. There are a couple of outlets, but this riverside one is the best.

Rookwood Pottery Bistro (☎ 513-721-5456, 1077 Celestial St; mains $7-14; 🕑 11:30am-8:30pm Sun-Thu, to 10:30pm Fri & Sat) Once a famous pottery factory known for its jewel-toned finishes, the Rookwood has for decades occupied a place high on the hill atop Mt Adams and high on the list of local diners. It offers a solid menu of sandwiches and inventive mains. Ask for a table in one of the beehive-shaped kilns.

Graeter's Ice Cream (☎ 513-381-0653; www.graeters.com; 41 E 4th St; dishes $2-4; 🕑 7am-6pm Mon-Fri, until 3pm Sat) Another local delicacy, this is the place for dessert. Other branches are located around the city.

Drinking

The city's German influence meant Cincinnati was once a beer drinkers' paradise – in the 1890s there were 1800 saloons for 297,000 people, guzzling two-and-a-half times more than the rest of the country. Mt Adams, Northside and Over-the-Rhine are still busy nightspots. Covington Landing has places on the river (in moored boats) that are refreshing on hot nights when there's a breeze.

Blind Lemon (☎ 513-241-3885; 936 Hatch St) Here's a sweet spot in Mt Adams, with an atmospheric courtyard. Live bands play outdoors on warm evenings. Inside, trains and other bric-a-brac hang from the ceiling.

Arnold's (☎ 513-421-6234; 210 E 8th St; 🕑 Mon-Sat) Arnold's is a downtown oldie but goodie dating from 1861. There's live music nightly from the front porch–like stage – often bluegrass.

Comet (☎ 513-541-8900; 4579 Hamilton Ave, Northside) The casual Comet has the city's best jukebox and bar food (try the burrito).

HofbrauHaus (☎ 859-491-7200; 200 E 3rd St, Newport) The legendary Munich beer hall comes to the US.

Entertainment

Check *CityBeat* (p616) for listings. The free **GLBT News** (www.greatercincinnatiglbtnews.com) has a bar and club guide.

LIVE MUSIC

Southgate House (☎ 859-431-2201; www.southgatehouse.com; 24 E 3rd St, Newport; 🕑 from noon) In an historic haunted mansion where the Tommy Gun was invented, this is a brilliant venue; big and small bands alike play.

Northside Tavern (☎ 513-542-3603; www.northside-tavern.com; 4163 Hamilton Ave, Northside) Touring indie bands plug in their amps here.

PERFORMING ARTS

Music Hall (☎ 513-721-8222; www.cincinnatiarts.org; 1241 Elm St) The acoustically pristine Music Hall is the city's classical music venue, where the symphony orchestra, pops orchestra, opera and ballet hold their seasons. This is not the best neighborhood, so be cautious and park nearby.

SPORTS

Great American Ballpark (☎ 513-765-7000; www.cincinnatireds.com; 100 Main St) Cincy, home of the Reds, is a great baseball town, with its modern riverside ballpark and an undying love for the home team (pro baseball's first).

Paul Brown Stadium (☎ 513-621-3550; www.bengals.com; 1 Paul Brown Stadium) The Bengals pro football team scrimmages a few blocks west of the ballpark.

Getting There & Around

TO/FROM THE AIRPORT

The **airport** (☎ 859-767-3501; www.cvgairport.com) is actually in Kentucky, 13 miles south. To get downtown, take the TANK bus ($1.25, see Public Transportation, below) from Terminal 1 or 3; a cab costs about $25.

BUS

Several buses travel daily with **Greyhound** (☎ 513-352-6012; 1005 Gilbert Ave) to Louisville ($20 to $30, two hours), Indianapolis ($17 to $28, 2½ hours) and Columbus ($17 to $25, two hours).

PUBLIC TRANSPORTATION

Metro (☎ 513-621-4455; 120 E 4th St; www.sorta.com) runs the local buses ($1) and links with the **Transit Authority of Northern Kentucky** (TANK; ☎ 859-331-8265; www.tankbus.org), which charges $1.25 per trip. The visitors center (p618) has route maps.

TRAIN

Sharing Union Terminal with Cincinnati Museum Center (p618), **Amtrak** (☎ 513-651-3337; 1301 Western Ave) has three trains a week to Indianapolis ($17 to $38, 3½ hours), Chicago ($33 to $79, eight hours) and Washington, DC ($50 to $121, 14½ hours). Trains depart in the middle of the night.

MICHIGAN

Location, location, location. If that's what it's all about, then Michigan's got it, baby, surrounded by four of the five Great Lakes (Superior, Michigan, Huron and Erie) and fringed by 3200 miles of shoreline. Highlights include lazing on Lake Michigan's golden beaches; cruising the colored sandstone cliffs of Pictured Rocks; backcountry hiking on remote, wildlife-rich Isle Royale; and slowing down on car-free Mackinac Island. Detroit is also a must-see, though be prepared for quizzically raised eyebrows from Americans when you reveal your plans to visit.

The state consists of two parts split by water: the larger Lower Peninsula, shaped like a mitten, and the smaller, lightly populated Upper Peninsula (UP), shaped like a slipper. They are linked by the awesome Mackinac Bridge, which spans the Straits of Mackinac (*mac*-in-aw).

History
Five major tribes – the Ojibwa, Ottawa, Miami, Potawatomi and Huron (or Wyandot) – were living off Michigan's rich land when the French arrived and staked the first European claim. That honor goes to Jesuit Père Jacques Marquette, who founded Sault Ste Marie in 1668, making it the third-oldest city in the USA. In 1701 the long-named French explorer Antoine de La Mothe, Sieur de Cadillac, established Detroit in a strategic position between Lakes Erie and Huron.

MICHIGAN FACTS

Nicknames Great Lakes State, Wolverine State
Population 10 million
Area 96,700 sq miles
Capital city Lansing (population 119,100)
Official motto If you seek a pleasant peninsula, look about you
Birthplace of Industrialists Henry Ford I (1863–1947) and Henry Ford II (1917–87), filmmaker Francis Ford Coppola (b 1939), singer Madonna (b 1958), tennis player Serena Williams (b 1984)
Famous for Cars, Cornflakes, the Motown sound, the typewriter, the Model T Ford

---

In 1763 the French settlements were taken over by the British, who used Michigan as a base for instigating Indian raids against the Americans during the Revolutionary War. They also built a fort on Mackinac Island in 1780. Its location in the straits between Lake Michigan and Lake Huron made it one of the most important ports in the North American fur trade, and a site the British and Americans battled over many times.

The car industry has dominated Michigan's economy seemingly forever. Today the manufacture of passenger cars and transportation equipment accounts for about one quarter of the state's annual gross product. General Motors (GM), Ford and the Chrysler Group of DaimlerChrysler all maintain their headquarters in or near Detroit.

Information
Michigan sales tax is 6%.

Check the following websites for statewide information:
Michigan highway conditions (☎ 800-381-8477; www.michigan.gov/mdot)
Michigan state park information (☎ 800-447-2757; www.michigandnr.com/parksandtrails) Park entry requires a vehicle permit (per day/year residents $6/24, nonresidents $8/29). Campsites cost $10 to $29; reservations accepted (fee $2). Some parks have wi-fi.
Travel Michigan (☎ 800-644-2489; www.michigan.org)

DETROIT
Detroit, quite frankly, looks like it has had the shit kicked out of it. Once-grand buildings lie boarded up with trash blowing about their bases, steam rises from the sewers (in winter) and wide swaths of downtown are downright vacant. It's like walking through a city on the post-apocalyptic Day After. But…ready for this? That's what makes it fascinating. Nowhere is the cautionary tale of the American Dream better told: Detroit used its wits to get rich, then lost it all. Now it's struggling to reclaim its place. Motown, the Wright Museum of African American History and the Henry Ford Museum/Greenfield Village are excellent, one-of-a-kind attractions, making America's 'black eye' city that much more appealing.

History
At the turn of the 20th century Detroit was a medium-sized city of 285,000, known as a manufacturing center for horse-drawn

GREAT LAKES

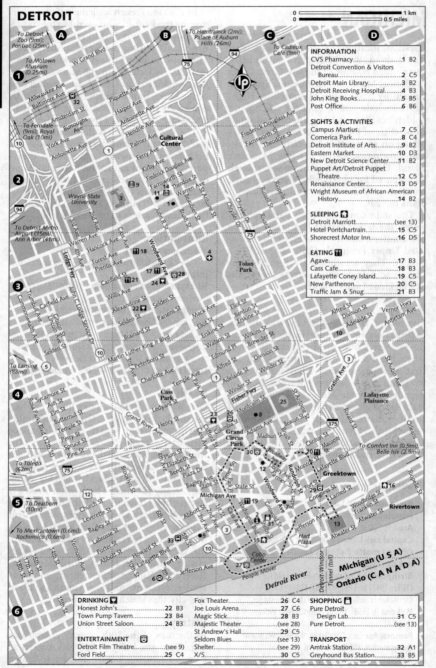

DETROIT

carriages and bicycles. Thanks in part to the massive iron and copper mines in the Upper Peninsula, cheap transport on the Great Lakes and enterprising souls, such as Henry Ford, the Dodge brothers and the Fisher brothers, Detroit quickly became the motor capital of the world. Ford in particular changed the fabric of US society. He didn't invent the automobile, as so many mistakenly believe, but he did perfect the assembly line manufacturing method and became one of the first industrialists to use mass production. The result was the Model T, the first car that the USA's middle class could afford to own.

Since its 1950s heyday, when Detroit's population exceeded two million, the city's fortunes have spiraled downwards. Racial tensions spurred a violent riot in 1967 and left blocks of the city smoldering. The oil shocks and inroads by Japanese carmakers in the 1970s rocked the auto industry, and many residents fled to the suburbs. The city entered an era of deep decline, with its population eventually dropping below one million.

Today 80% of the city's residents are black, and the Motor City remains an ethnically rich, national center for African American culture. Two recent sports events – the baseball All-Star game in 2005 and the Super Bowl in 2006 – spurred a fair bit of downtown development.

Orientation

The glossy Renaissance Center (aka 'RenCen'), GM's headquarters, dominates the skyline. Woodward Ave is the city's main boulevard and heads north from the plaza all the way to Pontiac. The Mile Roads are the major east–west arteries; 8 Mile (which entered the national consciousness thanks to local boy Eminem) forms the boundary between Detroit and the suburbs. Across the river lies Windsor, Canada. Detroit is a geographical oddity, as it's the only US city that looks south to Canada.

Information

BOOKSTORES
John King Books (☎ 313-961-0622; 901 Lafayette Blvd; ⏱ 9:30am-5:30pm Mon-Sat)

EMERGENCY
Crisis hotline (☎ 313-224-7000)
Fire, police, ambulance (☎ 911) Emergency.

INTERNET ACCESS
Free wi-fi at Campus Martius (p624), Town Pump Tavern (p626) and the RenCen lobby.
Detroit Main Library (☎ 313-833-1000; 5201 Woodward Ave) Free Internet access.

INTERNET RESOURCES
Detroit Yes (www.detroityes.com) A fantastic, artist-run website that examines Detroit's 'ruins' (ie decaying buildings); provides maps, too.
Look up Detroit (www.lookupdetroit.com) Loads of links to all things Motor City.

MEDIA
Detroit News (www.detnews.com) Daily.
Detroit Free Press (www.freep.com) Daily.
Metro Times (www.metrotimes.com) Distributed free on Wednesday, this is the best guide to the entertainment scene.
Between The Lines (www.pridesource.com) Free, weekly gay and lesbian paper.

WUOM-FM 91.7 is the newsy local NPR affiliate. WGRV-FM 105.1 plays soul music.

MEDICAL SERVICES
CVS (☎ 313-833-0201; 350 E Warren Ave; ⏱ 24hr) Pharmacy.
Detroit Receiving Hospital (☎ 313-745-3370; 4201 St Antoine Ave)

MONEY
ATMs are plentiful in and near the RenCen.
Travelex (☎ 734-942-4731; ⏱ 11am-7pm) Currency exchange in the Metro airport's LC Smith Terminal.

POST
Post office (☎ 313-226-8075; 1401 W Fort St; ⏱ 24hr)

TOURIST INFORMATION
Affirmations Lesbian/Gay Community Center
(☎ 248-398-7105; www.goaffirmations.org; 195 W 9 Mile Rd; ⏱ 9am-9pm Mon-Thu, 9am-11pm Fri & Sat) In Ferndale, northwest of the city center, near several gay-friendly venues.
Detroit Convention & Visitors Bureau (☎ 313-202-1800, 800-338-7648; www.visitdetroit.com; 10th fl, 211 W Fort St; ⏱ 9am-5pm Mon-Fri)

Dangers & Annoyances

The main streets (Woodward Ave, Jefferson Ave, Lafayette Blvd) with office buildings, restaurants, nightclubs and attractions are as safe as any other large USA city. Outside of the downtown core, use caution.

DETROIT IN...

Two Days

Visit the **Motown Museum** (below), **Wright Museum of African American History** (below), and the **Detroit Institute of Arts** (below), all within close proximity. Pick up sassy urban wares at **Pure Detroit** (opposite), then stuff your face with a heaping soul food dinner, followed by a late-night coney dog (remember to pack the antacids). Spend your second day in **Dearborn** (p628) wandering and wondering through the unbelievable collection of Americana at the **Henry Ford Museum** (p628) and adjacent **Greenfield Village** (p628) complex. Have dinner at one of Dearborn's many Middle Eastern restaurants on Michigan Ave.

Four Days

Follow the two-day itinerary. On your third day visit leafy **Ann Arbor** (p628) or cross under the river by tunnel to Canada (or do both – their proximity to Detroit makes it easy). On your fourth day get a final car fix at Auburn Hills' **Chrysler Museum** (p629), then view the city **'ruins'** (p623) en route to a **hockey, basketball, football** or **baseball game** (p627). At night, go dancing at a **techno club** (p626; techno originated in Detroit).

Sights & Activities

Some of the best attractions are in nearby Dearborn (p628), 10 miles west of the town center, and other suburbs (see p629). Places are commonly closed on Monday and Tuesday.

MOTOWN MUSEUM

The **Motown Museum** (☎ 313-875-2264; www.motownmuseum.com; 2648 W Grand Blvd; adult/child $8/5; 🕙 10am-6pm Tue-Sat) is a string of unassuming houses that became known as 'Hitsville USA' after Berry Gordy launched Motown Records here with an $800 loan in 1959. Stars that rose from the Motown label include Stevie Wonder, Diana Ross, Marvin Gaye, Gladys Knight and Michael Jackson. Gordy and Motown split for the glitz of Los Angeles in 1972, but you can still step into humble Studio A and see where the Four Tops and Smokey Robinson recorded their first hits.

CULTURAL CENTER

Two outstanding museums are in the area known as the Cultural Center, by Woodward and Kirby Aves. At the **Wright Museum of African American History** (☎ 313-494-5800; www.maah-detroit.org; 315 E Warren Ave; adult/child 3-12 $8/5; 🕙 9:30am-5pm Tue-Sat, 1-5pm Sun), the full-scale model of slaves chained up on an 18th-century slave ship will leave you chilled. Diego Rivera's mural *Detroit Industry*, fills a room at the renowned **Detroit Institute of Arts** (☎ 313-833-7900; www.dia.org; 5200 Woodward Ave; adult/child $4/1; 🕙 10am-4pm Wed & Thu,

10am-9pm Fri, 10am-5pm Sat & Sun) and reflects the city's blue-collar labor history.

ELSEWHERE

Detroit's melting pot is best experienced at the **Eastern Market** (Gratiot Ave & Russell St); on Tuesday and Saturday, the large halls are filled with bartering shoppers and vendors. Surrounding the open market are specialty shops, delis and restaurants. **Greektown**, centered on Monroe St, is another dynamic downtown area; it has restaurants, bakeries and a casino.

Campus Martius (www.campusmartiuspark.org; 800 Woodward Ave) is Detroit's newest communal hot spot. The 1.6-acre park sports an outdoor ice rink, eating areas and a stage for concerts. It has dulled the luster somewhat of the riverfront **Hart Plaza**, though Hart is still the site of many free, summer-weekend festivals and concerts.

Belle Isle, located 2.5 miles northeast of downtown at E Jefferson Ave and E Grand Blvd, is a very good spot for a picnic and walkabout. The city is building a riverfront path between Hart Plaza and Belle Isle, though it had not opened at the time of research.

The **People Mover** (☎ 313-962-7245; www.thepeoplemover.com), Detroit's 3-mile elevated rail system, appears forlornly unpractical, but it's cheap (50¢) and provides great views of the city and riverfront.

It's easy to pop over to **Windsor, Canada** (see p627), where there are bars, restaurants and a huge casino filled with pie-eyed slot-machine junkies.

Detroit for Children

Detroit is chockful of attractions for little ones. Purchase **Metro Parent Magazine** (www.metroparent.com) at any bookstore, or pick up a free copy of its miniguide *Going Places* at the Science Center or other kid-friendly venues.

DETROIT ZOO

At the **Detroit Zoo** (☎ 248-398-0900; www.detroitzoo.org; 8450 W 10 Mile Rd; adult/child 2-12 $11/7; ☷ 10am-5pm May-Oct, 10am-4pm Nov-Apr; ⓟ), enter the amazing Arctic Ring of Life and 'polar bear tube,' where the huge white creatures swim overhead. It's the world's largest polar exhibit and has first-rate displays on Inuit culture. The Penguinarium is a highlight, as is the National Amphibian Conservation Center. It's located just north in Royal Oak.

DETROIT PUPPET THEATER

Puppet ART/Detroit Puppet Theater (☎ 313-961-7777; www.puppetart.org; 25 E Grand River Ave; adult/child $7/5) is run by Soviet-trained puppeteers and artists who perform beautiful shows in their 70-person theater; a small museum displays puppets from different cultures. Shows are often held on Saturday afternoon; call for the schedule.

NEW DETROIT SCIENCE CENTER

The **New Detroit Science Center** (☎ 313-577-8400; www.detroitsciencecenter.org; 5020 John R St; adult/child

---

THE AUTHOR'S CHOICE

The local fashion house **Pure Detroit** (www.puredetroit.com) is the be-all/end-all for cool souvenirs. Its products reflect the city's culture and are created by local artists. The auto-centric outlet in the **Renaissance Center** (☎ 313-259-5100; in the Wintergarden; ☷ 10am-6pm Mon-Sat) offers clocks made out of pistons, belts tailored from seatbelts and handbags cut from Camaro upholstery. The downtown **Pure Detroit Design Lab** (☎ 313-961-8320; 156 W Congress St; ☷ 11am-7pm Tue-Thu, noon-8pm Fri & Sat, reduced hrs summer) features local fashionistas' wares, like hoodies collaged from vintage T-shirt scraps.

2-12 $7/6; ☷ 9am-3pm Tue-Fri, 10:30am-6pm Sat, noon-6pm Sun) has hands-on 'Matter & Energy' and 'Waves & Vibrations' laboratories among its arsenal, as well as an Imax cinema and planetarium.

COMERICA PARK

This **park** (☎ 313-471-2255; 2100 Woodward Ave) is a great place to see a baseball game with kids. Take them for a spin on the park's Ferris wheel or clever carousel equipped with tigers. Check for promotions that allow kids to run around the bases after Sunday games.

Festivals & Events

North American International Auto Show (☎ 248-643-0250; www.naias.com; tickets $12) It's autos galore for two weeks in mid-January at the Cobo Center.

Movement Festival (☎ 313-567-0080; www.movementfestival.com; admission free) The world's largest electronic music festival congregates in Hart Plaza over Memorial Day weekend in May.

Woodward Dream Cruise (☎ 888-493-2196; www.woodwarddreamcruise.com; admission free) Thousands of classic cars cruise down Woodward Ave on the third Saturday in August; 1.5 million people watch them.

Sleeping

Add 9% tax to the rates listed here.

BUDGET

Affordable motels abound in the Detroit suburbs. If you're arriving from Metro Airport, follow the signs for Merriman Rd when leaving the airport and take your pick.

Clarion Hotel (☎ 734-728-7900; www.choicehotels.com; 8600 Merriman Rd; r from $79; ⓟ ⚇) Nearby the Northwest Inn and a step up.

Northwest Inn (☎ 734-595-7400; 9095 Wickham Rd; s/d incl tax $57/68; ⓟ) Among the dozen motels in this area.

MIDRANGE

Shorecrest Motor Inn (☎ 313-568-3000, 800-992-9616; www.shorecrestmi.com; 1316 E Jefferson Ave; s/d $69/89; ⓟ) Shorecrest is the pick of the litter, with comfortable rooms just six blocks northeast of Hart Plaza. Friendly, helpful staff.

Comfort Inn (☎ 313-567-8888; www.choicehotels.com; 1999 E Jefferson Ave; r incl breakfast $89-139; ⓟ) Similar to the Shorecrest, though a few blocks further east, Comfort's prices reach

GREAT LAKES

the higher end of the spectrum when it's busy, usually in summer.

Hotel Pontchartrain (☎ 313-965-0200; www .hotelpontch.com; 2 Washington Blvd; r $79-169; P ☎) This is an historic, full-amenity hotel downtown by Cobo Center. There are good rates if business is slow; it's owned by Sheraton. Parking is $20.

TOP END

Detroit Marriott (☎ 313-568-8000; www.marriott .com; Renaissance Center; r $129-229; P) This is a mondo (1300 room) convention hotel, but it is kind of cool to be in the Renaissance Center, especially if you get a view-worthy room up toward the 72nd floor (request when booking; no extra charge). Rooms have high-speed Internet access; parking costs $15.

Eating

Detroit restaurants reward diners with reasonable prices. Note that many drinking and live music establishments also serve good food.

DOWNTOWN

Lafayette Coney Island (☎ 313-964-8198; 118 Lafayette Blvd; items $2-3; ☯ 24hr) Take care of late-night appetites at the legendary Lafayette, where the minimalist menu consists of hot dogs smothered with chili and onions (ie a 'coney'), burgers, fries, pies, donuts and beer. Cast-iron stomach required.

Southern Fires (☎ 313-393-4930; 575 Bellevue Rd; mains $8-12; ☯ 11am-7pm Mon, 11am-9pm Tue-Fri, noon-9pm Sat, noon-8pm Sun) You can choose from cornmeal-encrusted catfish, braised short ribs and the 3in-thick slab of meatloaf at this soul food restaurant. Sides are succulent collard greens, sweet potatoes and buttered cornbread. Southern Fires is located near Belle Isle.

New Parthenon (☎ 313-961-5111; 547 Monroe St; mains $7-12; ☯ 11am-3am) Flaming cheese and the cry of 'Opa!' are a Detroit tradition at this Greektown restaurant. The grape leaves reign supreme.

CULTURAL CENTER

Cass Café (☎ 313-831-1400; www.casscafe.com; 4620 Cass Ave; mains $5-9; ☯ 11am-11pm Sun-Thu, 11am-1am Fri & Sat) The Cass is an artsy eatery serving soups, sandwiches and veggie beauties, like the lentil walnut burger.

Traffic Jam & Snug (☎ 313-831-9470; www.traffic -jam.com; 511 W Canfield St; sandwiches $7-8, mains $11-18; ☯ 11am-10:30pm Mon-Thu, 11am-midnight Fri, noon-midnight Sat, noon-8pm Sun) Detroit's best brewpub food is all over the map – Ethiopian lentils, Indian curries and Vietnamese noodles, among others.

Agave (☎ 313-833-1120; www.agavedetroit.com; 4265 Woodward Ave; mains $9-18; ☯ 11am-2am Mon-Fri, 4pm-2am Sat & Sun) Chic Agave dishes up-market Mexican plates, such as seafood saffron rice and garlic salmon, as well as staples like enchiladas suizas. It turns more bar-ish late night and is famed for its margaritas.

ELSEWHERE

Mexicantown is along Bagley St, where you'll find inexpensive, authentic Mich-Mex food.

Xochimilco (☎ 313-843-0179; 3409 Bagley St; mains $5-12; ☯ 11am-2am) This place has been pulling crowds for years with its solid menu of burritos and other standards.

Cadieux Café (☎ 313-882-8560; www.cadieuxcafe .com; 4300 Cadieux Rd; mains $7-15; ☯ dinner) 'It's beautiful to be Belgian,' as they say at this Prohibition-era café. Great Belgian food (especially the mussels) and beer, plus feather bowling (kind of like Italian bocce). Located in east Detroit.

The walkable Ferndale area at 9 Mile Rd and Woodward Ave has many good restaurants and bars, as does Royal Oak just north of Ferndale on 10 Mile Rd.

Drinking

Town Pump Tavern (☎ 313-961-1929; 100 W Montcalm St) Seems like everyone's knocking one back at the Town Pump – must be the pleasing Euro-style decor and beer selection.

Honest John's (☎ 313-832-5646; 488 Selden St; ☯ 7am-2am) It's a spiffed up dive bar owned by a helluva character named John; good, cheap burgers and a jukebox.

Union Street Saloon (☎ 313-831-3965; 4145 Woodward Ave) This place has been around since the early 1900s and attracts a mod crowd.

Entertainment

LIVE MUSIC

Detroit may be Motown, but in recent years it's been rap, techno and hard-edged rock that have pushed the city to the forefront of the music scene; homegrown stars include the White Stripes and Eminem.

St Andrew's Hall (☎ 313-961-6358; www.stand rewshall.com; 431 E Congress St) A legendary alternative band venue; downstairs is Shelter, a smaller music/dance club.

Seldom Blues (☎ 313-567-7301; www.seldomblues .com; Renaissance Center) Upscale supper club, with jazz and blues acts sweetening the air nightly.

Fox Theatre (☎ 313-983-6611; 2211 Woodward Ave) The gloriously restored 1928 venue that large touring shows occupy.

X/S (☎ 313-963-9797; www.xsdetroit.com; 1500 Woodward Ave) This techno hothouse is Detroit's top downtown spot for dancing, in an old piano store.

Magic Stick (☎ 313-833-9700; www.majestic detroit.com; 4120 Woodward Ave) and larger **Majestic Theater** (☎ 313-833-9700; 4140 Woodward Ave) are side-by-side concert halls where indie rockers and rap DJs perform. The complex also has bowling, billiards, a pizza joint and café.

A couple of noted blues and jazz clubs are in Hamtrack, north of downtown, including **Baker's Keyboard Lounge** (☎ 313-345-6300; www.bak erskeyboardlounge.com; 20510 Livernois Ave), with soul food, and **Attic Bar** (☎ 313-365-4194; 11667 Jos Campau Ave), a true blues bar where customers take over the piano when a band isn't around.

CINEMA

Detroit Film Theatre (☎ 313-833-3237; 5200 Woodward Ave; tickets $8) Art flicks in the Detroit Institute of Arts.

SPORTS

Palace of Auburn Hills (☎ 248-377-0100; www.nba .com/pistons; 2 Championship Dr) The Palace hosts the mighty Pistons pro basketball team.

Joe Louis Arena (☎ 313-396-7444; www.detroitred wings.com; 600 Civic Center Dr) The much-loved Red Wings play pro hockey at this arena where, if you can wrangle tickets, you can witness the strange octopus-throwing custom.

Ford Field (☎ 313-262-2003; www.detroitlions.com; cnr Brush St & Adams Ave) The Lions pro football team plays here.

Comerica Park (☎ 313-471-2255; www.detroit tigers.com; 2100 Woodward Ave) Next door to Ford Field, the Tigers play pro baseball at this impressive venue.

Getting There & Around

It is best to have your own wheels to get around the Motor City; public transportation is lacking, much to the automakers' delight.

TO/FROM THE AIRPORT

The **Metro Airport** (☎ 734-247-7678; www.metroair port.com) is 15 miles southwest of Detroit. Transport options from the airport to the city are few: you can take a cab for about $40, or you can take a SMART bus ($1.50), but it takes 1½ hours to get downtown. Pick up is at the lower level of LC Smith Terminal; drop off is a few blocks from the Renaissance Center.

BUS

There are buses to more than 40 cities throughout Michigan with **Greyhound** (☎ 313-961-8011; 1001 Howard St), including Grand Rapids ($23 to $29, 3½ hours), Traverse City ($45 to $55, 7½ hours) and Marquette ($59 to $91, 14½ hours).

Transit Windsor (☎ 519-944-4111; www.citywind sor.ca/transitwindsor) operates the Tunnel Bus to Windsor, Canada. It costs $2.75 (American or Canadian) and departs from Detroit-Windsor Tunnel (on Randolph St, across from the Renaissance Center). Bring your passport.

CAR

Southeastern Michigan is one of the cheapest places in the country to rent a car. Avis, Hertz and other rental agencies have offices at the Metroairport (call from the courtesy phones) and around town. Check in the Transportation chapter (p1175) for contact details.

PUBLIC TRANSPORTATION

The **Detroit Department of Transportation** (DDOT; ☎ 888-336-8287; www.ci.detroit.mi.us/ddot) handles the local bus service ($1.50). The **Suburban Mobility Authority for Regional Transportation** (SMART; ☎ 313-962-5515; www.smartbus.org) handles the service to the 'burbs ($1.50). The public library has schedules.

TAXI

For cab service, call **Checker Cab** (☎ 313-963-7000).

TRAIN

Trains runs daily with **Amtrak** (☎ 313-873-3442; 11 W Baltimore Ave) to Kalamazoo ($21 to $40; three hours) and Chicago ($23 to $57; 5½ hours). You can also head east – to New York ($75 to $142; 16 hours) or destinations en route – but you'll first be bused to Toledo.

GREAT LAKES

MICHAEL MOORE TAKES 'EM ON

Local-boy-done-good Michael Moore launched his career with *Roger and Me* (1989), a documentary showing the tragic and surreal consequences that ensue when auto giant General Motors (GM) pulls up its stakes from Flint – where the company was born – and moves plant operations overseas. Thousands of people lost their jobs, and the local economy was devastated, though GM continued to turn a huge profit. Moore spends the film trying to track down Roger Smith, GM's chairman at the time, to have a chat. The revelation of the corporate conscience has never been more hilarious, or more sad.

Moore continues to challenge big business and government through his works, which include TV series (*TV Nation* and *The Awful Truth*) and books (*Stupid White Men* and *Dude, Where's My Country?*) in addition to films. In 2003 his film *Bowling for Columbine*, about America's gun culture and industry, won the Academy Award for Best Documentary. Moore grabbed headlines when he used his acceptance speech to take the American government to task for its war in Iraq. Next up was his film *Fahrenheit 9/11* (2004). Moore hit the big-time with this look at the Bush administration's actions after the September 11 terrorists attacks, and the links between the Bush and bin Laden families. The film – the highest-grossing documentary ever – prickled conservatives to the extent they began writing their own books with titles like *Michael Moore is a Big Fat Stupid White Man*. Keep up with Moore's doings at www.michaelmoore.com.

AROUND DETROIT
Dearborn
Ten miles west of downtown, Dearborn is home to one of the finest museum complexes in the country: the indoor **Henry Ford Museum** (☎ 313-982-6001; www.thehenryford .org; 20900 Oakwood Blvd; adult/child 5-12 $14/10; ☻ 9:30am-5pm) and the adjacent, outdoor **Greenfield Village** (☎ 313-982-6001; adult/child 5-12 $20/14; ☻ 9:30am-5pm daily mid-Apr–Oct, 9:30am-5pm Fri-Sun Nov & Dec), featuring historic buildings shipped in from all over the country, reconstructed and restored. The museums contain a fascinating wealth of American culture, such as the chair Lincoln was sitting in when he was assassinated, Edgar Allan Poe's writing desk, Thomas Edison's laboratory from Menlo Park and the bus on which Rosa Parks refused to give up her seat. (Don't worry: you'll get your car fix here, too.) You also can add on the **Rouge Factory Tour** (☎ 313-982-6001; adult/child 5-12 $14/10; ☻ 9:30am-5pm mid-Apr–Dec, closed Sun Jan–mid-Apr), and see F-150 trucks roll off the assembly line where Ford first perfected his self-sufficient, mass-production techniques.

All three attractions are separate, but you can get a combination ticket for one day and two attractions (adult/child five to 12 $26/20) or two days and all three attractions (adult/child five to 12 $48/38).

After the hours of gawking, refuel at one of Dearborn's Middle Eastern restaurants. The city has a huge Arab population and a wealth of eateries from which to choose; Michigan Ave is lined with them.

Ann Arbor
Forty-one miles west of Detroit, leafy, liberal and bookish, Ann Arbor is home to the University of Michigan. The walkable downtown is loaded with coffee shops, bookstores, brewpubs and cheap places in which to grab a bite.

The university provides the town's main attractions. The **Matthei Botanical Gardens** (☎ 734-998-7061; sitemaker.umich.edu/mbgna; outdoor gardens admission free, conservatory adult/child 5-18 $5/2; 1800 Dixboro Rd; ☻ 8am-dusk) offers 300 acres crisscrossed by walking paths, plus a cacti-filled greenhouse; it's about 5 miles east of downtown. The 'Arb' – **Nichols Arboretum** (☎ 734-998-7061; 1610 Washington Hts; admission free; ☻ dawn-dusk) – is another oasis of greenery for walking, jogging and Frisbee throwing; it's right by campus. The university also has free art and archaeology museums.

Ann Arbor's biggest events are the school's football games, a fall tradition attracting 115,000 fans per game. Tickets are nearly impossible to purchase, especially when nemesis Ohio State is in town. You can try, or obtain tickets to other sporting events, by calling the **U of M Ticket Office** (☎ 734-764-0247).

You'll find Middle Eastern dishes at **Jerusalem Garden** (☎ 734-995-5060; 307 S 5th Ave; mains $3-9; ☻ 10am-9pm Mon-Fri, 11am-10pm Sat, noon-8pm Sun). **Zingerman's Delicatessen** (☎ 734-663-3354; www.zingermans.com; 422 Detroit St; mains $7-12; 🕐 7am-10pm) is regarded as one of the Midwest's finest. **Fleetwood Diner** (☎ 734-995-5502; 300 S Ashley St; mains $5-7; 🕐 24hr) is an atmospheric round-the-clock greasy spoon that attracts the studious and down at heel.

When darkness falls, head to the **Blind Pig** (☎ 734-996-8555; www.blindpigmusic.com; 208 S 1st St) or the **Ark** (☎ 734-761-1800; www.a2ark.org; 316 S Main St), both nationally acclaimed venues for rock, blues and more. Handcrafted beer is found at **Arbor Brewing Company** (☎ 734-213-1393; 114 E Washington St).

HEARTLAND

Michigan's heartland is a 20-county region that lies at the center of the Lower Peninsula and includes agricultural and urban areas, farm fields and suburbs.

Lansing

Smallish Lansing is the state capital and home of Michigan State University (east of downtown, south of Grand River Ave). Between downtown and the school is Lansing's **River Trail**, which extends 7 miles along the shores of Michigan's longest river, the Grand. The paved path is popular with cyclists, joggers and in-line skaters, and links a number of attractions, including a children's museum, zoo and salmon ladder.

Downtown, the **Michigan Historical Museum** (☎ 517-373-3559; 702 W Kalamazoo St; admission free; 🕐 9am-4:30pm Mon-Fri, 10am-4pm Sat, 1-5pm Sun) features 26 permanent galleries, including a replica UP copper mine you can walk through and a three-story relief map of the state. The **RE Olds Transportation Museum** (see boxed text, below) will please car buffs.

The best selection of motels is found around Cedar St, exit 104 off I-96. In this area are **Days Inn** (☎ 517-393-1650; 6501 S Pennsylvania Ave; s/d incl breakfast from $59/69; 🅿 🐾) and **Econo Lodge** (☎ 517-394-7200; 1100 Ramada Dr; r incl breakfast weekday/weekend $45/49; 🅿 🐾). The downtown hotels feed off politicians and lobbyists, and are considerably more expensive.

Most of Lansing's best restaurants are clustered around the head of Michigan Ave. For meals try **Clara's** (☎ 517-372-7120; 637 E Michigan Ave; mains $12-18; 🕐 11am-11pm Mon-Thu, 11am-midnight Fri & Sat, 10am-10pm Sun), in the historic railroad depot, or **Kewpee's** (☎ 517-482-8049; 118 S Washington Sq; mains $2-6; 🕐 8am-6pm Mon-Fri, 11am-2pm Sat), renowned for its olive burgers.

CLASSIC CARS IN MICHIGAN

More than sand dunes, Mackinac Island fudge or even the Great Lakes, Michigan is synonymous with cars. You won't have to drive far to see a fleet of beauties, particularly around Detroit:

Henry Ford Museum (opposite) This Dearborn museum is loaded with vintage cars, including the first one Henry Ford ever built. In adjacent Greenfield Village you can ride in a Model T that rolled off the assembly line in 1923.

Automotive Hall of Fame (☎ 313-240-4000; 21400 Oakwood Blvd, Dearborn; adult/child 5-18 $6/3; 🕐 9am-5pm May-Oct, closed Mon Nov-Apr) Also in Dearborn, the Auto Hall is stocked with classic cars as well as a replica of the first gasoline automobile.

Motorsports Hall of Fame (☎ 800-250-7223; Novi Rd, Novi; adult/child under 12 $4/2; 🕐 10am-5pm Mon-Sun summer, 10am-5pm Thu-Sun rest of year) In the Novi Expo Center just off I-96, the Motorsports Hall has three-dozen vehicles that were driven by legendary racers.

Walter P Chrysler Museum (☎ 888-456-1924; 1 Chrysler Dr, Auburn Hills; adult/child 6-12 $6/3; 🕐 10am-6pm Tue-Sat, noon-6pm Sun) This museum, in the DaimlerChrysler Technical Center Campus, has 70 vehicles on display, including rare models of Dodge, DeSoto, Nash and Hudson.

Sloan Museum (☎ 810-237-3450; 1221 E Kearsley St, Flint; adult/child 4-11 $5/3; 🕐 10am-5pm Mon-Fri, noon-5pm Sat & Sun) The Sloan has two buildings housing more than 60 cars, including the oldest production-model Chevrolet in existence and a 1910 Buick 'Bug' raced by Louis Chevrolet.

Gilmore Car Museum (☎ 269-671-5089; Hickory Rd at Hwy 43, Hickory Corners; adult/child 7-15 $8/6; 🕐 9am-5pm Mon-Fri, 9am-6pm Sat & Sun, closed Nov-Apr) North of Kalamazoo along Hwy 43, this museum complex offers 22 barns filled with 120 vintage autos, including 15 Rolls Royces dating back to a 1910 Silver Ghost.

RE Olds Transportation Museum (☎ 517-372-0422; 240 Museum Dr, Lansing; admission $5; 🕐 10am-5pm Tue-Sat year-round, noon-5pm Sun Apr-Oct) In the old Lansing City Bus Garage are 20 vintage cars, from the first Oldsmobile, built in 1897, to an Indy 500 pace car.

The campus also has abundant restaurants, pubs and nightclubs.

Grand Rapids

The second-largest city in Michigan, Grand Rapids is known for office-furniture manufacturing, a conservative Dutch Reform attitude and the fact that it's only 30 miles from Lake Michigan's Gold Coast. The **visitors center** (☎ 800-678-9859; www.visitgrandrapids.org; 171 Monroe Ave NW, Suite 700; ⚇ 8:30am-5pm Mon-Fri) is downtown, with two better-than-you'd-think museums nearby.

The **Gerald R Ford Museum** (☎ 616-254-0400; 303 Pearl St NW; adult/child under 16 $5/free; ⚇ 9am-5pm) is dedicated to the country's only Michigander president (though he was born with a different name in Nebraska; see p699). Ford stepped into the Oval Office after Richard Nixon and his vice president, Spiro Agnew, resigned in disgrace. It's an intriguing period in US history, and the museum does an excellent job of covering it, right down to displaying the burglary tools used in the Watergate break-in. Nearby is the striking **Van Andel Museum Center** (☎ 616-456-3977; www.grmuseum.org; 272 Pearl St NW; adult/child 3-17 $7/2.50; ⚇ 9am-5pm Mon-Sat, noon-5pm Sun), dedicated to the history of Grand Rapids (including its role as furniture-maker) and west Michigan. The 118-acre **Frederik Meijer Gardens** (☎ 616-957-1580; www.meijergardens.org; 1000 E Beltline NE; adult/child 5-13 $10/6; ⚇ 9am-5pm Mon-Sat, noon-5pm Sun) features impressive blooms and sculptures.

Days Inn (☎ 616-235-7611; 310 Pearl St NW; s/d $76/83; P ⚇), downtown, is a good sleeping option. **Peaches B&B** (☎ 866-732-2437; www.peaches-inn.com; 29 Gay St SE; r $97; P) is in a comfy house a short walk from the city center.

At night, head to **Grand Rapids Brewing Company** (☎ 616-285-5970; 3689 28th St SE; mains $7-13; ⚇ 11am-10pm Sun-Thu, 11am-11pm Fri & Sat) or **Cottage Bar** (☎ 616-454-9088; 18 LaGrave St SE; mains $6-10; ⚇ Mon-Sat), a hip place downtown serving hamburgers, and outdoor seating when it's warm.

LAKE MICHIGAN SHORE

Michigan's west coast – aka its Gold Coast – is the place to come to watch incredible sunsets from atop towering sand dunes. The 300-mile shoreline features endless stretches of beach, and is dotted with coastal parks and small towns that boom during the summer tourist season. Note all state parks listed here take **campsite reservations** (☎ 800-447-2757; www.midnrreservations.com) and require a vehicle permit (per day/year $8/29), unless specified otherwise. For more in-depth exploration, get Lonely Planet's *Road Trip: Lake Michigan* book.

Saugatuck

This Lake Michigan resort town is a popular destination for gays, and is known for its strong arts community and numerous B&Bs.

The best thing to do in Saugatuck is also the most affordable. Jump aboard the **Saugatuck Chain Ferry** (Water St; $1), and the operator will pull you across the Kalamazoo River. On the other side you can huff up the stairs to the grand views atop **Mount Baldhead**, a 200ft-high sand dune. Then race down the north side to beautiful **Oval Beach**. The **Saugatuck Dune Rides** (☎ 269-857-2253; www.saugatuckduneride.com; 6495 Blue Star Hwy; adult/child $14.50/9.50; ⚇ 10am-5:30pm Mon-Sat, noon-5:30pm Sun May-Sep) provide a half-hour of good, cheesy fun.

Most of the town's B&Bs are in century-old Victorian homes, which cost $100 to $200 a night per couple in the summer high season. Try the charming **Bayside Inn** (☎ 269-857-4321; www.baysideinn.net; 618 Water St; r $75-180), a former boathouse with an outdoor tub, or **Twin Gables Inn** (☎ 269-857-4346, 800-231-2185; www.twingablesinn.com; 900 Lake St; r $90-210), which overlooks Lake Michigan. Mom-and-pop motels on the edge of the city, like the **Pines Motorlodge** (☎ 269-857-5211; www.thepinesmotorlodge.com; 56 Blue Star Hwy; r $125-165), have comfortable rooms.

Ludington & Manistee

The largest state park and one of the most popular along Lake Michigan is **Ludington State Park** (☎ 231-843-8671; campsites $18-25; ⚇ year-round), on M-116. It has a top-notch trail system, a renovated lighthouse to visit and miles of beach. To its north is **Nordhouse Dunes**, a 3000-acre federally designated wilderness with its own trail system. You enter Nordhouse Dunes through the Lake Michigan Recreation Area, a US Forest Service campground several miles south of Manistee.

The town of Ludington itself isn't that exciting, but you may find yourself here to catch the SS *Badger* ferry to Manitowoc,

Wisconsin (see p566). If so, have a beer at **Jamesport Brewing Co** (☎ 231-845-2522; 410 S James St). **Parkview Cottages** (☎ 231-843-4445; www.parkviewcottages.com; 803 W Fitch St; cottage $75-125) can put you up for the night.

Sleeping Bear Dunes National Lakeshore

This national park stretches from north of Frankfort just before Leland, on the Leelanau Peninsula. Stop at the park **visitors center** (☎ 231-326-5134; www.nps.gov/slbe; 9922 Front St; 9am-4pm winter, 8am-6pm summer) in Empire for information, trail maps and vehicle entry permits (week/annual $10/20).

Attractions here include the famous **Dune Climb** along Hwy 109, where you trudge up the 200ft-high dune and then run or roll down, and **Pierce Stocking Scenic Drive**, a 7-mile, one-lane road that passes stunning Lake Michigan vistas. The park also offers the best day hiking in the Lower Peninsula. Those seeking an overnight wilderness adventure should head to **North Manitou Island** or day-trip to **South Manitou Island** on the **ferry** (☎ 231-256-9061; www.leelanau.com/manitou; Leland). A round-trip costs $25/14 per adult/child under 13, with three to seven departures per week from May to November.

Feeling lazy? Plop your butt in an inner tube and float down the Platte River, which you can arrange through **Riverside Canoe Trips** (☎ 231-325-5622; www.canoemichigan.com; 5042 Scenic Hwy, Honor; tube/kayak/canoe $16/24/33; May–mid-Oct).

Traverse City

Michigan's Cherry Capital is the largest city in the northern half of the Lower Peninsula. It's got a bit of urban sprawl, but it's still beautiful, fun, and a great base from which to see Sleeping Bear Dunes, the Mission Peninsula and the area's other enticing outdoor attractions.

Two blocks from downtown along US 31 is Clinch Park, with a pretty beach, while nearby **Traverse City State Park** (☎ 231-922-5270; 1132 US 31 N; campsites $23) has 700ft of sugary sand. Between the two parks are dozens of resorts, motels, Jet Ski rental shops and parasail operators.

The most popular drive is to head north from Traverse City on Hwy 37 for 20 miles to the end of **Mission Peninsula**. Stop at the Chateau Grand Traverse or Chateau Chan-

tel wineries along the way and sample their chardonnay or pinot noir. If you purchase a bottle, you can take it out to Lighthouse Park beach, on the end of the peninsula, and enjoy it with the waves licking your toes.

Back in the city is the **Traverse Area Recreation Trail** (TART for short), an 11-mile paved path that makes its way along the bay. At **Brick Wheels** (☎ 231-947-4274; www.brickwheels.com; 736 E 8th St; skates/bike per day $17/30) you can rent mountain bikes or in-line skates and then jump on the trail outside.

For an indoor activity, hear rare, antique instruments played at the **Music House Museum** (☎ 231-938-9300; www.musichouse.org; 7377 US 31 N; adult/child 6-15 $9/3; 10am-4pm Mon-Sat, noon-4pm Sun May-Oct).

If you arrive in mid-July, head north on US 31 to Elk Rapids and beyond for roadside stands selling cherries and pies, and farms where you can pick your own fruit.

Traverse City has plentiful lodgings, but they are often full (and more expensive) on weekends.

Stop at the downtown **visitors center** (☎ 800-872-8377; www.mytraversecity.com; 101 W Grandview Pkwy; 9am-5pm Mon-Fri, 9am-3pm Sat, extended hrs Mon-Sun summer) for an accommodations list. Most resorts overlooking the bay cost $100 to $200 per night.

Park Shore Resort (☎ 877-349-8898; www.park shoreresort.com; 1401 US 31 North; r weekday/weekend from $75/100;) is a good one, where guests can rent Jet Skis and enjoy nightly bonfires. Motels on the other side of US 31 (away from the water) are more moderately priced, such as **Mitchell Creek Inn** (☎ 231-947-9330, 800-947-9330; www.mitchellcreek.com; 894 Munson Ave; r/cottage from $49/89), near the state park beach.

After a day of fun in the sun, refresh with sandwiches at foodie-favorite **Folgarelli's** (☎ 231-941-7651; 424 W Front St; sandwiches $6-8; 9:30am-6:30pm Mon-Fri, 9:30am-5:30 Sat, 9:30am-4:30 Sun) and cold, handcrafted beer and root beer at **North Peak Brewing Company** (☎ 231-941-7325; 400 W Front St).

Petoskey & Harbor Springs

Tucked away inside Little Traverse Bay, Petoskey and Harbor Springs are where Michigan's upper-crusters maintain summer homes. The downtown areas of both

---

FOLLOWING IN PAPA'S FOOTSTEPS

A number of writers have ties to northwest Michigan, but none are as famous as Ernest Hemingway, who spent the summers of his youth at his family's cottage on Walloon Lake. Hemingway buffs often tour the area to view the places that made their way into his writing.

In Petoskey, you can see the Hemingway collection at the **Little Traverse History Museum** (☎ 231-347-2620; www.petoskeymuseum.org; 100 Depot Ct; admission $1; ☺ 10am-4pm Mon-Fri, 1-4pm Sat Jun-Sep, 1-4pm Thu-Sat May & Oct-Dec), including rare 1st-edition books that the author autographed for a friend when he visited in 1947. Afterward, visit **City Park Grill** (☎ 231-347-0101; 432 E Lake St), where Hemingway, with his famous drinking habit, was a regular.

Next, head south on US 31 toward Charlevoix. Just before entering that town, turn east onto Boyne City Rd, which skirts beautiful Lake Charlevoix and eventually arrives at the **Horton Bay General Store**. Built in 1876 with a high false front, the store's most prominent feature is its large porch, with benches and stairs at either end. Hemingway idled away some youthful summers on that porch and fished nearby Horton Creek for trout. He was married in Horton Bay's Congregational Church, and the general store appeared in the opening of his short story 'Up in Michigan.'

The **Michigan Hemingway Society** (www.northquest.com/hemingway; PO Box 953, Petoskey, MI 49770) provides further information for self-guided tours. It also hosts a **Hemingway festival** for a weekend every October.

---

cities have gourmet restaurants and high-class shops, and the marinas are filled with yachts.

In Petoskey, **Stafford's Perry Hotel** (☎ 231-347-4000; www.theperryhotel.com; Bay at Lewis St; r from $80) is a grand historic place to stay. Between the two cities along M-119 is **Petoskey State Park** (☎ 231-347-2311; 2475 M-119; campsites $23-25; mid-Apr–Oct), with a beautiful beach.

STRAITS OF MACKINAC

This region, between the Upper and Lower Peninsulas, features a long history of forts and fudge shops. Car-free Mackinac Island is Michigan's premier tourist draw.

One of the most spectacular sights in the area is the 5-mile-long **Mackinac Bridge** (known locally as 'Big Mac'), which spans the Straits of Mackinac. The $2.50 toll is worth every penny, as the views from the bridge, which include two Great Lakes, two peninsulas and hundreds of islands, are second to none in Michigan.

Remember: despite the spelling, it's pronounced *mac*-in-aw.

Mackinaw City

At the south end of Mackinac Bridge, bordering I-75, is Mackinaw City, a tacky tourist town with a gift shop and fudge kitchen on every corner (fudge is Northern Michigan's most famous product). Mackinaw City is best known as one of two departure points

for Mackinac Island, but it does have a couple of interesting attractions of its own.

Right next to the bridge (its visitors center is actually beneath the bridge) is **Colonial Michilimackinac** (☎ 231-436-5563; www.mackinacparks.com; adult/child 6-17 $9.50/6; ☺ 9am-6pm summer, 9am-4pm May–mid-Oct), a National Historic Landmark that features a reconstructed stockade first built in 1715 by the French. Some 3 miles southeast of the city on US 23 is **Historic Mill Creek** (☎ 231-436-4226; www.mackinacparks.com; adult/child 6-17 $7.50/4.50; ☺ 9am-5pm summer, 9am-4pm May–mid-Oct), which has an 18th-century sawmill, historic displays and nature trails. A combination ticket for both sights, along with Fort Mackinac (opposite), is available at a discount.

The only things that outnumber fudge shops in Mackinaw City are motels, which line I-75 and US 23. Thanks to the popularity of Mackinac Island and a nearby casino, it's almost impossible to find a room for less than $100 during the summer. Exceptions being **Days Inn** (☎ 231-436-8961; www.daysinnmackinacbridge.com; 206 N Nicolet St; r weekday/weekend from $60/70; (P) (R)) and **Rainbow Motel** (☎ 231-436-5518; www.rainbowmotel.net; 602 S Huron St; r weekday/weekend from $47/60; ☺ mid-May–mid-Oct; (P) (R)).

St Ignace

At the north end of Mackinac Bridge is St Ignace, the other jumping-off point for Mackinac Island, and the second-oldest settlement in Michigan – Père Jacques Marquette founded a mission here in 1671. As soon as you've paid your bridge toll you'll pass a huge **Michigan Welcome Center** (☎ 906-643-6979; I-75N; ☺ 8am-6pm summer, 9am-5pm rest of year), with racks of brochures and lodging help.

Mackinac Island

From either St Ignace or Mackinaw City you can catch a ferry to Mackinac Island, Michigan's first tourist destination. The British built a fort atop the famous limestone cliffs in 1780 and then fought with the Americans for control of it during the War of 1812.

The most important date on this 2000-acre island was 1898 – the year cars were banned to encourage tourism. Today all travel on the island is by horses or bicycles; even the police use bikes to patrol the town. The crowds of tourists (called Fudgies by the islanders) can be crushing at times, particularly on summer weekends. If at all possible, spend a night on Mackinac Island; the real charm of this historic place emerges after the last ferry leaves in the evening.

SIGHTS & ACTIVITIES

Overlooking the downtown area is **Fort Mackinac** (☎ 906-847-3328; www.mackinacparks.com; adult/child 6-17 $9.50/6; ☺ 9:30am-7:30pm in summer, 9:30am-4:30pm May–mid-Oct), one of the best-preserved military forts in the country. The admission price is also good for six other museums in town, including the Dr Beaumont Museum (where the doctor performed his famous digestive tract experiments) and Benjamin Blacksmith Shop. Edging the shoreline of the island is Hwy 185, the only state highway in Michigan that doesn't permit cars. The best way to view the incredible scenery along this 8-mile road is by bicycle; bring your own on the ferry or rent one in town at any of almost a dozen bike shops for about $7 per hour plus a hefty deposit. The two best attractions – **Arch Rock** (a huge limestone arch that sits 150ft above Lake Huron) and **Fort Holmes** (the island's 'other fort') – are both free. You can also ride past the **Grand Hotel**, which boasts a veranda stretching halfway to Detroit. Unfortunately if you're not staying at the Grand (minimum $205 per night per person), it costs $10 to stroll its long porch and step inside the lobby. Not worth

it. However, if you purchase a ticket to Fort Mackinac, you can eat lunch at Fort Mackinac Tea Room. The outdoor tables feature a million-dollar view of downtown and the Straits of Mackinac.

SLEEPING

Rooms are booked far in advance on summer weekends. Call or stop by the **visitors center** (☎ 800-454-5227; www.mackinacisland.org; Main St; ☺ 9am-5pm) for help with lodging reservations. The lodging and restaurants listed here are open mid-May to mid-October only, unless noted otherwise.

Camping is not permitted anywhere on Mackinac Island. That means you have to spend a wad to spend the night. Most hotels and B&Bs charge at least $150 for two people. Exceptions include the four-room **Bogan Lane Inn** (☎ 906-847-3439; www.boganlaneinn.com; Bogan Lane; r incl breakfast $80-100; ☺ year-round); the 18-room **La Chance Cottage** (☎ 906-847-3526; www.lachancecottage.com; Main St; r incl breakfast $95-105); and **Pontiac Lodge** (☎ 906-847-3364; www.pontiaclodge.com; cnr Main & Hoban Sts; r incl breakfast from $110-150; ☺ year-round). All are walkable to downtown.

EATING & DRINKING

The best-known eateries on Mackinac Island are the dozen fudge shops, which use fans to blow the tempting aroma of the freshly made confection out onto Huron St. Hamburger and sandwich shops abound downtown.

French Outpost (☎ 906-847-3772; Cadotte Ave; mains $7-9; ☺ 11am-10pm) Enjoy salads or sandwiches along with a pint of beer at this quiet spot toward the Grand Hotel from downtown.

Horn's Bar (☎ 906-847-6154; Main St; mains $10-16; ☺ 11am-11pm) Horn's Bar serves good dinners and has live entertainment nightly.

Astor St Café (☎ 906-847-6031; Astor St; mains $9-15; ☺ lunch & dinner) Astor St fires up Midwestern specials, such as whitefish, roast turkey and meatloaf.

Brian's Barbeque (☎ 906-847-3526; Main St; items $2.50-8; ☺ lunch & dinner) Hot dogs, bratwursts and chicken are served on the front lawn of La Chance Cottage.

GETTING THERE & AROUND

Three ferry companies operate out of both Mackinaw City and St Ignace – **Arnold Line** (☎ 800-542-8528; www.arnoldline.com), **Shepler's**

(☎ 800-828-6157; www.sheplersferry.com) and **Star Line** (☎ 800-638-9892; www.mackinacferry.com) – and charge the same rates: round-trip adult/child five to 12/bicycle $18/9/6.50. The ferries run several times daily from May to October; Arnold Line runs longer, weather permitting. Once you're on the island, horse-drawn cabs will take you anywhere, or rent a bicycle.

UPPER PENINSULA

A visit to this rugged, wooded and isolated region is a Midwest highlight. The Upper Peninsula (UP) has only 45 miles of interstate highway and just a handful of cities, of which Marquette is the largest. Between the cities are miles of undeveloped shoreline (on Lakes Huron, Michigan and Superior), scenic two-lane roads, small rural towns and pasties, the local meat/vegetable pot pies brought over by Cornish miners 150 years ago. Michigan's two best wilderness areas – Isle Royale and the Porcupine Mountains – are here, at the UP's west end.

You'll find that it's a different world up north. Residents of the UP, aka 'Yoopers,' consider themselves distinct from the rest of the state – they've even threatened to secede in the past.

Sault Ste Marie & Around

Founded in 1668, Sault Ste Marie (Sault is pronounced 'soo') is the oldest city in Michigan and the third-oldest in the USA. The town is best known for its locks that raise and lower 1000ft-long freighters between the different lake levels. **Soo Lock Park** is at the end of Water St in the heart of downtown. It features an interpretive center and observation decks from where you can watch the action. To get closer to the boats, go down to the adjacent walkway.

Most of Sault Ste Marie's motels are along the I-75 Business Loop and Ashmun St. Try the pleasant **Plaza Motor Motel** (☎ 906-635-1881, 888-809-1881; www.plazamotormotel.com; 3901 I-75 Business; r $49-81), or the spiffy **Askwith Lockview Motel** (☎ 906-632-2491, 800-854-0745; www.lockview.com; 327 W Portage Ave; r $66-72; ◷ May–mid-Oct), across from Soo Locks.

To enjoy a carnivorous feast amid a gallery of stuffed animal heads, make your way to **Antlers** (☎ 906-632-3571; 804 E Portage Ave; mains $8-20; ◷ 11am-9pm). Huge steaks, burgers and ribs anchor the menu; animal rights

enthusiasts and vegetarians beware. **Cup of the Day** (☎ 906-635-7272; 406 Ashmun St; mains $5-7; ◷ 7:15am-6pm Mon-Fri, 8am-3pm Sat) serves breakfast and lunch.

An hour's drive west of Sault Ste Marie, via Hwy 28 and Hwy 123, is the eastern UP's top attraction: lovely **Tahquamenon Falls**, with tea-colored waters tinted so by upstream hemlock leaves. The Upper Falls in **Tahquamenon Falls State Park** (☎ 906-492-3415; campsite $15-17, per vehicle $8) are 200ft across with a 50ft drop, making them the third-largest falls east of the Mississippi River. The Lower Falls are a series of smaller cascades best viewed by renting a **boat** (☎ 906-492-3457, 906-492-3415) and rowing across the river to an island. The large state park also has camping and great hiking, and there's a brewpub near the park entrance. North of the park, beyond the little town of Paradise, is the fascinating **Great Lakes Shipwreck Museum** (☎ 906-635-1742; www.shipwreckmuseum.com; 18335 N Whitefish Point Rd; adult/child 5-17 $8.50/5.50; ◷ 10am-6pm May-Oct), where the intriguing displays include items trawled up from sunken ships. More than 300 ships have sunk nearby in the congested sea lanes and unpredictable weather of the 'Graveyard of the Great Lakes.'

Hwy 123 leads to Paradise, where family-owned **Curly's Paradise Motel** (☎ 906-492-3445; www.superiorsights.com/curleys/index.html; Hwy 123; r $80-99) sits right on the lake. There are numerous other well-kept mom-and-pop motels along this stretch of highway.

Pictured Rocks National Lakeshore

Sitting roughly mid-peninsula on the Lake Superior shoreline, Munising is the gateway to **Pictured Rocks National Lakeshore** (www.nps.gov/piro), a 110-sq-mile national park just to the east that holds the namesake colored sandstone bluffs. Most people view the 200ft-high cliffs on a 2½-hour boat tour with **Pictured Rock Boat Cruises** (☎ 906-387-2379; www.picturedrocks.com; adult/child 6-12 $29/12); boats depart hourly from downtown from 9am to 5pm in July and August (reduced trips rest of year). You also can drive to **Miners Castle Overlook**, 12 miles east of Munising off Rte 58, for a good view. The most scenic backpacking adventure in the state is the **Lakeshore Trail**, a four- to five-day, 43-mile trek from Grand Marais to Munising through the heart of the park. Stop in at the **Hiawatha National Forest/Pictured Rocks Visitors**

Center (☎ 906-387-3700; 400 E Munising Ave; ☽ 8am-6pm summer, 9am-4:30pm rest of year) at the corner of Hwy 28 and Rte 58 for maps, backcountry permits and other details.

Just offshore is **Grand Island**, part of the Hiawatha National Forest. Hop aboard the **Grand Island Ferry** (☎ 906-387-3503; www.grandislandmi.com; ☽ late May–mid-Oct) to get there (round-trip adult/child six to 12 $15/10), and rent a mountain bike ($30 per day) from the ferry company to zip around, or take the three-hour bus tour ($20).

Munising has lots of motels, such as the recommended **Alger Falls Motel** (☎ 906-387-3536; www.algerfallsmotel.com; Hwy 28 E; r $48-68). **Falling Rock Café & Bookstore** (☎ 906-387-3008; 104 E Munising Ave; items $2-6; ☽ 7am-9pm Mon-Fri, 8am-9pm Sat & Sun) has sandwiches, pasties and live music.

Marquette

From Munising, Hwy 28 heads west and hugs Lake Superior. This beautiful stretch of highway has lots of beaches, roadside parks and rest areas where you can pull over and enjoy the scenery. Within 45 miles you'll reach Marquette, a city that abounds with outdoor-recreation opportunities. Stop at the **Michigan Welcome Center** (☎ 906-249-9066; US 41/Hwy 28; ☽ 8am-7pm summer, 9am-5pm rest of year), in an impressive log lodge as you enter the city, and pick up brochures on hiking trails and waterfalls in the area.

Panoramic views are enjoyed on the easy **Sugarloaf Mountain Trail** or the harder, wilderness-like **Hogsback Mountain Trail**. Both are reached from County Rd 550, just north of Marquette. In the city, the high bluffs of **Presque Isle Park** make a great place to catch the sunset.

Marquette is the perfect place to stay put for a few days to explore the central UP. The alpine-like **Nordic Bay Lodge** (☎ 800-892-9376; www.nordicbay.com; 1880 US 41 S; r incl breakfast from $65; ☒ ☐), overlooking Lake Superior a few miles south of downtown, is in the woods with access to trails; it has a ski wax/bike maintenance room for winter/summer. **Value Host Motor Inn** (☎ 906-225-5000; 1101 US 41 W; r $55-65), with a sauna, is a few miles west of town.

Unbelievable but true: the tiny, one-table **Rice Paddy** (☎ 906-225-0368; 1720 Presque Isle Ave; mains $5-7; ☽ 11am-9pm Mon-Fri) serves the world's best pad thai and provides a dandy local-color snapshot; don't miss it.

Unique breakfast, lunch and dinner dishes are served at **Sweet Water Café** (☎ 906-226-7009; 517 N 3rd St; mains $6-10; ☽ 7am-3pm Mon & Tue, 7am-9pm Wed-Sun), with a large vegetarian selection.

Sample the local meat/veggie pie specialty at **Jean Kay's Pasties & Subs** (☎ 906-228-5310; 1639 Presque Isle Ave; items $3-4; ☽ 10am-9pm Mon-Fri, 10am-8pm Sat & Sun).

You'll get mighty fine handcrafted beer at **Vierling Saloon** (☎ 906-228-3533; 119 S Front St; ☽ 11am-10pm Mon-Sat).

Isle Royale National Park

Totally free of vehicles and roads, **Isle Royale National Park** (www.nps.gov/isro; user fee per day $4; ☽ mid-Apr–Oct), a 210-sq-mile island in Lake Superior, is certainly the place to go for peace and quiet – and to commune (cautiously) with moose and wolves. It is laced with 165 miles of hiking trails that connect dozens of campgrounds along Superior and inland lakes. You must be totally prepared for this wilderness adventure, with a tent, camping stove, sleeping bags, food and water filter. Or say 'to hell with that crap,' and stay at the **Rock Harbor Lodge** (☎ 906-337-4993; www.isleroyaleresort .com; r/cottage from $170/165). The **park headquarters** (☎ 906-482-0984; 800 E Lakeshore Dr; ☽ 8am-6pm Mon-Sat summer, 8am-4:30pm Mon-Fri rest of year) in Houghton can provide information.

From the dock outside the headquarters, the **Ranger III** (☎ 906-482-0984) departs at 9am on Tuesday and Friday for the six-hour boat trip (one way adult/child under 12 $52/24) to Rock Harbor, at the east end of the island. If you're looking for a quicker trip, **Royale Air Service** (☎ 877-359-4753; www.royaleairservice .com) flies from Houghton County Airport to Rock Harbor in 30 minutes (one way $170). Or head 50 miles up the Keweenaw Peninsula to Copper Harbor (a beautiful drive) and jump on the **Isle Royale Queen** (☎ 906-289-4437; www.isleroyale.com) for the 8am three-hour crossing (one way adult/child under 12 $58/29). Days of departure vary, so call for the schedule. You also can access Isle Royale from Grand Portage, Minnesota (p658). Bringing a kayak or canoe on the ferry costs an additional $25.

Porcupine Mountains Wilderness State Park

Michigan's largest state park, with 90 miles of trails, is another wilderness highlight of the Upper Peninsula, and it's a lot easier to reach than Isle Royale. 'The Porkies,' as they're called, are so rugged that loggers bypassed most of the range in the early 19th century, leaving the park with the largest tract of virgin forest between the Rocky Mountains and Adirondacks.

From Silver City, head west on Hwy 107 to reach the **Porcupine Mountains visitors center** (☎ 906-885-5208; 412 S Boundary Rd; ☉ 10am-6pm mid-May–mid-Oct), where you buy vehicle entry permits (per day/annual $8/29) and backcountry permits (per night for one to four people $10). Continue to the end of Hwy 107 and climb 300ft for the stunning view of **Lake of the Clouds**.

Winter is also a busy time at the Porkies, with downhill skiing (a 640ft vertical drop) and 26 miles of cross-country trails; check with the **ski area** (☎ 888-937-2411; www.skithepork ies.com) for conditions and costs.

The **Sunshine Motel** (☎ 888-988-2187; www .ontonagonmi.com/sunshine; 24077 Hwy 64; r $55, cabins $60-70), 3 miles west of Ontonagon, is near the park and makes a good base.

WISCONSIN

You might as well embrace your heritage, and Wisconsin's is cheese. Folks here refer to themselves as 'cheeseheads' and empha-size it by wearing foam rubber cheese-wedge hats for special occasions (most notably dur-ing Green Bay Packers football games). Lest there be any doubt about dairy pride, check out the state's quarter – yep, there's a cow and a big hunk of cheese right on the back.

So it's no surprise that much of the Dairy State is bucolic, cow-speckled farm-land. What does astonish are the craggy cliffs, lighthouses, and shimmering islands of Lakes Superior and Michigan, which crown Wisconsin to the north and east, respectively. Door County and the Apos-tle Islands are prime places to explore the coastal beauty. When an urban fix hits, make for Milwaukee, a down-to-earth city if ever there was one that admirably bal-ances Harleys and beer with world-class art and cultural festivals.

History

In 1634 Jean Nicolet landed near Green Bay, home of the Sioux-speaking Win-nebago people, and the French soon opened

---

> **WISCONSIN FACTS**
>
> **Nicknames** Badger State, America's Dairyland
> **Population** 5.5 million
> **Area** 65,500 sq miles
> **Capital city** Madison (population 218,000)
> **Official motto** Forward
> **Birthplace of** Author Laura Ingalls Wilder (1867–1957), architect Frank Lloyd Wright (1867–1959), painter Georgia O'Keeffe (1887–1986), Senator Joseph McCarthy (1908–57), actor Orson Welles (1915–85)
> **Famous for** First state to legislate gay rights

---

a trading post. Jesuits established missions in the region in the 1660s, but eventually French territorial claims passed to the Brit-ish and then to the new USA.

A lead-mining boom in the 1820s spurred development. The many miners who came from nearby states were called 'badgers' for their subterranean activities. Following statehood in 1848 and the Civil War, im-migrants poured in – from Germany and Scandinavia most notably. The Badger State was soon known for its beer, butter, cheese and paper.

While Wisconsin still leads the nation in the number of dairy farms and clings to the 'top cheesemaker' title, its role is under threat. Midsize farms here, as throughout the country, are having a tough time: al-most a third of Wisconsin's dairies have shut down in the past 10 years.

Information

Wisconsin sales tax is 5%, with many coun-ties tacking on an additional 1%.

Check the following websites for statewide information:

Wisconsin Department of Tourism (☎ 800-432-8747; www.travelwisconsin.com)

Wisconsin highway conditions (☎ 800-762-3947; www.dot.wisconsin.gov)

Wisconsin state park information (☎ 888-947-2757; www.dnr.state.wi.us/org/land/parks) Park entry requires a vehicle permit (per day/year residents $5/20, nonresidents $10/30). Campsites cost $9 to $20; reserva-tions accepted (fee $9.50).

MILWAUKEE

No one gives much consideration to Mil-waukee, standing as it does in Chicago's shadow, and that's a shame, because it's a city that really does have a lot going for it. Visitors can engage in earthy pleasures, such as beer and motorcycles, by touring Miller Brewery and Harley-Davidson's plant, then kick into high-culture gear at the stunning art museum. In summertime, a slew of festivals lets loose much revelry by the lake. Speaking of which: the Lake Express ferry makes Milwaukee quite a perfect jumping-off point before heading elsewhere in the Midwest. But before leaving, please, please go see the racing sausages at Miller Park.

History

First settled by Germans in the 1840s, Milwaukee has a German character that's still evident in its architecture (the Germanic City Hall and beer-bankrolled Pabst Theater, for example). Later waves of Italians, Poles, Irish, African Americans and Mexicans added to the varied culture.

German settlers started small breweries here in the mid-19th century, but the introduction of bulk brewing technology in the 1890s turned beer into a major Milwaukee industry. Schlitz ('the beer that made Milwaukee famous'), Pabst and Miller were all based here at one time, but among the majors, only Miller remains.

Orientation

Lake Michigan sits to the east of the city, and is rimmed by parkland. The inspired Riverwalk is a great system of redeveloped walking paths along both sides of the Milwaukee River downtown. Wisconsin Ave divides east–west streets. North–south streets are usually numbered and increase as they head west from the lake.

Information

BOOKSTORES
Harry Schwartz Books (☎ 414-332-1181; 2559 N Downer Ave)

EMERGENCY
Police, fire, ambulance (☎ 911) Emergency.

INTERNET ACCESS
The East Side neighborhood near the University of Wisconsin-Milwaukee boasts coffee shops with wi-fi.

Node Coffee Shop (☎ 414-431-9278; www.node coffee.com; 1504 E North Ave; per hr $4; ⏰ 24hr) is a vegan-friendly, night-owl place to surf.

INTERNET RESOURCES
Ethnic Wisconsin (www.ethnicwisconsin.org) Information on the state's varied ethnic groups, including self-guided neighborhood tours of Milwaukee.
On Milwaukee (www.onmilwaukee.com) Job listings, traffic and weather updates, plus restaurant and entertainment reviews.
Vicit Milwaukee (www.visitmilwaukee.org) Visitor center's website, sometimes with discount coupons for hotels and attractions.

MEDIA
Milwaukee Journal Sentinel (www.jsonline.com) The local daily.
Shepherd Express (www.shepherd-express.com) The free weekly entertainment paper; available at bookstores, coffee shops and entertainment venues.

Tune into WUWM-FM 89.7 for NPR, or WLZR-FM 102.9 for rock.

MEDICAL SERVICES
Froedtert Hospital (☎ 414-805-3000; 9200 W Wisconsin Ave)
Walgreens (☎ 414-272-2171; 1400 E Brady St; ⏰ 24hr) Pharmacy.

MONEY
US Bank (☎ 414-765-4035; 777 E Wisconsin Ave) ATM and foreign currency exchange available.

POST
Post office (☎ 800-275-8777; 345 W St Paul Ave)

TOURIST INFORMATION
Milwaukee LGBT Community Center (☎ 414-271-2656; www.mkelgbt.org; 315 W Court St, Suite 101; ⏰ 10am-10pm Mon-Fri, 6-10pm Sat) Has information on happenings; or search www.outinmilwaukee.com.
Visitors center (☎ 414-908-6205, 800-554-1448; www.visitmilwaukee.org; 400 W Wisconsin Ave; ⏰ 8am-5pm Mon-Fri) In the Midwest Airlines Center.

Sights

Sights are spread out, but usually accessible by public buses.

MILWAUKEE ART MUSEUM
This first-rate, lakeside **museum** (☎ 414-224-3200; www.mam.org; 750 N Lincoln Memorial Dr; adult/child 13-18 $8/4; ⏰ 10am-5pm, to 8pm Thu) features a truly stunning wing-like addition by the famous Spanish architect Santiago Calatrava. The museum's all-encompassing collection includes paintings from the 15th

century onward. There's a permanent display on Frank Lloyd Wright, and fabulous folk and outsider art galleries. Pick up the free, self-guided audio tour.

HARLEY-DAVIDSON PLANT

In 1903 William Harley and Arthur Davidson, local schoolmates, built and sold their first Harley-Davidson motorcycle. A century later the big bikes are a symbol of American manufacturing pride, and this **Harley-Davidson plant** (☎ 414-343-7850; www.harley-davidson.com; 11700 W Capitol Dr; admission free; ☼ usually 9:30am-1pm Mon-Fri), in the suburb of Wauwatosa (20 minutes' drive from downtown Milwaukee) is where engines are built. (Body assembly goes on in York, Pennsylvania, and Kansas City, Missouri.) The one-hour tours are kind of technical, but the ultimate payoff comes when you get to sit in the saddle of a vintage bike. No open shoes are permitted in the plant.

BREWERIES

Pabst and Schlitz have moved on, but Milwaukee is still known for its watery, working-class beer. Of course, that's not everyone's cup of tea, but it would be a shame not to join the legion of beer drinkers that line up for tours of the **Miller Brewing Company** (☎ 414-931-2337; www.millerbrewing.com; 4251 W State St; admission free; ☼ 10:30am-3:30pm Mon-Sat). A fascinating walk through the bottling and distribution areas will give you an idea of just how much brew the public consumes. Bring ID to participate in the tasting session.

For more swell times (and better beer), head out to the **Sprecher Brewing Company** (☎ 414-964-2739; www.sprecherbrewery.com; 701 W Glendale Ave), a microbrewery with a museum featuring memorabilia from long-gone breweries and a beer garden replete with oompah music. Tours ($3) are held at 4pm Friday; 1pm, 2pm and 3pm Saturday; and 1:30pm and 2:30pm Sunday. It's 5 miles north of downtown; reservations required.

MUSEUMS & MANSIONS

The **Eisner Museum of Advertising and Design** (☎ 414-847-3290; www.eisnermuseum.org; 208 N Water St; adult/child 12-18 $5/2.50; ☼ 11am-5pm Wed-Fri, 11am-8pm Thu, noon-5pm Sat, 1-5pm Sun) presents excellent exhibits on how the mediums influence today's culture.

The 1893 **Pabst Mansion** (☎ 414-931-0808; www.pabstmansion.com; 2000 W Wisconsin Ave; adult/child 6-17 $8/4; ☼ 10am-4pm Mon-Sat, noon-4pm Sun) is the well-appointed home of the former local brewmaster.

America's Black Holocaust Museum (☎ 414-264-2500; 2233 N 4th St; adult/student $5/3; ☼ 9am-5pm Tue-Sat) poignantly outlines the consequences of racism from slavery onward.

Activities

The parkland edging Lake Michigan is prime for walking and bicycling. For the latter, try **Milwaukee Bike & Skate Rental** (☎ 414-273-1343; www.milwbikeskaterental.com; Veteran's Park; bicycle per hr $8; ☼ 10am-7pm summer), near McKinley Marina.

Festivals & Events

Summerfest (☎ 800-273-3378; www.summerfest.com; day pass $12) is the granddaddy of festivals, with 11 days of music and merriment in late June/early July.

There's also **PrideFest** (www.pridefest.com), **Polish Fest** (www.polishfest.org), **Irish Fest** (www.irishfest.com), **German Fest** (www.germanfest.com) and a host of others. Call the visitors center for details.

Sleeping

Rates listed here are for summer, when you should book ahead; rooms can be 15% to 30% less in winter. The 14.6% tax is not included in the listed rates. For cheap chain lodging, try Howell Ave, south near the airport.

Astor Hotel (☎ 800-558-0200; www.theastorhotel.com; 924 E Juneau Ave; r incl breakfast $79-129; (P) (□)) The Astor, dating from 1918, has bright, spacious rooms, some with cool old furnishings, plus perks like free Internet and a shuttle to nearby sights. It's located near the lake, east of downtown's core. Parking costs $4.

Best Western Inn Towne Hotel (☎ 414-224-8400; www.inntownehotel.com; 710 N Old World 3rd St; s/d from $89/99; (P)) It's operated by a chain, but this old hotel, in the heart of downtown, has good-quality rooms with a vintage ambience. All rooms have free wi-fi. Parking is $10.

Howard Johnson (☎ 414-271-4656, 888-271-4656; www.howardjohnsonmke.com; 176 W Wisconsin Ave; r from $79; (P)) This property sports HoJo's typical, generic stylings, but it's one of the friendliest prices you'll find downtown. Parking is $9.

Pfister Hotel (☎ 414-273-8222; www.thepfisterhotel
.com; 424 E Wisconsin Ave; r from $199; P ﾐ) Built in
the 19th century, the gorgeous Pfister is Milwaukee's grande dame, as a stroll through
the lobby and peek at the Victorian painting
collection emphatically declare. Wi-fi costs
$9.95 daily. If business is slow, rooms rates
are significantly reduced. Parking is $14.

Eating
Good places to scope for eats include N Old
World 3rd St downtown; the fashionable
East Side by the University of Wisconsin-
Milwaukee; hip, Italian-based Brady St by
its intersection with N Farwell Ave; and the
gentrified Third Ward, anchored along N
Milwaukee St south of I-94.

The Friday night fish fry is a highly social
tradition observed throughout Wisconsin
and all over Milwaukee. One of the best
options follows.

American Serb Memorial Hall (☎ 414-545-6030;
www.serbhall.com; 5101 W Oklahoma Ave; meal $7-10;
☉ noon-9pm Fri) Southwest of downtown, a
large crowd of regulars come for its all-you-
can-eat baked cod.

African Hut (☎ 414-765-1110; 1107 N Old World
3rd St; mains $9-13; ☉ 11:30am-9:30pm Mon-Sat)
A wonderful place to go for exotic meat
and vegetarian dishes with ingredients like
pounded yam, cassava and cooked-down
peanuts blended with herbs, served amid
leopard-print walls.

Dancing Ganesha (☎ 414-220-0202; www.dan
cingganesha.com; 1692-94 N Van Buren St; mains $9-18;
☉ dinner) Lamb saag, turkey kheema and
pork vindaloo are but a few of the variations
on the usual Indian theme at this hip restaurant. Meals are complemented by a fine
drink menu that includes saffron martinis.

Benji's Deli (☎ 414-332-7777; 4156 N Oakland Ave;
mains $6-11; ☉ 7am-8pm) Seek out the hoppel
poppel – a local specialty of eggs, potatoes,
and sausage whipped together – among the
many meaty offerings at this famous deli in
Shorewood.

South of town a few blocks (over the
bridge and too far to walk), around S 5th
and 6th Sts, the Latin enclave of Walker's
Point holds several Mexican restaurants.

La Fuente (☎ 414-271-8595; 625 S 5th St; mains $7-
9; ☉ 10am-10pm) The good, inexpensive food
draws crowds weekend nights.

Milwaukee Public Market (☎ 414-336-1111;
www.milwaukeepublicmarket.org; 400 N Water St;

☉ 11am-7pm Tue-Sun) You can browse for fresh
foods at this Third Ward market.

A Milwaukee specialty is frozen custard,
like ice cream only smoother and richer.
Leon's (☎ 414-383-1784; 3131 S 27th St; ☉ 11am-
midnight) and **Kopp's** (☎ 414-961-2006; 5373 N Port
Washington Rd, Glendale; ☉ 10:30am-11:30pm) are
popular purveyors.

Drinking
The beer legacy guarantees that a thirst-
quenching array of golden nectar is available. Over a dozen bars and restaurants lie
around N Water and E State Sts. More bars
can be found in Walker's Point on 1st and
2nd Sts, and along Brady St between Astor
and Farwell Sts.

Von Trier (☎ 414-272-1775; 2235 N Farwell Ave)
The German Von Trier is a long-standing,
real-deal favorite, with plenty of good stuff
on tap and a biergarten.

Palm Tavern (☎ 414-744-0393; 2989 S Kinnickinnic
Ave) Located in the blossoming south side
neighborhood of Bay View, this warm,
quiet little bar has a good selection of beers
and single-malt scotches.

John Hawk's (☎ 414-272-3199; 100 E Wisconsin Ave)
Hawk's is a 'British' pub with a big choice
of beers, fish fries, sandwiches and live jazz
on Saturday. It occupies a prime spot on
the riverfront.

Entertainment
Miller Park (☎ 414-902-4000, 800-933-7890; www
.milwaukeebrewers.com; 1 Brewers Way) The Milwaukee Brewers play baseball at top-notch
Miller Park, which has a retractable roof
and real grass. It's famous for its 'Racing
Sausages,' ie a group of people in giant
sausage costumes who sprint down the
field at the end of the 6th inning. Located
near S 46th St.

Bradley Center (☎ 414-227-0400; www.nba
.com/bucks; 1001 N 4th St) The NBA's Milwaukee
Bucks dunk here.

Getting There & Around
TO/FROM THE AIRPORT
The **General Mitchell International Airport**
(☎ 414-747-5300; www.mitchellairport.com) is 8 miles
south of downtown.

Take the **Airport Connection van** (☎ 800-236-
5450; www.mkelimo.com) downtown (one way/
round-trip $11/20), or catch the public bus
No 80 ($1.75) or a cab ($25).

GREAT LAKES

BOAT

The **Lake Express ferry** (☎ 866-914-1010; www.lake -express.com) sails from downtown (the terminal is located a few miles south of the city center) to Muskegon, Michigan, and provides easy access to Michigan's beach-lined Gold Coast (p630). For ferry details, see p566.

BUS

Centrally located **Greyhound** (☎ 414-272-2156; 606 N James Lovell St) has frequent buses to Chicago ($13 to $28, two hours) and Minneapolis ($52 to $68, seven hours). Across the street, **Badger Bus** (☎ 414-276-7490; www.badgerbus.com; 635 N James Lovell St) goes to Madison ($15, 1½ hours).

CAR

National car-rental agencies have offices at the airport and around town; Hertz has one at the downtown train station. Check rental information in the Transportation chapter (p1175) for contact details.

PUBLIC TRANSPORTATION

The **Milwaukee County Transit System** (☎ 414-344-6711; www.ridemcts.com; 1942 N 17th Ave) provides efficient local bus service ($1.75) as well as a trolley-like bus – the 'Milwaukee Loop' ($2, valid all day) – that runs downtown in summer. The downtown train station has route maps.

TAXI

For cab service, call **Yellow Cab** (☎ 414-271-1800).

TRAIN

The *Hiawatha* train is run by **Amtrak** (☎ 414-271-0840; 433 W St Paul Ave) seven times a day to/from Chicago ($20, 1½ hours); catch it downtown or at Amtrak's airport train station. The *Empire Builder* stops in Milwaukee once daily on its route between Chicago and Seattle.

SOUTHERN WISCONSIN

This part of Wisconsin has some of the prettiest landscapes, particularly the hilly southwest. There is whimsy for all ages, from circus animals to the spaceship-like Forevertron. Madison, the green, laid-back capital, has great appeal, and architecture fans can be unleashed at Taliesin, the Frank Lloyd Wright *über*-sight.

Racine

Racine is an unremarkable industrial town 30 miles south of Milwaukee, but it has two key Frank Lloyd Wright sights, both of which offer tours that must be pre-booked. The first, the **Johnson Wax Company Administration Building** (☎ 262-260-2154; 1525 Howe St; admission free; ⊗ Fri only), dates from 1939 and is a magnificent space with tall, flared columns; call for the tour schedule. The other is the lakeside **Wingspread** (☎ 262-681-3353; 33 E Four Mile Rd; admission free; ⊗ 9:30am-3pm Tue-Thu), the last and largest of Wright's Prairie houses.

The **Racine Art Museum** (☎ 262-638-8300; www .ramart.org; 441 Main St; adult/child 12-18 $5/3; ⊗ 10am-5pm Tue-Sat, noon-5pm Sun) houses one of the continent's most significant craft collections, focusing on ceramics, fibers, glass, metals and wood.

Madison

Wonderfully ensconced on a narrow isthmus between Mendota and Monona lakes, Madison is an irresistible combination of small, grassy state capital and liberal, bookish college town.

The **visitors center** (☎ 608-255-2537, 800-373-6376; www.visitmadison.com; 615 E Washington Ave; ⊗ 8am-5pm Mon-Fri) is six blocks east of Capitol Sq; ask about the VisitorPass ($10) for savings at local businesses. **Isthmus** (www .thedailypage.com) is the free entertainment paper. Madison is also the birthplace of the cheeky, farcical newspaper, the **Onion** (www .theonion.com).

SIGHTS & ACTIVITIES

The heart of town is marked by the x-shaped **State Capitol** (☎ 608-266-0382; admission free; ⊗ 8am-6pm Mon-Fri, 8am-4pm Sat & Sun), the largest outside Washington, DC. Tours are available on the hour most days. On Saturday, Capitol Sq is overtaken by the **Dane County Farmer's Market** (www.dcfm.org; ⊗ May-Nov), a good place to sample the Wisconsin specialties of cheese curds and beer-cooked bratwursts.

By all means, take advantage of the city's lakes and trails. For rentals, try **Yellow Jersey** (☎ 608-257-4737; www.yellowjersey.org; 419 State St; bikes per day $10; ⊗ 10am-6pm Tue, Wed & Fri, 10am-8pm Mon & Thu, 9am-5pm Sat, noon-5pm Sun) for two-wheelers, and **Carl & John's Paddlin'** (☎ 608-284-0300; www.paddlin.com; 110 N Thornton St; kayak/canoe per day $30; ⊗ 10am-6pm Mon-Thu, 10am-

8pm Fri, 10am-5pm Sat & Sun) for lake-faring craft. Both are near Capitol Sq.

State St, the lengthy strip of student stores, bars and cafés, runs from the capitol west to the University of Wisconsin. The campus has its own attractions, including the **Chazen Museum of Art** (☎ 608-263-2246; www.chazen.wisc .edu; 800 University Ave; admission free; ☽ 9am-5pm Tue-Fri, 11am-5pm Sat & Sun) and the 1240-acre **Arboretum** (☎ 608-263-7888; 1207 Seminole Hwy; admission free; ☽ 7am-10pm), dense with lilac.

The impeccable **Monona Terrace Community Center** (☎ 608-261-4000; www.mononaterrace .com; 1 John Nolen Dr; admission free; ☽ 8am-5pm; P), two blocks from Capitol Sq, has a fabulous rooftop garden overlooking Lake Monona. It finally opened in 1997, 59 years after Frank Lloyd Wright designed it. Tours (adult/student $3/2) are offered at 1pm daily.

Beside Capitol Sq, the **Veterans Museum** (☎ 608-267-1799; http://museum.dva.state.wi.us; 30 W Mifflin St; admission free; ☽ 9am-4:30pm Mon-Sat, noon-4pm Sun) holds thoughtful displays that outline all of the country's war involvements. The nearby **Overture Center for the Arts** (☎ 608-258-4973; www.overturecenter.com; 201 State St) has a variety of performing arts venues and galleries inside.

SLEEPING

HI Madison Hostel (☎ 608-441-0144; www.mad isonhostel.org; 141 S Butler St; dm $18-21, r $41-44; ▣) The convenient hostel is a short walk from the capitol. The office is open from 8am to 11am and 5pm to 9pm, with extended hours in summer.

University Inn (☎ 608-285-8040, 800-279-4881; www.universityinn.org; 441 N Frances St; r $79-139; P) Right by the State St action downtown, this handy hotel offers free high-speed Internet access. Rates are highest on summer weekends.

Select Inn (☎ 608-249-1815; www.selectinn.com; 4845 Hayes Rd; r $51-56; P ▣) This Tyrolean knock-off, with free high-speed Internet access, stands out among the moderately priced motels off I-90/I-94. It's 6 miles from the town center. Other motels can be found off Hwy 12/18 and along Washington Ave.

EATING & DRINKING

State St holds an outstanding range of eating and drinking options, many with inviting patios. Cruising Williamson ('Willy')

St turns up good Lao, Jamaican, Caribbean and other eateries.

Himal Chuli (☎ 608-251-9225; 318 State St; mains $7-11; ☽ 11am-9pm Mon-Sat, noon-9pm Sun) This cheerful and cozy place serves up home-made Nepali fare, including vegetarian dishes.

Kabul (☎ 608-256-6322; 541 State St; mains $6-12; ☽ 11am-10:30pm Sun-Thu, 11am-11pm Fri & Sat) Head to Kabul for nicely done Afghani food.

Michelangelo's (☎ 608-251-5299; 114 State St; mains $2-5; ☽ 7am-11pm) Pop in and try Michelangelo's fair-trade coffees, sweets and sandwiches.

Memorial Union (☎ 608-265-3000; 800 Langdon St) For a beer, join the fun atmosphere at this bar located at the university. The lakeside patio is especially nice on warm afternoons.

GETTING THERE & AWAY

The central **Greyhound bus station** (☎ 608-257-3050; 2 S Bedford St) is also used by **Badger Bus** (☎ 414-276-7490; www.badgerbus.com; 635 N James Lovell St, Milwaukee) for trips to Milwaukee ($15, 1½ hours). For details, see opposite.

Around Madison
FRANK LLOYD WRIGHT SIGHTS

Forty miles west of Madison and 3 miles south of Spring Green, **Taliesin** was the home of native son Frank Lloyd Wright for most of his life and is the site of his architectural school. It's now a major pilgrimage destination for fans and followers. The house was built in 1903, the Hillside Home School in 1932, and the **visitors center** (☎ 608-588-7900; www.taliesinpreservation.org; Hwy 23; ☽ 9am-6pm May-Oct) was built in 1953. A wide range of guided tours ($15 to $80) cover various parts of the complex; reservations are required for the more lengthy ones. The two-hour walking tour ($15, no reservation needed) is a good introduction to Frank Lloyd Wright's work.

Spring Green has a B&B in town and half a dozen motels strung along Hwy 14, north of town. Small **Usonian Inn** (☎ 877-876-6426; www.usonianinn.com; E 5116 Hwy 14; r weekday/weekend $55/69; ☒) was designed by a Wright student; **Prairie House** (☎ 800-588-2088; E 4884 Hwy 14; r weekday/weekend $69/79) is larger, with a whirlpool and game room.

The **Spring Green General Store** (☎ 608-588-7070; www.springgreengeneralstore.com; 137 S Albany St;

items $5-7; 9am-6pm Mon-Fri, 8am-6pm Sat, 8am-4pm Sun) serves sandwiches and earthy lunch specials.

The **American Players Theatre** (608-588-2361; www.playinthewoods.org) stages productions at an outdoor amphitheater by the Wisconsin River.

QUIRKY SIGHTS

At his **Sculpture Park** (www.drevermor.com; admission free; 9am-5pm Mon & Thu-Sat, noon-5pm Sun), 11 miles northwest of Madison on US 12, Dr Evermor welds old pipes, carburetors and other salvaged metal into a hallucinatory world of futuristic creatures and structures. The crowning glory is the giant, egg-domed Forevertron, cited by *Guinness World Records* as the world's largest scrap metal sculpture. The good doctor himself – aka Tom Every – is often around and happy to chat about his birds, dragons and other pieces of folk art. A visit here is highly recommended; keep an eye out for sculptures along the highway that mark the entrance to the park.

Baraboo, 20 miles northwest of Madison, was once the winter home of the Ringling Brothers Circus. **Circus World Museum** (608-356-8341, 866-693-1500; www.circusworldmuseum.com; 550 Water St; adult/child 5-11 summer $15/8, winter $7/3.50; 9am-6pm summer, reduced hrs winter) preserves a nostalgic collection of wagons, posters and equipment from the touring big-top heydays. In summer, admission includes clowns, animals and acrobats doing the three-ring thing. In early July the little town holds its **Great Circus Festival** (608-356-8341, 866-693-1500) with a parade and big-top shows. Among numerous motels, sprawl-ing **Spinning Wheel** (608-356-3933; www.spinningwheelmotel.com; 809 8th St; r in summer $59-77) is decent.

Continue north on US 12 to the **Wisconsin Dells** (www.wisdells.com), a mega-center of kitschy diversions, including family theme parks, water-skiing thrill shows and super-minigolf courses – a jolting contrast to the natural appeal of the area with its scenic limestone formations carved by the Wisconsin River. To appreciate the original attraction, take a boat tour or walk the trails at Mirror Lake or Devil's Lake state parks; both have camping. For lodging, the area is chockful of sterling relics from the early 1960s, including **Bridge View Motel** (608-254-6114; www.bridgeviewmotel.com; 1020 River Rd; r $35-65;). Look for modest restaurants on Broadway Ave.

The **House on the Rock** (608-935-3639; www.thehouseontherock.com; 5754 Hwy 23; adult/child 5-12 $19.50/10.50; opening hrs vary), south of Taliesin, is one of Wisconsin's busiest attractions. The strange 'house,' one man's obsession, was built atop a rock column and sprawled to become a monument of the imagination. The vast collection of objects and wonderments overwhelm. Allow three to five hours to see it all.

Along the Mississippi River

The Mississippi River forms most of Wisconsin's western border, and alongside it run some of the most scenic sections of the Great River Rd (Hwy 35) – the designated route that follows Old Man River from Minnesota to the Gulf of Mexico.

From Madison, head west on US 18. You'll hit the River Rd at **Prairie du Chien**.

TOP FIVE GREAT LAKES QUIRKY FESTIVALS

Superman Celebration (800-949-5740; www.metropolischamber.com; Metropolis, Illinois; admission free) In early June, the town that adopted the caped superhero throws a whopping party in his honor.

Spam Jam (507-437-5100; www.spam.com; Austin, Minnesota; admission free) Sponsored by the Spam Museum (p656), on the third Sunday in June, the festival hosts bands, Spam-and-pancake breakfasts, and puppet shows depicting the canned meat's history.

Tour de Donut (www.bebikeclub.com; Staunton, Illinois; entry fee $10) It's a 30-mile bicycle race in mid-July, with donut stations en route; each glazed goodie eaten knocks five minutes off one's final time.

Lumberjack World Championships (715-634-2484; www.lumberjackworldchampionships.com; Hayward, Wisconsin; general admission adult $12-14, child $10-12) On the third or fourth weekend in July, Paul Bunyan types chop, speed saw and logroll for the world's top prize.

Cow Chip Throw (608-643-4317; www.wiscowchip.com; Prairie du Sac, Wisconsin; admission free) On the first weekend in September, 800 competitors fling dried manure patties as far as the eye can see; the record is 248ft.

Founded in 1673 as a French fur-trading post, the town's name quaintly honors the prairie dogs that once populated the area.

North of Prairie du Chien, the hilly river side wends through the scene of the final battle in the bloody Black Hawk War. Historic markers tell part of the story, which finished at the Battle of Bad Ax when Native American men, women and children were massacred trying to flee across the Mississippi.

Upstream, **La Crosse** is a fine riverside town with a historic center nestling restaurants and pubs. Grandad Bluff offers grand views of the river. It's east of town along Main St (which becomes Bliss Rd); follow Bliss Rd up the hill and then turn right on Grandad Bluff Rd. For area information, stop by the **visitors center** (☎ 608-782-2366, 800-658-9424; www.explorelacrosse.com; 410 Veteran's Memorial Dr; ✆ 8am-5pm Mon-Fri, extended hrs summer). To bed down, try the friendly **Guest House Motel** (☎ 608-784-8840, 800-274-6873; www.guesthousemotel .com; 810 S 4th St; r incl breakfast $80-140).

EASTERN WISCONSIN
Kettle Moraine & Oshkosh

Just north of West Bend, **Kettle Moraine State Forest** (☎ 262-626-2116; N 1765 Hwy G) is a regional highlight, and offers good walking and cross-country skiing opportunities. Note that Kettle Moraine has two parts: this north unit, and a south unit near Whitewater.

Further north, **Oshkosh** is home to the **Experimental Aircraft Association AirVenture Museum** (☎ 920-426-4800; www.airventuremuseum.org; off E Frontage Rd; adult/child 6-17 summer $12/9, reduced in winter; ✆ 8:30am-5pm Mon-Sat, 10am-5pm Sun), which shows its extensive collection of weird and wonderful winged things year-round. The museum is south of town on US 41. In late July the huge **Oshkosh Air Show** attracts some 300,000 aeronautical enthusiasts.

Green Bay

Founded in the 1660s as a fur-trading post, Green Bay boomed as a Lake Michigan port and later a terminus for Midwest railroads. Processing and packing agricultural products became a major industry, and gave name to the city's legendary pro football team: the Green Bay Packers. The franchise is unique as the only community-owned non-profit in the NFL; perhaps pride in ownership is what makes the fans so die-hard (and wear foam rubber cheese wedges on their head).

The **visitors center** (☎ 920-494-9507, 888-867-3342; www.packercountry.com; 1901 S Oneida St; ✆ 8am-4:30pm Mon-Fri) is by the football stadium, just off Lombardi Ave, south of downtown. The town core is on the east side of the Fox River around Walnut St.

While tickets are nearly impossible to get, you can always get in the spirit by joining a pre-game tailgate party, where fans fire up grills and set up tables by their cars. The generous flow of alcohol has led to Green Bay's reputation as a 'drinking town with a football problem.' Or visit the **Green Bay Packer Hall of Fame** (☎ 920-569-7512; www.pack ers.com; Lambeau Field; adult/child 6-11 $10/5; ✆ 9am-6pm, hrs vary during home games), which is indeed packed with memorabilia. It has football movies and interactive exhibits, plus tours of the newly expanded stadium.

Other sights of interest include the **National Railroad Museum** (☎ 920-437-7623; www .nationalrrmuseum.org; 2285 S Broadway; adult/child 4-12 May-Sep $9/6.50, Oct-Apr $8/5; ✆ 9am-5pm Mon-Sat, 11am-5pm Sun), which features some of the biggest steam and diesel locomotives ever to haul freight into Green Bay's vast yards; train rides are offered in summer. The **Oneida Nation Museum** (☎ 920-869-2768; www.oneidanation.org; W 892 Cty Rd EE; adult/child $3/2; ✆ 9am-5pm Tue-Sat summer, 9am-5pm Tue-Fri winter), 7 miles west of downtown, outlines the tribe's past and present.

Tidy, independent **Bay Motel** (☎ 920-494-3441; www.baymotelgreenbay.com; 1301 S Military Ave; r 39-70; P) is a mile from Lambeau Field.

Door County

With its rocky coastline, picturesque lighthouses, orchards and small 19th-century villages, you have to admit Door County is pretty damn lovely. The county is spread across a narrow peninsula jutting 60 miles into Lake Michigan. Despite considerable crowds in summer and increasing numbers of wealthy newcomers, development has remained essentially low-key and the atmosphere retains a certain highbrow gentility.

Visitors usually make a loop around the peninsula on its two highways. Hwy 57 runs beside Lake Michigan, and goes through Jacksonport and Bailey's Harbor. Hwy 42 borders Green Bay and passes through

GREAT LAKES

DEATH'S DOOR

Native Americans and early French explorers named the straights between Lake Michigan and Green Bay 'Death's Door' due to the treacherous currents and unpredictable waves that reached up and claimed boats of all sizes. More than 100 vessels were stranded or damaged going through in the fall of 1872 alone. Modern navigation aids have rendered the passage much less threatening today.

(from south to north) Egg Harbor, Fish Creek, Ephraim and Sister Bay. Gills Rock is perched at the peninsula's tip, decorated by a string of islands. No public buses serve the peninsula, and not much stays open from November to April.

The most attractive part of the loop begins at **Sturgeon Bay**, the peninsula's main town. As you enter it stop at the knowledgeable **Chamber of Commerce** (☎ 920-743-4456; www .doorcounty.com; 1015 Green Bay Rd; ✆ 8am-5pm Mon-Fri, 10am-4pm Sat & Sun mid-May–mid-Oct, reduced hrs rest of year); on the porch a kiosk is accessible 24 hours a day with lodging information.

The best accommodation choices are along the Green Bay shoreline. Prices listed are for July and August, the most expensive months; many places fill up early and have minimum-stay requirements. In Ephraim, **Trollhaugen Lodge** (☎ 800-854-4118; www.trollhau genlodge.com; 10176 Hwy 42; r from $75-100) is close to the action and has a hot tub. In Fish Creek, **Julie's Park Café and Motel** (☎ 920-868-2999; www.juliesmotel.com; 4020 Hwy 42; r $80-120; meals $7-14; ✗) is tidy and well run. In Sturgeon Bay, the kitschy **Chal-A-Motel** (☎ 920-743-6788; 3910 Hwy 42/57; r $64) lets you share the premises with 1000 Barbie dolls, mechanical elves and a DeLorean car in its shed of wonders. Camping and sunset-watching are available at **Peninsula State Park** (☎ 920-868-3258; campsites $10-12) by Fish Creek.

Many restaurants have a 'fish boil,' a regional specialty started by Scandinavian lumberjacks, in which whitefish, potatoes and onions are cooked in a cauldron. It's sedate, until the chef douses the flames with kerosene, and then whoosh! A fireball creates the requisite 'boil over' (which gets rid of the fish oil), signaling dinner is ready. Finish with Door's famous cherry pie.

Attractive **Summer Kitchen** (☎ 920-854-2131; Hwy 42, Ephraim; mains $6-17; ✆ 8am-8pm) serves tasty breakfast, lunch and dinner. At **Shipwrecked** (☎ 920-868-2767; 7791 Egg Harbor Rd, Egg Harbor; mains $12-16; ✆ 11am-10pm) you can wash down a good dinner with the house-made brew; try the cheese curds. Also, sample the smoked fish available around Gills Rock.

From the tip of the peninsula, daily **ferries** (☎ 920-847-2546; www.wisferry.com; Northport Pier) go to **Washington Island** (round-trip adult/child six to 11/ bike/car $10/5/4/22), which has 700 Scandinavian descendants, a couple of museums, beaches, bike rentals and carefree roads for cycling. Accommodations and camping are available. More remote is lovely **Rock Island**, a state park with no cars at all. It's a wonderful place for walking, swimming and camping. Get there via the eponymous **ferry** (☎ 920-535-0122), which departs Jackson Harbor on Washington Island (round-trip adult/child $9/5).

Returning on the peninsula's quiet east side, secluded **Newport State Park** offers trails, camping and solitude. **Whitefish Dunes State Park** has sandscapes and a wide beach (beware of riptides). At adjacent **Cave Point Park**, watch the waves explode into the caves beneath the shoreline cliffs.

NORTHERN WISCONSIN

The north is a thinly populated region of forests and lakes, appreciated for camping and fishing in summer, skiing and snowmobiling in winter. Scenic Hwy 70 cuts east–west. The entire region has abundant mom-and-pop motels, resorts and rental cottages.

Northwoods & Lakelands

Nicolet National Forest is a vast, wooded district ideal for outdoor activities. The simple crossroads of **Langlade** is a center for whitewater river adventures. **Bear Paw Outdoor Resort** (☎ 715-882-3502; www.bearpawoutdoors.com; 3494 Hwy 55) provides trips and accommodations.

In winter **Granite Peak Ski Resort** (☎ 715-845-2846; www.skigranitepeak.com; day pass adult/child $48/38) in **Wausau** perks up, offering 265 skiable acres and a 700ft vertical drop.

In **Lac du Flambeau**, stop at the **Ojibwe Museum & Cultural Center** (☎ 715-588-3333; www .ojibwe.com; 603 Peace Pipe Rd; adult/child $3/2; ✆ 10am-4pm Mon-Fri, 10am-2pm Sat May-Oct, reduced hrs rest of year) or, out of town on the reservation, visit **Waswagoning** (☎ 715-588-2615; www.waswagoning

.com; adult/child 5-12 $8/6; 10am-4pm Tue-Sat, mid-Jun–Aug), a re-creation of a traditional Ojibwe village.

Apostle Islands

Wisconsin ends at the rugged, glaciated littoral of awesome Lake Superior, fringed by a sprinkling of unspoiled islands.

Access to the emerald Apostle Islands is from **Bayfield**, a humming resort town with narrow, hilly streets, Victorian-era buildings, lake vistas and apple orchards. The **Chamber of Commerce** (☎ 715-779-3335; www.bayfield.org; 42 Broad St; 8:30-5pm Mon-Fri) has an attached visitors center, accessible at all times, with lodging information and a free phone. Storefront outfitters renting kayaks and bikes are easily found throughout town.

Bayfield has loads of B&Bs, cottages and other lodging, but reserve ahead in summer. **Tree Top House** (☎ 715-779-3293; www.air streamcomm.net/~treetop; 225 N 4th St; r $40-65) is a delightful B&B. Most rooms at **Seagull Bay Motel** (☎ 715-779-5558; www.seagullbay.com; cnr 7th St & Hwy 13; r summer $70-100, winter $40-70) have decks. **Old Rittenhouse Inn** (☎ 800-779-2129; www.rittenhouseinn.com; 301 Rittenhouse Ave; r $99-299) is by far the classiest place in town.

The **Big Top Chautauqua** (☎ 888-244-8368; www.bigtop.org) is a major regional summer event with big-name concerts and musical theater; call for schedule and prices.

Before exploring the 22 islands of **Apostle Islands National Lakeshore**, drop by the **visitors center** (☎ 715-779-3397; www.nps.gov/apis; 410 Washington Ave; 8am-4:30pm daily Jun-Sep, 8am-4:30pm Mon-Fri Oct-May). Campers can pick up the required camping permit here (it costs $15 no matter how long you stay). The islands have no facilities, and walking is the only way to get around. Various companies offer seasonal charter, sailing and ferry trips to and around the islands, and kayaking is very popular. **Apostle Islands Cruise Service** (☎ 715-779-3925; www.apostleisland.com; mid-May–mid-Oct), departing at 10am from Bayfield's City Dock, offers a three-hour narrated trip past sea caves and lighthouses (adult/child six to 12 $27/16). Other trips call at islands to drop off/pick up campers and their kayaks, which avoids the long, possibly rough paddle.

Inhabited **Madeline Island**, a fine day trip, is also reached by **ferry** (☎ 715-747-2051; www .madferry.com) from Bayfield (round-trip adult/child six to 11/bicycle/car $9.50/5/5/21.50). Its walkable village of La Pointe has some mid-priced places to stay and varying restaurants for a nosh. There's a **visitors center** (☎ 715-747-2801, 888-475-3386; www.madelineisland .com; Middle Rd; 9am-4pm Mon-Fri, reduced hrs winter) and a **historical museum** (☎ 715-747-2415; www.wisconsinhistory.org/madelineisland; adult/child 5-12 $5.50/2.75; 10am-5pm late May-early Oct), with fur-trade exhibits. Bus tours are available, and bikes and mopeds can be rented. **Big Bay State Park** (☎ 715-747-6425; campsites $10-12, vehicle $10) has a beach and trails.

Along Highway 13

This is a fine drive around the Lake Superior shore, past the Ojibwa community of **Red Cliff** and the Apostle Islands' mainland segment, which has a beach. Tiny **Cornucopia**, looking like a seaside village, has great sunsets. The road runs on through a timeless countryside of forest and farm reaching US 2 for the final miles into Superior.

MINNESOTA

Minnesota is the Great Lakes' most remote state, but it rewards intrepid travelers handsomely. Outdoor enthusiasts can wet their paddles in the spectacular Boundary Waters Canoe Area Wilderness, where nighttime brings a blanket of stars and lullaby of wolf howls. The pine-filled north boasts exceptional forests and fishing, while the scenic southeast flaunts eagles along the Mississippi River. If that all seems a bit too far-flung, stick to the Twin Cities of Minneapolis and St Paul, where you can't swing a moose without hitting something cool or cultural. And for those looking for middle ground – ie a cross between the big city and the woods – the dramatic, freighter-filled port of Duluth beckons.

History

The Eastern Sioux were the primary inhabitants when the first French trappers arrived in the 17th century. Starting in the early 18th century, Ojibwa bands (also called Chippewa) moved into northeast Minnesota and, armed with guns traded by the French, pushed the Sioux southwest onto the prairie.

GREAT LAKES

MINNESOTA FACTS

Nicknames North Star State, Gopher State
Population 5 million
Area 86,940 sq miles
Capital city St Paul (population 280,400)
Official bird Common loon
Birthplace of Author F Scott Fitzgerald (1896–1940), actress Judy Garland (1922–69), cartoonist Charles Schultz (1922–2000), songwriter Bob Dylan (b 1941), filmmakers Joel Coen (b 1954) and Ethan Coen (b 1957)
Famous for Introducing Spam, Lucky Charms cereal and Greyhound buses to the masses

---

Timber was the territory's first boom industry, and soon water-powered sawmills arose at Minneapolis, St Paul and Stillwater. Wheat from the prairies also needed to be processed, and the first flour mills were built along the river in the 1820s.

Shortly after its 1858 admission to the Union, Minnesota became the first state to send volunteers to fight the Civil War, but in 1862 an uprising of the displaced Sioux meant a series of bloody battles at home.

The population boomed in the 1880s, with mass immigration (especially from Scandinavia), development of the iron mines and expansion of the railroads. Since the 1920s depleted forests and larger farms have meant a declining rural population, but industry and urban areas have grown steadily.

Information

Minnesota sales tax is 6.5%, with municipalities adding up to 1% more.

Check the following websites for statewide information:

Minnesota highway conditions (☎ 800-542-0220; www.511mn.org)

Minnesota Office of Tourism (☎ 800-657-3700; www.exploreminnesota.com)

Minnesota state park information (☎ 866-857-2757; www.dnr.state.mn.us/state_parks) Park entry requires a vehicle permit (per day/year for residents & nonresidents $7/25). Campsites cost $11 to $23; reservations accepted (fee $8.50).

MINNEAPOLIS–ST PAUL

The sprawling Twin Cities display distinct personalities. Minneapolis is young, forward thinking and environmentally aware, with all the progressive prosperity trimmings – a cache of coffee shops, organic and ethnic eateries, rock and roll clubs and enough theaters to be nicknamed Mini-Apple (second only to the Big Apple, New York City, in per capita venues). St Paul is quiet and dignified, lorded over by a massive old cathedral and refined mansions. Together they represent pure US heartland – industrious, wholesome and friendly – the kind of place where the bus drivers tell everyone to 'Have a nice day,' rain or shine (or snow).

History

Belgian missionary Louis Hennepin preached to local Native Americans in 1680. Zebulon Pike explored the upper reaches of the Mississippi River in 1804, a year after the USA acquired the region in the Louisiana Purchase. Fort Snelling, the most remote outpost of the USA's Northwest Territory, was built in 1820.

Power harnessed from the St Anthony waterfall in the mid-19th century enabled Minneapolis to process wheat from the prairies and timber from the north, and the city's growth spurt began. Today St Paul's German-Irish-Catholic heritage is evident, whereas Minneapolis is more Nordic.

Orientation

The Twin Cities form a metropolis on both sides of the generally hidden Mississippi River. On the west side, downtown Minneapolis – the heart of the two cities – is a modern grid of high-rise buildings, many linked by a series of enclosed overhead walkways called 'Skyways' (very welcome in winter). Despite the name, Uptown is actually southwest of downtown, with Hennepin Ave the main axis. Central St Paul is 10 miles to the east on I-94.

Information

The metro region has multiple telephone area codes. To call from one to another, dial the area code and seven-digit number.

BOOKSTORES

Booksmart (Map pp648-9; ☎ 612-823-5612; 2914 Hennepin Ave S, Minneapolis) In Uptown.

EMERGENCY

Police, fire and ambulance (☎ 911) Emergency.
Victim crisis line (☎ 612-340-5400)

INTERNET ACCESS

Minneapolis has loads of Internet coffee shops, many with free wi-fi, like Spyhouse Coffee (p653).

Minneapolis Public Library (Map pp648-9; ☎ 612-630-6000; www.mplib.org; 300 Nicollet Mall, Minneapolis) Log on for free with a picture ID at this brand-spanking new facility, scheduled to open by this book's publication.

INTERNET RESOURCES

The visitors centers (right) have created easy-to-navigate websites with maps, and restaurant, lodging and attraction coupons (especially for St Paul). The Media listings (below) provide the entertainment lowdown.

MEDIA

City Pages (www.citypages.com) Weekly entertainment freebie.

Pioneer Press (www.twincities.com) St Paul's daily.

Star Tribune (www.startribune.com) The Minneapolis daily.

KNOW-FM 91.1 broadcasts NPR. Community station KFAI-FM 90.3 (106.7FM in St Paul) provides eclectic music and talk.

MEDICAL SERVICES

Fairview University Medical Center (Map pp648-9; ☎ 612-273-6402; 2450 Riverside Ave, Minneapolis)

Walgreens (☎ 612-789-6251; 2643 Central Ave NE, Minneapolis; ☾ 24hr) There many other outlets (not open 24 hourly) closer to downtown.

MONEY

The airport (p655) and Mall of America (p651) have currency-exchange facilities.

Wells Fargo Bank (Map pp648-9; ☎ 612-667-7990; cnr 6th St S & Marquette Ave, Minneapolis) Offers foreign exchange, as well as an ATM and regular bank services.

POST

Post office (Map pp648-9; ☎ 800-275-8777; 100 1st S, Minneapolis) In a stunning art deco building.

TOURIST INFORMATION

Minneapolis visitors center (Map pp648-9; ☎ 612-335-6000, 888-676-6757; www.minneapolis.org; 1301 2nd Ave S; ☾ 8am-4:30pm) In the Convention Center.

St Paul visitors center (Map p650; ☎ 651-265-4900, 800-627-6101; www.visitstpaul.com; 175 W Kellogg Blvd, Suite 502, St Paul; ☾ 8am-4:30pm Mon-Fri) In the RiverCentre.

Sights

Most attractions are closed Monday; many stay open late Thursday.

MINNEAPOLIS

The first-class, recently expanded **Walker Art Center** (Map pp648-9; ☎ 612-375-7622; www.walkerart .org; 725 Vineland Pl; adult/child 12-18 $8/5, Thu evening admission free; ☾ 11am-5pm Tue-Sun, 11am-9pm Thu & Fri) has a strong permanent collection of 20th-century art and photography, including big-name US painters and great US pop art.

Beside the Walker is the 7-acre **Minneapolis Sculpture Garden** (Map pp648-9; admission free;

MINNEAPOLIS–ST PAUL IN...

Two Days

Spend the first day in Minneapolis. Visit the **Walker Art Center** (above) and the **Minneapolis Sculpture Garden** (above). Walk the trail by **St Anthony Falls** (p648), the power source of the timber and flour mills that gave rise to the city. Have dinner and drinks in **Uptown** (p653), a hip punk-yuppie neighborhood. Still feeling frisky? Find a noisy rock club (the city is filled with them). The second day is for St Paul. Peek in the **Cathedral of St Paul** (p650), then stroll by the mansions of the **Summit-Selby** (p650) neighborhood, F Scott Fitzgerald's old stomping ground. Take a break at **Grand Avenue's** restaurants (p654). Stroll **Harriet Island** (p651), then take a tour of St Paul's **underground caves** (p652). Spend the evening at one of the myriad **theaters** (p654) of the Twin Cities.

Four Days

Follow the two-day itinerary. On your third day rent a bike or canoe and explore the city's parks and lakes, such as **Calhoun**, **Cedar** or **Harriet** (p651). You can't put it off any longer: on day four, shop at the **Mall of America** (p651), the country's largest. If you still have energy, visit the old mill city of **Stillwater** (p656).

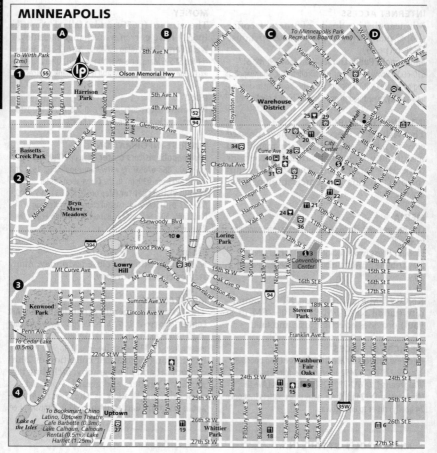

MINNEAPOLIS

6am–midnight), studded with contemporary works, like the oft-photographed spoon and cherry. The garden is connected to attractive Loring Park by a sculptural pedestrian bridge over I-94.

The **St Anthony Falls Heritage Trail** (Map pp648–9), on the north edge of downtown at the foot of Portland Ave, is a recommended 2-mile path that provides both interesting history (markers dot the route) and the city's best access to the banks of the Mississippi. View the cascading falls from the car-free Stone Arch Bridge. On the north side of the river, Main St SE has a stretch of redeveloped buildings housing restaurants and bars. Pick up a trail map and learn about the era when Minneapolis

led the world in flour milling at the **Mill City Museum** (Map pp648-9; ☎ 612-341-7555; www .millcitymuseum.org; 704 2nd St S; adult/child 6-17 $8/4; ☺ 10am-5pm Tue-Sat, 10am-9pm Thu, noon-5pm Sun). It's housed in an old mill, and offers rides inside an eight-story grain elevator ('the Flour Tower') and a baking lab.

The **Minneapolis Institute of Arts** (Map pp648-9; ☎ 612-870-3131; www.artsmia.org; 2400 3rd Ave S; admission free; ☺ 10am-5pm Tue-Sat, 10am-9pm Thu, 11am-5pm Sun) houses a veritable history of art, especially European. The Prairie School and Asian galleries are also highlights.

Within a mile or two of downtown, a ring of lakes circles the inner-city area. Cedar Lake, Lake of the Isles (Map pp648–9), Lake Calhoun and Lake Harriet are surrounded

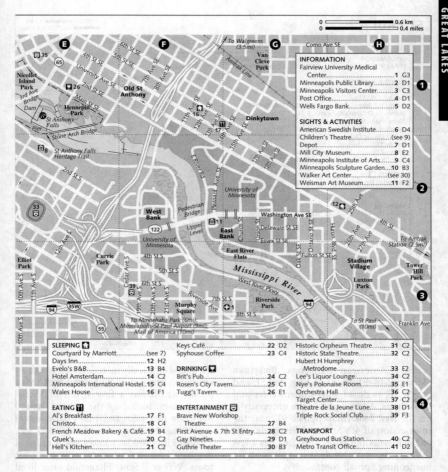

SLEEPING			Keys Café..........................**22** D2	Historic Orpheum Theatre........**31** C2
Courtyard by Marriott............(see 7)			Spyhouse Coffee..................**23** C4	Historic State Theatre..............**32** C2
Days Inn.....................**12** H2				Hubert H Humphrey
Evelo's B&B..................**13** B4			DRINKING	Metrodome....................**33** E2
Hotel Amsterdam...........**14** C2			Brit's Pub..........................**24** C2	Lee's Liquor Lounge..............**34** C2
Minneapolis International Hostel..**15** C4			Rosen's City Tavern..............**25** C1	Nye's Polonaise Room............**35** E1
Wales House..................**16** F1			Tugg's Tavern....................**26** E1	Orchestra Hall....................**36** C2
				Target Center....................**37** C2
EATING			ENTERTAINMENT	Theatre de la Jeune Lune........**38** D1
Al's Breakfast................**17** F1			Brave New Workshop	Triple Rock Social Club...........**39** F3
Christos.......................**18** C4			Theatre........................**27** B4	
French Meadow Bakery & Café..**19** B4			First Avenue & 7th St Entry....**28** C2	TRANSPORT
Gluek's.......................**20** C2			Gay Nineties....................**29** D1	Greyhound Bus Station..........**40** C2
Hell's Kitchen................**21** C2			Guthrie Theater.................**30** B3	Metro Transit Office..............**41** D2

by parks and comfortable suburbs. Cycling paths (cross-country ski trails in winter) meander around the lakes, where you can go boating in summer or ice-skating in winter. **Wirth Park**, just west of downtown, has the full gamut. **Thomas Beach**, on Lake Calhoun, is popular for swimming; for bicycling and canoeing, see p651. Also visit **Minnehaha Park**, 6 miles south of downtown, to view the falls made famous by Longfellow's epic poem *Hiawatha*, though Longfellow never actually visited. Call the **Parks Board** (☎ 612-230-6400; www.minneapolisparks.org) for recreation information.

The **American Swedish Institute** (Map pp648–9; ☎ 612-871-4907; www.americanswedishinst.org; 2600 Park Ave S; adult/child 6-18 $5/3; ☻ noon-4pm Tue-

Sat, noon-8pm Wed, 1-5pm Sun) is a magnificent Romanesque mansion, with artifacts and antiques from the time when Minneapolis had a bigger Swedish population than most cities in Sweden.

The **University of Minnesota** (Map pp648–9), by the river southeast of Minneapolis' center, is one of the USA's largest campuses, with over 50,000 students. Most of the campus is in the **East Bank** (Map pp648–9) neighborhood. A highlight in the area is the **Weisman Art Museum** (Map pp648–9; ☎ 612-625-9494; www.weisman.umn.edu; 333 E River Rd; admission free; ☻ 10am-5pm Tue-Fri, 10am-8pm Thu, 11am-5pm Sat & Sun), which occupies an angular, irregular, stainless-steel structure by architect Frank Gehry. Works inside include early 20th-

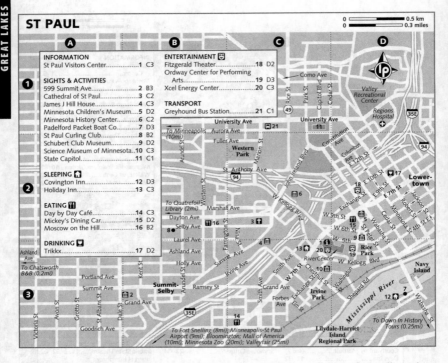

ST PAUL

0 _____ 0.5 km
0 _____ 0.3 miles

INFORMATION
St Paul Visitors Center...............1 C3

SIGHTS & ACTIVITIES
599 Summit Ave........................2 B3
Cathedral of St Paul..................3 C2
James J Hill House....................4 C3
Minnesota Children's Museum.....5 D2
Minnesota History Center..........6 C2
Padelford Packet Boat Co...........7 D3
St Paul Curling Club..................8 B2
Schubert Club Museum..............9 D2
Science Museum of Minnesota...10 C3
State Capitol..........................11 C1

SLEEPING
Covington Inn.........................12 D3
Holiday Inn............................13 C3

EATING
Day by Day Café......................14 C3
Mickey's Dining Car..................15 D2
Moscow on the Hill..................16 B2

DRINKING
Trikkx...................................17 D2

ENTERTAINMENT
Fitzgerald Theater....................18 D2
Ordway Center for Performing
Arts....................................19 D3
Xcel Energy Center...................20 C3

TRANSPORT
Greyhound Bus Station..............21 C1

century American paintings. **Dinkytown** (Map pp648–9), based at 14th Ave SE and 4th St SE, is dense with student cafés and bookshops. A small part of the university is on the **West Bank** (Map pp648–9), near the intersection of 4th St S and Riverside Ave, of the Mississippi river. This area has a few restaurants, some student hangouts and a burgeoning Somali community.

Uptown (Map pp648–9), based around the intersection of Hennepin Ave S and Lake St, is a punk-yuppie collision of shops and restaurants south of downtown. It stays lively until late.

ST PAUL

Smaller and quieter than Minneapolis, St Paul has retained more of its historic character, although construction continues to modernize it.

The **Cathedral of St Paul** (Map p650; ☎ 651-228-1766; www.cathedralsaintpaul.org; 239 Selby Ave; admission free; ☽ 7:30am-6pm) presides over the city from its hilltop perch and marks the attractive **Summit-Selby** (Map p650) neighborhood. This wealthy 19th-century dis-

trict, now ethnically mixed, is well worth an afternoon stroll. Follow **Summit Avek** (Map p650), which has a fine string of Victorian houses, including the palatial **James J Hill House** (Map p650; ☎ 651-297-2555; www.mnhs .org/hillhouse; 240 Summit Ave; adult/child 6-17 $8/4; ☽ 10am-3:30pm Wed-Sat, 1-3:30pm Sun), a railroad magnate's former mansion, now open for tours. Writer F Scott Fitzgerald once lived at **599 Summit Avenue** (Map p650), and authors Garrison Keillor and Sinclair Lewis have also called the area home. Literary buffs can pick up the *Fitzgerald Homes and Haunts* map at the St Paul visitors center. Restaurants and shops are bunched along Selby and Grand Aves.

From November through March stop in and watch the action at the **St Paul Curling Club** (Map p650; ☎ 651-224-7408; www.stpaulcurling .club.org; 470 Selby Ave). For those uninitiated in northern ways, curling is a winter sport that involves sliding a hubcab-sized 'puck' down the ice toward a bull's-eye.

The turreted 1902 Landmark Center, facing Rice Park, contains the **Schubert Club Museum** (Map p650; ☎ 651-292-3267; www.schubert

.org; basement, 75 W 5th St; admission free; ☒ 11am-3pm Mon-Fri, 1-5pm Sun), which has a brilliant collection of old pianos and harpsichords, some tickled by Mozart, Beethoven and the like.

The **Science Museum of Minnesota** (Map p650; ☎ 651-221-9444; www.smm.org; 120 W Kellogg Blvd; for exhibits only adult/child 4-12 $8.50/6.50; ☒ 9:30am-5pm Mon-Wed, 9:30am-9pm Thu-Sat, noon-5pm Sun) has the usual hands-on kids' exhibits and Omnimax theater, but the wacky quackery of the 'questionable medical devices' area takes it beyond the norm.

The **Minnesota History Center** (Map p650; ☎ 651-296-6126; www.mnhs.org; 345 W Kellogg Blvd; adult/child 6-17 $8/4; ☒ 10am-8pm Tue, 10am-5pm Wed-Sat, noon-5pm Sun, plus 10am-5pm Mon summer) caters to serious researchers, but has excellent public exhibits on native peoples and state history.

Revitalized **Harriet Island** (Map p650), running off Wabasha St S, is a lovely place to meander; it has a park, river walk, concert stages and fishing dock. **Padelford Packet Boat Co** (Map p650; ☎ 651-227-1100; www.riverrides .com) operates 1½-hour paddleboat tours (adult/child five to 12 $15/7.50) from the dock. Tours begin at noon and 2pm daily from June to August, and at 2pm Saturday and Sunday only in May and September.

The Cass Gilbert–designed **State Capitol** (Map p650; ☎ 651-296-2881; 75 Constitution Ave; admission free; ☒ 9am-5pm Mon-Fri, 10am-4pm Sat, 1-4pm Sun) has golden horses on its giant dome; tours are available.

SOUTHERN SUBURBS

In Bloomington, the **Mall of America** (☎ 952-883-8800; www.mallofamerica.com; off I-494 at 24th Ave; ☒ 10am-9:30pm Mon-Sat, 11am-7pm Sun) is the USA's largest shopping center. Yes, it's just a mall, filled with the usual stores, movie theaters and eateries. But there's also a roller coaster inside, and a large aquarium – all under one enormous roof. Take the Hiawatha light-rail from downtown. For details of its attractions for kids, see right.

East of the mall, **Fort Snelling** (☎ 612-726-1171; www.mnhs.org/places/sites/hfs; cnr Hwys 5 & 55; adult/child 6-17 $8/4; ☒ 10am-5pm Mon-Sat, noon-5pm Sun Jun-Aug, 10am-5pm Sat, noon-5pm Sun only May & Sep-Oct) is the state's oldest structure, established in the early 19th century as a frontier outpost in the remote Northwest Territory. Guides in period dress show restored buildings and re-enact pioneer life.

Activities

The parks around the Twin Cities and lakes offer plenty of ways to stay active, summer or winter.

BICYCLING

The parks are crisscrossed with bike paths. Get wheels at **Calhoun Rental** (☎ 612-827-8231; 1622 W Lake St; bicycle per hr $7.50; ☒ 10am-7pm Apr-Oct, extended hrs summer) in Uptown; credit card and driver's license required. Bike trails also line both sides of the Mississippi River; the **Minneapolis website** (www.ci.minneapolis.mn.us/citywork /public-works/transportation/bicycles/maps) has maps.

CANOEING

Lake of the Isles is a wonderful place to paddle away the day, and the **Minneapolis Park & Recreation Board** (☎ 612-370-4883; www .minneapolisparks.org; 3000 E Calhoun Pkwy, Minneapolis; canoe/kayak per hr $10/10; ☒ 10am-6pm daily late May-early Sep, 10am-6pm Sat & Sun only early Sep-Oct) rents a slew of vessels.

Minneapolis-St Paul for Children

Check the **Minneapolis-kids.com** (www.minne apolis-kids.org) website for the latest on kids' offerings.

MALL OF AMERICA

Prepare to spend a wad once you unleash the kids at the country's largest **mall** (☎ 952-883-8800; www.mallofamerica.com; off I-494 at 24th Ave, Bloomington; ☒ 10am-9:30pm Mon-Sat, 11am-7pm Sun). They will want to make a beeline to **Camp Snoopy** (☎ 952-883-8555; www.campsnoopy.com), the much-touted indoor amusement park. It features 25 rides, including a little roller coaster. To walk through will cost you nothing; a one-day, unlimited-ride wristband is $25, or you can pay for rides individually ($2.50 to $5). The kids will also discover **Lego Imagination Center** (admission free), which is located in the mall.

Underwater Adventures (☎ 952-883-0202; www .sharky.tv; adult/child 3-12/child 13-17 $15/9/13) is the state's largest aquarium, where children can touch sharks and stingrays.

The hours for each attraction correspond roughly to general mall hours. For more information, see left.

MINNESOTA CHILDREN'S MUSEUM

This **museum** (Map p650; ☎ 651-225-6000; www .mcm.org; 10 W 7th St, St Paul; admission $8; ☒ 9am-5pm

Tue-Sun, 9am-8pm Thu year-round, plus 9am-5pm Mon summer) has the usual gamut of hands-on activities, as well as a giant ant hill to burrow through, and the 'One World' intercultural community where kids can shop and vote.

OTHER SIGHTS

The **Minnesota History Center** (Map p650; ☎ 651-296-6126; www.mnhs.org; 345 W Kellogg Blvd; adult/child 6-17 $8/4; ◷ 10am-8pm Tue, 10am-5pm Wed-Sat, noon-5pm Sun, plus 10am-5pm Mon summer) educates with its 'A to Z' treasure hunt and climbable boxcar, while the **Science Museum of Minnesota** (Map p650; ☎ 651-221-9444; www.smm.org; 120 W Kellogg Blvd; for exhibits only adult/child 4-12 $8.50/6.50; ◷ 9:30am-5pm Mon-Wed, 9:30am-9pm Thu-Sat, noon-5pm Sun) pleases kids with its laser show and Omnimax. For more information about both sights, see p651 and p651 respectively.

The recently expanded **Children's Theatre** (Map p650; ☎ 612-874-0400; www.childrenstheatre.org; 2400 3rd Ave S) is so good it has won a Tony award for 'outstanding regional theater.'

The respected **Minnesota Zoo** (☎ 952-431-9500; www.mnzoo.org; 13000 Zoo Blvd; adult/child 3-12 $12/7; ◷ 9am-6pm summer, 9am-4pm winter; (P)), in suburban Apple Valley, 20 miles south of town, has naturalistic habitats for its 400-plus species, with an emphasis on cold-climate creatures. The rides at Camp Snoopy are child's play compared to what's out at **Valleyfair** (☎ 952-445-7600; www.valleyfair.com; 1 Valleyfair Dr; adult/child $34/18; ◷ from 10am daily Jun-Aug, from 10am Sat & Sun May & Sep, closing times vary), a full-scale amusement park 25 miles southwest in Shakopee.

Tours

Down In History Tours (☎ 651-292-1220; www.wabashastreetcaves.com; 215 S Wabasha St) One tour walks you through St Paul's underground caves ($5), which gangsters once used as a speakeasy. The company offers several other fun, offbeat tours, too. Call for the tour schedule.

Magical History Tours (☎ 952-888-9200; www.humanonastick.com) This company puts visitors on S egway scooters for a guided five-mile three-hour historical zip along the riverfront ($70).

Festivals & Events

St Paul Winter Carnival (☎ 651-223-4700; www.winter-carnival.com; admission varies depending on event) Ten days of ice sculptures, ice skating and ice fishing in January.

Minneapolis Aquatennial (☎ 612-376-7669; www.aquatennial.org; admission free) Ten days celebrating the ubiquitous lakes in mid-July.

Sleeping

You get good quality for your money in the Twin Cities. Rooms cost more in summer. The 13% tax is not included in the following prices.

MINNEAPOLIS
Budget

Minneapolis International Hostel (Map pp648-9; ☎ 612-871-3210; www.minneapolishostel.com; 2400 Stevens Ave S; dm $20-24, r $29-60; (P)) This homey hostel beside the Institute of Arts has antique furniture, wood floors and fluffy quilts on the beds. Reservations recommended; parking is $10.

Midrange

Wales House (Map pp648-9; ☎ 612-331-3931; www.waleshouse.com; 1115 5th St SE; r with/without bathroom $65/55; (P)) This cheery 10-bedroom home often caters to scholars at the nearby University of Minnesota. It has free wi-fi and welcoming common areas, like a season-round porch and lounge with fireplace.

Evelo's B&B (Map pp648-9; ☎ 612-374-9656; sevelo@mpls.k12.mn.us; 2301 Bryant Ave; r $65-85) Evelo's is in a quiet neighborhood between the Walker Art Center and Uptown. The Victorian home has beautiful woodwork, lots of windows and light, and three comfy rooms.

Days Inn (Map pp648-9; ☎ 612-623-3999; www.daysinn.com; 2407 University Ave SE; r $69-129; (P)) This is a high-end Days Inn that often caters to people in town for events (when prices move to the upper end of the spectrum).

Top End

Courtyard by Marriott (Map pp648-9; ☎ 612-375-1700; www.thedepotminneapolis.com; 225 3rd Ave S; r $189-229; (P)) This Courtyard is pretty sweet for a chain hotel. It's located in the historic riverfront Depot, which also houses an indoor ice rink and waterpark. Rooms have free high-speed Internet access, with wi-fi in the lobby. Parking costs $13.

ST PAUL
Midrange

Chatsworth B&B (Map p650; ☎ 651-227-4288; www.chatsworth-bb.com; 984 Ashland Ave; r $99-169; (P)) Sweetly situated in a Summit-area Victorian house dating from 1902, Chatsworth has serene gardens and cozy rooms, and is near Grand Ave's restaurants.

Holiday Inn (Map p650; ☎ 651-225-1515; 175 W 7th St; r $79-169; P ⊜) Adjacent to the RiverCentre. Parking is $13.

Top End

Covington Inn (Map p650; ☎ 651-292-1411; www.covingtoninn.com; Pier 1, Harriet Island; r $140-235; P) This charming B&B is on a tugboat floating in the Mississippi River, where you can watch the river traffic glide by while sipping your morning coffee. It's located across from St Paul's downtown.

Eating

Lots of fun, good-value options exist in both cities.

MINNEAPOLIS

Areas dense with restaurants include Nicollet Mall downtown; Nicollet Ave S between 14th and 29th Sts (otherwise known as 'Eat Street') lined with Vietnamese, Mexican and other ethnic eateries; and the campus area by Washington Ave and Oak St.

Downtown

Hell's Kitchen (Map pp648-9; ☎ 612-332-4700; www.hellskitcheninc.com; 89 10th St S; mains $9-14; ❤ breakfast & lunch) Spirited chefs and waitstaff bring you uniquely Minnesotan foods, like the walleye bacon-lettuce-tomato sandwich or bison burger, plus lemon-ricotta hotcakes for breakfast.

Keys Café (Map pp648-9; ☎ 612-339-6399; www.keyscafe.com; 821 Marquette Ave; mains $4-10; ❤ 6:30am-10pm Mon-Fri, 7am-10pm Sat, 8am-10pm Sun) The

bustling Keys, a local chain, dishes up luscious breakfasts and sandwiches; try the caramel rolls.

Gluek's (Map pp648-9; ☎ 612-338-6621; 16 6th St N; mains $7-16; ❤ 11am-2am Mon-Sat) Pot roast, macaroni-and-cheese with spaetzle and other good meals have emerged from the Gluek's German kitchen since 1902.

Uptown

Chino Latino (☎ 612-824-7878; www.chinolatino.com; 2916 Hennepin Ave S; shared plates $14-26; ❤ dinner) This shiny, spangled place is the Uptown scenester hangout. The food is Latin-Asian fusion, with novelties such as a satay bar and the large, shared *pupu* (Polynesian-influenced appetizer) platter.

French Meadow Bakery & Café (Map pp648-9; ☎ 612-870-7855; www.frenchmeadow.com; 2610 Lyndale Ave S; sandwiches $7-8, mains $14-18; ❤ 6:30am-10pm Sun-Thu, 6:30am-11pm Fri & Sat) French Meadow focuses on local and organic ingredients. On warm days (true, there aren't that many, so seize this opportunity when it comes), you can't beat a plate of Belgian waffles with fresh berries while sitting curbside in the sun.

Café Barbette (☎ 612-827-5710; www.barbette.com; 1600 W Lake St; mains $9-18; ❤ 8am-1am Sun-Thu, 8am-2am Fri & Sat) Intimate, Parisian-style Barbette welcomes with low booths and art-filled walls. It's good for wine, cheese and appetizers with friends, or for a romantic dinner with a date, but whatever you do, don't miss the warm chocolate cake.

Spyhouse Coffee (Map pp648-9; ☎ 612-871-3177; 2451 Nicollet Ave; items $2-4; ❤ 7am-midnight Mon-Fri,

---

GAY & LESBIAN TWIN CITIES

Minneapolis has the country's second-highest percentage of gay, lesbian, bisexual and transgender (GLBT) residents – second only to San Francisco – and the city enjoys strong GLBT rights. **OutFront Minnesota** (☎ 612-822-0127; www.outfront.org) provides information on GLBT-friendly local businesses and harassment incident reporting, among its many programs.

For venues and events, check the free, bi-weekly **Lavender** (www.lavendermagazine.com). The **Quatrefoil Library** (☎ 651-641-0969; www.quatrefoillibrary.org; 1619 Dayton Ave, St Paul; ❤ 7-9pm Mon-Fri, 10am-5pm Sat, 1-5pm Sun) has a large collection of GLBT books, periodicals and DVDs. The late-June **Pride Festival** (☎ 952-852-6100; www.tcpride.com; admission free), one of the USA's largest, draws about 400,000 revelers.

For sleeping, the European-style **Hotel Amsterdam** (Map pp648-9; ☎ 612-288-0459; 828 Hennepin Ave, Minneapolis; r $44-65; 🖳) bills itself as 'the inn that's out.' Rooms are located above a busy bar; they are utilitarian but clean, and all share a bath.

For nightlife, **Trikkx** (Map p650; ☎ 651-224-0703; www.trikkx.com; 490 N Robert St, St Paul; ❤ 5pm-2am) is a noted hot spot. At **Gay Nineties** (Map pp648-9; ☎ 612-333-7755; www.gay90s.com; 408 Hennepin Ave, Minneapolis), dancing, dining and drag shows attract both a gay and straight clientele.

8am-midnight Sat & Sun) Join the artsy crowd stopping in for coffee and baked goods.

Elsewhere
Al's Breakfast (Map pp648-9; ☎ 612-331-9991; 413 14th Ave SE; mains $3-6; ☺ 6am-1pm Mon-Sat, 9am-1pm Sun) It's the ultimate hole-in-the-wall: 15 stools at a tiny counter. Whenever a customer comes in, everyone picks up their plates and scoots down to make room for the newcomer. Fruit-full pancakes are the big crowd-pleaser.

Christos (Map pp648-9; ☎ 612-871-2111; www .christos.com; 2632 Nicollet Ave S; mains $14-19; ☺ 11am-9pm Sun-Thu, 11am-10pm Fri & Sat) Popular Christos is reminiscent of a Greek taverna, with moussaka, souvlakia and all the staples; lots of vegetarian options, too.

ST PAUL
Grand Ave between Dale and Victoria Sts is a worthy browse, with Algerian, Nepalese, Japanese and other eateries in close proximity. University Ave, west of the capitol, has dozens of cheap Southeast Asian restaurants.

Mickey's Dining Car (Map p650; ☎ 651-222-5633; 36 W 7th St; mains $3-7; ☺ 24hr) Mickey's is a downtown classic, the kind of place where the friendly waitress calls you 'honey' and satisfied regulars line the bar with their coffee cups and newspapers. The food has timeless appeal, too: burgers, malts and apple pie.

Moscow on the Hill (Map p650; ☎ 651-291-1236; www.moscowonthehill.com; 371 Selby Ave; mains $13-20; ☺ lunch Mon-Fri, dinner nightly) On cold gray days, come to Moscow for Eastern European comfort food (ie stews). Start with a traditional shot of Stoli and a little sweet-pickle garnish.

Day by Day Café (Map p650; ☎ 651-227-0654; 477 W 7th St; mains $5-7; ☺ 6am-8pm Mon-Fri, 6am-3pm Sat, 7am-3pm Sun) Read the paper while munching breakfast or soup/salad/sandwich staples at this bright café.

Drinking
Brit's Pub (Map pp648-9; ☎ 612-332-3908; 1110 Nicollet Mall) It's not every day you go to a drinking establishment with a lawn bowling green on its roof. And that isn't all: you will find that there's a large selection of Scotch, port and beer to boot.

Rosen's City Tavern (Map pp648-9; ☎ 612-338-1926; 430 1st Ave N) This is one of many busy

places in Minneapolis' Warehouse District that pours a fine brew.

Tugg's Tavern (Map pp648-9; ☎ 612-379-4404; 219 Main St SE) Tugg's draw is its swell outdoor patio on the Mississippi River's revitalized north-side strip.

Entertainment
With its large student population and thriving performing arts scene, the Twin Cities offer an active nightlife. Check **TC Tix** (☎ 612-288-2060; www.tctix.com) for same-day discounts.

THEATERS
The region is applauded for its huge range of performing arts companies, including dozens of fine theater troupes, dance companies and classical music groups. For listings, see the local print media (p647). In particular, look for events at the following venues (all in 'Mini-Apple' unless otherwise noted):

Brave New Workshop Theatre (Map pp648-9; ☎ 612-332-6620; www.bravenewworkshop.com; 2605 Hennepin Ave) An established venue for musical comedy, revue and satire.

Fitzgerald Theater (Map p650; ☎ 651-290-1221; www.fitzgeraldtheater.org; 10 E Exchange St, St Paul) Where Garrison Keillor tapes his Prairie Home Companion radio show.

Guthrie Theater (Map pp648-9; ☎ 612-377-2224; www.guthrietheater.org; 725 Vineland Pl) Quality classical and contemporary performances. The Guthrie is scheduled to open its jumbo new facility just east of Mill City Museum by this book's publication.

Historic Orpheum Theatre (Map pp648-9; ☎ 612-339-7007; www.hennepintheatredistrict.org; 910 Hennepin Ave) The usual venue for Broadway shows and touring acts.

THE AUTHOR'S CHOICE

Nye's Polonaise Room (Map pp648-9; ☎ 612-379-2021; www.nyespolonaise.com; 112 E Hennepin Ave, Minneapolis) Nye's serves traditional Polish foods, like pierogi and spare ribs, but the real draw is dancing to the World's Most Dangerous Polka Band from Thursday through Saturday. Slip away from your table, pass through the swinging doors with ship-style portholes and find an old-timer – male or female – to twirl you around the room. Join the crooning in the piano lounge the rest of the week.

Historic State Theatre (Map pp648-9; ☎ 612-339-7007; www.hennepintheatredistrict.org; 805 Hennepin Ave) Hosts Broadway shows and touring acts.

Orchestra Hall (Map pp648-9; ☎ 612-371-5656; www.minnesotaorchestra.org; 1111 Nicollet Mall) Superb acoustics, a great venue for recitals and concerts by the acclaimed Minnesota Symphony Orchestra.

Ordway Center for Performing Arts (Map p650; ☎ 651-224-4222; www.ordway.org; 345 Washington St, St Paul) A chamber music venue and home of the Minnesota Opera.

Theatre de la Jeune Lune (Map pp648-9; ☎ 612-333-6200; www.jeunelune.org; 105 1st St N) Features experimental French-American collaborations.

LIVE MUSIC

Acts such as Prince and proto-grunge bands, like Hüsker Dü and the Replacements, cut their chops here. All the clubs listed are in Minneapolis, which is where the action is.

First Avenue & 7th St Entry (Map pp648-9; ☎ 612-338-8388; www.first-ave.com; 701 1st Ave N) This is the bedrock of Minneapolis' music scene, and it still pulls in top bands and big crowds.

Triple Rock Social Club (Map pp648-9; ☎ 612-333-7499; www.triplerocksocialclub.com; 629 Cedar Ave) A popular punk/alternative club.

Lee's Liquor Lounge (Map pp648-9; ☎ 612-338-9491; www.leesliquorlounge.com; 101 Glenwood Ave) Rockabilly and country-tinged alt bands twang here.

CINEMAS

Uptown Theatre (☎ 612-825-6006; 2906 Hennepin Ave S, Minneapolis) Catch art-house flicks in Uptown.

SPORTS

Football and hockey are the big tickets in town.

Hubert H Humphrey Metrodome (Map pp648-9; 900 5th St S, Minneapolis) Both the **Vikings** (☎ 612-338-4537; www.vikings.com) pro football team and **Twins** (☎ 612-338-9467; www.minnesotatwins.com) major league baseball team play in the Metrodome.

Target Center (Map pp648-9; ☎ 612-337-3865; www.nba.com/timberwolves; 600 1st Ave N, Minneapolis) This is where the Timberwolves pro basketball team lays 'em up.

Xcel Energy Center (Map p650; ☎ 651-222-9453; www.wild.com; Kellogg Blvd, St Paul) The Wild pro hockey team skates here.

Getting There & Around

AIR

The **Minneapolis-St Paul International Airport** (☎ 612-726-5555; www.mspairport.com) is between the two cities to the south. It's the home of Northwest Airlines, which operates several direct flights to/from Europe.

The cheapest way to Minneapolis is via the Hiawatha light-rail line (25 minutes); to St Paul; take bus No 54 (25 minutes). See Public Transportation (below) for details.

SuperShuttle (☎ 612-827-7777; www.supershuttle.com) also runs to downtown Minneapolis and St Paul ($14 each). A cab to Minneapolis/St Paul costs $25/14.

BUS

From both cities there is a **Greyhound bus station** (Minneapolis ☎ 612-371-3325; 950 Hawthorne Ave; St Paul ☎ 651-222-0507; 166 W University Ave), with buses traveling daily to Milwaukee ($52 to $68, seven hours), Chicago ($60 to $80, nine hours) and Duluth ($25 to $40, three hours).

CAR

National car-rental agencies have offices at the airport and around town. Check rental information p1175 for contact details.

PUBLIC TRANSPORTATION

Metro Transit (☎ 612-373-3333; www.metrotransit.org) runs frequent and well-used buses throughout the area ($1.50, plus 50¢ for express or rush-hour buses), as well as the excellent Hiawatha light-rail line ($1.50) between downtown and the Mall of America. Express bus No 94 connects the Twin Cities. A day pass ($6) is available; pick it up with route maps at the downtown **Metro Transit Office** (719 Marquette Ave, Minneapolis; ☒ 7:30am-5:30pm Mon-Fri).

TAXI

For cab service, call **Yellow Taxi** (☎ 612-824-4000).

TRAIN

The **Amtrak station** (☎ 651-644-1127; 730 Transfer Rd), off University Ave SE, is between the Twin Cities. Trains go daily to Chicago ($59 to 105, eight hours) and Seattle ($205 to $270, 37 hours). The ride east to La Crosse, Wisconsin, is beautiful, skirting the Mississippi River and offering multiple eagle sightings.

SOUTHEASTERN MINNESOTA

Some of the scenic southeast can be seen on short drives from the Twin Cities. Better is a loop of a few days' duration, following the rivers and stopping in some of the historic towns and state parks.

A few miles east of St Paul, the **St Croix River** forms the border with Wisconsin. Northeast of the city along US 61, then east on US 8, attractive Taylors Falls marks the upper limit of navigation. Take a walk along the gorge in Interstate Park. Due east of St Paul, on Hwy 36, touristy **Stillwater**, on the lower St Croix, is an old logging town with restored 19th-century buildings, river cruises and antique stores. Larger **Red Wing** to the south on US 61, is a similar but less-interesting restored town, though it does offer its famous Red Wing Shoes (actually more like sturdy boots) and salt glaze pottery.

The best part of the **Mississippi Valley** area begins south of here, but on the Wisconsin side – cross the river on US 63 (see p642).

Maiden Rock, on Wisconsin Hwy 35 downstream from Red Wing, offers views from its 400ft Indian-legend namesake. A bit further south, a great stretch of Hwy 35 edges beside the bluffs around **Stockholm** (population 90).

Continuing south, cross back over the river to **Wabasha**, in Minnesota, which has a historic downtown and large population of bald eagles that congregate in winter. To learn more, visit the **National Eagle Center** (☎ 651-565-4989; www.nationaleaglecenter.org; 152 W Main St; admission free; ☼ 10am-4pm Tue-Sun). **Rivertown Café** (☎ 651-565-2202; 119 Pembroke St; dinners from $7; ☼ breakfast & lunch daily, dinner Wed, Fri & Sat) provides a taste of small-town America.

On the Wisconsin side again, Hwy 35 is very scenic heading south to **Alma**, offering superlative views from Buena Vista Park. Cross the river once again further downstream at **Winona**. This former port offers historical exhibits aboard the **Wilkie Steamboat Center** (☎ 507-454-1254; foot of Main St; adult/child 6-12 $3.50/2; ☼ 10am-4pm Wed-Sun early Jun-early Sep), as well as river cruises from adjacent Levee Park. Landlubbers can enjoy river views from Garvin Heights Park and eagle views in winter.

Inland and south, the Bluff Country is dotted with limestone bluffs, the southeast corner's main geological feature. **Lanesboro** is a gem and acts as an activity center. Cycling on rails-to-trails and canoeing are popular. Seven miles westward on County Rd 8 (call for directions), **Old Barn Resort** (☎ 507-467-2512; www.barnresort.com; dm/s/d $20/30/40, campsite/RV site $22/30 Apr-early Nov) is a pastoral hostel cum campground/restaurant/outfitter.

Harmony, south of Lanesboro, is the center of an Amish community, and another welcoming town. You can stay at **Selvig House B&B** (☎ 507-886-2200; www.selvighouse.com; 140 Center St E; r $110).

Head north on US 52 to **Rochester**, home of the famed **Mayo Clinic** (☎ 507-284-2511; 200 1st St SW), which attracts medical patients and practitioners from around the world. Free morning tours (at 10am weekdays) and a film outline the Mayo brothers' story and describe how the clinic developed its cutting-edge reputation.

Southwest of Rochester, on I-90, **Austin** is home to the **Spam Museum** (☎ 800-588-7726; www.spam.com; 1937 Spam Blvd; admission free; ☼ 10am-5pm Mon-Sat, noon-4pm Sun May-Aug, closed Mon Sep-Apr), where visitors can pay homage to the peculiar, revered tins of meat.

NORTHEASTERN MINNESOTA

Duluth

At the westernmost end of the Great Lakes, Duluth (with its neighbor, Superior, Wisconsin) is one of the busiest ports in the country, sporting over 40 miles of wharf and waterfront. Daniel Du Lhut brokered a peace agreement here in 1679 with the Ojibwa and Sioux nations, which enabled French adventurers to develop the fur trade. Duluth grew as a shipping point for timber and, later, for Minnesota's iron ore.

Duluth's dramatic location (it's built into a cliffside) is an excellent place to see changeable Lake Superior in action. It can shimmer like a cut diamond one minute, then send off ferocious, ice-capped waves the next. Attractions here naturally revolve around the water. Duluth's gritty maritime history, its ships and its shops make it an absorbing place to linger.

There is a year-round **visitors center** (☎ 218-722-4011; www.visitduluth.com; 21 W Superior St, Suite 100; ☼ 8:30am-5pm Mon-Fri), as well as a summer **visitors center** (☎ 218-722-6024; 350 Harbor Dr; ☼ 10am-5pm Sun-Fri, 10am-6:30pm Sat mid-May–Sep, reduced hrs Oct) in the Duluth Entertainment Convention Center (DECC), opposite the Vista dock.

SIGHTS & ACTIVITIES

The waterfront area is distinctive; mosey along the Lakewalk trail and the Canal Park/Lake St District. Look for the Aerial Lift Bridge, which rises to let ships through to the port area. The first-rate **Maritime Visitors Center** (☎ 218-720-5260; www.wsmma.com; 600 Lake Ave S; admission free; ☺ 10am-4:30pm Sun-Thu, 10am-6pm Fri & Sat spring & fall, 10am-9pm daily summer, 10:30am-4:30pm Fri-Sun winter) has a great view of the bridge, and exhibits on Great Lakes shipping and shipwrecks. Call the **boatwatchers' hotline** (☎ 218-722-6489) or check the computer screens outside the museum to learn when the big ones come and go; 1000 ships a year pass through here.

To continue the nautical theme, walk the **William A Irvin** (☎ 218-722-7876; www.williamairvin .com; 350 Harbor Dr; adult/child 3-12 $9/6; ☺ 9am-6pm Sun-Thu, 9am-8pm Fri & Sat Jun-Aug, 10am-4pm daily Sep–mid-Oct), a 610ft Great Lakes freighter. The interesting hour-long tour also includes a look aboard a Coastguard ice cutter.

The impressive **Great Lakes Aquarium** (☎ 218-740-3474; www.glaquarium.org; 353 Harbor Dr; adult/child 3-11 $13/7; ☺ 10am-6pm) is America's only freshwater aquarium; it has exhibits on Lake Superior. If you're grumpy, go look at the otters.

Back toward the city, in the fine old train station, is the **Depot** (☎ 218-727-8025; www.du luthdepot.org; 506 Michigan St; adult/child 6-13 $9/5; ☺ 10am-5pm Mon-Sat, 1-5pm Sun Sep–May, 9:30am-6pm Jun-Aug). It houses three museums: one for children, one on history and, perhaps of most interest, the Railroad Museum, which holds a good collection of old locomotives. Admission covers all three.

Other sights include **Stora Enso Paper Mills** (☎ 218-722-6024; 100 N Central Ave; admission free), which offers free tours on Monday, Tuesday and Friday from June to August; get tickets at the summer visitors center.

Local excursions include lakeside **rail trips** (adult $11 to $20, child $5 to $10) departing from the Depot, and **harbor cruises** (adult/child $12/6) from **Vista Fleet** (☎ 218-722-6218; www.vis tafleet.com; 323 Harbor Dr; ☺ mid-May–Oct). Call both places for schedules. For a spectacular view of the city and harbor, climb the rock tower in **Enger Park** (Skyline Pkwy by Enger Park Golf Course).

Skiing and snowboarding are the big winter activities, and **Spirit Mountain** (☎ 218-628-2891; www.spiritmt.com; 9500 Spirit Mountain Pl; per day adult/child 7-12 $45/35; ☺ 10am-9pm Mon-Fri, 9am-9pm Sat & Sun mid-Nov–Mar), 10 miles south of Duluth, is the place to go; rentals available. In summer, kayak next to freighters with the **University of Minnesota Duluth's outdoor program** (☎ 218-726-6533; www.umdrsop.org; kayak per person $40; ☺ Jul & Aug), which also offers a variety of other activities year-round; call for schedule. For swimming (if you dare brave the icy water) follow Lake Ave south across the Aerial Lift Bridge to Minnesota Point, where you'll find a public beach on the north side.

SLEEPING

This is a busy place in summer, and lodgings are often full (if so, try Superior).

London Rd, east of downtown, has a couple of inexpensive lodging options, like the **Chalet Motel** (☎ 218-728-4238, 800-235-2957; 1801 London Rd; r $55-80).

Voyageur Lakewalk Inn (☎ 218-722-3911, 800-258-3911; www.voyageurlakewalkinn.com; 333 E Superior St; s/d peak weekends $63/68) Right downtown with rooftop views, Voyageur Lakewalk Inn is a real find with cozy rooms.

Fitgers Inn (☎ 218-722-8826; www.fitgers.com; 600 E Superior St; cityside/lakeside r from $125/155) Occupying a former brewery, Fitgers is an interesting and plush inn with high-speed Internet access in rooms and wi-fi in public areas.

Spirit Mountain (☎ 218-624-8544; www.spiritmt .com; 9500 Spirit Mountain Pl; campsites/RV sites $15/25) Camping is available at Spirit Mountain, 10 miles south of town, where the best sites are the walk-ins.

EATING & DRINKING

The Canal Park waterfront area has eateries of all price ranges in restored commercial spaces. In the **DeWitt-Seitz Marketplace** (394 Lake Ave S), **Taste of Saigon** (☎ 218-727-1598; mains $6-10; ☺ 11am-8:30pm Sun-Thu, 11am-9:30pm Fri & Sat) creates scrumptious Vietnamese meals, including vegetarian dishes like mock duck, while **Amazing Grace** (☎ 218-723-0075; sandwiches $3-6; ☺ 7am-11pm) serves sandwiches in a comfortable café with folk music some evenings.

Fitgers Brewhouse & Grill (☎ 218-726-1392; 600 E Superior St; mains $7-10; ☺ 11am-10pm Sun & Mon, 11am-11pm Tue-Sat) makes its own beer and has tasty pub fare or you can try **Grandma's Saloon & Grill** (☎ 218-727-4192; 522 Lake Ave S; mains $13-17; ☺ 11am-10:30pm Sun-Thu, 11am-11:30pm Fri & Sat), which has filling down-home favorites, many including the local wild rice.

Check **Ripsaw** (www.ripsawnews.com), the local alternative paper, for entertainment

GREAT LAKES

happenings. Note most restaurants and bars reduce their hours in winter.

GETTING THERE & AROUND

Greyhound (☎ 218-722-5591; 4426 Grand Ave) has a couple of buses daily to Minneapolis-St Paul ($25 to $40, three hours) and Milwaukee ($55 to $85, 11 hours).

North Shore

Heading northeast, Hwy 61 is a wonderfully scenic strip of pavement along Lake Superior's shore. On its way to the Canadian border, the route passes numerous state parks, waterfalls, hiking trails (notably the long-distance Superior Hiking Trail) and low-key towns. Lots of weekend, summer and fall traffic make reservations essential.

Two Harbors has a museum, lighthouse and B&B. Just beyond town is the **Houle Information Center** (☎ 218-834-4005; www.lakecnty.com; 1330 Hwy 61; ☼ 9am-1pm), with area information.

Route highlights north of Two Harbors are Gooseberry Falls, Split Rock Lighthouse and Palisade Head. About 110 miles from Duluth, agreeable little **Grand Marais**, a burgeoning arts town, is a good base for exploring Superior National Forest, Boundary Waters Canoe Area Wilderness (BWCAW; see right) and the rest of the region. For information on the Boundary Waters, visit the **Gunflint Ranger Station** (☎ 218-387-1750; ☼ 6am-6pm May-Sep), just south of town, from where outfitters rent equipment and organize trips. The **visitors center** (☎ 218-387-2524; www.grandmarais.com; 13 N Broadway St; ☼ 9am-5pm Mon-Sat Jul-Sep, reduced hrs rest of year) is also a good resource.

Lodging options include camping, resorts and motels, like the **Harbor Inn** (☎ 218-387-

1191; www.bytheharbor.com; 207 Wisconsin St; r $75-120).

Sven and Ole's (☎ 218-387-1713; 7 Wisconsin St; sandwiches $3-7; ☼ 11am-8pm Sun-Thu, 11am-9pm Fri & Sat) is nearby for sandwiches; pizza and beer at the attached Pickled Herring Pub.

Hwy 61 continues to **Grand Portage National Monument**, beside Canada, where the early voyageurs had to carry their canoes around the Pigeon River rapids. This was the center of a far-flung trading empire, and the reconstructed 1788 trading post is well worth seeing. **Isle Royale National Park** in Lake Superior is reached by daily **ferries** (☎ 715-392-2100; www.grand-isle-royale.com; one way adult $39-65, child 4-11 $22-37) from May to October. (The park also is accessible from Michigan; see p635).

Boundary Waters

From Two Harbors, Hwy 2 runs inland to the legendary Boundary Waters Canoe Area Wilderness (BWCAW). This pristine region has more than a thousand lakes and streams in which to dip a paddle. It's possible to go just for the day, but most people opt for at least one night of camping, a wonderfully remote experience where it most likely will be you, the howling wolves, the moose who's nuzzling the tent and a sky full of stars. Beginners are welcome, and everyone can get set up with gear from local lodges and outfitters. **Permits** (☎ 877-550-6777; www.bwcaw .org; adult/child under 18 $10/5, plus $12 reservation fee) are required for overnight stays. Day permits, though free, are also required; call **Superior National Forest** (☎ 218-626-4300) for details.

Many argue the best BWCAW access is via the engaging town of **Ely**, northeast of the Iron Range area, which has accommodations, restaurants and scores of

---

TALKING MINNESOTAN, DONCHA KNOW

There is and isn't a Minnesota accent. Despite popular misconceptions and the influence of films, such as *Fargo* (just across the border in North Dakota), you can't really define a single local speech type. But there is a sort of language variation that residents employ for effect and humor based on the preceding generations of Swedes and Norwegians and *their* English. And certain expressions are used regularly that you don't hear elsewhere, such as 'alrighty,' 'doncha know,' 'you betcha' and 'hokey dokey,' which add a homey, casual flavor to conversation. 'That's different' is often said to avoid disagreement, hurt or insult over an opposite opinion. Best known of all is the wonderful, all-purpose 'uff da,' a Scandinavian term heard in a variety of situations and seen on bumper stickers. It conveys consternation and disgruntlement, but politely, sort of like 'oops' or 'oy vey.' Give it a try the next time you find a moose sniffing your car or another bird-sized mosquito diving toward your skin.

outfitters. The **Chamber of Commerce** (☎ 800-777-7281; www.ely.org; 1600 E Sheridan St; ☉ 9am-5pm Mon-Fri, plus 9am-5pm Sat, noon-3pm Sun summer) has general information and accommodation assistance. Don't miss the **International Wolf Center** (☎ 218-365-4695; www.wolf.org; 1369 Hwy 169; adult/child 6-12 $7.50/4; ☉ 9am-5pm daily, 9am-7pm Jul-Aug, 9am-5pm Sat & Sun only late Oct–mid-May), which offers intriguing exhibits and wolf-viewing trips. Also in the Wolf Center is **Kawishiwi Wilderness Station** (☎ 218-365-7561; ☉ 6am-6pm May-Sep), which offers expert camping and canoeing details, trip suggestions and required permits.

Iron Range District

An area of red-tinged scrubby hills rather than mountains, Minnesota's Iron Range District consists of the Mesabi and Vermilion Ranges, running north and south of US 169 from roughly Grand Rapids northeast to Ely. Iron was discovered here in the 1850s, and at one time more than three-quarters of the nation's iron ore was extracted from these vast open-pit mines. Visitors can see working mines and the terrain's sparse, raw beauty all along US 169.

In **Calumet**, a perfect introduction is the **Hill Annex Mine State Park** (☎ 218-247-7215; 880 Gary St; ☉ 9am-4pm Mon-Thu, 9am-5pm Fri-Sun), with its open-pit tour (adult/child five to 12 $9/6) and exhibit center; tours are held Friday to Sunday in summer. There's an even bigger pit in **Hibbing**, where a must-see **viewpoint** (admission free; ☉ 9am-6pm mid-May–mid-Sep) north of town overlooks the 3-mile-long Hull-Rust Mahoning Mine. The Greyhound bus company got its start in Hibbing, carrying miners to the pit. The **Greyhound Bus Museum** (☎ 218-263-5814; www.greyhoundbusmuseum.org; 1201 Greyhound Blvd; adult/child 6-12 $4/1; ☉ 9am-5pm Mon-Sat, 1-5pm Sun mid-May–Sep) tells the story with models, posters and antique buses. (Ironically, Greyhound cut its service to Hibbing several years ago.) Bob Dylan lived at 2425 E 7th Ave as a boy and teenager; the **Hibbing Public Library** (☎ 218-262-1038; www.hibbing.lib.mn.us; 2020 E 5th Ave; ☉ 9am-8pm Mon-Thu, 9am-5pm Fri & Sat, closed Sat in summer) has well-done Dylan displays. **Zimmy's** (☎ 218-262-6145; 531 E Howard St; sandwiches $6-8; ☉ 11am-1am) has more memorabilia, plus drinks and pub grub. For a bed, try **Hibbing Park Hotel** (☎ 218-262-3481; www.hibbingparkhotel.com; 1402 E Howard St; r $70-83; ☒).

Chisholm has the hodgepodge **Minnesota Museum of Mining** (☎ 218-254-5543; 900 Lake St W; adult/child $4/3; ☉ 9am-5pm Mon-Sat, 1-5pm Sun) and **Ironworld Discovery Center** (☎ 218-254-7959; www.ironworld.com; US 169; adult/child under 7 $6/free; ☉ 9:30am-5pm Jun-Aug), a theme park featuring open-pit mine tours and area ethnic displays.

Further east is **Virginia**, with more mine sites plus a giant loon, Minnesota's state bird. The **Ski View Motel** (☎ 218-741-8918; 903 N 17th St; s/d $44/48) could be the cleanest in the state. The Virginia area has the Range's best restaurant selection. The **Whistling Bird Café** (☎ 218-741-7544; 101 N Broadway Ave; ☉ dinner), a few miles south in Gilbert, serves Jamaican food.

Soudan has the area's only **underground mine** (☎ 218-753-2245; www.soudan.umn.edu; 1379 Stuntz Bay Rd; adult/child 5-12 $9/6, vehicle permit $7; ☉ 10am-4pm late May-early Sep) available for visiting; wear warm clothes.

International Falls & Canadian Border

North up US 53, the nondescript border town of International Falls is busy in summer due to its location. Beyond, Hwy 11 leads through forest to Lake of the Woods, bordering Ontario. For border-crossing information, see p1167.

Voyageurs National Park

In the 17th century French Canadian fur traders, or voyageurs, began exploring the Great Lakes and northern rivers by canoe. **Voyageurs National Park** (www.nps.gov/voya) covers part of their customary waterway, which became the border between the USA and Canada.

Twelve miles east of International Falls on Hwy 11 is **Rainy Lake visitors center** (☎ 218-286-5258; ☉ 9am-5pm summer, 9am-5pm Wed-Sun Oct-May), the main park office. Ranger-guided walks and boat tours are available here. Generally, though, park access is only by hiking or motorboat (the waters are mostly too wide and too rough for canoeing, though kayaks are becoming popular). A few access roads lead to campgrounds and lodges on or near Lake Superior, but these are mostly used by people putting in their own boats.

Some seasonal visitors centers can be found at **Ash River** (☎ 218-374-3221) and **Kabetogama Lake** (☎ 218-875-2111; ☉ 9am-5pm summer); call Ash River for opening hours. These areas have outfitters, rentals and services, plus some smaller bays for canoeing. At Kabetogama, **Carlson's Harmony Beach** (☎ 218-875-2811; www.harmonybeachresort.com; 10002 Gappa Rd; campsites $20, cottages $110-190) is a friendly resort, with camping, rooms and cabins.

For those seeking wildlife, canoeing or forest camping, the BWCAW is where you want to be (see p658).

NORTH-CENTRAL MINNESOTA

Wooded and lake-filled, this area is synonymous with outdoor activities and summer fun. Campsites and cottages abound, and almost everybody is fishing-crazy. The lake land begins at large, circular Mille Lacs Lake. Nearby **Mille Lacs Kathio State Park** (☎ 320-532-3523; campsites $11-19) offers camping, cabins, hiking trails, canoe rentals and small lakes to explore.

Chippewa National Forest Area

The 1036-sq-mile Chippewa National Forest is a mixed-use region with managed forests, old growth areas, Indian reservations and recreational opportunities.

Attractive **Walker** has a beach and makes a good spot for a break. For information on hiking, canoeing and camping, check in at the **Chippewa National Forest office** (☎ 218-547-1044; 201 Minnesota Ave E; ⏲ 8am-4:30pm Mon-Fri) either here, or in the town of Cass Lake, to the north.

Northwest of Walker, **Itasca State Park** (☎ 218-266-2100; off Hwy 71 N; campsites $15-19) is an area highlight. You can walk across the tiny headwaters of the mighty Mississippi, rent canoes or bikes, hike the trails and camp. The log **HI Mississippi Headwaters Hostel** (☎ 218-266-3415; www.himinnesota.org; dm $19-22, r from $36; ⏲ daily in summer) is in the park; call for schedule outside summer. Or if you want a little rustic luxury, try the venerable **Douglas Lodge** (☎ 866-857-2757; r $60), run by the park, which also has cabins and two good dining rooms.

On the western edge of the forest, neat and tidy **Bemidji** is an old lumber town with a well-preserved downtown and a giant statue of legendary logger Paul Bunyan and his faithful blue ox, Babe. The **visitors center** (☎ 218-759-1064; www.visitbemidji.com; 300 Bemidji Ave N; ⏲ 8am-5pm Mon-Fri, 10am-2pm Sat Sep-May, 8am-6pm Mon-Fri, 9am-5pm Sat, noon-5pm Sun Jun-Aug) display includes Paul's toothbrush. Stay by the lake and fish at **Taber's Log Cabins** (☎ 218-751-5781; www.taberslogcabins.com; 2404 Bemidji Ave N; cabins $59-69; ⏲ May-Oct). **Raphael's Bakery Café** (☎ 218-759-2015; 319 Minnesota Ave; items $3-5; ⏲ 6am-5:30pm Mon-Fri, 6am-2pm Sat) has fine light lunches, coffee and wild-rice bread.

Great Plains

Sure, you can blow through the Plains on I-70, I-80 or I-90. Most of the region is flat as a board and known to induce curses of 'enough wheat already!' But turn up your nose and you'll miss hearty bits of America such as South Dakota's ear-bedecked Corn Palace, the rigs at the World's Biggest Truck Stop in Iowa and Bobby Vinton crooning in Branson. The Plains' remote and wild parks top the list of must-sees, offering eerie Badlands, Black Hills and the stony faces of Mt Rushmore. The region is also the USA's best place to learn about Native America, where you can make arrowheads and shoot a blow gun at Oklahoma's Cherokee Heritage Center, or take in the sobering history of massacre sites like Wounded Knee.

The area retains its raw, frontier edge. This is, after all, the land where cowboys became cowboys, 60 million buffalo ran wild, pioneers blazed trails west and the heroic Plains Indians fought overpowering forces. These days the mantle has been passed to Stetson-hatted locals lassoing steers, cowgirls cursing over football and farmers grimacing at the sky (more rain? another tornado?) when they're not rattling along two-lane highways in their pickup trucks.

St Louis and Kansas City slake visitors' big-city fix. Route 66 provides dinky towns in which to pull up an ear of corn and plate of chicken-fried steak. Locals here may tell you they prefer their land wide and open so they can 'see if anyone's coming.' Why not let that someone be you?

HIGHLIGHTS

- Exploring the harsh, lunar landscape of **Badlands National Park** (p692)
- Drinking beer, bowling and watching baseball, baby – all under one tall arch in **St Louis** (p666)
- Driving the longest remaining stretch of **Route 66 between Tulsa and Oklahoma City** (p713)
- Veering off the interstates to view the **Corn Palace** (p690) in Mitchell, **Carhenge** (p701) in Alliance, and other Americana
- Seeing the disturbing, illuminating Wounded Knee massacre site at **Pine Ridge Indian Reservation** (p691)

North Dakota

Badlands National Park ★
South Dakota
★ Mitchell
★ Pine Ridge Indian Reservation
Alliance ★
Iowa
Nebraska

Kansas
Missouri
★ St Louis

Route 66 ★
Oklahoma

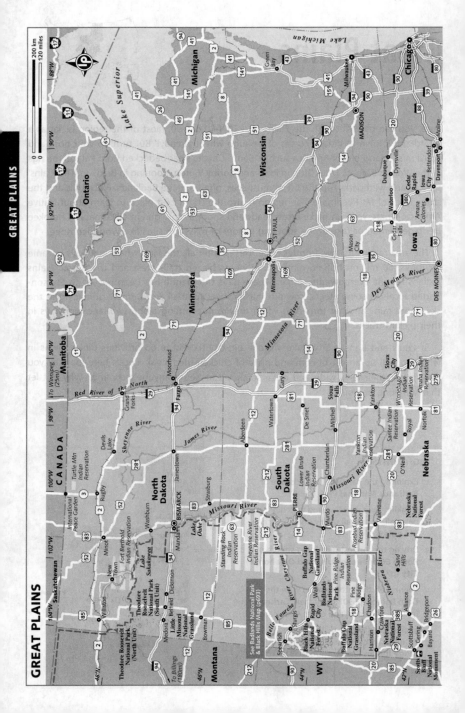

GREAT PLAINS

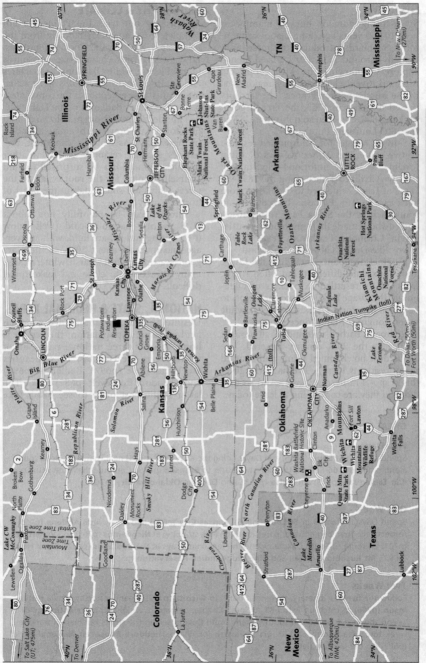

HISTORY

Spear-toting nomads hunted mammoths here 10,000 years ago, long before cannon-toting Spaniards introduced the horse (accidentally) around 1630. Fur-frenzied French explorers, following the Mississippi and Missouri Rivers, claimed a huge region west of the Mississippi for France. The territory passed to Spain in 1763, the French got it back in 1800, and then sold it to the USA in the 1803 Louisiana Purchase.

Settlers' hunger for land pushed resident Native American tribes westward, often forcibly, as in the notorious relocation of the Five Civilized Tribes along the 1838–39 'Trail of Tears,' which led to Oklahoma from back east (p715). Pioneers blazed west on trails such as the Santa Fe across Kansas, and cowboys made their myth on the cattle-drivin' Chisholm Trail from Texas to wild towns like Dodge City and Deadwood.

Original occupants, including the Osage and Sioux, had different, but often tragic, fates. Many resettled in pockets of Oklahoma (the Osage luckily found their plots to be above the world's richest oil wells), while others fought for lands once promised.

Railroads, barbed-wire and oil all brought change as the 20th century hovered. The 1930s dust bowl ruined farms and spurred many residents to say: 'I've had enough of this crap – I'm heading west.' And so they did; and they are continuing to leave today.

GEOGRAPHY & CLIMATE

Astonishing but true: the Plains are not completely flat and rise gradually from the Mississippi River to the Rocky Mountains. Low, rolling hills characterize Missouri's Ozark Plateau, while Oklahoma's Ouachitas and South Dakota's Black Hills sport actual mountains. One exception is the convoluted, below-the-plains Badlands of the Dakotas.

Thunderstorms, drought, blizzards and hailstorms all brew with equal abandon in these parts. As Dorothy can attest, tornadoes are the region's wildest weather manifestation. Don't be surprised to find yourself running for the root cellar, as the Great Plains are smack dab in the heart of 'tornado alley.'

Summer can be painfully hot (about 90°F), winter painfully cold (well below 0°F). Spring and fall are mild, with an average maximum of about 50°F, so these are good seasons to visit. Harsh winters cause many attractions to close and make travel difficult.

NATIONAL, STATE & REGIONAL PARKS

Despite the Plains' abundance of open land and sparse population, the region is home to only three national parks, all of which are in the Dakotas. These beauties are Wind Cave (p697), Badlands (p692) and Theodore Roosevelt (p687) parks. The latter is the best place to see bison (aka

---

GREAT PLAINS IN...

Five Days

Spend Day 1 in **St Louis** (p666) and Day 2 riding the **Katy Trail** (p675) near Hermann. Head south along old **Route 66** (ie I-44) through the Ozarks to **Branson** (p675). Continue the route with Day 4 in **Tahlequah** (p715) and **Tulsa** (p713), and Day 5 in **Oklahoma City** (p709).

One Week

Spend Days 1, 2 and 3 in **St Louis** (p666), **Kansas City** (p676) and lovely little **Abilene** (p705), respectively. Then begin the long trek north on I-83, stopping at **Nicodemus** (p705) and **Valentine** (p701) en route to South Dakota. Spend the remaining days at the **Badlands** (p692), **Black Hills** (p692), **Mt Rushmore** (p696) and **Pine Ridge Indian Reservation** (p691).

Two Weeks

Follow the five-day itinerary, then head north to **Wichita** (p702). Meander northwest via **Hutchinson** (p706) to catch up with I-83 to South Dakota, perhaps overnighting in **Valentine** (p701). Spend the next four days in southwestern South Dakota seeing the sights outlined in the one-week tour. Head north on I-85, via **Spearfish** (p695), to **Theodore Roosevelt National Park** (p687) for the last few days.

buffalo), creatures that once roamed the Plains 60-million strong but were killed off in wanton slaughters during the mid-19th century. Recent conservation efforts have restored the number to 150,000. South Dakota's Badlands and Black Hills National Forest (p693) as well as Oklahoma's Wichita Mountains Wildlife Refuge (p712) provide backdrops for further wildlife viewing.

Most of the prairie grasslands have gone by way of the farmer's plow; only 0.1% of the original tall grass survives. It can be seen in the Oglala (Nebraska), Buffalo Gap (South Dakota) and Little Missouri (in North Dakota, name notwithstanding) National Grasslands and the Tallgrass Prairie National Preserve in Kansas.

See individual state introductory sections for state park details. Contact the **National Park Service** (www.nps.gov) for indispensable trail pamphlets and other information.

GETTING THERE & AROUND
Air
The region's main airport is **Lambert-St Louis International** (☎ 314-426-8000; www.lambert-stlouis .com), but it has few direct international flights. Visitors from abroad may be better off getting a connection from O'Hare Airport in Chicago.

Bus
The car- or motorcycle-less brave won't be able to see much beyond the interstates. **Greyhound** (☎ 800-231-2222; www.greyhound.com) buses ply the major roads (I-40 across Oklahoma, I-70 across Missouri and Kansas, I-80 across Iowa and Nebraska, I-90 across South Dakota). Note if you're heading north–south through the Plains, some Greyhound routes go by way of Colorado (ie not direct). **Jefferson Lines** (☎ 888-864-2832; www.jeffersonlines.com) is a smaller carrier that specializes in Great Plains routes, handy for those north–south trips.

Car & Motorcycle
Driving sure beats public transport if you want to see the Great Plains' very best attractions. Six east–west interstate highways cross the region; north–south routes are fewer, less developed and less direct. I-44 has been built over and around the original Route 66 across Missouri and Oklahoma, and a small part of Kansas, but substantial stretches survive and are covered in the

Missouri (p674), Kansas (p706) and Oklahoma (p712) sections. US 50, the last surviving transcontinental route that is not a modern interstate, crosses Kansas and Missouri. The Great River Rd is a well-signed network of roads and highways that runs along the Mississippi River.

Train
Daily **Amtrak** (☎ 800-872-7245; www.amtrak.com) routes cross the Plains states, often at night.
Ann Rutledge Between Chicago and Kansas City (including St Louis).
California Zephyr Between Chicago and San Francisco via Iowa (including Osceola, south of Des Moines) and Nebraska (including Omaha and Lincoln).
Empire Builder Between Chicago and Seattle via North Dakota (including Fargo).
Heartland Flyer Between Fort Worth and Oklahoma City.
Kansas City Mule Between St Louis and Kansas City.
Southwest Chief Between Chicago and Los Angeles via Missouri (including Kansas City) and Kansas (including Newton, north of Wichita).
Texas Eagle & State House Between Chicago and St Louis.

MISSOURI

Missouri is the Great Plains' prize: it's the most consistently scenic state and berths the region's two largest cities (St Louis and Kansas City). The Ozark Mountains' plateaus, hills and valleys provide great recreational areas. If you happen to tire of nature and suddenly develop the urge to see Yakov Smirnoff and eat a funnel cake, then Branson awaits. Route 66 meanders past gems like the Jesse James Wax Museum and replica Stonehenge. Biking the Katy Trail through Missouri's Rhineland is another highlight.

History
Missouri was admitted to the Union as a slave state in 1821, per the Missouri Compromise (which permitted slavery in Missouri but prohibited it in any other part of the Louisiana Territory above the 36°30′ parallel). In 1846 Dred Scott, a slave from Missouri, filed suit on the grounds that temporary residence in free territory released him from slavery; he lost his case. The decision further divided Missouri's pro- and anti-slavery factions, and bitter feelings were stoked along the Missouri-Kansas border by Civil War time.

GREAT PLAINS

MISSOURI FACTS

Nickname Show Me State

Population 5.7 million

Area 69,710 sq miles

Capital city Jefferson City (population 39,000)

Official aquatic animal The paddlefish

Birthplace of Samuel Clemens (Mark Twain; 1835–1910), outlaw Jesse James (1847–82), writer TS Eliot (1888–1965), singer Sheryl Crow (b 1962), author Maya Angelou (b 1928)

Home of The world's largest BBQ contest (in Kansas City in October)

Famous for Gateway Arch, Budweiser, the first ice cream cone, hot dog and iced tea

---

The state's 'Show Me' nickname is attributed to Congressman Willard Duncan Vandiver, who said in an 1899 speech, 'I come from a state that raises corn and cotton and cockleburs and Democrats, and frothy eloquence neither convinces nor satisfies me. I am from Missouri. You have got to show me.' The name is now used to indicate locals' stalwart, not-easily-impressed character.

Information

Missouri sales tax is 4.2%; city and county taxes add up to 4.1% more.

Bed & Breakfast Inns of Missouri (☎ 800-213-5642; www.bbim.org) Information on 100 B&Bs statewide.

Missouri Division of Tourism (☎ 800-519-2100; www.visitmo.com)

Missouri highway conditions (☎ 800-222-6400; www.modot.state.mo.us)

Missouri state park information (☎ 800-334-6946; www.mostateparks.com) State parks are free to visit. Campsites cost $8-17; some accept reservations (fee $8.50).

ST LOUIS

The single-flash image of St Louis is its Arch, a simple silver beam that curves up toward the sky, then comes back to earth. It's uncomplicated, like the city itself. Beer, bowling and baseball provide some of the top attractions. Many music legends – Chuck Berry, Tina Turner and Miles Davis – got their start here in the 'Home of the Blues,' and the bouncy live music venues keep the flame burning. St Louis welcomes visitors by keeping costs reasonable, and many sights (Forest Park, the Bud tour) are free.

History

Fur-trapper Pierre Laclede knew prime real estate when he saw it, so he put down stakes pronto at the junction of the Mississippi and Missouri rivers, and established St Louis as a frontier outpost in 1764. The hustle picked up considerably when prospectors discovered gold in California in 1849, and St Louis became the jump-off point – aka 'Gateway to the West' – for get-rich-quick dreamers.

In 1904 St Louis hosted two international events – the World's Fair and Summer Olympics – and became known as a center of innovation. Aviator Charles Lindbergh furthered the reputation in 1927 when he flew the first nonstop, solo transatlantic flight in the 'Spirit of St Louis,' named for the far-sighted town that paid for the aircraft. The city retains its forward-thinking status

---

ST LOUIS IN...

Two Days

On Day 1, get underneath the hulking **Gateway Arch** (p668), then churn up the Mississippi River with a **steamboat ride** (p668). Drink beer and meet Clydesdales at the **Anheuser-Busch Brewery tour** (p668), then soak up the suds with fried ravioli and other Italian noshes in the **Hill** (p672). Finish off with a creamy, decadent **Ted Drewes frozen custard** (see Drink & Dine St Louis Style, p671) on old Route 66. Spend the second day in **Forest Park** (p669) – rent bicycles, paddleboats or ice skates and visit the free zoo and art museum. Dine in the stately **Central West End** (p672). Rock (perhaps with Chuck Berry) at **Blueberry Hill** (p672).

Four Days

On Day 3, visit the recycled **City Museum** (p670) and quirky **Bowling Museum** (p670). Catch a **Cardinals** (p672) game if they're in town; if not, view a movie at the **Moolah Theatre** (p673). On Day 4, hit the road to nearby **St Charles** (p673).

GREAT PLAINS

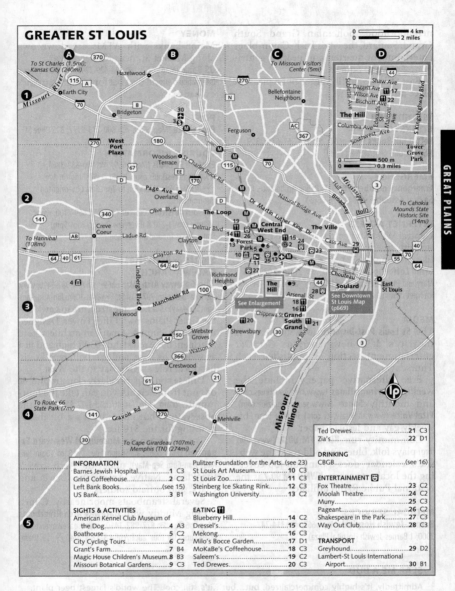

GREATER ST LOUIS

INFORMATION	
Barnes Jewish Hospital.................1 C3	
Grind Coffeehouse...................2 C2	
Left Bank Books....................(see 15)	
US Bank...........................3 B1	

SIGHTS & ACTIVITIES	
American Kennel Club Museum of	
the Dog........................4 A3	
Boathouse.........................5 C2	
City Cycling Tours..................6 C2	
Grant's Farm.......................7 B4	
Magic House Children's Museum.8 B3	
Missouri Botanical Gardens.........9 C3	

Pulitzer Foundation for the Arts..(see 23)	
St Louis Art Museum................10 C3	
St Louis Zoo.......................11 C3	
Steinberg Ice Skating Rink.........12 C2	
Washington University.............13 C2	

EATING 🍴	
Blueberry Hill.....................14 C2	
Dressel's.........................15 C2	
Mekong...........................16 C3	
Milo's Bocce Garden...............17 D1	
MoKaBe's Coffeehouse.............18 C3	
Saleem's.........................19 C2	
Ted Drewes......................20 C3	

Ted Drewes......................21 C3	
Zia's.............................22 D1	

DRINKING	
CBGB............................(see 16)	

ENTERTAINMENT 🎭	
Fox Theatre......................23 C2	
Moolah Theatre...................24 C2	
Muny.............................25 C3	
Pageant..........................26 C2	
Shakespeare in the Park...........27 C3	
Way Out Club.....................28 C3	

TRANSPORT	
Greyhound........................29 D2	
Lambert-St Louis International	
Airport...........................30 B1	

today, with several aerospace and high-tech companies based here.

Orientation

The landmark Gateway Arch is in the riverside Jefferson National Expansion Memorial. Just north is the Laclede's Landing restaurant-and-shopping precinct. To the west is downtown and its central artery, Market St. Just north is Washington Ave, a loft/arts district.

Neighborhoods of interest radiate out from this core, including Forest Park; the posh Central West End abutting the park; the buzzing-all-night Loop beside Washington University; the Hill, an Italian-American

GREAT PLAINS

neighborhood; bohemian Grand South Grand; Soulard, the city's Irish-Cajun-blues entertainment quarter; and nearby, gentrifying Lafayette Square.

East St Louis, in Illinois, is not a pleasant place after dark.

Information
BOOKSTORES
Left Bank Books (Map p667; ☎ 314-367-6731; 399 North Euclid, Central West End)

EMERGENCY
Emergency number (☎ 911) Police, ambulance, fire.
Sexual Assault (☎ 314-726-6665)

INTERNET ACCESS
Central West End coffee shops are popping up with free wireless access, as are eateries like Mekong (p672).
Grind Coffeehouse (Map p667; ☎ 314-454-0202; 56 Maryland Plaza, Central West End; ☺ 9am-3am) Free Internet terminal and wi-fi.

MEDIA
The **St Louis Post-Dispatch** (www.stltoday.com) is the city's daily newspaper; its *Get Out* entertainment section is published each Thursday.

Free alternative papers include the weekly **Riverfront Times** (www.riverfronttimes.com) and monthly **Sauce** (www.saucemagazine.com). **Vital Voice** (www.thevitalvoice.com) is the free, biweekly gay and lesbian paper.

Community-run **KDHX FM 88.1** (www.kdhx .org) plays folk, blues and odd rock; the website's 'calendar' does a bang-up job covering the local arts scene. **KWMU FM 90.7** is the National Public Radio affiliate.

MEDICAL SERVICES
Barnes-Jewish Hospital (Map p667; ☎ 314-747-3000; 1 Barnes-Jewish Hospital Plaza)

MONEY
Major banks with ATMs are downtown along Market St, near Kiener Plaza.
US Bank (Map p667; ☎ 314-429-1248; Lambert-St Louis International Airport) Best bet for foreign-currency exchange.

POST
Post office (Map p669; ☎ 800-275-8777; 815 Olive St)

TOURIST INFORMATION
Explore St Louis (Map p669; ☎ 800-888-3861; www.explorestlouis.com; 7th St & Washington Ave; ☺ 8:30am-5pm Mon-Fri, to 2pm Sat) City-oriented information.
Missouri Visitors Center (☎ 314-869-7100; www .visitmo.com; I-270 & Riverview Dr; ☺ 8am-5pm) Statewide maps and information.

Sights & Activities
GATEWAY ARCH
The **Gateway Arch** (Map p669; ☎ 877-982-1410; www .gatewayarch.com; 707 N 1st St; ☺ 8am-10pm Jun-Aug, 9am-6pm Sep-May) is a five-star structure to gawk at – the Great Plains' own Eiffel Tower. Designed in 1965 by Finnish-American architect Eero Saarinen, the Arch stands 630ft high and just as wide at its base, and symbolizes St Louis' historical role as 'Gateway to the West.'

Unless you're particularly claustrophobic or faint from heights, you can take the four-minute **tram ride** (adult/child 3-12 $10/3) to the observatory, but honestly, it's a bit disappointing for the $10 fee.

The subterranean **Museum of Westward Expansion** (Map p669; admission free; ☺ 8am-10pm Jun-Aug, 9am-6pm Sep-May), under the Arch, covers the Plains' Native Americans, Lewis and Clark, and buffalo soldiers.

Several steamboats moor nearby. Churn up Big Muddy with **Gateway Arch Riverboats** (Map p669; ☎ 877-982-1410; www.gatewayarchriver boats.com; 1hr tour adult/child 3-12 $10/4; ☺ 10:30am-

---

SLAP ME A BUD

Admittedly, it's highly commercialized, but...but...it's still cool. The world's largest beer plant, the historic **Anheuser-Busch Brewery** (Map p669; ☎ 314-577-2626; www.budweisertours.com; 12th & Lynch Sts; admission free; ☺ 9am-4pm Mon-Sat, 11:30am-4pm Sun Mar-Oct, to 5pm Jun-Aug, reduced Nov-Feb), gives free, super-slick tours. Would you expect less from the company that makes Budweiser and controls 50% of the domestic market? View the bottling plant and famous Clydesdale horses; note the tanks in the stock house – each one holds 200,000 six-packs. Bring ID to sample two free beers at the end. You'll get a third brew (plus a damn fine 'Honorary Beermaster' certificate) by volunteering for the 'taste test.'

GREAT PLAINS

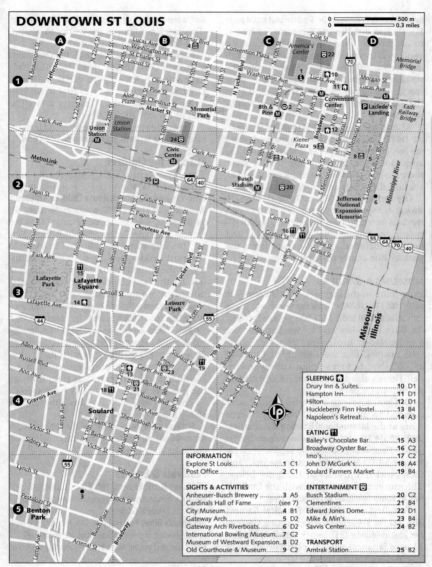

DOWNTOWN ST LOUIS

0   500 m
0   0.3 miles

INFORMATION
Explore St Louis.........................1 C1
Post Office.................................2 C1

SIGHTS & ACTIVITIES
Anheuser-Busch Brewery 3 A5
Cardinals Hall of Fame...........(see 7)
City Museum..............................4 B1
Gateway Arch.............................5 D2
Gateway Arch Riverboats............6 D2
International Bowling Museum.....7 C2
Museum of Westward Expansion..8 D2
Old Courthouse & Museum........9 C2

SLEEPING
Drury Inn & Suites....................10 D1
Hampton Inn.............................11 D1
Hilton......................................12 D1
Huckleberry Finn Hostel............13 B4
Napoleon's Retreat...................14 A3

EATING
Bailey's Chocolate Bar..............15 A3
Broadway Oyster Bar................16 C2
Imo's.......................................17 C2
John D McGurk's.......................18 A4
Soulard Farmers Market............19 B4

ENTERTAINMENT
Busch Stadium..........................20 C2
Clementines.............................21 B4
Edward Jones Dome..................22 D1
Mike & Min's............................23 B4
Savvis Center...........................24 B2

TRANSPORT
Amtrak Station.........................25 B2

4:30pm), just south of the Arch; a park ranger narrates the midday cruises.

FOREST PARK

New York City may have Central Park, but St Louis has the even bigger (by 500 acres) **Forest Park** (6am-10pm). The superb, 1300-acre spread was the setting of the 1904

World's Fair. On the grounds is the impressive **St Louis Art Museum** (Map p667; ☎ 314-721-0072; www.slam.org; 1 Fine Arts Dr; admission free; 10am-5pm Tue-Sun, to 9pm Fri), originally built for the fair and today holding 30,000 international works.

In warm weather, beeline to the **Boathouse** (Map p667; ☎ 314-367-2224; www.boathouse

forestpark.com; Government Dr; 4-person boat rental per hr $15; 11am-dusk Mon-Sat, 10am-sunset Sun Apr-Nov) to paddleboat over Post-Dispatch Lake. In cooler weather, make for the **Steinberg Ice Skating Rink** (Map p667; 314-367-7465; www.steinbergskatingrink.com; adult/child $6/4, skates per hr $2; 10am-9pm Sun-Thu, 10am-midnight Fri & Sat winter); it's on the east side of the park, near Kingshighway Blvd.

Also in the park is the **St Louis Zoo** (Map p667; 314-781-0900; www.stlzoo.org; 1 Government Dr; admission free; 9am-5pm, 8am-7pm summer). While the apes, lions and penguins are free to view, there is a charge to see the children's zoo ($4), sea lion show ($3) and insectarium ($2).

City Cycling Tours (Map p667; 314-616-5724; www.citycyclingtours.com; 3hr tour $30; daily year-round, call for times) offers excellent, guided 10-mile rides through the park; bicycles and helmets included. Tours depart from the park visitor center on Grand Dr.

MUSEUMS & GARDENS

Everything in the ingenious **City Museum** (Map p669; 314-231-2489; www.citymuseum.org; 701 N 15th St; adult/child under 3 $12/free; 9am-5pm Mon-Thu, 9-1am Fri, 10-1am Sat, 11am-5pm Sun, closed Mon & Tue Sep-May) is made from recycled industrial castoffs, like the Enchanted Caves in an old shoe factory's spiral conveyor tunnel. There's also an aquarium ($5 extra) and rooftop water park.

Did you know priests who sinned were damned to an eternity of bowling? Learn more at the **International Bowling Museum** (Map p669; 314-231-6340; www.bowlingmuseum.com; 111 Stadium Plaza; adult/child under 16 $7.50/6; 11am-4pm Tue-Sat Oct-Mar, 9am-5pm daily Apr-Sep), and then bowl free frames at the lanes below. The museum shares space with the **Cardinals Hall of Fame** (admission incl in museum fee).

The first-rate **Missouri Botanical Gardens** (Map p667; 314-577-9400; www.mobot.org; 4344 Shaw Ave; adult/child under 13 $7/free; 9am-5pm) holds a 14-acre Japanese garden, carnivorous plant bog and Victorian-style hedge maze.

The **American Kennel Club Museum of the Dog** (Map p667; 314-821-3647; 1721 S Mason Rd, near Kirkwood; adult/child 5-14 $5/1; 10am-4pm Tue-Sat, 1-5pm Sun) features doggie art from pre-Columbian pottery to William Wegman photos, plus the hall of fame with Lassie, Toto and other noted canines.

The **Pulitzer Foundation for the Arts** (Map p667; 314-754-1850; www.pulitzerarts.org; 3716 Washington Blvd; admission free; noon-5pm Wed, 10am-4pm Sat) showcases contemporary works in a stunning building by Tadao Ando.

Facing the Arch, the 1845 **Old Courthouse & Museum** (Map p669; 314-655-1600; 11 N 4th St; admission free; 8am-4:30pm) is where the famed Dred Scott slavery case was first tried. Galleries depict the trial's history, as well as that of the city itself.

Cross the river to see the World Heritage Site **Cahokia Mounds State Historic Site** (p598).

St Louis for Children

The city receives high praise for its kids' attractions. A survey by *Parenting* magazine ranked the **Magic House Children's Museum** (Map p667; 314-822-8900; www.magichouse.org; 516 S Kirkwood Rd, Kirkwood; adult/child under 2 $6.50/free; noon-5:30pm Tue-Thu, noon-9pm Fri, 9:30am-5:30pm Sat, 11am-5:30pm Sun, from 9:30am daily in summer) as the most child-appealing sight in the country. If the fitness safari doesn't tucker 'em out, try the face blender, gear wall, TV station or recording studio.

Grant's Farm (Map p667; 314-843-1700; www.grantsfarm.com; 10501 Gravois Rd; admission free; 9am-3:30pm Tue-Fri, 9am-4pm Sat, 9:30am-4pm Sun mid-May–mid-Aug, reduced hrs spring & fall, closed mid-Oct–mid-Apr; P) thrills tykes with its Clydesdale horses and 1000 other animals from six continents; take the trackless train through the preserve where the beasts roam freely.

The zoo (left) and City Museum (left) are also young crowd pleasers.

Sitters to the Rescue (314-863-9800; per hr $18, 4hr minimum) provides babysitters who will come to your hotel.

Festivals & Events

Whitaker Music Festival (314-577-5100; admission free) Wednesday evening concerts through June and July in the Botanical Gardens.

Big Muddy Blues Festival (314-241-5875; www.lacledeslanding.org/events/blues.html; admission free) Four stages of riverfront blues; held on Labor Day weekend.

Sleeping

Lower-priced options are at the airport (exit 236 off I-70) or exits off city-encircling I-270. Add 14.87% tax to the prices below.

BUDGET

Huckleberry Finn Hostel (Map p669; 314-241-0076; 1904-1908 S 12th St, Soulard; dm $20; closed Jan & Feb; P) In a fine old townhouse, this former

HI (now independent) hostel is well-sited near pubs and restaurants. Take bus No 52 to/from downtown.

MIDRANGE

Hampton Inn (Map p669; ☎ 314-621-7900, 800-426-7866; www.hamptoninnstlouis.com; 333 Washington Ave; r $109-129; P ⊠ ☐ ☒) The downtown, good-value Hampton provides standard rooms but crowns them with a fine batch of freebies: high-speed and wireless Internet access, hot breakfast, indoor pool and fitness center. Parking costs $10.

Drury Inn & Suites (Map p669; ☎ 314-231-8100, 800-378-7946; www.druryhotels.com; 711 N Broadway, in the Convention Center; r/ste from $95/116; P ⊠ ☐ ☒) The Drury has similar free amenities to the Hampton, plus free parking and free evening drinks. This is one of downtown's least expensive hotels; discount coupons are available at visitor centers for additional savings.

Napoleon's Retreat (Map p669; ☎ 314-772-6979, 800-700-9980; www.napoleonsretreat.com; 1815 Lafayette Ave; r $99-150; P ⊠ ☒) Off the beaten path but near Lafayette Square's burgeoning nightlife, this B&B has four rooms, each with private bath. Try the Burgundy Room. Wireless access is available.

TOP END

Hilton (Map p669; ☎ 314-436-0002, 888-302-4143; www .hilton.com; 400 Olive St; s $119-189, d $129-209; P ⊠ ☐ ☒) This new boutique-style property opened downtown in 2005. It caters to a business crowd with wi-fi in rooms, a business center with computers, comfy beds, indoor pool and fitness room. Parking is $15.

Eating

St Louis boasts the region's most diverse selection of food – so get your Mediterranean and Vietnamese fix here while you have the chance. The city is particularly proud of its Italian offerings.

DOWNTOWN

Laclede's Landing along the riverfront under the historic Eads railway bridge has several restaurants, though most are ho-hum.

Broadway Oyster Bar (Map p669; ☎ 314-621-8811; 736 S Broadway Ave; mains $8-13; ⊙ 11am-10pm Sun-Thu, to 11pm Fri & Sat) Serves lots of the namesake mollusks, plus Cajun food, beer and blues nightly.

SOULARD & LAFAYETTE SQUARE

Restaurants and pubs occupy most corners in Soulard, with plenty of live blues and Irish music. Lafayette Square is a few miles west, with eateries mostly along Park Ave.

Bailey's Chocolate Bar (Map p669; ☎ 314-241-8100; www.baileyschocolatebar.com; 1915 Park Ave; items $5-9; ⊙ 4pm-1am Tue-Sat) It's pure brilliance: specialize in chocolate desserts (fudgy truffle cake, anyone?), chocolate coffees and alcoholic beverages, with cheese plates and fancy pizzas thrown in to conceal the decadence.

John D McGurk's (Map p669; ☎ 314-776-8309; 1200 Russell Blvd; mains $7-19; ⊙ 11am-1am Mon-Sat, 3pm-midnight Sun) The city's favorite pub has traditional Irish dishes; Irish bands play most nights.

Soulard Farmers Market (Map p669; Lafayette Ave & 7th St; ⊙ Wed-Sat) Browse for fresh produce, meats, spices and baked goods.

DRINK & DINE ST LOUIS STYLE

The city cooks and brews local specialties:

- **Toasted ravioli** – They're coated in breadcrumbs, then deep fried. Zia's (opposite) makes memorable ones.

- **St Louis pizza** – It's square-shaped, thin-crusted, provolone cheese–based and sticks to the roof of your mouth. Local chain **Imo's** (Map p669; ☎ 314-421-4667; 742 S 4th St; pizzas $7; ⊙ 10am-midnight) bakes 'the square beyond compare.'

- **Frozen custard** – Don't dare leave town without gorging on the super-creamy soft ice cream (strangely called 'concrete') at **Ted Drewes** (Map p667; ☎ 314-481-2652; 6726 Chippewa St; cup $2-4; ⊙ 11am-11pm or so Feb-Dec). Lines are long on warm evenings, but move fast. There's a smaller branch at 4224 S Grand Blvd, open in summer.

- **Schlafly beer** – Look behind bar taps for this local microbrew.

GRAND SOUTH GRAND

Running along South Grand Blvd, this young, bohemian area thrives with Asian eateries and is good for vegetarian fare.

MoKaBe's Coffeehouse (Map p667; ☎ 314-865-2009; 3606 Arsenal St; sandwiches $5-7; ❤ 10am-1am Mon-Sat, from 9am Sun) Lesbian-friendly MoKaBe's is famous for its grilled veggie sandwich and huge, sprawling all-vegetarian Sunday brunch ($12).

Mekong (Map p667; ☎ 314-773-3100; 3131 S Grand Ave; mains $6-8; ❤ 11am-10pm Sun-Thu, to 11pm Fri & Sat) Mekong serves Vietnamese standbys like pho (noodle soup), egg rolls and various beef, chicken, pork and tofu dishes.

THE HILL

This trim, tiny-housed Italian neighborhood features innumerable pasta places.

Zia's (Map p667; ☎ 314-776-0020; www.zias.com; 5256 Wilson Ave; mains $8-17; ❤ lunch & dinner Mon-Sat) Big, family-style tables dominate traditional Zia's, which means plenty of space to hold fat plates of toasted ravioli.

Milo's Bocce Garden (Map p667; ☎ 314-776-0468; 5201 Wilson Ave; mains $7-14; ❤ 11am-1am) Enjoy the outdoor courtyard to eat sandwiches and pastas, drink and play bocce ball with old Italian guys.

CENTRAL WEST END

Lots of fine, midrange eateries line Euclid Ave in this dignified old neighborhood.

Dressel's (Map p667; ☎ 314-361-1060; 419 N Euclid Ave; mains $6-13; ❤ 11:30am-11pm) This classic Welsh pub serves rarebit, fish and chips and sandwiches in an atmosphere celebrating Wales' literary and drinking heritages.

THE LOOP

Near Washington University, 'the Loop' runs along Delmar Blvd with many international restaurants catering to a youthful crowd.

Saleem's (Map p667; ☎ 314-721-7947; 6501 Delmar Blvd; mains $7-16; ❤ lunch & dinner Mon-Sat) 'Where garlic is king' is the motto, and the herb shows up in bright-orange Saleem's kabobs, kofte, hummus and other Persian dishes.

Blueberry Hill (Map p667; ☎ 314-727-0880; www.blueberryhill.com; 6504 Delmar Blvd; mains $5-9; ❤ 11am-1:30am Mon-Sat, 11am-midnight Sun) It's a nostalgic city favorite, with heaps of rock memorabilia, good burgers and a whale of a jukebox.

Drinking

Most bars close at 1:30am, though some have 3am licenses. Laclede's Landing and Soulard are chock full o' drinkeries, most with live music on weekends.

Boathouse (p669) is a lovely, outdoor place to sit, sip and sunset watch.

Boozy barflies mix it up with hipsters at **CBGB** (Map p667; ☎ 314-773-9743; 3163 S Grand Blvd), a laid-back watering hole.

Dressel's, Milo's Bocce Garden and Bailey's Chocolate Bar are good places to drink as well as eat.

Entertainment

Check the **Riverfront Times** (www.riverfronttimes.com) for entertainment updates.

JAZZ, BLUES & ROCK

The city's best show is held once a month (on the third Thursday) when St Louis native Chuck Berry rocks the small basement bar at **Blueberry Hill** (see Eating, left). The $25 tickets sell out very quickly. The venue hosts smaller-tier bands on the other nights.

Pageant (Map p667; ☎ 314-726-6161; www.thepageant.com; 6161 Delmar Blvd, The Loop) This is where most touring bands perform.

Way Out Club (Map p667; ☎ 314-664-7638; www.wayoutclub-stl.com; 2525 S Jefferson Ave) Way Out is a worthy venue with punk, rockabilly and alt rock bands.

Mike & Min's (Map p669; ☎ 314-421-1655; 925 Geyer Ave, Soulard; ❤ closed Mon) You'll hear blues and jazz while sitting side-by-side with earthy locals chugging Bud Light.

SPORTS

Busch Stadium (Map p669; ☎ 314-421-2400; www.stlcardinals.com; btwn Broadway, Clark & 8th Sts) The much-loved Cardinals baseball team earned itself this shiny new stadium.

Edward Jones Dome (Map p669; ☎ 314-425-8830; www.stlouisrams.com; 901 N Broadway) This is where the NFL's Rams go deep.

Savvis Center (Map p669; ☎ 314-622-2583; www.stlouisblues.com; 1401 Clark Ave) The St Louis Blues play NHL hockey here.

PERFORMING ARTS

Grand Center, west of downtown, is the heart of St Louis's theater district. Purchase tickets through **MetroTix** (☎ 800-293-5949; www.metrotix.com).

Muny (Map p667; ☎ 314-361-1900; www.muny .com; Forest Park) The Municipal Opera (aka 'Muny') hosts nightly summer shows; some of the 12,000 seats are free.

Shakespeare in the Park (☎ 314-361-0101; www .sfstl.com; Forest Park; ☽ 8pm Wed-Mon late May-late Jun) It's one of the city's best events – and free.

Fox Theatre (Map p667; ☎ 314-534-1678; 527 N Grand Blvd) Catch a concert or Broadway show at this 1929 ornate beauty.

CINEMA

The wonderful, single-screen **Moolah Theatre** (☎ 314-446-6868; www.stlouiscinema.com/moolah; 3821 Lindell Blvd), housed in an old Masonic temple, shows mainstream movies amid upscale concessions like martinis and Ted Drewes custard; leather couches to sit on.

GAY & LESBIAN VENUES

Soulard and Grand South Grand have gay and lesbian venues. Women will find company at MoKaBe's Coffeehouse (opposite). Men will find friends at **Clementines** (Map p669; ☎ 314-664-7869; 2001 Menard St). Peruse the **Vital Voice** (www.thevitalvoice.com) for more.

Getting There & Around
TO/FROM THE AIRPORT

Lambert-St Louis International Airport (Map p667; ☎ 314-426-8000; www.lambert-stlouis.com) is the Great Plains' hub, with flights to all major regional and US cities. Located 12 miles northwest of downtown, the airport is connected by the light-rail MetroLink ($3), taxi (about $35) or the shuttle service **Trans Express** (☎ 314-428-7799, 800-844-1985; one-way $15).

BUS

Greyhound (Map p667; ☎ 314-231-4485, 800-231-2222; 1450 N 13th St) departs several times daily to Chicago ($30 to $40, 6½ hours), Memphis ($40 to $50, 6½ hours) and Oklahoma City ($80 to $95, 11 hours).

PUBLIC TRANSPORTATION

Metro (☎ 314-231-2345; www.metrostlouis.org; single ride with/without transfer $1.75/1.50, from airport $3, day pass $4) runs local buses and the MetroLink light-rail system. Ride free between Union Station and Laclede's Landing (weekdays only 11:30am to 1:30pm). Metro is extending the line from Forest Park south to Shrewsbury, slated for 2006 completion.

TAXI

St Louis County Cabs (☎ 314-993-8294)

TRAIN

Amtrak (Map p669; ☎ 314-331-3309, 800-872-7245; 550 S 16th St) travels three times daily to Chicago ($21 to $49, 5½ hours); there are also daily trains to Kansas City ($25 to $32, 5½ hours) and, with bus connection, Memphis ($73 to $100, 7½ hours).

RIVER TOWNS

Interesting towns that make popular weekend excursions for St Louisans lie north and south of St Louis on the Mississippi River and just west on the Missouri.

St Charles

This historic river town, founded in 1769 by the French, is on the Missouri River 20 miles northwest of St Louis, and is now almost a suburb. The **visitor center** (☎ 800-366-2427; www.historicstcharles.com; 230 S Main St; ☽ 8am-5pm Mon-Fri, 10am-5pm Sat, noon-5pm Sun) has information.

The picturesque, historic nine-block downtown is a few miles off the interstate and features the first **state capitol** (S Main St). The historic 26-block **Frenchtown neighborhood** (N Main St) is just north.

The days of Lewis and Clark are re-enacted in the third week of May, and the **Lewis & Clark Center** (☎ 636-947-3199; www.lewisandclark .net; 1050 Riverside Dr; adult/child $2/1; ☽ 10am-5pm Mon-Sat, noon-5pm Sun) has exhibits.

For cyclists, St Charles is the eastern gateway to the Katy Trail State Park (p675).

Along St Charles' three I-70 exits are newer, better-value motels than those in St Louis. The reliable **Red Roof Inn** (☎ 636-947-7770; 2010 Zumbehl Rd; s/d $59/64; P ☒) has decent rooms. St Charles has several good B&Bs, including **Boone's Lick Trail B&B** (☎ 636-947-7000, 888-940-0002; www.booneslick.com; 1000 S Main St; r $125-175; P ☒), a class act with claw-foot bathtubs and four-post beds.

Hannibal

Mark Twain's birthplace, 105 miles north of St Louis, is a bit weary these days. Still, for big-time fans, the scenes of Tom Sawyer and Huck Finn's great adventures are irresistible. You can see the white fence Tom didn't paint and the cave where he and Becky Thatcher got lost. The large **Mark**

Twain Boyhood Home & Museum (☎ 573-221-9010; www.marktwainmuseum.org; 208 Hill St; adult/child 6-12 $8/4; ☻ 8am-6pm, reduced in winter) features four replica buildings, two films and three gift shops. Afterward, float down the Mississippi on the **Mark Twain Riverboat** (☎ 573-221-3222; www.marktwainriverboat.com; Center St; 1hr cruise adult/child 5-12 $10/7; departures 11am, 1:30pm & 4pm May-Oct).

The **Hannibal Inn** (☎ 573-221-6610; www.hannibalinn.com; 4141 Market St; s/d $70/80; ⓟ ⓧ ⓡ), off Hwy 61, boasts a large, heated cloverleaf pool (with additional Jacuzzi and sauna) and a playground.

Cape Girardeau

Another pleasant river town, 115 miles downstream from St Louis, Cape Girardeau was a steamboat stop as early as 1835. Drop by the **visitor center** (☎ 800-777-0068; www.capegirardeaucvb.com; 100 Broadway; ☻ 8am-5:30pm Mon-Fri, 10am-4pm Sat) for brochures. Downtown's **Water Street** and the nearby **riverfront** are fine places for a stroll.

About 10 miles north, on Hwy 177, is **Trail of Tears State Park** (☎ 573-334-1711), a beautiful region that belies its sad past as part of the Cherokees' forced march to Oklahoma. There are trails, Mississippi overlooks and **camping** ($7-15).

CENTRAL MISSOURI

The central region's jewel is the Katy Trail, though there are a couple of other good parks as you go west.

So little is going on in the small state capital, **Jefferson City** ('Jeff City'), on US 50, that a law had to be passed requiring state officials to live here.

North of the capital on I-70, **Columbia** is a nice college town, home to the University of Missouri – the oldest university west of the Mississippi.

Boone's Lick State Historic Site (☎ 660-837-3330; admission free; ☻ 9am-dusk), northwest of Boonville on Hwy 87, is where Daniel Boone's sons manufactured salt from the 'licks,' natural saltwater springs. Just across the Missouri, and reached by Hwy 41, tiny **Arrow Rock State Historic Site** (☎ 660-837-3330) was first settled in 1810 and was later an important stopover on the Santa Fe Trail. It has more than a dozen historic buildings and a great **visitor center** (admis-

---

ROUTE 66: GET YOUR KICKS IN MISSOURI

The 'Show Me' state will show you a fat slice of the Mother Road. Meet the route in **St Louis** (p666), where it will take you past the **Gateway Arch** (p668), **International Bowling Museum** (p670) and **Ted Drewes Frozen Custard** (p671). On your way out of town, stop by the **Museum of Transportation** (☎ 314-965-7998; www.museumoftransport.org; 3015 Barrett Station Rd, off I-270 exit 8; adult/child 5-12 $4/2; ☻ 9am-4pm Tue-Sat, 11am-4pm Sun), which displays pieces of Route 66's Coral Court motel, a Streamline Moderne landmark.

Follow I-44 (the interstate is built over most of Route 66 in Missouri) west to **Route 66 State Park** (☻ 7am-½hr after dusk), with its **visitor center** (☎ 636-938-7198; ☻ 9am-4:30pm) inside a 1935 roadhouse. Back on the interstate, detour at Eureka to the folk-art **Black Madonna Shrine** (☎ 636-938-5151; donation $5; ☻ 9am-4pm year-round, to 7pm May-Sep).

Speed west again on I-44 to Stanton, then follow the signs to family-mobbed **Meramec Caverns** (☎ 800-676-6105; www.americascave.com; adult/child $14/7; ☻ 9am-7pm), as interesting for their Civil War history and hokey charm as for their stalactites; and the conspiracy-crazy **Jesse James Wax Museum** (☎ 573-927-5233; adult/child $6/2.50; ☻ 9am-6pm daily Jun-Aug, 9am-5pm Sat & Sun May & Sep). Further west, take Business 44 through **Rolla** to gawk at the mini **Stonehenge replica** on the University of Missouri's campus. Rejoin I-44 westbound.

Ready for a snooze? Get off I-44 at Lebanon at the 1940s **Munger Moss Motel** (☎ 417-532-3111; www.mungermoss.com; 1336 E Rte 66; r $31-43) – its motto 'here yesterday, today and tomorrow.'

West of Springfield, drive on Hwy 96 through towns with names like Albatross and Rescue. Roll on into Civil War–era Carthage's historic town square and catch a flick at the **66 Drive-In Theatre** (☎ 417-359-5959; 17231 Old 66 Blvd, Carthage; adult/child $5/2). In Joplin, get on Hwy 66, turning onto old Route 66 before the Kansas state line.

For more information, contact the **Route 66 Association of Missouri** (www.missouri66.org). See also p30.

sion free; (🕐 10am-4pm) which has information about the Boone's Lick region.

Katy Trail State Park

Katy Trail State Park (☎ 660-882-8196, 800-334-6946; www.katytrailstatepark.com) boasts a superb 225-mile biking and hiking trail that connects St Charles and Clinton, 65 miles southeast of Kansas City. The trail runs along the former Missouri–Kansas–Texas railroad (the 'Katy'). Along its eastern end, the trail snakes between high bluffs and the Missouri River. Some of its most scenic sections are west of Defiance, where wee German towns make up 'Missouri's Rhineland.' Among these are hilltop Hermann, home to wineries and the cozy rooms of **Acorn Bunk & Bagel** (☎ 573-486-4003, 877-486-4003; www.bbonline .com/mo/acorn; 236 W 4th St, Hermann; r $40-85; ✖ 🐾). Another highlight is the stretch between Jefferson City and New Franklin, including areas inaccessible to cars. Amtrak stops in Hermann, Jeff City and Sedalia, and bike rentals and accommodations are available in each (and also in Defiance); check the park website for contact information.

OZARK MOUNTAINS

Most of the Ozarks are in Arkansas, but the charming hill country extends into the southern quarter of Missouri and into eastern Oklahoma.

The **Ozark Trail** (☎ 573-751-2479; www.ozarktrail .com) is a 300-mile hiking trail through parts of the Mark Twain National Forest. One day it will run 500 miles from St Louis to Arkansas' Ozark Highland Trail.

About 70 miles southwest of St Louis, **Bonne Terre Mine** (☎ 314-731-5003; www.2dive.com; walking/boat tour $12.50/17.50; 🕐 10:30am-3:30pm, to 4:30pm Fri-Sun) is near the intersection of Hwy 47 and US 67. The water-filled, 80-sq-mile mine, built in 1864 to extract lead, is open for scuba diving on weekends only and requires a two-dive minimum. Dives start at $65.

Two unique parks lie south of the mine. At **Johnson's Shut-Ins State Park** (☎ 573-546-2450), 8 miles north of Lesterville on Hwy N, the swift Black River swirls through canyon-like gorges ('shut-ins'); there's a swimming area a quarter mile from the park office. At **Elephant Rocks State Park** (☎ 573-546-3454), on the northwest edge of Graniteville on Hwy 21, enormous, one-billion-year-old rocks

stand end-to-end like circus elephants; a gentle trail takes you through.

North of US 60, midway between Cape Girardeau and Springfield, the **Ozark Scenic Riverways** (☎ 573-323-4236) – Current River and Jack's Fork – boast 134 miles of splendid canoeing and tubing. There are six **camp grounds** along the Riverways. **Van Buren**, on Hwy 60, has motels and canoe rentals. Take the fun car ferry across the river, off Hwy KK near Rector.

Branson

Hokey Branson is a love-it-or-hate-it tourist town (population 6050). The main attractions are the 47 theaters hosting 100 country music and corny comedy shows. During peak season – June and July, and Labor Day to Christmas – the population swells to 150,000. About 65% of the visitors who pour in are seniors.

The neon-lit '76 Strip' (Hwy 76) is an Ozark Vegas with miles of motels, restaurants, wax museums, and music and comedy theaters putting on three shows daily. When shows let out, traffic crawls. Watch for the color-coded routes that bypass it.

The **visitor center** (☎ 417-334-4136, 800-272-6766; www.explorebranson.com; Hwy 248), just west of the US 65 junction, has town and lodging information. The scores of 'Visitor Information' centers around town offer free tickets to shows if you'll sit through a 90-minute time-share plug.

Many **theater shows** are associated with particular performers (often performing in peak season only), such as Wayne Newton, Andy Williams, the Osmond Brothers, Bobby Vinton, Yakov Smirnoff and Mel Tillis. Other shows include the long-running, cornball 'Baldknobbers Jamboree.' Prices range from about $25 to $45 a head; theaters usually run afternoon and evening shows, and sometimes morning ones. For tickets, call **Ozark Ticket & Travel** (☎ 888-493-1222; www.branson.com; service charge $2-3). Reserve a week in advance during peak season.

Two outdoor attractions, open since 1959, spurred the Branson boom. Huge **Silver Dollar City** (☎ 417-336-7180, 800-831-4386; www.silverdollar city.com; adult/child 4-11 $44/33; 🕐 9:30am-7pm, reduced hrs in winter), west of town, is an amusement park simulating the Mark Twain era with music shows, replica buildings and craft shops. The **Shepherd of the Hills** (☎ 417-334-4191,

GREAT PLAINS

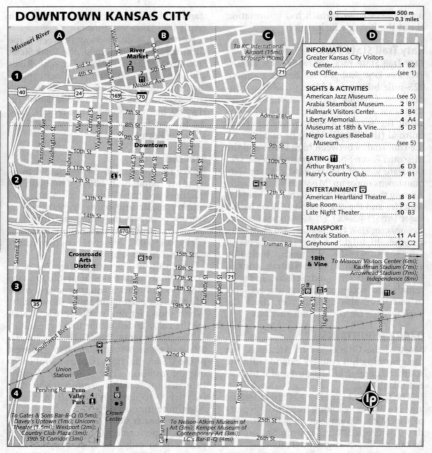

DOWNTOWN KANSAS CITY

| 0 | 500 m |
| 0 | 0.3 miles |

INFORMATION
Greater Kansas City Visitors
  Center...**1** B2
Post Office....................................(see 1)

SIGHTS & ACTIVITIES
American Jazz Museum.............(see 5)
Arabia Steamboat Museum............**2** B1
Hallmark Visitors Center................**3** B4
Liberty Memorial...............................**4** A4
Museums at 18th & Vine.................**5** D3
Negro Leagues Baseball
  Museum.......................................(see 5)

EATING
Arthur Bryant's.................................**6** D3
Harry's Country Club.......................**7** B1

ENTERTAINMENT
American Heartland Theatre.........**8** B4
Blue Room...**9** C3
Late Night Theater.........................**10** B3

TRANSPORT
Amtrak Station................................**11** A4
Greyhound.......................................**12** C2

800-653-6288; www.theshepherdofthehills.com; 5586 W Hwy
76; with dinner $38) is a show based on a home-
spun novel of Ozark life.

Branson fills up with package-tour visitors during peak times. To snare any of
the overpriced accommodations, you might
have to use a reservation service: **Branson
Hotline** (☎ 800-523-7589; www.bransonhotline.com)
books rooms for $50 and up, and **Branson
Vacation Reservations** (☎ 800-221-5692; www.bran
sonamerica.com) has package deals (three shows
and two nights for $239).

Table Rock Lake, southwest of town, is a
deservedly popular destination for boating, fishing, camping and other outdoor
activities. It also can have less expensive,
more scenic lodging. Try **Indian Trails Resort**

(☎ 417-338-2327; www.indiantrailsresort.com; Indian
Point Rd; cottages with kitchenettes from $51; ☒), on
the lake and 9 miles east of Branson.

KANSAS CITY

Big, open and inviting, Kansas City (KC)
is famed for its BBQ (90-plus joints slather
it on), fountains (second only to Rome in
quantity) and jazz. While the latter doesn't
swing as it once did, the Jazz Museum
can fill you in on what it was like when
Charlie Parker was around here blowing
notes. These days, KC has sobered up to
become more tax town than sax town – the
Internal Revenue Service and H&R Block's
headquarters tower over downtown – but
neighborhoods like Westport make KC a

perfectly pleasant place to while away a couple of days.

History
KC began life in 1821 as a trading post but really came into its own once westward expansion began. The Oregon, California and Santa Fe trails all pushed off from here, when the town was known as Westport.

Jazz exploded in the 1930s under mayor Tom Pendergast's Prohibition-era tenure, when he allowed alcohol to flow freely. At one time, KC had more than 100 nightclubs, dance halls and vaudeville houses swinging to the beat (and booze). The Jazz District alone had 60 clubs; and legends like Count Basie and Charlie Parker called KC home. The roaring good times ended with Pendergast's indictment on tax evasion and the clubs had mostly died out by 1944.

KC was a bustling farm-distribution and industrial center for generations – a serious 'cow town.' Its giant stockyards closed in 1991, but not without bestowing the legacy of KC's renowned BBQ.

Orientation
State Line Rd, running north–south, divides KC Missouri and KC Kansas (which has little to offer travelers, as it's mostly suburbs). KC Missouri has some distinct areas, including the historic River Market, centered on 5th St and Walnut St, north of downtown; the gallery-filled Crossroads Arts District by Baltimore and 20th Sts; and the historic African American Jazz District at 18th and Vine. Food and drink areas include Westport, on Westport Rd near Broadway, south of downtown; the 39th St Corridor, just west of Westport by the Kansas border; and the upscale, chain-store–laden Country Club Plaza (often shortened to 'the Plaza'), based on Broadway between 46th and 48th Sts.

Information
BOOKSTORES
Barnes & Noble (☎ 816-753-1313; 420 W 47th St; ◯ 9am-11pm) At the Plaza.

EMERGENCY
Emergency number (☎ 911) Police, ambulance, fire.

INTERNET ACCESS
Westport's cafés often have Internet access or wi-fi.

Westport Coffee House (☎ 816-756-3222; 4010 Pennsylvania St; per hr $6; ◯ 7:30am-11pm Mon-Thu, 7:30-1am Fri, 10am-1am Sat, 10am-10pm Sun) Provides Internet access.

INTERNET RESOURCES
Kansas City Arts Council (www.artskc.org) Provides the performing and visual arts low-down.
Barscoop (www.barscoop.com) Helps dedicated drinkers plot their evening.

MEDIA
The **Kansas City Star** (www.kansascity.com) is the daily paper; its *Preview* entertainment section comes out on Thursday. The **Pitch** (www.pitch.com) is a free weekly alternative paper.

MEDICAL SERVICES
Kansas University Medical Center (☎ 913-588-5000; 3901 Rainbow Blvd) In Kansas, just across the border from the 39th St Corridor.

POST
Post office (☎ 816-283-3460; 1100 Main St in City Center Sq)

TOURIST INFORMATION
Greater Kansas City Visitors Center (☎ 816-221-5242, 800-767-7700; www.visitkc.com; 22nd fl, 1100 Main St in City Center Sq; ◯ 8:30am-5pm Mon-Fri) City-oriented information.
Country Club Plaza Visitors Center (☎ 816-691-3866; 4907 Central St; ◯ 10am-6pm) Another city outlet.
Missouri Visitors Center (☎ 816-889-3330; www.visitmo.com; 4010 Blue Ridge Cutoff, off I-70, by the stadiums; ◯ 8am-5pm) Statewide maps and information.

Sights & Activities
The **Museums at 18th & Vine** (☎ 816-474-8463; 1616 E 18th St; adult for 1/2 museums $6/8, child 5-11 for 1/2 museums $2.50/4; ◯ 9am-6pm Tue-Sat, noon-6pm Sun) are well worth visiting. You can play drums to Sonny Rollins at the interactive **American Jazz Museum** (www.americanjazzmuseum.com), which also has displays on KC Kansas native Charlie Parker. Visit the **Negro Leagues Baseball Museum** (www.nlbm.com) to learn about African American teams (eg the KC Monarchs and New York Black Yankees) that flourished until baseball became fully integrated in 1959. Displays cover stars such as Satchel Paige and Jackie Robinson.

Giant badminton shuttlecocks (courtesy of Claes Oldenburg) absurdly surround

GREAT PLAINS

the **Nelson-Atkins Museum of Art** (☎ 816-561-4000; www.nelson-atkins.org; 4525 Oak St; admission free; ☻ 10am-4pm Tue-Thu, 10am-9pm Fri, 10am-5pm Sat, noon-5pm Sun; P). The grand, ever-expanding facility holds an excellent collection of American, European and Asian art, including a 14th-century Chinese temple. Nearby is the **Kemper Museum of Contemporary Art** (☎ 816-753-5784; www.kemperart.org; 4420 Warwick Blvd; admission free; ☻ 10am-4pm Tue-Thu, 10am-9pm Fri & Sat, 11am-5pm Sun). The museums are 5 miles south of downtown, two blocks east of Country Club Plaza.

Home to 200 tons of salvaged 'treasure' from a riverboat that was snagged and then sunk in 1856, the **Arabia Steamboat Museum** (☎ 816-471-4030; www.1856.com; 400 Grand Blvd; adult/child 4-12 $9.75/4.75; ☻ 10am-5:30pm Mon-Sat, noon-5pm Sun), located in River Market, offers insight to the crafty Missouri River, which claimed 289 steamboats.

The **Hallmark Visitors Center** (☎ 816-274-3613; www.hallmarkvisitorscenter.com; admission free; ☻ 9am-5pm Tue-Fri, 9:30am-4:30pm Sat) features not-terribly-interesting exhibits on how greeting cards are made, but hey, Hallmark is one of KC's biggest employers, so cut it some slack. It's located in the Crown Center shopping complex.

Across Main St is the towering **Liberty Memorial**, built for WWI veterans.

Festivals & Events
American Royal Barbecue (www.americanroyal.com) The world's largest BBQ contest takes place during the first weekend in October.

Sleeping
Downtown accommodations are costly and not well suited for optimal eats and drinks. Better value options are in Westport and the Plaza. The hotels listed below all provide free high-speed Internet access in rooms and wireless access in public areas. Add 14.85% tax to the rates.

Quarterage Hotel (☎ 816-931-0001; www.quarteragehotel.com; 560 Westport Rd; r from $84; P ✕) The locally-owned Quarterage is in Westport and about one mile from the Plaza. It offers modest, standard rooms with nice freebies like parking, hot breakfast and open-bar cocktails from 5pm to 7pm.

Embassy Suites (☎ 816-756-1720; www.embassysuites.com; 220 W 43rd St; r from $129; P ✕ ≋) It's the usual chain, but the prices and ameni-

ties – free hot breakfast, evening cocktails, indoor pool and parking – are good. It's a half block from Westport and three blocks from the Plaza.

Raphael Hotel (☎ 816-756-3800, 800-821-5343; www.raphaelkc.com; 325 Ward Pkwy at Wornall Rd; r from $140; P ✕) The Raphael is a swanky, European-style boutique hotel right on the Plaza. The 'traditional' rooms aren't huge, but the high-class service makes you forget about it.

Southmoreland Inn (☎ 816-531-7979; www.southmoreland.com; 116 E 46th St; r $130-190; P ✕) Southmoreland is an exceptionally nice, 12-room B&B in a big old mansion near the art museums and two blocks from the Plaza.

Eating & Drinking
Westport, 39th St and Country Club Plaza are your best bets for clusters of food and drink. Be sure and try a locally brewed Boulevard Beer, available at most alcohol-serving establishments. Bars stay open until 1:30am, some until 3am.

RIVER MARKET
Harry's Country Club (☎ 816-421-3505; www.harryscountryclub.com; 112 Missouri Ave; mains $5-11; ☻ 11-1:30am Mon-Sat) Harry's English-pub-meets-country-music ambience attracts a friendly crowd nibbling fried bologna sandwiches or pot roast, and swilling cans of Hamm's or glasses of whiskey.

WESTPORT
Pot Pie (☎ 816-561-2702; www.kcpotpie.com; 904 Westport Rd; mains $12-19; ☻ 11am-10pm Tue-Thu, 11am-11pm Fri, 5pm-11pm Sat) Check out the chalkboard inside because it announces what sort of fish, pork and beef dishes – and, of course, pot pies – are available daily. Lunch here is a good value.

Jerusalem Café (☎ 816-756-2770; 431 Westport Rd; mains $8-11; ☻ 11am-10pm Mon-Sat, 11am-8pm Sun) The menu carries all the Middle Eastern staples, both veg (hummus, baba ganouj) and nonveg (kabobs). You can smoke a hookah and drink coffee in the upstairs lounge.

39TH STREET CORRIDOR
D' Bronx (☎ 816-531-0550; 3904 Bell St; sandwiches $4-7; ☻ 10:30am-9pm Mon-Wed, 10:30am-10pm Thu, 10:30am-11pm Fri & Sat) It's a classic deli with 50 whopping hot and cold sandwiches to choose from, though the shining star is the crispy pizza.

'CUEING IT UP

Savoring hickory-and-oak smoked brisket, pork or ribs at one of the classic BBQ joints around town is a must for any meat eater. KC's own style of BBQ is pit-smoked and slathered with sauces ranging from sweet and tomato-based to tangy and vinegar-based. A juicy slab of ribs costs about $17 throughout the city. **Arthur Bryant's** (☎ 816-231-1123; www.arthurbryantsbbq.com; 1727 Brooklyn Ave; ⏰ 10am-9:30pm Mon-Thu, to 10pm Fri & Sat, 11am-8pm Sun) flops two handfuls of meat between outmatched slices of bread. Arguably the city's most famous BBQ is at **Gates & Sons Bar-B-Q** (☎ 816-753-0828; www.gatesbbq.com; 3201 Main St; ⏰ 10am-midnight), where it is assumed you'll want a frosted mug of beer with your brisket or turkey. Hole-in-the-wall **LC's Bar-B-Q** (☎ 816-923-4484; 5800 Blue Pkwy; ⏰ 11am-9pm Mon-Sat) is a modest joint that serves up immodest ribs.

Blue Koi (☎ 816-561-5003; 1803 W 39th St; mains $6-10; ⏰ 11am-9:30pm Mon-Thu, 11am-10:30pm Fri, noon-10:30pm Sun) This unpretentious Asian noodle shop doles out dumplings, soups and bubble teas (many of them spiked with alcohol) with West Coast panache.

Nichol's Lunch (☎ 816-561-5200; 39th St & Southwest Trafficway; mains $3-6; ⏰ closed Mon) This 24-hour greasy spoon kicks out breakfasts and burgers. It's best late-night when the people-watching perks up, and everyone from cowboys to transsexuals totter in for a fry-up.

COUNTRY CLUB PLAZA
Eden Alley (☎ 816-561-5415; www.edenalley.com; 707 W 47th St; mains $7-12; ⏰ 11am-9pm Mon-Sat) Those seeking respite from KC's BBQ will find vegetable-rich dishes like black bean quesadillas and spinach-mushroom loaf. Located in the Unity Temple's no-frills basement.

Entertainment

Check the **Pitch** (www.pitch.com) and other local media for listings.

LIVE MUSIC

Jazz, blues and rock venues are scattered across the city.

Davey's Uptown (☎ 816-753-1909; 3402 Main St) Local and regional alternative acts play nightly.

Blue Room (☎ 816-474-2929; 18th & Vine, in the Jazz Museum; admission $5) This slick club hosts jazz shows on Monday, Thursday, Friday and Saturday nights.

THEATER

KC's theater scene is more happening than you'd think.

Unicorn Theatre (☎ 816-531-7529; www.unicorn theatre.org; 3828 Main St) Unicorn stages contemporary, thought-provoking works.

Late Night Theater (☎ tickets 816-235-6222, theater 816-474-4568; www.latenighttheater.com; 1531 Grand Blvd) Silliness reigns at Late Night, ie 'Rock-ula,' a musical about a vampire hair band.

American Heartland Theatre (☎ 816-842-9999; www.ahtkc.com) The American Heartland Theatre mounts sizable regional productions; in Crown Center.

SPORTS

Arrowhead Stadium (☎ 816-920-9300; I-70 & Blue Ridge Cutoff) The NFL's **Chiefs** (www.kcchiefs.com) are the top ticket in town. When they're not kicking ass, the **Wizards** (www.kcwizards.com) pro soccer team plays at this stadium, east of downtown.

Kauffman Stadium (☎ 800-676-9257; I-70 & Blue Ridge Cutoff) Baseball's **Royals** (www.kcroyals.com) play at Kauffman, across the parking lot from Arrowhead.

Shopping

Music Exchange (☎ 816-931-7560; www.musicexchangekc.com; 4200 Broadway; ⏰ 10am-8pm Mon-Sat, to 9pm Fri, noon-6pm Sun) Westport's Exchange has a monstrous vinyl collection, including many old jazz records.

Getting There & Around

KC International Airport (☎ 816-243-5237; www.fly kci.com) is 17 miles northwest of downtown. A taxi into town costs about $42; call **Yellow Cab** (☎ 816-471-5000). Or take the cheaper **KCI Shuttle** (☎ 816-243-5000; $15).

Greyhound (☎ 816-221-2885; 1101 Troost St) sends buses daily to Omaha ($30, four hours), Chicago ($50, 13 hours) and St Louis ($32, five hours). **Amtrak** (☎ 816-421-3622) is just behind Union Station, with daily service to St Louis ($25 to $32, 5½ hours) and other cities.

Local transport is with **Metro buses** (☎ 816-221-0660; www.kcata.org; fare $1).

AROUND KANSAS CITY
Independence
Eight miles east of Kansas City, Independence was the home of Harry S Truman, US president from 1945 to 1953. The **Truman Presidential Library & Museum** (☎ 816-833-1400; www.trumanlibrary.org; 500 W US 24; adult/child 6-18 $7/3; ☺ 9am-5pm Mon-Sat, to 9pm Thu, noon-5pm Sun) exhibits more than 30,000 objects, from the presidential piano to the papers Truman signed authorizing the atomic bomb. See how Harry and Bess lived at the **Truman Home** (219 N Delaware St), packed with original belongings. Tour tickets are sold at the **visitor center** (☎ 816-254-9929; 223 N Main St; adult/child under 17 $4/ free; ☺ 8:30am-5pm, closed Mon winter). The courthouse where Harry began his political career is in nearby Independence Sq, as are mom-and-pop-type restaurants and stores. You'll also notice a huge, spiraling temple. Independence is the center of the Community of Christ, a Mormon splinter group.

Chain motels cluster around the junction of I-70 and Noland Rd (exit 12). **Serendipity B&B** (☎ 800-203-4299; www.bbhost.com/serendipitybb; 116 S Pleasant Ave; r $45-100), near Truman's home, is great value with six antique-like Victorian rooms and filling breakfasts.

St Joseph
For the best low-budget, interactive museum about mail delivery you'll ever see, head to St Joseph, 50 miles north of Kansas City. This is where, in 1860, the first Pony Express set out, carrying messages from 'St Jo' 1900 miles west to California. The service lasted just 18 months before going bust. The **Pony Express Museum** (☎ 816-279-5059; www.ponyexpress .org; 914 Penn St; adult/child 7-18 $4/2; ☺ 9am-5pm Mon-Sat, 1-5pm Sun) tells the story of the Express and its riders: 'skinny, wiry fellows' recruited to face death daily – 'orphans preferred.'

St Jo was also home to outlaw Jesse James (his last) and jazz great Coleman Hawkins, the namesake of a mid-June festival. Pick up a downtown walking-tour map at the **visitor center** (☎ 816-233-6688, 800-785-0360; www .stjomo.com; 109 S 4th St; ☺ 9am-6pm Mon-Fri, 8:30am-4pm Sat, noon-4pm Sun).

Housed in a former mental hospital, the large **Glore Psychiatric Museum** (☎ 816-364-1209; 3406 Frederick Ave; adult/child 7-18 $3/1; ☺ 10am-5pm Mon-Sat, 1-5pm Sun) is fascinating. Simple displays show how lobotomies accidentally began and how 'treatment' has advanced from the 'bath of surprise' to occupational therapy, such as painting.

Several chain motels are near I-29 exit 47.

IOWA

Author Bill Bryson jokes that he's from Iowa because 'someone has to be,' but Iowa has a few quirks up its sleeve. Yes, it's the state that has five hogs to every one person and the state whose recent contribution to science was the discovery that single-celled organisms have sex. But it's also the state that houses the writers' town of Iowa City; the commune-dwelling, refrigerator-builders of the Amana Colonies; Ozzy Osbourne's old (bat) chomping grounds of Des Moines; and the yogic-flying meditators of Vedic City.

See? And you thought it would be dull here.

History
After the 1832 Black Hawk War pushed local Native Americans westward, immigrants flooded into Iowa from all parts of the world and hit the ground farming. Some established experimental communities such as the Germans of the Amana Colonies (p683). Others spread out and kept coaxing the soil (95% of the land is fertile) until Iowa attained its current status as 'food capital of the world' and US leader in hog, corn and soybean production.

It ain't all about farming, though. This is the state that makes or breaks presidents. Ever since the early 1970s, the Iowa Caucus

---

IOWA FACTS

Nickname Hawkeye State
Population 2.9 million
Area 56,275 sq miles
Capital city Des Moines (population 196,100)
Official rock Geode
Birthplace of John Wayne (1907–79), author Bill Bryson (b 1951), *American Gothic* painter Grant Wood (1891–1942), actor Ashton Kutcher (b 1978)
Home of The world's first microwave oven (developed in Amana)
Famous for Madison County's bridges, John Deere tractors, hogs (No 1 in US pork production), Iowa Caucus that jumpstarts the presidential elections

has opened the national election battles and it's the first test that presidential candidates must pass en route to the White House. Lose Iowans' votes and your chances elsewhere dwindle considerably.

Information

Iowa sales tax is 5%, with many counties tacking on up to 2% more.

Iowa Bed & Breakfast Guild (☎ 800-743-4692; www.ia-bednbreakfast-inns.com)

Iowa highway conditions (☎ 800-288-1047, in Iowa 511; www.511ia.org)

Iowa state park information (☎ 515-281-5918; www.iowadnr.com) State parks are free to visit. Campsites cost $9 to $19; reservations not accepted.

Iowa Tourism Office (☎ 888-472-6035; www .traveliowa.com; 200 E Grand Ave, Des Moines, IA 50309)

DES MOINES

Des Moines, meaning 'of the monks' not 'corn' as the surrounding fields might suggest, is Iowa's spread-out capital and has a couple of good, free attractions. A fact not mentioned in the tourist brochures: before Ozzy Osbourne married Sharon and she started cooking for him, he bit the head off a bat here in 1982.

The Des Moines River slices through downtown. The Court Ave restaurant and entertainment district sits just west. East Village, at the foot of the capitol building and (yes) east of the river, is home to up-and-coming galleries, eateries and a few gay bars. Ingersoll Ave, west of the city center, is another hip area and one of the few places for late-night activity. I-80 and I-35 skirt Des Moines to the north; I-235 cuts through its middle.

Information

City View (www.dmcityview.com) Alternative online guide to eating, drinking, entertainment and politics.

Des Moines Register (www.dmregister.com) The local daily newspaper; its comprehensive *Datebook* entertainment guide comes out on Thursday.

Do Stuff (www.drake.edu/stuff2do.html) Drake University's online round-up of local entertainment and attractions.

Downtown post office (☎ 515-283-7730; 400 Locust St; 🕘 9am-5pm Mon-Fri)

Emergency number (☎ 911) Police, ambulance, fire.

FedEx Kinko's (☎ 515-282-5955; 100 Locust St, Ste 150; Internet per hr $12; 🕘 7am-8pm Mon-Fri, 9am-5pm Sat)

Iowa Methodist Medical Center (☎ 515-241-6212; 1200 Pleasant St)

Java Joe's (☎ 515-288-5282; 214 4th St; 🕘 7am-11pm Mon-Thu, 7am-midnight Fri & Sat, 9am-10pm Sun) Free wi-fi.

Visitor center (☎ 515-286-4960; www.destination desmoines.com; 405 6th Ave, off I-235 downtown; 🕘 8:30am-5pm Mon-Fri)

Sights & Activities

The **State Capitol** (☎ 515-281-5591; E 9th St & Grand Ave; admission free; 🕘 8am-4:30pm Mon-Fri, 9am-4pm Sat) must have been Liberace's favorite government building. Its every detail – from the sparkling gold dome to the smell of fried chicken wafting from the cafeteria – seems to strive to outdo the other. On no account miss the collection of first-ladies-of-Iowa dolls. The ambitious **Iowa Historical Building** (☎ 515-281-6412; 600 E Locust St; recommended donation adult/child $5/2; 🕘 9am-4:30pm Tue-Sat, noon-4:30pm Sun, open Mon Jun-Aug) has a 'favorite things of the 20th century' exhibit, which includes pacemakers and miniskirts.

The **Des Moines Art Center** (☎ 515-277-4405; 4700 Grand Ave; admission free; 🕘 11am-4pm Tue & Wed, 11am-9pm Thu, noon-4pm Sat & Sun), south of the I-235 42nd St exit, features a good contemporary collection, a sculpture garden and (on occasion) a talking 'butter cow.'

Sleeping

Nothing is terribly expensive in Des Moines. Then again, nothing is terribly cheap, either. Add 12% tax to the following rates.

Several chain motels are bunched at I-80/I-35 exit 131 in Urbandale, such as **Best Inn** (☎ 515-270-1111; www.bestinn.com; 5050 Merle Hay Rd; s/d $58/66; P ⊠ ⊠).

Cottage B&B (☎ 515-277-7559; www.thecottagedsm .com; 1094 28th St; r $89-109; P ⊠ ⊠) It's well-located near Drake University and a good value if you don't mind froofy, flowery colors and furnishings; private baths. Wireless Internet access available.

Ramada Inn (☎ 515-226-1600; 1600 114th St, exit 124 off I-80/I-35, in Clive; r from $64; P ⊠ ⊠) Offers continental breakfast where you can make your own waffles. Mmm, waffles.

Hotel Fort Des Moines (☎ 800-532-1466; www .hotelfortdesmoines.com; 1000 Walnut St; r/ste weekend $89/119, weekday $119/139; P ⊠ 🖵 ⊠) Everyone from Mae West to JFK has spent the night in the old-world Fort. Amenities include an indoor pool, business center with high-speed Internet and location next to frothy sips at Raccoon River Brewing Company. Parking costs $6.

Eating & Drinking

Downtown's Court Ave and East Village, as well as Ingersoll Ave to the west, are rich veins for gustatory satisfaction.

La Mie (☎ 515-255-1625; 841 42nd St; mains $14-21; ☺ lunch Mon-Sat, dinner Mon-Fri, brunch Sun) La Mie offers a bakery with a yum-filled pastry case up front, and a French-inspired bistro in back, where seasonal dishes range from trout meunière to a sausage-veal-and-white-bean concoction.

Java Joe's (☎ 515-288-5282; 214 4th St; items $3-7; ☺ 7am-11pm Mon-Thu, 7am-midnight Fri & Sat, 9am-10pm Sun) The small menu covers a lot of ground: sandwiches (corned beef, smoked turkey), Indian dishes (Madras lentils, ginger curry), vegetarian burritos, hummus and, of course, cupfuls of coffee. Live music on weekends.

Basil Prosperi (☎ 515-243-9819; 407 E 5th St; prix fixe $25; ☺ lunch Mon-Sat, dinner Fri & Sat) Basil's serves breads, baked goods and cheeses by day, but weekend nights are when the real action happens, ie a four-course, Continental extravaganza fit for royalty.

Vaudeville Mews (☎ 515-243-3270; www.vaudevillemews.com; 212 4th St; ✗) The Mews features a swell, turn-of-the-century bar and all the entertainment you care to chew, be it live music, indie films, poetry or experimental theater.

The Lift (☎ 515-288-3777; 222 4th St; ✗) The Lift is an artsy bar popular for its good beers and sassy martini list.

Getting There & Around

Des Moines International Airport (☎ 515-256-5100; www.dsmairport.com), southwest of downtown, offers limited air service. **Greyhound** (☎ 515-243-1773; 1107 Keosauqua Way) has buses leaving daily for Chicago ($42, 7½ hours) and Omaha ($26, 2½ hours). Amtrak's nearest stop is in Osceola, IA, 39 miles south.

MTA metro buses (☎ 515-283-8100; www.dmmta .com; 6th & Walnut Sts) run several local routes.

AROUND DES MOINES
Madison County

This sleepy county, about 30 miles southwest of the capital, slumbered for half a century until Robert James Waller's block-buster, tear-jerking novel *The Bridges of Madison County* and its movie version brought in scores of fans to check out the sites. The covered bridges where Robert and Francesca fueled their affair are here. Pick up a map at the Madison County **chamber of commerce** (☎ 515-462-1185, 800-298-6119; www .madisoncounty.com; 73 Jefferson St, Winterset; ☺ 9am-5pm Mon-Fri, 10am-4pm Sat, noon-4pm Sun). The **Covered Bridge Festival** is held in mid-October.

The **birthplace of John Wayne** (☎ 515-462-1044; 216 S 2nd St, Winterset; adult/child $3/1; ☺ 10am-4:30pm), aka Marion Robert Morrison, is in a humble dwelling.

Neal Smith National Wildlife Refuge

About 20 miles east of Des Moines, near Prairie City, this wonderful, 5000-acre wild-life refuge is the site of an unprecedented tallgrass reconstruction project. See the film and displays at the **Prairie Learning Center** (☎ 515-994-3400; www.tallgrass.org; Hwy 163; admission free; ☺ 9am-4pm Mon-Sat, noon-5pm Sun) to learn about the ecosystems that have vanished. Outside are herds of buffalo and elk, plus a 5-mile auto tour and 2-mile hiking trail.

Eldon

About 90 miles southeast of Des Moines, on Hwy 16, tiny Eldon lives in infamy as the source of Grant Wood's iconic (and often parodied) *American Gothic* (1930). You can see the house, on the subsequently named American Gothic St, and strike your own grimacing pose with whatever 'tool' you have on you. The actual painting is in the Art Institute of Chicago.

Fairfield & Vedic City

Hmm, where to go to meditate for world peace and practice yogic flying (where the body lifts up and moves forward in short bursts) with like-minded masses – San Francisco? LA? Try the cornfields of southern Iowa. Anchored by the Maharishi University of Management, founded by the Maharishi Mahesh Yogi – he who taught the Beatles transcendental meditation in India – Fairfield and Vedic City host an unusual (by Iowa standards) array of vegetarian restaurants, incense-wafting shops and ayurvedic spas. In hippie-trippy Vedic City all homes face east, with small domes on top and rooms oriented to correspond with sun and moon cycles.

The **Best Western Fairfield Inn** (☎ 641-472-2200; www.bestwesternfairfieldinn.com; 2200 W Burlington Ave; r $65-82; ✖ ✦) is good value compared to the towns' spa resorts. Pick up locally grown foodstuffs at **Everybody's** (☎ 641-472-5199; 501 N 2nd St; ✆ 6:30am-9:30pm Mon-Fri, 7:30am-9:30pm Sat & Sun), an organic grocery store with attached café. The gallery-hopping **Artwalk** draws crowds the first Friday of each month.

Fairfield is 105 miles southeast of Des Moines on Hwy 34; Vedic City is a few miles north on Hwy 1.

ALONG I-80

Most of Iowa's attractions are within an easy drive of I-80, which runs east–west across the state's center. Des Moines is midway along the road.

Quad Cities

Four cities straddle the Mississippi River by I-80 – Davenport and Bettendorf in Iowa, and Moline and Rock Island in Illinois. See p595 for Illinois-side details.

The **Iowa 80 Truckstop** (☎ 563-284-6961; www.iowa80truckstop.com; I-80 exit 284 in Walcott; ✆ 24hr) is the world's biggest, baby, complete with a Hall of Fame displaying actual rigs, a movie theater, chrome-laden store, truck wash and dentist's office to supplement the usual eateries and gas pumps. A more refined experience awaits at the new **Figge Art Museum** (☎ 563-326-7804; www.figgeartmuseum.org; 225 W 2nd St, Davenport; adult/child 3-12 $7/4; ✆ 11am-5pm Tue-Sun, to 9pm Thu), with unexpectedly good Haitian and Mexican Colonial collections and views of Big Muddy.

Iowa City

The former capital is now a busy student town. The University of Iowa campus spills across both sides of the Iowa River; on the east side (at Iowa Ave and Clinton St) it mingles with riverfront parks and downtown restaurants and bars. In summer (when the student-to-townie ratio evens out) bands often play at the pedestrian mall. The **visitor center** (☎ 319-337-6592, 800-283-6592; www.icccvb.org; 408 1st Ave; ✆ 8am-5pm Mon-Fri), in neighboring Coralville, has information.

Prairie Lights Books (☎ 319-337-2681; 15 S Dubuque St; ✆ 9am-10pm Mon-Sat, 9am-6pm Sun) hosts readings by famous authors practically every night, a testament to its connection to the university's prestigious Writer's Workshop.

Near Coralville Lake, the **Devonian Fossil Gorge** (☎ 319-338-3543; Dubuque St; admission free; ✆ dawn-dusk), 2.5 miles north of I-80 exit 244, is a Devonian-era seafloor with countless fossils, all exposed by the 1993 floods.

In West Branch, 11 miles east on I-80, is the worthwhile **Herbert Hoover Birthplace & Library** (☎ 319-643-5301; adult/child $5/free; ✆ 9am-5pm). Hoover served as president from 1928 to 1932 and was a famous relief administrator, but he's more remembered (deservedly or not) as the namesake of Depression-era 'Hoovervilles.'

A mile from the university, **Alexis Park Inn** (☎ 888-925-3947; www.alexisparkinn.com; 1165 S Riverside Dr; ste $60-100; ✖ ✦) provides nifty aviation-themed suites and free perks like laundry, breakfast delivered door-front and high-speed wireless access. Four-post beds and other antiques adorn the 1913 Dutch Colonial **Brown Street Inn** (☎ 319-338-0435; www.brownstreetinn.com; 430 Brown St; r $65-110; ✖ ✖ ▣), an easy walk from downtown.

It's food and beer galore around downtown. **Masala** (☎ 319-338-6199; 9 Dubuque St; mains $4-9; ✆ lunch & dinner) serves yummy vegetarian curries; try the well-stocked lunch buffet ($6.65). **Baldy's** (☎ 319-338-1010; 18 S Clinton St; wraps $5-7; ✆ 9am-7pm Mon-Fri, 9am-3pm Sat, 11am-3pm Sun) makes 50 different wrap sandwiches; bald people get a 5% discount. At **Dave's Foxhead Tavern** (☎ 319-351-9824; 402 E Market St) Nobel and Pulitzer prize-winning writers mingle with scraggly regulars under the namesake critter lording over the bar.

Infrequent buses depart from the **Greyhound station** (☎ 319-337-2127; 404 E College St) to Des Moines ($20 to $28, two hours) and Chicago ($29 to $43, 5½ hours).

Amana Colonies

These seven villages, 18 miles northwest of Iowa City, are stretched along a 15-mile loop. All were established as German religious communes in the 1850s by Inspirationists, who follow a belief in *Werkzeuge*, the divine revelation of inspired prophets. Unlike the Amish and Mennonite religions, Inspirationists embrace modern technology, evident in their booming refrigerator business (note the plant in Middle Amana).

Today the well-preserved villages offer a glimpse at this unique culture, and there are lots of arts, crafts, cheeses, baked goods and wines to buy. Stop at the Amana Colonies

GREAT PLAINS

visitor center (☎ 800-579-2294; www.amanacolonies
.com; 622 46th Ave, Amana; ☺ 9am-5pm Mon-Sat, 10am-
5pm Sun) for the essential guide map.

Museums are sprinkled throughout the villages. Popular stops include the **Amana Woolen Mill** (☎ 800-222-6430; 800 48th Ave, Amana; admission free; ☺ 8am-5pm Mon-Thu, 8am-6pm Fri & Sat, 11am-5pm Sun May-Oct, reduced Nov-Apr) and the **Barn Museum** (☎ 319-622-3058; 2 blocks north off Hwy 6, South Amana; adult/child/youth $3.50/1/1.75; ☺ 9am-5pm Apr-Oct), which has Henry Moore's collection of miniature replicas.

A $8 combo ticket ($15 for a family pass) gets you into the insightful **Amana Heritage Museum** (☎ 319-622-3567; 4310 220th Trail, Amana; ☺ 10am-5pm Mon-Sat, noon-4pm Sun Apr-Oct, 10am-5pm Sat Nov-Mar), the **Communal Kitchen & Cooper Shop Museum** (☎ 319-622-3567; J St, Middle Amana; ☺ noon-5pm Mon-Fri, 10am-5pm Sat, noon-4pm Sun May-Oct), the agricultural museum (South Amana), church museum and restored general store museum (both in Homestead). Get your ticket at any of these sites. Individually all cost $4, except the Heritage museum which costs $6; kids are free.

The villages are home to a campsite and many good-value B&Bs, including Homestead's timeless **Die Heimat** (☎ 319-622-3937, 888-613-5463; www.dheimat.com; 4434 V St; r $75-90; ☒ ☒), with its simple, elegant rooms and whopping buffet breakfast.

One of the Amanas' top draws is the hefty-portioned, home-cooked German cuisine. Closest to I-80 is **Zuber's Restaurant** (☎ 319-622-3911; 2206 44th Ave, Homestead; mains $11-16; ☺ lunch & dinner Mon-Sat, brunch & dinner Sun), which serves great pork chop and spaetzle meals. Keep an eye out for Millsteam wheat beer, brewed in these parts.

Loess Hills Byway

The well-signed Loess Hills Byway is an inviting 200-mile network of roads that run along Iowa's western edge, parallel to I-29. It's named for the rare loess (rhymes with Gus), a windblown glacier-ground soil that began piling up into unique formations about 18,000 years ago. Steep, terraced bluffs are the result today. Nowhere but China do loess hills reach these heights.

The most dramatic scenery is off I-29 (north of Council Bluffs), in Harrison and Monona Counties; exit I-29 at Hwy 183 and head north. In Moorhead, stop at the **Loess Hills Hospitality Association** (☎ 712-886-5441; www

---

BICYCLING & BOOZING THROUGH THE HEARTLAND

Described as a rolling Mardi Gras and held the last week in July, **Ragbrai** (Register's Annual Great Bike Ride Across Iowa) started in 1973 when a few guys from the *Des Moines Register* up and biked across the state. Today 8500 riders – young, old, in and out of shape – start with their back wheel in the Missouri River and pedal for seven days until their front wheel hits the ol' Mississip'. They camp in small host towns, inhale the down-home grub, drink beer and, above all, absorb the landscape and people-scape of Iowa. To submit a rider application, go to www.ragbrai.org and apply by April 1. Participants are chosen by lottery.

.loesshillstours.com; 119 Oak St; ☺ 9am-4:30pm Mon-Sat, 1-4:30pm Sun Apr-Nov, 1-4pm Mon-Sat Dec-Mar) for route maps and tips on hikes.

ALONG US 20

US 20 is Iowa's northern passage from Dubuque on the Mississippi River to Sioux City on the Missouri River.

Dubuque

Dubuque makes a great stop: 19th-century Victorian homes line its narrow, and surprisingly urban, streets between the Mississippi River and seven steep hills. Those seeking action can canoe on the area's rivers, cycle the 26-mile Heritage Trail or square dance.

Get information from the **visitor center** (☎ 563-556-4372; www.traveldubuque.com; 300 Main St; ☺ 9:30am-5pm, reduced in winter) near the river.

The **4th Street Elevator** (☎ 563-582-6496; 4th St & Fenelon; adult/child round-trip $2/1; ☺ 8am-10pm Apr-Nov) at the Fenelon Place Elevator Company climbs a steep hill for huge views. Ring the bell to begin the ride. Learn about 300 years of life on the Mississippi at the impressive **National Mississippi River Museum & Aquarium** (☎ 563-557-9545; 350 E 3rd St; adult/child 3-6/child 7-17 $9.75/4/7.50; ☺ 10am-5pm Sep-May, 10am-6pm Jun-Aug). Nearby, the **Spirit of Dubuque** (☎ 563-583-8093; www.dubuqueriverrides.com; 3rd St, at Ice Harbor; adult/child $14/8.50; ☺ May-Oct, call for schedule) offers Mississippi cruises. Bird-watchers may see the national bird at **Eagle Point Park**, north of downtown (take Rhomberg to Shiras).

The historic **Julien Inn** (☎ 800-798-7098; www .julieninn.com; 200 Main St; r $49-79, ste $85-120; ✖) is fun. The lobby flaunts its 1960s makeover; fleur-de-lis signs hang over carpeted doors; a little bedside bulb lights up when guests have a message. Dubuque has great B&Bs too, including the lovely **Richards House** (☎ 563-557-1492; www.therichardshouse.com; 1492 Locust St; r with shared bath $40-65, r with private bath $50-95; ✖ ✖).

Try to make it to **Breitbach's Country Dining** (☎ 563-552-2220; 563 Balltown Rd, Balltown; mains $9-16, weekend buffet $11; ☯ breakfast, lunch & dinner), a rewarding 17-mile drive north of Dubuque. Breitbach's has been serving gut-busting cod and chicken dinners since 1852. Back in town, **Shot Tower Inn** (☎ 563-556-1061; 390 Locust St; large pizza $16; ☯ 11am-11pm Sun-Thu, 11am-midnight Fri & Sat) is a pizza place by the elevator with a deck and pitchers of beer.

The physically and spiritually hungry alike will find sustenance at **Our Lady of the Mississippi Abbey** (☎ 563-582-2595; www.mississip piabbey.org; 8318 Abbey Hill Lane, 7 miles south of Dubuque off I-52), where Trappistine nuns stir up cream, butter, chocolate and God's love to create **Trappistine Creamy Caramels** (☎ 866-556-3400; www.trappistine.com). Mail order available.

Dyersville & Around
An otherwise quiet farm town, Dyersville attracts thousands of visitors each year for two reasons: baseball and toys. Run around the bases at the **Field of Dreams baseball diamond** (☎ 888-875-8404; www.fodmoviesite.com; 28963 Lansing Rd; admission free; ☯ 9am-6pm Apr-Nov), as seen in the 1989 film.

Dyersville's farm-toy show in November attracts more than 20,000 fans, and four farm-toy manufacturers are here. Plus there's the surprising **National Farm Toy Museum** (☎ 563-875-2727; www.nationalfarmtoymuseum .com; 1110 16th Ave; adult/child $4/2; ☯ 8am-6pm) with a fun film and 30,000 historic toy tractors and barns.

Waterloo & Around
Home of four John Deere tractor plants, Waterloo is the place to get one of those prized green-and-yellow caps that you've seen all over middle America. Fun tractor-driven tours (1½ hours) of the **John Deere Tractor Assembly** (☎ 319-292-7697; 3500 E Donald St; tours free; ☯ 8am, 10am & 1pm) show how these vehicles are made ('with pride'). Minimum age is 13 and reservations required.

The sleeping's just fine at **Heartland Inn** (☎ 319-235-4461; www.heartlandinnds.com; 1809 LaPorte Rd, I-380 exit 72; r $70-90; ✖ 🖳 🖳), which has an indoor pool, continental breakfast and free Internet access (lobby terminal and wireless in rooms).

NORTH DAKOTA

It's flat, cold and *way* up there – but North Dakota is definitely not the same old ordinary vacation everybody else is doing. In fact, it's the least-visited state in the US, though that has more to do with location than appeal. The vast, wide-open landscape lends itself to – well, firearms. Hunting is one of the state's main draws, as are fishing, bird-watching and wildlife-watching in general. Pheasants and geese are as common as houseflies, and the lakes teem with walleye. Hotels even offer discounted 'sportsmen's rates,' big-game freezer storage and boat parking areas. Raise the topic of whether hunting is politically correct at your own risk.

Outdoor pursuits, from hiking to water sports, are the highlight of North Dakota, and the best place for most of them is the renowned Theodore Roosevelt National Park. As for urban areas, don't miss Fargo, made famous by the Coen Brothers' movie. It has a newly revitalized downtown and surprising sophistication.

History
During their epic journey, Lewis and Clark spent more time in what is now North Dakota than any other state, meeting up with Shoshone guide Sacagawea on their way west. In the mid-19th century, smallpox epidemics came up the Missouri River, decimating the Arikara, Mandan and Hidatsa tribes, who affiliated and established the Like-a-Fishhook Village in the mid-19th century. When the railroad arrived in North Dakota in the 1870s, thousands of settlers flocked in to take up allotments under the Homestead Act. By 1889 the state population was more than 250,000, half foreign-born (one in eight were from Norway).

Young Theodore Roosevelt came here to ditch his city-slicker image and get himself roughened up; later he became the president who created the first national parks.

GREAT PLAINS

NORTH DAKOTA FACTS

Nicknames Peace Garden State, Roughrider State, Flickertail State

Population 642,400

Area 70,705 sq miles

Capital city Bismarck (population 55,532)

Official flower Wild prairie rose

Birthplace of Singer Peggy Lee (1920–2002), actress Angie Dickinson (b 1931), homerun hero Roger Maris (1934–85), cream of wheat

Home of Actress Angie Dickinson, singer Peggy Lee, basketball player and coach Phil Jackson, writer and philosopher William H Gass

Famous for World's largest buffalo and Holstein statues, Teddy Roosevelt's retreat, Mandan villages

Mining has increased in recent years, and many family farms have been taken over by big agricultural companies. Though North Dakota's job growth has slightly outpaced that of its downstairs neighbor, South Dakota's population is increasing while North Dakota's is set to remain static or even shrink.

Information

North Dakota's sales tax is 5%.

State Tourism Department (☎ 701-328-2525, 800-435-5663; www.ndtourism.com)

North Dakota Parks and Recreation (☎ 701-328-5357, Bismarck; campsite reservations ☎ 800-807-4723) Visitors to state parks will need to purchase a $4 daily vehicle permit.

Highway conditions (☎ 701-328-7623)

ALONG I-94

The quickest, if not exactly the most scenic, route across North Dakota, I-94 also provides easy access to most of the state's top attractions.

Fargo

Named for the Fargo of Wells Fargo Bank, North Dakota's biggest city had an important role in the economic development of the region. It's been a fur-trading post, a frontier town, a quick-divorce capital and a haven for folks in the Federal Witness Protection Program, not to mention the namesake of the Coen Brothers' film *Fargo* (though the movie was actually filmed in Minnesota). Its location along the Red River was chosen as a crossing point be-

hind closed doors by the folks who ran the Northern-Pacific Railway back in 1871. The history of the city's growth is told in an interesting photo display in the baggage room of the old **railroad depot** (7th & Main Sts; admission free; ✆ 7:30am-4:30pm Mon-Fri).

Housed in a grain elevator, the Fargo-Moorhead **visitor center** (☎ 701-282-3653, 800-235-7654; 2001 44th St; ✆ 7:30am-7pm Mon-Fri, 9am-6pm Sat, 10am-5pm Sun in summer, call for hr rest of year), off I-94 exit 348, has free popcorn, coffee and brochures.

The modern, ambitious **Plains Art Museum** (☎ 701-232-3821; www.plainsart.org; 704 1st Ave N; adult/child $3/2.50; ✆ 10am-5pm Tue-Sat, 10am-8pm Thu, 1-5pm Sun) features sophisticated programming and a striking polished-industrial interior. Recent exhibits included an Edward Weston photo retrospective, a series of experimental short films and a permanent collection that includes major works by regional Native American artists.

In the historic downtown, the gorgeous 1926 art-deco **Fargo Theatre** (☎ 701-235-4152; 314 Broadway) has an old Wurlitzer organ and screens independent films.

Across the river in Moorhead, MN, the **Heritage Hjemkomst Interpretive Center** (☎ 218-299-5511; 202 1st Ave; adult/child $6/4; ✆ 9am-5pm Mon-Sat, 9am-8pm Tue, noon-5pm Sun) tells the story of a high school guidance counselor named Robert Asp who single-handedly built a 76ft replica of a 9th-century Viking ship in Hawley, MN, and how his family, after his death, sailed it to Norway in 1982.

Not the kind of digs you'd expect to find in these parts, the **Hotel Donaldson** (☎ 701-478-1000; www.hoteldonaldson.com; 101 Broadway; s/d $149/159) is in a refurbished century-old building. Its 17 suites, each designed around the work of a different regional artist, have flat-screen TVs, Bose stereo systems, heated floors, Jacuzzis, plush linens – the works. The chic lounge and restaurant are worth stopping in for a bite or a drink.

Across from the theater, **Babb's Coffee House** (☎ 701-271-0222; 315 Broadway; snacks $1-4; ✆ breakfast, lunch & dinner) has espresso beans airlifted from Seattle, comfy living-room furniture and big windows for viewing local wildlife.

Bismarck

Bismarck, North Dakota's capital, may not be the most immediately attractive city, but it has a handful of sights and some great day trips that make it a nice stopover. There's a cute downtown core as well as good beaches and trails along the Missouri River.

The Bismarck-Mandan **visitor center** (☎ 701-222-4308, 800-767-3555; 1600 Burnt Boat Dr, Bismarck; ⏰ 8am-5pm Mon-Fri) has friendly staff and free coffee. Check your email downtown at **Cyberia Internet Café** (☎ 701-223-9570; www.cyberia bismarck.com; 405 E Broadway; per hr $3; ⏰ 7am-9pm Mon-Fri, 9am-9pm Sat, noon-6pm Sun).

The impressive 1930s art-deco **State Capitol** (☎ 701-328-2480; N 7th St; ⏰ 8am-5pm Mon-Fri, tours hourly) is often referred to as the 'skyscraper of the prairie' and looks something like a Stalinist school of dentistry. There's an observation deck on the 18th floor. Behind the Sacagawea statue, the huge **North Dakota Heritage Center** (☎ 701-328-2666; Capitol Hill; admission free; ⏰ 8am-5pm Mon-Fri, 9am-5pm Sat, 11am-5pm Sun) offers comprehensive displays of the state's history.

Fort Abraham Lincoln State Park (☎ 701-663-9571), 7 miles south of Mandan on SR 1806, is well worth the detour. Its **On-A-Slant Indian Village** has three re-created Mandan earthlodges. Nearby you can tour full-scale replicas of the fort's cavalry post.

In Bismarck, motels congregate around I-94 exit 159 and State St. The main drag – consisting primarily of malls and megastores – is along Bismarck Expressway Ave at S Washington St. Here you'll find the *Alphaville*-esque **Expressway Inn** (☎ 701-222-2900; 200 Bismarck Expressway Ave; s/d $49/59; 🅿 🖥), with businesslike rooms and close proximity to several chain restaurants.

For a sampling of authentic American cuisine, line up with the locals in the drive-through lane at **Big Boy** (☎ 701-223-4125; 2511 E Main Ave; cheeseburgers 99¢, shakes $1.65; ⏰ breakfast, lunch & dinner). Out-of-this-world BBQ and over-the-top Martian decor define **Space Aliens** (☎ 701-223-6220; 1304 E Century; ribs $10-16, burgers $7-9; ⏰ lunch & dinner). If you can't face another plate of red meat, try the **Rice Bowl** (☎ 701-663-1986; 609 W Main St, Mandan; mains $6-12; ⏰ lunch & dinner).

Around Bismarck

North of Bismarck are several worthwhile attractions near the spot where Lewis and Clark wintered with the Mandan in 1804–05. The best is the **North Dakota Lewis & Clark Interpretive Center** (☎ 701-462-8535; adult/child $5/3; ⏰ 9am-7pm summer, 9am-5pm rest of year)

in Washburn, where you can learn about the duo's epic expedition and the Native Americans who helped them. **Fort Mandan** (CR 17), a replica of the 30-acre fort built by Lewis and Clark, is 2.5 miles west (10 miles downstream from the flooded original site). Just north of Stanton, the **Knife River Indian Villages** (☎ 701-745-3309; CR 37; admission free; ⏰ 7:30am-6pm summer, 8am-4:30pm rest of year) feature the sites of three Hidatsa and Mandan villages that were occupied for at least 900 years. Sacagawea joined Lewis and Clark from here.

West of Bismarck on I-94, stop and see **Sue, the World's Largest Holstein Cow** (New Salem). In case the appeal of a giant cow statue isn't immediately apparent, there are also great views from the site.

In Dickinson, 65 miles west of Sue, the **Dakota Dinosaur Museum** (☎ 701-225-3466; adult/child $6/3; ⏰ 9am-5pm summer only) has several dinosaur reconstructions and a Triceratops guarding the doorway. Ask to speak with the friendly fossil finder, who is usually around.

South of Bismarck, scenic SR 24/1806 goes through Standing Rock Indian Reservation. The **burial site of Sitting Bull** is at Fort Yates, not far from Lake Oahe.

Theodore Roosevelt National Park

Undoubtedly North Dakota's highlight, **Theodore Roosevelt National Park** (person/vehicle $5/10) near the state's western border has two very different units. The South Unit, near I-94 at Medora, has rolling badlands and a 36-mile scenic loop. The remote North Unit, 68 miles north on US 85, offers a 14-mile drive and has fewer visitors. An extensive area around the units is protected as the **Little Missouri National Grassland**.

Wildlife is everywhere – around 200 species of bird, mule and whitetail deer, wild horses, bighorn sheep, elk, herds of bison and, of course, sprawling subterranean prairie dog towns.

Hikers can explore 85 miles of backcountry trails (a permit is required). You can hike, ride or cycle the 110-mile **Maah Daah Hey Trail** (☎ 701-225-5151) between the park units.

The park has three visitor centers, including the Medora **visitor center** (☎ 701-623-4466; ⏰ 8am-8pm summer, call for hrs rest of year), with Theodore Roosevelt's old cabin out back. Roosevelt described this area as 'a land of vast, silent spaces, of lonely rivers, and of plains, where the wild game stared at the passing horsemen,' and it's hard to describe the place better even today.

Accommodations in nearby Medora include the **Badlands Motel** (☎ 701-623-4444, 800-633-6721; 501 Pacific Ave; s/d $80/93, May-Oct; 🛇 🖵), a rustic-lodge style motel a block from downtown. The park itself has two developed **campgrounds** ($10) and free backcountry camping. Contact the visitor center for information.

ALONG US 2

The Great Northern Rd, US 2 has a wilder profile than I-94. Keep an eye out for **missile silos** buried in the prairie, particularly between Grand Forks and Devils Lake and around Minot; they're surrounded by chain-link fence and not open to the public.

Grand Forks

The birthplace of cream of wheat, Grand Forks is also home to the University of North Dakota (UND) and an air force base. During the Red River flood in 1997, the entire town was evacuated, and 75% of the buildings and houses were flooded. Recovery was swift, though you can still see signs of the damage.

Get brochures about local attractions at the **Greater Grand Forks Visitors Center** (☎ 701-746-0444, 800-866-4566; 4251 Gateway Dr; 🕒 8am-5pm Mon-Fri, 9am-5pm Sat & Sun).

Originally part of the university, the **North Dakota Museum of Art** (☎ 701-777-4195; Centennial Dr; admission free; 🕒 9am-5pm Mon-Fri, 1-5pm Sat & Sun) is now an independent operation that hosts a dozen or so traveling exhibits each year.

The natural-foods co-op **Amazing Grains** (☎ 701-775-4542; 214 Demers Ave; 🕒 9am-8pm Mon-Fri, 9am-6pm Sat, noon-6pm Sun) has organic produce as well as deli sandwiches and baked goods for takeout.

Devils Lake

Birders and hunters go crazy for this town and its namesake, one of the best areas for waterfowl hunting in the country. The **visitor center** (☎ 701-662-4903, 800-233-8048; Hwy 2 E; 🕒 8am-5pm Mon-Fri, 9am-5pm Sat & Sun) has information on supplies and licenses.

The Sioux originally called the lake Miniwakan ('Spirit Water'), which settlers later misinterpreted as 'Evil Spirits.' Today it's

surrounded by campgrounds and a few state parks.

The Spirit Lake Sioux Indian Reservation includes **Fort Totten** (☎ 701-766-4441; adult/child $4/1.50; 🕒 8am-5pm May-Sep, other times by appointment), south of town. Built in 1861–63 as a military post, it was later converted to a Native American school and health center.

New Town

About 15 miles south of Stanley (on US 2), in the Fort Berthold Indian Reservation, New Town is worth a detour. Drive up **Crow Flies High Butte**, 4 miles west of town, for views of Lake Sakakawea. Across the bridge, the splendid **Three Tribes Museum** (☎ 701-627-4477; admission $3; 🕒 10am-6pm Apr-Nov) explains how the Mandan, Hidatsa and Arikara peoples affiliated in the 19th century. The reservation is host to several summer powwows.

West to Montana

Along US 2 heading west from Minot, the bleak horizon is dotted with attractively decrepit little prairie settlements just shy of ghost-town status. South of US 2 about 15 miles along remote SR 1804, **Fort Buford** (☎ 701-572-9034; admission free; 🕒 9am-6pm Mon-Fri May-Sep) was the Army outpost where Sitting Bull surrendered; both he and Chief Joseph were held here at times. About 2 miles away, the **Fort Union Trading Post** (☎ 701-572-9083; admission free; 🕒 8am-8pm summer, 9am-5:30pm rest of the year) is a reconstruction of the American Fur Company post built in 1828. At Fort Union, if so inclined, you can cross the border between Montana and North Dakota on foot.

SOUTH DAKOTA

Some of the most arresting scenery in the entire country is found here, tucked away in this remote and wild state. The weirdly lunar formations of the Badlands, like an inverted Grand Canyon, are unmissable. Then there's the spectacular beauty of the Black Hills, full of forests, mountains, creeks, canyons, and some of the most important sites in Native American culture. Two of the country's most recognizable monuments – Mt Rushmore and Crazy Horse – are carved into mountainsides here. There's bountiful wildlife and, in between, a few pleasant cities to explore.

GREAT PLAINS

SOUTH DAKOTA FACTS

Nicknames Sunshine State, Mt Rushmore State
Population 754,844
Area 77,125 sq miles
Capital city Pierre (population 14,000)
Official fossil Triceratops
Birthplace of Sitting Bull (c 1831–90), Crazy Horse (c 1838–77), Black Elk (c 1863–50), Calamity Jane (c 1852–1903), Tom Brokaw (b 1940), Catherine 'Daisy Duke' Bach (b 1954)
Home of News anchor Tom Brokaw, TV's Mary Hart, Catherine Bach ('Daisy Duke')
Famous for Mt Rushmore, Black Hills, the Sioux, *Little House on the Prairie*

I-90 gives good access to the state's premier attractions, crossing the state from Sioux Falls in the east to Spearfish in the west. Get off the interstate to enjoy South Dakota's unique 'pink' two-lane highways, made from the state's abundant reddish quartzite.

History

When the USA acquired South Dakota with the 1803 Louisiana Purchase, the region was very much the domain of the Sioux and a few brave fur trappers. It wasn't until the 1850s that the rich Dakota soil attracted the interest of settlers.

The 1868 Fort Laramie Treaty between the USA and the Sioux promised the Sioux large tracts of land on which to roam freely. The treaty was broken in 1874 when Lt Col George Custer led an expedition into the Black Hills in search of gold – unfortunately for the Sioux, he found it. Miners and settlers soon streamed in illegally, and the Sioux retaliated in the biggest of the Indian Wars.

The Battle of Little Bighorn in 1876 (see boxed text, below), in which the great Crazy Horse defeated Custer, was the Plains Indians' last major victory over the invaders. Faced with overwhelming force, the tribes split up. Sitting Bull fled to Canada, Crazy Horse turned in his gun in 1877, and the railroads and settlers inched forward. The final decimation of Sioux resistance came at Wounded Knee in 1890, when the army reacted to a revival of the Ghost Dance religion and ruthlessly massacred some 300 men, women and children. Much later, in 1973, Oglala Sioux loyal to the American Indian Movement occupied Wounded Knee and kept federal officers at bay for 70 days. Today South Dakota is one of the poorest states in the USA, but it has a vibrant tourism industry.

Information

South Dakota sales tax is 4%. In the state's center, roughly along the Missouri River, Central Time changes to Mountain Time.
Road construction information (☎ 605-773-3571)
South Dakota Department of Tourism (☎ 800-732-5682; www.state.sd.us/tourism) Publishes a good information pack, including the *South Dakota Guide to Indian Reservations & Art* and *Lewis and Clark: the South Dakota Adventure*.
South Dakota state parks (☎ 800-710-2267)
Winter road conditions (☎ 605-394-2255)

SIOUX FALLS

Sioux Falls, at the intersection of I-90 and I-29, has an attractive historic district downtown with trolleys running along its streets. Beyond the core, South Dakota's biggest city is a regional center for agriculture, as well as for marketing, banking and gambling.

SHERMAN VS THE SIOUX

By the late 1870s, it became obvious to the emergent USA that there was one remaining obstacle to the unfettered development of the Plains: the independent Plains Indians. In 1876 the army's General Sherman, responding to the Native Americans' decision not to return to their reservations, planned to eliminate all opposition in a three-pronged attack. The Sioux and other tribes gathered at Rosebud to live their last great year on the Plains. Thousands of warriors came – including chiefs Crazy Horse, Sitting Bull, Red Cloud, Little Big Man and Two Moons. Sitting Bull entered a trance and foresaw the death of white soldiers. Sherman's three forces then converged on the Sioux and their allies. The charismatic chief Crazy Horse and 1,500 braves held off the southern force at Rosebud, killing 90. Shortly after, Crazy Horse led the charge that annihilated Custer and the 7th Cavalry at the Battle of Little Bighorn.

The Sioux Falls **visitor center** (☎ 605-336-1620, 800-333-2072; www.siouxfalls.com; 200 N Phillips Ave; ⊙ 8am-5pm Mon-Fri) is near the Prairie Star gallery, which trades in Native American artwork.

See the Big Sioux River splash over rocks at **Falls Park** off Weber Ave north of downtown; the park has a good **visitor center** (☎ 605-367-7430; ⊙ 9am-9pm daily Apr-Sep, 9am-5pm Sat & Sun Oct-Apr) with an observatory. The huge pink quartzite **Old Courthouse Museum** (☎ 605-367-4210; 6th St & Main Ave; admission free; ⊙ 9am-5pm Mon-Sat, noon-5pm Sun), a restored 1890s building, has three floors of exhibits including a good display on Plains Indians.

At I-29 exit 77, in the city's southwest, is the no-frills **Empire Inn** (☎ 605-361-2345; 4208 W 41st St; s/d from $40/45; ✷ ✷), with a sauna, extra-long beds and a substantial continental breakfast included.

Around Sioux Falls

About 80 miles southwest of Sioux Falls, **Yankton**, listed on the National Register, is a well-preserved town at the east end of Lewis and Clark Lake, a boaters' paradise. The **visitor center** (☎ 605-665-3636, 800-888-1460; www.yanktonsd.com; 218 W 4th St; ⊙ 8am-5pm Mon-Fri, 10am-3pm Sat & Sun summer) conducts group tours, including the Historic Walking and Driving Tour that takes in 40 sites. **Lewis & Clark Resort** (☎ 605-665-2680; 43496 Lake Shore Dr; r $86-95, cabins from $169; ✷ ✷) offers basic motel units and cabins lakeside. Or camp in one of 400 sites at the **Lewis & Clark Recreation Area** (☎ 605-668-2985; campsites & RV sites $10-15, cabins $37).

Dedicated *Little House on the Prairie* fans should head to Laura Ingalls Wilder's former home in **De Smet**. There are two original **Wilder homes** (☎ 605-854-3383, 800-880-3383; www.discoverlaura.org; adult/child $7/4; ⊙ 9am-6pm daily summer, Mon-Sat spring & fall, Mon-Fri Nov-Mar) – the one where the Wilders spent the first winter, and the Ingalls home 'Pa' built, accessible by a two-hour guided tour only. There's also a drive-by tour of sites featured in her books and an **outdoor play** (☎ 605-692-2108; adult/child $7/4) performed weekends in June and July.

ALONG I-90

Along the journey from Sioux Falls to Rapid City there's very little to interfere with your view of the horizon. North and south of here, though, are some of the state's most scenic parts.

Mitchell

Mitchell's claim to fame is the Taj Mahal of agriculture, the must-be-seen-to-be-believed **Corn Palace** (☎ 605-996-5031; 6th & Main Sts; admission free; ⊙ 8am-9pm daily summer, 8am-5pm daily May & Sep, 8am-5pm Mon-Fri rest of the year). Incredibly, the Moorish-style building is redecorated each year with 275,000 ears of corn. It serves as Mitchell's civic center, active all year. Stop by for a basketball game in winter.

The domed **Mitchell Prehistoric Indian Village Museum** (☎ 605-996-5473; 3200 Indian Village Rd; adult/child $6/4; ⊙ 8am-6pm summer, call for times rest of year), north of the palace, contains two unearthed 11th-century Mandan lodges.

Mitchell's lodging rates zoom in summer. You'll find basic rooms at the **Corn Palace Motel** (☎ 605-996-5559; 902 S Burr; s/d from $45/48; ✷), whose charmingly cheesy facade echoes its namesake in pastel plaster.

Chamberlain

Where I-90 crosses the Missouri River is the picturesquely situated Chamberlain, home to the excellent **Akta Lakota Museum & Cultural Center** (☎ 605-734-3452, 800-798-3452; admission free; ⊙ 8am-6pm Mon-Sat, 9am-5pm Sun May-Sep, 8am-5pm Mon-Fri rest of the year), at St Joseph's Indian School, with Sioux and other Native American artifacts. History buffs should pop into the hilltop visitor center, east of town, where the **Lewis & Clark Information Center** (☎ 605-734-4562; ⊙ 8am-6pm summer) has exhibits on the duo.

It's well worth taking the time for a detour onto the **Native American Scenic Byway** (SR 1806), which meanders crookedly for 100 miles from Chamberlain to Pierre, following the Missouri River through spectacular countryside, including the Crow Creek and the Lower Brule Indian Reservations.

Pierre

A pretty town situated at a bend in the Missouri River, South Dakota's capital is rich in history and opportunities for outdoor pursuits. It's situated 30 miles north of I-90 on US 83 but is more rewardingly approached from Chamberlain via Hwys 50 and 34, an 87-mile drive through the Crow Creek Indian Reservation. The area north of Pierre (pronounced '*peer*') was the setting for many scenes in the movie *Dances with Wolves*.

The Pierre **visitor center** (☎ 605-224-7361, 800-962-2034; 800 W Dakota Ave; ⊙ 8am-5pm Mon-Fri,

10am-5pm Sat, 1-5pm Sun) sits on the bank of the Missouri River and makes a good starting point for a riverside stroll.

The photogenic **State Capitol** (☎ 605-773-3765; 500 E Capitol Ave; ☻ 8am-10pm) has a self-guided tour available. Exhibits at the **South Dakota Cultural Heritage Center** (☎ 605-773-3458; 900 Governor's Dr; adult/child $3/free; ☻ 9am-4:30pm Mon-Fri, 1pm-4:30pm Sat & Sun) include a bloody ghost dance shirt from Wounded Knee. On the Missouri River, **Framboise Island** – where the Lewis and Clark expedition spent four days and was nearly derailed by inadvertently offending members of the local Brule tribe – has several hiking trails that begin just beyond the visitor center. Launching from the same place are river cruises on the **Capital City Queen** (☎ 800-962-2034; adult/child $12/7; tours 1:30 & 6:30pm Sat-Thu, 1:30pm & 5:30pm Fri, May-Sep). For genuine Americana, visit South Dakota's largest **livestock auction** (☎ 800-280-7210; www.ftpierrelivestock.com; ☻ hrs vary, check website for calendar), across the river in Ft Pierre. Half the fun is in trying to decode the auctioneer's high-speed singsong, but there's also usually BBQ and live country music.

The **Budget Host Inn/State Motel** (☎ 605-224-5896; 640 N Euclid St; s/d from $39/52; Ⓟ Ⓡ) has basic rooms close to the Capitol, with a sauna, laundry facilities and a recliner in each single room.

Rosebud Indian Reservation

At Murdo, detour 40 miles south on US 83 to **Rosebud Indian Reservation** (☎ 605-856-2538), the home of the Sicangu Lakota Oyate. Seven miles southwest of Rosebud, the **Buechel Memorial Lakota Museum** (☎ 605-747-2745; St Francis; ☻ 8am-5pm summer, by appointment winter) was temporarily closed at the time of research; displays include some Crazy Horse belongings.

Salt Camp Cabins & B&B (☎ 605-747-2206; BIA Hwy 7, Rosebud; r/cabin $75/100) overlooks the lovely Crazy Horse Canyon, which has a nice lake for a dip. If you stay as a guest of the B&B (not the cabins), you'll be treated to a hearty breakfast and dinner.

Back in Murdo, get your testosterone fix at the **Pioneer Auto Show** (☎ 605-669-2691; I-90 & US 83; adult/child $7/4; ☻ 8:30am-6pm Mon-Sat, 10am-6pm Sun), which has several barns full of classic cars and motorcycles, including Elvis' Harley-Davidson in a glassed-in shrine. It's pure Middle America cornball, but the mu-

seum does have some really cherry muscle cars capable of making grown men squeal and weep like little girls. Fun for the whole family!

Pine Ridge Indian Reservation

It's hard to visit Pine Ridge without being overwhelmed with emotion. Nearly everything in the area stands as a testament to the United States' often brutal history. Home to the Lakota Oglala Sioux, this reservation south of the Badlands is the nation's poorest 'county,' with an unemployment rate hovering between 70% and 80%, and the crime rate is among the highest per capita in the US. Average life expectancy here – 48 for men, 52 for women – is lower than in Bangladesh. Still, despite the problems, a spirit of community is palpable, and locals are friendly and welcoming to visitors.

Just how things got so dire is an ugly and complicated tale. The original 1868 treaty between the Lakota people and the US government, promising the Lakota a 60-million-acre reservation that stretched from the Missouri River in the east to the Bighorn Mountains in the west, was continuously violated by the government until all that was left of the reservation were fragments. In 1877, the discovery of gold in the Black Hills led Congress to confiscate this previously undisputed Lakota territory. This, combined with further encroachment by white settlers, led to the Battle of Little Bighorn, in which Indian warriors fighting under Crazy Horse and Sitting Bull defeated Custer.

But the victory was short-lived. On December 29, 1890, in what would become one of the most infamous atrocities in US history, the 7th US Cavalry attacked a group of Lakota at Wounded Knee, massacring some 300 men, women and children. Today, the **Wounded Knee Massacre Site**, 20 miles northeast of Pine Ridge town, is the reservation's top attraction. But it certainly isn't hyped in the tourist brochures, and the site is little more than a ramshackle cemetery and a faded roadside sign.

Tune in to what's going on now in the Pine Ridge area by listening to local radio station KILI 90.1 FM, 'the voice of the Lakota nation,' which broadcasts community events and plays some traditional music.

Off Hwy 18 in Pine Ridge town is the **Red Cloud Indian School** (☎ 605-867-5491), with Chief

Red Cloud's grave – in a hilltop cemetery with views of the Black Hills – and the Heritage Center (open seasonally), which has a shop selling art and Lakota flash cards. At the farmhouse **Wakpamni B&B** (☎ 605-288-1800; r from $60; 🈳 Ⓟ), 20 miles east of Pine Ridge, guests can enjoy a sweat-lodge ceremony, horseback-riding ($50) and sometimes the chance to talk with an Oglala guide.

Look for the locally produced *Welcome to the Oglala Lakota Nation* brochure, which includes listings of the area's frequent powwows.

Wall

Along with trucker caps, Wall Drug bumper stickers are inexplicably cool among hipsters these days, and billboards hyping the tourist trap infest South Dakota's highways. Once you get there, you might wonder what all the fuss was about. **Wall Drug** (☎ 605-279-2275; 510 Main St; 🕑 6am-10pm, 6:30am-6pm in winter) dominates the town, but it's scarcely more than an 'Olde West' facade and a block-long souvenir shop selling carnival-quality junk: Wild West toys, Black Hills gold, tacky western wear, books on Wall Drug, 'Wall Drug' bumper stickers, singing cowboy machines and big gorillas. There is 5¢ coffee, as advertised, and a few listless saloons across the street, but it's hardly worth going out of your way to visit. The town is on I-90, north of Pine Ridge Indian Reservation.

Badlands National Park

If Peter Jackson had decided New Zealand wasn't right for the evil realm of Mordor (for *The Lord of the Rings* movies), he could've filmed here instead. The otherworldly landscape, with barren walls and spikes stabbing the dry air, and evil crevices plunging into oblivion, was understandably named *mako sica* ('badland') by Native Americans. Looking over the bizarre formations from the corrugated walls surrounding the Badlands is like seeing an ocean someone burned all the water out of. Today the protected Badlands National Park includes a remnant of one of the world's greatest prairie grasslands, several species of Plains mammal and golden eagles – and the odd rattlesnake.

The park's north unit packs the most punch; the Hwy 240 loop road is easily reached from I-90 and you can see the park in a couple of hours if you're in a hurry.

The gravel Sage Creek Rim Rd goes west of the loop (for an additional fee), above the Badlands Wilderness Area, which is open for backcountry hiking and camping. The less-accessible south units are in Pine Ridge Indian Reservation.

The **Ben Reifel Visitors Center** (☎ 605-433-5361; Cedar Pass; 🕑 9am-4pm) is open all year, but **White River Visitors Center** (☎ 605-455-2878; 🕑 10am-4pm summer), in the southern section, is summer-only. If you visit in winter, watch for snowdrifts, and be prepared for swift and dramatic weather changes any time of year. A seven-day pass costs $10 for cars and $5 for hikers and cyclists.

The **Badlands Circle 10 Campground** (☎ 605-433-5451, 800-231-3617; campsites $15, RV sites $15-23) is half a mile south of I-90 exit 131. Motels can be found on I-90 in Kadoka and Wall, or stay at a cabin in the park at the Oglala Sioux-operated **Cedar Pass Lodge** (☎ 605-433-5460; r & cabins from $55; 🕑 Apr-Oct). Drop by the lodge's restaurant for an Indian taco made with fry bread and buffalo.

BLACK HILLS

The sacred, spiritual and ancestral home of the Lakota Sioux, this 8000-sq-mile region on the Wyoming–South Dakota border lures visitors with its tree-covered canyons and 7000ft peaks. The region's name – the 'Black' comes from the dark Ponderosa pine-covered slopes – was conferred by the Lakota Sioux. In the 1868 Fort Laramie Treaty, they were assured that the hills would be theirs for eternity, but the discovery of gold changed that, and the Sioux were pushed north and later into reservations. The Sioux continue their struggle to reclaim the lands.

You'll need several days to explore the area, which covers more ground than Rocky Mountain, Grand Canyon or Yosemite National Parks. Throughout are incredible back-road drives, rock climbing, mines, caves, Custer State Park, Mt Rushmore and Crazy Horse monuments, the Black Hills National Forest, outdoor activities (ballooning, cycling, boating, hiking, skiing and panning for gold) and heaps of tacky kitsch in between.

Between Memorial Day and Labor Day, room rates skyrocket – sometimes even 300% above off-season rates – and reservations are essential. In winter, some lodgings and most attractions are closed.

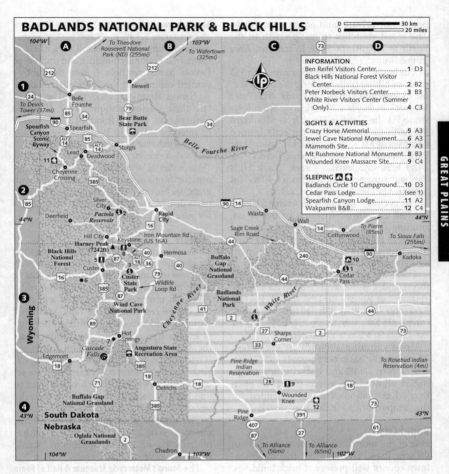

BADLANDS NATIONAL PARK & BLACK HILLS

0 ___ 30 km
0 ___ 20 miles

INFORMATION
Ben Reifel Visitors Center...................1 D3
Black Hills National Forest Visitor
  Center...2 B2
Peter Norbeck Visitors Center...........3 B3
White River Visitors Center (Summer
  Only)..4 C3

SIGHTS & ACTIVITIES
Crazy Horse Memorial......................5 A3
Jewel Cave National Monument.......6 A3
Mammoth Site.................................7 A3
Mt Rushmore National Monument....8 B3
Wounded Knee Massacre Site..........9 C4

SLEEPING
Badlands Circle 10 Campground.....10 D3
Cedar Pass Lodge.......................(see 1)
Spearfish Canyon Lodge...............11 A2
Wakpamni B&B............................12 C4

GREAT PLAINS

Orientation & Information

I-90 skirts the north of the Black Hills, and three major access roads head into the hills: US 14A, which loops from Spearfish to Sturgis via Deadwood; the US 385 Black Hills Parkway (initially US 85), which runs north–south the length of the hills; and US 16 (and US 16A), running east–west from Rapid City to the Jewel Cave National Monument via Mt Rushmore. Just south of Wall is the eastern half of the **Buffalo Gap National Grassland**, an area of prairie and badlands.

About half the 4½ million annual visitors choose one place as a base; others split their stay between the North Hills (Spearfish, Deadwood, Sturgis) and the more visited South Hills (Custer, Keystone, Hot

Springs). At the cusp of the hills stand the 'gateway' towns on I-90 (Rapid City, Sturgis, Spearfish).

Visitor centers and reservations:

Black Hills Central Reservations (☎ 800-529-0105; 68 Sherman St, Deadwood; ⏰ 6am-8pm Mon-Fri, 8am-5pm Sat & Sun) Last-minute motel and cabin vacancies.

Black Hills Visitors Center (☎ 605-355-3700; 1851 Discovery Circle, Rapid City; ⏰ 8am-8pm in summer)

National Grassland visitor center (☎ 605-279-2125; 708 Main St, Wall; ⏰ 8am-6pm summer) Interprets the history, flora and fauna of the region.

Black Hills National Forest

The majority of the Black Hills' attractions lie within this 1875-sq-mile mixture of protected and logged forest, perforated by pockets of private land along most roads. The forest stretches from Spearfish in the north to Angostura State Recreation Area in the south.

The best way to explore is on any of the 353 miles of hiking trails or along the many scenic byways and gravel 'fire roads.' The Peter Norbeck Byway is a 70-mile loop from Keystone via the Needles Hwy, Iron Mountain Rd (with tunnels offering perfectly framed glimpses of Mt Rushmore) and Custer State Park. Spearfish Canyon Scenic Byway (US 14A) follows Spearfish Creek. Black Hills Parkway runs north–south from I-90 to Hot Springs via Deadwood and Custer.

For cycling, the 114-mile **George S Mickelson Trail** cuts through much of the forest, running from Lead through Hill City and Custer to Edgemont. Deadwood's HI Penny Motel runs a shuttle to pick up or drop off cyclists at various points on the trail.

There are six ranger stations around the forest and a **visitor center** (near US 385 & Hwy 44; dawn-dusk Memorial Day-Labor Day) at Pactola Reservoir. The **Black Hills National Forest office** (☎ 605-673-9200; Hwy 16; 7:30am-5pm Mon-Fri, 8am-4:30pm Sat & Sun) is in Custer.

Good camping abounds in the forest. There are 30 basic **campgrounds** (☎ 877-444-6777; campsites $10-18) and backcountry camping is allowed anywhere (free; no open fires). Reservations are recommended for the campgrounds for summer weekends.

Rapid City

One of the more attractive urban centers in the area, Rapid City has a foot-friendly downtown core of well-preserved brick buildings, complete with signs posted along the wide sidewalks explaining the history and significance of the architecture. 'Rapid' nestles between the plains and the Black Hills – it's the main gateway town to the hills. The **visitor center** (☎ 605-343-1744; 444 Mt Rushmore Rd) has information on accommodations and restaurants, as well as Black Hills tour services.

If it's raining, visit the stone fortress like **Journey Museum** (☎ 605-394-6923; 222 New York St; adult/child $6/4; 10am-5pm Mon-Sat, 1-5pm Sun) for a trip through 2½ billion years of the history of the Black Hills, focusing on the Lakota Sioux.

Budget motels line North Street and surround I-90 exit 59. For something special right downtown, try the historic **Hotel Alex Johnson** (☎ 605-342-1210, 800-888-2539; www.alexjohnson.com; 523 6th St; s/d from $69/89), whose overwhelming design is based on a blend of Germanic Tudor architecture and traditional Lakota Sioux symbols – note the lobby's painted ceiling and the chandelier made of war lances. Rooms are modernized but maintain their original antique decor. If you're feeling brave, ask for Room 812, supposedly haunted by a 'Lady in White.'

The **Firehouse Brewing Co.** (☎ 605-348-1915; www.firehousebrewing.com; 610 Main St; mains $8-10; lunch Mon-Sat, dinner daily) is a popular hangout for home-brewed beer and good pub grub, including buffalo burgers and baked pasta dishes. There's an outdoor beer garden for sunny days and warm evenings.

Sturgis

This unassuming little town revs up big time for the annual **Sturgis Rally & Races** (☎ 605-720-0800; www.sturgismotorcyclerally.com; early Aug), a gathering of anything up to 500,000 Harley-Davidson motorcycle riders, fans and curious onlookers. During the rally, you can't swing a dead cat without hitting someone in leather fringe; saloons are crammed and the streets resemble rows of giant dominoes. (Ogle all you want, but touch the bikes at your own risk.) Temporary campsites are set up around town and motels boost rates to hundreds of dollars a night. Check the rally website for vacancies.

The **chamber of commerce** (☎ 605-347-2556; www.sturgis-sd.org; 2040 Junction Ave; 8am-5pm) has information on nearby attractions, scenic roads, the bike rally and more.

The **Sturgis Motorcycle Museum & Hall of Fame** (☎ 605-347-2001; 1344 Main St; adult/child $3/free; 8am-4pm Mon-Fri, 9am-4pm Sat & Sun) has some 40 classic Harleys, a couple dozen other vintage and custom bikes, and a basement dedicated to traveling exhibits on women in motorcycling. Get a discounted-admission coupon at the Harley shop across the street.

Standing stoically apart from the Black Hills, the namesake mountain of **Bear Butte State Park** (☎ 605-347-5240; person/car $3/5), 7 miles north of Sturgis on Hwy 79, juts 1400ft above the plains. Once the stronghold of Crazy Horse, it remains of great spiritual significance to the Plains Indians, evident in the hundreds of prayer cloths strung along the two-hour hike from the visitor center to the summit. Bear Butte is the northern end of the **Centennial Trail**, a 111-mile riding/hiking trail to Wind Cave National Park (p697). There are basic campsites ($6), horseback-riding and fishing on Bear Butte Lake.

Spearfish

A good base on I-90 is Spearfish, at the mouth of scenic **Spearfish Canyon Scenic Byway** (US 14A). The helpful, friendly **chamber of commerce** (☎ 605-642-2626; 106 W Kansas; ☼ 8am-5pm Mon-Fri, lobby always open) has a lobby stocked with all sorts of brochures. Ask about the self-guided tour of US 14A, which includes detailed information about numbered roadside markers. The office also has pamphlets on hikes in the area; the **Roughlock Trail** near Spearfish Canyon Lodge is an easy walk to a picnic spot, while the new, nearby '**76 Trail** is a more challenging ascent of the canyon wall. Both are highly recommended. In winter, skiers come to hit nearby downhill slopes and cross-country trails.

Chain motels cluster around I-90 exit 14, including **Howard Johnson Express Inn** (☎ 605-642-8105; 323 S 27th St; r/ste from $80/110; ✕ ✖ 🖳), with continental breakfast and heated pool. For a plush, 'rustic' treat in a wilder setting, try the **Spearfish Canyon Lodge** (☎ 605-584-3435; www.spfcanyon.com; 10619 Roughlock Falls Rd; r from $139, reservations recommended; ✕ ✖), 13 miles south of Spearfish near trails and streams, with a decadent ski-lodge atmosphere and 54 spacious, piney rooms. Rates for all lodging in the area plunge in the off season (basically October to May).

For camping, **Spearfish KOA** (☎ 605-642-4633; campsites $18-28, RV sites $18-40, cabins $45-47; ☼ closed winter; 🖳) is southwest of I-90 exit 10 near the creek.

Deadwood

Like Vegas meets Bonanza, Deadwood juxtaposes the bright neon jangling of slot machines with Wild West storefronts, re-enacted gunfights and eternal devotion to Wild Bill Hickok, who was shot in the back of the head here in 1876 while gambling. Settled illegally by anxious gold rushers in the 1870s, Deadwood (inspiration for the hit HBO series) is now a National Historic Landmark. Its Main St is lined with re-stored gold rush-era buildings. The town's hell-raisin' days are long gone, replaced by a gentler crowd of tour-bus poker players

taking advantage of legalized limited-stakes gambling, which jump-started the town's tourist appeal in the 1990s.

The Deadwood **visitor center** (☎ 605-578-1876, 800-999-1876; 735 Main St; ☼ 8am-5pm) has brochures, as does the more helpful **History & Information Center** (☎ 605-578-2507; Pine St & USA 85/14A; ☼ 8am-7pm), a block west of Main St, which also has exhibits and photos of the town's history.

Calamity Jane (also known as Martha Canary) and Hickok rest side by side up in Boot Hill at **Mount Moriah Cemetery** (admission $1; ☼ dawn-dusk).

Book accommodations well ahead in summer, particularly anytime close to the Sturgis motorcycle rally. Downtown, you can't beat the **Historic Franklin Hotel** (☎ 605-578-2241; 700 Main St; r from $92), with its antique furnishings, wood-paneled 1930s dining room and cocktail-hour balcony overlooking Main St. Rooms are named for celebrities who've stayed in them, including Teddy Roosevelt, John Wayne and – most recently – country music duo Big and Rich, who got their start down the street playing for beer.

Budget motels line Main St; top among these is the **HI Penny Motel** (☎ 605-578-1842, 877-565-8140; 818 Upper Main St; r from $46), which functions more like a hostel, though it no longer has hostel rooms available. It rents bicycles (from $16 per day), dispenses hiking advice and runs a shuttle service for the George S Mickelson Trail (see opposite).

You can load up on chicken wings and greasy pasta at the buffets run by most of the gambling houses, and saloons offer cheap pub grub to soak up the brews. A classier option is the **Deadwood Social Club** (☎ 800-952-9398; 657 Main St; ☼ lunch & dinner), above **Saloon No 10**. This is also hands-down the best saloon in Deadwood, with dark paneled walls, sawdust on the floor, locals at the bar, stuffed critters and wax busts of outlaws on the walls, and – most importantly – slot machines confined to a separate room. The original Saloon No 10, where Wild Bill took a serious loss at the gambling table, stood across the street, but the building burned to the ground. That spot is now home to **Wild West Winners** (☎ 605-578-1100; 622 Main St), with a small basement display on Hickok, but the current Saloon No 10 does a better job of re-creating its namesake's atmosphere. The other notable hooch house in town is the

Midnight Star (☎ 605-578-1555; www.themidnightstar .com; 677 Main St), owned by actor Kevin Costner and his brother. Souvenirs and costumes from his movies dot the building.

In nearby **Lead** (pronounced *leed*), peek at the 944ft-deep open cut of the **Homestake gold mine** (☎ 605-584-3110; 160 W Main St; tours adult/child $6/5; ☼ daily May-Sep) to see what mining will do to a mountain.

Mount Rushmore National Monument

Looking like they're either emerging from or being absorbed by the mountain, the stony faces of past presidents George Washington, Thomas Jefferson, Abraham Lincoln and Theodore Roosevelt – carved 60ft tall in the granite of a Black Hills outcrop – are one of the most famous images in the USA (the monument gets three million visitors each year). You can't help but be overwhelmed by its sheer scale and the massive physical effort of the team (led by sculptor Gutzon Borglum) that created it. If Washington were depicted from head to toe, he would be 465ft high. The site was dedicated in 1927 and 14 years of work commenced – Washington emerged in 1930, Jefferson in 1936, Lincoln in 1937 and Roosevelt in 1939. Borglum died in March 1941 and his son Lincoln supervised the completion in October 1941.

The monument is 3 miles south of Keystone via US 16A, and 25 miles southwest of Rapid City via US 16. The **visitor center** (☎ 605-574-2523; ☼ 8am-10pm summer, 8am-5pm winter) plays a good film and has exhibits on the construction at various stages. You pass through an avenue of all 50 state flags before reaching the Grand View Terrace. The **Presidential Trail** (admission free) loop leads near the monument – and offers some fine nostril views. There's a 9pm **light show** in summer that's worth planning your trip around. You can park near the center ($8) or, if you arrive early, at a small free lot 400yd further along Hwy 244, which curves behind the monument and offers some great profile views.

Keystone

The nearest lodging and restaurants to Mt Rushmore are in Keystone, a one-time mining town now solely devoted to the monument. You can learn more about Mt Rushmore's enigmatic creator by visiting the touristy **Rushmore-Borglum Story** (☎ 605-666-4448; US 16A; admission $7; ☼ 8am-7pm Mon-Sat, 9am-7pm Sun summer, call for hr rest of year).

For a budget option in town, try the resorty **Mount Rushmore's Royal Express Motel** (☎ 605-666-5070, 888-326-6695; r from $39; P ☎), off the highway. Rooms are spacious and interestingly furnished, with doors opening onto outdoor balconies or a central atrium containing an indoor pool and small video arcade.

Just north on US 16A is the comfortably rustic **Powder House** (☎ 605-666-4646, 800-321-0692; 24125 Hwy 16A; r $110, cabins $70-170; P), so named because it originally served as a cache of explosives and bootleg hooch. It's open May to September. Also lovely are the modernized log cabins at **Holy Smoke Resort** (☎ 605-666-4616, 866-530-5696; cabins $55-140; ☼ P), with microwaves, refrigerators, satellite TV and full baths in a secluded spot. Reservations are crucial at both.

Crazy Horse Memorial

The world's largest monument, 4 miles north of Custer, **Crazy Horse Memorial** (person/car $9/20) is, as author Ian Frazier describes, 'a ruin, only in reverse.' Onlookers at the 563ft work-in-progress can gawk at what will be – the Sioux leader astride his horse, pointing to the horizon saying, 'My lands are where my dead lie buried.'

Never photographed, defeated in battle or persuaded to sign a meaningless treaty, the great Crazy Horse was the obvious choice for a 'monument for all Native Americans.' Lakota Sioux elders hoped a monument would balance the presidential focus of Mt Rushmore, and in 1948 they asked Boston-born sculptor Korczak Ziolkowski to build it. Mostly alone except for a few mountain goats, he blasted at the rock until his death in 1982. His family continues the work. As formidable a figure as Crazy Horse was, Ziolkowski seems to have been no less of an indomitable spirit. The sheer will and hard labor required is astounding, as demonstrated in a movie shown at the visitor center.

No one is predicting when the sculpture will be complete. Depending on weather, you can see (and hear) blasts most days. A new **light show** tells the story of the monument and what it represents; it's splashed across the rock face in the evenings all summer.

The huge **visitor center** (☎ 605-673-4681; ☼ 8am-9pm) charts the progress, exhibits scale models and has a viewing deck. During the Volksmarch, held the first weekend of June, there are trips up to the mountain, which is lit nightly. Adjacent to the center is the impressive **Indian Museum & Cultural Center**, Ziolkowski's studio and the home in which his widow still lives. The studio and the Museum & Cultural Center are free with admission to the monument, and both are open same hours as the visitor center.

For the first time, the nonprofit foundation that manages the monument has recently launched a fund-raising drive (the goal, at time of research, was $26.5 million). Ziolkowski and his family refused federal funding, because they felt the people, not the government, should finance such a work.

You can stay in a teepee in view of Crazy Horse's profile at the hokey but friendly **Heritage Village** (☎ 605-673-4761, 888-428-3386; teepee/tent $22/14), 1 mile south.

Custer

Custer isn't much to look at, but it has a great location near Custer State Park. The **chamber of commerce** (☎ 605-673-2244; 615 Washington St; ☻ 9am-6pm Mon-Sat, 9am-2pm Sun) can dole out more information. Check your email – and enjoy a giant diner-style breakfast with the locals – at **Laube's Pastry Shoppe** (☎ 605-673-5003; www.laubespastry.com; 541 Mt Rushmore Rd; Internet per hr $2.50; ☻ 6:30am-3pm).

The yellow-and-red 1930s cottages at **Shady Rest Motel** (☎ 605-673-4478, 800-567-8259; 238 Gordon St; cabin $55-165; ☻), two blocks south of Mt Rushmore Rd, are comfortable and handily situated across the street from where the kids can pan for gold.

There are 17 campgrounds in the region. The popular **Flintstones Bedrock City** (☎ 605-673-4664; US 385; campsites/RV sites/cabins $18.50/24/42), 1 mile south of town, is treeless, but there's a wealth of activities for the kids at the attached theme park ($7, open May to September).

Custer State Park

This superb 114-sq-mile park is one of the state's highlights. The only reason it isn't a national park is the state grabbed it first. It boasts one of the largest free-roaming buffalo herds in the world (about 1500), the famous 'begging burros' (donkeys seeking handouts) and more than 200 species of bird. Elk, whitetail and mule deer, pronghorns, mountain goats, bighorn sheep, coyotes, mountain lions and bobcats may also be seen along the 18-mile Wildlife Loop Rd, Iron Mountain Rd and the incredible, 14-mile Needles Hwy.

Every year in October there is a roundup of the park's buffalo, and 500 are sold at the November auction (get yours for $500 to $1000).

The **Peter Norbeck Visitors Center** (☎ 605-255-4464; US 16A; person/car summer $5/10, rest of year $2/5; ☻ 8am-8pm summer, 9am-5pm rest of year), 15 miles east of Custer in the center of the park, has exhibits and offers activities.

Hiking through the prairie grassland and pine-covered hills is a great way to see wildlife. Trails such as Sylvan Lake Shore, Cathedral Spires, French Creek Natural Area and Centennial crisscross a variety of habitats. A popular hike is up the state's tallest mountain, Harney Peak; the trailhead is at Sylvan Lake. Swimming, fishing and boating on the park's lakes – as well as climbing on its jagged rock spires – are also popular.

You can pitch a tent in eight **campgrounds** (☎ 800-710-2267; www.campSD.com; campsites $13-18, no hook-ups) around the park. Reservations are recommended in summer.

The park has four impressive **resorts** (☎ 800-658-3530; www.custerresorts.com), each with cabins and campsites: the State Game Lodge, Sylvan Lake, the Blue Bell and the Legion Lodge. Summer rates for a lodge room or cabin start at $75. Book well ahead.

Wind Cave National Park

This park, filled with grassland and forest, just south of Custer State Park, covers nearly 47 sq miles. The **visitor center** (☎ 605-745-4600; ☻ 8am-7pm summer, 8am-5pm rest of year) has displays and conducts interpretive walks ($7, at 1:30pm and 3:30pm, one hour). The central feature is, of course, the cave, which is 98 miles long and growing (new tunnels are frequently discovered). The cave's foremost feature is its 'boxwork' calcite formations, which look like honeycomb and date back 60 to 100 million years. The strong gusts – felt at the entrance, but not inside – give the cave its name. There are a variety of tours offered, including elaborate spelunking adventures; call ahead to check schedules.

Hiking is a popular activity in the park, where you will find the southern end of the 111-mile **Centennial Trail**. There's first come, first served primitive **camping** ($12) in summer.

Jewel Cave National Monument

Another of the Black Hills' many fascinating caves is 125-mile-long Jewel Cave, 13 miles west of Custer on US 16. It's known for the nailhead calcite crystals that line its walls. Tours ($8 to $27) range in length and difficulty. Arrange your tour at the **visitor center** (☎ 605-673-2288; ◷ 8am-7:30pm summer, 8am-5:30pm spring, 8am-4:30pm Sep-Apr).

Hot Springs

This aptly named town, south of the main Black Hills circuit, boasts beautiful 1890s sandstone buildings and warm mineral springs. The **visitor center** (☎ 605-745-6974, 800-325-6991; N River St; ◷ 9am-7pm Mon-Fri, 9am-6pm Sat, noon-4pm Sun May-Sep) is in the old train depot.

The water at **Evans Plunge** (☎ 605-745-5165; 1145 N River St; adult/child $9/7; ◷ 5:30am-9pm Mon-Fri, 8am-9pm Sat & Sun summer, 5:30am-8pm Mon-Fri, 10am-8pm Sat & Sun rest of year), a giant indoor geothermal springs pool, is 87°F all year. Locals like to wade in **Fall River Park**, off S River St, or swim at **Cascade Falls** (warm all year), 10 miles south on US 71.

The remarkable **Mammoth Site** (☎ 605-745-6017; 1800 US 18; adult/child $6.75/4.75; ◷ 8am-8pm May 15-Aug 15, call for hr rest of year) is the country's only left-as-found mammoth fossil display. Hundreds of animals perished in a sinkhole here over several centuries about 27,000 years ago. Most of the 52 mammoths found so far are adolescents (and all are male!); in July you can cheer on paleontologists digging for more bones.

The hilltop **Historic Log Cabin Motel** (☎ 605-745-5166; US 385; cabins $45-115), north of town, has a petting zoo, hot tub, basketball court and bikes.

NEBRASKA

Nebraska has a number of hidden charms, not least of which is the weather. Storms roll in on short notice, instantly darkening the sky and painting drama all over previously unimpressive landscapes. The state's two major cities, Omaha and Lincoln, both have historic town centers with cobbled streets and well-preserved brick structures buzzing with vivid new life. And the Sand Hills are a unique phenomenon, of particular interest to birders, who come from all over to witness the sandhill crane migration.

The state's main thoroughfare is I-80, efficient but often dull. Those traveling to or from South Dakota's Black Hills should take the more scenic US 275 and US 20 northwest of Omaha, or Hwy 2 through the Sand Hills.

History

Lewis and Clark followed the Missouri along Nebraska's eastern fringe and met with Native Americans here in 1804. Some 20 years later, trappers latched onto the Platte River. Then in 1841, the first covered wagon passed through on its way to Oregon. The Platte Valley was soon swarming with hopeful settlers – around 400,000 – all looking to start a new life in the mythical West.

Transcontinental railroads such as the Union Pacific made covered wagons irrelevant, and the trail ruts succumbed to pasture as more settlers rushed in after the 1862 Homestead Act. The rich soils and abundant grasslands helped Nebraska develop into a productive agricultural state.

Information

Nebraska's sales tax is 5.5%, with some local areas adding up to 1 to 2% more.

Tourism information:

Nebraska Game & Parks Commission (☎ 800-826-7275; www.ngpc.state.ne.us; vehicle stickers per day/year $3/17) Stickers are good at any Nebraska state park.

Nebraska highway information (☎ 511 or ☎ 800-906-9069, out of state ☎ 402-471-4533)

Nebraska Travel & Tourism Division (☎ 402-471-3796, 800-228-4307; www.visitnebraska.org)

NEBRASKA FACTS

Nickname Cornhusker State
Population 1.7 million
Area 77,360 sq miles
Capital city Lincoln (population 232,362)
Official tree Cottonwood
Birthplace of Lakota leader Red Cloud (c 1822–1909), Malcolm X (1925–65), Gerald Ford (b 1913), author Willa Cather (1873–1947), Johnny Carson (1925–2005), Marlon Brando (1924–2004), Nick Nolte (b 1941)
Home of Gazillionaire Warren Buffett
Famous for First rodeo (1882), only unicameral state legislature (1934), Chimney Rock, football

OMAHA

It's easy to get the wrong idea about Omaha. Sure, it has its share of thicknecks and red-staters. But the revitalized Old Market neighborhood easily holds its own when it comes to aesthetics, energy and sophisticated dining and nightlife options. It's not all spurs and steaks here these days, no ma'am.

That's no surprise considering that the city began as a pioneering trade outpost. Its location on the Missouri River and proximity to the Platte made it an important stop on the Oregon and Mormon Trails. Fort Omaha was built in 1868 as a staging post for troops fighting in the Indian Wars. These days Omaha is in the nation's top 10 for millionaires-per-capita.

Information
Visitors center (☎ 402-444-4660, 866-937-6624; www.visitomaha.com; 1001 Farnam St; ☒ 9am-4:30pm Mon-Sat Sep-May, 9am-4:30pm Mon-Sat & 1:30-4:30pm Sun Jun-Aug)

Sights & Activities
It's possible, in fact recommended, to spend most of your Omaha visit exploring the **Old Market**, between 10th and 13th Sts and Farnam and Jackson Sts. This history-drenched, atmospheric core of the city has cobblestone streets and century-old warehouses constantly being converted into chic nightclubs, gourmet restaurants and funky decor shops.

One of Nebraska's top attractions owes its fortune to the state's location smack-dab in the center of the USA, which helped it become the headquarters of the Strategic Air Command (SAC). Midway between Omaha and Lincoln, the fascinating **Strategic Air & Space Museum** (☎ 402-827-3100, 800-358-5029; 28210 West Park Hwy; adult/child $7/3; ☒ 9am-5pm), at I-80 exit 426, boasts two massive hangars housing more than 30 aircraft (including the bomb-dropping B-36 Peacemaker) and 20 missiles.

The Art-Deco **Joslyn Art Museum** (☎ 402-342-3300; 2200 Dodge St; adult/child $6/3.50; ☒ 10am-4pm Tue-Sat, noon-4pm Sun) houses a great collection of Renaissance and 19th- and 20th-century American and European art.

The home where African American leader Malcolm X was born in 1925 no longer exists, but there's an information display and **historical marker** (☎ 402-444-5955; 3448 Pinkney St at Evans St; admission free; ☒ 7:30am-

dusk) set amid the 10 acres of forested land where the house once stood.

Housed in a landmark 1907 building, the **Great Plains Black Museum** (☎ 402-345-6817; 2213 Lake St; admission free; ☒ 10am-2pm Tue-Sun) recounts the role of African Americans in the West via photos, film, artifacts and music.

The swank **Gerald R Ford birth site** (☎ 402-444-5955; 32nd St & Woolworth Ave; admission free; ☒ 7:30am-9pm) commemorates the 38th president (born Leslie King) and is adjacent to the Gerald R Ford Conservation Center.

Sleeping
Motels abound along I-80 and I-680 N exits and over in Council Bluffs.

Best Western Redick Plaza Hotel (☎ 402-342-1500; 1504 Harney St; d from $99; ☒ ☒) A comfortable downtown hotel near the Old Market, this modern tower has spacious rooms designed for business travelers; rates include a free cooked breakfast.

Platte River State Park (☎ 402-234-2217; 25 miles south of I-80; teepees $15, cabins $30-90) There's no camping at the park, but there are lots of comfortable cabins, teepees and wild turkeys.

Eating & Drinking
M's Pub (☎ 402-342-2550; 422 S 11th; starters $5-8, mains $9-15; ☒ lunch & dinner to 1am) A prime example of how to rejuvenate an old industrial warehouse without destroying its rough-hewn charm, this unpretentious but classy restaurant serves tasty pizzas on unleavened lavosh bread, baked casseroles and creative salads.

Johnny's Café (☎ 402-731-4774; 4702 S 27th St; mains $13-25; ☒ lunch & dinner Mon-Sat) Still one of the best of the city's traditional steakhouses, Johnny's is next to the former stockyards (which closed in 1998). Its iron cow-sculpture doors open to meat-eating bliss.

Mister Toad's (☎ 402-345-4488; 1002 Howard St; pub fare $5-8) Walking into this old wood-lined pub is like putting on clothes right out of the dryer. There's live music most nights and a cozy back room full of books and stained glass.

Dubliner (☎ 402-342-5887; 1205 Harney) One of the city's more rollicking joints, this long, narrow basement pub has a convivial atmosphere and a massive beer selection; taste them all to get a commemorative Dubliner mug.

GREAT PLAINS

LINCOLN

Home to the historic brick-and-cobblestone Haymarket District, a lively bar scene and the state capital, Lincoln makes a good overnight stop. Named for 'Honest Abe' (the former US president), Nebraska's capital city has a friendly feel, thanks to a negligible crime rate, low cost of living and more city parks per capita than any other US city.

Information

Visitor center (☎ 402-434-5348, 800-423-8212; www .lincoln.org; 201 N 7th St; ⊗ 9am-8pm Mon-Fri, 8am-4pm Sat, noon-4pm Sun) Inside Lincoln Station in the Haymarket.

Sights & Activities

The remarkable 400ft-high **State Capitol** (☎ 402-471-0448; www.capitol.org; 14th & M Sts; hourly tours free; ⊗ 8am-5pm Mon-Fri, 10am-5pm Sat, 1-5pm Sun) represents the apex of phallic architecture. A continued restoration (to be finished in 2007) still mars the view, but it's worthwhile taking a tour of the 1932 art-deco interior. A 14th-floor observation deck is open to the public, weather permitting.

The **University of Nebraska State Museum** (☎ 402-472-2642; www.museum.unl.edu; Morrill Hall; adult/child $4/2; ⊗ 9:30am-4:30pm Mon-Sat, 1:30-4:30pm Sun) has a solid collection of elephant fossils, a planetarium with laser shows and mammoth bones supposedly dug up by a chicken.

The prized Nebraska Cornhuskers football team plays home games here in fall. On most weekdays, you can tour the team's field and hall of fame at **Memorial Stadium** (☎ 402-472-1905).

Sleeping

There are budget motels aplenty on W '0' St, near I-80 (exits 395, 396 and 397). Pickings are slightly better off I-80 at the Cornhusker Hwy (NW 12th St) exit.

Embassy Suites Hotel (☎ 402-474-1111; 1040 P St; ste from $120; P ⊠ ⌘) This enormous hotel adjacent to the Haymarket district has luxurious rooms, many with Jacuzzis, and a nine-story open atrium featuring two waterfalls. A cooked-to-order breakfast is included and parking costs $5.

HI Cornerstone Hostel (☎ 402-476-0926; http://in color.inebraska.com/gnelson/CornerstoneHostel.html; 640 N 16th St; member/nonmember $10/13) In a church between two fraternity houses, this small, quiet hostel has nine dorm beds, full kitchen and laundry facilities, and no lock-out time.

Eating

Lincoln's Haymarket District, a rejuvenated six-block warehouse area dating from the early 20th century, has a good variety of grub.

Mill (☎ 402-475-5522; 800 P St; snacks $1-5; ⊗ breakfast, lunch & dinner) University students and downtown workers soak in the afternoon sun on the dock of this nuevo-industrial café, which serves coffee and snacks, offers free wi-fi Internet access and has a newsstand.

Oven (☎ 402-475-6118; 201 N 8th St; mains $10-18; ⊗ dinner) An upscale Indian restaurant, Oven has more than a dozen vegetarian dishes on the menu.

Maggie's Vegetarian Wraps (☎ 402-477-3959; 311 N 8th St; $4-6; ⊗ lunch & dinner) This casual hangout serves vegan wraps, soups and baked goodies for dine-in or takeout.

ALONG I-80

Known as the Great Platte River Rd, I-80 is the shortest but least stimulating route across the Plains. It's hardly a thrill a minute but there are some worthwhile stops.

In Grand Island, near the junction of US 281, is the modern **Stuhr Museum of the Prairie Pioneer** (☎ 308-385-5316; www.stuhrmuseum.org; I-80 exit 312; adult/child $8/6; ⊗ 9am-5pm Mon-Sat, noon-5pm Sun), which contains the building where Henry Fonda was born and a slew of living-history exhibits.

At Grand Island, Hwy 2 branches northwest through Broken Bow to Alliance in the panhandle. Hwy 2 is slow but scenic. It passes through the **Sand Hills** – 20,000 sq miles of sand dunes covered in grass – one of the country's most isolated areas. Keep a full tank.

Causing no small amount of driver confusion, the **Great Platte River Road Archway Monument** (☎ 877-511-2724; www.archway.org; adult/child 6-12/student 13-18 $10/3/6; ⊗ 9am-6pm May-Sep, 9am-4pm Oct-Apr) hangs perilously over I-80 east of Kearney. The gadget-heavy museum traces Nebraska's history with cool multimedia exhibits and kid-friendly activities.

North Platte is home to the **Buffalo Bill Ranch State Historic Park** (☎ 308-535-8035; Scouts Rest Ranch Rd; admission free; ⊗ 8am-8pm daily summer, 9am-dusk Mon-Fri winter), six miles north of town, which celebrates Bill Cody, the father of rodeo and the famed Wild West Show.

To the west, near Paxton, Central Time changes to Mountain Time. You can spend the extra hour downtown at **Ole's Steakhouse**

& **Big Game Lounge** (☎ 308-239-4500; I-80 exit 145; mains $5-15; ☯ breakfast, lunch, dinner to 1am, to 10pm Sun), a cozy, wood-lined lodge with a blue-lit polar bear in a display case and more tusked heads on the wall than stools at the bar.

ALONG US 26 (OREGON TRAIL)

Branch off I-80 at **Ogallala** – a well-preserved historic town worth checking out – and follow the Oregon Trail along US 26 to the huge landmarks of Nebraska's panhandle. Near Bridgeport, 56 miles northwest, stands the **Courthouse & Jail Rocks**, the first of the major landmarks.

From Bridgeport, take a detour 40 miles north on US 385 to rural Alliance, the quiet, somewhat reluctant home to **Carhenge** (☎ 308-762-1520; admission free), in a field 3½ miles north of town along Hwy 87 (catch it at the east end of town). The Stonehenge replica is made from 34 discarded car bodies. It would be a lot cooler – though less funny – if to get there you didn't have to drive past thousands of auto graves in people's front yards that could pass for Carhenge prototypes. Still, it's a pretty effective visual gag and worth the 3-mile detour.

Continuing west on US 26, you'll find **Chimney Rock**, the most frequently mentioned trail landmark in pioneer diaries – and the model for the artwork on many Nebraska license plates. The excellent **visitor center** (☎ 308-586-2581; adult/child $3/free; ☯ 9am-5pm daily summer, 9am-5pm Tue-Sun Sep-May) interprets the pioneer trails. Dirt roads surround the center and allow for exploring.

Visible for miles, the most impressive Oregon Trail landmark is **Scotts Bluff National Monument** (☎ 308-436-4340; Hwy 92; admission per car $5), three miles west of Gering. The Sioux called it *me-a-pa-te* (hill that is hard to go around). Today you can drive up it in a flash, or take the 1.5-mile hike. The views of Wyoming's Laramie Peak 90 miles west and North Platte River 800ft below are outstanding. It also has a **visitor center** (☯ 8am-5pm, Summit Rd ☯ 8am-4:30pm).

ALONG US 20

The further west you go, the more space you'll see between towns, trees and pickup trucks. Get the free *Highway to Adventure: US 20* brochure, available at visitor centers.

Running on converted railroad lines, the **Cowboy Trail** (☎ 402-370-3374) is a network of cycling, hiking and horseback-riding trails. When completed, the route will run nearly 200 miles and it will connect Norfolk with Valentine.

At **Ashfall Fossil Beds State Historical Park** (☎ 402-893-2000; adult/child $3/2; ☯ 9am-5pm Mon-Sat, 11am-5pm Sun), off US 20 north of Royal, you can see unearthed prehistoric skeletons of more than 200 critters, buried 10 million years ago by ash from a Pompeii-like explosion in what is now Idaho.

Valentine

An absurdly cute town on the edge of the Sand Hills, the 'Cupid Capital of Nebraska' takes its name so seriously that even the street signs are red-and-white. It's a great (and romantic!) base for canoeing, kayaking and inner-tubing along the Niobrara River. If you're feeling more dangerous than cuddly, take a scenic drive along **Outlaw Road** (Hwy 12), which passes by the Fort Nebraska National Wildlife Refuge.

Get the scoop on outfitters at the hearts-and-flowers-themed **visitor center** (☎ 402-376-2969; US 20 & US 83; ☯ 9am-8pm Mon-Sat).

The red-brick **Valentine Motel** (☎ 402-376-2450; Main St; s/d $35/40) has cute rooms and a 1953 Ford parked out front.

Northern Panhandle

Wide-open spaces dotted with interesting attractions make the panhandle worth a visit.

The **Museum of the Fur Trade** (☎ 308-432-3843; adult/child $2.50/free; ☯ 8am-5pm summer), 3 miles east of Chadron on US 20, includes the restored Bordeaux Trading Post.

Northwest of Crawford, **Toadstool Geological Park** is a mini-badlands with a wide variety of fossils and a hiking trail. The nearby **Hudson-Meng Bison Bonebed** (☎ 308-665-3900; adult/child $4/1; ☯ 9am-5pm May-Sep) displays the site where 1000 bison enigmatically perished more than 10,000 years ago.

Fort Robinson State Park (☎ 308-665-2900; admission per vehicle $2.50; ☯ dawn-dusk), 4 miles west of Crawford, is where Crazy Horse was killed in 1877 while in captivity – a plaque marks the spot.

At Harrison, drive 23 miles south on Hwy 29 to reach **Agate Fossil Beds National Monument** (☎ 308-668-2211; 7-day pass adult/car $3/5; ☯ 8am-6pm summer, 8am-5pm rest of year), a rich source of unusual fossils dating back 10 to 20 million years.

GREAT PLAINS

GREAT PLAINS

KANSAS

Kansas is a state of superlatives, attractions Too Amazing to Be Believed – things like the World's Biggest Prairie Dog, Deepest Hand-Dug Well and Largest Ball of Twine. It may be the only state in the nation that needs its own circus barker. The name conjures up visions of wicked witches and yellow-brick roads, hot-air balloons over golden prairies, tornadoes powerful enough to catapult houses. On the other hand, it's best-known for wheat – hardly the most glamorous tourist attraction in the country.

But visitors are in for some surprises, and not just along the lines of six-legged cattle and talking scarecrows. From the healthy music scenes in Lawrence and Wichita to the oasis of well-preserved Victorian architecture in Abilene, from Hutchinson's space center to the otherworldly formations known as Monument Rocks, and from little Lindsborg to Nicodemus, there are hidden gems in this state just waiting to be discovered.

At the other end of the spectrum, Kansas' socio-political landscape also continues to astonish; at the time of research, a conservative legislature was debating the pros and cons of teaching creationism in schools instead of evolution.

History

Kansas' history has been pretty tumultuous. The state played a key role in sparking the Civil War when the Kansas-Nebraska Act of 1854 allowed settlers in the Kansas and Nebraska territories to vote on whether slavery would exist in each state. Immediately, swarms of settlers on all sides of the question flooded the two territories, hoping to swing the vote in their favor. Election fraud ran rampant, and clashing views led to widespread violence. In one example, a band of pro-slavery thugs dubbed 'Ruffians' ransacked Lawrence, causing forces led by abolitionist John Brown to strike back. Known as 'Bleeding Kansas,' this volatile era lasted until January 1861, when Kansas was admitted as a free state. The Civil War began 10 weeks later.

Growing pains continued: early settlers wiped out herds of buffalo and expelled the Native Americans (even the state's namesake Kansa relocated to Oklahoma in 1873).

KANSAS FACTS

Nickname Sunflower State

Population 2.7 million

Area 82,282 sq miles

Capital city Topeka (population 123,993)

Official state song 'Home on the Range'

Birthplace of Aviator of the 1920s and '30s Amelia Earhart (1897–1937); jazz legend Charlie Parker (1920–55); and silent film stars Roscoe 'Fatty' Arbuckle (1887–1933), Louise Brooks (1906–85) and Buster Keaton (1895–1966)

Home of Former Republican Senator Bob Dole

Famous for Fictional residents Dorothy and Toto (of *Wizard of Oz* fame), Turkey Red wheat

---

Before long – partly due to prohibitionist Carrie Nation, who swept through Kansas in 1900 wielding her axe against the evils of drink – the Sunflower State was transformed from rip-roaring open range into some of the world's most productive wheatlands. The children of Mennonites who emigrated from the steppes of Russia during the 1870s brought with them handfuls of the now-famous 'Turkey Red' wheat, which made itself thoroughly at home. The state's other big industry is aviation, with several major manufacturers based around Wichita.

Information

Kansas sales tax is 5.3%, and some cities and counties add 1% to 2% to that rate.

Travel information:

Kansas road conditions (☎ 866-511-5368; http://511.ksdot.org)

Kansas state park information (☎ 620-672-5911; www.kdwp.state.ks.us; daily vehicle permit Apr-Sep/Oct-Mar $6.50/5.50)

Kansas Travel & Tourism (☎ 785-296-4922, 800-252-6727; www.travelks.com; 1000 SW Jackson St, Ste 100, Topeka) The website has regional historical information and links to special-interest tourism guides.

WICHITA

Kansas' largest city, Wichita serves as *the* destination for entertainment and culture among folks who live in the outlying areas – somewhat to the bafflement of the city's residents. But there's a fair amount going on here, from arts and culture to underground music. The city is an attractive blend of historic Old Town architecture and modern industry.

History

This city on the confluence of the Big and Little Arkansas Rivers began in the 1860s as a cow-town on the Chisholm Trail. It took about a dozen cowboys to move a 100,000-strong herd of cattle through the town – and where there are cowboys there are cowgirls, con men, gamblers, gunslingers and prostitutes. When things got a bit too rowdy, Wichita passed laws that moved all the action over to the town of Delano across the river. While the Wichitans spent their Sunday mornings in church, folks in Delano were treated to naked-lady foot races. These days, Delano is a rather more sedate residential-commercial neighborhood in Wichita.

The railroad's arrival in 1872 triggered a boom, and burgeoning wheat and oil industries fanned its growth. Following WWI, Wichita began producing heaps of airplanes. The city's most recent notoriety came from being the home of Dennis Rader, the 'BTK' serial killer.

Orientation & Information

Wichita's historic Old Town is on the inner east side, with Delano across the Big Arkansas River and the parklike Museums on the River district occupying a triangle of green space between the Big and Little Arkansas Rivers.

Located inside the Wichita Boathouse, the **visitor center** (☎ 316-337-9088, 800-288-9424; www.visitwichita.com; 335 W Lewis; ⏰ 9am-5pm Mon-Sat, noon-4pm Sun) runs guided tours onboard Wichita's old-fashioned **trolleys** (☎ 316-337-9088 for reservations; adult/child $10/8; tours 10am Thu & Fri, 10am & noon Sat).

Vagabond Café (☎ 316-303-1110; 614 W Douglas Ave; ⏰ 7am-2am) has good coffee, beer, books, art and free Internet access.

Sights & Activities

Most of Wichita's points of interest are concentrated in the self-explanatory **Museums on the River** area.

The **Wichita Art Museum** (☎ 316-268-4921; www.wichitaartmuseum.org; 1400 W Museum Blvd; adult/child $5/2, admission free Sat; ⏰ 10am-5pm Tue-Sat, noon-5pm Sun) is home to a good collection of American art, including pieces by Edward Hopper and Mary Cassatt, and hosts frequent traveling exhibits. The Living Room wing was added in 2003.

Guarded by Wichita artist Blackbear Bosin's 44-foot statue 'The Keeper of the Plains,' the **Indian Center Museum** (☎ 316-262-5221; 650 N Seneca St; admission $6; ⏰ 10am-5pm Mon-Sat, 1-5pm Sun) has exhibits of Native American art and artifacts, a kiva and traditional Wichita-style grass house. Events are scheduled here year-round.

The sleek, modern **Exploration Place** (☎ 316-263-3373; www.exploration.org; 300 N McLean Blvd; adult/child $8/6; ⏰ 9am-5pm Mon-Fri, 10am-6pm Sat, noon-5pm Sun) has lots of kid-friendly science exhibits, including a touchable tornado, as well as a café and the CyberDome Theater.

Stroll through **Botanica – The Wichita Gardens** (☎ 316-264-0448; www.botanica.org; 701 Amidon; adult/child $6/3; ⏰ 9am-5pm Mon-Fri Nov-Mar, 9am-5pm Mon-Sat, 1-5pm Sun Apr-Oct), an attractively arranged maze of 24 themed botanic gardens in the Museums on the River district.

Old Cowtown (☎ 316-264-6398; 1871 Sim Park Dr; adult/child $7/5; ⏰ 10am-5pm Mon-Sat, noon-5pm Sun Apr-Oct) is an open-air museum that re-creates the Wild West, complete with pioneer-era buildings, staged gunfights and guides in cowboy costumes. It's cheesy but great for kids.

Frank Lloyd Wright designed the prairie-style **Allen-Lambe House** (☎ 316-687-1027; 255 N Roosevelt St; admission $8; ⏰ by appointment only on 10 days' notice) in 1915 and considered it one of his best. Don't miss the Japanese-influenced garden and koi pond. No one under age 16 is allowed on tours.

Old Town plaza hosts a weekly **farmers market** (☎ 316-992-0413; ⏰ 7am-noon Sat May-Oct).

Sleeping

Inn at the Park (☎ 316-652-0500; www.innatthepark .com; 3751 E Douglas; r weekday/weekend $99/140; Ⓟ) This three-story brick mansion was a private residence until 1955. Its large B&B rooms are individually decorated with elaborately plush furnishings and thematic touches like leaded-glass windows, pine floors, fireplaces, spa tubs and canopy beds.

Hotel at Oldtown (☎ 316-267-4800, 877-265-3269; www.hotelatoldtown.com; 830 1st St; d weekend/weekday $109/169; Ⓟ ✗) With the central square practically in its back yard, this place is ideally situated for exploring Wichita's historic core. The lobby and especially the piano bar have preserved the building's 1900s atmosphere. Suites all have kitchenettes and CD players.

Scotsman Inn Mark 8 (☎ 316-265-4679, 888-830-7268; www.scotsmaninnwichita.com; 1130 N Broadway;

GREAT PLAINS

d from $38; (P)) This basic budget inn has tidy rooms with refrigerators and data ports, and a great location near historic downtown.

Eating

Wichita is the home of Pizza Hut, but that's far from the pinnacle of the city's dining options.

Saigon (☎ 316-262-8134; 1103 N Broadway; mains $5-8; ☾ 9am-9pm Sun-Thu, 9am-10pm Fri & Sat) Possibly the world's best egg rolls are found at this family-run, authentic Vietnamese restaurant, which also serves some inventive vegetarian dishes and traditional *bun* noodles.

Artichoke Sandwich Bar (☎ 316-263-9164; 811 N Broadway; sandwiches $4-7; ☾ 11am-midnight Mon-Sat) The Reuben rules at this cute little pub and café, known for providing mobs of loyal locals with hefty sandwiches and live music.

Larkspur Restaurant (☎ 316-262-5275; 904 E Douglas, Old Town; dinner mains $16-22; ☾ 11am-10pm Mon-Thu, 11am-11pm Fri & Sat, 4-9pm Sun) Though the food might not be as consistently top-notch as it once was, this place is still a hotspot and the atmosphere and location are hard to beat. On sunny days, locals crowd the outside patio for pastas and steaks.

Drinking & Entertainment

River City Brewing Co (☎ 316-263-2739; www.rivercitybrewingco.com; 150 N Mosley, Old Town; burgers $7.50; ☾ 11am-10pm Sun-Thu, 11am-2am Fri & Sat) This brewery in Old Town serves five of its own microbrews along with regional pub fare such as buffalo steaks and Kansas-raised beef. It also has live music and DJ nights and an upstairs cocktail lounge.

Anchor (☎ 316-260-8989; 1109 E Douglas; ☾ 7am-2am Mon-Sat, 10am-2am Sun) An excellent artist-run café, the Anchor serves great coffee and a huge selection of bottled beers in a brick-lined room with low tables and a long bar. Weekly trivia nights, poetry readings and live music make it a local favorite. The same owners run the tattoo shop next door.

Kirby's Beer Store (☎ 316-685-7013; 3227 E 17th St N) This miniature dive has hosted some of the best underground rock shows in the state and still draws top touring bands, as well as local acts.

ALONG I-70

What it lacks in glamour, Kansas' 'main street' makes up for in efficiency. The ruler-straight interstate runs east–west from Kansas City to the Colorado border. Most of Kansas City's points of interest are in Missouri and are covered in that section (p676). West of Abilene, the landscape around I-70 stretches into rolling, wide-open plains, with winds strong enough to knock over an 18-wheeler. The scenery can be monotonous, but there are several interesting stops along the way.

Lawrence

Lawrence has been an oasis of progressive politics from the start. Founded by abolitionists in 1854 and an important stop on the Underground Railroad, it became a battlefield in the clash between pro- and anti-slavery factions. In 1863, the Confederate guerrillas of William Clarke Quantrill raided the town, killing more than 150 civilians and nearly burning the city to the ground. Survivors responded by building sturdier houses of brick and stone, many of which still survive.

INFORMATION

Visitor center (☎ 785-865-4499, 888-529-5267; www.visitlawrence.com; 402 N 2nd St; ☾ 8:30am-5:30pm Mon-Sat, 1-5pm Sun)

Nova Cyber Café (☎ 785-841-3282; 745 New Hampshire St; per hr $6)

SIGHTS & ACTIVITIES

Lawrence is home to **Kansas University** (KU), with a beautiful campus atop what many believe is Kansas' only hill, and the intertribal university **Haskell Indian Nations University**, where Olympians Jim Thorpe and Billy Mills studied. KU's **Spencer Museum of Art** (☎ 785-864-4710; www.ukans.edu/~sma; admission free; ☾ 10am-5pm Tue-Sat, noon-5pm Sun, to 9pm Thu) has a collection that includes work by glass sculptor Dale Chihuly, Harlem Renaissance painter Jacob Lawrence and several European masters.

The walkable downtown centers on **Massachusetts St**, one of the nicest streets in this part of the country for a leisurely stroll.

SLEEPING

Eldridge Hotel (☎ 785-749-5011; www.eldridgehotel.com; 701 Massachusetts St; ste from $89; (P) (X) (R)) The suites at this historic downtown hotel, built in 1926 and renovated in 2005, have plush antique furnishings with room service. There's also a hip lounge and classy restaurant.

Halcyon House B&B (☎ 785-841-0314; www.thehalcyonhouse.com; 1000 Ohio St; r with shared bath from $49, cottage from $129; (P)) The cute, oddly shaped bedrooms here have lots of natural light, and there's a landscaped garden and homemade baked goods served for breakfast in a glassed-in sunroom.

EATING & DRINKING

Teller's Restaurant (☎ 785-843-4111; 746 Massachusetts St; mains from $12; ⌚ 11am-10pm Sun-Thu, 11am-11pm Fri & Sat) One of the city's top options, Teller's serves Italian dishes, steak and pasta in a converted bank, with a good wine list, a gay-friendly atmosphere and a 'vault' bathroom.

Wheatfields Bakery & Café (☎ 785-841-5553; 904 Vermont St; breakfast $2-5.50; ⌚ 6:30am-8pm Mon-Sat, 7:30am-4pm Sun) This appropriately named and award-winning café serves excellent breads and is a local fave for breakfast.

Free State Brewing Co (☎ 785-843-4555; www.freestatebrewing.com; 636 Massachusetts St; ⌚ 11am-midnight Mon-Sat, noon-11pm Sun) Grab a pint or two at Kansas' first legal brewery in over a hundred years, which opened in 1989 in a trolley station.

ENTERTAINMENT

For live music, head to the **Bottleneck** (☎ 785-841-5483; 737 New Hampshire) or, for more sophisticated fare, the beaux-arts **Liberty Hall** (☎ 785-749-1972; 644 Massachusetts St), where Beat writer and long-time Lawrence resident William S Burroughs' funeral was held in 1997.

Topeka

Though most Kansans cringe when its name is mentioned, the state's aesthetically challenged capital city has some worthwhile attractions.

Start your exploration at the **visitor center** (☎ 785-234-1030, 800-235-1030; 1275 SW Topeka Blvd; ⌚ 8am-5pm Mon-Thu, 8am-4:30pm Fri), which books accommodations and can recommend restaurants.

The **Brown vs Board of Education National Historic Site** (☎ 785-354-4273; 15th & Monroe; admission free; ⌚ 9am-5pm), at the Monroe Elementary School, runs a very thorough tour and shows an informative video about the landmark 1954 Supreme Court decision that banned segregation in US schools.

With a dome a few feet higher than the one in Washington, DC, the **State Capitol** (☎ 785-276-8681; 10th & Jackson Sts; ⌚ 8am-5pm Mon-Fri, tours 9am-3pm Mon-Fri Jun-Jan) houses a John Steuart Curry mural of abolitionist John Brown.

Abilene

In the late 19th century, Abilene was a rowdy cow town at the end of the Chisholm Trail. Nowadays it's better known for liking Ike – former president Dwight D Eisenhower, who grew up here. With its compact core of historic brick buildings, well-preserved residential neighborhoods and a quiet location off the interstate, Abilene is one of the state's highlights.

The **visitor center** (☎ 785-263-2231, 800-569-5915; www.abilenekansas.org; 201 NW 2nd St; ⌚ 8am-5pm Mon-Sat, 1-4pm Sun) has loads of brochures plus free coffee and a recipe for Mamie Eisenhower's sugar cookies.

The **Eisenhower Center** (☎ 785-263-4751; www.eisenhower.archives.gov/exhibit; 200 SE 4th St; museum $3.50, other sites free; ⌚ 9am-4:45pm) includes Ike's boyhood home, a museum and library, and his and Mamie's graves, which are housed in a meditation center where you can contemplate the infinite dullness of mainstream life in the Eisenhower era (1953–61).

The **Kirby House Restaurant** (☎ 785-263-7336; www.kirby-house.com; 205 NE 3rd St; dinner mains $8-12; ⌚ 11am-2pm Mon-Sun, 5-8pm Mon-Sat) has a lace-curtained dining room in a historic home and a menu of staples like prime rib and country-fried steak plus more ambitious seafood and vegetarian options.

Hays

The town of Hays grew up around its namesake fort, built in the 1860s to protect railroad workers from Native Americans. Today, some original buildings and a re-creation of the officers' quarters stand at the **Fort Hays Historical Site** (☎ 785-625-6812; 4 miles south of I-70 on US 183; adult/student $3/2; ⌚ 9am-5pm Tue-Sat, 1-5pm Sun-Mon), where you'll also find a museum featuring a few Native American artifacts.

The domed **Sternberg Museum of Natural History** (☎ 877-332-1165; 3000 Sternberg Dr; adult/child $6/4; ⌚ 9am-7pm Tue-Sat, 1-7pm Sun) has an unusual fish-within-a-fish fossil and animated dinosaurs.

Off I-70

Founded in 1877 by African American settlers seeking a promised land, lonely but friendly **Nicodemus** (population 52), 59 miles northwest of Hays, has five historic buildings in one of the oldest surviving towns of its kind in the US. The **visitor center** (☎ 785-

GREAT PLAINS

ROUTE 66: GET YOUR KICKS IN KANSAS

A little more than 13 miles of the storied Route 66 pass through the southeast corner of Kansas.

The road starts ominously at the Missouri border, with **Hell's Half Acre**, where the land has been left ravaged by lead and zinc mining. This was the site of violent miners' strikes in the mid-1930s.

The next stop is the town of Galena. Turn left on Main St, then turn right seven blocks later on Old Route 66 and continue west. Look for the **Howard Litch Historical and Mining Museum** (☎ 620-783-2192; 319 W 7th St; ☷ hours vary, call ahead), a tribute to the folks who worked in the mining industry here.

Three miles down the road you will cross Spring River and enter the small town of Riverton, where you'll find the **Eisler Brothers Old Riverton Store** (☎ 316-848-3330). The 1920s general store sells groceries, deli sandwiches, souvenirs and all kinds of plants. It's also the headquarters of the **Kansas Historic Route 66 Association** (☎ 316-848-3330; www.route66.itgo.com/ks66.html).

Cross the four-lane highway and stay on old Route 66 to the 1923 **Marsh Rainbow Arch Bridge**, the last of its kind.

From the bridge, it's less than 4 miles south to **Baxter Springs**, the site of a Civil War massacre and numerous bank robberies. Veer left off Willow Ave onto 3rd St toward downtown, turning right onto Military Ave. The **Heritage Center & Historical Museum** (8th & East Aves; ☷ 10:30am-4:30pm Tue-Sat, 1-4:30pm Sun Apr-Oct, closed Mon-Fri Nov-Mar) has historical exhibits including a reconstructed blacksmith shop, pre–Civil War cabin and lead/zinc mine. There's an optional detour from here on a signposted loop of the older road before the highway rejoins US 69A and rolls into Oklahoma.

For more information, contact the association in Riverton. See also p30.

839-4233; ☷ 8:30am-5pm generally, call to confirm) shows a short film and gives free guided tours. Nicodemus' **Homecoming**, held the last weekend in July, is a big event.

The startling **Monument Rocks** (☎ 785-272-3840), 80ft chalk formations that look like a Jawa hangout in *Star Wars*, are about 30 miles southeast of I-70 on US 83. The public is welcome to explore, but it's private property, so if you find any fossils – not uncommon – leave them where they are, or call for further information.

ALONG US 50 & US 56

More attractive alternatives to I-70 across Kansas are US 50 and US 56. Both pass through the Flint Hills in the east, then meet out west and mosey into Dodge City arm-in-arm.

Fabled US 50 pairs up with I-35 southwest from Kansas City; after crossing I-135, it heads out on its own as it passes through Chase County, which William Least Heat-Moon examined in his book *Prairyerth*.

Hutchinson

Learn about the race into outer space in – of all places – Hutchinson, on US 50 west of I-135, home of the amazing **Cosmosphere &**

Space Center (☎ 620-662-2305, 800-397-0330; 1100 N Plum Ave; all-day pass adult/child $12.50/10, museum only $8/7.50; ☷ 9am-6pm Mon-Thu, 9am-9pm Fri & Sat, noon-6pm Sun; ⓟ), where you can see the original Apollo 13, Soviet cosmonaut outfits and a nuclear warhead that was found rotting in an Alabama warehouse.

Along US 56

Another route is US 56 southwest, which follows the old Santa Fe Trail (a little north of US 50). Council Grove used to be a good place to fix the Conestoga wagon. The **Cottage House Hotel** (☎ 620-767-6828, 800-727-7903; www.cottagehousehotel.com; 25 N Neosho; r $50-155), a turreted Victorian, has 28 squeaky-floored rooms with period furnishings and private baths.

The large Mennonite communities around **Hillsboro**, on US 56 west of Marion, are descendants of Russian immigrants who brought the Turkey Red strain of wheat to the Plains, where it thrived despite harsh conditions. Contact the **visitor center** (☎ 620-947-3506; 109 S Main; ☷ 9am-5pm Mon-Thu, 9am-4pm Fri) for information on tours.

Cute **Lindsborg**, about 15 miles north of US 56, on SR 4 west of I-135, flaunts its Swedish roots with themed events, restaurants, shops and hotels; and a collection of public-art sculptures of Dala horses, a classic Swedish icon. The **visitor center** (☎ 785-227-3706, 888-227-2227; www.lindsborg.org; 104 E Lincoln; ☒ 9am-4pm) has a schedule of events, books accommodations and recommends activities.

Back on US 56, continue west to Great Bend, then southwest to Larned, where you can see the **Santa Fe Trail Center Museum** (☎ 620-285-2054; adult/child $4/1.50; ☒ 9am-5pm Tue-Sun Labor Day-Memorial Day), a multicultural exploration of the world that developed along the two-way trail linking the US and Mexico. Just west of this is the restored **Fort Larned National Historic Site** (☎ 620-285-6911; 7-day pass $5; ☒ 8:30am-4:30pm), the only fort along the Santa Fe Trail.

Dodge City

Famous as the setting for the TV series 'Gunsmoke' (1955–75) and the Wild West vernacular it inspired, modern Dodge, on US 50/56 southwest of Larned, revels in the old days, though it's hard to see much evidence of the hell-raisin' days on the surface. Even if you just pass through, don't get the heck out of Dodge before trying some of the city's famous Mexican food, found in numerous spots up and down the main drag (Wyatt Earp Blvd). For recommendations, saunter into the **visitor center** (☎ 620-225-8186; 400 W Wyatt Earp Blvd; ☒ 8am-6:30pm summer, 8am-5pm Mon-Fri Sep-Apr), or just follow your nose.

Fort Dodge (☎ 620-227-2121; US 154; admission free; ☒ 10am-4pm), a mix of old and new buildings, is home to retired soldiers, a museum and a house where General Custer once spent a night. About 9 miles west of town on US 50 are Santa Fe Trail wagon-wheel ruts, most visible at dusk.

The cartoon–movie-set tourist draw of **Boot Hill Museum & Front Street** (☎ 620-227-8188; adult/child $7/free; ☒ 9am-5pm Mon-Sat, 1-5pm Sun) includes a cemetery, jail and saloon, where gunslingers re-enact high-noon shootouts all summer long while Miss Kitty and her dancing gals rustle up some chuck-wagon grub.

If you want to avoid the ubiquitous chain hotels, try **Thunderbird Motel** (☎ 620-225-4143; 2300 W Wyatt Earp Blvd; s/d $35/45), a comfy joint where each room has a mini refrigerator and microwave.

OKLAHOMA

Think of Oklahoma and you may conjure up images of cowboys and Indians riding across the plains. There's something to that – winds do blow on the western prairie and museums across the state celebrate both the bygone ranching-and-wrangling way of life and the state's many Native American tribal cultures. Today you can attend a rodeo or a powwow to see those legacies in action. But Oklahoma also has rolling woodlands and forested mountains in the east and southwest, a capital city that is growing and thriving, and 400 miles of Route 66. So stop at a roadside café, have a slice of pie and a chat: you won't regret it.

History

Archaeologists have found evidence of Native American settlement in the area from more than 11,000 years ago. Much later, Wichita, Arapaho, Comanche and Osage occupied or used the land. By 1834 the region (minus the panhandle) had been declared autonomous Indian Territory. Tribes from across the nation were relocated here, often at gunpoint. In one of the most dramatic examples, more than 4000 of 15,000 Cherokee perished in the cold and hunger while marching the 'Trail of Tears' to the territory in the winter of 1838–39.

In the 1880s, before the US gave the go-ahead to parcel out former Native American lands, eager homesteaders ('Sooners') crossed territory lines to stake claims. That's right:

OKLAHOMA FACTS

Nickname Sooner State

Population 3.5 million

Area 69,900 sq miles

Capital city Oklahoma City (population 519,040; metro area 1 million)

Official song 'Oklahoma!' (Rodgers & Hammerstein)

Birthplace of Woody Guthrie (1912–67), athlete Jim Thorpe (1887–1953), Will Rogers (1879–1935), Garth Brooks (b 1962), actor Brad Pitt (b 1963)

Home of Boy Scouts of America, parking meters (1935), bands Flaming Lips and Hanson

Famous for 1930s dust bowl, tornadoes, football, 1995 Oklahoma City bombing

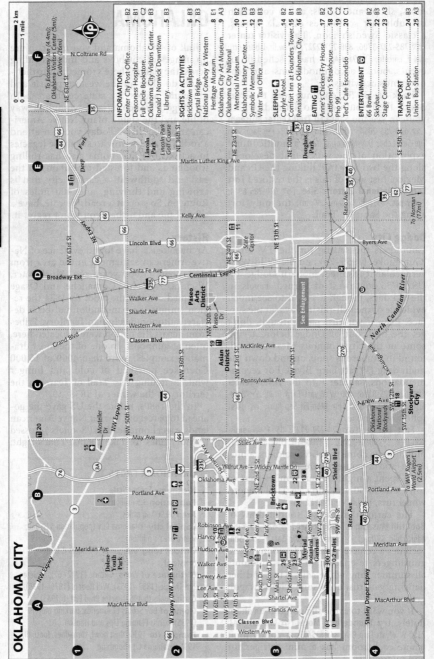

OKLAHOMA CITY

INFORMATION	
Center City Post Office................	1 B2
Deaconess Hospital.....................	2 B1
Full Circle Bookstore..................	3 C2
Oklahoma City Visitors Center....	4 B3
Ronald J Norwick Downtown	
Library.....................................	5 B3

SIGHTS & ACTIVITIES	
Bricktown Ballpark......................	6 B3
Crystal Bridge............................	7 B3
National Cowboy & Western	
Heritage Museum.......................	8 E1
Oklahoma City Art Museum.......	9 A3
Oklahoma City National	
Memorial Museum.....................	10 B2
Oklahoma History Center...........	11 D3
Symbolic Memorial.....................	12 B3
Water Taxi Office........................	13 B3

SLEEPING	
Carlyle Motel.............................	14 B2
Comfort Inn at Founders Tower..15 B1
Renaissance Oklahoma City.......	16 B3

EATING	
Anne's Chicken Fry House...........	17 B2
Cattlemen's Steakhouse.............	18 C4
Pho 99......................................	19 C2
Ted's Cafe Escondido.................	20 C1

ENTERTAINMENT	
66 Bowl.....................................	21 B2
Skkybar.....................................	22 B3
Stage Center.............................	23 A3

TRANSPORT	
Santa Fe Depot..........................	24 B3
Union Bus Station......................	25 A3

the Sooner State is named for law-breakers. In April of 1889 settlement to non-Indians was officially opened and towns emerged overnight in the Great Land Rush.

Statehood in 1907 was followed by another boom when oil was discovered in the 1920s, but the Depression and soil erosion affected the state badly. Thousands of 'Okie' farmers migrated west on the 'Mother Road' (Route 66) to find a better life. The state's agricultural industry eventually rebounded, due to greater care for the fragile Plains environment. And oil continues to play a role in the state's development.

Information

State sales tax is 4.5%. Hotel taxes are 2% to 5%.

Oklahoma Tourism & Recreation Department (☎ 405-521-2406, 800-652-6552; www.travelok.com) Operates 12 visitor centers, including one at either end of I-40. Call or go online to request a packet with guide and map.

Oklahoma visitor center (☎ 405-478-4637; www .travelok.com; Exit 137 I-35, at NE 122nd, Oklahoma City; ☺ 8:30am-5pm)

OKLAHOMA CITY

You can feel revitalization in the air as you walk down the streets of Oklahoma City (OKC). Within the past five years, among other improvements, a new capitol dome, a new convention center and a major new history museum have gone up. OKC is a manageable, friendly city that strives to hold onto its cowboy heritage, honor its tragic involvement with domestic terrorism, and attract visitors for the future. The 17-acre park in the middle of downtown and a renovated warehouse entertainment district do much to add to the town's appeal. And all this is set down in and around Route 66.

History

Oklahoma City literally sprang up overnight when 'unassigned' Indian Territory lands were opened to white settlement on April 22, 1889. More than 10,000 land claimants staked out their piece of the pie near the Santa Fe railroad station. The city yanked capital honors out from under Guthrie in 1910 and was catapulted into wealth in 1928 when OKC's first gusher erupted above a vast oil field. The vagaries

of oil and gas production continue to help fuel the city's economy today.

Orientation

The capitol is pretty darn central, so all the state's main interstates go through: I-44 runs northeast–southwest; I-35 travels due north–south (it's only four hours to Dallas); I-40 goes east–west. The NW Expressway branches off I-44 north of downtown.

Information

Bank of America (☎ 405-230-4003; 415 W Kerr Ave) **Daily Oklahoman** (www.dailyoklahoman.com) Newspaper.

Deaconess Hospital (☎ 405-604-6000, 24hr emergency room 405-604-6106; 5501 N Portland Ave) **Emergency number** (☎ 911) Police, ambulance, fire. **Full Circle Bookstore** (☎ 405-842-2900; 50 Penn Pl; ☺ 10am-9pm Mon-Sat, noon-5pm Sun) Independent bookstore with a good Route 66 selection.

King Country 93.3 FM Popular cowboy country songs, local event promotion.

Oklahoma City Visitor Center (☎ 405-297-8912, 800-225-5652; www.visitokc.com; 189 W Sheridan Ave; ☺ 8am-5pm Mon-Fri)

Oklahoma visitor center (☎ 405-478-4637; www .travelok.com; Exit 137 I-35, at NE 122nd; ☺ 8:30am-5pm) Has city info too, near I-44.

Post office (☎ 800-275-8777; 305 NW 5th St) **Ronald J Norwick Downtown Library** (☎ 405-231-8650; 300 Park Ave; ☺ 9am-9pm Mon-Thu, 9am-5pm Fri & Sat, 1-6pm Sun) Visitor's card allows 30 minutes free Internet access.

Sights & Activities

A couple of museums and the Oklahoma City bombing site are downtown, but the other attractions are spread around the town's edges. Stockyards City (p711), to the southwest, is an old-timey false-front town with restaurants and shops (and occasional cattle auctions). The entertaining Bricktown District is east of the center and the renowned cowboy museum lies to the northeast.

The city is still much defined by April 19, 1995, when the Alfred P Murrah Federal Building was bombed by domestic terrorists. Of the 168 people that died, 16 were children at day care. The stories of the victims and survivors are told at the touching, high-tech **Oklahoma City National Memorial Museum** (☎ 405-235-3313; www.oklahomacitynationalmemo rial.org; 605 N Harvey Ave; adult/senior & student $7/6;

9am-6pm Mon-Sat, 1-6pm Sun, box office closes 1hr earlier). The outdoor **Symbolic Memorial** (admission free; 24hr) is made up of large, empty chair sculptures set in the former building's footprint.

Sure the rambling **National Cowboy & Western Heritage Museum** (405-478-2250; www.nationalcowboymuseum.org; 1700 NE 63rd St; adult/child $8.50/4; 9am-5pm) has an excellent collection of western painting and sculpture, with many by Charles M Russell and Frederic Remington. But for more fun head straight to the rodeo or American cowboy galleries to watch parts of old Westerns and wander through the re-created frontier town of Prosperity Junction.

The huge new **Oklahoma History Center** (405-522-5248; www.ok-history.mus.ok.us; NW 23rd St & N Lincoln Blvd; adult/child under 6 $5/free; 9am-5pm Mon-Sat, noon-5pm Sun) opened across from the capitol in late 2005. Explore the history of the state's Native and African Americans, as well as that of the homesteaders who arrived during the late 1880s land rush.

Take a **Water Taxi** (405-234-8263; www.watertaxi.com; 3 Mickey Mantel Dr; per day $6; 10am-10pm Apr-Oct, reduced hrs winter) ride along the area canal, or enjoy a Saturday afternoon watching the Triple A Redhawks play at **Bricktown Ballpark** (405-281-1000; www.oklahomaredhawks.com; 2 Mickey Mantle Dr).

Downtown, the **Oklahoma City Art Museum** (405-236-3100; www.okcmoa.com; 415 Couch Dr; adult/child $7/5; 10am-5pm Tue-Sat, until 10pm Thu, 1-5pm Sun) focuses on mid-20th century American art, especially glasswork. A seven-story conservatory, **Crystal Bridge** (405-297-3995; Reno & Robinson Aves; adult/child $5/3.50; 10am-6pm Mon-Sat, noon-6pm Sun), contains three ecosystems and a waterfall amid the 17-acre **Myriad Gardens**.

Festivals & Events

Festival of the Arts (405-270-4848; www.artscouncilokc.com/festival; Hudson St & Reno Ave; admission free) Downtown streets fill with food and art vendors mid-April.

Red Earth Native American Cultural Festival (405-427-5228; www.redearth.org; State Fair Park, I-40 & NW 10th St; adult/child $10/7.50) American Indian tribe members come from across the nation to celebrate and compete in early June.

State Fair Park (405-948-6704; www.okstatefairpark.com; I-40 & NW 10th St; admission $10) The fair grounds hosts a horse- or rodeo-related event just about every month.

Sleeping

Many older motels are along I-35 south of town; newer chain properties stack up along the NW Expressway.

Comfort Inn at Founders Tower (405-810-1100; www.comfortinn.com; 5704 Mosteller Dr, off NW Expressway; r $62-79;) Comfy, quiet mini-suites have microwaves, mini-fridges, coffee makers, big desks and armchairs in pleasant plaids. Free expanded continental breakfast and high-speed Internet included.

Renaissance Oklahoma City (405-228-8000; www.marriott.com; 10 N Broadway Ave; r $119-$200;) The fountain in the lobby atrium adds to the peace and calm at this most upscale downtown hotel. Spa services are available near the indoor pool. Parking costs $16 and from here you will find that it's walking distance to Bricktown.

Budget-wise, the **Carlyle Motel** (405-946-3355; 3600 NW 39th St; r $32;) is dingy, but the little brick buildings are conveniently on Route 66. **Economy Inn** (405-478-9292; economyinnkenny@yahoo.com; 12005 N I-35 service rd; r $26-39;) has peeling paint outside and nice enough rooms inside.

Eating

Bunches of eateries cluster in Bricktown, and a small, scattered **Asian District** (near 23rd St & Classen Blvd) has reasonable Vietnamese noodle houses and Chinese restaurants.

Pho 99 (405-525-3579; 3009 N Classen Blvd; mains $4-7; 10am-8pm) Looking for home cooking Asian-style? This is where the resident Vietnamese go for pho. Try the salty lemonade with soda or a strawberry smoothie to drink.

Cattlemen's Steakhouse (405-236-0416; www.cattlemensrestaurant.com; 1309 S Agnew Ave; breakfasts $4-6, lunches $4-8, dinners $10-20; 6am-10pm Sun-Thu, 6am-midnight Fri & Sat) Everybody's favorite, this Stockyards City institution has been feeding cowpokes slabs of meat and hearty (though not necessarily heart-healthy) cookin' since 1910. The old-fangled booths and dark paneling suit the place.

Ted's Cafe Escondido (405-848-8337; 2836 NW 68th St; lunch specials $7-8, mains $10-16; 11am-10pm Mon-Thu, 11am-10:30pm Fri & Sat, 11am-8:30pm Sun) Chips and complimentary *queso* (spicy cheese dip) are so fresh, they arrive at the table almost before you do. Come early to enjoy the traditional Tex-Mex food; waits start weekends after 6:30pm.

Anne's Chicken Fry House (☎ 405-943-8915; 4106 NW 39th St; mains $4-11; ◷ 11am-9pm Tue-Sat) One of the few remaining Route 66 eateries, Anne's has a nostalgic mural and decor.

Entertainment

For listings, pick up the free weekly **Oklahoma Gazette** (www.okgazette.com) or just head to the renovated warehouses in the **Bricktown District** (www.bricktownokc.com; east of Broadway Ave & north of Reno Ave), which contain restaurants and bars.

Skkybar (☎ 405-272-9222; www.skkybar.com; 7 Mickey Mantle Dr) The fourth-floor martini bar/dance club pulses to a Top 40 and '80s and '90s beat, with occasional live music.

66 Bowl (☎ 405-946-3966; www.66bowl.com; 3810 NW 39th St; ◷ 8:30am-midnight) Live alternative rock bands play Friday and Saturday nights at this Route 66 bowling alley.

Stage Center (☎ 405-270-4801; www.stagecenter .com; 400 W Sheridan Ave) Two theaters and a cabaret room host contemporary plays, musicals and events.

Shopping

Numerous saddle shops, western wear stores and cowboy knick-knack outlets line the streets of **Stockyards City** (Agnew Ave at SW 12 St), adjacent to the still-active stockyards. The **Passeo Arts District** (east of Shartel, north of NW 23rd St) isn't much more than Passeo Dr itself, but there are several art galleries and boutiques in the Spanish colonial buildings.

Getting There & Around

Will Rogers World Airport (☎ 405-680-3200; www.fly okc.com) is 5 miles southwest of downtown. Take I-44 south from I-40, or I-240 west from I-35. The **Airport Express Shuttle** (☎ 405-681-3311) charges $16 to get downtown; in a **Yellow Cab** (☎ 405-232-6161) it costs about $20.

The Amtrak *Heartland Flyer* train goes from OKC's **Santa Fe Depot** (☎ 800-872-7245; 100 S EK Gaylord Blvd) to Fort Worth ($23, 4¼ hours). Buy your ticket on the train; there's no office here.

Greyhound buses depart daily from the **Union Bus Station** (☎ 405-235-6425; 427 W Sheridan Ave) for Tulsa ($19, two hours) and Dallas ($41, four hours), among other destinations. There is no direct bus to Kansas City.

Metro Transit's **Oklahoma Spirit Trolleys** (☎ 405-234-7433; www.gometro.org) connect downtown and Bricktown sights for a quarter per ride.

AROUND OKLAHOMA CITY

Guthrie

Brick-and-stone Victorian buildings line street after street of Oklahoma's first capital, 20 miles north of Oklahoma City. The well-preserved buildings in downtown contain shops, museums and eateries. The town teems with life summer weekends and during mid-April's **'89er Celebration**.

The **Guthrie Information Center** (☎ 405-282-1947; www.guthrieok.com; 212 W Oklahoma) has maps and can point out the small theme museums (banjo, sports, frontier drugstore, history) in town. Ask the **Bed & Breakfast Association of Guthrie** (☎ 405-282-8898, 888-551-1889; www.guthriebb.com) to help match you with one of the more than 12 landmark B&Bs in town. **Kate's Diner** (☎ 405-282-2462; 120 W Cleveland; breakfast $3-7, lunch & dinner mains $5-9; ◷ 6am-2pm Mon-Sat, 7am-7pm Sun) serves the best fluffy, buttery, homemade biscuits around.

WESTERN OKLAHOMA

West of Oklahoma City toward Texas the land opens into expansive prairie fields and Route 66 twists on and off I-40. To the southwest there are several Native American heritage sights and the unexpected Wichita Mountains, possible daytrips from OKC.

Route 66 – Oklahoma City to Texas Panhandle

From OKC to Texola, near the state line, is about 150 miles. In Clinton, 85 miles west of OKC, walk through six decades of history, memorabilia and music at the entertaining **Route 66 Museum** (☎ 580-323-7866; www.route66.org; 2229 W Gary Blvd; adult/child $3/1; ◷ 9am-7pm Mon-Sat, 1-6pm Sun, closed at 5pm Labor Day-Memorial Day, closed Sun-Mon Jan & Feb). An audio tour is available.

Thirty miles further west in Elk City, the **National Route 66 Museum** (☎ 580-225-6266; adult/child $5/4; ◷ 9am-5pm Mon-Sat, 2-5pm Sun) is more form than substance, but the entry price includes a re-created pioneer town and a farm museum.

The original kitschy neon sign at the **Western Motel** (☎ 580-928-3353; 315 NE Hwy 66; r $35; ☒) in Sayre, 18 miles west of Elk City, is quite photogenic. Take a 25-mile detour north to Cheyenne and the **Washita Battlefield National Historic Site** (☎ 580-497-2742; www .nps.gov/waba; Hwy 47, 2 miles east of US 283; admission free; ⏰ dawn-dusk), where George Custer's troops launched the 1868 attack on the slumbering (and peaceful) village of Chief Black Kettle.

Learn more at the **Black Kettle Museum** (☎ 580-497-3929; US 283 & Hwy 47, Cheyenne; admission free; ⏰ 10am-noon & 1-4pm Tue-Fri, 9am-5pm Sat & Sun).

Anadarko

West of I-44 via US 62, 60 miles southwest of OKC, Anadarko and the surrounding area are home to 64 Native American tribes. The town hosts powwows and other events almost monthly. Get a schedule from the Anadarko Visitor Center inside the **National Hall of Fame for Famous American Indians** (☎ 405-247-5555; www.anadarko.org; Hwy 62, 1 mile east of town; admission free; ⏰ 9am-5pm Mon-Sat, 1-5pm Sun), which has a 40-acre park with 43 bronze busts.

Take a guided tour of seven tribal lodgings (huts, mounds, teepees etc) re-created on a hillside at **Indian City USA** (☎ 405-247-5661; www.indiancityusa.com; Rte 8, 3 miles south of town; tours adult/child $8.50/5.50; ⏰ 9am-5pm). The 1950s-built sight (not Native American owned) has seen better days, but it's rare that different tribes are represented in one place. Dancers perform summer weekends.

Keep your eye out for signs advertising church suppers and benefits; these are the only places to get Native American food in town. Several shops do sell indigenous crafts.

Fort Sill

Established in 1869 as an outpost against Native Americans, Fort Sill is still an active army base north of Lawton (85 miles southwest of OKC). The **Fort Sill Museum Visitor Center** (☎ 580-442-5123; 435 Quanah Rd; admission free; ⏰ 8:30am-4:30pm Mon-Sun) has photos and a film of the African American troop that built the fort. Ask for a map to **Geronimo's grave**, a couple of miles away. You can walk through four of the old fort buildings, including a guardhouse where Geronimo was detained.

Wichita Mountains

More than 500 buffalo and a herd of longhorns roam the **Wichita Mountains Wildlife Refuge** (☎ 580-429-3222; http://wichitamountains.fws.gov; visitor center Hwy 49 & Hwy 115; ⏰ 8am-4:30pm Mon-Fri), 15 miles northwest of Lawton–Fort Sill. The mixed-grass prairie and lake areas are superb for hiking and wildlife spotting. Drive up Mt Scott (2464ft) for great views. Sites at the **Doris Campground** (☎ 580-429-3222; http://wichitamountains.fws.gov; without/with electricity $6/12), 2 miles west of the visitor center, are first come, first served.

Another extension of the Wichitas is 51 miles to the west at the 4500-acre **Quartz**

ROUTE 66: GET YOUR KICKS IN OKLAHOMA

Oklahoma's connection with America's Main Street runs deep: the road's chief proponent, Cyrus Avery, came from here; John Steinbeck's *Grapes of Wrath* told of the plight of depression-era Okie farmers fleeing west on Route 66; and Oklahoma has more miles of the original alignment than any other state. The **Oklahoma Route 66 Association** (www.oklahomaroute66.com) puts out a 95-page map booklet that you can pick up from **Oklahoma Tourism & Recreation Department** (www.travelok.com) visitor centers (a colorful brochure map is also available).

After you enter the state from Kansas and Missouri, the first **Big Blue Whale** (2705 N Hwy 66) you come to is in Catoosa, outside Tulsa. It's a bit hard to follow the route in Tulsa, but generally from Hwy 66 you take 193rd St south and turn west on 11th St, where you might stop at **Corner Café** (p714) for a bite or stay nearby at the **Hotel Ambassador** (opposite). Route 66 signs start again as you follow Hwy 244 southwest across the river. The souvenir menu and neon sign are enough reason to visit **Rock Café** (opposite) in Stroud, but the food is really excellent too. **Chandler** (opposite) has a few interesting gas stations and such; be sure to take pictures of the **Round Barn** (opposite) in Arcadia. You enter Oklahoma City and the route jogs south on Lincoln Blvd, west on NW 23rd St, north on May Ave, and west on NW 39th St – where you could play a game at **66 Bowl** (p711). Further along, Clinton is home to the rockin' **Route 66 Museum** (p711), with tons of stuff to see and buy. The **Western Motel** (p711) in Sayre is another kitschy sign photo-op before you get back on the road and head toward Amarillo.

For more in-depth info, check out Jim Ross' book, *Oklahoma Route 66*. See also p30.

Mountain Resort State Park (☎ 877-999-5567; www.quartzmountainresort.com; Hwy 44; r $84-109; P ⊠ ⊠) on Lake Altus-Lugert. Hiking trails, a golf course, swimming beaches, go-karts and a nature center provide plenty to do if you stay at the lodge.

ROUTE 66 – OKLAHOMA CITY TO TULSA

Route 66 between Oklahoma's two largest cities is the country's longest remaining continuous stretch of the Mother Road (about 110 miles). Take it and save the toll required for I-44, which Route 66 snakes around.

In Arcadia, 23 miles east of OKC, stop at the cavernous, red **Round Barn** (☎ 406-396-0824; admission free; ⏰ 10am-5pm Tue-Sun); inside are photos of other round barns from around the world. **Hillbillies Cafe and B&B** (☎ 405-396-2982; www.hillbillees.com; mains $4-8, r $65; ⏰ 11am-8pm Mon-Thu, 11am-10pm Fri & Sat, 11am-3pm Sun) has live country or blues weekends and quirky Old West rooms out back (no nonsmoking).

About midway between Oklahoma City and Tulsa, **Chandler** is a pleasant little town with a couple of old filling stations. The redwood cabin **Lincoln Motel** (☎ 405-258-0200; 740 E First St; r $40-45; ⊠) was first built in 1939. In Stroud, 14 miles east, **Rock Café** (☎ 918-968-3390; 114 W Main St; breakfasts $3-6, mains $4-8; ⏰ 6:30am-9pm Sun-Thu, 6am-10pm Fri & Sat; ⊠) serves some intense home cooking – pulled pork sandwiches, chicken-fried steak, even German schnitzel.

TULSA

A dowdy downtown flanked by a river that's been slowed to a trickle by industry, and highways with some serious chain store-itis, make Tulsa (population 393,049) seem less than stellar. The green rolling hills to the south, filled with oil money-bought mansions, make a prettier picture. Tulsa was billed as the 'Oil Capital of the World' in the early to mid-20th century, but the town actually didn't have much black gold – just oil companies reaping the rewards of statewide wells.

I-44 rolls through town and I-244 loops north around downtown. The **Tulsa Visitor Center** (☎ 918-585-1201; www.visittulsa.com; William Center Towers II, 2 W Second St) provides limited help. East of town is the nearest **Oklahoma**

Visitor Center (☎ 918-439-3212; www.travelok.com; I-44 at 161st E Ave; ⏰ 8:30am-5pm). The staff at the busy **Brookside Library** (☎ 918-745-1201; 1207 E 45th St; ⏰ 10am-8pm Mon-Thu, 10am-5pm Fri & Sat) can loan you an access number to log on to the Internet.

Sights & Activities

Northwest of downtown, off Hwy 64, the excellent **Gilcrease Museum** (☎ 918-596-2700; www.gilcrease.org; 1400 Gilcrease Museum Rd; donation $3; ⏰ 10am-5pm) sits on the estate of a Native American who discovered oil on his allotment. The impressive collection of American Western, Native American, and Central and South American fine art is accented by the deep colors of the display walls.

South of town, an oil magnate's Italianate villa houses the **Philbrook Museum of Art** (☎ 918-749-7941; www.philbrook.org; 2727 S Rockford Rd, east of Peoria Ave; adult/child $7.50/5.50; ⏰ Tue-Sun 10am-5pm, to 8pm Thu), with European, Asian and Ancient Egyptian art. It would have been more interesting as a house museum; nice gardens though.

Greenwood Cultural Center (☎ 918-596-1030; www.greenwoodculturalcenter.com; 322 N Greenwood Ave; admission free; ⏰ 9am-5pm Mon-Fri, 10am-1pm Sat) displays photos of the historic African American Greenwood District before and after a 1921 race riot, as well as pictures comprising the **Oklahoma Jazz Hall of Fame** (www.okjazz.org). The hall holds occasional concerts.

Named for the TV evangelist, **Oral Roberts University** (ORU) flaunts a retro-futuristic campus with a 200ft, UFO-like glass **Prayer Tower & Visitor Center** (☎ 918-495-7910; 7777 S Lewis Ave; admission free; ⏰ 10am-4:30pm Tue-Sat, 1-4:30pm Sun) – east of the huge praying hands.

Sleeping

Chain motels aplenty line Hwy 244 and I-44.

Cherokee Casino Resort (☎ 800-760-6700; www.cherokeecasino.com; 777 W Cherokee St, off Hwy 412; r $79; P ⊠ ⊠) East of downtown is the largest of the state's Native American casinos. Cherokee artwork and craftsmanship decorate the rooms at the shiny new full-service hotel, which has several bars and restaurants.

Hotel Ambassador (☎ 918-587-8200; www.hotelambassador-tulsa; 1324 S Main St; r $129-$189; P ⊠ ⊠ ⊡) Look for the old photos of this 1929 hotel before renovation in the guest library.

A location just south of downtown and a top-notch restaurant make the place ideal even if the neoclassical, boutiquey rooms can be a bit small by today's standards.

Victorian Inn (☎ 918-743-2009; 114 E Skelly Dr; s/d $26/36; P ⊠) The sunny yellow motel at I-44 exit 226, near riverside parks, has microwaves in-room.

Eating

Look for dining options in the Brookside neighborhood, on Peoria Ave between 31st and 51st Sts, and on Historic Cherry St (now 15th St) just east of Peoria Ave.

Corner Café (☎ 918-587-0081; 1103 S Peoria Ave; breakfasts $3-6, mains $4-9; ☺ 6am-9pm) Munch on diner fare along old Route 66 like breakfast regulars have been doing forever.

India Palace (☎ 918-492-8040; 6963 S Lewis Ave; lunch buffet $7, dinner mains $8-12; ☺ lunch & dinner) The lunch buffet is impressive, the cups of chai, bottomless. There's a solid vegetarian selection, too.

Jamil's (☎ 918-742-9097; 2831 E 51st St; mains $11-19; ☺ dinner Tue-Sun) Each monster steak or seafood dish comes with 'Lebanese' appetizers: tabouleh, hummus, crudités, a cabbage roll, ribs – and fried bologna.

Entertainment

Check the **Urban Tulsa Weekly** (www.urbantulsa .com) for what's going on. As well as being a hotel, the Cherokee Casino Resort has 24-hour gaming and live music weekends in the jazz piano lounge.

Full Moon Café (☎ 918-583-6666; 1525 E 15th St; ☺ 11am-2am Mon-Sat, 11am-midnight Sun) Casual food and live blues, jazz, rap or pop Tuesday to Friday. Saturday night is a '70s and '80s disco party.

Cain's Ballroom (☎ 918-584-2206; www.cainsball room.com; 423 N Main St) Today's rockers perform on the same floor where Bob Wills played western swing in the 1930s.

Discoveryland! (☎ 918-742-5255; www.discovery landusa.com; 5529 S Lewis Ave, Sand Springs; tickets $17; ☺ 8pm Mon-Sat Jun-Aug) Five miles northwest of Tulsa there's a dandy outdoor production of *Oklahoma!* put on.

Getting There & Around

Tulsa International Airport (☎ 918-838-5046; www .tulsaairports.com), off Hwy 11, is northeast of downtown. **Greyhound** (☎ 918-584-4428; 317 S Detroit Ave) has daily buses bound for Oklahoma

City ($19, two hours) and Kansas City ($68, five hours). **Tulsa Transit** (☎ 918-582-2100; www .tulsatransit.org) posts a map of the local metro buses online.

GREEN COUNTRY

Subtle forested hills, interspersed with lakes, cover Oklahoma's northeast corner, aka **Green Country** (www.greencountryok.com), which includes Tulsa. The area has a strong Native American influence as it is where several of the Five Civilized Tribes (Cherokee, Choctaw, Chickasaw, Creek and Seminole) were relocated in the 1830s. Most of the towns can be visited as day trips from Tulsa. Route 66 runs northeast from Tulsa, paralleling I-44 to the north, before jogging into Kansas and on to Missouri.

Bartlesville

Oil built the town of Bartlesville, 50 miles north of Tulsa, and Frank Phillips (Phillips Oil) poured a good deal of his fortune into the much-loved **Woolaroc** (☎ 918-336-0307; www.woolaroc.org; Rte 123, 12 miles south of town; adult/ child $5/free; ☺ 10am-5pm Tue-Sun, closed Tue early Sep-late May). The Wild West complex has a buffalo refuge, a mountain man camp, a Native American center, a museum and an oil patch to explore.

You can tour Frank Lloyd Wright's tallest skyscraper (with Wright-designed furnishings), the stunning, 221ft **Price Tower Arts Center** (☎ 918-336-4949; www.pricetower.org; 510 Dewey Ave; adult/child $4/free, tours $8/5; ☺ 10am-5pm Tue-Sat, noon-5pm Sun; tours 11am & 2pm). Even better, stay in one of the 21, upper-floor, Wright-inspired rooms that are the **Inn at Price Tower** (☎ 918-336-1000, 877-424-2424; www.innatpricetower .com; s/d $125/145, ste $245; ⊠ ⊠). Free breakfast, gallery admission and tour included. The restaurant is open to the public for lunch ($7 to $10) and dinner ($17 to $25) daily.

Claremore

Born in 1879, Will Rogers was a cowboy, a hilarious homespun philosopher, star of radio and movies, and part Cherokee. **Will Rogers Memorial Museum** (☎ 918-341-0719; www .willrogers.com; 1720 W Will Rogers Blvd, Claremore; donation adult/child $4/3; ☺ 8am-5pm), 30 miles northeast of Tulsa off Route 66, is as much about the American West's coming of age as it is the story of one man. The museum's huge.

STATE OF NATIVE AMERICA

In the mid-19th century the land north of the Red River and south of the Platte River wasn't Oklahoma at all, it was Indian Territory – autonomous lands granted by treaty to Indian nations in perpetuity (for what that was worth). Andrew Jackson's 1830 Indian Removal Act set the stage for the relocation of eastern tribes to the Territory. As terrible as the Trail of Tears was, subsequent years were high times for the Cherokee, Creek, Seminole, Chickasaw and Choctaw tribes (known as the Five Civilized Tribes). These woodland farmers combined Native American ways with Euro-American systems – property was community-owned but the nation also had its own constitution, public schools, newspapers, courts and law enforcement. Tribal authority lost ground during post–Civil War reconstruction and again when the 1887 Dawes Act brought an end to Indian nation land ownership. Individual tribe members were assigned an 'allotment' of 110-200 acres each, but through tax manipulation and skullduggery, many were cheated out of individual ownership, too. A degree of autonomy returned when 1970s and '80s court decisions held that no act of Congress had ever terminated tribal sovereignty, paving the way for tax-free gaming and an influx of money for some tribes.

When all was said and done, 67 Native American tribes had been moved to a land where six were indigenous. Indian nation capitol complexes are still scattered around the state today and most have small museums or cultural centers. Don't miss the excellent **Cherokee Heritage Center** (below), which does the best job of presenting a full picture of pre- and post-relocation life. Powwows and festivals take place in spring and summer, especially in **Andarko** (p712); the **Red Earth Native American Cultural Festival** (see p710) is in Oklahoma City in June.

Grab one of the few seats at **Dot's Café** (☎ 918-341-9718; 310 W Will Rogers Blvd; breakfasts $3-5, mains $5-8; ⏰ 7am-2pm Mon-Sat, to 8pm Thu) and enjoy good pie and a healthy dose of local gossip.

Trail of Tears Country

The area southeast of present-day Tulsa was, and in some cases still is, Creek and Cherokee land. For anyone interested in learning about Native American culture, this is a good place to start.

Do you remember the Merle Haggard song 'Okie from Muskogee?' Well, **Muskogee**, 49 miles southeast of Tulsa, is home to the **Five Civilized Tribes Museum** (☎ 918-683-1701; Agency Hill, Honor Heights Dr; adult/student $3/1.50; ⏰ 10am-5pm Mon-Sat, 1-5pm Sun) inside an 1875 Union Indian Agency house. Take the Muskogee Turnpike to Hwy 64 south.

Thirty miles west on Hwy 62 is **Tahlequah** (tal-*ah*-quaw), the Cherokee capital since 1839. A knowledgeable native guide at the **Cherokee Heritage Center** (☎ 918-456-6007; www.cherokeeheritage.org; 21192 Keeler Rd;

adult/child $8.50/7.50; ⏰ 10am-5pm Mon-Sat, 1-5pm Sun) leads tours through a re-creation of a pre-European contact woodland village (no teepees here), where you can learn to shoot a blow gun or play stick ball. A log cabin town represents Cherokee life during the mid-19th century. Summer nights the associated, outdoor **Tsa-La-Gi Amphitheater** (☎ 918-456-6007; www.cherokeeheritage.org; 21192 Keeler Rd; adult $10-20, child $5-10; ⏰ 8pm Thu-Sat Jul & Aug) stages a dramatization of the Trail of Tears (p371).

Take scenic Rte 10 north to where canoe outfitters line the **Illinois River**. Try **War Eagle Floats** (☎ 800-722-3834; www.shopoklahoma.com/war eagle; 13020 N Rte 10) for two-hour to two-day-long float trips.

Downtown **Okmulgee**, off I-75, looks a bit like the set of a 1950s film. The **Creek Council House Museum** (☎ 918-756-2324; 106 W 6th St; admission free; ⏰ 10am-4:30pm Tue-Sat) is in the former capital of the Muscogee (Creek) Nation, built in 1878. In August, the town hosts the **Okmulgee Invitational Rodeo** (☎ 800-355-5552), an African American rodeo.

Texas

Snow falls on a cactuslike plant high in the mountains, an oompah-band strikes up at a 100-year-old German *biergarten*, a whooping crane hunts for crawfish along a coastal marsh... these are all snapshots of Texas. If you pictured dusty trails and tumbleweeds, cowboys and oil derricks, widen your scope. In one very large state you can explore soaring pine forests, rapid-running rivers, 600 miles of beaches, devil-dry deserts and green rolling hills. The closeness of Mexico has meant an intermingling of food and language, culture and tradition statewide. But other settlers have made their mark as well: in the late 19th century, European immigrants arrived in large numbers and today you can eat at Czech bakeries and German meat markets across south-central Texas.

Of course, if you want to see the Old West, you can do that too. Mosey on over to Fort Worth's Stockyards District or to Bandera's dude ranches. Attend a rodeo, or drive through the big-sky and canyon country of the Panhandle Plains. In West Texas the broad, dusty flatlands are the picture of a rugged frontier but, even there, unexpected peaks rise up to 8,000ft and black bears forage in the Chisos Mountains. And did you know that good wineries dot the landscape near Lubbock and Fredericksburg? From Austin's swinging blues bars to Amarillo's old Route 66, Texas is full of surprising images.

HIGHLIGHTS

- Seeing contemporary art by day and two-stepping by night in **Fort Worth** (p754)

- Photographing the **Guadalupe Mountains** (p760) and **McKittrick Canyon Trail** (p760) in March, when the cacti is in bloom

- Getting your hands sticky eating smoky BBQ off butcher paper at **City Market** (p728) in Luling

- Floating down Hill Country's Guadalupe River to **Gruene** (p730) – you in one inner tube, your cooler in another

- Munching chips and salsa at one of El Paso's hole-in-the-wall Mexican joints like **L&J Café & Bar** (p762)

- Listening to big-name country acts up close and personal at the 1942 **John T Floore's Country Store** (p734) in Helotes, near San Antonio

- Driving the steep, winding Rio Grande road, **Route 170** (p765), through mountainous territory abutting Big Bend Ranch State Park

- Enjoying Tuesday-night blues with Toni Price at the **Continental Club** (p727) in Austin

- Seeing the **Art Car Museum** (p739) and other wacky folk installations in Houston

HISTORY

Caddo, Apache and Karankawa were among the Indian tribes that Spanish explorers encountered when they arrived to map the coast in 1519. Both Cabeza de Vaca and Francisco Vásquez wandered about the area in search of gold and riches. The Spaniards named their new territory *tejas* (*tay*-has), a corruption of the Caddo Indian word for 'friend.'

When the newly formed country of Mexico made Texas a state in 1821, the arrangement didn't sit well with independent-minded Texans. By 1835 they'd started the Texas War for Independence and captured San Antonio and the Alamo. An infamous siege put the fortified mission firmly back into the hands of Mexico's General Santa Anna. But Mexican troops were routed by Sam Houston's army at San Jacinto in 1836, and the Republic of Texas was born. Independence ended nine years later when Texas became the 28th state of the Union.

Cattle ranching formed the core of Texas' post–Civil War economy, but in 1910, when black gold gushed forth from Spindletop, near Beaumont, everything changed. WWII brought military bases to Texas, yet it was oil that again brought prosperity. During the energy crisis of the 1970s, petroleum prices tripled, gasoline prices quadrupled, and Texans – the biggest domestic oil suppliers, with many of the nation's largest refineries – laughed all the way to the bank. Boom time was big, but the bust in the 1980s was just as spectacular. A worldwide glut devastated the oil industry and towns seemed to empty overnight.

The early 1990s buzzword was diversification, as south-central Texas became a high-tech corridor and Houston built world-class medical research facilities. The 1994 North American Free Trade Agreement (Nafta) loosened trade restrictions between the US, Canada and Mexico, providing an economic shot in the arm for Texas. Former Texas governor George W Bush was re-elected to a second term as president of the United States in 2004, which must have made his father, George Bush Sr (the 41st president), mighty proud.

The many Texans still involved in the oil and gas industries have long extolled the bumper-sticker prayer: 'Lord, give me just one more boom and I promise I won't

---

TEXAS FACTS

Nickname Lone Star State

Population 22.5 million

Area 261,797 sq miles

Capital city Austin (population 680,899)

Other cities Houston (2 million), Dallas (1.2 million), San Antonio (1.2 million)

Official state small mammal Armadillo

Official state large mammal Longhorn steer

Birthplace of Buddy Holly (1936–59), Howard Hughes (1905–76), Janis Joplin (1943–70), Roy Orbison (1936–88), Dwight D Eisenhower (1890–1969), Lyndon B Johnson (1908–73), Steve Martin (b 1945), Renee Zellweger (b 1969), Matthew McConaughey (b 1969)

Home of George W Bush, Willie Nelson, AJ Foyt (racecar driver), Sandra Day O'Connor

Famous for Cowboys, the Alamo, wide-open spaces, and great BBQ

---

waste it.' As crude oil and petroleum prices continue to rise in 2005, it looks like their dreams just may have come true.

GEOGRAPHY & CLIMATE

Pine forests in the northeast give way to wetlands along the coast near Louisiana; further south along the Gulf Coast, the climate becomes semiarid and coconut palms grow at the state's furthest reaches. Wide, flat, dry valleys in the far west separate several mountain ranges (Guadalupe Peak at 8749ft is the highest peak). Verdant hills and meandering rivers characterize central Hill Country. Name any nasty weather phenomenon and part of the state may have to deal with it: drought in the west, tornadoes around Dallas–Fort Worth (mostly spring and summer), hurricanes along the Gulf Coast (from June to October).

July to August – even into September – Texas is *hot*. Temperatures stay in the 90s statewide and parts get unbearable. Big Bend in West Texas (102°F average) is best avoided unless you stay in the mountains, where it's 10 to 15 degrees cooler. Down on the Gulf Coast, the wind always blows off the water, keeping the temperature down in summer and up in winter. Corpus Christi rarely gets below 40°F (though there was that freak Christmas Eve snowstorm in 2004). Winter ice and snow are more common in the Panhandle Plains,

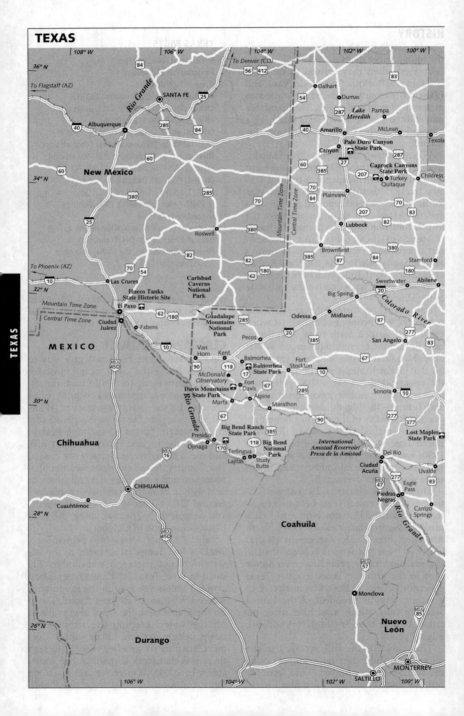

TEXAS

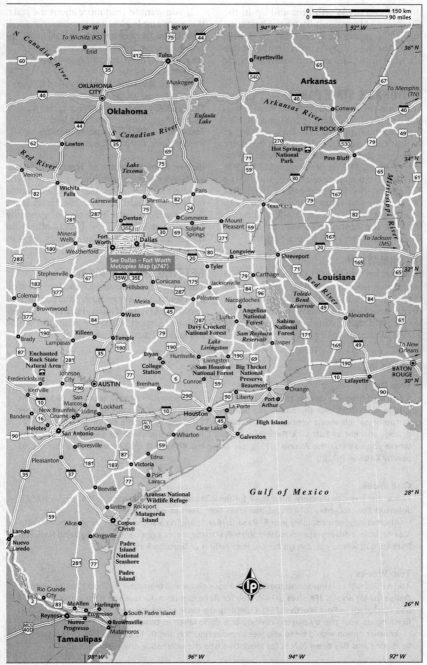

the Dallas–Fort Worth area and up in the Guadalupe Mountains. By far the best time to visit is spring (late February to April), when the humidity is low, temperatures are only in the 70s and the wildflowers are in bloom.

NATIONAL & STATE PARKS

Texas has two national parks in West Texas, Big Bend National Park (p763) and Guadalupe Mountains National Park (p760), as well as the Padre Island National Seashore (p745) on the Gulf Coast. **Texas Parks & Wildlife** (☎ 800-792-1112, central reservations 512-389-8900; www.tpwd.state.tx.us) puts out a free guide to the 125 state parks. Reservations for campsites ($4 to $16) and cabin rental ($40 to $90), where available, can be made online or through the central reservations number. Day-use fees are $1 to $5 per person.

INFORMATION

Texas Tourism (☎ 800-452-9292; www.traveltex.com) is one busy government agency: it produces the booklike annual *Texas State Travel Guide* (free), maintains an extensive website with lodging and sight listings, and runs 12 Texas Travel Information Centers.

If you want to read more about the state, there are ample glossy magazines:

Texas Highways (www.texashighways.com) Travels through the culture, history and landscape.

Texas Monthly (www.texasmonthly.com) Focuses on the personalities and the places.

Texas Music Magazine (www.txmusic.com) Well, you can probably guess what that's about.

TXT Newsmagazine (http://txtnewsmag.com) A gay and lesbian entertainment magazine for Texas.

Texas Parks & Wildlife Magazine (www.tpwmagazine.com) Covers all things outdoorsy.

Historic Accommodations of Texas (HAT; ☎ 800-428-0368; www.hat.org) produces a list of B&Bs statewide. State sales tax is 6.25%. Local taxes usually add another 2%. Hotel taxes differ from town to town in Texas but generally range from 14% to 17%. Unless otherwise noted, a child's admission price is for 4 to 12 years old; toddlers are usually free.

GETTING THERE & AWAY

The busiest international gateways to the state are Houston's George Bush Intercontinental Airport (IAH) and Dallas–Fort Worth International Airport (DFW). Austin, San Antonio and El Paso also have major airports.

TEXAS IN...

Five Days

If you only have five days in the big state of Texas, stay central. Start your tour with two days in **Austin** (opposite); pick the bands you want to see at the **Continental Club** (p727) or another of the many live-music venues, see the **bats** (p723) depart from the Congress Ave bridge at sunset, and eat at **Salt Lick Barbecue** (p726). Drive 80 miles south to **San Antonio** (p730), where you can visit the **Alamo** (p732), eat along the **Riverwalk** (p732), and take a day trip to nearby **Gruene** (p729).

One Week

Follow the five-day itinerary, then drive (or fly) 200 miles east to **Houston** (p735) to see NASA's **Johnson Space Center** (p743) and the Texas Gulf Coast at **Galveston** (p743).

Alternatively, you could fly into **El Paso** (p761), spending a night or two so you can pop into Mexico, before driving (approximately 300 miles) to the mountainous area near **Big Bend National Park** (p763), where you can go hiking, river rafting or horseback riding.

Two Weeks

Add a third night in Houston to the one-week tour above and then drive (or fly) 230 miles north to **Dallas** (p746) and its **JFK sites** (p749). Stay for three nights; make sure not to miss the museums and stockyards in **Fort Worth** (p754). Complete the circle by driving back to **Hill Country** (p728), finishing up your trip by playing cowboy at a dude ranch in **Bandera** (p729).

Another option would be to end week one in Houston and fly to **El Paso** (p761), the gateway to Mexico and **Big Bend** (p763) for week two (see the alternative one-week tour above).

FEEL THE LUV

Flight attendants strutted out in orange hot pants and white go-go boots at the launch of **Southwest Airlines** (☎ 800-435-9792; www.iflyswa.com) in 1971. Back then the outrageous fledgling flyer served only Houston, Dallas and San Antonio. Today Southwest connects 10 cities in Texas and 50 more across the country. In 2004 it carried more passengers than any other airline and celebrated 33 years of turning a profit. How'd it do it? Love.

One of the company's first ad campaigns declared 'Now there's someone else up there that loves you' and it chose LUV as its NY Stock Exchange ticker symbol. The corporate culture has maintained a dedication to keeping costs low, to having a sense of humor, and to putting its employees first (so they're happy serving you). Advance fare specials regularly run as low as $34 one way in-state, and your flight attendant might give the safety briefing as John Wayne, before impersonating Donald Duck or breaking into song. The go-go boots are gone, but tennis shoes and khaki shorts are now de rigueur.

Southwest has never served meals or assigned seats but, in addition to peanuts, attendants now hand out Nabisco 100-calorie snack packs. The possibility of a cheap seat, cookies and a laugh can help make the hassle of getting around a very big state a little more bearable.

Amtrak (☎ 800-872-7245; www.amtrak.com) has two main train routes through Texas. The *Sunset Limited* runs between Orlando, Florida and Los Angeles three times a week, with stops in Houston, San Antonio, Del Rio, Alpine (near Big Bend National Park) and El Paso. (At publication time, Hurricane Katrina had interrupted *Sunset Limited* service going east of Texas indefinitely.) The *Texas Eagle* runs between Chicago and San Antonio daily, with stops in Texarkana, Dallas–Fort Worth, Austin and San Marcos. Note that trains often have late-night arrivals/departures in Texas.

GETTING AROUND

Traveling by car lets you see small-town Texas, but make sure you check the daily mileage allowance of a hire car before you start a grand tour. Most companies slap you with a fee for one-way drop-off rentals; to avoid this, it's best to fly or bus between cities, where it's easy to rent a car from a national firm (see p1175 for details). Then you can make short overnight trips around the area.

Southwest Airlines (☎ 800-435-9792; www.iflyswa .com) services Houston, Dallas, San Antonio, Austin, El Paso, Midland-Odessa, Lubbock, Corpus Christi and Harlingen (South Padre Island). Continental and American Airlines are also headquartered in the state (in Houston and Dallas respectively).

Greyhound (☎ 800-231-2222; www.greyhound.com) and its partner **Kerrville Bus Lines** (☎ 800-474-3352; www.iridekbc.com) serve all but the tiniest

towns in the state, though it may take several transfers and twice as long as it would by car.

SOUTH-CENTRAL TEXAS

Floating down a clear river as it meanders under live oaks and past rolling hills just may be the best way to spend a day in south Texas. But there's much more to do in the Hill Country of south-central Texas. You can ride a horse at a dude ranch or two-step on an old wooden dance-hall floor. You can visit both small German- and Czech-settled towns and big cities. Austin, the state's capital, is a music epicenter extraordinaire. San Antonio, home of the Alamo, has the festive Riverwalk crowded with bars and restaurants. If you want to get to the heart of Texas and you only have a short time to do it, south-central is the way to go.

AUSTIN

You don't even have to go to a nightclub in Austin to hear live music; bands regularly play at supermarkets, record shops – even at the airport. Though this is the state capital, an artsy rather than a formal vibe prevails. Walking down the street you're as likely to see a woman wearing a 1950s dress, complemented by jet-black hair and tattoos, as you are to see someone in a business suit. Bumper stickers instruct residents to 'Keep Austin Weird.' More-conservative Texas towns are just fine with Austin's weirdness –

AUSTIN

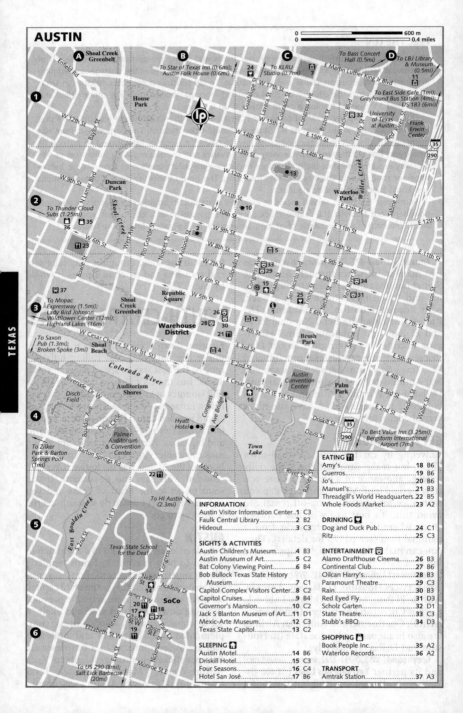

0 600 m
0 0.4 miles

INFORMATION
Austin Visitor Information Center..1 C3
Faulk Central Library.................2 B2
Hideout.................................3 C3

SIGHTS & ACTIVITIES
Austin Children's Museum...........4 B3
Austin Museum of Art................5 C2
Bat Colony Viewing Point...........6 B4
Bob Bullock Texas State History
   Museum...............................7 C1
Capitol Complex Visitors Center....8 C2
Capitol Cruises.........................9 B4
Governor's Mansion.................10 C2
Jack S Blanton Museum of Art.....11 D1
Mexic-Arte Museum..................12 C3
Texas State Capitol..................13 C2

SLEEPING
Austin Motel............................14 B6
Driskill Hotel...........................15 C3
Four Seasons...........................16 C4
Hotel San José.........................17 B6

EATING
Amy's....................................18 B6
Guerros..................................19 B6
Jo's.......................................20 B6
Manuel's.................................21 B3
Threadgill's World Headquarters..22 B5
Whole Foods Market..................23 A2

DRINKING
Dog and Duck Pub....................24 C1
Ritz......................................25 C3

ENTERTAINMENT
Alamo Drafthouse Cinema..........26 B3
Continental Club......................27 B6
Oilcan Harry's..........................28 B3
Paramount Theatre...................29 C3
Rain.......................................30 B3
Red Eyed Fly...........................31 D3
Scholz Garten..........................32 D1
State Theatre...........................33 C3
Stubb's BBQ............................34 D3

SHOPPING
Book People Inc........................35 A2
Waterloo Records......................36 A2

TRANSPORT
Amtrak Station.........................37 A3

as long as they keep it contained here and don't let it spread.

History

The second president of the Republic of Texas, Mirabeau Lamar, decided the fledgling country should have a grand capital; in 1839 he chose the bend in the Colorado River that would become Austin. A university was suggested that same year, but it wasn't until 1883 that classes began at the University of Texas (UT). Musically speaking, the early 1960s were big: Wednesday-night jam sessions at Threadgill's gas station and beer joint attracted musicians like the soon-to-be-famous rock diva, Janis Joplin. The legendary Armadillo World Headquarters became ground zero for the Cosmic Cowboy movement in the 1970s – *the* musical hangout for guys like Willie Nelson and Kinky Friedman and for seminal acts like the Clash and Van Morrison. Later Austin performers that have made their mark include the Butthole Surfers and Stevie Ray Vaughan. Though folk, country and rockabilly roots run deep here, there are just as many local artists and venues pounding out punk and indie rock these days.

Orientation

At the center of the center is Congress Ave, running north–south. East 6th St, between Congress Ave and I-35, is the notorious nighttime entertainment hub. Downtown ends and South Austin begins at Town Lake, really a dammed stretch of the Colorado River. S Congress Ave (SoCo) is home to quirky stores and several restaurants and hotels. North of downtown, Guadalupe St, or the Drag, parallels Congress Ave alongside the University of Texas. The Mopac

Expressway (Loop 1) is west of downtown, and area lake roads lead off that.

Information

Go wireless at the many, many bars, restaurants and cafés with free hot spots (check www.austinwirelesscity.org).

Useful local businesses:

Austin American-Statesman (www.statesman.com) Get your local news from this daily newspaper.

Austin Visitor Information Center (☎ 512-478-0098, 800-926-2282; www.austintexas.org; 209 E 6th St; ☯ 9am-6pm) Pick up neighborhood walking-tour maps.

Book People Inc (☎ 512-472-4288; 603 N Lamar Blvd; ☯ 9am-10pm) Austin's premier independent bookstore.

Faulk Central Library (☎ 512-974-7400; 800 Guadalupe St; ☯ 10am-9pm Mon-Thu, 10am-6pm Fri & Sat, noon-6pm Sun) Set up a free account with any ID and you can access the Internet.

Hideout (☎ 512-443-3688; 617 Congress Ave; per hr $6; ☯ 8am-10pm) This coffee shop has two Internet terminals and free wi-fi.

KLRU TV (www.klru.org) PBS-affiliate with local programming that includes the popular music show *Austin City Limits*.

Sights & Activities

Though music and E 6th St are the main draws, there are also a few good museums and loads of parks and lakes in and around town – Austinites like to spend lots of time outside.

DOWNTOWN

Wander along the hoof-marked ground of a cattle drive, look through rough-hewn slave cabins or duck into a movie theater beneath a 1930s-era marquee. The humongous **Bob Bullock Texas State History Museum** (☎ 512-936-8746; www.storyoftexas.com; 1800 N Congress Ave; adult/child $5/3, Texas Spirit $5/3, Imax $7/5; ☯ 9am-6pm Mon-Sat, 11-6pm Sun) is quite theatrical; high-tech

---

GOING BATTY

Every year, between April and October, up to 1.5 million Mexican free-tailed bats migrate to Austin to roost on a platform beneath the Congress Ave Bridge. This is a mating colony, so only mothers and their offspring are hanging around. It's become an Austin tradition to watch around sunset as the bats swarm out to feed nightly. Columns of these bats have been recorded as high as 10,000ft on radar. The best **bat colony viewing points** are the lawns on the riverbanks to the east of the bridge (though the balcony of the Four Season's bar, p725, has a certain appeal). A bat hotline is run by **Bat Conservation International** (☎ 512-416-5700 category 3636; www.batcon .org). **Capital Cruises** (☎ 512-480-9264; www.capitalcruises.com; 208 Barton Springs Rd; adult/child $8/5), behind the Hyatt, has bat-watching cruises on Town Lake, departing 30 minutes before sunset.

gizmos make many exhibits interactive, and there's also a Texas Spirit film and an Imax theater on-site.

The 1888, pink-granite **Texas State Capitol** (☎ 512-463-0063; cnr 11th St & Congress Ave; admission free; ⏰ 7am-10pm Mon-Fri, 9am-8pm Sat & Sun) stands 15ft taller than the US Capitol. The **Capitol Complex Visitors Center** (☎ 512-305-8400; www.tspb .state.tx.us; 112 E 11th St; ⏰ 9am-5pm Mon-Sat, noon-5pm Sun) has exhibits and provides information on capitol tours. Reservations are required to take the 20-minute tour of the nearby 1856 **Governor's Mansion** (☎ 512-463-5518; www .governor.state.tx.us/about/mansion; 1010 Colorado St; admission free; ⏰ tours 10am-noon Mon-Thu).

Austin's notable **Mexic-Arte Museum** (☎ 512-480-9373; www.mexic-artemuseum.org; 419 Congress Ave; adult/child $5/1; ⏰ 10am-6pm Mon-Thu, 10am-5pm Fri & Sat) has rotating exhibitions by Mexican artists and a killer gift shop. Traveling modern-art shows at the **Austin Museum of Art** (☎ 512-495-9224; www.amoa.org; 823 Congress Ave; adult/child $5/4; ⏰ 10am-8pm Tue-Sat, noon-5pm Sun) can be interesting, even if space is limited. At the **Austin Children's Museum** (☎ 512-472-2499; www.austinkids.org; 210 Colorado St; adult/child under 2 $4.50/2.50; ⏰ 10am-5pm Tue-Sat, noon-5pm Sun), kids can climb around the Time Tower to learn local history, or play toy guitars to videos in Kiddie City Limits.

UNIVERSITY OF TEXAS AT AUSTIN

Look back on LBJ's political life and his involvement with JFK, the Bay of Pigs incident, the Civil Rights movement and the Vietnam War at the **Lyndon B Johnson Library & Museum** (☎ 512-721-0200; www.lbjlib.utexas.edu; cnr 2313 Red River St & Martin Luther King Blvd; admission free; ⏰ 9am-5pm).

A snazzy new 50,000-sq-ft space for the 20th-century and Latin-American holdings of the **Jack S Blanton Museum of Art** (☎ 512-471-7324; www.blantonmuseum.org; cnr Martin Luther King Blvd & Congress Ave; admission free; ⏰ 10am-5pm Mon-Fri, to 7pm Thu, 1-5pm Sat & Sun) is scheduled to open by the time you read this.

You can tour the **KLRU Studio** (☎ 512-471-4811; www.klru.org/faqs; cnr 26th & Guadalupe Sts, 6th fl; admission free), where *Austin City Limits* is recorded, on Fridays at 10:30am. Tickets for tapings are given away at radio-announced locations and they run out fast; call the **hotline** (☎ 512-475-9077) for schedule information.

AUSTIN SOUTH

Just south of the Colorado River, 351-acre **Zilker Park** (☎ 512-472-4914; www.ci.austin.tx.us /zilker; 2201 Barton Springs Rd) has trails, a nature center, botanical gardens and **Barton Springs Pool** (☎ 512-476-9044; 2201 Barton Springs Rd; adult/child $3/1; ⏰ recreational swim 1-8pm late May–mid-Aug). This locally beloved swimming hole is spring-fed by chilly, sparkling clear waters.

Learn to identify the many indigenous plants in the botanical gardens and along the nature trails of **Lady Bird Johnson Wildflower Center** (☎ 512-292-4200; www.wildflower.org;

MARCH MADNESS

Musicians fly in to Austin from around the world in mid-March to play most every music style you've heard of, as well as some you haven't (country-metal? an all-female indie-pop quintet?). Music executives and record label representatives descend to find the next big thing. During five days, more than 1200 acts will be onstage at 50 or so venues during the **South by Southwest** (SXSW; ☎ 512-467-7979; www.sxsw.com) music festival. And there are as many unofficial bands playing unofficial venues as there are official ones. Hotels, of course, are booked solid up to a year in advance.

During the day, industry buffs head to the Austin Convention Center to talk shop and pick up free earplugs at a trade show. SXSW hosts a concurrent film festival and interactive Internet conference. Registering for a Platinum Badge ($520 to $810, depending how far ahead you buy it) gets you into all three trade shows, conferences, screenings, clubs and VIP lounges; a Music Badge ($345 to $545) allows entry into the music conference, trade show and nightly gigs (sold online starting in September). The cheapest way to get into the clubs during SXSW is to buy a wristband ($150) at **Waterloo Records** (p727) starting mid-February, but be forewarned; those with badges gain entrance first and venues fill up. If your heart's set on seeing someone, go early and wait through a couple of acts. Otherwise, make another choice – maybe you'll like that Tejano electric-funk band after all.

4801 La Crosse Ave; adult/child $6/2.50; ☺ 9am-5:30pm Tue-Sat, noon-5:30pm Sun), 12 miles south on Mopac Expressway.

Festivals & Events

First Thursdays on S Congress Ave (www.firstthursday.info) Local shops stay open late and restaurants host live music on the first Thursday each month.

South by Southwest (SXSW; ☎ 512-467-7979; www.sxsw.com) In mid-March, one of the American music industry's biggest gatherings (see March Madness, opposite).

Austin City Limits Music Festival (☎ 512-389-0315; www.aclfestival.com; 3-day pass $105) More than 125 bands on eight stages during three days in September.

Sleeping

Most of the chain hotels cluster on I-35, where it intersects US 290 E (north of downtown) and US 290 W (to the south). Avoid the extra-seedy motels on S Congress Ave south of Oltorf St.

BUDGET

HI Austin (☎ 512-444-2294; www.hiaustin.org; 2200 S Lakeshore Blvd; dm members/nonmembers $16.75/19.75; Ⓟ ☒ 🖳) This hostel on the lake has bike, canoe and kayak rentals. There is also occasional live music, a laundry, a kitchen and a common room, but there are no double rooms. Take I-35 south of downtown to Riverside Dr.

Best Value Inn (☎ 512-441-0143; www.bestvalue inn.com; 2525 S I-35, south of Oltorf St; s $39-44, d $48-54;

Ⓟ 🖳) New minifridges, microwaves and coffee makers – as well as free hot breakfast and high-speed Internet – make up for aging rooms. From here it's just a short drive to SoCo.

MIDRANGE

Austin Motel (☎ 512-441-1157; www.austinmotel.com; 1220 S Congress Ave; r $52-106; Ⓟ 🖳) A savvy thrift-shopper must have decorated these guest rooms – from funky '70s to grandma's extra bedroom-esque. Two-room poolside suites (micro, fridge, futon) are especially cool ($128).

Hotel San José (☎ 512-444-7322, 800-574-8897; www.sanjosehotel.com; 1316 S Congress Ave; r with shared bath $88-90, with private bath $145-195; Ⓟ ☒ 🖳) Zen-inspired sleek functionality and simple comfort define this hip hotel. In the evening, nibble upon appetizers in the wine-bar courtyard, and for breakfast order a bento box of granola, fruit and fresh juice. Free DVD and CD library and wi-fi are all included.

Run by fun, young Austinites, Sylvia and Chris, the comfy B&Bs **Star of Texas Inn** (☎ 512-472-6700, 866-472-6700; www.staroftex asinn.com; 611 W 22nd St; r $85-165; Ⓟ ☒ 🖳) and **Austin Folk House** (☎ 512-472-6700, 866-472-6700; www.austinfolkhouse.com; 506 W 22nd St; r $99-105; Ⓟ ☒ 🖳) are *the* places to stay if you want to be near UT. The Star's a bit larger, with porches for rocking and a dog and cat for petting. High-speed or wireless Internet is available at both.

TOP END

Four Seasons (☎ 512-478-4500; www.fourseasons.com; 98 San Jacinto Blvd; r $255-305; Ⓟ 🖳 🖳) Marblelike Texas limestone offsets oversized leather couches and chunky wood tables in the lobby; it's enough rustic elegance to make any oil tycoon feel at home. From lakeside rooms you can watch the bats depart from under Congress Ave bridge from April to October. Parking $14.

Also recommended:

Driskill Hotel (☎ 512-474-5911; www.driskillhotel.com; 604 Brazos St; r $200-350; Ⓟ 🖳) An 1886 hotel; ask for the *larger* historic rooms. Parking $17.

Lake Austin Spa Resort (☎ 512-372-7300, 800-847-5637; www.lakeaustin.com; 1705 S Quinlan Park Rd, off Rte 2222; 3-night packages from $1470; Ⓟ ☒ 🖳 🖳) Take W 1st St west to FM2222, turn left on Quinlan Park Rd and follow to lake.

TEXAS

Eating

The best eateries tend to be in central and south Austin, not near UT.

DOWNTOWN

Thunder Cloud Subs (☎ 512-479-6504; 2308 Lake Austin Blvd; subs $3-6; ⏲ 10:30am-9:30pm Mon-Sat, 11am-8:30pm Sun) A Hill Country chain born here in Austin, Thunder Cloud makes tasty subs, like NY Italian and Veggie Delight, as well as salads. This branch is in a renovated house across the street from Town Lake, west of the center.

Manuel's (☎ 512-472-7777; 310 Congress Ave; brunch $7-14, mains $8-18; ⏲ 10am-11pm Mon-Thu, 10am-midnight Fri & Sat, 10am-10pm Sun) Central Mexican food is served in modern surrounds – slick booths with black-and-red accents. A jazz band accompanies Sunday brunch and some happy hours have music.

SOUTH AUSTIN

Guerros (☎ 512-447-7688; 1412 S Congress Ave; mains $6-15; ⏲ 11am-10pm) A great Tex-Mex menu, a colorful interior and an outdoor picnic-table area help make this a local favorite. Come early; crowds overflow into the streets on weekend nights.

Threadgill's World Headquarters (☎ 512-472-9304; www.threadgills.com; 301 W Riverside Dr; mains $8-18; ⏲ 11am-10pm) An offshoot of the original roadhouse that attracted Willie Nelson, Threadgill's has tin signs and real Southern cooking. Live music plays in the large beer garden on weekends.

For a hot beverage and people-watching on S Congress, head to the outdoor café, **Jo's** (☎ 512-444-3800; 1300 S Congress Ave; ⏲ 7am-9pm, to 6pm Mon); across the street, **Amy's** (☎ 512-440-7488; 1301 S Congress Ave; ⏲ 11am-10pm, to 11pm Fri & Sat) sells insanely rich (sweet cream, Amaretto peach…) locally made ice cream.

AROUND TOWN

East Side Cafe (☎ 512-476-5858; 2113 Manor Rd, off I-35 N; mains $9-25; ⏲ lunch & dinner) Expect earth-fresh ingredients in the peach-strawberry soup or veggie enchiladas; you can walk through the herb and vegetable garden behind the whitewashed wood house. (Yes, there are meat dishes too.)

Salt Lick Barbecue (☎ 512-894-3117; www.saltlickbbq.com; 18300 FM 1826, off US 290, Driftwood; mains $10-15; ⏲ 11am-10pm) Take the 20-mile drive south of Austin through beautiful Hill Country to some of the best BBQ in the state. The massive open pits are a sight that tons of people come to see; expect to wait, for some time and bring along your own beer or wine.

Drinking

The line between bar, restaurant, grocery store and live music venue is blurred in Austin and you may find refreshment anywhere. Tourists frequent the notorious 6th St bars early evenings; as the night goes on, the crowd gets younger.

Want to play pool instead of listen to music? Hang out and chug a beer with UT's finest at the **Ritz** (☎ 512-474-2270; 320 E 6th St). The English-style **Dog & Duck Pub** (☎ 512-479-0598; 406 W 17th St; ⏲ 11am-2am, from noon Sun) not only has pool tables but a jukebox, a nice patio and free wireless access.

Entertainment

The free weekly **Austin Chronicle** (www.austinchronicle.com) lists live music and events, as does the XL entertainment section in Thursday's **Austin American-Statesman** (www.statesman.com). **Tune to Austin** (www.tunetoaustin.com) publishes a terrific illustrated map that lists clubs and restaurants; it's available at Book People Inc (p723).

THE AUTHOR'S CHOICE

Whole Foods Market (☎ 512-476-1206; www.wholefoods.com; 525 N Lamar Blvd; sandwiches $6-9, mains $6-15; ⏲ 8am-10pm, coffee bar opens 6am) OK, so ostensibly this is a grocery store. (Who knew there were five kinds of radish?) But the flagship of Austin-originated Whole Foods chain, opened March 2005, is also a gourmet seafood restaurant, a pasta trattoria, a sushi bar, a take-away café and a coffee shop. You can sit and eat at five in-house restaurant counters or line up at the take-away smorgasbord for Indian food, salads, Texan mains, sandwiches or pizzas. There are self-service tables inside, outside by an artificial creek and on the rooftop. The whole place is a free wireless zone, and there are regular concerts and cooking classes held. Not over-the-top enough for you? Head for the in-store chocolate fountain and ask for a hand-dipped homemade marshmallow.

LIVE MUSIC

On Friday or Saturday night, bands may be playing at any of the more than 150 clubs in town. But don't just look for music at bars; restaurants often host live tunes at least a few days a week.

Continental Club (☎ 512-441-2444; www.continentalclub.com; 1315 S Congress Ave; 6pm-2am Mon, 4pm-2am Tue-Fri, 3pm-2am Sat, 9pm-2am Sun) Small but classic, the Continental Club is quintessential Austin. Hipsters, suburban housewife-tourists and migrant farm workers sway together to hard-rockin' blues. Nightly live acts include sultry local blues singer Toni Price on Tuesdays. There's also happy hour and Saturday afternoon gigs too.

Stubb's BBQ (☎ 512-480-8341; www.stubbsaustin.com; 801 Red River St; 6pm-2am Tue-Sun) The backyard amphitheater regularly attracts big-name concerts (rock, blues, country); lesser star power plays in the downstairs theater-bar. Upstairs, the restaurant (open from 11am to 10pm) serves pretty good BBQ (the bottled sauce is sold nationally).

Broken Spoke (☎ 512-442-6189; www.brokenspokeaustintx.com; 3201 S Lamar Blvd; 6pm-2am Tue-Sat) Two-step at an authentic honky-tonk with live bands. Local act Cornell Hurd and artist Dale Watson play regularly.

Scholz Garten (☎ 512-474-1958; www.scholzgarten.net; 1607 San Jacinto Blvd; 11am-9pm) The original building still has long tables reminiscent when Scholz began as a beer hall back in 1866; there's also a restaurant. On weekends, including Saturday afternoon, music plays in the beer garden out back.

Saxon Pub (☎ 512-448-2552; www.thesaxonpub.com; 1320 S Lamar Blvd) A variety of music emanates from Saxon Pub seven nights a week – from folk to blues-rock.

Red Eyed Fly (☎ 512-474-1084; www.redeyefly.com; 715 Red River St) Serving up local hard-core rock, punk and alternative music on two stages; this is one of the more raucous venues.

Bergstrom International Airport (☎ 512-530-2242; www.ci.austin.tx.us/austinairport) Proving that Austin really is the live music capital of Texas, if not the world, the airport hosts a variety of bands outside terminal bars almost every afternoon.

CLASSICAL MUSIC & THEATER

The **Austin Theatre Alliance** (www.austintheatre.org) stages concerts, plays, comedy shows and films at the **Paramount Theatre** (☎ 512-472-5470;

713 Congress Ave) and the **State Theatre** (☎ 512-472-5470; 719 Congress Ave) next door.

Austin Symphony Orchestra (☎ 512-476-6064; www.austinsymphony.org), the **Austin Lyric Opera** (☎ 512-472-5992; www.austinlyricopera.org) and **Ballet Austin** (☎ 513-476-2163; www.balletaustin.org) all perform at **Bass Concert Hall** (☎ 512-471-1444; cnr 23rd & Trinity Sts) on the UT campus.

CINEMA

Alamo Drafthouse Cinema (☎ 512-867-1839; www.originalalamo.com; 409 Colorado St; admission $6.50) Eat dinner, down a brewski and watch cult classics and independent films at this old-time theater in the Warehouse District.

Shopping

Eclectic boutiques and thrift shops congregate along S Congress Ave. Surrounding the intersection of N Lamar Blvd and W 6th St, in the West End, are several big clothing stores and Whole Foods Market (see opposite). Catty corner across the street, choose from a large selection of Texan artists at **Waterloo Records** (☎ 512-474-2500; www.waterloorecords.com; 9am-10pm). In-store concerts are held regularly.

Getting There & Around

AIR

The **Bergstrom International Airport** (☎ 512-530-2242; www.ci.austin.tx.us/austinairport) is off Hwy 71, southeast of downtown. The Airport Flyer (bus 100, 50¢) runs to downtown (7th St and Congress Ave) and UT (Congress Ave and 18th St) every 40 minutes or so. **SuperShuttle** (☎ 512-258-3826; www.supershuttle.com) charges $10 from the airport to downtown. A taxi between the airport and downtown costs from $18 to $22. Most national rental car companies are represented at the airport.

BUS

The **Greyhound Bus Station** (☎ 512-458-4463; www.greyhound.com; 916 E Koenig Lane) is located on the north side of town off I-35; take bus 7 (Duval) to downtown. More than 10 buses a day leave for San Antonio ($14, one to two hours).

In addition to regular city buses, **Capital Metro** (☎ 512-474-1200; www.capmetro.org) runs free tourist-oriented 'Dillos, or trolleys; the five daytime and two nighttime routes connect downtown, SoCo and UT.

TEXAS

THE GREAT BBQ FEUD

Meat-market BBQ is a passionate subject in the small towns of south-central Texas. Every few years *Texas Monthly* heats up the debate by publishing their picks for the best 'Q, but the authority remains Robb Walsh's book, *Legends of Texas Barbecue Cookbook*. Don't expect many side dishes at local barbecue joints – it's just smoked brisket, ribs, sausage and other meats at their finest ($8 to $12 per pound).

Charles Kreuz (pronounced krites) opened his meat market in 1900 in Lockhart, 20 miles south of Austin on US 183; generations later a family feud split the legacy in two: **Kreuz Market** (☎ 512-398-2361; 619 N Colorado St; ⏲ 9am-6pm Mon-Sat) is a modern, barnlike place run by the son who inherited the family recipe (no forks, no sauce). **Smitty's** (☎ 512-398-9344; 208 S Commerce St; ⏲ 7am-6pm Mon-Sat, 9am-3pm Sun) sells BBQ in the original old Kreuz building, inherited by the daughter.

We may incite riot, but **City Market** (☎ 830-875-9019; 633 E Davis, off US 183; ⏲ 7am-6pm Mon-Sat) in Luling, 24 miles south of Lockhart, has the juiciest, most tender small-town BBQ of all. Line up in the smoky pit room to get your butcher paper slathered with meat. Don't ask for utensils or plates; there haven't been any since they opened in the 1930s. Why fix what ain't broke?

TAXI

Family-owned **Roy's Taxi** (☎ 512-482-0000), and others, charge $2 at flag fall and $2 per mile.

TRAIN

The *Texas Eagle* train, heading from San Antonio to Chicago, stops at Austin's **Amtrak Station** (☎ 512-476-5684; www.amtrak.com; 250 N Lamar Blvd). Take the Silver 'Dillo east into downtown.

AROUND AUSTIN

Northwest of Austin along the Colorado River are the six **Highland Lakes**. One of the most popular for recreation is the almost-19,000-sq-acre **Lake Travis**. Rent boats and jet skis at the marina, or overnight in posh digs at **Lakeway Inn Resort** (☎ 512-261-6600; www.lakewayinn.com; 101 Lakeway Dr, off Hwy 71; r $135-179; P ⏲ ☐). You must be older than 18 to enter **Hippie Hollow** (www.hippiehollow.com; day pass $8; ⏲ 9am-dusk Sep-May, 8am-dusk Jun-Aug), Texas' only official clothing-optional beach and a popular gay hangout. From FM 2222, take Rte 620 south 1.5 miles to Comanche Trail and turn right. The entrance is 2 miles ahead on the left.

HILL COUNTRY

More than a century ago, German and Czech settlers established roots in the rolling hills and valleys near the clear-running rivers of Hill Country. Take time to wander down dirt roads looking for wildflowers, or check into a dude ranch for a taste of the cowboy life. Small towns dot the landscape between Austin and San Antonio; most can be day trips from one or both cities.

Fredericksburg

The appeal of ornate Victorian architecture in this sizeable 1870s German town gets lost among the hordes of retirees (and their parents) wandering among the shops and cafés. The main road through town is the busy US 290, eliminating any peace. The **Fredericksburg Convention & Visitors Bureau** (☎ 830-997-6523; www.fredericksburg-texas.com; 302 E Austin St; ⏲ 8:30am-5pm Mon-Fri, 9am-5pm Sat, noon-5pm Sun) has a **wine-trail map** (www.texaswinetrail .com) of the 15 wineries scattered throughout Hill Country. **Fredericksburg Winery** (☎ 830-990-8747; www.fbgwinery.com; 247 W Main St; ⏲ 10am-5:30pm Mon-Thu, 10am-7:30pm Fri & Sat, noon-5:30pm Sun) makes wines and holds tastings right on Main St.

The fields in front of **Wildseed Farms** (☎ 800-848-0078; www.wildseedfarms.com; 100 Legacy Dr; admission free; ⏲ 9am-6:30pm), 7 miles east on US 290, have spectacular wildflower displays much of the year; walk along nature trails or buy seeds and giftware in the shop.

At **Enchanted Rock State Natural Area** (☎ 325/247-3903; www.tpwd.state.tx.us/park/enchanted_rock; Rte 965; adult/child $5/free; ⏲ 8am-10pm), 18 miles north of Fredericksburg, you can climb the 425ft solid, pink granite rock. Go early; gates close when the daily quota is reached.

Nearly 300 B&Bs do business in the county; the reliable **Gastehaus Schmidt Reservation Service** (☎ 830-997-5612, 866-427-8374;

www.fbglodging.com) helps sort them out. **Altdorf Biergarten Restaurant** (☎ 830-997-7865; 301 W Main St; mains $9-12; ☉ 11am-9pm Mon & Wed-Sat, 11am-4pm Sun) serves schnitzel and has a shady beer garden with keg tables.

Kerrville Bus Co (☎ 800-335-3722; www.iridekbc .com; Golden Convenience Store, 1001 S Adams St) sends three daily buses to and from San Antonio ($18, 1¾ hours). No buses run directly from Austin. Fredericksburg is 70 miles north of San Antonio and 78 miles west of Austin.

Luckenbach

The town of Luckenback is pretty much just the rickety old **General Store & Luckenback Bar** (☎ 830-997-3224; www.luckenbachtexas.com; ☉ 10am-9pm Mon-Sat, noon-10pm Sun), part mercantile and part beer joint, with an adjacent dance hall. The place has been a mecca for country music fans ever since Hondo Crouch bought the 'town' in 1970 and invited friends like Waylon and Willie to hang out. The store hosts concerts most weekends; other days you might find some good ol' boys pickin' and grinnin' under the oak tree. From Fredericksburg, take US 290 east to FM 1376 and go south about 3 miles.

Bandera

In Bandera, 30 miles southeast of Kerrville and 27 miles northwest of San Antonio, the locals take their horses – and their friendly, slow-paced lifestyle – seriously. It's little bit of the Old West in modern-day Texas. Wood-plank buildings on quiet Main St contain Western wear and rustic antique shops, and a handful of restaurants and honky-tonks. Wannabe cowpokes can saddle up at the many outlying dude ranches: lodging, meals and at least one ride per day are usually included ($95 to $125 per person per night). The superfriendly staff at **Bandera County Visitors Bureau** (☎ 800-364-3833; www .banderacowboycapital.com; 1206 Hackberry St; ☉ 9am-5pm Mon-Sat) provide ranch recommendations.

In addition to overnight packages, **Twin Elm Ranch** (☎ 830-796-3628; www.twinelmranch.com; cnr Rte 470 & Hwy 16; nonguests/guests $6/free; ☉ 8pm Tue & Fri) hosts local rodeos June through August. **Silver Spur Guest Ranch** (☎ 830-796-3037; www.ssranch.com; FM 1077), 10 miles south of Bandera, has day riding packages (one hour on horseback plus breakfast $40).

Having the rib-eye steak and eggs for breakfast at **OST Restaurant** (☎ 830-796-3836; 305 Main St; breakfast $3-7, mains $5-14; ☉ 6am-10pm, to 11pm Sat) just seems appropriate in cowboy country. Descend the stairs into **Arky Blue's Silver Dollar Saloon** (☎ 830-796-8826; 308 Main St; ☉ 10am-2am) and look for the table carved by Hank Williams Sr. This smoky, longtime honky-tonk has live country music Thursday through Sunday. Enjoy a beer on the outdoor patio at the **11th Street Cowboy Bar** (☎ 830-796-4849; 307 11th St; ☉ 10am-midnight Mon-Fri, 10am-1am Sat, noon-midnight Sun), with live country Friday through Sunday.

Gruene

The whole kit and caboodle of turn-of-the-20th-century Gruene (pronounced green), along the Guadalupe River, is on the National

TEXAS

TOP FIVE WILDFLOWER TRAILS

You know spring has arrived in Texas when you see cars pulling up roadside and families hiking out to take the requisite picture of their kids surrounded by bluebonnets, the state flower. Though the state has a beautiful array of natural blooms, the Department of Transportation (TXDOT) helps considerably by seeding highway right-of-ways. Peak season varies from February to May, depending on the region; check with TXDOT's **Wildflower Hotline** (☎ 800-452-9292) to find out what's blooming. Five of the top roadside views are:

US 290 (Hill Country; btwn Austin & Fredericksburg) The whole roadside blooms in April, but most dramatic are the fields at Wildseed Farms (opposite).

Route 16 and **FM 1323** (Hill Country; north from Fredericksburg, east to Willow City) Mid-April is a riot of color around every corner.

US 290 (Around Houston; east, btwn Chappel Hill & Brenham) Small, US 290 towns host festivals on April weekends to celebrate the area's fields of bluebonnets.

Route 3255 (West Texas; north of El Paso, off Hwy 54) Orangeish-gold poppies cover the hillsides in late March and early April.

Route 170 (West Texas; btwn Presidio & Terlingua, near Big Bend) Late-February bluebonnets rise an amazing 2ft tall.

Register of Historic Places. Though part of larger New Braunfels, only 25 miles northeast of San Antonio on I-10, the small rustic town somehow maintains its integrity. Arts and crafts and knickknacks are more quirky than mass-produced, and there's even a small music museum. **Gruene Hall** (☎ 830-606-1281; www.gruenehall.com; 1280 Gruene Rd; ☽ 11am-9pm Mon-Wed, 10am-midnight Thu & Fri, 10am-1am Sat, 10am-9pm Sun) to be claims Texas' oldest dance hall (c 1878). Country, Cajun or folk-rock bands play nightly in summer, and at least three nights a week the rest of the year.

You haven't been to south-central Texas if you haven't floated down a river in an inner tube. Put your plastic (not Styrofoam) cooler full of adult beverages (cans, no bottles) in the bottom-fortified tube next to you to really beat the heat. **Rockin' R River Rides** (☎ 888-883-5628; www.rockinr.com; 1405 Gruene Rd; per tube with/without bottom $16/14; ☽ 8am-2:30pm) buses you up the Guadalupe and you float the three to four hours back to Gruene.

Sit among the ruins of an old cotton gin at the **Gristmill Restaurant** (☎ 830-625-0684; 1287 Gruene Rd; mains $10-20; ☽ 11am-11pm), or out on decks high above the river. You'll pay more for a riverfront cottage room at **Gruene Mansion Inn** (☎ 830-629-2641; www.gruenemansioninn .com; r incl breakfast $149-179; ✕), but the view's worth it.

SAN ANTONIO

If San Antonio had a flavor, it would be Tex-Mex. This was one of the first areas colonized by the Spanish, the seat of government for the Mexican state of Tejas, and today more than 58% of the 1.2 million residents claim Hispanic heritage. The Alamo was also the sight of the most famous battle in the Texas War for Independence, in which many Mexican Texans played a part. What has evolved here is a lively multicultural town that fiestas one day and rodeos the next. Although San Antonio is the nation's eighth-largest city, the areas you'll most likely want to see are concentrated in a gentrified, walkable downtown core. More restaurants and bars than you could eat or drink at in a month crowd the Riverwalk, a flood canal that was developed to attract tourists. Boy has it worked: they come in droves. Don't be deterred, sure it's much-visited and a bit overdone in places, but it's also a whole lot of fun.

History

In the 18th century the Spanish established a string of missions in the area to encourage and protect colonization. San Antonio began as military garrison in 1718, and by 1731 Spanish settlers from the Canary Islands had founded a town here. Later in the century both Mexican and American settlers were attracted to the area after it became the northernmost state in newly independent Mexico in 1821. During the Texas War for Independence (1835–36), several battles were fought in the area. But it was the dramatic Texan loss at the Battle of the Alamo that created the famous rallying cry 'Remember the Alamo!' and helped the Texans win their independence. In 1845, the country became a state, and the town attracted a large influx of German immigrants. The city's growth in the 20th century was largely due to local military installations: Fort Sam Houston, Kelly, Lackland, Randolph and Brooks Air Force Base. Today tourism is San Antonio's bread-and-butter.

Orientation

The intersection of Commerce and Losoya Sts is the very heart of both downtown and the Riverwalk. The Alamo is several blocks northeast of this intersection. The King William Historic District is south along the river. I-10 (east–northwest) and I-35 (southwest–northeast) rope in the west and south sides of downtown and I-37 (north–south) contains it to the east.

The city's in a fairly accessible location: Austin and the Hill Country are an hour's drive northeast, Houston is a straight three hours along I-10 to the east, and Corpus Christi and the coast are just about 2½ hours to the south.

Information

Espuma Coffee & Tea Emporium (☎ 210-226-1912; 928 S Alamo St; per 20 min $2.50; ☽ 7am-3pm Mon-Thu, 8am-10pm Fri & Sat; 8am-4pm Sun) Two Internet terminals.

Riverwalk Medical Clinic (☎ 210-272-1741; 408 Navarro St) 24-hour clinic.

San Antonio Central Library (☎ 210-207-2500; 600 Soledad St; ☽ 9am-9pm Mon-Thu, 9am-5pm Fri & Sat, 11am-5pm Sun) Internet access.

San Antonio Express-News (www.mysa.com) The daily newspaper has good travel information on its website.

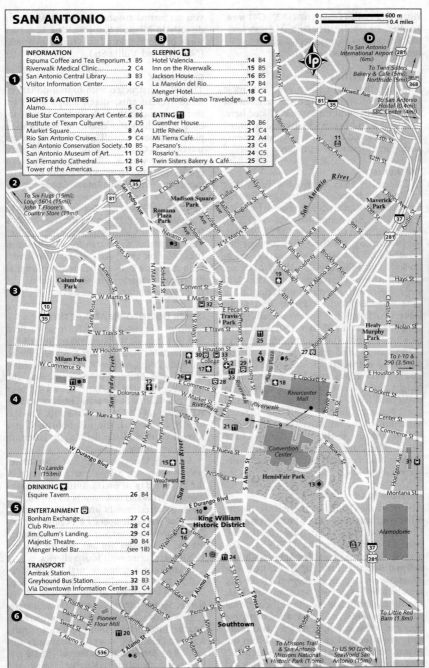

SAN ANTONIO

0 — 600 m
0 — 0.4 miles

INFORMATION
Espuma Coffee and Tea Emporium..1 B5
Riverwalk Medical Clinic.................2 C4
San Antonio Central Library...........3 B3
Visitor Information Center..............4 C4

SIGHTS & ACTIVITIES
Alamo...5 C4
Blue Star Contemporary Art Center.6 B6
Institute of Texan Cultures............7 D5
Market Square...............................8 A4
Rio San Antonio Cruises................9 C4
San Antonio Conservation Society..10 B5
San Antonio Museum of Art..........11 D2
San Fernando Cathedral................12 B4
Tower of the Americas..................13 C5

SLEEPING
Hotel Valencia..............................14 B4
Inn on the Riverwalk....................15 B5
Jackson House..............................16 B5
La Mansión del Rio.......................17 B4
Menger Hotel...............................18 C4
San Antonio Alamo Travelodge....19 C3

EATING
Guenther House...........................20 B6
Little Rhein..................................21 C4
Mi Tierra Café..............................22 A4
Paesano's....................................23 C5
Rosario's.....................................24 C5
Twin Sisters Bakery & Café..........25 C3

DRINKING
Esquire Tavern.............................26 B4

ENTERTAINMENT
Bonham Exchange........................27 C4
Club Rive.....................................28 C4
Jim Cullum's Landing....................29 C4
Majestic Theatre...........................30 B4
Menger Hotel Bar.....................(see 18)

TRANSPORT
Amtrak Station.............................31 D5
Greyhound Bus Station.................32 B3
Via Downtown Information Center.33 C4

To San Antonio International Airport (6mi)
To Twin Sisters Bakery & Cafe (5mi); Northside (5mi)
To San Antonio Hostel (0.4mi); SBC Center (4mi)
To Six Flags (15mi); Loop 1604 (15mi); John T Floore's Country Store (19mi)
To I-10 & 290 (3.5mi)
To Laredo (153mi)
To Little Red Barn (1.8mi)
To Missons Trail & San Antonio Missions National Historic Park (1.5mi)
To US 90 (2mi); SeaWorld San Antonio (15mi)

Madison Square Park
Romana Plaza Park
Columbus Park
Milam Park
Maverick Park
Healy Murphy Park
Travis Park
Alamo Plaza
Rivercenter Mall
Convention Center
HemisFair Park
Alamodome
King William Historic District
Pioneer Flour Mill
Southtown

TEXAS

Visitor Information Center (☎ 210-207-6748; www
.sanantoniovisit.com; 317 Alamo Plaza; ☑ 8:30am-6pm)
Slick, with tons of tourist magazines and volunteers on
busy street corners to direct you.

Sights & Activities

Although the city itself spreads out, most
sights are within strolling distance from the
Riverwalk. In addition to what's listed here,
there are a number of kitschy, kid-oriented
(and costly) oddity museums and theme
park–like rides in the same area.

THE ALAMO

In December 1835, during the Texas War
for Independence, Texan troops captured
San Antonio and occupied and fortified
the Mission San Antonio de Valero (1724),
better known as the **Alamo** (☎ 210-225-1391;
www.thealamo.org; 300 Alamo Plaza; admission free;
☑ 9am-5:30pm Mon-Sat, 10am-5:30pm Sun, to 7pm
Jun-Aug). On February 23, 1836, Mexican
general Antonio López de Santa Anna laid
siege. Even with several luminaries of the
time – James Bowie, William Travis and
Davy Crockett – the Texans couldn't beat
the odds (some say 2500 to 150). Santa Anna's troops took the Alamo after 13 days
of pounding, and executed most of the
surviving defenders. Bowie's and Travis'
black slaves (Sam and Joe, respectively)
fought alongside their masters during the
battle and lived. The Wall of History and
the 17-minute film in the Long Barrack
Museum tell the full story. The old church
is now a shrine to the fallen heroes of the
battle. The Daughters of the Republic of
Texas volunteer staff members are quite
knowledgeable.

MISSION TRAIL

About 2 miles south of the Alamo lie the
other four missions (from north to south):
Concepción (1731), San José (1720), San
Juan (1731) and Espada (1745-56). Together, these make up **San Antonio Missions
National Historical Park** (☎ 210-932-1001; www
.nps.gov/saan; visitor center, cnr Roosevelt & Napier Aves;
admission free; ☑ 9am-5pm). Mission San José,
the most beautiful, is the site of the national
park visitor center, which has an informative
film and a few exhibits. At least two tours
daily are offered at each mission. From the
Alamo, take S St Mary's St to Mission Rd.
Ongoing construction may mean detours; if
you get turned around, Roosevelt Ave leads
directly to Mission San José. Bus 42 serves
some of the Mission Trail from downtown
(Navarro and Villita Sts).

RIVERWALK

Though constructed with tourist dollars in
mind (restaurants, snack shops and bars
line every inch), the lush greenery and cool
breeze off the water make the Riverwalk a
pleasant place to stroll – and a must-see attraction. At Christmastime the whole place
gets strung with a zillion lights. You can
cruise along the river to the sound of a narrated tour with **Rio San Antonio Cruises** (☎ 210-
244-5700; www.riosanantonio.com; adult/child under 6
$6.50/1.50; ☑ 9am-10:30pm Sun-Thu, 9am-11:30pm Fri
& Sat mid-Mar–Oct, 10am-8pm Sun-Thu, 10am-9pm Fri &
Sat Nov–mid-Mar). Get tickets at the Rivercenter
Mall or across the water from the Hilton
(near Market and S Alamo Sts). The Riverwalk runs in a U shape below street level at
the center of town; signs throughout downtown point out access stairways.

OTHER DOWNTOWN ATTRACTIONS

South of the center, near E Durango Blvd
and St Mary St, the **King William Historic District** contains homes from the late 19th to
the early 20th century. Victorian, colonial-
revival and Queen Anne are among the
styles represented. Pick up a walking tour
map outside the **San Antonio Conservation Society** (☎ 210-224-6163; 107 King Williams St). Though
mostly residential, the neighborhood has
several B&Bs and the deliciously fattening
Guenther House (p734).

Across S Alamo St to the east is **Southtown**
(www.southtown.net), a small arts district. On
the first Friday of each month, shops, studios, galleries and restaurants stay open late,
serving refreshments and playing music.
The **Blue Star Contemporary Art Center** (☎ 210-
227-6960; www.bluestarartspace.org; 116 Blue Star; admission free; ☑ noon-6pm Wed-Sun) fills up a large
1920s warehouse with four galleries.

If you're not going to make it to Mexico on this trip, walk (or take the trolley)
seven blocks west of the Riverwalk to
Market Square (☎ 210-207-8600; 514 W Commerce
St; ☑ 10am-6pm, to 8pm Jun-Aug). This *mercado*
(market) has booths selling Mexican craftwork and clothing, as well as souvenirs and
food. The **San Fernando Cathedral** (☎ 210-227-
1297; www.sfcathedral.org; 115 Main Plaza; admission free;

6:15am-7pm), established in 1731 by Canary Island immigrants, is on the way back to the river from the market.

Explore 30 cultures, including Native American and Tejano (of mixed Mexican and Spanish descent), that made Texas what it is at the museum of the **Institute of Texan Cultures** (☎ 210-458-2300; www.texancultures.utsa .edu; 801 S Bowie St; adult/child $7/4; 10am-6pm Tue-Sat, noon-5pm Sun). In the same park you can also ride up to the observation deck of the recently renovated 750ft **Tower of the Americas** (☎ 210-207-8615; www.sanantonio.gov/sapar/hemisfair .asp; HemisFair Park; adult/child $4/1.50; 9am-10pm Sun-Thu, 9am-11pm Fri & Sat), which was due to reopen by this book's publication.

At the far north end of downtown, the **San Antonio Museum of Art** (SAMA; ☎ 210-978-8100; www.sa-museum.org; 200 W Jones Ave; adult/child $8/3; noon-8pm Tue, noon-5pm Wed-Sat, noon-6pm Sun) has an impressive collection of Spanish Colonial, Mexican and pre-Columbian works.

Further afield, summer fun seekers head toward **SeaWorld San Antonio** (☎ 210-523-3611; www.seaworld.com; 105000 SeaWorld Dr, off US 90; adult/child $44/34; 10am-9pm, to 10pm Sat) and the **Six Flags** (www.sixflags.com) amusement park with monster roller coasters and an attached water park. Both are on the outer Loop 1604.

Festivals & Events
Fiesta San Antonio (☎ 210-227-5191; www.fiesta -sa.org) is a mammoth, citywide party mid-to late April. For 10 days there are river parades, carnivals, Tejano music, dancing, tons of food and a 10km run to work it off.

The **San Antonio Stock Show & Rodeo** (☎ 210-225-5851; www.sarodeo.com; SBC center; ticket adult/child $5/3) comes to town for 16 days starting mid-February. Big concerts follow each night's rodeo.

Sleeping
A mind-boggling number and variety of lodgings blanket the city. Still, festivals and conventions fill them all. Unlike other, more business-oriented Texas towns, the high rates here are on weekends, not weekdays. Two-night stays are required at most B&Bs and the cheapest motels are on outer Loop 1604.

BUDGET
San Antonio Hostel (☎ 210-223-9426; 621 Pierce St, off Grason St; dm $18; P) Behind the Bullis House B&B (rooms $69 to $105) are two

makeshift buildings full of bunk-rooms that serve as the hostel, with a shared kitchen and common area. Great pool.

San Antonio Alamo Travelodge (☎ 210-222-1000; www.travelodge.com; 405 Broadway; r $59-89; P) Though you can easily cover the few blocks to the Alamo, there's a bus stop right outside the door. Free hot breakfast at the on-site diner.

MIDRANGE
Menger Hotel (☎ 210-223-4361, 800-345-9285; www .historicmenger.com; 204 Alamo Plaza; r $119-149; P) Legend has it that General Robert E Lee once rode his horse into the lobby of the Menger Hotel, built 300ft from the Alamo in 1859. This 316-room living museum-cum-luxury hotel is so welcoming that several spirits have decided not to leave. Parking $19.

Inn on the Riverwalk (☎ 210-225-6333, 800-730-0019; www.innonriver.com; 129 Woodward Pl; r without/ with Jacuzzi $99/119; P) Sixteen decorator-designed rooms are in three comfy old houses-turned-B&Bs. From what may be the best riverfront location in the city, you can walk the eight peaceful minutes north on the paved bank to get to the restaurants and bars. Wireless enabled.

Jackson House (☎ 210-225-4045; www.nobleinns .com; 102 Turner St; r $120-200; P) The stained-glass conservatory covering the pool adds to the Victorian appeal here. Afternoon refreshments are included at this King William District B&B.

TOP END
Hotel Valencia (☎ 210-227-9700; www.hotelvalencia .com; 150 E Houston St; r $199-259; P) Of the high-end Riverwalk lodgings, this is the most sleek-and-boutique. Parking $16.

La Mansión del Rio (☎ 210-518-1000, 800-292-7300; www.lamansion.com; 112 College St; r $189-319; P) Spanish-colonial élan drips from every fountain here. Rustic beams adorn ceilings, and dark-wood French doors open to waterfront balconies in some rooms. Parking $25.

Eating
Twin Sisters Bakery & Cafe (☎ 210-354-1559; 124 Broadway; breakfasts $2-7, lunches $4-10; breakfast & lunch Mon-Fri;) Tofu *ranchero* (with hot salsa) for breakfast and turkey burgers for lunch – Twin Sisters keeps it light and fresh. There's

another branch at **Northside** (☎ 210-822-0761; 6322 N New Braunfels Ave; breakfast $2-7, lunch $4-10, mains $7-15; ☺ 7am-9pm Mon-Fri, breakfast & lunch Sat, brunch Sun; ☒), which also has pastas and stir-frys for dinner.

Guenther House (☎ 210-227-1061; 205 E Guenther St; breakfast $4-7, lunch $5-8; ☺ breakfast & lunch) The Pioneer Flour Mill founder built this house next to his factory in 1860. Today the café in the home's lower level and garden uses the company's flour, cornmeal and tortillas to make delicious dishes like sweet Belgian waffles.

Mi Tierra Café (☎ 210-225-1262; 218 Produce Row, Market Sq; breakfasts $7-10, mains $7-13; ☺ 24hr) So well-loved that the defenders of the Alamo and the Mexican army would probably have shared breakfast here (if it had opened before 1941, that is). Expect classic Texas Mexican at its most ornate with red velvet, mariachis and all.

Also recommended:

Rosario's (☎ 210-223-1806; 919 S Alamo St; lunch $6-8, dinner $8-12) Modern Mexican, veggie options.

Little Red Barn (☎ 210-532-4235; 1836 S Hackberry; mains $7-14; ☺ lunch & dinner) Fun, fast-paced steakhouse about 2 miles southeast of the center.

Entertainment

The free weekly **San Antonio Current** (www.sacurrent.com) has listings of clubs, local music and cultural events.

Menger Hotel Bar (☎ 210-223-4361; 204 Alamo Plaza) This tiny dark-wood bar with subdued lighting is the perfect place for a rendezvous.

Bonham Exchange (☎ 210-271-3811; www.bonhamexchange.com; 411 Bonham St) Each Saturday go-go boys dance at this gay nightclub, located inside an 1891 community center.

Club Rive (☎ 210-222-4700; www.clubrive.com; 245 E Commerce St) Four nightclubs in one, here

you can smoke a hookah, dance to a techno beat, watch exotic dancers vibrate or listen to live music.

John T Floore's Country Store (☎ 210-695-8827; www.liveatfloores.com; 14492 Bandera Rd, off Hwy 16 in Helotes) Two miles northwest of outer Loop 1604, this dance hall was first opened by a friend of Willie Nelson's as a store 1942. Willie stops by to play an occasional concert.

THEATER

Majestic Theatre (☎ 210-554-1010; www.majesticempire.com; 224 E Houston St) Attend concerts and musicals in a 1929 movie theater that looks like someone's Moorish fantasy.

SPORTS

The **San Antonio Spurs** (☎ 210-554-7787; www.nba.com/spurs), the city's NBA basketball team, plays at the **SBC Center** (☎ 210-444-5000; SBC Center Parkway & Walters St, off I-35). Purchase tickets through **Ticketmaster** (☎ 210-224-9600; www.ticketmaster.com).

Getting There & Around

AIR

You can reach 28 US and Mexican cities nonstop from **San Antonio International Airport** (☎ 210-207-3411; www.sanantonio.gov/airport; off I-410, east of Hwy 281), 8 miles north of downtown. VIA city bus 2 (80¢) runs from the airport to downtown San Antonio (including Navarro at Villita Sts) about every 30 minutes. **SATrans** (☎ 210-281-9900; www.saairportshuttle.com) runs shuttle buses to downtown ($9); a cab will cost $18 to $20.

BUS

The **Greyhound Bus Station** (☎ 210-270-5824; www.greyhound.com; 500 N St Marys St) is shared by **Kerrville Bus Lines** (☎ 800-474-3352; www.iridekbc.com).

WALKING THE RIVER

Yes, the Riverwalk is touristy. But residents do frequent the walk; they just know where to go. Bypass the frat-party chains (Dick's Last Resort, Pat O'Brian's…) unless you want to get romping drunk and your hotel's within walking distance. Those in the know choose **Paesano's** (☎ 210-227-2782; 111 W Crockett; pastas $10-16, mains $18-29; ☺ 11am-10pm Sun-Thu, 11am-11pm Fri & Sat) for Italian and the **Little Rhein** (☎ 210-225-2111; 231 S Alamo St; mains $20-$30; ☺ dinner) for a special night out and some serious steak. Just looking for an interesting place for a cocktail? The **Esquire Tavern** (☎ 210-222-2521; 155 E Commerce St; ☺ 9am-12:30am) is a 1933 speakeasy with a catwalk balcony perched high over the water. Glide through the rest of your evening listening to live jazz (8pm nightly) at **Jim Cullum's Landing** (☎ 210-223-7266; www.landing.com; 123 Losoya St) and everyone will think you're a local.

Austin is 1½ hours ($14), Houston 3½ hours ($23) with Greyhound, and Fredericksburg takes just under two hours ($19) with Kerrville.

VIA Downtown Information Center (☎ 210-362-2020; www.viainfo.net; 260 E Houston St; ☿ 9am-6pm Mon-Fri, 9am-2pm Sat) is the place to buy a $3 day pass for the extremely tourist-friendly downtown streetcar routes (80¢ one way).

CAR & MOTORCYCLE
Parking in San Antonio can be a problem, but midrange lodgings downtown sometimes have free guest parking. There's a garage behind the visitor information center (p732). Major car rental agencies have offices at the airport.

TAXI
Taxi rates are $1.70 flag fall ($2.70 after 9pm) plus $1.80 per mile. The biggest company in town is **Yellow-Checker Taxi** (☎ 210-222-2222).

TRAIN
The *Sunset Limited* (Florida–California) and *Texas Eagle* (San Antonio–Chicago) trains stop a few days a week (usually late at night) at the **Amtrak Station** (☎ 210-223-3226; www.amtrak.com; 350 Hoefgen Ave).

HOUSTON

See a Broadway touring show, gaze at a 13th-century Cypriot fresco, eat in a world-class restaurant: Houston is the cultural capital of Texas. More than two million people call the nation's fourth-largest city home. You may wonder how, given the intense summer heat and humidity that can make breathing difficult, but air-conditioning was invented here (literally). You can cool off in the Gulf of Mexico in nearby Galveston, or take a day trip to Johnson Space Center and dream of soaring above it.

History
Shipping merchants Augustus and John Allen established Houston when they proved Buffalo Bayou, the river at the north of the city, was navigable in 1836. In 1914, construction on the Houston Ship Channel was completed and the city became the state's oil-export capital. US government contracts helped develop Houston's petrochemical and petroleum industries, making the city one of the wealthiest energy exporters in the world by the 1970s. A glut on the world market sent oil prices plummeting and in the mid-1980s the economy hit rock bottom. Since then, Houston's economy has branched into medical services and high-tech industries (including aerospace and computer-related industries). The increased oil prices in 2005 may hurt consumers at the pump but it is again fueling Houston's growing economy. When Hurricane Katrina hit in August 2005, more than 250,000 victims of the storm that hit Louisiana and Mississippi took refuge in Houston. The outpouring of city, state and private aid was massive and many of the evacuees may relocate permanently.

Orientation
Houston's downtown core is surprisingly traffic-free; that's because businesses, shops and residential districts sprawl out 50 miles in each direction. Where I-45 (northwest–southeast), I-59 (southwest–northeast) and I-10 (east–west) meet forms downtown. Main St, the route for the light-rail system, starts downtown and zooms south to the Museum District, Hermann Park, the Texas Medical Center and on to the behemoth Reliant Stadium.

Westheimer (lots of street names in town don't have modifiers like St, Rd or Dr) starts southeast of downtown in the Montrose area (it connects to Main St as Elgin St); you can take it through the wealthy River Oaks area and on to the I-610 West and shopping paradise at the Galleria mall. I-610 (the Loop) and the Sam Houston Tollway (Beltway 8) circle round the town. Just to confuse travelers completely, each highway has different names depending on what part of town you're in. I-10 east of town is called the East Fwy; to the west, it's the Katy Fwy. When asking for directions, always request the highway number in addition to the name.

Information
Houston has three area codes: ☎ 713, ☎ 281 and ☎ 832; dial all 10 digits for local calls.

BOOKSTORES
Brazos Bookstore (Map p736; ☎ 713-523-0701; 2421 Bissonnet St) Occasional poetry readings and book signings.

TEXAS

CENTRAL HOUSTON

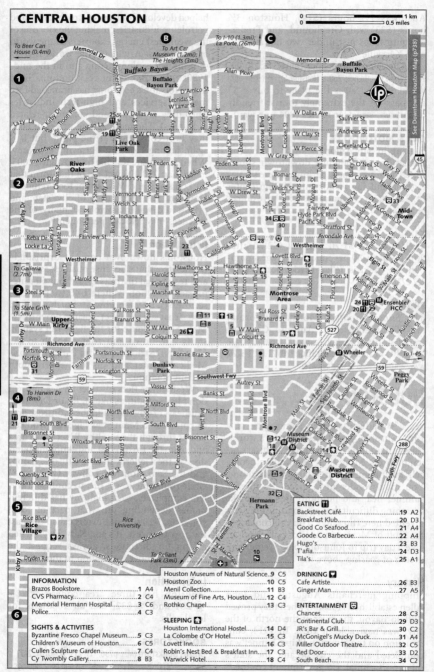

TEXAS

HOUSTON IN...

Two Days

Kick off the day with wings and waffles at the **Breakfast Klub** (p740) before heading to the Museum District to see the **Menil Collection** (below) and the **Museum of Fine Arts** (below). If you're staying downtown that night, check out the bars and restaurants around Main and Prairie Sts; if you're closer to the Montrose area, explore the nightlife there.

On day two you could wander through the **Houston Museum of Natural Science** (p738) and nearby **Hermann Park** (p738) or go see the fun and funky folk art at the **Orange Show Center for Visionary Art** (p739) and the **Art Car Museum** (p739) before attending whatever play or performance you've scored tickets for that night.

Four Days

Follow the two-day itinerary, then on your third day drive 25 miles south to the **Johnson Space Center** (p743) for a gander at the Apollo rockets and the nation's space program. On the fourth day, take another day trip, this time to **Galveston** (p743) on the Gulf Coast.

EMERGENCY

Police (Map p736; ☎ 713-529-3100; 802 Westheimer; 🕙 24hr)

Police, fire and ambulance (☎ 911) Emergency.

INTERNET ACCESS

Houston Public Library (Map p738; ☎ 713-236-1313; 500 McKinney St) Get a number from the desk, it's easy.

MEDIA

88.7 KUHT Classical music and NPR (National Public Radio) from the University of Houston.

91.7 KTRU Rice University college and indie rock.

94.5 KTBZ Alt rock and pop.

100.3 KILT Country.

Houston Chronicle (www.chron.com) The city's daily newspaper, with entertainment and dining sections each Thursday.

Houston Press (www.houstonpress.com) Houston's free weekly with event listings and great restaurant reviews.

MEDICAL SERVICES

Memorial Hermann Hospital (Map p736; ☎ 713-704-4000; 6411 Fannin) Part of the Texas Medical Center megacomplex.

CVS Pharmacy (Map p736; ☎ 713-897-8491; 1003 Richmond Ave; 🕙 24hr)

MONEY

Currency exchange is available at both Houston airports, as well as at the Chase Bank on Main St.

Chase Bank (Map p738; ☎ 713-216-4865; 712 Main St)

POST

Post office (Map p738; ☎ 713-226-3161; 401 Franklin St)

TOURIST INFORMATION

Greater Houston Convention & Visitors Bureau (Map p738; ☎ 713-437-5200, 800-446-8786; cnr Walker & Bagby Sts; 🕙 9am-4pm Mon-Sat, 11am-4pm Sun) Free parking on Walker St.

Sights & Activities

Some of the most interesting attractions are not in the city at all (see p743). Attractions in the city proper are concentrated in the Montrose area, Museum District and Hermann Park. In addition to what's listed here, there are small museums focusing on the Holocaust, printing history, funerary tradition and fire fighters.

The impressive collection at the **Museum of Fine Arts, Houston** (Map p736; ☎ 713-639-7300; www.mfah.org; 1001 Bissonnet; adult $7, child 6-18 $3.50, Thu free; 🕙 10am-5pm Tue & Wed, 10am-9pm Thu, 10am-7pm Fri & Sat, 12:15-7pm Sun) touches on every period of art from antiquity to the present, but is heavy on French Impressionism, photography, and post-1945 European and American paintings and sculpture. Across the street, the **Cullen Sculpture Garden** (Map p736; cnr Montrose Blvd & Bissonnet S; admission free) holds works by Rodin, Matisse and others.

The 15,000 art works once belonging to John and Dominique de Menil form the core of the **Menil Collection** (Map p736; ☎ 713-525-9400; www.menil.org; 1515 Sul Ross St; admission free; 🕙 11am-7pm Wed-Sun). The couple's taste ran from the medieval and Byzantine to the surreal; several rooms are devoted to the likes of René Magritte and Max Ernst. The **Cy Twombly Gallery** (Map p736; ☎ 713-525-9450; 1501

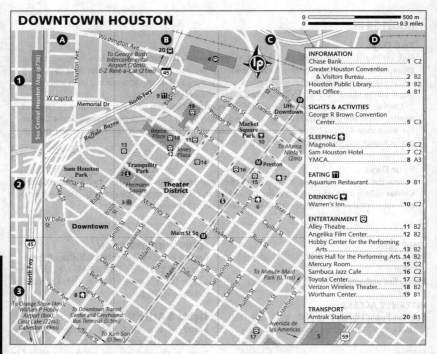

DOWNTOWN HOUSTON

Branard St; admission free; ☺ 11am-7pm Wed-Sun) annex contains very abstract art.

Dominique de Menil's acquisition of a 13th-century Cypriot fresco necessitated a bit of international diplomacy, but **Byzantine Fresco Chapel Museum** (Map p736; ☎ 713-521-3990; 4011 Yupon St; admission free; ☺ 11am-6pm Fri-Sun) now safely protects the treasure. Another meditative sanctuary, the **Rothko Chapel** (Map p736; ☎ 713-524-9839; www.rothkochapel.org; 3900 Yupon St; admission free; ☺ 10am-6pm), is more modern, with 14 large abstract paintings anchoring the space.

Delve into excellent traveling shows – often with shiny themes (treasures of Tsarist Russia, gold of the world) – at the **Houston Museum of Natural Science** (Map p736; ☎ 713-639-4629; www.hmns.org; 1 Hermann Circle; adult/child $6/3.50; ☺ 9am-5pm Mon & Wed-Sat, 11am-5pm Sun, 10am-8pm Tue). Dinosaurs and fossils, gems and minerals, chemistry and interactive experiments are all part of the permanent collections. Inside, the **Cockrell Butterfly Center** (adult/child $5/3.50; ☺ 9am-5pm Mon-Sat, 11am-5pm Sun, to 6pm Jun-Aug) is a conservatory where you can walk among thousands of butterflies.

Houston for Children

Young-uns getting restless? **Hermann Park** (☎ 713-524-5876; www.hermannpark.org; 600 Fannin) has playgrounds, a lake with paddle boats, and the revitalized **Houston Zoo** (Map p736; ☎ 713-533-6500; www.houstonzoo.org; 1513 N MacGregor; adult/child $7/3; ☺ 9am-5pm, to 6pm Jun-Aug). Out front of the zoo is the **Herman Park Miniature Train** (☎ 713-529-5216; per ride $2.35; ☺ 10am-5pm), which leaves the station every 30 minutes. The Miller Outdoor Theatre (p741) has kid-oriented matinees.

Walking distance from the park is the technicolor **Children's Museum of Houston** (Map p736; ☎ 713-522-1138; www.cmhouston.org; 1500 Binz St; admission $5; ☺ 9am-5pm Tue-Sat, to 8pm Thurs, noon-5pm Sun). Nonstop activities include making tortillas and learning Spanish in a Mexican village, and drawing in an open-air art studio.

Downtown, the **Aquarium Restaurant** (Map p738; ☎ 713-223-3474; 4120 Bagby St; kids' meals $6-7, mains $18-29; ☺ 11am-10pm Sun-Thu, 11am-11pm Fri & Sat) has a few amusement rides associated with it, as do its sister restaurants in Kemah (p743). South of town, on the I-610 loop, is a huge **Six Flags** (www.sixflags.com) theme park.

QUIRKY HOUSTON

Conservative Houston has a wacky art streak. Postman Jeff McKissack's outdoor, found-art tribute to his favorite fruit is today the **Orange Show Center for Visionary Art** (☎ 713-926-6368; www.orangeshow.org; 2402 Munger St, off I-45 S; admission free; ☽ 9am-1pm Wed-Fri, noon-5pm Sat & Sun). The center also keeps up the **Beer Can House** (222 Malone St, off Memorial Dr), a house/outdoor sculpture covered with 50,000 beer cans, and sponsors the **Art Car Parade** (www.orangeshow.org; Allen Parkway), when hundreds of painted, altered and augmented automobiles show off on the second Sunday in May. The **Art Car Museum** (☎ 713-861-5526; www.artcarmuseum.com; 140 Heights Blvd; admission free; ☽ 11am-6pm Wed-Sun) is a repository for more than 15 of the psychedelic, buglike, and Mad Max-esque vehicles.

Tours

Houston Tours (☎ 713-988-5900; www.houstontours.com; city tour $35) has bus tours hitting all the major districts in town as well as tours that will take you to the Johnson Space Center and Galveston. Some of Tom Bagby's **Experience Houston Tours** (☎ 713-465-7415; experiencehoustontours@att.net) downtown tours also include the Museum of Fine Arts and the Houston Museum of Natural Science.

Festivals & Events

February is when the **Houston Livestock Show & Rodeo** (☎ 832-667-1000; www.hlsr.com; ticket adult/child $6/3) rolls into **Reliant Park** (☎ 832-667-1400; www.reliantpark.com; 1 Reliant Park, I-610 S at Kirby Dr) for 20 days. The midway hums with rides and the halls are filled with prize animals, but the main event is the nightly rodeo followed by a major-name singer.

The hilarious **Art Car Parade** (above) takes place in May. Lots of ladies (and a few guys) turn up in town at the beginning of November for the **International Quilt Festival – Houston** (☎ 713-781-6864; www.quilts.com; admission $10). It's held at the **George R Brown Convention Center** (Map p738; 1001 Avenida de las Americas).

Sleeping

The coming of the light-rail is a part of a larger revival in the past few years that has included a number of hotels – chain and

otherwise – opening downtown (rates drop dramatically Friday and Saturday nights).

BUDGET

YMCA (Map p738; ☎ 713-758-9250; 1600 Louisiana St; s with bath $33, male-only s without bath $28-30; Ⓟ ⊠ 🖳) Only four blocks from the light-rail, between downtown and Montrose, the Y has a great, safe location. Rooms on floors eight to 10 have refrigerators and TVs (kitchen down the hall). All are singles.

Other budget options are the **Houston International Hostel** (Map p736; ☎ 713-523-1009; www.houstonhostel.com; 5302 Crawford St; dm $14.50; Ⓟ 🖳), in a slightly junky house near museums, and chain motels nearby on I-59 (Southwest Fwy).

MIDRANGE

Magnolia (Map p738; ☎ 713-221-0011; www.magnoliahotelhouston.com; 1100 Texas Ave; r $99-$159; Ⓟ 🔛) Just as sleek and sophisticated – in deep woods and modern neutrals – as her sister hotel in Dallas. Wrap up in the complimentary robe and head to the rooftop for a magnificent panorama and a dip in the pool. The whole place is wireless equipped. Parking $23.

Warwick Hotel (Map p736; ☎ 713-526-1991, 800-670-7275; www.warwickhotelhouston.com; 5701 Main St; r $99-159; Ⓟ 🔛 🔛) The elegance of a 1920 hotel, but with big, comfy rooms. Some packages include admission to the Museum of Fine Arts across the street. Parking $9.

Of B&Bs in the Montrose area, the **Lovett Inn** (Map p736; ☎ 713-522-5224; www.lovettinn.com; 501 Lovett Blvd; r $95-150; Ⓟ ⊠ 🔛) occupies a large, stately home and grounds; a bit more whimsical and overgrown is the rose-colored **Robin's Nest Bed & Breakfast Inn** (Map p736; ☎ 713-528-5821; www.therobin.com; 4104 Greeley St; s $86-145, d $126-175; Ⓟ ⊠).

TOP END

La Colombe d'Or Hotel (Map p736; ☎ 713-524-7999; www.lacolombedor.com; 3410 Montrose Blvd; r $195-275; Ⓟ ⊠) The museum-quality antiques and rare oil paintings seem right at home in this charming 1923 mansion. Each of the six suitelike rooms have sitting and dining areas. There's also a library and a French restaurant.

Sam Houston Hotel (Map p738; ☎ 832-200-8800; www.samhoustonhotel.com; 1117 Prairie St; r $155-225; Ⓟ) Flat-screen TVs, a complimentary DVD library and free high-speed Internet are all part of the modern luxury at the Sam Houston. The chic bar occasionally hosts art-reception happy hours. Parking $25.

Eating

Numerous enclaves of food and drink include Rice Village, the Montrose area and west Westheimer near the Galleria.

MIDTOWN

T'afia (Map p736; ☎ 713-524-6922; 3701 Travis St; mains $15-20; ☯ dinner Tue-Sat, brunch Sun) Chef Monica Pope uses fine, organic, local ingredients in her inventive American cuisine (some call it yuppie food).

RIVER OAKS & MONTROSE

Tila's (Map p736; ☎ 712-522-7654; 1111 S Shepherd Dr; mains $10-15; ☯ 11am-11pm Mon-Thu, 11am-2am Fri & Sat, 10am-11pm Sun) Central-Mexican recipes and interesting ingredients result in dishes like brie and pear quesadillas. The dining rooms have a rustic, faux-painted flair and there's a patio.

Local chef Hugo Ortega is involved in two huge successes: **Backstreet Cafe** (Map p736; ☎ 713-521-2239; 1103 S Shepherd; lunches $10-15, dinner mains $16-25; ☯ 11am-10pm Sun-Thu, 11am-11pm Fri & Sat) serves nouveau American; **Hugo's** (Map p736; ☎ 713-524-7744; 1600 Westheimer; lunches $10-15, dinner mains $14-25; ☯ 11am-10pm Sun-Thu, 11am-11pm Fri & Sat) produces upmarket Mexican and has the best tequila menu in town.

UNIVERSITY

Jim Goode first became a restaurant owner in 1977; now his character-filled Texas eateries number four, including **Goode Co Barbecue** (Map p736; ☎ 713-522-2530; 5109 Kirby Dr; plates $6-10; ☯ 11am-10pm) and **Good Co Seafood** (Map p736; ☎ 713-523-7154; 2621 Westpark Dr; po'boys $7-8, mains $13-16; ☯ 11am-10pm).

DOWNTOWN

Kim Son (Map p738; ☎ 713-222-2461; 2001 Jefferson St; mains $9-18; ☯ 11am-11pm, to midnight Fri & Sat) This legendary restaurant at the corner of Chartres and Jefferson Sts, just south of I-59, is run by the La family, who escaped in a boat from Vietnam in 1979. The enormous menu ranges from rice-noodle soup to jellyfish and lotus root.

Mama Ninfa's (☎ 713-228-1145; 2704 Navigation Blvd; mains $8-15; ☯ 11am-10pm) This original off-

neighborhood hole-in-the-wall spawned a Tex-Mex empire. Waiters in *guayaberas* (white embroidered shirts) are sincere when they say they're 'at your service.' Follow Franklin St southeast of downtown, under I-59, until it becomes Navigation Blvd.

THE GALLERIA & BEYOND

Steak is huge in Houston, both figuratively and literally, and all the national heavy-hitters are represented – Ruth's Chris, the Palm etc. They're mostly on Westheimer near the Galleria. The clubby, local **State Grille** (☎ 713-622-1936; 2925 Weslayan St, off W Alabama Ave; mains $15-30; ☯ lunch Mon-Fri, dinner Mon-Sat) has a monster veal chop, but also does seafood remarkably well.

Drinking

Warren's Inn (Map p738; ☎ 713-247-9207; 307 Travis St) Sip cheap, strong drinks at an antitrendy bar on old Market Sq.

Ginger Man (Map p736; ☎ 713-526-2770; 5607 Morningside Dr, Rice Village) This homey pub has 69 beers on tap (and siblings in Austin and Dallas). The beer garden out back is especially popular with university students.

Cafe Artiste (Map p736; ☎ 713-528-3704; 1601 W Main St; ☯ 7am-11pm Sun-Thu, 7am-1am Fri & Sat) There's no hurry to leave your table at this brewed-by-the-cup coffee house. It also serves beer and wine, OK food and has free wi-fi.

Entertainment

Houston's never really had an entertainment district per se, but downtown is growing one around the light-rail's Preston stop (on Main St between Prairie and Preston

Aves), where bars, restaurants and clubs cluster. The entertainment supplement to the **Houston Chronicle** (www.chron.com) comes out on Thursday; **Houston Press** (www.houstonpress.com) is another good source for listings.

NIGHTCLUBS & LIVE MUSIC

McGonigel's Mucky Duck (Map p736; ☎ 713-528-5999; www.mcgonigels.com; 2425 Norfolk St) Smoke-free music: how refreshing. Listen to live acoustic, Irish, folk and country performers nightly. Under-21s welcome with parents.

Continental Club (Map p736; ☎ 713-529-9899; www.continentalclub.com; 3700 Main St) This is the number two location of Austin's famed live-music venue, and it hasn't missed a beat with top-notch blues, rock and rockabilly at least five nights a week.

Sambuca Jazz Cafe (Map p738; ☎ 713-224-5299; www.sambucarestaurant.com; 900 Texas Ave) A swanky supper club, Sambuca serves live nightly jazz accompanied by an eclectic menu.

The **Bayou Place** (cnr Texas Ave & Smith St) complex has chain restaurants, dance clubs and the **Verizon Wireless Theater** (Map p738; ☎ 713-230-1600; www.verizonwirelesstheater.com; 520 Texas Ave), a prime concert venue.

Yet more choices:

Red Door (Map p736; ☎ 713-526-8181; www.reddoorhouston.com; 2416 Brazos St) No sign, just a hot DJ and the young and fabulous.

Mercury Room (Map p738; ☎ 713-225-6372; www.mercuryroom.com; 1008 Prairie) R&B, Motown and Latin-funk bands play in art deco surrounds.

THEATER

Downtown is home to several performing arts venues collectively known as the **Theater District** (www.houstontheaterdistrict.org).

Hobby Center for the Performing Arts (Map p738; ☎ 713-315-2525; www.thehobbycenter.org; 800 Bagby St) This modern complex is home to traveling Broadway shows and Theatre Under the Stars, which produces mostly musicals. It also hosts dancers and musicians, organized by the **Society for the Performing Arts** (SPA; ☎ 713-227-4772; www.spahouston.org).

Alley Theatre (Map p738; ☎ 713-228-8421; www.alleytheatre.org; 615 Texas Ave) A first-rate, local company performs contemporary and classic drama and comedies.

Miller Outdoor Theatre (Map p736; ☎ 713-284-8350; www.milleroutdoortheatre.com; 100 Concert Dr) Hermann Park's outdoor theater is a great place to lay out a blanket on a summer night and take in a free play, musical or concert.

CLASSICAL PERFORMANCE

Da Camera of Houston (☎ 713-524-7601; www.dacamera.com) Expanding the reach of classical music, Da Camera attracts stars and combines chamber music with literature.

Jones Hall for the Performing Arts (Map p738; ☎ 713-227-3974; www.houstontx.gov/joneshall; 615 Louisiana St) is home to the **Houston Symphony** (☎ 713-224-7575; www.houstonsymphony.org); some SPA events are also held here.

The **Houston Grand Opera** (☎ 713-228-6737; www.houstongrandopera.org) and **Houston Ballet** (☎ 713-227-2787; www.houstonballet.org) both play at the beautiful **Wortham Center** (Map p738; ☎ 713-250-3600; www.houstontx.gov/worthamcenter; 615 Texas Ave).

CINEMAS

Angelika Film Center (Map p738; ☎ 713-225-5232; www.angelikafilmcenter.com; 510 Texas Ave, Bayou Place) This downtown art theater shows a mix of first-run, foreign and independent films.

TEXAS

GAY & LESBIAN HOUSTON

Montrose has been the town's gathering place for gay men and women for decades, and the gay community is involved with many aspects of city life and the local art scene. That's not to say the town isn't pretty conservative; public displays of affection will probably turn heads. Every June, the **Pride Committee of Houston** (☎ 713-529-6979; www.pridehouston.org) sponsors a huge gay pride parade, with attendees arriving from all over the state. Related events stretch out all month. KPFT 90.1 FM is the home of Queer Voices radio, and the **Houston Voice** (www.houstonvoice.com) is the gay and lesbian newspaper.

In the Montrose area, **South Beach** (Map p736; ☎ 713-529-7623; www.southbeachthenightclub.com; 810 Pacific St) is the premier dance club, and attracts the prettiest boys; next door, **JR's Bar & Grill** (Map p736; ☎ 713-521-2519; www.jrsbarandgrill.com; 808 Pacific St) has a more laid-back, fern-bar style. The popular lesbian dance bar, **Chances** (Map p736; ☎ 713-523-7217; www.chancesbar.com; 1100 Westheimer) has limited parking (avoid Hollywood Video across the street; they tow).

SPORTS

Contained in **Reliant Park** (☎ 832-667-1400; www
.reliantpark.com; 1 Reliant Park, cnr I-610 S & Kirby Dr)
are Reliant Stadium, Reliant Arena and the
1963 Astrodome, once billed as the eighth
wonder of the world. Events take place year-
round. In 2004, Reliant Stadium, home to
the NFL **Houston Texans** (☎ 877-635-2002; www.
houstontexans.com), hosted Super Bowl XXVIII.
The park is the southernmost stop on the
light-rail system.

Houston Astros (☎ 713-259-8000; www.astros
.com) play pro baseball downtown at **Minute
Maid Park** (Map p738; 501 Crawford).

The **Toyota Center** (Map p738; 1510 Polk) is
home to three teams:
Houston Rockets (☎ 713-627-3865; www.houston
rockets.com) NBA basketball team.
Houston Comets (☎ 713-627-9622; www.houston
comets.com) WNBA basketball team.
Houston Aeros (☎ 713-627-2376; www.aeros.com) IHL
hockey team, sort of like Triple A in baseball.

Shopping

Galleria (☎ 713-622-0663; www.simon.com; 5075
Westheimer Rd, off I-610) The biggest collection
of shops in Houston are located in and
around the Galleria, a huge, mazelike mall
at the corner of Westheimer and Post Oak.
There are 375 stores, anchors like Macy's,
Foley's and Nordstrom, and a bevy of restaurants, not to mention hotels – and an
ice-skating rink.

Rice Village, the area on S Kirby Dr near
University Blvd, has a few unique stores and
even more upscale chain stores gathered
near restaurants and Rice University.

North of I-10, Waugh Dr turns into
Heights Blvd, the anchor of the **Heights** (www
.houstonheights.org) neighborhood. Shop for antiques here, especially on 19th St. Another
shopping area is on **Harwin Drive** (off I-59, Southwest Fwy), southwest of town. Look for discounts at the many Indian and Asian stores.

Getting There & Away

AIR

Twenty-two miles north of the city center,
George Bush Intercontinental Airport (IAH; ☎ 281-
230-3100; http://iah.houstonairportsystem.org; btwn I-45
& I-59 N) is served by many major domes-
tic and international carriers, and is home
base for Continental Airlines. Twelve miles
southeast of town, **William P Hobby Airport**
(HOU; ☎ 713-640-3000; http://hou.houstonairportsys

tem.org; off I-45 S) is a major hub for Southwest
Airlines and domestic travel. Read your
ticket closely, as some airlines, like Delta,
may fly out of either airport. Wi-fi service
is available at both airports.

BUS

Long-distance buses arrive at the **Greyhound
Bus Terminal** (Map p738; ☎ 713-759-6565; www.grey
hound.com; 2121 Main St), located between downtown and the Museum District, and two
blocks from the Downtown Transit Center
light-rail stop. Direct buses connect to New
Orleans ($51, eight hours), Dallas ($35, 4½
hours) and San Antonio ($23, 3½ hours),
among others.

TRAIN

The Orlando–Los Angeles train, the *Sunset Limited*, stops at the **Amtrak Station** (Map
p738; ☎ 713-224-1577; www.amtrak.com; 902 Washington Ave). It travels east Monday, Wednesday
and Friday nights, and travels west early
Sunday, Tuesday and Friday mornings.
Destinations include New Orleans ($51, 10
hours), San Antonio ($33, five hours) and
El Paso ($124, 20 hours).

Getting Around

Sprawling, spread-out Houston is all about
superhighways and racinglike speeds (or
parking lot–like traffic). The coming of the
light-rail, however, means that it's now possible to visit town car-free because most of
the sights are on the downtown, Museum
District–Reliant Park corridor. If you want
to venture further, say to the Galleria, you'll
need to rent a car.

TO/FROM THE AIRPORT

The Hobby Airport Express bus (No 101)
connects to downtown (and to the Downtown Transit Center light-rail stop) Monday
through Saturday ($1). Bus 102 is the Bush
IAH Express that will take you from Bush
Intercontinental to downtown or the transit
center. **Express Shuttle USA** (☎ 713-523-8888; www
.airportexpresshouston.com) provides service from
both Bush IAH ($18 to $28) and Hobby
($14 to $28) airports. A taxi to IAH/HOU
airports from downtown is about $37/20.

BUS

Houston's **Metropolitan Transit Authority** (Metro;
☎ 713-635-4000; www.ridemetro.org) runs a com-

plicated network of bus lines ($1) around town that is wholly inefficient for visitors.

CAR
Every major national rental agency can be found at either airport and at offices throughout town. The independent **E-Z Rent-A-Car** (☎ 281-442-7733; www.e-zrentacar.com; 15222 John F Kennedy Blvd) has weekend rates as low as $13 per day to outfox the big guys. It operates out of the Holiday Inn; take the hotel's shuttle from the airport.

TAXI
Cab rates are $3 flag fall and $1.50 for each additional mile. Note that Houston's breadth means your cab tab can quickly surpass car rental rates. Companies include **United** (☎ 713-699-0000) and **Yellow** (☎ 713-236-1111).

AROUND HOUSTON
If you come to Houston, don't miss the day trips. The Gulf Coast island of Galveston is less than 45 miles southeast on I-45. On the way you pass NASA's world-famous Johnson Space Center in Clear Lake (25 miles southeast of Houston) – both are must-sees.

Clear Lake
Parades of billowing sails pass by the many waterfront marinas. The **NASA/Clear Lake Convention & Visitors Bureau** (☎ 281-338-0333, 800-844-5253; www.nasaclearlaketexas.com; Suite 40, 20710 I-45, Webster; ☼ 9am-5pm Mon-Fri) has a great list of watersport operators on its website.

Located here also is one of the state's most popular tourist destinations, **Johnson Space Center**. The official NASA visitor center and museum is called **Space Center Houston** (☎ 281-244-2100; www.spacecenter.org; 1601 NASA Rd 1, off I-45 S; adult/child $18/14, ☼ 10am-5pm Mon-Fri, 10am-6pm Sat & Sun, later Jun-Aug; ℗). Most exhibits are really more for the kids than for the serious history buff, but you can see some of the actual workings of Johnson Space Center – shuttle training facilities, zero-gravity labs, the original mission control and Rocket Park – by taking the included tram tour that departs every 20 minutes. Book ahead online for a Level 9 Tour ($62, 16 and older), which gets you closer to the astronauts and into areas the general tour doesn't.

East on Galveston Bay, the **Kemah Boardwalk** (☎ 877-285-3624; www.kemah.com; cnr Bradford & 2nd Sts) is a Disney-wannabe, with theme restaurants, shops, carnival rides, amusements, and a miniature train; drive south of the Space Center on I-45, turn east onto FM 518/2094, after 7 miles jog north on Hwy 146, and the next quick right (east) brings you to the highly manipulated fun.

Galveston
The island of Galveston is part genteel Southern lady and part sunburned beach bum, with elaborate decorated-gingerbread pastel homes and windswept salt-damaged waterfront motels and restaurants. A killer hurricane hit here in 1900, engulfing the island and claiming 6000 lives (still the country's worst natural disaster in terms of lives lost). Recent storms have spared this coast, but residents know what is always possible. Maybe that's why they party like there's no tomorrow at annual Mardi Gras festivities.

The island (at the southeast end of I-45) is 30 miles long and no more than 3 miles wide. Seawall Blvd follows the gulf shore. The historic Strand district is bounded by 20th and 25th Sts, Mechanic St and Harborside Dr. **Galveston Island Visitors Center** (☎ 409-763-4311, 888-425-4753; www.galveston.com; 2428 Seawall Blvd; ☼ 8:30am-5pm) shows a film about the island.

Texas Seaport Museum (☎ 409-763-1877; www.tsm-elissa.org; Pier 21, cnr Harborside Dr & 21st St; adult/child under 18 $6/4; ☼ 10am-5pm) explores the town's 19th-century shipping heyday. Tour the *Elissa*, a beautiful 1877 Scottish tall ship. Next door, **Pier 21 Theatre** (☎ 409-763-8808; www.galvestonhistory.org/plc-pier21.htm; Pier 21; adult/child under 18 $3.50/2.50; ☼ 11am-6pm Sun-Thu, 11am-8pm Fri & Sat) shows a fascinating documentary about the great storm of 1900.

For sand and surf head to **Stewart Beach Park**, on the east end of Seawall Blvd at Broadway. Just off the seawall, there's a narrow spit of sand flanking the waves (if you can call them that). **Moody Gardens** (☎ 409-744-4673; www.moodygardens.com; 1 Hope Blvd; day pass $31, under 3 free; ☼ 10am-6pm Sun-Fri, 10am-8pm Sat, to 9pm Jun-Aug) is a bit of a tourist trap, with a 2-million-gallon aquarium, a butterfly rain forest and an Imax theater, all stuffed into glass pyramids.

It's easy to make Galveston a day trip from Houston, but if you decide to stay over, be warned that the surfside motels are generally old, overpriced, and completely booked on summer weekends. Inside the Sandpiper Motel on Stewart Beach, **HI Galveston Hostel** (☎ 409-765-9431; www.sandpipermotel.com; 201 E Seawall Blvd; dm members/nonmembers $18.50/21.50, r $50-200; P 🖥 🐶) has six-bed dorms and a common area with a TV. The 1922 Spanish colonial **Hotel Galvez** (☎ 409-765-7721; www.galveston.com/galvez; 2024 Seawall Blvd; r $98-249; P 🐶) is across from the Gulf further west.

Several chain eateries stand on the piers by the Strand, but the best seafood in town is at **Gaido's** (☎ 409-762-9625; 3800 Seawall Blvd; mains $12-35; 🕙 noon-9pm Mon-Thu, noon-10pm Fri-Sun), Galveston's oldest, family-owned restaurant (since 1911). Homemade breads form the foundation for super sandwiches at **Sunflower Bakery** (☎ 409-763-5500; 1527 Church St.; pastries $1-3, sandwiches $5-6.50; 🕙 7am-6pm Mon-Fri, 7:30am-4pm Sat).

Kerrville Bus Co (☎ 800-474-3352; www.iridekbc.com; 3825 Broadway) runs a morning bus and an evening bus ($16, one hour) to the Greyhound Bus Terminal (p742) in Houston. The **Galveston Island Rail Trolley** (☎ 409-763-4311; www.islandtransit.net) links the Strand with Seawall via 25th St ($1), with a small Strand loop.

La Porte

The 19th-century Texas War for Independence was won at the Battle of San Jacinto, where General Sam Houston routed Mexican general Antonio López de Santa Anna on April 21, 1836 (re-enacted annually). **San Jacinto Battleground State Historic Site** (☎ 281-479-2421; www.tpwd.state.tx.us/park/sanjac; 3523 Hwy 134; admission free; 🕙 8am-dark) preserves more than 1000 acres of the battleground. The 570ft **San Jacinto Monument** (museum free, observation deck adult/child $7/free; 🕙 8am-6pm) looks like the Washington Monument with a star on top (making it 12ft taller). You can also tour the vintage 1914 **Battleship Texas** (adult/child $7/free; 🕙 10am-5pm), a veteran of both World Wars. Follow I-10 east to Crosby-Lynchburg Rd south, take the Lynchburg ferry across the river and the park is half a mile further.

High Island

A major flyway for migratory birds crosses eastern coastal Texas, and the woods at High Island, 80 miles southeast of Houston, provide shelter for song birds during spring (mid-March to mid-May) and autumn (late September to October). Numbers are highest during fall-outs, when storm conditions force migrators to descend and rest. The preserve is run by the **Houston Audubon Society** (☎ 713-932-1639; www.houstonaudubon.org; cnr Hwys 124 & 87, off I-10; sanctuary day pass $5; 🕙 dawn-dusk).

Piney Woods

The Piney Woods are a quiet place where 100ft tall trees outnumber people. Nature is the attraction, but don't expect drama; here you'll find deserted trails, rare plants and excellent birding sites.

At **Big Thicket National Preserve** (☎ 409-246-2337; www.nps.gov/bith; cnr US 69 & Rte 420; 🕙 visitor center 9am-5pm), coastal plains meet desert sand dunes, and cypress swamps stand next to pine and hardwood forests. If you're lucky, you may see one of the 20 species of small wild orchids while hiking the 45 miles of trail. The eight park units are 100 miles northwest of Houston.

SOUTHERN GULF COAST

As you travel south along the Gulf on Hwy 35, you pass over bayous, rivers and bays; many migrating birds, including the whooping crane, call these mild-weather estuaries home in winter. Small towns with ports filled with shrimp boats dot the coast. Corpus Christi (population 260,000) is the largest, with a sizeable protected bay. Long stretches of island beaches, untouched except for a condo or two, lead into Padre Island National Seashore. Further south, almost to Mexico, South Padre Island is spring-break center, with the requisite miniature golf courses and bungee-jumping apparatus. Those wanting to pitch a tent on the beach, bird-watch, or simply relax at an ocean-front hotel could spend an eternity wandering the sands of the Southern Gulf Coast.

ROCKPORT

Thirty-five miles northeast of Rockport is Texas' premier birding site, the 70,504-acre **Aransas National Wildlife Refuge** (☎ 361-286-3559; FM 744, off Hwy 35; www.fws.gov/southwest/refuges/texas/aransas.html; per car $5; 🕙 park dawn-dusk, visitor center 8:30am-4:30pm), where 400-and-some whooping cranes (up from just 31 in 1951) winter from November through March. Year-round you also might see wild boars, alligators, armadillos, white-tailed deer and many other species.

Get even closer to the 5ft-tall white cranes by taking a boat from the artist colony and fishing village of Rockport; contact the **chamber of commerce** (☎ 800-242-0071; www.rockport-fulton.org). There's usually more birding activity on the morning boat tour with **Rockport Birding & Kayak Adventures** (☎ 877-892-4737; www.rockportadventures.com; tickets $35; ☎ tours 7:30am & 1:30pm Mar-Nov).

CORPUS CHRISTI

The salt breezes and palm tree–lined bayfront are pleasant enough, but hot summers and an almost antitourist attitude (residents want to keep their hometown to themselves) usually sends vacationers and Winter Texans further south. The National Seashore is the real reason to visit. **Corpus Christi Convention & Visitors Bureau** (☎ 361-881-1888, 800-678-6232; www.corpuschristi-tx-cvb.org; 1823 N Chaparral; ☼ 8:30am-5pm Mon-Fri) is a good source of lodging information. Just across the harbor bridge from downtown is the 900ft aircraft-carrier **USS Lexington** (☎ 361-888-4873; www.usslexington.com; 2914 N Shoreline Blvd; adult/child $12/7; ☼ 9am-5pm, to 6pm Jun-Aug), which is now a museum, and the **Texas State Aquarium** (☎ 361-881-1200; www.texasstateaquarium.org; 2710 N Shoreline; adult/child $13/8; ☼ 9am-5pm, to 6pm Jun-Aug), with exhibits focusing on the Gulf of Mexico and the Amazon.

PADRE ISLAND NATIONAL SEASHORE

Corpus Christi's city limits extend as far as **Padre Island**, which is 20 miles east of downtown on Hwy 358 (SPID). To reach this island (it's really North Padre Island, but no one calls it that), cross the JFK Causeway and the bridge. Here the sugar-sand beach backed by grass-strewn dunes is so undeveloped that you can drive on it (speed limit 15mph). The first 10 miles to the south of the bridge are still part of Corpus Christi, but the remaining 60 miles make up the **Padre Island National Seashore** (☎ 361-949-8068; www.nps.gov/pais; Park Rd 22; per car $10, Malaquite campsite $8; ☼ visitor center 8:30am- 4:30pm, to 6pm Jun-Aug). Endangered Kemp Ridley sea turtles nest in the park (steer clear and tell a ranger if you see a really big turtle on land.) In off-season, it's easy to find yourself alone if you hike a short distance away. The visitor center has the last available drinking water. Heed the 4WD-only warning; even locals get stuck. There's a semi-developed, paved Malaquite campground, and primitive beach camping is free with a permit (but be warned that the constant wind may carry the fine sand into body crevices you didn't know existed).

Holiday Inn Sunspree Resort (☎ 361-949-8041; www.holidayinns.com; 15202 Windward Dr; r $97-209; P ☒) is the only full-service hotel on the island. There are several chain motels lining the downtown bayfront. Chaparral and Water Sts are the hub of food and entertainment activity downtown. At **Executive Surf Club** (☎ 361-884-7873; www.executivesurfclub.com; 309 N Water St; ☼ lunch & dinner) you can eat a burger from a surfboard bar table inside or listen to live rock, folk and country…outside.

SOUTH PADRE ISLAND

Don't confuse the National Seashore with South Padre Island, a condo-crammed resort 3½ hours south of Corpus Christi on Hwy 77. Gulf currents make the water bluer and the winters warmer than in the rest of the state. For most of March the island crawls with partying college students (and all motels are booked solid at inflated prices). Want to parasail, bungee jump and drink yourself silly? You've come to the right place. For more information, and a list of condos you can rent, contact the **South Padre Island Visitor Center** (☎ 956-761-6433, 800-767-2373; 600 Padre Blvd; ☼ 9am-5pm). **Wings Birding Tours** (☎ 888-293-6443; www.wingsbirds.com) has several springtime birding tours along the southern Gulf coast and in the Rio Grande Valley.

DALLAS–FORT WORTH

Just 30 miles apart, Dallas and Fort Worth anchor a gigantic megalopolis known as the Metroplex. The two cities offer distinct takes on the Texas experience. Dallas lives up to its exported image: big and showy, rich and prosperous. It's a driven city, preoccupied with growth and status. Fort Worth seems more comfortable just being its down-to-earth self. Combining lots to see and do – excellent art museums, historic Old West stockyards – with an easy-to-manage layout, Fort Worth might be the state's best-kept secret.

TEXAS

DALLAS

Flashy TV-show millionaires and big hair are what Dallas is famous for, and the reality is not far off. Even in the materially minded US, the 'Big D' stands tall as a paragon of conspicuous consumption. Aside from JFK assassination sites, shopping is the city's main enticement. Museums are scattered and the gritty downtown feels deserted; those who do work there eat lunch at office-building lunch shops and then scatter to the many fabulous restaurants in uptown and beyond in the evening. Most residents are suburbanites and the real action for them is far from the center of town. Sure, visit for a day or two, but don't try to scratch the surface too deep – you'll come up empty.

History

Dallas was founded in 1839, but the town took off when oil was discovered nearby in 1930 and it became a petroleum industry financial center. President Kennedy's assassination sent the city reeling in November 1963. Larry Hagman's portrayal of scheming oil tycoon JR Ewing on *Dallas* in the 1980s, and the Dallas Cowboys' three Super Bowl victories in the 1990s helped Dallas regain its Texas swagger. Since then, it has become a town known for its business acumen, especially in banking, and as a technology and telecommunications center.

Orientation

Downtown Dallas is just east of the junction of I-30 and I-35 E; take the Commerce St exit off I-35. Uptown – with smart, trendy bars, restaurants and hotels – is north of downtown; follow Harwood St (or St Paul St, if you're taking the trolley) to McKinney Ave. Bars line Greenville Ave, northeast of downtown off Ross Ave. Deep Ellum, at the east end of Elm St, has become a bit scary, but it's still the nucleus of Dallas' live-music scene. I-20 connects to Fort Worth, 30 miles to the west.

Information

BOOKSTORES

Crossroads Market (☎ 214-521-8919; 3930 Cedar Springs Rd, off Dallas N Tollway) Gay-owned independent with café.

Half Price Books (☎ 214-379-8000; 5803 E Northwest Hwy, off I-75) The used-book empire began here in Dallas.

EMERGENCY

Police, fire and ambulance (☎ 911) Emergency.

INTERNET ACCESS

Central Library (☎ 214-670-1700; 1515 Young St; ⏰ 9am-9pm Mon-Thu, 9am-5pm Fri & Sat, noon-5pm Sun) Get a free Internet card at the desk.

Dallas CVB Visitor Center (☎ 214-571-1300; www .visitdallas.com; 100 S Houston St; ⏰ 8am-5pm Mon-Fri, 9am-5pm Sat & Sun) Three free terminals, 20 minutes max.

A BIG STATE OF MIND

A particular chest-puffing pride goes along with being the only US state ever to have been an independent nation. Oh, and Texas is BIG. Though half the size of Alaska, it has the largest inhabitable land area – larger than Germany, England, Scotland, Ireland, Northern Ireland, Belgium and the Netherlands combined. You can drive west across the border from Louisiana and not reach New Mexico for 14 hours, or drive north from Brownsville and be in Amarillo a mere 16 hours later. The memorial to Texas independence, the **San Jacinto Monument** (p744) stands 12ft taller than the Washington monument and the **Texas State Capitol** (p724) is 15ft taller than the one in DC. See a trend?

As full of their state as Texans may be, most are friendly folk who are quick to laugh and slow to speak. In their own take on the southern accent, one-syllable words can stretch out to three beats (*yea-ah-sss* = yes, *sh-ee-yit* = shit). Listen for colorful colloquialisms that pepper everyday conversation: something slick is *slipperier than awl sheeyit*, a comfy couch is *so soft it makes your ass laugh*. Terminology is different too: a *pit* is a BBQ or grill used to cook out, and *y'all* is the plural of you. A *good ol' boy* is a stand-up guy who likes guns or the outdoors, has a black-and-white sense of right and wrong, and will do anything in his power to protect those he loves (you decide if that sounds like President Bush or not).

As you travel around, remember, Texas isn't just a state, it's a BIG state of mind.

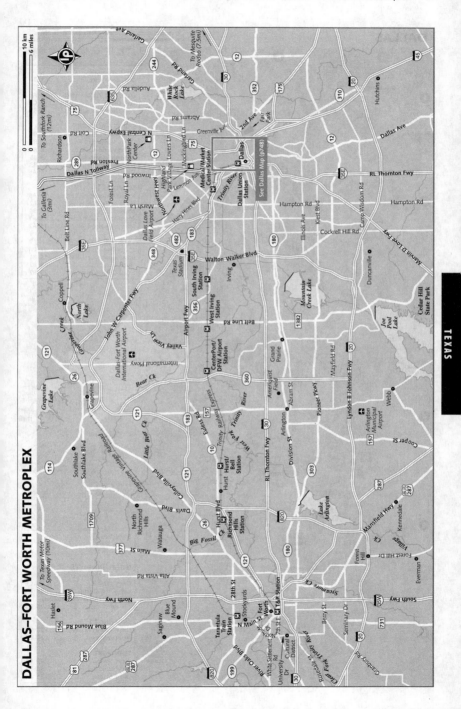

DALLAS–FORT WORTH METROPLEX

TEXAS

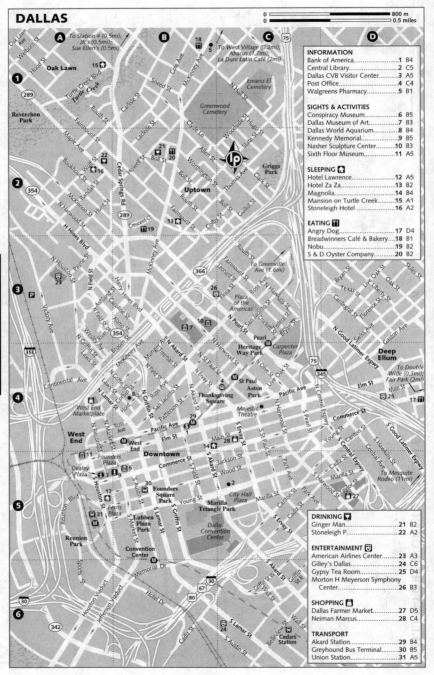

DALLAS

0 ———————————— 800 m
0 ———————————— 0.5 miles

TEXAS

INFORMATION
Bank of America	**1** B4
Central Library	**2** C5
Dallas CVB Visitor Center	**3** A5
Post Office	**4** C4
Walgreens Pharmacy	**5** B1

SIGHTS & ACTIVITIES
Conspiracy Museum	**6** B5
Dallas Museum of Art	**7** B3
Dallas World Aquarium	**8** B4
Kennedy Memorial	**9** B5
Nasher Sculpture Center	**10** B3
Sixth Floor Museum	**11** A5

SLEEPING
Hotel Lawrence	**12** A5
Hotel Za Za	**13** B2
Magnolia	**14** B4
Mansion on Turtle Creek	**15** A1
Stoneleigh Hotel	**16** A2

EATING
Angry Dog	**17** D4
Breadwinners Café & Bakery	**18** B1
Nobu	**19** B2
S & D Oyster Company	**20** B2

DRINKING
Ginger Man	**21** B2
Stoneleigh P	**22** A2

ENTERTAINMENT
American Airlines Center	**23** A3
Gilley's Dallas	**24** C6
Gypsy Tea Room	**25** D4
Morton H Meyerson Symphony Center	**26** B3

SHOPPING
Dallas Farmer Market	**27** D5
Neiman Marcus	**28** C4

TRANSPORT
Akard Station	**29** B4
Greyhound Bus Terminal	**30** B5
Union Station	**31** A5

DALLAS IN...

Two Days
Start your day downtown at Dealey Plaza and the **JFK sites** (below), stopping for lunch nearby in the West End. The afternoon could be spent at the **Nasher Sculpture Center** (below) and other museums of the **Arts District** (below), or shopping at the original **Neiman Marcus** (p752). For dinner, catch a McKinney Ave trolley going to uptown and restaurants and bars like **La Duni Latin Café** (p751) and **Ginger Man** (p752).

Day two, skip over to **Fort Worth** (p754) or shop some more: at **Highland Park Village** (p753), the **Galleria** (p753) or **NorthPark Center** (p753). That night, put on your Versace to see-and-be-seen at the Dragonfly restaurant of the **Hotel ZaZa** (p751).

MEDIA
88.1 KNTU University of North Texas jazz station.
90.1 KERA NPR and other public broadcasting.
102.1 The Edge A popular alt-rock station.
D Magazine (www.dmagazine.com) Monthly glossy with dining and events.
Dallas Morning News (www.dallasnews.com, www.guidelive.com) The city's daily; Guide Live is its Friday dining and entertainment supplement.
Dallas Observer (www.dallasobserver.com) Free alternative weekly; entertainment listings.

MEDICAL SERVICES
Parkland Memorial Hospital (☎ 214-590-8000; 5201 Harry Hines Blvd) Near Market/Medical Center Station.
Walgreens Pharmacy (☎ 214-922-9233; 3418 McKinney Ave; ⏰ 24hr)

MONEY
Foreign currency exchange is available at the airport.
Bank of America (☎ 214-508-6881; 1401 Elm St)

POST
Post office (☎ 214-468-8270; 400 N Ervay St)

TOURIST INFORMATION
Dallas CVB Visitor Center (☎ 214-571-1300; www.visitdallas.com; 100 S Houston St; ⏰ 8am-5pm Mon-Fri, 9am-5pm Sat & Sun) Occupies the Old Red Courthouse.

Sights
All things JFK-related are downtown, close to the visitor center and the West End tourist district. The city's art museums and symphony center are in the Arts District, on downtown's north edge. Fair Park, east off I-30, has a big collection of museums.

JFK SITES
President John F Kennedy's assassination here on November 22, 1963, changed the city, the country and, some even say, the world. From Dealey Plaza, walk along Elm St beside the infamous grassy knoll and look for the white 'X' in the road that marks the exact spot where he was shot. Turn around and look up at the top floor of the Texas School Book Depository from where Lee Harvey Oswald supposedly pulled the trigger. The fascinating and highly audio-visual **Sixth Floor Museum** (☎ 214-747-6660; www.jfk.org; Book Depository, 411 Elm St; adult/child under 6 $13/3; ⏰ 9am-6pm) explains in minute-by-minute detail what happened. A selection of films and audio clips add depth to the experience and all the conspiracy theories are succinctly summarized.

Do you want more proof that Oswald didn't act alone? The **Conspiracy Museum** (☎ 214-741-3040; 110 S Market St; adult/child $9/3; ⏰ 10am-6pm) looks a bit like a student's history fair project, but raises enough questions to make you think. Across N Market St is the **Kennedy Memorial**, a simple but profound sculpture by the architect Phillip Johnson.

ARTS DISTRICT
Modern installations are both inside and out at the **Nasher Sculpture Center** (☎ 214-242-5100; www.nashersculpturecenter.org; 2001 Flora St; adult/child $12/free; ⏰ 10am-6pm Tue-Sun, to 9pm Thu). The **Dallas Museum of Art** (☎ 214-922-1200; www.dallasmuseumofart.org; 1717 N Harwood St; adult/student $10/5; ⏰ 11am-5pm Tue-Sun, to 9pm Thu) is a high-caliber world tour of decorative and fine art befitting a big city.

Explore the watery Mayan world of a Central American jungle at the **Dallas World Aquarium** (☎ 214-720-2224; 1801 N Griffin St; adult/child $16/9; ⏰ 10am-5pm). There's also a rainforest exhibit with an unusual collection of underwater critters.

TEXAS

FAIR PARK

Created especially for the 1936 Texas Centennial Exposition, **Fair Park** (☎ 214-421-9600; www.fairpark.org; 1300 Cullum Blvd; adult/child passport $24/14) is chock-full of concrete art-deco architecture and museums. The park is also home to Cotton Bowl stadium and the Texas State Fair. Year-round sights include the **Dallas Museum of Natural History** (☎ 214-421-3466; ☷ 10am-5pm Mon-Sat, noon-5pm Sun), the **Woman's Museum** (☎ 214-915-0860; ☷ noon-5pm Tue-Sun) and **Science Place** (☎ 214-428-5555; ☷ 9:30am-4:30pm Tue-Fri, 9:30am-5:30pm Sat, 11:30am-5:30pm Sun). Be warned that Fair Park is not in the best neighborhood: it's perfectly safe during the day, but not as frequented as it otherwise might be. From downtown, it's easiest to take Commerce St east to 2nd Ave south; cross under I-30 and you'll run into the park.

AROUND TOWN

Though it hasn't been on for ages, people fondly recall the TV drama *Dallas* and remember **Southfork Ranch** (☎ 972-442-7800; www.southfork.com; 3700 Hogge Rd/FM 2551; adult/child 4-12 $9/6.50; ☷ 9am-5pm), the filming location. It's about 30 miles northeast of downtown; take I-75 north to Parker Rd, turn west and follow signs.

Tours

Hit Dallas' highlights with a four-hour tour by **All in One Tour Services** (☎ 214-698-0332; www.allinonetourservices.com; tours $53). The dramatic and committed **John Nagle** (☎ 214-674-6295; www.jfktours.com; tours $25; ☷ Sat & Sun) guides 1¼-hour walking tours of JFK assassination sites; a 22-page guide booklet is included (otherwise, it's $12.95 from the Conspiracy Museum).

Festivals & Events

The 52ft Big Tex statue towers over Fair Park (left) from late September through October during the **State Fair of Texas** (☎ 214-565-9931; www.bigtex.com). Come ride the tallest Ferris wheel in North America, eat corn dogs and fried Milky Ways, and browse among the prize-winning cows, sheep and quilts. Fair Park holds many other events during the year, including antique expositions, car shows and rodeos.

Sleeping

The best areas to stay in are uptown and downtown, but these are also among the most expensive. The further you get from the center, the cheaper the highway chain motels get.

BUDGET

Hearthside Suites (☎ 214-904-9666; www.hearthside.com; 10326 Finnell St, off I-35 E; r $35-69; ☷) All the rooms at this extended-stay hotel have a full-size fridge, microwave and stovetop. It's northwest of Dallas Love Field airport.

Super 8 Dallas Market Center (☎ 214-631-6633; www.super8.com; 9229 Hwy 183; r $39-59; ☷ ☷) Plain-Jane motel with laundry and business and fitness centers. A high-speed Internet room costs $5 extra. The Trinity Railway Express Market Center stop is a mile away.

MIDRANGE

Magnolia (☎ 214-915-6500; www.magnoliahotels.com; 1401 Commerce St; r $99-139; ☷ ☷) Upholstered headboards and blond-wood accents make the Magnolia chic; the complimentary cocktail hour and late-night milk-and-cookies make it loveable. In the evening you might soak in the Jacuzzi after a workout, read in

---

GAY & LESBIAN DALLAS

The Dallas Gay & Lesbian Alliance's **Resource Center of Dallas** (☎ 214-528-9254; www.resourcecenterdallas.org) can refer you to points of interest and gay-owned businesses in town. The **Dallas Voice** (www.dallasvoice.com) newspaper is the town's gay and lesbian advocate.

Dallas' gay and lesbian scene is centered on upper Cedar Springs Rd, near uptown; in fact, Caven Enterprises runs several nightclubs in one block (the Halloween street party is a must-attend).

Station 4 (☎ 214-559-0650; 3911 Cedar Springs Rd; www.caven.com) A Star Trek–inspired dance club, attracts a mixed gay-straight crowd.

JR's (☎ 214-528-1004; www.caven.com; 3923 Cedar Springs Rd; ☷ 11am-2am) For a guys night out, this is a fun place with darts and pool, food and wireless access.

Sue Ellen's (☎ 214-559-0650; www.caven.com; 3903 Cedar Springs Rd) Dallas' biggest lesbian bar.

THE AUTHOR'S CHOICE

Dream of being royalty? Step into the life of ease at the **Mansion on Turtle Creek** (☎ 214-559-2100; www.rosewoodhotels.com; 2821 Turtle Creek Blvd; r $200-490; P ⬛ 🐾). For every two guests there's one staff member attending. Classical music and complimentary beverages welcome you to the understated opulence of the 143-room hotel on 4.5 landscaped acres. Fresh flowers sit atop hand-carved European furniture in guest rooms. The original, marble-clad Italianate villa, built by Sheppard King in 1925, now serves as the Mansion on Turtle Creek Restaurant. Entrées show a strong Southern influence (such as baked lobster with Creole mustard) and the dinner tasting menu ($90) is a way to sample excellence. The mansion is full of stories – a wheelchair-size elevator next to the dining room, for example, was put in for wheelchair-bound Franklin D Roosevelt, the 32nd president.

---

the library or play pool in the club room. Parking $18.

Stoneleigh Hotel (☎ 214-871-7111; www.stoneleigh hotel.com; 2927 Maple Ave; r $89-169; P) A posh address at less-than-uptown prices (with a great bar across the street). Russet and gold fabrics warm the traditional furnishings at this 1923 hotel. Parking $6 to $12.

Hotel Lawrence (☎ 214-761-9090; www.hotellaw rencedallas.com; 302 S Houston St; r $125-170; P ⬛) This renovated downtown hotel (read small rooms) has neoclassical earth-tone designs and a restaurant. Last-minute online specials can be as little as $69. Parking $5 to $15.

TOP END

Hotel Za Za (☎ 800-597-8399; www.hotelzaza.com; 2332 Leonard St; r $195-290; P 🐾) Colorful, exotic silks and whimsical shapes characterize guest rooms, and the hip, themed suites – the Shag-a-delic, the Zen, the Medusa – are pure fun ($450 to $995). Be seen lounging poolside or eating at the Dragonfly restaurant, and you're in. Parking $18.

Eating

The young and beautiful in Dallas eat out often, so there are innumerable restaurants to feed them, especially in uptown. Greenville Ave, north of Ross Ave, also has a concentration of eateries as does Deep Ellum, known more for it's nightlife. At least the chain restaurants have an interesting setting in the downtown warehouse district, the **West End** (www.dallaswestend.org; N Market St & Ross Ave).

UPTOWN & KNOX-HENDERSON

In 2004, Dallas banned indoor smoking at restaurants and their attached bars.

Breadwinners Café & Bakery (☎ 214-754-4940; 3301 McKinney Ave; breakfast $6-9; sandwiches $8-11, din-

ner mains $17-26; ☽ breakfast & lunch daily, dinner Tue-Sun) Whether you have the tenderloin eggs Benedict for brunch, the veggie melt for lunch or the nut-crusted fish for dinner, be sure to save room for cookies.

La Duni Latin Café (☎ 214-520-7300; 4620 McKinney Ave; mains $10-18; ☽ lunch & dinner Tue-Sun, brunch Sat & Sun) Fried plantains topped with black beans and beef are just the beginning. All the dishes at this upmarket, modern eatery have a Spanish accent, if not a specific country of origin.

S&D Oyster Company (☎ 214-880-0111; 2701 McKinney Ave; mains $11-15; ☽ 11am-10pm) Barebones decor here means the focus is on really good seafood. Try the BBQ shrimp – if it doesn't run out before you get there.

Among the really fabulous (and fabulously priced) options, Kent Rathburn's **Abacus** (☎ 214-559-3111; www.abacus-restaurant.com; 4511 McKinney Ave; mains $29-39; ☽ dinner Mon-Sat) has settled into a comfortable rhythm, and the NY concept restaurant, **Nobu** (☎ 214-252-7000; www.noburestaurant.com; 400 Crescent Ct; mains $30-50; ☽ lunch & dinner) is the new kid on the block.

GREENVILLE AVE

Grape (☎ 214-828-1981; 2802 Greenville Ave; mains $15-25; ☽ lunch & dinner) Small room, red-check tablecloths, grapevine lights…romance is in the air. Many of the by-the-glass wine selections are chosen to pair with the changing daily specials on the chalkboard menu.

Also on Greenville:

Cafe Izmir (☎ 214-826-7788; 3711 Greenville Ave; mains $3-8; ☽ dinner) Middle Eastern tapas.

Central Market (☎ 214-234-7000; Greenville Ave & Lovers Ln; mains $3-8; ☽ 8am-10pm) Upscale grocery store with meals to go.

TEXAS

DEEP ELLUM

Angry Dog (☎ 214-741-4406; 2726 Commerce St; mains $5-9; ☺ 11am-midnight Sun-Thu, 11am-2am Fri & Sat) Of the places to eat, drink and listen in Deep Ellum, Angry Dog has the unbeatable burgers.

Drinking

The restaurant indoor smoking ban doesn't affect stand-alone bars.

Ginger Man (☎ 214-754-8771; www.gingermanpub .com; 2718 Boll St; ☺ 11am-2am Wed-Fri, 1pm-2am Sat-Tue) This pub in a spice-color house has a great, shady yard full of picnic tables out back and live music Saturday nights.

Stoneleigh P (☎ 214-871-2346; 2926 Maple Ave; ☺ 11am-2am) Plunk your quarter in the jukebox at this neighborhood bar and belly up to a former soda fountain.

Old Monk (☎ 214-821-1880; 2847 N Henderson Ave; ☺ 4pm-2am Mon-Fri, noon-2am Sat & Sun) Irish, German and Belgian brews on tap are served in a suitably dank, dark, smoky setting. To get here, take US 75 two miles north of uptown and exit on Henderson going south.

Entertainment

Check the **Dallas Observer** (www.dallasobserver .com) or **Guide Live** (www.guidelive.com) in Friday's *Dallas Morning News* for complete entertainment listings. A rise in alleged gang activity keeps a few people away, but **Deep Ellum** (www.deepellumtx.com; around Commerce St, east of I-75) is still live-music central.

LIVE MUSIC & NIGHTCLUBS

Gilley's Dallas (☎ 214-421-2021; www.gilleysdallas .com; 1135 S Lamar St; ☺ 6pm-2am Thu-Tue) Boot-scoot around 10,000 sq ft of dance floor or ride the mechanical bull from the movie *Urban Cowboy* – Gilley's is pure country. Live music Friday and Saturday.

In Deep Ellum, the beloved concert venue **Gypsy Tea Room** (☎ 214-744-9779; www .gypsytearoom.com; 2548 Elm St) hosts both big names and local punk and rock bands. **Double Wide** (☎ 214-887-6510; www.double-wide.com; 3510 Commerce St) is all redneck, trailer-livin' kitsch – from the wood-veneer paneling to the hooked-rug art. There's alt-rock live on weekends, DJs other nights.

On lower Greenville Ave, the **Whisky Bar** (☎ 214-828-0188; www.whisky-bar.com; 1930 Greenville Ave) has a rooftop patio, a DJ Friday and Sat-

urday, and live acoustic music Wednesday; **Muddy Waters** (☎ 214-823-1518; 1518 Greenville Ave) books blues, rockabilly and more.

SPORTS

Mesquite Rodeo (☎ 972-222-2855; www.mesquitero deo.com; 1818 Rodeo Dr; ☺ 8pm Fri & Sat Apr-Sep) Bronc-bustin', bull-ridin' cowboys square off at a weekend rodeo broadcast nationwide. Take I-30 15 miles east to Hwy 80.

Dallas Cowboys (☎ 972-579-5000; www.dallascow boys.com) 'America's Team' plays NFL football at Texas Stadium off Hwy 183 in Irving.

Dallas Stars (☎ 214-467-8277; www.dallasstars.com) This NHL hockey team plays at the American Airlines Center, between the Woodall Rodgers Fwy and I-35 E, just north of the West End.

Dallas Mavericks (☎ 972-988-3865; www.dallas mavericks.com) This NBA basketball team also plays at the American Airlines Center.

Texas Rangers (☎ 817-273-5100; www.texasrang ers.com) The Rangers play pro baseball at the Ameriquest Field in Arlington, between Dallas and Fort Worth.

Dallas Burn (☎ 214-979-0303; www.dallasburn .com) This team plays pro soccer at the Cotton Bowl in Fair Park (p750).

THEATER & CLASSICAL PERFORMANCES

Lakewood Theater (☎ 214-821-9084; www.lakewood theater.com; 1825 Abrams Parkway, off Greenville Ave) This renovated 1938 art-deco cinema holds film festivals, in addition to staging concerts, musicals and plays.

The **Dallas Symphony Orchestra** (☎ 214-692-0203; www.dallassymphony.com) performs at **Morton H Meyerson Symphony Center** (2301 Flora St) in the Arts District, and the **Dallas Opera** (☎ 214-443-1000; www.dallasopera.org) plays at Music Hall in Fair Park (p750).

Shopping

Dallas is the region's shopping mecca, where you can find pretty much anything you might want to buy and malls are as common as flies.

Neiman Marcus (☎ 214-741-6911, 800-937-9146; 1 Marcus Sq, on Ervay St btwn Main & Commerce Sts) A downtown landmark, this is the original Neiman Marcus store.

West Village (www.westvil.com; 3699 McKinney Ave at Lemmon) In the heart of uptown, West Village has trendy stores, a wine bar and an Asian bistro arranged streetside.

Highland Park Village (www.hpvillage.com; cnr Mockingbird Lane & Preston Rd) Shop at Kate Spade, Prada, Jimmy Choo and other high-end boutique stores.

Galleria (☎ 972-702-7100; www.galleriadallas .com; 13355 Noel Rd at I-635 & Dallas North Tollway) The daddy of all area malls; also has an ice rink and hotels.

NorthPark Center (☎ 214-361-6345; www.north parkcenter.com; 1030 Northpark Center, Northwest Hwy at Central Expressway) Has expansion plans to double in size (to more than 200 stores) by the end of 2006.

Dallas Farmers Market (☎ 214-670-5880; www .dallasfarmersmarket.org; cnr Marilla Blvd & S Harwood St; ☼ 7am-6pm) Buy produce directly from the growers, or shop for flowers and antiques at this large market.

Getting There & Away
AIR
American Airlines' homeport is **Dallas–Fort Worth International Airport** (DFW; ☎ 972-574-4420; www.dfwairport.com), 16 miles northwest of the city via I-35 E. Great Britain and Mexico are among the nonstop international destinations. Southwest Airlines uses smaller, more convenient **Dallas Love Field** (DAL; ☎ 214-670-6073; www.dallas-lovefield.com), just northwest of downtown (take Inwood Rd northeast from Harry Hines Blvd and turn left on Cedar Springs).

BUS
Greyhound buses make runs all over the country from the **Greyhound Bus Terminal** (☎ 214-655-7085; www.greyhound.com; 205 S Lamar St). Direct Greyhound buses connect Dallas with cities such as Austin ($27, 3½ hours) and Houston ($32, five hours).

CAR & MOTORCYCLE
Every major rental car company has an office at DFW, and many are at Love Field too.

TRAIN
Amtrak's San Antonio–Chicago *Texas Eagle* stops at downtown's **Union Station** (☎ 214-653-1101; www.amtrak.com; 401 S Houston St).

Getting Around
TO/FROM THE AIRPORT
Catch the Monday–Saturday Trinity Railway Express train to downtown's Union Station ($2.25). The Center Port/DFW Airport stop is actually in a parking lot; shuttle buses take you to the terminals. On weekdays, express bus 202 ($2.25) runs downtown from DFW and bus 39 ($1.25) heads downtown from Love Field.

It's easier to take a shuttle, especially on Sunday when there's no train service. **Yellow Checker Shuttle** (☎ 817-267-5150; www.yel lowcheckershuttle.com) and **SuperShuttle** (☎ 817-329-2000; www.supershuttle.com) run shuttles from DFW to downtown for around $16, and from Love Field for the same price. A taxi between DFW and central Dallas will cost $40 to $50.

BUS & LIGHT-RAIL
Dallas Area Rapid Transit (DART; ☎ 214-979-1111; www.dart.org) operates buses and an extensive light-rail system that connects Union Station and other stops downtown with outlying areas (single trip $2.25, day pass $4.50). Day passes are available from the station store at **Akard** (1401 Pacific Ave; ☼ 7:30am-5:30pm Mon-Fri); maps are also online. Travel uptown from down on the free McKinney Ave trolley, which runs daily between Ross Ave and St Paul St, near the Dallas Museum of Art, and McKinney Ave and Hall St.

CAR & MOTORCYCLE
If you do rent a car, be warned that rush-hour freeway traffic is *bad* and there's little free parking downtown; parking garages cost from $10 per day.

TAXI
Yellow Cab (☎ 214-426-6262) and **Checker Cab** (☎ 972-222-2000) have an initial $2 for each person that gets into the cab and 40¢ every quarter mile after that.

AROUND DALLAS
East Texas is full of small towns still organized around the courthouse square, where spring and fall festivals are as common as breathing. The lovely **rose festival** (www.texas rosefestival.com) in **Tyler** (www.tylertx.com; I-20 & US 69), which is located 100 miles east of Dallas, takes place in every year October, but the **rose museum** (☎ 903-597-3130; 420 Rose Park Dr; adult/child $3.50/1.50; ☼ 9:30am-4:30pm Mon-Fri, 10am-4:30pm Sat, 1:30-4:30pm Sun, closed Mon Nov-Feb) is open year-round – 14 acres of the beauties bloom in the municipal garden starting in April.

TEXAS

FORT WORTH

It's strange that three of the best art museums in the state are in a city nicknamed 'Cowtown' because of its historic stockyards. Never mind, that's one of the most endearing things about Fort Worth: there's a lot to do, but not a lot of pretense. You can see a mini cattle drive in the morning, spend the afternoon browsing sleek, minimalist art, and in the evening head downtown to eat, drink and make merry at Sundance Sq. Fort Worth has the feeling of a place that's alive and growing. With a population of 500,000, the town is far more user-friendly than Dallas, not to mention greener and cleaner. Why go next door at all?

Fort Worth became famous during the great open-range cattle drives of the late 19th century. More than 10 million head of cattle were trooped through the city on the Chisholm Trail, which ran north from Texas to Kansas. The late 19th and early 20th centuries saw rampant lawlessness: Butch Cassidy and the Sundance Kid hid out in town, as did Great Depression–era holdup artists Bonnie Parker and Clyde Barrow. The cattle business remained king here throughout the 1920s, even as major finds in nearby oil fields turned the city into an important petroleum-industry operations center. Amon Carter, oilman and early publisher of the *Star-Telegram*, put the city on the arts map when his will provided the resources for the Amon Carter museum (right) in what is today the Cultural District.

Orientation

Fort Worth is fairly compact and wonderfully easy to get around; I-30 runs south of downtown and I-35 W to the east. Downtown, the Cultural District and the Stockyards form a lopsided triangle. North Main St runs between downtown and the Stockyards, 7th St E Ave connects downtown to the Cultural District, and University Dr and Northside Dr connect the Cultural District to North Main St near the Stockyards.

Information

Central Library (☎ 817-871-7701; 500 W 3rd St; ♥ 9am-9pm Mon-Thu, 10am-8pm Sat, noon-5pm Sun) Internet access.

Fort Worth Convention & Visitors Bureau (www .fortworth.com) Downtown (☎ 817-336-8791; 415 Throckmorton St; ♥ 8:30am-5pm Mon-Fri, 10am-4pm Sat) Cultural District (☎ 817-882-8588; 3401 W Lancaster Ave; ♥ 10am-5pm Mon-Sat) Stockyards (☎ 817-624-4741; 130 E Exchange Ave; ♥ 9am-6pm Mon-Fri, 9am-6pm Sat, noon-5pm Sun) Produces spiffy 3-D maps.

Sights & Activities

The eminently walkable downtown, with Sundance Sq at its heart, is full of restaurants and bars, theaters and shops. Green and leafy, the Cultural District, south of 7th St E, forms a parklike setting for five major museums and the Will Rogers Memorial Center. North of downtown, up N Main St, cowboy-wear stores, museums and a rodeo arena occupy Old West–era buildings in the Stockyards. I-35 W runs north–south to the east of downtown (really), I-30 runs east–west and forms the southern boundary of downtown.

CULTURAL DISTRICT

Within easy walking distance are three world-class museums at the heart of the **Cultural District** (www.fwculture.com). You round a corner from womblike, concrete galleries to be confronted by the city skyline and outdoors through a wall of glass at the **Modern Art Museum of Fort Worth** (☎ 817-738-9215; www.themodern .org; 3200 Darnell St; adult/child $6/free; ♥ 10am-5pm Tue-Thu & Sat, 10am-8pm Fri, 11am-5pm Sun). Noteworthy works in the collection include paintings and sculpture by Picasso and Mark Rothko.

The **Amon Carter Museum** (☎ 817-738-1933; www.cartermuseum.org; 3501 Camp Bowie Blvd; admission free; ♥ 10am-5pm Mon-Wed & Fri, 10am-8pm, Sun noon-5pm) displays pre-1945 American painting, including one of the country's best compilations of work by Western artists Frederic Remington and Charles M Russell. There's also an extensive photography collection. European, pre-Colombian and other international art is the focus of the **Kimbell Art Museum** (☎ 817-332-8451; www.kimbell art.org; 3333 Camp Bowie Blvd; admission free; ♥ 10am-5pm Tue-Thu & Sat, noon-8pm Fri, noon-5pm Sun), across the street to the east.

Yee-ha! The **National Cowgirl Museum** (☎ 817-336-3375; www.cowgirl.net; 1721 Gendy St; adult/child $6/4; ♥ 10am-5pm Mon-Sat, noon-5pm Sun) rides high with state-of-the-art exhibits. Ride a slow-mo electronic bucking bronc and video magic makes it look like you're in a high-action Old West rodeo. Four small

---

COWBOY CENTRAL

One of the figures often romanticized in literary or cinematic history is the cowboy, who has come to symbolize the freedom of the plains and the industrious and untamable nature of the American people themselves. After the Civil War, westward expansion and the capture of new lands from the Indians made cattle drives common. Cowboys would herd together thousands of cattle to be driven north. Today you can experience the sights – and the smell – of a cattle auction at the **Western Stockyards** (p758) in Amarillo. The cowboy culture lives on in rodeos around Texas where guys and gals show off their riding (and roping) skills. One of the biggest is the February **Houston Livestock Show & Rodeo** (p739), but contests take place regularly in the Fort Worth **Stockyards** (below) and at the **Mesquite Rodeo** (p752) near Dallas. In Bandera, you can not only attend a rodeo at **Twin Elm Ranch** (p729), you can book a stay at one of the many dude ranches in town and ride yourself. Want a kinder, gentler Old West? Check into the historic **Gage Hotel** (p766) in the Big Bend area for pampering rustic style.

---

theaters on-site focus on women – one video is about Jessie in Pixar's *Toy Story* – but the museum's overall effect is more rugged frontiers-person than anything 'girly.' A **Cattle Raisers Museum** is being constructed across the street.

The **Museum of Science & History** (☎ 817-255-9300; www.fwmuseum.org; 1501 Montgomery St; combo ticket adult/child $13/11; ◷ 9am-5:30pm Mon-Thu, 9am-8pm Fri & Sat, 11:30am-5:30pm Sun) brims with fossils, dinosaurs and kid-friendly stuff to do. There's also a planetarium and an Omni Imax theater.

STOCKYARDS NATIONAL HISTORIC DISTRICT
Once the livestock industry's trading center, the **Stockyards** (www.fortworthstockyards.org) are now a tourist-oriented district with a few small museums, Western this-and-that shops and restaurants. City-paid cowboys on horseback roam the district, answering tourist questions and posing for photos. Twice a day, at 10am and 4pm, they drive a small herd of Texas longhorns (about 16 to 20) down the block in front of the visitor center. It's a *gol-dang* Kodak moment, pardner. **Cowtown Coliseum** (☎ 817-625-1025; www.stockyardsrodeo.com; 121 E Exchange Ave; adult/child rodeo $9/5.50; wild west show $8/4.50) hosts rodeos Friday and Saturday nights at 8pm year round; June to August, Pawnee Bill's Wild West Show is at 2:30pm and 4:30pm Saturday and Sunday.

The former sheep and hog pens of **Stockyards Station** (140 E Exchange Ave; www.stockyardsstation.com) now house a mall of sorts and the depot of the **Grapevine Vintage Railroad** (☎ 817-625-7245; www.tarantulatrain.com). The 3pm daily

Trinity River Run (adult/child $10/6) is a one-hour trek along the Chilsom Trail at the edge of downtown. Park free at the lot on the easternmost end of Exchange Ave.

DOWNTOWN
Colorful architecture, a host of bars, restaurants and hotels, a few art galleries, and a vibrant theater scene make the 14-block **Sundance Square** (www.sundancesquare.com; near Main & 3rd Sts) the best downtown core in Texas. The area is more than safe, it's downright friendly day or night; parking garages are free after 5pm and on weekends.

The small **Sid Richardson Collection of Western Art** (☎ 817-332-6554; www.sidrmuseum.org; 309 Main St) museum is expected to reopen after expansion in late 2006. Two miles south of downtown on Main St, taste the three microbrews (pale lager, red and black lager) to your heart's content after the short tour and beer tasting at **Rahr & Sons Brewing Co** (☎ 817-810-9266; 701 Galveston Ave, at S Main St; ◷ tours 1-3pm Sat).

AROUND TOWN
Twenty miles north of downtown, on I-35 W, Nascar races at **Texas Motor Speedway** (☎ 817-215-8565; www.texasmotorspeedway.com; Hwy 114 & I-35; tours adult/child $8/6; ◷ 9am-5pm Mon-Fri, 10am-5pm Sat, 10am-5pm Sun). You can ride (at 150-plus mph) along four laps for $105 or drive 10 laps for $345 in a Nascar stock car, with **Team Texas** (☎ 940-648-1043; www.teamtexas.com).

Festivals & Events
The town's biggest event is the **Fort Worth Stock Show & Rodeo** (☎ 817-877-2400; www.fwstockshow rodeo.com; grounds adult/child $8/6), held late January

TEXAS

or early February each year at **Will Rogers Coliseum** (1 Amon Carter Sq) in the Cultural District.

Sleeping

Revelers and passing freight trains can make a night in the Stockyards a bit noisy.

BUDGET

Ramada Inn Midtown (☎ 817-336-9311; www.ramada.com; 1401 S University Dr, off I-30; r $42-65; P 😤) The location, 2 miles south of Cultural District museums, makes this prime territory. Rooms were overhauled in 2005 and a restaurant is in the works.

MIDRANGE

Residence Inn (☎ 817-885-8250; www.residenceinn.com; 2500 Museum Way, off W 7th St; ste $109-169; P 🖳 😤) Even the smallest rooms have full kitchens and high-speed Internet. This Marriott property opened midway between downtown and the Cultural District in spring 2005.

Park Central Hotel (☎ 817-336-2011; www.parkcentralhotel.com; 1010 Houston St; r $79-99; P 😤) Standard rooms are just that, but double suites ($149) are slightly larger, with kitchenettes. Walking distance to Sundance Sq.

In the Stockyards, the brand-spankin' new **Amerisuites Stockyards** (☎ 817-626-6000; www.amerisuites.com; 132 E Exchange Ave; r $119-149; P 🖳) has kitchenettes and wi-fi; the 1907 **Stockyards Hotel** (☎ 817-625-6427; www.stockyardshotel.com; 109 E Exchange Place; r $140-150) has Western theme rooms (but no nonsmoking).

TOP END

Ashton Hotel (☎ 866-327-4866; www.theashtonhotel.com; 610 Main St; r $195-290; P 🚫) An 1890 and a 1915 building have been seamlessly melded into a 39-room boutique hotel. The retention of details like elaborate moldings and built-in bookshelves creates an expensive residential feel. Book ahead for dinner, served Wednesday through Saturday.

Eating

Prices in the Stockyards, especially for steak, can be inflated. Downtown has the largest concentration of eateries; there's not much in the Cultural District proper.

DOWNTOWN

Reata (☎ 817-336-1009; 310 Houston St; mains $15-36; 😋 lunch & dinner) Southwest specialties and rib-eyes crowd the menu at this downtown fave. The rooftop patio here is a great place to have drinks.

Zoë Italian (☎ 817-870-8885; 405 Throckmorton St; pizzas $8-12, pastas $5-12; 😋 lunch Mon-Fri, dinner Mon-Sat) The Italian menu is classic, but the neon light hangings and pale-wood tables are all modern hipness. Antipastos come in small and large sizes.

Del Frisco's Double Eagle Steak House (☎ 817-877-3999; 812 Main St; mains $25-40; 😋 lunch & dinner) The same dark wood with white tablecloths decorate this, like all clubby big-steak places. Unlike the others, Del Frisco's also serves smaller meat cuts, like a 6oz fillet.

STOCKYARDS

Esperanza's Panaderia y Café (JoT's Bakery; ☎ 817-626-4356; 2122 N Main St; breakfast $5-7, mains $7-15; 😋 6am-7pm) Breakfasts here are real Mexican – pulled chicken tops the breakfast *migas* (eggs scrambled with tortilla strips) or you could have your eggs topped with *machacado* (spiced dried beef).

AROUND TOWN

North of the Cultural District, **Angelo's Barbecue** (☎ 817-332-0357; 2533 White Settlement Rd; plates $7-12; 😋 10am-10pm Mon-Sat) has been serving since 1958; **Celebrity Bakery & Café** (☎ 817-332-3242; 1612 S University Dr; salads & sandwiches $6-9; 😋 8am-6:30pm Mon-Sat, 11am-5pm Sun) is in a strip mall to the south of the museums.

Drinking

All the restaurants around downtown's Sundance Sq have bars, and most of the bars have food.

THE AUTHOR'S CHOICE

Joe T Garcia's (☎ 817-626-4356; 2201 N Commerce St; lunch specials $6-12; 😋 lunch & dinner Mon-Thu, 11am-11pm Fri & Sat, 10am-10pm Sun) A city-block-long wall encloses the dining patio, where torch ginger and hibiscus grow, and colorful Mexican tiles ring bubbling fountains. Lunch is à la carte, but for dinner you choose between chicken or beef enchiladas ($11) or fajitas ($12) and they come with guacamole and chips, cheese nachos, two beef tacos and two cheese enchiladas. The great food is no secret; a line (no reservations taken) often stretches around the block.

TEXAS

Flying Saucer Emporium (☎ 817-336-7470; 111 E 4th St; ☺ 11am-1am Mon-Wed, 11am-2am Thu-Sat, noon-midnight Sun) Barmaids and barmen pull pints from 77 taps at this vast drinkery.

Entertainment

Fort Worth Weekly (www.fwweekly.com) lists entertainment goings-on – there's a surprising amount happening for a town this size.

NIGHTCLUBS & LIVE MUSIC

Billy Bob's Texas (☎ 817-624-7117; www.billybobstexas .com; 2520 Rodeo Plaza, Stockyards; ☺ 11am-2am Mon-Sat, noon-2am Sun) Top country-and-western stars, house bands and DJs play on two stages at Texas' largest honky-tonk in the Stockyards. No mechanical bull is good enough here – on Friday and Saturday night, a live bull-riding competition takes place at an indoor arena. Pool tables and games help make this a family place; under-18s are welcome with a parent.

8.0 Restaurant & Bar (☎ 817-336-0880; 111 E 3rd St, Sundance Sq) From spring through fall, the massive outdoor red-brick patio has live music almost nightly. It's like a free concert for all downtown.

White Elephant Saloon (☎ 817-624-1887; www .whiteelephantsaloon.com; 106 E Exchange Ave) The quintessential Stockyards cowboy bar hosts live country music nightly.

City Streets (☎ 817-335-5400; www.clubcitystreets .com; 425 Commerce St) This multistyle downtown nightclub has techno and hip-hop music, '70s and '80s tunes and a billiards room.

THEATER & CLASSICAL PERFORMANCES

Bass Performance Hall (☎ 817-212-4325; www .basshall.com; 555 Commerce St) Built in the late 1990s on a European opera house model, the glittery, domed Bass hall has several theaters that host everything from Alanis Morissette to the Will Rogers Folleys. The symphony, ballet and opera also make their home here.

Getting There & Around

For more information about airport arrival, see p753.

BUS

Eleven buses a day make the one-hour trip ($8) from the downtown **Greyhound Bus Terminal** (☎ 817-429-3089; www.greyhound.com; 901 Commerce St) to Dallas.

The **Fort Worth Transit Authority** (The T; ☎ 817-215-8600; www.the-t.com) runs bus 1 to the

Stockyards and bus 2 to the Cultural District from the Transfer Center at Jones and 9th Sts. The fare is $1.25 one way.

TRAIN

Texas Eagle stops at the **Amtrak Station** (☎ 817-332-2931; www.amtrak.com; 1501 Jones St) en route to San Antonio or Chicago. Monday through Saturday, **Trinity Railway Express** (TRE; ☎ 817-215-8600; www.trinityrailwayexpress.com; T&P Station, 1600 Throckmorton St) connects downtown Fort Worth with downtown Dallas ($2.25, 1¼ hours).

PANHANDLE PLAINS

The northwest Texas panhandle is a seemingly endless, flat landscape, punctuated only by utility poles and windmills, until a vast canyon materializes almost miragelike to play tricks on the horizon. The canyonlands, formed by eroding caprock (the layer of caliche, marl, chalk and gravel that lies beneath the plains), make for classic Western scenery, which continues once you get into the region's two cities: Amarillo, home to Route 66 and a fast-disappearing Texas of old, and Lubbock, where you'll find all things Buddy Holly.

AMARILLO

Get off the highway and beyond the strip malls to find remnants of the 1950s Amarillo (now population 109,000) that was a happening stop on the fabled Route 66. The town is still a convenient overnight for those driving cross-country. Remember this is cattle country, low and flat; if the wind is blowing just right, you can smell the stockyards.

Orientation & Information

The small downtown is north of I-40 and west of Hwy 87/27, the main north–south road through town. Loop 335 circles the city. Buy Texas souvenirs and get oriented at the **visitor information center** (☎ 806-374-8474; www .visitamarillotx.com; cnr 4th Ave & Buchanan St; ☺ 9am-6pm Mon-Fri, 10am-4pm Sat & Sun). Internet access is free to customers at **Schlotzsky's Deli** (☎ 806-353-7859; 3440 Bell Ave; ☺ 10:30am-9pm, to 10pm Fri & Sat).

Sights & Activities

The old Route 66 in Amarillo is most character-filled along **W 6th Avenue**, also known as the San Jacinto District. Shop-fronts from

TEXAS

ROUTE 66 – TEXAS

The Mother Road scoots across Texas for a mere 178 miles. The Panhandle Plains it crosses are flat and open – the big-sky country of the South – which makes it all the easier to see the wild thunderstorms and occasional tornadoes that affect the area. The state's claim to Route 66 fame is that it contains the road's center point. And though no official record exists, it probably also has the most cars planted in the dirt as art.

Entering Texas from Oklahoma, **McLean** is about 35 miles west of Texola. The **Devil's Rope Museum** (☎ 806-779-2225; www.barbwiremuseum.com; 100 Kingsley St, McLean; admission free; ○ 10am-4pm Tue-Sat) has a Route 66 exhibit and the **Texas Old Route 66 Association**, which posts a map online. There's also a gift shop and a museum cataloging barbed wire and cattle brands on site. Take a detour north on Hwy 207 in Conway (45 miles west of McLean) to spray paint your name on one of the VW Beetles planted nose-down at **Bug Ranch**.

As you approach **Amarillo**, it's hard to miss the giant cowboy waving from the **Big Texan Steak Ranch & Motel** (opposite). The place opened in 1959 on Route 66, but moved to I-40 in 1970. In Amarillo, the interesting stretch of old Route 66 is now **W 6th Avenue**. Go in search of the original partially buried cars at **Cadillac Ranch** (below) on what's now the southern I-40 access road, west of Loop 335. Fifty miles later, when you reach **Adrian**, you're halfway between Chicago and Los Angeles (though nearby Vega contests this).

the 1920s have everything from burgers and beer to books, hardware and antiques for sale. Every Tuesday at 10am, ranchers come to town to bid for steers, bulls and heifers at the **Western Stockyards** (☎ 806-373-7464; 101 & S Manhattan, at E 3rd Ave). Visitors are welcome; there's a little café open daily.

The late local eccentric Stanley Marsh created a sculptural salute to Route 66 at **Cadillac Ranch** (I-40 btwn exits 60 & 62). Park along the south feeder road, a couple of miles west of Loop 335, and walk the well-worn path to the 10 Cadillacs partially buried hood first. If there are spray-paint cans there, feel free to contribute to the art.

Take Rte 1541 the 25 miles from downtown Amarillo to **Palo Duro Canyon State Park** (☎ 806-488-2227; www.paloducanyon.com; Hwy 217; campsites $10-15, cabins $45-95, day pass $3), where a fork of the Red River carved its way through multicolor caprock to create the second largest canyon in the US. A good paved road leads down into the canyon and around a scenic 16-mile loop with hiking, camping and **horseback riding** (☎ 806-488-2821; $35 per hr) – reservations are required. Be warned – it's dang hot in summer. Canyon, 12 miles west of Palo Duro on Hwy 217, is home to the superb **Panhandle Plains Historical Museum** (☎ 806-651-2244; www.panhandleplains.org; 2401 4th Ave; adult/child $4/3; ○ 9am-5pm Mon-Sat, to 6pm Jun-Aug, 1-6pm Sun). Realistic exhibits explore the petroleum industry, pioneer life and the cultural history of the southern Great Plains.

Sleeping & Eating

Amarillo has every chain hotel and restaurant you can think of, and then some, along I-40 (those west of town are newer).

La Casita del Sol (☎ 806-342-3444; www.lacasitadelsol.com; 1607 S Harrison; r $105, ste $135; P ⊠) Bonnie Rodriguez has done an amazing job bringing a faded 1926 Spanish colonial home back to life as a B&B with whimsical faux painting and local art. The walled courtyard greenery shows off her talents as a gardener too.

Fiesta Motel (☎ 806-374-5599; 4104 I-40 E; r $26-35; P) The rooms are small and old-fashioned (think wagon-wheel wallpaper), but the owner here obviously cares about his clientele: 'No pets or prostitutes' allowed (the sign says so).

Golden Light Café (☎ 806-374-0097; 2908 W 6th Ave; mains $4-7; ○ 11am-10pm Mon-Wed, 11am-11pm Thu-Sat) In the San Jacinto District, this tiny greasy spoon has been serving burgers, home-cut fries and cold beer to crowds on Route 66 since 1956.

There are a whole bunch of BBQ places in town; of them, **Dyer's Bar-B-Que** (☎ 806-358-7104; 1619 Kentucky E526; mains $6-10; ○ 11am-10pm) has the best food, though it's not much on atmosphere.

Drinking & Entertainment

The **Amarillo Globe-News** (www.getout.amarillo.com) publishes a *Get Out* entertainment section on Friday, but W 6th Ave is where to go for an evening of imbibing.

Golden Light Cantina (☎ 806-374-0097; www .goldenlightcafe.com; 2908 W 6th Ave; ☺ closed Sun & Mon) This bar, next door to the Golden Light Café, has live music on Friday and Saturday.

Blue Gator Bar & Grill (☎ 806-372-7750; 2903 W 6th Ave; ☺ closed Sun & Mon) You can listen to live rock and blues here. Draft beer is $1.50 every day.

Globe-News Center for the Performing Arts (www.globenewscenter.org; cnr 5th Ave & Buchanan St) This modern, wave-shaped center, home for the city's symphony and opera, is scheduled to open in early 2006.

Getting There & Away

Coaches leave from the **Greyhound Bus Terminal** (☎ 806-374-5371; www.greyhound.com; 700 S Tyler St) for Lubbock ($26, 2½ hours). Southwest and Continental Airlines fly into Amarillo International Airport, located on the east edge of town north of I-40 via exit 76.

LUBBOCK

On the high plains, Lubbock sits between a few cotton farms, some ranches, a handful of vineyards (you heard right) and a whole lotta nothin'. Texas Tech University is the lifeblood of the town and some visitors come to pay homage to rock-and-roll's hero, Buddy Holly. Truth is, maybe Mac Davis had it right when he sang 'Happiness is Lubbock in my rearview mirror...'

THE AUTHOR'S CHOICE

Big Texan Steak Ranch & Motel (☎ 800-657-7177; www.bigtexan.com; 7700 I-40 E, exit 74; breakfasts $6-17, lunch specials $9, mains $13-25, s $45, d $60-65; P ☺) Stretch Cadillac limos with steer-horn hood ornaments wait out front, marquee lights blink above, a shooting arcade pings inside, and cowboy troubadours serenade diners: this former Route 66 roadside attraction is so cheesy you gotta love (or hate) it. Billboards advertising the free 72-oz steak start back in Oklahoma (if you can't eat it and all the sides in an hour, it costs $50). The steaks here are surprisingly tasty and quite reasonable. The mid-price motel has an over-the-top Old West theme with a Texas-shape swimming pool. You can even board your horse at the Horse Hotel. Looking for roadside kitsch? You've found it.

Information

The **Lubbock Convention & Visitor's Bureau** (☎ 806-747-5232; www.lubbocklegends.org; Ste 200, 1301 Broadway) is inside on the 2nd floor. Free Internet access is available at **Mahon Library** (☎ 806-775-2840; 1306 9th St; ☺ 9am-9pm Mon-Wed, 9am-6pm Thu-Sat, 1-5pm Sun); ask at the desk. The country radio station where Waylon Jennings DJ-ed in the 1950s (before playing with Buddy Holly) is **96.3 KLLL**.

Sights

The **Buddy Holly Center** (☎ 806-767-2686; www.bud dyhollycenter.org; 1801 Ave G; adult/child $5/3; ☺ 10am-5pm Mon, 10am-6pm Tue-Fri, 11am-6pm Sat) details the career of the rocker whose plane went down in an Iowa snowstorm in 1959. Fans still leave guitar picks at **Buddy Holly's grave** (Lubbock City Cemetery, 31st & Teak Ave). Take a right when you get in the cemetery and the modest headstone is on the left by the side of the road.

As odd as it may seem, on the vast plains south of Lubbock are two wineries producing wines better than any that come out of Hill Country: **Cap Rock Winery** (☎ 806-863-2704; www.caprockwinery.com; 408 E Woodrow Rd, east of Hwy 87; ☺ 10am-5pm Mon-Sat, noon-5pm Sun, tours noon-4pm) and **Llano Estacado Winery** (☎ 806-745-2258; www.llanowine.com; FM 1585 east of US 87; ☺ 10am-5pm Mon-Sat, noon-5pm Sun, last tour 4pm).

Sleeping

Whenever there's a big Texas Tech event, including any football game, motel prices may go up by as much as 40% and it can be hard to find a room at all; plan ahead.

Koko Inn (☎ 800-782-3254, 806-747-2591; www .lubbockhospitality.com/koko; 5201 Ave Q; s $45-50, d $50-55; P ☺) This older motel has been well kept by the local owners. Swim in the indoor atrium pool, or have a drink or a meal at the on-site bar and restaurant.

Woodrow House (☎ 806-793-3330, 800-687-5236; www.woodrowhouse.com; 2629 19th St; r $95; P ☒ ☺) Federal-style Woodrow House was created to be a B&B – one with a caboose out back ($115 a night). Not all rooms have a TV (common-room TV available) but all have wireless Internet.

Eating & Drinking

Skyviews (☎ 806-744-7462; www.hs.ttu.edu/skyviews; cnr 19th & University Sts, Bank of America Bldg, 6th fl; lunches $6-9, dinners $17-20 ☺ lunch Mon-Fri year-round, dinner Feb-Apr, late Jun-Jul & Sep-Nov) The culinary students of Texas Tech create evocative dinner menus (from Fijian to French) part of the year; reservations essential.

Head to **Café J** (☎ 806-743-5400; 2605 19th St; lunch mains $7-17, dinner mains $14-20; ☿ lunch Tue-Fri & Sun, dinner Tue-Sun) for upscale American, and **Gardski's Loft** (☎ 806-744-2391; 2009 Broadway; mains $7-10; ☿ 11am-10pm) for down-home choices like meatloaf.

The city's main nightlife happens in the **Depot District** (cnr Buddy Holly Ave, formerly Ave H, & 19th St), where there's a sports bar, a daiquiri bar, a brewpub, big dance clubs and eateries.

Getting There & Away
Seven miles north of town, **Lubbock International Airport** (☎ 806-775-3126; www.flylia.com; 5401 N Martin Luther King Blvd) is served by American Eagle, Continental and Southwest airlines. Buses depart from the possibly unlucky **Greyhound Bus Terminal** (☎ 806-765-6641; www.greyhound.com; 1313 13th St).

WEST TEXAS

The western reaches of the state are the Texas of the silver screen: tumble weeds roll across dusty ground, cacti grow out of desert sands and legends rise out of the frontier. Here is where you'll find Guadalupe Mountains National Park, home to the state's tallest mountain, and Big Bend National Park, a moonscape of desert mountains and deep arroyos. It's a river-running, mountain-biking and hiking paradise, and it's also one of the least visited national parks in the country. It's a delight to discover that the area around the park is also home to a cutting-edge arts installation and an uber-hip motel, in addition to historic Old West towns. West Texas is also home to El Paso, a city that's in many ways more like old Mexico than like the rest of Texas.

GUADALUPE MOUNTAINS NATIONAL PARK
At 8749ft, remote Guadalupe Peak is the highest point in Texas. Winter photos of snow-covered succulents seem incongruous and amazing. McKittrick Canyon has the state's best autumn foliage and impressive spring wildflower displays. If you seek high-desert splendor, this place is a must. That said, it's not easy to get here. The closest

motels are near Carlsbad Caverns National Park (p959) in White's City, about 35 miles to the north in New Mexico. El Paso is 120 miles to the west.

The **Headquarters Visitors Center** (☎ 915-828-3251; www.nps.gov/gumo; off US 62/180; 7-day pass $3, campsites $8; ☿ 8am-4:30pm, to 6pm Jun-Aug) at Pine Springs has RV and tent camping. Of the 80 miles of trail, the best day hike is **McKittrick Canyon Trail** (off US 62/180; ☿ 8am-4:30pm), which can be a 6.8-mile round-trip. The trailhead is 11 miles northeast of the visitor centre; make sure you're back by 4:30pm when the gates close. The strenuous trek from the visitor center parking lot to **Guadalupe Peak** is an 8.5-mile round-trip that gains 3000ft in elevation; ask at the visitor center about backcountry camping.

The park's north segment, **Dog Canyon**, is best reached from New Mexico and Hwy 137. Ten backcountry campsites dot the park, and overnight hikers must get a free permit at either Pine Springs visitor center or Dog Canyon. No water is available in the backcountry. No gasoline, dump stations, food or beverages are available in the park.

HUECO TANKS STATE HISTORIC SITE
About 32 miles east of El Paso off US 62/180, the Hueco Tanks (pronounced *wey-co*) have attracted humans for as many as 10,000 years. Three small granite mountains are pocked with depressions (*hueco* is Spanish for 'hollow') that hold rainwater, creating an oasis in the barren desert. Evidence of human habitation in the form of pictographs, potsherds and bits of worked flint is abundant, as is wildlife. The 860-acre park is also a magnet for rock climbers. **Park Headquarters** (☎ 915-849-6684, central reservations 512-389-8900; www.tpwd.state.tx.us/park/hueco; Rte 2775; day pass $4, campsite $10-12; ☿ 8am-6pm) has a small gift shop, a nearby interpretive center and 20 campsites (17 with electricity and water). To minimize human impact on the fragile park, a daily visitor quota is enforced; make reservations 24 hours in advance just to gain entry. You can explore the North Mountain area by yourself, but to hike deeper into the park – where the more interesting pictographs are – you have to book one of the free **pictograph tours** (☿ 9am & 11am Wed-Sun May-Sep; 9am, 9:30am, 10am & 2pm daily Oct-Apr). Bird-watching tours take place on the third Sunday of the month.

EL PASO

The Franklin Mountains rise up from desert flatlands to form a dramatic backdrop for the far West Texas town of El Paso (population 570,000). Standing here you are further west than most of New Mexico, and closer to Santa Fe than to Austin. Across the Rio Grande lies Ciudad Juárez (population two million), Mexico's fourth-largest city. Though the US Border Patrol tries to keep the two countries neatly separated, Mexican culture dominates and Spanish is the default language. (Though, even if they start in Spanish, many residents also speak perfect, unaccented English.)

El Paso is trying to shake its poor, downtrodden image and the downtown area is under some serious long-term reconstruction. A few sections still feel derelict and cars on the road are some of the oldest you'll see in the country. El Pasoans have an unpretentious, bicultural society with a strong independent streak and a low cost of living.

History

El Paso del Norte, the pass for which the city is named, was for centuries a key trading route across the Americas. Mexican revolutionary Pancho Villa holed up in El Paso for a time. It wasn't until the Mexican-American War of 1846 that the land north of the Rio Grande became permanently part of the United States. In 1881 the railroad arrived, bringing wealth and urban sophistication, as well as some of the Wild West's most colorful characters: gunfighter John Wesley Hardin lived and died here. The Chamizal Agreement in 1961 fixed border disputes that arose from a wandering Rio Grande and created a riverfront park. In recent years, low-cost wages have taken industry across the boarder into the free trade zone of Mexico.

Orientation

The Franklin Mountains pin the downtown area against the border and cleave the rest of the city into eastern and western sides. The airport is on the east, while the University of Texas at El Paso (UTEP) and the New Mexico border lie on the west. I-10 runs east–west between the mountains and downtown, and scenic Transmountain Rd traverses the Franklins further north. Downtown is bordered on the north by Yandell Dr, on the east by Cotton St and on the south and west by the border. Note that El Paso and the rest of far-west Texas are in the mountain time zone, one hour behind the rest of the state.

Information

Adelante (☎ 915-533-9875; www.rgadelante.org) A bilingual gay and lesbian information source.

El Paso Public Library (☎ 915-544-6772; 501 N Oregon; ⏲ 8:30am-8:30pm Mon-Thu, 8:30am-5:30pm Fri & Sat, 1-5pm Sun) Free Internet access.

El Paso Visitors Center (☎ 915-534-0601, 800-351-6024; www.visitelpaso.com; Civic Center, Santa Fe St; ⏲ 8am-5pm Mon-Fri) Small, but has knowledgeable local staff.

Sights & Activities

The soul of El Paso lies downtown by the border, where the streets are crowded with discount clothing stores and people waiting for buses. Local history has it that there once was a pond with live alligators where **San Jacinto Plaza** stands, and El Paso local Luis Jimenez' sculpture there celebrates this fact.

Crossing the border into **Ciudad Juárez** is just a matter of walking across the Santa Fe St bridge (25¢ for pedestrians); see p762 for requirements. The bridge leads onto Av Juárez, the city's main tourist strip. Stroll down to the cathedral area and back, passing restaurants and shops galore. The **El Paso-Juárez Trolley Co** (☎ 915-544-0061; www.borderjumper.com; 1 Civic Center Plaza; adult/child $12.50/9) operates the Border Jumper, a trolley looping from the Civic Center through Juárez and back, making 11 stops en route (get off and on at will). It departs on the hour from 10am to 4pm; the 10am trolley fills up, so it's best to make reservations. Most motels have arrangements with private guides who lead minivan tours ($15 per person, 3½ hours). Taking a car across the border is not recommended as theft is common and special insurance is required.

For a sweeping panorama of the Franklin Mountains, El Paso, sprawling Juárez and on into New Mexico, take the **Wyler Aerial Tramway** (☎ 915-566-6622; www.tpwd.state.tx.us/park/tram; 1700 McKinley Ave; adult/child $7/4; ⏲ noon-6pm Mon, Thu & Sun, noon-8pm Fri & Sat) to the top of 5632ft Ranger Peak. **Franklin Mountains State Park** (☎ 915-566-6441; www.tpwd.state.tx.us/park; Transmountain Rd, 4 miles east of I-10; day pass $3; ⏲ 8am-5pm, to 8pm Sat & Sun Apr-Oct) has a 118-miles network of hiking trails threading through

TEXAS

it. For more views head to **Scenic Drive** (off Alabama); the turnout above downtown is breathtaking at night when there's a sea of lights.

Die-hard history buffs might enjoy the lower valley's **Mission Trail**, a driving route southeast of town that connects the shells of several early Spanish missions on the Tigua Indian reservation. Take I-10 east to the Zaragoza exit, turn right and follow sights.

Sleeping

Compared to the rest of the state, lodging in El Paso is very affordable. Newer motels are spitting distance from New Mexico, west of the mountains on I-10.

La Hacienda Travelodge (☎ 915-772-4231; www .travelodge.com; 6400 Montana Ave; r $53-85; P 🖳 🕱) Barrel-tile roofs, courtyard greenery and wood-plank doors provide loads of Spanish character here. Many rooms have mini-fridges, microwaves and coffeemakers; all have free high-speed Internet. There's also a good Mexican restaurant on-site.

Holiday Inn Express Central (☎ 915-544-3333; 409 E Missouri; www.holidayinns.com; r $69-89; P 🕱) Coats of magenta, orange and yellow paint have considerably brightened this downtown hotel and its lobby. Renovated rooms remain pretty standard.

Camino Real (☎ 915-534-3000; www.caminoreal .com/elpaso; 101 S El Paso St; r Mon-Fri $115-150, Sat & Sun $89-120; P 🖳 🕱) A stained-glass dome soars above a two-story bar ceiling, a fountain bubbles in the courtyard, a pool graces the rooftop: luxury pervades the entire 1912 historic landmark hotel.

Budget digs include the good value **Coral Motel** (☎ 915-772-3263; 6308 Montana Ave; r $35-45; P 🖳 🕱), with free high-speed Internet; the faded 1922 **Gardner Hotel/El Paso International Hostel** (☎ 915-532-3661; www.gardnerhotel .com; 311 E Franklin Ave; dm $17.50, r $22-49), downtown, was last decorated in 1950 (no nonsmoking).

Eating & Drinking

Clearly, Mexican is the food of choice in El Paso; it's hard to go wrong.

Casa Jurado (☎ 915-532-6435; 226 Cincinnati Ave; lunches $5-7, dinner mains $6-15; 🕙 11am-10pm) Sleek art and furniture fills the room: this is Mexican gone modern. The menu lists standards, but also includes inventive and vegetarian options like *calabacita* (Mexican squash) enchiladas.

L&J Café & Bar (☎ 915-566-8418; 3622 E Missouri; mains $5-12; 🕙 10am-8pm kitchen, bar to 2am) Great salsa and fresh chips start you off, but everything served at this friendly bar is tasty. They'll even leave out the tortillas if you ask for the low-carb enchiladas.

Forti's Mexican Elder Restaurant (☎ 915-772-0066; 321 Chelsea St; mains $8-$18; 🕙 10am-10pm Mon-Thu, 10am-11pm Fri & Sat, to 8pm Sun) This long-time favorite is a bit like a Mexican steak house.

BORDERLANDS

Que paso? Nada. Texas is a bicultural experience and even gringos use a certain number of Mexican phrases in everyday life. All across the state you can get *migas* (eggs cooked with tortilla strips) or *taquitos* (scrambled eggs and fillings wrapped in a tortilla, *tacos* for short) for breakfast. The opportunity to cross into Mexico proper is a bonus for visitors to south and west Texas. Cross a bridge over the Rio Grande and within blocks you'll find Mexican folk-art markets and eateries. Shopping for silver jewelry, colorful pottery, embroidery, cheap alcohol and prescription drugs (technically illegal to bring back to the US) is big business.

It's tough to delve deep into Mexican culture along the border, but you'll be introduced to the food and music. US citizens need a picture ID and proof of citizenship (birth certificate, passport or voter's registration), Canadians need a passport or birth certificate, and other foreign nationals must have a passport and appropriate visas before both entering Mexico and returning to the USA. Avoid driving into Mexican border towns, where car theft is rampant.

Ciudad Juárez (p761) is a popular day's excursion from El Paso. Thirty miles southeast of South Padre Island, as far as you can go in Texas, **Brownsville** (☎ 800-626-2639; www.brownsville.org) is opposite **Matamoros** (www.visitmatamoros.com), Mexico. Further west by 35 miles, the small-town pair of **Progresso** and **Nuevo Progresso** is a favorite destination for South Texans who want to avoid urban grit and begging. Drug-related violence has exploded across the border from Laredo in Nuevo Laredo; stay away, it's not safe.

The *milanesa* (pounded, breaded and fried flank steak) is particularly good.

Also recommended:

H&H Car Wash (☎ 915-533-1144; 701 E Yandell Ave; mains $3-7; ☺ 7am-3pm) Tiny hole-in-the-wall diner attached to a car wash.

Ardovino's Pizza (☎ 915-760-6000; 206 Cincinnati St; mains $5-15; ☺ 11am-9pm Mon-Thu, 11am-10pm Fri & Sat, 11am-8pm Sun) Stone-oven pizzas.

Cafe Central (☎ 915-545-2233; 1 Texas Ct; mains $16-35; ☺ 11am-10pm Mon-Thu, 11am-11:30pm Fri & Sat) Upscale eclectic restaurant and bar with live music weekends; the bar is open until late on weekends.

Entertainment

For cultural and event listings, pick up the free weekly **What's Up** (www.whatsup-ep.com), the free monthly **El Paso Scene** (www.epscene.com) or the Friday *Tiempo* supplement to the **El Paso Times** (www.elpasotimes.com). Nightclub live music offerings are pretty limited. The closest thing El Paso has to an entertainment district is a single block of restaurants and bars on Cincinnati St between Mesa and Stanton, near the University of Texas El Paso.

Dome Bar (☎ 915-534-3000; Camino Real, 101 S El Paso St) Relax in elegant surrounds and listen to live jazz from Thursday to Saturday.

T Lounge (☎ 915-513-8227; www.thetlounge.com; 1218 Texas Ave) Blues, rock and alternative bands play Wednesday through Saturday.

Chamizal National Memorial (☎ 915-532-7273; www.nps.gov/cham; 800 S San Marcial St) The amphitheater at the park celebrating Mexican-American border resolution plays host to evening concert series and musical events.

Shopping

Mexican arts and crafts (ceramics, silver, woodwork, textiles) can be had both in town and across the border in Juárez. El Paso is also known for boot making: for custom creations ($250 to $2,500+), head to **Caboots** (☎ 915-544-1855; www.caboots.com; 501 S Cotton St; ☺ 9am-5pm Mon-Fri). The mega-manufacturer **Justin Boots** (☎ 915-779-5465; I-10 at Hawkins) has an outlet southwest of town.

Getting There & Around

El Paso International Airport (☎ 915-780-4749; www.elpasointernationalairport.com; off I-10), 8 miles northeast of downtown, has services to 16 American and two Mexican cities. Sun Metro bus 33 ($1) runs between the airport and downtown. A cab from the airport to downtown

costs $15 to $17. Several hotels have courtesy telephones for shuttle pickup.

Amtrak's Florida–California *Sunset Limited* stops at **Union Depot** (☎ 915-545-2247; www.amtrak.com; 700 San Francisco St). The **Greyhound Bus Station** (☎ 915-532-2365; www.greyhound.com; 200 W San Antonio St) sends coaches to Albuquerque, New Mexico ($38, six to eight hours) daily.

Sun Metro (☎ 915-533-3333; www.sunmetro.org) runs the extensive citywide bus service. A bus information booth is on the corner of Oregon and Main Ave, across from San Jacinto Plaza. Two entertainment trolley routes (25¢) transport folks around downtown and up to Cincinnati St.

BIG BEND

Look at a map of Texas. See the western elbow of land poking into Mexico? That's the Big Bend, where the Rio Grande, and consequently the border, curves. South of I-10, between Van Horn and Fort Stockton, flatlands give way to mountains and valleys, to Chihuahuan desert and limestone canyons. Rock climbing, hiking, rafting and glider rides are all possible here in this outdoor playground. Along the border are two excellent national and state parks, and about an hour and a half to the north there are little towns with thriving art colonies, Old West hotels, an observatory and more parks. The region is usually explored as a whole. Be warned, driving along the curvaceous, undulating roads past stunning views may make you wish you were astride a Harley.

This area has been likened to the devil's playground because of the summer heat. The best times to visit are February to April and October to November. Avoid July and August if at all possible. El Paso (220 miles to the northwest) and Midland-Odessa (150 miles northeast) are the closest airports. You can tell you're in the middle of nowhere because gasoline is expensive, cell-phone coverage is minimal, and Internet access is hard to find.

National Park

The Chisos Mountains rise up at the center of **Big Bend National Park** (☎ 432-477-2251; www.nps.gov/bibe; 7-day pass per vehicle $15, per motorcycle $5). To the west, the dramatic mesas and rock formations are the result of ancient volcanic activity. To the east of the mountains stretches desert habitat. The diverse geography makes for an amazing variety of wildlife: mountain lions, black bears, collared peccaries and white-tailed deer, as well as 56 species of reptiles and amphibians and more than 100 bird species. With more than 800,000 acres, the park is vast enough for a lifetime of hiking, but the 110 miles of paved road and 150 miles of dirt road make scenic driving the most popular activity. Short-term visitors can see a lot in a couple of days. Because of post–September 11 border restrictions, there's no access to Mexico from the park. Numerous outfitters lead river rafting, horseback riding and jeep tours in the park (see Getting Around Big Bend, below).

The **Panther Junction Visitors Center** (☎ 915-477-2251; 8am-6pm) is along the main park road, 29 miles from the Persimmon Gap entrance gate south of Marathon, and 26 miles from the Maverick entrance at Study Butte. Rangers there are glad to help you plot your trip, and gasoline is available nearby. Most of the 150-plus miles of hiking trails are in the Chisos Mountains, but the 1.5-mile **Santa Elena Canyon Trail**, 40 miles southwest of Panther Junction, is popular. It's rated easy, but you have to wade through a stream and climb stairs to get up above the river on the canyon wall. Near **Rio Grand Village**, 20 miles southeast of the main visitor center, you can hike around some old bathhouses to the shallow **hot springs**.

Drama takes hold as you wind your way up the narrow road through the red rock to **Chisos Mountain Lodge & Restaurant** (☎ 432-477-2291; lodge & motel r $88-99, cottages $101-$112; breakfasts $4-9, mains $7; breakfast, lunch & dinner). The attractive and rustic cottages are fairly secluded, situated on the hill above the main lodge; No 103 has the best view. The food is so-so – it's better to pack a cooler ahead of time. Also in the complex is a **visitor center** (8am-5pm), which sells a mountain-trail map, and a **camp store** (9am-9pm) with basic supplies.

Primitive **campgrounds** (☎ 877-444-6777; www .reserveusa.com; campsites $10) at Chisos Basin and Rio Grande Village have running water and flush toilets. A limited number of spots can be reserved ahead. **Rio Grand Village RV Park** (☎ 432-477-2293; 2-person RV sites $21) is the only place with hookups in the park. The 25 spaces are first come, first served.

Terlingua–Study Butte

The closest jumping-off points into the national park (just three miles to the east) are two small, dusty towns attached to each other near the junction of Hwy 118 and Route 170. This is outfitters paradise, where you can arrange river-rafting, jeep or horseback riding

---

GETTING AROUND BIG BEND

You don't ever have to get out of your car for a visit to the Big Bend area to be worthwhile – the scenery is epic. But if you're looking for a different perspective, outfitters oblige with any number of transportation options – horseback or jeep rides, river rafting or glider soaring.

The same company runs both **Big Bend Stables** (☎ 432-371-2212; www.lajitasstables.com; Rte 170 at Hwy 118; 2-hr rides $45, half day with lunch $70) and **Lajitas Stables** (17 miles west of Hwy 118 on Rte 170; 2-hr rides $55, half day with lunch $90) for horseback rides outside the national park. The Lajitas ride is more mountainous and challenging.

Arrange a river-float trip or jeep tour (multihour to multiday) with **Rio Grande Adventures** (☎ 432-371-2567, 800-343-1640; www.riograndeadventures.com; 3–4-hr float trip or jeep tour $70). It also rents jeeps ($125 per day) and canoes ($29 per person per day) and provides shuttle service to pick you up (or move your vehicle) downriver. **Far Flung Outdoor Center** (☎ 432-371-2633, 800-839-7238; www.farflungoutdoorcenter.com; Rte 170 at Hwy 118; 4-hr float trip $60, 3-hr jeep tour $55) has similar guided tours and rentals for both inside and outside the park. Jeep tours and half-day ATV tours ($125 per rider) on private land get further off paved roads into backcountry than park tours. More-active types should check out **Desert Sports** (☎ 888-989-6900, 432-371-2727; www .desertsportstx.com; Rte 170, 5 miles west of Hwy 118) for customized guided hikes, as well as biking (four-hour ride, $135 for two) and canoe tours ($125 per person per day) into the national and state parks. A three-day hike-bike-raft combo goes for $350 per person. Desert Sports also rents out mountain bikes and canoes, and provides shuttle service.

Marfa Gliders (☎ 800-667-9464; www.flygliders.com; Marfa airport, Hwy 17; glider ride $95) takes you soaring near the Davis Mountains. On clear days you can see Mexico. Reservations required.

trips (see Getting Around Big Bend, opposite). **Terlingua Ghost Town** (Rte 170 W) is a long-gone mining village where former shanties have been turned into minihomes and the old general store sells beer and souvenirs.

Forgo the Big Bend Inn and stay at the friendly **Longhorn Ranch Motel & Packsaddle Restaurant** (☎ 432-371-2542; www.terlinguatx.com/long horn.html; Hwy 118, 8 miles north of Rte 170; s/d $49/59, breakfast $3-6, mains $5-10; breakfast & dinner;). Former cinema **Starlight Theatre** (☎ 432-371-2326; Ivey St, Terlingua Ghost Town; mains $12-29; dinner), has been resurrected as a lively restaurant.

Lajitas to Presidio

West of the national park, **Route 170** hugs the Rio Grande through some of the most spectacular and remote scenery in the country. This river road takes you through a lunar landscape of low desert arroyos, sweeping vistas and rugged mountains (at one point there's a 15% grade, the maximum allowable). Leaving Terlingua, you first come to **Lajitas** (☎ 877-525-4827; www.lajitas.com; r $195-$330;), which looks like a town but is actually all one resort that you never have to leave. On-site outfitters arrange adventures, you can play golf (hitting the 19th hole across the river into Mexico) or rejuvenate at the spa, then choose between six dining options. There's even a private runway for your jet.

Bordering all that luxury is **Big Bend Ranch State Park** (☎ 432-229-3416; www.tpwd.state .tx.us/park/bigbend; off Rte 170; day pass $3, campsites $3), with interesting turnouts for hiking or picnicking along the river road. Take the easy 0.7-mile hike into narrow **Closed Canyon**, where the cliffs rise above you, blocking out the sun. This park is much less explored than its big brother, but is just as stunning. Camping is off Casa Piedra Rd; get the code for the gate at the visitor center for **Fort Leaton State Historic Site** (☎ 432-229-3613; www .tpwd.state.tx.us/park/fortleat; Rte 170; fort admission $2; 8:30am-4:30pm). Past the park, **Presidio** is a dreary border town with not much else to do other than cross into Mexico. From there, Marfa is 60 miles north on US 67.

Marfa

Just more than 100 miles north of Big Bend National Park is Marfa, the unlikely home to art and aliens (maybe). The **Chinati Foundation** (☎ 432-729-4362; www.chinati.org; off Hwy 67; adult/child $10/5; by tour only 10am & 2pm Wed-Sat), half a mile south of town, is a sprawling complex of minimalist art founded in 1986 by New York artist Donald Judd. The installation has helped make this small desert town an artists' enclave. Eight miles east of town on US 90, the **Marfa Lights Viewing Site** is where fans and fanatics watch for the mysterious moving balls of light that sometimes appear in the distance (first recorded in 1883). No one's been able to explain the phenomenon scientifically. Be prepared to wait all night; there's no schedule and no promises.

The town's original fame, however, came after James Dean, Elizabeth Taylor and Rock Hudson filmed *Giant* here in 1955. The cast and crew stayed a block off the main square at the gorgeous 1930s-era **Hotel Paisano** (☎ 866-729-3669; www.hotelpaisano.com; cnr N Highland & West Sts; r $80-150, ste $150-200). There's movie memorabilia off the lobby, a high-class dinner-only restaurant, and the nice desk clerks will let you poke around upstairs while the housekeepers are cleaning. New on the scene in 2005, the **Thunderbird** (☎ 432-729-1984; www.thunderbirdmarfa.com; US 90 W; standard r $95-110, deluxe w/daybed $115-125;) lures you in with hip retro appeal that has been called 'cowboy zen.'

The smoothies and sandwiches at **Squeeze** (☎ 432-729-4500; 215 N Highland Ave; sandwiches $4-6; 10am-6pm Tue-Sat) are mighty fresh, but the dark-chocolate frappé surpasses all. Pop into **Marfa Book Company** (☎ 429-729-2906; 105 S Highland Ave; 9am-9pm) to look for local titles or to have a coffee.

Fort Davis

At elevation 5000ft, Fort Davis is the highest town in Texas and the temperature can be 10 to 20 degrees cooler here than down at the national park. The small town, 20 miles north of Marfa on Hwy 17, has old false-front buildings and a few places to stay and eat. Sixteen steep miles north above Fort Davis is the stellar **McDonald Observatory** (☎ 432-426-3640; www.mcdonaldobservatory.org; Hwy 118; daytime pass adult/child $8/7; 9am-5pm Tue, Fri & Sat evenings). Take a guided tour of the facility and have a solar viewing in the daytime, or attend an evening **star party** (adult/child $10/8; 7:30pm Apr-Aug, 9:30pm Nov-Mar). For great views, drive up past the visitor center to the lookout points at the higher stations (map available at the gift shop).

TEXAS

THE AUTHOR'S CHOICE

Gage Hotel (☎ 432-386-4205, 800-884-4243; www.gagehotel.com; 101 Hwy 90, Marathon; r $70-190; ✕ ⬛)
The historic rooms here come straight out of a Wild West pulp novel, with wide wooden blinds
on the windows and saddle blankets on the raised log beds. Check in and you're welcomed with
a large chocolate-chip cookie. The bargain shared-bath rooms on the 1st floor ($79, no TV or
phone, bathrobes available) come with earplugs for a reason: you can hear everything that happens in the rich and ranchlike lobby down the hall. Newer cabana-style adobe suites next door
are nicer, with antique wooden doors, Mexican tile floors, fireplaces and outdoor patios facing a
lush courtyard. Another walled courtyard surrounds the oasislike pool. A few doors down, **Café
Cenzio** (mains $17-20; ☽ dinner) concocts gourmet renditions of Texas favorites – light poblano
pepper soup followed by hand-battered chicken-fried steak in jalapeno gravy with fresh asparagus.
This is roughing it luxury style. Marathon is 58 miles north of Big Bend National Park.

A mile or two west of town, on the way to
the observatory, **Fort Davis National Historic Site**
(☎ 432-426-3224; www.nps.gov/foda; Hwy 118; 7-day pass
$3; ☽ 8am-5pm) has 24 intact 1880s buildings.
You can hike (or drive) the 3 miles further
west from there to **Davis Mountains State Park**
(☎ 432-426-3337; www.tpwd.state.tx.us/park/davis; Hwy
118; day pass adult/child $3/free, campsites $9-16).

The best place to stay locally is at **Indian
Lodge** (☎ 432-426-3254; www.tpwd.state.tx.us/park/in
dian; Hwy 118; r $75-90; ✕ ⬛), inside the Davis
Mountains State Park. The 1930s adobe
buildings have been renovated beautifully, with pine-log ceilings that complement southwestern interiors. **Hotel Limpia**
(☎ 432-426-3237; www.hotellimpia.com; Hwy 118, Town
Sq; r $69-$110; ✕) is in an 1912 stone-front
building on the main street. **Murphy's Pizzeria & Cafe** (☎ 432-426-2020; Hwy 118, across from
courthouse; mains $5-9; ☽ 11am-9pm Mon-Sat) serves
personal-size pies as well as large pizzas,
pastas, sandwiches and salads.

Thirty-seven miles north of Fort Davis,
near I-10, **Balmorhea State Park** (☎ 432-375-
2370; Hwy 17; www.tpwd.state.tx.us/park/balmorhe; day
pass adult/child $3/free, motel r $50-60; ✕ ⬛) is built
around a huge spring-fed pool that's the best
swimming hole in the state. The motel was
built by the Civilian Conservation Corps.

Alpine

At population 8000, Alpine is the biggest city
in the Big Bend area, and the only one with
chain motels, restaurants, grocery stores
and public transportation. It's about 20
miles east of Marfa and west of Marathon
on US 90, 17 miles southeast of Fort Davis
on Hwy 118 and 90 miles north of Big Bend
National Park on US 385. Sul Ross State
University and the February **Cowboy Poetry
Gathering** (☎ 432-364-2490; www.cowboy-poetry.org)
also call Alpine home. The **chamber of commerce visitor center** (☎ 432-837-2326; www.alpine
texas.com; 106 N 3rd St; ☽ 9am-5pm Mon-Fri, 10am-2pm
Sun) has information about the whole region
and free Internet access.

The town has limited **Greyhound** (☎ 800-
231-2222; www.greyhound.com) bus service, and
the **Amtrak Station** (☎ 800-872-7245; www.amtrak
.com; 102 W Holland St) is a stop on the *Sunset
Limited* line. Buy tickets on board, as there's
no ticket office. Arrivals are often delayed
until the middle of the night by freight traffic. If you want to rent a car here, you're
stuck with **Alpine Auto Rental** (☎ 800-894-3463,
432-837-3463; www.alpineautorental.com; 414 E Holland
Ave; $39 & up). **Trans-Pecos Taxi** (☎ 432-940-1776;
$106 to Chisos Basin) will take you anywhere in
the national park.

The West

JOHN ELK III

California

The American Dream has always flowed west, lured by the promises of California. 'Eureka!' cried the gold miners in 1848 – 'I've found it.' 'Eureka!' cried naturalist John Muir and industrialist William Randolph Hearst. 'Eureka!' cried Steve Jobs and Marilyn Monroe. 'Eureka!' cry immigrants from China and Mexico. All see gold in the tawny hills and granite mountains, in a central valley drunk with topsoil, in towering forests and teeming high-tech cities.

By many measures, California remains the biggest, most dynamic, most diverse, most forward-thinking state in the nation. It has the most people, the largest economy (seventh-largest in the world, in fact), the most exports, the most immigrants, the most national parks (tied with Alaska), the most agriculture, the biggest trees. How do you measure innovation? Ask yourself where we'd be without the vacuum tube, personal computers, the Internet, Frisbees, fortune cookies, the seedless watermelon, McDonald's and Mickey Mouse.

But mainly, Californians just seem to have more fun. You can enjoy 1200 miles of the Pacific Coast. You can feast in temples of organic California cuisine while sipping Napa Valley wines, then go celebrity-spotting among the nightclubs of the world's movie capital. You can ski above azure Lake Tahoe or hike Yosemite's granite monoliths in the morning and be in artful, bohemian San Francisco by showtime.

HIGHLIGHTS

- Imbibing the hype, the horror, the hip and Hollywood in **Los Angeles** (p773)
- Negotiating the hairpin turns along the sublime coastal edge of **Big Sur** (p817)
- Engaging in lusty eating and drinking in 'Baghdad by the Bay,' **San Francisco** (p822)
- Contemplating the moody, towering elders of our world, the **coast redwoods** (p853)
- Raising a glass to sun, food, wine and art in **Wine Country** (p847)
- Listening to the wind whisper like a half-crazed miner in the ghost towns of **Gold Country** (p855)
- Skiing the snow-clad mountains near the sapphire jewel of **Lake Tahoe** (p860)
- Tackling the granite walls and waterfalls of the majestic, sublime **Yosemite National Park** (p862)
- Tippling martinis, just like Sinatra used to, in retro-chic **Palm Springs** (p808)
- Seeking desert solitude in the salt flats and sand dunes of **Death Valley National Park** (p811)

CALIFORNIA IN...

One week

Two strategies: the first is to spend four days experiencing the **San Francisco Bay Area** (p822) – including side trips to the **Wine Country** (p847) and **Monterey** (p818) – and spend three days in the **Sierra Nevada** (p860) at **Tahoe** (p860), **Yosemite** (p862) and **Sequoia National Park** (p864). Or spend a week taking in **San Francisco** (p822) and **Los Angeles** (p773), connecting them via the splendor of the **Central Coast** (p813) – **Monterey** (p818), **Big Sur** (p817) and **Hearst Castle** (p816).

Two weeks

Again, two strategies: first, make a loop circuit starting in **Los Angeles** (p773) and going up the **Central Coast** (p813) to **San Francisco** (p822), then east to the **Sierra Nevada** (p860), then south to **Death Valley National Park** (p811) and the **Mojave** (p810), and then back to **Los Angeles**. Or go from **San Francisco** up the rugged **North Coast** (p849) to **Redwood National Park** (p853), then east to **Lassen Volcanic National Park** (p860), then south through the **Sierra Nevada** (p860) and finally bust a move down I-5 to **Los Angeles** and, of course, **Disneyland** (p796)!

HISTORY

By the time the first European explorers arrived in the 16th century, California was home to about 300,000 indigenous people. The Pacific Coast being such a splendid place, conflict between native groups was almost nonexistent.

The Spanish explored California through the 1540s in search of a fabled 'city of gold.' When they didn't find it, they left the territory virtually alone. It wasn't until the Mission Period, from 1769 to 1810, that Spain made a serious attempt to settle the land, establishing 21 Catholic missions to convert the natives and building several military forts (presidios) to protect the territory from British and Russian interests.

After Mexico won independence from Spain in 1821, it ruled California briefly. But the young United States took over after defeating Mexico in the 1846–47 Mexican American War. By coincidence, within days of the US gaining official possession in 1848, gold was discovered in northern California – and the nation's manifest destiny was never more palpable. California's gold rush drew people from all over the world, and the state population exploded from 14,000 to 90,000 by the end of 1849. In 1850, California gained admission to the USA as a nonslave state.

In the mid-19th century, the effort to build the transcontinental railroad (whose eastern terminus was Sacramento) led to the arrival of some 15,000 Chinese laborers, who suffered

under a wave of anti-Chinese legislation once the railroad was completed in 1869.

Despite the bad omen of the 1906 San Francisco earthquake, the 20th century resulted in California growing exponentially in size, diversity and importance. From 1910 to 1960, the population steadily rose from 2.3 to 15.8 million people. Mexican immigrants arrived during the 1910–21 Mexican Revolution and again during WWII to fill labor shortages. During WWII, important military-driven industries developed, and anti-Asian sentiments resurfaced, leading to the internment of many Japanese Americans.

This confluence of wealth, size, heavy immigration and lack of tradition is probably why California remains at the forefront of social trends. Since the 1930s, Hollywood has mesmerized the nation with its dreams and fashions, while San Francisco has reacted against the banal complacency of post-WWII suburbia, spreading Beat poetry, hippie free love and gay pride. The Internet revolution, initially spurred by the high-tech pioneers in Silicon Valley, rewired the country and led to a 1990s gold rush in overspeculated stocks.

The stock bubble burst at the turn of the 21st century, plunging the state's economy into chaos, though by 2005, it had begun to stabilize despite state deficits. Californians, however, couldn't wait: in 2003 they voted to recall their elected governor, Gray Davis, and to replace him with actor-turned-politician Arnold Schwarzenegger. Dubbed

CALIFORNIA

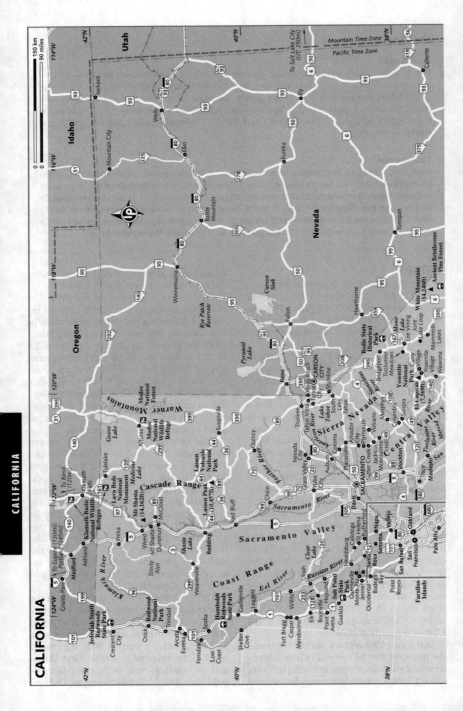

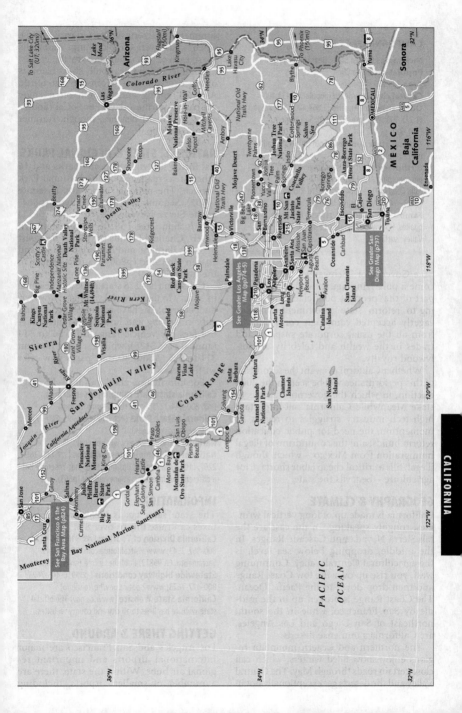

CALIFORNIA FACTS

Nicknames Golden State, Bear Flag Republic

Population 35.9 million

Area 155,959 sq miles

Capital city Sacramento (population 433,400)

Other cities Los Angeles (3,864,400), San Diego (1,275,100), San Jose (925,000), San Francisco (791,600)

Official state symbols Gold (mineral), California redwood (tree)

Birthplace of Writer John Steinbeck (1902–68), photographer Ansel Adams (1902–84), chef Julia Child (1912–2004), President Richard Nixon (1913–94), actor Marilyn Monroe (1926–62)

Famous for Disneyland, protests and earthquakes, Hollywood, hippie tree-huggers, Silicon Valley, surfing

'the Governator,' Schwarzenegger has become a polarizing figure: while playing the part of the 'people's politician' and pledging to 'reform' state government, he's also eagerly accepted campaign contributions from all the usual corporate suspects and trades in the wealth and celebrity of Hollywood royalty.

Whether Californians want the second act of this performance will be seen in the 2006 election, in which the governor's seat is at stake. Meanwhile, California's all-important high-tech industry struggles to regain its momentum, the need for public education reform builds, and the conundrum of illegal immigration from Mexico – which, though illegal, fills a critical cheap labor shortage for agriculture – bedevils the state.

GEOGRAPHY & CLIMATE

California is made up of long vertical wrinkles, roughly speaking. In the east are the tall Sierra Nevada and Cascade Ranges. In the middle, dropping below sea level, is the agricultural Central Valley. Continuing west, you rise up over the low Coast Range and then drop down to the Pacific Ocean. The Coast Range is broken up in the middle by San Francisco, while in the south, northeast of San Diego and Los Angeles, are California's immense deserts.

The northern and eastern mountain regions enjoy snow-filled winters, which can close certain roads through May. The Central Valley and the deserts get exceptionally hot in summer; the deserts are best in early spring, when wildflowers are blooming. Along the coast, each season is tempered by the Pacific; in summer, inland heat pulls chilly blankets of fog over the coast from Big Sur north. As such, spring and autumn often enjoy the coast's warmest days. For SoCal (Southern Californian) beaches, though, summer means surf's up.

NATIONAL, STATE & REGIONAL PARKS

California has eight national parks and 16 other areas managed by the National Park Service. The national parks are Yosemite (p862), Sequoia and Kings Canyon (p864) in the Sierra Nevada, Death Valley (p811) and Joshua Tree (p810) in the southern desert, Channel Islands (p813) off the coast of Santa Barbara, and Redwood (p853) and Lassen Volcanic (p860) National Parks in the north.

California has 278 state parks, some equal in beauty to their federal siblings. However, budget problems have meant rising fees and cuts in staffing and hours. Currently, day-use fees per vehicle range from $4 to $14 (annual pass $125), while camping fees run $11 to $25. About 80 state parks now offer wi-fi access.

For information check out the following:

California state park camping reservations (☎ 800-444-7275; www.reserveamerica.com)

California State Parks (☎ 916-653-6995, 800-777-0369; www.parks.ca.gov)

National Park Service (www.nps.gov)

National park camping reservations (☎ 800-365-2267; http://reservations.nps.gov) Note that Yosemite has a different toll-free reservations number (p863).

INFORMATION

The state sales tax is 7.25%; added local taxes can raise this to over 8%.

California Division of Tourism (☎ 916-444-4429, 800-862-2543; www.visitcalifornia.com; PO Box 1499, Sacramento, CA 95812) Publishes a free travel planner.

Statewide highway conditions (☎ 916-445-7623, 800-427-7623; www2.dot.ca.gov/hq/roadinfo)

California State Website (www.ca.gov) The official state website has links to all city and county websites.

GETTING THERE & AROUND

Los Angeles and San Francisco are major international airports and important regional air hubs. Within the state, there are a number of smaller airports, including

Sacramento, Oakland, San Jose, Burbank, Ontario, Orange County and San Diego.

The state's cities and major towns are served by **Greyhound** (☎ 800-231-2222).

Los Angeles, San Diego and San Francisco are probably the best places to rent a car, with many national and local operators. See p1173.

There are four main **Amtrak** (☎ 800-872-7245; www.amtrak.com) routes connecting California with the rest of the USA:

California Zephyr Daily service between Chicago and San Francisco (Emeryville), with stops in Denver, CO; Salt Lake City, UT; and Reno, NV.

Coast Starlight Daily service along the West Coast, from Seattle, WA, to Los Angeles, via Portland, OR; Sacramento; Oakland; and Santa Barbara.

Southwest Chief Daily service between Chicago and Los Angeles via Kansas City, MO; Albuquerque, NM; and Flagstaff, AZ.

Sunset Limited Service three times a week between Orlando, FL, and Los Angeles, via New Orleans, LA; San Antonio, TX; and Tucson, AZ.

Within the state, useful rail routes include the *Pacific Surfliner*, which links San Diego and Los Angeles, continuing on to San Luis Obispo; the *Capitol Corridor*, between San Jose, Oakland and Sacramento; and the *San Joaquins*, connecting the Bay Area to Bakersfield in Southern California, with connections to Yosemite.

LOS ANGELES

You'll find at least a kernel of truth in every stereotype, and this is certainly true of Los Angeles. The stars, the glitz, the flaky poseurs, those miles of 'endless summer' beaches packed with the buff and the beautiful. Sure, they're here. But LA is also a city where imagination and creativity rule absolutely and lots of really smart people crank out films, designs and an economy larger than that of most nations. Do a little social archaeology and you're going to find a true 'field of dreams' that will delight you.

Dazzling architecture and history are embodied in the revitalized Downtown area. The cuisine scene is extraordinary and the entertainment world-class. LA absolutely shines culturally with superb museums, concert halls and art scenes. It's a titanic, sprawling, brawling place – a patchwork of 88 separate towns conspiring to look like a city. But don't try to get your mind around it all. Simply pluck your favorite attractions and regions, move slowly against the overwhelming tide of daily life here, and you'll find LA at once as fascinating, relaxing, enjoyable and memorable as anywhere on earth. Just remember to relax and drink it all in, *slowly*.

History

LA's human history begins with the Gabrielino and Chumash Indians who roamed the area as early as 6000 BC. Their hunter-gatherer existence ended in the late 18th century with the arrival of Spanish missionaries and pioneers from Mexico. Known as El Pueblo de la Reina de Los Angeles, the first civilian settlement became a thriving farming community but remained a far-flung outpost for decades.

A series of seminal events caused LA's population to swell to two million by 1930: the collapse of the northern California gold rush in the 1850s, the arrival of the railroad in the 1870s, the growth of the citrus industry, the discovery of oil in 1892, construction of a harbor in San Pedro and the opening of the LA aqueduct in 1913.

During WWI, the Lockheed brothers and Donald Douglas established aircraft manufacturing plants in LA. Two decades later, the aviation industry – helped along by billions of federal dollars for military contracts – was among the industries that contributed to a real-estate boom and sparked suburban sprawl. Another, of course, was the film industry, which took root here as early as 1908.

Orientation

Los Angeles (population city four million, county 10 million) may be vast and amorphous, but the areas of visitor interest are fairly well defined. About 12 miles inland, Downtown combines great architecture and museums with global-village pizzazz thanks to such enclaves as Little Tokyo, Chinatown and El Pueblo de Los Angeles. Euro-flavored Pasadena lies northeast of Downtown, sprawling Hollywood northwest. South of Hollywood, Mid-City's main draw is Museum Row, while further west are ritzy Beverly Hills and the Westside communities of Westwood, home to UCLA; mansion-studded Bel-Air; and

GREATER LOS ANGELES

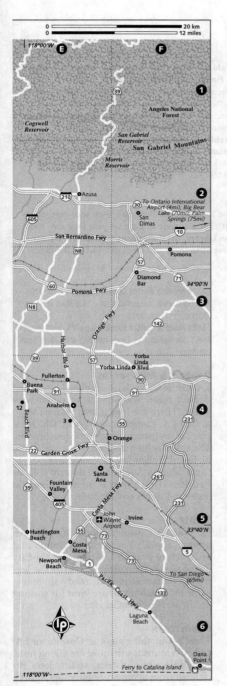

Brentwood with the hilltop Getty Center. Of the beach towns, Santa Monica is the most tourist-friendly; others include swish-but-low-key Malibu, bohemian Venice and bustling Long Beach.

Getting around is easiest by car, although public transport is usually adequate within specific neighborhoods. Lonely Planet also publishes a laminated, pocketsize map of the city.

For information on how to get to LA's various neighborhoods from the Los Angeles International Airport (LAX), see p794.

Information

BOOKSTORES
Book Soup (Map p783; ☎ 310-659-3110; 8818 Sunset Blvd, W Hollywood) Frequent celeb sightings.
California Map & Travel Center (Map p785; ☎ 310-396-6277; 3312 Pico Blvd, Santa Monica) Guidebooks galore.

EMERGENCY
Police, fire and ambulance (☎ 911) Emergency.
Police, nonemergency (☎ 800-275-5273)
Rape & battering hotline (☎ 800-656-4673; 🕑 24hr)

INTERNET ACCESS
For wi-fi hot-spot locations, check www.jiwire.com.
Cyber Java (Map p780; ☎ 323-466-5600; 7080 Hollywood Blvd, Hollywood; per 10min/wi-fi $1.75/free; 🕑 7am-11:30pm)
Interactive Café (Map p785; ☎ 310-395-5009; 215 Broadway, Santa Monica; per 10min $1; 🕑 6am-1am Sun-Thu, to 2am Fri & Sat)

INTERNET RESOURCES
At LA (www.at-la.com) Ultimate web portal to all things LA.
LA.com (www.la.com) Hip guide to shopping, eating and special events around town.
LA Blogs (www.lablogs.com) Gateway to LA-related blogs.
Visit Los Angeles (www.visitlosangeles.info) Official website of the Los Angeles Convention & Visitors Bureau.

MEDIA
KCRW 89.9 FM (www.kcrw.org) World music, intelligent talk, BBC and NPR.
LA Weekly (www.laweekly.com) Free alternative news and listings magazine.
Los Angeles Magazine (www.lamag.com) Monthly gossipy lifestyle glossy.
Los Angeles Times (www.latimes.com) Pulitzer Prize–winning daily.

CALIFORNIA

LOS ANGELES IN...

Two Days
Start your day with breakfast at the **Griddle Café** (p791) in West Hollywood, and then work off the carbs with a stroll along newly revitalized **Hollywood Boulevard** (p779). Afterward, it's off to **Beverly Hills** (p782) and Rodeo Dr via mansion-lined Sunset Blvd. From here, make a beeline to the **Getty Center** (p784) before concluding the day with dinner in **Santa Monica** (p791).

On the second day, weather permitting, spend the morning frolicking on the beach in Venice and checking out the mad scene along the famous **Ocean Front Walk** (p784), then hit the road for Downtown. Check out LA's origins at **El Pueblo de Los Angeles** (p778), the new **Cathedral of Our Lady of the Angels** (p778) and **Walt Disney Concert Hall** (p778), then get your cultural fix at the **MOCA Grand Avenue** (p778). Head back to Hollywood for pre-dinner drinks and sunset views at **Yamashiro** (p792), then let your belly tell you where to go for dinner.

Four Days
Make **Universal Studios Hollywood** (p539) the focus of your third day, then spot real movie stars over dinner at **Spago Beverly Hills** (p791). For a change of pace on your final day, head to **Pasadena** (p785) and the serene **Huntington Library, Art Collections & Botanical Gardens**. After dinner in Old Pasadena head to the **Sunset Strip** (p782) for one last night on the razzle.

MEDICAL SERVICES
Cedars-Sinai Medical Center (Map p783; ☎ 310-855-5000; 8700 Beverly Blvd, W Hollywood; ☯ 24hr emergency)
Los Angeles Free Clinic (appointments ☎ 323-462-4158) Hollywood (Map p780; 6043 Hollywood Blvd & 5205 Melrose Ave); Mid-City (Map p783; 8405 Beverly Blvd). Medical and dental care, and counseling.
Rite-Aid pharmacies (☎ 800-748-3243) Call for the branch nearest you.

MONEY
American Express (☯ 9am-6pm Mon-Fri, 10am-2pm Sat) Pasadena (Map pp774-5 ; ☎ 626-449-2281; 269 S Lake Ave); W Hollywood (Map p783; ☎ 310-659-1682; 8493 W 3rd St)
TravelEx (☯ 10am-5pm Mon-Fri) Beverly Hills (Map p783; ☎ 310-274-9177; 421 N Rodeo Dr); W Hollywood (Map p783; ☎ 310-659-6093; 806 Hilldale Ave)

POST
Post offices abound in Los Angeles. Call ☎ 800-275-8777 for the nearest branch.

TOURIST INFORMATION
California Welcome Center (Map p783; ☎ 310-854-7616; Beverly Center Mall, 8500 Beverly Blvd, W Holly-wood; ☯ 10am-6pm Mon-Sat, from 11am Sun)
Downtown Los Angeles Visitors Center (Map p777; ☎ 213-689-8822; www.visitlosangeles.info; 685 S Figueroa St; ☯ 9am-5pm Mon-Fri)
Hollywood Visitors Center (Map p780; ☎ 323-467-6412; Hollywood & Highland complex, 6801 Hollywood Blvd; ☯ 10am-10pm Mon-Sat, to 7pm Sun)

Santa Monica Visitor Center (Map p785; ☎ 310-393-7593; www.santamonica.com; 1920 Main St, Santa Monica; ☯ 10am-6pm)
Santa Monica Visitor Kiosk (Map p785; 1400 Ocean Ave, Santa Monica; ☯ 10am-4pm Sep-May, 10am-5pm Jun-Aug)

Dangers & Annoyances
LA crime rates have dropped, but that doesn't mean you should let down your guard. There are few, if any, reasons to go to East LA, Compton and Watts, which are plagued by gangs, drugs and prostitution. The risk of getting mugged, while low, is also higher in Hollywood or Venice than, say, in Santa Monica, Westwood, Beverly Hills or Pasadena. Downtown is pretty deserted at night and teems with homeless folks.

Sights
Each of LA's neighborhoods has its own unique appeal. For great museums and architecture head to Downtown, Mid-City or Pasadena. West Hollywood has the legendary Sunset Strip and trendy shopping, while the beach towns are great for soaking up the laid-back SoCal vibe.

DOWNTOWN
There's something afoot in Downtown LA, and adventurous urbanites are taking note. A budding arts district, stylish lofts reclaimed from aging office buildings, quirky

DOWNTOWN LOS ANGELES

0 _____ 1 km
0 _____ 0.5 miles

INFORMATION
Downtown Los Angeles Visitors
 Center...1 B4
Visitor Center....................................2 D4

SIGHTS & ACTIVITIES
Avila Adobe......................................3 D4
Bob Baker Marionette Theater...........4 B3
Bradbury Building..............................5 C4
Cathedral of Our Lady of the Angels..6 C3
Central Plaza.....................................7 D3
Chinese American Museum.................8 D4
City Hall..9 C4
Dorothy Chandler Pavilion...............10 C4
Grand Central Market.......................11 C4
Japanese American National
 Museum...12 D4
MOCA Geffen Contemporary...........13 D4
MOCA Grand Avenue.......................14 C4
Orpheum..15 B5
Union Station...................................16 C4
Walt Disney Concert Hall.................17 C4

SLEEPING
Figueroa Hotel.................................18 A5
Millennium Biltmore Hotel...............19 B4
Standard Downtown LA..............(see 26)
Stillwell Hotel..................................20 B5

EATING
Ciudad...21 B4
Empress Pavilion..............................22 D3
Patina..(see 17)
Philippe the Original........................23 D3
Water Grill.......................................24 B5
Zip Fusion..25 D5

DRINKING
Rooftop Lounge @ Standard
 Downtown LA................................26 B4

ENTERTAINMENT
Dodger Stadium...............................27 D2
East West Players.............................28 D4
Los Angeles Opera......................(see 10)

Los Angeles Philharmonic...........(see 17)
Mark Taper Forum...........................29 C3
Redcat...(see 17)
Staples Center.................................30 A5

TRANSPORT
Greyhound.......................................31 D6
Union Station/Gateway Transit
 Center..32 D4

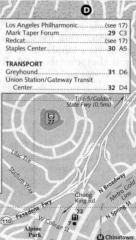

CALIFORNIA

bars and restaurants, and headline-grabbing architecture all fuel the buzz. If you're open-minded and don't mind a little grit and grime here and there, Downtown is your oyster. Park the car, then explore on foot or via a DASH minibus (p795). Parking is cheapest (about $5 all day) around Little Tokyo and Chinatown.

El Pueblo de Los Angeles & Around

Compact, colorful and car-free, this state historic park commemorates LA's founding and preserves the city's oldest buildings, most notably the 1818 **Avila Adobe** (Map p777; ☎ 213-680-2525; admission free; ☺ 10am-3pm). It's right on **Olvera Street**, a block-long, Mexican-flavored brick alley that's lined with tacky souvenir stalls and simple eateries. Pick up a self-guided tour pamphlet at the **visitor center** (Map p777; ☎ 213-628-1274; Sepulveda House, Olvera St; ☺ 10am-3pm).

Near El Pueblo, the 1939 Spanish Mission–style **Union Station** (Map p777; 800 N Alameda St) is the last of the grand railroad stations built in the US. It stands on the spot of LA's original Chinatown, whose residents were forcibly relocated a few blocks north to the area along Broadway and Hill St. Today's **Chinatown** is still a vibrant cultural and social hub of LA's Chinese Americans but of late has also begun registering on the radar of artists and hipsters from around town. Check out the galleries and eclectic stores in the historic **Central Plaza** (Map p777; 947 N Broadway) mall and on nearby **Chung King Road**. For more on the community, visit the new **Chinese American Museum** (Map p777; ☎ 213-485-8567; www.camla.org; 425 N Los Angeles St; suggested donation $3; ☺ 10am-3pm Tue-Sun).

Civic Center

LA's 1928 **City Hall** (Map p777; ☎ 213-978-0642; 200 N Spring St; admission free; ☺ 8am-5pm Mon-Fri) cameoed as the *Daily Planet* in the *Superman* TV series and got blown to bits in the 1953 sci-fi thriller *War of the Worlds*. If the smog isn't bad, you'll enjoy 360-degree views from the wraparound observation deck. Call for free tour times.

Northwest of here, the Frank Gehry–designed **Walt Disney Concert Hall** (Map p777; ☎ 213-972-4399, ext 5; http://wdch.laphil.com; 111 S Grand Ave; tours guided $10, audio adult/student/senior $10/8/8; ☺ tours guided 10-11:30am matinee days, audio 9am-3pm nonmatinee days) is a gravity-defying sculpture of curving and billowing stainless-steel walls that conjures visions of a ship adrift in a rough sea. Disney Hall is the new home of the Los Angeles Philharmonic, which used to play at the Dorothy Chandler Pavilion just east of here.

Also on Grand Avenue's 'cultural corridor' is **MOCA Grand Avenue** (Map p777; ☎ 213-626-6222; www.moca-la.org; 250 S Grand Ave; adult/child/student/senior $8/free/5/5, Thu free; ☺ 11am-5pm Mon & Fri, to 8pm Thu, to 6pm Sat & Sun), an Arata Isozaki–designed art museum that presents all the heavy hitters working from the 1940s to the present – Andy Warhol to Cy Twombly.

North of Disney Hall looms the new **Cathedral of Our Lady of the Angels** (Map p777; ☎ 213-680-5200; www.olacathedral.org; 555 W Temple St; admission & tours free; ☺ 6:30am-6pm Mon-Fri, from 9am Sat, from 7am Sun; tours 1pm Mon-Fri; P), a monumental work by Spanish architect José Rafael Moneo. Behind its austere ochre mantle awaits a vast hall of worship filled with plenty of original art and soft light filtering in through milky, alabaster windows. Gregory Peck is buried in the mausoleum. The cathedral store sells self-guided tour booklets.

Pershing Square & Around

A short stroll southwest of City Hall plunges you right into Downtown's historic core anchored by **Pershing Square** (Map p777), LA's oldest public park (1866) and flanked by the grand old **Millennium Biltmore Hotel** (p787). The forest of office high-rises just north of here marks the bustling Financial District.

Southwest of Pershing Sq, along Hill St, gold and diamonds are the main currency in the **Jewelry District**. For dazzling architecture head to nearby Broadway whose 1893 **Bradbury Building** (Map p777; ☎ 213-626-1893; 304 S Broadway; admission free; ☺ 9am-6pm Mon-Fri, to 5pm Sat & Sun) is the undisputed crown jewel. Its red-brick facade conceals a light-flooded, galleried atrium that has starred in such movies as *Blade Runner*. Across the street, the colorful and frenzied **Grand Central Market** (Map p777; ☎ 213-624-2378; 317 S Broadway; ☺ 9am-6pm) is great for a browse or a snack.

Broadway also earned a spot on the National Register of Historic Places for its 11 lavish **movie palaces**, built between 1913 and 1931 in a marvelous hodgepodge of styles, from Spanish Gothic to French baroque. Some, such as the **Orpheum** (Map p777; 842 Broadway), have been gloriously restored and are now used for special screenings, parties and other events.

Shopaholics should head south to the **Fashion District**, a 56-square-block area that's more Arabic bazaar than American mall. Bargains abound and haggling is ubiquitous.

Little Tokyo
Little Tokyo is the Japanese counterpart to Chinatown, with an attractive mix of traditional gardens, Buddhist temples, outdoor shopping malls and sushi bars. A great introduction to the area is the **Japanese American National Museum** (Map p777; ☎ 213-625-0414; www .janm.org; 369 E 1st St; adult/child/student/senior $8/ free/4/5, 5-8pm Thu free; ☼ 10am-5pm Tue-Sun, to 8pm Thu), whose permanent exhibit includes displays about WWII internment camps such as the one at Manzanar in the Eastern Sierra (p867).

The adjacent **MOCA Geffen Contemporary** (Map p777; ☎ 213-626-6222; www.moca-la.org; 152 N Central Ave; adult/child/student/senior $8/free/5/5, Thu free; ☼ 11am-5pm Mon & Fri, to 8pm Thu, to 6pm Sat & Sun) presents mostly large-scale installations.

In the gritty section southeast of Little Tokyo an **Arts District** is emerging ever so slowly. The young and adventurous types living and working in makeshift studios above abandoned warehouses support a growing number of cafés, restaurants and shops.

EXPOSITION PARK & AROUND
A couple of miles south of Downtown LA, the family-friendly **Exposition Park** (Map pp774–5) began as an agricultural fairground in 1872 and now contains three quality museums, a lovely **Rose Garden** (admission free; ☼ 9am-dusk mid-Mar–Dec) and the 1923 **Los Angeles Memorial Coliseum**. The latter hosted the 1932 and 1984 Summer Olympic Games, the 1959 baseball World Series and two Super Bowls. The **University of Southern California** (USC) campus is just north of the park, which is served from Downtown by DASH bus 'F' (p795). There's $6 parking on Figueroa at 39th St.

The **Natural History Museum of LA County** (Map pp774-5; ☎ 213-763-3466; www.nhm.org; 900 Exposition Blvd; adult/child/senior/student $9/2/6.50/6.50; ☼ 9:30am-5pm Mon-Fri, from 10am Sat & Sun) usually makes headlines with its special exhibits but also has interesting permanent halls filled with such crowd-pleasers as stuffed African elephants, a *Tyrannosaurus rex* skull and a super-rare megamouth shark.

There are plenty of buttons to push next door at the **California Science Center** (Map pp774-5; ☎ 323-724-3623; www.californiasciencecenter.org; 700 State Dr; admission free; ☼ 10am-5pm) where you can also watch baby chicks hatch, meet a giant techno-doll named Tess, ride out a simulated earthquake or watch a movie at the adjacent **IMAX** (☎ 213-744-7400; adult/child/ senior/student $7.50/4.50/5.50/5.50).

Steps away, the **California African American Museum** (Map pp774-5; ☎ 213-744-7432; www.caa museum.org; 600 State Dr; admission free; ☼ 10am-4pm Wed-Sat) presents a range of African American art and artifacts, especially by artists working in the western USA.

The area south of Exposition Park, along both sides of the I-110 (Harbor Fwy), is generally known as South Los Angeles, a largely bleak area that's no stranger to poverty and crime. Pretty much the only reason to venture down here is to see the amazing **Watts Towers** (Map pp774-5; ☎ 213-847-4646; 1765 E 107th St; adult/child/senior $5/free/3; ☼ 11am-2:30pm Fri, from 10:30am Sat, 12:30-3pm Sun), a superb example of folk art built entirely from found objects – green 7-Up bottles to seashells and pottery.

HOLLYWOOD
Aging movie stars know that a facelift can pump up a drooping career, and it seems the same can be done with LA neighborhoods. Legendary **Hollywood Boulevard** (Map p780) in particular has been groomed and spruced up in recent years, and even though it's still far from recapturing the glamour of its Golden Age (1920s to '40s), at least some of the seediness is gone.

The most interesting mile runs between La Brea Blvd and Vine St, along the **Hollywood Walk of Fame**, which honors more than 2000 celebrities with brass stars embedded in the sidewalk. For interesting tidbits about local landmarks keep an eye out for the big historic signs along here, or join a guided walking tour (p787).

The spark plug for the boulevard's rebirth was the construction of **Hollywood & Highland** (Map p780; ☎ 323-467-6412; www.hollywoodandhighland .com; 6801 Hollywood Blvd; admission free; ☼ 24hr), a big mall that's a perfect marriage of kitsch and commerce. Its **Kodak Theatre** (Map p780; ☎ 323-308-6363; www.kodaktheatre.com; adult/child/ senior/student $15/10/10/10; ☼ 10:30am-4pm Jun-Aug, to 2:30pm Sep-May) hosts the Academy Awards and other star-studded events.

CALIFORNIA

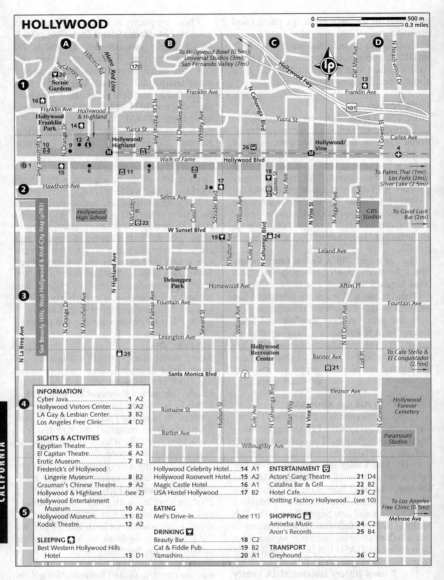

Hollywood & Highland basically dwarfs the 1927 **Grauman's Chinese Theatre** (Map p780; ☎ 323-464-6266; 6925 Hollywood Blvd), famous for its forecourt where screen legends have left their imprint in cement: feet, hands and – in the case of Jimmy Durante – a protruding proboscis. Other classic movie palaces along here include the flamboyant 1926 **El Capitan Theatre** (Map p780; ☎ 323-467-7674; 6838 Hollywood Blvd) and the 1922 **Egyptian Theatre** (Map p780; ☎ 323-466-3456; 6712 Hollywood Blvd).

One of the boulevard's newest attractions is the engaging **Hollywood Museum** (Map p780; ☎ 323-464-7776; www.thehollywoodmuseum.com; 1660 N Highland Ave; adult/child/senior $15/12/12; ☷ 10am-5pm Thu-Sun), a veritable shrine to the stars –

Chaplin to Leonardo. The basement holds Hannibal Lecter's original jail cell from *Silence of the Lambs*.

For more film and TV sets (from *Star Trek*, *X-Files* and *Cheers*) make a beeline to the **Hollywood Entertainment Museum** (Map p780; ☎ 323-465-7900; www.hollywoodmuseum.com; 7021 Hollywood Blvd; adult/student/senior $12/5/10; ☯ 10am-6pm late May–early Sep, 11am-6pm Thu-Tue mid-Sep–mid-May), which also offers a moderately interesting romp through the history and mystery of moviemaking.

East of Highland Ave, Hollywood Blvd's seedier side survives in numerous tattoo parlors and stripper supply stores, making it a suitable setting for the new **Erotic Museum** (Map p780; ☎ 323-463-7684; www.theeroticmuseum.com; 6741 Hollywood Blvd; adult/student/senior $13/10/10; ☯ noon-9pm Sun-Thu, to midnight Fri & Sat). Inside are naughty sketches by Picasso, nude pictures of Marilyn, early John Holmes porn and changing exhibits ranging from silly to saucy to sexy. And yes, you must be at least 18 to enter.

For more titillation drop by the **Lingerie Museum** (Map p780; ☎ 323-957-5953; 6608 Hollywood Blvd; admission free; ☯ 10am-9pm Mon-Sat, 11am-7pm Sun), a small collection of the stars' undies inside the original store of push-up bra pioneer Frederick's of Hollywood.

Lording it over the bustle, in its dignified hillside perch, looms LA's most recognizable landmark, the **Hollywood Sign**, built in 1923 as an advertising gimmick for a real-estate development called Hollywoodland. East of Hwy 101 (Hollywood Fwy), the neighborhoods of **Los Feliz** (loss *fee*-les) and **Silver Lake** are bohemian-chic enclaves with shopping, funky bars and a hopping cuisine scene.

The Metro Red Line (p794) serves central Hollywood and Los Feliz from Downtown LA and the San Fernando Valley. There's validated parking ($2 for four hours) at Hollywood & Highland.

GRIFFITH PARK

Sprawling **Griffith Park** (Map pp774-5; ☎ 323-913-4688; admission free; ☯ 6am-10pm, trails close at dusk) is a thick spread of California oak, wild sage and manzanita that is five times the size of New York's Central Park. Access is easiest via the Griffith Park Dr or Zoo Dr exits off I-5 (Golden State Fwy). Parking is plentiful and free. For information and maps stop by the **Griffith Park Ranger Station** (☎ 323-665-5188; 4730 Crystal Springs Dr).

The large park harbors numerous family-friendly diversions, notably the **Los Angeles Zoo** (Map pp774-5; ☎ 323-644-4200; www.lazoo.org; 5333 Zoo Dr; adult/child/senior $10/5/7; ☯ 10am-5pm,

---

STARGAZING

Hollywood hasn't been a promising place to bump into celebs since most of the studios moved north to the San Fernando Valley in the 1950s. To see particular TV stars, your best bet is to watch tapings of their shows. **Audiences Unlimited** (☎ 818-753-3470, ext 812; www.tvtickets.com) handles ticket distribution for dozens of shows, mostly sitcoms. Production season runs from August to March and tickets are free.

Tickets may also be picked up at the Entertainment Center inside **Universal Studios Hollywood** (Map pp774-5; ☎ 818-622-3801; www.universalstudioshollywood.com; 100 Universal City Plaza; admission over/under 48in $50/40; ☯ vary), one of the world's largest movie studios. Its movie-based theme park offers an entertaining mix of thrill rides, live action and audience participation shows (like the new Fear Factor Live), plus a studio backlot tram tour peppered with special effects. Adjacent to the park, **Universal City Walk** is a fantasy promenade of shops, restaurants, movie theaters and nightclubs.

For a more 'edu-taining' look at movie-making, join the guided tours run by **Warner Bros Studios** (Map pp774-5; ☎ 818-972-8687; www2.warnerbros.com/vipstudiotour; 3400 Riverside Dr, Burbank, San Fernando Valley; tours $39; ☯ 8:30am-4pm Mon-Fri; Ⓟ) or **Sony Pictures Studios** (Map pp774-5; ☎ 323-520-8687; 10202 W Washington Blvd, Culver City; tours $24; ☯ Mon-Fri; Ⓟ). Both take you to sound stages, outdoor sets and into such departments as wardrobe and makeup. Reservations are required; bring photo ID.

NBC Studios (Map pp774-5; ☎ 818-840-3537; 3000 W Alameda Ave, Burbank, San Fernando Valley; adult/child $7.50/4.50; ☯ 9am-3pm Mon-Fri) runs tours that include a stop at the *Tonight Show* set. For tickets to *Tonight Show* tapings, call or check www.nbc.com/nbc/footer/Tickets.shtml.

to 6pm Jul–early Sep) whose 1200 finned, feathered and furry friends rarely fail to enthrall visitors.

Those keen on learning how the West was won will hit the mother lode at the **Museum of the American West** (Map pp774-5; ☎ 323-667-2000; www.museumoftheamericanwest.org; 4700 Western Heritage Way; adult/child/senior/student $7.50/3/5/5; ♥ 10am-5pm Tue-Sun, to 8pm Thu). Its 10 galleries skillfully combine scholarship and showmanship and are a veritable gold mine of Old West memorabilia.

On the southern perimeter, the landmark 1935 **Griffith Observatory & Planetarium** (Map pp774-5; ☎ 323-664-1181; www.griffithobs.org; 2800 E Observatory Rd) has been undergoing a top-to-bottom overhaul and should by now be reprising its 'starring' role as a window to the universe. Call for times and prices.

WEST HOLLYWOOD

West Hollywood (WeHo) teems with clubs, bars, boutiques and elegant hotels and packs more personality into its minuscule 1.9 sq miles than most larger neighborhoods. Much of the action is concentrated along the famous **Sunset Strip** (Map p783, Sunset Blvd between Laurel Canyon Blvd and Doheny Dr), a favorite nighttime playground since the 1920s and easily recognized by its giant billboards. WeHo is also the heart of gay and lesbian life in LA, with most hangouts found along Santa Monica Blvd between Robertson and La Cienega Blvds.

Further south, near the western end of boutique-lined **Melrose Avenue**, the architecturally striking Pacific Design Center harbors the small **MOCA Pacific Design Center** (Map p783; ☎ 213-626-6222; www.moca-la.org; 8687 Melrose Ave; admission free; ♥ 11am-5pm Tue, Wed & Fri, 11am-8pm Thu, 11am-6pm Sat & Sun), whose rotating exhibits tend to revolve around architecture and design themes. The surrounding **Avenues of Art & Design** invite strolling, people-watching and gallery-hopping.

MID-CITY

East of WeHo, along Fairfax Ave, the **Fairfax District** (Map p783) lures visitors with its **Original Farmers Market** (6333 W 3rd St) and the adjacent **Grove**, an open-air shopping mall.

For a dose of culture, follow Fairfax south to Wilshire Blvd's Museum Row, anchored by the exquisite **Los Angeles County Museum of Art** (LACMA; Map p783; ☎ 323-857-6000; www.lacma.org;

5901 Wilshire Blvd; adult/child/senior/student $9/free/5/5, after 5pm free; ♥ noon-8pm Mon, Tue & Thu, to 9pm Fri, 11am-8pm Sat & Sun). One of the country's leading art museums, it brims with several millennia worth of paintings, sculpture and decorative arts from around the world and also hosts such blockbuster touring exhibits as the recent King Tut extravaganza.

LA's love affair with the automobile is celebrated at the **Petersen Automotive Museum** (Map p783; ☎ 323-930-2277; www.petersen.org; 6060 Wilshire Blvd; adult/child/senior/student $10/3/5/5; ♥ 10am-6pm Tue-Sun; Ⓟ), whose entertaining mock LA streetscape creatively chronicles how the automobile has helped shaped the city's growth. Parking $6.

Museum Row is also home to the **Page Museum** (Map p783; ☎ 323-934-7243; www.tarpits.org; 5801 Wilshire Blvd; adult/child/senior/student $7/2/4.50/4.50; ♥ 9:30am-5pm Mon-Fri, 10am-5pm Sat & Sun; Ⓟ), which displays the fossilized skeletons of long-extinct mammals that died in the adjacent **La Brea Tar Pits**, such as saber-toothed cats, ground sloths, mammoths and mastodons. Parking $6.

BEVERLY HILLS

The mere mention of Beverly Hills conjures images of fame and wealth, reinforced by film and TV. Fact is, the reality is not so different from the myth. Stylish and sophisticated, this is indeed where the well-heeled frolic. If you're into stargazing, you could take a guided bus tour (p787), buy a map to the stars' homes or bump into George Clooney at Spago Beverly Hills (p791). Several city-owned garages offer two hours of free parking.

Attractions in the downtown area include **Rodeo Drive**, a three-block ribbon of style for the Prada and Gucci brigade, and the nearby **Museum of Television & Radio** (Map p783; ☎ 310-786-1000; www.mtr.org; 465 N Beverly Dr; suggested donation adult/child/senior/student $10/5/8/8; ♥ noon-5pm Wed-Sun). At this enormous archive you can select your favorite broadcasts – sports to sitcoms, documentaries to cartoons – and then view or listen to them at your own private console.

About a mile south, the **Museum of Tolerance** (Map p783; ☎ 310-553-8403; www.museumoftolerance .com; 9786 W Pico Blvd; adult/child/student/senior $10/7/7/8; ♥ 11:30am-6:30pm Mon-Thu & to 3pm Fri Nov-Mar, to 5pm Fri Apr-Oct, 11am-7:30pm Sun) uses interactive technology to make visitors confront

BEVERLEY HILLS, WEST HOLLYWOOD & MID-CITY

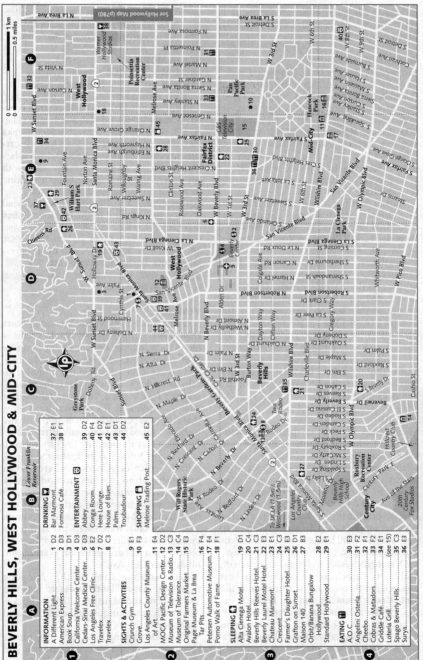

Will Rogers
State Historic
Park

To UCLA (1.5mi);
Westwood (1.5mi)

Los Angeles
Country
Club

0   1 km
0   0.5 miles

See Hollywood Map (p780)

West
Hollywood

Warner
Hollywood
Studios

Poinsettia
Recreation
Center

Pan
Pacific
Park

CBS
Television
City

Fairfax
District

Beverly
Center

West
Hollywood

Greystone
Park

Beverly Gardens Park

Beverly
Hills

Rexbury
Recreation
Center

Beverly
Hills High
School

Century
City

Hancock
Park

Mid-City

Lower Franklin
Reservoir

CALIFORNIA

racism and bigotry, although the focus is clearly on the Holocaust. Last entry is 2½ hours before closing.

WESTWOOD & AROUND

Just west of Beverly Hills, Westwood is defined by the vast campus of the **University of California, Los Angeles** (UCLA, Map pp774–5), one of the country's top universities. In Westwood Village, south of campus, the **UCLA Hammer Museum** (Map pp774-5; ☎ 310-443-7000; www.hammer.ucla.edu; 10899 Wilshire Blvd; adult/child/student/senior $5/free/free/3; ☺ 11am-7pm Tue, Wed, Fri & Sat, to 9pm Thu, to 5pm Sun; Ⓟ with validation $2.75) presents cutting-edge contemporary art exhibits.

Fans of Marilyn Monroe, Natalie Wood, Roy Orbison and other stars can pay them their final respects at the nearby **Westwood Memorial Park** (1218 Glendon Ave; admission free; ☺ 8am-dusk; Ⓟ).

Northwest of Westwood, high above the 405 (San Diego) Fwy, is one of LA's must-sees: the $1-billion **Getty Center** (Map pp774-5; ☎ 310-440-7300; www.getty.edu; 1200 Getty Center Dr; admission free; ☺ 10am-6pm Sun & Tue-Thu, to 9pm Fri & Sat; Ⓟ) The sprawling art campus presents triple delights: a respectable art collection (Renaissance to David Hockney), the fabulous architecture of Richard Meier and beautiful gardens. On clear days, you'll also be treated to breathtaking views of city and ocean. Parking $7.

MALIBU

Malibu hugs 27 miles of spectacular coastline, right where the Santa Monica Mountains plunge into the ocean. It has been a celebrity enclave since the early 1930s when money troubles forced landowner May Rindge to lease out property to her famous friends. Clara Bow and Barbara Stanwyck were among the first to stake out their turf in what became known as the **Malibu Colony** (Map pp774–5). It is still home to such A-list celebs as Tom Hanks and Barbra Streisand today.

Despite its wealth and high star quotient, Malibu is surprisingly low-key and best appreciated through its twin treasures: the **Santa Monica Mountains** and the beaches, including the famous **Surfrider Beach**.

Further east, the original Getty museum, the **Getty Villa** (Map pp774-5; www.getty.edu; 17985 Pacific Coast Hwy), was scheduled to reopen in early 2006 after an eight-year renovation. It will

showcase the institution's precious collection of Greek, Roman and Etruscan antiquities in a reconstructed Roman mansion.

SANTA MONICA

Santa Monica is LA's most agreeable seaside city, with wide beaches, a pedestrian-friendly downtown and plenty of shopping and dining, especially along **Third Street Promenade**, **Main Street** and **Montana Avenue** (Map p785). Kids love the venerable **Santa Monica Pier**, where diversions include a historic carousel, a small amusement park with a solar-powered Ferris wheel, and an aquarium with touch tanks. There's free two-hour parking in public garages on 2nd and 4th Sts.

Devotees of avant-garde art should head about 3 miles inland to the **Bergamot Station Arts Center** (Map p785; 2525 Michigan Ave, enter from Cloverfield Blvd; most galleries ☺ 10am-6pm Tue-Sat; Ⓟ), with over 30 galleries and the progressive **Santa Monica Museum of Art** (Map p785; ☎ 310-586-6488; www.smmoa.org; admission by donation; ☺ 11am-6pm Tue-Sat).

VENICE

If aliens landed on Venice's famous **Ocean Front Walk** (Map p785), they would probably blend right into the human zoo of wannabe Schwarzeneggers, a Speedo-clad 'snake man' and a roller-skating Sikh minstrel. Known locally as Venice Boardwalk, this is the place to get your hair braided, your skin tattooed or your aura adjusted. It's a surreal freak show that's best experienced on a hot summer weekend. Avoid the boardwalk after dark.

Venice was founded in 1905 by tobacco heir Abbot Kinney as an amusement park called 'Venice of America' where Italian *gondolieri* poled visitors around canals. Most canals vanished beneath roads later on, but some have been restored and are now flanked by flower-festooned homes. The **Venice Canal Walk** (Map p785) threads through this idyllic neighborhood, best accessed from either Venice or Washington Blvds, near Dell Ave.

Also worth a stroll is the mile-long stretch of **Abbot Kinney Boulevard** between Venice Blvd and Main St, which is chockablock with fun boutiques, galleries, bars and restaurants.

There are parking lots ($6 to $15) on the beach and near the Venice Boardwalk and street parking on Abbot Kinney Blvd.

SANTA MONICA & VENICE

INFORMATION	
California Map & Travel Center....**1**	D1
Interactive Café.............................**2**	A2
Santa Monica Visitor Center.......**3**	B2
Santa Monica Visitor Kiosk........**4**	A2

SIGHTS & ACTIVITIES	
Bergamot Station Arts Center....**5**	C1
Gold's Gym..................................**6**	B3
Magicopolis.................................**7**	A2
Puppet & Magic Center..............**8**	A2
Santa Monica Museum of Art...(see 5)	
Santa Monica Pier......................**9**	A2
Yoga Works.................................**10**	B2

SLEEPING	
Ambrose.....................................**11**	B1
Cal Mar Hotel Suites..................**12**	A1
Georgian Hotel...........................**13**	A2
HI Los Angeles–Santa Monica....**14**	A2
Inn at Venice Beach....................**15**	C4
Sea Shore Motel.........................**16**	B3

EATING	
Beechwood.................................**17**	D4
Counter......................................**18**	D1
JiRaffe.......................................(see 20)	
Mao's Kitchen............................**19**	C4
Real Food Daily..........................**20**	A2
Venice Cantina...........................**21**	C4

DRINKING	
Roosterfish.................................**22**	C4
Toppers......................................**23**	A1
Voda..**24**	A2

ENTERTAINMENT	
Temple Bar.................................**25**	B1

LONG BEACH

Long Beach's flagship attraction is the elegant and supposedly haunted British ocean liner **Queen Mary** (Map pp774-5; ☎ 562-435-3511; www.queenmary.com; 1126 Queens Hwy; adult/child/senior $23/12/20; ⏲ 10am-5pm Mon-Thu, to 6pm Fri-Sun, but vary by season; (P)). Larger and more luxurious than even the *Titanic*, it transported royals, dignitaries, immigrants and troops during its 1001 Atlantic crossings between 1936 and 1964. Moored next to the *Queen* is the **Scorpion** (adult/child/senior $10/9/9), an authentic Soviet submarine whose claustrophobic interior is open for self-touring. Parking $10.

Fans of watery zoos will love the **Aquarium of the Pacific** (Map pp774-5; ☎ 562-590-3100; www.aquariumofpacific.org; 100 Aquarium Way; adult/ child/senior $19/11/17; ⏲ 9am-6pm; (P)), a joyful, high-tech romp through an intriguing underwater world where sharks dart, jellyfish dance and sea lions frolic. Its 12,500 creatures hail from tepid Baja California, the frigid northern Pacific, tropical coral reefs and local kelp forests. You can even pet small sharks. Parking $6.

Long Beach can be easily reached from Downtown via the Metro Rail Blue Line. **Pine Avenue** is a major nosh and party strip.

PASADENA

Resting in the shadow of the lofty San Gabriel Mountains, northeast of Downtown, Pasadena is a genteel city with old-time mansions, superb architecture and fine art

CALIFORNIA

museums. Every New Year's Day, it is thrust into the national spotlight during the Rose Parade (opposite) and the ensuing football game played at the famous 1922 **Rose Bowl** stadium.

The city's main fun zone is **Old Pasadena**, a bustling shopping and entertainment district along Colorado Blvd, between Arroyo Seco Parkway and Pasadena Ave. A short walk west, the **Norton Simon Museum** (☎ 626-449-6840; www.nortonsimon.org; 411 W Colorado Blvd; adult/child/student/senior $6/free/free/3; ❧ noon-6pm Wed-Mon, to 9pm Fri; **P**) has a prized collection of European art from Renaissance to the 20th century, plus an exquisite sampling of 2000 years of Indian and Southeast Asian sculpture.

Nearby, the 1908 **Gamble House** (Map pp774-5; ☎ 626-793-3334; www.gamblehouse.org; 4 Westmoreland Pl; adult/child/student/senior $8/free/5/5; ❧ noon-3pm Thu-Sun; **P**), designed by Charles and Henry Greene, is a prime example of Craftsman architecture.

Urban LA feels a world away at the rarefied **Huntington Library, Art Collections & Botanical Gardens** (Map pp774-5; ☎ 626-405-2100; www.huntington.org; 1151 Oxford Rd; adult/child/student/senior $15/6/10/12; ❧ noon-4:30pm Tue-Fri, from 10:30am Sat & Sun; **P**), the former estate of railroad tycoon Henry Huntington. Don't miss the Japanese Garden, the Desert Garden and the 1455 Gutenberg Bible in the library. The art gallery focuses mainly on 18th-century British and French paintings.

Activities
CYCLING & IN-LINE SKATING
The nicest place for skating or riding is along the paved beach trail that travels 22 miles from Santa Monica to Torrance Beach, with a detour around the yacht harbor at Marina del Rey. Rental outfits are plentiful in all beach towns. Mountain bikers will find the Santa Monica Mountains a suitable playground. The website at www.labikepaths.com has lots of good information.

FITNESS CENTERS & GYMS
Many midrange and practically all top-end hotels have small fitness centers, but for group classes or a full-fledged workout, try one of these places:

Crunch Gym (Map p783; ☎ 323-654-4550; www.crunch.com; 8000 Sunset Blvd, W Hollywood; per day $24; ❧ 5am-midnight Mon-Fri, 7am-10pm Sat & Sun) High-tech gym with cutting-edge classes such as Disco Yoga and Cycle Karaoke.

Gold's Gym (Map p785; ☎ 310-392-6004; www.goldsgym.com; 360 Hampton Dr, Venice; per day $20; ❧ 4am-midnight Mon-Fri, 5am-11pm Sat & Sun) Pump it up at Arnold's old gym.

Yoga Works (Map p785; ☎ 310-393-5150; www.yogaworks.com; 2215 Main St, Santa Monica; per class $16) Popular place for doing the plough or sun salutation.

HIKING
Just a hop, skip and jump from frenzied Hollywood Blvd, **Runyon Canyon Park** (Map pp774-5) is a surprise slice of wilderness, while nearby **Griffith Park** is also laced by numerous trails. For longer rambles head to the Santa Monica Mountains, where **Will Rogers State Historic Park**, **Topanga State Park** and **Malibu Creek State Park** are all excellent gateways to beautiful terrain. Maps are available at park entrances. Admission is free, but parking costs $8.

SWIMMING & SURFING
Water temperatures become tolerable by late spring and peak at about 70°F (21°C) in August and September. Water quality varies; for updated conditions check the 'Beach Report Card' at www.healthebay.org. Good surfing spots include Malibu Lagoon State Beach, aka Surfrider Beach, and the Manhattan Beach pier (Map pp774-5).

Los Angeles for Children
Keeping the rug rats entertained should not be hard in LA. Many museums and attractions have kid-oriented exhibits, activities and workshops, but for a special treat head to the excellent new **Kidspace Children's Museum** (Map pp774-5; ☎ 626-449-9144; www.kidspacemuseum.org; 480 N Arroyo Blvd, Pasadena; admission $8, ❧ 9:30am-5pm; **P**), which has hands-on exhibits, outdoor learning areas and gardens.

Kids love animals, of course, making the sprawling Los Angeles Zoo (p781) in family-friendly Griffith Park a sure bet. Dinosaur fans gravitate to the Natural History Museum of LA County (p779), while budding scientists love the California Science Center (p779) next door.

The Santa Monica Pier (p784) has carnival rides and a small aquarium, but for a full 'fishy' immersion head south to the Aquarium of the Pacific (p785) in Long Beach, which also has the grand Queen Mary (p785), where teens might get a kick out of the ghost tours.

The adorable singing and dancing marionettes at **Bob Baker Marionette Theater** (Map p777; ☎ 213-250-9995; www.bobbakermarionettes.com; 1345 W 1st St, near Downtown; admission $10, reservations required; ☒ 10:30am Tue-Sat, 2:30pm Sat & Sun; ℗) have enthralled generations of Angelenos. A similarly magical experience awaits at **Puppet & Magic Center** (Map p785; ☎ 310-656-0483; www.puppetmagic.com; 1255 2nd St, Santa Monica; admission $6.50; ☒ 1pm Wed, 1pm & 3pm Sat & Sun). For real magic tricks, try nearby **Magicopolis** (Map p785; ☎ 310-451-2241; www.magicopolis.com; 1418 4th St, Santa Monica; matinee/evening $20/27; ☒ shows 8pm Fri & Sat, 2:30pm Sat & Sun).

Many hotels can provide referrals to reliable, qualified babysitter services.

Tours

Los Angeles Conservancy (☎ 213-623-2489; www.laconservancy.org) Thematic walking tours, mostly of Downtown LA, with an architectural focus. Reservations required.

Red Line Tours (☎ 323-402-1074; www.redlinetours.com) 'Edutaining' walking tours of Hollywood and Downtown using headsets that cut out traffic noise.

Spirit Cruises (☎ 310-548-8080; www.spiritcitycruises.com) Cruises and whale-watching excursions (January to March) departing from Marina del Rey, San Pedro and Long Beach.

Starline Tours (☎ 323-463-333, 800-959-3131; www.starlinetours.com) Narrated bus tours of the city, stars' homes and theme parks.

Festivals & Events

LA has a packed calendar of annual festivals and special events. Here are some of the blockbusters (in chronological order):

Rose Parade (☎ 626-449-4100; www.tournamentofroses.com) New Year's Day cavalcade of flower-festooned floats along Pasadena's Colorado Blvd, followed by the Rose Bowl football game.

Cinco de Mayo (☎ 213-625-5045; www.cityofla.org/elp; ☒) Free festivities in Downtown LA's El Pueblo de Los Angeles from late April to early May.

Sunset Junction Street Fair (☎ 323-661-7771; www.sunsetjunction.org) Street party celebrating Silver Lake's cultural wackiness with grub, libations and edgy bands in mid-August.

West Hollywood Halloween Carnival (☎ 323-848-6400; www.visitwesthollywood.com) Free rambunctious street fair with eccentric, and often X-rated, costumes on Santa Monica Blvd in West Hollywood on October 31.

Pasadena Doo Dah Parade (☎ 626-440-7379; www.pasadenadoodahparade.com) Wacky Rose Parade parody on the Sunday before Thanksgiving.

Hollywood Christmas Parade (☎ 323-469-2337; www.hollywoodchamber.net) On the Sunday after Thanksgiving, celebs ring in the season by waving at fans from flashy floats along Hollywood Blvd.

Sleeping

When picking a neighborhood for your stay, think about what type of experience you most want. For the beach life, base yourself in Santa Monica or Venice. Urban explorers will want to be close to West Hollywood, while Downtown is great for fans of history and architecture but pretty dead after dark. Central Hollywood provides easy access to the Metro Rail Red Line, but staying in posh Beverly Hills is certain to impress folks back home. Some bargains notwithstanding, hotel rates in Los Angeles are steep. We've listed peak rates, so prices should drop in the off-season. The lodging tax is 12% to 14%. Hotel parking is free unless noted otherwise.

DOWNTOWN

Stillwell Hotel (Map p777; ☎ 213-627-1151, 800-553-4774; 838 S Grand Ave; r $50-60; ☒) Nearly a century old, the Stillwell offers clean and no-nonsense rooms, good security and a bar so noir it seems to have leapt off the pages of a Raymond Chandler novel.

Figueroa Hotel (Map p777; ☎ 213-627-8971, 800-421-9092; www.figueroahotel.com; 939 S Figueroa St; r $120-225; ℗ ☒) This charmer near the Staples Center welcomes guests with a striking, Spanish-style lobby leading to a lovely pool and outdoor bar. The Moroccan-themed rooms are nice but not all are equal, so check out a few before picking your favorite. Parking $8.

Standard Downtown LA (Map p777; ☎ 213-892-8080; www.standardhotel.com; 550 S Flower St; r from $140; ℗ ☒ ☒) This hotel goes after the same young, hip and shag-happy crowd as its Sunset Strip sister (p789). The rooms feature platform beds and peek-through showers. Check out the intense rooftop bar (p792). Parking $25.

Millennium Biltmore (Map p777; ☎ 213-624-1011, 800-245-8673; www.millenniumhotels.com; 506 S Grand Ave; r $160-360, ste $460-3000; ℗ ☒ ☒) Presidents, royalty and celebrities have shacked up in this 1923 palatial landmark. Rooms, sheathed in soothing gold and blue, feature all the trappings, although some are quite small. Parking $24.

'OUT' & ABOUT IN LOS ANGELES

LA is one of the country's gayest cities, with the rainbow flag flying especially proudly along Santa Monica Blvd in West Hollywood (WeHo). Dozens of high-energy bars, cafés, restaurants, gyms and clubs flank this strip, turning it pretty much into a 24/7 fun zone. Beauty reigns supreme in 'Boystown,' while Silver Lake has a big leather and Levi's crowd. The beach towns have the most relaxed, neighborly scenes, especially in Santa Monica, Venice and Long Beach. For the latest news and insider tips, look for freebie magazines in gay-friendly establishments, including **A Different Light** (Map p783; ☎ 310-854-6601; 8853 Santa Monica Blvd, W Hollywood), the bastion of queer lit, nonfiction and magazines. The **LA Gay & Lesbian Center** (Map p780; ☎ 323-993-7400; www.laglc .org; 1625 N Schrader Blvd, Hollywood) is a one-stop service and health agency.

Here are our Top Five party places to get you started:

▪ **Abbey** (Map p783; ☎ 310-289-8410; 692 N Robertson Blvd, W Hollywood) WeHo's funnest, coolest and most varied club, bar and restaurant.

▪ **Here Lounge** (Map p783; ☎ 310-360-8455; 696 N Robertson Blvd, W Hollywood) Premier venue for S&M (standing and modeling).

▪ **Palms** (Map p783; ☎ 310-652-6188; 8572 Santa Monica Blvd, W Hollywood) Lesbian scene staple with legendary Beer Bust Sundays.

▪ **Roosterfish** (Map p785; ☎ 310-392-2123; 1302 Abbot Kinney Blvd, Venice) Timeless, friendly been-there-forever neighborhood bar.

▪ **Faultline** (Map pp774-5; ☎ 323-660-0889; 4216 Melrose Ave, Hollywood) Party central for manly men with nary a twink in sight; Beer Bust Sundays.

HOLLYWOOD

USA Hostel Hollywood (Map p780; ☎ 323-462-3777, 800-524-6783; www.usahostels.com; 1624 Schrader Blvd; incl breakfast & tax dm $22-25, r $59-65, discounts Oct-May; 🖳) Energetic, well-run and supercentral, this hostel is a convivial spot with plenty of parties and activities, a big kitchen, free linen and all-day coffee and tea. All rooms have their own bath.

Magic Castle Hotel (Map p780; ☎ 323-851-0800, 800-741-4915; www.magiccastlehotel.com; 7025 Franklin Ave; r $130-240; P ✕ 🖳 🐾) This fully revamped stand-by now sparkles with trendy blond-wood furniture and attractive art; the full-kitchen suites sleep up to six people. Start your day with fresh croissants and gourmet coffee on your balcony (some rooms) or by the pool. Parking $8.

Hollywood Celebrity Hotel (Map p780; ☎ 323-850-6464, 800-222-7017; www.hotelcelebrity.com; 1775 Orchid Ave; r incl breakfast $90-120; P 🖳) The sleek art deco–style lobby is a welcoming overture to this central, good-value property. The rooms can't quite carry the tune, but most are large, clean and have comfy beds; some have full kitchens.

Best Western Hollywood Hills Hotel (Map p780; ☎ 323-464-5181, 800-287-1700; www.bestwestern.com; 6141 Franklin Ave; r $90-160; P 🐾) A central loca-

tion, cleanliness and accommodating staff are among the winning attributes of this family-run hotel. For more space and quiet, get a room in the back, facing the sparkling tiled pool. The attached hipster coffee shop stays open until 3am.

Hollywood Roosevelt Hotel (Map p780; ☎ 323-466-7000, 800-950-7667; www.hollywoodroosevelt.com; 7000 Hollywood Blvd; r $160-330, ste $550-2500; P 🖳 🐾) A Hollywood favorite since the first Academy Awards were held here in 1929, this historic hotel pairs a palatial Spanish lobby with rooms sporting a sleek Asian contempo look. Marilyn Monroe shot her first commercial (for toothpaste) by the pool. Parking $18.

WEST HOLLYWOOD & MID-CITY

Orbit/Banana Bungalow Hollywood (Map p783; ☎ 323-655-1510, 800-446-7835; www.bananabungalow .com; 7950 Melrose Ave; incl tax dm $18-22, r $54-89; P 🖳) Mod decor, a hip location and dorms with private baths are among the assets of this convivial hostel, which also has plenty of space for lounging and socializing. A café serves inexpensive breakfasts and dinners, but self-caterers will find only a microwave to work with.

Alta Cienega Motel (Map p783; ☎ 310-652-5797; 1005 N La Cienega Blvd; r incl breakfast $60-70; P) The

'Lizard King' Jim Morrison once boozed and snoozed in room 32 of this plain-Jane motel back in the late 1960s.

Farmer's Daughter Hotel (Map p783; ☎ 323-937-3930, 800-334-1658; www.farmersdaughterhotel.com; 115 S Fairfax Ave; r $125-170; P ☒) After an extreme makeover, this LA fixture now sports a sleek 'urban cowboy' look, complete with denim bedspreads and high-speed and wi-fi access. Staff members are happy to clue you in about top spots at the Farmers Market and Grove mall across the street.

Standard Hollywood (Map p783; ☎ 323-650-9090; www.standardhotel.com; 8300 W Sunset Blvd; r $145-225, ste $450; P ☐ ☒) This *über*-hip hotel seems stuck in perpetual party mode, so don't come here for a quiet night's sleep. Surprises abound, including a pool fringed by Astroturf the color of lapis lazuli, a barber who doubles as a tattoo artist, and condoms in the minibar. Parking $18.

Beverly Laurel Motor Hotel (Map p783; ☎ 323-651-2441, 800-962-3824; 8018 Beverly Blvd; r $95-120; mains $4-10; P ☒) Those wanting to ride the retro wave on a slim budget should check into one of the arty rooms at this classic 1950s motel. The attached Swingers diner (dishes $4-10) crawls with hipsters until the wee hours.

Grafton on Sunset (Map p783; ☎ 323-654-4600, 800-821-3660; www.graftononsunset.com; 8462 W Sunset Blvd; r $200-230, ste $250-350; P ☐ ☒) We like this charismatic boutique hotel for its Feng Shui aesthetic, enormous swimming pool and cozy rooms. Staying here puts you within a whisker of the strip's high-velocity club scene (ask the concierge about VIP access). Parking $22.

BEVERLY HILLS

Beverly Hills Reeves Hotel (Map p783; ☎ 310-271-3006; 120 S Reeves Dr; r incl breakfast $90-100; P) Budget and Beverly Hills don't usually mix, except at this simple property on a quiet side street. New management is making some upgrades but promised that prices would hold steady.

Maison 140 (Map p783; ☎ 310-281-4000, 800-432-5444; www.maison140.com; 140 S Lasky Dr; r incl breakfast $170-240; P ☐) This sensuous gem in the former home of silent-movie siren Lillian Gish cleverly marries French frivolity and Asian understatement in rooms that skimp on size but not on luxury. Rates include an evening wine reception and pool privileges at the Avalon (right). Parking $18.

Crescent (Map p783; ☎ 310-247-0505; www.crescent bh.com; 403 N Crescent Dr; r $165-225; P ☒ ☐) New owners have spun this once-dowdy property into a mod hot spot with a buzzing lobby-lounge-bar and chic, if smallish, rooms outfitted with flat-screen TV, iPod mini and free wi-fi. Parking $20.

Avalon Hotel (Map p783; ☎ 310-277-5221, 800-535-4715; www.avalonbeverlyhills.com; 9400 W Olympic Blvd; r $200-370; P ☐ ☒) Midcentury modern meets amenities fit for the new millennium at this stylish boutique hotel where trendy types sip cosmos at the ultracool Blue on Blue restaurant-bar. Parking $24.

SANTA MONICA & VENICE

Sea Shore Motel (Map p785; ☎ 310-392-2787; www .seashoremotel.com; 2637 Main St; r $90-110, ste $125-225; P ☒) This family-owned motel is one of a dying breed: a clean, budget-priced place mere steps from the beach, bars, boutiques and restaurants. The Spanish-tiled rooms are attractive enough, but the new lofty suites with full kitchens and balconies are killers. Free wi-fi.

HI Los Angeles–Santa Monica (Map p785; ☎ 310-393-9913, 800-909-4776, ext 137; www.lahostels.org; 1436 2nd St; dm members/non-members $28/31, r without bath $69/72; ☐) It's low in the charm department, but the location – close to the beach and Third Street Promenade – is the envy of much fancier places.

Ambrose (Map p785; ☎ 310-315-1555, 877-262-7673; www.ambrosehotel.com; 1255 20th St; r incl breakfast $175-225; P ☒ ☐) This blissful boutique hotel about 20 blocks from the beach beautifully blends Craftsman and Asian aesthetics. The

---

THE AUTHOR'S CHOICE

Chateau Marmont (Map p783; ☎ 323-656-1010, 800-242-8328; www.chateaumarmont.com; 8221 W Sunset Blvd; r $315, ste $350-510, bungalow $1500; P ☒) Practically every celluloid luminary – Greta Garbo to Gwyneth Paltrow – has enjoyed breakfast or drinks in the lobby bar, trysted in a bungalow or swum laps in the pool of this Hollywood landmark. Howard Hughes used to spy on bikini beauties from the balcony of his suite, now Bono's favorite. The superstitious might want to stay clear of Bungalow No 2 where John Belushi tossed back his final speedball in 1982. Free wi-fi; parking $25.

spic-and-span rooms have high ceilings, dark-wood furniture and the latest in entertainment and communication gadgets.

Inn at Venice Beach (Map p785; ☎ 310-821-2557, 800-828-0688; www.innatvenicebeach.com; 327 Washington Blvd, Venice; r incl breakfast $140-210; **P**) Close to the beach, the Venice canals and bars and restaurants, this pleasant inn sports fresh and cheerful decor and plenty of amenities. The central courtyard is great for munching your morning muffins. Free wi-fi.

Cal Mar Hotel Suites (Map p785; ☎ 310-395-5555, 800-776-6007; www.calmarhotel.com; 220 California Ave; ste $160-200; **P** 🔄) The looks may be stuck in the disco decade, but who's to complain if a moderate tariff buys you a supercentral yet quiet location and a large suite with kitchen? It's a great choice for families and anyone in need of plenty of elbow room.

Georgian Hotel (Map p785; ☎ 310-395-9945, 800-538-8147; www.georgianhotel.com; 1415 Ocean Ave; r $200-340, ste $255-340; **P** 🔀 🔲) This eye-catching art deco landmark with its snug veranda for breakfast and sunset lounging has decor so Great Gatsby–esque that wearing a straw boater wouldn't look out of place. The rooms, decked out in soothing earth tones, are surprisingly modern. Cute factor: the rubber duckie in the tub. Parking $21.

Eating

One thing's for sure: Angelenos are curious epicureans. No matter whether you fancy Korean *bulgoki* (BBQ), Ethiopian *watt* (stew), Mexican carne asada (roasted beef) or maybe just a good old-fashioned hamburger, you'll be sure to find the real thing among the city's gazillion eateries. Trendy types currently lust after adventurous Asian, brassy Nuevo Latino and unfussy bistro fare, preferably served in small-plate portions perfect for grazers and waist-watchers. No matter which part of town you find yourself in, there's simply no excuse for not eatin' good.

DOWNTOWN

Patina (Map p777; ☎ 213-972-3331; 141 S Grand Ave; mains lunch $18-30, dinner $33-40; lunch Mon-Fri, dinner daily) The flagship restaurant of culinary wunderkind Joachim Splichal is now in stunning new digs at the Walt Disney Concert Hall. Tantalize your tongue with such unique compositions as blue-crab mango cannelloni or Peking duck with caramelized Belgian endives.

Zip Fusion (mains $8-17; lunch Mon-Fri, dinner Mon-Sat) Downtown (Map p777; ☎ 213-680-3770; 744 E 3rd St); West LA (Map pp774-5; ☎ 310-575-3636; 11301 W Olympic Blvd) The chatter of happy patrons usually wafts around the gallerylike dining room or the bougainvillea-filled patio of this Arts District favorite. Food magician Jason Ha composes boundary-pushing fusion fare that borrows from Asia, Europe and Latin America, largely with convincing results. Most dishes are candy for eyes and palate, especially the 'alba-cado', which features intricately spiced albacore tuna delicately wrapped by wafer-thin avocado slices. The seaweed salad and the spicy calamari are other good choices.

Ciudad (Map p777; ☎ 213-486-5171; 445 S Figueroa St; mains lunch $9-19, dinner $15-26; lunch Mon-Fri, dinner daily) Bold Latin fare has been the recipe for success at this Downtown outpost of TV chefs Susan Feniger and Mary Sue Milliken. The spirited decor is the perfect backdrop for such dishes as perky ceviche and wild mushroom empanadas. Great desserts and even better caipirinhas.

Water Grill (Map p777; ☎ 213-891-0900; 544 S Grand Ave; mains $25-40, lunch Mon-Fri, dinner daily) Only the brisk ocean breeze is missing from this first-rate seafood restaurant. Start with the 'fruits of the sea platter' before moving on to such piscatorial delights as ahi tuna tartare or dock-fresh Alaskan halibut. Try to leave room for the signature chocolate bread pudding.

Also recommended:

Empress Pavilion (Map p777; ☎ 213-617-9898; 3rd fl, Bamboo Plaza, 988 N Hill St; dim sum per plate $2-5, dinner $20-25; dim sum & lunch 9am-3pm, dinner 3-10pm) Dim sum to die for.

Philippe the Original (Map p777; ☎ 213-628-3781; 1001 N Alameda St; sandwiches $5; 6am-10pm) The original French dip sandwich: millions served since 1908. Cash only.

HOLLYWOOD

Café Stella (Map p780; ☎ 323-666-0265; 3932 W Sunset Blvd, Silver Lake; mains $14-24; dinner Tue-Sat) This darling bistro, tucked away in a secluded courtyard (look for the red star on the rooftop), would not look out of place on Paris' Left Bank. The blackboard menu features mostly classics such as tarragon chicken, escargot and onion soup.

Palms Thai (Map p780; ☎ 323-462-5073; 5273 Hollywood Blvd; mains $6-19; ✆ 11am-2am) For some of the best Thai food in town head to this supper club famous for its hilarious (and actually quite good) Elvis impersonator. The huge menu has all the usual favorites, but you'll be amazed by what they can do with frog, quail and jellyfish.

Cheebo (Map p783; ☎ 323-850-7070; 7533 W Sunset Blvd, Hollywood; mains breakfast $5-9, lunch $8-14, dinner $10-26; ✆ 8am-11:30pm) With its pumpkin-colored walls, paper-covered tables and cups of crayons, Cheebo screams 'tots-friendly.' Yummy organic pizzas are delivered piping hot on wooden boards. Lots of choices for vegetarians, and killer chocolate soufflé.

El Conquistador (Map p780; ☎ 323-666-5136; 3701 W Sunset Blvd, Silver Lake; mains $9-13.50; ✆ lunch Tue-Sun, dinner daily) This wonderfully campy Mexican cantina is perfect for launching yourself into a night on the razzle. One margarita is all it takes to drown your sorrows, so be sure to fill the belly with their yummy enchiladas and tacos.

Mel's Drive-in (Map p780; ☎ 323-465-2111; 1660 N Highland Ave; mains $7-10) Catch that *American Graffiti* vibe at this fun '50s diner in the historic Max Factor Building in central Hollywood. The epic menu features all the classics.

BEVERLY HILLS, WEST HOLLYWOOD & MID-CITY

Angelini Osteria (Map p783; ☎ 323-297-0070; 7313 Beverly Blvd; mains $10-34; ✆ lunch Tue-Fri, dinner Tue-Sun) Conversation flows as freely as the wine at this convivial eatery whose die-hard fans share a passion for great Italian food. Choose from soulful risottos, pungent pastas and delightful lamb chops with price tags to match all budgets.

Spago Beverly Hills (Map p783; ☎ 310-385-0880; 176 N Cañon Dr; mains lunch $14-27, dinner $26-36; ✆ lunch Mon-Sat, dinner daily) Wolfgang Puck's flagship emporium has long been tops for celebrity-spotting and fancy eating. Try to score a table on the lovely patio and prepare for cart-wheeling tastebuds. Reservations essential.

Cobras & Matadors (Map p783; ☎ 323-932-6178; 7615 W Beverly Blvd; tapas $4-12) Tables are squished together as tight as lovers at this trendy tapas bar. If you pick up a bottle of

vino at the shop next door, the corkage fee is waived.

Griddle Café (Map p783; ☎ 323-874-0377; 7916 W Sunset Blvd; dishes $6-9; ✆ 8am-3pm) If you've greeted the day by peeling your lids back from crusty, bloodshot eyes, this scenester joint's high-octane coffee, wagon-wheel-sized pancakes or tasty egg dishes will likely restore balance to your brain.

A.O.C. (Map p783; ☎ 323-653-6359; 8022 W 3rd St; dishes $4-14; ✆ dinner) The small-plate menu at this stomping ground of the rich, lithe and silicone-enhanced will have you noshing happily on sweaty cheeses, homemade charcuterie and such richly nuanced morsels as braised pork cheeks. Huge list of wines by the glass.

Other favorites:

Surya (Map p783; ☎ 323-653-5151; 8048 W 3rd St; mains $9-22; ✆ lunch Mon-Fri, dinner daily) Its curries are culinary poetry.

Lotería Grill (Map p783; ☎ 323-930-2211; Original Farmers Market, 6333 W 3rd St; dishes $2.50-9; ✆ 9am-9pm Mon-Sat, to 7pm Sun) Outstanding mole and other Mexican favorites.

SANTA MONICA & VENICE

Counter (Map p785; ☎ 310-399-8383; 2901 Ocean Park Blvd, Santa Monica; burgers from $6.50; ✆ 11am-10pm) Let your creativity fly at this crisp postmodern patty-and-bun joint where you can build your own gourmet burger by choosing your favorite bread, cheese, topping and sauce. The basket of delicious fries – a steal at just $2 – easily feeds two or three.

Beechwood (Map p785; ☎ 310-448-8884; 822 Washington Blvd, Venice; mains $15-25; ✆ dinner) With its warm woods and cool patio lounge with toasty fire pit, this sophisticated Venice hangout is clearly a winner in the looks department. The updated American bistro fare convinces too, especially the small-plate bar menu, although the service needs work.

Venice Cantina (Map p785; ☎ 310-399-8420; 23 Windward Ave; mains $8-22; ✆ lunch Sat & Sun, dinner daily) This high-octane hot spot just off the Venice Boardwalk usually fills with shiny happy patrons knocking back potent tequila and sinking teeth into intrepidly flavored Mexican fare.

JiRaffe (Map p785; ☎ 310-917-6671; 502 Santa Monica Blvd, Santa Monica; mains lunch $10-12.50, dinner $18-28) Surfer-chef Raphael Lunetta honed his culinary craft in Paris and now regales

CALIFORNIA

diners with flawless Cal-French cuisine. The menu changes regularly, but the signature roast-beet salad and caramelized pork chops never go out of fashion.

Also recommended:

Real Food Daily (Map p785; ☎ 310-451-7544; 514 Santa Monica Blvd, Santa Monica; mains $6-12) Excellent organic and vegan food.

Mao's Kitchen (Map p785; ☎ 310-581-8305; 1512 Pacific Ave, Venice; mains $5-10; ☙ 11:30am-10:30pm Sun-Thu, to 3am Fri & Sat) Fresh Chinese food: hot, cheap and heaps of it.

Drinking

Bar Marmont (Map p783; ☎ 323-650-0575; 8171 Sunset Blvd, W Hollywood) Everything drops into place as smoothly as an ice cube at this chic boîte with A-lister cachet. Sip your Cosmo underneath the butterfly ceiling or repair to the patio teeming with babes and beaus.

Formosa Café (Map p783; ☎ 323-850-9050; 7156 Santa Monica Blvd, Hollywood) The onetime watering hole of Bogart, Monroe and Gable is a cool place to sop up some Hollywood nostalgia along with your Mai Tai.

Voda (Map p785; ☎ 310-394-9774; 1449 2nd St, Santa Monica) Voda is chic, small and shimmering with flattering candlelight, making it a top date spot. Fruit-infused vodka drinks are the house specialty.

Cat & Fiddle Pub (Map p780; ☎ 323-468-3800; 6530 Sunset Blvd, Hollywood) London meets Hollywood at this bustling pub with its buzzing fountain courtyard where you can enjoy Sunday twilight jazz radio broadcasts.

Good Luck Bar (Map p780; ☎ 323-666-3524; 1514 Hillhurst Ave, Los Feliz) The clientele is cool, the music loud and the beverages seductively strong at this well-established watering hole with its Shanghai gangster-bar looks.

Toppers (Map p785; ☎ 310-393-8080; 1111 2nd St, Santa Monica) Watch the sun drop into the ocean, margarita in hand, during happy hour (4:30pm to 7:30pm) at this buzzing rooftop bar.

Also recommended:

Yamashiro (Map p780; ☎ 323-466-5125; 1999 N Sycamore Ave, Hollywood) Sake with a view from this romantic hilltop Japanese palace.

Beauty Bar (Map p780; ☎ 323-468-3800; 1638 N Cahuenga Blvd, Hollywood) Martinis and manicures.

Rooftop Lounge @ Standard Downtown LA (Map p777; ☎ 213-892-8080; 550 S Flower St, Downtown) Libidinous rooftop bar with waterbed pods for lounging and a pool for cooling off.

Entertainment

The freebie *LA Weekly* and the Los Angeles *Times* Calendar section (especially Thursday's tabloid-sized pull-out) are your best sources for plugging into the local scene. Buy tickets at the box office or through **Ticketmaster** (☎ 213-480-3232; www.ticketmaster.com).

LIVE MUSIC & NIGHTCLUBS

Knitting Factory Hollywood (Map p780; ☎ 323-463-0204; 7021 Hollywood Blvd, Hollywood) This all-ages bastion of indie bands offers up top-notch world music, progressive jazz and other alterna-sounds. Headliners take the main stage, the rest make do with the intimate AlterKnit Lounge.

Troubadour (Map p783; ☎ 310-276-6168; 9081 Santa Monica Blvd, W Hollywood; ☙ Mon-Sat) The Troub did its part in catapulting the Eagles and Tom Waits to stardom, and it's still a great place to catch tomorrow's headliners. The all-ages policy ensures a mixed crowd that's refreshingly low on attitude.

Catalina Bar & Grill (Map p780; ☎ 323-466-2210; 6725 W Sunset Blvd, Hollywood; ☙ Tue-Sun) LA's premier jazz club has moved into new, slicker and more spacious digs, but nothing has changed about Catalina Popescu's top-notch booking policy, which has included heavies like Wynton Marsalis and Chick Corea.

Spaceland (Map p774-5; ☎ 323-661-4380; 1717 Silver Lake Blvd, Silver Lake) Mostly local alt-rock, indie, skate-punk and electrotrash bands take the stage here in the hopes of making it big (Beck and the Eels played some early gigs here).

Conga Room (Map p783; ☎ 323-938-1696; www.congaroom.com; 5364 Wilshire Blvd, Mid-City; ☙ Thu-Sat) Watch ladies in spiky heels and nattily dressed gents whirl around to the salsa beat at this upscale club with the slightly decadent feel of prerevolution Havana. Come early for dance lessons or dinner at La Boca restaurant.

Temple Bar (Map p785; ☎ 310-393-6611; 1026 Wilshire Blvd, Santa Monica) At one of the more happening hangouts west of Hollywood the bands are hit-or-miss, but the drinks are strong, the crowd's heavy on the eye candy and the ambience fairly relaxed.

Babe & Ricky's (Map pp774-5; ☎ 323-295-9112; 4339 Leimert Blvd, Leimert Park) Mama Laura has presided over LA's oldest blues club for four decades. The Monday-night jam session, with free food, often brings the house down.

Also try the following:

Hotel Cafe (Map p780; ☎ 323-461-2040; 1623 1/2 N Cahuenga Blvd, Hollywood) Intimate space for handmade music by talented singer-songwriters.

Echo (Map p780; ☎ 213-413-8200; 1822 W Sunset Blvd, near Silver Lake) Divey hangout filled with Eastside hipsters hungry for an eclectic alchemy of sound.

House of Blues (Map p783; ☎ 323-848-5100; www.hob .com; 8430 W Sunset Blvd, W Hollywood) The original branch.

CLASSICAL MUSIC & OPERA

Los Angeles Philharmonic (Map p777; ☎ 323-850-2000; www.laphil.org; 111 S Grand Ave; tickets $15-120) Led by Esa Pekka-Salonen, the world-class LA Phil performs classics and cutting-edge works at the Walt Disney Concert Hall.

Hollywood Bowl (Map p780; ☎ 323-850-2000; www.hollywoodbowl.com; 2301 N Highland Ave, Hollywood; tickets $1-105; ❤ late Jun–Sep) This historic natural amphitheater is the LA Phil's summer home and also a stellar place to catch big-name rock, jazz, blues and pop acts. Do as the locals and come early for a pre-show picnic (alcohol is allowed).

Los Angeles Opera (Map p777; ☎ 213-972-8001; www.laopera.com; Dorothy Chandler Pavilion; 135 N Grand Ave, Downtown; tickets $30-190) Star tenor Plácido Domingo presides over the LA Opera, whose productions range from crowd-pleasers to rarely performed works.

Redcat (Map p777; ☎ 213-237-2800; www.redcat .org; 631 W 2nd St, Downtown) Part of the Walt Disney Concert Hall complex, this venue presents a global feast of avant-garde and experimental theater, performance art, dance, readings, film and video.

THEATER

Live theater thrives in Los Angeles thanks to an endless talent pool. Half-price tickets to many shows are sold online by **LAStageTIX** (www.theatrela.org).

Mark Taper Forum (Map p777; ☎ 213-628-2772; www.taperahmanson.com; 135 N Grand Ave, Downtown) The Taper is the home base of the Center Theatre Group, one of SoCal's leading resident ensembles. It has developed numerous new plays, most famously Tony Kushner's *Angels in America*.

Actors' Gang Theatre (Map p780; ☎ 323-465-0566; www.theactorsgang.com; 6209 Santa Monica Blvd, Hollywood) Cofounded by Tim Robbins, this socially mindful troupe presents daring and offbeat interpretations of classics and new works pulled from ensemble workshops.

Odyssey Theatre (Map pp774-5; ☎ 310-477-2055; www.odysseytheatre.com; 2055 S Sepulveda Blvd, near Westwood) This well-respected ensemble presents new work, updates the classics and develops its own plays in a ho-hum space that houses three 99-seat theaters under one roof.

Also check what's playing here:

East West Players (Map p777; ☎ 213-625-4397; 120 N Judge John Aiso St, Downtown) Pioneering Asian American ensemble.

Will Geer Theatricum Botanicum (Map pp774-5; ☎ 310-455-3723; www.theatricum.com; 1419 N Topanga Canyon Blvd, north of Santa Monica; tickets $11-25) Enchanting theater in the woods.

SPECTATOR SPORTS

Dodger Stadium (Map p777; ☎ 323-224-1448; www .dodgers.com; 1000 Elysian Park Ave, Downtown; tickets $6-60) LA's Major League Baseball team plays from April to September in this legendary stadium.

Staples Center (Map p777; 213-742-7340; www.staples center.com; 1111 S Figueroa St, Downtown) This state-of-the-art venue is home base for all three of LA's professional basketball teams – the LA Lakers, LA Sparks and LA Clippers – as well as the LA Kings NHL ice hockey team.

Shopping

No matter whether you're a penny-pincher or a power shopper, you'll find plenty of opportunity to drop some cash in LA. Fashionistas flock to **Robertson Blvd** (between Beverly and 3rd St) and **Melrose Avenue** (between San Vicente and La Brea), while bargain hunters haunt Downtown's **Fashion District**. Hollywood is ground zero for groovy tunes, most notably at **Amoeba Music** (Map p780; ☎ 323-245-6400; 6400 W Sunset Blvd) and **Aron's Records** (Map p780; ☎ 323-469-4700; 1150 N Highland Ave). East of here, Silver Lake is the place for cool kitsch and collectibles, especially around **Sunset Junction** (where Hollywood and Sunset Blvds meet). Santa Monica has good boutique shopping on **Montana Avenue** and **Main Street**, while the chain store brigade (Gap to Sephora) has taken over **Third Street Promenade**.

Good flea markets include the weekly **Melrose Trading Post** (Map p783; 7850 Melrose Ave, Hollywood; admission $2; ❤ 9am-5pm Sun), which brings out hipsters in search of retro treasure, and the monthly **Rose Bowl Flea Market** (Map pp774-5; Rose Bowl, 1001 Rose Bowl Dr, Pasadena; admission $7-20; ❤ 5am-4:30pm 2nd Sun of the month), the 'mother' of all flea markets with over 2200 vendors.

Getting There & Away

AIR

Los Angeles International Airport (LAX; Map pp774-5; ☎ 310-646-5252; www.lawa.org) is right on the coast, south of Santa Monica. Its eight terminals wrap around a two-level traffic loop, with ticketing and check-in on the upper (departure) level and baggage-claim areas on the lower (arrival) level. To travel between terminals, board the free Shuttle A on the lower level. Hotel shuttles stop here as well.

Regional airports such as Bob Hope Airport in Burbank, north of Hollywood, and Long Beach Airport, on the border with Orange County, handle mostly domestic flights.

BUS

The main bus terminal for **Greyhound** (Map p777; ☎ 213-629-8421; 1716 E 7th St) is in an unsavory part of Downtown, so avoid arriving after dark. Bus No 58 goes to the transit plaza at Union Station with onward service across town, including Metro Rail's Red Line to Hollywood. Some buses go directly to the terminal in **Hollywood** (Map p780; ☎ 323-466-6381; 1715 N Cahuenga Blvd).

CAR & MOTORCYCLE

All the major international car-rental agencies have branches at LAX and throughout Los Angeles (see p1173 for central reservation numbers). If you don't have a prebooking, use the courtesy phones in the arrival areas at LAX. Offices and lots are outside the airport, but each company provides free shuttles to take you there.

For Harley rentals, try **Eagle Rider** (Map pp774-5; ☎ 310-536-6777; 11860 S La Cienega Blvd; per day $75-135; ☼ 9am-5pm), near LAX.

TRAIN

Amtrak trains roll into Downtown's historic **Union Station** (Map p777; ☎ 800-872-7245; 800 N Alameda St). The *Pacific Surfliner* travels daily to San Diego ($26, three hours), Santa Barbara ($17, 2½ hours) and San Luis Obispo ($25, 5½ hours).

Getting Around

TO/FROM THE AIRPORT

Door-to-door shuttles, such as those operated by **Prime Time** (☎ 800-473-3743) and **Super Shuttle** (☎ 310-782-6600), leave from the lower level of all terminals. Typical fares to Santa Monica, Hollywood or Downtown are $18, $23 and $14, respectively.

Curbside dispatchers will summon a taxi for you. Fares average $20 to $25 to Santa Monica, $25 to $35 to Downtown or Hollywood and up to $80 to Disneyland.

Using public transportation is slower and less convenient but cheaper. From outside any terminal, catch a free Shuttle C bus to the LAX Transit Center, the hub for buses serving all of LA. Trip planning help is available at ☎ 800-266-6883 or online at www .metro.net.

Popular routes include the following:

Downtown Metro Bus Nos 42a or 439 West, 1½ hours, $1.25.

Hollywood Metro bus No 42a West to Overhill/La Brea, transfer to Metro bus No 212 North, 1½ hours, $2.50.

Venice & Santa Monica Big Blue Bus No 3, about 50 minutes, 75¢.

CAR & MOTORCYCLE

Unless you have plenty of time or you're strapped for some cash, you're going to want to spend some time behind the wheel, although this means contending with some of the worst traffic in the country. Avoid rush hour (7am to 9am and 3:30pm to 6pm).

Downtown Santa Monica, Beverly Hills and West Hollywood have public parking garages where the first two hours are free and rates low thereafter. Parking at motels and cheaper hotels is usually free, while fancier ones charge anywhere from $8 to $25 for the privilege. Valet parking at nicer restaurants and hotels is commonplace.

PUBLIC TRANSPORTATION

LA's main public transportation agency is **Metro** (☎ 800-266-6883; www.metro.net), which operates about 200 bus lines as well as four rail lines:

Blue Line Downtown to Long Beach.

Gold Line Union Station to Pasadena.

Green Line Norwalk to Redondo Beach.

Red Line Downtown LA's Union Station to North Hollywood, via central Hollywood and Universal Studios.

Tickets cost $1.25 per boarding or $3 for a day pass with unlimited rides. Bus drivers sell single tickets and day passes (exact fare required), while train tickets are available from vending machines at each station. Call the toll-free number or check the website for trip-planning help.

Some neighborhoods, including Downtown and Hollywood, are served by local **DASH minibuses** (☎ your area code + 808-2273; www.ladottransit.com; fare 25¢). Santa Monica–based **Big Blue Bus** (☎ 310-451-5444; www.bigbluebus.com) serves much of western LA, including Santa Monica, Venice, Westwood and LAX (75¢). Its express bus No 10 runs from Santa Monica to Downtown LA ($1.75).

TAXI
Except for those lined up outside airports, train stations, bus stations and major hotels, cabbies only respond to phone calls. Fares are metered and cost $2 at flag fall plus $1.80 a mile. Some companies:
Checker (☎ 800-300-5007)
Independent (☎ 800-521-8294)
Yellow Cab (☎ 800-200-1085)

AROUND LOS ANGELES
Catalina Island
Mediterranean-flavored Catalina Island is a world removed from the bustle of Los Angeles and a popular day trip or overnight getaway. Nearly all tourist activity is concentrated in the pint-sized port town of **Avalon**, a cluster of cutesy shops and restaurants fronted by a tiny beach. The latter sits right next to the Green Pier, where the **Catalina Visitors Bureau** (☎ 310-510-1520; www.visitcatalina.org, www.catalina.com; ☺ vary) dispenses brochures and information. Places to explore include the **Catalina Island Museum** (☎ 310-510-2414; adult/child/senior $4/1/3; ☺ 10am-4pm, to 5pm Jul & Aug, closed Tue Jan-Mar) inside the landmark **Casino**, a one-time dance and concert hall; and the **Wrigley Memorial & Botanical Garden** (☎ 310-510-2595; 1400 Avalon Canyon Rd; admission $5; ☺ 9am-4pm), about 1.5 miles inland, which commemorates chewing-gum magnate William Wrigley Jr (1861–1932), who once owned Catalina.

The best way to experience the island is in or on the water. Snorkeling and diving are both excellent, or you could rent a kayak to explore the rugged coast. Outfitters cluster on the Green Pier.

The only other settlement is remote **Two Harbors** in Catalina's largely undeveloped backcountry of sunbaked hillsides, valleys and canyons dotted with native flora. The interior is a protected nature preserve and may only be explored on foot or mountain bike (permits required, call ☎ 310-510-1421) or on an organized tour (from $30),

such as those offered by **Discovery Tours** (☎ 310-510-8687) and **Jeep Eco-Tours** (☎ 310-510-2595). A hinterland curiosity is the herd of bison, left behind from a 1924 movie shoot.

Catalina's main tourist season is June to September when prices soar and the island seems to sink from the load of day-trippers. Consider spending the night when the ambience goes from frantic to romantic in no time. The visitor bureau can help you find accommodation.

Catalina Express (☎ 310-519-1212, 800-481-3470; www.catalinaexpress.com; round-trip about $50, 1hr) operates frequent scheduled ferry service to Avalon from San Pedro, Long Beach and Dana Point (in Orange County) and to Two Harbors from San Pedro only. Reservations are recommended in summer.

Six Flags Magic Mountain
Velocity is king at **Six Flags** (Map pp774-5; ☎ 661-255-4111, 818-367-5965; www.sixflags.com/parks/magic mountain; 26101 Magic Mountain Pkwy, Valencia; adult/child under 4ft/senior $48/30/30; ☺ from 10am daily Apr–early Sep, Sat & Sun mid-Sep–Mar, closing times vary from 6pm-midnight), the ultimate roller-coaster park, where you can go up, down and inside out faster and in more baffling ways than anywhere besides a space shuttle.

SOUTHERN CALIFORNIA COAST

ORANGE COUNTY
You know you've joined the big leagues when they start making a TV series about you. That's just what happened to Orange County, that giant quilt of suburbia wedged between LA and San Diego. Disneyland may have put the place on the map more than 50 years ago, but every installment of the hit show *The OC* beams fresh images of local affluence, aspirations and anxieties across the globe. These days, Orange County is all about living large. Shopping is a major passion, and it's probably no coincidence that ritzy South Coast Plaza in Costa Mesa is the single biggest grossing mall in the entire country. But don't forget, when too much commercialism gets you down, there are always the beaches – all 42 glorious miles of them – to rejuvenate the spirit.

Disneyland Resort

Ever since Walt Disney opened the original **Disneyland** (☎ 714-781-4000 or 714-781-7290; www .disneyland.com; 1313 Harbor Blvd, Anaheim; one-day pass either park adult/child 3-9 $53/43, both parks $73/63; (P)) in 1955, the mother of all theme parks has captured the hearts, minds and wallets of millions of visitors (parking $10). It is divided into seven thematic 'lands,' including space-age Tomorrowland, jungle-themed Adventureland, and Fantasyland, where classic Disney characters make their home. The most popular rides include the wildly creative Indiana Jones Adventure, the endearing Pirates of the Caribbean and the redesigned white-knuckle Space Mountain.

Next door, **Disney's California Adventure** celebrates the natural and cultural glories of the Golden State. It's bigger and less crowded but lacks the density of attractions and depth of imagination. The best rides are Soarin' over California, a virtual hang-glide, and California Screamin', a roller coaster.

Also part of Disneyland Resort are three Disney hotels and **Downtown Disney**, a mall lined with corporate-owned chain stores, restaurants and entertainment venues.

You can see either park in a day, but it requires at least two days to go on all the rides (three if visiting both parks), especially in summer when lines are long – visit midweek and arrive before the gates open. When getting to the parks, familiarize yourself with the Fastpass system, which gives you pre-assigned boarding times for selected attractions, thereby significantly cutting waiting times.

A variety of multiday passes good at both parks is available. Check the website to buy tickets or check park hours. These vary daily, although in July and August the parks are usually open from 8am to midnight.

The surrounding city of Anaheim recently completed a $4.2 billion revamp and cleanup, and you'll find plenty of hotels and restaurants near the parks. Recommended independent properties are **Candy Cane Inn** (☎ 714-774-5284, 800-345-7057; www.candycaneinn.net; 1747 S Harbor Blvd; r $120-175; (P) 🍴 🏊) and the **Anabella** (☎ 714-905-1050, 800-863-4888; www.anabella hotel.com; 1030 Katella Ave; r $90-190; (P) 🍴 🖳 🏊).

Knott's Berry Farm

Smaller and less frantic than Disneyland, **Knott's Berry Farm** (☎ 714-220-5200; www.knotts.com; 8039 Beach Blvd, Buena Park; adult/child 3-11/senior $45/15/35; mains $15-20; (P)) was America's first theme park at its 1932 opening. It's essentially a high-tech amusement park with an Old West theme. Tame experiences such as gold-panning demonstrations and staged gunfights contrast with such gut-wrenching roller coasters as the wooden Ghost Rider and the new suspended Silver Bullet. Afterwards, treat your stomach to a classic fried-chicken dinner at Mrs Knott's Chicken Dinner Restaurant. Parking $9.

Orange County Beaches

Surfers, artists, retirees and rich matrons give many of Orange County's beach towns their distinct vibe. Just across the LA-OC county-line, **Seal Beach** is refreshingly non-commercial with its pleasantly walkable downtown, while newly gentrified **Huntington Beach** (aka Surf City, USA) epitomizes the California surfing lifestyle. Next up is the ritziest of the OC's beach communities: **Newport Beach**, which teems with Botoxed beauties, Hummer-driving hunks and bag-toting shopaholics. The main tourist area, on the Balboa Peninsula, has grand beaches, the 1905 Balboa Pier and a family-oriented amusement center.

Laguna Beach is the OC's most cultured and charming seaside town, where secluded beaches, glassy waves and eucalyptus-covered hillsides create a Riviera-like feel. Art is huge here, especially in July when the town hosts three art festivals.

Mission San Juan Capistrano (☎ 949-234-1300; cnr Ortega Hwy & Camino Capistrano; adult/child/senior $6/5/5; 🕑 8:30am-5pm), about 10 miles south and inland from Laguna, is one of California's most beautiful missions, featuring lush gardens and the charming Serra Chapel.

SAN DIEGO

Bright, bubbly, ebullient and sunny, San Diego is one of those cities as intoxicating as good champagne. When much of the nation shivers under blankets of rain and snow, San Diegans picnic in the park or 'hang 10' in the blue-green wash of the surf. Downtown's skyline keeps watch over a crescent-shaped bay that is one of the world's greatest natural harbors. And few can ignore the contagious energy of the Gaslamp Quarter, always abuzz with restaurants and bars, or the cultural smorgasbord of the Balboa

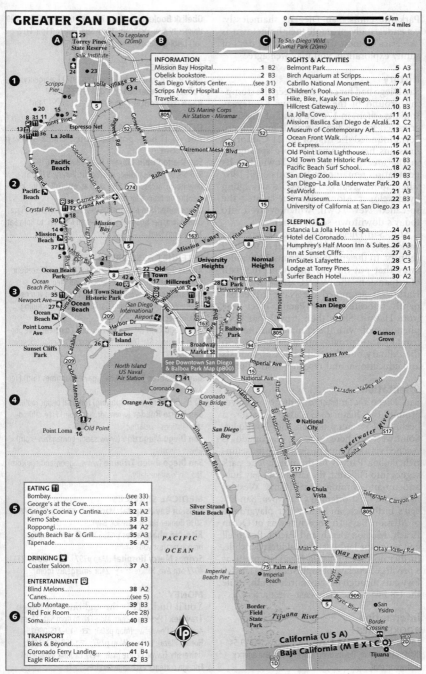

GREATER SAN DIEGO

| 0 | 6 km |
| 0 | 4 miles |

INFORMATION
Mission Bay Hospital.............................1 B2
Obelisk bookstore..................................2 B3
San Diego Visitors Center...............(see 31)
Scripps Mercy Hospital........................3 B3
TravelEx...4 B1

SIGHTS & ACTIVITIES
Belmont Park..5 A3
Birch Aquarium at Scripps...................6 A1
Cabrillo National Monument...............7 A4
Children's Pool.......................................8 A1
Hike, Bike, Kayak San Diego...............9 A1
Hillcrest Gateway.................................10 B3
La Jolla Cove...11 A1
Mission Basilica San Diego de Alcalá..12 C2
Museum of Contemporary Art...........13 A1
Ocean Front Walk................................14 A2
OE Express...15 A1
Old Point Loma Lighthouse................16 A4
Old Town State Historic Park.............17 B3
Pacific Beach Surf School....................18 A2
San Diego Zoo......................................19 B3
San Diego–La Jolla Underwater Park.20 A1
SeaWorld...21 A3
Serra Museum.......................................22 B3
University of California at San Diego.23 A1

SLEEPING 🛏
Estancia La Jolla Hotel & Spa.............24 A1
Hotel del Coronado.............................25 B4
Humphrey's Half Moon Inn & Suites.26 A3
Inn at Sunset Cliffs..............................27 A3
InnSuites Lafayette..............................28 C3
Lodge at Torrey Pines.........................29 A1
Surfer Beach Hotel...............................30 A2

EATING 🍴
Bombay...(see 33)
George's at the Cove...........................31 A1
Gringo's Cocina y Cantina..................32 A2
Kemo Sabe..33 B3
Roppongi...34 A2
South Beach Bar & Grill.......................35 A3
Tapenade...36 A2

DRINKING 🍷
Coaster Saloon.....................................37 A3

ENTERTAINMENT 🎭
Blind Melons..38 A2
'Canes...(see 5)
Club Montage.......................................39 B3
Red Fox Room..................................(see 28)
Soma..40 B3

TRANSPORT
Bikes & Beyond...............................(see 41)
Coronado Ferry Landing......................41 B4
Eagle Rider..42 B3

To Legoland (20mi)
To San Diego Wild Animal Park (20mi)

Torrey Pines State Reserve
Salk Institute
Scripps Pier
La Jolla Village Dr
Espresso Net
Torrey Pines
La Jolla
Pacific Beach
US Marine Corps Air Station - Miramar
Clairemont Mesa Blvd
La Jolla Blvd
Balboa Ave
Pacific Beach
Crystal Pier
Garnet Ave
Grand Ave
Mission Bay
Linda Vista Rd
Mission Beach
Ocean Beach Park
Mission Valley
Friars Rd
University Heights
Normal Heights
North Park
Hillcrest
El Cajon Blvd
University Ave
Ocean Beach Pier
Newport Ave
Old Town State Historic Park
Ocean Beach
Point Loma Ave
San Diego International Airport
Washington St
5th Ave
Balboa Park
East San Diego
Lemon Grove
Akins Ave
Sunset Cliffs Park
Harbor Dr
Harbor Island
Broadway
Market St
Imperial Ave
National Ave
Point Loma
Old Point
North Island US Naval Air Station
Coronado
Orange Ave
Coronado Bay Bridge
San Diego Bay
National City
Paradise Valley Rd
Sweetwater River
Chula Vista
Telegraph Canyon Rd
Silver Strand State Beach
PACIFIC OCEAN
Main St
Otay River
Otay Valley Rd
Imperial Beach Pier
Imperial Beach
Palm Ave
San Ysidro
Border Field State Park
Tijuana River
Beyer Blvd
Border Crossing
California (USA)
Baja California (MEXICO)
Tijuana

See Downtown San Diego & Balboa Park Map (p800)

CALIFORNIA

LP

Park museums. San Diegans shamelessly, yet endearingly, promote their hometown as 'America's Finest City.' After a few days of sunny exploration, you may well agree.

History

San Diego had for centuries been the stomping ground of the indigenous Kumeyaay Indians when, in 1769, a band of missionaries led by the Franciscan friar Junípero Serra founded the first of the 21 California missions here. A small pueblo sprung up in the area of today's Old Town, but its population remained minuscule until 1867 when some creative real estate wrangling by developer Alonzo Horton created the so-called 'New Town,' which evolved into today's downtown south of here.

Still, San Diego languished as a relative backwater through the first half of the 20th century. In the end it was events 3000 miles away that put the city firmly on the path of expansion: the WWII attack on Pearl Harbor. It prompted the Navy to permanently relocate the US Pacific Fleet here from Hawaii. Since then growth has been phenomenal, with the climate and the seafront location proving attractive not only to the military but also to businesses, tourists and educational and research institutions.

Orientation

San Diego's compact downtown revolves around the historic Gaslamp Quarter, a beehive of restaurants, bars and boutiques. Southwest of here, upscale Coronado is reached via a stunning bridge, while museumrich Balboa Park is to the north. The park segues into Hillcrest, the city's lesbi-gay hub, and up-and-coming North Park. West of here are tourist-oriented Old Town, San Diego's birthplace, and the water playground of Mission Bay. The beach towns of Ocean Beach, Mission Beach and Pacific Beach all epitomize the laid-back SoCal lifestyle while, further north, La Jolla (la-*ho*ya) sits pretty as a privileged enclave of sophistication. The I-5 Fwy cuts through the city north–south, while the I-8 Fwy is the main east–west artery.

Information

BOOKSTORES

Le Travel Store & STA Travel (Map p800; ☎ 619-544-0005; 745 4th Ave, Downtown) Travel books and agency under one roof.

Obelisk Bookstore (Map p797; ☎ 619-297-4171; 1029 University Ave; ⌚ 10am-10pm Sun-Thu, to 11pm Fri & Sat) Lesbi-gay books, mags and merchandise.

EMERGENCY

Police, fire and ambulance (☎ 911) Emergency.
Police, nonemergency (☎ 619-531-2000)
Rape crisis center (☎ 888-272-1767; ⌚ 24hr)

INTERNET ACCESS

For wi-fi hot-spot locations, check www.jiwire.com.
San Diego Public Library (Map p800; ☎ 619-236-5800; www.sandiego.gov/public-library; 820 E St, Downtown; access free) Free wi-fi access. Call or check the website for branch locations.
Cyberzone (Map p800; ☎ 619-239-4263; Horton Plaza, Downtown; per hr $4; ⌚ 10am-9pm Mon-Fri, to 8pm Sat, 11am-8pm Sun)

INTERNET RESOURCES

Access San Diego (www.accesssandiego.com) Excellent source for barrier-free travel around San Diego.
Gaslamp.org (www.gaslamp.org) Everything you need to know about the bustling Gaslamp District, including parking secrets.
San Diego.com (www.sandiego.com) Comprehensive portal to all things San Diegan, from fun stuff to serious business.

MEDIA

Gay & Lesbian Times (www.gaylesbiantimes.com) Free weekly.
KPBS 89.5 FM (www.kpbs.org) National public radio.
San Diego Reader (www.sdreader.com) Free tabloid-sized listings magazine.
San Diego Magazine (www.sandiegomagazine.com) Glossy monthly.
San Diego Union-Tribune (www.signonsandiego.com) The city's major daily.

MEDICAL SERVICES

Mission Bay Hospital (Map p797; ☎ 858-274-7721; 3030 Bunker Hill St, Mission Bay)
Rite-Aid pharmacies (☎ 800-748-3243) Call for branch nearest you.
Scripps Mercy Hospital (Map p797; ☎ 619-294-8111; 4077 5th Ave, Hillcrest; ⌚ 24hr emergency room)

MONEY

You'll find ATMs throughout San Diego.
Travelex (⌚ 10am-6pm Mon-Fri, to 4pm Sat, 11am-4pm Sun) Downtown (Map p800; ☎ 619-235-0901; Horton Plaza); La Jolla (Map p797; ☎ 858-457-2412; University Towne Centre mall, 4417 La Jolla Village Dr) Foreign currency exchange services.

POST

Post offices abound in San Diego. Call
☎ 800-275-8777 or log onto www.usps.com
for the nearest branch.

Post office (Map p797; ☎ 619-232-8612; 815 E St,
Downtown)

TOURIST INFORMATION

San Diego Visitors Center (☎ 619-236-1212, 800-
350-6205; www.sandiego.org) Downtown (Map p800; cnr
W Broadway & Harbor Dr; ☯ 9am-5pm daily Jun-Aug,
9am-4pm Thu-Tue Sep-May); La Jolla (Map p797; 7966 Her-
schel Ave; ☯ 11am-5pm Jun-Aug, reduced hr Sep-May)

Sights

DOWNTOWN

San Diego's downtown covers the 'New
Town' area first subdivided by Alonzo Horton in 1867. Its main street, 5th Ave, was once
a notorious strip of saloons, gambling joints
and bordellos known as the Stingaree. These
days, the beautifully restored **Gaslamp Quarter** is Downtown's heart and soul, a bustling
playground of restaurants, bars, clubs, shops
and galleries. For the full historical picture,
peruse the exhibits inside the 1850 **William
Heath Davis House** (Map p800; ☎ 619-233-4692; www
.gaslampquarter.org; 410 Island Ave; suggested donation $3,
walking tours adult/senior & student $8/6; ☯ 10am-6pm
Tue-Sat, 11am-3pm Sun, tours 11am Sat), which also
offers guided walking tours of the quarter.

Downtown's newest landmark building,
the shiny **Petco Park** (p797; ☎ 619-795-5011; www
.petcoparkevents.com; 100 Park Blvd; tours adult/child/sen-
ior $9/5/6; tours ☯ 10:30am, 12:30pm & 2:30pm Tue-Sun;
Ⓟ) home of the San Diego Padres base-
ball team, is just a quick stroll east of the
Gaslamp.

A commercial focal point of the area is
the postmodern **Horton Plaza** (Broadway & 4th St;
Ⓟ with validation 3hr free), a mazelike shopping
mall. West of here, adjacent to the historic
Santa Fe Depot railroad station, the **Museum
of Contemporary Art** (Map p800; ☎ 619-234-1001; www
.mcasd.org; 1001 Kettner Blvd; admission free; ☯ 11am-
5pm Thu-Tue; Ⓟ per hr $2) puts the emphasis on
minimalist and pop art, as well as conceptual
works and cross-border art from Tijuana. A
second branch is in La Jolla (p802).

The museum is little more than a Frisbee-
toss away from the Embarcadero waterfront, where you can catch a harbor cruise
or the Coronado Ferry (right). The main
attraction, though, is the new **San Diego Aircraft Carrrier Museum** (Map p800; ☎ 619-544-9600;

www.midway.org; Navy Pier; adult/child/senior/student
$13/7/10/10; ☯ 10am-5pm; Ⓟ) aboard the de-
commissioned USS *Midway*, the Navy's
longest-serving aircraft carrier (1945–91).
A self-guided audio-tour takes in such areas
as the berthing spaces, the galley, the sick
bay and, of course, the flight deck with its
restored aircraft, including an F-14 Tomcat.
Allow at least two hours. Parking $10.

Other salty Embarcadero sights include
the historic sailing vessels of the **Maritime
Museum** (Map p800; ☎ 619-234-9153; www.sdmaritime
.com; 1492 N Harbor Dr; adult/child/senior $8/5/6; ☯ 9am-
8pm), most notably the 1863 *Star of India*.
Further south, tacky **Seaport Village** (☯ 10am-
9pm; Ⓟ 2hr free) is a tourist-geared cluster of
novelty shops, gift shops and snack bars.

In northern downtown, **Little Italy** (Map
p800; www.littleitalysd.com) has evolved into one
of the city's hippest places to live, eat and
shop. India St is the main drag.

CORONADO

Joined to the mainland by a boomerang-
shaped bridge, the Coronado peninsula's
main draw is the **Hotel del Coronado** (Map
p797, p804), famous for its buoyant Victorian architecture and illustrious guest book,
which includes Thomas Edison, Brad Pitt
and Marilyn Monroe. The hourly **Coronado
Ferry** (Map p797; ☎ 619-234-4111; round-trip $4.50;
☯ 9am-10pm) shuttles between the Broad-
way Pier on the Embarcadero to the ferry
landing at the foot of Orange Ave, where
Bikes & Beyond (Map p797; ☎ 619-435-7180; rental
per hr from $5; ☯ 9am-7pm) rents bicycles. North
Island US Naval Air Station occupies most
of northern Coronado.

BALBOA PARK

Balboa Park is a treat for all the senses, an
urban oasis brimming with a dozen museums,
gorgeous gardens and architecture, performance spaces and the big and famous zoo. The
area was little more than a dirt patch when
horticulturalist Kate Sessions put her green
thumb to work back in 1892. Two world fairs
in the first half of the 20th century added
the ornate Beaux Arts and Spanish Colonial
buildings grouped around plazas connected
by the central east–west El Prado promenade.
Be cautious if strolling after dark. Parking
is free. Balboa Park is easily reached from
Downtown on bus Nos 7, 7A and 7B. A free
tram shuttles visitors around.

CALIFORNIA

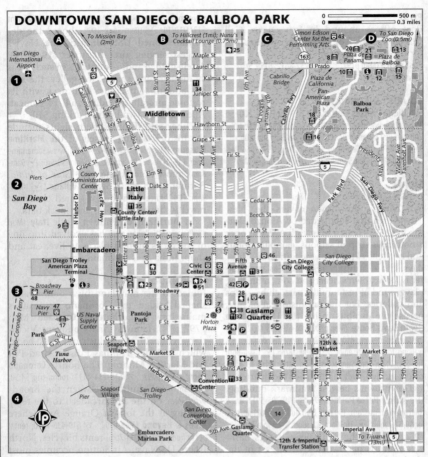

DOWNTOWN SAN DIEGO & BALBOA PARK

The **Balboa Park Visitors Center** (Map p800; ☎ 619-239-0512; www.balboapark.org; 1549 El Prado; ⏱ 9:30am-4:30pm), in the House of Hospitality, sells park maps and the Balboa Passport ($30, with zoo admission $55), which allows onetime entry to 13 of the park's museums within one week. Museums offer free admission Tuesday on a rotating schedule.

The most scenic park approach is from the west across Cabrillo Bridge, which drops you at Plaza de California, dominated by the flamboyant **California Building**. Inside, the **Museum of Man** (Map p800; ☎ 619-239-2001; www.museumofman.org; adult/child/senior $6/3/5; ⏱ 10am-4:30pm) has a world-class collection of pottery, jewelry, baskets and other artifacts that illuminate the cultural history of human-

kind. Behind the museum are the **Old Globe Theaters** (p806).

Further east, a trio of museums rings Plaza de Panama, including the **San Diego Museum of Art** (Map p800; ☎ 619-232-7931; www.sdmart.org; adult/child/student/senior $9/4/7/7; ⏱ 10am-6pm Tue-Sun, to 9pm Thu), which gets accolades for its European old masters but also has good collections of American and Asian art. The **Mingei International Museum** (Map p800; ☎ 619-239-0003; www.mingei.org; adult/child/student $6/3/3; ⏱ 10am-4pm Tue-Sun) exhibits folk art from around the globe, while the small but exquisite **Timken Museum of Art** (Map p800; ☎ 619-239-5548; www.timkenmuseum.org; 1500 El Prado; admission free; ⏱ 10am-4:30pm Tue-Sat, from 1:30 Sun, closed Sep) showcases European and

American heavies, from Rembrandt to Cézanne and John Singleton Copley.

East along El Prado, the **Museum of Photographic Arts** (Map p800; ☎ 619-238-7559; www.mopa .org; adult/child/student/senior $6/free/4/4; ⏰ 10am-5pm, to 9pm Thu) exhibits fine-art photography and hosts an ongoing film series. Next up is Plaza de Balboa, flanked by the **Reuben H Fleet Science Center** (Map p800; ☎ 619-238-1233; www.rhfleet .org; adult/child/senior $6.75/5.50/6; ⏰ 9:30am-varies), a family-oriented hands-on museum cum **Imax theater** (extra admission). Opposite is the **Natural History Museum** (Map p800; ☎ 619-232-3821; www.sdnhm.org; adult/child/student/senior $9/5/6/6; ⏰ 10am-5pm), where dinosaur skeletons, an impressive rattlesnake collection and an earthquake exhibit captivate visitors. Admission includes nature-themed movies shown in a giant-screen cinema.

Buildings around Pan-American Plaza in the park's southern section date from the 1935 Pacific-California Exposition. It's all about polished chrome and cool tailfins at the **San Diego Automotive Museum** (Map p800; ☎ 619-231-2886; www.sdautomuseum.org; adult/child/senior $7/3/6; ⏰ 10am-5pm), a must for fans of vintage cars and motorcycles. Next door, the **San Diego Aerospace Museum** (Map p800; ☎ 619-234-8291; www .aerospacemuseum.org; adult/child/student/senior $9/4/7/7; ⏰ 10am-5:30pm Jun-Aug, to 4:30pm Sep-May) offers a fun-filled look at the history and mystique of flight. Highlights include an original Blackbird SR-71 spy plane and a replica of Charles Lindbergh's *Spirit of St Louis*.

If it slithers, crawls, stomps, swims, leaps or flies, chances are it makes its home in the world-class **San Diego Zoo** (Map p797; ☎ 619-231-1515; www.sandiegozoo.org; adult/child $21/14, with guided bus tour & aerial tram ride $32/20; ⏰ vary) in northern Balboa Park. Arrive early, when the animals are most active. Combination tickets to the zoo and the San Diego Wild Animal Park (p807) cost adult/child $55/34.

North of Balboa Park, **Hillcrest** is queer central, but anyone will feel welcome in its buzzing restaurants, boutiques, bookstores, bars and cafés. Start a stroll at the **Hillcrest Gateway** (Map p797), a neon arch near 5th and University Ave.

PRESIDIO HILL & OLD TOWN

When Junípero Serra first stumbled into San Diego, he picked today's Presidio Hill as the site of his first California mission. The spot turned out to be less than ideal, and only a few years later the mission moved a few miles upriver, closer to a steady water supply and fertile land. **Mission Basilica San Diego de Alcalá** (Map p797; ☎ 619-281-8449; www .missionsandiego.com; 10818 San Diego Mission Rd at Friars Rd; adult/child $3/2; ⏰ 9am-5pm) is a modest rectangle embracing a tranquil garden. In place of the original now stands the handsome **Serra Museum** (Map p797; ☎ 619-297-3258; 2727 Presidio Dr; adult/child/student/senior $5/2/4/4; ⏰ 10am-4:30pm), which is less about the man himself than about life during the city's rough-and-tumble early period.

For more on the theme, head downhill to the **Old Town State Historic Park** (Map p797; ☎ 619-220-5422; San Diego Ave at Twiggs St; visitor center ⏰ 10am-5pm; **P**), which preserves several original adobe buildings and several more recreated structures, including a schoolhouse and a newspaper office, from the first pueblo. Most now contain museums, shops or restaurants.

CALIFORNIA

The **visitor center** at the northwestern end of the central plaza operates free tours.

POINT LOMA

This peninsula wraps protectively around the entrance to crescent-shaped San Diego Bay like an arm drapes around a shoulder. Enjoy stunning bay panoramas from the **Cabrillo National Monument** (Map p797; ☎ 619-557-5450; www.nps.gov/cabr; per car $5; ☺ 9am-6:15pm Jul & Aug, 9am-5:15pm Sep-Jun; **P**), which commemorates the man who led the first Spanish exploration of the West Coast. In winter enjoy the good whale-watching and tide-pooling. The nearby 1854 **Old Point Loma Lighthouse** helped guide ships until 1891 and is now a museum. Access to the point is via Catalina Blvd or on bus No 6A from Downtown.

MISSION BAY & THE BEACHES

After WWII, coastal engineering turned the swampy San Diego River mouth into a 7-sq-mile playground of parks, beaches and bays. Attractions run the gamut from free outdoor activities to luxurious resort hotels. Kite flying is popular, along with water sports and cycling on miles of paved bike paths.

Also here is **SeaWorld** (Map p797; ☎ 619-226-3901; www.seaworld.com/seaworld/ca; 500 SeaWorld Dr; adult/child 3-9 $51/41; ☺ 9am-11pm Jul-Aug, shorter hr rest of year; **P**), one of San Diego's top-flight attractions. The biggest crowds turn out for the live animal shows, most notably the Shamu Adventure, which has the world's most famous killer whale leaping, diving, gliding and interacting with the audience. There are also zoolike animal exhibits and a few amusement-park-style rides, such as the wet and wild Journey to Atlantis, a combination flume ride and roller coaster. Lines can get long in summer and around holidays. Parking $7.

San Diego's three major beaches are ribbons of hedonism where armies of tan, taut bodies frolic in the sand and surf. South of Mission Bay, hippie-flavored **Ocean Beach** (OB) has a fishing pier, beach volleyball, sunset BBQs and good surf. Newport Ave is chockablock with bohemian bars, eateries and shops selling beachwear and surf gear.

West of Mission Bay, **Mission Beach** (MB) and its northern neighbor, **Pacific Beach** (PB), are connected by the car-free **Ocean Front Walk**, which swarms with skaters, joggers and cyclists year-round. **Belmont Park** in MB beckons with a wooden roller coaster, a large indoor pool and other such diversions. Garnet Ave in PB teems with good restaurants and nightlife.

LA JOLLA

Snuggling against one of Southern California's loveliest sweeps of coast, La Jolla is a ritzy suburb with shimmering beaches and a tight downtown packed with upscale anything. Noteworthy sights include the **Children's Pool**, **La Jolla Cove** and, marked by buoys, the offshore **San Diego–La Jolla Underwater Park**, a great spot for scuba diving (see below). For cutting-edge art head to the sleek **Museum of Contemporary Art** (Map p797; ☎ 858-454-3541; www.mcasd.org; 700 Prospect St; adult/student/senior $6/2/2; ☺ 11am-7pm Thu, to 5pm Fri-Tue), the sister venue of the Downtown branch (p799).

La Jolla is also home to the University of California, San Diego (UCSD), and its renowned research facilities. The **Birch Aquarium at Scripps** (Map p797; ☎ 858-534-3474; http://aquarium.ucsd.edu; 2300 Exhibition Way; adult/child/student/senior $10/6.50/7/8.50; ☺ 9am-5pm; **P**) has fish galore in a spectacular oceanfront setting. Up the coast, the **Torrey Pines State Reserve** (Map p797; ☎ 858-755-2063; www.torreypine.org; ☺ 8am-dusk; **P**) protects the endangered Torrey pine and is perfect for leisurely ocean-view strolls. Parking $6.

Activities

Water babies will be in their element in San Diego. Surfing and windsurfing (surf report ☎ 619-221-8824) are both excellent, although in some areas territorial locals are a major irritation. First-timers can learn to hang 10 at the **Pacific Beach Surf School** (Map p797; ☎ 858-373-1138; www.pacificbeachsurfschool.com; 4150 Mission Blvd; lessons $55-70). The best snorkeling and scuba diving is in the **San Diego–La Jolla Underwater Park** (Map p797), where you'll come face-to-fin with glowing orange garibaldi flitting around giant kelp forests. For gear or instruction, try **OE Express** (Map p797; ☎ 858-454-6195; www.oeexpress.com; 2158 Avenida de la Playa) in La Jolla.

Tours

Hike, Bike, Kayak San Diego (Map p797; ☎ 858-551-9510, 866-425-2925; www.hikebikekayak.com; 2246 Avenida de la Playa, La Jolla) Just what it says.

Old Town Trolley Tours (☎ 619-298-8687; www.historictours.com; adult/child $25/15) Hop-on, hop-off loop tour to the main attractions; also land-and-water SEAL tours with military emphasis.

San Diego Harbor Excursion (Map p797; ☎ 619-234-4111; www.sdhe.com; 1050 N Harbor Dr; adult/child from $15/7.50) A variety of bay and harbor cruises.

Sleeping

Rates skyrocket in summer when reasonably priced empty rooms may be scarce, especially in the beach towns. The San Diego Conventions & Visitor Bureau runs a **room reservation line** (☎ 800-350-6205; www.sandiego.org). The room tax is 10.5%.

DOWNTOWN

La Pensione Hotel (Map p800; ☎ 619-236-8000, 800-232-4683; www.lapensionehotel.com; 606 W Date St, Downtown; r $75-95; **P**) Staying at this Little Italy gem puts you within a pizza toss of cafés and restaurants and close to a trolley station and many attractions. Rooms are handsome, if small, and street noise can be an issue (bring ear plugs), but it's still a great bargain.

USA Hostel San Diego (Map p800; ☎ 619-232-3100, 800-438-8622; www.usahostels.com; 726 5th Ave, Downtown; dm/d $22/57; **▢**) In a former Victorian-era hotel, this convivial Gaslamp Quarter hostel has cheerful rooms, a full kitchen and a lounge for chilling. Rates include linen, lockers and pancakes in the morning.

500 West Hotel (Map p800; ☎ 619-234-5252, 866-500-7533; www.500westhotel.com; 500 W Broadway, Downtown; r without bath $60-90; **✕**) Rooms are shoebox-sized and baths down the hallway, but hipsters on a budget love the fun decor, flat-screen TVs and communal kitchen.

Bristol Hotel (Map p800; ☎ 619-232-6141, 800-662-4477; www.thebristolsandiego.com; 1055 1st Ave, Downtown; r $120-190; **P ▢**) Fresh flowers, original pop art and snappy colors throughout give this property an upbeat, jazzy feel. The good-sized rooms feature such pleasant perks as plush bathrobes, free high-speed DSL and a CD player. Parking $18.

Prava (Map p800; ☎ 619-233-3300; www.pravahotel.com; 911 5th Ave, Downtown; r $140-180; **P**) This classy boutique hotel has huge sparkling rooms with pullout sofas for extra guests, kitchenettes with blenders for cocktails and king-sized beds draped in Egyptian cotton. There's also a restaurant and a 24-hour gym.

BALBOA PARK & HILLCREST

InnSuites Lafayette (Map p797; ☎ 619-296-2101, 800-468-3531; http://sandiego.innsuites.com; 2223 El Cajon

Blvd, N Park; r incl breakfast $100-125; **P ▢ ☟**) In the up-and-coming neighborhood of North Park (east of Hillcrest), this Colonial-style mansion used to be a major Hollywood celeb hangout. The nicely furnished units wrap around a huge pool designed by Johnny 'Tarzan' Weissmuller. Free wi-fi in the lobby.

Britt Scripps Inn (Map p797; ☎ 619-230-1991, 888-881-1991; www.brittscripps.com; 406 Maple St; r incl breakfast $325-575; **P ✕ ▢**) This Victorian belle of Banker Hill, near Balboa Park, offers a rare alchemy of high-tech and tradition. Vintage fixtures and furnishings seamlessly pair with wi-fi, flat-screen TVs and multiline phones. Rates include a wine-and-cheese reception in the cozy parlor.

BEACHES

Inn at Sunset Cliffs (Map p797; ☎ 619-222-7901, 866-786-2543; www.innatsunsetcliffs.com; 1370 Sunset Cliffs Blvd, Ocean Beach; r $150-250, ste $400-475; **P ✕ ☟**) Wake up to the sound of surf crashing onto the rocky shore at this charmer wrapped around a flower-bedecked courtyard with small heated pool. The breezy rooms are a bit on the small side, so go for one of the suites (some with full kitchens) if you need more space. Ask about discounts.

Surfer Beach Hotel (Map p797; ☎ 858-483-7070, 800-787-3373; www.thesurferbeachhotel.com; 711 Pacific Beach Dr, Pacific Beach; r $160-200, ste $225-250; **P ☟**) A makeover has taken rooms here from drab to fab. Most come with ocean-view patio, perfect for watching the sunset, cold beer in hand, after a hard day on the beach. The larger units are great for families. Parking $6.

Humphrey's Half Moon Inn & Suites (Map p797; ☎ 619-224-3411, 800-345-9995; www.halfmooninn.com; 2303 Shelter Island Dr, Point Loma; r $150-210, ste $260-500;

ⓟ ⊠ ▣ ▨) Fans of boating, jazz and Polynesian style will feel at home in this waterfront resort. Newly spruced-up rooms, many with marina-view balconies, run the gamut of comforts.

Lodge at Torrey Pines (Map p797; ☎ 858-453-4420, 800-995-4507; www.lodgetorreypines.com; 11480 N Torrey Pines Rd, La Jolla; r $325-625; ⓟ ⊠ ▣ ▨) Luxury is taken seriously at this genteel Craftsman-style property overlooking the famed Torrey Pines Golf Course. Other 'playgrounds' include a vast heated swimming pool, a full-service spa and sumptuous beds made up with the finest linens. The gourmet restaurant is tops. Parking $17.

Other lush choices:

W San Diego (Map p800; ☎ 619-231-8220, 877-946-8357; www.whotels.com/sandiego; 421 W B St; r $260-400; ⓟ ▣ ▨) Sassy, urban, stylish. Parking $26

Hotel del Coronado (Map p797; ☎ 619-435-6611; www.hoteldel.com; 1500 Orange Ave, Coronado; r $290-400; ⓟ ⊠ ▣ ▨) A classic. Parking $18.

Eating

With more than 6000 restaurants, San Diego's cuisine scene is likely to please everyone from fast-food junkies to adventurous eaters. Wonderful ethnic restaurants abound and there are plenty of young, creative chefs standing by to give your belly a workout. Reservations are advised at dinnertime, especially on weekends.

DOWNTOWN

Croce's Restaurant & Jazz Bar (Map p800; ☎ 619-233-4355; 802 5th Ave; mains breakfast & lunch $7-19, dinner $23-35; ⦿ breakfast & lunch Sat & Sun, dinner daily) Empty tables are a rare sight at this sizzling restaurant, Ingrid Croce's tribute to her late

---

THE AUTHOR'S CHOICE

Roppongi (Map p797; ☎ 858-551-5252; 875 Prospect St, La Jolla; tapas $10-25, mains $18-32; ⦿ 11:30am-9:30pm) Fusion really shines at this gorgeous eatery with clever lighting that makes everyone look good. Most people like to build their meals from a selection of ambitious tapas that take their cue mostly from Asian flavors. The Polynesian crab stack, piled high and tossed at table, is a killer choice, and the ahi tuna with watermelon a surprising flavor bomb. Great wines and sakes, too

---

husband, singer Jim Croce. The contemporary American menu has few false notes, and neither do the musicians who perform nightly at the jazz bar.

Indigo Grill (Map p800; ☎ 619-234-6802; 1536 India St; lunch $7-14, dinner $17-28; ⦿ lunch Mon-Fri, dinner daily) This Little Italy jewel wows adventurous diners with boundary-pushing cuisine that blends the flavors of Alaska, the American Southwest and Mexico into perky dishes that tickle all the senses.

Café Cérise (Map p800; ☎ 619-595-0153; 1125 6th Ave; mains lunch $8-12, dinner $25-28; ⦿ lunch Mon-Fri, dinner Tue-Sat) Every ingredient sings with freshness at this contempo Parisian-style bistro whose menu is constantly evolving. The chef even makes his own pâtés and sausages.

Pokéz (Map p800; ☎ 619-702-7160; 947 E St; mains under $6; ⦿ 10am-9pm Mon-Fri, to 7pm Sat & Sun) Pokéz manages to serve the seemingly impossible: healthful Mexican food that actually tastes good. Seasoned tofu and vegan chorizo make appearances alongside classic beef and chicken. Cash only.

BALBOA PARK & HILLCREST

Kemo Sabe (Map p797; ☎ 619-220-6902; 3958 5th Ave, Hillcrest; mains $13-26; ⦿ dinner) Prepare to send your tastebuds on a bold journey at this Hillcrest favorite where Asia meets the American Southwest, both in the decor and on the plate. The Thai jerk smoked duck salad is typical of chef Deborah Scott's audacious fusion fare.

Bombay (Map p797; ☎ 619-298-3155; 3975 5th Ave, Hillcrest; mains $11-17; ⦿ lunch & dinner) Subdued art and an indoor waterfall form a soothing backdrop for Bombay's tantalizing curries and zesty tandoori dishes. Those with an asbestos palate can ask the chef to turn up the heat. Budget gourmets come for the $10 lunch buffet.

Hob Nob Hill (Map p800; ☎ 619-239-8176; 2271 1st Ave; dishes $5-17; ⦿ 7am-9pm) It serves lunch and dinner, sure, but it's really the prospect of this retro diner's scrumptious hot breakfasts that helps us get out of bed. No sweat if you've overslept: they're served all day.

BEACHES

George's at the Cove (Map p797; ☎ 858-454-4244; 1250 Prospect St, La Jolla; mains $26-42; ⦿ lunch & dinner) The Euro-Cal food is as dramatic as the oceanfront location thanks to the bottomless imagination and restless palate of champion chef Trey Foshee. Complex flavors, choice ingredients, dazzling presentation and impeccable service have been a winning formula at this classy outpost for two decades.

Gringo's Cocina y Cantina (Map p797; ☎ 858-490-2877; 4474 Mission Blvd, Pacific Beach; mains lunch $8-14, dinner $12-20; ☺ lunch & dinner) Upbeat, contempo and vast, this kicky Mexican cantina serves up a roster of regional classics, from Oaxacan mole chicken to mango mustard–glazed salmon from Yucatán. The weekend brunch is popular too.

South Beach Bar & Grill (Map p797; ☎ 619-226-4577; 5059 Newport Ave, Ocean Beach; meals $5-10; ☺ 11am-2am) This funky pub close to the ocean is famous for its hefty mahimahi tacos ($3) and other fresh fishy fare. Come for primo people watching and a cool jukebox that lets you download your favorite tune from the Internet. Cash only.

Tapenade (Map p797; ☎ 858-551-7500; 7612 Fay Ave, La Jolla; mains lunch $13.50-18.50, dinner $19-36) Consistently voted one of San Diego's top restaurants, Tapenade dazzles diners with its inspired seasonal French cuisine and diet-busting desserts. Gourmets on a budget should try the two-course lunch for $20 or the three-course sunset dinner for $28 (5:30pm to 6:30pm).

Drinking

Onyx Room & Thin (Map p800; ☎ 619-235-6699; 852 5th Ave, Downtown) Come for cocktails and conversations to the ultracool, industrial-look Thin or the plushier, candlelit Onyx in the basement. The latter also has a dancefloor.

Nunu's Cocktail Lounge (Map p800; ☎ 619-295-2878; 3537 5th Ave, Hillcrest) Dark and divey, this hipster haven started pouring when JFK was president and still looks the part with its curvy booths, big bar and lovably kitsch decor. Smoking patio.

Red Fox Room (Map p797; ☎ 619-297-1313; 2223 El Cajon Blvd, North Park) This dimly lit restaurant-lounge was retro long before retro went hip. Grizzled vets, pretty young things and mom and pop all feel welcome here. It's attached to the InnSuites Lafayette (p803).

Airport Lounge (Map p800; ☎ 619-685-3881; 2400 India St, Downtown/Little Italy) The clientele is cool, the drinks are strong and the servers are dressed like flight attendants at this buzzy watering hole right in the flight path of the San Diego Airport.

Coaster Saloon (Map p797; ☎ 858-488-4438; 744 Ventura Pl, Mission Beach) This old-fashioned neighborhood bar has front-row views of the Belmont Park roller coaster and draws an unpretentious crowd with its beer selection and good margaritas.

Entertainment

Check the San Diego *Reader* or the Night and Day section in the Thursday edition of the San Diego *Union-Tribune* for the latest happenings around town. **Arts Tix** (☺ 11am-6pm Tue-Thu, 10am-6pm Fri & Sat, 10am-5pm Sun), in a kiosk on Broadway outside Horton Plaza, has half-price tickets for same-day evening or next-day matinee performances and full-price tickets to all types of other events. **Ticketmaster** (☎ 619-220-8497; www.ticketmaster.com) is another vendor.

LIVE MUSIC & NIGHTCLUBS

Casbah (Map p800; ☎ 619-232-4355; 2501 Kettner Blvd; cover $7-15) Liz Phair, Alanis Morissette and the Smashing Pumpkins have all rocked this funky Casbah on their way up the charts and it's still a good place to catch tomorrow's headliners.

4th & B (Map p800; ☎ 619-231-4343; 345 B St, Downtown) This midsized venue has music lovers head-bobbing with an eclectic mix of talent, from unsigned hopefuls to big names like BB King and Elvis Costello. The lounge is great for resting feet and eardrums.

On Broadway (Map p800; ☎ 619-231-0011; www.obec.tv; 615 Broadway; cover $20; ☺ Fri & Sat) San Diego's sexiest dance spot is a sprawling double-decker affair where DJs mix it up on – count them – five dancefloors. Dress to impress, or forget about making it past the velvet-rope goons.

Soma (Map p797; ☎ 619-226-7662; www.somasd.com; 3350 Sports Arena Blvd, near Old Town; cover $7-14) This all-ages venue (no booze) puts the spotlight on up-and-coming local bands of the alterna-rock and punk persuasion. It's electric and edgy with fiercely loyal crowds.

Other places to get down:

Blind Melons (Map p797; ☎ 858-483-7844; 710 Garnet Ave, Pacific Beach) Edgy.

'Canes (Map p797; ☎ 858-488-1780; 3105 Ocean Front Walk, Mission Beach) Tropical.

House of Blues (Map p800; ☎ 619-299-2583; 1055 5th Ave, Downtown) Predictable.

Club Montage (Map p797; ☎ 619-294-9590; 2028 Hancock St, near Old Town; ☺ Fri & Sat) Gay.

CLASSICAL MUSIC & OPERA

San Diego Symphony (Map p800; ☎ 619-235-0804; www .sandiegosymphony.com; 750 B St) For serious music lovers, there's no finer place than the Copley Symphony Hall, where this accomplished orchestra presents classical and family concerts. In summer, it moves to **Navy Pier** (Map p800; 960 N Harbor Dr) for more light-hearted fare.

San Diego Opera (Map p800; ☎ 619-570-1100; www.sdopera.com; Civic Theatre, 3rd & B St) High-quality, eclectic programming is the hallmark of the city's opera ensemble, which occasionally draws international guest stars such as Cecilia Bartoli.

Old Globe Theaters (Map p800; ☎ 619-234-5623; www.theglobetheaters.org; Balboa Park) High-caliber theater is performed in three venues, including a replica of Shakespeare's eponymous London stage.

Getting There & Away

San Diego International Airport (Map p800; ☎ 619-231-2100; www.san.org) sits right in the middle of the city, about 3 miles west of Downtown.

TIJUANA: CHAOS, CLASS & CULTURE CLASH

Rita Hayworth was discovered here. Carlos Santana's career began in its nightclubs. And one of the world's great culinary inventions, the Caesar salad, hails from nowhere other than…drum roll please…yes! Tijuana, that grubby, noisy, frenzied, yet oddly tantalizing city of two million right across the border from San Diego.

During Prohibition in the 1920s, Tijuana (TJ, for short) was the darling of the Hollywood crowd. These days, tequila and beer exert their siren song on college students, Navy boys and other revelers who each weekend descend upon the rollicking bars and nightclubs of **Avenida Revolución** (La Revo), the main tourist strip and only a 15-minute walk from the border. By day, it's the shops that lure bargain hunters in search of everything from cheap liquor to shoes to pharmaceuticals. Alas, competition is fierce and the constant hustle from storefront vendors can quickly grate on your nerves. Nearly all businesses accept US dollars.

Once you've 'done' La Revo, be sure to venture beyond for a more interesting and often surprisingly sophisticated side of Tijuana. Pick up a map from a **visitor center** (☎ 664-683-1405; www.tijuanaonline.org) that shows the precise locations of all the places mentioned below. There are branches right by the pedestrian and car border crossings as well as on La Revo between Calles 3a and 4a.

The winemakers of **LA Cetto** (☎ 664-685-3031; www.lacetto.com; Avenida Cañón Johnson 2108; ☽ 10am-6pm Mon-Fri, 10am-5pm Sat) prove that Mexico is not just tequila country. In their tasting room you can sample vintages grown in Baja's Valle de Guadalupe rarely available outside of Mexico. Architecture fans may want to steer towards the **Catedral de Nuestra Señora de Guadalupe** (Avenida Niños Héroes & Calle 2a), Tijuana's oldest church. For a cultural fix, make a beeline to the excellent **Museo de las Californias** (☎ 664-687-9600; Paseo de los Héroes & Miña; admission $2; ☽ 10am-6pm Tue-Fri, to 7pm Sat & Sun), whose engaging exhibits chronicle Baja California's often-intriguing history. The museum is part of the **Centro Cultural de Tijuana**, whose schedule of classical concerts, theater and dance recitals goes a long way towards undermining the city's image as a cultural wasteland. Nearby, **Mercado Hidalgo** is a fun indoor/outdoor market where the locals stock up on such basics as rice, beans, and chili from pussycat mild to hellishly hot.

TJ has an excellent cuisine scene. Good choices on or near La Revo include the casual **Café La Especial** (☎ 664-685-6654; Avenida Revolución 718; breakfast & lunch $5, dinner $10-15), in the basement below Hotel Lafayette, where you can wash down tasty carne asada, enchiladas and tacos with some of the best margaritas on the strip. **La Costa** (☎ 664-685-3124; Calle 7a btwn Avenidas Revolución & Constitución; mains $10-23; ☽ 10am-10pm) is often packed to the gills with fans of fresh fish and seafood. Beyond La Revo, direct your tastebuds to the classy **La Diferencia** (☎ 664-634-7078; Blvd Sánchez Taboada 10611; mains $15-30; ☽ noon-1:30am) to feast on such exotic morsels as squash-blossom soup or duck with hibiscus sauce in a beautifully columned dining room.

The easiest way to get to Tijuana is by taking the San Diego Trolley and then walking across the border or taking a Mexicoach shuttle ($5 round-trip) from the Border Station Parking lot. Due to heightened security, expect long lines when returning to the US. See Visas (p1158) and Customs (p1146) for border requirements.

Greyhound (Map p800; ☎ 619-239-8082; 120 W Broadway) has hourly direct buses to Los Angeles ($16, 2½ to four hours).

Amtrak's *Pacific Surfliner* makes several trips daily to Los Angeles ($27, three hours) and Santa Barbara ($32, 5½ hours) from the **Santa Fe Depot** (Map p800; ☎ 619-239-9021; 1055 Kettner Blvd, Downtown). Coaster commuter trains to northern San Diego County also come through here.

All major car-rental companies have desks at the airport, or call the national toll-free numbers (p1173). **Eagle Rider** (Map p797; ☎ 619-222-8822, 877-437-4337; 3655 Camino del Rio W) rents motorcycles.

Getting Around
Bus No 992, nicknamed the Flyer ($2.25, 5am to 1am), operates at 10- to 15-minute intervals between the airport and Downtown, with stops along Broadway. Airport shuttle services include **Cloud 9 Shuttle** (☎ 800-974-8885) and **Xpress Shuttle** (☎ 800-900-7433). A taxi to Downtown from the airport costs between $8 and $13.

Local buses and the San Diego Trolley, which travels south to the Mexican border, are operated by **Metropolitan Transit System** (MTS; ☎ 619-233-3004; www.sdcommute.com). The **Transit Store** (Map p800; ☎ 619-234-1060; Broadway & 1st Ave) has available route maps, tickets and one/two/three/four-day Day Tripper passes for $5/9/12/15, respectively. Taxi flag fall is $1.70 with $2 charged for each additional mile.

AROUND SAN DIEGO
San Diego Wild Animal Park
Take a walk on the 'wild' side at this 1800-acre **open-range zoo** (Map p797; ☎ 760-747-8702; www.sandiegozoo.org; 15500 San Pasqual Valley Rd, Escondido; adult/child $28.50/17.50; ☼ 9am-10pm mid-Jun–early Sep, to 5pm mid-Sep–mid-Jun), where you can watch giraffes graze, lions lounge and rhinos romp more or less freely on the valley floor. For that instant safari feel, board the Wgasa Bush electric tram that will hurtle you from East Africa to the Asian Plains and the Mongolian Steppe in 50 minutes. Combination tickets with the San Diego Zoo are $55/34.

The park is in Escondido, about 30 miles north of downtown San Diego. Take the I-15 Fwy to the Via Rancho Parkway exit, then follow the signs.

Legoland
Legoland (Map p797; ☎ 760-918-5346; www.lego.com/legoland/california; 1 Legoland Dr, Carlsbad; adult/child/senior $45/38/38; ☼ 10am-5pm, extended hrs Jul & Aug) is an enchanting fantasy environment of rides, shows and attractions mostly suited for the elementary-school set. Tots can dig for dinosaur bones, pilot helicopters and earn their driver's license, while mom and pop will probably get a kick out of Miniland, which recreates such American landmarks as the White House and the Golden Gate Bridge entirely of Lego blocks. Legoland is about 32 miles north of downtown San Diego. Take the I-5 Fwy north to the Cannon Rd E exit, then follow the signs.

CALIFORNIA DESERTS

The desert is a magical place, so empty and yet so full. It may seem barren and boring at first, but spend a little time and you'll feel your senses sharpen to reveal a different kind of beauty – subtle, intimate, restorative. Weathered volcanic peaks, subliminally erotic sand dunes, purple-tinged mountains, groves of cacti, tiny wildflowers pushing up from caramel-colored soil for their brief lives, lizards scurrying beneath colossal boulders. These are just some of the elements that create the irresistible mystique of the desert.

ANZA-BORREGO DESERT STATE PARK
Shaped by an ancient sea and tectonic forces, Anza-Borrego holds the record for largest state park in the USA outside Alaska. Framing the park's only settlement – tiny Borrego Springs (pop 2535) – are 600,000 acres of mountains, canyons and badlands; a fabulous variety of plants and wildlife; and intriguing relics of native tribes, Spanish explorers and gold-rush pioneers. The wildflower-blooming season (usually March to May; call ☎ 760-767-4684 for updates) is a great time to visit, right before the Hades-like heat makes exploring dangerous.

Borrego Springs has stores, restaurants, motels and a public library with free Internet access. The park's excellent **visitor center** (☎ 760-767-5311, 760-767-4205; www.anzaborrego.statepark.org; 200 Palm Canyon Dr; ☼ 9am-5pm Oct-May, Sat & Sun only Jun-Sep) is 2 miles west of here.

You'll need your own wheels to explore the park. A passenger car will get you to

CALIFORNIA

many interesting spots, but only a 4WD can tackle many of the 500 miles of back-country dirt roads. To truly get a sense of the place, get out on a hiking trail (pack plenty of water). Good – and fairly easy – options include the **Borrego Palm Canyon Trail** (3-mile round-trip) to a native palm grove and waterfall; the **Cactus Loop Trail** (1 mile) with great views; and the **Pictograph Trail** (2 miles) for close-ups of native rock art and a restored stagecoach stop.

The park's three developed and eight primitive campgrounds rarely fill up, but you can also camp for free anywhere you wish as long as you keep at least 100ft away from water. Open ground fires and gathering vegetation (dead or alive) are prohibited.

Accommodations in Borrego Springs include the well-kept **Palm Canyon Resort** (☎ 760-767-5341, 800-242-0044; 221 Palm Canyon Dr; r $70-195, mains $10-20; ✖ ✖), which also has a good restaurant; and the adobe-style **Borrego Valley Inn** (☎ 760-767-0311, 800-333-5810; www.borregovalleyinn.com; 405 Palm Canyon Dr; r incl breakfast $135-200; ✖ ✖ ✖), which has lovely rooms with Southwestern decor.

For a casual meal served with a side of local color try **Carlee's Place** (☎ 760-767-3262; 660 Palm Canyon Dr; meals $10-25), while gourmet fare awaits at **La Casa del Zorro** (☎ 760-767-5323; 3845 Yaqui Pass Rd; r from $265, dinner mains $30-40).

PALM SPRINGS

Change is afoot in Palm Springs. Once the swinging hangout of Sinatra and Elvis and other rollicking stars, the city went gray, conservative and dreary in the 1980s. But the pendulum of popularity has swung back as a new generation of celebs and hipsters latches onto the city's retro-chic charms: kidney-shaped pools, midcentury steel-and-glass bungalows, boutique hotels with stylish vintage decor and piano bars serving perfect martinis.

Old-style glamour is definitely back.

But even if all that in-and-out-and-in-again grooviness leaves you cold, there's plenty to do in Palm Springs, the oldest and ritziest of the nine cities in the Coachella Valley. You could hike along palm-studded canyons or ski through silky snow (or both in the same day), play a round of golf, explore museums or straddle a giant earthquake fault line. The city is also a major gay and lesbian getaway.

The best time to visit is from October to April, but Palm Springs stays reasonably busy even in summer when hotel rates drop and temperatures rise above 100°F (38°C).

Palm Springs' compact downtown flanks Palm Canyon Dr (the continuation of Hwy 111, the main road into town), which runs north–south. The parallel Indian Canyon Dr runs one-way south to north.

Information

Access Internet at the **public library** (☎ 760-322-7323; 300 S Sunrise Way; access free; ✖ Mon-Sat).

In town are **Desert Regional Medical Center** (☎ 760-323-6511; 1150 N Indian Canyon Dr; ✖ 24hr) and a **post office** (333 E Amado Rd).

Both visitor centers make room reservations and are stocked with information, including free guides for the mobility-impaired and gay and lesbian travelers (also check www.palmspringsgay.com) as well as *A Map of Palm Springs Modern* ($5) for architecture fans:

Tramway Visitors Center (☎ 760-778-8418, 800-347-7746; www.palm-springs.org; 2901 N Palm Canyon Dr; ✖ 9am-5pm, seasonal variations possible) North of town, at the tramway turnoff, in a 1965 Albert Frey–designed gas station.

Uptown Visitors Center (☎ 760-327-2828; 777 N Palm Canyon Dr, Suite 101; ✖ 10am-5pm)

Sights & Activities

Escape the summer heat aboard the **Palm Springs Aerial Tramway** (☎ 760-325-1449; www.pstramway.com; 1 Tramway Rd; adult/child/senior $21/14/19, after 3pm $18/11/11; ✖ 10am-10pm Mon-Fri, from 8am Sat & Sun), whose rotating cars whisk you from sunbaked desert to pine-scented Alpine wonderland in only 10 minutes. The mountain station at 8516ft offers sweeping views and access to 54 miles of hiking trails through the wilderness of **Mount San Jacinto State Park**, including a 5.5-mile trek to the summit. In winter, you can comb through the forest on snowshoes or cross-country skis, available for rent at the **Adventure Center** (open Thursday to Sunday) near the mountain station.

Another chilling-out option is **Knott's Soak City** (☎ 760-327-0499; www.knotts.com/soakcity/ps; 1500 S Gene Autry Trail; adult/child $26/15, after 3pm $16/12; ✖ vary), a water park with slides, tube rides and wave pools.

In the cooler months, especially during the spring wildflower season, don't miss a ramble around the **Indian Canyons** (☎ 760-325-

3400; www.indian-canyons.com; adult/child/student/senior $6/2/4.50/4.50; 8am-5pm), rare veins of green once inhabited by the native Cahuilla people. Bring a picnic and find your favorite spot by a palm-shaded stream or beneath towering rock formations. Nearby **Tahquitz Canyon** (760-416-7044; www.tahquitzcanyon.com; 500 W Mesquite; adult/child $12.50/6; 7:30am-5pm) is famous for its 60ft waterfall and ancient rock art.

Culture buffs flock downtown to the **Palm Springs Desert Museum** (760-325-7186; www.psmuseum.org; 101 Museum Dr; adult/child/senior $7.50/3.50/6.50; 10am-5pm Tue-Sat, to 8pm Thu, noon-5pm Sun) for its art collection, natural science exhibits and events.

At the airport, the **Palm Springs Air Museum** (760-778-6262; www.air-museum.org; 745 N Gene Autry Trail; adult/child/senior $10/5/8.50; 10am-5pm) shows off some great vintage planes, including the amazing WWII-era B-17 (the 'Flying Fortress').

Tours

Celebrity Tours (760-770-2700; Rimrock Shopping Center, 4751 E Palm Dr; 1hr tour adult/child/senior $22/12/14, 2½hr tour $27/14/25) Palm Springs gossip – past and present.

Desert Adventures (760-324-5337; www.red-jeep.com; 2/3/4hr tours $69/89/99) Snappily narrated and information-packed jeep tours through shake, rattle and roll country along the San Andreas Fault.

PS Modern Tours (760-318-6118; tour $55) For fans of Frey, Neutra, Lautner and other midcentury architects.

PS Windmill Tours (760-320-1365; adult/child/senior $23/10/20) Learn all about the grove of whirring windmills surrounding Palm Springs. Reservations required.

Sleeping

Chase Hotel (760-320-8866, 877-532-4273; www.chasehotelpalmsprings.com; 200 W Arenas Rd; r incl breakfast $80-140, ste $120-170;) This midcentury motel complex in downtown gets top marks for its uncluttered, oversized rooms (some with kitchenettes), warm staff, and extras like the generous breakfast, fresh afternoon cookies and immaculate pool area. *Great* value.

Casa Cody (760-320-9346, 800-231-2639; www.casacody.com; 175 S Cahuilla Rd; r incl breakfast $100-160, ste $170-360;) Tucked behind billowing bougainvillea, this lovely country inn has units draped in desert-themed decor, including some with full kitchens, wood-burning fireplaces and private patios.

Pepper Tree Inn (760-318-9850, 866-887-8733; www.peppertreepalmsprings.com; r $100-170, ste $210-280;) A massive renovation has morphed this former flophouse into a stylish boutique hotel right in the heart of town. Rooms are swathed in earth tones and wrap around a big pool.

Other good choices:

Alpine Gardens Hotel (760-323-2231, 888-299-7455; www.alpinegardens.com; 1586 E Palm Canyon Dr; r $60-85, with kitchen $115-125;) Primo budget pick.

Caliente Tropics (760-327-1391, 866-468-9595; www.calientetropics.com; r $50-300;) Polynesian-style motor lodge where Elvis once splashed poolside.

Parker Palm Springs (760-770-5000, 888-450-9488; www.theparkerpalmsprings.com; 4200 E Palm Canyon Dr; r from $300;) Posh full-service resort with whimsical decor by designer *du jour* Jonathan Adler.

Eating

Fisherman's Market & Grill (760-327-1766; 235 S Indian Canyon Dr; mains $6-14; 11:30am-9pm) Shrimp to cod to sea bass – the ocean fare at this self-service shack is so fresh, you half expect waves lapping at your ankles. The fish-and-chips is a classic.

Wang's (760-325-9264; 424 S Indian Canyon Dr; mains $10-15; dinner) This swank Pan-Asian outpost, mood-lit and complete with indoor koi pond, is the darling of the in-crowd, even though the menu plays it safe with pad thai, kung pao chicken and other classics.

Blue Coyote Grill (760-327-1196; 445 N Palm Canyon Dr; mains $10-20; 10am-10pm) Romantic and convivial, this indoor-outdoor cantina delivers with solid Mexican fare and margaritas so strong they should be served with a seat belt to keep you in your chair.

Now (760-327-0550; 476 N Palm Canyon Dr; mains $22-32; dinner Thu-Tue) The name stands for 'never on Wednesday', which is the one day the chef does not tease diners with such ambitious American bistro fare as quail fricassee, lobster fondue or pepper-seared tuna.

Also recommended:

Native Foods (760-416-0070; 1775 E Palm Canyon Dr; mains $7-12; 11:30am-9:30pm) Tasty vegan fare.

Le Vallauris (760-325-5059, 385 W Tahquitz Canyon Way; mains lunch $15-26, dinner $23-38; lunch & dinner) French haute cuisine.

Getting There & Around

Palm Springs International Airport (760-318-3800; www.palmspringsairport.com; 3400 E Tahquitz Canyon Way) is served directly from major US cities, including Houston, Atlanta and Chicago. **Greyhound** (760-325-2053; 311 N Indian

Canyon Dr) has direct buses to Los Angeles ($21, 2½ to four hours). Slow-moving local service is provided by **SunBus** (☎ 760-343-3451; www.sunline.org; ticket/day pass $1/3).

JOSHUA TREE NATIONAL PARK

Like figments from a Dr Seuss book, the whimsical Joshua trees (actually tree-sized yuccas) welcome visitors to this sprawling park. It's popular with rock climbers and day hikers, especially in spring when many trees dramatically send up a huge single cream-colored flower. The mystical quality of this stark, boulder-strewn landscape has inspired many artists, most famously the band U2 who named its 1987 album after the Joshua tree.

Park highlights include **Hidden Valley** with its dramatic piles of golden, sculpted boulders; **Keys View**, with vistas as far as Mexico (best at sunset); and the **Cholla Cactus Garden**. An excellent short hike is the 1.1-mile **Barker Dam loop trail**, which takes in all that makes Joshua Tree special: weathered rock piles, a historic dam, Indian petroglyphs and, of course, the trees themselves. For a greater physical challenge, head to the **Fortynine Palm Oasis** (3-mile round-trip) or the **Lost Palms Oasis** (7.5-mile round-trip).

The park has two **visitor centers** (☎ 760-337-5500; www.nps.gov/jotr; Main (National Monument Rd, Twentynine Palms; ⌚ 8am-5pm); Smaller (S entrance, Cottonwood Springs; ⌚ 8am-4pm). In emergencies call ☎ 909-383-5651.

Park admission is $10 per vehicle, good for seven days and comes with a map and the useful *Joshua Tree Guide* newspaper. There are no facilities besides restrooms, so gas up and bring food and plenty of water.

Sleeping & Eating

Of the park's nine campgrounds only **Black Rock Canyon** (☎ 800-365-2267; sites $10) and **Indian Cove** (☎ 800-365-2267; sites $10) have reservable sites. Cottonwood also costs $10, while the other five charge $5. Only Black Rock Canyon and Cottonwood have water. Backcountry camping is permitted as long as it's 1 mile from the road and 500ft from any trail; registration is required at one of the 12 backcountry boards throughout the park.

If camping is not your thing, base yourself in Twentynine Palms (home of the world's largest US Marine base), Joshua Tree or Yucca Valley, all north of the park.

Standouts from among the run-of-the-mill motels along 29 Palms Hwy: **Twentynine Palms Inn** (☎ 760-367-3505; www.29 palmsinn.com; 73950 Inn Ave, Twentynine Palms; r incl breakfast $75-195, mid-Jun–mid-Sep $50-160; mains lunch $6-9, dinner $12-23; 🍽 🔲) Historic adobe-and-wood cabins and respected restaurant around an oasis. **Spin & Margie's Desert Hideaway** (☎ 760-366-9124; www.deserthideaway.com; 64491 29 Palms Hwy, Joshua Tree; ste $105-140; 🔲 🍽) Charming Southwestern-style cabins with kitchen and private patio.

For sustenance your best bet is the funky-cool **Crossroads Café** (☎ 760-366-5414; 61715 29 Palms Hwy, Joshua Tree; dishes $4-10; ⌚ 7am-8pm). For coffee, sandwiches, salads, live music and Internet access drop by the nearby **Beatnik Cafe** (☎ 760-366-2090; 61597 29 Palms Hwy, Joshua Tree; meals under $10, Internet per 15min $2; ⌚ 7am-midnight).

Around Joshua Tree National Park

North of the park, **Pioneertown** (www.pioneer town.com; Hwy 247) was built in 1946 as a Western movie set and is now home to the legendary **Pappy's & Harriet's Pioneertown Palace** (☎ 760-365-5956; www.pappyandharriets.com; mains $8-25; ⌚ Thu-Mon), a happening honky-tonk with live music, cheap beer and great BBQ. The owners also operate a small **hotel** (☎ 760-365-4879; r $55-65).

MOJAVE NATIONAL PRESERVE

If you're on a quest for the 'middle of nowhere,' you'll find it in the desert wilderness of the **Mojave National Preserve** (www.nps.gov /moja; admission free), a 1.6 million–acre jumble of sand dunes, mountains, Joshua trees, volcanic cinder cones and sculptured rock formations. No services or facilities are available within the preserve.

From Baker, Kelbaker Rd crosses a ghostly landscape of cinder cones before arriving at **Kelso Depot**, a handsome Spanish-style railroad station built in 1924. It houses a sparkling new **visitor center** (☎ 760-252-6161; ⌚ 9am-5pm) with interesting desert-demystifying exhibits. From here it's another 11 miles south to the majestic **Kelso Dunes** that rise up to 700ft and, when conditions are right, emanate a low 'booming' sound caused by shifting sands. The dunes' quiet and graceful presence is nothing short of magical. Hiking to the top of the tallest one takes about two hours round-trip.

ROUTE 66: GET YOUR KICKS IN CALIFORNIA

Ah, California. For down-on-their-luck Okies and post-WWII baby boomers, Route 66 was the highway of dreams leading to the promised land. The route enters the Golden State at the Colorado River, near Needles, traverses the Mojave Desert and culminates at the ocean in Santa Monica. Turn-by-turn driving directions are available for free at www.historic66.com. For trip planning, try the **California Route 66 Preservation Foundation** (☎ 760-868-3320; www.cart66pf.org).

From Needles, the National Old Trails Hwy barrels headlong through largely uninhabited desert towns that died off when the I-40 was built. The most interesting are **Goffs**, one of the best-preserved desert settlements in the Mojave, and **Amboy**, the turnoff to **Joshua Tree National Park** (opposite). Stop in Newberry Springs for refreshments at the quirky **Bagdad Café** (☎ 760-257-3101; 46548 National Trails Hwy), where much of Percy Adlon's eponymous 1988 film was shot.

Signs of civilization re-emerge in **Barstow**, a railroad settlement where the **Casa Del Desierto**, a historic Harvey House (railway hotels and restaurants by English immigrant Fred Harvey in the late 19th century), harbors the **Route 66 'The Mother Road' Museum** (☎ 760-255-1890; www .route66museum.org; donations welcome; 681 N 1st St; ☉ 11am-4pm Fri-Sun). Follow the Old National Trails Hwy through Lenwood and Helendale. Nearby the **Exotic World Burlesque Museum** (☎ 760-243-5261; www.exoticworldusa.org; admission $5; ☉ 10am-4pm Tue-Sun) is a paean to the world's va-va-va-voom 'movers and shakers.'

In Victorville, the small **California Route 66 Museum** (☎ 760-951-0436; www.califrt66museum .org; 16825 D St; donations welcome; ☉ 10am-4pm Thu-Mon) is another stop for 'route warriors.' Drive over dramatic Cajon Pass on I-15 and plunge down into the suburban LA maelstrom. Follow Foothill Blvd west of San Bernardino, which has the **First McDonald's Museum** (☎ 909-885-6324; www.route-66.com/mcdonalds; 1398 N E St; admission free; ☉ 10am-5pm), past the kooky **Wigwam Motel** (☎ 909-875-3005; www.wigwammotel.com; 2728 W Foothill Blvd, Rialto; d $50-80) and the **Giant Orange** (15395 Foothill Blvd). Rancho Cucamonga has retro restaurants like the rustic **Sycamore Inn** (☎ 909-982-1104; 8318 Foothill Blvd) and the **Magic Lamp Inn** (☎ 909-981-8659; 8189 Foothill Blvd) with its fabulous neon sign.

Foothill Blvd turns into Colorado Blvd as it moves into **Pasadena** (p785), where you can stop at the nostalgic soda fountain of **Fair Oaks Pharmacy** (☎ 626-799-1414; 1526 Mission St) before braving traffic on the final stretch through LA. Head south on the I-110 Fwy, north on Sunset Blvd and west on Santa Monica Blvd, which will deliver you straight to road's end at the ocean in **Santa Monica** (p784).

At Kelso Depot, Kelbaker Rd intersects with the northbound Cima Rd, which meets back up with I-15 after 32 miles. En route it skirts **Cima Dome**, a 1500ft hunk of granite whose slopes are smothered in one of the world's largest and densest **Joshua tree forests**. For a close-up look, hike up the Teutonia Peak Trail (4 miles round-trip).

East of Cima Rd, Mojave Rd takes you to the preserve's two first-come, first-served campgrounds (sites $12) set amid a volcanic landscape at Mid Hills and Hole-in-the-Wall. The latter also has a small **visitor center** (☎ 760-928-2572; ☉ 9am-4pm Wed-Sun Oct-Apr, Fri-Sun May-Sep). Roads in this area are unpaved but navigable. South of Hole-in-Wall, **Mitchell Caverns** (☎ 760-928-2586; adult/child $4/2; tours ☉ 1:30pm Mon-Fri, 10am, 1:30pm & 3pm Sat & Sun Sep-May, 1:30pm Sat & Sun Jun-Aug) is a subterranean world of quirky limestone formations.

Free backcountry and roadside camping is permitted throughout the preserve in areas that have been previously used for this purpose. If you need a roof over your head, choices include three grotty motels in Baker, each with rooms around $60. Much better, albeit a bit off-the-beaten-path, is the B&B-style **Nipton Hotel** (☎ 760-856-2335; www.nipton.com; r $75, tent cabins $63; ☒ ☒ ☐) in a century-old adobe villa in the railroad outpost of Nipton northeast of the preserve. The owners also offer tent cabins, free wi-fi, a café and a well-stocked trading post.

DEATH VALLEY NATIONAL PARK

The name itself evokes all that is harsh and hellish – a lifeless place hotter than Satan's hoof. Well, not quite. Closer inspection reveals Death Valley as a timeless medley of canyons, sand dunes, oases and sculpted

CALIFORNIA

mountains. It holds the US records for hottest temperature (134°F, or 56°C, measured in 1913), lowest point (Badwater, 282ft below sea level) and largest national park outside Alaska (4687 sq miles). Bring plenty of water for yourself and your vehicle. Wildflower groupies will want to visit in March and April (hotline ☎ 760-786-3200).

Orientation & Information

Centrally located Furnace Creek has a general store, restaurants, lodging, gas station, a golf course and a **visitor center** (☎ 760-786-3200; www .nps.gov/deva; ☺ 8am-5pm). In Stovepipe Wells Village, about 24 miles northwest of here, there's a store, gas station, motel-restaurant and ranger station. Gas and sustenance are also available at Scotty's Castle, in the north, and Panamint Springs, on the park's western edge. The entrance fee ($10 per vehicle; valid for seven days) must be paid at self-service pay stations located throughout the park. For a free map and newspaper present your receipt at the visitor center.

There's Internet access just south of the park in Shoshone at **Café C'est Si Bon** (☎ 760-853-4307; 118 Hwy 127, dishes $2-6, Internet per hr $6; ☺ usually 8am-4pm Wed-Mon), a charming solar-powered café serving tasty vegetarian fare.

Sights & Activities

A good place to start your explorations is in Furnace Creek, from where it's a quick drive up to **Zabriskie Point** for spectacular valley views across golden badlands eroded into waves, pleats and gullies. At **Dante's View**, another 20 miles south, you can simultaneously see the highest (Mt Whitney) and lowest (Badwater) points in the contiguous USA.

Badwater itself, a foreboding landscape of crinkly salt flats, is a 17-mile drive south of Furnace Creek along Badwater Rd (Rte 178). Attractions along the way include narrow **Golden Canyon**, easily explored on a 2-mile round-trip walk, and **Devil's Golf Course**, where salt has piled up into saw-toothed miniature mountains. A 9-mile detour along **Artists Drive** is best done in the late afternoon when the hills erupt in fireworks of color.

Near Stovepipe Wells Village, north of Furnace Creek, you can scramble along the smooth marble walls of **Mosaic Canyon** or marvel at the interplay of light and shadow at the undulating **Sand Dunes**. Another 36

miles north is **Scotty's Castle** (☎ 760-786-2392; adult/child/senior $11/6/9; ☺ 9am-5pm), where costumed guides bring to life the strange tale of a lovable con-man named Death Valley Scotty and his friend, benefactor and victim, Chicago insurance magnate Albert Johnson. About 8 miles west of here, giant **Ubehebe Crater** is the result of a massive volcanic eruption. Hiking to the bottom and back takes about 30 minutes. Another 27 miles south via a rough dirt road (high clearance required) takes you to the eerie **Racetrack**, where slow-moving rocks leave faint tracks in the dry lakebed.

The most popular backcountry adventure, though, is the 27-mile trip along unpaved **Titus Canyon Road**, which climbs, curves and plunges through the Grapevine Mountains past a ghost town, petroglyphs and spectacular canyon narrows. It's a one-way road accessible only from Hwy 374 near Beatty; the entrance is about 2 miles outside park boundaries.

Sleeping & Eating

During wildflower season accommodations are often booked solid and campgrounds full by midmorning, especially on weekends.

Furnace Creek Inn (☎ 760-786-2345; www.furnace creekresort; r $250-390; mains lunch $10-14, dinner $21-29; ☺ mid-Oct–mid-May; ✗ ☺ ☻) At this elegant, mission-style hotel you can count the colors of the desert while unwinding by the spring-fed pool or sample a fine meal in the gourmet restaurant (dinner dress code).

Furnace Creek Ranch (☎ 760-786-2345; www .furnacecreekresort.com; r $108-182; ✗ ☺ ☻) is a rambling 224-unit resort with dated, if comfortable, rooms, many with patios or balconies. It offers less exalted belly-filling options. Its **Wrangler Restaurant** (mains breakfast/lunch $9/11, dinner $19-29; ☺ 6am-9.30pm) puts out buffet breakfasts and lunches and turns into a steakhouse at night. Next door, the **Forty-Niner Café** (mains $6-19; ☺ 7am-9pm) cooks up American standards, although for the juiciest burgers mosey over to the **19th Hole Bar & Grill** (burgers $7; ☺ lunch Oct-May).

Stovepipe Wells Village (☎ 760-786-2387; www .stovepipewells.com; r $63-103, mains breakfast & lunch $4-8, dinner $10-23; ☻ ☐ ☻) The standard motel-style rooms here are small and worn and the air-con noisy, but those with private patio are great for sipping cocktails under the stars.

Campers will find public showers ($3) at Furnace Creek Ranch and Stovepipe Wells Village, where the fee includes pool access. Free backcountry camping permits are available from the visitor center.

The most central camping options are the following:

Furnace Creek (☎ 800-365-2267; http://reservations .nps.gov; Furnace Creek area; campsites $10-16; ☽ year-round) Pleasant grounds, including some shady sites.

Sunset (Furnace Creek area; sites $10; ☽ Oct-Apr) RV-oriented and the largest, with over 1000 spots.

Stovepipe Wells (Stovepipe Wells Village; sites $10; ☽ Oct-Apr) Parking-lot style, but close to the sand dunes.

Texas Spring (Furnace Creek area; sites $12; ☽ Oct-Apr) The best for tents; nice hillside location.

Around Death Valley

Your accommodation choices widen if you're willing to overnight outside the park. The pit stops of Ridgecrest and Beatty, Nevada, are your best bet for budget and midrange motels. En route to the latter, the ghost towns of **Rhyolite** and **Goldwell Open-Air Museum** are intriguing roadside attractions.

Shoestringers should steer south to the small and friendly **HI Desertaire Hostel** (☎ 760-852-4580, 877-907-1265; www.desertairehostel.com; 2000 Old Spanish Trail Hwy, Tecopa; dm/r $15/40, nonmembers $18/50; ☒ ☒). It's in Tecopa, a dusty blink-and-you-missed-it outpost best known for its public **hot spring mineral baths** (☎ 760-852-4420; admission $5; ☽ 6am-9pm).

CENTRAL COAST

California's Central Coast stretches from Ventura north to Monterey Bay, and it includes nearly 300 miles of prime shoreline. Hwy 101 is the region's main artery, but coastal drives don't get much sweeter than the Pacific Coast Hwy (Hwy 1) between San Luis Obispo and Monterey.

VENTURA & THE CHANNEL ISLANDS

Ventura, an agricultural town and gateway to Channel Islands National Park, has a charming downtown with an assortment of cafés, restaurants and antique shops.

Ventura Harbor, southwest of Hwy 101, is the main departure point for boat trips to the Channel Islands, whose unique flora and fauna have garnered them the nickname 'California's Galápagos.' Five of the eight

islands in the chain, which stretches from Newport Beach to Santa Barbara, comprise **Channel Islands National Park**. The NPS **visitor center** (☎ 805-658-5730; www.nps.gov/chis; 1901 Spinnaker Dr; ☽ 8:30am-5pm) is in Ventura Harbor. The islands are preserved as virtual wilderness, so they have few facilities but offer unbeatable swimming, snorkeling, diving, kayaking, hiking and bird-watching. The islands also have primitive **campgrounds** (☎ 800-365-2267; sites $10); bring food and water.

Anacapa, the closest island to the mainland, is best for half- or single-day trips, with short, easy trails and unforgettable views. Santa Cruz, the largest island, is also convenient for single-day trips, though its longer, more strenuous hikes invite extended explorations. The other three islands require longer channel crossings and are best visited as three-day camping trips: San Miguel is often shrouded in fog; Santa Barbara supports a sizable elephant seal colony; and Santa Rosa is home to many bird species and archaeological sites and offers beach camping.

One air service and two boat operators offer camper transportation and a variety of day trips and packages. Expect to pay about $42/25 per adult/child for an eight-hour boat trip to Anacapa Island:

Channel Islands Aviation (☎ 805-987-1301; www.flycia.com; 305 Durley Ave, Camarillo; adult/child $130/105) Flights to Santa Rosa Island from airports in Camarillo and Santa Barbara.

Islands Packers (☎ 805-642-1393; www.islandpackers .com; 1691 Spinnaker Dr, Ventura) Next to the NPS visitor center. Takes campers and offers whale-watching trip.

Truth Aquatics (☎ 805-962-1127; www.truthaquatics .com; 301 W Cabrillo Blvd, Santa Barbara) Emphasizes scuba diving; more limited schedule.

SANTA BARBARA

Pretty, affluent Santa Barbara – with its white stucco, red tile–roofed homes perched on green hillsides over tawny beaches – recalls a Mediterranean port town. You won't regret slowing down to explore its fine art and history museums and its munificent ocean. Balancing its yachting and retirement communities are five colleges, including the University of California at Santa Barbara (UCSB), which provide a youthful buzz.

State St is downtown's main artery and Lower State St (south of Ortega St) is bar central, while upper State St has most of the attractive shops and museums.

CALIFORNIA

Information

Outdoors Santa Barbara Visitor Center (☎ 805-884-1475; www.outdoorsb.noaa.gov; 4th fl, 113 Harbor Way; ☺ 11am-5pm, to 6pm summer) Comprehensive public lands information, including the Channel Islands.

Pacific Travelers Supply (☎ 800-546-8060; www .pactrav.com; 12 W Anapamu St; ☺ 10am-7pm Mon-Sat, to 6pm Sun) Maps and guidebooks.

Visitor center (☎ 805-965-3021; www.santabarbaraca .com; 1 Garden St; ☺ 9am-5pm, to 6pm Jul & Aug, to 4pm Nov-Jan) Has lodging availability.

Sights & Activities

The visitor center has a free, self-guided walking tour of downtown's historic buildings.

Start your explorations at the exquisite **Santa Barbara County Courthouse** (☎ 805-962-6464; 1100 Anacapa St; ☺ 8:30am-4:45pm Mon-Fri, from 10am Sat & Sun). Built in Spanish-Moorish Revival style with hand-painted ceilings and Tunisian tiles, it's an absurdly beautiful place to be on trial. Don't miss the murals in the Old Assembly Room or the clock tower's panoramic view. Free tours available. The nearby **Santa Barbara Museum of Art** (☎ 805-963-4364; www.sbma .net 1130 State St; adult/child 6-17 $9/6, Sun free; ☺ 11am-5pm Tue-Sun) is sophisticated and eclectic, with strong exhibits on Asian art plus American and European expressionism and classical sculpture. The fascinating **Karpeles Manuscript Library Museum** (☎ 805-962-5322; www.karpeles.com; 21 W Anapamu St; admission free; ☺ 10am-4pm) displays a mind-boggling array of original manuscripts. Einstein, Darwin, Abraham Lincoln and Wagner are here, just to drop names.

In 1786, Padre Junípero Serra founded **Mission Santa Barbara** (☎ 805-682-4713; 2201 Laguna St; adult/child under 12 $4/free; ☺ 9am-5pm). Not for nothing is it nicknamed 'Queen of the Missions' – it's one gorgeous lady indeed, plus there are good historical displays (including exhibits on the Native Chumash) and a moody cemetery.

A quarter-mile north (follow signs), the **Museum of Natural History** (☎ 805-682-4711; www .sbnature.org; 2559 Puesta del Sol Rd; adult/child 2-12 $8/5; ☺ 10am-5pm) has beautiful architecture and grounds and equally tidy, attractive exhibits. Another mile north, **Santa Barbara Botanic Garden** (☎ 805-682-4726; www.sbbg.org; 1212 Mission Canyon Rd; adult/child 5-12 $7/1; ☺ 9am-5pm Mon-Fri, to 6pm Sat & Sun) is a real treat. Bring a picnic and enjoy the 5.5 miles of trails devoted to California's native flora, including cacti, redwoods and wildflowers.

Back on the waterfront, **Stearns Wharf** is a rough wooden pier at the base of State St with a few restaurants and shops, while the busier harbor contains the **Santa Barbara Maritime Museum** (☎ 805-962-8404; www.sbmm.org; 113 Harbor Way; adult/child 6-17 $6/3; ☺ 10am-5pm, to 6pm in summer), which has fun, briny exhibits, including a scale model of the oil derricks plunked on the horizon outside.

From the harbor, a paved trail skirts the beach for miles, and concessionaires here and at the end of State St rent bikes (per hour $7) and surreys (per two hours $24). At the harbor, **Paddle Sports** (☎ 805-899-4925; www.kayaksb.com; per 2hr from $20) rents kayaks and runs Channel Island kayak tours ($179). **Sea Landing** (☎ 805-882-0088) runs whale-watching (per adult/child $75/40) and other trips and has watersports rentals.

Sleeping

It's hard to economize in Santa Barbara, though off-season sees good discounts. Cheaper chain motels cluster along upper State St, near Las Positas Rd, several miles north of downtown (bus Nos 6 or 11).

Franciscan Inn (☎ 805-963-8845; www.franciscan inn.com; 109 Bath St; r midweek $115-150, weekend $125-170; ☒) Ivy-covered railings, spacious rooms (some with kitchenettes) and attractive floral decor set this gracious hotel apart. It's a good deal in a great location near the beach.

Mason Beach Inn (☎ 805-962-3203; www.mason beachinn.com; 324 W Mason St; r midweek/weekend from $115/180; P ☒ ☐ ☒) Dependably pleasant and well kept, this is also near the beach. Its hidden courtyard pool is an asset.

Cabrillo Inn (☎ 805-966-1641; www.cabrillo-inn .com; 931 E Cabrillo Blvd; r midweek $120-180, weekend $160-230; P ☒ ☒) This nondescript motel has five-star positioning across from the beach, with windows and large decks perfectly framing the sunset.

Hotel State Street (☎ 805-966-6586; www.hotel statestreet.com; 121 State St; r $60-90; P ☒) The best budget in town is next to the Amtrak station (bring ear plugs). Simple but very clean private rooms have sinks and share well-kept hall facilities.

Santa Barbara Tourist Hostel (☎ 805-963-0154; www.sbhostel.com; 134 Chapala St; dm $20-23, r $65-85; P ☒ ☐) Neat freaks and light sleepers may have a hard time at this busy hostel. Ask about separate cottages. Internet $1 per 5 minutes.

Eating & Drinking

La Super Rica (☎ 805-963-4940; 622 N Milpas St; dishes $4-7; 🕑 11am-9pm) Wow. Julia Child said it first and made this unassuming little shack famous, but man was she right. It's the best Mexican anywhere, served on paper plates. Don't fret the line – get in it.

Brophy Brothers (☎ 805-966-4418; mains $7-18; 🕑 11am-10pm) At the harbor, Brophy's stays hopping with loyal locals who appreciate the clam chowder ($5) and fresh seafood. Nice views upstairs, too.

Reds (☎ 805-966-5906; 211 Helena at State St; 🕑 6:30am-6pm Mon-Fri, 7am-5pm Sat, 8am-1pm Sun) Chill at this funky coffeehouse with free wi-fi, decent sandwiches, music and art events, and Wednesday and Saturday BBQs.

Palazzio (☎ 805-564-1985; www.palazzio.com; 1026 State St; mains $12-20; 🕑 lunch & dinner) Students pack in for guaranteed filling portions of above-average Italian pastas. The reproduction of the Sistine Chapel ceiling sets the mood.

Bouchon (☎ 805-730-1160; www.bouchonsantabarbara.com; 9 W Victoria St; mains $24-30; 🕑 dinner) For a romantic gourmet meal in a rustically elegant dining room, try the California cuisine at Bouchon. From the wine list to the cheese course to the garnish, everything is local, fresh and fine.

Entertainment

James Joyce (☎ 805-962-2688; 513 State St) Along with darts, a pool table, peanut shells underfoot and real warmth, the James Joyce offers live Dixieland jazz on Saturday nights.

Elsie's (☎ 805-963-4503; 117 W de la Guerra) Escape the State St scene and grab a comfy couch at this locals' bar. There's no sign or hard alcohol, but plenty of friendly conversation.

Getting There & Around

Greyhound (☎ 805-965-7551; 34 W Carrillo St) has daily buses to Los Angeles and San Francisco, while **Amtrak** (☎ 805-963-1015; State St) has a direct train and coach service to Los Angeles and San Luis Obispo.

The **Downtown-Waterfront Shuttle Bus** (25c; 🕑 10am-6pm) runs two routes: along State St to Stearns Wharf, and along Cabrillo Blvd from the yacht harbor to the zoo.

SANTA BARBARA TO SAN LUIS OBISPO

Just north of Santa Barbara on Hwy 101 are two recommended state beaches, **El Capitan** and **Refugio**, which have great **campgrounds** (☎ 800-444-7275; day use/camping $8/25); Refugio's sites edge the sand and are ridiculously popular. Further north, take the turnoff for **Solvang** (www.solvangusa.com), a postcard-cute, mock-Danish village that bakes authentic shortbread cookies. Nearby in Buellton, the **Hitching Post II** (☎ 805-688-0676; www.hitchingpost2.com; 406 E Hwy 246; mains $19-41; 🕑 dinner) was made famous in the movie *Sideways* and warrants the acclaim for its steaks, fries and wine.

Speaking of wine, the **Santa Barbara wine country** (www.sbcountywines.com) is along Hwy 154 north of the city, making it an attractive alternate route; the wineries are cradled in the bucolic Santa Ynez Valley, and the Santa Barbara visitor center has free winery maps.

All roads eventually rejoin Hwy 101 north of Santa Maria and Vandenberg Air Force Base at **Pismo Beach**, a perfectly sun-faded, saltwater-taffy beach town. The sand goes on forever with very friendly surf. If you find it hard to leave, try the scuffed but acceptable **Ocean Breeze Inn** (☎ 805-773-2070; www.oceanbreezeinn.net; 250 Main St; r $100-160; ⊠ 🐾) or the more polished, chain-quality **Sandcastle Inn** (☎ 805-773-2422; www.sandcastleinn.com; 100 Stimson Ave; r without/with view from $100/$160; ⊠).

SAN LUIS OBISPO

San Luis Obispo, or SLO, is lively yet low-key with a high quality of life and community spirit. Like so many other California towns, it grew up around a mission, founded in 1772 by Junípero Serra. There's not much to see, tourist-wise, but it makes an enjoyable base for area explorations. The **visitor center** (☎ 805-781-2777; www.visitslo.com; 1039 Chorro St; 🕑 10am-5pm, to 7pm Fri & Sat) is off Higuera St. The best day to visit is Thursday, when the local **farmers market** (🕑 6-9pm) turns Higuera St into a fantastic street party, complete with live bands and open-air BBQs.

Sights

SLO's attractions cluster around **Mission Plaza**, a shady oasis with restored adobes overlooking San Luis Creek, where kids can splash; all these sites are free or by donation. The plaza is lorded over by the simple but charming **Mission San Luis Obispo De Toloso** (☎ 805-543-6850; 🕑 9am-5pm Apr-Oct, to 4pm Nov-Mar). The **San Luis Obispo County Historical Museum** (☎ 805-543-0430; 696 Monterey St; 🕑 10am-4pm Wed-Sun) is no bigger than a minute, while the **San Luis Obispo Art Center** (☎ 805-543-8562;

1010 Broad St; 11am-5pm Wed-Mon) showcases the local talent. The quirkiest SLO attraction is **Bubblegum Alley**, a narrow passageway accessed between 733 and 737 Higuera St covered with wads of discarded chewing gum. It's just what it sounds like.

Sleeping & Eating

SLO's motel row is north of downtown along Monterey St.

Los Padres Inn (805-543-5017; 1575 Monterey St; r midweek $90-110, weekend $100-120; P) One of the better deals on Monterey St, the newly renovated rooms have attractive Mission-style decor.

HI Hostel Obispo (805-544-4678; 1617 Santa Rosa St; dm $18-20, r $45-55; closed 10am-4:30pm; P) These clean, small dorm rooms are in a nice Victorian one block from the train station. Internet $1 per 15 minutes.

Big Sky Café (805-545-5401; www.bigskycafe.com; 1121 Broad St; sandwiches $8, mains $12-15; 7am-9pm, from 8am Sun) The world cuisine menu boasts Thai, African, Cajun and American Southwest influences, all served with a down-home touch. It's a perennial favorite.

Café Roma (805-541-6800; www.caféromaslo.com; 1020 Railroad Ave; mains $14-25; dinner Mon-Sat) A more romantic choice is this SLO classic across from the Amtrak station, which dishes up old-country rustic Italian.

THE AUTHOR'S CHOICE

Madonna Inn (805-543-3000, 800-543-9666; www.madonnainn.com; 100 Madonna Rd; r $150-250; (steaks $25-30; restaurant dinner; P) The Madonna Inn is as fabulously gaudy as any Vegas hotel, while remaining an authentic original. Each of the 108 rooms was individually designed by the owners, whose 'rock rooms' achieve only-in-America status: stone floors, stone walls, stone ceilings, stone showers, stone commodes and many more surprises. Standouts are Caveman, Old World, Hide-A-Way and Yahoo. The pure tack-o-rama of the inn's Gold Rush restaurant is eye-blinding: effervescent pink booths, fake trees and Christmas lights, with gilded mirrors reflecting it infinitely. Plus, there's dancing to old-fashioned bands (Wednesday to Saturday), an all-day café and a brand-new, rock-tastic swimming pool.

Getting There & Away

Greyhound (805-543-2121; 150 South St) has frequent buses to Los Angeles, Santa Barbara and San Francisco. Amtrak's *Pacific Surfliner* has daily service to Santa Barbara, LA and San Diego. The *Coast Starlight* between Seattle and LA also stops at the train station at the southern end of Santa Rosa St.

MORRO BAY TO HEARST CASTLE

North of San Luis Obispo on Hwy 1, the first town you meet is **Morro Bay**. Its namesake **Morro Rock**, a 578ft volcanic peak jutting pugnaciously skyward, is the first indication of the coast's upcoming drama, though Morro Bay itself won't make you linger.

The area has some great state parks, however, with marvelous hiking and camping (800-444-7275 for reservations). South of town, **Morro Bay State Park** (805-772-7434; campsites/RV sites $25/35) has a natural-history museum and a heron-rookery reserve. Further south, and even better, is the largely undeveloped **Montaña de Oro State Park** (805-528-0513; campsites $11), featuring coastal bluffs, sand dunes and a 4-mile sand spit separating Morro Bay from the Pacific. North of town, **Morro Strand State Beach** (805-772-8812; campsites $25) is a nice length of sand.

About 20 miles north of Morro Bay, the self-proclaimed artists' village of **Cambria** is the best town to lay off the gas. It features an unusual monument to one man's architectural ambition: **Nitt Witt Ridge** (805-927-2690; 881 Hillcrest Dr), a house built entirely from found materials and junk – like abalone shells, beer cans and toilet seats. There are several tours daily; call to confirm times.

In Cambria, the **Bridge Street Inn** (805-927-7653; www.bridgestreetinncambria.com; 4314 Bridge St; dm $23, r $40-70; P) is a 'European-style guest house' that sleeps like a hostel but acts like a B&B. It's bright but tiny, all rooms have shared baths, and the friendly owners make you feel at home. For no-frills, midrange motels, try San Simeon, north of Cambria along the highway. **Linn's** (805-927-1499; 2277 Main St, Cambria; dishes $6-14; 7:30am-9pm) is a casual eatery famous for its pies and desserts. For a finer meal, slip into the back patio at **Robin's** (805-927-5007, 4095 Burton Dr; mains $13-18; 11am-9pm) and choose from the eclectic, pan-Asian menu.

The main attraction along the highway, though, is **Hearst Castle** (800-444-4445; www

.hearstcastle.org; tours day adult/child 6-17 $24/12, night $30/15; ☷ 8:20am-3:20pm, later in summer). Overlooking the Pacific, it is California's most famous monument to wealth and ambition. William Randolph Hearst, the newspaper magnate, created an estate that sprawls over 127 acres of lushly landscaped gardens, accentuated by shimmering pools and statues from ancient Greece and Moorish Spain. A visit is worthwhile; Hearst's ostentation was on a par with European royalty. Four daytime estate tours and one evening tour are offered; the day tour is best for first-time visitors. All tours last about 1½ hours, including the ride up to the castle and back to the visitor center. Reservations are recommended in summer.

About 4.5 miles north of Hearst Castle, Point Piedras Blancas is home to California's largest **elephant-seal colony**, which comes to breed, molt and sleep. The main viewpoint has interpretative panels. The seals are here year-round but the, er, mating period is between December and February.

CCAT (☎ 805-541-2228) operates a bus service between San Luis Obispo, Morro Bay and San Simeon/Hearst Castle.

BIG SUR

The 90-odd miles between Cambria and the Monterey Peninsula were first called El Sur Grande by the Spanish, the Big South. It's easy to see why. The coastline here is an awe-inspiring symphony of nature, and at times Hwy 1 seems to clutch at the cliffs as if in desperation above a ravenous sea. Services are few and far between, but vista points appear every few hundred yards. For more information, contact the **Big Sur Chamber of Commerce** (☎ 831-667-2100; www.bigsurcalifornia.org).

It's about 25 miles from Hearst Castle to **Gorda**, a 'town' that's just a gas station, a basic deli and store, and an overpriced restaurant and inn. Yet on the cliffs above town is the very cool **Treebones Resort** (☎ 877-424-4787, www.treebonesresort.com; yurt incl breakfast from $120, campsite $45; dinner $14-19; ☒ ☷). This collection of 14 yurts – spacious, round, canvas-sided tents with wood floors, queen beds and decks overlooking the ocean – combines the adventure of camping (which you can also do) with the comforts of a hotel. Shared bathrooms are spotless and a BBQ dinner is served nightly. Nos 7 to 10 occupy prime spots.

The next 12 miles contain several good excuses to pull over: **Plaskett Creek Campground**

(☎ 800-444-7275 reservations; www.reserveamerica.com; camping $20); Sand Dollar Beach ($5) across the highway; Kirk Creek Campground ($20), and **Limekiln State Park** (831-667-2403; camping $25, day use $6).

Another 12 miles gets you to the **Esalen Institute** (☎ 831-667-3000; www.esalen.org), where the scent of burning sage wafts over the expensive New Age workshops. The best way to experience Esalen without enrolling is to make a same-day reservation for either a massage ($90 to $115), which includes time in their famous hot springs, or for 'night bathing' from 1am to 3am ($20).

Julia Pfeiffer Burns State Park ($8 day use), 3 miles north of Esalen, has two highlights: the first is the quarter-mile hike to view 50ft McWay Falls, which drops into the sea. The second is Julia Pfeiffer's pair of environmental campsites ($13 to $20), secluded high above the surging waves; you can, and should, reserve them up to seven months in advance (☎ 800-444-7275; www.reserveamerica.com).

Seven miles further is cozy **Deetjen's Big Sur Inn** (☎ 831-667-2377; www.deetjens.com; r without/with bath from $90/180; breakfast $6-11, dinner $17-27; ☒). Eclectic, quirky and rustic, this historic homestead exemplifies the Big Sur spirit. Tiny rooms are quiet, romantic retreats without TVs or phones, and the restaurant is just as atmospheric, serving gourmet country meals daily.

Just north of Deetjen's, the **Henry Miller Memorial Library** (☎ 831-667-2574; www.henrymiller.org; ☷ 11am-6pm Wed-Mon) is, in essence, a sophisticated bookstore emphasizing Miller's works, but more importantly, it strives to keep the author's iconoclastic spirit alive amid a gale of 21st-century conservatism. Call for events.

Big Sur Center, 2 miles north, contains a clutch of traveler services: the post office, a gas station, and the region's best grocery store and **deli** (☎ 831-667-2225; sandwiches $5-6; ☷ 7:30am-8pm). The best bakery on the coast is also here: **Big Sur Bakery & Restaurant** (☎ 831-667-0520; www.bigsurbakery.com; pizza $12-15, entrees $17-32; ☷ 8am-3pm Tue-Sun, dinner Tue-Sat). Come early; pastries run out fast. If you're late, the excellent restaurant has sandwiches, wood-fired pizzas and steaks.

Big Sur Center is also the start of the 6-mile string of services along the highway that constitutes the 'town' of Big Sur.

CALIFORNIA

In less than a mile is the **USFS Big Sur Ranger Station** (☎ 831-667-2315; 🕑 8am-4:30pm, to 6pm summer), a comprehensive public-lands office that covers all the Big Sur parks and can recommend hikes and camping; it issues backcountry permits for the Ventana Wilderness. Note that one $8 fee allows same-day access to three state parks: Julia Pfeiffer Burns, Pfeiffer Big Sur and Andrew Molera. While here, ask for directions to the rugged, wheelchair-accessible **Pfeiffer Beach** (separate entry fee $5); locals keep taking the sign down.

Immediately north of the ranger station, **Pfeiffer Big Sur State Park** (day use $8) occupies 680 acres and has plenty of coastal hiking trails; the 1.4-mile round-trip to Pfeiffer Falls provides a fine experience of redwoods. There is a large, 218-site **campground** (☎ 800-444-7275; www.reserveamerica.com; campsites $20-35) and **Big Sur Lodge** (☎ 800-424-4787; www .bigsurlodge.com; r from $184; 🏊). This quiet complex of modern, recently renovated, single-story attached buildings makes for a relaxing overnight.

Ventana Wilderness is extremely popular with backpackers; get overnight parking permits ($4), free backcountry permits and trail information from the Big Sur Ranger Station (above). The most popular adventure is the 10-mile hike to Sykes hot springs.

In another mile or so, the Mexican-influenced **Big Sur Roadhouse** (☎ 831-667-2264; mains $12-20; 🕑 dinner Wed-Mon) serves tasty, affordable dinners of enchiladas, sea bass and steak.

Further on, **Big Sur River Inn** (☎ 831-667-2700; www.bigsurriverinn.com; s/ste $135/250) offers simple but clean motel rooms and delightful family suites; neither have TV or phones. Its popular restaurant is open all day and has a deck overlooking the river – or take your sandwich and claim one of the river chairs.

Andrew Molera State Park (day use $8), about 4.5 miles north of Pfeiffer Big Sur, features a gentle mile-long trail that leads to a beautiful beach and a small, first-come, first-served campground ($9).

Point Sur, 3 miles north, is that compelling hump of volcanic rock jutting into the ocean. The only way to visit it is to take the three-hour tour of its 1899 **Point Sur Light Station** (☎ 831-625-4419; adult $8; 🕑 Sat & Sun year-round, extra days in summer). It's about another 20 miles to Carmel.

CARMEL & AROUND

Carmel-by-the-Sea became a bohemian retreat after San Francisco's 1906 earthquake forced artists to find a cheaper place to live. Today, it remains a quintessential example of a self-ordered California community, one driven by the dreams of a sophisticated upper class. Local bylaws ensure that it remains rustic and modestly picturesque – there are no streetlights, sidewalks or mail delivery service – even as refinement and wealth drips from every awning and abode. Simply driving the narrow streets and admiring the homes – a cornucopia of cedar shingles, stone and terra-cotta tiles – is entertainment enough. Ocean Ave is the main thoroughfare, sloping down past tony shops, galleries and eateries to a pristine white-sand beach.

The **San Carlos Borromeo del Rio Carmelo Mission** (☎ 831-624-3600; www.carmelmission.org; 3080 Rio Rd; adult/child $5/1; 🕑 9:30am-5pm Mon-Sat, from 10:30am Sun) was founded by Padre Junípero Serra in 1770. An oasis of calm and solemnity, the mission is one of the most complete in California, and the museum is full of dusty surprises. Mass is held in the gorgeous vaulted basilica at weekends.

Point Lobos State Reserve (☎ 831-624-4909; http:// ptlobos.org; per car $8; 🕑 9am-5pm, to 7pm summer), 3.5 miles south of Carmel, is a scenic jewel of the state park system. Its rocky coastline encompasses 554 aboveground acres and 750 submerged acres that are ideal for scuba diving. Gorgeous, easy hikes crisscross the point, from where you can spot whales, sea lions and otters. A small whaling museum pays homage to this once-vital industry.

Carmel and Monterey are linked by Hwy 1 and by the spectacular **17-Mile Drive**. This road is justifiably famous, taking in Pebble Beach's signature Lone Cypress, exclusive mansions, crumbled coastline and peerless golf courses. There are five entry gates to **Pebble Beach** (www.pebblebeach.com; cars $8.50); entering by bicycle is free.

MONTEREY & AROUND

Monterey enjoys an enviable position at the edge of the uniquely diverse Monterey Bay, now protected as the nation's largest marine sanctuary. In addition, the city's rich Latino heritage – dating back to the 18th century – is well preserved in numerous museums and restored adobe buildings from California's Spanish and Mexican periods. Most of these are concentrated in downtown 'Old Monterey,' while the aquarium and Cannery Row are just northwest in 'New Monterey.'

The helpful **visitor center** (☎ 831-657-6400; www.montereyinfo.org; ☻ 9am-6pm Mon-Sat, 10am-5pm Sun, shorter hrs in winter), at Camino El Estero and Franklin St, provides peninsula-wide information and lodging availability. The center is part of El Estero Park, with a lake and a great kids' playground.

BayBooks (☎ 831-375-0277; www.montereybaybooks.net; 316 Alvarado St; ☻ 7:30am-10pm) is a good independent bookseller with a coffeeshop and free wi-fi.

Sights
MONTEREY STATE HISTORIC PARK
Located downtown, this park is a collection of Monterey's finest historical buildings. The **Pacific House Museum** (☎ 831-649-7118; admission free; ☻ 10am-3pm Mon, Wed & Fri-Sun), at Custom House Plaza near the wharf, contains the park's headquarters, offers free guided tours and has excellent exhibits on the region's human and natural history. Several dozen historic buildings can be visited by following the self-guided tour: most are open to the public, but hours vary among them, so check with before setting out. All are free.

Also at Custom House Plaza, the **Maritime Museum of Monterey** (☎ 831-372-2608; adult/child 13-17 $8/5; ☻ 10am-5pm Thu-Tue) features seafaring exhibits, extremely detailed model ships and a mighty lighthouse lens. Across from

the plaza, **Fisherman's Wharf** is a low-key tourist trap of restaurants and gift shops.

MONTEREY BAY AQUARIUM
The **Monterey Bay Aquarium** (☎ 831-648-4800, tickets (☎ 800-756-3737;); www.montereybayaquarium.org; 886 Cannery Row; adult $20, child 3-12 $11, reservation transaction fee $3; ☻ 10am-6pm) is the temple to Monterey's epic underwater universe – and among the country's best aquariums. Highlights include the two-story Kelp Forest tank, the million-gallon Outer Bay tank where sea turtles and ponderous sunfish glide by, the kid-friendly Splash Zone, and feeding time with the sea otters. The aquarium receives nearly two million visitors a year. To avoid queues, reserve tickets in advance.

MONTEREY MUSEUM OF ART
The **Monterey Museum of Art** (☎ 831-372-5477; admission $5; ☻ 11am-5pm Wed-Sat, 1-4pm Sun) has two downtown branches; both are small but satisfying. The **Civic Center** (559 Pacific St) collection emphasizes Californian artists and photographers, while **La Mirada** (720 Via Mirada) sprinkles its enticing art galleries around a historic home with a pretty rose garden.

CANNERY ROW
In its heyday **Cannery Row** (www.canneryrow.com) was a hectic, smelly place, and John Steinbeck's eponymous novel made it famous. In the 1950s, the once-thriving sardine-canning industry crashed in a hurry due to climate

---

THE VOICE OF TOM JOAD

The novels of John Steinbeck (1902–68), and even the man himself, exemplify a particular American grain, a plainspoken, gimlet-eyed dignity. Tough, funny, brash – a Stanford dropout who would win a Nobel Prize for Literature – Steinbeck's mark on American letters is as thorough as Mark Twain's. He captured the troubled spirit of rural and working class America, and Tom Joad was the protagonist of his Pulitzer Prize–winning *The Grapes of Wrath*. Like Huck Finn, Joad's spirit still roams the land – though his Okie accent is today decidedly Mexican.

A fitting tribute to Salinas' famous son is its state-of-the-art **National Steinbeck Center** (☎ 831-775-4721; www.steinbeck.org; 1 Main St/Hwy 68, Salinas; adult/child 6-12 $11/6; ☻ 10am-5pm). Smack in the middle of the flat, fertile valley that was Steinbeck's home and passion, it has interactive exhibits that bring each novel to life, including short clips from movie adaptations. One cherished possession is Rocinante, the camper Steinbeck drove across America while writing *Travels with Charley*. A short biographical film helps weave together all the strands of the novelist's life.

Included in the center is the Valley of the World exhibit, where video interviews with local farmers and activities like 'The Produce Game' take you from field to table to learn how modern agriculture works.

For the complete Steinbeck experience, visit during the first week in August for the National Steinbeck Festival.

changes and overfishing. Nowadays Cannery Row nets only tourists with a carousel, a wax museum, a kids' play space and a seine's worth of fish houses and souvenirs.

MONARCH GROVE SANCTUARY
In Pacific Grove, follow signs from Lighthouse Ave to find the sanctuary, an October-to-March overwintering site for Monarch butterflies. Volunteer guides are on hand. Call ☎ 831-648-3116 for information.

Activities
A favorite activity is walking or biking the paved Recreation Trail, which edges the coast through Monterey and ends at Lovers Point beach in Pacific Grove.

Bay Bikes (☎ 831-655-2453; www.baybikes.com; 585 Cannery Row; per hr/day $6/27) rents a full range of bikes. **Adventures by the Sea** (☎ 831-372-1807; per day $30) Alvarado (201 Alvarado St); Cannery (299 Cannery Row) rents bikes and kayaks. Knowledgeable and friendly, **Monterey Bay Kayaks** (☎ 800-649-5357; www.montereybaykayaks.com; 693 Del Monte Ave; per day $30) rents kayaks and offers three-hour guided trips ($55) and lessons (from $65).

Monterey Bay Dive Center (☎ 831-656-0454; www.montereyscubadiving.com; 225 Cannery Row; kits per day snorkel/scuba $40/70) rents kits for snorkeling and scuba diving and offers a PADI certification course ($300) and guided trips (from $60).

Several outfits run whale-watching trips year-round from the wharf, but only the recommended **Monterey Bay Whale Watch** (☎ 831-375-4658; www.gowhales.com; 3-5hr trips $28-41) has marine biologists for guides; reservations required.

For an affordable taste of the peninsula's world-famous golf, try the **Pacific Grove Municipal Golf Course** (☎ 831-648-5777; 77 Asilomar Blvd; 18 holes $34-40); reserve one week ahead.

Festivals & Events
Among the many special events that send hotel rates skyrocketing:
AT&T Pebble Beach Pro-Am golf tournament (www.attpbgolf.com) February.
Concours d'Elegance car show (www.pebblebeach concours.net) August.
Monterey Jazz Festival (www.montereyjazzfestival.org) September.

Sleeping
High-season rates listed here can drop by a third or more in winter, while at any time special-event weekends might be half again as much. Call ahead to see what you're in for! Many places have a two-night minimum stay at summer weekends.

Monterey Hotel (☎ 831-375-3184, 800-727-0960; www.montereyhotel.com; 406 Alvarado St; r from $140; ☒ Ⓟ) For affordable romance right downtown, this historic 1904 hotel is decked out in reproduction antiques, ornate carved headboards and marble bathrooms. Ask about packages. Parking $15.

Asilomar (☎ 831-372-8016; www.visitasilomar.com; 800 Asilomar Ave; r incl breakfast $130-145; ☒ 🖳 ☙) The heart of this Pacific Grove retreat was designed by famous architect Julia Morgan. Newer buildings mimic her Arts and Crafts style, though historic rooms (no phones or TVs) are recommended and cheaper. You'll share the grounds with conferences, but so what. A gorgeous beach is steps away, and year-round rates make this the best summer or festival deal on the peninsula.

Bide-a-Wee Motel (☎ 831-372-2330; www.bide aweeinn.com; 221 Asilomar Ave, Pacific Grove; r from $100-160; ☒) Also hidden near the coast, this nice little motel with the cute name is a good value. Some rooms have full kitchens. Great off-season rates.

HI Monterey Hostel (☎ 831-649-0375; www.monterey hostel.org; 778 Hawthorne St; dm $22-25; Ⓟ ☒ 🖳) Only four blocks from Cannery Row, this simple, clean hostel is just the ticket for backpackers. Internet $1 per 10 minutes.

Relatively economical motels and chains line downtown Monterey's Munras Ave and N Fremont St, east of Hwy 1 (Casa Verde exit). Two nice independents are the **Cypress Gardens Resort Inn** (☎ 831-373-2761, 877-922-1150; www.cypressgardensinn.com; 1150 Munras Ave; r from $80; Ⓟ ☒ 🖳 ☙) and the **Lone Oak Lodge** (☎ 831-372-4924, 800-283-5663; www.loneoaklodge.com; 2221 N Fremont; midweek/weekend from $80/100; Ⓟ); both are consistently friendly and comfortable.

Eating
If you aren't choosy, there are seafood shacks aplenty crowding Cannery Row and Fisherman's Wharf.

Old Monterey Cafe (☎ 831-646-1021; 489 Alvarado St; meals $6-12; ☙ 7am-2:30pm daily, 4:30-9pm Thu-Sat) This local institution is *mucho* popular for its generous breakfasts and Californian- and Mexican-influenced diner menu.

Monterey's Fish House (☎ 831-373-4647; 2114 Del Monte Ave; mains $14-17, specials $19-22; ☙ lunch

Mon-Fri, dinner nightly) Here it is. You found it. The perfect, family-owned seafood restaurant where the fish is just off the boat, every preparation divine, and the bill – affordable! Ignore the menu and wait for the specials, though the crab cakes and crab ravioli deserve some sort of prize. Make reservations, or squeeze into the bar and make friends.

Passionfish (☎ 831-655-3311; www.passionfish.net; 701 Lighthouse Ave, Pacific Grove; mains $14-20; ☽ dinner) For a more refined romantic experience, the international gourmet cuisine, wine list and service here are tops.

Mucky Duck (☎ 831-655-3031; 479 Alvarado St; ☽ 11am-1:30am) No pretensions, just English pub fare and a rowdy back beer garden.

Getting There & Around

Monterey-Salinas Transit (MST; ☎ 831-899-2555; www.mst.org; tickets $1.75-7) operates buses around the peninsula to Carmel and Pacific Grove, north to Salinas and Watsonville, and south to Big Sur. The Monterey Transit Plaza, at the south end of Alvarado St, is the main MST terminal. In summer, free shuttles connect downtown Monterey and Cannery Row.

SANTA CRUZ

Santa Cruz is where southern California beach culture meets northern California counterculture. As the home of the University of California at Santa Cruz (UCSC) and its 13,000 left-of-center students, it is far more youthful, hip and political than touristy Monterey, and with over one-sixth of the county composed of state parks, it offers ample opportunities to walk among the redwoods.

While some locals worry that SC's weirdness quotient is dropping, judging by attendance at Wednesday's **Farmers Market** (☎ 831-454-0566; www.santacruzfarmersmarket.org; Cedar & Lincoln Sts; ☽ 2:30-6:30pm), it's okay, dude.

Orientation & Information

Pacific Ave, lined with shops and restaurants, is the main drag. For the beach and Boardwalk, head south on parallel Front St and turn left on Beach St. The on-the-ball **visitor center** (☎ 831-425-1234, 800-833-3494; www.santacruz.org; 1211 Ocean St; ☽ 9am-5pm Mon-Sat, 10am-4pm Sat, 11am-3pm Sun) has accommodations availability; book online through their website.

Bookshop Santa Cruz (☎ 831-423-0900; 1520 Pacific Ave; ☽ 10am-10pm) is as busy on a Friday

night as any bar, as is **Logos** (☎ 831-427-5100; 1117 Pacific Ave; ☽ 10am-10pm).

Sights

The classic 1906 **Boardwalk** (☎ 831-426-7433; www.beachboardwalk.com; 400 Beach St; rides $2-4, all-day ticket $35; ☽ daily mid-April–mid-Nov, Sat & Sun mid-Nov–mid-April) is the oldest beachfront amusement park on the West Coast, with a 1923 Giant Dipper coaster and a 1911 Looff carousel – both National Historic Landmarks; hours vary weekly.

The **Surfing Museum** (☎ 831-420-6289; admission free; ☽ noon-4pm Mon & Wed-Sun, closed Wed in winter) is a teeny-tiny paean to the history and art of wave riding. It's at Lighthouse Point on W Cliff Dr and overlooks Steamer's Lane, Santa Cruz' most popular surfing break.

Natural Bridges State Beach (☎ 831-423-4609; 2531 W Cliff Dr; admission $6; ☽ dawn-dusk), just north of Santa Cruz, has a good beach, tidal pools and trees where monarch butterflies hibernate from October to March.

Established in 1902, **Big Basin Redwoods State Park** (☎ 831-338-8860; www.bigbasin.org; per car $6; ☽ 6am-10pm), 23 miles north of Santa Cruz via Hwys 9 and 236, is the birthplace of California's conservation movement. It has 20,000 acres of redwood forest and 80 miles of trails, one of which drops to the Pacific.

Some locals swear Bigfoot, or his cousins, live in the Santa Cruz Mountains, and the **Bigfoot Discovery Museum** (☎ 831-335-4478; www.bigfootdiscoveryproject.org; 5497 Hwy 9, Felton; ☽ 1-6pm Wed-Fri, from 11am Sat & Sun) has gathered all the facts and the *National Enquirer* covers to prove it. Give him 20 minutes, and Mike Rugg will make you a believer.

Another classic bit of oddball Americana is the **Mystery Spot** (☎ 831-423-8897; www.mysteryspot.com; adult $5; ☽ 9am-5pm), 3 miles north of Santa Cruz on Branciforte Dr. Who can explain how the buildings lean and balls roll uphill? Don't forget your bumper sticker.

Finally, meditate on local weirdness at the Oriental-style **Tea House Spa** (☎ 831-426-9700; www.teahousespa.com; 112 Elm St; private hot-tub r per person per hr $10-15; ☽ 11am-midnight).

Activities

Hiking or biking on the beautiful W Cliff Dr is satisfying anytime, but particularly at sunset. Check Beach St for bike-rental shops. **Kayak Connection** (☎ 831-479-1121; 413 Lake Ave; kayak per 4hr $27) has kayak rentals.

CALIFORNIA

SURFING

Recommended beginner breaks are Cowell's – which is next to famous, experts-only Steamer Lane – and 38th Ave, which is near several popular intermediate breaks, like 26th Ave and the Hook. For better rentals from knowledgeable staff, head to Capitola, where ladies can make waves for the women-owned **Paradise Surf Shop** (☎ 831-462-3880; www.paradisesurf.com; 3961 Portola Dr; boards ½/full day $15/30), which has board rentals and lessons ($80). Dudes can get suited up at **O'Neill Surf Shop** (☎ 831-475-4151; www.oneill.com; 1115 41st Ave; boards per day $12-20, wetsuits $10-12).

The venerable **Richard Schmidt Surf School** (☎ 831-423-0928; www.richardschmidt.com; 849 Almar Ave; 2hr group lesson $80) is a great place to learn.

Sleeping & Eating

Hotel prices creep up in summer. For midrange motels and chains, try Riverside Ave and Ocean St.

Seaway Inn (☎ 831-471-9004; www.seawayinn.com; 176 W Cliff Dr; r midweek/weekend $130/170; P ✗) For a cozy, attractive motel near the beach, this is a solid choice.

Carousel Motel (☎ 831-425-7090, 800-214-7400; www.santacruzmotels.com; 110 Riverside Ave; r midweek/weekend from $110/140; P) The family-oriented Carousel has attractive rooms and Boardwalk packages. Kids under 16 stay free.

Brookdale Lodge (☎ 831-338-6433; www.brookdalelodge.com; 11570 Hwy 9; midweek/weekend from $80/100; P ☀) Escape to the Santa Cruz Mountains at Brookdale Lodge, 14 miles north. It's great for families (huge pool); rooms are standard, but well cared for. In its Brook Room restaurant, you dine next to a burbling stream.

HI Carmelita Cottages Hostel (☎ 831-423-8304; 321 Main St; dm $19-22; 🖳) This is one of the busiest hostels on the coast, which is perhaps why rooms and attitudes get a little frayed. Internet $1 per 20 minutes.

Camping (☎ 800-444-7275; campsites $25) You can camp among the redwoods in nearby Henry Cowell and Big Basin State Parks, north of town off Hwy 9, and at New Brighton State Beach, about 4 miles south of Santa Cruz near Capitola. Reservations are advised. Big Basin also has excellent, simple **tent cabins** (☎ 831-338-4745, 800-874-8368; www.bigbasintentcabins.com; cabin $50), for those who didn't bring gear.

Downtown Santa Cruz, especially Pacific Ave and Front St, is chockablock with eateries of all stripes.

Saturn Cafe (☎ 831-429-8505; 145 Laurel St at Pacific Ave; mains $6.50-8.50; ☽ 11:30am-3am) A Santa Cruz classic, the decor of the late-night Saturn Cafe is an evolving pop-culture freak show, while the menu could pass for a greasy-spoon diner if it wasn't entirely vegetarian and vegan.

Zachary's (☎ 831-427-0646; 819 Pacific Ave; mains $5-11; ☽ 7am-2:30pm Tue-Sun) This is consistently voted the best breakfast in town.

Attic (☎ 831-460-1800; www.theatticsantacruz.com; 931 Pacific Ave; mains $6-9; ☽ 11am-9pm) This self-described 'art lounge' is a calm oasis of healthy salads and sandwiches, an armlong list of teas, and various artful happenings.

Gelato Mania (☎ 831-426-7117; Pacific Ave at Church St; ☽ 11am-10pm) Spend your $5 on creamy gelato or on 10 minutes of scented oxygen. Decisions, decisions…

Entertainment

Check the weekly *Metro Santa Cruz* for schedules. **Kuumbwa Jazz Center** (☎ 831-427-2227; www.kuumbwajazz.org; 320 Cedar St) books big-name jazz musicians, while **Catalyst** (☎ 831-423-1336; www.catalystclub.com; 1011 Pacific Ave) is the most popular live-music nightclub.

Club Dakota (☎ 831-335-5882; www.clubdakota.net; 1209 Pacific Ave) is a happening gay and lesbian bar with dancing, DJs, and events.

Getting There & Away

Santa Cruz Metropolitan Transit (☎ 831-425-8600; www.scmtd.com) operates from the **Santa Cruz Metro Transit Center** (920 Pacific Ave; ticket/day pass $1.50/4.50) and serves the greater Santa Cruz region. The Hwy 17 Express ($3.50) connects to the train station in San Jose. At the Transit Center, **Greyhound** (☎ 831-423-1800) runs daily buses to/from San Francisco ($11) and Los Angeles ($43).

SAN FRANCISCO & THE BAY AREA

SAN FRANCISCO

A rogue, a cad, an imp. San Francisco would have you believe it's all feather boas and leather miniskirts, just a gaudy, naughty good time looking for a cute sailor on shore leave. Don't believe it. San Francisco is surely charming, and when you see it from across the tousled waters of the bay or from atop one of its impossible hills, it's hard to imagine any other American city looking so damn attractive. It has row upon row of gorgeously restored Victorian homes (this town's true 'painted ladies'), acres of forested urban parks and long sandy strands offering picture-postcard views of the brick-red Golden Gate Bridge. But like the hooker with a heart of gold, who'll steal your money and make you love her anyway, it's San Francisco pugnacious spirit not her good looks that will make you swoon. The city's willing embrace of eccentrics and misfits, its thriving ethnic neighborhoods, its abiding devotion to creativity and innovation, its Mediterranean climate, its scrappy little big city-ness – these are the things that make you wish for one more night at the center of her world.

History

San Francisco's true birthday is 1848. Although native populations had inhabited the peninsula for at least six centuries and the Spanish arrived in 1769, the peninsula hadn't been a prosperous place. That changed in 1848. Over a matter of days, Mexico ceded California to the USA and gold was discovered in the Sierra Nevada foothills – and before you could shout 'Westward, ho!' this pitiful outpost became a true and necessary American city that would shimmer in the public imagination.

By the end of 1849, San Francisco's population had grown from 800 to 25,000, many of them rich, at least for an afternoon. Casinos, saloons, brothels, opium dens: there were numerous ways for a free-spending miner to become poor again. Dirty living and reckless criminality marked the city's 'Barbary Coast' (now Jackson Sq), where sailors were routinely knocked out, robbed and 'Shanghai'd' – awaking to find themselves indentured to a ship that was already out to sea.

These decades cemented the city's wild reputation, even as it matured in the face of devastating trials. The 1906 earthquake and fire leveled nearly everything, and frantic years of construction followed. During the Great Depression in the 1930s, large-scale public-works projects gave the region a lift – the most outstanding examples being the San Francisco–Oakland Bay Bridge (1936) and the Golden Gate Bridge (1937).

During WWII the Bay Area became a major launching pad for military operations in the Pacific theater. During the postwar years, military spending drove the local economy even as counterculture movements arose: the Beats spearheaded the '50s poetry movement and free-love hippies ushered in the '60s, while San Francisco's nascent gay community coalesced and established itself.

In the 1980s, growing prosperity mellowed San Francisco's freakier elements, and in 1989, another major earthquake hit. Then the late 1990s dot-com revolution seemed to rewrite the rules of commerce and economics. Internet-crazy stock speculation made people rich (rich!), and in a greedy delirium, rents and real estate skyrocketed, refashioning the city's social landscape.

The inevitable bust has been swift and left the city gasping financially and a little unsure of its identity. Many artists and middle-class

---

SAN FRANCISCO IN...

Two Days

On day one, follow the **walking tour** (p833), ending your day among the **North Beach hot spots** (p827). On day two, stroll or bicycle the north edge of the city – through the **Wharf** (p827), **Fort Mason** (p831), **the Marina** (p830), **Crissy Field** (p831), and over the **Golden Gate Bridge** (p833). Include a trip to **Angel Island** (p843). Reward yourself for all that hoofing with an elegant dinner and a swanky nightcap at the **Starlight Room** (p839).

Four Days

On day three, tackle the **Asian Art Museum** (p826), the **SF Moma** (p826), and/or the new **De Young** (p831). Chill out in **Yerba Buena Gardens** (p826), or **Golden Gate Park** (p831). Then sample some funky nightlife: start in a **Mission** or **Haight Street bar** (p839) and continue with nightclubs in the **Castro** or **SoMa** (p839). On day four, slip out of the city for a taste of **Wine Country** (p847), then end your stay with a smile by attending **Beach Blanket Babylon** (p840).

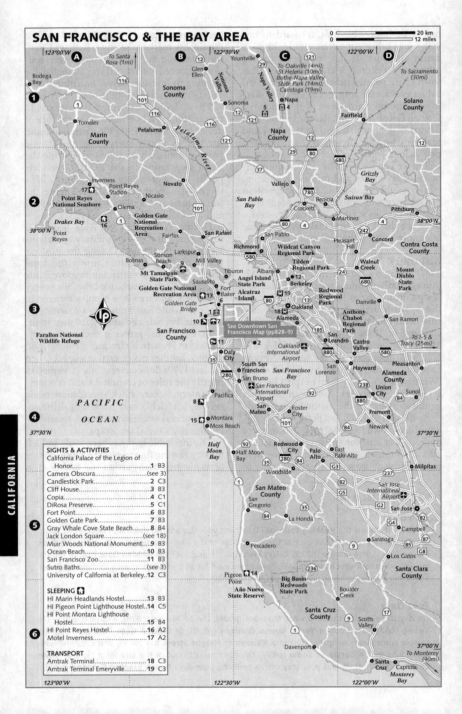

SAN FRANCISCO & THE BAY AREA

CALIFORNIA

SIGHTS & ACTIVITIES

California Palace of the Legion of Honor..**1** B3	
Camera Obscura.........................(see 3)	
Candlestick Park..........................**2** B3	
Cliff House...................................**3** B3	
Copia..**4** C1	
DiRosa Preserve..........................**5** C1	
Fort Point...................................**6** B3	
Golden Gate Park........................**7** B3	
Gray Whale Cove State Beach.......**8** B4	
Jack London Square....................(see 18)	
Muir Woods National Monument....**9** B3	
Ocean Beach..............................**10** B3	
San Francisco Zoo......................**11** B3	
Sutro Baths................................(see 3)	
University of California at Berkeley.**12** C3	

SLEEPING

HI Marin Headlands Hostel............**13** B3	
HI Pigeon Point Lighthouse Hostel..**14** C5	
HI Point Montara Lighthouse Hostel..**15** B4	
HI Point Reyes Hostel..................**16** A2	
Motel Inverness..........................**17** A2	

TRANSPORT

Amtrak Terminal..........................**18** C3	
Amtrak Terminal Emeryville...........**19** C3	

families have been driven out, and the poor marginalized further. Today, San Francisco swaggers a little less as it tries to fix a rampant homelessness problem, keep the streets clean and improve underperforming schools.

But it is not without panache. In 2004, its young mayor Gavin Newsom jumped into the ongoing nationwide gay-marriage controversy (p832) with both feet, and in 2005 San Francisco became the state's headquarters for stem-cell research and the growing biotech industry. The future may continue to be born here, after all.

Orientation

Compact San Francisco covers the tip of a 30-mile peninsula, with the Pacific Ocean to the west and the San Francisco Bay to the north and east. The city can be divided into three sections. The downtown district is in the northeast between Van Ness Ave, Market St and the bay, and includes the Embarcadero, Union Sq, the Financial District, Civic Center, the Tenderloin, Chinatown, North Beach, Nob Hill, Russian Hill and Fisherman's Wharf.

The South of Market District, or SoMa, is a trendy warehouse zone that leads south into the Mission, the city's Latino quarter. The Castro, the city's gay quarter, is west of the Mission.

The residential western part of the city stretches from Van Ness Ave all the way to the Pacific Ocean, encompassing the upscale Marina and Pacific Heights, Japantown, the Haight, the Richmond and Sunset Districts, and Golden Gate Park.

From San Francisco International Airport, take Hwy 101 north. See p841.

Information
BOOKSTORES

City Lights Bookstore (Map pp828-9; ☎ 415-362-8193; www.citylights.com; 261 Columbus Ave; ☻ 10am-midnight) Poetic and progressive.

A Clean Well-Lighted Place for Books (Map pp828-9; ☎ 415-441-6670; www.bookstore.com; 601 Van Ness Ave; ☻ 10am-11pm Mon-Sat, to 9pm Sun) Lots of author readings.

A Different Light Bookstore (Map pp828-9; ☎ 415-431-0891; www.adlbooks.com; 489 Castro St; ☻ 10am-11pm) The USA's largest gay bookseller.

Get Lost (Map pp828-9; ☎ 415-437-0529; www.getlostbooks.com; 1825 Market St; ☻ 10am-6pm Mon-Sat, 11am-5pm Sun) Specializes in travel.

Green Apple (Map pp828-9; ☎ 415-387-2272; www.greenapplebooks.com; cnr Clement & 6th Ave; ☻ 10am-10:30pm) A mecca for used and new books.

EMERGENCY
Police, fire and ambulance (☎ 911) Emergency.
Fire department (☎ 415-558-3268)
Police (☎ 415-553-0123)
SF Rape Treatment Center (☎ 415-437-3000)

INTERNET ACCESS
Free wi-fi hotspots are at Union Sq and the Metreon (p826). Walgreens (below) can burn digital photos onto a CD ($2.99).
Apple Store (Map pp828-9; ☎ 415-392-0202; 18 Ellis St; access free; ☻ 10am-9pm Mon-Sat, 11am-6pm Sun)
Cafe.com (Map pp828-9; ☎ 415-433-4001; www.sf-cafe.com; 120 Mason at Eddy; per 30min $3.50; ☻ 7am-10pm Mon-Sat, 7:30am-9pm Sun) Full-service Internet café.

INTERNET RESOURCES
SF Station (www.sfstation.com) Comprehensive SF listings and events.
Mister SF (www.mistersf.com) City trivia, history and people.
Sfist (www.sfist.com) A local blog.

LAUNDRY
Brain Wash (Map pp828-9; ☎ 415-255-4866; www.brainwash.com; 1122 Folsom near 7th; ☻ 7am-11pm) Food, beer, entertainment, free wi-fi, Internet terminals ($3 per 20 minutes), coin laundry and a dry-cleaning service – go get clean!

MEDIA
KPFA 94.1 FM Alternative news and music.
KQED 88.5 FM Local NPR affiliate.
San Francisco Bay Guardian (www.sfbg.com) Free weekly; alternative news and entertainment.
San Francisco Chronicle (www.sfgate.com) Main daily newspaper; great website.
San Francisco Examiner (www.examiner.com) Free daily tabloid.
SF Weekly (www.sfweekly.com) Free weekly; alternative news and entertainment.

MEDICAL SERVICES
San Francisco General Hospital (Map pp828-9; ☎ 415-206-8000; 1001 Potrero Ave)
Walgreens (Map pp828-9; ☎ 415-861-6276; 498 Castro; ☻ 24hr) Dozens of locations.

MONEY
Bank of America (Map pp828-9; ☎ 415-262-4760; www.bankamerica.com; downstairs, 1 Powell St)

POST

Rincon Center post office (Map pp828-9; ☎ 800-275-8777; www.usps.com; 180 Steuart, San Francisco, CA 94105)

TOURIST INFORMATION

San Francisco's Visitor Information Center (Map pp828-9; ☎ 415-391-2000; www.sfvisitor.org; Market & Powell Sts; ☒ 9am-5pm Mon-Fri, to 3pm Sat & Sun, closed Sun in winter) Lower level of Hallidie Plaza.

California Welcome Center (Map pp828-9; ☎ 415-981-1280; Pier 39; ☒ 10am-5pm)

Dangers & Annoyances

Use your city smarts anywhere, but be especially wary in the rough Tenderloin and after dark in SoMa and the Mission, particularly near the 16th St and 24th St BART stations.

Sights

San Francisco is a cornucopia of distinct, ethnically diverse neighborhoods spread over 43 breathtaking hills. Public transit covers the city well, but walking and biking are the best ways to travel.

UNION SQUARE

Nothing says San Francisco like the rattle and clang of a cable car. That, plus the city's largest shopping and hotel district, leads folks to Union Sq, whose centerpiece is a spacious granite plaza dominated by the 97ft-high **Dewey Monument** (Map pp828–9), erected in 1903 to commemorate the Spanish–American War. Along ritzy Maiden Lane is the **Folk Art International Building** (Map pp828-9; 140 Maiden Lane), the city's only Frank Lloyd Wright building (now a gallery; closed Sun). Powell St can become quite the scene – shoppers, buskers and tourists lined up at the **cable-car turnaround**. San Francisco's Theater District lies immediately southwest of Union Sq.

CIVIC CENTER

The Civic Center area is a study in contrasts, as the city's high culture collides with its pressing homelessness problem. The **Asian Art Museum** (Map pp828-9; ☎ 415-581-3500; www.asianart.org; 200 Larkin St; adult/child 13-17 $10/6; ☒ 10am-5pm Tue-Sun, to 9pm Thu), housed in the former main library, is a stunning architectural blend of old and new. The Asian art collection itself is one of the world's largest and is smartly and dramatically laid out.

Next door to it, the stylish **Main Library** (Map pp828-9; ☎ 415-557-4400; www.sfpl.org; cnr Larkin

& Grove Sts; ☒ hours vary) contains interesting educational centers dedicated to San Francisco's history. Across the plaza, the 1915 beaux arts–style **City Hall** (Map pp828-9; ☎ 415-554-4000; 400 Van Ness Ave; ☒ 8am-5pm Mon-Fri) sports a grand foyer and staircase (popular for weddings) and some cute historical exhibits.

On the opposite side of City Hall, the 1932 **War Memorial Opera House** is where the city's opera and ballet companies perform (p840). Nearby **Hayes Valley**, along Hayes St between Franklin and Laguna Sts, is a mix of trendy restaurants, hip stores and boutiques.

SOMA

South of Market, or SoMa, refers to the vast, largely industrial area from Market St to China Basin. Hot nightclubs brings sections to life after dark.

Yerba Buena Gardens (☎ events 415-543-1718; www.ybgf.org; Mission St), between 3rd and 4th Sts, is a relaxing urban green space bordered by cultural institutions and containing a wealth of activities for families (p834). From May to October it hosts free outdoor concerts and events.

San Francisco Museum of Modern Art (SFMOMA; Map pp828-9; ☎ 415-357-4000; www.sfmoma.org; 151 3rd St; adult/child under 12 $10/free; ☒ 11am-6pm Thu-Tue, to 9pm Thu) This rakish red-brick landmark is one of the nation's premier modern-art showcases. Its strength is American abstract expressionism, but all the great American and European modern artists are represented, and it has a distinguished collection of American photography, including Ansel Adams, Edward Weston and Dorothea Lange.

The **Yerba Buena Center for the Arts** (Map pp828-9; ☎ 415-978-2787; www.ybca.org; 701 Mission St; art gallery admission $6; ☒ noon-5pm Tue-Sun, to 8pm Thu-Sat) has an excellent modern art gallery, plus theaters for avant-garde performances and films. Also here, the **Metreon** (Map pp828-9; ☎ 415-369-6000; www.metreon.com; 101 4th St; ☒ 10am-10pm) is an up-to-the-minute entertainment complex and shopping center.

The 20-year-old **Cartoon Art Museum** (Map pp828-9; ☎ 415-227-8666; www.cartoonart.org; 655 Mission St; adult/child 6-12 $6/2; ☒ 11am-5pm Tue-Sun) has been called 'the best comic art museum in the world' by none other than Art Spiegelman. He should know, right?

The **California Academy of Sciences** (Map pp828-9; ☎ 415-321-8000; www.calacademy.org; 875 Howard at 4th St; adult/child 4-11 $7/2; ☒ 10am-5pm) houses the famed Steinhart Aquarium and the Natural History Museum. In 2008, it will move to its snazzy new home in Golden Gate Park.

FINANCIAL DISTRICT

The financial district was once part of the notorious Barbary Coast. Except for the banking trade, the debauchery is long gone. Buildings that controversially altered but now define the San Francisco skyline include the 761ft **Bank of America building** (Map pp828-9; 555 California St), whose top-floor **Carnelian Room** (☎ 415-433-7500) provides amazing views, and the 853ft **Transamerica Pyramid** (Map pp828-9; 600 Montgomery St), completed in 1972 and still San Francisco's tallest building.

For the city's best chronicle of the gold rush era, head, of course, to another bank: the **Wells Fargo bank museum** (Map pp828-9; ☎ 415-396-2619; 420 Montgomery St; admission free; ⊙ 9am-5pm Mon-Fri).

At the base of Market St along the Embarcadero, the refurbished **Ferry Building** (p837) is now a magnet for tourists and gourmands. Ferries also run from here to points around the bay.

CHINATOWN

A steady stream of Chinese immigrants has kept this the city's most vibrant, crowded and authentic ethnic neighborhood. Cantonese remains the first language for many. **Grant Avenue**, between Bush and Jackson Sts, is the main thoroughfare, but Chinatown is best experienced by wandering its side streets and alleys – many of which, in the late 1800s, were notorious for brothels, opium dens and gambling parlors; see p833 for more.

The **Chinese Historical Society of America Museum** (Map pp828-9; ☎ 415-391-1188; www.chsa.org; 965 Clay St; adult/child 6-17 $3/1; ⊙ noon-5pm Tue-Fri, to 4pm Sat & Sun) has a superb collection of Chinese American artifacts. Its graceful exhibits make this the best place to get a feel for the Chinese American experience, then and now.

Portsmouth Square, at Kearny and Washington Sts, was the heart of San Francisco during the gold rush, and to neighborhood residents it's still Chinatown's 'living room.' Children romp in the park's playground and older folks gamble on the benches. Across the stone overpass, the **Chinese Culture Center** (Map pp828-9; ☎ 415-986-1822; www.c-c-c.org; 750 Kearny St, 3rd fl, Holiday Inn; admission free; ⊙ 10am-4pm Tue-Sat) has displays and a small art gallery.

NORTH BEACH

Like Chinatown, the city's Italian quarter makes for an atmospheric ramble (p833). The adopted home of writers Jack Kerouac and Allen Ginsberg, North Beach was the birthplace of the '50s Beat movement, and it remains a center for poetry and politics. Along Broadway, another San Francisco institution thrives, that of nude dancing.

Washington Square (Map pp828-9), North Beach's playground, is a green swatch perfect for lounging, while nearby, atop Telegraph Hill, is the 210ft **Coit Tower** (Map pp828-9; ☎ 415-362-0808; admission free, elevator rides adult $3.75; ⊙ 10am-6:30pm), one of San Francisco's most prominent landmarks. The tower's lobby is adorned with superb WPA murals. Elevator rides to the top are worth it.

RUSSIAN HILL & NOB HILL

West of North Beach, the steep streets of Russian Hill offer some scenic stairway gardens and the oft-photographed 1000 block of **Lombard Street** (Map pp828-9) between Hyde and Leavenworth Sts – aka 'the world's crookedest street.'

The cable car was invented by Andrew Hallidie after he witnessed a horse-drawn carriage crash trying to reach the summit of Nob Hill. This effort is recounted in the **Cable Car Barn & Museum** (Map pp828-9; ☎ 415-474-1887; www.cablecarmuseum.com; 1201 Mason St; admission free; ⊙ 10am-5pm, to 6pm summer), which also showcases the noisy meeting of the cables.

Progressive **Grace Cathedral** (Map pp828-9; ☎ 415-749-6300; www.gracecathedral.com; 1100 California St) is a 20th-century building of soaring Gothic proportions. Highlights include bronze casts of Ghiberti's Gates of Paradise, two labyrinths (one outside, one inside) and the AIDS Interfaith Memorial Chapel, with a triptych by Keith Haring. A popular time to visit is when the choir sings (11am Sunday and 5:15pm Thursday).

FISHERMAN'S WHARF

For San Francisco as theme park, the city's famous wharf is an almost obligatory stop. Both the views and the tack-o-rama are sublime, and there's enough real nautical history to make you feel you've learned something.

The Hyde St cable car is the arrival method of choice, dropping you between **Ghirardelli Square** (Map pp828-9), a former chocolate factory, and the **Cannery**, a former

CALIFORNIA

DOWNTOWN SAN FRANCISCO

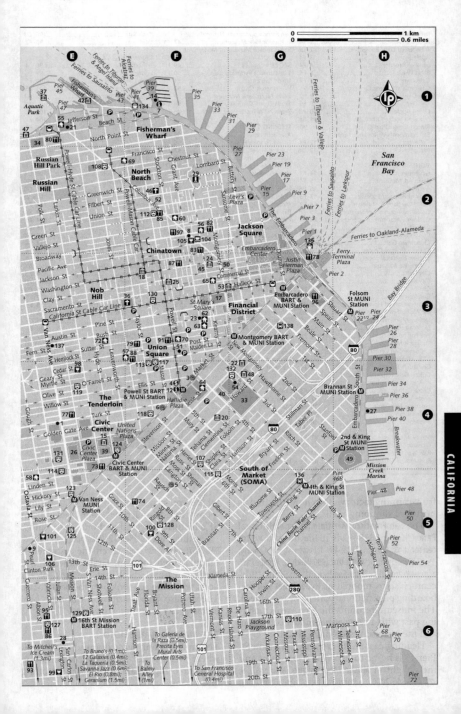

CALIFORNIA

fruit-canning factory. Both now function as nostalgic shopping malls.

The **San Francisco Maritime National Historical Park** (Map pp828–9) is made up of a **visitor center** (☎ 415-561-7100; 499 Jefferson St, the Cannery; ⏰ 9:30am-5pm); a **museum** (900 Beach St, Aquatic Park; admission free; ⏰ 10am-5pm), and six late-19th-century ships moored at **Hyde Street Pier** ($5 boarding pass; national park passes accepted). The museum recounts the Bay Area's seafaring past with a remarkable model collection, and the historic vessels bring it to life.

Heading east along crowded Jefferson St, Pier 45 is home to two WWII-era ships and the delightful **Musée Méchanique** (Map pp828-9; ☎ 415-346-2000; admission free; ⏰ 10am-7pm),

where you can crank up over 300 antique 'penny arcade' machines, many saved from SF's historic Playland and old Sutro Baths.

Further east is **Pier 39** (Map pp828-9; ☎ 415-981-7437; www.pier39.com), surely the epicenter of manufactured tourism. Grab chowder in a bread bowl and check out the herd of sea lions, who long ago took over the boat docks. There's also an aquarium, a carousel, performers, bay tours and souvenirs.

THE MARINA & PRESIDIO

To improve your peace of mind, head west, where green parks, sandy beaches and one singular bridge make for dreamy strolling and biking.

Adjoining Aquatic Park, **Fort Mason** (Map p824; ☎ 415-441-3400; www.fortmason.org) is a former Spanish and US military fort that today is a hive of artistic and progressive civilian activity, housing nonprofit organizations, art galleries, theaters and several small, excellent cultural museums. It's also home to the **Golden Gate National Recreation Area headquarters** (Map pp828-9; ☎ 415-556-0560; www.nps.gov/goga; bldg 201), the nation's most-visited urban park.

The Marina was born out of reclaimed marshland in time for the 1915 Panama-Pacific International Exposition. One surviving Expo structure is Bernard Maybeck's stately **Palace of Fine Arts** (Map pp828-9), off Baker St bordering the Presidio. Today it contains the **Exploratorium** (Map pp828-9; ☎ 415-561-0356; www.exploratorium.edu; 3601 Lyon St; adult/child 4-12 $12/8; ☷ 10am-5pm Tue-Sun), a great hands-on science museum.

The **Presidio** (☎ 415-561-4323) is another former military base that's been converted to civilian uses and parkland. **Crissy Field** (☎ 415-561-7690; www.crissyfield.org) is lined with gorgeous beaches and contains a very welcome café and bookstore aptly named the **Warming Hut** (☎ 415-561-3040; sandwiches & salads $6; ☷ 9am-5pm). Further on is **Fort Point** (Map p824; ☎ 415-561-4395; www.nps.gov/fopo) and the view of the Golden Gate Bridge that Alfred Hitchcock made famous in *Vertigo*. Along the Presidio's west side, picturesque **Baker Beach** is popular; its north end is considered 'clothing optional.'

THE MISSION
The city's Latino district is by turns gritty, family-oriented, hip and political. It's got some of the best cheap meals and bars, particularly around 16th St between Mission and Guerrero and along the 'Valencia St Corridor,' between 20th and 24th Sts.

The 1791 adobe **Mission Dolores** (Map pp828-9; ☎ 415-621-8203; Dolores & 16th Sts; admission $3; ☷ 9am-4:30pm) was the sixth California mission founded by Father Junípero Serra, and it's the oldest building in the city. The adjoining 1918 basilica has exceptional stained glass and tilework, and the historic cemetery is interesting. The grassy slopes of **Mission Dolores Park**, a couple of blocks south, are popular sunning grounds.

Galería de la Raza (Map pp828-9; ☎ 415-826-8009; 2857 24th St; www.galeriadelaraza.org; admission free; ☷ noon-6pm Wed-Sat) is a small gallery hosting diverse exhibits of traditional, political and

urban Latino art. It has the pulse on Mission district events and runs the adjacent Latino arts store **Studio 24** (☷ noon-6pm Wed-Sun).

The neighborhood is noted for its bounty of colorful murals. Two prime spots are **Clarion Alley** (off Valencia near 17th) and **Balmy Alley** (off 24th St near Folsom).

THE CASTRO
The compact Castro, the gay center of San Francisco, is great for strolling, shopping and dining – as well as for satisfying any transgressive urges. The magnificent **Castro Theatre** (p840), where the city's most important film festivals are held, is the primary landmark on busy Castro St. See Entertainment for a sampling of the neighborhood's nightlife.

THE HAIGHT
San Francisco's Summer of Love, ushered in by Golden Gate Park's Human Be-In in 1967, was a short, idealistic moment that crumbled under the weight of drug abuse and increasing violence, a legacy that haunts this neighborhood. It was here that San Francisco's psychedelic sound emerged, epitomized by bands like the Grateful Dead and Jefferson Airplane. Today, Haight St is more about fashion and nightlife than free love, but it maintains a unique aura.

The **Upper Haight** (Map pp828-9), also known as Haight-Ashbury, stretches from Golden Gate Park to Buena Vista Park and is lined with funky clothing shops, cafés and cheap restaurants. On Haight St east of Divisadero St, the **Lower Haight** (Map pp828-9) is a scruffy few blocks of music clubs, cafés and top-notch bars.

GOLDEN GATE PARK & AROUND
San Francisco's biggest park was designed in 1871 by 24-year-old William Hammond Hall, who transformed 1017 acres of windswept dunes into the world's largest city park. For info, contact the **McLaren Lodge office** (Map pp828-9; ☎ 415-831-2700; www.sfpt.org; ☷ 8am-5pm Mon-Fri), near the park's Fell St entrance.

The 1879 **Conservatory of Flowers** (Map pp828-9; ☎ 415-666-7001; adult/child 5-11 $5/1.50; ☷ 9am-4:30pm Tue-Sun) was modeled after the Kew Gardens in London; it's a gorgeous glass greenhouse resplendent with foliage of all varieties. Still being completed at press time, the new **De Young Fine Arts Museum** (Map pp828-9; ☎ 415-863-3330; www.thinker.org/deyoung) already looks like an

SAN FRANCISCO: THE QUEEREST PLACE ON EARTH

In spring 2004, SF Mayor Gavin Newsom married at city hall 4037 same-sex couples, who came from 46 states and eight countries – an event that put San Francisco in the thick of yet another watershed moment in US gay history. The weddings were performed in defiance of California law, and their legality is being challenged – their fate will, in all likelihood, be decided by the US Supreme Court. To forestall a possible victory and to stop states (like Massachusetts) from approving these unions, conservative politicians are now demanding a federal constitutional amendment banning gay marriage.

Besides unleashing a societal hissy fit, these simple declarations of love are also a striking example of the maturation and complexity of gay life in San Francisco. Fifty years ago, in the early 1950s, gays first organized to demand if not acceptance, then equality and fairness. The Mattachine Society, the first serious homosexual-rights organization in the USA, sprang up in San Francisco, as did the Daughters of Bilitis, the nation's first lesbian organization.

Through the 1950s and into the 1960s, SF gay life revolved mainly around bars, which were routinely and publicly raided by police. Gay citizens were blacklisted. Eventually, this blatant persecution raised the public's ire, and it was largely stopped.

In 1977 gay activist Harvey Milk was elected to the Board of Supervisors, and recognition of the gay-rights movement reached a new peak. Then, the following year, Milk and Mayor George Moscone were assassinated by Dan White, an antigay former police officer. This tragedy was followed in the 1980s by the AIDS epidemic, which forever solidified the city's gay community.

Today, gays are elected to public office without comment, and clearly, they are getting married, having children and building families. The Bay Area's gay youth, meanwhile, keep only clothes in their closets. They are remaking the previous generation's gay/lesbian/transgender categories to fit their nuanced experiences of gender and sexuality, identifying themselves as 'bois,' 'trannydykes,' 'genderqueers,' and 'heteroflexibles,' if they aren't disposing of labels entirely.

Experiencing San Francisco gay life today involves much more than visiting bars, but for some of these, see p839 and p839. Also, check out the Bay Area Reporter (www.ebar.com) and the Bay Times.

Dubbed the 'queer Smithsonian,' the **GLBT Historical Society** (Map pp828-9; ☎ 415-777-5455; www.glbthistory.org; 657 Mission St, Suite 300; ☽ gallery 1-5pm Tue-Sat) has the country's largest gay and lesbian archive (open by appointment) and rotating exhibits of queer art and life. Call first, as they may relocate. **Theatre Rhinoceros** (Map pp828-9; ☎ 415-861-5079; www.therhino.org; 2926 16th St) is the nation's longest-running gay-and-lesbian theater company, while **New Conservatory Theatre Center** (Map pp828-9; ☎ 415-861-8972; www.nctcsf.org; 25 Van Ness Ave at Market) presents an 11-month 'Pride Season.'

For more guerrilla antics, see what the **Sisters of Perpetual Indulgence** (☎ 415-820-9697; www .thesisters.org) are up to. This charitable organization is a San Francisco institution.

Kicking off Gay Pride Week at the end of June is the **San Francisco Gay & Lesbian Film Festival** (☎ 415-703-8650; www.frameline.org), two intense weeks of international queer cinema.

Other queer-ific celebrations beyond the Pride Parade and Halloween include late September's huge **Folsom Street Fair** (☎ 415-861-3247; www.folsomstreetfair.com), known for nudity, chaps and chains, and early October's milder **Castro Street Fair** (☎ 415-841-1824; www.castrostreetfair.org).

abandoned rusting freighter, but its tower contains a spectacular viewing platform. Thankfully unrusted, its excellent fine-art collection focuses primarily on the Americas. Nearby, the **Japanese Tea Garden** (☎ 415-752-4227; adult/child 6-12 $3.50/1.25; ☽ 8:30am-6pm) is an immaculate garden with a stylized pagoda and a horseshoe-shaped footbridge.

In addition, the park has a lovely and extensive Botanical Garden (free), miles of hiking and biking trails, a challenging nine-hole golf course, sports fields and picnicking. Rowboats and pedal boats can be rented on **Stow Lake** (☎ 415-752-7869; per hr boats $13-17, surreys/bikes/in-line skates $20/8/6).

Along the western edge of the park is popular Ocean Beach. It's ideal for sunning and wading, but is too cold and rough for proper swimming. At the north end, along the Great Hwy, is the landmark, rebuilt **Cliff**

House (Map p824; ☎ 415-386-3330; www.cliffhouse.com; 1090 Point Lobos); the original opened in 1863. A wide deck takes in the view and overlooks the bones of the old Sutro Baths next door, which burnt down in 1966. Inside, a pricey restaurant and café have positioned every seat for sunset over the Pacific Ocean. Also here is the fun **Camera Obscura** (☎ 415-750-0415; adult/child $3/2; ☽ daily, hrs vary; to dusk on weekends), an ancient invention and historic Playland attraction.

From here, a highly recommended, easy trail leads to Lands End, providing photogenic views of the Marin Headlands and the Golden Gate Bridge.

The **California Palace of the Legion of Honor** (Map p824; ☎ 415-863-3330; www.thinker.org; adult/child 12-17 $8/5, Tue free; ☽ 9:30am-5pm Tue-Sun), in Lincoln Park north of Golden Gate Park, is San Francisco's other premier fine-art museum. Its world-class collection covers European art from medieval times to the early 20th century.

SAN FRANCISCO BAY
Designed by Joseph Strauss and constructed between 1933 and 1937, the beautiful **Golden Gate Bridge** (Map p824; ☎ 415-921-5858), 2 miles in length with a main span of 4200ft, links San Francisco with Marin County. At the time of completion it was the longest suspension bridge in the world. A prime starting point for bridge gazing is **Fort Point Lookout**, on Marine Dr at the bridge's southern end. Cars pay a $5 toll for southbound (Marin to San Francisco) travel; pedestrians and cyclists can cross for free via the sidewalk along the bridge's east side.

From 1933 to 1963, the 12-acre rocky island located in the middle of San Francisco Bay was the nation's most famous penitentiary, supposedly escape-proof and home to such notorious convicts as Al Capone, 'Machine Gun' Kelly and Robert Stroud (the 'birdman of Alcatraz'). **Alcatraz** did 'lose' a few inmates, though it's never been established if any made it to land alive. **Blue & Gold Ferries** (Map pp828-9; ☎ 415-773-1188, reservations 705-5555; www.blueandgoldfleet.com; adult/child 5-11 $16/11) runs to the island from Pier 41. Tickets include an audio tour; book ahead.

Activities
For bicycle rentals, **Avenue Cyclery** (Map pp828-9; ☎ 415-387-3155; 756 Stanyan St) is on the eastern edge of Golden Gate Park, while **Blazing**

Saddles (☎ 415-202-8888; www.blazingsaddles.com; per hr/day $7/28) has several locations along Fisherman's Wharf.

To get *in* the bay, rent kayaks at **City Kayak** (Map pp828-9; ☎ 415-357-1010; www.citykayak.com; Pier 38, Embarcadero at Townsend St; per hr $15-25) or take a 1½-hour catamaran cruise with **Adventure Cat** (Map pp828-9; ☎ 415-777-1630; www.adventure cat.com; Pier 39; adult from $25).

Ocean Beach is a popular but very challenging place to surf, with cold swells rising 12ft or higher. The folks at **Wise Surfboards** (☎ 415-750-9473; 800 Great Hwy) are very knowledgeable and maintain an updated surf report (☎ 415-273-1618).

For whale-watching and trips to the Farallon Islands, contact **Oceanic Society Expeditions** (Map pp828-9; ☎ 800-326-7491; www.oceanic-society .org; Fort Mason, bldg E; adult $61-82).

Walking Tour

> **WALK FACTS**
>
> Distance: 1.8 miles
> Duration: ½ – full day

Ah, San Francisco's hills – you can curse them, circumnavigate them, surmount them, but you can't deny them. Their views beckon and so you climb, finally grateful. Here are two of San Francisco's best neighborhoods – Chinatown and North Beach – and one of its most famous hills. The walk is around 1.8 miles long and will take half a day to a full day, depending on pace.

At Grant Ave and Bush St, the stone dragons and jade-green awnings of the **Chinatown Gate (1)** announce the official entrance to Chinatown. Walk north on bustling Grant Ave, which is the place to shop for pocket Buddhas, samurai swords, kimonos and medicinal ginseng.

At Sacramento St, turn left and then right onto Waverly Pl, an alley lined with brightly painted, filigreed open balconies. On the corner is **Clarion Music Center (2;** ☎ 415-391-1317; www.clarionmusic.com; 816 Sacramento St), chock-full of amazing Asian instruments.

At Clay St, turn west uphill. At the corner of Stockton St, the **Kong Chow Temple (3;** 4th fl, 855 Stockton St) showcases a surreal, ancient altar. As with Tin How Temple (p834), leaving a donation is polite, and no pictures are allowed.

CALIFORNIA

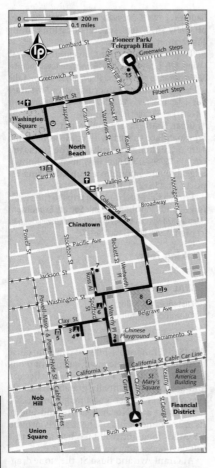

Next door, the dramatic **Chinese Consolidated Benevolent Building** (4; 843 Stockton St) is Chinatown's 'city hall' (closed to the public).

One block west up Clay St is the **Chinese Historical Society of America Museum** (5; p827), which is housed in the historic Chinese YWCA building.

Return east on Clay St and continue heading north along Waverly Pl. Four floors up and hidden from the street is perhaps the oldest Chinese altar in America, **Tin How Temple** (6; 125 Waverly, 4th fl). The otherworldly altar is redolent with burning incense, the ceiling crowded with paper lanterns and fortunes.

At Washington St, jog left and enter Ross Alley, a hidden pedestrian walkway that's been featured in several films. At the end, the

Golden Gate Fortune Cookie Factory (7; 56 Ross Alley) is an unadorned shop front where Chinese women at two old-fashioned machines produce fortune cookies, a San Francisco invention. Try a hot sample and then buy a bag!

Return to Washington St and walk east to **Portsmouth Square** (8; p827); sit for a spell and watch the action unfold in Chinatown's living room, then peruse the **Chinese Culture Center** (9; p827) across the stone bridge.

Now, it's good-bye Chinatown and hello North Beach. Turn north on Kearny St and left up Columbus Ave (just a *small* hill). At Broadway, **City Lights Bookstore** (10; p825) is owned by Lawrence Ferlinghetti, a Beat poet who opened the store in 1953. A publisher and bookseller, City Lights remains a vital San Francisco countercultural institution.

If the need strikes, rejuvenate at the much-loved **Caffe Trieste** (11; ☎ 415-982-2605; www.caffetrieste.com; 601 Vallejo; 🕐 6:30am-10pm, to midnight Fri & Sat); definitely don't miss the Saturday afternoon accordion jam.

Further on Columbus, the beautiful **National Shrine of St Francis of Assisi** (12; 610 Vallejo St) is one of California's first churches (free concerts 4pm Sun).

Inside the US Bank is the tiny, proud **North Beach Museum** (13; 1435 Stockton St; admission free; 🕐 9am-5pm Mon-Fri, to 1pm Sat), with an eclectic mix of artifacts and photos.

Washington Sq is anchored by the ornate 1924 **Saints Peter & Paul Church** (14; 666 Filbert St), whose majestic altar is a match for the Chinese temples. From here, head east up Filbert St, which gets progressively steeper (*this* is a hill) until you reach the top of Telegraph Hill and **Coit Tower** (15; p827). The tower was financed by the eccentric Lillie Hitchcock Coit, who asked that a third of her estate be used to 'add to the beauty of the city I have always loved.'

Finally, either return to North Beach via the shops and restaurants of Grant Ave, or continue east down the precipitous Filbert steps, which are lined with urban gardens. At the bottom, Sansome St and the Embarcadero are flat and easy.

San Francisco for Children
American Child Care (☎ 415-285-2300; www.americanchildcare.com; 580 California St, Ste 500)
Exploratorium (p831) All ages will enjoy this large and thought-provoking museum of art, science and human perception. Book ahead for the fun Tactile Dome.

CALIFORNIA

KINKY SF

From gold rush–era brothels to the Mr Natural '60s to the bathhouse '70s to today's era of webcams and celebrity porn stars – San Francisco has always been kinky, and as many a parade attests, citizens still enjoy letting it all hang out. Here are some ways to join them.

Good Vibrations (Map pp828-9; ☎ 415-522-5460; www.goodvibes.com; 603 Valencia; ◔ 11am-7pm Sun-Wed, to 8pm Thu-Sat) This women-owned, sex-positive shop is as bright, clean and good-natured as a cable-car ride for nudists. Its humorous antique vibrator 'museum' is almost as fascinating as the displays for sale.

Image Leather (Map pp828-9; ☎ 415-621-7551; 2199 Market St; ◔ 9am-10pm Mon-Sat, 11am-7pm Sun) This Castro shopfront has everything for the hard-core leather fetishist. You can't miss the sign leading to the 'dungeon' – but do you dare? The faint-of-heart can simply buy a leather-clad teddy bear.

Asia SF (Map pp828-9; ☎ 415-255-2742; www.asiasf.com; 201 9th St; set-price meals $25-37; ◔ dinner) At this raucous restaurant, the bawdy, short-skirted, transgender servers, or 'gender illusionists,' lip-synch songs between courses on the spaghetti strap–thin bar. 'Asian-fusion' also describes the menu.

Center for Sex & Culture (☎ 415-255-1155; www.sexandculture.org) The center sponsors studious explorations of sexuality, with lectures, classes and films. A 'Firecracker' rating system gauges events for explicitness. Four firecrackers – such as for the Masturbate-a-thon fundraiser – and you know it's a corker.

Power Exchange (Map pp828-9; ☎ 415-487-9944; www.powerexchange.com; 74 Otis St at Mission; men $15-75, couples $10-20, women free; ◔ 9pm-4am Thu-Sun) When you're ready to go all the way, come to this balls-to-the-wall sex club. One floor is gay men only, another is for everyone and all persuasions.

Exotic Erotic Ball (☎ 415-567-2255; www.exoticeroticball.com) For the sex-positive crowd, this 20-year-old, mid-October event is Christmas, New Year's and Halloween all rolled into one kinky, lubed party. Don't be a looki-loo; come dressed to impress in your own secret fantasy.

Fire Engine Tours (☎ 415-333-7077; www.fireengine tours.com; Beach St, the Cannery; adult/child 12 & under $35/25; ◔ 1pm Wed-Mon) Tours on a 1955 open-air Mack fire engine go over Golden Gate Bridge. For some, heaven is a big red truck.

Golden Gate Park (p831) Buffaloes, a carousel, playgrounds, picnicking, pedal boats, a beach: you can't miss.

Precita Eyes Mural Arts Center (Map pp828-9; ☎ 415-285-2287; www.precitaeyes.org; 2981 24th St; 1-2hr classes $10; ◔ store 10am-5pm Mon-Fri, noon-4pm Sat & Sun) Bring your budding urban artist here for a lesson in real street-art and mural painting.

San Francisco Zoo (Map p824; ☎ 415-753-7080; www .sfzoo.org; Sloat Blvd at 47th Ave; adult/child 3-11 $11/5; ◔ 10am-5pm) This above-average city zoo has all your favorites.

Yerba Buena Gardens (p826) Families could spend all day here. In addition to the surrounding cultural fare, it has an outdoor children's playground, an **ice-skating & bowling center** (☎ 415-777-3727; www.skatebowl .com), a **historic carousel** (admission $2; ◔ 11am-6pm) and the supercool **Zeum Art & Technology Center** (☎ 415-777-2800; www.zeum.org; 221 4th St; adult/child 4-18 $7/5; ◔ 11am-5pm Wed-Sun, plus Tue in summer), where kids can make their own clay-animation and karaoke-music videos, among other creative endeavors. Plus, Yerba Buena is bordered by the **Metreon** (p826), with cheap eats, a high-tech video arcade and Hollywood movies.

Tours

Chinese Culture Center (☎ 415-986-1822; www.c-c-c .org) Chinese history ($17) and Chinese cuisine ($40, with lunch).

Cruisin' the Castro (☎ 415-550-8110; adult $45; May-Nov) The fabulous Trevor Hailey strolls through gay history.

Mission Trail Mural Walk (☎ 415-285-2287; www .precitaeyes.org; adult $10-12; ◔ weekends) Takes in 50 to 70 fantastical Mission murals.

Public Library City Guides (☎ 415-557-4266; www .sfcityguides.org) Wide range of free walking tours by local historians.

Festivals & Events

Chinese New Year Parade (☎ 415-391-9680; www .chineseparade.com) One of the nation's largest, this winds through Chinatown in January or early February.

SF International Film Festival (☎ 415-561-5000; www .sffs.org) The nation's oldest film festival occurs in late April.

Bay to Breakers (☎ 415-359-2800; www.baytobreakers .com; race registration $30-40) This mid-May classic exemplifies SF's adorably strange side – technically a 12km foot race, but actually a roving street party with elaborate costumes, nudity and kegs on wheels.

SF Gay Pride Month June begins with the Gay & Lesbian Film Festival and the last weekend of the month (Saturday and Sunday respectively) sees the **Dyke March** (☎ 415-241-8882; www.dykemarch.org) and the **Lesbian, Gay,**

CALIFORNIA

Bisexual & Transgender Pride Parade (☎ 415-864-3733; www.sfpride.org), which makes a spectacle of itself along Market St in front of a million people.

SF AIDS Walk (☎ 415-615-9255; www.aidswalk.net) This 10km walk, the state's largest AIDS fundraising event, occurs in mid-July.

Halloween (www.halloweensf.com; tickets $5) San Francisco's high holy day has become an overwhelming Castro and Civic Center street party.

SF Jazz Festival (☎ 415-788-7353; www.sfjazz.org) The main jazz festival is in late October, while a spring season runs March through June.

Sleeping

Foggy summer is high season in expensive San Francisco; doubles from $100 to $180 are considered 'midrange.' The **San Francisco Visitor Information Center** (p826) runs a **reservation line** (☎ 888-782-9673; www.sfvisitor.org) or you can book online. **Bed & Breakfast SF** (☎ 415-899-0060; www.bbsf.com) is a local B&B/apartment service. At a pinch, Lombard St (Hwy 101) is packed with chains and motels. The city's hotel tax is 14%.

UNION SQUARE & CIVIC CENTER

Halcyon Hotel (Map pp828-9; ☎ 415-929-8033, 800-627-2396; www.halcyonsf.com; 649 Jones St; d per night/week from $90/500; P) These 25 crisp little efficiencies (with microwaves and wet bars) retain attractive touches of the 1912 building. Coin laundry makes weekly stays convenient *and* cheap. Parking $15.

Hayes Valley Inn (Map pp828-9; ☎ 415-431-9131, 800-930-7999; www.hayesvalleyinn.com; 417 Gough St; d $60-80) This is the type of modest, attractive budget stay you hope for but don't expect

---

THE AUTHOR'S CHOICE

San Remo Hotel (Map pp828-9; ☎ 415-776-8688, 800-352-7366; www.sanremohotel.com; 2237 Mason St; r $60-80, penthouse $155; P) This greenery-festooned jewel at the top of North Beach is one of the city's best deals. Cheapest rooms face the interior, and all have double or twin beds and share facilities – but these potential flaws come off like charming quirks. Eclectic, unfussy antique decor and relaxed, helpful staff members draw Europeans by the bucket-load. The attractive bathrooms are vintage morsels, and the rooftop penthouse is a secluded, highly prized roost. Parking $10-14.

---

in SF. Good-sized rooms share tiny, clean bathrooms and a kitchen.

Hotel des Arts (Map pp828-9; ☎ 415-956-3232; www.sfhoteldesarts.com; 447 Bush St; r without/with bath $120/140; P) Contemporary artists have individually designed each of the 51 rooms, and hallways are chockablock with art – it's like living in a gallery where you're the installation. Unforgettable. Parking $24.

York Hotel (Map pp828-9; ☎ 415-885-6800; www.yorkhotel.com; 940 Sutter St; r $100-140; P) Hitchcock's *Vertigo* was filmed here, and the York's subdued, retro-modern stylings look equally good today. Management often works a deal, and the cool Plush Room (☎ 415-885-2800; www.empireplushroom.com) has cabaret shows nightly. Parking $25. Internet $2 per 15 minutes.

Mosser (Map pp828-9; ☎ 415-986-4400, 800-227-3804; www.themosser.com; 54 4th St; r with bath $110-150, without bath $80; P) All rooms are small and dressed in the same clean-lined modern decor, so opt for the bargains with sparkling shared bath. Parking $29.

Hotel Triton (Map pp828-9; ☎ 415-394-0500, 800-800-1299; www.hoteltriton.com; 342 Grant Ave; r from $170; P) This funky designer hotel celebrates a cheeky sense of humor: from upholstered headboards, crushed velvet spreads and blown-glass chandeliers to ecocelebrity suites and a rubber-duck mascot. Parking $33.

Sir Francis Drake (Map pp828-9; ☎ 415-392-7755; www.sirfrancisdrake.com; 450 Powell at Sutter; r from $180; P) For Union Sq fun, the Olde-English-with-a-twist Sir Francis is great. Rooms are comfy and stylish, while the Beefeaters out front are pure kitsch. Parking $37.

NORTH BEACH & FINANCIAL DISTRICT

Pacific Tradewinds (Map pp828-9; ☎ 415-433-7970, 888-734-6783; www.sanfranciscohostel.org; 680 Sacramento St; dm $18-24;) Newly renovated with unshakable bunks and nautical trim, this is the city's smallest, most attractive hostel. Egregiously nice, travel-savvy staff.

Green Tortoise Hostel (Map pp828-9; ☎ 415-834-1000; www.greentortoisehostel.com; 494 Broadway, off Columbus; dm $20-23, r $52-60;) Metaphorically, this tour company simply pulled the wheels off the bus. Scuffed rooms are forgettable, but the ballroom is abuzz with activity.

Hotel Bohème (Map pp828-9; ☎ 415-433-9111; www.hotelboheme.com; 444 Columbus Ave; r $150-170;) Iron bed frames, gauzy netting and ceiling lights covered by Oriental paper umbrellas create a moody atmosphere that lovingly recalls the Beat era.

FISHERMAN'S WHARF

HI San Francisco Fisherman's Wharf (Map pp828-9; ☎ 415-771-7277; Fort Mason Bldg 240; dm/d $26/76; P ✖ 🖳) Superbig dorms and communal showers lack privacy, but otherwise this hostel has it all: an unmatched setting in a national park, great public rooms and a café. Internet $1 per 10 minutes.

Hotel del Sol (Map pp828-9; ☎ 415-921-5520, 877-433-5765; www.thehoteldelsol.com; 3100 Webster at Lombard; r from $150; P ✖ 🖳) Sunshine-bright decor and free parking make this nicely renovated 1950s motor court a more interesting choice than other Lombard St fare.

Argonaut Hotel (Map pp828-9; ☎ 415-563-0800, 866-415-0704; www.argonauthotel.com; 495 Jefferson St; r from $180; P 🖳) Everything is shipshape at the Argonaut, which highlights modern nautical decor and the original beams and brick of the historic Cannery building. Costly but killer views take in Alcatraz and the Golden Gate Bridge. Parking $36.

HAIGHT-ASHBURY

Red Victorian (Map pp828-9; ☎ 415-864-1978; www.redvic.com; 1665 Haight St; r with bath $120-126, without bath $86-110; ✖) Idiosyncratic and heartfelt, owner Sami Sunchild's remarkable B&B transcends every Summer of Love cliché. Each comfortable room is a work of art, and shared facilities are wild. Breakfast is included.

San Francisco Zen Center (Map pp828-9; ☎ 415-863-3136; www.sfzc.org; 300 Page St near Laguna; s $66-100, d $88-120; ✖) Great for singles. Comfortable, homey rooms (some with shared bath) are simplicity itself. Zen participation is not expected, but you can join residents for the 5am prayer bell if you like.

CASTRO

Parker House (Map pp828-9; ☎ 415-621-3222, 888-520-7275; www.parkerguesthouse.com; 520 Church St at 17th Sts; r without bath $120-140, with bath $150-200; P ✖ 🖳) The city's best gay B&B has luxurious decor, with a steam bath and gardens. Limited parking; reserve ahead. Parking $15.

Willows Inn (Map pp828-9; ☎ 415-431-4770; www.willowssf.com; 710 14th St; r $115-135; ✖) This relaxed gay B&B draws international guests. Summery bent-willow furniture gives the inn its name; all rooms have shared baths. Breakfast and afternoon cocktails included.

Eating

The 1990s dot-com revolution spurred a culinary renaissance in the city that continues unabated despite the recent drop in expense-account write-offs. You can sample a smorgasbord of international cuisines, but most particularly you'll find ethereal Asian, Latin American, Italian and French cooking – all cross-pollinated with the fresh approach of California cuisine.

Ferry Building (Map pp828-9; ☎ 415-693-0996; www.ferrybuildingmarketplace.com), at the foot of Market St, is now a gourmet heaven: its high-quality restaurants and shops form an end-to-end banquet of delicacies. Time your visit for the outdoor **farmers market** (☎ 415-291-3276; www.cuesa.org; ⏱ 10am-2pm Tue, from 8am Sat year-round, 4-8pm Thu, 10am-2pm Sun in summer).

UNION SQUARE & THE FINANCIAL DISTRICT

Tiny Belden St, near Kearny between Pine and Bush Sts, is lined with smart bistros with outdoor seating; it's a great destination for lunch or dinner.

Sears Fine Foods (Map pp828-9; ☎ 415-986-1160; www.searsfinefood.com; 439 Powell St; items $7-10; ⏱ 6:30am-10pm) This renovated SF classic – a straight-up diner – is better than ever. The Swedish pancakes really are good.

Yank Sing (Map pp828-9; ☎ 415-957-9300; www.yanksing.com; 101 Spear St, Rincon Center; dishes $3.50-8; ⏱ lunch) The carts keep comin' – laden with the city's best dim sum. Let your eyes feast, but watch out – items tally quick!

Fleur de Lys (Map pp828-9; ☎ 415-673-7779; www.fleurdelyssf.com; 777 Sutter St at Jones; set-price dinners $68-88; ⏱ dinner Mon-Sat) A romantic atmosphere is created by the tented ceiling, while the menu is a meditation on truffles and foie gras. Love is two spoons and warm chocolate soufflé.

CIVIC CENTER

California Culinary Academy (Map pp828-9; ☎ 415-216-4329; 625 Polk St; set-price lunch $16-22, dinner $24-38; ⏱ lunch & dinner Tue-Fri) Place yourself in the hands of tomorrow's great chefs. The most fun is Thursday and Friday's 'grand buffet.'

CHINATOWN

House of Nanking (Map pp828-9; ☎ 415-421-1429; 919 Kearny St; meals $7-12; ⏱ 11am-10pm Mon-Fri, from noon Sat, noon-7:30pm Sun) Once cramped and rude, it's now expanded, more amenable, and just as undeniably delicious. Expect a line.

CALIFORNIA

TOP VEGETARIAN

San Francisco – a mecca for vegetarian cuisine – is to lentils and brown rice what filet mignon is to a Big Mac.

Millennium (Map pp828-9; ☎ 415-345-3900; www.millenniumrestaurant.com; 580 Geary; mains $20-22; ☯ dinner) No sissy crudites here. Dishes are more complex than the human genome, and the gourmet results are generous, rich and robust. Mushrooms get starring roles. The wine list is all organic.

Greens (Map pp828-9; ☎ 415-771-6222; www.greensrestaurant.com; Fort Mason, Bldg A; lunch $9-14, dinner mains $12-25, fixed-price Sat $46; ☯ lunch Tue-Sun, dinner Mon-Sat) Since 1979, venerable Greens has combined elegant, Mediterranean-influenced cuisine and one of the city's best views to wide acclaim. The takeout lunch counter is handy.

Lucky Creation (Map pp828-9; ☎ 415-989-0818; 854 Washington St; mains $5-7; ☯ 11am-9:30pm Thu-Tue) This unpretentious, simple Buddhist restaurant is a star in the heart of Chinatown. The wheat-gluten puffs would fool a carnivore; clay pots are recommended.

Ananda Fuara (Map pp828-9; ☎ 415-621-1994; www.anandafuara.com; 1298 Market St; mains $6-11; ☯ 8am-8pm Mon-Sat, to 3pm Wed) Run by students of guru Sri Chinmoy, Ananda Fuara is vegetarian food to calm body, soul and wallet. Yum-ilicious drinks include yogi tea, *lhassi* (Indian yogurt drink), and the unusual teeccino.

Geranium (Map pp828-9; ☎ 415-647-0118; www.geraniumrestaurant.com; 615 Cortland Ave; mains $13-15; ☯ dinner Tue-Sun, brunch Sat & Sun) In Bernal Heights, affordable Geranium delivers – as promised – high-quality 'vegetarian comfort food.'

Fleur de Lys (p837) Reserve a table at the most refined vegetarian restaurant in town. Fleur de Lys creates a dedicated, four-course ($68) vegetarian meal nightly. It's three air kisses and a squeeze divine.

Yuet Lee (Map pp828-9; ☎ 415-982-6020; 1300 Stockton St at Broadway; mains $4.50-11; ☯ 11am-3am Wed-Mon) It looks like nothing, but everything is fresh, fast and perfect. The salt-and-pepper squid is ecstasy. A great late-night choice.

NORTH BEACH

L'Osteria del Forno (Map pp828-9; ☎ 415-982-1124; 519 Columbus Ave; mains $11-17; ☯ 11:30am-10pm Wed-Mon) The place and menu are small, but you can't miss with the fresh, handmade raviolis and pizzas.

Helmund (Map pp828-9; ☎ 415-362-0641; 430 Broadway; mains $11-18; ☯ dinner, also lunch Tue-Fri) Delicious Afghan food is served by a gracious staff at this old favorite – try the lamb and the aromatic pumpkin dishes. Lunch is a buffet.

FISHERMAN'S WHARF

There's nothing wrong with the older Italian American establishments along the wharf – just expect the view to trump the cooking, and be grateful when it doesn't.

Gary Danko (Map pp828-9; ☎ 415-749-2060; www.garydanko.com; 800 North Point St; set-price menu $60-80; ☯ dinner) Gary Danko's New French American cuisine tops most gourmet dance cards. The cheese cart – a don't-miss event – has made discerning palates weep. Decor is

smooth and service impeccable without being snooty. It's worth every penny.

THE MARINA

Chestnut St, the Marina's main drag, is lined with dining choices.

Pacific Catch (Map pp828-9; ☎ 415-440-1950; 2027 Chestnut at Fillmore; items $3.50-10; ☯ 11am-10pm) This tiny grill is cheap, fast and great. Seared ahi and salmon grace rice bowls and tacos, and the Hawaiian poke is swell.

Isa (Map pp828-9; ☎ 415-567-9588; 3324 Steiner St at Chestnut St; plates $8-17; ☯ dinner Mon-Sat) 'Small plates' are all the rage, and the inventive morsels of French cuisine at Isa are prepared by one of the nation's up-and-coming chefs, Luke Sung. Head for the relaxed back patio.

THE MISSION

Tartine Bakery (Map pp828-9; ☎ 415-487-2600; www.tartinebakery.com; 600 Guerrero; sandwiches $7-8; ☯ 8am-7pm, to 8pm Thu-Sun) With heavenly smashwiches, fancified croque monsieurs, and pastries so profoundly delicious you might die, expect crowds.

Bruno's (Map pp828-9; ☎ 415-648-7701 www.brunoslive.com; 2389 Mission at 20th; plates $6-11; ☯ dinner Tue-Sat) The decor feels retro because Bruno's has knocked around, but the Cajun-inspired small plates – a bevy of rapturous, fried morsels – are of-the-moment sinful. Live jazz nightly makes it a scene easily repeated.

Limón (Map pp828-9; ☎ 415-252-0918; www.limon-sf.com; 524 Valencia; mains $14-20; ❷ lunch & dinner Mon-Fri, noon-10pm Sat & Sun) The hip lime interior sets the mood for smart updates of traditional Peruvian cuisine; the *ceviche* and *lomo saltado* are rave-worthy.

Also recommended:

La Taquería (Map pp828-9; ☎ 415-285-7117; 2889 Mission St at 25th; burritos $4-6; ❷ 11am-9pm) The perfect carnitas burrito, *sin arroz*.

Ti Couz (Map pp828-9; ☎ 415-252-7373; www.ticouz16.com; 3108 16th St; crepes $4.50-8; ❷ 5-10pm Tue-Thu, 11am-10pm Fri-Mon) French crepes, sweet and savory.

Mitchell's Ice Cream (Map pp828-9; ☎ 415-648-2300; 688 San Jose Ave at 29th; cones $2-4; ❷ 11am-11pm) Ice cream so good there are lines in the fog.

THE CASTRO

Cafe Flore (Map pp828-9; ☎ 415-621-8579; 2298 Market St at Noe; mains $7-11; ❷ 7am-10pm) This relaxed café, aka 'Cafe Hairdo,' is a classic Castro meeting place where the good food is second to the moving scenery.

Bagdad Café (Map pp828-9; ☎ 415-621-4434; 2295 Market at 16th; mains $10-14; ❷ 24hr) In need of quality comfort food at 4am? Set a course for this 24-hour diner. Cash only.

THE HAIGHT

Rosamunde Grill (Map pp828-9; ☎ 415-437-6851; 545 Haight St; sausages $4; ❷ 11:30am-10pm) Just the one item, executed perfectly: gourmet sausage sandwiches.

Pork Store Café (Map pp828-9; ☎ 415-864-6981; www.porkstorecafe.com; 1451 Haight St; items $5-9; ❷ 7am-3:30pm Mon-Fri, 8am-4pm Sat & Sun) The hangover-curing grub at this classic Haight St greasy spoon is worth the weekend wait.

Thep Phanom (Map pp828-9; ☎ 415-431-2526; www.thepphanom.com; 400 Waller St; mains $9-12; ❷ dinner) This dependable, atmospheric Lower Haight favorite serves some of San Francisco's best Thai food – focus on the specials.

THE RICHMOND

Straits Cafe (Map pp828-9; ☎ 415-668-1783; www.straitsrestaurants.com; 3300 Geary Blvd at Parker Ave; mains $11-20; ❷ lunch & dinner Mon-Thu, noon-10pm Fri-Sun) Singapore cuisine is the original pan-Asian fusion: part Chinese, Thai, Malaysian and Indian. It's served here with the proper tropical drinks and atmosphere.

Chapeau! (Map pp828-9; ☎ 415-750-9787; 1408 Clement St at 15th; mains $14-19; ❷ dinner Tue-Sun) A perfect neighborhood restaurant: the greeting is always friendly and the well-prepared French cuisine is affordable – it's hard to beat.

Kabuto (Map pp828-9; ☎ 415-752-5652; www.kabutosushi.com; 5121 Geary Blvd at 15th; sushi $4-10; ❷ dinner Tue-Sat) San Francisco is a sushi-lover's town, and creative Kabuto is always covered with kisses. Why, oh why, must it be so tiny?

Drinking

The Mission, the Haight and North Beach are famous for their bars and pubs.

Edinburgh Castle (Map pp828-9; ☎ 415-885-4074; www.castlenews.com; 950 Geary St) British beers, single-malt whiskies, authentic fish-and-chips and an upstairs music and performance space: what's not to like?

Zeitgeist (Map pp828-9; ☎ 415-255-7505; 199 Valencia St) The back beer garden (with evening BBQ) is the in spot for city bikers and punk hipsters.

Lone Star Saloon (Map pp828-9; ☎ 415-863-9999; 1354 Harrison St) Bears, daddies and leathermen sidle up to this famous gay bar.

Lexington Club (Map pp828-9; ☎ 415-863-2052; www.lexingtonclub.com; 3464 19th St; ❷ Mon-Sat) This is *the* lesbian hangout in the Mission.

Plough & the Stars (Map pp828-9; ☎ 415-751-1122; www.theploughandstars.com; 116 Clement St at 2nd) Homesick Irish can pine over a pint and SF's best Irish music. Good Irish jukebox, too.

Martuni's (Map pp828-9; ☎ 415-241-0205; 4 Valencia at Market) This classy gay piano bar draws a diverse crowd for glittering cocktails, tinkling ivories and conversation.

Toronado (Map pp828-9; ☎ 415-863-2276; www.toronado.com; 547 Haight St) A venerable Haight watering hole. Beer mavens dig the 50+ microbrews on tap; punks love the jukebox.

Entertainment

The *San Francisco Bay Guardian* and *SF Weekly* have extensive entertainment listings, as does www.sfarts.com. For tickets to the theater, big music acts and other shows, call **BASS** (☎ 415-776-1999; www.tickets.com). **TIX Bay Area** (☎ 415-433-7827; www.theatrebayarea.org; ❷ Tue-Sun), at Union Sq, also sells half-price show tickets.

NIGHTCLUBS

Harry Denton's Starlight Room (☎ 415-395-8595; www.harrydenton.com; 450 Powell St) On the top floor

CALIFORNIA

of the Sir Francis Drake Hotel, Harry Denton's has views and nightly dancing.

Tonga Room (☎ 415-772-5278; www.tongaroom.com; 950 Mason St) Polynesian kitsch in the Fairmont Hotel. Great happy hour (5pm to 7pm Monday to Friday) includes a $7 buffet.

El Rio (Map pp828-9; ☎ 415-282-3325; www.elriosf.com; 3158 Mission St at Cesar Chavez) Perfectly diverse in every aspect, from music to patrons, El Rio is a lesson in Mission hip.

Café (Map pp828-9; ☎ 415-861-3846; www.cafésf.com; 2367 Market St) This lively Castro club draws a mixed gay and lesbian crowd onto its dancefloor and street-view deck.

Savanna Jazz (Map pp828-9; ☎ 415-285-3369; www.savannajazz.com; 2937 Mission St at 25th; mains $11-15; ☺ Tue-Sun) Live jazz should always be like this – warm and intimate, with a long bar and a close stage. Serves African-influenced soul food.

LIVE MUSIC

Bottom of the Hill (Map pp828-9; ☎ 415-621-4455; www.bottomofthehill.com; 1233 17th St) Oddballs, newcomers and punks crowd the nightly lineup. It's essential listening, with real character.

Boom Boom Room (Map pp828-9; ☎ 415-673-8000; www.boomboomblues.com; 1601 Fillmore St) This historic Fillmore haunt serves blues and funk.

12 Galaxies (Map pp828-9; ☎ 415-970-9777; www.12galaxies.com; 2565 Mission at 22nd) Up-and-coming bands rock this comfy, two-level space.

Independent (Map pp828-9; ☎ 415-771-1421; www.theindependentsf.com; 628 Divisadero at Hayes) Stripped-down interior and established indie rock bands.

Also recommended:

Bimbo's 365 Club (Map pp828-9; ☎ 415-474-0365; www.bimbos365club.com; 1025 Columbus at Chestnut) Gorgeous space.

Great American Music Hall (Map pp828-9; ☎ 415-885-0750; www.gamh.com; 859 O'Farrell at Polk)

Fillmore (Map pp828-9; ☎ 415-346-6000; www.thefillmore.com; 1805 Geary at Fillmore) Holy house of '60s music.

DANCE CLUBS

EndUp (Map pp828-9; ☎ 415-357-0827; www.theendup.com; 401 6th St) One of the city's most popular clubs. 'Fag Fridays' start the weekend, which finishes with Sunday's daylong T-dance.

Stud (Map pp828-9; ☎ 415-252-7883; www.studsf.com; 399 9th St) This legendary all-persuasions gay dance club hosts numerous theme nights. Don't miss 'Trannyshack' Tuesdays.

1015 Folsom (Map pp828-9; ☎ 415-431-7444; www.1015.com; 1015 Folsom St) A very happening, multilevel club – Saturday's 'Club Release' is extremely popular.

Milk (Map pp828-9; ☎ 415-387-6455, www.milksf.com; 1840 Haight St) Sweat to hip-hop, funk, dancehall and more.

CLASSICAL MUSIC & OPERA

Yerba Buena Center for the Arts (Map pp828-9; ☎ 415-978-2787; www.ybca.org; 701 Mission St) Yerba Buena hosts first-class modern music, dance and theater.

Davies Symphony Hall (Map pp828-9; ☎ 415-864-6000; www.sfsymphony.org; 201 Van Ness Ave) The San Francisco Symphony performs here from September to May.

Both the acclaimed San Francisco Opera and the **San Francisco Ballet** (☎ 415-861-5600; www.sfballet.org) perform at the **War Memorial Opera House** (Map pp828-9; ☎ 415-864-3330; www.sfopera.com; 301 Van Ness Ave).

THEATER

San Francisco has numerous small theater companies and one major company, the **American Conservatory Theater** (ACT; www.act-sf.org).

Geary Theater (Map pp828-9; ☎ 415-749-2228; 415 Geary St) ACT performs primarily here.

MagicTheatre (Map pp828-9; ☎ 415-441-8822; www.magictheatre.org; Fort Mason, Bldg D) Made famous by Sam Shepard, this is an important breeding ground for new playwrights.

Club Fugazi (Map pp828-9; ☎ 415-421-4222; www.beachblanketbabylon.com; 678 Green St; seats $35-65) Showcases the ribald, hilarious *Beach Blanket Babylon* – a quintessentially San Franciscan theater-comedy extravaganza.

Catch touring Broadway productions:

Curran Theatre (Map pp828-9; ☎ 415-551-2000; 445 Geary St)

Golden Gate Theatre (Map pp828-9; ☎ 415-551-2000; 1 Taylor St)

Orpheum Theatre (Map pp828-9; ☎ 415-551-2000; 1192 Market St)

CINEMA

Castro Theatre (Map pp828-9; ☎ 415-621-6120; www.castrotheatresf.com; 429 Castro St) This grand old-style cinema has the city's best calendar of art, independent and foreign films.

Also recommended for funky, whacked celluloid:

Red Vic (Map pp828-9; ☎ 415-668-3994; www.redvicmoviehouse.com; 1727 Haight St)

Roxie Cinema (Map pp828–9; ☎ 415-863-1087; www
.roxie.com; 3117 16th St)
Screening Room (Map pp828–9; ☎ 415-978-2787) At
Yerba Buena Center for the Arts (p826).

SPORTS
San Francisco 49ers (☎ 415-656-4900; www.sf49ers
.com) The city's NFL football team plays at
Candlestick Park (Map p824).
San Francisco Giants (☎ 415-478-2277; http://san
francisco.giants.mlb.com) The major-league base-
ball club plays at the stunning SBC Park
(Map pp828–9).

Shopping
Shopping in San Francisco is part blood
sport, part cultural experience. For the latter, browse North Beach's Grant Ave from
Bush to Filbert Sts – go from Chinatown
to North Beach, from silk kimonos to rare
vinyl. In Hayes Valley, Hayes St from Franklin to Laguna Sts is an upscale, stylish mash
of galleries, boutiques and intriguing wares.
Upper Haight's Haight St from Masonic Ave
to Golden Gate Park is a scene worth tripping through once – there are great clothes,
and it's not all tie-dye and Doc Martens.
Similarly, the Castro has interesting clothes
aplenty, plus other blush-worthy wares. For
recycled clothes and furniture, literature and
other bric-a-brac, head for the Mission's Valencia St between 16th and 24th Sts.

For shopping as fashionista blood sport,
take a credit card in each hand and enter
Union Sq.

Getting There & Away
AIR
San Francisco International Airport (SFO; Map p824;
☎ 650-821-8211; www.flysfo.com) is 14 miles south
of downtown off Hwy 101. Most domestic
and international carriers fly in and out of
SFO. SFO's AirTrain, an automated people
mover, connects the terminals, parking garages, rental-car center and BART station.

BUS
The **Transbay Terminal** (Map pp828–9; 425 Mission St), at
1st St in SoMa, is the major bus station. Take
AC Transit (☎ 510-891-4777; www.actransit.org) buses
to the East Bay, **Golden Gate Transit** (☎ 415-455-
2000; www.goldengate.org) buses north into Marin
and Sonoma Counties, and **SamTrans** (☎ 800-
660-4287; www.samtrans.com) buses south to Palo
Alto and along the Pacific Coast.

> **HOT CORNER**
> Bar-hopping doesn't get better than this half-
> block of Columbus Ave (Map pp828–9).
>   **Vesuvio** (Map pp828–9; ☎ 415-362-3370;
> www.vesuvio.com; 255 Columbus Ave) Start at
> this Beat haven for drinking poets and po-
> etic drunks.
>   **Tosca Cafe** (Map pp828–9; ☎ 415-986-9651;
> 242 Columbus Ave) Next, order a 'house cappuc-
> cino' with the politicos and local celebrities
> at this North Beach institution.
>   **Jazz at Pearl's** (Map pp828–9; ☎ 415-291-
> 8255; www.jazzatpearls.com; 256 Columbus Ave;
> tapas $6-12; cover $5-15) Having booked ahead,
> eat dinner and enjoy top-flight '30s-era jazz
> at this elegant, intimate nightclub. Dress up;
> it's a knockout.
>   **Specs'** (Map pp828–9; ☎ 415-421-4112; 12
> W Saroyan Pl) Finally, unwind at this weird,
> cranky old dive where everything, even
> patrons, feels dropped in amber.

Greyhound (☎ 415-495-1569, 800-231-2222; www
.greyhound.com) has several buses daily to Los
Angeles ($45, from eight hours), to Truc-
kee near Lake Tahoe ($58 round-trip, 5.5
hours) and other destinations. Buses leave
from the Transbay Terminal.

TRAIN
CalTrain (☎ 800-660-4287; www.caltrain.com) operates down the Peninsula. From the depot
at 4th and King Sts in San Francisco, it
links to Millbrae (connecting to BART and
SFO, 30 minutes), Palo Alto (one hour) and
San Jose (1½ hours). **Amtrak** (☎ 800-872-7245;
www.amtrakcalifornia.com) runs free shuttle buses
to San Francisco's Ferry Building and Cal-
Train station from its terminals in Emeryville and Oakland's Jack London Sq.

Getting Around
Operated by the Metropolitan Transportation Commission, www.511.org is an excellent resource, covering transit options for
the entire nine-county Bay Area. You can
also call ☎ 511, an automated Bay Area
transit information service.

TO/FROM THE AIRPORT
BART (Bay Area Rapid Transit; ☎ 415-989-2278; www
.bart.gov) has direct service from the airport
to downtown San Francisco ($4.95). Or take

SamTrans (☎ 800-660-4287) express bus No KX ($3.50, 30 minutes) to San Francisco's Transbay Terminal.

The **SFO Airporter** (☎ 650-246-2768; www.sfoairporter.com; adult $15) bus departs from the baggage claim areas and stops at major hotels. Door-to-door shuttles cost around $14 to $17; try **SuperShuttle** (☎ 415-558-8500; www.supershuttle.com) or **Lorrie's** (☎ 415-334-9000). Depending on where you're going to in San Francisco, the trip can take 20 to 40 minutes.

Taxis to downtown San Francisco cost $35 to $45.

BOAT

Blue & Gold Ferries (Map pp828-9; ☎ information 415-773-1188, sales 415-705-5555; www.blueandgoldfleet.com) runs the Alameda–Oakland ferry from Pier 41 and the Ferry Building. It also serves Alcatraz and Angel Islands. **Golden Gate Ferry** (☎ 415-455-2000; www.goldengate.org) has regular service from the Ferry Building to Larkspur and Sausalito in Marin County.

CAR & MOTORCYCLE

If you can, avoid driving in San Francisco: street parking is competitive and tickets are expensive. However, convenient downtown parking lots are at the Embarcadero Center, at 5th and Mission Sts and at Sutter and Stockton Sts.

National car-rental agencies have 24-hour offices at the airport and regular offices downtown. See p1173 for toll-free contact information.

City Rent-a-Car (Map pp828-9; ☎ 415-359-1331; www.cityrentacar.com; 1433 Bush St) is a consistently reliable and competitively priced independent city agency.

PUBLIC TRANSPORTATION

San Francisco's **Municipal Transit Agency** (MUNI; ☎ 415-673-6864; www.sfmuni.com) operates comprehensive bus and streetcar lines and three cable-car lines; two cable-car lines leave from Powell and Market Sts, and one leaves from California and Markets Sts. A detailed MUNI Street & Transit Map ($2.50) is available at newsstands and the Powell St MUNI kiosk. The general fare for buses or streetcars is $1.50; cable-car fare is $5. A MUNI Passport (one-/three-/seven-day $11/18/24) allows unlimited travel on all MUNI transport, including cable cars; it's sold at San Francisco's Visitor Information Center (p826) and

at the TIX Bay Area kiosk at Union Sq. A seven-day City Pass ($43) includes transit and admission to six attractions.

The **Bay Area Rapid Transit system** (BART; ☎ 415-989-2278; www.bart.gov; tickets $1.25-7.45) is the commuter train system linking San Francisco with the East Bay. In the city, BART runs beneath Market St, down Mission St and south to SFO and Millbrae, where it connects with CalTrain.

TAXI

Fares run about $2.25 per mile. Here are some of the major cab companies:
DeSoto Cab (☎ 415-970-1300)
Veteran's Taxicab (☎ 415-648-1313)
Yellow Cab (☎ 415-626-2345)

MARIN COUNTY

Just across the Golden Gate Bridge, wealthy, laid-back **Marin** (www.visitmarin.org) is as warm and green as San Francisco is foggy and urban. **Sausalito** (Map p824), the first town you encounter, is a pleasant bayside community; it makes a good destination for bike trips over the bridge (take the ferry back). At the harbor, the **San Francisco Bay-Delta Model** (☎ 415-332-3871; www.baymodel.org; 2100 Bridgeway Blvd; admission free; ☼ 9am-4pm Tue-Fri, 10am-6pm Sat & Sun, closed Sun winter) is a geeky fun, 1.5-acre hydraulic re-creation of the entire bay and delta.

Marin Headlands

These hilly, windswept headlands are laced with hiking trails and offer spectacular views of San Francisco. To reach the **visitor center** (☎ 415-331-1540; www.nps.gov/goga/mahe/; ☼ 9:30am-4:30pm), take the Alexander Ave exit from the Golden Gate Bridge and head west on Conzelman Rd. Attractions include the **Point Bonita lighthouse** (☼ Sat-Mon), the Cold War–era **Nike missile site** (☼ Wed-Fri) and **Rodeo Beach**, plus there's *free* walk-in camping on the cliffs at Bicentennial. At Fort Baker, the **Bay Area Discovery Museum** (☎ 415-339-3900; www.baykidsmuseum.org; 557 McReynolds Rd, Sausalito; adult/child 1-17 $8.50/7.50; ☼ 9am-4pm Tue-Fri, 10am-5pm Sat & Sun) is an ideal destination for kids.

Near the visitor center, the **HI Marin Headlands Hostel** (Map p824; ☎ 415-331-2777, 800-909-4776; dm $18-22, r from $54; P ☑) occupies two historic 1907 buildings. Private rooms in the commanding officer's house are sweet. Internet $1 per 10 minutes.

Mount Tamalpais State Park

Majestic 2571ft Mt Tamalpais, or Mt Tam, is a tiny mountain that lords it over the Bay Area with breathtaking views. **Mount Tamalpais State Park** (Map p824; ☎ 415-388-2070; www.mttam.net; per car $6) encompasses 6300 acres of wilderness plus more than 200 miles of trails; don't miss East Peak. Panoramic Hwy climbs from Hwy 1 through the park to Stinson Beach, itself a nice town with a pretty beach. **Park headquarters** are at **Pantoll Station** (801 Panoramic Hwy; campsites $15), where there are trailheads and a first-come, first-served campground.

Near park headquarters, **Mountain Home Inn** (☎ 415-381-9000; www.mtnhomeinn.com; 810 Panoramic Hwy; r $175-325; lunch $10-13, 3-course dinner $38; ✗ ▯) occupies a secluded perch. Appealing, outdoorsy rooms bring in the view, while the restaurant's open-air deck makes the perfect lunch or dinner stop (open Wednesday to Sunday).

Muir Woods National Monument

The slopes of Mt Tam were once carpeted with mighty redwoods. The only surviving remnant is 550-acre **Muir Woods** (☎ 415-388-2595; www.nps.gov/muwo; per car $3). A national monument since 1908, it was named after Sierra Club founder John Muir. The easy 1-mile Main Trail Loop leads past the splendor of the 1000-year-old trees at Cathedral Grove and returns via Bohemian Grove. Muir Woods is 12 miles north of the Golden Gate Bridge via Hwy 101 (take the Hwy 1 exit and follow signs). No camping or picnicking is allowed.

Point Reyes National Seashore

The triangular peninsula of **Point Reyes National Seashore** (Map p824) comprises 110 sq miles of blustery beaches, lagoons and forested cliffs. The westernmost point of the peninsula, Point Reyes Headlands, is crowned by the **Point Reyes Lighthouse** (☻ Thu-Mon), a great spot for onshore whale-watching, while the peninsula's northern tip is home to a herd of tule elk. The **Bear Valley Visitors Center** (☎ 415-464-5100; www.nps.gov/pore) is just past Olema and has trail maps and park displays. Point Reyes has four hike-in **campsites** (☎ reservations 415-663-8054; campsites $15), two near the beach.

The **West Marin chamber of commerce** (☎ 415-663-9232; www.pointreyes.org) can lead you to numerous cozy inns and cottages. **Motel Inverness** (Map p824; ☎ 415-669-1081; www.motelinverness.com; 12718 Sir Francis Drake Blvd; r $100-175) is an appealing, nicely managed midrange motel; its 24-hour lodge is warmed by a great fireplace. The economy-minded can bunk at **HI Point Reyes Hostel** (☎ 415-663-8811; dm $14-16), off Limantour Rd, 8 miles from the Bear Valley Visitors Center.

If you like oysters, beeline for **Johnson Oyster Company** (☎ 415-669-1149; oysters $9-30;

ANGEL ISLAND

Looming over Alcatraz in San Francisco Bay, Angel Island has 740 acres of some of the region's best hiking, biking and camping, plus its own dramatic history. During the Civil War, the US military used it as a fort, and later the island became a notorious immigration station, where boatloads of would-be Chinese immigrants remained stranded for months, only to be denied entry because of the 1882 Chinese Exclusion Act. Many immigrants literally carved their despair and dreams on the station walls.

Now a state park, **Angel Island** (Map p824; ☎ 415-435-1915; www.angelisland.org; ☻ 8am-dusk) has a 5-mile paved rim road and trails leading to its windy, scenic peak. Ayala Cove, where the ferries dock, contains bike rentals (per hour/day $10/30), one-hour tram tours (adult/child $12.50/7.50), a simple **café** (☎ 415-897-0715), a picnic area with a small beach, and a **visitor center**. Historic buildings, like the Immigration Station, are mainly open weekends, but hours can expand in summer; check ahead.

Camp and enjoy the twinkling San Francisco skyline all night long; campsite Nos 4 and 5 have the prime views. Reserve ahead for **campsites** (☎ 800-444-7275; www.reserveamerica.com; reservation fee/campsite $7.50/15). Sites have chemical toilets, water nearby, BBQ grills and picnic tables. There is even a beachside kayak camp.

Blue & Gold Ferries (reservations ☎ 415-705-5555; information 415-773-1188; www.blueandgoldfleet.com; round-trip adult/child 6-12 $13.50/8) departs daily for Angel Island from Pier 41 (weekends only off-season). Or take an Alcatraz/Angel Island combo tour (adult/child $42/27.25).

8am-4:30pm), off Sir Francis Drake Blvd in the park. This is where they farm them, so just pluck, shuck and suck. Nearby, Point Reyes Station is a pleasant small town for a meal or picnic supplies. Or enjoy the exquisite, artful cuisine at **Manka's** (☎ 415-669-1034; www.mankas.com; set-price meal $58-88; dinner Thu-Sun), an unforgettable, special-occasion destination off Sir Francis Drake Blvd north of Inverness (look for signs).

OAKLAND

Oakland is a largely working-class city that's not a prime tourist destination, but its rich history and lively restaurant and nightclub scene make it an interesting day trip.

For maps and self-guided walking tours, head to the **Oakland Convention & Visitors Bureau** (☎ 510-839-9000; www.oaklandcvb.com; 463 11th St at Broadway, in the Marriott; 8:30am-5pm Mon-Fri); nearby, the City Center mall contains the convenient 12th St BART station.

Sights & Activities

A few blocks south, along 9th St, is the center of **Old Oakland**, a haven of Victorian architecture. Within walking distance, east of Broadway between Franklin and Webster Sts, is Oakland's bustling **Chinatown**, not yet dolled up for tourists. The 1931 **Paramount Theatre** (☎ 510-465-6400; www.paramounttheatre.com; 2025 Broadway at 21st St) is a gorgeous art deco movie theater that screens films and hosts performances by the Oakland Ballet and Oakland East Bay Symphony.

Oakland's main site is the **Oakland Museum of California** (☎ 510-238-2200; www.museumca.org; 10th & Oak Sts; adult/child 6-17 $8/5; 10am-5pm Wed-Sat, from noon Sun). This excellent, state-focused museum encapsulates the entirety of California history, culture, ecology and art.

The **African American Museum & Library** (☎ 510-637-0198; www.oaklandlibrary.org/aamlo; 659 14th St; noon-5:30pm Tue-Sat) has a free gallery with changing exhibits on the African American experience in northern California.

On the waterfront, **Jack London Square** (Map p824), at the south end of Broadway, has been remade into an attractive tourist zone filled with restaurants, shops and clubs. The square is named for local hero Jack London (1876–1916), who supposedly wrote portions of the *Sea Wolf* and *Call of the Wild* in the tiny 1880 watering hole **Heinhold's First & Last Chance Saloon** (☎ 510-839-6761; 48

Webster). This National Literary Landmark is open daily for inspirational drinking.

Eating & Drinking

In Oakland, quality, inexpensive Asian restaurants abound.

Le Cheval (☎ 510-763-8495; 1007 Clay St; meals $7-11; 11am-9:30pm Mon-Sat, dinner Sun) Tops for Vietnamese cuisine.

Battambang (☎ 510-839-8815; 850 Broadway; meals $6-10; 11am-9:30pm Mon-Sat) A less hectic, well-regarded choice for Cambodian.

Nan Yang (510-655-3298; 6048 College Ave; meals $6-16; lunch & dinner Tue-Fri, noon-9:30pm Sat & Sun) For Indian-influenced Burmese food, go here, along the pleasant retail corridor near Rockridge BART. The curried chicken-noodle soup and the ginger and green-tea salads are unusual.

Jack London Sq is a center for nightlife. Elegant and intimate **Yoshi's** (☎ 510-238-9200; www.yoshis.com; 510 Embarcadero West; meals $15-20) is one of the country's top jazz clubs; it has an attached Japanese restaurant. **Kimball's Carnival** (☎ 510-444-6979; www.kimballscarnival.com; 522 Second St) is a cavernous space with R & B dancing mainly on weekends. **Mingles** (☎ 510-835-3900; www.minglesoakland.com; 370 Embarcadero) is smaller, sweatier and largely R & B.

Getting There & Around

For comprehensive Bay Area transit information, visit www.transitinfo.org. From **Oakland International Airport** (Map p824; ☎ 888-435-9625; www.oaklandairport.com), shuttle buses ($2) to the Coliseum BART station run about every 15 minutes until midnight. **SuperShuttle** (☎ 415-558-8500, 800-258-3826) offers door-to-door service to Oakland ($18) and San Francisco ($25). A taxi to downtown Oakland costs about $25, to San Francisco about $55.

Oakland's **Greyhound station** (☎ 800-229-9424; 2103 San Pablo Ave) is rather seedy. **AC Transit** (☎ 510-817-4777; www.actransit.org) operates local buses between San Francisco and Oakland ($3); bus No O is the most convenient. There is an **Amtrak station** (☎ 800-872-7245) at Jack London Sq. From San Francisco, take **BART** (www.bart.gov) to the 12th St station in downtown Oakland ($2.55). Far more pleasant is the **Alameda–Oakland ferry** (☎ 510-522-3300; www.eastbayferry.com), which operates from two locations in San Francisco (Pier 39 and the Ferry Building) to Jack London Sq nine to 12 times daily ($5.50 one way).

BERKELEY

The entire Bay Area is a liberal enclave, but its radical core is **Berkeley** (www.visitberkeley.com). Though it has mellowed since the 1960s hey-day of the student-led free-speech movement and anti–Vietnam War protests, it remains an iconoclastic fiefdom. Strolling its attractive university and surrounding streets is both enjoyable and politically enlightening.

Sights & Activities

Founded in 1868, the **University of California at Berkeley** (Map p824) – or just 'Cal' – is one of the country's top universities and home to 33,000 diverse, politically conscious students. The university's **Visitor Services center** (☎ 510-642-5215; www.berkeley.edu; 101 University Hall, 2200 University Ave at Oxford St; ⏰ 8:30am-4:30pm Mon-Fri, tours 10am Mon-Sat, 1pm Sun) has information and leads free campus tours. Cal's landmark is the 1914 Sather Tower (also called the 'Campanile'), with rides (adult $2) to the top. The Bancroft Library displays the small gold nugget that started the California gold rush in 1848.

Other campus highlights include the **Berkeley Art Museum** (☎ 510-642-0808; www.bampfa.berkeley.edu; 2626 Bancroft Way; admission $8; ⏰ 11am-5pm Wed-Sun, to 7pm Thu), east of Telegraph Ave. It may resemble a concrete bunker, but its galleries help sharpen the cutting edge of modern art. Also here, the highly respected **Pacific Film Archive** (☎ 510-642-1124) screens little-known independent and avant-garde films, while **Cafe Muse** (☎ 510-548-4366; ⏰ lunch, to 7pm Thu) features a 'raw' menu.

Leading to the campus's main south gate, **Telegraph Avenue** is as far-out and gritty as San Francisco's Haight Ave, and even more crowded with cafés, cheap eats, record stores and bookstores – including the peer-less **Cody's Books** (☎ 510-845-7852; www.codysbooks.com; 2454 Telegraph Ave; ⏰ 10am-10pm).

For an urban escape, head for **Tilden Park** (☎ 510-562-7275; www.ebparks.org) in the Berke-ley hills, which includes hiking trails, picnic areas, swimming at Lake Anza, and plenty of kid stuff, such as pony rides and a steam train. Most activities charge a small fee.

Sleeping

Basic and midrange motels are clustered west of campus along University Ave.

Bancroft Hotel (☎ 510-549-1000, 800-549-1002; www.bancrofthotel.com; 2680 Bancroft Way; r $129; P ✗) Across from campus, this old-fashioned 22-roomer is on three floors (no elevator). Parking $10.

Hotel Durant (☎ 510-845-8981, 800-238-7268; www.hoteldurant.com; 2600 Durant Ave; r $160-175; P ⬚) The 140-room Durant is more modern and polished in decor and service, with a ground-floor restaurant and bar. Parking $10.

Eating & Drinking

Chez Panisse (☎ 510-548-5525; www.chezpanisse.com; 1517 Shattuck Ave; set-price menu $45-75, café mains $15-18; ⏰ closed Sun) Genuflect at the birthplace of California cuisine; Alice Waters' formal res-taurant downstairs is open only for set-price dinners. Upstairs, a more relaxed café serves lunch and dinner. Why all the fuss over fresh, organic, local produce? Reserve a table (up to a month ahead) and find out.

Also in the Gourmet Ghetto, which is along Shattuck Ave north of University Ave, are **Cheese Board Pizza** (☎ 510-549-3055; 1512 Shat-tuck Ave; ⏰ 11:30am-2pm, 4:30-7pm Tue-Sat) and the adjacent **Cheese Board Collective** (☎ 510-549-3183; 1504 Shattuck Ave; ⏰ 10am-6pm Tue-Fri, to 5pm Sat). Both serve treats that are a food lover's dream.

Still, gourmet doesn't have to empty your wallet. **Vik's Chaat Corner** (☎ 510-644-4412; 726 Allston Way at 4th St; items $3.50-6; ⏰ 11am-6pm Tue-Sun) is off-the-chart good, but nothing more than a warehouse-district Indian cafeteria.

A prime student pick is **Café Intermezzo** (2442 Telegraph Ave; meals $4-6; ⏰ 8am-10pm).

To begin exploring Berkeley's bar scene, you could do much worse than the back patio at **Jupiter** (☎ 510-843-8277; 2181 Shattuck Ave).

Getting There & Around

AC Transit (☎ 510-817-1717; www.actransit.org) runs local buses in Berkeley as well as between Berkeley/Oakland ($1.50) and San Francisco ($3). From San Francisco, it's a short trip on **BART** (www.bart.gov) to the Downtown Ber-keley station ($3.05), which is four blocks from the main Cal campus gate.

PENINSULA & SOUTH BAY

San Francisco is the tip of a 30-mile penin-sula sandwiched between the Pacific Ocean and San Francisco Bay. Do you know the way to San Jose? Head south along either Hwy 101 or the more scenic I-280.

Along Hwy 1

Far more scenic than either freeway is nar-row, coastal Hwy 1, along which beaches are

CALIFORNIA

strung like pearls. North of Montara State Beach, unsigned **Gray Whale Cove State Beach** is notable as a clothing-optional strand.

Just south, the **HI Point Montara Lighthouse Hostel** (Map p824; ☎ 650-728-7177; dm $18-21, r $51-57), on Hwy 1 at 16th St, is a scuffed, clean and popular hostel with a private beach. Follow signs to **Moss Beach Distillery** (☎ 650-728-5595; 140 Beach Way; sandwiches & mains $12-16; ☽ noon-8pm), a historic spot with good fish-and-chips and an ocean-view deck that's da bomb at sunset.

Quiet **Half Moon Bay** (Map p824) is rimmed by a long, attractive state beach ($6 day use), and its Pillar Point Harbor has several good restaurants and a brewpub.

Ten miles south and 1 mile east on Hwy 84, the friendly **San Gregorio General Store** (☎ 650-726-0565; Hwy 84 & Stage Rd; ☽ 9am-7pm) has a saloon, cowboy hats, poetry, nostalgic odds and ends, and live music on weekends – when its distinctive northern California ambience really comes alive.

Five miles south, **Pescadero** is a good stop for picnic supplies, and it's home to the locally renowned **Duarte's Tavern** (☎ 650-879-0464; www.duartestavern.com; 202 Stage Rd; ☽ 7am-9pm; lunch $6-11), where the creamy artichoke soup, fresh baked bread and olallieberry (like a raspberry) pie constitute the perfect meal.

Another 5 miles south, beds at **HI Pigeon Point Lighthouse Hostel** (Map p824; ☎ 650-879-0633; dm $19-23, r $56-59) are in constant demand, but it remains well managed. It's a quiet, windswept coastal perch.

Three miles south, **Costanoa** (☎ 650-879-1100, 877-262-7848; www.costanoa.com; 2001 Rossi Rd at Hwy 1; tent/RV $40-55, bungalow $115-145, cabin $170-185, lodge $195-255) is posh personified. Tents, canvas bungalows and cabins share 'comfort stations,' with showers, fireplaces *and* saunas. Lodge rooms have private baths, and all rates include a buffet breakfast at the café.

Año Nuevo State Reserve (☎ 650-879-0227; $6 day use; ☽ 8am-dusk, closed Dec 1-14), 3 miles south of Costanoa, is highly recommended for its year-round elephant-seal colony. During the mating and birthing season (December 15 to March 31), visitors are allowed only on heavily booked guided tours (☎ reservations 800-444-4445; per person $5); otherwise, visitation is not restricted.

Palo Alto

Palo Alto is the northern edge of Silicon Valley, the epicenter of the country's high-tech industry, and the home to Stanford University. Affluent and conservative, Palo Alto is still a college town at heart.

Stanford University opened in 1891, just two years before founder Leland Stanford's death. The lovely campus was built on the Stanford family homestead and, as a result, is still called 'the farm.' From downtown Palo Alto, University Ave, the town's main drag, spears straight into the heart of the spacious campus. **Visitor Information Services** (☎ 650-723-2560; www.stanford.edu) is in Memorial Hall, across from Hoover Tower, which you can climb for $2. The gorgeous **Cantor Arts Center** (☎ 650-723-4177; admission free; ☽ 11am-5pm Wed-Sun), on Museum Way, displays classical and contemporary art.

A few blocks from campus, **Cardinal Hotel** (☎ 650-323-5101; www.cardinalhotel.com; 235 Hamilton Ave; r with bath $135-165, without bath $70-90; ☒ ▯) offers guests graciously old-fashioned lodgings. Shared facilities are spotless, making the bathless rooms an excellent deal.

SAN JOSE

Perpetually in the shadow of its more eccentric neighbors, San Jose has a reputation for dull, sprawling conformity, but really, it's not so bad. In fact, as the undisputed 'capital' of Silicon Valley, it has grown astonishingly fast in recent years and is California's third-largest city. Especially if you have kids, San Jose's handful of stellar sites deserves an excursion from San Francisco.

Downtown San Jose is at the junction of Hwy 87 and I-280. The **visitor center** (☎ 408-295-9600; www.sanjose.org; 408 Almaden; ☽ 8am-5pm Mon-Fri) is inside the convention center.

Sights

If Silicon Valley's tech gurus poured all their mojo into one place, painted it neon, and charged admission, it would look remarkably like the **Technology Museum of Innovation** (☎ 408-294-8324; www.thetech.org; 201 S Market St; adult $9.50, child 3-12 $7; ☽ 10am-5pm, Tue-Sun winter). Exploring inventions and creativity in every discipline, interactive exhibits embody the scope and future of the computer revolution. Don't tell slack-jawed adults this was built for the kids.

Children's Discovery Museum (☎ 408-298-5437; www.cdm.org; 180 Woz Way, San Jose; admission $7; ☽ 10am-5pm Mon-Sat, from noon Sun, Tue-Sun winter) Got kids too young for the Tech? Bring them here. This enormous interactive play space will keep them busy all day.

The underappreciated **San Jose Museum of Art** (☎ 408-294-2787; www.sanjosemuseumofart.org; 110 S Market St; admission free; ☺ 11am-5pm Tue-Sun) has a small collection focused on Bay Area and West Coast modern artists.

An anachronism in this high-tech town, the **Rosicrucian Egyptian Museum & Planetarium** (☎ 408-947-3635; www.egyptianmuseum.org; Naglee & Park Aves; adult/child 5-10 $9/5; ☺ 10am-5pm Mon-Fri, 11am-6pm Sat & Sun) has the largest collection of Egyptian artifacts on display west of the Mississippi River. Highlights include real mummies and a re-created Egyptian tomb.

Sleeping & Eating

Arena Hotel (☎ 408-294-6500, 800-954-6835; www .pacifichotels.com; 817 The Alameda; r weekend/midweek $80/90; ⓟ ▣ 🐾) Just west of downtown San Jose, the Arena offers spacious, amenity-laden rooms, every bath is a Jacuzzi, and a buffet breakfast *and* dinner are included. It's a great deal.

Original Joe's (☎ 408-292-7030; 301 S First St; pasta $11-14, mains $17-25; ☺ 11am-1am). 'Institution' is an overused word, but nothing else fits Joe's. Tuxedoed waiters treat you like the Godfather at a sit-down, while the huge portions of traditional Italian cooking would test even Marlon Brando. Recommendations? Veal parm, chicken cacc, or fresh ravioli.

71 Saint Peter (☎ 408-971-8523; www.71saintpeter .com; 71 N San Pedro Square; sandwiches $9-12, mains $15-22; ☺ lunch Mon-Fri, dinner Mon-Sat) An attractive choice for Italian cuisine and a touch of romance. Other options line the street.

NORTHERN CALIFORNIA

Mountains ring California, forming a sort of bath tub. The Coastal Range in the west, and the mighty Sierra Nevada at the state's eastern edge cradle the vast, sea-level Central Valley, one of America's breadbaskets. Famous sights near the coast include redwood trees and California's fabled Wine Country; in the Sierra you'll find Yosemite and Lake Tahoe.

WINE COUNTRY

A patchwork of vineyards covers toast-colored hills in pastoral Wine Country, which extends from the cool, foggy Pacific coast to the hot, inland Sonoma and Napa Valleys. One of the world's premier viticulture regions, it invites comparison with some of France's greatest terroirs. There are over 500 wineries in Napa and Sonoma Counties, but quality, not quantity, sets the region apart.

Wine Country is an easy day trip from San Francisco, but stay overnight if you can; the heavy afternoon summer traffic is a buzz-kill. Free tastings exist no more in fancy Napa; a 'flight' of several varieties runs $5 to $15, but as high as $30. In down-to-earth Sonoma, tastings range from free to $5, and you'll probably meet the vintner's family dog. Wineries are open 10am to 4pm or 5pm daily. Some reduce hours in winter; call ahead. A cushy, if touristy, way to see Wine Country is on the **Napa Valley Wine Train** (☎ 707-253-2111, 800-427-4124; www.winetrain.com; adult/child under 12 $48/24, plus lunch $30-43/23 or dinner $48-68/23), which offers three-hour trips daily.

Napa Valley

Over 200 wineries crowd 30-mile-long Napa Valley along two main arteries: busy St Helena Hwy (Hwy 29) and curvy Silverado Trail, a mile or two east.

Downtown Napa is decidedly plain. Follow signs for the **Napa Valley Visitors Bureau** (☎ 707-226-7459; www.napavalley.com; 1310 Napa Town Center; ☺ 9am-5pm), which has brochures, lodging updates and the free *Inside Napa Valley*, with a comprehensive winery guide. Check e-mail at **Napa Library** (☎ 707-253-4241; www.co.napa.ca.us; 580 Coombs St; ☺ 10am-9pm Mon-Thu, to 5:30pm Fri, to 5pm Sat, 2-9pm Sun).

SIGHTS

Napa is known for cabernet sauvignon; seek out the boutique wineries. The following are listed south to north.

Sample tiny-scale-production cult wines at supercool **Vintners' Collective** (☎ 707-255-7150; www.vintnerscollective.com; 1245 Main St; ☺ Wed-Mon).

Don't miss **Copia** (☎ 707-259-1600; www.copia .org; 500 1st St; adult/child 13-20/under 12 $13/5/free; ☺ 10am-5pm Wed-Mon), a cultural center that brings together all things Wine Country in one heady package. From the interactive exhibits about America's culinary habits to the primer on wine tasting, to cooking demonstrations, to a restaurant and café, to films and concerts: a visit will leave you sated.

West of town in the Carneros district, see modern art at 217-acre **DiRosa Preserve**

CALIFORNIA

(☎ 707-226-5991; www.dirosapreserve.org; 5200 Carneros Hwy; admission $3; ☿ Tue-Fri 9:30am-3pm, tours by appointment Tue-Sat), then visit the **Artesa Winery** (☎ 707-224-1668; www.artesawinery.com; 1345 Henry Rd) for top-of-the-world vistas, stunning architecture and bubbly.

North of town, wine and art merge at **Hess Collection** (☎ 707-255-1144; www.hesscollection .com; 4411 Redwood Rd). Works by Francis Bacon, Louis Soutter and others are spread over three floors, with the tasting room downstairs. For earthy sangiovese and fruit-forward pinot grigio, visit **Luna Vineyards** (☎ 707-255-2474; www.lunavineyards.com; 2921 Silverado Trail). Chef-owned **Robert Sinskey** (☎ 707-944-9090; www.robertsinskey.com; 6320 Silverado Trail) does wine-and-cheese parings (call ahead).

In Rutherford, definitely visit ever-so-fun **Frog's Leap** (☎ 707-963-4704; www.frogsleap .com; 8815 Conn Creek Rd), which is free, but you *must* call ahead. Francis Ford Coppola's **Niebaum-Coppola Winery** (☎ 707-968-1100; www .niebaum-coppola.com; 1991 St Helena Hwy; tour $25) has a free movie 'museum,' including a Tucker car and Coppola's *Godfather* Oscars; the optional $25 tour focuses on the dramatic 1887 Inglenook chateau.

St Helena is the Beverly Hills of Napa. The **Culinary Institute of America** (☎ 707-967-2320; www2.ciachef.edu/greystone; 2555 Main St; cooking demonstration $12.50; ☿ 10am-5pm), a graduate school for chefs, occupies the Christian Brothers' 1889 chateau and features exhibits and twice-daily cooking demos. Cookbook lovers: Visit the campus store. The attached, well-regarded **Wine Spectator Greystone restaurant** (☎ 707-967-1010; mains $17-29) serves less-pricey appetizers in its bar and lovely garden.

Near Calistoga, architecture, art and wine harmonize at **Clos Pegase** (☎ 707-942-4981; www .clospegase.com; 1060 Dunaweal Lane), which has a $65 million modern-art collection.

Calistoga is the best town for lingering, particularly in its famous **thermal spas** or mud baths. **Indian Springs** (☎ 707-942-4913; 1712 Lincoln Ave) and Golden Haven (right) are both good picks; packages last an hour and start around $75, not including extras like massages. For the complete Northern California, clothing-optional experience, head for **Harbin Hot Springs** (☎ 707-987-2477; www.harbin.org; day use midweek/weekend $25/30, dm $35/50, r $60-120/90-180), 4 miles north of Middletown, which is 12 miles north of Calistoga. There's a vegetarian restaurant; bring linen for dorms.

SLEEPING & EATING

Napa has midrange chain-style motels – Chablis Inn, John Muir Inn, Redwood Inn, Discovery Inn, Travelodge – but otherwise valley lodgings are expensive, particularly on weekends. Your best bet for sleeping is Calistoga.

Calistoga Inn (☎ 707-942-4101; www.calistogainn .com; 1250 Lincoln Ave, Calistoga; r without bath midweek/ weekend $75/125) Rooms don't have TVs or phones. Amble downstairs to the friendly restaurant and bar.

El Bonita Motel (☎ 707-963-3216, 800-541-3284; www.elbonita.com; 195 Main St; r $135-249) Book in advance to secure a room at this sought-after St Helena motel.

Golden Haven (☎ 707-942-6793; www.goldenhaven .com; 1713 Lake St, Calistoga; r midweek/weekend from $79/99) Nothing-special rooms at great prices.

Bothe-Napa Valley State Park (☎ 707-942-4575, reservations 800-444-7275; www.reserveamerica.com; campsites $15-20; ☒) For camping; gorgeous hiking beneath redwoods.

French Laundry (☎ 707-944-2380; www.french laundry.com; 6640 Washington St, Yountville; fixed-price menu $175; ☿ dinner nightly, lunch Fri-Sun) The pinnacle of California dining, the French Laundry is epic, a high-wattage culinary experience on par with the world's best. Book two months ahead at 10am sharp.

Gordon's Cafe & Wine Bar (☎ 707-944-8246; 6770 Washington St, Yountville; sandwiches & salads $5-10; ☿ to 3pm) Hang with locals at this unpretentious midvalley breakfast and lunch spot.

Oakville Grocery (☎ 707-944-8802; www.oakville grocery.com; 7856 St Helena Hwy, at Oakville Crossroad) *The* place for stinky cheeses, crusty breads, sandwiches and picnics.

All Seasons Bistro (☎ 707-942-9111; www.allseasons napavalley.net; 1400 Lincoln Ave, Calistoga; ☿ lunch Fri-Sun, dinner nightly) For eclectic Euro-Cal bistro fare; winemakers eat here.

Sonoma Valley

Seventeen-mile-long Sonoma Valley is less commercial than Napa and has about 60 wineries, most just off Hwy 12. Unlike Napa, most Sonoma wineries allow picnicking.

Kick-back-casual **Sonoma** anchors the valley's southern end. The **visitor center** (☎ 707-996-1090, 800-576-6662; www.sonomavalley.com; 453 1st St E; ☿ 9am-5pm) is on historic Sonoma Plaza, which is surrounded by restaurants and shops. Check e-mail at **Adobe Net Cafe** (☎ 707-935-0390; www.adobenetcafé.com; 135 W Napa St).

SIGHTS & ACTIVITIES

Sonoma State Historical Park (☎ 707-938-1519; www.parks.ca.gov; adult/child under 17 $2/free; ⏰ 10am-5pm) includes the 1823 Sonoma Mission, Sonoma Barracks, Vallejo home 0.5 miles away and Petaluma Adobe (15 miles west near suburban Petaluma), a wonderful vision of 19th-century California.

Down a quiet country road in Sonoma, **Gundlach-Bundschu** (☎ 707-938-5277; www.gunbun .com; 2000 Denmark St) feels like a storybook castle, with its own lake, picnicking and hiking.

Just west of charming **Glen Ellen,** on the road to Jack London State Historic Park, **Benziger** (☎ 707-935-3000, 888-490-2739; www.benziger .com; 1883 London Ranch Rd; tours $10) is a great place to learn about winemaking with tractor-driven vineyard tours. Taste Syrah in a garage at tiny, Aussie-owned **Loxton Cellars** (☎ 707-935-7221; www.loxtonwines.com; 11466 Dunbar Rd). In Kenwood, meet the whacko winemaker at **Kaz Winery** (☎ 707-833-2536; www .kazwinery.com; 233 Adobe Canyon Rd; ⏰ Fri-Mon).

There's nothing special about sprawling **Santa Rosa**, at the valley's northern end, but it's convenient and affordable. The best reason to visit is the **Charles M Schulz Museum** (☎ 707-579-4452; www.schulzmuseum.org; 2301 Hardies Lane; adult/child $8/5; ⏰ noon-5pm Mon & Wed-Fri, 10am-5pm Sat & Sun), dedicated to Santa Rosa's native son and his creation, Charlie Brown and the Peanuts gang. Warm-hearted exhibits remind you why 'Sparky' was without peer among cartoonists; next door there's an **ice-skating rink** (☎ 707-546-7147; adult/child $9-12/7.50-10); call for times.

SLEEPING

The town of Sonoma makes a convenient base.

Sonoma Hotel (☎ 707-996-2996, 800-468-6016; www.sonomahotel.com; 110 W Spain St, Sonoma; r incl breakfast midweek/weekend from $145/195; ✗) On Sonoma Plaza, this historic hotel has stylish furnishings. Several small rooms are cheaper.

El Pueblo Inn (☎ 707-996-3651, 800-900-8844; www.elpuebloinn.com; 896 W Napa St, Sonoma; r old/new midweek $110/165, weekend $150/185; P ✗ ⚲) One mile west of downtown Sonoma, El Pueblo has comfy older motel rooms and fresher-looking newer ones.

Jack London Lodge (☎ 707-938-8510; www.jack londonlodge.com; 13740 Arnold Dr, Glen Ellen; r midweek/weekend $120/170; P ✗ ⚲) Book ahead for these better-than-average motel rooms.

Sugarloaf Ridge State Park (☎ 707-833-5712, reservations 800-444-7275; www.reserveamerica.com; campsites $15-20) North of Kenwood on Adobe Canyon Rd.

If you're conserving cash, Santa Rosa's Cleveland Ave has several chain motels: **Sandman Hotel** (☎ 707-544-8570; 3421 Cleveland Ave; s/d $85/90; P ⚲)

Hillside Inn (☎ 707-546-9353; www.hillside-inn.com; 2901 Fourth St; s/d/q $73/76/88; P ⚲) Town's best-kept motel is closest to Sonoma Valley, too; add $4 for kitchens.

EATING

Cafe la Haye (☎ 707-935-5994; www.cafelahaye.com; 140 E Napa St, Sonoma; mains $15-23; ⏰ dinner Tue-Sat) Attached to an arts center, Cafe La Haye serves big-city cooking in a tiny bistro.

Sonoma Market (☎ 707-996-3411; 500 W Napa St, Sonoma) Get picnic supplies here.

Fig Cafe (☎ 707-938-2130; www.thefigcafe.com; 13690 Arnold Dr, Glen Ellen; mains $11-17; ⏰ dinner nightly, brunch Fri-Sun) Euro-Cal comfort food in a casual café worth seeking out.

Getting There & Around

Wine Country is 90 minutes north of San Francisco via Hwy 101 or I-80. Buses get you to the valleys but aren't ideal for vineyard-hopping. For transit information, dial ☎ 511. **Greyhound buses** (☎ 800-231-2222; www.greyhound .com) run from San Francisco to Santa Rosa ($15.50). **Golden Gate Transit** (☎ 415-923-2000; www.goldengate.org) runs from San Francisco to Petaluma ($6.90) and Santa Rosa ($7.60), where you connect with **Sonoma County Transit** (☎ 707-576-7433; www.sctransit.com).

For Napa, take BART trains (p842) from San Francisco to El Cerrito, and transfer to **Vallejo Transit** (☎ 707-648-4666; www.vallejotransit .com) to Vallejo; **Napa Valley Vine** (☎ 707-255-7631, 800-696-6443; www.napavalleyvine.net) buses run between Vallejo, Napa and Calistoga.

Bicycles cost about $30 per day. Rent in Yountville (and book tours) at **Napa Valley Bike Tours** (☎ 707-944-2953, 800-707-2453; www.napavalley biketours.com; 6488 Washington St), in Calistoga at **Calistoga Bike Shop** (☎ 707-942-9687, 866-942-2453; www.calistogabikeshop.com; 1318 Lincoln Ave) and in Sonoma at **Sonoma Valley Cyclery** (☎ 707-935-3377; www.sonomavalleycyclery.com; 20093 Broadway).

NORTH COAST

The craggy North Coast is marked by fog-shrouded coves, rocky cliffs, timber-strewn beaches and redwood forests. Highway 1

CALIFORNIA

twists and turns up the coast, while US 101 zips through fertile valleys east of the coastal mountains. The two roads join at Leggett, the beginning of redwood country.

Bodega Bay to Fort Bragg

Winding above crashing surf, along narrow cliffs and grassy flatlands, Hwy 1 along the Sonoma and Mendocino coast may be the most beautiful – and hard-to-drive – stretch of main road in Northern California. Take it easy. And pack a sweater: summertime fog means chilly daytime temperatures. The beaches are gorgeous, but obey signs: frigid water and rip tides make swimming dangerous. November to April, gray whales migrate down the coast; look for whale-watching trips. Budget four hours without stops.

Bodega Bay is a small fishing town; a series of fantastic state beaches extends north to Jenner. Head inland 3 miles to tiny Bodega, which you'll recognize from Hitchcock's 1963 thriller *The Birds*. **Bodega Bay Sportfishing** (☎ 707-875-3495; 1410 Bay Flat Rd; adult $30) runs whale-watching trips. **Bodega Bay Surf Shack** (☎ 707-875-3944; www.bodegabaysurf.com; surfboards per day $13, kayaks per 4 hr $45) rents surfboards and kayaks.

Jenner is perched on picturesque coastal hills at the mouth of the Russian River, above a resident harbor-seal colony; look for them from Hwy 1 turnouts north of town.

The centerpiece of **Fort Ross State Park** (☎ 707-847-3286, 707-847-3708; www.parks.ca.gov; per car $6, campsites $15) is a reconstructed 1812 Russian trading post with interesting historical exhibits. There's also primitive, first-come, first-served camping.

Salt Point State Park (☎ 707-847-3221, reservations 800-444-7275; www.reserveamerica.com; per car $4, campsites $10-25) has hiking trails, tide pools, two campgrounds and Gerstle Cove Marine Reserve and Kruse Rhododendron State Reserve, where pink blooms spot the green, wet woods in springtime.

Gualala (wah-*la*-la), founded in 1858 as a lumber mill, has a breathtaking coastal location. A mile south, **Gualala Point Regional Park** (☎ 707-785-2377, reservations 707-565-2267; www.sonoma-county.org/parks; per car $4, campsites $17) has a redwood-forested campground, windswept beach and hiking trails.

Pretty **Point Arena** has a cute main street and an ugly fishing pier. Just north, ascend the 1908 **Point Arena Lighthouse & Museum**

(☎ 707-882-2777;   www.pointarenalighthouse.com; adult/child $5/1) for knockout coastal views.

Eight miles north of Elk, **Van Damme State Park** (☎ 707-937-5804, reservations 800-444-7275; www.reserveamerica.com; per car $6, campsites $25) has popular **Fern Canyon Trail**, passing through a pygmy forest, and good camping.

The definitive North Coast town, **Mendocino** puts the 'Q' in quaint. Perched on a jaw-droppingly beautiful headland, 'Mendo' is known for Cape Cod–style architecture, galleries, fine restaurants, cutesy shops and *no* McDonald's. Plan to stroll. The **visitor center** (☎ 707-937-5397; www.gomendo.com; 11am-4pm) is in the Ford House on Main St. The **Mendocino Art Center** (☎ 707-937-5818; www.mendocinoartcenter.org; 45200 Little Lake St; 10am-5pm) is the cultural hub.

Though it's getting gentrified, **Fort Bragg** is more blue collar, with an inviting downtown and cheaper food and lodging. Fort Bragg's pride and joy is the 1885 **Skunk Train** (☎ 704-964-6371; 866-457-5865; www.skunktrain.com; adult/child 3-11 $35/20), whose diesel and steam engines make half-day trips into the woods. Join fishing and whale-watching trips at Noyo Harbor, at the south end of town.

SLEEPING & EATING

The **Bodega Harbor Inn** (☎ 707-875-3594; www.bodegaharborinn.com; 1345 Bodega Ave; r $60-95;), in Bodega Bay, has affordable cottage-style rooms. Food-savvy art freaks dine at **Seaweed Café** (☎ 707-875-2700; www.seaweedcafe.com; 1580 Eastshore Dr; mains dinner $18-27, lunch $10-18; Sat & Sun lunch, Thu-Sun dinner).

The historic **Gualala Hotel** (☎ 707-884-3441; www.thegualalahotel.com; r without/with bath $55/85-105), on Hwy 1 in Gualala, has bare-bones basic rooms above a saloon. Also in Gualala, gorgeous and quirky **St Orres** (☎ 707-884-3303; www.saintorres.com; Hwy 1; r without bath incl breakfast $90-105, cottages from $135; dinner mains $40) has a hand-hewn Russian-style redwood main hotel, secluded cottages and a dramatic Cal-cuisine restaurant. Or you could splurge on dinner at **Pangaea** (☎ 707-884-9669; www.pangaeacafe.com; 39165 S Hwy 1; mains $22-35; dinner Wed-Sun). Just north, ever-so-charming **Mar Vista Cottages** (☎ 707-884-3522, 877-855-3522; www.marvistamendocino.com; 35101 S Hwy 1; cottages from $140;) has the North Coast's sweetest cottages.

Mendocino is a lovely, but expensive, place to stay. The visitor center website has complete listings. **Sweetwater Spa & Inn**

(☎ 800-300-4140, 707-937-4076; www.sweetwaterspa .com; 44840 Main St; r $125-220) runs dozens of attractive lodgings; all rates include use of the spa, which can also be enjoyed on its own.

Unfussy travelers should head for **Jughandle Creek Farm** (☎ 707-964-4630; http://jughandle .creek.org; r/cabins adult $27-35, student $21-30, child $11, camping $11), in Caspar, opposite Jug Handle State Reserve. Hostel-like private rooms and cabins share baths (bring sleeping bags); the farmhouse has a kitchen. Call ahead to arrange work-stay discounts.

Fort Bragg has many nondescript midrange motels. The best bargain is the **Colombi Motel** (☎ 707-964-5773; www.colombimotel.com; 647 Oak St; r $45-70). For a B&B, try the 1886 **Weller House** (☎ 707-964-4415, 877-893-5537; www.weller house.com; 524 Stewart St; r incl breakfast $115-180), with its rooftop hot tub. The **North Coast Brewing Co** (☎ 707-964-3300; 444 N Main St) serves its award-winning brews in its pub and restaurant. Local musicians play at always-fun **Headlands Coffeehouse** (☎ 707-964-1987; 120 E Laurel St).

GETTING THERE & AWAY

Mendocino Transit Authority (MTA; ☎ 800-696-4682; www.4mta.org) operates bus No 65 daily from Fort Bragg south to Santa Rosa via Willits and Ukiah ($16, 3 hours); at Santa Rosa, catch San Francisco–bound bus No 80 ($7.60), operated by **Golden Gate Transit** (☎ 415-923-2000; www.goldengate.org). Neither Greyhound nor Amtrak serves towns along Hwy 1.

Russian River

In western Sonoma County, two hours north of San Francisco (via Hwys 101 and 116), the Russian River winds through vineyards, redwood forests and small, honky-tonk vacation towns, which get packed in summer. **Guerneville** is the biggest. It's popular with gays and lesbians, young families and Harley-Davidson riders. Canoeing is a favorite activity. The **visitor center** (☎ 707-869-3533; www.russianriver.com; 16209 1st St; ☼ 10am-5pm, to 4pm Sun) has maps and lodging updates.

The 805-acre **Armstrong Redwoods State Reserve** (☎ 707-869-2015; per car $4, campsites $15), two miles north of Guerneville, protects magnificent old-growth redwoods. Camp at nearby Austin Creek.

For lazy down-river floats, *everyone* rents canoes from **Burke's Canoe Trips** (☎ 707-887-1222; www.burkescanoetrips.com; 8600 River Rd; canoes $55), 7 miles east of town; make reservations.

South of town, taste bubbly in a hilltop barn at **Iron Horse Vineyards** (☎ 707-887-1507; www.ironhorsevineyards.com; 97786 Ross Station Rd; ☼ 10am-3:30pm).

Nine miles west of Guerneville, tiny, über-quaint **Duncans Mills** has kayak rentals and the always-good **Cape Fear Café** (☎ 707-865-9246; 25191 Hwy 116; breakfast & lunch $8-15, dinner $16-24). The **Blue Heron** (☎ 707-865-9135; ☼ Tue-Sun) is *the* spot for music, microbrews and pub grub.

The **Bohemian Highway**, south of Monte Rio, winds south to some nifty discoveries in **Occidental**.

Healdsburg to Scotia

Sophisticated **Healdsburg** is centered on a green, Spanish-style plaza; plan to window-shop. Over 90 wineries within a 30-mile radius dot the Russian River, Dry Creek and Alexander valleys. Get a Wine Country map from the **Healdsburg Visitors Center** (☎ 707-433-6935, 800-648-9922; www.healdsburg.org; 217 Healdsburg Ave; ☼ 9am-5pm Mon-Fri, to 3pm Sat, 10am-2pm Sun). **Getaway Adventures** (☎ 707-763-3040, 800-499-2453; www.getawayadventures.com) leads bicycle tours.

Near the Russian River, check out pop art and sip zinfandel and chardonnay at oh-so-cool **Roshambo Winery** (☎ 707-433-7165; www .roshambowinery.com; 3000 Westside Rd). At the north end of Dry Creek Valley are two great bike-to wineries. Cute-as-a-button **Preston Vineyards** (☎ 707-433-3327, 800-305-9707; www.prestonvineyards .com; 9282 W Dry Creek Rd) is a 19th-century organic farm that makes sauvignon blanc, Rhône varietals, homemade bread and olive oil. Always-fun **Bella Vineyards** (☎ 707-473-9171, 866-572-3552; www.bellawinery.com; 9711 W Dry Creek Rd) serves big reds in a hillside cave.

For a detour, head to pastoral **Anderson Valley**, which is studded with vineyards and apple orchards; take winding Hwy 128 northwest to tiny **Boonville**, then return via Hwy 253 northeast to Ukiah. Cute **Hopland**, 15 miles south of Ukiah on Hwy 101, has Old West–style buildings and wine-tasting rooms. **Real Goods Solar Living Center** (☎ 707-744-2017; www .solarliving.org; 13771 S Hwy 101; admission by donation $1-5; ☼ 10am-6pm) is a 12-acre demonstration site for permaculture, environmentally friendly building methods and alternative-energy sources. **Fetzer winery** (☎ 800-846-8637; www.fetzer .com; 13601 E Side Rd) has gorgeous gardens.

Ukiah is the region's largest town, but has few attractions. The **visitor center** (☎ 707-462-4705; www.gomendo.com; 200 S School St; ☼ 9am-5pm

Mon-Fri) has countywide information. **Orr Hot Springs** (☎ 707-462-6277; hotwater@pacific.net; day use $22, dm $55-65, r & cottages $115-185; ☯ 10am-10pm), 15 miles west of Ukiah (Hwy 101 to N State St exit), is an earthy, clothing-optional hot springs (reservations required). Facilities include hot tubs, dorm rooms, private rooms, cottages and a communal kitchen.

North of tiny **Leggett** on Hwy 101, lose yourself under giant redwoods at **Richardson Grove State Park** (☎ 707-247-3318, reservations 800-444-7275; www.reserveamerica.com; per car $6, campsites $20). The summer-only **visitor center** (☯ 9am-5pm) has good exhibits. Campsites sit beside the Eel River.

Garberville and its ragged sister Redway, 2 miles away, became famous in the 1970s for the sinsemilla marijuana grown in the surrounding hills. Today Garberville is a quiet, one-street town with basic services, cheap motels and diners.

The **Lost Coast** became 'lost' when the state's highway system bypassed the rugged mountains of the King Range, which rise 4000ft within several miles of the ocean. The region is largely undeveloped; the scenery is stunning. From Garberville it's 23 miles along a rough road to Shelter Cove, a seaside subdivision with a deli, restaurant and motels. Talk to locals before venturing along back roads.

Along Hwy 101, 80-sq-mile **Humboldt Redwoods State Park** (☎ 707-946-2409, reservations 800-444-7275; www.reserveamerica.com; campsites $15-20) protects some of the world's oldest redwoods. The awe-inspiring **Avenue of the Giants**, a 32-mile, two-lane road winding through wonderful old-growth forests, runs parallel to Hwy 101. Book ahead for magnificent campsites near the informative **visitor center** (☎ 707-946-2409; ☯ 9am-5pm).

Ferndale, at the northern tip of the Lost Coast, has beautifully restored Victorians and a small-town sensibility epitomized by the Kinetic Sculpture Race every Memorial Day weekend. Or visit the **Kinetic Sculpture Museum** (☎ 707-786-9259; 580 Main St; admission free; ☯ 10am-5pm Mon-Sat, noon-4pm Sun).

Scotia is a rarity in the modern world: a 'company town' entirely owned and operated by the Pacific Lumber Company. It's a creepy place (smile: you're being watched). Stop by the **Scotia Museum & Visitors Center** (☎ 707-764-2222; www.palco.com; admission free; ☯ 8am-4:30pm Mon-Fri summer only), on Main St, and see if they're offering mill tours.

SLEEPING & EATING

Healdsburg's motels include the **L&M Motel** (☎ 707-433-6528; www.landmmotel.com; 70 Healdsburg Ave; r $100-120; ☒ ☒ ☒) and the nicer **Best Western Dry Creek** (☎ 707-433-0300, 800-222-5784; www.drycreekinn.com; 198 Dry Creek Rd; r $120-140; ☒ ☒).

Foodies: the venerable French Laundry (p848) now has competition in swanky **Cyrus** (☎ 707-433-3311; www.cyrusrestaurant.com; fixed-price menus $52-85; ☯ dinner Wed-Mon), an ultrachic dining room in the great tradition of the French-country auberge. **Bear Republic** (☎ 707-433-2337; 345 Healdsburg Ave; mains $7-11) is a lively brewpub.

In Hopland, look for the 1890 Hopland Inn, temporarily closed at the time of writing. The **Hopland Brewery Tavern** (☎ 707-744-1015; ☯ noon-7pm Thu-Mon) is the nation's oldest brewpub with awesome beer by the Mendocino Brewing Company, but no food.

In Ukiah, chain motels, such as Motel 6, Super 8 and Discovery Inn, line S State St. The best value is **Sunrise Inn** (☎ 707-462-6601; 650 S State St; r $48-68; ☒). Seven hundred–acre **Vichy Springs Resort** (☎ 707-462-9515; www.vichysprings.com; 2605 Vichy Springs Rd; day use $22-38, r incl breakfast s $115-165, d $155-205; ☒ ☒ ☒) has comfy lodge rooms, great hiking and wonderful carbonated mineral baths.

The historic Tudor-style **Benbow Inn** (☎ 707-923-2124, 800-355-3301; www.benbowinn.com; r $130-200), just south of Garberville off Hwy 101, indulges guests with complimentary decanted sherry in each lovely room; consider a riverside room if you're splurging. The white-tablecloth restaurant and wood-paneled bar are particularly inviting on foggy evenings.

Along the Avenue of the Giants, tiny Miranda has several eateries and **Miranda Gardens Resort** (☎ 707-943-3011; www.mirandagardens.com; cottages without kitchen $105-135, with kitchen $145-185; ☒). Stand-alone, roomy cottages are perfect for families and long stays.

In Ferndale, the four rooms at the restored **Hotel Ivanhoe** (☎ 707-786-9000; www.hotel-ivanhoe.com; 315 Main St; r $95-145; ☒) are done to the Victorian nines. There are also a decent Italian restaurant and lively saloon.

GETTING THERE & AROUND

Greyhound (☎ 800-231-2222; www.greyhound.com) operates from San Francisco to Ukiah ($25). The **Redwood Transit System** (☎ 707-443-0826; www.hta.org) operates buses Monday through Saturday between Scotia and Trinidad ($1.95, 2.5 hours).

Eureka to Crescent City

The largest town before Oregon, **Eureka** looks like nothing special from Hwy 101, just more American strip malls. But venture to Old Town and you'll find fabulous Victorians, inviting shops and good restaurants. The **Eureka visitor center** (☎ 707-442-3738, 800-356-6381; www.eurekachamber.com; 2112 Broadway; ☼ 8:30am-5pm Mon-Fri, 10am-4pm Sat) has maps and information. In Old Town, **Going Places** (☎ 707-443-4145; 328 2nd St) is a great travel bookstore.

The **Clarke Memorial Museum** (☎ 707-443-1947; 3rd & E Sts; admission by donation; ☼ 11am-4pm Tue-Sat) has impressive American Indian collections. One of only seven of its kind in the nation, **Blue Ox Millworks** (☎ 707-444-3437; www.blueoxmill.com; adult/child 6-12 $7.50/3.50; ☼ 9am-4pm Mon-Sat) hand-mills Victorian detailing using traditional carpentry and authentic 19th-century equipment. Fascinating, self-guided tours let you watch the craftsmen work. At this writing, there were plans to move; call for the current address. Cruise the harbor aboard the 1910 **Madaket** (☎ 707-445-1910; www.humboldtbaymaritimemuseum.com; adult/child 5-12/senior/teen $15/7.50/13/13; ☼ May-Oct), which departs from the foot of C St.

Nine miles north of Eureka, **Arcata** is a hippie-dippie university town with the same leftie-alternative bent as San Francisco's Haight St. Downtown's Arcata Plaza is the center of the scene. On the northeast side of town, **Humboldt State University** (☎ 707-826-3011; www.humboldt.edu) has an attractive campus and a good art gallery. The blissful **Finnish Country Sauna & Tubs** (☎ 707-822-2228; 5th & J Sts; per hr $15) has a café and outdoor tubs.

At the junction of Hwys 299 and 101 is a **California Welcome Center** (☎ 707-822-3619; www.arcatachamber.com; ☼ 9am-5pm), with tons of area information. See p858 for more on Hwy 299, the Trinity Scenic Byway.

Trinidad, about 12 miles north of Arcata, is a working fishing town perched above a spectacular bay. Follow Edward St to the harbor, where there's a wonderful beach and short hikes on dramatic Trinidad Head. Nearby Luffenholtz Beach is popular (but unpatroled) for surfing, and north of town, Patrick's Point Rd is dotted with lodging and campgrounds tucked into the forest. **Patrick's Point State Park** (☎ 707-677-3570; reservations 800-444-7275; www.reserveamerica.com; day use $6, campsites $15-20) has stunning rocky headlands, tide pools and camping.

On Hwy 101 a mile south of tiny **Orick** is the **visitor center for Redwood National & State Parks** (☎ 707-464-6101, ext 5265; www.nps.gov/redw; ☼ 9am-5pm). Together, Redwood National Park and Prairie Creek, Del Norte and Jedediah Smith State Parks are a designated World Heritage Site and contain almost half of the remaining old-growth redwood forests in California. The national park is free; the state parks have a reciprocal $6 day-use fee in some areas. Only the state parks have developed campsites ($20), all highly recommended. The visitor center has information about all the parks and free permits for backcountry camping and to visit Tall Trees Grove.

The highlights at Redwood National Park are **Lady Bird Johnson Grove** and **Tall Trees Grove**, home to several of the world's tallest trees, as well as roaming elk herds.

Prairie Creek Redwoods State Park (☎ 707-464-6101, ext 5301) has famous Fern Canyon, a sheer 60ft fissure overgrown with ferns. It's free to drive the 8-mile **Newton B Drury Scenic Parkway**, which passes through virgin redwood forests and runs parallel to Hwy 101.

There's little in **Klamath** except a giant redwood carving of Paul Bunyan at the entrance to the tourist trap **Trees of Mystery** (☎ 800-638-3389; www.treesofmystery.net; adult/senior/child $13.50/10/6.50; ☼ 9am-5pm, later in summer), though its **End of the Trail Museum** (admission free) has a collection of American Indian artifacts. Several miles north, **Del Norte Coast Redwoods State Park** (☎ 707-464-6101, ext 5120) contains redwood groves and 8 miles of unspoiled coastline.

On a crescent-shaped bay, **Crescent City** is the only sizable coastal town north of Arcata. It has few old buildings, as over half the town was destroyed by a tidal wave in 1964. The 1865 **Battery Point Lighthouse** (☎ 707-464-3089; admission $3; ☼ 10am-4pm Wed-Sun Apr-Oct), at the south end of A St, is accessible whenever the tide is out.

Jedediah Smith Redwoods State Park (☎ 707-464-6101, ext 5112), 5 miles northeast of Crescent City, is less crowded than the other parks but no less beautiful and lush. Its **Hiouchi Information Center** (☎ 707-464-6101, ext 5067; ☼ summer only) is on Hwy 199, 5 miles east of Hwy 101.

SLEEPING & EATING

Dozens of plain-Jane motels line Hwy 101 in Eureka; the cheapest are found south of downtown. On a hill above the highway is the family-run **Bayview Motel** (☎ 707-442-1673,

866-725-6813; www.bayviewmotel.com; 2844 Fairfield St; r $85; mains $20-34; ✕), a bright, clean mid-range choice. In Old Town, luxurious **Carter House Inns** (☎ 707-444-8062, 800-404-1390; www .carterhouse.com; 301 L St; r incl breakfast $190-210; ✕) runs a cushy hotel and several Victorian properties across the street. Its fashionable Restaurant 301 is famous for New French-Cal cuisine and a magnificent wine list.

On the nearby Samoa Peninsula, the ever-popular **Samoa Cookhouse** (☎ 707-442-1659; all-you-can-eat meals $10-15) is the dining hall of an 1893 lumber camp. It's a fun, atmospheric place where grub with all the fixin's is served on long, oilcloth-covered tables.

In Arcata, the 1915 **Hotel Arcata** (☎ 707-826-0217, 800-344-1221; www.hotelarcata.com; 708 9th St; r $79-105) isn't ornate, but the rooms are comfortable. Restaurants are on the square.

In Klamath, the wonderful 1914 **Requa Inn** (☎ 707-482-1425, 866-800-8777; www.requainn .com; 451 Requa Rd; r $85-135; ✕) has country-style rooms overlooking the river. The **HI Redwood Hostel** (☎ 707-482-8265; www.norcalhostels.org; 14480 Hwy 101; dm/r $20/45), 8 miles north of Klamath, occupies a stunningly beautiful spot.

A mile south of Crescent City, **Crescent Beach Motel** (☎ 707-464-5436; www.crescentbeachmotel .com; 1455 Hwy 101 S; s/d $81-90/86-96) has simple, plain rooms and million-dollar ocean views.

GETTING THERE & AROUND

Greyhound (☎ 800-231-2222; www.greyhound.com) serves Arcata; from San Francisco budget $35/7 hours. **Redwood Transit buses** (☎ 707-443-0826; www.hta.org) serve Arcata and Eureka on their Monday through Saturday Trinidad–Scotia routes ($1.95, 2½ hours).

SACRAMENTO

Sacramento – surrounded by suburbs and the flat, agricultural Central Valley – is often casually dismissed by California's sophisticated coast-dwellers. What provincialism! Actually, if you want to soak in California's gold rush and pioneer history, the state capital can't be beat. Its Old Sacramento is unadulterated touristy fun, an authentic if sanitized patch of the Old West with raised wooden sidewalks, parking meters for hitching posts, and real steam trains. Sacramento's stellar museums are a must-stop if you have kids or are headed to the Gold Country.

In 1839, Swiss immigrant John Sutter established a fort and pioneer community in present-day Sacramento – making it the area's first European settlement. After gold was discovered in the nearby foothills in 1848, the fort was quickly overrun by fortune-hungry miners. In 1854, after several years of legislative indecision, the riverfront settlement became California's permanent capital.

The **visitor center** (☎ 916-442-7644; www.discover gold.org; 1004 2nd St; ☯ 10am-5pm), in Old Sacramento can recommend hotels.

Sights

The gorgeous, 19th-century **state capitol** is at 10th St and Capitol Mall. It's worth seeing, and includes the **Capitol Museum** (☎ 916-324-0333; www.statecapitolmuseum.com; admission free; ☯ 9am-5pm), which conducts tours and has several period-furnished rooms. Don't miss the Assembly and Senate rooms, which are open to the public even when in session.

Along the Sacramento River, **Old Sacramento** (Old Sac; www.oldsacramento.com) contains California's largest concentration of historic buildings on the National Register, tons of restaurants and atmosphere, and three great museums. The **California State Railroad Museum** (☎ 916-323-9280, 916-445-6645; www.californiastate railroadmuseum.org; 125 I St; adults/children 6-17 $6/2; ☯ 10am-5pm) is the locomotive mother lode. It lets you get in, under, and over 20 enormous, meticulously restored engines and cars, plus ride a steam train ($6) on summer weekends. Next door, the **Discovery Museum** (☎ 916-264-7057; 101 I St; www.thediscovery.org; adults/child 13-17/child 4-12 $5/4/3; ☯ 10am-5pm, closed Mon in winter) brings to life gold rush-era Sacramento.

Nearby, Judge Edwin B Crocker's jaw-dropping Victorian home contains his visionary collection of 19th-century paintings, now the eponymous **Crocker Art Museum** (☎ 916-264-5423; www.crockerartmuseum.org; 3rd & O Sts; adult/child 7-17 $6/3; ☯ 10am-5pm Tue-Sun, to 9pm Thu).

Restored to its 1850s appearance, **Sutter's Fort** (☎ 916-445-4422; cnr 27th & L Sts; adult/child 6-16 $6/3; ☯ 10am-5pm) fills with costumed 'reen-actors' daily in summer, some Saturdays other times. Adjacent to the fort, the well-done **California State Indian Museum** (☎ 916-324-0971; admission $2; ☯ 10am-5pm) is small but very informative, with Ishi artifacts.

Sleeping & Eating

HI Sacramento Hostel (☎ 916-443-1691; 925 H St; dm $24, r $30-60; Ⓟ ✕ 🖳) What a gem! The public areas in this restored Victorian mansion are B&B quality, spacious dorms are clean, and staff members are aces, plus it's convenient to Old Sac. Parking $5. Internet $1 per 5 minutes.

Downtown has a glut of midrange chain hotels, including Quality Inn, Holiday Inn, Travelodge and Best Western.

Delta King (☎ 916-444-5464, 800-825-5464; www .deltaking.com; r incl breakfast midweek/weekend from $119/169; ⓟ ⓧ ⓧ) For some romance, try the beautiful, teeny-tiny cabins in this refurbished 1927 paddlewheeler docked on the river in Old Sac. Riverside (add $15) is best. Three ghosts included. Parking $12.

For restaurants, try Old Sac and J St north of 16 St.

Firehouse (916-442-4772; www.firehouseoldsac.com; 1112 2nd St; lunch mains $10-16, dinner $20-39; ☼ lunch & dinner Mon-Fri, dinner Sat) This venerable Old Sac favorite is a cut above, with a hidden courtyard, notable wine list, and gourmet tweaks to its steak-and-seafood menu. The portobello tower is tasty.

Rubicon (916-448-7032; 2004 Capitol Ave; items $6-8; ☼ 11am-11:30pm Mon-Thu, to 12:30am Fri & Sat, to 10pm Sun) For award-winning beer (try the IPA) and decent pub grub, join the locals at Rubicon.

Getting There & Around

Sacramento is 91 miles east of San Francisco via I-80, and 386 miles north of LA via I-5.

Sacramento International Airport (☎ 916-929-5411; www.sacairports.org), 15 miles north of downtown off I-5, is serviced by most major airlines.

Greyhound (☎ 800-231-2222; 7th & L Sts) serves San Francisco ($15, two hours), Los Angeles ($44, nine hours), Seattle ($75, 17½ hours) and other major towns.

Sacramento's **Amtrak** (☎ 800-872-7245; at 5th & l Sts) depot is near downtown. Trains leave daily for Oakland ($17, two hours), Los Angeles ($59, 14 hours), and Seattle ($90, 20½ hours).

Sacramento Regional Transit (☎ 916-321-2877; www.sacrt.com) runs a bus system (fare $1.50), a free downtown DASH trolley, and a light-rail commuter line.

GOLD COUNTRY

Hugging the western Sierra Nevada, California's Gold Country winds 300 scenic miles north to south along Hwy 49; the most interesting stretch, the one covered here, is from Nevada City to Sonora. The route is an atmospheric time-capsule: as some ramshackle mining towns decay into the foothills, others provide a modern taste of the Victorian good life with magnificently restored 19th-century hotels and saloons. Plus, there's a notable wine region (p857) and lots of outdoor activities.

The gold rush started on January 24, 1848, when James Marshall was inspecting the lumber mill he was building for John Sutter, near present-day Coloma. From the mill's tailrace water Marshall pulled out a gold nugget 'roughly half the size of a pea' – an inauspicious beginning to a legendary era.

The first true rush came from San Francisco in the spring of 1848. At first, men found gold so easily they thought nothing of spending (or gambling) all they had in one night. By the end of 1848 over 30,000 people had come, and by 1849 the real gold rush was on, with an additional 60,000 people (known as the 49ers) migrating to California in search of the 'Mother Lode.'

Gold Country is the start for many rafting trips on the American, Tuolumne, Kings and Stanislaus Rivers. **Whitewater Connection** (☎ 800-336-7238; www.whitewaterconnection.com), on Hwy 49 in Coloma, offers half-day trips (from $90) and longer excursions. **Wolf Creek Wilderness** (☎ 530-477-2722; www.wolfcreekwilderness .com; 595 E Main St, Grass Valley; kayaks per day from $40) has kayak rentals and lessons ($65 to $300).

Outside of Auburn off I-80, exit 121, is a **California Welcome Center** (☎ 530-887-2111; 13411 Lincoln Way; www.auburncwc.com; ☼ 9:30am-4:30pm Mon-Fri, 9am-3pm Sat, from 11am Sun) with statewide information, or contact the **Gold Country Visitors Association** (☎ 800-225-3764; www.calgold.org).

Northern Mines

Hwy 50 is the dividing line between the Southern and Northern Mines, which stretch south from Nevada City to Placerville.

Bright as a silver dollar, touristy **Nevada City** has polished up its once-rough streets with organic cafés, gourmet restaurants, and boutiques. Small museums trace the area's mining and immigrant history. For self-guided walking tours, visit the **chamber of commerce** (☎ 530-265-2692, 800-655-6569; www.nevadacitychamber.com; 132 Main St; ☼ 9am-5pm Mon-Fri, 11am-4pm Sat). The **Tahoe National Forest Headquarters** (☎ 530-265-4531; ☼ 8am-4:30pm Mon-Fri, plus Sat in summer), on Hwy 49 at the north end of Coyote St, has hiking and backcountry information. There's great exploring in the surrounding forest.

About 5 miles southwest, **Grass Valley** is historic but less precious; area locals – a mix of artists, hippies, farmers and ranchers – come here to buy groceries. Two miles east of town off Hwy 49, the **Empire Mine State Historic Park** (☎ 530-273-8522; www.empiremine.org; adults/children 6-16 $3/1; ☻ 9am-6pm summer, 10am-5pm winter) sits atop 367 miles of mine shafts that, from 1850 to 1956, produced six million ounces of gold. In summer, living-history weekends are a highlight; an underground tour of the main shaft is due to open in late 2006.

Auburn is one of Gold Country's most visited towns because its historic center is right off I-80. Within walking distance is the fine **Placer County Museum** (☎ 530-889-6500; 101 Maple St; admission free; ☻ 10am-4pm Tue-Sun) in the stately courthouse.

In summer, have a swim at the confluence of the North and South Forks of the American River, 3 miles south of Auburn on Hwy 49. Ask by the bridge for the best spots.

At **Coloma** is the **Marshall Gold Discovery State Historic Park** (☎ 530-622-3470; per car $5; ☻ park 8am-dusk). It contains a replica of Sutter's Mill, restored buildings, a museum (hours vary) and short hikes. Historic demonstrations occur daily, and the pretty riverside park makes a delightful picnic spot.

SLEEPING & EATING

In Nevada City, the **Outside Inn** (☎ 530-265-2233; www.outsideinn.com; 575 E Broad St; r $69-140; ☒ ☒ ☒) caters to outdoor enthusiasts; cute rooms are artistically rustic and whimsically painted. It's dog friendly and has wi-fi. Just outside of town, **Northern Queen Inn** (☎ 530-265-5824; www.northernqueeninn.com; 400 Railroad Ave; r $80-110; ☒ ☒) is an affordable, well-kept 86-room motel. Separate cottages have kitchens and are good for families.

For eats in town, **Citronée** (☎ 530-265-5697; www.citroneebistro.com; 320 Broad St; dinner mains $10-32; ☻ lunch & dinner Mon-Fri, plus dinner Sat) serves a good plate. The cross-pollinated French-California menu of seared ahi and steak frites, rabbit and ribs, is cheaper downstairs, fancier upstairs. Or park next to the pickups at the **Northridge** (☎ 530-478-0470; 773 Nevada St; pizza $8-15; ☻ noon-10pm), an unkempt roadside bar and pizza joint that's a plain ole good time.

In downtown Grass Valley, the restored, 1852 **Holbrooke Hotel** (☎ 530-273-1353, 800-933-7077; www.holbrooke.com; 212 W Main St; r from $85/95 midweek/weekend; ☒ ☒) has 28 Victorian-style rooms, with exposed brick, iron bedframes, elaborate wallpapers and wi-fi. It has its own recommended restaurant and bar and is near other good eats.

Also in Grass Valley, the coolest renovation of a historic property is the **Swan Levine House** (☎ 530-272-1873; www.swanlevinehouse.com; 328 S Church St; r $90-110; ☒ ☒), a rambling 19th-century hospital turned into a modern-art gallery. An attached printmaking studio is open for guests' use. Four huge, funky rooms are doily-free.

Along I-80 near Auburn, at exit 121, is **Ikedas** (☎ 530-885-4243; www.ikedas.com; 13500 Lincoln Way; ☻ 8am-7pm, to 8pm weekends), a decent market with excellent homemade pies, fast-food hamburgers and milkshakes. It's popular with Tahoe-bound travelers.

Southern Mines

The Southern Mines extend from Placerville south to Sonora and contain the most atmospheric gold rush–era towns. Some, like **Plymouth** ('Ole Pokerville'), **Amador City** and **Mokelumne Hill** (Moke Hill) are virtual ghost towns – a line of abandoned shopfronts slowly crumbling into photogenic oblivion. Others, like **Jackson**, **Murphys** and **Sutter Creek**, are doing quite well, thank you, but retain an unhurried, rural charm despite tourist makeovers. This section of Hwy 49 is a great place to be unhurried, yourself.

Talk about a time capsule: Jackson's **Amador County Museum** (☎ 209-223-6386; 225 Church St; admission free; ☻ 10am-4pm Wed-Sun) is the type of local history museum they don't make anymore. Quaint and personal, it dusts off the community's pride.

For an antidote to gold-rush fever, take Hwy 88 north to **Chaw'Se Indian Grinding Rock State Historic Park** (per car $6; campsites $20; ☻ dawn-dusk), which remains sacred ground for the local Miwok Indians. The magnificent 'grinding rock' is covered with ancient petroglyphs and mortar holes called chaw'ses. The park's **Regional Indian Museum** (☎ 209-296-7488; ☻ 11am-3pm Mon-Fri, 10am-4pm Sat & Sun) is excellent, and good camping is available.

On the way to Grinding Rock, **Black Chasm Cavern** (☎ 866-762-2837; www.caverntours.com; ☻ 9am-6pm daily, 10am-5pm winter; adults/children 3-13 $12/6) is so stunning *The Matrix* used it for a set, while 9 miles east of San Andreas, the granddaddy

---

FRUIT OF THE GOLD COUNTRY

The Gold Country contains one of California's *other* wine regions, and it's laid-back and inviting in the way Napa and Sonoma were 20 years ago – you know, when tastings were mostly free and the focus was on the grapes, not the lifestyle.

More than 50 family-run wineries dot the foothills east of Hwy 49 between Placerville and Plymouth. Many have growing reputations, and the region couldn't be prettier. Wineries are generally open year-round for tastings, from 10am or noon to 5pm daily; many have picnic areas. For complete listings and maps, contact **Amador County** (☎ 888-655-8614; www.amadorwine.com) and **El Dorado County** (☎ 800-306-3956; www.eldoradowines.org). Shenandoah Rd east of Plymouth leads to the region's heart.

In Plymouth, **Amador Vintage Market** (☎ 209-245-3663; www.amadorvintagemarket.com; 9393 Main St; ☎ 10am-7pm) makes a perfect pretrip stop. You can pick up gourmet picnic fixings, get wine country maps and even taste local vintages at its wine bar.

Then there's **Apple Hill** (☎ 530-644-7692; www.applehill.com). East of Placerville and north of Hwy 50 (take exit 54), the rolling countryside is a patchwork of fruit orchards, vineyards and Christmas-tree farms, and in late summer and autumn it comes alive. You can pick your own fruit, sample fresh pies, enjoy pony and hay rides and much more. One of the few orchards open year-round is **Boa Vista Orchards** (☎ 530-622-5522; www.boavista.com; 2952 Carson Rd; ☽ 8am-5pm).

---

of area caves is the spectacular **California Cavern** (☎ 209-736-2708, 888-818-7462; www.caverntours.com; admission $10; ☽ 10am-4pm mid-April–Nov), described by John Muir 'graceful flowing folds deeply pleated like stiff silken drapery.'

Fifteen miles north of Murphys on Hwy 4, **Calaveras Big Trees State Park** (☎ 209-795-2334; per car $6, campsites $20) protects giant sequoia groves; if you aren't continuing to Yosemite, make sure to see them. Calaveras has the region's best camping and hikes.

Columbia (☎ 209-536-1672; www.columbiacalifornia .com) is now a state historic park, with four square blocks of authentic 1850s buildings and concessionaires in period costumes conjuring the Old West. It's crazy with kids panning for gold, but that's part of the fun. The park itself doesn't close, but most businesses are open 10am to 5pm.

Today, **Sonora** is the biggest town in the Southern Mines, but it lacks historic ambience. The **visitor center** (☎ 209-533-4420, 800-446-1333; www.thegreatunfenced.com; 542 S Stockton Rd; ☽ 9am-7pm Mon-Fri, 10am-6pm Sat) will help with Gold Country accommodations.

SLEEPING & EATING

In Sutter Creek, the romantic **Sutter Creek Inn** (☎ 209-267-5606; www.suttercreekinn.com; 75 Main St; r incl breakfast $90-170, weekends plus $20; ✖) has 17 cozy, secluded rooms, some with swinging beds. Or opt for the dependable **Days Inn** (☎ 209-267-9177; 271 Hanford St; midweek $79-99, weekend $89-109; ✖ ✖ ✖).

Nearby, the **Sutter Creek Coffee Roasting Co** (☎ 209-267-5550; 20 Eureka St; ☽ 6:30am-5pm Mon-Sat, 8am-2pm Sun) is a friendly coffeehouse with a sunny patio ideal for writing postcards.

On Hwy 49 in Sutter Creek, **Zinfandels** (☎ 209-267-5008; mains $16-20; ☽ dinner Thu-Sun) dishes up seasonal cuisine that's more interesting than the typical steak-and-potato fare. Service is unpolished but eager.

A great get-away-from-it-all choice is **Hotel Leger** (☎ 209-286-1401; www.hotelleger.com; 8304 Main St; r midweek $55-75, weekend $65-125; ✖ ✖ ✖ ✖) in tiny Mokelumne Hill. Eclectic, sometimes amazing antiques stuff the refurbished, some say haunted, rooms (no TV or phone). There's an atmospheric bar and restaurant (☽ dinner Thu-Sun). Midweek is a steal.

The lauded, 1862 **St George Hotel** (☎ 209-296-4458; www.stgeorgehotel.com; 16104 Main St, Volcano; r incl breakfast $85-110; ✖ ✖ ✖) is enough reason for driving to Volcano – or even the Gold Country. Attractive rooms in the grand main building share baths, while six bungalows have private baths. Locals flock to the renowned dinner-only restaurant and its vintage saloon (open Thursday to Sunday) – a favorite watering hole serving burgers.

In Murphys, **Murphys Historic Hotel & Lodge** (☎ 209-728-3444, 800-532-7684; www.murphyshotel.com; 457 Main St; r midweek $60-90, add $20 weekends; ✖ ✖) offers plain-spun Victorian rooms with shared bath and modern, bath-equipped motel rooms. Stop for a pint in the antler-festooned saloon.

CALIFORNIA

In Columbia, the co-run **City Hotel & Fallon Hotel** (☎ 209-532-1479, 800-532-1479; www.cityhotel .com; r incl breakfast, Fallon Hotel from $75-130, City Hotel $110-130, meals $14-30; ⊙ dinner Tue-Sun, brunch Sun) have the most authentic Victorian restorations of all. The 24 stunning rooms are museum-worthy. The City Hotel has an acclaimed restaurant and Fallon Hotel hosts a repertory theater. Ask about packages.

In busy Sonora, there are plenty of mid-range hotels, but for the same price, stay at the lovely, old-fashioned **Gunn House Hotel** (☎ 209-532-3421; www.gunnhousehotel.com; 286 S Washington St; r midweek $76-96, add $10 weekends; P X Ⓡ Ⓡ). Rear rooms avoid street noise.

Getting There & Around

About 26 miles northeast of Sacramento, Hwy 49 intersects I-80 in the town of Auburn. Local bus systems include **Gold Country Stage** (☎ 530-477-0103), which links Nevada City, Grass Valley and Auburn (fare $1 to $2), and **Placer County Transit** (☎ 530-885-2877). No public transit serves the Southern Mines on Hwy 49.

NORTHERN MOUNTAINS

Sparsely populated, the Northern Mountains region is a little-explored wonder of lakes, alps, rivers and desert. From the heights of Lassen Peak and snowcapped Mt Shasta to the scorched badlands of Lava Beds National Monument, the area captivates with landscapes of drama and grace.

Redding to Yreka

Once only a pit stop on the road to more scenic locales, **Redding** now vies for attention as a destination in its own right. And the recently completed **Sundial Bridge**, designed by Spanish architect Santiago Calatrava, is a strong lure. The unique bridge/sundial is a glass-deck pedestrian overpass that spans the Sacramento River and is part of the greater **Turtle Bay Exploration Park** (☎ 800-887-8532; 840 Auditorium Drive; www.turtlebay.org; ⊙ 9am-5pm, Wed-Mon Nov-Feb; adults $11, ages 15 & under $6). Comprehensive visitor information for the entire area is available at **Shasta-Cascade Wonderland Association** (☎ 530-365-1180, 800-474-2782; www.shastacascade.org; ⊙ 9am-6pm Mon-Sat, from 10am Sun) located 10 miles south of Redding in the Shasta Factory Outlets Mall off I-5.

A recommended side-trip from Redding is to historic **Weaverville**, 45 miles west on Hwy 299 (the Trinity Scenic Byway), where the gold rush–era Taoist temple **Joss House** still stands, as does the lovingly refurbished **Weaverville Hotel** (☎ 530-623-2222; www.weaverville hotel.com; 203 Main St; d from $130). **Weaverville Ranger Station** (☎ 530-623-2121; 210 N Main St; ⊙ 8am-4:30pm Mon-Fri) issues backcountry permits to surrounding **Trinity Alps**, a barely touched wilderness of mountain lakes and rivers.

North of Redding, I-5 crosses **Shasta Lake**, California's largest reservoir. Hiking trails lace the 365 miles of shoreline and campgrounds are plentiful. The lake exists solely because of colossal **Shasta Dam** (☎ 530-275-4463; www.usbr.gov; ⊙ 8:30am-4:30pm, free tours 9am-4pm). High in the limestone megaliths at the north end of the lake are the prehistoric caves of **Lake Shasta Caverns** (☎ 530-238-2341, 800-795-2283; www.lakeshastacaverns.com; tours adult/child 3-11 $20/12).

Cozy **Dunsmuir**, a historic railroad town, has been caringly gentrified, offering culture – music, theatre, art, cuisine – without sacrificing its authentic rusticity. If for no other reason, stop to fill your water bottle from the public fountain; locals claim theirs is 'the best water on earth.'

Mount Shasta city draws mountain climbers as well as spiritual trekkers who believe the majestic mountain imbues the region with numinous power. Whatever you're seeking, this lovely town makes a perfect base for explorations. The **Mount Shasta Visitor Center** (☎ 530-926-4865, 800-926-4865; www.mtshastachamber .com; 300 Pine St; ⊙ 9am- 5:30pm Mon-Sat, to 4pm Sun) provides information on sites and activities. Tiny **Sisson Museum** (☎ 530-926-5508; www.mount shastasissonmuseum.org; admission free; ⊙ 1-4pm Apr-Sep, from 10am Jun-Sep, closed Jan-Mar) is full of curiosities. Next-door is **Mount Shasta Fish Hatchery** (☎ 530-926-2215; 1 N Old Stage Rd; ⊙ 8am-dusk), the oldest operating hatchery in the West.

Visitors to Mt Shasta city aren't usually on a pilgrimage to the fish hatchery however; they're here to meet the mountain itself. Looming and snow-shrouded, **Mount Shasta** (14,162ft) owns the horizon. As pioneer poet Joaquin Miller described: 'Lonely as God, and white as a winter moon, Mount Shasta starts up sudden and solitary from the heart of the great black forests…'

Everitt Memorial Hwy goes up the mountain to 7900ft; to access it, simply head east from town on Lake St and keep going. Rangers will suggest a number of good hiking trails, according to both your condition and the weather's. To climb higher than 10,000ft, obtain a $15 Summit Pass from the **Mount Shasta Ranger Station** (☎ 530-926-4511; 204 W Alma St; ⏰ 8am-4:30pm Mon-Sat, 9am-3pm Sun). Campers note: even in summer, temperatures on and around the mountain drop below freezing. On the south slope, off Hwy 89, **Mount Shasta Board & Ski Park** (☎ 530-926-8610, 800-754-7427; www.skipark.com) offers skiing and snowboarding in winter, mountain biking and chairlift rides in summer.

McCloud, an atmospheric, historic mill town, is 10 miles east of I-5 on Hwy 89 at the foot of Shasta's southern slope. You can access the surrounding creeks and waterfalls on the many peaceful trails.

Until recently the main attraction in **Yreka** (y-*ree*-kuh), inland California's northernmost city, was the Blue Goose excursion train. Train service no longer runs, but the historic downtown still merits a visit.

SLEEPING & EATING
Clustered near major thoroughfares, lodgings in Redding tend to be noisy. North of downtown on N Main are a few clean, quiet motels. Simple **Value Inn & Suites** (☎ 530-241-2252; 533 N Market St; d from $60; 🖳) offers extras like refrigerator and wi-fi. Also north of town is quaint **Tiffany House B&B** (☎ 530-244-3225; www .tiffanyhousebb.com; 1510 Barbara Rd; d from $100).

For something different (and kitschy) sleep in a vintage caboose at **Railroad Park Resort** (☎ 530-235-4440, 800-974-7245; www.rrpark .com; d from $95; 🖳 🛋), off I-5 just south of Dunsmuir. Among Dunsmuir's good eateries is Thai restaurant **Sengthongs** (☎ 530-235-4770; www.sengthongs.com; 5843 Dunsmuir Ave; mains $11-20; ⏰ lunch & dinner).

Mt Shasta's serene **Strawberry Valley Inn** (☎ 530-926-2052; 1142 S Mt Shasta Blvd; d from $75; 🗶 🗶) has tastefully understated, generously appointed rooms; full breakfast included. Get wired (on caffeine and Internet) at **Has Beans Coffeehouse** (☎ 530-926-3602; 1011 S Mt Shasta Blvd; 🖳).

For its tiny size, McCloud has a disproportionate number of B&Bs – all charming. Most celebrated is **McCloud Bed & Breakfast Hotel** (☎ 530-964-2822, 800-964-2823; www.mccloud hotel.com; 408 Main St; d from $120; 🗶), a regal, block-long Victorian property. The on-site restaurant serves breakfast (free to guests) and dinner. The intensely scenic three-hour **Shasta Sunset Dinner Train** (☎ 800-733-2141; www

.shastasunset.com; set-price meals $88, tax/drinks extra; ⏰ 6pm) departs weekends from McCloud.

Several comfortable motels line Yreka's Main St, including the **Klamath Motor Lodge** (☎ 530-842-2751, 800-551-7255; 1111 S Main St; d $65; 🗶 🛋). For strong coffee and light meals try **Nature's Kitchen** (☎ 530-842-1136; 412 S Main; dishes $8; ⏰ 8am-3pm).

GETTING THERE & AROUND
Amtrak trains (☎ 800-872-7245; www.amtrak.com) service Redding and Dunsmuir; **Greyhound buses** (☎ 800-231-2222; www.greyhound.com) serve Redding and Yreka. **Stage buses** (☎ 530-842-8295, 800-2478243) cover Siskiyou County from Dunsmuir to Yreka, weekdays only. By car, San Francisco to Redding is 215 miles (4 hours); Redding to Yreka is 98 miles (1hour 45 minutes). For updated road conditions call **Siskiyou County** (☎ 530-842-4438).

Northeast Corner
Eerie and very beautiful, **Lava Beds National Monument** commemorates turbulent history: recent geologic and ancient human. The volcanic park features lava flows, craters, cones and over 500 lava tubes. This charred land was site of the Modoc War, one of the last major Indian Wars. The Indians maintain a strong presence here today. And their ancestors' petroglyphs adorn some of the park's cave walls. Information, good maps and free flashlights (for cave exploration) available at the **visitor center** (☎ 530-667-8113; www.nps.gov /labe; 1 Indian Well; ⏰ 8am-6pm May-Oct, to 5pm Nov-Sep) off Hwy 161 at the park's south entrance. Nearby is the park's only campground ($10). The simple sites (no showers) are suitable for tents and small RVs. Free wilderness camping is available; ask at the visitor center.

Just north is **Klamath Basin National Wildlife Refuges** – a reserve consisting of six separate refuges. This Pacific Flyway safe haven is a prime stopover for migrating birds. It's an important wintering site for bald eagles. The **visitor center** (☎ 530-667-2231; http://klamath basinrefuges.fws.gov; 4009 Hill Rd; ⏰ 8am-6pm May-Oct, 8:30am-5pm Nov-Sep) is along the road to Lava Beds Monument on Hwy 161. Self-guided 10-mile auto tours ($3 per car) of the Lower Klamath and Tule Lake reserves provide excellent viewing; better still are the self-guided canoe tours ($30). Inquire at visitor center.

Overall, this area has few commercial services, though there is the friendly, tidy **Ellis**

Motel (☎ 530-667-5242; r $40-45, with kitchen plus $5), 1 mile north of Tulelake on Hwy 139. One of the most popular (and one of the only) restaurants around is **Captain Jack's Stronghold** (☎ 530-664-5566; mains $7-12; ☺ Tue-Sun), located 5 miles south of Tulelake on Hwy 139.

Modoc National Forest covers almost 3125 sq miles of California's northeast corner. **Medicine Lake**, 14 miles south of Lava Beds Monument on Hwy 49, is a beautiful crater lake surrounded by pine forest, volcanic formations and campgrounds.

Alturas, at the junction of Hwys 299 and 395, is the Modoc County seat and primarily serves local ranchers. The Modoc National Forest **Supervisor's Headquarters** (☎ 530-233-5811; 800 W 12th St; www.fs.fed.us/r5/modoc; ☺ 8am-5pm Mon-Fri) has hiking information and maps. The **Modoc National Wildlife Refuge** (☎ 530-233-3572; http://modoc.fws.gov; ☺ 7:30am-4pm Mon-Fri) is 3 miles southeast of Alturas. Just 24 miles east of Alturas, on the California–Nevada border, is the high desert of **Surprise Valley**, gateway to the wild **Warner Mountains**.

Further south is one of the region's most lauded natural attractions, **Lassen Volcanic National Park** (per car $10, campsites $10-16). In addition to Lassen Peak (10,457ft), the world's largest plug-dome volcano, the park features steaming Yellowstone-type geothermal sulfur pools and cauldrons. The park has two entrances, both with visitor centers: the smaller on Hwy 44 at Manzanita Lake, and the main one south off Hwy 89, where **park headquarters** (☎ 530-595-4444; www.nps.gov/lavo; ☺ 8am-4:30pm daily Jul-Sep, Mon-Fri Oct-Jun) is located. Hwy 89 through the park is open to cars June to October (and to cross-country skiers in winter). All camping is first-come, first-served. Outside the park lodges and cabins line Hwy 89 between Hat Creek and Old Station.

SIERRA NEVADA

In the mighty Sierra Nevada – dubbed the 'Range of Light' by John Muir – nature has been as prolific and creative as Picasso in his prime. This 400-mile phalanx of craggy peaks, chiseled and gouged by glaciers and erosion, is a patchwork of landscapes that welcome and challenge outdoors fans. Cradling no fewer than three national parks (Yosemite, Sequoia and Kings Canyon), the Sierra is quite literally a wonderland of superlatives, home to the contiguous USA's highest mountain, North America's tallest waterfall and the world's biggest tree.

LAKE TAHOE

Shimmering softly in myriad Technicolor shades of blue and green, Lake Tahoe is the nation's second-deepest lake with an average depth of 1000ft. Generally speaking, the north shore is quiet and upscale, the west shore rugged and old-timey, the east shore undeveloped and the south shore busy and tacky with aging motels and flashy casinos. The horned peaks surrounding the lake are a recreational heaven.

Tahoe gets packed in summer, around holidays and on winter weekends when reservations are essential. **Lake Tahoe Central Reservations** (☎ 530-583-3494, 888-434-1262; www.mytahoevacation.com) is among the agencies that can help with rooms and packages. Overall, room rates tend to be lowest in South Lake Tahoe. There's also lots of camping in the state parks and at USFS sites.

North Shore & East Shores

As the north shore's commercial hub, **Tahoe City** is great for grabbing supplies at supermarkets and information at the **visitor center** (☎ 530-581-6900; 380 N Lake Tahoe Blvd; ☺ 9am-5pm Mon-Fri, to 4pm Sat & Sun). It is also the closest lake town to **Squaw Valley USA** (☎ 530-583-6985; www.squaw.com; off Hwy 89; adult/child/teen $62/5/31), a megasized ski resort that hosted the 1960 Winter Olympic Games. The après-ski crowd often gathers for beer and burgers at the venerable **Bridgetender** (☎ 530-583-3342; 65 W Lake Blvd; dishes $8-10) in Tahoe City.

Overall, though, the little towns east of here tend to be more attractive. **Tahoe Vista** and **Kings Beach** have good swimming and kayaking in summer. For a taste of old Tahoe, spend a night at **Rustic Cottages** (☎ 530-546-3523, 888-778-7842; 7449 N Lake Blvd, Tahoe Vista; www.rusticcottages.com; cabins incl breakfast $59-199; ✗), whose storybook cabins blend seamlessly into the pine forest. Kings Beach has some great eats, including satisfying pastas at **Lanza's** (☎ 530-546-2434; 7739 N Lake Blvd; mains $10-18; ☺ dinner) and unpretentious American fare at **Jason's Beachside Grille** (☎ 530-546-3315; 8338 N Lake Blvd; mains lunch $6-10, dinner $8-19), whose lake-view deck is perfect for sunset drinks.

Further east, Hwy 28 barrels into Nevada at Crystal Bay, where you can try your luck at any of its casinos, including the **Cal-Neva Resort** (☎ 775-832-4000, 800-225-6382; www.calnevaresort .com; 2 Stateline Rd; r $60-110; ⓧ), whose onetime owner Frank Sinatra entertained Kennedy, Monroe and mobsters in the early 1960s.

The main draw of Tahoe's relatively undeveloped eastern shore is the **Lake Tahoe-Nevada State Park** (☎ 775-831-0494; http://parks.nv.gov /lt.htm), a popular playground with beaches, lakes and miles of trails. In summer, crowds frolic in the brilliant turquoise water of **Sand Harbor**.

Truckee & Donner Lake

Cradled by mountains and the Tahoe National Forest, **Truckee** is a thriving little town steeped in Old West history. There's superb dining in the historical downtown near the Amtrak train depot, which also houses the **visitor center** (☎ 530-587-2757, 866-443-2027; www .truckee.com; 10065 Donner Pass Rd; ☉ 9am-5:30pm). The sophisticated **Moody's** (☎ 530-587-8688; 10007 Bridge St; mains lunch $10-16, dinner $18-25) is a favorite of Paul McCartney. Ski hounds can hit the slopes at several resorts, including **Sugar Bowl** (☎ 530-426-9000; www.sugarbowl.com; Hwy 40 near Soda Springs/Norden exit off I-80; adult/teen $59/44), which was cofounded by Walt Disney. It's near Donner Summit, where the Donner Party pioneers became trapped during the fierce winter of 1846. More than half of the group's 89 members died; the rest survived by eating the dead bodies. The grisly tale is chronicled at the **Emigrant Trail Museum** (☎ 530-582-7892; admission $2; ☉ 9am-4pm, to 5pm summer), on the eastern shore of Donner Lake, which has great swimming and boating.

South Lake Tahoe & West Shore

With dozens of motels, eateries and stores lining busy Hwy 50, South Lake Tahoe projects an urban vibe that contrasts sharply with the natural charisma of other lake towns. Gambling in Stateline, just across the Nevada border, is a major draw, as is the world-class ski resort **Heavenly** (☎ 775-586-7000, 800-4328-3659; www.skiheavenly.com; tickets adult/child lift $65/29, gondola $22/14). A trip to the top aboard the sleek new gondolas pretty much guarantees fabulous views of the lake and the **Desolation Wilderness** (www.fs.fed.us/r5/eldorado/wild/deso). This stark and beautiful landscape of raw granite peaks, glacier-carved valleys and alpine lakes extends south and west of the lake and is a hiker's delight. Pick up maps, information and wilderness permits (required for overnight trips) at the **USFS Visitors Center** (☎ 530-543-2674; Hwy 89; ☉ May-Oct). It's about 3 miles north of the 'Y' (the intersection of Hwys 50 and 89) right at the **Tallac Historic Site** (☎ 530-541-5227; admission by donation; ☉ 10am-4pm Jun-Sep), which preserves several early-20th-century estates that now contain exhibits. The nearby **Camp Richardson Resort** (☎ 530-542-6584, 800-544-1801; www.camprichardson.com) has lodging, a lakeside restaurant-bar, a full-service marina and, in winter, cross-country trails.

North of here, Hwy 89 sinuously threads along the densely forested western shore to **Emerald Bay State Park** (☎ 530-541-3030; day-use fee $6; ☉ late May-Sep), where granite cliffs and pine trees frame a fjordlike inlet that truly lives up to its name. A steep 1-mile trail leads down to **Vikingsholm Castle** (adult/child $5/3; ☉ 10am-4pm), a 1928 Scandinavian-style mansion that is open for touring. The castle also marks one end of the fabulous **Rubicon Trail**, which ribbons north along the lakeshore for 4.5 mostly gentle miles to **DL Bliss State Park** (☎ 530-525-7277; day-use fee $6), famous for its sandy beaches. There's **camping** (reservations ☎ 800-444-7275; www.reserveamerica.com; sites $20-35) in both parks. Also, check out the darling cabins of **Tahoma Meadows B&B Cottages** (☎ 530-525-1553, 866-525-1533; www.tahoma meadows.com; 6821 W Lake Blvd; cottages $95-190; ⓧ).

Getting There & Around

Major commercial airlines serve **Reno-Tahoe International Airport** (☎ 775-328-6400), from where **Tahoe Casino Express** (☎ 800-446-6128) runs frequent shuttles to South Tahoe (one-way/ return $20/26, 1½ hr).

Greyhound has daily buses to Reno ($10.50, 50 minutes), Sacramento ($21, three hours) and San Francisco ($30, five to six hours). Amtrak stops in Truckee.

Local buses operated by **Tahoe Area Rapid Transit** (TART; ☎ 530-550-1212; www.laketahoetransit .com) run between Tahoma on the western shore to Incline Village on the northern shore as well as to Truckee. South Lake Tahoe is served by **BlueGO** (☎ 530-541-7149; www.bluego.org), which, in summer, also operates the Nifty Fifty Trolley to Camp Richardson and Emerald Bay.

In winter, Hwy 89 (Emerald Bay Rd) is usually closed, and tire chains are often required on I-80 and Hwy 50; for road information, call ☎ 800-427-7623.

CALIFORNIA

YOSEMITE NATIONAL PARK

If you've never been to Yosemite, you're in for the treat of a lifetime. America's third-oldest national park packs such a surreal amount of beauty that it makes even Switzerland look like God's practice run. While the downside is that the park attracts an astonishing four million visitors a year, it is impossible not to find your heart touched by its splendor. The haughty profile of Half Dome, the hulking presence of El Capitan, the drenching mist of Yosemite Falls and countless other unforgettable sights will have you burning up the pixels in your digicam. Come in spring to see the spectacular waterfalls at their fullest, and to avoid summer's crushing crowds and campfire smog. Autumn is also tranquil, and after a fresh winter snow the park looks as tranquil and quiet as a pharaoh's tomb.

Orientation

Yosemite's entrance fee ($20 per vehicle, $10 for those on bicycle or foot) is valid for seven days. There are four primary entrances: South Entrance (Hwy 41), Arch Rock (Hwy 140), Big Oak Flat (Hwy 120 west) and Tioga Pass (Hwy 120 east). Hwy 120 traverses the park as Tioga Rd (see boxed text, opposite), connecting Yosemite Valley with Mono Lake via 9945ft Tioga Pass.

Visitor activity concentrates in the valley's Yosemite Village, home to the main visitor center, a post office, a museum, eateries and other infrastructure. Curry Village is another hub. Considerably less busy, Tuolumne (*twol-uh-mee*) Meadows, towards the eastern end of Tioga Rd, draws primarily hikers, backpackers and climbers. Wawona, near the southern entrance, has a hotel, store, pioneer museum and giant sequoias.

Gas up year-round at Wawona and Crane Flat inside the park or at El Portal on Hwy 140 just outside its boundaries. In summer, gas is also sold at Tuolumne Meadows.

Information

Public library (☎ 209-372-4552; Girls' Club Bldg; Yosemite Valley; access free; ☺ vary)
Yosemite Lodge (per min 25 ¢, wireless per day $10)
Emergency Care (☎ 911)
Yosemite Medical Clinic (☎ 209-372-4637; ☺ vary)

The stores in Yosemite Village, Curry Village and Wawona have ATMs. Extended summer hours may apply.

Post office (Yosemite Village)
Yosemite Valley Visitor Center (☎ 209-372-0299; www.nps.gov/yose; ☺ 9am-5pm year-round)
Tuolumne Meadows Visitor Center (☎ 209-372-0263; ☺ 9am-5pm late spring-early autumn)
Big Oak Flat Information Station (☎ 209-379-1899; ☺ 9am-5pm Apr-Oct)
Wawowa Information Station (☎ 209-375-9531; ☺ 8:30am-4:30pm late May-early Oct)

Sights
YOSEMITE VALLEY

Meadow-carpeted Yosemite Valley is 7 miles long, bisected by the rippling Merced River and hemmed in by some of the most spectacular chunks of granite nature has wrought anywhere on earth. The most famous are, of course, the monumental **El Capitan** (7569ft), one of the world's largest monoliths and an eldorado for rock climbers, and **Half Dome** (8842ft), a perfectly rounded granite dome and the park's spiritual centerpiece. You'll have great views of both from the valley floor but for the classic photo-op, head up Hwy 41 to **Tunnel View**. With a little sweat, you'll have even better postcard panoramas – sans the crowds – from the **Inspiration Point Trail** (2.6 miles round-trip), which starts at the tunnel.

Yosemite's waterfalls mesmerize even the most jaded traveler, especially when the spring runoff turns them into thunderous cataracts. Most are reduced to a mere trickle by late summer. **Yosemite Falls** is considered the tallest in North America, dropping 2425ft in three tiers. A slick new wheelchair-accessible trail leads to the bottom of this cascade or, if you prefer solitude and different perspectives, you can also clamber up the grueling trail to the top of the falls (6.8 miles round-trip). No less impressive are nearby **Bridalveil Fall** and others scattered throughout the valley.

Any aspiring Ansel Adams should head up the 1-mile paved trail to **Mirror Lake** early or late in the day to catch the ever-shifting reflection of Half Dome in the still waters. The lake all but dries up by late summer.

GLACIER POINT & WAWONA

Soaring 3200ft above the valley floor, **Glacier Point** offers one of the park's most glorious views and practically puts you at eye level with Half Dome. It's about an hour's drive up Glacier Point Rd off Hwy 41 or a strenuous hike along the **Four-Mile Trail** (9.2 miles round-trip). If you don't want to backtrack, reserve a seat on the hiker's shuttle bus (p864).

In Wawona, the park's historical center, the main attraction is the **Mariposa Grove of Giant Sequoias**, where the 2700-year-old Grizzly Giant and other gargantuan trees make their home.

TUOLUMNE MEADOWS
Approximately 55 miles from Yosemite Valley, Tuolumne Meadows, at 8600ft, is the largest subalpine meadow in the Sierra. It provides a dazzling contrast to the valley, with lush, open fields, clear blue lakes, ragged granite peaks and domes, and cooler temperatures. Hikers and climbers will find a paradise of options, and campgrounds are less crowded. Access is via the Tioga Rd (Hwy 120; see boxed text, right), where you'll find a store, lodge and visitor center.

Activities
HIKING
With over 800 miles of hiking trails, Yosemite is a delight for trekkers of all abilities. Easy valley-bottom trails can get as jammed as a U2 concert, but it's easy to escape the teeming masses by simply continuing up any of the steep walls. The ultimate hike, of course, is to the top of **Half Dome** (17 miles round-trip), but be warned: it is strenuous, difficult and best tackled in two days. The less ambitious or physically fit will still have a ball following the same trail as far as **Vernal Fall** (2.6 miles round-trip), the top of **Nevada Fall** (6.5 miles round-trip) or idyllic **Little Yosemite Valley** (8 miles round-trip). The route partly follows the famous John Muir Trail.

Free wilderness permits are required year-round for overnight trips and a quota system limits the number of people leaving from each trailhead. You can make **reservations** (☎ 209-372-0740; www.nps.gov/yose/wilderness/permits.htm; per person $5) from 24 weeks to two days before your trip or try grabbing a permit at a park wilderness center on the day of your planned hike.

ROCK CLIMBING
With sheer spires, polished domes and soaring monoliths, Yosemite is rock-climbing nirvana. **Yosemite Mountaineering School** (☎ 209-372-8344; www.yosemitemountaineering.com; all-day class from $117), in Curry Village, offers top-flight

---

> ### IMPASSABLE TIOGA PASS
> Hwy 120 is the only road connecting Yosemite National Park with the Eastern Sierra, and it climbs through the mountains' highest pass, Tioga Pass at 9945ft. Most California maps mark this road 'closed in winter,' which while literally true is also misleading. Tioga Rd is usually closed from the first heavy snowfall in October until May or even June. If you are planning a trip through Tioga Pass in the spring, you're likely to be out of luck. According to the park's official policy, the earliest date that the road through the pass will be plowed is April 15, yet the pass has only been open in April once since 1980. So call ahead (☎ 209-372-0200) for road and weather conditions before heading for Tioga Pass.

---

instruction for rock hounds from novice to advanced, plus guided climbs and equipment rental.

WINTER SPORTS
In winter the action converges on **Badger Pass** (☎ 209-372-1000; www.badgerpass.com), whose gentle slopes are perfect for beginning skiers and snowboarders. Cross-country skiers can schuss around the forest on 40km of groomed tracks and another 140km of marked trails. There are additional trails at Crane Flat and the Mariposa Grove. Equipment rental is available at the ski schools and the Yosemite Mountaineering School (see left).

Sleeping & Eating
Lodging reservations (☎ 559-252-4848; www.yosemitepark.com) can be made up to 366 days in advance and are critical from May to early September. Rates – and demand – drop from mid-November to mid-March. Unless noted, all lodging listed here is in the valley.

Yosemite Lodge at the Falls (r $113-161; 🖳 🖾) Rooms at this central complex sport a fresh new look and upgraded amenities as well as patios or balconies overlooking Yosemite Falls, meadows, cliffs or the parking lot. There's fine dining at the Mountain Room (mains $16-30), an all-day food court (meals under $10) and a lively lounge with open-pit fireplace for toasting marshmallows.

Curry Village (canvas cabins $70, cabins without/with bath $85/108; r $113; breakfast/dinner buffets $9.50/12, patio mains $6-20; 🖭) Founded in 1899 as a summer camp, Curry has hundreds of units squished together beneath towering evergreens. The canvas cabins are basically glorified tents, so for more privacy get a small but cozily furnished cabin. Food options include all-you-can-eat breakfast and dinner buffets and the outdoor Pizza Patio, which turns into a chatty après-hike hangout in the evenings.

Ahwahnee (r $360; dinner mains $22-39; 🖭) The rich, royal and renowned regularly reside in the sumptuous rooms at this historic property. The rest of us can soak up the ambience during afternoon tea in the cathedral-like Great Lounge, over a drink in the bar or at a gourmet meal in the grand dining room.

Wawona Hotel (r without/with bath $113/170; dinner mains $14-25; 🕑 mid-Mar–Nov, Dec holidays; 🗙 🖭) Filled with ghosts and character, this genteel property is a Victorian-era throwback with wide porches and manicured lawns. About half the 104 rooms share baths. The dining room serves delicious fare with a Southwestern touch.

Simple canvas tent cabins sleeping up to four people are in the valley at cramped **Housekeeping Camp** ($67) and, in summer, at **Tuolumne Meadows Lodge** ($75) and **White Wolf Lodge** ($71) in the high country. The latter two have dining halls serving breakfast and dinner (mains from $7 to $20).

From May to September, these **campgrounds** (☎ 301-722-1257, 800-436-7275; http://reservations.nps .gov) are crammed, noisy and booked to bulging, especially **Upper**, **Lower** and **North Pines** (sites $18) in the valley. All three require reservations, which can be made months in advance; check the website for details.

Overnighters looking for a quieter, more rugged experience are better off in smaller, nonvalley spots like **Bridalveil Creek** (sites $12), **Yosemite Creek** (sites $8) and **Porcupine Flat** ($8). These are first-come, first-served and usually full by noon. All campgrounds have bear boxes, picnic tables, fire rings, water and either flush or vault toilets. The Yosemite Mountaineering School (p863) rents camping gear.

OUTSIDE YOSEMITE NATIONAL PARK

Yosemite Bug Lodge & HI Hostel (☎ 209-966-6666, 866-826-7108; www.yosemitebug.com; dm $18, tent cabins $30-50, r $55-115, r without bath $40-70; 🖵) Tucked into a leafy dell in Midpines, about 20 miles from the park on Hwy 140, the folksy Bug usually hosts a United Nations of visitors of all ages, who appreciate the clean rooms, delicious meals and sensible prices. The Yarts bus stops right outside.

Narrow Gauge Inn (☎ 559-683-7720, 888-644-9050; www.narrowgaugeinn.com; 48571 Hwy 41, Fish Camp; r incl breakfast $80-110 Nov-Mar, $130-195 Apr-Oct; mains $16-36; restaurant 🕑 Wed-Sun May-Oct; 🗙 🖭) At this friendly country retreat, cedar-shingled facades conceal 26 good-sized rooms, each with balcony or patio and radiating comfort. The restaurant is one of the finest around. The inn is about 4 miles south of the park.

Getting There & Around

The nearest Greyhound and Amtrak stations are in Merced, where you can transfer to buses operated by **Yarts** (☎ 209-388-9589, 877-989-2787; www.yarts.com), which travel to the park along Hwy 140, stopping in towns along the way. In summer, another Yarts route runs from Mammoth Lakes (p866) along Hwy 120 via the Tioga Pass. Tickets are $20 one-way from either Merced or Mammoth Lakes, less if boarding in between.

In winter, valley roads are plowed and the highways to the parks are kept open (except Tioga Rd/Hwy 120, p863), although snow chains may be required.

Free shuttle buses loop around Yosemite Valley and the Tuolumne Meadows and Wawona areas. There are also hiker's buses from the valley to Glacier Point (one-way/round-trip $15/29.50) and Tuolumne Meadows (round-trip $23).

Bike rentals (per hour/day $7.50/24.50) are available at Yosemite Lodge and Curry Village.

SEQUOIA & KINGS CANYON NATIONAL PARKS

At this celebrated twin park you'll find yourself in the company of giants. Giant sequoias, that is, which grow bigger, stronger and more abundantly here than anywhere else in the world. There are giant mountains, too, most famously Mt Whitney, at 14,494ft the tallest in the lower 48 states. And finally there's giant Kings Canyon, gored out of granite by the powerful Kings River. They are what lure the vast majority of the 1.5 million annual visitors here, but those seeking quiet and solitude need only to hit the trail to quickly find themselves in breathtakingly beautiful wilderness.

Orientation & Information

Sequoia was designated a national park in 1890 (the second in the USA after Yellowstone), Kings Canyon in 1940. The two parks, though distinct, are operated as one unit with a single admission (valid for seven days) of $10 per carload or $5 for individuals arriving on bicycle or foot. For the latest updates, as well as general information, call the park at ☎ 559-565-3341 (24-hour recorded information) or check the website at www.nps.gov/seki.

From the west, Hwy 180 leads to the parks' Big Stump Entrance before plunging down into Kings Canyon. Coming from the south, Hwy 198 enters Sequoia at the Ash Mountain Entrance from where it ascends as the incredibly narrow and zigzagging Generals Hwy.

Grant Grove Village (☎ 559-565-4307), in Kings Canyon, and **Lodgepole Village** (☎ 559-565-4436), in Sequoia, are the two hubs. Each has a year-round **visitor center** (☼ 8am-6pm mid-Jul–Sep, shorter hrs winter), market, showers, a post office and ATM. Also open all year is the **Foothills Visitors Center** (☎ 559-565-3135; ☼ 8am-5pm), at the Ash Mountain Entrance. **Cedar Grove Visitors Center** (☎ 559-565-3793) and the **Mineral King Ranger Station** (☎ 559-565-3768) are only open in summer. For 24-hour recorded information, call ☎ 559-565-3341.

Gas is available at Hume Lake (year-round) and Stony Creek (summer), both outside park boundaries on national forest land.

Sights

SEQUOIA NATIONAL PARK

Novice tree-huggers should make a beeline to the **Giant Forest**, a 5-sq-mile grove that protects the park's most massive and impressive specimen, including the world's biggest, the bulky **General Sherman Tree**. Snap a picture, then lose the crowds by venturing on any of the trails leading further into the forest.

For a primer on the big trees, head 2 miles south to the excellent **Giant Forest Museum** (☎ 559-565-4480; admission free; ☼ 9am-4:30pm), which also provides access to more good trails, one of them wheelchair accessible. For mind-boggling views of the Great Western Divide, climb the steep quarter-mile staircase up **Moro Rock**.

Discovered in 1918, **Crystal Cave** (☎ 559-565-3759; www.sequoiahistory.org; adult/child/senior $11/6/9; ☼ 11am-4pm mid-May–Oct) has limestone formations estimated to be 10,000 years old. The 45-minute tour covers half a mile of chambers; tickets are available at the Lodgepole and Foothills visitor centers, *not* at the cave.

KINGS CANYON NATIONAL PARK

Just north of Grant Grove Village, **General Grant Grove** brims with majestic giants. Beyond here, Hwy 180 begins its jaw-dropping 36-mile descent into **Kings Canyon**, serpentining past violently chiseled rock walls tinged by moss and decorated with waterfalls. Near **Boyden Cavern** (☎ 209-736-2708; adult/child/senior $10/5/9; ☼ May-Oct) the road meets the Kings River, its thunderous roar ricocheting off granite cliffs soaring up to 8000ft high, making Kings Canyon one of the deepest canyons in North America.

Offering camping, simple lodging, food and information, remote **Cedar Grove Village** is the last outpost of civilization before the rugged grandeur of the backcountry. A popular day hike meanders for 4 miles to roaring **Mist Falls** from Roads End. The less ambitious can amble along a fern-fringed trail to **Zumwalt Meadow**, a lovely picnic spot.

Activities

With 800 miles of marked trails the parks are a hiker's dream. Cedar Grove and Mineral King offer the best backcountry access. Trails are usually open by mid-May,

---

GIANT SEQUOIAS: KINGS OF THE FOREST

In California you can stand under the world's oldest trees (in the Ancient Bristlecone Pine Forest, p867) and its tallest (the coastal redwoods in Redwood National Park, p853), but the record for biggest in terms of volume belongs to the giant sequoias (*Sequoiadendron giganteum*). They grow only on the Sierra's western slope and are most abundant in Sequoia and Kings Canyon and Yosemite national parks. John Muir called them 'Nature's forest masterpiece' and anyone who's ever craned their neck to take in their soaring vastness has done so with the awe usually reserved for Gothic cathedrals. Trees can grow to 300ft tall and 40ft in diameter with bark over 2ft thick. The Giant Forest Museum (left) in Sequoia National Park has excellent exhibits about their fascinating history and ecology.

although there's hiking year-round in the Foothills area. Overnight backcountry trips require wilderness permits ($15), which are subject to a quota system. For details, see www.nps.gov/seki/bcinfo.htm.

In winter, you can cross-country ski or snowshoe among the snow-draped trees of Grant Grove and the Giant Forest. Equipment rental is available at Grant Grove Village and the Wuksachi Lodge (see below).

Sleeping

John Muir Lodge (☎ 559-335-5500, 866-522-6966; www.sequoia-kingscanyon.com; Grant Grove Village; r $160; ☒) Quiet, classy and modern, this woodsy lodge has good-sized, if somewhat generic, rooms and a lovely lobby with stone fireplace, books and board games.

Wuksachi Lodge (☎ 559-253-2199, 888-252-5757; www.visitsequoia.com; near Lodgepole Village; r $100-220; dinner mains $18-28) Named after a local Native American tribe, this elegant and modern mountain lodge has spacious rooms dressed in subdued forest colors and equipped with TV and telephone (a rarity in either park).

Grant Grove Cabins (☎ 559-335-5500, 866-522-6966; www.sequoia-kingscanyon.com; cabins $45-125; ☒) Match your comfort needs to the various cabin types dotted around Grant Grove Village, from tent cabins to nicely furnished historical cottages with private bathrooms.

Cedar Grove Lodge (☎ 559-335-5500, 866-522-6966; www.sequoia-kingscanyon.com; Cedar Grove Village; r $109-125; ☿ May-Oct; ☒) The 21 motel-style rooms are frill-free but comfortable enough and the only noncamping option for staying within earshot of the Kings River.

Camping reservations (☎ 301-722-1257, 800-365-2267; http://reservations.nps.gov) are accepted only at Dorst and Lodgepole in Sequoia with the other dozen or so campgrounds being first-come, first-served (they rarely fill up). Most have flush toilets, and sites cost between $17 and $20. Those in Cedar Grove and the Foothills are best in spring and autumn when the ones at the higher elevations get nippy at night. Only Lodgepole, Azalea and Potwisha are open year-round.

Outside Sequoia's southern entrance, several independent and chain motels line Hwy 198 in the town of Three Rivers.

Eating

Self-caterers have a limited and pricey selection of food to choose from at the markets in Grant Grove Village, Lodgepole Village and Cedar Grove Village. The latter two also have snack bars serving burgers, sandwiches, hot dogs and other no-nonsense food for less than $10.

Grant Grove Village Restaurant (☎ 559-335-5500; breakfast & lunch $5-9, dinner $9-17; ☿ year-round) For more selection, these all-American classics may not make you euphoric but should at least fill the tummy nicely.

Demanding palates should head to the Wuksachi Lodge (see left), which is open for breakfast, lunch and dinner and serves delicious fare with a healthy bent, including meat-free options.

EASTERN SIERRA

Vast, empty and majestic, the Eastern Sierra is where jagged peaks plummet down into the arid expanse of the Great Basin desert, a dramatic juxtaposition that makes for a potent cocktail of scenery. Hwy 395 runs the entire length of the range, with turnoffs leading to pine forests and shaggy meadows, alpine lakes, simmering hot springs and glacier-gouged canyons. Hikers, cyclists, fishers and skiers all have a ball here. The main towns are Bridgeport, Mammoth Lakes and Bishop.

For a glimpse of the gold-rush era, detour to **Bodie State Historic Park** (☎ 760-647-6445; admission $2; ☿ 8am-7pm Jun-Aug, 9am-4pm Sep-May), which preserves one of the West's largest unrestored ghost towns. Stop by the museum, then stroll around the buildings that sit frozen in time on a windswept plain. To get there, head east for about 13 miles (the last three unpaved) on Hwy 270 about 7 miles south of Bridgeport. Although the park is open year-round, the road is often closed in winter.

South of here, quiet and mysterious **Mono Lake** is famous for its unearthly tufa towers, which rise from the alkaline water like drip sand castles. The most photogenic concentration is at the **South Tufa Reserve** (admission $3), on the lake's southern rim. The **Mono Basin Scenic Area Visitors Center** (☎ 760-647-3044; ☿ 9am-4:30pm) has excellent exhibits.

From the nearby town of Lee Vining, Hwy 120 heads west into Yosemite National Park via the Tioga Pass, although the road is only open in summer (see boxed text, p863).

As you continue south, you can detour around the scenic 16-mile **June Lake Loop** or head on to **Mammoth Lakes**, a fast-growing four-season resort town framed by breathtaking scenery and guarded by 11,053ft **Mammoth Mountain** (☎ 760-934-0745, 800-626-6684; www.mammothmountain.com; ski-lift tickets $57), a top-notch ski area. The slopes morph into a mountain-bike park in summer, when there is also wonderful camping, fishing and day hiking in the Mammoth Lakes Basin and the Reds Meadow area. While here, swing by the near-vertical, 60ft-high basalt columns of the **Devil's Postpile National Monument**, which were formed by volcanic activity. Hot-springs fans can soak in the roiling pools of the **Hot Creek Geological Site** (admission free; ☿ dawn-dusk) south of town. Be sure to pay attention to posted signs to avoid getting scalded. The **Mammoth Lakes Visitor Center & Ranger Station** (☎ 760-934-5500, 888-466-2666; www.visitmammoth .com; Hwy 203; ☿ 8am-5pm) has maps and information about any of these sites.

South of Mammoth, Hwy 395 descends into the Owens Valley, soon arriving in charismatic **Bishop**, where sights include an interesting railroad museum and a Paiute-Shoshone cultural center. Its busy main street features covered sidewalks and vintage neon signs and is lined with restaurants, cafés, bookstores, galleries, motels and outdoor-supply stores. Bishop provides access to the best fishing and rock climbing in the entire eastern Sierra and is also the main gateway for horse-pack trips into the mountains.

If you'd like to meet some of the earth's oldest living things, budget a half-day or so for a trip up to the **Ancient Bristlecone Pine Forest** (☎ 760-873-2500). These gnarled, otherworldly-looking trees grow above 10,000ft on the slopes of the parched and seemingly inhospitable White Mountains. The oldest tree – called Methuselah – is estimated to be over 4700 years old. The road (closed November to April) is paved to the top, where there are hikes of varying length, primitive camping and a visitor center. From Hwy 395 take Hwy 168 east for 13 miles, then head uphill for another 10 miles at the marked turnoff.

Hwy 395, meanwhile, barrels on south to Independence and the **Manzanar National Historic Site** (☎ 760-878-2194; www.nps.gov/manz; admission free; ☿ 9am-4:30pm), which commemorates the war relocation camp where some 10,000 Japanese Americans were interned during WWII following the attack on Pearl Harbor. A short film shown at the brand-new interpretive center vividly chronicles life at the camp, as do the excellent exhibits.

South of here, in Lone Pine, you can finally catch a glimpse of **Mount Whitney**, at 14,494ft the highest mountain in the lower 48. Climbing to its peak is hugely popular but requires a permit issued on a lottery basis. For full details, consult www.fs.fed.us/r5/inyo. West of Lone Pine, the bizarrely shaped coyote-colored boulders of the **Alabama Hills** have enchanted artists, climbers and filmmakers, who used them as a backdrop for such classics as *How the West Was Won*. For information, stop by the **Interagency Visitor Center/Mount Whitney Ranger Station** (☎ 760-876-6222; ☿ 8am-5pm) at the Hwy 395/136 junction.

Sleeping & Eating

Campgrounds abound in the Eastern Sierra. Backcountry camping requires fire permits, even for a camp stove, available for free at any ranger station. Mammoth Lakes and Bishop are your best bet for chain motels.

Redwood Motel (☎ 760-932-7060, 888-932-3292; www.redwoodmotel.net; 425 Main St, Bridgeport; d from $73; ☿ mid-Mar–Nov; ✗) A cow in a Hawaiian shirt and other wacky farm-animal sculptures provide a cheerful welcome to this spotless motel. Your host, a professional artist and clown, will shower you with local area tips.

Mammoth Country Inn (☎ 760-934-2710, 866-934-2710; www.mammothcountryinn.com; 75 Joaquin Rd, Mammoth Lakes; r incl breakfast $85-185; ✗) This enchanting B&B has seven rooms with artist-designed beds, fluffy robes, a TV/DVD combo and sparkling new baths. Free wi-fi.

Winnedumah Hotel (☎ 760-878-2040; www.winne dumah.com; 211 N Edwards St, Independence; r $50-80; ✗) This 1927 country-style inn was once a popular movie star hangout when the cameras were rolling in the nearby Alabama Hills.

Whoa Nellie Deli (☎ 760-647-1088; near junction of Hwys 120 & 395, Lee Vining; mains $7-18; ☿ 7am-9pm late Apr-Oct) Great food in a gas station? Come on… No, really, you gotta try this amazing kitchen where chef Matt 'Tioga' Toomey feeds delicious fish tacos, wild buffalo meatloaf and other tasty morsels to clued-in passers-by.

Whiskey Creek (☎ 760-934-2555; cnr Minaret Rd & Main St, Mammoth Lakes; mains $16-26) For great fish and meat dishes, try this rambling restaurant whose bar pours locally crafted brews.

Erick Schat's Bakkery (☎ 760-873-7156; 763 N Main St, Bishop; sandwiches $3.50-7) The best place along Hwy 395 to feed cravings for freshly made sandwiches – served on their own breads – or tasty cookies and pastries.

Southwest

Other than perhaps Alaska and Hawaii, few places in America generate more iconic imagery than the Southwest. Think classic cowboy movie sets, towering stands of saguaro cactus, Georgia O'Keeffe's colorful canvases or Ansel Adams' monochromatic photographs. It's hard to ignore the Southwest's expansive sense of freedom – of movement, of expression, of the open road. Nature's effects, too, are unavoidably writ large: eons of wind and torrents of water have carved grand canyons and wild buttes.

Southwest mythology has been forged by ancestral Indians (whose legends and customs still thrive), Spanish missionaries (whose churches still survive), rough-and-ready miners (whose former towns stand ready for exploration) and Billy the Kid–style outlaws (whose Wild West aura still prevails). Because of the region's sheer size and diverse influences, you'll have a tough time deciding what to do. Mountain biking in southern Utah, downhill skiing in northern Utah and rafting the Taos 'box' have few equals. Rock climbing on monolithic mesas, camping under the stars and hiking in canyon country leave you breathless.

But it's not all nature, all the time. Sophisticated cities like Santa Fe, Las Vegas and Phoenix are abuzz with galleries, four-star dining, museums and bed-and-breakfasts. Start tumbling like a weed through Indian country and painted deserts. You'll never look back.

HIGHLIGHTS

- Visiting the Southwest without seeing the **Grand Canyon** (p901) is like leaving your house without your keys
- Rafting the **Colorado River** (p902) is a must-do-before-you-die experience
- Exploring Utah's out-of-this-world beautiful **Monument Valley** (p931)
- Experiencing solitude at **Grand Staircase–Escalante National Monument** (p933), amid two million acres of desert
- Getting hip in **Park City** (p923), the coolest small town in Utah, with the Torrey (p932) and Boulder (p932) tying for second place
- Dropping your jaw at the view in **Dead Horse Point** (p930)
- Soaking in waters at New Mexico's classic **Ojo Caliente** (p951), or radiating heat at the luxe digs at **Sierra Grande Lodge & Spa** (p955) in Truth or Consequences
- Knocking back margaritas at the **Adobe Bar** (p953) at the Taos Inn
- Watching bats fly out for a dusky dinner at **Carlsbad Caverns National Park** (p959)
- Living the high life on the **Las Vegas Strip** (p875)

Utah
★ Park City

Nevada

Grand Staircase–Escalante National Monument ★
★ Dead Horse Point
★ Colorado River

Las Vegas ★
★ Monument Valley

Grand ★ Canyon
Ojo Caliente ★ ★ Taos

Arizona
New Mexico

Truth or Consequences ★
Carlsbad Caverns National Park ★

SOUTHWEST

HISTORY

The history of human habitation in the Southwest dates back 12,500 years. But by AD 100, three dominant and fascinating cultures had emerged: the Hohokam, the Mogollon and the Ancestral Puebloans (formerly known as the Anasazi).

The Hohokam lived in the Arizona deserts from 300 BC to AD 1450, and created an incredible canal irrigation system, earthen pyramids and a rich heritage of pottery. But they mysteriously disappeared in the mid-15th century. From 200 BC to AD 1450 the Mogollon people lived in the central mountains and valleys of the Southwest, and left behind the Gila Cliff Dwellings National Monument (p956).

The Ancestral Puebloans left the richest heritage of archaeological sites, like that at Chaco Culture National Historic Park (p954). Today descendants of the Ancestral Puebloans are found in the Pueblo Indian groups throughout New Mexico. The Hopi are descendants, too, and their village Old Oraibi (p907) may be the oldest continuously inhabited settlement in North America.

In 1540 Francisco Vásquez de Coronado led an expedition from Mexico City to the Southwest. Instead of riches, his party found Indians, many of whom were then killed or dislocated. More than 50 years later, Juan de Onate established the first capital of New Mexico at San Gabriel. Great bloodshed resulted from Onate's attempts to control Indian pueblos and he left in failure in 1608. Santa Fe (p943) was established as a new capital the following year.

Development in the Southwest expanded rapidly during the 19th century, mainly due to railroad and geological surveys. As the US pushed west, the army forcibly removed whole tribes of Native Americans in often horrifyingly brutal Indian Wars. Gold and silver mines drew fortune seekers, and practically overnight the lawless mining towns of the Wild West mushroomed. Capitalizing on the development, the Santa Fe Railroad lured an ocean of tourists fascinated by the West's rugged beauty and Indian culture.

Modern settlement is closely linked to water use. Following the Reclamation Act of 1902, huge federally funded dams were built to control rivers, irrigate the desert and encourage development. Rancorous debates and disagreements over water rights continue today, especially with the phenomenal boom in residential development. The Southwest has been drawing newcomers from around the country because of a relaxed lifestyle, friendly folks, open space and a lower cost of living.

GEOGRAPHY & CLIMATE

The Southwest is jam-packed with one of the world's greatest concentrations of remarkable rock formations. Thanks to the area's soft and widespread sedimentary layers, rain and erosion readily carve them into fantastic shapes. The rich colors that imbue the landscape come from the unique mineral compositions of each rock type.

Although the Colorado Plateau encompasses a series of plateaus located between 5000ft and 8000ft in elevation and separated by deep canyons, the greatest among them is the Grand Canyon (p901).

While mountains are snowcapped in winter, most of the Southwest receives little annual rainfall. During the summer, temperatures can soar over 90°F; although it's dry heat, it's still uncomfortable. Nights are usually cooler, and spring and fall can be pleasant.

NATIONAL, STATE & REGIONAL PARKS

Not to exaggerate, but the Southwest arguably has *the* most fabulous concentrations of national parks and monuments in North America. Don't overlook, though, the luring but less crowded state parks.

One of the national park system's most popular destinations is the Grand Canyon National Park (p901) in Arizona. Other Arizona parks include Monument Valley Navajo Tribal Park (p907), a desert basin with towering sandstone pillars and buttes; Canyon de Chelley National Monument (p907), with ancient cliff dwellings; Organ Pipe Cactus National Monument (p914), in the pristine Sonoran Desert; the odd mix of Painted Desert and fossilized logs at Petrified Forest National Park (p908); and the pristine desert and giant cactus at Saguaro National Park (p913).

The southern red-rock canyon country in Utah includes Arches (p929), Canyonlands (p930), Zion (p935) and Bryce (p933). Grand Staircase-Escalante National Monument (p933) is a mighty region of undeveloped desert, while Capitol Reef

SOUTHWEST

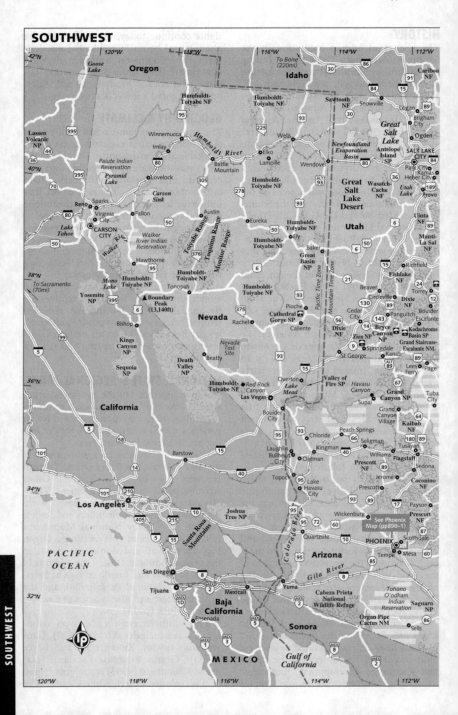

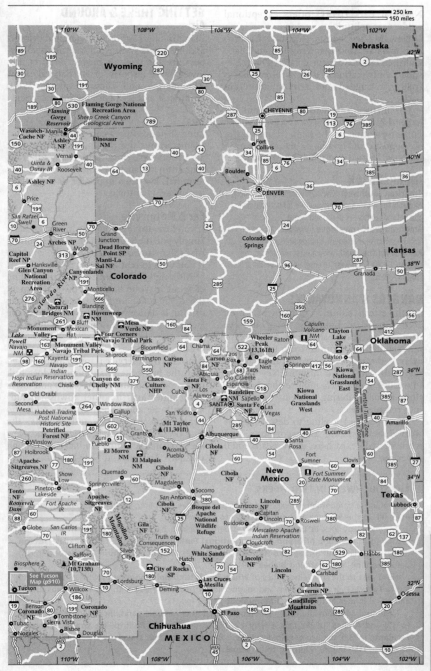

National Park (p931) offers exceptional wilderness solitude.

New Mexico boasts Carlsbad Caverns National Park (p959) and mysterious Chaco Culture National Historic Park (p954). Nevada's only national park is Great Basin (p887), a rugged and remote mountain oasis.

For further information, check out the **National Park Service** (NPS; www.nps.gov) website. For information on the region's state parks, see opposite for Nevada, p916 for Utah, p936 for New Mexico and p888 for Arizona.

INFORMATION

American Southwest (www.americansouthwest.net) Arguably the most comprehensive site for national parks and natural landscapes of the Southwest.

American West Travelogue (www.amwest-travel .com) A selective reading list, photographs and more.

Notes from the Road (www.notesfromtheroad.com) Click on 'Desert Southwest' to enter another world; it'll be hard to return.

DANGERS & ANNOYANCES

Southwestern summer rainstorms, often accompanied by lightning, can come out of nowhere, and flash floods occur regularly, sometimes from a storm many miles away. A dry riverbed or wash can become a raging torrent within minutes. Never camp in washes, and always inquire about conditions before entering canyons or driving into remote areas.

Many people traveling to desert regions worry about snakes and scorpions, and while they do exist here, chances are you'll never see one.

GETTING THERE & AROUND

Air

Phoenix Sky Harbor International Airport and Las Vegas' McCarran International Airport are the region's busiest airports, followed by the airports serving Salt Lake City, Albuquerque and Tucson. America West, Southwest and Delta are the main carriers.

Bus

Long-distance buses can get you to major points within the region, but don't serve all national parks or important, off-track tourist towns, such as Moab. Be aware, bus terminals are often in poorer or more dangerous areas of town.

Car & Motorcycle

If you love driving, you'll be in heaven here. Simply put, the Southwest has more stunning roads than any other region in the country. If you wish to rent a car, see p1175.

Although little compares to the feeling of wind in your hair and the freedom of the open road, long-distance motorcycle driving is dangerous because of the fatigue factor. Use caution during long hauls.

Train

Amtrak's train service is much more limited than the bus system, although it does link many major Southwestern towns and offers bus connections to other towns (including Santa Fe and Phoenix). The *California Zephyr* traverses Utah and Nevada; the *Southwest Chief* stops in Arizona and New Mexico; and the *Sunset Limited* cuts through southern Arizona and New Mexico.

THE SOUTHWEST IN TWO WEEKS

This region is gargantuan. To experience a representative sampling, you'll need to unfurl a good map, fill up the gas tank and put the pedal to the metal.

Try your lady luck in **Las Vegas** (p874) before kicking back in funky **Flagstaff** (p896) and venturing to the edge of **Grand Canyon National Park** (p901). Hang out in collegiate **Tucson** (p909) or mellow out at **Saguaro National Park** (p913). Sling some guns in **Tombstone** (p915) before settling into charming **Bisbee** (p915).

Head east to the sprawling dunes of **White Sands National Monument** (p957), then sink into **Santa Fe** (p943), a foodie haven and magnet for art mavens. Hang with hippies in **Taos** (p951) and stand in awe at the colossal **Monument Valley** (p931).

Head into southern Utah for a stunning collection of national parks, including **Canyonlands** (p930) and **Arches** (p929). Cruise **Hwy 12** (p931) near **Capitol Reef** (p931), **Grand Staircase-Escalante** (p933), the candy-colored spires at **Bryce Canyon** (p933) and the sheer red-rock walls at **Zion** (p935), before returning to Las Vegas.

NEVADA

Welcome to the dark side of your dreams. It's time to lose your inhibitions; unleash your inner rebel. Pump the gas and pound the desert pavement, because you're on a full-throttle, reckless journey into sinful oblivion. Tonight you're living on the edge, allowed to break all the rules. You're a boozer, a gambler, a Gucci-clad glam girl, a down-and-out, chain-smoking drunk bum. That's you throwing quarters in the slot machine at the grocery store. That's you slamming a beer in some slightly sleazy middle of nowhere town as the rising sun turns the sky pink. You're blazing a trail across the Las Vegas Strip, stunned by its opulence; its over-the-top, almost appallingly ridiculous, yet oh so irresistible, decadence. You're on a wild adventure, screaming down the vast emptiness of the 'Loneliest Road in America,' feeling like a Wild West outlaw on a quest for something. You're flying over rugged countryside, past breathtaking desert valleys, up snowcapped peaks. And when you tire of being bad, recharge on the blue shores of Lake Tahoe and pitch a tent under a star-studded sky, some remote location that's so quiet it's almost unnerving.

History

Nevada's first inhabitants were the Paiute and Ancestral Puebloan people. Though claimed by Spain, Nevada was scarcely touched by Europeans until the 1820s, when trappers ventured into the Humboldt River Valley. Most 19th-century emigrants passed straight through Nevada to the California gold fields. But in 1859 the Comstock Lode – the largest silver deposit ever mined – was discovered south of Reno.

As the Comstock Lode was mined out, Nevada's population declined. In the early 20th century, new mineral discoveries temporarily revived the state's fortunes, but the Great Depression brought an end to those dreams. So, in 1931 the state government legalized gambling and created agencies to tax it, turning an illegal activity into a revenue source and tourist attraction.

Since WWII Nevada's wide-open spaces have been used to test nuclear weapons and military aircraft; its next controversial industry may be nuclear-waste storage. Today

NEVADA FACTS
Nicknames Silver State, Sagebrush State
Population 2.4 million
Area 109,826 sq miles
Capital city Carson City (population 52,500)
State flower Sagebrush
Birthplace of First lady Thelma 'Pat' Nixon (1912–93); Andre Agassi (b 1970)
Home of Nevada Test Site
Famous for Las Vegas, the Comstock Lode at Virginia City, UFOs, legal prostitution

the state thrives on tourism, with most revenues coming from the ubiquitous casinos.

Although the US government stopped exploding nuclear bombs underground at the Cold War–era Nevada Test Site in 1992, the end of a possible nuclear future for state residents isn't so clearcut. In 1998, a US Department of Energy report – which took 18 years and more than $5 billion to research – recommended Yucca Mountain, near the test site and 100 miles northeast of Las Vegas, as the best possible location for the nation's only long-term high-level nuclear waste repository. Nevada officials, including Vegas mayor Oscar Goodman, have fought the proposed waste dump tooth and nail, but Congress approved President Bush's Yucca Mountain Project proposal on 23 July 2002. Waste storage is scheduled to begin as early as 2010.

Information

Las Vegas Convention & Visitors Authority (☎ 702-892-0711; www.lasvegas24hours.com; 3150 Paradise Rd, Las Vegas, NV 89109) A helpful organization.

Nevada Commission on Tourism (☎ 800-638-2328; www.travelnevada.com; 401 N Carson St, Carson City, NV 89701) Sends free books, maps and information on accommodations, campgrounds and events.

Nevada Division of State Parks (☎ 775-687-4384; www.parks.nv.gov; 1300 South Curry St, Carson City, NV 89703-5202) Information about Nevada state parks.

Note that prostitution is definitely illegal in Clark County (which includes Las Vegas) and Washoe County (which includes Reno), though there are legal brothels in many smaller counties.

Nevada is on Pacific Standard Time, and has two areas codes: Las Vegas and vicinity is ☎ 702, while the rest of the state is ☎ 775.

LAS VEGAS

A surreal apparition rising out of barren desert sands, at first glance Las Vegas appears a shimmering mirage, a figment of your imagination. An otherworldly, schizophrenic, bold and blazing creation of some demented cartoon artist. An alternate universe, where the globe's most famous sights – ancient Egypt's pyramids, Paris' Eiffel Tower, the canals of Venice – tumble together, bathed in an ethereal neon glow. Fused by greed, driven by lust, pulsating with passion, Las Vegas embodies the shady side of the American Dream. It's a place where inhibitions are temporarily lost, sins forgotten and fate decided by the spin of a roulette wheel. Reality is skewed, the obscure becomes mainstream. There's a bible-toting Elvis bumming smokes from the guy hawking his first hip-hop album in what appears to be Tuscany. At the strip joint off the strip the drunken guy on his last fling is throwing dollars at the perky-breasted gal dancing on the pole. She's telling him the money's so good she commutes from the West Coast.

Las Vegas never stops pumping. Exuding frenetic electricity, time is irrelevant. There are no clocks. The booze always flows. A visit to this seedy, yet decadent, fantasyland is like embarking on a choose-your-own adventure story where anything can happen (and something always does).

History

Contrary to Hollywood legend there was much more at the dusty crossroads than a gambling parlor and some tumbleweeds the day mobster Ben 'Bugsy' Siegel rolled in and erected a glamorous, tropical-themed casino, the Flamingo, under the searing sun.

Speared into the modern era by the completion of a railroad linking Salt Lake City to Los Angeles in 1902, Vegas boomed in the 1920s thanks to federally sponsored construction projects. The legalization of gambling in 1931 then carried Vegas through the Great Depression. WWII brought a huge air-force base and big aerospace bucks, plus a paved highway to Los Angeles. Soon after, the Cold War justified the Nevada Test Site. It proved to be the textbook case of 'any publicity is good publicity': monthly above-ground atomic blasts shattered casino windows downtown, while the city's official Miss Mushroom Cloud mascot promoted atomic everything in tourism campaigns.

A building spree sparked by the Flamingo in 1946 led to mob-backed tycoons upping the glitz ante at every turn. Big-name entertainers, like Frank Sinatra, Liberace and Sammy Davis Jr, arrived on stage at the same time as topless French showgirls.

The high-profile purchase of the Desert Inn in 1966 by eccentric billionaire Howard Hughes gave the gambling industry a much-needed patina of legitimacy. The debut of the MGM Grand in 1993 signaled the dawn of the era of the corporate 'megaresort.'

An oasis in the middle of a final frontier, Sin City continues to exist chiefly to satisfy the needs and desires of visitors. Hosting over 35 million visitors a year, Las Vegas is the engine of North America's fastest growing metropolitan area and the last liberty port of opportunity for countless people seeking their fortune.

Orientation

Downtown Las Vegas is the original town center, and home to the city's oldest hotels and casinos. The main drag is Fremont St, four blocks of which is now a covered pedestrian mall.

Las Vegas Blvd is the main north–south drag, running from North Las Vegas south toward the airport. South of the city limits, this boulevard is famously known as 'the Strip,' where you'll find most of the gargantuan hotel-casinos. More casinos are found east of the Strip along Paradise Rd, and just west of I-15 near the intersection of Flamingo Rd and Valley View Blvd.

The Greyhound bus station is within easy walking distance of downtown hotels.

Information

BOOKSTORES

Waldenbooks (☎ 702-733-1049; 3200 Las Vegas Blvd) Inside the Fashion Show Mall.

EMERGENCY

Emergency number (☎ 911)
Gamblers Anonymous (☎ 702-385-7732) May help with gambling concerns.
Police Department (☎ 702-229-3111)

INTERNET ACCESS

Cyber Stop (☎ 702-736-4782; Hawaiian Marketplace, Polo Towers Plaza, 3743 S Las Vegas Blvd; per hr $12)

INTERNET RESOURCES

Vegas.com (www.vegas.com) Travel information with booking service

Las Vegas.com (www.lasvegas.com) City of Las Vegas website

City of Las Vegas (www.ci.las-vegas.nv.us) Travel services

MEDIA

Las Vegas Review-Journal (☎ 702-383-0211; www.lvrj.com) Daily paper with a weekend guide on Friday.

Las Vegas Weekly (☎ 702-990-2400; www.lasvegasweekly.com) Free weekly with good entertainment and restaurant listings.

MEDICAL SERVICES

Sunrise Hospital & Medical Center (☎ 702-731-8000; 3186 S Maryland Parkway)

University Medical Center (☎ 702-383-2000; 1800 W Charleston Blvd)

MONEY

Every hotel-casino, bank and most convenience stores have ATMs.

American Express (☎ 702-739-8474; MGM Grand, 3799 S Las Vegas Blvd) Changes currencies at competitive rates.

POST

Post office (☎ 702-735-8519; 3100 S Industrial Rd) Just west of the strip.

TOURIST INFORMATION

Las Vegas Visitor Information Center (☎ 702-892-0711; www.vegasfreedom.com; 3150 Paradise Rd; ⏰ 8am-5pm) Official tourist office.

Dangers & Annoyances

The major tourist areas are safe. However, Las Vegas Blvd between downtown and the Strip gets pretty shabby, and Fremont St east of downtown is definitely unsavory. If you're staying at the USA Hostels Las Vegas, which is east of downtown, avoid walking alone or at night.

Sights

The following attractions are our favorites, but represent only a small sample of Vegas' offerings.

CASINOS

Opulent, yet elegant, the **Bellagio** (☎ 702-693-7111; www.bellagio.com; 3600 S Las Vegas Blvd) was built to dazzle. Its Tuscan architecture and 8-acre artificial lake, complete with choreographed dancing fountains, are mesmerizing. The hotel's lobby features an 18ft ceiling adorned with a backlit glass sculpture composed of 2000 hand-blown flowers in vibrant colors. The **Bellagio Gallery of Fine Art** (☎ 702-693-7871; admission $15; ⏰ 9am-9pm) showcases temporary exhibits by fantastic artists.

Hand-painted ceiling frescoes, roaming mimes and full-scale reproductions of famous Venice landmarks are found at the romantic **Venetian** (☎ 702-414-1000; www.venetian.com; 3355 S Las Vegas Blvd; gondola rides adult/child/private from $12.50/5/50). A gondola ride down the Grand Canal is a highlight. So is a visit to the stunning **Guggenheim Hermitage**

LAS VEGAS IN...

Two Days

Start by exploring the **Strip** (above), visiting landmark casinos, like the **Venetian** (above), **Luxor** (p878) and **Bellagio** (above). Spend the afternoon poolside or indulging in some spa pampering. Come nightfall, wander the Strip casinos again and gawk at the volcanic eruptions and sizzling fountain shows.

The next day, indulge your glitzy side with a trip to the **Liberace Museum** (p879). Then head downtown to see the **Neon Museum** (p878) and the **Fremont Street Experience** (p878), catching a drink afterwards in a vintage casino like **Main Street Station** (p878). At night hit a hot dance club, like **Ra** (p882) or **Rain** (p882) or visit **Sapphire** (p882), an over-the-top strip club, for a truly Vegas experience.

Four Days

Follow the itinerary for two days, then explore **Hoover Dam** (p883) and drive along Lake Mead's North Shore Rd up to **Valley of Fire State Park** (p883); you can also take a short hike at **Red Rock Canyon** (p883). Back in Vegas, check out the **Guggenheim Hermitage Museum** (p877), and maybe indulge in a gourmet meal or a **Cirque du Soleil** (p882) performance.

SOUTHWEST

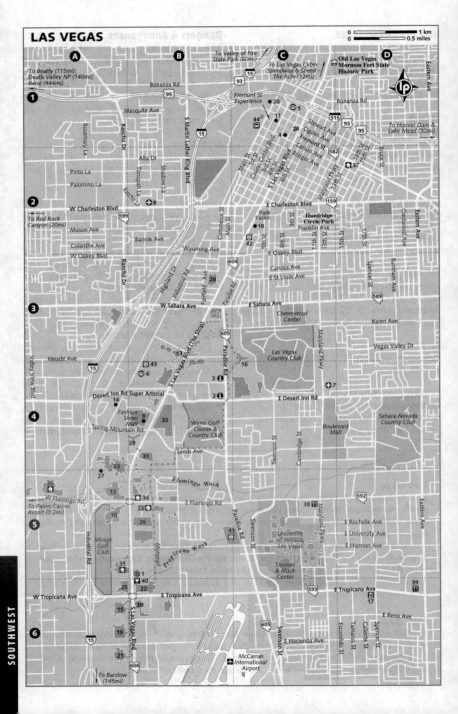

LAS VEGAS

SOUTHWEST

Museum (☎ 702-414-2440; www.guggenheimlasvegas.org; adult/child $15/7; ☽ 9.30am-8.30pm).

Quintessentially Las Vegas, **Caesars Palace** (☎ 702-731-7110; www.caesarspalace.com; 3570 S Las Vegas Blvd) is a Greco-Roman fantasyland featuring marble reproductions of classical statuary, including a not-to-be-missed four-ton Brahma shrine near the front entrance. Towering fountains, goddess-costumed cocktail waitresses and the swanky, haute couture **Forum Shops** all ante up the glitz.

Not trying to be any one fantasy, tropically themed **Mandalay Bay** (M-Bay; ☎ 720-632-7777; www.mandalaybay.com; 3950 S Las Vegas Blvd) really feels likes a classy resort. Standout attractions include the multilevel **Shark Reef** (☎ 702-632-7000; adult/child $15/10; ☽ 10am-11pm), an aquarium complex home to thousands of submarine beasties with a shallow pool where you can pet pint-sized sharks.

Though traces of the original swashbuckling skull-and-crossbones theme linger at **Treasure Island** (TI; ☎ 702-894-7111; www.treasureisland.com; 3300 S Las Vegas Blvd), the new-look terra-cotta-toned resort now strives for an 'elegant Caribbean hideaway' feel – with 'leave the kids at home' implied. The spiced-up **Sirens of Treasure Island** (admission free) is a mock sea battle pitting sultry temptresses against renegade freebooters. You can see it every 90 minutes from 7pm to 11.30pm Monday to Saturday.

Keeping true to its Hollywood roots (it's owned by movie mogul Metro Goldwyn Mayer), the **MGM Grand** (MGM; ☎ 702-891-1111; www.mgmgrand.com; 3799 S Las Vegas Blvd) is a gigantic, glitzy 'City of Entertainment.' Out front is the USA's largest bronze statue, a 45ft tall, 100,000lb lion perched atop a 25ft pedestal, ringed by lush landscaping, fountains and Atlas-themed statues.

The captivating **Mirage** (☎ 702-791-7111; www.mirage.com; 3400 S Las Vegas Blvd) is tropically themed, replete with a giant jungle foliage atrium, meandering creeks and soothing cascades. At the casino's south entrance, the **royal white tiger habitat** permits a glare-free view of a parade of big cats 24 hours a day. Out front, the fiery trademark **faux volcano** erupts frequently.

Evoking the gaiety of the City of Light, **Paris-Las Vegas** (☎ 702-946-7000; www.parislv.com; 3655 S Las Vegas Blvd) strives to capture the essence of the grande dame by re-creating her landmarks. Fine likenesses of the Opéra House, the Arc de Triomphe, Champs-Élysées, and even the River Seine frame the property. Just like in the French capital, the signature attraction is the ersatz Eiffel Tower.

New York-New York (☎ 702-740-6969; www.nynyhotelcasino.com; 3790 S Las Vegas Blvd) is a mini-megapolis featuring scaled-down replicas of the Empire State Building (47 stories or 529ft); the Statue of Liberty, ringed by a September 11 memorial; a mini version of the Brooklyn Bridge; and renditions of the Chrysler, AT&T and CBS buildings. Manhattan-a-phobes beware: it really can feel like Central Park on a sunny Sunday afternoon.

NEW KID ON THE STRIP

The Strip's famous skyline has a different look these days, thanks to the brand new $2.7 billion **Wynn Las Vegas** (☎ 702-770-7100; www.wynnlasvegas.com; 3131 Las Vegas Blvd), opened in May 2005. The most expensive hotel-casino built to date, it upholds the city's decadent reputation. With a 50-story curved tower covered in bronze glass, the facility is as swanky as it gets. The entire place exudes an air of secrecy – the entrance is obscured from the Strip by a $130-million man-made mountain, which rises seven-stories tall in some places. Inside, the Wynn resembles a natural paradise – with mountain views, tumbling waterfalls, fountains and other special effects. Perks include a golf course, 2716 guest rooms and 111,000-sq-ft of gaming space. Acclaimed director Franco Dragone has created a water-themed production show, **Le Reve**, in a specially constructed theater-in-the-round, which includes a 1-million gallon pool doubling as the stage.

Perhaps the most impressive resort on the Strip, the focus at **Luxor** (☎ 702-262-4000; www.luxor.com; 3900 S Las Vegas Blvd) is its 30-story pyramid, cloaked in black glass from base to apex. The atrium is so voluminous it can accommodate nine 747 jetliners and 50 Cessna's. A 10-story-high crouching sphinx and a sandstone hieroglyphics etched obelisk guard the pyramid. The **King Tut Museum** (☎ 702-262-4000; admission $5; 🕙 9am-midnight) features exquisite reproductions of ancient artifacts.

At 1149ft, the white, three-legged $550 million **Stratosphere** (☎ 702-380-7777; www.stratospherehotel.com; 2000 S Las Vegas Blvd) is the tallest building west of the Mississippi. Atop the elegantly tapered tower you'll find indoor and outdoor viewing decks, offering the most spectacular 360-degree panoramas in town.

The **Hard Rock Hotel & Casino** (☎ 702-693-5000; www.hrhvegas.com; 4455 Paradise Rd) is home to one of the world's most impressive collections of rock and roll memorabilia. The pool complex is a constant throbbing (literally, there are underwater speakers!) meat-market party with a capital P.

OTHER ATTRACTIONS

The most charming of downtown's establishments, **Main Street Station** (☎ 702-387-1896; www.mainstreetcasino.com; 200 N Main St) re-creates Victorian opulence with detailed craftsmanship, old-fashioned elegance, and an extensive collection of antiques, architectural artifacts and collectibles.

A four-block pedestrian mall topped by an arched steel canopy filled with computer-controlled lights, the **Fremont Street Experience** (☎ 702-866-373-5200; www.vegasexperience.com; Fremont St), between Main St and Las Vegas Blvd, has brought life back to downtown. Five times nightly, the canopy becomes a six-minute light-and-sound show enhanced by 550,000 watts of wraparound sound.

The crown jewel of a downtown redevelopment effort, **Neonopolis** (☎ 702-477-0470; www.neonopolis.com; 450 Fremont St; 🕙 11am-11pm) is most notable for its collection of vintage neon signs. At the alfresco **Neon Museum** (☎ 702-387-6366; www.neonmuseum.org; cnr Fremont & 3rd Sts; admission free; 🕙 24hr) plaques tell the story of the assemblage.

Activities

At the **Las Vegas Cyber Speedway & Speed** (☎ 702-733-7223; www.nascarcafelasvegas.com; Sahara, 2535 S Las Vegas Blvd; admission Cyber Speedway $8, re-ride $4, Speed $13; 🕙 Cyber Speedway noon-9pm Sun-Thu, 11am-10pm Fri & Sat, Speed 11am-midnight, 11am-1am Fri & Sat) the Indy car simulators, with 20ft wraparound screens, are so authentic they excite real Formula One drivers. Speed is an electromagnetic rollercoaster that slingshots to a top of 70mph.

The highlight of a ride on the **Manhattan Express Rollercoaster** (☎ 702-740-6969; www.nynyhotelcasino.com; New York-New York, 3790 S Las Vegas Blvd; admission $12.50, re-ride $6; 🕙 10am-midnight) is a heartline twist-and-dive maneuver, producing a sensation similar to one felt by a pilot during a barrel roll in a fighter plane.

At the **Stratosphere Tower** (☎ 702-380-7777; www.stratospherehotel.com; Stratosphere, 2000 S Las Vegas Blvd; admission per ride $19; 🕙 10am-1am Sun-Thu, 10am-2am Fri & Sat), the Big Shot straps riders into completely exposed seats that zip up and down the tower's pinnacle for 12 seconds.

Las Vegas for Children

Now that sin is in again, few places in Vegas bill themselves as family-friendly. As state law prohibits people under 21 from loitering in gaming areas, the only megaresorts that cater to children are **Circus Circus** (☎ 702-734-0410; www.circuscircus.com; 2880 S Las Vegas Blvd) and **Excalibur** (☎ 702-597-7777; www.excalibur.com; 3050 S Las Vegas Blvd). There's still some stuff for kids, however. See right for details.

Kids will dig a visit to **Siegfried & Roy's Secret Garden & Dolphin Habitat** (☎ 702-791-7188; www.mirage.com; Mirage, 3400 S Las Vegas Blvd; admission $12, child under 10 free; ⊗ 11am-7pm Mon-Fri, 10am-7pm Sat & Sun). Exotic and endangered lions, tigers, jaguars and an elephant roam in a lush zoo setting. Up-close-and-personal Atlantic bottlenose dolphin interactions are the highlights of the super-sized aquarium.

The **Circus Circus Midway** (☎ 702-734-0410; www.circuscircus.com; Circus Circus, 2880 S Las Vegas Blvd; admission free; ⊗ 11am-midnight) features animals, acrobats and magicians performing on center stage; shows are held every 30 minutes.

Quirky Las Vegas

For connoisseurs of over-the-top extravagance, the **Liberace Museum** (☎ 702-798-5595; www.liberace.org; 1775 E Tropicana Ave; adult/child $12/8; ⊗ 10am-5pm Mon-Sat, 1-5pm Sun) is a must-do. The home of 'Mr Showmanship' houses the most flamboyant art cars, outrageous costumes and ornate pianos you'll ever see.

The largest private collection of Elvis memorabilia is displayed at the **Elvis-A-Rama Museum** (☎ 702-309-7200; www.elvisarama.com; 3401

Industrial Rd; admission $10; ⊗ 10am-8pm). It's gaudy, cheesy and over-the-top, but then so was the man himself.

Sleeping

There's no shortage of places to stay in Vegas. Options range from filthy fleapits east of downtown to exquisite penthouse suites overlooking the Strip. Whatever you do, don't arrive without a reservation, at least for the first night. You'd be amazed how often every standard room in town is booked.

BUDGET

Barbary Coast (☎ 702-737-7111; www.barbarycoastcasino.com; 3595 S Las Vegas Blvd; r from $40; P ✗) With cheap rooms smack bang mid-Strip, the Barbary is great value and it's often hard to secure a bed. Rooms feature charming Victorian-era decor.

Circus Circus (☎ 702-734-0410; www.circuscircus.com; 2880 S Las Vegas Blvd; r from $40; P ✗ ✉) Most standard rooms at this family favorite have sofas and balconies. The decor is tasteful and many rooms are nonsmoking. Avoid the motel-style Manor rooms out back. Children under 18 stay free.

Also recommended:

Excalibur (☎ 702-597-7777; www.excalibur.com; 3050 S Las Vegas Blvd; r from $50; P ✗ ✉)

USA Hostels Las Vegas (☎ 702-385-1150; 1322 Fremont St; dm/s/d $15/35/45; ✗ ✉)

GOING TO THE CHAPEL, GOING TO GET MARRIED

Spontaneous weddings have always been a Vegas trademark. It must be part of that slightly naughty, lose your inhibitions, what happens in Vegas stays in Vegas theme, because more than 100,000 couples choose to say their vows here each year! Whether it's a planned affair, or a spur-of-the moment decision, Las Vegas offers more than 30 different places to tie the knot. There's no waiting period and you don't need a blood test. You just have to be at least 18 years old and show up at the **Marriage License Bureau** (☎ 702-455-4415; 200 S Third St; ⊗ 8am-midnight Mon-Thu, 24hr Fri-Sun). Once you have the certificate, it's off to the chapel.

For an out-of-this world marriage experience, head to the **Las Vegas Hilton** (☎ 702-697-8751; 3000 Paradise Rd; chapel ⊗ 8am-5pm), where you'll be tying the knot Star Trek–style. Intergalactic music plays as you cross the bridge of the USS *Enterprise,* and you'll even have a Klingon or Ferengi for your witness. If you want to keep it short-and-sweet, you'll pay about $500. More elaborate packages cost $1000 to $3000.

For something a little more traditional, try the **Little White Wedding Chapel** (☎ 702-382-5943; www.littlewhitechapel.com; 1301 S Las Vegas Blvd; ⊗ 24hr). It's welcomed thousands of couples since opening in 1946, and is a favorite spot for celebs to say 'I Do.' Demi Moore and Bruce Willis were hitched here. So was Michael Jordan. And who can forget Britney Spears? You can have an Elvis impersonator officiate or have the affair broadcast over the Internet. If you really *can't* wait to get married, the chapel will pick you up and take you to its sister property, the Tunnel of Vows Drive-Thru. Weddings ceremonies start at $60; packages cost $200 to $800.

MIDRANGE

Mandalay Bay (☎ 702-632-7777; www.mandalaybay
.com; 3950 S Las Vegas Blvd; r from $125; P X X)
The ornately appointed rooms at Mandalay Bay have a South Seas theme; amenities
include floor-to-ceiling windows and luxurious bathrooms. The sprawling pool complex, which includes a sand-and-surf beach
and the Euro-style Moorea Beach Club and
ultralounge, is one of its best assets.

Hard Rock Hotel & Casino (☎ 702-693-5000;
www.hardrockhotel.com; 4455 Paradise Rd; r from $125;
P X X) French doors reveal expansive
views and portraits of rockers grace the
stylish Euro-minimalist rooms. Suites have
large-screen TVs, wi-fi and jet tubs. The
action revolves around the lush pool area,
with a sexy sandy beach, whirlpools and
private cabanas.

Luxor (☎ 702-362-4000; www.luxor.com; 3900 S Las
Vegas Blvd; r $75-125; P X X) Featuring art-
deco and Egyptian furnishings and marble
bathrooms, Luxor's rooms are one of Vegas'
best midrange deals. Rooms in the newer
tower have better views than pyramid digs.

Monte Carlo (☎ 702-730-7777; www.monte-carlo
.com; 3770 S Las Vegas Blvd; r from $125; P X X)
Hardly Monaco, but traditional European
style permeates the spacious rooms. The
swimming complex is cool and the spa is
something to behold, with Chinese marble,
Indian stone, Italian porcelain, Indonesian
ceramics and Saudi Arabian granite.

Caesars Palace (☎ 702-731-7110; www.caesarspalace
.com; 3570 S Las Vegas Blvd; r from $125; P X X)
Caesars' standard rooms are some of the
most luxurious in town. Subtle design accents, like Pompeian mural wall treatments,
enhance the spaciousness.

THE AUTHOR'S CHOICE

Palms Casino Resort (☎ 702-942-7777; www
.palms.com; 4321 W Flamingo Rd; r from $125;
P X X) Off-Strip and originally aimed
at young locals, the post–*Real World* Palms
now attracts a flashier MTV-influenced
crowd and is a favorite with celebs like Paris
Hilton and Britney Spears. Standard rooms
are generous. Request an upper floor to
score a Strip view. For true luxury, rent the
Real World Suite (from $7500), where the
gang lived during filming. The 2900-sq-ft
suite looks just like it did in the TV show.

Also recommended:

New York-New York (☎ 702-740-6969; www
.nynyhotelcasino.com; 3790 S Las Vegas Blvd; r from $80;
P X X)
Mirage (☎ 702-791-7111; www.mirage.com; 3400 S Las
Vegas Blvd; r from $125; P X X)
Paris-Las Vegas (☎ 702-946-7000; www.parislv.com;
3655 S Las Vegas Blvd; r from $125; P X X)
Bally's (☎ 702-739-4111; www.ballyslv.com; 3645 S Las
Vegas Blvd; r from $125; P X X)
Rio (☎ 702-777-7777; www.playrio.com; 3700 W
Flamingo Rd; ste from $125; P X X)
Main Street Station (☎ 702-387-1896; www.main
streetcasino.com; 200 N Main St; r from $75; P X)

TOP END

True luxury comes cheaper here than almost anywhere else in the world. If you
drop wads of cash around the casino, expect
to be comped a sumptuous suite.

Venetian (☎ 702-414-1000; www.venetian.com;
3355 S Las Vegas Blvd; r from $300; P X X) Fronted
by flowing canals and graceful arched
bridges, the Venetian's standard rooms are
the largest and most luxurious in town, with
oversized Italian marble baths and canopy-
draped bedchambers.

THEhotel (☎ 702-632-7777; www.mandalaybay
.com; Mandalay Bay, 3950 S Las Vegas Blvd; ste from $300;
P X X ▢) From the moment you enter
the intimate lobby, you feel a world away
from the Strip's hustle-bustle. The expansive suites boast broadband Internet, wet
bars, plasma TVs, separate living areas and
cosmo NYC chic decor.

Four Seasons (☎ 702-632-5000; www.fourseasons
.com/lasvegas; Mandalay Bay, 3960 S Las Vegas Blvd;
r from $300; P X X ▢) This nongaming re-
sort, on Mandalay Bay's 35th through 39th
floors, emphasizes quiet comfort and 24/7
concierge coddling. In-room high-speed
Internet, a full-service spa and twice-daily
housekeeping seal the deal.

Eating

Sin City is an unmatched eating adventure.
Since Wolfgang Puck brought Spago to Caesars in 1992, celebrity Iron Chefs have taken
up residence in nearly every megaresort.
Cheap buffets and loss-leader meal deals
still exist, mostly downtown, but the gourmet quotient is high with prices to match.
Reservations are a must for fancier restaurants; book as far in advance as possible.
Every major casino has a 24-hour café and

at least a couple of restaurants. Vegas' restaurants alone could be fodder for an entire book; we've listed some of our favorites.

BUDGET

Victorian Room (☎ 702-737-7111; Barbary Coast, 3595 S Las Vegas Blvd; dishes $5-10; 🕑 24hr) Deep red leather booths, stained glass and polished brass add ambience to this lively and central coffee shop. Graveyard specialties like New York steak-and-eggs ($5.95) and 24/7 T-bone or prime rib deals make it a favorite after-hours hangout.

Siena Deli (☎ 702-736-8424; 2250 E Tropicana Ave; dishes $6-10; 🕑 8am-6:30pm Mon-Sat) Mama mia, Siena is the best deli in town, hands down. Make a meal out of Sicilian-style flat pizza and the housemade tiramisu. Or grab a mouthwatering hot or cold deli sandwich.

Paymon's Mediterranean Café & Hookah Lounge (☎ 702-731-6030; 4147 S Maryland Parkway; dishes $5-10; 🕑 breakfast, lunch & dinner) One of the city's few veggie spots. It serves items such as baked eggplant with fresh garlic, baba ganoush, tabouleh and hummus. The adjacent Hookah Lounge is a tranquil place to chill with a water pipe and fig-flavored cocktail.

MIDRANGE

808 (☎ 877-346-4642; Caesars Palace, 3570 S Las Vegas Blvd; dishes $15-35; 🕑 5:30-10:30pm Sun-Thu, 5:30-11pm Fri & Sat) Many locals regard this tropical island–themed delight as the city's top seafood stop. Chef Jean-Marie Josselin's creative menu mixes elements of French, Mediterranean, Indian and Pacific Rim cuisines with fabulous results.

Café Bellagio (☎ 702-693-7111; Bellagio, 3600 S Las Vegas Blvd; dishes $10; 🕑 24hr) Among the best eateries in town, the menu offers exciting twists on traditional American favorites.

THE AUTHOR'S CHOICE

Bellagio (☎ 702-693-7111; www.bellagio.com; 3600 S Las Vegas Blvd; r from $300; P ⊗ ⊛) If anything in Vegas is truly 'spectacular,' this luxe five-diamond destination is it. Oversize, lavish bathrooms feature Italian marble, plush robes and deep soaking tubs. Updated guestrooms are styled with original artwork and picture windows overlooking the lush grounds. The stately Spa Tower suites elevate luxury to a new level.

Big draws are the delicious coffee drinks, flowery setting, and gorgeous views of the swimming pool and garden areas.

House of Blues (☎ 702-632-7600; Mandalay Bay, 3960 S Las Vegas Blvd; dishes $10-20; 🕑 lunch & dinner) The swampy bayou atmosphere and down home southern cuisine at this homey roadhouse (think burgers, salads and BBQ) is enhanced by eccentric outsider folk art. Skip church: the uplifting Sunday Gospel Brunch includes unlimited champagne.

Zeffirino (☎ 702-414-3500; Grand Canal Shoppes, Venetian, 3355 S Las Vegas Blvd; dishes $12-15; 🕑 lunch & dinner) Housemade breads and seafood prepared with Venetian techniques are the highlights. Handcrafted furnishings accent the elegant dining room, with porch seating overlooking the canal.

Buffet at Bellagio (☎ 702-693-7111; casino level, Bellagio, 3600 S Las Vegas Blvd; breakfast $12, brunch $15, dinner $25-35) The Bellagio rightfully takes top honors for Vegas' best live-action buffet. The sumptuous all-you-can-eat spread includes such crowd-pleasers as smoked salmon, roast turkey, and innumerable creative Chinese, Japanese and Italian dishes.

TOP END

Picasso (☎ 702-693-7223; Bellagio, 3600 S Las Vegas Blvd; dishes from $30; 🕑 6-9:30pm Wed-Mon) Five-star chef Julian Serrano delivers artistic Franco-Iberian fusion in a museumlike setting. Original eponymous masterpieces complement main dishes, like the signature sautéed fallow deer medallions and seafood boudin. Linger on the patio over a digestif. Prix fixe ($85) and degustation ($95) menus recommended. Jacket and tie suggested. Reservations are essential but difficult.

Red Square (☎ 702-632-7407; Mandalay Bay, 3960 S Las Vegas Blvd; dishes $20-25; 🕑 5:30-10:30pm) How post-perestroika: a headless Lenin invites you to join your comrades for a tipple behind the red curtain in this postmodern Russian restaurant. There's a solid ice bar, heaps of caviar, a huge selection of frozen vodkas and infusions – and loaner sable fur coats for when you step into the locker!

Bally's Steakhouse (☎ 702-967-7999; Bally's, 3645 S Las Vegas Blvd; brunch $58; 🕑 brunch, lunch & dinner) Indulge at the best, and most expensive, Sunday brunch in town. Ice sculptures and lavish flower arrangements abound at the Sterling Brunch, as do food stations featuring roast duckling, steak Diane, seared salmon with beet butter sauce – you get the idea.

Drinking

Vegas has its share of fantastic watering holes that lure even the most hard-core gamblers away from the tables.

Ghost Bar (☎ 702-942-7777; Palms Casino Resort, 4321 W Flamingo Rd; admission $10-20) A clubby crowd, often thick with celebs, packs the Palms' 55th-floor watering hole. It's up-to-the-minute hot, glam to the max. DJs spin groovy tunes while patrons sip overpriced cocktails amid the sky-high 360-degree panoramas and smart sci-fi decor. Dress to kill.

V Bar (☎ 702-414-3200; Venetian, 3355 S Las Vegas Blvd) Glam young thangs meet and greet in this beautiful minimalist lounge. The acid jazz and low-key house music are mere accoutrements since low lighting and secluded sitting areas (and sturdy martinis) encourage intimate behavior.

Hush (☎ 702-261-1000; Polo Towers, 3745 S Las Vegas Blvd, 19th fl; admission $5-20) Tucked away high atop a timeshare condo complex, this lounge is best known by a hip younger crowd for its 180-degree Strip view. The rooftop pool, private Moroccan cabanas and oversize, elevated beds open up for uptempo DJ nights.

Entertainment

Las Vegas has no shortage of entertainment on any given night. For tickets to many major concerts and sports events (including fights), contact **Ticketmaster** (☎ 702-474-4000).

CLUBS & LIVE MUSIC

Little expense has been spared to bring clubs at the Strip's megaresorts up to par with counterparts in New York and Los Angeles.

Ra (☎ 702-262-4949; Luxor, 3900 S Las Vegas Blvd; cover $10-30; 🕙 10pm-dawn Wed-Sat) Vegas' most spectacular club is fit for the ancient Egyptian god of the sun. Wednesday's Pleasuredome/Flaunt brings fashion shows, deep house and an old-school mix. The dress code is glam, the crowd young and sybaritic.

Rain (☎ 702-942-7777; Palms, 4321 W Flamingo Rd; cover $20-40; 🕙 11pm-late Thu-Sat) Britney Spears once threw an impromptu concert while partying at this hot, hot club. Enter through a futuristic tunnel and immediately get lost in color and motion. The bamboo dancefloor

appears to float on a bed of water, undulating amid fog and pyrotechnic displays.

Body English (☎ 702-693-4000; Hard Rock, 4455 Paradise Rd; cover $20; 🕙 10:30pm-4am Fri-Sun) The Hard Rock's elegant Euro-style club emphasizes VIP pampering. Booth reservations require one bottle ($300 minimum) per foursome, but there's a big bar upstairs. Famous folk hang out in the VIP rooms, while the lesser-knowns dance to mainstream house, hip-hop and rock tunes below.

House of Blues (☎ 702-632-7600; Mandalay Bay, 3950 S Las Vegas Blvd; cover $10-100) Blues is the tip of the hog at this Mississippi Delta juke joint. Seating is limited, so arrive early (shows from 6pm). Sight lines are good and the outsider folk-art decor is übercool.

PRODUCTION SHOWS

There are hundreds of shows to choose from in Vegas.

Perpetually popular is Cirque du Soleil's aquatic show, **O** (☎ 702-796-9999; admission $99-150; 🕙 7:30pm & 10:30pm), performed at the Bellagio. Cirque du Soleil also presents **Mystère** (☎ 702-796-9999; admission $95, limited seats for $60; 🕙 7pm & 10pm Wed-Sun), at Treasure Island (aka TI), and the adult-themed **Zumanity** (☎ 866-606-7111; admission $65-125; 🕙 7:30pm & 10:30pm Fri-Tue), at New York-New York.

Folies Bergère (☎ 800-829-9034; Tropicana, 3801 S Las Vegas Blvd; admission $49 & $59) Las Vegas' longest-running production show is a tribute to the Parisian Music Hall featuring some of the most beautiful showgirls in town. Shows (topless) are performed at 10:30pm Monday, Wednesday, Thursday and Saturday, and at 8:30pm Tuesday and Friday. On each of these nights a 'covered' show is performed at 7:30pm.

STRIP CLUBS

Prostitution may be illegal, but there are plenty of places offering the illusion of sex on demand.

Sapphire (☎ 702-796-6000; 3025 S Industrial Rd; cover $20) Vegas' largest adult entertainment complex, featuring a massive multilevel main stage and a story-high martini display.

Olympic Garden (☎ 702-385-9361; 1531 S Las Vegas Blvd; cover $20; 🕙 24hr) Wins high marks from topless club aficionados. Up to 50 dancers work at any given time, thus there's something to please everyone. Studs strip upstairs Wednesday through Sunday.

Getting There & Around

Just south of the major Strip casinos and easily accessible from I-15, **McCarran International Airport** (☎ 702-261-5743) has direct flights from most US cities, and some from Canada and Europe. **Bell Trans** (☎ 702-739-7990) offers shuttle service ($4.25) between the airport and the Strip. Downtown destinations are slightly higher.

The **Greyhound bus station** (☎ 702-384-9561; 200 S Main St), downtown, has regular buses to and from Los Angeles ($37, six hours), San Diego ($47, eight hours) and San Francisco ($70, 15 hours). **Amtrak** (☎ 800-872-7245) does not run trains to Las Vegas, although it does offer a connecting bus service from Los Angeles ($35, six hours).

Citizens Area Transport (☎ 702-228-7433) operates local buses ($1.25 to $2). Bus No 301 runs frequently 24 hours daily between the Strip and downtown.

The **Strip Trolley** (☎ 702-382-1404) does a loop from Mandalay Bay to the Stratosphere and out to the Las Vegas Hilton every 25 minutes until 2am ($1.65).

A monorail connects the Sahara to the MGM Grand, stopping at major Strip megaresorts along the way, and operating from 7am to 2am. A single ride costs $3; a day pass is $10.

Dozens of agencies rent cars for competitive prices, including **Dollar** (☎ 800-800-4000), which has windows in numerous Strip casinos.

Contact the **Nevada Department of Transport** (☎ 877-687-6237; www.nvroads.com) for conditions on the roads.

AROUND LAS VEGAS
Red Rock Canyon

The dramatic natural splendor of this **park** (☎ 702-363-1921; admission $5; ☽ 8am-dusk) is the perfect anecdote to Vegas' artificial brightness. A 20-mile drive west of the Strip, the canyon is actually more like a valley with the steep, rugged red rock escarpment rising 3000ft on its western edge. There's a 13-mile, one-way scenic loop with access to hiking trails and **camping** (campsites $10) 2 miles east of the visitor center.

Lake Mead & Hoover Dam

Lake Mead and Hoover Dam are the most-visited sites within the **Lake Mead National Recreation Area** (☎ 702-293-8907), which encompasses 110-mile-long Lake Mead, 67-mile-long Lake Mohave and many miles of desert around the lakes. The excellent **Alan Bible Visitors Center** (☎ 702-293-8990; ☽ 8:30am-4:30pm), on Hwy 93 halfway between Boulder City and Hoover Dam, has information on recreation. From there, North Shore Rd winds around the lake and makes a great scenic drive.

The graceful curve and art-deco style of the 726ft **Hoover Dam** contrasts superbly with the stark landscape. Originally called Boulder Dam, this New Deal project was completed in 1935 at a cost of $175 million. It's original intent was flood control, but it now helps supply Colorado River water (and hydroelectric power) to thirsty cities, including Las Vegas. Visitors are limited to surface tours (adult/child $10/4), and tickets are sold at the **visitor center** (☎ 702-294-3517; ☽ 9am-4:30pm). Note that commercial trucks and buses are not allowed to cross the dam.

Valley of Fire State Park

A masterpiece of desert scenery filled with psychedelically shaped sandstone outcroppings, this **park** (admission $5) makes for another great Vegas escape. Near the north end of Lake Mead National Recreation Area, it's easily accessible from Las Vegas. Hwy 169 runs right past the **visitor center** (☎ 702-397-2088; ☽ 8:30am-4:30pm), which has hiking information and excellent desert-life exhibits. The winding side road to **White Domes** is especially scenic. The valley is at its most fiery at dawn and dusk, so consider staying overnight in one of the park's two year-round **campgrounds** (campsites $8).

Laughlin

On the banks of the Colorado River, Laughlin is the poor man's Vegas. The casinos lining the strip sport familiar names – Flamingo, Harrahs – but the look is more blue jeans than bling-bling. Laughlin's a down home gambling type of place – think burgers, Budweiser and penny slots. It attracts an older more sedate crowd, the kind of folks looking to gamble in the city without all the sin.

One reason Laughlin has become so popular is that it boasts some of the cheapest hotel rates in the West – and while rooms are fairly bland, these are no fleapits. Try the very pleasant **Colorado Belle** (☎ 702-298-4000,

800-477-4837; www.coloradobelle.com; r from $20; 🔀 🛒 🖭), with a Mississippi River boat theme. Right on the river, the **River Palms** (☎ 702-298-2242, 800-835-7903; www.rvrpalm.com; r from $20; 🔀 🛒) has a nonsmoking gambling room and quite a few restaurants to choose from.

WESTERN NEVADA

The western corner of the state is where modern Nevada got its start. It was the site of the state's first trading post, first farms and the famous Comstock silver lode in and around Virginia City, which spawned towns, financed the Union side in the Civil War and earned Nevada its statehood. For information about the Nevada side of Lake Tahoe, see p861.

Reno

'The Biggest Little City in the World,' Reno's a slightly hokey cowpoke type of country town trying hard to upgrade its image to Vegaslike proportions, building a handful of flashier casinos and an impressive art museum. But Reno's greatest asset is its lack of pretentiousness. Its charm derives from the fact that it *isn't* Vegas. A visit to the little city with big dreams provides insight into working-class Nevada life, an experience that's gritty, real and refreshingly void of Hollywood gloss.

Reno's downtown is north of the Truckee River and south of I-80. Most of the action is along Virginia St, between 1st and 6th Sts. You'll also find a **visitor center** (☎ 775-827-7600; www.renolaketahoe.com; 300 N Center St; ⏰ 8am-5pm Mon-Fri).

SIGHTS & ACTIVITIES
Casinos
Few of Reno's casinos have the flash of Vegas, though some do try. The attention-grabbing **Silver Legacy** (☎ 775-329-4777; 407 N Virginia St) shows off with a 19th-century streetscape plus sound-and-light shows inside a 120ft dome. One of the city's newest, and nicest, casinos is the **Siena** (☎ 775-337-6260; 1 S Lake St), just south of the Truckee River, which has Tuscan styling and a more subdued atmosphere. Veteran downtown establishments include **Fitzgeralds** (☎ 800-535-5825; 255 N Virginia St), with its silly and outdated 'lucky leprechaun' theme, the nearby **Eldorado** (☎ 775-786-5700; 345 N Virginia St) and **Club Cal Neva** (☎ 877-777-7303; cnr 2nd & N Virginia Sts).

Away from downtown are the flashy **Peppermill** (☎ 775-826-2121; 2707 S Virginia St); the huge **Reno Hilton** (☎ 775-789-2000; 2500 E 2nd St), east of downtown near Hwy 395; and **John Ascuaga's Nugget** (☎ 775-356-3300; 1100 Nugget Ave), off I-80 in nearby Sparks.

Other Attractions
You'll find a mix of contemporary art and historical exhibitions at the **Nevada Museum of Art** (☎ 775-329-3333; 160 W Liberty St; adult/student $7/5; ⏰ 11am-6pm Tue-Sun, 11am-8pm Thu). In an eye-catching black structure, allegedly inspired by the Black Rock Desert, it takes Reno architecture (and local art exhibition) to new, intriguing levels.

The **National Automobile Museum** (☎ 775-333-9300; 10 Lake St; adult/child $8/3; ⏰ 9:30am-5:30pm Mon-Sat, 10am-4pm Sun) has an impressive collection of one-of-a-kind vehicles, including James Dean's 1949 Mercury and a 1938 Phantom Corsair.

Reno's cutting edge **National Bowling Stadium** (☎ 775-334-2695; 300 N Center St; admission free; ⏰ 6am-2:30am), the 'Taj Mahal of Tenpins,' has 78 lanes and a 450ft scoreboard. Check it out from the spectator stage or get in the swing of things with a private lesson.

SLEEPING
The casinos are cheapest Sunday through Thursday. Weekend rates can be much higher and hotels do sell out, so phone ahead.

Siena (☎ 775-337-6260; 1 S Lake St; www.sienareno .com; r from $60; 🅿 🔀 🛒) Reno's newest hotel is also one of its most luxurious, with cozy, nicely appointed rooms. Midweek prices can be surprisingly affordable, making it one of Reno's best bargains.

Silver Legacy (☎ 775-329-4777; www.silverlegacy reno.com; 407 N Virginia St; r from $60; 🅿 🔀 🛒) The Victorian-themed rooms at this large hotel-casino right downtown are basic, but very clean and comfortable. If you like a view, ask for a room high in the tower facing the mountains.

Seasons Inn (☎ 775-322-6000; www.seasonsinn .com; 495 West St; r $50-100; 🅿 🔀) This reliable motel has clean, fairly quiet rooms close to the casino action.

Sundowner (☎ 775-786-7050; www.sundowner -casino.com; 450 N Arlington St; r $35-70; 🅿 🔀 🛒) Consistently one of Reno's cheapest hotel options, rooms are adequate but hardly exciting.

SOUTHWEST

EATING & DRINKING

Most casinos have all-you-can-eat buffets, although the quality of food isn't great. Check casino coffee shops and restaurants for dining deals.

Peg's Glorified Ham & Eggs (☎ 775-329-2600; 420 S Sierra; dishes $5-11; ☯ 6:30am-2pm) Locally regarded for serving the best breakfast in town, Peg's offers tasty comfort food that's not too greasy. It's the perfect place to sit outside and read the Sunday paper while munching on an overstuffed omelet.

Harrah's Steakhouse (☎ 775-788-2929; 219 N Center St; dishes $20-30; ☯ lunch & dinner) This elegant restaurant has a romantic atmosphere – think roses, linen and low lighting. The recipient of numerous local awards for fine dining, it serves the requisite big juicy steaks along with other meat and seafood options. There's a decent selection of salads, but not much else for vegetarians.

Lexie's (☎ 775-337-6260; dishes $10-20; ☯ lunch & dinner) Elegant Lexie's, inside the Siena, faces the Truckee River, and offers gourmet beef, seafood and other dishes with Italian overtones. It also has a huge selection of wines.

Brew Brothers (☎ 775-786-5700; 345 N Virginia St; dishes $6-12; ☯ breakfast, lunch & dinner) In the Eldorado, this slightly hipper-than-average casino eatery serves good pizza and truly tasty microbrews. The place gets packed and loud, though, when the nightly bands kick in.

Deux Gros Nez (☎ 775-786-9400; 249 California Ave; dishes $4-7; ☯ breakfast, lunch & dinner) This quirky café serves strong coffee and healthy fare, including smoothies, sandwiches, breakfast egg dishes and vegetarian pasta dinners.

Bubinga Lounge (☎ 775-786-5700; 345 N Virginia St) Reno's hottest nightspot, the Bubinga boasts two separate themed bars, a big dancefloor and fun cocktails. It's a good place to flirt. Look for it in the Eldorado.

GETTING THERE & AROUND

The **Reno-Tahoe International Airport** (☎ 775-328-6870) is a few miles southeast of downtown. **Greyhound** (☎ 775-322-8801; 155 Stevenson St) has frequent buses to San Francisco ($33, six hours) and Los Angeles ($62, 12 hours), and one daily to Las Vegas ($72, 10 hours). **Amtrak** (☎ 775-329-8638; 135 E Commercial Row) has daily service to Sacramento ($65, five hours) and Oakland ($71, 9½ hours).

Many hotels offer free shuttles to and from the airport. Local bus system **Citifare**

(☎ 775-348-7433) covers the metropolitan area (adult/child $1.50/1.25); the main transfer station is at E 4th and Center Sts.

Pyramid Lake

A piercingly blue expanse in an otherwise barren landscape, Pyramid Lake, 25 miles north of Reno on the Paiute Indian Reservation, is a stunning sight. Popular for recreation and fishing, the shores are lined with beaches and interesting tufa formations (a porous rock formed by water deposits). Near the lake's eastern shore, Anaho Island is a bird sanctuary for the American white pelican. Permits for **camping** (campsites per night $9) and **fishing** (per person $7) are available at the **ranger station** (☎ 775-476-1155; ☯ 8am-6pm Mon-Wed, 7am-5pm Thu-Sun), on Hwy 446 in Sutcliffe.

Carson City

Handsome old buildings and pleasant tree-lined streets abound in Nevada's state capital, a small but fast-growing town. It's a refreshing, underwhelming place offering quiet retreat from big city clutter. The casinos are sedate, and there are a few worthwhile historical museums to discover.

Hwy 395/Carson St is the main drag. The **visitor center** (☎ 775-882-1565; www.carson citychamber.com; 1900 S Carson St; ☯ 8am-5pm Mon-Fri), a mile south of downtown, gives out a local map with interesting historical walking and driving tours. For hiking and camping information, stop by the United States Forest Service's (USFS) **Carson Ranger District Office** (☎ 775-882-2766; 1536 S Carson St; ☯ 8am-4:30pm Mon-Fri).

Housed inside the 1869 US Mint building, the excellent **Nevada State Museum** (☎ 775-687-4810; 600 N Carson St; admission $3; ☯ 8:30am-4:30pm) has dioramas showing Native American life and, in the basement, a re-created gold mine.

On downtown's northern fringe you can't miss the neon cowboy outside the **Frontier Motel** (☎ 775-882-1377; 1718 N Carson St; r from $35; Ⓟ ⊠), a classic roadside spot with clean, basic rooms. Just south of downtown is the nicely maintained **Desert Hills Motel** (☎ 775-882-1932; www.deserthillsmotel.com; 1010 S Carson St; r from $60; Ⓟ ⊠). Hungry bargain hunters will enjoy the prime rib and other discounted dinners at the **Carson Nugget** (☎ 775-882-1626; 507 N Carson St; dishes $5-15; ☯ breakfast, lunch & dinner).

Greyhound (☎ 775-882-3375; 1718 N Carson St) buses stop at the Frontier Motel on the way to and from Reno ($12, one hour) and Las Vegas ($72, nine hours).

Virginia City

During the 1860s gold rush Virginia City was a high-flying, rip-roaring Wild West boomtown. Newspaperman Samuel Clemens, alias Mark Twain, spent some time in this raucous place during its heyday; years later his eyewitness descriptions of mining life were published in a book called *Roughing It*. Good times came to an end in 1875, when a fire destroyed more than 2000 buildings. Virginia City was miraculously rebuilt within a year, but never again achieved its former rough-and-tumble glory.

There's not much going on in Virginia City today, but the town is a National Historic Landmark, with a main street of Victorian buildings, wooden sidewalks and some hokey but fun 'museums.' The main drag is C St, with the **visitor center** (☎ 775-847-0311; 86 S C St; ☺ 9am-5pm Mon-Fri) in the historic Crystal Bar.

Many of the town's attractions are seriously silly, though some are true gems, such as the quirky **Way It Was Museum** (☎ 775-847-0766; 113 N C St; admission $3; ☺ 10am-6pm). It's a fun, old-fashioned place offering good background information on mining the lode. The half-hour tour of the **Chollar Mine** (☎ 775-847-0155; adult/child $5/2; ☺ noon-5pm summer), at the south end of F St (hours vary, call to confirm), is also worthwhile. To see how the mining elite lived, stop by the **Mackay Mansion** (D St) and the **Castle** (B St). Dozens of played-out miners are buried at the picturesque **Silver Terrace Cemetery**, off Carson St.

Virginia City has a few peaceful places to sleep. A mile south of town, the **Gold Hill Hotel** (☎ 775-847-0111; www.goldhillhotel.net; Hwy 342; r $55-130; ☒) is a great choice. Claiming to be Nevada's oldest hotel, rooms in the original hotel are more unique, featuring brass and canopy beds, and even a sleigh-shaped bed.

The vegetarian friendly **Mandarin Garden** (☎ 775-847-9288; 30 B St; dishes $4-8; ☺ lunch & dinner) serves cheap and tasty noodle-and-rice plates.

If you're thirsty, C St offers a number of creaky but cool taverns, including the crusty **Red Dog Saloon** (☎ 775-847-0202; 76 N C St), where psychedelic-rock pioneers the Charlatans were the house band in 1965.

NEVADA GREAT BASIN

Outside Nevada's major cities, the land is largely empty, textured with range after range of mountains and arid valleys. It's big country out here – wild, remote and quiet. A trip across Nevada's Great Basin is a serene, almost haunting, experience. But those on the quest of the 'Great American Roadtrip' will relish the fascinating historic towns and quirky diversions tucked away along lonely desert highways.

Along I-80

This is the old fur trappers' route, which followed the Humboldt River from northeast Nevada to Lovelock, near Reno. Heading east from Reno, **Winnemucca** is the first worthwhile stop. It boasts a vintage downtown, shops, and numerous motels and restaurants. Some 50 miles north, the Santa Rosa Mountains offer rugged scenery and ghost towns. For information, stop by the **chamber of commerce** (☎ 775-623-2225; 30 W Winnemucca Blvd; ☺ 8:30am-4:30pm Mon-Fri) or the USFS **Santa Rosa Ranger Station** (☎ 775-623-5025; 1200 E Winnemucca Blvd; ☺ 8:30am-4:30pm Mon-Fri).

Southwest of Winnemucca is the folk-art sculpture garden **Thunder Mountain**, directly off I-80 in Imlay. Built by WWII veteran Chief Rolling Mountain Thunder as a monument to the injustices against Native Americans, it's full of curious figures, buildings and other structures. Self-guided tours are free and available anytime.

The culture of the American West is most diligently cultivated in **Elko**. Aspiring cowboys and cowgirls should visit the **Western Folklife Center** (☎ 775-738-7508; 501 Railroad St; admission free; ☺ 9-5pm Mon-Fri), which offers art and history exhibits, and also hosts the popular **Cowboy Poetry Gathering** each January. At the town center, **Stockmen's Casino & Hotel** (☎ 800-648-2345; www.fh-inc.com; 340 Commercial St; r from $40; ☒ ☒) is a fine place to stay, with clean, remodeled rooms.

To the south of Elko, the **Ruby Mountains** are a superbly rugged range. The picture-perfect village of **Lamoille** has food and lodging, and one of the most-photographed rural churches in the USA.

Along Highway 50

On 'the loneliest road in America' barren brown hills collide with big blue skies. The highway goes on forever, crossing solitary Great Basin terrain. Town's are few and far between, the only sounds the hum of the engine or the whisper of wind. Once part of the Lincoln Hwy, lonesome Hwy 50 follows the route of the Overland Stagecoach, the Pony Express and the first transcontinental telegraph line. It's a wonderful desert drive, a soothing relief from Nevada's pulsating neon cities.

Fallon is an agricultural and military town, home to a naval air base. The **Lariat** (☎ 775-423-3181; 850 W Williams St; r $44; ⚄ ⚃) offers comfortable motel rooms. Three miles west on Hwy 50, **Bob's Root Beer Drive Inn** (☎ 775-867-2769; 4150 Reno Hwy; dishes from $5; ☽ closed winter) is a vintage drive-in, serving salads, soups, sandwiches and very tasty root beer floats.

Heading east, the next substantial town is **Austin**, rundown since its 1880s heyday but still interesting. The mountainous area around it is lovely, and Austin's **USFS office** (☎ 775-964-2671; 100 Midas Rd; ☽ 8am-4:30pm Mon-Fri), just off Hwy 50, can recommend hikes and driving loops. **Mountain biking** is also popular. Stop by the friendly **Tyrannosaurus-Rex** (☎ 775-964-1212; 270 Maine St) shop, just east of town, for maps, frozen yogurt and bike rentals (from about $25 a day).

To the southwest of Austin, the **Berlin-Ichthyosaur State Park** (☎ 775-964-2440; admission $3) features the ghost town of Berlin and the fossil remains of half a dozen ichthyosaurs (carnivorous marine reptiles that lived here 225 million years ago). Daily fossil tours are offered in summer (adult/child $2/1), and there's a good year-round **campground** (campsites $11).

During the late 19th century, $40 million worth of silver was extracted from the hills near **Eureka**. The town is now fairly well preserved, possessing a handsome courthouse, the interesting **Eureka Sentinel Museum** (☎ 775-237-5010; 10 N Monroe St; admission free; ☽ 10am-6pm), a beautifully restored 1880 opera house and a few well-kept motels.

Larger **Ely**, another silver- and copper-mining town, is worth a stop. The downtown has beautiful historic murals and great old neon signs, along with some decent motels.

Near the Nevada–Utah border is the awesome, uncrowded **Great Basin National Park**. It encompasses 13,063ft Wheeler Peak, rising abruptly from the desert. Hiking trails near the summit take in superb country with glacial lakes, ancient bristlecone pines and even a permanent ice field. Admission is free; the park **visitor center** (☎ 775-234-7331) arranges guided tours of **Lehman Caves** (admission $2-8), which are richly decorated with rare limestone formations. There are four developed **campgrounds** (campsites $10) within the park.

Along Highway 95

Hwy 95 goes roughly north–south through the western part of the state, the southern section is starkly scenic as it passes the Nevada Test Site (where more than 720 nuclear weapons were exploded in the 1950s). In Beatty, the gracious **HI Happy Burro Hostel** (☎ 775-553-9130; happyburro@pcweb.net; 100 Main St; dm/d $18/35; Ⓟ ☐) is a real gem, located inside a beautiful refurbished antique motel.

Along Highways 375 & 93

Hwy 375, dubbed the 'Extraterrestrial Hwy,' intersects Hwy 93 near top-secret **Area 51**, part of Nellis Air Force Base and a supposed holding area for captured UFOs. In the tiny town of **Rachel**, on Hwy 375, **Little A'Le'Inn** (☎ 775-729-2515; www.aleinn.com; r $45) accommodates earthlings and aliens alike, and sells extraterrestrial souvenirs.

Continuing east, Hwy 93 passes through a gorgeous Joshua-tree grove before arriving in **Caliente**, a former railroad town with a mission-style 1923 depot. Area attractions include **Cathedral Gorge State Park**, with campsites amid badlands-style cliffs. Twenty miles north, **Pioche** is an attractive mining town overlooking beautiful Lake Valley.

ARIZONA

Sure it's cheesy to proclaim, but Arizona is a state that puts the *grand* in Grand Canyon. A land of magnificent purple sunsets, it's a place where you can kick off your boots and sing by the campfire amid looming saguaro cacti. A place where leathery old-timers spin yarns about the bad old days – shootouts and outlaws, ladies of the night and the thrill of striking gold. It's a state rich in history, much of it tragic, where Native Americans were persecuted for many years, pushed off their land onto barren reservations. And it's a place filled with hope, where the heart of the Old West still beats strong, where somehow Native American tribes have managed to survive, and where tourists can learn about their long, tumultuous history.

Arizona is graced with larger-than-life sights; you might not know exactly where they're located, but everyone's seen the photos of the drop-your-jaw-in-awe canyon, watched the movies where cowboys gallop past Monument Valley's fiery red spindles and orange buttes, heard the stories about Doc Holliday and the shootout at the OK Corral. Nestled amid all the open space, are sprawling cities known for their silky green golf courses, retirement villages and spas. And small shabby chic boomtowns that never quite busted, artsy places where you can step back in time for a day and ponder what life must have been like in the times that inspired the legends.

History

Native American tribes inhabited Arizona for centuries before Spanish explorer Francisco Vásquez de Coronado launched a Southwest expedition here from Mexico City in 1540. Settlers and missionaries followed in his wake, and by the mid-19th century the US controlled Arizona. The Indian Wars, in which the US Army battled Indians to 'protect' settlers and claim land for the government, officially ended in 1886 with the surrender of Apache warrior Geronimo.

Railroad and mining expansion grew. In 1912 President Theodore Roosevelt's support for damming the territory's rivers led to Arizona becoming the 48th state. After WWII growth exploded, as more and more folks discovered it was a great place to live.

Today Arizona is a state in transition. Fifty years of rapid growth have taken a toll on the state's limited natural resources. Scarcity of water remains among the foremost issues for Arizona lawmakers, who continue the desperate search for water needed to supply the burgeoning cities.

Arizona has the third-largest population of Native Americans in the USA. Issues pertaining to poverty and positive assimilation of these peoples into equitable positions in society are also front-and-center topics, yet to be fully concluded.

More illegal immigrants sneak across the border from Mexico into Arizona than any other US state, and illegal immigration and problems with lax border control are hot topics. In August, 2005, Arizona Governor Janet Napolitano declared a border emergency in four Arizona counties and has moved to release up to $1.5 million in state funding to tighten border security in these counties. The money will be used for overtime pay for law enforcement officers, to repair border fences and, among other things, to meet costs related to deaths of illegal immigrants.

Information

Arizona's state sales tax is 5.6%, though the actual rate fluctuates from city to city. Generally speaking, lodging rates in southern Arizona (including Phoenix, Tucson and Yuma) are much higher in winter and spring, which are considered the state's 'high season.'

Arizona Office of Tourism (☎ 602-230-7733, 800-842-8257; www.arizonaguide.com; 2702 N 3rd St, Ste 4015, Phoenix, AZ 85004) Free state information.

Arizona Public Lands Information Center (☎ 602-417-9300; www.publiclands.org; 222 N Central Ave, Phoenix, AZ 85004) Information about USFS, NPS, Bureau of Land Management (BLM) and state lands and parks.

PHOENIX

Golf courses and strip malls, palm trees, strange sandy mountains and tall buildings, an endless maze of tangled freeways – at first glance the Greater Phoenix Metropolitan Area appears a confusing jumble. Covering almost 2000 sq miles, the metropolis is easily the largest in the Southwest and incorporates dozens of bedroom communities,

SOUTHWEST

WHAT'S THE TIME?

Arizona is on Mountain Standard Time, but is the only western state that does not observe daylight saving time from spring to early fall. The exception is the Navajo Reservation, which *does* observe daylight saving time.

with Scottsdale, Mesa and Tempe the most appealing. Boasting more than 300 days of sunshine a year, Phoenix is searing hot in summer (think above 110°F) but delightful in winter. Many visitors start their Southwest vacations here, and pause for a few days to check out the sights. Major museums, superlative shopping, relaxing resorts, delectable dining, spectator sports and golfing greens (where do they get that water?) abound. Relaxed sophistication is the city's hallmark. A cowboy hat and jeans are rarely out of place, ties seldom required.

History

Until the completion of Theodore Roosevelt Dam in 1911, northeast of town on the Salt River, modern Phoenix didn't amount to much more than a desert outpost. The Hohokam people lived here as early as 300 BC and developed a complex system of irrigation canals, only to mysteriously abandon them around AD 1450. The US Army built Fort McDowell northeast of Phoenix in the mid-1860s, and the railway arrived in 1887. Once Theodore Roosevelt Dam was built, however, the region began to boom. The Central Arizona Project (CAP), a $4 billion project completed in the early 1990s amid much controversy, brought more water to the region from the Colorado River via a series of canals and pipelines that run 336 miles from Lake Havasu to Tucson.

Orientation

Most of the valley sits approximately 1100ft above sea level, though it's ringed by mountains that range from 2500ft to more than 7000ft in elevation. Central Ave runs north–south through Phoenix, dividing west addresses from east addresses; Washington St runs west–east dividing north address from south addresses.

Scottsdale, Tempe and Mesa are east of the airport. Scottsdale Rd runs north–south between Scottsdale and Tempe. The airport is 3 miles southeast of downtown.

Information

BOOKSTORES

Book Store (☎ 602-279-3910; 4230 N 7th Ave) Large selection of books and magazines.
Wide World of Maps (☎ 602-279-2323; 2626 W Indian School Rd) Dedicated to maps and guidebooks.

EMERGENCY

Emergency number (☎ 911)
Phoenix Police Department (☎ 602-262-6151; 620 W Washington St)
Scottsdale Police Department (☎ 480-312-5000; 9065 E Via Linda Ave)

INTERNET ACCESS

Central Phoenix Library (☎ 602-262-4636; 1221 N Central Ave; 🕑 10am-9pm Mon-Thu, 10am-6pm Fri & Sat, noon-6pm Sun) Free Internet access.

MEDIA

Arizona Republic (☎ 602-444-8000; www.azcentral.com) Arizona's largest newspaper; publishes free entertainment guide, the *Rep,* every Thursday.
Phoenix New Times (☎ 602-271-0400; www.phoenixnewtimes.com) The major Phoenix free weekly; lots of event and restaurant listings.

MEDICAL SERVICES

Arizona Dental Association (☎ 602-957-4777) Dental referrals.
Banner Good Samaritan Medical Center (☎ 602-239-2000; 1111 E McDowell Rd; 🕑 24hr emergency)

MONEY

Foreign exchange is available at the airport and major bank branches.

POST

Post office (☎ 602-253-9648; 522 N Central Ave)

TOURIST INFORMATION

Downtown Phoenix Visitor Information Center (☎ 602-254-6500; www.visitphoenix.com; 50 N 2nd St; 🕑 8am-5pm Mon-Fri) Main office of the Phoenix Convention & Visitors Bureau (CVB).
Mesa Convention & Visitors Bureau (☎ 480-827-4700, 800-283-6372; www.mesacvb.com; 120 N Center St; 🕑 8am-5pm Mon-Fri)
Scottsdale Convention & Visitors Bureau (☎ 480-421-1004; www.scottsdalecvb.com; 4343 N Scottsdale Rd, Ste 170; 🕑 8:30am-6pm Mon-Fri, 9am-1pm Sat)

SOUTHWEST

PHOENIX

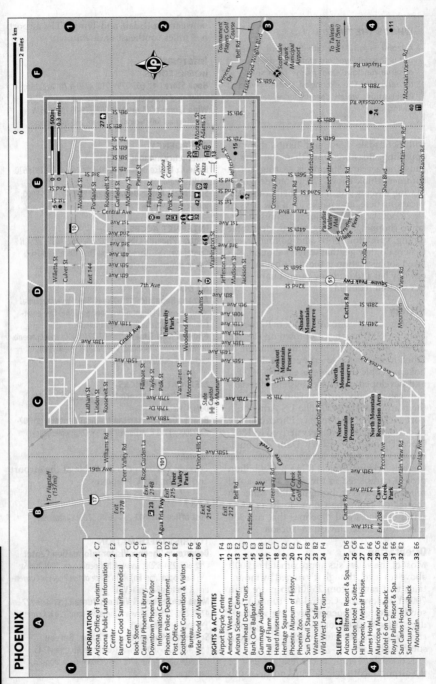

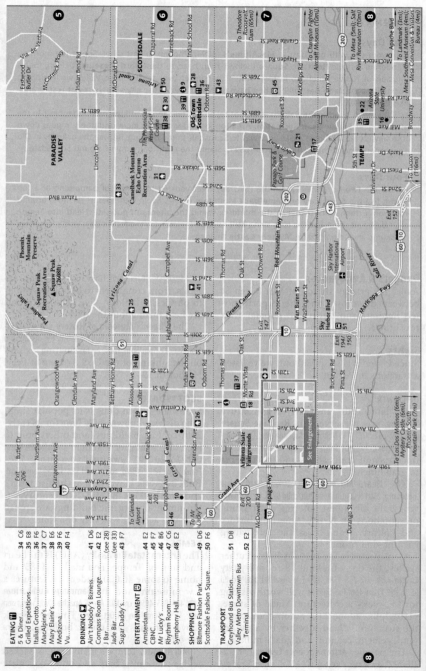

PHOENIX IN...

Two Days

Start your day with breakfast at **MacAlpine's** (p894), Phoenix' oldest diner. Spend the morning wandering historic **Heritage Square** (below), then head to the **Heard Museum** (below), for an infusion of Native American history. Watch the sunset over the Paradise Valley while sipping cocktails at the **Jade Bar** (p895), then have dinner at one of the city's classy resort restaurants, like **Vu** (p894).

If it's warm, head to the **Salt River** (opposite) on day two and spend the morning tubing. In the afternoon hit **Squaw Peak Recreation Area** (opposite) for a hike. Linger until the sun goes down (the sunsets are fabulous). Make your way to Scottsdale in the evening. Browse the galleries in Old Town then dine at the **Italian Grotto** (p895). Spend the night barhopping around Scottsdale.

Four Days

Follow the two-day itinerary. On the third day treat yourself to a night of pampering at a top resort, like the **Sanctuary on Camelback Mountain** (p894). Explore the desert environs around town on a themed 4WD tour in the morning; spend the afternoon poolside. Head into Tempe after dark and check out the bars along **Mill Avenue** (below). On the fourth day, visit a few more museums, including bizarre **Mystery Castle** (below).

Dangers & Annoyances

Avoid the grungy stretch of Van Buren St between downtown and the airport; motels here are run down and popular with prostitutes.

Sights

Since Phoenix is so spread out, we've listed attractions by region.

PHOENIX

Eight late- 19th- and early-20th-century houses are preserved in **Heritage Square** (☎ 602-262-5071; 115 N 6th St; admission free; ⊙ 10am-4pm Tue-Sat, 12-4pm Sun), which also features fine arts and crafts shops and great places to grab lunch.

The **Heard Museum** (☎ 602-252-8840; www .heard.org; 2301 N Central Ave adult/child $7/3; ⊙ 9:30am-5pm) is the city's best, offering outstanding presentations on Native American history and culture. Don't miss the fascinating kachina-doll room.

Constructed in the 1930s by Boyce Luther Gulley, the one-of-a kind 18-room **Mystery Castle** (☎ 602-268-1581; 800 E Mineral Rd; adult/child $5/3; ⊙ 11am-4pm Tue-Sun) is well worth visiting for its wacky architecture. Made of stone, petroglphs, adobe and automobile parts, the structure is held together by a mix of sand, cement, calcium and goat's milk.

The popular **Arizona Science Center** (☎ 602-716-2000; www.azscience.org; 600 E Washington St; adult/child $9/7; ⊙ 10am-5pm) has 350 hands-on exhibits, from computers to bubbles, weather to physics to biology. Live demonstrations are held throughout the day.

The **Phoenix Museum of History** (☎ 602-253-2734; 105 N 5th St; adult/child $5/2.50; ⊙ 10am-5pm Mon-Sat, 12-5pm Sun) has a fascinating exhibit on the sinking of the USS *Arizona* at Pearl Harbor in 1941.

SCOTTSDALE

Scottsdale's main draw is its popular shopping district, known as **Old Town** for its early-20th-century buildings (and others built to look old). Another highlight is **Taliesin West** (☎ 480-860-2700; www.franklloydwright.org; 12621 Frank Lloyd Wright Blvd; adult/child $18/5; ⊙ 9am-5pm). Built by Frank Lloyd Wright (he also taught and lived here) in the mid-20th-century, environmentally organic buildings are spread over 600 acres. It's worthy of a tour.

TEMPE

The **Arizona State University** (ASU) is the heart and soul of Tempe. Founded in 1885 and home to some 46,000 students, it features a few museums and the **Gammage Auditorium** (☎ 480-965-4050; cnr Mill Ave & Apache Blvd; admission free; ⊙ 1-4pm Mon-Fri Oct-May). This was Frank Lloyd Wright's last major building; tours are offered.

Mill Avenue, Tempe's main drag, is packed with restaurants, bars and other collegiate hangouts. It's a fun place to wander and look for old records or vintage dresses.

MESA

Animated dinosaurs, dioramas, a territorial jail, gold panning and changing art shows are some of the displays and interactive exhibits at the **Mesa Southwest Museum** (☎ 480-644-2230; 53 N MacDonald; adult/child $7/5; ☁ 10am-5pm Tue-Sat, 1-5pm Sun). One of the world's largest collections of fighter aircraft is displayed at the **Champlin Fighter Aircraft Museum** (☎ 480-830-4540; Falcon Field Airport, 4800 E McKellips Rd; adult/child $7/5; ☁ 8:30am-3:30pm Jun-Aug, 10am-5pm Sep-May).

Activities

Mountains ring the city, and there are numerous city and regional parks to hike and bike through. **Phoenix South Mountain Park** (☎ 602-495-0222; 10919 S Central Ave) offers more than 40 miles of trails, great views and dozens of Native American petroglyph sites.

For fabulous desert views, especially at sunset, head to **Squaw Peak Recreation Area** (☎ 602-262-7901; Squaw Peak Dr). The trek to the 2608ft summit of Squaw Peak is one of Phoenix' most popular outdoor endeavors.

Mountain and road biking is possible in both parks, with many designated trails. If you need to pick up peddles, try the **Airport Bicycle Center** (☎ 480-596-6633; 8666 E Shea Blvd, Scottsdale; per day from $25).

Floating down the Salt River in an inner tube is loads of fun, and a great way to relax and cool down in summer. Near Mesa, **Salt River Recreation** (☎ 480-984-3305; 1320 N Bush Hwy; tubes $12) rents tubes and provides van shuttles to good starting points. Tubing season is mid-April through September.

Phoenix for Children

Phoenix is a great family town. If your child loves animals, head to the **Phoenix Zoo** (☎ 602-273-1341; 455 N Galvin Parkway; adult/child $10/5; ☁ 9am-5pm Sep-Jun). A wide variety of animals, including some rare ones, are housed in several distinct and natural-looking environments. Don't miss the petting zoo.

The **Hall of Flame** (☎ 602-275-3473; 6101 E Van Buren St; adult/child $5/3; ☁ 9am-5pm Mon-Sat, noon-4pm Sun), exhibiting more than 90 fully restored fire-fighting machines from 1725 to the present day, is another kiddy favorite.

To cool off in summer, visit **Waterworld Safari** (☎ 623-581-1947; 4243 W Pinnacle Peak Rd; adult/child $20/16; ☁ 10am-8pm Mon-Thu, 10am-9pm Fri & Sat, 11am-7pm Sun Jun-Aug), with a six-story-high water slide, acres of swimming pools and a wave-making machine.

Tours

Vaughan's Southwest (☎ 602-971-1381; www.south westtours.com) offers 4½ hour city tours ($45), as well as a 14-hour Grand Canyon tour ($115) for people with very limited time. The company does hotel pick-ups.

Arrowhead Desert Tours (☎ 602-942-3361; 841 E Paradise Lane, Phoenix) and **Wild West Jeep Tours** (☎ 480-922-0144; 7127 E Becker Lane, Scottsdale) offer a variety of themed 4WD tours into the desert from $75.

Festivals & Events

Phoenix' most popular event is the **Fiesta Bowl football game** (☎ 480-965-8777; www.tostitos fiestabowl.com) held on New Year's Day at the ASU Sun Devil stadium. It's preceded by one of the largest parades in the southwest.

The **Arizona State Fair** (☎ 602-252-6771; www .azstatefair.com) takes place at the Arizona State Fairgrounds during the first two weeks of October, and offers the typical rodeo and midway action.

Sleeping

From basic motels to ritzy resorts, the valley's hundreds of places to stay have one thing in common – prices plummet in summer.

BUDGET

HI Phoenix, Metcalf House (☎ 602-254-9803; 1026 N 9th St; dm/d $17/35; ⓟ) Popular with young travelers, this friendly hostel occupies a nondescript house in a working-class neighborhood north of downtown (too far to walk). It has kitchen and laundry facilities, but does not accept reservations. Parking costs $3.

Motel 6 on Camelback (☎ 480-946-2280; www .motel6.com; 6848 E Camelback Rd, Scottsdale; r $52; ⓟ ⓧ ⓡ) Yes, it's a standard chain, but conveniently located smack dab in the middle of upscale Scottsdale, only a quick drive from Old Town.

MIDRANGE

Clarendon Hotel + Suites (☎ 602-252-7363; www .theclarendon.net; 401 W Clarendon Ave; r from $110; ⓟ ⓧ ⓡ) A boutique joint, rates are absurdly cheap for an establishment as classy as this (but it just opened, so prices could skyrocket). Rooms are sparse with dark wood furniture and original art.

San Carlos Hotel (☎ 602-253-4121; www.hotel sancarlos.com; 202 N Central Ave; r $140; P X ⊠) Big on character, this 1928 downtown property is an Italian Renaissance-inspired beauty that's been nicely restored. Rooms are small, but atmospheric, and there's a restaurant, bar and exercise room.

Maricopa Manor (☎ 800-292-6403; www.maricopa manor.com; 15 W Pasadena Ave; r from $130; P X ⊠) This small, elegant place has seven beautiful suites, many with French doors onto a deck overlooking the pool, garden and fountain areas. You won't find a more intimate resort experience.

TOP END

The most elegant and expensive places to stay are the resorts. These aren't just places to sleep, they are destinations within themselves (some make an entire vacation out of it). We've quoted peak-season rates here; they plummet in the summer.

Sanctuary on Camelback Mountain (☎ 480-948-2100; www.sanctuaryoncamelback.com; 5700 E McDonald Dr, Paradise Valley; r from $300; P X ⊠) This swanky spa resort offers massage under the stars ($130), and is a trendy and romantic choice. Some rooms are sleek and elegant, others minimally sparse. All feature very comfortable beds.

Royal Palms Resort & Spa (☎ 602-840-3610; www .royalpalmsresortandspa.com; 5200 E Camelback Rd; r from $355; P X ⊠) President Bush chose to stay here twice in 2004. Spanish-colonial style rooms range from minimalist to gilded, depending on how much you shell out. Homemade cookies, truffles or candy are part of the nightly turndown service.

Arizona Biltmore Resort & Spa (☎ 602-955-6600; www.arizonabiltmore.com; 24th St & E Missouri Ave;

r $350-530, ste from $680; P X ⊠) Frank Lloyd Wright influenced much of the design for the city's first luxury resort (opened in 1929). A beautiful and historically interesting place, facilities include two golf courses, several swimming pools, an athletic club, health spa, children's program and two very good restaurants.

Eating

Phoenix has the largest selection of restaurants in the Southwest. About two-thirds of the places listed here are in the valley, and some of the very best are in the resorts, although you don't have to stay to dine. All addresses are in Phoenix, unless indicated.

BUDGET

MacAlpine's (☎ 602-252-3039; 2303 N 7th St; dishes from $5; ☺ 6:30am-2:30pm) The oldest diner in Phoenix, it serves huge breakfasts and features an authentic soda fountain with genuine sundaes. Every Friday from 6pm it hosts a lively swing dance party, complete with dance lessons and buffet dinner.

5 & Diner (☎ 602-264-5220; 5220 N 16th St; dishes $5-10; ☺ breakfast, lunch & dinner) A visit here is lots of fun, featuring inexpensive food, friendly service and a '50s setting. The menu is the predictable pre-nouvelle American cuisine – burgers, fries, tuna melts, shakes, etc.

Los Dos Molinos (☎ 602-243-9113; 8646 S Central Ave; dishes $7-12; ☺ lunch & dinner Tue-Sat) Known for its cheap and tasty fare, the food at this New Mexican–influenced restaurant is delicious, especially if you have a taste for chilies.

MIDRANGE & TOP END

Grilled Expeditions (☎ 480-317-0600; cnr 7th & Mill Aves, Tempe; dishes $10-20; ☺ lunch & dinner) Melt-in-your-mouth steaks, Cajun dishes and a large salad selection are served in bright, modern environs or outside on the packed patio. Anything beef is a good choice; the house specialty is the 1200 Series NY Strip ($25). It's been buried in 1200°F mesquite coals – delicious.

Vu (☎ 480-991-3388; 7500 E Doubletree Ranch Rd, Scottsdale; dishes $25-30; ☺ 5pm) Inside the Hyatt Regency Scottsdale, this swanky and vibrant restaurant is mod to the max. Dishes are contemporary steak and seafood oriented, and tables overlook a lagoon and lush gardens.

THE AUTHOR'S CHOICE

James Hotel (☎ 480-308-1100; www.james hotel.com; 7353 E Indian School Rd, Scottsdale; r from $160, ste $520; P X ⊠) Paris Hilton has slept here, along with a host of other celebs. It's a very hip place with bright modern decor and giant flat screen TVs on the walls. This swanky boutique joint is *the* place to see and be seen in town.

THE AUTHOR'S CHOICE

Medizona (☎ 480-947-9500; 7214 E 4th Ave, Scottsdale; dishes $24; ☽ dinner) One of Phoenix' top restaurants, this place has won numerous local awards. It combines Mediterranean and southwestern cuisine with excellent results – the menu is unique, the food enchanting, the environs intimate and romantic.

Italian Grotto (☎ 480-994-1489; 3915 N Scottsdale Rd, Scottsdale; dishes $10-20; ☽ lunch & dinner) The lounge interior is dark and lit by candles. Modern art graces brushed metal walls and cozy half-circle black leather booths abound, making it a romantic spot for an Italian meal. Try the lasagna; it's a steal at $11.

Landmark (☎ 480-962-4652; 809 W Main St, Mesa; dishes $10-20; ☽ lunch & dinner) One of Mesa's best restaurants, this place has been serving homestyle American food for about 25 years. Built as a Mormon church in the early 1900s, the restaurant is decorated with antiques and photos, and has a huge salad bar.

Mary Elaine's (☎ 480-423-2530; 6000 E Camelback Rd; dishes from $25; ☽ 5pm) Posh and very elegant, this restaurant inside the Phoenician has earned a well-deserved stellar reputation for serving delicious and creative Southwestern and French cuisine. Jackets required for men.

Drinking

Scottsdale has the greatest concentration of trendy bars and clubs, while Tempe attracts the student crowd.

Jade Bar (☎ 480-948-2100; 5700 E McDonald Dr) A luscious place inside the Sanctuary on Camelback Mountain, it overlooks the sparkling Paradise Valley. Order a cantaloupe martini as the sun sinks low on the horizon.

J Bar (☎ 480-308-1100; 7353 E Indian School Rd) Swanky and seductive, this sleek joint is a big city bar with a long list of specialty drinks. It's a place to see and be seen. Look for it inside the James Hotel.

Sugar Daddy's (☎ 480-970-6556; 3102 N Scottsdale Rd, Scottsdale; cover $2) Live music rocks this casual, and often rowdy, local pick nightly. If your ears are ringing, make your way outside, as Sugar Daddy's has one of the best

patios in town. You'll be fighting for personal space, but that could be a good thing if you've come to flirt (as many have).

Compass Room Lounge (☎ 602-252-1234; 122 N 2nd St) Spectacular 360-degree views of downtown are the reason to visit this rotating bar on the 24th floor of the Hyatt Regency Phoenix. It's great for a sunset drink. The decor is richly posh, the lighting low.

Ain't Nobody's Bizness (☎ 602-224-9977; 3031 E Indian School Rd) A friendly lesbian bar that's been popular for years. It's a low-key place, perfect for meeting locals.

Entertainment

Rhythm Room (☎ 602-265-4842; 1019 E Indian School Rd, Scottsdale) Live blues and jazz are spotlighted at this local favorite. It attracts a mixed, often eclectic, crowd looking for a good time.

CBNC (☎ 480-990-3222; 1420 N Scottsdale Rd, Scottsdale) DJs spin excellent hip-hop, R & B and dance tunes at this popular club. You may even spot a big name celeb on the dancefloor. Ladies get in free most nights.

Mr Lucky's (☎ 602-246-0686; 3660 NW Grand Ave) Grab your boots and spurs, pardoner, and ride on down to Mr Lucky's for live country music and dancing. The outside corral has bull-riding competitions on weekends (with real bulls, not the mechanical kind).

Amsterdam (☎ 602-258-6122; 718 N Central Ave) Swanky and seductive, gay men flock to this throbbing alternative lifestyle club to strut their stuff on the crowded dancefloor.

Symphony Hall (☎ 602-262-7272; 225 E Adams) Both the **Arizona Opera** (☎ 602-266-7464) and the **Phoenix Symphony Orchestra** (☎ 602-495-1999) perform here.

SPECTATOR SPORTS

The men's basketball team, the **Phoenix Suns** (☎ 602-379-7867), and the women's team, the **Phoenix Mercury** (☎ 602-252-9622), play at the America West Arena. Football team **Arizona Cardinals** (☎ 602-379-0102) plays at Sun Devil Stadium in Tempe. The **Arizona Diamondbacks** (☎ 602-514-8400) play baseball at the Bank One Ballpark.

Shopping

The question is not so much what to buy (you can buy just about anything) but where to go. Scottsdale is the art gallery capital of Arizona.

SOUTHWEST

Heard Museum (☎ 602-252-8840; www.heard.org; 2301 N Central Ave) The bookshop here has the best range of books about Native Americans, and the most reliable, excellent and expensive selection of Native American arts and crafts.

The valley has several notable shopping malls. For more upscale shopping, visit the **Scottsdale Fashion Square** (cnr Camelback & Scottsdale Rds, Scottsdale) and the even more exclusive **Biltmore Fashion Park** (cnr Camelback Rd & 24th St, Phoenix).

Getting There & Around

Phoenix' **Sky Harbor International Airport** (☎ 602-273-3300) is 3 miles southeast of downtown. Valley Metro's Red Line operates buses from the airport to Tempe, Mesa and downtown Phoenix ($1.25).

Greyhound (☎ 602-389-4200; 2115 E Buckeye Rd) runs regular buses to Tucson ($16, two hours), Flagstaff ($23, 3½ hours), Los Angeles ($37, seven hours) and other destinations.

Valley Metro (☎ 602-253-5000; www.valleymetro .org) operates buses ($1.25) all over the valley. On weekdays it also runs the free Flash service around the ASU area and free Dash service around downtown Phoenix.

CENTRAL ARIZONA

The gateway to the Grand Canyon, this region offers cool relief from summer heat amid mountains and forests. The fun college town of Flagstaff is here. So is funky, artsy Jerome. Beautiful Sedona, with its stunning red-rock scenery, is a center for the New Age and a major tourist hub.

Flagstaff

A funky, vibrant town filled with college kids attending Northern Arizona University (NAU), Flagstaff boasts cool mountain air, ponderosa pines and even a mountain to ski. Microbreweries, interesting hotels and hip restaurants are housed in historic brick buildings lining the pleasant streets. There are plenty of outdoorsy adventures to keep you busy – hiking and biking trails are abundant. Less than a two-hour drive from the Grand Canyon, Flagstaff makes a great regional base.

The **visitor center** (☎ 928-774-9541; www.flag staff.az.us; 1 E Route 66; ☿ 9am-5pm) is inside the historic Amtrak train station.

SIGHTS

If you have time for only one sight in Flagstaff, head to the **Museum of Northern Arizona** (☎ 928-774-5211; www.musnaz.org; 3001 N Fort Valley Rd; adult/student/senior $5/3/4; ☿ 9am-5pm). It features exhibits on local Native American archaeology, history and customs, as well as geology, biology and the arts.

The **Lowell Observatory** (☎ 928-774-2096; www.lowell.edu; 1400 W Mars Hill Rd; admission $4; ☿ 9am-5pm Apr-Oct, noon-5pm Nov-Mar) witnessed the first sighting of Pluto in 1920. Weather permitting, visitors can stargaze through the telescope (9pm Monday to Saturday from June to August, varying times rest of the year).

The Sinagua cliff dwellings at **Walnut Canyon National Monument** (☎ 928-526-3367; www.nps.gov/waca; admission $3; ☿ 9am-6pm) are set in nearly vertical walls of a small limestone butte amid a forested canyon. A short hiking trail descends past many cliff-dwelling rooms. The monument is 11 miles southeast of Flagstaff off I-40 exit 204.

The 1000ft-tall volcano cone at the **Sunset Crater Volcano National Monument** (☎ 928-526-0502; www.nps.gov/sucr; admission $5; ☿ 8am-6pm), located on a loop road 12 miles north of Flagstaff along Hwy 89, was formed by volcanic eruptions in AD 1064. An interpretive trail grants visitors a firsthand look at volcanic features. Follow the loop road from the crater to nearby **Wupatki National Monument** (☎ 928-679-2365; www.nps.gov/wupa; admission $5, free if already paid at Sunset Crater; ☿ 8am-6pm), which has hundreds of Ancestral Puebloan historic sites, five of which are easily accessible.

ACTIVITIES

If you want to say you've skied Arizona, head to the small, but lofty, **Arizona Snowbowl** (☎ 928-779-1951, snow report 928-779-4577; www.ari zonasnowbowl.com; Snowbowl Rd; half/full day $34/42; ☿ mid-Dec–mid-Apr). Four lifts service 30 runs (beginner through expert) at elevations between 9200ft to 11,500ft. The skiing is not world class, but this is a state known for its deserts, not its snow.

Arizona's highest mountain, the 12,663ft **Humphreys Peak**, is a reasonably straightforward, though strenuous, hike in summer. The trail begins at the Arizona Snowbowl and winds through forest, eventually coming out above the timberline. The total

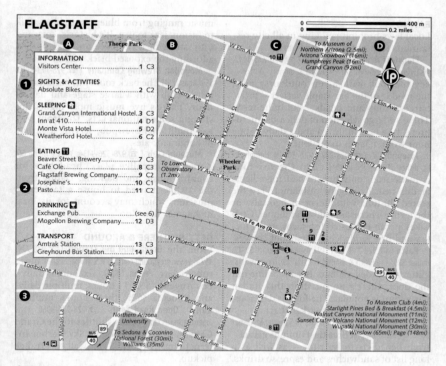

FLAGSTAFF

INFORMATION	
Visitors Center	1 C3

SIGHTS & ACTIVITIES	
Absolute Bikes	2 C2

SLEEPING	
Grand Canyon International Hostel	3 C3
Inn at 410	4 D1
Monte Vista Hotel	5 D2
Weatherford Hotel	6 C2

EATING	
Beaver Street Brewery	7 C3
Café Ole	8 C3
Flagstaff Brewing Company	9 C2
Josephine's	10 C1
Pasto	11 C2

DRINKING	
Exchange Pub	(see 6)
Mogollon Brewing Company	12 D3

TRANSPORT	
Amtrak Station	13 C3
Greyhound Bus Station	14 A3

distance is 4½ miles one-way; allow six to eight hours round-trip.

Absolute Bikes (☎ 928-779-5969; 18 N San Francisco; half/full-day rental from $15/25) rents mountain, road and children's bikes, and has trail maps and information.

SLEEPING

Flagstaff provides the best cheap and moderate lodging in this region. Summer is high season and prices rise.

Weatherford Hotel (☎ 928-779-1919; www .weatherfordhotel.com; 23 N Leroux; r from $60; ✷) Flagstaff's most historic hotel is fantastic value, keeping its rates year-round. A charming place with a turn-of-the-19th-century feel in its eight rooms (no TV or telephone), it boasts numerous lounges for relaxing. A real find.

Inn at 410 (☎ 928-774-0088, 800-774-2008; www .inn410.com; 410 N Leroux; r $135-190; ✷ ✗) Elegant and very romantic, this fully renovated 1907 house offers nine spacious, beautiful bedrooms. Most come with a fireplace or whirlpool bath, and a full gourmet breakfast and afternoon snacks are included.

Two units have adjoining rooms suitable for two children.

Grand Canyon International Hostel (☎ 928-779-9421; www.grandcanyonhostel.com; 19 S San Francisco; dm/d from $15/30; 🖳) Housed in a historic building with hardwood floors and southwestern decor, dorms are clean and small. There's a kitchen, laundry facilities, TV lounge and a host of backpacker-geared tours on offer.

Starlight Pines Bed & Breakfast (☎ 928-527-1912; www.starlightpinesbb.com; 3380 E Lockett Rd; r from $120; ✷ ✗) Shadowed by Mt Elden, the four rooms come with fireplaces, handmade soaps and vintage clawfoot bathtubs. A romantic place, it will even serve you breakfast in bed.

Monte Vista Hotel (☎ 928-779-6971; www .hotelmontevista.com; 100 N San Francisco; r $60-120; ✷) Scenes from the movie *Casablanca* were filmed at this c 1927 hotel, where many of the 50 rooms and suites are named after the film stars who slept in them. Rooms are comfortable and old-fashioned, but not luxurious (John Wayne and Humphrey Bogart handled it just fine).

SOUTHWEST

EATING

Local laws prohibit smoking in all city restaurants (but not restaurant/bars).

Flagstaff Brewing Company (☎ 928-773-1442; 16 E Route 66; dishes $8; ☒ lunch & dinner) A low-key brewpub with a fun outdoorsy vibe, the food is of the bar-staple variety – pizza, burgers, soup and salads – but quite tasty. There's a large selection of delicious microbrews (the best in town) and a daily happy hour from 4:30pm to 6:30pm.

Josephine's (☎ 928-779-3400; 503 N Humphreys St; dishes $15-20; ☒ lunch & dinner) Creative food is made from only the freshest ingredients at this casually elegant restaurant. Try the seared ahi tuna with ginger mango salsa or the tortilla-encrusted halibut at dinner. Crab cakes, pecan-encrusted fish tacos, and a turkey and Brie sandwich are standout choices.

Pasto (☎ 928-779-1937; 19 E Aspen Ave; lunch $9-12, dinner $20; ☒ lunch & dinner) With yellow walls, glittery chandeliers, faux ivy and a line out the door, there's no question this Italian pasta joint is popular. The food is delicious, and the place emits upmarket charm.

La Bellavia (☎ 928-774-8301; 18 S Beaver St; dishes $6-8; ☒ 6:30am-2pm) Breakfast options galore – from benedicts to burritos – as well as a long list of sandwiches and espresso drinks. The atmosphere is old school, no frills dining, which makes the lack of charm almost charming. Service is friendly and quick.

Café Ole (☎ 928-774-8272; 119 S San Francisco St; dishes $5-11; ☒ 5-9pm Tue-Sat) A friendly, family-run place serving some of the best New Mexican cuisine in the region, green and red chili sauce is featured prominently. Everything is fresh and healthy (no lard in the beans; minimal frying).

Beaver Street Brewery (☎ 928-779-0079; 11 S Beaver St; dishes $8-11; ☒ lunch & dinner) Grub is of the burger and pizza variety with a few eclectic twists, like basil-and-sundried tomato burgers and margarita chicken sandwiches. It's a local fave for its excellent microbrews (five handmade ales are usually on tap).

DRINKING & ENTERTAINMENT

From quiet bars to live music joints to rowdy pubs, Flagstaff is as big on variety as the microbrews it produces. The brewpubs listed under Eating (above) are also popular at night.

Exchange Pub (☎ 928-779-1919; 23 N Leroux St) Inside the Weatherford Hotel, it has live music ranging from bluegrass to blues, folk to fusion, jazz to jive. It's historic, cozy and intimate with a fireplace and old posters adorning the exposed brick walls.

Mogollon Brewing Company (☎ 928-773-8950; 15 N Agassiz St) The back room has been turned into a club with a large stage and dancefloor. There's live music most nights, including some national acts. The front part is a traditional brewpub, serving a variety of handmade ales.

Museum Club (☎ 928-526-9434; 3404 E Route 66) A popular barnlike place, head here for country music and dancing. Dating from the 1920s, it used to house a taxidermy museum, which may account for its local nickname, 'The Zoo.'

GETTING THERE & AROUND

From the **Greyhound bus station** (☎ 928-774-4573; www.greyhound.com; 399 S Malpais Lane) buses run to Las Vegas ($50, six hours, daily), Los Angeles ($53, 11 hours, multiple daily) and Phoenix ($25, three hours, multiple daily). **Open Road Tours** (☎ 928-226-8060; www.openroadtours.com) offers shuttles to the Grand Canyon ($20) and Phoenix Sky Harbor International Airport ($31). Call to arrange pickup.

Operated by **Amtrak** (☎ 928-774-8679; www.amtrak.com), the *Southwest Chief* stops in Flagstaff on its daily run between Chicago and Los Angeles.

Williams

With Old Route 66 running through its center, Williams epitomizes Main St America. Literally a two-street town, it seems like nothing much has changed here over the decades. Most tourists visit to ride the turn-of-the-19th-century **Grand Canyon Railway** (☎ 928-773-1976; www.thetrain.com; Railway Depot, 200 W Railroad Ave; round-trip adult/child from $58/25) to the South Rim (departs 10am). Even if you're not a train buff, a trip on this historic steam locomotive can be lots of fun. Characters in period costumes provide historical and regional narration, and banjo folk music sets the vibe.

Williams has sleeping options for all budgets. The **Sheridan House Inn** (☎ 928-635-9441; 460 E Sheridan Ave; d/ste $145/210; ☒ Mar-Dec; ☒ ☒) is our favorite place. While not historic, the rooms are well appointed, with full marble baths. Rates include a hot breakfast and buffet-style dinner. If you just need a place to crash, the **Highlander Motel** (☎ 928-635-2541, 800-800-8288; 533 W Route 66; r from $35; 🞫) is clean and good value.

Route 66 fans will dig the eclectic decor at **Cruiser's Café 66** (☎ 928-635-2445; 233 W Route 66; dishes $8-15; 🕑 4-10pm), from the giant stuffed buffalo at the entrance to the vintage gas pumps, old signs and murals eulogizing America's most famous highway. It's a fun place, serving BBQ and other American fare inside a 1930s filling station.

The **World Famous Sultana Bar** (☎ 928-635-2028; 301 W Route 66) served as a basement speakeasy during prohibition. Today it's a saloon from another era, where the smoke is thick and the talk boisterous. There's sometimes live music.

Greyhound (☎ 928-635-0870; www.greyhound .com; 1050 N Grand Blvd) stops at Chevron gas station. **Open Road** (☎ 928-226-8060, 800-766-7117; Railway Depot, 200 W Railroad Ave) offers two daily shuttles to the Grand Canyon ($10) and Flagstaff ($10).

Sedona

If the scenery looks familiar in picture perfect Sedona, it's probably because you've seen it on the silver screen. With spindly towers, grand buttes and flat-topped mesas, it's easy to understand why Hollywood found these splendid crimson sandstone formations so enticing. Though Sedona was founded in the 19th century, the discovery of energy 'vortexes' here in the 1980s turned this once modest settlement into a bustling New Age destination. Today the combination of scenic beauty and mysticism attracts throngs of tourists year-round. You'll find all sorts of alternative medicine practices in town, along with art galleries, gourmet

restaurants and more than one top-end resort.

In the middle of town, the 'Y' is the junction of Hwys 89A and 179. Businesses are spread along both roads. The **Gateway Visitors Center** (☎ 928-282-9119; www.redrockcountry.org; Forest Rd at Hwy 89A; 🕑 8:30am-5pm Mon-Sat, 9am-3pm Sun) has tourist information and vortex maps.

SIGHTS & ACTIVITIES

New Agers believe Sedona's rocks, cliffs and rivers radiate electromagnetic energy. The earth's four best-known vortexes are here, and include **Bell Rock** near Village of Oak Creek east of Hwy 179, **Cathedral Rock** near Red Rock Crossing, **Airport Mesa** along the Airport Rd and **Boynton Canyon**.

Sedona's stunning scenery is best experienced from the back of a jeep. Many companies offer 4WD jeep tours, but **Pink Jeep Tours** (☎ 928-382-5000, 800-873-3662; www.pinkjeep .com; 204 N Hwy 89A) is the most esteemed. Tours (from $95) take you alongside adrenaline pumping drop-offs, past panoramic vistas and archeological sites.

SLEEPING

Sedona hosts many beautiful B&Bs, creek-side cabins and full-service resorts; pickings are slim for budget travelers.

Inn on Oak Creek (☎ 928-282-7896; www .innonoakcreek.com; 556 Hwy 179; r incl breakfast $195-290; 🞫 🞩) Casual elegance on the water is the theme at Sedona's most charming and intimate sleeping option. Try the Restive Rooster Room, which has a tub with a view, or the Western-themed Bunkhouse Room. The breakfast takes place over four courses and is as gourmet as it gets.

Sky Ranch Lodge (☎ 928-282-6400; www.skyranch lodge.com; Airport Rd; r $80-160; 🞫 🞭) Spacious

---

OAK CREEK CANYON & SURROUNDING BACKCOUNTRY DRIVES

For something truly magical take Hwy 89A northeast into **Oak Creek Canyon**. It's a drive that won't soon be forgotten. The canyon is at its narrowest here, and the red, orange and white cliffs at their most dramatic. Giant cottonwoods crowd the creek sides, providing a scenic shady backdrop for trout fishing and swimming. Stop at **Grasshopper Point** (admission $7), about 2 miles into the drive, to cool off. It's a great swimming hole. Then continue for 5 miles until reaching **Slide Rock State Park** (☎ 928-282-3034; admission per vehicle $8; 🕑 8am-6pm). Here you can unpack the picnic basket and have lunch. Afterwards let the creek sweep you down its natural rock shoot – it's fun for kids and adults alike.

Head back into town around sunset and turn off at **Airport Road**. The setting sun makes for a trippy picture – the rocks blaze psychedelic red and orange against a bright pink and purple sky.

motel rooms on six landscaped acres; some include balconies, fireplaces, kitchenettes or refrigerators. Cottages ($190) with vaulted ceilings, kitchenettes and private decks are also available. The views are fantastic.

EATING & DRINKING
The caliber of cooking is fantastic in Sedona. Even the budget places serve fresh, innovative dishes.

Coffeepot Restaurant (☎ 928-282-6626; 2050 W Hwy 89A; dishes $5-8; ☯ 6am-2pm) For breakfast and lunch, this has been the place to go for decades. The menu is huge and offers more types of omelets than most restaurants have menu items (it claims 101, including peanut butter and jelly!).

Oak Creek Brewing Company (☎ 928-204-1300; 2050 Yavapai Dr; dishes $9-15; ☯ lunch & dinner) The American menu features burgers, pizza, sandwiches and delicious wings. Food is served inside casual light wood environs with copper brewing vessels at the bar. There are nine beers on tap, many of which were gold medal winners at the Great American Beer Festival.

Shugrue's Hillside Grill (☎ 928-282-5300; 671 Hwy 179; dishes $25-30; ☯ lunch & dinner) A great choice for an upscale meal, Shugrue's serves consistently excellent food along with panoramic views. The menu offers everything from steak to ravioli, but is best known for its well-prepared seafood. A jazz ensemble plays on weekends.

Historic Rainbow's End Restaurant & Nightclub (☎ 928-282-1593; 3235 W Hwy 89A; ☯ lunch & dinner) Locals dig the scarred wood bar and pool tables in this smoky old saloon. There's a small jukebox and neon beer signs on the walls. Live music rocks the place Friday and Saturday nights.

GETTING THERE & AROUND
The **Sedona-Phoenix Shuttle** (☎ 928-282-2066; www.sedona-phoenix-shuttle.com; 2545 W Hwy 89A) runs between Phoenix Sky Harbor International Airport and Sedona eight times daily ($40). Call to make reservations.

Jerome
Precariously perched on a steep hillside, tiny Jerome has a European feel – as if someone took a French country village and transported it to the Arizona desert. Shabby chic and eclectically enticing, the

old mining town emits an untouristy and altogether romantic vibe. Known as the 'Wickedest Town in the West' during its late-1800s mining heyday, today Jerome's historic buildings have been lovingly restored; turned into galleries, restaurants, saloons and B&Bs.

The **chamber of commerce** (☎ 928-634-2900; www.jeromechamber.com; Hull Ave; ☯ 10am-4pm summer) offers tourist information.

At the top of the town, the 1917 **Surgeon's House B&B** (☎ 928-639-1452; 101 Hill St; r incl full breakfast $100-150; ☒) is a funky place covered in gnarled old vines. The three suites come with great views. The coolest asset is the back garden, with lounge chairs, fountains and even a beach motif.

Delicious nouveau American fare is served at the **Asylum Restaurant** (☎ 928-639-3197; 200 Hill St; lunch/dinner $10/20; ☯ lunch & dinner) inside the Jerome Grand Hotel. Deep red walls, lazy fans, gilded artwork, jazz music and views, views, views provide the ambience. There's a very long wine list.

Dark and smoky, the **Spirit Room Bar** (☎ 9280-634-5006; 164 Main St) is the town's liveliest watering hole.

Prescott
Arizona's first territorial capital boasts a historic Victorian-era downtown with a colorful history. Along the plaza is **Whiskey Row**, an infamous strip of old saloons that still serve plenty of booze today. Residents are an intriguing mix of hippies, retirees and cowboy-style conservatives, with artsy types and outdoor enthusiasts contributing further to the bohemian quality of this intriguing town.

The **chamber of commerce** (☎ 928-445-2000; www.prescott.org; 117 W Goodwin; ☯ 9am-5pm Mon-Fri) has tourist information.

The restored **Hassayampa Inn** (☎ 928-778-9434; www.hassayampainn.com; 122 E Gurley St; r incl full breakfast $100-200; ☒) features a vintage hand-operated elevator, original furnishings, hand-painted wall decorations and a lovely dining room. An evening cocktail is included.

Quaint, homey rooms with quilts are found at the charming **Hotel Vendome** (☎ 928-776-0900; www.vendomehotel.com; 230 S Cortez St; d from $80; ☒). Try for the room with the sunset tub.

The tiny **Rose Restaurant** (☎ 928-777-8308; 235 S Cortez; dishes from $20; ☯ dinner Wed-Sun) boasts Prescott's most celebrated chef. Seafood, meat and pasta make up the gourmet menu. Microbrews are served at the crowded, and charismatic, **Prescott Brewing Company** (☎ 928-771-2795; 130 Gurley St; dishes $7-20; ☺ lunch & dinner), which also does decent English- and American-style pub food.

Prescott Transit Authority/Greyhound (☎ 928-445-5470; 820 E Sheldon St) has buses to Phoenix ($24, 2½ hours, 13 daily) and Flagstaff ($22, 1½ hours, daily).

GRAND CANYON NATIONAL PARK

A trip to Grand Canyon National Park is an iconic American experience. Initially dismissed as little more than an obstacle to exploration, the canyon first drew 19th-century miners bent on exploiting its rich natural resources. Native American resistance and the lack of water slowed development, but by the time Frederick Jackson Turner declared the end of the American frontier in 1893, entrepreneurs had transformed the canyon into one of the country's most celebrated destinations. At the dawn of the industrial revolution, people flocked here in search of the romanticized wilderness ideal and embraced its sublime beauty. They still do. Today the park attracts five million visitors from around the world each year.

The Grand Canyon's dramatic scenery enthralls even the most jaded visitors and leaves all who witness it somehow changed. Its dimensions are mind-blowing. The Grand Canyon is a mile deep and averages 10 miles wide. Snaking along its floor are 277 miles of the Colorado River, which has carved the canyon over the past six million

years and exposed ro[...] years old – half of Ear[...]

The two rims of the [...] quite different experie[...] more than 200 mile[...] rarely visited on the [...] tors choose the South Rim, which boasts easy access, the bulk of services and the panoramic vistas for which the park is famous. The quieter North Rim has its own charms; at 8200ft elevation (1000ft higher than the South Rim), its cooler temperatures support wildflower meadows and tall, thick stands of aspen and spruce.

Orientation

The park's most developed area is Grand Canyon Village, 6 miles north of the South Rim Entrance Station. The only entrance to the North Rim lies 30 miles south of Jacob Lake on Hwy 67.

Information

Most visitor facilities are clustered around Grand Canyon Lodge (p905). The entrance ticket for the **park** (vehicle/bicyclists & pedestrians $20/10) is valid for seven days and can be used at both rims.

Canyon View Information Plaza (☎ 928-638-7644; www.nps.gov/grca; ☺ 8am-6pm) At the village's northeast end, this is the main visitor center.

North Rim Visitor Center (☎ 928-638-9875; ☺ 8am-6pm) Adjacent to the Grand Canyon Lodge.

WHEN TO GO

June is the driest month, July and August the wettest. January has average overnight lows of 13°F to 20°F and daytime highs

---

SAFE CANYON HIKING

Hiking into the canyon is a favorite park pastime, offering the chance to experience this majestic natural wonder from a different perspective. But while hiking below the rim can be a sublime experience, it can also be dangerous. Summer heat, in this harsh and arid environment, can be crippling. Attempting to hike from the rim to the Colorado River and back in one day is *stupid*, and should not be attempted by even the fittest hikers – people have died down here before, and more will die in the future. However, if you follow a few simple rules, your hike will likely be a highlight of your Grand Canyon trip. First, water is vital. Carry at least 4L (quarts) of water per person per day; on super hot days double that figure. Even if you're just going for a 'short jaunt' down 'a little way' on the Bright Angel Trail, take water. Other items to bring include a full-brimmed hat and waterproof sunscreen. Second, pace yourself. You may not feel tired on the way down, but remember you still have to come *up*. Before hitting the trail, visit a ranger station for advice. Park rangers can suggest hikes to match your fitness level. For more hiking tips see Lonely Planet's *Hiking in the USA*.

40°F. Summer temperatures inside canyon regularly soar above 100°F. While the South Rim is open year-round, most visitors come between late May and early September. The North Rim is open from mid-May to mid-October.

BACKCOUNTRY PERMITS

All overnight hikes in the park require a permit. The **Backcountry Information Center** (☎ 928-638-7875; www.nps.gov/grca/backcountry; ☷ 8am-noon & 1-5pm) accepts applications for backpacking permits ($10 plus $5 per person per night) for the current month and following four months only. Your chances are decent if you apply early and provide alternative hiking itineraries. If you arrive without a permit, don't despair. Head to the Back Country Information Center, by Maswik Lodge (p904), and get on the waiting list. You'll likely get a permit within one to six days, depending on the season and itinerary.

South Rim

Camera-toting tourists pack the park's most popular rim each summer, most staying only long enough to ogle from the easily accessible scenic viewpoints. It's little secret why this rim is so popular – most of the park's infrastructure is here and the dramatic, sweeping canyon views are endless and usually unobscured. To escape the crowds, visit during the fall or winter.

SIGHTS & ACTIVITIES

Two **scenic drives** follow the rim on either side of the village – **Hermit Road** to the west and **Desert View Drive** to the east. The rim dips in and out of view as the road passes through the piñon-juniper and ponderosa stands of Kaibab National Forest. Pullouts along the way offer spectacular views, and interpretive signs explain canyon features and geology.

Hiking along the South Rim is among park visitors' favorite pastimes, with options for

---

RUNNING THE COLORADO

The King Kong of rivers, a run down the Colorado River is an epic, adrenaline-pumping adventure. While 'normal' rapids are rated I through V (with five being pretty damn tuff), the 160-plus rapids on the Colorado merit their own scale, I to X, with many rapids a V or higher and two classified as 10s. This is not a river to take for granted – people die here. You should always wear your life vest, listen closely to your guide and give this river the respect it deserves. If you do, you'll likely finish unscathed.

Unless you're already on the waiting list for a permit, it's not possible to run the Colorado on a private trip. Therefore you'll need to join a commercial voyage. Here the biggest decision is picking a boat – oar, paddle or motorized. Motorized trips are generally the least scary option. The huge inflatable boats go twice as fast and tend to be more stable. Oar boats are the most common vessels on the river. They give you the excitement of riding a smaller raft, but the guide does all the rowing – thus retaining control on the big rapids. For heart-attack fun, join a paddle trip (meaning everyone in the boat rows). Flipping is pretty much guaranteed, and you're completely dependent on fellow shipmates' paddling skills (depending on your attitude, it's either bad news or the ultimate rush).

River nights are spent camping (gear provided) under the stars on sandy beaches. It's not as primitive as it sounds – guides are legendary for their combination of white-water abilities, gastronomy and information.

Given two or three weeks, you can run the entire 279 miles of river through the canyon. Three shorter sections (each 100 miles or less) take four to nine days. Oar and paddle trips cost $200 to $300 per day, motorboats $225 to $325. Book six to 12 months in advance. Recommended outfitters:

- **Arizona River Runners** (☎ 602-867-4866; www.raftarizona.com; PO Box 47788, Phoenix, AZ 85068) Motorboat trips.

- **OARS** (☎ 209-736-2924; www.oars.com; PO Box 67, Angels Camp, CA 95222) Oar-powered trips; paddle trips on request.

- **Outdoors Unlimited River Trips** (☎ 928-526-454; www.outdoorsunlimited.com; 6900 Townsend Winona Rd, Flagstaff, AZ 86004) Specializes in paddle trips.

every skill level. The **Rim Trail** is the most popular, and easiest, walk in the park. It connects a series of scenic points and historical sights over 13 miles and portions are paved. Every viewpoint is accessed by one of the three shuttle routes.

The most popular of the corridor trails is the beautiful **Bright Angel**. The steep and scenic 8-mile descent to the Colorado is punctuated with four logical turnaround spots. Summer heat can be crippling, day hikers should either turn around at one of the two resthouses (a 3- to 6-mile round-trip) or hit the trail at dawn to safely make the longer hikes to Indian Garden and Plateau Point (9.2 and 12.2 miles round-trip). Hiking to the river in one day is not an option. The trailhead starts at the Grand Canyon Village.

The **South Kaibab** is arguably one of the park's prettiest trails, combining stunning scenery and unobstructed 360-degree views with every step. Steep, rough and wholly exposed, summer ascents can be dangerous and during this season rangers discourage all but the shortest day hikes. Turn around at **Cedar Ridge**, perhaps the park's finest short day hike. It's dazzling, particularly at sunrise, when the deep ruddy ambers and reds of each canyon fold seem to glow from within.

TOURS

Park tours are run by **Xanterra** (☎ 303-287-2757, 888-297-2757; www.beautiful-places-on-earth.com/xanterra/default.asp), which has information desks at the visitor centers and Bright Angel, Maswik and Yavapai Lodges. Various daily **bus tours** (tickets from $16) are offered.

Mule trips into the canyon depart daily from the corral west of Bright Angel Lodge. Choose from the seven-hour day trip ($129) or the overnight trip ($350), which includes a lodging at Phantom Ranch and all meals. Riders must be at least 4ft 7in tall, speak fluent English and weigh less than 200lbs. Keep in mind, this is no carnival ride – these journeys are hot, dusty and bumpy.

SLEEPING

The South Rim's six lodges are operated by **Xanterra** (☎ 888-297-2757; www.beautiful-places-on-earth.com/xanterra/default.asp) – use this phone number to make advance reservations (highly recommended) at any of the places (including Phantom Ranch) listed here.

For sai
switchboard accommodation
Tusayan (at South (31 miles south), Came
or Williams (about 60 miles

Bright Angel Lodge (Grand Canyon Vill
$49-241; ⊠) Built in 1935, the log-and
Bright Angel offers historic charm and
cently refurbished rooms. The least expensive doubles are simple, with shared baths. More expensive rooms are brighter, airier and big on character.

Phantom Ranch (dm/cabin $23/78) At the bottom of the canyon, it offers basic cabins sleeping four to 10 people and segregated dorms. Most cabins are reserved for overnight mule tours, but hikers may make reservations if space is available. The ranch serves hearty family-style meals at dinner ($25) and breakfast ($18), and box lunches ($9). If you lack a reservation, show up at the Bright Angel Lodge transportation desk at 6am to snag any canceled bunks.

Mather Campground (☎ 800-365-2267; http://reservations.nps.gov; Grand Canyon Village; campsites $15-40; ⊗ year-round) Offers well-dispersed, relatively peaceful sites amid piñon and juniper trees. There are pay showers, laundry facilities, drinking water, toilets, grills and a small general store.

Desert View Campground (☎ 800-365-2267; http://reservations.nps.gov; campsites $10; ⊗ mid-May–mid-Sep) Near the East Entrance, 25 miles east of Grand Canyon Village, this first-come,

THE AUTHOR'S CHOICE

El Tovar Hotel (Grand Canyon Village; d/ste $125/285; ⊠) With replica Remington bronzes, arts and crafts–style chairs, stained glass and exposed beams, this quintessential 1905 national park lodge attracts visitors seeking more than a roadside motel. Wide inviting porches wreathe around the rambling wood structure, offering pleasant spots to people-watch and admire canyon views. Even if you're not a guest, stop by to relax with a book on the porch swing or a drink on the patio. The public spaces hint at the genteel elegance of the park's heyday. Standard rooms are on the small side, but offer high standards of comfort. Suites are fantastic.

SOUTHWEST

...day reservations call the
...638-2631). If you can't find
... in the national park, try
...trance Station), Valle
... (53 miles east)
... or & cabins
...stone
...nd
...South Rim
... is full.

... RV sites
... 103;

Yava...
Apr-Oc... ... n and
juniper forest.

EATING & DRINKING

El Tovar and Bright Angel Lodge offer creative menus and surprisingly good food.

El Tovar Dining Room (☎ 928-638-2631; El Tovar Lodge; dishes $12-22; ☯ breakfast, lunch & dinner; ✗) White linen covered tables set with china and huge picture windows with canyon views create a memorable ambience. The service is excellent, the menu creative, the portions big and the food is really very good. Reservations required for dinner.

Arizona Room (☎ 928-638-2631; Bright Angel Lodge; dishes $8-21; ☯ 4:30-10pm) With a wonderful balance between casual and upscale, this restaurant is another fantastic option. Antler chandeliers hang from the ceiling, and picture windows overlook the canyon. Mains include steak, chicken and fish dishes. Reservations are not accepted, and there's often a wait.

Bright Angel Restaurant (☎ 928-638-2631; Bright Angel Lodge; dishes $8-13; ☯ breakfast, lunch & dinner) This family-style restaurant serves burgers, fajitas, lasagna, roast turkey and other simple dishes. With few windows and no canyon views, it's a bit dark and the least inviting full-scale dining restaurant.

Also recommended:

Maswik & Yavapai Cafeterias (☎ 928-638-2631; dishes $6-10; ☯ breakfast, lunch & dinner) Based in their respective lodges, expect cafeteria food, service and seating.

Deli at Marketplace (☎ 928-631-2262; Grand Canyon Village; dishes $5-8; ☯ breakfast, lunch & dinner) Fresh takeaway sandwiches and hot dishes.

GETTING THERE & AROUND

Most people arrive at the canyon in private vehicles or on a tour. **Open Road Tours** (☎ 928-226-8060; www.openroadtours.com) runs shuttles

m Phoenix Sky Harbor International Airport ($50) and Williams ($15).

Free shuttles operate along three routes: around the Grand Canyon Village, west along Hermits Rest Route and east along Kaibab Trail Route. Buses run at least twice per hour.

Havasu Canyon

In the heart of the Havasupai Indian Reservation, about 195 miles west of the South Rim, the hidden valley around Havasu Canyon has four gorgeous, spring-fed waterfalls and enchanting, azure swimming holes. The falls lie 10 miles below the rim, accessed via a moderately challenging hiking trail, and trips require an overnight stay in the village of Supai (near the falls). Do not try to hike down and back in one day – not only is it dangerous, but it also doesn't allow time to see the falls.

Supai offers two sleeping options, and reservations must be secured before starting out. The **Havasupai Lodge** (☎ 928-448-2111; r $80) has motel rooms with canyon views. A café serves breakfast, lunch and dinner. The **Havasupai Campground** (☎ 928-448-2121; campsites $10), two miles past Supai, has primitive campsites along a creek. After a night in Supai, continue through Havasu Canyon to the waterfalls and sparkling blue-green swimming holes. If you don't want to hike to Supai, call the lodge or campground to arrange for a mule or horse ($150 roundtrip) to carry you there. Rides depart from Hualapai Hilltop, where the hiking trail begins. The road to Hualapai Hilltop is 7 miles east of Peach Springs off Route 66. Look for the marked turn-off and follow the road for 62 miles.

North Rim

On the Grand Canyon's North Rim, solitude reigns supreme. Rugged and remote (it's only 10 miles from the South Rim as the crow flies, but a 215-mile, five-hour drive on winding desert roads from Grand Canyon Village), this rim boasts meadows thick with wildflowers and dense clusters of willowy aspen and spruce trees. The air is often crisp, the skies vast and blue. If the crowds on the South Rim make you cringe, this is where to head for wild isolation. In fact, the area is so remote it sees only 10% of park visitors.

Facilities on the North Rim are closed from mid-October to mid-May, although you can drive into the park and stay at the campground until the first snow closes the road from Jacob Lake.

SIGHTS & ACTIVITIES

The short and easy paved trail (0.3 miles) to **Bright Angel Point** is a canyon must. Beginning from the back porch of Grand Canyon Lodge, it goes to a narrow finger of an overlook with fabulous views. It's popular for sunrise and sunset walks, but visit after dusk for unparalleled stargazing.

The **North Kaibab Trail** is the North Rim's only maintained rim-to-river trail and connects with trails to the South Rim. The first 4.7 miles are the steepest, dropping well over 3000ft to **Roaring Springs** – a popular all-day hike. If you prefer a shorter day hike below the rim, walk just 0.75 miles down to **Coconino Overlook** or a mile to the **Supai Tunnel** to get a flavor for steep inner-canyon hiking.

Canyon Trail Rides (☎ 435-679-8665; www.canyon rides.com; Grand Canyon Lodge) offers one-hour mule trips ($20) along the rim and half- or full-day trips into the canyon. The full-day, seven-hour trip ($95, minimum age 12 years) departs at 7:25am. Lunch and water are provided. Half-day trips ($45, minimum age eight years) leave at 7:25am and 12:25pm.

SLEEPING, EATING & DRINKING

North Rim accommodations are limited to one lodge and one campground. If these are booked, try your luck 80 miles north in Kanab, UT, or 84 miles northeast in Lees Ferry.

Grand Canyon Lodge (☎ 928-638-2612; www .grandcanyonnorthrim.com; r & cabins $91-116; ☒ mid-May–mid-Nov; ☒) By far our favorite sleeping option in the park (perhaps in any US national park), this lodge made of wood, stone and glass is the kind of place you imagine should be perched on the rim. The canyon views are stunning, the lobby regal. Rustic, yet modern, cabins comprise the majority of accommodations. Reserve far in advance.

North Rim Campground (☎ 800-365-2267; http:// reservations.nps.gov; campsites $15) This campground, 1.5 miles north of Grand Canyon Lodge, offers pleasant sites on level ground blanketed in pine needles. There is water, a store, a snack bar, and coin-operated show-

ers and laundry, but no hookups. Reservations accepted.

Grand Canyon Lodge Dining Room (☎ 928-638-2612; dishes $9-20; ☒ breakfast, lunch & dinner) Some people get downright belligerent if they can't get a window seat at this wonderful spot with panoramic views. The windows are so huge, however, it really doesn't matter where you sit. The solid menu includes several vegetarian options. Dinner reservations required.

Rough Rider Saloon (☎ 928-638-2612) For a drink and a browse of the Teddy Roosevelt memorabilia, visit this popular watering hole adjacent to the Grand Canyon Lodge. The stone patio offers rough-hewn rocking chairs facing the rim and a blazing fire on chilly nights. Rangers offer talks (sometimes even providing telescopes for stargazing).

GETTING THERE & AROUND

The **Transcanyon Shuttle** (☎ 928-638-2820; Grand Canyon Lodge) departs for the South Rim (one way/round-trip $65/110; cash only) at 7am. Reserve at least a week in advance. Children under 12 get a discount. A hikers' shuttle (from $2) to the North Kaibab Trail departs at 5:20am and 7:20am from Grand Canyon Lodge. You must sign up the night before at the front desk.

NORTHEASTERN ARIZONA

Some of Arizona's most beautiful and photogenic landscapes lie in the northeastern corner of the state. Between the fabulous buttes of Monument Valley, the shimmering blue waters of Lake Powell and the fossilized logs of the Petrified Forest National Park are lands locked in ancient history. Inhabited by Native Americans for centuries, much of this region is reservation land belonging to the Navajo and Hopi Indians.

Lake Powell

Popular with families and college kids alike, Lake Powell is the country's second-largest artificial reservoir and part of the Glen Canyon National Recreation Area (which stretches between Utah and Arizona). Set amid striking red-rock formations, sharply cut canyons and dramatic desert scenery, it's a water lover's heaven.

The region's central town is **Page**. Hwy 89 forms the main strip. The **Carl Hayden Visitor Center** (☎ 928-608-6404; ☒ 8am-7pm late May early

Sep, 8am-5pm rest of year) is located at the dam, 2 miles north of Page. Free one-hour tours (occurring multiple times daily) take you inside the dam.

Wahweap Marina (☎ 928-645-2433; www.lake powell.com), six miles north of Page, has lodging, restaurants and every type of boat rental imaginable.

To visit photographic **Antelope Canyon** (it's the slot canyon in all the regional picture books), you'll need to join a tour. **Roger Ekis's Antelope Canyon Tours** (☎ 928-645-9102; www.antelopecanyon.com; 22 S Lake Powell Blvd) is recommended.

Clean, basic and overpriced chain hotels line Hwy 89 in Page. **Uncle Bill's** (☎ 928-645-1224; www.canyon-country.com/unclebill; 117 8th Ave; r $40-150; 🔀) is a welcoming place where you are encouraged to feel at home – throw a steak on the grill, leaf through books in the library or just hang out. The cheapest rooms share baths.

The only hotel with a direct view of the lake, **Lake Powell Resort** (☎ 928-645-2433; www .lakepowell.com; 100 Lake Shore Dr; d $140-160; 🔀 🔊) offers basic rooms, a great pool and a dining room with panoramic views.

For breakfast, the **Ranch House Grille** (☎ 928-645-1420; 819 N Navajo Dr; dishes $4-9; ☉ 5am-3pm) has good food, huge portions and fast service. BBQ dinners are featured at the cavernous **Gunsmoke Saloon** (☎ 928-645-2161; 644 N Navajo Dr; dishes $6-19; ☉ 5-9pm), which becomes a popular bar late night.

Navajo Indian Reservation

The wounds are healing but the scars remain, a testament to the nastiest, most embarrassing part of US history – the relocation of thousands of Native Americans to reservations. From the rusting trailers and social services buildings in small nowhere towns to hand-made roadside signs promising handicrafts sold by 'Friendly Indians,' the evidence of hard times is everywhere, as innocuous as the copper sand lining the desolate highways. At times the Navajo Reservation resembles a wasteland. But amid all the nothingness is some of North America's most spectacular scenery, including Monument Valley.

A visit to the reservation is more than just personally rewarding. The Navajo rely on tourist dollars to survive; help keep their heritage alive by choosing to stay on reservation land or purchasing their renowned crafts.

HOUSEBOATING ON LAKE POWELL

Houseboats give water rats the opportunity to not only play in the lake, but also sleep, eat and drink on it. Despite hosting hundreds of houseboats, the Lake Powell is big enough to boat for several days and rarely see anyone else. Summer rates cost $1106 to $3354 for three days to $1854 to $6450 for a week, in boats ranging from 36ft to 59ft that sleep between eight and 12 people. Rates drop by 40% between October and April. Contact **Aramark** (☎ 800-528-6154; www .lakepowell.com) for details and reservations.

The Navajo Reservation, unlike Arizona, does observe Mountain daylight saving time. Thus during summer, the reservation is one hour ahead of Arizona.

WINDOW ROCK

The tribal capital is at Window Rock, a bustling little place at the intersection of Hwys 264 and 12. Information about the whole reservation is available from **Navajo Tourism Office** (☎ 928-871-6436; www.navajo.org; ☉ 8am-5pm Mon-Fri) in the center of town.

The **Navajo Nation Museum & Library** (☎ 928-871-7941; cnr Hwy 264 & Post Office Loop Rd; admission free; ☉ 8am-5pm Mon-Sat, 8am-8pm Wed) features permanent collections, changing shows and the tribal library.

The **Annual Navajo Nation Fair**, held for several days in early September, is one of the word's largest Native American events, with an intertribal powwow, Indian rodeo, and traditional song and dance displays.

Rooms at the **Navajo Nation Inn** (☎ 928-871-4108; www.navajonationinn.com; Hwy 264 east of Hwy 12; r from $70; 🔀 🔊) feature Southwestern motifs. The on-site restaurant serves Navajo and American fare.

The **Navajo Transit System** (☎ 928-729-4002; www.navajotransitsystem.com) runs buses from Window Rock to Gallup, New Mexico ($2.50, one hour, four daily Monday to Saturday) and Tuba City ($13, four hours, daily Monday to Friday), via the Hopi Indian Reservation.

HUBBELL TRADING POST NATIONAL HISTORIC SITE

Thirty miles west of Window Rock in the town of Ganado, this **trading post** (☎ 928-755-

3475; admission free; ✆ 8am-6pm May-Sep, 8am-5pm Oct-Apr), now a National Historic Site, looks much as it would have after John Lorenzo Hubbell established it in 1878. It sells local crafts, specializing in top-quality Navajo weavings.

CANYON DE CHELLY NATIONAL MONUMENT

This many-fingered canyon contains several beautiful Ancestral Puebloan sites important to Navajo history. Families still farm the land, wintering on the rims then moving to hogans on the canyon floor in spring and summer. The canyon is private Navajo property administered by the NPS. Only enter hogans with a guide and don't photograph people without their permission.

Most of the bottom of the canyon is off-limits to visitors unless you take a 4½ hour guided hike ($15), held twice daily from May to September. Find out more at the **visitor center** (✆ 928-674-5500; ⊙ 8am-5pm) in the small village of Chinle. **Justin Tso's Horseback Tours** (✆ 928-674-5678), near the visitor center, has horses available for $10 per person per hour, plus $10 an hour for the guide.

Also near the visitor center, **Cottonwood Campground** (campsites free) has sites on a first-come, first-served basis. The **Thunderbird Lodge** (✆ 928-674-5841; www.tbirdlodge.com; d $100-150; ❄) has comfortable rooms, and an inexpensive cafeteria serving tasty Navajo and American food.

FOUR CORNERS NAVAJO TRIBAL PARK

Put a foot into Arizona and plant the other in New Mexico. Slap a hand in Utah and place the other in Colorado. This is the only place in the USA where four states come together at one point, although you'll have to cough up the $2.50 admission fee if you want to say you've done it.

MONUMENT VALLEY NAVAJO TRIBAL PARK

If you get serious déjà vu from the scenery here, it's probably because you've seen it a hundred times before. Hollywood can't seem to get enough of Monument Valley's fiery red spindles and grand buttes, and they've been showcased in hundreds of films and commercials.

Great views are had from the **scenic drive** along Hwy 163, but to really get up close and personal, you'll need to visit the

Monument Valley Navajo Tribal Park (✆ 435-727-3287; admission per person $5; ⊙ 7am-7pm May-Sep, 8am-4:30pm Oct-Apr). The visitor center houses exhibits, a restaurant and tour companies. From the visitor center, a rough unpaved loop road covers 17 miles of stunning valley views. You can drive it in your own vehicle or take a tour ($30, 2½ hours). The advantage here is that tours enter areas private vehicles can't. If you want to play John Wayne in your own Western, join a horseback ride ($30). To sign up, head to the visitor center.

The only place to stay near Monument Valley is Goulding's Lodge (see p931), just inside Utah.

NAVAJO NATIONAL MONUMENT

The exceptionally well preserved Ancestral Puebloan sites of Betatkin and Keet Seel in the **Navajo National Monument** (✆ 928-672-2700; Hwy 564; admission free; ⊙ 8am-5pm late May-Sep) are well worth a visit. Thanks to the effort it takes to reach them (it's a 5-mile round-trip hike to Betatkin and a 17-mile round-trip slog to Keet Seel), the sites don't attract busloads of tourists. Daily hiking permits are free, but limited. Call to reserve one in advance or stop by the visitor center, 9 miles north of Hwy 160 along Hwy 564. Both sites can only be visited on ranger-guided tours. There's a **campground** (campsites free) at the visitor center.

Hopi Indian Reservation

The oldest, most traditional and religious tribe in Arizona (if not the entire continent), the Hopi are a private people who have received less outside influence than most other tribes. Villages, many built between AD 1400 and AD 1700, dot the isolated mesas. **Old Oraibi**, inhabited since the early 12th century, vies with Acoma Pueblo in New Mexico for the title of oldest continuously inhabited town in North America.

Hwy 264 runs past the three mesas (First, Second and Third Mesa) that form the heart of the reservation. There are no banks, and cash is preferred for most transactions. Photographs, sketching and recording are not allowed – *don't even ask*.

At the end of First Mesa, the tiny village of **Walpi** (c 1600) juts out into space from the top of a spectacularly narrow mesa;

it's the most dramatic of the Hopi villages. The friendly **tourist office** (☎ 928-737-2262) can arrange guided walking tours (adult/child $8/5) several times daily. To reach Walpi, look for signs to First Mesa from Hwy 264 (around Mile 392), and follow the road to the parking area at the top of the mesa.

The Hopi are known for their kachina dolls, and these and other crafts can be purchased from individual artists in the villages and at roadside galleries.

The **Hopi Cultural Center Restaurant & Inn** (☎ 928-734-2401; www.hopiculturalcenter.com; r $90-95; dishes $6-8; ☽ breakfast, lunch & dinner; ☒), in Second Mesa, is the reservation's only hotel. The restaurant serves burgers, salads and Hopi dishes, such as *noqkwivi* (lamb and hominy stew). The Cultural Center's **museum** (☎ 728-734-6650; admission free; ☽ 8am-5pm Mon-Fri) is a good first stop, with informative exhibits on Hopi history.

Winslow

'Standing on a corner in Winslow, Arizona, such a fine sight to see…' Sound familiar? Thanks to the Eagles catchy '70s tune 'Take It Easy,' otherwise nonmemorable Winslow has gained some serious name recognition. A small plaza on Route 66 at Kinsley Ave, in the heart of old downtown, pays homage to the band with a life-sized bronze statue of a hitchhiker backed by a trompe l'oeil wall mural of the girl in a flatbed Ford.

Just 60 miles south of the Hopi mesas, Winslow makes a good regional base. About a dozen old motels are found along Route 66. The historic hacienda-style **La Posada** (☎ 928-289-4366; www.laposada.org; 303 E 2nd; r/ste $79/99; ☒) is the best choice.

Petrified Forest National Park

Comprised of broken, horizontal fossilized logs pre-dating the dinosaurs, this **national park** (☎ 928-524-6228; www.nps.gov/pefo; admission per vehicle $10) is a strange site. The park's appeal is heightened by the stunning landscape of the Painted Desert, which changes color as the sun shifts across the sky. The kaleidoscope of reds, pinks and oranges combined with the 225 million-year-old pieces of wood is a beautiful, almost haunting, site.

The park straddles I-40 at exit 311, 25 miles east of Holbrook. From this exit, a 28-mile paved park road offers a splendid **scenic drive**. Apart from short trails at some of the pullouts, there are no maintained trails, campsites or accommodations.

WESTERN ARIZONA

The Colorado River is alive with sun-worshippers at Lake Havasu City, while Route 66 offers well-preserved stretches of classic highway near Kingman. South of I-10, the wild, empty landscape is among the most rugged in the West.

Kingman & Around

Back when Route 66 was still the Mother Rd, Kingman was a bigger deal. Today it's just another fast-fading relic, a few decades

---

ROUTE 66: GET YOUR KICKS IN ARIZONA

Route 66 enthusiasts will find 400 miles of pavement stretching across Arizona – including the longest uninterrupted portion of old road left in the country, between Seligman and Topock. The Mother Rd connects the dots between Winslow's windblown streets, Williams' 1940s-vintage downtown, Kingman's mining settlements and gunslinging Oatman, each a glimpse of a bygone era. Unpaved dirt segments, long forgotten towns and notorious bits of old highway provide a taste of old-school motoring. It's a blast from the past all right, where decades collide and time often seems to standstill. In Kingman (above), it's as if the clock stopped in the mid-1950s and never started ticking again. Aging motels with fading paint, classic American diners and rusting long abandoned gas pumps line the broad streets. Towns like Oatman (above) transport you even further back in history. Wander unpaved roads past weathered buildings, have a smoke on a creaky porch with a leathery old-timer and listen to his yarns or down whiskey with locals in the one saloon. And just when you're thoroughly confused as to what year it is, the road zips you back into modern day. With funky pubs, classy restaurants and loads of outdoor activities, Flagstaff (p896) reminds you this tour isn't just about the past. For more info on the old highway, contact the **Historic Route 66 Association of Arizona** (☎ 928-753-5001; www.azrt66.com).

past its prime. Run-down motels, ugly billboards and gas stations galore grace its main drag. But several turn-of-the-19th-century buildings remain. If you're following the Route 66 trail, or looking for cheap lodging, it's worth a stroll.

Pick up self-guided driving tour maps at the **Powerhouse Visitor Center** (☎ 928-753-6106; 120 W Andy Devine Ave; 9am-6pm, 9am-5pm Dec-Feb), which has a **Route 66 museum** (admission $3) opposite Locomotive Park.

The atmospheric 1909 **Hotel Brunswick** (☎ 928-718-1800; www.hotel-brunswick.com; 315 E Andy Devine Ave; r $30-60) has 12 old-fashioned cowboy/girl rooms with single beds and shared baths. More expensive digs have larger beds, TVs and private baths. Its on-site restaurant, **Hubbs Café** (dishes $15-19, 5-9pm), is a genteel Southwest bistro serving pasta, steaks and a few international plates.

A former gold-mining town, **Oatman**, southwest of Kingman, is now a hokey but spirited tourist haunt, with gunfights at high noon and wild burros roaming the streets. At the century-old **Oatman Hotel** (☎ 928-768-4408; 181 N Main St; r $35-55), the simple rooms remain almost unchanged since Clarke Gable and Carole Lombard honeymooned here in the 1930s.

Lake Havasu City

When the city of London auctioned off its 1831 bridge in the late 1960s, developer Robert McCulloch bought it for $2.5 million, disassembled it into 10,276 granite slabs, transported the 10,000 tons of stone and reassembled it at Lake Havasu City, which sits along a dammed-up portion of the Colorado River. The place attracts hordes of young spring breakers and weekend warriors who come to play in the water and party hard. An 'English Village' of pseudo-British pubs and gift shops (it's more drab than wacky) surrounds the bridge. **Lake Havasu Marina** (☎ 928-855-2159), in the English Village, rents a variety of boats.

With pools, nightclubs, hot tubs and restaurants, **London Bridge Resort** (☎ 928-855-0888; www.londonbridgeresort.com; 1477 Queens Bay Rd; ste $100-300; ☒ ☒) attracts a playful crowd. Units feature either one or two bedrooms with kitchenettes.

Fresh seafood is the main draw at popular **Shugrues** (☎ 928-453-1400; 1425 McCulloch Blvd; dishes $10-30; lunch & dinner). **Mudshark Brewing Co** (☎ 928-453-2981; 210 Swanson Ave; dishes $8-18; lunch & dinner) serves excellent handcrafted brews and classic pizza and burger choices.

Yuma

The sun is always blazing in Arizona's sunniest, driest and third-largest metropolitan area. With winter temperatures around 70°F, Yuma lures retirees by the thousands to the scores of trailer parks around town. But despite its popularity with snowbirds (retired winter visitors), Yuma doesn't offer much for travelers. However, if it's freezing in Tucson, you might just want to shack up here for a few days.

The **Convention & Visitors Bureau** (☎ 928-783-0071; www.visityuma.com; 377 S Main St; 9am-5pm Mon-Fri) has all the area information. The town's number one tourist attraction is the **Yuma Territorial Prison State Historic Park** (☎ 928-783-4771; www.pr.state.az.us; 1 Prison Hill Rd; adult/child $4/2; 8am-5pm). Between 1876 and 1909, it housed 3069 of Arizona's most feared criminals, including 29 women. Today it's a slightly gruesome, mildly historic, offbeat attraction suitable for the whole family.

For sleeping, try **La Fuente Inn & Suites** (☎ 928-329-1814; www.lafuenteinn.com; 1513 E 16th St; r $80-100; ☒ ☒ ☐). In a modern, Spanish colonial–style building surrounded by gardens, the spacious rooms are mainly one- or two-room suites. A continental breakfast, evening cocktail hour and exercise room are pluses.

Dark and eclectically decorated, **Lutes Casino** (☎ 928-782-2192; 221 Main St; dishes $3-5; breakfast, lunch & dinner) is a local favorite offering pool tables and arcade games. Order a cheeseburger and smother it with Lute's own secret-recipe hot sauce. Kids are welcome.

TUCSON

A bustling college town where old West meets south of the border, Tucson is attractive, fun and one of the most culturally invigorating places in the Southwest. Set in a flat valley surrounded by craggy, odd-shaped mountains, it's Arizona's second-largest city, but has a distinct small-town vibe. Rich in Hispanic heritage (more than 20% of the population is of Mexican or Central American descent), Spanish slides easily off most tongues and high-quality Mexican restaurants abound. The eclectic shops toting vintage garb, scores of funky restaurants and

SOUTHWEST

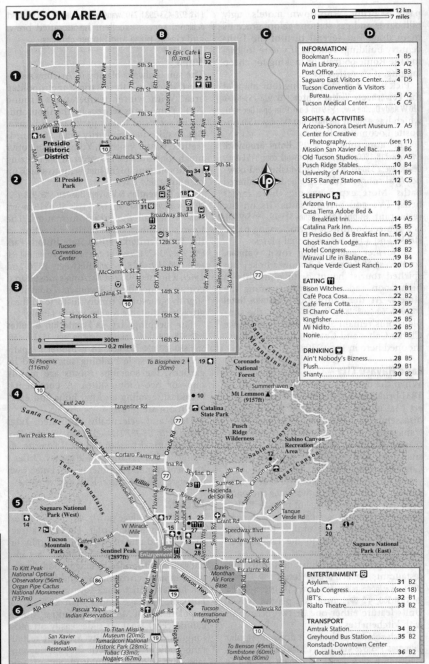

TUCSON AREA

| 0 | 12 km |
| 0 | 7 miles |

INFORMATION
Bookman's.....................................**1** B5
Main Library.................................**2** A2
Post Office....................................**3** B3
Saguaro East Visitors Center......**4** D5
Tucson Convention & Visitors
　Bureau..**5** A2
Tucson Medical Center..............**6** C5

SIGHTS & ACTIVITIES
Arizona-Sonora Desert Museum..**7** A5
Center for Creative
　Photography.......................(see 11)
Mission San Xavier del Bac.......**8** B6
Old Tucson Studios.....................**9** A5
Pusch Ridge Stables..................**10** B4
University of Arizona.................**11** B5
USFS Ranger Station.................**12** C5

SLEEPING
Arizona Inn..................................**13** B5
Casa Tierra Adobe Bed &
　Breakfast Inn..........................**14** A5
Catalina Park Inn.........................**15** B5
El Presidio Bed & Breakfast Inn..**16** A2
Ghost Ranch Lodge......................**17** B5
Hotel Congress...........................**18** B2
Miraval Life in Balance...............**19** B4
Tanque Verde Guest Ranch.......**20** D5

EATING
Bison Witches.............................**21** B1
Café Poca Cosa...........................**22** B2
Café Terra Cotta.........................**23** B2
El Charro Café.............................**24** A2
Kingfisher....................................**25** B5
Mi Nidito.....................................**26** B5
Nonie...**27** B5

DRINKING
Ain't Nobody's Bizness...............**28** B5
Plush..**29** B1
Shanty...**30** B2

ENTERTAINMENT
Asylum...**31** B2
Club Congress.......................(see 18)
IBT's...**32** B1
Rialto Theatre............................**33** B2

TRANSPORT
Amtrak Station...........................**34** B2
Greyhound Bus Station..............**35** B2
Ronstadt-Downtown Center
　(local bus).................................**36** B2

dive bars don't let you forget Tucson is a college town at heart, home turf to the 35,000-strong University of Arizona (U of A).

Orientation

Downtown Tucson and the historic district are east of I-10 exit 258. About a mile northeast of downtown is the U of A campus; 4th Ave is the main drag here, and is packed with cafés, bars and funky shops.

Information

BOOKSTORES

Bookman's (☎ 520-325-5657; 1930 E Grant Rd) Great selection of used books, music and magazines.

EMERGENCY

Emergency number (☎ 911)
Police (☎ 520-791-4444; 270 S Stone Ave)

INTERNET ACCESS

Library (☎ 520-791-4393; 101 N Stone Ave) Free Internet access.

MEDIA

The local newspapers are the morning *Arizona Daily Star*, the afternoon *Tucson Citizen* and the free *Tucson Weekly*, full of great entertainment and restaurant listings.

MEDICAL SERVICES

There are 10 hospitals and many smaller health-care facilities in Tucson.
Tucson Medical Center (☎ 520-327-5461; 5301 E Grant Rd; ◷ 24hr emergency)

MONEY

ATMs are abundant. Foreign exchange is available at most banks; $5 is charged if you don't have an account. The Tucson International Airport doesn't exchange currency.

POST

Post office (☎ 800-275-8777; 141 S 6th Ave)

TOURIST INFORMATION

Tucson Convention & Visitors Bureau (☎ 520-624-1817; www.visittucson.org; Ste 7199, 110 S Church St; ◷ 8am-5pm Mon-Fri, 9am-4pm Sat & Sun)

Sights & Activities

The 19th-century buildings and craft stores in the **Presido Historic District**, between Court and Main Aves and Franklin and Alameda Sts, are worth a wander.

The internationally renowned **Center for Creative Photography** (☎ 520-621-7968; www.creativephotography.org; 1030 N Olive Ave; admission free; ◷ 9am-5pm Mon-Fri, noon-5pm Sat & Sun), on the University of Arizona Campus, has a great collection of works by American photographers, interesting gallery shows and a remarkable archive (including most of Ansel Adams' and Edward Weston's work).

The **Santa Cantalina Mountains** are the best-loved and most visited of Tucson's many mountain ranges. Head to the area around Sabino Canyon, where you'll find the **USFS ranger station** (☎ 520-749-8700; admission per vehicle $5; ◷ 8am-4:30pm Mon-Fri, 8:30am-4:30pm Sat & Sun). Maps, hiking guides and information are available.

To **horseback** ride amid cacti and scrub brush, visit one of several stables offering excursions by the hour, half-day or longer. Summer trips tend to be short breakfast or sunset rides. One of the most reputable companies is **Pusch Ridge Stables** (☎ 928-825-1664; 13700 N Oracle Rd; rides from $25), which also offers overnight pack trips.

Festivals & Events

The **Tucson Gem and Mineral Show** (☎ 520-332-5773; www.tgms.org), in early February, is the largest of its kind in the world. The **Fiesta de los Vaqueros** (Rodeo Week; ☎ 520-741-2233; www.tusconrodeo.com) is held during the last week of February, and the huge nonmotorized parade is a locally famous spectacle.

Sleeping

Lodging prices vary considerably, with higher rates in winter and spring.

BUDGET & MIDRANGE

Hotel Congress (☎ 520-622-8848; 311 E Congress St; dm/s/d $42/62/72; P ⊠ ☐) Downtown's very popular, beautifully restored hotel dates from the 1920s and many of its fine rooms have period furnishings. Downstairs there's a hip music club, café and bar, so expect some noise at night; if you can't deal with that, ask for a room at the far end of the hotel.

Casa Tierra Adobe Bed & Breakfast Inn (☎ 520-578-3058; www.casatierratucson.com; 11155 W Calle Pima; r from $135; closed Mid-Jun–mid-Aug; P ⊠) For those seeking romantic, secluded desert abodes, this modern adobe home on the western edge of Saguaro National Park is well worth considering. Surrounded by

5 acres of cacti and Palo Verde trees, the sunsets are breathtaking; the outdoor whirlpools perfect for stargazing.

El Presidio Bed & Breakfast Inn (☎ 520-635-6151; 297 N Main Ave; r incl full breakfast $105-135; P) In Tucson's most attractive historic district, the inn boasts a mix of Victorian and adobe architectural styles. Rooms feature antique furniture and original art. Afternoon drinks are included. Credit cards not accepted.

Catalina Park Inn (☎ 520-792-4541; www .catalinaparkinn.com; 309 E First St; r incl full breakfast from $135; P) Much time was spent restoring this 1927 home, which has many unique and creative touches. Try the basement-Catalina room. It's giant, resembles a classic adobe and has a whirlpool in a former cedar closet. No children under 12.

Ghost Ranch Lodge (☎ 520-791-7565; www .ghostranchlodge.com; 801 W Miracle Mile; r from $55; P) Designed in part by Georgia O'Keefe, this 1940s place sits in 8 acres of cactus-filled desert and citrus gardens. Rooms have lots of character, with wooden rafter ceilings.

TOP END

Tucson's ranches and resorts are often destinations in themselves. We've listed just a few; there are many more. Rates can drop dramatically in the summer.

Arizona Inn (☎ 520-325-1541; www.arizonainn .com; 2200 E Elm St; r from $260; P) The grande dame of Tucson hotels, this sedate and beautiful pink-stucco place provides tranquil respite from city life. Exuding grace and old-Arizona charm, rooms are

---

THE AUTHOR'S CHOICE

Tanque Verde Guest Ranch (☎ 520-296-6275; www.tanqueverderanch.com; 14301 E Speedway Blvd; r $290-480; P) Tucson's most luxurious ranch allows you to play cowboy by day and debutante by night. Fifteen miles east of town in the Rincon Mountains, it offers breakfast and cookout rides, along with pools, tennis courts and a spa. Digs are big and cozy, with fireplaces and patios in many units. The newest casitas are some of the most luxurious lodging in the state. Dinners are impressive buffet affairs. Rates include all meals and activities.

---

spacious and decorated with original antiques or well-done reproductions.

Miraval Life in Balance (☎ 520-825-4000; www .miravalresort.com; 500 E Via Estancia Dr; r $770-1100; P) One of the country's most exclusive health spas, Miraval focuses on alternative healing, stress management and self-discovery. Activities include yoga, meditation and tai chi, as well as horseback riding, tennis and swimming. Rates include all meals, classes and a $95 per day spa credit. No children.

Eating

Tucson has a well-deserved reputation for Mexican food, and you'll be pleasantly surprised by the caliber of cooking.

El Charro Café (☎ 520-622-1922; 311 N Court Ave; dishes $15-20; ☉ lunch & dinner) The oldest place in town, they say it has been in the same family since 1922. Its *carne seca* (dried beef) used to be dried on the roof in the old days. Today the Mexican food is innovative, mouthwatering and fresh, making it popular with tourists and locals alike.

Bison Witches (☎ 520-740-1541; 526 4th Ave; dishes $6; ☉ lunch & dinner) College students pack this small restaurant daily, and for good reason. The sandwiches are humongous, excellent value and filled with all sorts of tasty ingredients. The environs are trendy, with bright walls and TVs showing sports. There's a good microbrew selection.

Café Terra Cotta (☎ 520-577-8100; 3500 E Sunrise Dr; dishes $12-24; ☉ lunch & dinner) This restaurant gets consistently high ratings for its wood-fired pizza, spicy pork tenderloin and other upscale Southwestern fare. The appetizers sound so appetizing that many people order two and forgo a main dish.

Mi Nidito (☎ 520-622-5081; 1813 S 4th Ave; dishes $6-10; ☉ lunch & dinner) Frequently gets rave reviews for its Mexican fare. There's often a wait; it doesn't take reservations. Bill Clinton ate here when he was president.

Kingfisher (☎ 520-323-7739; 2564 E Grant Rd; dishes $20; ☉ lunch & dinner) Modern and sophisticated with great decor, this is the kind of place you'll want to linger. The menu is short, but everything is creative and delicious. Try the baby back ribs with prickly pear BBQ sauce ($19).

Nonie (☎ 520-319-1965; 2526 E Grant Rd; dishes $12-15; ☉ lunch & dinner) A New Orleans bistro serving authentic French Creole and Cajun

---

THE AUTHOR'S CHOICE

Café Poca Cosa (☎ 520-622-6400; Clarion Hotel, 88 E Broadway Blvd; dishes $20; ☯ lunch & dinner) Dark and intimate, this award-winning place serves Nuevo-Mexican to rave reviews. The excellent food incorporates many regions of Mexico, and the menu changes twice daily. Food is freshly prepared, innovative and beautifully presented. Try the chef's choice; it changes with each plate and features three different entrees. The *mole* (classic Mexican chocolate sauce) and margaritas are also superb.

---

cuisine, its classy, cozy and comfortable. If crawfish, jambalaya, alligator and fried pickles are your idea of good food, this is a great place to indulge.

Drinking & Entertainment

Downtown 4th Ave, near 6th St, is a good place to barhop. Clubs showcase everything from DJs to live music.

Plush (☎ 520-798-1298; cnr 4th Ave & 6th St; cover $5) One half is a chill lounge and wine bar with multi-colored low lights, plush couches and funky art. The other half is a dark, smoky club showcasing live music. It has a mix of tables and standing room.

Shanty (☎ 520-623-2664; cnr 4th Ave & 9th St) The beer menu takes you around the world at this light and airy pub, with copper pillars, pool tables and free popcorn. If it's warm, sit on the patio by the fountain.

Ain't Nobody's Bizness (☎ 520-318-4838; 2900 E Broadway Blvd, Ste 118) Tucson's favorite lesbian bar for years running. Escape the chaos around the pool tables and on the dancefloor by heading to the quiet smoke-free room.

Club Congress (☎ 520-622-8848; Congress St) Live and DJ music are found at this very popular dance club. It attracts everyone from college kids to well-dressed professionals to guests staying at Hotel Congress upstairs.

Asylum (☎ 520-882-8949; 121 E Congress St; cover $5) DJs spin most nights at this downtown dance club. The decor is dark and edgy, with Gothic art and photos on the walls. Black is the color du jour on the dancefloor.

Rialto Theater (☎ 520-798-3333; 318 E Congress St; cover $10-35) This renovated 1919 vaudeville theater is Tucson's main venue for big-name bands. Expect acts on national tours.

IBT's (☎ 520-882-3053; 616 N 4th Ave) Tucson's best gay dance club, the theme changes nightly – from drag shows to dance mixes to karaoke.

Getting There & Around

The **Tucson International Airport** (☎ 520-573-8000) is 9 miles south of downtown. The taxi fare from the airport to downtown is around $15. **Greyhound** (☎ 520-792-3475; 2 S 4th Ave) runs buses to Phoenix ($16, two hours, daily) among other destinations. **Amtrak** (☎ 800-872-7245; 400 E Toole Ave) has trains to Los Angeles ($32, 9½ hours, three weekly).

The **Ronstadt-Downtown Center** (cnr Congress St & 6th Ave) is the major local transit center. From here **Sun Tran** (☎ 520-792-9222) buses serve metropolitan Tucson ($1). There are no night buses.

AROUND TUCSON

The places listed here are less than an hour's drive from town and make great day trips.

Arizona-Sonora Desert Museum & Old Tucson Studios

Javelinas, coyotes, bobcats, snakes and just about every other local desert animal are displayed in natural-looking outdoor settings at this excellent living **museum** (☎ 520-883-2702; www.desertmuseum.org; 2021 N Kinney Rd; adult/child $10/2; ☯ 8:30am-5pm) off Hwy 86, about 12 miles west of Tucson. A perennial local favorite, it's one of Tucson's crown jewels. The grounds are thick with desert plants, and docents are on hand to answer questions.

A few miles southeast of the museum, the **Old Tucson Studios** (☎ 520-883-0100; www.oldtucson .com; 201 S Kinney Rd; adult/child $15/10; ☯ 10am-6pm) were once an actual Western film set. Today the popular studios have been converted into a Western theme park (a must for kids) complete with shootouts and stage-coach rides.

Saguaro National Park

Although you see these towering succulents throughout the region, large stands of the majestic saguaro and their associated habitat and wildlife are protected in this **national park** (☎ 520-733-5153; www.nps.gov/sagu; admission $6; ☯ 8:30am-5pm).

The park has two separate units, east and west of Tucson. The **Saguaro East Visitors Center** is 15 miles east of downtown. It has information on day hikes, horseback riding and park camping (free permits must be obtained by noon on the day of your hike). This section of the park boasts about 130 miles of trails, including the **Tanque Verde Ridge Trail**, which climbs to the summit of Mica Mountain (8666ft).

Two miles northwest of the Arizona-Sonora Desert Museum is the **Saguaro West Visitors Center**. Although night hiking is permitted in this portion of the park, camping is not. The **Bajada Loop Drive** is an unpaved 6-mile loop that begins 1½ miles west of the visitor center and provides fine views of cactus forests, several picnic spots and access to trailheads. The **King Canyon trailhead**, just outside the park boundary (almost opposite the Arizona-Sonora Desert Museum), stays open until 10pm and is a great sunset or stargazing hike.

Mission San Xavier del Bac

Dating back to 1692, **Mission San Xavier del Bac** (☎ 520-294-2624; 1950 W San Xavier Rd; admission by donation; ☯ 7am-5pm) is Arizona's oldest European building still in use. A graceful blend of Moorish, Byzantine and late Mexican Renaissance architecture, the building has been restored but work is always continuing on the frescoes inside.

Biosphere 2

Built to be completely sealed off from Biosphere 1 (that would be earth), **Biosphere 2** (☎ 520-896-6200; www.bio2.edu; adult/child $13/9; ☯ 8:30am-5pm) is a 3-acre glassed dome housing seven separate microhabitats designed to be self-sustaining. In 1991, eight bionauts entered Biosphere 2 for a two-year tour of duty, during which they were physically cut off from the outside world. They emerged thinner, but in fair shape. Although this experiment could be used as a prototype for future space stations, it was privately funded and controversial. Heavy criticism came after the dome leaked gases and was opened to allow a bionaut to emerge for medical treatment. Columbia University now operates the facility, and gives public tours. Biosphere 2 is about 30 miles north of Tucson on Hwy 77.

WEST OF TUCSON

From Tucson, Hwy 86 heads west into some of the driest and emptiest parts of the Sonoran Desert. West of Sells, the **Kitt Peak National**

Optical Observatory (☎ 520-318-8726; www.noao.edu/kpno; Hwy 86; admission $2; ☯ 9am-3:45pm) is the largest optical observatory in the world, featuring 22 telescopes, one of which is used to study the sun. Guided tours (10am, 11:30am and 1:30pm) last about an hour. The three-hour nightly stargazing ($36) sessions are a real treat. These are very popular and should be booked weeks in advance.

If you want solitude in stark, quiet and beautiful desert surroundings, visit **Organ Pipe Cactus National Monument** (☎ 520-387-6849; Hwy 85; admission $5; ☯ 8am-5pm). Two unpaved loop drives (21 and 53 miles) and six hiking trails take you through the park, which has three types of large columnar cacti, and an excellent variety of other desert flora and fauna. There is a **campground** (campsites $10) by the visitor center.

SOUTH OF TUCSON

South of Tucson, I-19 is the main route to Nogales, Arizona and Mexico. Along the way are several interesting stops.

At exit 69, the **Titan Missile Museum** (☎ 520-574-9658; 1580 W Duval Mine Rd; adult/child $7.50/4; ☯ 9am-5pm Nov-Apr, closed Mon & Tue May-Oct) features an underground launch site for Cold War–era intercontinental ballistic missiles. Tours are informative and leave frequently.

If history and/or shopping for crafts interest you, visit the small village of **Tubac** (I-19 exit 34), with more than 80 galleries.

At exit 29, **Tumacácori National Historic Park** (☎ 520-398-2341; www.nps.gov/tuma; admission $5; ☯ 8am-5pm) is the well-preserved ruin of a never-completed Franciscan church started in 1800.

Nogales

Arizona's most important gateway into Mexico sees a constant flow of foot and vehicle traffic sliding across the border separating Nogales, Arizona, from Nogales, Sonora, Mexico. US citizens slip into Mexico to shop for bargains on handicrafts, pharmaceuticals and tequila, while Mexican citizens cross over to buy products not available in their country.

The **Nogales-Santa Cruz County Chamber of Commerce** (☎ 520-287-3685; www.nogaleschamber.com; 123 W Kino Park; ☯ 8am-5pm Mon-Fri) has all the usual tourist information. The **Mexican Consulate** (☎ 520-287-2521; 571 Grand Ave) is in town if you need it.

Chain motels are found off I-19 at exit 4. Mariposa Rd has the usual assortment of fast-food restaurants and a supermarket.

Greyhound (☎ 520-287-5628; 35 N Terrace St) has regular services to Tucson ($8, two hours). From the bus terminal, about 3 miles south of the border, there are frequent bus departures further into Mexico and a train to Guadalajara and Mexico City.

Drivers into Mexico can obtain car insurance from friendly, helpful **Sanborn's** (☎ 520-281-1873; www.sanbornsinsurance.com; 2921 N Grand Ave; ☽ 8am-5pm Mon-Fri, 8am-4pm Sat & Sun). The cost is determined by the value of the car and length of your stay, but there's a $22 minimum charge.

SOUTHEASTERN CORNER

Cochise County is a land rich with cowboys, Indians, ranchers, miners, gunslingers and all manner of Western lore. It's also an area of rugged, scenic beauty.

Rural **Benson** is a quiet travelers' stop with a few motels. Don't miss the fantastic **Kartchner Caverns State Park** (☎ 502-586-4100; Hwy 90; ☽ 7:30am-6pm), 9 miles south of town. It's a 2.5-mile-long wet limestone cave, touted as one of the world's best 'living' caves. Two tours (adult/child $23/13) are offered and these can sell out months in advance, so reserve ahead.

Small and remote **Chiricahua National Monument** (☎ 520-824-3560; admission $5), in the Chiricahua Mountains, offers strangely eroded volcanic geology and abundant wildlife. The **Bonita Canyon Scenic Drive** takes you 8 miles to Massai Point at 6870ft, and there are numerous hiking trails. The monument is 40 miles southeast of Willcox off Hwy 186.

Tombstone is a formerly rip-roaring, 19th-century silver-mining town, and the site of the famous 1881 shootout at the OK Corral. Now a National Historic Landmark, it attracts crowds of tourists to its old Western buildings, stagecoach rides and gunfight reenactments. It's hokey, sure, but also a fun place to grab a beer in an old saloon. The **Visitor & Information Center** (☎ 520-457-3929; www.tombstone.org; cnr 4th & Allen Sts; ☽ 9am-1pm Mon-Fri) will get you oriented.

Bisbee

Built into the steep walls of Tombstone Canyon, Bisbee is one of Arizona's most endearing and best-preserved historic towns.

Oozing old-fashioned ambience, its elegant Victorian buildings line narrow twisting streets, and house classy galleries, sumptuous restaurants and charming hotels.

Most businesses are found in the Historic District (Old Bisbee), along Subway and Main Sts. The **chamber of commerce** (☎ 520-432-5421; www.bisbeearizona.com; 31 Subway St; ☽ 9am-5pm Mon-Fri, 10am-4pm Sat & Sun) has tourist information.

Bisbee owes its existence to the ore found in the surrounding hills. To learn how it was collected visit the **Queen Mine** (☎ 520-432-2071; 119 Arizona St; adult/child $12/5; ☽ 9am-3:30pm). Retired miners give the hour-long tours, which descend deep underground (it's a chilly 47°F down here so bring warm clothes).

The charming Victorian-era **Bisbee Grand Hotel** (☎ 520-432-5900; www.bisbeegrandhotel.com; 61 Main St; r $75-150; ✿) is by far the best place to sleep. Try one of the themed suites – the Old Western is our favorite, featuring a converted covered wagon for a bed.

Hip **Cafe Roka** (☎ 520-432-5153; 35 Main St; dishes $13-25; ☽ 5-9pm Wed-Sat) serves innovative gourmet American fare. There's live Jazz on Friday and Saturday night. For casual dining, head to **Bisbee Grille** (☎ 520-432-6788; 2 Copper Queen Plaza; dishes $8-11; ☽ breakfast, lunch & dinner).

UTAH

Go outside and play. Isn't that what parents used to say? In Utah, it could well be a marketing moniker. The rugged terrain of this little-populated state really does beg to be biked, hiked, skied and otherwise actively pursued. Its dazzling display of grandeur leaves visitors a bit awestruck and dumbfounded. The panoply of colors, colors everywhere, as far as the eye can see, is more varied than a 64-pack of crayons. The temptation to simply sit still and watch the ever-changing kaleidoscope runs in opposition to hiking where no one (literally) has hiked before. This haunting topography is *that* vast.

The southern Utah landscape is defined by five national parks with towering mountain peaks, plunging canyons, sweeping sandstone domes and seemingly endless expanses of undulating desert. Northern Utah is marked by the Great Salt Lake, forested mountains in the snow-covered

Wasatch Range (where the 2002 Olympic Winter Games where held) and the wild Uinta Mountains.

Utah is also defined by modern Mormons, whose social and political influence reverberates throughout the state. When the Mormon pioneers reached the area in 1847, they, too (like the Indians 7000 years before them), felt a spiritual response and claimed it as their new home (their Zion). No matter your belief system, the magical landscape of Utah will feel like heaven on earth.

History

Utah gets its name from the nomadic Ute people who, along with the Paiute and Shoshone, lived in the Great Basin desert more than 8000 years ago. Europeans arrived as early as 1776, but Indians inhabited the region freely until the mid-19th century. Led by Brigham Young, the Mormons fled religious persecution to Utah, establishing Salt Lake City on July 24, 1847. They called their state Deseret, meaning 'honeybee,' according to the Book of Mormon.

After the US acquired the Utah Territory from Mexico, the Mormons petitioned Congress for statehood six times. Their petitions were consistently rejected because of Mormon polygamy (the practice of having more than one spouse at the same time), which was outlawed by the US government. Tensions grew between the Mormons and the federal government until 1890, when Mormon Church President Wilford Woodruff announced that God had told him that Mormons should abide by US law. Polygamy was discontinued and, soon afterward, Utah became the 45th state in 1896. Today Mormons remain in the majority in

> ### UTAH FACTS
> **Nicknames** Beehive State, Mormon State
> **Population** 2.3 million
> **Area** 82,144 sq miles
> **Capital city** Salt Lake City (population 182,000)
> **Official insect** Honeybee
> **Birthplace of** Donny (b 1957) and Marie (b 1959) Osmond; beloved bandit Butch Cassidy (1866-1908)
> **Home of** Winter Olympic Games 2002
> **Famous for** Mormons, red-rock canyons

Utah and continue to exert a powerful conservative influence on life in the state.

Information

State sales in Utah tax is 6.6%. Note: it's difficult to change currency outside Salt Lake City; see opposite.

Gay & Lesbian Community Center of Utah (☎ 801-539-8800, 888-874-2743; www.glccu.com; 361 N 300 West, Salt Lake City, UT 84103) This helpful center offers advice, activities and classes.

Natural Resources Map & Bookstore (www.maps .state.ut.us) Has detailed maps of all the stellar places to explore.

Utah! (www.utah.org) Consult for statewide information. It has information on lodging, camping and outdoor activities.

Utah Travel Council (☎ 801-538-1030, 800-200-1160; www.utah.com; Council Hall, Capitol Hill, Salt Lake City, UT 84114; ☯ 8am-5pm Mon-Fri, 10am-5pm Sat & Sun) Publishes the free *Utah Travel Guide*. The council's **bookstore** (☎ 801-538-1398) sells guides and maps.

Utah State Parks & Recreation Department (☎ 801-538-7220; www.stateparks.utah.gov; 1594 W North Temple, Salt Lake City, UT 84114) Sells multiple-park permits ($70 annual) and arranges camping reservations.

DRINKING IN UTAH

Can you get a drink in Utah? Absolutely. Simply head for one of the state's so-called 'private clubs,' which are full bars selling all manner of alcoholic drinks; they stop serving nightly at 1am. To become a temporary 'member' it costs $5 for two weeks and entitles you to bring up to five guests. You can also get 'sponsored' by another member; don't worry, it's common practice, and anyway, there's usually a watchful doorman or bartender who'll do the asking for you.

Restaurants can serve wine, beer or liquor with food. 'Taverns' sell low-alcohol (3.2%) beer only. This same 3.2% beer can be purchased at grocery and convenience stores, while hard alcohol and wine can only be purchased at state liquor stores.

For the most part, you won't even notice these laws. That's because Utah has a huge range of bars, taverns and brewpubs – and no shortage of folks to keep the doors swinging and the stools warm.

SALT LAKE CITY

Don't be lulled by your preconceptions about Salt Lake City (SLC). Ever since the Winter Olympics came to town, Utah's state capital has become ever so slightly cosmopolitan. There's even a hint of counterculturalism in the air – albeit faint. Though Salt Lake is headquarters of the Mormon Church, only about half its citizens are Latter-day Saints (LDS; see p920). The result is a broader public discourse than in other Utah cities and towns. Sure, SLC is conservative by coastal standards, but at least there's an ongoing conversation about identity.

Be sure to see Temple Sq, but remember there's a big secular city beyond the church walls, with enticing museums, a thriving university and dynamic arts scene. And when the trail beckons, you're only 45 minutes' drive from the towering Wasatch Mountains' brilliant hiking and world-class skiing.

Orientation

SLC is laid out in a spacious grid with streets aligned north–south or east–west. (Interestingly, streets were originally built 132ft wide so that four oxen pulling a wagon could turn around.) Because streets are so wide, there are mid-block pedestrian crossings downtown. Carry the orange flags, available at these crossings, for increased visibility. Everything radiates from Temple Sq: the corner of South Temple (east–west) and Main (north–south) is the zero point for streets and addresses. Eight blocks equals one mile.

Two major interstates cross at SLC. I-15 runs north–south, I-80 east–west and I-215 loops the city.

Information

BOOKSTORES

Sam Weller Books (☎ 801-328-2586, 800-333-7269; 254 S Main; ⏰ 10am-8pm Mon-Sat, 10am-4pm Sun) The city's biggest independent bookstore, with the best selection of travel books, guides and maps.

EMERGENCY

Emergency number (☎ 911)
Police (☎ 801-799-3000; 315 E 200 South)

INTERNET ACCESS

Library (☎ 801-524-8200; www.slcpl.lib.ut.us; 210 E 400 South; ⏰ 9am-9pm Mon-Thu, 9am-6pm Sat, 1-5pm Sun) Free Internet access and excellent periodicals.

INTERNET RESOURCES

Salt Lake Tourist & Visitors Center (www .saltlakecityutah.org) An online travel planner with a wealth of historical information.
TravelWest (www.travelwest.net/cities/saltlake) Information on camping, parks, lodging, area attractions and more.

MEDIA

City Weekly (☎ 801-573-7003; www.slweekly.com) Free alternative weekly with good restaurant and entertainment listings; publishes the useful *City Guide* three times annually.
Salt Lake Metro (☎ 801-323-9500; www.slmetro.com) SLC's free, gay newspaper.
Salt Lake Tribune (☎ 801-257-8742; www.sltrib.com) Utah's largest-circulation paper; not Mormon-owned, but conservative.

MEDICAL SERVICES

Salt Lake Regional Medical Center (☎ 801-350-4111; 1050 E South Temple; ⏰ 24hr emergency)
University Hospital (☎ 801-581-2121/291; 50 N Medical Dr; ⏰ 24hr emergency)

MONEY

On weekends visit the Salt Lake City International Airport to change money.
Wells Fargo (☎ 801-246-2677; 79 S Main)

POST

Post office (☎ 800-275-8777; www.usps.com; 230 W 200 South)

TOURIST INFORMATION

Salt Lake Ranger Station (☎ 801-733-2660; ⏰ 8am-5pm Mon-Fri) No walk-ins accepted but telephone information on the Wasatch-Cache National Forest is provided.
Visitor Information Center (☎ 801-521-2822, 800-541-4955; www.visitsaltlake.com; 90 S West Temple; ⏰ 8:30am-5pm Mon-Fri year-round, 9am-5pm Sat & Sun summer) The center, within the Salt Palace Convention Center, publishes the free *Salt Lake Visitors Guide*.

Sights

DOWNTOWN

The city's most famous sight, **Temple Square** (☎ 801-240-2534, 800-537-9703; www.visittemplesquare .com; admission free; ⏰ 9am-9pm) occupies a 10-acre block and is surrounded by 15ft-high walls. Docents at the **visitor centers** inside the two entrances (on S and N Temple) give free, 30-minute tours. The **Tabernacle** is the

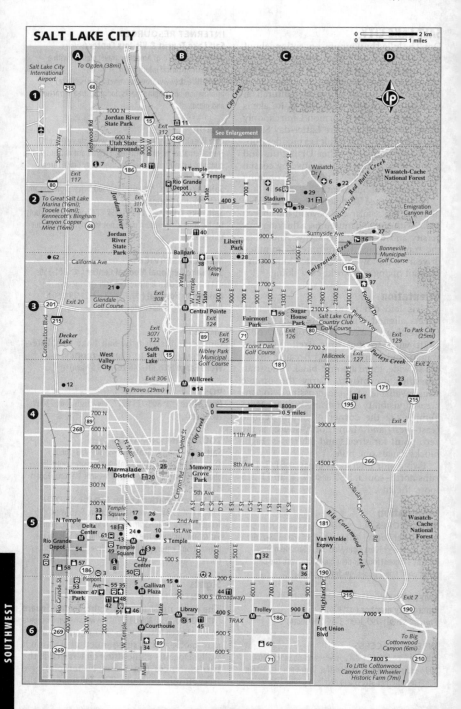

SALT LAKE CITY

highlight of Temple Sq, but it is closed until mid-2007 for renovations.

Lording over the square, the 210ft **Salt Lake Temple** is topped with a golden statue of the angel Moroni who appeared to LDS-founder Joseph Smith. Temple ceremonies are secret and open only to LDS 'in good standing.'

Adjoining Temple Sq, the **Museum of Church History and Art** (☎ 801-240-3310; 45 N West Temple; admission free; 🕑 9am-9pm Mon-Fri, 10am-7pm Sat & Sun) has impressive exhibits of pioneer history and fine art. Research your genealogy at the **Family History Library** (☎ 801-240-2331; 35 N West Temple; 🕑 7:30am-10pm Tue-Sat, 7:30am-5pm Mon).

Brigham Young lived in the **Beehive House** (☎ 801-240-2671; 67 E South Temple; admission free) until his death in 1877, and the house has been meticulously maintained with period furnishings and artwork. Tours are held 9:30am to 4:30pm Monday to Saturday and 10am to 1pm Sunday. The **LDS Conference Center** (☎ 801-240-0075; 60 W North Temple; 🕑 9am-9pm) offers great views from its rooftop gardens.

Daughters of Utah Pioneers (DUP) museums are located throughout Utah, but the **Pioneer Memorial Museum** (☎ 801-532-6479; 300 N Main; admission free; 🕑 9am-5pm Mon-Sat year-round, 1-5pm Sun summer) is by far the best, a vast four-story treasure trove of thousands of pioneer artifacts.

Just north of Temple Sq, the walls of the impressive **State Capitol** (☎ 801-538-1563; www.utahstatecapitol.utah.gov; 123 State Capitol; 🕑 8am-8pm)

are normally covered with historical murals, but the building is being renovated until mid-2007.

BEYOND DOWNTOWN

The **University of Utah** (☎ 801-581-7200; www.utah.edu; 200 South), or 'U of U' as it's more commonly called, was the site of the Olympic Village in 2002. The **Olympic Legacy Cauldron Park** (☎ 801-581-8849, 866-659-7275; www.olyparks.com; 3000 Bear Hollow Park) has giant panels detailing the games; check out the heavy-handed but heartfelt film (adult/child $3/2), with artificial fog and booming sound effects. It's screened from 10am to 6pm Monday to Saturday.

SLC's best art museum, the **Utah Museum of Fine Arts** (☎ 801-581-7332; www.umfa.utah.edu; 410 Campus Center Dr; adult/child $4/2; 🕑 10am-5pm Tue & Thu-Fri, 10-8pm Wed, 11am-5pm Sat & Sun) has soaring galleries, cherry-wood floors, and permanent collections of tribal, Western and modern art; it also books important international traveling shows.

In the nearby Wasatch Foothills, the lovely 150-acre **Red Butte Gardens** (☎ 801-581-4747; Wakara Way; adult/child & senior $5/3; 🕑 10am-5pm Nov-Apr, 9am-8pm May-Oct) has trails, 25 acres of gardens and gorgeous valley views.

Dedicated to the 1847 arrival of the Mormons, **This Is The Place Heritage Park** (☎ 801-582-1847; www.thisistheplace.org; 2601 E Sunnyside Ave/800 South; 🕑 9am-6pm) encompasses **Old Deseret Village** (adult/child $6/4; 🕑 10am-5pm late May-early Sep), a 450-acre living-history museum, with costumed docents depicting life in the

---

SING PRAISES

The members of the Church of Jesus Christ of Latter-Day Saints (LDS; www.lds.org or www .mormon.org) – or Mormons – prize family above all else, and Mormon families tend to be large. Hard work and strict obedience to church leaders are very important. Smoking, and drinking alcohol, tea or coffee, are forbidden. Women are forbidden to take leadership roles, as were African Americans until 1978.

The faith considers missionary service important, and many young adults go on missions to spread the faith around the world. Women are called Sisters during their service, and the men are called Elders. There are now around 11 million Mormons worldwide.

The **Mormon Tabernacle Choir** (801-240-4150; www.mormontabernaclechoir.com) is one of the world's foremost choirs. When they sing fortissimo, the sheer power of the 360-voice ensemble will blow you away. Alas, the 1867 Tabernacle (p917), the acoustically bright, ringing hall where they normally sing, is being renovated until mid-2007. In the meantime, you can attend their famous Sunday morning radio broadcast, *Music and the Spoken Word* (the oldest continuous radio broadcast in America), in the LDS Conference Center (p919) at Temple Sq at 9:30am; arrive by 9am. Or attend their Thursday evening rehearsal at 8pm.

---

mid-19th century. Some of the 41 buildings are replicas, others originals, including Brigham Young's farmhouse. You'll feel anachronistic in your khaki pants. Self-guided tours cost $2.

Activities

Millcreek, Big Cottonwood and Little Cottonwood canyons, all on the east side of the Wasatch Mountains and within easy reach of SLC, offer excellent opportunities for hiking, mountain biking, camping and cross-country skiing. The **Utah State Parks & Recreation Department** (801-972-7800; www .slcgov.com; 1965 W 500 South; 8am-5pm Mon-Fri) has tons of information about city parks.

REI (801-486-2100, 800-426-4840; www.rei.com; 3285 E 3300 South; 10am-9pm Mon-Fri, 9am-7pm Sat, 11am-6pm Sun) rents camping equipment, climbing shoes, kayaks and most winter-sports gear. The well-regarded **Guthrie Bicycle** (801-363-3727; 156 E 200 South; 9:30am-7pm Mon-Fri, 9:30am-6pm Sat) rents road and mountain bikes ($30 per day) for plenty of in-town trails.

The **Utah Heritage Foundation** (801-533-0858; www.utahheritagefoundation.com; 485 N Canyon Rd) offers tours of SLC's historic landmarks and distributes free self-guided walking tour brochures.

Salt Lake City for Children

There's lots for tots in SLC; the Visitor Information Center has an A-Z list. The wonderful hands-on exhibits at the **Children's Museum of Utah** (801-328-3383; www.childmuseum.org; 840 N 300 West; admission $4; 10am-5pm Mon-Sat, 10am-8pm Fri, closed Mon winter) stimulate imaginations and senses.

Wheeler Historic Farm (801-264-2241; www .wheelerfarm.com; 6351 S 900 East; admission free, wagon rides $2, tours $2; dawn-dusk, visitor center 9:30am-5:30pm), in South Cottonwood Regional Park, dates from 1886. Kids can help farm hands milk cows, churn butter and feed animals. There's also blacksmithing, quilting and wagon rides in summer.

The **Hogle Zoo** (801-582-1631; 2600 E Sunnyside Ave; adult/child & senior $7/5; 9am-6:30pm Jun-Sep, 9am-5:30pm in winter) takes folks face-to-face with tigers, wolves, gorillas and even elephants (well, sort of face-to-face). Kids love the petting zoo and miniature-train rides ($1).

For a sure-to-please treat, slip down the water slides at **Raging Waters** (801-972-3300; www.ragingwatersutah.com; 1700 S 1200 West; adult/child $18/14; 10:30am-7:30pm Mon-Sat, noon-7:30pm Sun May-Sep).

The **Tracy Aviary** (801-322-2473, 801-596-8500; 589 E 1300 South; adult/child $5/3; 9am-6pm summer, 9am-4:30pm winter) delights bird lovers with displays of world-wide winged creatures. Kids can feed ducks, colorful lories and parrots.

Tours

Grayline (801-534-1001; www.saltlakecitytours.org; 3359 S Main, Ste 804) offers 4½ hour Mormon Tabernacle Choir tours for $30.

Passage to Utah (801-534-1001; www.saltlake citytours.org; Ste 804, 3359 S Main) provides some eco-sensitive walking tours and science and nature tours in SLC and the surrounding area.

Festivals & Events

Crowds come for the **Utah Arts Festival** (www.uaf .org), in late June, and **Days of '47** (☎ 801-254-4656; www.daysof47.com), the 'Mormon Mardi Gras,' from mid- to late July, which has everything from a rodeo to an enormous parade.

Sleeping

SLC's lodgings are primarily chain properties, many clustered on W North Temple near the airport and along S 200 West near 500 South and 600 South. Rates are lowest during the spring and fall, and spike when there's a convention. At top-end hotels, rates are lowest on weekends. Summertime prices plunge at ski resorts (p923), about 45 minutes' drive from downtown.

BUDGET

Skyline Inn (☎ 801-582-5350; www.skylineinn.com; 2475 E 1700 South; r $55-69; P ☎ 🖳) This modest, well-maintained hotel overlooking downtown is a great off-the-beaten-path choice. Near Big and Little Cottonwood Canyons, it's especially good for skiers and hikers.

City Creek Inn (☎ 801-533-9100, 866-533-4898; www.citycreekinn.com; 230 W North Temple; r $48-58; P) One of SLC's best budget choices is located right downtown, next to Temple Sq. It's simple, attractive and family owned.

Ute Hostel (☎ 801-595-1645; www.infobytes .com/utehostel; 21 E Kelsey Ave; dm/d $15/35; P ☒) Ute Hostel is small and homey, and is set among attractive Craftsman houses.

MIDRANGE

Peery Hotel (☎ 801-521-4300, 800-331-0073; www .peeryhotel.com; 110 W 300 South; r $80-120; P 🖳 ☒) If you like historic hotels, this one's a charmer. The small but impeccably maintained rooms have thick bedspreads, gilt-framed mirrors, heavy wooden furniture, and up-to-date bathrooms with pedestal sinks and aromatherapy soaps.

Anton Boxrud (☎ 801-363-8035, 800-524-5511; www.antonboxrud.com; 57 S 600 East; r $78-140; P ☒) You'll feel like a guest in a friend's home at this seven-room, meticulously restored 1901 Victorian on a tree-lined street, walkable to downtown. The charming innkeeper always has cookies and drinks on hand and serves a full breakfast.

THE AUTHOR'S CHOICE

Grand America (☎ 801-258-6000, 800-621-4505; www.grandamerica.com; 555 S Main; r $210-330; P 🖳 🖳 ☒) SLC's only true luxury hotel towers over the city like a 24-story wedding cake. The retro-fancy lobby sports over-the-top custom fixtures, including Murano-glass chandeliers. Rooms are decked out with Italian-marble bathrooms, English-wool carpeting, tasseled damask draperies and other cushy touches. Sunday brunch (adult/child $32/16) is equally lavish.

Saltair B&B (☎ 801-533-8184, 800-733-8184; www .saltlakebandb.com; 164 S 900 East; r incl full breakfast $80-110, cottages $130-150; P ☒) Inside a 1903 Victorian on a pretty (but busy) residential street, this B&B provides a range of rooms and cottages (with kitchens).

Eating

The food scene here is vast and varied, with a huge, impressive assortment of ethnic restaurants.

BUDGET

Salt Lake Roasting Company (☎ 801-363-7572; 320 E 400 South; ⏱ 7am-midnight Mon-Sat) For pastries, soups, quiches, sandwiches and room to spread out, you can't beat this two-story café.

Cafe Trang (☎ 801-539-1638; 818 S Main; mains $5-11; ⏱ lunch & dinner) This hole-in-the-wall with table service has rice-noodle bowls and aromatic Vietnamese specialties.

MIDRANGE

Lugano (☎ 801-412-9994; 3364 S 2300 East; mains $10-20; ⏱ dinner; P) Bright, dynamic flavors are the hallmarks at this bellissimo chef-owned, modern-northern-Italian trattoria, where there's nary a tourist. Share specialties from the wood-fired oven. It's a great après-ski location, well worth the 15-minute drive from downtown.

Sage's Café (☎ 801-322-3790; 473 E Broadway; mains $12-15; ⏱ dinner Wed-Fri, 9am-9pm Sat & Sun) Everything at this comfy spot, retro-fitted into a former home, is vegan, organic and made in-house (including the root beer).

Red Iguana (☎ 801-322-1489; 736 W North Temple; dishes $7-12; ⏱ lunch & dinner) You'll find no better *mole* (classic Mexican chocolate sauce)

THE AUTHOR'S CHOICE

Metropolitan (☎ 364-3472; 173 W Broadway; mains $18-28; ☽ dinner Mon-Sat) If Salt Lake had celebs, they'd hang out at Metropolitan, where the culinary craftsmanship is so good and the flavors so sparkling, they merit comparison with big-city restaurants in California. The sexy concrete-and-velvet dining room complements the chef's artistry. You can always order small plates from the bistro menu ($8 to $12) while swilling martinis at the bar.

than at this top pick for Mexican. The room ain't much, but with food this good and great margaritas, who cares.

Bombay House (☎ 581-0222; 1615 S Foothill Dr; mains $8-16; ☽ dinner Mon-Sat) East of downtown, Bombay's Indian cooking is vibrant and fiery. Arrive early; it gets packed.

Drinking

Squatter's Pub Brewery (☎ 801-363-2739; www.squatters.com; 147 W Broadway) Squatter's has some great microbrews to choose from; try the smooth Vienna Lager or its lighter St Provo Girl.

Red Rock Brewing Company (☎ 801-521-7446; www.redrockbrewing.com; 254 S 200 West) Also vying for best-brewpub honors, Red Rock jams on weekends. The extensive menu includes good salads and wood-fired pizza ($8 to $15).

Port O' Call (☎ 801-521-0589; 68 W 400 South) If it's liquor you're after, this large, full-service bar spreads across four floors in a cool 1912 building. It's quiet during the day, but at night crowds can pack in for DJs and bands.

Entertainment

The **Salt Lake City Arts Council** (☎ 801-596-5000; www.slcgov.com/arts; 54 Finch Lane) has a complete cultural-events calendar listing theater, dance, opera, symphony and free outdoor concerts. The historic **Capitol Theater** (☎ 801-355-2787; www.finearts.slco.org/facilities/capitol/capitol.html; 50 W 200 South), dramatic **Rose Wagner Performing Arts Center** (☎ 801-355-2787; www.finearts.slco.org/facilities/rose/rose.html; 138 W 300 South) and acoustically rich **Abravanel Hall** (☎ 801-533-6683; www.finearts.slco.org/facilities/abravanel/abravanel.html; 123 W South Temple) are primary venues. For tickets call **ArtTix** (☎ 801-355-2787, 888-451-2787; www.arttix.org).

SLC has Utah's only gay scene; the free *Salt Lake Metro* has up-to-the-minute listings. For dancing, **Club Sound** (☎ 801-328-0255; 579 W 200 South; ☽ Wed-Sat) hosts gay Fridays; **Club Naked** (☎ 801-521-9292; 326 S West Temple; ☽ Wed-Sat) is popular with over-21 dance bunnies on Saturday.

Cup of Joe (☎ 801-363-8322; 353 W 200 South St; ☽ 7am-midnight Mon-Fri, 9am-midnight Sat, 9am-8pm Sun) Acoustic music Friday and open-mike-poetry night Saturday (8pm to 10pm) take place at this cool, artsy coffeehouse in an old brick warehouse (with free wi-fi, too).

SPORTS

Utah Jazz (www.nba.com/jazz), the men's professional basketball team, plays at the **Delta Center** (☎ 801-355-3865; www.deltacenter.com; 301 W South Temple). The International Hockey League's **Utah Grizzlies** (☎ 801-988-7825; www.utahgrizzlies.com) play at the **E Center** (☎ 801-988-8888; www.theecenter.com; 3200 South Decker Lake Dr, West Valley City), which hosted most of the men's ice hockey competitions during the Olympics.

Shopping

The best downtown major-label shopping is at the diverse indoor-outdoor **Gateway** (☎ 801-456-0000; www.shopthegateway.com; 200 South to 50 North, 400 West to 500 West; ☽ 10am-9pm Mon-Thu, 10am-10pm Fri & Sat, noon-5pm Sun). Nearby, you'll find artists' studios, indie boutiques and funky second-hand stores at **Artspace** (Pierpont Ave, btwn 300 West & 400 West) in SLC's warehouse district. **Sugarhouse** (2100 South, btwn 900 East & 1300 East) looks like Main St USA and has a good mix of indie shops and mall stores. For more brand names, head to the 100 stores inside the converted trolley barns at **Trolley Square** (☎ 801-521-9877; btwn 600 South & 700 East).

Getting There & Around
AIR

The **Salt Lake City International Airport** (☎ 801-575-2400; www.slcairport.com; 776 N Terminal Dr) is 6 miles west of downtown. Numerous door-to-door shuttle vans are available at the airport; a trip downtown costs $10 to $15. Call the airport's **transportation desk** (☎ 801-575-2477) for details.

BUS

There are several daily buses with **Greyhound** (☎ 801-355-9579; www.greyhound.com; 160 W South Temple) south through Provo and St George to Las Vegas, Nevada ($53, 8½ hours); west to San Francisco ($79, 16 hours); east to Denver ($61, 10 to 12 hours); and north to Seattle ($101, 20 to 24 hours).

UTA (☎ 801-743-3882, 888-743-3882; www.rideuta .com) buses ($1.30) serve SLC and the Wasatch Front area until about midnight (there's limited service on Sunday). TRAX, UTA's light-rail system, runs east from the Delta Center to the university ($1.25). The center of downtown SLC is a free-fare zone.

UTA buses also go to Provo, Tooele, Ogden and other Wasatch Front-area cities and suburbs ($2.50); during ski season they serve the four local resorts and Sundance, near Provo (all $6, round-trip).

CAR
Rugged Rental (☎ 801-977-9111, 800-977-9111; www .ruggedrental.com; 2740 W California Ave) specializes in 4WDs and SUVs, and has good service and better rates than the majors.

TRAIN
Amtrak's *California Zephyr* stops daily at the **Union Pacific Rail Depot** (☎ 801-322-3510, 800-872-7245; www.amtrak.com; 340 S 600 West) going east to Chicago ($112 to $219, 35 hours) and west to Oakland, California ($59 to $15, 18 hours).

AROUND SALT LAKE CITY
Once part of prehistoric Lake Bonneville, the **Great Salt Lake** today covers 2000 sq miles and is far saltier than the ocean; you can easily float on its surface.

The pretty, 15-mile-long **Antelope Island State Park** (☎ 801-773-2941; I-15 exit 335; per vehicle $8; ☼ 7am-10pm), 40 miles northwest of SLC, has the best beaches for lake swimming, as well as nice hiking. It's also home to one of the largest bison herds in the country, and the fall corralling of these animals is a great wildlife spectacle. A basic **campground** (campsites $11) is open year-round.

Century-old **Kennecott's Bingham Canyon Copper Mine** (☎ 801-252-3234; www.kennecott.com; 8362 W 10200 S; $4 per vehicle; ☼ 8am-8pm Apr-Oct) is the world's largest factitious excavation and, still operational, it's only getting bigger. The 2.5-mile-wide and 0.75-mile-deep gash, in the Oquirrh Mountains west of SLC, is the only man-made sight on Earth, other than the Great Wall of China, that's visible from outer space.

Within 40 minutes' drive of SLC, four world-class ski resorts in Little Cottonwood and Big Cottonwood Canyons receive about 500in of powdery snow annually. **Snowbird Ski Area** (☎ 801-933-2222, 800-453-3000; www.snowbird.com; Little Cottonwood Canyon; adult/child $59/47) has excellent snowboarding, while laid-back **Alta Ski Area** (☎ 801-359-1078, 888-782-9258; www.alta.com; Little Cottonwood Canyon; adult/child $47/20) is the skier's choice. Two more choices are **Brighton Ski Area** (☎ 801-532-4731, 800-873-5512; www.brightonresort.com; Big Cottonwood; adult/child under 10/senior $41/free/10 and **Solitude Ski Area** (☎ 801-534-1400; www.skisolitude.com; Big Cottonwood Canyon; adult/senior/child $47/10/26).

WASATCH MOUNTAINS & NORTH
Utah has awesome skiing, some of the best anywhere in North America. Its fabulous low-density, low-moisture snow – between 300in and 500in annually – and thousands of acres of high-altitude terrain helped earn Utah the honor of hosting the 2002 Winter Olympics. This mountainous region, within 55 miles of SLC, is home to 11 ski resorts, and offers abundant hiking, camping, fly-fishing and mountain biking.

Park City
About 30 miles east of SLC via I-80, Park City (elevation 6900ft) skyrocketed to international fame when it hosted the downhill, jumping and sledding events at the 2002 Winter Olympics. Not only is Park City the Southwest's most popular ski town, it also serves as home to the US Ski Team. Come spring, the town gears up for hiking and mountain-biking season in the high peaks towering over Park City.

A silver-mining community during the 19th century, its attractive Main St is remarkably well preserved, and lined with galleries, shops, hotels, restaurants and bars. And despite the sea of pre-fab housing that has spread across the valley and surrounding hills, the town remains relatively charming.

Park City also hosts the **Sundance Film Festival** (☎ 801-328-3456; www.sundance.org), in January, bringing independent films and their makers, stars and fans to town for two weeks. Tickets often sell out in advance.

The **Visitor Information Center** (www.parkcityinfo .com; ☼ generally 9am-6pm Mon-Sat, 11am-4pm Sun; Park City Museum ☎ 435-649-6104, 435-615-9559; 528

Main St; Kimball Junction ☎ 435-658-9616; Hwy 224 & Olympic Blvd) is helpful, but information is also available at the **Park City Historic Museum** (☎ 435-658-9625; www.parkcityhistory.org; 528 Main St; ☸ 10am-7pm Mon-Sat, noon-6pm Sun), with mining and history exhibits.

ACTIVITIES
Park City boasts three of Utah's pre-eminent ski resorts. An in-town chairlift whisks skiers to **Park City Mountain Resort** (☎ 435-649-8111; www.parkcitymountain.com; 1310 Lowell Ave), host of the 2002 Winter Olympic giant slalom and snowboarding events. Posh **Deer Valley Resort Deer Valley** (☎ 435-649-1000, 800-424-3337; www.deervalley.com; adult/child/senior $73/41/51) is for skiers only, and **Canyons** (☎ 435-649-5400; www .thecanyons.com; adult/child & senior $71/42) is Utah's largest resort. All three host **summer activities**, like mountain biking and hiking.

Olympians may be long gone from **Utah Olympic Park** (☎ 435-658-4200, 866-659-7275; www .utaholympicpark.com; Hwy 224; adult/child/teen & senior $8/4/6), but you can tour the facilities where it all happened and, if you're lucky, watch the pros practice (call for rates, schedules and reservations). From mid-November to mid-March, Park City's most thrilling offering is an 80mph **bobsled ride** ($200) with an incredible 4Gs of centrifugal force. Visitors can also take classes in **ski jumping** and **luge riding**.

SLEEPING
There are more than 100 condo complexes, upscale hotels and B&Bs in Park City, and while winter rates quoted here are very high, prices drop in summer.

Washington School Inn (☎ 435-649-3800, 800-824-1672; www.washingtonschoolinn.com; 543 Park Ave; r $255-285; P ⌨ ✕) These sumptuous rooms are located in a restored schoolhouse that survived a major Park City fire in 1898.

Edelweiss Haus (☎ 435-649-9432, 800-245-6417; www.pclodge.com/properties/edelweiss-haus/index.htm; 1482 Empire Ave; r $170-360; ☸ ⌨ P ✕) This modern condo complex offers standard hotel rooms, as well as one- and two-bedroom apartments.

Chateau Après Lodge (☎ 435-649-9372, 800-357-3556; www.chateauapres.com; 1299 Norfolk Ave; dm $30, r $85-105; ✕ P) Located near the ski lifts, this reasonably priced 1963 lodge is popular with budget travelers. Rooms are basic and sleep from one to four people.

EATING
Park City has more than enough dining options to suit any palette.

Uptown Fare (☎ 435-615-1998; 227 Main St; dishes $5-7; ☸ lunch) Only your mom could fix a more comforting meal than you'll find at this cozy spot. Try the homemade soups, sandwiches (house-roasted turkey) and chocolatey scratch brownies.

Morning Ray Café & Bakery (☎ 435-649-5686; 268 Main St; breakfast mains $5-9, dinner mains $11-19; ☸ 7am-2pm, dinner Wed-Sun) Locals call it the 'Morning Wait,' but it's worth it for the strong coffee, veggie scrambles, homemade granola and bona fide New York bagels, flown in par-boiled and baked on-site. Dinners are good (pot roast and pasta and the like), but breakfasts are best.

Chimayo (☎ 435-649-6222; 368 Main St; mains $26-36; ☸ dinner) Every plate is perfect at Chimayo, which combines the earthy flavors of Southwestern cooking with European-culinary techniques. The room is one of the prettiest in town, adorned with wrought-iron chandeliers, carved wooden beams and Mexican tiles.

Renee's Bar & Cafe (☎ 435-615-8357; 136 Heber Ave; lunch mains $7-11, dinner mains $10-14; ☸ lunch & dinner) You don't have to be vegetarian to appreciate the imaginative menu at PC's top spot for herbivores. Savory standouts include the portobello-mushroom Rueben, gruyere cannelloni, and macaroni and cheese.

Cafe Terigo (☎ 435-645-9555; 424 Main St; lunch mains $12-15, dinner mains $17-28; ☸ lunch & dinner Mon-Sat) Tops for lunch (especially on the flower-festooned patio in summer), Terigo makes terrific salads and pasta, meats and seafood.

Wasatch Brew Pub (☎ 435-649-0900; 250 Main St; meals $8-16; ☸ 4-11pm Mon-Fri, 11am-11pm Sat & Sun) The Polygamy Porter goes down easy with good pub grub. Stick around for TV sports, billiards and darts.

ENTERTAINMENT
A half-dozen crowded clubs, most with live music, line Main St.

Renée's (☎ 435-615-8357; 136 Heber Ave) Drink martinis with laid-back locals while tapping your toe to live music. Tuesday is Tecate-and-tacos night.

Spur (☎ 435-615-1618; 350 Main St) Live bands play on weekends here, a favorite of fresh-faced 30- and 40-somethings.

Egyptian Theatre Company (☎ 435-649-9371; www.egyptiantheatrecompany.org; 328 Main St) The restored 1926 theater is a primary venue for Sundance; the rest of the year it hosts plays, musicals and concerts.

GETTING THERE & AROUND

Several companies run vans from Salt Lake City International Airport and hotels to Park City; make reservations. **Park City Transportation** (☎ 435-649-8567, 800-637-3803; www .parkcitytransportation.com) operates shared rides ($30), while **Powder for the People** (☎ 435-649-6648, 888-482-7547; www.powderforthepeople.com) has private-charter vans ($87 for one to three people, $29 each additional passenger); reservations required.

Free buses operated by **Park City Transit** (☎ 435-615-5350; www.parkcityinfo.org) run three to six times an hour from 8am to 11pm, with diminished service from 6am to 8am and 11pm to 2am. The excellent system covers most of Park City, including the three ski resorts, and makes it easy not to rent a car.

Heber City & Around

About 45 miles southeast of SLC, Heber City is fairly utilitarian, but it's an affordable base for exploring the Wasatch Mountains. Most businesses are along Hwy 40 (Main St).

The 1904 **Heber Valley Historic Railroad** (☎ 435-654-5601; www.hebervalleyrr.org; 450 S 600 West; adult/child/senior $26/16/21) offers family-friendly scenic trips through gorgeous Provo Canyon.

About 15 miles southwest of Heber City, scenic Hwy 189 squeezes through the steep-walled **Provo Canyon** on its way to Provo, home to clean-cut Brigham Young University, but not really worth a stop. For information on camping and hiking in the Uinta National Forest, contact the **Uinta National Forest Heber Ranger Station** (☎ 435-654-0470; 2460 S Hwy 40; ☽ 8am-5pm Mon-Fri).

Consider driving the attractive **Alpine Loop Road**. From Hwy 189, head north onto narrow and twisting Hwy 92, which leads to Robert Redford's **Sundance Resort** (☎ 385-225-4107, 800-892-1600; www.sundanceresort.com; Alpine Loop Rd), an elegant, rustic and environmentally conscious getaway located in a wilderness setting with excellent skiing, a year-round arts program, spa and summer hiking, and mountain biking.

Three beautiful caves in **Timpanogos Cave National Monument** (☎ 801-756-5239/8; www.nps.gov /tica; Alpine Scenic Loop; per vehicle $3; ☽ May-Sep) are accessible on ranger-led tours; call ahead.

SLEEPING & EATING

Heber City motels are basic, but far cheaper than accommodations in Park City. You can also camp in the surrounding forest and nearby state parks.

Swiss Alps Inn (☎ 435-654-0722; www.swissalpsinn .com; 167 S Main; r $65-80; ☒) This quaint motel is one of the best in town.

Snake Creek Grill (☎ 435-654-2133; www.snake creekgrill.com; 650 Hwy 113; mains $14-20; ☽ dinner Wed-Sun) One of northern Utah's best restaurants looks like a saloon from an old Western. But the all-American Southwest-style menu features dishes like blue-cornmeal-crusted trout and finger-lickin' ribs.

Ogden

After the completion of the first transcontinental railway in 1869, Ogden became an important railway town. Today its restored-mid-19th-century downtown is a major draw. During its heyday, historic 25th St between Union Station and Grant Ave was lined with brothels and raucous saloons; now it has the city's nicest selection of restaurants and bars. Ogden lies about 38 miles north of SLC. And since people in SLC and Park City look down their noses at Ogden, the slopes here are luxuriously empty.

The restored **Union Station** houses the **visitor center** (☎ 801-627-8288, 800-255-8824; www .ogdencvb.org; 25th St & Wall Ave; ☽ 8am-4:30pm Mon-Fri); it's also home to several worthy **museums** (☎ 801-393-9886; www.theunionstation.org; adult/child $5/3; ☽ 10am-5pm Mon-Sat), with vintage trains, firearms, cars and more.

The steep-walled **Ogden Canyon** heads 40 miles northeast through the Wasatch Mountains to Monte Cristo Summit (9148ft), passing the following ski areas: **Snowbasin Ski Area** (☎ 801-620-1000, 888-437-5488; www.snowbasin .com; Hwy 226; adult/child $58/35), a 3200-acre resort that hosted downhill and super-G skiing events in the 2002 Winter Olympics; and the appropriately named **Powder Mountain Ski Area** (☎ 801-745-3772; www.powdermountain.net; adult/child/senior $43/25/35).

Millstream Motel (☎ 801-394-9425; 1450 Washington Blvd; r $40-45; ℗) retains the flavor of its 1940s heyday.

SOUTHWEST

Logan & Around

Logan, founded in 1859, is a quintessential old-fashioned American community with strong Mormon ties and home to Utah State University. Situated in bucolic Cache Valley, it offers year-round outdoor activities – hiking, camping, snowmobiling and cross-country skiing. Get oriented at the **Cache Valley Tourist Council** (☎ 435-752-2161, 800-882-4433; www .tourcachevalley.com; 160 N Main St; ☻ 9am-5pm Mon-Fri).

The **Wellsville Mountain range**, one of the world's highest to rise from such a narrow base, is best explored with information and maps from the **Logan Ranger Station** (☎ 435-755-3620; 1500 E Hwy 89; ☻ 8am-4:30pm Mon-Fri).

The 40-mile drive through **Logan Canyon** (Hwy 89 to Garden City) is beautiful any time of year, but in the fall it's jaw-dropping. You'll enjoy hiking and biking trails, rock climbing, fishing spots and seasonal campgrounds.

Perhaps the best of its kind, the **American West Heritage Center** (☎ 435-245-6050; www.awhc .org; 4025 S Hwy 89; adult/child/family $6/4/25; ☻ 10am-5pm Mon-Sat May-Sep) recreates 19th-century frontier communities with plenty of hands-on activities. It hosts the popular weeklong **Festival of the American West** in July, a must for frontier buffs.

SLEEPING & EATING

Beaver Creek Lodge (☎ 435-946-3400, 800-946-4485; www.beavercreeklodge.com; Hwy 89, Mile 487; r summer $80-90, winter $100-130; ✖) This lodge has TVs (but no phones), and offers horseback riding and snowmobiling packages.

Caffe Ibis (☎ 435-753-4777; 52 Federal Ave; dishes under $6; ☻ 8am-4pm) Popular with the university crowd, this café serves gourmet coffees and sandwiches.

Bluebird Restaurant (☎ 435-752-3155; 19 N Main St; dishes $4-8; ☻ lunch & dinner Mon-Sat) The 1920s-style Bluebird is classic.

NORTHEASTERN UTAH

Despite being hyped as 'Utah's Dinosaur land,' the main attraction is actually the high wilderness terrain. All towns are a mile above sea level and the rugged Uinta Mountains make for great trips.

Mirror Lake Highway

This alpine route (Hwy 150) begins in **Kamas**, about 12 miles east of Park City, and covers 65 miles as it climbs to eleva-

tions of more than 10,000ft into Wyoming. The highway provides breathtaking vistas of the western Uinta Mountains, while passing by scores of lakes, campgrounds and trailheads. Contact the **Ranger Station** (☎ 435-783-4338; 50 E Center St; ☻ 8am-4:30pm Mon-Fri) for general information on the Wasatch-Cache National Forest.

Uinta Mountains

The only way to access the 800-sq-mile, east–west-trending High Uintas Wilderness Area is by foot or horse – it's tough going, but the rewards are great. The high country has hundreds of lakes, most of which are stocked annually with trout and whitefish. Come for the excellent fishing and the rare experience of wild, remote wilderness. The Ashley National Forest's **Roosevelt Ranger Station** (☎ 435-722-5018; www.fs.fed.us/r4/ashley/rec reation; 244 W Hwy 40, Roosevelt; ☻ 8am-5pm Mon-Fri) has information.

In addition to wilderness **campgrounds** (campsites $8-10), you can stay at **Defa's Dude Ranch** (☎ 435-848-5590; www.defasduderanch.com; UT 35, Hanna; cabins $30-40; ☻ May-Oct; ✖), which has rustic cabins in a beautiful, remote setting; bring your own bedding (or request it). There's also a café, saloon and horseback riding ($20 per hour).

Vernal

The region's largest town has plenty of services. The **visitor center** (☎ 435-789-3799; www .dinoland.com; 496 E Main St; ☻ 9am-5pm) includes a good **natural history museum** (with a garden full of life-size dinosaurs) and offers driving tour brochures; the Red Cloud Loop and Petroglyphs tour is a highlight. The **Vernal Ranger Station** (☎ 435-789-1181; 355 N Vernal Ave; ☻ 8am-5pm Mon-Fri) has details on camping and hiking.

Twelve miles northeast of Vernal, **Red Fleet State Park** (☎ 435-789-4432; www.stateparks .utah.gov; Hwy 191; per vehicle $5; campsites $11) offers boating, camping and an easy hike to a series of fossilized dinosaur tracks.

The Green and Yampa Rivers have satisfying rapids for white-water enthusiasts, as well as calmer areas for gentler float trips. Trips cost $65 to $800 for one to five days; the visitor center has a list of outfitters.

Sage Motel (☎ 435-789-1442, 800-760-1442; www .vernalmotels.com; 54 W Main St; s/d $49/55) is a simple, but friendly and welcoming place to stay.

Flaming Gorge National Recreation Area

Named for its fiery red sandstone, the gorge area (day use $2) has 375 miles of reservoir shoreline, fly-fishing and rafting upon the Green River, trout fishing, hiking and cross-country skiing. Visit the **Flaming Gorge Headquarters** (☎ 435-784-3445; www.fs.fed .us/r4/ashley/recreation; 25 W Hwy 43; ☻ 8am-4:30 daily summer, 8.30am-4.30pm Mon-Fri rest of year) or **Flaming Gorge Dam Visitors Center** (☎ 435-885-3135; US 191; ☻ 8am-6pm summer, limited hrs winter).

Sheep Creek Canyon, a dramatic 13-mile paved loop through the Sheep Creek Canyon Geological Area, leaves Hwy 44 about 15 miles west of Greendale Junction.

The **campgrounds** (☎ 877-444-6777; www.reser veusa.com; campsites $14-18) in and around Flaming Gorge are mostly open mid-May to mid-October; reserve ahead. **Red Canyon Lodge** (☎ 435-889-3759; www.redcanyonlodge.com; 790 Red Canyon Rd; cabins $95-125; ☐) provides rustic and luxury cabins without TVs; **Flaming Gorge Lodge** (☎ 435-889-3773; www.fglodge.com; 155 Greendale, Hwy 191; r/condo $83/123; ☒) rents motel rooms and modern condominiums.

Dinosaur National Monument

One of the largest dinosaur fossil beds in North America was discovered here in 1909. The quarry was enclosed and hundreds of bones were exposed but left in the rock. Apart from the quarry, you can drive, hike, backpack and raft through the national monument's dramatic, starkly eroded canyons. The monument straddles the Utah–Colorado state line. Headquarters are in tiny Dinosaur, Colorado, while the **dinosaur quarry** (☎ 435-789-2115; www.nps.gov/dino; per vehicle $10; ☻ 8am-6pm summer, 8am-4:30pm Mon-Fri winter) is in Utah, about 15 miles east of Vernal via Hwys 40 and 149.

SOUTHEASTERN UTAH

Soaring snow-capped peaks lord over blue-hued mesas and plunging red-rock river canyons in the most desolate corner of Utah, appropriately nicknamed Canyonlands. The terrain is so inhospitable that it was the last region to be mapped in the continental US. It will challenge your capacity for wonder.

Over 65 million years, water carved serpentine, sheer-walled gorges along the course of the Colorado and Green Rivers, which define the borders of Canyonlands National Park, Utah's largest. Nearby Arches National Park encompasses more rock arches than anywhere else worldwide. Between the parks lies Moab, the state's premier destination for mountain biking, river-running and 4WD-ing South of Moab, ancestral Puebloan sites are scattered among wilderness areas and parks, most famously Monument Valley, which extends into Arizona (p907).

Tread lightly; millions of footsteps are taking their toll on this deceptively fragile environment.

This section is organized roughly north to south, beginning with Green River, on I-70, and following US 191 into the southeast corner of the state.

Green River

The 'world's watermelon capital,' Green River offers a good base for river running on the Green and Colorado Rivers, or exploring the nearby San Rafael Swell.

The **San Rafael Information Center** (☎ 435-564-3605; www.johnwesleypowell.com; 120 E Main St; ☻ 8am-6pm Mon-Sat) has information about adventuring in the area.

The Colorado and Green Rivers were first explored in 1869 and 1871 by the legendary one-armed Civil War veteran, geologist and ethnologist John Wesley Powell. Learn about his amazing travels at **John Wesley Powell River History Museum** (☎ 435-564-3427; www.jwprhm.com; 885 E Main St; adult/child $2/1; ☻ 8am-8pm Apr-Oct, 8am-4pm Nov-Mar), which also has exhibits on the Fremont Indians, geology and local history.

Local outfitters run **white-water rafting** day trips (adult/child $60/40), including lunch and transportation; ask about multiday excursions. Call **Holiday Expeditions** (☎ 435-564-3273, 800-624-6323; www.bikeraft.com; 1055 E Main St) or **Moki Mac River Expeditions** (☎ 435-564-3361, 800-284-7280; www.mokimac.com; 100 Silliman Lane).

SLEEPING & EATING

Budget choices include the first two options, then the choices slide up the fee scale. Ray's Tavern is far and away the best place to eat in town.

Robbers Roost Motel (☎ 435-564-3452; www .robbersroost-motel.com; 225 W Main St; r $30-50; ☻)

Bookcliff Lodge (☎ 435-564-3406, 800-493-4699; www.bookclifflodge.com; 395 E Main St; r $40-45; ☒ ☐)

SOUTHWEST

Best Western River Terrace (☎ 435-564-3401, 800-528-1234; www.bestwestern.com; 880 E Main St; r $80-90; 🐾 ✕ 🖳)

Holiday Inn Express (☎ 435-564-4439, 877-531-5084; www.holidayinn.com; 965 E Main St; r $65-75; 🐾 ✕ 🖳)

Ray's Tavern (☎ 435-564-3511; 25 S Broadway; steaks $11-20; ☾ lunch & dinner)

GETTING THERE & AWAY

There are buses with **Greyhound** (☎ 435-564-3421, 800-231-2222; www.greyhound.com; 525 E Main St) to SLC ($37, four hours) and Las Vegas ($64, 7½ hours); buses stop at the Rodeway Inn. **Amtrak** (☎ 435-872-7245, 800-872-7245; www.amtrak.com; 250 S Broadway) runs daily to Denver, Colorado ($42 to $78, 11 hours). It's the only stop in southeastern Utah.

Moab

If you've been jonesing for civilization, Moab is a sight for sore eyes. Shop for groceries till midnight, browse the shelves at two indie bookstores, sit down for dinner at nine o'clock and still find several places open for a beer afterward. All this culture comes at a price: chain motels line Main St, T-shirt shops abound, and neon signs blot out the stars. If you're coming from the wilderness, Moab is jarring.

But there's a distinct sense of fun in the air. Moab bills itself as Utah's recreation capital, and it delivers. From the hiker to the jeeper, recreational enthusiasm borders on fetishism.

Southeastern Utah's largest town, Moab has almost lost its small-town rural roots, and some fear it's becoming the next Vail, Colorado. It won't ever become a sprawling suburb (it's surrounded by state and federal lands), but it gets overrun spring through fall, and the impact of all those feet, bikes and 4WDs on the fragile desert is a serious concern. People disagree on what to do. Talk to anyone and you'll fast learn that Moab's polarized political debates are yet another high-stakes extreme sport.

INFORMATION

Most businesses are along Hwy 191, also called Main St. **Moab Information Center** (☎ 800-635-6622; www.discovermoab.com; Main & Center; ☾ 8am-8pm) serves walk-in visitors only. You'll find books and maps, and comprehensive information on everything from campgrounds

and permits to astronomical data and river conditions. The free, opinionated newspaper *Canyon Country Zephyr* is published six times annually. Pick up a copy from **Back of Beyond** (☎ 435-259-5154; 83 N Main; ☾ 9am-10pm), an excellent downtown bookstore.

ACTIVITIES

The **Moab Area Travel Council** (☎ 435-259-8825, 800-635-6622; www.discovermoab.com; cnr Main & Center; ☾ 8am-5pm Mon-Fri) has information about rafting, biking, hiking and 4WD vehicles.

Outfitters take care of everything, from permits to food to setting up camp to transportation. Among the best:

Adrift Adventures (☎ 435-259-8594, 800-874-4483; www.adrift.net; 378 N Main)

Canyon Voyages (☎ 435-259-6007, 800-733-6007; www.canyonvoyages.com; 211 N Main)

OARS (☎ 435-259-5919, 800-342-5938; www.oars.com; 2540 S Hwy 191)

Sheri Griffith Expeditions (☎ 435-259-8229, 800-332-2439; www.griffithexp.com; 2231 S Hwy 191)

SLEEPING

Despite tons of hotels, B&Bs and campgrounds, the town is packed from spring to fall; reservations are advised. The **BLM office** (☎ 435-259-2100; www.blm.gov/utah/moab; 82 E Dogwood; ☾ 8am-4:30pm Mon-Fri) has camping information.

Camelot Adventure Lodge (☎ 435-260-1783; www.camelotlodge.com; per person $125-145; ✕) On 50 rugged riverside acres beneath Hurrah Pass, the five-room Camelot is a bona fide backcountry lodge, unlike anyplace else. The only way to get here is via 4WD or boat. Ride camels, play disc golf, hike and mountain bike without driving anywhere. Rates include three down-home meals (BYOB). Do yourself a favor and stay two nights at this unforgettable retreat for athletically inclined friends.

Landmark Inn (☎ 435-259-6147, 800-441-6147; www.landmarkinnmoab.com; 168 N Main; d $62-78; ✕ 🐾) Kids love the waterslide at this almost-downtown motel. Rooms are scrupulously maintained and slightly kitsch. Amenities include great bathtubs and a hot tub.

Castle Valley Inn (☎ 435-259-6012; www.castlevalleyinn.com; Castle Valley Rd; r $95-125, bungalows $160-175; ✕) Moab's best midrange B&B lies 15 miles northwest of downtown. The setting is idyllic, the reception warm, the style relaxed and the hot tub hot. Choose a standard room or a freestanding bungalow with kitchen. Breakfasts include fruit picked fresh from on-site trees.

EATING

There's no shortage of restaurants in Moab, from backpacker coffeehouses to proud gourmet dining rooms. Many restaurants are closed in winter, so call ahead.

Mondo Café (☎ 435-259-5551; McStiff's Plaza, 59 S Main; ☾ 6:30am-7pm) Get jacked on caffeine, check email, then play hackeysack with the dudes.

Center Café (☎ 435-259-4295; 60 N 100 West; bistro dishes $6-11, mains $16-28; ☾ dinner) Hands down southern Utah's best restaurant, the Center Café is what you'd expect of Mendocino, not Moab. The chef-owner cooks with confidence, drawing inspiration from regional American and Mediterranean cuisines: there's everything from grilled prawns with cheddar-garlic grits to pan-roasted lamb with balsamic-port reduction. The desserts are truly superb.

Buck's Grill House (☎ 435-259-5201; 1393 N Hwy 191; mains $9-24; ☾ dinner) The best in its class, Buck's serves good steaks and Southwestern specialties, like duck tamales, buffalo meatloaf and elk stew. Portions are huge, and it serves good burgers.

Eddie McStiff's (☎ 435-259-2337; 59 S Main St; dishes $7-15; ☾ 5:30pm-midnight Mon-Fri, 11:30am-midnight Sat & Sun) Moab's biggest restaurant serves pizza, steaks, pasta, salads, burgers and bar food. McStiff's also brews tasty microbrews.

Fat City Smokehouse (☎ 435-259-4302; 100 W Center; dishes $11-18; ☾ lunch & dinner) Behind Club Rio, Fat City serves big plates of Texas-style BBQ and great beef tri-tip. Caveat: Smoke from the bar wafts into the dining room.

GETTING THERE & AROUND

There are flights available from SLC with **Salmon Air** (☎ 435-259-0566, 800-448-3413; www .salmonair.com) to **Canyonlands Airport** (☎ 435-259-7421; www.moabairport.com), 16 miles north of town, via Hwy 191.

Bighorn Express (☎ 888-655-7433; www.big hornexpress.com) operates scheduled van service to and from SLC and Green River, while **Roadrunner Shuttle** (☎ 435-259-9402; www.roadrunnershuttle.com) operates on-demand service.

For hiker-biker shuttles, contact **Acme Bike Shuttle** (☎ 435-260-2534; 702 S Main) or **Coyote Shuttle** (☎ 435-259-8656; 55 W 300 South).

Arches National Park

The Southwest has a string of jeweled parks and this popular **national park** (☎ 435-719-2299; www.nps.gov/arch; off Hwy 191; per vehicle $10; ☾ visitor center 8am-4:30pm, extended hrs spring-fall) is one of its most remarkable gems, boasting the world's greatest concentration of sandstone arches. That means that Arches, five miles north of Moab on Hwy 191, is often very crowded. Even so, a visit is always worthwhile (try it under moonlight, when the rocks are spooky and the place eerily empty). Many arches are easily reached by paved roads and relatively short hiking trails. Highlights include **Balanced Rock**, the oft-photographed **Delicate Arch**, the spectacularly elongated **Landscape Arch** and popular, twice-daily ranger-led trips into the **Fiery Furnace** (adult/child $8/4; reservations recommended).

As you casually stroll beneath these monuments to nature's power, listen carefully, especially in winter, and you may hear spontaneous popping noises in distant rocks – the sound of arches forming. (If you hear popping noises *overhead*, run like the dickens!)

THE BARD OF MOAB

Edward Abbey (1927–89), one of America's great Western prose writers, worked as a seasonal ranger at Arches National Monument in the 1950s, before it became a national park. In his essay collection, *Desert Solitaire: A Season in the Wilderness*, Abbey wrote of his time here and describes the simple beauty and subtle power of the vast landscape. In perhaps the book's most famous essay, he bemoaned what he dubbed 'Industrial Tourism,' the exploitation of the natural environment by big business acting in cahoots with government, turning the National Monument into a 'Natural Money-Mint.' Many of Abbey's predictions have come true – you need only arrive at Arches on a busy weekend and get stuck in a line of SUVs to know that he was, in his way, a prophet. After reading his book, you'll comprehend the desert in new, unexpected ways.

Because of heat and a scarcity of water, few visitors backpack, though this is allowed with free permits (available from the visitor center). The scenic **Devils Garden Campground** (☎ 877-444-6777, 518-885-3639; www .reserveusa.com; Hwy 191; campsites $10) is 18 miles from the visitor center.

Dead Horse Point State Park

Whatever you do, don't pass by this tiny **state park** (☎ 435-259-2614; www.stateparks.utah .gov; Hwy 313; per vehicle $7; ☽ dawn-dusk), with walloping and mesmerizing views of the Colorado River, Canyonlands National Park and the distant La Sal Mountains. It's located just off Hwy 313 (the road to Canyonlands), and it's absolutely worthwhile. If you only have time for one major viewpoint, this is it. The 21-site **Kayenta Campground** (☎ 801-538-7220, 800-322-3770; www.stateparks.utah.gov; Hwy 313; campsites $14) provides limited water, RV hookups and a dump station.

Canyonlands National Park

Covering 527 sq miles, **Canyonlands** (☎ 435-719-2313; per vehicle $10) is Utah's largest and wildest park. Indeed, parts of it are as rugged as almost anywhere on the planet. Need proof? Just check the view from Dead Horse Point, where canyons are rimmed with white cliffs tumbling to the river 2000ft below. Arches, bridges, needles, spires, craters, mesas, buttes – Canyonlands is a crumbling, decaying beauty, a vision of ancient earth.

You can hike, raft and 4WD (Cataract Canyon offers some of the wildest white water in the West), but be sure that you have plenty of gas, food and water before leaving Moab. Difficult terrain and lack of water render this the least developed and visited of the major Southwestern national parks.

The canyons of the Colorado and Green Rivers divide the park into three districts. **Island in the Sky** is most easily reached and offers amazing views. There's a helpful **visitor center** (☎ 435-259-4712; www.nps.gov/cany /island; Hwy 313; ☽ 8am-4:30pm, extended hrs spring-fall) here and some excellent short hikes (the mile-long trail to Grand View Overlook takes you right along the canyon's edge). This park section is 32 miles south of Moab; head north along Hwy 191 and then west on Hwy 313.

Needles is on Hwy 211, which heads west from US 191, 40 miles south of Moab; you'll find more great views here and a smaller **visitor center** (☎ 435-259-4711; www.nps.gov/cany /needles; Hwy 211; ☽ 8am-4:30pm, extended hrs Mar-Oct). And then there's the **Maze**, one of the wildest and most remote areas in the Southwest, accessible by 4WD only. Within **Horseshoe Canyon**, along the 32-mile-long road from Hwy 24 to the Maze, you'll find Great Gallery, with superb life-size rock art left by prehistoric Indians.

In addition to entrance fees, permits are required for overnight backcountry camping, backpacking, mountain biking, 4WD trips and river trips. Reserve at least two weeks ahead, by fax or mail only, with the **NPS Reservations Office** (☎ 435-259-4351; fax 435-259-4285; www.nps.gov/cany/permits.htm; 2282 SW Resource Blvd, Moab, UT 84532). Or just show up, although reservations are recommended in spring and fall.

Natural Bridges National Monument

Forty miles west of Blanding via Hwy 95, this **monument** (☎ 435-692-1234; www.nps.gov /nabr; Hwy 275; per vehicle $6; ☽ 7am-dusk) became Utah's first NPS land in 1908. The highlight is a dark-stained, white sandstone canyon containing three easily accessible natural bridges. The oldest, the Owachomo Bridge, spans 180ft but is only 9ft thick. Basic **camping** (campsites $10) is available.

Hovenweep National Monument

Beautiful, little-visited **Hovenweep** (☎ 970-560-4282; www.nps.gov/hove; Hwy 262; per vehicle $6; ☽ visitor center 8am-5pm), meaning 'deserted valley' in the Ute language, contains six sets of prehistoric ancestral Puebloan Indian sites, five of which require long hikes to reach. You'll find a visitor center, ranger station and basic **campground** (campsites $10), but no facilities. The main access is east of Hwy 191 on Hwy 262 via Hatch Trading Post, more than 40 miles from Bluff or Blanding.

Bluff

Surrounded by red rock, tiny Bluff was founded by Mormon pioneers in 1880 and makes a comfortable, laid-back base for regional exploring. It sits at the junction of Hwys 191 and 163, along the San Juan River. **Wild Rivers Expeditions** (☎ 435-672-2244;

www.riversandruins.com; 101 Main St) has been guiding trips since 1957 (day trips adult/child $125/75). **Far Out Expeditions** (☎ 435-672-2294; www.faroutexpeditions.com; 7th & Mulberry Sts) arranges off-the-beaten-track trips to Monument Valley ($105) and other locations.

Bluff has good lodgings, including the favored and hospitable **Recapture Lodge** (☎ 435-672-2281; www.bluffutah.org/recapturelodge; Hwy 191; r $46-60; ☒), a rustic, cozy property pleasantly shaded between the highway and the river.

Stop by friendly **Cow Canyon Trading Post** (☎ 435-672-2208; Hwys 191 & 163; mains $11-18; ☯ dinner Thu-Mon Apr-Oct), with terrific regionally inspired meat and vegetarian dinners, and good salads. The trading post has rugs, baskets, pottery, jewelry and good books.

Moki Dugway & Mule Point

The **Moki Dugway** (Hwy 261) heads south from Hwy 95 to connect with Hwy 163 at Mexican Hat. Along the way is a turnoff to **Mule Point Overlook** – don't miss this cliff-edge viewpoint, one of the country's most sweeping, encompassing Monument Valley and other landmarks.

Back on Hwy 261, the pavement ends and the Moki Dugway suddenly descends a whopping 1100ft along a series of fist-clenching hairpin turns. At the bottom, a dirt road heads east into the **Valley of the Gods**, a 17-mile drive through mind-blowing monoliths of sandstone. Near the southern end of Hwy 261, a 4-mile paved road heads west to **Goosenecks State Park**, a small lookout with memorable views of the San Juan River, 1100ft below.

Monument Valley

From the village of **Mexican Hat** (named after a sombrero-shaped rock), Hwy 163 winds southwest and enters the Navajo Indian Reservation and, after about 30 miles, Monument Valley Navajo Tribal Park (p907).

Just inside the Utah border, **Goulding's Lodge** (☎ 435-727-3231; www.gouldings.com; Hwy 163; r $170; ☒ ☒) is the only hotel near Monument Valley; each room has a balcony with a million-dollar view of the colossal red buttes. A full-service outpost, Goulding's also has a restaurant, museum, store, gas and **campground** (tent sites $18, RV sites $26-32), and also offers tours.

SOUTH-CENTRAL & SOUTHWESTERN UTAH

Locals call it 'color country,' but the cutesy label hardly does justice to the eye-popping hues that saturate the landscape. From the deep-crimson canyons of Zion National Park, to the delicate pink-and-orange minarets at Bryce Canyon, to the swirling yellow-white domes of Capitol Reef, the land is so spectacular that it encompasses three national parks and the gigantic Grand Staircase-Escalante National Monument (GSENM).

This section is organized roughly northeast to southwest: from Hanksville, along Hwy 24 through Capitol Reef National Park and southwest along Hwy 12, which passes the Grand Staircase-Escalante National Monument and Bryce Canyon. Quite simply, it's one of the most scenic roads in the country. From Hwy 12, US 89 goes south to Kanab (and continues to the North Rim of the Grand Canyon). Further west are Cedar City, St George and gorgeous Zion National Park.

Hanksville

Conveniently situated at the junction of Hwys 95 and 24, Hanksville offers up a **BLM office** (☎ 435-542-3461; 406 S 100 West; ☯ 8am-4:30pm Mon-Fri), with information on the **Henry Mountains**, a remote, 11,000ft-high range. **Goblin Valley State Park** (☎ 435-564-3633; Hwy 24; per vehicle $5; ☯ 7am-10pm), full of delightful and alien rock formation, has **camping** (☎ 800-322-3770; www.stateparks.utah.gov; campsites $14). About 20 miles west near Caineville, **Luna Mesa Oasis** (☎ 435-456-9122; Hwy 24; dishes $5-15; ☯ 8am-8pm Mon-Sat) is a friendly spot to grab a meal.

Capitol Reef National Park

Not as crowded as its compatriots but equally scenic, Capitol Reef contains much of the 100-mile **Waterpocket Fold**, created 65 million years ago when the earth's surface buckled up and folded, exposing a cross-section of geologic history that is downright painterly in its colorful intensity. Hwy 24 cuts grandly through the park, but take the park's own scenic drive ($5) starting from the **visitor center** (☎ 435-425-3791; www.nps.gov/care; Hwy 24 & Scenic Dr; ☯ 8am-4:30pm, extended hrs summer), where there's grassy, basic **camping** (campsites $10).

SOUTHWEST

THE STORY OF EVERETT RUESS

Artist, poet, writer and adventurer Everett Ruess (1914–34) is a local legend in southern Utah. At 20 years old, he set out into the desert on his burro, somewhere near the Escalante River Canyon, never to be seen again. But he left behind scores of letters detailing his 'restless fascination' with the land, letters that paint a vivid portrait of life in canyon country before man and his machines forever altered the landscape. Most people have never heard of Everett Ruess, but in many ways he is to the Southwest what John Muir is to the Sierra Nevada – explorer, chronicler and ardent lover of nature.

Pick up a copy of *Everett Ruess: A Vagabond for Beauty*, which includes his letters and an afterword by Edward Abbey. Find this and all of Ruess' posthumously published works at Escalante Outfitters (below), where you can also inquire about the October **'Everett Ruess Days' festival** (www.everettruessdays.org), which includes plein air art shows, speakers and workshops.

Torrey

This little village makes a good stopping point for lodging, as well as providing surprisingly great meals. The **Capital Reef Country Visitors Center** (☎ 435-425-3365, 800-858-7951; www.capitolreef.org; Hwys 12 & 24; ☼ 11am-5:30pm Apr-Oct) is quite helpful.

Capitol Reef Inn & Cafe (☎ 435-425-3271; www.capitolreefinn.com; 360 W Main St; r $48; ☼ Apr-Oct; ✗) These 10 comfortable rooms are outfitted with hand-crafted wood furniture. Climb the giant kiva to watch the sunset and then hop into the hot tub.

Pine Shadows Bungalows (☎ 435-425-3939, 800-708-1223; www.pineshadowcabins.net; 195 West 125 South, Teasdale; cabins $69-75; ✗) Tucked between piñon pines beneath white cliffs, these five spacious cabins have vaulted ceilings and kitchenettes. They make for a great hideaway and excellent value just outside of town.

Cafe Diablo (☎ 435-425-3070; 599 W Main St; mains $17-28; ☼ 5-10pm Apr-Oct; ✗) One of southern Utah's best eateries, Diablo serves outstanding highly stylized Southwestern cooking – including succulent vegetarian dishes – bursting with flavor and towering on the plate.

Boulder

Tiny Boulder is 32 miles south of Torrey on Hwy 12. From here, the attractive **Burr Trail** heads east as a paved road across the northeastern corner of the Grand Staircase-Escalante National Monument, winding up at Bullfrog Marina on Lake Powell. Consider taking a one-day, child-friendly excursion with knowledgeable **Earth Tours** (☎ 435-691-1241; www.earth-tours.com; ☼ spring-fall), which offers half-/full-day tours for $50/75; or a multiday backcountry trek with the equally

recommended **Escalante Canyon Outfitters** (☎ 435-335-7311, 888-326-4453; www.ecohike.com; ☼ spring-fall), which offers four- to six-day all-inclusive treks for $770 to $1175.

The comfortable, modern rooms at **Boulder Mountain Lodge** (☎ 800-556-3446; www.boulder-utah.com; Hwy 12; r $90-168; P ☐) are among the nicest accommodations along Hwy 12.

If you've given up on eating well in southern Utah, take heart: the must-visit **Hell's Backbone Grill** (☎ 435-335-7464; Hwy 12 at Burr Trail, Boulder Mountain Lodge; breakfast mains $4-8, dinner mains $12-22; ☼ breakfast & dinner Apr-Oct) serves soulful, earthy preparations of locally raised meats and organically grown produce from its own garden.

Escalante

This quiet, small town provides gateway access to the Grand Staircase-Escalante National Monument (GSENM). With a whopping population of about 850 people, it's the largest outpost for almost 75 miles in any direction.

The **Escalante Interagency Office** (☎ 435-826-5499; www.ut.blm.gov/monument; 775 W Main St; ☼ 7:30am-5:30pm) is a superb resource center with complete information on all area public lands. Fifteen miles east on Hwy 12, **Calf Creek Recreation Area** (☎ 435-826-5499; www.ut.blm.gov/monument; per vehicle $2; campsites $7; ☼ year-round) has pleasant, basic camping and a recommended 3-mile hike to Lower Calf Creek Falls.

Escalante Outfitters, Inc (☎ 435-826-4266; 310 W Main St; ☼ 8am-10pm) is a great travelers' oasis, selling maps, books, camping supplies, liquor, espresso and the best homemade pizza ($12 to $22) you'll find in Utah; no kidding.

Overnighters stay in cute, cozy, clean **cabins** ($45) out back.

Grand Staircase-Escalante National Monument

This 2656-sq-mile **monument** (www.ut.blm.gov/monument), established in 1996, is tucked between Bryce, Capitol Reef and Glen Canyon National Recreation Area. Tourist infrastructure is minimal, leaving a vast, remote desert for adventurous travelers who have the time and necessary outdoor equipment to explore.

Three unpaved roads, Skutumpah/Johnson Canyon Rd (the least used and most westerly route), Cottonwood Canyon Rd and Smoky Mountain Rd – cross the monument roughly north to south between Hwys 12 and 89. A fourth unpaved road (the Hole-in-the-Rock Rd) begins from Hwy 12 and dead-ends at the Glen Canyon National Recreation Area. Roads get slick and impassable when wet. Wilderness camping is allowed with a required permit. Before heading out, obtain current road and travel information from the Escalante Interagency Office (opposite), the visitor centers in Kanab (p934) or **Cannonville** (☎ 435-826-5640; 10 Center St, Cannonville; 🕑 8am-4:30pm, closed winter).

Kodachrome Basin State Park

Dozens of red, pink and white sandstone chimneys highlight this colorful **state park** (☎ 435-679-8562; www.stateparks.utah.gov; Cottonwood Canyon Rd; per vehicle $5). A **campground** (☎ 801-322-3770, 800-322-3770; campsites incl park entrance fee $14) and several **cabins** (☎ 435-679-8536, 435-679-8787; www.brycecanyoninn.com; cabins $65; 🕑 Apr-Nov; ⊠) are available during summer, as are horseback rides ($16 per hour).

Bryce Canyon National Park

The Grand Staircase, a series of steplike uplifted rock layers stretching north from the Grand Canyon, culminates at this very popular **national park** (☎ 834-5322; www.nps.gov/brca; Hwy 63; on foot $10, per vehicle $20; 🕑 8am-8pm May-Oct, 8am-4:30pm Nov-Mar, 8am-6pm Apr) in the Pink Cliffs formation. It's full of wondrous pinnacles and points, steeples and spires, and odd formations called 'hoodoos.' The 'canyon' is actually an amphitheater eroded from the cliffs.

From Hwy 12, Hwy 63 heads 4 miles south to Rim Rd Dr (8000ft), an 18-mile dead-end road that follows the rim of the canyon, passing the visitor center, lodge, viewpoints (don't miss Inspiration Point) and trailheads, ending at Rainbow Point at 9115ft elevation. You can whisk in and out in a few hours, but for a richer experience, numerous trails will take you out among the spires and deeper into the heart of the landscape. There is a free (voluntary) shuttle system from Hwy 12.

The park's only licensed outfitter is **Canyon Trail Rides** (☎ 679-8665; www.canyonrides.com; Hwy 63; 2hr/half-day $40/55), which operates out of Bryce Canyon Lodge (p934); rides head into Bryce Amphitheater, past dramatic hoodoos, on horses and mules (mules give a smoother ride).

The NPS operates **North Campground** (☎ 877-444-6777; www.reserveusa.com; Bryce Canyon Rd; campsites $10, plus reservation fee May 15-Sep 30 $9) and **Sunset Campground** (2 miles south of visitor center; campsites $10; 🕑 late spring-fall); both have toilets and water. Sunset is more wooded, but has fewer amenities. For laundry, showers and groceries, visit North Campground. During summer, sites fill by noon; no reservations are taken.

STICK 'EM UP!

Nearly every town in southern Utah claims a connection to Butch Cassidy (1866–?) the Old West's most famous bank and train robber. As part of the Wild Bunch, Cassidy (né Robert LeRoy Parker) pulled 19 heists from 1896 to 1901. Most accounts describe him with a breathless romanticism, comparing him with Robin Hood. All stories usually have one thing in common: a dilapidated shack or a canyon, just over yonder, that served as his hideout. But the itty-bitty town of Circleville, 28 miles north of Panguitch, is the honest-to-goodness boyhood home of the gun-slingin' bandit. The house still stands, partially renovated, 2 miles south of town on the west side of Hwy 89. Nobody is sure where Cassidy fled, but most believe he died in South America in 1908. But ask around, and you're sure to hear a lot of conflicting, tall tales. For the Hollywood version, rent *Butch Cassidy and the Sundance Kid* (1969), with Robert Redford and Paul Newman at their sexiest.

...ryce Canyon Lodge (☎ summer 435-...ter 435-772-3213, reservations 888-297-2757; ...ycecanyonlodge.com; Hwy 63; r $108-136, cabins ...o; ◷ Apr-Oct; ✕) exudes rustic mountain charm. Rooms are in satellite buildings and range from modern hotel-style units with up-to-date furnishings and balconies, to romantic, slightly dated, free-standing cabins with gas fireplaces and front porches. If you can secure a reservation, it's worth every penny.

A couple of standard motels sit at the junction of Hwys 63 and 12, including **Bryce View Lodge** (☎ 435-834-5180, 888-279-2304, www.bryceviewlodge.com; 991 S Hwy 63; r $65), geared to budget travelers with smaller rooms and fewer extras.

Panguitch & Around

Simple little Panguitch is a popular stop on Hwy 89. It's surrounded by knockout scenic drives, has several good motels and is convenient to both Bryce Canyon (24 miles) and Zion (70 miles) National Parks. **Garfield County Travel Council** (☎ 435-676-1160, 800-444-6689; www.brycecanyoncountry.com; 55 S Main St; ◷ 9am-5pm) has regional information. **Panguitch Lake** lies southwest on Hwy 143.

Situated at 10,400ft, **Cedar Breaks National Monument** (☎ 435-586-9451; www.nps.gov/cebr; Hwy 148; per vehicle $3; ◷ 8am-6pm) is an absolutely stunning amphitheater featuring wonderfully eroded, almost neon-colored spires. South of the park, scenic **Highway 14** crosses the beautiful Markagunt Plateau between I-15 and Hwy 89.

The cute little **Blue Pine Motel** (☎ 435-676-8197; 130 N Main St; r $45-50; Ⓟ) is open year-round.

Kanab

Vast expanses of rugged desert extend everywhere around the remote outpost of Kanab, and until the advent of roads, Kanab was an isolated Mormon community. Don't be surprised if it all looks familiar now, though. Hollywood Westerns were shot here, and John Wayne and other gun-slingin' celebs helped earn Kanab the nickname 'Utah's Little Hollywood.'

Hwy 89 snakes through town, and a good selection of motels and restaurants lie along it, making it a popular travelers' stopover.

Kanab Visitor Center (☎ 435-644-4680; www.ut.blm.gov/monument; 745 E Hwy 89; ◷ 8am-4:30pm, Mon-Fri Nov-Mar) provides road, trail and weather updates for Grand Staircase-Escalante National Monument (p933). The **Kane County Office of Tourism** (☎ 435-644-5033, 800-733-5263; www.kaneutah.com; 78 S 100 E; ◷ 8am-8pm Mon-Fri, 9am-5pm Sat, 9am-1pm Sun summer, 8:30am-5pm Mon-Sat, 1-5pm Sun winter) is the main source for area information; it hosts a special kids' website: www.kane4kids.com.

The historic and centrally located **Parry Lodge** (☎ 435-644-2601, 800-748-4104; www.parrylodge.com; 89 E Center St; r $51-73; ☻), the finest property around, is beautifully landscaped. Back in the day, all the actors stayed here, but the rambling motel has become a faded dowager of the leading lady she once was. Rooms are clean and well kept, and the lodge has a restaurant and bar on-site.

Cedar City

Less than an hour's drive northeast of Zion on I-15, Cedar City is a natural stopping place. Offering free Internet access, the **Cedar City & Brian Head Tourism & Convention Bureau** (☎ 435-586-5124, 800-354-4849; www.scenicsouthernutah.com; 581 N Main St; ◷ 8am-5pm Mon-Fri year-round, 9am-1pm Sat summer) shares space with the **chamber of commerce** (☎ 435-586-4484). From June to September, the nationally renowned **Shakespearean Festival** (☎ 435-586-7878, 800-752-9849; www.bard.org) keeps the town buzzing.

For basic accommodations, **Abbey Inn** (☎ 435-586-9966, 800-325-5411; www.abbeyinncedar.com; 940 W 200 N; r $86-100; ☻) offers a nice decor and full breakfast.

St George

A spacious Mormon town with wide streets, an eye-catching temple and pioneer buildings, St George is popular with retirees and visitors to Zion and other nearby parks. The main source for town information is the **chamber of commerce** (☎ 435-628-1658; www.stgeorgechamber.com; 97 E St George Blvd; ◷ 9am-5pm Mon-Fri, 10am-2pm Sat). The **Interagency Information Center** (☎ 435-688-3246; 345 E Riverside Dr; ◷ 7:45am-5pm Mon-Fri, 10am-3pm Sat) provides information on USFS and BLM lands, state parks and the Arizona Strip.

Nine miles north of town, **Snow Canyon State Park** (☎ 435-628-2255; www.stateparks.utah.gov; Hwy 18; per vehicle $5) has volcanic landscapes, petroglyphs and hiking trails to lava caves.

St George has the biggest selection of accommodations in southern Utah; most are chains, though, and many line St

George Blvd. For a nicer abode try **Green Gate Village** (☎ 435-628-6999, 800-350-6999; www .greengatevillageinn.com; 76 W Tabernacle St; r incl full breakfast $80-180, weekends add $20; ☒ ☒). Grassy lawns separate nine historic buildings that comprise this attractive B&B inn. All rooms feature lovely antiques, TVs, refrigerators and private baths.

Painted Pony (☎ 435-634-1700; 2 W St George Blvd, Ancestor Sq; sandwiches $8, dinner mains $17-25; ☺ 11:30am-10pm Mon-Sat), with Southwestern-style dishes marked by subtlety and nuance, offers the best dining in St George. Standouts include rib-eye steak, pan-roasted escolar and the grilled portobello sandwich. The decor complements the cooking, with Navajo prints, tin sconces and colorful contemporary art. Make reservations.

Greyhound (☎ 435-673-2933, 800-231-2222; www .greyhound.com; 1235 S Bluff) departs from the local McDonald's, with buses to SLC ($55, six hours) and Las Vegas ($30, two hours).

Springdale

Many travelers pass through heading to Zion National Park, as Springdale sits along Hwy 9 just outside the park's southern entrance. It's a pleasant, relaxed community, catering mostly to park visitors; the **visitors bureau** (☎ 888-518-7070; www.zionpark.com) can answer questions.

Springdale has an abundance of good restaurants and nice lodging options, including the basic and pleasant **Terrace Brook Lodge** (☎ 435-772-3932, 800-342-6779; www .terracebrooklodge.com; 990 Zion Park Blvd; 1-/2- bed r $50/63, family unit $80-94; ☒).

Springdale's only bar rates among the region's best. **Bit & Spur Restaurant & Saloon** (☎ 435-772-3498; 1212 Zion Park Blvd; mains $10-14, specials $18-24; ☺ dinner) is a local institution and the liveliest spot in town, offering up occasional live music. Southwest-influenced seafood and steak specials are worth every penny.

Families like the order-at-the-counter **Zion Pizza & Noodle Company** (☎ 435-772-3815; www.zionpizzanoodle.com; 868 Zion Park Blvd; dishes $10-14; ☺ 4-10pm) and its Utah microbrews.

Zion National Park

The white, pink and red rocks of **Zion** (☎ 435-772-3256; www.nps.gov/zion; UT 9; ☺ 8am-7pm summer, 8am-6pm spring & fall, 8am-5pm winter) are huge, overpowering and magnificent – you're guaranteed to be awed upon your first glimpse of the place. Of the three roads that access the park, the middle road, Kolob Terrace Rd, lacks services, is paved only halfway and closes in winter. From April through October, the park operates very frequent Zion Shuttles – two free, linked shuttle loops that depart from the visitor center from at least 6:45am to 10pm daily.

The **Zion Canyon Visitor Center** (☎ 435-772-3256; www.nps.gov/zion; per vehicle $20; ☺ 8am-7pm summer, 8am-6pm spring & fall, 8am-5pm winter) is quite informative, with lots of books, and maps, weather and river conditions and campground information. Ask about ranger-led activities, which include nature walks, and interpretive talks on flora, fauna, ecology and geology. The center also houses the **backcountry desk** (☎ 435-772-0170; ☺ 7am-7pm in summer, 7am-6pm in spring & fall), which dispenses permits the day before your hike.

More than 100 miles of trails offer everything from leisurely strolls to wilderness backpacking and camping. The most famous backpacking trip is through the **Narrows**, a 16-mile journey through dramatic canyons along the Virgin River (June to September).

At the south gate, two basic **campgrounds** (☎ 800-365-2267; http://reservations.nps.gov; campsites $16-18) have more than 300 first-come, first-served campsites, but come early. A few campsites can be reserved.

Zion Lodge (☎ 435-772-3213, 888-297-2757, reservations 303-297-2757; www.zionlodge.com; r/cabin/ste $125/133/$147; ☺ year-round; ☒ ☒) Smack in the middle of Zion Canyon, the park's only lodge has 81 well-appointed motel rooms and 40 cabins with gas fireplaces. All have wooden porches with stellar views. There are no TVs, but there's a good restaurant. Book up to 23 months in advance, or try for a **same-day reservation** (☎ 928-638-2631). The rates listed are for summer.

There's so much to see that entire books have been written about Zion, including Lonely Planet's very own *Zion & Bryce Canyon National Parks*.

NEW MEXICO

Blazing red ristras hang from hacienda doorways carved hundreds of years ago. Stunningly simple adobe pueblos stand proudly, constructed with techniques so perfect they are still employed today. For centuries, too,

Indian markets have drawn thousands lured by famed black-on-black pottery or Navajo weavings. Adding to the melting pot, silhouetted crosses top centuries-old Spanish Catholic and missionary churches. Nowhere else in the United States do three such distinct cultures – Indian, Hispanic and Anglo – intersect so pointedly and profoundly. Unlike any other state license plate in the country, the New Mexico plate says 'USA,' a reminder that New Mexico is indeed a part of the contiguous 48. There will be times when you don't quite believe it.

From abstract mountain folds and endless horizons to surreal mesa tops and sacred ceremonial places, it's no surprise that so many artists have given into its undeniable pull. Unquenched in a seemingly parched desert, your spirit will soar beneath New Mexico's piercing skies.

When more pedestrian desires take over, go skiing at Taos, spelunking at Carlsbad, camping amid the yucca and gypsum at White Sands, clamoring up steep ladders into abandoned cliff dwellings. Explore the origins of the Atomic Age in Los Alamos or the mysteries of aliens in Roswell. Follow in the footsteps of outlaw Billy the Kid or float down the romantic Rio Grande. Then head back to a palpable timelessness that infuses this land of enchantment.

History

People roamed the land here as far back as 10,500 BC, but by Coronado's arrival in the 16th century, Pueblos were the dominant communities. Santa Fe was established as the colonial capital in 1610, after which Spanish settlers and farmers fanned out across northern New Mexico, and missionaries began their often violent efforts to convert the area's Pueblo Indians to Catholicism. After a successful revolt, Indians occupied Santa Fe until 1692, when Diego de Vargas recaptured the city.

In 1851 New Mexico became US territory. Indian wars, settlement by cowboys and miners, and trade along the Santa Fe Trail further transformed the region, and the arrival of the railroad in the 1870s created an economic boom.

Painters and writers set up art colonies in Santa Fe and Taos in the early 20th century. In 1943 a scientific community descended on Los Alamos and developed the atomic

---

NEW MEXICO FACTS

Nickname Land of Enchantment
Population 1.8 million
Area 121,356 sq miles
Capital city Santa Fe (population 62,200)
Official bird Roadrunner
Birthplace of Outlaw William Bonney, aka Billy the Kid (1859–81); Smokey Bear
Home of US's oldest road (the Camino Real), public building (Santa Fe Governors' Palace, 1610)
Famous for Chilies, ancient pueblos, the first atomic bomb (1945)

---

bomb (see p950). These days big issues include water rights (whoever owns the water has the power) and immigration (the state has one of the highest percentages of Hispanic residents in the country).

Information

Sales tax hovers around 6%, with an additional tax placed on accommodations in some counties.

New Mexico Culture (www.nmculture.org) For statewide information.

New Mexico Net (www.nmnet.org)

New Mexico Tourism Department (Map p944; ☎ 505-827-7400, 800-545-2040; www.newmexico.org; 491 Old Santa Fe Trail, Santa Fe, NM 87503) For statewide visitor information and a free *Vacation Guide*.

Public Lands Information Center (☎ 505-438-7542, 877-276-9404; www.publiclands.org; 1474 Rodeo Rd, Santa Fe, NM 87507) Provides camping and recreation information.

ALBUQUERQUE

Depending on your perspective, New Mexico's most populous city is simply another dot on the map of Route 66 as it snakes its way from Los Angeles to Chicago, or it's a distinctive and vibrant mix of university students, Native Americans, Hispanics, and gays and lesbians. You'll find square dances and tai chi classes flyered with equal enthusiasm. You'll find cowboys and chiropractors chowing down at hole-in-the-wall taquerias as well as retro cafés. Albuquerque may not knock your socks off with sparkle, but it'll get under your skin with sincerity. It exudes a 'realness' that's hard to find in Santa Fe any more and a 'normalcy' that somehow bypassed Taos.

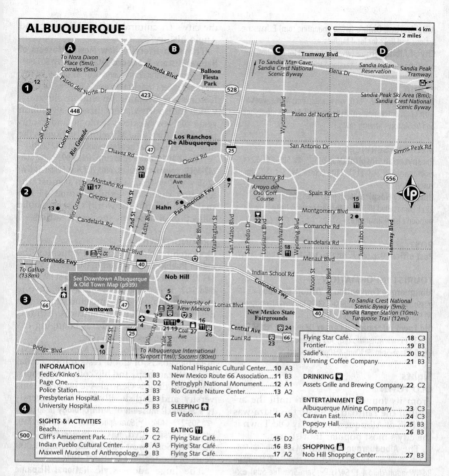

ALBUQUERQUE

INFORMATION	
FedEx/Kinko's	1 B3
Page One	2 D2
Police Station	3 B3
Presbyterian Hospital	4 B3
University Hospital	5 B3

SIGHTS & ACTIVITIES	
Beach	6 B2
Cliff's Amusement Park	7 C2
Indian Pueblo Cultural Center	8 A3
Maxwell Museum of Anthropology	9 B3

National Hispanic Cultural Center	10 A3
New Mexico Route 66 Association	11 B3
Petroglyph National Monument	12 A1
Rio Grande Nature Center	13 A2

SLEEPING	
El Vado	14 A3

EATING	
Flying Star Café	15 D2
Flying Star Café	16 B3
Flying Star Café	17 A2

Flying Star Café	18 C3
Frontier	19 B3
Sadie's	20 B2
Winning Coffee Company	21 B3

DRINKING	
Assets Grille and Brewing Company	22 C2

ENTERTAINMENT	
Albuquerque Mining Company	23 C3
Caravan East	24 C3
Popejoy Hall	25 B3
Pulse	26 B3

SHOPPING	
Nob Hill Shopping Center	27 B3

Orientation

Albuquerque's major boundaries are Paseo del Norte Dr to the north, Central Ave to the south, Rio Grande Blvd to the west and Tramway Blvd to the east. Central Ave is the city's main artery. Also known as old Route 66, it passes through Old Town, downtown, the university and Nob Hill. The city is divided into four quadrants (NW, NE, SW and SE), and the intersection of Central Ave and the railroad tracks just east of downtown serves as the center point of the city.

Information

BOOKSTORES

Page One (Map p937; ☎ 505-294-2026; www .page1books.com; 11018 Montgomery Blvd NE;

✆ 9am-10pm Mon-Sat, 9am-8pm Sun) Huge and comprehensive.

EMERGENCY

Emergency number (☎ 911)
Police (Map p939; ☎ 505-256-8368; 2901 Central Ave NE)

INTERNET ACCESS

FedEx/Kinko's (Map p937 ☎ 505-255-9673; 2706 Central Ave SE; per min 20¢; ✆ 24hr)
Library (Map p939; ☎ 505-768-5140; 501 Copper Ave NW; ✆ 10am-6pm Mon-Sat, 10am-7pm Tue & Wed) Free Internet access after purchasing a $3 library card.

INTERNET RESOURCES

Albuquerque.com (www.albuquerque.com) Attraction, hotel and restaurant information.

SOUTHWEST

Albuquerque Online (www.abqonline.com) Exhaustive listings and links for local businesses.

City of Albuquerque (www.cabq.gov) Information on public transport, area attractions and more.

MEDIA

Alibi (☎ 505-346-0660; www.alibi.com) A free weekly with good entertainment listings; available in coffee shops and bookstores around town.

MEDICAL SERVICES

Presbyterian Hospital (Map p937; ☎ 505-841-1234, emergency 505-841-1111; 1100 Central Ave SE; ✆ 24hr emergency)

University Hospital (Map p937; ☎ 505-272-2411; 2211 Lomas Blvd NE; ✆ 24hr emergency) Head here if you don't have insurance.

POST

Post office (Map p939; ☎ 505-346-1674;201 5th St SW)

TOURIST INFORMATION

Albuquerque Convention & Visitors Bureau (Map p939; ☎ 505-842-9918, 800-733-9918; www.itsatrip.org; 20 First Plaza; ✆ 8am-5pm Mon-Fri)

Old Town Information Center (Map p939; ☎ 505-243-3215; www.itsatrip.org; 303 Romero St NW; ✆ 9:30am-5pm, 9:30am-4:30pm Oct-Apr)

Sights

OLD TOWN

From its foundation in 1706 until the arrival of the railroad in 1880, the Plaza was the hub of Albuquerque; today Old Town is the city's most popular tourist area.

The **Albuquerque Museum** (Map p939; ☎ 505-242-4600; www.albuquerquemuseum.com; 2000 Mountain Rd NW; adult/child 4-12 $4/1; ✆ 9am-5pm Tue-Sun) exhibits New Mexican artists, and explores the city's tri-cultural Indian, Hispanic and Anglo history.

The teen-friendly **New Mexico Museum of Natural History & Science** (Map p939; ☎ 505-841-2800; www.nmnaturalhistory.org; 1801 Mountain Rd NW; adult/child under 11/student & senior $6/3/5; ✆ 9am-5pm) features an Evolator (evolution elevator), which transports visitors through 38 million years of New Mexico's geologic and evolutionary history. The Museum also houses the huge-screen **DynaTheater** (adult/child 3-12 $6/3).

The **Rattlesnake Museum** (Map p939; ☎ 505-242-6569; www.rattelsnakes.com; 202 San Felipe St NW; $2.50; ✆ 10am-5pm), Old Town's most interesting diversion, exhibits some 45 live snakes and claims the world's largest public collection of different species of rattlers.

AROUND TOWN

Operated by New Mexico's 19 pueblos, the **Indian Pueblo Cultural Center** (Map p937; ☎ 505-843-7270; www.indianpueblo.org; 2401 12th St NW; adult/child $4/2; ✆ 9am-5pm) is a must for anyone visiting pueblos. The museum traces the development of Pueblo cultures, exhibits customs and crafts, features changing exhibits and serves Pueblo fare.

The University of New Mexico (UNM) area has loads of good restaurants, casual bars, offbeat shops and hip college hangouts. The main drag is Central Ave between University and Carlisle Blvds. The university's **Maxwell Museum of Anthropology** (Map p937; ☎ 505-277-4404; ✆ 9am-4pm Tue-Fri, 10am-4pm Sat), off University Blvd, has an interesting 'People of the Southwest' exhibit depicting 11,000 years of the region's cultural history.

The huge adobe-style **National Hispanic Cultural Center** (Map p937; ☎ 505-246-2261; www

---

TURQUOISE TRAIL

The Turquoise Trail, a National Scenic Byway, has been a major trade route since at least 2000 BC. Today it's the scenic back road between Albuquerque and Santa Fe, lined with quirky communities and other diversions. Stop in **Cedar Crest** at the highly recommended **Tinkertown Museum**, an inspiring assortment of towns, circuses and other scenes. Continue through **Golden**, with an art gallery and lots of gorgeous desert scenery.

Madrid (pronounced MAA-drid), a bustling coal-mining company town in the 1920s and '30s, was all but abandoned after WWII. Now the town attracts more bikers than New Agers. Check out the **Old Coal Mine Museum** with preserved old mining equipment, pretty much right where the miners left it. Next stop: **Cerrillos**, a photographer's dream, relatively unchanged since the 1880s. The town includes the first mine in North America, built to extract turquoise around AD 100.

Continue north on NM 14 until you hit I-25, which takes you into Santa Fe.

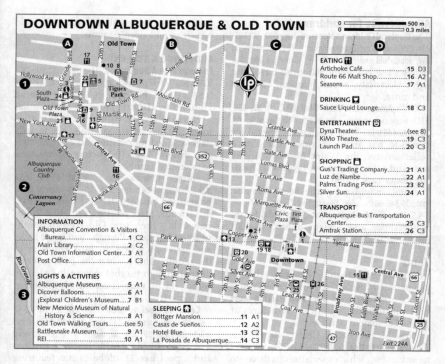

DOWNTOWN ALBUQUERQUE & OLD TOWN

EATING 🍴	
Artichoke Café	15 D3
Route 66 Malt Shop	16 A2
Seasons	17 A1

DRINKING 🍷	
Sauce Liquid Lounge	18 C3

ENTERTAINMENT 🎭	
DynaTheater	(see 8)
KiMo Theatre	19 C3
Launch Pad	20 C3

SHOPPING 🛍	
Gus's Trading Company	21 A1
Luz de Nambe	22 A1
Palms Trading Post	23 B2
Silver Sun	24 A1

TRANSPORT	
Albuquerque Bus Transportation Center	25 C3
Amtrak Station	26 C3

INFORMATION	
Albuquerque Convention & Visitors Bureau	1 C2
Main Library	2 C2
Old Town Information Center	3 A1
Post Office	4 C3

SIGHTS & ACTIVITIES	
Albuquerque Museum	5 A1
Dicover Balloons	6 A1
¡Explora! Children's Museum	7 B1
New Mexico Museum of Natural History & Science	8 A1
Old Town Walking Tours	(see 5)
Rattlesnake Museum	9 A1
REI	10 A1

SLEEPING 😴	
Böttger Mansion	11 A1
Casas de Sueños	12 A2
Hotel Blue	13 C2
La Posada de Albuquerque	14 C3

.nhccnm.org; 1701 4th St SW; adult/child $3/free; 🕐 10am-5pm Tue-Sat) houses a visual arts building, a performance center, and three galleries of Hispanic art, history and culture.

Rich with birdlife, the 270-acre **Rio Grande Nature Center** (Map p937; ☎ 505-344-7240; www.nmparks.com; 2901 Candelaria Rd NW; per vehicle $3; 🕐 park 8am-5pm, visitor center 10am-5pm) also offers gentle hiking and biking trails that wind through meadows and groves of trees.

The 2.7-mile **Sandia Peak Tramway** (☎ 505-856-7325; www.sandiapeak.com; Tramway Blvd; adult/child $15/10; 🕐 9am-8pm Wed-Sun, 5-8pm Tue) starts in the desert realm of cholla cactus and soars to the pines atop 10,678ft Sandia Peak. The High Finance Restaurant & Tavern is a popular, albeit touristy, destination at the top.

Northwest of downtown, **Petroglyph National Monument** (Map p937; ☎ 505-899-0205; www.nps.gov/petr; per vehicle Mon-Fri $1, Sat & Sun $2) offers three trails of varying degrees of difficulty that encircle upwards of 15,000 rock etchings that date from AD 1300. Head west on I-40 across the Rio Grande and take exit 154 north.

Activities

The omnipresent Sandia Mountains and the less crowded Manzano Mountains offer outdoor activities, including **hiking**, **skiing** (downhill and cross-country), **mountain biking** and camping. The **Sandia Ranger Station** (Map p937; ☎ 505-281-3304; 11776 Hwy 337; 🕐 8am-5pm, closed Sun Oct-Apr), off I-40 exit 175 south, has maps and information. For equipment, try **REI** (Map p939; ☎ 505-247-1191; 1905 Mountain Rd NW).

Reach the top of the Sandias via the eastern slope along the lovely **Sandia Crest National Scenic Byway** (I-40 exit 175 north), which passes several trailheads; or take the Sandia Peak Tramway (left); or take NM 165 from Placitas (I-25 exit 242), a dirt road through Las Huertas Canyon that passes the prehistoric dwelling of **Sandia Man Cave**.

Atop of the Sandia Peak Tramway, the **Sandia Peak Ski Area** (☎ 505-242-9052; www.sandiapeak.com; half-/full day lift tickets adult $29/40, child & senior $30/22) remains open during summer weekends and holidays (May to October) for mountain bikers.

SOUTHWEST

Albuquerque for Children

The !Explora! Children's Museum (Map p939; ☎ 505-224-8300; www.explora.mus.nm.us; 1701 Mountain Rd NW; adult/child under 12 $7/3; ☽ 10am-6pm Mon-Sat, noon-6pm Sun) has demonstrations involving light, electricity, sound, motion, anatomy and more.

Cliff's Amusement Park (Map p937; ☎ 505-881-9373; www.cliffsamusementpark.com; 4800 Osuna NE Rd; adult/child $21/18; ☽ Apr-Sep), a great reward for the kids, has about 25 rides, including a roller coaster, the Water Monkey, a play area and other traditional favorites. Opening hours vary widely.

Adults might enjoy the Beach (Map p937; ☎ 505-345-6066; 1600 Desert Surf Circle; adult/child 5-9 $27/11; ☽ May-Sep) as much as kids. Seven water slides and a giant pool create 5ft swells for body surfers.

Tours

From mid-April to mid-November, the Albuquerque Museum (p938) offers informative, free and guided Old Town walking tours of 17 historically significant structures at 11am Tuesday to Sunday.

New Mexico native Christy Rojas runs Aventura Artística (☎ 800-808-7352; www.newmexicotours.com), which specializes in three- to four-day tours of the Albuquerque–Santa Fe area.

Festivals & Events

A million spectators are drawn to magical hot-air-balloon ascensions at the International Balloon Fiesta (☎ 505-821-1000, 888-422-7277; www.aibf.org) in early October. Several companies offer rides over the city and the Rio Grande, including Discover Balloons (☎ 505-842-1111; www.discoverballoons.com; per person $140).

The New Mexico Gay Rodeo Association (www.nmgra.com) hosts the Zia Regional Rodeo on the second weekend of August.

Sleeping

Central Ave (aka Route 66) is lined with vintage motels. Look for accommodations west of downtown along Central Ave near Rio Grande Blvd, or along Central Ave in the UNM district.

BUDGET

El Vado (Map p937; ☎ 505-243-4594; 2500 Central Ave SW; r $32; P) Built with adobe bricks in 1936 and claiming to be the purest surviving Route 66 motel in Albuquerque, El Vado has clean and simple rooms.

MIDRANGE & TOP END

La Posada de Albuquerque (Map p939; ☎ 505-242-9090, 800-777-5732; www.laposada-abq.com; 125 2nd St NW; r $70-90; P) Built in 1939 by Conrad Hilton, this Historic Hotel of America has a relaxed lobby bar, with weekend jazz, tiled fountains, white stucco walls rising to a dark-wooded mezzanine and gaslight-style chandeliers. The 110 spacious rooms have handcrafted furniture.

Böttger Mansion (Map p939; ☎ 505-243-3639, 800-758-3639; www.bottger.com; 110 San Felipe St NW; r incl breakfast & extras $110-169; P) Built in 1912, this friendly place retains its original Victorian style – there's no Old West or Southwestern feel here! Perhaps you'll get lucky and arrive on a first or third Thursday of the month. That's when the B&B serves a delightful high tea that may include lemon sorbet, melon soup, cheese and leek quiche, and dessert.

Casas de Sueños (Map p939; ☎ 505-247-4560; www.casasdesuenos.com; 310 Rio Grande Blvd SW; r incl full breakfast $119-189; ☒ ☐ P) This lovely and peaceful place with luscious gardens and a pool has 22 adobe casitas featuring handcrafted furniture and original artwork. Some casitas have a kitchenette, fireplace and/or private hot tub.

Hotel Blue (Map p939; ☎ 505-924-2400; www.thehotelblue.com; 717 Central Ave NW; s/d $79/89; ☒ P) This stylish boutique hotel close to downtown has 145 rooms and suites on six floors.

Eating

Albuquerque offers plenty of good eateries, particularly if you like Southwestern cuisine.

THE AUTHOR'S CHOICE

Nora Dixon Place (☎ 505-898-3662, 888-667-2349; www.noradixon.com; 312 Dixon Rd; r incl full breakfast $95-155) In nearby Corrales, a charming farming village 8 miles north of downtown Albuquerque, this friendly B&B has three lovely rooms nestled in the Rio Grande Bosque. They all face an enclosed courtyard with views of the Sandias. As you might hope, the architecture is pure adobe New Mexican territorial style.

SOUTHWEST

THE AUTHOR'S CHOICE

Sadie's (Map p937; ☎ 505-345-5339; 6230 4th St NW; lunch dishes $5-7, dinner dishes $7-11) A massive place with a barnlike atmosphere (and a big-screen TV in the bar), Sadie's is a local institution. We make this our first stop in Albuquerque – bar none. Recite along with us: 'a carafe of grand gold margaritas and the enchilada dinner, please, with blue corn, rolled, chicken, green vegetarian, no onions and a side of guac. Great. Thanks.'

Route 66 Malt Shop (Map p939; ☎ 505-242-7866; 1720 Central Ave SW; dishes $5; ☽ lunch & dinner Mon-Sat) This nostalgic and friendly place only has a tiny counter with four stools, one table and one booth. But it serves great green-chili cheeseburgers, hot pastrami and other sandwiches.

Winning Coffee Company (Map p937; ☎ 505-266-0000; 111 Harvard Dr NE; dishes $4-6) Flavorful, strong coffee is the key draw at this large, laid-back coffeehouse, a favorite with locals and students due to its proximity to UNM.

Seasons (Map p939; ☎ 505-766-5100; 2031 Mountain Rd NW; lunch $7-14, dinner $14-28; ☽ lunch & dinner Mon-Fri, dinner Sat & Sun) With refreshingly bright yellow walls, high ceilings, fresh flowers and a creative menu, this contemporary place provides welcome relief from the usual Old Town atmosphere. Try the hearty red-chili-dusted chicken burgers or Baja tacos either inside or on the rooftop cantina.

Artichoke Café (Map p939; ☎ 505-243-0200; www.artichokecafe.com; 424 Central Ave SE; dishes $9-29; ☽ lunch Mon-Fri, dinner nightly) The unpretentious service here belies the fact that the eatery has been voted an Albuquerque favorite many times. The back outdoor patio offers relief from Central Ave traffic.

Flying Star Café (Map p937; ☽ 6:30am-11pm Sun-Thu, 6:30am-midnight Fri & Sat) Central Ave (☎ 505-255-6633; 3416 Central Ave SE); Juan Tabo Blvd (☎ 275-8311; Juan Tabo Blvd NE); Rio Grande Blvd (☎ 344-6714; 4026 Rio Grande Blvd NW); Menaul Blvd (☎ 293-6911; 8001 Menaul Blvd NE) With four constantly packed locations, this is the place to go for homemade soups, muffins, breads, innovative main dishes, desserts and ice cream.

Frontier (Map p937; ☎ 505-266-0550; 2400 Central Ave SE; dishes $3-7; ☽ 24hr) An Albuquerque tradition, the Frontier boasts enormous cinnamon rolls and the best huevos rancheros ever. The food, people-watching and Western art collection are outstanding.

Drinking

Assets Grille & Brewing Company (Map p937; ☎ 505-889-6400; 6910 Montgomery Blvd NE; dishes $6-14; ☽ lunch & dinner Mon-Sat, bar open nightly) Serving fresh-brewed micro beer along with a broad menu, this place has a fun bar brimming with young professionals.

Sauce Liquid Lounge (Map p939; ☎ 505-242-5839; 405 Central Ave NW; ☽ Tue-Sat) A hip little place with a bit of a New York-lounge feel. A DJ plays house music on the weekend, but it's not so loud that you can't just hang and talk.

Entertainment

La Posada de Albuquerque (Map p939; ☎ 505-242-9090, 800-777-5732; 125 2nd St NW) Pop into this place for weekend jazz.

Many live-music clubs and bars are concentrated downtown.

Launch Pad (Map p939; ☎ 505-764-8887; 618 Central Ave SW) A retro-modern place grooving to alternative sounds.

Caravan East (Map p937; ☎ 505-265-7877; 7605 Central Ave NE) The perfect place to practice your two-step or line dancing with live country-and-western bands.

Albuquerque Mining Company (Map p937; ☎ 505-255-4022; 7209 Central Ave NE), a most venerable institution, and the more hip **Pulse** (Map p937; ☎ 505-255-3334; 4100 Central Ave SE) are the city's two most popular gay and lesbian nightclubs.

Popejoy Hall (Map p937; ☎ 505-277-4569; www.unmtickets.com; cnr Central Ave & Cornell St SE) and the historic **KiMo Theatre** (Map p939; ☎ 505-768-3544; 423 Central Ave NWi) are the primary venues for big-name national acts, as well as local opera, symphony and theater. The KiMo Theatre runs tours from 9am to 4pm Monday to Friday.

Shopping

For Native American crafts and informed salespeople, stop by the **Palms Trading Post** (Map p939; ☎ 505-247-8504; 1504 Lomas Blvd NW; ☽ Mon-Sat) or **Gus's Trading Company** (Map p939; ☎ 505-843-6381; 2026 Central Ave SW).

Luz de Nambe (Map p939; ☎ 505-242-5699; 328 San Felipe St NW; ☽ Mon-Sat) Sells discounted and famed Nambeware.

QUIRKY NEW MEXICO

There are some places in New Mexico you just won't find anywhere else:

- **International UFO Museum & Research Center, Roswell** (p958) Revisit the Roswell Crash of 1947
- **Very Large Array** (p955) Searching for signs of intelligent life
- **Earthships, Taos** (p952) Living 'off the grid'
- **Bisti Badlands and De-Na-Zin Wilderness** (p954) A trippy, surreal landscape of colorful rock formations
- **Montezuma's Castle, Las Vegas** (p950) An eye-popping structure with hot springs bubbling at its feet

---

Silver Sun (Map p939; ☎ 505-242-8265; 2042 South Plaza NW) A reputable spot for turquoise.

If you walk east from the university down and around Central Ave in Nob Hill until you reach the Nob Hill Shopping Center at Carlisle Ave, you'll find an eclectic and unusual mix of shops (from a tattoo parlor to a herbal medicine shop to a toy store) located here.

Getting There & Around

AIR

Though the **Albuquerque International Sunport** (☎ 505-244-7700; www.cabq.gov/airport; 2200 Sunport Blvd) is New Mexico's biggest airport, it's still relatively small. Most major US airlines service Albuquerque, though **Southwest** (☎ 800-435-9792) has the largest presence.

Cabs between the airport and downtown cost about $8.

BUS

The **Albuquerque Bus Transportation Center** (Map p939; 300 2nd St SW) houses **Greyhound** (☎ 505-243-4435, 800-231-2222; www.greyhound.com), which serves destinations throughout New Mexico.

SunTran (☎ 505-243-7433; www.cabq.gov/transit; ❂ 6am-9pm, some lines run until 6pm), the public bus system, covers most of Albuquerque on weekdays and hits the major tourist spots daily (adult/child $1/35¢). SunTran Route 50 connects the airport with downtown (there's no Sunday or evening service). **Sandia Shuttle** (☎ 505-243-3244; www.sandiashuttle .com) runs daily shuttles to many Santa Fe hotels between 8am and 5pm ($23).

Twin Hearts (☎ 505-751-1201, 800-654-9456) leaves four times daily for Santa Fe ($20), Taos ($45), Red River ($55) and Angel Fire ($55).

TRAIN

The Southwest Chief stops daily at Albuquerque's **Amtrak station** (Map p939; ☎ 800-872-7245; www.amtrak.com; 214 1st St SW), heading east to Kansas City, Missouri ($113, 18 hours) and beyond, or west through Flagstaff, Arizona (from $94, five hours) to Los Angeles (from $106, 15 hours). Service to Santa Fe ($36, 2½ hours) involves transferring to a bus in Lamy, 18 miles south of Santa Fe.

ALONG I-40

Although you can zip between Albuquerque and Flagstaff, AZ, in less than five hours, the national monuments and pueblos along the way are well worth a visit. For a scenic loop, take Hwy 53 southwest from Grants, which leads to all the following sights, except Acoma. Hwy 602 brings you north to Gallup.

Acoma Pueblo

The dramatic mesa-top 'Sky City' sits 7000ft above sea level and 367ft above the surrounding plateau. One of the oldest continuously inhabited settlements in North America, pottery-making people have lived here since the later part of the 11th century. Guided tours (adult/child 6-17 $10/7) leave from the **visitor center** (☎ 505-469-1052, 800-747-0181) at the bottom of the mesa. From I-40 take exit 108, about 50 miles west of Albuquerque.

El Malpais National Monument

Meaning 'bad land' in Spanish, eerie El Malpais encompasses about 200 sq miles of lava flows. The **information center** (☎ 505-783-4774; www.nps.gov/elma; Hwy 53; ❂ 8:30am-4:30pm), 22 miles southwest of Grants on Hwy 53, has hiking and primitive (free) camping details.

El Morro National Monument

The 200ft sandstone outcropping at this **monument** (☎ 505-783-4226; www.nps.gov/elmo; adult/child $3/free; ☗ 9am-7pm summer, 9am-5pm rest of year), also known as 'Inscription Rock,' has been a travelers' oasis for millennia. Thousands of carvings – from petroglyphs in the pueblo at the top (c 1250) to elaborate inscriptions by the Spanish conquistadors and the Anglo pioneers – offer a unique means of tracing history. Look for it about 38 miles southwest of Grants via Hwy 53.

Zuni Pueblo

The Zuni are known worldwide for their delicately inlaid silverwork, which is sold in stores lining Hwy 53. Walk past stone houses and beehive-shaped mud ovens to the massive **Our Lady of Guadalupe Mission**, featuring impressive murals. The **Ashiwi Awan Museum & Heritage Center** (☎ 505-782-4403; Ojo Caliente Rd; admission by donation; ☗ 9am-5pm Mon-Fri) displays early photos and other tribal artifacts.

The friendly **Inn at Halona** (☎ 505-782-4547, 800-752-3278; www.halona.com; 1 Shalaka Dr; r with/without breakfast $85/79; ☒), decorated with local Zuni arts and crafts, is the only place to stay on the pueblo.

Gallup

Because Gallup serves as the Navajo and Zuni peoples' major trading center, you'll find many trading posts, pawnshops, jewelry stores, and crafts galleries in the historic district. It's arguably the best place in New Mexico for top-quality goods at fair prices. Gallup is another classic Route 66 town, with loads of vintage motels and businesses.

The **Gallup Cultural Center** (☎ 505-863-4131; www.southwestindian.com; Hwy 66 ☗ 8am-5pm) houses a small but well-done museum with Indian art, including excellent collections of both contemporary and old kachina dolls, pottery, sand painting and weaving. A tiny theater screens films about Chaco Canyon and the Four Corners region. Contact the **Gallup Visitor Information Center** (☎ 505-863-3841, 800-242-4282; www.gallupnm.org; 701 Montoya Blvd; ☗ 8am-5pm Mon-Fri) for details.

The town's lodging jewel is **El Rancho** (☎ 505-863-9311, 800-543-6351; www.elranchohotel.com; 1000 E Hwy 66; s/d/ste $42/55/80). Many of the great actors of the '40s and '50s stayed here – including Humphrey Bogart, Katharine Hepburn and John Wayne. El Rancho features a superb Southwestern lobby, restaurant, bar and an eclectic selection of simple rooms.

The small, casual **El Metate Tamale Factory** (☎ 505-722-7000; 610 W Mesa Ave; dishes $4-7; ☗ breakfast, lunch & dinner Mon-Sat) makes flavorful (and affordable) tamales and other specialties.

SANTA FE

In the last decade Santa Fe style has become synonymous with laid-back sophistication, abstract adobe architecture, carved wooden furniture and doorways. No matter where you're from, you've probably already encountered the ubiquitous, iconic images: howling coyotes and flute-playing Kokopellis; well-to-do Anglo women (probably from either US coast) with graying hair wearing long black skirts and silver necklaces; and art, art and more art – everywhere you look. These images are certainly ever present and they might seem like clichéd images, but take

---

ROUTE 66: GET YOUR KICKS IN NEW MEXICO

New Mexico revels in all 475 miles of its Route 66 legacy. From east to west, cruise through the yesteryear towns of **Tucumcari**, 173 miles from Albuquerque, with its **Mesalands Dinosaur Museum** (☎ 505-461-3466; www.mesalands.edu/museum/museum.htm; 222 E Laughlin St; adult/child $5/2.50; ☗ 10am-6pm Tue-Sat Mar–Aug, noon-5pm Tue-Sat Sep-Feb) that showcases real dinosaur bones and has hands-on exhibits. It's well worth a visit. Then stop in **Santa Rosa**, 50 miles further, at the **Route 66 Auto Museum** (☎ 505-472-1966; 2766 Old Route 66; adult/child under 12 $5/free; ☗ 7:30am-7pm May-Aug, 7:30am-5pm Sep-Apr), which pays homage to this mother of all cross-country roads. Next up: lovely **Las Vegas** (p950), sophisticated **Santa Fe** (above), sprawling **Albuquerque** (p936), dramatic **Acoma Pueblo** (opposite), the boom, bust, bust, boom town of **Grants** and hard-edged **Gallup** (opposite). In addition to publishing a quarterly magazine, the active **New Mexico Route 66 Association** (Map p937; ☗ 505-224-2802; www.rt66nm.org; 1415 Central Ave NE, Albuquerque) has archives, news and event calendars on its website.

SOUTHWEST

SANTA FE

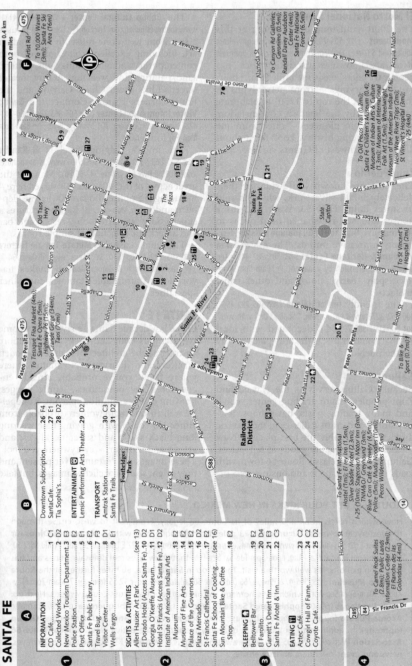

heart – there's no more aesthetically alluring cliché in America. Enjoy them. But also
stroll down the narrow streets behind the
plaza and across the railroad tracks to find
an area rich with Hispanic influence, a colorful place bursting with a life force as red as
ristras and as fiery as a New Mexico sunset.

Orientation

Cerrillos Rd (I-25 exit 278), a 6-mile strip
of hotels and fast-food restaurants, enters
town from the south; Paseo de Peralta circles the center of town; St Francis Dr (I-
25 exit 282) forms the western border of
downtown and turns into US 285, which
heads north toward Española, Los Alamos
and Taos. Alameda St follows the canal
east–west through the center of town, and
Guadalupe St is the main north–south
street through downtown. Most downtown
restaurants, galleries, museums and sites
are either on or east of Guadalupe St and
are within walking distance of the plaza, in
the center of town.

Information

BOOKSTORES

Collected Works (☎ 505-988-4226; 208B W San
Francisco St) A good selection of regional travel books.
Travel Bug (☎ 505-992-0418; www.mapsofnewmexico
.com; 839 Paseo de Peralta) More travel books and maps.

EMERGENCY

Emergency number (☎ 911)
Police (☎ 505-955-5000; 2515 Camino Entrada)

INTERNET ACCESS

CD Café (☎ 505-986-0735; 301 N Guadalupe St; per hr
$10) Sip coffee or listen to CDs while you surf.
New Mexico Department of Tourism (☎ 505-
827-7336; www.newmexico.org; 491 Old Santa Fe Trail;
🕑 8am-5pm) Free Internet access.
Santa Fe Public Library (☎ 505-955-6781; 145
Washington Ave) Make reservations for a free half-hour
of access.

INTERNET RESOURCES

Santa Fe Chamber (www.santafechamber.com) Listings
and links for local businesses.
Santa Fe Information (www.santafe.org) Official online
visitors guide to the city of Santa Fe.

MEDIA

The New Mexican (☎ 505-988-5541; www.santa
fenewmexican.com) Daily paper with breaking news.

Santa Fe Reporter (☎ 505-988-5541; www.sfreporter
.com) Free alternative weekly; Friday section has thorough
listings of what's going on.

MEDICAL SERVICES

St Vincent's Hospital (☎ 505-820-5247; 455 St
Michael's Dr; 🕑 24hr emergency)

MONEY

Wells Fargo (☎ 505-984-0424; 241 Washington Ave)
Changes foreign currency.

POST

Post office (☎ 800-275-8777; 120 S Federal Pl)

TOURIST INFORMATION

New Mexico Tourism Department (☎ 505-827-
7400; www.newmexico.org; 491 Old Santa Fe Trail;
🕑 8am-5pm) has brochures, a hotel reservation line, free
coffee and free Internet access.
Public Lands Information Center (☎ 505-438-7542;
www.publiclands.org; 1474 Rodeo Rd; 🕑 9am-4:30pm
Mon-Fri) This helpful place has lots of maps and information.
Visitor Center (☎ 505-955-6200, 800-777-2489; www
.santafe.org; 201 W Marcy St; 🕑 8am-5pm Mon-Fri) At
the Sweeny Convention Center. Small and
convenient.

Sights

The four museums administered by the
Museum of New Mexico (☎ 505-827-6463; 1 museum $7, 4-day pass to all 4 $15, children under 16 free;
🕑 10am-5pm Tue-Sun) are recommended: the
Palace of the Governors (☎ 505-476-5100; www
.museumofnewmexico.org; 100 Palace Ave), with regional history inside one of the country's
oldest buildings; the **Museum of Fine Arts**
(☎ 505-476-5072; www.museumofnewmexico.org; 107
Palace Ave), with tours at 1:30pm; the **Museum
of Indian Arts & Culture** (☎ 505-476-1250; www
.miaclab.org; 710 Camino Lejo); and the **Museum of
International Folk Art** (☎ 505-476-1200; www.moifa
.org; 706 Camino Lejo).

Possessing the world's largest collection
of her work, the **Georgia O'Keeffe Museum**
(☎ 505-946-1000; www.okeeffemuseum.org; 217 Johnson
St; adult/child $8/free; 🕑 10am-5pm Sat-Thu, 10am-8pm
Fri, galleries closed Wed Nov-Jun) features the artist's paintings of flowers, bleached skulls
and adobe architecture. Tours of O'Keeffe's
house (p951) require advance reservations.

The **St Francis Cathedral** (☎ 505-982-5619; 131
Cathedral Pl; 🕑 8am-5pm) houses the oldest Madonna statue in North America. This cathedral is also important for another reason:

SANTA FE IN...

Two Days

By day, hit the nearby **Georgia O'Keeffe Museum** (p945), **Museum of Fine Arts** (p945) and **Palace of the Governors** (p945), packing in a quick burrito for lunch. Linger over a special dinner at **Geronimo** (p948).

On the second day, chill out over a coffee and magazines at **Downtown Subscription** (p948), then stroll down Canyon Rd, visiting as many art galleries as you want. If you've got time left, check out the **Museum of International Folk Art** (p945) or the **Museum of Indian Arts & Culture** (p945). Head back to the plaza for dinner and drinks – perhaps a sunset cocktail on the rooftop **Belltower Bar** (p948) at La Fonda.

Four Days

Follow the two-day itinerary, then on the third day, visit the museums you haven't already seen. Otherwise, stroll south to the state capitol, hike around the **Bandelier National Monument** (p950). On the fourth day, take an early morning **cooking class** (opposite) and an afternoon day trip to either **Los Alamos** (p950) or **Las Vegas** (p950).

Jean Baptiste Lamy was sent to Santa Fe by the Pope with orders to tame the wild Western outpost town through culture and religion. Convinced that the town needed a focal point for religious life, he began construction of this cathedral in 1869. Lamy's story has been immortalized in Willa Cather's *Death Comes for the Archbishop*. Mass is held at 7am and 5pm Monday to Saturday, and 8am, 10am, 5pm and noon on Sunday.

Primarily showing student and faculty work, the esteemed four-year **Institute of American Indian Arts Museum** (☎ 505-983-8900; www.iaia.edu; 108 Cathedral Place; adult/child $4/2; ☉ 9am-5pm) features the finest offerings of Native American artists from around the country. The attached **Allen Hauser Art Park** also has sculptures by Michael Naranjo and others.

The **Santa Fe Children's Museum** (☎ 505-989-8359; www.santafechildrensmuseum.org; 1050 Old Pecos Trail; admission $4; ☉ 10am-5pm Wed-Sat, noon-5pm Sun) features hands-on exhibits on science and art for young children. The museum runs daily two-hour programs (usually at 10am or 2:30pm), which tackle subjects like solar energy and printmaking.

In 1937 Mary Cabot established the **Wheelwright Museum of the American Indian** (☎ 505-982-4636; www.wheelwright.org; 704 Camino Lejo; admission free; ☉ 10am-5pm Mon-Sat, 1-5pm Sun) to showcase Navajo ceremonial art. While its strength continues to be Navajo exhibits, it now includes contemporary Native American art and historical artifacts as well.

In La Cienega, about 15 miles south of Santa Fe, **El Rancho de las Golondrinas** (☎ 505-471-2261; www.golondrinas.org; 334 Los Pinos Rd, La Cienega; adult/child $5/2; ☉ 10am-4pm Wed-Sun Jun-Sep) shows off Spanish Colonial history made real. It's a great place for kids.

Activities

Check 'Pasatiempo' (the Friday section of the free daily *New Mexican* newspaper) for its 'Bring the Kids' column, with a rundown on area events for children.

The Pecos Wilderness and Santa Fe National Forest, east of town, have over 1000 miles of **hiking** trails, several of which lead to 12,000ft peaks. Summer storms are frequent, so prepare for hikes by checking weather reports. For maps and details, contact the Public Lands Information Center (p945).

The **Santa Fe Ski Area** (☎ 505-982-4429, snow report 505-983-9155; www.skisantafe.com; lift tickets adult/child $47/34; ☉ 9am-4pm Thanksgiving-Easter) is a half-hour's drive from the plaza up Hwy 475. From the 12,000ft summit you can admire 80,000 sq miles of desert and mountains. On weekends from June through August and for a couple weeks during fall foliage, the chairlift is open (one way/round-trip $4/6).

Busloads of people head up to the Taos Box (p952) for white-water river running, but there are also mellow float trips throughout New Mexico and overnight guided rafting trips. Contact **New Wave River Trips** (☎ 505-984-1444, 800-984-1444; www.newwaverafting.com;

1101 Cerrillos Rd). Stay cool on day trips through the **Rio Grande Gorge** (adult/child half day $47/44, full day $84/77) or Taos Box ($100), or go for a three-day Rio Chama float ($400).

Sun Mountain Bike & Coffee Shop (☎ 505-982-8986; www.sunmountainbikeco.com; 102 E Water St) has information about regional trails, rents bikes and can drop you off at trailheads. **Bike & Sport** (☎ 505-820-0809; www.nmbikensport.com; 1829 Cerrillos Rd) rents mountain bikes from $22 a day.

Several hiking trails, particularly those at **Randall Davey Audubon Center** (☎ 505-983-4609; www.nm.audubon.org; 1800 Upper Canyon Rd; trail use $2; 9am-4pm Mon-Fri, 9am-2pm Sat), are perfect for active children.

The Japanese-style **10,000 Waves** (☎ 505-982-9304; www.tenthousandwaves.com; 3451 Hyde Park Rd; communal tubs $14, private tubs per person $19-27; 9:15am-10pm Wed-Mon, 4-10pm Tue), with land-scaped grounds concealing 10 attractive tubs in smooth Zen design, offers waterfalls, cold plunges, and hot and dry saunas.

If you develop a love for New Mexican cuisine, try cooking lessons at the **Santa Fe School of Cooking** (☎ 505-983-4511; www.santafeschoolofcooking.com). Classes, with over 20 options including traditional New Mexican and Southwestern breakfast, are 2½ hours long and cost $58 to $75, including the meal.

Tours

Access Santa Fe (☎ 505-988-2774; www.accesssantafe.com; trips 9:30am & 1:30pm), a 'destination management company,' departs from the lobbies of the El Dorado Hotel and Hotel

---

EXPLORING CANYON ROAD

At one time Canyon Rd was a dusty street lined with artists' homes and studios, but today most of the artists have fled to cheaper digs and the private homes have been replaced with a flock of upscale galleries. Today it's a can't-miss attraction: over 90 galleries at the epicenter of the nation's healthiest art scene display rare Indian antiquities, Santa Fe School masterpieces and wild contemporary work. It's a little overwhelming, but soothe your battered brain with wine and cheese on Friday (at 5pm or so), when glittering art openings clog the narrow street with elegant collectors.

St Francis for a two-hour walking tour of the city. The tours are held at 9:30am and 1:30pm and cost $10 (under 12 free).

Outback Tours (☎ 888-772-3274; www.outbacktours.com) focuses on the region's geology, ecology and history on 4WD day, overnight and evening tours to Taos ($96), Jemez ($85) and Abiquiu ($85).

Festivals & Events

Following are Sante Fe's biggest festivals:
Spanish Market (☎ 505-982-2226; www.spanishmarket.org) In late July, traditional Spanish colonial arts, from retablos and bultos to handcrafted furniture and metalwork, make this juried show an artistic extravaganza.
Santa Fe Indian Market (☎ 505-983-5220; www.swaia.org) On the weekend after the third Thursday in August, the plaza is packed with the finest Native American artisans from all over North America.
Santa Fe Fiestas (☎ 505-988-7575) Two weeks of events in early September, including concerts, a carnival, parades and a candlelight procession.

Sleeping

The **visitor center** (www.santafe.org) website lists helpful reservation services. Cerrillos Rd is lined with lots of chains and independent motels.

BUDGET

Silver Saddle Motel (☎ 505-471-7663; www.motelsantafe.com; 2810 Cerrillos Rd; s/d $59/65; P X) Inspired Southwestern comfy-rustic decor, including some rooms with attractively tiled kitchenettes and lots of kitschy appeal, reveals Americana at its finest.

Santa Fe International Hostel (☎ 505-988-1153; santafehostel@quest.net; 1412 Cerrillos Rd; dm $15, s/d with shared bath $25/35, s/d with private bath $33/43; P X) An outdoor patio and grill, murals done by visiting artists, free continental breakfast, a communal kitchen, linens and no lockout all adds up to one fine hostelling experience.

MIDRANGE

El Rey Inn (☎ 505-982-1931, 800-521-1349; www.elreyinnsantafe.com; 1862 Cerrillos Rd; r $79-119, ste $120-199; P X) This is a highly recommended classic courtyard hotel, with super rooms, a great pool and even a kids' playground scattered around five acres of greenery.

Camel Rock Suites (☎ 505-989-3600, 877-989-3600; www.camelrocksuites.com; 3007 S St Francis Dr; ste $109; P X) Huge suites – apartments, really –

THE AUTHOR'S CHOICE

El Farolito (☎ 505-988-1631, 888-634-8782; www.farolito.com; 514 Galisteo St; r $180-225; P ✕) Intimate and elegant, each of the seven comfy adobe casitas (some including patios) comes with a stocked fridge, VCR and all the amenities you expect from a fine B&B. Whether it's through the use of folk art, Native American detailing or lodge decor, the feel is luxe Southwest par excellence. Farolitos, by the way, are warm little lights that line walkways and rooftops. This place will warm your soul in similar fashion.

with full kitchens, dining room and fold-out sofas make this place a fantastic deal.

Santa Fe Motel & Inn (☎ 505-982-1039, 800-930-5002; 510 Cerrillos Rd; r $99; P ✕ 🐾) This motel has just 23 rooms, but they're well put together and attractive, many detailed in Southwestern style in what were once historic residences.

Stagecoach Motor Inn (☎ 505-471-0707; 3360 Cerrillos Rd; r incl breakfast $78-150; P ✕) With heaps more character than most Cerrillos Rd entries, this nice spot has huge, beautifully decorated rooms and a shady courtyard.

Garrett's Desert Inn (☎ 505-982-1851, 800-888-2145; www.garrettsdesertinn.com; 301 Old Santa Fe Trail; r $99-139, ste $119-149; P ✕ 🐾) These basic rooms and spacious suites right next to the plaza, are far more attractive than their counterparts on Cerrillos Rd.

Eating

Whole books have been written on dining in Santa Fe; it's hard to go wrong here.

BUDGET

Downtown Subscription (☎ 505-983-3085; 376 Garcia St; snacks $2-7; � 6am-7pm) Excellent coffee, 31 types of tea, pastries and a few savory offerings are complimented by a truly spectacular newsstand and flagstone patio.

Aztec Café (☎ 505-820-0025; 317 Aztec St; sandwiches $6; � 7am-dark Mon-Sat, 8am-dark Sun) This cozy café keeps the tattoos-and-climbing-gear crowd fed with sandwiches and malteds served beneath art that pales in comparison to the people-watching.

Tia Sophia's (☎ 505-983-9880; 210 W San Francisco St; dishes $3-7; � 7am-2pm Mon-Sat) The plaza workforce joins knowledgeable collectors

for this top spot's fabulous lunch specials and other great New Mexican offerings.

MIDRANGE

Geronimo (☎ 505-982-1500; 724 Canyon Rd; lunch dishes $9-22, dinner dishes $25-35; � lunch Tue-Sun, dinner nightly) Housed in a 1756 adobe, a meal at Geronimo is a splurge you won't soon forget, as it's among the finest and the most romantic restaurants in town.

Mudu Noodles (☎ 505-983-1411; 1494 Cerrillos Rd; dishes $12-19; � 5:30-9pm Mon-Sat; P) Pan-Asian organic dishes, like salmon dumplings, Vietnamese spring rolls and tofu laksa, inspire lines out the door of this lovely spot; the noodles and specials are recommended, and almost everything has a vegan version.

Cowgirl Hall of Fame (☎ 505-982-2565; 319 S Guadalupe St; dishes $8-13; � lunch Mon-Fri, 8:30am-2am Sat, 8:30am-midnight Sun, kitchen closes 11pm) Winner of both Best Bar and Best Place for Kids in a survey, thanks to a great playground and live music after 9pm. The Hall of Fame has fabulous food too. Try the salmon tacos, butternut squash casserole or anything mesquite grilled – all served with Texas caviar and Western-style feminist flair.

TOP END

Coyote Café (☎ 505-983-1615; 132 Water St; dishes $21-42; � dinner Fri-Mon & Thu) Chef Mark Miller's interpretations of New Mexican cuisine – try the buttermilk corncakes with chipotle prawns or pecan-wood grilled rib chop – remain a highlight of any foodie's visit.

Drinking

Belltower Bar (☎ 505-982-5511; 100 E San Francisco St) Atop La Fonda, you can enjoy a cold beer or killer margarita while watching one of those patented New Mexico sunsets.

THE AUTHOR'S CHOICE

SantaCafé (☎ 505-984-1788; 231 Washington Ave; lunch dishes $8-16, dinner dishes $19-37; � lunch Mon-Sat, dinner daily; P) Chef David Sellars is practically an international celebrity for dishes like goats cheese–stuffed free-range chicken with confit tamales (get the green chili mashed potatoes on the side). You want more? Give up wanting; there's nothing more to want.

Blue Corn Café & Brewery (☎ 505-438-1800; 4056 Cerrillos Rd; dishes $7-15; ☽ 11am-10pm Sun-Thu, 11am-11pm Fri & Sat) This cavernous brewpub has won awards for its Atomic Blonde Ale and Cold Front Coffee Stout, served alongside tapas, burgers and Chuy's chalupas.

Entertainment

Cowgirl Hall of Fame (☎ 505-982-2565; 319 S Guadalupe St; cover $1-5) In addition to being a fine and rustic-with-a-vengeance venue for catching live shows (despite the name, rarely country), it also has microbrews, great food and nonsmoking events.

Lensic Performing Arts Theater (☎ 505-984-1370; www.lensic.com; 1050 Old Pecos Trail) This beautifully renovated 1930s movie house hosts eight different performance groups and a weekly classic film series.

Santa Fe Opera (☎ 505-986-5900, 800-280-4654; www.santafeopera.org; tickets $24-142; ☽ late Jun-late Aug) Opera fans (and those who've never seen or heard an opera in their life) come to Santa Fe for this alone: an architectural marvel, with views of wind-carved sandstone wilderness crowned with sunsets and moonrises, and at center stage (and what a stage!) internationally renowned vocal talent performing humanity's masterworks of aria and romance. Best of all? You can wear jeans!

Shopping

From carved howling coyotes to turquoise jewelry to fine art, Santa Fe attracts shoppers of all budgets. Don't forget Canyon Rd galleries (p947).

Plaza Mercado (☎ 505-988-5792; www.plazamercado .com; 112 W San Francisco St) A swish spot packed with art galleries, antique stores and Santa Fe–style clothing.

Tesuque Flea Market (US 84/285; ☽ 9am-4pm Fri, 8am-5pm Sat & Sun Mar-Nov) An outdoor market a few minutes' drive north of Santa Fe at Tesuque Pueblo, offering deals on high-quality rugs, jewelry, art and clothing.

Getting There & Around

TNM&O/Greyhound (☎ 505-471-0008; www.grey hound.com; St Michael's Dr) has four daily buses to Albuquerque ($11, 80 minutes) and two daily buses to Taos ($16 to $18, 1½ hours). **Twin Hearts Shuttle** (☎ 800-654-9456; www.twin heartsexpress.com) runs between Santa Fe and the Albuquerque Sunport ($20), Taos ($25),

Española ($15), Red River ($30) and Questa ($25) daily; make reservations in advance.

Amtrak (☎ 800-872-7245; www.amtrak.com) stops at Lamy; from where buses continue 17 miles to Santa Fe.

Santa Fe Trails (☎ 505-955-2001; www.santafenm .gov; Sheridan Ave; ☽ 6am-11pm Mon-Fri, 8am-8pm Sat, 10am-7pm Sun), between Palace and Marcy Aves, provides local bus service (adult/child $1/50¢ per ride or day pass $2).

AROUND SANTA FE

As if there weren't enough to keep you happy for a week *within* the town limits of Santa Fe, she has to go and tempt you *outside* her borders. The red rocks, pine forest and streams of this region offer an embarrassment of hiking riches, natural hot springs and pueblos. Within miles of each other, Bandelier National Monument and Los Alamos evidence the iconographic geological, human and atomic history of the American West.

Pueblos

North of Santa Fe is the heart of Pueblo Indian lands. The **Eight Northern Pueblos** (ENIPC; ☎ 505-852-4265) publish the excellent and free *Eight Northern Indian Pueblos Visitors Guide*, available at area visitor centers.

Eight miles west of Pojoaque along Hwy 502, the ancient **San Ildefonso Pueblo** (per vehicle $3, camera/sketching/video permits $10/25/20; ☽ 8am-5pm) was the home of Maria Martinez, who in 1919 revived a distinctive traditional black-on-black pottery style. Several exceptional potters (including Maria's direct descendants) work in the pueblo; stop at the **Maria Poveka Martinez Museum** (admission free; ☽ 8am-4pm Mon-Fri), which sells the pueblo's pottery.

Española

In some ways Española is the gateway to the real New Mexico, separating the tourist-choked wonderland of Santa Fe from the reality of the rural. Much of the surrounding area is farmland, and much has been deeded to Hispanic land-grant families since the 17th century. Though the town itself doesn't offer much beyond a strip with fast-food restaurants and a disproportionate number of hair salons, it has a couple of stars. Contact the **chamber of commerce** (☎ 505-753-2831; www .espanolanmchamber.com; 710 Paseo de Oñate; ☽ 9am-5pm Mon-Fri) for more information.

Just northwest of town, on the road to Ojo Caliente (opposite), **Rancho de San Juan** (☎ 505-753-6818; www.ranchodesanjuan.com; Hwy 285; r & ste $225-525; ☒) is a small gem with first-class rooms, a spa, great service and a spectacular setting for dining on New Mexican classics, at two nightly seatings.

Ranchito San Pedro B&B (☎ 505-753-0583; www .janhart.com; Hwy 581; cabins $95; ☒), an adobe 'art dude ranch,' in a surprisingly pastoral neighborhood, is about as relaxing as they come.

Las Vegas

Not to be confused with the glittery city to the west, this Vegas is one of the loveliest towns in New Mexico, and one of the largest and oldest towns east of the Sangre de Cristo Mountains. Its eminently strollable downtown has a pretty Old Town Plaza and some 900 historic buildings listed in the National Register of Historic Places. It's architecture is a mix of Southwestern and Victorian. Ask for a walking-tour brochure from the **chamber of commerce** (☎ 505-425-8631, 800-832-5947; www.lasvegasnewmexico.com; 701 Grand Ave; ☽ 9am-5pm Mon-Fri).

Built in 1882 and carefully remodeled a century later, the renovated **Plaza Hotel** (☎ 505-425-3591, 800-328-1882; www.plazahotelnm .com; 230 Old Town Plaza; s & d incl breakfast $88-116; ☐) is Las Vegas' most celebrated and historic lodging. The elegant building now offers 36 comfortable accommodations in antique-filled rooms.

Indulge in a good New Mexican meal at **Estella's Café** (☎ 505-454-0048; 148 Bridge St; lunch dishes $5-7, dinner dishes $7-12; ☽ 11am-3pm Mon-Wed, 11am-8pm Thu-Fri, 11am-7pm Sat). Estella's devoted patrons treasure their homemade red chili, *menudo* (tripe and grits) and scrumptious enchiladas.

From the plaza, Hot Springs Blvd leads 5 miles north to Gallinas Canyon and the massive **Montezuma's Castle**, an eye-popping structure on the flanks of the Sangre de Cristo Mountains; once a hotel, it's now the United World College of the West. Along the road are a series of **hot spring pools** (admission free; ☽ 5am-midnight).

Los Alamos

Los Alamos, hugging the national forest and perched on mesas overlooking the desert, offers a fascinating dynamic in which souvenir T-shirts emblazoned with atomic explosions and 'La Bomba' wine are sold next to books on pueblo history and wilderness hiking.

You can't actually visit the **Los Alamos National Laboratory**, where the first atomic bomb was conceived, but you can visit the well-designed **Bradbury Science Museum** (☎ 505-667-4444; www.lanl.gov/museum; Central Ave; admission free; ☽ 10am-5pm Tue-Sat), which covers atomic history. The **Los Alamos Historical Museum** (☎ 505-662-4493; www.losalamos.com/his toricalsociety; 1921 Juniper St; admission free; ☽ 9:30am-4:30pm Mon-Sat, 11am-5pm Sun) features atomic-age popular culture artifacts and exhibits on the social history of life 'on the hill' during the secret project. Pick up one of its self-guided downtown **walking tour** pamphlets.

Bandelier National Monument

Because of its convenient location and spectacular landscape, **Bandelier** (☎ 505-672-3861; per vehicle $10, campsites $10; ☽ dawn-dusk) is an excellent choice for folks interested in ancient pueblos. Rio Grande Puebloans lived here until the mid-1500s. Although none of the sites are restored, there are almost 50 sq miles of protected canyons

---

ATOMIC NEW MEXICO

In 1943 Los Alamos (then a boys school perched on a 7400ft mesa) was chosen as the top-secret headquarters of the Manhattan Project – the code name for research and development of the atomic bomb. Accessed by two dirt roads, the site had no gas or oil lines, only one wire service, and was surrounded by thick forest. Many of those who lived on 'the hill' – including scientists' spouses, army personnel, and local Hispanics and Native Americans recruited to work in the labs and homes – had no idea what kind of work was being done.

On July 16, 1945, Manhattan Project scientists first detonated an atomic bomb at the Trinity Site in southern New Mexico, now part of White Sands Missile Range (p956). After atomic bombs destroyed Hiroshima and Nagasaki, Los Alamos was finally exposed to the public. Today the lab is still the backbone of the town, and tourism embraces the town's atomic history.

offering backpacking trails and camping at Juniper Campground, set among the pines near the monument entrance. It has about 100 campsites.

Abiquiu

The tiny community of Abiquiu (sounds like barbecue), on Hwy 84 about 45 minutes' drive northwest of Santa Fe, is famous because the renowned artist Georgia O'Keeffe lived and painted here permanently from 1949 until her death in 1986. With the Chama River flowing through farmland and spectacular rock landscape, the ethereal landscape continues to attract artists, and many live and work in Abiquiu. O'Keeffe's adobe house is open for limited visits: her **foundation** (www .georgiaokeeffe.org) offers one-hour **tours** (☎ 505-685-4539) on Tuesday, Thursday and Friday from April to November ($22), often booked months in advance.

An area institution, the peaceful and lovely **Abiquiú Inn** (☎ 505-685-4378, 800-447-5621; www.abiquiuinn.com; US 84; RV sites $18, s & d $89-149, 4-person casitas $189; ✗) is a sprawling collection of shaded adobes; some spacious rooms have kitchenettes. The very professional staff also runs the on-site **Abiquiú Cafe** (dishes $7-16; ✆ 7:30am-9pm). Stick to the Middle Eastern menu – falafel, dolmas and gyros are all winners – and you can't go wrong.

Ojo Caliente

Billed as America's oldest health resort, **Ojo Caliente** (☎ 800-222-9162; www.ojocalientespa.com; 50 Los Baños Dr; s/d $74/110, cottages s/d $90/145; ✗), which means 'hot eye' in Spanish, offers five springs, plus a charmingly tattered, family-owned resort with pleasant if not luxurious rooms and casitas. The on-site **Artesian Restaurant** (dishes $5-25; ✆ 7:30am-2:30pm & dinner) prepares organic and local ingredients with aplomb, including fresh trout encrusted with pine nuts in a cilantro-jalapeño butter. It's about 40 miles north of Santa Fe on US 285.

Cuba

Set in 360 beautiful acres in the Nacimiento Mountains, the friendly and recommended **Circle A Ranch Hostel** (☎ 505-289-3350; www .circlearanch.info; dm $20, r $35-55; ✆ May–mid-Oct), just off Hwy 550, is a gem. The lovely old adobe lodge, with exposed beams, grassy grounds, hiking trails and a classic kitchen, is a peaceful and relaxing place to hang out. Choose between private bedrooms (some with quilts and iron bedsteads) and shared bunkrooms.

TAOS

This tiny town has a big reputation. Isolated Taos boasts – with a pleasant but ever-so-disinterested tone – a long history of luring artists with its fabled clear light, a stunning multistory adobe pueblo inhabited by dignified souls and a magnificent mountain setting.

It's an eccentric place, full of bohemians and mainstream dropouts, solar-energy enthusiasts, fine chefs, acculturated B&B owners and old-time Hispanic families who still farm hay fields. It's rural and worldly, a place where grazing horses and a disproportionate number of artists hold equal sway.

Information

Magic Circle Bagels Cyber Cafe (☎ 505-758-0045; 710 Paseo del Pueblo Sur; snacks $3-6; ✆ 6:30am-4pm Mon-Fri, 7am-2pm Sat & Sun) Head here for Internet access.
Taos Guide (www.taosguide.com) Great links.
Taos Link (www.taoslink.com)
Visitor center (☎ 505-758-3873, 800-732-8267; www .destinationtaos.com; Paseo del Pueblo Sur at Paseo del Cañon; ✆ 9am-5pm) Can help you get your bearings.

Sights

Built around AD 1450 and continuously inhabited ever since, **Taos Pueblo** (☎ 505-758-1028; www.taospueblo.com; Taos Pueblo Rd; adult/child $10/5, photography or video permit $5; ✆ 8am-4pm, closed for 10 weeks around Feb & Mar) is the largest existing multistoried pueblo structure in the US and one of the best surviving examples of traditional adobe construction. Whatever else you do, don't miss it.

Taos Historic Museums (☎ 505-758-0505; www .taoshistoricmuseums.com; adult/child $6/3; ✆ 9am-5pm summer, shorter hrs winter) runs two great houses: the **Blumenschein Home** (222 Ledoux St), with spectacular art, and the **Martínez Hacienda** (Ranchitos Rd), a colonial trader's former home.

The **Millicent Rogers Museum** (☎ 505-758-2462; www.millicentrogers.org; Millicent Rogers Museum Rd; adult/child $7/6; ✆ 10am-5pm, closed Mon Nov-Mar), filled with pottery, jewelry, baskets and textiles, has one of the best collections of Indian and Spanish colonial art in the US.

Housed in a historic mid-19th-century adobe compound, the **Harwood Foundation** (☎ 505-758-9826; www.harwoodmuseum.org; 238 Ledoux St; admission $6; ☺ 10am-5pm Tue-Sat, noon-5pm Sun) features paintings, drawings, prints, sculpture and photography by northern New Mexico artists, both historical and contemporary.

The marvelous, adobe **Fechin Institute** (☎ 505-758-2690; www.fechin.com; 227 Paseo del Pueblo Norte; admission $5; ☺ 10am-4pm Wed-Sun) exhibits the Russian artist Nicolai Fechin's private collection, as well as much Asian art.

Four miles south of Taos in Ranchos de Taos, the oft-photographed **San Francisco de Asis Church** (☎ 505-758-2754; St Francis Plaza; ☺ 9am-4pm Mon-Fri) was built in the mid-18th century but didn't open until 1815. It's been memorialized in numerous Georgia O'Keeffe paintings and Edward Weston photographs.

At 650ft above the Rio Grande, the steel **Rio Grande Gorge Bridge** is the second-highest suspension bridge in the US; the view down is eye-popping. Just west of the bridge is a fascinating community of **Earthships** (☎ 505-751-0462; http://earthship.org; US 64; admission $5; ☺ 10am-4pm), self-sustaining, environmentally savvy houses built with recycled materials, that survive completely off the grid. Self-guided tours ($5) are worthwhile, as are overnight accommodations (see above).

Activities

During the summer, **white-water rafting** is popular in the Taos Box, the steep-sided cliffs that frame the Rio Grande. Day-long trips begin at around $90 per person; contact the visitor center for local outfitters. **Hiking** is plentiful here; trailheads line the road to the ski valley.

With a peak elevation of 11,819ft and a 2612ft vertical drop, **Taos Ski Valley** (☎ 800-347-7414; www.skitaos.org; adult/child $57/35) offers some of the most challenging skiing in the US and yet remains low-key and relaxed.

Sleeping

Doña Luz Inn (☎ 505-758-4874, 800-758-9187; www .ladonaluz.com; 114 Kit Carson Rd; r $60-199; ☒) The fabulous location is just the beginning at this historic, 200-year-old inn. Rooms range from the tiny La Luz to the three-level Rainbow Room suite, which features a hot tub on the rooftop sundeck. All are decorated in colorful Spanish-colonial style and with a cheerful clutter of amazing art.

> **THE ENCHANTED CIRCLE**
>
> For a scenic driving tour, this 84-mile loop road takes you north and east of Taos through barren windswept high desert, alpine forests and mountain streams. Follow Hwy 522 north to Questa; head east on Hwy 38 through Red River to Eagle Nest; then return on Hwy 64. West of Questa is the spectacular **Wild Rivers Recreation Area** (☎ 505-770-1600; admission $3), at the confluence of the Rio Grande and Red River, which have cut 800ft canyons into the plateau.

Laughing Horse Inn (☎ 505-758-8350, 800-776-0161; www.laughinghorseinn.com; 729 Paseo del Pueblo Norte; r $54-118, ste $130-160; ☒) Narrow adobe rooms are furnished with chili-shaped Christmas lights, piñon incense, hand-hewn furniture – it's how Taoseños actually live! The communal atmosphere continues with a hot tub under the stars, kitchen privileges and a huge penthouse. The vibe reminds you why you travel in the first place.

Taos Inn (☎ 505-758-2233, 800-826-7466; www .taosinn.com; 125 Paseo del Pueblo Norte; r $85-225; ☒ ☏) Parts of this landmark date to the 17th century, which is why it's on the National Register of Historic Places. Even though it's not the plushest place in town, it's fabulous, with a cozy lobby, heavy wood furniture, a sunken fireplace and lots of live local music at its famed Adobe Bar.

Earthship Rentals (☎ 505-751-0462; US 64; r $150-200) Want to experience life off the grid (ie forgoing TV and phone)? Stay in an earthship, a 100% solar-powered dwelling with a gray-water system and beautifully biotectured interior.

Adobe Wall Motel (☎ 505-758-3972; 227 E Kit Carson Rd; r $56-66; ☒) For almost 100 years, this shady courtyard motel has been accommodating travelers in big, slightly tattered rooms with wonderful fireplaces.

Eating

Taos Pizza Out Back (☎ 505-758-3112; 712 Paseo del Pueblo Norte; slices $4-6, medium pies $15-25; ☺ 11am-9pm) Enjoy every possible ingredient under the sun (for example, we recommend the Vera Cruz, which has chicken breast and veggies marinated in a honey-chipotle sauce) on pizza pies or slices the size of a small country.

Apple Tree (☎ 505-758-1900; 123 Bent St; lunch dishes $6-10, dinner dishes $13-25; ☺ 11:30am-3pm & 5-10pm) It's fancy, taking full advantage of its fabulous location and historic adobe with fine art, candles, a lovely patio, a huge wine list and gourmet twists on New Mexican classics. Picnic-style lunch fare is a real deal.

Mainstreet Bakery (☎ 505-758-9610; Guadalupe Plaza; dishes $4-7; ☺ 7am-2pm Mon-Fri, 7am-noon Sat & Sun) Its bread and butter is baking for natural grocers, but grab some breakfast treats, or try the lunch special: a bowl of black beans, green chili, red onions, tomatoes and cornbread.

Orlando's (☎ 505-751-1450; NM 522; dishes $7-11; ☺ 10:30am-3pm & dinner) This is it: the best New Mexican food in town, period. Those chicken enchiladas, huge burritos, all dressed to perfection and served up in the beautiful dining room.

Drinking

Adobe Bar (☎ 505-758-2233; 125 Paseo del Pueblo Norte; ☺ from noon) There's something about this place: the chairs, the Taos Inn's history, the casualness, the vibe, the tequila. It's true, the packed streetside patio has some of the state's finest margaritas, along with an eclectic lineup of great live music, like Manzanares and Madi Soto, and there's almost never a cover.

Eske's Brew Pub & Eatery (☎ 505-758-1517; 106 Des Georges Lane; pub grub $6-10; ☺ 4-10pm Mon-Thu, 11am-10pm Fri-Sun) This crowded hangout rotates more than 25 microbrewed ales. Live local music, from acoustic guitar to jazz, is usually free but national acts might charge a cover.

Alley Cantina (☎ 505-758-2121; 121 Terracina Lane; pub grub $6-14) It figures that the oldest building in Taos is a comfy bar. Nowadays you can catch live music ranging from zydeco to rock and jazz almost nightly.

Shopping

Taos has historically been a mecca for artists, and the huge number of galleries and studios in and around town are evidence of this.

Twining Weavers (☎ 505-758-9000; 133 Kit Carson Rd) Features handwoven rugs, tapestries and pillows.

El Rincón Trading Post (☎ 505-758-9188; 114 Kit Carson Rd) Even if you're not looking to buy anything, stop in here to browse through the dusty museum of artifacts, including Indian crafts, jewelry and Old West memorabilia.

Getting There & Around

From Santa Fe, take either the scenic 'high road' along Hwy 76 and Hwy 518, with galleries, villages and sites worth exploring, or follow the Rio Grande on straightforward Hwy 68.

Greyhound (☎ 505-758-1144, 800-231-2222; www .greyhound.com; 1386 Paseo del Pueblo Sur) has daily bus service to Albuquerque ($28 to $30, 2¼ hours) and Santa Fe ($16 to $18, 1½ hours), with stops at Pilar and Española.

Faust (☎ 505-758-3410, 888-830-3410) leaves the Albuquerque Sunport daily at 1:30pm; the return shuttle leaves Taos for Albuquerque at 8am. Times are subject to change.

NORTHWESTERN NEW MEXICO

Dubbed 'Indian Country' for good reason – huge swaths of land fall under the aegis of the Navajos, Pueblo, Zuni, Apache and Laguna tribes – this quadrant of New Mexico showcases remarkable ancient Indian sites alongside modern, solitary Native American settlements. From excavated dwellings at Chaco Culture National Historical Park to unexcavated ones at Aztec Ruins National Monument, the mysteries of the land are carried on the wind. It's not all Native Americans, though. In Chama, it's all aboard. The Cumbres and Toltec Scenic Railroad transports travelers to the mid-19th century on a classic locomotive train trip through the mountains.

Farmington & Around

The largest town in New Mexico's northwestern region, Farmington makes a good base from which to explore the Four Corners area. The **Convention & Visitors Bureau** (☎ 505-326-7602, 800-448-1240; www.farmingtonnm .org; Farmington Museum at Gateway Park, 3041 E Main St; ☺ 8am-5pm Mon-Fri) has more information.

Shiprock, a 1700ft-high volcanic plug that rises eerily over the landscape to the west, was a landmark for the Anglo pioneers and is a sacred site to the Navajo. The Navajo community of Shiprock hosts an annual **Northern Navajo Nation Fair**, in late September or early October, featuring a rodeo, pow-wow and traditional dancing.

An ancient pueblo, **Salmon Ruin & Heritage Park** (☎ 505-632-2013; adult/child 6-16 $3/1; ☺ 8am-5pm

Mon-Fri, 9am-5pm Sat & Sun) features a large village built by the Chaco people in the early 1100s. Abandoned, resettled by people from Mesa Verde and again abandoned before 1300, the site includes the remains of a homestead, petroglyphs, a Navajo hogan, an early Puebloan pithouse, a teepee and a wickiup (a rough brushwood shelter). To reach it, take Hwy 64 east toward Bloomfield.

Fourteen miles northeast of Farmington, the 27-acre **Aztec Ruins National Monument** (☎ 505-334-6174; www.nps.gov/azru; adult/child 17 & under $4/free; ☺ 8am-5pm, 8am-6pm Jun-Aug) features the largest reconstructed kiva in the country, with an internal diameter of almost 50ft. Let your imagination wander as you sit inside the Great Kiva. During the summer months rangers give early afternoon talks at the c 1100 site about ancient architecture, trade routes and astronomy. They're very informative.

About 35 miles south of Farmington along Hwy 371, the undeveloped **Bisti Badlands & De-Na-Zin Wilderness** is a trippy, surreal landscape of strange, colorful rock formations – it's like stepping onto a science-fiction film set; desert enthusiasts shouldn't miss it. The Farmington **BLM office** (☎ 505-599-8900; 1235 La Plata Hwy; ☺ 9am-5pm Mon-Fri) dispenses information.

SLEEPING & EATING

Silver River Spa Retreat & Adobe B&B (☎ 505-325-8219, 800-382-9251; www.silveradobe.com; 3151 W Main St; r $115) This lovely two-room place offers a peaceful respite among the trees on the San Juan River. Fall asleep to the sound of the river, wake to organic blueberry juice and enjoy a morning walk to the prairie dog village.

Three Rivers Eatery & Brewhouse (☎ 505-324-2187; 101 E Main St; dishes $5-12; ☒) Managing to be both trendy *and* kid-friendly, this hippish place has good food and its own microbrews. Try the homemade potato skins, but keep in mind that the steaks are substantial. Spiffy sandwiches and soups are served at lunchtime.

Chama

Nine miles south of the Colorado border, Chama's **Cumbres & Toltec Scenic Railway** (☎ 505-756-2151, 888-286-2737; www.cumbresandtoltec .com) is both the longest (64 miles) and highest (over the 10,015ft-high Cumbres Pass)

authentic narrow-gauge steam railroad in the US. It's a beautiful trip, particularly in September and October during fall foliage, through mountains, canyons and high desert.

Gandy Dancer B&B (☎ 505-756-2191, 800-424-6702; www.gandydancerbb.com; 299 Maple Ave; r $99-129; ☒) Ensconced in an early 1900s house, this ultra tasteful place offers seven pristine and stylish rooms, an outdoor hot tub and views. The helpful hosts provide information, breakfast, reservations and dinners (November to March) or box lunches on request.

Village Bean (☎ 505-756-1663; 425 Terrace Ave; dishes under $8; ☺ 7am-2:30pm Mon-Fri, 7am-3:30pm Sat & Sun) This lively space offers excellent coffee and tasty baked goods. Lunchtime sandwiches are served with homemade bread; soups and salads are made with equally fine attention.

Chaco Culture National Historic Park

Featuring massive Ancestral Puebloan buildings set in an isolated high-desert environment, intriguing **Chaco** (per vehicle $8; ☺ dawn-dusk) contains evidence of 5000 years of human occupation. At its prime, the community at Chaco Canyon was a major trading and ceremonial hub for the region – and the city the Pueblan people created here was masterful in its layout and design. Pueblo Bonito is four stories tall and may have had 600 to 800 rooms and kivas. Apart from taking the self-guided loop tour, you can hike various **backcountry trails**.

The **visitor center** (☎ 505-786-7014; www.nps.gov /chcu; ☺ 8am-6pm late Jun-early Sep, 8am-5pm early Sep-late Jun) is in a remote area approximately 80 miles south of Farmington. **Gallo Campground** (campsites $10, no RV sites) is 1.5 miles from the visitor center.

NORTHEASTERN NEW MEXICO

East of Santa Fe, the lush Sangre de Cristo Mountains give way to high and vast rolling plains. Dusty grasslands stretch to infinity and further – to Texas. Cattle and dinosaur prints dot the landscape, a land of extremes with formerly fiery volcanoes in Capulin and hot springs in Montezuma (p950). Ranching is an economic mainstay, and on many stretches of the road you'll see more cattle than cars.

The Santa Fe Trail, along which pioneer settlers rolled in wagon trains, ran from New Mexico to Missouri. You can still see the wagon ruts in some places off I-25 between Santa Fe and Raton. If you're looking for a bit of the Old West without a patina of consumer hype, this is the place.

Cimarron

Cimarron was a Wild West town following Anglo settlement; today it's very quiet. If you're driving here to or from Taos, you'll pass through gorgeous **Cimarron Canyon State Park**, a steep-walled canyon with several hiking trails, excellent trout fishing and camping.

A saloon in 1873, the **St James Hotel** (☎ 505-376-2664, 800-748-2694; www.stjamescimarron .com; Hwy 21; historic r $90-120, modern r $60-100) was converted into a hotel in 1880 and renovated 100 years later. It's a toss up between the 14 simple historical rooms or the modern annex, which has 10 rooms equipped with TVs and phones. Within the hotel, you'll find a decent midrange restaurant and a cozy bar with a pool table.

Capulin Volcano National Monument

Rising 1300ft above the surrounding plains, **Capulin** (☎ 505-278-2201; www.nps.gov/cavo; per vehicle $5) is the most accessible of several volcanoes in the area. From the visitor center, a 2-mile road spirals up the mountain to a parking lot at the crater rim (8182ft), where trails lead around and into the crater. The entrance is 3 miles north of the Capulin village, which itself is 30 miles east of Raton on Hwy 87.

SOUTHWESTERN NEW MEXICO

The Rio Grande Valley unfurls from Albuquerque down to the bubbling hot springs of funky Truth or Consequences. Crops, while plentiful, grow on a wing and a prayer. Illegal aliens creep across the border with Mexico on the same wing and prayer. Residents are few and far between, except in lively Las Cruces, the state's second-largest city.

I-10 cuts through the Chihuahua Desert, dominated by yucca and agave. This is ranching country, though the cattle are sparse. North of the desert and west of I-25, the rugged Gila National Forest is wild with backpacking and fishing adventures. The very wildness of Southwestern New Mexico is perhaps its greatest attraction, but the breadth of these attractions may surprise you.

Socorro & Around

Socorro, believe it or not, was for a short time during the 19th century New Mexico's biggest town, thanks to gold and silver mining. Today its Victorian buildings are testament to that brief boom period. The **chamber of commerce** (☎ 505-835-0424; www .socorro-nm.com; 101 Plaza; ☯ 8am-5pm Mon-Fri, 10am-noon Sat) has area information.

At the **Economy Inn** (☎ 505-835-4666; 400 California St NE; r $30-50; ☒), clean and reasonably well-kept rooms have microwaves and small refrigerators.

Martha's Black Dog Coffeehouse (☎ 505-838-0311; 110 Manzanares Ave; dishes under $10) serves tasty coffees and desserts, but don't stop there. Enjoy bountiful breakfast dishes (perhaps a burrito), a vegetarian Mediterranean plate at lunchtime, a complex soup or a healthy green salad.

Endangered whooping cranes winter in the 90 sq miles of fields and marshes at **Bosque del Apache National Wildlife Refuge** (☎ 505-835-1828; admission per vehicle $3; ☯ dawn-dusk), south of Socorro near San Antonio. There's a visitor center and driving tour. Refuge visitors often stop by the **Owl Bar Cafe** (☎ 505-835-9946; 215 San Antonio St; dishes $6-15; ☯ breakfast, lunch & dinner Mon-Sat), 0.5 miles east of I-25 near San Antonio, for acclaimed green chili cheeseburgers.

For those heading west into Arizona from Socorro, Hwy 60 makes a remote, scenic alternative to I-40. Past the town of Magdalena, and 47 miles west of Socorro, is the **Very Large Array** (VLA; 4 miles south of US 60 off Hwy 52; www.vla.nrao.edu; admission free; ☯ 8:30am-dusk) radio telescope facility, a complex of 27 huge antenna dishes sprouting like giant mushrooms in the high plains. To get there, drive 4 miles south of US 60 off Hwy 52.

Truth or Consequences

Built on the site of natural hot springs in the 1880s, this funky little town once known as Hot Springs was renamed Truth or Consequences (or 'T or C') in 1950, after a popular radio program of the same name. Wander around the little hole-in-the-wall cafés, check out the junk shops and definitely take a dip in one of the town's hot spring spas. The **chamber of commerce** (☎ 505-894-3536; www .truthorconsequencesnm.net; 400 W 4th St; ☯ 9am-5pm Mon-Fri, 9am-1pm Sat) has local listings.

Many local motels double as spas. The **Sierra Grande Lodge & Spa** (☎ 505-894-6976;

www.sierragrandelodge.com; 501 McAdoo St; r $105-135; dinner dishes $15-25; 🖳) is an oasis, not a mirage. It's real and refined, and occupies a masterfully renovated 1920s lodge. Guest rooms and suites are luxe and tranquil; mineral bath privileges are included with the room. Spa treatments radiate warmth, as does the contemporary kitchen, which prepares rack of lamb, stuffed free range chicken, and other sophisticated and seasonal dishes. Dinner is served 5pm to 10pm Wednesday to Sunday.

Riverbend Hot Springs (☎ 505-894-6183; 100 Austin St; per person with/without HI or AYH card $18/20, d $36-47, r with kitchenette $62), a riverside hostel, offers dormitory-style accommodations in cabins, trailers and teepees. Hot-spring tubs are available morning and evening, and are free for guests.

Las Cruces & Around

The second-largest city in New Mexico is home to New Mexico State University (NMSU), which keeps things somewhat lively with about 15,000 students. The **Convention & Visitors Bureau** (☎ 505-541-2444, 800-343-7827; www.lascrucescvb.org; 211 N Water St, Las Cruces) has information.

For many, a visit to neighboring **Mesilla** is the highlight of their time in Las Cruces. Wander a few blocks beyond the plaza to gather the essence of a mid-19th-century Southwestern town of Hispanic heritage.

White Sands Missile Test Center Museum (☎ 505-678-2250, 505-678-8824; www.wsmr-history.org; Bldg 200, Headquarters Ave; admission free; ⏱ 8am-4pm Mon-Fri, 10am-3pm Sat & Sun), about 25 miles east of Las Cruces along Hwy 70, has been a major military testing site since 1945. It still serves as an alternate landing site for the space shuttle.

In Las Cruces, **Lundeen Inn of the Arts** (☎ 505-526-3326, 888-526-3326; www.innofthearts.com; 618 S Alameda Blvd; s $58-64, d $75-85, ste incl breakfast $85-105; ✗), a large, turn-of-the-19th-century Mexican territorial-style inn, has 20 guest rooms (all wildly different), an airy living room with soaring ceilings (made of pressed tin) and an art gallery.

Join the university crowd at **Spirit Winds Coffee Bar** (☎ 505-521-1222; 2260 S Locust St; dishes $3-6; ⏱ 7am-8pm Mon-Sat, 10am-6pm Sun) for excellent cappuccino, good sandwiches, salads, soups and pastries. **Nellie's Cafe** (☎ 505-524-9982; 1226 W Hadley Ave; dishes $4-6; ⏱ 8am-4pm Tue-Sat) is the favored local Mexican restaurant. Shoot some pool and down some brews at

Brew Ha Ha (☎ 505-647-3348; 2500 S Valley Dr) or belly up to the bar at **El Patio Restaurante & Cantina** (☎ 505-524-0982), located on the plaza.

Greyhound/TNM&O (☎ 505-524-8518; www.greyhound.com; 490 N Valley Dr) has buses traversing the two interstate corridors (I-10 and I-25), as well as buses to Roswell and beyond.

Silver City & Around

Silver City's downtown streets are dressed with lovely old brick and cast-iron buildings, some Victorian ones, a few adobes and a Wild West air. Billy the Kid spent some of his boyhood here, and a few of his haunts can be seen. Silver is also the gateway to outdoor activities in the Gila National Forest, which is rugged country suitable for remote cross-country skiing, backpacking, camping, fishing and other activities.

The **chamber of commerce** (☎ 505-538-3785, 800-548-9378; www.silvercity.org; 201 N Hudson St; ⏱ 9am-5pm Mon-Sat) publishes a gallery map. **Gila National Forest Ranger Station** (☎ 505-388-8201; www.fs.fed.us/r3/gila; 3005 E Camino De Bosque; ⏱ 8am-4:30pm Mon-Fri) has area information.

Up a winding 42-mile road north of Silver City, the **Gila Cliff Dwellings National Monument** (☎ 505-536-9461; admission $3; ⏱ 8am-5pm summer, 8am-4:30pm rest of year) was occupied in the 13th century by Mogollon Indians. Mysterious, relatively isolated and accessible, these remarkable cliff dwellings look very much like they would have at the turn of the first millennium.

Rounded volcanic towers make up the **City of Rocks State Park** (☎ 505-536-2800; Hwy 61; campsites $10-14), where you can camp among the towers in secluded campsites with tables and fire pits. Head 24 miles northwest of Deming along Hwy 180, then 3 miles northeast on Hwy 61.

Nearby, lovely **Faywood Hot Springs** (☎ 505-536-9663; www.faywood.com; 165 Hwy 61; adult/child per day $12/6, campsites $29-34, cabins $96; ⏱ 10am-10pm) has both public and private pools, as well as camping and private cabins.

For a sliver of Silver City's history, the **Palace Hotel** (☎ 505-388-1811; www.zianet.com /palacehotel; 106 W Broadway; d $38-49, ste $62, incl breakfast; ✗) has 18 rooms and an Internet café. **Diane's Restaurant & Bakery** (☎ 505-538-8722; 510 N Bullard St; lunch dishes $7-11, dinner dishes $18-28; ⏱ lunch & 5-8:30pm Tue-Fri, 9am-2pm Sat & Sun) employs elegant touches like white linens to complement the fine eclectic specialties.

SOUTHEASTERN NEW MEXICO

With the exception of the forests surrounding the resort towns of Cloudcroft and Ruidoso, Southeastern New Mexico is marked by seemingly endless horizons and grassy plains. It's also marked by awesome White Sands National Monument and magnificent Carlsbad Caverns National Park. Spend dusk at both places if you can. It's all here, from the quirky to the diverse: alien sightings in Roswell, Billy the Kid at Fort Sumner and in Lincoln, Smokey Bear and oil rigs the further east you go.

Alamogordo & Around

Despite a dearth of amenities, Alamogordo is the center of one of the most historically important space and atomic research programs in the country. The four-story **New Mexico Museum of Space History** (☎ 505-437-2840, 877-333-6589; www.spacefame.com; Hwy 2001; adult/child 4-12 $2.50/2; ☼ 9am-5pm) has excellent exhibits on space research and flight. Its **Tombaugh IMAX Theater & Planetarium** (adults/children $6/4.50) shows outstanding films on a huge wraparound screen on anything from the Grand Canyon to the dark side of the moon.

Sixteen miles southwest of Alamogordo (15 miles southwest of Hwy 82/70), gypsum covers 275 sq miles to create a dazzling white landscape at crisp, stark **White Sands National Monument** (☎ 505-679-2599; www.nps.gov /whsa; adult/child 16 & under $3/free; ☼ 8am-7pm Jun-Aug, 8am-5pm Sep-May). These captivating windswept dunes are a highlight of any trip to New Mexico. Backcountry campsites, with no water or toilet facilities, are a mile from the scenic drive. Pick up permits (adult/child 16 and under $3/1.50) in person at the visitor center one hour before sunset.

Numerous motels stretch along White Sands Blvd, including **Best Western Desert Aire Motor Inn** (☎ 505-437-2110; www.bestwestern.com; 1021 S White Sands Blvd; r $62-109; ☒), with standard-issue rooms and suites (some with kitchenettes), along with a sauna and whirlpool. The **Plaza Pub** (☎ 505-437-9495; cnr S White Sands Blvd & 10th St; dishes $4-6), a truly local place to kick back, has good burgers and green chili stew.

The **TNM&O/Greyhound Bus Station** (☎ 505-437-3050, 800-231-2222; www.greyhound.com; 601 N White Sands Blvd) has several daily buses to Albuquerque ($38, 4½ hours), Roswell ($25, 2½ hours), Carlsbad ($37, 4½ hours) and El Paso ($22, two hours).

Cloudcroft

Pleasant Cloudcroft, with turn-of-the-19th-century buildings, offers lots of outdoor recreation, a good base for exploration and a low-key feel. Situated high in the mountains, it provides welcome relief from the lowlands heat to the east. The **chamber of commerce** (☎ 505-682-2733; www.cloudcroft.net; ☼ 10am-5pm Mon-Sat) is on Hwy 82.

The **Lodge Resort & Spa** (☎ 505-682-2566, 800-395-6343; www.thelodgeresort.com; 1 Corona Place; r $109-189, pavilion r $99-129, ste $179-319; ☒ 🖳) is one of the Southwest's best historic hotels. Rooms in the main Bavarian-style hotel are furnished with period and Victorian pieces. Within the Lodge, **Rebecca's** (☎ 505-682-3131; breakfast $6-11, lunch $7-17, dinner $18-34; ☼ breakfast, lunch & dinner) offers by far the best food in town.

Ruidoso

You want lively? For these parts? You want Ruidoso. Downright bustling in the summer and big with racetrack bettors, resorty Ruidoso has an utterly pleasant climate thanks to its lofty and forested perch near Sierra Blanca (12,000 ft). It's spread out along Hwy 48 (known as Mechem Dr or Sudderth Dr), the main drag. The **chamber of commerce** (☎ 505-257-7395, 800-253-2255; www .ruidoso.net; 720 Sudderth Dr; ☼ 8:30am-5pm Mon-Thu, 9am-5pm Fri-Sun) gets you oriented.

Serious horse racing happens at the **Ruidoso Downs Racetrack** (☎ 505-378-4431; www .ruidosodownsracing.com; Hwy 70; admission free, grandstand seats & boxes $2.50-$8.50; ☼ races Thu-Sun late May-early Sep, casino 11am-11pm year-round). The fine **Hubbard Museum of the American West** (☎ 505-378-4142, www.hubbardmuseum.org; 841 Hwy 70 W; admission $6; ☼ 9am-5pm) displays more than 10,000 Western-related items, including Old West stagecoaches, saddles and American Indian pottery.

The best ski area south of Albuquerque is **Ski Apache** (☎ 505-336-4356, snow conditions 257-9001; www.skiapache.com; Hwy 48, exit 532; all-day passes adult $49-52, child $31-34; ☼ 8:45am-9pm), 18 miles northwest of Ruidoso on the slopes of beautiful Sierra Blanca Peak (about 12,000ft).

SLEEPING & EATING

Numerous motels, hotels and cute little cabin complexes line the streets.

Ruidoso Lodge Cabins (☎ 505-257-2510, 800-950-2510; www.ruidosolodge.com; 300 Main Rd; cabins $149-159) Attractively set along the river.

Sitzmark Chalet (☎ 505-257-4140, 800-658-9694; www.sitzmark-chalet.com; 627 Sudderth Dr; r $65-105; 🖳 ⊠) Offers 17 simple but nice rooms. The hot tub comes in handy after a day of hiking.

Cornerstone Bakery (☎ 505-257-1842; 359 Audeth Dr; dishes under $8; 🕑 7:30am-2pm) Stay around long enough and this eatery may become your touchstone. Everything on the menu, from omelettes to croissant sandwiches, is worthy.

Casa Blanca (☎ 505-257-2495; 501 Mechem Dr; dinner dishes $6-20) Dine on Southwestern cuisine in a renovated Spanish-style house. The chili rellenos are to die for.

Circle the wagons and ride over to **Flying J Ranch** (☎ 505-336-4330; Hwy 48; adult/child 4-12 $19/10; 🕑 nightly May-Aug, Sat Sep-Oct), about 1.5 miles north of Alto, for a meal. This 'Western village' stages gunfights and offers pony rides with its cowboy-style chuckwagon.

Lincoln & Capitan

Fans of Western history won't want to miss little Lincoln. Twelve miles east of Capitan along the **Billy the Kid National Scenic Byway** (www.billybyway.com), this is where the gun battle that turned Billy the Kid into a legend took place. The whole town is beautifully preserved in close to original form; modern influences (such as neon-lit motel signs, souvenir stands, fast-food joints) are not allowed.

At the **Anderson Freeman Visitors Center & Museum** (☎ 505-653-4025; Hwy 380; admission to 4 sites $6; 🕑 8:30am-4:30pm), exhibits on the Buffalo soldiers, Apaches and the Lincoln County War explain the town's history.

For overnighters, the **Ellis Store Country Inn** (☎ 505-653-4609, 800-653-6460; www.ellisstore.com; MM 98, Hwy 380; r $89-99, r incl breakfast $90-120) offers three antique-filled rooms (complete with wood stove) in the main house; five additional rooms are located in a historic mill on the property. From Thursday to Sunday, the host offers a six-course dinner ($70 per person) served in the lovely and cozy dining room.

Like nearby Lincoln, cozy Capitan is surrounded by the beautiful mountains of **Lincoln National Forest**. The main reason to come is so the kids can visit **Smokey Bear Historical State Park** (☎ 505-354-2748; admission $1; 🕑 9am-5pm), where Smokey (yes, there actually was a real Smokey Bear) is buried.

Fort Sumner State Monument

Use a moment to spare at Fort Sumner. The little village that sprang up around old Fort Sumner gets more than a footnote in the history books for two reasons: the disastrous Bosque Redondo Indian Reservation and Billy the Kid's last showdown with Sheriff Pat Garrett. The area is brimming with Indian and outlaw history. The **monument** (☎ 505-355-2573; www.nmmonuments .org; Hwy 272; admission $1; 🕑 Wed-Mon) interprets the Bosque Redondo tragedy.

Roswell

Conspiracy theorists and *X-Files* fanatics descend from other worlds onto Roswell, which has built a tourist industry around the alleged July 1947 UFO crash. The military quickly closed the area and allowed no more information for several decades (although later they claimed it was a weather balloon). Roswellians, though, have fun with the concept: even the downtown street lights are adorned with alien eyes.

Stop by the **Hispano Chamber & Visitors Bureau** (☎ 505-624-0889, 888-767-9355; www.roswell-usa.com; 426 N Main St; 🕑 8am-5pm Mon-Fri) to get oriented.

Serious followers of UFO phenomena should duck into the **International UFO Museum & Research Center** (☎ 505-625-9495; www .iufomrc.org; 114 N Main St; admission free; 🕑 9am-5pm). Original photographs and witness statements form the 1947 Roswell Incident Timeline explain the great cover-up.

The annual **Roswell UFO Festival** happens over the July 4 weekend; the International UFO Museum & Research Center can supply details.

About 36 miles south of Roswell, **Heritage Inn** (☎ 505-748-2552; www.artesiaheritageinn.com; 209 W Main St, Artesia; r $65-75; 🖳 ⊠) offers 11 Old-West–style rooms and is the nicest lodging in the area. The **Wellhead** (☎ 505-746-0640; 332 W Main St, Artesia; dishes $6-15; 🕑 lunch & dinner Mon-Sat), housed in a 1905 building and decorated with an oil-drilling theme, has the area's best food.

Nuthin' much compares to **Nuthin' Fancy Café** (☎ 505-623-4098; 2103 N Main St; dishes $9-15; 🕑 6am-9pm) for blue plate specials and diner food. In a nod to modern times, it also has an espresso bar and upward of 15 beers on tap.

The **TNM&O/Greyhound Bus Depot** (☎ 505-622-2510; www.greyhound.com; 1100 N Virginia Ave) has daily buses to Carlsbad ($18, 1½ hours),

Albuquerque ($37, four hours) and beyond. From Tuesday to Saturday a bus heads to Santa Fe at 7am ($40, 5¾ hours). Buses also go to El Paso, Texas.

Carlsbad

Travelers use Carlsbad as a base for visits to nearby Carlsbad Caverns National Park and the Guadalupe Mountains (see p760). The **chamber of commerce** (☎ 505-887-6516, 800-221-1224; www.carlsbadchamber.com; 302 S Canal St; 9am-5pm Mon, 8am-5pm Tue-Fri, 9am-3pm Sat May-Sep) has information on both.

On the northwestern outskirts of town, **Living Desert State Park** (☎ 505-887-5516; 1504 Miehls Dr, off Hwy 285; adult/child 7-12 $3/5; 8am-8pm May-Aug, 9am-5pm Sep-Apr) is a great place to see and learn about cacti, coyotes and wildlife. The park has a good 1.3-mile trail that showcases different habitats of the Chihuahuan Desert.

The **Quality Inn** (☎ 505-887-2861; www.quality inncarlsbad.com; 3706 National Parks Hwy; r incl full breakfast $60;) has attractively landscaped grounds, a courtyard patio and hot tub, and live entertainment and dancing in the lounge.

Locals and visitors crowd **Lucy's** (☎ 505-887-7714; 701 S Canal St; dishes under $10; lunch & dinner Tue-Sun) for cheap, tasty New Mexican meals.

TNM&O/Greyhound (☎ 505-887-1108; www.grey hound.com; 1000 Canyon St) buses depart daily for Albuquerque ($45, five hours) and El Paso, Texas ($39 to $41, three hours).

Carlsbad Caverns National Park

Established initially as a national monument in 1923, and as a World Heritage Site in 1995, this truly impressive **national park** (☎ 505-785-2232, 800-967-2283; www.nps.gov /cave; 3225 National Parks Hwy; 8am-5pm, 8am-7pm late May–mid-Aug) covers 73 sq miles and includes almost 100 caves. Visitors can take a 2-mile subterraneous walk from the cave mouth to an underground chamber 1800ft long, 255ft high and over 800ft below the surface.

But wait, there's more. The cave's other claim to fame is the 250,000-plus Mexican free-tail bat colony that roost here from April to October. Visitors flock here at sunset to watch them fly out to feast on a smorgasbord of bugs.

Rocky Mountains

The Rocky Mountain states undulate to their own unique rhythm. The wind's soft whisper, a gushing river's boisterous roar, an elk's bugle, the crunch of footsteps on icy white snow all create a soothing harmony. Supremely beautiful, rugged, wild and free, road trips were invented for states like these. The long meandering kind, where you drift down the byways of Colorado, Wyoming, Montana and Idaho, and get lost in the natural beat. It's a region that humbles and astonishes even the most cynical of skeptics, a soulful place where the Old West's heart still pumps. Big blue skies stretch on forever, roads slip through alpine valleys, past windswept prairies, between lofty snowcapped peaks.

There's an adventure waiting around every turn – be it broncos and bulls at the Cheyenne rodeo, catapulting through the Salmon River's raging rapids, champagne powder skiing at Vail or a blissful night under the stars in the Absaroka Beartooth Wilderness, we guarantee you'll never be bored. And whether you're wandering the streets of big city Denver, barhopping in boisterous Boise or geyser-gawking in Yellowstone, you'll find friendly folks, plenty of sunshine and as much fresh air as you can gulp.

HIGHLIGHTS

- Doing the movie-star glam ski thing in **Aspen** (p986) or **Sun Valley** (p1025)

- Tubing the creek then jiving over microbrews with locals in progressive **Boulder** (p972)

- Hiking past towering peaks in **Rocky Mountain National Park** (p975)

- Savoring the mountain vibes while rocking out to bluegrass in **Telluride** (p993)

- Deciphering the mystery behind ancient cliff dwellings at **Mesa Verde National Park** (p992)

- Viewing gushing geysers and wondrous wildlife in **Yellowstone National Park** (p1004)

- Exploring the **Grand Tetons** (p1007) jagged granite spires

- Living it up in lively **Missoula** (p1016), bursting with outdoor adventures

- Staring into a sublime blue lake in **Glacier National Park** (p1020)

- Going gaga for the views in stunning **Hells Canyon National Recreation Area** (p1027)

HISTORY

Before the late 18th century when French trappers and Spaniards stepped in, the Rocky Mountain area was a land of many tribes, including the Nez Percé, the Shoshone, the Crow, the Lakota and the Utes.

Meriwether Lewis and William Clark claimed their enduring fame after the USA bought almost all of present-day Montana, Wyoming and eastern Colorado in the Louisiana Purchase in 1803. The two explorers set out to survey the land, covering 8000 miles in three years. Their success urged on other adventurers, and soon the migration was in motion. Wagon trains voyaged to the mountainous lands into the 20th century, only temporarily slowed by the completion of the Transcontinental Railroad across southern Wyoming in the late 1860s.

To accommodate settlers, the USA purged the western frontier of the Spanish, British and, in a truly shameful era, most of the Native American population. The government signed endless treaties to defuse Native American objections to increasing settlement, but always reneged and shunted tribes onto smaller reservations. Gold miners' incursions into Native American territory in Montana and the building of US Army forts along the Bozeman Trail ignited a series of wars with the Lakota, Cheyenne, Arapaho and others.

Gold and silver mania preceded Colorado's entry to statehood in 1876. Statehood soon followed for Montana (1889), Wyoming (1890) and Idaho (1890). Along with miners, white farmers and ranchers were the people with power in the late 19th century.

Mining, grazing and timber played major roles in the area's economic development, sparking the growth of cities and towns to provide financial and industrial support. They also subjected the region to boom-and-bust cycles by unsustainable use of resources, and left a legacy of environmental disruption.

After the economy boomed post-WWII, the national parks started attracting vacationers. Tourism is now a leading industry in all four states.

GEOGRAPHY & CLIMATE

While complex, the physical geography of the region divides conveniently into two principal features: the Rocky Mountains

---

TOP FIVE SKI SPOTS

Aspen, CO (p986) A range of mountains for the glitzy and humble, pro and novice.

Crested Butte, CO (p989) So little pretension, such gorgeous slopes.

Jackson Hole, WY (p1009) A vertical rise that will make your jaw drop.

Sun Valley, ID (p1025) Top-of-the class skiing meets celebrity glam.

Vail, CO (p984) One of the world's favorites; offers reams of top terrain.

---

proper and the Great Plains. Extending from Alaska's Brooks Range and Canada's Yukon Territory all the way to Mexico, the Rockies sprawl northwest to southeast, from the steep escarpment of Colorado's Front Range westward to Nevada's Great Basin. Their towering peaks and ridges form the Continental Divide: to the west, waters flow to the Pacific; to the east, toward the Atlantic and the Gulf of Mexico.

For many travelers, the Rockies are a summer destination, and it starts to feel summery around June. The warm weather generally lasts until about mid-September. The winter, which brings in packs of powder hounds, doesn't usually hit until late November, though snowstorms can start in the mountains as early as September. Winter usually lasts until March or early April. In the mountains, the weather is constantly changing (snow in summer is not uncommon), so always be prepared. Fall, when the aspens flaunt their fall gold, or spring, when wildflowers bloom, are wonderful times to visit.

NATIONAL & STATE PARKS

The region is home to some of the USA's biggest national parks. In Colorado there is Rocky Mountain National Park, offering awesome hiking through alpine forests and tundra, and Mesa Verde National Park, primarily an archaeological preserve with elaborate cliffside dwellings.

Wyoming has Grand Teton National Park, with dramatic granite spires, and Yellowstone National Park, the world's first national park, a wonderland of volcanic geysers, hot springs and forested mountains. In Montana you'll find Glacier National Park, with high sedimentary peaks,

www.lonelyplanet.com

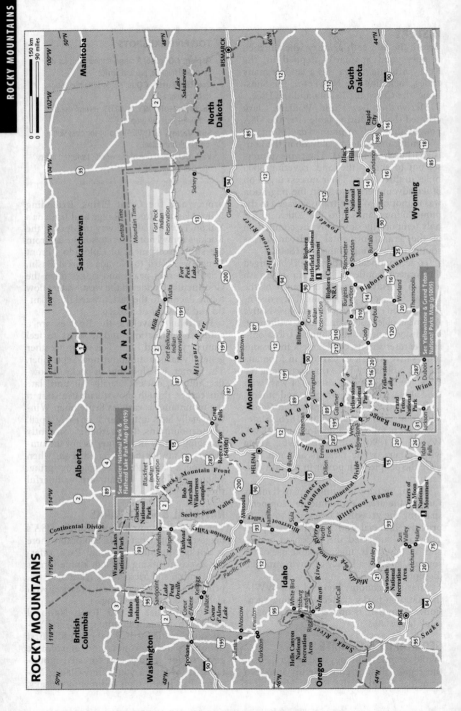

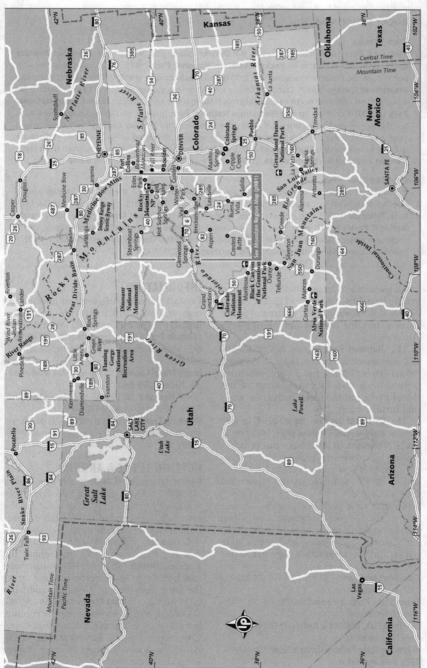

ROCKY MOUNTAINS

ROCKY MOUNTAINS IN...

Two Weeks

Start your Rocky Mountain odyssey in the **Denver** (p966) area. Visit progressively hip **Boulder** (p972) and soak up vistas in **Rocky Mountain National Park** (p975). Next head west on I-70, and play in the mountains around **Vail** (p984) and **Breckenridge** (p982) before visiting charming **Steamboat Springs** (p980). Cross the border into Wyoming, stop in outdoorsy **Lander** (p1003) for a night, then continue north to chic **Jackson Hole** (p1009) and fabulous **Grand Teton National Park** (p1007). Continue on to **Yellowstone National Park** (p1004); you'll need a few more days for this geyser-packed wonderland. Cross the state line into 'big sky country' and slowly make your way northwest through Montana, stopping in funky **Bozeman** (p1012) and lively **Missoula** (p1016) before visiting **Flathead Lake** (p1018). Head west to Idaho. Get your outdoor fix in **Hells Canyon National Recreation Area** (p1027). End your trip in up-and-coming **Boise** (p1023).

One Month

A month will allow you to explore the region in more depth. Follow the itinerary for two weeks, but dip southwest in Colorado before visiting Wyoming. Check out glitzy **Aspen** (p986), laid-back **Telluride** (p993), and unpretentious **Crested Butte** (p989) and **Ouray** (p996). **Mesa Verde National Park's** (p992) eerie ruins and happening **Durango** (p990) should not be missed. Other must-sees include **Glacier National Park** (p1020) and **Bob Marshall Wilderness Complex** (p1020) in Montana, and **Sun Valley** (p1025) and **Ketchum** (p1025) in Idaho.

small glaciers and lots of wildlife, including grizzly bear. Idaho is home to Hells Canyon National Recreation Area, where the Snake River carves the deepest canyon in North America.

The **National Park Service** (NPS; ☎ 303-969-2500; www.nps.gov; Intermountain Region, 12795 Alameda Parkway, Denver, CO 80225) has a comprehensive website with state-by-state listings of national parks, monuments, recreation areas and historic trails.

The **US Forest Service** (☎ 303-275-5350; www.fs.fed.us; Rocky Mountain Regional Office, 740 Simms St, Box 25127 Lakewood, CO 80225) has visitors information on its website. Reserve Forest Service campsites at www.reserveusa.com, or by calling ☎ 877-444-6777. A reservation fee ($9) is charged.

To find state park information, consult one of the following organizations. Also, online camping reservations can be made for Colorado, Wyoming and Idaho state parks, but no reservations are taken for Montana's state parks.

Colorado State Parks (☎ 303-470-1144, 800-678-2267; www.parks.state.co.us)
Idaho State Parks & Recreation (☎ 208-334-4199; www.idahoparks.org)
Montana Fish, Wildlife & Parks (☎ 406-444-2535; www.fwp.state.mt.us)
Wyoming State Parks & Historic Sites (☎ 877-996-7275; www.wyo-park.com)

INFORMATION

Contact the following tourism-information organizations, which provide free state-highway maps and statewide information.

Colorado Travel & Tourism Authority (☎ 800-265-6723; www.colorado.com; PO Box 3524, Englewood, CO 80155)
Idaho Travel Council (☎ 800-635-7820; www.visitid.org; PO Box 83720, Boise, ID 83720)
Travel Montana (☎ 800-847-4868; www.visitmt.com; PO Box 200533, Helena, MT 59620)
Wyoming Travel & Tourism (☎ 800-225-5996; www.wyomingtourism.org; I-25 at College Dr, Cheyenne, WY 82002)

GETTING THERE & AROUND

Denver International Airport (DIA; www.flydenver.com; 8500 Peña Blvd) is the main hub. From here you can fly to the small airports dotting the area. Salt Lake City (p922) also has connections with destinations in all four states.

Greyhound (☎ 800-231-2222; www.greyhound.com) has fixed bus routes throughout the Rockies. **TNM&O** (☎ 719-635-1505; www.greyhound.com) is affiliated with Greyhound, and serves the same lines through Colorado and parts of Wyoming. **Powder River Coach USA** (☎ 800-442-3682) primarily serves eastern Wyoming, but also goes to Denver, Billings and Rapid City, South Dakota. **Rimrock Stages** (☎ 800-255-7655; www.rimrocktrailways.com) also serves Montana destinations.

The following **Amtrak** (☎ 800-872-7245; www
.amtrak.com) services run to and around the
region:

California Zephyr Daily between Emeryville, California
(in San Francisco Bay Area), and Chicago, with six stops in
Colorado, including Denver, Fraser-Winter Park, Glenwood
Springs and Grand Junction.

Empire Builder Daily from Seattle, Washington, or
Portland, Oregon, to Chicago, with 12 stops in Montana
(including Whitefish and East and West Glacier) and one
stop in Idaho at Sandpoint.

Southwest Chief Links Los Angeles and Chicago, with
stops in the southern Colorado towns of Trinidad, La Junta
and Lamar.

The Rockies are vast and public transport
is limited, so it's most convenient to have
your own wheels.

COLORADO

The secret's been out for years now (often
to the dismay of locals) – Colorado's a great
place to live. Once you've visited and experienced its funky mountain charm, it's
pretty hard to say goodbye. And why would
you want to? This is a state that has it all. A
place where lofty snowcapped peaks tumble
into sophisticated cities. Where the air is
always crisp and clean, the sky a sunny blue.
A place where you can spend the morning
in the office, the afternoon on a mountain
bike and the evening sipping creamy microbrews at a cozy bar.

Rich in Wild West history, there's a fascinating story behind every Colorado town.
The plotline is always meaty; the characters
rough-and-tumble miners, gun-totting outlaws, ladies of the night and even visitors
from outer space.

A casual laid-back vibe pervades the
state, and locals pride themselves on having
a great quality of life. Winters are reserved
for skiing; in summer outdoor fiends turn
to fishing, rafting, hiking, biking, or simply placing their inner tube in the closest
stream and letting it rip.

Boasting 54 'fourteeners' (peaks rising
over 14,000ft), the 'Rocky Mountain state'
is blissfully beautiful. And despite the constant influx of people, it never feels crowded.
There's always a remote mountain lake or
craggy summit free to ponder life's riches.
Chic ski towns, such as Aspen and Vail,

draw celebrities and powder hounds alike
to their pristine bowls, designer shops and
glossy picture-perfect mountain ambience.
Ultra-liberal Boulder, located just a stone's
throw from famous Rocky Mountain National Park, attracts hippies, artists, rad-
icals and vacationers to its pleasant outdoor
cafés, brew houses and unique shops. The
southwestern corner of the state is home
to mysterious Mesa Verde National Park,
historic Durango, and other national parks
with sand dunes to climb and dark canyons
to discover.

History
Six bands of Utes once resided in a vast area
stretching between the Yampa and San Juan
Rivers. When white miners entered their
lands, the Utes did not give in so easily. Chief
Ouray (1833–80), remembered for paving
the way to peace between the two parties,
actually had little choice but to eventually
give up most of the Ute territory.

The mining era was launched with the
discovery of gold west of Denver in 1859,
but by the 1870s silver took center stage.
Mountain smelter sites, such as Leadville
and Aspen, turned into thriving population
centers almost overnight.

The state relied heavily on its abundant
natural resources, and the 20th century was
economically topsy-turvy. Tourism, as well
as the high-tech industry, have come to the
rescue and made Colorado the most prosperous of the Rocky Mountain states.

Information
Colorado Road Conditions (☎ 877-315-7623; www
.state.co.us) Highway advisories.

COLORADO FACTS

Nickname Centennial State
Population 4.7 million
Area 104,247 sq miles
Capital city Denver (population 2.6 million)
State insect Colorado Hairstreak Butterfly
Birthplace of Florence Sabin (1871–1953), one
of the first prominent female scientists; Douglas
Fairbanks (1883–1939), star of silent films; Paul
Whiteman (1890–1967), the 'King of Jazz'
Home of Ski slopes, hot springs, bighorn sheep
Famous for Rocky mountain oysters (fried bull's
testicles), microbreweries

ROCKY MOUNTAINS

DENVER IN...

Two Days

Start your day with breakfast at the **Walnut Café** (p970), Denver's favorite morning fuel stop. Spend the rest of the morning wandering the pedestrian-only **16th Street Mall** (p968); don't miss the **Tattered Cover Bookstore** (below). Have lunch at **Pizza Colore** (p970), then head to the unique **Black American West Museum & Heritage Center** (p968). Visit funky **LoDo** (p968) in the early evening for boutique browsing and happy hour at **Cuba Cuba Café & Bar** (p969). Spend the night barhopping around LoDo. On your second day, head out of the city for a few hours and visit the **Coors Brewing Company** (p972) in Golden. Return for happy hour; try **Mynt Lounge** (p970) this time, or see if there's a professional **football** or **baseball game** (p970) playing.

Four Days

Follow the two-day itinerary, then do some more exploring outside city limits. Take a trip to **Idaho Springs** (p972) for hot-spring soaking, or visit ultra-hip **Boulder** (p972), packed with trendy microbreweries, outdoorsy shops and hiking trails. You'll also have time to visit a few more Denver attractions, such as the **Denver Art Museum** (p968). If it's summer, get tickets to see a show at **Red Rock's Park & Amphitheater** (p968) – the acoustics are as good as the views.

Colorado Travel & Tourism Authority (☎ 800-265-6723; www.colorado.com; PO Box 3524, Englewood, CO 80155) Statewide tourism information.

Denver Post (www.denverpost.com) Major newspaper available statewide.

Rocky Mountain News (www.rockymountainnews.com) Major Colorado newspaper.

DENVER

The region's only urban metropolis, the 'Mile High City' is the friendliest of state capitals. Set against a brilliant Rocky Mountain backdrop, Denver effortlessly blends the Old West with cosmopolitan hipness. Top-notch restaurants, grassy city parks, funky boutiques, and bars and clubs for all tastes abound. The city isn't huge by US standards, and is pleasant to explore on foot. It also makes a good regional base.

Orientation

Most of Denver's sights are in the downtown district, which comprises a square defined to the south and east by Colfax Ave and Broadway. The 16th St Mall is the focus of most retail activity, while Lower Downtown ('LoDo'), which includes historic Larimer Sq near Union Station, is the heart of Denver's nightlife scene. To access LoDo and the 16th St Mall exit I-25 at Speer Blvd.

If you're arriving in Denver by bus, you'll be dropped off at Denver Bus Station on 19th St. From here it's an easy walk to the 16th St Mall. Turn right on Curtis St and follow it to 16th St.

Information
BOOKSTORES

Book Garden (☎ 303-399-2004; 2625 E 12th Ave) Books for women, and gay and lesbian readers.

Tattered Cover Bookstore (☎ 303-436-1070; 1628 16th St) Denver's most loved bookstore.

EMERGENCY

In the event of a city-wide emergency, AM radio station 850 KOA is a designated point of information.

Denver Police/Fire/Paramedics Communications Center (☎ 720-913-2000)

Police Headquarters (☎ 720-913-2000; 1331 Cherokee St)

INTERNET ACCESS

Denver Public Library (☎ 720-865-1111; 10 W 14th Ave) Free Internet access.

MEDIA

The mainstream newspapers are the *Denver Post* and the *Rocky Mountain News*. The best source for local events is the free weekly *Westword*. Monthly glossy-mag *5280* has a comprehensive dining guide.

MEDICAL SERVICES

Denver Health Medical Center (☎ 303-436-6000; 777 Bannock St)

University Hospital (☎ 303-399-1211; 4200 E 9th Ave)

MONEY

American Express (☎ 303-383-5050, 800-291-9598; 555 S 17th St)

Wells Fargo Bank (☎ 303-861-8811; 1740 Broadway)

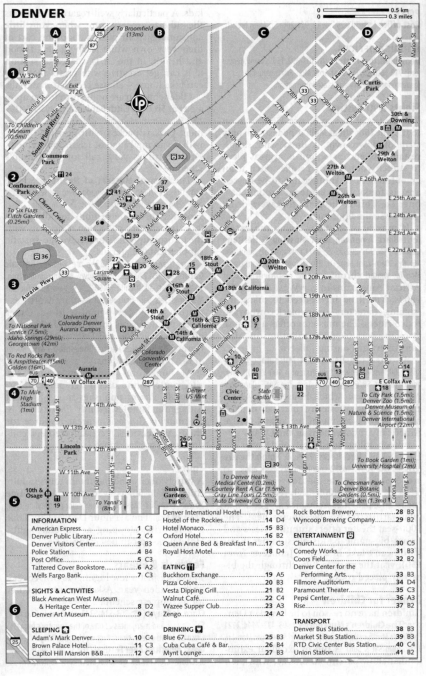

DENVER

POST
Post office (☎ 303-296-4692; 951 20th St) Main branch.

TOURIST OFFICES
Denver visitors center (☎ 303-892-1505; www.denver
.org; 918 16th St; ◷ 9am-5pm Mon-Fri) Invaluable
resource for both city and state information.

Sights & Activities
The best way to experience Denver is on
foot. The **16th Street Mall**, a pedestrian-only
strip of downtown, is lined with shops,
restaurants and bars, and is a great place
to stretch your legs or people-watch from
an outdoor café. Another not-to-be missed
area is funky **LoDo**, centered around Larimer Sq. This is the place to have a drink
or browse the boutiques.

If museums are your thing, the excellent **Black American West Museum & Heritage
Center** (☎ 303-292-2566; 3091 California St; admission
$5; ◷ 10am-2pm Mon-Fri, 10am-5pm Sat & Sun, closed
Mon-Tue winter) chronicles the explorations of
African Americans in the West during the
1800s. You'll be introduced to many intriguing characters – from black cowboys to
rodeo riders. The museum offers a glimpse
at often overlooked contributions of African Americans during this era.

Also try the **Denver Art Museum** (☎ 720-
865-5000; www.denverartmuseum.org; 100 W 14th Ave;
adult/student $8/6; ◷ 10am-5pm Tue-Sat, 10am-9pm
Wed, noon-5pm Sun), which houses fine Asian,
European and Western American departments, as well as one of the largest Native
American art collections in the USA.

Fifteen miles southwest of Denver on
Hwy 93 is **Red Rocks Park & Amphitheatre**
(☎ 303-640-2637; 16352 County Rd 93; park admission
free; ◷ 5am-11pm). The outdoor amphitheatre is set between 400ft-high red sandstone
rocks and provides acoustics so good that
many artists record live albums here. The
9000-seat theater offers stunning views and
draws big-name bands all summer. Even
if you can't take in a show (concerts from
$30), visit the park to hike through the bi-
zarrely placed rocks.

Denver for Children
Children have no reason to be bored in Denver. The **Children's Museum** (☎ 303-433-7444; 2121
Children's Museum Dr; admission $6; ◷ 9am-4pm Mon-Fri,
10am-5pm Sat & Sun) is full of excellent exhibits that allow parents to interact with their

kids. A particularly well-regarded section is
the kid-size grocery store, where your little
consumerists can push a shopping cart of
their very own while learning about food
and health. In the 'Arts à la carte' section
kids can get creative with crafts that they
can take home – all use recycled materials.

Older children are unlikely to frown upon
a day at **Six Flags Elitch Gardens** (☎ 303-595-4386;
2000 Elitch Circle; adult/child $40/22). This amuse-
ment park is packed with nearly 50 rides,
with a varying range of fright inducement.
Opening times vary; call for the season's
schedule.

The **Denver Museum of Nature & Science**
(☎ 303-322-7009; 2001 Colorado Blvd; museum adult/
child $9/6, museum & Imax $13/9; ◷ 9am-5pm) also
provides absorbing exhibits for all ages in
its extraordinary collection. Check in with
the information desk to receive age-specific
supplemental materials.

For greenery, the 23-acre **Denver Botanic
Gardens** (☎ 720-865-3500; www.botanicgardens.org;
1005 York St; adult/child $8.50/5; ◷ 9am-8pm Tue-Sat
May–mid-Sep, 9am-5pm rest of year) are worth exploring with your botanists-to-be. Other
green picnic spaces include **City Park** (home
of the Denver Zoo and Denver Museum of
Nature & Science) and **Cheesman Park**, west
of the Botanic Gardens.

At bookstores and sites around the
city, you can find useful free publications.
Colorado Parent publishes monthly event
listings for families. *Family Phone Book &
Destination Guide* is a great resource for
child-care services, recreation centers, children's classes and more.

Tours
A variety of city and mountain tours (adult/
child $25/12.50) is available with **Gray Line
Tours** (☎ 303-289-2841; www.coloradograyline.com;
3000 E 1st Ave). The 3½-hour Denver City Tour
is a favorite, stopping at popular sights.
Hotel pick-up can be arranged.

Festivals & Events
These are just a few highlights of Denver's
festival-laden year. Ask the visitors center
for a complete schedule.
Cinco de Mayo (☎ 303-534-8342; www.newsed.org)
Salsa music and margaritas at one of the country's biggest
Cinco de Mayo celebrations; first weekend in May.
Great American Beer Festival (☎ 303-447-0816; www
.beertown.org) A whole gamut of brew; early September.

Taste of Colorado (☎ 303-295-6330; www.atasteof colorado.com) More than 50 restaurants cook up their specialties at various food stalls. In addition there's booze, live music, and arts and crafts vendors at this Labor Day festival.

Sleeping

Besides the places mentioned here, there are various chain and independent motels scattered throughout the city with rooms starting at $50. The closest campground is 15 miles north of the city in Broomfield.

BUDGET

Hostel of the Rockies (☎ 303-861-7777; 1530 Downing St; dm from $16, r $40) It's the busiest hostel in town, offering same-sex dorms that are slightly spacious, with just four beds to a room. A free, basic breakfast is available daily.

Denver International Hostel (☎ 303-832-9996; www.youthhostels.com; 630 E 16th Ave; dm $9) With the cheapest beds in town, this hostel offers very fine value. The same-sex rooms are a little cramped but cheerful, and there are rarely more than five people in a dorm.

Royal Host Motel (☎ 303-831-7200; 930 E Colfax Ave; r $50; (P) (X)) A little run-down and slightly sleazy, but quite secure, and near a popular music venue and bar strip. Some rooms don't have a phone, so request one if needed.

MIDRANGE

Queen Anne Bed & Breakfast Inn (☎ 303-296-6666; www.queenannebnb.com; 2147 Tremont Pl; r from $90; (P) (X) (X)) In two late-1800s Victorian houses, this romantic B&B is a great choice. Chamber music plays softly in the public areas, and fresh flowers abound. Rooms are decorated with period antiques, and some boast fantastic hand-painted murals. Rates include a full breakfast and evening wine tasting.

Capitol Hill Mansion B&B (☎ 303-839-5221; www.capitolhillmansion.com; 1207 Pennsylvania St; r from $95; (P) (X) (X)) Stained-glass windows, original 1890s woodwork and turrets all make this Romanesque mansion a special place to stay. Rooms are elegant, uniquely decorated and not-too-frilly. Some of the special features, which vary by room, include a solarium, a canopy bed and whirlpool tubs. The included breakfast is sumptuous; there's evening wine and refreshments.

Oxford Hotel (☎ 303-628-5400; www.theoxford hotel.com; 1600 17th St; r from $135; (P) (X)) In a sim-

ple red sandstone building, this classy hotel exudes elegance. Marble walls, stained-glass windows, frescos and sparkling chandeliers adorn the public spaces. Rooms are large and decked out with imported English and French antiques. The Art Deco Cruise Room Bar is one of Denver's swankiest cocktail lounges. Hotel parking is $21.

Adam's Mark Denver (☎ 303-893-3333; www .adamsmark.com; 1550 Court Pl; r Sun-Thu from $80, Fri & Sat $120; (P) (X) (X)) This huge hotel boasts a great downtown location and amenities, such as a fitness room and sauna. It's well set up for business travelers, though others can reap the rewards of discounted weekends. Parking ranges from $15 to $22.

TOP END

Brown Palace Hotel (☎ 303-297-3111; www.brown palace.com; 321 17th St; r from $235; (P) (X)) This distinguished historic landmark is *the* place to stay in Denver. Within walking distance of restaurants and nightlife, the Brown Palace is elegantly decorated and provides old-world atmosphere and excellent service. It has hosted everyone over the years – from the Beatles to Winston Churchill. Hotel parking is $22.

Eating

Denver has restaurants for all tastes and budgets. Cheap street meals can be found on the 16th St Mall.

Cuba Cuba Café & Bar (☎ 303-605-2882; 1173 Delaware St; dishes $10-20; (✸) lunch & dinner) We get dreamy just thinking about the mango

---

THE AUTHOR'S CHOICE

Hotel Monaco (☎ 303-296-1717; www.monaco -denver.com; 1717 Champa St; r from $210; (P) (X)) Hip and ultra-stylish, this boutique gem features Art Deco and French designs. The modern rooms have bold color schemes and feather beds. It's a favorite with the Hollywood set, and many celebrities stay here when in town. A unique perk is the evening 'Altitude Adjustment Hour,' when guests enjoy free wine and five-minute massages. One hundred percent pet friendly, staff will even deliver a named goldfish to your room upon request. Discounts are routinely offered and parking costs from $7 to $21.

THE AUTHOR'S CHOICE

Yanni's (☎ 303-692-0404; 2225 S Monaco Pkwy; dishes $11-20; ☽ lunch & dinner) Flavors explode in your mouth, and you won't be able to put your fork down at this atmospheric Greek restaurant with generous portions. As if that's not enough, the owner comes by frequently with complimentary Ouzo shots. It's well worth the effort it takes to reach this family-run south Denver restaurant.

---

mojito at this swanky Cuban joint serving finger-lickin' BBQ spareribs, flavor-packed fried yucca and a sumptuous coconut-crusted tuna. The back patio offers fantastic sunset city views; the bright blue-walled environs emit an island vibe.

Zengo (☎ 720-904-0965; 1610 Little Raven St; dishes $20; ☽ dinner) From Kobe beef on a seared stone to a concoction of tuna, mint, lime, papaya and coconut known as Bangkok ceviche, this elegant fusion restaurant really delivers. Dishes are innovative, service is attentive and the decadent cocktails are potent.

Pizza Colore (☎ 303-534-6884; 1512 Larimer St; dishes from $6; ☽ lunch & dinner) Big portions of inexpensive pasta and wood-oven pizzas are served at this casual Italian restaurant. The food is delicious (especially considering the price). There's ample outdoor seating if the weather cooperates.

Vesta Dipping Grill (☎ 303-296-1970; 1822 Blake St; mains $15-25; ☽ dinner) Pick a type of meat, then choose from 30 different sauces to dip it into. It's a simple concept that works exceedingly well. The melt-in-your mouth quality of the creative dishes – many Asian inspired – makes Vesta one of Denver's favorite restaurants. The atmosphere is relaxed yet funky.

Buckhorn Exchange (☎ 303-534-9505; 1000 Osage St; dishes from $18) Meat-lovers will dig the Buckhorn's eclectic offerings – from rattlesnake to alligator tails to buffalo prime rib. Steaks are big and juicy, and you can start your meal with a platter of Rocky Mountain oysters (fried bull's testicle – it's a Colorado thing). The upstairs saloon has been serving booze for more than 140 years and is perfect for a predinner cocktail.

Wazee Supper Club (☎ 303-623-9518; 1600 15th St; dishes $7-9, pizza $10-18) Once you step into Wazee,

there's little chance you'll turn around – it smells that delicious. Known for some of the best pizza in the city, this longtime local favorite is a friendly, buzzing place.

Walnut Café (☎ 303-832-5108; 338 E Colfax Ave; dishes $5-7; ☽ breakfast & lunch) This is *the* breakfast spot in the 'hood,' with a diverse range of offerings, from American standards such as waffles and egg variations to breakfast burritos; healthy lunches are also served. Get here early, or be patient.

Drinking

Most bars and nightspots are in LoDo, though you'll also find action on the grittier E Colfax Ave, east of the State Capitol. The biweekly gay newspaper *Out Front,* found in coffee shops and bars, has entertainment listings.

Mynt Lounge (☎ 303-825-6968; 1424 Market St) This offers one of the best happy hours in town – from 3pm to 9pm the martinis are just $3, and there is a massive list to choose from. Mynt is an ultra-swank white-themed minimalist lounge with a very sexy vibe.

Wyncoop Brewing Company (☎ 303-297-2700; 1634 18th St) The big Wyncoop is arguably the city's most rocking brewery. It offers an interesting selection of beers. There are more than 20 pool tables upstairs.

Rock Bottom Brewery (☎ 303-534-7616; 1001 16th St) This place has people-packed booths, a bustling bar, sports-screening TVs and an outdoor patio prime for sunny afternoons with a pitcher.

Blue 67 (☎ 303-260-7505; 1475 Lawrence St) The true-blue draw at this suave bar and restaurant is the drink – it offers more than 60 styles of martini. Flavors include chocolate, strawberry, Japanese pear and a token 'cowboy martini.' Live jazz plays nightly from about 9:30pm.

Entertainment

To find out what's happening with music, theater and other performing arts, pick up a free copy of *Westword*. In town, the main venues for national acts are **Paramount Theater** (☎ 303-534-8336; 1621 Glenarm Pl) and **Fillmore Auditorium** (☎ 303-837-0360; 1510 Clarkson St).

Rise (☎ 303-383-1909; 1909 Blake St; cover $10) One of Denver's hottest clubs, the music changes nightly. Downstairs the atmosphere is trippy light show, and go-go dancers, scantily clad waitresses and Chinese pole dancers. Upstairs it's more sedate with a tranquil lounge and outdoor palm-lined patio. Locals say Rise is one of Denver's best spots for singles.

Church (☎ 303-832-3538; 1160 Lincoln St; cover $10) There's nothing like ordering a stiff drink inside an old cathedral. Yes, this club, which draws a large and diverse crowd, is in a former house of the Lord. There are three dance floors, a couple of lounges and even a sushi bar! Arrive before 10pm Friday through Sunday to avoid the cover charge. On Thursday the club opens its doors to the 18-plus crowd.

Denver Center for the Performing Arts (☎ 303-893-4100; www.denvercenter.org; 1245 Champa St) Occupying four city blocks, this complex is the world's second-largest performing-arts center. It hosts resident Colorado Symphony Orchestra, Opera Colorado, Denver Center Theater Company, Colorado Ballet and touring Broadway shows.

Comedy Works (☎ 303-595-3637; www.comedyworks .com; 1226 15th St) For some merriment, head to this top-rated comedy club, which snickers and snorts with world-class stand-up acts.

Denver is a city known for manic sports fans and boasts five pro teams. The **Colorado Rockies** (☎ 303-762-5437) play baseball at the highly rated **Coors Field** (2001 Blake St). The **Pepsi Center** (☎ 303-405-1111; 1000 Chopper Pl) hosts the Denver Nuggets basketball team and the Colorado Avalanche hockey team. The much-lauded **Denver Broncos football team** (☎ 720-258-3333) and the **Colorado Rapids soccer team** (☎ 303-299-1599) play at **Mile High Stadium** (☎ 720-258-3000; 1805 S Bryant St), 1 mile west of downtown.

Getting There & Away
AIR
The **Denver International Airport** (DIA; www.fly denver.com; 8500 Peña Blvd) is served by around 20 airlines and offers flights to nearly every major US city. Located 24 miles east of downtown, DIA is connected with I-70 exit 238 by the 12-mile-long Peña Blvd.

Tourist and airport information is available at a **booth** (☎ 303-342-2000) in the terminal's central hall.

BUS
Greyhound buses stop at the **Denver Bus Station** (☎ 303-293-6555; 1055 19th St), which runs services to Cheyenne ($19, three hours) and

Billings ($95, 14 hours). **Powder River Coach USA** (☎ 800-442-3682) and **TNM&O** (☎ 806-763-5389) also stop here.

TRAIN
Amtrak's *California Zephyr* runs daily between Chicago and San Francisco via Denver. Trains arrive and depart from **Union Station** (☎ 303-825-2583; 17th & Wynkoop Sts). For recorded information on arrival and departure times, call ☎ 303-534-2812. **Amtrak** (☎ 800-872-7245) can also provide schedule information and train reservations.

Denver's **Ski Train** (☎ 303-296-4754; www.skitrain .com) to Winter Park operates on weekends throughout the ski season, as well as in July and August. Same-day round-trip tickets cost $45; discounted tickets for children ($20) are available for Sunday trips only.

Getting Around
TO/FROM THE AIRPORT
All transportation companies have booths near the baggage-claim area. **Public Regional Transit District** (RTD; ☎ 303-299-6000; www.rtd -denver.com) buses runs a SkyRide service to the airport from downtown Denver hourly ($8, one hour). RTD also goes to Boulder ($10, 1½ hours) from the Market St Bus Station. Taxis to downtown Denver charge a flat $45, excluding tip. **Super Shuttle** (☎ 303-370-1300, 800-258-3826) offers van services (from $18) from downtown Denver and around to the airport, and vice versa.

CAR & MOTORCYCLE
Street parking can be a pain, but there are slews of pay garages in downtown and LoDo. Nearly all the major car-rental firms have counters at DIA, though a few have offices in downtown Denver; check the *Yellow Pages*.

For those lacking a credit card, **A-Courtesy Rent A Car** (☎ 303-733-2218; 270 S Broadway; ⌚ 7:30am-5pm Mon-Fri) accepts cash deposits, but the vehicles cannot be driven outside the state.

PUBLIC TRANSPORTATION
RTD provides public transportation throughout the Denver and Boulder area. Local buses cost $1.15 for local services, $2.50 for express services. Useful free shuttle buses run along the 16th St Mall.

RTD also operates a light-rail line serving 16 stations on a 12-mile route through downtown. Fares are the same as for local buses.

ROCKY MOUNTAINS

TAXI

For 24-hour cab service, call:
Freedom Cab (☎ 303-292-8900)
Metro Taxi (☎ 303-333-3333)
Yellow Cab (☎ 303-777-7777)

AROUND DENVER
Golden

The masses descend upon Golden, a city with a small historic district and a few engaging sites, to tour the **Coors Brewing Company** (☎ 303-277-2337; cnr 13th & Ford Sts; admission free). Visiting the vat-laden facilities is a bit like volunteering to step into a Coors ad, but there are free samples (three glasses worth!) at the end. Tours are held from 10am to 4pm Monday to Saturday. Kids and train-spotters will get a better buzz from the **Colorado Railroad Museum** (☎ 303-279-4591; 17155 W 44th Ave; adult/child $6/3; ⊙ 9am-5pm), with its 50 locomotives and train cars on display.

About 5 miles west of Golden, **Lookout Mountain Park**, the gateway to the Denver Mountain Parks system, has – no surprise – great views. Fun **mountain-bike trails** are in Matthews/Winters Park, south of I-70 along Hwy 26, and the White Ranch Open Space Park, a few miles north of town.

The **Golden Visitors Center** (☎ 303-279-3113; www.goldencochamber.org; 1010 Washington Ave; ⊙ 8:30am-5pm Mon-Fri, 10am-4pm Sat & Sun) has the lowdown on sites and accommodations.

RTD (☎ 303-299-6000; www.rtd-denver.com) bus Nos 14, 16 and 16L run between Golden, from the corner of Washington and 10th Sts, and downtown Denver (corner of California and 15th Sts).

Idaho Springs & Georgetown

Nestled into steep mountain walls, these two small towns west of Denver along I-70 have a historical air born from their 19th-century mining pasts. Idaho Springs and Georgetown sit pretty with antique shops, galleries and restaurants against the dramatic backdrop of the rising Rockies. Relaxation is for sale at the inviting **Indian Springs Resort** (☎ 303-989-6666; www.indianspringsresort.com; 302 Soda Creek Rd; campsites $18, r $55-95) in Idaho Springs. The resort has indoor and outdoor private baths (per hour $15), a geothermal vapor cave with soaking pools ($15), a covered swimming pool ($10) and mud baths in 'Club Mud' ($10).

Late May to mid-September, drive to the 14,264ft summit of **Mount Evans** via the Mt Evans Hwy, off I-70 exit 240 at Idaho Springs. Near the exit, the **USFS Clear Creek Ranger Station** (☎ 303-567-3000; ⊙ 8am-5:30pm) has information on campgrounds.

FRONT RANGE

The front range of the Rockies stretches from Colorado Springs north to Fort Collins along I-25 and includes a stretch of cities and towns, many little more than satellite communities of Denver. We've included a few places west of the interstate – such as Rocky Mountain National Park and Cripple Creek – because they are easy day trips from Front Range cities.

Boulder

Rebellious Boulder revels in its liberalism, and residents are quick to say they live in the 'People's Republic of Boulder.' Always good for a national controversy or two – from football recruiting sex scandals to freedom of speech – Boulderites are forward-thinking individualists with an ongoing love affair for the outdoors. The main roads are always packed with mountain bikers, the endless city parks bustling with hikers. A mix of hippies, well-heeled young professionals and hard-drinking college kids (the 30,000-student strong University of Colorado is here – with a reputation of party, party, party) all give the city its unique vibe. Hang out on the pedestrian-only Pearl St Mall – packed with boutiques, restaurants and bars, bars, bars – and catch a street performance. Down a pint or two at one of the microbreweries or pick up a six-pack and tube down the Boulder Creek on a summer day.

ORIENTATION

Boulder's two areas to see and be seen are the downtown Pearl St Mall and the University Hill district (next to campus), both off Broadway. Overlooking the city from the west are the Flatirons, an eye-catching rock formation. Boulder is north of Denver. From I-25 exit at Hwy 36 (it's a left-hand exit) and follow this road for about 20 miles into town.

INFORMATION

Boulder Bookstore (☎ 303-447-2074; 1107 Pearl St) Large selection of travel guides and recent fiction.
Boulder Visitors Center (☎ 303-442-2911; www.boul dercoloradousa.com; 2440 Pearl St; ⊙ 8:30am-5pm Mon-Thu, 8:30am-4pm Fri) Offers information and Internet access.

SCENIC DRIVE – PEAK TO PEAK HIGHWAY

Stretching some 40 miles between Nederland and Estes Park, this route takes you past a series of breathtaking mountains, including the 14,255ft Long's Peak, lush valleys and grassy meadows. You can break up the ride by stopping at one of the little towns along the way. Our favorite is Ward. Just opposite the turnoff for Ward is a road leading up to Brainard Lake. The lake itself is tiny, but in a gorgeous setting and there are some great hiking trails leading from it. Afterwards stop in at the Millsite Inn, just north of the turnoff. On sunny fall days it's packed with colorful characters, and features greasy hamburgers and dripping cold microbrews in an old crumbling wooden structure with a creaky porch. To reach the Peak To Peak Hwy from Boulder drive west on Hwy 119 until you reach Nederland, then take Hwy 72. Allow between three and five hours.

SIGHTS & ACTIVITIES

Shop, hike, bike and drink until you drop. The main feature of downtown Boulder is the **Pearl Street Mall**, a vibrant pedestrian zone filled with bars, galleries and restaurants.

Head west on Arapahoe Ave until it dead-ends into Eben G Fine Park. Here you'll find Boulder Creek. In the summer everyone buys tubes at the **Conoco Gas Station** (☎ 303-442-6293; 1201 Arapahoe Ave; tubes $14) and floats down the creek – it just might be the best urban do-it-yourself float trip in the country! The rapids are mild to slightly wild – there's a few small waterfalls sure to flip your tube, and there are good swimming holes. Cross over the bridge in the park and follow one of the numerous hiking trails for high-above-the-city views and red rock scrambles.

From the popular Chautauqua Park, at the west end of Baseline Rd, **hiking** trails head in many directions, including up to the Flatirons. Other nice hikes head up Gregory Canyon and Flagstaff Mountain. The easy Mesa Trail runs north 7 miles from Chautauqua to Eldorado Canyon and offers access to more difficult routes, such as Shadow Canyon, Fern Canyon and Bear Canyon, which leads up to Bear Peak (8461ft).

The 16-mile Boulder Creek Trail is the main cycling route in town and leads west on an unpaved streamside path to Four Mile Canyon. Challenge-seekers can also ride 4 miles up Flagstaff Rd to the top of Flagstaff Mountain. Bike rentals, maps and information are available from **University Bicycles** (☎ 303-444-4196; 839 Pearl St) and **Full Cycle** (☎ 303-440-7771; 1211 13th St).

Eldorado Canyon State Park (☎ 303-494-3943; visitors center ⊙ 9am-5pm) is one of the country's most favored rock-climbing areas, offering Class 5.5 to 5.12 climbs. The park entrance is on Eldorado Springs Dr, west of Hwy 93.

Information is available from **Boulder Rock Club** (☎ 303-447-2804; 2829 Mapleton Ave).

In winter city buses leave from the corner of 14th and Walnut Sts (round-trip $7) and take you to **Eldora Mountain Resort** (☎ 303-440-8700; www.eldora.com; Hwy 130; lift ticket $50), where you can spend the day skiing and snowboarding on decent terrain – it's not as big as some of Colorado's resorts, but it's cheaper.

SLEEPING

Boulder has numerous lodging options, although most are on the pricey side.

Hotel Boulderado (☎ 303-442-4344, 800-433-4344; www.boulderado.com; 2115 13th St; r winter/summer from $120/170; ❉) The charming Boulderado is in an exquisitely restored 1909 brick building with antique-furnished digs. Choose from small but quaint historic rooms or more spacious, wheelchair-friendly, modern abodes.

Boulder Victoria (☎ 303-938-1300; 1305 Pine St; r from $150; ❌) Just minutes' walk from the Pearl St Mall, rooms at this elegant B&B feature antiques, brass beds, down comforters and fabulous wallpaper. The manicured, flower-filled grounds are perfect for strolling. No children under 12.

Boulder Outlook Hotel & Suites (☎ 303-443-3322; www.boulderoutlook.com; 800 28th St; r $90; ❉ ▣) This unique hotel with a funky paint job has a fitting motto: 'cure for the common hotel.' There's a large indoor pool with rocks for scrambling and a Jacuzzi. Rooms are big and modern.

Boulder International Youth Hostel (☎ 303-442-0522; www.boulderhostel.com; 1107 12th St; dm $17, s/d with shared bathroom $39/45; ▣) Near all the action on University Hill, this tidy place has the town's cheapest accommodation, and boasts a kitchen and laundry facilities. There's a three-day limit on the dorms, and room rates are reduced after the first night.

ROCKY MOUNTAINS

Boulder Mountain Lodge (☎ 303-444-0882; www .bouldermountainlodge.com; 91 Four Mile Canyon Rd; campsites $14, r winter/summer from $60/70; 🖫 🖫) Set in a shady canyon, 4 miles west of Boulder on Hwy 119, this lodge is gorgeously placed amid pines and cottonwood trees. It offers shady camping, as well as clean, motel-style rooms.

Foot of the Mountain Motel (☎ 303-442-5688; www.footofthemountainmotel.com; 200 Arapahoe Ave; r winter/summer from $60/70; 🖫) For both remoteness and convenience to the city, this attractive motel may be ideal. Near the entrance to Boulder Mountain Park, it has cozy wood-paneled rooms.

EATING

Boulder has all sorts of restaurants, many as fine as those you'd find in a big city. If you're on a budget, eat during happy hour. Many restaurants feature these between 3pm and 6pm when everything – from appetizers to burgers – is on bargain-basement sale.

Bacaro Ristorante (☎ 303-444-4888; 921 Pearl St; dishes $8-20; 🕑 lunch & dinner) This oft-packed, classy Italian joint does dirt-cheap tapas during its 4pm to 7pm daily happy hour (the best deal in town). Dinner mains, especially seafood, pasta and very reasonably priced personal pizzas (from $6, big enough for two), are mouthwatering. Sidewalk seating and a rooftop bar are pluses. Late night, Bacaro turns into a pumping dance club.

Sherpa's Adventurers Restaurant & Bar (☎ 303-440-7151; 825 Walnut St; dishes $3-13; 🕑 lunch & dinner) Part restaurant, part travel adventure center, this place, run by a Nepalese sherpa, has a large menu consisting of bits of Tibet, portions of Nepal and a few pinches of India. Plates are enormous – the saag appetizer ($5) alone can make a meal.

Lucille's Creole Cafe (☎ 303-442-4743; 2142 14th St; dishes $4-8; 🕑 breakfast & lunch) Boulder's favorite breakfast spot – lines form early, but the wait is worth it. There's a Creole lunch menu, but everyone orders breakfast. Try the Eggs Sardou ($7) or the daily special.

Boulder Dushanbe Teahouse (☎ 303-442-4993; 1770 13th St; dishes $8-14; 🕑 breakfast, lunch & dinner) Incredible Tajik craftsmanship envelops the phenomenal interior of this teahouse presented by Boulder's Russian sister city, Dushanbe. The international fare ranges from Amazonian to Mediterranean to, of course, Tajik.

Mediterranean Restaurant (☎ 303-444-5355; 1002 Walnut St; dishes from $12; 🕑 lunch & dinner) The best all-round restaurant in town, 'The Med' offers a varied European-influenced menu – from tapas to flavor-packed pasta. The wine list is long, the cocktails delicious, the atmosphere cozy.

Rio Grande (☎ 303-444-3690; 1101 Walnut St; dishes $8-15; 🕑 lunch & dinner) Tex Mex favorites are devoured by hungry hordes nightly (expect lengthy weekend waits at this perennial favorite). The margaritas are potent, the beef fajitas superb. Always loud and chaotic, the Rio appeals to first-date couples and large families alike.

Mountain Sun Pub & Brewery (☎ 303-546-0886; 1535 Pearl St; dishes $6-9; 🕑 lunch & dinner) A rainbow of brews is available in this tapestry-lined pub, including fruity beers. The place manages to feel relaxed even when busy with its usual eclectic mix of students and locals. The burgers are large and juicy.

DRINKING

Boulder likes to party, and there are plenty of bars to keep you lubricated well through the night.

Pearl Street Pub (☎ 303-939-9900; 1108 Pearl St) Sorrows are drowned by multiple pints at the scarred wooden bar upstairs, where the vibe is shabby chic meets Old West. Downstairs, 20-something locals pound shots by the pool tables, soaking up the smoky, beer-drenched atmosphere. Boulder's favorite trendy dive.

Reef Piano Bar & Grill (☎ 303-209-3740; 1801 13th St) This super trendy piano bar is one of Boulder's hottest nightspots, the kind of place where dress-to-impress locals strut their stuff on the dance floor to the tunes of the dueling pianos.

Catacombs Bar (☎ 303-443-0486; 2115 13th St) One of the few places in Boulder where you can have a cigarette with your drink (the town has a no-smoking ordinance in bars and restaurants), it's full of young college kids looking to get rowdy and hook up, and there are daily, very cheap, happy hours.

GETTING THERE & AROUND

Frequent bus service is available with **RTD** (☎ 303-299-6000; www.rtd-denver.com) both in and around Boulder ($1.25); maps are available at **Boulder Station** (14th & Walnut Sts). RTD buses (route B) operate between Boulder Station and Denver's Market St Bus Station ($3.50, one hour). RTD's SkyRide bus (route AB) heads to Denver International Airport ($10, 1½ hours, hourly). **Super Shuttle** (☎ 303-444-0808) provides hotel ($19) and door-to-door ($25) shuttle service from the airport.

Rocky Mountain National Park

Teeming with stunning natural beauty, from towering peaks to wide-open alpine tundra, a visit to Rocky Mountain National Park is a Colorado must-do. It's so alluring, in fact, that more than three million visitors mosey in annually. Breathe in crisp mountain air, hike through grassy meadows or between snowcapped peaks, and keep an eye out for elk, bighorn sheep, moose, marmots and bear. Most visitors stay near **Trail Ridge Road** (last Mon in May–mid-Oct), which winds through spectacular alpine tundra environments. Those who prefer communing with nonhuman nature should venture on foot away from the road corridor; the reward is quiet, superlative scenery.

Late-19th-century hotel and road construction in the settlement of Estes Park prompted naturalist Enos Mills to campaign in 1909 to protect the area. He faced opposition from private grazing and timber interests, but in early 1915 Congress approved the bill creating Rocky Mountain National Park.

ORIENTATION

Trail Ridge Rd (US 34) is the only east–west route through the park; the US 34 eastern approach from I-25 and Loveland follows the Big Thompson River Canyon. The most direct route from Boulder follows US 36 through Lyons to the east entrances. Another approach from the south, mountainous Hwy 7, provides access to campsites and trailheads (including Longs Peak) on the east side of the Continental Divide. Winter closure of US 34 through the park makes access to the west side dependent on US 40 at Granby.

Two entrance stations are on the east side: at Fall River (US 34) and Beaver Meadows (US 36). The Grand Lake Station (US 34) is the sole entry on the west side.

INFORMATION

Three of the park's five visitors centers are actually outside the park's entrances.
Beaver Meadows visitors center/Park Headquarters (☎ 970-586-1206; US 36; ☺ 8am-6pm Jun-Aug, 8am-5pm rest of year)

Kawuneeche visitors center (☎ 970-627-3471; US 34; ☺ 8am-5:30pm Jun-Aug, 8am-4:30pm rest of year) A mile north of Grand Lake.
Lily Lake visitors center (☎ 970-586-5128; Hwy 7; ☺ 9am-4:30pm May-Nov) South of Estes Park.

Within the park are **Fall River visitors center** (☎ 970-586-1415; ☺ 9am-5pm Jun-Aug, Sat & Sun Sep-May) and **Alpine visitors center** (☎ 970-586-8881; ☺ 10:30am-4:30pm May-Oct).

Entry to the park (vehicles $15, hikers and cyclists $5) is valid for seven days. Backcountry permits ($15) are required for overnight trips. The **Backcountry Office** (☎ 970-586-1242; Rocky Mountain National Park, Estes Park, CO 80517; ☺ 7am-7pm) is east of the Park Headquarters. Reservations can be made by mail or in person from March to the end of December, or by phone from March to mid-May and November to April.

ACTIVITIES

The bustling Bear Lake Trailhead offers easy **hikes** to several lakes and beyond. Another busy area is Glacier Gorge Junction Trailhead. The free Glacier Basin–Bear Lake shuttle services both.

Forested Fern Lake, 4 miles from the Moraine Park Trailhead, is dominated by craggy Notchtop Peak. You can complete a loop to the Bear Lake shuttle stop in about 8.5 miles for a rewarding day hike, or head into the upper fern creek drainage to explore the backcountry. The strenuous **Flattop Mountain Trail** is the only cross-park trail, linking Bear Creek on the east side with either Tonahutu Creek Trail or the North Inlet Trail on the west side.

Families might consider the moderate hikes to **Calypso Cascades** in the Wild Basin or to **Gem Lake** in the Lumpy Ridge area.

One of the easiest peak climbs in the area is the 1.5-mile trail up **Lily Mountain** (great views), 6 miles south of Estes Park on Hwy 7. At the other extreme is the strenuous hike to the 14,255ft summit of **Longs Peak**, which usually doesn't open till July. An easier option near here is the hike to Chasm Lake (11,800ft).

Trail Ridge Rd crosses the Continental Divide at **Milner Pass** (10,759ft), where trails head 4 miles (and up 2000ft!) southeast to Mt Ida, which offers fantastic views.

Trails on the west side of the park are quieter and less trodden than those on the

ROCKY MOUNTAINS

east side. Try the short and easy East Inlet Trail to **Adams Falls** (0.3 miles) or the more moderate 3.7-mile Colorado River Trail to the **Lulu City** site.

Before July, many of the trails are snowbound, and high water runoff makes passage difficult.

All **cycling** is restricted to paved surfaces, such as Trail Ridge Rd and the Horseshoe Park/Estes Park Loop. The only exception is the 9-mile, 3000ft climb up Fall River Rd (head back down on Trail Ridge Rd).

On the east side, the Bear Lake and Glacier Gorge Junction Trailheads offer good routes for **cross-country skiing** and **snowshoeing**. **Backcountry skiing** is also possible; check with the visitors centers.

SLEEPING

The only overnight accommodations in the park are at campgrounds; the majority of motel or hotel accommodations are around Estes Park (right) or Grand Lake (opposite).

The park has five formal campgrounds. All have a seven-day limit during summer; all but Longs Peak take RVs (no hookups). Fees are $18 ($10 in winter, when the water supply is off).

Aspenglen (54 sites) Five miles west of Estes Park on US 34.

Glacier Basin (150 sites) Seven miles west of Beaver Meadows visitors center.

Longs Peak (26 sites) Twelve miles south of Estes Park on Hwy 7; provides Longs Peak hikers with an early trail start.

Moraine Park (247 sites) Two and a half miles from Beaver Meadows visitors center.

Timber Creek (100 sites) Seven miles north of Grand Lake.

The Moraine Park, Longs Peak and Timber Creek campgrounds are open year-round. Moraine Park and Glacier Basin campgrounds accept credit-card reservations up to five months in advance through the **National Park Reservation Center** (☎ 800-365-2267; http://reservations.nps.gov; PO Box 85705, San Diego, CA 92186-5705). The other three campgrounds are first-come, first-served.

GETTING AROUND

A free shuttle bus provides frequent summer service from the Glacier Basin parking area to Bear Lake. Another shuttle operates between Moraine Park campground and the Glacier Basin parking area. Shuttles run daily from mid-June to early September, and thereafter on weekends only until mid-October.

Estes Park

Without question, Estes Park is a tourist trap. It's a place teeming with camera-toting visitors, and more often than not meandering elk. As the more popular gateway to the loved Rocky Mountain National Park, Estes Park's population skyrockets on summer weekends and offers nearly any convenience a traveler might need – think countless motels and a surfeit of places to purchase souvenir T-shirts, ice cream cones and taffy.

Try the **Estes Park visitors center** (☎ 970-586-4431; www.estesparkresort.com; 500 Big Thompson Ave; ☺ 9am-8pm Jun-Aug, 8am-5pm Mon-Fri, 9am-5pm Sat, 10am-4pm Sun Sep-May), just east of the US 36 junction, for help with lodging; note that many places close in winter.

From Denver International Airport, **Estes Park Shuttle** (☎ 970-586-5151; www.estesparkshuttle.com) runs four times daily to Estes Park ($39, 1¾ hours).

SLEEPING

Most of the budget motels are east of town along US 34 or Hwy 7.

Stanley Hotel (☎ 970-586-4964; www.stanleyhotel.com; 333 Wonderview Ave; r from $150; ☒ ☒) Stephen King was inspired to write *The Shining* after staying here. The grand dame of northern Colorado historic resort hotels, it has great mountain views, splendid dining and ghost tours of the building on weekend nights. Speaking of which, you should book room No 401 if you want to increase your chances of ghost spotting – staff consider it the 'most haunted.'

Black Canyon Inn (☎ 970-586-8113; www.blackcanyoninn.com; 800 MacGregor Ave; cabins from $160; ☒ ☒) On 14 lovely forested acres, this inn offers cabins with kitchenette and fireplace, and some with Jacuzzi. Its restaurant is known for quality steak dinners.

Allenspark Lodge Bed & Breakfast (☎ 303-747-2552; www.allensparklodge.com; 184 Main St; r $70-140) Made from ponderosa pine logs, this elegant B&B offers rooms with views and handmade 1930s pine furniture. There's a library, large sunroom, hot tub, and beer and wine bar. The included hot breakfast is served family style. No children under 14.

Discovery Lodge (☎ 970-586-3336; www.estesdiscoverylodge.com; 800 Big Thompson Ave; r $60) One of the most likable budget options. It has a playground, fishing pond and plenty of green lawn, so it's a good choice for families.

Colorado Mountain School (☎ 970-586-5758; www.cmschool.com; 351 Moraine Ave; dm $25) Located in town, the dorms here are a great choice if there's space. Reservations are advised. It also runs climbing courses and offers guide services.

YMCA of the Rockies (☎ 970-586-3341; www.ymca rockies.org; 2515 Tunnel Rd; r/cabin from $100/120; 🖭) On the town outskirts, the YMCA offers abundant accommodations on its peaceful 860-acre grounds. The roomy cabins, which sleep between four and 10 people, work especially well for families.

Mary's Lake Campground (☎ 970-586-4411; marys lake@aol.com; 2120 Mary's Lake Rd; campsites/RV sites $24/36; 🖭) A good camping choice.

EATING
Notchtop Bakery & Cafe (☎ 970-586-0272; 457 E Wonderview Ave; dishes $4-7; 🕑 breakfast & lunch) In the Stanley Village shopping center, this is one of the best spots in town for tasty and healthy meals. Fill up on fair-trade coffee and scrumptious baked goods.

Dunraven Inn (☎ 970-586-6409; 2470 Colorado 66; dishes $9-30; 🕑 dinner) This place has a very eclectic decor showcasing many versions of the *Mona Lisa*. The Italian menu offers loads of pasta, seafood and vegetarian plates to choose from, along with a children's menu. It's an intimate restaurant perfect for a special evening.

Grand Lake
The other gateway to Rocky Mountain National Park, Grand Lake is less chaotic and more charming than Estes Park – although it still rakes in tourists by the thousands during summer. The downtown is pleasant, the namesake lake handsome. The **Grand Lake Visitors Center** (☎ 970-627-3402; www.grand lakechamber.com; 🕑 9am-5pm) is at the junction of US 34 and W Portal Rd.

The **Arapaho National Forest**, to the west of town, has some good mountain-biking trails; get a map from the **Grand Lake Metro Recreation District** (☎ 970-627-8328; 928 Grand Ave, Ste 204; 🕑 8am-5pm Mon-Fri). **Rocky Mountain Sports** (☎ 970-627-8124; 900 Grand Ave) rents and sells outdoor equipment. Several Rocky Mountain National Park **hiking** trailheads are just outside the town limits, including those to the Tonahutu Creek Trail and the Cascade Falls/North Inlet Trail, both near Shadowcliff Lodge.

Sit on the front porch of the **Grand Lake Lodge** (☎ 970-627-3967; www.grandlakelodge.com; 15500 Hwy 34; cabins from $85; 🕑 closed mid-Sep–May; 🗙 🖭) and feel your troubles melt away. Perhaps the establishment's greatest asset, the porch offers sweeping town, lake and mountain views. Delightfully rustic accommodations are in quaint cabins scattered about the property. The restaurant is another treat, with large picture windows and an enclosed porch (both offering fabulous views). It serves a fantastic Rocky Mountain trout.

Overlooking Grand Lake, the nonprofit **HI Shadowcliff Lodge** (☎ 970-627-9220; www.shadow cliff.org; 405 Summerland Park Rd; dm/r/cabin $18/45/100; 🕑 Jun-Sep) boasts a beautiful setting. Cabins, which accommodate six to eight people, have kitchen, fireplace and porch. Reservations are essential.

Peacefully situated under the trees next to the Tonahutu River, **Historic Rapids Lodge** (☎ 970-627-3707; www.rapidslodge.com; 209 Rapids Lane; r & condos from $75) has lovely, if slightly frilly, rooms and condos for groups. The lodge rooms cater to adults only.

EG's Garden Grill (☎ 970-627-8404; 1000 Grand Ave; dishes $10-20; 🕑 lunch & dinner) serves good grub from salads to seafood; its fish tacos make for a very satisfying lunch. Nearby, the big and casual **Pancho & Lefty's** (☎ 970-627-8773; 1120 Grand Ave; dishes $7-12; 🕑 lunch & dinner) dishes up a commendable mix of American and Mexican classics.

Home James Transportation Services (☎ 970-726-5060; www.homejamestransportation.com) runs door-to-door shuttles to Denver International Airport ($58, 2½ hours); reservations are a must.

Colorado Springs
Evangelical conservatives, tourists and military installations comprise the bizarre demographics of Colorado's second-largest city. Home to a large military base, the US Air Force Academy and the North American Radar Air Defense (the command center monitoring US and Canadian airspace; it's located in a hollowed-out mountain and is where the president would weather a nuclear missile strike), it's also the city where bibles were recently distributed with the Sunday paper! In a picture-perfect location below the famous Pikes Peak, Colorado Springs offers a runaway train of listed attractions: hike through Garden of the Gods'

ROCKY MOUNTAINS

strange red rock formations, take a ride on the cog railway or browse the shops in the low-key downtown area.

The I-25 bisects the sprawling metropolitan area. To the east is the central business district, centered around Tejon St between Kiowa St and Colorado Ave. Here you will find restaurants, bars, clubs and shops. To the west of the I-25 are Old Colorado City, Garden of the Gods and Manitou Springs.

The **Colorado Springs visitors center** (☎ 719-635-7506; www.coloradosprings-travel.com; 515 S Cascade Ave; ❤ 8:30am-5pm) has all the usual tourist information.

SIGHTS & ACTIVITIES

The bewitching red sandstone formations at the **Garden of the Gods** (the rocks are smack in the middle of town and seem so out of place you won't quite believe your eyes) draw around two million visitors each year to see highlights such as Balanced Rock, High Point and Central Garden. Soak up the beauty on one of the park hiking trails.

Travelers have been making the trip on the **Pikes Peak Cog Railway** to the summit of Pikes Peak (14,110ft) since 1891. Katherine Lee Bates was so impressed with her 1893 trip to the summit, she was inspired to write 'America the Beautiful.' Swiss-built trains smoothly make the round-trip in 3¼ hours, which includes 40 minutes at the top. Trains depart from the **Manitou Springs depot** (☎ 719-685-5401; www.cograilway.com; 515 Ruxton Ave, Manitou Springs; admission $26; ❤ Apr-Jan). The depot is 6 miles from downtown Colorado Springs. Take US 24 west to Manitou Ave; head westward on Manitou Ave, from where you'll make a left onto Ruxton Ave. The small town

of **Manitou Springs** is well known for its nine soda-water springs and historic downtown area.

The tough 12.5-mile **Barr Trail** to the summit is a local favorite. From the trailhead, just above the Manitou Springs depot, the path climbs 7300ft. Fit hikers should reach the top in about eight hours. Leave in the early morning, as afternoon thunderstorms can prove deadly. Make sure your body is acclimated to the altitude before setting out. It's easy to hitch a ride down the mountain once you reach the top.

From the town of Divide, west of Manitou Springs on US 24, you can drive the **Pikes Peak Toll Road** (per person/car $10/35; ❤ 9am-3pm winter, 7am-7pm summer) to the summit. Due to weather, it's sometimes closed in winter.

SLEEPING

El Colorado Lodge (☎ 719-685-5485; www.pikes-peak .com/elcolorado; 23 Manitou Ave; d/q from $60/95; Ⓟ ⓧ) You may start hallucinating tumbleweeds if you spend too much time in this comfortable Southwest-style adobe. Most of the cabins have a fireplace, and the larger ones (for up to six people) are split-level.

Garden of the Gods Motel (☎ 719-636-5271; 2922 W Colorado Ave; r winter/summer from $45/80; Ⓟ ⓧ ⓢ) With spacious rooms, an indoor pool and a sauna, this motel is good value. Conveniently situated within walking distance of Old Colorado shops and restaurants, it's popular with families.

J's Motor Hotel (☎ 719-635-8539; 820 N Nevada; r from $45; Ⓟ ⓧ ⓢ) Within walking distance of downtown nightlife, this place is clean and plain, and will do for a night if you just want to sleep.

Garden of the Gods Campground (☎ 719-475-9450; www.coloradocampground.com; 3704 W Colorado Ave; campsites $28, cabins $40; Ⓟ ⓢ) For camping close to town you could do worse than this place. There are only a few trees, and most of the area is paved, but the pool is refreshing and the basic cabins not bad value.

EATING & DRINKING

The Tejon strip downtown is the place to eat and drink in Colorado Springs.

32 Bleu (☎ 719-955-5664; 32 S Tejon St; lunch $7-9, dinner $13-24; ❤ lunch & dinner) Downstairs, this snazzy place offers 32 different glasses of wine to accompany its internationally influenced nosh. Upstairs, the nightclub books

---

THE AUTHOR'S CHOICE

Broadmoor (☎ 719-634-7711; www.broadmoor .com; 1 Lake Ave; r from $270; Ⓟ ⓧ ⓢ) One of the top five-star resorts in the USA, the Broadmoor sits in a picture-perfect location against the blue-green slopes of Cheyenne Mountain. Everything about the property is exquisite: acres of lush grounds and a shimmering lake to stroll past, world-class golf, ornately decorated grandiose public spaces, a myriad of bars and restaurants, a fantastic spa and uber-comfortable European-styled guestrooms.

national acts and live bands perform nightly (admission $3 to $20).

Phantom Canyon Brewing Co (☎ 719-635-2800; 2 E Pikes Peak Ave; dishes from $6; ☺ lunch & dinner) In an old exposed warehouse building, this local brewery serves a variety of pints and American cuisine in a casual atmosphere. The appetizers can be large enough for a meal. Locals flock to the upstairs bar for pool and socializing at night.

Western Omelet (☎ 719-636-2286; 16 S Walnut St; dishes $4-8; ☺ breakfast & lunch) If you're hungover after a big night, do as the locals do and head here for a green chili cure. The Mexican breakfast dishes, such as huevos rancheros (with green chili, of course), are greasy spoon fare. It's a big place completely lacking in character, which oddly gives it its charm.

Poor Richard's (☎ 719-632-7721; 324 N Tejon St; dishes $6-8, pizza $12-14; ☺ lunch & dinner) Since the mid-1970s, this colorful low-key space has served great vegetarian meals, pizza and beer. If you've forgotten what tofu is, you can remedy that here. There's a kids' room in the back with a small play area.

Tony's (☎ 719-228-6566; 311 N Tejon St; dishes $4-7; ☺ lunch & dinner) For greasy sandwiches or mac and cheese, you can't get much cheaper than Tony's (and the quality is not bad either). Pretty much an institution since it opened, Wisconsin-themed Tony's is a neighborhood bar that serves the cheapest pitchers in town. There's often live music at night.

Hotel Bar (☎ 719-577-5733; Broadmoor Hotel, 1 Lake Ave) On a warm summer afternoon there's no better spot for a drink with a view than this bar overlooking a private lake. Order a chilled glass of wine and a cigar, and sit back and watch the ducks pass by. When the weather turns cool the outdoor stone fireplaces are lit.

Rum Bay (☎ 719-634-3522; 20 N Tejon St; cover $5) There are seven clubs in one at this very popular and absolutely giant place. Dance to pulsating techno, sing karaoke, listen to live jazz or two-step the night away. The cover charge allows entrance to the equally popular Tequila's across the street.

GETTING THERE & AROUND
The **Colorado Springs Municipal Airport** (☎ 719-550-1900; 7770 Drennan Rd) offers a viable alternative to Denver International Airport. The **Yellow Cab** (☎ 719-634-5000) fare from the airport to the city center is between $20 and $25.

TNM&O buses between Cheyenne, Wyoming and Pueblo stop daily at the **depot** (☎ 719-635-1505; 120 Weber St). The **transportation center** (☎ 719-385-7433; 127 E Kiowa St; ☺ 8am-5pm Mon-Fri) offers schedule information and route maps for all 31 city bus lines.

Cripple Creek

Just an hour from Colorado Springs, yet worlds away, a visit to Cripple Creek is like stepping back into the Wild West of lore. The booze still flows and gambling still thrives, but yesteryear's saloons and brothels have been converted into tasteful casinos. Despite the flashing neon signs, Cripple Creek manages to retain a lot of its old charm, with most casinos tucked inside original century-old buildings.

At the turn of the 20th century the city was one of the most important in the state – producing $340 million worth of gold between 1891 and 1916, and a staggering $413 million worth by 1952.

If nothing else, Cripple Creek is a wonderful day trip from Colorado Springs. The road climbs quickly as you head west into the mountains and the last 18 miles, especially in the fall when the trees turn golden, are quite breathtaking.

As far as casinos go, try **Womack's Hotel & Casino** (☎ 719-689-0333; 210 E Bennett Dr) for something classy, **JP McGills** (☎ 719-689-2446; 232 E Bennett Dr) for something reminiscent of Las Vegas and the **Brass Ass** (☎ 719-689-2104; 264 E Bennett Dr), with a giant brass donkey in the doorway, for an Old West gambling experience.

For dancing, darts and pool try the **Horseshoe Saloon** (☎ 719-689-7463; 123 E Bennett Dr), which retains the charm of a turn-of-the-century booze hall with a wine-red carpet and old photographs stretched mural-like across the walls.

Cripple Creek is 50 miles southwest of Colorado Springs on Hwy 67. Catch the **Ramblin' Express** (☎ 719-590-8687; www.ramblinexpress .com) from Colorado Springs ($22). The bus departs hourly between 7am and 10pm from the 8th St Depot and leaves from JP McGills casino hourly between 8:30am and 2:10am.

CENTRAL MOUNTAIN REGION

Colorado's northern mountains are well known for the plethora of ski resorts located within them. In summer they offer numerous opportunities for hiking and white-water rafting. The southern reaches of Colorado's Rockies offer never-ending mountain views, world-class ski resorts and the sprawling San Luis Valley, rich in Hispanic heritage and home to the scenic wonders of the Great Sand Dunes National Park and the Sangre de Cristo Mountains.

Steamboat Springs

Tantalizingly charming, Steamboat's character is as alluring as the mountains it offers for skiing. Powdery white slopes meet the quaint historic downtown, still a major ranching center, and no matter the season, there's always something outdoorsy to do.

Steamboat Springs' two major areas are Old Town and, 5 miles south, the curving streets at Steamboat Village, centered on the ski resort. US 40 is known as Lincoln Ave through Old Town.

The **Steamboat Springs Visitors Center** (☎ 970-879-0880; www.steamboat-chamber.com; 1255 S Lincoln Ave; ☯ 8am-5pm Mon-Fri, 10am-3pm Sat) and the **USFS Hahn's Peak Ranger District** (☎ 970-879-1870; 925 Weiss Dr; ☯ 8am-5pm Mon-Fri, 9am-noon Sat) can set you up with information.

With a well-earned reputation for consistently satisfying powder skiing, **Steamboat Ski Area** (☎ 970-879-6111; www.steamboat.com; lift ticket adult/child $64/39) features a 3600ft vertical drop.

For **mountain biking**, pick up a trails map at the visitors center; there are also bike trails accessible by the gondola at the ski resort. A popular activity in the area is whitewater rafting. In fact, a stretch of the Yampa River swings right through town. **Bucking Rainbow** (☎ 970-879-8747; 402 Lincoln Ave) offers rafting and fly-fishing trips on the Yampa, Colorado, Eagle and Arkansas Rivers.

SLEEPING

Steamboat Central Reservations (☎ 970-879-0740; www.steamboat.com) helps book accommodations and ski-stay packages.

Hotel Bristol (☎ 970-879-3083; www.steamboat hotelbristol.com; 917 Lincoln Ave; r from $100; ☐) An elegant Old West hotel, the Bristol offers good-value rooms in ambient environs. Digs are small, but sophisticated, with dark wood and brass furnishings and Pendleton wool blankets on the beds. There's a ski shuttle, a six-person indoor whirlpool and a cozy restaurant.

Inn at Steamboat (☎ 970-879-2600; www.innat steamboat.com; r $90-150; ☒ ☒ ☐ ☒) Convenient to the ski resort, this friendly lodge offers comfortably furnished rooms and excellent amenities, including a sauna, laundry facilities and a free shuttle to Steamboat Ski Area. Ski packages are available.

Strawberry Park Hot Springs (☎ 970-879-0342; www.strawberryhotsprings.com; 44200 County Rd; campsites/cabins/caboose $40/50/80; ☒) Synonymous with relaxation, these woodsy grounds offer camping, basic cabins and even a caboose, plus hot pools, a cool creek, waterfalls and massage therapists. The sandy-bottomed, rock-lined soaking pools are fantastic on moonlit evenings; clothing is optional after dark. If you just want to soak, the springs are open daily from 10am to 10:30pm; admission is $10 for adults, $5 for children. Vehicles without 4WD are required to use chains from November to April for the 3-mile steep road up to the resort.

Nordic Lodge Motel (☎ 970-879-0531; 1036 Lincoln Ave; r $50-130; ☒) Steamboat's best-value motel, it has large rooms and a very nice indoor hot tub. Convenient to downtown shops and bars, the local bus stops right out front.

EATING & DRINKING

Harwigs/L'Apogee at 911 Lincoln Ave (☎ 970-879-1919; 911 Lincoln Ave; dishes from $20; ☯ dinner) A fine-dining favorite, this place serves Asian-influenced French fare in elegant environs. Candles and piano music set the mood, there's an award-winning wine cellar and service is top-notch. The menu changes frequently, the food is consistently delicious.

Cugino's Pizzeria (☎ 970-879-5805; 825 Oak St; dishes $6-15; ☯ lunch & dinner) A pretty little place, Cugino's has an amiable staff and a wide variety of Italian-food options, from hoagies and pasta to calzones and pizza.

Johnny B Good's Diner (☎ 970-870-8400; 738 Lincoln Ave; dishes $5-7; ☯ breakfast, lunch & dinner) If Marilyn and milkshakes make you go 'mmm,' hop onto a stool at this swell diner for burgers, sandwiches and 'belly stuffers,' such as meatloaf and spaghetti.

Level'z (☎ 970-870-9090; 1860 Ski Times Sq; ☐) This multilevel place offers something for everyone. There's an Internet café on the 1st floor, a sports bar on the 2nd and a popular dance club on the 3rd. With live nightly entertainment, pool tables and 20 beers on tap, Level'z is a hot after-dark hangout.

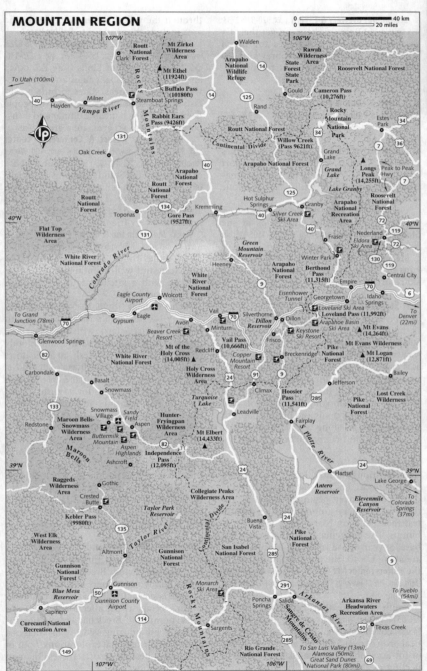

MOUNTAIN REGION

Steamboat Brewery & Tavern (☎ 970-879-2233; 435 Lincoln Ave) Beer drinkers can get their fix at this brewery, which serves top-notch amber ales and other microbrews. It's a low-key watering hole perfect for dissecting the day's skiing adventures.

GETTING THERE & AROUND

The **Yampa Valley Regional Airport** (☎ 970-276-3669), located 22 miles west, serves Steamboat Springs.

Alpine Taxi (☎ 970-879-8294, 800-343-7433) serves both the Yampa Valley Regional Airport (adult/child $27/14) and Denver International Airport (adult/child $70/35, four hours).

Greyhound's US 40 service between Denver and Salt Lake City stops at the **Stockbridge Center** (☎ 970-870-0504; 1505 Lincoln Ave), about 0.5 miles west of town.

Steamboat Springs Transit (☎ 970-879-3717) runs free buses between Old Town and the ski resort year-round.

Hot Sulphur Springs

The primary draw in Hot Sulphur Springs is the inviting and gorgeously situated **Hot Sulphur Springs Resort & Spa** (☎ 970-725-3306; www.hotsulphursprings.com; 5617 County Rd 20; spa use adult/child $17/12; r & cabin from $100; ✕), where you can either stop for a soak or spend the night. TV is out of the question (rooms are without), so is smoking and alcohol. The resort features 22 pools and private baths in natural settings, along with a range of spa services – from massage to body wraps.

Winter Park

Unpretentious Winter Park is a favorite local ski resort. Located less than a two-hour drive from Denver, beginners can frolic on miles of powdery groomers while experts test their skills on Mary Jane's world-class bumps. The congenial town is a wonderful base for year-round romping. Most services are along US 40 (the main drag), including the **visitors center** (☎ 970-726-4118; www.winterpark -info.com; 78841 Hwy 40; ☉ 8am-5pm Mon-Fri, 9am-5pm Sat & Sun).

South of town, **Winter Park Resort** (☎ 970-726-5514; www.skiwinterpark.com; lift ticket adult/child $65/35) covers four mountains and has a vertical drop of over 2600ft. It also has 45 miles of lift-accessible **mountain-biking** trails connecting to a 600-mile trail system running

through the valley. Other fine rides in the area include the road up to **Rollins Pass**.

The cozy **Arapahoe Ski Lodge** (☎ 970-726-8222; www.arapahoeskilodge.com; 78594 Hwy 40; r $75-110; ✕ 🛏), just north of Lions Gate Rd, offers an indoor sauna, spa, games and fireplace-warmed lounge areas. Rates include breakfast. The ski-season packages (for two people from $215), which include dinner and transportation to the ski area, are a great deal.

The **Vintage Resort & Conference Center** (☎ 970-726-8801; www.vintagehotel.com; 100 Winter Park Dr; r from $80; ✕ 🛏 🛢) is right at the base of the mountain. Standard rooms are smallish, but have high ceilings, big windows and comfortable decor. The on-site restaurant and bar serves decent food. Service is efficient and very friendly.

Rocky Mountain Inn & Hostel (☎ 970-726-8256; www.therockymountaininn.com; Hwy 40; dm/r from $19/50; 🛏), 2 miles from Winter Park in Fraser, is a clean and well-maintained hostel-inn, stocked with a kitchen, laundry facilities and common space.

Higher Grounds (☎ 970-726-0447; Hwy 40; dishes $8-12; ☉ breakfast, lunch & dinner), a café and martini lounge, starts with breakfast and brunch (think Belgian waffles and Bloody Marys) and ends with fresh tapas; it hosts a weekly gay night. **Pepe Osaka's** (☎ 970-726-0455; Hwy 40; mains $10-20; ☉ lunch & dinner) comes recommended by locals for its sushi. If you don't do raw, fear not – it also serves Mexican and Thai dishes, as well as steak.

Home James Transportation Services (☎ 970-726-5060, 800-359-7535) runs shuttles to Denver International Airport ($40, two hours). Amtrak's *California Zephyr* stops daily in Fraser (near Winter Park), while the scenic **Ski Train** (☎ 303-296-4754; ☉ 9am-4pm Tue-Fri) links Denver with Winter Park (see p971). Greyhound buses stop at the Winter Park visitors center and at the Amtrak station in Fraser.

Breckenridge & Around

With a 19th-century mining feel, it's hard to resist fun-loving 'Breck.' It's as appealing to family vacationers as it is to university grads partaking in that great Colorado coming-of-age ritual affectionately known as 'ski bumming.' Breck has a reputation for partying, but boozing aside, it also makes a great base for regional explorations. Four of Colorado's best ski resorts are less than an hour's drive away.

The **visitors center** (☎ 970-453-6018; www.go breck.com; 309 N Main St; ✆ 9am-5pm) has information on accommodations.

ACTIVITIES

In winter it's all about the snow. **Breckenridge** (☎ 800-789-7669; www.snow.com; lift ticket $63), spanning 600 acres over four mountains, features some of the best beginner and intermediate terrain around (the green runs are flatter than most in Colorado), as well as killer steeps and chutes for experts, and a renowned snowboard park (it has the USA's largest half-pipe and plenty of jumps).

North America's highest resort, **Arapahoe Basin Ski Area** (☎ 970-468-0718; www.arapahoebasin .com; lift ticket $50) is smaller and less commercial, and you can ride A-Basin until mid-June. Full of steeps, walls and backcountry terrain, it's a local favorite because it doesn't draw herds of package tourists. The outdoor bar is a great place to kick back with a cold microbrew, and people are always grilling burgers and socializing at impromptu tailgate parties in the parking lot (known as 'the beach').

Keystone Ski Resort (☎ 970-496-2316; www.key stoneresort.com; lift ticket $61) is another option and has night skiing.

In summer there are loads of **hiking** and **mountain-biking** opportunities. Ride up and bike down the trails at Breckenridge (single/day $12/28). The resort rents bikes (half/full day $20/28).

SLEEPING

The main form of accommodations in Breckenridge is in condos. **Breckenridge Resort Central Reservations** (☎ 970-453-2918; 311 S Ridge St) can help with bookings.

Fireside Inn B&B and Hostel (☎ 970-453-6456; www.firesideinn.com; 114 N French St; dm $30, r summer/ winter from $65/100; ▯) This welcoming hostel offers a very comfortable stay, as well as ski and bike storage and a hot tub. Breakfast is free for private-room guests, $3 for dorm dwellers.

Abbett Placer B&B (☎ 970-453-6489, 888-794-7750; www.abbettplacerbnb.com; 205 S French St; r $85-130) In a restored Victorian home, this is a personable choice. It is well run, has a hot tub and most rooms have a fireplace.

EATING & DRINKING

Most of the eating and drinking in Breck takes place along a few blocks of Main St.

Downstairs at Eric's (☎ 970-453-1401; 111 S Main St; lunch special $5, dishes from $6; ✆ lunch & dinner) Say you're a local to score the lunch special – a soft drink with small pizza, burger or sandwich and a side. A basement joint, Eric's is a colorful and lively place with filling pub grub that keeps locals returning. There are more than 120 beers to choose from.

Fatty's (☎ 970-453-9802; 106 S Ridge Rd; pizza from $13; ✆ lunch & dinner) The pizzas feed at least two. Locals frequent the bar, so it can get rowdy at night. In summer sit outside on the patio and people watch.

Hearthstone (☎ 970-453-1148; 130 S Ridge St; happy-hour appetizers $5, dishes from $20; ✆ lunch & dinner) In a beautiful red sandstone building, the Victorian-era influences the dining-room decor at this elegant restaurant. The nouveau-American cuisine is fresh and altogether excellent. Those on a budget should visit during the 4pm to 6pm happy hour, when the mouthwatering jumbo jalapeno breaded shrimp go for 75¢ a piece – after four or five you'll be full.

Cecilia's (☎ 970-453-2243; 520 S Main St) Breckenridge's most popular late-night hangout, Cecilia's packs in crowds all week long. There's a large dance floor with mostly DJ music, a few pool tables and a corner couch or two.

Sherpa & Yettis (☎ 970-547-9299; 320 S Main St) A popular nightclub, this one in a basement, Sherpa's is a trendy place with mod art on the walls. Saturday is hip-hop night, with lots of drink specials; other nights feature live bands, including some big names.

GETTING THERE & AROUND

Breckenridge is off I-70, 104 miles west of Denver. The **Resort Express** (☎ 970-468-7600) offers service between Breck and Denver International Airport ($53, two hours, multiple trips daily). To get between the resorts hop on the free **Summit Stages** (☎ 970-668-0999) buses, which connect Breckenridge with the rest of Summit County and Vail. It's also easy to hitchhike during the ski season. While this is never entirely safe, most people don't have a problem in this region.

Leadville

At 10,200ft the air is thin in Leadville, but delectably crisp and clean – just the way the locals like it. Perfect for ambling, it's a scenically refreshing town with a dramatic mining legacy.

For area advice, head to the **visitors center** (☎ 719-486-3900; www.leadvilleusa.com; 809 Harrison Ave; ☼ 9am-5pm) or the **USFS Leadville Ranger Station** (☎ 719-486-0749; 2015 Poplar St; ☼ 8am-4:30pm Mon-Fri), at the north end of town.

Historic **mining areas** are a short drive away and can also be viewed via a 2½-hour ride on the **Leadville, Colorado & Southern Railroad** (☎ 719-486-3936; 326 E 7th St; adult/child $24/13; ☼ 8:30am-5pm Jun-Sep).

For **hiking**, the stunning mountains surrounding Leadville include two 14,000ft peaks, Mt Massive and Mt Elbert, the latter being Colorado's highest (14,433ft). There's also good mountain biking – rent bikes at **Bill's Sport Shop** (☎ 719-486-0739; 225 Harrison Ave). **Ski Cooper** (☎ 719-486-2277; www.skicooper.com; lift ticket $33), 9 miles north of Leadville, is a small mountain with 26 trails.

Right downtown, **Delaware Hotel** (☎ 719-486-1418; www.delawarehotel.com; 700 Harrison Ave; r from $70; ✗) is a carefully restored building with Victorian rooms, attentive service and a locally lauded restaurant.

Leadville Hostel & Inn (☎ 719-486-9334; www.leadvillehostel.com; 500 E 7th St; dm/d $15/25; ⌨) is a great-value, low-key choice with a laundry, pool table and loads of common space. Movies are screened nightly on a big TV, and there's no curfew.

In town, pitch your tent at **Leadville RV Corral** (☎ 719-486-3111; 135 W 2nd St; campsites $18-24, RV sites $28).

For pasta, pizza, seafood and even a few Thai dishes, head to the cheerful and spotless **Tennessee Pass Café** (☎ 719-486-8101; 222 Harrison Ave; dishes $8-12; ☼ lunch & dinner). Vegetarians should find plenty of fresh and savory fare to keep their appetites stimulated here.

Some other busy eateries include **Quincy's** (☎ 719-486-9765; 416 Harrison; dishes $7-15; ☼ lunch & dinner) for filet mignon and prime ribs, and **Casa Blanca** (☎ 719-486-9969; 118 E 2nd St; dishes $5-8; ☼ 11:30am-8:30pm Mon-Sat) for no-frills Mexican food.

Dee Hive Tours & Transportation (☎ 719-486-2339; 506 Harrison Ave) provides service to Denver International Airport ($135, additional passenger $68).

Vail

Synonymous with swank, Vail is a favorite winter playground for the world's rich and famous. This is where the movie stars ski, and it's not odd to see Texans in 10-gallon hats and ladies in mink coats zipping down the slopes. A resort town in every sense of the word, the compact Vail Village offers restaurants, bars and boutiques of high standard. The glitz factor is certainly up there, but the place is more laid back and less pretentious than Colorado's other high-octane resort, Aspen. For terrain, Vail is our favorite mountain in the state. Wide open and immense, the back bowls (which cater to intermediate and expert skiers) are nothing short of spectacular, especially on a powder day. Locals must agree, because they flock here by the SUV-load each weekend. Those not shopping and skiing can hike, bike and explore the surrounding alpine country.

ORIENTATION

Vail Village is the principal center of activity. Motorists must park at the Vail Transportation Center & Public Parking garage before entering the pedestrian mall area near the chairlifts. About 0.5 miles to the west, Lionshead is a secondary center and lift.

INFORMATION

Vail Visitors Center (☎ 970-479-1385; www.visitvailvalley.com; Transportation Center; ☼ 9am-5pm)

White River National Forest Holy Cross Ranger District (☎ 970-827-5715; I-70 exit 176 & US 24; ☼ 8am-5pm Mon-Fri)

ACTIVITIES

Vail Mountain (☎ 970-476-9090; vail.snow.com; lift ticket adult/child $70/40), with more than 5200 skiable acres, has 193 trails. Experts will go gaga, but other ability levels are well taken care of, too.

Cross-country skiers can head to the **Cordillera Nordic Center** (☎ 970-926-5100; www.cordillera-vail.com; 650 Clubhouse Dr, Edwards), 15 miles west of Vail. Check with the White River National Forest Holy Cross Ranger District for details on nearby backcountry ski routes such as Shrine Pass.

The Holy Cross Wilderness Area is rich with **hiking** opportunities, such as the strenuous Notch Mountain Trail, affording great views of Mt of the Holy Cross. The Half Moon Pass Trail leads up Mt of the Holy Cross. The Eagles Nest Wilderness Area – in particular, Booth Falls, Gore Lake and Two Elk Pass – is another great place to lace up those boots.

On the south side of I-70, a paved **cycling** route extends through Vail and continues east to the Ten Mile Canyon Trail over Vail Pass to Frisco, the hub of Summit County bike trails. Another popular but demanding ride climbs over Tennessee Pass to Leadville on the narrow shoulders of US 24.

VAIL FOR CHILDREN

So the kids don't want yet another day of ski school, while you sparkle down your black diamonds? Fret not. There are plenty of other things to keep children busy in Vail.

At mountaintop **Adventure Ridge** (☎ 970-476-9090) youth can enjoy mountain biking, disc golf, volleyball and tramp lining in summer, and tubing, snowmobiling, snowshoeing and laser tag in winter. 'Kids Night Owl' ($60) is for people aged seven to 14 years who desire a parent-free evening of dinner and activities.

In summer, **Gore Range Natural Science School** (☎ 970-827-9725; www.gorerange.org) hosts various multiday and overnight educational programs (courses $230 to $350) in wildlife, ecology and environmental sciences for students from first to twelfth grades. See its website for a schedule.

Vail Recreation District (☎ 970-479-2279; www.vailrec.com; 395 E Lionshead Circle) runs year-round activities for all ages, including basketball, gymnastics, ice-skating and junior golf. Teens might want to disappear into the '20 Below Club' for its pool tables, movies and skateboarding.

SLEEPING

Don't expect any budget lodgings near Vail.

Vail Cascade Resort & Spa (☎ 970-476-7111; www.vailcascade.com; 1300 Westhaven Dr; r from $260; P 🐾 🍸) An award-winning swanky property, this is the place to go for luxurious pampering. Rooms feature lots of cherrywood furnishings and marble vanities. Two movie theaters show first-run films, and a restaurant, athletic club and full spa complete the package. Child care and a children's program is also available. Rates drop dramatically in summer and parking is $12.

Tivoli Lodge (☎ 970-476-5615; www.tivolilodge.com; 386 Hanson Rd; 🐾 🍸) Under renovation when we stopped by, this is a friendly European-style place just one block from four lifts in Vail Village. In a stone castlelike building, the lodge offers cozy rooms, most

with balcony, as well as a hot tub and sauna. Call or check the website for rates.

Roost Lodge (☎ 970-476-5451; www.roostlodge.com; 1783 N Frontage Rd; r $50-100; 🐾 🍸) This lodge in West Vail is great value, providing a very clean and comfortable stay, though the rooms are on the small side. Rates include continental breakfast and a shuttle to the slopes.

Gore Creek Campground (campsites $13) This forested USFS campground, located 6 miles from Vail Village at the east end of Bighorn Rd, has 25 first-come, first-served campsites from June to September.

EATING & DRINKING

Billy's Island Grill (☎ 970-476-8811; Lionshead Mall; dishes $15-25; ☽ lunch & dinner) This restaurant, with a great deck for cocktail sipping, brings the ocean to the mountains with a handsome-looking selection of seafood, plus steaks, chicken, pizza and vegetarian options.

Sweet Basil (☎ 970-476-0125; 193 E Gore Creek Dr; lunch $10-15, dinner $25) The menu changes seasonally at this creative American restaurant with big picture windows and contemporary art on the walls. The eclectic fare, which includes favorites such as Colorado leg of lamb with white bean ratatouille, is consistently good.

Joe's Famous Deli (☎ 970-479-7580; 288 Bridge St; dishes $5-8; ☽ breakfast, lunch & dinner) A casual, counter-service joint, Joe's does a great sandwich – if you don't like one of the 20 grilled and cold varieties, create your own. Kids will delight in the ice cream possibilities.

Tap Room & Sanctuary (☎ 970-479-0500; 333 Bridge St) A favorite stop with hipsters on the barhopping circuit, the Tap Room has a giant selection of beers, fabulous margaritas and a cigar lounge. Upstairs, the Sanctuary is a hot club that's popular with a fashionable, younger crowd.

GETTING THERE & AROUND

From December to early April only, the **Eagle County Airport** (☎ 970-524-9490), 35 miles west of Vail, has direct jet services to destinations across the country.

Colorado Mountain Express (☎ 970-926-9800; www.cmex.com) shuttles to/from Denver International Airport ($62, 2½ hours). Greyhound buses stop at the **Vail Transportation Center** (☎ 970-476-5137; 241 S Frontage Rd) en route to Denver ($23, 2¼ hours) or Grand Junction ($18, 3¼ hours).

ROCKY MOUNTAINS

Vail's free **buses** (☎ 970-477-3456; http://vailgov .com/transit) stop in West Vail, East Vail and Sandstone; most have bike racks.

Glenwood Springs

Located just outside a spectacular canyon, Glenwood Springs is a pleasurable place to kick up your heels. Aside from its world-famous hot springs, it offers outdoor escapades ranging from the adventurous to soothing.

For area information, hit the **visitors center** (☎ 970-945-6589; www.glenwoodchamber.com; 1102 Grand Ave; ☺ 9am-5pm Mon-Fri, 10am-5pm Sat & Sun).

The **Hot Springs Lodge & Pool** (☎ 970-947-2955; www.hotspringspool.com; 401 N River St; admission $10; ☺ 9am-10pm) is one of Colorado's favorite family vacation spots. It's not a secluded retreat, but there is much to keep you happy – ample shallow areas, deeper areas with diving boards, waterslides and minigolf.

There's tiptop road and mountain biking, as well as tons of hiking around Glenwood Springs; pick up a free trails guide at the visitors center. Rent bikes at **BSR Sports** (☎ 970-945-7317; 210 7th St).

Glenwood Canyon offers Class III and IV white-water rafting below the Shoshone Dam, 7.5 miles east of town. Try **Rock Gardens Rafting** (☎ 970-945-6737) for guided tours ($20 to $64).

About 20 motels and hotels are in the Glenwood area, and those closest to the town center fill up quickly in summer. There is also a string of mildly cheaper motels in West Glenwood, 1 to 2 miles from town on Hwy 6. **Hotel Denver** (☎ 970-945-6565; www.thehotel denver.com; 402 7th St; r from $75; ☒) is a modern hotel with spacious rooms. It's an easy stroll to the hot springs and the town center.

Glenwood Springs Hostel (☎ 970-945-8545; 1021 Grand Ave; dm/r from $12/19; ☐) is a welcoming and relaxed place, with kitchens, common lounges and more than 3000 records for your listening pleasure. Discounts for hostel guests are available at some restaurants and sites in the area.

Glenwood Canyon Brewing Company (☎ 970-945-1276; Hotel Denver, 402 7th St; dishes from $7; ☺ lunch & dinner) is a cozy place with wooden tables, a pressed tin ceiling and a lively atmosphere. The large menu has great standouts – try the beer and chili basted ribs or the cheddar beer soup. There are about 10 local brews on tap.

Before hitting the trails, fuel up at the **Glenwood Cafe** (☎ 970-945-2639; 311 8th St; dishes $4-8; ☺ breakfast & lunch). Breakfast is of the eggs, hash browns and hotcakes variety, but not greasy enough to leave you comatose.

Colorado Mountain Express (☎ 970-926-9800; www.cmex.com) offers daily shuttle service to and from Denver International Airport ($75, four hours). Amtrak's *California Zephyr* stops daily at the **train depot** (☎ 970-945-9563; 413 7th St). Greyhound buses leave from the **bus station** (☎ 970-945-8501; 118 W 6th St).

Roaring Fork Transit Authority (☎ 970-920-1905; www.rfta.com) has buses that connect Glenwood with Aspen.

Aspen

Unbashfully posh Aspen is Colorado's glitziest high-octane resort, playing host to some of the wealthiest skiers in the world. The handsome historic red-brick downtown is as alluring as the glistening slopes, but Aspen's greatest asset is its scenery. The magnificent alpine environment, especially in fall when the aspen trees put on a spectacular display, adds extra sugary eye candy to an already glittering jewel.

Aspen visitors center (☎ 970-925-1940; www.aspen chamber.org; 425 Rio Grande Pl; ☺ 8am-5pm Mon-Fri) has all the usual information.

ACTIVITIES
Skiing & Snowboarding

Aspen Skiing Company (☎ 970-925-1220; www.aspen snowmass.com; lift ticket $70) operates the area's four ski resorts. **Aspen** (or Ajax) is an athlete's mountain, offering more than 3000ft of steep vertical drop. **Aspen Highlands** has outstanding extreme skiing and breathtaking views. **Buttermilk Mountain** provides gentle slopes for beginners and intermediate skiers. **Snowmass** offers mixed terrain and boasts the longest vertical drop in the USA (4400ft).

The best cross-country skiing in the area is at **Ashcroft** (☎ 970-925-1971), in the beautiful Castle Creek Valley, with 20 miles of groomed trails passing through a ghost town. For backcountry skiing, the **10th Mountain Division Hut Association** (☎ 970-925-5775; www.huts .org; 1280 Ute Ave) offers nearly 300 miles of trails connecting 22 overnight cabins. Getting to the cabins requires both skill and advance reservations. The office also handles bookings for the Braun Hut System, which covers Aspen, Vail, Leadville and Hunter Creek.

Other Activities

The three wilderness areas that surround Aspen offer bountiful **hiking** trails. The Hunter Valley Trail leads through wildflower meadows and into the Hunter-Fryingpan Wilderness Area. Hot springs are the reward after 8.5 miles of moderate climbing on the Conundrum Creek Trail. Another awesome area to hike is the stunningly beautiful Maroon Bells-Snowmass Wilderness Area.

Plenty of heavily used mountain biking routes ply Aspen Mountain and Smuggler Mountain. Hunter Valley and the Sunnyside trails provide a challenging single-track loop north of town. The Montezuma Basin and Pearl Pass rides offer extreme cycling experiences, well above timberline, south of town from Castle Creek Rd. The **Hub** (☎ 970-925-7970; 315 E Hyman Ave) rents bikes.

ASPEN FOR CHILDREN

Aspen offers organized activities for the younger set year-round, as well as heaps for teens who might prefer less-structured activities, such as swimming or ice-skating.

A summertime site to consider is **Anderson Ranch Arts Center** (☎ 970-923-3181; www.anderson ranch.org; Snowmass Village), a nonprofit arts institution recommended for its wonderful array of five-day summer courses (from $165) focusing on crafts and creativity.

The **Aspen Center for Environmental Studies** (ACES; ☎ 970-925-5756; www.aspennature.org; 100 Puppy Smith St) runs great day programs in summer for children aged five to 10, which can include hiking, storytelling, playing and even some learning; rates vary. Summer evenings here feature a free Sunset Beaver Walk – splendid for families.

The **Aspen Recreation Center** (☎ 970-544-4100; www.aspenrecreation.com; 895 Maroon Creek Rd) is loaded with facilities, including pools, an ice-skating rink and climbing wall, and provides childcare referrals. Its **Aspen Youth Center** (☎ 970-925-7091) runs activities for children aged eight to 18.

SLEEPING

Hotel Jerome (☎ 800-331-7213, www.hoteljerome .com; 330 E Main St; r from $265; 🖳 🖵) Superb service and relaxed elegance are the trademarks at the historic Hotel Jerome. Rooms feature period antiques, marble baths with big tubs and thick down comforters on the beds. A classic Old West bar, ski concierge and a heated outdoor pool are extra perks.

Little Nell (☎ 970-920-4200; www.thelittlenell.com; 675 E Durant Ave; r from $260; 🖳 🖵) Beautiful and relaxing, Little Nell exudes elegant European ambience. Gas-burning fireplaces, high-thread-count linens and rich color schemes make up the bedroom decor. The Greenhouse Bar is perfect for après-ski unwinding.

St Moritz Lodge (☎ 970-925-3220; www.stmoritz lodge.com; 334 W Hyman Ave; dm $30, r $60-175; 🖵 🖵) Neat and congenial, this European-style lodge offers a wide variety of options, from nice dorms to two-bedroom condos. Continental breakfast is served, and the pool and steam room are for all guests. The cheapest rooms share baths.

Mountain Chalet (☎ 970-925-7797; www.mountain chaletaspen.com; 333 E Durant Ave; r from $85; 🖵) Stay here for convenience to both the lifts and town center. Some rooms have a mountain view, and the lounge is well suited for lounging. Amenities include a hot tub and sauna. The **USFS White River National Forest's Aspen Ranger District** (☎ 970-925-3445; 806 W Hallam; 🕑 8am-4:30pm Mon-Fri winter, plus 8am-4:30pm Sat summer) operates nine **campgrounds** (campsites $14).

EATING & DRINKING

Mother Lode (☎ 970-925-7700; 314 E Hyman Ave; dishes $15-25; 🕑 dinner) This highly praised longtimer has been serving innovative Italian cuisine to the masses since 1959. The menu is equal parts salad, pasta, and meat-and seafood-focused specialty dishes.

Explore Booksellers & Bistro (☎ 970-925-5338; 221 E Main St; dishes $10-14; 🕑 breakfast, lunch & dinner) Two of life's greatest joys – good books and good grub – join forces at this great spot. The upper-floor bistro is suited for slow dining, deep conversing and cups of tea. Everything is vegan, save for the eggs, which are free-range. After dining, explore the bookstore's well-stocked nooks.

Main St Bakery (☎ 970-925-6446; 201 E Main St; dishes $6-10; 🕑 breakfast & lunch) It's a hit, especially at breakfast time, for its gamut of sweet and savory goods – from granola and pancakes to chicken pot pie – in its convivial room and outdoor patio.

Red Onion (☎ 970-925-9043; 420 E Cooper Ave; dishes $8-12; 🕑 lunch & dinner) Aspen's oldest saloon, first opened in 1892, is a longstanding favorite of the local ski patrol. There's the usual pub grub to eat.

ROCKY MOUNTAINS

THE AUTHOR'S CHOICE

Woody Creek Tavern (☎ 970-923-4285; 2 Woody Creek Plaza; ☿ closes 11pm) If you can make it down valley about 8 miles, do so. This local hangout was the favorite watering hole of late gonzo journalist Hunter S Thompson, and quite a few other celebrities, too. There's cheap beer on tap, walls jam-packed with stuff, and a vibe that's just like the bar back home.

Cooper St Bar (☎ 970-925-7758; 508 E Cooper Ave; dishes $7-12; ☿ lunch & dinner) A good place to start your night, with a pint and a burger and maybe shoot a little pool. The place gets rowdy early.

Double Diamond (☎ 970-920-6905; 450 S Galena St; admission from $5) When live-music acts – from rock and blues to salsa and reggae – come into town, they play at this spacious club. It's seen George Clinton, G-Love and many others. Shows generally get rocking at 10pm.

GETTING THERE & AROUND
Four miles north of Aspen on Hwy 82, **Sardy Field** (☎ 970-920-5380) has commuter flights from Denver, and nonstops to Phoenix, Los Angeles, San Francisco, Minneapolis and Memphis. **Colorado Mountain Express** (☎ 970-947-0506; www.cmex.com) offers frequent services to Denver International Airport ($100, four hours).

Roaring Fork Transit Agency (☎ 970-920-1905; www.rfta.com) buses connect Aspen with the ski mountains and Glenwood Springs.

Buena Vista & Salida

Buena Vista and Salida won't stick in your mind after you leave, but shooting the rapids of the Arkansas River or soaking in a hot spring under the stars sure will. A bit of a jumping-off point, the area, south of Leadville on US 24, is certainly worth at least a day of your time.

For rafting, stop by **Wilderness Aware Rafting** (☎ 719-395-2112; www.wildernessaware.com; trips from $40). You'll want to run Brown's Canyon (class III-IV), the Narrows (III-IV) or the Numbers (IV-V), and the earlier in the season the better (try for late April or early May when the river is bloated with snow run-off and the rapids are much more intense). The company is located at the junc-

tion of Hwys 285 and 24 at Johnson Village, 2 miles south of Buena Vista.

After a day on the river, forget the bruises incurred when the boat flipped with a soak in the five pools at **Cottonwood Hot Springs Inn & Spa** (☎ 719-395-6434; 18999 County Rd 306; admission $15, r from $90). The pools are rustic with fantastic views (the stars can be amazing). Clothing is optional after dark between October and May, and the resort discourages children. The hot springs are about 6 miles south of Buena Vista.

West of Buena Vista the USFS operates scenic **Cottonwood Lake campground** (campsites $10) on the South Cottonwood Creek about 5 miles down USFS Rd 344 from the County Rd 306 turnoff (near the hot springs). Mountain goats are often spotted on the way to the camp.

In Buena Vista and Salida you'll find a string of motels and lodges with rooms from about $80 in summer, less in winter. Contact the **Buena Vista visitors center** (☎ 719-395-6612; www.buenavistacolorado.org; 343 S US 24; ☿ 9am-5pm Mon-Sat, 11am-3pm Sun Jun-Aug, 9am-5pm Mon-Fri Sep-May) and the **Salida visitors center** (☎ 719-539-2068; www.salidachamber.org; 406 W US 50; ☿ 9am-5pm Mon-Sat).

There is no public transport to Buena Vista.

Great Sand Dunes National Park

Landscapes collide in a shifting sea of sand at the **Great Sand Dunes National Park** (☎ 719-378-2312; 11999 Hwy 150; admission $3; visitors center ☿ 9am-5pm), making you wonder whether a space ship has whisked you to another planet. In the vast San Luis Valley, squeezed between the jagged 14,000ft peaks of the Sangre de Cristo and San Juan Mountains and flat, arid scrub brush, are 30 sq mile of dunes, the tallest of which rises 700ft from the valley floor.

Plan your visit to the USA's newest national park around a full moon. Stock up on supplies, stop by the visitors center for your free back-country camping permit, then hike into the surreal landscape and set up your tent in the middle of nowhere. You won't be disappointed.

There are numerous **hiking trails**, or the more adventuresome can try **sandboarding** (where you ride a snowboard down the dunes). You'll need your own equipment, but Colorado is jam-packed with snowboard rental shops. Spring is the best time for boarding, when the dunes are at their most moist. For the slickest boarding arrive a few hours after it rains – when the dunes are wet underneath, but dry on top. Try riding down Star Dune, roughly 750ft high. It's a strenuous 3-mile hike from the Dunes parking lot. The High Dune, about 650ft tall, is another option. Be sure to bring lots of water. Walking in loose sand is difficult, and summer temperatures on the dunes can exceed 130°F.

There is a **campground** (campsites $12) in the preserve. Otherwise, just south of the entrance you'll find the **Great Sand Dunes Oasis** (☎ 719-378-2222; 5400 Hwy 150; campsites $14, cabins $35; May-Oct). Cabins are rustic one-room affairs with shared facilities. The place has a restaurant and grocery store. Also near the monument's entrance, the **Great Sand Dunes Lodge** (☎ 719-378-2900; www.gsdlodge.com; 7900 Hwy 150 N; r from $80;) is a peaceful motel-style place; rooms have back-porch areas for dune gazing.

The sand dunes are about 35 miles northeast of Alamosa, and 250 miles south of Denver. From Denver, take I-25 south to Hwy 160 west and turn onto Hwy 150 north. There is no public transport.

Crested Butte

Remote and beautiful, Crested Butte feels real. Despite being one of Colorado's best ski resorts (some say *the* best), it doesn't put on airs. There's nothing haughty, or even glossy, about the town – just lovely fresh mountain air, a laid-back attitude and friendly folk.

Most everything in town is on Elk Ave, including the **visitors center** (☎ 970-349-6438; www .crestedbuttechamber.com; 601 Elk Ave; 9am-5pm).

Crested Butte Mountain Resort (☎ 970-349-2333; www.skicb.com; lift ticket $60) sits 2 miles north of the town at the base of the impressive mountain of the same name. Surrounded by forests, rugged mountain peaks, and the West Elk, Raggeds and Maroon Bells-Snowmass Wilderness Areas, the scenery is wet-your-pants beautiful. It caters mostly to intermediate and expert riders.

Crested Butte is also a mountain-biking mecca, full of excellent high-altitude single-track trails. For maps, information and mountain-bike rentals visit the **Alpineer** (☎ 970-349-5210; 419 6th St).

The attractive **Crested Butte International Hostel** (☎ 970-349-0588; www.crestedbuttehostel.com; 615 Teocalli Ave; dm $20-27, r with shared bathroom from $60) is one of Colorado's nicest. Bunks come with reading lamps and lockable drawers, and the communal area is mountain rustic with a stone fireplace and comfortable couches.

For more privacy try the handsome cedar-flavored **Inn at Crested Butte** (☎ 970-349-1225; www.innatcrestedbutte.com; 510 Whiterock Ave; r from $70). It has comfy doubles and triples, an outdoor hot tub and a free shuttle to the ski resort.

The closest large campground to Crested Butte is the reservable USFS **Lake Irwin** (campsites $12), west of town before Kebler Pass.

Certainly not a secret, the **Secret Stash** (☎ 970-349-6245; 21 Elk Ave; pizza $13-17; dinner) is an enticing pizza place with a joyful interior. Sit on the floor upstairs, or park yourself on a velvety chair.

ALIEN ENCOUNTERS

The sand dunes may have you thinking you've left the planet, but to really watch for outer space visitors you have to stop by the **UFO Watchtower & Campground** (☎ 719-378-2271; www .ufowatchtower.com; admission by donation; campsites $10; 11am-10pm) on Hwy 17, 2.5 miles north of Hooper.

Judy Messoline built the watchtower and opened her property up to UFO fanatics in 2000 after her cattle-ranching endeavors failed. The San Luis Valley is known for its high levels of UFO activity. Those who believe in the paranormal say the area is a giant antenna that attracts alien life forms, while Indian legend says it's a window to other worlds. There have been hundreds of unexplained sightings – everything from mile-long crafts to fireballs filling the night sky.

Today people from all over the country make the pilgrimage to Judy's humble dome with a 2nd-story viewing deck. In August hundreds gather for an annual night of close encounters with the third kind. A visit is definitely a unique, and if you're lucky, otherworldly, experience. If nothing else, the sunsets are phenomenal.

ROCKY MOUNTAINS

Cheap and filling meals are served at the pleasant **Paradise Cafe** (☎ 970-349-6233; cnr 4th St & Elk Ave; dishes $4-7; ☼ breakfast & lunch). If you have a hankering for Thai or Vietnamese, head to **Ginger Cafe** (☎ 970-349-7291; 313 3rd St; dishes $8-12; ☼ lunch & dinner).

Crested Butte has an interesting music scene year-round, and the lively **Eldo** (☎ 970-349-6125; 215 Elk Ave) is where most out-of-town bands play. From the great outdoor deck you can peep at street life below. The **Princess Wine Bar** (☎ 970-349-0210; 218 Elk St) is an intimate bar perfect for sitting and chatting a while. First-rate live music of the local singer-songwriter flavor is on show nightly.

Crested Butte's air link to the outside world is **Gunnison County Airport** (☎ 970-641-2304), 28 miles south of the town. **Alpine Express** (☎ 970-641-5074) meets all commercial flights in winter, but requires reservations in summer. The fare to Crested Butte is $25.

The free **Mountain Express** (☎ 970-349-7318) connects Crested Butte with Mt Crested Butte every 15 minutes in winter, less often in other seasons; check times at bus stops.

Black Canyon of the Gunnison National Park

Here a dark narrow gash above the Gunnison River leads down a 2000ft-deep chasm that's as eerie as it is spectacular. No other canyon in America combines the narrow openings, sheer walls and dizzying depths of the Black Canyon, and a peek over the edge evokes a sense of awe (and vertigo) for most. Head to the 6-mile long South Rim Rd, which takes you to 11 overlooks at the edge of the canyon, some reached via short trails up to 1.5-miles long. To challenge your senses, cycle along the smooth pavement running parallel to the rim's 2000ft drop-off. You get a better feel for the place than if you're trapped in a car.

More information can be had at the **visitors center** (☎ 970-249-1914; S Rim Dr; ☼ 8am-6pm, 8am-4pm winter), 2 miles from the entrance point. Entry to the park (bicycle or motorcycle per person $4, car or RV per vehicle $7) is good for seven days.

South Rim Campground (campsites $10) has 88 campsites. **North Rim Campground** (campsites $10), closed in winter, offers 13 sites.

SOUTHWESTERN COLORADO

The southwestern corner of the state boasts lots of stunning alpine scenery along with charming old mining towns brimming with Wild West lore. The mysterious Ancient Puebloan ruins, preserved in Mesa Verde National Park, are also here.

Durango

The region's most happening and attractive attraction, Durango is nothing short of delightful. It's one of those archetypal old Colorado mining towns, filled with graceful old hotels, Victorian-era saloons and mountains as far as the eye can see. If the town alone doesn't whet your appetite, dip into Durango's goody bag of adventures to get the glands really salivating. Meander through the historic district and listen for a shrill whistle, then watch the steam billow as the old train pulls in. Rent a bike and explore the trails, or get out the skis and head up the road for miles upon miles of powdery white bowls and tree-lined glades.

ORIENTATION

Most visitors' facilities are along Main Ave, including the 1882 Durango & Silverton Narrow Gauge Railroad Depot (at the south end of town). Motels are mostly north of the town center. The downtown is compact and easy to walk in a few hours.

INFORMATION

Maria's Bookshop (☎ 970-247-1438; 960 Main Ave) A good general bookstore.

Mercy Medical Center (☎ 970-247-4311; 375 E Park Ave)

Public Library (☎ 970-385-2970; 1118 E 2nd Ave) Free Internet access.

Visitors Center (☎ 800-525-8855; www.durango.org; 111 S Camino del Rio) South of town at the Santa Rita exit from US 550.

SIGHTS & ACTIVITIES
Durango & Silverton Narrow Gauge Railroad

Climb aboard the steam-driven **train** (☎ 970-247-2733, 888-872-4607; www.durangotrain.com; adult/child $65/31) for a scenic 45-mile trip north to Silverton, a National Historic Landmark. In continuous operation for 123 years, the train carries passengers behind vintage locomotives. The dazzling trip, which relives the sights and sounds of yesteryear, takes 3½ hours each way, and allows two hours for exploring Silverton. It is only offered from May through October. In winter the train runs to

Cascade Canyon (adult/child $45/22), where you will learn about native flora and fauna.

Skiing & Snowboarding

The town's other main drawcard is **Durango Mountain Resort** (☎ 970-247-9000, 800-693-0175; www .durangomountainresort.com; adult/child lift ticket $55/28), 25 miles north on US 550. The resort, also known as Purgatory, offers 1200 skiable acres of varying difficulty and boasts 260in of snow per year. Two terrain parks offer plenty of opportunities to catch some big air.

Rafting

The **Rivers West** (☎ 970-259-5077; 520 Main St; half/full-day from $40/60) is one of numerous companies that offer a variety of rafting trips down the Animas River. Beginners should check out the one-hour introduction to rafting, while the more adventurous can try the combination trip. It includes a ride to Silverton on the narrow gauge railroad and a run down the upper Animas, which boasts Class III to V rapids.

SLEEPING

Summer rates are high and rooms fill quickly, so it's always best to book ahead. Visit in winter, however, and you're in for a treat – some rates drop by 50%. There is a string of cheap motels north of town on Hwy 550 that go for around $60 in summer, and as little as $30 in winter.

General Palmer Hotel (☎ 970-247-4747; www .generalpalmer.com; 567 Main Ave; r from $105; 😮) A Victorian landmark built in 1898, the hotel features pewter, brass or wood four-poster beds along with quality linens and a teddy bear for snuggling. Rooms are small, but elegant, and if you tire of TV there's a collection of board games at the front desk. The entire place is reminiscent of a time long past. Check out the cozy library or the relaxing solarium.

Siesta Motel (☎ 970-247-0741; fax 970-247-0971; 3475 N Main Ave; s/d from $45/55; 😮) This family-owned hotel is one of the town's cheapest options. It's a welcoming place offering spacious and comfortable rooms. There's a little courtyard with a BBQ grill.

Leland House (☎ 970-385-1920; www.leland-house .com; 721 E 2nd Ave; r from $150) The 10 charming rooms in this 1927 restored brick apartment house are named after historic figures associated with the building, and decked

THE AUTHOR'S CHOICE

Strater Hotel (☎ 970-247-4431; www.strater .com; 699 Main St; r $200; 😮) A lovely old-world place with courteous staff and a museumlike interior. Check out the Stradivarius violin or the gold-plated commemorative Winchester. Romantic and peaceful rooms are furnished with antiques, crystal and lace. Beds are super comfortable, the linens impeccable. It's a fantastic deal in winter, when rooms with king-sized beds can go for as little as $79. The Strater runs summertime melodrama theater and operates the historic Diamond Belle Saloon – perfect for a late afternoon cocktail. The hot tub is a major romantic plus, it can be reserved by the hour.

out with their memorabilia and biographies. All rooms have kitchen facilities, and a gourmet breakfast is included.

Rochester House (☎ 970-385-1920; www.rochester hotel.com; 721 E 2nd Ave; r from $150) Next door to Leland House, and run by the same folks, this newly renovated place features spacious rooms with high ceilings. The decor is influenced by old Westerns, and movie posters and marquee lights adorn the hallways. It's a little bit of old Hollywood in the new west.

EATING

From the budget diner to the top-end steakhouse to mouthwatering microbreweries, Durango offers a surprisingly diverse collection of restaurants for a town its size.

East by Southwest (☎ 970-247-5533; 160 E College Dr; sushi $4-13, dishes $12-20; 😊 lunch & dinner) Thai, Vietnamese, Indonesian and Japanese cuisine, including a full sushi bar, is served in a congenial low-key setting. The food is delicious and can be washed down with a creative martini or sake cocktail. Locals rave.

Steamworks (☎ 970-259-9200; 801 E 2nd Ave; dishes $9-15; 😊 lunch & dinner) Industrial meets ski lodge at this popular microbrewery, with high sloping rafters and metal pipes. There's a large bar area, separate dining room and a Cajun-influenced menu. The homemade brews are excellent. At night there are DJs and live bands.

Carver Brewing Co (☎ 970-259-2545; 1022 Main Ave; dishes $5-15; 😊 lunch & dinner) A local institution, this relaxed brewery churns out 1000 barrels of beer annually. Enjoy a pint with burgers and sandwiches in the outdoor beer garden.

Randy's (☎ 970-247-9083; 152 E College Dr; dishes $20-25; ☯ dinner) A fine-dining establishment serving an eclectic menu of mainly seafood and steak, it's an intimate place just perfect for that special meal. Eat between 5pm and 6pm and get the same menu for $12 to $14. Locals say this is a superb restaurant for top-end dining.

Ore House (☎ 970-247-5707; 147 E College Dr; dishes $20-30; ☯ dinner; ✗) The best steakhouse in town, food is served in casual and rustic environs. Order a hand-cut aged steak, or try the steak, crab leg and lobster combo known as the Ore House Grubsteak ($40). It's easily big enough for two people. There's also a large wine cellar.

DRINKING

With a mix of college students and ski bums, it's little surprise that Durango has an active night scene. See earlier reviews for Carver Brewing Co and Steamworks; both microbreweries are popular after-dark watering holes. Live and DJ music is featured nightly at Steamworks.

Ska Brewing Company (☎ 970-247-5792; 545 Turner Dr) Big on flavor and variety, we think these are the best beers in town. Mainly a production facility, this small friendly place has a tasting-room bar usually jam-packed with locals catching up on gossip over an end-of-the-day pint. The brewmaster often doubles as the bartender, and the atmosphere is refreshingly relaxed.

Diamond Belle Saloon (☎ 970-376-7150; 699 Main Ave) A period place right down to the wait-

ress dressed in Victorian-era garb – fishnets and a garter with a feather in her hair. Cozy and elegant, the piano player pumps out ragtime tunes and takes requests. There are half-price appetizers and drink specials from 4pm to 6pm.

Lady Falconburgh's (☎ 970-582-9664; 640 Main Ave) With the largest selection of microbrews and imports in the Four Corners region, it's no secret that this place is popular. There's a brick and brass theme with original murals on the walls and more than 100 beers on offer – 38 of which are on tap. Voted Durango's best pub by locals, it's a great place for mingling. You won't feel out of place alone.

GETTING THERE & AROUND

The **Durango-La Plata County Airport** (☎ 970-247-8143) is 18 miles southwest of Durango via US 160 and Hwy 172. Greyhound/TNM&O buses run daily from the **Durango Bus Center** (☎ 970-259-2755; 275 E 8th Ave), north to Grand Junction and south to Albuquerque, New Mexico.

Durango lies at the junction of US 160 and US 550, 42 miles east of Cortez, 49 miles west of Pagosa Springs and 190 miles north of Albuquerque.

Mesa Verde National Park

Shrouded in mystery, Mesa Verde is a fascinating, if slightly eerie, national park to explore. It is here that a civilization of Ancestral Pueblo Indians appears to have vanished in AD 1300, leaving behind a complex civilization of cliff dwellings. Mesa Verde is unique among parks for its focus on preserving this civilization's cultural relics so that future generations may continue to interpret the puzzling settlement, and subsequent abandonment, of the area.

Ancestral Puebloan sites can be found throughout the canyons and mesas of the park, perched on a high plateau south of Cortez and Mancos. If you have time for only a short visit, check out the Chapin Mesa Museum and walk through the Spruce Tree House, where you can climb down a wooden ladder into the cool chamber of a kiva.

Mesa Verde rewards travelers who set aside a day or more to take the ranger-led tours of Cliff Palace and Balcony House, explore Wetherill Mesa, simply linger in the Chapin Mesa museum or participate in one of the campfire programs.

THE AUTHOR'S CHOICE

Jean Pierre Bakery (☎ 970-385-0122; 601 Main Ave; dishes $5-12; ☯ breakfast & lunch) Visit this charming patisserie on a cold winter day (or any day for that matter) for a taste of France in Colorado. The mouthwatering delicacies are made from scratch. Don't miss the soup and sandwich lunch special ($12), which includes a sumptuous French pastry chosen from the large counter display. Service could use a little improvement, but once you taste the food you'll forget how long it took to arrive. Well worth at least one meal.

Preserving the Ancestral Puebloan sites while accommodating ever-increasing numbers of visitors continues to challenge the NPS. The NPS strictly enforces the Antiquities Act, which prohibits removal or destruction of any such items and also prohibits public access to many of the approximately 4000 known Ancestral Puebloan sites.

The park entrance is off US 160 midway between Cortez and Mancos. From the entrance it is 21 miles to the **Park Headquarters** (☎ 970-529-4461; www.nps.gov/meve; 7-day park entry per vehicle $10, bicyclists, hikers & motorcyclists $5), which has road information and the word on park closures (many areas are closed in winter).

The **Chapin Mesa Museum** (☎ 970-529-4631; admission free; ☒ 8am-6:30pm, 8am-5pm winter) is near the Chief Ranger's office. Along the way are panoramic **Park Point** (10 miles from the entrance) and the **Far View visitors center** (☎ 970-529-5034; ☒ 8am-5pm), 15 miles from the entrance, where visitors must stop for tickets ($2.50) for tours of the magnificent Cliff Palace or Balcony House.

The largest concentration of Ancestral Puebloan sites in the area is at **Chapin Mesa**, including the densely clustered Far View Site and the large Spruce Tree House. At **Wetherill Mesa**, the second-largest concentration, visitors may enter stabilized surface sites and two cliff dwellings, including the Long House, open late May through August. South from Park Headquarters, the 6-mile **Mesa Top Road** connects excavated mesa-top sites, accessible cliff dwellings and vantages of inaccessible dwellings from the mesa rim.

The park concessionaire, **Aramark Mesa Verde** (☎ 970-529-4421; www.visitmesaverde.com; PO Box 277, Mancos, CO 81328; adult/child from $36/25), offers guided tours to excavated pit homes, cliff dwellings and the Spruce Tree House daily from May to mid-October.

The nearby towns of Cortez and Mancos have plenty of midrange places to stay. Within the national park, visitors must choose between two extremes: camping or staying at a top-end lodge. An overnight stay in the park allows convenient access to the many sites during the best viewing hours, participation in evening programs and the sheer pleasure of watching the sun set over Ute Mountain from the quiet of the mesa top. The **Far View Lodge** (☎ 970-529-4421; r $100; ☒ mid-Apr-Oct; ☒) is perched on the mesa top, 15 miles from the park entrance.

Rooms have Southwestern furnishings, private balconies and outstanding views.

Campers can head to **Morefield Campground** (☎ 970-529-4421; campsites/RV sites $19/25; ☒ May-mid-Oct), 4 miles from the park entrance. With 445 campsites, this place has plenty of capacity for the peak season. Grassy tent sites at Navajo Loop are conveniently located near Morefield Village (which offers a general store, gas station, restaurant, showers and laundry). Free evening campfire programs take place nightly from Memorial Day to Labor Day at the Morefield Campground Amphitheater.

The best dining option is the **Metate Room** (☎ 970-529-4421; Far View Lodge; dishes $15-25; ☒ dinner), which features an innovative menu inspired by Native American food and flavors. Palates are titillated with mains such as oven-roasted chicken breast with green chili stuffing and buffalo fajitas.

Telluride

It's been a hunting ground for the Utes, a saloon-swinging mining mecca and a ghost town. But nowadays folks flock to this archetypal mountain town for outdoor adventures galore, festivals and an all around laid-back feel. Easy on the eyes, Telluride boasts not only a well-preserved Victorian downtown, but also perfect mountain views.

ORIENTATION

Colorado Ave, also known as Main St, is where you'll find most of the restaurants, bars and shops. The town's small size means you can get everywhere on foot, so leave your car at the intercept parking lot at the south end of Mahoney Dr (near the visitors center) or wherever you are staying.

From town you can reach the ski mountain via two lifts and the gondola. The latter also links Telluride with Mountain Village, the true base for the Telluride Ski Area. Located 7 miles from town along Hwy 145, Mountain Village is a 20-minute drive east, but only 12 minutes' away by gondola (free for foot passengers).

INFORMATION

Bookworks (☎ 970-728-0700; 191 S Pine St) The town's biggest bookstore.

Telluride Medical Center (☎ 970-728-3848; 500 W Pacific Ave)

Visitors center (☎ 970-728-3041; www.telluride.com; 398 W Colorado Ave; ☒ 9am-5pm)

TELLURIDE'S FABULOUS FESTIVALS

Telluride has two giant festivals each year.

The **Telluride Bluegrass Festival** (☎ 800-624-2422; www.planetbluegrass.com; admission per day $55) sells out months in advance and attracts thousands for a weekend of top-notch rollicking blue-grass in a fantastic outdoor setting. Held in late June, it's an awesome party. Stalls sell all sorts of food and local microbrews to keep you happy. When the sun goes down revelers kick it up a notch, dancing wildly to the day's most anticipated acts. Many folks choose to camp, and if you purchase your ticket early enough you can get a four-day festival and camping pass for $240. This combo allows you to pitch your tent at Warner Field, within walking distance of the festival. If this option is sold out, you can camp at Ilium Campground, a beautiful site on the river, 7 miles west of Telluride. During the festival a four-day pass costs $45 per person and includes frequent shuttle service between the site and festival. There are numerous other campgrounds within 15 miles of Telluride that cost about $12 per site (see below). All campgrounds fill up quickly during festival week, so arrive early. Tickets and camping passes can be purchased on the festival website.

Telluride's other blow-out event is the increasingly popular, and esteemed, **Telluride Film Festival** (☎ 603-433-9202; www.telluridefilmfestival.com; admission $20-650), held in early September. National and international films are premiered at venues throughout the town, and the event attracts big-name stars. The only way to guarantee you'll see your first-choice film is to purchase a pass. These start at $325 and include priority entrance to numerous pictures. Admission to individual films costs $20; however, these tickets are only made available right before show time and passholders get first dibs. For more information on the relatively complicated pricing scheme, visit the film festival website.

SIGHTS & ACTIVITIES

Covering three distinct areas, **Telluride Ski Resort** (☎ 970-728-6900; www.tellurideskiresort.com; lift ticket $70) is served by 16 lifts. Much of the terrain is for advanced and intermediate skiers, but there's still ample choice for beginners.

There are public cross-country trails in Town Park, as well as along the San Miguel River and the Telluride Valley floor west of town. Instruction and rentals are available from the **Telluride Nordic Center** (☎ 970-728-1114; 800 E Colorado Ave). Experienced Nordic skiers will appreciate the **San Juan Hut Systems'** (☎ 970-626-3033; www.sanjuanhuts.com; hut per night $25) series of crude huts along a 206-mile route stretching from Telluride west to Moab, Utah. In summer these huts, which are equipped with bunks and cooking facilities, are popular with mountain bikers. Book well in advance, as huts fill quickly.

While on the subject, mountain biking is big news in Telluride. The surrounding peaks offer awesome single-track routes and, of course, stupendous scenery. Beginners should try the easy and smooth gravel **River Trail** that connects Town Park with Hwy 145 for a total trail distance of about 2 miles. If you want a bit more of a workout, continue up **Mill Creek Trail**, west of the Texaco gas sta-

tion near where the River Trail ends. After the initial climb, the trail follows the contour of the mountain and ends at the Jud Wiebe Trail (hikers only) where you'll have to turn back. To rent some gear, visit **Easy Rider Mountain Sports** (☎ 970-728-4734; 101 W Colorado Ave), which has a variety of bikes to choose from, as well as maps and information.

Hiking is also popular in the region. The **Jud Wiebe Trail**, a 2.7-mile loop from town, offers views after a 1300ft climb and is the only trail near Telluride dedicated to foot travel. Take Oak St north to Tomboy Rd and continue up the gated road on your left to reach the signed trailhead. The return portion of the loop ends at Aspen St.

The **Bear Creek Trail** is slightly more than 2 miles and ascends 1040ft to a beautiful cascading waterfall. From this trail you can access the strenuous **Wasatch Trail**, a 12-mile loop that heads west across the mountains to **Bridal Veil Falls**. The Bear Creek trailhead is at the south end of Pine St, across the San Miguel River.

SLEEPING

Camel's Garden (☎ 970-728-9300; www.camelsgarden .com; 250 W San Juan Ave; r from $275; 🖳) A modern and luxurious choice located at the base of the gondola. The lobby is filled with local artwork, and the large rooms feature custom crafted furniture and Italian-marble bathrooms with oversized tubs. Don't miss the giant 25ft outdoor hot tub. The complex also features restaurants, bars and spa treatments.

Victorian Inn (☎ 970-728-6601; www.tellurideinn .com; 401 W Pacific Ave; r from $80) It's exterior doesn't look very Victorian, but this inn has comfortable rooms (some with kitchenettes) emitting a hint of the era. There's a hot tub and sauna outside.

Oak Street Inn (☎ 970-728-3383; 134 Oak St; r from $66) Rooms are rather spartan, but it's the budget option in town and not bad value if money is tight. The cheapest rooms share baths.

Telluride Town Park Campground (☎ 970-728-2173; 500 W Colorado Ave; campsites $10; ☯ mid-May–mid-Sep) Right in the center of town, it has 20 sites with shower access ($1.50 for a hot shower). It fills up quickly in the high season.

Matterhorn Campground (☎ 970-327-4261; Hwy 145; campsites from $12, vehicle pass $6; ☯ mid-May–mid-Sep) Ten miles south of Telluride, this forest service campground has well-maintained sights, as well as shower and toilet blocks. It's a good option if you arrive during a festival and other lodging options are full.

EATING
Cosmopolitan (☎ 970-728-1292; 300 W San Juan Ave; dishes from $20; ☯ dinner) Can you resist a menu that includes Himalayan yak ribeye and lobster corn dogs? Chef Chad Scothorn has won numerous awards for his culinary aptitude, and his restaurant, inside the Hotel Columbia, certainly boasts the most unique menu in town. Influenced by the cuisines of France, Southwest USA and Thailand, the menu changes weekly, but the food is always excellent. Complement your meal with a bottle of fine wine – there are 200 vintages to choose from.

Baked in Telluride (☎ 970-728-4775; 127 S Fir St; dishes $6-10; ☯ breakfast, lunch & dinner) For a fill-up on pizza, sandwiches, salads and calzones head to this very casual place. The front deck is where to sit if you're looking to see or be seen.

221 South Oak (☎ 970-728-9505; 221 S Oak St; dishes $25; ☯ dinner) An intimate restaurant in a historic home, it has a small but innovative menu mixing world flavors with

excellent results. Dishes are meat, fish and seafood based with lots of fresh vegetables. Vegetarians shouldn't be frightened by all the meaty choices – a veggie menu is available upon request.

Fat Alley (☎ 970-728-3985; 128 S Oak St; dishes $6-9; ☯ lunch & dinner) For BBQ, bourbon and beer try this low-key restaurant. BBQ is the specialty of the house, but there are also burgers, Southwestern dishes and veggie options. It's a good place to bring the kids – the restaurant bills itself as 'family oriented.'

DRINKING
Last Dollar Saloon (☎ 970-728-4800; 100 E Colorado Ave) For a splash of local color with your cocktail head to this Telluride favorite. With the best selection of imported beers in town, as well as pool tables and darts, it's no wonder this creaky wooden bar is so popular.

Fly Me to the Moon Saloon (☎ 970-728-6666; 132 E Colorado Ave) Let your hair down and kick up your heels to the tunes of live bands at this saloon, the best place in Telluride to groove.

Smugglers Brewpub & Grille (☎ 970-728-0919; 225 South Pine St) Beer-lovers will feel right at home at casual Smugglers, a great place to hang out in any season. With at least seven beers on tap, this brewpub is big on variety. Try the chocolaty Two Plank Porter or the Smuggler's Scottish Strong Ale.

GETTING THERE & AROUND
Commuter aircraft serve the mesa-top **Telluride Airport** (☎ 970-778-5051; www.telluride airport.com), 5 miles east of town – weather permitting. At other times planes fly into Montrose, 65 miles north. **Telluride Express** (☎ 970-728-6000; www.tellurideexpress.com) runs shuttles to Montrose airport (adult/child $42/20); call to arrange pick-up.

THE AUTHOR'S CHOICE

Hotel Columbia (☎ 970-728-0660; www .columbiatelluride.com; r from $135; ☒) A real gem, each of the hotel's rooms has a balcony, fireplace and a mountain view. Baths are larger than average and breakfast is included. Other highlights include a rooftop Jacuzzi, library and fitness room. Plus, the hotel is right across the street from the gondola.

Ouray & The Million Dollar Highway

Between Silverton and Ouray, US 550 is known as the Million Dollar Hwy because the roadbed fill contains valuable ore. One of the state's most memorable drives, it's a breathtaking stretch of pavement that passes old mine head-frames and larger-than-life Alpine scenery – at some points the spectacular peaks are so close they seem ready to grab you. The road is scary when raining or snowing, so take extra care.

Sandwiched between imposing peaks, tiny Ouray just might be that little bit of paradise John Denver waxes lyrical about in *Rocky Mountain High*. Here the mountains don't just tower over you, they actually embrace you – the peaks surrounding Ouray leave barely 0.25 miles of valley floor in town. 'Awesome' just doesn't do the place justice.

The **visitors center** (☎ 970-325-4746; www.ouray colorado.com; 1220 Main St; ☯ 9am-5pm) is at the hot-springs pool.

SIGHTS & ACTIVITIES

Ouray's stunning scenery isn't the only ace up the town's sleeve. The **Ouray Hot Springs** (☯ 970-325-4638; 1220 Main St; admission $8; ☯ 10am-10pm Jun-Aug, call for hrs rest of year) is the perfect place for a healing soak. The crystal-clear natural spring water is free of the sulfur smells plaguing other hot springs, and the giant pool features a variety of soaking areas at temperatures from 96°F to 106°F.

Climbing the face of a frozen waterfall can be a sublime experience. To try it, head to the **Ouray Ice Park** (☎ 970-325-4061; www.ouray icepark.com; admission free; ☯ 7am-5pm mid-Dec–March), a 2-mile stretch of the Uncompagre Gorge that has been dedicated to public ice climbing. The first in the world, the park draws enthusiasts from around the globe to try their hand at climbs for all skill levels. For information on its festival, see below. **San Juan Mountain Guides** (☎ 970-325-4925; www.ouray climbing.com; two-/three-day courses $305/455) offers a weekend two-day introduction course and a three-day advanced course. All equipment is included, but check its website for dates. If you already know your stuff and just need to pick up some gear, stop by **Ouray Mountain Sports** (☎ 970-325-4284; 722 Main St).

FESTIVALS & EVENTS

Every year in mid-January Ouray holds the **Ouray Ice Festival** (☎ 970-325-4288; www.ourayice festival.com), which doubles as a fundraiser for the Ouray Ice Park. The festival features four days of climbing competitions, dinners, slide shows and clinics. You can watch the competitions for free, but to check out the evening events you'll need to make a $15 donation to the ice park. Once inside you'll get free brews from popular Colorado microbrewer New Belgium.

SLEEPING & EATING

Some of Ouray's lodges are destinations within themselves.

Beaumont Hotel (☎ 970-325-7000; www.Beaumont Hotel.com; 505 Main St; r $180-350) Ouray's classiest lodging option, this small hotel offers 12 rooms elegantly appointed with period furnishings. Established in 1886, the hotel was closed for more than 30 years before undergoing extensive renovations and reopening five years ago. It also boasts a spa and three unique boutiques.

Box Canyon Lodge and Hot Springs (☎ 970-325-4931; www.boxcanyonouray.com; 45 3rd Ave; s/d from $70/80) Offers geothermally heated rooms that are spacious and accommodating. The real treat here are the four wooden springs-fed hot tubs for guests – just perfect for a romantic stargazing soak.

Wiesbaden (☎ 970-325-4347; www.wiesbadenhot springs.com; cnr 6th Ave & 5th Ave; r from $120; ☒) This hotel's star lure is a natural indoor vapor cave, free for guests. It's another cozy spot to spend the night, with hot springs just outside.

Historic Western Hotel, Restaurant & Saloon (☎ 970-325-4645; www.historicwesternhotel.com; 210 7th Ave; r $35-95) Old Wild West meets Victorian elegance at this place, one of the largest remaining wooden structures on Colorado's western slope. It offers rooms for all budgets; the cheapest have shared baths. The open-air 2nd-floor verandah commands stunning views of the Uncompagre Gorge, while the Old West Saloon serves affordable meals and all sorts of drinks in a timeless setting.

Amphitheater Forest Service Campground (☎ 877-444-6777; US 550; campsites $12) A mile south of town, this USFS campground offers pleasing tent sites.

Tundra Restaurant at the Beaumont (☎ 970-325-7040; 505 Main St; dishes from $20; ☯ dinner) This elegant restaurant has won several awards for its wine cellar and does Thursday evening tastings. Billing itself as serving 'High Altitude' cuisine, it focuses on regional specialties with great results.

Outlaw Restaurant (☎ 970-325-4366; 610 Main St; dishes $14-22; lunch & dinner) Appetizing steaks and seafood, as well as a host of other dishes – from pasta to nightly specials – are served in a relaxing atmosphere. There's live piano music, a full bar and loads of regional memorabilia on the walls.

Silver Nugget Café (☎ 970-325-4100; 746 Main St; dishes $7-20; lunch & dinner) A busy, contemporary eatery in a historic building, Silver Nugget features a very large breakfast menu as well as deli-style sandwiches at lunch. Dinner offerings include deep-fried Rocky Mountain rainbow trout, and liver and onions.

GETTING THERE & AROUND
Ouray is 24 miles north of Silverton along US 550 and best reached by private vehicle.

Grand Junction
Western Colorado's main urban hub, Grand Junction has a pleasant downtown district. Most travelers just stop here for a night on their way to Utah's national parks – it's on I-70, just east of the Utah border. But the town also makes a great base for exploring the scenic wonders of Colorado National Monument and the Grand Mesa.

And if you linger, you'll learn a local secret: some of Colorado's finest mountain biking can be found around here, particularly near Fruita, 13 miles west. **Ruby Canyon Cycles** (☎ 970-241-0141; 301 Main St) rent bikes from $20.

Tourist information is available at the **visitors center** (☎ 970-244-1480; www.visitgrand junction.com; 740 Horizon Dr; 8:30am-8pm Jun-Aug, 8:30am-5pm Sep-May) and the **USFS Grand Junction** (☎ 970-242-8211; 2777 Crossroad Blvd; 8am-5pm Mon-Fri) office.

The historic **Hotel Melrose** (☎ 970-242-9636; www.hotelmelrose.com; 337 Colorado Ave; dm $20, r $33-45) is full of character and very close to downtown.

Two Rivers Inn (☎ 970-245-8585; 141 N 1st St; s/d $50/55;), along a traffic-heavy street, is a basic motel with comfortable enough rooms. It has a hot tub and pool.

The innocently attractive **Crystal Cafe & Bake Shop** (☎ 970-242-8843; 314 Main St; dishes $4-8; breakfast & lunch), with low muzak playing

and wine glasses on the table, is where locals come for their sweets injection; it also serves excellent breakfasts and lunches.

Visit **Rockslide Brewery** (☎ 970-245-2111; 401 Main St; dishes $9-15; lunch & dinner) for food and beer.

Walker Field (☎ 970-244-9100; www.walkerfield .com), Grand Junction's commercial airport, is 8 miles northeast of downtown (I-70 exit 31), and offers daily flights to Denver, Phoenix and Salt Lake City. Buses leave the **Greyhound depot** (☎ 970-242-6012; 230 S 5th St) for Denver ($40, 5½ hours) and other destinations. Amtrak's daily *California Zephyr* stops at the **train depot** (☎ 970-241-2733; 339 S 1st St).

Around Grand Junction
An 'island in the sky,' **Grand Mesa** is a lava-capped plateau rising more than 11,000ft above sea level at its highest point. Its broad summit offers a refresher from the Grand Valley's summer heat, as well as beautiful alpine scenery and an interesting four-hour loop drive from Grand Junction (via I-70, Hwy 65 and US 50). Get maps and information at the **Grand Mesa Byway Welcome Center** (☎ 970-856-3100; 9am-4pm Mon-Sat, 1-4pm Sun mid-May–mid-Oct), on Hwy 65 in Cedaredge, or from several smaller information stations atop the mesa. In winter test the fine powder and intermediate runs of **Powderhorn Ski Area** (☎ 970-268-5700; www.powderhorn.com; lift ticket adult $40), on the mesa's northern slope.

The 32-sq-mile scenic wonder called **Colorado National Monument** (hiker/car $3/5) is one of the most rewarding side trips possible off an interstate highway – well worth a driving detour year-round but more stellar for backcountry exploration. With about half a dozen accessible colorful sandstone canyons precipitously descending to the flatlands, this beauty is exceptional for hiking and camping, as well as biking on Rim Rock Rd, which links the eastern and western entrances. The monument is 4 miles west of Grand Junction, though its western entrance is closer to Fruita. The **visitors center** (☎ 970-858-3617; 8am-6pm Jun-Aug, 9am-5pm Sep-May) is 7 miles south of Fruita, on the plateau at the north end of the park. **Saddlehorn Campground** (campsites $10), near the visitors center, has the only formal campsites within the park. Backcountry camping is free (permits required).

WYOMING

From the craggy peaks of the Grand Tetons to the windswept prairies around Cheyenne, Wyoming is the kind of state that inspires country musicians to write cowboy ballads. With much of its beauty derived from its romantic emptiness, it's the kind of place you'd expect to find that lonesome cowboy riding the range, whistling a melancholy tune, embracing the solitude. Sparsely populated, Wyoming feels vast: miles upon miles of forested mountains, untrodden, arid basins, windswept cattle-strewn fields dotted with dilapidated barns. The people residing here are an independent and unhurried lot, adamantly tied to the land.

Galloping with rodeos and pageants, the pioneer past is alive and kicking in the 'Cowboy State.' Its unbroken northwestern corner epitomizes both the myth and reality of the Wild West. Sure, the high-noon shoot-outs are now staged, but plenty of charismatic wildlife still roams the Lower 48's most remote regions. Outdoor enthusiasts are spoiled for choice around stupendous, geyser-packed Yellowstone or the majestic Grand Tetons. And gateway towns, such as chic Jackson Hole and progressive Lander, are ideal launch pads for epic hiking, camping, climbing and skiing adventures. In other parts of the state, just hearing the lyrical names of the natural attractions – Bighorn Mountains, Devil's Tower, Medicine Bow, Wind River Range – is enough to have you itching to visit. Once you arrive, you'll likely be left slack-jawed and gaping at the majestic, often lonely, landscape you've journeyed too.

History

Home to native tribes, including the Arapaho and Shoshone who now reside on the 1.7 million-acre Wind River Indian Reservation, Wyoming was opened up to settlers in the 1860s after the construction of the Transcontinental Railroad.

In 1869 legislators granted women 21 years and older the right to vote and hold office, and Wyoming was later known as the Equality State. Some of the lawmakers thought it a clever way to attract much-needed female settlers – in 1870 adult men outnumbered women six to one.

In the late 19th century disputes that sometimes erupted in shoot-outs arose between big cattle barons and the small-time ranchers on the frontier. The Johnson County Cattle War of 1892 remains one of the most contemplated events in the region's history. In 1903 infamous range detective Tom Horn (who worked for the cattle companies) was hanged in Cheyenne for a murder that many still say he did not commit.

The 20th century saw economic development for the state based largely on extractive industries, such as mining. Uranium was discovered in 1918; trona was found in 1939. An economic mainstay for Wyoming and its surrounding states has long been Yellowstone National Park, which has lured large wads of tourist dollars since the end of WWII.

Today Wyoming remains a rural state where most folk either work on the family ranch or have jobs in the energy agency. One of the hottest issues in the state today pertains to trying to keep the younger generation in the state following university – recent census numbers show Wyoming's under-50-year-old population is quickly declining. To entice people to stay, or to interest other 20-somethings to move to the state, politicians are offering cheap plots of land if residents agree to live and work in small towns for a set number of years. The state is also concentrating on boosting tourism revenues.

Information

Wyoming's state sales tax is 7%.

Wyoming Road Conditions (☎ 307-772-0824, 888-996-7623)

Wyoming Travel & Tourism (☎ 800-225-5996; www.wyomingtourism.org; I-25 at College Dr, Cheyenne, WY 82002)

CHEYENNE

Many a country tune has been penned about Cheyenne, Wyoming's state capital and largest city. On the edge of the Great Plains, it's a cowboy town desperately clinging to the spirit of its frontier past. It doesn't offer much for visitors (it's a place where people live, rather than travel too), but its location at the junction of I-25 and I-80 makes it an obvious pit stop.

The **Cheyenne Visitors Center** (☎ 307-778-3133; www.cheyenne.org; 1 Depot Sq; ☼ 8am-5pm Mon-Fri, 9am-5pm Sat, 11am-5pm Sun, closed Sat & Sun winter) is a great resource. **City News** (☎ 307-638-8671; 1722 Carey Ave) stocks a fair range of publications, including regional titles.

Sights & Activities

If you're traveling with the kids in summer, head to Gunslinger Sq for an old-fashioned shoot-out. The **Cheyenne Gunslingers** (☎ 307-635-1028; cnr Lincolnway & Carey Ave; admission free) are a nonprofit group of actors that put on a great show – from near hangings to slippery jail-breaks. Stars include corrupt judges, smiling good guys and, of course, the badass villains. It's lively, if not exactly accurate, Old West entertainment. Show times are 6pm daily and at noon on Saturday from June to July.

Tour Cheyenne's major attractions, including the Wyoming State Capital, Governor's Mansion and late-19th-century homes of wealthy cattle barons, on the historic **Cheyenne Street Railway Trolley** (☎ 307-778-3133; 121 W 15th St; adult/child $8/4; ☼ 10am-4pm Mon-Sat, 1:30pm Sun mid-May–mid-Sep). The hop-on hop-off tours allow you to tour the attractions on your own and give a taste for old Cheyenne.

For a peek into what life was like in the old days, visit the lively **Frontier Days Old West Museum** (☎ 307-778-7290; 4601 N Carey Ave; adult/child $5/free; ☼ 8am-6pm Mon-Fri, 9am-5pm Sat & Sun summer, 9am-5pm Mon-Fri, 10am-5pm Sat & Sun winter) at I-25 exit 12. It is chockful of rodeo memorabilia – from saddles to trophies – and also houses other Wild West mementos.

Festivals & Events

Beginning late July, the city stages Wyoming's largest celebration, **Cheyenne Frontier Days** (☎ 307-778-7222; 4501 N Carey Ave). It's 10 days of rodeos (admission $10 to $22), concerts, dances, air shows, chili cook-offs and other shindigs that draw big crowds from across the Rockies.

Sleeping

Reservations are a must during Frontier Days, when rates double and everything within 50 miles is booked. If you're reserving ahead for that time, the visitors center's website can tell you which hotels in the area still offer rooms. Rates drop during winter. A string of cheap motels line noisy Lincolnway (I-25 exit 9).

Nagle Warren Mansion Bed & Breakfast (☎ 307-637-3333; www.naglewarrenmansion.com; 222 E 17th St; r from $120; P 🐾) This lavish spread is a fabu-

> ## WYOMING FACTS
> **Nicknames** Equality State, the Cowboy State
> **Population** 505,907
> **Area** 97,914 sq miles
> **Capital city** Cheyenne (population 51,507)
> **State mammal** Bison
> **Birthplace of** Abstract expressionist artist Jackson Pollock (1912–56)
> **Famous for** Yellowstone, homes where buffalo roam, agriculture, dude ranches

lous find. In a quickly going hip neighborhood, it offers very luxurious abodes decked out with late-19th-century regional antiques. Spacious and elegant, the mansion also boasts a small health club, Jacuzzi and massage treatments. Considering the glitz factor, it's a great deal.

Lincoln Court (☎ 307-638-3302; 1720 W Lincolnway; r from $50; P 🐾 🐾 🐾) It has decent rooms and is the best-value motel in summer, when it shares facilities with the pricier Best Western next door, including an indoor pool, fitness room and Jacuzzi.

Little America Hotel (☎ 307-775-8400; www.littleamerica.com; 2800 W Lincolnway; r from $75; P 🐾 🐾) This sprawling chain hotel west of I-25 has a golf course and large rooms with extras, such as bigger-than-standard TVs and hair dryers. The public areas are tastefully decorated with Navajo rugs and a big fireplace.

AB Camping (☎ 307-634-7035; abcamping@juno.com; 1503 W College Dr; campsites/RV sites $14/23; ☼ Mar-Oct) This tidy place offers the closest camping to Cheyenne. It's off I-25 at exit 7.

Eating

Whalen's Deli (☎ 307-637-7400; 318 W 17th St; dishes $3-6; ☼ 6am-8pm Mon-Sat) Run by a lovely couple, this is an attractive café and deli, with quality coffee and great deals on healthy sandwiches, soup, bagels, waffles and more.

Sanford's Grub & Pub (☎ 307-634-3381; 115 E 17th St; dishes $7-16; ☼ lunch & dinner) Walls aflutter with sports bric-a-brac and road signs, the fun Sanford's has a novella-length menu of tasty eats, including burgers, chicken and even a range of 'porker' dishes. Beer is served in ice-cold glasses.

Little Bear Inn (☎ 307-634-3684; 700 Little Bear Rd; dishes $12-20; ☼ dinner) A Cheyenne classic, the Little Bear serves hearty portions of quality steaks and sumptuous seafood in elegant Old

West surroundings. Adventurous diners can try the Rocky Mountain Oysters (fried bull's testicles). The restaurant is off I-25 exit 16.

Getting There & Around

The **Cheyenne Airport** (☎ 307-634-7071; www .cheyenneairport.com; 200 E 8th Ave) has daily flights to Denver. Greyhound and Powder River buses depart the **bus depot** (☎ 307-634-7744; 222 E Deming Dr) daily for Billings ($80, 11 hours) and Denver ($19, three hours), among other destinations.

On weekdays, the **Cheyenne Transit Program** (CTP; ☎ 307-637-6253; ◷ 8am-5pm Mon-Fri) operates six local bus routes ($1).

LARAMIE

Culturally vibrant Laramie is a college town, home to Wyoming's only four-year university. It's got a bit more spunk, and a heck of a lot more funk, than most Wyoming towns. Assets include a thriving historic area, lively nightspots and charming coffeehouses.

The **Laramie Visitors Center** (☎ 307-745-7339; 800 S 3rd St; ◷ 8am-5pm Mon-Fri) can help plan your stay. For outdoor info visit the **USFS Medicine Bow-Routt National Forest & Thunder Basin National Grassland Headquarters** (☎ 307-745-2300; 2468 Jackson St; ◷ 8am-5pm Mon-Fri).

Sights

It's easy to spend an afternoon wandering around Laramie's interesting 1860s-era **historic district**, packed with craft and jewelry shops and hip bookstores. For an infusion of culture, check out one of the museums on the **University of Wyoming** (UW; ☎ 307-766-4075) campus. We like the **University of Wyoming Art Museum** (☎ 307-766-6622; 2111 Willett Dr; admission free; ◷ 10am-5pm Mon-Sat), which has a range of paintings, sculptures and other rotating works from the 17th to 21st centuries. If you're traveling with the kids, stop by the **Wyoming Territorial Prison & Old West Park** (☎ 307-745-616; www.wyoprisonpark.org; 975 Snowy Range Rd; adult/child $11/free; ◷ 9am-6pm May-Oct, 10am-5pm Sat & Sun Nov-Mar, closed Apr). It's a curious restoration of an early prison and frontier town. The on-site **Horse Barn Theater** (adult/child $30/20) presents nightly melodramas and music revues at 6pm that include dinner.

Sleeping

Reservations are recommended (and rates much higher) for UW graduation (mid-May), Fourth of July, Cheyenne Frontier Days (p999) and fall UW football weekends. Numerous budget options are found off I-80 exit 313.

Gas Lite Motel (☎ 307-742-6616; 960 N 3rd St; r $65; ✖ ☒) This motel's rooms are decorated with playful renditions of the Old West; cowboy murals wall the indoor pool and caricatures color the parking lot. On a more practical note, the spic-and-span rooms are well equipped with a fridge, microwave and iron. Pets are welcome.

Veer Bar Guest Ranch (☎ 307-745-7036; www.vee-bar.com; 2081 Hwy 130; r day/week $150/1450; ☒) For the true Wyoming cowboy experience you can't beat a week at this guest ranch. It sits pretty on 800 acres, 21 miles west of Laramie, Single-night stays are possible on Saturday in summer and other nights during the rest of the year. Most guests stay for a week, partaking in horseback rides, fishing expeditions, river tubing and overnight campouts. Rates include all meals and activities. Digs are in comfortable, rustic and old-fashioned cabins. Dinners are steak and seafood affairs.

Sunset Inn (☎ 307-742-3741; 1104 S 3rd St; r $65; ✖ ☒) A comfortable place with spacious rooms, a pool and hot tub. It has a few wheelchair-friendly rooms available, along with a couple of cheaper bare-bones rooms for those on a real budget.

The best camping options are **USFS sites** (campsites $10) in the Pole Mountain area, just 10 miles east of town.

Eating & Drinking

Laramie has some of Wyoming's better restaurants, as well as a few boisterous bars.

Jeffrey's Bistro (☎ 307-742-7046; 123 Ivinson Ave; dishes $6-14; ◷ 11am-8pm Mon-Wed, 11am-9pm Thu-Sat) This long-established place boasts a zesty menu of fresh and innovative salads, sandwiches and pasta dishes. Everything is homemade and on the wholesome side.

Sweet Melissa's Vegetarian Cafe (☎ 307-742-9607; 213 S 1st St; dishes $4-6; ◷ lunch & dinner) A mellow student hangout, it's a comforting place with lots of nonmeaty foods for protein intake: fakin' BLT and even Italian-sausage lasagna. Fill up on coffee or chai and a hunk of yummy dessert.

Old Buckhorn Bar (☎ 307-742-3554; 114 Ivinson St) This rowdy place is where to go for live country-and-western music, along with a drink or three.

3rd St Bar & Grill (☎ 307-742-5522; 220 Grand Ave) Smoky, but quieter, it's a good place to start or end an evening.

Getting There & Around

Located 4 miles west of town via I-80 exit 311, **Laramie Regional Airport** (☎ 307-742-4164) has daily flights to Denver. **Greyhound** (☎ 307-742-5188) and **Powder River** (☎ 800-442-3682) buses stop at the **Tumbleweed Express gas station** (4700 Bluebird Lane) at the east end of town (I-80 exit 316).

MEDICINE BOW MOUNTAINS & SNOWY RANGE

The Snowy Range's lovely, lofty summits cap the rugged Medicine Bow Mountains west of Laramie. Southwest are the Sierra Madre and the Continental Divide – the Medicine Bow National Forest stretches across both. It's a fantastically wild and scenic region that's perfect for anyone seeking less-trodden paths.

The 29-mile **Snowy Range Scenic Byway** (Hwy 130) traverses Snowy Range Pass (10,830ft; open Memorial Day to mid-October) between Centennial and Saratoga. Wildflowers and wildlife are abundant, as are overlooks, trails, rafting, fishing areas and campgrounds. Pick up a map at the **Centennial Visitors Center** (☎ 307-742-6023; ☽ 9am-4pm Jun-Aug, Sat & Sun Sep-May), a mile west of Centennial on Hwy 130.

DEVILS TOWER NATIONAL MONUMENT

Rising a dramatic 1267ft above the placid Belle Fourche River, this nearly vertical monolith is an awesome site. Known as Bears Lodge by some of the 20-plus Native American tribes who consider it sacred, the **Devils Tower National Monument** (☎ 307-467-5283; www.nps.gov/deto; hiker/car $5/10) is a must-see for those traveling between the Black Hills (on the Wyoming–South Dakota border) and western Wyoming's parks. The nation's first national monument, established in 1906, it drew international curiosity in 1941 when parachutist George Hopkins was stuck atop the monument for six days. In 1977 it was the point of alien contact in Stephen Spielberg's *Close Encounters of the Third Kind*. Covering only about 2 sq miles, the park offers hiking, bird-watching, picnicking and camping. Rock climbing is also popular, though climbers are asked not to indulge in June, when Native American ceremonies take place.

The **visitors center** (☎ 307-467-5283; ☽ 8am-8pm Jun-Aug, 8:30am-4:30pm Apr & May, 9am-5pm Sep & Oct) is 3 miles beyond the entrance. The **Belle Fourche Campground** (campsites $12; ☽ Apr-Oct) fills early. Camping is also available in the Bearlodge Mountains, Black Hills and in the sleepy burg of Sundance.

SHERIDAN

In the shadow of the Bighorn Mountains, where the Rockies rise up from the plains, Sheridan is a charming small town with a well-preserved historic district. Century-old buildings, once home to Wyoming cattle barons, line Main St. Popular with adventure fanatics who come to play in the Bighorns, Sheridan is an upbeat place getting more popular each year. If dude ranching is your thing, there are plenty of places outside town to get in some serious saddle time.

Get information at the **Sheridan Visitors Center** (☎ 307-672-2485; www.sheridanwyomingchamber .org; E 5th St at I-90 exit 23; ☽ 8am-7pm Jun-Aug, 8am-5pm Mon-Fri Sep-May).

World-renowned for their hand-tooled leather goods, **King's Saddlery and Museum** (☎ 307-672-2702; 184 N Main St; admission free; ☽ 8am-5pm Mon-Sat) sells all the cowboy necessities. The adjacent museum houses one of the largest collections of Native American artifacts and cowboy memorabilia in the region, and is well worth a wander.

Most motels are along Main St north of 5th St, and along Coffeen Ave. You'll notice the good-value **Apple Tree Inn** (☎ 307-672-2428; 1552 Coffeen Ave; s/q $45/65; ✕) from a distance, thanks to its cheerful 'Prussian green' paint job. The single rooms are snug, but quads are much more spacious.

Fifteen miles west of town, **Spahn's Big Horn Mountain Bed and Breakfast** (☎ 307-674-8150; www.bighorn-wyoming.com; Hwy 335; r from $100; ✕ ✕) is Wyoming's oldest B&B. In a four-story log cabin, rooms are rustic with patchwork quilts and claw-foot tubs. The big deck is a great asset, with prairie views stretching out for miles. Highlights of a stay include nightly wildlife safaris, where guides take guests on a search for moose and elk.

If you've worked up an appetite, head to **Paolo's** (☎ 307-672-3853; 123 N Main St; dishes $7-14; ☽ lunch & dinner). The restaurant knows its dough, and it makes for scrumptious pizza. Also on offer are authentic pasta dishes and olive oil–drizzled salads.

For something a little meatier, visit the locally acclaimed **Golden Steer** (☎ 307-674-9334; 2071 N Main St; dishes $5-20; ⏰ lunch & dinner). The juicy sirloins are cooked anyway you like them, and plates of fried shrimp satisfy fatty cravings. There's usually live music on Friday and Saturday nights.

The **Sheridan County Airport** (☎ 307-672-8861), at the south end of town via Big Horn Ave (Hwy 332), has daily flights to Denver. Northbound and southbound **Powder River** (☎ 800-442-3682) buses stop twice daily at **Boogie's Texaco** (588 E 5th St).

BIGHORN MOUNTAINS

With vast grassy meadows, seas of wildflowers and peaceful conifer forests, the Bighorn Mountains are truly an awe-inspiring range. Factor in gushing waterfalls and abundant wildlife and you've got a stupendous natural playground. Hundreds of miles of marked trails offer boundless opportunities for hiking, mountain biking, snowshoeing and even snowmobiling. Three scenic east–west roads cross the mountains: US 16 (Cloud Peak Skyway), between Buffalo and Worland via Powder River Pass (9666ft), skirts the pristine Cloud Peak Wilderness Area; US 14 (Bighorn Scenic Byway), between Ranchester and Greybull, conquers Granite Pass (8950ft); and US 14 Alternate (Medicine Wheel Passage) traverses Baldy Pass (9430ft), connecting Burgess Junction with Lovell. Along the way, you'll pass Medicine Wheel National Historic Landmark, a mysterious and sacred site for Native Americans.

Along all three routes you'll find hiking trails, picnic areas, scenic vistas, fishing streams, and dozens of inviting USFS and Bureau of Land Management (BLM) campgrounds. If you just want to explore for a day, nearby Sheridan makes a good base and has plenty of lodging. Also in Sheridan, **Big Horn Mountain Sports** (☎ 307-672-6866; 334 N Main St) has loads of information on musts for hiking, biking, fishing and camping. The following ranger stations also have detailed information.

Bighorn National Forest Buffalo Ranger District (1415 Fort St; ⏰ 8am-4:30pm Mon-Fri)
Bighorn National Forest Headquarters (☎ 307-674-2600; 2013 Eastside 2nd St; ⏰ 8am-5pm Mon-Fri)

Buffalo Area BLM (☎ 307-684-1100; 1425 Fort St; ⏰ 8am-4:30pm Mon-Fri)

CODY

Raucous Cody likes to capitalize on its Wild West image (it's named after legendary William F 'Buffalo Bill' Cody). With a streak of yeehaw, the town happily relays yarns (not always the whole story, mind you) about its past. Summer is high season, and Cody puts on quite an Old West show for the throngs of visitors making their way to Yellowstone National Park, 52 miles to the west. From Cody, the approach to geyserland is dramatic to say the least. President Teddy Roosevelt once said this stretch of pavement was 'the most scenic 50 miles in the world.'

The **visitors center** (☎ 307-587-2777; 836 Sheridan Ave; ⏰ 8am-6pm Mon-Sat, 10am-3pm Sun Jun-Aug, 8am-5pm Mon-Fri Sep-May) and the **USFS Shoshone National Forest Wapiti Ranger District** (☎ 307-527-6921; 203A Yellowstone Ave; ⏰ 8am-4:30pm Mon-Fri) are logical starting points.

Cody's major tourist attraction is the superb **Buffalo Bill Historical Center** (☎ 307-587-4771; 720 Sheridan Ave; adult/child $15/4; ⏰ 7am-8pm Jun-Aug, 10am-3pm Tue-Sun Sep-May). A sprawling complex, it showcases everything Western: from posters, grainy films and other lore pertaining to Buffalo Bill's world-famous Wild West shows, to galleries showcasing frontier-oriented artwork to museums dedicated to Native Americans. Its newest wing, the Draper Museum of Natural History, explores the Yellowstone region's ecosystem with excellent results. Also popular is the **Cody Nite Rodeo** (☎ 307-587-2992; Stampede Park, 421 W Yellowstone Ave; adult/child from $12/6), which giddyups nightly from June to August.

Twenty miles west of Cody, the North Fork Shoshone River is a favorite among white-water rafting fans. A variety of wildlife, including elk and moose, are often seen from the river. Trips start at around $30. Check out **Wyoming River Trips** (☎ 307-587-6661; www.wyomingrivertrips.com; 1701 Sheridan Ave) in town.

Built by ol' Mr Bill in 1902, **Irma Hotel** (☎ 307-587-4221; www.irmahotel.com; 1192 Sheridan Ave; r from $80; 🖧) offers historic rooms in the main building or more modern, less-expensive motel-style rooms. Don't miss the on-site Silver Saddle Saloon; the ornate cherry-wood bar was a gift from Queen Victoria.

The pleasing **Gateway Campground** (☎ 307-587-2561; gateway@gatewaycamp.com; 203 Yellowstone Ave;

campsites/RV sites $12/19, r & cabins $55-65; 😵 💻) has a nice range of accommodations: shady sites for camping, cozy cabins and motel rooms.

Maxwell's Fine Food & Spirits (☎ 307-527-7749; 937 Sheridan Ave; dishes $8-17; 🕑 11am-9pm Mon-Sat) has a comfortable interior devoid of trophy animal heads, and a good selection of sandwiches, pasta, pizza and more; vegetarians will do just fine here.

For yummy burgers or a game of pool head to the **Silver Dollar Bar** (☎ 307-527-7666; 1313 Sheridan Ave). It's a historic place with lots of TV screens and live music nightly.

Yellowstone Regional Airport (☎ 307-587-5096; www.flyyra.com), 1 mile east of Cody, offers daily flights to Salt Lake City and Denver. **Powder River** (☎ 800-442-3682) buses stop at **Palmer's Outpost** (1521 Rumsey Ave) en route to Casper or Billings, Montana.

LANDER & AROUND

Just a stone's throw from the Wind River Indian Reservation, small town Lander is packed with outdoor enthusiasts (along with a healthy serving of longtime ranchers). The presence of the reputable National Outdoor Leadership School (NOLS) lends an interesting flavor and a college-town feel.

Explore your options at the **Lander visitors center** (☎ 307-332-3892; www.landerchamber.org; 160 N 1st St; 🕑 9am-5pm Mon-Fri) and the **USFS Shoshone National Forest Washakie District Ranger Station** (☎ 307-332-5460; 333 E Main St; 🕑 8am-4:30pm Mon-Fri).

Lander's great location at the foot of the glaciated Wind River Range (comprising Wyoming's highest mountains) makes it a perfect base for rock climbing and mountaineering. The rugged areas around Lander are also reputed for mountain biking, **hiking** and **fishing**.

Wild Iris Mountain Sports (☎ 307-332-4541; 333 Main St) is the climbers' mecca, while cyclists and powder hounds head to **Freewheel Ski & Cycle** (☎ 307-332-6616; 378 W Main St).

Sinks Canyon State Park, 6 miles south of Lander on Sinks Canyon Rd (Hwy 131), is a beautiful park with perplexing natural features. The Middle Fork of the Popo Agie River flows through the narrow canyon, disappears into the soluble Madison limestone called the Sinks, and pops up faster and warmer 0.25 miles downstream in a pool called the Rise. The summer-only **visitors center** (☎ 307-332-3077; 3079 Sinks Canyon

Rd; 🕑 9am-6pm Jun-Aug) is near two scenic **campgrounds** (campsites $8).

For lodging, one of the better returns for your money is **Pronghorn Lodge** (☎ 307-332-3940; www.pronghornlodge.com; 150 Main St; r from $60; 😵), which has faultless and spacious rooms, plus a hot tub.

For something a little more personal, try **Blue Spruce Inn** (☎ 307-332-8253; www.bluespruceinn.com; 677 S 3rd St; s/d $70/85; 😵 😵). The B&B features four individually decorated guestrooms with decor collected from the host's journeys around the world.

Camping is free (three-night maximum) at **Lander City Park** (☎ 307-332-4647; 405 Fremont St), but you can shower and use a hot tub if you tent up on the riverfront spots at **Holiday Lodge** (☎ 307-332-2511; 210 McFarlane Dr; per person $8).

Pizza, sandwiches and salads go down well on the outdoor deck at **Gannett Grill** (☎ 307-332-8228; 126 Main St; dishes $5-8; 🕑 lunch & dinner), especially when the sun is out. Special kids' meals ($4.50) come with a toy.

Cowfish (☎ 307-333-8227; 148 Main St; dishes $10-17; 🕑 lunch & dinner) is a Western restaurant for the new millennium, serving a range of innovatively seasoned 'cows, pigs and chickens'; interesting seafood selections are also on offer.

Wind River Transportation Authority (☎ 307-856-7118; www.wrtabuslines.com) provides scheduled Monday to Friday service between Lander, Riverton, Dubois, Rock Springs and Riverton Regional Airport ($15).

RESERVATION RADIO

In central Wyoming, home of the Wind River Indian Reservation, tune in to KWRR (89.5FM) for music and talk radio revolving around Native American issues. You might drop in on some Arapahoe music or even Shoshone-language lessons. The program **Native American Calling** (NAC; www.nativecalling.org) is a central feature that focuses on preserving and celebrating Native culture – its diverse topics touch upon activism, politics, current events, literature and music. Started by Native Koahnic Broadcast Corporation in Alaska, NAC is broadcast over 60 stations on the continent, mostly in the western half of the USA. KWRR also broadcasts local news and National Public Radio (NPR) programs.

ROCKY MOUNTAINS

YELLOWSTONE NATIONAL PARK

You just can't visit Wyoming without checking out the state's flagship attraction. Spectacular Yellowstone National Park, the world's first, is home to half the world's geysers and the Lower 48's motliest concentration of free-roaming wildlife. And when you factor in the plethora of alpine lakes, rivers and waterfalls you'll quickly realize you've stumbled across one of Mother Nature's most fabulous creations. This natural cornucopia attracts up to 30,000 visitors daily in summer and three-million gate-crashers annually. To escape the crowds, take a hike.

When John Colter became the first white man to visit the area in 1807, the only inhabitants were Tukadikas, a Shoshone Bannock people who hunted bighorn sheep. Colter's reports of the soaring geysers and boiling mud holes (at first dismissed as tall tales) brought in expeditions and tourism interest. The park was established in 1872 to preserve Yellowstone's spectacular geography: the geothermal phenomena, the fossil forests and Yellowstone Lake.

Orientation

The 3472-sq-mile park is divided into five distinct regions (clockwise from the north): Mammoth, Roosevelt, Canyon, Lake and Geyser Countries.

Of the park's five entrance stations, only the North Entrance, near Gardiner, Montana, is open year-round. The others, typically open May to October, are the Northeast Entrance (Cooke City, Montana), the East Entrance (Cody), the South Entrance (north of Grand Teton National Park) and the West Entrance (West Yellowstone, Montana). The park's main road is the 142-mile Grand Loop Rd scenic drive.

Information

The park is open year-round, but most roads close during winter. Park entrance permits (hiker/vehicle $10/20) are valid for seven days for entry into both Yellowstone and Grand Teton National Parks (p1007). Summer-only visitors centers are evenly spaced every 20 to 30 miles along Grand Loop Rd.

Albright Visitors Center & Park Headquarters
(☎ 307-344-2263; www.nps.gov/yell; Mammoth; ⊙ 8am-7pm Jun-Aug, 9am-5pm Sep-May)

NPS Backcountry Office (☎ 307-344-2160; PO Box 168, Yellowstone NP, WY 82190, Mammoth; ⊙ 8am-7pm Jun-Aug, 9am-5pm Sep-May)
Old Faithful Visitors Center (☎ 307-545-2750; Grand Loop Rd; ⊙ 9am-5pm mid-Apr–May, 8am-8pm Jun–mid-Apr)

Sights & Activities

Known for its fossil forests and geothermal areas at Mammoth Hot Springs and Norris Geyser Basin, **Mammoth Country** is North America's most volatile and oldest-known continuously active (115,000 years) thermal area. The peaks of the Gallatin Range rise to the northwest, towering above the lakes, creeks and the area's numerous hiking trails.

Fossil forests, the commanding Lamar River Valley and its tributary trout streams, Tower Falls and the Absaroka Mountains' craggy peaks are the highlights of **Roosevelt Country**, the park's most remote, scenic and undeveloped region. Several good hikes begin near the Tower Junction.

A series of scenic overlooks and a network of the Grand Canyon of the Yellowstone rim trails highlight the beauty of **Canyon Country**. South Rim Dr leads to the canyon's most spectacular overlook, at Artist Point. Mud Volcano is Canyon Country's primary geothermal area. Notable trails include the Seven Mile Hole Trail, which descends from the north rim into the canyon and tracks up Mt Washburn, the park's highest peak (10,243ft).

Yellowstone Lake, the centerpiece of **Lake Country** and one of the world's largest alpine lakes, is also home to the country's largest inland population of cutthroat trout. The often snowcapped Absaroka Mountains rise east and southeast of the lake.

Geyser Country has the most geothermal features in the park. Upper Geyser Basin contains 180 of the park's 200 to 250 geysers. The most famous is **Old Faithful**, which spews from 3700 to 8400 gallons of water 100ft to 180ft into the air every 1½ hours or so. The Firehole and Madison Rivers offer superb fishing and wildlife viewing.

Hikers can explore Yellowstone's backcountry from more than 85 trailheads that give access to 1200 miles of **hiking** trails. A free backcountry-use permit, available at visitors centers and ranger stations, is required for overnight trips. Backcountry

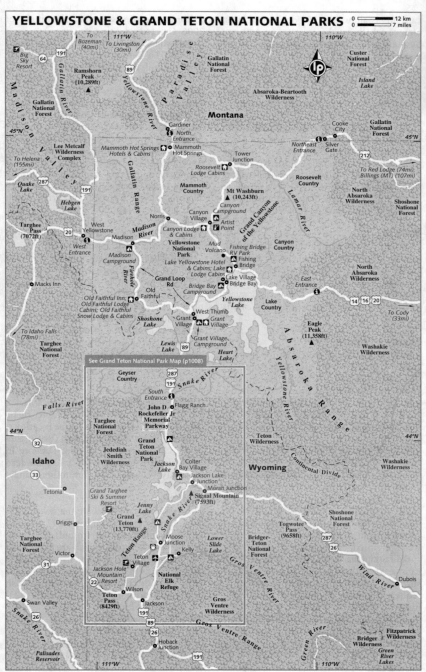

YELLOWSTONE & GRAND TETON NATIONAL PARKS

0 — 12 km
0 — 7 miles

To Bozeman (40mi)
To Livingston (30mi)

111°W   110°W

Big Sky Resort   64   191

Ramshorn Peak (10,289ft)

89

Gallatin River

Paradise Valley

Gallatin National Forest

Custer National Forest

Island Lake

Absaroka-Beartooth Wilderness

Montana

45°N

Gallatin National Forest   Cooke City

Madison Valley

Lee Metcalf Wilderness Complex

To Helena (155mi)

287

Quake Lake

Hebgen Lake

Targhee Pass (7072ft)

20

West Yellowstone

191

Mammoth Hot Springs Hotels & Cabins   Mammoth Hot Springs

Gardiner   North Entrance

Gallatin Range

Gallatin River

Roosevelt Lodge Cabins

Tower Junction

Northeast Entrance   Silver Gate

45°N

To Red Lodge (74mi); Billings (MT) (107mi)

212

North Absaroka Wilderness

Shoshone National Forest

Mammoth Country

Mt Washburn (10,243ft)

Lamar River

Roosevelt Country

Macks Inn

West Entrance   Madison

Madison River

Norris

Canyon Campground   Canyon Village

Canyon Lodge & Cabins

Artist Point

Grand Canyon of the Yellowstone

Canyon Country

Madison Campground

Firehole River

Yellowstone National Park

Mud Volcano

Fishing Bridge RV Park   Fishing Bridge

Lake Yellowstone Hotel & Cabins; Lake Lodge Cabins

Lake Village   Bridge Bay

North Absaroka Wilderness

To Idaho Falls (78mi)

Old Faithful Inn; Old Faithful Lodge Cabins; Old Faithful Snow Lodge & Cabins

Grand Loop Rd

Old Faithful

Bridge Bay Campground

Yellowstone Lake

East Entrance

14   16   20

To Cody (33mi)

Targhee National Forest

Shoshone Lake

Lewis Lake

Grant Village

West Thumb   Grant Village

Grant Village Campground

Lake Country

Eagle Peak (11,358ft)

Absaroka Range

Washakie Wilderness

Yellowstone River

89

Heart Lake

See Grand Teton National Park Map (p1008)

Falls River

44°N

32

Idaho

33

Tetonia

Driggs

Geyser Country

South Entrance   Flagg Ranch

287
191

Snake River

John D Rockefeller Jr Memorial Parkway

Targhee National Forest

Grand Teton National Park

Jedediah Smith Wilderness

Jackson Lake

Colter Bay Village

Jackson Lake Junction   Moran Junction

Teton Wilderness

44°N

Washakie Wilderness

Continental Divide

Grand Targhee Ski & Summer Resort

Jenny Lake

Grand Teton (13,770ft)

Teton Range

Snake River

Signal Mountain (7593ft)

Moose Junction   Kelly

Lower Slide Lake

Gros Ventre River

Bridger-Teton National Forest

Togwotee Pass (9658ft)

287

26

Shoshone National Forest

Wind River

Victor

31

Jackson Hole Mountain Resort

22

Teton Village

Wilson

Teton Pass (8429ft)

Jackson

National Elk Refuge

Gros Ventre Wilderness

Gros Ventre Range

Dubois

Swan Valley

26

Snake River

191
89

26

Hoback Junction

191

Gros Ventre River

Green River

Bridger Wilderness

Fitzpatrick Wilderness

Green River Lakes

Palisades Reservoir

111°W   110°W

camping is allowed in 300 designated sites, 60% of which can be reserved in advance by mail; a $20 fee applies regardless of the number of nights.

Cycling is best from April to October, when the roads are usually snow-free. Cyclists can ride on public roads and a few designated service roads, but not on the backcountry trails.

Most park trails are not groomed, but unplowed roads and trails are open for **cross-country skiing**. The rapids of Yankee Jim Canyon on the Yellowstone River host white-water rafting day-trippers. **Yellowstone Raft Company** (☎ 800-858-7781; www.yellowstone raft.com) offers a range of guided adventures out of Gardiner starting in late May.

Sleeping

NPS and private campgrounds, along with cabins, lodges and hotels, are all available in the park. Reservations are essential in summer. Contact the park concessionaire **Xanterra** (☎ 307-344-7311; www.travelyellowstone .com) to reserve a spot at its campsites, cabins or lodges.

CABINS & LODGES

Xanterra-run cabins, hotels and lodges are spread around the park and open from May or June to October. Mammoth Hot Springs Hotel and Old Faithful Snow Lodge are the exceptions; these lodges are also open mid-December through March. All places are nonsmoking and none have air-con, TV or Internet hook-ups.

Lake Yellowstone Hotel & Cabins (Lake Country; cabins $85-115, r $170-410) Oozing grand 1920s Western ambience, this historic hotel is Yellowstone's classiest lodging option. The stylish lounge was made for daydreaming; it offers big picture windows with lake views, lots of natural light and a live string quartet serenading in the background. Rooms are well appointed, cabins more rustic.

Old Faithful Inn (Geyser Country; r $75-350) Built right next to the signature geyser, it's little surprise that Old Faithful is in the most requested lodging in the park. A national historic landmark, it embodies everything a national park lodge should. The immense lobby, with its huge stone fireplaces, is the sort of place you'd imagine early railroad barons lingering in. The inn is currently undergoing a major restoration and plans

a shorter operating season in the summer of 2006. Call to make sure its open.

Old Faithful Snow Lodge & Cabins (Geyser Country; r $75-150) The newest sleeping option in the park, it's built to resemble a great Old Western lodge (think lots of timber). Wildlife-themed, the place tries to incorporate classic park motifs. Rooms are stylish and modern.

Roosevelt Lodge Cabins (Roosevelt Country; cabins $55-90) These pleasant cabins are good for families. With a cowboy vibe, the place offers nightly 'Old West dinner cookouts.' Guests travel by horse or wagon to a large meadow 3 miles from the lodge for open-air buffets.

Lake Lodge Cabins (Lake Country; cabins $55-115) The main lodge boasts a large front porch with lakeside mountain views and a cozy great room with two fireplaces. Choose from rustic 1920s wooden cabins, or more modern motel-style modules.

Grant Village (Lake Country; r $95-110) Near the southern edge of the park. this place has attractive motel-style rooms. Two nearby restaurants have fabulous lake views and provide easy access to sustenance.

Mammoth Hot Springs Hotel & Cabins (Mammoth Country; cabins $60-90, r $70-280) Wide variety of sleeping options, including cheap cabins and simple rooms with shared baths. The more expensive digs are still simple, but more comfortable. Elk are often seen grazing on the front lawn.

Old Faithful Lodge Cabins (Geyser Country; cabins $55-75) Views of Old Faithful; simple, rustic cabins. Good value for its prime location.

Canyon Lodge & Cabins (Canyon Country; cabins $40-115, r $135) Centrally located. Lodging in 1950s-era rustic cabins or more modern motel-style rooms. Tidy, but nothing fancy.

CAMPING

The best budget options are the seven NPS-run campgrounds (campsites $12 to $14), in Mammoth (open year-round), Roosevelt and Geyser Countries, which are first-come, first-served. Xanterra runs five reservable campgrounds (per night for up to six people $18), all with cold-water bathrooms, flush toilets and drinking water. RV sites ($23) are also available.

Bridge Bay Campground (Lake Country) Near the west shore of Yellowstone Lake. There are 431 sites.

Canyon Campground (Canyon Country) Centrally located, with pay showers and coin laundry nearby. There are 272 sites.

Fishing Bridge RV Park (Lake Country) Full hook-ups for hard-shell RVs only ($32). Pay showers and coin laundry. There are 346 sites.

Grant Village Campground (Lake Country) On Yellowstone Lake's southwest shore. Pay showers and coin laundry nearby. There are 425 sites.

Madison Campground (Geyser Country) Generator-free, tent-only area. There are 280 sites.

AROUND YELLOWSTONE

Plentiful accommodations can be found in the gateway towns of Cody (p1002), Gardiner and West Yellowstone.

In West Yellowstone, **Sleepy Hollow Lodge** (☎ 406-646-7707; www.sleepyhollowlodge.com; 124 Electric St; cabins from $80) is a real gem, with small log cabins sporting kitchens; it has BBQ grills and picnic tables for use.

Also in West Yellowstone, historic **Madison Motel** (☎ 406-646-7745; 139 Yellowstone Ave; dm $20, r $50-75; ☻ May-Oct; ✖ ▣) has rooms with or without bath, as well as dorm accommodations (although there is no kitchen).

In Gardiner, a very good choice is **Hillcrest Cottages** (☎ 406-848-7353; www.hillcrestcottages.com; 200 Scott St; cottages $60-100; ✖). The lovely little cottages come with kitchenettes, and one is wheelchair accessible.

Eating

Snack bars, delis, burger counters and grocery stores are scattered around the park. Breakfast buffets, salad bars and lunches at the hotel restaurants and cafeterias are decent value, but dinners at the fancier lodge dining rooms are rather overpriced for the quality of food. Dinner reservations are required at **Lake Yellowstone Hotel** (☎ 307-242-3899), **Old Faithful Inn** (☎ 307-545-4999) and **Grant Village** (☎ 307-242-3499).

Getting There & Away

The closest year-round airports are: Yellowstone Regional Airport in Cody (52 miles); Jackson Hole Airport (56 miles); Gallatin Field Airport (Bozeman, 65 miles); and Idaho Falls Regional Airport (107 miles) in Idaho. The airport in West Yellowstone, Montana, is usually open June to September. It's often more affordable to fly into Salt Lake City, Utah (390 miles), or Denver, Colorado (563 miles), and then rent a car.

No public transport exists to or within Yellowstone National Park. During summer commercial buses operate from Jackson and Cody. Buses operate to West Yellowstone and Gardiner from Bozeman year-round.

GRAND TETON NATIONAL PARK

It's hard to stop gawking at the jagged granite spires of the Teton Range, the centerpiece of spectacular Grand Teton National Park. Twelve glacier-carved summits rise above 12,000ft, crowned by the singular Grand Teton (13,770ft). The park is less crowded and more intimate than neighboring Yellowstone, offering boundless opportunities to get off-the-beaten track. Numerous hiking trails wind through alpine scenery, past rushing streams and around translucent lakes that mirror the soaring peaks. Bear, elk and moose roam this 40-mile-long range; the chance of spotting wildlife is good.

Orientation

The park has two entrance stations: Moose (south), on Teton Park Rd west of Moose Junction; and Moran (east), on US 89/191/287 north of Moran Junction. The park is open year-round, although some roads and entrances close from around November to May 1, including part of Moose-Wilson Rd, restricting access to the park from Teton Village.

Information

Park entrance permits (hiker/vehicle $10/20) are valid for seven days for entry into both Yellowstone and Grand Teton National Parks.

The **Park Headquarters** (☎ 307-739-3600; www.nps.gov/grte; ☻ 8am-7pm Jun-Aug, 8am-5pm rest of year) shares a building with **Moose Visitors Center** (☎ 307-739-3399, for backcountry permits 307-739-3309; Teton Park Rd; ☻ 8am-7pm Jun-Aug, 8am-5pm rest of year), 0.5 miles west of Moose Junction. Summer-only visitors centers are at Jenny Lake and Colter Bay.

Three concessionaires operate accommodations, restaurants and activities:

Dornan's (☎ 307-733-2522; www.dornans.com)

Grand Teton Lodge Company (☎ 307-543-2811, 800-628-9988; www.gtlc.com)

Signal Mountain Lodge (☎ 307-543-2831, 800-672-6012; www.signalmtnlodge.com)

Sights & Activities

The 5-mile **Signal Mountain Summit Road**, east of Teton Park Rd, goes to Signal Mountain's summit; it's generally closed to vehicles in

ROCKY MOUNTAINS

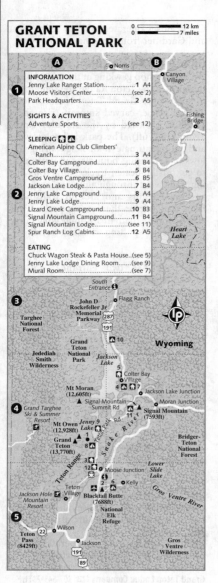

backcountry-use permit, available at visitors centers, is required for overnight trips, though reservations can be made from January to May by writing to park headquarters (p1007). The north–south **Teton Crest Trail**, which runs just west of the main summits, can be accessed from trailheads that wind up steep canyons.

The Tetons offer great rock climbing. Excellent short routes abound, as well as classic longer summits, such as Grand Teton, Mt Moran and Mt Owen. The **Jenny Lake Ranger Station** (☎ 307-739-3343; ☻ 8am-6pm Jun-Aug) is ground zero for climbing information. For instruction and guided climbs, contact **Exum Mountain Guides** (☎ 307-733-2297; www.exumguides.com).

Adventure Sports (☎ 307-733-3307), located at Dornan's Market in Moose Village, has maps, rents bikes, and can suggest road- and mountain-biking routes.

Fishing is also a draw – several species of whitefish and cutthroat, lake and brown trout thrive in the park's rivers and lakes. Get a license at the Moose Village store, Signal Mountain Lodge or Colter Bay Marina.

Cross-country skiing and **snowshoeing** are the best ways to take advantage of winter in the park. Pick up a brochure at Moose Visitors Center detailing routes.

Sleeping

The park features NPS campgrounds and private cabins, lodges and motels. Most campgrounds and accommodations are open May to October, weather depending. Lodges and cabins do not have TVs or radios.

Jenny Lake Lodge (☎ 307-543-3100; www.gtlc .com; cabins from $450; ☻ Jun-Sep) The most exclusive lodging in the park, Jenny Lake is in a quiet location amid pine forests. Digs are in 37 historic Western-styled cabins. Each is beautifully decorated with thick down comforters and handmade quilts. Rates include breakfast, a five-course dinner, horse riding and biking.

Jackson Lake Lodge (☎ 307-543-3100; www.gtlc .com; r $175-250; ☻ Jun-Sep; ☻) A full-service resort with 365 guestrooms perched on a bluff overlooking Jackson Lake. The grand lobby features Native American art and 60ft picture windows with fabulous Teton views. Rooms are fashionable, and the lodge can arrange everything from horseback riding to float trips.

winter. Another nice route is the **Jenny Lake Scenic Loop Road**, which abuts Grand Teton.

There are interesting **historic buildings** to be found at Menor's Ferry, 0.5 miles north of Moose Village, and along Mormon Row, east of Blacktail Butte.

The park has 200 miles of **hiking trails**; pick up maps at the visitors centers. A free

Signal Mountain Lodge (☎ 307-543-2831; www
.signalmtnlodge.com; cabins from $100, r $135; ❧ May–
mid-Oct) At the edge of Jackson Lake, this
spectacularly located place offers a variety
of accommodation options – from cozy
well-appointed cabins to rather posh rooms
with stunning lake and mountain views.

Colter Bay Village (☎ 307-543-3100; www.gtlc
.com; canvas tents $36, cabins $40-115; ❧ Jun-Sep)
Cozy log and tent cabins on the shores of
Jackson Lake. Rustic, yet comfortable, this
is a good choice for families and budget
travelers. There are two restaurants, a marina and grocery store on the premises.

Spur Ranch Log Cabins (☎ 307-733-2522; cabins
$155-230) In Moose, located on the banks of
the Snake River in a big wildflower laden
meadow, the 12 spacious cabins are decked
out with down comforters and handcrafted
lodge pole furniture. There's an on-site restaurant and bar. The place stays open year-
round; rates are reduced in winter.

American Alpine Club Climbers' Ranch (☎ 307-
733-7271; www.americanalpineclub.org; dm $10; ❧ mid-
Jun–mid-Sep) Budget travelers not wishing to
camp should check out the dorms at this
place, 4 miles north of the Moose Visitors
Center. It offers the best in-park deals, although you can't reserve bunks in advance.

The **NPS** (☎ 307-739-3603) operates the park's
five **campgrounds** (campsites $12), all first-come,
first-served. Demand for sites is high from
early July to Labor Day. Most campgrounds
fill by 11am (Jenny Lake fills much earlier;
Gros Ventre rarely fills up). Colter Bay and
Jenny Lake have tent-only sites reserved for
backpackers and cyclists.

Colter Bay Campground (Near Jackson Lake Junction)
There are 350 sites.

Gros Ventre Campground (Near Gros Ventre Junction)
There are 3360 sites, 100 tent-only.

Jenny Lake Campground (Near Moose Junction) There
are 349 tent-only sites.

Lizard Creek Campground (Near Colter Bay Village)
There are 360 sites.

Signal Mountain Campground (Near Jackson Lake
Junction) There are 386 sites.

Eating

Several reasonably priced restaurants are
in and around Colter Bay Village, Jackson
Lake Lodge and Moose village.

Mural Room (☎ 307-543-1911; dishes $20-30;
❧ breakfast, lunch & dinner) In the Jackson Lake
Lodge, this upscale place features wall murals

and giant picture windows with great Teton
views. The food is well prepared and rather
gourmet. Dinner reservations suggested.

Jenny Lake Lodge Dining Room (☎ 307-543-
3352; 5-course meal per person $50; ❧ breakfast, lunch &
dinner) Unwind before dinner with a drink on
the porch. Dinner is an intimate 5-course
experience served in a quaint log dining
room. Breakfast is also fixed-price menu.
Lunch is a more casual à la carte affair.
Dinner and breakfast reservations required;
jackets suggested for men at dinner.

Chuck Wagon Steak & Pasta House (☎ 307-543-
2811; dishes from $6; ❧ breakfast, lunch & dinner) A
family-friendly restaurant, this low-key place
in Colter Village serves big buffet breakfasts
and pasta, steak and all-you-can eat salad
bar–oriented lunches and dinners.

JACKSON HOLE

Jackson Hole is as jet setting as Wyoming
gets. The handsome town, set against
a stellar Teton backdrop, is the kind of
place where cowboy meets couture. Where
moose, elk and bison cruise the valley floor
and powder hounds swish down world-class
ski slopes. The vibe is playful and slightly
glam, but never pretentious. Wander into
the Mangy Moose Saloon, packed with ski-
bums, tourists, hipsters, ranchers and even
the occasional movie star, and you'll get
the idea. Jackson Hole buzzes year-round,
and summer visitors can hike, bike, raft and
roam to their heart's content.

Orientation

The region known as Jackson Hole is a valley bounded by the Gros Ventre and Teton
Ranges to the east and west, respectively.
Most of the area's amenities are concentrated in the town of Jackson. Teton Village, 12 miles northwest of Jackson, is home
to the wintertime mecca of Jackson Hole
Mountain Resort.

Information

Jackson Hole Wyoming (www.jacksonholenet.com) A
good website for information on the area.

USFS Bridger-Teton National Forest Headquarters
(☎ 307-739-5500; 340 N Cache Dr; ❧ 8am-4:30pm
Mon-Fri)

Valley Bookstore (☎ 307-733-4533; 125 N Cache St)
Has a superb selection of books, as well as regional maps.

Visitors Center (☎ 307-733-3316; www.jacksonhole
chamber.com; 532 N Cache Dr; ❧ 9am-5pm)

Sights

Downtown Jackson has a handful of **historic buildings** and, in summer, the **town square shoot-out** (admission free) is a hokey tourist draw; it takes place at 6:15pm Monday to Saturday. For more substance, visit the **National Elk Refuge** (☎ 307-733-9212; www.nationalelkrefuge.fws.gov/; Hwy 89; admission free; ⏰ 8am-5pm Sep-May, 8am-7pm Jun-Aug), about 2 miles northeast of town via Elk Refuge Rd. The refuge protects thousands of wapiti from November to March. A highlight of a winter visit is taking a 45-minute **horse-drawn sleigh ride** (adult/child $13/9; ⏰ 10am-4pm mid-Dec–Mar). The rides weave between the elk and offer great photo opportunities.

Activities

One of the USA's top ski destinations, **Jackson Hole Mountain Resort** (☎ 307-733-2292; www.jacksonhole.com; lift ticket adult/child $64/35), known as 'the Village,' boasts the USA's greatest continuous vertical rise – from the 6311ft base at Teton Village to the 10,450ft summit of Rendezvous Mountain. The terrain is mostly advanced, boasting lots of fluffy powder and rocky ledges made for jumping. When the snow melts the resort offers hiking, aerial tram rides ($16), mountain biking and horseback riding.

THE AUTHOR'S CHOICE

Amangani (☎ 307-734-7333; www.amangani.com; 1535 NE Butte Rd; r from $700; 🅿 🉐) The theme at the ultra-posh Amangani is understated elegance. Built into the edge of a mountain, the place blends effortlessly into its environment. Classy to the core, guest privacy is paramount. The hotel prides itself on its discerning service and eclectic ambience. Slate and redwood play prominently into interior design; rooms are rustic yet luxurious.

Snake River Lodge (☎ 307-732-6000; www.snakeriverlodge.com; 7710 Granite Loop Rd; r $175-400; 🅿 🉐) Gorgeously situated at the bottom of Jackson Hole Mountain Resort, it has a beautiful pool, spa facilities and a fitness room with a view. Wooden walls, stone slab floors and big fireplaces create the vibe. Rooms are well stocked with down comforters, exposed wood-beamed ceilings and lots of other luxury trappings.

Smack bang in town, the year-round 400-acre **Snow King Resort** (☎ 307-733-5200; www.snowking.com; lift ticket adult/child $35/25) offers night skiing, ice skating ($5) and snow tubing ($10). In summer you can mountain bike or ride the alpine slide or scenic chairlift.

If you're interested in mountain biking, head to **Teton Cyclery** (☎ 307-733-4386; 175 N Glenwood St) for advice. This excellent shop has knowledgeable service and bike rentals.

Rendezvous River Sports (☎ 307-733-2471; www.jhkayakschool.com; 945 W Broadway) offers kayak instruction. For rig rentals, try **Leisure Sports** (☎ 307-733-3040; 1075 S US89). Singles seeking a climbing partner swear by the bulletin board at **Teton Mountaineering** (☎ 307-733-3595; 170 N Cache Dr).

Sleeping

Reservations are essential in summer and winter. Cheaper rates are available from October 1 until the first big snowfall, and from early April to Memorial Day weekend. **Jackson Hole Central Reservations** (☎ 800-443-6931) is the one-stop shop for lodgings.

Virginian Lodge (☎ 307-733-2792; www.virginianlodge.com; 750 W Broadway; winter/summer r from $55/95; 🅿 🉐) This cheerful place is one of the best-value motels in town. It's not exactly posh, but rooms are clean and comfortable, and the big grassy pool area is a real plus. Push through the swinging doors of the smoky old saloon and you're in for a fun night.

Hostel X (☎ 307-733-3415; www.hostelx.com; 3315 McCollister Dr; d/q $55/70) Teton Village's only budget option is a relaxed place, offering basic rooms with private bathroom (and maid service), plus a full-on entertainment room. There's a five-night minimum in winter, when the fireplace is blazing, the place hopping and reservations advised. The hostel closes from early April to late May and from October through November.

Bunkhouse (☎ 307-733-3668; www.anvilmotel.com/bunkhouse; 215 N Cache Dr; dm $25, r from $49; 🉐) The Anvil Motel's 25-bed hostel is the only in-town budget option. The basement-level space has clean dorm beds, a laundry, ski lockers, a TV lounge and a basic kitchen. It's quiet most of the year, but becomes party central when the powder is fresh. Hostellers can use the motel's hot tub.

Wagon Wheel Village (☎ 307-733-4588; www.wagonwheelvillage.com; 435 N Cache Dr; campsites/RV sites $24/45) Popular with climbers, these cramped creek-side campsites encourage socializing with your neighbors. When busy, they can really be lots of fun.

Eating

Jackson is home to Wyoming's most sophisticated food.

Rendevous Bistro (☎ 307-739-1100; 380 S Broadway; dishes $13-18; ☽ dinner) Locals love this bustling bistro with a smart interior that serves the best-value top-end food in town – from steak to lobster. Environs are intimate, the service excellent.

Snake River Brewing Co (☎ 307-739-2337; 265 S Millward St; dishes $5-11; ☽ lunch & dinner; ✕) Popular with the local ski crowd, its pub grub (think wood-fired pizza and juicy burgers) stands up well to the smooth homemade microbrews. Happy-hour pints ($2.50) and lunch specials ($6) make it a local favorite.

Harvest Bakery & Cafe (☎ 307-733-5418; 130 W Broadway; dishes $3-7; ☽ breakfast, lunch & dinner) This natural-foods store – filled with organic produce, fresh breads and baked goods – serves up wholesome soups, sandwiches and smoothies from its café.

Bubba's Bar-B-Que (☎ 307-733-2288; 515 W Broadway; dishes $5-15; ☽ breakfast, lunch & dinner) Get the biggest, fluffiest breakfast biscuits for miles at this friendly and energetic BYOB eatery. Later on, it's got a decent salad bar, and serves a ranch of ribs and racks.

Drinking

Like all resort towns with restless bunches of seasonal workers and play-hard visitors, Jackson has an animated nightlife.

Mangy Moose Saloon (☎ 307-733-9779; Teton Village) This lively place hosts a wide variety of live shows, from free local bands to big-name national touring acts. A favorite après-ski spot, it attracts hordes of locals and tourists. It's an intimate venue where the stage is visible from two levels.

Stagecoach Bar & Grill (☎ 307-733-4407; 5755 W Hwy 22) This bar is worth the 5-mile drive from Jackson, particularly on Tuesday for free pool, Wednesday for DJ'd reggae or Thursday for disco hits. Herb tokers and cowpokers mingle here more than any other place in the Wild West. Horse parking is available outside.

Rancher (☎ 307-733-3886; 20 E Broadway) Overlooking the square, this pool hall is the hard drinkin' local happy-hour hangout.

THE AUTHOR'S CHOICE

Snake River Grill (☎ 307-733-0557; 84 E Broadway; dishes from $20; ☽ dinner) Locally adored for its gourmet grub, this place isn't afraid to get creative. The award-winning menu, featuring much seafood along with some game entries, is as good as the world-class wine list. Even the pizza is special – they're topped with fancy ingredients such as Portobello mushrooms or duck sausage.

Million Dollar Cowboy Bar (☎ 307-733-2207; 25 N Cache Dr) Everyone should saddle up (at least briefly) to this entertaining landmark, which has a chop shop that dishes decent Philly cheesesteaks.

Getting There & Around

The **Jackson Hole Airport** (☎ 307-733-7682) is 7 miles north of Jackson off US 26/89/191 within Grand Teton National Park. Daily flights serve Denver, Salt Lake City, Dallas and Houston, while weekend flights connect Jackson with Chicago.

Alltrans' Jackson Hole Express (☎ 307-733-1719; www.jacksonholebus.com) buses depart at 6:30am daily from Jackson's Exxon Station (cnr Hwy 89 S & S Park Loop Rd) for Salt Lake City ($56, 5½ hours). **Southern Teton Area Rapid Transit** (☎ 307-733-4521; www.startbus.com) buses connect Jackson and Teton Village.

MONTANA

Like an addictive drug, once you've had a hit of Montana's bountiful offerings you'll crave a hell of a lot more. There's nothing quite like that first Montana high – a soul-soothing experience that words can't justify. Maybe it's the sky, which seems bigger and bluer here than anywhere else. Maybe it's the air, intoxicatingly crisp, fresh and scented with pine. Maybe it's the way the mountains melt into undulating grasslands, or the sight of a shaggy grizzly sipping from an ice-blue glacier lake. Maybe it's the frontier spirit, wild and free and oh-so-American, that earned Montana its 'live and let live' state motto. Whatever the cause, Montana's the kind of place that remains alive in nostalgia long after you've left its beautiful wilds behind.

ROCKY MOUNTAINS

MONTANA FACTS

Nickname Treasure State

Population 930,698

Area 147,045 sq miles

Capital city Helena (population 27,340)

State fossil Duck-billed dinosaur

Birthplace of Gary Cooper (1901–61), Hollywood star of 1930s to '50s; Evel Knievel (b 1938), legendary motorcycle daredevil

Famous for Big sky, fly-fishable rivers, snow, rodeos, bears

Once the untamed domain of ranchers, miners, explorers and Native Americans, modern-day state demographics are shifting quickly. Artists, writers, real-estate developers, students and movie stars, hooked on the fabulous Montana high, are migrating here in droves. Scruffy, nowhere towns are going glam; mom-and-pop shops and dusty old saloons are competing with chic boutiques, slick microbreweries and fusion restaurants. However, the vibe remains refreshingly unpretentious.

Montana's a laid-back state, a place where folks are down-to-earth and love the outdoors. And despite the influx of transplants, Montana never feels crowded: the livestock to human ratio is still 12:1! From trout-filled rivers made for fly-fishing to rugged and pristine wilderness areas, there's plenty of space to get away. Even the state's biggest attractions, Glacier National Park and Flathead Lake, offer quiet beauty and opportunities for remote exploration.

History

If these lands could talk. Montana has seen many a historical conflict between white settlers and Native American tribes, including battles of the Big Hole and Rosebud. The gold frenzy hit in 1863, with a discovery near Bannack. Marcus Daly struck the world's largest and purest copper vein in Butte, which was mined for the next 100 years.

In 1889 Montana became the 41st state of the Union. Though tourism began to sweep through the Rockies in the late 19th century, the boom didn't really hit Montana until the 1980s. Now the state's attractions support the economy. The tourism industry has yet to prove completely reliable though, as was shown by the forest fires of summer 2003. The blazes in northwest Montana affected thousands of acres as well as the local economy.

Information

Montana does not have a state sales tax.

Montana Road Conditions (☎ 800-226-7623, within Montana 511; www.mdt.state.mt.us)

Travel Montana (☎ 800-847-4868; www.visitmt.com; PO Box 200533, Helena, MT 59620)

BOZEMAN

Bozeman is kind of like Montana's version of Los Angeles – a hip place to be. It may have small town agricultural roots, but today it's a vibrant, fast-growing hub, where ranchers rub shoulders with hipster college students in the trendy boutiques and funky restaurants lining Main St. Rumped up against the Bridger Mountains, Bozeman is blessed with famous Montana beauty and a slightly bohemian air.

The **visitors center** (☎ 406-586-5421; www.bozemanchamber.com; 1003 N 7th Ave; ☙ 8am-5pm Mon-Fri) can provide information on lodging and attractions.

Montana State University's **Museum of the Rockies** (☎ 406-994-2251; www.museumoftherockies.org; 600 W Kagy Blvd; adult/child $9.50/6.50; ☙ 8am-8pm) is the most entertaining natural history museum in Montana, with dinosaur exhibits, early Native American art and laser shows.

With every passing digital year the calculating dinosaurs (slide rules, room-sized electronic computers, key punch machines) at the **American Computer Museum** (☎ 406-582-1288; www.compustory.com; 2304 N 7th Ave; admission $4; ☙ 10am-4pm Jun-Aug, 10am-4pm Tue, Wed, Fri & Sat Sep-May) seem more comical. Don't miss the prototypes of first-run video games.

South of town, Hyalite Canyon is great for climbing, trail running and mountain biking. North of town, the Bridger Mountains offer excellent hiking and skiing at **Bridger Bowl Ski Area** (☎ 406-587-2111; www.bridgerbowl.com; 15795 Bridger Canyon Rd; lift ticket $35) and **Bohart Ranch Cross-Country Ski Center** (☎ 406-586-9070; 16621 Bridger Canyon Rd). For maps, trail guides and gear rental drop by **Barrel Mountaineering** (☎ 406-582-1335; 240 E Main St).

Soak away your aches and pains in the pools, sauna and steam room at **Bozeman Hot Springs** (☎ 406-586-6492; admission $5; ☙ 8am-1pm Sun-Thu, 8am-midnight Fri & Sat), 8 miles west of Bozeman off US 191.

Sleeping

The full gamut of chain motels lies north of downtown on 7th Ave, near I-90. There are also a few options east of downtown on Main St.

Voss Inn (☎ 406-587-0982; www.bozeman-vossinn .com; 319 S Wilson St; s/d $110/130; ✗) Offering six carefully restored rooms, this Victorian-era B&B is a charming place to stay. Big beds, old-fashioned charm and terry cloth robes heighten its appeal.

Bozeman Backpacker's Hostel (☎ 406-586-4659; 405 W Olive St; dm/r $16/35) This Aussie-run independent hostel's casual approach means a relaxed vibe, friendly folk and no lockout – but also wavering cleanliness and uncomfortable beds. It's *the* place to rendezvous with active globestompers.

Lewis & Clark Motel (☎ 406-586-3341; www .lewisandclarkmotel.net; 824 W Main St; s/d $60/70; ✗ ☒) For a drop of Vegas in your Montana, stay at this flashy motel with casino games and cold beers in the lobby. The large rooms have floor-to-ceiling front windows, and there's a pool, Jacuzzi and sauna on-site.

Bear Canyon Campground (☎ 800-438-1575; www.bearcanyoncampground.com; campsites $15, RV sites $20-25; ✓ May-Oct; ☒) Three miles east of Bozeman off I-90 exit 313, this campground has pleasant sites and RV hook-ups.

Eating

Mint (☎ 406-388-1100; Belgrande, 27 E Main St; dishes $10-30; ✓ lunch & dinner) Boasting a fabulous wine list, this local landmark offers more sophistication than the typical Montana roadhouse. Located 8 miles west of town, the menu is meat-oriented with juicy steaks featured prominently. Sleek booths, old cowboy photos and a mounted longhorn head create the ambience. Those on a budget will appreciate the cheaper bar menu; veggies can chow on a daily meatless plate.

John Bozeman's Bistro (☎ 406-537-4100; 125 W Main St; dishes $10-25; ✓ lunch & dinner) The innovative menu changes constantly at this popular upscale dining haunt. The eclectic offerings circumnavigate the globe, include lots of veggie options and are consistently delicious.

Cateye Café (☎ 406-587-8844; 23 N Tracy Ave; meals $5-8; ✓ 7:30am-2:30pm Wed-Mon) Heaping hot plates of eggs and more are served up at this popular breakfast joint. Even vegans are accounted for, with nondairy veggie

options on the menu. Wash it all down with a bubbling mimosa.

Community Food Co-Op (☎ 406-587-4039; 908 W Main St; ✓ 9am-9pm) The co-op has all the fixings for a splendid meal, plus a deli ($3 to $6). Head to the 2nd-floor café for gorgeous desserts, accompanied by fair-trade coffee and mountain views. There's sometimes live music.

Drinking

No joke: barhopping is one of the most popular majors at Montana State University (MSU).

Molly Brown (☎ 406-586-9903; S 8th St) Popular with students, this noisy dive bar offers 20 beers on tap and eight pool tables for getting your game on.

Zebra (☎ 406-585-8851; 15 N Rouse St) Inside the Bozeman Hotel, this place is the epicenter of the local live music scene.

Getting There & Away

The **Gallatin Field Airport** (☎ 406-388-6632) is 8 miles northwest of downtown. **Karst Stage** (☎ 406-388-2293; www.karststage.com) runs buses daily, December to April, from the airport to Big Sky ($27, one hour) and West Yellowstone ($37, two hours); summer service is by reservation only.

Greyhound and Rimrock Trailways depart from the **bus depot** (☎ 406-587-3110; 1205 E Main St), 0.5 miles from downtown, and service all Montana towns along I-90.

GALLATIN & PARADISE VALLEYS

Outdoor enthusiasts can explore the expansive beauty around the Gallatin River for days. **Big Sky Resort** (☎ 800-548-4486; www.big skyresort.com; lift ticket adult/child $60/45), with three mountains, 400in of annual powder and Montana's longest vertical drop (4350ft), is the valley's foremost destination for skiing. In summer it offers gondola-served hiking and mountain biking. For backpacking and backcountry skiing, head to the **Lee Metcalf Wilderness Complex**, which covers 389 sq miles of Gallatin and Beaverhead National Forest land west of US 191. Numerous scenic USFS campgrounds snuggle up to the Gallatin Range on the east side of US 191.

Fisherfolk will prefer to tie their flies in the Paradise Valley, which is full of blue-ribbon **fishing** access sites. Rafts, kayaks and canoes take to the river June to August.

Twenty miles south of Livingston, off US 89 en route to Yellowstone, unpretentious **Chico Hot Springs** (☎ 406-333-4933; www .chicohotsprings.com; r from $80, pool for nonguests $6.50; 🖫) has a couple of suave year-round soaking pools, and its lively bar hosts swinging county-and-western dance bands on weekends. The on-site restaurant (mains $20 to $30) is known around the region for its fine steak and seafood fare.

BILLINGS

It's hard to believe laid-back Billings is Montana's largest city – it feels much more like a small town. A friendly ranching and oil center, it offers big city conveniences without big city stress. Though it's not an absolute must-see, it's a worthwhile place to break your journey. The historic downtown, with squat brown buildings, wide streets, cozy cafés and interesting little knick-knack shops, is hardly cosmopolitan, but emits a certain endearing charm. Cultural sites worth visiting include the **Yellowstone Art Museum** (☎ 406-256-6804; 401 N 27th St; adult/child $7/5; 🕙 10am-5pm Tue-Sat), which has the largest publicly held Will James collection, as well as a diverse range of Western art, and the small but interesting **Western Heritage Center** (☎ 406-256-6809; 2822 Montana Ave; admission free; 🕙 10am-5pm Tue-Sat).

Billing's landmark hotel, the **Historic Northern Hotel** (☎ 406-245-5121; www.thenorthern hotel.com; cnr Broadway & 1st Ave; r $90; 🅿 🍴 🖳) does a great job of blending cowboy with contemporary. Rooms are elegant, the vibe casual Old West. Its saloon is popular at night, when locals show up for pints and live music. For budget accommodations, the welcoming **Big 5 Motel** (☎ 406-245-6646; 2601 N 4th Ave; s/d $35/40; 🅿 🍴) is a good bet – it has a convenient location and tidy rooms.

Wake up at the chipper **McCormick Cafe** (☎ 406-255-9555; 2419 Montana Ave; meals $4-7; 🕙 7am-4pm Mon-Fri, 8am-3pm Sat; 🖳), where you can get a steaming cup of coffee and heaping plates of bacon and eggs. Soups, salads and pizza are served at lunch. It's a downhome no-frills dining experience.

Pug Mahon's (☎ 406-259-4190; 3011 1st Ave N; lunch & brunch $6-8, dinner $9-15; 🕙 lunch & dinner) is a friendly Irish pub, with good food, great beer, and a Sunday champagne brunch that brings in the crowds.

For a slice of authentic Americana, catch a minor league **Billings Mustangs** (☎ 406-252-1241; Cobb Field, 901 N 27th St; tickets $5; 🕙 Jun-Sep) baseball game.

Logan International Airport (☎ 406-238-3420), 2 miles north of downtown, has direct flights to Salt Lake City, Denver, Minneapolis, Seattle, Phoenix and destinations within Montana. The **bus depot** (☎ 406-245-5116; 2502 1st Ave N; 🕙 24hr) has services to Bozeman ($27, three hours), Butte ($40, five hours) and Missoula ($53, eight hours).

ABSAROKA BEARTOOTH WILDERNESS

The fabulous, vista-packed Absaroka Beartooth Wilderness – stretching more than 943,377 acres – is perfect for a solitary adventure. Thick forests, jagged peaks and marvelous, empty stretches of alpine tundra are all found in this wilderness, saddled between Paradise Valley in the west and Yellowstone National Park in the south. The thickly forested Absaroka Range dominates the area's west half and is most easily reached from Paradise Valley or the Boulder River Corridor. The Beartooth Range's jagged peaks are best reached from Hwy 78 and US 212 near Red Lodge. Because of its proximity to Yellowstone, the Beartooth portion gets two-thirds of the area's traffic. A plethora of uncrowded alpine tundra awaits in the rugged interior.

A picturesque old mining town with fun bars and restaurants and a good range of places to stay, **Red Lodge** offers great day hikes, backpacking and, in winter, skiing right near town. The **Red Lodge visitors center** (☎ 406-446-1718; 601 N Broadway Ave; 🕙 9am-5pm Jun-Aug, 9:30am-4:30pm Mon-Fri Sep-May) has accommodation information, while the **Beartooth Ranger Station** (☎ 406-446-2103; 6811 Hwy 212 S; 🕙 8am-4:30pm Mon-Fri), about a mile south of Red Lodge, has maps and outdoor info.

The awesome **Beartooth Highway** (US 212; 🕙 Jun–mid-Oct) connects Red Lodge to Cooke City and Yellowstone's north entrance by an incredible 68-mile journey that passes soaring peaks and wildflower-sprinkled tundra. There are five reservable USFS campgrounds along the highway, within 12 miles of Red Lodge.

BUTTE

Blue Collar Butte feels a bit past its prime, like a decade-old pair of jeans you've long forgotten. With a skyline of massive mining headframes and a plethora of vacant ornate buildings, Butte appears frozen in hard times. Get past the rotting porches and dilapidated houses, however, and you'll quickly see these jeans have a lot more life left in them. Folks are friendly and often eccentric, the surrounding scenery is appealing, the vibe historic. Once a raucous late-19th-century boom town, Butte's a bit more staid these days, but the town – and its fascinating bars – still carry an air of political intrigue.

Grab a free Uptown Butte walking-tour map of one of the USA's largest historic districts from the **visitors center** (☎ 406-723-3177; www.butteinfo.org; 1000 George St; ☘ 8am-8pm Jun-Aug, 9am-5pm Mon-Fri Sep-May), north of I-15/I-90, or just stroll along Granite, Broadway and Park Sts and read the National Register of Historic Places plaques.

The largest quartz crystal ever found in Montana, the 'Big Daddy,' is just one of many minerals on display at the worthwhile **Mineral Museum** (☎ 406-496-4414; 1300 W Park St; admission free; ☘ 9am-6pm Jun-Aug, 9am-4pm Sep-May) on the Montana Tech campus. It's easy to spend an hour or two exploring interesting exhibits and a replica of an old mining town at the **World Museum of Mining** (☎ 406-723-7211; 155 Museum Way; adult/child $7/5; ☘ 9am-5:30pm Apr-Oct).

Don't judge the place by its slightly shabby exterior – inside the **Copper King Mansion** (☎ 406-782-7580; 219 W Granite St; r from $65; ☒) is elegantly Elizabethan. Filled with ornate period antiques, masterfully carved woodwork, and a private collection of late-19th-century clothing and memorabilia, the Copper King is a unique B&B. Rooms are large and furnished with antiques, but the B&B's greatest charm is derived from its opulent work-of-art public areas.

The historic **Finlen Hotel & Motor Inn** (☎ 406-723-5461; www.finlen.com; 100 E Broadway; r from $45; ☒) has a friendly staff and well-maintained rooms (request one with a view).

For more than decent Italian food, visit **Spaghettini's** (☎ 406-782-8855; 26 N Main St; dishes $10-17; ☘ lunch & dinner). The lingering aroma and intimate festive atmosphere will transport you to a quaint trattoria. A diverse range of pastas, polenta etc is served. There are oodles of choices for vegetarians.

Gamer's (☎ 406-723-5453; 15 W Park St; dishes $4-8; ☘ breakfast & lunch) is a local favorite for big American breakfasts and pasties (compact

---

DETOUR: LITTLE BIGHORN BATTLEFIELD

Ensconced within the boundless prairies and pine-covered hills of Montana's southwest Plains, the Crow Indian Reservation is home to the **Little Bighorn Battlefield National Monument** (☎ 406-638-3224; admission per car $10; ☘ 8am-6pm). One of the USA's most well-known Native American battlefields, this is where General George Custer made his famous 'last stand.' Custer, and 272 soldiers, messed one too many times with Plains Indians (including Crazy Horse of the Lakota Sioux), who overwhelmed the force in a frequently painted massacre. A visitors center tells the tale. The entrance is a mile east of I-90 on US 212.

---

yet hearty pies native to Cornwall, England, filled with meat, onions and potatoes or turnips). It has a congenial atmosphere.

Butte's watering holes retain a gritty, authentic feel and deserve museum status. Highlights include the iconic, 100-plus-year-old **M&M Bar** (19 N Main St) and the **Irish Times** (☎ 406-782-8142; cnr Main & Galena Sts), which has draft Guinness and live music most weekends.

Rimrock Bus and Greyhound use Butte's **bus depot** (☎ 406-723-3287; 103 E Front St) en route to Bozeman, Missoula and Helena.

HELENA

Luring politicians, outdoor enthusiasts and artists, Montana's state capital is an agreeable city where business mixes easily with pleasure. During the week it's a bustling place where politicos and lobbyists pound out legislature. On weekends it becomes a veritable ghost town, as almost every seems to take to the mountains for a little playtime. Once a vibrant mining haunt, Helena, at the foot of the Rockies, remains an upbeat place, with trendy galleries and interesting restaurants lining pleasant streets.

For information, visit the following:
Helena National Forest Ranger District (☎ 406-449-5490; 2001 Poplar St; ☘ 7:30am-6pm Mon-Fri, 8:30am-5pm Sat Jun-Aug, 7:30am-5pm Mon-Fri Sep-May)
Helena visitors center (☎ 406-442-4120; www. helenachamber.com; 225 Cruse Ave; ☘ 8am-5pm Mon-Fri)
Summer-only visitors center (☎ 406-447-1540; 2003 Cedar St; ☘ 9am-5pm)

Many of Helena's sites are free, including the neoclassical **State Capitol** (☎ 406-444-4789; cnr Montana Ave & 6th St; ☹ 8am-6pm Mon-Fri), the elegant old buildings along Last Chance Gulch (Helena's pedestrian shopping district) and the **Holter Museum of Art** (☎ 406-442-6400; 12 E Lawrence; ☹ 10am-5pm Mon-Sat Jun-Aug, 11:30am-5pm Tue-Fri, noon-5pm Sat & Sun Sep-May), which exhibits modern pieces by Montana artists.

For something a bit unexpected, visit **Kumamoto Plaza** (☎ 406-449-7904; 34 N Last Chance Gulch; admission free; ☹ 9am-5pm), a small Japanese-arts gallery and cultural center, established to link Montana with its sister state, Kumamoto, Japan. Be sure to also visit the **Archie Bray Foundation** (☎ 406-443-3502; 2915 Country Club Ave; admission free; ☹ 10am-5pm Mon-Sat, 1-5pm Sun), one of the nation's top training grounds for ceramics and pottery artists.

Nine **hiking** and **mountain biking** trails wind through Mt Helena City Park, including one that takes you to the 5460ft-high summit of Mt Helena.

East of downtown near I-15 is a string of chain motels – most have free continental breakfast, pool and Jacuzzi for $60 to $85.

Our favorite place to stay in town, **Sanders** (☎ 406-442-3309; 328 N Ewing St; www.sandersbb.com; r $100-120; ℗ 🐾), is a beautiful B&B. It boasts exquisite vintage furnishings, much of it from the late-19th-century original owners. Each room is unique, and thoughtfully decorated.

Though it may not ooze with personality, **Jorgenson's Inn & Suites** (☎ 406-442-1770; www.jorgensonsinn.com; 1714 11th Ave; r from $60; ℗ 🐾 🖳 🕿) is a good midrange choice with modern, well-equipped rooms and a restaurant/lounge.

Fire Tower Coffee House (☎ 406-495-8840; 422 Last Chance Gulch; ☹ breakfast, lunch & dinner; 🖳) is where to go for coffee, light meals and sometimes live music on Friday evenings. **No Sweat Café** (☎ 406-442-6954; 427 N Last Chance Gulch; dishes $4-7; ☹ breakfast & lunch) is a feel-good spot with art-lined walls, and mostly organic hearty egg dishes, sandwiches and Mexican fare; the juice is very fresh.

Also good, for its beer as much as its food, is **Bert & Ernie's** (☎ 406-443-5680; 361 N Last Chance Gulch; dishes $6-16; ☹ lunch & dinner) serving standard American fare.

The **Helena Regional Airport** (☎ 406-442-2821; www.helenaairport.com), 2 miles north of downtown, operates flights to most other airports in Montana, Salt Lake City, Spokane and Minneapolis. Rimrock Stages leave from Helena's **bus depot** (☎ 406-442-5860; 3100 E Hwy 12), 7 miles east of town on US 12, where at least daily buses go to Missoula ($21, 2¼ hours), Billings ($37, 4¾ hours) and Bozeman ($18, two hours).

MISSOULA

Missoula is a hip college town (home to the University of Montana) that's growing more popular with each year (and that's not just our opinion – transplants are flocking here by the bus load). The dreadlocks, global import shops and veggie restaurants near the university add a great dash of cultural flavor to this intellectually stimulating place. A milder-than-usual climate and a gorgeous location along the Clark Fork River make Missoula the perfect outdoor playground. It's within spittin' distance of the Rattlesnake Recreation Area and the Bitterroot Range, and a river actually runs through it!

Information

Tune in to University of Montana stations KUFM (89.1FM) and KUKL (89.9FM) for National Public Radio (NPR), quirky local news and groovy free-form alternative music mixes.

Trail Head (☎ 406-543-6966; www.trailheadmontana .net; 110 E Pine St; ☹ 9.30am-8pm Mon-Fri, 9am-6pm Sat, 11am-6pm Sun) Maps, abundant advice, camping and kayaking rental gear.

USFS Northern Region Headquarters (☎ 406-329-3511; 200 E Broadway; ☹ 8:30am-4:30pm Mon-Fri)

Visitors center (☎ 406-532-3250; www.missoulacvb .org; 1121 E Broadway; ☹ 8am-5pm Mon-Fri)

Sights & Activities

Downtown, the contemporary installations at the **Art Museum of Missoula** (☎ 406-728-0447; 335 N Pattee St; admission free; ☹ 10am-7pm Tue, 10am-6pm Wed-Fri, 10am-4pm Sat) are worthy of a wander. Seven miles west of downtown, the **Smokejumper Center** (☎ 406-329-4900; W Broadway; admission free; ☹ 10am-4pm Jun-Aug) is the active base for the heroic men and women who parachute into forests to combat raging wildfires. Its visitors center has thought-provoking audio and visual displays that do a great job illustrating the life of the Western firefighter.

One of the area's most accessible **hikes** is along the south side of Clark Fork from McCormick Park (west of the Orange St bridge) into Hellgate Canyon. At sunset join the steep pilgrimage from the football stadium to the 'M' on 5158ft Mt Sentinel for spectacular views.

Advanced skiers love **Snowbowl Ski Area** (☎ 406-549-9777; www.montanasnowbowl.com; lift ticket adult/child $35/16), 17 miles north of Missoula, for its 2600ft vertical drop. **10,000 Waves** (☎ 406-549-6670; www.10000-waves.com; 1311 E Broadway) runs a range of rafting and kayaking trips ($35 to $80) on the Class III and IV rapids of Alberton Gorge (of the Clark Fork River), as well as scenic trips on the gentler Blackfoot and Bitterroot Rivers.

Sleeping

Most lodging is on Broadway between Van Buren and Orange Sts, within walking distance of the campus and downtown.

Goldsmith's Bed & Breakfast (☎ 406-728-1585; www.goldsmithsinn.com; 809 E Front St; r $80-140; 🖳) This delightful B&B, with comfy rooms, is a pebble's toss from the river. The outdoor deck overlooking the water is the perfect place to kick back with a good novel. Rooms are attractive, featuring Victorian furniture. Some come with private sitting rooms, fireplaces and reading nooks.

Campus Inn (☎ 406-549-5134; www.campusinn missoula.com; 744 E Broadway; r $85; 🖳 🖳) This solid-value place has spacious rooms with ample amenities. Some rooms are inside the main building; others are motel-style.

City Center Motel (☎ 406-543-3193; 338 E Broadway; r $45; 🖳 🖳) With subtle Western accents (such as the swinging wooden door leading to the bath), this motel is good value. Its comfortable rooms come with a fridge and microwave.

Eating

Tipu's (☎ 406-542-0622; 1151/2 S 4th St; dishes $6-12; 🖳 lunch & dinner) Missoula's only all-vegetarian restaurant offers flavorful chai and East Indian chow that's tasty and filling. Don't miss the fresh chutneys.

Two Sister's (☎ 406-327-8438; 127 W Alder St; dishes $5-20; 🖳 breakfast, lunch & dinner) A relative newcomer, Two Sister's has locals raving about its eclectic menu and charismatic atmosphere. The creative offerings are geared towards herbivores and carnivores alike, with tasty benedicts at breakfast and chipotle BBQ chicken and linguini with clams at lunch and dinner.

Bernice's Bakery (☎ 406-728-1358; 190 S 3rd St; dishes $2-5; 🖳 6am-10pm Sun-Thu, 6am-11pm Fri & Sat) Fabulous organic coffee and tea, sink-your-teeth into 'em good sweets and yummy breakfasts are all staples at this revered Missoula institution. Don't miss the homemade granola.

Food For Thought (☎ 406-721-6033; 540 Daly Ave; mains $4-7; 🖳 7am-10pm) This crunchy joint, across from the University of Montana, packs in lots of college students for heaped portions of health-conscious food.

Drinking & Entertainment

In Missoula, barhopping ranks right up there with hiking, rodeo, disco dancing and cowtipping. For live music listings, browse the **Independent** (www.missoulanews.com) or the Entertainment section of Friday's *Missoulian*.

Iron Horse Brewpub (☎ 406-728-8866; 501 N Higgins St) An upbeat student favorite with plenty of places to sit and sip, including an outdoor patio.

Top Hat (☎ 406-728-9865; 134 W Front St) Bluegrass, blues and rock bands, plus pool and table tennis, get this big open space grooving at night.

Old Post (☎ 406-721-7399; 103 W Spruce St) This cozy wood-walled number draws crowds with its happy-hour specials and upscale pub grub. Jazz and blues bands saunter in on weekends.

Other Side (☎ 406-543-3405; 1100 Strand Ave) It's worth the trek west of town for poker, cheap booze and live shows, some all ages.

Wilma Theatre (☎ 406-728-2521; 131 S Higgins St; admission $7) Screens independent, art-house and foreign flicks.

Getting There & Around

Missoula County International Airport (☎ 406-728-4381) is located 5 miles west of Missoula on US 12 W.

Greyhound buses serve Montana's four corners from the **depot** (☎ 406-549-2339; 1660 W Broadway), 1 mile west of town.

BITTERROOT VALLEY

Bursting with wonderful hiking trails, tranquil fishing holes, ski slopes and bike paths, the Bitterroot valley is contoured some with dramatic and beautiful canyons. East Side Rd – the scenic route known as the 'back road' – is parallel to Hwy 93 and offers a glimpse of the Bitterroot's agricultural soul as well as a few historical sites, including **St Mary's Mission** (☎ 406-777-5734; 315 Charlos St, Stevensville; adult/child $3/1; 🕑 10am-5pm Jun-Aug, 10am-4pm Mon-Sat, 10am-2pm Sun Sep-May).

About halfway down the valley in Hamilton, the **Bitterroot Visitors Center** (☎ 406-363-2400; 105 E Main St; 🕑 8am-6pm Mon-Fri Jun-Aug, 8am-5pm Sep-May) provides area information. For a relaxing soak and a night in the wilderness, visit the very soothing **Lost Trails Hot Springs Resort** (☎ 406-821-3574; www.losttrailhot springs.com; 8321 S Hwy 93; adult/child pool $6/4, cabin & r $55-110; 🏊) in Sula. The outdoor pool is lovely and accommodations are rustic, but quite comfortable.

FLATHEAD LAKE

Thanks to picture-pretty bays and 128 miles of wooded shoreline, fish-filled Flathead Lake is one of Montana's most favored attractions. The **Flathead Lake Marine Trail** makes paddling from one access point to another a fun way to travel; two marine **campsites** (☎ 406-751-4577; campsites $8) are available. You can easily drive around the lake in four hours. Make sure to spend time lingering along the shores and stopping at roadside fruitstands.

On the Indian Reservation at the lake's south end, fast-growing **Polson** (visitors center ☎ 406-883-5969; www.polsonchamber.com; 4 2nd Ave E; 🕑 8am-4pm Mon-Fri, 9am-4pm Sat, 10am-3pm Sun Jun-Aug, Mon-Fri 10am-2pm Sep-May) is the region's biggest service center, with several gas stations, fast-food restaurants and motels.

At the opposite end of the lake, **Bigfork** (visitors center ☎ 406-837-5888; www.bigfork.org; 8155 Hwy 35; 🕑 9am-5pm Jun-Aug, 10am-2pm Mon-Fri Sep-May) is an artsy village with good grub and funky shops. The **Swan Lake Ranger District Station** (☎ 406-837-5081; 200 Ranger Station Rd; 🕑 8am-4:30pm Mon-Fri), west of Bigfork, has camping details.

Between Polson and Bigfork are lakefront campgrounds, summer camp-style resorts, and, on the lake's east side, orchards festooned with plump cherries. In either town you can join a boat tour to visit **Wild Horse Island**, where wild mares and steeds roam. Watch for Flathead Nessie, said to be a distant cousin to the Loch Ness Monster, who has been lurking around since the 1930s. **Flathead Raft Co** (☎ 406-883-5838; www.flathead raftco.com) runs kayaking and river-rafting trips (from $40). Call for directions.

WHITEFISH & KALISPELL

With hip bars, slick restaurants and oh-so-cool boutiques, up-and-coming Whitefish has perfected that new West look. It's also got a lot going for it: it's a fabulous gateway to Glacier National Park (p1020) and sits in the shadow of one of Montana's premier year-round resorts, **Big Mountain** (☎ 406-862-2900; www.bigmtn.com; lift ticket adult/child $50/36), with winter downhill skiing, and gondola-served hiking and mountain biking in summer. To rent some wheels, visit **Glacier Cyclery** (☎ 406-862-6446; 326 2nd St). The mind-boggling **Miracle of America Museum** (☎ 406-883-6804; 58176 Hwy 93; adult/child $3/1; 🕑 8am-8pm Jun-Aug, 8:30am-5pm Mon-Sat, 1:30-5pm Sun Sep-May), located just 2 miles south of Polson, is definitely worth seeing. By turns random and fascinating, its cluttered Americana includes motorcycles, military displays and the largest buffalo ever recorded in the state.

Though not as charming, Kalispell, 13 miles south, is Flathead Valley's cheapest place to resupply.

Kalispell Area visitors center (☎ 406-758-2800; www.kalispellchamber.com; 15 Depot Park; 🕑 8am-5pm Mon-Fri) and **Whitefish visitors center** (☎ 406-862-3501; www.whitefishrvpark.com; 520 E 2nd St; 🕑 9am-5:30pm Mon-Sat Jun-Aug, 9am-5pm Mon-Fri Sep-May) have all the usual information. **Tally Lake Ranger Station** (☎ 406-862-2508; 1335 Hwy 93 N; 🕑 8am-4:30pm Mon-Fri) has camping details and maps.

Places fill fast in both towns, so reservations are recommended. A string of chain motels lines US 93 south of Whitefish. Here you'll also find the cheerful **Chalet Motel** (☎ 406-862-5581; www.whitefishlodging.com; 6430 Hwy 93 S; r $75; 🍴 🖥 🏊), about a mile from town. It offers spacious rooms and has a hot tub. At the south edge of town, the peaceful **Duck Inn** (☎ 406-862-3825; www.duckinn.com; 1305 Columbia Ave; r $70-110; 🍴 🐕) is a lovely wooden lodge overlooking Whitefish River. The 10 big, airy rooms feature fireplaces and lots of character.

Budget travelers will find basic bunks at the **Downtowner Motel** (☎ 406-862-2535; www .downtownermotel.cc; 224 Spokane Ave; dm $20, r from $45; 🖥), in Whitefish. Rates include use of the adjacent gym and sauna.

For satisfying shady campsites, try **Whitefish RV Park** (☎ 406-862-7275; www.whitefishrvpark .com; 6404 Hwy 93 S; campsites/RV sites $16/27), a mile south of town.

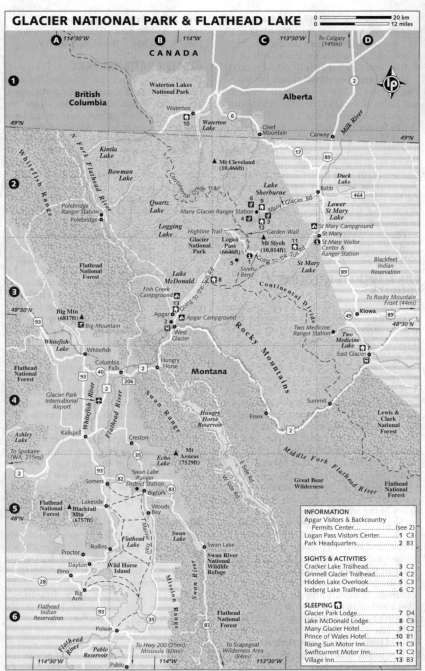

GLACIER NATIONAL PARK & FLATHEAD LAKE

0 ——— 20 km
0 ——— 12 miles

INFORMATION
Apgar Visitors & Backcountry
  Permits Center.........................(see 2)
Logan Pass Visitors Center...........**1** C3
Park Headquarters.......................**2** B3

SIGHTS & ACTIVITIES
Cracker Lake Trailhead..................**3** C2
Grinnell Glacier Trailhead.............**4** C2
Hidden Lake Overlook...................**5** C3
Iceberg Lake Trailhead..................**6** C2

SLEEPING
Glacier Park Lodge.......................**7** D4
Lake McDonald Lodge...................**8** C3
Many Glacier Hotel.......................**9** C2
Prince of Wales Hotel...................**10** B1
Rising Sun Motor Inn.....................**11** C3
Swiftcurrent Motor Inn..................**12** C2
Village Inn..................................**13** B3

ROCKY MOUNTAINS

In Kalispell, the **Kalispell Grand Hotel** (☎ 406-755-8100; www.kalispellgrand.com; 100 Main St; r from $70; ⊠) has smallish modern rooms and high-speed Internet access for those with laptop in tow. Rates include continental breakfast.

Glacier Park International Airport (☎ 406-257-5994; 4170 Hwy 2), halfway between Whitefish and Kalispell on US 2, has flights to various destinations around the USA. The **Airport Shuttle Service** (☎ 406-752-2842) serves Whitefish ($18) and Kalispell ($7.50).

Amtrak stops at Whitefish's **railroad depot** (☎ 406-862-2268; 500 Depot St) enroute to West Glacier ($10) and East Glacier ($24). Intermountain Transport connects the **Kalispell bus station** (☎ 406-755-4011; 1301 S Main St) to Whitefish's railroad depot; buses also run to Missoula, Helena, Bozeman and Seattle.

The free Shuttle Network of Whitefish (SNOW) runs between Whitefish and Big Mountain during ski season.

BOB MARSHALL WILDERNESS COMPLEX

Let's just say, if the state had a perfume, its essence would be bottled from the wilds around Bob Marshall. Running roughly from the southern boundary of Glacier National Park in the north to Rogers Pass (on Hwy 200) in the south, three designated wilderness areas hum within the complex. A medley of geology, plants and wildlife, Great Bear, Bob Marshall and Scapegoat are scintillating. National forest lands begirding the complex offer campgrounds, road access to trailheads and quieter country when 'the Bob' hosts hunters in fall. The core lands encompass 2344 sq miles, with 3200 miles of trails and sections that are a 40-mile slog from the nearest road.

Access the Bob from the Seeley-Swan Valley in the west, Hungry Horse Reservoir in the north, the Rocky Mountain Front in the east or off Hwy 200 in the south. The easiest (and busiest) access routes are from the Benchmark and Gibson Reservoir trailheads in the Rocky Mountain Front.

Trails generally start steep, reaching the wilderness boundary after around 7 miles. It takes another 10 miles or so to really get into the Bob's heart. Good day hikes run from all sides. Two USFS districts tend to the Bob: **Flathead National Forest Headquarters** (☎ 406-758-5204; www.fs.fed.us/r1/flathead; 1935 3rd Ave E, Kalispell; ⊗ 8am-4:30pm Mon-Fri)

Lewis & Clark National Forest Supervisors (☎ 406-791-7700; www.fs.fed.us/r1/lewisclark; 1101 15th St N, Great Falls; ⊗ 8am-4:30pm Mon-Fri)

GLACIER NATIONAL PARK

Dramatically beautiful, Glacier National Park is Montana's most revered attraction. The park's rugged and desolate alpine terrain is full of lush valleys, clear crystal lakes and rushing waterfalls. Wildlife enthusiasts will have a field day in Glacier. Spotting animals is common: cougars, grizzlies, black bears and elk all roam freely. Most visitors tend to stick to developed areas and short hiking trails, but take some time to explore off-the-beaten path routes in this gem.

Those who don't have the time to explore the remote reaches can still get a dose of divine scenery by driving Going-to-the-Sun Rd, which displays examples of glacial activity and often mountain goats and bighorn sheep. In winter, when Going-to-the-Sun Rd is closed but surrounding access roads lead to snowshoe and cross-country ski trails, the park is left to wildlife and the adventurous.

Created in 1910, Glacier's spectacular landscape continues uninterrupted north into Canada, where it is protected in less crowded Waterton Lakes National Park. Together the two parks comprise Waterton-Glacier International Peace Park. In 1995 the parks were declared a World Heritage Site for their vast cross section of plant and animal species. Although the name evokes images of binational harmony, in reality each park is operated separately, and entry to one does not entitle you to entry to the other.

In 2003, 15% of the park's acreage was scorched by wildfires. The park is open year-round; however, most services are only open from mid-May to September.

Orientation

Glacier's 1562 sq miles are divided into five regions, each centered on a ranger station: Polebridge (northwest); Lake McDonald (southwest), including the West Entrance and Apgar village; Two Medicine (southeast); St Mary (east); and Many Glacier (northeast). The 50-mile Going-to-the-Sun Rd is the only paved road that traverses the park.

Information

Visitors centers and ranger stations in the park sell field guides and hand out hiking maps. Those at Apgar and St Mary are open daily May to October; the visitors center at Logan Pass is open when Going-to-the-Sun Rd is open. The Many Glacier, Two Medicine and Polebridge Ranger Stations close at the end of September. **Park headquarters** (☎ 406-888-7800; www.nps.gov/glac; ☼ 8am-4:30pm Mon-Fri), in West Glacier between US 2 and Apgar, is open year-round.

Entry to the park (vehicles/individuals $10/5) is valid for seven days. Day hikers don't need permits, but overnight back-packers do (May to October only). Half of the permits (per person per day $4) are available on a first-come, first-served basis from the Apgar Backcountry Permit Center (which is open May 1 to October 31), St Mary Visitor Center, and the Many Glacier, Two Medicine and Polebridge Ranger Stations.

The other half can be reserved at the Apgar Backcountry Permit Center, St Mary and Many Glacier visitors centers, and Two Medicine and Polebridge Ranger Stations. Advance reservations ($20) can be made at the permit centers or after April 1 by writing to: Backcountry Reservations, Glacier National Park, West Glacier, MT 59936.

Sights & Activities

Starting at Apgar, the phenomenal **Going-to-the-Sun Road** skirts shimmering Lake McDonald before angling sharply to the Garden Wall – the main dividing line between the west and east sides of the park. At Logan Pass you can stroll 1.5 miles to **Hidden Lake Overlook**; heartier hikers can try the 7.5-mile **Highline Trail**. About halfway between the pass and St Mary's Lake, the **Continental Divide Trail** crosses the road at Siyeh Bend, a good starting point for multiday hikes.

Busier routes include the 5-mile **Grinnell Glacier Trail**, which climbs 1600ft to the base of the park's most visible glacier, and the 6-mile **Cracker Lake Trail**, a 1400ft climb to some of the park's most dramatic scenery. For more solitude, try trails in the North Fork or Two Medicine areas. North of the Canadian border, the approaches to spec-tacular hikes are much shorter.

Mountain bikes are prohibited on park trails. Road bikes can ply the park's pave-ment, but they are banned from parts of Going-to-the-Sun Rd from 11am to 4pm in summer.

Glacier Park Boat Co (☎ 406-257-2426; www.glacierparkboats.com) rents kayaks and canoes, and runs popular guided tours ($12) from five locations in Glacier National Park. For rafting excursions, guided day hikes and backpacking trips, contact **Glacier Wilderness Guides** (☎ 406-387-5555; www.glacierguides.com) in West Glacier.

Young naturalists (aged six to 12) should request the *Junior Ranger Newspaper* at the Apgar or St Mary visitors centers or the Many Glacier or Two Medicine Ranger Stations.

ICEBERG LAKE HIKE

The five- to six-hour 9-mile day hike to Ice-berg Lake is justifiably a favorite. Enclosed by stunning 3000ft vertical headwalls on three sides, it's one of the most impressive glacial lakes in North America. The 1200ft ascent is gentle and the approach is mostly at or above treeline, affording awesome views. Wildflower fiends will delight in the meadows around the lake.

Iceberg Lake was named in 1905 by George Grinnell, who saw icebergs calving from the glacier at the foot of the headwalls. The glacier is no longer active, but surface ice and avalanche debris still provide size-able flotillas of bergs as the lake melts in early summer. Scientists predict that if glo-bal climate-warming trends continue, all of the park's 50-some moving ice masses will be completely melted by 2030, so there's no better time than now to see some of the ancient ice for yourself. The hike begins and ends at Iceberg Lake trailhead near the Many Glacier Ranger Station.

Sleeping

Within the park, campgrounds and lodges are mainly open from mid-May to the end of September. East Glacier and West Glacier offer overflow accommodations year-round.

LODGES

Dating from the early 19th century, Glacier's seven historic lodges are now operated by **Glacier Park, Inc** (☎ reservations 406-892-2525; www.glacierparkinc.com). All are completely nonsmok-ing, and rooms do not have air-con or TV.

Glacier Park Lodge (☎ 406-226-5600; www.bigtree hotel.com; East Glacier; r $140-500; ☼ late May-Sep; ✕) The park's flagship lodge, this gracefully el-egant place features interior balconies sup-ported by Douglas fur timbers and a massive

ROCKY MOUNTAINS

stone fireplace in the lobby. It's an aesthetically appealing, historically charming and very comfortable place to stay. Pluses include nine holes of golf and cozy reading nooks.

Prince of Wales Hotel (☎ 403-859-2231; www .princeofwaleswaterton.com; Prince of Wales Rd, Waterton townsite, Waterton Lakes National Park; r from $260 Canadian; ☉ mid-May–Sep; ☒) On the Canadian side, the venerable Prince of Wales Hotel is a national historic site perched on a rise overlooking the lake. Though photogenic from a distance (we're talking cover-model material), up close the hotel looks smaller and much more genteel. Nevertheless, the views alone are worth the price.

Lake McDonald Lodge (☎ 406-888-5431; www.lake mcdonaldlodge.com; Lake McDonald Valley; cottage $95-140, r $100-150; ☉ Jun-Sep; ☒) Built in 1913, this old hunting lodge is adorned with stuffed animal trophies and exudes relaxed ambience. The 100 rooms are in lodge-, chalet- or motel-style digs. Nightly park ranger talks and lake cruises are popular activities.

Many Glacier Hotel (☎ 406-732-4411; www.many glacierhotel.com; Many Glacier Valley; r $115-200; ☉ mid-Jun–mid-Sep; ☒) Modeled after a Swiss chalet, Many Glacier is the park's largest hotel with 208 rooms. Panoramic mountain views and a pretty location on the edge of Swiftcurrent Lake add to its appeal.

Also recommended:

Rising Sun Motor Inn (☎ 406-732-5523; www.rising sunmotorinn.com; St Mary Valley; r $95-110; ☉ mid-Jun–mid-Sep)

Swiftcurrent Motor Inn (☎ 406-732-5531; www.swift currentmotorinn.com; Many Glacier Valley; cottage $45-75, r $95-110; ☉ mid-Jun–mid-Sep)

Village Inn (☎ 406-888-5632; www.villageinnatapgar .com; Apgar; r $110-170; ☉ Jun-Sep)

CAMPING

Of the 13 **NPS campgrounds** (☎ 406-888-7800; reservations.nps.gov; campsites $12-17), only sites at Fish Creek and St Mary can be reserved in advance (up to five months). Sites fill by mid-morning, particularly in July and August. Only Apgar campground and St Mary campground offer winter camping ($7.50).

AROUND GLACIER

AYH Brownie's (☎ 406-226-4426; Hwy 49; dm/s/d $16/21/29; ☉ May-Sep; ☐) In East Glacier, above Brownie's Grocery & Deli, this friendly place is always in demand, but gets mixed reviews.

It offers dorm and private rooms, a coin laundry and a kitchen.

Northfork Hostel & Squarepeg Ranch (☎ 406-888-5241; www.nfhostel.com; dm $15, cabins $30-65) In Polebridge, this ultra-rustic (no electricity) year-round option has bunks, cabins, a kitchen and the veggie-friendly Northern Lights Café next door. Guests can use the hostel's mountain bikes, cross-country skis, snowshoes and kayaks for free. Pickup is available from West Glacier Amtrak station (summer/winter $30/35).

Glacier Highland Resort Motel (☎ 406-888-5427; Hwy 2; r from $75; ☒) In West Glacier, opposite the train station, this motel has 33 units and a hot tub.

Glacier Campground (☎ 406-387-5689; off Hwy 2; campsites/RV sites $18/24, cabin $30-40) One mile west of West Glacier, this campground has sites on 40 acres of lovely wooded grounds, as well as a cute cluster of basic wooden cabins.

Eating

In summer there are grocery stores with limited camping supplies in Apgar, Lake McDonald Lodge, Rising Sun and at the Swiftcurrent Motor Inn. Most lodges have on-site restaurants, although the quality of food varies.

Dining options in West Glacier are unexciting. If you can, head to Whitefish.

Serrano's Mexican Restaurant (☎ 406-226-9392; 29 Dawson Ave; dishes $7-12; ☉ lunch & dinner) In East Glacier, Serrano's serves good Mexican food in casual environs both inside and outside on its deck.

Getting There & Around

Amtrak's Empire Builder stops at East Glacier (Glacier Park Station) and West Glacier (Belton Station). **Glacier Park, Inc** (☎ 406-892-2525) runs shuttles over Going-to-the-Sun Rd, including the unreservable Hiker's Shuttle ($8 to $24), which originates in West Glacier or Many Glacier.

IDAHO

If you're craving one of those adrenalin-racing, memory-making, no-holds-barred adventures, head to Idaho to get your fix. A virtual supermarket for wilderness enthusiasts, this state stocks just about every outdoor excursion out there. Sandwiched between the Pacific Northwest and the Rockies, Idaho is second only to Alaska for most national forests and wilderness areas. It also boasts the deepest gorge on the continent (Hells Canyon) and the densest lake population of any state in the West. Factor in heaps of mountains, raging rivers and a sprinkling of progressively hip towns, and you'll quickly discover it's a serious smorgasbord of heart-pumping natural delights.

River rats will dig the big white water on the Salmon and Snake Rivers. Skiers will relish the glitzy slopes at Sun Valley and Ketchum. Solitude seekers will find plenty of tantalizingly tranquil territory off the state's numerous scenic byways. Even city slickers won't feel lost. Funky Boise boasts slick shops and happening nightlife; glam Sun Valley is where to do the movie-star thing. Wherever you travel in Idaho, be it 'up a crick,' through the rapids or down the slopes, the spectacular scenery is always diverse and never wavering.

History

Idaho was not really settled until gold was struck at Pierce in 1860. Miners rushed to Idaho's mountains, establishing gold camps and trade centers, such as Boise and Lewiston. Rich silver and lead veins spurred further growth, and by the late 19th century a homesteading boom had begun.

The Shoshone people were once the West's dominant Indian group. Some Shoshone peoples, along with the Bannock, now live on the Fort Hall Indian Reservation in the southeast.

Information

Idaho Road Conditions (☎ 208-336-6600, within Idaho 888-432-7623)
Idaho Tourist Information (☎ 800-635-7820; www .visited.org)
Idaho Travel Council (☎ 800-635-7820; www.visitid .org; PO Box 83720, Boise, ID 83720)

BOISE

Boise is positively buzzing these days. Not only is it Idaho's largest city and capital, it's also young, hip and quite fun. With an outdoors slant and hassle-free vibe, the city is more than a gateway to Idaho's wilder climes – it holds its own as a destination. Much of its late-19th-century architecture remains, cafés and restaurants stay open

---

IDAHO FACTS

Nickname Gem State
Population 1.4 million
Area 83,575 sq miles
Capital city Boise (population 192,170)
State motto *Esto perpetua* (Let it be perpetual)
Birthplace of Sacagawea, Shoshone woman on Lewis and Clark expedition; Gutzon Borglum (1867–1941), sculptor of Mt Rushmore; Picabo Street (b 1971), Olympic skiing medalist
Famous for Spuds, wilderness, white water, hunting

---

late, and crowds from nightspots spill onto the streets on hot summer nights. Locals consider Boise a gay-friendly city, and it has an active gay and lesbian community.

Orientation

Delve into the main business district, bounded by State, Grove, 4th and 9th Sts. Restaurants and nightspots are found downtown in the brick-lined pedestrian plaza of the Grove, the gentrified former warehouse district at 8th St Marketplace and in Old Boise, just east of downtown.

Information

Stop by the **visitors center** (☎ 208-344-5338; www .boise.org; 850 Front St; ✆ 10am-5pm Mon-Fri, 10am-2pm Sat Jun-Aug, 9am-4pm Mon-Fri Sep-May).

Sights

Boise has the largest population of Basque descendents outside of Europe's Basque country. Along Grove St between 6th St and Capitol Blvd, the Basque Block has sites commemorating early Basque pioneers. You can learn about Basque ancestry at the **Basque Museum & Cultural Center** (☎ 208-343-2671; www.basquemuseum.com; 611 Grove St; admission free; ✆ 10am-4pm Tue-Fri, 11am-3pm Sat).

Built in 1905, the architecturally impressive **state capitol** (☎ 208-334-5174; 700 W Jefferson St) is the only US statehouse heated by geothermal water. It's worth strolling past. Riverfront Julia Davis Park contains the **Idaho Historical Museum** (☎ 208-334-2120; 610 N Julia Davis Dr; adult/child $2/1; ✆ 9am-5pm Mon-Sat, 1-5pm Sun), which is great for a real look into the Old West. The **Boise Art Museum** (☎ 208-345-8330; 670 Julia Davis Dr; adult/child $8/4; ✆ 10am-5pm Tue-Wed, Fri & Sat, 10am-8pm Thu, noon-5pm Sun) has

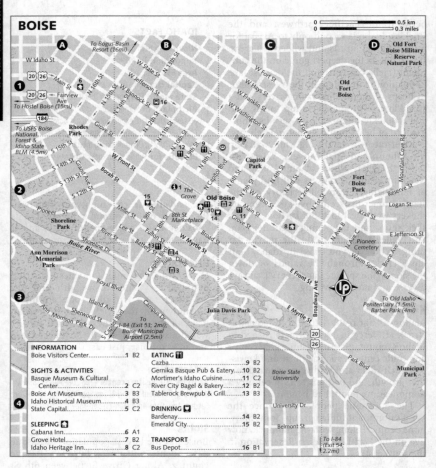

BOISE

INFORMATION
Boise Visitors Center....................1 B2

SIGHTS & ACTIVITIES
Basque Museum & Cultural
  Center.......................................2 C2
Boise Art Museum........................3 B3
Idaho Historical Museum.............4 B3
State Capital.................................5 C2

SLEEPING
Cabana Inn...................................6 A1
Grove Hotel..................................7 B2
Idaho Heritage Inn.......................8 C2

EATING
Cazba...9 B2
Gernika Basque Pub & Eatery....10 B2
Mortimer's Idaho Cuisine...........11 C2
River City Bagel & Bakery..........12 B2
Tablerock Brewpub & Grill.........13 B3

DRINKING
Bardenay....................................14 B2
Emerald City..............................15 B2

TRANSPORT
Bus Depot..................................16 B1

lots of 19th-century pieces by American artists.

East of Broadway Ave off Warm Springs Rd is the fascinating, but rather chilling, **Old Idaho Penitentiary** (☎ 208-368-6080; 2445 Old Penitentiary Rd; adult/child $4/3; ☒ noon-5pm Sep-May, 10am-5pm Jun-Aug).

Activities

Boise is bursting with outdoor adventures, from hiking to skiing to swimming. In the foothills above town, the **Ridge to Rivers Trail System** (www.ridgetorivers.org) offers 75 miles of scenic to strenuous hiking and biking trails. In summer everyone loves to float down the Boise River. Rent tubes or rafts at **Barber Park** (☎ 208-343-6564; Warm Spring Rd; tube rental $5; ℗)

and float 5 miles downstream. Parking here costs $4. A shuttle bus ($2) runs from the take-out point. The skiing at **Bogus Basin Resort** (☎ 208-332-5100; www.bogusbasin.com; 2405 Bogus Basin Rd; lift ticket $40), 16 miles north of Boise, isn't as fabulous as other state resorts, but has plenty of powder and short lift lines. There are also 37 miles of cross-country trails.

Festivals & Events

Gene Harris Jazz Festival (www.geneharris.org) Smooth jazz by masters; held the first week in April.
Boise River Festival (☎ 208-338-8887) Parades, sporty fun and lots for kids; held the last weekend in June.
Snake River Stampede (☎ 208-466-8497; www .snakeriverstampede.com) Action-packed pro rodeo in Nampa; held late July.

Art in the Park (☎ 208-345-8330) Outdoor art fest held the weekend after Labor Day.

Sleeping

Idaho Heritage Inn (☎ 208-342-8066; www.idheritage inn.com; 109 W Idaho St; r $75-110; P ✗) This wonderfully charming, family-run B&B offers six cozy rooms with varying amenities. The private baths run geothermally heated water.

Hostel Boise (☎ 208-467-6858; 17322 Canada Rd, Nampa; www.hostelboise.com; dm/s/d $14/31/35; P ▢) This country-style hostel's rooms have a max of four beds each. Located just outside town, there's a BBQ on the back patio, and lots of yard space for lying around and digesting after grilling up those tasty Boca Burgers. Lifts from the airport cost $10.

Cabana Inn (☎ 208-343-6000; cabanainn@interplus .net; 1600 Main St; r $40; P ✗) A few hops west of downtown, this motel run by helpful folk offers well-kept rooms with microwaves. It's nothing special, but a solid budget bet.

Eating

Tablerock Brewpub & Grill (☎ 208-342-0944; 705 Fulton St; dishes $7-16; ☯ 11am-11pm Mon-Sat, 11am-10pm Sun) This hopping place cranks out handcrafted brews and hefty pub food in congenial environs. It's popular for dinner or just drinks. Try the White Bird Wheat.

Mortimer's Idaho Cuisine (☎ 208-338-6550; 110 S 5th St; dishes from $20; ☯ 5-10pm Tue-Sat) For a special meal, head to this unique place, which specializes in innovative cuisine from around the region, with an emphasis on local ingredients. It offers everything from Kobe beef to elk chops to fresh Idaho cheeses.

Cazba (☎ 208-381-0222; 211 N 8th St; mains $12-20; ☯ 11am-9.30pm Mon-Fri, 7am-9.30pm Sat & Sun) The popular Cazba is a fine place to catch up on missed meals. Its large platefuls of delightful food – gyros bigger than the Med – will leave everyone (including vegetarians) satisfied and very full.

Gernika Basque Pub & Eatery (☎ 208-344-2175; 202 S Capitol Blvd; dishes $6-8; ☯ lunch & dinner) This friendly bar on the Basque Block is where to head for the likes of pork tenderloin sandwiches and chorizo, as well as draft beers and Basque wine. 'Beef tongue Saturday' commences at 11:30am.

River City Bagel & Bakery (☎ 208-338-1299; 908 Main St; dishes $2-6; ☯ breakfast & lunch) A good place for morning fuel, this amiable eatery offers a range of bagels and sandwiches,

---

THE AUTHOR'S CHOICE

Grove Hotel (☎ 208-333-8000; www.grovehotel boise.com; 245 S Capital Blvd; r from $110; P ✗ ✦) European style influences the decor at this classy hotel with warm color tones and plush furnishings. With cocktail lounges, restaurants and cozy public areas, this is one of Boise's best bets for upscale accommodation.

---

plus espresso, chai and more. It has sidewalk seating and an attached bookstore.

Drinking

Emerald City (☎ 208-342-5446; 415 S 9th St) Proud to be 'straight friendly,' this gay bar and nightclub is a convivial spot to swill some drinks and live a little on the dance floor. DJs spin nightly except Saturday, when a show gets the spotlight.

Bardenay (☎ 208-426-0538; 610 Grove St) One of Boise's most unique watering holes, Bardenay was the USA's very first 'distillery-pub.' Today it serves its own homebrewed vodka, rum and gin in casual, airy environs.

Getting There & Around

The **Boise Municipal Airport** (☎ 208-383-3110; I-84 exit 53) has daily flights to Denver, Las Vegas, Phoenix, Portland, Salt Lake City, Seattle and Spokane. Greyhound and Northwestern Trailway services depart from the **bus station** (☎ 208-343-3681; 1212 W Bannock St) and travel along three main routes: I-84, US 95 and I-15/20/287/91.

Boise Urban Stages (BUS; ☎ 208-336-1010) operates local buses, including an airport route (No 13).

KETCHUM & SUN VALLEY

Thanks to the highly rated Sun Valley ski resort, Ketchum and Sun Valley are Idaho's premier destinations and the most happening cluster of towns in Idaho. A longtime favorite with highflyers, Sun Valley frequently takes top honors as the best ski resort in the USA. Trophy homes of the truly rich and famous dot the hilltops, and it's not uncommon to see a shining Hollywood face cruising down a slope. But despite the swank appeal, this is no LA. These year-round destinations, nestled among resplendent natural beauty, are also places to get away from it all.

Ketchum is the main commercial hub, with many restaurants, hotels and boutiques. Nobel-prize winning author (and avid sportsman) Ernest Hemingway (1899–1961) was a frequent visitor to the area, and spent his last years in Ketchum, where he's buried. Twelve miles south on Hwy 75, Hailey (lived in and half-owned by Bruce Willis) is where most seasonal workers and ski bums live.

Information

Sun Valley/Ketchum Visitors Center (☎ 208-726-3423; www.visitsunvalley.com; 411 Main St; ☾ 9am-6pm)

USFS Sawtooth National Forest Ketchum Ranger Station (☎ 208-622-5371; 206 Sun Valley Rd; ☾ 8am-5pm Mon-Fri)

Activities

Famous for its prime powder and excellent slopes, **Sun Valley Resort** (☎ 800-786-8259; www.sunvalley.com; lift ticket winter/summer $46/20) is west of Ketchum. World-class **Bald Mountain** (☎ 208-622-6136; lift ticket winter/summer $66/20) has mostly advanced terrain, while older **Dollar Mountain** (☎ 208-622-2242; Elkhorn Rd; lift ticket winter/summer $50/25) features easier runs. In summer all offer **hiking** and **mountain biking**. These activities are also popular along the well-maintained **Wood River Trail System** (WRTS), winding 20 miles through Ketchum and Sun Valley. Other excellent trails near Ketchum, which also permit mountain biking, include the 5.5-mile **Adams Gulch loop** and **Fox Creek**, a 5-mile loop with mountain views.

Sleeping

Tamarack Lodge (☎ 208-726-3344; www.tamaracksunvalley.com; 500 E Sun Valley Rd; r $110; ☒ ☒) Tasteful rooms complete with fireplace, balcony and many amenities are offered at this well-maintained lodge. The Jacuzzi and indoor pool are definite assets. Discounts are often available mid-week and off-season.

Lift Tower Lodge (☎ 208-726-5163; ltowerl@micron.net; 703 S Main St; r $65-90) This friendly small motel in downtown Ketchum offers free continental breakfasts and a hot tub. It sits next to a landmark exhibition chairlift c 1939.

Sun Valley Lodge (☎ 208-622-2001; www.sunvalley.com; r from $180; ☒) Hemingway completed *For Whom the Bell Tolls* in this lodge, which offers comfy rooms, the cheapest of which

are smallish in size. Amenities include a fitness facility, games room, bowling alley and sauna.

Meadows RV Park (☎ 208-726-5445; 13 Broadway Run, Hwy 75; campsites/RV sites $15/27) About 2 miles south of Ketchum, it offers decent camping.

Boundary Campground (campsites $11) Reservations are not accepted at this USFS site off Trail Creek Rd, 3 miles east of the Ketchum Ranger Station.

Eating & Drinking

Ketchum Grill (☎ 208-726-4660; 520 East Ave; dishes $10-17; ☾ dinner) A local favorite, Ketchum Grill boasts a creative menu bursting with fresh fare. The elegant offerings include lots of seafood, along with plenty of veggie options.

Bigwood Bread (☎ 208-726-2034; 270 Northwood Way; dishes $4-8; ☾ 7am-5pm Mon-Fri) With a cheery and upbeat atmosphere, this art-lined café has hearty breads, baked goods, sandwiches, salads and healthy-start offerings, such as organic muesli ($2.50).

Desperado's (☎ 208-726-3068; 211 4th St; dishes $7-9; ☾ 11:30am-10pm Mon-Sat) Despo's is a bright, busy and colorful eatery specializing in reasonably priced Mexican food. Fill up on burritos, chimichangas, tacos and quesadillas. A pitcher of margaritas is $17.

Grumpy's (860 Warm Springs Rd; dishes $4-8) Decorated with old beer cans, this small place is big in personality. It sizzles a damn fine burger, and on clear days locals flock to the decks to down schooners in the sun.

Whiskey Jacques (☎ 208-726-5297; 251 Main St) Make a night of it at this spacious, no-frills local institution: catch the game on TV, play a round of pool or Foosball, cut loose to live bands and DJs, or just drink till the cows come home.

Getting There & Around

The region's airport is Hailey's **Friedman Memorial Airport** (☎ 208-788-4956), 12 miles south of Ketchum. **A-1 Taxi** (☎ 208-726-9351) offers rides to the airport from Ketchum ($19).

Ketchum Area Rapid Transit (KART; ☎ 208-726-7576; ☾ 8am-6pm Mon-Fri) operates free daily bus service between Ketchum and Sun Valley.

Around Ketchum

A one-hour drive southeast of Ketchum, **Craters of the Moon National Monument** (☎ 208-527-3257; vehicle/hiker or cyclist $4/2; ☾ 8am-4:30pm Sep-May, 8am-6pm Jun-Aug) is an 83-sq-mile volcanic showcase. Lava flows and tubes and cinder cones are found along the 7-mile **Crater Loop Road**, accessible by car or bicycle from April to November. In winter it's popular with skiers and snowshoers. Short trails lead from Crater Loop Rd to crater edges, onto cinder cones and into tunnels and lava caves. A surreal **campground** (campsites $10) near the entrance station has running water only in summer.

North of Ketchum, Hwy 75 follows the Salmon River and winds past timbered slopes for 30 miles before ascending Galena Summit (8701ft), which offers truly breathtaking views. The 1180-sq-mile **Sawtooth National Recreation Area** spans the Sawtooth, Smoky, Boulder and Salmon River mountains and has 40 peaks over 10,000ft, more than 300 high-alpine lakes, 100 miles of streams and 750 miles of trails. The adjacent 340-sq-mile Sawtooth Wilderness Area centers on the rugged Sawtooth Range. Though most tourists come in summer and winter, boundless recreation is possible year-round.

The **area headquarters** (☎ 208-727-5000; Hwy 75; ☺ 8am-4:30pm Sep-May, 8am-5pm Jun-Aug), 8.5 miles north of Ketchum, refers visitors to guides for climbing, fishing and backcountry skiing, and has information on yurt rentals and camping. It also sells Trailhead Parking Passes (three-day/year passes $5/15), required for parking in the recreation area.

MCCALL

More rustic than glitz, wonderfully scenic McCall sits along Payette Lake's southern shore at the northern end of Long Valley. It's a year-round community with an air of seclusion. Residents enjoy a relaxing pace of life, and visitors take advantage of water sports, great skiing at nearby **Brundage Mountain** (☎ 208-634-4151; www.brundage.com; lift tickets $34), mountain biking, and good restaurants and lodgings. The **McCall Visitors Center** (☎ 208-634-7631; 102 N 3rd St; ☺ 8am-5pm Mon-Fri) is one block south of W Lake St. Detailed recreation information is available from the USFS Payette National Forest offices: **McCall Ranger District** (☎ 208-634-0400; 102 W Lake St; ☺ 7:30am-4:30pm Mon-Fri) and **Forest Krassel Ranger District** (☎ 208-634-0600; 500 N Mission St; ☺ 7:30am-4:30pm Mon-Fri).

The fabulous **Whitetail Club** (☎ 208-634-2244; www.whitetailclub.com; 501 W Lake St; r from $250;

☒ ☒) is a swanky place to stay. Blending with the natural environment, buildings are made from lodgepole pine, stone and shiny marble. Old black-and-white photos, antiques, deep couches and picture windows with lake views provide a classy, yet rustic ambience. The 70-plus suites are lavish affairs with private decks, deep mahogany furniture and thick tapestries. All sorts of activities can be arranged, and two on-site restaurants offer innovative menus.

HELLS CANYON NATIONAL RECREATION AREA

Plunging down 8913ft from Mt Oore's He Devil Peak on the east rim to the Snake River at Granite Creek, awe-inspiring Hells Canyon is North America's deepest gorge – thousands of feet deeper than the Grand Canyon. The remote 652,488-acre Hells Canyon National Recreation Area is one of the state's premier natural attractions, a must-see on any Idaho itinerary. Fishing, swimming, camping and dramatic views of the gorge and surrounding mountains are just a few of the highlights.

The **Snake National Wild & Scenic River** winds through the canyon, and is a favorite spot for rafting and jet-boat trips. Nearly 900 miles of **hiking trails** traipse by riverbanks, past mountain peaks and along canyon walls decorated with ancient petroglyphs. Wildflowers color meadows, and much wildlife resides here.

The Hells Canyon NRA spans the Idaho–Oregon state line, but the Oregon section is not readily accessible from Idaho. US 95 parallels its eastern boundary; a few unpaved roads lead from US 95 between the tiny towns of Riggins (a big rafting center) and White Bird into the NRA. Only one road leads from US 95 to the Snake River itself, at Pittsburg Landing.

The **Hells Canyon NRA Riggins** (☎ 208-628-3916; ☺ 8am-5pm Mon-Fri) has maps and information on campgrounds, roads, trails and fishing. The unstaffed **Salmon River Visitors Center** (☎ 208-628-3778; www.rigginsidaho.com; Riggins City Park, Hwy 95; ☺ 9am-5pm Mon-Sat) has brochures on the area's outfitters; the narrow strip of land called Riggins prides itself on being Idaho's white-water capital and is the base for rafting on the Lower Salmon River.

Travelers with time (and high-clearance vehicles) can drive to the canyon rim on unpaved roads for dramatic views. USFS

ROCKY MOUNTAINS

WILD & WOOLEY ESCAPADES ON THE SALMON'S MIDDLE FORK

A river junkie's wet dream, a trip down the Middle Fork of the Salmon River is a voyage that won't soon be forgotten. Part of the Lower 48's longest undammed river system, the rugged remote Middle Fork is often rated as one of the world's top 10 white-water and fly-fishing trips. The three- to eight-day journey begins its 3000ft vertical drop (an average descent of 28ft per mile) surrounded by conifer forest at 6000ft at the Boundary Creek put-in outside Stanley. There are more than 100 rapids (Class II to IV plus) and no roads reach the river's banks for 100 miles, until the confluence with the Main Fork of the Salmon.

Unique highlights along the way include visits to early 20th-century homesteader cabins, several soakable hot springs, wildlife-watching opportunities, day hikes to well-preserved rock art sites, and blue-ribbon catch-and-release angling in gin-clear riffles for native cut-throat and rainbow trout. Once on the river, few folks complain about being served coffee in their sleeping bag, and having guides whip up eggs Benedict and Dutch-oven desserts while they float, fish, soak and dream their cares away.

Early season (late May to mid-June) features peak flow and thrilling, chilly white water, while mid-season (mid-June to August) means warmer water and better fishing. Late season (mid-August to September) trips offer lower water and specialized fishing and hiking itineraries.

For details about Middle Fork trips, contact Idaho's premier river outfitter Coeur d'Alene–based **River Odysseys West** (ROW; ☎ 208-765-0841; www.rowinc.com). All-inclusive rates (excluding pre- and post-trip transportation to and from the put-in and take-out) start at $200 per day.

Andrew Dean Nystrom & Becca Blond

Rd 517 (open July to October), 0.25 miles south of the Hells Canyon Riggins office on US 95, climbs 17 miles to the rim and ends 2 miles later at the breathtaking **Heaven's Gate Lookout**.

IDAHO PANHANDLE

Tipping up toward Canada, this alluring region is speckled with resorts, lakes and old mining haunts. **Coeur d'Alene**, **Kellogg** and **Sandpoint** are prime destinations for skiers, anglers and water-sports enthusiasts, while the old silver-mining town of **Wallace** exudes preserved Western flavor. Sixty lakes lie within 60 miles of Coeur d'Alene, including Hayden, Priest and Pend Oreille, all surrounded by campgrounds. Outdoor activities are ubiquitous – white-water rafting the Class III run of the St Joe National Wild and Scenic River, jet-skiing on Lake Coeur d'Alene, backpacking through the primeval forest around Priest Lake.

The Panhandle has a reputation – often inflated by the media – as a base for neo-Nazi, white-supremacist groups. However, you're far more likely to meet wildlife than wildly irrational people. The **Coeur d'Alene Visitors Center** (☎ 208-665-2350; 115 Northwest Blvd; ☺ 10am-5pm Jun-Aug, 10am-3pm Tue-Sat rest of year) is a good regional information starting point.

For lodging in Coeur d'Alene, try the **Flamingo Motel** (☎ 208-664-2159; 718 Sherman Ave; r $70-85 ☒). It's a pink-door darling with spotless, charming rooms.

In Sandpoint, **Lakeside Inn** (☎ 208-263-3717; lakeside@televar.com; 106 Bridge St; r $65-95; ☒) has a good waterfront location, plus a Jacuzzi and comfortable rooms.

Pacific Northwest

The rumors are true – it rains a lot up here. But the skies are gray far less often than the region's protective locals would have you believe, and rarely during peak travel season, and even if Oregon and Washington really did suffer the round-the-clock monsoons of popular myth, they would probably still be worth visiting. It's hard to imagine an area with a greater concentration and wider variety of attractions than the Pacific Northwest. Within a day or so's drive, travelers will come across volcanoes and caves, moss-draped rainforests and sun-baked deserts, the wild Pacific coastline and placidly meandering rivers, high-walled canyons and snow-capped mountain peaks.

And that's just the scenery. This region is also home to two of the more dynamic cities in the US: high-strung Seattle and laid-back Portland. Major trends, both economic and artistic, have sprouted here and spread across the nation, even internationally – Nike, Starbucks, grunge rock, Amazon.com, microbreweries, just to name a few. The Pacific Northwest is also home to a number of traditional and contemporary indigenous cultures whose museums and casinos both welcome visitors.

Politically, the region tends to lean toward green, though Washington is a bit more conservative than its southern neighbor, and in both states there's a fairly sharp division between the urban left and the rural right. Count it as just another example that, in the Pacific Northwest, opposites attract.

HIGHLIGHTS

- Exploring the pristine beauty of the **San Juan Islands** (p1054)

- Camping at long, slender **Lake Chelan** (p1056) and being surrounded by glacier-carved mountains

- Tapping into the cultural nerve center that is **Seattle** (p1034)

- Discovering a small-town feel and big-city perks in young, hip **Portland** (p1058) while exploring its walkable, urban core

- Teetering on the rim of the achingly blue **Crater Lake** (p1071), Crater Lake National Park

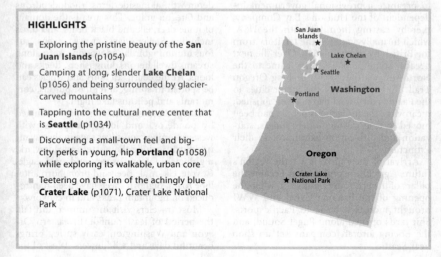

HISTORY

Native American societies including the Chinook and the Salish had long established coastal communities by the time Europeans arrived in the Pacific Northwest in the 18th century. Inland, on the arid plateaus between the Cascades and the Rocky Mountains, the Spokane, Nez Percé and other tribes thrived on seasonal migration between river valleys and temperate uplands.

Three hundred years after Columbus landed in the New World, Spanish and British explorers were probing the northern Pacific coast, still seeking the fabled Northwest Passage. In 1792, Capt George Vancouver was the first explorer to sail the waters of Puget Sound, claiming British sovereignty over the entire region. At the same time, an American, Capt Robert Gray, found the mouth of the Columbia River. In 1805 the explorers Lewis and Clark crossed the Rockies and made their way down the Columbia to the Pacific Ocean, extending the US claim on the territory.

In 1824 the British Hudson's Bay Company established Fort Vancouver in Washington as headquarters for the Columbia region. This opened the door to waves of settlers but had a devastating impact on the indigenous cultures, assailed as they were by the double threat of European diseases and alcohol.

In 1843 settlers at Champoeg, on the Willamette River south of Portland, voted to organize a provisional government independent of the Hudson's Bay Company, thereby casting their lot with the USA, which formally acquired the territory from the British by treaty in 1846. Over the next decade, some 53,000 settlers came to the Northwest via the 2000-mile-long Oregon Trail. By 1860 most of the major cities in the Pacific Northwest had been established; meanwhile the indigenous people had been moved to reservations, where illness, starvation and dislocation led almost to their extinction.

Arrival of the railroads set the region's future. Agriculture and lumber became the pillars of the economy until 1914, when the opening of the Panama Canal and WWI brought increased trade to Pacific ports. Shipyards opened along Puget Sound, and the Boeing aircraft company set up shop near Seattle.

Big dam projects in the 1930s and '40s provided cheap hydroelectricity and irrigation. WWII offered another boost for aircraft manufacturing and ship-building, and agriculture continued to thrive. In the postwar period Washington's population, especially around Puget Sound, grew to twice that of Oregon. But hydroelectricity production and the massive irrigation projects along the Columbia have nearly destroyed the river's ecosystem. Logging has also left its scars, especially in Oregon. The environment remains a contentious issue in the Northwest; flash points are the logging of old-growth forests and the destruction of salmon runs in streams and rivers.

In the 1980s and '90s, the economic emphasis shifted again as the high-tech industry, embodied by Microsoft in Seattle and Intel in Portland, took hold in the region. But this boom, too, was followed by a dramatic collapse, and unemployment in the Northwest soared until 2004, when it slowly began to level off.

GEOGRAPHY & CLIMATE

The major geographical regions are the coastal mountains and islands, the Cascade Range, and the plateaus stretching from east of the Cascades to the Rocky Mountain foothills. The mighty Columbia River drains nearly all of Oregon, Washington and Idaho. West of the Cascades, forests are fast-growing and dense. Wild berries proliferate in the undergrowth, alongside ferns, rhododendrons and Oregon grape. This area is the domain of mule deer, elk and black bears, and birds including Steller's jays, crows, ravens, rufous hummingbirds and woodpeckers; along streams dwell herons, kingfishers, ducks and loons. At the coast, sea lions and whales can be spotted in spring, and gulls, puffins, cormorants and pelicans take flight.

East of the Cascades, forests are dominated by ponderosa and lodgepole pines, with western juniper and silver sage in the savannas. Birds include the western meadowlark, nighthawk, falcon, osprey and bald eagle. Coyote, elk, mule deer and pronghorn antelope roam. Bighorn sheep have been reintroduced on mountain peaks and in canyons.

Most travelers visit in summer and fall, the period of least rainfall. In eastern Oregon and Washington, early spring brings beautiful days and wildflowers. West of the

---

PACIFIC NORTHWEST IN...

Four days
In four days you can hit both major cities. Start with **Seattle** (p1034) – check out Pioneer Square, Belltown, the art museum and a restaurant or two. Spend the next day on the water – take a scenic ferry ride to **Bainbridge Island** (p1046), **Vashon** (p1046), or the **San Juan Islands** (p1055). Drive south on day three, stopping at **Mount St Helens** (p1047) before digging into **Portland** (p1058). On day four, drive up the historic highway through **Columbia River Gorge** (p1076), stopping whenever a trailhead or waterfall catches your fancy.

One week
Follow the four-day itinerary, spending the fourth night in the Gorge. Next morning, head south to **Bend** (p1074) for outdoor recreation and microbrewed refreshments. Continue south to spend the sixth day exploring **Crater Lake** (p1071). From here you can choose to catch a play in **Ashland** (p1070) or meander back up north via the **McKenzie River** (p1073) area or along the **coast** (p1077).

Cascades, the precipitation doesn't subside until after May, but after that the summer days are almost uniformly bright and mild.

NATIONAL, STATE & REGIONAL PARKS
Oregon has one national park, Crater Lake; Washington has three – Olympic, North Cascades and Mt Rainier. Maps and passes are available at ranger stations or through Nature of the Northwest (see below). There are 240 state parks in Oregon and 215 in Washington.

INFORMATION
Oregon and western Washington have a 10-digit dialing system for local calls. To make a local call within the ☎ 206, ☎ 253, ☎ 425, ☎ 360 and ☎ 564 area codes in Washington, and throughout Oregon, dial the area code first (without a 1).

Nature of the Northwest (☎ 503-872-2750, 800-270-7504; www.naturenw.org/forest-directory.htm; Suite 177, 800 NE Oregon St, Portland, OR 97232; ⏱ 9am-5pm Mon-Fri) Recreational information on national forests and state parks of the region; sells the Northwest Forest Pass (per day/year $5/30), required at many parks, trailheads, visitor centers and boat launches.

Oregon road conditions (☎ 800-977-6368, ☎ 503-588-2941 from out of state)

Oregon State Parks & Recreation Dept (☎ 503-378-6305, 800-551-6949; www.oregonstateparks.org; 1115 Commercial St NE, Salem, OR 97310)

Oregon Tourism Commission (☎ 503-986-0000, 800-547-7842; www.traveloregon.com; 775 Summer St NE, Salem, OR 97301; ⏱ 8am-5pm Mon-Fri) Sends out information and brochures on accommodations, camping, state parks and recreation outfitters.

Washington road conditions (☎ 206-368-4499 in Seattle, ☎ 800-695-7623 elsewhere in the state)

Washington State Parks & Recreation Commission (☎ 360-902-8844, 800-233-0321; www.parks.wa.gov; PO Box 42650, Olympia, WA 98504)

Washington State Tourism Office (☎ 360-725-5052; www.tourism.wa.gov; ⏱ 7am-7pm) Useful website; 'travel counselors' give advice by phone.

GETTING THERE & AWAY
AIR
Seattle-Tacoma (Sea-Tac) is the main airport in the Northwest, with daily service to Europe, Asia and points throughout the US and Canada. Portland International Airport (PDX) serves the US, Canada and has nonstop flights to Frankfurt, Germany and Guadalajara, Mexico. See p1163 for a listing of major airlines.

BUS
Greyhound (☎ 800-229-9424; www.greyhound.com) provides service along the I-5 corridor and the main east–west routes, with links to some smaller communities.

TRAIN
More pleasant and scenic than the bus, and comparably priced, **Amtrak** (☎ 800-872-7245; www.amtrak.com) runs trains to, from and around the Northwest, including the following:

Cascades Four trains a day connect Portland and Eugene with Seattle and Vancouver, BC.

Coast Starlight Runs daily along the West Coast between Seattle and Los Angeles via Portland and Oakland, CA.

Empire Builder Runs daily between Chicago and either Seattle or Portland; train divides in Spokane.

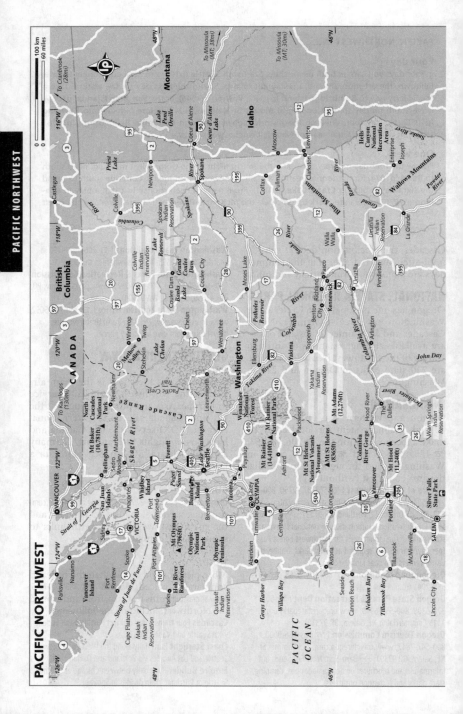

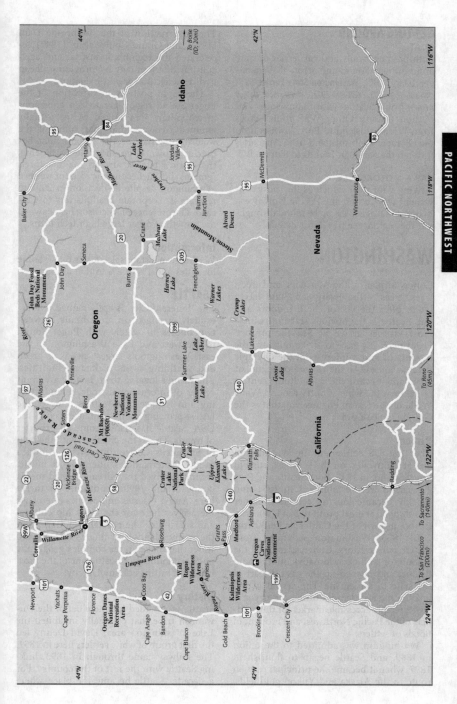

GETTING AROUND

BOAT

Both passenger-only and car ferries operate around Puget Sound and across to Vancouver Island, BC. **Washington State Ferries** (WSF; ☎ 206-464-6400, 888-808-7977; www.wsdot.wa.gov /ferries) links Seattle with Bainbridge and Vashon Islands. Other WSF routes cross from Whidbey Island to Port Townsend on the Olympic Peninsula, and from Anacortes through the San Juan Islands to Sidney, BC.

CAR & MOTORCYCLE

Driving your own vehicle is the most convenient way to tour the Pacific Northwest. Major rental agencies can be found throughout the region; see p1175 for details.

WASHINGTON

Coffee, airplanes, the Mariners, and trees, trees, trees – the Evergreen State has a lot to offer the visitor, both indoors and out. Seattle is the obvious starting point – most visitors arrive at Sea-Tac airport. From here, it's easy to strike out into the mountains and rainforests of the Olympic Peninsula, head to the rugged coastline, or go inland toward the agricultural centers of Yakima, the wine country around Walla Walla or the feat of engineering that is the Grand Coulee Dam.

History

The first US settlement in Washington was at Tumwater, on the southern edge of Puget Sound, in 1845. Both Seattle and Port Townsend were established in 1851 and quickly became logging centers. Lumber was shipped at great profit to San Francisco, the boomtown of the California gold rush.

In 1853, Washington separated from the Oregon territory. Congress reduced the amount of land open to native hunting and fishing, and opened up the eastern part of the state to settlement. The arrival of rail links in the last decades of the century created a readily accessible market for the products of the Pacific Northwest and brought in floods of settlers.

Washington was admitted to the union in 1889, and Seattle began to flourish in 1897, when it became the principal port en route to the Alaska and Yukon goldfields.

The construction of the Bonneville Dam (1937) and Grand Coulee Dam (1947) accelerated the region's industrial and agricultural development by providing cheap hydroelectric power and irrigation.

The rapid postwar urbanization of the Puget Sound region created an enormous metropolitan area linked by perpetually jammed freeways that mar some of the waterfront vistas. Seattle in particular has quickly grown large and affluent. Boeing, the world's biggest aircraft manufacturer, remains the chief economic force of western Washington despite its decision in 2001 to relocate its corporate headquarters to Chicago. The presence of Microsoft has spawned the growth of other large high-tech firms.

Information

Washington's state sales tax is 6.5%. Some localities add 1% to 2% to that amount.

SEATTLE

The 'Emerald City' is aptly named. Picturesquely arranged on an isthmus between two bodies of water, with Puget Sound to the west and Lake Washington to the east, Washington's largest city is as green and sparkling as its nickname indicates. The former logging town is now a vibrant center of international trade, manufacturing and high-tech industries. One of the fastest-growing metropolitan areas in the USA, Seattle has also become an exporter of trends. This is the city that, with the help of Starbucks Coffee, introduced America to the Americano. Underground music, having survived the Nirvana-fueled media circus of the 1990s, continues to thrive here. And TV series and movies often base themselves here for the city's hip cultural and social life. The coastal mountains and the many islands and fingers of land and water that make up the complex geography of Puget Sound give Seattle one of the most beautiful settings of any US city.

History

Seattle was named for the chief of the Duwamish tribe that originally inhabited the Lake Washington area. David Denny led the first group of white settlers here in 1851. The railway came through in 1893, linking Seattle with the rest of the country. For a decade, Seattle became the place where prospectors headed for the Yukon gold territory would stock up on provisions. It also served as the banking center for the fortunes they brought back.

The boom continued through WWI, when Northwest lumber was in great demand and the Puget Sound area prospered as a shipbuilding center. In 1916 William Boeing founded the aircraft manufacturing business that would become one of the largest employers in Seattle, attracting tens of thousands of newcomers to the region during WWII.

In more recent years, the growth of Microsoft and other software developers has made it difficult to find anyone in town who isn't a contractor, caterer or car dealer for the Microsoft crowd.

A series of calamitous events around the turn of the millennium seemed to deflate the confidence of even the most upbeat Seattleites. In November 1999, the city drew attention as protesters and police clashed violently outside a World Trade Organization summit. In June 2000 a federal judge ruled that Microsoft should be split up as a result of its monopolistic business practices (the decision was later overturned). And on February 28, 2001, a 6.8-magnitude earthquake near the state capital caused billions of dollars worth of damage (though, miraculously, little loss of life). Just a few weeks later came the ultimate kick in the teeth: Boeing announced its intention to relocate its headquarters to Chicago. The aircraft manufacturer has kept many jobs in the area, but its move called attention to the vulnerability of Seattle's less than diverse economy.

Orientation

Seattle's Sea-Tac Airport is some 13 miles south of the city. Amtrak trains use the King St Station, north of the new Seahawks stadium, just south of Pioneer Sq. Greyhound's bus terminal is at 8th Ave and Stewart St, on the north edge of downtown.

Seattle is very neighborhood-oriented; locals give directions in terms of Capitol Hill, Belltown, Fremont etc, which can be confusing if you don't know the layout. Basically, heading north from downtown, Capitol Hill and the U District lie to the east of I-5, while the historic downtown core, Seattle Center, Fremont and Ballard lie to the west. Aurora Ave (Hwy 99) is a major north–south artery.

> ### WASHINGTON FACTS
>
> **Nicknames** Evergreen State, Chinook State
> **Population** 5.9 million
> **Area** 66,544 sq miles
> **Capital city** Olympia (population 42,514)
> **Birthplace of** Novelist and social critic Mary McCarthy (1912–89); Jimi Hendrix (1942–70); *Far Side* cartoonist Gary Larson (b 1950); Kurt Cobain (1967–94); Bill Gates (b 1955)
> **Famous for** Lumber, Microsoft, grunge rock, Starbucks

To reach Fremont from downtown, take 4th Ave to the Fremont Bridge; from here, hang a left on NW 36th Ave (which becomes Leary) to reach Ballard. Eastlake Ave goes from downtown to the U District.

MAPS
Seattle has anything but a tidy grid layout and can be confusing to get around – a good map is essential. Head to Metsker Maps (see below) for a good selection.

Information
BOOKSTORES
Beyond the Closet Books (☎ 206-322-4609; 518 E Pike St) Gay-focused bookstore.
Bulldog News & Espresso (☎ 206-632-6397; 4208 University Way NE) A very thorough newsstand.
Elliott Bay Book Company (☎ 206-624-6600; 101 S Main St) Labyrinthine store in historic Pioneer Sq has readings almost nightly.
Left Bank Books (☎ 206-622-0195; 92 Pike Pl) Socialist intellectual heaven.
Metsker Maps (☎ 206-623-8747; 702 1st Ave) Great selection of maps & travel guides.

EMERGENCY
Community Info Line (☎ 206-461-3200) Information on emergency services, housing, legal advice etc.
Police, fire and ambulance (☎ 911)
Seattle Police (☎ 206-625-5011)
Seattle Rape Relief (☎ 206-632-7273)
Washington State Patrol (☎ 425-649-4370)

INTERNET ACCESS
Seattle is one big wi-fi hotspot. For laptop-free travelers, there are several good Internet cafés (most of which offer 30 minutes free if you buy a coffee or snack).
Online Coffee Company (☎ 206-328-3731; 1720 E Olive Way; ☼ 8am-midnight Mon-Sat, 9am-midnight Sun)

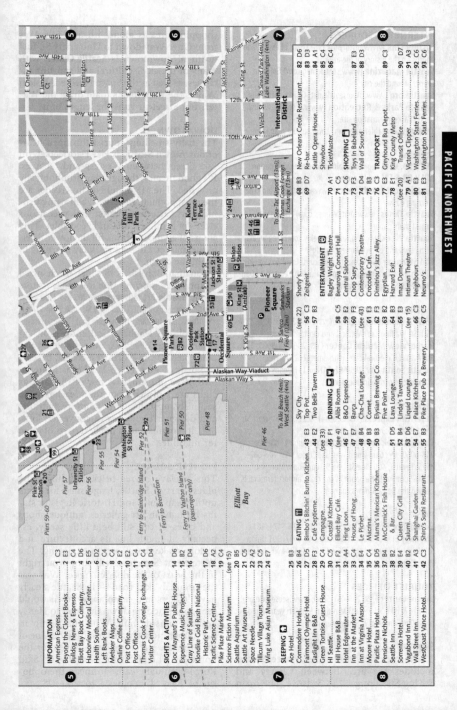

INTERNET RESOURCES

History Link (www.historylink.org) Loads of essays and photos on the history of the area.

Seattle Magazine (www.seattlemag.com) Guide to events around the city.

Seattle.org (www.cityofseattle.net) Official website.

Seattle Parks & Recreation (www.ci.seattle.wa.us/parks) Parks information site.

Tablet (www.tabletmag.com) Local culture magazine.

MEDIA

KEXP 90.3 FM Legendary alt-rock community station.

KPLU 88.5 FM Public radio.

Seattle Post-Intelligencer (www.seattlepi.com) The morning daily.

Seattle Times (www.seattletimes.com) The state's largest daily paper.

Seattle Weekly (www.seattleweekly.com) Free weekly with news and entertainment listings.

The Stranger (www.thestranger.com) Excellent weekly with in-your-face news and entertainment, edited by Dan Savage of 'Savage Love' fame.

MEDICAL SERVICES

45th St Community Clinic (☎ 206-633-3350; 1629 N 45th St, Wallingford) Medical and dental services.

Harborview Medical Center (☎ 206-731-3000; 325 9th Ave) Full medical care, with emergency room.

Health South (☎ 206-682-7418; 1151 Denny Way) Walk-in clinic for nonemergencies.

MONEY

American Express (☎ 206-441-8622; 600 Stewart St; ☼ 8:30am-5:30pm Mon-Fri)

Thomas Cook Foreign Exchange Airport (☎ 206-248-6960; ☼ 6am-8pm) Westlake Center (☎ 206-682-4525; Level 3, 400 Pine St; ☼ 9:30am-6pm Mon-Sat, 11am-5pm Sun) The booth at the main airport terminal is behind the Delta Airlines counter.

POST

Post office Broadway Station (☎ 206-324-5474; 101 Broadway E) Main branch (☎ 206-748-5417; 301 Union St) University Station (☎ 206-675-8114; 4244 NE University Way, U District)

TOURIST OFFICES

Visitor center (☎ 206-461-5840; www.seeseattle.org; 7th Ave & Pike St; ☼ 8:30am-5pm Mon-Fri year-round, plus 10am-4pm Sat & Sun in summer)

Sights

The historic downtown area, **Pioneer Square**, includes the area between Cherry and S King Sts, along 1st to 3rd Ave. The main shopping area is along 4th and 5th Aves from Olive Way down to University St. Just north of downtown is **Seattle Center**, with many of the city's cultural and sporting facilities, as well as the Space Needle. Alaskan Way is the **Waterfront**'s main drag; the Waterfront Streetcar runs the length of it.

DOWNTOWN

The fishy-smelling, tourist-thronged heart of downtown Seattle is **Pike Place Market**, on Pike Street between Western and 1st Aves. It's good theater, though claustrophobically crowded. The Main and North Arcades are the most popular areas, with bellowing fishmongers, arts and crafts, and precarious stacks of gemlike fruits and vegetables. Tiny shops of all descriptions fill the lower levels of the market. Go on a weekday morning to avoid the crush.

Jonathan Borofsky's 48ft-high mechanized sculpture *Hammering Man* welcomes visitors to the **Seattle Art Museum** (☎ 206-654-3100; www.seattleartmuseum.org; 100 University St; adult/child $7/free; ☼ 10am-5pm Tue-Sun, 10am-9pm Thu). The museum's John H Hauberg Collection is an excellent display of masks, canoes, totems and other pieces from Northwest coastal tribes.

North of Pike Place Market is **Belltown**, birthplace of grunge. A few of the famous clubs are still here, but the area has gone seriously upscale, with fancy restaurants and designer boutiques in converted lofts. Still, it remains one of the best parts of town for nightlife.

PIONEER SQUARE

This enclave of red-brick buildings, the oldest part of Seattle, languished for years until cheap rents and Historic Register status brought in art galleries, antique shops and cafés. It can still be a little seedy, especially at night, but its architecture and history make it well worth exploring. The Waterfront Streetcar will drop you right in the heart of the district. Yesler Way was the original 'skid road' – in Seattle's early days, loggers in a camp above town would send logs skidding down the road to Henry Yesler's pierside mill. With the slump in the timber industry and resulting decline of the area, the street became a haven for the homeless. The nickname Skid Rd (or 'Skid Row') eventually came to mean the opposite of 'Easy St' in cities across the US

SEATTLE IN...

Two days

Start with a leisurely latte at **Zeitgeist** (p1045). Then explore historic **Pioneer Square** (opposite) and the totem poles in **Occidental Park** (below). Don't miss the chance to duck into **Elliott Bay Book Company** (p1035), Seattle's best bookstore. Nosh at the café downstairs, or follow your nose to a tasty meal in the International District. That evening, catch a **Mariners** (p1046) or **Seahawks** (p1046) game or – if you have wheels – cruise over to **Ballard Avenue** (p1044) for nightlife. The next day, hit **Pike Place Market** (opposite), then take the monorail over to **Seattle Center** (below) for a close-up view of the **Space Needle**. Stop into the EMP's **Liquid Lounge** (p1044) during happy hour, or go bar-hopping in Belltown.

Four days

Follow the two-day itinerary, then, the next morning, catch a ferry to **Bainbridge Island** (p1046) and breathe in the salt air. Enjoy a tasting at the **Bainbridge Island Winery** (p1047) before your return trip. In the evening, head to **Capitol Hill** (p1040). The next day, explore quirky **Fremont** (p1040) or the **U District** (p1040) – or both – then take a walk or rent a bicycle and ride along the nearby **Burke-Gilman Trail** (p1041).

Just south of Pioneer Sq, on Occidental Ave S, **Occidental Park** has totem poles carved by Chinookan artist Duane Pasco. Between S Main and Jackson Sts, the park turns into a tree-lined pedestrian mall bordered by galleries, sculptures and coffee shops.

At the **Klondike Gold Rush National Historic Park** (☎ 206-553-7220; 117 S Main St; admission free; ☉ 9am-5pm), one of the few *indoor* national parks in the country, learn what kind of provisions you would've needed were you to stake a claim in the Yukon territory.

INTERNATIONAL DISTRICT

East of Pioneer Sq (take S Jackson St), Asian groceries and restaurants line the streets. The **Wing Luke Asian Museum** (☎ 206-623-5124; www.wingluke.org; 407 7th Ave S; adult/child $4/2; ☉ 11am-4:30pm Tue-Fri, noon-4pm Sat & Sun) documents the often difficult and violent meeting of Asian and Western cultures in Seattle with artwork, special exhibits, historic photographs, a replica of a WWII Japanese-American internment camp and recorded interviews with internees.

The district's **Jackson Street** was once home to a thriving jazz scene. As teens in the late '40s and early '50s, Quincy Jones and Ray Charles used to hustle their way into jazz clubs here and play into the wee hours of the morning.

SEATTLE CENTER

In 1962, Seattle hosted a World's Fair, a summer-long exhibition that enticed nearly 10 million visitors to view the future, Seattle style. The vestiges, which 40 years later look simultaneously futuristic and retro, are on view at the **Seattle Center** (☎ 206-684-8582; www.seattlecenter.com; 400 Broad St). **Space Needle** (☎ 206-905-2100; adult/child $13/6; ☉ 10am-10pm Sun-Thu, 10am-midnight Fri & Sat) is a 605ft-high observation station with a revolving restaurant (p1044). The **monorail** (round-trip adult/child $3/1.50), a 1.5-mile experiment in mass transit, runs every 10 minutes daily from downtown's Westlake Center right through a crumple in the smashed-guitar hull of the Experience Music Project.

It's hard not to be astounded by Microsoft cofounder Paul Allen's **Experience Music Project** (EMP; ☎ 206-367-5483; www.emplive.com; 325 5th Ave N; adult/child $20/15, with Science Fiction Museum $27/20; ☉ 10am-8pm in summer, 10am-5pm Sun-Thu, 10am-9pm Fri & Sat in winter). The lovechild of a fat wallet and a rock 'n' roll heart, the EMP is worth a look for the architecture alone; whether it's worth the admission price depends on how old and music-obsessed you are (the younger the better – EMP's fun quotient peaks around age 13). The shimmering, abstract building, designed by Frank Gehry, houses 80,000 music artifacts, including handwritten lyrics by Nirvana's Kurt Cobain and a Fender Stratocaster demolished by Jimi Hendrix. Kids will love the chance to record and mix their own song or make a video. To serious music fans, the exhibits may seem a little basic, although the video archive is excellent. A recent addition to the

EMP is the **Science Fiction Museum** (☎ 877-367-5483; 325 5th Ave N; adult/child $13/9; ☒ 10am-8pm in summer, 10am-5pm Sun-Thu, 10am-9pm Fri & Sat in winter), with displays of actual light sabers, phaser guns, Capt Kirk's chair and a host of otherworldly video clips. The Sky Church theater, Liquid Lounge bar and Turntable restaurant are accessible free of charge.

CAPITOL HILL

This stylish, irreverent neighborhood could star in its own episode of *Queer Eye for the Straight City* – it displays all the panache and vitality that comes with being Seattle's main gay and lesbian stronghold. The junction of Broadway and E John St (the continuation of Olive Way) is the core of activity – ie restaurants, bars, shops and plenty of sidewalk theater. Continue north to stately **Volunteer Park**, on E Prospect St, which was originally Seattle's cemetery. Here the **Seattle Asian Art Museum** (☎ 206-654-3100; 1400 E Prospect St; adult/child $3/free; ☒ 10am-5pm Wed-Sun, 10am-9pm Thu; P) houses an extensive collection of paintings, sculptures, ceramics and textiles of Japan, China and Korea. It was undergoing an extensive renovation at the time of writing. Also in Volunteer Park is the glass-sided Victorian **conservatory** (admission free), filled with palms, cacti and tropical plants.

Capitol Hill is about 1.5 miles northeast of downtown. Take bus No 7 or 10 and get off at Broadway. If you're driving, there is also a pay parking lot on Harvard Ave E, behind the Broadway Market.

FREMONT

The off-kilter neighborhood of Fremont, about two miles north of Seattle Center, is known for wacky public sculpture, junk stores, hippies and a summer **outdoor film festival** (☎ 206-781-4230; www.fremontoutdoormovies.com; Phinney Ave N at 36th St; tickets $5; ☒ Jun-Aug). Fremont Ave N is the main strip. Probably the most discussed piece of public art in the city, *Waiting for the Interurban* (N 34th St at Fremont) is a cast aluminum statue of people awaiting a train that never comes; the Interurban linking Seattle and Everett stopped running in the 1930s (it started up again in 2001 but the line no longer passes this way). Check out the human face on the dog; it's Armen Stepanian, once Fremont's honorary mayor, who made the mistake of objecting to the sculpture. Beware the scary-eyed *Fremont Troll,* a mammoth cement figure devouring a VW bug beneath the Aurora Bridge at 36th St.

THE U DISTRICT

The 700-acre University of Washington campus sits at the edge of Lake Union in a hopping commercial area about 3 miles northeast of downtown. The main streets are University Way, known as the 'Ave,' and NE 45th St, both lined with coffee shops, restaurants and bars, cinemas and bookstores. The core of campus is **Central Plaza**, known as Red Square because of its brick base. Get information and a campus map at the **visitor center** (☎ 206-543-9198; 4014 University Way; ☒ 8am-5pm Mon-Fri).

Near the junction of NE 45th St and 16th Ave is the **Burke Museum** (☎ 206-543-5590; adult/child $6.50/4; ☒ 10am-5pm), with an excellent collection of Northwest coast Indian artifacts. At the corner of NE 41st St and 15th Ave is the **Henry Art Gallery** (☎ 206-543-2280; adult/child under 14 $8/free, admission free Thu; ☒ 11am-5pm Tue-Sun, 11am-8pm Thu), a sophisticated space centered on a remarkable permanent exhibit by light-manipulating sculptor James Turrell, as well as various temporary and touring collections.

BALLARD

The community of Ballard, settled by Scandinavian fishermen in the early 20th century, feels like your average *lutefisk*-flavored blue-collar neighborhood – until you turn down Ballard Ave, where a row of hip bars, restaurants and brewpubs appears. This cobbled street has suddenly become a hotbed of nightlife worth exploring.

Northwest of Seattle, the waters of Lake Washington and Lake Union flow through the 8-mile-long Lake Washington Ship Canal and into Puget Sound. Construction of the canal began in 1911; today 100,000 boats a year pass through the **Hiram M Chittenden Locks** (☎ 206-783-7059; 3015 NW 54th St; admission free; ☒ 10am-4pm Thu-Mon in winter, 10am-6pm in summer), about a half mile west of Ballard off NW Market St. Tours are provided from March to November. On the southern side of the locks, you can watch from underwater glass tanks or from above as salmon struggle up a **fish ladder** on their way to spawning grounds in the Cascade headwaters of the Sammamish River, which feeds Lake Washington.

Activities

Seattle's location lends itself to **hiking**, **bicycling** and all kinds of **water sports**. Both hikers and cyclists enjoy the 16.5 mile **Burke-Gilman Trail**, an abandoned railroad corridor that starts at the impressive industrial skeleton of Gas Works Park on Lake Union and ends up on the north side of Lake Washington.

HIKING

There are great hiking trails through old-growth forest at Seward Park, which dominates the Bailey Peninsula that juts into Lake Washington, and longer but fairly flat hikes in 534-acre Discovery Park, northwest of Seattle at the mouth of Chittenden Locks. The **Sierra Club** (☎ 206-523-2019) leads day-hiking and car-camping trips on weekends; most day trips are free.

CYCLING

Circling Green Lake is a popular weekend activity. Rent a bicycle at **Gregg's Greenlake Cycle** (☎ 206-523-1822; 7007 Woodlawn Ave NE; $20-30 per day).

ON THE WATER

On Lake Union, **Northwest Outdoor Center Inc** (☎ 206-281-9694, 800-683-0637; www.nwoc.com; 2100 Westlake Ave N; kayaks $10-15 per hr) rents kayaks and offers tours and instruction in sea and whitewater kayaking. The **UW Waterfront Activities Center** (☎ 206-543-9433), at the southeast corner of the Husky Stadium parking lot off Montake Blvd NE, rents canoes and rowboats for about $8 per hour. Bring ID or a passport.

In the right conditions, Green Lake and Lake Washington are popular for windsurfing. **Greenlake Boat Rentals** (☎ 206-527-0171; 7351 E Green Lake Dr) provides lessons and rentals.

Seattle for Children

The whole of Seattle Center will fascinate youngsters, but they'll get the most out of the **Pacific Science Center** (☎ 206-443-2001; 200 2nd Ave N; adult/child $10/7; ☺ 10am-6pm in summer, 10am-5pm Mon-Fri in winter; **P**). It entertains and educates with virtual-reality exhibits, laser shows, holograms, an Imax theater and a planetarium – parents won't be bored either. Parking $5 to $10.

Downtown on Pier 59 is the entrancing **Seattle Aquarium** (☎ 206-386-4320; www.seattle aquarium.org; adults $12, children $5-8; ☺ 10am-5pm in winter, 9:30am-7pm in summer), another fun way to learn about the natural world of the Pacific Northwest. Its centerpiece is the Dome, a spherical underwater room where you can see deepwater denizens from all angles; don't miss the daily feeding frenzy at 1:30pm.

Next door is the **Imax Dome** (☎ 206-622-1868; www.seattleimaxdome.com; adult/child $7/6), a 180-degree surround-screen theater, where you can see *The Eruption of Mt St Helens* as if you were sitting on top when it blew; call for film schedule.

Tours

Bill Speidel's Underground Tour (☎ 206-682-4646; adult/child $10/5) Explores a network of subterranean chambers that predate the Great Fire and subsequent rebuilding of the district above the tide flats; reservations advised. Tours leave daily from Doc Maynard's Public House, 610 1st Ave.

Gray Line of Seattle (☎ 206-626-5208, 800-426-7505; www.graylineofseattle.com; 800 Convention Pl; 3hr tour $29) City Sights Tour runs year-round.

Show Me Seattle Tours (☎ 206-633-2489; www.show meseattle.com; adult/child $38/25) Daily shuttle tours in small groups.

Festivals & Events

Chinese New Year (☎ 206-382-1197; www.inter nationaldistrict.org) January or late February. Parades, fireworks and food in the International District.

Northwest Folklife Festival (☎ 206-684-7300; www.nwfolklife.org) Memorial Day weekend in May. International music, dance, crafts, food and family activities at the Seattle Center.

Seafair (☎ 206-728-0123; www.seafair.com) Late July and August. Huge crowds attend this festival on the water, with hydroplane races, a torchlight parade, an air show, music and a carnival.

Bumbershoot (☎ 206-281-8111; www.bumbershoot .com) Labor Day weekend in September. A major arts and cultural event at Seattle Center, with live music, author readings, theatrical performances and lots of unclassifiable fun.

Sleeping

The **Seattle Hotel Hotline** (☎ 206-461-5882, 800-535-7071) has a free reservation service with winter Super Saver Packages. For a list of B&B inns, try the **Seattle B&B Association** (☎ 206-547-1020, 800-348-5630; www.lodginginseattle.com). The prices listed below are average high-season rates; generally, prices drop on weekends and plummet in winter.

BUDGET

Moore Hotel (☎ 206-448-4851; www.moorehotel.com; 1926 2nd Ave; r with shared bath $45; s/d with private bath

$62/69) Rooms at this once-grand hotel next to the elegant Moore Theater are nothing fancy, but they have plenty of old-world charm, and you can hardly beat the price for this location. Don't miss the adjoining Limelight, an unpretentiously retro lounge.

HI Seattle (☎ 206-622-5443, 888-622-5443; www.hiseattle.org; 84 Union St; dm $19-26, r $54) This gigantic hostel is clean, friendly, open 24 hours, and unbeatably convenient to the Waterfront and Pike Place Market. The dining room has a great view.

Green Tortoise Guest House (☎ 206-340-1222, 888-424-6783; www.greentortoise.com; 1525 2nd Ave; dm from $24) A slightly grungier option, but relaxed and friendly, this backpacker's hostel is also right in the middle of the action. It has six- and eight-bed dorms and free breakfast.

Commodore Hotel (☎ 206-448-8868, 800-714-8868; www.commodorehotel.com; 2013 2nd Ave; s/d with shared bath $49/55, with private bath $59/69, ste $124-144) The rates at this newly renovated and very friendly hotel include a continental breakfast.

MIDRANGE

Ace Hotel (☎ 206-448-4721; www.theacehotel.com; 2423 1st Ave; r with shared/private bath from $75/140) Hands-down Seattle's hippest hotel, the Ace sports minimal, futuristic decor (everything's white or stainless steel, even the TV), antique French army blankets, condoms instead of pillow mints and a Kama Sutra in place of the Bible.

Pensione Nichols (☎ 206-441-7125, 800-440-7125; www.seattle-bed-breakfast.com; 1923 1st Ave; s/d/ste $90/110/195) Ideally situated between Pike Place Market and Belltown, this charming haven has 10 European-style rooms and a common room overlooking the market.

Wall Street Inn (☎ 206-448-0125, 2507 1st Ave; s/d from $120/135) The innkeepers at this Belltown B&B live on-site with their kids, giving the place a friendly family atmosphere. Rooms are furnished with quilts and antiques, and some have views of the Space Needle. The location is great, although it can mean some street noise.

Gaslight Inn B&B (☎ 206-325-3654; 1727 15th Ave E; r with shared/private bath $80/100, ste from $130) This Capitol Hill B&B is a restored turn-of-the-century house with a warm, dark-wood atmosphere, 15 rooms, a pool and a hot tub. The owners have amassed an impressive art collection over the years.

Inn at Virginia Mason (☎ 206-583-6453, 800-283-6453; 1006 Spring St; r from $115) This hotel on First Hill just above downtown is part of the Virginia Mason hospital complex. It has quiet rooms and a nice rooftop garden with views.

Vagabond Inn (☎ 206-441-0400, 800-522-1555; www.vagabondinn.com; 325 Aurora Ave N; r $95-105; P ⊠) Kids under 18 stay free with their parents at this functional chain hotel near Seattle Center.

Also recommended:

Hill House B&B (☎ 206-720-7161, 800-720-7161; www.seattlebnb.com; 1113 E John St; r without/with bath $80/95) In a restored 1903 home in Capitol Hill.

Pacific Plaza Hotel (☎ 206-623-3900, 800-426-1165; 400 Spring St; r from $110) A business-oriented hotel with a great central location.

Seattle Inn (☎ 206-728-7666, 800-255-7932; 225 Aurora Ave N; r from $79; P ⊠) Spacious and disconcertingly pastel rooms and a complimentary breakfast.

WestCoast Vance Hotel (☎ 206-441-4200; www.westcoasthotels.com/vance; 620 Stewart St; r from $120) Large European-style hotel; ask about reduced B&B rates in winter.

TOP END

Inn at the Market (☎ 206-443-3600, 800-446-4484; 86 Pine St; r $190-380; P) A luxuriously serene little enclave right in the thick of Pike Place but insulated from the street noise by wads of cash. (A suite can run you up to $600.) The ivy-beribboned courtyard is precious and most rooms have views over Puget Sound. Parking $15.

Sorrento Hotel (☎ 206-622-6400, 800-426-1265; www.hotelsorrento.com; 900 Madison St; r $250, ste from $280; P) For atmospheric lodging in the center of town, check out the city's oldest ultraswank hotel. The Italian Renaissance–style building was renovated to its present decadence in 1980. Parking $19.

Fairmont Olympic Hotel (☎ 206-621-1700, 800-223-8772; 411 University St; s/d from $395/405; P) Huge and imposing, this opulent 1924 hotel looks more like a government building or a European bank from the outside. Its 450 rooms don't come cheap, but guests are treated like movie stars. Parking $20.

Hotel Edgewater (☎ 206-728-7000, 800-624-0670; www.edgewaterhotel.com; 2411 Alaskan Way; waterfront r from $325; P) This luxury hotel on Pier 67 is the only one that faces onto Elliott Bay. You're no longer allowed to fish from the windows, but you can sit by the fireplace and reel in the salty air and views of Puget

Sound. Rates vary greatly depending on views, amenities and season. Parking $16.

Eating
BUDGET

Head to Pike Place Market to forage for fresh produce, baked goods, deli items and take-out ethnic foods.

Elliott Bay Café (☎ 206-682-6664; 101 S Main St; snacks $5-6; ☽ breakfast, lunch & dinner) Beneath Elliott Bay Book Company is this cozy place for soup, salad and sandwiches. It also serves the beloved Top Pot handcrafted doughnuts.

Bimbo's Bitchin' Burrito Kitchen (☎ 206-329-9978; 506 E Pine St; $4.25-7.95; ☽ lunch & dinner) It looks like a hipster exploded in here, with over-the-top Mexi-kitsch decor covering every inch of the tiny space. The food is cheap, fresh and massive, and served until 2am on weekends. Don't miss **happy hour** ($2.50 drinks; ☽ 4-7pm) at the adjoining **Cha-Cha Lounge**, a cool, comfortable tiki bar.

Mama's Mexican Kitchen (☎ 206-728-6262; 2234 2nd Ave; mains $5-8; ☽ lunch & dinner) Mama's is always enjoyably packed, thanks to huge combo plates, cheap burritos and some great happy-hour margaritas. A good place to stop and refuel on the Belltown bar circuit.

Two Bells Tavern (☎ 206-441-3050; 2313 4th Ave; burgers $6-7; ☽ lunch & dinner; ✗) This venerable nonsmoking pub is a comfortable, welcoming place to enjoy one of Seattle's best burgers.

Salumi (☎ 206-621-8772; 309 3rd Ave S; from $5; ☽ lunch until 4pm Tue-Fri) The only place in Seattle where you can adopt and eat your own ham, this tiny deli is a meat-eater's dream. There's always a line at lunchtime, but the sandwiches and meat plates are worth the wait.

Also recommended:

Macrina (☎ 206-448-4032; 1st Ave at Battery St; lunch $8-14; ☽ breakfast, lunch) Locals line up for Macrina's pastries, artisan bread, panini sandwiches and light lunches.

Schultzy's Sausages (☎ 206-548-9461; 4142 University Way NE; ☽ lunch & dinner) It's hotdog heaven (there's even a veggie option!) at this longtime U District favorite.

Top Pot (☎ 206-728-1966; 2124 5th Ave; $1-3; ☽ breakfast, lunch & dinner) Doughnuts to die for.

MIDRANGE

Palace Kitchen (☎ 206-448-2001; 2030 5th Ave; starters $6-8, mains $20; ☽ dinner until 1am) Owned by semi-celebrity chef Tom Douglas, Palace Kitchen is a late-night hot spot that fills up

PACIFIC NORTHWEST

when the cocktail crowd gets peckish. Its bar snacks are anything but ordinary.

Shiro's Sushi Restaurant (☎ 206-443-9844; 2401 2nd Ave; sushi from $4, mains $16-20; ☽ dinner) Get a seat at the bar and watch the maestro prepare some of the freshest sushi rolls in town.

House of Hong (☎ 206-622-7997; 409 8th Ave S; dinner $10-15; ☽ 10am-5pm) Some of the best dim sum in the city is served here, so you don't even have to rush out of bed to get your fix.

Madame K's (☎ 206-783-9710; 5327 Ballard Ave NW, Ballard; pizzas from $12; ☽ dinner) An elegant, red-and-black pizza parlor with shades of its former life as a bordello, this chic place is packed at dinner. It's also popular for drinks, and the desserts are appropriately sinful.

Old Town Ale House (☎ 206-782-8323; 5233 Ballard Ave NW, Ballard; sandwiches $8-10, appetizers $3-6; ☽ lunch & dinner) This cavernous, warmly lit, red-brick pub serves great giant sandwich 'wedges', massive stacks of delicious fries and microbrewed beer.

Café Septieme (☎ 206-860-8858; 214 E Broadway; mains $8-14; ☽ breakfast, lunch & dinner) This trendy, modern French-inspired space serves fancy drinks, gourmet salads and light meals.

Other recommendations:

Coastal Kitchen (☎ 206-322-1145; 429 15th Ave E; dishes from $8; ☽ breakfast, lunch & dinner) Eclectic mix of Mediterranean and Mexican inspirations.

Hing Loon (☎ 206-682-2828; 628 S Weller St; garlic prawns $9.25; ☽ lunch & dinner) Specializes in seafood dishes.

Le Pichet (☎ 206-256-1499; 1933 1st Ave; lunch $6-10, dinner $16-18; ◔ breakfast, lunch & dinner, until 2am Sat & Sun) An adorable French bistro that combines elegance with a relaxed, homey atmosphere.

Shanghai Garden (☎ 206-625-1688; 624 6th Ave S; mains from $13; ◔ lunch & dinner) Hand-shaved noodles are the specialty here.

TOP END

Cactus (☎ 206-324-4140; 4220 E Madison St; lunch $8-10, dinner $10-15; ◔ lunch & dinner Mon-Sat, 4-10pm Sun) This popular neighborhood place is half tapas bar, half Southwestern Mexican fine dining. Hollywood stars have reportedly been spotted cuddling over giant mojitos here.

Campagne (☎ 206-728-2800; 86 Pine St; mains $25-35; ◔ dinner) In the courtyard at the Inn at the Market, this is Seattle's best traditional French restaurant; for a more casual option, try the downstairs café (mains $12 to $16).

Queen City Grill (☎ 206-443-0975; 2201 1st Ave; starters $9-15, mains $18-25; ◔ lunch & dinner until 2am) This longtime Belltown favorite serves daily seafood specials and menus that change to reflect the use of seasonal ingredients; don't miss the goat cheese appetizer or the grilled ahi. The room is warmly lit and cozy, yet sophisticated, and service is all class.

McCormick's Fish House & Bar (☎ 206-682-3900; 722 4th Ave; mains $15-23; ◔ lunch & dinner) This old-fashioned oyster and cigar bar is the flagship in a local chain; it's recommended for fresh daily seafood specials.

Sky City (☎ 206-443-2111; Seattle Center; appetizers $10-15, mains $30-45; ◔ lunch & dinner, plus breakfast Sat & Sun) If you're planning on dinner in the

---

THE AUTHOR'S CHOICE

Agua Verde Cafe (☎ 206-545-8570; 1303 NE Boat St; taco plates $7; ◔ lunch & dinner Mon-Sat, takeout only Sun) On the shores of Portage Bay at the southern base of University Ave, Agua Verde Cafe is a wonderful little gem that overlooks the bay and serves mouth-watering, garlic-buttery tacos of fish, shellfish or portabella mushrooms, plus all kinds of other Mexican dishes. There's usually a wait to get in, but you can order from the takeout window, or relax on the deck with a beer until a table opens up. You can also rent kayaks downstairs in the same building, in case you want to work off your dinner with a sunset paddle.

Space Needle's rotating restaurant, be aware that although the ride up is free if you have reservations, and the views are spectacular if it's clear, the menu prices might make your head spin in tandem with the restaurant.

Drinking

For late-night action, head to Capitol Hill's Pike-Pine Corridor, extending from Broadway to about 12th Ave, home to a plethora of arty live-music clubs and taverns. For a less-vigorous but still very busy bar scene, check out the pubs along Ballard Ave.

BARS

Alibi Room (☎ 206-623-3180; 85 Pike Pl) The perfect place to hide from the perfect crime, the Alibi attracts a crowd of mysterious strangers hunched behind cigarettes, savoring dangerous drinks and killer views.

Five Point (☎ 206-448-9993; 415 S Cedar St; ◔ 24hrs) Not retro, just old, the Five Point has been around since 1929, as have many of the regulars at its black tuck-and-roll bar chairs. The men's bathroom has a periscope view of the Space Needle.

Liquid Lounge (☎ 206-770-2777; 325 5th Ave N) Upstairs at the EMP (p1039), the Liquid Lounge, with its sleek high-tech atmosphere, is perhaps the best way to experience the EMP. The Lounge has DJs or live music most nights, and happy hour bargains on food and drink. Don't worry, it's not your gin and tonic that's making the ceiling go all wonky.

Shorty's (☎ 206-441-5449; 2222 2nd Ave) A totally unpretentious oasis in a block of très-chic lounges, Shorty's has cheap beer and hotdogs, alcoholic slurpees and a back room that's pure pinball heaven.

Monkey Pub (☎ 206-523-6457; 5303 Roosevelt Way NE) Off the beaten track, between the U District and Green Lake, this friendly punk-rock bar has a great jukebox, pool tables and occasional bands.

Comet (☎ 206-323-9853; 922 E Pike St) A no-frills institution with cheap beer and loyal locals, the Comet is a longstanding, comfy dive that hosts bands and occasionally very bad karaoke/open mike performances by local scene celebs.

Also recommended:

Barca (☎ 206-325-8263; 1510 11th Ave) A sexy, becur-tained space with the decadence of an opium den.

Lava Lounge (☎ 206-441-5660; 2226 2nd Ave) Fiery den with massive hipster cachet.

Linda's Tavern (☎ 206-325-1220; 707 E Pine St) Amazingly popular hipster hangout with a tiki-themed patio and $1.50 cans of Black Label.

Lock & Keel Tavern (☎ 206-781-9092; 5144 Ballard Ave NW, Ballard) A long, skinny saloon with a seafaring feel, popular for after-work drinks.

BREW PUBS

Jolly Roger Taproom (☎ 206-782-6181; 1514 NW Leary Way; lunch $4-7, dinner $10-12) A secret treasure tucked away off busy Leary, the Jolly Roger's a tiny, pirate-themed bar with a nautical chart painted onto the floor. Best of all, its delicious handcrafted beer comes in real, 20-ounce pints ($3.75), or you can try a sampler of five types ($7). Most of the food has beer in it and the menu pairs each meal with a suggested brew.

Hale's Ales Brewery (☎ 206-706-1544; www.halesales.com; 4301 Leary Way NW) Though quite short on atmosphere, the Hale's Brewery offers a self-guided tour, friendly service and, of course, great beer. Get an imperial pint for $4 or tasters for $1 each.

Pike Place Pub & Brewery (☎ 206-622-6044; 1415 1st Ave) The Pike Place Market-area pub serves great burgers and awesome brews – try the Kilt Lifter, Naughty Nellie's or the XXXXX Stout – in a funky neo-industrial multi-tiered space.

Elysian Brewing Co (☎ 206-860-1920; 1221 E Pike St) This spacious Capitol Hill pub has comfortable booths across from a massive central bar, plus communal tables in a sunken side room. The huge windows are great for people-watching – or being watched, if your pool game's good enough.

COFFEEHOUSES

This is the city that birthed Starbucks, and the homegrown-turned-overgrown chain also owns Seattle's Best Coffee and Torrefazione Italia, making it difficult to avoid. But small independent coffeehouses abound.

B&O Espresso (☎ 206-322-5028; 204 Belmont Ave E) A pleasant spot for some postcard scribbling on Capitol Hill.

Café Allegro (☎ 206-633-3030; 4214 University Way NE) The university is home to this two-story coffee house, supposedly the city's first espresso bar.

Zeitgeist (☎ 206-583-0497; 171 S Jackson St) A high-ceilinged, brick-walled café with great coffee and pastries, plus data ports for the 'working artist' crowd.

Entertainment

Consult the *Stranger, Seattle Weekly* or the daily papers for listings. Tickets for big events are available at **TicketMaster** (☎ 206-628-0888), which operates a **discount ticket booth** (☎ 206-233-1111) at Westlake Center.

LIVE MUSIC

Crocodile Cafe (☎ 206-441-5611; 2200 2nd Ave) A beloved institution in Belltown and famous as a launching pad for the grunge scene, the Croc still hosts great local and touring bands.

Neumo's (☎ 206-709-9467; 925 E Pike St) The 'new Moe's,' this club fills the big shoes of its long-gone namesake in booking some of the best local and touring rock shows in town.

Chop Suey (☎ 206-324-8000; 1325 E Madison St) A dark, high-ceilinged space with a ramshackle faux-Chinese motif, this venue has some of the best live rock shows in town.

Tractor Tavern (☎ 206-789-3599; 5213 Ballard Ave NW, Ballard) This spacious, amber-lit venue in Ballard mainly books folk and acoustic acts.

Other recommendations:

Central Saloon (☎ 206-622-0209; 207 1st Ave S) The city's premier blues club.

Dimitriou's Jazz Alley (☎ 206-441-9729; 2033 6th Ave) Prestigious jazz club.

New Orleans Creole Restaurant (☎ 206-622-2563; 114 1st Ave S) Jazz club near Pioneer Sq.

Showbox (☎ 206-628-3151; 1426 1st Ave) Big rock venue for touring bands.

CINEMAS

At opposite ends of Capitol Hill are two of the city's best art cinemas, the **Egyptian** (☎ 206-323-4978; 805 E Pine St) and the **Harvard Exit** (☎ 206-323-8986; 807 E Roy St). Both are key venues during the three-week **Seattle International Film Festival** (☎ 206-464-5830; www.seattlefilm.com), in late May and early June.

THEATER & PERFORMING ARTS

Seattle boasts one of the most vibrant theater scenes on the West Coast. Check the local newspapers for picks and schedules.

Bagley Wright Theatre (☎ 206-443-2222) The Seattle Repertory Theatre performs at the Bagley. Both the Bagley and the Intiman Playhouse front on Mercer St, the north side of Seattle Center.

Seattle Symphony (☎ 206-215-4747) The symphony is a major regional ensemble; it plays at the Benaroya Concert Hall, downtown at 2nd Ave and University St.

PACIFIC NORTHWEST

Seattle Opera (☎ 206-389-7676) The Seattle Opera isn't afraid to tackle weighty or non-traditional works. Performances are at the Seattle Opera House in Seattle Center.

A Contemporary Theatre (ACT; ☎ 206-292-7676; 700 Union St) Located at Kreielsheimer Pl, this theater produces excellent performances.

Intiman Playhouse (☎ 206-269-1900) The Intiman Theatre Company, Seattle's oldest, takes the stage at this theater.

Pacific Northwest Ballet (☎ 206-441-9411) The ballet is based at the Seattle Opera House.

SPECTATOR SPORTS

Tickets for most of the following sports are sold through **TicketMaster** (☎ 206-628-0888).

Seattle Mariners (☎ 206-628-3555) Check out this baseball team, which plays in Safeco Field just south of downtown.

Seattle Seahawks (☎ 206-827-9777) Watch the Seahawks play pro football in the avant-garde new Seahawks Stadium.

Supersonics (☎ 206-283-3865) Seattle's National Basketball Association franchise, Supersonics draws huge crowds at Seattle Center's Key Arena.

Huskies (☎ 206-543-2200) The Huskies are the enormously popular University of Washington football team.

GAY & LESBIAN VENUES

Re-bar (☎ 206-233-9873; 1114 Howell St) This storied dance club, where many of Seattle's defining cultural events happened (Nirvana album releases etc), welcomes gay, straight, bi or undecided revelers to its dance floor.

Neighbours (☎ 206-324-5358; 1509 Broadway Ave E) For the gay club scene and its attendant glittery straight girls, check out this longstanding dance factory that's always packed, though no one ever admits going.

Shopping

The main shopping area is downtown from 3rd to 6th Aves and University to Stewart Sts. The streets around Pike Place Market are a maze of arts-and-crafts stalls, galleries and small shops. Pioneer Sq and Capitol Hill also have some interesting, locally owned gift shops. For bookstores, see p1035. There are a few great, only-in-Seattle shops to seek out:

Archie McPhee's (☎ 206-297-0240; 2428 NW Market St, Ballard) This place really does have something for just about everyone.

Toys in Babeland (☎ 206-328-2914; 707 E Pike St; ☼ 11am-10pm Mon-Sat, noon-7pm Sun) The answer to the question 'Where can I buy pink furry handcuffs and a glass dildo?'

Wall of Sound (☎ 206-441-9880; 315 E Pine St) Has a staff of friendly experts and a great selection of hard-to-find magazines.

Getting There & Away

AIR

Seattle's airport, **Seattle-Tacoma International Airport** (Sea-Tac; ☎ 206-433-5388; www.portseattle.org), 13 miles south of Seattle on I-5, has daily service to Europe, Asia, Mexico and points throughout the USA and Canada, with frequent flights to and from Portland and Vancouver, BC. Small commuter airlines link Seattle to the San Juan Islands, Bellingham, Wenatchee, Yakima and Spokane.

BOAT

Clipper Navigation (☎ 206-448-5000) runs the passenger-only *Victoria Clipper,* which departs Pier 69 for Victoria (adult/child round trip $133/66, three hours, four times daily in summer); first departure stops at San Juan Island.

Washington State Ferries (☎ 206-464-6400, in Washington ☎ 888-808-7977; www.wsdot.wa.gov/ferries) runs ferries from Seattle to Bremerton (passenger/car $6.10/13.30, 60 minutes, daily) and to Bainbridge Island (passenger/car $6.10/13.30, 35 minutes, daily); both ferries leave from Pier 52, at Alaskan Way and Marion St. It also runs a passenger-only ferry from Seattle to Vashon Island ($8.10 round trip, 25 minutes), leaving from Pier 50.

BUS

Greyhound (☎ 206-628-5526; 8th Ave & Stewart St) has daily connections to Portland ($23, 4½ hours) as well as points east.

Quick Shuttle (☎ 800-665-2122; www.quickcoach.com) runs five daily express buses between Seattle and Vancouver, BC (4½ hours) from Sea-Tac Airport ($45).

TRAIN

Amtrak (☎ 800-872-7245, 303 S Jackson St) serves the following locations (fares vary; these are average):

Chicago $220, two days, one daily.
Portland $25, 3½ hours, four daily.
Oakland $100, 23 hours, one daily.
Vancouver, BC $30, four hours, one daily.

Getting Around

TO/FROM THE AIRPORT

Gray Line runs an **Airport Express** (☎ 206-626-6088, 800-426-7532) between Sea-Tac and major downtown hotels every 30 minutes from 5am to 11pm (one way/round-trip $10.25/17). Or, catch Metro Transit bus No 174 or 194 ($1.25, 30 minutes) outside the baggage claim area. Cabs cost $30 to $35.

CAR & MOTORCYCLE

Seattle traffic has been among the worst in the country for years and isn't improving. Add to that the steep one-way streets, expensive parking and high taxes on rental cars, and you might consider relying on public transit. If you do drive, take a friend: some Seattle freeways have High-Occupancy Vehicle (HOV) lanes for vehicles carrying two or more people. National rental agencies have offices at the airport and around town.

PUBLIC TRANSPORTATION

Metro Transit (☎ 206-553-3000, in Washington ☎ 800-542-7876) serves the greater Seattle metropolitan area. All bus rides are free from 6am to 7pm in the area between 6th Ave and the Waterfront, and between Pioneer Sq and Battery St in Belltown (note that Seattle Center is not within the ride-free zone). Fares are $1.50 peak (6am to 9am and 3pm to 6pm) and $1.25 off-peak. Buy tickets in advance and get a system map at the **King County Metro Transit office** (☎ 206-553-3000; transit.metrokc.gov; 201 S Jackson St) or at the Westlake Center bus tunnel station.

Vintage Australian streetcars run along the waterfront from Broad Street (a 10-minute walk from Seattle Center) to South Main and branch east to the International District. Fares are the same as for Metro buses.

TAXI

Farwest Taxi (☎ 206-622-1717)
Yellow Cabs (☎ 206-622-6500)

Around Seattle

The Washington State Ferry to Winslow, the primary town of **Bainbridge Island**, is popular for the great views of Seattle it offers as it crosses Elliott Bay. The **Bainbridge Island Winery** (☎ 206-842-9463; Hwy 305; ◷ noon-5pm), north of Winslow, is popular with cyclists and wine lovers. Ferries leave from Pier 52 (passenger/car $6.10/13.30, 35 minutes, hourly).

Another outing is the four-hour tour of the waterfront and **Blake Island** operated by **Tillicum Village Tours** (☎ 206-933-8600, 800-426-1205; adult/child $69/25). Boats depart from Pier 55 in Seattle for the island's Northwest Coast Indian Cultural Center and Restaurant. The package includes a traditional Indian salmon bake, dancing and a film about Northwest Native Americans. There's time for a short hike after the meal.

SOUTH CASCADES

Mighty peaks, spectacular hikes and rugged scenery make the mountains of the Cascade Range an outdoor enthusiast's heaven. Summer days can turn blustery in an instant, so pack a warm sweater and rain gear.

Mount Adams

As easily accessible as it is beautiful, Mt Adams (12,276ft) is one of the most inviting of the Cascade peaks. A unique activity in the area is huckleberry picking (permits required). For information on berry picking, hiking or climbing, inquire at the **Trout Lake ranger station** (☎ 509-395-3400; 2455 Hwy 141; ◷ 8am-4:30pm Mon-Fri, plus Sat & Sun in summer). There are numerous campgrounds around Mt Adams, and B&Bs on Trout Lake. Maps cost $4.25 at the ranger station.

The eastern slope is part of the Yakama Indian Reservation and mostly closed to nontribal members. A notable exception is the 3-mile **Bird Creek Meadow Trail**, one of the best-loved hikes in the Northwest, which gently climbs to an alpine meadow showered by waterfalls and ablaze with wildflowers. It begins in a small, western portion of the reservation that is open to non-Yakamas ($10 vehicle fee). Near Bird Creek Meadows are three lakeside **campgrounds** (☎ 509-865-2405).

The easiest access to Mt Adams is from the Columbia River Gorge, from either I-84 or Hwy 14. Take Hwy 141 to Trout Lake, the focal point of recreation in the area.

Mount St Helens National Volcanic Monument

On May 18, 1980, Mt St Helens erupted with the force of a 24-megaton blast, leveling hundreds of square miles of forest and blowing 1300ft off its peak. It's calmed down since then, but the danger isn't completely past (see the boxed text, p1049). Slowly recovering from the devastation, the

171 sq miles of volcano-wracked wilderness makes an easy but dramatic day trip from Portland or Seattle.

The **Mount St Helens Visitor Center** (☎ 360-274-2100; ☒ 9am-5pm), just off I-5 exit 49 near Castle Rock, presents an overview of the site's history and geology. At the end of State Hwy 504, in the heart of the blast zone, the **Johnston Ridge Visitors Center** (☎ 360-274-2131; ☒ 10am-6pm) provides views into the mouth of Mt St Helens' north-facing crater. A more remote vista point, with good views of the lava dome inside the crater, is on the northeastern side of the mountain along **Windy Ridge**, the terminus of USFS Rd 99 (closed in winter). Admission for a single/multiple-site pass is $3/6 ($1/2 for kids).

Mount Rainier National Park

At 14,410ft Mt Rainier, 95 miles southeast of Seattle, is the highest peak in the Cascades. The park has four entrances: Nisqually, on Hwy 706 via Ashford, near the park's southwest corner; Ohanapecosh, via Hwy 123; White River, off Hwy 410; and Carbon River, the most remote entryway, at the northwest corner. Only the Nisqually entrance is open in winter, when it's used by cross-country skiers. Call ☎ 800-695-7623 for road conditions.

For some detailed information about the park, contact the **superintendent's office** (☎ 360-569-2211 ext 3314; www.nps.gov/mora). Maps and trail descriptions can be downloaded from the website. Park entry is $10/5 per car/pedestrian (free for those under 17). For overnight trips, get a wilderness camping permit (free) from ranger stations or visitor centers. The six campgrounds in the park have running water and toilets, but no RV hookups. **Reservations** (☎ 800-365-2267; www.mount.rainier.national-park.com/camping.htm; reserved campsites summer/off-season $15/12, unreserved campsites $10) are strongly advised during summer months and can be made up to two months in advance by phone or online.

The most popular route up to the summit of Mt Rainier starts in Paradise, near the Nisqually entrance. **Rainier Mountaineering** (☎ 253-627-6242, summer only ☎ 360-569-2227; www.rmiguides.com; 2-day climb $551) has guided summit climbs. Pick up your trail information and backcountry permits at the **Longmire Hiker Information Center** (☎ 360-569-2211 ext 3317; ☒ summer only) and the **Jackson Visitor**

Center (☎ 360-569-2211 ext 2328; ☒ May-Oct) at Paradise.

In addition to several campgrounds, **Longmire National Park Inn** (☒ year-round) and **Paradise Inn** (☒ late May-early Oct) have rooms from $82; for reservations, call ☎ 360-569-2275 or go to www.guestservices.com/rainier.

Packwood (on US 12) is the closest town to the White River and Ohanapecosh entrances, both of which have campsites ($15). The **Packwood Ranger Station** (☎ 360-494-0600) is near the east end of town. The **Cowlitz River Lodge** (☎ 888-305-2185; 3069 Hwy 12, Packwood; r $47-55 in winter, $60-70 in summer) has 32 modern rooms, a hot tub and a herd of elk that hang out on the lawn.

The remote Carbon River entrance gives access to the park's inland rain forest. The ranger station (☎ 360-829-9639), just inside the entrance, is open daily in summer.

The **Rainier Shuttle** (☎ 360-569-2331) runs between Sea-Tac Airport and Ashford ($40, three times daily) or Paradise ($46, daily). **Gray Line** (☎ 206-624-5077; www.graylineseattle.com) runs tours from Seattle ($54, 10 hours).

SOUTHEASTERN & CENTRAL WASHINGTON

The wide-open farmlands around Walla Walla, southeastern Washington's financial center, are speckled with farmhouses and wineries. The bucolic landscape belies the violence that occurred just outside of town, where visitors can tour the site of the 1847 Whitman Mission massacre. The Yakima Valley is an arid agricultural region; old US 12, the Yakima Valley Hwy, parallels the freeway east of Yakima city and provides a pastoral alternative to I-82.

Walla Walla

Home of Whitman College and one of the most significant enclaves of historic architecture in eastern Washington, Walla Walla has a small downtown core that's cute enough to take home. More than 30 wineries grace the Walla Walla valley; sample their chardonnays at several tasting rooms on Main St. For information try the **chamber of commerce** (☎ 509-525-0850; www.wwchamber .com; 29 E Sumach St; ☒ 8:30am-5pm Mon-Fri, 9am-5pm Sat & Sun). **Coffee Connection Cafe** (☎ 509-529-9999; 226 E Main St) serves as a community center with Internet access ($5 per hour), games and magazines.

THE NOT-QUITE-SLEEPING GIANT

Just when you thought it was safe… Mt St Helens hadn't made much noise since its devastating eruption of May 18, 1980. Experts had warned, though, that further eruptions would come. Still, after almost 25 years of peace and quiet, locals may have grown a bit complacent. So when the mountain started to rumble in September 2004, starting hundreds of tiny earthquakes in the surrounding areas, the nervous excitement among volcano-watchers was palpable.

It turned out to be not much of an eruption after all. But it certainly put the blasted-out peak back on everyone's mind for a while.

There were warnings before the 1980 eruption, too. That March, small steam clouds built above the mountain and earthquakes rocked the area. Initially, geologists thought the pyrotechnics were simply the result of ground water reaching the molten core of the mountain and didn't realize until quite late that a major eruption was imminent.

Molten rock was rising toward the surface, heavily infused with water pressurized at temperatures of more than 660°F. As the piston of lava and its explosive charge of superheated steam pushed closer and closer to the surface, a bulge formed on the north side of the peak, growing larger and more unstable every day.

On May 18, the mountain gave way and a mass of rock, ash, steam and gas blasted 15 miles into the air. The entire north face of Mt St Helens disintegrated and collapsed in what geologists believe was the largest landslide in recorded history. A 200mph rush of mud, snow, ice and rock consumed Spirit Lake and engulfed 17 miles of the North Fork Toutle River valley. Poisonous gases exploded north of the crater, leveling 150 sq miles of forest in an instant.

Huge deposits of mud and ash closed shipping channels on the Columbia River for weeks, and several inches of ash settled between Yakima and Spokane. Many years later, drifts of ash left by the region's snowplows were still visible along the roadsides. You can see 100ft banks of dredged white ash, now covered with gorse, along the Toutle River near I-5 exit 52.

Nearby residents were given ample warning – perhaps too much, as quite a few returned to their homes when the volcano did not erupt on cue. Some 59 people were killed when it finally blew. The most famous casualty was Harry Truman – not the US president but the proprietor of a resort on Spirit Lake – who had lived in the area for many years and simply refused to leave. His lodge and all of Spirit Lake were buried 200ft of mud, ash and debris.

Geologists concur that another explosion is only a matter of time, an assessment brought dramatically home by the mountain's recent activity.

As you wander the main drag, don't miss Wayne Chabre's oddly amusing sculpture exploring the chicken-vs-egg debate at the corner of Main and Palouse Sts. Further down, note the pastel facade of the old cinema that now houses a Macy's; its interior is heartbreakingly drab-retail, but the storefront is lovely.

The remains of the 1836 **Whitman Mission** are 7 miles west of Walla Walla off US 12. Marcus Whitman and 14 other missionaries died when, in 1847, after a measles epidemic killed half the tribe, a band of Cayuse Indians attacked the 11-year-old mission. When news of the uprising reached Washington, DC, Congress established the Oregon Territories, the first formal government west of the Rockies. The **visitor center** (☎ 509-522-6357; adult/family $3/5; ☼ 8am-4:30pm) has exhibits and maps.

A good place to get a taste of the local wine country is **Fort Walla Walla Cellars** (☎ 509-520-1095; 127 E Main St; ☼ noon-4pm Fri-Sun & by appointment), housed in a cute brick building downtown with an outdoor patio. Alternatively there's the well-regarded **Waterbrook** (☎ 509-522-1262; 31 E Main St; ☼ 10:30am-4:30pm).

The **Mill Creek Brew Pub** (☎ 509-522-2440; 11 S Palouse; burgers $6-8; ☼ 11am-midnight) has seven microbrews, good burgers and a nice patio. The vast, comfy interior caters to a younger crowd, with both tables and counter/bar seating and a private back room for groups.

Yakima & Around

Yakima is the trading center of an immense and rather bleak agricultural area. The main reason to stop is the excellent **Yakima Valley Museum** (☎ 509-248-0747; 2105 Tieton Dr; admission $6; ☼ 11am-5pm Tue-Sun), with exhibits on native Yakama culture, tons of artifacts and a hands-on learning center for kids.

Numerous wineries lie between Yakima and Benton City; pick up a map at the **visitor center** (☎ 509-248-2021; www.yakima.org; 10 N 9th St; ⊗ 8:30am-5pm Mon-Fri).

This valley is home to the Yakama Indian Reservation, the state's largest. The huge **Yakama Indian Nation Cultural Center** (☎ 509-865-2800; adult/child $4/1; ⊗ 8am-5pm), off Hwy 97 at Toppenish, has displays on traditional life. Toppenish is also known for its murals depicting events from Yakama and Northwest history, visible on many buildings around town.

OLYMPIA

Olympia is something of a countercultural mecca, home to the fiercely alternative Evergreen State College, the liberal arts school where Simpsons creator Matt Groening studied. The diminutive state capital also gave birth to riot grrrl, Sleater-Kinney and K Records. Situated at the southern end of Puget Sound, Olympia and the neighboring towns of Lacey and Tumwater constitute an urban entity known as the South Sound.

The **State Capitol Visitors Center** (☎ 360-586-3460; 14th Ave & Capitol Way; ⊗ 8am-5pm Mon-Fri, plus 10am-4pm Sat & Sun in summer) provides information on the capitol campus and the Olympia area.

At the Washington State Capitol campus is the vast, domed 1927 **Legislative Building** (tours free; ⊗ hourly 10am-3pm, except Christmas and Thanksgiving). Visitors can also tour the **campus** (admission free; ⊗ 1:30pm Jun-Aug) and visit the Temple of Justice and Capitol Conservatory, housing a large collection of tropical plants.

The **State Capital Museum** (☎ 360-753-2580; 211 W 21st Ave; admission $2; ⊗ 10am-4pm Tue-Fri, noon-4pm Sat) has exhibits on the Nisqually Indians. The fun **Olympia Farmers Market** (☎ 360-352-9096; ⊗ 10am-3pm Thu-Sun Apr-Oct, Sat & Sun Nov-Dec), at the north end of Capitol Way, has fresh local produce, crafts and food booths.

Golden Gavel Motor Hotel (☎ 360-352-8533, 800-407-7734; 909 Capitol Way S; r from $55) is a carefully maintained downtown motel. Also try the **Carriage Inn Motel** (☎ 360-943-4710; 1211 Quince St SE; r from $50), off I-5 exit 105.

The **Urban Onion** (☎ 360-943-9242; 116 Legion Way E; lunch $7-9; ⊗ breakfast, lunch & dinner), a classy vegetarian haunt in an old hotel, serves cheap breakfast and affordable lunch

(salads and quiche), but prices soar for dinner. The **Spar Bar** (☎ 360-357-6444; 114 4th Ave E; breakfast $4-5, lunch $5-8; ⊗ breakfast, lunch & dinner) is a stylish old café/cigar store with a purple-glazed facade and a cozy back-room bar called the Highclimber. For a quick fix, hit **Oldschool Pizzeria** (☎ 360-786-9640; 108 Franklin St; pizzas $8.50-19; ⊗ lunch & dinner).

Catch live local bands at the **4th Avenue Tavern** (☎ 360-786-1444; 210 4th Ave E). **Fishbowl Brewpub** (☎ 360-943-3650; 515 Jefferson St SE) has home-brewed English-style ales and fine pub fare.

TACOMA

Tacoma gets a bad rap as a beleaguered mill town known mostly for its distinctive 'Tacom-aroma,' a product of the nearby paper mills. Its nickname, 'City of Destiny', because it was the Puget Sound's railroad terminus, once seemed like a grim joke. But destiny has started to come through for Tacoma. A renewed investment in the arts and significant downtown revitalization make it a worthy destination on the Portland–Seattle route. The city's setting, backed up against the foothills of Mt Rainier and facing onto the fjords of Puget Sound and the jagged peaks of the Olympic Mountains, isn't half-bad either.

Find information at the **visitor center** (☎ 253-305-1000, 800-272-2662; www.traveltacoma .com; 1001 Pacific Ave; ⊗ 8:30am-5pm Mon-Fri).

Tacoma's tribute to native son Dale Chihuly, the **Museum of Glass** (☎ 253-396-1768; 1801 E Dock St; adult/child $10/4; ⊗ 10am-5pm Tue-Sat, noon-5pm Sun, 10am-8pm Thu in summer), with its slanted tower called the Hot Shop Amphitheater, has art exhibits and glassblowing demonstrations. Chihuly's characteristically elaborate and colorful **Bridge of Glass** walkway connects the museum with downtown's enormous copper-domed neobaroque **Union Station** (1911), designed by the folks who built New York's Grand Central Station. Renovated in the early 1990s, the station now houses the federal courts (and still more insanely flowery Chihuly pieces). Next door is the **Washington State History Museum** (☎ 888-238-4373; 1911 Pacific Ave; admission $7; ⊗ 10am-5pm Tue-Sat, noon-5pm Sun), with good exhibits on the tribes of the Northwest Coast.

The **Tacoma Art Museum** (☎ 253-272-4258; 1701 Pacific Ave; adult/child under 6 $7/free; ⊗ 10am-5pm Mon-Sat, noon-5pm Sun, closed Mon in winter) has moved to new quarters and strengthened its collection of regional art; you won't see a lot of big names here, but you'll get a well-chosen cross-section of work by significant Pacific Northwest artists. The ornate **Pantages Theater** (☎ 253-591-5894; 901 Broadway), once an elaborate vaudeville hall, is Tacoma's premier performance stage. Directly north of 9th St on Broadway is **Antique Row**, a maze of collectibles shops.

Take Ruston Way out to **Point Defiance** (☎ 253-591-5337; zoo admission adult/child $9/7; 🕑 9:30am-5pm, 9:30am-6pm in summer), a 700-acre park complex with free-roaming bison and mountain goats, a logging museum, zoo and aquarium, and miles of forested trails.

For B&B inns, call the **Greater Tacoma B&B Reservation Service** (☎ 253-759-4088, 800-406-4088). About the least expensive lodging near the center is **Travel Inn Motel** (☎ 253-383-8853; 2512 Pacific Ave; r from $45). Other moderately priced options are scattered south of the center between I-5 exits 128 and 129.

Harmon Pub & Brewery (☎ 253-383-2739; 1938 Pacific Ave S; mains $9-14), opposite the history museum, draws its own homemade ales, some of which go into hearty dishes. The bayside **Harbor Lights** (☎ 253-752-8600; 2761 Ruston Way; dinner $9-17) is a longstanding favorite for seafood. **Antique Sandwich Company** (☎ 253-752-4069; 5102 N Pearl St; lunch & snacks $4-7) is a funky luncheonette and coffee shop beloved by the locals.

Sound Transit bus routes 590 and 594, which use the station behind the **Tacoma Dome** (510 Puyallup Ave), are a cheap way to reach Seattle ($3). The free Downtown Connector service makes a loop between the station and Seattle city center every 15 minutes. **Amtrak** (☎ 253-627-8141; 1001 Puyallup Ave) links Tacoma to Seattle and Portland. For a taxi, call **Yellow Cab** (☎ 253-472-3303).

OLYMPIC PENINSULA

Perhaps the highlight of a trip to Washington – at least for nature lovers – the Olympic Peninsula is a pristine example of the benefits of wilderness preservation. It's a rugged, remote area characterized by wild coastlines, deep old-growth forests and craggy mountains. Seafaring Native Americans have lived here for thousands of years. Only one road, US 101, rings the peninsula. Although the highway is in excellent condition, distances are bigger than they look on

a map, and visitors often find it takes a lot longer than expected to get where they're going. From Seattle, the fastest access to the peninsula is by ferry and bus via Bainbridge Island or on Washington State Ferries from Keystone on Whidbey Island.

Olympic National Park

One of the most popular US national parks, the Olympic National Park is noted for its wilderness hiking, dramatic scenery and varying ecosystems. The heavily glaciated Olympic Mountains rise to nearly 8000ft. Few roads penetrate more than a few miles into the park proper, but visitors willing to hike a bit will find waterfalls, alpine meadows, moss-bearded forests and lakes. Most lower valley trails are passable year-round, but expect rain, or clouds, at any time.

INFORMATION

Park entry fee is $5/10 per person/vehicle, valid for one week, payable at park entrances. Many park visitor centers double as USFS ranger stations, where you can pick up permits for wilderness camping ($5 per group, valid up to 14 days, plus $2 per person per night).

Forks Visitor Information Center (☎ 360-374-2531, 800-443-6757; 1411 S Forks Ave; 🕑 10am-4pm) Suggested itineraries and seasonal information.

Olympic National Park Visitor Center (☎ 360-565-3130; 3002 Mt Angeles Rd; 🕑 9am-5pm) Very helpful center at the Hurricane Ridge gateway, a mile off Hwy 101 in Port Angeles.

Wilderness Information Center (☎ 360-565-3100; 🕑 7:30am-6pm Sun-Thu, 7:30am-8pm Fri & Sat in summer, 8am-4:30pm in winter) Directly behind the visitor center, you'll find maps, permits and trail information.

EASTERN ENTRANCES

The graveled Dosewallips River Rd follows the river from US 101 for 15 miles to **Dosewallips Ranger Station**, where the trails begin; call ☎ 360-565-3130 for road conditions. Even hiking smaller portions of the two long-distance paths – with increasingly impressive views of heavily glaciated **Mount Anderson** – is reason enough to visit the valley. Another eastern entry for hikers is the **Staircase Ranger Station** (☎ 360-877-5569; 🕑 summer only), just inside the national park boundary, 15 miles from Hoodsport on US 101. Two state parks along the eastern edge of the national park are popular with campers:

Dosewallips State Park and **Lake Cushman State Park** (☎ 888-226-7688; campsites/RV sites $18/25). Both have running water, flush toilets and some RV hookups.

WESTERN ENTRANCES

Isolated by distance and inclement weather, and facing the Olympic Coast National Marine Sanctuary, the Pacific side of the Olympics remains its wildest. Only US 101 offers access to its noted temperate rain forests and wild coastline. The **Hoh River Rain Forest** can get 12ft to 14ft of annual precipitation. Trails from the **visitor center and campground** (☎ 360-374-6925; ☼ 9am-4:30pm, 9am-6pm Jul & Aug), at the end of 19-mile Hoh River Rd, plunge into thick clusters of old-growth trees wearing green moss sweaters. If you want to reenact *The Lord of the Rings,* this is the place.

The **Queets River Valley** is the most remote, and hence pristine, part of the park. A gentle, 3-mile day hike starts at primitive **Queets Campground and Ranger Station** (☎ 360-962-2283; campsites $8-10).

Lake Quinault is a beautiful glacial lake surrounded by forested peaks; it's popular for fishing, boating and swimming. A number of short trails begin just below **Lake Quinault Lodge** (☎ 360-288-2900; www.visitlakequinault.com; r from $120), an antique hideaway on South Shore Rd with heated pool and sauna, fireplace rooms and lake-view dining. Or try **Rain Forest Resort Village** (☎ 360-288-2535; www.rfrv.com; 516 South Shore Rd; r/cabins $95/135).

The **Enchanted Valley Trail** climbs up to a large meadow (a former glacial lakebed) that's resplendent with wildflowers and copses of alder trees. The 13-mile hike to the aptly named valley begins from the Graves Creek Ranger Station at the end of the South Shore Rd, 19 miles from US 101.

NORTHERN ENTRANCES

The higher you go along the 18-mile road toward the dizzying vistas at **Hurricane Ridge,** the smaller you feel. At the top, there's an interpretive center in a flower-strewn meadow from which you can see Mt Olympus and dozens of other peaks (on a clear day). The road begins at the visitor center in Port Angeles. The closest campground is **Heart O' the Hills** (☎ 360-956-2300; campsites $10), 5 miles south of Port Angeles on Hurricane Ridge Rd.

Popular for boating and fishing is **Lake Crescent.** From **Storm King Information Station**

(☎ 360-928-3380; ☼ summer only) on the lake's south shore, a 1-mile hike climbs through old-growth forest to Marymere Falls. Along the Sol Duc River, the **Sol Duc Hot Springs Resort** (☎ 360-327-3583; www.northolympic.com/solduc; campsites/RV sites/cabins $15/20/120; ☼ closed Oct-Mar) has lodging, dining, massage ($65) and, of course, hot-spring pools (adult/child $10/8), as well as great day hikes.

Port Angeles

Despite its aesthetic deficiencies and the prevalence of stripmalls, Port Angeles makes an excellent base for exploring the Olympic Peninsula – it may be a less-than-attractive town, but everything around it is drop-dead gorgeous. The **visitor center** (☎ 360-452-2363; 121 E Railroad Ave; ☼ 8am-8pm May-Oct, 10am-4pm in winter) is adjacent to the ferry terminal. Rent outdoor gear at **Olympic Mountaineering** (☎ 360-452-0240; 140 W Front St).

Pitch a tent at **Salt Creek County Park** (☎ 360-928-3441; www.clallam.net; campsites $14), 16 miles west on Hwy 112, with stunning views of the Strait of Juan de Fuca. The amiably managed **Thor Town Hostel** (☎ 360-452-0931; www.thortown.com; 316 N Race St; dm/r $15/30) has lodging in a homey, casual setting. Or try the **Tudor Inn B&B** (☎ 360-452-3138; www.tudorinn.com; 1108 S Oak St; r from $85).

First Street Haven (☎ 360-457-0352; 107 E 1st St; breakfast $5-7) is the place for hearty country breakfasts with local old-timers. **Thai Peppers** (☎ 360-452-4897; 222 N Lincoln St; mains $8-10) is a good destination for vegetarians.

Two ferries run from Port Angeles to Victoria, BC: the **Coho Vehicle Ferry** (☎ 360-457-4491; passenger/car $9/33), taking 1½ hours, and the passenger-only **Victoria Express** (☎ 360-452-8088; adult/child $13/8; ☼ May-Sep), which takes one hour.

Olympic Bus Lines (☎ 360-417-0700) runs twice daily to Seattle from the public transit center at the corner of Oak and Front Sts (one way/round-trip $30/50). **Clallam Transit buses** (☎ 360-452-4511) go to Forks and Sequim. **Budget Rent-a-Car** (☎ 360-457-4246) is at Fairchild International Airport and across from the ferry terminal; Horizon Air flies to Fairchild daily. For a taxi, call **Blue Top** (☎ 360-452-2223).

Northwest Peninsula

Several Indian reservations cling to this corner of the continent, and they welcome respectful visitors. The most remote and storied is the Makah Indian Reservation, centered on Hwy 112 in Neah Bay, 75 miles west of Port Angeles. The Makah has gained attention recently by winning the battle to re-establish its traditional whaling practices, a struggle entertainingly documented in Robert Sullivan's book *A Whale Hunt*. The out of the way but fascinating **Makah Cultural & Research Center** (☎ 360-645-2711; admission $5; ✹ 10am-5pm in summer, closed Mon & Tue in winter) is the sole repository of artifacts from nearby Ozette; the museum's exhibits document the day-to-day life of the ancient Makah. Seven miles beyond, a short boardwalk trail leads to **Cape Flattery**, a 300ft promontory that marks the most northwesterly point in the lower 48 states.

Convenient to the Hoh Rain Forest and the Olympic coastline is **Forks**, 57 miles from Neah Bay. Stay at the Waltons-esque **Hoh Humm Ranch** (☎ 360-374-5337; 171763 Hwy 101; r from $40), a B&B in a working farmhouse where balconies gaze over riverside herds of sheep, cattle and llamas. Or crash at the remote **Rain Forest Hostel** (☎ 360-374-2270; www.rainforesthostel .com; dm/d $12/25), on US 101 8 miles south of the turnoff for the Hoh Rain Forest.

Port Townsend

Ferrying in to Port Townsend, one of the best-preserved Victorian-era seaports in the USA, is like sailing into a sepia-toned old photograph. The city experienced a building boom in 1890 followed by an immediate bust, leaving its architectural splendor largely intact. For information try the **visitor center** (☎ 360-385-2722; www.ptchamber .org; 2437 E Sims Way; ✹ 9am-5pm Mon-Fri, 9am-4pm Sat & Sun). Internet access is available uptown at **Port Townsend Library** (1220 Lawrence St).

Historic **Fort Worden** (☎ 360-385-4730), located 2 miles north of the ferry landing (take Cherry St from uptown), was featured in the film *An Officer and a Gentleman*. Within the complex are the Commanding Officer's Quarters, a restored **Victorian-era home** (☎ 360-385-4730; admission $1; ✹ 10am-5pm Jun-Aug, 1-4pm Sat & Sun only Mar-May & Sep-Oct), and the **Coast Artillery Museum** (☎ 360-385-0373; admission $2; ✹ 11am-4pm Jun-Aug, Sat & Sun only Mar-May & Sep-Oct).

Within **Fort Worden State Park**, the **HI Olympic Hostel** (☎ 360-385-0655; olyhost@olympus.net; 272 Battery Way; dm $14-17, r from $50) has impeccable if spartan quarters in a former barracks; it's up the hill behind the park office. The **Waterstreet Hotel** (☎ 360-385-5467, 800-735-9810; 635 Water St; r with shared/private bath from $60/75), in the center of town, offers old-world charm at reasonable rates. The turreted, Prussian-style **Manresa Castle** (☎ 360-385-5750, 800-732-1281; www .manresacastle.com; 7th & Sheridan Sts; r from $99), built in 1892, was later expanded to house Jesuit priests. Even if you don't stay here, it's worth taking a self-guided tour; note the former chapel, truncated to form a breakfast room and banquet room. Rates drop in winter.

Port Townsend's main drag is lined with trendy cafés and restaurants. For a no-nonsense breakfast, join the local marina folk at **Landfall Restaurant** (☎ 360-385-5814; 412 Water St; breakfast $5-7; ✹ breakfast & lunch). **Sirens** (☎ 360-379-1100; 832 Water St) is a dimly lit, romantic upstairs bar with a balcony overlooking the port.

To reach Port Townsend, take the ferry from downtown Seattle to Bainbridge Island ($6.10). At the ferry dock catch the No 90 bus to Poulsbo ($1, 20 minutes), then pick up a No 7 bus to Port Townsend ($1, one hour). **Washington State Ferries** (☎ 206-464-6400) goes to and from Keystone, on Whidbey Island (car and driver/passenger $9/2, 35 minutes). For a cab, call **Peninsula Taxi** (☎ 360-385-1872).

NORTHWEST WASHINGTON

One of the highlights of any trip to the Pacific Northwest are Puget Sound's quiet, pastoral San Juan Islands, accessible only by ferry and air. Also lovely, and simpler to reach, Whidbey Island contains beautiful Deception Pass State Park and the quaint, oyster-rich village of Coupeville. Back on the mainland is the lively university town of Bellingham.

Whidbey Island

Green, low-lying Whidbey Island snakes 41 miles along the Washington mainland from the northern suburbs of Seattle to Deception Pass – so named because, on discovering the treacherous chasm that separates Whidbey from Fidalgo Island to the north, Captain George Vancouver realized he had been 'deceived' in thinking Whidbey was attached to the mainland. **Deception Pass State Park**, with forest trails, lakes and more than 17 miles of shoreline, encompasses the narrow channel traversed by a dramatic bridge that links the two islands.

Historic **Coupeville**, 10 miles south of Oak Harbor, Whidbey's main town, has an attractive seafront, antique stores and old inns. For information try the **visitor center** (☎ 360-678-5434; 107 S Main St; ◷ 10am-5pm). The Victorian-era **Inn at Penn Cove** (☎ 360-678-8000; 702 N Main St; r from $65) has B&B-style rooms. Sample oysters and mussels at the **Captain's Galley** (☎ 360-678-0241; 10 Front St; ◷ lunch & dinner).

Harbor Airlines (☎ 800-359-3220; www.harborair .com) has daily links from Oak Harbor Airport to Sea-Tac Airport and the San Juan Islands. **Washington State Ferries** link Clinton to Mukilteo (car and driver/passenger $8/4, 20 minutes, every 30 minutes) and Keystone to Port Townsend (car and driver/passenger $9/2, 30 minutes, every 45 minutes). **Island Transit buses** (☎ 360-678-7771, 800-240-8747) run the length of Whidbey every hour daily except Sunday, from the Clinton ferry dock.

Anacortes

Though most people leave it immediately, Anacortes on Fidalgo Island is worth looking around. The tiny town has some interesting old buildings along its main street. Mostly, though, it's known as the departure point for the San Juan Island ferries. For information, stop by the **chamber of commerce** (☎ 360-293-3832; 819 Commercial Ave; ◷ 9am-5pm Mon-Fri, noon-5pm Sat & Sun).

Various lodgings line Hwy 20. Downtown is **Cap Sante Inn** (☎ 360-293-0602, 800-852-0846; 906 9th St; r from $75), cozy and close to the eponymous marina. **Rockfish Grill/Anacortes Brewery** (☎ 360-588-1720; 320 Commercial Ave; pizza $7-10; ◷ lunch & dinner) has good wood-fired pizzas.

The **Bellair Airporter Shuttle** (☎ 800-423-4219; www.airporter.com) links Anacortes to the I-5 corridor at Mount Vernon ($10) and to connections for Bellingham and Sea-Tac airport. **Skagit Transit** (☎ 360-757-4433) bus No 410 travels hourly between Anacortes (10th St and Commercial Ave) and the San Juan ferry terminal.

Bellingham

The handsome port city of Bellingham, 18 miles south of the US-Canada border, is home to Western Washington University, a busy nightlife scene and plenty of good restaurants. Its action is divided between the port-centric downtown, grouped around

Commercial and Holly Sts, and Fairhaven, a cluster of red-brick buildings 3 miles to the south. Find information at the **visitor center** (☎ 360-671-3990, 800-487-2032; www.bellingham.org; 904 Potter St; ◷ 8:30am-5:30pm), off I-5 exit 253.

Victoria/San Juan Cruises (☎ 360-738-8099, 800-443-4552) has whale-watching trips to Victoria, BC, via the San Juan Islands (adult/child $70/30, three hours). Boats leave from the Bellingham Cruise Terminal in Fairhaven.

Most of the inexpensive motels are on Samish Way, off I-5 exit 252. Downtown are the remodeled **Shangri-La Downtown Motel** (☎ 360-733-7050; 611 E Holly St; r from $55) and similarly priced **Bellingham Inn** (☎ 360-734-1900; 202 E Holly St).

For organic produce, go to the **Community Food Co-op** (☎ 360-734-0542; 1220 N Forest St). **Old Town Cafe** (☎ 360-671-4431; 316 W Holly St; breakfast $3-6) serves cheap breakfast until 3pm. In Fairhaven, **Colophon Cafe** (☎ 360-647-0092; 1208 11th St; sandwiches $6-8), at Village Books, has scrumptious pastries and big sandwiches. **Henderson Books** (☎ 360-734-6865; 116 Grand Ave) is another great place to sit with a cup of joe and a good book.

Three Bs Tavern (☎ 360-734-1881; 1226 N State St) is a raucous student hangout with live music on the weekends. In Fairhaven, the **Archer Ale House** (☎ 360-647-7002; 1212 10th St; snacks $5-8) is a smoke-free pub with tempting seafood specials and a wide selection of draft beer.

San Juan Islands Shuttle Express (☎ 360-671-1137, 888-373-8522) offers daily summer service to Orcas and the San Juan Islands. **Alaska Marine Highway Ferries** (☎ 360-676-0212, 800-642-0066; www.state.ak.us/ferry/) go to Skagway and other southeast Alaskan ports. The **Bellair Airporter Shuttle** (☎ 800-423-4219; www.airporter.com) runs to Sea-Tac airport with connections en route to Anacortes and Whidbey Island.

SAN JUAN ISLANDS

The San Juan archipelago sprawls across 750 sq miles of Pacific waters where Puget Sound and the Straits of Juan de Fuca and Georgia meet. Long considered an inaccessible backwater of farmers and fishers, the islands today are economically dependent on tourism, but they somehow retain their bucolic charm. Late May to September is the best time to visit.

For information on the islands, contact the San Juan Islands **visitor center** (☎ 360-468-3663; www.guidetosanjuans.com). During July and

August, accommodation reservations are essential; try **All Island Reservations** (☎ 360-378-6977).

Sea kayaks, a popular means of exploring the shores of the San Juans, are available for rent on Lopez, Orcas and San Juan Islands. Expect a guided half-day trip to cost $30 to $45. Note that most beach access is barred by private property, except at state or county parks.

Airlines serving the San Juan Islands include **Harbor Air Lines** (☎ 800-359-3220; www.harbor air.com), **Kenmore Air** (☎ 800-543-9595) and **West Isle Air** (☎ 800-874-4434). Public transport is pretty much nonexistent, but most motels will pick up guests at the ferry landing with advance notice, and bike rentals are available.

Washington State Ferries (☎ 206-464-6400, in Washington ☎ 800-843-3779; www.wsdot.wa.gov/ferries) leave Anacortes for the San Juans; some continue to Sidney, BC, near Victoria. Ferries run to Lopez Island (45 minutes) and to Friday Harbor on San Juan Island (75 minutes). Fares vary by season; the cost of the entire round-trip is collected on westbound journeys only (except those returning from Sidney, BC). To visit all the islands, it's cheapest to go to Friday Harbor first and work your way back through the other islands.

Lopez Island

The most agricultural of the San Juan Islands, Lopez is also the closest to the mainland. For pastoral charm, it's a hard place to beat. South of the ferry landing (1.3 miles) is **Odlin County Park** (☎ 360-468-2496; campsites from $15).

San Juan Island

San Juan offers the most hospitable blend of sophisticated amenities and rural landscapes. The main settlement is **Friday Harbor**, where the **visitor center** (☎ 360-378-5240; 9:30am-4:30pm Mon-Fri, noon-4:30pm Sat & Sun) is at Front and Spring Sts. **San Juan Island National Historical Park** (☎ 360-378-2240; 8:30am-4pm), commemorating a mid-19th-century British-US territorial conflict, consists of two former military camps on opposite ends of the island. Both of these day-use sites contain remnants of the old officers' quarters; the American Camp, on the island's southeast end, features a splendid hike up Mt Finlayson, from which three mountain ranges can be glimpsed on a clear

day. On the western shore, **Lime Kiln Point State Park** (☺ 8am-5pm Oct-Mar, 6:30am-10pm Apr 1-Oct 15) is devoted to whale-watching.

Wayfarer's Rest (☎ 360-378-6428; www.rockisland .com/~wayfarersrest; 35 Malcolm St; dm/cabins $25/50) in Friday Harbor is a backpackers' hostel. **Roche Harbor Resort** (☎ 360-378-2155, 800-451-8910; www.rocheharbor.com; r from $85) is a splendid seaside village on the island's northwest corner. Friday Harbor has several great places to eat near the ferry landing.

Orcas Island

Ruggedly beautiful Orcas Island is the largest of the San Juans. The ferry terminal is at Orcas Landing, 13.5 miles south of the main population center, Eastsound. On the island's eastern lobe is **Moran State Park** (☎ 360-376-2326), dominated by Mt Constitution (2409ft), with 40 miles of trails; get a map at headquarters.

For help with accommodations, call the **Orcas lodging hotline** (☎ 360-376-8888; www.orcas -island.com/lodging.html). The romantic **Turtleback Farm Inn** (☎ 360-376-4914, 800-376-4914; 1981 Crow Valley Rd; d $90-225) is a restored farmhouse on a secluded 80 acres. The backwoods hippie hangout **Doe Bay Village Resort & Retreat** (☎ 360-376-2291; www.doebay.com; r $25-140), on the island's easternmost shore, has cabins with or without kitchens, yurts and hostel beds, plus hot tubs, guided tours and other fringe benefits.

Cafe Olga (☎ 360-376-5098; 11 Point Lawrence Rd, Olga; pies per slice $5; ☺ 9am-6pm Mon-Fri, 9am-8pm Sat & Sun, closed Wed Mar-Apr), in the village of the same name, is tucked inside a barn alongside a crafts gallery. It specializes in pie and seafood – in that order. Expect to wait for a table.

NORTH CASCADES

The North Cascades offer some of the most dramatic points in the state, from the visitor-friendly faux-German village of Leavenworth through to the rocky, glacier-topped crests of mountain ridges and the trails that wind among them. Only one road, Hwy 20, cuts through the 781-sq-mile North Cascades National Park, and the route is usually closed from late November to April. Pick up maps and backcountry permits at **park headquarters** (☎ 360-856-5700; 2105 Hwy 20; ☺ 8am-4:30pm) in Sedro Woolley, well to the west of the mountains.

Leavenworth

Cuter than a Nutcracker's button nose, little Leavenworth, notched into the mountains along the Wenatchee River, would be a worthy stop even without its Bavarian shtick. Schlager music blares in the streets, and even the gas stations are dressed up like Tyrolean cottages. There's not much going on here after dark, but you'll need the rest anyway for hiking or rafting in neighboring Wenatchee National Forest.

Find information at the **visitor center** (☎ 509-548-5807; www.leavenworth.org; 220 9th St; ✆ 8am-5pm Mon-Fri, 10am-5pm Sat, 10am-4pm Sun). For information on hiking or white-water rafting, contact the **US Forest Service office** (☎ 509-548-6977; 600 Sherbourne St; ✆ 7:45am-4:30pm).

Mrs Anderson's Lodging House (☎ 509-548-6173, 800-253-8990; www.quiltersheaven.com; 917 Commercial St; r from $55), with antique-decorated B&B rooms above a quilt shop, is so comfortable it's almost womblike. The **Blackbird Lodge** (☎ 509-548-5800, 800-446-0240; www.blackbirdlodge.com; r from $100) does a more upscale version of the German inn theme, with fireplaces and complimentary room-service breakfast.

For the obligatory brats-and-beer, head to **King Ludwig's** (☎ 509-548-6625; 921 Front St; sausage plates $8-10) or, for a more casual take, **Gustav's** (☎ 509-548-4509; 617 Hwy 2; burgers/brats $3/4).

Lake Chelan

Long, slender Lake Chelan is central Washington's playground. **Lake Chelan State Park** (☎ 509-687-3710), on South Shore Rd, has 144 campsites; a number of lakeshore campgrounds are accessible only by boat. The town of Chelan, at the lake's southeastern tip, is the primary base for accommodation and services. It has a **USFS ranger station** (☎ 509-682-2549; 428 Woodin Ave). **Link Transit buses** (☎ 509-662-1155; www.linktransit.com) connect Chelan with Wenatchee and Leavenworth ($1).

Beautiful **Stehekin** (or 'the way through'), on the northern tip of Lake Chelan, is accessible only by **boat** (☎ 509-682-4584; www.ladyofthelake.com; one way/round-trip $18/28 plus variable fuel surcharge), **seaplane** (☎ 509-682-5555; round-trip from Chelan $120) or a long hike across Cascade Pass, 28 miles from the lake. Most facilities are open mid-June to mid-September.

Methow Valley

The Methow (met-how) River valley has hiking, biking, rafting and fishing, but it's best known for cross-country skiing. Snows block Hwy 20 between Marblemount and Mazama from mid-November to mid-April (call ☎ 888-766-4636 for updates), so Methow-bound skiers approach from western Washington by taking US 2 to Wenatchee, then heading north to Twisp. Three USFS campgrounds are just off Hwy 20 on Early Winters Creek. Inquire at the **USFS visitor center** (☎ 509-996-4000; ✆ 9am-5pm), west of Winthrop, about conditions. For other lodgings, call **Methow Valley Central Reservations** (☎ 509-996-2148; www.methow.com/lodging).

North Cascades National Park

Hundreds of great backcountry hikes crisscross this park. Campgrounds abound, with 19 facilities accessible from Hwy 20, but bring food and supplies. **Newhalem**, a damworker's town, is the jumping-off point for recreation; the **visitor center** (☎ 206-386-4495; ✆ 9am-5pm) has information on trails and camping as well as rafting on the Skagit River. The **National Park Service** (www.nps.gov/noca) is another good resource.

Upper Skagit River Valley

Hwy 20 makes its subtle ascent east along this pretty Cascade river valley from Sedro Woolley toward North Cascades National Park. **Concrete**, 23 miles east of Sedro Woolley, has motels and is a base for exploring 10,781ft Mt Baker. **Rockport**, at the junction of Hwys 20 and 530, is a prime bald eagle viewing site. Stop for gas and snacks at Marblemount, where the **Wilderness Information Center** (☎ 360-873-4500 ext 39; ✆ 8am-4:30pm Mon-Fri) issues backcountry permits.

NORTHEASTERN WASHINGTON

The far-western foothills of the Rockies and the rugged landscape of the Columbia Basin afford a dramatic backdrop for the massive Grand Coulee Dam hydroelectric project. Spokane, just inside the border with Idaho, is a bustling metropolitan center.

Grand Coulee Dam

Construction of the Grand Coulee Dam, 225 miles from Seattle, started in 1933 as a WPA project. The dam disrupted the Columbia River's ecology and displaced the Colville Confederated Tribes from their riverfront land; it now provides irrigation to farmland and is the world's third-largest hydropower producer. The town of Coulee Dam is the best bet for a motel room.

The **Grand Coulee Visitor Arrival Center** (☎ 509-633-9265; ☼ 9am-5pm Sep-Nov, 8:30am-10:30pm summer, closed Dec), has historical exhibits and films on the dam's construction and regional geology. There are also nighttime laser shows in summer, screened on the dam's smooth, angled slope. There are free 30-minute tours hourly from 10am to 5pm.

Spokane

Visitors might be surprised to discover that Spokane has a lot of style. The largest city between Seattle and Minneapolis, it consists of an appealing juxtaposition of urban industrial grit and a whole lot of neon. Even farm-supply shops here have giant neon signs. The city does sprawl out in a less than attractive manner, but the downtown core is cool, especially when cloaked in darkness and allowed to shine.

Find information at the **visitor center** (☎ 509-747-3230; www.visitspokane.com; 201 W Main St; ☼ 8:30am-5pm Mon-Fri, 9am-5pm Sat, 10am-4pm Sun). Internet access is free at the Spokane Public Library, downtown at the corner of Lincoln and Main Sts.

Developed for the 1974 World's Fair and Exposition, **Riverfront Park** features gardens, playgrounds and a vintage carousel. A gondola at the park's west end glides over the multitiered **Spokane Falls**, but it's almost as vertiginously thrilling to cross the river on a footbridge. For a lesson in creative recycling, check out **Steam Plant Square**, a 1916 steam generator newly converted into an industrial-chic space with offices, shops, cafés and the **Steam Plant Grill** (☎ 509-777-3900; 159 S Lincoln St). Peer up into one of the plant's 225ft-tall smokestacks.

Spokane's **wineries** produce renowned merlots; the visitor center has a map of the top spots.

Chain motels line both Division St and Sunset Blvd. By far your best bet, though, is the crescent-shaped **Trade Winds Motel** (☎ 509-838-2091; 907 W 3rd Ave; r from $45) – it's tacky-cool, with a retro feel and big, balconied rooms. The **Budget Inn** (☎ 509-838-6101; 110 E 4th Ave; s/d from $50/55; [P] [Ⓡ]), off exit 281, is a roadside mammoth handy to downtown. For camping try **Riverside State Park** (☎ 509-465-5064; 9711 W Charles Rd; campsites $14), 6 miles northwest off Hwy 291.

Frank's Diner (☎ 509-747-8798; 1516 W 2nd Ave; breakfast $6-8; ☼ 6am-8pm), inside a vintage railway car, is a must for breakfast. **Europa Pizzaria & Bakery** (☎ 509-455-4051; 125 S Wall St; pasta $9-15, pizza $10-20; ☼ lunch & dinner) serves Italian comfort food until midnight in an exposed-brick salon.

A comfortably grubby rock bar, the **B-Side** (☎ 509-624-7638; 230 W Riverside) boasts an interesting smorgasbord of local musical talent and some seriously evocative bathroom graffiti. Follow the locals to **Mootsy's** (☎ 509-838-1570; 406 W Sprague Ave) for happy hour, where pints of Pabst cost $1 and the city's oddest characters entertain strangers at no charge.

Buses and trains depart from the **Spokane Intermodal Transportation Station** (221 W 1st Ave). **Amtrak** (☎ 509-624-5144) has daily service to Seattle ($33, 7½ hours), Portland ($31, 9½ hours) and Chicago ($134, 14½ hours).

OREGON

Oregon's landscape and its population are equally difficult to pigeonhole. The landscape combines rugged coastline and thick evergreen forests with barren, fossil-strewn deserts, volcanoes and glaciers. And as for the population, you name it – Oregonians run the full gamut from pro-logging, anti-gay conservatives to tree-hugging, dope-growing, ex-hippie liberals. The one thing they all have in common is a fierce devotion to where they live.

History

Oregon started as an ad hoc collection of New England missionaries and French and British trappers, officially becoming a US territory in 1848 and a state in 1859. Settlers populated most of the coastal and central region by the 1860s, many having made the arduous six-month journey across the continent on the Oregon Trail.

The new Oregonians proceeded to appropriate the homelands of the various Native American groups. In what came to be called the Rogue River Wars, one such group – the Takelma, dubbed *coquins*, or 'rogues,' by French beaver trappers early in the 19th century – attacked immigrant parties and refused to negotiate with the army to allow passage through their land. Tensions

PACIFIC NORTHWEST

OREGON FACTS

Nickname Beaver State

Population 3.4 million

Area 95,997 sq miles

Capital city Salem (population 142,940)

Birthplace of Short-story writer Raymond Carver (1938–88); radical journalist John Reed (1887–1920); chef James Beard (1903–85); scientist, antinuclear activist and double Nobel laureate Linus Pauling (1901–94); The Simpsons creator Matt Groening (b 1954)

Famous for Forests, the Oregon Trail, recycling (the 'Bottle Bill'), Nike

mounted, and butchery escalated on both sides. Eventually the Takelma retreated into the canyons of the western Rogue Valley, but they surrendered after several winter months of skirmishing with little food or shelter. They were sent north to the Grand Ronde Reservation on the Yamhill River, and they weren't alone. By the late 1850s, most of the Native Americans in the region had been confined to reservations.

The railroad reached Portland in 1883, and by 1890 the city was one of the world's largest wheat-shipment points. The two world wars brought further economic expansion, much of it from logging. In the postwar era, idealistic baby boomers flooded into Oregon from California and the eastern states, seeking alternative lifestyles and natural surroundings. These arrivals brought pace-setting policies on many environmental and social issues.

Since the 1960s, Portland and western Oregon have been particularly influenced by the new, politically progressive settlers, while small towns and rural areas have remained conservative. Its ballot-initiative system gives Oregonians the opportunity to advance citizen-proposed laws to the ballot box, and Oregon has become a stage for political dramas on divisive issues – such as physician-assisted suicide and gay marriage – in which the whole country has an interest.

Information

Oregon has no state sales tax.

Highway and road construction information
(☎ 800-977-6368; www.odot.state.or.us/highways.asp)

Oregon State Tourism (☎ 800-547-7842; www.travel oregon.com)

PORTLAND

Combining the sparkling waterfront beauty and lefty social vibe of Seattle with a small-town feel and a walkable urban core, Portland is a great place to spend a few days. It's a young, hip city with a thriving cultural scene that includes everything from opera to karaoke, hotdog stands to haute cuisine, and rock climbing to indie rock.

History

The Portland region was first settled in 1829 by retired trappers from the fur-trading post at nearby Fort Vancouver. The name was chosen when one party of settlers won a coin toss (the other choice was 'Boston'). With its prime location at the confluence of two rivers, the city soon became a center of shipping in the Northwest. During the 20th century it grew steadily, thanks in part to a WWII-fuelled shipbuilding boom.

The port and shipping operations have since moved north of downtown, and much of the city's rough-and-tumble waterfront feel went with it. The Old Town has been substantially revitalized, and the once-industrial Pearl District now brims with expensive lofts. The high-tech industry drove a lot of the area's economic growth in the past decade, and the industry's recent crash had a profound effect on Portland – the city's unemployment rates led the nation, and schools and social programs have suffered. This doesn't seem to have deterred newcomers, however; Portland's population, like its reputation as a city planner's dream, continues to grow.

Orientation

The Willamette River divides the city into east and west sides; Burnside St divides north from south, giving rise to the city's four quadrants. Downtown is in Southwest Portland. The historic Old Town, Chinatown, trendy 23rd Ave and the chic post-industrial Pearl District are in Northwest Portland. The Portland Streetcar connects Northwest to downtown, while Tri-Met's MAX light-rail system links the city center with Southeast Portland and the airport.

Northeast and Southeast Portland include a mix of late-19th-century residential neighborhoods and commercial developments. Close to downtown in Northeast is Lloyd Center, the nation's first full-blown shopping mall, and the historic residential Irvington neighborhood. A few miles north of that, NE Alberta St runs through the city's most dynamic neighborhood, with hipsters and first-time homeowners cramming an ever-shifting landscape of galleries, shops and restaurants. In Southeast, the Hawthorne District, between 30th and 45th Aves, is upscale bohemian. Less obvious neighborhoods worth checking out include SE Belmont St around 33rd Ave, SE Clinton St at 26th Ave, and the intersection of E Burnside St and 28th Ave. Southeast of downtown is Sellwood, an antique-store haven.

Information
BOOKSTORES

CounterMedia (☎ 503-226-8141; 927 SW Oak St) Gorgeous books on fringe culture and highbrow erotica.
Gai-Pied (☎ 503-331-1125; 2544 NE Broadway) Bookstore catering to gay men.
In Other Words (☎ 503-232-6003; 3734 SE Hawthorne Blvd) Feminist bookstore and resource center.
Powell's City of Books (☎ 503-228-4651; www .powells.com; 1005 W Burnside St) Legendary shop with a whole city block of new and used titles.
Reading Frenzy (☎ 503-274-1449; 921 SW Oak St) A DIY zine emporium; upstairs is the Independent Publishing Resource Center (☎ 503-827-0249), with a zine library and self-publishing resources.

EMERGENCY

Oregon State Police (☎ 503-378-3720)
Police, fire and ambulance (☎ 911)
Portland Police (☎ 503-823-3333)
Portland Women's Crisis Line (☎ 503-235-5333)

INTERNET ACCESS

Backspace (☎ 503-248-2900; www.backspace.bz; 115 NW 5th Ave; per hr $6; ☽ 7am-2am Mon-Fri, 10am-2am Sat, noon-midnight Sun) This youth-oriented hangout has arcade games, coffee and snacks, art exhibits and Internet access.

INTERNET RESOURCES

Gay Oregon (gaypdx.com) A resource for Portland's gay and lesbian communities.
PDX Guide (pdxguide.com) Evocative bar reviews written by a guy who knows, plus other happenings around town.
PDX History (pdxhistory.com) A photographic record of people and moments in Portland's past.
Portland Communique (communique.portland.or.us) Local news blog known for stirring up debate.
Portland Independent Media Center (portland .indymedia.org) Community news and lefty activism.

PORTLAND IN...

Two days

Grab the MAX to **Pioneer Courthouse Square** (p1062) for prime people-watching. Hit a museum or two on the **South Park Blocks** (p1062), then catch a streetcar down SW 10th Ave to the literary buffet of **Powell's City of Books, Reading Frenzy** and **CounterMedia** (above). If it's raining, nestle into the dungeon of **Ringlers Annex** (p1067) with your new treasures and sip a pint of local brew. If the weather's fine, visit the **Classical Chinese Garden** (p1063), chow down at **Veganopolis** (p1066) and retire to **Hung Far Low** (p1066) for a nightcap. Next day, get a postcard view of Portland from the **Washington Park International Test Rose Garden** (p1063); squeeze in some shopping along **NW 23rd** (p1068) or, if you're up for it, a hike in **Forest Park** (p1063); and relax with dinner at **Higgins** (p1066).

Four days

Follow the two-day itinerary, then, next morning, stroll along **Tom McCall Waterfront Park** (p1063) – through Saturday Market if it's a weekend – and across the Steel Bridge to the **Eastbank Esplanade** (p1063). Take the kids to **Oregon Museum of Science & Industry** (p1063), where they can explore the scientific world while you see the splendors of ancient Egypt in the Omnimax theater. Catch the No 14 bus to **Hawthorne Boulevard** (p1068) for shopping, snacks, microbrews and patchouli-scented people-watching.

On day four, get a jumpstart with **Stumptown Coffee** (p1067), then explore some of the **wine-tasting rooms** (p1069) just outside of town. For dinner, pair your newly acquired knowledge of the vine with delicious small plates at **Navarre** (p1066). Afterwards, catch an offbeat film at the **Clinton Street Theater** (p1068) or shoot pool and scope out the artwork at the couch-strewn **Nightlight Lounge** (p1067).

PACIFIC NORTHWEST

PORTLAND

INFORMATION
CounterMedia...............................1 D3
Legacy Good Samaritan Hospital.....2 A1
Portland/Oregon Visitors
   Association...............................3 D4
Powell's City of Books...................4 C3
Reading Frenzy.............................5 D3

SIGHTS & ACTIVITIES
Chinatown Gates...........................6 E3
Classical Chinese Garden................7 E2
Oregon History Center....................8 C4
Oregon Museum of Science &
   Industry...................................9 F6
Pioneer Courthouse......................10 D4
Portland Art Museum....................11 C4
Portland Building.........................12 D4
Portland River Company................13 E6
Salmon Street Springs Fountain......14 E5
Saturday Market..........................15 E3
Skidmore Fountain.......................16 E3
Whitsell Auditorium....................(see 11)

SLEEPING
Benson......................................17 D3
Heathman Hotel..........................18 D4
Hotel Lucia................................19 D3
Jupiter Hotel..............................20 H3
Mallory Hotel.............................21 B3
Mark Spencer Hotel......................22 C3
Northwest Portland International
   Hostel....................................23 B2

EATING
Higgins......................................24 C4
Jake's Famous Crawfish................25 C3
La Casita...................................26 G4
Veganopolis...............................27 E3

DRINKING
BridgePort Brew Pub....................28 C1
Hung Far Low.............................29 E2
Lucky Labrador Brewing Company...30 H5
Rimsky-Korsakoffee House.............31 H4
Ringlers Annex............................32 C3
Towne Lounge............................33 B3

ENTERTAINMENT
Backspace..................................34 E3
Berbati's Pan..............................35 E3
Cinema 21..................................36 A2
Crystal Ballroom.........................37 C3
Dante's.....................................38 E3
Darcelle XV................................39 E2
Dirty Duck.................................40 E3
Doug Fir................................(see 20)
Ground Kontrol..........................41 E3
Hobo's......................................42 E2
Holocene...................................43 H4
Imago Theater............................44 G3

Jimmy Mak's..............................45 D2
Loveland...................................46 G3
Scandals....................................47 D3

SHOPPING
3 Monkeys.................................48 A1
Just Be Toys..........................(see 34)
Ozone 03...................................49 A1
Seaplane...................................50 A1

TRANSPORT
Citybikes Annex..........................51 G3
Greyhound Bus Station..................52 D2

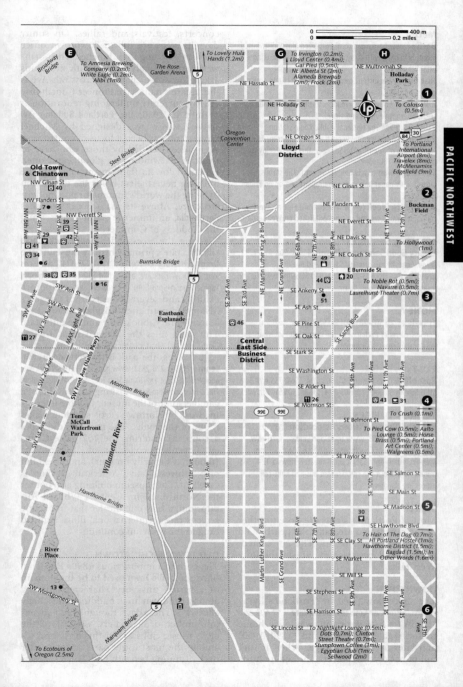

MEDIA

Barfly (www.barflymag.com) Pint-sized glossy distributed monthly in bars, with sassy, spot-on reviews of drinking establishments.

Just Out (www.justout.com) Serves the Portland area's gay community.

KBOO 90.7 FM Progressive local station run by volunteers; alternative news and views.

KOPB 91.5 FM The National Public Radio station

Portland Mercury (www.portlandmercury.com) The local sibling of Seattle's the *Stranger,* this free weekly is published on Thursday.

The Oregonian (www.oregonlive.com) The state's largest daily paper has an entertainment section on Friday (*The A&E*).

Willamette Week (www.wweek.com) Free alt-weekly covering local news and culture, published on Wednesday.

MEDICAL SERVICES

Legacy Good Samaritan Hospital (☎ 503-413-7711; www.legacyhealth.org; 1015 NW 22nd Ave)

Walgreens (☎ 503-238-6053; 940 SE 39th Ave) This location has a 24-hour pharmacy.

MONEY

Travelex (☎ 503-281-3045; ⊗ 5:30am- 4:30pm) Foreign-currency exchange in the main ticket lobby at Portland International Airport.

POST

Post office main branch (☎ 503-294-2564; 715 NW Hoyt St) University Station (☎ 503-274-1362; 1505 SW 6th Ave)

TOURIST OFFICES

Portland/Oregon Visitors Association (☎ 503-275-8355, 877-678-5263; www.travelportland.com; 701 SW 6th Ave in Pioneer Courthouse Sq; ⊗ 8:30am-5:30pm Mon-Fri, 10am-4pm Sat) A small theater shows a 12-minute film about the city. Tri-Met bus and light-rail offices are also here.

Sights

Most of Portland's sights are close together in the downtown area and the nearby Old Town-Chinatown nexus. The city's main parks – and best views – are in the lofty West Hills.

DOWNTOWN

The space now filled by 'Portland's living room,' **Pioneer Courthouse Square** (☎ 503-223-1613; SW 6th Ave & Morrison St), was once home to the regal Hotel Portland (1890–1950) and later a parking garage. When it isn't full of hackeysack players, the square hosts concerts, festivals and rallies. On sunny days its steps are full of downtown office workers enjoying their lunches. The northwest corner usually swarms with street kids asking for spare change. Across 6th Ave is the square's namesake Pioneer Courthouse (1875), currently undergoing renovations.

Built in 1980, the **Portland Building** (SW 5th Ave & Main St) was designed by Michael Graves and has been a focus of controversy ever since. Derided by those who have to work in its windowless gloom, and often ridiculed for its flamboyant exterior, the building nevertheless holds the distinction of being the world's first major postmodern structure. Above its main doors crouches **Portlandia**, an immense statue representing the Goddess of Commerce.

Along the tree-shaded **South Park Blocks** sits the state's primary history museum, the **Oregon History Center** (☎ 503-222-1741; www.ohs .org; 1200 SW Park Ave; adult/child $10/5; ⊗ 10am-5pm Tue-Sat, noon-5pm Sun). As well as temporary exhibits and several objects from Oregon's history on permanent display, there's a research library, bookshop and helpful staff. You can't miss the Richard Haas *trompe l'oeil* mural that covers the building.

Just across the park is the **Portland Art Museum** (☎ 503-226-2811; www.pam.org; 1219 SW Park Ave; adult/child $10/6; ⊗ 10am-5pm Tue, Wed, Sat, 10am-8pm Thu & Fri, noon-5pm Sun). Visiting can be a bit of a gamble; some of the museum's more interesting work by Northwest artists seldom makes it out of the vaults. The museum did score a coup in acquiring the 152-piece Clement Greenberg collection of American art (though it's usually on tour), and its exhibit of Northwest Native American carvings is excellent. The museum building also houses the Northwest Film Center's Whitsell Auditorium, a first-rate theater that frequently screens rare or international films. Plans to expand the museum continue.

OLD TOWN & CHINATOWN

The core of rambunctious 1890s Portland, once-seedy **Old Town** used to be the domain of assorted unsavory characters lurking among rundown brick buildings and smelly alleyways. These days, though, disco queens outnumber drug dealers. Several of the city's music clubs are in this area, and it's among the most lively parts of town after dark. Running beneath Old Town's streets are the **shanghai tunnels** (☎ 503-622-4798; tours by appointment; adult/child $11/6), a series of underground corridors through which unscrupulous and profiteering ship captains used to 'shanghai' drunken sailors, drugging or beating them and dragging them aboard as indentured workers.

The ornate **Chinatown Gates** on Burnside St at SW 4th Ave welcome visitors to this tiny ethnic neighborhood. The authentic Suzhou-style **Classical Chinese Garden** (☎ 503-228-8131; NW 3rd Ave & Everett St; adult/child $7/5.50; ☿ summer 9am-6pm, winter 10am-5pm) is a one-block haven of tranquility with a teahouse in the 'Tower of Cosmic Reflections.' Tours (free with admission) leave at noon and 1pm. Wheelchair accessible.

A preserve of Victorian-era architecture, the district that surrounds **Skidmore Fountain** (SW 1st Ave & Ankeny St) bustles from March to December with **Saturday Market** (☿ 10am-5pm Sat, 11am-4:30pm Sun), complete with buskers, food carts and tie-dye T-shirts.

Two-mile-long **Tom McCall Waterfront Park**, which flanks the west bank of the Willamette River from SW Clay St to the Steel Bridge, was a freeway until 1974, when it was torn up and replaced with a grassy riverside promenade. The park is now a venue for summer festivals and concerts. In warm weather, the computer-controlled **Salmon Street Springs** fountain swarms with frolicking kids. The walking/bicycling/skating/jogging route along the waterfront was extended in 2002 across the Steel Bridge to the **Eastbank Esplanade**, a 1-mile walkway with good views of downtown occasionally dampened by freeway noise.

WEST HILLS & WASHINGTON PARK

Behind downtown Portland are the West Hills, a ridge of ancient volcanic peaks that divide the city from its westerly suburbs. Labyrinthine trails link the various sites; ask for a map at the visitor center. The huge Washington Park complex contains the **International Rose Test Gardens** (☎ 503-823-3636; admission free; ☿ dawn-dusk) with 400 types of rose, including many rare varieties. Further uphill is the lush **Japanese Garden** (☎ 503-223-1321; www.japanesegarden.com; adult/child $6.75/4; ☿ 10am-4pm Oct-Mar, 10am-7pm Apr-Sep, closed until noon Mon; P). Prettiest in the fall, **Hoyt Arboretum** (☎ 503-228-8733; 4000 Fairview Blvd; admission free; ☿ trails 5am-10pm, visitor center 9am-4pm; P) is wheelchair-accessible

---

PECULIAR PORTLAND?

You see it on bumper stickers all over town: 'Keep Portland Weird!' Good idea, but how do you do it? And who's asking? Turns out that a group of small-business owners, eager to preserve the city's oddball character and resist chain-store blandification, got together some years ago to encourage folks to frequent quirky local places over malls and big-box stores. Want to help keep Portland weird? Visit www.keepportlandweird.com for the whole story and a list of participating businesses (one of which is the excellent art-house Cinema 21, p1068).

---

and has 10 miles of hiking trails that wind through 900 species of tree.

You can feel like old-money Portland without even paying admission at **Pittock Mansion** (☎ 503-823-3624; www.pittockmansion.com; 3229 NW Pittock Dr; adult/child $6/3; ☿ 11am-4pm Jun-Aug, noon-4pm Sep-May, closed Jan; P). The grounds, encouragingly dotted with picnic tables, offer stunning views across the valley.

Activities

Hiking and **mountain biking** are two of the most popular and easily enjoyable outdoor activities in Portland.

Hikers will find more than 50 miles of trails in **Forest Park**. Pick up a map of the park at the Hoyt Arboretum Visitor Center. The Wildwood Trail starts in the zoo/Children's Museum complex at the arboretum and winds through 30 miles of forest. Another easily accessible entry point is in Macleay Park at NW Thurman St and 26th Ave.

Head uphill to the western end of NW Thurman St and continue past the gate onto Leif Erikson Dr, an old dirt logging road leading 11 miles into Forest Park (obey posted signs or prepare to be scolded by fellow hikers). For maps, contact the **Oregon Department of Transportation** (☎ 503-986-3602; www.odot.state.or.us/techserv/bikewalk/mapsinfo.htm) or any cycle shop.

Portland for Children

Kids and their parents both love **Oregon Museum of Science & Industry** (OMSI; ☎ 503-797-4000; www.omsi.edu; 1945 SE Water Ave; adult/child museum or theater $9/7, planetarium or submarine $5.50, all-museum pass $19/15; ☿ 9:30am-5:30pm Tue-Sun), which has

PACIFIC NORTHWEST

GAY & LESBIAN PORTLAND

In its customary role as a proving ground for progressive social issues, Portland has become a hotbed of debate over the gay-marriage issue. The latest round was sparked in March 2004, when the chair of the Multnomah County Commission quietly ruled that forbidding gays to marry is discriminatory. Activists celebrated the decision as a leap forward, and local gay and lesbian couples rushed to get married. Around the same time, gay-rights advocates filed a lawsuit challenging Oregon's marriage law as unconstitutional. The combination of these two developments during an election year caused a predictable reaction by folks on the other side of the argument. In November's election, 57% of Oregon voters passed Measure 36, defining marriage as between a man and a woman.

Gay-rights group Basic Rights Oregon responded with a two-pronged attack: a lawsuit arguing that Measure 36 violates the state constitution, and a bill in the Oregon Legislature that would allow 'civil unions,' a marriagelike contract, for gay and lesbian couples. At the time of writing, both were still pending. The battle is far from over. Many gay-rights advocates are dissatisfied with the idea of civil unions, seeing them as a compromise that implies second-tier status. But even if Measure 36 were overturned, there would most likely be a backlash and another antigay measure – and probably just in time for the next big election.

hands-on science exhibits, an Omnimax theater, planetarium shows and the USS *Blueback* submarine.

In summer, the Zoo Train connects the Washington Park Rose Garden with the **Oregon Zoo** (☎ 503-226-1561; www.oregonzoo.org; 4001 SW Canyon Rd; adult/child $9.50/6.50; ☺ 9am-4pm Oct-Mar, 9am-6pm Apr-Sep; **P**), which has one of the world's most successful elephant breeding programs; inquire about summer concerts on the zoo's lawns. Parking $1.

Parents rave about the **Children's Museum** (☎ 503-223-6500; www.portlandcm2.org; 4015 SW Canyon Rd; admission $6; ☺ 9am-5pm Mon-Thu & Sat, 9am-8pm Fri, 11am-5pm Sun; **P**) near the zoo, with hands-on learning activities and exhibits. To get here, take the MAX or bus No 63.

Tours

Ecotours of Oregon (☎ 503-245-1428, 888-868-7733; www.ecotours-of-oregon.com; 3127 SE 23rd Ave; tours $40-60; ☺ scheduled on demand) Naturalist tours of northwest Oregon, notably Mt St Helens.

Portland River Company (☎ 503-229-0551; www.portlandrivercompany.com; 315 SW Montgomery St; tours $43-47) Year-round kayak tours of the Willamette River.

Portland Walking Tours (☎ 503-774-4522; www.portlandwalkingtours.com; adult/child $15/12) The 'A Walk Through Time' tour highlighting Old Town leaves at 3pm from Pioneer Sq every Friday, Saturday and Sunday.

Festivals & Events

Watch locals and suburbanites stake out prime parade-viewing territory by chaining lawn chairs to downtown sidewalks days in

advance of the **Portland Rose Festival** (☎ 503-227-2681; www.rosefestival.org), which runs from late May to June. Other highlights of the city's biggest celebration include a seedy riverfront carnival in Tom McCall Waterfront Park, roaming packs of wild-eyed sailors, beauty queens and blooming roses.

March through downtown with dykes on bikes and 10,000 others during Portland's **Gay Pride Parade** (☎ 503-295-9788; www.pridenw.org) in late June.

The **Oregon Brewers Festival** (☎ 503-778-5917; www.oregonbrewfest.com), held in Waterfront Park, is a summer highlight in late July. A winter version in a Pioneer Sq tent warms the huddled masses with heavier, cold-weather microbrews in early December (www.holidayale.com).

Sleeping

Most of central Portland's midrange hotels are downtown, with a plethora of chain options clustered around the Lloyd District and convention center in Northeast. Freeway exits around the outskirts of town are good places for budget options. Downtown hotels generally have valet parking only, at $10 to $20 a night. Make summer reservations well in advance. A 12.5% bed tax will be added to the room rate listed, which, unless noted, is for high season.

BUDGET

White Eagle (☎ 503-335-8900, 866-271-3377; 836 N Russel St; dm $30, r $40-50) A legendary musicians' haunt that may actually be haunted, the White Eagle is a top choice for music fans and heavy sleepers. Its 11 basic rooms above a brick-lined bar in a newly hip industrial neighborhood have shared baths and are named for songs by semi-legendary local band the Holy Modal Rounders. The hotel, once a brawl-friendly dockworkers' hangout nicknamed the 'Bucket of Blood,' was opened in 1905 by two Polish immigrants and allegedly had all the amenities a gentleman might need – brothel upstairs, opium den below.

HI Portland Hostel (☎ 503-236-3380, 866-447-3031; www.portlandhostel.org; 3031 SE Hawthorne Blvd; dm $16-21, f $38-48) This popular hostel is in a fun area and has good facilities. Check out the ecofriendly 'living roof.' Guests traveling by bicycle get a $3 discount. Take bus No 14 from downtown.

Northwest Portland International Hostel (☎ 503-241-2783; www.oregonhostels.com; 1818 NW Glisan St; dm/s/d $18/46/52) Quieter and more adult-friendly than the Hawthorne location, this hostel in a tree-lined residential area is another good base, right between the Pearl District and Northwest Portland.

MIDRANGE
Jupiter Hotel (☎ 503-230-9200; www.jupiterhotel.com; 800 E Burnside St; r from $75) The Jupiter is designed as a hipster hangout; room decor is minimal, with Scandinavian-sleek furnishings and furry throw pillows. The attached Doug Fir Lounge has live music nightly, and guests chatter on the outdoor patio into the wee hours (so if you want a quiet night, look elsewhere). After midnight, if there's a vacancy, you can get a room for $59.

Mallory Hotel (☎ 503-223-6311; www.mallory hotel.com; 729 SW 15th Ave; r $95-155; P) A local favorite, this classic boutique hotel has an understated charm, with luxurious common areas and plainer rooms. The impeccably retro lounge will have you rattling your ice cubes Rat Pack–style.

Hotel Lucia (☎ 503-225-1717, 877-225-1717; www .hotellucia.com; 400 SW Broadway; r from $125) The service entrance bears a lofty 'mission statement' and the lobby feels like a sleek techno nightclub, but the rooms in this newly facelifted hotel, though smallish, have old-world elegance, and the service is tops.

Mark Spencer Hotel (☎ 503-224-3293; www.mark spencer.com; 409 SW 11th Ave; r from $100) This is a great deal for anyone staying several days, as all the well-furnished rooms have kitchenettes. It's smack in the middle of the Stark St nightlife action, which is always fun to watch.

TOP END
Heathman Hotel (☎ 503-241-4100; www.heathman hotel.com; 1001 SW Broadway; r $140-210, ste from $300) A Portland institution, the Heathman has topnotch service and one of the best restaurants in the city. The hotel has its own librarian who stocks its lending library with books signed by authors who have stayed here. There's high tea in the afternoons, jazz in the evenings, and each simple, spacious room is decorated with original Northwest art.

Benson (☎ 503-228-2000, 888-523-6766; www.ben sonhotel.com; 309 SW Broadway; r from $125) Rock stars and politicos – including Vice-President Dick Cheney – stay at the Benson when in town. Built in 1912 by a lumber tycoon, the hotel radiates decadence – check out the lobby bar even if you're not staying. Some of the rooms have whirlpool tubs and pianos, and all have Tempur-Pedic or pillowtop mattresses and plenty of work space.

THE AUTHOR'S CHOICE

McMenamins Edgefield (☎ 503-669-8610; www.mcmenamins.com; 2126 SW Halsey St, Troutdale; dm/s $25/55, d $85-105, ste $115-130, f $200) How many golf courses have a watering hole at every hole? At McMenamins Edgefield, a former county poor farm restored by Portland's McMenamin Brothers, you can do a multibar pub crawl amid squirrels and bunnies, enjoy some pitch-and-putt golf (from $10), taste the local wine, watch a movie ($3) and then collapse in your own bed mere steps away. The best spot here for sampling a scrumptious microbrew (whether or not you're in the midst of your round of golf) is the Little Red Shed, perhaps the single most adorable drinking establishment ever created. Only a handful of people fit inside the Beatrix Potter-ish hut, and those who do tend to curl up by the fire with a cigar and a glass of scotch, so plan ahead. But you won't miss out: there are half a dozen other bars on the complex, and if you're staying the night here, there's no reason not to try them all! To get here, drive east on Hwy 84 to the Troutdale exit, then take a right onto Halsey.

PACIFIC NORTHWEST

Eating

Portland is rapidly becoming a gourmand's dream, with hot new restaurants opening all the time. Self-catering is an easy budget option, with multiple choices for organic grocery shopping. Vegan and vegetarian options also abound. Most of the upscale joints are in Northwest and the Pearl District, and even at the snootiest of them you can wear jeans and tennis shoes. Downtown is full of food carts (especially around SW 5th Ave at Stark St) offering a world tour of cheap lunches.

BUDGET

Veganopolis (☎ 503-226-3400; www.veganopolis. com; 412 SW 4th Ave; $4-6; ☯ 8am-6pm Mon-Sat) Only in Portland would you find a popular cafeteria-style restaurant dedicated to nothing but vegan cuisine. It's cheap and tasty, and there's free wi-fi!

La Casita (☎ 503-234-8894; 607 SE Morrison St; mains $1-5; ☯ 7am-4am) Open almost all night, this friendly taqueria buzzes with the postbar crowd in the small hours.

MIDRANGE

Navarre (☎ 503-232-3555; 10 NE 28th Ave; plates $2-20; ☯ 5pm-10pm) Combining a fun dining style with a jolly atmosphere and well-designed space, wild-haired chef John Taboada sends foodies into flavor heaven with small plates of inventive Italian-French-Spanish cuisine (try anything with beets in it).

Lovely Hula Hands (☎ 503-445-9910; www.lovely hulahands.com; 938 Cook St; starters $6-8, mains $8-17; ☯ 5-11pm Tue-Sun) This newcomer in a restored pink house with flowery wallpaper and a homey, Southern feel has won devotion from locals for its eclectic menu, weird cocktails (milk punch? Talulah's Bathwater?) and quirky attitude. Don't miss the Thai flatiron steak.

Jake's Famous Crawfish (☎ 503-226-1419; 401 SW 12th Ave; happy-hour snacks $2-4, mains $8-18; ☯ 11:30am-10pm Sun-Thu, until midnight Fri & Sat, happy hour 3-6pm Mon-Fri) The best reason to visit this old-school seafood and steak establishment, besides the classy interior, is the cheap happy-hour menu; arrive early to beat the suits to a table.

TOP END

Higgins (☎ 503-222-9070; 1239 SW Broadway; mains $12-30; ☯ lunch & dinner Mon-Fri, dinner 4pm-2:30am Sat, 4pm-midnight Sun) Chef Greg Higgins consistently wins restaurant-of-the-year honors for his innovative preparation of fresh, locally grown organic ingredients, especially mushrooms and seafood. The less expensive bar menu includes downtown's best burger.

Drinking

Portland is rightly famous for its microbrews and brewpubs, but there are also any number of places to sip in style.

BARS

In general, bars are open from around 5pm until 2am.

Alibi (☎ 503-287-5335; 4024 N Interstate Ave) Vehemently tiki-themed, this karaoke favorite has peppy servers and absurdly complicated tropical drinks. Show up before 9pm to avoid the karaoke, and shortly thereafter if you want a turn at the mike.

Hung Far Low (☎ 503-223-8686; 112 NW 4th Ave) Beyond the cruelly fluorescent-lit Chinese restaurant is a dark and cozy hideout, blessed by Buddha and a bartender who knows that quantity trumps quality. This is where your liver wants to go when it dies.

Dots (☎ 503-235-0203; 2521 SE Clinton St; ☯ 11am-2am) A Portland classic, Dots serves mountains of cheese fries to hipsters amid kitschy

---

THE AUTHOR'S CHOICE

Noble Rot (☎ 503-233-1999; 2724 SE Ankeny; ☯ dinner Mon-Sat) In his Southeast Portland neo-industrial wine bar, local media darling and Noble Rot chef Leather Storrs has established himself as a serious contender on the restaurant scene by backing up his flamboyant, in-your-face attitude with mad skills in the kitchen. The culinary wonders he produces – drool-worthy grilled panini, decadent macaroni and cheese, a savory caramelized onion tart and the fantastically named Apples Carl Sagan – allow him to get away with things like wearing an 'I heart foie gras' T-shirt on the front page of the daily newspaper at the height of the gourmet goose-liver debate. The restaurant also regularly offers 'flights' of wine, which are like miniature samplers paired with specific dishes for a set price. With Noble Rot, Storrs demonstrates not only that food and wine can be fun as well as serious, but also that a business can have as strong a personality as its owner.

art and velvet-brocade wallpaper in near-total darkness.

Nightlight Lounge (☎ 503-731-6500; 2100 SE Clinton St; ⏱ 3pm-2:30am) This artist-run neighborhood bar has copper-topped tables, a back room full of couches, great local art on the walls and a drinks menu that reads like a comic novel. No smoking until 8pm.

Colosso (☎ 503-288-3333; 1932 NE Broadway) Seduction incarnate, this velvet-and-concrete tapas bar pairs its amazing cocktails – try the signature 'Zirkpatrick' – with luscious food.

Towne Lounge (☎ 503-241-8696; www.townelounge.com; SW 20th Place & Morrison St) A 'secret' bar marked only by the bare green light bulb at its entrance (look for the Greek columns), this funereal, art-deco hideout encourages going incognito. Live music most nights.

Ground Kontrol (☎ 503-796-9364; www.groundkontrol.com; 511 NW Couch St; ⏱ noon-10pm Sun-Thu, noon-midnight Fri & Sat, bar from 7pm) A bar/arcade with vintage videogames and a stairway to pinball heaven, Ground Kontrol is a fun place to indulge your inner child.

Also recommended:

Aalto Lounge (☎ 503-235-6041; 3356 SE Belmont St; ⏱ closed Sun) A friendly wine bar with gorgeous bartenders, an outdoor patio and a clean-lined design that echoes the style of its namesake.

Horse Brass (☎ 503-232-2202; 4534 SE Belmont St; ⏱ 11am-2:30am Mon-Fri, 10am-2:30am Sat & Sun) An authentic English pub, the 'horse's ass' has great beer, darts, football matches and impenetrable clouds of smoke.

Ringlers Annex (☎ 503-525-0520; 1223 SW Stark St) A multitiered bar in a triangular building, with a candlelit crypt in the basement.

BREW PUBS

Hair of the Dog (☎ 503-232-6585; 4509 SE 23rd Ave) The best local microbrewery, Hair of the Dog doesn't have its own brewpub, but it gives tours by appointment.

BridgePort Brew Pub (☎ 503-241-7179; www.bridgeportbrew.com; 1313 NW Marshall St) Portland's oldest microbrewery is undergoing remodeling (set to reopen January 2006), which will leave the place brighter and the menu more upscale. The widely available beer is top-notch (try the great Black Strap Stout or the flagship Blue Heron).

Lucky Labrador Brewing Company (☎ 503-236-3555; 915 SE Hawthorne Blvd) Quintessentially Portland, this is a friendly brew hall in industrial Southeast with a cool patio out back that invites people to bring their dogs.

Amnesia Brewing Company (☎ 503-281-7708; 832 N Beech St; ⏱ 4-10pm; ✕) This industrial space off Mississippi complements its brews with free-range burgers grilled on the patio.

Alameda Brewpub (☎ 503-460-9025; 4765 NE Fremont; ⏱ 11am-11pm) Live music, creative dishes and at least a dozen beers on tap – plus its own – make this Northeast brewpub a favorite.

COFFEEHOUSES

Stumptown Coffee (☎ 503-230-7797; 3377 SE Division St; coffee & snacks $1-5) The locally owned Stumptown is generally acknowledged to make the best coffee in town.

Pied Cow (☎ 503-230-4866; 3244 SE Belmont St; coffee & snacks $3-9) This elegant historic mansion has loads of atmosphere, gourmet munchies and lovely outdoor garden seating.

Rimsky-Korsakoffee House (☎ 503-232-2640; 707 SE 12th Ave; coffee & snacks $3-5) Once you get past its unmarked facade (it looks like a private home), you'll find rotating tabletops and classical music blasting like it's thrash metal.

Entertainment

Check the *Mercury* or *Willamette Week* for listings and cover charges.

LIVE MUSIC

Dante's (☎ 503-226-6630; 1 SW 3rd Ave) National acts and vaudeville shows heat up this steamy red bar, with an intimate stage, toasty fire pit and frosty barmaids.

Berbati's Pan (☎ 503-248-4579; 10 SW 3rd Ave; ✕) Big and buzzing, this newly remodeled space books some of the more interesting music in town.

Doug Fir (☎ 503-248-4579; 10 SW 3rd Ave; ✕) The lounge attached to the new Jupiter Hotel looks like something designed by a sensitive lumberjack and books top touring and local bands. Packed on weekends.

Loveland (☎ 503-234-5683; 230 SE 2nd Ave) This gigantic, revamped industrial brick building is one of the few places to host all-ages rock shows.

Holocene (☎ 503-239-7639; 1001 SE Morrison St) This industrial-chic club in an unprepossessing warehouse has an Asian-themed bar and DJs or live music most nights.

Crystal Ballroom (☎ 503-778-5625; 1332 W Burnside St) Major bands play at this (usually all-ages) historic ballroom; the 'floating' dance floor bounces at the slightest provocation.

Jimmy Mak's (☎ 503-295-6542; 300 NW 10th Ave) This is the city's longstanding live jazz venue, serving excellent Greek food.

GAY & LESBIAN VENUES

Crush (☎ 503-235-8150; 1412 SE Morrison St) Some of the best cocktails in town are mixed at this semiswank but low-key, newly expanded bar. There's a 'vice room' for smokers.

Scandals (☎ 503-227-5887; 1038 SW Stark St) This large-windowed, energetic club is a lynchpin of Portland's gay nightlife, which centers on SW Stark St at 11th Ave downtown.

Egyptian Club (☎ 503-236-8689; 3701 SE Division St) Lesbians of all stripe gather at this Southeast Portland bar for dancing, pool and karaoke.

Also recommended:

Darcelle XV (☎ 503-222-5338; 208 NW 3rd Ave)
Portland's landmark drag club.

Dirty Duck (☎ 503-224-8446; 439 NW 3rd Ave)
Working-class bear den, with pool tables.

Hobo's (☎ 503-224-3285; 120 NW 3rd Ave) Stylish piano bar.

CINEMAS

Clinton Street Theater (☎ 503-238-8899; 2522 SE Clinton St; admission $4-6) The Clinton books the coolest and weirdest films in town, from Japanese horror to provocative documentaries, and has recently opened Portland's smallest brewery. Geeks and goths pack the place for ritual viewings of 'Rocky Horror' Saturdays at midnight.

Cinema 21 (☎ 503-223-4515; 616 NW 21st Ave; admission $4-6) This huge, well-established arthouse has helped nurture Portland's appreciation for independent cinema.

Hollywood (☎ 503-493-1128; 4122 NE Sandy Blvd; admission $4-6) Looking like something that fell off a cake, this ornate old theater shows a great selection of indie and arthouse films.

Also recommended:

Bagdad (☎ 503-232-6676; 3702 SE Hawthorne Blvd; admission $3) A faux-Moorish theater showing second-run films, with beer and pizza.

Laurelhurst Theater (☎ 503-232-5511; 2735 E Burnside St; admission $3) Locally owned and newly remodeled theater showing several second-run films a night, plus beer and pizza.

THEATER & PERFORMING ARTS

Chamber Music Northwest (☎ 503-223-3202; www .cmnw.org; tickets $19-40) Check out the summer series of chamber music concerts.

Imago Theater (☎ 503-231-9581; 17 SE 8th Ave; adult/child $25/15) This theater company is well-regarded for its innovative puppet theater, which appeals as much to adults as to children, including the long-running 'Frogz, Lizards, Orbs and Slinkys.'

Oregon Ballet Theatre (☎ 503-222-5538; www.obt .org) Portland's resident dance troupe performs classical and contemporary programs.

Portland Art Center (PAC; ☎ 503-239-5481; www .portlandart.org; 2045 SE Belmont St; ☾ noon-6pm Wed-Sat) A newly established space, PAC hosts performances and installations by several local artists and theater groups.

SPECTATOR SPORTS

Portland Timbers (☎ 503-553-5400; admission $10) This minor-league soccer team plays in PGE Park; head for Section 107, where beer and testosterone flow freely and local boys practice their British hooligan accents.

Portland Trail Blazers (☎ 503-231-8000) This pro basketball team plays at the Rose Garden Arena, but tickets sell out quickly.

Portland Winter Hawks (☎ 503-238-6366) Check out this pro hockey team, which also plays in the Rose Garden.

Shopping

The city's high-end mecca for shopping is Northwest, the neighborhood north of Burnside St bisected by NW 21st and 23rd Aves. The Pearl District is crammed with galleries and chic interior-design shops. Hawthorne Blvd is funkier, while Sellwood is full of antique stores. For locally made clothing, arts and crafts, head to NE Alberta St.

Just Be Toys (☎ 503-796-2733; 107 NW 5th Ave) Pick up some Asian-import comics, clothes, shoes, toys, games and obscure videos and DVDs at this fun shop – don't miss the art gallery upstairs.

Ozone 03 (☎ 503-227-1975; 701 E Burnside St) A great little record store in a booming neighborhood, this place carries new and used local and national albums as well as a good magazine selection.

Seaplane (☎ 503-234-2409; 827 NW 23rd Ave) Hipster fashion has recently taken off in Portland, and Seaplane, a collectively run shop featuring local designers, is leading the charge.

Clear Creek Distillery (☎ 503-248-9470; 1430 NW 23rd Ave) Take a tour of the distillery, then pick up a bottled gift or two to bring home – eau-de-vie and Oregon brandy are among the favorite souvenirs.

Frock (☎ 503-595-0379; 2940 NE Alberta) This Northeast Portland shop has vintage clothes for sale, as well as locally designed clothing and accessories.

3 Monkeys (☎ 503-222-9894; 803 NW 23rd Ave; ☽ 11am-6pm Mon-Tue, 11am-7pm Wed-Sat, noon-6pm Sun) Monkeys galore, plus weird kitschy household decor and other stuff you never knew you needed.

Getting There & Away
AIR
Portland International Airport (PDX; ☎ 877-739-4636; www.flypdx.com) has daily flights all over the country. **Lufthansa** (☎ 800-645-3880) offers direct flights to Frankfurt, Germany, with connections to other European cities.

BUS
Greyhound (☎ 503-243-2310; 550 NW 6th Ave) connects Portland with cities along I-5 and I-84. Regular service includes the following destinations: San Francisco (17 to 20 hours); Seattle (three to four hours); and Vancouver, BC (8 to 10 hours).

TRAIN
Amtrak (☎ 503-241-4290, 800-872-7245) serves Union Station, NW 6th Ave at Hoyt St. Trains run regularly to and from the following destinations: Seattle (four hours, four daily), Los Angeles (30 hours, one daily) and Chicago (two days, two daily, one nonstop). It's worth investigating Amtrak's *Coast Starlight* train, which leaves Portland daily for Seattle, Vancouver, San Francisco and LA.

Getting Around
TO/FROM THE AIRPORT
Tri-Met's MAX light-rail train runs between the airport lobby and downtown ($1.70, 45 minutes); in the reverse direction, catch it northbound along SW Yamhill St. Taxis from the airport cost about $30.

BICYCLE
Rent a bike at **Citybikes Annex** (☎ 503-239-6951; 734 SE Ankeny St; per day/week $20/75; ☽ 11am-7pm Mon-Fri, 11am-5pm Sat & Sun) or **Fat Tire Farm** (☎ 503-222-3276; 2714 NW Thurman St; per day $20-40; ☽ 11am-7pm Mon-Fri, 10am-5pm Sat & Sun). Both shops have maps of metro-area bike routes.

CAR & MOTORCYCLE
Major car-rental agencies have outlets at PDX airport and around town. Oregon law prohibits you from pumping your own gas. Most of downtown is metered parking; a free option is to park along an inner-Southeast street and walk across a bridge to the city center. If you use a SmartPark garage (95¢ per hour), remember to move your car after four hours (even if just around the block and back in), or your costs will double.

PUBLIC TRANSPORTATION
Local buses and the MAX light-rail system are run by Tri-Met, which has an **information bureau** (☎ 503-238-7433; www.trimet.org; ☽ 8:30am-5:30pm Mon-Fri) at Pioneer Courthouse Sq. A streetcar runs from Portland State University, south of downtown, through the Pearl District to NW 23rd Ave. Within the downtown core, public transportation is free; outside downtown, fares run from $1.40 to $1.70. Irritatingly, buses and light-rail both stop running at 1:30am, so make alternate plans to get home if you're staying out until closing time.

TAXI
Order cabs by phone (or ask a bartender to call you one); you can't hail them from the street.
Broadway Cab (☎ 503-227-1234)
Radio Cab (☎ 503-227-1212)

Around Portland
A short and scenic drive from Portland are some of the best wineries in the state, mostly scattered around the towns of Dundee and McMinnville along Hwy 99W. To get started, contact **Willamette Valley Wineries Association** (☎ 503-646-2985; www.willamettewines.com).

Meandering through plush green hills on winding country roads from one wine-tasting room to another is a delightful way to spend an afternoon (just make sure you designate a driver). More than 30 wineries are dotted along Hwys 99W and 18; blue signs point the way to each. If you only have time for a quick sampling, head for the **Oregon Wine Tasting Room** (☎ 503-843-3787; ☽ 11am-6pm), 9 miles south of McMinnville on Hwy 18, where you'll find many of the area's wineries represented. The **Grape Escape** (☎ 503-282-4262) specializes in wine-country tours departing from Portland.

Also nearby, infamous eccentric Howard Hughes' **Spruce Goose**, the world's largest wood-framed airplane, is housed in the **Evergreen Aviation Museum** (☎ 503-434-4180; www .sprucegoose.com; 3850 SW Three Mile Lane; adult/child $9.50/5.50; ☉ 9am-5pm).

Complement your tour through wine country with a spectacular meal at the **Joel Palmer House** (☎ 503-864-2995; www.joelpalmerhouse .com; 600 Ferry St, Dayton; starters $5-10, mains around $20; ☉ 5-9pm Tue-Sat), one of the most renowned restaurants in the area. It's famous for its rack of lamb and masterful treatment of wild mushrooms collected by hand from the surrounding woods.

SOUTHERN OREGON

The valleys of the Rogue and Umpqua Rivers and the Klamath Basin hold some of Oregon's most incredible sights, including Crater Lake. The city of Ashland hosts a renowned Shakespeare festival. Siskiyou Pass, on I-5 between Oregon and California, is known for treacherous winter driving; call ☎ 800-977-6368 for a road report.

Oregon Caves National Monument

In the Illinois River valley, the 'Oregon Caves' (there's actually only one) feature 3 miles of chambers with a fast-moving stream, the River Styx, running the length of the cave. The only way to see it is by taking one of the National Park Service's 90-minute **guided tours** (adult/child $8/5.50; ☉ hourly 10am-4pm Mar-Nov, 9am-5pm May-Aug). Dress very warmly and be prepared to get a little wet. In summer, guides have offered a four-hour 'off-trail' cave tour ($25); however, these might not continue if studies show they have a negative environmental impact on the caves. Call the **Illinois Valley Visitor Information Center** (☎ 541-592-4076; 201 Caves Hwy) in Cave Junction for updates.

From Grants Pass, take US 199 south 28 miles to Cave Junction, then travel 20 miles east on Hwy 46. The road to the caves is steep and narrow; ask about road conditions at the visitor center.

Ashland

If you like Stratford-upon-Avon, you'll love Ashland. It used to be all about the Bard in this quaint, Elizabethan-fronted Rogue River Valley town. But Ashland is rapidly becoming a haven for wine lovers and a popular spot for the vacation homes of baby boomers. It's an attractive, genteel place with pockets of old-school granola liberals.

INFORMATION

Southern Oregon Reservation Center (☎ 541-488-1011, 800-547-8052; www.sorc.com) Room reservations, tickets and recreation packages.
Visitor center (☎ 541-482-3486; www.ashlandchamber .com; 110 E Main St; ☉ 9am-5pm)

SIGHTS & ACTIVITIES

The **Oregon Shakespeare Festival** (OSF) puts on 11 plays a year from February to October. It made its reputation on Shakespearean and Elizabethan drama, but recently the emphasis has shifted to bolder, more contemporary plays, many of which the OSF commissions itself. There are three festival theaters: the 1200-seat outdoor Elizabethan Theatre, the Angus Bowmer Theatre and the intimate New Theatre. Reservations are encouraged, but it's sometimes possible to get last-minute tickets by waiting at the **box office** (☎ 541-482-4331; www.osfashland.com; 15 S Pioneer St; tickets $22-65) for unclaimed seats, released at 9:30am and 6pm daily (noon for matinees).

Downtown Ashland is a pleasant place to stroll and window-shop. Swans glide across the pond at **Lithia Park**, which serves as a venue for summer concerts and events; a trail along the creek leads to picnic spots.

The visitor center has a list of wineries open for tours and tastings. A handy place to start is the unpretentious **Ashland Vineyards & Winery** (☎ 541-488-0088; 2775 E Main St; ☉ 11am-5pm Tue-Sun Apr-Oct, call for hrs rest of year), just 2 miles from downtown (take I-5 exit 14).

SLEEPING

Ashland is loaded with quaint Victorian B&Bs, though they fill up fast in summer. Rates drop dramatically in the off season. The **Ashland B&B Clearinghouse** (☎ 541-488-0338, 800-588-0338; www.bbclearinghouse.com) can help locate a B&B. If you get stuck for accommodations, try Medford, just 12 miles north.

Ashland Hostel (☎ 541-482-9217; www.ashland hostel.com; 150 N Main St; dm/s $21/50) Mere blocks from downtown, this convivial hostel has a fireplace in the common room, a spacious kitchen, clean dorms and attractive family rooms with shared baths. The front porch looks out to a street lined with Victorian houses.

Columbia Hotel (☎ 541-482-3726, 800-718-2530; www.columbiahotel.com; 262½ E Main St; r $64-115) This small, European-style hotel is a block from the theaters.

Timbers Motel (☎ 541-482-4242; www.ashlandtim berslodging.com; 1450 Ashland St; r $75-105; ⌨) This friendly, functional, modern motel has family suites and some rooms with a refrigerator and microwave.

EATING & DRINKING

Ashland has a restaurant tax of 5%. The restaurants listed here are all open for lunch and dinner daily.

Siskiyou Brew Pub (☎ 541-482-7718; 31 Water St) This comfortable hangout, a local favorite, serves its own microbrews and upscale pub food on a comfy outdoor patio by the river. There's live music most nights.

Black Sheep (☎ 541-482-6414; 51 N Main St; mains $8-15) Stick to the Elizabethan theme at this atmosphere-drenched English pub, where you can get a proper pint of Guinness, check your email, play board games or curl up by the fire and watch the city through giant second-story windows. It's nonsmoking until 11pm and serves food until 1am nightly.

Thai Pepper (☎ 541-482-8058; 84 N Main St; mains $11-15) This creekside Asian restaurant is a favorite for giant portions of spicy cuisine.

Ashland Creek Bar & Grill (☎ 541-482-4131; 92½ N Main St) Ninety percent deck, this is an ideal spot for sipping a microbrew by the creek on a sunny afternoon or warm evening.

GETTING THERE & AROUND

Ashland is 350 miles north of San Francisco and 285 miles south of Portland along I-5.

Wild Rogue Wilderness Area

Just northwest of Ashland, the Wild Rogue Wilderness lives up to its name, with the turbulent Rogue River cutting through 40 miles of untamed, roadless canyon. The area is known for hardcore whitewater rafting (classes III and IV) and long-distance hikes.

Grants Pass is the gateway to adventure along the Rogue. The **visitor center** (☎ 541-476-7717; 1995 NW Vine St; ☼ 8am-5pm Mon-Fri, 9am-5pm Sat), near I-5 exit 58, and the **Siskiyou National Forest supervisor's office** (☎ 541-471-6500; 200 Greenfield Dr) has information on recreational activities. For raft permits and backpacking advice, head to the Bureau

of Land Management's **Rand Visitor Center** (☎ 541-479-3735; www.or.blm.gov/rogueriver; 14335 Galice Rd, Merlin; ☼ 7am-4pm); take the Merlin exit off I-5 and drive 14 miles west on Merlin-Galice Rd.

Rafting the Rogue is not for the faint of heart; a typical trip takes three days and costs upward of $500. Outfitters include **Rogue River Raft Trips** (☎ 541-476-3825, 800-826-1963; www.rogueriverraft.com), **Rogue Wilderness Inc** (☎ 541-479-9554, 800-336-1647; www.wildrogue.com) and **Sundance River Center** (☎ 541-479-8508, 888-777-7557; www.sundanceriver.com).

The 40-mile **Rogue River Trail** was once a supply route from Gold Beach. The full hike takes about five days; day hikers might aim for Whiskey Creek Cabin, a 7-mile round-trip from the Grave Creek trailhead. The trail is dotted with rustic lodges; advance reservations are required. Lodging averages $75 per person, usually including dinner and a packed lunch. Try **Black Bar Lodge** (☎ 541-479-6507) or **Marial Lodge** (☎ 541-474-2057). There are also primitive campgrounds along the way.

Greyhound and Amtrak Thruway buses run daily to Portland and elsewhere from the **station** (☎ 541-476-4513; 460 NE Agness Ave).

Crater Lake National Park

Eerily symmetrical and uncannily blue, **Crater Lake National Park** offers unbelievable vistas, hiking and cross-country skiing trails, a boat ride to a rugged island and scenic drives around the lip of the crater. The park can be reached from Medford (72 miles) or Klamath Falls (73 miles) on Hwy 62. The popular south entrance is open year-round, although it can be rough going in winter; chains are advised.

Most facilities are closed from October to late May, but people still come for cross-country skiing. In summer, a $10 vehicle fee is charged to enter the park. For information, contact **park headquarters** (☎ 541-594-2211; PO Box 7, Crater Lake, OR 97604).

Most travelers do a day trip from Medford, Roseburg or Klamath Falls. In the park choose between **Mazama Village Motor Inn** (south entrance off Hwy 62; s/d $103; ☼ Jun-Oct) and, perched on the lake's rim, the majestic old **Crater Lake Lodge** (r from $123; ☼ late May-Oct). For reservations at either place, or to find out about cruises, call ☎ 541-830-8700 or visit www.crater-lake.com. If park lodging is booked up, try lodges and United States Forest Service (USFS) campgrounds around Union Creek and Prospect, west on Hwy 62. **Mazama Village Campground** (☎ 541-830-8700; campsites/RV sites $14.75/15.75), near the park's south entrance, has 200 first-come, first-served sites.

Steens Mountain

Steens Mountain, the highest peak in southeastern Oregon (9670ft), is part of a massive, 30-mile fault-block range. On the west slope of the range, Ice-Age glaciers bulldozed massive U-shaped valleys into the flanks of the mountain. To the east, delicate alpine meadows and lakes flank 'the Steens,' dropping off dizzyingly into the Alvord Desert 5000ft below.

Beginning in Frenchglen, the 66-mile gravel **Steens Mountain Loop Road** offers access to Steens Mountain Recreation Area; it's open from late June to November, depending on the weather; call the **Bureau of Land Management** (☎ 541-573-4557, 541-573-4400; ☉ 7:45am- 4:30pm Mon-Fri) for information.

Tiny **Fish Lake campground** (☎ 541-573-4400; campsites $10) is 20 miles from **Frenchglen**; 2 miles further is the 36-site **Jackman Park** (campsites $8). The old-fashioned **Frenchglen Hotel** (☎ 541-493-2825; s/d with shared bath $65; ☉ Apr-Nov) has small, austere rooms and friendly service – it's popular with bird-watchers.

WILLAMETTE VALLEY

Pioneers along the Oregon Trail were aiming for this, the incredibly fertile Willamette Valley between what are now Portland and Eugene. Salem, the state capital, is about an hour's drive from Portland in the northern valley, and most of the other attractions in the area make easy day trips as well. Toward the south, the small college towns of Corvallis and Eugene are both dynamic and engaging.

Eugene

Eugene is paradoxically the birthplace of Nike – Oregon's most obvious corporate success story and consequently a lightning rod for debates on fair-labor practices – and a stronghold of radical left-wing activism. Its annual Earth Day festivities are the most enthusiastic in the region, and the high proportion of students means there's a constant supply of fresh blood to infuse the old hip-

pies with new energy. Beyond the political implications, though, the student population gives Eugene a carefree and youthful energy that makes it an enjoyable stopover.

INFORMATION

Check the *Eugene Weekly*, free in cafés and boxes across town, for event listings.

Lane County Convention & Visitors Association (☎ 541-484-5307, 800-547-5445; www.cvalco.org; Ste 190, 115 W 8th Ave; ☉ 8am-5pm Mon-Fri)

Sip & Surf Cybercafé (☎ 541-343-9607; Olive St & 10th Ave; per hr $6; ☉ 7:30am-6pm Mon-Fri, noon-5pm Sat) Fifteen minutes of computer time free with a $1 purchase.

SIGHTS & ACTIVITIES

At E 5th Ave between Pearl and High Sts, **Fifth Street Public Market** is the heart of a small but lively shopping and café district. The famous **waffle iron** used to make the first Nike soles is displayed at the **Nike Factory Store** (☎ 541-342-5155; 296 E 5th Ave; ☉ 10am-6pm).

Housed in a replica of a Native American longhouse, the University of Oregon's **Museum of Natural History** (☎ 541-346-3024; 1680 E 15th Ave; admission $2; ☉ noon-5pm Wed-Sun) has an impressive display of Native American artifacts, including the country's oldest pair of shoes and an interesting analysis of early architecture.

Festivals & Events

The **Oregon Country Fair** (☎ 541-343-4298), in July, is a riotous three-day celebration of Eugene's folksy, hippie past and present. It's held on a farm 13 miles west of Eugene on Hwy 126, near Veneta.

SLEEPING

Eugene International Hostel (☎ 541-349-0589; 2352 Willamette St; dm/r $19/36; ☉ closed 11am-5pm) More friendly than tidy, this laid-back hostel is just outside of downtown in a quiet residential neighborhood; take buses 24 or 25. The kitchen is vegetarian-only.

Downtown Motel (☎ 541-345-8739, 800-648-4366; 361 W 7th Ave; s/d from $35/45) A great bargain, the Downtown is much nicer than you might think at first glance, with spacious rooms, helpful staff who can recommend restaurants, and a good location.

Courtesy Inn (☎ 541-345-3391; 345 W 6th Ave; r from $59) The friendly managers and great location make this basic motel a good choice; rooms have a refrigerator and microwave.

EATING & DRINKING

Fifth Street Market has a great bakery and a number of small restaurants, and there's a string of small, cheap cafés along 13th Ave by the university.

Ring of Fire (☎ 541-344-6475; 1099 Chambers St; appetizers $8.50, mains $11-16; ☻ lunch & dinner) Guard your tongue at this Thai place, or order one of the fancy cocktails to counteract the heat on your heaped plate of pineapple seafood red curry; the stylish lounge serves food until 1am on weekends.

Cafe Zenon (☎ 541-343-3005; 898 Pearl St; lunch $7-10, dinner $8-15; ☻ 8am-11pm Sun-Thu, 8am-midnight Fri & Sat) Zenon's sophisticated Mediterranean cuisine made with fresh Northwest ingredients keeps it packed, especially for late night dinner.

Two of Eugene's best bets for live music also have great food: **Sam Bond's Garage** (☎ 541-431-6603; 407 Blair Blvd; mains $6-8; ☻ lunch & dinner) serves great vegetarian fare, and **Cafe Paradiso** (☎ 541-484-9933; 115 W Broadway; sandwiches $3.75-6; ☻ breakfast, lunch & dinner), home to Eugene's longest-running open-mike night (8pm Tuesday), has good coffee, sandwiches and pasta.

GETTING THERE & AROUND

Amtrak (☎ 541-687-1383; E 4th Ave & Willamette St)
Bus station (☎ 541-344-6265; 987 Pearl St)

McKenzie River Valley

One of the most stunning natural areas in the state, the McKenzie River Valley is also one of the easiest to visit. The town of McKenzie Bridge, a cluster of campgrounds and cabins 50 miles east of Eugene on Hwy 126, is the gateway. Great fishing, easy hikes and fun rafting trips are highlights; for details, contact the **visitor center** (☎ 541-896-3330; 44643 Hwy 126) in Leaburg.

In summer, take the hair-raising **Old McKenzie Highway** (Hwy 242) over the 5325ft, lava-laden mountain pass to the **Dee Wright Observatory** for spectacular views of volcanoes in the adjoining Three Sisters Wilderness. The scenic, 26-mile **McKenzie National Recreation Trail** follows the river north from McKenzie Bridge to Fish Lake and is dotted with campgrounds. The old highway and pass are closed November to June, but you can access the trail year-round from Hwy 126.

From Eugene, take bus No 91 ($1) to reach the trailhead across from the **McKenzie River**

Ranger Station (☎ 541-822-3381; 57600 Hwy 126). The aptly named but often crowded **Paradise Campground** (☎ 877-444-6777; campsites $14; ☻ open May-Oct), 4 miles east of McKenzie Bridge on Hwy 126, has campsites in a mossy old-growth forest alongside the river.

Corvallis

Small and quiet, Corvallis makes a convenient base for exploring the Willamette Valley. Oregon State University anchors the west side of town. The tree-lined downtown district along the Willamette River has cafés, bookstores, bars and nice restaurants. There's a newly established riverside walkway lined with park benches and fountains. For maps, stop by the **visitor center** (☎ 541-757-1544; 420 NW 2nd St; ☻ 9am-5pm Mon-Fri).

The area around Corvallis has some excellent mountain-biking trails; ask at the visitor center for information, or stop by **Peak Sports** (☎ 541-754-6444; 135 NW 2nd St; ☻ 9am-6pm Mon-Thu, 9am-8pm Fri, 9am-6pm Sat, noon-5pm Sun) for maps and trail guides.

Several inexpensive chain motels line SW 4th and 2nd Sts downtown. **Towne House Motor Inn** (☎ 541-753-4496; 350 SW 4th St; r $35-75; Ⓟ) is close to everything and has laundry facilities and a funky lounge.

The upscale, quasi-rustic waterfront **Big River Restaurant** (☎ 541-757-0694; 101 NW Jackson St; mains $16-22; ☻ lunch & dinner) has an eclectic menu that changes nightly. Get amped up at the **Sunnyside Up Cafe** (☎ 541-758-3353; 116 NW 3rd St; drinks $1-3, breakfast $2-6; ☻ 6am-7pm), a cheery yellow-walled coffeehouse. At **Natalia & Cristoforo's Italian Deli** (☎ 541-752-1114; 351 NW Jackson St 2; sandwiches $6-8; ☻ 10am-6pm Mon-Sat), the energetic owners prepare takeout hoagies and muffuletta sandwiches ideal for a picnic or bike ride.

Avalon Cinema (☎ 541-752-4161; 2nd & Jackson Sts; admission $5-7) shows independent films in a small vintage theater.

Salem

Salem's main draws are the capitol building and Willamette University. It's also the most convenient base for exploring Silver Falls State Park and the Oregon Garden. Find information at the **visitor center** (☎ 503-581-4325; 1313 Mill St SE).

The highlight of a trip to the capital is Willamette University's **Hallie Ford Museum of Art** (☎ 503-370-6300; 900 State St; admission $3;

10am-5pm Tue-Sat), which has, hands down, the state's best collection of regional art in the Carl Hall Gallery (named for the artist and Willamette professor whose work has fueled the museum's growth). The museum also hosts traveling exhibits and maintains a print archive.

The 1938 **Oregon State Capitol** (☎ 503-986-1388; 900 Court St NE; admission free; tours 9am-3pm on the hr in summer) looks like a sci-fi film director's vision of an Orwellian White House. Rambling 19th-century **Bush House** (☎ 503-363-4714; 600 Mission St SE; adult/child $4/2; ☯ noon-5pm Tue-Sun) is an Italianate mansion now preserved as a museum within a nice public garden.

Silver Falls State Park (☎ 503-873-8681; car $3 per day) is 26 miles east of Salem on Hwy 214 (via Hwy 22). The South Falls, a 177ft waterfall you can hike behind, provides instant gratification just a few feet from the main parking lot. You can also hike a 7-mile loop and see all 10 falls on the site, or ride the 4-mile paved bike path. Camping and swimming are available. Horseback riding can be organized through the **Adaptive Riding Institute** (☎ 503-873-3890; www.open.org/horses88/; ☯ May-Sep), which offers riding for people with disabilities.

Fifteen miles northeast of Salem on Hwy 213 (Silverton Rd) is the **Oregon Garden** (☎ 503-874-8100; www.oregongarden.org; 879 W Main St; adult/child $8/6; ☯ 9am-6pm in summer, 9am-3pm winter). The garden, prettiest in late May, nurtures vast numbers of rare and native plant species, and its wetlands act as a natural water-filtration system that recycles the city of Silverton's waste water. It's also home to Oregon's only building designed by architect Frank Lloyd Wright; the **Gordon House** (tours $2) was set to be demolished by a wealthy but oblivious Portland-area homeowner when the Wright Conservancy intervened and moved it to its current site.

CENTRAL & EASTERN OREGON

Volcanic eruptions and persistent erosion have turned central and eastern Oregon into an eerie moonscape, from the pastel ribbons of rock at the John Day Fossil Beds to the dramatic gouging of Hells Canyon and the gentle hills around Warm Springs.

Bend & Mount Bachelor

An active, outdoorsy city in the midst of a rapid growth spurt, Bend has tons of outdoor fun right in its backyard. Don't let the Hwy 97 strip fool you – just off the main thoroughfare, the walkable downtown is lined with cool restaurants, shops and bars. The **visitor center** (☎ 541-389-8799; 63085 N US 97; ☯ 8am-5pm Mon-Fri) is in a huge building at the north end of town.

Perhaps the best museum in the state, Bend's **High Desert Museum** (☎ 541-382-4754; www.highdesertmuseum.org; 59800 S Hwy 97; adult/child $12/7; ☯ 9am-5pm; **P**) has impeccable exhibits on early cultural life and the fascinating natural history of the High Desert, including live animals in their typical habitats. Get an up-close glimpse of the famous spotted owl at the raptor center. Tickets are good for two days.

Lava Lands Visitor Center (☎ 541-593-2421; admission free; ☯ 9am-5pm May-Sep), on US 97 about 11 miles south of Bend, has exhibits revealing the geology, wildlife and archeology of the **Newberry National Volcanic Monument**. Nearby is Lava Butte, rising 500ft above the surrounding lava flows.

Twenty-two miles southwest of Bend, 9065ft **Mt Bachelor** (☎ 541-382-2442, 800-829-2442; www.mtbachelor.com; adult/child from $50/30; ☯ 9am-4pm Mon-Fri, 8am-4pm Sat & Sun) has Oregon's best skiing, with 3100ft of vertical and more than 300 inches of snow per year; it's known for fine dry powder. The season begins in November and can last until June.

Central Oregon Reservation Center (☎ 541-382-8334; ☯ 8am-5pm Mon-Fri) can help with accommodations. There's a motel strip along US 97 (here called 3rd St), where both **Sonoma Lodge** (☎ 541-382-4891; 450 SE 3rd St; d from $35) and the similarly priced **Chalet Motel** (☎ 541-382-6124; 510 SE 3rd St) are clean and friendly; doubles have in-room microwaves and refrigerators.

For good food, try Wall or Bond Sts downtown. Squeeze into the **Deschutes Brewery & Public House** (☎ 541-382-9242; 1044 NW Bond St; sandwiches $8) for a pint and an upscale pub meal – if it's crowded, which it usually is, grab a pint of the brewery's signature Mirror Pond ale and wait at the bar.

Warm Springs Indian Reservation

Home to three groups, the Wasco, the Tenino and the Northern Paiute (the Confederated Tribes), Warm Springs Reservation stretches east and west from the banks of the **Deschutes River** to the peaks of the Cascades. Contact the **Confederated Tribes of the Warm Springs Reservation** (☎ 541-553-1161; www.warmsprings.com) if you want to learn more about the reservation's residents and events. For information on **rafting** the Deschutes, stop at the north end of the eye-blink-long town of Maupin, at the **chamber of commerce** (☎ 541-395-2599; www .maupinoregon.com; PO Box 220, Maupin, OR 97037).

The **Warm Springs Museum** (☎ 541-553-3331; adult/child $6/3; ☯ 10am-5pm), on Hwy 26 just west of Warm Springs, evokes traditional Native American life and culture with artifacts, audiovisuals and re-created villages. The **Kah-Nee-Ta Resort** (☎ 541-553-1112; r from $145), 11 miles north of Warm Springs on Simnasho Rd, has a giant hot-springs-fed **swimming pool** (day passes adult/child $10/5; Ⓟ), parking $5, as well as a casino, spa, restaurant and lodgings in hotel rooms or teepees.

John Day Fossil Beds National Monument

You can't help feeling a bit like an alien visitor in the otherworldly landscape surrounding the John Day Fossil Beds. Within this vast, beautifully desolate section of the state, the monument encompasses 22 sq miles with three entry points. Services are few and far between, so fill your gas tank and have plenty of water on hand.

Only the Sheep Rock Unit has a staffed **visitor center** (☎ 541-987-2333; ☯ 9am-6pm, closed Sat & Sun in winter), 10 miles northwest of Dayville on Hwy 19, with maps, pamphlets and displays of fossils found in the area. Be sure to take the short hike up the **Blue Basin trail**, which will make you feel like you've just landed on the sunny side of the moon. The Painted Hills Unit, near the town of Mitchell, consists of low-slung, colorfully banded hills formed about 30 million years ago. The Clarno Unit exposes mud flows that washed over an Eocene-era forest and eroded into distinctive, sheer-white cliffs topped with spires and turrets of stone.

Two nice campgrounds, **Lone Pine** (☎ 541-416-6700; campsites $8) and **Big Bend** (☎ 541-416-6700), are on the North Fork John Day River near the Sheep Rock Unit. **Service Creek Stage Stop B&B** (☎ 541-468-3331; www.servicecreek stagestop.com; 38686 Hwy 19; s/d from $40/60) has a general store, a friendly greasy-spoon and raft rentals in case you want to float the placid John Day.

Hells Canyon & the Wallowa Mountains

The Wallowa Mountains are among the most beautiful natural areas in Oregon, with their glacier-hewn peaks and crystalline lakes; the only drawback is the huge number of visitors who flock here in summer. Escape the hordes on one of several remote, overnight hikes into the **Eagle Cap Wilderness Area**, accessible from Wallowa Lake. Just north of the mountains, in the Wallowa Valley, Enterprise and Joseph are two small towns off Hwy 82 with lodging and food. Joseph is a miniature arts-and-crafts mecca known for its bronze galleries.

Wilder adventures and an even more dramatic landscape are found at **Hells Canyon**, where the Snake River has been carving out an 8000ft-deep trench for about 13 million years. The white-water action starts just below Hells Canyon Dam, 28 miles north (downriver) from the small campground community of Copperfield, a nexus of activity on the river. **Hells Canyon Adventures** (☎ 541-785-3352, 800-422-3568; www.hellscanyon adventures.com; 4200 Hells Canyon Dam Rd), in Oxbow, runs daylong **raft trips** ($150 per person) as well as less expensive, but noisy, **jet-boat tours** (adult/child $30/10). For perspective, drive up to the spectacular lookout at **Hat Point** (USFS Rd 4240), 23 miles from Imnaha, with views of the Wallowa Mountains, Idaho's Seven Devils, the Imnaha River and the wilds of Hells Canyon. The road is open from late May until snowfall; allow two hours and call ☎ 541-426-5546 first for conditions.

The **Wallowa Mountains Visitor Center** (☎ 541-426-5546; 88401 Hwy 82; ☯ 8am-5pm Mon-Sat, noon-5pm Sun in summer), in Enterprise, has information on both areas and is a good source for trail maps and backcountry hiking tips.

Copperfield Park Campground (☎ 541-785-3323; www.idahopower.com/riversreccopperfield.htm; Hwy 86; campsites/RV sites $8/12), just below Oxbow Dam at the beginning of Hells Canyon, has 62 riverside campsites. Or stay in Joseph at the popular **Indian Lodge Motel** (☎ 541-432-2651, 888-286-5484; 201 S Main; s/d from $40/50).

MOUNT HOOD

Visible from much of northern Oregon on a sunny day, the state's highest peak is 11,240ft Mt Hood. It can be reached year-round (barring temporary road closures due to snow) via US 26 from Portland and via Hwy 35 from Hood River. Together with the Columbia River Hwy, these routes constitute the **Mount Hood Loop**, one of the finest scenic-road excursions in the USA. The weather changes quickly; call ☎ 800-977-6368 to check road conditions, and carry chains in winter even if it's sunny when you set out.

Barely-there **Government Camp**, 56 miles from Portland and 44 miles from Hood River at the pass, has some food and lodging. The **Mount Hood Information Center** (☎ 503-622-4822, 888-622-4822; 65000 E Hwy 26; ☷ 8am-6pm in summer, 8am-4:30pm in winter) is in Welches next to Mt Hood Village.

A masterpiece of the Works Progress Administration era, the 1930s **Timberline Lodge** was built and decorated in grand rustic style as a hotel, ski resort and restaurant. It's 5 miles north of US 26 from Government Camp. The horror movie *The Shining* used some exterior shots of the hotel and surroundings. The **ski area** (☎ 503-622-0717) is open almost year-round most years. **Mount Hood Meadows** (☎ 503-337-2222; lift tickets adult/child $50/30), 76 miles from Portland, is the largest ski area on Mt Hood and often has the best conditions. **SkiBowl** (☎ 503-272-3206; lift tickets adult/child $35/25), off US 26 just west of Government Camp, has night skiing.

Hikers should get the free USFS pamphlet *Day Hikes Around Mt Hood*. After Japan's Mt Fuji, Mt Hood is the world's most-climbed peak over 10,000ft, with a typical route from Timberline Lodge taking about 10 to 12 hours round-trip (for experienced climbers). **Timberline Mountain Guides** (☎ 541-312-9242; www .timberlinemtguides.com; 2 days from $385) is a well-established guide service and climbing school. Climbing is best from May to mid-July.

Huckleberry Inn (☎ 503-272-3325; 88611 E Government Camp Loop; r from $65) has standard rooms and an adjoining greasy-spoon diner. For rustic decadence, treat yourself to a room at the **Timberline Lodge** (☎ 503-231-5400; 800-547-1406; www.timberlinelodge.com; dm $80, r from $120). There's feverish competition for campsites around Mt Hood; try **Still Creek** (☎ 503-622-7674; campsites $14), 1 mile east of Government Camp on Hwy 26, or the postcard-perfect **Trillium Lake** (☎ 503-622-4822; campsites $14); turn right 1 mile east of Government Camp on Hwy 26, drive 2 miles south to the entrance. **Mount Hood RV Village** (☎ 503-622-4011; www.mthood village.com; 65000 E Hwy 26; RV sites from $35) is a huge resort complex near Brightwood.

COLUMBIA RIVER GORGE
The enormous canyon of the Columbia River, which divides Washington and Or-

egon, is one of the Pacific Northwest's most dramatic and scenic destinations. On the Oregon side, river-level I-84 is the quickest route that provides access to the most popular sites. A slower but more scenic route is the historic Columbia River Hwy (US 30), from Troutdale to Warrendale. Washington's Hwy 14, though again slower going than I-84, offers spectacular vistas. Campers will find state parks on both sides of the river, although campsite places are scarce on summer weekends and traffic noise can be bothersome.

Historic Columbia River Highway
The first paved road in the Northwest and America's first scenic highway, this lushly forested, winding highway between Troutdale, just east of Portland, and Hood River opened in 1915. To reach it, take exit 17 or 35 off I-84. Famous as the western entry to the gorge, the **Vista House at Crown Point** (☎ 503-695-2230; admission free; ☷ 9am-6pm) interpretive center sits atop a craggy cliff of basalt.

Bike, walk or jog along two stretches of the old highway that have been renovated for nonautomotive use. The western section of the trail runs between Tanner Creek (at the Bonneville Dam exit from I-84) and Eagle Creek; another, longer stretch runs 4.5 miles from Hood River to Mosier (the parking lots in this section require a $3 day-use fee).

Waterfalls and hiking trails line the Oregon side of the gorge. Stop at **Multnomah Falls** to ogle the 642ft, two-tiered falls and hike to the top (about one hour). The **Forest Service visitor center** (☎ 503-695-2372; ☷ 9am-5pm) next door to the gift shop is a good place to get information on other gorge hikes.

Hood River & Around
The town of Hood River, 63 miles east of Portland on I-84, is a slender wedge of bike and ski shops, cafés and a few hotels. The Columbia River here is famous as a windsurfing hot spot, and there's great mountain biking south of town off Hwy 35 and Forest Rd 44. The **visitor center** (☎ 541-386-2000; 405 Portway Ave; ☷ 9am-5pm Mon-Fri) is across I-84 from the city center.

The **Bingen School Inn** (☎ 509-493-3363; cnr Cedar & Humbolt Sts; dm/r from $15/45, linens extra), across the Columbia in Bingen, Washington, has lodging in an old schoolhouse. The **Vagabond Lodge** (☎ 541-386-2992; www.vagabondlodge

.com; 4070 Westcliffe Dr; r from $50) has river-view motel rooms. **Viento State Park** (☎ 541-374-8811; campsites/RV sites $14/16), 8 miles west of Hood River, is popular with windsurfers.

Tillicum Cafe (Oak St & 2nd Ave; breakfasts $6-9; 🕙 11am-close Mon-Fri, 8am-close Sat & Sun) warns that it is 'not responsible for bypass surgery' resulting, presumably, from its massive Gold Old Boy breakfast special and similar hearty fare. Nearby, the **Full Sail Brewery** (☎ 541-386-2247; 506 Columbia St; burgers $5-6; 🕙 noon-8pm, tours hourly 1-4pm) has a cozy tasting room bar with a small pub menu. Free 20-minute brewery tours end up here.

OREGON COAST

Oregon's most famous beach resorts are between the Columbia River and Newport. Much of the southern coast, from Florence to the California border, approaches pristine wilderness. Oregon's beaches are open to the public, even in developed areas, and the coastline is dotted with state parks.

Brookings & Gold Beach

Some 6 miles north of the California line on US 101 is the balmy harbor town of Brookings. There's not much to it beyond the **visitor center** (☎ 541-469-3181, 800-535-9469; www.brookingsor.com; 16330 Lower Harbor Rd; 🕙 9am-5pm Mon-Fri), but it's minutes from rugged coastline and redwood forest.

Roads along the Chetco River lead inland from Brookings to the western edge of remote **Kalmiopsis Wilderness Area**, the state's largest. Oregon's only redwood forests, as well as old-growth myrtle, are found here, notably in **Alfred A Loeb State Park** (☎ 541-469-2021, 800-551-6949; campsites/cabins $16/35), 10 miles east of Brookings on N Bank Chetco Rd. North of town is **Samuel H Boardman State Park**, with 11 miles of Oregon's most beautiful coastline.

Zip up the Rogue River to the Wild Rogue Wilderness Area in a jet boat from Gold Beach, 27 miles north of Brookings. **Jerry's Rogue Jets** (☎ 541-247-4571, 800-451-3645; www.roguejets.com) offers scenic trips (from $35) and whitewater adventures ($35 to $80). For about the same price you can ride to the town of Agness on a **mail boat** (☎ 541-247-7033, 800-458-3511; www.mailboat.com). The visitor center is at the **Gold Beach Ranger Station** (☎ 541-247-7526, 800-525-2334; www.goldbeach.org; 29279 S Ellensburg Ave; 🕙 9am-5pm Mon-Fri).

Gold Beach Resort (☎ 541-247-7066, 800-541-0947; 29232 Ellensburg, Hwy 101; r from $110; P 🔊) has 39 deluxe beachfront rooms, all with ocean views, in-room refrigerator and microwave. There are also campgrounds upriver.

Bandon

A good base for golf, Bandon has a nice setting and a well-preserved old town full of cafés, gift shops and taverns. The **visitor center** (☎ 541-347-9616; www.bandon.com; 🕙 9am-5pm) is at 300 2nd St and can provide details about local golf courses and other activities. Beach Loop Dr leads south of town to Bandon's best beaches, with towering sea stacks (coastal rock pillars that have resisted the surrounding erosion) and monoliths that host large numbers of seabirds. **Coquille Point**, at the end of 11th St, is a popular place to spot migrating whales in winter and spring.

The **HI Sea Star Hostel** (☎ 541-347-9632; 375 2nd St; dm $18, r from $40), in Old Town, has an adjoining café with heavenly coffee and a great breakfast. **Table Rock Motel** (☎ 541-347-2700, 800-457-9141; www.tablerockmotel.com; 840 Beach Loop Rd; r from $45, with view from $75), on a shrubby bluff, has rooms and apartment-style quarters with kitchenettes.

Harp's (☎ 541-347-9057; 130 Chicago Ave; seafood $14-17; 🕙 closed Sun & Mon) is recommended for bay-view dining.

Oregon Dunes National Recreation Area

Fifty miles of shifting sand between Florence and Coos Bay form the largest expanse of coastal dunes in the USA. Hiking trails, bridle paths, and boating and swimming areas have been established, and the entire region has abundant wildlife, especially birds. Unfortunately, dune buggies and dirt bikes scream up and down the dunes, especially the stretch south of Reedsport (see the boxed text, p1078). Reedsport is also home to the coast's biggest skate park, at 20th St along US 101.

Oregon Dunes National Recreation Area Headquarters (☎ 541-271-3611; 855 Highway Ave; 🕙 8am-4:30pm Mon-Fri) is based in logged-out Reedsport. This town hosts chainsaw-carving championships in June.

The popular **Jessie M Honeyman State Park** (☎ 541-997-3641, 800-452-5687; campsites/RV sites $18/25), 3 miles south of Florence on US 101, is handy for recreation in the dunes.

Umpqua Lighthouse State Park (☎ 503-271-4118, 800-452-5687; campsites/cabins/yurts $12/35/45) has deluxe yurts with TV/VCR and refrigerators a mile south of Winchester Bay. USFS campgrounds like **Eel Creek** (☎ 541-759-4462, 800-452-5687; campsites $15), 10 miles south of Reedsport, offer the best dune access.

Yachats

Volcanic intrusions south of Yachats form some of Oregon's most beautiful shoreline. Surf explodes against the shore to create dramatic features like the Devil's Churn and the Spouting Horn at **Cape Perpetua**, where visitors can prowl among intertidal rocks and sandy inlets or hike or drive up to a fantastic viewpoint. Ten miles south of Yachats the **Heceta Head Lighthouse**, built in 1894, perches above the churning ocean; a trail leads there from enchanting Devil's Elbow State Park. Taking the elevator down to the **Sea Lion Caves** (☎ 541-547-3111; www.sealion caves.com; 91560 Hwy 101; adult/child $7/4.50), filled with glossy, wriggling Steller's sea lions, is a highlight of the central Oregon coast.

Try camping at **Cape Perpetua Campground** (☎ 541-547-3289, 800-452-5687; campsites $12). Six miles south of Yachats is the **See Vue Motel** (☎ 541-547-3227; www.seevue.com; 95590 Hwy 101; r from $75), an old charmer with ocean-view rooms. There's good food and a friendly atmosphere at the **Drift Inn** (☎ 541-547-4477; mains $8-10), a wood-lined watering hole along Hwy 101.

Newport

It's hard not to like Newport. The scruffy little port town has lively, old-fashioned seafood markets facing Yaquina Bay, some excellent marine-life museums and the pic-

---

turesque and historic Nye Beach, which has just emerged sparkling after a three-year, $2 million makeover. Grab a map at the **visitor center** (☎ 541-265-8801, 800-262-7844; 555 SW Coast Hwy; ☉ 8:30am-5pm Mon-Fri, 10am-4pm Sat during May).

The **Oregon Coast Aquarium** (☎ 541-867-3474; 2820 SE Ferry Slip Rd; adult/child $10.75/6.50; ☉ 10am-5pm in winter, 9am-6pm in summer) has arresting marine exhibits such as an enormous Plexiglas tunnel through a shark tank and a fascinating pair of seahorses that look like the offspring of a dragon and a houseplant. Also interesting is the nearby **Hatfield Marine Science Center** (☎ 541-867-0271; 2030 S Marine Science Dr; suggested donation $2; ☉ 10am-5pm in summer, 10am-4pm Thu-Mon in winter), with a touch pool and exhibits.

The **Sylvia Beach Hotel** (☎ 541-265-5428; www .sylviabeachhotel.com; 267 NW Cliff St; dm $30, r from $85), named for the proprietor of Paris' Shakespeare and Co bookstore, has rooms decorated after famous writers; the Edgar Allan Poe is inspired, with a raven in the corner and a pendulum swinging over the bed. Next door, the **Nye Beach Hotel** (☎ 541-265-3334; www.nyebeach.com; 219 NW Cliff St; r from $75) is a faux-historic inn built in 1992; it has ocean-view rooms and a good café. For camping, **South Beach State Park** (☎ 541-867-4715, 800-452-5687; campsites $21), 2 miles south of Newport on US 101, is right on the beach.

The **Rogue Ales Brewery** (☎ 541-265-3188; 748 SW Bay Blvd; pub fare $8-10) brews two of the best beers on the whole planet, the award-winning Shakespeare Stout and the decadent Chocolate Stout, as well as some mean fish-and-chips. If you can't bear to leave, you're in luck: there are a few **guest rooms** (s/d $80/120) over the pub. For seafood, drop anchor at the over-the-top nautically themed **Whale's Tale** (452 SW Bay Blvd; seafood $8-18).

Cannon Beach

Miles of sandy beaches, broken by immense basalt promontories and rocky tide pools, stretch north and south of Cannon Beach, 9 miles south of Seaside. For information try the **visitor center** (☎ 503-436-2623; 2nd St; ☉ 10am-5pm Mon-Sat, 11am-4pm Sun). The town itself is attractive but touristy, especially along Hemlock St; all those souvenir shops will be hard-pressed to coax you off the beautiful beach.

Park free at Tolovana Beach (take the third Cannon Beach exit off Hwy 101) for access to the deservedly much-photographed **Haystack**

DUNE BUGGY DANGER

Designated off-road vehicle (ORV) and non-ORV areas are set up to restrict ORVs, not hikers (who have full freedom to explore any public areas of the dunes). However, hikers venturing into ORV territory need to remain keen to the direction of ORV traffic. Climbing toward the crest of a high dune is an especially bad place to be when a dune buggy comes flying over the top. Red (sometimes orange) flags waving above the dunes indicate oncoming ORVs.

Rock. Stunning views grace the Oregon Coast Trail over Tillamook Head between Cannon Beach and Seaside in Ecola State Park. On the renowned Sandcastle Day, held in June, teams compete for originality and execution in sand sculpture.

Blue Gull Inn Motel (☎ 503-436-2714, 800-507-2714; 632 S Hemlock St; r from $80) is pleasant. Budget travelers can stay in Seaside, 10 minutes south on Hwy 101, at the **Seaside International Hostel** (☎ 503-738-7911; 930 N Holladay Dr; dm/r from $18/40).

Use the handy wheelbarrows to haul your gear to campsites at **Oswald West State Park** (☎ 503-368-5154; campsites $10-14), 10 miles south of Cannon Beach on Hwy 101.

For fresh seafood, try **Dooger's** (☎ 503-436-2225; 1371 S Hemlock; lunch $5-10, dinner $14-18). **Pizza a Fetta** (☎ 503-436-0333; 231 N Hemlock; slice $2-3, pie $18-28) is a good budget option – provided you go for one of the huge slices, rather than a less economical whole pie.

Astoria

Astoria sits at the mouth of the Columbia River, where the 4.1-mile **Astoria Bridge** crosses over to Washington. John Jacob Astor and his Pacific Fur Trading Company established a small fort here in the spring of 1811, making this the first US settlement in the West. Find information at the **visitor center** (☎ 503-325-6311; 111 W Marine Dr; ☿ 9am-5pm).

Astoria has some of the most lovingly restored and precipitously poised Victorian homes outside of San Francisco. Its visual appeal is frequently confirmed by film companies who set movies here; most recently, Astoria played the background in the horror flick *The Ring II*. Cult-film fans can check out the **'Goonies house'** (368 38th St), from Spielberg's 1984 pirate-kids movie. Tour the ornate **Flavel House** (☎ 503-325-2203; 441 8th St; adult/child $5/2; ☿ 11am-4pm) to get a feel for the city's magnificent residences, dating back to the 1880s.

Reconstructed **Fort Clatsop** (☎ 503-861-2471; admission $3; ☿ 8am-5pm), 8 miles south of Astoria off US 101, is worth a stop. The Lewis and Clark party spent a miserable winter here in 1805-06. The fort was named after a local Native American community who befriended them.

On Clatsop Spit and close to the beaches in Hammond is **Fort Stevens State Park** (☎ 503-861-1671, 800-452-5687; campsites/RV sites/yurts $13/17/29); don't miss the photogenic wreck of an English sailing ship on the beach.

Clementine's B&B (☎ 503-325-2005, 800-521-6801; www.clementines-bb.com; 847 Exchange St; r $85-150) occupies an 1888 Italianate mansion right across from Flavel House; rooms have featherbeds and balconies. Or act like Astorian royalty for a day at the downtown **Hotel Elliott** (☎ 503-325-2222, 877-378-1924; www.hotelelliott.com; 357 12th St; r $110-275), built in 1924 and renovated fabulously a few years back.

Big ships float by the cannery-turned-sophisticated seafood restaurant **Gunderson's Cannery Cafe** (☎ 503-325-8642; 1 6th St; lunch $8-10, dinner $12-25), which overlooks the river. **Brown Baggers Deli** (☎ 503-325-0325; 1269 Commercial St; sandwiches $3-5) and the next-door **Rusty Cup** (☎ 503-325-8265; 1213 Commercial St) are both good for sandwiches, coffee and snacks.

Alaska

It's the longest sidetrip in the USA and probably the most expensive. It takes a week on the road, two to three days on a ferry or, from much of the country, a $700 to $800 airline ticket to reach Alaska. Still, most travelers to the USA either consider it or at least dream about it, and those who find the time and money to visit the 49th state rarely regret it.

Many are initially drawn to Alaska by its colorful reputation, then are stunned by the grandeur of what they see once they arrive. There are mountains, glaciers and wildlife in other parts of North America, but few are on the same scale or as overpowering as those in Alaska. To see hundreds of bald eagles gather at a river filled with thousands of salmon, or to watch a 5-mile-wide glacier continually calve ice off its extremities are natural experiences that can permanently change your way of thinking.

Alaska is big, and so is everything about it: the tallest mountain in North America (Mt McKinley), the third-longest river in the USA (the Yukon) and more than 5000 glaciers – including one larger than Switzerland (Bering Glacier). Towns and cities in Alaska are small, but what is wild is plentiful. The brown bears on Kodiak Island have been known to stand 10ft tall; the king salmon in the Kenai River often weigh 70lb or more. A 50ft-long humpback whale breaching totally out of the water is not something easily missed.

HIGHLIGHTS

- Cruising around **Glacier Bay National Park** (p1093) to watch glaciers shed icebergs the size of cars

- Hiking along the **Mendenhall Glacier** (p1092) on the West Glacier Trail in Juneau

- Chugging high into the mountains on the historic **White Pass & Yukon Railroad** (p1095) from Skagway

- Learning to love Spam and laughing at Alaskan cuisine during the 'Whale-Fat Follies' at **Mr Whitekeys Fly by Nite Club** (p1103) in Anchorage

- **Whale-watching** on a marine wildlife tour in Kenai Fjords National Park (p1105), reached from Seward

- Exploring the **Kennicott Copper Mine** ruins near the funky town of McCarthy (p1109)

- Riding the shuttle bus in **Denali National Park** (p1111) to view wildlife and Mt McKinley, the tallest peak in North America

- Enjoying a cold beer and a hot soak at **Chena Hot Springs** (p1113)

- Driving through the **Brooks Range** (p1114) along the rugged Dalton Hwy

HISTORY

Indigenous Alaskans – the Athabascans, Aleuts and Inuit, and coastal tribes of Tlingits and Haidas – migrated over the Bering Strait land bridge 35,000 years ago. In the 18th century, waves of Europeans arrived, first British and French explorers, then Russian whalers and fur traders, naming land formations, taking otter pelts and leaving the cultures of Native Alaskans in disarray.

With the Russians' finances badly over-extended by the Napoleonic Wars, in 1867 US Secretary of State William H Seward was able to purchase the territory from them for $7.2 million – less than 2¢ an acre. There was uproar over 'Seward's Folly,' but the land's riches soon revealed themselves; first whales, then salmon, gold and finally oil.

After Japan bombed one Aleutian island and occupied another in WWII, the military built the famous Alcan (Alaska–Canada) Hwy, which linked the territory with the rest of the USA. The 1520-mile Alcan was built in less than nine months and contributed greatly to the postwar development of Alaska, which became a state in 1959. An earthquake in 1964 left Alaska in shambles, but recovery was boosted when oil deposits were discovered under Prudhoe Bay. Soon construction of a 789-mile pipeline to the port of Valdez was underway.

With Prudhoe Bay's oil reserves drying up and the battle over drilling in the Arctic National Wildlife Refuge (ANWR) still being fought in Washington, DC, Alaska suffers from budget deficits and an unemployment rate of more than 7%, the highest in the country. Whether the build-and-boom takes place in the ANWR and bails out the state's dismal economy is yet to be seen. But one thing's for sure: tourists will experience increased fees at parks, campgrounds and museums as public funds disappear. What won't disappear is the grandeur of this land, the abundance of wildlife, and Mt McKinley on fire from the alpenglow of a clear evening in Alaska.

GEOGRAPHY & CLIMATE

Alaska's extremely variable climate is the result of its huge size. At latitudes spanning the Arctic Circle, the main body of Alaska is about 800 sq miles, with the arc of the Aleutian Islands chain stretching some 1600 miles south and west, and a 'panhan-

---

ALASKA FACTS

Nickname Last Frontier
Population 655,435
Area 591,004 sq miles
Capital city Juneau (population 31,283)
Other cities Anchorage (270,951), Fairbanks (82,214), Kodiak (13,811), Ketchikan (13,548)
Official state symbols forget-me-not (flower), North to the Future (motto), mushing (sport)
Birthplace of Singer and poet Jewel (b 1974), cartoonist Virgil F Partch (1916–84)
Home of The Iditarod; the 'Last Great Race' is the world's longest dogsled event
Famous for Its size (if split in half, Alaska would still be the largest two states in the USA), Eskimos (Inuit)

---

dle' strip running 600 miles southeast down the North American coast.

Alaska's weather is famous for being unpredictable. The Interior can top 90°F during the summer, while the Southeast and Southcentral maritime regions will average 55°F to 70°F. In the Southeast it rains almost daily from late September through October, while even a good week of weather in the summer will include a day or two when you need to pull out your rain gear. In winter, residents experience long nights, -50°F temperatures and the fantastic northern lights.

The peak tourist season is early July to mid-August, when the best-known parks are packed, and it's essential to make reservations for ferries and accommodations. May and September still have mild weather, with less crowds and lower prices. Hours and prices in this chapter are for the summer season unless otherwise noted.

WILDLIFE

Despite its 'frozen wasteland' reputation, Alaska is rich in flora and fauna. The coastal regions have lush coniferous forests, while the Interior is dominated by boreal forest of white spruce, cottonwood and birch. Further north is a taiga zone – a moist, subarctic forest characterized by muskeg, willow thickets and stunted spruce – then the treeless Arctic tundra, with grass, mosses and a variety of tiny flowers thriving briefly in summer.

A great variety of wildlife can be easily seen, notably moose, deer and bears. Harder to spot are caribou, which inhabit the Interior

ALASKA

ALASKA

ALASKA

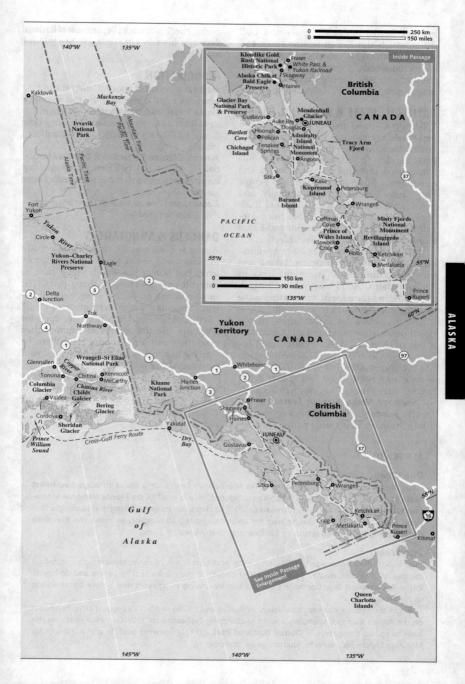

ALASKA

in large herds; mountain goats and Dall sheep, which also live in remote areas; and wolves, which are reclusive by nature. Marine life includes seals, porpoises, whales, sea otters and walruses. During summer, millions of spawning salmon fill rivers and streams.

NATIONAL, STATE & REGIONAL PARKS

Wilderness – land free of strip malls and McDonald's restaurants – is the main attraction of Alaska. Within the state the National Park Service (NPS) administers 54 million acres as national parks, preserves and monuments. More than two million people visit Alaska's national parks annually, and popular parks include Klondike Gold Rush National Historical Park in Skagway, Denali National Park in the Interior and Kenai Fjords National Park near Seward.

State parks account for another 3 million acres, and most offer camping, hiking and even opportunities for overnight treks in the mountains. At 773 sq miles, Chugach State Park (on the edge of Anchorage) is the third-largest state park in the country.

The best place for information on national parks, state parks and all public land is one of the four Alaska Public Lands Information Centers (APLICs). Anchorage has the largest **APLIC** (☎ 907-271-2737; www.nps .gov/aplic/center; 605 W 4th Ave, Suite 105). If arriving by ferry, the APLIC in Ketchikan is the **Southeast Alaska Discovery Center** (☎ 907-228-6234; 50 Main St). The **NPS** (www.nps.gov) has information on all national parks. For state

parks, check out **Alaska Department of National Resources** (www.dnr.state.ak.us/parks). See p92 for an overview.

INFORMATION

Alaska One (www.alaskaone.com) Travel and tourist information, as well as bus, ferry, air and train schedules.
Alaska Travel Industry Association (www.travel alaska.com) Produces the free, annual Alaska State Vacation Planner, and distributes state maps and railroad and ferry schedules.
Alaska Wilderness Recreation & Tourism Association (☎ 907-258-3171; www.awrta.org) A group of tour companies and outfitters committed to responsible tourism and minimizing visitor impact.
Alaskan.com (www.alaskan.com) Tourist information; also has transport schedules.

DANGERS & ANNOYANCES

Alaska is notorious for its biting insects. In the cities and towns you'll have few problems, but out in the woods you'll have to contend with a variety of flying pests. The most effective protection is an insect repellent containing a high percentage of DEET (diethyltoluamide). Unfortunately, repellents are more effective against mosquitoes than black flies and 'no-see-ums.' Foil them by wearing light colors, tucking the legs of your pants into your socks and wearing a hat.

The greatest fear for most backcountry visitors is encountering a bear on the trail. When in bear country use common sense: clap when traveling through thick bush; leave pets at home; hang your food at least 10ft

---

ALASKA IN...

One Week

From Washington state, hop on the Alaska Marine Hwy ferries for a cruise through **Southeast Alaska** (p1086). Spend a day in Ketchikan to squeeze in a tour of **Misty Fjords National Monument** (p1088), and three days in **Juneau** (p1091) to check out its great hiking and many glaciers. Jump back on the Alaska Marine Hwy for an overnight trip to Skagway to relive the **Klondike Gold Rush** (p1095), then return to Juneau to depart Alaska by plane.

Two Weeks

Take a flight to **Anchorage** (p1096), rent a car and beat it out of town. Head south and follow the beautiful Seward Hwy to **Seward** (p1104), to take in the Alaska SeaLife Center and go kayaking in Resurrection Bay. Continue the road trip by driving to artsy Homer before backtracking to Anchorage.

Begin the second week with two days exploring and hiking in Alaska's biggest city, then jump on the Alaska Railroad, spending a night in charming **Talkeetna** (p1110). Continue north on the train to spend three days in **Denali National Park** (p1111), viewing wildlife and hopefully Mt McKinley before returning to Anchorage on the train.

DRILLING FOR OIL IN THE LAST GREAT WILDERNESS

Alaska is a battleground for many environmental issues, but none tug more at the nation's conscience than the push to drill for oil in the Arctic National Wildlife Refuge (ANWR). Yellowstone National Park sees more visitors in a weekend than this refuge does in a year, yet the battle over oil has turned the ANWR into a sacred icon as America's last great wilderness.

And either you're for drilling in the refuge or you're not. There's no middle ground in this debate.

The refuge was created under President Eisenhower in the 1950s and expanded to 19.6 million acres by President Carter in 1980. It's often labeled by environmentalists as America's Serengeti, a pristine wilderness inhabited by 45 species of mammals, including grizzly bears, polar bears and wolves. Millions of migratory birds use the refuge to nest and every spring the country's second-largest caribou herd, 120,000-strong, gives birth to 40,000 calves there.

But there is also oil in the refuge, concentrated in the fragile coastal plains that span 1.5 million acres along the Beaufort Sea. Geologists believe the ANWR has the largest untapped reserve in the country, rivaling the massive Prudhoe Bay fields to the west when they were first explored. The US Geological Survey has estimated the amount of recoverable oil falls between 5.6 million and 16 billion barrels.

The oil industry, salivating over such a large field, contends that only 8% of the refuge would be affected by its infrastructure: roads, pipelines, trucks, drilling platforms, an entire town to house workers, an occasional spill. And, according to the American Petroleum Institute, once fully developed the ANWR would produce 1.5 million barrels a day for 20 years – as much as the USA imports from Saudi Arabia.

Environmentalists contend that drilling the refuge would not put the country on a course of 'energy independence.' They argue that the refuge would never quench more than 2% of the country's thirst for oil and that simply increasing gasoline mileage requirements on vehicles, particularly gas-guzzling SUVs, would result in bigger (and quicker) energy savings than the ANWR ever could provide.

The battle raged from the earliest days of President Reagan in the 1980s until 2005. But a combination of high gas prices at the pump and a persistent President George W Bush, an oil man from Texas, finally convinced the US Senate, which had long opposed developing the ANWR, to include it in an energy bill.

It now appears that drilling is inevitable, and one columnist compared such an industrial invasion with addicts hocking 'the family heirlooms to keep their drug habit going.' The heroin happens to be oil, and many fear that opening the ANWR will encourage the oil industry to campaign for drilling rights in other areas presently closed: the California coast, the Great Lakes or even the Rocky Mountains.

Ironically, the ANWR would have no effect on today's high gas prices as it would take at least 10 years for the first Arctic oil to reach refineries. By then the coastal plain, a marshy tableland that supports the park's greatest concentration of wildlife and is the biological heart of the refuge, could be forever marred with the thumbprint of a dig-and-drill president and a nation addicted to oil.

ALASKA

off the ground; and never take any food (or toothpaste, lotions or anything with a scent) into your tent. At the same time, don't let paranoia keep you out of the wilderness – bears only attack if they feel trapped, are enticed by food or their cubs are threatened.

ACTIVITIES

Alaska's biggest drawcard is the outdoors. Hiking trails are boundless and they're the best way to escape the summer crowds in places like Juneau and the Kenai Peninsula. For hiking and backpacking opportunities throughout the state, turn to Lonely Planet's *Hiking in Alaska*. Mountain biking is allowed on many trails, and bikes can be rented throughout the state. You can also rent kayaks in coastal towns like Ketchikan, Sitka, Juneau, Seward and Valdez, where paddlers enjoy sea kayaking in protective fjords, often within view of glaciers. Other popular outdoor activities are white-water rafting, wildlife watching, canoeing, fishing, and just pulling over on the road and admiring the scenery.

GETTING THERE & AROUND

Air

Anchorage is the major regional air hub. **Alaska Airlines** (☎ 800-252-7522; www.alaskaair.com) has direct flights to Anchorage from Seattle ($250 round-trip), Chicago ($600) and many West Coast cities. Other airlines also offer direct flights, including **Northwest** (☎ 800-225-2525; www.nwa.com) from Minneapolis ($580), **Delta** (☎ 800-221-1212; www.delta.com) from Atlanta ($575) and **American Airlines** (☎ 800-443-7300; www.aa.com) from Dallas ($670). Within the state, Alaska Airlines serves many towns, while 'bush planes' can be chartered to the most remote areas.

Boat

The **Alaska Marine Highway** (☎ 800-642-0066; www.ferryalaska.com) connects Bellingham, WA, with 14 towns in Southeast Alaska and is a very popular way to travel to this roadless region. The ferries also service six towns in Southcentral Alaska, and make a special run once a month from Kodiak to Unalaska in the Aleutian Islands ($258, 55 hours).

Bus

Bus services link all the main towns in Alaska, with connections to the Lower 48. Traveling by bus is not cheaper than flying, but you do get to experience the Alaska Hwy. From Seattle, WA, **Greyhound** (☎ 206-628-5526; www.greyhound.com; cnr 8th Ave & Stewart St) can get you to Whitehorse, Canada ($149, 47 hours), via Vancouver. From Whitehorse, **Alaska Direct** (☎ 800-770-6652; 509 Main St) leaves three days a week for Anchorage ($180, 18 hours).

Car

Allow at least a week to drive from northern USA through Canada to Fairbanks on the mostly paved Alcan Hwy. It's not worth the time it takes unless you can make some stops on the way and spend a few weeks in Alaska. Local rental cars are handy to get around the countryside; they start at $40 a day, commonly with 100 miles free.

Train

The **Alaska Railroad** (☎ 907-265-2494, 800-544-0552; www.akrr.com) offers service between Seward and Anchorage ($59 one way) and from Anchorage to Denali ($129), before ending in Fairbanks ($179). Book seats early on this popular train.

SOUTHEAST ALASKA

The Southeast is the closest slice of Alaska to continental USA. It's possible to fly to the panhandle for a quick visit, but a better option is to cruise the Inside Passage, a waterway made up of thousands of islands, glacier-filled fjords and a mountainous coastline. You can jump on a state ferry and stop at a handful of the 14 ports along the way for sightseeing, hiking, kayaking and whale-watching.

Getting There & Around

AIR

Alaska Airlines (☎ 800-252-7522; www.alaskaair.com) has daily northbound and southbound flights year-round, with stops at all main towns. Round-trip advance-purchase fares include Seattle–Juneau ($390 to $500), Anchorage–Juneau ($270) and Ketchikan–Juneau ($250). Smaller airlines serving the region include **LAB Flying Service** (☎ 907-766-2222; www.labflying.com), **Taquan Air** (☎ 907-225-8800, 800-770-8800; www.taquanair.com) and **Wings of Alaska** (☎ 907-789-0790; www.wingsofalaska.com).

BOAT

Alaska Marine Highway (☎ 800-642-0066; www.ferryalaska.com) calls on the main towns almost daily in summer. The complete trip, from Bellingham, WA, to Haines ($210 per person) stops at ports along the way and must be scheduled in advance. Trips within the Inside Passage include Ketchikan–Petersburg ($52), Petersburg–Sitka ($39), Sitka–Juneau ($39) and Juneau–Haines ($33). Alaska Marine Hwy ferries are equipped to handle cars (Bellingham–Haines $407) but space must be reserved months ahead.

You can also pick up the state ferries from Prince Rupert, British Columbia, to Ketchikan ($52, six hours), or twice a month join the special runs across the Gulf of Alaska from Juneau to Whittier ($194).

TRAIN

The narrow-gauge 1890s **White Pass & Yukon Railroad** (☎ 800-343-7373; www.whitepassrailroad.com)

links Skagway and Fraser, British Columbia, with a bus connection to Whitehorse, which is situated on the Alcan Hwy ($95, five hours).

KETCHIKAN

The Alaska Marine Hwy's first Alaskan stop is Ketchikan, a fishing town with frontier character.

Ketchican Visitors Bureau (☎ 907-225-6166, 800-770-3300; www.visit-ketchikan.com; 131 Front St; ☑ 7am-5pm) Arranges tours and has city bus information.

Southeast Alaska Discovery Center (☎ 907-228-6220; 50 Main St; adult/child $5/free; ☑ 8am-5pm) Houses an impressive exhibit hall; provides details of outdoor activities.

Surf City (☎ 907-225-5475; 425 Water St; per 20min/1hr $5/10; ☑ 8am-4pm) Access the Internet here.

Sights & Activities

Learn about all things salmon from the observation decks of the **Deer Mountain Tribal Hatchery & Eagle Center** (☎ 907-225-5158, 800-252-5158; 1158 Salmon Rd; adult/child $9/free; ☑ 8am-4:30pm). The eagle center allows you to get up close and personal with a pair of injured eagles who can no longer fly.

The star of the former red-light district of Creek St is **Dolly's House** (☎ 907-225-6329; 24 Creek St; adult/child $5/free; ☑ 10am-10pm), the parlor of Ketchikan's most famous madam, Dolly Arthur. The **Totem Heritage Center**

(☎ 907-225-5900; 601 Deermont St; adult/child $5/free; ☑ 8am-5pm) features a collection of priceless 19th-century totem poles.

The 3-mile **Deer Mountain Trail** begins near the city center and provides access to the alpine world above the tree line and wonderful views of the town. There are more trails in the **Ward Lake Recreation Area**. **Southeast Sea Kayaks** (☎ 907-225-1258, 800-287-1607; www.kayak ketchikan.com; 1007 Water St; single/double kayak per day $45/60, day trip $79-149) rents kayaks by the day.

Sleeping

Gilmore Hotel (☎ 907-225-9423, 800-275-9423; www .gilmorehotel.com; 326 Front St; r $115-155; 🖵) Built in 1927, the Gilmore has 38 rooms that still retain a historical flavor but also include cable TV, coffeemakers and hair dryers.

New York Hotel (☎ 907-225-0246, 866-225-0246; www.thenewyorkhotel.com; 207 Stedman St; s/d $109/119, multiple nights less $5; ✗) Another historic inn in the heart of town; rooms have cable TV and complimentary coffee.

Captain's Quarters (☎ 907-225-4912; www.ptialaska .net/~captbnb; 325 Lund St; r $90-95) Has three rooms a short walk from downtown, one with a full kitchen.

HI-AYH Ketchikan Hostel (☎ 907-225-3319; 400 Main St; members/nonmembers $12/15; ✗) Bustling but basic, with lockout 9am to 6pm.

The closest camping is at three rustic USFS campgrounds 10 miles north of Ketchikan

ALASKA

ALASKA'S FOREST SERVICE CABINS

The US Forest Service (USFS) cabin program offers more than shelter in the mountains or cheap lodging in this land of high prices. When you rent a USFS cabin ($25 to $50 a night), you're renting your own personal wilderness.

Although some cabins can be reached on foot or by boat, the vast majority require a flight on a floatplane, ensuring that your party will be the only one in the area until the next group is flown in. The fishing can be outstanding, the chances of seeing wildlife excellent and your wilderness solitude guaranteed.

This is Alaskan wilderness at its easiest and cheapest, but remember that a USFS cabin is not a suite at the Hilton. The cabin provides security from the weather, a wood-burning stove, an outhouse and, often, a small rowboat, but you need to pack sleeping bags, food, a water filter and a cooking stove.

Of the 190 USFS cabins, 150 are in **Tongass National Forest** (www.fs.fed.us/r10/tongass), which covers most of Southeast Alaska, and the other 40 are in **Chugach National Forest** (www.fs.fed.us /r10/chugach), in the Prince William Sound area. Check the websites to see what each cabin offers. Cabins can be reserved 180 days in advance through the **National Recreation Reservation Service** (☎ 877-444-6777, 518-885-3639; www.reserveusa.com).

In addition to the nightly fee, you need to budget for the cost of the floatplane and paying a bush pilot for both a drop-off and a pickup. For cabins within 15 or 20 minutes of major towns such as Juneau or Ketchikan, expect to pay $300 to $400 for a party of two or three.

in the Ward Lake Recreation Area: **Signal Creek**, **Last Chance** and **Three C** are all located on Ward Lake Rd and cost $10.

Eating & Drinking

Bar Harbor Restaurant (☎ 907-225-2813; 2813 Tongass Ave; lunch $9-12, dinner $15-19; ☺ 11am-2:30pm & 4:30-9pm Mon-Sat; ✗) A cozy place between downtown and the ferry terminal with a menu that is intriguingly eclectic – from burritos to coconut prawns with a marmalade sauce – and a back deck for outdoor dining when the sun is out.

Streamers on the Dock (☎ 907-225-1600; 76 Front St; dinner mains $15-30; ☺ 10am-9pm) Upscale dining with a great waterfront view if there isn't a five-story cruise ship docked in front.

That One Place (207 Stedman St; breakfast $7-10, lunch $8-13; ☺ 8am-4pm; ✗) A wonderful café at the New York Hotel, where practically everything on the lunch menu is seafood-related. Let's face it, if you're in Alaska long enough you'll eventually order halibut tacos. You might as well do it here where the locals rave about them.

Safeway (2417 Tongass Ave; ☺ 5am-midnight) Next to the Plaza Mall, Ketchikan's largest supermarket has a salad bar, ready-to-eat items and a Starbucks.

First City Saloon (☎ 907-225-1494; 830 Water St) A sprawling place with giant-screen TVs, 20 beers on tap, pool tables and live music.

Getting There & Around

Alaska Airlines and Alaska Marine Hwy ferries service Ketchikan (see p1086).

The **M/V Prince of Wales** (☎ 907-826-4848, 866-308-4848; www.interislandferry.com; adult/child $30/18) sails to Hollis on Prince of Wales Island twice a day June through August. For wheels, try **Alaska Car Rental** (☎ 907-225-5123, 800-662-0007; 2828 Tongass Ave; per day $49; ☺ 8am-5pm).

AROUND KETCHIKAN

Two miles south of Ketchikan, **Saxman Native Village** (☎ 907-225-4421; www.capefoxtours.com; tour adult/child $35/17; ☺ 8am-5pm) is a village of indigenous Tlingit people. Its **Totem Park** (admission free) has the world's largest standing collection of totem poles, as well as a cultural center. Ten miles north of Ketchikan, **Totem Bight State Historical Park** (☎ 907-247-8574; admission free; ☺ 6am-10pm) contains 14 restored totem poles and a historic **longhouse** (admission free; ☺ 8am-8pm).

Misty Fjords National Monument begins 22 miles east of Ketchikan, offering wildlife-watching and spectacular views of 3000ft sheer granite walls rising from the ocean. **Alaska Cruises** (☎ 907-225-6044, 800-228-1905; www.mistyfjord.net; adult/child $150/125) runs a six-hour trip around the monument. **Island Wings** (☎ 907-225-2444, 888-854-2444; www.islandwings.com; tour $200) combines flightseeing and hiking in the monument's lush old-growth forests.

PRINCE OF WALES ISLAND

Real Alaska is only a three-hour ferry ride away from the cruise-ship madness of Ketchikan. Prince of Wales Island, the third-largest island in the USA, features Native Alaskan villages, the Southeast's most extensive road network and a lot of clear-cuts, but no cruise ships. For information, the island's **chamber of commerce** (☎ 907-755-2626; www.princeofwalescoc.org; Klawock Bell Tower Mall, Craig-Klawock Hwy; ☺ 10am-3pm Mon-Fri) is in Klawock and a **USFS office** (☎ 907-826-3271; 900 9th St; ☺ 8am-5pm Mon-Fri) is in Craig.

Bring a mountain bike and you can spend a week or more exploring the 300 miles of paved and graded gravel roads or the 1800 miles of shot-rock logging roads. Bring a kayak and you can do the same along 990 miles of contorted coastline. Or rent either one from **Alaska Kustom Kayaks** (☎ 907-755-2800; www.alaskakustomkayaks.com; Klawock Bell Tower Mall, Craig-Klawock Hwy; bike per day $20, single/double kayak $50/70).

In Craig, stay at **Ruth Ann's Hotel** (☎ 907-826-3378; cnr Main & Water Sts; r $90-125; ✗) or the delightful **Inn of the Blue Heron** (☎ 907-826-3606; 406 9th St; s $79-99, d $94-114; ✗).

The **M/V Prince of Wales** (☎ 866-308-4848; www.interislandferry.com; adult/child $30/18) makes the Hollis–Ketchikan run twice a day. The main communities of Klawock and Craig are 25 miles and 31 miles southwest of Hollis. In 2006, *M/V Stikine* will begin service between Wrangell and Coffman Cove at the northern end of the island. **POW Ferry Shuttle** (☎ 907-957-2224; $12) runs a Hollis–Craig service. Rental cars are available in Craig and Klawock, or can be brought from Ketchikan on the ferry (from $34).

WRANGELL

Founded by Russians, leased to the British and then taken over by Americans with the purchase of Alaska, the town of Redoubt St

---

THE RISE & FALL OF TOTEMS

Ironically, Europeans first stimulated and then almost ended the Native Alaskan art of carving totems in the Southeast region. Totems first flourished in the late 18th century, after clans had acquired steel knives, axes and other cutting tools through the fur trade with white explorers.

The art form was almost wiped out between 1880 and the 1950s, when potlatches were outlawed – a decision that banned the ceremony for which most totems were carved. When the law was repealed in 1951, a revival of totem carving took place and the practice still continues.

Generally, the oldest totems are 50 to 60 years old. Once they reach this age, the heavy precipitation and acidic muskeg soil of Southeast Alaska takes its toll on the cedar pole, until the wood rots and the totem finally tumbles.

Dionysius was renamed Fort Wrangell in 1868. This is one of the few ports where the state ferries dock downtown, so it's possible to have a look around during the hour the ship takes to unload. The **visitor center** (☎ 907-874-3901, 800-367-9745; www.wrangell.com; 296 Outer Dr; ⏱ 10am-4pm Mon-Fri) is in the new Nolan Center. There's a local **USFS office** (☎ 907-874-2323; 525 Bennett St; ⏱ 8am-4:30pm Mon-Fri), and **Practical Rent-A-Car** (☎ 907-874-3975), at Wrangell airport, is open when flights arrive.

Learn about Tlingit culture, gold-rush Wrangell or about when Wyatt Earp filled in as the town's deputy marshal for 10 days at the new **Wrangell Museum** (☎ 907-874-3770; 296 Outer Dr; adult/child/family $5/3/12; ⏱ 10am-5pm Mon-Sat) in the Nolan Center. In the middle on the harbor is **Chief Shakes Island**, with six totems and a tribal house.

There are several local B&Bs.

Rooney's Roost (☎ 907-874-2026; www.rooneysroost .com; 206 McKinnon St; r $75-95; ✕) has five rooms and a full breakfast.

Hardings Old Sourdough Lodge (☎ 907-874-3613, 800-874-3613; www.akgetaway.com; 1104 Peninsula St; s/d $89/99; ✕) has a sauna and Jacuzzi, home-style meals and free ferry and airport transfers.

Stikine Inn (☎ 907-874-3388, 888-874-3388; 107 Stikine Ave; s/d $95/106; ✕) is the largest hotel in town. It's near the ferry dock and convenient to the Front St business district. All 33 rooms have private bathrooms, and there's a restaurant on site. Rooms with a view of the water are $10 extra.

Wrangell Hostel (☎ 907-874-3534; 220 Church St; dm $15; ✕) is in the Presbyterian church, while the **City Park Campground** (Zimovia Hwy; campsite free), 1.75 miles south of the ferry terminal, is a delightful place to pitch a tent.

The **Garnet Room** (☎ 907-874-2353; 107 Stikine Ave; lunch $6-10, dinner $11-25; ⏱ 5:30am-9:30pm; ✕)

at the Stikine Inn offers local seafood and a panoramic view of Zimovia Strait.

Diamond C Café (☎ 907-874-3677; 223 Front St; breakfast $4-10; ⏱ 6am-3pm; ✕) is where locals head for breakfast, while **Bob's IGA Supermarket** (223 Brueger St; ⏱ 8am-6pm Mon-Sat) has a deli and bakery.

Mingle with locals at **Totem Bar** (☎ 907-874-3533; 116 Front St), or head there when a cruise ship is in port to watch the local troupe of cancan dancers.

PETERSBURG

At the north end of spectacular Wrangell Narrows lies the picturesque community of Petersburg, a town known for its Norwegian roots and home to Alaska's largest halibut fleet.

The **Petersburg Chamber of Commerce** (☎ 907-772-4636; www.petersburg.org; cnr Fram & 1st Sts; ⏱ 9am-5pm Mon-Sat, noon-4pm Sun) has B&B and USFS information. You can also visit the **USFS office** (☎ 907-772-3871; Federal Bldg, Nordic Dr; ⏱ 8am-5pm Mon-Fri).

The center of old Petersburg was **Sing Lee Alley**, which winds past weathered homes and boathouses perched on pilings above the water. The **Clausen Memorial Museum** (☎ 907-772-3598; 203 Fram St; adult/child $3/free; ⏱ 10am-5pm Mon-Sat) features local artifacts and fishing relics, and a small but excellent museum store.

There are kayaking opportunities, ranging from day paddles to week-long adventures. **Tongass Kayak Adventures** (☎ 907-772-4600; www .tongasskayak.com; single/double kayak $55/65) offers rentals and drop-off transportation, as well as several guided paddles, including a day paddle at LeConte Glacier ($200).

Tides Inn (☎ 907-772-4288, 800-665-8433; www.tides innalaska.com; 307 1st St; s/d $75/95; 💻) is a centrally located motel with 45 rooms. It provides a continental breakfast.

ALASKA

Scandia House (☎ 907-772-4281, 800-722-5006; www.scandiahouse.com; 110 N Nordic Dr; r $100-135; ☐) is Petersburg's most upscale hotel, with a view of the harbor, a courtesy van to pick you up and freshly baked muffins in the morning.

Alaska Island Hostel (☎ 907-772-3632, 877-772-3632; www.alaskaislandhostel.com; 805 Gjoa St; dm $20; ☒ ☐) is in a cozy spot 1.5 miles from the ferry terminal. It offers four-person dorm rooms, a laundry, a kitchen and an outdoor grill in case you hook a big one.

Rooney's Northern Lights Restaurant (☎ 907-772-2900; 203 Sing Lee Alley; breakfast $4-10, dinner $15-30; ☽ 6am-10pm; ☒) overlooks a bustling harbor; all the crab, halibut and shrimp on its seafood platter is locally caught. Also try **Coastal Cold Storage** (306 Nordic Dr; ☽ 6am-5:30pm Mon-Sat, 7am-2pm Sun) for its halibut beer bits, a local specialty.

Locals shoot pool at **Harbor Bar** (☎ 907-772-4526; 310 Nordic Dr), while **Kito's Kave** (☎ 907-772-3207; 11 Sing Lee Alley) has live music and dancing, and can get wild at times.

To see the scenery and sights on the Mitkof Hwy, stop at **Tides Inn** (☎ 907-772-4288, 800-665-8433; 307 1st St), which rents cars from $83 a day.

SITKA

Russians established Southeast Alaska's first nonindigenous settlement here in 1799, and the town flourished on fur. Today Sitka sees itself as the cultural center of the Southeast and its most beautiful city, because it's the only one on the Pacific Ocean.

The **Sitka Convention & Visitors Bureau** (☎ 907-747-5940; www.sitka.org; 330 Harbor Dr; ☽ 8am-5pm Mon-Fri) is located across the street from St Michael's Cathedral, and also staffs a desk in the Centennial Building. The **USFS office** (☎ 907-747-6671; 204 Siginaka Way; ☽ 8am-4:30pm Mon-Fri) can provide hiking and kayaking information for the area.

Sights & Activities

Sitka National Historical Park has a gorgeous trail that winds past 15 totem poles, while its **visitor center** (☎ 907-747-0110; Lincoln St; adult/child $4/free; ☽ 8am-5pm) features Russian and indigenous artifacts, and traditional carving demonstrations. **St Michael's Cathedral** (☎ 907-747-8120; 240 Lincoln St; admission $2; ☽ 9am-4pm Mon-Fri) is a replica of the original 1840s Russian Orthodox cathedral destroyed by fire in 1966; priceless treasures were salvaged by residents. Castle Hill is the site of **Baranof's Castle**, where Alaska was officially transferred from Russia to the USA. Built in 1842, the **Russian Bishop's House** (☎ 907-747-6281; Lincoln St; adult/child $4/free; ☽ 9am-5pm) is Sitka's oldest intact Russian building. **Sheldon Jackson Museum** (☎ 907-747-8981; 104 College Dr; adult/child $4/free; ☽ 9am-5pm), on the college campus, houses an excellent indigenous-culture collection. The colorful **Katlian St fishing quarter**, at the west end of town, is a photographer's delight.

Sitka has superb hiking, and the **Gaven Hill Trail** into the mountains is accessible from the downtown area. There are also many kayaking trips around Baranof and Chichagof Islands. **Sitka Sound Ocean Adventures** (☎ 907-747-6365; www.ssoceanadventures.com; single/double kayak $50/60) rents kayaks and runs guided day trips ($125); its office is in a blue bus at the Centennial Building. Thanks to Sitka's ocean location, marine wildlife boat tours have mushroomed in the town. **Allen Marine Tours** (☎ 907-747-8100, 888-747-8101; www.allenmarinetours.com; adult/child $79/40; ☽ 8:30-11:30am Sat & Sun) offers three-hour tours.

Sleeping

The Sitka area has almost 30 B&Bs; the visitor center keeps an updated list.

Shee Atiká Totem Square Inn (☎ 907-747-3693, 866-300-1353; www.sheeatika.com; 201 Katlian St; r $119;

ALASKAN MUSIC FESTIVALS

What makes you tap your toes? For three weeks in June, Sitka hosts the **Sitka Summer Music Festival** (www.sitkamusicfestival.org; half series adult/child $50/25, single concert $15/10), when more than 20 internationally known musicians arrive for a series of chamber music concerts at Centennial Hall, renowned for its breathtaking views of Sitka Sound. The highly acclaimed event is so popular that tickets need to be booked in advance.

If that's too much culture for you, in early August there's the **Talkeetna Bluegrass Festival** (www.talkeetnabluegrass.com; ticket $35), a four-day campout north of town at Mile 102 George Parks Hwy. Tickets cover the entire event, when more than 30 bluegrass bands from around the country jam for 20 of the 24 hours a day. This is wild fun under the midnight sun.

▢ ☒) Recently renovated, the inn has 66 rooms, free continental breakfast and a full kitchen on the 4th floor. Its best feature, however, is the view from the rooms, which overlook either the historic square or the ocean.

Sitka Hotel (☎ 907-747-3288; www.sitkahotel.com; 118 Lincoln St; s/d with shared bath $60/65, with private bath $80/85; ▢) This venerable hotel has 60 rooms, which are small but well kept. The hotel also offers cable TV, laundry and luggage storage.

Karras Day Rental (☎ 907-747-3978; 230 Kogwanton St; s/d $55/80; ☒) A few blocks from downtown, there are four cozy rooms with shared bath in this private home.

There are two USFS campgrounds: **Starrigavan** (Halibut Point Rd; campsites $12-30), less than a mile north of the ferry terminal, and **Sawmill Creek** (Blue Lake Rd; campsites free), 6 miles east of Sitka.

Eating & Drinking

Ludvig's Bistro (☎ 907-966-3663; 256 Katlian St; dinner mains $19-30; ☖ 2-10pm; ☒) Sitka's newest restaurant is European-quaint; seven tables and a handful of stools at a brass-and-blue-tile bar. The women who run it describe their seafood-laden menu as 'rustic Mediterranean fare' and it's by far the most innovative cooking in Sitka.

Back Door Café (☎ 907-747-8856; 104 Barracks St; meals under $5; ☖ 6:30am-5pm Mon-Sat, 9am-2pm Sun; ☒) This is a very calm eye in the cruiseship storm.

Little Tokyo (315 Lincoln St; lunch $8-10, fish & tempura rolls $6-12; ☖ 11am-9pm Mon-Fri, noon-9pm Sat & Sun; ☒) Even crew members from the commercial fleet, who know a thing or two about raw fish, say Sitka's only sushi bar is a good catch.

Bayview Restaurant (☎ 907-747-5440; 407 Lincoln St; breakfast $6-10, lunch $8-11, dinner mains $16-27; ☖ 5am-9pm Mon-Sat, 5am-3pm Sun; ☒) Serves gourmet hamburgers with a view of the boat harbor.

Lakeside Grocery (☎ 907-747-3317; 705 Halibut Point Rd) Has sandwiches, soups, a salad bar and a small eating area.

Pioneer Bar (☎ 907-747-3456; 212 Katlian St) This is the most interesting place to have a beer in Sitka, and is one of Alaska's classic bars. The walls are covered with photos of boats, their crews and big fish, while hanging over the bar is a ship's brass bell. Don't ring it unless you're ready to buy a round.

Getting There & Away

Sitka Airport, on Japonski Island, is served by **Alaska Airlines** (☎ 800-252-7522; www.alaskaair .com). **Northstar Rental** (☎ 907-966-2552; Sitka Airport; ☖ 8am-6pm) has compacts for $50 per day. **Alaska Marine Highway** (☎ 907-747-8737, 800-642-0066; www.ferryalaska.com) ferries stop almost daily at the terminal, which is 7 miles north of town. **Ferry Transit Bus** (☎ 907-747-8443; one way/round-trip $6/8) will take you into town.

SECONDARY PORTS

The **LeConte ferry** (☎ 800-642-0066) services small ports between Sitka and Juneau, offering a chance to experience a Southeast Alaska not overrun by cruise-ship passengers. **Wings of Alaska** (☎ 907-789-0790; www.wingsofalaska.com) and **LAB Flying Service** (☎ 907-766-2222; www .labflying.com) also fly to these places.

On Kupreanof Island, the Native Alaskan beachfront community of **Kake** boasts Alaska's tallest totem pole. Rustic **Tenakee Springs** (population 105) is known for its relaxed pace, alternative lifestyle and public bathhouse, built around a 108°F hot spring. Twice monthly, the *LeConte* travels to the lively fishing town of **Pelican**, on Chichagof Island, a unique day trip from Juneau ($62). Built on pilings over tidelands, Pelican's main street is a mile-long wooden boardwalk.

JUNEAU

Occasionally referred to as 'Little San Francisco,' downtown Juneau clings to a mountainside and has narrow streets, a bustling waterfront and snowcapped mountains, while the rest of the city spreads north into the Mendenhall Valley. Alaska's scenic capital is also the gateway to many attractions, including Glacier Bay National Park (p1093) and Admiralty Island National Monument (p1093).

The **Juneau Convention & Visitors Bureau** (☎ 907-586-2201, 800-587-2201; www.traveljuneau.com; 101 Egan Dr; ☖ 8am-5pm) is in Centennial Hall. There is also a direct phone link to the **Juneau ranger's station** (☎ 907-586-8751, 907-586-8800; 8461 Old Dairy Rd; ☖ 8am-4:30pm Mon-Fri) for detailed information on cabins, Glacier Bay, Admiralty Island and Tongass National Forest. The **Juneau Library** (☎ 907-586-5249; 292 Marine Way; ☖ 11am-9pm Mon-Thu, noon-5pm Fri-Sun) provides Internet access.

ALASKA

Sights & Activities

The **Alaska State Museum** (☎ 907-465-2901; 395 Whittier St; adult/child $5/free; ☉ 8:30am-5:30pm) has historical displays and indigenous artifacts, plus a full-size eagle's nest atop a two-story tree.

The **Juneau-Douglas City Museum** (☎ 907-586-3572; 114 W 4th St; adult/child $3/free; ☉ 9am-5pm Mon-Fri, 10am-5pm Sat & Sun) highlights the area's gold-mining history. The **Last Chance Mining Museum** (☎ 907-586-5338; 1001 Basin Rd; admission $4; ☉ 9:30am-12:30pm & 3:30-6:30pm) is an impressive complex of railroad lines, ore cars and repair sheds. The short hike to **Treadwell Mine ruins**, just south of Douglas, is also very interesting.

About 3 miles north of downtown, the **Macaulay Salmon Hatchery Visitor Center** (☎ 907-463-4810, 877-463-2468; 2697 Channel Dr; adult/child $3/1.50; ☉ 10am-6pm Mon-Fri, 10am-5pm Sat & Sun) has underwater viewing windows that allow you to see fish spawning. Displays explain the salmon life cycle and hatchery operations.

The area's numerous glaciers include **Mendenhall Glacier**, the famous 'drive-in' glacier; the informative **visitor center** (☎ 907-789-0097; Glacier Spur Rd; admission $3; ☉ 8am-7:30pm) is 13 miles from the city. **Mendenhall Glacier Transport** (☎ 907-789-5460; one way $5) runs a bus from downtown to the visitor center.

Hiking is the most popular activity in the area, and some trails access USFS cabins. The most stunning scenery is along the **West Glacier Trail**, which sidles along Mendenhall Glacier. **Juneau Parks & Recreation** (☎ 907-586-5226; 155 S Seward St; ☉ 8am-4:30pm) offers free organized hikes. The **Mt Roberts Trail** is the most popular hike to the alpine country above Juneau. Or skip the hike; the **Mt Roberts Tram** (☎ 907-463-3412, 888-461-8726; 490 S Franklin St; adult/child $22/13; ☉ 9am-9pm) takes passengers from the dock to the treeline, where there is a nature center and a restaurant.

The area is wonderful for kayaking day trips and longer paddles. **Alaska Boat & Kayak** (☎ 907-789-6886; 11521 Glacier Hwy; single/double kayak $45/60; ☉ 9am-6pm) rents boats, and **Alaska Discovery** (☎ 800-586-1911; www.akdiscovery.com; 5310 Glacier Hwy; 3-day trip $495) runs paddles in Berners Bay.

The steep-sided Tracy Arm fjord, 50 miles southeast of Juneau, makes an excellent day trip. **Adventure Bound Alaska** (☎ 907-463-2509, 800-228-3875; 215 Ferry Way; $105-115) runs day cruises.

Sleeping

Downtown accommodations are heavily booked during summer but Juneau has more than 50 B&Bs; stop at the visitor center to find one.

Alaska's Capital Inn (☎ 907-586-6507, 888-588-6507; www.alaskacapitalinn.com; 113 W 5th St; r $125-219; ✗) A stay in this gorgeously restored 1906 mansion is a real treat. Soak away your cares in the clothing-optional deck hot tub. There's a two-night minimum.

Alaskan Hotel (☎ 907-586-1000, 800-327-9347; www.ptialaska.net/~akhotel; 167 S Franklin St; r with/without bath $60/80; ✗) This lovely historic hotel is located in the heart of the Franklin St nightlife district – great news if you want to party, less so if you're a light sleeper.

Driftwood Lodge (☎ 907-586-2280, 800-544-2239; www.driftwoodalaska.com; 435 Willoughby Ave; r $89-119; ✗ ▯) The rooms are no-frills but clean, and most have kitchenettes. There's a courtesy airport/ferry van, a coin laundry and bike rental.

Other recommendations:

Silverbow Inn (☎ 907-586-4146, 800-586-4146; www.silverbowinn.com; 120 2nd St; r $118-149; ✗) A charming boutique inn located above Juneau's best bakery.

Juneau International Hostel (☎ 907-586-9559; www.juneauhostel.org; 614 Harris St; dm adult/child $10/5; ✗ ▯) Alaska's best hostel is a five-minute walk from the state capitol.

Eating & Drinking

Fiddlehead Restaurant (☎ 907-586-3150; 429 W Willoughby Ave; dinner $17-24; ☉ 7am-9:30pm; ✗) This restaurant serves seafood and Juneau's best vegetarian cuisine. Upstairs – and more upscale – is the Italian dining room Di Sopra, which serves dinner ($19 to $28) from 5:30pm to 9:30pm.

Doc Water's Pub (☎ 907-586-3627; 2 Marine Way; Merchant's Wharf; dinner $11-27; ☉ 10:30am-11pm; ✗) If the sun is shining, grab a table outside, watch floatplanes take off and enjoy the best beer-battered halibut in town.

Thane Ore House (☎ 907-586-3442; 4400 Thane Rd; dinner mains $23; ✗) Juneau's best salmon bake, 4 miles south of town, is an all-you-can-eat affair in a rustic setting. There's courtesy van transportation and a small mining museum.

Rainbow Foods (☎ 907-586-6476; 224 4th St; ☉ 9am-7pm Mon-Sat, 9am-6pm Sun; ✗) A cool natural-foods store with a deli that makes a happening lunch spot.

Silverbow Inn Bakery (☎ 907-586-4146; 120 2nd St; sandwiches $7-8; ⏱ 7am-6pm; ✗) Fresh-baked bagels and sandwiches.

Island Pub (☎ 907-364-1595; 1102 2nd St; ⏱ 4-10pm Sun-Thu, 4pm-midnight Fri & Sat) Across the channel in Douglas is the capital city's newest restaurant, serving good foccacia and gourmet pizza accompanied by a mountainous view.

Safeway (☎ 907-523-2000; cnr Vintage Blvd & Egan Hwy) A supermarket with prepared foods and a salad bar.

South Franklin St is Juneau's drinking sector. The (in)famous **Red Dog Saloon** (☎ 907-463-3658; 278 S Franklin St) has a sawdust floor and relic-covered walls. Hidden in **Alaskan Hotel** (☎ 907-586-1000, 800-327-9347; www.ptialaska .net/~akhotel; 167 S Franklin St) is a unique bar with historic ambience and occasional music.

Getting There & Around

The main airline serving Juneau is **Alaska Air** (☎ 800-252-7522; www.alaskaair.com). Smaller companies like **Wings of Alaska** (☎ 907-789-0790; www.wingsofalaska.com) provide service to isolated communities.

The ferry terminal is located 14 miles from downtown; **M/V LeConte** (☎ 907-465-3941) runs to Hoonah ($29, four hours), Angoon ($33, 11 hours), and Tenakee Springs ($31, eight hours), while the high-speed **M/V Fairweather** (☎ 907-465-3941) connects to Skagway ($44, 2½ hours) and Haines ($33, two hours).

Juneau's public bus system, **Capital Transit** (☎ 907-789-6901; fare $1.50; ⏱ 8am-5pm Mon-Fri), can take you from the airport to the city center, but not the ferry terminal. Numerous car-rental places offer pick up/drop off and unlimited mileage. Compacts at **Rent-A-Wreck** (☎ 907-789-4111; 888-843-4111; 2450 C Industrial Blvd) are $35, while **Evergreen Ford** (☎ 907-790-1340; 8895 Mallard St) rents them for $48.

ADMIRALTY ISLAND NATIONAL MONUMENT

Fifteen miles southeast of Juneau, this island has 1406 sq miles of designated wilderness, featuring brown bears, eagles, whales, harbor seals and sea lions. Stock up on supplies in Juneau and information from the **Juneau Ranger District office** (☎ 907-586-8790; 8465 Old Dairy Rd; ⏱ 8am-5pm Mon-Fri) in Mendenhall Valley.

The single settlement on Admiralty Island, **Angoon**, is a dry community with only one café. It's the starting point for the 32-mile Cross Admiralty Canoe Rte to Mole Harbor.

Favorite Bay Inn (☎ 907-788-3123, 800-423-3123; www.favoritebayinn.com; s/d $99/139; ✗) has rooms with shared bath, and will pick up from the ferry terminal.

The best bear-viewing area in Southeast Alaska is at **Pack Creek**, on the eastern side of Admiralty Island. The bears are most abundant July to August, when the salmon are running, and visitors can watch them feed from an observation tower. The tower is reached by a mile-long trail, usually as part of a guided tour. **Alaska Discovery** (☎ 800-586-1911; www.akdiscovery.com; 5310 Glacier Hwy, Juneau) offers a one-day tour from Juneau ($550 per person) and a three-day trip ($1050).

GLACIER BAY NATIONAL PARK & PRESERVE

Sixteen tidewater glaciers spill from the mountains and fill the sea with icebergs around the famous wilderness of **Glacier Bay National Park & Preserve**. To see the glaciers, most visitors board the **Baranof Winds** (☎ 888-8229-8687; $159) for an eight-hour cruise up the West Arm of Glacier Bay.

The only developed hiking trails are in Bartlett Cove, but there is excellent kayaking; rent equipment from **Glacier Bay Sea Kayaks** (☎ 907-697-2257; www.glacierbayseakayaks.com; single/ double kayak per day $40/50). **Alaska Discovery** (☎ 800-586-1911; www.akdiscovery.com) and **Spirit Walker Expeditions** (☎ 907-697-2266, 800-529-2937; www.sea kayakalaska.com) offer day paddles for $125.

The **park headquarters** (☎ 907-697-2230; www .nps.gov/glba; 1 Park Rd; ⏱ 8am-4:30pm Mon-Fri) in Bartlett Cove maintains a free campground and a **visitor center** (☎ 907-697-2627; ⏱ 7am-9pm) at the dock, which provides backcountry permits and maps. The park is served by the settlement of **Gustavus** (www.gustavusak.com), which has lodging, restaurants and supplies.

Glacier Bay Lodge (☎ 888-229-8687; www.visitgla cierbay.com; 199 Bartlett Cove Rd; r $180-205; ✗) is the only hotel and restaurant at Bartlett Cove.

Bear's Nest B&B (☎ 907-697-2440; www.gustavus .com/bearsnest; 2 White Dr; cabins $115; ✗), where you can stay in the Round House or an A-frame cabin, is a delightful experience. Prepare breakfast in your cabin from the organic food of your choice.

Gourmet meals are included with your stay at **Gustavus Inn** (☎ 907-697-2254, 800-649-5220; www.gustavusinn.com; 1 Mile Gustavus Rd; r $165;

⊠), while **Puffin B&B** (☎ 907-697-2260; www
.puffintravel.com; Wilson Rd; r from $100; ⊠) is the
place to rent a cabin.

A quarter-mile south of the Salmon River
Bridge is **Beartrack Mercantile** (☎ 907-697-2358;
Dock Rd; ☾ 9am-7pm Mon-Sat, 10:30am-6pm Sun),
which has groceries – but for a less expensive option, bring your own.

Alaska Airlines (☎ 800-252-7522; www.alaskaair
.com) has daily flights between Gustavus and
Juneau ($149 round-trip). The Glacier Bay
Lodge bus meets flights for $12. **Glacier Bay
Express** (☎ 907-789-0081, 888-289-0081; 13391 Glacier
Hwy, Juneau) uses a high-speed catamaran for
transport between Auke Bay and Bartlett
Cove ($149 round-trip).

HAINES

Haines is a scenic departure point for Southeast Alaska and a crucial link to the Alcan
Hwy. Every summer thousands of travelers,
particularly RVers, pass through this slice
in the mountains on their way to Canada's
Yukon Territory and Interior Alaska. The
Northwest Trading Company arrived here
in 1878, followed by missionaries, gold
prospectors and the US Army, which built
its first permanent post in Alaska, Fort Seward, in 1903. The events of WWII – and
the resulting construction of Haines Hwy
and the Alcan – meant that Haines was finally connected to the rest of America.

Collect information from the **Haines Convention & Visitors Bureau** (☎ 907-766-2234, 800-
458-3579; www.haines.ak.us; cnr 2nd Ave & Willard St;
☾ 8am-7pm Mon-Fri, 9am-6pm Sat & Sun).

Sights & Activities

The **Sheldon Museum** (☎ 907-766-2366; 11 Main
St; adult/child $3/free; ☾ 10am-5pm Mon-Fri, 2-5pm
Sat & Sun) features indigenous artifacts and
a gift shop upstairs, and gold-rush relics
downstairs. The **American Bald Eagle Foundation** (☎ 907-766-3094; 113 Haines Hwy; adult/child $3/1;
☾ 10am-6pm) displays more than 100 species
of animals, including almost two dozen eagles, in their natural habitat. For something
quirky, hit the **Hammer Museum** (☎ 907-776-
2374; 108 Main St; adult/child $3/free; ☾ 10am-5pm Mon-
Fri), a 1200-hammer monument to owner
Dave Pahl's obsession with the tool.

Get walking-tour maps of the **Fort Seward**
national historical site from the visitor
center. Within the fort, the **Alaska Indian Arts
Center** (☎ 907-766-2160; Historical Bldg 13; admission

free; ☾ 9am-5pm Mon-Fri) has carving and weaving demonstrations.

Haines offers two major hiking trail systems (the visitor center has details) and
numerous rafting trips. **Chilkat Guides** (☎ 907-
766-2491; www.raftalaska.com; adult/child $79/62) runs
a four-hour Chilkat River float, while **Alaska
Kayak Supply** (☎ 907-766-2427, 800-552-9257; www
.seakayaks.com; 425 Beach Rd; single/double kayak per day
$35/65) rents kayaks.

Sleeping

Hotel Hälsingland (☎ 907-766-2000, 800-542-6363;
www.hotelhalsingland.com; 13 Fort Seward Dr; r $69-109;
⊠) Housed in a classic, recently renovated
building with a pleasant restaurant and bar.
Some rooms have fireplaces and claw-foot
bathtubs.

Fort Seward Lodge (☎ 800-478-7772; www.ftseward
lodge.com; 39 Mud Bay Rd; s/d with shared bath $50/60, with
private bath $70/80; ⊠) Features a large restau-
rant, cocktail lounge and some of the most
affordable rooms in Haines.

Captain's Choice Motel (☎ 907-766-3111, 800-
478-2345; www.capchoice.com; 108 2nd Ave; s/d $107/117;
⊠ 🖳) Nicest motel in town, with a huge
sun deck that overlooks the bay.

On the Beach Inn (☎ 907-766-2131, 800-766-3992;
www.onthebeachinn.com; 6.5 Mile Lutak Rd; r $75-125,
cabins $65; ⊠) Near the ferry terminal, this
B&B has a great view of Lynn Canal and a
long porch to enjoy them from.

For a cabin in a wooded setting, head out
of town to **Bear Creek Cabins & Hostel** (☎ 907-
766-2259; www.bearcreekcabinsalaska.com; Small Tract
Rd; campsites/dm/cabins $14/18/48; ⊠) or **Salmon
Run Campground** (☎ 907-766-3240; www.salmonrun
adventures.com; 6.5 Mile Lutak Rd; campsites/RV sites
$14/26, cabins $55-65).

Eating & Drinking

Chilkat Restaurant & Bakery (☎ 907-766-3653;
Dalton St at 5th Ave; breakfast $5-8, lunch $6-8; ☾ 7am-
3pm Mon-Tue & Thu-Sat; ⊠) Follow your nose to
this bakery, which is a local favorite for its
homemade pies and soups.

Fireweed Restaurant (☎ 907-766-3838; Blacksmith
St; pasta $13-19, pizza $10-20; ☾ 11am-10pm Tue-Sat;
⊠) A bright, laid-back bistro with produce
straight from the restaurant's own garden.

Grizzly Greg's Pizzeria (☎ 907-766-3622; 126
Main St; small pizzas $12; ☾ 11am-9pm; ⊠) The
best pizza in town; try the Grizzly Combo
calzone stuffed with eight toppings. Big
enough to feed a grizzly.

Mountain Market & Deli (☎ 907-766-3340; 151 3rd Ave S; sandwiches $6.25; ⊗ 7am-7pm Mon-Fri, 7am-6pm Sat & Sun; ☒) Great coffee, innovative wraps, cool atmosphere.

Haines is a hard-drinking town: **Fogcutter Bar** (☎ 907-766-2555; Main St) and **Harbor Bar** (☎ 907-766-2444; 2 Front St) get lively at night, while Fort Seward has the more serene **Hotel Hälsingland Pub** (☎ 907-766-2000; 13 Fort Seward Dr).

Getting There & Away

Several air-charter companies service Haines, the cheapest being **Wings of Alaska** (☎ 907-789-0790; www.wingsofalaska.com). Also check with **LAB Flying Service** (☎ 907-766-2222, 800-426-0543; www.labflying.com), which offers an hour of Glacier Bay National Park flightseeing for $140 (minimum two people).

Chilkat Cruises (☎ 907-766-3395, 888-766-2103; one way adult/child $22/12) will get you to and from Skagway.

Eagle Nest Car Rentals (☎ 907-766-2891, 800-354-6009; 1183 Haines Hwy), in the Eagle Nest Motel, has cars available for $45 to $50 with 100 miles included.

AROUND HAINES

The 75-sq-mile **Alaska Chilkat Bald Eagle Preserve**, along the Chilkat River, protects the world's largest-known gathering of bald eagles. The greatest numbers of birds are spotted in December and January, but you can see eagles here any time during summer. Lookouts on the Haines Hwy between Miles 18 and 22 allow motorists to glimpse the birds. **Alaska Nature Tours** (☎ 907-766-2876; www.kcd.com/aknature; 103 2nd Ave S) offers a three-hour tour of the preserve (adult/child $55/40).

SKAGWAY

The northern terminus of the Alaska Marine Hwy, Skagway was a gold-rush town infamous for its lawlessness. In 1887 the population was two; 10 years later it was Alaska's largest city, with 20,000 residents. Today, Skagway survives entirely on tourism and gets packed when the cruise ships pull in and passengers converge on the town like in the gold-rush days.

The **Skagway Convention & Visitors Bureau** (☎ 907-983-2854, 888-762-1898; www.skagway.com; cnr Broadway St & 2nd Ave; ⊗ 8am-6pm) is in the Arctic Brotherhood Hall – just look for the thousands of driftwood pieces tacked on to

its front. The **Klondike Gold Rush National Historical Park Visitors Center** (☎ 907-983-2921, 907-983-9223; 154 Broadway St; ⊗ 8am-6pm) provides information on the Chilkoot Trail (Alaska's most popular hiking trail because it was used by stampeders during the Klondike Gold Rush), local trails and camping.

Sights & Activities

The **Klondike Gold Rush National Historical Park** is a seven-block corridor along Broadway St that features 15 restored buildings, false fronts and wooden sidewalks from Skagway's golden era as a boomtown. Thanks to the cruise ships, it's the most popular national park in Alaska. To best appreciate this amazing moment in Skagway's history, join a free, ranger-led walking tour that begins at the park visitor center on the hour from 9am to 3pm, except at noon.

The **Skagway Museum** (☎ 907-983-2420; Skagway City Hall, cnr 7th Ave & Spring St; adult/child $2/1; ⊗ 9am-5pm Mon-Fri, noon-4pm Sat & Sun) was renovated in 2002 and its gold-rush relics are now some of the most interesting exhibits in town. **Moore's Cabin** (cnr 5th Ave & Spring St; admission free; ⊗ 10am-5pm) is the town's oldest building, while **Mascot Saloon** (290 Broadway St; admission free; ⊗ 8am-6pm) is a museum devoted to Skagway's heyday as the 'roughest place in the world.' The best tour is a three-hour Summit Excursion on the **White Pass & Yukon Railroad** (☎ 907-983-2217, 800-343-7373; www.whitepassrailroad.com; 231 2nd Ave; adult/child $89/45), which climbs the high White Pass in a historic narrow-gauge train.

Sleeping

At the White House (☎ 907-983-9000; www.atthewhitehouse.com; cnr Main St & 8th Ave; r $120-145; ☒) Step into the past with a night at this 10-room inn, built in 1902 and filled with antiques. The rooms are comfortable and every morning begins with a delicious breakfast buffet.

Skagway Bungalows (☎ 907-983-2986; www.aptalaska.net/~saldi; Mile 1 Dyea Rd; cabins $99; ☒) A world away from the bustling downtown (but only a mile out from the road) are these log cabins nestled in the woods. In the morning a basket of baked goods is delivered to your porch.

Sgt Preston's Lodge (☎ 907-983-2521, 866-983-2521; 370 6th Ave; s $70-108, d $80-118; ☒ ▢) A quiet, single-level motel just far enough

ALASKA

from Broadway St to escape most of the cruise-ship crush.

Near the ferry terminal is **Pullen Creek RV Park** (☎ 907-983-2768, 800-936-3731; www.pullen creekrv.com; campsites/RV sites $14/25), while **Skagway Mountain View RV Park** (☎ 907-983-3333; 1450 Broadway St; campsites $15, RV sites $18-26) has laundry facilities.

Eating & Drinking

Sweet Tooth Café (☎ 907-983-2405; cnr Broadway St & 3rd Ave; breakfast & lunch $5-9; ⏱ 6am-2pm; ✗) You'll get a pile of pancakes here.

Glacial Smoothies & Espresso (☎ 907-983-3223; 336 3rd Ave; breakfast $4-7; ⏱ 6am-6pm; ✗) Serves lattes and great Belgian waffles, and has Internet access.

Stowaway Café (☎ 907-983-3463; 205 Congress Way; dinner $16-21; ⏱ 4-10pm ✗) Funky and fantastic, near the Harbor Master's office.

Sabros (☎ 907-983-2469; Broadway St; lunch $6-9; ⏱ 6am-4pm; ✗) This small café – just four tables outside, four inside – is easy to miss but shouldn't be. Its vegetarian choices are extensive and its halibut chowder is the best on Broadway.

Red Onion Saloon (☎ 907-983-2222; 205 Broadway St) This former brothel is now Skagway's liveliest bar. Naturally.

Getting There & Away

LAB Flying Service (☎ 907-983-2471; www.labflying .com), **Wings of Alaska** (☎ 907-983-2442; www.wings ofalaska.com) and **Skagway Air** (☎ 907-983-2218; www.skagwayair.com) have regular flights between Skagway and Juneau, Haines and Glacier Bay; Skagway Air is generally cheapest, at $90, $45 and $120 respectively.

Alaska Marine Highway (☎ 907-983-2941, 800-642-0066; www.ferryalaska.com) has ferries departing every day in summer, and **Chilkat Cruises & Tours** (☎ 888-766-2103; www.chilkatcruises .com; one way adult/child $22/12) runs twice daily to Haines.

Sourdough Car Rentals (☎ 907-983-2523; cnr Broadway St & 6th Ave; ⏱ 8am-5pm) has both cars ($50) and bikes ($10).

Alaska Direct (☎ 800-770-6652) connects Skagway with Fairbanks three times a week ($220), with buses stopping at Whitehorse along the way ($55).

The **White Pass & Yukon Railroad** (☎ 800-343-7373; www.whitepassrailroad.com) goes to Fraser, British Columbia, where there's a bus connection to Whitehorse (adult/child $95/48).

SOUTHCENTRAL ALASKA

Southcentral Alaska has mountains, glaciers, good fishing, great hiking and state ferries, just like the Southeast. But it has one thing that most of Alaska does not: roads between towns and other regions of the state. This alone makes Southcentral Alaska one of the most accessible and popular areas for travelers.

ANCHORAGE

Anchorage offers the comforts (and challenges) of a large US city, within 30 minutes' drive of the Alaskan wilderness. Founded in 1914 as a work camp for the Alaska Railroad, the city was devastated by the 1964 Good Friday earthquake. The oil boom made it an industry headquarters, and oil money paid for everything from concert halls to 122 miles of bike paths. Today almost half the state's residents live in or around the city, as Anchorage has become the economic and political heart of Alaska.

Orientation

A surveyor was obviously in charge of laying out Anchorage. Its downtown is pedestrian-friendly, with numbered avenues running east–west and lettered streets north–south. East of A St, street names continue alphabetically, beginning with Barrow.

MAPS

The best free city map is the *Alaska Activities Map*, distributed all over town. For more detail there's Rand McNally's *Anchorage* ($4). The best selection of maps is at Cook Inlet Book Company (below) or the Alaska Public Lands Information Center (opposite).

Information

BOOKSTORES

Cook Inlet Book Company (☎ 907-258-4544; 415 W 5th Ave) Downtown bookstore with one of the best selections of Alaska-related titles anywhere.

Title Wave Books (☎ 888-598-9283; Northern Lights Center, 1360 W Northern Lights Blvd) A huge bookstore with an Internet café, specializing in used and bargain books.

ANCHORAGE IN...

Two Days

After a stick-to-yer-ribs breakfast at **Snow City Café** (p1102), hike up **Flattop Mountain** (p1100) to get a lay of the land or possibly a peak of Mt McKinley. Then let yourself wander for hours in the excellent **Anchorage Museum of History & Art** (below). Enjoy an evening stroll to the monuments and parks on downtown's west side before settling into one of the many nearby gourmet and ethnic eating spots. Finally, join Alaskans making fun of themselves in the 'Whale-Fat Follies' at **Mr Whitekeys Fly by Nite Club** (p1103).

On the second day, drive down scenic Seward Hwy to **Portage Glacier** (p1104) and explore the visitor center or join a cruise to the retreating ice floe. Along the way, look for beluga whales in Turnagain Arm. In the afternoon, ride the tram at **Alyeska Resort** (p1103) and wander in the alpine region. Finish the day off with wine back at **Seven Glaciers** (p1104) on top of Mt Alyeska.

EMERGENCY

Anchorage Police (☎ 907-786-8500; 4501 S Bragaw St) For nonemergencies.

Crisis hotline (☎ 907-276-7273) In the rare event of sexual assault, contact this 24-hour line.

INTERNET ACCESS

Cyber City (☎ 277-7601; 1441 W Northern Lights Blvd; per hr $4) Open to 2am for late-night gamers.

ZJ Loussac Public Library (☎ 907-343-2975; 3600 Denali St) Free Internet access.

MEDIA

Anchorage Daily News (www.adn.com) This top-rate paper has the largest daily circulation in the state.

Anchorage Press (www.anchoragepress.com) The city's free weekly newspaper is your source for events listings and social commentary.

KNBA 90.3 For Native Alaskan music and current events.

KRUA 88.1 For local news.

MEDICAL SERVICES

Alaska Regional Hospital (☎ 907-276-1131; 2801 DeBarr Rd) For emergency care.

Physician referral service (☎ 800-265-8624) Free service.

Providence Alaska Medical Center (☎ 907-562-2211; 3200 Providence Dr)

MONEY

Key Bank (☎ 907-257-5500, 800-539-2968; 601 W 5th Ave; ☽ 10am-5pm Mon-Fri) Only exchanges Canadian dollars.

Wells Fargo (☎ 800-869-3557; 301 W Northern Lights Blvd; ☽ 10am-6pm Mon-Fri, 10am-3pm Sat) Can exchange the most common foreign currencies.

POST

Post office (344 W 3rd Ave) Downtown in the village at Ship Creek Center.

TOURIST INFORMATION

Alaska Public Lands Information Center (☎ 907-271-2737; www.nps.gov/aplic/center; 605 W 4th Ave, Suite 105; ☽ 9am-5pm) Has park, trail and cabin information as well as excellent displays.

Log Cabin & Downtown Visitor Information Center (☎ 907-274-3531 for recorded event information, 907-276-3200; www.anchorage.net; 524 W 4th Ave; ☽ 7:30am-7pm) Distributes a visitor guide and walking-tour map.

Sights & Activities

The **Alaska Native Heritage Center** (☎ 800-315-6608; 8800 Heritage Center Dr; adult/child $21/16; ☽ 9am-6pm) is spread over 26 acres, and has a theater and exhibition space devoted to the history, lifestyle and arts of Native Alaskans. In open studios, artists carve baleen or sew skin-boats, and surrounding a small lake in the center are five replica village settings – Athabascan, Yupik, Inupiat, Aleut and Tlingit/Haida – with Native Alaskans involved in such traditional activities as splitting and drying salmon, tanning hides or building kayaks.

The impressive **Anchorage Museum of History & Art** (☎ 907-343-4326; 121 W 7th Ave; adult/child $6.50/2; ☽ 9am-6pm) is the largest museum in Alaska, with a permanent collection of 17,500 objects. The much smaller **Heritage Library Museum** (☎ 907-265-2834; 301 W Northern Lights Blvd; admission free; ☽ noon-5pm Mon-Fri) displays Native Alaskan costumes, weapons and artwork.

Another excellent Native Alaskan culture experience is the **Alaska Native Medical Center** (☎ 907-563-2662; 4315 Diplomace Dr; admission free; ☽ 6am-9pm), near Tudor Rd and Boniface Parkway, which has a collection of artifacts. The 1st-floor **craft shop** (☎ 907-729-1122;

ANCHORAGE

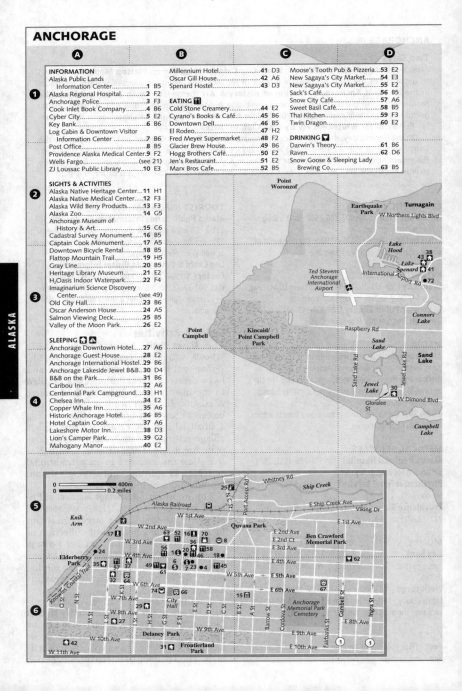

INFORMATION
Alaska Public Lands
  Information Center.........................1 B5
Alaska Regional Hospital.................2 F2
Anchorage Police...........................3 F3
Cook Inlet Book Company..............4 B6
Cyber City.......................................5 E2
Key Bank...6 B6
Log Cabin & Downtown Visitor
  Information Center 7 B6
Post Office..8 B5
Providence Alaska Medical Center.9 F2
Wells Fargo..............................(see 21)
ZJ Loussac Public Library.............10 E3

SIGHTS & ACTIVITIES
Alaska Native Heritage Center...11 H1
Alaska Native Medical Center.....12 F3
Alaska Wild Berry Products.........13 F3
Alaska Zoo..................................14 G5
Anchorage Museum of
  History & Art.............................15 C6
Cadastral Survey Monument......16 B5
Captain Cook Monument...........17 A5
Downtown Bicycle Rental...........18 B5
Flattop Mountain Trail................19 H5
Gray Line....................................20 B5
Heritage Library Museum...........21 E5
H₂Oasis Indoor Waterpark..........22 F4
Imaginarium Science Discovery
  Center................................(see 49)
Old City Hall...............................23 B6
Oscar Anderson House................24 A5
Salmon Viewing Deck.................25 B5
Valley of the Moon Park.............26 E2

SLEEPING
Anchorage Downtown Hotel.......27 A6
Anchorage Guest House..............28 E2
Anchorage International Hostel...29 B6
Anchorage Lakeside Jewel B&B..30 D4
B&B on the Park.........................31 B6
Caribou Inn.................................32 A6
Centennial Park Campground.....33 H1
Chelsea Inn.................................34 E2
Copper Whale Inn.......................35 A6
Historic Anchorage Hotel............36 B5
Hotel Captain Cook....................37 A6
Lakeshore Motor Inn...................38 D3
Lion's Camper Park.....................39 G2
Mahogany Manor........................40 E2

Millennium Hotel........................41 D3
Oscar Gill House.........................42 A6
Spenard Hostel...........................43 D3

EATING
Cold Stone Creamery...................44 E2
Cyrano's Books & Café................45 B6
Downtown Dell...........................46 B5
El Rodeo.....................................47 H2
Fred Meyer Supermarket.............48 F2
Glacier Brew House.....................49 B6
Hogg Brothers Café.....................50 B5
Jen's Restaurant..........................51 E2
Marx Bros Cafe...........................52 B5

Moose's Tooth Pub & Pizzeria....53 E2
New Sagaya's City Market...........54 E3
New Sagaya's City Market...........55 E2
Sack's Café..................................56 B5
Snow City Café............................57 A6
Sweet Basil Café.........................58 F3
Thai Kitchen................................59 F3
Twin Dragon................................60 E2

DRINKING
Darwin's Theory..........................61 B6
Raven..62 D6
Snow Goose & Sleeping Lady
  Brewing Co................................63 B5

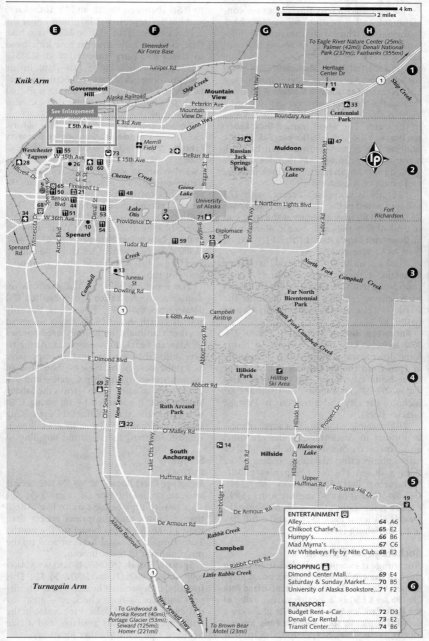

ALASKA

ENTERTAINMENT 😃
Alley...**64** A6
Chilkoot Charlie's...................**65** E2
Humpy's....................................**66** B6
Mad Myrna's............................**67** C6
Mr Whitekeys Fly by Nite Club..**68** E2

SHOPPING 🛍
Dimond Center Mall................**69** E4
Saturday & Sunday Market.......**70** B5
University of Alaska Bookstore..**71** F2

TRANSPORT
Budget Rent-a-Car...................**72** D3
Denali Car Rental.....................**73** E2
Transit Center..........................**74** B6

10am-2pm Mon-Fri) sells fine pieces on consignment, and most of the money goes back to the person who carved the ivory earrings, wove the baleen basket or sewed the sealskin slippers.

The **Cadastral Survey Monument** (cnr E St & W 2nd Ave) traces Anchorage's development as a city. Nearby, **Captain Cook Monument** (Resolution Park) marks the 200th anniversary of Cook's visit to Cook Inlet and offers great views of the water. The wood-framed **Oscar Anderson House** (☎ 907-274-2336; Elderberry Park, 420 M St; adult/child $3/1; ⊙ noon-4pm) was built in 1915, a year after Anchorage was founded, and its guided tours are an interesting look into the early days of Alaska.

The city is a cyclist's dream, with 122 miles of paved paths; the 11-mile **Tony Knowles Coastal Trail**, which begins at the west end of 2nd Ave, is the most scenic. Rent bikes at **Downtown Bicycle Rental** (☎ 907-279-5293; cnr W 4th Ave & C St; per day $29).

Alaska's most-climbed peak is **Flattop Mountain**, a three- to five-hour, 3.4-mile round-trip from a trailhead on the outskirts of Anchorage. Maps are available at the Alaska Public Lands Information Center (p1097).

Anchorage Historic Properties (☎ 907-274-3600; adult/child $5/1) takes visitors on hour-long downtown walking tours beginning at 1pm from the **Old City Hall** (W 4th Ave). For three-hour city tours ($46), try **Gray Line** (☎ 907-277-5581; 745 W 4th Ave). Its 10-hour tour includes the city and a trip out to Portage Glacier ($99).

'Flightseeing' – touring in a small plane – is popular in Anchorage. Tours are short and expensive, but if time is limited they offer a glimpse into Alaska's grandeur. More than a dozen charter companies peddle flightseeing; **Rust's Flying Service** (☎ 907-243-1595, 800-544-2299) has 30-minute tours ($89), a three-hour flight to view Mt McKinley in Denali National Park ($269) and a full day of fly-in fishing ($369).

Anchorage for Children

Anchorage is exceptionally kid-friendly – a third of the city's 125 free parks boast play-scapes. Close to downtown, **Frontierland Park** (cnr 10th Ave & E St) is a local favorite. **Valley of the Moon Park** (cnr Arctic Blvd & W 17th St) makes a delightful picnic spot. **Delaney Park**, known locally as the 'Park Strip,' stretches from A

to P Sts (between W 9th and W 10th Aves) and has an impressive playground near the corner of E St. If the Flattop Mountain hike (left) is overly ambitious for your kids, head to **Alaska Wild Berry Products** (☎ 907-562-8858; 5525 Juneau St; admission free; ⊙ 10am-11pm). Inside the sprawling gift shop is a chocolate waterfall; outside there's a short nature trail that leads to a handful of reindeer that kids can feed and pet.

To add some science to Alaska's nature, check out the **Imaginarium Science Discovery Center** (☎ 907-276-3179; 737 W 5th Ave; adult/child $5.50/5; ⊙ 10am-6pm Mon-Sat, noon-5pm Sun). This award-winning center features creative, hands-on exhibits that explain the northern lights, earthquakes, oil exploration and other Alaskan topics. Had enough learning? Nothing will make your kids' adrenaline pump like the Master Blaster Water Coaster at the **H₂Oasis Indoor Waterpark** (☎ 907-522-4420; 1520 O'Malley Rd; adult/child $20/15; ⊙ 10am-10pm). Feel free to just watch from the grown-ups-only hot tubs.

The unique wildlife of the Arctic is on display at the **Alaska Zoo** (☎ 907-346-1088; 4731 O'Malley Rd; adult/child $9/5; ⊙ 10am-5pm), the only zoo in North America that specializes in northern animals, including three species of Alaskan bears, snow leopards, Amur tigers and Tibetan yaks. Just as impressive as a polar bear is the view of thousands of salmon spawning up Ship Creek – and anglers trying to catch them – from the **Salmon Viewing Deck**. It's reached by following C St north from the Alaska Railroad Depot. King salmon arrive in early June; silvers follow in August. So many fish it's mind-boggling.

Sleeping

BUDGET

Anchorage Guest House (☎ 907-274-0408; www.akhouse.com; 2001 Hillcrest Dr; dm $28, r from $78; ✉ ▯) This beautiful place feels more like a B&B than a hostel, and the prices reflect that. Rent a bike ($2.50 per hour) for the nearby Tony Knowles Coastal Trail, or soak up the midnight sun in the sunroom.

Spenard Hostel (☎ 907-248-5036; www.alaskahostel.org; 2845 W 42nd Pl; dm/r $18/72; ✉ ▯) This friendly, independent hostel is near the airport and has 24-hour check-in – great for red-eye arrivals to Alaska. Free coffee in the morning, bike rentals available and a ride board to find a lift to other locations.

Anchorage International Hostel (☎ 907-276-3635; www.anchorageinternationalhostel.org; 700 H St; dm/r $20/50; ✗) A cheap but colorless downtown option with less-than-salubrious quarters.

The city maintains two campgrounds. The **Centennial Park Campground** (☎ 907-343-6986; 8300 Glenn Hwy; campsites $17) is 4.5 miles from downtown, and **Lion's Camper Park** (☎ 907-343-6992; 5300 DeBarr Rd; campsites $17) is in Russian Jack Springs Park .

MIDRANGE

B&Bs (from $90) have blossomed; inquire at the visitor center or try the **Anchorage Alaska B&B Association** (☎ 907-272-5909, 888-584-5147; www.anchorage-bnb.com).

Oscar Gill House (☎ 907-279-1344; www.oscargill.com; 1344 W 10th Ave; r $99-125; ✗) This historic home features a fantastic breakfast and free bikes. Book this one months in advance.

Chelsea Inn (☎ 907-276-5002; 3836 Spenard Rd; s/d with shared bath $69/79, with private bath $79/89; ▣ P) This small European-style inn has comfortable rooms with a communal kitchen, Internet access, continental breakfast and free transportation from the airport. What more could you want?

Anchorage Lakeside Jewel B&B (☎ 907-245-7321, 866-539-3555; www.anchoragelakesidejewel.com; 8840 Gloralee St; d $99-139; ▣ ✗) Overlooking Jewel Lake, you can swim, kayak and fish without leaving this B&B. Or just lounge in the large common area and watch the sunset.

B&B on the Park (☎ 907-277-0878, 800-353-0878; www.bedandbreakfastonthepark.net; 602 W 10th Ave; r $125; ✗) All five rooms in this beautifully restored 1946 log church have their own private bath. Family-style breakfast is served at 8am sharp, so no lollygagging in bed!

Caribou Inn (☎ 907-272-0444, 800-272-5878; 501 L St; r with/without bath $99/89; ✗ P) Ideal downtown location, and the rooms, though small and a bit worn around the edges, are definitely acceptable. There's free transportation from the airport.

Brown Bear Motel (☎ 907-653-7000; Mile 103 Seward Hwy; r from $52; ✗) Well out of town, the rooms are clean, but get noisy when the adjacent Brown Bear Saloon is hopping. Tip a few with the locals and then hit the sack.

Other recommendations:

Lakeshore Motor Inn (☎ 907-248-3485, 800-770-3000; www.lakeshoremotorinn.com; 3009 Lakeshore Dr; r $129-159; ✗ P) Laundry facilities and free airport transportation.

Anchorage Downtown Hotel (☎ 907-258-7669; www.anchoragedowntownhotel.com; 826 K St; r $139-169; ✗ ▣ P) Discounts if you stay three nights or longer.

TOP END

Mahogany Manor (☎ 907-278-1111, 888-777-0346; www.mahoganymanor.com; 204 E 15th Ave; d $199-249, ste $249-339; ✗) Perched above the city, the manor is surrounded by woods that obscure the city's skyline in summer. The common areas – replete with floor-to-ceiling windows, numerous decks, huge fireplaces and 19ft whirlpool – are a tad more impressive than the rooms themselves.

Millennium Hotel (☎ 907-243-2300, 866-866-8086; www.millenniumhotels.com; 4800 Spenard Rd; r $260-290; ✗ ▣ ✍) Four miles from downtown and right on Lake Spenard, the world's busiest floatplane base, this sprawling hotel has rustic-chic rooms and a lobby filled with stuffed bears. Babysitting service, 24-hour room service, even a private floatplane dock, are a few of the countless perks.

Hotel Captain Cook (☎ 907-276-6000, 800-843-1950; www.captaincook.com; cnr W 4th Ave & K St; r $255-405; ▣ ✍) The swanky grand dame of Anchorage pampers guests with hot tubs, fitness clubs, a beauty salon, Web TV and the famed Crow's Nest Bar, where you gaze upon Cook Inlet in one direction and the Chugach Mountains in the other. For the price, the standard rooms aren't all that swanky though.

Historic Anchorage Hotel (☎ 907-272-4553, 800-544-0988; www.historicanchoragehotel.com; 330 E St; r $209-249; ▣ ✗) Anchorage's premier boutique hotel is in the heart of downtown, and combines gracious service with its historic past. Will Rogers and Wiley Post stayed here two days before their fateful flight to Barrow.

Copper Whale Inn (☎ 907-258-7999; www.copperwhale.com; cnr W 5th Ave & L St; r $145-185; ✗) Just blocks from the city center, the rooms are no-frills but tidy, and your view of Cook Inlet and the Alaska Range is the highlight of breakfast.

Eating

Anchorage boasts a variety of international cuisines you'll be hard-pressed to find in the Bush. Fill up while you can!

BUDGET

Hogg Brothers Café (☎ 907-276-9649; 1049 W Northern Lights Blvd; breakfast & lunch $6-9; ⏲ 6:30am-4pm; ✗) This bizarre, pig-obsessed joint serves

THE AUTHOR'S CHOICE

Snow City Café (☎ 907-272-2489; 1034 W 4th Ave; mains $5-10; ☺ 7am-4pm Mon-Fri; ✗) Serves up wholesome, slightly trendy grub, and you can get breakfast all day. The bread is crusty and homemade, the cups of coffee are generous and their Ship Creek Benedict (two poached eggs and salmon cakes on an English muffin) is the Alaskan way to start the day. Locals invade on Wednesday evenings to play Irish music and drink beer.

all-day breakfasts, including 20 kinds of omelettes.

Cyrano's Books & Café (☎ 907-274-2599; 413 D St; meals $5-9; ☺ noon-10pm Tue-Sun; ✗) This is the place to lose yourself in a paperback over French and Mediterranean sweets, soups, salads and wraps. Or come in the evening for a glass of wine and poetry, or a performance in the Cyrano's Off-Center Playhouse ($15).

Sweet Basil Café (☎ 907-274-0070; 335 E St; sandwiches $7; ☺ 8am-3pm Mon-Fri, 9am-3pm Sat; ✗) Inexpensive, healthy cuisine (as well as decidedly unhealthy but recommended desserts), fruit smoothies and coffee in the heart of the tourist quarter.

Downtown Deli (☎ 907-276-7116; 525 425 W 4th Ave; dinner $12-16; ☺ 6am-10pm; ✗) This fabulous spot, owned by former governor Tony Knowles, is famed for its reindeer stew and Philly cheesesteak.

Cold Stone Creamery (☎ 907-569-0305; 2813 Dawson St) Deliciously explains why Alaskans eat more ice cream per capita than anyone else in the USA.

New Sagaya's City Market (3900 W 13th Ave) Specializing in Asian fare, this eclectic upscale grocery store stocks lots of organic goodies and has a great deli. There's another location at 3700 Old Seward Hwy.

Fred Meyer supermarket (1000 E Northern Lights Blvd) The widest selection and best prices in town.

MIDRANGE

El Rodeo (☎ 907-338-5393; 385 Muldoon Rd; lunch & dinner $7-15; ☺ 11am-9:30pm Mon-Thu, 11am-10pm Fri, 11:30am-10pm Sat, 11:30am-9pm Sun; ✗) This little Mexican restaurant gets packed at night, but the wait for a table is well worth it. For more than 10 years this has been the best and most affordable Tex-Mex in Anchorage.

Sack's Café (☎ 907-274-4022; 328 G St; lunch $9-13, dinner $18-40; ☺ 11am-2:30pm & 5-9:30pm Mon-Thu, 11am-2:30pm & 5-10:30pm Fri & Sat, 10:30am-3pm Sun; ✗) Call it Asian-Mediterranean-Alaskan fusion. Lunch items include tiger prawns and avocado sandwich, and chicken curry. For dinner try the popular chicken and Alaskan scallops with shitake mushrooms and Asian black bean salsa.

Moose's Tooth Pub & Pizzeria (☎ 907-258-2537; 3300 Old Seward Hwy; pizza $7-25; ☺ 11am-11pm Mon-Thu, 11am-midnight Fri & Sat, noon-11pm Sun; ✗) Take your pick from the impressive menu of veg, meat or seafood pizzas. Wash your pizza down with one of the award-winning brews on tap.

Twin Dragon (☎ 907-276-7535; 612 E 15th Ave; lunch/dinner $9/12; ☺ 11am-10pm Mon-Thu, 11am-10:30pm Fri & Sat, noon-9:30pm Sun; ✗) The all-you-can-eat Mongolian barbecue buffet is a bargain.

Thai Kitchen (☎ 907-561-0082; 3405 Tudor Rd; dinner $8-12; ☺ 11am-3pm & 5-9pm; ✗) This kid-friendly place comes highly recommended, with more than 100 items on the menu, dozens of which are vegetarian.

TOP END

Marx Bros Cafe (☎ 907-278-2133; 627 W 3rd Ave; mains $29-50; ☺ 5:30-10pm Tue-Sat; ✗) Soak up the views of Cook Inlet while enjoying Anchorage's finest dining with all the trimmings: white tablecloths, stemware filled with your choice of 500 vintages, macadamia-crusted halibut and justly famous Caesar salad.

Jen's Restaurant (☎ 907-561-5367; 701 W 36th Ave; dinner $18-36; ☺ 11:30am-2pm Mon-Fri, 6-10pm Tue-Sat; ✗) Innovative, Scandinavian-accented cuisine emphasizing fresh ingredients and elaborate presentation. There's also a tapas bar.

Glacier Brew House (☎ 907-274-2739; 737 W 5th Ave; dinner $17-26; ☺ 11am-9:30pm Mon, 11am-10pm Tue-Thu, 11am-11pm Fri & Sat, noon-9:30pm Sun; ✗) Sample handcrafted beers, slurp down seafood pastas and gnaw on wood-grilled chops and ribs.

Drinking

Raven (☎ 907-276-9672; 708 E 4th Ave) Mingle with the locals over a game of pool at this well-lit but smoky neighborhood hangout. The perfect place to kick off your evening.

Snow Goose & Sleeping Lady Brewing Co (☎ 907-277-7727; 717 W 3rd Ave) If the sun is setting over

Cook Inlet and the Alaska Range, head to the rooftop deck of this brewpub. Only the beer is better than the view.

Darwin's Theory (☎ 907-277-5322; 426 G St) People-watching is the activity of choice at this favorite local bar, with free popcorn and a good mixed crowd.

Entertainment

Check the *Anchorage Press* and Friday's *Anchorage Daily News* for the latest entertainment listings.

Mr Whitekeys Fly by Nite Club (☎ 907-279-7726; 3300 Spenard Rd; ✗) Best known for the low-brow but uproarious 'Whale-Fat Follies' musical act ($13 to $19, reservations required) and an infatuation with Spam. It also features jazz, blues and rock.

Mad Myrna's (☎ 907-276-9762; 530 E 5th Ave; cover Sat & Sun $5-10; ✗) A fun, cruisy bar with line-dancing Thursday, drag shows on Friday and dance music most other nights after 9pm.

Chilkoot Charlie's (☎ 907-272-1010; 2435 Spenard Rd) 'Koots,' as locals call this beloved landmark, is big and brash, with 10 bars, four dance floors and sawdust everywhere. It's amazing the bands that have played here: Doobie Brothers, Blue Oyster Cult and Green Day among others.

Alley (☎ 907-646-2222; 900 W 5th Ave; cover $3) Has a dance floor presided over by Anchorage DJs spinning techno, trance and hip-hop.

Humpy's (☎ 907-276-2337; 610 W 6th Ave) Live music nightly from around 9pm, running the gamut from acoustic folk to ska to disco retrospective. All of it can be enjoyed with more than 40 beers on tap, the most of any bar in Anchorage.

Shopping

Dimond Center Mall (☎ 907-344-2581; 800 E Dimond Blvd; ☽ 10am-9pm Mon-Fri, 10am-7pm Sat, noon-6pm Sun) Pretty much every consumer item you'd need.

Saturday & Sunday Market (☎ 907-272-5634; www.anchoragemarkets.com; cnr W 3rd Ave & E St; ☽ 10am-6pm Sat & Sun) A fun place for souvenir shopping, cheap food and local entertainment.

REI (☎ 907-272-4565; 1200 W Northern Lights Blvd; ☽ 10am-9pm Mon-Sat, 10am-6pm Sun) There are scores of wilderness outfitters, but this shop has a huge selection of backpacking, kayaking and camping gear.

University of Alaska Bookstore (☎ 907-786-1151; 2905 Providence Dr; ☽ 8:30am-7pm Mon-Thu, 8:30am-6pm

Fri) Head here for clothes; it has an interesting selection you won't find anywhere else.

Getting There & Around

Ted Stevens Anchorage International Airport (☎ 907-266-2525; www.dot.state.ak.us/anc/index.shtml) has frequent inter- and intrastate flights. Terminals are off International Airport Rd. **Alaska Airlines** (☎ 800-252-7522; www.alaskaair.com) flies to 19 Alaskan towns, including Fairbanks, Juneau, Nome and Barrow. **Era Aviation** (☎ 800-866-8394; www.flyera.com) flies to Cordova, Valdez, Kodiak and Homer. **Pen Air** (☎ 800-448-4226; www.penair.com) serves southwest Alaska.

Alaska Shuttle (☎ 907-338-8888) offers door-to-door transportation between the airport and downtown (one to three people $12) and outlying areas of Anchorage (one to three people $20). The city's bus service (People Mover) picks up from both terminals (bus 7A) on a route that heads back downtown.

Denali Car Rental (☎ 907-276-1230; 1209 Gambell St; ☽ 9am-5pm Mon-Fri, 10am-4pm Sat) also has subcompacts (daily/weekly $45/270) with 150 miles included. Most other car-rental companies, including **Budget Rent-A-Car** (☎ 907-243-0150, 800-248-3765; 511 Spenard Rd), charge $55 per day. Avoid picking up a car at the airport as you will be hit with a 33% rental tax, as opposed to 18% in the city.

Alaska/Yukon Trails (☎ 800-770-7275) goes to Fairbanks ($79, nine hours) via Denali ($59, five hours) and Dawson City in Canada ($219, 19 hours). **Seward Bus Lines** (☎ 907-563-0800; www.sewardbuslines.net) goes to Seward ($40, 2½ hours), while **Homer Stage Lines** (☎ 907-868-3914) will take you to Homer ($55, five hours).

Alaska Railroad (☎ 907-265-2494, 800-544-0552; www.akrr.com) goes south to Whittier ($52, 2½ hours) and Seward ($59, four hours), and north to Denali ($129, eight hours) and Fairbanks ($179, 12 hours).

People Mover (☎ 907-343-6543; www.peoplemover.org; adult/child $1.50/75¢) is the local bus service; its main terminal is at the **Transit Center** (cnr W 6th Ave & G St).

AROUND ANCHORAGE

Seward Hwy runs south of Anchorage, squeezed between the mountains and Turnagain Arm, where motorists often pull over to watch beluga whales. At **Alyeska Resort** (☎ 907-754-1111; www.alyeskaresort.com; 1000 Arlberg

Ave; r $175-210; 🖥 🍴 ⊠) in Girdwood, you can ride a tram to explore the alpine area, and then enjoy its mountaintop **Seven Glaciers** (dinner $32-52; ⊙ 5:30-9:30pm) restaurant before heading back down.

At Portage, a short railroad/toll road runs to Whittier for the ferry to Valdez. Portage Glacier Access Rd leads to the **Begich-Boggs Visitors Center** (☎ 907-783-2326; ⊙ 9am-6pm), 5 miles south of Portage, and **Portage Glacier**. **Gray Line** (☎ 907-277-5581) offers hour-long cruises ($25), the only way to see the entire glacier. There are two USFS campgrounds along Portage Glacier Access Rd: **Black Bear Campground** (campsites $10) and **Williwaw Campground** (1/2 people $13/20).

North of Anchorage, Glenn Hwy runs 13 miles to Eagle River Rd – a beautiful mountainside trip. The **Eagle River Nature Center** (☎ 907-694-2108; 32750 Eagle River Rd; ⊙ 10am-5pm; P) offers wildlife displays and scenic hiking. Parking costs $5. Near Palmer, 42 miles north, **Hatcher Pass** is an alpine paradise, with hiking, parasailing, gold-rush artifacts and panoramas of the Takeetna Mountains. Stay at **Hatcher Pass Lodge** (☎ 907-745-5897; www.hatcherpasslodge.com; Mile 17.5 Hatcher Pass Rd; r $110, cabins $160; ⊠) or **Motherlode Lodge** (☎ 907-745-6171, 877-745-6171; www.motherlodelodge.com; Mile 14 Hatcher Pass Rd; r $129; ⊠). Both have restaurants.

KENAI PENINSULA

This wonderful region, broken up by mountains, fjords and glaciers and laced with hiking trails and rivers filled with salmon, is a popular playground for both tourists and locals. More than half the population of the state lives within a two-hour drive of Kenai Peninsula. Don't like crowds? Then plan on tying on the hiking boots or renting a kayak.

Seward

This scenic town is flanked by rugged mountains and overlooks salmon-filled Resurrection Bay. Founded in 1903 as an ice-free port at the southern end of the Alaska Railroad, Seward prospered as the beginning of the gold-rush trail to Nome and was later devastated by the 1964 Good Friday earthquake.

The downtown **visitor center** (www.sewardak.org; cnr Jefferson St & 3rd Ave; ⊙ 9am-5pm) is in a Pullman railroad car. There's also a **USFS office** (☎ 907-224-3374; cnr 4th Ave & Jefferson St;

⊙ 8am-5pm Mon-Fri). The **Seward Library** (☎ 907-224-3646; 238 5th Ave; ⊙ 1-8pm Mon-Fri, 1-6pm Sat) offers free Internet access. The **Kenai Fjords National Park visitor center** (☎ 907-224-3175; www.nps.gov/kefj; 1212 4th Ave; ⊙ 8am-7pm) has information on hiking and paddling.

SIGHTS & ACTIVITIES

Alaska SeaLife Center (☎ 907-224-3080, 800-224-2525; 301 Railway Ave; adult/child $14/11; ⊙ 8am-7pm) is the only cold-water marine-science facility in the western hemisphere; it's home to 1000 fish, nearly all from Alaskan waters, and is the top attraction on the Kenai Peninsula. Plan to spend an afternoon here watching puffins, otters and 1000lb Steller sea lions glide past giant viewing windows.

Six miles south of town is **Caines Head State Recreation Area**, which was fortified during WWII to guard the entrance of Resurrection Bay after the Japanese bombed the island of Unalaska. Exploring the bunkers, gun emplacements and surrounding alpine country makes for an intriguing way to spend a day. You can access the area on foot at low tide along the Coastal Trail, or paddle to it with **Kayak & Custom Adventures** (☎ 907-224-3960, 800-288-3134; 328 3rd Ave; single/double kayak per day $35/45, day trip $99; ⊙ 8am-7pm), which offers guided day trips and kayak rentals. **Miller's Landing Campground** (☎ 907-224-5739, 866-541-35739; www.millerslandingak.com; Lowell Point Rd; one way/round-trip $35/45) also runs a water taxi to the state park.

Seward's other great hike is the **Mt Marathon Trail**, a 3-mile walk (round-trip) to spectacular views on the mountain overlooking Seward.

SLEEPING

Van Gilder Hotel (☎ 800-204-6835; www.vangilderhotel.com; 308 Adams St; d with shared/private bath $109/149, ste $219; ⊠) A 1916 historic hotel, which means two things: tiny rooms and lots of ghosts. Gossips say poltergeists haunt the 1st floor and some employees won't go in the laundry room at night; on-the-clock staff refused to confirm either way.

Farm B&B (☎ 907-224-5691; www.alaskan.com/thefarm; Mile 0.3 Salmon Creek Rd; r $75-100, cottages $90; ⊠) Indulge your sylvan fantasies in this sprawling family farmhouse, just off Exit Glacier Rd. Choose a room in the house, or curl up in one of the cottages nestled on the wooded property.

Seward Windsong Lodge (☎ 907-224-7116, 888-959-9590; www.sewardwindsong.com; Mile 0.5 Exit Glacier Rd; r/ste $199/239; ▯ ✕) Snowcapped mountains rise above Seward's most luxurious lodge, while just down the road is a glacier. Sure, you're 4 miles from Seward, but there's free shuttle transportation whenever you want to go downtown.

Motels in the Small Boat Harbor area include **Murphy's Motel** (☎ 907-224-8090, 800-686-8191; 911 4th Ave; r $100-149; ✕) and **Breeze Inn** (☎ 907-224-5237, 888-224-5237; 1306 Seward Hwy; s/d from $129/139; ✕), a better choice with larger and cleaner rooms.

Other recommendations:

Moby Dick Hostel (☎ 907-224-7072; 432 3rd Ave; dm $17.50, r $50-65; ✕) Friendly staff, well located and clean enough for seasoned budget travelers.

Snow River Hostel (☎ 907-440-1907; Mile 16 Seward Hwy; dm/d $15/40; ✕) Out of town, but highly recommended for its sauna and wood-fired stove.

Waterfront Campground (☎ 907-224-3331; Ballaine Blvd; campsites $8, RV sites $12-25; ✕) Between downtown and the boat harbor.

EATING & DRINKING

Terry's Fish & Chips (☎ 907-224-8807; 1210 4th Ave; $7-13; ◷ 24hr; ✕) Rated as the best cheapie fish stand at the harbor.

Ray's Waterfront (☎ 907-224-5606; 1316 4th Ave; lunch $9-16, dinner $15-35; ◷ 11am-11pm; ✕) The best seafood in town, also boasting legendary breakfast casseroles and a picture-perfect view.

Sue's Teriyaki Kitchen (☎ 907-224-4593; 303 S Harbor St; dinner $8-15; ◷ 11:30am-8pm; ✕) It may not look like much, but the kimchi is great and the sushi even better.

Yukon Bar (☎ 907-224-3063; cnr 4th Ave & Washington St) and **Tony's Bar** (☎ 907-224-3045; 135 4th Ave) have live music and can get loud at night. Head to **Resurrect Art Gallery & Coffee House** (☎ 907-224-7161; 320 3rd Ave; ✕) for a latte and a quieter atmosphere, though Tuesday is acoustic night.

GETTING THERE & AWAY

From the **ferry terminal** (☎ 907-224-5485; 913 Port Ave), ferries go to Kodiak ($73, 13 hours), Valdez ($77, 11 hours) and Homer ($126, 23 hours) every few days. **Seward Bus Lines** (☎ 907-224-3608) runs daily to Anchorage ($40, 2½ hours). **Alaska Railroad** (☎ 800-544-0552; www.akrr.com) takes a spectacular daily route to Anchorage ($59, four hours).

Kenai Fjords National Park

South of Seward is Kenai Fjords National Park. The park's main features are the 917-sq-mile **Harding Icefield** and the tidewater glaciers that calve into the sea. Even through it's making a fast retreat, **Exit Glacier**, at the end of Exit Glacier Rd, is still the most popular attraction. There's a visitor center and a paved 0.25-mile trail to a glacier overlook. Hikers can climb a difficult 5 miles to the edge of the ice field – worth it for spectacular views. The park visitor center is in Seward (opposite).

The best marine-wildlife cruises in the state are the tour boats that run into Kenai Fjords. **Major Marine Tours** (☎ 907-224-8030, 800-764-7300; www.majormarine.com) offers a half-day Resurrection Bay tour (adult/child $69/34) and a full-day tour viewing Holgate Arm ($122/61), both of which include a national park ranger on every boat. The latter tour is the best way to view seals, whales and other marine wildlife.

Sterling Hwy

Paved Sterling Hwy makes an arc around the Kenai Peninsula, passing **Kenai National Wildlife Refuge**, where you might see wildlife and a plague of anglers. Head to **Kenai**, which has good views and some Russian history, and continue on to Captain Cook Strait Recreation Area, which is off the fishing circuit. South of Soldotna, the scenic highway hugs the coastline, passing through small villages with campgrounds and great clamming beaches. Scenic **Ninilchik** has a Russian accent, and **Eagle Watch Hostel** (☎ 907-567-3905; Mile 3 Oil Well Rd; adult/child $13/7; ✕) is 3 miles east in a gorgeous rural setting.

Homer

Charming, colorful Homer, at the end of Sterling Hwy, sits on beautiful Kachemak Bay amid awe-inspiring mountains. The town began attracting alternative types in the 1960s, and is now home to artists and aging hippies. The **visitor center** (☎ 907-235-7740; www.homeralaska.org; 201 Sterling Hwy; ◷ 9am-7pm Mon-Fri, 10am-6pm Sat & Sun) has courtesy phones to book rooms or tours. The **library** (☎ 907-235-3180; 141 W Pioneer Ave; ◷ 10am-6pm Mon, Wed, Fri & Sat, 10am-8pm Tue & Thu) has Internet access.

SIGHTS & ACTIVITIES

The **Pratt Museum** (☎ 907-235-8635; 3779 Bartlett St; adult/child $6/3; ◷ 10am-6pm) features 'Darkened

Waters,' the best display anywhere on the *Exxon Valdez* oil spill, an event that still haunts the residents of Homer.

Homer Spit is a 4.5-mile sand bar with clamming, beach camping and a small boat harbor. The best hiking is along the beaches, particularly the Shoreline Rte west of Main St, and at Kachemak Bay State Park, located across Kachemak Bay.

SLEEPING

B&Bs have mushroomed all over town. Call **Homer's Finest B&B Network** (☎ 907-235-4983, 800-764-3211; www.homeraccommodations.com) or **Cabins & Cottages Network** (☎ 907-235-0191, 888-364-0191; www.cabinsinhomer.com).

Old Town B&B (☎ 907-235-7558; www.oldtown bedandbreakfast.com; 106 W Bunnell St; r $95-115; ☒) A classy and friendly number, with three beautiful rooms and great views.

Driftwood Inn (☎ 907-235-8019, 800-478-8019; www.thedriftwoodinn.com; 435 W Bunnell Ave; RV sites $28-31, s $59-155, d $69-165; ☒) Quiet yet centrally located, it has rooms ranging from tiny 'ship quarters' to large rooms with all the amenities. Fall asleep to the sound of the waves.

Alaskan Suites (☎ 907-235-1972, 888-239-1972; www.alaskansuites.com; 3255 Sterling Hwy; cabins $195) This is Alaska – you need to spend a night in a log cabin. These luxurious cabins come with a porch where you can grill dinner while watching the sunset.

Skyline B&B (☎ 907-235-3832; www.skylinebb.com; 60855 Skyline Dr; r $85-120) Features beautiful views of Grewingk Glacier, and blueberry sourdough pancakes in the morning.

Chocolate Drop Inn (☎ 907-235-3668, 800-530-6015; www.chocolatedropinn.com; r $125-195) A stunning log cabin with five rooms, a sauna inside and a hot tub outside – the only way to watch the northern lights.

Homer Hostel (☎ 907-235-1463; www.homerhostel.com; 304 W Pioneer Ave; dm $22, r $47-57) Within an easy walk of everything in town, location alone makes this the better of the two hostels in Homer.

There's (often rowdy) beach camping at **Homer Spit Public Campground** (Homer Spit Rd; campsites/RV sites $6/10) but **Karen Hornaday Memorial Campground** (Bartlett St; campsites/RV sites $6/10) is a better bet for families.

EATING & DRINKING

Two Sisters Bakery (☎ 907-235-2280; 233 W Bunnell Ave; light meals $5-9; ☻ 7am-6pm Mon-Sat, 9am-4pm

Sun; ☒) One of Homer's many excellent coffee houses, with tables on a porch overlooking the bay.

Smoky Bay Natural Foods (☎ 907-235-7252; 248 W Pioneer Ave) A co-op with organic veggies, groceries, herbs, a great bulk-foods selection and a deli (mains $5 to $9) that is open from 9:30am to 3pm and serves soups, quiches and healthy mains daily.

Café Cups (☎ 907-235-8330; 162 W Pioneer Ave; lunch $8-12, dinner $18-24; ☻ 11am-10pm Mon-Fri, 5-10pm Sat; ☒) With a bizarre coffee-cup exterior and pleasant interior, this café does creative fine dining – silver salmon with strawberry *pico de gallo*, for instance – served with scores of different wines and 23 types of hot sauce.

Homestead (☎ 907-235-8723; Mile 8.2 E End Rd; mains $21-32; ☻ 5-9pm; ☒) The finest restaurant in Homer. You must make a reservation to enjoy the steaks, king crab and Sonoran seafood stew, alongside any brilliant choice from the eclectic wine list.

Glacier Drive-In (☎ 907-235-7148; 11-8 Homer Spit Rd; mains $5-10; ☻ 11am-8pm Tue-Sun; ☒) is one of the better cheap eateries, while nearby is the **Salty Dawg Saloon** (☎ 907-235-6718; Homer Spit Rd), Homer's best-known watering hole.

GETTING THERE & AWAY

Era Aviation (☎ 907-235-7565, 800-866-8394; www.flyera.com) flies frequently from Anchorage ($115, 50 minutes). The ferry **M/V Tustumena** (☎ 907-235-8449; www.ferryalaska.com) goes twice weekly to Seldovia ($28, 1½ hours) and Kodiak ($65, 9½ hours). **Polar Car Rental** (☎ 800-876-6417; Homer airport terminal; ☻ 24hr) rents subcompacts for $55 a day. **Homer Stage Line** (☎ 907-235-2252; www.homerstageline.com) provides a bus service to Anchorage ($55, five hours).

PRINCE WILLIAM SOUND

Prince William Sound is the northern extent of the Gulf of Alaska, flanked by mountains and featuring abundant wildlife, including whales, sea lions, harbor seals, otters, eagles and bears. Bring your raincoat – annual rainfall averages more than 100in. Don't pass through without splurging on a marine-wildlife boat tour or a kayak adventure.

Whittier

At the western end of Prince William Sound, Whittier was built by the military as a WWII warm-water port. Rail tunnels were drilled west through solid rock to con-

HIGH-SPEED ALASKA

There's still no wireless Internet on the Alaska Marine Hwy, but the venerable state ferries entered the era of high-speed connection anyhow when the *M/V Fairweather* was christened in November 2003. The $40 million ferry is the first aluminum passenger-and-vehicle catamaran built for the state ferry system and is capable of speeds of up to 32 knots – that's 40mph for you landlubbers. The catamaran was placed in service between Juneau and Skagway and makes the run between the capital city and Haines in less than three hours. By comparison, the *M/V Columbia* needs more than six hours for the same run.

Passengers loved the high-speed service so much that in 2005 the *M/V Chenega*, the Alaska Marine Hwy's second catamaran, was put into service between Whittier, Valdez and Cordova in Prince William Sound. With daily high-speed service across the Sound, Cordova is now an easy sidetrip from Anchorage for tourists pondering what to do with the last two days of their vacation.

nect with the main line of the Alaska Railroad. In 2000, the tunnel was converted to handle vehicles as well, and the first luxury hotel has already been built in Whittier. More are undoubtedly on their way.

Alaska Sea Kayakers (☎ 907-472-2534, 877-472-2534; www.alaskaseakayakers.com; Whittier Boat Harbor; single/double kayak per day $40/55, trip $79-300) has rentals and guided trips for paddlers to explore the fjords and glaciers near Whittier.

If you're looking for a place to stay, **Anchor Inn** (☎ 907-472-2354, 877-870-8787; 100 Whittier St; s/d $85/95; ✗) also offers food and drink, and the **Inn at Whittier** (☎ 907-472-7000, 866-472-5757; www.innatwhittier.com; 1 Harbor Loop Rd; r $109-349; ✗) has luxury suites and a grand view of the boat harbor from its restaurant and lounge. Camp at **Glacier View Campground** (Glacier St; campsites $10).

A train leaves Whittier daily for Anchorage ($52, 2½ hours). The *M/V Bartlett* ferry travels east to Valdez ($77, 2¾ hours) and Cordova ($77, 3¼ hours) daily.

Valdez

Just 25 miles east of Columbia Glacier, the ice-free port of Valdez is the southern terminus of the Trans-Alaska Pipeline. Valdez first boomed when 4000 gold seekers passed through, heading for the Klondike. After the 1964 earthquake, the city was rebuilt 4 miles further east.

The **Valdez Convention & Visitors Bureau** (☎ 907-835-4636; www.valdezalaska.org; 200 Fairbanks Dr; ☻ 8am-7pm Mon-Sat, 9am-6pm Sun) has information about the area and courtesy phones to book accommodations. The **library** (☎ 907-835-4632; 212 Fairbanks St; ☻ 10am-6pm Mon & Fri, 10am-8pm Tue-Thu, noon-5pm Sat) has free Internet access.

SIGHTS & ACTIVITIES

Though the *Exxon Valdez* oil spill was an environmental disaster, the cleanup created a cash bonanza when Exxon hired fishing boats and locals to clean beaches. Many opportunists became known as the 'spillionaires.' The **Valdez Museum** (☎ 907-835-2764; 217 Egan Dr; adult/child $3/2; ☻ 9am-6pm) is packed with displays, including oil-spill exhibits and a model of the pipeline. Bustling **Small Boat Harbor** has a scenic mountain backdrop and pleasant boardwalk where in the evening you can watch charter fishing boats unload catches of halibut.

The magnificent **Columbia Glacier** is retreating, but its 3-mile-wide face can still be seen from Alaska Marine Hwy ferries going to or from Whittier. For a longer and much closer look, **Stan Stephens Glacier & Wildlife Cruises** (☎ 907-835-4731, 866-867-1297; www.stanstephenscruises.com; 112 N Harbor Dr) runs seven-hour boat tours to Columbia Glacier (adult/child $88/45) and a nine-hour tour that also includes Meares Glacier (adult/child $128/65).

Although not blessed with the hiking that Anchorage and Juneau possess, Valdez still offers a number of scenic trails. **Shoup Bay Trail** is a 12.8-mile hike to its namesake bay that includes walk-in campsites halfway there. For white-water enthusiasts, **Keystone Raft & Kayak Adventures** (☎ 907-835-2606, 800-328-8460; www.alaskawhitewater.com; half-day $75) runs raft trips on the Class IV Tsaina River, while kayakers can explore the icebergs, seals and kittiwake colony of Shoup Bay. **Anadyr Adventures** (☎ 907-835-2814, 800-865-2925; www.anadyradventures.com; 225 Harbor Dr; single/double kayak per day $45/65) rents kayaks and offers guided day trips.

ALASKA

SLEEPING

There are more than 30 B&Bs around town, starting at $70/80 per single/double; the visitor center has listings and a speed-dial phone for bookings.

Blueberry Mary B&B (☎ 907-835-5015; 810 Salmonberry Way; r $90-100; ✗) A mile from downtown, this B&B has a gorgeous view of the bay, a sauna for after the hike and, yes, blueberries on your waffles at breakfast.

Downtown Inn (☎ 907-835-2791, 800-478-2791; 113 Galina Dr; r with shared/private bath $85/100; ✗) Rooms are clean, and breakfast is included.

Aspen Hotel (☎ 907-835-4445, 800-478-4445; www.aspenhotelsak.com; 100 Meals Ave; standard r $159; ▢ ▨ ✗) Valdez's newest hotel is also its largest and nicest, with wi-fi and an indoor pool and spa.

Bear Paw RV Campground (☎ 907-835-2530; 101 N Harbor Dr; campsites $17-20, RV sites $25-30) Cute wooded campsites near Small Boat Harbor.

EATING

Totem Inn Restaurant (☎ 907-835-4443; 144 E Egan Dr; breakfast & lunch $5-9, dinner $15-32; ◷ 5am-11pm; ✗) The best breakfast in town; you can find decent burgers and seafood here the rest of the day.

Alaskan Halibut House (☎ 907-835-2788; 208 Meals Ave; mains $4-9; ◷ 6am-10pm; ✗) has halibut, chips and salad; **Mike's Palace** (☎ 907-835-2365; 201 N Harbor Dr; mains $10-20; ◷ 11am-11pm; ✗) has been serving Greek dishes, pasta and seafood for 35 years in Valdez; and **Fu Kung** (☎ 907-835-5255; 207 Kobuk St; lunch $8, dinner $12-15; ◷ 11am-11pm Mon-Sat, 4-11pm Sun; ✗) has sushi and killer Chinese.

GETTING THERE & AWAY

Era Aviation (☎ 907-266-8394, 800-866-8394; www.flyera.com) makes the 40-minute flight daily to Anchorage for $110 to $160, depending on when you book. **Alaska Marine Highway** (☎ 907-835-4436; www.ferryalaska.com) ferries sail regularly to Whittier ($77, 2¾ hours), Seward ($77, 11 hours), Homer ($178, 34 hours) and Cordova ($43, 2¾ hours).

Cordova

At the eastern end of the sound, this beautiful little town's population of 2600 doubles in summer with fishing and cannery workers. First settled by the nomadic Eyak, who lived on the enormous salmon runs, Cordova became a fish-packing center in 1889.

The **Cordova Chamber of Commerce** (☎ 907-424-7260; www.cordovachamber.com; 404 1st Ave; ◷ 10am-5pm Mon-Fri, 10am-2pm Sat) has pamphlets and tips, but the **library** (☎ 907-424-6667; 622 1st Ave; ◷ 10am-8pm Tue-Fri, 1-5pm Sat) has the most useful visitor information, including B&B listings. The **USFS office** (☎ 907-424-7661; 612 2nd St; ◷ 8am-5pm Mon-Fri) has free maps to hiking trails accessible from the road.

The interesting **Cordova Museum** (☎ 907-424-6666; 622 1st Ave; admission $1; ◷ 10am-6pm Mon-Fri, 1-5pm Sat, noon-3pm Sun), in the Centennial Building, offers cassettes for self-guided town tours and will store your pack during the day. It has displays on history, marine life and mining.

Activity centers on the small boat harbor during summer. The most stunning scenery, which includes **Childs Glacier** calving into the Copper River, is along the 50-mile Copper River Hwy. **Alaska River Rafters** (☎ 907-424-7238, 800-776-1864; www.alaskarafters.com; Mile 13 Copper River Hwy) offers a full-day bus tour to Childs Glacier or a half-day raft and hike adventure to **Sheridan Glacier** ($85/65 adult/child).

Prince William Motel (☎ 907-424-3201, 888-796-6835; 502 2nd St; s/d $90/100; ✗) has huge, clean rooms, while **Reluctant Fisherman Inn** (☎ 907-424-3272, 877-770-3272; 407 Railroad Ave; r $110-130; ✗) is as close to luxurious as Cordova gets.

Alaskan Hotel & Bar (☎ 907-424-3299; 600 1st St; r with shared/private bath $40/60; ✗) is a bit tattered, but a decent choice.

You'll find **Odiak Camper Park** (☎ 907-424-6200; Whitshed Rd; campsites/RV sites $5/20) half a mile east of town, but it can be dismal.

Don't pass up **Baja Taco Wagon** (☎ 907-424-5599; Harbor Loop; dinner $7-12; ◷ 7am-7pm Mon-Fri, 8am-8pm Sat & Sun), a funky converted school bus across from the harbor; this is the place to enjoy some of the best tacos north of San Diego.

Killer Whale Café (☎ 907-424-7733; 507 1st St; dinner $8-10; ◷ 11am-8:30pm Sun-Thu, 11am-9pm Fri & Sat; ✗) has sandwiches and vegetarian-friendly meals. The best dining and freshest catch is at **Reluctant Fisherman Inn** (☎ 907-424-3272; 407 Railroad Ave; dinner $12-17; ◷ 6:30am-9pm), where you dine with a full view of the boat harbor and Orca Inlet. **Powder House Bar** (☎ 907-424-3529; Mile 1.5 Copper River Hwy) features folk and country music along with its grub and drinks.

Alaska Airlines (☎ 907-424-7151, 800-252-7522; www.alaskaair.com) flies daily from Anchorage ($110, one hour) and Juneau ($290, two hours). In summer, the *M/V Bartlett* ferry arrives every couple of days from Valdez ($43, 2¾ hours) or Whittier ($77, 3¼ hours). Rent a car at **Cordova Auto Rentals** (☎ 907-424-5982, Smith Airport, Mile 12 Copper River Hwy) for $77.

Wrangell-St Elias National Park

Part of a 31,250-sq-mile wilderness area, this park is a crossroads of mountain ranges: Wrangell, Chugach and St Elias. Extensive ice fields and 100 major glaciers spill from the peaks, including one bigger than the state of Rhode Island. This park is more difficult to visit than Denali National Park but, to those who make the effort to experience it, no less impressive.

From Valdez, the Richardson Hwy is a jaw-dropping scenic route to Glennallen, past canyons, mountain passes and glaciers. The Wrangell-St Elias National Park **visitor center** (☎ 907-822-7440; www.nps.gov/wrst; Mile 106.8 Richardson Hwy; ☺ 8am-6pm) is in Copper Center.

A side road at Tonsina goes southeast to Chitina, which has the last place to fill up your tank. Nearby are a grocery store, two restaurants and some campgrounds. From there, the rugged Mt McCarthy Rd follows former railroad tracks 60 miles east through the stunning Chugach Mountains and across the mighty Copper River to the Kennicott River. Here a footbridge is used to cross the river and access historic McCarthy and the abandoned copper-mining town of Kennicott, which is in the national park.

McCarthy & Kennicott

Scenic and funky little McCarthy was the Wild West counterpart of the Kennicott company town and, to a degree, still is today.

In 1900 miners discovered the rich Kennicott copper deposit, and a syndicate built 196 miles of railroad through the wilderness to take the ore to Cordova. For 30 years Kennicott worked around the clock, but in 1938 management closed the mine, giving workers two hours to catch the last train out. Despite some pilferage, Kennicott remains a remarkably preserved piece of US mining history. The **Kennicott Visitor Center** (Kennicott Railroad Depot; ☺ 9am-5:30pm) is staffed by the NPS during the summer, and has displays and maps of the company town.

There's some good hiking around the glaciers, peaks and mines, as well as rafting on the Kennicott River. **St Elias Alpine Guides**

(☎ 907-544-4445, 888-933-5427; www.steliasguides.com) offers day trips from McCarthy for historical tours of Kennicott ($25). **Wrangell Mountain Air** (☎ 907-554-4411, 800-478-1160; www.wrangell mountainair.com) offers a variety of scenic-flight tours, beginning with its 35-minute Glacier Tour for $70.

Kennicott River Lodge & Hostel (☎ 907-554-4441; www.kennicottriverlodge.com; dm/cabin/ste $28/100/150; ☒) is a beautiful log lodge on the west side of the river with a 12-person sauna. **Ma Johnson's Hotel** (☎ 907-554-4402; www.mccarthylodge.com; s/d $109/159; ☒), in a renovated 1916 building, offers round-trip transportation from the footbridge and a wholesome breakfast. There's also **Kennicott Glacier Lodge** (☎ 800-582-5128, within Alaska 800-478-2350; www.kennicottlodge.com; s/d $169/189), which offers superb views of the Kennicott Glacier from its long front porch. **McCarthy Lodge** (☎ 907-554-4402; breakfast $10, lunch $5-9, dinner $10-30; ☒) is run by the same folks as Ma Johnson's, offering outstanding meals, showers ($6.50) and cold beer ($4). Only in Alaska would a shower cost more than a beer.

Backcountry Connection (☎ 907-822-5292, within Alaska 866-582-5292; www.alaska-backcountry-tours.com) buses leave Glennallen most days for McCarthy via Chitina ($70). In McCarthy there's a four-hour layover to visit Kennicott; this long day trip costs $99. **McCarthy Air** (☎ 907-554-4440; www.mccarthyair.com) can fly you into McCarthy from Chitina for $250 for three people, and $375 from Valdez.

KODIAK ISLAND

Southwest of Kenai Peninsula, Kodiak Island is most famous for Kodiak brown bears, which grow huge gorging on salmon. Accommodations and transportation are expensive, but camping gear and a mountain bike can make Kodiak affordable.

The **Kodiak Island Convention & Visitor's Bureau** (☎ 907-486-4782, 800-789-4782; www.kodiak.org; 100 Marine Way; ☺ 8am-5pm Mon-Sat) has lists of accommodations (including 20 B&Bs), and trail guides for hikers ($5) and mountain bikers ($4). The **Homes Johnson Library** (☎ 907-486-8686; 319 Lower Mill Rd; ☺ 10am-9pm Mon-Fri, 10am-5pm Sat, 1-4pm Sun) has free Internet access.

Bear-watching is best from July to September, but usually involves a charter flight to a remote salmon stream through a company like **Sea Hawk Air** (☎ 800-770-4295; www.seahawkair.com; per person $420). **Mythos Expeditions**

ALASKA

Kodiak (☎ 907-486-5536; www.thewildcoast.com) offers guided kayak day trips for whale-watching ($200 to $300).

Kodiak B&B (☎ 907-486-5367; 308 Cope St; s/d $90/100; ✗) is convenient to downtown with two clean rooms, a friendly owner and a pleasant deck that overlooks the boat harbor. A block away is **Kodiak Inn** (☎ 907-486-5712; 236 Rezanof Dr W; s $139-149, d $149-159; ▯), the city's best motel.

Alaska Airlines (☎ 800-252-7522; www.alaskaair.com) has two flights and **Era** (☎ 907-487-4363, 800-866-8394; www.flyera.com) has five flights daily from Anchorage. The ferry **M/V Tustumena** (☎ 907-486-3800; www.ferryalaska.com) connects Kodiak three times weekly with Homer ($65, 9½ hours) and Seward ($73, 13 hours).

THE INTERIOR

The big, broad land of Alaska's Interior is a central plateau drained by great rivers and bordered by the rugged Alaska Range to the south and the Brooks Range to the north. Alaska's major highways (rarely more than two-lane roads) crisscross the region, providing affordable access.

The main route is George Parks Hwy (Hwy 3), which winds 358 miles from Anchorage to Fairbanks, passing Denali National Park, while the Richardson Hwy (Hwy 4) extends 366 miles south from Fairbanks to Valdez. The Glenn Hwy (Hwy 1) completes this Interior triangle by extending 189 miles from Anchorage to the George Parks Hwy near Palmer and finally to the Richardson Hwy at Glennallen. All the Interior roads are lined with turnoffs, campgrounds, hiking trails and wildlife-spotting possibilities. Towns are small service centers with gas stations, motels and cafés, but a few have retained their rustic, gold-rush frontier flavor.

GEORGE PARKS HWY

North of Anchorage, George Parks Hwy passes through the 'bedroom' community of Wasilla (where almost all the residents work and shop in Anchorage), just past the Glenn Hwy (Hwy 1) turnoff. A dramatic detour, the Fishook-Willow Rd between Palmer and Willow, goes through **Hatcher Pass** (see p1104), an alpine paradise with foot trails, gold-mining artifacts and panoramas of the Talkeetna Mountains.

Talkeetna

At Mile 98.7, a side road heads north to this interesting town. It was a miners' supply center in 1901, and later a riverboat station and railroad-construction headquarters. Since the 1950s, Mt McKinley mountaineers have made Talkeetna their staging post, and today the town is the most interesting along the George Parks Hwy by far. The **Talkeetna/ Denali Visitors Center** (☎ 907-733-2688, 800-660-2688; www.alaskan.com/talkeetnadenali; George Parks Hwy; ☯ 7am-8pm) has information about the area.

The **Mountaineering Ranger Station** (☎ 907-733-2231; cnr 1st & B Sts; ☯ 8am-6pm) handles expeditions to Mt McKinley and has displays that will interest even those who have no desire to stand on North America's highest peak. The four restored buildings of the **Talkeetna Historical Society Museum** (☎ 907-733-2487; admission $3; ☯ 10am-6pm) are a block south of Main St and house exhibits on bush pilots and McKinley climbs.

For scenic flights to view Mt McKinley ($140 to $250), check out **Doug Geeting Aviation** (☎ 907-733-2366, 800-770-2366; www.alaskaairtours.com), **Hudson Air Service** (☎ 907-733-2321, 800-478-2321; www.hudsonair.com) or **K2 Aviation** (☎ 907-733-2291, 800-764-2291; www.flyk2.com). If the day is clear, be prepared for a long wait and an unforgettable flight.

Talkeetna Motel (☎ 907-733-2323; B St; r $76-94) has simple but clean rooms and is away from the hustle of Main St. **Latitude 62 Lodge/ Motel** (☎ 907-733-2262; Mile 13.5 Talkeetna Spur Rd; s/d $63/74) is a bit more upscale, while the **Talkeetna Alaskan Lodge** (☎ 907-733-9500, within Alaska 888-959-9590; www.talkeetnalodge.com; Mile 12.5 Talkeetna Spur Rd; r $269-379) is one of Alaska's most stunning lodges, where a third of the rooms have a view of Mt McKinley. **Talkeetna Hostel International** (☎ 907-733-4678; www.talkeetnahostel.com; I St; dm/s/d $27/60/75; ✗ ▯), a wonderful hostel, is a 10-minute stroll from Main St.

Talkeetna Roadhouse (☎ 907-733-1351; Main St; breakfast $11; ☯ 6am-3pm & 5-9pm; ✗) is the best spot for a hearty breakfast, while in the evening it serves soup and light fare. Across the street, **Mountain High Pizza Pie** (☎ 907-733-1234; Main St; pizza $13-25; ☯ 11:30am-11pm Sun-Thu, 11:30am-midnight Fri & Sat; ✗) serves cold beer on tap and hot pizzas straight from the oven.

Café Michele (☎ 907-733-5300; Talkeetna Spur Rd & 2nd St; dinner $17-29; ☯ 11am-10pm; ✗) serves up the town's best food and has the most up-scale atmosphere. Try the superb signature soy-ginger salmon.

The **Alaska Railroad** (☎ 800-544-0552; www.akrr .com) from Anchorage stops at Talkeetna daily in summer ($80, 3½ hours) and heads north to Denali National Park ($75, four hours) and Fairbanks ($103, 8½ hours). **Talkeetna Shuttle Service** (☎ 907-733-1725, 888-288-6008) has two runs a day between Anchorage and Talkeetna ($55, three hours).

Denali National Park

This breathtakingly brilliant wilderness area, which includes North America's highest mountain, attracts one million visitors a year. A single road curves 91 miles through the heart of the park, lined with off-trail hiking opportunities, wildlife and stunning panoramas. The Denali Park Rd can be used only by official shuttle buses, which have limited seating. Numbers of overnight backpackers in the wilderness zones are also strictly limited. This means Disneyland-like crowds at the entrance, but relative solitude once you're inside.

Wildlife, including mammals such as marmot and moose, is easy to spot. Caribou, wolves and brown bears are crowd favorites. However, the main attraction is magnificent Mt McKinley, a high pyramid of rock, snow and glaciers rising from the valley floor. Clouds will obscure McKinley more often than not, so be prepared to wait for the big picture.

INFORMATION

The park entrance is at Mile 237.3 George Parks Hwy. Entry costs $10/20 per person/family, and is good for a week. The highway north and south of the park entrance is a touristy strip of private campgrounds, lodges, restaurants and facilities.

The new **Visitor Access Center** (VAC; ☎ 907-683-2294; www.nps.gov/dena; Mile 1.5 Denali Park Rd; ☽ 9am-9pm) is the place to organize your trip into the park, pick up permits and purchase maps. If possible, plan the exact days you will be in the park, and reserve bus seats and campsites through **Denali National Park Reservations** (☎ 907-272-7275, 800-622-7275; www .reservedenali.com).

Shuttle buses provide access for day hiking and sightseeing, and can be reserved from late February for that summer. In the backcountry you can get on or off buses along their routes. Buses leave the VAC regularly (6am to 2pm) for various stops, including Polychrome Pass Rest Area ($18.50, three hours) and Wonder Lake ($32.50, 6½ hours). Special camper shuttle buses, with space for backpacks and mountain bikes, charge $23.75 to any point on the road.

ACTIVITIES

For day hiking, get off the shuttle bus at any valley, riverbed or ridge that takes your fancy (no permit needed). For a guided walk, book at the VAC one or two days ahead.

For backcountry camping, you must get a backcountry permit from the VAC one day in advance. The park is divided into 43 zones, each with a regulated number of visitors. Some are more popular than others. Watch the Backcountry Simulator Program video at the VAC – it covers bears, rivers and backcountry safety – and check the quota board for an area you can access. You then go to the counter to book a camper shuttle bus and buy your maps.

Most cyclists book campsites at the VAC and then carry their bikes on the camper shuttle. Cycling is only permitted on roads. Rent bikes from **Denali Outdoor Center** (☎ 907-683-1925, 888-303-1925; www.denalioutdoorcenter.com; Mile 238.5 Parks Hwy; per day $40).

Several rafting companies offer daily floats on the Nenana River. **Denali Raft Adventures** (☎ 907-683-2234, 888-683-2234; www.denaliraft .com; Mile 238 Parks Hwy) offers a wild canyon run through the gorge, as well as a milder Mt McKinley float ($69).

SLEEPING

Carlo Creek Lodge (☎ 907-683-2576; www.alaskaone .com/carlocreek; Mile 224 George Parks Hwy; campsites $16, cabins $77-129) About 13 miles south of the park entrance, this lodge offers a variety of creek-side accommodations.

Denali Mountain Morning Hostel (☎ 907-683-7503; www.hostelalaska.com; Mile 224 George Parks Hwy; dm/r $25/65, cabins $75-130; ✗ ▣) Recommended accommodation where you can stash your gear (or rent some), and you can shuttle between the park entrance and hostel for free. Make reservations!

Denali River Cabins (☎ 907-683-8000, 800-230-7275; www.denalirivercabins.com; Mile 231 George Parks Hwy, Denali Village; cabins $139-169; ✗) Modern cabins and a restaurant-bar, but no TV or phone.

Denali Sourdough Cabins (☎ 907-683-2773, 800-544-0970; www.denalisourdoughcabins.com; Mile 238.8 George Parks Hwy; cabins $145; ✖) Small, cozy cabins near the park entrance.

Denali Grizzly Bear Campground (☎ 907-683-2696, 866-583-2696; www.denaligrizzlybear.com; Mile 231 George Parks Hwy; campsites $19, tent cabins $26-30, cabins $52-188) Has a hot shower, laundry services and, most importantly, a beer store.

Campsites inside the park cost $9 to $19, and most can be reserved for a $4 fee. That includes Riley Creek, just inside the park entrance, which is usually overrun by RVers. Other campgrounds are spaced along the park road, the most lovely being **Wonder Lake** (Mile 85 Park Rd; campsites $16), with 26 spots looking onto Mt McKinley. **Sanctuary River** (Mile 23 Park Rd; campsites $9) is for tents only, but makes a great day-hike area. It can be difficult to get a place in the campground of your choice, so take anything available and change campgrounds when you can.

EATING
Overlook Bar & Grill (☎ 907-683-2723; Mile 238.5 George Parks Hwy; dinner $10-29; ☽ 11am-11pm) This is a cozy place for a meal of steak, seafood or pasta at the Crow's Nest Inn; it's also the best bar in the greater Denali area.

Henry's (☎ 907-683-2863; Mile 4 Stampede Rd; light meals $7-15; ☽ 7-9:30am & 5:30-9pm; ✖) is an excellent coffeehouse at the EarthSong Lodge near Healy, serving breakfast bagels and just-baked goods in the morning, pizza and salads in the evening, and espresso drinks and smoothies in between.

Just outside the park, **Lynx Creek Pizza & Pub** (☎ 907-683-2547; Mile 238.6 George Parks Hwy; pizza $14-24; ☽ 11am-midnight) has excellent offerings, including beer on tap and huge pizzas, while **Denali Park Salmon Bake & Cabins** (☎ 907-683-2733; Mile 238.5 George Parks Hwy; cabins $59, mains $20) offers Alaskan salmon dinners and the most affordable cabins in the area.

The only food inside the park entrance area is at McKinley Mercantile, which sells fresh, dried and canned food. It's better to stock up on supplies in Fairbanks, Anchorage or Wasilla.

GETTING THERE & AWAY
From the VAC inside the park, **Alaska/Yukon Trails** (☎ 800-770-7275; www.alaskashuttle.com) departs for Anchorage ($76, six hours) and Fairbanks ($46, three hours).

The **Alaska Railroad** (☎ 907-265-2494, 800-544-0552; www.akrr.com) departs from a depot near Riley Creek campground; it's expensive but very scenic. The trip to Fairbanks is $54 and to Anchorage, $129. It also has a three-day package out of Anchorage for $621 that includes two nights' lodging and a bus tour inside the park.

FAIRBANKS
A spread-out, low-rise city, Fairbanks features extremes of climate, colorful residents and gold fever. In a city that can hit -60°F in the winter, summer days average 70°F and occasionally top 90°F. Downtown is roughly centered on Golden Heart Park, and Cushman St is more or less the main street. Downtown motels, B&Bs and restaurants are 15 minutes' walk from the train station.

Fairbanks was founded in 1901, when a trader could not get his riverboat any further up the Chena River. A gold strike made Fairbanks a boom town, with 18,000 residents by 1908, but by 1920 it had slumped to 1000. WWII, the Alcan Hwy and military bases produced minor booms, but the town took off as a construction base for the Trans-Alaska Pipeline and still serves as a gateway to the North Slope. Just north of the city is Fort Knox, Alaska's largest gold mine.

Information
The **Log Cabin & Downtown Visitor Information Center** (☎ 907-456-5774, 800-327-5774; www.explorefairbanks.com; 550 1st Ave; ☽ 8am-8pm) overlooks the Chena River and has courtesy phones to motels and B&Bs, and free Internet access. The **Alaska Public Lands Information Center** (☎ 907-456-0527; 250 Cushman St; ☽ 9am-6pm) has maps, information and displays on parks, wildlife refuges and recreation areas.

Sights & Activities
Pioneer Park (☎ 907-459-1087; cnr Airport Way & Peger Rd; admission free; ☽ 11am-9pm) is a 44-acre park and the city's biggest attraction. Formerly known as Alaskaland, it has historical displays such as an old sternwheeler, the railroad car that carried President Warren Harding to the golden spike ceremony in 1923 and a century-old working carousel.

The University of Alaska unveiled its newly expanded **Museum of the North** (☎ 907-474-7505; 907 Yukon Dr; adult/child $5/3; ☽ 9am-7pm) in the fall of 2005; it's now Alaska's most impressive museum. The $32 million expansion doubled the size of the existing museum and added an art gallery as well as geology and history exhibits, including Blue Babe, a 36,000-year-old bison found preserved in the permafrost.

For hiking, head out to Chena River State Recreational Area, which has short walks, or the 29-mile Chena Dome Trail. At **Chena Hot Springs Resort** (☎ 907-451-8104, 800-478-4681; www.chenahotsprings.com; Mile 56.5 Chena Hot Springs Rd; campsites/RV sites $20, cabins $65-200) you can soak those mosquito bites all day or get ambitious and do a guided activity such as horseback riding. The resort also has comfortable cabins, a good restaurant and a bar where you can drink with locals or study the Yukon Quest Sled Dog memorabilia on the walls. Canoeing options range from afternoon paddles to overnight trips; ask at **7 Bridges Boats & Bikes** (☎ 907-479-0751; www.7gablesinn.com; 4312 Birch Lane; canoe per day $35), at 7 Gables Inn. Alternatively, cruise the calm Chena River with a 3½-hour tour on the historic sternwheeler **Riverboat Discovery** (☎ 907-479-6673; www.riverboatdiscovery.com; 1975 Discovery Dr; adult/child $45/30; ☯ 8:45am & 2pm).

Sleeping

Contact the visitor center for information on Fairbanks' 100-plus B&Bs, mostly priced from $75/85 per single/double. Most of those with reasonable rates are either less than desirable or quite far from downtown. At the other end of the lodging scale, Fairbanks also has several hostels. Fairbanks exacts an 8% tax on hotels.

Ah, Rose Marie B&B (☎ 907-456-2040; 302 Cowles St; r $65-80; ☒) On the south side of the river, this longtime B&B has comfortable rooms and is within easy walking distance of everything downtown.

7 Gables Inn (☎ 907-479-0751; www.7gablesinn.com; 4312 Birch Lane; r $65/130; ☐) Has a variety of rooms, many with Jacuzzis, and outstanding full breakfasts. After breakfast you can borrow a canoe and paddle the Chena River.

Bridgewater Hotel (☎ 907-452-6661, 800-528-4916; www.fountainheadhotels.com; 723 1st St; r $159; ☐) Overlooking the Chena River and conveniently located downtown is one of Fairbanks' more plush hotels. Rates include transportation from the airport or train station.

Billie's Backpackers (☎ 907-456-4944; www.alaska hostel.com; 2895 Mack Rd; dm $25; ☐) A friendly hostel that is a 10-minute walk from the university and has bikes, Internet access and free storage.

Golden North Motel (☎ 907-479-6201, 800-447-1910; www.goldennorthmotel.com; 4888 Old Airport Rd; s/d $69/74) Smallish rooms with private bath and cable TV.

Eating & Drinking

Soapy Smith's (☎ 907-451-8380; 543 2nd Ave; dinner $9-21; ☯ 11am-10pm; ☒) Good burgers, salads, sandwiches and chowder are served in a saloon atmosphere.

LaVelle's Bistro (☎ 907-450-0555; 575 1st Ave; dinner $16-32; ☯ 4:30-9pm Sun-Mon, 4:30-10pm Tue-Sat; ☒) Fine dining in Fairbanks? LaVelle's fits the bill with the city's best wine cellar and a menu to match. Try the potato-crusted salmon.

Gambardella's Pasta Bella (☎ 907-457-4992; 706 2nd Ave; dinner $16-25; ☯ 11am-9pm Mon-Thu, 11am-10pm Fri & Sat, 4:30-9pm Sun; ☒) Some of the best homemade pizzas in the Interior, in a delightful outdoor setting.

Thai House (☎ 907-452-6123; 526 5th Ave; dinner mains $13-17; ☯ 11am-10pm Mon-Sat; ☒) Veg-friendly restaurant, south on Cushman St.

Palace Theatre & Saloon (☎ 907-456-5960; Pioneer Park; adult/child $16/7) Honky-tonk piano and cancan dancers in its Golden Heart Revue show.

Getting There & Around

Alaska Airlines (☎ 907-474-0481, 800-252-7522; www.alaskaair.com) has 10 daily flights to Anchorage (one way/round-trip $180/205), with occasional bargains. For travel into Arctic Alaska, contact **Frontier Flying Service** (☎ 907-474-0014, 800-478-6779; www.frontierflying.com).

Rent-A-Wreck (☎ 907-452-1606, 800-478-1606; 2105 S Cushman St; ☯ 8am-5:30pm Mon-Fri, 9am-noon Sat) will rent you a compact for $39 a day, and at **Go North Alaska Travel Center** (☎ 907-479-7272, 866-236-7272; 3500 Davis Rd; ☯ 8am-5pm) you can rent campers for $83 to $143 per day with 100 free miles.

Alaska Direct Bus Lines (☎ 800-770-6652) runs from Fairbanks to Whitehorse ($165, 15 hours), with buses stopping at Tok ($65, five hours). **Alaska/Yukon Trails** (☎ 800-770-7275; www.alaskashuttle.com) offers daily connections to Denali National Park ($46, 2½ hours) and Anchorage ($91, eight hours). It also services Dawson City ($162, 10 hours).

The **Alaska Railroad** (☎ 800-544-0552; www.akrr.com) departs at 8:15am daily for Denali

ALASKA

National Park ($54, three hours) and Anchorage ($179, 12 hours).

The **Metropolitan Area Commuter Service** (☎ 907-459-1011) provides a local, weekday bus service (single fare/day pass $1.50/3).

THE BUSH

The Bush is the vast area of Alaska that is not readily accessible by road or ferry. It includes Arctic Alaska, the Brooks Range, the Alaska Peninsula–Aleutian Islands chain and the Bering Sea coast. Traveling to the Bush usually involves small, expensive chartered aircraft. Facilities for travelers are also pricey and very limited. If you're planning to visit small, isolated communities, it's best to be accompanied by a local contact or tour guide.

To visit **Arctic Alaska**, take the Dalton Hwy, a rough gravel road that goes 490 miles north from Fairbanks to Deadhorse, near Prudhoe Bay. You can tour the oil complex at Prudhoe, but you can't camp on the shores of the Arctic Ocean. The highlight of the long drive is the **Arctic Circle** and **Atigun Pass** (4752ft) in the Brooks Range, 300 miles from Fairbanks, for the views of the North Slope. **Dalton Hwy Express** (☎ 907-474-3555; www.daltonhighwayexpress.com) makes the run to Prudhoe Bay three times a week. It's $120 round-trip from Fairbanks to the Arctic Circle (six hours one way), and $290 to Prudhoe Bay (16 hours one way). **Arc-**

tic Outfitters (☎ 907-474-3530; www.arctic-outfitters.com) offers a self-drive package to Prudhoe Bay for $848, which includes a car, three nights' lodging and an Arctic Ocean tour.

The Dalton Hwy passes the remote **Gates of the Arctic National Park**, which has great hiking and paddling, but the park is best accessed from the town of **Bettles**, which can be reached only by air. For information, contact the **National Park Ranger Station** (☎ 907-692-5494; wwwnps.gov/gaar). For guided and unguided trips into the park, contact **Sourdough Outfitters** (☎ 907-692-5252; www.sourdoughoutfitters.com).

On the Bering Sea coast, the storied goldrush town of **Nome** is friendly and interesting. The **visitor center** (☎ 907-443-6624; www.nomealaska.org; ☼ 9am-9pm) has information about accommodations and trips in the surrounding area. You can camp on **Golden Sands Beach** (campsite free), where gold is still being panned. An advance-purchase **Alaska Airlines** (☎ 800-252-7522; www.alaskaair.com) ticket runs $380 to $500 round-trip from Anchorage.

Isolated settlements on the **Aleutian Islands** can be reached by the ferry **M/V Tustumena** (☎ 800-526-6731; www.ferryalaska.com), which makes a monthly trip along the archipelago every summer. It's a superbly scenic trip when the weather is clear, and the ferry stops at five ports for just long enough to look around. It costs $618 round-trip from Homer to Dutch Harbor. If you want to stay longer at Dutch Harbor, and you should, fly back ($462) on Peninsula Airways; you'll need to book the ticket through Alaska Airlines.

ALASKA

Hawaii

Catch the sunrise over lunarlike Haleakala Crater, one of the world's largest volcanoes. Kayak among dolphins and sea turtles along the south Maui coast. Watch fiery red lava light up the night sky on the Big Island. Take a surfing lesson from one of the celebrated pros along Waikiki Beach. Or go to untouristed Moloka'i and see what the islands used to be like.

Hawaii is diverse and jaw-droppingly beautiful. Intrepid traveler Mark Twain referred to the archipelago as 'the loveliest fleet of islands that lies anchored in any ocean.' Naturally, much has changed since Twain's day, and some critics write Hawaii off as overdeveloped and spoiled. But anyone who truly dislikes Hawaii probably hasn't been here. Sure there are megaresorts where you can just lounge around all day, but there are also plenty of unspoiled niches – quiet beaches, back trails and sleepy towns – just waiting to be explored.

And the landscapes are like no place else in the USA. Sunseekers will discover beaches ranging from gleaming white to jet black. Land-lovers will find lava-strewn trails, lush green rain forests, deep red canyons and mountains high enough to don winter snowcaps. The water world is equally extraordinary. Hawaii has some of the planet's top surfing and windsurfing conditions, with both death-defying waves for pros and protected bays for beginners. Brilliant fish and corals provide stunning diving and snorkeling. Two-thirds of all the humpback whales in the North Pacific winter near Hawaii's coastline, frolicking to the thrill of onlookers.

And then there are the people. Hawaiians are friendly and laid-back, always ready to strike up a conversation – or, as they say on the islands, 'talk story.' The weather is as steady as the people, warm and comfortable all year round. Be quiet and listen: the twang of a steel-string guitar, the whisper of plumeria-scented breezes, the laughter of children playing in the surf – there really is magic in the land of aloha.

HAWAII

HIGHLIGHTS

- Riding the monster surf on **O'ahu's North Shore** (p1128)
- Watching majestic humpback whales breaching along **Maui's Coast** (p1134)
- Experiencing the fiery lava of **Hawai'i Volcanoes National Park** (p1131)
- Exploring quiet **Moloka'i** (p1137) on the back of a mule
- Hiking the sea cliffs on Kaua'i's spectacular **Na Pali Coast** (p1136)

Na Pali Coast ★
O'ahu's North Shore ★
Moloka'i ★
Maui's Coast ★
Hawaii
Hawai'i Volcanoes National Park ★

HAWAII

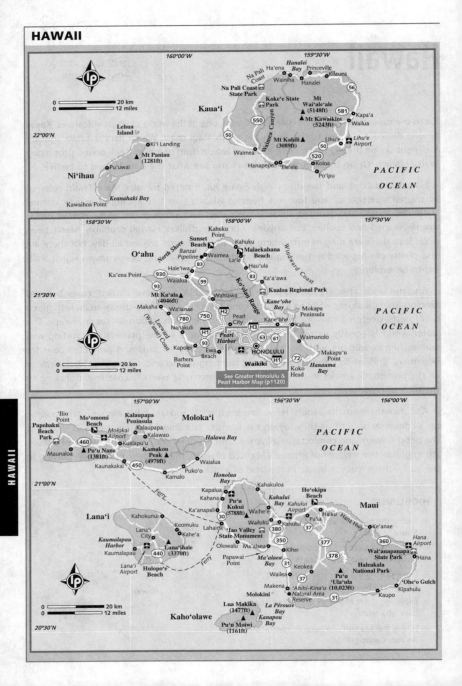

HAWAII

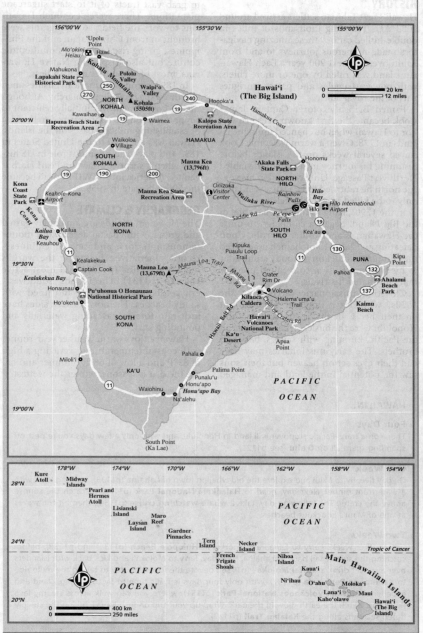

HISTORY

Hawaii's first Tahitian settlers arrived around 1000 AD. Traveling thousands of miles in double-hulled canoes, these amazing navigators made numerous journeys to and from Tahiti over the next 200 years. Each Hawaiian island was ruled by one or more chiefs, with power struggles and palace intrigues part of the royal fabric.

Famed British explorer Captain James Cook became the first known Western visitor to Hawaii when he chanced upon the islands in 1778. Given a warm welcome, Cook stayed several weeks on the islands before resuming his journey in search of the fabled Northwest Passage. Unsuccessful in his voyage north he returned to Hawaii a year later, only to be killed in a freak melee.

In the 1790s, King Kamehameha, chief of the Big Island, began a campaign to unite the Hawaiian islands under his rule. Upon defeating an island, Kamehameha sacrificed the conquered chief on a bloody stone altar to his war god Ku – a convenient practice that eliminated his rivals.

Christian missionaries arrived in the 1820s, with New England whalers hot on their heels. In the 1840s, Lahaina and Honolulu were the busiest whaling towns in the Pacific, bursting with sailors, bars and brothels. The early missionaries may have had their eyes set on heaven but their sons saw the potential in the land and managed to grab vast tracts of it to start sugarcane plantations. There weren't enough Hawaiians to work the fields, so immigrants were brought in from China, Japan and the Philippines, giving rise to Hawaii's multiethnic culture but also displacing Native Hawaiians, most of whom became landless.

In 1893 a group of American businessmen overthrew the Hawaiian monarchy. Although the US government was initially reluctant to support the coup, it soon warmed to the idea of establishing military bases on the islands. Hawaii was annexed to the United States in 1898 and played an infamous role in US history when a surprise attack on Pearl Harbor vaulted America into WWII. Hawaii became the 50th US state in 1959.

GEOGRAPHY & CLIMATE

The Hawaiian islands are amazingly varied and grand, with coastal deserts and mountainous interiors, and several Guinness-record superlatives, including the world's highest sea cliffs (p1137) and most active volcano (p1131). The islands' southwestern coasts are sunny, dry and lined with sandy beaches. The northeastern sides have lush rain forests, cascading waterfalls and pounding surf.

Hawaii enjoys warm weather year-round, with coastal temperatures averaging a high of 83°F and a low of 68°F. Summer and fall are the driest seasons, winter the wettest.

HAWAII IN...

Four Days

Those on a trans-Pacific stopover will land in Honolulu, and with only a few days you're best off spending them all on **O'ahu** (see p1121).

One Week

On day five, fly to Maui and explore the old whaling town of **Lahaina** (p1133), capping it off with a waterfront dinner. Next day, head to **Haleakala National Park** (p1136) to catch the sunrise above the crater. The following day, take a **whale-watching cruise** (p1134), then hit the waves at one of Maui's knockout beaches.

Two Weeks

Got another week? Ferry to Lana'i and snorkel at **Hulopo'e Beach** (p1138) and (p1138), before catching the sunset sail back to Lahaina. Next day, ferry to Moloka'i and kick back with islanders over a sunset drink at **Hotel Moloka'i** (p1138); devote the following day to taking the mule ride to **Kalaupapa Peninsula** (p1137). With only four days left, it's time to fly to the Big Island and experience **Hawai'i Volcanoes National Park** (p1131), where you can walk across steamy lava flows and watch the earth glow in the dark! Wrap up your trip on lush Kaua'i, hiking the steeply fluted sea cliffs along the **Kalalau Trail** (p1137).

NATIONAL, STATE & REGIONAL PARKS

Both of Hawaii's national parks are volcano intensive. On the Big Island, **Hawai'i Volcanoes National Park** (p1131) is an awesome mélange of wilderness environments ranging from tropical beaches to subarctic mountaintops, centered on two active volcanoes. On Maui, **Haleakala National Park** (p1136) focuses on Haleakala Crater, which so resembles the lunar surface that astronauts have trained there.

Hawaii's many state parks range from beachfront sites with full facilities to undeveloped wilderness. For information on state parks and to make camping reservations, contact the **Division of State Parks** (Map p1122; ☎ 808-587-0300; www.hawaii.gov/dlnr/dsp; 1151 Punchbowl St, Honolulu).

LANGUAGE

English and Hawaiian are the official state languages. About 9000 people speak Hawaiian, and Hawaiian words and phrases pepper the speech of most Hawaiian residents.

INFORMATION

To explore the islands in more depth, pick up a copy of Lonely Planet's comprehensive *Hawaii* guide. Hawaii's sales tax is 4.16% and there's an additional 7.25% room tax.
Alternative Hawaii (www.alternative-hawaii.com) This culturally sensitive ecotourism site is an excellent resource.
Hawaii Visitors & Convention Bureau (www.gohawaii.com) This bureau covers Hawaii thoroughly.

GETTING THERE & AWAY

Honolulu is a major Pacific air hub and an intermediate stop on many flights between the US mainland and Asia, Australia and the South Pacific. Passengers on any of these routes can often make a free Honolulu stopover. From Europe, ask about an add-on fare from the US West Coast or perhaps a round-the-world ticket. From the US mainland, the cheapest fares often start at around $600 from the East Coast, $400 from California. Most major US airlines fly to Honolulu and Maui; some also fly directly from the mainland to the Big Island.

GETTING AROUND

Hawaiian Airlines (☎ 808-838-1555, 800-367-5320; www.hawaiianair.com) and **Aloha Airlines** (☎ 808-484-1111, 800-367-5250; www.alohaairlines.com) are the main carriers flying between Hawaiian

HAWAII FACTS

Nickname Aloha State
Population 1.2 million
Area 10,930 sq miles
Capital city Honolulu
State fish Humuhumunukunukuapua'a (rectangular triggerfish)
Birthplace of Surfing
Home of Ukuleles, America's only royal palace
Famous for Hula dancing, the world's most active volcano

islands. Service is frequent, flight times are short and fares cost from $63 to $103 one way; flights are usually cheaper early in the morning and late in the day.

Currently, the only ferry services in the state operate from Maui to Lana'i and Moloka'i. If environmental concerns are adequately addressed, a new high-speed ferry service between O'ahu, Kaua'i, Maui and the Big Island could begin in 2007; see **Hawaii Superferry** (www.hawaiisuperferry.com) for the latest.

O'ahu is the only island that can be explored extensively by public bus. Maui, the Big Island and Kaua'i have limited bus service between major towns, but no service to most sightseeing destinations.

Rental cars are available on all the main islands and typically cost $35 to $50 a day, $175 to $250 a week. It's wise to book a car before you arrive; browse websites of the major rental companies to find the best price.

On the larger islands, half- and full-day sightseeing bus tours are available for $50 to $100. Specialized tours include whale-watching cruises, bicycle tours, snorkeling trips, overnight tours and helicopter tours. All can be booked after arrival in Hawaii.

O'AHU

When most people think of Hawaii, it's typically O'ahu locales – like Waikiki, Pearl Harbor and Sunset Beach – that spring to mind. O'ahu is where the action is, whether you're looking for nightlife or surf meets. Honolulu and Waikiki offer a vibrant city scene, but that's just one side of the island. Just beyond the city you'll find rolling hills carpeted in pineapples, fluted mountains cut by cascading waterfalls, and turquoise

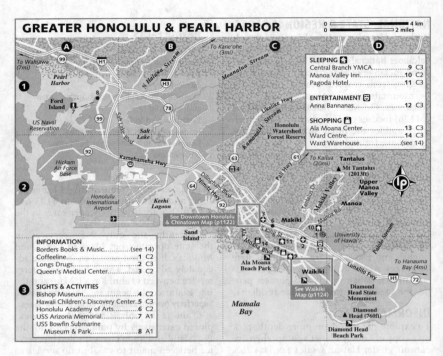

GREATER HONOLULU & PEARL HARBOR

0 _____ 4 km
0 _____ 2 miles

SLEEPING
Central Branch YMCA...............9 C3
Manoa Valley Inn....................10 C2
Pagoda Hotel..........................11 C3

ENTERTAINMENT
Anna Bannanas........................12 C3

SHOPPING
Ala Moana Center....................13 C3
Ward Centre............................14 C3
Ward Warehouse...................(see 14)

INFORMATION
Borders Books & Music.............(see 14)
Coffeeline...............................1 C2
Longs Drugs............................2 C3
Queen's Medical Center............3 C2

SIGHTS & ACTIVITIES
Bishop Museum........................4 C2
Hawaii Children's Discovery Center.5 C3
Honolulu Academy of Arts..........6 C2
USS Arizona Memorial................7 A1
USS Bowfin Submarine
  Museum & Park.....................8 A1

bays remote enough to provide the backdrop for the TV series *Lost*. Yep, that show about a remote South Pacific isle is shot right on O'ahu's undeveloped North Shore, and the jungles the castaways run through are none other than O'ahu trails.

Getting Around

O'ahu's extensive public bus system, **TheBus** (☎ 808-848-5555; www.thebus.org), has some 80 routes that collectively cover most of O'ahu; all fares are $2. From Honolulu International Airport to Waikiki, take bus 19 or 20. Buses 2, 19 and 20 connect Waikiki with downtown Honolulu and Chinatown.

The major car rental companies have booths at the airport, and several also have branches in Waikiki. **Blue Sky Rentals** (Map p1124; ☎ 808-947-0101; 1920 Ala Moana Blvd), in Waikiki, rents mopeds for $40 per day.

HONOLULU & WAIKIKI

In Honolulu, East meets West with a delightful diversity of sights, scents and flavors. You can explore the only royal palace in the USA, feast on savory Pacific Rim cuisine and spend the evening listening to Hawaiian music on the beach.

With its phenomenal oceanfront setting, sunny year-round weather and a plethora of things to do, it's little wonder why Waikiki has become one of America's top vacation destinations. Its two gorgeous miles of sandy beach are a venue for anything to do with the water – from swimming and surfing to sunbathing and people-watching.

History

Shortly after King Kamehameha conquered O'ahu in the 1840s, foreign ships began stopping in Honolulu (Sheltered Harbor) and a harborside trading village sprang up. To keep track of the trade and get his cut of the action, Kamehameha moved his royal court to Honolulu and a palace was erected a few blocks from the waterfront. In 1901 tourism was introduced to Waikiki with the opening of the first oceanfront hotel, and a tram was built to connect Honolulu to its beachside suburb. With the advent of jet travel in the 1960s, tourism took off and never looked back.

HAWAII

Orientation

The airport is on the outskirts of Honolulu; airport buses pass through Honolulu's city center on their way to Waikiki. Diamond Head, the extinct volcano looming above the eastern side of Waikiki, is such a major landmark that islanders typically say 'go Diamond Head' when they give directions.

Information

BOOKSTORES

Bestsellers (Map p1124; ☎ 808-953-2378; Hilton Hawaiian Village, 2005 Kalia Rd, Waikiki; ⏰ 8am-10pm)
Borders Books & Music (Map p1120; ☎ 808-591-8995; Ward Centre, 1200 Ala Moana Blvd, Honolulu; ⏰ 9am-10pm or later)

EMERGENCY

Police, fire and ambulance (☎ 911) Emergency.

INTERNET ACCESS

Coffeeline (Map p1120; ☎ 808-778-7909; cnr University & Seaview Aves, Honolulu; ⏰ 7am-3:45pm Mon-Fri, 8am-noon Sat) Free wi-fi at this café near the university.
Daily Buzz Internet Cafe (Map p1124; ☎ 808-924-2223; 150 Kaiulani Ave, Waikiki; 1st 10 min $3, then per min 15¢; ⏰ 6am-2pm)

MEDIA

Honolulu Advertiser (www.honoluluadvertiser.com) Hawaii's largest daily newspaper.
Honolulu Weekly (www.honoluluweekly.com) This progressive free paper has an extensive entertainment section.
KINE (105.1 FM) Tune in here for Hawaiian music any time of the day.

MEDICAL SERVICES

Longs Drugs (Map p1120; ☎ 808-949-4781; 2220 S King St, Honolulu; ⏰ 24hr) The nearest all-night pharmacy to Waikiki, between McCully St and University Ave. Other Longs with varying hours are found around the city, including at Ala Moana Center.
Queen's Medical Center (Map p1120; ☎ 808-538-9011; 1301 Punchbowl St, Honolulu; ⏰ 24hr) A major full-service hospital.

MONEY

Bank of Hawaii (Map p1124; ☎ 808-543-6900; 2228 Kalakaua Ave, Waikiki) In central Waikiki.
First Hawaiian Bank (Map p1122; ☎ 808-525-6888; 2 N King St, Honolulu) In downtown Honolulu.

POST

Post office downtown (Map p1122; ☎ 800-275-8777; 335 Merchant St); Waikiki (Map p1124; ☎ 808-973-7515; 330 Saratoga Rd) Downtown branch in the Old Federal Building.

TOURIST INFORMATION

Hawaii Visitors & Convention Bureau (Map p1124; ☎ 808-923-1811; www.gohawaii.com; Waikiki Business Plaza, 2270 Kalakaua Ave, Suite 801)
O'ahu Visitors Bureau (☎ 877-525-6248; www.visit-oahu.com) Phone and online information on Honolulu and all of O'ahu.

Sights & Activities

DOWNTOWN HONOLULU

At the heart of downtown Honolulu, the 19th-century **'Iolani Palace** (Map p1122; ☎ 808-522-0832; www.iolanipalace.org; cnr S King & Richards Sts; tour $20; ⏰ 9am-2pm Tue-Sat) offers a unique glimpse into

---

O'AHU IN...

Two Days

Congratulations! You've made it to Hawaii, so go ahead and hit the beach. If you've never tried your hand at surfing, take a lesson from one of the surfers at **Waikiki Beach** (p1122). A sunset dinner at a waterfront restaurant like **Shore Bird Beach Broiler** (p1126) makes a perfect finale. On day two, stroll through **Chinatown** (p1122), slurp a bowl of noodles with the locals at **To Chau** (p1125) and explore the fascinating historical quarters of **downtown Honolulu** (above).

Four Days

Follow the two-day itinerary and then take your sightseeing back to the water on day three – spend the morning snorkeling among tropical fish at **Hanauma Bay Nature Preserve** (p1127) and the afternoon windsurfing at **Kailua Beach** (p1127). Alternatively, if you prefer your thrills on land, hike up to the summit of **Diamond Head** (p1127) for a good workout and a bird's-eye city view.

Set day four aside for a tour round O'ahu, taking in the **Sunset Beach** (p1128) scene and stopping for lunch with the surfer crowd at **Café Hale'iwa** (p1128).

HAWAII

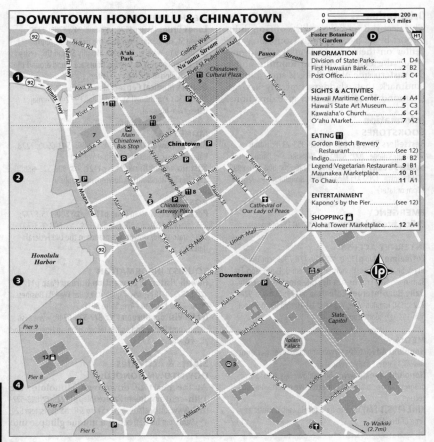

DOWNTOWN HONOLULU & CHINATOWN

INFORMATION	
Division of State Parks...............**1** D4	
First Hawaiian Bank.....................**2** B2	
Post Office.......................................**3** C4	
SIGHTS & ACTIVITIES	
Hawaii Maritime Center.............**4** A4	
Hawai'i State Art Museum.........**5** C3	
Kawaiaha'o Church.....................**6** C4	
O'ahu Market................................**7** A2	
EATING	
Gordon Biersch Brewery	
Restaurant...............................(see 12)	
Indigo...**8** B2	
Legend Vegetarian Restaurant...**9** B1	
Maunakea Marketplace..............**10** B1	
To Chau...**11** A1	
ENTERTAINMENT	
Kapono's by the Pier..................(see 12)	
SHOPPING	
Aloha Tower Marketplace...........**12** A4	

Hawaii's intriguing history. At the adjacent
State Capitol, visitors can wander through the
rotunda without charge. Built of coral slabs,
the nearby **Kawaiaha'o Church** (Map p1122; ☎ 808-
522-1333; 957 Punchbowl St; admission free; ☒ 8am-4pm
Mon-Fri) is O'ahu's oldest church (1838).

Another central piece of the island art
scene, the **Hawai'i State Art Museum** (Map p1122;
☎ 808-586-0900; www.state.hi.us/sfca; 250 S Hotel St;
admission free; ☒ 10am-4pm Tue-Sat), showcases
the work of Hawaiian artists.

The **Hawaii Maritime Center** (Map p1122;
☎ 808-523-6151; www.holoholo.org/maritime; Pier 7;
admission $7.50; ☒ 8:30am-5pm) offers an evoca-
tive look at Hawaii's maritime history, from
the arrival of the first Polynesian settlers to
the whaling era.

CHINATOWN

A walk through Chinatown, immediately
north of downtown Honolulu, takes you
through one of the more intriguing quarters
of the city. You can get tattooed, consult a
herbalist, explore temples and antique shops,
and feast on superb Asian food. A good place
to start is colorful **O'ahu Market** (Map p1122;
cnr Kekaulike & N King Sts) – the bustling heart of
Chinatown for more than a century.

WAIKIKI

Waikiki is all about the beach. Catamarans
and outriggers pull up onto the sand offering rides, and all along the beach there are
concession stands renting surfboards, boogie boards, kayaks and windsurfing gear at

very reasonable prices. And if you need just a little bit of help in perfecting your technique, lessons are readily available as well.

GREATER HONOLULU

Bishop Museum (Map p1120; ☎ 808-847-3511; www .bishopmuseum.org; 1525 Bernice St; admission $15; ☺ 9am-5pm), considered the finest Polynesian anthropological museum in the world, offers impressive displays on Hawaii's multiethnic history.

The exceptional **Honolulu Academy of Arts** (Map p1120; ☎ 808-532-8700; www.honoluluacademy .org; 900 S Beretania St; admission $7; ☺ 10am-4:30pm Tue-Sat, 1-5pm Sun) has solid collections of Asian, European and Pacific artwork.

There are several hiking trails and lookouts with sweeping city views in the Tantalus area, the lush Upper Manoa and Makiki Valleys, and in the hills above the University of Hawai'i. Some trailheads are accessible by bus. Guided hikes are offered on weekends by the **Sierra Club** (☎ 808-538-6616; www.hi.sierraclub.org; hikes $5).

If you want a great place to swim without the tourist crowds, head to **Ala Moana Beach Park** (Map p1120; 1201 Ala Moana Blvd), between downtown and Waikiki.

Honolulu & Waikiki for Children

O'ahu spills over with activities for *keiki* (children). To check out the wild side, head to the petting area of the **Honolulu Zoo** (Map p1124; ☎ 808-971-7171; 151 Kapahulu Ave; adult/child $6/1; ☺ 9am-4:30pm). Across the street, the **Waikiki Aquarium** (☎ 808-923-9741; 2777 Kalakaua Ave; adult/child $9/2; ☺ 9am-5pm) has a touch tank geared especially for kids.

Of course there's an array of fun things to do right on Waikiki Beach, from outrigger-canoe rides to surfing lessons. And when the sun fails to shine, the hands-on **Hawaii Children's Discovery Center** (Map p1120; ☎ 808-524-5437; 111 Ohe St; adult/child $8/6.75; ☺ 9am-1pm Tue-Fri, 10am-3pm Sat & Sun) is the perfect place to spend an afternoon.

Tours

A variety of reasonably priced sightseeing tours of Honolulu and the rest of the island are offered by **Discover Hidden Hawaii Tours** (☎ 808-737-3700, 800-946-4432; www.discoverhawaii tours.com) and **Roberts Hawaii** (☎ 808-539-9400, 800-831-5541; www.robertshawaii.com).

Festivals & Events

King Kamehameha Day, a state holiday on June 11, is celebrated with festivities at 'Iolani Palace, hula shows, music and crafts. Watch the world's top surfers chase the world's highest waves during the **Triple Crown of Surfing**, November to December on the North Shore. See www.calendar.gohawaii.com for more on festivals and events.

Sleeping

O'ahu boasts nearly half of the hotel rooms in Hawaii, with the lion's share in sunny Waikiki.

HONOLULU

If you're not up for the hustle and bustle of Waikiki, there are some pleasant options elsewhere in Honolulu.

Manoa Valley Inn (Map p1120; ☎ 808-947-6019; www .manoavalleyinn.com; 2001 Vancouver Dr; r with shared/private bath from $99/140; ℗ ✗) This restored Victorian, on the National Register of Historic Places, exudes colonial charm. It's as atmospheric as it gets, as long as you don't mind being near the university rather than the beach.

Pagoda Hotel (Map p1120; ☎ 808-941-6611, 800-367-6060; www.pagodahotel.com; 1525 Rycroft St; r from $95; ℗ ☎) Return visitors flock to this place for its good-value, comfortable digs. Midway between Waikiki and downtown, it's

HAWAII

GAY & LESBIAN WAIKIKI

Waikiki is the heart of Honolulu's well-developed gay scene. For more information on gay-friendly establishments, visit www.gayhawaii.com.

Waikiki's top gay venue, **Hula's Bar & Lei Stand** (Map p1124; ☎ 808-923-0669; 134 Kapahulu Ave; ☺ 10am-2am), is a cheery open-air bar and the place to meet. Other good spots are **Angles Waikiki** (Map p1124; ☎ 808-926-9766; 2256 Kuhio Ave; ☺ 10am-2am), a bar by day and a nightclub after dark; **Fusion Waikiki** (Map p1124; ☎ 808-924-2422; 2260 Kuhio Ave; ☺ 10pm-4am), which features karaoke and female impersonator shows; and **In-Between** (Map p1124; ☎ 808-926-7060; 2155 Lau'ula St; ☺ 4pm-2am), a gay karaoke bar where drama reigns.

best suited for visitors with a car. Check out the hotel's namesake pagoda-style restaurant and surrounding koi pond. Parking $5.

Central Branch YMCA (Map p1120; ☎ 808-941-3344; www.centralymcahonolulu.org; 401 Atkinson Dr; s/d with shared bath $33/45, with private bath $41/55; 🅿 🚫 🛗) Opposite a lovely beach just outside Waikiki, the YMCA has 114 straightforward rooms. Those with private bath are open to men and women; shared bath are for men only. Guests have access to Y facilities, including a sauna. Parking $5.

WAIKIKI

If you want to be in the midst of the action, Waikiki is the place to stay. Generally, the closer to the beach, the pricier it gets.

Kalakaua Ave, the main beachfront strip, is lined with swanky hotels and $300-plus rooms. Better value can be found at the smaller hostelries on the backstreets, in the Kuhio Ave area and up near the Ala Wai Canal, all a short walk from the beach.

Waikiki Prince Hotel (Map p1124; ☎ 808-922-1544; www.waikikiprince.com; 2431 Prince Edward St; r $45-55, with kitchenette $60-75; 🅿 🚫) One of Waikiki's best-kept secrets, this friendly place offers simple but comfortable rooms at unbeatable prices. Parking $5.

Ilima Hotel (Map p1124; ☎ 808-923-1877, 800-801-9366; www.ilima.com; 445 Nohonani St; r $135-165; 🅿 🛗) The perfect choice for those who want to prepare their own meals – all 99 rooms in this hotel have full kitchens.

Hostelling International Waikiki (Map p1124; ☎ 808-926-8313; www.hostelsaloha.com; 2417 Prince Edward St; dm/d $23/54; ⊗ reception 7am-3am; P 💻) Just minutes from the beach, this 60-bed hostel is a great place to meet other travelers, but reserve ahead as it is often booked solid. Parking $5.

Cabana at Waikiki (Map p1124; ☎ 808-926-5555, 877-902-2121; www.cabana-waikiki.com; 2551 Cartwright Rd; ste incl breakfast $139-175; P 💈) This gay-friendly hotel with cool tropical decor has 15 apartments, each of which can sleep up to four people. Parking $8.

Outrigger Hotels & Resorts (Map p1124; ☎ 808-921-6870, 800-462-6262; www.outrigger.com, www.ohana hotels.com; r from $90; P 💈) This chain operates roughly 25% of the hotels in Waikiki. Essentially, the Ohana-named ones are off the beach and hence cheaper, the Outrigger ones closer to the water and pricier. The character can be a bit cookie-cutter but the amenities are good and the standards high. Discounts abound – check the web page. Four of the chain's hotels are marked on the Waikiki map:

Ohana Reef Lanai (☎ 808-923-3881; 225 Saratoga Rd)
Ohaha Royal Islander (☎ 808-922-1961; 2164 Kalia Rd)
Ohana Waikiki Malia (☎ 808-923-7621; 2211 Kuhio Ave)
Outrigger Waikiki (☎ 808-923-0711; 2335 Kalakaua Ave)

Eating

Whether you fancy unassuming ethnic eateries or fine dining on the beach, the city's a treat for the tastebuds.

HONOLULU & CHINATOWN

Indigo (Map p1122; ☎ 808-521-2900; 1121 Nu'uanu Ave; mains $16-26; ⊗ lunch Tue-Fri, 6-9:30pm Tue-Sat) On the Chinatown-downtown border, Indigo's a favorite of locals and visitors alike for its innovative Eurasian cuisine and cheery courtyard setting.

To Chau (Map p1122; ☎ 808-533-4549; 1007 River St; soup $4-7; ⊗ 8am-2:30pm) The perfect place to join Chinatown residents over a steamy bowl of *pho*, a delicious Vietnamese soup spiced with heaps of fresh basil.

Maunakea Marketplace (Map p1122; N Hotel St; meals $5; ⊗ 7am-3:30pm) Mom-and-pop vendors dish out homestyle Chinese, Filipino and Thai fare in this Chinatown marketplace – the ultimate local grinds.

Gordon Biersch Brewery Restaurant (Map p1122; ☎ 808-599-4877; 1 Aloha Tower Dr; mains $10-23; ⊗ 11am-11:30pm Sun-Thu, 11:30am-1am Fri & Sat)

THE AUTHOR'S CHOICE

Sheraton Moana Surfrider (Map p1124; ☎ 808-922-3111, 800-325-3535; www.moana-surfrider.com; 2365 Kalakaua Ave; r from $270; P 💈) If you love colonial-style hotels, you're in for a treat. Hawaii's first beachfront hotel (since 1901), this grand establishment has been authentically restored right down to the carved columns of the porte cochere. Hawaiian quilts and artwork adorn the airy lobby, and even the guest rooms retain their period appearance with modern conveniences discreetly concealed behind armoire doors. Parking $10.

You'll find a good water view, fresh seafood and O'ahu's finest local brew on tap at this bistro in the Aloha Tower Marketplace.

Legend Vegetarian Restaurant (Map p1122; ☎ 808-532-8218; Chinatown Cultural Plaza; mains $7-12; ⊗ 10:30am-2pm Thu-Tue) Tofu in the guise of meat is the specialty at this health-conscious Chinese lunch spot.

WAIKIKI

Duke's Canoe Club (Map p1124; ☎ 808-922-2268; 2335 Kalakaua Ave; breakfast & lunch buffet $12, dinner mains $15-27; ⊗ 7am-11:30pm) Named after surfing legend Duke Kahanamoku, this waterfront restaurant packs a crowd for its island atmosphere and reliable food.

Ono Hawaiian Food (Map p1124; ☎ 808-737-2275; 726 Kapahulu Ave; meals $8-10; ⊗ 11am-7:45pm Mon-Sat) The best place to try traditional fare – go for the kalua pig plate, served with several Hawaiian side dishes.

Banyan Veranda (Map p1124; ☎ 808-922-3111; 2365 Kalakaua Ave; 3-course meal $52; ⊗ dinner) This

---

BEACH SKINNY

Different sections of Waikiki's long, glorious beach have different names and personalities. From northwest to southeast: **Kahanamoku Beach** offers calm waters, **Fort DeRussy Beach** has the best windsurfing, **Gray's Beach** is a favorite for swimmers, **Central Waikiki** is the place to be seen, **Kuhio Beach Park** is where the surfers hang, **Queen's Surf Beach** is a haunt for gay beachgoers and **Kapiolani Beach Park** is an ideal spot for picnicking.

HAWAII

THE AUTHOR'S CHOICE

Shore Bird Beach Broiler (Map p1124; ☎ 808-922-2887; 2169 Kalia Rd; dinners $10-20; ✆ 6pm-1am) At this fun open-air restaurant you grill your own steak, chicken or fish on a communal barbie as you chat with fellow diners. Dinners include a solid buffet of salads and sides. To top it off, the beachfront setting here is second to none. Come at sunset for a memorable experience.

---

courtyard veranda at the century-old Sheraton Moana Surfrider offers classic Pacific Rim and French cuisine in a thoroughly romantic setting.

Keo's (Map p1124; ☎ 808-922-9355; 2028 Kuhio Ave; mains $10-18; ✆ 5-11pm) A favorite of visiting celebs, this Thai restaurant has a full page of vegetarian options as well as all the usual fish and meat versions.

Irifune's (Map p1124; ☎ 808-737-1141; 563 Kapahulu Ave; mains $10-15; ✆ lunch & dinner Tue-Sat) Follow the locals to this bustling Japanese eatery where fresh fish is artistically prepared – the *tataki 'ahi* (seared tuna) is to die for.

Saint Germain (Map p1124; ☎ 808-924-4305; 2301 Kuhio Ave; mains $3-6; ✆ 7am-9pm) Come here for a tasty variety of soups, salads and hearty baguette sandwiches.

Fatty's Chinese Kitchen (Map p1124; ☎ 808-922-9600; 2345 Kuhio Ave; mains $4-6; ✆ 10:30am-10:30pm) Who says Waikiki has to be expensive? This hole-in-the-wall eatery serves fresh Chinese fare at bargain prices.

Food Pantry (Map p1124; ☎ 808-923-9831; 2370 Kuhio Ave; ✆ 6am-1am) The best place to get groceries in Waikiki.

Drinking

Moana Terrace Bar (Map p1124; ☎ 808-922-6611; 2552 Kalakaua Ave; ✆ 11am-1am) The Waikiki Beach Marriott's mellow poolside bar mixes a decent mai tai and has live Hawaiian music in the evenings.

Coconut Willy's Bar (Map p1124; ☎ 808-923-9454; International Market Place, 2330 Kalakaua Ave; ✆ 11am-1am) Willy's tends to be loud, but it's a great people-watching spot.

Entertainment

Honolulu and Waikiki rock, gyrate, croon, romance and mellow out. The free *Honolulu Weekly* has full details on what's happening.

Wave Waikiki (Map p1124; ☎ 808-941-0424; 1877 Kalakaua Ave; admission $5; ✆ 8pm-4am) Waikiki's hottest dance club with an emphasis on trance, hip-hop, hard rock and alternative music.

Moose McGillycuddy's (Map p1124; ☎ 808-923-0751; 310 Lewers St; admission $3-5; ✆ 9pm-1am Mon-Sat) Another hopping spot, this Waikiki restaurant-nightclub features Top 40 music.

Kapono's by the Pier (Map p1122; ☎ 808-536-2100; Aloha Tower Marketplace; ✆ 9pm-2am Tue-Sat) The best place to head for big-name Hawaiian music acts.

Anna Bannanas (Map p1120; ☎ 808-946-5190; 2440 S Beretania St; ✆ 9pm-2am Thu-Sat) Near the university, this is a hot weekend dance venue.

Waikiki abounds in Hawaiian-style entertainment. Bask in the aloha with performances by local hula troupes at the city-sponsored **Kuhio Beach Torch Lighting & Hula Show** (admission free; ✆ 6:30-7:30pm) at Kuhio Beach Park (Map p1124). Many beachfront hotels offer evening Hawaiian music at their outdoor bars; plop down with a tropical drink, or stroll along the shore and enjoy it for free. Two excellent places to start are the beachside Sheraton Moana Surfrider (p1125) and Duke's Canoe Club (p1125).

Shopping

International Market Place (Map p1124; ☎ 808-971-2080; 2330 Kalakaua Ave; ✆ 10am-10pm) Nearly a hundred stalls sell everything from seashell necklaces to sarongs – all set under a sprawling banyan tree in central Waikiki.

Bailey's Antique Shop (☎ 808-734-7628; 517 Kapahulu Ave) For antiques and used aloha shirts, this is a great place to browse – almost like a museum.

You'll find shops selling quality crafts, Hawaiian food items and island-style clothing in Honolulu's main shopping centers:

Ala Moana Center (Map p1120; 808-955-9517; 1450 Ala Moana Blvd; ✆ 9am-9pm Mon-Sat, 10am-7pm Sun)

Aloha Tower Marketplace (Map p1122; ☎ 808-566-2337; 1 Aloha Tower Dr; ✆ 9am-9pm Mon-Sat, 9am-7pm Sun)

Ward Centre (Map p1120; ☎ 808-591-8411; Ward Ave; ✆ 10am-9pm Mon-Sat, 10am-6pm Sun) Adjacent to Ward Warehouse.

PEARL HARBOR

The very name Pearl Harbor conjures up images of the December 7, 1941, Japanese attack that took 2500 lives, sank 21 ships and catapulted the US into WWII. Today more than 1.5 million people a year 're-member Pearl Harbor' by visiting the **USS Arizona Memorial** (Map p1120).

From the memorial, which sits directly over the sunken *Arizona,* visitors can look down at the shallow wreck that became the tomb for 1177 sailors. The **visitor center** (☎ 808-422-2771; www.nps.gov/usar; admission & tour free; 🕑 7:30am-5pm) runs 1¼-hour tours that include a documentary on the attack and a boat ride out to the memorial. Tours run on a first-come, first-served basis; arrive early to beat the queues. No purses, fanny packs or large cameras are allowed, but storage ($2) is available in the parking lot.

If you have to wait for your tour to start, walk over to the adjacent **USS Bowfin Submarine Museum & Park** (Map p1120; ☎ 808-423-1341; admission free, submarine tour $8; 🕑 8am-5pm), where you can poke around grounds dotted with WWII relics or clamber down into a retired submarine. Bowfin is also the departure point for a shuttle bus to the **USS Missouri** (Map p1120; ☎ 808-973-2494; tour $16; 🕑 9am-5pm), whose deck hosted the Japanese surrender that ended WWII.

From Waikiki, bus 42 goes to Pearl Harbor ($2) or take the **VIP Shuttle** (Map p1120; ☎ 808-839-0911; one way $4), which picks up from Waikiki hotels and is slightly faster, taking about 45 minutes.

SOUTHEAST O'AHU

The southeast coast abounds in dramatic scenery and offers plenty of activity options. For a sweeping view of the area make the 1.5-mile climb up **Diamond Head** (Map p1120; Diamond Head Rd; admission $1; 🕑 6am-6pm), the 760ft extinct volcano that forms the famous backdrop to Waikiki.

You'll find O'ahu's most popular snorkeling at **Hanauma Bay Nature Preserve** (Map p1120; ☎ 808-396-4229; Hwy 72; admission $5; 🕑 6am-6pm Wed-Mon, to 7pm Apr-Oct; Ⓟ), a gorgeous bay of turquoise waters set in a rugged volcanic ring. For the best conditions head to the outer reef; if you don't have snorkel gear you can rent it ($6) on site. Parking $1.

Long and lovely **Sandy Beach**, along Hwy 72 about a mile north of Hanauma, offers challenging bodysurfing with the kind of punishing shorebreaks and strong rips that makes it a favorite of pros – exhilarating action even for spectators!

An 18ft-deep tropical aquarium and choreographed dolphin shows are the highlight at **Sea Life Park** (Map p1120; ☎ 808-259-7933; 41-202 Hwy 72; adult/child $26/13; 🕑 9:30am-5pm), Hawaii's only marine park.

The favorite restaurant in these parts is unquestionably **Roy's** (Map p1120; ☎ 808-396-7697; Hawaii Kai Corporate Plaza, Hwy 72; mains $20-30; 🕑 dinner), which has superbly prepared Pacific Rim cuisine.

To get to any of these places from Waikiki, take bus 22 ($2).

BE YOUR OWN TOUR GUIDE

If you don't have a car, don't fret – it's possible to make a fun day excursion circling the island by public bus. As a matter of fact, one bus (52, Wahiawa–Circle Island) goes up through Haleiwa, circles the entire North Shore and Windward Coast, and comes down the scenic Pali Hwy back to Honolulu. If you were to sit on the bus nonstop it would take about four hours round-trip from Honolulu and, like all bus rides, it costs just $2. For each stop you make along the way, you'll need to buy a new $2 ticket – but at, say, $10 for a five-break journey, you've got yourself a deal of an island tour.

WINDWARD COAST

The deeply scalloped Ko'olau mountains form a scenic backdrop for the entire windward coast. Trade winds whipping in from the northeast rebound off the mountains, creating ideal conditions for windsurfing.

The **Nu'uanu Pali Lookout** (1200ft), on Hwy 61, offers a panoramic view of the coast. It's also the site of the last stand made by O'ahuans when King Kamehameha invaded the island – so many warriors were pushed over the precipice that a century after the battle 500 skulls were found at the base of the cliffs.

Beneath the windswept *pali* (cliffs) sits beautiful **Kailua Beach**, the island's top **windsurfing** spot. Just beyond the beach, the bird sanctuary of **Popoia Island** is a popular destination for kayakers. Kayak and windsurfing gear rentals, as well as windsurfing lessons, are available weekdays on the beach – no reservations necessary.

Other notable beaches on the windward coast are **Kualoa Regional Park**, which has a scenic setting and an ancient stone fish-pond, and **Malaekahana Beach**, a sandy beach good for swimming and surfing.

The **Polynesian Cultural Center** (☎ 808-293-3333; www.polynesia.com; Hwy 83, La'ie; admission $35; ☺ noon-9pm Mon-Sat) pulls in more visitors than anyplace else on O'ahu except Pearl Harbor. Pacific Island students from the nearby Brigham Young University help pay their tuition by demonstrating crafts in seven theme villages representing Samoa, New Zealand, Fiji, Tahiti, Tonga, the Marquesas and Hawaii.

NORTH SHORE

Surf-mania prevails on O'ahu's legendary North Shore. The massive 30ft winter swells at Sunset Beach, the Banzai Pipeline and Waimea Bay attract the best surfers in the world. So it's not surprising that the North Shore hosts some of the most awesome surf competitions on the planet, including the famed Triple Crown, which is held in December with prize purses reaching six figures.

The gateway to the North Shore, **Hale'iwa** is the only real town in this region – along its main road you'll find a funky surf museum, shops selling surfing paraphernalia and rusty pickup trucks with surfboards tied to the roof. When the surf's up, folks really do drop what they're doing and hit the waves. And they don't have to go far, as **Hale'iwa Ali'i Beach Park**, right in town, sees towering north swells.

The North Shore's most popular beach, **Waimea Bay Beach Park**, flaunts a dual personality. In summer the water can be as calm as a lake and ideal for swimming and snorkeling, while in winter it rips with the highest waves on the island.

A few miles to the north, the **Banzai Pipeline** breaks over a shallow reef, creating a death-defying ride for the pros hitting the action here. Next up is **Sunset Beach Park**, O'ahu's classic winter surf spot, famous for its incredible surf and tricky breaks; it's also a popular sunbathing locale for those strutting the latest in beachwear.

Café Hale'iwa (☎ 808-637-5516; 66-460 Kamehameha Ave; breakfast $3-7, lunch $5-8; ☺ 7am-2pm), a haunt for local surfers, makes the perfect North Shore meal stop.

HAWAI'I (THE BIG ISLAND)

It's certainly no misnomer that locals call their home the Big Island. Big it is – more than twice the size of all the other Hawaiian Islands combined. It encompasses a diverse geography that includes active volcanoes, coastal deserts, lush rain forests and snowy mountains. The beaches range in color from jet black to bone white, with scores of hidden gems among them. Whether you opt to camp at the edge of a smoldering volcano, relax in a century-old B&B or soak up the rays at a beachfront resort, you'll never be longing for something to do on the Big Island.

Getting There & Around

The island's two major airports, in Kailua and Hilo, both have taxi stands and car-rental booths.

Hele-On (☎ 808-961-8744; www.co.hawaii.hi.us/mass _transit/heleonbus.html), the public bus system, offers limited service between Hilo and Kailua from Monday to Saturday; some

---

DA KINE LINGO

Hawaiian surfer lingo approaches the status of a separate language. Here are some terms you might hear while riding the waves:

brah – friend, surfing buddy

da kine – great wave, top quality

goofy-footing – surfing with the right foot forward

kaha – traditional Hawaiian term for board surfing

kaha nalu – bodysurfing

keiki waves – small, gentle waves suitable for kids

macker – huge wave, big enough to drive a Mack truck through

malihini – newcomer, tenderfoot

pau – quitting time

snake – to steal (eg 'that dude's snaking my wave')

stick – surfboard

wahine – female surfer

wipeout – get knocked down by a big wave

buses take a northerly route via Waimea and others a southerly route via Captain Cook and Volcano. Fares between the towns range from $3 to $5.25. Service is infrequent, so call ahead for schedules.

KAILUA

On the sunny Kona coast, Kailua served as a summer home for Hawaiian royalty long before mainland tourists turned it into the largest vacation destination on the Big Island. At first glance the town can seem overwhelmed by kitschy shops, but on closer examination you'll discover a treasure trove of curious sights – from old temples to fishers casting their nets from the shoreline as the sun sets. It's also home to the Ironman Triathlon, which attracts 1500 international athletes to compete in the most challenging swimming, running and cycling event to be found anywhere.

Sights & Activities

The grounds of King Kamehameha's Kona Beach Hotel at **Kamakahonu** beach were once the site of Kamehameha the Great's royal residence. They include the **Ahu'ena Heiau**, a temple Kamehameha once used for human sacrifice.

Minutes away on Ali'i Dr is the lava-rock **Moku'aikaua Church** (☎ 808-329-0655; Ali'i Dr; admission free; ☼ 8am-5pm), built in 1836 by Hawaii's first Christian missionaries. Get a peek at how royalty used to live at **Hulihe'e Palace** (☎ 808-329-1877; 75-5718 Ali'i Dr; admission $6; ☼ 9am-4pm), built in 1838 and packed with curious Hawaiian artifacts. For the island's best easy-access snorkeling, head to **Kahalu'u Beach** on Ali'i Dr in Keauhou at the south side of Kailua; inexpensive gear rental is available on site.

Sleeping

Kona Tiki Hotel (☎ 808-329-1425; www.konatiki .com; 75-5968 Ali'i Dr; r incl breakfast from $61; ☒) The rooms are straightforward at this vintage place, but it's one sweet deal for being right on the ocean. One caveat – it's popular with return visitors so book ahead.

Hale Kona Kai (☎ 808-329-2155, 800-421-3696; hkk.kona@verizon.net; 75-5870 Kahakai Rd; 1-bedroom units $125-135; ☒) This condo has all the modern comforts that you will need, and it's so close to the water's edge the surf will lull you to sleep at night.

Eating

Ocean View Inn (☎ 808-329-9998; 75-5683 Ali'i Dr; meals $5-10; ☼ 6:30am-2:45pm & 5:15-9pm Tue-Sun) An eclectic menu of Chinese, Japanese and Hawaiian food reflects Hawaii's delightful diversity.

Island Lava Java (☎ 808-327-2161; 75-5799 Ali'i Dr; light eats $4-8; ☼ 6am-10pm; ▣) Come for the irresistible combo of real Kona coffee, good sandwiches and fascinating people-watching. There's Internet access ($3 per 15 minutes) too.

Kona Inn (☎ 808-329-4455; 75-5744 Ali'i Dr; lunch $10, dinner $17-28; ☼ 11:30am-9:30pm) This delightful steak and seafood restaurant hails from 1929 and makes the perfect choice for waterfront dining.

Entertainment

Happy-hour specials abound in the open-air restaurants along Ali'i Dr.

Huggo's (☎ 808-329-1493; 75-5828 Kahakai Rd; ☼ 5:30pm-midnight) For Kailua's music and dance scene, head to this waterfront spot at the south side of town.

SOUTH KONA COAST

Although many visitors overlook this area, it offers superb water adventures, fascinating historical sites and scenic hillside villages punctuated by little coffee farms.

A side road off Hwy 11 leads to the sparkling waters of mile-wide **Kealakekua Bay**. **Kealakekua Bay State Historical & Underwater Park** is at the bay's south end, while an obelisk at its north end marks the spot where Captain Cook was killed. The bay's north end has splendid **snorkeling**, but can be reached only by sea or by a 1½-hour hike along a dirt trail. The best snorkeling tour is by **Fairwind** (☎ 808-322-2788, 800-677-9461; www.fair-wind.com; 3½-hr cruise $65), which departs from Keauhou.

Run by the same family since 1917, **Manago Hotel** (☎ 808-323-2642; www.managohotel.com; 82-6155 Hwy 11; r with shared/private bath $31/51), in the town of Captain Cook, offers simple rooms and the town's favorite restaurant (closed Monday).

South of Kealakekua Bay, the incredible **Pu'uhonua O Honaunau National Historical Park** (☎ 808-328-2288; www.nps.gov/puho; admission per car $5; ☼ 6-8pm Mon-Thu, 6am-11pm Fri-Sun), also called 'Place of Refuge', includes several ancient temples and a *pu'uhonua* (a sanctuary where defeated warriors could have their lives spared). There's terrific diving

HAWAII

THE KONA COFFEE SCOOP

Aromatic Kona joe enjoys a faithful following in the world's niche coffee market. It's hands-down the most successful coffee grown in the USA. Commercial coffee grows on the other Hawaiian islands, but only Kona-grown coffee has gourmet cachet.

So, what's the scoop? Well, for starters, the upland hills of South Kona, where the coffee thrives, have the ideal coffee-growing climate of sunny mornings, cloudy afternoons and cool nights. And then there's the fertile volcanic soil. But that's only part of the picture. There are no large plantations here. The average coffee farm is under 5 acres and family-run. The berries are allowed to ripen naturally. As they don't all turn a ripe red at the same time, they must be picked by hand several times during the season, which extends from August to November. The coffee berries are roasted in small batches, with 8lbs of raw coffee beans producing a single pound of dry coffee. For the 600-plus coffee farms that dot the Kona district, it's a labor of love. During the season you'll find farm stands along the roadside proudly selling their backyard harvest. Expect to pay about $20 a pound – which, all factors considered, is a real bargain!

and snorkeling near the small boat ramp immediately north of the park.

NORTH KONA COAST

Beautiful secluded beaches lie on the north Kona Coast. Most are accessible only by foot, but visitors can reach the sparkling sands of pristine **Kona Coast State Park** (Hwy 19; admission free; ☉ closed Wed) by car. The Big Island's fanciest resorts are further north, in the Waikoloa area of the South Kohala district. South Kohala was an important area in Hawaiian history, and it shelters *heiau* (ancient stone temples), fishponds, petroglyphs and ancient trails that can be fun to explore. The island's most popular beach, **Hapuna Beach State Recreation Area** (Hwy 19; admission free), renowned for its bodysurfing, is the place to see and be seen.

NORTH KOHALA

The northwest tip of the Big Island is dominated by a central ridge, the Kohala Mountains. The remains of a 600-year-old deserted fishing village can be explored at **Lapakahi State Historical Park** (Hwy 270; admission free; ☉ 8am-4pm except holidays). **Mo'okini Heiau**, on the island's desolate northern tip, is one of the oldest and most historically significant temples in Hawaii. A stone enclosure nearby marks the birth site of King Kamehameha. Hwy 270 ends at a viewpoint overlooking scenic **Pololu Valley** and its fluted coastal cliffs.

SADDLE RD

True to its name, the 50-mile Saddle Rd (Hwy 200), Hawaii's most remote thoroughfare, cuts across the 'saddle' between the island's towering mountains, Mauna Kea and Mauna Loa. Not surprisingly the air is crisp and the views majestic. Although the road is paved, most car-rental contracts prohibit travel on it because there are no gas stations or other facilities along the route.

Hawaii's highest mountain, **Mauna Kea** (13,796ft), is topped with a cluster of world-class astronomical observatories. The visitor center at the **Onizuka Center for International Astronomy** (☎ 808-961-2180; www.ifa .hawaii.edu/info/vis; admission free; ☉ 9am-10pm) offers displays, free astronomy presentations, stargazing and summit tours. A rugged 6-mile hiking trail from the visitor center to the summit of Mauna Kea begins at 9300ft and takes 10 hours round-trip; start early, bring warm clothing and be prepared for severe weather conditions.

HAMAKUA COAST

The island's rugged Hamakua Coast offers some of the Big Island's most spectacular scenery – a mélange of deep ravines, lush jungle valleys and cascading waterfalls.

At the end of Hwy 240 you'll find a dramatic overview of **Waipi'o Valley**, the largest of seven magnificent amphitheater valleys on the windward coast. The 45-minute hike down from the lookout to the valley floor is steep, but will reward you with a close-up view of ancient taro patches and a beautiful black-sand beach. Another option is to take a mule-drawn wagon tour with **Waipi'o Valley Wagon Tours** (☎ 808-775-9518; www.waipio valleywagontours.com; 1½-hr tour $45; ☉ 4 times daily Mon-Sat).

'Akaka Falls State Park (Hwy 220) has the Big Island's most impressive accessible waterfall, with a couple of stunning lookouts along a short rain-forest loop trail. **Pepe'ekeo Scenic Dr** makes for a delightful 4-mile detour, cutting through a thick forest of flowering tulip trees on the way south to Hilo.

HILO

In terms of lush natural beauty, Hilo, the island capital, beats Kailua any day – the only catch is finding a dry one. The rainiest city in the entire USA may dampen some spirits, but it also feeds the area's tumbling waterfalls, junglelike valleys and copious gardens. Indeed, Hilo is Hawaii's top spot for growing orchids, which are exported to florists around the world. Thanks in part to its soggy reputation, tourist traffic is light and the city remains affordable, attracting an ethnically diverse community of back-to-the-earth folks.

Information

Big Island Visitors Bureau (☎ 808-961-5797; www .gohawaii.com/bigisland; 250 Keawe St; ◷ 8am-4:30pm Mon-Fri) Stocks tourist brochures for the whole island.

Bytes & Bites (☎ 808-935-3520; 223 Kilauea Ave; per 15 min $2.50; ◷ 10am-10pm) Hilo's best Internet spot, right downtown.

Sights & Activities

With its waterfront of century-old buildings, downtown Hilo brims with historic charm. Pick up a walking-tour map at the tourist office and explore the town's intriguing nooks and crannies. The splendid **Lyman Museum** (☎ 808-935-5021; www.lymanmuseum.org; 276 Haili St; admission $10; ◷ 9:30am-4:30pm Mon-Sat) showcases Hawaii's natural and cultural history.

Don't miss Hilo's waterfalls. Morning is the best time to see rainbows at **Rainbow Falls**, off Waianuenue Ave. Another 1.5 miles up the same avenue, **Pe'epe'e Falls** drops down a sheer rock face into bubbling pools known as the Boiling Pots.

Sleeping & Eating

Dolphin Bay Hotel (☎ 808-935-1466, 877-935-1466; www.dolphinbayhilo.com; 333 Iliahi St; r from $79) Find out for yourself why this friendly place is a perennial favorite among return visitors. All rooms have kitchens.

Shipman House B&B (☎ 808-934-8002, 800-627-8447; www.hilo-hawaii.com; 131 Kaiulani St; r incl breakfast $199-219; ✕) Immerse yourself in history at this graceful Victorian mansion whose guest list has included Hawaii's Queen Lili'uokalani and author Jack London.

Arnott's Lodge (☎ 808-969-7097; www.arnott slodge.com; 98 Apapane Rd; campsites $10, dm/s/d with shared bath $20/42/52; ▯) This budget lodge is the perfect place to meet other travelers.

Miyo's (☎ 808-935-2273; 400 Hualani St; mains $8-12; ◷ lunch & dinner Mon-Sat) With superb homemade Japanese meals served in a rustic teahouse setting, Miyo's is simply as good as it gets.

Café 100 (☎ 808-935-8683; 969 Kilauea Ave; meals $4-6; ◷ 6:45am-8:30pm Mon-Sat) This legendary drive-in popularized *loco moco*, which is rice topped with hamburger, fried egg and a cardiac-arresting amount of brown gravy; the rest of the menu follows suit.

HAWAI'I VOLCANOES NATIONAL PARK

One of a kind, **Hawai'i Volcanoes National Park** (☎ 808-985-6000; www.nps.gov/havo; week pass per car $10) encompasses an awesome and constantly changing landscape. Centered on Kilauea, the world's most active volcano, the place is a wonderland of volcanic sites. You can walk across steaming crater floors, see hillsides of molten lava light up the night sky and explore a terrain that ranges from tropical beaches to the subarctic Mauna Loa summit (13,679ft).

Rangers at the **Kilauea Visitor Center** (☎ 808-985-6017; ◷ 7:45am-5pm), near the park entrance, can provide the latest on trail conditions, volcanic activity and guided walks.

Sights & Activities

Many of the park's most amazing sights are along the 11-mile **Crater Rim Dr** that skirts the entire rim of Kilauea Caldera with stops at steam vents and crater lookouts. Short trails and trailheads provide starting points for longer hikes into and around the caldera. Along the way don't miss the **Jaggar Museum** (☎ 808-985-6049; admission free; ◷ 8:30am-5pm) with its seismographic displays and bird's-eye view of Halema'uma'u Crater.

The Halema'uma'u Overlook, perched on the crater rim, is at the start of the **Halema'uma'u Trail**, which runs 3 miles across steamy Kilauea Caldera. Crater Rim Dr continues across the barren Ka'u Desert and then through the fallout area of the 1959 eruption of Kilauea Iki Crater. **Devastation**

HAWAII

Trail is a fascinating half-mile walk across a former rain forest devastated by cinder and pumice from that eruption. Another unique 15-minute walk is through tunnel-like **Thurston Lava Tube**, which is almost big enough to run a train through.

The park's **Chain of Craters Rd** stands as a testimony to the power of Madame Pele (the goddess of volcanoes). Once a major road to Hilo, it now dead-ends abruptly near the coast, where recent eruptions have buried it in lava. At the road's end you can see steam plumes shooting up as the molten lava flows into the sea, and if you wait till dark the hillside glows a fiery red. It's a good paved road, but there are no services along the entire 20-mile stretch, so bring water and check the gas tank before striking out.

Sleeping

Kilauea Lodge (☎ 808-967-7366; www.kilauealodge .com; Old Volcano Rd; r incl breakfast $140-160; ✗) This cozy lodge offers a variety of solid, upmarket options, including some with fireplaces (yep, it gets cold up here at night!).

Volcano House (☎ 808-967-7321; www.volcano househotel.com; 1 Crater Rim Dr; r $95-225) The park's only hotel overlooks Kilauea Caldera and offers suitably simple rooms; it also houses a pricey restaurant with ordinary fare.

HI Holo Holo In (☎ 808-967-7950; www.enable .org/holoholo; 19-4036 Kalani Honua Rd; dm $17-19, r $44; ▣) For a good budget choice head to this friendly little hostel in the village of Volcano, just outside the park.

The park maintains two roadside campgrounds: **Namakanipaio** (Hwy 11; free), which is 3 miles north of the visitor center, and Kulanaokuaiki (free), 3.5 miles down Hilina Pali Rd, off Chain of Craters Rd; there's no registration or reservation system. Free hiking shelters and primitive camping areas are available along backcountry trails – for

these, overnight hikers must register at the visitor center no more than one day ahead.

Eating

Kiawe Kitchen (☎ 808-967-7711; cnr Old Volcano & Haunani Rds; mains $9-12; ☸ lunch & dinner Thu-Tue) Gourmet pizza, baguette sandwiches and Big Island microbrews are sold here.

Lava Rock Café (☎ 808-967-8526; Old Volcano Rd; mains $6-12; ☸ 7:30am-4pm or later) Serves the best breakfast in the village.

MAUI

Maui lures more visitors to its shores than any other Neighbor Island (the Hawaiian islands other than O'ahu). It's not just its glorious beaches, world-class windsurfing and romantic inns; Maui has something for everyone. There's top-notch conditions for anything to do with the ocean, from snorkeling and swimming to kayaking and whale-watching. If you prefer your thrills on land you can hike to the bottom of the world's largest sleeping volcano or meander your way over 54 one-lane bridges on the jungly road to Hana.

Of course if you just want to lie back, there are plenty of beachside resorts where you can while away the afternoon with a piña colada in hand.

And as if there's not enough to do, Maui has the advantage of being a gateway to its sister islands of Moloka'i and Lana'i, which can be visited via convenient boat shuttles.

Getting There & Around

Although there are smaller airports in Kapalua and Hana, most travelers to Maui arrive at **Kahului International Airport** (OGG; ☎ 808-872-3830), the busiest airport in Hawaii outside Honolulu. The major international car-rental companies have booths at the airport, and there are shuttle-bus services to the main tourist destinations. **Executive Shuttle** (☎ 808-669-2300) has the best prices, charging $20 to Kihei and $35 to Lahaina for the first person and $3 more for each additional person.

If you really want to explore Maui and get to off-the-beaten-path sights, you'll need your own wheels as public transportation is limited to the main towns and tourist

---

MOVE OVER SUSHI

If you like sushi, you'll love *'ahi poke,* a zesty island favorite made of cubed raw tuna *('ahi)* marinated in soy sauce, sesame oil, green onions and chili pepper. It goes great with beer and can be readily found on the appetizer section of island menus and at the deli counter of supermarkets.

resorts. The **Maui Public Transit System** (☎ 808-270-7511; www.co.maui.hi.us/bus; fares $1-2; ☾ Mon-Sat) operates buses from the town of Kahului to Lahaina, Wailuku, Kihei and Wailea.

LAHAINA & KA'ANAPALI
The condos may be clustered in Kihei, the mega-hotels in Ka'anapali, but make no mistake about it, Lahaina is the place everyone flocks to in their waking hours. An old whaling town that's retained many of its period buildings, Lahaina not only boasts plenty of sightseeing options but also harbors a plethora of restaurants that includes some of the best in Hawaii.

Sights & Activities
The focal point of Lahaina is its bustling small-boat harbor, backed by the historic **Pioneer Inn** and Banyan Tree Sq – the latter is home to the largest **banyan tree** in the US. The main drag and tourist strip is Front St, which runs along the ocean and is lined with shops, galleries and restaurants.

All of Lahaina's main sightseeing attractions are within walking distance of the waterfront. They include the former homes of early missionaries, prisons built for rowdy sailors and the remains of a royal palace. To get started, pick up a free walking-tour map at the **Lahaina Visitor Center** (☎ 808-667-9193; www.visitlahaina.com; 648 Wharf St; ☾ 9am-5pm), inside the old courthouse at Banyan Tree Sq.

If you're looking for beaches, forget Lahaina and head 3 miles north instead, to the resort community of Ka'anapali, which is fronted by one sandy beach after another. The gem among them, **Kahekili Beach Park**, boasts swaying palms and fantastic snorkeling and swimming. While in Ka'anapali, visit the evocative **Whaling Museum** (☎ 808-661-4567; 2345 Ka'anapali Parkway; admission free; ☾ 9:30am-10pm) in the Whalers Village mall. The Akina West Maui Shuttle connects Lahaina and Ka'anapali ($1, 25 minutes) throughout the day.

Sleeping
Plantation Inn (☎ 808-667-9225, 800-433-6815; www.theplantationinn.com; 174 Lahainaluna Rd; r incl breakfast $160-255; ☒ ☙) The crème de la crème of Lahaina's upscale inns, this central place beams with period charm.

Makai Inn (☎ 808-662-3200; www.makaiinn.net; 1415 Front St; r $75-130) On the northern out-skirts of town, this family-run gem sports a waterfront location, full kitchens and lots of aloha.

Pioneer Inn (☎ 808-661-3636, 800-457-5457; www.pioneerinnmaui.com; 658 Wharf St; r from $120; ☙) You couldn't be closer to the action than at this harborside hotel, though the rooms themselves don't pack as much character as the rest of the building.

Eating
Café O'Lei Lahaina (☎ 808-661-9491; 839 Front St; lunches $7-10, dinner mains $15-21; ☾ 10:30am-9:30pm) A standout among the oceanfront restaurants lining Front St, this breezy place offers everything from organic salads and foccacia sandwiches to a luscious blackened mahimahi.

Pacific'O (☎ 808-667-4341; 505 Front St; lunches $10-15, dinner mains $20-30; ☾ 11am-4pm & 5:30-10pm) Lahaina's top fine-dining spot offers innovative Pacific Rim cuisine and an unbeatable beachside setting.

David Paul's Lahaina Grill (☎ 808-667-5117; 127 Lahainaluna Rd; mains $26-39; ☾ from 6pm) This award-winning restaurant expertly mixes Hawaiian and continental influences, with the likes of seared tuna crusted in Maui onions and Kona coffee–roasted rack of lamb.

Breakwall Café (☎ 808-661-7220; 505 Front St; light eats $3-6; ☾ 7am-2pm Mon-Sat) Friendliest café around; if you have your own laptop you can use the wi-fi connection free, or log on to one of the café's computers for 20¢ per minute.

Drinking
Pioneer Inn (☾ 808-661-3636; 658 Wharf St; ☾ 11am-10pm) With its whaling-era atmosphere and harborside veranda, this is unquestionably the most popular place for a drink in Lahaina.

Aloha Mixed Plate (☎ 808-661-3322; 1285 Front St; ☾ 10:30am-10pm) Dig your toes into the sand at this fun beach shack on the north side of town. Come at sunset for cool tropical drinks, savory *pupu* (snacks) and Hawaiian music.

Entertainment
Old Lahaina Lu'au (☎ 808-667-4332; www.oldlahainaluau.com; 1251 Front St; adult/child $85/55; ☾ 5:15-8:15pm) If you want a night out to remember, this beachside luau is unsurpassed for its authenticity and all-around aloha – the hula

HAWAII

troupe is first-rate and the feast superb. Book ahead, as it often sells out.

MA'ALAEA BAY

Ma'alaea Bay runs along the low isthmus separating the mountain masses of west and east Maui. Prevailing winds from the north funnel between the mountains, creating strong midday gusts and some of the best **windsurfing** conditions on Maui.

The superb **Maui Ocean Center** (☎ 808-270-7000; www.mauioceancenter.com; 192 Ma'alaea Rd, Ma'alaea; adult/child $21/14; �८ 9am-5pm, to 6pm Jul & Aug), the largest tropical aquarium in the USA, offers a feast for the eyes. Dedicated to Hawaiian marine life, the variety and brilliance of the fish and coral is nothing short of dazzling. Highlights include a 'living reef' section focusing on colorful fish you might see while snorkeling, and an enormous walk-through tank where gliding eagle rays and reef sharks literally encircle you. It's as close as you can get to being underwater without donning dive gear!

A fantastic harbor view, attentive service and excellent seafood make **Ma'alaea Grill** (☎ 808-243-2206; Ma'alaea Harbor; lunch $7-11, dinner $15-21; �८ 10:30am-3pm Mon, to 9pm Tue-Sun) one of Maui's best seafood restaurants.

KIHEI

Fringed with sandy beaches its entire length and gleaming in near-constant sunshine, there's little secret as to why Kihei hosts more visitors than any other place on Maui.

Kihei has good water conditions for swimming, windsurfing and kayaking. **South Pacific Kayaks** (☎ 808-875-4848; www.mauikayak .com; 2439 S Kihei Rd; single/double kayak per day $30/40, tour $55-90; �८ 8am-5pm) rents kayaks and leads adventurous paddles tours in the 'Ahihi-Kina'u Natural Area Reserve, where sea turtles and dolphins frequent the waters.

Sleeping

Kihei has scores of condo complexes, hotels and inns.

Nona Lani Cottages (☎ 808-879-2497, 800-733-2688; www.nonalanicottages.com; 455 S Kihei Rd; r $95, cottages $105) The scent of plumeria fills the air at this little cottage cluster, whose friendly hosts make leis from the flowers grown out back.

Maui Sunseeker (☎ 808-874-3131, 800-399-3885; www.mauisunseeker.com; 551 N Kihei Rd; studios

$120-170) Soak up the rays on the clothing-optional rooftop deck of this gay-friendly inn. The dozen studios here sport a tasteful decor that outshines other places in its price range.

Mana Kai Maui (☎ 808-879-2778, 800-367-5242; www.crhmaui.com; 2960 S Kihei Rd; r $100, 1-bedroom units $180; ☒) You won't find a better sunset view than at this complex perched on the ocean edge. You can snorkel right out the door.

Eating

KKO (☎ 808-875-1007; 2511 S Kihei Rd; mains $10-17; �८ 8am-midnight) This spirited restaurant has Hawaiian-style torches blazing nightly and a menu centering on innovative seafood dishes. The spicy fish quesadilla is a treat to be relished.

Sansei Seafood Restaurant & Sushi Bar (☎ 808-879-0004; 1881 S Kihei Rd; appetizers $3-14, mains $16-30; �८ dinner; ☒) This is the trendiest place in town, but worth the wait for a table. The Japanese-Hawaiian fare covers the gamut from traditional sashimi to seared snapper in white truffle sauce.

Entertainment

Hapa's Night Club (☎ 808-879-9001; 41 E Lipoa St; admission $5-8; ☒) Maui's hottest dance spot has something for everyone. It hosts the gay community on 'ultra-fab' Tuesday, does an aloha jam on Wednesday and has top live bands other nights.

WHALE OF A TAIL

Come in the winter and you're in for the sight of your life. That's when humpback whales cruise the waters along the western coast of Maui, the main birthing grounds for these awesome creatures. As a safeguard against shark attacks, the whales like to stay in shallow waters when they have newborn calves. Consequently, you can spot them performing their acrobatic breaches and tail slaps right from the beach.

To get an even closer look at these amazing creatures, take a whale-watching cruise with the nonprofit **Pacific Whale Foundation** (☎ 808-249-8811, 800-942-5311; www.pacificwhale.org; adult/child $30/15; �८ Dec-Apr), which sails out of both Lahaina and Ma'alaea harbors.

WAILEA & MAKENA

As Maui's most upscale seaside community, Wailea boasts million-dollar homes and extravagant resorts with four-figure room rates. Along its coastline you'll find attractive golden-sand beaches that lure swimmers, divers and sunbathers. The mile-long **Wailea Beach Path** is a superb place to enjoy shoreline whale-watching in winter.

South of Wailea, Makena has two knockout undeveloped beaches – **Big Beach** and the secluded **Little Beach** – as well as the **'Ahihi-Kina'u Natural Area Reserve**, which encompasses trails, historic ruins and hidden coves ideal for snorkeling.

KAHULUI & WAILUKU

Kahului and Wailuku, Maui's two largest communities, flow together in one urban sprawl. Kahului hosts Maui's windsurfing shops, whose employees give lessons at breezy **Kanaha Beach**.

The more historic Wailuku makes for a good stroll and lunch break. On the outskirts of Wailuku, **'Iao Valley State Monument** ('Iao Valley Rd; admission free; 7am-7pm) centers on the picturesque 'Iao Needle rock pinnacle, which rises 1200ft from the valley floor.

Information

Maui Memorial Hospital (808-244-9056; 221 Mahalani St, Wailuku; 24hr) The island's main hospital.

Maui Visitors Bureau (808-872-3893; www.visit maui.com; Kahului Airport; 7:45am-10pm) Pick up free tourist magazines and brochures from the racks nearby. A staffed booth in the airport's arrivals area.

Wow-Wee Maui's Café (808-871-1414; 333 Dairy Rd, Kahului; per min 20¢; 6am-6pm) A fun place for Internet access.

Sleeping & Eating

Old Wailuku Inn (808-244-5897, 800-305-4899; www .mauiinn.com; 2199 Kaho'okele St, Wailuku; r $120-180) Step back into the 1920s in this elegant period home, built by a wealthy banker and authentically restored by its friendly innkeepers. Rooms are large and comfy with traditional Hawaiian quilts warming the beds.

Asian Star (808-244-1833; 1764 Wili Pa Loop, Wailuku; mains $6-12; 10am-9:30pm) This is the place to feast on classic Vietnamese fare like *pho* noodle soup and *banh hoi*, a rice-paper wrap chock-full of goodies and garnished with mint.

PA'IA

Pa'ia is an old sugar town with a fresh coat of paint. In the 1980s, windsurfers began discovering nearby **Ho'okipa Beach**, and Pa'ia soon picked up a new identify as the 'Windsurfing Capital of the World.' It now boasts an eclectic international community and an ever-growing variety of superb restaurants.

With a French chef, **Moana Bakery & Café** (808-579-9999; 71 Baldwin Ave; breakfast & lunch $6-12, dinner $12-29; 8am-9pm) has terrific croissants and a creative fusion of French and Hawaiian offerings. **Pa'ia Fish Market Restaurant** (808-579-8030; 2A Baldwin Ave; meals $9-15; 11am-9:30pm) is the place to go for fresh fish sandwiches. **Livewire Café** (808-579-6009; 137 Hana Hwy; per min 15¢; 6am-10pm Sun-Thu, to midnight Fri & Sat) is a great place to surf the Internet while enjoying homemade pastries and heady coffee.

HANA HIGHWAY

The most spectacular coastal drive in all Hawaii, the Hana Hwy (Hwy 360) winds its way deep into jungle valleys and back out above a rugged coastline. Not for the faint of heart, the road is a real cliff-hugger with scores of one-lane bridges, roadside waterfalls and head-spinning views.

Along the way, the **YMCA Camp Ke'anae** (808-248-8355; www.mauiymca.org; 13375 Hana Hwy, Ke'anae; campsites & dm $17, cottages $125) offers hostel-style beds in cabins; advance reservations are required. **Wai'anapanapa State Park**, just north of Hana, shelters two impressive lava-tube caves with clear mineral waters; there's tent **camping** (808-984-8109; campsites free) on a knoll above the stunning black-sand beach. Call ahead for a permit.

HANA & AROUND

Hana, protected by its isolation, is one of the most unchanged communities in the state, with many of its residents of Native Hawaiian descent. Surfers head to **Waikoloa Beach**, while sunbathers favor **Kaihalulu (Red Sand) Beach**, reached by a trail at the end of Uakea Rd.

The road south from Hana is incredibly beautiful. 'Ohe'o Stream cuts its way through **'Ohe'o Gulch** as an Eden-like series of wide pools and waterfalls, each tumbling into the one below. Just past the gulch is the sleepy village of **Kipahulu**, burial site of aviator Charles Lindbergh.

HAWAII

Surrounding a stone fishpond, **Hana Hale Malamalama** (☎ 808-248-7718; www.hanahale.com; Uakea Rd; studios $160, cottages from $185) is one of the most atmospheric places to stay in Maui. The seven units include a 'treehouse cottage.' **Joe's Place** (☎ 808-248-7033; www.joesrentals.com; 4870 Uakea Rd; r $45-55) has a friendly manager, clean comfortable rooms and shared kitchen facilities – it's a magnet for budget travelers. Join Hana folk at **Tutu's** (☎ 808-248-8224; 174 Hana Bay; meals $4-7; ☼ 8am-4pm), a simple grill fronting Hana Beach Park.

HALEAKALA NATIONAL PARK

No trip to Maui is complete without visiting **Haleakala National Park** (www.nps.gov/hale; 7-day entry pass per car $10, per person on foot, bicycle or motorcycle $5), the mighty volcano that gave rise to East Maui. The volcano's floor measures a whopping 7.5 miles wide, 2.5 miles long and 3000ft deep – more than enough to swallow the entire isle of Manhattan. From its towering rim there are dramatic views of its lunarlike surface. But the adventure needn't stop at the viewpoints – with a good pair of hiking boots you can walk down into the crater on trails that meander around eerie cinder cones, and peer up at towering walls.

For an unforgettable experience, arrive in time to see the sunrise – an event that Mark Twain called the 'sublimest spectacle' he'd ever seen. Check on weather conditions and sunrise times (☎ 808-877-5111) before driving up. **Park headquarters** (☎ 808-572-4400; ☼ 8am-4pm) can give you details on free guided hikes and nature talks.

Free tent camping is allowed at Hosmer Grove, near the main entrance (three-night maximum); no permit required. Permits (first-come, first-served, from the park headquarters) are required for the two backcountry campgrounds on the crater floor. There are primitive cabins in the crater, but demand is so high they hold a monthly lottery (write to Cabin Lottery Request, Haleakala National Park, Box 369, Makawao, HI 96768 two months in advance).

KAUA'I

This island has been the darling of honeymooners ever since Elvis tied the knot here in *Blue Hawaii*. And it's no secret why. Kaua'i boasts majestic mountains and sea cliffs, towering waterfalls and so much lush greenery it's been dubbed 'The Garden Isle.' It's a mecca for hikers, kayakers and other outdoor enthusiasts. The razorback Na Pali cliffs, on the rugged north shore, are Hawaii's foremost trekking destination.

Getting There & Around

Kaua'i's commercial airport is in Lihu'e. All the major car rental companies maintain booths there, and taxis line up outside the arrival area. Kaua'i has a limited public **bus service** (☎ 808-241-6410; all routes $1.50; ☼ Mon-Sat), which serves most towns but doesn't go to destinations like Kilauea Point and Koke'e State Park.

LIHU'E

This former plantation town is Kaua'i's capital and commercial center. Seek information at the **Kaua'i Visitors Bureau** (☎ 808-245-3971; www.kauaivisitorsbureau.org; 4334 Rice St; ☼ 8am-4:30pm Mon-Fri). The insightful **Kaua'i Museum** (☎ 808-245-6931; www.kauaimuseum.org; 4428 Rice St; admission $7; ☼ 9am-4pm Mon-Fri, 10am-4pm Sat) traces the island's intriguing history.

Garden Island Inn (☎ 808-245-7227; www.gardenislandinn.com; 3445 Wilcox Rd; r from $85) offers comfortable rooms just minutes from the beach. Rub shoulders with the locals at **Hamura Saimin** (☎ 808-245-3271; 2956 Kress St; noodle soups $4; ☼ 10am-9:30pm or later), which has been serving homemade noodles here since the 1920s.

NA PALI COAST & NORTH SHORE

Unspoiled and unhurried, Kaua'i's mountainous north shore features incredible scenery. Be sure to stop at **Kilauea Point Wildlife Refuge** (☎ 808-828-0383; Kilauea Rd, Kilauea; admission $3; ☼ 10am-4pm) to enjoy its historic lighthouse and thriving seabird sanctuary.

The village of **Hanalei**, on a magnificent bay, has sports shops renting kayaks for paddling up the Hanalei River. **Historic B&B** (☎ 808-826-4622; www.historicbnb.com; 5-5067 Hwy 56; r incl breakfast from $85), in a converted Buddhist temple, features a Japanese-style decor that'll soothe the soul. **Hanalei Gourmet** (☎ 808-826-2524; Hwy 56; meals $10-23; ☼ 8am-9:30pm) serves reliable island-style food including fresh fish specials.

Marking the western end of Hwy 56, at the little village of **Ha'ena**, is lovely **Ke'e Beach**, which has excellent snorkeling. Camping is allowed (with a permit) at nearby **Ha'ena**

Beach Park (☎ 808-241-6660; campsites $3), close to the Kalalau trailhead.

The challenging but oh-so-rewarding 11-mile **Kalalau Trail** runs along the steeply fluted Na Pali cliffs and winds up and down a series of lush valleys in **Na Pali Coast State Park**. The scenery is breathtaking, with sheer green cliffs dropping into brilliant turquoise waters. You'll need a **permit** (☎ 808-274-3444) for hiking beyond the first valley, as well as for camping ($10), which is allowed in three valleys. This is rugged backcountry – give yourself at least three days to do it without rushing.

SOUTH SHORE

Sunny **Po'ipu**, Kaua'i's main resort area, fronts a fabulous run of sandy beaches. It's good for swimming and snorkeling year-round and for surfing in summer. **Koloa Landing Cottages** (☎ 808-742-1470; www .koloa-landing.com; 2704B Ho'onani Rd; r $95-110) offers well-equipped accommodations and plenty of aloha. Perched above the ocean, **Gloria's Spouting Horn Bed & Breakfast** (☎ 808-742-6995; www.gloriasbedandbreakfast.com; 4464 Lawa'i Beach Rd; r incl breakfast $325; 🖳) pampers those looking for a romantic stay. **Roy's Poipu Bar and Grill** (☎ 808-742-5000; 2360 Kiahuna Plantation Dr; mains $19-25; 🕑 dinner) specializes in creative Hawaiian regional dishes using impeccably fresh island ingredients.

WEST SIDE

The top destinations here are **Waimea Canyon**, a mini Grand Canyon with cascading waterfalls and spectacular gorges, and the adjacent **Koke'e State Park**. Both feature breathtaking views and a vast network of hiking trails. Waimea Canyon Dr (Hwy 550) starts in the town of Waimea and is peppered with scenic lookouts along the way to the park. Pick up information on trails at the park's **Koke'e Museum** (☎ 808-335-9975; www.kokee.org; 3600 Koke'e Rd; donation $1; 🕑 10am-4pm).

MOLOKA'I

This sleepy rural island makes the perfect choice for those itching to get off the beaten track. More traditionally Hawaiian than its neighboring islands, nearly half of Moloka'i's population is of Native Hawaiian

ancestry. Thanks to its resistance to would-be developers, the island is free of high-rise buildings, shopping centers and large resorts. As a matter of fact, Moloka'i has barely changed at all for tourism, and that's part of the appeal here. You can walk the quiet sands of the longest beach in Hawaii, take a mule ride down a death-defying cliff to an old leprosy colony and watch the sun set over ancient fishponds. And though Moloka'i may be overshadowed by its larger neighbors, the scenery here is just as awesome – especially along the North Shore, from Kalaupapa to Halawa, which features the world's highest sea cliffs (3300ft).

SIGHTS & ACTIVITIES

Kaunakakai, Moloka'i's central town, has a post office, a bakery, a pharmacy and one of just about everything else a small island needs. The stores along its dusty main street have old wooden false fronts, giving Kaunakakai the appearance of a frontier town. Neon, traffic lights and fast-food chains are nowhere to be found, and the town's tallest object remains the church steeple.

The incredibly scenic 28-mile south-coast drive from Kaunakakai to Halawa Valley takes about 1½ hours one way and rewards you with delightful glimpses of old homesteads, fishponds and waterfalls. The last part of the road is very narrow, with lots of hairpin bends and coastal views, winding up to a picture-perfect panorama of **Halawa Bay**. The road then runs down to a challenging surfing spot, **Halawa Beach Park**.

In the central part of the island you'll find windswept **Mo'omomi Beach**, whose dunes are home to several species of endangered plants; the former plantation town of **Kualapu'u**, where you can stop for a cup of locally grown coffee; and **Kamakou Preserve**, where lush rain forests harbor native birds and the island's highest point, **Kamakou Peak** (4970ft).

The **Kalaupapa Peninsula**, separated from the rest of Moloka'i by formidable cliffs, has served as a settlement for people with leprosy since the 19th century. Although it's still home to an aging population of patients, the peninsula has been designated as the **Kalaupapa National Historical Park** (www .nps.gov/kala). It's an amazing place to visit, but can only be entered with a guide. The most adventurous way to get there is to

HAWAII

ride a mule down a switchbacking cliffside trail with **Moloka'i Mule Ride** (☎ 808-567-6088, 800-567-7550; www.muleride.com; tour $165; ☉ Mon-Sat); the cost includes lunch and a tour of the peninsula.

At the west end of the island, Moloka'i's magnificent **Papohaku Beach Park** offers 2½ unbroken miles of golden sand and crashing surf. It also has Moloka'i's best camping, but pick up a permit ($3) in advance at the **county office** (☎ 808-553-3204; Mitchell Pauole Center, Ainoa St; ☉ 8am-4pm Mon-Fri) in Kaunakakai.

SLEEPING & EATING

Hotel Moloka'i (☎ 808-553-5347, 800-535-0085; www .hotelmolokai.com; Kamehameha V Hwy, Kaunakakai; r $90-140; ☒) Friendly staff, a Polynesian design and great stargazing make this aging hotel the most atmospheric place to stay in Moloka'i. Opt for a 2nd-story unit for the best ocean views.

Hula Shores (☎ 808-553-5347; Hotel Moloka'i, Kamehameha V Hwy, Kaunakakai; breakfast & lunch $5-8, dinner $14-20; ☉ breakfast, lunch & dinner) If you were any closer to the water you'd need to wear a bathing suit. A perennial favorite, this open-air place has macadamia-nut pancakes, good burgers and salads, and fresh fish dinners. Also an ideal spot for a sunset drink.

GETTING THERE & AWAY

In the center of the island, Moloka'i Airport (also called Ho'olehua Airport) has limited car rentals, so book early. You can also get to the island via a passenger ferry, which is used mostly by Moloka'i residents commuting to jobs in Lahaina, Maui. The **Molokai Princess** (☎ 808-662-3355; www.molokai ferry.com; adult/child $40/20) makes the 1¾-hour journey from Kaunakakai Wharf to Lahaina at 5:30am and 2:30pm Monday to Saturday, and at 3pm on Sunday. In the other direction, the ferry leaves Lahaina at 6:30am Monday to Saturday and daily at 5:15pm.

LANA'I

Once the world's largest pineapple plantation, in the 1990s Lana'i abandoned its agricultural roots in exchange for a new identity as an exclusive getaway destination. It now boasts two of Hawaii's most elite resorts, one on beautiful Hulopo'e

Beach at the southern tip of the island and the other on the edge of Lana'i City.

The center of Lana'i remains **Lana'i City** – not a city at all, but merely a little town of tin-roofed houses that's home to almost all of the island's residents. The people are as friendly as it gets and the pace is relaxingly S-L-O-W. Other than soaking up the small-town charm, there isn't much to see in Lana'i City. Most of Lana'i's sights, which include obscure archaeological ruins and Hawaii's last native dryland forest, are in remote areas along dirt roads that require a 4WD vehicle.

Not surprisingly, visiting Lana'i can be quite expensive. One of the easiest ways to get a little taste of the good life is to take the ferry over from Maui in the morning, snorkel in the dolphin-rich waters of **Hulopo'e Beach**, and take the boat back in the late afternoon. Or extend your stay and enjoy a night in island-style character.

SLEEPING

Hotel Lanai (☎ 808-565-7211, 800-795-7211; www .hotellanai.com; 828 Lana'i Ave; r $105-135) Built by Jim Dole (as in Dole pineapples) in 1923 to house plantation guests, this restored 10-room hotel is a delightful throwback to an earlier era.

Four Seasons Resort Lana'i at Manele Bay (☎ 808-565-2000, 800-321-4666; www.fourseasons .com/lanai; r $350-695, ste from $725) Shortly after it opened, the world's richest man, Bill Gates, booked the entire hotel to host his wedding – need we say more? The place simply exudes elegance.

EATING

Blue Ginger Café (☎ 808-565-6363; 409 7th St; breakfast & lunch $5-8, dinner $10-14; ☉ 6am-8pm, to 9pm Fri & Sat) Enjoy a meal with Lana'ians at this unpretentious bakery-café that serves up three square meals a day, including scrumptious fresh-fish dinners.

Formal Dining Room (☎ 808-565-7300; Lodge at Koele; mains $40-45; ☉ 6:30-9:30pm) Lana'i's fanciest restaurant has steep prices, but food and service live up to the bill. Lana'i venison is a specialty; men will need a jacket but loaners are available at the front desk.

GETTING THERE & AWAY

There's an airport on the outskirts of Lana'i City but almost everyone takes the ferry to Lana'i – it's not only cheaper but you'll also often see whales and spinner dolphins en route. **Expeditions** (☎ 808-661-3756; www.go-lanai .com; adult/child $25/20) runs a passenger ferry five times daily between Maui and Lana'i. The first boat leaves Lahaina Harbor for Lana'i at 6:45am and the last boat departs Lana'i for the return to Maui at 6:45pm.

OTHER ISLANDS

KAHO'OLAWE

This uninhabited island, 7 miles off the southwest coast of Maui, was used exclusively by the US military as a bombing target from WWII until 1990. Since then, the military has spent millions of dollars trying to clean up Kaho'olawe, but it continues to be off-limits to casual visitors because of the stray ammunition that still peppers the island and its surrounding waters.

Kaho'olawe has spiritual significance to Native Hawaiians, who hope to revitalize the island's many cultural and natural resources. To learn more about the island, browse the website of **Protect Kaho'olawe 'Ohana** (www.kahoolawe.org).

NI'IHAU

The smallest of the inhabited Hawaiian Islands and a Native Hawaiian preserve, Ni'ihau has long been closed to outsiders, earning it the nickname 'The Forbidden Island.' No other place in Hawaii has more successfully turned its back on change. The island's 250 residents still speak Hawaiian as a first language and Ni'ihau has no paved roads, no airport, no islandwide electricity and no telephones.

NORTHWESTERN HAWAIIAN ISLANDS

Also known as the Leeward Islands, these 10 tiny island clusters are scattered across nearly 1300 miles of ocean to the northwest of Kaua'i. They include atolls, each with a number of low sand islands formed on top of coral reefs, as well as single-rock islands.

All of the islands except Kure Atoll (a state seabird sanctuary) and the Midway Islands are part of the **Hawaiian Islands National Wildlife Refuge** (pacificislands.fws.gov), which was established in 1909 and is the oldest and largest US wildlife refuge. Midway, the site of a pivotal WWII battle between Japanese and American naval forces, has been set aside as the **Midway Atoll National Wildlife Refuge** (midway.fws.gov).

The Northwestern Hawaiian Islands are home to endangered Hawaiian monk seals, 15 million seabirds and four species of land birds that exist nowhere else on earth. Because of their fragile ecosystems, visitors aren't allowed on the Northwestern Hawaiian Islands without a special permit, and those are typically limited to biologists and research scientists.

HAWAII

Directory

CONTENTS

ACCOMMODATIONS

This guide includes recommendations for all budgets, but it emphasizes midrange accommodations. Unless otherwise noted, 'budget' is considered under $80, 'midrange' $80 to $200 and 'top end' over $200.

In text, accommodation rates are based on standard double-occupancy in high season. These rates are a general guide only. Special events, busy weekends, conventions and holidays can drive prices higher, and in most places, low-season rates will be lower, sometimes significantly. Prices do not include hotel tax, which can add 10% to 15%.

Since nearly every US hotel has nonsmoking rooms, the nonsmoking icon (⊠) is used only when a hotel bans smoking entirely.

For all but the cheapest places and the slowest seasons, reservations are advised. In high-season tourist hotspots, every room might be booked months ahead. Walking in off the street without a reservation only gets you the best deal when things are really dead. In general, many hotels offer specials on their websites, but low-end chains sometimes give a moderately better rate over the phone. Chain hotels also increasingly have frequent flyer mileage deals; ask when booking.

Good websites for hotel discounts include the following:

Trip Advisor (www.tripadvisor.com)
Priceline.com (http://travel.priceline.com)
Hotels.com (www.hotels.com)
Travelocity (www.travelocity.com)
Orbitz (www.orbitz.com)
Hotwire (www.hotwire.com)

B&Bs

In the USA, B&Bs are usually high-end romantic retreats. They are often restored historic homes with lovely furnishings run by personable, independent innkeepers, and they include delicious breakfasts. Most have a theme – Victorian, rustic, Cape Cod and so on – and amenities range from merely comfortable to hopelessly indulgent. Rates normally top $100, and the best run $200 to $300+ a night; some have minimum-night-stay requirements on weekends.

Outside of tourist hotspots, B&Bs may be plainer, cheaper and geared more toward average folks or families. These may be rooms in someone's home.

B&Bs often close out of season and may require reservations, which are essential for top-end places. Baths may be shared or private, and young children are not always welcome; always ask on both counts. Recommended local B&B agencies are sprinkled throughout this guide. National guides include *Bed & Breakfast USA* and the *Complete Guide to American Bed & Breakfasts*. On the Internet, check **Select Registry** (www.selectregistry.com) and **BnB Finder** (www.bnbfinder.com).

Camping

Most national forests, state and national parks, and **Bureau of Land Management** (BLM; www.blm.gov) lands offer camping. 'Primitive' campsites offer no facilities and usually cost $5 to $8 a night, first-come, first-served. 'Basic' sites usually provide toilets (flush or pit), drinking water, fire pits and picnic benches; they run $5 to $15 a night, and some or all may be reserved in advance. 'Developed' campsites, usually in national or state parks, have nicer facilities and more amenities: hot showers, BBQs, RV sites, coin laundry and so on. These run $12 to $25 a night, and most can be reserved in advance. The all-purpose **Recreation.gov** (www.recreation .gov) can get you started.

Here are the main ways to reserve:
National Park Service (NPS; ☎ 800-365-2267, outside the USA ☎ 301-722-1257; http://reservations.nps.gov) Sites can be booked up to five months ahead.
National Recreation Reservation Service (NRRS; ☎ 877-444-6777, outside the USA ☎ 518-885-3639; http://reserveusa.com; $10 reservation fee) Handles a range of NPS, US Forest Service (USFS) and BLM campgrounds. Reserve campsites 240 days in advance, cabins 360 days in advance.
ReserveAmerica (www.reserveamerica.com) Handles many state park campgrounds, and publishes **Camping Life** (www.campfirechronicle.com), a newsletter with advice, kids' stuff, and more.

Private campgrounds tend to cater to RVs and families (tent sites may be few and lack character), and facilities may include playgrounds, convenience stores, swimming pools and other activities and supplies. Many also have camping cabins: either tent cabins with canvas walls and a wooden floor, hard-sided cabins with screened windows and cots or plank beds, or fully equipped cabins with proper beds, heating and private baths.

KOA (Kampgrounds of America) is a national network of private campgrounds with a full range of facilities. You can order KOA's free annual **directory** (☎ 406-248-7444; http://koa .com; PO Box 30558, Billings, MT 59114; shipping fee $5).

Hostels

In the USA, hostels are clustered mainly in the northeast, the Northwest, California and the Rocky Mountains. Large cities might have a dozen choices, but across portions of the Midwest it's hard to find even one.

PRACTICALITIES

News & Entertainment

- National newspapers: *New York Times, USA Today, Wall Street Journal*
- Mainstream news magazines: *Time, Newsweek, US News & World Report*
- Radio news: National Public Radio (NPR), lower end of FM dial
- Broadcast TV: ABC, CBS, NBC, FOX and PBS (public broadcasting)
- Major cable channels: CNN (news), ESPN (sports), HBO (movies) and the Weather Channel

Video System

- NTSC standard (not compatible with PAL or SECAM)

Electricity

- AC 110V is standard; must buy AC adapters to run most non-US electronics

Weights & Measures

- Weight: ounces (oz), pounds (lb), tons
- Liquid: oz, pints, quarts, gallons
- Distance: feet (ft), yards, miles

To convert weights, liquid measures and distances to the metric system, see the inside front cover.

Hostelling International USA (HI-USA; ☎ 202-783-6161; www.hiusa.org) runs over 100 hostels in the US. Most have gender-segregated dorms, a few private rooms, shared baths and a communal kitchen, provide linen free or for a small fee (sleeping bags not allowed), prohibit alcohol and smoking, and organize social activities. In big cities, hostels may be open 24 hours and forgo 'chores,' while others close in the afternoon (usually 10am to 5pm) and ask guests to do some cleaning. Dorm prices can sometimes be as low as $10, but they usually run $20 to $35.

Reservations are accepted and advised during the high season, when there may be a maximum stay of three nights. Contact HI-USA for their handbook ($3). If you're in the US, you can reserve most affiliated hostels through the central **booking service** (☎ 888-464-4872).

The USA has many independent hostels not affiliated with HI-USA. For listings of these, check the following:

Hostel Handbook (www.hostelhandbook.com) Good links page and hosteling advice; the handbook costs $4.

HostelWorld (www.hostelworld.com) Covers the US and the rest of the world.

Hostels.com (www.hostels.com) Has reader ratings and travel insurance.

Backpackers.com (www.backpackers.com) Lots of other backpacking advice.

If you're hosteling, you might also consider the inexpensive accommodations run by the **Young Men's Christian Association** (YMCA; www.ymca.net). These are same-sex dorms or private rooms in or near downtown in larger cities; while geared mainly for temporary residents, they are open to travelers. 'Y's have a lot of differing restrictions for overnight guests, and they vary greatly in quality; some are seedy and located in run-down neighborhoods. Always check out the facilities in person first. YWCAs (for women only) are much less common and rarely have traveler facilities.

Hotels

Hotels in the USA range from the most opulent to the most humble. Chains have come to dominate in many places, but that doesn't mean you can't also find delightfully funky boutique properties as well as smaller, family-run establishments. In this guide, standard chains are usually only reviewed when they are particularly notable or are an area's only recommended option.

Hotels in all categories usually include phones, TVs (usually with cable), alarm clocks, private baths and a simple continental breakfast. Many midrange properties will also include minibars, microwaves, hairdryers, Internet access, air-conditioning/heating (depending on region), pools and writing desks, while top end hotels add fitness and business centers, concierge services, restaurants and bars and much more.

Chain hotels offer the comfort of always knowing what you'll get.

BUDGET

Days Inn (☎ 800-329-7466; www.daysinn.com)
Econo Lodge (☎ 877-424-6423; www.econolodge.com)

Motel 6 (☎ 800-466-8356; www.motel6.com)
Super 8 Motel (☎ 800-800-8000; www.super8.com)

MIDRANGE

Best Western (☎ 800-780-7234; www.bestwestern.com)
Clarion Hotel (☎ 877-424-6423; www.clarionhotel.com)
Comfort Inn (☎ 877-424-6423; www.comfortinn.com)
Fairfield Inn (☎ 800-228-2800; www.fairfieldinn.com)
Hampton Inn (☎ 800-426-7866; http://hamptoninn .hilton.com)
Holiday Inn (☎ 800-465-4329; www.holiday-inn.com)
Howard Johnson (☎ 800-446-4656; www.hojo.com)
La Quinta (☎ 866-725-1661; www.lq.com)
Quality Inn (☎ 877-424-6423; www.qualityinn.com)
Red Roof Inn (☎ 800-733-7663; www.redroof.com)
Rodeway Inn (☎ 877-424-6423; www.rodewayinn.com)
Sleep Inn (☎ 877-424-6423; www.sleepinn.com)
Travelodge (☎ 800-578-7878; www.travelodge.com)

TOP END

Hilton (☎ 800-445-8667; www.hilton.com)
Hyatt (☎ 888-591-1234; www.hyatt.com)
Marriott (☎ 888-236-2427; www.marriott.com)
Radisson (☎ 800-333-3333; www.radisson.com)
Ramada (☎ 800-272-6232; www.ramada.com)
Sheraton (☎ 800-598-1753; www.starwoodhotels .com/sheraton)
Westin (☎ 800-937-8461; www.starwoodhotels.com /westin)

Independent and family-run hotels can vary greatly in decor (even room to room) and cleanliness; it's prudent to ask to see your room before paying, particularly at cheaper places. In general, rooms will have one king-size bed or two double or queen-size beds, and rates will cover two adults, with small surcharges for a third or fourth person. Even if children 'sleep free,' cots or rollaway beds may cost extra. Also, always ask about the hotel's policy for telephone calls; all charge exorbitantly for long distance, but some also charge for local calls and toll-free numbers.

Motels

The distinction between a motel and a hotel sometimes exists in name only. However, motels originated as 'drive-up rooms' along the highway, where you parked your car outside your door, and this is still usually the case. Motels tend to cluster around interstate exits and along main routes into towns, and be single- or double-story structures with exterior corridors surrounding a parking lot. Many remain less-expensive 'mom-and-pop' operations rather than chains; breakfast is rarely included (and when it is, usually equals burnt coffee and donuts); and amenities might top out at a phone and a TV (maybe with cable), but some have a few rooms with simple kitchenettes. Exteriors don't always predict room decor or cleanliness; some places may look tired from the outside but be well-kept and cared for, or the situation could be decidedly reversed. Always ask to see your room before you commit.

University Accommodations

During vacations, some universities and colleges offer accommodations in student dormitories. Generally meant for those attending summer courses, this is not a popular option for independent travelers. Dorm accommodations are not well publicized, services are minimal, booking conditions can be restrictive and perhaps most of all, campuses are not very lively during vacations.

ACTIVITIES

There is so much to do outdoors in the USA that this guide devotes a whole chapter to it (see p101). This section focuses on practical details and contact information for national outdoors organizations. See the regional chapters for local groups and outfitters.

Perhaps the best all-around Internet resource is the **Great Outdoor Recreation Pages** (GORP; http://gorp.away.com), which has community boards, advice and sales. A great general interest magazine is **Outside** (http://outside .away.com). If you just need gear, two national retailers are **REI** (www.rei.com) and the **Sports Authority** (www.thesportsauthority.com).

The USA has a wealth of public lands. Here are the main federal agencies and information sources:

Recreation.gov (www.recreation.gov) Links to all federal and state agencies.
Bureau of Land Management (www.blm.gov)
National Park Service (www.nps.gov)
US Fish & Wildlife Service (www.fws.gov)
US Forest Service (www.fs.fed.us)
Wilderness.net (www.wilderness.net) Provides a description and contact information for each national wilderness area.

Courses

For comprehensive instruction in a range of outdoor skills, contact the **National Outdoor Leadership School** (NOLS; ☎ 800-710-6657; www.nols

.edu; 284 Lincoln St, Lander, WY 82520). **Outward Bound** (☎ 866-467-7651; www.outwardbound.org; 100 Mystery Point Rd, Garrison, NY 10524) is also famous for its courses emphasizing wilderness skills and personal growth.

Cycling & Mountain Biking

Bike rental companies exist nearly everywhere and are recommended throughout this guide. See the Transportation chapter (p1171) for advice on touring the USA by bicycle and on transporting your own bicycle to the States. If you bring your own bike, bring a heavy-duty lock too; bicycle theft is a big business.

Note that bikes are often banned from designated wilderness areas and national park trails, though they are allowed on paved or dirt roads within these preserves, and they can generally be used on national forest and BLM single-track trails. Trail etiquette requires that cyclists yield to other users; otherwise, bicycles are subject to the same rules of the road as automobiles.

Useful bike organizations:
League of American Bicyclists (LAB; ☎ 202-822-1333; www.bikeleague.org; 1612 K St NW, Ste 800, Washington, DC 20006) This national advocacy group publishes **Bicycling** magazine (www.bicycling.com); its excellent website has links, touring advice and a database of rides. Members get discounts and state-by-state resources (in its annual *Almanac*).
Adventure Cycling Association (☎ 406-721-1776, 800-755-2453; www.adventurecycling.org; 150 E Pine St, PO Box 8308, Missoula, MT 59807) Organizes tours, sells great bike routes and publishes *Adventure Cyclist* magazine.
Backroads (☎ 510-527-1555, 800-462-2848; www.back roads.com; 801 Cedar St, Berkeley, CA 94710) Wide variety of tours nationwide, from cushy to strenuous.
Bike (www.bikemag.com) A hip mag aimed at the fat-tire crowd.
Cycle America (☎ 800-245-3263; www.cycleamerica .com; Box 485, Cannon Falls, MN 55009) This tour company specializes in cross-country rides.

Hiking & Backpacking

With very few exceptions, all of America's parks and preserves are open to hikers. The best-maintained trails are usually in national and state parks, where they can range from easy, paved, wheelchair-accessible paths to day- and weeklong wilderness journeys.

For planning day hikes in national and state parks, free park trail maps are usually adequate. For backpacking and other lands, topographic maps may be useful and even necessary; see Maps p1154. Before hiking on any trail, always ask at a ranger station or visitor center about current conditions. If you are backpacking, you are usually required to get a permit or register with park rangers a day ahead. Whether free or costing a few dollars, backcountry permits are usually limited; in popular national parks they book up months ahead. In sensitive areas, backcountry use may have lots of restrictions.

For advice on low-impact camping and wilderness etiquette, see p89. The **Leave No Trace Center** (☎ 800-332-4100; www.lnt.org) is a great hiker's resource, while the nonprofit **'Tread Lightly' program** (☎ 800-966-9900; www.tread lightly.org) emphasizes vehicular etiquette.

Be prepared for a wilderness journey and know what to do if things go wrong. **Survive Outdoors** (www.surviveoutdoors.com) dispenses tons of safety, first-aid and commonsense tips, from dealing with bee stings to identifying poisonous snakes and spiders. For true wilderness survival, pick up the classic *How to Stay Alive in the Woods* (1956/2001) by Bradford Angier.

This guide is chock-full of specific hiking recommendations and local resources. Some useful national resources include the following:

American Hiking Society (www.americanhiking.org) Lists local hiking clubs nationwide and has links for hiking gear and guides.

Backpacker (www.backpacker.com) A mag for, well, backpackers!

Rails-to-Trails Conservancy (☎ 202-331-9696; www.railtrails.org) Converts abandoned railroad corridors into public biking and hiking trails; sells a nationwide trail guide. Also lists and reviews trails at www.traillink.com.

The continental USA's three mountain systems are traversed by legendary, epic trails, which can be broken up into smaller segments. Contact the following:

Appalachian Trail Appalachian Trail Conference (☎ 304-535-6331; www.appalachiantrail.org; PO Box 807, Harpers Ferry, WV 25425)

Continental Divide Trail Continental Divide Trail Alliance (☎ 888-909-2382; www.cdtrail.org; PO Box 628, Pine, CO 80470); Continental Divide Trail Society (☎ 410-235-9610; www.cdtsociety.org; 3704 N Charles St, Suite 601, Baltimore, MD 21218)

Pacific Crest Trail Pacific Crest Trail Association (☎ 916-349-2109; www.pcta.org; 5325 Elkhorn Blvd, Suite 256, Sacramento, CA 95842)

Rafting, Kayaking & Canoeing

If a river or body of water in the US can support watercraft, an outfitter or rental operation will invariably be found nearby. In national parks, river running always requires a permit, and in some cases – for instance, the whitewater sections of the Colorado River – waitlists for individual permits are years long. In these cases, book in advance with an organized tour (see the regional chapters for more information). The following websites are helpful resources:

American Canoe Association (ACA; ☎ 703-451-0141; www.acanet.org; 7432 Alban Station Blvd, Suite B-232, Springfield, VA 22150) ACA publishes **Paddler magazine** (www.paddlermagazine.com) and is a great all-around resource.

American Whitewater (☎ 866-262-8429; www .americanwhitewater.org; 204B Philadelphia Ave, Takoma Park, MD 20912) This nonprofit is dedicated to preserving America's remaining wild rivers.

Canoe & Kayak (www.canoekayak.com) This magazine's website has great resource links.

Kayak Online (www.kayakonline.com) Good resource for kayak gear; links to outfitters nationwide.

Paddling.net (www.paddling.net)

Sea Kayaker (www.seakayakermag.com) Glossy mag focuses on plying America's oceans.

Rock Climbing & Canyoneering

For a general rock climbing resource, **Climbing magazine** (www.climbing.com) is a good start. Canyoneers should contact the **American Canyoneering Association** (☎ 435-590-8889; www .canyoneering.net).

Skiing & Snowboarding

Most of the USA's ski resorts are all-inclusive experiences: they offer equipment rental, lessons, restaurants, kids' programs and often lodging and day care. Ski season is normally mid-December to April, though some resorts have longer seasons. In summer many resorts are great places to mountain bike and hike. Ski packages (including airfare, hotel and lift tickets) are easy to find through resorts and travel agencies; they can be a good deal if your main goal is to ski.

Virtually every ski resort has its own website. *Skiing America* by Charles Leocha has overviews of North America's big ski resorts. Here are some good magazines and websites:

Ski (www.skimag.com)

Skiing (www.skiingmag.com)

Powder (www.powder.com)
SnoCountry Mountain Reports (www.snocountry
.com) Snow reports for all of North America.
Snowboard.com (www.snowboard.com) A community
website for snowboarders; lots of unvarnished advice.

CROSS-COUNTRY SKIING

Cross-country skiing (otherwise known as
Nordic skiing) is just as popular as downhill.
Most downhill ski resorts have cross-country
trails, and in winter many national park and
forest hiking trails, city parks and golf
courses become cross-country ski areas. For
more information, try the following:
Cross-Country Ski Areas Association (www.xcski.org)
Comprehensive information for North America.
Colorado Cross Country Ski Association (www.colorado
-xc.org) Covers Rocky Mountain cross-country ski centers.
Cross Country Skier (www.crosscountryskier.com)

Surfing

Pick up a copy of **Surfer magazine** (☎ 949-
661-5147; www.surfermag.com). *Surfer*'s travel reports cover just about every break in the
USA; order copies by phone or on the web.
Stormrider Guide North America is also
recommended.

BUSINESS HOURS

Unless otherwise noted, standard business
hours in this guide are as follows. Businesses are open from 9am to 5pm Monday
to Friday. Banks are open 8:30am to 4:30pm
Monday to Thursday, till 5:30pm Friday.
Some post offices and banks are also open
from 9am to noon or 1pm on Saturday.

Stores are open 10am to 6pm Monday
to Saturday, noon to 5pm Sunday. In malls
and major downtown shopping areas,
hours may be extended to 8pm or 9pm.
Supermarkets are generally open from 8am
to 8pm, and most cities have a few 24-hour
supermarkets. Note that in some parts of
the country, all businesses except a few restaurants may close on Sunday.

Hours for restaurant meals in this guide
are as follows: breakfast is 7am to 10am,
lunch 11:30am to 2:30pm, dinner 5pm to
9:30pm or later on Friday and Saturday.
If restaurant hours deviate from this by
more than a half hour, the specific hours
are noted. Bars and pubs are usually open
from 5pm to midnight daily, extending to
2am on Friday and Saturday. Nightclubs
and dance clubs open at 9pm and close at

2am Wednesday to Saturday. Hours may
be longer in larger cities and deviations are
noted in text.

CHILDREN

Most large cities in this guide have a 'City
for Children' section that lists the area's
best kids' activities and resources, including
dependable childcare services for travelers
where they exist.

Practicalities

Most facilities in the USA are ready to accommodate a child's needs. Nearly all restaurants (even the most expensive) have
high chairs, and if a restaurant doesn't have
a specific children's menu, it can make a
kid-tailored meal. Many diners and family
restaurants break out paper placemats and
crayons for drawing. Most public toilets – in
airports, stores, malls, movie theaters and so
on – have a baby changing table, even in the
men's toilet, and public places increasingly
have gender-neutral 'family' facilities.

Motels and hotels commonly have rooms
with two beds, which are ideal for families.
They also have 'roll-away beds' or 'cots' that
can be brought into the room for an extra
charge. Some have 'kids stay free' programs,
which range up to 12, and sometimes 18,
years old. Some B&Bs, to preserve a romantic atmosphere, don't allow children;
ask when reserving.

Every car rental agency should be able
to provide an appropriate child seat or re-
straint, since these are required in every
state; request one when booking. Airlines
also sometimes offer 'kids fly free' promotions, and they usually offer steep discounts
for traveling infants.

In addition, most tourist bureaus list
local resources for children's programs,
childcare facilities and so on.

Sights & Activities

The USA is full to bursting with hands-
on science museums, playgrounds, theme
parks and fun centers. For a smattering of
some of the nation's top spots, see 'Oh, To
Be a Kid Again' (p38).

It bears reminding that nearly every national and state park gears a certain number
of exhibits, trails and programs (such as national park Junior Ranger kits) for kids and
families. *Kids in the Wild: A Family Guide*

to *Outdoor Recreation* (2000) by Cindy Ross and Todd Gladfelter will help ensure successful family camping trips. For all-around information and advice, check out Lonely Planet's *Travel with Children*. Other useful resources:

Family Travel Times (www.familytraveltimes.com) Newsletter fosters travel that pleases the entire family, not just the kids.

Go City Kids (www.gocitykids.com) Excellent coverage of kid-centric play and resources in major US cities.

Kids.gov (www.kids.gov) Eclectic national resource; download songs and creative activities.

CLIMATE CHARTS

For general advice on climate and when to travel in the USA, see p24. Every regional chapter also has a When to Go section with more specific regional information. The climate charts (p1147) provide a snapshot of the USA's weather patterns.

CUSTOMS

For a complete list of US customs regulations, visit www.customs.gov. Or visit the official portal for US Customs and Border Protection, www.cbp.gov.

US Customs allows each person to bring 1L of liquor (provided you are 21 years old or older), 100 cigars and 200 cigarettes duty-free into the USA. US citizens are allowed to import, duty-free, $800 worth of gifts and purchases from abroad, while non-US citizens are allowed to bring in $100 worth.

US law permits you to bring in, or take out, as much as $10,000 in US or foreign currency, traveler's checks or letters of credit without formality. There's no maximum limit, but larger amounts of money must be declared to customs.

There are heavy penalties for attempting to import illegal drugs. It's also forbidden to bring in to the US drug paraphernalia, lottery tickets, items with fake brand names, and goods made in Cuba or Iraq. Any fruit, vegetables, or other food or plant material must be declared or left in the bins in the arrival area. Most food items are prohibited to prevent the introduction of pests or diseases.

The USA, like 140 other countries, is a signatory to CITES, the Convention on International Trade in Endangered Species. As such, it prohibits the import and export of products made from species that may be endangered in any part of the world, including ivory, tortoiseshell, coral, and many fur, skin and feather products. If you bring or buy a fur coat, snakeskin belt, alligator-skin boots or bone carving, you may have to show a certificate when you enter and/or leave the USA that states your goods were not made from an endangered species.

DANGERS & ANNOYANCES

Despite its seemingly Babylon-like list of dangers – guns, violent crime, earthquakes, tornadoes, hurricanes – the USA is actually a very safe country to visit. Perhaps the single greatest danger for travelers is posed by car accidents on America's highways (buckle up – it's the law). The two greatest annoyances will be auto traffic in the cities and crowds at popular sites.

Outdoor activities have their own sets of dangers and annoyances, but these vary with the terrain and the sport. The best advice is to talk to rangers about any risks posed by wildlife or the elements, and whether bugs and mosquitoes will be a particular problem when you'll be visiting.

Crime

For the traveler, petty theft is the biggest concern, not violent crime. When withdrawing money from an ATM, try to do so during the day or at night in well-lit, busy areas. If you are driving, don't pick up hitchhikers, and lock valuables in the trunk of your car; leaving bags and cameras lying in plain sight invites 'smash-and-grab' thieves. The same is true in hotels: use hotel safes when available, or otherwise hide and lock expensive items.

Other standard safety precautions are never to open your hotel door to a stranger (if someone seems suspicious, call the front desk to verify who they are), and in cities drive with your car doors locked.

Guns are in the news and would seem to be everywhere in the USA, but are not really (except perhaps Alaska). During hunting season, however, wear bright colors if you hike in the woods.

Scams

There are no scams unique to the USA. All prey on the gullibility of people or their eagerness to get rich quick. Travelers are most likely to encounter three-card monte card games (they are always rigged) and

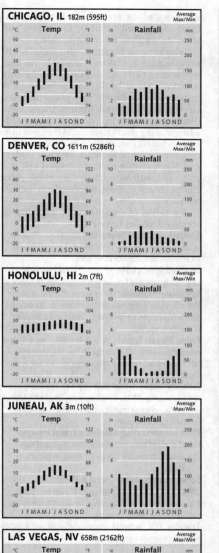

CHICAGO, IL 182m (595ft)

DENVER, CO 1611m (5286ft)

HONOLULU, HI 2m (7ft)

JUNEAU, AK 3m (10ft)

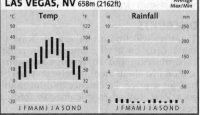

LAS VEGAS, NV 658m (2162ft)

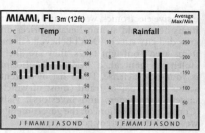

MIAMI, FL 3m (12ft)

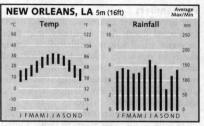

NEW ORLEANS, LA 5m (16ft)

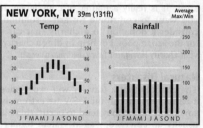

NEW YORK, NY 39m (131ft)

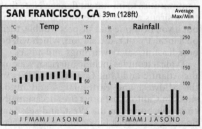

SAN FRANCISCO, CA 39m (128ft)

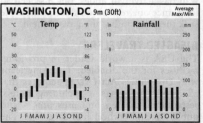

WASHINGTON, DC 9m (30ft)

expensive electronics, watches and designer items being sold at unbelievable prices on crowded city streets. Don't believe it; if the items aren't outright fakes, they are likely stolen. In general, a healthy skepticism is your best defense. For a list of current scams and types of fraud (most of which target homeowners and investors), visit 'Consumer Protection' on the government's website, http://firstgov.gov.

Panhandlers

The homeless are an unfortunate fact of life in almost every American city, and even in some small towns. Panhandlers set up camp on sidewalks asking for change, and these pleas are upsetting and sometimes annoying but almost never dangerous. If you don't wish to give any change, a firm no usually ends the solicitation.

There's an argument that giving to panhandlers only encourages them to target tourist areas. It is really a matter of conscience. If you want to contribute toward a solution, consider a donation to a charity that cares for the urban poor. For help finding a charity, visit **Charity Navigator** (www.charitynavigator.org).

Natural Disasters

The chances that a traveler will experience a natural disaster in the USA are extremely small, but where they tend to occur, there is usually an emergency siren system to alert communities to imminent danger. Note that these sirens are tested periodically at noon, but if you hear one and suspect trouble, turn on a local TV or radio station, which will be broadcasting safety warnings and advice.

Typical troubles include hurricanes along the Atlantic and Gulf Coasts, tornadoes in the Midwest and earthquakes and mudslides in California. Forest fires occasionally endanger homes in the West, and seasonal flooding can wreak havoc in the South. Hawaii has active volcanoes, but it's been so long since one really blew that most people seek them out rather than avoid them.

DISABLED TRAVELERS

The USA is a world leader in providing facilities for the disabled. The Americans with Disabilities Act (ADA) requires that all public buildings – including hotels, restaurants, theaters and museums – and public transit be wheelchair accessible. The more populous areas have the best and most widespread facilities, but always call ahead to confirm what is available.

Telephone companies are required to provide relay operators – available via teletypewriter (TTY) numbers – for the hearing impaired. Many banks now provide ATM instructions in Braille. All major airlines, Greyhound buses and Amtrak trains assist disabled travelers; just describe your needs when making reservations, and they will help make whatever arrangements are necessary.

Some car rental agencies – such as Budget and Hertz – offer hand-controlled vehicles and vans with wheelchair lifts at no extra charge, but you must reserve them well in advance.

A number of organizations specialize in serving disabled travelers:

Access-Able Travel Source (☎ 303-232-2979; www .access-able.com; PO Box 1796, Wheat Ridge, CO 80034) An excellent website with many links.

Disabled Sports USA (☎ 301-217-0960; www.dsusa .org; 451 Hungerford Drv, Suite 100, Rockville, MD 20850) Nationwide organization run by Access-Able Travel Source that offers sports and recreation programs for the disabled, selects US athletes for Paralympic Games and publishes *Challenge* magazine.

Flying Wheels Travel (☎ 507-451-5005; www.flying wheelstravel.com; 143 W Bridge St, Box 382, Owatonna, MN 55060) A full-service travel agency specializing in disabled travel.

Mobility International USA (☎ 541-343-1284; www.miusa.org; PO Box 10767, Eugene, OR 97440) Advises disabled travelers on mobility issues and runs an educational exchange program.

Moss Rehabilitation Hospital's Travel Information Service (www.mossresourcenet.org/travel.htm) This hospital provides a concise list of useful contacts on its website.

Society for Accessible Travel & Hospitality (SATH; ☎ 212-447-7284; www.sath.org; 347 Fifth Ave, Suite 610, New York, NY 10016) Lobbies for better facilities and publishes *Open World* magazine.

Travelin' Talk Network (www.travelintalk.net) A global network of service providers.

DISCOUNTS

Travelers will find a plethora of ways to shave costs on hotel rooms, meals, rental cars, museum and attraction admissions, and on just about anything else that can be had for a price. Persistence and ingenuity go a long way when it comes to finding deals in the USA.

Students and seniors (who are generally considered age 62 and up) are not issued separate discount cards, but they benefit from savings of all kinds. Simply carry proof of age or student status; international students should consider getting an **International Student Identity Card** (ISIC; www.isiccard.com), which provides its own discounts and should convince any dubious merchants of your student status. Then, as a matter of policy, ask about a discount every time you book a room, reserve a car, order a meal or pay an entrance fee. Most of the time this saves 10% or so, but sometimes the saving is significant, like 50%. American seniors should seriously consider getting a National Park Golden Age Passport, which allows free access to national lands and 50% off use fees like camping.

American Automobile Association (AAA; www.aaa .com) membership comes with a raft of discounts, and it has reciprocal agreements with several international auto associations. Other people whose status might lead to discounts are war veterans, the disabled, business travelers and foreign visitors. These discounts may not be advertised – it always pays to ask.

Discount coupons float around everywhere. Some aren't worth the paper they are printed on, but scour tourist agencies for publications, brochures, books and flyers with discount coupons and you'll find a few good ones. Highway welcome centers and even gas stations often stock cheap-looking newsprint coupon booklets; coupon flyers accompany Sunday newspapers. Coupons usually have restrictions and conditions, so read the fine print.

Online, get hotel discount coupons through **Roomsaver.com** (www.roomsaver.com).

Finally, children usually receive a discounted price, and public museums usually have free or discounted hours once a week or month.

EMBASSIES & CONSULATES
US Embassies & Consulates
The **US Department of State Bureau of Consular Affairs website** (http://travel.state.gov) has links for all US embassies abroad:

Australia Sydney (☎ 02-9373-9200; Level 59 MLC Center, 19-29 Martin Place, Sydney NSW 2000); Melbourne (☎ 03-9526-5900; 553 St Kilda Rd, Melbourne, Victoria 3004); Perth (☎ 08-9202-1224; 16 St George's Tce, 13th fl, Perth, WA 6000)

Austria Vienna (☎ 43-1-313-390; Boltzmanngasse 16, A-1091, Vienna)

Belgium Brussels (☎ 32-508-2111; Regentiaan 27 Blvd du Regent, B-1000, Brussels)

Canada Ottawa (☎ 1-613-238-5335; 490 Sussex Dr, Ottawa, Ontario, K1N 1G8); Vancouver (☎ 1-604-685-4311; 1095 W Pender St, Vancouver, BC, V6E 2M6); Montreal (☎ 1-514-398-9695; 1155 Rue St-Alexandre, Montreal, Quebec, H3B 3Z1); Ontario (☎ 1-416-595-1700; 360 University Ave, Toronto, Ontario M5G 1S4)

Denmark Copenhagen (☎ 45-3341-7100; Dag Hammar-skjölds Allé 24, 2100 Copenhagen)

Finland Helsinki (☎ 358-9-616-25730; Itäinen Pulstotie 14B, Helsinki)

France Paris (☎ 01-4312-2222; 2 Av Gabriel, 75382 Paris Cedex 08)

Germany Berlin (☎ 030-8305-0; Neustädtische Kirchstrasse 4-5, 10117 Berlin)

Greece Athens (☎ 30-210-721-2951; 91 Vasilissis Sophias Ave, 10160 Athens)

India New Delhi (☎ 011-2419-8000; Shantipath, Chanakyapuri 110021, New Delhi)

Ireland Dublin (☎ 01-668-8777; 42 Elgin Rd, Ballsbridge, Dublin 4)

Israel Tel Aviv (☎ 972-03-519-7617; 71 Hayarkon St, Tel Aviv, 63903)

Italy Rome (☎ 39-06-46741; Via Vittorio Veneto 119A, 00187 Rome)

Japan Tokyo (☎ 03-3224-5000; 1-10-5 Akasaka, Minato-ku, Tokyo 107-8420)

Kenya Nairobi (☎ 363-6000; United Nations Ave, PO Box 606, Village Market, 00621 Nairobi)

Korea Seoul (☎ 2-397-4114; 32 Sejongno, Jongno-gu, Seoul 110-710)

Malaysia Kuala Lumpur (☎ 60-3-2168-5000; 376 Jalan Tun Razak, Kuala Lumpur)

Mexico Mexico City (☎ 01-55-5080-2000; Paseo de la Reforma 305, Col Cuauhtémoc, 06500 Mexico City)

Netherlands The Hague (☎ 070-310-9209; Lange Voorhout 102, 2514 EJ The Hague); Amsterdam (☎ 020-575-5309; Museumplein 19, 1071 DJ Amsterdam)

New Zealand Wellington (☎ 04-462-6000; 29 Fitzherbert Terrace, Thorndon, Wellington)

Norway Oslo (☎ 47-22-44-85-50; Drammensveien 18, 0244 Oslo)

Russia Moscow (☎ 7-095-728-5000; Bolshoy Deviatinsky Pereulok 8, 121099 Moscow)

Singapore Singapore (☎ 65-6476-9100; 27 Napier Rd, Singapore 258508)

South Africa Pretoria (☎ 27-12-431-4000; 877 Pretorius St, Box 9536, Pretoria 0001)

Spain Madrid (☎ 91-587-2200; Calle Serrano 75, 28006 Madrid)

Sweden Stockholm (☎ 46-8-783-5300; Dag Hammar-skjölds Vag 31, SE-115 89 Stockholm)

Switzerland Bern (☎ 031-357-70-11; Jubilaumsstrasse 93, CH-3005 Bern)

Thailand Bangkok (☎ 66-2-205-4005; 95 Wireless Rd, Bangkok 10330)

UK London (☎ 020-7499-9000; 24 Grosvenor Sq, London W1A 1AE); Edinburgh (☎ 0131-556-8315; 3 Regent Tce, Edinburgh, Scotland EH7 5BW); Belfast (☎ 028-9038-6100; Danesfort House, 223 Stranmillis Rd, Belfast, Northern Ireland BT9 5GR)

Embassies & Consulates in the USA

Just about every country in the world has an embassy in Washington, DC. Call ☎ 202-555-1212 for embassy phone numbers, or visit www.embassy.org for links to all international embassies. Many countries also have consulates in other large cities. Look under 'Consulates' in the yellow pages. Most countries have an embassy for the UN in New York City.

FESTIVALS & EVENTS

The national festivals and events listed here are celebrated almost everywhere, though with much more fanfare in some places than others. In addition, hundreds of state and county fairs, multicultural events, pioneer days and harvest celebrations fill state and local calendars. Contact state tourist offices to find out what's happening. For more festival highlights, see 'Hoedowns and Hootenannies' under Top Tens (p26) and see 'Festivals' sections in regional chapters; also see Holidays (opposite).

JANUARY
Chinese New Year Two weeks at the end of January. The first day is celebrated with parades, fireworks and lots of food. San Francisco's parade is notable.

TRAVEL ADVISORIES

■ **Australia** (☎ 1300-139-281; www.smartraveler.gov.au)

■ **Canada** (☎ 800-267-6788; www.voyage.gc.ca)

■ **Germany** (☎ 030-5000-0; www.auswaertiges-amt.de)

■ **New Zealand** (☎ 04-439-8000; http://mft.govt.nz/travel)

■ **UK** (☎ 0870-606-0290; www.fco.gov.uk)

■ **USA** (☎ 202-647-5225; www.travel.state.gov)

FEBRUARY
Black History Month African American history is celebrated nationwide.

Valentine's Day The 14th. For some reason, St Valentine is associated with romance.

Mardi Gras In late February or early March, the day before Ash Wednesday. Parades, revelry and abandonment accompany the culmination of Carnival. New Orleans is the most legendary.

MARCH
St Patrick's Day The 17th. The patron saint of Ireland is honored. Huge celebrations occur in New York, Boston and Chicago. You should wear green – if you don't, you could get pinched.

Easter In late March or April, the Sunday following Good Friday (which is not a public holiday). Churches are full in the morning, followed by the kid-popular Easter egg hunt.

MAY
Cinco de Mayo The 5th. The day the Mexicans wiped out the French Army in 1862. In the South and the west, city parades celebrate their Mexican heritage.

Mother's Day The second Sunday. Children send cards and flowers and call Mom. Restaurants will be busy.

JUNE
Father's Day The third Sunday. Same idea, different parent.

Gay Pride Month (www.interpride.org) In some cities, this lasts just a week, but in San Francisco, festivities run for a month. The last weekend in June culminates with parades.

JULY
Independence Day The 4th. Parades and fireworks erupt nationwide to commemorate American independence. Strangely, Chicago pulls out all the stops on the 3rd.

OCTOBER
Halloween The 31st. Kids dress in costumes and go door-to-door trick-or-treating for candy. Adults dress in costumes and act out alter egos at parties. New York and San Francisco are the wildest.

NOVEMBER
Day of the Dead The 2nd. Observed in areas with Mexican communities, this is a day to honor deceased relatives; candy skulls and skeletons are popular.

Election Day The second Tuesday. Annual ritual where Americans engage in participatory democracy.

Thanksgiving The fourth Thursday. A latter-day harvest festival where family and friends gather for daylong meals, traditionally involving roasted turkey. New York City hosts a huge parade.

DECEMBER
Chanukkah Date determined by the Hebrew calendar, but usually begins before Christmas. This eight-day Jewish holiday (also called Hanukkah or the Feast of Lights) commemorates the victory of the Maccabees over the armies of Syria.
Christmas The 25th. The weeks leading up to Christ's birth include a range of religious and secular rituals: tree-lighting ceremonies, church choir concerts, church services, caroling in the streets and, of course, shopping.
Kwanzaa (www.officialkwanzaawebsite.org) From the 26th to the 31st. This African American celebration is a time to give thanks for the harvest.
New Year's Eve The 31st. People drink champagne, make new year's resolutions, watch the festivities on TV, then the next day nurse hangovers and watch college football.

FOOD
In this book, prices for restaurants usually refer to an average main dish at dinner; unless otherwise indicated, prices do not include drinks, appetizers, desserts, taxes or tips, and the same dish at lunch will usually be cheaper. When price categories are used in text, 'budget' means a meal under $10, 'midrange' means most dinner mains are $8 to $15, and 'top end' means most dinner mains are over $20. Within neighborhood and price sections, restaurants are listed by author preference. See 'Business Hours,' p1145, for the standard restaurant meal hours referred to in this guide, and remember that most US restaurants now ban or restrict smoking.

For the skinny on US cuisine, customs and table manners, see the Food & Drink chapter, p109.

GAY & LESBIAN TRAVELERS
Most major US cities have a visible and open gay community that is easy to connect with. For highlights, see 'We're Here, We're Queer' (p38). Also check out the boxed texts on gay life in San Francisco (p832), Los Angeles (p788), New York (p154), Philadelphia (p199), Portland (p1064), Chicago (p591), Minneapolis (p653), Boston (p238), Washington, DC (p320), Richmond (p350), Atlanta (p386), South Florida (p496), New Orleans (p422), Austin (p725), Dallas (p750), Houston (p741) and Waikiki (p1123).

The level of acceptance nationwide varies greatly. Gay and lesbian travelers should avoid hand-holding and outward displays of affection unless acceptance is obvious and

unmistakable. In some places, there is absolutely no tolerance whatsoever, and in others tolerance and acceptance is predicated on gays and lesbians not 'flaunting' their sexual preference.

Damron (☎ 415-255-0404, 800-462-6654; www.damron.com) publishes several excellent travel guides, including *Men's Travel Guide*, *Women's Traveller* and *Damron Accommodations*. *The Queerest Places: A Guide to Gay and Lesbian Historic Sites* by Paula Martinac is full of juicy details and history, and covers the country.

Other useful national resources:
Advocate (www.advocate.com) Gay news.
Gay.com (www.gay.com) Comprehensive resource; lots of travel information and guides 'powered' by *Out & About* magazine.
Gay & Lesbian National Hotline (☎ 888-843-4564; www.glnh.org) A national hotline for help, counseling, information and referrals; see website for hours.
Gay & Lesbian Yellow Pages (☎ 800-697-2812; www.glyp.com) Has listings for 25 US cities.
Gay Travel News (www.gaytravelnews.com) Lists gay-friendly destinations, travel agencies and hotels.
National Gay/Lesbian Task Force (☎ 202-393-5177; www.thetaskforce.org) A national advocacy group; website has current news and lists of referrals.
Out Traveler (www.outtraveler.com) Gay travel magazine.
Purple Roofs (www.purpleroofs.com) Lists queer accommodations, travel agencies and tours worldwide.

HOLIDAYS
On the following national public holidays, banks, schools and government offices (including post offices) are closed, and transportation, museums and other services operate on a Sunday schedule. Many stores, however, maintain regular business hours. Holidays falling on a weekend are usually observed the following Monday.

National public holidays:
January 1 New Year's Day.
Third Monday in January Martin Luther King Jr Day.
Third Monday in February Presidents' Day.
Last Monday in May Memorial Day.
July 4 Independence Day (or the Fourth of July).
First Monday in September Labor Day.
Second Monday in October Columbus Day.
November 11 Veterans' Day.
Fourth Thursday in November Thanksgiving.
December 25 Christmas Day.

Special mention should be made of **Spring Break**, when university students get one week off from school so they can overrun beach towns with wild shenanigans. Colleges don't all choose the same week, so spring breaks occur throughout March and April. To seek out or avoid these gatherings, see www.spring breakworld.com.

INSURANCE
No matter how long or short your trip, make sure you have adequate travel insurance, purchased before departure. At a minimum, you need coverage for medical emergencies and treatment, including hospital stays and an emergency flight home if necessary. Medical treatment in the USA is of the highest caliber, but the expense could kill you. See p1180 for complete information.

You should also consider coverage for luggage theft or loss, and trip cancellation insurance. If you already have a homeowner's policy, see what it will cover and consider getting supplemental insurance to cover the rest. If you have prepaid a large portion of your trip, cancellation insurance is a worthwhile expense.

A comprehensive travel insurance policy that covers all these things should cost about 5% to 7% of the total cost of your trip.

Finally, if you will be driving, it's also essential that you have liability insurance. Car rental agencies offer insurance that covers damage to the rental vehicle and separate liability insurance (which covers damage to people and other vehicles). See p1175 for details.

In addition to student travel agencies (p1163), here are some agencies offering comprehensive travel policies:

Insure.com (☎ 800-556-9393; www.insure.com) An independent site that compares quotes among 200 insurance companies and gives advice about the different types of coverage. In the UK, they run Quoteline Direct, www .quotelinedirect.co.uk; in Canada, Kanetix, www.kanetix.ca.

Travelex (☎ 888-457-4602; www.travelex.com) A major insurer with offices worldwide.

Travel Guard (☎ 800-826-1300; www.travelguard.com)

Access America (☎ 866-807-3982; www.access america.com)

INTERNET ACCESS
The USA is as tech-savvy as they come. Travelers will have few problems staying connected.

In text, the Internet icon (🖳) in hotel listings means the hotel provides a public Internet terminal for guests; if there is a cost, this is noted. These days nearly every midrange and up hotel has in-room dial-up or high-speed access for connecting your own equipment, and an increasing number of budget hotels provide this too. Ask when reserving. Many hotels and city neighborhoods also now offer wi-fi hotspots (see 'Look Ma, No Wires,' below).

For quick Internet surfing and email, another dependable bet is a public library. Nearly every branch has public terminals, though they will have time limits, and occasionally out-of-state residents are charged a small fee ($1 to $2). Even small towns have

---

LOOK MA, NO WIRES
By one count, the USA has nearly 10,000 wi-fi hotspots, or a third of all the wi-fi hotspots in the world. That doesn't yet cover the continent, but you'll be hard-pressed to find any town that doesn't have at least one café offering 'wireless fidelity' access. If you're in a city or a college town, you can almost count on civic-sponsored neighborhood hotspots as well, and some states (like California and Michigan) have provided access at certain state parks. About as many of these wi-fi hotspots are free as charge for access.

A growing number of websites provide extensive wi-fi hotspot lists by US city, and they also provide lots of 'what it is' and 'how to access' information – in addition to retail links if you need gear. Here are a few:

- **www.wi-fi.com** Run by the Wi-Fi Alliance, a nonprofit association promoting wi-fi standards. Get lists of certified products and of 'official,' Alliance-certified Wi-Fi Zones.

- **www.hotspot-locations.com** This Swiss company lists all wi-fi hotspots, whether pay or free, and has a wealth of info on tech (such as wi-fi sniffers), operators and books for sale.

- **www.wififreespot.com** Focuses exclusively on free wi-fi hotspots in the US.

- **www.wi-fihotspotlist.com** Another good US hotspot list.

at least one Internet café or copy center (rates run $10 to $20 per hour) and cities have dozens; under cities in this guide, 'Internet Access' sections list the best options. In addition to providing Internet access, full-service Internet cafés let you hook up your own peripherals to upload photos and/or burn them onto CDs (see also 'Photography,' p1155).

If you're not from the US, remember that you will need an AC adapter and a plug adapter for US sockets. See p27 for Internet resources.

LEGAL MATTERS

In everyday matters, if you are stopped by the police, bear in mind that there is no system of paying traffic or other fines on the spot. Attempting to pay a fine to an officer is frowned upon at best and may result in a charge of bribery. For traffic offenses, the police officer or highway patroller will explain the options to you. There is usually a 30-day period to pay a fine, but the officer has the authority to take you directly to a magistrate to pay immediately.

If you are arrested for a more serious offense, you have a legal right to an attorney, and you are allowed to remain silent. There is no legal reason to speak to a police officer if you don't wish, but never walk away from an officer until given permission. All persons who are arrested are legally allowed the right to make one phone call. If you don't have a lawyer, friend or family member to help you, call your embassy. The police will give you the number upon request. As a matter of principle, the US legal system presumes a person innocent until proven guilty.

Each state has its own civil and criminal laws, and what is legal in one state may be illegal in others. Federal laws are applicable to the postal service, US government property and many interstate activities.

A new wrinkle in all of this is the USA Patriot Act, which was passed in the wake of September 11 to improve national security. Among other things, it expanded the federal government's ability to detain foreign visitors and immigrants for an extended period of time without submitting charges or bringing them to trial. Ostensibly, this can only be done once a judge has been shown that the person is connected to terrorism or an identified terrorist organization, but

---

> **THE LEGAL AGE FOR...**
>
> - Drinking: 21
> - Driving: 16
> - Heterosexual consensual sex: 16–18
> - Homosexual consensual sex: where legal, 16–18
> - Voting: 18
>
> The age of consent varies by state; see www.ageofconsent.com for state-by-state details.

---

the standards of proof and oversight are not clear. While this should be taken seriously by all foreign visitors, it is extremely unlikely that it will affect you. For more information and referrals for help, visit the website of the **American Civil Liberties Union** (ACLU; www.aclu.org/safeandfree).

Driving

In all states, driving under the influence of alcohol or drugs is a serious offense, subject to stiff fines and even imprisonment. For more information on driving and road rules, see p1176.

Drinking

Bars and stores often ask for photo identification to prove you are of legal drinking age. Being 'carded' is standard practice and shouldn't be taken personally. The sale of liquor is subject to local government regulations, and some counties ban liquor sales on Sunday, after midnight or before breakfast. In 'dry' counties, liquor sales are banned altogether.

Drugs

Recreational drugs are prohibited by federal and state laws. Some states, such as California and Alaska, treat possession of small quantities of marijuana as a misdemeanor, though it is still punishable with fines and/or imprisonment.

Possession of any drug, including cocaine, ecstasy, LSD, heroin, hashish or more than an ounce of pot, is a felony punishable by lengthy jail sentences, depending on the circumstances. For foreigners, conviction of any drug offense is grounds for deportation.

MAPS

If you're driving, a good road atlas is essential. **Rand McNally's** (www.randmcnally.com) maps are excellent, as are its Thomas Brothers city guides; both can be found in most bookstores and many gas stations. You can also order them online. If you are a member of **AAA** (www.aaa.com) or one of its international affiliates, you can get AAA's high-quality free maps from any regional office. Both Rand McNally's and AAA's websites also provide driving directions and free downloadable maps, as does **Google Maps** (http://maps.google.com).

If you will be backpacking, a good topographical (topo) map could be essential. The **US Geological Survey** (USGS; ☎ 888-275-8747; www.usgs.gov) produces a series of 1:24,000 scale maps (or 7.5-minute maps) that cover the entire country and are ideal for hiking. The USGS also publishes a separate series of topo maps of all the national parks. These can be found at many national park information centers, ranger stations and outdoor stores; the USGS website has a comprehensive list of retailers that stock its maps. The USFS publishes 1:126,720 scale (2 inches = 1 mile) topo maps of the national forests, but they aren't quite as useful as the USGS maps.

The **University of Texas** (www.lib.utexas.edu/maps/index.html) maintains an extensive online map library that covers the US and the world.

Another fantastic map service is provided by **National Geographic** (www.nationalgeographic.com). Their online Map Machine is a great tool for creating customized, downloadable (but relatively small) highway and topo maps, while its online store has all the products you'd want, including GPS maps. GPS gear and software can also be purchased from **Magellan** (www.magellangps.com) and **Garmin** (www.garmin.com).

MONEY
Cash

The stable US dollar – aka greenback, simoleon or buck – is the only currency generally accepted in the country, though a few places near the Canadian border also accept Canadian dollars.

The US dollar is divided into 100 cents (¢). Coins come in denominations of 1¢ (penny), 5¢ (nickel), 10¢ (dime), 25¢ (quarter), the seldom-seen 50¢ (half-dollar) and the $1 coin. Quarters are most commonly used in vending machines and parking meters. Bills come in $1, $2 (rare), $5, $10, $20, $50 and $100 denominations.

ATMS

ATMs are available 24 hours a day at almost every bank, and in shopping centers, airports, grocery stores and casinos. Withdrawing cash from an ATM using a credit card usually incurs a fee ($1 to $3), but if your home bank account is affiliated with one of the main worldwide ATM networks (Plus, Cirrus, Exchange, Accel), you can sometimes avoid the fee by using your bank card. The exchange rate on ATM transactions is usually as good as you'll get.

Check with your bank or credit card company for exact information about using its cards in stateside ATMs. If you will be relying on ATMs (not a bad strategy), bring more than one card and keep them separate.

Credit Cards

Major credit cards are accepted nearly everywhere throughout the USA. In fact, it's almost impossible to rent a car or make phone reservations without one. (Though, strangely, some airlines require your credit card billing address to be in the USA – a hassle if you're booking domestic flights once here.) It's highly recommended that you carry at least one credit card, and if it's only one, make it Visa or MasterCard, which are more widely accepted.

Carry copies of your credit card numbers separately. If your credit cards are lost or stolen, contact the company immediately. Here are the main credit card toll-free numbers:
American Express (☎ 800-528-4800; www.americanexpress.com)
Diners Club (☎ 800-234-6377; www.dinersclub.com)
Discover (☎ 800-347-2683; www.discovercard.com)
MasterCard (☎ 800-622-7747; www.mastercard.com)
Visa (☎ 800-847-2911; www.visa.com)

Currency Exchange

Banks are the best places to exchange foreign currencies. Currency exchange counters at the airport and in tourist centers usually have the worst rates. Most large city banks offer currency exchange, but not always banks in rural areas. **Travelex** (☎ 888-457-4602; www.travelex.com) is a major currency exchange company.

For a list of exchange rates at the time this guide went to press, see the inside front cover.

Taxes

Sales tax varies by state and county; see each region's 'Information' section for specifics. Or, check out state sales taxes on the **Sales Tax Clearinghouse** (http://thestc.com/STRates.stm). Hotel taxes vary by city, and these are listed under city 'Sleeping' sections.

Tipping

Tipping is standard practice across America. In city restaurants, tipping 15% of the bill is expected; less is okay in an informal diner, while top end restaurants expect 20%. Bartenders expect $1 per drink. Taxi drivers and hairdressers expect 10% to 15%.

Skycaps at airports and porters at nice hotels expect $1 a bag or so. It's polite to leave a few dollars for the hotel maid, especially if you spend several nights. In big city coffee shops and sandwich counters, 'tip jars' appear like mushrooms after the rain; leave your change if you're inclined.

Traveler's Checks

Because of ATMs, traveler's checks are becoming obsolete except as a trustworthy backup. If you decide to carry them, buy them in US dollars; local businesses may not cash ones in a foreign currency. Keep a separate record of their numbers in case they are lost or stolen. American Express traveler's checks are the most widely accepted.

PHOTOGRAPHY

Print film is available everywhere, and digital camera memory cards in almost as many places – try drugstores, chain retailers like Target or Circuit City and camera stores. Specialized camera batteries may only be available in camera stores. For advice on picture-taking, see Lonely Planet's *Travel Photography*.

Drugstores and supermarkets are good places to get your print film processed cheaply – around $6 for a roll of 24 exposures. One-hour processing services are more expensive, usually from around $11. Walgreens and Wal-Mart are two major chains where you can burn digital photos onto a CD ($3 to $5).

About the only caution when it comes to photography concerns people. Always ask permission if you want to photograph someone close up. Some Native American reservations prohibit photography and video

completely; when it's allowed, photo subjects expect a small tip (about $1).

POST

The US Postal Service (USPS) is the busiest postal service in the world; it's also inexpensive and reliable. Still, for urgent and important documents, some people prefer the more expensive door-to-door services of **Federal Express** (FedEx; ☎ 800-463-3339; www.fedex.com) or **United Parcel Service** (UPS; ☎ 800-742-5877; www.ups.com).

Postal Rates

As of July 2005, the postal rates for 1st-class mail within the USA were 37¢ for letters weighing up to one ounce (23¢ for each additional ounce) and 23¢ for postcards. First-class mail goes up to 13oz, and then priority-mail rates apply.

International airmail rates (except to Canada and Mexico) are 80¢ for a 1oz letter and 70¢ for a postcard. To Canada and Mexico it's 60¢ for a 1oz letter and 50¢ for a postcard. Aerograms are 70¢ to all countries.

For 24-hour postal information, call ☎ 800-275-8777 or check www.usps.com. You can get zip (postal) codes for a given address, the rules about parcel sizes, and the location and hours of any post office.

Sending & Receiving Mail

If you have the correct postage, you can drop mail weighing less than 16oz into any blue mailbox. To send a package 16oz or heavier, go to a post office. There are branch post offices and post office centers in many supermarkets and drugstores.

General delivery mail (ie poste restante) can be sent to you c/o General Delivery at any post office that has its own zip code. Mail is usually held for 10 days before it's returned to the sender; you might request your correspondents to write 'Hold for Arrival' on their letters. You'll need photo identification to collect general delivery mail. In some big cities, general delivery mail is not held at the main post office, but at a postal facility away from downtown.

SHOPPING

American consumerism knows no bounds. For proof, wander the corridors of any megagiant-super mall. Most visitors won't want to leave before procuring a little brand-name

American kitsch. No worries here, mate – you'll find it's merely abundant when it isn't truly bizarre. Some tacky roadside souvenirs achieve the status of folk art, and if nothing else, they prove that Americans really do have a sense of humor about themselves.

But actually, many regions in America are known for excellent local handicrafts or native artwork and goods. Traditional quilts, Pueblo jewelry, Navajo blankets, traditional or modern pottery, Gullah sweetgrass baskets and tooled leather cowboy boots are just a few of the things to look for. Good pieces will be expensive; if they are cheap, they are probably not authentic.

Another popular item in America is antiques, and there is a booming trade in old stuff. As with handicrafts, real antiques will be expensive; bargains are rare and sometimes suspect. The most popular types – anything colonial, Victorian, Amish, Shaker, art deco or '50s moderne – are guaranteed to have a hefty price tag.

If you're on the hunt for cool, unusual souvenirs, try modern art museum stores, which specialize in items that play off the museum's collection. They also often sell high-quality original designs by local artists. Even a plastic bag from the MoMA has its own cachet.

Finally, bargain hunters should track down local factory outlets. These are usually malls near a freeway exit on the outskirts of a city where brand-name stores sell their damaged, left over or out-of-season stock at discounts ranging from modest to practically giveaway. Service will be minimal and choices limited, but for some the chance to find half-price Levi's, Nike shoes or Polo shirts is a siren song.

SOLO TRAVELERS

There are no particular problems or difficulties traveling alone in the USA.

Many hotels offer lower rates for a single person, but not all do. These rooms tend to be small and badly located, so if you want more comfort, make a reservation for a double. Similarly, restaurants often shunt single diners to cramped corners. To avoid this, make a reservation for two, and after being seated for a while, look disappointed that your friend isn't coming and order your meal; more than likely, the waitstaff will become extra helpful because of your plight. Or, if you want to meet people, eat at the bar if that is available.

Some issues of safety are slightly different for women than they are for men; women should see p1161 for more-specific advice. For anyone, hitchhiking is always risky and not recommended, *especially* hitchhiking alone. And don't pick up hitchhikers when driving.

In general, don't advertise where you are staying, or even that you are traveling alone, if someone strikes you as suspicious. Americans tend to be friendly and very eager to help and even take in solo travelers, and this is one of the pluses of traveling this way. However, don't take all offers of help at face value. If someone who seems trustworthy invites you to his or her home, let someone know where you're going (even your hotel manager). This advice also applies if you go for a long hike by yourself. If something happens and you don't return as expected, you want to know that someone will notice and know where to begin looking for you.

TELEPHONE

The US phone system comprises numerous regional phone companies, plus competing long-distance carriers and lots of smaller mobile-phone and pay-phone companies. Overall, the system is very efficient, but it can be confusing and expensive. Avoid making long-distance calls on a hotel phone or on a pay phone. It's always cheaper to use a regular landline.

STAYING IN TOUCH

Too busy to write postcards? Too poor to call? Too lazy for email?

Don't worry. Stay in touch with friends and family easily by creating a personal blog of your travels, which everyone can read. See 'Blogs, Vlogs and Podcasting,' p63 for information.

Or, sign up for **Locating Me** (www.locatingme.com): this web service lets you post your current whereabouts and contact info (hourly, if you wish) so you can be reached in case of an emergency back home. You can also post your own medical information, which could be useful if *you* have an emergency.

Mom will be ever so relieved.

Note that most telephone books are fantastic resources: in addition to complete calling information, they list community services, public transportation and things to see and do. Online, a good resource for phone numbers is www.yellowpages.com.

Cell Phones

In the USA cell phones use GSM 1900 or CDMA 800, operating on different frequencies from systems in other countries. The only foreign phones that will work in the USA are tri-band models, operating on GSM 1900 as well as other frequencies. If you have a GSM tri-band phone, check with your service provider about using it in the USA. Make sure to ask if roaming charges apply; these will turn even local US calls into pricey international calls.

You may be able to take the SIM card from your home phone, install it in a rented mobile phone that's compatible with the US systems, and use the rental phone as if it were your own phone – same number, same billing basis. Ask your mobile phone company about this. You can rent a phone for about $45 per week, but rates vary.

You can also rent a GSM 1900 compatible phone with a set amount of prepaid call time. **T-Mobile** (www.t-mobile.com) is one US company that provides this service, but it ain't cheap.

Finally, huge swaths of rural America don't pick up a signal. Make sure your provider covers your route.

Dialing Codes

If you're calling from abroad, the international country code for the USA is ☎ 1 (the same as Canada, but international rates apply between the two countries). To make an international call from the USA, dial ☎ 011, then the country code, followed by the area code (usually without the initial '0') and the phone number.

All phone numbers within the USA consist of a three-digit area code followed by a seven-digit local number. If you are calling a number within the same area code, just dial the seven-digit number. If you are calling long distance, dial ☎ 1 plus the area code plus the phone number. New area codes are added and changed all the time, so if a number doesn't work, that may be the reason.

For local directory assistance, dial ☎ 411. For directory assistance outside your area code, dial ☎ 1 plus the three-digit area code of the place you want to call plus 555-1212; this is charged as a long-distance call. For international assistance, dial ☎ 00.

The 800, 888, 877 and 866 prefixes are for toll-free numbers. Most can only be used within the USA, some only within the state, and some only outside the state. To find an organization's 800 number, call ☎ 800-555-1212.

The 550, 554, 900, 920, 940, 976 codes and some other prefixes are for calls charged at a premium rate – phone sex, horoscopes, jokes etc.

Pay Phones

Local calls cost 35c to 50c at pay phones for the first few minutes; talking longer costs more money. Only put in the exact amount, since phones don't give change. Local-call charges only apply to a small area. If the number you're trying to call is beyond this area, a synthetic voice will tell you to insert more money. Local calls from pay phones get expensive quickly, and long-distance calls are prohibitive. If you can't avoid it, use a prepaid phone card, a phone credit card, or the access line of a major carrier, such as **AT&T** (☎ 800-321-0288) or **MCI** (☎ 800-888-8000).

Phone Cards

Phone cards are now almost essential for travelers using the US phone system. There are two basic types.

A phone credit card bills calls to your home phone number. Some cards issued by foreign phone companies will work in the USA – inquire before you leave home.

A prepaid phone card is a good alternative for travelers and widely available in big cities and major retailers. Always check the card's connection fees (see if it has a toll-free access number from pay phones) in addition to the rate. AT&T sells a reliable phone card that's available at many retailers.

TIME

America subscribes to daylight savings time (DST): on the first Sunday in April, clocks are set one hour ahead ('spring ahead'). Then, on the last Sunday of October, clocks are turned back one hour ('fall back'). Just to keep you on your toes, Arizona, Hawaii and most of Indiana don't use DST.

Foreigners are sometimes confused by the US date system, which is written as month/day/year. Thus, 8 June 2006 becomes 6/8/06. Got it?

See p1192 for a map of time zones.

TOURIST INFORMATION

There is no national office promoting US tourism. However, the federal government provides a good resource: under the 'Travel and Recreation' page on its official web portal (http://firstgov.gov), there are links to all the nation's state travel bureaus, plus a wealth of links to other recreation information.

In this guide, state tourism bureaus are listed in each regional chapter's 'Information' section, while city and county tourist bureaus are listed throughout.

Any tourist office worth contacting has a website and will, on request, send out a swag of free promotional material. They also field phone calls; some local tourist offices maintain lists of hotel room availability, updated daily, but very few offer reservation services. All tourist offices have self-service racks of brochures and discount coupons to local attractions. Some also sell maps and books.

Some of the most comprehensive tourist information sources are state-run 'welcome centers,' which are usually placed along interstates. Their materials cover wider territories, and the offices are usually open longer hours, including weekends and holidays.

Many cities have an official convention and visitors bureau (CVB); these sometimes double as tourist bureaus, but since their main focus is drawing the convention trade, CVBs can be less useful for independent travelers.

Keep in mind that, in smaller towns, when the local chamber of commerce runs the tourist bureau, the lists of hotels, restaurants and services they provide usually only mention chamber members; the town's cheapest options may be missing.

Similarly, in prime tourist destinations, some private 'tourist bureaus' are really agents who book hotel rooms and tours on commission. They may offer excellent service and deals, but you'll get what they're selling and nothing else.

VISAS

As the USA continues to fine-tune its national security guidelines post-September 11, US entry requirements will evolve as well. It is imperative that travelers double- and triple-check current regulations before coming to the USA.

The main portal for US visa information is www.unitedstatesvisas.gov; this website is comprehensive, providing all the information here, plus forms, US consulates abroad and even visa wait times calculated by country. The **US State Department** (www.travel.state.gov) also maintains comprehensive visa information. The website maintained by **US Citizenship and Immigration Services** (USCIS; http://uscis.gov) focuses on immigrants not temporary visitors.

Visa Application

Apart from Canadians and those entering under the Visa Waiver Program (see opposite), foreign visitors need to obtain a visa from a US consulate or embassy. In most countries, you must now schedule a personal interview, to which you must bring all your documentation and proof of fee payment. Wait times for interviews vary, but afterward, barring problems, visa issuance takes from a few days to a few weeks. The US consular office should also inform you if you must follow the National Security Entry/Exit Registration System (NSEERS) registration procedures upon arrival (p1160).

Your passport must be valid for at least six months longer than your intended stay in the USA (some countries have exemptions from this), and you'll need to submit a recent photo (2in by 2in) with the application; there is a $100 processing fee, and in a few cases an additional visa issuance reciprocity fee (check the main US visa website for details). In addition to the main nonimmigrant visa application form (DS-156), all men aged 16 to 45 must complete an additional form (DS-157) that details their travel plans.

In almost all cases, visa applicants are required to show documents of financial stability (or evidence that a US resident will provide financial support), a round-trip or onward ticket and 'binding obligations' that will ensure their return home, such as family ties, a home or a job.

Because of these requirements, those planning to travel through other countries before arriving in the USA are generally better off applying for a US visa while they are still in their home country, rather than while on the road.

The most common visa is a nonimmigrant visitor's visa, type B1 for business purposes, B2 for tourism or visiting friends and relatives. A visitor's visa is good for multiple entries over one or five years, and specifically prohibits the visitor from taking paid employment in the USA. The validity period depends on what country you are from. The length of time you'll be allowed to stay in the USA is determined by US immigration at the port of entry (see p1160).

If you're coming to the USA to work or study, you will need a different type of visa, and the company or institution to which you are going should make the arrangements. Other categories of nonimmigrant visas include an F1 visa for students undertaking a recognized course; an H1, H2 or H3 visa for temporary employment; a J1 visa for exchange visitors in approved programs; a K1 visa for the fiancé or fiancée of an American citizen; and an L1 visa for intracompany transfers.

VISA WAIVER PROGRAM

Under the Visa Waiver Program, citizens of certain countries may enter the USA without a US visa for stays of 90 days or less; no extensions are allowed. Currently, 27 countries are included: Andorra, Australia, Austria, Belgium, Brunei, Denmark, Finland, France, Germany, Iceland, Ireland, Italy, Japan, Liechtenstein, Luxembourg, Monaco, the Netherlands, New Zealand, Norway, Portugal, San Marino, Singapore, Slovenia, Spain, Sweden, Switzerland and the UK.

Under this program, visitors must produce at the port of entry all the same evidence as for a nonimmigrant visa application: ie they must demonstrate that the trip is for a limited time, and that they have a round-trip or onward ticket, adequate funds to cover the trip and binding obligations abroad. You don't need a visa if: your passport was issued before October 26, 2005, but is 'machine readable' (with two lines of letters, numbers and <<< at the bottom); if it was issued on or after October 26, 2005, and includes a digital photo as well as being machine readable; or if it was issued on or after October 26, 2006, and contains a digital photo and 'biometric data,' such as digital iris scans and fingerprints. Confirm

with your passport issuing agency that your passport meets current US standards. You'll be turned back if it doesn't, even though you belong to a VWP country.

In addition, the same 'grounds for exclusion' apply (see following), except that you will have no opportunity to appeal the grounds or apply for an exemption. If you are denied under the Visa Waiver Program at a US point of entry, you will have to use your onward or return ticket on the next available flight.

GROUNDS FOR EXCLUSION & DEPORTATION

If on your visa application form you admit to being a subversive, smuggler, prostitute, junkie or an ex-Nazi, you may be excluded. You can also be refused a visa or entry to the USA if you have a 'communicable disease of public health significance,' a criminal record or if you've ever made a false statement in connection with a US visa application. However, if these last three apply, you can request an exemption; many people are granted them and then given visas.

US immigration has a very broad definition of a criminal record. If you've ever been arrested or charged with an offense, that's a criminal record, even if you were acquitted or discharged without conviction. Don't attempt to enter through the Visa Waiver Program if you have a criminal record of any kind; assume US authorities will find out about it.

Communicable diseases include tuberculosis, the Ebola virus, SARS and most particularly HIV. US immigration doesn't test people for disease, but officials at the point of entry may question anyone about his or her health. They can exclude anyone whom they believe has a communicable disease, perhaps because they are carrying medical documents, prescriptions or AIDS/HIV medicine. Being gay is not a ground for exclusion; being an IV drug user is. Visitors may be deported if US immigration finds that they have HIV but did not declare it. Being HIV-positive is not a ground for deportation, but failing to provide accurate information on the visa application is.

Often USCIS will grant an exemption (a 'waiver of ineligibility') to a person who would normally be subject to exclusion, but this requires referral to a regional immigration office and can take some time (allow at least two months). If you're tempted to conceal something, remember that US immigration is strictest of all about false statements. It will often view favorably an applicant who admits to an old criminal charge or a communicable disease, but it is extremely harsh on anyone who has ever attempted to mislead it, even on minor points. After you're admitted to the USA, any evidence of a false statement to US immigration is grounds for deportation.

Prospective visitors to whom grounds of exclusion may apply should consider their options *before* applying for a visa.

Entering the USA

If you have a non-US passport, you must complete an arrival/departure record (form I-94) before you reach the immigration desk. It's usually handed out on the plane along with the customs declaration. For the question, 'Address While in the United States,' give the address where you will spend the first night (a hotel address is fine).

No matter what your visa says, US immigration officers have an absolute authority to refuse admission to the USA or to impose conditions on admission. They will ask about your plans and whether you have sufficient funds; it's a good idea to list an itinerary, produce an onward or round-trip ticket and have at least one major credit card. Showing that you have over $400 per week of your stay should be enough. Don't make too much of having friends, relatives or business contacts in the USA; the immigration official may decide that this will make you more likely to overstay. It also helps to be neatly dressed and polite. If they think you're OK, a six-month entry is usually approved.

REGISTRATION

The Department of Homeland Security's registration program – called **US-VISIT** (www.dhs.gov/us-visit) – is now almost completely phased in. It includes every port of entry and every foreign visitor to the USA.

For most visitors, registration consists of having your photo taken and having electronic (inkless) fingerprints made of each index finger; the process takes less than a minute. The same registration procedure is followed when you exit the USA.

A 'special registration' called NSEERS (the National Security Entry/Exit Registration System) currently applies to citizens of certain countries that have been deemed particular risks. These countries are mainly in the Middle East and Africa; visit www.unitedstatesvisas.gov for a complete list. Registration in these cases also includes a short interview in a separate room and computer verification of all personal information supplied on travel documents. US officials can require this separate interview of any traveler.

Visa Extensions

If you want, need or hope to stay in the USA longer than the date stamped on your passport, go to the local USCIS office (call ☎ 800-375-5283 or look in the local white pages telephone directory under 'US Government') to apply for an extension well *before* the stamped date. If the date has passed, your best chance will be to bring a US citizen with you to vouch for your character, and to produce lots of other verification that you are not trying to work illegally and have enough money to support yourself. However, if you've overstayed, the most likely scenario is that you will be deported.

Short-Term Departures & Reentry

It's quite easy to make trips across the border to Canada or Mexico, but upon return to the USA, non-Americans will be subject to the full immigration procedure. Always take your passport when you cross the border. If your immigration card still has plenty of time on it, you will probably be able to reenter using the same one, but if it has nearly expired, you will have to apply for a new card, and border control may want to see your onward air ticket, sufficient funds and so on.

Traditionally, a quick trip across the border has been a way to extend your stay in the USA without applying for an extension at a USCIS office. This can still be done, but don't assume it will work. First, make sure you hand in your old immigration card to the immigration authorities when you leave the USA, and when you return make sure you have all the necessary application documentation from when you first entered the country. US immigration will be very suspicious of anyone who leaves for a few days and returns immediately hoping for a new six-month stay; expect to be questioned closely.

Citizens of most Western countries will not need a visa for Canada, so it's really not a problem at all to cross to the Canadian side of Niagara Falls, detour up to Quebec or pass through on the way to Alaska. Travelers entering the USA by bus from Canada can be closely scrutinized. A round-trip ticket that takes you back to Canada will most likely make US immigration feel less suspicious. Mexico has a visa-free zone along most of its border with the USA, including the Baja Peninsula and most of the border towns, such as Tijuana and Ciudad Juárez. You'll only need a Mexican visa or tourist card if you want to go beyond the border zone. For more, see 'Border Crossings,' p1167.

VOLUNTEERING

Volunteer opportunities abound in the USA, and they can be a great way to break up a long trip. They can also provide some of your most memorable experiences: you will interact with Americans, society and the land in ways you never would just passing through.

Most programs charge a fee; this usually runs from $200 to $500 or so, depending on the length of the program and the type of food and lodging it provides. None cover travel to the USA.

In addition to the groups here, all of the trail alliances under 'Hiking,' p1144, use volunteers:

Global Volunteers (☎ 800-487-1074; www.global volunteers.org; 375 E Little Canada Rd, St Paul, MN 55117)
Habitat for Humanity (☎ 229-924-6935, ext 2551; www.habitat.org; 121 Habitat St, Americus, GA 31709) Focuses on housing and homelessness.
Volunteer America (www.volunteeramerica.net) Publishes a free newsletter, a good general resource.
Volunteers for Peace (VFP; ☎ 802-259-2759; www .vfp.org; 1034 Tiffany Rd, Belmont, VT 05730)
Wilderness Volunteers (☎ 928-556-0038; www .wildernessvolunteers.org) Weeklong trips helping maintain America's parks and wildlands.

WOMEN TRAVELERS

Women traveling by themselves or in a group should not encounter any particular problems in the USA. Indeed, there are a number of excellent resources that facilitate just this.

The community website www.journey woman.com helps women talk to each other, and it has links to other sites. As for guides, try the inspirational *A Journey of One's Own* (1992) by Thalia Zepatos; the pocketsize expertise of *Gutsy Women: Travel Tips and Wisdom for the Road* (1996) by Marybeth Bond; or the irreverent, equally portable *The Bad Girl's Guide to the Open Road* (1999) by Cameron Tuttle.

These two national advocacy groups might also be helpful:

National Organization for Women (NOW; ☎ 202-628-8669; www.now.org; 1100 H St NW, 3rd fl, Washington, DC 20005)
Planned Parenthood (☎ 800-230-7526; www .plannedparenthood.org) Offers referrals to medical clinics throughout the country.

In terms of safety issues, single women need to exhibit the same street smarts and city savvy as any solo traveler (p1156), but they are sometimes more often the target of unwanted attention or harassment. Some women like to carry a whistle, mace or cayenne-pepper spray in case of assault. If you purchase a spray, contact a police station to find out about local regulations. Laws regarding sprays vary from state to state; federal law prohibits them being carried on planes.

If you are assaulted, it may be better to call a rape-crisis hotline before calling the **police** (☎ 911); telephone books have listings of local organizations, or contact the **Rape, Abuse & Incest National Network** (☎ 800-656-4673; www.rainn.org), a 24-hour hotline. Or, go straight to a hospital. Police can sometimes be insensitive with assault victims, while a rape-crisis center or hospital will advocate on behalf of survivors and act as a link to other services, including the police.

WORK

If you are a foreigner in the USA with a standard nonimmigrant visitor's visa, you are expressly forbidden to take paid work in the USA and will be deported if you're caught working illegally. In addition, employers are required to establish the bona fides of their employees or face fines, making it much tougher for a foreigner to get work than it once was.

To work legally, foreigners need to apply for a work visa before leaving home. A J1 visa, for exchange visitors, is issued to young

DIRECTORY

people (age limits vary) for study, student vacation employment, work in summer camps, and short-term traineeships with a specific employer. The following organizations will help arrange student exchanges, placements and J1 visas:

American Institute for Foreign Study (AIFS; ☎ 800-727-2437; www.aifs.com; River Plaza, 9 West Broad St, Stamford, CT 06902-3788)

BUNAC (☎ 020-7251-3472; www.bunac.org; 16 Bowling Green Lane, London EC1R 0QH)

Camp America (☎ 020-7581-7373; www.campamerica .co.uk; 37A Queens Gate, London SW7 5HR)

Council on International Educational Exchange (CIEE; ☎ 800-407-8839; www.ciee.org; 7 Custom House St, 3rd fl, Portland, ME 04101)

InterExchange (☎ 212-924-0446; www.interexchange .org; 161 Sixth Ave, NY, NY 10013) Camp and au pair programs.

International Exchange Programs (IEP) Australia (☎ 1300-300-912; www.iep-australia.com; Level 3, 362 La Trobe St, Melbourne, VIC 3000; Level 3, 333 George St, Sydney, NSW 2000); New Zealand (☎ 0800-443-769; www.iepnz.co.nz; Level 10, 220 Queen St, Auckland)

For nonstudent jobs, temporary or permanent, you need to be sponsored by a US employer who will have to arrange one of the various H-category visas. These are not easy to obtain, since the employer has to prove that no US citizen or permanent resident is available to do the job. Seasonal work is possible in national parks, tourist sites and especially ski areas. Contact park concessionaires, local chambers of commerce and ski-resort management. Lonely Planet's *Gap Year Book* is another good resource for ideas on how to combine work and travel.

Transparency

Transportation

GETTING THERE & AWAY

ENTERING THE USA

The USA is working hard to counter any lingering 'Fortress America' image post-September 11, and in fact its security procedures run fairly smoothly – it's not significantly more complicated or time-consuming to enter the country now than it was pre-September 11. That said, US officials are strict and vigilant (particularly at land border crossings). It's best to look neat, be polite and have all your papers in order, whether arriving by land, air or sea. For details on forms and current registration procedures, see Entering the USA, p1160.

If you are flying to America, the first airport that you land in is where you must go through immigration and customs, even if you are continuing on the flight to another destination.

Once you go through immigration, you collect your baggage and pass through customs. If you have nothing to declare, you'll probably clear customs quickly and without a baggage search, but don't assume this. For details on customs, see p1146. If you are continuing on the same plane or connecting to another one, it is your responsibility to get your bags to the right place. Normally, airline representatives are just outside the customs area to help you.

If you are a single parent, grandparent or guardian traveling with anyone under 18, it is a good idea to carry proof of legal custody or a notarized letter from the non-accompanying parent(s) authorizing the trip. The USA is concerned with thwarting child abduction, and not having authorizing papers could cause delays or even result in being denied admittance to the country.

Passport

Currently, all foreign visitors except Canadians must bring their passports. Canadians must have proof of citizenship, such as a citizenship card with photo identification, or a passport. Unless visitors qualify for the Visa Waiver Program (see p1159), visitors must also have a visa.

In 2008, however, the US plans to require all people entering the country, even returning US citizens, to carry a passport.

AIR
Airports & Airlines

The USA has over 400 domestic airports, and a baker's dozen are the main international gateways. Many other airports are called 'international' but most have only a few flights from other countries – typically links to Mexico or Canada. Even travel to an international gateway sometimes requires a connection in another gateway city. For example, many of the London–Los Angeles flights involve a transfer connection in Chicago.

Airports in the USA:

Atlanta Hartsfield International (ATL; ☎ 404-209-1700; www.atlanta-airport.com)

Boston Logan International (BOS; ☎ 800-235-6426; www.massport.com/logan)

Chicago O'Hare International (ORD; ☎ 800-832-6352; www.ohare.com/ohare/home.asp)

Dallas–Fort Worth (DFW; ☎ 972-574-8888; www.dfwairport.com)

Honolulu (HNL; ☎ 808-836-6413; www.honoluluairport.com)

Houston George Bush Intercontinental (IAH; ☎ 281-230-3000; www.houston-iah.com)

Los Angeles (LAX; ☎ 310-646-5252; www.lawa.org/lax/laxframe.html)

Miami (MIA; ☎ 305-876-7000; www.miami-airport.com)

New York John F Kennedy (JFK; ☎ 718-244-4444; www.panynj.gov/aviation/jfkframe.htm)

Newark (EWR; ☎ 973-961-6000; www.panynj.gov/aviation/ewrframe.htm)

San Francisco (SFO; ☎ 650-821-8211; www.flysfo.com)

Seattle Seattle-Tacoma International (SEA; ☎ 206-433-5388; www.portseattle.org/seatac/default.htm)

Washington, DC Dulles International (IAD; ☎ 703-572-2700; www.metwashairports.com/dulles/)

The national airlines of most countries have flights to the USA, and the USA has several airlines serving the world. Here is a list of the main international carriers. You can also check the website www.smilinjack.com/airlines.htm for links to international airlines worldwide.

Airlines flying to/from the USA:

Aer Lingus (EI; ☎ 800-474-7424; www.aerlingus.com; hub Dublin)

Aerolíneas Argentinas (AR; ☎ 800-333-0276; www.aeroargentinas.com; hub Buenos Aires)

Air Canada (AC; ☎ 888-247-2262; www.aircanada.com; hub Toronto)

Air France (AF; ☎ 800-237-2747; www.airfrance.com; hub Paris)

Air India (AI; ☎ 800-223-7776; www.airindia.com; hub Delhi)

Air New Zealand (NZ; ☎ 800-262-1234; www.airnewzealand.com; hub Auckland)

Alitalia (AZ; ☎ 800-223-5730; www.alitalia.com; hub Milan)

American Airlines (AA; ☎ 800-433-7300; www.aa.com; hub Dallas)

British Airways (BA; ☎ 800-247-9297; www.britishairways.com; hub London)

Cathay Pacific (CX; ☎ 800-233-2742; www.cathaypacific.com; hub Hong Kong)

Continental Airlines (CO; ☎ 800-231-0856; www.continental.com; hubs Houston, Cleveland, Newark)

Delta Air Lines (DL; ☎ 800-241-4141; www.delta.com; hub Atlanta)

El Al (LY; ☎ 800-223-6700; www.elal.com; hub Tel Aviv)

Garuda Indonesia (GA; ☎ 800-342-7832; www.garuda-indonesia.com; hub Jakarta)

Iberia (IB; ☎ 800-772-4642; www.iberia.com; hub Madrid)

Icelandair (FI; ☎ 800-223-5500; www.icelandair.com; hub Keflavik Airport, Iceland)

Japan Airlines (JL; ☎ 800-525-3663; www.jal.com; hub Tokyo)

KLM (KL; ☎ 800-447-4747; www.klm.com; hub Amsterdam)

Korean Air (KE; ☎ 800-438-5000; www.koreanair.com; hub Seoul)

Kuwait Airways (KU; ☎ 800-458-9248; www.kuwait-airways.com; hub Kuwait)

Lufthansa (LH; ☎ 800-645-3880; www.lufthansa.com; hub Frankfurt)

Northwest Airlines (NW; ☎ 800-447-4747; www.nwa.com; hubs Minneapolis/St Paul, Memphis, Detroit)

Polynesian Airlines (PH; ☎ 800-264-0823; www.polynesianairlines.com; hub Samoa)

Qantas (QF; ☎ 800-227-4500; www.qantas.com.au; hub Sydney)

Scandinavian Airlines (SAS; ☎ 800-221-2350; www.scandinavian.net; hubs Copenhagen, Helsinki, Oslo, Stockholm)

Singapore Airlines (SQ; ☎ 800-742-3333; www.singaporeair.com; hub Singapore)

South African Airways (SA; ☎ 800-722-9675; www.flysaa.com; hub Johannesburg)

Thai Airways International (TG; ☎ 800-426-5204; www.thaiair.com; hub Bangkok)

United Airlines (UA; ☎ 800-538-2929; www.ual.com; hub Los Angeles)

US Airways (US; ☎ 800-622-1015; www.usairways.com; hubs Philadelphia, Charlotte)

Virgin Atlantic (VS; ☎ 800-821-5438; www.virgin-atlantic.com; hub London)

Tickets

Getting a cheap airline ticket is a matter of good research, reserving early – at least three to four weeks in advance – and timing. Flying midweek and in the off-season (normally, fall to spring, excluding holiday periods) is always less expensive, and fare wars crop up anytime. As a general rule, online travel agencies have cheaper fares than you can get from the airlines directly, while living, breathing travel agents are excellent resources if your plans are long and/or complicated.

Keep in mind your entire US itinerary when shopping for flights. Some deals for travel within the USA can only be purchased overseas in conjunction with an international air ticket. These include various air passes, Greyhound bus line's international Ameripass, and some Amtrak rail passes. Also, you can often get domestic flights within the USA as an inexpensive add-on to your international airfare.

Most airline company websites offer discounts for online ticket sales (conversely, some airlines charge a small fee for phone sales). In addition to researching the online commercial agencies below, a handy tool is the search engine provided by **ITA Software** (www.itasoftware.com); this sorts results among agencies by price while also alerting you to potential downsides like long layovers, tight connections and so on (though it doesn't sell tickets). Remember, the cheapest flight might not always be the best flight.

Online commercial agencies:

Atevo Travel (www.atevo.com)
Cheap Tickets (www.cheaptickets.com)
Expedia.com (www.expedia.com)
Hotwire (www.hotwire.com)
Info Hub Specialty Travel Guide (www.infohub.com) Theme travel.
LowestFare.com (www.lowestfare.com)
Orbitz (www.orbitz.com)
Priceline (www.priceline.com)
STA Travel (www.statravel.com) Student travel.
Travelocity.com (www.travelocity.com)
Yahoo! Travel (www.travel.yahoo.com)

COURIER FLIGHTS

Some firms provide very cheap fares to travelers who will be couriers, hand-delivering documents or packages. Courier opportunities are not easy to come by, and they are unlikely to be available on other than principal international routes (they are nonexistent on domestic routes). The traveler is usually allowed only one piece of carry-on baggage, with the checked-baggage allowance being taken by the item to be delivered. Two agencies to try are the **International Association of Air Travel Couriers** (www.courier.org) and the **Air Courier Association** (www.aircourier.org); both require membership and don't guarantee you'll get a courier flight.

INTERCONTINENTAL (RTW) TICKETS

Round-the-world (RTW) tickets are great if you want to visit other regions besides the USA. They're usually more expensive than a simple round-trip ticket, but the extra stops are good value. They're of most value for trips that combine the USA with Europe, Asia and/or Australasia. RTW itineraries that include South America or Africa as well as North America are more expensive.

RTW tickets go by different names depending on their itineraries (such as Pacific Circle, and so on); they use the routes of an airline alliance, such as **Star Alliance** (www.staralliance.com) and **One World** (www.oneworld.com); and they are valid for a fixed period, usually a year. Most RTW fares restrict the number of stops in the USA and Canada. The cheapest fares permit only one stop; others allow two or more. Some airlines 'black out' a few heavily traveled routes (like Honolulu to Tokyo). In most cases a 14-day advance purchase is required. After the ticket is purchased, dates can usually be changed without penalty, and tickets can be rewritten to add or delete stops for an extra charge.

For RTW tickets, try the following:

Air Brokers (www.airbrokers.com)
Air Treks (www.airtreks.com)
Circle the Planet (www.circletheplanet.com)
Just Fares (www.justfares.com)

Africa

A few cities in West and North Africa have direct flights to the USA – Abidjan (Côte d'Ivoire), Accra (Ghana), Cairo (Egypt), Casablanca (Morocco) and Dakar (Senegal). Apart from South African Airways flights from Johannesburg to New York, most flights from Africa to the USA go via a European hub, most commonly London.

Agents serving Africa:

Flight Centre South Africa (☎ 0860-400-727; www .flightcentre.co.za)
STA Travel South Africa (☎ 0861-781-781; www.sta travel.co.za)

Asia

Bangkok, Singapore, Kuala Lumpur, Hong Kong, Seoul and Tokyo all have good connections to the US West Coast. Many flights to the USA go via Honolulu and allow a stopover. Bangkok is the discounted fare capital of the region, though its cheapest agents can be unreliable.

Agents serving Asia:

Four Seas Tours Hong Kong (☎ 2200-7848; www.four seastravel.com)

No 1 Travel Japan (☎ 03-3205-6073; www.no1-travel .com)

STA Travel Bangkok (☎ 662-236-0262; www.statravel .co.th); Singapore (☎ 65-6737-7188; www.statravel.com .sg); Hong Kong (☎ 852-2736-1618; www.hkst.com.hk /statravel/); Japan (☎ 03-5391-2922; www.statravel.co.jp)

Australia

Some flights go from Sydney and Melbourne direct to Los Angeles and San Francisco. Flights to other US cities will usually involve a stop in Los Angeles, or possibly San Francisco or Honolulu. Qantas, Air New Zealand and United are the main airlines on the route. Fares from Melbourne, Sydney, Brisbane and sometimes Adelaide and Canberra are 'common rated' (the same for all cities). From Hobart and Perth, there'll be an add-on fare.

Low season is roughly February, March, October and November. High season is mid-June to mid-July and mid-December to mid-January. The rest of the year is considered shoulder season. Discounted tickets have minimum- and maximum-stay provisions.

Agents serving Australia:

Flight Centre (☎ 1300-133-133; www.flightcentre .com.au)

STA Travel (☎ 1300-733-035; www.statravel.com.au)

Trailfinders (☎ 1300-780-212; www.trailfinders.com.au)

Travel.com (☎ 1300-130-482; www3.travel.com.au)

Travel Shop (☎ 1300-767-908; www.travelshop.com.au)

Canada

Daily flights go from Vancouver, Toronto, and many smaller cities to all the big US centers. Commuter flights to cities such as New York and Chicago can be very expensive. Some of the best deals are charter and package fares to sunny destinations such as Florida, California and Hawaii, with higher prices in the winter peak season.

It may be much cheaper to travel by land to the nearest US city, then take a discounted domestic flight. For example, round-trip fares to New York are much cheaper from Seattle, Washington, than from Vancouver, BC, only 130 miles away.

Agents serving Canada:

Expedia (www.expedia.ca)

Travel Cuts (☎ 866-246-9762; www.travelcuts.com)

Travelocity (www.travelocity.ca)

Continental Europe

There are nonstop flights to many US cities, but the discounted fares often involve indirect routes and changing planes. The main airlines between Europe and the USA are Air France, Alitalia, British Airways, KLM, Continental, United, American, Delta, Scandinavian Airlines and Lufthansa. Sometimes an Asian or Middle Eastern carrier will have cheap deals on flights in transit to the USA, if you can get a seat. Also try Icelandair connections via London.

BELGIUM

Airstop (☎ 070-233-188; www.airstop.be)

Connections (☎ 070-233-313; www.connections.be)

FRANCE

Anyway.com (☎ 0892-302-301; http://voyages.anyway .com)

Lastminute (☎ 0899-78-50-00; www.fr.lastminute.com)

Nouvelles Frontieres (☎ 0825-000-747; www.nouvelles -frontieres.fr)

OTU Voyages (☎ 0820-817-817; www.otu.fr) Specializes in student travel.

Voyageurs du Monde (☎ 0892-688-363; www.vdm .com)

GERMANY

Just Travel (☎ 089-747-3330; www.justtravel.de)

Last Minute (☎ 01805-284-366; www.lastminute.de)

Reiseboerse.com (☎ 030-2800-2800; www.reise boerse.com)

STA Travel (☎ 069-7430-3292; www.statravel.de)

ITALY

CTS Viaggi (☎ 06-441-111; www.cts.it) Student and youth travel.

NETHERLANDS

Air Fair (☎ 020-620-5121; www.airfair.nl)

SCANDINAVIA

Kilroy Travels (www.kilroytravels.com); Sweden (☎ 0771-545-769); Denmark (☎ 70-15-40-15); Norway (☎ 026-33)

SPAIN

Barcelo Viajes (☎ 902-116-226; www.barceloviajes.com)

New Zealand

Air New Zealand has regular flights from Auckland direct to Los Angeles. Flights from Christchurch and Wellington require a plane change in Auckland or the Pacific Islands.

TRANSPORTATION

You'll find that low, shoulder and peak seasons are roughly the same as for Australia.

Agents serving New Zealand:

Flight Centre (☎ 0800-24-35-44; www.flightcentre.co.nz)
STA Travel (☎ 0508-782-872; www.statravel.co.nz)
Travel.co.nz (☎ 0800-468-332; www.travel.co.nz)

Latin America

The main gateway from Central and South America is Miami, but there are also many direct flights to Los Angeles and Houston. Check the national airlines of the countries you want to connect to as well as US airlines such as United and American. At times, it can be much cheaper to fly to a Mexican border town than to the adjacent town on the US side. A flight from Mexico City to Tijuana can cost quite a bit less than a flight to San Diego, just a few miles north on the US side.

Agents serving Latin America:

Asatej (☎ 0810-777-2728; www.asatej.com) Argentina.
IVI Tours (☎ 0212-993-6082; www.ividiomas.com) Venezuela.
Mundo Joven (☎ 5518-1755; www.mundojoven.com) Mexico.
Student Travel Bureau (☎ 3038-1555; www.stb .com.br) Brazil.
Viajo.com (☎ 1084-0450; www.viajo.com) Mexico.

UK & Ireland

One of the busiest and most competitive air sectors in the world is from the UK to the USA, with hundreds of scheduled flights by British Airways, American Airlines, United, Delta, Northwest, Continental, Kuwait, Air India and discount specialist Virgin Atlantic.

Discount air travel is big business in London. Advertisements for many travel agencies appear in the travel pages of the weekend broadsheet newspapers, in *Time Out*, the *Evening Standard* and in the free magazine *TNT*. Discounted fares are highly variable, volatile and subject to various conditions and restrictions. From UK regional airports, discounted flights may be routed via London, Paris or Amsterdam, and will probably not fly direct to smaller US cities such as Las Vegas or Denver.

Most British travel agents are registered with ABTA (the Association of British Travel Agents), which will guarantee a refund or an alternative if you've paid money to an agent who goes out of business. Using an unregistered agent is not recommended.

Agents serving the UK and Ireland:

Ebookers.com (☎ 0800-082-3000; www.ebookers.com)
Flight Centre (☎ 0870-499-0040; www.flightcentre .co.uk)
North-South Travel (☎ 01245-608-291; www.north southtravel.co.uk) Donates part of its profit to projects in the developing world.
Quest Travel (☎ 0870-442-3542; www.questtravel.com)
STA Travel (☎ 0870-160-0599; www.statravel.co.uk) Discount and student travel specialist.
Trailfinders (☎ 0845-058-5858; www.trailfinders.co.uk)
Travel Bag (☎ 0800-082-5000; www.travelbag.co.uk)
Travelocity (☎ 0870-111-7061; www.travelocity.co.uk)

LAND
Border Crossings

The USA shares long land borders with Canada in the north and Mexico in the south. It is relatively easy crossing from the USA into either country; it's getting into the USA that can pose problems if you haven't brought all your documents. See Entering the Country, p1160. The **US Customs & Border Protection Agency** (http://apps.cbp.gov/bwt/) tracks current wait times at every border crossing. Some borders are open 24 hours, but most are not.

The USA has 22 official border crossings with Canada. Busy entry points include those at Detroit/Windsor (Michigan), Buffalo/Fort Erie (New York), Niagara Falls (New York) and Blaine/Québec (Washington). The downside to choosing a quiet border crossing is that officers have plenty of time to take apart your luggage. For border wait times returning to Canada, visit www .cbsa-asfc.gc.ca/general/times/menu-e.html.

The USA has over 40 official entry points with Mexico. The main ones are San Diego/ Tijuana (California), Nogales (Arizona), El Paso/Ciudad Juárez (Texas) and Brownsville/Matamoros (Texas). As always, have your papers in order, act polite and don't make jokes or casual conversation – officers take a dim view of friendliness.

Canada
BUS

Greyhound has direct connections between main cities in Canada and the northern USA, but you may have to transfer to a different bus at the border. Note that **Greyhound US** (☎ for customer service 214-849-8966, for reservations 800-231-2222; www.greyhound.com) and **Greyhound Canada** (☎ 800-661-8747; www.greyhound.ca) are different companies. Greyhound's Ameripass is not valid for travel within Canada, but you can use it when crossing into Canada via certain routes – from Boston or New York to Montreal (around $70), from Detroit to Toronto ($50) or Seattle to Vancouver ($30) – and back to the USA by the same routes.

CAR & MOTORCYCLE
If you're driving into the USA from Canada, don't forget the vehicle's registration papers, liability insurance and your home driver's license. Canadian auto insurance is valid in the USA. Canadian driver's licenses are valid and an international driver's permit is a good supplement.

If your papers are in order, taking your own car across the US–Canadian border is usually quick and easy, but occasionally the authorities of either country decide to search a car *thoroughly*. On weekends and holidays, especially in summer, traffic at the main border crossings can be very heavy, and waits can be long.

TRAIN
Amtrak (☎ 800-872-7245; www.amtrak.com) and Canada's **VIA Rail** (☎ 888-842-7245; www.viarail.ca) run daily services from Montreal to New York, Toronto to New York via Niagara Falls, Toronto to Chicago, and Vancouver to Seattle. See p1179 for information on Amtrak's North American Rail Pass, which includes Canadian travel. Customs inspections happen at the border, not on boarding.

Mexico
BUS
Greyhound US (☎ for reservations 800-231-2222, customer service 214-849-8966; www.greyhound.com) and **Greyhound Mexico** (☎ in US 800-229-9424, in Mexico 800-710-8819; www.greyhound.com.mx) have cooperative service, with direct buses between main towns in Mexico and the USA. Northbound buses can take some time to cross the US border, as sometimes US immigration insists on checking every person on board.

There are numerous domestic Mexican bus companies. **Ticketbus** (☎ in US 800-950-0287, in Mexico 800-702-8000; www.ticketbus.com.mx) is an alliance of several.

CAR & MOTORCYCLE
If you're driving into the USA from Mexico, don't forget the vehicle's registration papers,

liability insurance and your home driver's license. Mexican driver's licenses are valid and an international driver's permit is a good supplement. Very few car rental companies will let you take a car from the US into Mexico.

US auto insurance is not valid in Mexico, so even a short trip into Mexico's border region requires you to buy Mexican car insurance, available for about $15 per day at most border crossings, as well as from the **American Automobile Association** (AAA; ☎ 800-874-7532; www.aaa.com). At some border towns, including Tijuana or Ciudad Juárez, there can be very long lines of vehicles waiting to re-enter the USA. For a short visit, it's usually more convenient to leave your car in a lot on the US side and walk or bus across the border. For a longer driving trip into Mexico, beyond the border zone or Baja California, you'll need a Mexican *permiso de importación temporal de vehículos* (temporary vehicle import permit). See Lonely Planet's *Mexico* guide for the tedious details, or call the Mexican tourist information number in the USA (☎ 800-446-3942).

TRAIN
Amtrak gets close to the Mexican border at San Diego, California, and El Paso, Texas, but there are currently no cross-border services. All of the Mexican train services to towns on the US border have been closed.

SEA
Cargo Ship/Freighter
It is possible to travel to and from the USA on a freighter, though it will be much slower than a cruise ship (opposite), and while amenities have improved, you won't enjoy cruise ship comforts either. Nevertheless, freighters aren't as spartan as they sound, and they are much cheaper (sometimes by half) than cruise ships. Trips range from a week to two months, and stops at interim ports are usually quick. Excellent sources of information are the **Cruise & Freighter Travel Association** (☎ 800-872-8584; www.travltips.com) and **Freighter World Cruises** (☎ 800-531-7774; www.freighterworld.com).

TOURS
Group travel can be an enjoyable way to go, particularly for single travelers or those wanting a big outdoor adventure with a

minimum of planning. See p1177 for more tours once you're in the USA.

If you're interested in taking a **cruise ship** to America – as well as to other interesting ports o' call – a good specialized travel agency is **Cruise Web** (☎ 800-377-9383; www.cruiseweb.com). Or just book a bunk ($2,500 and up) on the *QE2*, run by **Cunard** (☎ in US 800-728-6273, in UK 0845-071-0300; www.cunardline.com). The standard London–New York run is six days, but Cunard has two other luxury liners and oodles more options.

Reputable tour companies:

American Holidays (☎ 01-673-3840; www.american -holidays.com) This Ireland-based company specializes in tours to North America; all types of arrangements.

Elderhostel (☎ 877-426-8056; www.elderhostel .org) This venerable, nonprofit organization runs 'learning adventures' around the world for those 55+ years young; trips run from easy to active.

North America Travel Service (☎ 0207-499-7299; www.northamericatravelservice.co.uk) This UK-based tour operator specializes in US trips of all kinds.

Trek America (☎ 800-221-0596 in US, 0870-444-8735 in UK; www.trekamerica.com) Specializing in active, some-times strenuous outdoor adventures; Trek America will book flights from the UK only. Group sizes are small and activities include hiking, camping, canoeing, climbing and more.

GETTING AROUND

AIR

Flying is the only practical way to get around the USA if your time is limited. The domestic air system is extensive and reliable, with dozens of competing airlines, hundreds of airports and thousands of scheduled flights every day. Flying is usually more expensive than traveling by bus, train or car, but a special airfare deal can make the cost very competitive. All the advice for buying an international airline ticket applies to domestic flights as well.

Main 'hub' airports include all of the international gateways (p1163) plus a number of other large cities. Most cities and towns have a local or county airport, but you usually have to travel via a hub airport to reach them.

If you need to park your car while you fly somewhere else, one useful website is www .parkingaccess.com, which offers information, reservations and discounts on parking at most major airports.

YOU MAY NOW BOARD YOUR FLIGHT

US airport security measures overall are efficient, though they continue to be tweaked. For up-to-date information, contact the **Transportation Security Administration** (TSA; ☎ 866-289-9673; www.tsa.gov/public), which provides average security wait times by airport and time of day (20 minutes is standard).

All passengers must first check in with their airline and collect a boarding pass; present the pass and your photo ID (required) at the security gate. At a minimum, you must de-belt and de-shoe, pass through a metal detector and have your carry-on luggage x-rayed. About a third of all passengers are asked to undergo a second screening; this involves hand wand and pat down checks and opening your bags. You can request a private room.

Avoid wearing hidden body piercings or underwire bras. Don't wrap gifts, since they may need to be opened. And laptop computers may need to be turned on. If you get stopped because your name appears on the TSA Watch List, afterward you can file a Passenger Identity Verification Form (see the TSA website); this doesn't remove your name from the list, but it establishes that you are not the 'John Doe' they want, and it will expedite screening next time.

All checked luggage is screened for explosives; TSA may open your suitcase for visual confirmation. Either leave your bags unlocked or use a TSA-approved lock, purchased from **Travel Sentry** (www.travelsentry .org) or **Safe Skies** (www.safeskieslocks.com); otherwise, TSA will break your lock. As for how to pack checked luggage: don't check undeveloped film, since some screening machines damage it. Don't stack books or papers, avoid packing food and drinks, and put personal items in clear plastic bags if you don't want them handled.

The TSA website has a full list of prohibited carry-on items. Here are some.

- Pocketknives, even keychain-size
- Straight razors (safety razors OK)
- Scissors (blunt-tipped OK)
- Lighters (safety matches OK)
- All sports equipment
- Carpentry tools

TRANSPORTATION

Airlines in the USA

Domestic air travel is increasing again – in 2004, 630 million passengers flew on nearly 10 million flights – but the US airline industry remains in financial turmoil. Since September 11, several smaller airlines have gone out of business, while four major ones (Delta, Northwest, United and US Airways) have filed for bankruptcy but continue to operate as they sort out their finances and negotiate with their unions. Consequently, travelers can expect more changes to routes and service, and they should double-check all arrangements.

That said, discount airlines are doing well. Southwest, JetBlue and AirTran have been profitable, and Delta recently introduced its low-cost Song fleet. One of the biggest service changes is food, as many airlines do away with free meal service and replace it with for-purchase sandwiches and other items.

Overall, air travel in the USA is very safe (much safer than America's highways); for comprehensive details by carrier, check out **Airsafe.com** (www.airsafe.com), which also has good advice on current airport security procedures (see the boxed text, p1169).

Here are the main domestic carriers:

AirTran (☎ 800-247-8726; www.airtran.com) Atlanta-based airline primarily serves Midwest and eastern US.

Alaska Airlines (☎ 800-252-7522; www.alaskaair .com) Serves Alaska and western US, with flights to East Coast cities.

America West (☎ 800-235-9292; www.americawest.com) Service nationwide from hubs in Phoenix and Las Vegas.

American Airlines (☎ 800-433-7300; www.aa.com) Nationwide service.

ATA Airlines (☎ 800-435-9282; www.ata.com) Connects major US cities; shares routes with Southwest.

Continental Airlines (☎ 800-523-3273; www .continental.com) Nationwide service.

Delta Air Lines (☎ 800-221-1212; www.delta.com) Nationwide service.

Frontier Airlines (☎ 800-432-1359; www.frontier airlines.com) Denver-based airline with nationwide service, including Alaska.

Hawaiian Airlines (☎ 800-367-5320; www.hawaiian air.com) Serves Hawaiian Islands and West Coast, with America West connections elsewhere.

JetBlue (☎ 800-538-2583; www.jetblue.com) Nonstop connections between East and West Coast cities and Puerto Rico.

PRINCIPAL AIR ROUTES

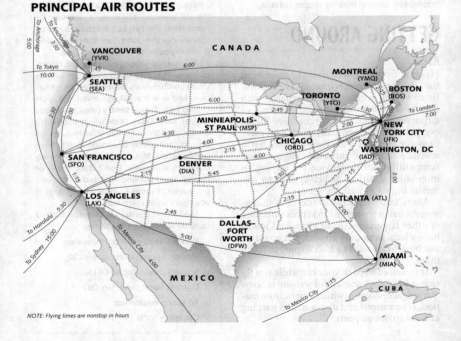

NOTE: Flying times are nonstop in hours

Midwest Express (☎ 800-452-2022; www2.midwest express.com) Milwaukee-based carrier serves major US cities.

Northwest Airlines (☎ 800-225-2525; www.nwa .com) Nationwide service, including Alaska and Hawaii.

Song (☎ 800-359-7664; www.flysong.com) Delta's low-cost airline connects major East and West Coast cities.

Southwest Airlines (☎ 800-435-9792; www.iflyswa .com) Service across continental USA.

Spirit Airlines (☎ 800-772-7117; www.spiritair.com) Serves eastern seaboard, Florida and Caribbean.

Ted (☎ 800-225-5833; www.flyted.com) United's low-cost service connects major cities nationwide, including Los Angeles, Chicago, Washington DC, Las Vegas, New Orleans etc.

United Airlines (☎ 800-864-8331; www.ual.com) Nationwide service, including Alaska and Hawaii.

US Airways (☎ 800-428-4322; www.usairways.com) Primarily serves eastern United States, Midwest and Caribbean.

Air Passes

International travelers who plan on doing a lot of flying in the USA might consider buying an air pass, which could save you money. Air passes are available only to non-US citizens, and they must be purchased in conjunction with an international ticket. Conditions and cost structures can be quite complicated, but all include a certain number of domestic flights (from three to 10) that must be used within 60 days. Sometimes you must plan your itinerary in advance, but sometimes dates (and even destinations) can be left open; if seats are available, you could reserve a flight as late as a day ahead. It might be worth talking with a travel agent to evaluate if an air pass is right for you.

Air passes take advantage of particular airline networks. Two of the biggest are **Star Alliance** (www.staralliance.com) and **One World** (www.oneworld.com).

BICYCLE

Traveling, or touring, by bicycle is popular and accessible. No matter the distance, it's possible to stay almost entirely on quiet backroads (which is necessary and advisable since bicycles are not permitted on freeways), and most cities have some system of bike lanes, however minimal. Cyclists are required to follow the same rules of the road as automobiles, but don't expect drivers to always respect the right of way of

cyclists. **Better World Club** (☎ 866-238-1137; www .betterworldclub.com) offers a bicycle roadside assistance program.

For a list of bicycling associations, tour groups and magazines, see p1143, and turn to p102 for a general overview of where to cycle in the USA. For epic cross-country journeys, you will want the support of a tour operator; from east to west (or reverse) is about two months of dedicated pedaling.

If you are transporting your own bike to or around the USA, the best resource for information is the **League of American Bicyclists** (LAB; ☎ 202-822-1333; www.bikeleague.org; 1612 K St NW, Ste 800, Washington, DC 20006), which lists bike regulations by airline and has lots of other advice on its website. In general, most international and domestic airlines will carry bikes as checked baggage without charge if they're in a box. If they aren't disassembled, many impose an oversize-baggage charge (up to $50). Amtrak trains and Greyhound buses will transport bikes within the USA, sometimes charging extra.

Otherwise, buy a bike once you get here and resell it before you leave. Every city has bike shops; larger ones will have many, selling every type and quality of bike. If you prefer a cheaper, used bicycle, try local flea markets, garage sales and the notice boards at hostels and colleges. These are also the best places to sell your bike, though stores selling used bikes may also buy from you. If you're not too finicky about price, then selling a bike is a snap.

Long-term bike rentals are also easy to find; recommended rental places are listed throughout this guide. Rates run from $100 per week and up, and a credit card authorization for several hundred dollars is usually necessary as a security deposit.

BOAT

There is no river or canal public transportation system in the USA, but there are many smaller, often state-run, coastal ferry services, which provide economical, efficient and scenic links to the many islands off the US coasts. Most larger ferries will transport private cars, motorcycles and bicycles. For details, see the regional chapters. The most spectacular coastal ferry runs are on the south coast of Alaska and along the Inside Passage (p1086). The Great Lakes have a number of islands that can be visited only by boat, such as Mackinac Island, Michigan (p633); the Apostle Islands, off Wisconsin (p645); and the remote Isle Royale National Park (p658). Or check out the **Delta Queen Steamboat Co** (☎ 800-543-1949; www.deltaqueen .com) – three luxurious steamboats make three- to 12-day excursions on the Mississippi, Missouri, Tennessee and Ohio Rivers, from Minneapolis to New Orleans.

BUS

For cheap, efficient travel between major towns and cities, buses are a reliable choice. If you're on a tight budget and want to tour long distances, making up your itinerary as you go, buses are the best way to travel. Gotta-go middle class Americans prefer to fly or drive, but buses let you see the countryside and meet citizens along the way. As a rule, buses are clean and comfortable, with air-conditioning, reclining seats, onboard lavatories and no smoking permitted.

Greyhound (☎ for reservations 800-231-2222, for customer service 214-849-8966; www.greyhound.com) is the major long-distance bus company, with routes throughout the USA and to the Canadian cities of Montreal, Toronto and Vancouver. In 2005, Greyhound eliminated service to many seldom-visited small towns to improve the efficiency (and profitability) of its main service to larger towns. In general, routes now just trace major highways; you may need to transfer to local or county bus systems to get to small towns off these thoroughfares. Greyhound will usually have their contact information.

Competing with Greyhound are the 50-plus franchises of **Trailways** (☎ 703-691-3052; www.trailways.com). Trailways may not be as useful as Greyhound for long trips, but fares are generally a little lower. Here are a few of the regional Trailways bus companies:

Atlantic Coast Trailways (☎ 800-548-8584; www .atlanticcoastcharters.com) On the Atlantic Coast.

Pacific Trailways of Southern California (☎ 714-892-5000; www.pacificcoachways.com) On the Pacific Coast.

Peter Pan Trailways (☎ 800-237-8747; www.peter panbus.com) In the Northeast.

Most baggage has to be checked in; label it properly and loudly to avoid it getting lost. Larger items, including skis and bicycles, can be transported, but there may be an extra charge. Call to check.

The frequency of bus service varies from several times a week to every hour, every day. Despite the elimination of many tiny destinations, nonexpress Greyhound buses still stop every 50 to 100 miles to pick up passengers, and long-distance buses stop for meal breaks and driver changes.

Some bus stations can be in dodgy areas, so if you arrive in the evening, spend the money on a taxi. Others are quite clean and safe, while in some towns there is just a flag stop. If you are boarding at one of these, pay the driver with exact change.

Bus Passes

Greyhound offers a range of national and regional passes ($4 purchase fee) that can make cross-country travel a bargain. Greyhound's **North American Discovery Pass** (www.discoverypass .com/) allows unlimited travel for periods from seven to 60 consecutive days. Consider buying two short-term passes if you want to stop in one place for a while. The pass allows short side trips to Montreal, Toronto and Vancouver. For longer journeys inside Canada, a combined pass is available.

An International Discovery Pass, or Ameripass, is slightly cheaper and available only to international visitors, not to US or Canadian citizens/residents. International visitors can buy the pass through their home travel agent, on the Internet (on the Discovery Pass website), or by calling **Greyhound** (☎ outside US 214-849-8100, 212-971-0492 Greyhound International Office). There are a range of types of International Discovery Passes, some including stops in Mexico and Canada.

Costs

Substantial ticket discounts can be had if you purchase seven days in advance, and special promotional fares are regularly offered. If you're traveling with a friend, ask about Greyhound's companion fares, where the second traveler gets 50% off with a three-day advance purchase.

As for other discounts: tickets for children ages two to 11 are 40% off the standard fare. People over 62 can get a 5% discount, or join the Greyhound Seniors Club and get 10% off. A companion for a disabled passenger gets 50% off the standard fare. Students who purchase the Student Advantage Discount Card ($20) will get 15% off most routes.

Here are some samples of standard (non-seven-day-advance) Greyhound fares: New York to San Francisco ($170, three days); Los Angeles to San Francisco ($45, eight hours); Boston to Philadelphia ($55, eight hours); New York to Miami ($115, 28 hours).

Reservations

Tickets for some Trailways and other buses can only be purchased immediately prior to departure. Greyhound bus tickets can be bought over the phone or on the Internet with a major US credit card (they don't accept international credit cards); tickets will be mailed to you if purchased 10 days in advance, or you can pick them up at the terminal with proper identification. Greyhound terminals also accept traveler's checks and cash. International visitors will need to visit a stateside Greyhound agency in person to use an international credit card.

On Greyhound, a prepurchased ticket no longer reserves or guarantees a seat on a bus. All seating is first-come, first-served. Greyhound recommends arriving an hour before departure to get a seat.

CAR & MOTORCYCLE

The USA is a car-mad society, but for at least one practical reason: driving a car is the most flexible, most convenient way to cover the continent's long distances, and to get to all of its small towns and wide-open spaces. Independence costs you, though, as rental rates and gas prices can eat a good chunk of a travel budget. Large cities are places to expressly avoid having a car.

This guide's Highlights recommend a few highly scenic drives; check the **National Scenic Byways** (www.byways.org) website for more.

Automobile Associations

The **American Automobile Association** (AAA; ☎ 800-874-7532; www.aaa.com) is the main US auto club, and it has reciprocal membership agreements with several international auto clubs (check with AAA and bring your membership card). An eco-friendly alternative to AAA is the **Better World Club** (☎ 866-238-1137; www.betterworldclub.com). The central member benefit in either organization is 24-hour emergency roadside assistance anywhere in the USA. Both clubs also offer trip planning and free maps, travel agency services and a range of discounts (car rentals, hotels etc).

The main difference is that Better World donates 1% of earnings to assist environmental cleanup and offers ecologically sensitive choices for every service. Better World also has a roadside assistance program for bicycles. AAA, on the other hand, offers travel insurance, its popular tour books, diagnostic centers for used car buyers and a greater number of regional offices.

Bring Your Own Vehicle

For details on driving your own car over the border, see p1168 and p1168. Unless you're moving to the USA, don't even think about freighting your car.

Drive-Away Cars

For flexible travelers, 'drive-away cars' can be a dream come true: you can cover the long distances between A and B for the price of gas. Timing and availability are key.

To be a driver you must be at least 23 years old with a valid driver's license (non-US citizens should have an International Driving Permit); you'll also need to provide a $300 to $400 cash deposit (which is refunded upon safe delivery of the car), sometimes a printout of your driving record, a major credit card and/or three forms of identification (or a passport). The auto transport company provides insurance; you pay for gas. The stipulation is that you must deliver the car to its destination within a specified time and mileage, which usually requires that you drive about six hours a day along the shortest route. Availability depends on demand. Coast-to-coast routes at holiday times are the easiest to arrange.

Two of the larger drive-away companies are **Auto Driveaway** (☎ 323-666-6100; www.auto driveawayla.com) and **Auto Driveaway Co** (☎ 800-346-2277; www.autodriveaway.com).

Driver's License

Visitors can legally drive in the USA for up to 12 months with their home driver's license. However, it is recommended that you also get an International Driving Permit (IDP); this will have more credibility with US traffic police, especially if your home license doesn't have a photo or is in a foreign language. Your automobile association at home can issue an IDP, valid for one year, for a small fee. You must carry your home license together with the IDP.

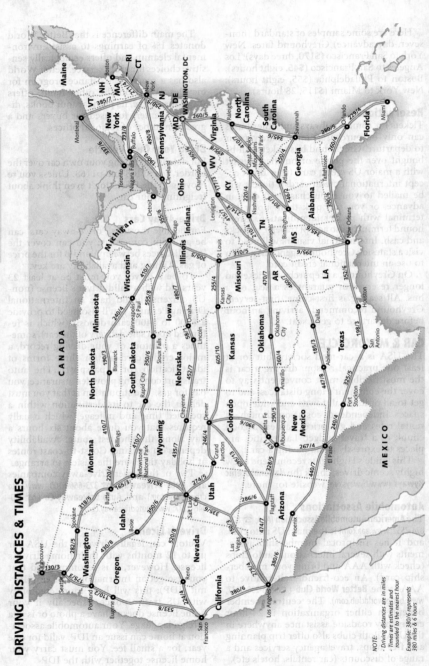

NOTE:
- Driving distances are in miles
- Times are estimates and rounded to the nearest hour

Example: 380/6 represents
380 miles & 6 hours

Insurance

Don't put the key into the ignition if you don't have insurance. You risk financial ruin if there's an accident and you don't have any. If you already have auto insurance (even overseas), or if you buy travel insurance, make sure that the policy has adequate liability coverage for a rental car where you will be driving; it probably does, but most states specify a minimum level of coverage.

Rental car companies will provide liability insurance, but most charge extra. Always ask; if liability insurance is included in the rental, don't be hustled into paying extra. Rental companies almost never include collision damage insurance for the vehicle. Instead, they offer an optional Collision Damage Waiver (CDW) or Loss Damage Waiver (LDW), usually with an initial deductible of $100 to $500. For an extra premium, you can usually get this deductible covered as well. However, most credit cards now offer collision damage coverage for rental cars if you rent for 15 days or less and charge the total rental to your card. This is a good way to avoid paying extra fees to the rental company, but note that if there's an accident, you sometimes must pay the rental car company first and then seek reimbursement from the credit card company. Check your credit card policy. Paying extra for some or all of this insurance increases the cost of a rental car by as much as $10 to $30 a day.

Purchase

Buying a car is usually much more hassle than it's worth, particularly for foreign visitors and trips under six months. Foreigners will have the easiest time arranging this if they have stateside friends or relatives who can provide a fixed address for registration, licensing and insurance, or by working with one of the companies below.

Newspapers and dealers are prime sources for autos. To evaluate prices, check the **Kelley Blue Book** (www.kbb.com); also check the car with an independent auto mechanic before you buy. Once purchased, the car's transfer of ownership papers must be registered with the state's Department of Motor Vehicles (DMV) within 10 days; you'll need the bill of sale, the title (or 'pink slip') and proof of insurance. Some states also require a 'smog certificate.' This is the seller's responsibility; don't buy a car without a certificate. A dealer will submit the paperwork to the DMV for you.

For foreigners, getting independent liability insurance is the toughest part; it is difficult to virtually impossible to arrange without a US driver's license. A car dealer or AAA may be able to suggest an insurer who will do this. Even with a local license, insurance can be expensive and difficult to obtain if you don't have evidence of a good driving record. Bring copies of your home auto insurance policy if it helps establish that you are a good risk. All drivers under 25, and especially those under 21, will have problems getting insurance.

Finally, selling a car can become a desperate business. Selling to dealers gets you the worst price but involves a minimum of paperwork. Otherwise, fellow travelers and college students are the best bets – but be sure the DMV is properly notified about the sale, or you may be on the hook for someone else's parking tickets.

Based in Seattle, Washington, **Auto Tour USA** (☎ 206-999-4686; www.autotourusa.com) specializes in helping foreign US visitors purchase, license and insure a car (they claim, in as fast as a day). While **Adventures on Wheels** (☎ 800-943-3579; www.adventuresonwheels.com) offers a six-month buy-back program: you buy one of their cars, they register and insure it; when your trip's done, they buy it back for a pre-established price.

Rental

Car rental is a huge, very competitive business in the USA. Most rental companies require that you have a major credit card, that you be at least 25 years old and that you have a valid driver's license (your home license will do). Alamo, Thrifty, Enterprise and Rent-A-Wreck may rent to drivers between the ages of 21 and 24 for an additional charge. Those under 21 are usually not permitted to rent at all.

Good independent agencies are listed in this guide, in the local yellow pages and by **Car Rental Express** (www.carrentalexpress.com), which rates and compares independent agencies in US cities; it's particularly useful for searching out cheaper long-term rentals.

Here are the major national companies:

Alamo (☎ 800-462-5266; www.alamo.com)
Avis (☎ 800-230-4898; www.avis.com)
Budget (☎ 800-527-0700; www.budget.com)

TRANSPORTATION

Dollar (☎ 800-800-4000; www.dollar.com)
Enterprise (☎ 800-261-7331; www.enterprise.com)
Hertz (☎ 800-654-3131; www.hertz.com)
National (☎ 800-227-7368; www.nationalcar.com)
Rent-a-Wreck (☎ 800-535-1391; www.rent-a-wreck
.com)
Thrifty (☎ 800-847-4389; www.thrifty.com)

Companies specializing in RV or camper rentals include:

Adventures on Wheels (☎ 800-943-3579; www.adven
turesonwheels.com)
Cruise America (☎ 800-327-7799; www.cruiseamerica
.com)
Happy Travel Camper Rental & Sales (☎ 800-370-
1262; www.camperusa.com)

Car rental prices vary widely and sometimes wildly; it pays to shop around. Airport locations may have cheaper rates but higher fees; city center offices may do pickups and drop-offs; and adjusting the days of your rental can completely change the rate. Weekend and weekly rates are usually cheaper. On average, the daily rate for a small car ranges from $35 to $50, while weekly rates are $175 to $250. If you belong to an auto club or a frequent-flier program, you may get a discount (or earn frequent-flier miles), so ask. Or, see about arranging a cheaper fly-drive package before you travel. No matter what, advance reservations are always recommended.

Some other things to keep in mind: Most national agencies make 'unlimited mileage' standard on all cars, but independents might charge a few dollars extra for this; limited mileage plans rarely work out unless you aren't going far. Some rental companies let you pay for your last tank of gas upfront; this is almost never a good deal. Tax on car rentals varies by state and agency location; always ask for the total cost with tax. Most agencies charge more if you pick the car up in one place and drop it off in another (they add a 'drop off' charge); only nationals even offer this option. Be careful about adding extra days or turning in a car early; extra days may be charged at a premium rate, and an early return may jeopardize the low weekly or monthly deal you originally arranged.

Motorcycle

To drive a motorcycle, you need a US state motorcycle license or an International Driv-

ing Permit endorsed for motorcycles. A state DMV can give you the rules relating to motorcycle use. Helmets are required in almost every state.

Motorcycle rental and insurance is expensive. But if you dream of straddling a Harley across America, contact **EagleRider** (☎ 888-900-9901; www.eaglerider.com), which has offices in major cities nationwide and also rents other kinds of adventure vehicles.

Road Conditions & Hazards

For nationwide traffic and road closure information, visit www.fhwa.dot.gov/traffic
info/index.htm.

Overall, America's highways are adequately maintained, but not always. Potholes, city commuter traffic and 'road rage' – the nationwide epidemic of impatient, bird-flipping drivers – are the main road hazards. Caution, foresight and courtesy will usually get you past them.

Winter driving is an issue in the north and in the mountains, where many cars are fitted with steel-studded snow tires; snow chains can sometimes be required in mountain areas. Driving off road, or on dirt roads, is often forbidden by rental car companies, and it can be very dangerous in wet weather.

In deserts and range country, drivers should watch for livestock trying to share the road with you. High-risk areas are signed as Open Range or with the silhouette of a steer. Deer and other wild animals can be a hazard in suburban and rural areas; high-risk areas are signed with the silhouette of a leaping deer. Take these signs seriously, particularly at night.

Road Rules

In the USA, cars drive on the right side of the road. The use of seat belts and child safety seats is required in every state.

The speed limit is generally 55mph or 65mph on highways, 25mph in cities and towns and as low as 15mph in school zones (strictly enforced during school hours). On interstate highways, the speed limit is sometimes raised to 75mph. It's forbidden to pass a school bus when its lights are flashing.

Most states have laws against littering along the highway. If you are caught, you can be fined $1000 and, most embarrassingly, be forced to pick up what you discarded.

Penalties are very severe for 'DUI' – driving under the influence of alcohol and/or drugs. Police can give roadside sobriety checks to assess if you've been drinking or using drugs. If you fail, they'll require you take a breath test, urine test or blood test to determine the level of alcohol or drugs in your body. Refusing to be tested is treated as if you'd taken the test and failed. The maximum legal blood alcohol concentration is 0.08%.

In some states it is illegal to carry 'open containers' of alcohol in a vehicle, even if they are empty. Containers that are full and sealed may be carried, but if they have ever been opened, they must be carried in the trunk.

HITCHHIKING

Hitchhiking in the USA is potentially dangerous and definitely not recommended. Indeed, drivers have heard so many lurid reports they tend to be just as afraid of those with their thumbs out. Hitchhiking on freeways is prohibited. You'll see more people hitchhiking (and stopping) in rural areas and in Alaska, and these places aren't any safer than anywhere else, but with sparse traffic, you may well get stranded.

In and around national parks, hitching to and from hiking trailheads is more common, but avoid it for the same reasons. Instead, check ride-share boards at ranger stations and hostels. You might get lucky at **Planet Carpool** (www.autotaxi.com), an online ride-share bulletin board.

LOCAL TRANSPORTATION

Except in large US cities, public transit is rarely the most convenient option for travelers, and coverage can be sparse to outlying towns and suburbs. However, it is usually cheap, safe and reliable. For regional details, see the Getting Around sections in the main cities. In addition, about half the states in the nation have adopted ☎ 511 as the all-purpose local transit help phone line.

Airport Shuttles

Shuttle buses provide inexpensive and convenient transport to/from airports in most cities. Most are 12-seat vans; some have regular routes and stops (which include the main hotels) and some pick up and deliver passengers 'door to door' in their service area; costs are $10 to $15 per person.

Bicycle

Some cities are much more amenable to bicycle transport than others, but generally, bicycle rentals are everywhere (and listed throughout this guide), most towns have dedicated bike lanes and paths, and bikes can usually be carried on public transportation. See p1171 for more on cycling in the USA.

Bus

Most cities and larger towns have dependable local bus systems. Most are designed for commuters and provide limited service in the evening and on weekends. Costs range from free to around $1 per ride.

Subway

Some cities have underground subways or elevated metropolitan rail systems, which provide the best local transport. The largest systems are in New York, Washington, DC, Chicago and the San Francisco Bay Area. Other cities have small, one- or two-line rail systems that mainly serve downtown.

Taxi

Taxis are metered, with charges from $1 or $2 to start, plus at least $1.20 per mile. They charge extra for handling baggage, and drivers expect a 10% to 15% tip. Taxis cruise the busiest areas in large cities, but if you're anywhere else, it's easiest to call and order one.

TOURS

Companies offer all kinds of tours in the USA; most focus on regions or cities. See Tours in the city sections for other recommendations, or p1172 for tours on the Delta Queen Steamboat Co.

Recommended tour companies:

Backroads (☎ 510-527-1555, 800-462-2848; www .backroads.com; 801 Cedar St, Berkeley, CA 94710) Primarily emphasizing bicycle tours, Backroads also creates a range of active, multisport trips for all abilities and budgets.

Gray Line (☎ 800-826-0202; www.grayline.com) For those short on time, Gray Line offers a comprehensive range of fairly standard tours.

Green Tortoise (☎ 800-867-8647; www.greentortoise .com) Offering budget adventures for independent travelers, Green Tortoise is famous for its sleeping-bunk buses and camaraderie. Most trips leave from San Francisco, traipsing through the West, across the country and to Central America.

TRANSPORTATION

TRANSPORTATION

TRAIN

Amtrak (☎ 800-872-7245; www.amtrak.com) has an extensive rail system throughout the USA, with Amtrak Thruway buses providing convenient connections to and from the rail network to some smaller centers and national parks. Compared to other modes of travel, trains are rarely the quickest, cheapest or most convenient option, but they can be close on all counts, and in themselves they are a very scenic, comfortable and social way to travel.

Nevertheless, Amtrak – a for-profit federal corporation – is continually threatened by Congress with steep budget cuts that would mean the end of its long-distance routes and perhaps even of the entire system. Would the federal government really allow Amtrak, the only national passenger railroad, to fail? Probably not, but travelers should confirm railroad routes when making plans.

Amtrak has several long-distance lines traversing the nation east to west, and even more running from north to south, and in total these connect all of America's biggest cities and many of its smaller ones. Long-distance services (on named trains) run daily on most routes, but some run only three to five days per week. See Amtrak's website for detailed route maps, and see the Getting There & Around sections in this guide's regional chapters.

Amtrak's commuter trains provide fast and more frequent service on shorter routes, especially along the Northeast corridor from Boston to Washington, DC. High-speed (but troubled) Acela trains on these routes are the fastest and most expensive. Other commuter rail lines serve the Lake Michigan shore near Chicago, the main cities on the California coast and the Miami area. Many are included in an Amtrak rail pass (see opposite).

Classes & Costs

Fares vary according to type of train and seating; on long-distance lines, you can travel in coach seats, business class, or 1st class, which includes all sleeping compartments. Sleeping cars include simple bunks (called 'Roomettes'), bedrooms with private facilities and suites sleeping four with two bathrooms. Sleeping car rates include meals in the dining car, which offers everyone sit-down meal service (pricey if not included). Commuter lines offer only business or 1st class seating; food service, when it exists, consists of sandwich and snack bars. Bringing your own food is allowed, and recommended, on all trains.

Various one-way, round-trip and touring fares are available, with discounts of 15% for seniors age 62 and over and for students (with a 'Student Advantage' card, $20), and 50% discounts for children ages two to 15. Fares are generally lower on all tickets from early January to mid-June and from late August to mid-December. Web-only 'Weekly Specials' offer deep discounts on certain undersold

---

ALL ABOARD!

Dozens of historic narrow-gauge railroads operate as attractions rather than as transport. Most only run in the warmer months, and they can be extremely popular – so book ahead. Who doesn't enjoy the steamy puff and whistle of a mighty locomotive as America's most glorious scenery streams by?

Here are some of the best:

Big Trees and Roaring Camp Railroad (www.roaringcamprr.com) Through the mountains around Santa Cruz, CA.

Cass Scenic Railroad Appalachian Mountains in West Virginia (p368).

Grand Canyon Railway Williams, AZ, to south rim of Grand Canyon (p898).

Cumbres & Toltec Scenic Railroad Chama, NM, into Colorado's Rocky Mountains (p954).

Durango & Silverton Narrow Gauge Railroad Ends at Silverton mining town in Colorado's Rocky Mountains (p990).

Great Smoky Mountains Railroad (www.gsmr.com) From Dillsboro to Bryson City, NC, through the Great Smoky Mountains.

Mount Hood Railroad (www.mthoodrr.com) Through the Hood River Valley outside Portland, OR.

Skunk Train Fort Bragg north past California coast redwoods (p850).

White Pass & Yukon Railroad Skagway, Alaska, to Fraser, British Columbia (p1095).

routes. To get many standard discounts, you need to reserve three days ahead.

Generally, the earlier you book, the lower the price. If you want to take an Acela or Metroliner train, avoid peak commuter times and aim for weekends.

Amtrak offers vacation packages that include rental cars, hotels, tours and attractions; call ☎ 800-805-9114 for details. Air-Rail packages offer train travel in one direction and a plane trip going the other way.

Here are some examples of Amtrak's long-distance services, fares (standard price, one way, coach class) and the travel times:

New York to Chicago $140, 19 hours
New York to Los Angeles $270, 62 hours
Los Angeles to San Antonio $220, 31 hours
Seattle to Oakland $155, 23 hours
Chicago to New Orleans $120, 20 hours
Washington, DC to Miami $220, 26 hours

Reservations

Reservations can be made any time from 11 months in advance to the day of departure; since space on most trains is limited, it's a good idea to reserve as far in advance as you can. This also gives you the best chance of getting fare discounts.

Train Passes

A USA Rail Pass is available only to international travelers (not to US or Canadian residents). The pass offers unlimited coach-class travel within a specific region for either 15 or 30 days, with the price depending on region, number of days and season traveled (fares range from $210 to $550).

Present your pass at an Amtrak office to buy a ticket for each trip. Reservations should be made as well, as far in advance as possible. You can get on and off the train as often as you like, but each sector of the journey must be booked. At some rural stations, trains will only stop if there's a reservation. Tickets are not for specific seats, but a conductor on board may allocate you a seat. First-class or sleeper accommodations cost extra and must be reserved separately.

A North America Rail Pass ($480 to $750) is offered by Amtrak in conjunction with Canada's VIA Rail. It allows unlimited travel on US and Canadian railways for 30 consecutive days, and it's available to American and Canadian residents as well as foreign visitors. The Explore America Pass ($290 to $515) is similar, lasts 45 days, but only includes US train travel.

TRANSPORTATION

Health Dr David Goldberg

CONTENTS

The North American continent encompasses an extraordinary range of climates and terrains, from the freezing heights of the Rockies to tropical areas in southern Florida. Because of the high level of hygiene here, infectious diseases will not be a significant concern for most travelers, who will experience nothing worse than a little diarrhea or a mild respiratory infection.

BEFORE YOU GO

INSURANCE

The USA offers possibly the finest health care in the world. The problem is that, unless you have good insurance, it can be prohibitively expensive. It's essential to purchase travel health insurance if your regular policy doesn't cover you when you're abroad.

Bring any medications you may need in their original containers, clearly labeled. A signed, dated letter from your physician that describes all medical conditions and medications, including generic names, is also a good idea.

If your health insurance does not cover you for medical expenses abroad, consider supplemental insurance. Check the Travel Links section of the **Lonely Planet website** (www.lonelyplanet.com) for more information. Find out in advance if your insurance plan will make payments directly to providers or reimburse you later for overseas health expenditures.

RECOMMENDED VACCINATIONS

No special vaccines are required or recommended for travel to the USA. All travelers should be up-to-date on routine immunizations. See the box below.

ONLINE RESOURCES

There is a wealth of travel health advice on the Internet. The World Health Organization publishes a superb book, called *International Travel and Health,* which is revised annually and is available online at no cost at www.who.int/ith. Another website of general interest is **MD Travel Health** (www.mdtravel health.com), which provides complete travel health recommendations for every country, updated daily, also at no cost.

It's usually a good idea to consult your government's travel health website before departure, if one is available:
Australia (www.smarttraveller.gov.au)
Canada (www.hc-sc.gc.ca/pphb-dgspsp/tmp-pmv /pub_e.html)
UK (www.phac-aspc.gc.ca/tmp-pmv/pub_e.html)
USA (www.cdc.gov/travel)

Vaccine	Recommended for	Dosage	Side effects
tetanus-diphtheria	all travelers who haven't had booster within 10 years	one dose lasts 10 years	soreness at injection site
measles	travelers born after 1956 who've had only one measles vaccination	one dose	fever; rash; joint pains; allergic reactions
chicken pox	travelers who've never had chicken pox	two doses a month apart	fever; mild case of chicken pox
influenza	all travelers during flu season (Nov through Mar)	one dose	soreness at injection site; fever

MEDICAL CHECKLIST

Recommended items for a personal medical kit:

- acetaminophen (Tylenol) or aspirin
- adhesive or paper tape
- antibacterial ointment (eg Bactroban) for cuts and abrasions
- antihistamines (for hay fever and allergic reactions)
- anti-inflammatory drugs (eg ibuprofen)
- bandages, gauze, gauze rolls
- DEET-containing insect repellent for the skin
- pocket knife
- permethrin-containing insect spray for clothing, tents and bed nets
- scissors, safety pins, tweezers
- steroid cream or cortisone (for poison ivy and other allergic rashes)
- sun block
- thermometer

IN THE USA

AVAILABILITY & COST OF HEALTH CARE

In general, if you have a medical emergency, the best bet is to find the nearest hospital and go to its emergency room. If the problem isn't urgent, you can call a nearby hospital and ask for a referral to a local physician, which is usually cheaper than a trip to the emergency room. You should avoid stand-alone, for-profit urgent care centers, which tend to perform large numbers of expensive tests, even for minor illnesses.

Pharmacies are abundantly supplied, but you may find that some medications that are available over-the-counter in your home country require a prescription in the USA, and, as always, if you don't have insurance to cover the cost of prescriptions, they can be shockingly expensive.

INFECTIOUS DISEASES

In addition to more common ailments, there are several infectious diseases that are unknown or uncommon outside North America. Most are acquired by mosquito or tick bites.

Giardiasis

This parasitic infection of the small intestine occurs throughout the world. Symp-

toms may include nausea, bloating, cramps and diarrhea, and may last for weeks. To protect yourself from Giardia, avoid drinking directly from lakes, ponds, streams and rivers, which may be contaminated by animal or human feces. The infection can also be transmitted from person-to-person if proper hand washing is not performed. Giardiasis is easily diagnosed by a stool test and readily treated with antibiotics.

HIV/AIDS

As with most parts of the world, HIV infection occurs throughout the USA. You should never assume, on the basis of someone's background or appearance, that they're free of this or any other sexually transmitted disease. Be sure to use a condom for all sexual encounters.

Lyme Disease

This disease has been reported from many states, but most documented cases occur in the northeastern part of the country, especially New York, New Jersey, Connecticut and Massachusetts. A smaller number of cases occur in the northern Midwest and in the northern Pacific coastal regions, including northern California. Lyme disease is transmitted by deer ticks, which are only 1mm to 2mm long. Most cases occur in the late spring and summer. The Center for Disease Control (CDC) has an informative, if slightly scary, web page on **Lyme disease** (www.cdc.gov/ncidod/dvbid/lyme).

The first symptom is usually an expanding red rash that is often pale in the center, known as a bull's-eye rash. However, in many cases, no rash is observed. Flu-like symptoms are common, including fever, headache, joint pains, body aches and malaise. When the infection is treated promptly with an appropriate antibiotic, usually doxycycline or amoxicillin, the cure rate is high. Luckily, since the tick must be attached for 36 hours or more to transmit Lyme disease, most cases can be prevented by performing a thorough tick check after you've been outdoors. For information, see Tick Bites (p1183).

Rabies

Rabies is a viral infection of the brain and spinal cord that is almost always fatal. The rabies virus is carried in the saliva of infected

HEALTH

animals and is typically transmitted through an animal bite, though contamination of any break in the skin with infected saliva may result in rabies. In the USA, most cases of human rabies are related to exposure to bats. Rabies may also be contracted from raccoons, skunks, foxes, and unvaccinated cats and dogs.

If there is any possibility, however small, that you have been exposed to rabies, you should seek preventative treatment, which consists of rabies immune globulin and rabies vaccine, and is quite safe. In particular, any contact with a bat should be discussed with health authorities, because bats have small teeth and may not leave obvious bite marks. If you wake up to find a bat in your room, or discover a bat in a room with small children, rabies prophylaxis may be necessary.

West Nile Virus

These infections were unknown in the USA until a few years ago, but have now been reported in almost all 50 states. The virus is transmitted by culex mosquitoes, which are active in late summer and early fall, and generally bite after dusk. Most infections are mild or asymptomatic, but the virus may infect the central nervous system, leading to fever, headache, confusion, lethargy, coma and sometimes death. There is no treatment for West Nile virus. For the latest update on the areas affected by West Nile, go to the **US Geological Survey website** (http://westnilemaps.usgs.gov).

ENVIRONMENTAL HAZARDS
Bites & Stings

Common sense approaches to these concerns are the most effective: wear boots when hiking to protect from snakes, wear long sleeves and pants to protect from ticks and mosquitoes. If you're bitten, don't overreact. Stay calm and follow the recommended treatment.

ANIMAL BITES

Do not attempt to pet, handle or feed any animal, with the exception of domestic animals known to be free of any infectious disease. Most animal injuries are directly related to a person's attempt to touch or feed the animal.

Any bite or scratch by a mammal, including bats, should be promptly and thoroughly cleansed with large amounts of soap and water, followed by application of an antiseptic, such as iodine or alcohol. The local health authorities should be contacted immediately for possible post-exposure rabies treatment, whether or not you've been immunized against rabies. It may also be advisable to start an antibiotic, since wounds caused by animal bites and scratches frequently become infected.

MOSQUITO BITES

When traveling in areas where West Nile or other mosquito-borne illnesses have been reported, keep yourself covered (wear long sleeves, long pants, hats and shoes rather than sandals) and apply a good insect repellent, preferably one containing DEET, to exposed skin and clothing. In general, adults and children over 12 should use preparations containing 25% to 35% DEET, which usually lasts about six hours. Children between two and 12 years of age should use preparations containing no more than 10% DEET, applied sparingly, which will usually last about three hours. Neurologic toxicity has been reported from DEET, especially in children, but appears to be extremely uncommon and generally related to overuse. DEET-containing compounds should not be used on children under age two.

Insect repellents containing certain botanical products, including oil of eucalyptus and soybean oil, are effective but last only 1½ to two hours. Products based on citronella are not effective.

Visit the **Center for Disease Control's website** (CDC; www.cdc.gov/ncidod/dvbid/westnile/prevention_info.htm) for prevention information.

SNAKE BITES

There are several varieties of venomous snakes in the USA, but unlike those in other countries they do not cause instantaneous death, and antivenins are available. First aid is to place a light constricting bandage over the bite, keep the wounded part below the level of the heart and move it as little as possible. Stay calm and get to a medical facility as soon as possible. Bring the dead snake for identification if you can, but don't risk being bitten again. Do not use the mythic 'cut an X and suck out the venom' trick; this causes more damage to snakebite victims than the bites themselves.

SPIDER & SCORPION BITES

Although there are many species of spiders in the USA, the only ones that cause significant human illness are the black widow, brown recluse and hobo spiders. The black widow is black or brown in color, measuring about 15mm in body length, with a shiny top, fat body, and distinctive red or orange hourglass figure on its underside. It's found throughout the USA, usually in barns, woodpiles, sheds, harvested crops and bowls of outdoor toilets. The brown recluse spider is brown in color, usually 10mm in body length, with a dark violin-shaped mark on the top of the upper section of the body. It's usually found in the South and southern Midwest, but has spread to other parts of the country in recent years. The brown recluse is active mostly at night, lives in dark sheltered areas, such as under porches and in woodpiles, and typically bites when trapped. Hobo spiders are found chiefly in the northwestern USA and western Canada. The symptoms of a hobo spider bite are similar to those of a brown recluse, but milder.

If bitten by a black widow, you should apply ice or cold packs and go immediately to the nearest emergency room. Complications of a black widow bite may include muscle spasms, breathing difficulties and high blood pressure. The bite of a brown recluse or hobo spider typically causes a large, inflamed wound, sometimes associated with fever and chills. If bitten, apply ice and see a physician.

The only dangerous species of scorpion in the USA is the bark scorpion, which is found in the southwestern part of the country, chiefly Arizona. If stung, you should immediately apply ice or cold packs, immobilize the affected body part and go to the nearest emergency room. To prevent scorpion stings, be sure to inspect and shake out clothing, shoes and sleeping bags before use, and wear gloves and protective clothing when working around piles of wood or leaves.

TICK BITES

Ticks are parasitic arachnids that may be present in brush, forest and grasslands, where hikers often get them on their legs or in their boots. Adult ticks suck blood from hosts by burrowing into the skin and can carry infections such as Lyme disease.

Always check your body for ticks after walking through high grass or thickly forested area. If ticks are found unattached, they can simply be brushed off. If a tick is found attached, press down around the tick's head with tweezers, grab the head and gently pull upwards – do not twist it. (If no tweezers are available, use your fingers, but protect them from contamination with a piece of tissue or paper.) Do not rub oil, alcohol or petroleum jelly on it. If you get sick in the next couple of weeks, consult a doctor.

Glossary

The best primer in what has happened to the English language since its arrival on the continent is Bill Bryson's *Made in America* (1994), which tackles American slang and expressions (and good dollops of history) from the *Mayflower* onwards. For Southernisms, turn to our 'Crash Course in Southern Slang,' p375.

4WD – four-wheel-drive vehicle

9/11 – September 11, 2001; the date of the Al-Qaeda terrorist attacks, in which hijacked airplanes hit the Pentagon and destroyed New York's World Trade Center

24/7 – 24 hours a day, seven days a week

AAA – the American Automobile Association, also called Triple A

Acela – high-speed trains operating in the northeast

adobe – a traditional Spanish-Mexican building material of sun-baked bricks made with mud and straw; a structure built with this type of brick

aka – also known as

alien – official term for a non-US citizen, visiting or resident in the USA (as in 'resident alien,' 'illegal alien' etc)

Amtrak – national government-supported passenger railroad company

Angeleno/Angelena – a resident of Los Angeles

antebellum – of the period before the Civil War; pre-1861

antojito – an appetizer, snack or light meal (Spanish)

Arts and Crafts – an architecture and design movement that gained popularity in the USA at the turn of the 20th century; the style emphasizes simple craftsmanship and functional design; also called (American) craftsman

ATF – Bureau of Alcohol, Tobacco & Firearms, a federal law enforcement agency

ATM – automated teller machine

ATV – all-terrain vehicle, used for off-road transportation and recreation; see also *OHV*

back east – a West Coast reference to the East Coast

backpacker – one who hikes or camps out overnight; less commonly, a young, low-budget traveler

bling-bling – hip-hop term for expensive jewelry and goods, the status symbols of success

BLM – Bureau of Land Management, an agency of the federal Department of the Interior that manages certain public land for resources and recreation

blog – short for web log; a personal diary available online

blue book – the *Kelley Blue Book*, a used-car pricing guide

bluegrass – a form of Appalachian folk music that evolved in the bluegrass country of Kentucky and Tennessee

bodega – especially in New York City, a small local store selling liquor, food and other basics

boomtown – as during the gold rush, a town that experiences rapid economic and population growth

booster – an avid promoter of a town or university; sometimes has parochial connotations

brick-and-mortar – a business' actual location, as opposed to its Internet presence

burro – a small donkey used as a pack animal

Bush, the – the greater part of Alaska, inaccessible by road or sea; to get there, charter a 'bush plane'

BYOB – bring your own booze; a staple of party invitations

Cajun – corruption of 'Acadia'; refers to Louisiana people who descended from 18th-century French-speaking Acadian exiles from eastern Canada

camper – pickup truck with a detachable roof or shell fitted out for camping

carded – to be asked to show your ID to buy liquor or cigarettes, or to enter a bar

carpetbaggers – exploitative Northerners who migrated to the South following the Civil War

CCC – Civilian Conservation Corps, a Depression-era federal program established in 1933 to employ unskilled young men

CDW – collision damage waiver; optional insurance against damaging a rental car

cell – cellular or mobile phone

chamber of commerce – COC; an association of local businesses that often provides tourist information

Chicano/Chicana – a Mexican-American man/woman

CNN – Cable News Network, a 24-hour cable TV news station

coach class – an economical class of travel on an airplane or train

coed – coeducational, open to both males and females; often used in noneducational contexts (eg hostel dorms)

conch (pronounced konk) – pink mollusk eaten as seafood; also a nickname for long-term Key West residents (new Key Westers are Freshwater Conchs)

conestoga – a big covered wagon drawn by horses or oxen, the vehicle of westward migration; also called a prairie schooner

Confederacy – the 11 Southern states that seceded from the USA in 1860–61

contiguous states – all states except Alaska and Hawaii; also called the lower 48

cot – camp bed (babies sleep in cribs)

country and western – an amalgam of rock and folk music of the southern and western USA

coyote – a small wild dog, native to the central and western North American lowlands; also a person who assists illegal immigrants to cross the Mexican border into the USA

cracker – in the South, a derogatory term for a poor white person

CVB – convention and visitors bureau, a city-run organization promoting tourism and assisting visitors

DEA – Drug Enforcement Agency, the federal body responsible for enforcing US drug laws

Deep South – in this book, the states of Louisiana, Mississippi and Alabama

Dixie – the South; the states south of the *Mason-Dixon Line*

DIY – do it yourself, as in DIY crafts or DIY magazines

DMV – Department of Motor Vehicles, the state agency that administers the registration of vehicles and the licensing of drivers

docent – a guide or attendant at a museum

dog, to ride the – to travel by Greyhound bus

downtown – the center of a city, central business district; in the direction of downtown (eg a downtown bus)

Dubya – George W Bush, the nation's current and 43rd president

DUI – driving under the influence of alcohol or drugs or both; sometimes called DWI (driving while intoxicated)

East – generally, the states east of the Mississippi River

efficiency – a small furnished apartment with a kitchen, often for short-term rental

Emancipation – refers to Abraham Lincoln's 1863 Emancipation Proclamation, which nominally freed all slaves in the Confederate-controlled states; in 1865 the US Constitution's 13th Amendment officially abolished slavery

entrée – the main course of a meal

express bus/train – bus/train that stops only at selected stations, and not at 'local' stations

express stop/station – stop/station served by express buses/trains as well as local ones

fanzine – a DIY magazine, often written by obsessive 'fanboys'

flag stop – a place where a bus stops only if you flag it down

foldaway – portable folding bed in a hotel

forty-niners – immigrants to California during the 1849 gold rush; also, San Francisco's pro-football team (49ers)

funnel cake – a specialty of the Pennsylvania Dutch, these deep-fried, spiral-shaped pastries are served dusted with powdered sugar, usually at outdoor fairs

gallery – a commercial establishment selling artwork; institutions that exhibit art collections are usually called museums

gated community – walled upscale residential area accessible only through security gates

general delivery – poste restante

Generation X – 1980s disaffected youth, replaced by Generations Y & Z

gimme cap – promotional baseball cap with company logo; often used pejoratively to refer to rural or lower-class white culture

GLBT – gay, lesbian, bisexual, transgender; *aka* inclusive of all nonheterosexuals

GOP – Grand Old Party, nickname of the Republican party

graduate study – advanced-degree study, after completion of a bachelor's degree

green card – technically, a Registration Receipt Card, issued to holders of immigrant visas; it's actually pink, and it allows the holder to live and work legally in the USA

hip-hop – rap music; also black urban youth culture generally

Hispanic – of Latin American descent or culture (often used interchangeably with *Latino/Latina*)

HI-USA – Hostelling International USA; refers to US hostels affiliated with Hostelling International, a member group of International Youth Hostel Federation (IYHF)

hookup – at campgrounds, refers to *RV* connections for electricity, water and sewage; in social situations, refers to a romantic coupling

Imax – specialized, giant-screen theaters and movies

INS – Immigration & Naturalization Service; as of 2002 replaced by the *USCIS* and no longer operating

interstate – an interstate highway, part of the national, federally funded highway system

IRS – Internal Revenue Service, the branch of the US Treasury Department that oversees tax collection

Jim Crow laws – in the post-Civil War South, laws intended to limit the civil or voting rights of Blacks; Jim Crow is an old pejorative term for a black person

Joshua tree – a tall, treelike type of yucca plant, common in the arid Southwest

kiva – a round underground chamber built by Southwestern American Indian cultures for ceremonial and everyday purposes

KOA – Kampgrounds of America, a private chain of campgrounds throughout the USA

Latino/Latina – a man/woman of Latin American descent (often used interchangeably with *Hispanic*)

LDS – from the Church of Jesus Christ of Latter-Day Saints, the formal name of the Mormon church

live oak – a hardwood, evergreen oak, native to the South; dead live oaks make excellent boat-building timber

local – a bus or train that stops at every bus stop or station; see also *express bus/train*

lower 48 – the 48 *contiguous states* of the continental USA; all states except Alaska and Hawaii

Mason-Dixon Line – the 1767 delineation between Pennsylvania and Maryland that was later regarded as the boundary between free and slave states in the period before the Civil War

MLB – Major League Baseball

MLS – Major League Soccer

mohito – sweet rum drink laden with mint

moonshine – illegal liquor, usually corn whiskey, associated with backwoods stills in the Appalachian Mountains

morteros – hollows in rocks used by American Indians for grinding seeds; also called mortar holes

NAACP – National Association for the Advancement of Colored People

National Guard – each state's federally supported military reserves, used most often in civil emergencies

National Recreation Area – National Park Service areas of scenic or ecological importance that are also reserved for recreation; they often incorporate public works, such as dams

National Register of Historic Places – the National Park Service list of historic sites; designation restricts modifications to help preserve the integrity of original buildings

NBA – National Basketball Association

NCAA – National Collegiate Athletic Association, the body that regulates intercollegiate sports

New Deal – wide-ranging domestic program of public works and regulations introduced by President Franklin D Roosevelt to counteract the effects of the Depression

NFL – National Football League

NHL – National Hockey League

NHS – National Historic Site

NM – National Monument

NOW – National Organization for Women, a political organization dedicated to promoting women's rights and issues

NPR – National Public Radio, a noncommercial, listener-supported national network of radio stations; notable for news and cultural programming

NPS – National Park Service, the division of the Department of the Interior that administers US national parks and monuments

NRA – National Recreation Area; also National Rifle Association, an influential pro-gun lobbyist

NWR – National Wildlife Refuge

OHV/ORV – off-highway vehicle or off-road vehicle

out west – the opposite of *back east;* any place west of the Mississippi River

outfitter – business providing supplies, equipment, transport, guides etc for fishing, canoeing, rafting and hiking trips

panhandle – a narrow piece of land projecting from the main body of a state (eg the Florida panhandle); also, to beg from passersby

parking lot/garage – paved area/building for parking cars (the word 'car park' is not used)

PBS – Public Broadcasting System, a noncommercial TV network; the TV equivalent of *NPR*

PC – politically correct; also personal computer

petroglyph – a work of rock art in which the design is pecked, chipped or abraded into the surface of the rock

PGA – Professional Golfers' Association

pickup – small truck with an open bed

pictograph – work of rock art in which the design is painted on a rock surface

po'boy – a fat sandwich on a bread roll

pound symbol – in the USA, the symbol #, not £

powwow – gathering of American Indian people

pueblo – American Indian village of the Southwest, with adjoining dwellings of *adobe* or stone

ranchero – a Mexican rancher; a Mexican-American musical style blending German and Spanish influences

rancho – a small ranch (Mexican Spanish)

raw bar – a restaurant counter that serves raw shellfish

Reconstruction – a period after the Civil War, when secessionist states were placed under federal control before they were readmitted to the Union

redneck – derogatory term for an extremely conservative, working-class or rural person

ristra – chili tied on a string and hanging vertically

RV – recreational vehicle, also known as a motor home

scalawags – Southern Whites with Northern sympathies who profited under *Reconstruction* after the Civil War

schlep – carry awkwardly or with difficulty (Yiddish)

schlock – cheap, trashy products (Yiddish)

shotgun shack – a small timber house with rooms arranged in a line, so you could fire a shotgun straight through from front to back; once-common dwellings for poor Whites and Blacks in the South

sierra – mountain range (Spanish)

snail mail – stamped letter, as opposed to email

snowbirds – term for wealthy retirees who travel to southern US vacation spots each winter

SoCal – Southern California

soul food – traditionally cuisine of Southern black Americans (such as chitterlings, ham hocks and collard greens)

SSN – social security number, a nine-digit ID code required for employment

stick, stick shift – manually operated gearshift; a car with manual transmission ('Can you drive a stick?')

strip mall – any collection of businesses and stores arranged around a parking lot

SUV – sports utility vehicle

swag – free promotional items given away to function as advertisements

terroir – a French term used in California wine country to specify the region in which grapes are grown and in which wine is made

trailer – transportable dwelling; a trailer park is a collection that doesn't move and provides low-cost housing

TTY, TDD – telecommunications devices for the deaf

two-by-four – standard-size timber, 2in thick and 4in wide

Union, the – the United States; in a Civil War context, the Union refers to the northern states at war with the southern Confederate states

USAF – United States Air Force

USCIS – US Citizenship & Immigration Services, the agency within the Department of Homeland Security that oversees immigration, naturalization and visa processing

USFS – United States Forest Service, the division of the Department of Agriculture that manages federal forests for resources and recreation

USGS – United States Geological Survey, an agency of the Department of the Interior responsible for, among other things, creating detailed topographic maps of the country

USMC – United States Marine Corps

USN – United States Navy

wash – a watercourse in the desert, usually dry but subject to flash flooding

Wasp – White, Anglo-Saxon Protestant; often used to refer to white-bread middle-class values

well drinks – bar drinks with less-expensive, generic-brand hard liquor, as opposed to name-brand 'top-shelf' drinks

WNBA – Women's National Basketball Association

wonk – a person overly obsessed with minute details, usually pejorative; equivalent to political nerd or computer geek

WPA – Works Progress (later, Works Projects) Administration; a Depression-era, New Deal program to increase employment by funding public works projects

zip code – a five- or nine-digit postal code; refers to the Zone Improvement Program, which expedited delivery of US mail

Behind the Scenes

THIS BOOK

For this 4th edition of *USA* Jeff Campbell coordinated a skilled team of authors comprising Glenda Bendure, Becca Blond, Jim DuFresne, Lisa Dunford, Ned Friary, Kim Grant, Beth Greenfield, Alex Hershey, Catherine Le Nevez, Debra Miller, Becky Ohlsen, Suzanne Plank, Andrea Schulte-Peevers, John A Vlahides and Karla Zimmerman. Contributions were also made by Ryan Ver Berkmoes, Virginie Boone, Edward Nawotka, Axel Alonso, Karen Levine, TophOne, Zoë Elton, Jeff Greenwald, Tara Duggan and Dr David Goldberg. The Hawaii chapter was based on text taken from *Hawaii 7*, *Hawai'i the Big Island 2* and *Maui 2*, written by Glenda Bendure, Michael Clark, Ned Friary, Conner Gorry, Kim Grant, Kristin Kimball, Alan Tarbell and Luci Yamamoto. James Lyon coordinated the 2nd edition of *USA* and Jeff Campbell coordinated the 3rd. This guidebook was commissioned in Lonely Planet's Oakland office, and produced by the following:

Commissioning Editors Sam Benson, Heather Dickson, Emily K Wolman
Coordinating Editors Holly Alexander, Julia Taylor, Lauren Rollheiser
Coordinating Cartographer Emma McNicol
Coordinating Layout Designer David Kemp
Managing Cartographer Alison Lyall
Assisting Editors Sarah Bailey, Brooke Clarke, Jackey Coyle, Emma Gilmour, Thalia Kalkipsakis, Brooke Lyons, Lucy Monie, Kristin Odijk
Assisting Proofreaders David Andrew, Kim Noble, Laura Stansfeld, Simon Williamson

Assisting Cartographers David Connolly, Herman So, Amanda Sierp, Simon Tillema, Joshua Geoghegan, Helen Rowley, Jacqueline Nguyen
Assisting Layout Designer Carol Jackson
Cover Designer Julie Rovis
Colour Designer Tom Delamore
Project Manager Rachel Imeson

Thanks to Jay Cooke, Erin Corrigan, Melanie Dankel, Suki Gear, Aimée Goggins, Martin Heng, Rebecca Lalor, Vivek Wagle, Gabbi Wilson

THANKS
JEFF CAMPBELL

First, my co-authors made my task easy, and I owe you all a round. At Lonely Planet, Sam Benson set our ship sailing, and Heather Dickson and Emily Woman steered her home, while Erin Corrigan was an angel on our shoulders: thanks to you all.

For keeping me on the right path with tips, advice and good humor, I owe a huge debt to Anne Hayes, Kate Hoffman, Mark Nigara, Karen Levine, David Holmes, Bill Metke, Brechin Flournoy, Alicia D, Kim Quinones, Roy Cairo, Suzie Birkeland and Heikkie Dean.

Not one word would have been written without my family's support: bright-eyed Miranda, ever-ready Jackson, and my eagle-eyed, patient wife, Deanna, who's so way smarter than I am. This one's for you, bubba.

BECCA BLOND

Thanks to all my friends for providing great travel tips on the region. Big thanks also to Aaron for his

---

THE LONELY PLANET STORY

The story begins with a classic travel adventure: Tony and Maureen Wheeler's 1972 journey across Europe and Asia to Australia. There was no useful information about the overland trail then, so Tony and Maureen published the first Lonely Planet guidebook to meet a growing need.

From a kitchen table, Lonely Planet has grown to become the largest independent travel publisher in the world, with offices in Melbourne (Australia), Oakland (USA) and London (UK). Today Lonely Planet guidebooks cover the globe. There is an ever-growing list of books and information in a variety of media. Some things haven't changed. The main aim is still to make it possible for adventurous travelers to get out there – to explore and better understand the world.

At Lonely Planet we believe travelers can make a positive contribution to the countries they visit – if they respect their host communities and spend their money wisely. Every year 5% of company profit is donated to charities around the world.

BEHIND THE SCENES

unwavering love and support and ability to put up with having a travel writer for a girlfriend. To my family – David, Patricia, Jessica, Jennie, Vera and John – thank you for always believing in me. At Lonely Planet, I'd like to thank all my co-authors, and commissioning editors Sam Benson and Heather Dickson for giving me the chance to work on this great project. Thanks also to all the editors and cartographers I worked with during queries – you guys are the best!

LISA DUNFORD

Thanks to all the friends, family, and family of friends who helped me, guided me and just plain told me where to go on the road in Texas and Oklahoma. I'm especially indebted to: George and Carol Springs, Tara Hrbacek, Anna and Seth Sosolik, Lisa Tanner, Daryn Polanco, Bernie Duncan, Cheryl Spoor, Stephanie and Kenny Johnson, Larry Smith, Dr David Valdez, Joe Kulbeth, Jeannette Stone, Pablo Sanchez, Meredith Hood, Nancy Shropshire and my mom, Mary Kay Dunford. I'd also like to express my gratitude for all the great LP people who I worked with on this project, including Sam Benson, Erin Corrigan, Heather Dickson, Alison Lyall, Jeff Campbell and Karla Zimmerman. Billy, as always, thanks for encouraging me to fly.

NED FRIARY & GLENDA BENDURE

Thanks to Erin Corrigan, Heather Dickson and Sam Benson at LP for their suggestions and encouragement. And thanks also to the many people along the way who provided the inside scoop on their favorite haunts, especially Susan Milton in Provincetown and Namita Raina in Boston.

KIM GRANT

It takes a pueblo to pull these books together. I'm grateful beyond measure that my world overflows with the kindness and good grace of others. Thanks to Sam Benson, Colby Cedar Smith, Catherine Direen, Becca Blond and my Albuquerque friends. You all know what you've done.

BETH GREENFIELD

Many thanks to Julia Buryk and John Fleenor for their expert guidance through the wilds of Pittsburgh. Thank you also to Kathryn and Thomas White of the Beechmont in Hanover, PA; Aimee Szparaga and Richard Nocera of the Villa at Saugerties; Carole Braden for her Catskills tips; Suzanne Ely for tipping me off to Easton and other PA gems; my clutch of NYC cohorts who know every inch of the city; Mom and Dad both

for their NJ knowledge and their love and support. Thank you to Kiki for being the best travel partner ever.

ALEX HERSHEY

First to my father, Robert D Hershey Jr, for letting me mooch off him again for two months. To CE–author extraordinaire Sam Benson for allowing me this excuse to hit the road, and to Jeff Campbell, Heather Dickson and the production team for keeping it together in the background. Ed from Helen's Garden and Robb Miller pointed me in the right directions in Rehoboth and C-ville, respectively. Bawlmer tips were proffered by David and Debbie Schwartz and Ted Wedel. Officer Clarke, your enthusiasm for Richmond is infectious. Paul Meyers and Tom Hyde made fabulous guides through DC's gay scene, and Sean Brandt soothed my colicky laptop. I credit the state of West Virginia for my conversion to the Church of Bluegrass. Another shout-out to TGOS. And, finally, to Krist.

CATHERINE LE NEVEZ

Huge thanks to all who helped on my journey, including numerous travel and hospitality professionals throughout the state, and thanks especially to Paul in Tallahassee, Bob Serata in the Keys and Jay in St Augustine; and to Linda in Miami and Owhnn in the Everglades. Thanks too to Erin, Elaine, Conrad and Helen in London for Miami info. At Lonely Planet, major thanks to Sam Benson for giving me the gig; my fellow *Florida* guide authors Loretta Chilcoat, Kim Grant and Beth Greenfield, and Commissioning Editor Jay Cooke, who all had a bearing on this chapter; Managing Cartographer Alison Lyall; Jennye Garibaldi; and Commissioning Editor Heather Dickson, Jeff Campbell and the *USA* 4 crew. And heartfelt thanks to the gentleman who helped me recover my research notes as they scattered across I-75 in Ocala: an amazing testament to the kindness of strangers. Most of all, thanks to my family for their unfailing support.

DEBRA MILLER

Many people, most of whom will never meet each other, came together to help my research. From bartenders to booksellers, boat captains to concierges – I give most of my thanks to you. It's always the casual conversations that reveal the best insider scoop. Thanks to the countless helpful professionals who staff visitors centers throughout the region – I'm continually amazed at how much you people know, and how willing you are to help. A huge thanks to the Atlanta crew, for keeping my ass in gear, sharing stories, contacts and plenty of wine. To my husband, Rob, who is always up for a road trip: you simply rock my world. Finally, a huge shout-out to Jeff Campbell, who manages this monstrous task with amazing grace.

BECKY OHLSEN

Thanks to my parents, Joel and Christina, and grandparents, Bob and Dorothy Ohlsen. Thanks also to Carrie and Broc Gorges and family, Karl and Natalie Ohlsen, Mark Miller, Julian Thompson, Audrey van Buskirk, Zach Hull, Patrick Leyshock, Andrew Pignataro, Seth Sonstein and the Sandy Hut.

SUZANNE PLANK

Thanks Suki Gear for including me on this project. Sam Benson, thanks for the super clear brief. Jeff Campbell, I knew you were out there if I needed you. Thanks. Heather Dickson, you're a joy; stay State-side! Among the many helpful, warm souls I met on the road, I am especially grateful to Susan and Brady Stewart, Teresa and (phantom chef extraordinaire) Greg Ramsey, Carter Fleming, Kerrie Wilson and Judy Judy Yzquierdo Morris. My deepest appreciation goes to my brilliant,

SEND US YOUR FEEDBACK

We love to hear from travelers – your comments keep us on our toes and help make our books better. Our well-traveled team reads every word on what you loved or loathed about this book. Although we cannot reply individually to postal submissions, we always guarantee that your feedback goes straight to the appropriate authors, in time for the next edition. Each person who sends us information is thanked in the next edition – and the most useful submissions are rewarded with a free book.

To send us your updates – and find out about Lonely Planet events, newsletters and travel news – visit our award-winning website: **www.lonelyplanet.com/feedback**.

Note: We may edit, reproduce and incorporate your comments in Lonely Planet products such as guidebooks, websites and digital products, so let us know if you don't want your comments reproduced or your name acknowledged. For a copy of our privacy policy visit www.lonelyplanet.com/privacy.

hilarious sidekick, editor, navigator and favorite friend Marty Jones for making my planet far from lonely.

ANDREA SCHULTE-PEEVERS

On the home front, a deep heartfelt thanks to David for being such a wonderful and loving companion on the road of life. Big thanks also to Sam Benson for entrusting me with this gig and for doling out tips, data and encouragement. Other capable folks who've shared their knowledge and wisdom include Cay Lepre, Kirstin Cattell, Katrina Paz, Ronele Klingensmith, Mary Ann McAuliffe, Erin Wallace, Kerri Holden, Alexandra Picavet, Joe Timko, Jeff Hocker, Caroline McGrath and Douglas Shaw – great big thanks to all of you.

JOHN A VLAHIDES

Thanks, Andy Moore: without you, I'd not have gotten my first travel-writing gig. I'm also grateful to Sam Benson, Heather Dickson and Jeff Campbell at Lonely Planet for their help and support. And if anyone cares to know who else matters to me, read my acknowledgments in any other Lonely Planet title I've written. I'm keeping this one short.

KARLA ZIMMERMAN

Thanks to the following people for sharing their considerable knowledge of all things local: Megan Bagnall, Lisa Beran, Tim Bewer, Peter Bognanni, John Boyle, Marie Erdman, Kelly Faulkner, Junita Gustafson, Jing He, Jonathon Hofley, JoAnn Hornak, Barbara and Andy Hurt, Val and Jeff Johnson, Mike Kirda, Amanda Powell, Danny Regan, Patrick Regan, Betsy Riley, Mary Riley, Rosemary Rowney, Diana Slickman, Bob Stockfish, Carrie Biolo Thompson, Amy and Brian Waterman, Brian Z, Don and Karen Zimmerman, Sara Zimmerman and the helpful workers in the Midwest's visitors centers. My gratitude to fellow USAers Sam Benson, Jeff Campbell, Heather Dickson, Lisa Dunford and Becky Ohlsen for their help and encouraging nudges. Thanks most of all to Eric Markowitz, who is, quite simply, the world's best partner.

OUR READERS

Many thanks to the hundreds of travelers who used the last edition and wrote to us with helpful hints, useful advice and interesting anecdotes:

A Bruce Abrahams, Catherine Allen, Scott Alquist, Nicholas Anchen, Jessica Andrews, Josée Andrews, Clare Angle, Ian Avery **B** Lella Baker, Lori Balbi, Joshua Taylor Barnes, Gary Bartolacci, Rick

Bauer, Terra Beaton, Michelle Belacic, Cecilia Bergold, Libby Bergstrom, Greg Bessoni, Mark Blackburn, Gill Blyth, Paul Boland, Rosemarie Brickley, C Nicole Brisebois, Michael Brown, Bruce Burton **C** Briar Campbell, Ruth Campbell, Gregory E Carpenter, Suzie Cavallaro, Mary Cerveny, Laura Chaddock, Michael Chang, Robert Clayton, Kenneth Cochran, Roger Conant, Michael Conroy, William & Mary Ann Corum, Katie Coulson, Dean Cracknell, Gene Crestia **D** Roberta Dal Cero, Richelle Daniel, Wim de Boer, Martin de Lange, Y De Meo, Saskia de Rover, Natalie Dixon, Owen Dyer **E** Michael Easker, Patrick Easterling, Barry Ehrlich, Susan El Abbas, Greg Enderby, Diane Evans, John M Evans **F** Roberto Filange, Zita Flatley, Heine Frifeldt, Michele Froidevaux **G** Robbie Garcia, Peter Garvey, Tom Gee, Manfred Gerrits, Cathy Godfrey, Ofir Goldberger, David Goldblum, Tony Goodbody, Russell Goodman, Malcolm Graham, Laura Green, Jessica Gregory, Kimberly Griffin, Robin Guenzel, Alex Guild, Shriman Gurung, Paul Guzyk **H** Peter Hafner, Robert Hajek, David Hall, Liz Hamblyn, Gareth Hammond, Mary Anne Harrar, Robert Hart, James Hawkins, Tracey Helman, Ian Hicks, Jackie Hill, John Hill, Matt Hodson, John Hoffmann, Perry Hoffman, Alyson Hogarth, Elizabeth Hogg, Thng Hui Hong, Jared Hopkinson, Clara Hori, Jeanne Howard, Rachel Howlett, Trevor Humphreys **I** Sonne Idleshon **J** Susann Jaretzke **K** Lila Kahn, Beth A Kaplan, Matthew Kennedy, Becky Kenny, Rebecca Kirby, Thomas Kuipers **L** S W Lam, Andrea Lamprecht-Van Vliet, Roxanne Lang, William H Langeman, Emilie Larsson, Peter Lawton-Harris, Saekyun Lee, Elizabeth Lehr, Abraham A Leib, Robert Leslie, Steve Lewis, Liesbeth Lindenbergh, Sofia Lizzio, Sara Logie, Charles T Lomatsch, Kellie Lord-Zieba, Don Lotze, Richard & Kirsty Ludbrook **M** Daniel Mann, Gina Manning, Marty Margeson, Conrad Matt, Ian McCahon, Nina McKenna, Raymond McLean, Jared Millar, Heather Monell, Barbara Moore, Will Moore, Keith Morris, Gerome Mortelecque, Brenda Murray, Ross & David Murray **N** Ulrich Naef, Felicity Neilson, Jen Nestington, William Newcomb, Tim Newton **P** Marianne Pak, Tim Parris, Val Perry, Genevieve Peterson, Yvonne Petersson, Ethan Phelps, Denny Pierce, Helen Pinkney, David Platter, Anna Price, Ronald Primas **R** Tanya Ragan, Kale Rahul, Edward Roberts, Alison Roche, Leon Roche, Juliana Rodriguez, Kelly Ross, Jeff Rothman, Virginia & Gilbert Roy **S** Rose St John, Jane Salty, Albert Scarpulla Jr, Roland Schmidt, Elisha Schoonmaker, Chris Sheehan, Jennifer Elise Sheehan, Daniel Sherlock, Jonathon Sibtain, Flavia Sindici, Kellee Slater, Mark Smalley, Laurie Smith, Vicki Smith, Terrance Soanes, Martin Sobek, Stefano Spaggiari, Ron Squires, Tammy Steinert, Joachim Stern, Alexander Stevenson, Lynette Stewart, Ian C Story, Nick Strickland, Morten Stryhn, Marian Sumner **T** George W Thagard, Bunny Thiele, Paul Thompson, Bruce Thomson, Brian Tiernan, Jane Toon, Michael Travica, Sam Trenchi, Jemma Triance, Craig Tubman **V** Michiel van Amelsfort, Thomas van der Veer, Paolo Venturini, Natalie Vincent **W** Kate Waters, David Watkin, Victor Weaver, Darien Werfhorst, Dylan Wiliam, Chris Willett, Brian Williams, Edward Williams, Chris Wills **Y** Jason Yelowitz, Andrew Young

ACKNOWLEDGMENTS

Many thanks to the following for the use of their content:

Globe on back cover © Mountain High Maps 1993 Digital Wisdom, Inc.

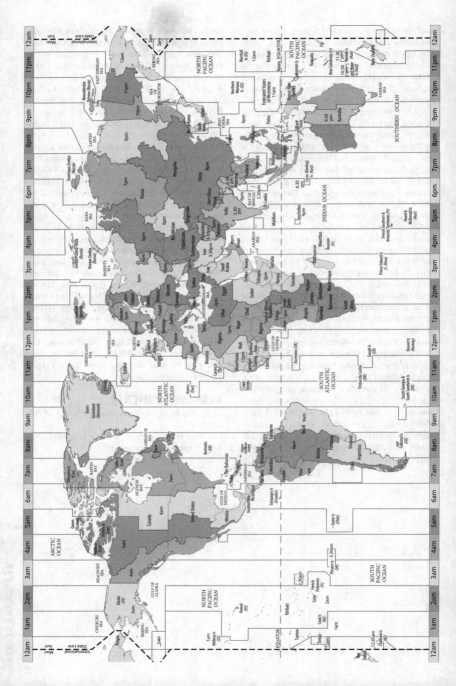

Index

000 Map pages
000 Location of photographs

MAP LEGEND
ROUTES

Tollway		One-Way Street
Freeway		Street Mall/Steps
Primary Road		Tunnel
Secondary Road		Walking Tour
Tertiary Road		Walking Tour Detour
Lane		Walking Trail
Under Construction		Walking Path
Track		Pedestrian Overpass
Unsealed Road		

TRANSPORT

Ferry	MBTA Subway Stop
Metro	Rail
Monorail	Rail (Underground)
CTA Station	Tram

HYDROGRAPHY

River, Creek	Canal
Intermittent River	Water
Swamp	Lake (Dry)
Mangrove	Lake (Salt)
Reef	Mudflats
Glacier	

BOUNDARIES

International	Regional, Suburb
State, Provincial	Ancient Wall
Marine Park	Cliff

AREA FEATURES

Airport	Land
Area of Interest	Mall
Beach, Desert	Market
Building	Park
Campus	Reservation
Cemetery, Christian	Sports
Forest	Urban

POPULATION

CAPITAL (NATIONAL)	CAPITAL (STATE)
Large City	Medium City
Small City	Town, Village

SYMBOLS

Sights/Activities
- Beach
- Castle, Fortress
- Christian
- Jewish
- Monument
- Museum, Gallery
- Point of Interest
- Pool
- Ruin
- Skiing
- Trail Head
- Zoo

Eating
- Eating

Drinking
- Drinking
- Café

Entertainment
- Entertainment

Shopping
- Shopping

Sleeping
- Sleeping
- Camping

Transport
- Airport, Airfield
- Bus Station
- Gas Station
- General Transport
- Parking Area

Information
- Bank, ATM
- Embassy/Consulate
- Hospital, Medical
- Information
- Internet Facilities
- Police Station
- Post Office
- Telephone

Geographic
- Lighthouse
- Lookout
- Mountain, Volcano
- National Park
- River Flow
- Waterfall

LONELY PLANET OFFICES

Australia
Head Office
Locked Bag 1, Footscray, Victoria 3011
☎ 03 8379 8000, fax 03 8379 8111
talk2us@lonelyplanet.com.au

USA
150 Linden St, Oakland, CA 94607
☎ 510 893 8555, toll free 800 275 8555
fax 510 893 8572
info@lonelyplanet.com

UK
72-82 Rosebery Ave,
Clerkenwell, London EC1R 4RW
☎ 020 7841 9000, fax 020 7841 9001
go@lonelyplanet.co.uk

Published by Lonely Planet Publications Pty Ltd
ABN 36 005 607 983